Birnbaum's 97 United States

A BIRNBAUM TRAVEL GUIDE

Alexandra Mayes Birnbaum
EDITORIAL CONSULTANT

Lois Spritzer
Editorial Director

Laura L. Brengelman
Managing Editor

Mary Callahan
Beth Schlau
Senior Editors

Patricia Canole
Gene Gold
Susan McClung
Associate Editors

Jonathan Goodnough
Map Coordinator

Susan Cutter Snyder
Editorial Assistant

HarperPerennial
A *Division* of HarperCollins*Publishers*

For Sam and Edith Grafton, who were there at the beginning.

FIRST EDITION

ISSN 0749-2561 (Birnbaum Travel Guides)
ISSN 0896-8683 (United States)
ISBN 0-06-278257-6 (pbk.)

97 98 99 ❖/RRD 5 4 3 2 1

BIRNBAUM TRAVEL GUIDES

Bahamas, and Turks & Caicos
Bermuda
Canada
Cancun, Cozumel & Isla Mujeres
Caribbean
Country Inns and Back Roads
Disneyland
Hawaii
Mexico
Miami & Ft. Lauderdale
United States
Walt Disney World
Walt Disney World for Kids, By Kids
Walt Disney World Without Kids

Contributing Editors

Sherry Amatenstein
Meg Beasley
Vicki L. Blanchfield
Gene Bourg
Margaret Bowen
Betsy Braden
John Braden
Diana Brubaker
Bob Butler
Kim Christ
Anne Christopherson
Dan Christopherson
James Cortese
Jane Hershey Cuozzo
Teresa Day
Brenda Fine
Connie Goddard
Kathryn Gress
H. Constance Hill
Rosemary Peters Hinkle
Martin Hintz
Arline Inge
Kathy Kaplan
Laura Kelly
Lea Lane
Cat Milan
JoAnn Milivojevic
Marilyn A. Moore
Rob Musial
Alanna Nash
Jane Ockershausen
Donna Peck
Patti Covello Pietschmann
Richard J. Pietschmann
Patricia Tunison Preston
Holly Rizzo
June Naylor Rodriguez
Frank Rosci
Genevieve Rowles
Dale Salm
William Schemmel
Joan Scobey
Art Siemering
Tracy A. Smith
Janet Steinberg
Ginny Turner
Tom Weiner
Loralee Wenger
Leslie Westbrook
Christine Zust

Maps

Mark Carlson
Susan Carlson
B. Andrew Mudryk
Paul J. Pugliese
Mark Stein Studios

Contents

Getting Ready to Go

Practical information for planning your trip.

The Cities

Thorough, qualitative guides to each of the 42 cities most often visited by vacationers and businesspeople. Each section offers a comprehensive report on the city's most compelling attractions and amenities—highlighting our top choices in every category.

Diversions

A selective guide to active and/or cerebral vacation themes, pinpointing the best places to pursue them.

Unexpected Pleasures and Treasures

For the Experience

For the Mind

For the Body

Directions

This country's most spectacular routes and roads, most arresting natural wonders, most magnificent parks and forests, all organized into 64 specific driving tours.

Foreword

We have tried to create a guide to the United States that's specifically organized, written, and edited for today's demanding traveler, one for whom qualitative information is infinitely more desirable than mere quantities of unappraised data.

This book, along with the other guides in our series, represents a generation of travel guides that is especially responsive to contemporary needs and interests. Large numbers of specific questions have provided the real editorial structure of this book. The volume of mail we regularly receive emphasizes that today's travelers want very precise information. Readers who want to know the name of the best restaurant in Chicago or Santa Fe or the best tennis camp for improving an erratic backhand will have no trouble whatever extracting that data from this guide.

We realize that it's impossible for any single travel writer to visit thousands of restaurants (and nearly as many hotels) in any given year and provide accurate appraisals of each. And even if it were physically possible for one human being to survive such an itinerary, it would of necessity have to be done at a dead sprint, and the perceptions derived therefrom would probably be less valid than those of any other intelligent individual visiting the same establishments. It is, therefore, both impractical and undesirable (especially in an annually revised and updated guidebook series such as we offer) to have only one person provide all the data on the entire world. Instead, we have chosen what we like to describe as the "thee and me" approach to restaurant and hotel evaluation and, to a somewhat more limited degree, to the sites and sights we have included in the other sections of the text. What this really reflects is personal sampling tempered by intelligent counsel from informed local sources.

This guidebook is directed to the "visitor," and such elements as restaurants have been specifically picked to provide the visitor with a representative, enlightening, and, above all, pleasant experience.

Other evidence of how we've tried to tailor our text to reflect modern travel habits is apparent in the section we call DIVERSIONS. Where once it was common for travelers to spend an urban visit seeing only the obvious sights, today's traveler is more likely to want to pursue a special interest or to venture off the beaten path. In response to this trend, we have collected a series of special experiences so that it is no longer necessary to wade through a pound or two of superfluous prose just to find exceptional pleasures and treasures.

Finally, I should point out that every good travel guide is a living enterprise; that is, no part of this text is carved in stone. In our annual revisions, we refine, expand, and further hone all our material to serve your travel needs better. To this end, no contribution is of greater value to us than your personal reaction to what we have written, as well as information reflecting your own experiences while using the book. Please write to us at 10 E. 53rd St. New York, NY 10022.

We sincerely hope to hear from you.

Alexandra Mayes Birnbaum

ALEXANDRA MAYES BIRNBAUM, editorial consultant to the *Birnbaum Travel Guides*, worked with her late husband, Stephen Birnbaum, as co-editor of the series. She has been a world traveler since childhood and is known for her travel reports on radio on what's hot and what's not.

United States

Pacific Time Zone
Mountain Time Zone
Cent
Seattle
WASHINGTON
Portland
OREGON
MONTANA
NORTH DAKOTA
SOUTH DAKOTA
IDAHO
WYOMING
NEBRASKA
NEVADA
Salt Lake City
UTAH
San Francisco
Denver
COLORADO
KANSAS
CALIFORNIA
Las Vegas
Los Angeles
San Diego
ARIZONA
Phoenix
Santa Fe
NEW MEXICO
OKL
Fort Wor
TEXAS
San Antoni
Alaska
N
0 mi 400
Hawaiian Islands
Kauai
Oahu
Maui
Hawaii
0 mi 400

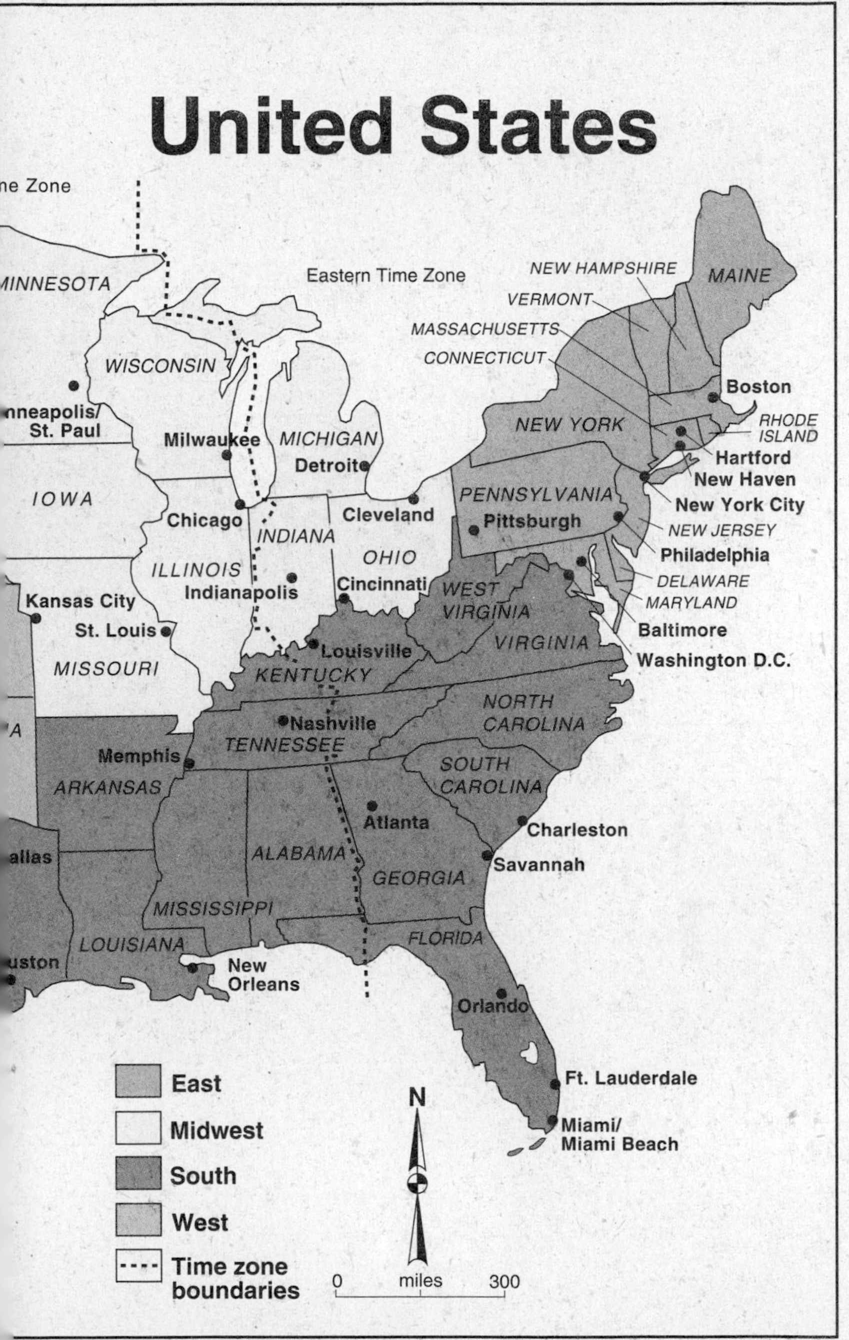
United States
Eastern Time Zone
WISCONSIN
St. Paul
Milwaukee
MICHIGAN
Detroit
IOWA
Chicago
ILLINOIS
INDIANA
Indianapolis
OHIO
Cleveland
Cincinnati
Kansas City
St. Louis
MISSOURI
KENTUCKY
Louisville
TENNESSEE
Nashville
Memphis
ARKANSAS
MISSISSIPPI
ALABAMA
Atlanta
GEORGIA
LOUISIANA
New Orleans
FLORIDA
Orlando
Ft. Lauderdale
Miami/
Miami Beach
SOUTH
CAROLINA
Charleston
Savannah
NORTH
CAROLINA
VIRGINIA
WEST
VIRGINIA
PENNSYLVANIA
Pittsburgh
Philadelphia
NEW JERSEY
DELAWARE
MARYLAND
Baltimore
Washington D.C.
NEW YORK
New York City
CONNECTICUT
Hartford
New Haven
RHODE
ISLAND
MASSACHUSETTS
Boston
VERMONT
NEW HAMPSHIRE
MAINE
East
Midwest
South
West
Time zone
boundaries
N
0
miles
300

How to Use This Guide

A great deal of care has gone into the special organization of this guidebook, and we believe it represents a real breakthrough in the presentation of travel material.

Our text is divided into four basic sections in order to present information in the best way on every possible aspect of an American vacation. Our aim is to highlight what's where and to provide basic information—how, when, where, how much, and what's best—to assist you in making the most intelligent choices possible.

Here is a brief summary of what you can expect to find in each section. We believe that you will find both your travel planning and en route enjoyment enhanced by having this book at your side.

GETTING READY TO GO

A mini-encyclopedia of practical travel facts with all the precise data necessary to create a successful trip to and through America. Here you will find how to get where you're going, plus selected resources—including useful publications, and companies and organizations specializing in discount and special-interest travel—providing a wealth of information and assistance useful both before and during your trip.

THE CITIES

Our individual reports on the 42 US cities most visited by tourists and businesspeople include a short-stay guide, with an essay introducing each city as a historic entity and a contemporary place to visit; an *At-a-Glance* section that's a site-by-site survey of the most important, interesting, and unique sights to see and things to do; *Sources and Resources,* a concise listing of pertinent tourist information, such as the address of the local tourist office, which sightseeing tours to take, where to find the best nightspot, which are the shops that have the finest merchandise and/or the most irresistible bargains, and where the best museums and theaters are to be found; and *Best in Town,* which lists our collection of cost-and-quality choices of the best places to eat and sleep on a variety of budgets.

DIVERSIONS

This section is designed to help travelers find the best places in which to engage in a variety of exceptional experiences, without having to wade through endless unrelated text. In every case, our particular suggestions are intended to guide you to that special place where the quality of experience is likely to be highest.

DIRECTIONS

Here are 65 American itineraries, from Maine's coastal islands to Hawaii's hidden beaches, to take you along this country's most beautiful routes and roads, past its most spectacular natural wonders, and through its most magnificent national parks and forests.

Each entry includes a guide to sightseeing highlights, a cost-and-quality guide to accommodations along the road (small inns, country hotels, bed and breakfast establishments, and detours to off-the-main-road discoveries), plus hints and suggestions for activities.

To use this book to full advantage, take a few minutes to read the table of contents and random entries in each section to get a firsthand feel for how it all fits together. You will find that the sections of this book are building blocks designed to help you put together the best possible trip. Use them selectively as a tool, a source of ideas, a reference work for accurate facts, and a guide to the best buys, the most exciting sights, the most pleasant accommodations, and the tastiest food—*the best travel experience* you can possibly have.

Getting Ready to Go

Getting Ready to Go

When to Go

With its vast range of topography and climate, the US provides year-round travel opportunities. Traditionally, the most popular vacation time is summer, when children are out of school and the weather is temperate throughout much of the country. Wintertime exceptions include Hawaii, southern California, and Florida, and other parts of the south and southwest, as well as ski resorts and other winter sports facilities across the US. In the spring and fall, driving tours to view the seasonal changes are popular.

Travel during the off-seasons (which vary throughout the country) and shoulder seasons (the months immediately before and after the peak months) can offer relatively fair weather and smaller crowds. During these periods, travel also often is less expensive—although high season rates may prevail because of a holiday or an important local event.

CLIMATE

The following chart lists average temperature ranges (in °F) in the US cities covered in this guide. For more detailed weather information, see the *Climate* entry in the individual city chapters in THE CITIES.

	January	*April*	*July*	*October*
Atlanta	33–51	50–73	69–88	51–73
Baltimore	24–41	43–65	67–87	46–68
Boston	23–36	41–57	65–82	47–63
Charleston, South Carolina	37–59	53–76	72–89	55–77
Chicago	14–29	39–59	63–83	43–64
Cincinnati	20–37	42–64	65–86	44–67
Cleveland	19–33	38–58	61–82	44–63
Dallas	34–54	55–77	75–98	56–80
Denver	16–43	34–61	59–88	37–67
Detroit	16–31	37–58	61–83	41–63
Ft. Lauderdale	57–76	66–83	75–90	70–85
Ft. Worth	34–54	55–77	75–98	56–80
Hartford	17–34	38–60	62–85	41–64
Honolulu	65–80	69–83	73–87	72–87
Houston	41–62	58–79	73–94	58–82
Indianapolis	18–34	42–63	65–85	43–66
Kansas City, Missouri	17–35	44–65	69–89	47–68
Las Vegas	33–56	50–77	76–105	54–82
Los Angeles	47–67	52–71	63–84	59–79
Louisville	24–41	46–68	68–88	46–69

Memphis	31–48	52–73	73–92	51–75
Miami–Miami Beach	59–75	68–82	76–89	72–84
Milwaukee	11–26	36–54	61–80	42–60
Minneapolis–St. Paul	2–20	36–56	63–83	39–60
Nashville	28–46	48–71	69–90	48–72
New Haven	22–36	40–57	66–82	47–64
New Orleans	43–62	59–79	74–91	59–79
New York City	26–38	44–61	68–85	50–66
Orlando	49–72	60–84	73–92	65–84
Philadelphia	24–39	43–63	67–86	47–67
Phoenix	39–65	53–83	80–105	59–88
Pittsburgh	19–34	39–61	61–83	42–63
Portland, Oregon	34–44	41–60	56–80	45–64
St. Louis	20–38	45–67	69–89	47–69
Salt Lake City	20–37	37–61	62–93	39–67
San Antonio	39–62	59–80	74–95	59–82
San Diego	48–65	55–68	65–76	60–75
San Francisco	42–57	47–63	53–71	51–70
Santa Fe	15–40	33–64	58–86	36–65
Savannah	38–60	54–78	72–91	56–78
Seattle	34–45	41–58	54–75	45–60
Washington, DC	22–43	41–67	64–88	43–69

If you have a touch-tone phone, you can call *The Weather Channel Connection* (phone: 900-WEATHER) for current weather forecasts. This service, available from *The Weather Channel* (2600 Cumberland Pkwy., Atlanta, GA 30339), costs 95¢ per minute; the charge will appear on your phone bill.

Traveling by Plane

SCHEDULED FLIGHTS

Airlines offering flights in the US include *AirTran, America West, American, American Trans Air, Continental, Delta, Frontier, Midway, Northwest, Southwest, TWA, United, USAir,* and *Western Pacific.* Numerous other discount, regional, and commuter carriers provide service on selected routes.

FARES The great variety of airfares can be reduced to the following basic categories: first class, business class, coach (also called economy or tourist class), excursion or discount, and standby, as well as various promotional fares. For information on applicable fares and restrictions, contact the airlines or ask your travel agent. Most airfares are offered for a limited time and sell out quickly. Once you've found the lowest fare for which you can qualify, purchase your ticket as soon as possible.

RESERVATIONS Reconfirmation is not generally required on domestic flights, although it is wise to call ahead to make sure that the airline has your reservation and any special requests in its computer.

SEATING You usually can reserve a specific seat when purchasing your ticket; otherwise, seats are assigned on a first-come, first-served basis at check-in. Seating charts may be available from airlines and are included in the *Desktop Flight Guide* (Official Airline Guides, PO Box 51703, Boulder, CO 80321; phone: 800-323-3537 for orders; 708-574-6000 for information; fax: 708-574-6565).

SMOKING US law prohibits smoking on flights scheduled for six hours or less within the US and its territories on both US and foreign carriers. In addition, most of the major US carriers have banned smoking on *all* domestic flights–including those to Alaska and Hawaii. A free wallet-size guide that describes the rights of nonsmokers under current regulations is available from *ASH* (*Action on Smoking and Health;* DOT Card, 2013 H St. NW, Washington, DC 20006; phone: 202-659-4310).

SPECIAL MEALS When making your reservation, you can request one of the airline's alternate menu choices for no additional charge. Though not always required, it's a good idea to reconfirm your meal request the day before departure.

BAGGAGE On major airlines, passengers usually are allowed to carry on board one or two bags that will fit under a seat or in an overhead compartment and to check two bags in the cargo hold. Specific regulations regarding dimensions and weight restrictions vary among airlines, but a checked bag usually cannot exceed 62 inches in combined dimensions (length, width, and depth) or weigh more than 70 pounds. There may be charges for additional, oversize, or overweight luggage, and for special equipment or sporting gear. Note that baggage allowances may be more limited on regional and commuter airlines. When checking your bags, make sure that the tags the airline attaches are correctly coded for your destination.

CHARTER FLIGHTS

By booking a block of seats on a specially arranged flight, charter operators frequently can offer travelers bargain airfares. If you do fly on a charter, however, read the contract's fine print carefully. Federal regulations permit charter operators to cancel a flight or assess surcharges of as much as 10% of the airfare up to 10 days before departure. You usually must book in advance, and once booked, you may not be able to change your flight—a good reason to buy trip cancellation insurance (see *Insurance,* below). Also, make your check out to the company's escrow account, which provides some protection for your investment in the event that the charter operator fails. Additional information on charter flights is provided in the publication *Jax Fax* (397 Post Rd., Darien, CT 06820; phone: 800-952-9329 for subscriptions; 203-655-8746 for information; fax: 203-655-6257).

DISCOUNTS ON SCHEDULED FLIGHTS

CONSOLIDATORS AND BUCKET SHOPS These companies buy blocks of tickets from airlines and sell them at a discount to travel agents or directly to consumers. Since many bucket shops operate on a thin margin, be sure to check a company's record with the *Better Business Bureau*—before parting with any money.

Cheap Tickets (6151 W. Century Blvd., Los Angeles, CA 90045; phone: 800-377-1000; fax: 800-454-2555).

Discount Travel International (169 W. 81st St., New York, NY 10024; phone: 212-362-3636; fax: 212-362-3236).

Fare Deals Travel (9350 E. Arapahoe Rd., Suite 330, Englewood, CO 80112; phone: 800-878-2929 or 303-792-2929; fax: 303-792-2954).

Southwest Travel Systems (1001 N. Central Ave., Suite 575, Phoenix, AZ 85004; phone: 800-STS-TRAVEL or 602-255-0234; fax: 602-255-0220).

STT Worldwide Travel (9880 SW Beaverton Hillsdale Hwy., Beaverton, OR 97005; phone: 800-348-0886 or 503-641-8866; fax: 503-641-2171).

Unitravel (1177 N. Warson Rd., St. Louis, MO 63132; phone: 800-325-2222 or 314-569-0900; fax: 314-569-2503).

LAST-MINUTE TRAVEL SERVICES These are clubs or agencies that provide members or clients with information on imminent trips and other bargain travel opportunities. Some of the clubs charge an annual fee; others offer free membership. Note that despite the names of some of the services listed below, you don't have to wait until literally the last minute to make travel plans.

Discount Travel International (address above).

FLY ASAP (PO Box 9808, Scottsdale, AZ 85252-3808; phone: 800-FLY-ASAP or 602-224-9504; fax: 602-224-9533).

Last Minute Travel (1249 Boylston St., Boston, MA 02215; phone: 800-LAST-MIN or 617-267-9800; fax: 617-424-1943).

Moment's Notice (7301 New Utrecht Ave., Brooklyn, NY 11204-5137; phone: 718-234-6295; fax: 718-234-6450).

Spur of the Moment Cruises (411 N. Harbor Blvd., Suite 302, San Pedro, CA 90731; phone: 800-4-CRUISE or 310-521-1070 in California; 800-343-1991 elsewhere in the US; 24-hour hotline: 310-521-1060; fax: 310-521-1061).

Traveler's Advantage (3033 S. Parker Rd., Suite 900, Aurora, CO 80014; phone: 800-835-8747 for member services; 800-548-1116 for information; fax: 303-368-3985).

Vacations to Go (1502 Augusta Dr., Suite 415, Houston, TX 77057; phone: 713-974-2121 in Texas; 800-338-4962 elsewhere in the US; fax: 713-974-0445).

Worldwide Discount Travel Club (1674 Meridian Ave., Miami Beach, FL 33139; phone: 305-534-2082).

GENERIC AIR TRAVEL These organizations offer a service similar to airline standby, except that they sell seats on not one but several scheduled and charter airlines. One pioneer of generic flights is *Airhitch* (2472 Broadway, Suite 200, New York, NY 10025; phone: 212-864-2000 in New York City; 800-326-2009 elsewhere in the US; fax: 212-864-5489).

BARTERED TRAVEL SOURCES Barter—the exchange of commodities or services in lieu of cash payment—is a common practice among travel suppliers. Companies that have obtained travel services through barter may sell these services at substantial discounts to travel clubs, which pass along the savings to members. One organization offering bartered travel opportunities is *Travel World Leisure Club* (225 W. 34th St., Suite 909, New York, NY 10122; phone: 800-444-TWLC or 212-239-4855; fax: 212-564-5158).

CONSUMER PROTECTION

Passengers whose complaints have not been satisfactorily addressed by the airline can contact the *US Department of Transportation* (*DOT;* Consumer Affairs Division, 400 Seventh St. SW, Room 10405, Washington, DC 20590; phone: 202-366-2220). Also see *Fly Rights* (*Consumer Information Center,* Department 133B, Pueblo, CO 81009; phone: 719-948-3334; fax: 719-948-9724). If you have safety-related questions or concerns, write to the *Federal Aviation Administration* (*FAA;* 800 Independence Ave. SW, Washington, DC 20591) or call or fax the *FAA Consumer Hotline* (phone: 800-322-7873; fax: 202-267-5087).

Traveling by Ship

Your cruise fare usually includes all meals, recreational activities, and entertainment. Shore excursions are available at extra cost, and can be booked in advance or once you're on board. An important factor in the price of a cruise is the location (and sometimes the size) of your cabin. Charts issued by the *Cruise Lines International Association* (*CLIA;* 500 Fifth Ave., Suite 1407, New York, NY 10110; phone: 212-921-0066; fax: 212-921-0549) provide information on ship layouts and facilities, and are available at some *CLIA*-affiliated travel agencies.

The *US Public Health Service (PHS)* inspects all passenger vessels calling at US ports. For the most recent summary or a particular inspection report, write to the *National Center for Environmental Health* (Attention: Chief, Vessel Sanitation Program, 1015 N. America Way, Room 107, Miami, FL 33132; phone: 305-536-4307; fax: 305-536-4528). Most cruise ships have a doctor on board, plus medical facilities.

Note that the ships of most of the international cruise lines are registered in foreign countries (such as the Bahamas or Panama), and US regulations do not permit ships of foreign registry to transport passengers between two US ports unless the following conditions are met: 1) Passengers must have boarded the ship at a foreign port, and 2) either the ultimate destination of the cruise must be a foreign port, or the ship must call at a foreign port between stops in the US. In order to meet these requirements, cruises offered by the major international cruise lines often begin and/or end in Canadian, Mexican, or other international ports, and passengers from the US are flown or otherwise transported to and from these ports. In addition, companies offering around-the-world cruises that call at US ports sometimes allow US passengers to join one leg of the cruise.

US companies plying the nation's coastal and inland waterways offer a wide range of cruises and shorter excursions—everything from whale watching to river tours and gambling cruises aboard historic paddle wheelers. Vacationers who enjoy being on the water but prefer staying in one place also might consider renting a houseboat.

For further information on cruises and cruise lines, consult *Ocean and Cruise News* (PO Box 92, Stamford, CT 06904; phone/fax: 203-329-2787). And for a free list of travel agencies specializing in cruises, contact the *National Association of Cruise Only Agencies* (*NACOA;* 3191 Coral Way, Suite 630, Miami, FL 33145; phone: 305-446-7732; fax: 305-446-9732). Additional information on local excursions can be obtained from local and state tourist offices.

Cruise Lines

Alaska Sightseeing/Cruise West (Fourth and Battery Building, Suite 700, Seattle, WA 98121; phone: 800-426-7702 or 206-441-8687; fax: 206-441-4757).

Alaska's Glacier Bay Tours and Cruises (520 Pike St., Suite 1400, Seattle, WA 98101; phone: 800-451-5952 or 206-623-2417; fax: 206-623-7809).

American Canadian Caribbean Line (PO Box 368, Warren, RI 02885; phone: 401-247-0955 in Rhode Island; 800-556-7450 elsewhere in the US; fax: 401-247-2350).

American Hawaii Cruises (2 N. Riverside Plaza, Chicago, IL 60606; phone: 800-765-7000 or 312-466-6000; fax: 312-466-6001).

Carnival Cruise Lines (3655 NW 87th Ave., Miami, FL 33178-2428; phone: 800-327-9501 or 305-599-2600; fax: 305-471-4740).

Clipper Cruises (7711 Bonhomme Ave., St. Louis, MO 63105-1956; phone: 800-325-0010 or 314-727-2929; fax: 314-727-6576).

Costa Cruises (80 SW Eighth St., Miami, FL 33130; phone: 800-462-6782; fax: 305-375-0676).

Crystal Cruises (2121 Ave. of the Stars, Los Angeles, CA 90067; phone: 800-446-6620 or 310-785-9300; fax: 310-785-0011).

Cunard (555 Fifth Ave., New York, NY 10017; phone: 800-5-CUNARD, 800-221-4770, or 212-880-7300; fax: 718-786-2353).

Dolphin Cruise Line (901 South America Way, Miami, FL 33132-2073; phone: 800-222-1003 or 305-358-2111; fax: 305-358-4807).

Holland America Line/West Tours (300 Elliot Ave. W., Seattle, WA 98119; phone: 800-426-0327 or 206-281-3535; fax: 800-628-4855 or 206-281-7110).

Norwegian Cruise Line (95 Merrick Way, Coral Gables, FL 33134; phone: 800-327-7030 or 305-445-0866; fax: 305-448-6406).

P&O Cruises (2815 Second Ave, Suite 400, Seattle, WA 98121; phone: 800-340-7674 for reservations; 800-774-6237 for information; fax: 206-728-3982).

Princess Cruises (10100 Santa Monica Blvd., Los Angeles, CA 90067; phone: 800-421-0522 or 310-553-1770; fax: 310-284-2844).

Royal Caribbean Cruise Lines (1050 Caribbean Way, Miami, FL 33132; phone: 800-327-6700 or 305-539-6000; fax: 800-722-5329).

Seabourn Cruise Line (55 Francisco St., Suite 710, San Francisco, CA 94133; phone: 800-929-9595 or 415-391-7444; fax: 415-391-8518).

Special Expeditions (720 Fifth Ave., New York, NY 10019; phone: 800-762-0003 or 212-765-7740; fax: 212-265-3770).

World Explorer Cruises (555 Montgomery St., Suite 1400, San Francisco, CA 94111; phone: 800-854-3835 or 415-393-1565; fax: 415-391-1145).

Shorter and Specialty Sailings

A Admiral's Sight-Seeing Cruise Line (PO Box 811493, Chicago, IL 60681; phone: 312-641-7245; fax: 312-641-7246).

Argosy Cruises (Pier 55, Suite 201, Seattle, WA 98101; phone: 206-623-1445; fax: 206-623-5474).

Bay State Cruise Company (67 Long Wharf, Boston, MA 02110; phone: 617-723-7800; fax: 617-457-1425).

Blue & Gold Fleet (Pier 39, PO Box Z-2, San Francisco, CA 94133-1011; phone: 800-426-8687 in California; 415-705-5555 elsewhere in the US; 415-705-5444 for recorded information; fax: 415-392-3610).

Boston Harbor Cruises (1 Long Wharf, Boston, MA 02110; phone: 617-227-4320; fax: 617-723-2011).

Camelot Cruises (1 Marine Park, Haddam, CT 06438; phone: 800-52-CRIME or 860-345-8591; fax: 860-345-3856).

Chicago from the Lake (455 E. Illinois St., Suite 361, Chicago, IL 60611; phone: 312-527-2002; fax: 312-527-2313).

Circle Line (Circle Line Marina, Pier 83, W. 42nd St. at the Hudson River, New York, NY 10036; phone: 212-563-3200; fax: 212-563-3347).

Circle Line Statue of Liberty Ferry (17 Battery Pl., Suite 715, New York, NY 10004-1102; phone: 212-269-5755; fax: 212-425-2215).

Clearwater (112 Market St., Poughkeepsie, NY 12601; phone: 914-454-7673; fax: 914-454-7953).

Community Boating (21 Embankment Rd., Boston, MA 02114; phone: 617-523-1038; fax: 617-523-6959).

Delta Queen Steamboat Co. (Robin St. Wharf, 1380 Port of New Orleans Pl., New Orleans, LA 70130-1890; phone: 800-543-1949 for reservations; 504-586-0631 for information; fax: 504-585-0630).

Dolphin Fleet of Provincetown (PO Box 243, Provincetown, MA 02657; phone: 800-826-9300 or 508-349-1900; fax: 508-349-1789).

Flamingo Lodge (1 Flamingo Lodge Hwy., Flamingo, FL 33034-6798; phone: 800-600-3813 or 941-695-3101; fax: 941-695-3921).

Harbor Tours (End of Bay St., Portsmouth, VA 23704; phone: 804-393-4735; fax: 804-397-6609).

Hornblower Dining Yachts (Pier 3, *Ferryboat Santa Rosa,* San Francisco, CA 94111; phone: 415-788-8866 or 310-301-9900; fax: 415-394-8444).

Lake George Steamboat Co. (Steel Pier, Beach Rd., Lake George, NY 12845; phone: 800-553-BOAT or 518-668-5777; fax: 518-668-2015).

Looney's Tavern Productions (PO Box 70, Double Springs, AL 35553; phone: 800-LOONEYS or 205-489-5000; fax: 205-489-3500).

Los Angeles Harbor Cruise (Village Boat House, Berth 78, Ports o' Call Village, San Pedro, CA 90731; phone: 310-831-0996; fax: 310-831-0599).

Maid of the Mist (151 Buffalo Ave., Suite 204, Niagara Falls, NY 14303; phone: 800-261-7801 or 716-284-8897; fax: 716-284-5446).

Maine Windjammer Cruises (PO Box 617, Camden, ME 04843; phone: 800-736-7981 or 207-236-2938; fax: 207-236-3229).

Mercury Chicago's Skyline Cruise Line (Michigan Ave. and Wacker Dr., SW corner of the Michigan Ave. Bridge, Chicago, IL 60601; phone: 312-332-1353 for recorded information).

Mid Lakes Navigation (PO Box 61, Skaneateles, NY 13152; phone: 800-545-4318 or 315-685-8500; fax: 315-685-7566).

Mississippi Belle II (PO Box 1234, Clinton, IA 52733; phone: 800-457-9975 or 319-243-9000; fax: 319-243-4020).

Mystic Seaport Museum (75 Greenmanville Ave., Mystic, CT 06355; phone: 203-572-0711; fax: 203-572-5328; mailing address: PO Box 6000, Mystic, CT 06355-0900).

National Women's Advisory Board on Sailing (c/o *Offshore Sailing School,* 16731 McGregor Blvd., Suite 110, Ft. Myers, FL 33908; phone: 800-221-4326 or 813-454-1700; fax: 813-454-1191).

Nautical Heritage Society (24532 Del Prado Ave., Dana Point, CA 92629; phone: 800-432-2201 or 714-661-1001; fax: 714-240-7842).

New England Aquarium Whale Watch (Central Wharf, Boston, MA 02110-3399; phone: 617-973-5281; fax: 617-720-5098).

New Orleans Paddlewheels (690 Port of New Orleans Pl., New Orleans, LA 70130; phone: 800-445-4109 or 504-529-4567; fax: 504-524-6265).

New Orleans Steamboat Company (2 Canal St., Suite 1300, New Orleans, LA 70130; phone: 800-233-BOAT, 800-365-BOAT, or 504-586-8777; fax: 504-587-0708).

The Oceanic Society (Fort Mason Center, Building E, San Francisco, CA 94123; phone: 800-326-7491 or 415-474-3385; fax: 415-474-3395).

Odyssey Cruises (17 W. 642 Butterfield Rd., Oakbrook Terrace, IL 60181; phone: 800-946-7245 or 708-990-0800; fax: 708-990-3356 or 708-990-7620).

Potomac Riverboat Company (205 The Strand, Alexandria, VA 22314; phone: 703-548-9000; fax: 703-548-9001).

Provincetown Whale Watch (29 Standish St., Provincetown, MA 02657; phone: 800-992-9333 or 508-487-3322; fax: 508-487-1834).

Red & White Fleet (Pier 41, Fisherman's Wharf, San Francisco, CA 94133; phone: 800-BAY-CRUISE, 415-546-BOAT, or 415-546-2700; fax: 415-546-2623).

Riverboat Romance (433 N. Palmetto Ave., Sanford, FL 32771; phone: 800-423-7401 in Florida; 407-321-5091 elsewhere in the US; fax: 407-330-7043).

San Diego Harbor Excursion (1511 Marine Way, Coronado, CA 92118; phone: 800-4-CRUISE or 619-234-4111; fax: 619-552-6165 or 619-552-6150).

Shoreline Sightseeing (474 N. Lakeshore Dr., Suite 3511, Chicago, IL 60611; phone: 312-222-9328; fax: 312-321-0632).

Spirit Cruises (Pier 4, Sixth & Water Sts. SW, Washington, DC 20024; phone: 202-554-8000; fax: 202-484-1330).

Spirit of Chicago (455 E. Illinois St., Suite 461, Chicago, IL 60611; phone: 312-836-7899; fax: 312-836-7889).

Spirit of Philadelphia (Pier 3 at Penn's Landing, Delaware and Market Sts., Philadelphia, PA 19106; phone: 215-923-1419; fax: 215-923-8556).

Wendella Sightseeing Boats (400 N. Michigan Ave., Chicago, IL 60611; phone: 312-337-1446; fax: 312-728-0220).

Yacht Ship Cruise Line (520 Pike St., Suite 1400, Seattle, WA 98101; phone: 800-451-5952 or 206-623-7110; fax: 206-623-7809).

Houseboat Rentals

Afton Cruise Lines (3291 S. St. Croix Trail, Afton, MN 55001; phone: 612-436-8883; fax: 612-436-6859).

Cottonwood Cove Resort & Marina (PO Box 1000, Cottonwood Cove, NV 89046; phone: 800-255-5561; phone/fax: 702-297-1464).

Forever Resorts (PO Box 52038, Phoenix, AZ 85072-2038; phone: 800-255-5561 or 602-968-4349; fax: 602-968-4355).

Great River Houseboats (1009 E. Main, PO Box 247, Wabasha, MN 55981; phone: 612-565-3376).

Holiday Harbor (PO Box 112, O'Brien, CA 96070; phone: 800-776-2628 or 916-238-2383; fax: 916-238-2102).

Lake Powell Resorts & Marinas (PO Box 56909, Phoenix, AZ 85079-6909; phone: 800-528-6154 or 602-278-8888; fax: 602-331-5258).

Minnesota Voyageur Houseboats (10326 Ash River Trail, Orr, MN 55771; phone: 800-253-5475 or 218-374-3571; fax: 218-374-4428).

Northwest Marine Charters (1500 Westlake Ave. N., Suite 110, Seattle, WA 98109; phone: 800-659-3048 or 206-283-3040; fax: 206-283-3041).

Roosevelt Recreational Enterprises (PO Box 5, Coulee Dam, WA 99116; phone: 800-648-5253 or 509-633-0136; fax: 509-633-1026).

Seven Crown Resorts (PO Box 16247, Irvine, CA 92713; phone: 800-752-9669 or 714-474-2100; fax: 714-833-3541).

Silverthorn Resort (PO Box 4205, Redding, CA 96099; phone: 800-332-3044 in California; 916-275-1571 elsewhere in the US; fax: 916-275-1573).

Voyagaire Houseboats (7576 Gold Coast Rd., Crane Lake, MN 55725; phone: 800-882-6287 or 218-993-2333; fax: 218-993-2268).

Traveling by Train

Almost all regularly scheduled passenger trains in the US (other than regional commuter lines) are run by *Amtrak* (phone: 800-USA-RAIL), which serves many major cities across the country. Publications with information on fares, schedules, stations, and routes can be obtained at *Amtrak* ticket offices, by calling the toll-free number above, or by writing to the *Amtrak Distribution Center* (PO Box 7717, Itasca, IL 60143-7717).

Tickets can be purchased at *Amtrak* offices and some commuter railway stations, as well as through travel agents. In some cases, tickets also can be purchased aboard the train (although there usually is a surcharge). For longer trips, two classes of tickets are sold—sleepers and coach—and reservations are required for both. Reservations also are required on some of *Amtrak*'s express inter-city trains, such as the *Metroliner,* which operates between New York City and Washington, DC, with stops in Baltimore (Maryland), Philadelphia (Pennsylvania), and Wilmington (Delaware). On longer routes, many trains have dining cars and bar cars; on shorter routes, there often is a snack bar or "cafe" car.

On long-distance trips, each passenger can bring two carry-on bags aboard, and can check three pieces of luggage, with a weight limit of 50 pounds per bag. Passengers with luggage exceeding these weight limits are charged an excess baggage fee (usually $7 per bag). Additional luggage can be checked for $10 per item. *Amtrak* stations in major cities often have attendants or redcaps to help with luggage.

The *Sunset Limited* train provides direct transcontinental service, via New Orleans (Louisiana), between Los Angeles (California) and Miami

(Florida). For all other transcontinental routes, passengers must make connections. The *Auto Train,* a special train that carries passengers and automobiles, provides daily nonstop service between Lorton (Virginia, near Washington, DC) and Sanford (Florida); separate fares are charged for passengers and vehicles.

Amtrak's "All Aboard America" fares include round-trip transportation between any two *Amtrak* stations within specified zones in the continental US. Up to three stopovers are allowed, as long as travel is completed within 45 days of the scheduled departure date. *Amtrak*'s *Great American Vacations* division (phone: 800-321-8684) offers rail/hotel packages that may include airfare and rental cars; information on tours also is provided.

Tours geared to visitors sometimes also are offered by regional lines, and various companies and organizations offer rail packages. Some packages feature luxury accommodations aboard private or chartered cars; others include excursions aboard particular railways and other travel services. Additional information on rail excursions is provided in *Rail Ventures: Complete Guide to Train Travel in North America,* by Jack Swanson and Jeff Karsh (Travis Isle, PO Box 583, Niwot, CO 80544; phone: 206-282-3254).

Tour Companies and Organizations

Accent on Travel (112 N. Fifth St., Klamath Falls, OR 97601; phone: 503-885-7330).

American Association of Private Railroad Car Owners (*AAPRCO;* Attention: Diane Elliott, 106 North Carolina Ave. SE, Washington, DC 20003; phone: 202-547-5696; fax: 202-546-3419).

Key Holidays (1141 Bont La., Walnut Creek, CA 94596; phone: 800-783-0783 or 510-945-8938; fax: 510-256-7597).

Slotsy Tours and Travel (1821 W. Commonwealth Ave., Suite B, Fullerton, CA 92633; phone: 800-336-2844 or 714-870-8641; fax: 714-870-8241).

Trains Unlimited Tours (PO Box 1997, Portola, CA 96122; phone: 800-359-4870 or 916-836-1745; fax: 916-836-1748).

Traveling by Bus

Buses are the most frequently used and economical mode of mass transportation in the US. *Greyhound Lines* (phone: 800-231-2222) and many smaller independent companies comprise the country's most comprehensive transportation network.

Tickets are purchased at bus stations, from a central office, or (in smaller towns) from a local business acting as an agent. On rural routes, tickets also can be bought from the bus driver (exact change may be required). Tickets are sold on a first-come, first-served basis. Reservations are not required, although tickets (but not specific seats) often can be reserved.

Greyhound's economical "Ameripass" permits unlimited travel for specified periods (7, 15, or 30 days) on the company's routes—and often the routes of smaller, connecting bus lines. Various promotional fares also are offered from time to time, although these discounted fares usually are not available on holidays. On many long-distance trips, passengers can stop off en route and continue their trip aboard another bus, as long as the entire journey is completed before the ticket expires. Most interstate long-distance buses have air conditioning, heating, toilets, adjustable seats, and reading lamps.

Traveling by Car

Driving is the most flexible way to explore the country. With its vast network of roads, the US is especially well suited for touring by car.

MAPS

Good maps often are available free from state and local tourist offices. Maps of all kinds—from interstate touring to detailed topographical maps–can be ordered from *Map Link* (25 E. Mason St., Suite 201, Santa Barbara, CA 93101; phone: 805-965-4402; fax: 800-MAP-SPOT or 805-962-0884).

Among the best resources for planning a driving route in the US are the following:

AAA US Road Atlas (*American Automobile Association;* 1000 AAA Dr., Heathrow, FL 32746-5063; phone: 407-444-7000; main fax: 407-444-7380; travel department fax: 407-444-4584).

Atlas and Gazetteer map series (DeLorme Mapping, PO Box 298, Lower Main St., Freeport, ME 04032; phone: 800-227-1656 or 207-865-4171; fax: 207-865-9291).

Rand McNally Road Atlas: US, Canada and Mexico (Rand McNally, 8255 N. Central Park Ave., Skokie, IL 60076; phone: 800-333-0136 or 847-329-8100; fax: 847-673-0813).

USA: The East and *USA: The West* atlases (Hildebrand, Schönberger Weg 15-17, Frankfurt 60488, Germany; phone: 49-69-762031).

AUTOMOBILE CLUBS AND BREAKDOWNS

To protect yourself in case of breakdowns while driving, and for travel information and other benefits, consider joining a reputable automobile club. Before joining any club, make sure it provides services throughout the US.

Automobile Clubs

Allstate Motor Club (Customer Service, PO Box 3094, Arlington Heights, IL 60006; phone: 800-347-8880).

American Automobile Association (*AAA;* 1000 AAA Dr., Heathrow, FL 32746-5063; phone: 407-444-7000; main fax: 407-444-7380; travel department fax: 407-444-4584).

Amoco Motor Club (PO Box 9043, Des Moines, IA 50369-9045; phone: 800-334-3300 or 515-226-5700; fax: 515-226-5735).

Exxon Travel Club (PO Box 3633, Houston, TX 77253; phone: 800-833-9966; fax: 713-680-5047).

Ford Auto Club (Membership Services Division, PO Box 224688, Dallas, TX 75222-4688; phone: 800-348-5220; fax: 214-541-3508).

Montgomery Ward Auto Club (200 N. Martingale Rd., Schaumburg, IL 60173; phone: 800-621-5151 or 708-605-3000).

Motor Club of America (95 Route 17 S., Paramus, NJ 07653-0931; phone: 800-242-0332 or 201-291-2000; fax: 201-291-2132).

United States Auto Club (Motoring Division, PO Box 660460, Dallas, TX 75266-0460; phone: 800-348-5058 or 800-2-FIX-CAR; fax: 214-541-3991).

INFO ON THE GO

Some car rental companies (such as *Avis* and *Hertz*) offer the new satellite tracking system in certain models. This system allows travelers to identify their location on a computer-generated map and plot a route to the desired destination. In addition, *Traveler's Checklist* (335 Cornwall Bridge Rd., Sharon, CT 06069; phone: 800-842-3064 or 860-364-0144; fax: 860-364-0369) sells the *Road Whiz Ultra,* a hand-held computer that provides information on restaurants, motels, gas stations, sources of medical assistance, and other services located near major highways, as well as useful statewide numbers.

RENTING A CAR

You can rent a car through a travel agent or national rental firm before leaving home, or from a regional or local company upon arrival. Reserve in advance.

Most car rental companies require a credit card, although some will accept a substantial cash deposit. The minimum age to rent a car is set by the company; some also may impose special conditions on drivers above a certain age. Electing to pay for collision or loss damage waiver (CDW or LDW) protection will add to the cost of renting a car, but releases you from full financial liability for the vehicle. Note that optional CDW/LDW insurance is not offered in states such as Illinois and New York, where companies are required by law to include such coverage in the basic rental package. Additional costs may include drop-off charges or one-way service fees.

National Car Rental Companies

Ace Rent-A-Car (phone: 800-242-7368).

Agency Rent-A-Car (phone: 216-349-1000).

Alamo Rent A Car (phone: 800-327-9633).

Avis Rent A Car (phone: 800-331-1212).

Budget Rent A Car (phone: 800-527-0700).

Dollar Rent A Car (phone: 800-800-4000).
Enterprise Rent-A-Car (phone: 800-325-8007).
Hertz Rent A Car (phone: 800-654-3131).
Holiday Autos (phone: 800-422-7737 or 909-949-1737).
National Car Rental (phone: 800-CAR-RENT).
Payless Car Rental (phone: 800-PAYLESS).
Sears Rent A Car (phone: 800-527-0770).
Snappy Car Rental (phone: 800-669-4802).
Thrifty Car Rental (phone: 800-367-2277).
U-Save Auto Rental (phone: 800-272-USAV).
Value Rent-A-Car (phone: 800-327-2501).

NOTE

Rent-A-Wreck **(call 800-421-7253 for the locations of franchises nationwide) rents cars that are well worn but (presumably) mechanically sound. Other rental and leasing agents specialize in luxury models—check the local yellow pages.**

Package Tours

A package tour is a collection of travel services that can be purchased in a single transaction. Its principal advantages are convenience and economy—you don't have to make individual arrangements for each service, and the cost usually is lower than that of the same services purchased separately. Tour programs generally can be divided into two categories: escorted or locally hosted (with a set itinerary) and independent (which usually are more flexible).

When considering a package tour, read the brochure *carefully* to determine exactly what is included and any conditions that may apply, and check the company's record with the *Better Business Bureau.* The *United States Tour Operators Association* (*USTOA;* 211 E. 51st St., Suite 12B, New York, NY 10022; phone: 212-750-7371; fax: 212-421-1285) also can be helpful in determining a package tour operator's reliability. As with charter flights, to safeguard your funds, always make your check out to the company's escrow account.

Many tour operators offer packages focused on special interests such as the arts, nature study, or specific sports. *All Adventure Vacations* (5589 Arapahoe, Suite 208, Boulder, CO 80303; phone: 800-537-4025 or 303-440-7924; fax: 303-440-4160) represents such specialized packagers. Many also are listed in the *Specialty Travel Index* (305 San Anselmo Ave., Suite 313, San Anselmo, CA 94960; phone: 415-459-4900 in California; 800-442-4922 elsewhere in the US; fax: 415-459-4974).

Below is a list of tour operators offering packages in the US. Note that companies described as wholesalers accept bookings only through travel agents. For information on companies and organizations that offer local sightseeing tours, see *Sources and Resources,* in THE CITIES, or contact the local tourist authorities.

Package Tour Operators

ABEC (1550 Alpine Vista Court, Fairbanks, AK 99712; phone: 907-457-8907; fax: 907-457-6689).

Abercrombie & Kent (1520 Kensington Rd., Suite 212, Oak Brook, IL 60521; phone: 800-323-7308 or 708-954-2944; fax: 708-954-3324). Wholesaler.

Above the Clouds Trekking (PO Box 398, Worcester, MA 01602; phone: 800-233-4499 or 508-799-4499; fax: 508-797-4779).

Adventure Center (1311 63rd St., Suite 200, Emeryville, CA 94608; phone: 510-654-1879 in northern California; 800-227-8747 elsewhere in the US; fax: 510-654-4200).

Adventure Golf Holidays (815 North Rd., Westfield, MA 01085; phone: 800-628-9655 or 413-568-2855; fax: 413-562-3621).

Adventure Vacations (10612 Beaver Dam Rd., Hunt Valley, MD 21030-2205; phone: 410-785-3500 in the Baltimore area; 800-638-9040 elsewhere in the US; fax: 410-584-2771). Wholesaler.

Adventures in Golf (11 Northeastern Blvd., Suite 360, Nashua, NH 03062; phone: 603-882-8367; fax: 603-595-6514).

Alaska Airlines Vacations (PO Box 68900, Seattle, WA 98168-0900; phone: 800-468-2248; fax: 206-433-3374).

Alaska Sightseeing/Cruise West (Fourth and Battery Building, Suite 700, Seattle, WA 98121; phone: 800-426-7702 or 206-441-8687; fax: 206-441-4757).

Allegro Enterprises (900 West End Ave., Suite 12C, New York, NY 10025; phone: 800-666-3553 or 212-666-6700; fax: 212-666-7451).

American Airlines FlyAAway Vacations (offices throughout the US; phone: 800-321-2121).

American Museum of Natural History Discovery Tours (Central Park W. at 79th St., New York, NY 10024; phone: 800-462-8687 or 212-769-5700; fax: 212-769-5755).

American Wilderness Experience (PO Box 1486, Boulder, CO 80306; phone: 800-444-0099 or 303-444-2622; fax: 303-444-3999).

Anglers Travel (3100 Mill St., Suite 206, Reno, NV 89502; phone: 800-624-8429 or 702-324-0580; fax: 702-324-0583).

Angling Travel and Tours (c/o *John Eustice & Associates,* 1445 SW 84th Ave., Portland, OR 97225; phone: 800-288-0886 or 503-297-2468; fax: 503-297-3048).

Any Mountain Tours (1012 S. Cleveland St., Arlington, VA 22204; phone: 800-296-2000 or 703-979-4300; fax: 703-979-2395).

Apple Vacations East (7 Campus Blvd., Newtown Sq., PA 19073; phone: 800-727-3400 or 610-359-6500; fax: 610-359-6524). Wholesaler.

Backcountry (PO Box 4029, Bozeman, MT 59772; phone: 800-575-1540 or 406-586-3556; fax: 406-586-4288).

Backroads (1516 Fifth St., Berkeley, CA 94710; phone: 800-462-2848 or 510-527-1555; fax: 510-527-1444).

BCT Scenic Walking (7777 Fay Ave., Suite 100, La Jolla, CA 92037; phone: 800-473-1210 or 619-456-2277; fax: 619-456-2299).

Bike & Cruise Tours (2130 NE Hogan Dr., Gresham, OR 97030; phone: 503-667-4053; fax: 503-669-8251).

Biss Tours (62-85 Woodhaven Blvd., Rego Park, NY 11374; phone: 800-964-BISS in New Jersey; 718-426-4000 elsewhere in the US).

Brendan Tours (15137 Califa St., Van Nuys, CA 91411; phone: 800-421-8446 or 818-785-9696; fax: 818-902-9876). Wholesaler.

Brooks Country Cycling (140 W. 83rd St., New York, NY 10024; phone: 212-874-5151 in New York, New Jersey, and Connecticut; 800-284-8954 elsewhere in the US; fax: 212-874-5286).

Butterfield & Robinson (70 Bond St., Suite 300, Toronto, Ontario M5B 1X3, Canada; phone: 800-387-1147 or 416-864-1354; fax: 416-864-0541).

California Academy of Sciences (Attention: Travel Division, Golden Gate Park, San Francisco, CA 94118; phone: 415-750-7222; fax: 415-750-7346).

Call of the Wild (2519 Cedar St., Berkeley, CA 94708; phone: 800-742-9494 or 510-849-9292; fax: 510-644-3811).

Capitol Tours (PO Box 4241, Springfield, IL 62708; phone: 800-252-8924 for reservations; 217-529-8166 for information; fax: 217-529-5831).

Caravan Tours (401 N. Michigan Ave., Chicago, IL 60611; phone: 800-CARAVAN or 312-321-9800; fax: 312-321-9810). Wholesaler.

Cartan Tours (3033 Ogden Ave., Lisle, IL 60532; phone: 800-422-7826 or 708-571-1400; fax: 708-778-0310). Wholesaler.

Ceiba Adventures (PO Box 2274, Flagstaff, AZ 86003; phone: 520-527-0171; fax: 520-527-8127).

Central Holidays *and* ***Steve Lohr's Holidays*** (206 Central Ave., Jersey City, NJ 07307; phone: 800-935-5000 or 201-798-5777; fax: 201-963-0966).

Certified Vacations (110 E. Broward Blvd., Ft. Lauderdale, FL 33301; phone: 800-233-7260 or 954-522-1440; fax: 954-357-4672).

Classic Adventures (PO Box 153, Hamlin, NY 14464-0153; phone: 800-777-8090 or 716-964-8488; fax: 716-964-7297).

Classic America *and* ***Classic Hawaii*** (1 N. First St., San Jose, CA 95113; phone: 800-221-3949 or 408-287-4550; fax: 408-287-9272). Wholesaler.

Collette Tours (162 Middle St., Pawtucket, RI 02860; phone: 800-752-2655 in New England; 800-832-4656 elsewhere in the US; fax: 401-727-4745).

Contiki Holidays (300 Plaza Alicante, Suite 900, Garden Grove, CA 92640; phone: 800-266-8454 or 714-740-0808; fax: 714-740-0818). Wholesaler.

Continental Vacations (offices throughout the US; phone: 800-634-5555).

Corliss Tours (436 W. Foothill Blvd., Monrovia, CA 91016; phone: 800-456-5717 or 818-359-5358; fax: 818-359-0724).

Creative World Rallies and Caravans (4005 Toulouse St., New Orleans, LA 70119; phone: 800-732-8337 or 504-486-7259; fax: 504-483-8830).

Dailey-Thorp (330 W. 58th St., New York, NY 10019-1817; phone: 212-307-1555; fax: 212-974-1420).

Dan Dipert Tours (PO Box 580, Arlington, TX 76004-0580; phone: 800-433-5335 or 817-543-3710; fax: 817-543-3728).

Delta's Dream Vacations (PO Box 1525, Ft. Lauderdale, FL 33302; phone: 800-872-7786).

Domenico Tours (751 Broadway, Bayonne, NJ 07002; phone: 800-554-8687, 201-823-8687, or 212-757-8687; fax: 201-823-9855).

Dvorak's Kayak and Rafting Expeditions (17921 US Hwy. 285, Nathrop, CO 81236; phone: 800-824-3795 or 719-539-6851; fax: 719-539-3378).

Earthwatch (680 Mt. Auburn St., PO Box 403BG, Watertown, MA 02272; phone: 800-776-0188 or 617-926-8200; fax: 617-926-8532).

Edwards & Edwards (50 Main St., Third Floor, White Plains, NY 10606; phone: 800-223-6108 or 914-328-2150; fax: 914-328-2752).

Equitour (PO Box 807, Dubois, WY 82513; phone: 307-455-3363 in Wyoming; 800-545-0019 elsewhere in the US; fax: 307-455-2354).

Experience Plus (1925 Wallenberg Dr., Ft. Collins, CO 80526; phone/fax: 800-685-4565 or 970-484-8489).

Eye of the Whale/Hawaiian Adventure Tours (PO Box 1269, Kapa'au, HI 96755; phone: 800-659-3544 or 808-889-0227; fax: 808-889-0227).

Far Flung Adventures (PO Box 377, Terlingua, TX 79852; phone: 800-359-4138 or 915-371-2489; fax: 915-371-2325).

Far Horizons (PO Box 91900, Albuquerque, NM 87199-1900; phone: 800-552-4575 or 505-343-9400; fax: 505-343-8076).

Fishing International (4775 Sonoma Hwy., Santa Rosa, CA 95409; phone: 800-950-4242 or 707-539-3366; fax: 707-539-1320).

FITS Equestrian (685 Lateen Rd., Solvang, CA 93463; phone: 800-666-3487 or 805-688-9494; fax: 805-688-2943).

Forum Travel International (91 Gregory La., Suite 21, Pleasant Hill, CA 94523; phone: 510-671-2900; fax: 510-671-2993 or 510-946-1500).

Frontiers International (100 Logan Rd., Wexford, PA 15090-0959; phone: 412-935-1577 in Pennsylvania; 800-245-1950 elsewhere in the US; fax: 412-935-5388).

Funjet Vacations (PO Box 1460, Milwaukee, WI 53201-1460; phone: 800-558-3050 for reservations; 800-558-3060 for customer service). Wholesaler.

Gadabout Tours (700 E. Tahquitz Canyon Way, Palm Springs, CA 92262; phone: 800-952-5068 or 619-325-5556; fax: 619-325-5127).

Globetrotters SuperCities (139 Main St., Cambridge, MA 02142; phone: 800-333-1234 or 617-621-9911; fax: 617-577-8380). Wholesaler.

Globus** and **Cosmos (5301 S. Federal Circle, Littleton, CO 80123-2980; phone: 800-221-0090 for reservations; 800-851-0728 for information; or 303-797-2800; fax: 303-798-5441). Wholesaler.

Golf International (275 Madison Ave., Suite 1819, New York, NY 10016; phone: 212-986-9176 in the New York City metropolitan area; 800-833-1389 elsewhere in the US; fax: 212-986-3720).

Golfing Holidays (10 Rollins Rd., Millbrae, CA 94030; phone: 800-652-7847 or 415-697-0230; fax: 415-697-8687).

Golfpac (417 Whooping Loop, Suite 1701, Altamonte Springs, FL 32701; phone: 800-327-0878 or 407-260-2288; fax: 407-260-8989).

Grand Slam Tennis Tours (222 Milwaukee St., Suite 407, Denver, CO 80206; phone: 800-289-3333 or 303-321-1760; fax: 303-321-1771).

Gray Line Tours (offices throughout the US; phone: 800-243-8353).

Hiking Holidays (PO Box 750, Bristol, VT 05443-0750; phone: 800-537-3850 or 802-453-4816; fax: 802-453-4806).

Horizon Air Holidays (PO Box 48309, Seattle, WA 98148; phone: 800-547-9308; fax: 206-248-6336).

International Bicycle Tours (PO Box 754, Essex, CT 06426; phone: 203-767-7005; fax: 203-767-3090).

INTRAV (7711 Bonhomme Ave., St. Louis, MO 63105-1961; phone: 800-456-8100 or 314-727-0500; fax: 314-727-9354).

Jefferson Tours (1206 Currie Ave., Minneapolis, MN 55403; phone: 800-767-7433 or 612-338-4174; fax: 612-359-3491).

Joseph Van Os Photo Safaris (PO Box 655, Vashon Island, WA 98070; phone: 206-463-5383; fax: 206-463-5484).

Kerrville Tours (PO Box 79, Shreveport, LA 71161-0079; phone: 800-442-8705 or 318-227-2882; fax: 318-227-2486).

Le Ob's Tours (4635 Touro St., New Orleans, LA 70122-3933; phone: 800-827-0932 or 504-288-3478; fax: 504-288-8517).

Liberty Travel (for the nearest location, contact the central office: 69 Spring St., Ramsey, NJ 07446; phone: 201-934-3500; fax: 201-934-3888).

Lismore Tours (106 E. 31st St., New York, NY 10016; phone: 212-685-0100 in New York State; 800-547-6673 elsewhere in the US; fax: 212-685-0614).

M.A.D. World Adventure Club (PO Box 400, Ingersoll, Ontario N5C 3V3, Canada; phone: 519-485-1306).

Marathon Tours (108 Main St., Boston, MA 02129; phone: 800-444-4097 or 617-242-7845; fax: 617-242-7686).

Maupintour (PO Box 807, Lawrence, KS 66044; phone: 800-255-4266 or 913-843-1211; fax: 913-843-8351). Wholesaler.

Mayflower (1225 Warren Ave., PO Box 490, Downers Grove, IL 60515; phone: 800-323-7604 or 708-960-3430; fax: 708-960-3575).

Mountain Travel-Sobek (6420 Fairmount Ave., El Cerrito, CA 94530; phone: 510-527-8100 in California; 800-227-2384 elsewhere in the US; fax: 510-525-7710).

MountainFit (PO Box 6188, Bozeman, MT 59771; phone: 800-926-5700 or 406-585-3506; fax: 406-585-3481).

Nantahala Outdoor Center Adventure Travel (13077 Hwy. 19 W., Bryson City, NC 28713-9114; phone: 800-232-7238 for reservations; 704-488-2175 for information; fax: 704-488-2498).

National Outdoor Leadership School (288 Main St., Lander, WY 82520; phone: 307-332-6973; fax: 307-332-1220).

Natural Habitat Adventures (2945 Center Green Court S., Boulder, CO 80301; phone: 800-543-8917 or 303-449-3711; fax: 303-449-3712).

Nature Expeditions International (PO Box 11496, Eugene, OR 97440; phone: 800-869-0639 or 503-484-6529; fax: 503-484-6531).

New England Hiking Holidays (PO Box 1648, N. Conway, NH 03860; phone: 800-869-0949 or 603-356-9696).

New England Vacation Tours (PO Box 560, W. Dover, VT 05356; phone: 800-742-7669 or 802-464-2076; fax: 802-464-2629). Wholesaler.

Northwest World Vacations (c/o *MLT,* 5130 Hwy. 101, Minnetonka, MN 55345; phone: 800-328-0025 or 612-989-5000; fax: 612-474-0725). Wholesaler.

Oceanic Society Expeditions (Ft. Mason Center, Building E, San Francisco, CA 94123; phone: 800-326-7491 or 415-441-1106; fax: 415-474-3395).

Olson Travelworld (1145 Clark St., Stevens Point, WI 54481; phone: 800-421-2255, 800-826-4026, or 715-345-0505; fax: 715-345-2394). Wholesaler.

Outdoor Bound (18 Stuyvesant Oval, Suite 1A, New York, NY 10009; phone: 800-724-8801 or 212-505-1020; fax: 212-979-5342).

Outland Adventures (PO Box 16343, Seattle, WA 98116; phone/fax: 206-932-7012).

PanAngling Travel Service (180 N. Michigan Ave., Room 303, Chicago, IL 60601; phone: 800-533-4353 or 312-263-0328; fax: 312-263-5246).

Panorama Tours (600 N. Sprigg St., Cape Girardeau, MO 63701; phone: 800-962-8687 in Missouri and adjacent states; 314-335-9098 elsewhere in the US; fax: 314-335-7824).

Perillo Tours (577 Chestnut Ridge Rd., Woodcliff Lake, NJ 07675; phone: 800-431-1515 or 201-307-1234; fax: 201-307-1808).

Pleasant Holidays (2404 Townsgate Rd., Westlake Village, CA 91361; phone: 800-242-9244 or 818-991-3390; fax: 805-495-4972).

Progressive Travels (224 W. Galer Ave., Suite C, Seattle, WA 98119; phone: 800-245-2229 or 206-285-1987; fax: 206-285-1988).

Questers Tours & Travel (581 Park Ave. S., Suite 1201, New York, NY 10016; phone: 800-468-8668 or 212-251-0444; fax: 212-251-0890).

REI Adventures (PO Box 1938, Sumner, WA 98390-0800; phone: 800-622-2236 or 206-891-2631; fax: 206-395-4744).

Rocky Mountain Worldwide Cycle Tours (PO Box 1978, Canmore, Alberta T0L 0M0, Canada; phone: 800-661-2453 or 403-678-6770; fax: 403-678-4451).

See & Sea Travel (50 Francisco St., Suite 205, San Francisco, CA 94133; phone: 415-434-3400 in California; 800-348-9778 elsewhere in the US; fax: 415-434-3409).

Sierra Club Outings (730 Polk St., San Francisco, CA 94109; phone: 415-923-5630).

Slickrock Adventures (PO Box 1400, Moab, UT 84532; phone: 800-390-5715; phone/fax: 801-259-6996).

Smithsonian Associates Study Tours (1100 Jefferson Dr. SW, Room 3045, Washington, DC 20560; phone: 202-357-4700; fax: 202-786-2315).

Sportsworld International (3350 Cumberland Circle, Suite 1940, Atlanta, GA 30339; phone: 770-850-3260; fax: 770-850-3261). Wholesaler.

Steppingstone Environmental Education Tours (PO Box 373, Narberth, PA 19072; phone: 800-874-8784 or 610-649-3891; fax: 610-649-3428).

Steve Currey Expeditions (PO Box 1574, Provo, UT 84603; phone: 800-937-7238; phone/fax: 801-224-5715).

Sunmakers (S. Tower, 100 W. Harrison, Suite 350, Seattle, WA 98119; phone: 800-841-4321 or 206-216-2900; fax: 800-323-2231 or 206-216-2906). Wholesaler.

Tauck Tours (PO Box 5027, Westport, CT 06881; phone: 800-468-2825 or 203-226-6911; fax: 203-221-6828).

Thomas Cook Vacations (100 Cambridge Park Dr., Cambridge, MA 02140; phone: 800-846-6272 or 617-868-2666; fax: 617-349-1094).

TNT Vacations (2 Charlesgate W., Boston, MA 02215; phone: 800-262-0123 or 617-262-9200; fax: 617-638-3445).

Tours and Travel Odyssey (230 E. McClellan Ave., Livingston, NJ 07039; phone: 800-527-2989 or 201-992-5459; fax: 201-994-1618).

Tours by Andrea (2838 Touro St., New Orleans, LA 70122; phone: 800-535-2732 or 504-942-5708; fax: 504-942-5737).

Travel Impressions (465 Smith St., Farmingdale, NY 11735; phone: 800-284-0044 or 516-845-8000). Wholesaler.

TravelTours International (250 W. 49th St., Suite 600, New York, NY 10019; phone: 800-767-8777 or 212-262-0700; fax: 212-944-5854). Wholesaler.

TravelWild International (PO Box 1637, Vashon Island, WA 98070; phone: 800-368-0077 or 206-463-5362; fax: 206-463-5484).

Trek America (PO Box 189, Rockaway, NJ 07866; phone: 800-221-0596 or 201-983-1144; fax: 201-983-8551).

Tropical Adventures Travel (111 Second Ave. N., Seattle, WA 98109; phone: 800-247-3483 or 206-441-3483; fax: 206-441-5431).

TWA Getaway Vacations (Getaway Vacation Center, 10 E. Stow Rd., Marlton, NJ 08053; phone: 800-GETAWAY; fax: 609-985-4125).

United Vacations (PO Box 24580, Milwaukee, WI 53224-0580; phone: 800-328-6877; fax: 414-351-5256).

Vermont Bicycle Touring (PO Box 711, Bristol, VT 05443-0711; phone: 800-245-3868 or 802-453-4811; fax: 802-453-4806).

Victor Emanuel Nature Tours (PO Box 33008, Austin, TX 78764; phone: 800-328-VENT or 512-328-5221; fax: 512-328-2919).

Voyagers International (PO Box 915, Ithaca, NY 14851; phone: 800-633-0299 or 607-257-3091; fax: 607-257-3699).

Wide World of Golf (PO Box 5217, Carmel, CA 93921; phone: 800-214-4653 or 408-624-6667; fax: 408-625-9671).

Wilderness: Alaska/Mexico (1231 Sundance Loop, Department BB, Fairbanks, AK 99709; phone/fax: 907-479-8203).

Wilderness Travel (801 Allston Way, Berkeley, CA 94710; phone: 800-368-2794 or 510-548-0420; fax: 510-548-0347).

Wildland Adventures (3516 NE 155th St., Seattle, WA 98155; phone: 800-345-4453 or 206-365-0686; fax: 206-363-6615).

Willard's Adventure Club (PO Box 10, Barrie, Ontario L4M 4S9, Canada; phone: 705-737-1881; fax: 705-737-5123).

Yamnuska (PO Box 1920, Canmore, Alberta T0L 0M0, Canada; phone: 403-678-4164; fax: 403-678-4450).

Yankee Holidays (435 Newbury St., Suite 210, Danvers, MA 01923-1065; phone: 800-225-2550 or 508-750-9688; fax: 508-750-9692). Wholesaler.

Insurance

The first person with whom you should discuss travel insurance is your own insurance broker. You may discover that the insurance you already carry protects you adequately while traveling and that you need little additional coverage. If you charge travel services, the credit card company also may provide some insurance coverage (and other safeguards). Below is a list of the basic types of travel insurance and some of the companies specializing in such policies.

Types of Travel Insurance

Automobile insurance: Provides collision, theft, property damage, and personal liability protection while driving.

Baggage and personal effects insurance: Protects your bags and their contents in case of damage or theft at any point during your travels.

Default and/or bankruptcy insurance: Provides coverage in the event of default and/or bankruptcy on the part of the tour operator, airline, or other travel supplier.

Flight insurance: Covers accidental injury or death while flying.

Personal accident and sickness insurance: Covers cases of illness, injury, or death in an accident while traveling.

Trip cancellation and interruption insurance: Guarantees a refund if you must cancel a trip; may reimburse you for additional travel costs incurred in catching up with a tour or traveling home early.

Combination policies: Include any or all of the above.

Travel Insurance Providers

Access America International (PO Box 90315, Richmond, VA 23230; phone: 800-284-8300 or 804-285-3300; fax: 804-673-1491).

Carefree (c/o *Berkely Care,* Arm Coverage, 100 Garden City Plaza, Fifth Floor, PO Box 9366, Garden City, NY 11530; phone: 800-645-2424 or 516-294-0220; fax: 516-294-0268).

NEAR Services (PO Box 1339, Calumet City, IL 60409; phone: 708-868-6700 in the Chicago area; 800-654-6700 elsewhere in the US; fax: 708-868-6706).

Tele-Trip (c/o *Mutual of Omaha,* 3201 Farnam St., Omaha, NE 68131; phone: 800-228-9792 or 402-351-5754; fax: 402-351-2456).

Travel Assistance International (c/o *Worldwide Assistance Services,* 1133 15th St. NW, Suite 400, Washington, DC 20005-2710; phone: 800-821-2828 or 202-331-1609; fax: 202-331-1530).

Travel Guard International (1145 Clark St., Stevens Point, WI 54481; phone: 800-826-1300 or 715-345-0505; fax: 800-955-8785).

Travel Insured International (PO Box 280568, East Hartford, CT 06128-0568; phone: 800-243-3174 or 860-528-7663; fax: 860-528-8005).

Disabled Travelers

Make travel arrangements well in advance. Specify to all services involved the nature of your disability to determine if there are accommodations and facilities that meet your needs.

Publications

Access Travel: A Guide to the Accessibility of Airport Terminals (Consumer Information Center, Department 575A, Pueblo, CO 81009; phone: 719-948-3334; fax: 719-948-9724).

Air Transportation of Handicapped Persons (Publication #AC-120-32; *US Department of Transportation,* Distribution Unit, Utilization and Storage Section, M-45.3, 33-410 75th Ave., Landover, MD 20785; phone: 301-322-4961; fax: 301-386-5394).

The Diabetic Traveler (PO Box 8223 RW, Stamford, CT 06905; phone: 203-327-5832; fax: 203-975-1748).

Directory of Travel Agencies for the Disabled *and* ***Travel for the Disabled,*** both by Helen Hecker (Twin Peaks Press, PO Box 129, Vancouver, WA 98666; phone: 800-637-2256 for orders; 360-694-2462 for information; fax: 360-696-3210).

The Disabled Driver's Mobility Guide (*American Automobile Association,* Traffic Safety Department, 1000 AAA Dr., Heathrow, FL 32746-5063; phone: 407-444-7961; fax: 407-444-7956).

Handicapped Travel Newsletter (PO Drawer 269, Athens, TX 75751; phone: 941-540-7612; fax: 941-540-7238).

Handi-Travel: A Resource Book for Disabled and Elderly Travellers, by Cinnie Noble (*Easter Seals/March of Dimes National Council,* 90 Eglinton Ave. E., Suite 511, Toronto, Ontario M4P 2Y3, Canada; phone/TDD: 416-932-8382; fax: 416-932-9844).

On the Go, Go Safely, Plan Ahead (*American Diabetes Association,* National Service Center, 1660 Duke St., Alexandria, VA 22314; phone: 800-232-3472 or 703-549-1500; fax: 703-549-6995).

Travel for the Patient with Chronic Obstructive Pulmonary Disease (c/o Dr. Harold Silver, 1601 18th St. NW, Washington, DC 20009; phone: 202-667-0134; fax: 202-667-0148).

Travel Tips for Hearing-Impaired People (*American Academy of Otolaryngology,* 1 Prince St., Alexandria, VA 22314; phone: 703-836-4444; fax: 703-683-5100).

Travel Tips for People with Arthritis (*Arthritis Foundation,* 1314 Spring St. NW, Atlanta, GA 30309; phone: 800-283-7800 or 404-872-7100; fax: 404-872-0457).

The Travelin' Talk Newsletter (*Travelin' Talk,* PO Box 3534, Clarksville, TN 37043-3534; phone: 615-552-6670; fax: 615-552-1182).

Traveling Like Everybody Else: A Practical Guide for Disabled Travelers, by Jacqueline Freedman and Susan Gersten (Modan Publishing, PO Box 1202, Bellmore, NY 11710; phone: 516-679-1380; fax: 516-679-1448).

The Wheelchair Traveler, by Douglass R. Annand (123 Ball Hill Rd., Milford, NH 03055; phone: 603-673-4539).

Wheelchair Vagabond, by John Nelson (Twin Peaks Press, PO Box 129, Vancouver, WA 98666; phone: 800-637-CALM for orders; 360-694-2462 for information; fax: 360-696-3210).

Organizations

ACCENT on Living (PO Box 700, Bloomington, IL 61702; phone: 800-787-8444 or 309-378-2961; fax: 309-378-4420).

Access: The Foundation for Accessibility by the Disabled (1109 Linden St., Valley Stream, NY 11580; phone/fax: 516-568-2715).

American Foundation for the Blind (11 Penn Plaza, Suite 300, New York, NY 10001; phone: 800-232-5463 or 212-502-7600; fax: 212-502-7777).

Mobility International (main office: 25 Rue de Manchester, Brussels B-1070, Belgium; phone: 32-2-410-6297; fax: 32-2-410-6874; US address: *MIUSA,* PO Box 10767, Eugene, OR 97440; phone/TDD: 503-343-1284; fax: 503-343-6812).

MossRehab Hospital Travel Information Service (telephone referrals only; phone: 215-456-9600; TDD: 215-456-9602).

National Rehabilitation Information Center (8455 Colesville Rd., Suite 935, Silver Spring, MD 20910-3319; phone: 301-588-9284; fax: 301-587-1967).

Paralyzed Veterans of America (*PVA;* PVA/Access to the Skies Program, 801 18th St. NW, Washington, DC 20006-3585; phone: 202-872-1300 in Washington, DC; 800-424-8200 elsewhere in the US; fax: 202-785-4452).

Society for the Advancement of Travel for the Handicapped (*SATH;* 347 Fifth Ave., Suite 610, New York, NY 10016; phone: 212-447-7284; fax: 212-725-8253).

Package Tour Operators

Accessible Journeys (35 W. Sellers Ave., Ridley Park, PA 19078; phone: 800-846-4537 or 610-521-0339; fax: 610-521-6959).

Accessible Tours/Directions Unlimited (Attention: Lois Bonanni, 720 N. Bedford Rd., Bedford Hills, NY 10507; phone: 800-533-5343 or 914-241-1700; fax: 914-241-0243).

Beehive Travel (77 W. 200 S., Suite 500, Salt Lake City, UT 84101; phone: 800-777-5727 or 801-578-9000; fax: 801-297-2828).

Classic Travel Service (275 Madison Ave., Suite 2314, New York, NY 10016-1101; phone: 212-843-2900; fax: 212-944-4493).

Dahl's Good Neighbor Travel Service (124 S. Main St., Viroqua, WI 54665; phone: 800-338-3245 or 608-637-2128; fax: 608-637-3030).

Flying Wheels Travel (PO Box 382, Owatonna, MN 55060; phone: 800-535-6790 or 507-451-5005; fax: 507-451-1685).

The Guided Tour (7900 Old York Rd., Suite 114B, Elkins Park, PA 19027-2339; phone: 800-783-5841 or 215-782-1370; fax: 215-635-2637).

Hinsdale Travel (201 E. Ogden Ave., Hinsdale, IL 60521; phone: 708-325-1335; fax: 708-325-1342).

MedEscort International (*Lehigh Valley International Airport,* PO Box 8766, Allentown, PA 18105-8766; phone: 800-255-7182 or 610-791-3111; fax: 610-791-9189).

Prestige World Travel (5710-X High Point Rd., Greensboro, NC 27407; phone: 800-476-7737 or 910-292-6690; fax: 910-632-9404).

Sprout (893 Amsterdam Ave., New York, NY 10025; phone: 212-222-9575; fax: 212-222-9768).

Weston Travel Agency (134 N. Cass Ave., PO Box 1050, Westmont, IL 60559; phone: 708-968-2513; fax: 708-968-2539).

NOTE

***Wheelchair Getaways* (PO Box 605, Versailles, KY 40383; phone: 800-536-5518 or 606-873-4973; fax: 606-873-8039), which rents vans designed to accommodate wheelchairs, has franchises nationwide.**

Single Travelers

The travel industry is not very fair to people who vacation by themselves—they often end up paying more than those traveling in pairs. There are services catering to single travelers, however, that match travel companions, offer travel arrangements with shared accommodations, and provide information and discounts. Helpful information for those traveling alone also is provided in the newsletter *Going Solo* (Doerfer Communications, PO Box 123, Apalachicola, FL 32329; phone/fax: 904-653-8848).

Organizations and Companies

Contiki Holidays (300 Plaza Alicante, Suite 900, Garden Grove, CA 92640; phone: 800-266-8454 or 714-740-0808; fax: 714-740-0818).

Gallivanting (515 E. 79th St., Suite 20F, New York, NY 10021; phone: 800-933-9699 or 212-988-0617; fax: 212-988-0144).

Globus** and **Cosmos (5301 S. Federal Circle, Littleton, CO 80123-2980; phone: 800-221-0090 for reservations; 800-851-0728 for information; or 303-797-2800; fax: 303-798-5441).

Jane's International Travel** and **Sophisticated Women Travelers (2603 Bath Ave., Brooklyn, NY 11214; phone: 800-613-9226 or 718-266-2045; fax: 718-266-4062).

Jens Jurgen's Travel Companion Exchange (PO Box 833, Amityville, NY 11701; phone: 800-392-1256 or 516-454-0880; fax: 516-454-0170).

Marion Smith Professional Singles (611 Prescott Pl., N. Woodmere, NY 11581; phone: 800-698-TRIP, 516-791-4852, 516-791-4865, or 212-944-2112; fax: 516-791-4879).

Partners-in-Travel (11660 Chenault St., Suite 119, Los Angeles, CA 90049; phone: 310-476-4869).

Solo Flights (612 Penfield Rd., Fairfield, CT 06430; phone: 800-266-1566 or 203-256-1235).

Travel Companions (*Atrium Financial Center,* 1515 N. Federal Hwy., Suite 300, Boca Raton, FL 33432; phone: 561-393-6448 in Florida; 800-383-7211 elsewhere in the US; fax: 561-393-6448).

Travel in Two's (239 N. Broadway, Suite 3, N. Tarrytown, NY 10591; phone: 914-631-8301 in New York State; 800-692-5252 elsewhere in the US).

Umbrella Singles (PO Box 157, Woodbourne, NY 12788; phone: 800-537-2797 or 914-434-6871; fax: 914-434-3532).

Older Travelers

Special discounts and more free time are just two factors that have given older travelers a chance to see the world at affordable prices. Many travel suppliers offer senior discounts—sometimes only to members of certain senior citizens organizations (which may offer travel benefits of their own).

When considering a particular package, make sure the facilities—and the pace of the tour—match your needs and physical condition.

Publications

The Mature Traveler (GEM Publishing Group, PO Box 50400, Reno, NV 89513-0400; phone: 702-786-7419).

The Senior Citizen's Guide to Budget Travel in the US and Canada, by Paige Palmer (Pilot Books, 103 Cooper St., Babylon, NY 11702; phone: 516-422-2225; fax: 516-422-2227).

Take a Camel to Lunch and Other Adventures for Mature Travelers, by Nancy O'Connell (Bristol Publishing Enterprises, PO Box 1737, San Leandro, CA 94577; phone: 510-895-4461 in California; 800-346-4889 elsewhere in the US; fax: 510-895-4459).

Unbelievably Good Deals & Great Adventures That You Absolutely Can't Get Unless You're Over 50, by Joan Rattner Heilman (Contemporary Books, 180 N. Stetson Ave., Suite 1200, Chicago, IL 60601; phone: 800-621-1918 or 312-540-4500; fax: 800-998-3103 or 312-540-4687).

Organizations

American Association of Retired Persons (*AARP;* 601 E St. NW, Washington, DC 20049; phone: 202-434-2277).

Mature Outlook (Customer Service Center, 6001 N. Clark St., Chicago, IL 60660; phone: 800-336-6330; fax: 312-764-5036).

National Council of Senior Citizens (1331 F St. NW, Washington, DC 20004; phone: 202-347-8800; fax: 202-624-9595).

Package Tour Operators

Elderhostel (75 Federal St., Boston, MA 02110-1941; phone: 617-426-7788).

Gadabout Tours (700 E. Tahquitz Canyon Way, Palm Springs, CA 92262; phone: 800-952-5068 or 619-325-5556; fax: 619-325-5127).

Grand Circle Travel (347 Congress St., Boston, MA 02210; phone: 800-221-2610 or 617-350-7500; fax: 617-346-6700).

Grandtravel (6900 Wisconsin Ave., Suite 706, Chevy Chase, MD 20815; phone: 800-247-7651 or 301-986-0790; fax: 301-913-0166).

Interhostel (*University of New Hampshire,* Division of Continuing Education, 6 Garrison Ave., Durham, NH 03824; phone: 800-733-9753 or 603-862-1147; fax: 603-862-1113).

Mature Tours (10 Greenwood La., Westport, CT 06880; phone: 800-266-1566 or 203-256-1235; fax: 203-259-7113).

OmniTours (104 Wilmot Rd., Deerfield, IL 60015; phone: 800-962-0060 or 708-374-0088; fax: 708-374-9515).

Saga International Holidays (222 Berkeley St., Boston, MA 02116; phone: 800-343-0273 or 617-262-2262; fax: 617-375-5950).

Traveling with Children

Sharing the excitement and discovery of travel with your family can bring special meaning to any trip. Although traveling with your children requires some additional preparation and planning, it does not have to be a burden or an excessive expense. An increasing number of hotels and other travel services cater to families and offer family packages and discounts for children. In addition, there are numerous publications that provide valuable information on family travel.

Publications

Adventuring with Children: An Inspirational Guide to World Travel & the Outdoors, by Nan and Kevin Jeffrey (Menasha Ridge Press, 3169 Cahaba Heights Rd., Birmingham, AL 35243; phone: 800-247-9437 or 205-967-0566; fax: 205-967-0580).

The Best Bargain Family Vacations in the USA, by Laura Sutherland and Valerie Wolf Deutsch (St. Martin's Press, 175 Fifth Ave., New York, NY 10010; phone: 800-288-2131 or 212-674-5151; fax: 212-677-6487 or 212-254-8175).

Best Places to Go: A Family Destination Guide to the World, by Nan Jeffrey (Menasha Ridge Press, address above).

Birnbaum's Disneyland (Hearst Business Publishing and Hyperion, 114 Fifth Ave., New York, NY 10011; phone: 212-633-4400; fax: 212-633-4811).

Birnbaum's Walt Disney World (Hearst Business Publishing and Hyperion, address above).

Birnbaum's Walt Disney World for Kids, By Kids (Hearst Business Publishing and Hyperion, address above).

Birnbaum's Walt Disney World Without Kids (Hearst Business Publishing and Hyperion, address above).

Disneyland and Southern California with Kids, by Kim Wright Wiley (Prima Publishing, PO Box 1260BK, Rocklin, CA 95677; phone: 800-632-8676 or 916-632-7400; fax: 916-632-4405).

Doing Children's Museums: A Guide to 265 Hands-On Museums, by Joanne Cleaver (Williamson Publishing, PO Box 185, Charlotte, VT 05445; phone: 800-234-8791 or 802-425-2102; fax: 802-425-2199).

The Explorer's Guide series (The Countryman Press, PO Box 175, Woodstock, VT 05091; phone: 800-245-4151 or 802-457-1049; fax: 802-457-3250).

The Family Travel Guide: An Inspiring Collection of Family-Friendly Vacations, by Carole T. Meyers (Carousel Press, PO Box 6061, Albany, CA 94706; phone: 800-990-9386 or 510-527-5849; fax: 800-990-9386).

Family Travel Times newsletter (*Travel with Your Children; TWYCH;* 40 Fifth Ave., New York, NY 10011; phone: 212-477-5524; fax: 212-477-5173). Subscription includes copy of "Airline Guide" issue (also available separately).

Farm, Ranch & Country Vacations, by Pat Dickerman (Adventure Guides, 7550 E. McDonald Dr., Scottsdale, AZ 85250; phone: 800-252-7899 or 602-596-0226; fax: 602-596-1722).

50 Great Family Vacations: Eastern North America, by Candyce H. Stapen (Globe Pequot Press, 6 Business Park Rd., PO Box 833, Old Saybrook, CT 06475; phone: 800-243-0495 or 203-395-0440; fax: 203-395-0312).

50 Great Family Vacations: Western North America, by Candyce H. Stapen (Globe Pequot Press, address above).

Flying with Baby: A Parent's Guide to Making Air Travel with an Infant or Toddler Easy, by Scott R. Weinberger (Third Street Press, PO Box 261250, Littleton, CO 80126-1250; phone: 813-360-0795; fax: 414-332-2193).

Fun Family Vacations in the Southeast, by Kent and Sharron Hannon (Peachtree Publishers, Ltd., 494 Armour Circle NE, Atlanta, GA 30324; phone: 800-241-0113 or 404-876-8761; fax: 800-875-8909).

Hawai'i, The Big Island: Making the Most of Your Family Vacation, by John Penisten (Prima Publishing, address above).

Maui and Lana'i: Making the Most of Your Family Vacation, by John Penisten (Prima Publishing, address above).

Me & You & the Kids Came Too, by Dawn and Robert Habgood (Dawbert Press, PO Box 2758, Duxbury, MA 02331; phone: 800-93-DAWBERT or 617-934-7202; fax: 617-934-2945).

100 Best Family Resorts in North America, by Jane Wilford with Janet Tice (Globe Pequot Press, address above).

Places to Go with Children series (Chronicle Books, 275 Fifth St., San Francisco, CA 94103; phone: 800-722-6657 for orders; 415-777-7240 for information; fax: 800-858-7787).

Recommended Family Resorts in the United States, Canada, and the Caribbean: 100 Quality Resorts with Leisure Activities for Children and Adults, by Jane Wilson, with Janet Tice (Globe Pequot Press, address above).

Super Family Vacations, by Martha Shirk and Nancy Klepper (HarperCollins Publishers, PO Box 588, Dunmore, PA 18512; phone: 800-331-3761; fax: 800-822-4090).

Taking the Kids series, by Eileen Oglintz (HarperCollins Publishers, address above).

Travel with Children, by Maureen Wheeler (Lonely Planet Publications, 155 Filbert St., Suite 251, Oakland, CA 94607; phone: 800-275-8555 or 510-893-8555; fax: 510-893-8563).

Trouble-Free Travel with Children: Helpful Hints for Parents on the Go, by Vicki Lansky (The Book Peddlers, 18326 Minnetonka Blvd., Deephaven, MN 55391; phone: 800-255-3379 or 612-475-3527; fax: 612-475-1505).

When Kids Fly (*Massport,* Public Affairs Department, 10 Park Plaza, Boston, MA 02116-3971; phone: 617-973-5600; fax: 617-973-5611).

Money Matters

CREDIT CARDS AND TRAVELER'S CHECKS

Most major credit cards enjoy wide domestic and international acceptance; however, not every hotel, restaurant, or shop in the US accepts all (or in some cases any) credit cards. It's also wise to carry traveler's checks while on the road, since they are replaceable if stolen or lost and are accepted throughout the US. You can buy traveler's checks at banks, and some are available by mail or phone. Keep a separate list of all traveler's checks (noting those that you have cashed) and the names and numbers of your credit cards. Both traveler's check and credit card companies have numbers to call for information or in the event of loss or theft.

CASH MACHINES

Automated teller machines (ATMs) are increasingly common, and most banks participate in ATM networks such as *MasterCard/Cirrus* (phone: 800-4-CIRRUS) and *Visa/PLUS* (phone: 800-THE-PLUS). Using a card—with an assigned Personal Identification Number (PIN)—from an affiliated bank or credit card company, you can withdraw cash from any machine in the same network. The *MasterCard/Cirrus ATM Location Directory* and the *Visa/PLUS International ATM Directory 1997* provide the locations of network ATMs nationwide and are available from banks and other financial institutions.

SENDING MONEY

Should the need arise, you often can have money sent to you via the services provided by *American Express MoneyGram* (phone: 800-926-9400 for information; 800-866-8800 for money transfers) or *Western Union Financial Services* (phone: 800-325-6000 or 800-325-4176). You also often can have money wired to you via a direct bank-to-bank transfer. Arrangements can be made with the participating institutions.

Accommodations

For specific information on hotels, resorts, and other selected accommodations, see *Checking In* in THE CITIES, sections throughout DIVERSIONS, and *Best en Route* in DIRECTIONS.

RELAIS & CHÂTEAUX

Founded in France, the *Relais & Châteaux* association has grown to include establishments in numerous countries. At the time of this writing, there were 28 members in the US. All maintain very high standards in order to retain their memberships, as they are reviewed annually. An illustrated catalogue of properties is available from *Relais & Châteaux* (11 E. 44th St., Suite 704, New York, NY 10017; phone: 212-856-0115; fax: 212-856-0193).

BUDGET MOTELS

At the other end of the scale, budget motels are designed to offer no-frills accommodations at economical prices. Many are listed in the *1997–1998 National Directory of Budget Motels* (Pilot Books, 103 Cooper St., Babylon, NY 11702; phone: 516-422-2225; fax: 516-422-2227). Local tourist offices also can provide information on motels and other economical lodgings in their areas. Another source of information is the local yellow pages. (Also see "Accommodations Discounts," below.)

BED AND BREAKFAST ESTABLISHMENTS

Commonly known as B&Bs, bed and breakfast establishments provide exactly what the name implies. A private bath isn't always offered, so check before you reserve. Although some hosts may be contacted directly, many prefer that arrangements be made through a reservations service.

For lists of B&B reservations services throughout the US, contact the *American Bed and Breakfast Association* (PO Box 1387, Midlothian, VA 23113; phone: 800-769-2468 or 804-379-2222; fax: 804-379-3627), *Bed & Breakfast: The National Network* (PO Box 4616, Springfield, MA 01101; no phone), and *Bed & Breakfast Reservations Services World-Wide* (*A Trade Association;* PO Box 14841, Baton Rouge, LA 70898-4841; phone: 504-336-4035; fax: 504-343-0672).

Publications

America's Wonderful Little Hotels and Inns: USA and Canada, by Sandra W. Soule (St. Martin's Press, 175 Fifth Ave., New York, NY 10010; phone: 800-288-2131 or 212-674-5151; fax: 212-677-6487 or 212-254-8175).

Bed & Breakfast Goes Hawaiian, by Evie Warner and Al Davis (Island Bed & Breakfast Hawaii, 4-1380 Kulio Hwy., Suite 202, Kapa'a, HI 96746; phone: 800-733-1632 or 808-822-7771; fax: 808-822-2723).

Bed & Breakfast in the Mid-Atlantic States, by Bernice Chesler (Globe Pequot Press, PO Box 833, Old Saybrook, CT 06475; phone: 800-243-0495 or 203-395-0440; fax: 203-395-0312).

Bed & Breakfast in New England, by Bernice Chesler (Globe Pequot Press, address above).

Bed & Breakfast North America: A Directory of Small Urban Hotels, Historic Victorian Inns, Country Inns, Guesthouses & Reservation Services, by Norma S. Buzan (Betsy Ross Publications, 24406 S. Ribbonwood Dr., Sun Lakes, AZ 85248; phone: 602-895-2795).

Bed & Breakfast Northwest–Pacific Rim: A Guide to Historic Victorian Inns, Scenic Country Inns, Individual Guesthouses, Ranches, Working Farms & Reservation Services, by Norma S. Buzan (Betsy Ross Publications, address above).

Bed & Breakfasts and Country Inns (American Historic Inns, PO Box 669, Dana Point, CA 92629; phone: 800-397-4667 or 714-499-8070; fax: 714-499-4022).

Birnbaum's Country Inns and Back Roads (HarperCollins Publishers, PO Box 588, Dunmore, PA 18512; phone: 800-331-3761; fax: 800-822-4090).

The Complete Guide to Bed & Breakfasts, Inns, & Guesthouses in the United States and Canada, by Pamela Lanier (Lanier Publishing International, Drawer D, Petaluma, CA 94953; phone: 707-763-0271; fax: 707-763-5762).

Gracious Stays & Special Places (Person to Person Travel Productions, 2856 Hundred Oaks St., Baton Rouge, LA 70808; phone/fax: 504-343-0672).

Inn Spots and Special Places, by Nancy Webster and Richard Woodworth (Wood Pond Press, 365 Ridgewood Rd., W. Hartford, CT 06107; phone: 860-521-0389; fax: 860-313-0185).

Recommended Country Inns series (Globe Pequot Press, address above).

Recommended Romantic Inns of America (Globe Pequot Press, address above).

Waterside Escapes, by Nancy Webster and Richard Woodworth (Wood Pond Press, address above).

RENTAL OPTIONS

An attractive accommodations alternative for the visitor content to stay in one spot is a vacation rental. For a family or group, the per-person cost can be reasonable. To have your pick of the properties available, make inquiries at least six months in advance. The *Worldwide Home Rental Guide* (3501 Indian School Rd. NE, Suite 303, Albuquerque, NM 87106; phone: 800-299-9886 or 505-255-4271; fax: 505-255-0814) lists rental properties and managing agencies.

Rental Property Agents

Barclay International Group (150 E. 52nd St., New York, NY 10022; phone: 212-832-3777 in New York City; 800-845-6636 elsewhere in the US; fax: 212-753-1139).

Condo World (4230 Orchard Lake Rd., Suite 3, Orchard Lake, MI 48323; phone: 800-521-2980 or 810-683-0202; fax: 810-683-5076).

Creative Leisure (951 Transport Way, Petaluma, CA 94954; phone: 800-4-CONDOS or 707-778-1800; fax: 707-763-7786).

Europa-Let (92 N. Main St., Ashland, OR 97520; phone: 800-462-4486 or 503-482-5806; fax: 503-482-0660).

Global Home Network (1110-D Elden St., Suite 205, Herndon, VA 22070; phone: 800-528-3549 for reservations; 703-318-7081 for information; fax: 703-318-7086).

Hawaiian Condo Resorts (444 Hovron Rd., Suite V-2B1, Honolulu, HI 96815; phone: 800-487-4505 or 808-949-4505; fax: 808-944-2507).

Hideaways International (767 Islington St., Portsmouth, NH 03801; phone: 800-843-4433 or 603-430-4433; fax: 603-430-4444).

Hometours International (PO Box 11503, Knoxville, TN 37939; phone: 800-367-4668 or 423-588-8722).

Keith Prowse & Co. (USA) Ltd. (234 W. 44th St., Suite 1000, New York, NY 10036; phone: 800-669-8687 or 212-398-1430; fax: 212-302-4251).

Property Rentals International (1 Park W. Circle, Suite 108, Midlothian, VA 23113; phone: 800-220-3332 or 804-378-6054; fax: 804-379-2073).

Rent a Home International (7200 34th Ave. NW, Seattle, WA 98117; phone: 800-488-7368 or 206-789-9377; fax: 206-789-9379).

Rent a Vacation Everywhere (*RAVE;* 135 Meigs St., Rochester, NY 14607; phone: 716-256-0760; fax: 716-256-2676).

VHR Worldwide (235 Kensington Ave., Norwood, NJ 07648; phone: 201-767-9393 in New Jersey; 800-633-3284 elsewhere in the US; fax: 201-767-5510).

Villa Leisure (PO Box 30188, Palm Beach, FL 33420; phone: 800-526-4244 or 407-624-9000; fax: 407-622-9097).

HOME EXCHANGES

For comfortable, reasonable living quarters with amenities that no hotel could possibly offer, consider trading homes with another family. The following companies provide information on exchanges:

Home Base Holidays (7 Park Ave., London N13 5PG, England; phone: 44-181-886-8752; fax: 44-181-482-4258).

HomeLink USA (PO Box 650, Key West, FL 33041; phone: 800-638-3841; phone/fax: 305-294-1448).

Intervac US/International Home Exchange (PO Box 590504, San Francisco, CA 94159; phone: 800-756-HOME or 415-435-3497; fax: 415-435-7440).

Loan-A-Home (7 McGregor Rd., Woods Hole, MA 02543; phone: 508-548-4032).

Worldwide Home Exchange Club (806 Brantford Ave., Silver Spring, MD 20904; phone: 301-680-8950).

HOME STAYS

United States Servas (11 John St., Room 407, New York, NY 10038; phone: 212-267-0252; fax: 212-267-0292) maintains a list of hosts throughout the US (and worldwide) willing to accommodate visitors free of charge. The aim of this nonprofit program is to promote cultural exchange, and *Servas* emphasizes that member travelers should be interested mainly in their hosts, not in sightseeing, during their stays.

ACCOMMODATIONS DISCOUNTS

Regardless of a hotel's price range, ask about weekly rates, corporate rates, weekend or midweek discounts, and other special promotions. In addition, various companies offer discounts on accommodations (and sometimes other travel services as well), although these discounts may be available only in certain cities. For instance, *Express Reservations* (3800 Arapahoe

Rd., Boulder CO 80301; phone: 800-356-1123; fax: 303-440-0166) offers discounts on hotel accommodations in Los Angeles and New York City.

The following organizations offer discounts of up to 50% on accommodations throughout the US:

Carte Royale (1 Premier Plaza, 5605 Glenridge Dr., Suite 300, Atlanta, GA 30342; phone: 800-218-5862 or 404-250-9940; fax: 404-252-9162).

Encore Marketing International (4501 Forbes Blvd., Lanham, MD 20706; phone: 800-638-0930 or 301-459-8020; fax: 301-731-0525).

Entertainment Publications (2125 Butterfield Rd., Troy, MI 48084; phone: 800-445-4137 or 810-637-8400; fax: 810-637-2035).

Great American Traveler (*Access Development Corp.,* PO Box 27563, Salt Lake City, UT 84127-0563; phone: 800-548-2812 or 801-262-2233; fax: 801-262-2311).

Hotel Express International (*International Concepts Group,* 14681 Midway Rd., Dallas, TX 75244; phone: 800-866-2015, 800-770-2015, or 214-497-9792; fax: 214-770-3575).

Impulse (6143 S. Willow Dr., Suite 410, Englewood, CO 80111; phone: 800-730-2457 or 303-741-2457; fax: 303-721-6011).

International Travel Card (6001 N. Clark St., Chicago, IL 60660; phone: 800-342-0558 or 312-465-8891; fax: 312-764-8066).

Privilege Card (3391 Peachtree Rd. NE, Suite 110, Atlanta, GA 30326; phone: 800-236-9732 or 404-262-0255; fax: 404-262-0235).

Quest International (402 E. Yakima Ave., Suite 1200, Yakima, WA 98901; phone: 800-742-3543 or 509-248-7512; fax: 509-457-8399).

Quikbook (c/o *Travelplanners,* 381 Park Ave. S., New York, NY 10016; phone: 800-789-9887 or 212-532-1660; fax: 212-532-1556).

Time Zones

The 48 contiguous states are divided into four time zones—eastern, central, mountain, and pacific. From east to west, the time becomes one hour earlier from one time zone to the next. Thus, when it is 12 noon in New York, it is 11 AM in Chicago, 10 AM in Denver, and 9 AM in Los Angeles. Alaska is one hour earlier than pacific time; Hawaii is two hours earlier. The map in the front of this guide indicates where these time zones divide the country (this information also is provided in most US telephone directories). Except in Arizona, Hawaii, and parts of Indiana, daylight saving time is observed throughout the country from the first Sunday in April until the last Sunday in October.

Business and Shopping Hours

Most businesses in the US are open weekdays from 9 AM to 5 PM. Retail stores usually are open weekdays and Saturdays from around 9 or 10 AM to 5:30 or

6 PM; in larger cities and tourist areas, stores may stay open later. Some stores also are open on Sundays. Malls and department stores often stay open at least one night a week until 8 or 9 PM (or later). Note that blue laws, which mandate that stores, bars, restaurants, and other establishments close on Sundays, are set by state or local governments and vary from place to place.

Banking hours traditionally have been weekdays from 9 AM to 3 PM. The trend is toward longer hours, however, and some banks may open at 8 or 8:30 AM and stay open until 5 or 6 PM (or later) at least one day a week. Banks also may be open for business on Saturday mornings. Automated teller machines, providing basic banking services, usually are available 24 hours a day.

Holidays

Banks, post offices, libraries, some museums, and many businesses are closed on most national holidays. Below is a list of these holidays and the dates they will be observed this year. (Note that the dates of some holidays vary from year to year; others occur on the same day every year.)

New Year's Day (January 1)
Martin Luther King Jr. Day (January 20)
Presidents' Day (February 17)
Memorial Day (May 30; observed May 26)
Independence Day (July 4)
Labor Day (September 1)
Columbus Day (October 12; observed October 13 in most states)
Veterans' Day (November 11)
Thanksgiving Day (November 27)
Christmas Day (December 25)

Mail

In major cities, main post offices often are open (or provide self-service sections) 24 hours a day. Although exact hours vary, branch offices usually are open weekdays from around 8 or 9 AM to between 5 and 6 PM. Many branch offices also are open on Saturdays, usually from around 8 AM to between noon and 1 PM (branch offices in larger cities may stay open until 2 or 3 PM).

Stamps also can be purchased at hotel desks, as well as at some supermarkets, pharmacies, and other stores. For rapid delivery, use overnight services such as *Express Mail* (available at post offices), *DHL Worldwide Express* (phone: 800-225-5345), *FedEx* (phone: 800-GO-FEDEX), or *United Parcel Service* (*UPS;* phone: 800-PICK-UPS).

You can have mail sent to you care of your hotel (marked "Guest Mail, Hold for Arrival") or to a post office (often only the main post office; the address should include "c/o General Delivery"). Some *American Express* offices also will hold mail for customers ("c/o Client Letter Service"). Information on this service is provided in the pamphlet *Worldwide Travelers' Companion,* available from any *American Express* travel office.

Telephone

To make a long-distance call, dial 1 + the area code + the local number. The nationwide number for information is 555-1212; in most areas, you also can dial 411 for local information. If you need a number in another area code, dial 1 + the area code + 555-1212. If you don't know an area code, dial 555-1212 or 411 for directory assistance (in Hawaii, dial 0 for a local operator). In most of the US, the number to call in an emergency is 911; in some rural or remote areas, you may need to dial 0 for an operator, who will connect you to the police or other emergency services.

Also available are combined telephone calling/bank credit cards, such as the *AT&T Universal Card* (PO Box 44167, Jacksonville, FL 32231-4167; phone: 800-423-4343). Similarly, *Sprint* (8140 Ward Pkwy., Kansas City, MO 64114; phone: 800-226-8472) offers *VisaPhone,* through which you can add phone card privileges to your existing *Visa* card.

Among the companies offering long-distance phone cards (without additional credit card privileges) are the following:

AT&T (295 N. Maple Ave., Basking Ridge, NJ 07920; phone: 800-CALL-ATT).

Executive Telecard International (4260 E. Evans Ave., Suite 6, Denver, CO 80222; phone: 800-950-3800).

LDDS/Worldcom (1 International Center, 100 NE Loop 410, Suite 400, San Antonio, TX 78216; phone: 800-275-0200).

MCI (323 Third St. SE, Cedar Rapids, IA 52401; phone: 800-444-4444; and 12790 Merit Dr., Dallas, TX 75251; phone: 800-444-3333).

Sprint (address above; phone: 800-PIN-DROP).

All of these companies also offer "prepaid" phone debit cards. These are similar to their other long-distance calling cards, except that the customer purchases a specific dollar amount of credit in advance. Charges for calls made with the card are debited from the credit purchased, and when the credit is used up the card is thrown away. Instructions for using such cards are provided by the issuing companies.

Hotels routinely add surcharges to the cost of phone calls made from their rooms. Long-distance telephone services that may help you avoid this added expense are provided by a number of companies, including *AT&T* (International Information Service, 635 Grant St., Pittsburgh, PA 15219; phone: 800-874-4000), *Executive Telecard International, LDDS/Worldcom, MCI,* and *Sprint* (addresses above). Note that some of these services can be accessed only with the companies' long-distance calling cards (see above).

In addition, even when you use such long-distance services, some hotels still may charge a fee for line usage.

Useful telephone directories for travelers include the *AT&T Toll-Free 800 National Shopper's Guide* and the *AT&T Toll-Free 800 National Business Guide* (phone: 800-426-8686 for orders), the *Toll-Free Travel & Vacation Information Directory* (Pilot Books, 103 Cooper St., Babylon, NY 11702; phone: 516-422-2225; fax: 516-422-2227), and *The Phone Booklet* (Scott American Corporation, PO Box 88, W. Redding, CT 06896; no phone).

Staying Healthy

Travelers in the US face few serious health risks. Tap water generally is clean and potable throughout the country. Fruit, vegetables, meat, fish, and dairy products also usually are safe. Note, however, that because serious gastrointestinal infections can result from the consumption of undercooked meat, poultry, and eggs, some caution should be exercised about what—and where—you eat.

Even in northern parts of the US, sunburn can be a problem. When spending any length of time outdoors, take appropriate precautions—including the use of a sunscreen with a Sun Protection Factor (SPF) of 15 or higher.

When swimming in the ocean, be careful of the undertow (the water running back down the beach after a wave has washed ashore), which can knock you off your feet, and riptides (currents running against the tide), which can pull you out to sea. Sharks sometimes are found in coastal waters but rarely come close to shore. Depending on the area, jellyfish—including Portuguese men-of-war—may be found, as well as eels and sea urchins. And remember that coral reefs (though limited in US waters) can be razor sharp.

Scorpion stings and the bites of centipedes, spiders, snakes, or any wild animal can be serious and must be treated immediately. If a welt or a rash develops around an insect bite or you subsequently experience flu-type symptoms, you may have been bitten by a tick carrying Lyme disease and should consult a physician.

Competent health professionals equipped to handle most medical problems can be found throughout the US. Most cities and towns of any size have at least one hospital in the area, and even the smallest of towns has a medical clinic or private physician nearby. Hospitals in most areas have emergency rooms, and many hospitals also have walk-in clinics for less serious medical problems.

Most drugstores are open from 8 AM to around 6 PM, weekdays and Saturdays, and some are open on Sundays as well. Major cities often have at least one drugstore that stays open 24 hours a day. In some areas, night duty may rotate among pharmacies. Your hotel concierge, a local hospital or medical clinic, or the police may be able to provide the location of the nearest all-night or on-call pharmacy. This information also may appear in the yellow pages, as well as in local newspapers.

Should you need non-emergency medical attention, ask at your hotel for the house physician or for help in reaching a doctor. Particularly in major cities, hospitals also may offer physician referral phone services. **In an emergency: Dial 911 for assistance or 0 for an operator, or go directly to the emergency room of the nearest hospital.**

Additional Resources

International SOS Assistance (8 Neshaminy Interplex, Suite 207, Trevose, PA 19053-6956; phone: 800-523-8930 or 215-244-1500; fax: 215-244-2227).

Medic Alert Foundation (2323 Colorado Ave., Turlock, CA 95382; phone: 800-ID-ALERT or 209-668-3333; fax: 209-669-2495).

Travel Care International (PO Box 846, Eagle River, WI 54521; phone: 800-5-AIR-MED or 715-479-8881; fax: 715-479-8178).

Traveler's Emergency Network (*TEN;* PO Box 238, Hyattsville, MD 20797-8108; phone: 800-ASK-4-TEN; fax: 301-559-5167).

U S Assist (2 Democracy Center, Suite 800, 6903 Rockledge Dr., Bethesda, MD 20817; phone: 800-895-8472 or 301-214-8200; fax: 301-214-8205).

Legal Aid

If you don't have, or cannot reach, your own attorney, most cities offer legal referral services maintained by county bar associations. These services ensure that anyone in need of legal representation gets it and usually can match you with a local attorney. Legal referral services, as well as individual lawyers, are listed in the local yellow pages. If you must appear in court, you are entitled to court-appointed representation if you can't obtain a lawyer or can't afford one.

For Further Information

State tourist authorities are the best sources of travel information. Main offices generally are open on weekdays during normal business hours. Smaller offices, providing on-the-spot information, often are open on weekends and holidays.

State Tourist Offices

Alabama: *Alabama Bureau of Tourism and Travel,* walk-in office: 401 Adams Ave., Montgomery, AL 36103 (phone: 800-ALABAMA or 334-242-4169; fax: 334-242-4554); mailing address: PO Box 4309, Montgomery, AL 36104.

Alaska: *Alaska Division of Tourism,* PO Box 110801, Juneau, AK 99811-0801 (phone: 907-465-2010; fax: 907-465-2287).

Arizona: *Arizona Office of Tourism,* 2702 N. Third St., Suite 4015, Phoenix, AZ 85004 (phone: 800-842-8257 or 602-542-8687; fax: 602-240-5475).

Arkansas: *Arkansas Department of Parks and Tourism,* Department 3732, 1 Capitol Mall, Little Rock, AR 72201 (phone: 800-NATURAL or 501-682-1511; fax: 501-682-1364).

California: *California Trade and Commerce Agency, Division of Tourism,* walk-in office: 801 K St., Suite 1600, Sacramento, CA 95814 (phone: 800-TO-CALIF or 916-322-2881; fax: 916-322-3402); mailing address: PO Box 1499, Sacramento, CA 95812.

Colorado: At the time of this writing, the Colorado state office of tourism remained closed due to budget cuts. However, travelers can obtain tourist information and make hotel reservations through the *Colorado Travel and Tourism Authority* (3554 N. Academy Blvd., Denver, CO 80917; phone: 800-COLORADO to order publications; 800-777-6880 for hotel reservations; fax: 719-591-7068).

Connecticut: *Connecticut Department of Economic Development, Tourism Division,* 865 Brook St., Rocky Hill, CT 06067-3405 (phone: 800-CT-BOUND or 860-258-4355; fax: 860-258-4275).

Delaware: *Delaware Tourism Office,* PO Box 1401, Dover, DE 19903 (phone: 800-441-8846 or 302-739-4271; fax: 302-739-5749).

District of Columbia: *Washington, DC, Convention and Visitors Association,* main office: 1212 New York Ave. NW, Suite 600, Washington, DC 20005 (phone: 202-789-7000; fax: 202-789-7037).

Florida: *Florida Department of Commerce, Division of Tourism,* 107 W. Gaines St., Suite 501D, Tallahassee, FL 32399-2000 (phone: 904-487-1462; fax: 904-921-9158).

Georgia: *Georgia Department of Industry, Trade, and Tourism, Tourist Division,* walk-in office: Marriott Marquis Two Tower, 285 Peachtree Center Ave. NE, Suite 1000, Atlanta, GA 30303-1230 (phone: 800-VISIT-GA or 404-656-3590; fax: 404-651-9063); mailing address: PO Box 1776, Atlanta, GA 30301.

Hawaii: *Hawaii Visitors Bureau*

Mainland Office: 350 Fifth Ave., Suite 808, New York, NY 10018 (phone: 800-353-5846 or 212-947-0717; fax: 212-947-0725).

Island Offices: main office: 2270 Kalakaua Ave., Suite 801, Honolulu, HI 96815 (phone: 808-923-1811; fax: 808-924-2120); additional offices: 250 Keawe St., Hilo, HI 96720 (phone: 808-961-5797; fax: 808-961-2126); 75-5719 W. Alii Dr., Kailua-Kona, HI 96740 (phone: 808-329-7787; fax: 808-326-7563); 3016 Umi St., Suite 207, Lihue, HI 96766 (phone: 808-245-3971; fax: 808-246-9235); 1727 Wili Pa Loop, Wailuku, HI 96793 (phone: 808-244-3530; fax: 808-244-1337).

Idaho: *Idaho Department of Commerce, Division of Tourism Development,* 700 W. State St., Boise, ID 83720-2700 (phone: 800-635-7820 or 208-334-2470; fax: 208-334-2631).

Illinois: *Illinois Bureau of Tourism,* James R. Thompson Center, 100 W. Randolph St., Suite 3-400, Chicago, IL 60601 (phone: 800-223-0121 or 312-814-4733; fax: 312-814-6175).

Indiana: *Indiana Department of Commerce, Tourism Division,* 1 N. Capitol Ave., Suite 700, Indianapolis, IN 46204-2288 (phone: 800-289-6646 or 317-232-8860; fax: 317-233-6887).

Iowa: *Iowa Department of Economic Development, Division of Tourism,* 200 E. Grand Ave., Des Moines, IA 50309 (phone: 800-345-IOWA or 515-242-4705; fax: 515-242-4749).

Kansas: *Kansas Department of Commerce and Housing, Travel and Tourism Development Division,* 700 SW Harrison St., Suite 1300, Topeka, KS 66603-3712 (phone: 800-252-6727 or 913-296-2009; fax: 913-296-6988).

Kentucky: *Kentucky Department of Travel Development,* Capital Plaza Tower, 500 Mero St., 22nd Floor, Frankfort, KY 40601 (phone: 800-225-TRIP or 502-564-4930; fax: 502-564-5695).

Louisiana: *Louisiana Office of Tourism,* PO Box 94291, Baton Rouge, LA 70804-9291 (phone: 800-33-GUMBO or 504-342-8119; fax: 504-342-8390).

Maine: *Maine Publicity Bureau,* PO Box 2300, Hallowell, ME 04347 (phone: 800-533-9595 or 207-623-0363; fax: 207-623-0388).

Maryland: *Maryland Department of Economic and Employment Development, Office of Tourism Development,* 217 E. Redwood St., Ninth Floor, Baltimore, MD 21202 (phone: 800-543-1036, 800-445-4558, or 410-767-3400; fax: 410-333-6643).

Massachusetts: *Massachusetts Office of Travel and Tourism,* 100 Cambridge St., 13th Floor, Room 1305, Boston, MA 02202 (phone: 800-447-MASS, ext. 500 to order publications; 617-727-3201 for information; fax: 617-727-6525).

Michigan: *Michigan Travel Bureau,* PO Box 3393, Livonia, MI 48151 (phone: 800-543-2937 or 517-373-0670; fax: 517-373-0059).

Minnesota: *Minnesota Office of Tourism,* 100 Metro Sq., 121 Seventh Pl. E., St. Paul, MN 55101-2112 (phone: 800-657-3700 or 612-296-5029; fax: 612-296-7095).

Mississippi: *Mississippi Division of Tourism Development,* PO Box 1705, Ocean Springs, MS 39566-1705 (phone: 800-927-6378 or 601-359-3297; fax: 601-359-5757).

Missouri: *Missouri Division of Tourism,* Truman State Office Building, PO Box 1055, Jefferson City, MO 65102 (phone: 800-877-1234 or 314-751-4133; fax: 314-751-5160).

Montana: *Travel Promotion Division, Montana Department of Commerce,* 1424 Ninth Ave., Helena, MT 59620 (phone: 800-VISIT-MT or 406-444-2654; fax: 406-444-1800).

Nebraska: *Nebraska Department of Economic Development, Travel and Tourism Division,* walk-in office: 700 S. 16th St., Lincoln, NE 68509 (phone: 800-228-4307 or 402-471-3796; fax: 402-471-3026); mailing address: PO Box 94666, Lincoln, NE 68509-4666.

Nevada: *Nevada Commission on Tourism,* Capitol Complex, 5151 S. Carson St., Carson City, NV 89710 (phone: 800-NEVADA-8, 800-237-0774, or 702-687-4322; fax: 702-687-6779).

New Hampshire: *New Hampshire Office of Travel and Tourism,* PO Box 1856, Concord, NH 03302-1856 (phone: 800-FUN-IN-NH or 603-271-2343; fax: 603-271-2629).

New Jersey: *New Jersey Department of Commerce and Economic Development, Division of Travel and Tourism,* walk-in office: 20 W. State St., Trenton, NJ 08625-0826 (phone: 800-JERSEY-7 or 609-292-2470; fax: 609-633-7418); mailing address: CN 826, Trenton, NJ 08625-0826.

New Mexico: *New Mexico Department of Tourism,* walk-in office: 491 Old Santa Fe Trail, Santa Fe, NM 87503 (phone: 800-545-2040, or 505-827-7400; fax: 505-827-7402); mailing address: PO Box 20003, Santa Fe, NM 87503.

New York: *New York State Department of Economic Development, Division of Tourism,* 1 Commerce Plaza, Room 301, Albany, NY 12245 (phone: 800-CALL-NYS or 518-474-4116; fax: 518-486-6416).

North Carolina: *North Carolina Travel and Tourism Division,* 430 N. Salisbury St., Raleigh, NC 27603 (phone: 800-VISIT-NC or 919-733-4171; fax: 919-733-8582).

North Dakota: *North Dakota Department of Tourism,* Liberty Memorial Building, 604 East Blvd., Bismarck, ND 58505 (phone: 800-435-5663 or 701-328-2525; fax: 701-328-4878).

Ohio: *Ohio Division of Travel and Tourism,* PO Box 1001, Columbus, OH 43266-0101 (phone: 800-BUCKEYE or 614-466-8844; fax: 614-466-6744).

Oklahoma: *Oklahoma Recreation and Tourism Division,* 2401 N. Lincoln Blvd., Suite 500, Oklahoma City, OK 73105 (phone: 800-652-6552 or 405-521-2409; fax: 405-521-3992).

Oregon: *Tourism Division, Oregon Economic Development Department,* 775 Summer St. NE, Salem, OR 97310 (phone: 800-547-7842 or 503-986-0000; fax: 503-986-0001).

Pennsylvania: *Pennsylvania Department of Commerce, Office of Travel and Tourism,* Forum Building, Room 453, Harrisburg, PA 17120 (phone: 800-VISIT-PA or 717-787-5453; fax: 717-234-4560).

Rhode Island: *Rhode Island Economic Development Corporation,* 7 Jackson Walkway, Providence, RI 02903 (phone: 800-556-2484 to order publications; 401-277-2601 for information; fax: 401-277-2102).

South Carolina: *South Carolina Department of Parks, Recreation and Tourism, Division of Tourism,* walk-in office: 1205 Pendleton St., Room 106, Columbia, SC 29201 (phone: 803-734-0122; fax: 803-734-0133); mailing address: PO Box 71, Columbia, SC 29201-0071.

South Dakota: *South Dakota Department of Tourism,* 711 E. Wells Ave., Pierre, SD 57501-3369 (phone: 800-S-DAKOTA or 605-773-3301; fax: 605-773-3256).

Tennessee: *Tennessee Department of Tourist Development,* PO Box 23170, Nashville, TN 37202-3170 (phone: 800-836-6200 or 615-741-2158; fax: 615-741-7225).

Texas: *Texas Department of Transportation, Travel Division,* walk-in office: 112 E. 11th St., Austin, TX 78701 (phone: 800-452-9292 or 512-483-3705; fax: 512-483-3793); mailing address: PO Box 5064, Austin, TX 78763.

Utah: *Utah Travel Council,* Council Hall, Capitol Hill, Salt Lake City, UT 84114 (phone: 800-UTAH-FUN or 801-538-1030; fax: 801-538-1399).

Vermont: *Vermont Department of Travel and Tourism,* 134 State St., Montpelier, VT 05601-1471 (phone: 800-VERMONT or 802-828-3236; fax: 802-828-3233).

Virginia: *Virginia Division of Tourism,* 1021 E. Cary St., 14th Floor, Richmond, VA 23219 (phone: 800-VISIT-VA or 804-786-4484; fax: 804-786-1919).

Washington State: *Washington State Tourism,* walk-in office: 101 General Administration Building, Olympia, WA 98504 (phone: 800-544-1800 or 360-586-2088; fax: 360-753-4470); mailing address: PO Box 42500, Olympia, WA 98504-2500.

West Virginia: *Division of Tourism,* 2101 Washington St. E., Charleston, WV 25305 (phone: 800-CALL-WVA or 304-558-2766; fax: 304-558-0077).

Wisconsin: *Wisconsin Division of Tourism,* PO Box 7606, Madison, WI 53707-7606 (phone: 800-432-TRIP or 608-266-2161; fax: 608-264-6150).

Wyoming: *Wyoming Division of Tourism,* I-25 and College Dr., Cheyenne, WY 82002 (phone: 800-225-5996 or 307-777-7777; fax: 307-777-6904).

The Cities

Atlanta

In a relatively scant 160 years, Atlanta has mushroomed from a backwoods wilderness into the cosmopolitan capital of Georgia and the financial, transportation, and communications hub of the southeastern United States. Futuristic towers vie with the magnificent pines and hardwoods that impart a park-like ambience. Asphalt arteries overlie north Georgia's famous red clay soil and weave through historic neighborhoods, ever-burgeoning suburbs, and self-contained "mini cities" along I-285, the perimeter highway that encircles the city. Museums, shopping malls, art galleries, theater venues, musical offerings, dining spots, and sporting options abound. Atlanta's increasing stature in the international arena was capped by its hosting of the *1996 Summer Olympic Games.* More than $2 billion in construction projects marked the massive refurbishing; among the tangible legacies are the 20-acre *Centennial Olympic Park* downtown and an 18-mile biking and pedestrian corridor to *Georgia's Stone Mountain Park.* In addition, the planting of thousands of trees and bushes has further enhanced the already lush landscape.

The spirited transformation was the latest of three major restructurings of Atlanta's skyline. In the early 1800s, Creek Indians and pine tree forest prevailed. In 1837, when officials proposed a rail route linking the area to Tennessee, surveyors for the *Western & Atlantic Railroad* staked the southern end of the new right of way near where *CNN Center* now stands. Originally called Terminus, then Marthasville, in 1847 the town was incorporated as Atlanta.

By the eve of the War Between the States, the once rough and rowdy railhead had settled into its place as a prosperous community whose 10,000 citizens ran banks and stores and produced munitions, food, and clothing for the Confederacy. For its strategic importance, Atlanta paid dearly. Following a 117-day siege in 1864, Atlanta fell to General William T. Sherman's Union forces. Before continuing the infamously destructive March to the Sea across middle Georgia, the occupying troops torched the town. Only weeks later, returning citizens and carpetbaggers from the North began raising a new city from the ashes. In 1868 Atlanta became the capital of the state. Much later, in the 1960s, architect-developer John Portman orchestrated an inner-city rebirth, beginning with the imaginative *Peachtree Center.*

Today's Atlanta, held together by an overburdened network of freeways, is home to the offices and production facilities of all but a handful of *Fortune* magazine's 500 largest corporations; about 10 of them are headquartered here. So are the American Cancer Society, CARE, CNN/Turner Broadcasting System, the federal Centers for Disease Control and Prevention (CDC), *Delta Air Lines, Georgia-Pacific,* Holiday Inn Worldwide, and UPS.

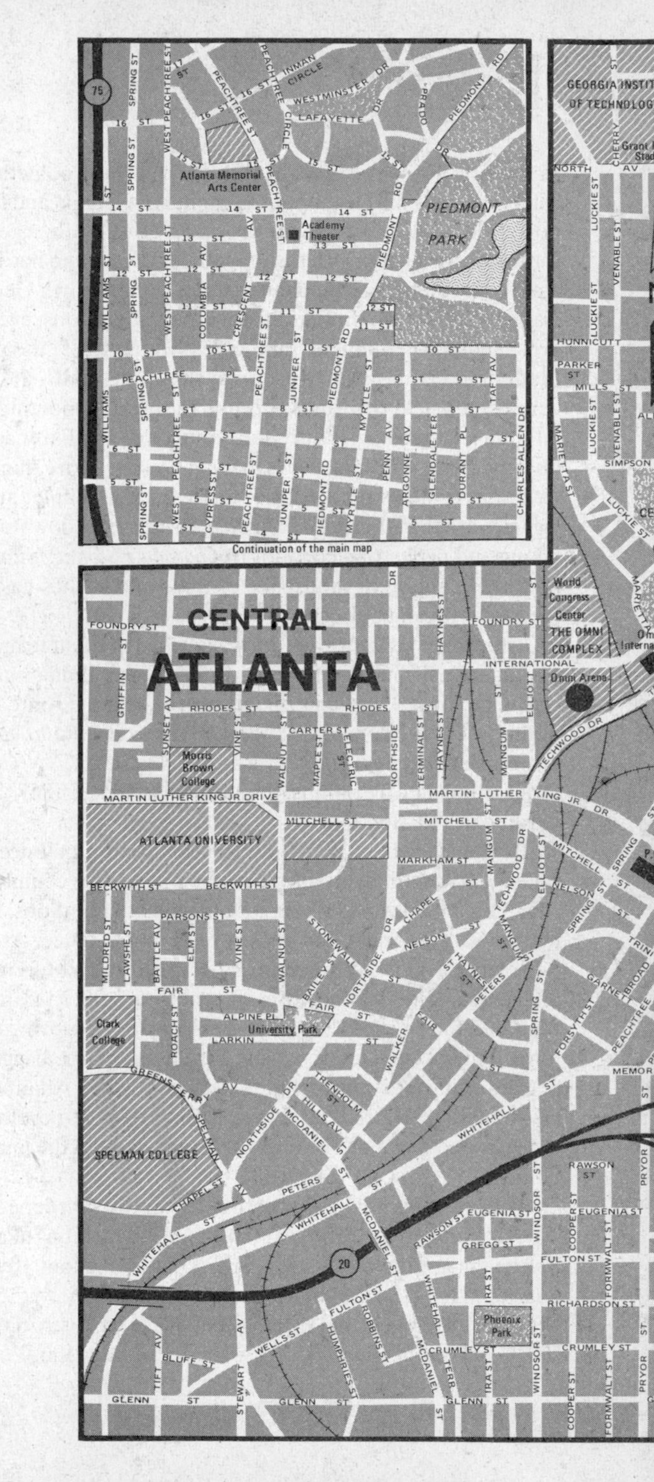

Continuation of the main map

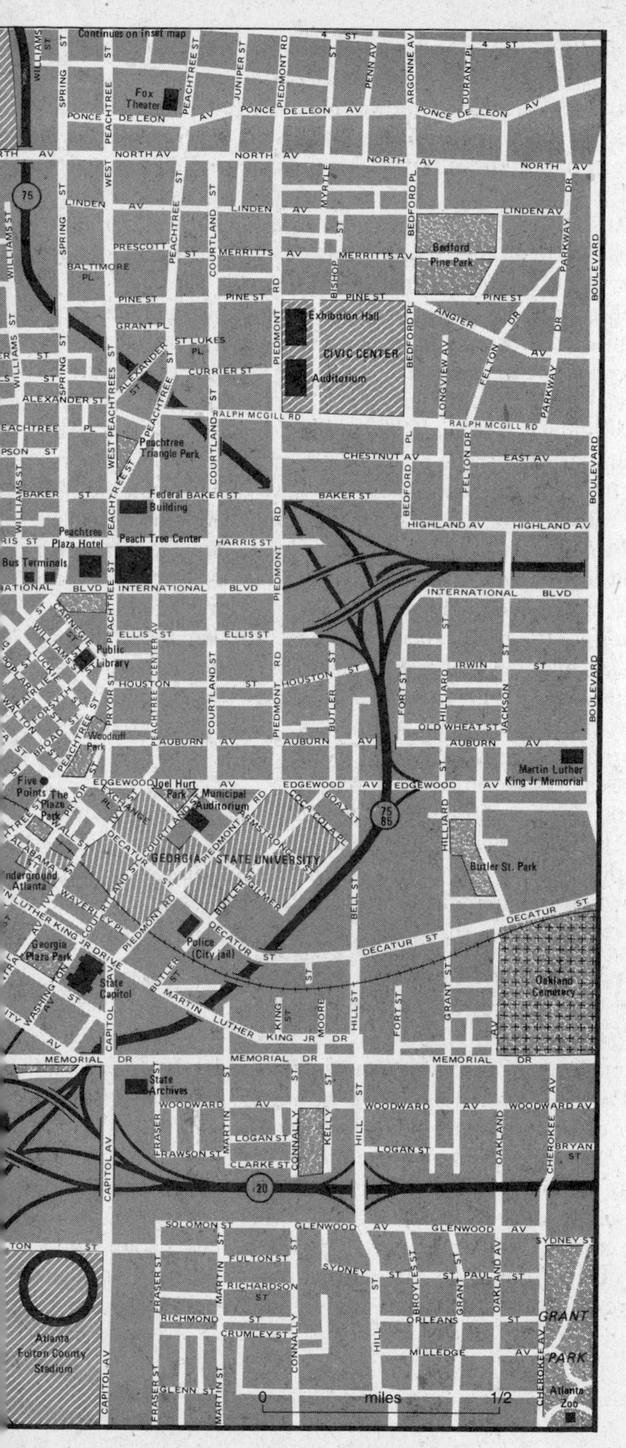
Continues on inset map
Fox Theater
PONCE DE LEON AV
NORTH AV
LINDEN AV
MERRITTS AV
Bedford Pine Park
PINE ST
ANGIER AV
Exhibition Hall
CIVIC CENTER
Auditorium
RALPH MCGILL RD
Peachtree Triangle Park
CHESTNUT AV
EAST AV
Federal Building
BAKER ST
HIGHLAND AV
Peachtree Plaza Hotel
Peach Tree Center
HARRIS ST
Bus Terminals
INTERNATIONAL BLVD
ELLIS ST
Public Library
HOUSTON ST
IRWIN ST
OLD WHEAT ST
AUBURN AV
Woodruff Park
EDGEWOOD AV
Joel Hurt Park
Municipal Auditorium
Martin Luther King Jr Memorial
Five Points
The Plaza Park
GEORGIA STATE UNIVERSITY
Underground Atlanta
Butler St. Park
DECATUR ST
Police (City jail)
Georgia Plaza Park
State Capitol
Oakland Cemetery
MARTIN LUTHER KING JR DR
MEMORIAL DR
State Archives
WOODWARD AV
LOGAN ST
RAWSON ST
CLARKE ST
BRYAN ST
75
85
20
SOLOMON ST
GLENWOOD AV
SYDNEY ST
FULTON ST
RICHARDSON ST
RICHMOND ST
CRUMLEY ST
ORLEANS ST
MILLEDGE AV
GLENN ST
GRANT PARK
Atlanta Zoo
Atlanta Fulton County Stadium
0 miles 1/2
BOULEVARD
PIEDMONT RD
PEACHTREE ST
CAPITOL AV

A drawing card for businesses and visitors alike is *Hartsfield Atlanta International Airport,* with the world's largest airport terminal.

Atlanta's international recognition owes much to Ted Turner's Cable News Network (CNN) and Turner Broadcasting System (TBS), which have propelled the city to the forefront of the communications industry. CNN and TBS, as well as superstation WTBS, are beamed across the country and to Europe, Australia, Latin America, and Asia. As a result, Turner's Atlanta *Braves* baseball team and Atlanta *Hawks* basketball team have fan clubs in some very unlikely out-of-hemisphere locales.

Atlanta may be a hard-headed business giant, but it's also a big-hearted town where enlightened urban planning has integrated human needs and priorities. *Underground Atlanta* is a case in point, a central "town center" where everyone can shop, recreate, and enjoy a good time. Older neighborhoods such as Midtown, Virginia/Highland, and Inman Park have been revitalized by young Atlantans who thrive on urban diversity. Newcomers, too, from across the US and around the world have radically altered the city's personality with their varied lifestyles and cultures. Philosophically, Atlantans span the spectrum from button-down conservative to ultra-hip.

A once-provincial town where seldom was heard a non-Southern word, the sound of Korean or Thai or the sight of a sari no longer turns a surprised head. That's not to say that the natives have forsaken their passion for *Varsity Drive-In* chili dogs and fried peach pies, or the barbecue and Brunswick stew at *Harold's,* only that it's far easier now to sample ethnic dishes than it is to find a traditional Southern meal. Attesting to its new image as an international crossroads and melting pot, about 53 nations operate consulates and trade offices in the city.

Atlantans, both natives and transplants, wouldn't want to live anywhere else, even after acknowledging the city's serious problems with the homeless, drugs, and crime. And in early spring, when dogwood and azalea blossoms brighten the hillsides, there truly is no city like it on earth.

Atlanta At-a-Glance

SEEING THE CITY

The 360° panorama from the revolving *Sun Dial Restaurant, Bar, and View* atop the *Westin Peachtree Plaza* hotel (see *Checking In*) is spectacular. On a clear day, your eye sweeps from the planes arriving and taking off at *Hartsfield Atlanta International Airport* to the Blue Ridge Mountains. Almost as breathtaking is the ride in a glass-enclosed elevator on the exterior of the cylindrical tower. Passengers arrive on the 72nd-floor observation level, where those who come to sightsee (there is a charge) receive a color guide to the landmarks below. Bar and restaurant patrons proceed to the 71st and 73rd floors, respectively. Peachtree St., at International Blvd. (phone: 589-7506).

SPECIAL PLACES

Downtown Atlanta is fairly compact, but the streets don't follow an orderly grid; rather, many were constructed over former Indian trails and others were wedged in among the early railroad tracks. It may sometimes seem that half of Atlanta's street names include the word "Peachtree," despite the fact that there are relatively few of the flowering trees. ("Peach" may be a corruption of "pitch," the resin of the ubiquitous pine tree.) Bear in mind, also, that the names of a number of streets change at least once along their length. *MARTA,* the public transportation system, is excellent, especially for sights downtown or near Peachtree Street (see *Getting Around*). For more widespread sightseeing, a car is necessary.

DOWNTOWN

GEORGIA CAPITOL Completed in 1889 and crowned by a dome of North Georgia gold, the neoclassic-style building contains the governor's office (with rotating art exhibitions in the lobby) and the eclectic *Museum of Science and Industry.* Visitors may watch the *General Assembly* in action from January through mid-March. Guided tours on weekdays. No admission charge. 206 Washington St. (phone: 656-2844).

UNDERGROUND ATLANTA Enhancing the historic commercial district where the city took root, this six-block area functions as a "town center" and gathering spot. Located below *and* above the turn-of-the-century system of viaducts, and anchored by a 138-foot light tower, the old streets encompass a variety of shops, restaurants, fast-food establishments, bars, and nightclubs. Open daily. Peachtree St. and Upper Alabama St. (phone: 523-2311).

WOODRUFF PARK Located downtown between *Peachtree Center* and *Underground Atlanta,* this urban oasis contains a horizontal waterfall, a geyser-type fountain, and a sculpture of a woman and phoenix entitled "Atlanta From the Ashes." At historic Five Points, where Peachtree, S. Peachtree, Decatur, and Marietta Sts. and Edgewood Ave. intersect.

MARTIN LUTHER KING JR. NATIONAL HISTORIC SITE On three blocks of Auburn Avenue are sites associated with the late Nobel Peace Prize winner. These are his birthplace; *Ebenezer Baptist Church;* his tomb; and the *King Center* (449 Auburn Ave.; phone: 524-1956). *National Park Service* rangers conduct guided tours of the neighborhood from a recently completed welcome center (450 Auburn Ave.; phone: 331-5190; no charge), which also offers orientation materials and exhibits on Dr. King.

CNN CENTER Within the vast headquarters of Ted Turner's cable empire, visitors may tour the Cable News Network studios, watch CNN newscasts, and observe the daily "TalkBack Live" program. Around the 14-story atrium, boutiques sell Atlanta *Braves* and *Hawks* sports paraphernalia, MGM movie memorabilia, and photographs and videotapes of visitors on a mock news set. The *Omni at CNN Center* hotel (see *Checking In*) is within the complex. Marietta St. and Techwood Dr. For free "TalkBack Live" tickets phone: 800-410-4CNN.

CENTENNIAL OLYMPIC PARK A legacy of the *1996 Summer Olympic Games,* these 20 acres adjacent to the *Georgia World Congress Center* feature grassy areas, brick-paved promenades, and a fountain in the form of the five Olympic rings. Bounded by Techwood Dr. and Marietta, Luckie, and Baker Sts.

GEORGIA DOME, GEORGIA WORLD CONGRESS CENTER, AND OMNI COLISEUM Grouped at the western edge of downtown, the three mammoth, multi-purpose structures are linked by a landscaped pedestrian plaza. The *Georgia Dome* (phone: 223-9200) fields the Atlanta *Falcons* football team and offers tours daily except Monday if no event is scheduled; there is a charge. The *Georgia World Congress Center* (phone: 223-4000) is Atlanta's major convention complex. At press time, it was learned that the *Omni Coliseum* (phone: 681-2100), home of the Atlanta *Hawks,* would be razed in the near future to make way for a new facility. No date had been set for completion of this project.

PEACHTREE CENTER This contemporary complex consists of six office towers; the *Hyatt Regency Atlanta, Marriott Marquis,* and *Westin Peachtree Plaza* hotels; and the *Peachtree Center Gallery,* with shopping, dining, and entertainment. All are linked by landscaped plazas and glass-enclosed, aerial skyways; these extend across several streets to connect with the huge *Atlanta Market Center. MARTA*'s *Peachtree Center* rapid-rail station serves the complex.

WELCOME SOUTH VISITORS CENTER Stop here for information and services that include currency exchange and an ATM machine. Be sure to view the 13-minute film on the South narrated by Johnny Cash, and explore the exhibits on Georgia and surrounding states; there's also a bookstore stocked with Southern literature. Open daily. No admission charge. 200 Spring St. and International Blvd. (phone: 224-2000).

FOX THEATER One of the last of the opulent 1920s "picture palaces," the *Fox*'s 4,518 seats make it the country's second-largest operating theater after New York City's *Radio City Music Hall.* The beautifully restored structure blends Egyptian, Moorish, and Byzantine design elements, a perfect backdrop for the concerts and touring Broadway musicals that fill its calendar. The *Atlanta Preservation Center* (phone: 876-2041) offers tours year-round; there is a charge. At other times, admission varies with the event. Peachtree St., at Ponce de Leon Ave. (phone: 881-2100).

ENVIRONS

ATLANTA NEIGHBORHOODS Scenic, historic, and friendly, each of Atlanta's in-town neighborhoods has a unique character; all are good places to meet and mingle with the local citizenry. The *Atlanta Preservation Center* (156 Seventh St.; phone: 876-2040) sponsors seasonal walking tours of Ansley Park,

Atlanta University Center, Downtown, Druid Hills (of *Driving Miss Daisy* fame), Inman Park, *Piedmont Park,* Sweet Auburn Avenue/*Martin Luther King Jr. Historic District, Underground Atlanta,* and West End.

SIX FLAGS OVER GEORGIA This wholesome, well-maintained theme park sports more than 100 rides, including six roller coasters. Talented young people present Broadway-style shows, special areas cater to kiddies, and big-name entertainers perform in an 8,000-seat amphitheater. Closed November through early March; closed weekdays early March through mid-May and September through October. Admission charge. Twelve miles west of Atlanta on I-20 (phone: 770-948-9290).

ZOO ATLANTA A replica of an 1863 train makes regular circuits around this 40-acre sanctuary where hundreds of birds, mammals, and reptiles are exhibited in natural habitats. Among the favorites is the silverback gorilla Willie B., named for a longtime mayor of Atlanta. Open daily. Admission charge. 800 Cherokee Ave. in *Grant Park* (phone: 624-5600).

ATLANTA CYCLORAMA While the audience gallery revolves, the dramatic circular painting of the Civil War Battle of Atlanta (50 feet high and 400 feet in circumference) comes alive with sound, light, and narration. A film explains the campaign to capture Atlanta and a museum exhibits the vintage steam engine *Texas* and Civil War memorabilia. Admission charge. Open daily. 800 Cherokee Ave. in *Grant Park* (phone: 658-7625).

STONE MOUNTAIN PARK This 3,200-acre complex holds something for everybody: train rides; hiking trails; a lake for riverboating, canoeing, and fishing; two golf courses; and 20 tennis courts, 16 of which were built for last year's *Summer Olympic Games.* In addition, there are a seasonal laser show; a grouping of antebellum plantation buildings; and the southern equivalent of *Mt. Rushmore.* Three equestrian Confederate heroes, three acres wide, have been sculpted across the sheer face of the 825-foot-high mountain that is the world's largest mass of exposed granite. Facilities include campgrounds, restaurants, and hotels. Major events and festivals are held each month. Open daily. Admission charge. Seventeen miles east of Atlanta on Rte. 78 (phone: 770-498-5702).

PIEDMONT PARK Atlanta's "urban backyard" in Midtown is a 180-acre green space for tennis, jogging, walks, and picnics. People watching is especially good during the *Atlanta Dogwood Festival* in late April and the *Atlanta Arts Festival* in mid-September. The *Atlanta Symphony Orchestra* presents free outdoor concerts here in summer.

ATLANTA BOTANICAL GARDEN Commune outdoors with nature and her embellished bounty, or meander indoors among tropical plants and rare succulents in this 30-acre horticultural paradise tucked into one corner of *Piedmont Park.* Closed Mondays. Admission charge. 1345 Piedmont Ave. (phone: 876-5859).

WOODRUFF ARTS CENTER Commanding an imposing site in Midtown, this multi-building complex is home to the internationally acclaimed *Atlanta Symphony Orchestra,* the *Alliance Theater,* the *Atlanta College of Art,* and the *High Museum of Art* (see *Museums*). 1280 Peachtree St. (phone: 733-5000).

WHITE WATER PARK For relief during Atlanta's steamy summers, this clean, well-run oasis offers more than 40 cooling experiences ranging from relaxing to high-thrill. There are lockers, showers, snack bars, and a picnic area. Closed October through April. Admission charge. 250 N. Cobb Pkwy., Marietta (phone: 770-424-9283).

KENNESAW MOUNTAIN NATIONAL BATTLEFIELD PARK The mountain and surrounding 2,884-acre park were the scene of one of the most important engagements in the 1864 Battle of Atlanta campaign. The site has a small Civil War museum and remnants of earthwork defenses; the grounds are great for picnicking and hiking. Open daily. No admission charge. 900 Kennesaw Mountain Dr., off I-75, 25 miles north of downtown, near Marietta (phone: 770-427-4686).

SMALLTOWN SOUTH A number of small towns surrounding Atlanta retain their courthouse squares, antebellum and Victorian homes, Civil War sites, and an Old South ambience. Among the nearby communities and tourist offices worth seeking out are Conyers (phone: 770-483-7049), Covington (phone: 770-787-3868), Decatur (phone: 378-2525), Fayetteville (phone: 770-461-9983), Jonesboro (phone: 770-478-4800; 800-662-STAY), Marietta (phone: 770-429-1115), McDonough (phone: 770-957-5786), Monroe (phone: 770-267-6594), and Roswell (phone: 770-640-3253).

EXTRA SPECIAL

Lake Lanier Islands, **a state-run resort 45 miles northeast of Atlanta, encompasses four islands and 1,200 acres of hills and woods. Amenities include a beach, a water park, tennis, golf, houseboating, horseback riding, sailing, and camping. Activities include concerts and a lavish holiday lights display during December. There are also two hotels:** ***Renaissance Pine Isle Resort*** **(9000 Holiday Rd.; phone: 770-945-8921) and** ***Lake Lanier Islands Hilton Resort*** **(7000 Holiday Rd.; phone: 770-945-8787), which has a challenging golf course. Open year round. On I-985, Exit 1 (phone: 770-932-7200; 800-840-5253).**

Callaway Gardens, about 70 miles southwest of Atlanta, is a 2,500-acre Garden of Eden. Walking and biking trails, and roadways, wind through lushly planted areas, while more fragile blooms flourish in an enchanting conservatory. The glass-enclosed butterfly center is one of North America's largest. A manmade lake and swimming beach are open during the summer months, when ***Florida State University's Flying Circus*** **is in residence; during December, the grounds are ablaze with thousands of holiday lights.**

Three outstanding golf courses and a variety of accommodations and restaurants serve visitors. Open daily. Admission charge (Pine Mountain, GA via I-85, I-185, and US 27; phone: 706-663-2281; 800-CALLAWAY).

Sources and Resources

TOURIST INFORMATION

For general information, brochures, and maps, contact the *Georgia Tourist Division* (Box 1776, Atlanta, GA 30301-1776; phone: 656-3590; 800-VISIT-GA; 800-813-1433) or the *Atlanta Convention and Visitors Bureau (ACVB*; 233 Peachtree St., Suite 2000, Atlanta 30303; phone: 222-6688; 521-6600), both closed weekends. After arriving in Atlanta, information can be obtained at *ACVB Visitor Centers* at the *Georgia World Congress Center, Hartsfield Atlanta International Airport,* Lenox Square, Peachtree Center, *Underground Atlanta,* and the *Welcome South Visitors Center* (200 Spring St. and International Blvd; phone: 224-2000).

LOCAL COVERAGE *Atlanta Constitution,* morning daily; *Atlanta Journal,* evening daily; *Atlanta Journal/Constitution Leisure Guide*, Saturdays; *Atlanta* magazine, monthly; *Creative Loafing* newspaper, weekly.

TELEVISION STATIONS WSB Channel 2–ABC; WAGA Channel 5–FOX; WGTV Channel 8–PBS; WXIA Channel 11–NBC; WTBS Channel 17–TBS; WPBA Channel 30–PBS; WGNX Channel 46–CBS.

RADIO STATIONS AM: WPLO 610 (country); WGST 640 (news/talk); WSB 750 (news/talk); WGKA 1190 (classical). FM: WABE 90.1 (public radio, classical music); WCLK 91.9 (jazz); WZGC 92.9 (classic rock); WFOX 97.1 (oldies); WSB 98.5 (adult contemporary); WKHX 101.5 (country).

TELEPHONE The area code for *most* of Atlanta inside the I-285 perimeter is 404; it's 770 for the city's suburban areas.

SALES TAX The sales tax is 6%; the hotel tax is 7%.

CLIMATE Spring and fall weather is crisp and comfortable, summers are hot and humid, and winters generally are mild, although temperatures can drop to below freezing, with occasional sleet and light snow. At an altitude of 1,050 feet in the foothills of the Blue Ridge Mountains, Atlanta gets about 50 inches of rainfall annually. May, September, October, and November tend to be the sunniest months.

GETTING AROUND

AIRPORT Atlanta is served by *Hartsfield Atlanta International Airport,* the world's second busiest. The two terminals (North and South), the five domestic concourses, and the international concourse comprise the world's largest air passenger complex. The layout is straightforward and buildings are connected by a fast and efficient subway system. Except during rush hours, it's about a 20-minute drive between the airport and downtown. *Atlanta Airport Shuttle* provides van transportation to downtown hotels and suburban areas such as *Emory University* and Lenox Square (phone: 524-3400). The same company also serves Roswell, Stone Mountain, and Windy Hill on I-75 North (phone: 768-7600). Travelers without much luggage can take *MARTA (Metropolitan Atlanta Rapid Transit Authority)* trains from the airport to downtown in about 15 minutes for $1.50 one way.

MARTA (METROPOLITAN ATLANTA RAPID TRANSIT AUTHORITY) A combination of bus and rapid rail service, *MARTA* is Atlanta's public transportation system. Bus routes lace the city and feed into 36 rapid rail stations on the East-West, North-South, and Northeast lines, connecting at the *Five Points* station downtown. Each station was designed by a different architect and features original artwork, some of it quite stunning. The fare for bus or rail is $1.50 and transfers between the two are free; exact change or a token is required. *MARTA* maintains information booths at the intersection of Peachtree and West Peachtree Streets near the *Hyatt Regency Atlanta* hotel, and at Broad and Walton Streets at the *Five Points* station (phone: 848-4711).

CAR RENTAL All major national firms are represented.

TAXI Atlanta's reputation for shoddy taxi service is due mainly to the vehicles and drivers that congregate at the airport. Elsewhere, taxicabs usually are clean, safe, and efficient. *Yellow Cab* (phone: 521-0200), *Checker Cab* (phone: 351-1111), and *Buckhead Safety Cab* (233-1152) are among the companies that provide 24-hour, radio-dispatched service.

SPECIAL EVENTS

One of the best times to visit Atlanta is during the April *Dogwood Festival* (phone: 329-0501). The *Atlanta Steeplechase* (phone: 237-7436) occurs later in the month, as does the *Georgia Renaissance Festival,* on weekends through the first week in June (and again in October through the first week in November; phone: 770-964-8575). May brings the *Atlanta Peach Caribbean Carnival* (phone: 220-0171), and the *Atlanta Jazz Festival* (phone: 817-6815). The July 4 *Peachtree Road Race* (phone: 231-9064) is the largest 10k race in the world, and is followed by evening fireworks at Lenox Square and *Georgia's Stone Mountain Park* (phone: 770-498-5600). The latter hosts a major festival every month of the year. The *Montreaux Atlanta Music Festival* is held during the *Labor Day* weekend (phone: 817-6815). The *Arts Festival of Atlanta* (phone: 885-1125) takes place in September; as does the *Atlanta Greek Festival* (phone: 633-5870). The lighting of the Great Tree at *Underground Atlanta* on *Thanksgiving* night kicks off the holiday season. College football's *Peach Bowl* is played at the end of December.

MUSEUMS

In addition to those described in *Special Places,* Atlanta has a number of notable museums.

ATLANTA HERITAGE ROW: THE MUSEUM AT UNDERGROUND This interactive museum offers one of the best overall orientations to the city. Visitors here can experience the shelling of a Civil War bunker, hop aboard an old trolley car, and sit in the cockpit of a Convair 880 while absorbing Atlanta's past, present, and future. Closed Mondays. Admission charge. 55 Upper Alabama St. in *Underground Atlanta* (phone: 584-7879).

ATLANTA HISTORY CENTER Within this lushly wooded complex lie a number of attractions. The *Atlanta History Museum* imaginatively segments the years since 1837 into eras of growth, and sponsors rotating exhibitions. The *Tullie Smith House* is an authentic 1840s "plantation plain" Georgia farmhouse and outbuildings. *Swan House* is a handsomely furnished Anglo-Palladian–style mansion that was built in 1928. Also within the 32 acres are the former coach house (now a popular lunch spot, gift shop, and art gallery) and a marked nature trail. Open daily. Admission charge. 3101 Andrews Dr. (phone: 814-4000).

MUSEUM OF THE JIMMY CARTER LIBRARY Memorabilia of President Carter's *White House* years (1977–81) include a re-creation of the Oval Office, elaborate state gifts, a film on the presidency, and interactive videos. The museum occupies one of the five circular buildings that form the *Carter Presidential Center* and is the only one open to the public. Set on 30 acres, the complex also contains a gift shop and a restaurant overlooking a quiet Japanese garden. Open daily. Admission charge. One Copenhill Ave. (phone: 331-3942).

FERNBANK SCIENCE CENTER This entertaining center has one of the nation's largest planetariums, an observatory (open Thursday and Friday evenings), a paved trail through 65 acres of unspoiled forest, and an Apollo Six Command Module in the museum. Open daily. Admission charge for planetarium shows only. 156 Heaton Park Dr., Decatur (phone: 378-4311).

FERNBANK MUSEUM OF NATURAL HISTORY The largest natural history museum south of the *Smithsonian,* this stunning building houses an IMAX theater and comprehensive exhibits on the evolution of Georgia and the universe. The dinosaurs, of course, are the biggest draw. Open daily. Admission charge. 767 Clifton Rd., Decatur (phone: 378-0127).

HERNDON HOME This Beaux Arts mansion was built in 1910 by Alonzo Herndon, a former slave and founder of the nation's second-largest, black-owned life insurance company. Closed Sundays and Mondays. No admission charge. 587 University Pl. (phone: 581-9813).

HIGH MUSEUM OF ART The building is a masterpiece of modern architecture, with an exterior of dazzling white tiles and a central atrium flooded with natural light. It houses collections of American, European, and African art and a fine assemblage of decorative arts. Closed Mondays. No charge on Thursday afternoons. 1280 Peachtree St. (phone: 733-4444). The *High Museum of Art Folk Art and Photography Galleries* downtown house additional displays. Closed Sundays. No admission charge. 30 John Wesley Dobbs Ave. (phone: 577-6940).

MARGARET MITCHELL HOUSE The building where Margaret Mitchell wrote most of *Gone With the Wind* is the only remaining tangible connection with Atlanta's most famous author. Recent restoration reflects two eras: the single-family home that was built in 1899 and the unit in which Ms. Mitchell and her husband lived (1925-32) after the house was converted to apartments. Admission charge. Peachtree and Tenth Sts. (phone: 249-7012).

MICHAEL C. CARLOS MUSEUM Architect Michael Graves designed the witty interior of this large and well-laid-out repository of the wealth of ancient lands: artifacts of Egyptian, Greek, Roman, pre-Columbian, Near and Middle Eastern, and sub-Saharan origin. Major rotating exhibitions come as loans from other institutions and from the museum's vast collection of prints and drawings dating to the Middle Ages. Open daily. Donations accepted. N. Decatur and Oxford Rds. on the Quadrangle of the *Emory University* campus (phone: 727-4282).

ROAD TO TARA MUSEUM This large collection of *Gone With the Wind* book and movie memorabilia, as well as genuine Civil War items, thrills "Windies" and history buffs alike. The museum is located in the renovated *Georgian Terrace,* the former hotel where Margaret Mitchell turned the epic manuscript over to her publisher. Open daily. Admission charge. 659 Peachtree St. (phone: 897-1939).

SCITREK–THE SCIENCE AND TECHNOLOGY MUSEUM OF ATLANTA Applying the principles of science is fun and then some at this hands-on playground where more than 150 machines, gadgets, and learning stations thrill and amuse children and adults alike. Open daily. Admission charge. 395 Piedmont Ave. (phone: 522-5500).

WREN'S NEST This Victorian house, named for a family of birds that took refuge in the mailbox, was the home of Joel Chandler Harris, an author and journalist best known as the chronicler of the *Uncle Remus* tales, featuring Br'er Fox and Br'er Rabbit. Storytelling sessions, many of them focusing on African folktales, are scheduled regularly. Closed Mondays. Admission charge. 1050 Ralph David Abernathy Blvd. (phone: 753-8535).

WORLD OF COCA-COLA The exterior design of the three-story building next to *Underground Atlanta* features clever take-offs on Coke's signature logo and green glass bottle. Inside is a wealth of soft drink memorabilia and commercials, capped off with free drinks. Open daily. Admission charge. 55 Martin Luther King Jr. Dr. (phone: 676-5151).

SHOPPING

Atlanta offers a taste of Fifth Avenue, Rodeo Drive, and the rainbow's end. Huge malls, department stores, designer boutiques, art galleries, food and flea markets, antiques centers, and outlet malls offer tempting merchandise. In the affluent Buckhead neighborhood, about 7 miles north of downtown, are clustered local branches of such upscale emporia as *Gucci, Abercrombie & Fitch,* and *Brooks Brothers.* Buckhead also is the antiques and art gallery epicenter. In *Underground Atlanta*'s festival-style complex downtown, scores of shops and vending carts feature food, apparel, and gifts. The in-town neighborhood of Virginia/Highland is a place to shop for cutting-edge clothing, offbeat items, and original art. Little Five Points is Atlanta's Bohemia, with shops and street life to match.

LENOX SQUARE Located in Buckhead, Atlanta's largest mall is where *Rich's, Macy's, Neiman Marcus, FAO Schwarz, Benetton,* and numerous other specialty shops reside. There are plenty of restaurants, too, plus concierge service and valet parking. 3393 Peachtree Rd. (phone: 233-6767).

PHIPPS PLAZA Anchored by *Saks Fifth Avenue, Lord & Taylor,* and *Parisian,* the high-fashion shops at this glamorous mall include *Armani, Tiffany,* and the only *Nike Town* in the southeast. Concierge service, valet parking, and a range of popular restaurants add to the experience. 3500 Peachtree Rd. (phone: 262-0992).

SPORTS AND FITNESS

A major league city, Atlanta fields four professional sports teams.

BASEBALL The Atlanta *Braves* play in the reconfigured stadium built for the *1996 Summer Olympic Games* (Capital Ave. at Ralph David Abernathy Blvd.; phone: 522-7630). The *Georgia Tech Yellow Jackets* play on campus in *Russ Chandler Field* (phone: 894-5447).

BASKETBALL The Atlanta *Hawks* host home games at an interim venue (phone: 827-DUNK for location) while a new arena is under construction. *Georgia Tech* tips off in *Alexander Memorial Coliseum* (10th St. and I-75/85; phone: 894-5447).

BICYCLING Bikes may be rented at *Skate Escape* (1086 Piedmont Ave., across from *Piedmont Park;* phone: 892-1292).

FISHING There's good fishing at Lakes Allatoona, Lanier, and Jackson. Fishing permits (necessary) can be purchased at *KMart, Wal-Mart,* and at hunting and fishing supply stores.

FITNESS CENTERS The *YMCA* (phone: 588-9622) has modern health centers throughout the metro area. Many of the city's private fitness clubs allow non-members use of their facilities for a nominal daily rate.

FOOTBALL The Atlanta *Falcons* host their *NFL* opponents at the *Georgia Dome* (1 Georgia Dome Dr.; phone: 223-8000). *Georgia Tech* plays at *Bobby Dodd Stadium* (North Ave. and I-75/85; phone: 894-5447).

GOLF Of hundreds of courses in the metro area, about 40 are open to non-members. Within the I-285 perimeter, the best public facilities are *Sugar Creek* (phone: 241-7671) and *North Fulton* (phone: 255-0723). The top suburban courses are at *Georgia's Stone Mountain Park* (phone: 770-498-5715); *Chateau Elan* (phone: 770-932-0900); *City Club Marietta* (phone: 770-528-0555); *Eagle Watch* (phone: 770-591-1000); *White Columns* (phone: 770-740-1111); and *Metropolitan* (phone: 770-981-5325).

JOGGING From downtown, run along Peachtree Street or Piedmont Road to *Piedmont Park*, about 1½ miles; roads in the park are closed to traffic. There is a bike and jogging trail around the *Carter Presidential Center* (see *Museums*). The Cochran Shoals unit of the *Chattahoochee River National Recreation Area* contains a 3-mile jogging and fitness trail with 22 exercise stations (1978 Island Ford Pkwy.; phone: 770-952-4419). For more information, call the *Atlanta Track Club* (phone: 231-9064).

MOTOR RACING Year-round races at the *Atlanta Motor Speedway* (US 19/41, Hampton, GA; phone: 770-707-4211) are highlighted by NASCAR competitions in March and November. Sports cars and motorcycles race from March through November at *Road Atlanta* (5300 Winder Hwy., Braselton, GA; phone: 770-967-6143).

RIVER RAFTING Rafting on the Chattahoochee River, on Atlanta's northern periphery, is a popular warm weather pastime. Equipment may be rented seasonally at the *Chattahoochee Outdoor Center* (1990 Island Ford Pkwy.; phone: 770-395-6851).

TENNIS The best public clay courts are at the *Bitsy Grant Tennis Center* (2125 Northside Dr.; phone: 351-2774), which also has hard courts. Other excellent public courts are at the *Blackburn Tennis Center* (3501 Ashford-Dunwoody Rd.; phone: 770-451-1061) and the *DeKalb Tennis Center* (1400 McConnell Dr., Decatur; phone: 770-325-2520). At *Georgia's Stone Mountain Park* (phone:770-498-5702), the public may play on 20 courts, 16 of which were built for the *1996 Summer Olympic Games.*

THEATER

For complete performance schedules, check the publications listed in *Local Coverage* above. Among the long-standing theatrical companies are the *Alliance Theater* and *Studio Theater* (phone: 733-5000) and the *Theatrical Outfit* (phone: 872-0665), both in Midtown, and *Theatre in the Square* in Marietta (phone: 770-422-8369). *Horizon Theater* (phone: 584-7450); *Jomandi Productions* (phone: 876-6346); and *Seven Stages Theater* offer productions as well. Touring Broadway companies often perform at the *Fox Theatre* (phone: 881-2100). The *Center for Puppetry Arts* (1404 Spring St.; phone:

873-3089) has performances, exhibitions, and a museum. And the *Atlanta Ballet* stages classical and contemporary works at the *Fox Theater* (Peachtree St. and Ponce de Leon Ave.; phone: 873-5811).

MUSIC

The *Atlanta Symphony Orchestra* plays a fall-through-spring schedule at the *Woodruff Arts Center* (1280 Peachtree St.; phone: 733-5000) as well as a summer pops series with touring entertainers at *Chastain Amphitheater.* Chamber music groups include the *Atlanta Virtuosi* (*Oglethorpe University Museum*; 4484 Peachtree Rd.; phone: 770-938-8611) and *Atlanta Chamber Players* (*Georgia State University Concert Hall;* phone: 651-1228). *Emory University* (phone: 727-6666) sponsors a number of musical series. Big-name groups and entertainers perform regularly at the *Georgia Dome* and other large concert venues.

NIGHTCLUBS AND NIGHTLIFE

Atlanta's nightlife covers the spectrum, with most places open until 3 or 4 AM. The intersection of Peachtree and East Paces Ferry Roads in Buckhead is the nucleus of the greatest concentration of evening and late-night entertainment in town. Jazz is featured at *Otto's* (265 E. Paces Ferry Rd.; phone: 233-1133) and *Dante's Down the Hatch* (*Underground Atlanta;* phone: 577-1800 and 3380 Peachtree Rd.; phone: 266-1600). Blues heads the menu at *Blind Willie's* (828 N. Highland Ave.; phone: 873-2583). *Somber Reptile* (842 Marietta St.; phone: 881-9701) features a combination of blues and jazz. The high-energy set flocks to *Oxygen* (3065 Peachtree Rd.; phone: 816-6522); *Chameleon Club* (3179 Peachtree Rd.; phone: 261-8004); and *Star Community Bar* (437 Moreland Ave.; phone: 681-9018). Big-name comedians play *The Punch Line* (280 Hildebrand Dr.; phone: 252-LAFF). Good places to meet and mingle are *Jellyrolls Dueling Pianos and Sing-A-Long* (295 E. Paces Ferry Rd.; phone: 261-6841); *Johnny's Hideaway* (3771 Roswell Rd.; phone: 233-8026); and *John Harvard's Brew House* (3041 Peachtree Rd.; phone: 816-2739). The most convivial old-fashioned neighborhood bar is *Manuel's Tavern* (602 N. Highland Ave.; phone: 525-3447). *Mama's Country Showcase* (3952 Covington Hwy.; phone: 288-6262) is the place for live country-western swing and two-step.

Best in Town

CHECKING IN

Atlanta visitors can pick and choose from among one of the broadest accommodations assortments in the country. The largest selections are in the downtown convention district; the uptown Buckhead commercial/shopping/entertainment area; near *Hartsfield Atlanta International Airport* and in commercial areas such as I-285/*Perimeter Mall* and I-285/*Cumberland Mall/Galleria.* Remember to book early from fall through spring, when major conventions may have everything virtually locked up. Most of Atlanta's major hotels have complete facilities for the business traveler. Those listed below as having "business services" usually offer such conveniences as meeting rooms, photocopiers, computers, translation services, and express check-out, among others. Call the individual hotel for additional information. Expect to pay $150 or more per night for a double room in hotels we've classified as very expensive; from $110 to $150 at those listed as expensive; and between $80 and $110 at those categorized as moderate; there are no exceptional inexpensive hotels in the city. But it is possible to stay inexpensively in bed and breakfast establishments. For information and reservations, contact *Bed & Breakfast Atlanta* (1801 Piedmont Ave., Suite 208, Atlanta 30324; phone: 875-0525; fax 875-9672). Unless otherwise noted, hotel rooms have air conditioning, private baths, TV sets, and telephones.

All hotels below are in Atlanta and telephone and fax numbers are in the 404 area code unless otherwise indicated.

VERY EXPENSIVE

Grand Hotel Atlanta A decidedly European feel pervades this luxury midtown establishment, where 264 lavishly decorated rooms and suites have separate showers and tubs, and hair dryers. A valet and a concierge are available. Recreational facilities include a health club with a sauna and an indoor lap pool; there are two restaurants (including the elegant *Florencia*), a bar, and a lounge. Business services are available. 75 14th St. (phone: 881-9898; 800-952-0702; fax: 873-4692).

Hyatt Regency Atlanta This downtown hotel sparked the interior atrium craze in the mid 1960s. Its recently refurbished 1,279 rooms and 58 suites now feature a rich burgundy, cream, and green color scheme. A new wing has been added to house downtown's largest hotel meeting facility. The Regency Club level contain upgraded amenities, 24-hour concierge service, and access to a private lounge that serves complimentary breakfast and cocktails. Amenities include a new health club, 34 specially designed to accommodate the disabled, a concierge, and business services. 265 Peachtree Rd. (phone: 577-1234; 800-233-1234; fax: 588-4137).

Nikko Atlanta Asian elegance and restrained luxury flavor this 440-room, Japanese-owned hotel in Buckhead. A traditional Japanese garden offers respite and the *Kamagowa* restaurant features Japanese fare that can be served in an authentic tatami room. Facilities include a health club and a pool, and there is 24-hour room service, a concierge, and complimentary transportation within a 2-mile radius. Business services are available. 3300 Peachtree Rd. (phone: 365-8100; 800-645-5687; fax: 233-5686).

Omni at CNN Center The 458 rooms here sport contemporary American decor and many have balconies overlooking all or part of the 14-story, five-and-one-half-acre atrium that forms the center of the *CNN Center* mega-structure.

There is a restaurant; other amenities include a concierge desk, an adjoining health club, and business services. Marietta St. and International Blvd. (phone: 659-0000; 800-843-6664; fax: 525-5050).

Renaissance Waverly In the heart of the suburban I-285/*Galleria* shopping and office complex, this deluxe, 521-room property is connected to the Galleria Convention Center on two levels. The hotel offers first class dining, including a 150-item Sunday brunch buffet. Amenities include indoor-outdoor pools, a Jacuzzi, a health club, 24-hour room service, a concierge, and business services. 2450 Galleria Pkwy. (phone: 770-953-4500; 800-468-3571; fax: 770-953-0740).

Ritz-Carlton, Atlanta With its European decor and elegant extras, this luxury property with 447 rooms is especially attractive to those whose business takes them to the nearby downtown financial district and the *Georgia World Congress Center.* The hotel's restaurant is one of the city's leading dining spots (see *Eating Out*), and the cafe is the scene of power breakfasts and lunches. Other amenities include 24-hour room service, a concierge, a fitness center, and business services. 181 Peachtree St. (phone: 659-0400; 800-241-3333; fax: 688-0400).

Ritz-Carlton, Buckhead In the heart of the city's most upscale neighborhood, this is probably Atlanta's most fashionable stopping place. The dining room (see *Eating Out*) and lounge are *the* places to see and be seen, and afternoon tea is the city's most elegant. Service is flawless, the 553 rooms and suites are handsomely appointed, and facilities include an indoor pool, a health club, 24-hour room service, a concierge, and business services. 3434 Peachtree Rd. (phone: 237-2700; 800-241-3333; fax: 239-0078).

Swissôtel Atlanta Elegant, efficient hotel-keeping and Biedermeier-style furnishings classify this 358-room property as first-rate. Its location within walking distance of *Lenox Square* and *Phipps Plaza* shopping malls is a big plus. The *Palm* steakhouse restaurant features a good beef and seafood menu. Amenities include 24-hour room service, a concierge, and business services. 3391 Peachtree Rd. (phone: 365-0065; 800-253-1397; fax: 365-8787).

Westin Peachtree Plaza Among the 1,068 pie-shaped guest rooms in this tall, round, downtown landmark are 14 rooms specially equipped for business travelers. The revolving *Sun Dial* restaurant (see *Eating Out*), and bar on the top three levels of the 73-story building offer a 360-degree view of the surrounding region. The *Savannah Fish Company* (see *Eating Out*) is another of the property's three eating places. Amenities include health facilities, an outdoor pool with retractable roof, 24-hour room service, a concierge, and business services. 210 Peachtree St. (phone: 659-1400; 800-228-3000; fax: 589-7424).

EXPENSIVE

Gaslight Inn This 1913 Craftsman-style bungalow in the popular Virginia/Highland neighborhood has been extravagantly renovated into a bed and breakfast inn with unique gas-burning fixtures and accents. The unusually large amount of public space includes a formal living room, a formal dining room where a complimentary continental breakfast is served, an airy den, a screened porch, and a walled garden with a fountain. One of three suites contains a Jacuzzi, a wet bar, and a private deck. The three smaller guest rooms fall in the moderate price range. Business services are available. Major credit cards are accepted. 1001 St. Charles Ave. (phone: 875-1001).

MODERATE

Days Inn The Atlanta-based chain offers clean, few-frills accommodations at very reasonable rates. Most have a pool, playground, and family restaurant; some have kitchenettes. Of the 12 Atlanta locations, the *Days Inn Downtown* (300 Spring St.; phone: 523-1144; fax: 577-8495) may be one of the best downtown values. A Midtown bargain is the 12-story, 144-room *Days Inn–Peachtree Street* (683 Peachtree St.; phone: 874-9200; fax: 873-4245), opposite the *Fox Theater.* Occupying a 1920s building, it has no restaurant but adjoins a fast-food eatery. Call 800-325-2525 for information on the others.

Shellmont Bed & Breakfast Lodge This imposing, 1891 home, trimmed with elaborate architectural details, contains five rooms furnished with Victorian antiques. A landscaped garden separates the main structure from a two-room carriage house that can sleep up to four. 821 Piedmont Ave. (phone: 872-9290; fax: 872-5379).

EATING OUT

Atlanta's hundreds of restaurants, cafés, and trendy grills and bistros serve everything from traditional Southern cooking to American regional dishes and an astonishing variety of international cuisines. Expect to pay between $100 and $140 for dinner for two at restaurants we've described as very expensive; between $70 and $100 at those in the expensive category; between $35 and $70 at dining spots rated moderate; and under $35 at our inexpensive choices. Prices do not include wine, drinks, tax, or tips. All telephone numbers are in the 404 area code, unless otherwise indicated.

Unless otherwise noted, restaurants are open for lunch and dinner.

VERY EXPENSIVE

Bone's This is the choice of those who wish to impress a guest. Impeccable service is the keynote in this clubby-style dining room. Choice steaks (five cuts, seven sizes), chops, veal, and seafood are the menu stars. Side dishes, such as grit fritters, sautéed snow peas, and steamed broccoli enhance meals.

Open daily; open weekends for dinner only. Reservations advised. Major credit cards accepted. 3130 Piedmont Rd. (phone: 237-2663).

Dining Room at The Ritz-Carlton, Buckhead Dining in this lovely room is a carefully orchestrated affair composed by chef Guenter Seeger, who insists on using only the freshest ingredients; he rises before dawn to prowl the markets. The menu, which changes daily, carries such creative and memorable dishes as roasted spiny lobster with artichoke risotto. The professional staff efficiently patrol the mahogany-paneled room that's hung with museum-quality art and furnished with comfortable, silk-upholstered banquettes. Open for dinner only; closed Sundays. Reservations advised. Major credit cards accepted. 3434 Peachtree Rd. (phone: 237-2700).

Restaurant at The Ritz-Carlton, Atlanta One of the best continental restaurants in the city, this dining room offers an elegant ambience complete with fine crystal chandeliers. Chef Daniel Schaffhauser adds unexpected flourishes to perfectly cooked dishes: Bass filet is embellished with roasted sesame-seed and soy-ginger vinaigrette, salmon is paired with Vidalia onion corn bread *gallette,* and roasted roe deer loin shares a plate with a vegetable napoleon, made of layers of potato, mushrooms, and spaghetti squash. Dinner only; closed Sundays. Reservations advised. Major credit cards accepted. 181 Peachtree St. (phone: 659-0400).

Sun Dial Located on the 71st floor of the *Westin Peachtree Plaza,* this restaurant offers unequaled views of the city with a menu to match. Enjoy sautéed Dungeness crab cakes and filet mignon with red onion marmalade. Sunsets are especially beautiful from this vantage point. Reservations advised. Major credit cards accepted. 210 Peachtree St. (phone: 659-1400).

EXPENSIVE

1848 House This Greek Revival–style plantation home, which is listed in the National Register of Historic Places, provides a taste of the Old South. Choose from such favorites as Charleston she crab soup, pan-roasted quail, and loin of lamb all perfectly prepared and served with imaginative side dishes. Open daily for dinner; Sunday brunch. Reservations advised. Major credit cards accepted. 780 S. Cobb Dr., Marietta (phone: 770-428-1848.

Hedgerose Heights Inn An intimate, refined setting makes a fitting backdrop for superb dishes complemented by a fine wine list and very good service. Open for dinner only; closed Sundays and Mondays. Reservations advised. Major credit cards accepted. 490 E. Paces Ferry Rd. (phone: 233-7673).

Savannah Fish Company Located in the *Westin Peachtree Plaza,* seafoodies can choose from Maine lobster, shrimp, oysters, clams, chowder, crab cakes, and scallops; beef eaters have a few selections as well. In the end, though, hardly anything tops the taste of that smoked bluefish dip, or the stunning setting with a horizontal waterfall and pool. Open daily for dinner.

Reservations advised. Major credit cards accepted. 210 Peachtree St. at International Blvd. (phone: 589-7456).

La Grotta Located on the lower level of an upscale Buckhead apartment building, the subdued, intimate space opens onto a surprising vista of a charming garden hidden among the neighboring high-rises. Pasta dishes such as *ravi-olini con caprino* (ravioli stuffed with goat cheese, apples, and celery in a buttery sun-dried tomato sauce) are first-rate. Veal and lamb cooked with garlic, shallots, and fresh herbs are house specialties. Open for dinner only; closed Sundays. Reservations advised. Major credit cards accepted. 2637 Peachtree Rd. (phone: 231-1368).

MODERATE

Abruzzi Classic Italian dishes, and those from the Abruzzi region, make this restau-rant a favorite. Veal osso buco, lobster *fra diavolo,* and delicately baked fish top the menu; venison, hare, quail, and wild boar appear in season. If nothing on the menu appeals, tell Nico Petrucci and he will have the kitchen whip up something special. Closed Sundays; open Saturdays for dinner only. Reservations advised. Major credit cards accepted. 2355 Peachtree Rd. (phone: 261-8186).

Atlanta Fish Market A 60-foot-high fish clad with copper scales stands on its tail outside the entrance to one of the city's premiere seafood restaurants. In the cavernous interior, which resembles a cross between a fish shack and an Art Deco train station, the numerous offerings are displayed in a gro-cery store–style counter in front of an open kitchen. The menu changes daily but you always can count on a large grilled Carolina mountain salmon trout filet, the house speciality. The Dungeness crab cocktail or salmon quesadilla makes a good starter. Open daily; open Sundays for dinner only. Reservations advised. Major credit cards accepted. 265 Pharr Rd. (phone: 262-3165).

Brasserie Le Coze After an initial struggle to overcome the effects of its mall loca-tion (there's also an outside entrance), the restaurant instituted by the famous Maguy Le Coze and her late brother Guy, of New York *Le Bernardin* fame, has caught on. The menu is varied and features *croque monsieurs* (grilled ham and swiss cheese sandwiches); out-of-this-world mussels in a white wine, shallot, and parsley broth; and yellowfin tuna carpaccio. Business lunchers might opt for coq au vin. Desserts include rum-flavored bananas in phyllo pastry topped with white chocolate mousse, vanilla *vacherin* (a meringue shell filled with ice cream and fruit) with *crème anglais,* and warm chocolate soufflé cake. Closed Sundays. Reservations advised. Major credit cards accepted. 3393 Peachtree Rd. (phone: 266-1440).

Buckhead Diner Gleaming stainless steel, neon, and leather distinguish this snazzy eatery that is a magnet for young fashionables and hip out-of-towners. The menu is a trendy array of old-fashioned favorites, such as a grilled salmon

BLT, and veal and wild mushroom meatloaf. No reservations. Major credit cards accepted. 3073 Piedmont Rd. (phone: 262-3336).

Curry House Chef Sohrab Khan subtly combines spices to produce consistently delicious Indian dishes. These include the mild chicken *moghli* and the spicier chicken *tikka masala* (tandoori chicken cooked with nuts in a mild cream sauce). Equally memorable are the vegetable dishes. Open daily for dinner. Reservations unnecessary. Major credit cards accepted. 451 Moreland Ave. (phone: 688-0005).

Mi Spia Pasta in general, and angel hair pasta in particular, is the speciality at this stylish trattoria in the upscale *Park Place Shopping Center.* The Mediterranean-Italian menu also lists beef, lamb, venison, and pork. Open daily; open weekends for dinner only. Reservations advised. Major credit cards accepted. 4505 Ashford-Dunwoody Rd. (phone: 770-393-1333).

Nava Pano Karatassos has done it again. When the Southwestern cuisine craze finally made it to Georgia, the restaurateur with the Midas touch brought in eight Santa Fe craftsmen to create an eatery with an authentic pueblo look. Even better, he lured chef Kevin Rathbun here from Dallas to turn out perfect sun-corn–crusted snapper, tuna served rare after being cured with lemon and cilantro, and other palate pleasers. Open daily for dinner. Reservations advised. Major credit cards accepted. 3060 Peachtree Rd. (phone: 240-1984).

Pano's & Paul's For 18 years, chef Paul Albrecht has kept this classy restaurant on the culinary cutting edge. A few favorites are yellowfin grouper wrapped in crisped potatoes, jumbo cold-water lobster tail, smoked and grilled Atlantic salmon, and roast American rack of lamb with garlic-mustard glaze. Eighteen appetizers run the gamut from Maine lobster bisque to beluga caviar. While the service is impeccable, the level of formality is a bit unnerving. The decor—fringed lamp shades, antique chandeliers, and velvet booths—is almost laughably opulent, but somehow manages to seem rather dear. Open for dinner only; closed Sundays. Reservations advised. Major credit cards accepted. 1232 W. Paces Ferry Rd. (phone: 261-3662).

Partners Morningside Café In a small, noisy room decorated with artwork, an upwardly mobile crowd dines on delicious seafood, steak, and pasta. Open daily for dinner only. No reservations. Major credit cards accepted. 1397 Highland Ave. (phone: 876-8104).

Veni Vidi Vici The accent is Northern Italian, with handmade pasta and breads brought in daily from another of his successful ventures, the *Buckhead Bread Company.* Plus there's a wood-burning rotisserie for spit-roasted pork, chicken, lamb, and duck. Specialties include suckling pig with chive mashed potatoes, braised cabbage, and crackling; crisp duck with onions, spicy lentils, and orange grappa sauce is another delicious choice. There are also menu items low in fat, cholesterol, and sodium, and a decent wine list. Open daily for dinner; open weekends for dinner only. Reservations advised. Major credit cards accepted. 41 14th St. (phone: 875-8424).

INEXPENSIVE

Pasta da Pulcinella Modest black-and-white photographs and line drawings are proof positive that profits are not frittered away on decor but go toward improving the already perfect pasta. Go for the *tortelli di mele* (ravioli filled with Granny Smith apples, sausage, and parmigiano cheese) or the *ravioli sardi di melanzane* (stuffed with eggplant, bell peppers, walnuts, ricotta, basil, and mint, and topped with a tomato-basil sauce), a vegetarian's delight. Closed Sundays; closed Saturdays for lunch. No reservations. No credit cards accepted. 1027 Peachtree St. (phone: 892-6195).

Rio Bravo These cantiñas, with campy Old Mexico decor, serve very good Tex-Mex victuals. No reservations. Major credit cards accepted. Six locations include the convivial Buckhead branch at 3172 Roswell Rd. (phone: 262-7431).

Sundown Café Southwestern and Mexican dishes never tasted so good. Don't miss the shrimp cakes in *chipotle* sauce with a cactus base and do finish with the chocolate *chimichanga* in a tequila cream sauce. Closed Sundays; open Saturdays for dinner only. No reservations. Major credit cards accepted. 2165 Cheshire Bridge Rd. (phone: 321-1118).

Varsity It's a scene right out of *American Graffiti*—a drive-in with car hops, an air of bedlam, and an all-American menu of hot dogs, hamburgers, and fried peach pies. No reservations. No credit cards accepted. 61 North Ave. (phone: 881-1706).

Vortex With service that sometimes seems accidental and a background tape that's deafening, the burgers, nevertheless, are the best. The all-American fare is complemented by a choice of 100 beers and 50 single malt Scotches by the glass. Open for dinner daily. No reservations. Major credit cards accepted. 1041 W. Peachtree St. (phone: 875-1667).

Baltimore

Baltimore has spent much of its life being unjustly ignored. The world found it easy to overlook this metropolis that lay quietly between the more dazzling cities of the Atlantic seaboard. Commerce between Washington, Philadelphia and New York bypassed Baltimore so smoothly and efficiently via its Beltway and Harbor Tunnels, that the city went virtually unnoticed.

But now Baltimore—a winning combination of big-city razzle-dazzle and small-town charm—is a vibrant link in the chain connecting Boston, New York, and Washington. It has acquired a cosmopolitan atmosphere while retaining the intimacy of traditional Southern hospitality. This waterfront treasure offers a sparkling harbor, promenades, marinas, world class museums, a modern business district, and a vast collection of culinary specialties—but still, it is the hospitality of locals that most impresses visitors.

Charles Center, Baltimore's business heart, along with historic *Fort McHenry,* the tiered iron stacks of the *Peabody Library,* and its famous medical institutions—including *Johns Hopkins University*—give the city an urbane, contemporary atmosphere, as well as a link to history. But perhaps the best single thing in Baltimore is its food—hard- or soft-shell crabs, oysters (raw, fried, and stewed), clams, and shad roe—prepared in traditional Maryland style.

Baltimore's deep-water port on the Chesapeake Bay—the major Atlantic port for grain, coal, and spices—has always provided an important commercial link to the rest of the country. Now its 45 miles of waterfront are further enhanced by a bright centerpiece—the *Inner Harbor.* This complex is the proud achievement of a long and concerted campaign to turn the city's decaying dock and pier area into Baltimore's biggest asset. Once full of derelict warehouses, debris, and pollution, the *Inner Harbor* is now the site of *Harborplace*—a pair of double-decker glass pavilions that enclose about 135 restaurants, cafés, and specialty shops—as well as the spectacular *National Aquarium,* with its wonderful displays of marine life and even a tropical rain forest.

Surrounding the historic harbor are some 200 individual neighborhoods, each with its own unique character: Fell's Point, the oldest working maritime district in the nation; Mt. Vernon Place, the city's most elegant square and site of the country's first monument to George Washington; Little Italy, whose many restaurants are within walking distance of *Harborplace;* Antique Row; Guilford; and Federal Hill. (For those interested in a glimpse of Baltimore as it was in the 1950s and 1960s, Barry Levinson, filmmaker and native son, used the city as a backdrop for three of his movies: *Diner, Tin Men,* and *Avalon.*)

The modern five-sided *World Trade Center,* designed by I. M. Pei, and *One Charles Center,* designed by Mies van der Rohe—blends in harmo-

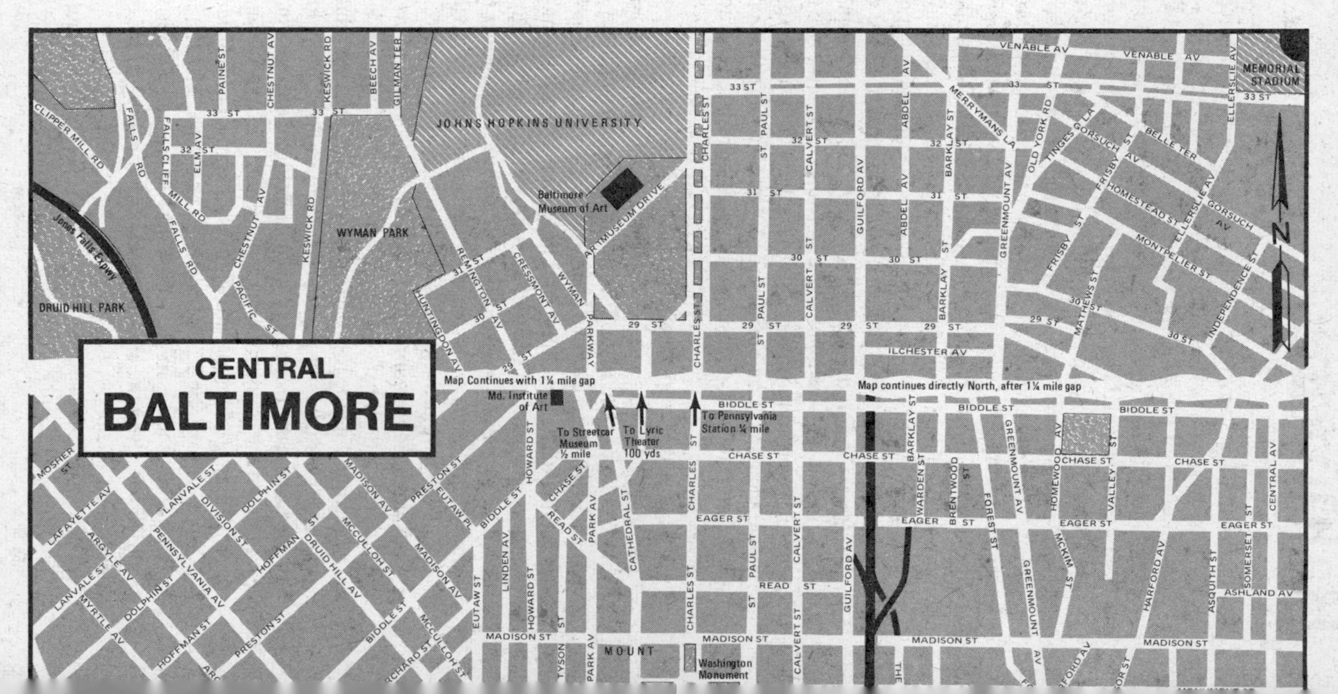
CENTRAL
BALTIMORE
JOHNS HOPKINS UNIVERSITY
Baltimore Museum of Art
WYMAN PARK
DRUID HILL PARK
MEMORIAL STADIUM
Jones Falls Expwy
Md. Institute of Art
Map Continues with 1¼ mile gap
Map continues directly North, after 1¼ mile gap
To Streetcar Museum ½ mile
To Lyric Theater 100 yds
To Pennsylvania Station ¼ mile
Washington Monument
MOUNT
N
CHARLES ST
ST PAUL ST
CALVERT ST
GUILFORD AV
ABDEL AV
BARKLAY ST
GREENMOUNT AV
33 ST
32 ST
31 ST
30 ST
29 ST
VENABLE AV
ELLERSLIE AV
MERRYMANS LA
OLD YORK RD
TINGES LA
GORSUCH AV
BELLE TER
FRISBY ST
HOMESTEAD ST
MONTPELIER ST
MATHEWS ST
INDEPENDENCE ST
ILCHESTER AV
ART MUSEUM DRIVE
WYMAN PARKWAY
CRESSMONT AV
REMINGTON AV
HUNTINGDON AV
PACIFIC ST
CHESTNUT AV
KESWICK RD
BEECH AV
GILMAN TER
PAINE ST
ELM AV
FALLS CLIFF
MILL RD
FALLS RD
CLIPPER MILL RD
BIDDLE ST
CHASE ST
EAGER ST
MADISON ST
HOWARD ST
LINDEN AV
EUTAW ST
EUTAW PL
PRESTON ST
MADISON AV
McCULLOH ST
DRUID HILL AV
HOFFMAN ST
DOLPHIN ST
DIVISION ST
PENNSYLVANIA AV
LANVALE ST
LAFAYETTE AV
ARGYLE AV
MYRTLE AV
MOSHER ST
READ ST
PARK AV
CATHEDRAL ST
TYSON ST
WARDEN ST
BRENTWOOD ST
FOREST ST
HOMEWOOD AV
McKIM ST
VALLEY ST
HARFORD AV
ASQUITH ST
SOMERSET ST
ASHLAND AV
CENTRAL AV

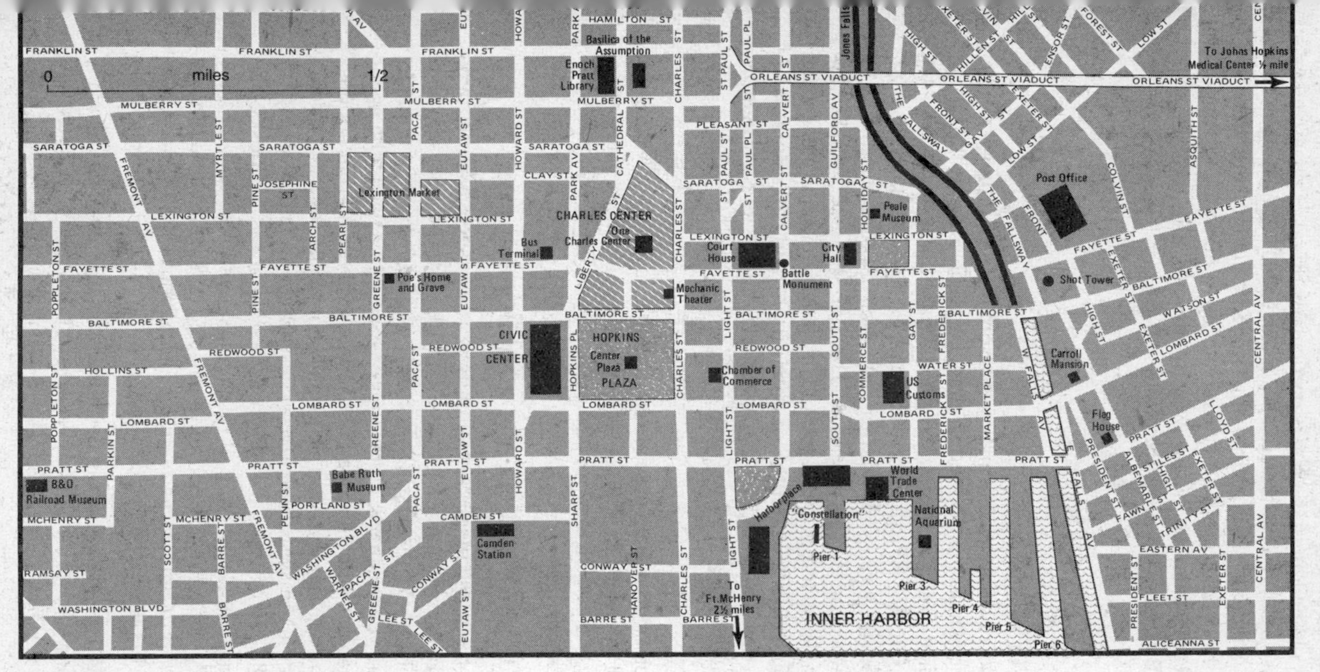
0
miles
1/2
To Johns Hopkins Medical Center ½ mile
ORLEANS ST VIADUCT
Basilica of the Assumption
Enoch Pratt Library
CHARLES CENTER
One Charles Center
Lexington Market
Bus Terminal
Poe's Home and Grave
Mechanic Theater
Court House
Battle Monument
City Hall
Peale Museum
Post Office
Shot Tower
CIVIC CENTER
HOPKINS PLAZA
Center Plaza
Chamber of Commerce
US Customs
Carroll Mansion
Flag House
World Trade Center
National Aquarium
"Constellation"
Harborplace
Pier 1
Pier 3
Pier 4
Pier 5
Pier 6
INNER HARBOR
To Ft. McHenry 2½ miles
Babe Ruth Museum
B&O Railroad Museum
Camden Station
Jones Falls
FRANKLIN ST
MULBERRY ST
SARATOGA ST
LEXINGTON ST
FAYETTE ST
BALTIMORE ST
REDWOOD ST
LOMBARD ST
PRATT ST
CAMDEN ST
CONWAY ST
BARRE ST
FREMONT AV
WASHINGTON BLVD
CHARLES ST
LIGHT ST
HOWARD ST
EUTAW ST
PACA ST
GREENE ST
THE FALLSWAY
CENTRAL AV
EASTERN AV
ALICEANNA ST

niously with the old and ornate, giving Baltimore an interesting and varied skyline. Of its old buildings, the city is particularly proud of the architecturally impressive *City Hall,* completed in 1875 in French Empire style. For the building's centennial, Baltimore spent some $11 million renovating the interior. Like the building itself, the city's assets can be perceived and appreciated most readily from the inside—which is probably why so many people who visit Baltimore like what they find.

Baltimore At-a-Glance

SEEING THE CITY

Baltimore offers its finest panoramic view from the *Top of the World,* an observation deck/museum devoted to changing displays about the city in the World Trade Center at the *Inner Harbor* (Pratt St., between South and Gay Sts.; phone: 837-4515); admission charge. Downstream lies *Fort McHenry,* where the successful American repulsion of British forces in 1814 inspired Francis Scott Key to compose "The Star-Spangled Banner." To the northwest, the buildings and plazas of Charles Center stand out against the surrounding cityscape. To the east lie Little Italy, Fell's Point, and Canton. A 7½-mile promenade links Canton on the east with Key Highway on the west and includes the *Inner Harbor.*

SPECIAL PLACES

As most notable sights in Baltimore are concentrated in a few nicely designed areas, the best way to see the city is by walking. Buses and taxis, which serve the entire city, are convenient, but parking in the lots downtown is neither difficult nor expensive.

INNER HARBOR AND ENVIRONS

HARBORPLACE The dazzling kingpin in Baltimore's renaissance. A plethora of shops, restaurants, and market stalls—about 135 in all—fill its two glass-enclosed pavilions. On the first floor of the *Light Street Pavilion* is a marketplace where vendors hawk all manner of comestibles, while the upper level is chockablock with small eateries serving everything from hot dogs to knishes. And whether you want a crab mallet or a collector's comic book, chances are it's in the *Sam Smith Market* (also on the second floor), where merchants sell a raft of unusual wares from their pushcarts and kiosks. The *Pratt Street Pavilion* has its share of restaurants, boutiques, and specialty stores. Directly across Pratt Street, and connected by an aboveground walkway, is the *Gallery at Harborplace* featuring an additional 75 shops and eateries. Pratt and Light Sts. (phone: 332-4191).

NATIONAL AQUARIUM The aquarium has an impressive series of audiovisual displays on marine life, with a total of 9,000 specimens on five different levels. The *Marine Mammal Pavilion* features Atlantic bottle-nosed dolphins, along with educational presentations and audiovisual displays. "Movelators" carry visitors between levels, which house shark and sting ray pools, puffins living in a reproduction of their natural habitat, one of the largest coral reefs in the US, and a replica of the northeast coast with a display of shellfish and other shoreline creatures which can be handled. Finally, visitors can wander through a tropical rain forest. Open daily. Admission charge. Pier 3, *Inner Harbor* (phone: 576-3810).

FORT McHENRY NATIONAL MONUMENT AND HISTORIC SHRINE In 1814, a young Maryland lawyer watched American forces successfully resist heavy British mortar bombardment and was so inspired by the sight of the Stars and Stripes still fluttering against the morning sky that he wrote "The Star-Spangled Banner." Visitors can see the fort, the old powder magazine, the officers' quarters, the enlisted men's barracks, and then walk along Francis Scott Key's famed ramparts overlooking the harbor. During the summer on weekend afternoons, drills and military ceremonies modeled after those of 1814 are performed by uniformed soldiers and sailors. Closed *Christmas* and *New Year's Day.* Admission charge. South of *Inner Harbor,* at the end of East Fort Ave. (phone: 962-4299).

MARYLAND SCIENCE CENTER AND PLANETARIUM Featured here are hundreds of hands-on activities, live demonstrations, and interactive displays ranging from a simulated space station control center to displays on sight, sound, magnetism, light, and mechanics. There is a 390-seat IMAX movie theater with a five-story screen capable of producing such vivid sensations of movement that viewers feel as if they are part of the action. Closed *Thanksgiving* and *Christmas.* Admission charge. At the southwest corner of the *Inner Harbor* (phone: 685-5225).

CHARLES CENTER AND DOWNTOWN

CHARLES CENTER Built during the past two decades, Charles Center is a 33-acre plot of office buildings, luxury apartment towers, overhead walkways, fountains, and plazas. It's bordered by Lombard Street on the south, Saratoga Street on the north, Hopkins Place and Liberty Street on the west, and Charles Street on the east. (One of the city's oldest and grandest thoroughfares, Charles Street has been revitalized in recent years with shops and restaurants to encourage new business.) Within the complex is *One Charles Center,* a 24-story tower of bronze-covered glass designed by Mies van der Rohe. Star performers, such as Jason Robards, Lauren Bacall, and the late Rudolf Nureyev and Jessica Tandy have performed at its *Morris Mechanic Theatre.* Charles and Baltimore Sts. (phone: 625-4230).

Hopkins Plaza (between Hopkins Pl., Charles St., Baltimore St., and Lombard St.) is the scene for many events, including performances by jazz ensembles and chamber groups. Center Plaza (north of Fayette St. between Liberty and Charles Sts.) features a 33-foot bronze sculpture in the shape of a flame, designed by Francesco Somaini and presented to the city by the

Gas and Electric Company. Skywalks link the Inner Harbor to the *Convention Center* (1 W. Pratt St.; phone: 659-7000). The neighboring *Baltimore Arena* (201 W. Baltimore St.; phone: 347-2010) hosts sporting and entertainment events as well.

EDGAR ALLAN POE HOUSE AND GRAVE Poe lived here in the 1830s; he visited Baltimore again in 1849 long enough to die and be buried. His grave is nearby, in the *Westminster Presbyterian Church Cemetery* at Fayette and Greene Streets. Call ahead for schedule and hours. Admission charge. 203 N. Amity St. (phone: 396-7932 for information). Graveyard tours are given on the first and third Friday evenings of the month and on Saturday mornings from April through November (phone: 706-2070).

CITY HALL Still in use, the domed building is a monument to mid-Victorian design and craftsmanship. 100 N. Holliday St. (phone: 837-5424 for tour information).

LEXINGTON MARKET Since 1782 this colorful indoor marketplace, covering two city blocks, has provided stalls for independent merchants. Today, more than a hundred kiosks and shops are in operation. Lunch on Maryland seafood at its best at *John W. Faidley Seafood* (see *Eating Out*). 400 W. Lexington and Paca Sts. (phone: 685-6169).

MOUNT VERNON PLACE ENVIRONS

This 19th-century bastion of Baltimore aristocracy now houses much of the 20th century's counterculture, with boutiques, restaurants, and natural food shops. Reminders of bygone days remain in the lovely 19th-century merchant prince housefronts, stately squares, and cultural institutions.

WALTERS ART GALLERY This extensive collection, owned by the Walters family (who also owned railroads) and bequeathed to the city, offers an impressive span of art from ancient Near Eastern, Byzantine, and classical archaeological artifacts to medieval European illuminated manuscripts and painted panels, Italian Renaissance paintings, and French Impressionist works. The gallery's collection of Indian, Japanese, Chinese, and Southeast Asian art is displayed in *Hackerman House,* a historic 1850s mansion overlooking Mount Vernon Place. Closed Mondays. Admission charge. 600 N. Charles St. (near Centre St). (phone: 547-9000).

ANTIQUE ROW The 800 block of Howard Street and the area around the corner on West Read Street are an antiques-browser's paradise. About 65 shops here sell items ranging from antique furniture to various forms of artwork. Among the best are *Amos Judd & Son* (841 N. Howard St.; phone: 462-2000), which carries paintings by European artists and bronze sculpture; *Dubey's Art and Antiques* (807 N. Howard St.; phone: 383-2881), with Oriental, English, and American furniture of the 17th and 18th centuries; and *Imperial Half Bushel* (831 N. Howard St.; phone: 462-1192), featuring American silver pieces from the 19th century.

MARYLAND HISTORICAL SOCIETY Home of Francis Scott Key's original handwritten manuscript of "The Star-Spangled Banner," it features 18th- and 19th-century clothing, furniture, and silver. Its library is rich in genealogical material. Closed Mondays. Admission charge. 201 W. Monument St. (phone: 685-3750).

PEABODY INSTITUTE AND CONSERVATORY OF MUSIC Worth a visit simply for a look at the magnificently designed library. Amid pillars and balconies, this 19th-century interior holds 300,000 volumes on tiered iron stacks that spiral upward six stories. Free student concerts are held frequently. Library open daily. No admission charge. Mount Vernon Pl. at Monument and N. Charles Sts. (phone: 659-8163; 659-8124 for concert information).

WASHINGTON MONUMENT AND MUSEUM The very first Washington Monument, designed by Robert Mills, it was completed in 1829 and recently restored. Visitors can climb the 228 steps to the top, where a statue of Washington rests. Closed Mondays and Tuesdays. Donation suggested. Mount Vernon Pl. (phone: 396-0929).

NORTH

BALTIMORE CITY CONSERVATORY Seasonal displays highlight this collection of 3,000 species of tropical plants and flowers. Closed Mondays through Wednesdays. No admission charge. In *Druid Hill Park* at Gwynns Falls Pkwy. and McCulloh St. (phone: 396-0180).

BALTIMORE ZOO More than 1,500 species of mammals, reptiles, and birds live here. A children's zoo and *Chimpanzee Forest* are very popular. Closed *Christmas.* Admission charge. *Druid Hill Park* (phone: 396-7102 or 396-6165).

BALTIMORE MUSEUM OF ART This museum is strong on 20th-century art, thanks to the *Cone Collection*—paintings, prints, and sculptures by Matisse, Picasso, and other post-Impressionists donated by the two wealthy Cone sisters of Baltimore. It also has period rooms that highlight the architectural and artistic development of Maryland from the 1700s through furniture and decorative art objects; the *Wurtzburger Collection* of African, Native American, pre-Columbian, and Oceanic art; a vast print collection; fine 19th- and 20th-century American paintings and sculpture; the spectacular outdoor *Levi* and *Wurtzburger Sculpture Gardens;* a stunning wing with galleries for changing exhibitions and a café overlooking the garden; a wing for modern and contemporary art; and the *Jacobs Wing* of Old Masters paintings. Closed Mondays and Tuesdays. No admission charge on Thursdays. Art Museum Dr. near N. Charles and 31st Sts. (phone: 396-7100).

EXTRA SPECIAL

Just 30 miles south of Baltimore on Route 2 (Ritchie Hwy.) lies Annapolis, Maryland's capital, where the charm of the first peacetime capital of the US is still preserved. Around town are lovely 18th-century buildings, includ-

ing the old *State House* (State Circle; phone: 974-3400), still in use today; the *Hammond-Harwood House* (19 Maryland Ave.; 269-1714), a Georgian home designed by William Buckland; and the campus of *St. John's College,* which appears much as it did to its most famous alumnus, Francis Scott Key. Also interesting is the *US Naval Academy,* which offers guided walking tours (phone: 263-6933). The remains of John Paul Jones lie in the crypt of the chapel. In town, the harbor is flanked by boutiques and restaurants, and sailing vessels can be seen coming and going.

Sources and Resources

TOURIST INFORMATION

The *Baltimore Area Convention and Visitors Association* offers useful tourist information, such as directions, maps, and brochures, as well as a listing of daily events. It's located at 301 East Pratt Street (phone: 837-4636; 800-282-6632; closed Sundays in January and February). Contact the *Maryland Tourism Office* (217 E. Redwood St., Baltimore, MD 21202; phone: 767-3400; 800-543-1036) for maps and calendars of events.

LOCAL COVERAGE The *Baltimore Sun,* published twice daily and on Sundays, lists upcoming events. The weekly *City Paper,* which is free, offers a refreshing alternative and great classifieds. *Baltimore* is a monthly magazine with features on city life, restaurant listings, and calendars of events. All are available at newsstands. *Baltimore Quick Guide* magazine is a comprehensive tourist publication, available for free in hotels and from the *Baltimore Area Visitors Center.*

TELEVISION STATIONS WMAR Channel 2–ABC; WBAL Channel 11–NBC; WJZ Channel 13–CBS; WMPB Channel 67–PBS; WBFF Channel 45–Fox; and WNUV–54 UPN.

RADIO STATIONS AM: WBAL 1090 (news/talk); WJFK 1300 (pop music); and WWIN 1400 (urban contemporary). FM: WJHU 88.1 (public radio); WERQ 92.3 (urban contemporary); and WLIF 101.9 (easy listening/news).

TELEPHONE All telephone numbers are in the 410 area code unless otherwise indicated.

SALES TAX The state sales tax is 5%; the hotel room tax is 7½% in the city.

CLIMATE Baltimore weather is fickle, neither the rigorous clime of the North nor the mildness of the South. Unpredictable rainfall makes umbrellas advisable. In the summer, the weather can be hot and muggy, though the Chesapeake Bay exerts a modifying influence and brings relief with nighttime breezes. The winter is cold with moderate snowfall. Spring is windy and pleasant.

GETTING AROUND

AIRPORT *Baltimore/Washington, DC International Airport* (phone: 859-7111; 800-I-FLY-BWI) is usually a 20-minute ride from downtown Baltimore via the Baltimore-Washington Expressway. *Maryland Rail Commuter (MARC)* train service (phone: 800-325-7245) is available weekdays from the airport to the city's *Penn Station;* a shuttle bus transfers passengers from the air terminal to the airport train station. Trains run from 7 AM to 10 PM. *SuperShuttle* offers van service between the airport and major downtown hotels every half hour from 6 AM to 11:30 PM (phone: 859-0803; 800-809-7080).

BUS The *Mass Transit Administration,* an inter-connecting system of buses, subway, and the *Light Rail,* covers the entire metropolitan area. Bus route information and maps are available at the *MTA*'s main office (300 W. Lexington St. at Eutaw St.); phone: 539-5000; 800-543-9809 in MD; 539-3497, for the hearing-impaired). The basic fare is $1.25; an all-day fare good on all public transport is $3.

CAR RENTAL All the major national firms are represented.

LIGHT RAIL AND SUBWAY The *Light Rail* runs from Glen Burnie in the south of the city to Timonium in the north. It operates from 6 AM to 11 PM weekdays, from 6 AM to 11 PM Saturdays, and from 11 AM to 7 PM Sundays; the base fare is $1.35. The subway system, called the *Metro Rail,* offers limited access to much of the downtown area. Trains operate from 5 AM to midnight on weekdays and from 8 AM to midnight on Saturdays. Base fare is $1.35. There is an additional charge for trips into the outer zones (phone: 539-5000). Free parking and bus shuttle service is available from the outlying stations.

TAXI Cabs may be hailed on the street but are usually called by phone. Major companies are *Yellow Sun Cab* (phone: 685-1212), *Diamond* (phone: 947-3333), and *BWI Airport Cab* (phone: 859-1103).

SIGHTSEEING TOURS

BUS/TROLLEY Guided tours are available from *Baltimore Rent-a-Tour* (phone: 653-2998). *Baltimore Trolley Tours* (phone: 724-0077) has 17 boarding locations for all-day touring daily during the summer, and on weekends in winter. The 30-minute tours begin at 10 AM and end at 4 PM.

CRUISES For those intrigued by the thought of a cruise along Chesapeake Bay, one of the country's most scenic waterways, there are many charter boat companies in the area. *Chesapeake Marine Tours* (Box 3350, Annapolis, MD 21403; phone: 410-268-7600) has a variety of cruises; its day-long trip starts at Annapolis on the west side of the bay and sails to St. Michaels on the eastern shore, where passengers can delve into Chesapeake's maritime history, have lunch, and meander about. *Harbor Cruises* (phone: 727-3113; 800-695-2628) and *Baltimore Patriot* (phone: 745-9216) also offer cruises, and the *Water Taxi* (phone: 563-3901; 800-658-8947) allows passengers unlimited on/off privileges all day at all the waterfront attractions on its route.

SPECIAL EVENTS

Though the city boasts a rich, year-round calendar of events, one is an odds-on favorite.

AND THEY'RE OFF!

The Preakness One of America's oldest horse races, it's the middle jewel of thoroughbred racing's Triple Crown. The race is run the third Saturday in May for more than $500,000 at a 1³⁄₁₆-mile dirt track at the *Pimlico Race Course.* The race started in 1873 and attracts the nation's best three-year-old thoroughbreds—not to mention crowds of over 90,000. *Preakness Festival Week,* held the week before, features outdoor concerts, exhibitions, and performances. For more information, contact the *Maryland Jockey Club, Pimlico Race Course,* 5201 Park Heights Ave. near Hayward and Winner Aves. (phone: 542-9400; 800-638-3811).

From the last week of April through mid-May, the *Maryland House and Garden Pilgrimage* lavishly demonstrates Baltimoreans' pride in their own backyards. This statewide event for garden lovers is a series of self-guided tours through a group of outstanding homes and gardens. For details, contact the *Maryland House and Garden Pilgrimage* offices (1105A Providence Rd., Baltimore, MD 21286; phone: 821-6933). Numerous ethnic fairs take place in warm weather and are held at a variety of locations (see newspapers for listings). Concerts from symphony to pop are held every summer from June through September at the 4,300-seat *Pier Six Concert Pavilion* (Pier 6 at Eastern and President Sts.; phone: 625-3100 or 481-SEAT)

MUSEUMS

In addition to those described in *Special Places,* Baltimore has several other museums of note.

BABE RUTH BIRTHPLACE MUSEUM Cooperstown may have the fame, but baseball buffs will find everything authentic here, from photos of the Babe to taped interviews and *Orioles* memorabilia. Open daily. Admission charge. 216 Emory St. off W. Pratt St. (phone: 727-1539).

BALTIMORE CITY LIFE MUSEUMS Baltimore has organized its small museums into an integrated collection; each museum represents a facet of the city's culture and history. At the *Peale Museum* (225 Holliday St.; phone: 396-1149), enjoy the collection of the Peale family, featuring works by Early American portrait painters (including some Baltimoreans), as well as several changing exhibits. Get acquainted with Baltimore's most famous literary son at the *H. L. Mencken House* on Union Square (1524 Hollins St.; phone: 396-7997). A number of other nearby museums at 800 East Lombard Street is known as *Museum Row*. These include *Carroll Mansion,* the elegant townhouse of a signer of the Declaration of Independence; the *Center of Urban Archaeology,* where you can dig into the city's past; the *1840 House,* which offers a visit to a 19th-century middle class family through a dramatic living history presentation; and the *Morton K. Blaustine Exhibtion Center,* which provides a sense of the city's diverse character. Call ahead for hours. Admission charge (phone: 396-3279 for information).

BALTIMORE MARITIME MUSEUM The submarine USS *Torsk,* the *US Coast Guard* cutter *Roger B. Taney,* and the *Lightship Chesapeake* are open for tours daily in summer; Saturdays and Sundays in winter. Admission charge. Pier 3, *Inner Harbor* (phone: 396-3453).

BALTIMORE PUBLIC WORKS MUSEUM A representation of what goes on beneath the street is one of several exhibits on the history of public works. Closed Mondays and Tuesdays. Admission charge. 751 Eastern Ave. (phone: 396-5565).

BALTIMORE STREETCAR MUSEUM Home of the nation's first electric streetcar, this museum features a mile-and-a-quarter ride on a vintage streetcar, an exploration of the original carhouse, and exhibits of antique vehicles. Open Sundays; also Saturdays from June through October. Admisssion charge. 1901 Falls Rd. (phone: 547-0264).

B&O RAILROAD MUSEUM The most extensive collection of railroad memorabilia in the US and the second largest in the world. It includes the nation's first passenger and freight station as well as related exhibits. Closed *Thanksgiving* and *Christmas.* Admission charge. 901 W. Pratt St. (phone: 752-2490).

LACROSSE FOUNDATION AND HALL OF FAME MUSEUM Baltimore is the cradle of lacrosse, and displayed here are memorabilia and records relating to all levels of play. Closed weekends July through February; closed Sundays March through June, when it is open Saturdays. Admission charge. On *Johns Hopkins University*'s Homewood Campus, 113 W. University Pkwy. (phone: 235-6882).

STAR-SPANGLED BANNER FLAG HOUSE Once the home of Mary Pickersgill, who made the flag that flew over *Fort McHenry,* it's furnished with 18th- and 19th-century antiques. Closed Sundays and Mondays. Admission charge. 844 E. Pratt St. (phone: 837-1793).

SPORTS AND FITNESS

BASEBALL The *Orioles* play their home games at *Camden Yards,* a 48,272-seat stadium near the harbor. Tickets for good seats may be hard to get. 333 W. Camden St. (phone: 685-9800; 800-551-7328).

BICYCLING A brochure and map describing nearby bicycle routes are available from the *Maryland State Highway Administration*'s Bicycle Hotline (phone: 800-252-8776). Bicycles can be rented from *Race Pace* (11612 Reistertown Rd., Reistertown; phone: 833-4444).

BOATING *Middle Branch Park* is the site of the *Baltimore Rowing and Resource Center* (phone: 396-3838), which includes boat storage and a fishing pier.

FITNESS CENTER The *Downtown Athletic Club* (210 E. Centre St.; phone: 332-0906) opens its pool and equipment to guests at nearby hotels.

FOOTBALL The *National Football League*'s *Baltimore Ravens* touchdown at *Memorial Stadium* (1000 E. 33rd St. at Ellerslie Ave.; phone: 554-1010).

GOLF The best public course is the 18-hole *Pine Ridge,* 2 miles north on Dulaney Valley Road (exit 27B on the Baltimore Beltway; phone: 252-1408). There are others at *Forest Park* (Hillsdale and Forest Park Aves.; phone: 448-4653) and *Carroll Park* (Monroe and Washington Blvds.; phone: 685-8344).

HORSE RACING The year-round season alternates between *Laurel Park Race Course* (Race Track Rd., Laurel; phone: 301-725-0400; 800-638-1859) and *Pimlico* race course. The high point is the *Preakness* held at *Pimlico Race Course* (Belvedere and Park Heights Aves.; phone: 542-9400; 800-638-3811) the third Saturday in May (see *Special Events*).

LACROSSE The *Johns Hopkins Blue Jays* (*Homewood Field,* Charles St. and University Pkwy.; phone: 516-7490) are among the best of the college teams in the country. Seats usually are available.

SOCCER Watch the *Baltimore Spirit* indoors from October through April at the *Baltimore Arena* (201 W. Baltimore; phone: 625-2320).

STEEPLECHASE Point-to-point races (with timber barrier jumps) are run in the valleys north of the city (Western Run, Worthington, Long Green) on Saturday afternoons during April.

TENNIS The *Greenspring Racquet Club* (10803 Falls Rd.; phone: 821-5683) is a large indoor facility; non-members may use courts for a fee.

THEATER

For complete listings, see the publications listed in *Local Coverage.* Baltimore's theatrical offerings range from Broadway tryouts or road shows at the *Morris Mechanic Theatre* (Charles Center; phone: 625-1400) to resident productions at *Center Stage,* the state theater of Maryland (700 N. Calvert St.; phone: 332-0033), to the *Vagabond Players,* the oldest continuously operated "little theater" in the US (806 S. Broadway; phone: 563-9135), and experimental works at the *Baltimore Theatre Project* (45 W. Preston St.; phone: 752-8558). There are also eight dinner-theaters that present Broadway shows. Try *Burn Brae Dinner Theatre* (3811 Blackburn Rd., Burtonsville; phone: 792-0290) or *F. Scott Black's Towson Dinner Theater* (100 E. Chesapeake Ave., Towson; phone: 321-6595).

MUSIC

The highly regarded *Baltimore Symphony Orchestra* performs throughout the year at the *Joseph Meyerhoff Symphony Hall* (1212 Cathedral St.; phone: 783-8000). *The Baltimore Opera Company* performs in the *Lyric Opera House* (140 W. Mt. Royal Ave.; phone: 727-6000). The *Baltimore Museum of Art* (Art Museum Dr.; phone: 396-7100) also hosts dance and music programs. Other concerts are presented by well-known visiting artists; check the newspapers.

NIGHTCLUBS AND NIGHTLIFE

Shamrock Pub (102 Water St.; phone: 576-8558) presents stand-up comics from New York and LA, including those from top late-night TV shows. *Buddies Pub* (313 N. Charles St.; phone: 332-4200) has a jazz quartet Thursday through Saturday nights. *Bertha's* (734 S. Broadway; phone: 327-5795) features jazz Tuesdays, Wednesdays, Fridays, and Saturdays. *Eight by Ten* (10 E. Cross St.; phone: 625-2000) offers rhythm and blues, jazz, and alternative music.

Best in Town

CHECKING IN

There is an increasing number of luxury hotels and several less costly ones downtown. Most of Baltimore's major hotels have complete facilities for the business traveler. Those listed below as having "business services" usually offer such conveniences as meeting rooms, photocopiers, computers, translation services, and express checkout, among others. Call the individual hotel for additional information. Expect to pay $140 or more per night for a double room at hotels we list as very expensive, $100 to $140 at expensive places, and $65 to $100 at moderate hotels; there are no exceptional inexpensive hotels in the city. Note that there is free parking at many of the hotel chains downtown. For bed and breakfast accommodations, contact *Amanda's Bed and Breakfast Reservation Service* (1428 Park Ave.; phone: 225-0001; 800-899-7533). Unless otherwise noted, hotel rooms have air conditioning, private baths, TV sets, and telephones.

All hotels below are in Baltimore and telephone and fax numbers are in the 410 area code unless otherwise indicated.

VERY EXPENSIVE

Harbor Court The modest exterior of this brick hotel facing the *Inner Harbor* belies the elegance that can be found inside. Exquisitely decorated with marble floors, reproductions of 18th-century furnishings, and Chinese art, it is Baltimore's most luxurious property. Most of the 203 rooms and suites have views of the harbor or downtown; amenities include two-line telephones, 24-hour room service, and a concierge. In addition to a coffee shop, there are two restaurants, including the excellent *Hampton's* (see *Eating Out*) and *Brighton's,* featuring American cuisine. There is a complete fitness center, a rooftop croquet court, a beauty salon, and business services. 550 Light St. (phone: 234-0550; 800-824-0076; fax: 659-5925).

Hyatt Regency, Baltimore A glossy waterfront hostelry with 487 rooms, 29,200 square feet of meeting space, and a skywalk connecting it to *Harborplace* and the *Baltimore Convention Center.* It's also only a short walk to the *National Aquarium* and the *Maryland Science Center.* Recreational facilities include tennis courts, a fitness center, a jogging track, and an outdoor pool. There's *Bistro 300* for casual fare and the more formal *Barry and Elliot's* dining on the rooftop level. Room service is available until 12:30 AM, and a concierge desk and business services are available. 300 Light St., *Inner Harbor* (phone: 528-1234; 800-233-1234; fax: 685-3362).

Renaissance Harborplace This recently renovated elegant high-rise features 622 rooms and suites on the *Inner Harbor* at *Harborplace.* It is convenient to the aquarium, science center, and other attractions. *Windows* restaurant looks out over the harbor and features local seafood and continental dishes; there are also two lounges (one with a piano bar). Room service is available 24 hours a day. Other amenities include a concierge desk and business services. 202 E. Pratt St. (phone: 547-1200; 800-325-5000 or 800-HOTELS-1; fax: 539-5780).

EXPENSIVE

Admiral Fell Inn A historic establishment with 80 rooms of various shapes and sizes carved out of eight connected buildings. All rooms are named for famous city residents; most feature king-sized beds. *The Point* serves a menu of English-pub fare. There's a free van to town and a summer ferry to *Inner Harbor.* Business services are available. Fell's Point, 888 S. Broadway (phone: 522-7377; 800-292-4667; fax: 522-0707).

Baltimore Marriott Inner Harbor Within walking distance of *Harborplace* downtown, this 525-room property is ideal for business travelers and, due to its convenient location, also a good bet for tourists. It has a restaurant and a lounge with entertainment. Room service is available until 11 PM, and a concierge desk and business services round out the list of conveniences. Pratt and Eutaw Sts. (phone: 962-0202; 800-228-9290; fax: 962-0202).

Clarion Hotel at Mount Vernon Square The same people who restored Washington, DC's *Hay-Adams* have brought similar distinctive qualities to this former *Latham* property. The Europen-style hotel offers fine service and old-fashioned decor in all 103 rooms. Although there was no restaurant at press time, there is room service until midnight. A concierge and business services also are available. 612 Cathedral St. (phone: 727-7101; 800-292-5500; 789-3312).

Mr. Mole Bed and Breakfast A truly lovely bed and breakfast establishment set in a late 19th-century home, it is named after a character from the story *The*

Wind in the Willows. Inside is an elegant world of crystal chandeliers, touches of Italian marble, and period antiques; the five rooms and suites are equally sumptuous. There is no restaurant, but a Dutch-style buffet breakfast is served in the breakfast room. The inn is located in a historic uptown residential neighborhood with its own private security patrol. It also provides garages with automatic door openers for its guests. No smoking allowed. 1601 Bolton St. (phone: 728-1179).

MODERATE

Biltmore Suites This 1880s Victorian mansion is now a 26-suite hotel. Spacious rooms have high ceilings and antique furnishings, and connecting doors facilitate a variety of room arrangements. Guests can enjoy a generous European breakfast and an early evening wine and lager tasting; there is no restaurant. 205 W. Madison St. (phone: 728-6550; 800-868-5064; fax: 728-5829).

Days Inn Inner Harbor A property that is a favorite for its location near the city's most popular attractions, it has 250 rooms and a restaurant; guests may use a nearby fitness center that has a pool and exercise equipment. Business services are available. 100 Hopkins Pl. (phone: 576-1000; 800-325-2525; fax: 576-9437).

Holiday Inn Inner Harbor Its convenient location one block from the *Inner Harbor* is unusual for such a moderately priced hotel. Don't be put off by the rather unappealing exterior; inside, things brighten up considerably. There are 375 guestrooms. *McKenna's* is a large restaurant and lounge, and other amenities include an indoor pool, a fitness center, and business services. 301 W. Lombard St. (phone: 685-3500; 800-HOLIDAY; fax: 727-6169).

Tremont Four blocks south of Mount Vernon Square (and *not* to be confused with the nearby *Tremont Plaza*), the 60-suite hotel caters to celebrities and executives wanting the privacy and amenities of an all-suite hotel. There is a restaurant and an outdoor pool. Another attractive feature is guest privileges at nearby *Baltimore Sports and Fitness.* Room service is available until 10 PM, and business services are offered. 8 E. Pleasant St. (phone: 576-1200; 800-873-6668; fax: 244-1154).

EATING OUT

Dedicated eaters find happiness in Baltimore. From its regional specialties, seafood in the rough and crab cakes, to the authentic dishes of its Little Italy, there are restaurants to suit most palates and pocketbooks. Our selections range in price from $60 to $80 for a dinner for two in the expensive category, $30 to $60 in the moderate category, and $30 or less in the inexpensive category. Prices do not include drinks, wine, tax, or tips. All restaurants are in the 410 area code unless otherwise indicated.

Unless otherwise noted, restaurants serve lunch and dinner.

EXPENSIVE

Hampton's The premier restaurant at the *Harbor Court* hotel is also one of the best in the city. Elegance is the watchword here, with fresh flowers, fine napery, china, silverware, and glowing candlelight. The menu, which changes seasonally, might include medaillons of monkfish, glazed filet of salmon, or smoked sea bass. There's also a champagne brunch on Sundays. Jacket and tie required for men. Open for dinner only; closed Mondays. Reservations recommended. Major credit cards accepted. 550 Light St. (phone: 234-0550).

Prime Rib A hangout for figures in the city's political and entertainment worlds. Its prime ribs are great, but no more so than the crab imperial. Jackets required for men. Open daily for dinner only. Reservations advised. Major credit cards accepted. 1101 N. Calvert (at Chase St)., in *Horizon House* (phone: 539-1804).

Tio Pepe The Spanish food here has rated highly among locals year after year, which means it's usually crowded; you might have to order another pitcher of sangria before your table is available. Some good bets include the roast suckling of pig, paella, and shrimp with garlic. Reservations (and jackets for men) necessary for dinner. Major credit cards accepted. 10 E. Franklin St. (phone: 539-4675).

MODERATE

Maison Marconi Here, the artistry is on the plate rather than in the decor. The specialty is filet of sole prepared in a variety of delicious ways. Other top favorites include lobster with sherry cream and mushroom sauce and broiled sweetbreads. Closed Sundays and Mondays. Reservations advised. Major credit cards accepted. 106 W. Saratoga St. (phone: 727-9522).

Olde Obrycki's Crab House Roll back your sleeves, put on your bib, grab a mallet, and get ready to battle steamed crabs. The warm family atmosphere adds to the enjoyment of seafood feasts. Open daily; closed mid-November through mid-March. Reservations advised. Major credit cards accepted. 1727 E. Pratt St., Upper Fell's Point. (phone: 732-6399).

Orchid Baltimore's only French and Oriental restaurant offers an award-winning menu of fresh meat, seafood, and crisp vegetables, in a marriage that combines the best of both worlds—creamy French sauces and fresh Oriental seasonings. Open daily Tuesdays through Fridays, dinner Saturdays and Sundays. Reservations necessary. Major credit cards accepted. Downtown near all attractions, 419 N. Charles St. (phone: 837-0080).

INEXPENSIVE

Chiapparelli's This restaurant in Little Italy is popular for its casual atmosphere and prompt service. Homemade ravioli stuffed with ricotta and spinach is a specialty. Reservations necessary on weekends. Major credit cards accepted. 237 S. High St. (phone: 837-0309).

John W. Faidley Seafood One of the world's largest raw oyster bars; in the past 100 years, it has established itself as the place for oysters, crabs, and clams brought in fresh daily from the bay. The downtown lunch crowd regards a visit to its branch in *Lexington Market*—a vast assemblage of butchers and merchants—as the ultimate adventure. Closed Sundays. No reservations. Major credit cards accepted. Paca at Lexington St. (phone: 727-4898).

HARBORPLACE

In addition to numerous food stalls, where visitors can find everything from Buffalo wings to chocolate-covered strawberries, the following restaurants have good food, harbor views, and moderate prices. In the *Light Street Pavilion* are *City Lights,* featuring seafood, pasta dishes, and homemade desserts (phone: 244-8811); *Phillips Harborplace,* with Chesapeake Bay seafood and a piano bar (phone: 685-6600); and *Wayne's Bar-B-Que,* with homemade soups (the crab soup is particularly good), salads, and desserts in addition to barbecued ribs and chicken (phone: 539-3810). In the *Pratt Street Pavilion* are *Bamboo House,* for Chinese food (phone: 625-1191) and *Tex-Mex* (phone: 783-2970) for south-of-the-border fare including burritos, tacos, and enchiladas.

Boston

No matter how you approach Boston, you'll be struck by the beauty of its location. Jutting into the island-studded harbor, the city graces the banks of the Charles River with riverside parks and a distinctive skyline. Here are the narrow cobblestones where Boston's colonists walked, the *Common* where their cattle grazed, and the churches where they prayed. Here, too, are the bold buildings of government, the fortresses of finance, the colorful chaos of the open market, and the free-wheeling spirit of the waterfront.

Anyone walking briskly could traverse this history-soaked terrain in an hour, but take the time to explore Boston at leisure, keeping an eye out for odd quirks of architecture and bright spots of whimsy. Spend some time in the North End, wandering along twisting streets barely wider than the ancient cowpaths they follow, or in the Back Bay, strolling down the broad Commonwealth Avenue mall lined with stately townhouses. Look for the famous brass nameplates and gas lamps of Beacon Hill, the intricate wrought-ironwork along Marlborough Street, and the grasshopper atop *Faneuil Hall*—the site of many Revolutionary protest meetings.

The 19th century saw the rise of commerce in Boston and a simultaneous flowering of arts and letters—represented by such figures as Emerson, Hawthorne, Longfellow, and Thoreau. The boom of population and wealth prompted the city fathers to fill in the increasingly noxious Back Bay wetlands to provide land for the city's expansion. Today, that barren landscape has been transformed by a century's growth of elms, magnolias, and fruit trees, and Back Bay buildings are prized as exceptional examples of Victorian architecture in America.

After surviving half a century of neglect and deterioration, Boston experienced a renaissance, beginning in the 1960s with the creation of *Government Center* and the restoration of the city's historic neighborhoods. During the 1970s, *Faneuil Hall Marketplace* became the prototype for a new concept of urban retail development (see *Special Places,* below). More recently, *Copley Place* and the renewed *Prudential Center* have added vitality to the city.

Yet a civilized sense of ease combined with an abundance of cultural opportunity remains. Boston's art museums are among the finest in the world, and its galleries—on Newbury Street, along Fort Point Channel, and the up-and-coming South Street and South End—are worth a day in themselves. Its music scene thrives as well, and the *Boston Symphony* is but the beginning. Baroque chamber music concerts often are sold out, jazz fans can sit through three sizzling sets in intimate cafés, and the biggest names in folk, country, and rock return faithfully to sing in the clubs that gave them their start. There's also the ever-popular *Boston Pops,* a symphony orchestra with a crowd-pleasing repertoire of popular and classical music.

The *Boston Ballet* is world-renowned, and a variety of contemporary dance companies present frequent, innovative programs. Broadway shows may get their start here, and local theater groups stage everything from Shakespeare to experimental plays. Besides the many commercial movie houses showing first- and second-run films, local colleges and cultural centers are always sponsoring film festivals where you can catch obscure movies from Eastern Europe or your favorite Chaplin, D. W. Griffith, or Bogart classics.

These same colleges and cultural centers provide virtually unlimited opportunities for education and self-improvement, from the large academic communities of *Harvard,* the *Massachusetts Institute of Technology (MIT), Boston University* , and *Northeastern* University, to the dozens of smaller institutions. The list of lectures open to the public on any given day is overwhelming.

For many people, Boston is, above all, a sports town. It's easy for *Red Sox* fans to indulge themselves at *Fenway Park*—one of the last of the great old urban ballparks. Basketball and hockey fans have their beloved *Celtics* and *Bruins* in the *Fleet Center,* and football followers have the *New England Patriots.* Visitors should bear in mind that loyalties are intense in Boston. If you must cheer for the opposition, do so softly.

Politics often seems like another favorite sport in Boston. Mayor James Michael Curley will live forever in the novel *The Last Hurrah,* and the grandson of another mayor, "Honey Fitz" Fitzgerald, became the 35th President of the US, John F. Kennedy. Such names as Elliot Richardson and Henry Cabot Lodge loom large in our national consciousness, as does that of the late Thomas P. "Tip" O'Neill, a North Cambridge native and formidable Speaker of the *US House of Representatives.*

Boston has long been known as "the home of the bean and the cod," though it isn't easy to find authentic baked beans. Local fishermen, however, provide Boston's tables with plenty of fresh fish and shellfish, and scrod (as cooked cod filets are called here) is found on many menus. Ethnic eateries of all kinds have proliferated in recent years, complementing the long-established restaurants and groceries in Chinatown and the Italian North End with Thai, Japanese, Portuguese, Indian, Mexican, and Greek foods, among others. There are also many restaurants dedicated to creative nouvelle cuisine using seasonal produce. Bostonians bargain for their own at *Haymarket* (see "Blackstone Block" in *Special Places*).

Thanks to the genius of Frederick Law Olmsted, Boston enjoys several miles of continuous parkland known as the *Emerald Necklace,* an 8-mile chain of parks that is the longest stretch of urban parkland in the United States. Perhaps the prettiest jewel of them all is the *Public Garden,* with its ever-changing displays of luxuriant blooms and its graceful Swan Boats cruising the quiet pond. Next to the *Public Garden* is *Boston Common,* the nation's oldest public park. The path along the *Charles River Esplanade,* which provides plenty of aquatic as well as terrestrial scenery, is popular

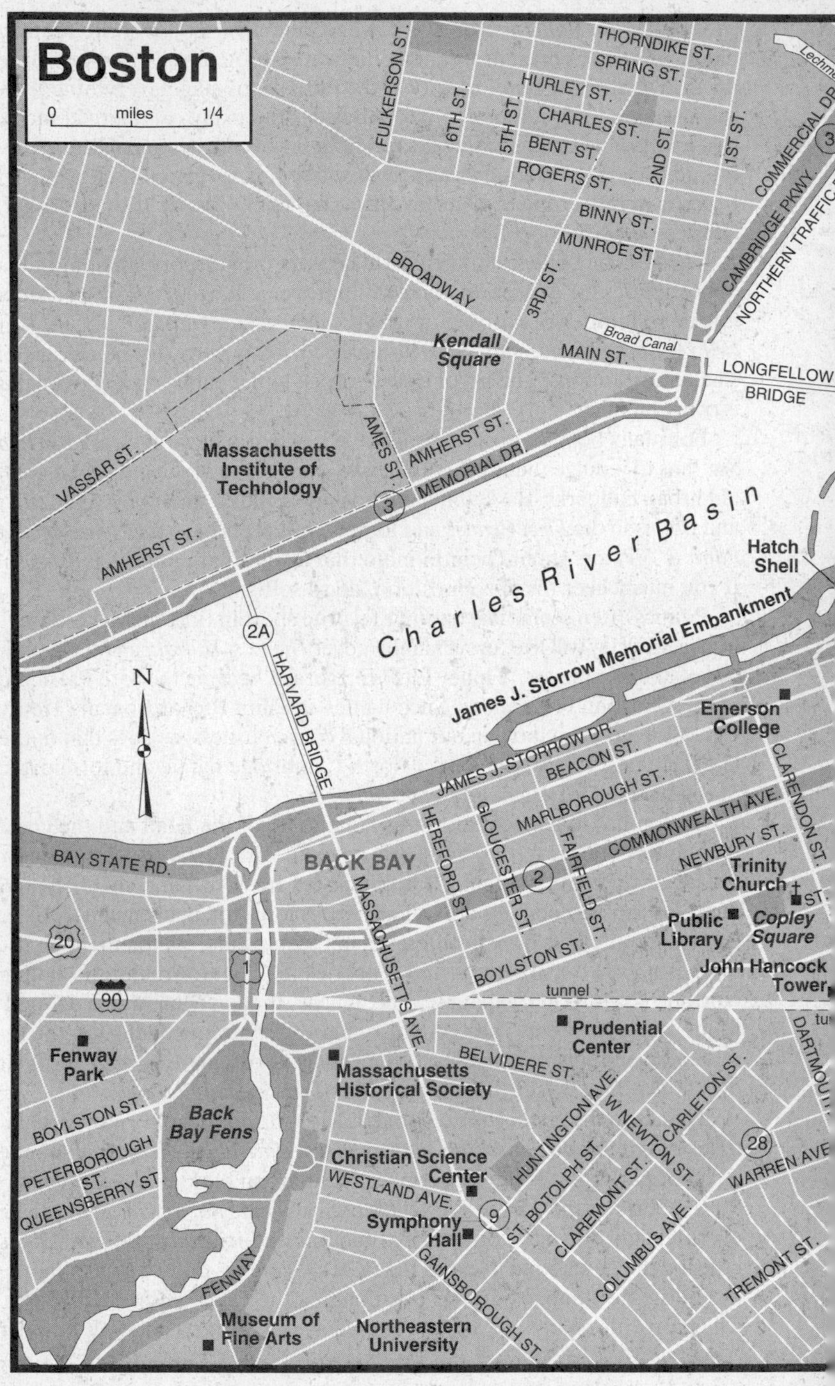

Boston
0 miles 1/4
THORNDIKE ST.
SPRING ST.
HURLEY ST.
CHARLES ST.
BENT ST.
ROGERS ST.
BINNY ST.
MUNROE ST.
FULKERSON ST.
6TH ST.
5TH ST.
3RD ST.
2ND ST.
1ST ST.
COMMERCIAL DR.
CAMBRIDGE PKWY.
NORTHERN TRAFFIC
Lechmere
BROADWAY
Broad Canal
Kendall Square
MAIN ST.
LONGFELLOW BRIDGE
AMES ST.
AMHERST ST.
MEMORIAL DR.
VASSAR ST.
Massachusetts Institute of Technology
AMHERST ST.
Charles River Basin
Hatch Shell
James J. Storrow Memorial Embankment
HARVARD BRIDGE
N
JAMES J. STORROW DR.
BEACON ST.
MARLBOROUGH ST.
COMMONWEALTH AVE.
NEWBURY ST.
Emerson College
CLARENDON ST.
BAY STATE RD.
BACK BAY
HEREFORD ST.
GLOUCESTER ST.
FAIRFIELD ST.
Trinity Church
ST.
Public Library
Copley Square
John Hancock Tower
MASSACHUSETTS AVE.
BOYLSTON ST.
tunnel
Prudential Center
DARTMOUTH
Fenway Park
BELVIDERE ST.
Massachusetts Historical Society
BOYLSTON ST.
Back Bay Fens
PETERBOROUGH ST.
QUEENSBERRY ST.
HUNTINGTON AVE.
W NEWTON ST.
CARLETON ST.
Christian Science Center
WESTLAND AVE.
WARREN AVE.
ST. BOTOLPH ST.
CLAREMONT ST.
Symphony Hall
COLUMBUS AVE.
TREMONT ST.
FENWAY
GAINSBOROUGH ST.
Museum of Fine Arts
Northeastern University
3
2A
2
20
1
90
9
28

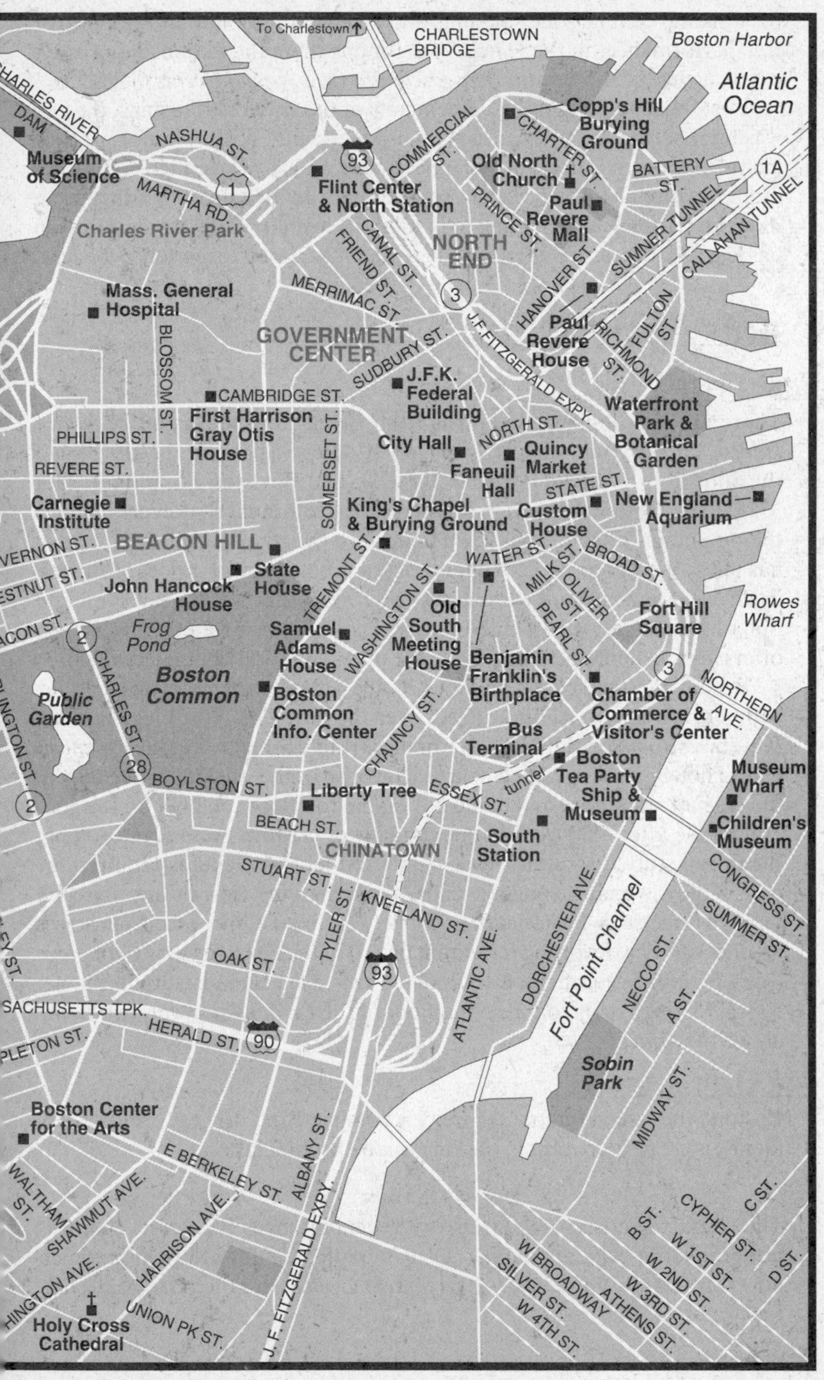

To Charlestown
CHARLESTOWN BRIDGE
Boston Harbor
Atlantic Ocean
CHARLES RIVER DAM
Museum of Science
NASHUA ST.
MARTHA RD.
Charles River Park
Flint Center & North Station
COMMERCIAL ST.
Copp's Hill Burying Ground
CHARTER ST.
Old North Church
BATTERY ST.
PRINCE ST.
Paul Revere Mall
NORTH END
CANAL ST.
FRIEND ST.
MERRIMAC ST.
SUMNER TUNNEL
CALLAHAN TUNNEL
HANOVER ST.
Mass. General Hospital
GOVERNMENT CENTER
SUDBURY ST.
J.F. FITZGERALD EXPY.
Paul Revere House
RICHMOND ST.
FULTON ST.
BLOSSOM ST.
CAMBRIDGE ST.
J.F.K. Federal Building
First Harrison Gray Otis House
PHILLIPS ST.
REVERE ST.
SOMERSET ST.
City Hall
NORTH ST.
Faneuil Hall
Quincy Market
Waterfront Park & Botanical Garden
STATE ST.
Custom House
New England Aquarium
Carnegie Institute
King's Chapel & Burying Ground
BEACON HILL
VERNON ST.
ESTNUT ST.
State House
John Hancock House
TREMONT ST.
WASHINGTON ST.
WATER ST.
MILK ST.
BROAD ST.
OLIVER ST.
PEARL ST.
ACON ST.
Frog Pond
Samuel Adams House
Old South Meeting House
Benjamin Franklin's Birthplace
Fort Hill Square
Rowes Wharf
CHARLES ST.
Boston Common
Boston Common Info. Center
Public Garden
INGTON ST.
CHAUNCY ST.
Chamber of Commerce & Visitor's Center
NORTHERN AVE.
Bus Terminal
Boston Tea Party Ship & Museum
Museum Wharf
Children's Museum
tunnel
BOYLSTON ST.
Liberty Tree
ESSEX ST.
BEACH ST.
South Station
CHINATOWN
STUART ST.
KNEELAND ST.
TYLER ST.
CONGRESS ST.
SUMMER ST.
DORCHESTER AVE.
Fort Point Channel
NECCO ST.
OAK ST.
ATLANTIC AVE.
A ST.
SACHUSETTS TPK.
HERALD ST.
PLETON ST.
Sobin Park
MIDWAY ST.
Boston Center for the Arts
E BERKELEY ST.
ALBANY ST.
WALTHAM ST.
SHAWMUT AVE.
HARRISON AVE.
J. F. FITZGERALD EXPY.
B ST.
CYPHER ST.
C ST.
W 1ST ST.
W 2ND ST.
W 3RD ST.
D ST.
W BROADWAY
SILVER ST.
ATHENS ST.
W 4TH ST.
HINGTON AVE.
Holy Cross Cathedral
UNION PK ST.

for walking, cycling, roller blading, and jogging. In summer, it is the site of free performances at the *Hatch Shell,* among them the famous *July Fourth* extravaganza of the *Boston Pops Orchestra* (see *Special Events*).

First inhabited largely by descendants of the very first Puritans, the city was later settled by Irish- and Italian-Americans. With the more recent arrival of Eastern European, Asian, Hispanic, and African emigrés, Boston's ethnic texture has grown richer over the years. In making the journey from its staid, Puritanical beginning to its vibrant, cosmopolitan present, Boston has learned to treasure its past while remaining eager to experience the new.

Boston At-a-Glance

SEEING THE CITY

There are two unparalleled posts from which to view Boston: the *John Hancock Tower*'s 60th-floor *Observatory* (Copley Sq.; phone: 247-1977) and the 50th-floor *Prudential Center Skywalk* (800 Boylston St.; phone: 236-3318). The *Observatory* offers a spectacular panorama that even includes the mountains of southern New Hampshire (weather permitting). It also has telescopes, recorded commentaries, a topographical model of Boston in 1775 (this is a must—we promise you'll be surprised), and a seven-minute film of a helicopter flight over the city. The newly renovated *Skywalk* also offers an excellent 360° view. Both are open daily and charge admission.

Boston also has several fabulous rooms with views where you can relax with a drink and watch the sun set over the city. The most elegant is the *Bay Tower Room* on the 33rd floor of the 60 State Street tower, near *Faneuil Hall.* Though it is a private club and a favorite of the working lunch crowd, the elegant restaurant and piano bar on the top floor are open to the general public after 4:30 PM. The menu features creative American cooking; the baked stuffed lobster is especially succulent. A jacket is required for men. Enjoy live music on weekends, and a dizzying view of the cityscape through three-story-high windows (phone: 723-1666). Other excellent choices are the 360° view revolving restaurant on top of the *Hyatt Regency Cambridge* (see *Checking In*) or the smartly updated *Top of the Hub* restaurant (phone: 536-1775; open daily) on the 52nd floor of the *Prudential* tower, two floors above the *Skywalk.*

SPECIAL PLACES

Boston is best seen on foot. The city is compact, and driving, even for residents, is often hair-raising; parking can be problematic.

DOWNTOWN

The confusing crisscross of narrow streets that gives Boston its charm is nowhere more evident than in the city's cradle, the downtown area, which now consists of *Faneuil Hall, Government Center,* and the financial, retail, and waterfront districts.

BOSTON COMMON This pastoral green, established in 1634, is the nation's oldest park. The earliest Bostonians brought their cows and horses here to graze. Today, you'll find their descendants engaging in free-form pastimes that range from playing music to playing baseball. We suggest starting your tour of the city here—but don't walk alone at night, as the *Common* is often inadequately patrolled. The lovely *Public Garden* is adjacent to the *Common,* across Charles Street. For information about attractions and activities throughout Boston, stop at the *Boston Common Visitors Center* (no phone) open daily 8:30 AM to 6 PM. For phone information, call the *Greater Boston Convention and Visitors* (phone: 536-4100) or *Boston By Phone* (phone: 800-374-7400), which has an extensive menu of recorded visitor information 24 hours daily). You can park at *Motor Mart* on Stuart Street, at the *57 Park Plaza* hotel (200 Stuart St.), or the *Boston Common Underground Garage* on Charles Street.

FREEDOM TRAIL The city has made it both easy and fun to track down the important sites from its colonial and Revolutionary past. Just follow the red brick (or red paint) line set into the sidewalks that connects them through downtown Boston and the North End and then across the river into Charlestown. The trail may be followed only on foot; it takes about two hours to walk its length without stops or side trips. To begin, take the *Green* or *Red Line* to Park Street and walk down Tremont Street to the *Visitors' Information Center* on the *Common,* which has maps.

PARK STREET CHURCH Built in 1809, the church witnessed William Lloyd Garrison's famous first anti-slavery address in 1829 and heard the first singing of "My country, 'tis of thee" three years later. It's open Tuesdays through Saturdays in July and August; otherwise by appointment. 1 Park St. (phone: 523-3383).

OLD GRANARY BURYING GROUND In this 1660 cemetery, next door to the *Park Street Church,* are the graves of such Revolutionary notables as John Hancock, Samuel Adams, Paul Revere, and the victims of the Boston Massacre, as well as the parents of Benjamin Franklin. Open daily (phone: 635-4505, ext. 6516).

KING'S CHAPEL AND BURYING GROUND Founded as the Massachusetts Bay Colony's first Anglican church in 1686, *King's Chapel* was the place of worship for British officers and the royal governor. Since the colonists had fled England to escape the Anglican Church, the church's founding was taken as an insult. The ornate *Governor's Pew,* the church's centerpiece, was removed from the church in 1826, only to be restored a century later after it was clear that the colony had rid itself of British elitism. The cemetery next door, established in 1631, is the city's oldest and contains the graves and tombstones of many revered old Bostonians, including John Winthrop, the first Governor of the Massachusetts Bay Colony; William Dawes, who was Paul Revere's companion on his famous ride; and Mary Chilton, the first woman Pilgrim from the Plymouth Colony to go to Boston. The church hosts free chamber music and other concerts year-round on Tuesdays just after noon. Open Mondays through Saturdays mid-June through *Labor Day;* Mondays, Fridays, and Saturdays mid-March through mid-June and *Labor Day* through October; Saturdays only the rest of the year. Tremont St. at School St. (phone: 227-2155).

DOWNTOWN CROSSING A great meeting place. Winter meets Summer Street, the *Red Line* meets the *Orange Line,* and the display windows of the two giants of Boston retailing, *Filene's* and *Jordan Marsh,* face each other across a brick, pedestrian-only street. On Saturdays, when the shoppers, vendors, and street performers are out in force, this intersection resembles Mecca at the end of *Ramadan,* which may be why a good proportion of the world's lesser-known religions are represented here, looking for new members or donations. Business is brisk for the vending carts, which sell everything from T-shirts to llama-skin luggage. At the intersection of Winter and Washington Streets.

OLD SOUTH MEETING HOUSE This *Freedom Trail* monument was scheduled to reopen as we went to press following a comprehensive renovation of the entire building, and an expansion of its displays and shop. Though this well-preserved church was built in 1729 to serve Boston's Puritan congregation, its greatest hour was secular. When dissent began to rumble in the colonies before the Revolution, it was here that patriots flocked to debate the issues of the day. It was here that, after failing to persuade the royal governor to send back to England three ships that were filled with dutiable tea and moored in the harbor, Samuel Adams announced, in December 1773, "Taxation without representation is tyranny." And it was from here that an incensed mob, some disguised as Indians, set out to dump the tea in the harbor and write a crucial chapter in the birth of this nation. In addition, Ben Franklin, who was born across the street, was baptized here when he was only hours old. An award-winning permanent audio exhibit re-creates the Tea Party and other exciting moments from Boston's past. Also on display are rare colonial artifacts and a scale model of early Boston. Costumed players reenact a town meeting on Saturday afternoons in the summer, and from October through April, there's a Thursday noon lecture series on American history. Open daily; admission charge. 310 Washington St. (phone: 482-6439).

GLOBE CORNER BOOKSTORE Formerly the *Old Corner Bookstore,* this venerable landmark was long the hub of Boston's literary scene. The building that first stood on this site belonged to the family of Anne Hutchinson, a religious dissident whose unorthodox beliefs became so popular in the 1630s that she was banished from the colony by an intimidated Governor Winthrop (he later conceded that he was about the only one in town who didn't like her opinions). The present building was constructed in 1718 after the Hutchinson home was destroyed in the Great Boston Fire of 1711. For years, it was the office of eminent publishers *Ticknor and Fields,* where editor Jamie Fields attracted such names as Emerson, Hawthorne, Holmes,

Longfellow, Lowell, and Thoreau to his stable of writers. Fields's office was a center of literary discussion. It is now a working bookstore with abundant travel titles, as well as books about New England and by New England authors. 3 School St. (phone: 523-6658).

OLD STATE HOUSE Boston's 18th-century seat of government served both the English colony and the American state of Massachusetts until the *State House* was completed in 1798. Now dwarfed by modern towers of law and finance, the present building was erected in 1713. The *Old State House* served as the council chambers of the royal governors sent from England. As the conflict between England and the colonies became more pointed, so did the goings-on about the *Old State House.* When edicts and proclamations were read from the east balcony, the colonists would adjourn to local taverns to work themselves into a fury and then return, emboldened, to protest. The Boston Massacre was staged in front of the building's east side. In 1776, the Declaration of Independence was first read in Boston from the balcony, as it continues to be every July 4. It's now a museum, tracing Boston's history from early to contemporary times. Open daily. Admission charge. 206 Washington St. (phone: 720-3290).

CITY HALL The focal point of the *Government Center* plaza, Boston's looming, concrete *City Hall* (1968), designed by Kallman, McKinnell & Knowles, is considered a landmark of modern architecture, although the local populace loves to revile it. *City Hall* sits in the middle of an eight-acre plaza that is often the scene of civic celebrations and politicking. Congress St. (phone: 635-4000).

FANEUIL HALL MARKETPLACE The market takes its official name from adjacent *Faneuil* (rhymes with "flannel") *Hall,* a historic meeting house. It is also known as *Quincy Market,* which is the name of the three stone market buildings. When it opened in 1826, this was the site of the city's meat and produce markets (11 of the original tenants still do business here). Redesigned between 1976 and 1978 by Benjamin Thompson and the Rouse Company, the market has become a much-copied prototype of urban renewal. Now a lively gathering place, it has performers and street vendors outside and eateries, trinket shops, and boutiques inside. Over a million people a month visit its stalls, restaurants, and shops. Open daily. Off I-93 between Clinton and Chatham Streets (phone: 338-2323).

WATERFRONT

There's much to do and see along Boston's waterfront. Walk along *Waterfront Park,* (officially *Christopher Columbus Park)* with its invigorating views of the harbor; browse in the many shops set in the renovated wharf buildings; or take a sightseeing tour by water from Long Wharf (see *Getting Around,* below). Also here is the *New England Aquarium* (see below). Just over the Congress Street Bridge, past the *Boston Tea Party Ship and Museum* and into the commercial district of South Boston—some call it Wallpaper Row—are the popular *Computer Museum* and *Children's Museum.* They are located on the park-like *Museum Wharf,* home of the enormous red-and-white H. P. Hood Milk Bottle, a vintage 1930s highway lunch stand that is 40 feet high.

NEW ENGLAND AQUARIUM One of the world's top collections of marine life—more than 2,000 species in all—it houses exhibits re-creating a tide pool, northern waters, and tropical marine environments. Of particular note is the four-story saltwater tank, girded by a spiral viewing ramp from which visitors can view the resident sharks, sea turtles, moray eels, and wide variety of fish. Divers regularly feed the underwater multitudes so they don't dine on each other. Penguins cavort in their own habitat, and seals and dolphins perform aboard the floating pavilion *Discovery,* next door to the main building. Get to watch harbor seals at play in their outdoor pool in front of the aquarium year-round. Films are shown in the auditorium, and there's an interesting gift shop. Open daily. No admission charge for children under three. Central Wharf, Waterfront (phone: 973-5200).

BOSTON TEA PARTY SHIP AND MUSEUM Board the *Brig Beaver II,* a full-size working replica of one of the three original ships at the Boston Tea Party, and throw a little tea into Boston Harbor. The adjacent museum houses documents relevant to the period as well as films and related exhibits. Open daily late-March through *Thanksgiving.* Admission charge. Congress Street Bridge at Fort Point Channel (phone: 338-1773).

CHILDREN'S MUSEUM Formerly an old woolens warehouse, this kid-pleasing place has a number of hands-on exhibits, including *Grandmother's Attic,* and an assembly line that teaches children how a factory operates. Open Tuesdays through Sundays; closed Mondays except during school holiday weeks and between July 1 and *Labor Day.* Admission charge. 300 Congress St., *Museum Wharf* (phone: 426-8855).

COMPUTER MUSEUM The first of its kind in the US, this museum harbors several floors of gadgetry, interactive exhibits, and educational programs that trace the history and the future of what is probably the 20th century's greatest contribution to technology. A veritable circus of computerized equipment performs dazzling feats: coloring a map of the US at your verbal command, providing your piano playing with the appropriate orchestral accompaniment, even altering the contours of your face on screen. A walk-through computer allows a visitor to examine a computer's components from the inside bit by bit (or is that byte by byte?). Open Tuesdays through Sundays; closed Mondays except Boston public school holidays. Admission charge; free for children under four. Within sight of the *Boston Tea Party Ship* at 300 Congress St., *Museum Wharf* (phone: 426-2800).

BEACON HILL

Here is the heart of old Boston, including the *State House,* Mt. Vernon Street, and Louisburg Square with its stately old townhouses that were (and still are) the pride of the first families of Boston. The cobblestone Acorn

Street, parallel to Mt. Vernon and Chestnut Streets, is the most photographed street in town.

BLACK HERITAGE TRAIL This 1.6-mile walking tour explores the history of Boston's black community throughout the 18th and 19th centuries. Free guided tours, led by *National Park Service* rangers, pass 14 sites of historic importance on Beacon Hill, including the *African Meeting House,* the oldest black church in the country, the homes of well-known abolitionists, and the *Robert Gould Shaw Memorial,* which honors the first US black regiment, which served under Shaw during the Civil War. (The tour also may be self-guided; pick up the brochure from the *National Park Service Visitor Center* at 46 Joy St.) Tours are conducted daily from *Memorial Day* through *Labor Day;* by appointment at other times of the year. Registration is not required, but it's advisable to call ahead (phone: 742-5415).

STATE HOUSE Designed by Charles Bulfinch, the gold-domed *State House* dates from 1795. Oliver Wendell Holmes (the author and doctor, not his son, the justice) remarked that the "Boston State House is the hub of the solar system," a remark that spawned the city's nickname, "the Hub." The original *State House* building is the ornate, red brick structure with white marble trim and a great golden dome. The wings are uninspired afterthoughts by comparison. If you squint just right you can block them out of view and see the building as James Monroe did in 1817. The president was so impressed that he put Bulfinch in charge of the reconstruction of the nation's *Capitol* in Washington, DC, where the architect repeated the rotunda and dome motif. Some final notes about the dome: Its original whitewashed shingles were replaced with copper in 1802 by a Grand Master of the Masons, a fellow by the name of Paul Revere. Gold leaf was added to the dome in 1866, though it was painted gray during World War II to hide the building from possible Axis bomb attacks. Enter through the side door of the right wing (the main door is hardly ever used). Pick up informational pamphlets or join a weekday guided tour in *Doric Hall,* which features busts, statues, memorials, and paintings of famous Americans. Also worth a visit are *Memorial Hall* (also known as the *Hall of Flags*), the *Chamber of the House of Representatives,* the *Senate Chamber,* the *Senate Reception Room,* and a library. Closed weekends. No admission charge. On Beacon St. facing the entrance to the *Common* (phone: 727-3676).

BOSTON ATHENAEUM One of the oldest libraries in the country, founded in 1807, is now housed here. This five-story National Historic Landmark building (the first three floors date from 1847–49; the top two from 1913–15) is a temple to civility. From its marble, mahogany, and ornate table lamps to its endless sea of volumes, the *Athenaeum* has the feel of a study in a colonial mansion, sumptuous yet studious. Once an art gallery whose exhibits were the foundation of the collection that became the *Museum of Fine Arts,* the *Athenaeum* still has a permanent collection of American and European works, from which it mounts exhibits in its second-floor gallery. In addition, it contains more than 600,000 titles, including the *King's Chapel Library* collection, sent in 1698 by England's William III; works from the *John Quincy Adams Library;* and part of George Washington's personal library. Look for a book written by Oliver Wendell Holmes, a former member of the *Athenaeum,* that has been edited in spots with a pen. The author, it is said, made a couple of later-than-last-minute corrections while leafing through the volume on a visit to the library. Asked why a visitor to the city should come here, a library administrator said it all: "Because it's just so darned Bostonian." Guided tours of the library are given Tuesdays and Thursdays at 3 PM; reservations necessary. At other times, the library is open only to members, scholars, and qualified researchers. There's no admission charge. 10½ Beacon St. (phone: 227-0270).

MT. VERNON STREET Henry James once called it the "only respectable street in America." This Beacon Hill street, which runs from behind the *State House* to Charles Street and beyond, is lined with homes that have rich historical associations—and owners. Look for the famous brass knockers, the charming carriage houses, and the intimate backyard gardens. Midway up the hill is Louisburg Square, a rectangle of terribly proper houses facing a tiny park that was once home to Louisa May Alcott and Jenny Lind. The most history-intensive part of this area is between Louisburg Square and Joy Street, where you will find the *Nichols House Museum,* the only Beacon Hill home open to the public. Closed January. Admission charge. 55 Mt. Vernon St. (phone: 227-6993).

CHARLES STREET Beacon Hill's one true commercial street stretches from Beacon Street to Cambridge Street. The street began as a seawall; before the Back Bay was filled in, Charles Street marked Beacon Hill's western shoreline, where tides rose nearly 15 feet. Along with lower Chestnut Street, Charles Street today forms Boston's "Antiques Row" and is home to a number of restaurants, shops, and pubs. The street's most interesting building, the *Charles Street Meeting House,* was built in 1807 as a Baptist church (it has since been converted into office and retail space). George Grant, the first black graduate of *Harvard* and the inventor of the wooden golf tee, lived at 108 Charles Street.

NORTH END

The *Paul Revere House* and *Old North Church* are both snugly tucked away among the narrow red brick streets of the North End, a colorful, Italian-American community with a lively street life and some excellent little restaurants (see *Eating Out*). To experience *la dolce vita,* stop at the *Caffè Dello Sport* (308 Hanover St.; phone: 523-5063) for cannoli, cappuccino, and good people watching.

PAUL REVERE HOUSE Home to the legendary Revolutionary War hero, this is the oldest wooden house in Boston. Revere moved here in 1770 with his wife, mother, and five children. He had eleven more children with his second wife, which is why his house was the only one on the block that didn't have to quarter British soldiers. On the night of April 18, 1775, after getting the nod from Joseph Warren in Boston that British troops were moving (British troops had already mustered in North Square), Revere quietly slipped into his house to change into his boots. From here he was rowed by friends across the Charles River, within sight of a British gunship. Borrowing a horse from Deacon John Larkin in Charlestown, the silversmith-cum-patriot galloped off on the ride that earned him a permanent place in American history. William Dawes and Samuel Prescott also rode forth with the news (as did many other area patriots). Although Revere completed his mission, which was to bring word to the town of Lexington, he decided to ride on to Concord; on the way he was captured by the British, questioned, then released. The exhibits inside the house, which include Revere's saddlebags, revolver, portraits, and the account of the ride in his own words, are sure to clear up some misconceptions about the man and his famous ride. Closed Mondays January through March; open daily except major holidays the rest of the year. Admission charge. 19 North Sq. (phone: 523-1676).

OLD NORTH CHURCH Affectionately known as "Old North," this structure, built in 1723, is officially named *Christ Church.* On the night of April 18, 1775, sexton Robert Newman hung two lanterns in the steeple to warn Bostonians that the British were coming by sea. His action and Paul Revere's famous ride were later immortalized by Henry Wadsworth Longfellow's poem. (The line you will want to remember is: "One if by land, two if by sea.") The church's original clock still ticks in the back, and services are still held every Sunday. Open daily. 193 Salem St. (phone: 523-6676).

BLACKSTONE BLOCK On the other side of the expressway, near *City Hall,* the city's first commercial district was named after Boston's first settler, William Blaxton (or Blackstone). Though most of the original 17th-century dwellings are gone, several from the 18th century remain, including the *Union Oyster House* restaurant (41 Union St.; phone: 227-2750) and the *Ebenezer Hancock House* (10 Marshall St.). Ebenezer's brother, John Hancock, actually owned the building; Ebenezer lived there from 1764 to 1785. As paymaster of the colonial troops, Ebenezer kept in the basement the two million silver crowns sent by France to help pay the Revolutionary troops (a deal artfully crafted by Benjamin Franklin). The *Boston Stone,* a millstone brought from England by a painter in the 1600s, is set in the foundation of a shop on Marshall Street. Originally used to grind colored powder into paint, it became to Boston what its counterpart, the London stone, was to that city—the official point from which all distances from Boston were measured. In back of the block is Blackstone Street, a malodorous little thoroughfare that should be avoided except on Fridays and Saturdays, when it is the site of *Haymarket,* the city's colorful outdoor produce market. Just north of *Faneuil Hall.*

Arlington is the first of an alphabetically ordered series of streets created when the Back Bay was filled in during the mid-1800s. Broad streets and avenues were laid out in an orderly fashion, and along them wealthy Bostonians built palatial homes, churches, and public institutions. This area is a joy to walk and gives a better feeling of Victorian Boston than any other part of the city.

PUBLIC GARDEN A gem among city parks and a Boston treasure since 1861, the garden has fountains, formal plantings, a pond, and a variety of native and European trees that are labeled for identification. Abundant flowers grow along the garden's many footpaths. The carefully tended beds are changed with the seasons—the spring tulips are particular favorites among locals and visitors alike. The flowers are not the only providers of color here: From the dark suits of the financiers en route between office and home to the brilliant hues of the tie-dyed T-shirts worn and sold here in summer, the *Public Garden* attracts an array of humanity that represents all of Boston. Treat yourself to a ride on the fabled, pedal-driven Swan Boats, which leisurely cruise the pond, with its live resident swans and ducks. Rides are offered daily, from mid-April to mid-September except on extremely windy or rainy days. There's a fee for rides; group rates are available (phone: 635-4505). Whether boating or walking, you may want to bring bread scraps for the resident ducks. In the winter, hardy locals tour the pond on ice skates. Adjacent to *Boston Common,* and bordered by Beacon, Charles, Boylston, and Arlington Sts.

COMMONWEALTH AVENUE Intended to replicate the broad boulevards of 19th-century Paris, with their stately, mansard-roofed homes, Commonwealth Avenue ("Comm. Ave." to the locals) has fulfilled its early promise. Stroll down the shady center mall, with its statues of famous Bostonians. In April, the magnolias are magnificent. On the corner of Clarendon Street stands the *First Baptist Church,* a splendid Romanesque structure designed by H. H. Richardson and completed in 1872. Open Tuesdays through Fridays, 10 AM to 1 PM, or by prior arrangement. No admission charge. 110 Commonwealth Ave. (phone: 267-3148).

ESPLANADE This strip of parkland runs between Storrow Drive and the Charles River in the vicinity of Back Bay. Formerly just a 2-mile walkway, it was expanded into a park with money donated by Mrs. James Storrow, widow of a wealthy Boston banker. A plush, clean, and relatively safe stretch of parkland, it is a convenient place for runners, cyclists, roller bladers, and the rest of the Back Bay cardiovascular crowd—not to mention sunbathers. Several footbridges lead to the *Esplanade* from the Back Bay, over Storrow Drive, where Bostonians display their maniacal driving habits.

COPLEY SQUARE Seagoing vessels used to drop anchor in Copley Square; now it harbors H. H. Richardson's magnificent 19th-century *Trinity Church,* (open daily), where there are free half-hour organ recitals every Friday from

September through June at 12:15 PM (phone: 536-0944). A perfect reflection of the church can be seen in the blue glass façade of the *John Hancock Tower,* a mirrored marvel designed by I. M. Pei that contains more than 13 acres of glass. When the building opened in 1975, the glass windows began popping out, much to the alarm of pedestrians who had to traverse the streets below. Just as all the glass was finally replaced, employees in the upper floors complained of a terrifying sway when the wind blew. The building underwent a massive shoring up, but the saga continued when the construction of the tower was found to have done serious structural damage to the beloved *Trinity Church.* Nonetheless, the *Tower*'s 60th floor *Observatory* offers spectacular views of the city and beyond (see *Seeing the City*). On Dartmouth Street across from the square is the main branch of the *Boston Public Library,* the oldest municipally supported library in the country (it was founded in 1852). Completed in 1895, the building is considered one of the first outstanding examples of the Renaissance Beaux Arts style in the US. The huge bronze doors just inside the outer doors were created by Daniel Chester French, sculptor of the *Lincoln Memorial.* The blocky addition in back, designed by Philip Johnson, was built in 1972. Step inside the Copley Square entrance for a quiet moment in the library's lovely central courtyard. Call for a schedule of weekly guided tours of the library's artistic treasures, many of which have been recently restored (phone: 536-5400). Near the fountain on *Copley Square* sits an outdoor sculpture, "The Tortoise and the Hare," which is a tribute to the thousands who participate in the *Boston Mararthon* and cross its finish line. Also on Dartmouth Street (on the other side of Huntington Ave.) is *Copley Place* (phone: 375-4400), a complex of hotels, fashionable shops (*Neiman Marcus, Tiffany, Godiva Chocolatiers,* and the like), restaurants, an 11-screen movie theater (phone: 266-1300), and an indoor waterfall.

NEWBURY STREET This is where fashionable Bostonians shop. There are many art galleries and boutiques, as well as a variety of restaurants and a number of outdoor cafés. It begins, sedately, where Arlington Street borders the *Public Garden* and the *Ritz-Carlton* and the *Burberry*'s store hold sway. (Just one block away from the *Ritz-Carlton,* on Boylston Street, is the *Heritage on the Garden* complex, which has high-end, international stores, such as *Escada, Hermès,* and *Waterford-Wedgwood.* Here's where you also find *Biba,* one of Boston's trendiest restaurants, and *The Spa* at the *Heritage,* the perfect antidote to a hard day of shopping.) But continue down Newbury Street toward Massachusetts Avenue and the boutiques gradually give way, ending in the mammoth *Tower Records* and the outrageous *Allston Beat.*

NEW ENGLAND HISTORIC GENEALOGICAL SOCIETY Since Bostonians are extremely curious about their lineage, it is fitting that one of the country's most exhaustive collections of family history is located here. The collection, which covers primarily the 17th through 19th centuries, includes 17th-century diaries and journals documenting the lives of New Englanders, and some documentation on other parts of the US and Canada. Closed Sundays and Mondays. There's no admission fee to look around; there is a small fee for using the society's research facilities. 101 Newbury St. (phone: 536-5740).

INSTITUTE OF CONTEMPORARY ART Exciting contemporary artwork by local artists as well as touring exhibitions in several media can be seen at the *ICA,* one of Boston's most important showplaces. An interesting film series is shown in the gallery, which was converted from a 19th-century police station. Open Wednesdays through Sundays. Admission charge. 955 Boylston St. (phone: 266-5152).

THE FIRST CHURCH OF CHRIST, SCIENTIST, IN BOSTON (CHRISTIAN SCIENCE CHURCH WORLD HEADQUARTERS) The world headquarters of the religion founded in the 19th century by the American religious reformer Mary Baker Eddy, this 15-acre complex houses several interesting attractions. Mrs. Eddy's original granite *First Church of Christ, Scientist,* built in 1894, is visible, although enveloped by an overpowering Byzantine and Renaissance edifice erected in 1906. The rectangular reflecting pool, tucked between two modern buildings designed by I. M. Pei, is good for a quiet walk and a view of the Boston skyline. Most interesting is the *Mapparium,* a 30-foot stained glass globe built in 1935 (and reflecting the world as it was in 1935, with only 70 countries), through which you walk on a glass bridge that is also an echo chamber. The *Mapparium* is located in the *Christian Science Publishing Society Building,* the editorial home of the *The Christian Science Monitor,* a newspaper with a truly global focus. The *Mapparium* is closed Sundays and holidays. Free tours of the complex are available. Massachusetts and Huntington Aves. (phone: 450-2000).

KENMORE SQUARE Formerly a fashionable area, this square is now notorious for traffic jams and college students (*Fenway Park* and *Boston University* are nearby). A cherished Boston landmark, the *Citgo* sign, has evaded demolition several times and it looks as if it is here to stay. Except when it was turned off during the energy-conservation drive of the late 1970s, it has splashed Kenmore Square with blue, white, and red lights for decades.

THE FENWAY

Some of the city's finest medical, educational, and cultural institutions are located in this former marshland in southwest Boston. The *Museum of Fine Arts* and the *Isabella Stewart Gardner Museum* are located on *The Fens,* as are *Simmons College, Emmanuel College,* and *Northeastern University. Symphony Hall,* home of the *Boston Symphony Orchestra* and the *Boston Pops Orchestra,* is here as well, and the *New England Conservatory of Music* and *Harvard Medical School* (located in the world-renowned Longwood Medical Area) are nearby.

THE FENS Landscape designer Frederick Law Olmsted crafted this serene parkland out of mud flats, while preserving some of the area's original environment. In this 12-acre park are footbridges, statuary, reed-bound pools, rows of magnolias, a rose garden, community gardens, and a running path, all surrounded by the still-marshy Fens. *Note:* Avoid this area after dark.

MUSEUM OF FINE ARTS This is one of the world's great art museums, with comprehensive exhibits from every major period and in every conceivable medium. Noteworthy are the collection of Impressionist paintings (with more Monets than anywhere outside Paris); the decorative arts and sculpture from the colonial period to the present; the most outstanding assemblage of Egyptian art outside of Cairo; the greatest collection of Asiatic art under one roof; an exhaustive gathering of American art, including numerous works by Homer, Copley, Sargent, and Hopper; and an impressive classical collection with artifacts from the 6th, 5th, and 4th centuries BC, and the early Roman Imperial period. The wares of silversmiths on display at the *MFA* will prove that the patriot Paul Revere had many valuable talents on top of riding fast on a horse and disturbing the peace. The main building was built in 1909; the airy West Wing, designed by renowned architect I. M. Pei, was added in 1981. It houses additional exhibition space, as well as a cafeteria, restaurant, café, and museum shop; special shows are often mounted here. Outside is the *Tenshin Garden,* which features New England flora and Japanese landscape design. Closed Mondays, though open Monday holidays; open late Wednesdays (the West Wing also is open late Thursdays and Fridays). Admission charge except Wednesdays from 4 to 9:45 PM. Directly in back of *The Fens,* 465 Huntington Ave. (phone: 267-9300).

ISABELLA STEWART GARDNER MUSEUM This marble Venetian palazzo houses one of the world's magnificent private art collections, and its enclosed flower-filled courtyard in prized as one of Boston's most special places. Isabella Stewart came to Boston in 1860 to marry John Lowell Gardner, a wealthy Brahmin industrialist. While she was a friend of some of the most famous folks of the era—art critic Bernard Berenson advised her on her collection, and artist John Singer Sargent painted her portrait—her flashy dress and spirited manner quickly made her suspect in the eyes of most proper Bostonians. The art Gardner collected during her worldwide travels is housed in a 15th-century–style Italianate mansion, built between 1899 and 1903, that remains furnished as it was during her lifetime. As a result, objects with as much sentimental as aesthetic value are exhibited next to several Rembrandts, Titian's *Rape of Europa,* a number of Tintorettos, Manets, Botticellis, Whistlers, and one Corot. (Because the art is arranged haphazardly and the museum signs and labels are not particularly detailed, it's a good idea to purchase the museum guide, sold at the main entrance.) When your feet are tired, you can take lunch or tea at a pleasant café on the premises. Every Saturday and Sunday at 1:30 PM from September through May, the museum hosts classical concerts. Closed Mondays and holidays. No admission charge for children under 12. 280 The Fenway (phone: 566-1401).

SOUTH END

Though it contains few recognizable tourist attractions, this reclaimed wetland is interesting for its architecture and its ethnic diversity.

UNION PARK A residential block of Victorian townhouses that were among the first built during the mid-19th-century development of the South End, this is a favorite spot in the Hub for many Bostonians. There are fountains, foliage, and a strip of greenery dividing the two rows of houses that give this pocket of civility a quiet, lazy feel. It is studded with magnolias during spring months.

SOUTHWEST CORRIDOR This pleasant, well-manicured footpath stretches from the Back Bay station on the *Orange Line* (just behind *Neiman Marcus*) to Massachusetts Avenue and beyond, affording a leisurely sampling of South End architecture, good people watching, and a view of Boston's skyline.

CHARLESTOWN

The Puritans first settled here in 1629 in their quest for a "city upon a hill." Charlestown's Breed's Hill was thought to be just fine, until a scarcity of safe drinking water forced the settlers to cultivate the marshy peninsula to the south that became Boston. The *Battle of Bunker Hill* was fought here, and Monument and Winthrop Squares are laced with excellent examples of 18th- and 19th-century architecture. City Square is where Paul Revere began his famed midnight ride. Nearby are the *Charlestown Navy Yard* and the USS *Constitution.*

BUNKER HILL MONUMENT This 221-foot granite obelisk was built in the 1800s to mark the site of the first major battle of the Revolutionary War. On June 17, 1775, on this hill overlooking the Boston Harbor, the British won the Battle of Bunker Hill—but hundreds of their soldiers were killed or wounded. Climb the 294 steps to the top of the monument (there's no elevator), or visit the information center below, which has exhibits and dioramas on the battle and the monument. Open daily; no admission charge. On Breed's Hill, in the center of Monument Square (phone: 242-5641).

USS *CONSTITUTION* This is the famous "Old Ironsides," Boston-built in 1797, proud victor in 40 sea battles, the oldest commissioned warship in the world, and still part of the fleet of the *US Navy.* It recently underwent extensive renovations for its 200th anniversary to be celebrated this year. An adjacent shoreside museum (phone: 426-1812) displays related memorabilia and a slide show. City Square bus stop. Open daily. Admission charge for museum; none for the *Constitution. Charlestown Navy Yard,* Charlestown (phone: 242-5670).

BUNKER HILL PAVILION Witness a vivid multimedia reenactment of the Battle of Bunker Hill on 14 screens, with seven sound channels. Open daily, with shows every half hour from April through November. Admission charge. Adjacent to USS *Constitution* (phone: 241-7576).

CAMBRIDGE

HARVARD SQUARE Just across the Charles River from Boston, Cambridge has always had an ambience all its own. Catering to the academic and professional communities, the square is a lively, "upscale" combination of the trendy and the traditional. It has the greatest concentration of bookstores in the country, many of which are open until late into the evening; movie options that range from vintage films to the latest from Hollywood and abroad; and the ever-present street musicians. When hunger pangs strike, everything from muffins to nouvelle cuisine awaits—with an authentic Italian ice to top it off. Take the *Red Line* toward Alewife and get off at the Harvard Square stop.

HARVARD YARD This tree- and lawn-filled enclave is the focal point of the oldest (1636) and most prestigious university in the country (the *Law School* is nearby, the *Business School* just across the river, and the *Medical School* a bus ride away in Boston). Notice especially *Massachusetts Hall* (1720; *Harvard*'s oldest building), Charles Bulfinch's *University Hall,* and, in the adjoining quadrangle, *Widener Library* and H. H. Richardson's *Sever Hall.* Campus tours are given year-round; check at the information office in *Holyoke Center* (phone: 495-1573).

WEEKS MEMORIAL BRIDGE This graceful footbridge was built to link *Harvard*'s Cambridge campus with the school's *Graduate School of Business Administration,* on the Boston side of the Charles River. It offers a splendid view of the white, crimson, and gold *Harvard* steeples and the *Harvard* crew team's practices.

HARVARD UNIVERSITY ART MUSEUMS *Harvard*'s impressive collection of paintings, drawings, prints, sculpture, and silver is housed in three fine museums. The *Arthur Sackler Museum* (485 Broadway) houses ancient Roman, Egyptian, and Islamic antiquities, as well as traveling exhibitions, in a 1985 post-modern building designed by James Stirling. Nearby is the neo-Georgian building of the *Fogg Museum* (32 Quincy St.), which features European and American art from the Middle Ages to the present. Connected to the *Fogg* is the *Busch-Reisinger Museum,* the only museum in the US that specializes in the art of Germanic language-speaking countries. All three are open daily. Admission charge (phone: 495-9400).

HARVARD UNIVERSITY NATURAL HISTORY MUSEUMS On a short block parallel to Oxford Street is this complex housing the *Comparative Zoology, Peabody, Mineralogical and Geological,* and *Botanical Museums.* The *Peabody* houses extensive anthropological and archaeological collections, with an emphasis on South American Indians, as well as a fine gift shop. The *Botanical* houses a famous collection of glass flowers handmade for *Harvard* between 1887 and 1936 by Leopold and Rudolph Blaschka, a German father and son, and renowned for their scientific accuracy as well as their beauty. Renowned *Harvard* professor Stephen Jay Gould often lectures at

Comparative Zoology, a natural history museum, and the *Mineralogical and Geological* museum displays rocks of all kinds. Reservations must be made for tours of any of the museums. Open daily. Admission charge except on Saturdays from 9 to 11 AM. 26 Oxford St. (phone: 495-3045).

RADCLIFFE YARD One of the Seven Sister colleges, *Radcliffe* has evolved from its historical role as "*Harvard*'s Annex" to its current position, with its undergraduates fully integrated with *Harvard*'s. *Radcliffe* offers alternative programs for women at the graduate level and those interested in career changes. Its *Schlesinger Library* has one of the country's top collections on the history of women in America, as well as an important culinary collection. Closed weekends. No admission charge. 3 James St. (phone: 495-8647).

OLD BURYING GROUND This historic cemetery, also known as *God's Acre,* is on Garden Street just past *Christ Church.* The graves date back to 1635, and a number of Revolutionary War heroes and *Harvard* presidents are buried here. On the Garden Street fence, there's a mileage marker dating to 1754.

BRATTLE STREET This elegant Cambridge street was known in the 1770s as "Tory Row" because seven mansions owned by supporters of King George were located here (a couple still stand today). William Brattle, a Loyalist who fled Boston in 1774, lived at 42 Brattle, an 18th-century gambrel-roofed Colonial home that later became the home of Margaret Fuller, an early feminist. The building is now the headquarters of the *Cambridge Center for Adult Education* (phone: 547-6789). The yellow clapboard *Pratt House* at No. 56 is where Dexter Pratt, Longfellow's "Village Blacksmith," lived and plied his trade. It now houses the tiny *Blacksmith House Café and Bakery* (phone: 876-2725). Though the "spreading chestnut tree" that Longfellow referred to is long gone, a plaque on the corner of Brattle and Story Streets preserves its memory. Longfellow lived just down the street from 1837 until his death in 1882. That house (105 Brattle St.; phone: 876-4491), built in 1759, served as the headquarters for General Washington during the British siege of Boston. Occasional concerts are held there in summer, and guided tours are available. Open Wednesday through Sundays from mid-May through mid-October; admission charge.

MASSACHUSETTS INSTITUTE OF TECHNOLOGY The foremost scientific and technological school in the country, *MIT* opened its doors in Boston in 1865 and moved across the river to its present Cambridge campus in 1916. In addition to its world-famous laboratories and graduate schools in engineering and science, its professional schools include the *Sloan School of Management,* the *Joint Center for Urban Studies* (with *Harvard*), and the *School of Architecture.* Architect I. M. Pei is an alumnus; next to his *Green Building* for the earth sciences stands Calder's stabile *The Big Sail,* part of a superb collection of outdoor sculptures on the campus. Also worth noting are Eero Saarinen's chapel and his *Kresge Auditorium,* just across from the main entrance on Massachusetts Avenue. The main *MIT Museum* (265

Massachusetts Ave.; phone: 253-4444) contains permanent collections and changing exhibits of contemporary art and technology. Closed Mondays and holidays; admission charge. The *Compton Gallery* (77 Massachusetts Ave.; phone: 253-4444) features changing technical exhibitions. Closed weekends; no admission charge. The *Wiesner Building* (20 Ames St.) is another I. M. Pei landmark, worth a visit for its arresting interior and the often provocative changing exhibitions at its *List Visual Arts Center* located there. Open September through June; no admission charge (phone: 253-4680). The *MIT Shop* (265 Massachusetts Ave., phone: 258-9118) is closed Mondays. *MIT* campus tours are given year-round on weekdays at 10 AM and 2 PM. *Red Line,* Kendall Square/MIT stop, or No. 1 Dudley bus, headed toward Harvard Square. 77 Massachusetts Ave. (phone: 253-1875).

MT. AUBURN CEMETERY The first garden cemetery in the United States, this rural retreat on the outskirts of Cambridge is bliss to the senses. Founded in 1831, *Mt. Auburn*'s 170 beautifully landscaped acres include hills, ponds, more than 3,500 magnificent trees (including 575 varieties), and an observation tower. An hour's stroll here might be the pinnacle of a sightseeing day—especially for bird watchers. Among the many famous people buried here are Mary Baker Eddy, Henry Wadsworth Longfellow, Julia Ward Howe, Oliver Wendell Holmes, and Winslow Homer. Open daily during daylight; tower open in fair weather from early spring to late fall. Stop for a map at the main entrance. 580 Mt. Auburn St. (phone: 547-7105).

OTHER SPECIAL PLACES

CHINATOWN This neighborhood has one of the largest Chinese-American populations in the country. Tucked between the "Combat Zone" (the city's rapidly shrinking enclave of pornography shops and clubs), the leather merchants' district, and the Southeast Expressway, Chinatown is a pocket of faithfully preserved Chinese culture. There are frequent festivals in celebration of Chinese holidays, including a big bash for *Chinese New Year* (see *Special Events*). This is an interesting place for strolling, although most visitors are attracted by Chinatown's many restaurants, which garner most of the city's late-night business. Try *Ho Yuen Ting* (13A Hudson St.; phone: 426-2316) or *Chau Chow* (52 Beach St.; phone: 426-6266) for excellent Cantonese food served with minimal fuss and minimalist decor. The latter stays open until 4 AM on weekends. The best approach to the neighborhood is through the Chinese arch at the head of Beach Street, where it meets Atlantic Avenue.

JOHN F. KENNEDY LIBRARY Designed by architect I. M. Pei, this presidential library sits on the edge of a point of land projecting into Dorchester Bay, with a magnificent view of the Boston skyline and out to sea. There's an exhibit of documents, photographs, films, and memorabilia that may conjure up a bit of nostalgia even if you voted for Nixon. Recent exhibits seek to keep JFK's legacy alive for the nearly 50% of the population born since his assassination in 1963. His famed rocking chair is here, as are the desk at which he presided over nearly three years as president and the documents of the Kennedy administration. The museum also houses a section devoted to Robert F. Kennedy and, by special arrangement, the papers of Ernest Hemingway, which occupy an entire floor. Open daily except major holidays. No admission charge for children under 6. By car, take the Southeast Expressway south to the JFK Library/UMass exit. Or take the *MBTA Red Line* (Ashmont train to the JFK/UMass stop; a shuttle bus will take you the rest of the way). From *Memorial Day* through *Labor Day* there is water shuttle service available from *Boston Harbor Cruises* at the foot of State Street in downtown Boston. Off Morrissey Blvd. next to the *University of Massachusetts* campus, in Dorchester. (phone: 929-4523).

COMMONWEALTH MUSEUM Next door to the *John F. Kennedy Library,* this museum has audiovisual presentations on the history of the people, places, and politics of Massachusetts. The state archives are also stored here; several exhibits are always on a rotating display. Closed Sunday, holidays, and holiday weekends. No admission charge. 220 Morrissey Blvd. (phone: 727-9268).

MUSEUM OF SCIENCE AND THE CHARLES HAYDEN PLANETARIUM Sitting astride the Charles River Dam and overlooking its boat locks is a cluster of modern buildings that make up one of Boston's greatest educational institutions. The *Museum of Science* includes over 400 interactive exhibits covering every aspect of science from medicine to geology to space exploration. Old favorites include the "Transparent Woman," whose internal organs light up as their functions are explained; the lightning exhibition, where lightning—and a resulting clap of thunder—are created before your very eyes; and the *Charles Hayden Planetarium.* The planetarium features a $2-million Zeiss planetarium projector and a multi-image program on cosmic discoveries, as well as laser light shows with computer animation and brilliant laser graphics. At the museum's *Omni Theater,* a 70-foot domed screen envelops the viewer in the ultimate film experience. The museum has a wonderful gift shop and a couple of cafeterias. Take the *MBTA Green Line* to *Science Park.* Open daily. Admission charge for the museum; additional charge for the *Omni Theater;* advance reservations are advised for the *Omni Theater. Science Park,* on O'Brien Hwy. at the eastern end of Storrow Dr. (phone: 723-2500).

ARNOLD ARBORETUM Contained in these 265 acres of beautifully landscaped woodland and park are over 14,000 trees, shrubs, and vines, most of them labeled by their assiduous *Harvard* caretakers. The visitors' center shop has a large selection of books on botany and horticulture. Open daily, sunrise to sunset. No admission charge. By car, the main gate and visitors' center are 100 yards south of the rotary junction of Routes 1 and 203. Or take the *E* train (*Green Line*), the Arborway bus No. 39 from the Copley Square stop, or the *Orange Line,* Forest Hills stop. Six miles southwest of downtown Boston on The Arborway, Jamaica Plain (phone: 524-1717).

FRANKLIN PARK ZOO The highlight of this facility is an exciting rain forest exhibit in which jungle animals prowl in areas resembling their natural habitats. In the middle of the huge, climate-controlled, hangar-like structure is the gorilla area, where six mountain gorillas frolic over the rocky terrain and where birds fly free (sort of) under the soaring roof. Other animals—dwarf forest buffalos, crocodiles, a dwarf hippo, storks, and even scorpions—roam in a separate space; the zoo also boasts four waterfalls and the largest collection of tropical plants in New England. Other sections include *Bird's World, Hooves and Horns,* and a *Children's Zoo.* Open daily; admission charge except on Tuesdays after noon. Take Route 1 (VFW Parkway) to Route 203 East, or take Bus No. 16 from the Forest Hills stop on the *Orange Line* or the Andrew stop on the *Red Line.* Rte. 203, *Franklin Park,* Dorchester (phone: 442-4896).

FREDERICK LAW OLMSTED NATIONAL HISTORIC SITE This house was occupied by Olmsted, the premier 19th-century landscape designer, and his two sons after the death of his wife. Best known as the designer of New York City's *Central Park,* Olmsted also designed Boston's 8-mile *Emerald Necklace* of green spaces, which ties the city to the suburbs. Tours are conducted of the house and of the grounds, which illustrate the principles of Olmsted's designs, and archives on the site include plans, drawings, and photographs of his work. Open Fridays through Sundays from 10 AM to 4:30 PM. No admission charge. 99 Warren St., Brookline (phone: 566-1689).

EXTRA SPECIAL

About 18 miles north of Boston on Route 107 is the town of Salem. It was the capital of the Massachusetts Bay Colony from 1626 to 1630, and again, briefly, in 1774, when the British closed Boston Harbor after the Boston Tea Party. However, Salem earned a bitter name in American history as the scene of the witch trials, in which a group of more than 100 villagers were accused of witchcraft. The hysterical allegations resulted in the deaths of 25 of the accused. Salem is also the site of Nathaniel Hawthorne's 1668 *House of the Seven Gables* (54 Turner St.; phone: 508-744-0991). Open daily. Admission charge. Hawthorne worked in the *Salem Custom House* and wrote his masterpiece, *The Scarlet Letter,* at 14 Mall Street. Like Boston, Salem has a history trail winding through its streets and port. Visit the *Salem Maritime National Historic Site* (174 Derby St.; phone: 508-745-1470), run by the *National Park Service,* for information, maps, and a variety of seasonal tours. It's open daily.

Stop at the *Witch Museum* (19½ Washington Sq. N.; phone: 508-744-1692). It's closed *Thanksgiving, Christmas,* and *New Year's Day;* there's an admission charge. The *Witch House* (310½ Essex St.; phone: 508-744-0180), site of some of the interrogations, radiates a spooky feeling when you pass it at night. It's open daily, mid-March through November; there's

an admission charge. Get in the mood for this tour by reading Arthur Miller's play *The Crucible.*

The *Peabody Essex Museum* (E. India Sq.; phone: 508-745-9500) has fascinating scrimshaw carvings and nautical regalia from the early days of shipping and from far-off ports. Closed Mondays from November through *Memorial Day.* Admission charge. *Pier Transit Cruises* offers harbor tours that leave from *Salem Willows Pier* (phone: 508-744-6311 or 800-696-6311).

Sources and Resources

TOURIST INFORMATION

For tourist information, maps, and brochures, visit the visitors' information center at *Boston Common.* It's open daily. The *Greater Boston Convention and Visitors Bureau* (*Prudential Center*; phone: 536-4100) has multilingual maps and brochures and is open weekdays. The *Massachusetts Office of Travel and Tourism* (100 Cambridge St.; phone: 727-3201) also can provide maps, calendars of events, health updates, travel advisories, and other tourist information; it's open weekdays. Another good source is the *Boston National Historical Park Downtown Visitor Center* (15 State St.; phone: 242-5642), located across from the *Old State House,* which has maps, brochures, books, and a slide show on the historic sites of Boston. In addition, park rangers here answer questions, offer advice, and lead walking tours. It's open daily.

The 24-hour Visitor's Channel of the Panorama Television Network, Channel 12 on local hotel television sets, provides weather updates every 15 minutes as well as travel advisories, traffic information, and half-hour bulletins on attractions within Boston and day trips outside the city.

COMPUTER GUIDES

Interactive video machines placed on various street corners assist visitors trying to get their bearings. Enter the name of a particular spot in the area or ask for a selection of shops and restaurants, and the machine will display detailed information. Other computer terminals located at *Logan Airport* provide information on cultural and tourist events throughout New England.

LOCAL COVERAGE *Boston Globe,* morning daily; *Boston Herald,* morning daily; *The Christian Science Monitor,* weekday mornings; *Boston Phoenix,* weekly; *The Tab,* weekly; *Boston* magazine, monthly; *Bostonia* magazine, quarterly.

A comprehensive guidebook is *In and Out of Boston (With or Without Children),* by Bernice Chesler (Globe Pequot Press; $15.95). Also good is *Historic Walks in Old Boston,* by John Harris (Globe Pequot Press; $12.95). For restaurant listings, see *Robert Nadeau's Guide to Boston Restaurants* by

Mark Zanger (World Food Press; $3.95). Also pick up a copy of *ACCESS Boston* (HarperCollins; $18.50).

TELEVISION STATIONS WBZ Channel 4–CBS; WCVB Channel 5–ABC; WHDH Channel 7–NBC; WGBH Channel 2–PBS; WXNE Channel 25–Fox; WSBK Channel 38; WLVI Channel 56.

RADIO STATIONS AM: WRKO 680 (talk); WJIB 740 (adult contemporary); WBZ 1030 (talk); WEEI 850 (sports). FM: WGBH 89.7 (classical/National Public Radio); WBUR 90.9 (news/talk/National Public Radio); WFNX 101.7 (contemporary/new wave); WCRB 102.5 (classical); WBCN 104.1 (rock/pop).

TELEPHONE The area code for Boston is 617. Some areas surrounding Boston are served by the 508 area code.

SALES TAX The state sales tax is 5%; the hotel room tax is 9.7%; state meal tax in restaurants is 5%.

CLIMATE Autumn may be the best time to see Boston. Days are generally clear and brisk, with temperatures in the 50s and 60s. At night it can drop into the 40s, with chilly winds. Winter can be formidable, with icy winds, snow, and sleet. If you intend to drive, make sure your car is properly equipped. Spring may be brief and cool, and temperatures are usually in the 50s and low 60s. In summer, the mercury climbs into the 80s and 90s (sometimes even higher) and it is often humid, although nights can be breezy and cooler.

GETTING AROUND

AIRPORT Just 3 miles from the center of the city, *Logan International Airport* handles both international and domestic traffic. The ride from the airport to downtown usually takes from 10 to 30 minutes (or longer), depending on time of day and traffic. *City Transportation* (phone: 561-9000) runs minibuses between *Logan* and Back Bay hotels from 6:30 AM to 8 PM. daily on the hour and half hour. *Peter Pan Trailways* (phone: 800-343-9999) provides bus service between the airport and the company's bus station at 555 Atlantic Avenue daily from noon to 7:10 PM.

The most practical means of getting to *Logan* from virtually anywhere in the Boston area—if you aren't carrying much luggage—is by the *MBTA (Massachusetts Bay Transit Authority) Blue Line* trains, which cost 85¢ and run every 10 to 12 minutes (every 15 minutes on Sundays) from 5:30 AM to about 12:45 AM. There are free shuttle buses from airport terminals to the *Blue Line* airport stop, from which the trip to *Government Center Station* at City Hall Plaza takes under 15 minutes. A water shuttle operated by the *Massachusetts Port Authority* also connects Rowes Wharf (400 Atlantic Ave.) with *Logan* (for information, call 800-23-LOGAN). The trip takes about seven minutes.

BUS/TROLLEY/TRAIN The *MBTA* operates a network of trolleys and subways (referred to by locals as "the *T*") with four major lines, the *Red, Blue, Green,* and *Orange.*

The *MBTA* also runs the city's bus system. *MBTA* service is fairly frequent during the day, less frequent at night, and nonexistent after about 12:30 AM. *MBTA* stations are marked with large, white circular signs bearing a giant "T." For schedules, directions, timetables, maps, and help in planning travel routes, call the *Travel Information Center* at 722-3200 or 800-392-6100 between 6 AM and 11:30 PM on weekdays and until 9 PM on weekends.

Compared to the mass transit systems in most major American cities, Boston is still a bargain: 60¢ for buses and 85¢ for the *T* within the underground sections of the system. Exact change is required for the buses. Three-day visitors' passes are $9, and seven-day passes are $18. They entitle holders to free rides on all *MBTA* conveyances—trolleys, subways, trains, and buses—and to $50 worth of discounts on entertainment, restaurants, and other attractions around the city.

The *T* is the cheapest and often the fastest way to travel between downtown and the airport. Take the *Blue Line* to the airport stop (the *Green Line* connects with it at the *Government Center* stop); from there, a free *MBTA* shuttle bus will take you to your terminal. Warning: Don't try this at rush hour with several suitcases. *MBTA* commuter trains are an excellent way of getting to Boston's suburbs. From *South Station* (Atlantic Ave. at Summer St.; no phone), a gorgeous and sprawling train station inside an ornate 19th-century façade, there are commuter trains to points south and west of Boston, including Framingham and Stoughton, as well as Providence, New Haven, and Stamford. *South Station* is also Boston's link with *Amtrak* (phone: 482-3660; for information and reservations 800-872-7245), which makes frequent runs to Providence, Rhode Island, Connecticut, and New York City. *North Station* (on Causeway St., just behind the former *Boston Garden* now the *Flint Center*; no phone) is the point of departure for commuter trains north and west, including Concord, Gardner, Lowell, Ipswich, and other points on the North Shore.

CAR RENTAL All major national firms are represented.

TAXI You can hail a taxi on the street, pick one up at a taxi stand downtown, or call *Boston Cab* (phone: 536-5010); *Independent Taxi Operators Association* (phone: 426-8700); *Red and White Cab* (242-2300); *Town Taxi* (phone: 536-5000); *Checker Taxi* (phone: 536-7000); *Cambridge Taxi* (Cambridge; phone: 547-3000 and 492-1100).

SIGHTSEEING TOURS

CRUISES *Bay State Cruise Company* (phone: 723-7800) provides service from *Memorial Day* through *Columbus Day* (and sometimes on warm weekends during the winter) out of two locations, Long Wharf and Commonwealth Pier. Boats take passengers on day trips to Georges Island (the site of *Fort Warren,* which was used as a Civil War prison) and the Inner Harbor; to Nantasket Beach and the Outer Harbor; across on whale watching trips; and a ferry crosses Cape Cod Bay to Provincetown.

The *Spirit of Boston* (phone: 457-1450) offers 2½-hour lunch and three-hour dinner cruises departing from Rowes Wharf. *Boston Harbor Cruises* (phone: 227-4320) runs whale watches from May through September, and harbor cruises of historical sites from April through mid-October, departing from Long Wharf. It also runs the *Navy Yard* water shuttle to Charlestown year-round. For $1, this is a great way to get from the *Aquarium* to the *Charlestown Navy Yard.* In season there is also a water shuttle to the *John F. Kennedy Library* on Dorchester Bay.

Massport (phone: 800-235-6426) runs a water shuttle from Rowes Wharf to *Logan Airport* (a seven-minute ride) year-round except Saturdays and holidays.

TROLLEY Boston's various trolley sightseeing tours have gained a reputation for colorful—albeit not always accurate—information. The major ones are *Old Town Trolley Tours* (phone: 269-7010), fully narrated tours of more than 100 historic Boston sites, as well as tours of Cambridge and brewpub tours; *Boston Trolley* (phone: TRO-LLEY; fax: 269-0678), which has a number of boarding and reboarding stops at major Boston hotels; and *Brush Hills Tours/Gray Line Boston* and *Beantown Trolley* (phone: 236-2148; fax: 986-0167).

SPECIAL EVENTS

The *Chinese New Year* is celebrated annually on every street in Chinatown in January or February, depending on the Chinese calendar. The one-day event, from noon to 6 PM, features a dragon and lion dance, firecrackers, and lots of food. Don't miss the *International Cultural Festival* at the *Ritz-Carlton* (see *Grand Hotels*) from the first week in January through the third week in March, featuring cuisine by various chefs and political and cultural lectures; each week a different country is highlighted. *St. Patrick's Day* and *Evacuation Day* (when the British fled Boston in 1776) are both celebrated in South Boston on March 17. *Patriots Day,* featuring a number of parades, reenactments of Revolutionary skirmishes, and other events, is observed in and around Boston (in Concord, Lexington, and so on) on the third Monday in April and the weekend before. The *Boston Marathon,* the oldest (its centennial was in 1996) and most celebrated marathon in the US is also held that Monday, with the front-runners usually crossing the finish line near Copley Square around 2 PM. The *Big Apple Circus,* sponsored by the *Children's Museum* (phone: 426-8855), comes to town from early April through mid-May, giving two performances daily. *Lilac Sunday,* the annual viewing of over 300 varieties of lilacs at the *Arnold Arboretum* (phone: 524-1718), is held on the third Sunday in May. The *Cambridge International Fair,* a celebration of summer and the arts with theater, dance, music, and food, is held in Central Square in early June. June is also the month of colorful neighborhood street fairs, with the *Back Bay Street Fair* and the *Bay Village Fair* on the first Saturday, and the *St. Botolph Street Fair* in the South End on the third Saturday. The *Boston Globe Jazz Festival* (phone: 929-2000), a week-long series of jazz performances and free midday concerts, is held each year in mid-June, kicking off in the plaza of the *Charles* hotel in Cambridge and concluding at the *Hatch Shell* on the *Esplanade*. Boston is filled with color and pageantry during the annual *Fourth of July* celebrations. On *July 4,* the waterfront comes alive with *Harborfest,* a series of events on land and water: The Declaration of Independence is read from the balcony of the *Old State House* at 10 AM; the annual turnaround of the USS *Constitution,* "Old Ironsides," commences at 10:30 AM; and the *Boston Pops* holds its beloved annual holiday concert at the *Hatch Shell* in the evening, which features a sing-along of all-American favorites and culminates with its rousing rendition of the *1812 Overture* underneath a dazzling display of fireworks. North End *Italian Festas,* a series of saint's day celebrations, always begin and end with religious services and processions, and feature a lot of food, games, dancing, and general festivity in between. They are held on nearly every weekend throughout July and August. The oldest American professional tennis championship, the nine-day *US Pro Tennis Championships at Longwood,* begins the third week of July and features many tennis greats (phone: 731-4500). Rowers from around the world and from a variety of American colleges compete in the annual *Head of the Charles Regatta*—which starts on the Charles near the Boston University Bridge and goes upstream to *Harvard* and beyond—on the last Sunday in October. In even-numbered years, the *Harvard-Yale Football Game* is held in Cambridge (phone: 495-2207). Boston's best *Christmas* tradition, the presentation of the *Handel & Haydn Society's Messiah,* is on five evenings in early December (phone: 266-3605). At the *Tea Party Reenactment* (Congress St. Bridge; phone: 338-1773), uniformed participants throw chests of tea off the *Tea Party Ship* on the Sunday closest to December 16. The *First Night Celebration,* a series of musical, culinary, theater, and film events that draws more than 500,000 people to Boston's Back Bay and downtown, is held on *New Year's Eve* (phone: 542-1399).

MUSEUMS

In addition to those described in *Special Places,* other fine museums worth visiting include the following:

BOSTON CENTER FOR THE ARTS Multi-use arts complex in a city block of historic buildings. Open Wednesdays through Sundays from noon to 4 PM. No admission charge. 539 Tremont St. (phone: 426-5000).

CARPENTER CENTER FOR THE VISUAL ARTS Part of *Harvard University,* this is Le Corbusier's only building in the US. Rotating exhibitions and film series are presented throughout the school year. The center is open daily; the *Sert Gallery* on the third floor is open Tuesday through Sunday afternoons. No admission charge. 24 Quincy St., Cambridge (phone: 495-3251).

FIRST HARRISON GRAY OTIS HOUSE The house was designed in the late 18th century by Charles Bulfinch for Otis, a lawyer, congressman, and Boston mayor. It is now the headquarters of the *Society for the Preservation of New England*

Antiquities. Guided tours are available Tuesdays through Saturdays. Admission charge. 141 Cambridge St. (phone: 227-3956).

GIBSON HOUSE A Victorian-era home. Open Wednesdays through Sundays May through October, and on weekends only from November through April. Admission charge. 137 Beacon St. (phone: 267-6338).

MUSEUM OF AFRO-AMERICAN HISTORY The museum's changing exhibits focus on both historical and contemporary issues and personalities. It's located in the *African Meeting House,* the oldest black church in the country, which was built by free black labor in 1806. Closed weekends. No admission charge. 46 Joy St. (phone: 742-5415).

MUSEUM OF THE ANCIENT AND HONORABLE ARTILLERY COMPANY OF MASSACHUSETTS Chartered in 1638 to protect the early settlers, the *Ancient and Honorable* is America's oldest military outfit. On display are firearms, artifacts, flags, cannons, uniforms, and other memorabilia. Closed weekends. No admission charge. *Faneuil Hall,* third floor (phone: 227-1638).

CONCORD MUSEUM Here are 15 galleries featuring the history of Concord from Native American habitation through the American Revolution period and the 19th century including displays of decorative arts from these periods. Open daily except major holidays. Admission charge. 200 Lexington Rd., Concord (phone: 508-369-9763).

MUSEUM OF OUR NATIONAL HERITAGE A museum and library of American history, it often hosts traveling exhibits of folk art and other artifacts. Open daily. No admission charge. 33 Marrett Rd., Lexington (phone: 861-6559).

RALPH WALDO EMERSON MEMORIAL HOUSE The former home of the essayist, philosopher, and poet. Open Thursdays through Sundays, mid-April through October; closed the rest of the year. Admission charge. 28 Cambridge Tpke., Concord (phone: 508-369-2236).

SPORTS MUSEUM Features memorabilia, photographs, equipment, temporary exhibits, interactive video presentations, and other artifacts of New England's rich sports history. Open daily. Admission charge. In the *Cambridgeside Galleria,* Memorial Dr., Cambridge (phone: 787-7678).

SHOPPING

Boston is a browser's paradise, with plenty of elegant and one-of-a-kind stores in a small area. Newbury Street is the place to go if your tastes run to art galleries, designer clothing, fine jewelry, expensive antiques, and outdoor cafés. Even if your preferences are more eclectic than elegant, don't rule out this pretty, European-looking venue. For atmosphere, walk the length of Charles Street, just across the *Public Garden* from the *Ritz.* The curving, gaslit street contains antiques shops, art and print galleries, and several intimate cafés. Just two blocks south of Newbury Street is *Copley Place,* a glitzy shopping mall just off Copley Square, that is connected by a glass-enclosed walkway to the recently redesigned *Prudential Center.* The

Downtown Crossing area has the city's two best-known department stores—*Jordan Marsh* and *Filene's*—surrounded by blocks of so-so shops. And finally, *Faneuil Hall Marketplace* remains one of the city's foremost shopping centerpieces. Below is a list of some of Boston's best emporia.

Allston Beat Blue jeans, leather, and metal, much loved by teens and collegians. 348 Newbury St. (phone: 421-9555).

Autre Fois The focus here is on French country furniture, although there is also furniture from Italy and England, plus a variety of decorative accessories. 125 Newbury St. (phone: 424-8823).

Avenue Victor Hugo Offers a wide range of used books and magazines. 339 Newbury St. (phone: 266-7746).

Betsey Johnson The wild, 1960s-inspired fashions of this New York designer enliven this street. 201 Newbury St. (phone: 236-7072).

Brattle Book Shop This Dickensian-style bookstore, located near the *Boston Common,* is an antiquarian book lover's Elysian Fields. More than 350,000 used, out of print, and rare books populate the three-story building, with original manuscripts and authors' autographs for sale. Closed Sundays. 9 West St. (phone: 542-0210 or 800-447-9595).

Cuoio Shoes This little shop (pronounced *kwao*) has some of the most unusual and elegant women's shoes around. 115 Newbury St. (phone: 859-0636).

DeLuca's Market When almost every food emporium is now either part of a chain or homogenized to anonymity, here's a friendly, family-run food market devoted to high quality and personal service. 11 Charles St. (phone: 523-4343) and 239 Newbury St., Back Bay (phone: 262-5990).

Escada Elegant, colorful clothing by German designer Margaretha Ley. 308 Boylston St., at *Heritage on the Garden* (phone: 437-1200).

FAO Schwarz This huge children's funhouse is almost as large as the New York City flagship. The centerpiece is the singing, two-story clock with moving figurines, a singing giraffe, and a bear tea party on top. 440 Boylston St. (phone: 262-5900).

Filene's A fine department store with a full line of clothing, accessories, and housewares. It is located above the famous *Filene's Basement,* but the two stores now have different owners. *Downtown Crossing,* 426 Washington St. (phone: 357-2100).

Filene's Basement Here you'll find the best bargains in town, with markdowns from every state in the union and nearly every country in the world. *Downtown Crossing.* 426 Washington St. (phone: 542-2011).

Firestone and Parsons An elegant jewelry store, this establishment carries what may be the city's finest estate gems. 8 Newbury St. (phone: 266-1858).

George Gravert Orderly and uncluttered, this establishment specializes in 18th- and 19-century continental antiques. There's a good selection of French country furniture, decorative accessories, and even some 19th-century garden statuary. 122 Charles St. (phone: 227-1593).

Giorgio Armani This understated emporium is a fitting venue for this Italian designer's understated and elegant clothing for men and women. 22 Newbury St. (phone: 267-3200), and at 210 Newbury St. (phone: 262-7300).

Hermès This boutique specializes in elegant and expensive French apparel and accessories for Boston's Brahmins. 22 Arlington St., at *Heritage on the Garden* (phone: 482-8707).

HMV There is a vast selection of CDs here, with an unbeatable World Music section. For other types of music, however, it may be worth going elsewhere, as prices tend to be on the high side. 1 Brattle Sq., Cambridge (phone: 868-9696).

Joan & David The well-known shoe designers have a boutique stocked with their beautiful, unique shoes and a small line of their clothing. *Copley Place* (phone: 536-0600).

Jordan Marsh New England's largest department store, this 19th-century landmark carries clothing, including most of the top designer labels, accessories, and housewares. There's a bargain basement, but it is not as highly esteemed as *Filene's Basement* across the street. 450 Washington St. (phone: 357-3000).

Joseph Abboud Native Bostonian Abboud went to New York, went national with his line of classic, earthy menswear, and returned to build this lovely, three-story boutique. 37 Newbury St. (phone: 266-4200).

Kakas Furriers An elegant fur and leather store near the *Public Garden* where older fashionable Bostonians like to shop. 93 Newbury St. (phone: 536-1858).

Louis, Boston Trendy, elegant menswear designed to make a statement. Also in the graceful old building is a floor of women's clothing, *Café Louis,* a continental bistro, and the *Mario Russo* hair salon . 234 Berkeley St., Back Bay (phone: 262-6100).

Marika's Antiques Loaded with tapestries, paintings, vases, and furniture from the US, Europe, and the Orient, this shop specializes in jewelry. 130 Charles St. (phone: 523-4520).

Newbury Comics All kinds of comic books, from classic to counterculture. 332 Newbury St. (phone: 236-4930) and seven other locations.

Nostalgia Factory A huge collection of original vintage ads, collectible prints, posters, and postcards is for sale here; there are also monthly exhibitions of such specialities as elections memorabilia and sheet music. 336 Newbury St. (phone: 236-8754).

Oilily Rainbows look dull next to the brightly colored children's clothing in this Dutch company's Boston store. 31 Newbury St. (phone: 247-9299).

Out of Town News A periodical lover's dream, staffed by folks who know when and where every journal under the sun is published, from a Des Moines Sunday paper to a magazine from Cairo. Harvard Sq. (phone: 354-7777).

Priscilla: The Bride's Shop This exclusive bridal shop has been making gowns for society brides for decades. 137 Newbury St. (phone: 267-9070).

Rosie's Bakery and Dessert Shop A brightly lit storefront bakery in Cambridge's Inman Square, it's known for its prize-winning brownie, an indescribably rich concoction delicately named a "Chocolate Orgasm," and the best poppyseed cake you'll find anywhere. A great place to order cakes for special occasions, too, should you find yourself in Boston with something to celebrate. 243 Hampshire St., Cambridge (phone: 491-9488).

Shreve, Crump & Low One of Boston's oldest and finest jewelry stores, it also stocks crystal, clocks, silver, and a fine collection of American and English antiques from the 18th and 19th centuries. 330 Boylston St. (phone: 267-9100).

Society of Arts and Crafts Talented craftspeople have always gravitated to New England, and for the past 95 years, the *Society* has been carrying their works of furniture, jewelry, housewares, and clothing. 175 Newbury St. (phone: 266-1810) and 101 Arch St. (phone: 345-0033).

Strutters Fans of vintage clothing and accessories should check out the high-quality goods here. 257 Newbury St. (phone: 247-7744).

Tiffany & Co. The prestigious house for jewelry and more. *Copley Place* (phone: 353-0222).

Toscanini's Rumor has it that Bostonians eat more ice cream per capita than the residents of any other city, and this is one of their favorite places to get it—in a blizzard or in balmy weather, it's packed. The ice cream is made on the premises and features exotic foreign flavors such as Italian *nocciola* (hazelnut) and *gianduia* (chocolate cream), and Indian cardamom-pistachio, mango, and saffron. 899 Main St., Central Sq., Cambridge (phone: 491-5877), and also in the *MIT Student Center,* on Mass. Ave. (phone: 494-1640).

Tower Records CDs, tapes, and LPs are housed in this dazzling three-story space at 360 Newbury St., on the corner of Massachusetts Ave. (phone: 247-5900). A second *Tower* store is near *Harvard* at 95 Mt. Auburn St. (phone: 876-3377).

Victorian Bouquet Ltd. More than just another flower shop, it has spectacular flower arrangements and a cordial, thoughtful staff. 53A Charles St. (phone: 367-6648).

Vose Galleries The specialty here is 18th-, 19th-, and early 20th-century American paintings. 238 Newbury St. (phone: 536-6176).

Waterstone's Booksellers Housed in an ornate old theater building, with about 150,000 titles, this is one of the largest bookstores in the city. 26 Exeter St. (phone: 859-7300). There's another branch in *Faneuil Hall Marketplace* (phone: 589-0930).

Women's Educational and Industrial Union Since 1877, the *WEIU* has been providing training and support for working women. Despite its age, the gift shop has a modern collection of housewares, children's clothes and toys, and knickknacks. There is an extensive needlework and crafts section, too. 356 Boylston St. (phone: 536-5651).

Wordsworth Bookstore A bookworm and gift-giver's paradise packed with every hard- and softcover book you can imagine, all discounted 10% to 30%. 30 Brattle St., Cambridge, near Harvard Sq. (phone: 354-5201).

SPORTS AND FITNESS

No doubt about it, Boston is one of the all-time great professional sports towns.

BASEBALL The *Red Sox* play at *Fenway Park* (4 Yawkey Way; phone: 267-1700). *Green Line,* Kenmore stop.

BASKETBALL The *Celtics* play their home games at the *Fleet Center* (150 Causeway St.; phone: 624-1000). *Green* or *Orange Line, North Station* stop.

BICYCLING A good place to rent a mountain or touring bicycle is the *Community Bike Shop* (490 Tremont St.; phone: 542-8623), which offers 12-speed Nishiki and Jakara bikes. (You'll need identification.) Bicycle tours in and beyond the city are conducted in season by *American Youth Hostels* (Activities Hotline phone: 730-8294) and the *Appalachian Mountain Club* (phone: 523-0636), among others.

BILLIARDS Some know it or its variations as pool or even snooker. Whatever the nomenclature, it is making a glorious comeback in Boston. The city's best-known place for billiards is *Jillian's Billiard Club* (145 Ipswich St.; phone: 437-0300), a staid pool hall near *Fenway Park* that is furnished like an English gentleman's library. Some think the *Boston Billiard Club* (126 Brookline Ave.; phone: 536-7665) is even classier. Both offer cocktail service, snacks, billiards, pool, snooker, darts, and backgammon.

FISHING *Boston Harbor Clambakes and Barbecues* (619 E. Broadway, South Boston; phone: 268-2244) offers fishing charters, clambakes, and evening cruises; *Yankee Fishing Fleet* (75 Essex Ave., Gloucester; phone: 508-283-0313 or 800-942-5464) runs charters from April through November; *Boston By Sail* (Long Wharf; phone: 742-3313) organizes deep-sea fishing excursions in season; and *Captain's Fishing Parties and Boat Livery* (Plum Island Pier, Newburyport; phone: 508-465-7733) features half- and full-day charters.

FITNESS CENTERS Try *Fitcorp Fitness and Physical Therapy Center* (133 Federal St.; phone: 542-1010 and at the *Prudential Center;* phone: 262-2052) which have a track and workout equipment; *Wellbridge Center* (1079 Commonwealth Ave., Brighton; phone: 254-1711; and 695 Atlantic Ave., Boston; phone: 439-9600), which has workout equipment, a pool, and a steamroom and sauna; or *Le Pli at the Charles* (5 Bennett St., Charles Sq., Cambridge; phone: 547-4081 and *Le Pli at Heritage on the Garden,* Boylston St,; phone: 426-6999), which have workout equipment, a sauna, a pool, and steamrooms. Many Boston hotels have fitness centers for guests. The *Boston Athletic Club* (653 Summer St.; phone: 269-4300) offers daily memberships to those with a local hotel room key. The *Greater Boston YMCA* (316 Huntington Ave.; phone: 536-7800) operates nine locations around the city; different branches have different equipment. All are open to non-members for a fee.

FOOTBALL Football (*New England Patriots*) and some soccer matches are played at *Foxboro Stadium* (Rte. 1, Foxboro; phone: 508-543-0350).

GOLF There's a city course in *Hyde Park,* where the *Parks and Recreation Department* offers golf instruction. Contact *George Wright Pro Shop* (420 West St., *Hyde Park;* phone: 361-8313); you also can play or take lessons at the *Fresh Pond Golf Club* (691 Huron Ave., Cambridge; phone: 349-6282).

HOCKEY The *Bruins* hockey team faces off at the *Fleet Center* (150 Causeway St.; phone: 624-1000 or 624-1050 for tickets), which replaced the *Boston Garden. Green* or *Orange Line, North Station* stop.

JOGGING Run along the banks of the Charles River on Memorial Drive (in Cambridge) or along Storrow Drive (in Boston). Many bridges over the river make loops of varying lengths possible.

RACING Greyhounds race at *Wonderland Park,* Revere (on the *Blue Line;* phone: 284-1300).

SAILING Befitting its history as a port city, Boston offers several options for visitors interested in skippering their own skiffs on the Charles or serving as crew members on larger vessels in the harbor and beyond.

Those who want to go it alone can rent boats at the *Boston Sailing Center* (54 Lewis Wharf; phone: 227-4198), *Boston by Sail* (66 Long Wharf; phone: 742-3313), and *Community Boating Inc.* (21 Embankment Rd.; phone: 523-1038).

SKIING There's cross-country skiing at *Weston Ski Track* on *Leo J. Martin Golf Course* (Park Rd., Weston; phone: 891-6575). *Lincoln Guide Service* (152 Lincoln Rd., Lincoln; phone: 259-9204) and *Pro-Motion* (111 South St., Bedford; phone: 275-1113) offer lessons daily. Within a two-hour drive of the city are a number of small downhill skiing areas: *Blue Hills Ski Area* in Canton (phone: 828-5070); *Boston Hill* in North Andover (phone: 508-683-2734); *Wachusett Mountain Ski Area* in Princeton (phone: 508-464-2300 and 800-754-1234); and *Nashoba Valley Ski Area* in Westford (phone: 508-692-3033).

TENNIS There are courts at the *Charles River Park Tennis Club* (35 Lomasney Way; phone: 742-8922). The *Metropolitan District Commission (MDC)* also operates a number of well-maintained tennis courts throughout the city. All are available on a first-come, first-served basis except the *Charlesbank Courts,* which include two unlit courts on the bank of the Charles River and two lighted courts on the southwestern section of *Boston Common.* These require a permit, which may be picked up a few days in advance; for more information, contact *MDC Lee Memorial Pool* (20 Somerset St.; phone: 523-9746). *Hyde Park,* another cluster of *MDC* courts, has six tennis courts, four of which are lighted. Unlit courts are open until dusk, lighted courts until 11 PM. For further details, contact the *MDC* (phone: 727-8865).

Only members and their guests may play at the *Longwood Cricket Club,* but, as the home of the *US Pro Tennis Championships at Longwood,* this is Boston's primary site of competitive tennis. The championship, which takes place for approximately nine days in the latter half of July, draws some of the top names in tennis. Information: *Longwood Cricket Club,* 564 Hammond St., Brookline, MA 02167 (phone: 731-2900; 731-4500 for tickets to the *US Pro* matches).

THEATER

Catch a Broadway show before it gets to Broadway. Trial runs often take place at the *Shubert Theater* (265 Tremont St.; phone: 426-4520), the *Colonial Theatre* (106 Boylston St.; phone: 426-9366), the *Wilbur Theater* (246 Tremont St.; phone: 423-4008), and the *Wang Center for the Performing Arts* (270 Tremont St.; phone: 482-9393). Or check out the *Charles Playhouse* (74 Warrenton St.; phone: 426-5225), a much smaller and often livelier place that hosts interesting contemporary plays. Currently in an open-ended run here is the long-running hit play *Shear Madness,* a participatory thriller in which the audience is invited to guess whodunit. The *New Theater* (140 Clarendon St.; phone: 247-7388) features new works with provocative themes. The *Lyric Stage* (140 Clarendon St.; phone: 437-7172) performs first-time, experimental works—often satiric and political—with aplomb. The *American Repertory Theater* (64 Brattle St., Cambridge; phone: 547-8300), one of the East Coast's premier repertory companies, is based at *Harvard*'s *Loeb Drama Center* and performs both classic and new plays during the school year. In addition, there are dozens of smaller theater groups, including several affiliated with colleges, such as the *Huntington Theatre Company* (264 Huntington Ave., Back Bay; phone: 266-7900) of *Boston University.* The *Boston Ballet Company* gives performances at the *Wang Center* (see above; call 695-6950 for ballet information). Tickets for theatrical and musical events can be purchased through the *Out of Town Ticket Agency* (on the mezzanine level of the *Red Line*'s *Harvard Square Station;* phone: 492-1900); *TicketMaster* (phone: 244-8400 for *TicketMaster* locations; 931-2000 to order tickets by phone); or, on the day of the play at reduced prices from *Bostix* at *Faneuil Hall Marketplace* and at *Copley Square*

(Boylston and Dartmouth Sts.; phone: 723-5181 for both locations). For information on performance schedules, check the local publications listed above.

MUSIC

Almost every evening, Bostonians can choose from among several classical and contemporary musical performances, ranging from the most delicate chamber music to the most ferocious alternative rock. The *Boston Symphony Orchestra,* usually under the baton of director Seiji Ozawa, performs at *Symphony Hall* (301 Massachusetts Ave.; phone: 266-1492) September through April; in summer, it's at the *Tanglewood Music Festival* in Lenox, Massachusetts. Selected members of the *Boston Symphony* make up the *Boston Pops Orchestra,* which performs less weighty orchestrations of popular music. In addition to performing at *Symphony Hall* (see above) from April through July, the *Boston Pops* gives free outdoor concerts in the *Hatch Shell* on the *Charles River Esplanade* in June and July. Both the *Handel & Haydn Society* (300 Massachusetts Ave.; phone: 266-3605) and *Boston Baroque* in Cambridge (phone: 641-1310) perform historically correct music on period instruments. The *Boston Lyric Opera* performs a full season of classical operas at the *Emerson Majestic Theater* (219 Tremont St.; phone: 248-8660). Several colleges and universities also offer classical concerts: *Harvard*'s *Sanders Theater* (Kirkland and Quincy Sts., Cambridge; phone: 495-5595); *MIT*'s *Kresge Auditorium,* in a peculiar building on the West Campus that has a curved roof resting on only three points (77 Massachusetts Ave., Cambridge; phone: 253-2826); and the *Boston University Concert Hall* (855 Commonwealth Ave.; phone: 353-3345).

Soothing piano music can be found in the *Plaza* bar of the *Copley Plaza* hotel and energetic sing-alongs at *Diamond Jim's Piano Bar* at the *Lenox* hotel (see *Checking In* for both hotels). The premier jazz club in the area is the super-elegant *Regattabar* in Cambridge's *Charles* hotel (see *Checking In*), which showcases both local and national talent. Top-name blues and pop musicians play here, too. For more jazz, try the bustling, intimate *Ryles* (Inman Sq., Cambridge; phone: 876-9330) or the mixed bag, from avant-garde to beebop, at *Scullers Jazz Lounge* in *Doubletree Guest Suites* (see *Checking In*), which showcases both national and local talent.

The *Rathskeller,* a.k.a. "The Rat" (528 Commonwealth Ave.; phone: 536-2750), is a head-banging Boston institution (many would contend its patrons belong in institutions) that relishes its role as the scourge of Kenmore Square. Here you'll find an endless stream of such bands as *The Queers* or *Slaughter Shack,* as well as nearby *Boston University*'s "existential" crowd. For some of the finest Irish music this side of Dublin, go to the *Purple Shamrock* (1 Union St.; phone: 227-2060); the *Black Rose* (160 State St.; phone: 742-2286); or the *Green Briar* (304 Washington St., Brighton; phone: 789-4100) on Monday nights. The *Tam O' Shanter* (1648 Beacon St., Brookline; phone: 277-0982) is an excellent venue for folk, blues, and the occasional jazz performance, as is the *Plough and Stars* (912 Massachusetts Ave., Cambridge; phone: 492-9653), where they pack them in cheek-to-jowl and serve some of the finest ales in the city. Also try the *House of Blues* (96 Winthrop St., Cambridge ; phone: 491-2583). For folk music in a coffeehouse atmosphere, visit *Passim* (47 Palmer St., Cambridge; phone: 492-7679); for bluegrass, drop in at *Harpers Ferry* (156 Brighton Ave.; phone: 254-9743). The *Western Front* (343 Western Ave., Cambridge; phone: 492-7772) is Boston's focal point for reggae music. Once you step in the door, you'll think you're in Kingston, Jamaica.

NIGHTCLUBS AND NIGHTLIFE

A sophisticated and well-heeled crowd gathers nightly in the elegant *Plaza* bar at the *Copley Plaza* hotel (see *Checking In*) or at the *Palm Court* at *Cricket's* (101 *Faneuil Hall Marketplace;* phone: 720-5570). If dancing disco is your passion, try the sumptuous *Roxy* (279 Tremont St.; phone: 338-7699). *The Last Hurrah,* downstairs at the *Omni Parker House* (see *Checking In*), also has live jazz bands on weekends, with no cover charge. Thursday through Saturday nights, there's dancing to pop music at *Club Nicole,* a spot in the *Back Bay Hilton* (40 Dalton St.; phone: 236-1100) reminiscent of the old *Stork Club* in New York. Among the trendiest clubs are *Avalon* (15 Lansdowne St.; phone: 262-2424); *Alley Cat* (1 Boylston Pl.; phone: 351-2510); *Karma* (7 Lansdowne St.; phone: 421-9595); *Zanzibar* (1 Boylston Pl., off Boylston St.; phone: 351-2560); and the *Scullers Lounge* in the *Doubletree Guest Suites* hotel (see *Checking In*). A rather disheartening sight is the *Bull & Finch* pub (84 Beacon St.; phone: 227-9605) of television's "Cheers" fame, which still draws crowds of tourists despite an expansion from the basement to the first floor and a general lack of atmosphere. Only the façade of this tourist trap was used for the show; the interior is filled with kitsch.

COMEDY CLUBS Sometimes it seems that nearly everybody in Boston is a comedian—or wants to be. Those who have decided to turn professional can be found at one of the area's many comedy clubs. Big-name comics can be found at *Nick's Comedy Stop* (100 Warrenton St.; phone: 482-0930). Another popular laugh is *Comedy Connection* (*Faneuil Hall Marketplace;* phone: 617-248-9700).

Best in Town

CHECKING IN

Boston has some gracious old hotels with the history and charm you'd expect to find in this dignified New England capital. But Boston experienced a hotel building boom in the 1980s, and there are now many modern places as well, offering standard contemporary accoutrements. Expect to pay $150 or more for a double room (including private bath, air conditioning, TV set, and phone, unless otherwise indicated) at those places noted as expensive; between $100 and $150 for those in the moderate category; and under $100 in places listed as inexpensive. Many of the more pricey properties offer special weekend packages at up to 50% discounts. Reservations always are required, so write or call well in advance. Most of Boston's major hotels have complete facilities for the business traveler. Those hotels listed below as having "business services" usually offer such conveniences as meeting rooms, photocopiers, computers, translation services, and express checkout, among others. Call the hotel for additional information.

For bed and breakfast accommodations in the Boston area, write to the *Massachusetts Office of Travel and Tourism* (100 Cambridge St., 13th Floor, Boston, MA 02202; phone: 727-3201) for its *Spirit of Massachusetts Bed & Breakfast Guide* or contact *Bed & Breakfast Associates of Bay Colony* (PO Box 57166, *Babson Park,* Boston, MA 02157; phone: 449-5302; 800-347-5088; fax: 449-5958); *Greater Boston Hospitality* (PO Box 1142, Brookline, MA 02146; phone: 277-5430); *Bed and Breakfast Cambridge & Greater Boston* (PO Box 1344, Cambridge, MA 02138; phone: 576-1492; 800-888-0178l; fax: 576-1430); *Host Homes of Boston* (PO Box 117, Waban, MA 02168 phone: 244-1308; fax: 244-5156); *New England Bed and Breakfast, Inc.* (P.O. Box 9100, Suite 176, Newton, MA 02159; phone: 244-2112); or *Bed & Breakfast Agency of Boston* (47 Commercial Wharf, Boston, MA 02110; phone: 720-3540, 800-248-9262, Fax: 523-5761).

All hotels below are in Boston and telephone and fax numbers are in the 617 area code unless otherwise indicated.

EXPENSIVE

Boston Harbor This distinctive, 16-story property, one of Boston's best hostelries, offers the most dramatic entry to the Hub. From *Logan Airport,* visitors are whisked by water taxi across Boston Harbor to dock within an anchor's throw of the hotel at Rowes Wharf, with its enormous eight-story golden arch that opens onto Atlantic Avenue and downtown Boston. The North End and the *Faneuil Hall Marketplace* are all within walking distance. The property's 230 spacious guestrooms (some with balconies) have views of either the city or the harbor. *Foster's Rotunda,* a copper-domed observatory atop the arch, boasts mesmerizing views. Amenities include a spa, saunas, and a 60-foot indoor pool, as well as 24-hour room service and a concierge. There's also the glass-enclosed *Harborview Lounge,* a casual, outdoor café (in summer), and the elegant *Rowes Wharf* bar and restaurant, specializing in seafood prepared in unusual ways. Business services are also available. 70 Rowes Wharf (phone: 439-7000 or 800-752-7077; fax: 330-9450).

Bostonian Understated and small (152 rooms), this beautifully appointed hotel is across from *Faneuil Hall Marketplace* and just two blocks from the North End and the revitalized waterfront. Its glass-enclosed, rooftop *Seasons* restaurant, which serves fine continental fare, discreetly overlooks the colorful bustle below. Other amenities include 24-hour room service, a concierge, and business services. North and Blackstone Sts. at *Faneuil Hall Marketplace* (phone: 523-3600; 800-343-0922; fax: 523-2454).

Charles This 296-room property just off *Harvard Square* is Cambridge's most distinquished hotel. The interior exudes a warmth from its decor of New England antiques and paintings by local artists. Guestrooms feature quilts, as well as TV in the bathroom, and a bar. Two restaurants serve fine fare including the distinquished *Rialto* for its Mediterranean cuisine. Facilities include full spa services; swimming pool, 24-hour room service, and the popular *Regattabar* jazz club. 1 Bennett St., Cambridge (phone: 864-1200; 800-882-1818; fax 864-5715.

Copley Plaza Recently acquired by Fairmont Hotels, this historic bowfront property is undergoing a $10 million renovation. Although it has 373 splendid guestrooms, its public areas are what make this hotel truly great. Corporate Boston fills the seats of the *Plaza* bar, which has been compared to a British officers' club in India. Adjacent to the bar is the airy tea court, which is painted in the precise Victorian technique of photographic realism, creating the illusion that you're outdoors. There are two restaurants: The elegant *Plaza* (see *Eating Out*) has a French menu, and *Copley's* serves excellent American/New England fare in richly decorated Victorian-style rooms. The multilingual staff is refined and helpful. Other amenities include 24-hour room service, a concierge, and business services. 138 St. James Ave., Copley Sq. (phone: 267-5300; 800-822-4200; fax: 247-6681).

Doubletree Guest Suites A distinctive property on the Charles River, it has 10 conventional guestrooms and 310 luxurious suites. There's a restaurant, and complimentary breakfast is served on weekends. Its *Scullers Jazz Lounge* (see *Nightlife*) is one of the city's premier jazz venues, and there's a health club with a pool, a whirlpool bath, a sauna, and exercise machines. Other amenities include room service until 11 PM, a concierge, and business services. 400 Soldiers Field Rd., at the Cambridge/Allston exit of I-90 (phone: 783-0090; 800-424-2900; fax: 783-0897).

Eliot This all-suite Back Bay establishment was built in 1925 as the nearby *Harvard Club* guest facilities. After a $4.3-million renovation several years ago, the elegant lobby and all the rooms shine in a classic European manner; each of the 93 suites has a marble bath, antique furnishings, French doors between rooms, and a private pantry. Guestrooms away from bustling Commonwealth Avenue are quieter. Dual-line room telephones include modems, and writing desks are larger than usual. Amenities include continental breakfast, mini-bars, and concierge service. Business services are also available. The popular bar of the same name next door is not part of the hotel. 370 Commonwealth Ave. (phone: 267-1607; 800-44-ELIOT; fax: 536-9114).

Four Seasons Service is this hotel's strong suit—which is not to say that the place is lacking in ambience. On the contrary: The 288 guestrooms, each with a bar and two to three phones, resemble a gracious Beacon Hill residence, with cherry furniture, floral prints, and marble vanities. This is one of only two Boston hotels that overlook the *Public Garden;* half the guestrooms enjoy leafy (or snow-swept) garden views. The hotel's formal restaurant, *Aujourd'hui* (see *Eating Out*), features an American-continental menu. The more informal *Bristol Lounge* offers live entertainment most nights and a Viennese dessert buffet Friday and Saturday nights. The location is convenient as well as attractive: Most of the city's popular sites are within walking distance. The full-service health club includes a pool, sauna, and whirlpool baths. Children get their own bathrobes, board games, Nintendo, milk and cookies, and food for the *Public Garden* ducks. Other amenities include 24-hour room service, a concierge, and business services. 200 Boylston St. (phone: 338-4400; 800-332-3442; fax: 423-0154).

Hyatt Regency, Cambridge Surrounding the atrium and glass-walled elevators are 469 rooms. The revolving rooftop restaurant offers a spectacular view of Boston, especially at sunset. The health club includes an indoor pool, a sauna, a whirlpool bath, and a steamroom. Other amenities include 24-hour room service, a concierge, and business services. On the Charles River, near *MIT* and *Harvard* (not easily accessible by public transportation). 575 Memorial Dr., Cambridge (phone: 492-1234; 800-233-1234; fax: 491-6906).

Lenox Built in 1900 and modeled after New York City's *Waldorf-Astoria,* this property has 214 guestrooms with high ceilings and rocking chairs (the corner rooms have fireplaces). Each is decorated in either French provincial or colonial style. The lobby is handsomely decorated in blue with gold trim and a fireplace—always blazing in the winter—that evokes the feel of a country inn. There also are two restaurants—the casual *Samuel Adams Brew House* and the more formal *Upstairs Grill.* Other amenities include room service until midnight, a concierge, and business services. 710 Boylston St. (phone: 536-5300; 800-225-7676; fax: 266-7905).

Marriott, Long Wharf A striking five-story atrium is the centerpiece of this big downtown property (400 rooms) at the foot of State Street. The *Harbor Terrace Sea Grille* requires a jacket and tie; the more casual *Rachel's Lounge* provides taped contemporary music for dancing nightly. A ballroom, indoor-outdoor pool, and health club offer diversions. Other amenities include room service until midnight, a concierge, and business services. 296 State St. (phone: 227-0800; 800-228-9290; fax: 227-2867).

Le Meridien The stylish French-owned hotel chain has created a small and delightful Gallic world in this splendid 1922 Renaissance Revival structure in downtown's Post Office Square. The 326 guestrooms, each with a small sitting area with a writing desk, are decorated in 150 different styles, from fin de siècle to modern. The elegant *Julien* restaurant offers a classical Gallic-inspired menu (see *Eating Out*)—the creation of consulting chef Marc Haeberlin of the three-Michelin-star *L'Auberge de L'Ill* in Alsace. Also on the premises is *Café Fleuri,* a French bistro housed in a leafy six-story atrium. The hotel hosts a delectable all-you-can-eat buffet of chocolate desserts on Saturday afternoons; Sunday brunch is wonderful here as well. *La Terrasse,* an informal outdoor café, serves breakfast, lunch, and cocktails. There's also a health club, an indoor pool, lobby shops, 24-hour room service, and a concierge. Business services are also available. 250 Franklin St., Post Office Sq. (phone: 451-1900; 800-543-4300; fax: 423-2844).

Omni Parker House When it opened in 1855, the elegant *Parker House* became a Boston institution almost immediately; it was here that Charles Dickens would dwell during his heavily publicized Boston visits. The 535 rooms are richly decorated with dark wood and tapestries, and the building, located on the historic *Freedom Trail,* is within walking distance of the *King's Chapel,* the *Park Street Church,* Beacon Hill, *Boston Common,* and the *Faneuil Hall Marketplace.* Boston cream pie and Parker House rolls were born at *Parker's,* the hotel's main restaurant (which still features both on its contemporary continental menu). The restaurant was once the meeting place of the *Saturday Club,* a 19th-century literary association whose members included such luminaries as Longfellow, Emerson, and Oliver Wendell Holmes. Other amenities include room service until midnight, a concierge, and business services. 60 School St. (phone: 227-8600; 800-THE-OMNI; fax: 742-5729).

Park Plaza and Towers Just south of the *Public Garden,* between Back Bay and the theater district, this venerable establishment has 960 rooms; 80 are located in the *Towers,* offering more luxurious quarters, a concierge, and continental breakfast. Guests enjoy fine dining at *Legal Sea Foods* (see *Eating Out*), and *Café Rouge,* with respectable American dishes. Other amenities include 24-hour room service, a health club, shops, and business services. 64 Arlington St. (phone: 426-2000; 800-966-7926; fax: 654-1999).

Ritz-Carlton This grande dame of Boston hotels has reigned since 1927. Strategically located near most of Newbury and Boylston Streets' smart shops, it overlooks the *Public Garden,* with the windows on the north side of the building offering views of the magnolia-lined *Commonwealth Avenue Mall.* All 278 guestrooms are traditionally furnished and decorated with 17th- to 19th-century paintings. The rooms in the hotel's older section are the fanciest. Afternoon tea in the upstairs lounge is a Boston institution. The large and lovely *Ritz* dining room serves excellent continental fare (see *Eating Out*), and the serene *Ritz* bar makes the best martini in town; both look out over the garden. Legions of staff members do their best to serve you. Other amenities include 24-hour room service, a concierge, and business services. 15 Arlington St. (phone: 536-5700; 800-241-3333; fax: 536-1335).

Royal Sonesta This flagship of the Sonesta chain boasts 400 tastefully decorated rooms and five elegant suites, along with an outpost of *Davio's* (see *Eating Out*), one of the area's best northern Italian restaurants. There's also a fully outfitted health club with a pool. Business services are available. 5 Cambridge Pkwy. (near Kendall Sq.), Cambridge (phone: 491-3600; 800-SONESTA; fax: 661-5956).

Westin, Copley Place This opulent 36-story, 804-room property is one of two hotels in *Copley Place,* located at one corner of Copley Square. Its *Turner Fisheries* restaurant serves award-winning clam chowder in a town renowned for its chowder. There's also a fully outfitted health club with a pool, saunas, and masseuse. Other amenities include 24-hour room service, a concierge, and business services. 10 Huntington Ave. (phone: 262-9600; 800-228-3000; fax: 424-7483).

MODERATE

Inn at Harvard With 113 rooms and a central atrium, this modern building is noted for a homey, collegiate feel. Each room is decorated with replicas of art from Harvard's museums. Although it was built by the university to host its many visitors, the inn is also open to the public. Updated New England–style food is served in the atrium for breakfast and dinner. Business services also are available. 1201 Massachusetts Ave., Cambridge (phone: 491-2222; fax: 491-6520).

Newbury Guest House A brick and brownstone townhouse that has been converted into an urban bed and breakfast establishment. Its location—in the heart of Back Bay, on a street of boutiques, cafés, and galleries—is perfect for city-philes who prefer country living. The 32 rooms in three adjoining townhouses are decorated in a simple, 19th-century style. A continental breakfast is served in the parlor and on the streetside patio in the summertime. 261 Newbury St. (phone: 437-7666, 800-437-7668; fax: 262-4243).

INEXPENSIVE

Chandler Inn Modest and comfortable, and conveniently located between Copley and Park Squares, near *Copley Place,* it has 56 rooms and provides a complimentary continental breakfast in the lobby. 26 Chandler St. at Berkeley St. (phone: 482-3450; 800-842-3450; fax: 542-3428).

Howard Johnson's Fenway A perfect location for *Fenway Park,* and not far from the *Museum of Fine Arts and* the *Isabella Stewart Gardner Museum.* The 94-room property has a restaurant, lounge, outdoor pool, valet service, bellhops, and a multilingual staff. 1271 Boylston St. (phone: 267-8300; fax: 267-2763).

Midtown In Back Bay, across the street from the *Christian Science World Headquarters* and near the *Prudential Center,* this low-rise property, flanked by ritzier lodgings on either side, is a darling of tour groups. All 159 rooms feature cable TV. 220 Huntington Ave. (phone: 262-1000; 800-343-1177; fax: 262-8739).

EATING OUT

Boston doesn't have a reputation as a culinary capital, but the 1980s brought a wealth of sophisticated restaurants—both expensive and moderately priced—opened by talented young chefs, many of whom actively sought to develop a more innovative New England–style cuisine. Bostonians' appetites and culinary standards rose to the occasion, and the city now supports a vital restaurant community. Visitors have their pick of many wonderful dining spots. Expect to pay $100 or more for two at one of the places we've noted as expensive; between $50 and $100 at those rated moderate; and $50 or under at those listed as inexpensive. Prices do not include drinks, wine, or tips. All telephone numbers are in the 617 area code unless otherwise indicated.

Unless otherwise noted, restaurants are open for lunch and dinner.

EXPENSIVE

Anago Bistro An understated, tranquil space enlivened by bouquets of fresh flowers, it serves some of the city's best continental fare from a menu that changes constantly. Specialties include crab and scallop casserole, braised venison, maple barbecued chicken, and wild mushroom stew. Dinner only. Closed Sundays and Mondays. Reservations advised. Major credit cards accepted. 798 Main St., Kendall Sq., Cambridge (phone: 492-9500).

Armani Express This upscale dining emporium offers dishes as finely tailored as the suits in the adjacent *Armani* boutique: Try chef Roberto Saracino's *pansoti* (triangular ravioli) *al funghi porcini* sautéed in a butter and sage sauce, or any of the consistently wonderful seasoned rice dishes such as the *risotto al pescatore,* with seafood and a light tomato broth. There is a trattoria downstairs, with a busy oak bar, and the refined, Italianate upstairs dining room was designed by Armani himself. Major credit cards accepted. Reservations advised. 214 Newbury St. (phone: 437-0909).

Aujourd'hui The lovely, second-story centerpiece of the *Four Seasons,* this hotel dining room has few peers for ambience, food, or wine. The American-cum-continental menu, which changes seasonally, features appetizing "alternative cuisine" specials, the creation of chef David Fritclay, that are both good and good for you. Excellent service. Open daily for all three meals. Reservations advised. Major credit cards accepted. 200 Boylston St. (phone: 338-4400).

Bay Tower Room Featuring a breathtaking view of Boston Harbor from 33 stories up, this restfully elegant dining room is the perfect setting for special-occasion suppers and banquets. The American and continental specialties change seasonally. Piano music is featured during early evening hours, with a live combo taking over later on Fridays and Saturdays. Open Mondays through Saturdays for dinner only; open on Sundays for private functions. Reservations necessary. Major credit cards accepted. 60 State St. (phone: 723-1666).

Biba Facing the *Public Garden,* this dramatic two-level restaurant and bar is the creation of Lydia Shire, one of Boston's most admired and interesting chefs. The inventive, six-part menu affords amazing choices for varying appetites and changing seasons. The sweetbreads are heavenly, and the wine list is remarkable in both range and price. Open daily, 11:30 AM to 9:30 or 10:30 PM (no lunch on Saturdays; snack menu available at bar). Reservations necessary. Major credit cards accepted. 272 Boylston St. (phone: 426-7878).

Le Bocage Some of the most consistently delectable French food available in New England is served in this elegant establishment, located in a suburb west of Boston. Both Gallic regional and classic entrées grace the menu, which changes to suit the season. A bright, efficient staff and a fine wine cellar add to the pleasurable dining. Open daily for dinner only. Reservations advised. Major credit cards accepted. 72 Bigelow Ave., Watertown (phone: 923-1210).

Café Budapest Decorated in the lavish Eastern European tradition, it is renowned for fine continental and Hungarian cooking. This is a wonderful place to linger over superb strudel and some of the best coffee anywhere. Reservations advised. Major credit cards accepted. 90 Exeter St. (phone: 266-1979).

Davide Though on the edge of the North End, it's far from the typical neighborhood red-checked tablecloth and red sauce place. Specialties include rack of lamb *valdostana,* a lightly breaded veal chop stuffed with prosciutto and fontina cheese, and pasta, which is hand-rolled by Davide himself. Closed at lunchtime on weekends. Reservations advised. Major credit cards accepted. 326 Commercial Ave. (phone: 227-5745).

Davio's This northern Italian eatery offers regional and continental entrées that are consistently well prepared, highlighted by veal chops, homemade pasta, and "upscale" pizza combinations. Good wines, good service, elegant surroundings. Outdoor seating in season. Reservations advised. Major credit cards accepted. 269 Newbury St. (phone: 262-4810). Also in the *Royal Sonesta,* 5 Cambridge Pkwy., Cambridge (phone: 661-4810).

L'Espalier When money is no object, Bostonians visit this contemporary French restaurant. Among devotees' favorites are the salad of Maine lobster with corn fritters, tempura soft-shelled crab, grilled Atlantic salmon, morels and minted peas, and maple cheesecake. The fixed price menu offers many choices for a three-course meal. Chef Frank McClelland now features simpler dishes and larger portions, but he has not tampered with the impressive 150-item wine list. This eatery resides in a beautiful Back Bay townhouse with three elegant, intimate dining rooms. Open for dinner only; closed Sundays. Reservations advised. Major credit cards accepted. 30 Gloucester St. (phone: 262-3023).

Hamersley's Bistro Ambitious in cuisine, modest in decor, this restaurant is one of the most appealing in the city. In the open kitchen, chef Gordon Hamersley turns out favorites inspired by French country cooking—golden roast chicken, sirloin with mashed potatoes, bouillabaisse, cassoulet—as well as more adventurous dishes such as roasted salmon with oysters, bacon, and hollandaise sauce. Open daily for dinner only. Reservations advised. Major credit cards accepted. 553 Tremont St. (phone: 423-2700).

Hampshire House Thoroughly evocative of 19th-century Boston is this former mansion turned tavern, restaurant—and tourist trap. The *Oak Room Lounge* is a paneled, clubby café-bar with moose heads on the wall and a fire blazing in the winter. It offers a simple American menu and a range of lighter fare. In the cozy and elegant *Library Grill* dining room overlooking the *Public Garden,* more eclectic American and continental offerings are served. The *Bull & Finch* pub was the inspiration for (but not the actual setting of) the television series "Cheers" (see *Nightclubs and Nightlife*). Reservations necessary. Major credit cards accepted. 84 Beacon St. (phone: 227-9600).

Julien The grandeur of the decor, with its high ceilings, gilded walls, and graceful Queen Anne chairs, creates a wonderful dining atmosphere. Situated in the old Members Court of the former *Federal Reserve Bank Building* (now the *Meridien* hotel), this dining spot produces light Alsatian cuisine such as homemade terrine of foie gras and ragout of sea scallops and sea urchins. Closed Saturday luncheon and Sundays. Reservations advised. Major credit cards accepted. 250 Franklin St. (phone: 451-1900).

Locke-Ober Café A splendid, albeit somewhat stuffy tradition in one of Boston's classic dining places. Though it was once an exclusive male bastion, today both sexes can eat in the handsome *Men's Grill,* with its glowing mahogany bar lined with massive silver tureens, its stained glass, snowy linen, and indefatigable gray-haired waiters. The food is identical in the less distinguished upstairs room—heavy on continental/American dishes and seafood; try the lobster bisque or the chicken Richmond under glass. Open daily; dinner only weekends. Reservations advised. Major credit cards accepted. 3 Winter Pl. (phone: 542-1340).

Maison Robert Among the finest French restaurants in the city, with first-rate food, drink, ambience, and service. Owner-chef Lucien Robert, one of the founding fathers of Boston's culinary revolution, has taught many of the city's chefs and continues to prepare unusual sauces for his fish, fowl, and meat dishes. Two dining areas, *Ben's Café* downstairs (on the patio in summer) and the elegant *Bonhomme Richard* upstairs, are open for lunch and dinner. Closed Sundays. Reservations necessary. Major credit cards accepted. 45 School St., in the *Old City Hall* (phone: 227-3370).

Plaza The space and decor are the height of Victorian splendor, the menu is classic American cuisine featuring beef, lamb, and chicken, and the service is exquisitely correct. A great place to go when you want to impress someone. Open for dinner Tuesdays through Saturdays. Reservations advised. Major credit cards accepted. *Copley Plaza Hotel,* 138 St. James St. (phone: 267-5300).

Ritz-Carlton Large, lovely, and serenely elegant in its old-fashioned formality, this second floor main restaurant overlooks Boston's *Public Garden*. The cuisine is continental, very good, and served by an expert staff. Men must wear jackets and ties at dinner. Reservations advised. Major credit cards accepted. *Ritz-Carlton Hotel,* 15 Arlington St. (phone: 536-5700).

Upstairs at the Pudding Set in the old upstairs dining room of *Harvard*'s famous *Hasty Pudding Club* (the walls are lined with original, hand-painted show bills from the club's productions of years past), this elegant place is truly Old Ivy, but the food is decidedly contemporary—and first-rate. Subtle northern Italian fare is featured. The veal scaloppine is excellent. Order from the à la carte menu, or choose the prix fixe tasting menu, which allows you to choose one dish from each of the four courses offered. The outdoor terrace, situated in the herb garden, offers a savory dining experience on warm summer nights. *Harvard* singing groups frequently perform at Sunday brunch. Open daily for dinner year-round; open for lunch from mid-April through December. Reservations advised. Major credit cards accepted. 10 Holyoke St., Cambridge (phone: 864-1933).

MODERATE

Blue Diner Among the city's trendy eateries, this place offers delicious diner fare including barbecued meat and Southern-style specialties. The tables in the lounge area are especially interesting—dioramas under glass, they were created by local artists especially for this place, and each one is different. Reservations advised. Major credit cards accepted. 150 Kneeland St. (phone: 695-0087).

The Blue Room Despite the name, the latest inspiration of local restaurateurs Chris Schlesinger and Stan Frankenheimer feels as warm and cozy as a red brick oven, thanks to the open kitchen, glowing grills, and exposed brick walls. The house specialties are grilled and roasted meat and seafood, such as rabbit mole, black-and-blue T-bone steaks, Persian spiced duck, and peanut-crusted tuna steaks. Their *pupu* platter—an assortment of exotic salads, pickles, and noodles—is a real treat. Open for dinner only Mondays through Saturdays; brunch on Sundays. Reservations necessary. Major credit cards accepted. 1 Kendall Sq. (phone: 494-9034).

Broadway Deli The Boston–New York "deli wars" have found a savory, satisfying harmony in this bright, bustling little eatery in the theater district. From corned beef and chopped liver to authentic egg creams and ultra-rich cheesecake, all the required deli delights are available at tables and for takeout. Open for breakfast, lunch, and dinner. No reservations. Major credit cards accepted. 275 Tremont St. (phone: 426-1400).

Café Lampara This is the place to get excellent and unusual pizza and pasta, although the café's popular roasted half chicken is the item many favor. Reservations advised. Major credit cards accepted. 916 Commonwealth Ave. (phone: 566-0300).

Casa Romero Though most people don't link Boston with Mexican food, the city does boast a couple of good Mexican eateries. The food here is authentic–marinated tenderloin of pork, *enchiladas verdes,* garlic soup, and *mole poblano.* The tile tables and wrought iron give this place enough of a Latin American feel to let you forget for a moment that when Bostonians think of south of the border, they're thinking Rhode Island. Open daily; dinner only Saturdays and Sundays. Reservations advised. Major credit cards accepted. 30 Gloucester St. (phone: 536-4341).

Changsho The food served in the relocated home of this Cambridge institution is still the best Chinese cooking you'll find outside New York's Chinatown. The restaurant has moved from its tiny, crowded storefront into a strikingly elegant—and much larger—space a block away. No reservations. Major credit cards accepted. 1712 Massachusetts Ave., Cambridge (phone: 547-6565).

Chart House In the oldest building on Boston's waterfront, its interior is a strikingly handsome arrangement of lofty spaces, natural wood, exposed red brick, and comfortable captain's chairs. The menu consists of abundant portions of steaks and seafood, with all the salad you can eat included in the reasonable prices. The award-winning clam chowder is superb. Dinner only. Reservations advised on weekend nights. Major credit cards accepted. 60 Long Wharf (phone: 227-1576).

Cornucopia on the Wharf Delicious food and views of Boston Harbor and *Christopher Columbus Park* are two excellent reasons to come here. Choose from broiled scrod with roasted garlic mashed potatoes and braised leeks, almonds, and green beans, or tea-smoked chicken with crispy sesame noodles and orange-star anise sauce. The bread pudding is outstanding. Patio seating in season. Open daily for dinner year-round, lunch April through November. Reservations necessary. Major credit cards accepted. 100 Atlantic Ave. (phone: 367-0300).

Dali Garlic braids hanging from the ceiling, white plaster walls daubed with kitschy swirls, and waiters in red jackets and black cummerbunds are not the only things that make this *tapas* bar not far from *Harvard* seem authentic: The kitchen turns out Spanish specialties seldom seen outside Iberia. From the marinated olives served with drinks to the changing list of *tapas* (hors d'oeuvres) and entrées such as *pescado al sal* (whole snapper baked in a salt crust) or *conejo escabechado* (rabbit braised in red wine with juniper berries), dining here is a delicious adventure. There's usually a wait for a table, but if you're not in a hurry, order a pitcher of sangria and have another dish of olives. Open daily for dinner only. No reservations. Major credit cards accepted. 415 Washington St., Somerville (phone: 661-3254).

David's This restaurant's decor reflects its theater district location, as does its pre- and post-theater dinner service. The menu is heavily influenced by the flavors of the Mediterranean, with an imaginative pasta selection and entrées such as lamb kebabs with couscous and minted chutney. In fine weather, there is limited outdoor seating as well. Closed Sundays and Mondays. Reservations advised. Major credit cards accepted. 123 Stuart St. (phone: 367-8405).

Durgin-Park Though famed for generous servings of roast beef, pot roast, prime ribs, fresh fish,oyster stew, Boston baked beans, corn bread, and Indian pudding, this historic place is visited equally for its unique sand-dusted floor atmosphere. Its long, communal tables are crowded with convivial diners attended by sharp-witted waitresses who like to give patrons a rough time (it's partly an act). No reservations. No credit cards. 340 *Faneuil Hall Marketplace* (phone: 227-2038).

Icarus For some reason, this respected restaurant is never crowded, making it a great place for a quiet, intimate meal. The room resembles a Brahmin's drawing room with dark wood, green walls, and oversize sculptures. The contemporary American food is always imaginative and well prepared. The menu, which is predominantly seafood, changes every six weeks. On Sunday nights, the wine café offers *tapa*-size portions and wine by the glass. Open daily for dinner; there is also brunch on Sundays. Reservations advised. Major credit cards accepted. 3 Appleton St. (phone: 426-1790).

Jimmy's Harborside Located about a whale's tail from the Fish Pier, this is an incredibly popular seafood spot with a solid reputation. Every seat in the main dining room has an excellent view of Boston Harbor. The traditional seafood menu has been expanded to include some Italian dishes, veal, and tenderloin. The wine list is replete with fine American wines. Don't mistake *Jimmy's* for *Jimbo's,* a less engaging place across the street. Reservations advised. Most major credit cards accepted. 242 Northern Ave. (phone: 423-1000).

Legal Sea Foods If you don't mind waiting in line, you'll find fresh and well-prepared seafood. No reservations. Major credit cards accepted. Several locations: *Park Plaza Hotel,* corner of Columbus Ave. and Arlington St. (phone: 426-4444); in the *Chestnut Hill Shopping Mall,* 43 Boylston St. (phone: 277-7300); 5 Cambridge Center, Kendall Sq., Cambridge (phone: 864-3400); *Copley Place* (phone: 266-7775), and *Prudential Center* (phone: 266-6800).

Magnolia's A gathering place for those seeking such Cajun staples as blackened fish, jambalaya, sweet potato pie, and other Southern fare. Open for dinner Tuesdays through Saturdays. Reservations advised. Major credit cards accepted. 1193 Cambridge St., Inman Sq., Cambridge (phone: 576-1971).

Mirabelle Beautifully adorned with murals and warms woods, this place is the pride of catering wizard Stephen Elmont. Chefs are adept at many cuisines. Open daily for breakfast, lunch, and dinner. Reservations advised. Major credit cards accepted. 85 Newbury St. (phone: 859-4848).

Olives Superb Tuscany-influenced Italian food is served here in a soothing dove-colored dining room with comfortable banquettes. Try the grilled lobster with white bean *raviolone* and artichoke sauce or the *tortelli* of butternut squash with brown butter and sage. Open for dinner Tuesdays through Saturdays. Reservations for groups of six or more only. MasterCard and Visa accepted. 67 Main St., Charlestown (phone: 242-1999).

Rebecca's In this comfortable, modern place, the walls are decorated with hand-painted flowers and accented by exposed brick and works by local artists. The menu, described as "new American," borrows from French, Greek, Indian, and Italian cuisines. No reservations. Major credit cards accepted. 21 Charles St. (phone: 742-9747).

Rocco's The decor in this theater district dining place is as dramatic as the neighborhood's atmosphere, with stage-scale curtains, murals on the ceiling, and two-story picture windows overlooking the street. The menu offers an eclectic choice of Italian fare. Closed Sunday dinner. Reservations advised. Major credit cards accepted. 5 S. Charles St. (phone: 723-6800).

Skipjack's With a dazzling aquarium-like decor, this mariner's delight features an extensive array of innovative seafood dishes. The wine list is extensive and carefully assembled, and the Sunday jazz brunch is a treat. Reservations advised. Major credit cards accepted. 199 Clarendon St., Copley Sq., Back Bay (phone: 536-3500). Also at 2 Brookline Pl., Brookline (phone: 232-8887).

Sonsie Owner Patrick Lyons has made a splash with his restaurant on this busy shopping thoroughfare by offering a menu as inviting as the atmosphere. The dining room, with spacious booths (total dining room capacity is 90) is graciously accented with Oriental rugs, and bird's-eye maple paneling; the paintings on the walls were commissioned for the restaurant. Some of the menu choices are grilled pork loin, salmon cooked in sake, and pizza with lime guacamole chicken and jack cheese. Open for breakfast, lunch, and dinner. Reservations strongly advised. Major credit cards accepted. 327 Newbury St. (phone: 351-2500).

Toscano Authentic northern Italian food is served in this elegant room with brick walls and red tiles. The menu changes daily, but you'll always find excellent risotto, homemade pasta, and fresh truffles in season. Closed Sunday lunch. Reservations necessary. American Express accepted. 41 Charles St. (phone: 723-4090).

West Street Grill Off the beaten track, between the *Common* and *Lafayette Place,* this trendy meeting place is the historic home of the Peabody family. Here Nathaniel Hawthorne married Sophia, and Elizabeth opened the bookstore that became the meeting place for such literati as Emerson and

Thoreau. Today, it has been renovated to accommodate a striking restaurant (formerly *Cornucopia*) and bar. The menu changes seasonally, but always relies heavily on pasta and grilled dishes. Closed Saturdays for lunch and Sundays. Reservations advised. Major credit cards accepted. 15 West St. (phone: 423-0300).

Ye Olde Union Oyster House It's the real thing: Boston's oldest restaurant. Daniel Webster himself used to guzzle oysters at the wonderful mahogany bar, where skilled shuckers still pry them open before your eyes. Full seafood lunches and dinners are served upstairs, amid well-worn colonial ambience. (One booth is dedicated to John F. Kennedy, once a frequent diner.) Don't miss the seafood chowder. Reservations advised. Major credit cards accepted. 41 Union St. (phone: 227-2750).

INEXPENSIVE

Addis Red Sea Boston's best Ethiopian restaurant (it doesn't have a lot of competition). Patrons sit on tiny, handwoven benches and (the fulfillment of everybody's secret dream) eat only with fingers without social demerit. You just scoop up piles of *watts* (stew) with *injera,* the spongy Ethiopian pancake. Portions are large, the music and ambience are quietly mesmerizing, and the Ethiopian red wine is a delight. Open daily for dinner and for lunch on weekends. Reservations advised. Major credit cards accepted. 544 Tremont St. (phone: 426-8727).

The Barking Crab At the city's only urban clam shack, customers sit at picnic tables under a tent, look out over a none-too-scenic channel of water, and order fresh seafood—fried clams, grilled fish, and boiled lobsters—from a take-out window. Don't miss the homemade clam chowder (New England, natch) and coleslaw. It's rustic, but that doesn't stop legions of suited businesspeople from the nearby financial district from stopping in for a summertime lunch. No reservations. No credit cards accepted. 88 Sleeper St. (phone: 426-2722).

Boca Grande If Tex-Mex is what you crave, this eatery is one of the best food values in Boston. Black bean tostadas, generous handmade tamales, and burritos are the favored fare. Reservations unnecessary. Major credit cards accepted. Two locations: 1728 Massachusetts Ave. (phone: 354-7400) and 149 First St., Cambridge (phone: 354-5550).

La Groceria Northern Italian cooking in an old house with several dining rooms, each with a distinct character (the intimate top floor is recommended). The pasta is homemade, as are the cheesecake and cannoli. The veal dishes and antipasto, hot and cold, are excellent. Extensive wine list. Open daily for dinner. Reservations advised for large parties. Major credit cards accepted. 853 Main St., Cambridge (phone: 547-9258 or 876-4162).

Jae's Café The food is Korean in inspiration and healthy in preparation. You can find *yukhai* (Korean raw beef), pan-fried dumplings stuffed with shrimp, and several light, mild curries. Every dish has lots of fresh vegetables and little oil. There's also a sushi bar downstairs. Reservations advised. Major credit cards accepted. 520 Columbus Ave. (phone: 421-9405).

No-Name Restaurant The name was not a conscious decision. Beginning as a ramshackle joint that counted only the local fishermen as its clientele, this has become a Boston institution serving the freshest seafood in the city (though the folks at *Jimmy's* might dispute this point) to tourists, businesspeople, and the ancient mariners who still frequent the place. With a view of the harbor, this nameless place is also frill-less: Expect Formica tables, paper napkins, and plastic cups. But that's its charm. Though the waitresses are a tad surly, they will fetch some of the finest fried seafood, boiled lobster, and broiled scallops on record. No reservations. No credit cards accepted. 15½ Fish Pier, just off Northern Ave. (phone: 338-7539).

Rubin's Kosher Delicatessen One of only a few kosher restaurants in the Boston area. Its chopped liver, potato *latkes* (pancakes), and lean pastrami (hot or cold) are the genuine articles. Closed Saturdays, and on Fridays after 2 PM. Reservations unnecessary. Major credit cards accepted. 500 Harvard St., Brookline (phone: 566-8761).

S&M New York Deli This large, bright, and bustling delicatessen is filled with the financial district crowd at lunchtime. The food is authentically New York–style, and the sandwiches (try the Reuben) rival the Big Apple's best. There are about 10 stools along a front counter and 20 tables in the back, or take your order out and have a picnic on *Boston Common,* a short walk up Beacon Street. Closed Sundays. No reservations. No credit cards accepted. 12 Beacon St. (phone: 523-8776).

NORTH END RESTAURANTS

This Old World, predominantly Italian district boasts dozens of restaurants crowded into a few square blocks, ranging in quality and price. For cozy, homemade meals, try tiny *Artu*, (6 Prince St., phone: 742-4336; no reservations; no credit cards). For great seafood Italian-style, try the *Daily Catch,* which specializes in calamari (squid) dishes, cooked in an open kitchen (323 Hanover St.; phone: 523-8567; no reservations; no credit cards). Similar in spirit but less well known is *Giacomo's* (355 Hanover St.; phone: 523-9026; no reservations; American Express accepted). Many locals swear by the crunchy, crusty pizza at *Pizzeria Regina* (11½ Thatcher St., phone: 227-0765; no reservations; no credit cards accepted). Don't leave the North End without experiencing *la dolce vita*—that's short for how sweet life seems when you're sitting at a sidewalk café, sipping espresso, savoring a cannoli or gelati, watching the world go by. The best espresso and sweets are at *Caffè Dello Sport* (308 Hanover St.; phone: 523-5063) and the most atmosphere at *Caffè Vittoria* (296 Hanover St.; phone: 227-7606). Neither accepts reservations or credit cards.

Charleston, South Carolina

Standing on a peninsula formed by the Ashley and Cooper Rivers as they flow into the Atlantic, Charleston faces *Fort Sumter* across the harbor, where the first shots of the Civil War were fired. With its architecturally gracious historic buildings and its magnificent gardens, the city retains the flavor and quiet charm of the Old South. In fact, residents used to joke that their city was "the best-preserved secret on the Eastern seaboard."

In the mid-1970s, however, tourism began to increase, and with a quarter-million-dollar revitalization campaign, abandoned warehouses near Market Street were converted into boutiques, art galleries, studios, restaurants, and expensive townhouses. *Market Square* was created and acted as a forerunner for similar projects.

About that time, Gian Carlo Menotti wandered into Charleston. He felt that the residents' obvious pride in their past made the city the perfect site for an American version of his internationally acclaimed *Festival of Two Worlds* in Spoleto, Italy. From its inaugural in 1977, *Spoleto Festival USA*—with its varied offerings of opera, chamber music, dance, and theater—has been a resounding success. (Regulars know it's best to secure tickets in January for the May-June performances.)

Today, Charleston greets about five million visitors annually, who spend nearly $785 million. Thus, more than any other industry, tourism has changed the lives of the area's 570,000 residents (81,000 live in the city itself). At the *Public Market,* where meat and vegetables once were sold, the restored arcades feature vendors and shops. Across the street is *Charleston Place,* a posh arcade of boutiques and restaurants.

Joseph R. Riley Jr., the popular five-term mayor, was once quoted as saying, "We won't let tourism take Charleston over. This is a real city, and excellent real cities are diverse." But despite the mayor's sentiments and the tax and economic incentives being offered, other industries have not yet moved here in any numbers. Environmentalists oppose razing choice property for industrial parks, and proud Charlestonian's have chosen to put their wealth into restoring what remains of their heritage.

Charleston At-a-Glance

SEEING THE CITY

Charleston is set in that sea level area of southeastern South Carolina known as the Low Country. There are no hills from which to get a good view of the city. Charleston has been nicknamed "the Holy City" because of its many churches; the best view of it is from the ground looking up, especially at night, when floodlights illuminate the church spires.

SPECIAL PLACES

The Old City is approximately 7 square miles, and even a five-day visit could be spent walking without covering the same street twice. An evening stroll is most popular with residents.

FORT SUMTER The fort where the first shots of the Civil War were fired in 1861 sits on a small manmade island at the entrance to Charleston's harbor. *Fort Sumter* withstood federal attacks between 1863 and early 1865. To the Union, it represented treachery; to the Confederates, it meant courageous resistance to oppression. The fort can be reached only by boat. *Fort Sumter Tours* leave *City Marina* (17 Lockwood Blvd.) daily at 1:30 PM in winter, three times daily in summer. One tour leaves *Patriot's Point* daily at 2:30 PM; three times daily in summer. Admission charge (phone: 722-1691).

CHARLES TOWNE LANDING Charleston was called Charles Towne in 1670 by the first permanent English settlers. Now a state park, *Charles Towne Landing* has restored houses, a full-scale replica of a 17th-century trading vessel, an open-air pavilion with archaeological artifacts, and a forest with indigenous animals. There are plenty of picnic tables, bike trails, and tram tours, too. The interpretive center offers several displays, including maps and Indian artifacts. Open daily. Admission charge. 1500 Old Towne Rd. (phone: 852-4200).

MAGNOLIA PLANTATION AND GARDENS Listed in the *National Register of Historic Places, Magnolia Plantation* has been the home of the Drayton family since the 1670s. World famous for its abundance of colors and scents, *Magnolia Gardens'* 30 acres abound with 900 varieties of camellias, 250 varieties of azaleas, and dozens of exquisite plants, shrubs, and flowers. In addition to the boat tours, a small zoo, and a ranch exhibiting a breed of miniature horse, *Magnolia Gardens* offers canoeing, bird watching, and bike trails through its 400-acre wildlife refuge. Another attraction here is the *Audubon Swamp Garden,* a separate, very secluded, 60-acre cypress swamp. Closed *Christmas.* Admission charge. Ten miles northwest of downtown on Rte. 61 (phone: 571-1266).

BOONE HALL This lovely 738-acre estate, formerly a cotton plantation settled by Major John Boone in 1681, closely resembles an MGM movie set. Although several original slave houses are here, true history buffs may be disappointed by the fact that the main building has been extensively reconstructed—not once, but twice. Closed *Thanksgiving* and *Christmas.* Admission charge. Seven miles north on Rte. 17 (phone: 884-4371).

DRAYTON HALL The only pre-Revolutionary mansion remaining on the Ashley River, this National Historic Landmark is one of the finest surviving exam-

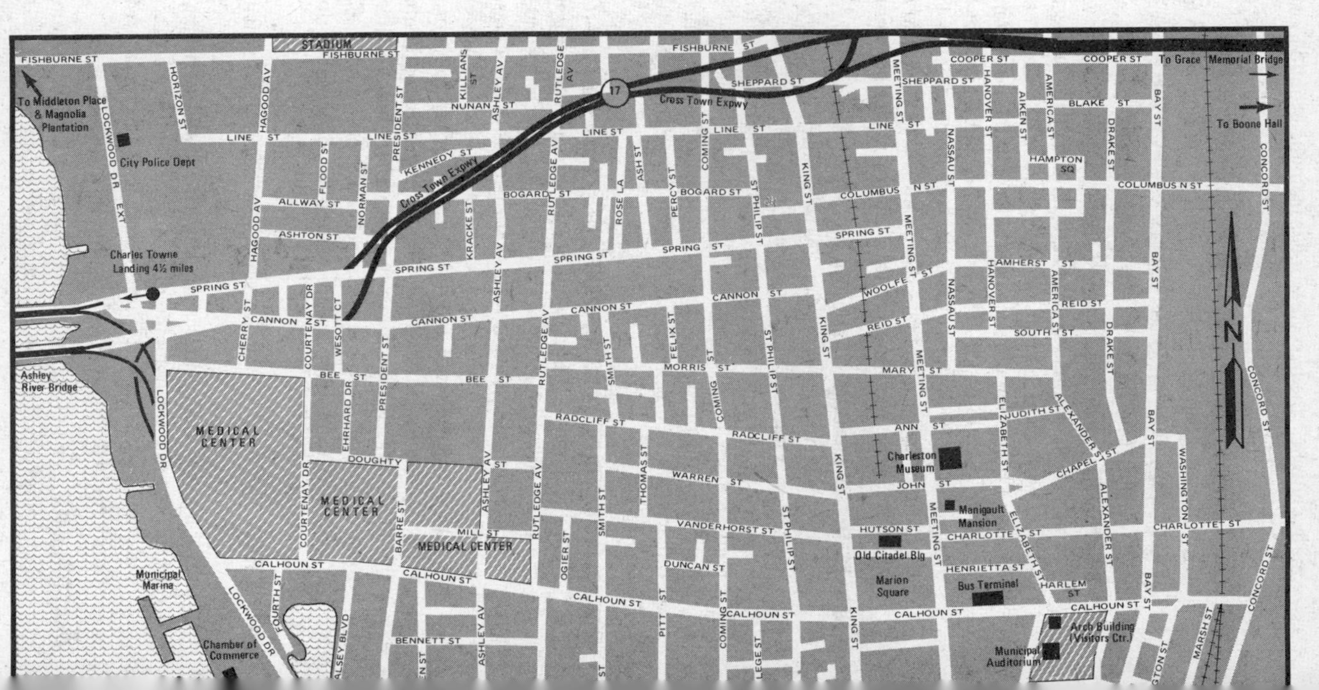

STADIUM
FISHBURNE ST
To Middleton Place & Magnolia Plantation
City Police Dept
HORIZON ST
LOCKWOOD DR EXT
HAGOOD AV
LINE ST
Charles Towne Landing 4½ miles
SPRING ST
CANNON ST
CHERRY ST
COURTENAY DR
WESOTT CT
Ashley River Bridge
LOCKWOOD DR
MEDICAL CENTER
Municipal Marina
Chamber of Commerce
FOURTH ST
HALSEY BLVD
FLOOD ST
ALLWAY ST
ASHTON ST
NORMAN ST
PRESIDENT ST
EHRHARD DR
BEE ST
DOUGHTY ST
BARRE ST
MILL ST
CALHOUN ST
BENNETT ST
KILLIANS ST
NUNAN ST
ASHLEY AV
KENNEDY ST
Cross Town Expwy
KRACKE ST
RUTLEDGE AV
17
BOGARD ST
ROSE LA
ASH ST
PERCY ST
COMING ST
ST PHILIP ST
SMITH ST
FELIX ST
MORRIS ST
OGIER ST
THOMAS ST
RADCLIFF ST
WARREN ST
VANDERHORST ST
DUNCAN ST
PITT ST
SHEPPARD ST
KING ST
COLUMBUS N ST
WOOLFE ST
REID ST
MARY ST
ANN ST
Charleston Museum
JOHN ST
Manigault Mansion
HUTSON ST
Old Citadel Blg
Marion Square
MEETING ST
NASSAU ST
HANOVER ST
AMHERST ST
SOUTH ST
AMERICA ST
AIKEN ST
ELIZABETH ST
JUDITH ST
ALEXANDER ST
CHAPEL ST
CHARLOTTE ST
HENRIETTA ST
Bus Terminal
HARLEM ST
Arch Building (Visitors Ctr.)
Municipal Auditorium
COOPER ST
BLAKE ST
HAMPTON SQ
DRAKE ST
BAY ST
WASHINGTON ST
MARSH ST
CONCORD ST
N
To Grace Memorial Bridge
To Boone Hall

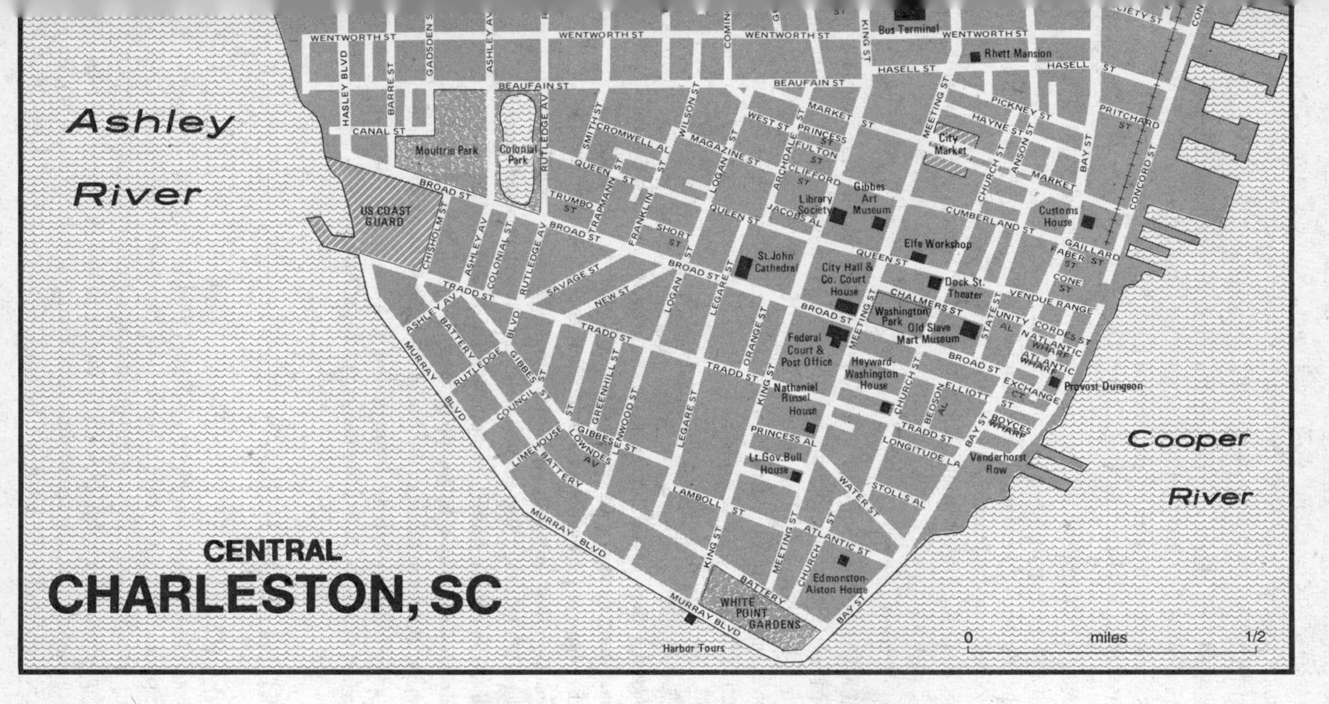
CENTRAL
CHARLESTON, SC
Ashley River
Cooper River
0 miles 1/2
Bus Terminal
Rhett Mansion
City Market
Customs House
Gibbes Art Museum
Library Society
Elfe Workshop
Dock St. Theater
St. John Cathedral
City Hall & Co. Court House
Washington Park
Old Slave Mart Museum
Federal Court & Post Office
Heyward-Washington House
Nathaniel Russel House
Provost Dungeon
Vanderhorst Row
Lt. Gov. Bull House
Edmonston-Alston House
WHITE POINT GARDENS
Harbor Tours
Moultrie Park
Colonial Park
US COAST GUARD
WENTWORTH ST
BEAUFAIN ST
HASELL ST
KING ST
MEETING ST
BROAD ST
TRADD ST
BAY ST
CHURCH ST
QUEEN ST
MURRAY BLVD
BATTERY
CONCORD ST

ples of Georgian Palladian architecture. The mansion is unfurnished, but its guided tour offers a special look at colonial South Carolina. Closed *Thanksgiving, Christmas,* and *New Year's Day.* Admission charge. Nine miles northwest of downtown on Rte. 61 (phone: 766-0188).

CHARLESTON MUSEUM This oldest municipal museum in the country has impressive collections of arts, crafts, furniture, textiles, and implements from South Carolina's early days, as well as occasional films. Closed major holidays. Admission charge. 360 Meeting St. (phone: 722-2996).

OLD EXCHANGE AND PROVOST DUNGEON During the Revolutionary War, the British imprisoned American patriots in the *Provost Dungeon,* which dates to 1780 and is in the historic *Old Exchange* building; today, exhibits show how the prisoners were treated during their detention. Attached to the *Provost* are excavations from the Half Moon Battery (ca. 1690), the original city wall built by the British. Closed major holidays. Admission charge. East Bay St. at Broad (phone: 727-2165).

WATERFRONT PARK This beautiful city park in the Historic District features swinging benches and a striking pineapple-shaped fountain with a pool where children cavort on hot days. Tall palmettos line the promenade along the Cooper River, and harbor breezes cool the air. On the corner of Concorde St. and Vendue Range on the southeast side of the downtown area.

EXTRA SPECIAL

At *Middleton Place,* about 15 miles north of Charleston via Route 61, the self-sustaining world of a Carolina Low Country plantation is re-created daily by people in 18th-century costume. Built in 1755, *Middleton Place* features the oldest landscaped gardens in the country, laid out by Henry Middleton in 1741. The 1,000-year-old Middleton Oak and the oldest camellias in the New World flourish on the lush grounds. Arthur Middleton, a signer of the Declaration of Independence, is buried here. A National Historic Landmark, *Middleton House* is the site of the *Spoleto Festival Finale* in June and *Plantation Days* (a dramatization of life on a plantation) in November. Open daily. Admission charge (phone: 556-6020).

Sources and Resources

TOURIST INFORMATION

The Charleston Convention and Visitors Bureau (375 Meeting St.; Charleston, SC 29401; phone: 853-8000) offers advice and brochures on tours, hotels, and restaurants. The staff will assist you in making reservations. It's open daily. A 25-minute multimedia show on the city's heritage, *Forever Charleston,* is shown frequently at the bureau; admission charge (phone: 724-7474). In the Historic District, the *Preservation Society of Charleston* (147 King St. at

Queen St.; phone: 723-4381) also offers information and tours, as well as a gift shop. It's closed Sundays.

For information on events and performance schedules, call the *Charleston Convention and Visitors Bureau* or the *Charleston County Parks and Recreation Commission* (phone: 762-2172). Contact the South Carolina state tourism hotline (phone: 803-734-0122) for maps, calendars of events, health updates, and travel advisories.

LOCAL COVERAGE *The Post & Courier,* morning daily; *Charleston* magazine, a monthly.

TELEVISION STATIONS WCBD Channel 2–ABC; WCIV Channel 4–NBC; WCSC Channel 5–CBS; and WITV Channel 7–PBS.

RADIO STATIONS AM: WTMA 1250 (country). FM: WSCI 89.3 (classical/jazz); WAVF 96.1 (rock); and WXLY 102 (classic rock).

TELEPHONE The area code for Charleston is 803.

SALES TAX The sales tax in Charleston is 6%; the hotel room tax is 4%.

CLIMATE Charleston's average temperature is 65F. Winters are mild, summers hot. March and April, when everything is abloom, are the best spring months to visit. In fall, October and November are ideal.

GETTING AROUND

AIRPORT *Charleston International Airport* is a 20-minute drive from downtown. *LowCountry Limousine* (phone: 767-7117) provides van service from the airport to the downtown hotels. Reservations are advised.

BUS The *South Carolina Electric and Gas Company* (665 Meeting St.; phone: 747-0922) operates the city bus system; the fare is 75¢. The *Downtown Area Shuttle* (*DASH*; phone: 724-7420) operates from 8 AM to 9 PM. The fare is 75¢, or $2 for an all-day pass.

CAR RENTAL Major national agencies are represented at the airport.

TAXI Cabs are inexpensive and a better bet than buses; they must be ordered by phone. Call *Yellow Cab* (phone: 577-6565).

SIGHTSEEING TOURS

BUS Guided bus or van tours are available from *Adventure Sightseeing* (phone: 762-0088) and *Gray Line Bus Tours* (phone: 722-4444). To see the city from the harbor, take a *Gray Line* water tour, departing at 2 PM daily (more often in summer) from the *City Marina* (17 Lockwood Blvd.; phone: 722-1112). It's also possible to rent a tape cassette from the gift shop at the *Mills House* hotel (see *Checking In*) for a walking or driving tour.

HORSE-DRAWN CARRIAGE Narrated tours in horse-drawn carriages are provided by *Charleston Carriage Co.* (phone: 577-0042), *Palmetto Carriage Tours* (phone: 723-8145), and *Old South Carriage Co.* (phone: 723-9712).

WALKING Walking tours are conducted by *Charleston Tea Party* (phone: 577-5896) and *Civil War Walking Tours* (phone: 722-7033). Or take a bicycle tour with a map and a bike from *The Bicycle Shop* (phone: 722-8168).

SPECIAL EVENTS

The *Southeastern Wildlife Exposition* draws over 40,000 visitors to its conservation and wildlife artwork exhibits during the second week of February, at 15 different downtown locations (phone: 723-1748 for information). During the *Festival of Houses and Gardens,* from mid-March to mid-April, more than 100 private homes and gardens are open to the public (phone: 723-1623 for information). The annual *Spoleto Festival USA,* two weeks of chamber music, dance, jazz, opera, and theater, begins in late May (phone: 722-2764 for schedule information). An array of local events, many free, make up *Piccolo Spoleto,* which coincides with the main festival (phone: 724-7305). The *Preservation Society* conducts *Candlelight Tours of Homes and Gardens* in September and October (phone: 722-4630).

MUSEUMS

In addition to those described in *Special Places,* other notable museums include the following:

GIBBES MUSEUM OF ART A fine collection by 18th- and 19th-century American painters, local and regional art, and portrait miniatures. Closed Sunday and Monday mornings. Admission charge. 135 Meeting St. (phone: 722-2706).

PATRIOTS POINT MARITIME MUSEUM This US naval history museum features the aircraft carrier *USS Yorktown,* among other ships. Closed *Christmas.* No admission charge for children under six. On Hwy. 17N, just across the Cooper River (phone: 884-2727).

HISTORIC HOUSES

Except where noted, the houses listed below are open daily except holidays. All charge admission and offer guided tours.

AIKEN-RHETT HOUSE (1817) 48 Elizabeth St. (phone: 723-1159).

CALHOUN MANSION (1876) Closed January and Mondays through Wednesdays. 16 Meeting St. (phone: 722-8205).

EDMONDSTON-ALSTON HOUSE (1828) 21 E. Battery St. (phone: 722-7171).

HEYWARD-WASHINGTON HOUSE (1770) 87 Church St. (phone: 722-0354).

JOSEPH MANIGAULT HOUSE (1803) 350 Meeting St. (phone: 723-2926).

NATHANIEL RUSSELL HOUSE (1808) 51 Meeting St. (phone: 724-8481).

SHOPPING

Charleston's Historic District offers the best and most varied places to shop in the city, ranging from stores carrying "Prehistoric Charleston" T-shirts to boutiques with high-fashion European-designed clothing to antiques shops. The *Public Market,* with its main entrance on Meeting at Market Streets, is a prime focus of attention. Open-air stalls feature works by local artisans, including sweetgrass baskets, a local tradition that harks back several generations. Other items sold here are hand-packaged red rice, a traditional Low Country side dish made with tomato sauce and spices, as well as the more prosaic T-shirts and paperweights. Flanking the *Public Market* along Market Street are gift shops that carry art prints of Charleston and home accessories.

Almost directly across from the market is *Charleston Place,* a hotel with an arcade of upscale shops such as *Godiva Chocolates, Victoria's Secret,* and several designer boutiques. Nearby is *Christian Michi* (220 King St.; phone: 723-0575), a boutique whose high-fashion clothing and eclectic home furnishings have attracted such celebrity clients as Melanie Griffith and Carly Simon.

Also in the Historic District, the *Historic Charleston Foundation Museum Shop* (108 Meeting St.; phone: 724-8484) sells books, furniture, jewelry, and other souvenirs, and offers a permanent exhibit on preservation. *Historic Charleston Reproductions* (105 Broad St.; phone: 723-8292) sells licensed reproductions of furniture and jewelry.

The three-block stretch of King Street north of Queen Street is the city's antiques area. The following are just a few of the assorted shops here: *Geo. C. Birlant & Co.* (191 King St.; phone: 722-3842), the largest in the city, features 18th- and 19th-century American and English furniture, dishes, glassware, and clocks; *American Sterling Galleries* (185 King St.; phone: 723-7197) offers antique silver, flatware, and holloware (teapots, creamers, and the like); and *Livingstons Antiques* (163 King St.; phone: 723-9697) imports turn-of-the-century English porcelain and furniture, as well as old books. In addition to its King Street location, there is also a branch at 2137 Savannah Highway (phone: 556-6162). *Joint Venture* (185 King St.; phone: 722-6730) sells estate jewelry. It's fun to poke around, but you probably won't be able to negotiate many bargains: The shopkeepers know what their wares are worth.

SPORTS AND FITNESS

BICYCLING *James Island County Park* (Rte. 17S and Rte. 171S; phone: 795-7275) is a 10-minute drive west of the Historic District. It has miles of bike trails (and bike rentals) and also has canoe and kayak rentals, a water park, and a fishing dock. There is an admission charge.

FISHING The best fishing is in the estuarine creeks that teem with bass, sheepshead, flounder, and trout (in fall and winter). In summer and fall, the creeks are full of crabs. Fishing for crabs and oysters, as well as creek fishing, is especially good on Capers, Dewees, Bulls, Kiawah, and Seabrook Islands. There are some public oyster beds closer to Charleston. For really good surf fishing, try Capers and Dewees Islands. For fishing and hunting regulations, write to the *South Carolina Wildlife Resources Department* (PO Box 167, Columbia, SC 29202).

FITNESS CENTERS *Life Quest* (35 Folly Rd.; phone: 571-2828) has Reflex fitness equipment, a sauna, and two aerobic workout studios.

GOLF There are public courses at *Patriots Point Links* (Hwy. 17, Mt. Pleasant; phone: 881-0042) and the *Shadowmoss Plantation Golf and Country Club* (20 Dunvegan Dr.; phone: 556-8251). Kiawah and Seabrook Islands have fine golf courses, but one of the most popular golfing areas in the country, Myrtle Beach, is only 98 miles north of Charleston on Route 17. This year-round resort town has 28 golf courses, many of them first rate. Even better is Hilton Head Island, 167 miles south of Charleston, with more than 20 golf courses, including *Harbour Town Golf Links* at *Sea Pines Plantation.* Hilton Head's accommodations are classier and more comfortable than those in the Myrtle Beach area. For more information, see *Golf: The Greening of America,* in DIVERSIONS. Daufuskie Island, reached by ferry from Hilton Head, is another first-rate golfing destination.

JOGGING Run around Colonial Lake, on Ashley Avenue. Or, for a nice 5-mile loop, run from Lockwood Drive to Battery, up East Bay Street, turn left onto Broad Street, right onto Meeting Street, and left onto Calhoun, which intersects with Lockwood.

SAILING Both crewed and bareboat sailboat charters, as well as sport fishing excursions, are available through *Bohicket Yacht Charters* (20 miles from Charleston, between Kiawah and Seabrook Islands; phone: 768-7294).

SWIMMING Near the city, Sullivan's Island and the Isle of Palms have fairly nice beaches, crowded in summer. North of Charleston, Capers and Dewees Islands have more secluded beaches, probably because they're only accessible by boat. Both are state wildlife refuges.

TENNIS The courts at the resorts on Kiawah and Seabrook Islands are open to the public but can be expensive, and resort guests have priority. Try *Shadowmoss Plantation Golf & Country Club* (20 Dunvegan Dr.; phone: 556-8251) for inexpensive public courts.

THEATER

Built in 1736, the 463-seat *Dock Street Theater* (on the corner of Church and Queen Sts.; phone: 965-4032) is the oldest in the country. It stages frequent performances of original drama, Shakespeare, Broadway, and 18th-century classics. Call in advance for up-to-date information and performance times. Tours of the theater are conducted sporadically during the week; admission charge. The *Robert Ivey Ballet* (1910 Savannah Hwy.; phone: 556-1343) presents major performances in the spring and fall at the *College of Charleston*'s *Sottile Theater* and at other venues around the city and state.

MUSIC

For *Community Concert Association* and *Symphony Orchestra* schedules, call the visitors' bureau (see *Tourist Information*). The *Spoleto Festival USA,* 12 days of chamber music, dance, jazz, opera, and theater, begins every year in late May (see *Special Events*).

NIGHTCLUBS AND NIGHTLIFE

The *Jukebox* (4 Vendue Range; phone: 723-3431) offers music from the 1960s and 1970s in the early evenings and changes to Top 40 later. For a quieter atmosphere, try the *Best Friend Bar* in the *Mills House* hotel (see *Checking In*). *Acme Bar & Grill* (5 Faber St.; phone: 577-7383) hosts rock, reggae, and jazz groups. *East Bay Trading Company* (corner of E. Bay and Queen Sts.; phone: 722-0722) is filled with fun antiques and an unusual bar. For jazz and blues, head to *Chef & Clef* (102 N. Market St.; phone: 722-0732). *Arizona Bar & Grill* (14 Chapel St.; phone 577-5090) has a Tex-Mex menu and live weekend entertainment. *Market Street Mill* (99 Market St.; phone: 722-6100) features pizza, pasta, and prime ribs, with live entertainment four nights a week. The best nightspot north of town is the *Windjammer* (1008 Ocean Blvd.; phone: 886-8596), a beer-and-billiards beach bar on the Isle of Palms with live music on weekends.

Best in Town

CHECKING IN

Expect to pay $200 or more per night for a double room at hotels we list as very expensive, $150 to $200 at expensive places, and $100 to $150 at those categorized as moderate; there are no exceptional inexpensive hotels in the Historic District. Most of Charleston's major hotels have complete facilities for the business traveler. Those listed below as having "business services" usually offer such conveniences as meeting rooms, photocopiers, computers, translation services, and express checkout, among others. Call the individual hotel for additional information. For bed and breakfast accommodations, contact *Historic Charleston Bed & Breakfast* (43 Legare St., Charleston, SC 29401; phone: 722-6606). Unless otherwise noted, hotel rooms have air conditioning, private baths, TV sets, and telephones.

All hotels below are in Charleston and telephone and fax numbers are in the 803 area code unless otherwise indicated.

VERY EXPENSIVE

John Rutledge House Inn This property has been meticulously restored, right down to the intricately carved mantels. The former home of a signer of the Constitution, its 19 rooms and three suites boast lovely parquet floors and antique reproductions. Relax in the ballroom with complimentary sherry. There is no restaurant, but amenities include turn-down service and breakfast served in the courtyard or delivered to your room with a morning newspaper. 116 Broad St. (phone: 723-7999; 800-476-9741; fax: 720-2615).

Charleston Place This glitzy hotel is the centerpiece of an impressive arcade of stylish shops and restaurants in the Historic District. It has 440 rooms, plus an indoor pool, a spa, and fitness facilities. The *Palmetto Café* features fine continental dining, and *Louis' Bar & Grill* is open for dinner. Amenities include 24-hour room service, a concierge, and business services. 130 Market St. (phone: 722-4900; 800-611-5545; fax: 722-0728).

Mills House A topnotch 214-room property operated by Holiday Inn, it is a Charleston classic. The antebellum decor reflects its 19th-century history, and, fittingly, it's in the center of the Historic District. The *Barbados Room* specializes in tableside preparation of continental food; you'll definitely want to make reservations for the famous Sunday buffet. Amenities include room service until 10 PM, a concierge, and business services. 115 Meeting St. (phone: 577-2400; 800-874-9600; fax: 722-2112).

EXPENSIVE

Battery Carriage House On the Battery facing the harbor, this sophisticated 11-room inn provides guests with four-poster beds, continental breakfast in bed, and turn-down service. There's no restaurant, but you can sip complimentary wine in the hospitality room or in the wisteria-draped, walled garden. 20 S. Battery (phone: 727-3100 between 10 AM and 5 PM).

Hawthorne Suites at the Market An elegant property in the heart of the Historic District. One of its many beauties is the entranceway, an 1874 portico. Its 164 one- and two-bedroom suites, furnished with antique reproductions, also have kitchens. Other niceties are the heated pool, concierge service, fitness facilities, and breakfast delivered to your room. There's no restaurant. Business services are available. 181 Church St. (phone: 577-2644; 800-527-1133; fax: 577-2697).

Lodge Alley Inn Quiet and tasteful, this hostelry is in Charleston's best shopping and sightseeing area. It has 34 rooms, each with a fireplace, as well as 37 one- and two-bedroom suites and a penthouse. The *French Quarter* restaurant serves country French fare, and the *Charleston Tea Party Lounge* is a lovely place to sip an aperitif. Amenities include room service (available only for breakfast) and business services. 195 E. Bay St. (phone: 722-1611; 800-845-1004; fax: 722-1611, ext. 7777).

Maison Du Pré At the northern end of the Historic District, three 19th-century single houses and two carriage houses have been fashioned into a warm, elegant inn. All 12 rooms and three suites have Oriental rugs, antique armoires, and marble-and-tile bathrooms. There's no restaurant, but continental breakfast and afternoon tea are included in the rate. 317 E. Bay St. (phone: 723-8691; 800-844-4667; fax: 723-3722).

Two Meeting Street Inn A real "find" in Charleston, built in 1891 and much like a European pension, it has been a guesthouse for more than 60 years. Nine spacious rooms and a wide second-floor verandah overlook *White Point Gardens* and the harbor. It's furnished with family antiques, silver, and Oriental rugs. No credit cards accepted. 2 Meeting St. (phone: 723-7322).

MODERATE

Best Western King Charles Inn In the center of the Historic District, it reflects old Charleston in the decor of its 90 rooms. There's free parking, a pool, and a dining room for breakfast only. 237 Meeting St. (phone: 723-7451; 800-528-1234; fax: 723-2041).

Days Inn Meeting St. The best deal in the Historic District: 124 rooms, a restaurant, and a pool. Free parking. 155 Meeting St. (phone: 722-8411; 800-325-2525; fax: 723-5361).

Hampton Inn Historic District Right next to the visitors' bureau (with its easy access to the Historic District by shuttle), this property in a former warehouse offers 166 rooms and five suites decorated with antique reproductions, and an attractive garden courtyard. There's no restaurant. Amenities include an outdoor pool, complimentary newspapers, and continental breakfast. 345 Meeting St. (phone: 723-4000; 800-HAMPTON; fax: 722-3725).

EATING OUT

A large number of good restaurants have sprung up in Charleston over the past several years—so many, in fact, that a visitor would have to stay here a long time to sample them all. Expect to pay $100 or more for dinner for two at places listed as very expensive; $70 to $100 at those categorized as expensive; $30 to $70 at places listed as moderate; and less than $30 at inexpensive eateries. Prices do not include drinks, wine, tax, or tips. All restaurants are in the 803 area code unless otherwise indicated.

Unless otherwise noted, restaurants are open for lunch and dinner.

VERY EXPENSIVE

Restaurant Million One of Charleston's dining gems, this nouvelle French establishment is housed in a beautifully restored old tavern. Two prix fixe menus offer such sumptuous dishes as smoked salmon ravioli and squab with herbs. There's à la carte dining as well. Open for dinner only; closed Sundays. Reservations necessary. Major credit cards accepted. 2 Unity Alley (phone: 577-7472).

EXPENSIVE

Louis' Charleston Grill Owner-chef Louis Osteen's menu features new Southern cuisine, such as mountain trout in herb-citrus crust and cashew-crusted grouper. A jazz combo lends a festive air. Open daily for dinner only.

Reservations advised. Major credit cards accepted. 224 King St. (phone: 577-4522).

MODERATE

Anson's Decorated with antique beveled-glass doors and ironwork, this eatery combines elegance with a friendly, casual ambience. Seafood is the specialty—cashew-crusted grouper is a particular favorite—but steaks are also offered. Open daily for dinner only. Reservations advised. Major credit cards accepted. 12 Anson St. (phone: 577-0551).

Carolina's A varied menu featuring game, beef, and pasta dishes is served in a contemporary-style dining room. Smoked Carolina quail is a popular entrée, as is the filet of beef served with crabmeat. Open daily for dinner only. Reservations advised. Major credit cards accepted. 10 Exchange St. (phone: 724-3800).

Celia's Porta Via As cozy as a visit to an Italian relative, this small place offers seafood dishes and homemade pasta; its fresh-baked bread draws raves. Closed Sundays; dinner only on Saturdays. Reservations advised. Major credit cards accepted. 49 Archdale St. (phone: 722-9003).

82 Queen Nestled in a lovely 18th-century townhouse with a garden court, this spot specializes in seafood and boasts three bars; the *Wine Bar* makes a nice spot for a pre- or post-dinner glass of wine. One of its noteworthy seasonal specials is sautéed veal in sun-dried-tomato butter. Reservations advised. Major credit cards accepted. 82 Queen St. (phone: 723-7591).

Garibaldi's This small café serves Italian home cooking with big-city service. A wide range of pasta dishes is offered daily, as are regular specials, including veal and seafood. Open daily for dinner only. Reservations advised. Major credit cards accepted. 49 S. Market St. (phone: 723-7153).

Magnolia's Once the city's *Customs House,* it's now a popular restaurant boasting Tex-Mex and Cajun dishes prepared with Low Country flair, such as grilled salmon served over grits with dill and shallot butter. Reservations necessary. Major credit cards accepted. 185 E. Bay St. (phone: 577-7771).

McCrady's A local favorite, this eatery is housed in an 18th-century tavern with many of its original pewter dishes and utensils on display. The menu selection runs from delicious grilled steaks to seafood prepared to order. Closed Sundays. No reservations. Major credit cards accepted. 2 United Alley (phone: 853-8484).

Poogan's Porch Fresh seafood and Low Country fare in an old Charleston house, with floral wallpaper and ceiling fans. Grilled alligator is a popular appetizer. Reservations necessary. Major credit cards accepted. 72 Queen St. (phone: 577-2337).

Slightly North of Broad A maverick Southern kitchen that specializes in seafood including sautéed flounder stuffed with deviled crab. A special menu encourages the sampling of Low Country dishes with smaller portions. Closed Sundays. No reservations. Major credit cards accepted. 192 E. Bay St. (phone: 723-3424).

INEXPENSIVE

Gaulart & Maliclet A local hangout, this tiny bistro serves simple French fare emphasizing fresh ingredients—seafood, a variety of healthful salads, and sandwiches on baguettes and croissants are some of the items on the menu. Closed Sundays; lunch only on Mondays. No reservations. Major credit cards accepted. 98 Broad St. (phone: 577-9797).

Pinckney Café and Espresso A mom-and-pop café whose seafood gumbo is highly touted by the artists and musicians who make up a good part of the clientele. Closed Sundays and Mondays. Reservations accepted for groups of six or more. No credit cards accepted. 18 Pinckney St. (phone: 577-0961).

Shem Creek Grilled seafood, chicken, and prime ribs make this place a local favorite. Desserts are exceptional. Open daily with late-night offerings from 10:30 PM to 2 AM. No reservations. Major credit cards accepted. 508 Mill St. (phone: 884-8102).

Chicago

There is a unique allure to Chicago. The third-largest city in the country (the city proper has just under three million people; the metropolitan area, more than six million), it is a vibrant, hip smorgasbord of theaters, award-winning restaurants, blues bars, museums, after-hours clubs, and world class hotels that stretch like a long, beckoning finger north along Lake Michigan, from the Loop (downtown Chicago's central business district) past Lincoln Park. This great city has inspired a Broadway musical, scores of stories and poems, and countless popular songs, and has been the subject of endless numbers of Hollywood films—all of which may seem especially ironic if you consider that nobody really knows whether the Indian word *checagou* means "great and powerful," "wild onion," or "skunk."

Chicago spreads along 29 miles of carefully groomed lakeshore. Respecting Lake Michigan, the people of Chicago have been careful not to destroy the property near the water with heavy manufacturing or industry. The lake is a source of water, as well as a port of entry for steamships and freighters coming from Europe via the St. Lawrence Seaway. Tens of millions of tons of freight are handled by Chicago's ports every year, and the city is still one of the world's largest railroad centers. The *Chicago Board of Trade* is the nation's most important grain market, and *O'Hare International,* its busiest airport.

Nuclear research and the electronics industry came of age here. In 1942, the world's first self-sustaining nuclear chain reaction was achieved at the *University of Chicago.* Half the radar equipment used during World War II was made here, too.

Chicago is *Second City,* the comedy club that spawned John Belushi, Joan Rivers, and Bill Murray, among others. Chicago is *Wrigley Field* and the long-suffering *Cubs.* Chicago is the *Goodman Theatre* and the *Hubbard Street Dance Company* and the symphony and bold Helmut Jahn architecture. It is barbecued ribs and stuffed pizza, David Mamet and John Malkovich, Mike Royko and Oprah Winfrey. It is Buddy Guy wailing the blues.

People from all over the world have come here to live. In 1890, 80% of all Chicago residents were immigrants or children of immigrants. There are more Poles in Chicago than in any Polish city except Warsaw, as well as sizable contingents from Germany, Italy, Sweden, Ireland, Asia, and Eastern Europe. People talk about "ethnic Chicago," which means you can find neighborhoods that will make you think you're in a foreign country. Nearly every nationality has a museum, and at least some of its customs have become public domain as well. There's a splendid array of inexpensive ethnic restaurants where you can get a whole meal for the price of an appetizer in a ritzier place.

This cosmopolitan center had unprepossessing beginnings. Jacques Marquette and Louis Joliet, the French explorers who provided the first record of the area, knew it as the Chicago Portage, one landmark on their route to Lake Michigan from the Mississippi. A trading post was established in 1679. In the 1812 Fort Dearborn Massacre, 53 people were killed by Indians. Eighteen years later, the first parcels of land were sold—$40 to $60 per 15,000-square-foot plot. The city, incorporated in 1837, began to look as if it might amount to something when the *Union Pacific Railroad* connected it to San Francisco in 1869; two years later, on October 8, 1871, it was in ashes. Burning at the rate of 65 acres per hour ($125,000 of damage per minute) and aided by a furious southwest wind, the Great Fire took 250 lives, made 90,000 homeless, melted 15,000 water service pipes, and left 1,688 acres in rubble. The total damage was estimated at $196 million.

As San Francisco would do after its 1906 earthquake, Chicago simply began to rebuild. And in the process, over the next 50 years, a new urban architecture was born. Building quickly and furiously upon four square miles of charcoal, and abetted by clients whose aesthetics derived from their interest in the profits to be gained from efficient buildings rather than the glory to be garnered from neoclassical palaces, Chicago architects *invented* the skyscraper. Frank Lloyd Wright then pioneered the ground-hugging, Prairie-style house that has become the prototype for the suburban, single-family dwelling units we know today. In 1909, architect Daniel Burnham laid out an elegant plan for the city, whose motto became *urbs in horto* ("city in a garden"). Today, 550 parks (including 29 clean public beaches) stretch across 7,332 acres, and there are 66,993 acres of trail-crossed forest preserves on the city's outskirts.

That the beaches are still clean and the forest acreage still pretty much unspoiled is a credit to the city planners, who have, over the years, managed to keep Chicago vibrant even as other downtown areas around the country have declined. While buildings elsewhere were pulled down to make way for parking lots, Chicago built a handful of skyscrapers set on pedestrian plazas studded with magnificent pieces of sculpture by Alexander Calder, Marc Chagall, Pablo Picasso, Claes Oldenburg, Joan Miró, and others.

If you haven't seen Chicago for a while, you're likely to be astounded. During the 1980s, the city underwent the greatest building boom it had seen since the 1920s. Along the lakeshore, new apartment buildings testify to the growing number of wealthy Chicagoans who are returning to live downtown (it's the departure of the working class that accounts for the city's drop in population). In the Loop, postmodern office buildings compete with the steel and glass towers of a generation ago and with the classics that gave Chicago its tradition of architectural distinction. The *Harold Washington Library Center,* built in 1991 and named for the former mayor, has added to the city's architectural reputation with its combination of Beaux Arts design and the powerful, heavy masonry that traditionally has

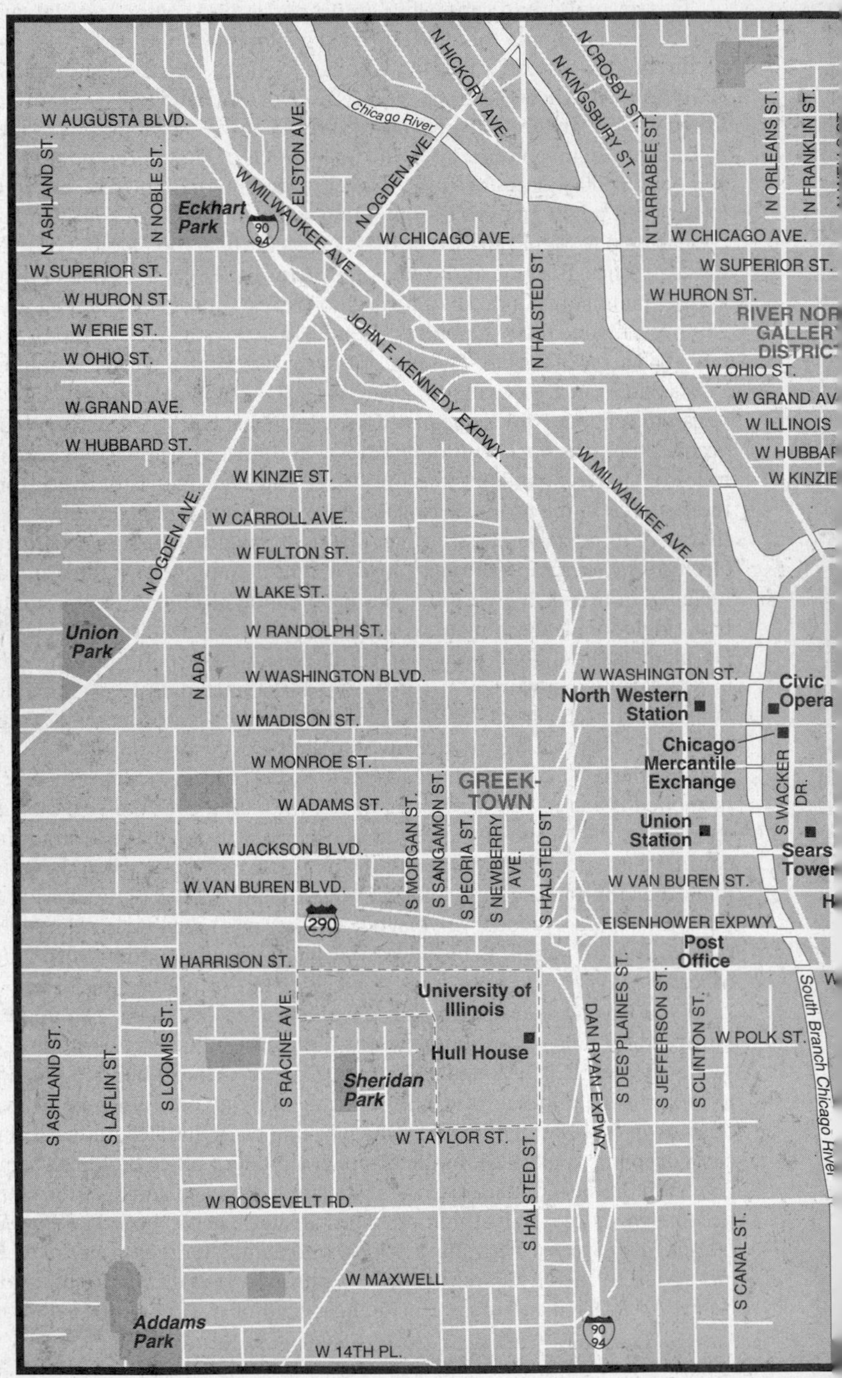
W AUGUSTA BLVD.
N ASHLAND ST.
N NOBLE ST.
Eckhart Park
ELSTON AVE.
Chicago River
N HICKORY AVE.
N OGDEN AVE.
W MILWAUKEE AVE.
N CROSBY ST.
N KINGSBURY ST.
N LARRABEE ST.
N ORLEANS ST.
N FRANKLIN ST.
W CHICAGO AVE.
W SUPERIOR ST.
W HURON ST.
W ERIE ST.
W OHIO ST.
W GRAND AVE.
W HUBBARD ST.
N HALSTED ST.
JOHN F. KENNEDY EXPWY.
RIVER NOR
GALLER
DISTRIC
W ILLINOIS
W HUBBAR
W KINZIE
W KINZIE ST.
W CARROLL AVE.
W FULTON ST.
W LAKE ST.
W RANDOLPH ST.
N OGDEN AVE.
Union Park
N ADA
W WASHINGTON BLVD.
W WASHINGTON ST.
North Western Station
Civic Opera
W MADISON ST.
W MONROE ST.
Chicago Mercantile Exchange
GREEK-TOWN
W ADAMS ST.
Union Station
S WACKER DR.
W JACKSON BLVD.
Sears Tower
W VAN BUREN BLVD.
W VAN BUREN ST.
S MORGAN ST.
S SANGAMON ST.
S PEORIA ST.
S NEWBERRY AVE.
S HALSTED ST.
290
EISENHOWER EXPWY.
Post Office
W HARRISON ST.
University of Illinois
Hull House
S ASHLAND ST.
S LAFLIN ST.
S LOOMIS ST.
S RACINE AVE.
Sheridan Park
DAN RYAN EXPWY.
S DES PLAINES ST.
S JEFFERSON ST.
S CLINTON ST.
W POLK ST.
South Branch Chicago River
W TAYLOR ST.
W ROOSEVELT RD.
S CANAL ST.
W MAXWELL
Addams Park
W 14TH PL.
90
94

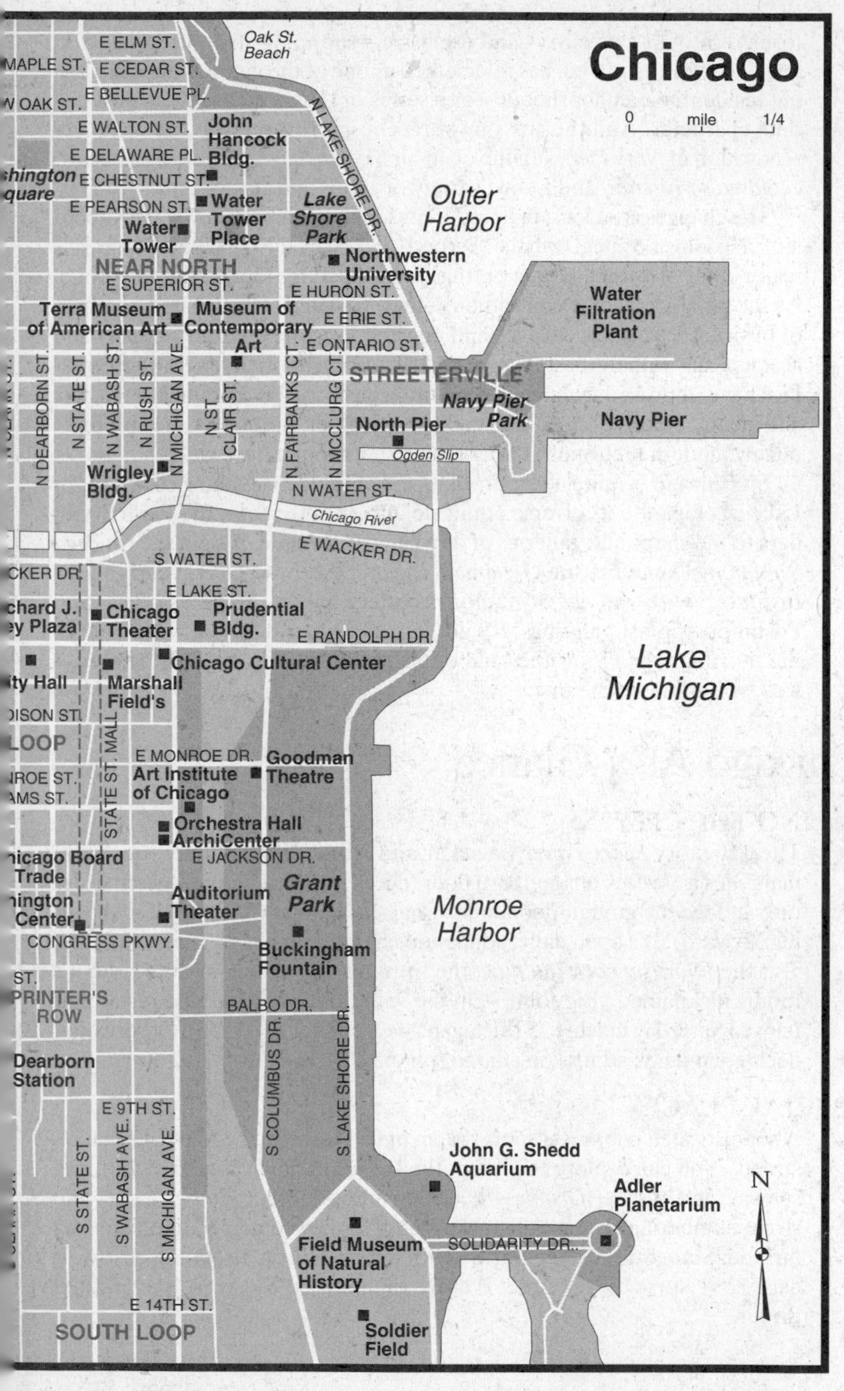

Chicago
0 mile 1/4
E ELM ST.
MAPLE ST.
E CEDAR ST.
E BELLEVUE PL.
OAK ST.
E WALTON ST.
E DELAWARE PL.
E CHESTNUT ST.
E PEARSON ST.
John Hancock Bldg.
Water Tower Place
Water Tower
Oak St. Beach
N LAKE SHORE DR.
Lake Shore Park
Outer Harbor
Northwestern University
NEAR NORTH
E SUPERIOR ST.
E HURON ST.
Terra Museum of American Art
Museum of Contemporary Art
E ERIE ST.
E ONTARIO ST.
Water Filtration Plant
STREETERVILLE
N DEARBORN ST.
N STATE ST.
N WABASH ST.
N RUSH ST.
N MICHIGAN AVE.
N ST. CLAIR ST.
N FAIRBANKS CT.
N MCCLURG CT.
Navy Pier Park
Navy Pier
North Pier
Ogden Slip
Wrigley Bldg.
N WATER ST.
Chicago River
E WACKER DR.
S WATER ST.
E LAKE ST.
Chicago Theater
Prudential Bldg.
E RANDOLPH DR.
Chicago Cultural Center
Marshall Field's
Lake Michigan
LOOP
STATE ST. MALL
E MONROE DR.
Goodman Theatre
Art Institute of Chicago
Orchestra Hall
ArchiCenter
E JACKSON DR.
Auditorium Theater
Grant Park
Monroe Harbor
CONGRESS PKWY.
Buckingham Fountain
PRINTER'S ROW
BALBO DR.
Dearborn Station
S COLUMBUS DR.
S LAKE SHORE DR.
E 9TH ST.
S STATE ST.
S WABASH AVE.
S MICHIGAN AVE.
John G. Shedd Aquarium
Adler Planetarium
N
Field Museum of Natural History
SOLIDARITY DR.
E 14TH ST.
SOUTH LOOP
Soldier Field

characterized Chicago edifices. North Michigan Avenue has been transformed into an extensive—and exclusive—shopping strip. Lincoln Park, once sleepy and isolated, has re-emerged as one of the nation's most intriguing residential neighborhoods—or a series of them, each with its own distinct character. And the city's most recent improvement is the complete renovation of *Navy Pier,* with the open-air *Skyline Stage Theater,* the *Chicago Children's Museum,* and a wide variety of shops and restaurants.

The changes aren't just in how the city looks, but also in how it feels about itself. No longer content with the "Second City" label, the directors of Chicago's major cultural attractions are putting on productions that do the city proud. As the nation's leading convention center, Chicago attracts large numbers of businesspeople. Its colleges and universities compete intellectually and academically with the best Eastern and Western schools. Even Chicago's politics have improved with age; though raucously inclined political reporters and incompetent aldermen still feed on each other, the city is run like a thoroughly modern metropolis rather than the fiefdom it once was.

So Chicago is quite a city, from its tony Gold Coast along the shore of Lake Michigan to its diverse ethnic neighborhoods; from the Rush Street bars to the shops and galleries of its Magnificent Mile. It's got the *Chicago Symphony Orchestra,* the *Goodman Theatre,* the *Lyric Opera,* and the *Art Institute,* with its world-famous collection of Impressionist and Postimpressionist paintings. It's got jazz and blues until the wee hours of the morning. And if it's the kind of place that makes you want to sing—well, you won't be the first.

Chicago At-a-Glance

SEEING THE CITY

The 110-story *Sears Tower* (Wacker and Adams Sts.; phone: 875-9696) maintains a *Skydeck* on the 103rd floor (check out the Calder *Universe* sculpture and see the ground-floor audiovisual show about Chicago before heading skyward). It's open daily; admission charge. For a view from the north, visit the *John Hancock Building*; the fifth-tallest building in the world, it's fondly nicknamed "Big John." On the 95th floor are a bar and restaurant (closed Saturday lunch; 875 Michigan Ave.; phone: 787-9596). Observation deck open daily; admission charge (phone: 751-3681).

SPECIAL PLACES

A sophisticated public transport system makes it easy to negotiate Chicago's streets. You can explore the Loop, the lakefront, and suburbs by El train, subway, and bus (see *Getting Around*). In addition, Chicago's grid plan and street numbering system even make it easy for newcomers to find their way around. State Street is the north-south axis, Madison Street the east-west axis: 1200 North on any street is at Division Street; 800 West is at Halsted Street.

THE LOOP/DOWNTOWN

The Loop generally refers to Chicago's central business district, which is circled by the elevated train known as the "El."

GRANT PARK A favorite spot for free summer music festivals, the park, located south of Randolph Street (bordered by Randolph Street, Lake Shore Drive, Michigan Avenue, and Roosevelt Road), offers an incredible view of the Chicago skyline. Near the intersection of Columbus Avenue and Congress Parkway, stop by the *Buckingham Fountain,* the world's largest lighted fountain—with a computerized 135-foot-high water display that spouts daily from May through September. The fountain was modeled after the *Latona Fountain* at *Versailles,* but it is twice the size; the formal gardens are just steps away. Between S. Michigan Ave. and Lake Shore Dr., south of Randolph St. (phone: 294-2307).

CHICAGO MERCANTILE EXCHANGE AND INTERNATIONAL MONETARY MARKET The spectacle is much the same as at the *Board of Trade,* only here you can sit down. It was opened in 1898 as the Butter and Egg Board; today more than 4,000 traders and staff crowd the trading floor daily. Visitors can watch the auction from a fourth-floor gallery and simulate trading at several interactive, multilingual exhibits. Each commodity has its own opening and closing times. Free tours are available and must be scheduled in advance. Closed weekends. No admission charge. 30 S. Wacker Dr. (phone: 930-8249).

SEARS TOWER At 1,454 feet and 110 stories, it's the world's tallest building; it also boasts the world's fastest elevator (it travels more than 20 miles per hour and takes only 55 seconds to get to the 103rd floor). Some 16,500 people use the building each day. The tower, which consists of nine staggered square tubes, was completed in 1974. The arched glass entryway was added in 1985 and generated another of Chicago's seemingly endless architectural controversies. Some thought the plaza too stark without the addition; others, particularly architectural purists, thought it glitzed up a building that made a strong enough statement on its own. Check out the Calder *Universe* sculpture and see the ground-floor audiovisual show about Chicago before heading for the *Skydeck* on the 103rd floor. The *Skydeck* is open daily; admission charge. 233 S. Wacker Dr., between Adams St. and Jackson Blvd. (phone: 875-9696, *Skydeck*).

CHICAGO BOARD OF TRADE The largest grain exchange in the world, this Art Deco treasure was built in 1930 and, half a century later, gained a new trading floor to accommodate expanding markets. Stand in the visitors' gallery and watch traders gesticulating on the floor, runners in colored jackets delivering orders, and an electronic record of all the trades displayed overhead. Free tours and a 15-minute movie run throughout the morning. Closed afternoons and weekends. No admission charge. 141 W. Jackson Blvd. at LaSalle St. (phone: 435-3590).

CHICAGO THEATER Restored to its 1920s splendor, this stage offers pop music concerts, contemporary dramas, and musicals against a Baroque backdrop of marble and crystal chandeliers. Even if you aren't going for the show, stop by for a look at its interior. 175 N. State St. (phone: 443-1130).

MARSHALL FIELD'S Chicago's most famous department store. When it was built in 1892—before electric lighting was common—it was designed in sections, with shopping areas on balconies overlooking a skylit central courtyard. Later, the skylights were covered, one with a vivid blue and gold Louis Tiffany mosaic visible by entering on the corner of Washington and State Streets. On the seventh floor is a marvelous food court, including the famed *Walnut Room* (a special treat at *Christmas*) and the *Crystal Palace,* which serves unbelievable ice cream sundaes (Frango mint ice cream—a subtle mix of coffee, chocolate, malt, and mint—is a tradition, as are its chocolate candies). Open daily. Wabash, State, Randolph, and Washington Sts. (phone: 781-1000).

HAROLD WASHINGTON LIBRARY CENTER Named for the city's late Mayor Washington, it's the largest municipal library facility in the world (in square footage); it's also expansive and comfortable to use and chock-full of an amazing array of contemporary art. The ornamental rose-brick façade has received its share of criticism as well as praise, but it does add warmth to a dreary corner of the Loop. There's a children's library with storytelling hours, as well as a gift shop with interesting mementos of Chicago. Open daily. No admission charge. 400 S. State St. (phone: 747-4999).

CHICAGO CULTURAL CENTER This 1897 Italian Renaissance-style building originally served as the *Chicago Public Library.* Its impressive interior, including green and white marble, elaborate mosaics, and a Louis Tiffany stained glass dome, is a fitting backdrop for a continuous schedule of dance performances, concerts, art exhibits, photography shows, lectures, and films. The city presents more than 500 free programs and exhibits at the *Center* annually. The *Museum of Broadcast Communications* is also housed here (see below). Open daily. No admission charge. 78 E. Washington St. (phone: 346-3278 for recorded message; 744-6630 for general information).

ART INSTITUTE OF CHICAGO El Greco's *Assumption of the Virgin,* Seurat's *Sunday Afternoon on the Island of La Grande Jatte–1884,* and Grant Wood's *American Gothic* are among the works in this museum's outstanding collections, which also include excellent Impressionist and Postimpressionist works, Japanese prints, Chinese sculpture and bronzes, European and American prints and drawings, decorative arts and sculpture, and more are housed in the impressive *Rice Building.* The *American Galleries* are wonderfully conceived to show off the development of US culture; the Chagall stained glass windows and the *Trading Room,* from the old *Chicago Stock Exchange Building,* are not to be missed. The photography department is one of the most sophisticated facilities of its kind in the world. The renovated *Galleries of Modern*

Art 1900–1950 display outstanding examples of European and American art, including Edward Hopper's *Nighthawks,* Vincent van Gogh's *Bedroom at Arles,* and Toulouse-Lautrec's *Ballet Dancers,* as well as one of the major Surrealist collections in the world. Open daily. No admission charge on Tuesdays. Michigan Ave. at Adams St. (phone: 443-3600 or 443-3500 for recorded information).

AUDITORIUM THEATER Brilliant Chicago architect Louis Sullivan died penniless, but this 104-year-old landmark, one of his most important works, still stands. Hand-painted murals and gold leaf abound here, and the interior—which houses a 2,412- to 3,661-seat theater (depending on the production), a hotel, and an office center—features 55 million pieces of mosaic tile. There's not a bad seat in the house. During World War II, this theater was turned into a bowling alley, but a major fund-raising effort in the mid-1960s brought about a restoration. It's now used for a variety of cultural functions, from stage plays to pop concerts. Tours are offered for groups of 10 or more, but individuals can join, if space is available. There's a charge for the tours. 50 E. Congress Pkwy. (phone: 922-4046 or 559-1212 for performance information).

CHICAGO ARCHITECTURE FOUNDATION The *Exhibition Gallery* has changing shows that span a wide range of architectural topics. The Foundation offers a variety of tours, including a walking tour of the Loop (daily, year-round) and other neighborhoods at various times throughout the year. The three-hour "Chicago Highlights" tour bus runs every Saturday March through November, and the first and third Saturdays December through February. There's a charge for the tours. Santa Fe Bldg., 224 S. Michigan Ave. (phone: 922-3432).

NAVY DEVELOPMENT/SKYLINE STAGE THEATER At the beginning of this century, the *Navy Pier* was the place where Chicago families boarded boats for a summer outing. Long neglected, the pier has been extensively renovated and is enjoying a renaissance, this time as a multipurpose development that includes the 1,500-seat *Skyline Stage Theater,* site of stage shows and concerts plus ballet performances and children's theater. Among the other additions to the complex are the *Family Pavilion,* with shops and restaurants, a 15-story Ferris wheel, and a carousel. *Navy Pier,* 600 E. Grand St. (For theater tickets, phone *Ticketmaster* at 559-1212; for information on the pier, dial 791-PIER).

CHICAGO CHILDREN'S MUSEUM This hands-on museum for youngsters has innovative exhibits on a variety of subjects, including recycling, environmentally responsible garbage disposal, and family relationships. Children can learn about architecture, try out a fully equipped mini-kitchen, videotape a "newscast," and climb, ride, and fly in a "Fantasy Vehicle." There is one room filled with nothing but Lego building blocks. Closed Mondays. Admission charge. *Navy Pier,* 600 E. Grand St. (phone: 527-1000).

PRINTER'S ROW Architecture buffs will find a haven among the restored buildings, jazz and blues clubs, bookstores, and galleries just south of the Loop on South Dearborn Street and South Plymouth Court. The *Hyatt Printer's Row,* housed in a building on the *National Register of Historic Places,* also graces the area. Every June along South Dearborn Street and South Plymouth Court, there is a two-day *Printer's Row Book Fair* with exhibits dedicated to all aspects of printing and publishing. While in the neighborhood, stop for a drink or an elegant dinner at the *Printer's Row* restaurant.

MUSEUM OF BROADCAST COMMUNICATIONS This facility traces the city's role in the broadcast industry using an extensive tape library and exhibits. In the museum's *Kraft Television Theatre,* you can watch old commercials and vintage prime-time shows. On weekends, visitors to the museum's news center can "anchor" a newscast, then watch it on video (call ahead to reserve camera time). The museum's shop, *Commercial Break,* sells ABC Sports jackets and David Letterman T-shirts, along with other media-related items. Open daily. No admission charge. In the *Chicago Cultural Center,* 78 E. Washington St. (phone: 629-6000).

PRAIRIE AVENUE HISTORIC DISTRICT This area of 19th-century mansions, along Prairie Avenue, between 18th and Cullerton Streets, is where Chicago's wealthy citizens once lived. The buildings that remain have been restored to their former elegance, and other historic buildings have been moved here. Standouts are the *Glessner House*, built by architect H. H. Richardson in 1886, and the *Henry B. Clark House*, the city's oldest building, built in 1836. The *Chicago Architecture Foundation* (phone: 922-3432) runs tours of the homes every Friday, Saturday, and Sunday.

FIELD MUSEUM OF NATURAL HISTORY Not only do the outstanding collections of more than 19 million artifacts and specimens on more than nine acres make this one of the largest public museums in the US, but through ongoing fieldwork and basic research, the museum has become an international center for scientific study and public learning. The museum's public exhibitions have shifted over the years from conventional displays to a strategy of introductory exhibits, major thematic exhibits, and resource centers. One of its most famous attractions is the pair of fighting elephants in the *Main Hall.* Other must-sees include an exhibit on Africa featuring an authentic, walk-through re-creation of a native village; a full-scale model of a Pawnee earth lodge, where there are daily programs on Indian life; and a full-size, three-level ancient Egyptian tomb. The *Hall of Chinese Jade* and the display of Japanese lacquerware are also outstanding. Closed *Thanksgiving, Christmas,* and *New Year's Day.* No admission charge on Wednesdays. S. Lake Shore Dr. at Roosevelt Rd. (phone: 922-9410).

JOHN G. SHEDD AQUARIUM The largest aquarium in the world, it has more than 200 fish tanks and a collection of over 7,000 specimens: sturgeon from

Russia, Bahamian angelfish, Australian lungfish, and a coral reef where divers feed the fish several times a day. The *Oceanarium* re-creates a Pacific Northwest coastal exhibit with whales, seals, dolphins, and otters. There's also a program called "Shedd's Family Overnight," which allows families to spend a night in the aquarium. Closed *Christmas* and *New Year's Day.* No admission charge on Thursdays. Museum Point at 1200 S. Lake Shore Dr. (phone: 939-2426; 939-2438 for the *Oceanarium*).

ADLER PLANETARIUM Exhibitions here include everything from surveying and navigating instruments to modern space exploration devices, plus a real moon rock and an antique instrument collection that is considered the best in the Western Hemisphere and one of the top three in the world. You can see it all before or after the sky show, which is the reason that most people come. There are new shows every six months, one for adults and one for children five years old and younger. Open daily. No admission charge on Tuesdays. 1300 S. Lake Shore Dr. on Museum Point. (phone: 322-0304).

NORTH MICHIGAN AVENUE

WATER TOWER PLACE This incredible, vertical shopping mall gets busier and better every year. Asymmetrical glass-enclosed elevators shoot up through a seven-story atrium, past shops selling dresses, books, and gift items, plus restaurants and a movie theater. Branches of *Marshall Field's, FAO Schwarz,* and *Lord & Taylor* are here, along with the elegant *Ritz-Carlton* hotel, reaching 20 stories above its 12th-floor lobby in the tower. The hotel's skylit *Greenhouse* is great for tea or cocktails after a hard day of shopping. N. Michigan Ave. at Pearson St.

WATER TOWER AND WATER TOWER PUMPING STATION Now landmarks, these distinctive matching castle-like structures are the only survivors of the Great Fire of 1871. The *Water Tower* (N. Michigan Ave. and Pearson St.), which masks a 135-foot-tall standpipe, now houses the *Chicago Office of Tourism* (see *Tourist Information,* below). Across Michigan Avenue is the *Water Tower Pumping Station* (803 N. Michigan Ave.), which now is the home of *Here's Chicago,* a multimedia show about the city. The show is presented daily except holidays; there's an admission charge (phone: 467-7114).

TERRA MUSEUM OF AMERICAN ART The permanent collection here reads like a *Who's Who in American Art* over the past two centuries, including works by Mary Cassatt, Winslow Homer, John Singer Sargent, William Merritt Chase, Samuel F. B. Morse, Edward Hopper, and Andrew Wyeth. Morse, inventor of the Morse code, painted the *Gallery of the Louvre,* a huge canvas recreating dozens of paintings from the *Louvre.* One of the few museums in the country dedicated solely to American art and artists, it also has visiting exhibits. Closed Mondays. No admission charge on Tuesdays and the first Sunday of every month. 666 N. Michigan Ave. (phone: 664-3939).

PEACE MUSEUM The only one of its kind in the US, it features exhibits and special programs at a variety of sites throughout the city on issues related to war, peace, and nonviolence. Closed Sundays and Mondays. No admission charge on Wednesdays. 350 W. Ontario St. (phone: 440-1860).

MUSEUM OF CONTEMPORARY ART Lively changing exhibitions—retrospectives of contemporary artists as well as surveys of 20th-century art movements and avant-garde phenomena—are featured here. The museum also mounts shows by Chicago artists and sponsors symposia and other special events. Closed Mondays. No admission charge on Tuesdays. 220 E. Chicago Ave. (phone: 280-5161).

NORTH SIDE

CHICAGO HISTORICAL SOCIETY Pioneer crafts demonstrations and a slide show about the Chicago Fire make this one of the city's most fascinating museums. New galleries focus on Chicago's beginnings and explore 19th-century American life through furniture and decorative objects. Closed *Thanksgiving, Christmas,* and *New Year's Day.* No admission charge on Mondays. 1629 N. Clark St. at North Ave. (phone: 642-4600).

LINCOLN PARK ZOO The best thing about this zoo is that it has the largest group of great apes in captivity, all happily coexisting in the *Great Ape House.* There's also a *Lion House,* a *Bird House,* and the standard houses of monkey, tiger, bear, and bison, plus the zoo's popular farm. Next door, a building restored to its early 20th-century charm now houses the *Café Brauer* (phone: 294-4660), with a fine view of the park and the Chicago skyline, as well as an office for bike and skate rentals, a small cafeteria, and the *Ice Cream Shoppe,* which dishes out old-fashioned ice cream creations. Open daily. No admission charge. 2200 Cannon Dr., *Lincoln Park* (phone: 294-4660).

LINCOLN PARK CONSERVATORY This botanical delight features changing floral displays and a magnificent permanent collection that includes orchids, a 50-foot African fiddle-leaf rubber tree with giant leaves, fig trees, and more ferns than you can shake a stick at. Closed *Christmas.* No admission charge. In *Lincoln Park,* Stockton Dr. at Fullerton Ave. (phone: 294-4770).

CHICAGO ACADEMY OF SCIENCES This museum features particularly lively exhibitions about the natural history of the Great Lakes area; the reconstruction of a 300-million-year-old forest that once stood near the present site, complete with gigantic insects and carnivorous dragonflies, is especially interesting. A "walk-through" cave and canyon and hands-on children's gallery are lots of fun for youngsters. Closed *Christmas.* No admission charge on Tuesdays. *North Pier,* 435 E. Illinois St., Level 3 (phone: 871-2668).

BIOGRAPH THEATRE A legend, although not as a theater, it was here in 1934 that the Lady in Red (Anna Sage) turned bank robber John Dillinger over to federal agents who then shot him, ending a massive manhunt for the FBI's

"Public Enemy No. 1." Today, the theater shows foreign and contemporary films. 2433 N. Lincoln Ave. (phone: 348-4123).

GRACELAND CEMETERY Buried here are hotel barons, steel magnates, architects Louis Sullivan and Daniel Burnham—enshrined in tombs and miniature temples, and overlooking islands, lakes, hills, and other scenic views. The ranks of Chicago's rich and famous interred here also include George Pullman, inventor of the sleeper railcar, Cyrus McCormick, who invented the harvester, and merchant Marshall Field. The *Getty Tomb,* designed by Sullivan, is a must stop. On most Sundays in August, September, and October, the *Chicago Architecture Foundation* sponsors two-hour tours of the cemetery. There's a charge for the tour. Call the foundation in advance for details (phone: 922-3432). N. Clark St. and Irving Park Rd.

LILL STREET With more than 40 professional potters working in dozens of studios, this is the largest ceramics center in the Midwest. Visitors can watch the artisans or buy some of their work. *Lill Street* potters offer classes, including a one-day family clay workshop. 1021 W. Lill St. (phone: 477-6185).

SOUTH SIDE

MUSEUM OF SCIENCE AND INDUSTRY Chicago's most popular attraction has computers to question, buttons to push, rides to ride, and much more. There are some 2,000 exhibitions in 75 major halls examining the principles of science and technology (as well as other subjects). High points: Colleen Moore's fairy castle of a dollhouse, and the Sears circus exhibit, full of dioramas of circus scenes, piped-in circus music, and a dynamic short film (the kind you want to sit through twice in a row). The working coal mine, the walk-through human heart, and the German *U-505* submarine are every bit as much fun as they always have been. And there also are exhibits on chemistry, physics, geology, the brain, the post office, anesthesiology, and the life sciences, as well as a *Business Hall of Fame* and an exciting section on computers. The *Henry Crown Space Center* features the *Omnimax Theater* and space exhibitions. (Be warned, it's a madhouse on weekends.) Closed *Christmas.* No admission charge Thursdays. S. Lake Shore Dr. at E. 57th St. (phone: 684-1414).

UNIVERSITY OF CHICAGO Guided walking tours of this illustrious university, founded in 1892 by John D. Rockefeller, include a stop at the *Robie House* (5757 S. Woodlawn Ave.), a fine example of the Prairie School of architecture, designed by Frank Lloyd Wright (as was its furniture) in 1909. The campus also has a marker commemorating the site of the world's first controlled atomic test in 1942 and *Rockefeller Chapel;* anecdotes about the chapel invariably involve famous statesmen, politicians, and celebrities. Free campus tours are conducted Mondays through Saturdays at 10 AM; call in advance for the meeting place. Also on campus is the *Smart Museum of Art,* a permanent collection that spans 5,000 years of Western and Asian art. The campus is in Hyde Park, a neighborhood bounded by Cottage Grove Ave., 55th St., Dorchester Ave., and 61st St. (phone: 702-8374).

ORIENTAL INSTITUTE MUSEUM This collection of art, archaeological artifacts, and textiles from the ancient Near East boasts a colossal statue of Tutankhamen and a winged bull with a human head from Assyria. Run by the *University of Chicago,* the museum offers guided tours and free films on Sunday afternoons. Closed Mondays. No admission charge. 1155 E. 58th St. (phone: 702-9521).

PULLMAN COMMUNITY Founded by George Pullman in 1880 as the nation's first company town, this early example of comprehensive urban planning is now a city, state, and national landmark. Walking tours conducted on the first Sunday of the month from May through October tell the story in detail; at other times, find the *Greenstone Church* and other important sites on maps available at the *Florence* hotel, a Pullman-era structure that serves as a visitors' center of sorts (and provides lunch on weekdays, breakfast and lunch on Saturdays, and brunch on Sundays). A number of the privately owned row houses are open for special tours held annually on the second weekend in October. West of the Dan Ryan Expwy. between 111th and 115th Sts. (phone: 785-8181).

WEST SIDE

HALSTED STREET If you have time to get to know only one Chicago street, make it Halsted; locals claim that you could live your entire life perfectly well without ever leaving here. Spanning 20 miles of metropolitan Chicago—from 3766 North to 12961 South and on through West Pullman and Calumet—it boasts hundreds of restaurants, bars, and nightclubs, 30 churches, 50 liquor stores, and offbeat shops you won't find on Michigan Avenue. West of the Loop on Halsted Street is Chicago's Greektown area with restaurants such as the *Neon Greek Village* (310 S. Halsted St.; phone: 648-9800), offering great Greek food—and even belly dancing. Theaters also line some blocks of Halsted Street, as do jazz and blues bars.

MEXICAN FINE ARTS MUSEUM The first Mexican museum in the Midwest, and the largest in the country, pays tribute to the wide and varied Mexican culture with exhibits, theatrical performances, and workshops. The museum's gift shop specializes in Mexican folk art and multilingual publications. Closed Mondays. No admission charge. 1852 W. 19th St. (phone: 738-1503).

HULL HOUSE Social welfare pioneer Jane Addams founded *Hull House* as a community service organization working for political reform and to improve garbage collection, to end sweatshops, and to protect abused children. Only two of the original *Hull House* buildings still exist, nestled into the modernist *University of Illinois* campus, with exhibits commemorating Addams, who was a peace activist, a humanitarian, and the first North American woman to win the Nobel Peace Prize. There are also exhibits commemorating her associates and the neighborhood they served. Closed Saturdays. No admission charge. 800 S. Halsted St. (phone: 413-5353).

OUTSKIRTS

OAK PARK Twenty-five buildings in this suburb, most of them remarkably contemporary looking, show the development of Frank Lloyd Wright's Prairie style of architecture. In addition to the architect's residence-workshop (see below), Wright's *Unity Temple* (875 Lake St., Oak Park; phone: 708-848-6225) is open to the public. There are daily tours (except on holidays); admission charge. The homes of Edgar Rice Burroughs and Ernest Hemingway (see *Museums*) are here, too, along with numerous gingerbread and turreted Queen Anne mansions. The *Oak Park Tour Center,* based in the *Frank Lloyd Wright Home and Studio,* operates most area walking tours as well as a visitors' center, where you can see photo exhibitions and take in an orientation program. At the *Wright Plus Festival,* the third Saturday in May, many private homes are open to the public. For more information, call the *Oak Park Visitor Center* (158 Forest St.; phone: 708-848-1976).

FRANK LLOYD WRIGHT HOME AND STUDIO In Oak Park, approximately 10 miles west of the city, this home and studio, designed by the master himself, was the birthplace of the so-called Prairie School of architecture and is a fine example of that style. At the center of the home is a fireplace around which the rest of the rooms are spread. Wright, who was self-taught, also designed the furniture—perhaps in his two-story, octagon-shaped, cantilevered drafting room. Open daily. Admission charge. Guided tours are required. 951 Chicago Ave., Oak Park (phone: 708-848-1500). This is also the headquarters of the *Oak Park Tour Center,* which operates architectural tours of the town, which is home to several other Wright buildings (see *Oak Park,* above).

MORTON ARBORETUM Sterling Morton ran a salt company ("when it rains, it pours"), but he was more fond of trees than salt (his birthday, April 26, is now recognized as *Arbor Day*), and therefore his niece established an arboretum in his name. A 1,500-acre living museum of roads and trails through an extraordinary array of flora—4,000 species at a recent count—its highlights include a Japanese garden, a prairie fragrance garden, a pinetum of conifers, dwarf shrubs, and every other kind of green that can be coaxed to grow in Illinois's harsh climate and clay soil. Open daily. Admission charge. Located about 25 miles west of downtown, easily accessible on I-88, where it intersects with Rte. 53 (phone: 708-719-2466).

BROOKFIELD ZOO Some 200 acres divided by moats and natural-looking barriers make this one of the most modern zoos in the country. There is an indoor rain forest, special woods for wolves, a bison prairie, a replica of the Sahara, and a dolphin show. *Tropic World* features South American, Asian, and African birds, primates, and other animals. Open daily. No admission charge on Tuesdays and Thursdays. 1st Ave. at 31st St. in Brookfield, 15 miles west of the Loop. Take Rte. 290 or I-55 to the 1st Ave. exit (phone: 242-2630 or 708-485-0263).

CHICAGO BOTANIC GARDEN This 300-acre collection of plants, trees, and shrubs from around the world is open year-round—except *Christmas Day.* Its special attractions include a three-island Japanese garden, a rose garden, 10 greenhouses, and a mile-long nature trail. There also is a tram tour of the gardens, an exhibit hall, a library, the *Museum of Floral Arts,* a gift shop, and a café. Admission charge to park your car, only. Half a mile east of the Edens Expwy. at Lake Cook Rd. in Glencoe (phone: 708-835-5440).

FOX RIVER CASINOS Gambling has come to the Chicago area, if not yet to the city itself. A couple of cities along the Fox River on the Chicago area's western edge have welcomed the arrival of floating casinos—boats that cruise the river for two and a half hours once a group of gamblers is onboard. Sailings are scheduled throughout the day and night. In Aurora, *Hollywood Casino,* which offers slots, blackjack, craps, and poker, is open daily, all day (one of its restaurants offers breakfast). There's an admission charge and reservations are necessary for the casino on weekends. The casino is docked in Aurora, 35 miles southwest of the Loop on I-88, along New York Street at the Fox River (phone: 708-801-7000). In the waters off Joliet, the *Empress River Casino* also offers the usual games of chance and numerous places to eat. Its sessions last two hours and departures are throughout the day. The casino is open daily; there's an admission charge. Reservations are necessary on weekend evenings. To get there, take I-55 south of Joliet to the Chanahon exit; the casino is docked along Empress Drive. (phone: 815-744-9400).

LIZZADRO MUSEUM OF LAPIDARY ART Located 45 minutes from Chicago, it has one of the most extensive collections of Oriental jade carvings in the US. About 150 exhibits show off cameos, gemstones, minerals, and fossils. Closed Mondays. No admission charge on Fridays. 220 Cottage Hill Rd., Elmhurst (phone: 630-833-1616).

RAVINIA FESTIVAL It's the place where musical talent, such as the *Chicago Symphony Orchestra* and Ray Charles, is drawn from around the world for open-air concerts in the summer. Locals relish an evening on the 36-acre lawn, to which they bring their own picnics, wine, and candles. There is also a variety of restaurants where visitors can carry out all that's needed for a memorable picnic under the stars or dine in style before taking their seats in the covered pavilion. Open June through *Labor Day.* Admission charge to the park; additional charge for pavilion seats. Reservations advised for pavilion seats. Located on Green Bay and Lake Cook Roads, it's about an hour's drive from the city. Take Edens Expwy., then Rte 41, north to the Ravinia exit; better yet, take the 40-minute ride on *Metra's* Northwestern line, which has a stop right in the park (phone: 847-433-8800).

SIX FLAGS GREAT AMERICA An extravagant roller coaster and a double-tiered carousel are the highlights of this theme park featuring more than 130 rides, shows, and attractions. Musical shows are performed throughout the season, and there's a giant participatory play area for kids, complete with merry-go-rounds and rides. It also is home to the world's largest IMAX movie theater. Open weekends only in May and September; open daily *Memorial Day* through *Labor Day.* Admission charge. Located one hour and fifteen minutes from Chicago, it is off I-94 at Rte. 132 in Gurnee (phone: 847-249-1776).

EXTRA SPECIAL

You don't have to go very far from downtown to reach the North Shore suburbs. Take Sheridan Road north through the lovely old suburbs of Evanston and Winnetka, or follow US 41 or I-94 north. US 41 goes through Lake Forest, an exquisite residential area, and Lake Bluff, site of the *Great Lakes Naval Station.* Along the way, there are several excellent restaurants, especially *Carlos'* (429 Temple Ave., Highland Park; phone: 847-432-0770) and *Froggy's* (306 Green Bay Rd., Highwood; phone: 847-433-7080). In the working-class town of Waukegan, *Mathon's* seafood restaurant has been delighting seafood addicts since before World War II (from Sheridan Rd. turn east on Mathon St., then one block south to Clayton St.; phone: 847-662-3610; closed Mondays). A few miles north on Sheridan Road is the *Illinois Beach State Park,* with a nature refuge offering miles and miles of unspoiled beach (Sheridan and Wadsworth Rds., Zion; phone: 847-662-4811). Heading inland from Waukegan on Route 120 leads directly to lake country. Although the area is not a state park, there are many lakes in the region after Route 120 becomes Route 134. Three large lakes near the Wisconsin border—Fox, Pistakee, and Grass—offer water sports, fishing, golf, and tennis. Right on the Wisconsin border, the 4,900-acre *Chain O'Lakes State Park* has campsites and boat rentals. Pick up Wilson Road north at Long Lake, which is on Route 134, then take Route 132 past Fox Lake. This leads to US 12, which runs to Spring Grove and the state park (phone: 847-587-5512).

Sources and Resources

TOURIST INFORMATION

The *Chicago Visitor Information Center,* in the historic *Water Tower* (N. Michigan Ave. and Pearson St., Chicago, IL 60611; phone: 744-2400), distributes a downtown map that pinpoints major attractions and hotels. You may also get information from the *Chicago Cultural Center* (77 E. Randolph St.; phone: 744-2400). For more information on Illinois, contact the state hotline (phone: 800-223-0121). The *Mayor's Office of Special Events* provides information on listings of special events (phone: 744-3315). Free visitor information packets are available by calling 1-800-2CONNECT.

LOCAL COVERAGE Chicago newspapers are the *Sun-Times* and the *Tribune;* both are morning dailies. Other local publications include the *Reader* and *New City,* two weekly newspapers that have complete listings of events and reliable reviews, and *Chicago* magazine, a monthly whose section of restaurant reviews is the most up-to-date local source on where and what to eat. Also useful are the following *Chicago Transit Authority* publications, available at El and subway stations: the *Chicago Street Directory,* which locates streets by their distance from State Street or Madison Street; the *CTA Route Map* of bus, subway, and El routes; and the *CTA Downtown Transit Map.*

For self-guided walking tours, see Ira J. Bach's architecturally oriented *Chicago on Foot* (Chicago Review; $16.95). For information on ethnic areas, we recommend *Chicago, City of Neighborhoods* by Dominic A. Pacyga and Ellen Skerrett (Loyola University; $22.95). Also, pick up a copy of *ACCESS Chicago* (HarperCollins; $18.50).

TELEVISION STATIONS WBBM Channel 2–CBS; WMAQ Channel 5–NBC; WLS Channel 7–ABC; WGN Channel 9–superstation; WTTW Channel 11–PBS; WFLD Channel 32–Fox.

RADIO STATIONS AM: WMAQ 670 (news); WGN 720 (talk/sports); WBBM 780 (news); WLUP 1000 (rock). FM: WBEZ 91.5 (public radio for Chicago); WNUA 95.5 (smooth jazz); WBBM 96.3 (top 40 dance music); WLUP 97.9 (rock); WFMT 98.7 (classical); WKQX 101.1 (classic rock); WGCI 107.5 (pop/rap).

Chicago also has four 24-hour Spanish language stations: WOJO 105.1 FM, and AM stations WIND 560, WOPA 1200, and WTAQ 1300.

TELEPHONE The area code for Chicago is 312. The area code for the near north and northwest suburbs is 847; for near-west and near-south suburbs, the area code is 708. Unless otherwise indicated, the telephone numbers in this chapter are in the 312 area code.

SALES TAX City sales tax is 9%, and there is a 14.9% hotel tax.

CLIMATE They don't call it the Windy City for nothing. The winter winds are fierce, and wind-chill factors occasionally measure 60F below zero! The optimal visiting season is autumn, when temperatures are in the 50s and 60s F; second-best is spring. Summers are humid, although the temperatures usually don't get higher than the mid-80s.

GETTING AROUND

AIRPORTS *O'Hare International Airport* is about 20 miles northwest of the Loop and, depending on traffic, a 30- to 60-minute ride by cab. *Continental Air Transport* (phone: 454-7800) has van service to the airport from 24 city locations (including all the major hotels) that run approximately every 30 minutes. Ask your hotel concierge for *Continental*'s return schedule; some hotels require that reservations be made in advance. *Chicago Transit Authority* (phone: 836-7000) *O'Hare Blue Line* trains run from several downtown locations on Dearborn Street to *O'Hare's* main terminal in approximately 45 minutes (available daily, 24 hours).

Midway Airport, which handles an increasing volume of domestic traffic, is nine miles south of the Loop. A taxi ride to *Midway* from the Loop will take 20 to 30 minutes. *Chicago Transit Authority* (phone: 836-7000) *Midway Orange Line* trains (available daily from 5:36 AM through 11:36 PM) run on the Loop elevated platform. The trip from the Loop to Midway via train takes about 35 minutes. *Continental Air Transport* (phone: 454-7800) also provides van service to the airport from all major hotels, but reservations must be made in advance. The run to the airport takes 30 to 45 minutes, and the cost is $9.50. There's also a direct *O'Hare Line* train to *Midway Airport;* for information about current fare and schedules, call 836-7000.

BUS/EL/SUBWAY/TRAIN *Chicago Transit Authority* operates bus, subway, and El services (phone: 836-7000). The basic fare is $1.50 (there are discounts for off-hour trips and for seniors). Packs of 10 tokens are available at most currency exchanges and cost only $12.50.

Metra (phone: 322-6900) offers commuter service between various stations in the city and its suburbs. Trains depart from the *North Western Station* (500 W. Madison St.) to the north and northwest suburbs; from *Union Station* (210 S. Canal St.) to the west and southwest suburbs; and from the *Randolph Street Station* (151 E. Randolph St.) and the *LaSalle Street Station* for the south suburbs (phone: 322-6777). *Amtrak* trains (phone: 800-872-7245) depart from *Union Station.*

CAR RENTAL All the major national firms are represented.

TAXI Cabs can be hailed in the street or picked up at stands in front of the major hotels. You also can call one of Chicago's taxi services: *American United* (phone: 248-7600); *Flash Cab* (phone: 561-1444); or *Yellow and Checker Cabs* (phone: TAXI-CAB).

SIGHTSEEING TOURS

BOAT For a river view, *Wendella Sightseeing Boats* (phone: 337-1446), *Mercury Cruise Line* (phone: 332-1353), and the *Odyssey Cruises* (phone: 708-990-0800) offer boat trips on the Chicago River and Lake Michigan daily from mid-April through mid-October. A charter craft, *Engine Company #41,* runs sightseeing excursions on a 92-foot fireboat; call the *Chicago Fire Boat Cruise Company* (phone: 579-1988). The *Spirit of Chicago,* at *Navy Pier* (455 E. Illinois St.; phone: 836-7899), has dining, dancing, and moonlight cruises, as well as narrated tours. Other sightseeing cruise lines include *A Admiral's Sight-Seeing Cruise Line* (phone: 641-7245), *Chicago from the Lake* (phone: 527-2002), and *Shoreline Sightseeing* (phone: 222-9328). The *Chicago*

Architecture Foundation (*CAF;* phone: 922-3432) conducts boat tours of the Chicago River from May through October. Days and times vary and some weekday tours are included, so it is best to call in advance for information on the current schedule (phone: 527-1977). The 90-minute tours leave from North Pier (phone: 922-TOUR for recorded information).

BUS Several private firms offer bus tours around Chicago; call *American Sightseeing Tours* (phone: 251-3100), the *Chicago Gray Line* (phone: 251-3107), and the *Chicago Motor Coach Company* (phone: 922-8919). There's also a do-it-yourself tour by public bus. The No. 151 bus route starts in the Loop, goes through *Lincoln Park,* past the *Historical Society,* and into New Town. When you've had your fill, get off and catch the same bus going in the opposite direction. *Untouchable Tours* (phone: 881-1195) offers a two-hour bus ride through neighborhoods once frequented by Chicago's notorious gangsters. Tours depart from the *Water Tower Pumping Station* (in winter, tours are held only on Wednesdays and weekends). *Chicago Supernatural Tours* (phone: 708-499-0300) offers tours of lurid and legendary sites, including haunted houses, sites of notorious murders, and gangster hideouts. The *Chicago Architecture Foundation* (*CAF,* see above) conducts about 50 different architectural tours of the city. The *CAF* Saturday bus tours depart from 224 South Michigan Avenue (phone: 922-3432). The four-hour tours may be booked in advance, although walk-in visitors are accepted if space is available.

HORSE-DRAWN CARRIAGE If a horse and buggy ride strikes your fancy, contact *J. C. Cutters,* which has a carriage stand at the corner of Superior Street and Michigan Avenue (phone: 664-6014); or *Antique Coach and Carriage* (236 W. Division St.; phone: 735-9400). For a guided tour that highlights Chicago's literary and cultural history, call Leah Axelrod's *My Kind of Tour* (Box 924, Highland Park, IL 60035; phone: 708-432-7003).

HELICOPTER For an aerial view of Chicago, there are helicopter tours, including sunset flights, run by *Head West Sky Operations* (at *Palwauke Regional Airport*; phone: 847-546-3333)

SPECIAL EVENTS

Chicago is a city of year-round festivals, and every season brings a variety of shows and celebrations, many with a special ethnic or cultural focus. If no information number is provided for a particular event, call the city's *Department of Special Events* (phone: 744-3315) for up-to-the-minute details.

The first ethnic celebration of the year is *Chinese New Year* in late January or early February, when all Chinatown turns out for its dragon parade, fireworks, and other festivities.

February brings the *Chicago Folk Festival,* sponsored by the *University of Chicago* and featuring folk music, arts, crafts, and food (phone: 702-9793). February is also *Black History Month,* which is celebrated with special exhibits at the *DuSable Museum* and other cultural institutions throughout the city.

In March, the entire city plunges wholeheartedly into *St. Patrick's Day,* even dyeing the river green for the occasion. The official *St. Patrick's Day Parade,* which runs along Dearborn Avenue from Wacker Drive to Van Buren Boulevard, is held on March 17 (phone: 263-6612). On the Saturday closest to March 17, there is the separate *South Side Irish St. Patrick's Day Parade* (phone: 238-1969).

April ushers in the *Easter Flower Show* held at the *Garfield Park Conservatory* (phone: 294-4770). In heavily Mexican Pilsen, *Easter* is observed with a reenactment of Christ's walk to Calvary on *Good Friday.* In May, the same neighborhood holds a *Cinco de Mayo* (fifth of May) festival celebrating Mexico's successful (if only temporary) repulsion of invading French forces in 1862. Downtown on the first weekend of May, three international art expositions attract dealers from around the world; and the *International Theater Festival,* also in May, draws top international and domestic productions.

In June, the festival season gets into full swing with the two-day *Gospel Festival,* followed a week later by the *Chicago Blues Festival,* both in *Grant Park* (phone: 744-3315). June also brings the *Old Town Art Fair,* which fills block after block of charming Lincoln Park residential streets with artists and craftspeople selling their wares. On *Father's Day,* it's time for the *Printer's Row Book Fair,* when hundreds of new and used book dealers line the streets of the South Loop.

The week-long *Taste of Chicago* begins in June and ends on July 3 with an immense fireworks display. Restaurateurs fill several acres of *Grant Park* with booths offering samples of their wares, and popular radio stations broadcast the nearly continuous music performed on stages up and down the main thoroughfare. The *Chicago Country Music Festival* adds to the festivities, which end with a rousing *Fourth of July* celebration, when the *Grant Park Symphony* performs the "1812 Overture" accompanied by a dazzling fireworks display.

Another event during *Fourth of July* weekend is the *Motorola Western Open Golf Tournament* (phone: 847-724-4600) at Cog Hill in suburban Lemont. Mid-July brings the *Air and Water Show,* which features a display of precision flying; the best place to watch it is North Avenue Beach.

In August, lovely old *Oz Park* (so named because *Wizard of Oz* writer Frank Baum lived there) gives a party that's geared toward children. Other August events are the *Gold Coast Art Fair,* now held in the River North gallery district; the *Venetian Night* parade of colorfully lighted boats through Monroe Street Harbor; the *Bud Billiken Day Parade,* a noisy and joyful celebration of the city's African-American community, held on the South Side (phone: 225-2400); and the *Midwest Buddhist Temple Ginza Holiday,* held in Old Town. On the turf course at *Arlington International Racecourse,* the world's top thoroughbreds compete in the prestigious and colorful *Arlington Million* (phone: 847-255-4300).

Highlights of *Labor Day* weekend include the *Chicago Jazz Festival* (phone: 744-3370); performers at the four-day event have included Ray Charles. Later in September, *"Viva! Chicago,"* a two-day celebration of Latin music, attracts lovers of salsa, merengue, mambo, and samba to *Grant Park* (phone: 744-3315). There's also a celebration modeled after the German *Oktoberfest,* sponsored by the *Berghoff* restaurant (phone: 427-3170) and held on Adams Street from State Street to Dearborn Avenue. During the last weekend of the month, the *Latino Film Festival* runs for 10 days at theaters around the city. Call for locations and film listings (phone: 431-1330 or 935-5744).

October features the last of the year's major parades on *Columbus Day* in the Loop. This is also the month when the city hosts a two-week *International Film Festival,* an annual tradition since 1965. Various theaters on the North Side participate (phone: 644-3400).

November marks the start of the *Michigan Avenue Holiday Lights Festival* (from the Saturday before *Thanksgiving* through December 31); processions of horse-drawn carriages and fireworks add to the festivities along the Magnificent Mile, which glows with holiday lights. During the holiday season, State Street windows get dressed up and the *Goodman Theatre* (phone: 443-3800) presents its now-classic *Christmas Carol.* And, finally, December brings the *Nutcracker* ballet to the *Arie Crown Theater* at *McCormick Place* (phone: 791-6000).

MUSEUMS

In addition to those described in *Special Places,* other museums of interest include the following:

BALZEKAS MUSEUM OF LITHUANIAN CULTURE This unique museum has dolls, textiles, folk art, antique weapons, and a hands-on children's museum. Open daily. Admission charge. 6500 S. Pulaski Rd. (phone: 582-6500).

DUSABLE MUSEUM OF AFRICAN-AMERICAN HISTORY Chicago more than likely is the country's only major city whose first permanent resident was of African descent. Set in the South Side's *Washington Park,* the museum is named after Jean-Baptiste Point duSable, a fur trader from Haiti who settled on the banks of the Chicago River in 1789.

Among the museum's major features are a 10-foot-high carved mahogany mural depicting highlights of African-American history; there also is a large display of African artifacts. Among the changing exhibits are depictions of life in the Caribbean. Open daily. No admission charge on Thursdays. 57th St. at S. Cottage Grove (phone 947-0600).

ERNEST HEMINGWAY MUSEUM Located in suburban Oak Park where the author was born and raised, the museum mounts major exhibitions on Hemingway's life and times and work. Closed Mondays, Tuesdays, Thursdays, and Fridays. Admission charge. 200 N. Oak Park Ave. (phone: 708-848-2222).

MUSEUM OF HOLOGRAPHY More than 150 three-dimensional images created by lasers are displayed. Closed Mondays and Tuesdays. Admission charge. 1134 W. Washington Blvd. (phone: 226-1007).

POLISH MUSEUM OF AMERICA Offers 350 paintings by Polish and Polish-American artists, costumes, and a 30,000-volume library. Closed *Christmas Eve* and *Christmas Day.* No admission charge. 984 N. Milwaukee Ave. (phone: 384-3352).

SPERTUS MUSEUM OF JUDAICA The collection here features displays that span 3,500 years of Jewish history; there's also a display aimed at children that re-creates an archaeological dig. Closed Saturdays, Jewish holidays, and some federal holidays. Admission charge. 618 S. Michigan Ave. (phone: 922-9012).

SWEDISH-AMERICAN MUSEUM Historic documents plus works of famous Swedish artists, including Carl Larson and Anders Zorn; at *Christmas,* there is a traditional Swedish *Festival of Lights* complete with candles, *Christmas* decorations, and songs. Closed Mondays. No admission charge for children under 12. 5211 N. Clark St. (phone: 728-8111).

UKRAINIAN NATIONAL MUSEUM A large collection of folk art, including Ukrainian ceramics, *Easter* eggs, and costumes. Closed Mondays through Wednesdays. Admission charge. 721 N. Oakley Blvd. (phone: 421-8020).

In addition, great sculpture and art can be seen in the plazas of downtown skyscrapers: Harry Bertoia's spellbinding *Sounding Sculpture,* at the *Standard Oil Building* (200 E. Randolph St.); *Flamingo,* a stabile by Alexander Calder, at Federal Center Plaza (Adams and Dearborn Sts.); Calder's gaily colored mobile *Universe,* in the *Sears Tower* lobby (Wacker Dr. and Adams St.); sculptor Claes Oldenburg's 101-foot-high baseball bat, *Batcolumn* (600 W. Madison St.); Marc Chagall's *Four Seasons* mosaic, at First National Plaza (Monroe and Dearborn Sts.); and *Chicago's Picasso* (its formal title because no one could agree on a name), a giant sculpture on the Richard J. Daley Plaza (Washington and Clark Sts.).

And don't miss Chicago's roof art. There are four wind-powered sculptures, each weighing more than a ton, atop the city's *Sporting Club* (211 N. Stetson Dr. near the *Fairmont* hotel). *Children of the Sun,* by Japanese artist Shingu, is made of stainless-steel pipe and punched metal.

MUSIC TO MUNCH BY

If you're at Richard J. Daley Plaza (on Washington and Clark Sts.) at lunchtime, you might catch a free concert. There are noon music and dance performances under the giant *Chicago's Picasso* sculpture two or three days a week from June through September, weather permitting (phone: FINE-ART, i.e., 346-3278, for schedule information).

SHOPPING

Some of Chicago's best sights are indoors, along the aisles of the city's many shops and department stores. While Los Angeles boasts Rodeo Drive and New York has Fifth Avenue, in Chicago the chic shopping district is known as the Magnificent Mile, the blocks along North Michigan Avenue between the Chicago River and Oak Street. Along the Magnificent Mile is *900 North Michigan Avenue,* an enclosed mall of elegant stores; a block away is *Water Tower Place,* another elegant indoor shopping center; and *Chicago Place,* an eight-level enclave of upscale shops, is at 700 North Michigan Avenue. Oak Street, just west of Michigan Avenue, is lined with international designer shops. State Street in the Loop is the setting for *Marshall Field's. T. J. Maxx, Filene's Basement,* and *Toys R Us* are also on this famed shopping street.

North Pier Chicago, a renovated multi-use building that was formerly a shipping terminal, has three floors filled with dozens of unusual shops and restaurants as well as museums and gamerooms. Locals looking for fine jewelry at good prices head for the *Mallers Building* (5 N. Wabash St.), which features 16 floors of retail and wholesale jewelry stores. And Hyde Park, a neighborhood near the *University of Chicago,* is the place for bookworms.

Avid shoppers also trek to the River North district's boutiques (north of the river, west of LaSalle St.); the Armitage/Halsted/Sheffield shops; the stores along Clark Street (in the Fullerton area); and the *Century Mall* (Diversey Pkwy./Clark St.), which was once a movie theater. The *Merchandise Mart,* between Orleans and Wells Streets and the Chicago River, has stores from many of the national chains. Here are some of our favorite Windy City shops.

Accent Chicago Every item in stock has "Chicago" imprinted on it—and we mean everything. *Water Tower Place,* Level 7 (phone: 944-1354); *Sears Tower* (phone: 993-0499); and the *Chicago Hilton and Towers* (phone: 360-0115).

Chicago Architecture Foundation The museum/office has one of the most complete gift shops for those seeking architecture-theme souvenirs. Its book collection is especially impressive. *Santa Fe Bldg.*, 224 S. Michigan Ave. (phone: 922-3431/2); and a store at the *John Hancock Center*, 875 N. Michigan Ave. (phone: 922-3432).

Avventura Some of the showiest men's shoes anywhere, plus more traditional footwear, ties, and belts. It's worth a trip here just to see the giant black cowboy boots with the red bull on front and No. 23 on back, custom designed for Michael Jordan. *Water Tower Place,* Level 4 (phone: 337-3700).

Bloomingdale's The Midwest flagship store for this legendary New York retailer has six floors of merchandise plus four spas and two restaurants. The Art Deco touches are a plus. *900 North Michigan Avenue* (phone: 440-4460).

Bogner A branch of the German retailer specializing in high-end skiwear, cashmere, and leather goods. 56 E. Oak St. (phone: 664-6466).

Bottega Veneta Fine Italian leather items, carefully crafted and tastefully displayed. Everything from luggage to desk accessories, plus a small selection of women's shoes and scarves. 107 E. Oak St. (phone: 664-3220).

C. D. Peacock This landmark, founded the same year as Chicago, in 1837, has purveyed silver, crystal, jewelry, and fine china to Chicagoans ever since. With chandeliers, fine cabinetry, and bronze peacock doors, it's known for its service (and for its expert repair shop). In *Northbrook Court* on Lake Cook Rd., Northbrook (phone: 847-564-8030).

Carson Pirie Scott and Company You can't get any more Chicago than this department store, whose Windy City tradition stretches back more than 130 years. Even if you aren't in a spending mood, stop by to see the elegant building designed at the turn of the century by architect Louis Sullivan (note the distinctive iron ornamentation on the northwest corner). 1 S. State St. (phone: 641-7000).

Cartier The Midwest outpost of the fine French jeweler. 630 N. Michigan Ave. (phone: 266-7440).

Chanel Classic clothes and accessories from this world-famous name. 940 N. Michigan Ave. (phone: 787-5500).

Chiasso Euro-design (largely Italian and contemporary) in fine home furnishings and gifts. *Chicago Place,* 700 N. Michigan Ave. (phone: 642-2808); 231 S. LaSalle St. (phone: 357-0437); and 303 W. Madison St. (phone: 419-1121).

City of Chicago The place for memorabilia and souvenirs, this store carries everything from tote bags to a Chicago manhole cover to the ever-popular Chicago street signs. Pick up one in stock or special order a custom-made sign. 401 E. Illinois St. (phone: 467-1111).

City Source In a century-old building, this shop is chock-full of upscale housewares and decorative items, including photo frames, needlepoint pillows, and pottery. 28 E. Huron (phone: 664-5499).

Crate & Barrel Ten Chicago area stores that purvey everything for the home, from pie plates to pine furniture. The flagship store is a five-story knockout at 646 N. Michigan Ave. (phone: 787-5900).

Elements The last word in designer housewares and jewelry by international artisans. 102 E. Oak St. (phone: 642-6574).

Famous Fido's Just about everything for dogs and cats, including the "Famous Fido's Doggie Deli" with a dining area and carryout of all-natural dog food, pet treats, and cakes. 1533 W. Devon Ave. (phone: 973-3436).

Fannie May Chicago's favorite chocolates for more than seven decades are sold in more than 100 shops around the city. Best-known outlet: *Water Tower Place* (phone: 664-0420).

FAO Schwarz Kiddie heaven, with dolls, stuffed animals, and video games galore. Grownups don't have a bad time here, either. *Water Tower Place,* Level 2 (phone: 787-8894) and 840 N. Michigan Ave. (phone: 587-5000).

Flashback Retro collectibles from television shows of the 1960s and 1970s, including "Lost in Space" and "Rocky and Bullwinkle" lunch boxes, "I Dream of Jeannie" dolls, and the poster that made Farrah Fawcett an overnight pinup girl. 3450 N. Clark St. (phone: 929-5060).

Gianni Versace This Italian designer's two-story boutique is stocked with his latest European fashions. 101 E. Oak St. (phone: 337-1111).

Giorgio Armani The noted Milanese designer offers his beautifully tailored *haute* threads to fashion-savvy devotees of both sexes. This is the only source of Armani *couture* collections between the coasts. 113 E. Oak St. (phone: 427-6264).

Godiva Chocolatier For those with a taste for sumptuous sweets. If chocolate is not your fatal attraction, try the rich cappuccino and espresso at this shop in *Water Tower Place,* Level 3 (phone: 280-1133).

Gucci The fine Italian leather emporium, with merchandise ranging from men's and women's sportswear and shoes to key rings. *900 North Michigan Avenue* (phone: 664-5504).

Hammacher Schlemmer Everything imaginable in elegant and unique gifts, from heated pet beds to a personalized Wurlitzer to a wide variety of kitchen and electronic gadgets. 445 N. Michigan Ave. (phone: 527-9100).

Henri Bendel Designer women's fashions, including sportswear, business clothing, and eveningwear. *900 North Michigan Avenue* (phone: 642-0140).

Illinois Artisans Shop A wide variety of items made by the state's top craftspeople. *Thompson Building,* 100 W. Randolph St. (phone: 814-5321).

Isis Unusual fashions for women, all in one-size-fits-all, including hand-painted items, fringed jackets, and parachute-silk skirts. 38 E. Oak St. (phone: 664-7076).

Krivoy Named for her grandmother, Cynthia Hadesman's shop offers dresses, skirts, and hats whose styles run the gamut from contemporary to antique. 1145 W. Webster Ave. (phone: 248-1466).

Mallers Building This 21-story office building has 16 floors of retail and wholesale jewelers. Here shoppers can buy diamonds, get a watch repaired, sell silver and gold, and have a favorite piece engraved. Stop on the third floor to visit a genuine old-time deli with great cheese blintzes and potato pancakes. 5 N. Wabash St.

Marshall Field's This Chicago landmark offers everything from rare books and Frango mints to wardrobe coordinators and foreign language translators.

111 N. State St. (phone: 781-1000). A second downtown location is at *Water Tower Place* (phone: 781-1000). See also *Special Places*.

Material Possessions Designer table settings, unique jewelry, and one-of-a-kind home accessories, all presented in chic surroundings. 54 E. Chestnut St. (phone: 280-4885).

Museum Shop of the Art Institute of Chicago Mobiles, stained glass, books, note cards, calendars, and a variety of high-quality gifts, including faithful reproductions of works in the museum's collection, are sold. An extensive stock of jewelry is especially worth inspecting. On *Valentine's Day*, a calligrapher is on hand to personalize cards. N. Michigan Ave. at Adams St. (phone: 443-3534).

NBC Store The *NBC Tower* houses a shop that carries NBC memorabilia, plus T-shirts emblazoned with the names of your favorite TV shows. 454 N. Columbus Dr. (phone: 836-5555).

Nicole Miller Novelty print silk scarves and ties, plus eveningwear for men and women. 61 E. Oak St. (phone: 664-3532).

Nike Town The latest in shoes and sportswear in a visually dramatic setting, surely worth a visit if not a purchase. 669 N. Michigan Ave. (phone: 642-6363).

North Beach Leather Trendy leather fashions for men and women; repair service, too. *Water Tower Place*, Level 3 (phone: 280-9292).

Nuts on Clark Nuts, coffee, wine, exotic teas, fruit, and chocolate are featured at this 30,000-square-foot store, just two blocks north of *Wrigley Field*. 3830 N. Clark (phone: 549-6622).

Pavo Real Boutique Sweaters from Peru and Bolivia plus handmade jewelry crafted by local and international artists. *900 North Michigan Avenue* (phone: 944-1390).

Sony Gallery of Consumer Electronics For sampling and buying the latest in electronic marvels for business and entertainment. 633 N. Michigan Ave. (phone: 943-3334).

Tiffany & Co. The Midwest branch of the place where Audrey Hepburn breakfasted. 715 N. Michigan Ave. (phone: 944-7500).

Ultimo Men's designer fashions; plus women's apparel, shoes, and jewelry. 114 E. Oak St. (phone: 787-0906).

A Unique Presence Exceptional crafts and gifts in a year-round art fair atmosphere. Unusual items from more than 300 North American artists. 2121 N. Clybourn Ave. (phone: 929-4292).

Waterstone's One of the two US branches of the famous British bookseller specializing in literature, art and travel books, history, and biography. 840 N. Michigan Ave. (phone: 587-8080).

Women & Children First The only truly feminist bookstore in the city offers regular book signings and special events linked to feminism in literature. 5233 N. Clark St. (phone: 769-9299).

WTTW Store of Knowledge Affiliated with the local public television station, this store sells fun, learning-focused games, books, and videos. *Water Tower Place,* Level 7 (phone: 642-6826).

CLOSE ENCOUNTERS

If you don't want to traipse but still want to take advantage of Chicago's chic stores, call any of the city's major department stores for personal shoppers. The personal shoppers at *Neiman Marcus* even make house (or hotel) calls. *Bloomingdale's* has separate personal shopper services for men and women.

SPORTS AND FITNESS

There's plenty of professional sports action in town year-round.

BASEBALL The *White Sox* play at *Comiskey Park* (35th and Shields, off the Dan Ryan Expwy.; phone: 924-1000). Seating 43,500 spectators, this state-of-the-art park is equipped with efficient escalators and elevators, plus numerous services and concessions for the fans. The *Cubs* play at *Wrigley Field* (Addison and Clark Sts.; phone: 404-2827), now also at night.

BASKETBALL The *NBA*'s Chicago *Bulls* play at the *United Center* (1800 W. Madison St.; phone: 733-5300).

BICYCLING Chicago has a glorious bike path along the shore of Lake Michigan, running from the Loop to the North Side—about six miles. You can rent bikes in summer from *Village Cycle Center,* 1337 N. Wells St. (phone: 751-2488). For more information about cycling, contact the *Chicagoland Bicycle Federation* (phone: 427-3325).

BOCCE Remember how good Marlon Brando looked playing this Italian bowling game in *The Godfather*? Nearly 400 members of the *Highland Bocce Club* gather at *Highwood Bocce Court* (440 Bank La.; phone: 847-432-9804), beneath an Italian deli and the train tracks, to play in good weather. There are also *bocce* courts at three city parks: *McGuane* (290 S. Poplar Ave.), *Riis* (6110 W. Fullerton Ave.), and *Smith* (2526 W. Grand Ave.).

BOWLING Turn back the clock 35 years and try *Southport Lanes* (3325 N. Southport Ave.; phone: 472-1601), where boys still set pins for the four alleys. Some Chicagoans rate this as the best of its kind. For 24-hour-a-day bowling, try *Waveland* (3700 N. Western Ave.; phone: 472-5900).

CRICKET Games sponsored by the *United Cricket Conference* (phone: 684-6530) are played Sundays at noon from mid-May through mid-September in *Washington Park* (55th St. and King Dr.; phone: 684-6530).

FISHING In summer, people flock to the rocks and piers along the shore, casting lines for a variety of fresh fish. In April, the smelt run draws hundreds to the shore with their nets. The rocks around *Northwestern University at Evanston* are especially popular.

FITNESS CENTERS *Combined Fitness Centre* (1235 N. LaSalle St.; phone: 787-8400) admits non-members for a fee, as does the health club at the *Chicago Hilton and Towers* hotel (see *Checking In*).

FOOTBALL The *NFL Bears* (phone: 294-2200) play at *Soldier Field* (Lake Shore Dr. south of Roosevelt Rd.; phone: 663-5922).

GOLF Chicago has 18 public golf courses, some along the lakeshore. The most accessible municipal courses are *Marowitz,* traditionally known as *Waveland,* a nine-hole course in *Lincoln Park* (3700 N. Waveland Ave.); and *Illinois Center Golf* (221 N. Columbus Dr.; phone: 616-1234), a new nine-hole course downtown. *Illinois Center Golf* and the *Chicago Park District* (phone: 753-8670) both offer lessons.

HIKING The *Forest Preserve District* for Cook and Du Page Counties offers numerous places to hike (phone: 847-366-9420). The *Sierra Club* (506 S. Wabash St.; phone: 431-0158) also organizes outings.

HOCKEY The *NHL Blackhawks* play in the *United Center* (1800 W. Madison St.; phone: 733-5300).

HORSE RACING Thoroughbreds race at four tracks in the Chicago area: *Arlington Park* (Euclid Ave. and Wilke Rd., Arlington Heights; phone: 847-255-4300); *Hawthorne* (3501 S. Laramie, Cicero; phone: 708-780-3700); *Maywood Park* (North and 5th Aves., Maywood; phone: 626-4816); and *Sportsman's Park* (3301 S. Laramie, Cicero; phone: 708-652-2812).

ICE SKATING Once temperatures dip below 45F, ice skating begins at Daley Bicentennial Plaza (337 E. Randolph St.; phone: 294-4790) and *Block 37* in the Loop (State and Washington Sts.; phone: 744-2893). There also is ice skating year-round at the indoor rink at *McFetridge Sports Center* (3843 N. California Ave.; phone: 478-0211). Skate rentals are available at all three.

JOGGING There's a jogging path along the entire lakeshore from *Jackson Park* north to *Lincoln Park,* accessible via numerous pedestrian walkways.

POLO Matches are held in the summer at the *Oak Brook Polo Club* (3500 Midwest Ave., Oak Brook; phone: 708-990-POLO).

SAILING Lake Michigan offers superb sailing, but as experienced sailors can tell you, the lake is deceptive. Storms with winds of up to 40 knots can blow in suddenly. Check with the Coast Guard before going out (phone: 708-251-0185).

SKIING There are more than 50 ski clubs in the Chicago area. For information, contact the *Chicago Metro Ski Council* (PO Box 7926, Chicago, IL 60680; phone: 346-1268).

SOCCER Montrose, with four fields, is *the* soccer place. Walk up the 32-foot Cricket Hill for a bird's-eye view of the games. The *International Soccer League* plays on Sundays; the less popular, though equally enthusiastic, *Central American Soccer League* plays Saturdays. Weekend games start in the summer and run through October.

SWIMMING Beaches line the shore of Lake Michigan. Those just to the north of the Loop off Lake Shore Drive are the most popular and often the most crowded. *Oak Street Beach* (at the top of Michigan Avenue) and *North Beach* (1600 North Ave.) afford swimming with skyscrapers as a backdrop; admission is free. If you go farther north, you'll find fewer people. The most accessible public beach outside the city is in north suburban Wilmette. There's an admission charge.

TENNIS The city has 708 outdoor municipal courts, including two downtown facilities. The better of the two (by far) consists of 12 well-lit clay courts at Daley Bicentennial Plaza, in the northern end of *Grant Park* (337 E. Randolph St.) near several residential high-rises. The courts are open daily. Reservations are necessary; there's a court fee (phone: 294-4790).

TOBOGGANING The *Cook County Forest Preserve District* operates 14 slides at five locations daily when the weather allows. Equipment rentals are available (phone: 708-366-9420).

THEATERS

For schedules and tickets, call the *League of Chicago Theatres' Hot Tix Hotline* (phone: 977-1755), or visit a *Hot Tix* booth (108 N. State St.; in Evanston, at the Sherman Ave. municipal parking garage between Church and Davis Sts.; in Oak Park, at 158 Forest Ave.; in Arlington Heights, at the *Metra* train station at 19 E. Northwest Hwy.; and at many *Rose Records* stores throughout the Chicago area). Full-price, advance-sale tickets are available by phone or at a *Hot Tix* booth. Half-price day-of-sale tickets are sold for cash only at the booths on Mondays through Saturdays (Wednesdays through Saturdays at Evanston, Arlington Heights, and Oak Park locations); half-price Sunday tickets are sold at the booths the day before. *Ticketmaster's Chicago Arts Line* (phone: 902-1500) takes phone orders for full-price, advance-sale tickets for an additional surcharge—which varies depending on the specific show.

Chicago's thriving theater scene breaks down into two camps: eclectic showcases for homegrown talent, and Broadway-caliber commercial houses. Listed below are two of our favorite Chicago venues.

CENTER STAGE

Goodman Theatre The second-oldest regional theater in the country, the *Goodman* mounts frequent productions of works by living writers, brings classics in eye-opening ways, and stages that colorful favorite, *A Christmas Carol,* at the end of the year. There are actually two theaters housed here: the *Studio,* which seats 135, and the *Mainstage,* which seats 683. Between the two theaters, eight to 10 plays are produced annually; because the productions are usually well received (and have long runs), the season extends throughout the year. 200 S. Columbus Dr. (phone: 443-3800).

Organic Theater Dedicated to producing world premiere theater, from the science fiction trilogy *Warp!* to the pirate epic *Bloody Bess,* award-winning *Adventures of Huckleberry Finn,* baseball comedy *Bleacher Bums, Do the White Thing, E/R Emergency Room* (which ran for four years), and an adaptation of Clive Barker's horror tale *In the Flesh,* the *Organic* has explored the full range of theatrical expression. David Mamet's *Sexual Perversity in Chicago* started out here, too. Every Saturday morning brings the *Cookie Crumb Club,* a participatory sing-along for young audiences and their grown-up friends. Closed Mondays. 3319 N. Clark St. (phone: 327-5588).

Steppenwolf Theatre Chicago's acclaimed pipeline to both Hollywood and Broadway, this homegrown company launched the careers of John Malkovich and Emmy-winner Laurie Metcalf (of "Roseanne" fame); Garry Marshall and Steve Martin have developed original plays for the cutting-edge *Steppenwolf* troupe. The company's production of *The Grapes of Wrath* won it a Tony, and its New York production of *The Song of Jacob Zulu* (which featured the South African group *Ladysmith Black Mambazo*) earned raves. In addition to its excellent ensemble, *Steppenwolf* boasts one of the city's finest (and newest) theaters. Each year the company produces five or six mainstage shows and a smattering of smaller workshop performances. 1650 N. Halsted St. (phone 335-1650).

Other Chicago theatrical troupes include the *Victory Gardens Theater* (2261 N. Lincoln Ave.; phone: 871-3000), dedicated to staging plays by such local playwrights as James Sherman (*Beau Jest*) and John Logan (*Hauptmann*); the funky *Remains Theatre* (phone: 335-9595), known for its talented artists as well as its laid-back attitude; the *Pegasus Players* (1145 W. Wilson Ave.; phone: 271-2638), renowned for their productions of Stephen Sondheim musicals; *Shakespeare Repertory* (1016 N. Dearborn St.; phone: 642-2273), which focuses exclusively on the Bard's works; and *City Lit Theater Company* (410 S. Michigan Ave.; phone: 913-9446), which specializes in adapting works of literature for the stage. Several local troupes share space in the *Theatre Building* (1225 W. Belmont Ave.; phone: 327-5252); it's worth a quick call to find out what's playing there.

The main commercial theaters are the *Auditorium Theater* (50 E. Congress Pkwy.; phone: 922-4046; 922-2110 for performance information);

the *Shubert* (22 W. Monroe St.; phone: 977-1700); the *Apollo Theater Center* (2540 N. Lincoln Ave.; phone: 935-6100); the *Briar Street Theatre* (3133 N. Halsted St.; phone: 348-4000); and the *Wellington Theater* (750 W. Wellington St.; phone: 975-7171). The *Mayfair Theatre* at the *Blackstone* hotel (636 S. Michigan Ave.; phone: 786-9120) presents *Shear Madness,* a comedic mystery involving audience participation, nightly except Tuesdays.

Dinner-theaters include the *Drury Lane South* (2500 W. 95th, Evergreen Park; phone: 708-422-0404); *Marriott's Lincolnshire Theatre* (10 Marriott Dr., Lincolnshire; phone: 708-634-0200); *Pheasant Run* (*Pheasant Run Lodge,* Rte. 64, St. Charles; phone: 708-584-6300); and the *Candlelight Playhouse,* the nation's first dinner-theater (5620 S. Harlem Ave. in Summit; phone: 708-496-3000).

Chicago's arts and theater community in recent years has given more attention to poets with innovative forums called "Poetry Slams." In the best beat tradition, Chicago's top performance poets listen, read, and compete at the nationally recognized *Uptown Poetry Slam,* held Sundays at the *Green Mill* cocktail lounge (4802 N. Broadway; phone: 878-5552). The *West Side Poetry Slam* is geared toward a more genteel audience, which is encouraged to participate on Tuesdays at *Fitzgerald's* (6615 W. Roosevelt Rd. in Berwyn; phone: 708-788-2118).

Fans of classic, foreign, or art films will find them at *Facets Multimedia* (1517 W. Fullerton Ave.; phone: 281-4114); the *Film Center of the Art Institute* (Columbus Dr. at Jackson Blvd.; phone: 443-3737); and *Fine Arts Theater* (418 S. Michigan Ave.; phone: 939-3700). For a golden-age film experience, try the *Music Box,* with its mammoth screen, sky ceiling with twinkling stars and moving clouds, dramatic lobby—and great popcorn. Films shown here are Hollywood standards, foreign fare, and some independents (3733 N. Southport Ave.; phone: 871-6604). The *Biograph,* where John Dillinger was gunned down, also still shows films (2433 N. Lincoln Ave.; phone: 348-4123).

MUSIC

Good music (and lots of it) abounds all over the city. The world-renowned *Chicago Symphony Orchestra,* under the baton of Daniel Barenboim, can be heard from late June at *Orchestra Hall,* a National Landmark building (220 S. Michigan Ave.; phone: 435-6666). The orchestra also plays at the *Ravinia Festival* (1575 Oakwood Ave.; phone: 708-433-8800) outside the city in Highland Park during the summer months; also see *Music Festivals: Summers of Sound,* in DIVERSIONS. Don't miss the *Grant Park Symphony,* which plays four times weekly in the summer under the stars along Lake Michigan. Concerts are free; audiences usually pack picnic dinners and sit out on the lawn. Another favorite is the *Chicago Sinfonietta,* a professional orchestra that performs classical, romantic, and contemporary music at *Orchestra Hall* on the campus of *Rosary College* (7900 W. Division St. in River Forest; phone: 708-366-1062).

Some of the hottest tickets in town from September through February are for performances of the *Lyric Opera of Chicago,* which stages classics and new productions at the *Civic Opera House* (20 N. Wacker Dr.; phone: 332-2244). *Performing Arts Chicago* (phone: 242-6237) presents classical and avant-garde music concerts at venues throughout the city. From February through May, you can hear the *Chicago Opera Theater* (4140 W. Fullerton Ave.; phone: 292-7578), which performs operas in English.

As for dance, *Ballet Chicago* presents classical ballet; the *Hubbard Street Dance Company* and the *Joel Hall Dance Company* are known for jazz; modern dance is the forte of the *Joseph Holmes Dance Company*; and the *Chicago Repertory Dance Ensemble* stages classical and modern dance. Each spring the *Civic Theater* (20 N. Wacker Dr.; phone: 332-2244) presents a series of dance performances featuring local troupes and internationally renowned companies, such as the *American Ballet Theater.* The *Dance Center of Columbia College* (4730 N. Sheridan; phone: 271-7928) highlights contemporary, modern, and avant-garde dance performances throughout the year. For the current schedule of dance events, call the *Chicago Dance Coalition*'s 24-hour information line (phone: 419-8383).

NIGHTCLUBS AND NIGHTLIFE

Don't leave the Windy City without taking in some of its fine blues, jazz, reggae, and folk music. Or try an offbeat bar, a neighborhood sports pub, or a comedy club in one of the few Midwest cities where nightlife lasts until dawn.

Chicago's blues tradition is revered, and some of the country's finest blues performers can be found in a handful of clubs around the city. *Blue Chicago* (736 N. Clark St.; phone: 642-6261) books a lot of notable female performers, as does its sister bar, *Blue Chicago on Clark* (536 N. Clark St.; phone: 661-0100). Crowded *B.L.U.E.S.* (2519 N. Halsted St.; phone: 528-1012) is built around solid blues acts and a lively environment; its roomier relative, *B.L.U.E.S. Etcetera* (1124 W. Belmont Ave.; phone: 525-8989), books major acts like Bo Diddley and Albert King. At *Buddy Guy's Legends,* in the former home of Chess Records (754 S. Wabash Ave.; phone: 427-0333), bluesman Guy holds court over new and veteran performers. But Chicago's standout blues club is *Kingston Mines* (2548 N. Halsted St.; phone: 477-4646), where local blues musicians—and celebrities—go after other clubs have closed. Blues enthusiasts may also want to venture to the South Side's haven, the *Checkerboard Lounge* (423 E. 43rd St.; phone 624-3240), or to the West Side to check out *Rosa's* (3420 W. Armitage Ave.; phone: 342-0452), Chicago's friendliest blues bar.

As strong as the city's blues legacy is its love of jazz. At *Andy's Lounge,* (11 E. Hubbard St.; phone: 642-6805) patrons dressed in anything from T-shirts to pinstripes enjoy jazz at lunchtime (live music starts at noon) and after work (sets start at 5 PM). The *Cotton Club* (1710 S. Michigan Ave.; phone: 341-9787) is decorated with photos of the stars of the original Harlem club. Joe Segal's *Jazz Showcase* at the *Blackstone* hotel (636 S. Michigan Ave.; phone: 427-4846) draws such top jazz performers as McCoy Tyner and Dorothy Donegan. The *Green Mill* cocktail lounge (4802 N. Broadway; phone: 878-5552) looks like the Al Capone haunt it once was, with an ornate interior and live jazz six nights a week. As its name suggests, the *Gold Star Sardine Bar* (680 N. Lake Shore Dr.; phone: 664-4215) is ultra-tiny, but attracts big names—Liza, Tony, and Frank have all stopped by to give unannounced performances.

Jazz also reigns supreme at *Pops for Champagne* (2934 N. Sheffield Ave.; phone: 472-1000), an upscale jazz club with a formal French garden and a choice of champagnes to sip while you relax and listen. The crowd from *Pops* pops across the street for more jazz and acoustic rock at *Oz* (2917 N. Sheffield; phone: 975-8100). *Toulouse* (49 W. Division St.; phone: 944-2606) has an intimate piano bar, and *Yvette* (1206 N. State St.; phone: 280-1700) features enthusiastic twin piano duets, while its sister establishment, *Yvette Wintergarden* (311 S. Wacker Dr.; phone: 408-1242), offers combos for dancing. The intimate *Toulouse Cognac Bar* (2140 N. Lincoln Park W.; phone: 665-9071 or 665-9073) is a cozy haven for jazz lovers, with award-winning violinist Johnny Frigo taking requests on Monday evenings.

North Clark Street is to reggae what North Halsted Street is to blues. A Caribbean pub-crawl might begin at the *Wild Hare* (3530 N. Clark; phone: 327-4273). Cross the street to find *Exedus II* (3477 N. Clark St.; phone 348-3998). Local and international reggae bands perform at both bars seven nights a week.

The *Old Town School of Folk Music* (909 W. Armitage Ave.; phone: 525-7793) is Chicago's premier folk music venue and also sponsors frequent concerts by musicians from South America, Africa, and Europe. The *Abbey Pub* (3420 W. Grace St.; phone: 478-4408) is the place for traditional Irish music, and at *No Exit* (6970 N. Glenwood St.; phone: 743-3355), folk musicians perform while the crowd sips java and plays chess (6970 N. Glenwood; phone: 743-3355).

Chicago's lively dance spots range from the mega-clubs (huge playhouses with separate rooms for dancing, live music, games, or conversing) housed in warehouses west of the Loop to little neighborhood bars. The most chic of the big clubs is *Drink* (541 W. Fulton St.; phone: 441-0818), where Chicago's celebrities and "beautiful people" go to be seen. Hammocks swing from the ceiling, and there's a VIP room with a cozy fireplace. *Ka-Boom!* (747 N. Green St.; phone: 243-8600) has a two-level dance floor and a kooky cabaret lounge with giant teacup-shape booths. A giant dance floor dominates *Crobar* (1543 N. Kingsbury; phone: 587-1313). Salsa aficionados will love *De Cache* (2047 W. Milwaukee Ave.; phone: 489-9600).

Smaller but equally lively dance clubs abound. The DJs at the *Artful Dodger* (1734 W. Wabansia Ave.; phone: 227-6859) spin everything from 1960s British rock to world beat to high-energy dance tracks. *Red Dog* (1958 W. North Ave.; phone: 278-1009) is a spacious second-story dance club that overlooks the funkiest intersection in artsy *Wicker Park. Neo* (2350 N. Clark St.; phone: 528-2622) offers a different theme each night. *Berlin* (954 W. Belmont Ave.; phone: 348-4975) draws an especially flamboyant crowd. Though primarily a restaurant, *Bossa Nova* (see *Eating Out*) has a small dance floor and live reggae and salsa music nightly.

More informal pubs and taverns include *Sheffield's Wine and Beer Garden* (3258 N. Sheffield Ave.; phone: 281-4989), which has an extensive selection of exotic and imported and domestic micro-brewed beers; the fireplace in the back café and poolroom keeps things cozy in wintertime. Also try *John Barleycorn Memorial Pub* (658 W. Belden; phone: 348-8899) where classical music soothes patrons trying any of 30 imported beers against a backdrop of prints of famous paintings and sculptures; in the summer, it has the city's most attractive outdoor beer garden. *Lucky's* (213 W. Institute Pl.; phone: 751-7777) is the trendy hangout of the young and beautiful, most of whom show up in something expensive and black. Sports bars are also plentiful. In the shadow of *Wrigley Field, Hi-Tops* (3551 N. Sheffield Ave.; phone: 348-0009) is the largest in town. There's also *Justin's* (3358 N. Southport Ave.; phone: 929-4844), with two satellite dishes and six TV sets; and *McGee's* (950 W. Webster; phone: 871-4272) where the folks behind the bar say you can request any game you want on the projection TV set in the back room.

Though the video sing-along craze started in Japan, *karaoke* (which means "empty orchestra") has caught on here in the Midwest. The most popular *karaoke* bars in Chicago are *Who's Next* (711 N. State St.; phone: 943-8780) and *Kerrigan's* (2310 W. Lawrence Ave.; phone: 334-0620).

Two-steppers and line-dancing fans can strut their spurs at several country music clubs about town. The clubs offer free lessons at least one night a week. *Bub City* (901 W. Weed St.; phone: 266-1200) and *Whiskey River* (1997 N. Clybourn Ave.; phone: 528-3400) are the premier country dance bars in the city; *Cadillac Ranch* (1175 W. Lake St., Bartlett; phone: 708-830-7200) is another fun place.

COMEDY CLUBS

Chicago has been a comedy center since the 1959 founding of the *Second City* comedy club, whose graduates include Joan Rivers, David Steinberg, and much of the cast of "Saturday Night Live," including the Belushi brothers and Bill Murray. *Second City* and its spin-off, *Second City E.T.C.,* are located at 1608 and 1616 North Wells Street, respectively (phone: 337-3992). Meanwhile, the *Comedy Womb* is a star-making club above the *Pines* restaurant (8030 W. Ogden St. in Lyons; phone: 708-442-0200), and *Zanies* (1548 N. Wells St.; phone: 337-4027) offers the best of the locals as well as such national talent as Richard Lewis. The *Improv* (504 N. Wells St.; phone: 782-6387), with 400 seats, features national acts as well as up-and-coming talent. Said to be giving *Second City* stiff competition is the *Annoyance Theater* (3747 N. Clark St.; phone: 929-6200), a group of loonies who put on such bizarre productions as *Manson: The Musical* and *Coed Prison Sluts* at their makeshift theater.

Best in Town

CHECKING IN

There are quite a number of interesting hotels in Chicago, varying in style from the intimate clubbiness of the *Tremont* and the *Talbott* to the super-modern elegance of the *Four Seasons, Ritz-Carlton,* and *Sutton Place.* Unless otherwise noted, all listed here have at least one restaurant; the choice of eating places normally increases with the price of a room and the size of the hotel. Big hotels have shops, meeting places, and nightly entertainment. All hotels have air conditioning, private baths, TV sets, and telephones unless otherwise mentioned. Most of Chicago's major hotels have complete facilities for the business traveler. Those hotels listed below as having "business services" usually offer such conveniences as meeting rooms, photocopiers, computers, translation services, and express checkout, among others. Call the hotel for additional information.

Rates in Chicago are higher than in most other Midwestern cities: Expect to pay \$180 to \$250 for a double room in expensive hotels; \$100 to \$160 in those classified as moderate; and from \$50 to \$90 in those listed as inexpensive. If money is no object, ask for a room with a view. North Michigan Avenue hotels are close to the Gold Coast, *Lincoln Park,* and *Water Tower Place;* Loop locations (about 10 minutes away by taxi) are convenient to businesses and the fine old downtown department stores.

For bed and breakfast accommodations, contact *Bed and Breakfast Chicago* (PO Box 14088, Chicago, IL 60614; phone: 951-0085). They also rent homes and apartments while their owners are away. Units are available in the downtown, Near North, Lakeshore, Lincoln Park, and nearby neighborhoods at prices starting at \$55 per person per night.

The city government, in conjunction with dozens of hotels, offers special winter rates from September through March. The *Chicago Office of Tourism* (phone: 744-2400) can provide a list of hotels with reduced rates or special packages for visitors during the winter (or off-season). There are also many hotels in the suburbs, most located near office complexes and major highway interchanges. The major chains have hotels at or near *O'Hare Airport* and along the TriState Tollway; a few are listed below. Rates tend to be lower outside the city limits.

All hotels below are in Chicago and telephone and fax numbers are in the 312 area code unless otherwise indicated.

EXPENSIVE

Ambassador West: A Grand Heritage Hotel This historic hotel on the Gold Coast was built in 1924; its 216 rooms were renovated in 1989. Staying here offers a taste of living in Chicago's most elegant neighborhood; down the street and around the corner are blocks of turn-of-the-century homes; you're also steps away from the nightlife on Division Street and a brisk walk from North Michigan Avenue. Amenities include a restaurant, a concierge, a gift shop, business services, room service, and parking (for an additional fee). Weekend packages are available year-round and include a horse-drawn carriage ride. 1300 N. State Pkwy. (phone: 787-3700; 800-437-4824; fax: 640-2967).

Chicago Hilton and Towers This elegantly renovated 30-story hotel features 1,620 rooms, the most lavish of which is the two-story Conrad Hilton Suite for $4,000 a night. Restored to their 1927 grandeur are the Great Hall and the Versailles-inspired Grand Ballroom. Facilities include an extensive fitness center and a computerized business center. Large groups of enthusiastic conventioneers can make it difficult to feel comfortable without a name tag. There are five restaurants including *Kitty O'Shea's Pub* for authentic Irish fare and music, too. There's a 140,000-square-foot convention center and a self-parking garage. Amenities include 24-hour room service, a concierge, and family-oriented activities. Business services are available. In the South Loop area. 720 S. Michigan Ave. (phone: 922-4400; 800-HILTONS; fax: 922-5240).

Claridge With 174 rooms and six suites (three with wood-burning fireplaces), this well-situated property is 10 minutes from the Gold Coast and steps away from Astor Street's elegance and Division Street's bars. For fine international cuisine try the hotel's *Passports* restaurant. Health club facilities are available nearby. Business services are also available. 1244 N. Dearborn St. (phone: 787-4980; 800-245-1258; fax: 266-0978).

Drake A 535-room institution, with a graciousness not often found in hotels these days. The *Cape Cod Room* (see *Eating Out*) is a favorite seafood eatery, and the *Oak Terrace* has a fine view of the Gold Coast. The hotel has 24-hour room service, a concierge, and business services. In the North Michigan Avenue area. 140 E. Walton St. (phone: 787-2200; 800-55-DRAKE; fax: 787-1431).

Fairmont Opulent and sophisticated, its 700 rooms and suites overlook the city skyline and Lake Michigan. Located in *Illinois Center* between the Chicago River and *Grant Park*, it features such appointments as marble bathrooms equipped with TV sets, telephones, and lighted dressing tables. Amenities include 24-hour room service, two restaurants including the superb *Entre Nous* for its fine French cuisine, an elegant nightclub, a concierge, and business services. In the Loop. 200 N. Columbus Dr. (phone: 565-8000; 800-527-4727; fax: 856-9020).

Four Seasons One of the city's most luxurious hotels occupies 19 floors of a stunning high-rise that also is home to the local branch of *Bloomingdale's* and numerous other classy emporia. There are 344 rooms (more than a third boast separate sitting rooms), an opulent Presidential Suite, and 16 residential apartments in this member of what is arguably the best-managed hotel group in the world. *Seasons* restaurant serves exquisitely prepared nouvelle American dishes (see *Eating Out*). Guest facilities include two-line telephones, lighted makeup mirrors, a spa, a sauna, and an indoor swimming pool. Other amenities are 24-hour room service, a concierge, and business services. This is a luxury hotel worthy of the adjective. In the North Michigan Avenue area. 120 E. Delaware Pl. (phone: 280-8800; 800-332-3442; fax: 280-9184).

Hyatt on Printer's Row A *National Register of Historic Places* building in the Printer's Row District, it boasts an elegant green-and-black lobby. Each of the 161 rooms has 13-foot ceilings, large loft-style windows, and an oversize bathroom of travertine marble, complete with a phone and color TV. Guests can enjoy dining at the first-rate *Prairie* restaurant (see *Eating Out*). Other amenities include a concierge, complimentary morning newspaper, and business services. In the South Loop area. 500 S. Dearborn St. (phone: 986-1234; 800-233-1234; fax: 939-2468).

Hyatt Regency Chicago With 2,019 rooms in two ultramodern towers, this leading convention hotel is conveniently located between the Loop and North Michigan Avenue, just south of the Chicago River. There's fine dining at *All-Seasons Café,* and the *Big Bar* has the city's most intoxicating view. Amenities include 24-hour room service, a concierge, and business services. 151 E. Wacker Dr. (phone: 565-1234; 800-233-1234; fax: 565-2966).

Inter-Continental A restoration has enhanced the sophisticated Biedermeier-style rooms and suites that distinguished the old *Medinah Athletic Club.* Built during the crash of 1929, the club has been transformed into a 341-room hotel overlooking Michigan Avenue. Butlers serve afternoon tea in a lobby sitting room. Guests may use the health club, which boasts a mosaic-tiled indoor swimming pool that was once the training site for Olympic gold medalist and future Tarzan Johnny Weissmuller. The hotel's first-floor bar and salon serve cocktails; the latter also serves afternoon tea. During summer, a sidewalk café off the salon serves lunch and light supper. The luxurious *Boulevard Restaurant* overlooks the lobby. There's a concierge desk and business services. 505 N. Michigan Ave. (phone: 944-4100; 800-327-0200; fax: 944-3050).

Nikko Chicago This elegant, 425-room hotel overlooking the Chicago River was built by Nikko Hotels International, Japan's largest hotel chain. Japanese touches abound, with landscaped indoor gardens and Japanese artwork—some suites even have tatami sleeping rooms. Its *Celebrity Café* overlooks the Chicago River and offers American food; the *Benkay* is a fine Japanese restaurant. Other pluses are 24-hour room service, a concierge, a health club, and business services. In the Loop. 320 N. Dearborn St. (phone: 744-1900; 800-NIKKO-US; fax: 527-2650).

Omni Ambassador East The only Chicago member of the Historic Hotels of America, it boasts a gleaming green-and-white Italian marble lobby with German crystal chandeliers. Those who stay in one of the 275 rooms and suites enjoy at no extra charge daily newspapers, temporary membership at nearby health clubs, and limousine rides to downtown. It still houses the famous *Pump Room* restaurant (see *Eating Out*), a Chicago institution whose entryway is lined with photos of famous guests, who always dined in Booth No. 1. Amenities include 24-hour room service, a concierge, and business services. Conveniently located in the Gold Coast area, close to *Lincoln Park,* Rush Street, and the Magnificent Mile of Michigan Avenue. 1301 N. State Pkwy. (phone: 787-7200; 800-THE-OMNI; fax: 787-4760).

Park Hyatt Opulent, contemporary elegance characterizes this hotel. The 355 guest rooms are done in tones of deep green or peach and feature marble-topped rosewood furnishings. Its excellent *Jaxx* restaurant looks out on the *Water Tower* and is the place for power breakfasts and other elegant meals; its lounge is comfortable for coffee or cocktails. The hotel offers 24-hour room service, a concierge, and business services. 800 N. Michigan Ave. (phone: 280-2222; 800-233-1234; fax: 280-1963).

Ritz-Carlton Contemporary and chic, this beautifully appointed 431-room luxury establishment rises 20 stories above its 12th-floor lobby; the beautifully proportioned fountain is a signature centerpiece. Housed in the spectacular *Water Tower Place* complex, it has all the accoutrements of elegance, including a fine health club and skylit indoor swimming pool. *The Dining Room* offers first-rate continental fare in a lush setting. Amenities include 24-hour room service, a concierge, and business services. In the North Michigan Avenue area. 160 E. Pearson St. (phone: 266-1000; 800-241-3333; fax: 266-1194).

Sutton Place This former *Le Meridien* offers luxury, from the striking glass and gray granite exterior to the Art Deco–inspired interior, the three story atrium bar to the state-of-the-art remote-controlled boardroom. All 247 rooms and 41 suites have CD players and VCRs. Its *Brasserie Bellevue* restaurant offers unusual interpretations of traditional dishes; also check out its weekend chocolate buffet. Health club facilities are available nearby. 21 E. Bellevue Pl. (phone: 266-2100; 800-543-4300).

Tremont This small, attractive hotel was renovated in 1985 in the style of an English manor. The brass-and-wood-detailed lobby has the comfortable feel of a men's club, and the 137 rooms and penthouse suites have period furnishings. There's a concierge, multilingual staff, and turndown service complete with cognac, and *Café Gordon,* featuring fine continental fare. In the North Michigan Avenue area. 100 E. Chestnut St. (phone: 751-1900; 800-621-8133; fax: 280-1304).

Westin Chicago Though popular with conventioneers, this gray concrete slab houses 740 recently refurbished rooms in muted color schemes, most with spectacular views of Lake Michigan. Amenities include 24-hour room service, a mini-bar, coffee maker, a health club, and VCR. The Executive Level offers additional perks: a welcome gift, complimentary continental breakfast, and hors d'oeuvres. There are three restaurants, one of which often features live jazz in the evening. 909 N. Michigan Ave (at E. Delaware Pl.). (phone: 943-7200, 800/228.3000; fax 649.7447).

MODERATE

Allerton Close to museums and shopping on Michigan Avenue and 10 minutes from the Loop, this 450-room property is an economical but quite pleasant choice—and a steal in this location. There's a restaurant, called *The Avenue,* which offers moderately priced American dishes. Business services are available. 701 N. Michigan Ave. (phone: 440-1500; fax: 440-1819).

Bismarck Recently renovated, this property offers 525 rooms and some nice suites. The *Crown Room* and *Gate 3½* restaurants are open for lunch and dinner, and business services are available. 171 W. Randolph St. at LaSalle St. (phone: 236-0123; fax: 236-3177).

Chicago Marriott This convention hotel dates from the 1960s, but its 1,172 rooms were extensively renovated several years ago. Located right on Michigan Avenue, it's within walking distance of the *Water Tower, North Pier,* and both of the city's major gallery districts, and not far from the Loop. Its spacious lobby includes a cocktail area and piano bar where guests can watch each other come and go. There are three restaurants, including *J. W.'s Steakhouse,* two lounges, 24-hour room service, an extensive health club and pool, business services, and shopping. Parking is available for a fee. 540 N. Michigan Ave. (phone: 836-0100; 800-228-9290; fax: 836-6139).

Clarion Executive Plaza Offering 415 rooms all with wonderful city views. *Florid's* restaurant offers fine continental cooking; and guests can use nearby health club facilities. Catering to members of the international business community, it offers a special telephone system that allows access to dialing and travel instructions in various foreign languages. Other business services are available as well, as is valet parking. 71 E. Wacker Dr. (phone: 346-7100; 800-621-4005; fax: 346-1721).

Holiday Inn O'Hare Convenient to the airport and the many offices nearby, it has 507 rooms and offers weekend packages. The hotel's "Holidome" has indoor and outdoor pools, a health club, saunas, a tanning salon, and a gameroom. Other amenities include free parking, three restaurants, two bars, and business services. 5440 River Rd., Rosemont (phone: 708-671-6350; 800-HOLIDAY).

Raphael This extremely reasonably priced 172-room hotel is perfect for those looking for intimacy and tastefully furnished rooms. The two-story lobby boasts cathedral windows, and the quaintly decorated rooms have sitting areas, stucco walls, and beamed ceilings. The hotel is within walking distance of Michigan Avenue's Magnificent Mile and *Water Tower Place.* Amenities include 24-hour room service, a restaurant, and some business services. 201 E. Delaware Pl. (phone: 312-943-5000; 800-821-5343; fax: 943-9483).

Sheraton Chicago and Towers The 34-story hotel boasts 1,200 guestrooms bordering the Chicago River. The Towers section offers upgraded accommodations and services on four private floors. Guests can use the private health club or take advantage of easy access to bike and jogging trails. The *Streeterville Grill* service fine Italian-style fare, while *Waves* offers nightly entertainment. 301 E. North Water St. (phone: 464-1000; 800-325-3535; fax: 329-7045).

INEXPENSIVE

Days Inn Lake Shore Drive Convenient to North Michigan Avenue and Lake Shore Drive, this 33-story, 580-room hotel offers marvelous views, an outdoor pool, standard business services, on-premises parking, and all laundry services, plus a revolving banquet hall on the top floor. Its *Gold Star Sardine Bar* is one of the city's popular after-hours spots, offering cabaret singers nightly. 644 N. Lake Shore Dr. (phone: 943-9200; 800-325-2525).

EATING OUT

The city's restaurant business is booming, and some of the finest cooking in America can be found here. Expect to pay $70 or more for a meal for two at those restaurants we've described as expensive; between $50 and $70 at places in the moderate category; and less than $40 at our inexpensive choices. Prices do not include drinks and wine, tips, or taxes. All telephone numbers are in the 312 area code unless otherwise indicated.

Unless otherwise noted, all restaurants are open for lunch and dinner.

EXPENSIVE

Ambria Everything about this place charms, from the comfortable setting to the menu's sophisticated variations on nouvelle cuisine. Chef Gabino Sotelino's imaginative menu subtly blends East and West in such dishes as Japanese *mizuna* greens salad with warm, creamy, goat-cheese dressing. The dinner menu has wonderful seafood dishes, such as charcoal-grilled sea bass served on tomato *coulis* with sautéed thinly sliced potatoes. Desserts are magnificent. Closed Sundays. Reservations necessary. Major credit cards accepted. 2300 N. Lincoln Park W. (phone: 472-5959).

Arun's One of the city's most elegant Thai dining spots, it offers such daily specials as quilted shrimp with fried rice cracker and curry sauce, prawns with garlic-lime sauce, and catfish curry. End the meal with fragrant layered rice custard and Thai iced coffee. Open for dinner only; closed Mondays. Reservations advised. Major credit cards accepted. 4156 N. Kedzie Ave. (phone: 539-1909).

Bice Trendsetters and beautiful people pack this trattoria, a branch of a growing international chain, where the contemporary decor is as sleek as the patrons. The menu is extensive, with a good selection of pasta, risotto, veal, and chicken prepared in a variety of ways. The best people watching is in the bar and, in good weather, the sidewalk café. Closed Sunday lunch. Reservations advised. Major credit cards accepted. 158 E. Ontario St. (phone: 664-1474).

Cape Cod Room Once the city's premier seafood house, this cozy New England–style spot with red-checkered tablecloths and nautical decorations remains popular. The Bookbinder soup, red snapper in a tomato-vegetable broth enhanced with sherry, is a signature item. Also try the fresh pompano, lobster, and other finny fare. Closed *Christmas.* Reservations advised. Major credit cards accepted. *Drake Hotel,* 140 E. Walton St. (phone: 787-2200).

Charlie Trotter's The menu changes daily in this adventuresome, two-room nouvelle cuisine restaurant, home of some of the city's most imaginative dishes. Appetizers range from caviar-topped sea scallops to sweetbreads with *pancetta,* radicchio, shredded potato, sweet peppers, and sharp cilantro butter presented in a crisp potato shell. Entrées are equally varied: tender venison and smoked quail with hazelnuts. Service is excellent; the wine list is extensive. Closed Sundays and Mondays. Reservations necessary; the most popular table is in the kitchen where you can watch the master chef at work. Major credit cards accepted. 816 W. Armitage Ave. (phone: 248-6228).

Everest Room This elegant French restaurant has a commanding view from atop the *Chicago Stock Exchange Building* in Chicago's financial center. The cornucopia of original dishes reflect the chef's Alsatian roots. Among the outstanding entrées are roast filet of sea bass wrapped in crisp shredded potatoes, black squid risotto, and salmon soufflé. Desserts are delectable, and the wine list is very good, with a strong selection of white wines. Service is impeccable, and even the waiters' trays are graced with fresh flowers. Closed Sundays and Mondays. Reservations necessary. Major credit cards accepted. 440 S. LaSalle St. (phone: 663-8920).

Le Français For years, Jean Banchet made this one of America's finest French restaurants. Today, the kitchen is in the hands of Roland and Mary Beth Liccioni, and the still-excellent fare has a somewhat lighter touch. Standouts include rack of lamb served with tiny fresh vegetables and couscous, stuffed Dover sole, Lyonnaise sausage served *en croûte* with port wine sauce, and crayfish bisque. The pastries are superb. Closed Sundays. Reservations necessary. Major credit cards accepted. 269 S. Milwaukee Ave., Wheeling; take Kennedy Expwy. to Rte. 294 north, Willow exit (phone: 708-541-7470).

Frontera Grill and Topolobampo A pair of upscale Mexican dining rooms. At *Frontera,* the ever-changing menu often includes the house specialty, *tacos al carbón,* chicken, duck, or skirt steak folded into a homemade tortilla. Or try the mahimahi with two sauces or Yucatecán-style marinated venison in a spicy sauce of fresh tomatoes, *habanero* chilies, and sour orange juice. *Topolobampo* offers, among other treats, roast pork loin with red-chili apricot sauce and pumpkin purée. Closed Sundays and Mondays. Reservations advised. Major credit cards accepted. 445 N. Clark St. (phone: 661-1434).

Gordon When owner Gordon Sinclair's culinary imagination ignites, the results are superlative. On any given night, you're likely to find artichoke fritters with béarnaise sauce, beef tenderloin with sweet potatoes, or rare seared tuna. Top off the meal with a great dessert like the flourless chocolate cake. Reservations advised. Major credit cards accepted. 500 N. Clark St. (phone: 467-9780).

Madison's The perfect place to stop either before or after attending a sports event at the nearby *United Center,* where hearty menu items such as filet mignon stuffed with prosciutto, mozzarella, garlic, and butter tempt patrons. Reservations advised. Major credit cards accepted. 1330 W. Madison St. (phone: 455-0099).

Morton's of Chicago The renowned steak chain began right here, and it's still the best steak in the whole city (if not the entire country). The double filet mignons, 24-ounce porterhouses, 20-ounce strip steaks, and other generous cuts are perfectly prepared to order. Choose from steaming baked potatoes, crisp hash browns, or toasted potato skins, all extra on the à la carte menu. Seafood dishes are just as delicious. Reservations advised. Major credit cards accepted. 1050 N. State St. (phone: 266-4820). There are more moderately priced versions in suburban Westchester (1 Westbrook Corporate Center; phone: 708-562-7000), and in Rosemont (9525 W. Bryn Mawr Ave.; phone: 708-678-5155).

Prairie Quite possibly where the term "Midwestern cooking" was coined, this intimate spot offers fine regional fare. The decor is elegant and uncluttered, and the chef Stephen Langlois's open kitchen is a fine place to pick up new cooking techniques as you watch your food being prepared. Whitefish smothered with onions, crisp bacon, puréed squash, and smoked whitefish caviar is just one of the thoughtfully prepared entrées, and those willing to chance an extra pound should try the warm carrot raisin cake with bourbon glaze and sugarplums. Reservations advised. Major credit cards accepted. 500 S. Dearborn St. (phone: 663-1143).

Pump Room A winning formula of fine food, diligent service, and lovely decor have made this a legend among Chicago restaurants. The wide-ranging menu features such house specialties as prime ribs and crispy roasted duck. A free Happy Hour buffet Mondays through Fridays is one of the best such spreads in the city. Live entertainment is presented nightly, and there's dance music on weekends. Reservations necessary. Major credit cards accepted. *Omni Ambassador East Hotel,* 1301 N. State Pkwy. (phone: 266-0360).

Seasons The menu, which changes with the seasons (naturally), features light preparations, among them delicious fish and fowl dishes and crisp fresh vegetables. Signature dishes include braised Maine lobster and Kobe beef. The wine list is extensive, and the surroundings are elegant, with dark woodwork and warm, red-patterned carpets. Request a table overlooking the lake. Reservations necessary. Major credit cards accepted. *Four Seasons Hotel,* 120 E. Delaware Pl. (phone: 649-2349).

Spiaggia The prices may empty your pocketbook, but this handsome bi-level restaurant, with its dramatic floor-to-ceiling windows overlooking the lake, is a winner, thanks partly to the knowledgeable staff. Thin-crust boutique pizzas are among the best starters, main courses range from succulent roast chicken and other game birds to inventively garnished meats and fish. Next door, the *Spiaggia Café* serves pizza, salads, pasta, and other Italian favorites in a more casual setting (no reservations). Restaurant closed for Sunday lunch. Reservations advised. Major credit cards accepted. 980 N. Michigan Ave. (phone: 280-2750 or 280-2764).

Yoshi's Café French technique and Japanese mastery combine to produce a menu featuring such inventive dishes as striped sea bass stuffed with herbs and served with lobster cream sauce, sautéed veal medallions on homemade buckwheat pasta, and tuna tartare on a bed of guacamole. Open for dinner only; closed Mondays. Reservations advised. Major credit cards accepted. 3257 N. Halsted St. (phone: 248-6160).

MODERATE

Bella Vista This vast place was once a bank, and the restaurant's owners (who are also responsible for *Bacino's* popular pizza places) took full advantage of the space with lush trompe l'oeil murals on all the walls; the tableware picks up both the color and floral motifs of the murals. The menu is contemporary Italian; diners can walk through the glassed-in wine rooms. Reservations advised. Major credit cards accepted. Somewhat out of the way, but convenient to *Wrigley Field* and *Lincoln Park;* also a block away from an elevated stop on the Howard Line. 1001 W. Belmont Ave. (phone: 404-0111).

Bistro 110 Garlic lovers will find paradise in this bustling spot the instant they sample a buttery roasted bulb spread on good French bread. Wood-oven–roasted meats, fish, and fowl are pungent with garlic and herbs. The decor is bright, with polished light wood floors and murals by Judith Rifka. Reservations advised. Major credit cards accepted. 110 E. Pearson St. (phone: 266-3110).

Blackhawk Lodge Many years ago, co-owner Doug Roth's father ran the *Blackhawk Inn,* a stylish and hearty favorite in the Loop. Now Roth *fils* has teamed with first-generation restaurateur Larry Levy to create a version of a Wisconsin summer camp for grown-ups. The rustic decor is reminiscent of a comfortable North Woods hunting retreat. Signature starters include crab cakes and cheese grits with a fresh mushroom sauce. Choose from a wide variety of such comfort foods as roast turkey, ribs, steak, and fish. Crowds move out to the screened-in porch in the summer. Reservations advised. Major credit cards accepted. 41 E. Superior St. (phone: 280-4080).

Blue Mesa Southwestern cooking is one of this city's latest dining crazes, and Santa Fe style reigns in this comfortable room with whitewashed adobe and bleached pine. Lovers of wonderfully pulpy guacamole and steaks smothered in green chilies and onions will be quite content. Reservations necessary for parties of eight or more. Major credit cards accepted. 1729 N. Halsted St. (phone: 944-5990).

Bub City A rollicking, mammoth, down-home Texas eating house, featuring shrimp and crab barbecue and "Big Easy" (read, New Orleans) bayou music to wash it all down. This is one loud, entertaining joint. Wear denim. Reservations advised. Major credit cards accepted. There's lots of parking near this out-of-the-way spot where Halsted Street and North Avenue meet. 901 W. Weed St. (phone: 266-1200).

Bukhara This Indian place claims its recipes go back 1,000 years. The focus is on marinated fresh seafood, poultry, beef, and lamb roasted in tandoors (hollow clay ovens). Try the tandoori chicken in pomegranate juice or the shish kebab with cumin-flavored lamb. Finish with a pudding of dates, almonds, and milk. Reservations advised. Major credit cards accepted. 2 E. Ontario St. (phone: 943-0188).

Café Ba-ba-Reeba! Everything about this place is festive and upbeat. The emphasis on *tapas* gives diners an opportunity to sample lots of dishes, although entrée-size options are also available. Selections change, but the menu usually includes such specialties as octopus in vinaigrette, grilled sausage, paella, and flan for dessert. Closed for lunch Mondays and in January and February. Reservations unnecessary. Major credit cards accepted. 2024 N. Halsted St. (phone: 935-5000).

Carson's Probably the best spareribs in the city. Salads with a creamy, anchovy-flavored dressing and tangy au gratin potatoes are the other lures. Don't dress up because bibs (supplied) are essential. No reservations, so expect to wait. Major credit cards accepted. 612 N. Wells St. (phone: 280-9200); 5970 N. Ridge Rd. (phone: 271-4000); 400 E. Roosevelt Rd., Lombard (708-627-4300).

Geja's Café This restaurant has good food—from fondue to seafood—and a romantic atmosphere, with flamenco and classical guitar played every night of the week. There's a superb wine list. Reservations advised. Major credit cards accepted. 340 W. Armitage Ave. (phone: 281-9101).

Hat Dance Kicky, as the name suggests: Aztec decor, Mexican food with a Japanese accent. Closed at lunch weekends. Reservations advised. Major credit cards accepted. 325 W. Huron St. (phone: 649-0066).

Italian Village Visitors to Chicago may wonder why there are so few restaurants in the Loop; likely because executives go to private clubs and office workers do fast food or company cafeterias. But the *Italian Village* offers three, right in the middle of the downtown area. Downstairs is the clubby and casual *La Cantina;* on the second floor is a country restaurant called the *Village Room;* both are reasonably priced and offer a standard selection of Italian fare. *Vivere,* on the main floor, serves far more sophisticated, and pricey, regional Italian dishes in a dramatic setting. *La Cantina* and the *Village Room* are closed Sunday lunch; *Vivere* is closed Saturday lunch and Sundays. Reservations advised. Major credit cards accepted. 71 W. Monroe St. (phone: 332-7005, *La Cantina* and *Village Room;* 332-4040, *Vivere*).

Kinzie Street Chophouse Serving steaks, chops and seafood in a bright friendly bistro. Closed Sunday lunch. Reservations advised. Major credit cards accepted. 400 N. Wells St. (phone: 822-0191).

Klay Oven Savor Delicious Indian cuisine in a formal setting. Excellent starters include *samosas* and *pakoras* served with fresh chutneys. Entrees include tandoori chicken, lamb, and quail. Reservations accepted. Major credit cards accepted. 414 N. Orleans St. (phone: 527-3999).

Maggiano's A Chicago hot spot, it packs them in nightly. The menu features hearty Italian fare served on heaping platters meant to be shared. Breads from the *Corner Bakery* (right next door) are not to be missed. Reservations advised. Major credit cards accepted. 516 N. Clark St. (phone: 644-7700).

Redfish Funky New Orleans antiques line the walls at this Cajun/Creole restaurant. The red beans and rice are perfect, spiced just enough to make the tongue tingle. In addition to traditional gumbo, *étouffée* and jambalaya, the menu has tasty blackened chicken with herbed goat cheese and a fine blackened redfish. The portions here are quite generous. The festive atmosphere continues in the adjoining *Voodoo Lounge* where a live jazz/blues/Dixieland band entertains Thursday through Saturday nights; late night snacks are available until midnight. Reservations advised. Major credit cards accepted. Open daily, Saturday and Sunday dinner only. 400 N. State St. at Kinzie (phone: 467-1600).

Santorini's The elegant decor draws the elite of Chicago's Greek community; the menu, featuring lamb chops wrapped in phyllo and several seafood dishes, is equally classy. Reservations advised. Major credit cards accepted. 138 S. Halsted St. (phone: 829-8820).

Shaw's Crab House This is a mammoth, immensely popular pre-World War II-style seafood house. Don't miss the stone or soft-shell crabs if they're "in season." The pecan pie may be Chicago's best. Reservations advised. Major credit cards accepted. 21 E. Hubbard St. (phone: 527-2722). *Shaw's Blue Crab Lounge* (660 Lake Cook Rd., Deerfield; phone: 847-948-1020) is a similar, but more casual, enterprise under the same ownership.

Tucci Milan The menu is a sophisticated variation on the one at sister eatery *Tucci Benucch* on the Magnificient Mile. Thin-crust pizzas are blanketed with a variety of innovative toppings; pastas range from the traditional to the au courant; and risottos include shrimp, fennel, cucumber, chives, and basil. Herb-roasted chicken and grilled swordfish in sun-dried tomato sauce are among the numerous satisfying entrées. Closed Sunday lunch. Reservations advised. Major credit cards accepted. 6 W. Hubbard St. (phone: 222-0044).

Tuscany Drawing crowds to Little Italy west of the Loop, this stylish northern Italian trattoria offers innovative pasta dishes and an extensive wine list. Rack of lamb, rotisserie chicken, and risotto are specialties. Reservations advised. Major credit cards accepted. 1014 W. Taylor St. (phone: 829-1990).

INEXPENSIVE

Ann Sather's There actually are three, but the original (on W. Belmont Ave.) may be the world's only Swedish restaurant housed in a former funeral home. The menu varies from time-honored Swedish dishes to hearty American fare: pork sausage patties and rich country gravy, and beefsteak and eggs with cinnamon rolls. Brunch is particularly good. Reservations unnecessary. MasterCard and Visa accepted. 929 W. Belmont Ave. (phone: 348-2378); 5207 N. Clark St. (phone: 271-6677); and 1329 E. 57th St., Hyde Park (phone: 947-9323).

Berghoff Another Chicago tradition—and one sometimes thinks it's the only local restaurant visitors have ever heard of. Favorites include German classics such as Wiener schnitzel and sauerbraten. Wash down your meal with a mug of Berghoff light or dark beer on tap. The *Berghoff Café,* a stand-up bar on the east end of the main floor, offering freshly carved roast beef, turkey, and corned beef sandwiches on fresh Berghoff's bread, is a fun and inexpensive spot for a quick lunch. Closed Sundays. Reservations accepted for five or more. Major credit cards accepted. 17 W. Adams St. (phone: 427-3170).

Billy Goat Tavern This journalists' hangout was the inspiration for the late John Belushi's "cheebugga, cheebugga" short-order routines on "Saturday Night Live." Otherwise, it's an underground greasy spoon serving merely adequate hamburgers. It's located on Lower Michigan Avenue; access is down the stairs from North Michigan Avenue. No reservations. No credit cards accepted. 430 N. Michigan Ave. (phone: 222-1525).

Emperor's Choice Located in historic Chinatown, this eatery is one of the best places in town for Szechuan food. Ink-on-silk portraits of emperors throughout Chinese history grace the walls. Chef Ron Moy's distinctive cuisine is showcased here and includes plump oysters or fresh sole lightly seasoned with ginger, cilantro, and black beans. Order the outstanding Peking duck a day in advance. Reservations advised. Major credit cards accepted. 2238 S. Wentworth Ave. (phone: 225-8800).

Greek Islands You can find thoughtfully prepared dishes such as gyros, squid, lamb, and fresh broiled red snapper at this simple eatery. The decor is pleasant, with blue-and-white-checkered cloths, and it's particularly popular with faculty at the nearby *University of Illinois.* Reservations unnecessary. Major credit cards accepted. 200 S. Halsted St. (phone: 782-9855).

Hard Rock Café Yes, Chicago has one, too. The walls of this hip hamburger emporium are covered with an assortment of rock music artifacts and declarations of world peace. Chili and grilled burgers lead the menu. Wash it all down with a fruit-and-honey "health shake." At the very least, it's the place to pick up an essential addition to any trendy T-shirt collection. No reservations. Major credit cards accepted. 63 W. Ontario St. (phone: 943-2252).

Helmand Come here for savory Afghan baby pumpkin and lamb Kabuli in an exotic, attractive setting. Top off the meal with cheese-like *burfee* or baklava baked with ground pistachios. The service is as good as the food. Open daily for dinner only. Reservations advised. Major credit cards accepted. 3201 N. Halsted St. (phone: 935-2447).

Ina's Kitchen Ever since Ina Pinkney opened this cozy spot in Lincoln Park in 1991, there have been lines out the door. Breakfast is served until 3 PM, when the kitchen closes. Lunch is added to the menu at 11 AM. Specials include a noodle and vegetable frittata, corn and black-bean scrapple, whole-wheat oatmeal pancakes, and a full range of pastries. Open for breakfast and lunch only. Closed Mondays. No Smoking. No reservations. No credit cards accepted. 934 W. Webster Ave. (phone: 525-1116).

Jane's This casual dining spot offers Chinese chicken salad with roasted cashews and other unusual fare. For dessert try the homemade mixed berry pie. Reservations advised. Major credit cards accepted. 1655 W. Cortland Ave. (phone: 862-JANE).

Lou Mitchell's For those who consider the idea of awakening before noon a barbaric proposal, make an exception and head for this outstanding breakfast spot. Freshly squeezed orange juice is followed by perfectly prepared pancakes, omelettes served in the pan, biscuits baked that morning, and fantastic coffee. Formica tabletops, eccentric waitresses, and a low-key clientele complete the picture. Lunch is served here, too, but breakfast has made this place a landmark on the city's restaurant scene. The doors open at 5:30 AM. No reservations. Major credit cards accepted. 563 W. Jackson Blvd. (phone: 939-3111).

The Lucky Platter This looks like a 1950s diner, but tastes delightfully 1990s with an eclectic menu of Caribbean pumpkin soup, Thai catfish, curried chicken salad, and sides of chilled sesame noodles and Oaxacan corn relish. Reservations for six or more accepted weeknights only. Major credit cards accepted. 514 Main St., Evanston (phone: 847-869-4064).

Medici on 57th Wooden floors and comfy booths accented with Italian tiles, classical music playing in the background, and windows overlooking a courtyard make for an informal setting at this chain's most upscale location. Thin-crusted pizza and the half-pound hamburger Medici with a choice of 10 toppings are specialties. Open for breakfast, lunch, and dinner. No reservations. No credit cards accepted. 1327 E. 57th St. (phone: 667-7394).

Pasteur This attractive corner storefront is among the best of some two dozen Vietnamese restaurants in the city. Recommended entrées are whole fried red snapper topped with sweet-salty sauce with scallions and lime or the charming nest of crispy fried egg noodles filled with seafood and vegetables. Closed Monday lunch. Reservations advised on weekends. Major credit cards accepted. 4759 N. Sheridan Rd. (phone: 271-6673).

Reza's Though the decor of this eatery is nothing special, this is Chicago's most popular Persian restaurant, mainly because it serves huge portions of tasty dishes such as broiled salmon and green peppers stuffed with spinach or mushrooms. This place is very popular with families. Reservations advised. Major credit cards accepted. Three locations: 5255 N. Clark St. (phone: 561-1898); 432 W. Ontario (phone: 664-4500); and the *Presidential Towers,* 555 W. Madison Ave. (phone: 902-2900).

Wishbone A fun spot that serves up some terrific down-home Southern cooking. Chicken is the thing here: grilled until juicy, Southern-fried, or Louisiana-blackened in a salad. Don't miss dessert, either: marble cheesecake, pecan pie served plain or oozing chocolate, and custard like Mom used to make. Open for breakfast, lunch, and dinner; closed Saturday lunch and Sunday lunch and dinner. No reservations. Credit cards accepted at Washington Street location only. 1001 W. Washington St. (phone: 850-2663) and 1800 W. Grand Ave. (phone: 829-3597).

HOT DOG! (AND PIZZA, TOO)

If all of the above fails to appeal to your culinary sensibilities, *Michael's* (1946 N. Clark St.; phone: 787-DOGS) is a terrific alternative. It's also just the spot for those with the I-can't-get-a-good-hot-dog blues. The special here is the "chardog," a half pound of spicy beef on a soft bun with onions, tomatoes, cucumbers, pickles, mustard, relish, and perhaps the kitchen sink. (If you're not in the mood for a hot dog, *Michael's* also offers an incredible salad bar, stuffed baked potatoes, grilled sandwiches, and world-famous cheddar fries.)

Hamburger and hot dog fans would be remiss to miss *Gold Coast Dogs* (2100 N. Clark St.; phone: 327-8887; 418 N. State St.; phone: 527-1222; and 325 S. Franklin St.; phone: 939-2624), where they can sample a real Chicago hot dog (it comes with fresh onions and peppers, not soggy sauerkraut). For funky 1950s fare, *Byron's* (850 W. North Ave.; phone: 266-3355) will take you back to the days of the drive-in, as will *Portillo* in the suburbs (806

W. Dundee Rd., Arlington Heights; phone: 847-870-0870; 611 E. Golf Rd. Schaumburg; phone: 847-884-9020; and 950 S. Barrington Rd., Streamwood; phone: 847-213-6656).

Finally, a visit to this city's eating establishments wouldn't be complete without a taste of Chicago's famous deep-dish pizza—layer upon layer of toppings baked in a deep pan. The pioneer of this pizza fit for Goliath is *Pizzeria Uno* (29 E. Ohio St.; phone: 321-1000), a place whose food more than makes up for its lack of atmosphere. Also in the area is *Pizzeria Due* (619 N. Wabash Ave.; phone: 943-2400), under the same ownership and serving the same hearty fare. *Gino's East* (160 E. Superior St.; phone: 943-1124) uses cornmeal crusts to vary the flavor. Other places to try this local delicacy are *Giordano's of Lincoln Park* (1840 N. Clark St.; phone: 944-6100); *Bacino's* (75 E. Wacker Dr.; phone: 263-0070; and 2204 N. Lincoln; phone: 472-7400); and *Edwardo's Natural Pizza* (1321 E. 57th St.; phone: 241-7960; and 9300 Skokie Blvd., Skokie; phone: 847-674-0008). The latter also serves another local favorite, stuffed pizza—a thick, gooey, pie-like creation. All of the above eateries are open daily; reservations are unnecessary and major credit cards are accepted.

Cincinnati

For the benefit of people unfamiliar with Ohio's geography, we'd like to establish that Cincinnati is not Cleveland. While Cleveland is in the north, on Lake Erie, Cincinnati sits on the Ohio River in the southwestern corner of the state, surrounded by tree-lined hills crowned with stately homes. Though resolutely businesslike and the headquarters of an unusually large number of well-known companies for a city its size (1.7 million people in the metropolitan area), Cincinnati is not as industrial as the cities of northern Ohio.

Originally called Losantiville, Cincinnati was founded in 1788. It was renamed in 1790 in honor of the Society of the Cincinnati, a patriotic organization of Revolutionary War officers, by General Arthur St. Clair, who happened to be passing through as the new governor of the Northwest Territory. "Losantiville!" he reportedly exclaimed. "What an awful name." The rest, as they say, is history.

Like most river cities, Cincinnati has a lusty past. Soldiers were dispatched to protect its earliest settlers from the Indians, but the soldiers soon proved to be the greater menace. William Henry Harrison visited not long before he became president and pronounced it "the most debauched place I ever saw." As late as 1901, Carrie Nation arrived on a temperance crusade, but failed to smash a single saloon window, saying "I would have dropped from exhaustion before I had gone a block." But eventually, somehow, seemliness got the upper hand.

Dubbed by Longfellow the "Queen City of the West," Cincinnati has received commendations from many, including Sir Winston Churchill, who said it was "the most beautiful of America's inland cities." This is partly the result of efforts by the business community and civic-minded citizens. Today's residents enjoy a variety of festivals and events, museums and galleries. Also a big sports town, Cincinnati is home to the *NFL Bengals* and the *Reds,* the first professional baseball team, organized here in 1869.

In the center of town is 20th-century Fountain Square, which surrounds the majestic 19th-century *Tyler-Davidson Fountain.* Modern office buildings and ground-level shops line Fountain Square on the north and east. Across the street, *Fountain Square South,* one of the city's most ambitious private projects, is a high-rise complex with offices, hotels, and shops. The compact downtown area is easy to navigate on foot because of its generally uncrowded streets and the 16-block-square Skywalk that connects many buildings. Numerous small restaurants, bars, and fast-food establishments exist to succor the foot-weary. Also within easy walking distance from downtown are *Riverfront Stadium* (where the *Reds* and the *Bengals* play) and *Riverfront Coliseum* (host to circuses, ice shows, rock concerts, and *University of Cincinnati* basketball).

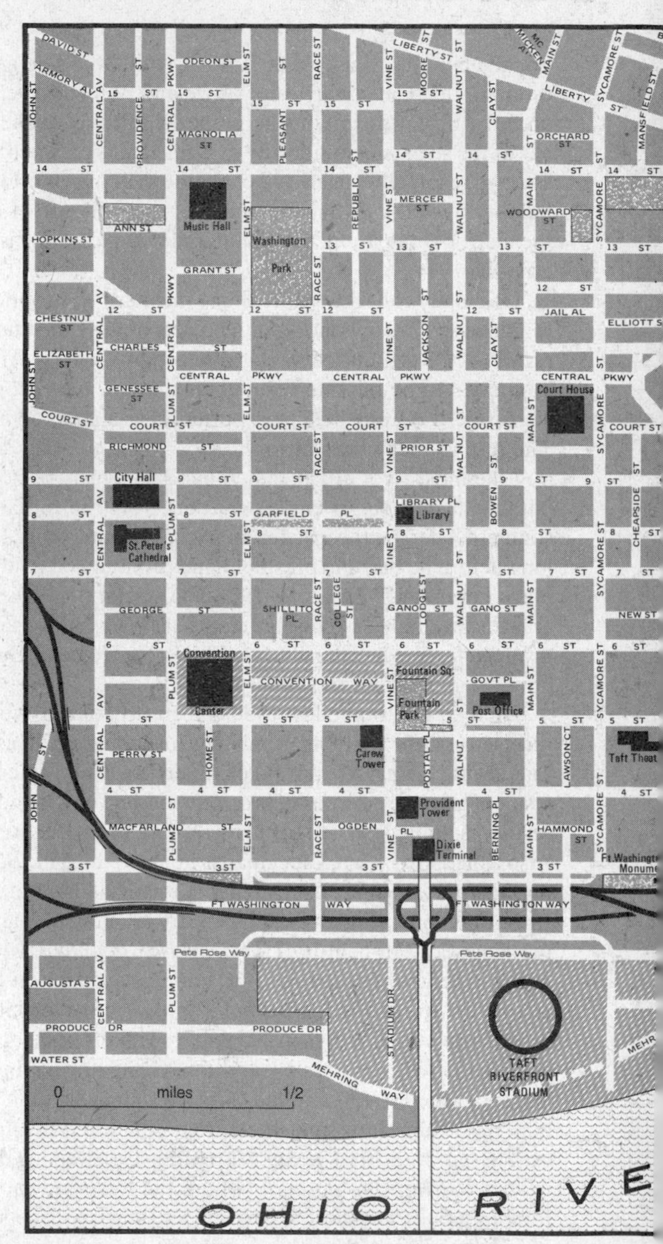

DAVID ST
ARMORY AV
JOHN ST
CENTRAL AV
PROVIDENCE ST
CENTRAL PKWY
ODEON ST
MAGNOLIA ST
ELM ST
PLEASANT ST
RACE ST
VINE ST
MOORE ST
LIBERTY ST
WALNUT ST
CLAY ST
MC MICKEN AV
MAIN ST
SYCAMORE ST
MANSFIELD ST
15 ST
14 ST
13 ST
12 ST
ORCHARD ST
REPUBLIC ST
MERCER ST
WOODWARD ST
ANN ST
Music Hall
Washington Park
HOPKINS ST
GRANT ST
JACKSON ST
JAIL AL
ELLIOTT ST
CHESTNUT ST
ELIZABETH ST
CHARLES ST
CENTRAL PKWY
GENESSEE ST
Court House
COURT ST
RICHMOND ST
PRIOR ST
PLUM ST
9 ST
City Hall
LIBRARY PL
Library
BOWEN ST
8 ST
GARFIELD PL
St. Peter's Cathedral
CHEAPSIDE ST
7 ST
GEORGE ST
SHILLITO PL
COLLEGE ST
GANO ST
LODGE ST
NEW ST
6 ST
Convention Center
CONVENTION WAY
Fountain Sq.
Fountain Park
GOVT PL
Post Office
5 ST
PERRY ST
HOME ST
Carew Tower
POSTAL PL
LAWSON CT
Taft Theat
4 ST
Provident Tower
MACFARLAND ST
OGDEN PL
Dixie Terminal
BERNING PL
HAMMOND ST
Ft.Washington Monume
3 ST
FT WASHINGTON WAY
Pete Rose Way
AUGUSTA ST
STADIUM DR
PRODUCE DR
WATER ST
MEHRING WAY
TAFT RIVERFRONT STADIUM
0 miles 1/2
OHIO RIVE

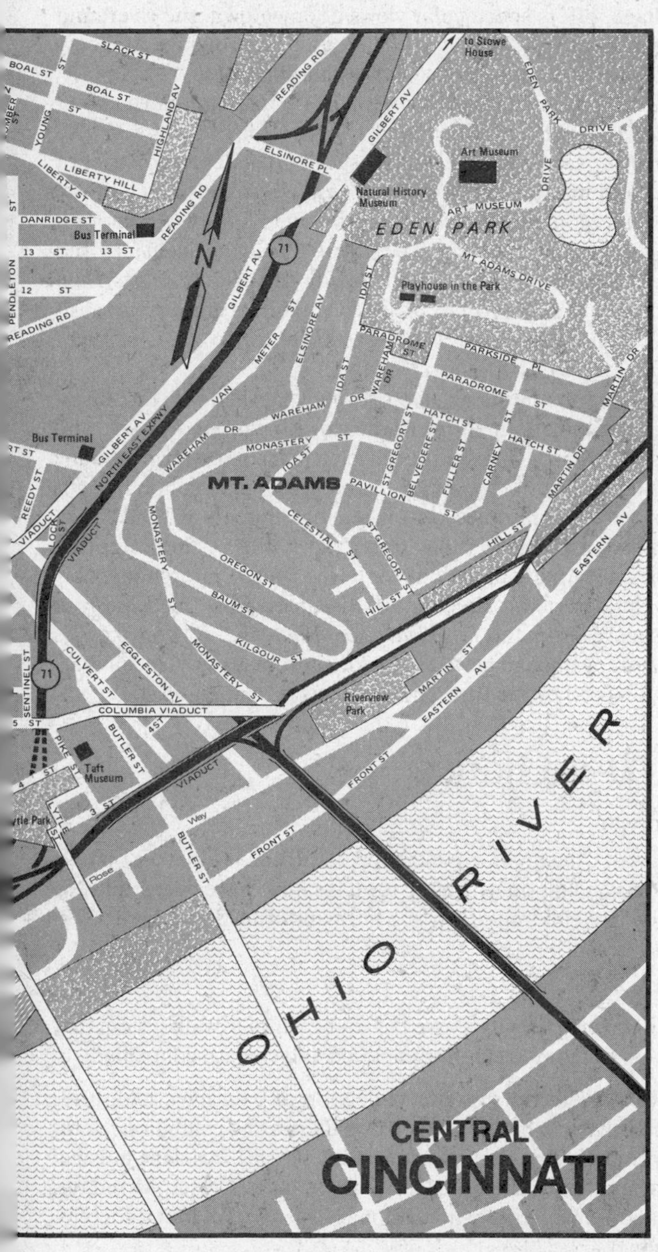
CENTRAL
CINCINNATI
EDEN PARK
MT. ADAMS
OHIO RIVER
Art Museum
Natural History Museum
Playhouse in the Park
Bus Terminal
Bus Terminal
Taft Museum
Riverview Park
Lytle Park
to Stowe House
71
71
N
SLACK ST
BOAL ST
BOAL ST
YOUNG ST
HIGHLAND AV
LIBERTY HILL
LIBERTY ST
DANRIDGE ST
13 ST
13 ST
12 ST
PENDLETON ST
READING RD
READING RD
READING RD
ELSINORE PL
GILBERT AV
GILBERT AV
GILBERT AV
NORTH EAST EXPWY
EDEN PARK DRIVE
ART MUSEUM DRIVE
MT. ADAMS DRIVE
IDA ST
ELSINORE AV
VAN METER ST
PARADROME ST
PARKSIDE PL
PARADROME ST
WAREHAM DR
WAREHAM DR
HATCH ST
HATCH ST
MONASTERY ST
ST GREGORY ST
BELVEDERE ST
FULLER ST
CARNEY ST
PAVILLION ST
CELESTIAL ST
MARTIN DR
MARTIN DR
HILL ST
HILL ST
EASTERN AV
EASTERN AV
MONASTERY ST
OREGON ST
BAUM ST
KILGOUR ST
MONASTERY ST
EGGLESTON AV
CULVERT ST
SENTINEL ST
COLUMBIA VIADUCT
VIADUCT
VIADUCT
VIADUCT
LOCK ST
REEDY ST
4ST
BUTLER ST
BUTLER ST
PIKE ST
5 ST
4 ST
3 ST
LYTLE ST
MARTIN ST
FRONT ST
FRONT ST
Way
Rose

Many of the city's 385,000 residents live on the hillsides that surround the business district. Mt. Adams, Cincinnati's version of New York's Greenwich Village, offers spectacular views of downtown, the river, and the "blue" hills of Kentucky. This is bohemia at a price: Its slopes are covered with restored row houses, shops, and restaurants.

Adjacent *Eden Park* is where the *Cincinnati Art Museum, Playhouse in the Park,* and *Krohn Conservatory* are found. Clifton is the site of the 36,000-student *University of Cincinnati,* a campus set in a residential district of baronial homes and interesting shops. Between Mt. Adams and Clifton, Mt. Auburn is undergoing extensive restoration in an effort to recapture some of the area's previous grandeur. The superb *Cincinnati Symphony* and *Cincinnati Opera Company* enchant audiences in the historic *Music Hall.* The university's *College Conservatory of Music* also offers impressive musical programs. The *Aronoff Center for the Arts* is home to the *Cincinnati Ballet.*

Cincinnatians are friendly but reserved, sedately satisfied with their lives. Although there are excellent shops in the downtown, Hyde Park, and Kenwood areas, "fashionably dressed" in Cincinnati is conservative by many other big-city standards. Also, you may hear a few unique colloquialisms during your stay here. For instance, the expressions "three-way" and "four-way" refer to chili toppings rather than traffic signs. "Please" indicates that the listener does not understand you. "Square" is used interchangeably with "block" when describing directions or distances, as in "the *Riverfront Stadium* is 4½ squares from the *Tyler-Davidson Fountain.*" A "pony keg" is a convenience store. Although newcomers or visitors may say "Cincinnata," the pronunciation used by the true Cincinnatians is "Cin-cin-*na*-ti."

Cincinnati At-a-Glance

SEEING THE CITY

For the best view of Cincinnati, go to the top of the *Carew Tower.* You may see the original seven hills on which the town is said to have been built. No admission charge for children under six. Fifth and Vine Sts. (phone: 579-9735).

SPECIAL PLACES

Pedestrians can traverse the city above the traffic via a Skywalk system that is totally covered. In many areas, it is enclosed and climate-controlled.

CINCINNATI ART MUSEUM This outstanding collection of paintings, sculpture, prints, and decorative arts fills more than 80 galleries and exhibition rooms (with an exceptionally fine section on ancient Persia). Ancient musical instruments, costumes, and textiles also are on view. Closed Mondays, *Thanksgiving,* and *Christmas.* No admission charge for children under 18. *Eden Park* (phone: 721-5204).

between the airport and major hotels. Buses shuttle between the airport and downtown hotels every half hour.

BUS *Queen City Metro* operates an excellent bus service. The bus stop signs carry numbers of the routes that stop there. The fare, which varies by destination, is less than $1. Route maps are available from *Queen City Metro* (122 West Fifth St.; phone: 621-4455).

CAR RENTAL Major car rental agencies are represented at the airport.

TAXI Call *Yellow Cab* (phone: 241-2100), or go to any of the major hotels, where cabs line up.

SIGHTSEEING TOURS

HORSE-DRAWN CARRIAGES Several companies operate carriages in the Fountain Square area. Board at Fountain Square.

RIVERBOAT Another popular way to see the city is from the water. *BB Riverboats*'s vessels are available for one- to two-hour trips; luncheon, dinner, and moonlight cruises; or day-long adventures. Boats are moored at Madison Avenue at *Covington Landing* (just across the river from Cincinnati; phone: 606-261-8500). Also try *Celebration Riverboats* (Ludlow, KY; phone: 606-581-0300).

SPECIAL EVENTS

Ever since 1873, Cincinnati has celebrated its annual *May Festival:* This series of concerts, often featuring opera superstars, is the oldest continuing choral festival in the Western Hemisphere. It is held at the *Music Hall* (1241 Elm St.; phone: 721-8222) during the last two weekends in May. The *Golf Center at Kings Island* (6042 Fairway Dr., Mason) hosts the *Senior PGA Tour Classic* each summer (phone: 398-5742) and the annual *ATP Tournament* in August (phone: 651-2872). In mid-September, Cincinnati celebrates its German heritage with an *Oktoberfest,* similar to the famous Munich festival, in and around Fountain Square.

SHOPPING

Cincinnati has its share of today's marketplaces, malls filled with department stores, chain shops, eateries, and entertainment. Enclaves of commerce with more individuality, however, also are easy to come by—and get to. Museum shops are an excellent source of quality gifts and mementos.

SPORTS AND FITNESS

Cincinnati is one of the country's most enthusiastic baseball cities, and it favors football as well.

BASEBALL The *Reds* play at *Riverfront Stadium* (201 E. Pete Rose Way; phone: 421-REDS).

BASKETBALL The *University of Cincinnati Bearcats* play in *Shoemaker Hall* on campus in Clifton (Clifton Ave.; phone: 556-2287), and the *Xavier University*

Musketeers play at the *Cincinnati Gardens* (2250 Seymour Ave.; phone: 745-3411).

BICYCLING There is a 6.2-mile (10-km) bike trail at *Airport Playfield, Lunken Airport* (Wilmer Ave.; phone: 321-6500). In summer months, call to see if rental bikes are available.

FISHING There's moderately good fishing at Lake Isabella, Winton Woods (the largest of the country lakes), and in the Ohio River. Serious Cincinnati sport fishers drive four hours to Lake Cumberland and Kentucky Lake in southern Kentucky.

FITNESS CENTER The *Central Parkway YMCA* (1105 Elm St.; phone: 241-5348) provides a pool, sauna, equipment, and an indoor running track, as well as an outdoor jogging map; it is open to non-members for a fee.

FOOTBALL The *NFL Bengals* play at *Riverfront Stadium* (201 E. Pete Rose Way; phone: 621-3550).

GOLF For spectators and golfers, the *Golf Center at Kings Island* (6042 Fairway Dr., Mason; phone: 398-5200) is among the best. Also consider the *Glenview* (10965 Springfield Pike) and *Neumann* (7215 Bridgetown Rd.) city courses or county links in *Winton Woods* and *Sharon Woods* parks.

HORSE RACING Enthusiasts should check out the action at *River Downs* (6301 Kellogg Ave.; phone: 232-8000) and *Turfway* racecourses (7500 Turfway Rd., Florence, KY; phone: 606-371-0200; 800-733-0200).

JOGGING For a 6-mile jaunt, follow tree-lined Central Parkway to Ludlow Street and come back; or run back and forth across the Ohio River Suspension Bridge, designed by Brooklyn Bridge builder John A. Roebling. The *Cincinnati Recreation Commission* publishes a free brochure, *Healthline Fitness Course,* available at the convention and visitors bureau.

SWIMMING A good public pool is *Sunlite Pool* at Coney Island just before *River Downs* (on Rte. 50; phone: 231-7801); call ahead. There are lake beaches at nearby Hueston Woods in Butler County and Caesar's Creek in Warren County.

THEATER

We start with our favorite place in Cincinnati for live theater.

CENTER STAGE

The Aronoff Center for the Arts The newest jewel in the Queen City's crown has revitalized downtown Cincinnati. It houses three theaters, an art gallery, restaurant, and gift shop. The powerful Cesar Pelli–designed structure is also the permanent home of the *Cincinnati*

Ballet; the center also hosts touring shows, pop concerts, and dance recitals. Seventh and Walnuts Sts. (phone: 621-2787).

The *Cincinnati Playhouse in the Park,* a highly-praised regional professional theater, presents world premieres of plays by new American playwrights, classics, rarely presented works, musicals, and comedies on its two stages from September through June. Its lavish production of Dickens's *A Christmas Carol* is an annual yuletide tradition. (The two theaters are wheelchair accessible and have a sound-enhancement system, large-print *Playbills,* and signed and audio-described performances.) Mt. Adams Circle, *Eden Park* (phone: 421-3888; 800-582-3208 in Ohio).

MUSIC

The internationally famous *Cincinnati Symphony Orchestra,* founded in 1895, has a September to May season at the *Music Hall* (1241 Elm St; phone: 381-3300); its summer home is the *Riverbend Music Center* (6295 Kellogg Ave.; phone: 381-3300 or 232-6220). The *College Conservatory of Music* is one of the nation's oldest and most prominent professional music schools; it offers frequent concerts and recitals on the *University of Cincinnati* campus (Corbett Dr.; phone: 556-4183). The *Cincinnati Opera* (phone: 241-ARIA), the second-oldest opera company in the US, performs at the downtown *Music Hall.* The *Cincinnati Ballet*'s new home is the *Aronoff Center for the Arts* (see above), although the company does return to the *Music Hall* for its traditional holiday performance of *The Nutcracker.*

NIGHTCLUBS AND NIGHTLIFE

Cincinnati is pretty much a couples' town. The most popular nightspots are *Caddy's* (phone: 721-3636) and *Flanagan's Landing* (phone: 421-4055); both are on West Pete Rose Way. Just across the Ohio River, on the Kentucky riverfront, are *Covington Landing Entertainment Complex* (1 Madison Ave., Covington, KY; phone: 606-291-9992) with a variety of nightclubs, bars, and eateries, including *Howl of the Moon Saloon* (phone: 606-491-7733) and *Gumbo Charlies* (phone: 606-491-3100). Another swinging Kentucky spot is the *Waterfront's* bar *Fusion* (phone: 606-581-1414). Cincinnati hotel bars that swing into the wee hours include *Fifth and Vine Street Bar (Westin), Champs Sports Bar (Hyatt), Palm Court (Omni Netherland Plaza),* the *Cricket (Cincinnatian),* and the *High Spirits Bar* atop the *Regal Cincinnati* (see *Checking In*). There also are numerous nightspots at the top of Mt. Adams, including *Rookwood Pottery* (see *Eating Out), Adrica's* (phone: 721-5329), *Longworth's* (phone: 579-0900), *Café Vienna* (phone: 621-6655), and *Mt. Adams Bar & Grill* (phone: 621-3666).

CHECKING IN

Cincinnati's accommodations rival those of any other comparably sized US city. Most of Cincinnati's major hotels have complete facilities for the business traveler. Those listed below as having "business services" usually offer such conveniences as meeting rooms, photocopiers, computers, translation services, and express checkout, among others. Call the individual hotel for additional information. Expect to pay between $100 and $195 per night for a double room at hotels listed as expensive, and $70 to $100 at moderate places; there are no exceptional inexpensive hotels in the city. For bed and breakfast accommodations, contact *Ohio Valley Bed and Breakfast* (11577 Taylor Mill Rd., Independence, KY 41051; phone: 606-572-9666). Unless otherwise noted, hotel rooms have air conditioning, private baths, TV sets, and telephones.

All hotels below are in Cincinnati and telephone and fax numbers are in the 513 area code unless otherwise indicated.

EXPENSIVE

Cincinnatian This restored 114-year-old landmark provides European-style elegance that has made it the city's premier hotel. There are 147 well-appointed rooms, some with balconies overlooking an eight-story atrium. Its elegant *Palace* restaurant (see *Eating Out*) serves American regional food, while the casual *Cricket Lounge* serves a light menu and offers afternoon tea. Amenities include full health and fitness center, 24-hour room service, a concierge, and business services. One block from the *Aronoff Center for the Arts* at 601 Vine St. (phone: 381-3000; 800-942-9000; fax: 651-0256).

Embassy Suites Cincinnati at Rivercenter All 226 deluxe suites are well-appointed and feature a microwave, refrigerator, coffee maker, and wet bar. The *E-Room* restaurant, featuring fresh American cuisine including pasta, beef, and seafood, was voted the "Best Room With a View" by *Cincinnati* magazine. Amenities include health club and sauna, indoor pool, and Jacuzzi, as well as complimentary full cooked-to-order breakfast, and parking. Located adjacent to *Covington Landing Entertainment Complex*. 10 E. Rivercenter Blvd., Covington, KY (phone: 606-261-8400; 800-EMBASSY; fax: 606-261-8486).

Hyatt Regency It has 485 rooms, 12 suites, and a health club with an indoor pool. *Champs Italian Chop House* (see *Eating Out)* features Italian specialties, seafood dishes, and steaks; *Findlay's* has more casual dining and breakfast and lunch buffets daily. Amenities include room service until midnight, a concierge, and business services. There's also valet parking. 151 W. Fifth St. (phone: 579-1234; 800-233-1234; fax: 579-0107).

Omni Netherland Plaza One of the city's finest, this *National Trust for Historic Preservation*'s Historic Hotel of America is connected by the skywalk to *Saks Fifth Avenue,* the *Convention Center*, with lots of meeting space of its own (18 meeting rooms; capacity for 1,200), and to the *Tower Place Shopping Mall* and downtown attractions. In addition to its 610 rooms, there are 11 suites. Dining can be either formal at *Orchids at the Palm Court* (see *Eating Out)* or a bit more casual at the *Café at the Palm Court.* Amenities include a fully equipped health club with an indoor pool, 24-hour room service, a concierge, and business services. 35 W. Fifth St. (phone: 421-9100; 800-THE-OMNI; fax: 421-4291).

Westin Overlooking Fountain Square, this 17-story downtown property has 448 rooms and 18 suites. There's also a pool, a fitness center, a whirlpool, and sauna. Additional amenities include a restaurant, 24-hour room service, a concierge, and business services. Fountain Sq. (phone: 621-7700; 800-228-3000; fax: 852-5670).

MODERATE

Regal Cincinnati Business travelers and conventioneers stay at this very modern, 888-room downtown place with a heated outdoor pool, health club, sauna, two lounges, two restaurants, barber, and valet parking. Diners can get a panoramic view from its award-winning restaurant, *Seafood 32,* the city's only rooftop revolving restaurant, and *Elm Street Grill* tops the menu with American dishes. Amenities include room service until midnight, a concierge, and business services. Connected by the Skywalk to the *Convention Center, Saks Fifth Avenue,* and downtown shopping and attractions. 150 W. Fifth St. (phone: 352-2100; 800-876-2100; fax: 352-2148).

EATING OUT

Cincinnati's most notable gastronomic eccentricity is its chili, which usually is served over spaghetti, to which may be added cheese ("three-way"), cheese and raw onions ("four-way"), or cheese, raw onions, and beans ("five-way"). Many of the city's finest restaurants are found in its hotels. At restaurants listed as expensive, expect to pay at least $50 to $75 for dinner for two; between $25 and $50 at those places designated as moderate; and under $25 at places listed as inexpensive. Prices do not include drinks, wine, tax, or tips. All restaurants are in the 513 area code unless otherwise indicated.

Unless otherwise noted, restaurants are open for lunch and dinner.

EXPENSIVE

Maisonette It may be in an unlikely spot, but it's one of the best French restaurants in the country. Its food has consistantly won major awards, and the service is friendly and warm. Specialties include an appetizer of sautéed duck liver with quinoa papaya *galette* and a main course of red deer chop with pepper sauce. Closed Sundays; dinner only on Saturdays and Mondays. Reservations necessary. Major credit cards accepted. 114 E. Sixth St. (phone: 721-2260).

Morton's of Chicago Award-winning steaks and Maine lobsters (flown in daily) are the specialty of this elegant, club-like restaurant. Its intimate mahogany bar is one of Cincinnati's "in" spots. Oriental rugs and mahogany walls decorate the stunning boardroom. Closed major holidays for dinner only. Reservations advised. Major credit cards accepted. *Tower Place Shopping Mall,* at Fourth and Race Sts. (phone: 241-4104).

Orchids at the Palm Court Diners can feast on well-prepared, sophisticated Midwestern fare, including grilled steaks presented with a variety of exquisite sauces in a splendidly restored Art Deco setting. Start with the ostrich scaloppine with herbed-forest mushrooms. Reservations advised. Major credit cards accepted. *Omni Netherland Plaza,* 35 W. Fifth St. (phone: 421-9100).

Palace This highly acclaimed restaurant in the *Cincinnatian* epitomizes elegance. The menu changes each season, but it often features exquisite versions of rack of lamb, veal steaks, and seafood dishes. Delicious appetizers include duck breast served with caramelized onion compote, roasted pepper vinaigrette, and goat cheese. Open daily for breakfast, lunch, and dinner. Reservations advised for dinner. Major credit cards accepted. 601 Vine St. (phone: 381-3000).

Waterfront Afloat directly across the Ohio River from downtown, it offers a spectacular skyline view along with its gustatory specialties—fresh grilled seafood, a raw bar, and steaks. Try an appetizer of pan-fried crab cakes with wok-charred green beans or Vietnamese spring rolls. Upstairs, classic northern Italian dishes are served at *Spazzi* with an authentic trattoria-style antipasti bar. Open daily for dinner only. Reservations advised. Major credit cards accepted. 14 Pete Rose Pier, Covington, KY (phone: 606-581-1414).

MODERATE

Champs Italian Chop House Regional Italian specialties, steaks (try the *bistecca Toscanna,* marinated in olive oil, herbs, tomato, and onion), and fresh seafood dishes such as *farfalle con salmone* (grilled salmon with asparagus, artichokes, bowtie pasta, and cream sauce) are the mainstays of the menu. An unusual attraction here is the exposed kitchen, so diners can watch their food being prepared. Closed Sundays. *Hyatt Regency* Hotel, 151 W. Fifth St. (phone: 579-1234).

China Gourmet Since its opening in 1977, it's been considered the very best. Lobster stir-fry in black bean sauce with Szechuan string beans and pike steamed in ginger are among the favorites. Closed Sundays. Reservations advised. Major credit cards accepted. 3340 Erie Ave. (phone: 871-6612).

Forest View Gardens Waiters and waitresses sing your favorite show tunes and serve tasty German and American food in a garden setting. Be sure to sample some of the homemade dishes—the sauerkraut ball appetizer and the apple strudel dessert. The *Dining Room/Showplace* is open for dinner only; closed Mondays through Wednesdays. Reservations necessary. The *Edelweiss Room* is open for lunch on weekdays and for dinner Tuesdays through

Sundays. Reservations advised for parties of six or more. Special luncheon show on the third Thursday of the month; reservations advised. Major credit cards accepted. 4508 N. Bend Rd., a 15-minute drive from downtown (phone: 661-6434).

Gumbo Charlies Offering a Florida-like atmosphere with a fabulous view of the Cincinnati skyline and Ohio River, this place specializes in seafood and pasta, with special emphasis on crab and Cajun preparations. Open daily April through October; open for dinner only and closed Mondays November through March. Reservations advised. Major credit cards accepted. 1 Madison Ave. at *Covington Landing Entertainment Complex* (phone: 606-491-3100).

Mallorca This authentic Spanish restaurant serves gargantuan portions of ambitious dishes, including *paella valenciana,* clams in green sauce, and broiled Spanish sausage. There are also seafood dishes, veal, and marinated baby goat. Reservations advised. Major credit cards accepted. 124 E. Sixth St. (phone: 723-9506).

Mike Fink An authentic riverboat, moored on the Kentucky side of the Ohio River, it is famous for its raw bar. Other options include the halibut Natchez or the peppercorn steak. Open daily; breakfast served on Sundays. Reservations advised. Major credit cards accepted. At the foot of Greenup St., Covington, KY (phone: 606-261-4212).

Montgomery Inn at the Boathouse This is the jewel in the crown of Ted Gregory, Cincinnati's restaurant king. The barbecued loin back ribs and chicken are laudable, and the wonderful view attracts celebrities. The sampler platter of appetizers is a must. There's an extensive wine list. Reservations advised. Major credit cards accepted. 925 Eastern Ave., adjacent to Sawyer Point (phone: 721-7427).

La Normandie Grill Adjacent to the *Maisonette* (see above), this steakhouse is renowned for its chops and fresh seafood. Good choices are broiled New Zealand rack of lamb and salmon with kiwi barbecue sauce. Casual conviviality is its hallmark. Closed Sundays and major holidays; dinner only on Saturdays. Reservations advised. Major credit cards accepted. 118 E. Sixth St. (phone: 721-2761).

Pigalls Café This fine restaurant is located in a downtown landmark building near the *Convention Center.* The atmosphere is casual and the bar is lively. Don't miss the goat cheese pizza with artichoke hearts and olive-walnut pesto. Closed Sundays. Reservations advised. Major credit cards accepted. 127 West Fourth St. (phone: 651-2233).

Precinct Located in a turn-of-the-century police precinct house, five minutes from downtown, this award-winning place is a good choice for an evening of dining and chatting with friends over what some say are the best steaks in town.

Two possibilities are steak Collinsworth (filet mignon with crab meat and asparagus) or steak Diane. Other selections include veal, pasta, and fresh seafood. Open daily for dinner only. Reservations advised. Major credit cards accepted. 311 Delta Ave. at Columbia Pkwy. (phone: 321-5454).

INEXPENSIVE

Carol's Corner Café This homey Betty Boop–themed café exudes the warm, cheerful personality of owner Carol Sherman-Jones, whose culinary art would satisfy even the toughest critic. Don't miss "Elner's Mighty Mushroom," a red wine—-braised portobello atop garlicky, pesto-laced eggplant. Closed *Easter, Thanksgiving,* and *Christmas.* Major credit cards accepted. 825 Main St. (phone: 651-BOOP).

Rookwood Pottery Atop Mt. Adams, in the original kilns of the historic *Rookwood Pottery* building, patrons devour gigantic burgers and overindulge at the do-it-yourself ice-cream sundae bar. Reservations unnecessary. Major credit cards accepted. 1077 Celestial St. (phone: 721-5456).

Longhorn Steaks A relaxed atmosphere in which to kick back and chow down on cowboy grub. All steaks are fresh (never frozen), and the Canadian salmon is marinated in a secret recipe and grilled to perfection. Open daily; dinner only weekends. Major credit cards accepted. 713 Vine St. (phone: 421-9696).

WHAT'S HOT

Sensational, soul-satisfying chili, rich with meat, kidney beans, tomato sauce, and spices, has been a mainstay of the Cincinnati diet ever since immigrant Greek restaurant owners started cooking a batch in case they ran out of other fare. Now there are innumerable chains devoted exclusively to this hearty dish, including *Skyline Chili* (4180 Thunderbird La.; phone: 874-1188) and *Goldstar Chili* (5204 Beechmont Ave.; phone: 231-4541). The secret behind the unique taste may never be revealed, for chili makers everywhere guard their recipes, but rumor has it that chocolate is the latest ingredient. Since 1994, Mexican-style chili restaurants have taken a stronghold: Try *Don Pablo's* (401 Riverboat Row; phone: 261-7100) on the Kentucky side of the river.

Cleveland

Cleveland is a working city, and it always has been. Laid out in 1796 with strict attention to order and propriety by the surveyors of the Connecticut Company (led by Moses Cleaveland), its tidy New England pattern of straight streets around a public square was knocked into a cocked hat with the coming of industrialization. Cleveland's location at the confluence of Lake Erie and the Cuyahoga River provided a waterway that stimulated the growth of heavy industry—shipping, steel, iron, and construction. The city sprawled. Successful entrepreneurs flourished: oil baron John D. Rockefeller; shipping magnates Sam Mather and Mark Hanna; and the Van Sweringen brothers, who created a vast railroad and construction empire. But behind all this boom, and most of the money, was the muscle power of a largely immigrant work force.

Today's Cleveland is something of a bellwether among mid-size industrial US cities. For one thing, heavy industry is no longer the only game in town; Cleveland is among the top four US cities for Fortune 500 corporate headquarters. Real estate development and restoration work are booming as well. The headquarters of Rockefeller's Standard Oil (now BP America) on Public Square is part of a $7-billion building surge in downtown Cleveland. *Tower City Center* is a $400-million project that includes *Terminal Tower* and its surrounding riverfront area. There's the 57-story *Society Center* building, designed by noted architect Cesar Pelli; *Playhouse Square Center*, the largest restoration of its kind in the country, which has revived four 1920s theaters; and the restoration of historic buildings in the Flats/Warehouse District, which in turn has led to the addition of shops, lofts, and cafés in that area. The *Nautica* riverfront development has brought life to the "left bank" of the Cuyahoga River. The *North Coast Harbor* area is developing as well; the 176-acre patch of land beside Lake Erie is home to the *Rock and Roll Hall of Fame and Museum* and the *Great Lakes Science Center.* And the $362-million *Gateway* complex, *Jacobs Field* open-air ballpark, and *Gund Arena* are home to major league baseball's *Indians*, as well as *NBA Cavaliers* games and *Lumberjacks* hockey.

Today, Cleveland has a population of 505,600; Cuyahoga County, which includes Cleveland and a ring of wealthy suburbs, has over two million people. Among the county's 59 suburbs is Shaker Heights, one of the most affluent areas in the country. There, where the Shakers once threw off American industrial life to set up a rural commune, reside the most prosperous industrial and business leaders.

But don't think Cleveland is getting effete or abandoning its heritage. A drive along the Detroit-Superior Bridge over the Flats shouldering the twists and turns of the Cuyahoga River, past steel mills belching flames into the sky, and barges plowing up and down the river, shows Cleveland's mus-

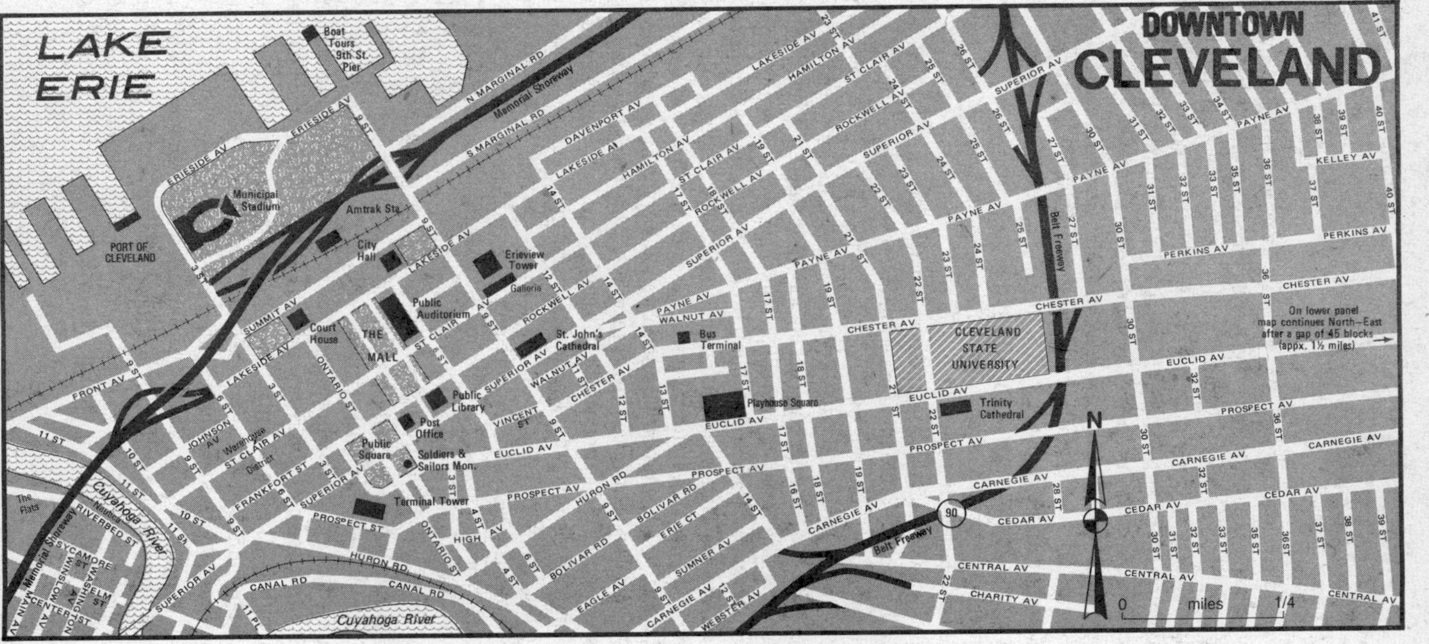

DOWNTOWN
CLEVELAND
LAKE
ERIE
Boat Tours 9th St. Pier
PORT OF CLEVELAND
Municipal Stadium
Amtrak Sta.
City Hall
Court House
THE MALL
Public Auditorium
Erieview Tower
Galleria
St. John's Cathedral
Bus Terminal
Playhouse Square
Public Library
Post Office
Public Square
Soldiers & Sailors Mon.
Terminal Tower
Warehouse District
The Flats
Cuyahoga River
CLEVELAND STATE UNIVERSITY
Trinity Cathedral
Memorial Shoreway
Belt Freeway
90
N
0 miles 1/4
On lower panel map continues North-East after a gap of 45 blocks (appx. 1½ miles)
N MARGINAL RD
S MARGINAL RD
ERIESIDE AV
LAKESIDE AV
HAMILTON AV
ST CLAIR AV
ROCKWELL AV
SUPERIOR AV
PAYNE AV
KELLEY AV
PERKINS AV
CHESTER AV
WALNUT AV
EUCLID AV
PROSPECT AV
CARNEGIE AV
CEDAR AV
CENTRAL AV
CHARITY AV
DAVENPORT AV
SUMMIT AV
FRONT AV
JOHNSON AV
FRANKFORT ST
ONTARIO ST
VINCENT ST
HURON RD
BOLIVAR RD
ERIE CT
SUMNER AV
EAGLE AV
WEBSTER AV
HIGH AV
CANAL RD
RIVERBED ST
SYCAMORE ST
WINSLOW AV
WASHINGTON
ELM ST
CENTER ST
MAIN AV
11 PL

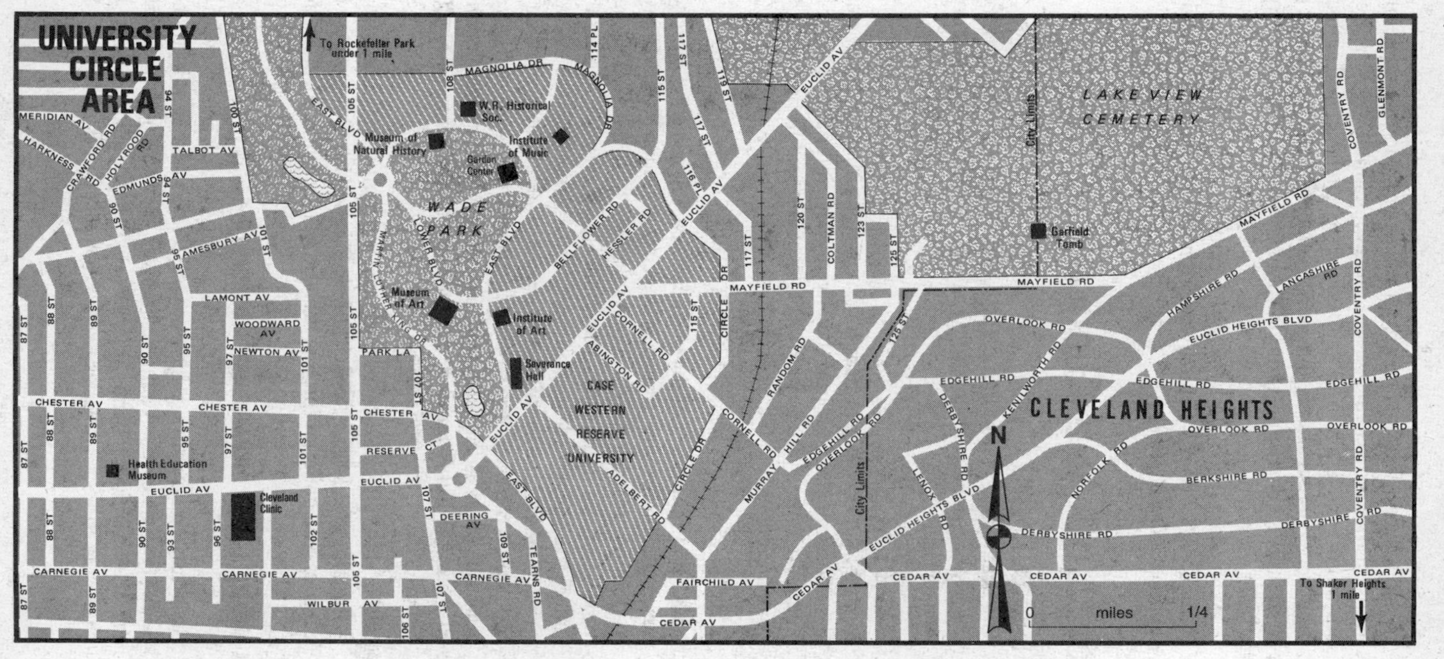
UNIVERSITY CIRCLE AREA
To Rockefeller Park under 1 mile
W.R. Historical Soc.
Museum of Natural History
Institute of Music
Garden Center
WADE PARK
Museum of Art
Institute of Art
Severance Hall
CASE WESTERN RESERVE UNIVERSITY
Health Education Museum
Cleveland Clinic
LAKE VIEW CEMETERY
Garfield Tomb
City Limits
CLEVELAND HEIGHTS
To Shaker Heights 1 mile
N
0 miles 1/4
EUCLID AV
MAYFIELD RD
CHESTER AV
CARNEGIE AV
CEDAR AV
EAST BLVD
MAGNOLIA DR
MARTIN LUTHER KING DR
EUCLID HEIGHTS BLVD
OVERLOOK RD
EDGEHILL RD
DERBYSHIRE RD
COVENTRY RD

cles still flexing. Ethnocentricity is still strong and the old neighborhoods live on. Little Italy is an east side enclave; Chinatown is on the fringes of downtown; and Tremont is a mixed ethnic neighborhood with a bewildering number of religious denominations and faiths. When you get right down to it, there's something genuinely American about the crazy-quilt ambience of Cleveland's neighborhoods. It's truly a city of the American Dream.

What does it all add up to? With cultural diversity, and interesting history, plenty of energy, and a very friendly citizenry, Cleveland definitely deserves a closer look.

Cleveland At-a-Glance

SEEING THE CITY

The best vantage point in the city is from the *Terminal Tower*'s 42nd-floor observation deck (Public Sq.; phone: 621-7981). Open weekends; admission charge.

SPECIAL PLACES

Many of Cleveland's most interesting sights are served by public transportation, but stroll around the city anyway, particularly in the University Circle area, the cultural heart of Cleveland, and in the lovely suburbs of Shaker Heights and Chagrin Falls.

DOWNTOWN

PUBLIC SQUARE In the heart of the business area, this is a good place to get one's bearings. Statues pay tribute to the city's founder Moses Cleaveland and to populist reform mayor Tom Johnson; and the *Soldiers and Sailors Monument* commemorates Cleveland's Civil War dead. Dominating the square are the world headquarters of BP America, the 57-story *Society Center* building, and the 52-story *Terminal Tower* built by the Van Sweringen brothers on the eve of the stock market crash that leveled their vast empire. *Terminal Tower* is the nucleus of *Tower City Center*, which connects to the *Ritz-Carlton* and *Renaissance Cleveland* hotels. Bounded by Euclid Ave., Superior Ave. and Ontario St.

THE ARCADE This 19th-century marketplace is a multitiered structure topped by a stunning block-long skylight of steel and glass. Bookstores, boutiques, eateries, and galleries line the arcade. At lunchtime, local musicians offer free classical, pop, and jazz concerts. 401 Euclid Ave. (phone: 621-8500).

ROCK AND ROLL HALL OF FAME AND MUSEUM Designed by renowned architect I. M. Pei, this museum chronicles the history of rock and roll with tributes to the artists, songwriters, radio broadcasters, and other industry notables. In addition to its extensive music archives, memorabilia, and *Hall of Fame*, there are numerous hands-on interactive displays. Open daily. Admission charge. E. 9th St. and Erieside Ave. (phone: 781-ROCK).

UNIVERSITY CIRCLE AREA

CLEVELAND MUSEUM OF ART A major American museum, and one of the few that is still free to the public, this private institution boasts an enviable collection of more than 30,000 works of art representing all periods and cultures—ancient Egypt, Greece, and Rome; the Near and Far East; India; Europe; America; Africa; and the pre-Columbian Americas. Galleries are organized chronologically, with decorative arts pieces displayed alongside paintings and sculpture of the same period and place. The Asian collection is one of the finest in the Western world, and the museum has particularly fine medieval, European painting, and decorative arts collections. In recent years, the museum has been developing its collection of contemporary art and photography. Throughout the year there are frequent concerts and films, with gallery talks every afternoon except Mondays. The original 1916 building overlooks a garden and lagoon; a 1970 wing, designed by Marcel Breuer, houses special exhibition galleries, the musical arts department, and the education department (one of the largest professionally staffed education departments in the country). The *Museum Café* connects to an outdoor sculpture garden. A number of Cleveland's other cultural institutions face the museum across a grassy oval. Closed Mondays. 11150 East Blvd. at University Circle (phone: 421-7340).

WESTERN RESERVE HISTORICAL SOCIETY The largest collection of Shaker memorabilia in the world is here, including inventions such as the clothespin, the ladder-back chair, and farming implements and furnishings. There is also an extensive genealogical collection, exhibitions on Indians and pioneers, and a gift shop. At the same location is the *Crawford Auto-Aviation Museum*, with 200 antique autos and old airplanes; displays trace the evolution of the automobile and describe Cleveland's prominence as an early car manufacturing center. Visit the museum's restoration shop. Open daily. Admission charge. 10825 East Blvd. (phone:721-5722).

CLEVELAND MUSEUM OF NATURAL HISTORY Exhibitions of armored fish and sharks preserved on Ohio shales, a 70-foot mounted dinosaur, skeletons of mastodon and mammoth, and *Lucy*, the most complete fossil of one of the ancestors of *Homo sapiens*, are all here. The museum also has a planetarium and observatory. Open daily. Admission charge. Wade Oval Dr. at University Circle (phone: 231-4600).

CLEVELAND PLAY HOUSE More than 80 years old and designed by renowned architect Philip Johnson, this is reputed to be one of the finest theaters in the nation, with productions that range from Shakespearean tragedies to contemporary plays, including Broadway tryouts. No tours are offered. 8500 Euclid Ave. (phone: 795-7000).

CLEVELAND CENTER FOR CONTEMPORARY ART The major works of American-born, internationally acclaimed artists such as Roy Lichtenstein, Jasper Johns, Red Grooms, and Andy Warhol are exhibited in this stunning gallery.

A spiral staircase leads up to a balcony where you can get a bird's-eye view of the open space with its pristine white walls and hardwood floors. Closed Mondays. Admission charge. 8501 Carnegie Ave. (phone: 421-8671).

KARAMU HOUSE Founded in 1915, America's first interracial cultural center has hosted many of the country's finest African-American performers. Productions have included *Dreamgirls, Ain't Misbehavin',* and *Black Nativity*, a version of the *Christmas* tale by Langston Hughes that has become an annual yuletide tradition in Cleveland. 2355 E. 89th St. (phone: 795-7070).

THE HEALTH MUSEUM Exhibitions on the workings of the human body and health maintenance intrigue adults and children alike. See everything from a walk-through model of a human eye to *Juno,* the transparent woman, and the inspiring *Wonder of New Life* display. Open daily. Admission charge. 8911 Euclid Ave. (phone: 231-5010).

CLEVELAND CHILDREN'S MUSEUM Permanent and temporary exhibits explore science and nature. Closed Mondays. No admission for children under two. At 10730 Euclid Ave. (phone: 791-KIDS).

LAKE VIEW CEMETERY The plantings are beautiful, the view fine, and the company illustrious. Among the natives buried here are President Garfield (you can't miss the monument); Mark Hanna, a shipping magnate and US senator; John Hay, secretary of state under McKinley; and John D. Rockefeller, founder of the fortune. The *Garfield Monument* offers a great view of downtown. Closed November through March. 12316 Euclid Ave. (phone: 421-2665).

ROCKEFELLER PARK This 296-acre park features the *Cultural Gardens* (between East Blvd. and Martin Luther King Jr. Dr.), a series of gardens with sculptures representing the 20 nationalities that settled the city. The *City Greenhouse* has a *Japanese Garden,* tropical plants, and a *Talking Garden* (with audio descriptions). Open daily. 750 E. 88th St. (phone: 664-3103).

LITTLE ITALY This ethnic neighborhood, just around the corner from University Circle, is filled with artists' galleries and studios, especially along Murray Hill Road. Gallery walks are held here regularly. For fresh, hot doughnuts, visit *Presti's* (1211 Mayfield Rd.).

SHAKER HEIGHTS

One of the most affluent suburbs in America, Shaker Heights was developed in the early 1900s by brothers O. P. and M. J. Van Sweringen and now houses Cleveland's elite in lovely old homes on wide, winding, tree-lined streets. The area was originally Shaker Lakes, the rural commune established by the 19th-century religious sect that left American industrial life for a religious regime featuring strict celibacy. Today, all that remains of the Shakers are the *Shaker Historical Museum* (16740 South Park; phone: 921-1201) and the *Shaker Cemetery* (Lee Rd. at Chagrin Blvd.).

WEST SIDE MARKET One of the largest Old World indoor markets in the country, it offers fresh produce, meat, and baked goods year-round. Closed Tuesdays, Thursdays, and Sundays. 1979 W. 25th St. at Lorain Ave. (phone: 664-3386).

CLEVELAND METROPARKS ZOO AND THE RAIN FOREST Among the oldest zoos in America (and, at 165 acres, one of the largest in the Midwest), its exhibits include *Birds of the World,* an indoor/outdoor aviary with feathered friends from the seven continents; *Northern Trek,* with Bactrian camels, white-lipped deer, and other animals from the northern plains of Asia; and a greenhouse with 300 different plant species. The $30-million *Rain Forest* features more than 600 species of animals and insects from the seven continents and simulates a tropical thunderstorm every 20 minutes or so. Closed *Christmas* and *New Year's Day.* No admission charge for children under two. 3900 Brookside Park Dr. (phone: 661-6500).

NASA LEWIS RESEARCH CENTER The NASA complex and its visitors' center offer exhibitions, lectures, and films on aeronautics, energy, space travel, and communications. There also are tours of a propulsion systems laboratory and a supersonic wind tunnel. Open daily. No admission charge. 21000 Brookpark Rd. (phone: 267-1187).

EXTRA SPECIAL

The *Pro Football Hall of Fame* (2121 George Halas Dr. NW; phone: 330-456-8207; 330-456-7762 for recorded information) is in Canton, 53 miles south of Cleveland on I-77. Inside are mementos of the game and its players, as well as a research library. Open daily. Admission charge. On the way, you may want to stop at *Hale Farm Village* (2686 Oak Hill Rd., Bath; phone: 575-9137 in Cleveland; 330-666-3711 in Akron), where you'll find homesteads, crafts shops, and a working farm typical of those of the Western Reserve between 1825 and 1850. Closed Mondays. Admission charge.

You can also stop in Akron for a tour of the *Stan Hywet Hall and Gardens* (714 N. Portage Path; phone: 330-836-5533), an excellent example of Tudor Revival architecture with 70 acres of gardens. Closed Mondays. Admission charge for house tour. Also check out the *Akron Art Museum* (70 E. Market St.; phone: 330-376-9185), a gem of a collection featuring contemporary exhibitions from video art to sculpture. Closed Mondays. No admission charge. *Inventure Place* is Akron's hands-on science center that explores inventions. It is also home of the *National Inventors Hall of Fame.* Closed Mondays. Admission charge. (221 S. Broadway St., Akron; phone: 330-762-4463). In Kirtland, a town about 30 miles east of Cleveland, is *Holden Arboretum* (9500 Sperry Rd.; phone: 946-4400), one of the largest of its kind in the country. Closed Mondays. Admission charge. Another

attraction here is *Lake Farmpark* (8800 Euclid-Chardon Rd., phone: 256-2122), a working farm with agricultural exhibits and activities, a restaurant, and a gift shop. Open daily. Admission charge.

Sources and Resources

TOURIST INFORMATION

The *Convention and Visitors Bureau of Greater Cleveland* (50 Public Sq., Suite 3100, Cleveland, OH 44113; phone: 621-4110; 621-8860 for events), which is closed weekends, is best for brochures, maps, and other information. For the latest information on events around the city, call the visitor information hotline (phone: 800-321-1004). Contact the Ohio state tourism hotline (phone: 800-BUCKEYE) for maps, calendars of events, health updates, and travel advisories.

LOCAL COVERAGE *Cleveland Plain Dealer,* morning daily; *Northern Ohio LIVE,* monthly; and *Cleveland* magazine, monthly. All are available at newsstands.

TELEVISION STATIONS WKYC Channel 3–NBC; WEWS Channel 5–ABC; WOIO Channel 19–CBS; WJW Channel 8–FOX; and WVIZ Channel 25–PBS.

RADIO STATIONS AM: WWWE 1100 (talk/sports) and WERE 1360 (talk). FM: WCLV 95.5 (classical) and WMMS 100.7 (rock).

TELEPHONE The area code for Cleveland is 216. For the Akron-Canton vicinity, the area code is 330.

SALES TAX The city sales tax is 3%; the hotel room tax is 11.5%.

CLIMATE Cleveland has cold and snowy winters, followed by brief springs and humid summers. Fall is generally the most pleasant season, with mild, sunny weather that often extends through November.

GETTING AROUND

AIRPORT *Cleveland Hopkins International Airport* is a 20- to 30-minute drive from downtown. The *Regional Transit Authority's Airport Rapid Transit* train runs from the airport to downtown's *Terminal Tower* in the same amount of time; the fare is $1.50.

BUS *Regional Transit Authority (RTA)* serves both downtown and the outlying areas. The fare is $1.25 for local buses; $1.50 for express buses. Complete route and tourist information is available from the downtown office. 615 W. Superior Ave. (phone: 621-9500).

CAR RENTAL Cleveland is served by the major national firms.

TAXI Cabs can be hailed in the street in the downtown area around Public Square or ordered on the phone. *Yellow Cab* (phone: 623-1500) and *AmeriCab* (phone: 881-1111) are the major operators.

SIGHTSEEING TOURS

BOAT The *Goodtime III* boat tour (phone: 861-5110) is the best introduction to "the Flats"—the industrial valley along the river basin where Rockefeller and shipping magnates Sam Mather and Mark Hanna made their fortunes—and the lakefront. The 1,000-passenger boat departs daily from May through October from the *East Ninth Street Pier* and goes down the Cuyahoga as far as the steel mills. The *Nautica Queen* (phone: 696-5511) offers lunch and dinner cruises of the lake and riverfront April through December, and departs from the *Powerhouse* in the Flats.

TROLLEY Year-round, *Trolley Tours* (phone: 771-4484) takes visitors on city excursions in buses that resemble trolley cars; reservations are necessary.

TRAIN *Rapid Transit* trains (fare $1.50) serve the city's east and west sides. Also, the *Waterfront* rail system (fare $1.50) offers transportation around the downtown area.

SPECIAL EVENTS

The *Cleveland Performance Art Festival* is held in March, and the *Tri-C Jazz Fest* and the *Cleveland International Film Festival* in April. Among the events in June are the *Boston Mills Art Festival;* the *Ohio Derby* horse race at *Thistledown Park* in Warrensville Heights (phone: 662-8600); and *Parade the Circle* (phone: 791-3900), a festival celebrating the performing arts institutions in University Circle. The *Cleveland Grand Prix, Annual Rib Burn-Off,* and *River Expo* are held in July. August sees the *Feast of the Assumption* in Little Italy, and fall festivities include the *Cleveland Air Show* and *Oktoberfest.* Annual *Holiday Lighting* takes place the day after *Thanksgiving* on Public Square.

MUSEUMS

In addition to the museums listed in *Special Places*, 45 miles southeast of Cleveland, in Kent, is the *Kent State University Museum* (Rockwell Hall, Main St.; phone: 330-672-3450), one of the finest collections of haute couture clothing in the country. Closed Mondays and Tuesdays. Admission charge.

SHOPPING

You can buy anything you want in Cleveland because, somewhere, someone is selling it. Besides the revitalized downtown shopping district, with its upscale *Galleria* and dazzling *Tower City Center,* there's Coventry Road in Cleveland Heights, which resembles New York's Greenwich Village, and *Beachwood Place*, a posh shopping mall in the suburb of Beachwood.

SPORTS AND FITNESS

BASEBALL The *American League's* Cleveland *Indians* play at *Jacobs Field* (2401 Ontario St.; phone: 420-4200) from April through early October.

BASKETBALL The *NBA Cavaliers* play at the *Gund Arena* (400 Huron Rd.; phone: 420-2000), from mid-October through early April.

BICYCLING Rent from *U-Rent-Um of America* (15400 Brookpark Rd.; phone: 676-6776) or *Easy Rider Bicycle Shop* (3974 E. 131st St.; phone: 752-1555). The nearby *Cuyahoga Falls Reservation* has good biking trails.

FITNESS CENTERS The *13th Street Sports Club* (1901 E. 13th St.; phone: 696-1365) has exercise equipment and a track. It is open to guests of area hotels for a fee. The *Athletic Club* (1375 E. Ninth St.; phone: 621-0770) has a track, a pool, and exercise equipment. It is open to guests of the *Sheraton* and other hotels (check with your hotel).

GOLF *Punderson State Park* (Rtes. 44 and 87; phone: 564-5465) has the best public 18-hole golf course.

HIKING The *Cleveland Metroparks* circle the city, offering 19,000 acres with trails for the ambitious hiker. Also, the *Cuyahoga Valley National Recreation Area* links Cleveland and Akron with 22 miles of paths and walkways (phone: 526-5256).

HOCKEY The *International Hockey League Lumberjacks* play at the *Gund Arena* (400 Huron Rd.; phone: 420-0000).

JOGGING Run along Euclid Avenue to Public Square and on to the Flats; stop in at *Koening Sporting Goods* at the *Galleria* (phone: 575-9900). Run at *Cleveland State University* (Euclid and E. 24th St.).

SOCCER The *National Professional Soccer League* Cleveland *Crunch* play at the *Cleveland State University Convocation Centre* (2000 Prospect Ave.; phone: 349-2090).

TENNIS The best public courts are at *Cain Park* (Superior Rd. at Lee Rd., Cleveland Heights; phone: 371-3000).

THEATER

For current offerings and performance times, check the publications listed in *Local Coverage* above. Cleveland has a variety of theatrical offerings, some locally produced, others traveling shows, including some pre-Broadway tryouts. Best bets for shows: *Cleveland Play House* and *Karamu House* (see *Special Places); Great Lakes Festival, Ohio Theatre* (1501 Euclid Ave.; phone: 241-5490) for traditional drama from Shakespeare to Arthur Miller; *Eldred Theatre* (2070 Adelbert Rd.; phone: 368-6262) for an eclectic selection of 20th-century drama. *Hanna Theatre* offers cabaret-style entertainment (E. 14th St.; phone: 771-1664); *Cleveland Public Theatre* (6415 Detroit Ave.; phone: 631-2727) offers avant-garde performances. For big-name entertainment, try the *Playhouse Square Center* (1519 Euclid Ave.; phone: 241-6000). Also, the *Cleveland Ballet* (1 Playhouse Sq.; phone: 621-2260) is a must for dance lovers, and the *Cleveland Opera* performs at the *State Theatre* (1519 Euclid Ave.; phone: 575-0900).

NIGHTCLUBS AND NIGHTLIFE

Favorites are *Peabody's* (2140 S. Taylor Rd.; phone: 321-4072) for folk or blues; *Club Isabella* (2025 University Dr.; phone: 229-1177) for jazz; *Wilbert's Bar and Grille* (1360 W. Ninth St.; phone: 771-2583) for an eclectic mix of music; and the *Whiskey* (1575 Merwin Ave.; phone: 522-1575), a trendy spot. At *Mirage on the Water* (2510 Elm St.; phone: 348-1135), view the stars through a 20-foot retractable roof; or try *Trilogy Night Club* (2325 Elm St.; phone: 241-1444) for futuristic music in a restored warehouse. For comedy, try the *Improv,* in the *Powerhouse in the Flats* entertainment complex (2000 Sycamore St.; phone: 696-4677), or the *Hilarities Comedy Hall* (1230 W. Sixth St.; phone: 781-7733), which offers local and national talent. Dueling pianos bring something different to the bar of *Howl at the Moon (Powerhouse in the Flats* complex, 2000 Sycamore St.; phone: 861-4695). Reggae fans should try the *Splash Nite Club* (1545 Merwin Ave.; phone: 589-9797) which has live bands and dancing.

Best in Town

CHECKING IN

Cleveland has a number of attractive and reasonably priced accommodations. Most of Cleveland's major hotels have complete facilities for the business traveler. Those listed below as having "business services" usually offer such conveniences as meeting rooms, photocopiers, computers, translation services, and express checkout, among others. Call the individual hotel for additional information. As an alternative to the major hotels, a company called *Private Lodgings* (PO Box 18590, Cleveland, OH 44118; phone: 321-3213) finds accommodations in private residences in a variety of price ranges. Expect to pay $150 or more per night for a double room at the hotels listed in the very expensive category; $110 to $150 at those listed as expensive; $60 to $110 at those categorized as moderate; and less than $60 at the inexpensive places. Unless otherwise noted, hotel rooms have air conditioning, private baths, TV sets, and telephones.

All hotels below are in Cleveland and telephone and fax numbers are in the 216 area code unless otherwise indicated.

VERY EXPENSIVE

Omni International An elegant property 10 minutes from downtown, it has 330 guestrooms and 14 suites. All of the beautifully appointed rooms have large work desks, and the suites feature Jacuzzis and sitting areas with wet bars. *Classics* (see *Eating Out*) offers fine dining in a formal setting, and *Le Bistro* and *Le Café* serve more casual fare. A concierge, complimentary shuttle service to downtown and University Circle, and business services are available. 2065 E. 96th St. (phone: 791-1900; 800-THE-OMNI; fax: 231-3329).

Ritz-Carlton Conveniently located in the *Tower City Center* complex, it has 208 rooms and 19 suites with panoramic views of the city. The *River View Room* offers elegant dining overlooking the riverfront, and high tea is served every afternoon in the lounge. There are banquet facilities, a ballroom, and a fitness center with pool, sauna, steamroom, and spa. Twice-daily maid service, a concierge, and business services are available. 1515 W. Third St. (phone: 623-1300; 800-241-3333; fax: 623-1492).

Renaissance Cleveland This member of the *National Trust for Historic Preservation*'s Historic Hotels of America has 493 rooms and luxury suites, as well as two restaurants, one of which, *Sans Souci,* offers exquisitely prepared Mediterranean food. Special feature: a 10-story atrium complete with waterfall and swimming pool. Other amenities include 24-hour room service, a concierge, and business services. 24 Public Sq. (phone: 696-5600; 800-325-5000 or 800-HOTELS-1; fax: 696-3102).

EXPENSIVE

Marriott Society Center This 25-story hotel has 402 comfortably appointed rooms, a restaurant, a bar that serves light meals, a fitness center, and a gift shop. Business services are offered. 127 Public Sq. (phone: 696-9200; 800-228-9290; fax: 696-0966).

Marriott West Near the airport, Cleveland's best motor inn has 374 rooms, an indoor pool, a therapy pool, a sauna, miniature golf, a putting green, volleyball, and badminton. There is also *J. W.'s Steakhouse, Duke's* restaurant, and a lounge with entertainment. Other amenities include a concierge desk, a free airport bus, and business services. 4277 W. 150th St. (phone: 252-5333; 800-228-9290; fax: 251-1508).

Wyndham Playhouse Square This 205-room triangular-shaped hotel is ideally situated in the heart of the historic theater district. Amenities include a health club, a pool, room service, valet parking, and express checkout. The *Windsor* restaurant features a fine continental menu. Business services are available. 1260 Euclid Ave. (phone: 615-7500; 800-WYNDHAM; fax: 615-3355).

MODERATE

Embassy Suites The only all-suite downtown hotel, its 252 units have kitchens and work areas. There's also a pool, a restaurant, and a fitness center. There is a concierge, and business services are offered. 1701 E. 12th St. (phone: 523-8000; 800-362-2779; fax: 523-1698).

Glidden House This stately mansion on University Circle, a short walk from the city's cultural center, has been transformed into an elegant bed and breakfast inn with 52 rooms and eight suites. Business services are available. 1901 Ford Dr. (phone: 231-8900; fax: 231-2130).

INEXPENSIVE

Alcazar A European-style property nestled in the trendy Cedar Hill area, 4 miles east of downtown. There are 110 rooms and 180 suites. Features include a full-service restaurant, heated garage, beauty salon, and laundromat. 2450 Derbyshire Rd., Cleveland Heights (phone: 321-5400).

EATING OUT

Restaurants reflect the huge ethnic diversity of the city. Expect to pay $60 or more for dinner for two at places listed as expensive, $30 to $60 at those categorized as moderate, and less than $30 at inexpensive places. Prices do not include drinks, wine, tax, or tips. All restaurants are in the 216 area code unless otherwise indicated.

Unless otherwise noted, restaurants are open for lunch and dinner.

EXPENSIVE

Classics This award-winning restaurant in the *Omni* hotel is known for its rack of lamb *persille* and steak Diane (both prepared at your table) and its special desserts. The inviting, intimate atmosphere, with live jazz and classical music playing in the background, perfectly complements the sophisticated fare. Closed Sundays; dinner only on Saturdays. Reservations advised. Major credit cards accepted. E. 96th St. and Carnegie Ave. (phone: 791-1300).

Giovanni's Pasta is prepared in delectable ways, and the veal and sweetbreads are equally satisfying. Among the specialties are Maryland crab-and-shrimp cakes and chilled, marinated sweetwater prawns with asparagus. The decor is quite elegant; people tend to dress to complement the surroundings. Closed Sundays. Reservations necessary. Major credit cards accepted. 25550 Chagrin Blvd., Beachwood (phone: 831-8625).

Hyde Park Grille This is the place for hearty meat eaters. Choose from steaks, filet mignon with king crab and béarnaise sauce, or an elegant chateaubriand for two, all served with delicately deep-fried onion crisps. Dark green upholstery and dark paneling complete the clubhouse atmosphere. There's jazz on weekends. Reservations advised. Major credit cards accepted. 1825 Coventry Rd., Cleveland Heights (phone: 321-6444).

Johnny's Bar This tavern's trendiness belies its location—an old residential neighborhood. The menu features veal and shrimp with linguine, bell pepper pasta with shrimp, veal steaks, and filet mignon. Closed Sundays. Reservations advised. Major credit cards accepted. 3164 Fulton Rd. (phone: 281-0555).

Parker's Flavorful French fare is prepared from fresh, organically grown ingredients. Specialties include medallions of pork, Belgian Blue beef, and free-range chicken. A delicate lemon soufflé is the house specialty dessert. Closed

Sundays; prix fixe dinner only on Saturdays. Reservations necessary. Major credit cards accepted. 2801 Bridge Ave. in Ohio City (phone: 771-7130).

Sammy's Wooden beams and brick walls make this 116-year-old converted warehouse a real gem. The adventurous offerings include chicken in phyllo with vegetables, and rack of lamb with pistachio nut coating and black currant sauce. For dessert, there is *boule de neige*, a rum and chocolate espresso cake with whipped cream. This eatery also has one of the best raw seafood bars in the city and live jazz nightly. Closed Sundays. Reservations advised. Major credit cards accepted. 1400 W. 10th St. (phone: 523-5560).

MODERATE

Great Lakes Brewing Company A block from the *West Side Market*, this eatery is popular for lunch. As befits a brewery, beer is the main attraction, with a golden Dortmunder-style lager and a darker, porter-style ale among the award-winning selections. Homemade soups, walleye, perch, and other fish dishes give you something to go with the brews. Reservations advised for dinner. Major credit cards accepted. 2516 Market Ave. (phone: 771-4404).

López y González Hearty portions of Mexican favorites—*tacos al carbón*, for example—are washed down with Mexican beer or oversize margaritas. Mesquite-smoked game hen, tequila chicken, and fresh fish round out the menu. Closed Sundays. Reservations advised. Major credit cards accepted. 2066 Lee Rd., Cleveland Heights (phone: 371-7611).

Pearl of the Orient Chinese food is carefully presented here. Worth noting are the house specialties: Peking duck and hot and sour soup. Reservations necessary. Major credit cards accepted. 20121 Van Aken Blvd., Shaker Heights (phone: 751-8181).

That Place on Bellflower Set in a charming century-old carriage house, this is the jewel of the city's French restaurants. Specialties are veal Oscar, *escalope* of veal, and fresh salmon renaissance (a combination of chopped salmon, onions, and spinach in pastry). In the summer, dining is alfresco. Closed Mondays, dinner only on Sundays. Reservations advised. Major credit cards accepted. 11401 Bellflower Rd., at University Circle (phone: 231-4469).

INEXPENSIVE

Balaton The atmosphere isn't much—bright lights and paper placemats—but the Hungarian food is the real thing. Popular favorites include Wiener schnitzel and Hungarian goulash. No alcoholic beverages are served. Closed Sundays and Mondays. No reservations. MasterCard and Visa accepted. 12523 Buckeye Rd. (phone: 921-9691).

Ruthie and Moe's A refurbished 1920s railroad dining car is the unusual setting for this friendly, comfortable eatery dishing up down-home cooking. Homemade matzoh ball soup, chicken gumbo, and daily specials make this a hot spot both for business lunches and family outings. The Thai chicken salad is also popular. Closed Saturdays and Sundays. No reservations. MasterCard and Visa accepted. 4002 Prospect Ave. (phone: 431-8063).

Tommy's Hearty soups, salads, creative sandwiches, and tasty spinach pies are the vegetarian fare here, all served fast and hot. The decor is simple. No reservations or credit cards accepted. 1820 Coventry Rd., Cleveland Heights (phone: 321-7757).

Dallas

Dallas is a paradox—both big city and small town. Gleaming glass monolithic structures loom over the downtown area, but Dallasites are just down-home folks at heart.

That is, if you can find a native Texan. Migration from the north (led by such major corporations as JC Penney, MCI, and Exxon) has doubled Dallas's population over the past two decades or so. The city that started as a cabin on the banks of the Trinity River about 150 years ago has grown to a metropolitan area of 4.1 million (counting neighboring Ft. Worth and surrounding suburbs). If Texas were a nation, Dallas would be its capital. Some residents claim the city is quintessential Texas—the epitome of ostentation—but that reputation has earned it some enmity in other parts of the state.

A few statistics: Dallas has more shopping space per shopper than any other American city, and it has even more restaurants per capita than New York. The *Dallas Market Center,* which supplies apparel and furnishings to stores across the country, averages about $50 billion a year in retail sales, and the airport Dallas shares with Ft. Worth is larger than the island of Manhattan. These facts point to one thing: extraordinary wealth. Where does it come from? Oil, cotton, electronics, banking, clothing, and insurance. This wealth greatly determines what might be called the Dallas lifestyle. At its best, it has generated a number of progressive civic programs; at its worst, it's led to tasteless extravagance and a preoccupation with money and power above all else.

The 1990s have seen a resurgence in extravagance and, once again, an acceptance of wealth as the norm. Medical research is a bigger business than ever, real estate is revitalized as retail businesses and housing development boom yet again, and tourism escalates beyond all expectations. The owner of a professional football team bought the world's best talent and gave Dallas an unprecedented three Super Bowl championships in four years—a feat that gives the city an intensified sense of pride.

There is a dark side to the dream, however—a shadow that has hung over the city for over 30 years. To millions of people throughout the world, Dallas is where President John F. Kennedy was assassinated in November 1963. Memphis and Los Angeles were the sites of similar tragedies—the murders of Martin Luther King Jr. and Robert F. Kennedy—but they bear no equivalent notoriety. Sadly, however, the words "Dallas" and "assassination" are likely to be linked for some time to come.

Dallas was founded in 1841 by a Tennessee lawyer named John Neely Bryan, who built a cabin at the junction of three forks of La Santísima Trinidad (Most Holy Trinity) River, and then promoted the area into a city with circulars and word-of-mouth advertising—within nine years, 430 people had joined him. With the help of a lot of oil, cattle, manufacturing, and several fortuitous technological revolutions, the growing metropolis eventually became the eighth-largest city in the country. In recent years, it also has gained respect in cultural and culinary circles: The $100-million *Morton H. Meyerson Symphony Center* has enhanced the city's Arts District, and a number of chefs from Dallas restaurants have achieved acclaim among national food critics.

But not everything is perfect beneath the Dallas sun. The crime rate is alarmingly high, and racial tensions smolder and steam on the south side of the city, in stark contrast to the manicured lawns of affluent North Dallas.

Perhaps it is not so surprising then to discover that the city's characteristic self-promotion conceals an uncertainty about its real nature. Dallas is Texan, no doubt (the rest of the country can see that even if Texans can't), and it is certainly American in its problems, successes, and prospects. But the city as a whole is something more than the sum of its obvious parts. And this intangible "more" fascinates residents and visitors alike.

Dallas At-a-Glance

SEEING THE CITY

For the best view of Dallas, go to the top of *Reunion Tower* (300 Reunion Blvd.; phone: 651-1234 or 741-3663), alongside the huge mirror-faced *Hyatt Regency* hotel, also a Dallas landmark. The tower has a revolving cocktail lounge, restaurant, and observation deck. Admission charge.

SPECIAL PLACES

Although attractions in Dallas are spread out, most of the museums are clustered at *Fair Park.*

FAIR PARK

Three miles east of downtown Dallas, *Fair Park* is the site of 24 attractions, including seven museums of science, history, and technology; the *Cotton Bowl Stadium,* site of the *New Year's Day* college football game; and *Fair Park Coliseum* (1300 Robert B. Cullum Blvd., two blocks south of I-30). Some 150 events take place throughout the park annually, but the biggest of them is the *State Fair of Texas* (phone: 565-9931; 800-375-1839), which lasts for three incredibly jammed weeks in October. Grand Ave. (phone: 670-8400 for a 24-hour information line).

MUSEUM OF NATURAL HISTORY In order to attract the *Texas Centennial Exposition* to Dallas in 1936, the city fathers built a group of museums at *Fair Park.* The *Museum of Natural History,* a neoclassical, cream limestone building, contains a variety of fauna and flora from the Southwest's 600-million-year history. There are some interesting zoological and botanical exhibitions, too. Open daily. Admission charge. *Fair Park,* 3535 Grand Ave. (phone: 421-DINO).

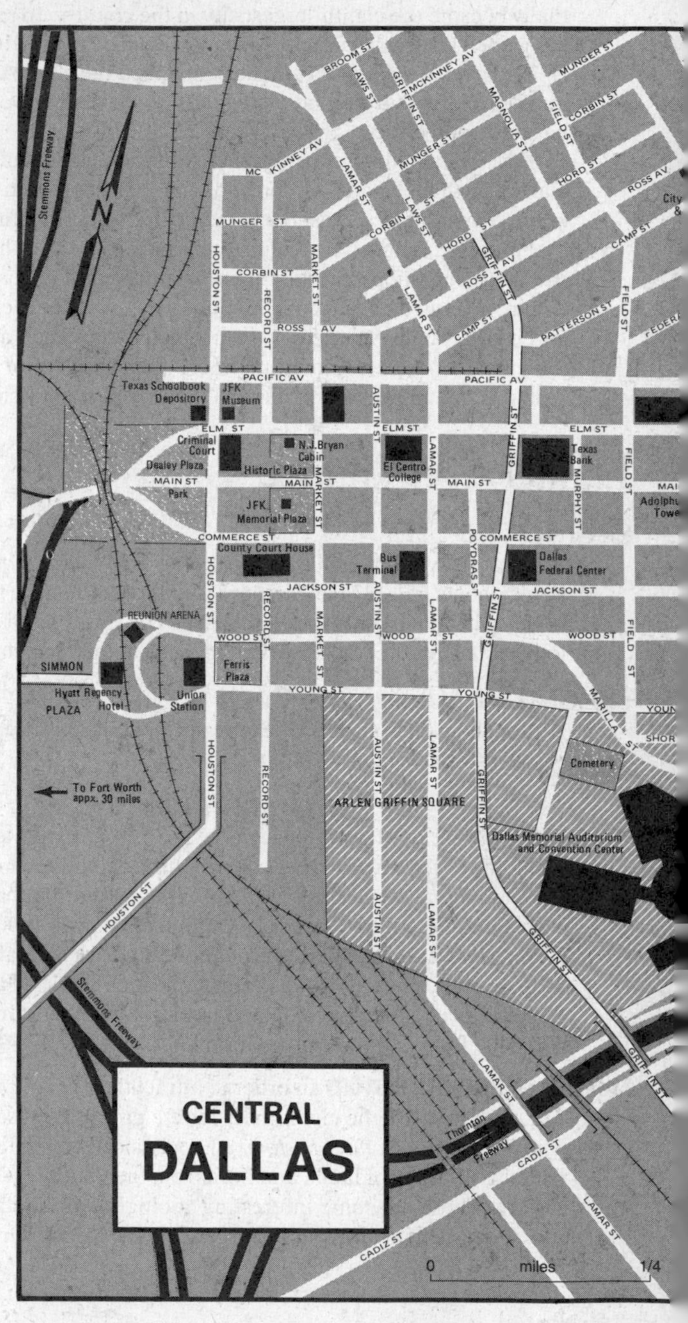

CENTRAL
DALLAS
Stemmons Freeway
N
BROOM ST
LAWS ST
GRIFFIN ST
McKINNEY AV
MAGNOLIA ST
MUNGER ST
FIELD ST
CORBIN ST
MC KINNEY AV
LAMAR ST
MUNGER ST
HORD ST
ROSS AV
MUNGER ST
CORBIN ST
LAWS ST
HORD ST
CAMP ST
HOUSTON ST
MARKET ST
CORBIN ST
RECORD ST
ROSS AV
GRIFFIN ST
ROSS AV
LAMAR ST
CAMP ST
FIELD ST
PATTERSON ST
ROSS AV
PACIFIC AV
PACIFIC AV
Texas Schoolbook Depository
JFK Museum
ELM ST
ELM ST
ELM ST
Criminal Court
N.J.Bryan Cabin
AUSTIN ST
El Centro College
LAMAR ST
GRIFFIN ST
Texas Bank
MURPHY ST
FIELD ST
Dealey Plaza
Historic Plaza
MAIN ST
Park
MAIN ST
MAIN ST
JFK Memorial Plaza
Adolphus
COMMERCE ST
POYDRAS ST
COMMERCE ST
County Court House
Bus Terminal
Dallas Federal Center
JACKSON ST
JACKSON ST
REUNION ARENA
WOOD ST
WOOD ST
WOOD ST
Ferris Plaza
SIMMON
Hyatt Regency Hotel
PLAZA
Union Station
YOUNG ST
YOUNG ST
MARILLA ST
Cemetery
To Fort Worth appx. 30 miles
ARLEN GRIFFIN SQUARE
Dallas Memorial Auditorium and Convention Center
HOUSTON ST
Stemmons Freeway
Thornton Freeway
CADIZ ST
CADIZ ST
0 miles 1/4

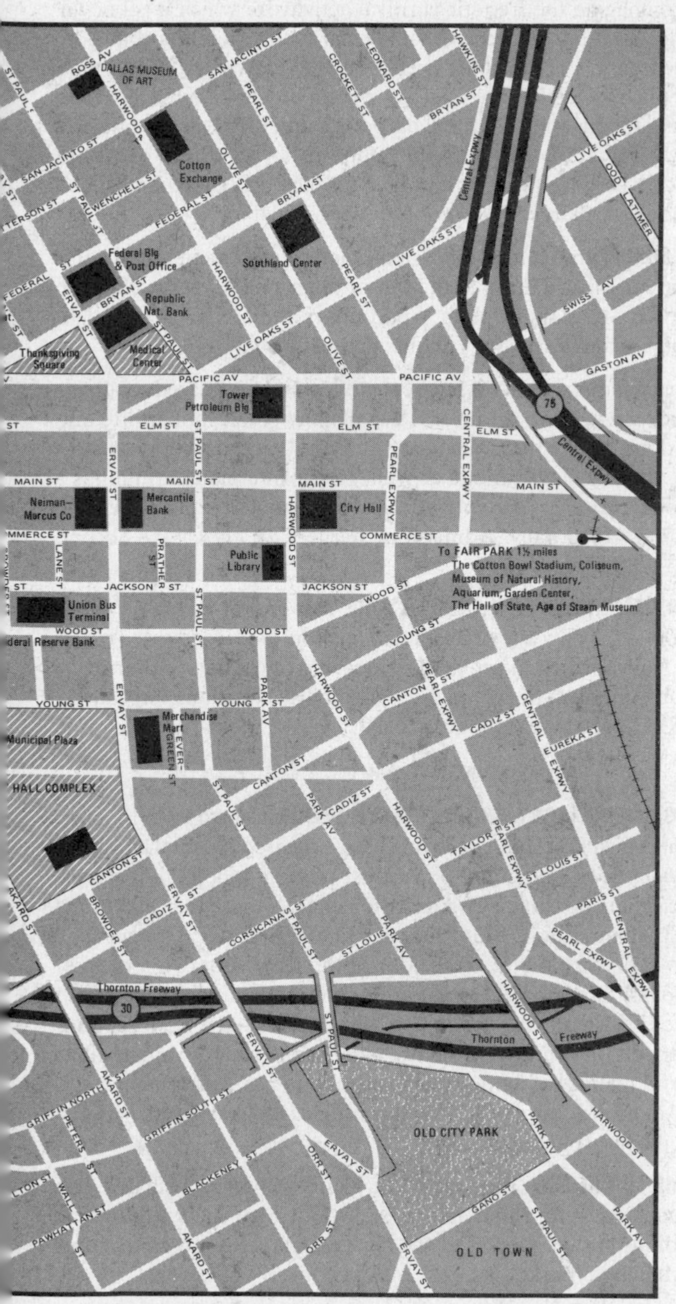

ROSS AV
DALLAS MUSEUM OF ART
SAN JACINTO ST
HARWOOD
PEARL ST
CROCKETT ST
LEONARD ST
HAWKINS ST
BRYAN ST
Central Expwy
LIVE OAKS ST
LATIMER
Cotton Exchange
OLIVE ST
EWENCHELL ST
FEDERAL ST
ST PAUL ST
Southland Center
Federal Blg & Post Office
Republic Nat. Bank
HARWOOD ST
ERVAY ST
SWISS AV
Thanksgiving Square
Medical Center
PACIFIC AV
GASTON AV
Tower Petroleum Blg
75
ELM ST
CENTRAL EXPWY
PEARL EXPWY
MAIN ST
Neiman-Marcus Co
Mercantile Bank
City Hall
COMMERCE ST
LANE ST
PRATHER ST
Public Library
JACKSON ST
WOOD ST
To FAIR PARK 1½ miles
The Cotton Bowl Stadium, Coliseum,
Museum of Natural History,
Aquarium, Garden Center,
The Hall of State, Age of Steam Museum
Union Bus Terminal
Federal Reserve Bank
YOUNG ST
CANTON ST
CADIZ ST
EUREKA ST
Municipal Plaza
Merchandise Mart
EVERGREEN ST
PARK AV
HALL COMPLEX
TAYLOR ST
ST LOUIS ST
PARIS ST
AKARD ST
BROWDER ST
CORSICANA ST
Thornton Freeway
30
Thornton Freeway
GRIFFIN NORTH ST
GRIFFIN SOUTH ST
PETERS ST
OLD CITY PARK
ORR ST
BLACKENEY ST
WALL ST
PAWHATTAN ST
GANO ST
OLD TOWN

MIDWAY AND THE TEXAS HALL OF STATE As you walk along the *Midway,* you will find it hard to imagine the frenetic carnival activity for which it is known. But during the *State Fair* or occasional special events, you'll probably be swept into the frenzy, stopping only long enough to try your luck at a shooting gallery or pitch 'n' toss. There is an assortment of scream-inducing rides, as well as great food stands—Greek, barbecue, and Mexican. At one end of the *Midway,* the *Texas Hall of State* (phone: 421-4500) has paintings devoted to Texas heroes. It was built in 1936 for the *Texas Centennial.* Open daily. No admission charge. *Fair Park* (phone: 670-8400).

AGE OF STEAM MUSEUM With steam engines and other railroad memorabilia, this museum is sure to bring a lump to the throat of anyone who ever loved an old train. Closed Mondays through Wednesdays. Admission charge. *Fair Park,* Washington and Parry Sts. (phone: 428-0101).

SCIENCE PLACE Permanent exhibits on science and technology geared to all age groups include *Body Tech,* an interactive display about human life and health; an exhibit of live bees busily at work; and electricity demonstrations. There are traveling exhibits as well. An on-site planetarium has a variety of shows, classes, and demonstrations designed to explore the mystery of the stars. Open daily. Admission charge. *Fair Park,* 1318 Second Ave. (phone: 428-5555).

MUSEUM OF AFRICAN-AMERICAN LIFE AND CULTURE This 38,000-square-foot heritage repository is the only one of its kind in the Southwest, dedicated exclusively to the study, preservation, and showcasing of exhibits and artifacts of the African-American people. Closed Mondays. No admission charge. *Fair Park,* 3536 Grand Ave. (phone: 565-9026).

DOWNTOWN

TEXAS SCHOOL BOOK DEPOSITORY AND THE SIXTH FLOOR Known to millions as the place from which Lee Harvey Oswald allegedly fired the fatal gunshots, the *Texas School Book Depository* is the most-photographed site in Texas. Open daily except major holidays. Admission charge; there is an additional charge for a 35-minute audio tour (phone: 633-6659; 653-6657 for groups). The *Sixth Floor* (located on the sixth floor of the Depository), a project of the *Dallas County Historical Foundation,* is a permanent exhibition which examines the life, death, and legacy of John F. Kennedy. Historic photographs, artifacts, interpretive displays, videos, and award-winning films evoke powerful feelings of an unforgettable chapter in American history. Open daily. Admission charge. 411 Elm St.; entrance on Houston St. between Elm and Pacific Sts. (phone: 653-6666).

JOHN F. KENNEDY MEMORIAL Near the spot where Kennedy was assassinated, this monument consists of four unconnected, 30-foot-high walls defining an area for meditation that is open to the sky and marked only by a center stone slab. Main and Market Sts.

UNION STATION This renovated 1916 rail station, which currently houses a grand hall and banquet rooms, a snack bar, and a visitors' center, is such a treat that travelers passing through town on *Amtrak* trains sometimes disembark just to view it. 400 S. Houston (phone: 653-1101).

MORTON H. MEYERSON SYMPHONY CENTER Designed by I. M. Pei, who was also the architect for Dallas's cantilevered *City Hall,* the center is a major facility for music and other performing arts. A computer was used in designing the unusual structural shapes and supports, which were intended to "uplift" audiences. Flora and Pearl Sts. (phone: 670-3600).

DALLAS MUSEUM OF ART The keystone of Dallas's downtown Arts District houses a permanent collection of pre-Columbian art, African sculpture, and 19th-century modern and contemporary works. The *Sculpture Garden,* featuring works by Henry Moore and Ellsworth Kelly, is an urban oasis, replete with cascades and shade trees. The *Reves Collection,* hung in a reconstructed Italian villa, and the *Bybee Collection* (furniture) are worth investigating. Also inside is the *Museum of the Americas,* with 4,000 works from North, South, and Central America, dating from pre-Columbian days. The Dallas skyline is an impressive backdrop to the building designed by Edward Larrabee Barnes. Closed Mondays. No admission charge, except for the *Reves Collection* and special exhibits. 1717 N. Harwood (phone: 922-1200).

DALLAS WORLD AQUARIUM This revolutionary aquarium has garnered rave reviews for its exhibits, including a representation of a coral reef. You can walk through a triangular-shape tunnel tank where sea horses, giant clams, ribbon eels, and sharks swim around you, and there is a terrarium with black-foot penguins. Open daily. Admission charge. 1801 N. Griffin St. (phone: 720-2224).

WEST END MARKETPLACE In the West End Historical District, this onetime warehouse boasts more than 125 shops, pushcart vendors, and refreshment stands. Open daily. 603 Munger Ave. (phone: 748-4801).

FARMERS' MARKET Here's an urban spin on rural Texas. From 6 AM on, farmers drive into town in their trusty pickups to sell the fruit—and vegetables—of their labor. The market consists of a tin-roof shelter and dozens of stalls staffed by colorful characters. The vegetables are fresher and a bit cheaper than anywhere else in town; the flowers are outstanding, too. In May there's a flower festival, in September a fall harvest, and in November an arts and crafts fair. Open daily. 1010 S. Pearl (phone: 670-5879).

DALLAS COUNTY HISTORICAL PLAZA A fascinating range of history and architectural styles is found in several buildings in this area. The *Old Red Courthouse* is a Romanesque marvel with leering gargoyles; also check out the *John Neely Bryan Cabin* and the *Kennedy Memorial.* Bordered by Market, Elm, Houston, and Commerce Sts.

DEEP ELLUM This former industrial neighborhood has been transformed into a funky collection of restaurants, nightclubs, galleries, and boutiques. East of downtown, bounded by the Central Expwy. and Elm and Commerce Sts.

THANKSGIVING SQUARE Designed by Philip Johnson and funded by an interfaith educational foundation, this meditation space has a garden, fountains, a spiral chapel, and a horizontal stained glass window. Melodious bells ring to mark the hour. Open daily. No admission charge. Pacific, Bryan, and Ervay Sts. (phone: 969-1977).

NEIMAN MARCUS The shrine of commercial elegance, this specialty store has been known to induce orgies of spending. Designer clothing and the finest china, crystal, and home furnishings make it a standout. If you have an insatiable craving for a wave-making machine or a biorhythm calculator, this is the place to satisfy it. These toys, however, are among the more conservative items in stock. The really exotic stuff is offered in the *Christmas* catalogue. Three locations: 1618 Main St. (phone: 741-6911); *NorthPark Center* (phone: 363-8311); and the *Prestonwood Mall* (phone: 233-1100).

ELSEWHERE

Outside the central business district lie many other attractions that make Dallas a place of never-ending excitement, from the battlefield of the Dallas *Cowboys* to the re-created natural environments of the *Dallas Zoo.*

DALLAS ARBORETUM Sixty-six acres on the eastern shore of White Rock Lake are dedicated to horticultural displays, education, and research. Just minutes from downtown are fragrant gardens, rolling green lawns, and tall shade trees. Admission charge. 8525 Garland Rd. (phone: 327-8263).

INFOMART This copy of London's 19th-century *Crystal Palace* exposition hall is one of the city's most distinctive architectural works. It's also a computer marketplace, so you can go shopping after admiring the façade. 1950 Stemmons Fwy. (phone: 746-3500).

MEADOWS MUSEUM Within *Southern Methodist University*'s School of Fine Arts is a prestigious assembly of Spanish paintings, drawings, and prints dating from the 16th century to the present. Closed Wednesdays. No admission charge. On campus, Bishop at Binkley (phone: 768-2516).

FRONTIERS OF FLIGHT MUSEUM This aviation museum at *Love Field Airport* highlights the history of flight in Dallas from *Fair Park*'s turn-of-the-century barnstormers to *Dallas/Ft. Worth*'s current position as one of the nation's leading airports. Closed Mondays. Admission charge. Located just above the main terminal lobby. Mockingbird La., *Love Field* (phone: 350-1651).

BIBLICAL ARTS CENTER Paintings by the Old Masters, contemporary spiritual works, and archaeological artifacts are used to help people understand the places, people, and events portrayed in the Bible. Closed Mondays. No admission charge. 7500 Park La. (phone: 691-4661).

MEMORIAL CENTER FOR HOLOCAUST STUDIES An outstanding exhibit of photographs, artifacts, documentary films, and videos tells the tragic story of the Holocaust, including tales of local survivors. There's a memorial room and a library as well. Closed Saturdays. No admission charge. 7900 Northaven St. (phone: 750-4654).

SWISS AVENUE HISTORIC DISTRICT Opulent mansions grace this grand boulevard, the most prestigious address in town almost a century ago. The buildings that are in the best shape are in the Wilson Block Historic District, within the 2800 and 2900 blocks of Swiss Avenue.

WAGON WHEEL RANCH Close to the airport, this is a family fun place offering horse rentals and group night rides, as well as barbecues, country entertainment, and hayrides, on 300 acres of wooded trails and picnic areas. Riding lessons, Western or English style, are offered. Reservations necessary. Northwest of Dallas in Grapevine (phone: 817-481-8284).

DALLAS ZOO About 1,400 mammals, reptiles, and birds live comfortably within this 70-acre zoo. The *Wilds of Africa* section provides several species of African animals with 25 acres that simulate their natural habitat. A monorail carries visitors along the treetops high over the *Wilds of Africa* for a prime view of the animals in their environment. Open daily. Admission charge. *Marsalis Park,* 621 E. Clarendon Dr. (phone: 670-5656).

LONE STAR PARK Pari-mutuel horse racing can be found at the *Dallas–Fort Worth Metroplex* with this huge, new complex in Grand Prairie. Live, on-site racing is offered April through *Labor Day,* and live racing via simulcast is offered the rest of the year. Just south of I-30 in Grand Prairie (phone: 263-RACE).

STUDIOS AT LAS COLINAS As the film industry in Texas booms, so does the production business at this state-of-the-art movie and television complex. For a behind-the-scenes look at the complex where films such as *RoboCop, Trip to Bountiful,* and *JFK* were made, take a guided tour, which includes the *National Museum of Communications.* Closed Sundays through Tuesdays. Admission charge. 6301 N. O'Connor Rd. at Royal Ln., Irving (phone: 869-FILM).

TEXAS STADIUM *Cowboys* fans go crazy here. This 64,000-seat stadium packs 'em in during home games. It's constructed to give you the sense of being in a theater or auditorium rather than a stadium, but critics point out that with the dome partially open, part of the field is always in shadow. Tours of the *Cowboys'* locker room, players' tunnel, pressbox, and some private suites are offered daily for a fee; reservations necessary. Hwy. 183 at Loop 12 in Irving (phone: 554-1804).

SOUTHFORK RANCH The Ewing family ranch, as seen on TV's "Dallas," has had an uneasy existence since the show was canceled. It closed after going bankrupt in 1991, but it has reopened after a $1-million renovation. A tram tour offers an overview of the property, including longhorn cattle and horses, and there are several restaurants, a visitors' center, and a gift shop. Open daily. Admission charge. Follow US Hwy. 75 north from Dallas about 35 miles to Parker Rd., Plano, then continue east 5½ miles to Farm Rd. 2551 (phone: 442-7800).

ARLINGTON

SIX FLAGS OVER TEXAS Located midway between Dallas and Ft. Worth, this family entertainment center covers 205 acres and offers over 100 rides, shows, and attractions. The $5-million *Looney Tunes Land* is a special children's area featuring the park's celebrity host, Bugs Bunny, and his Warner Brothers cartoon friends. The musical revue in the *Southern Palace Music Hall* and the country-style show in the *Crazy Horse Saloon* help to draw nearly three million visitors here each year. Summers are hot—but nearly everything that can be air conditioned is. Open weekends spring and fall; daily June through August. No admission charge for children under two. I-30 at Hwy. 360 (phone: 817-640-8900).

THE BALLPARK IN ARLINGTON The former *Arlington Stadium* is gone, replaced by a facility designed to evoke the feel of baseball's past. Built of Texas pink granite and red brick, with tiered balconies, it is decorated with icons of the Texas *Rangers*—both the police officers and the baseball players. The complex also features a hall of fame, an amphitheater, Little League fields, picnic grounds, numerous stores, and several restaurants. Nolan Ryan Expwy., at I-30 and Pennant Dr., Arlington (phone: 817-273-5100).

WET 'N' WILD This Texas-size recreation park attracts huge crowds on blistering summer weekends (weekdays are a bit less jammed). Water slides, inner-tube chutes, body-surfing pools, and children's play areas provide heat relief for all ages. Closed November through April, and weekdays in May and September. Admission charge. Across I-30 from *The Ballpark at Arlington* at 1800 E. Lamar Blvd. (phone: 817-265-3356).

EXTRA SPECIAL

Before the advent of its skyscrapers and highways, Dallas was a simpler place where architecture combined Victorian grace with the less refined Prairie School influence. One of the few places still able to convey a sense of those earlier, unhurried days is *Old City Park,* an oasis of greenery and history close to downtown. Restored Victorian houses, a railroad depot, pioneer log cabins, and other historically significant structures have been moved in from various locales in North Texas and are open for exploration. Closed Mondays. Admission charge. Gano and St. Paul (phone: 421-5141).

Safari buffs should consider taking a side trip to the *Fossil Rim Wildlife Center* (phone: 897-2960 for information) in the town of Glen Rose, about a one-and-a-half-hour drive south from the *Dallas/Ft. Worth Airport.* The center is a 2,900-acre safari camp where you can watch wildebeest, water

buck, and the endangered oryx and addax. Nearly 30 other species are in residence here, including giraffes, zebras, gazelles, gemsbok, kudus, and other antelope.

Sources and Resources

TOURIST INFORMATION

For brochures, maps, and general information, contact the *Dallas Convention and Visitors Bureau* (1201 Elm St., Suite 2000, Dallas, TX 75270; phone: 746-6677), which is closed weekends. There are three *Dallas Visitor Information Centers,* all open daily: at *West End MarketPlace* (603 Munger; phone: 880-0405); 1303 Commerce St. (phone: 746-6665); and *NorthPark Center* (phone: 368-5164). Call the Special Events Info-Line (phone: 746-6679) for daily information on Dallas events. Contact the Texas state tourism hotline (phone: 800-8888-TEX) for maps, calendars of events, health updates, and travel advisories.

LOCAL COVERAGE *Dallas Morning News,* daily (see *Guide,* a section in Friday's paper, for entertainment information); and *Dallas Observer,* weekly. The Dallas restaurant guide in *Texas Monthly* magazine is useful for food listings.

TELEVISION STATIONS KTVT Channel 11–CBS; KXAS Channel 5–NBC; WFAA Channel 8–ABC; and KERA Channel 13–PBS.

RADIO STATIONS AM: WBAP 820 (full service); KRLD 1080 (news); KVIL 1150 (contemporary); and KLIF 570 (talk). FM: KERA 90.1 (eclectic); KSCS 96.3 (country); WRR 101.1 (classical); KDMX 102.9 (light rock); and KVIL 103.7 (contemporary).

TELEPHONE The area code for Dallas is 214.

SALES TAX There is an 8.25% sales tax on most goods and services, including dining; the hotel room tax is 13%.

CLIMATE Summers are blisteringly hot and humid, with temperatures sometimes climbing to over 100F. Sudden thunderstorms punctuate the dry, blazing heat. From October through December, the weather is mild, although it can be in the 70s one day and in the 30s the next. From January through March, there are occasional sharp cold snaps and high winds (and once in a great while, some ice and snow), and between March and June you can expect rain and dust storms. (For local weather, call 787-1111. For temperature—and time—call 844-4444.)

GETTING AROUND

AIRPORT *Dallas/Ft. Worth Airport (D/FW),* one of the country's largest, is in Ft. Worth, approximately 20 miles from downtown Dallas. In light traffic, the drive into the city takes about a half hour. The inner-city *Love Field Airport* serves Texas and surrounding states. Most major hotels offer shuttle service. Companies providing transportation to area hotels include *SuperShuttle* (phone: 817-329-2000 in Ft. Worth).

BUS *Dallas Area Rapid Transit (DART)* (phone: 979-1111) operates the bus service; the fare is 75¢.

CAR RENTAL A car is necessary in Dallas; all major national firms are represented.

McKINNEY AVENUE TROLLEY Serving downtown, the Arts District (including the *Dallas Museum of Art* and the *Morton H. Meyerson Symphony Center*), and the McKinney strip, the trolley makes stops along the 2.8-mile route on McKinney Avenue and St. Paul Street. The fare is $1.50; a one-day pass costs $2; a three-day pass costs $5. The trolley runs daily (phone: 855-0006).

TAXI There are taxi stands at most major hotels, but the best way to get one is to call *Yellow Checker Cab* (phone: 565-9132).

SIGHTSEEING TOURS

BUS *Gray Line*'s "All About Dallas" tour covers downtown Dallas. Motorcoach pickups are available at major downtown hotels (phone: 824-2424).

SPECIAL EVENTS

College football teams face off in the *Cotton Bowl* on *New Year's Day* (phone: 638-7525). The *Scarborough Faire* (phone: 214-938-3247) is a six-weekend, 16th-century English fair held in nearby Waxahachie during April and May with 400 entertainers and plenty of food and drink; the *Byron Nelson Golf Classic* (phone: 717-1200) occurs in mid-May; and *Artfest* (phone: 361-2011) is held at *Fair Park* during *Memorial Day* weekend. The *Shakespeare Festival of Dallas* (phone: 559-2778) takes place during the last week in June through July. *Dallas Summer Musicals* are held from June through August at *Fair Park Music Hall* (phone: 421-0662 or 691-7200). The *State Fair of Texas* (phone: 565-9931; 800-375-1839) is held for three weeks in October in *Fair Park.*

SHOPPING

Despite stereotypes of Texan attire, from the 10-gallon hat on downward, cosmopolitan chic decidedly has replaced cowboy dandy, and shopping in Dallas has emerged as a tony pastime. Cowboy boots, however, are fashionable everywhere, and there may not be a better selection anywhere than in Dallas. Would-be Texans should stop at *Cavender's Boot City* (5539 LBJ Freeway; phone: 239-1375), with 30 stores in Texas, billed as the world's largest boot dealer, specializing in handmade Lucchese boots, jeans, and other Westernwear. Also try *Boot Town* (5909 Belt Line Rd. at Preston Rd.; phone: 385-3052), with shelves piled high with discounted boots by Acme, Tony Lama, Justin, Nocona, and Lucchese.

The city can be split into four shopping districts—downtown, uptown, Park Cities, and North Dallas. Dallas's two top malls are *NorthPark Center,* with *Neiman Marcus, Lord & Taylor,* and *Barney's New York,* and the *Galleria,* home to *Nordstrom, Marshall Field, Saks Fifth Avenue, Tiffany & Co.,* and *Gianni Versace.*

DOWNTOWN

Dallas Museum of Art Costume jewelry, gold earrings encrusted with semi-precious stones, and clay ornaments are enticing, as is the vast collection of art books, posters, and children's books. 1717 N. Harwood (phone: 922-1271).

Neiman Marcus Top-drawer goods have long been de rigueur at this venerable flagship store (see *Special Places*). 1618 Main St. (phone: 741-6911).

West End Marketplace This renovated factory houses more than 80 interesting shops and pushcarts (see *Special Places*). 603 Minger (phone: 748-4801).

Wild Bill's Official Western Wear Those who crave Western gear can try on a pair of Roy Rogers fringed leather gloves or a Texas belt buckle. Less orthodox, but guaranteed to garner notice, are the snakeskin tennis shoes. In the *West End MarketPlace* (phone: 954-1050).

UPTOWN

Adams-Middleton Gallery Renowned for its fine collections of paintings and sculpture. 3000 Maple (phone: 871-7080).

Afterimage Gallery Local photographers and artists display and sell their works here. At the *Quadrangle,* 2828 Routh St. (phone: 871-9140).

Aldredge Book Store Treasured tomes dateing as far back as the 16th century attract lovers of old bindings, marbleized endpapers, and silk bookmarks. Out of print and second-hand books are also available. 2909 Maple (phone: 871-3333).

Gerald Peters Gallery The work of noted contemporary artists, including sculptures, oil paintings, and drawings, is displayed and sold here. In addition, there are often special exhibits. 2913 Fairmount (phone: 969-9410).

Lady Primrose's English Countryside Devotees of English antiques will find an amazing selection from the remotest corners of Great Britain. 2200 Cedar Springs, in the *Crescent* hotel complex (phone: 871-8333).

La Mariposa Mexican and South American clothing is all the rage here. Also notable is the collection of folk art. 2817 Routh St. (phone: 871-9103).

Militaria This military arts gallery offers such items as a Royal Irish Rifleman's uniform, modern toy soldiers, historical statuettes, and books from all over the world. 2615 Fairmount (phone: 871-1565).

Stanley Korshak European designer men's and women's clothing, including Giorgio Armani, is available here. 2200 Cedar Springs, in the *Crescent* hotel complex (phone: 871-3600).

PARK CITIES

Anteks Southwestern, Texan, and Western home accessories—with emphasis on ranch antiques and reproductions—are packed into this store. Even such unusual items as antler candelabras and hand-crafted and -painted headboards can be found here. 5814 Lovers La. (phone: 528-5567).

Collector's Covey The bronze wildlife sculptures, decoys, and limited edition animal and bird prints here are very appealing. 15 *Highland Park Village* (phone: 521-7880).

La Crème Coffee and Tea The delicious scent of hand-blended coffees fill the air. Unusual teas also are available, as are a variety of coffee makers, teapots, and mugs. 4448 Lovers La. (phone: 369-4188).

Highland Park Village Built in 1931 and purported to be America's oldest shopping center, it is Dallas's equivalent of Rodeo Drive. Among its more famous boutiques are *Ann Taylor, Chanel, Godiva Chocolatier, Hermès, Polo/Ralph Lauren, Victor Costa,* and *William Noble Jewels.* Mockingbird and Preston Sts. (phone: 559-2740).

NORTH DALLAS

The Galleria This enormous, four-level, skylit mall boasts lots of stylish shops, including *Saks Fifth Avenue, Tiffany & Co.,* and *Marshall Field.* Best of all, valet parking is available at the *Westin* hotel on the mall's west side. *Gerlo Scherer* features the chic fashion of German designer Jil Sander, who specializes in silk and cashmere suits for women. Handsome stationery, sleek desk accessories, and fine writing implements are sold at *William Ernest Brown,* and *Optica* has a great selection of eyewear, including frames from Porsche, Ferre, and Paloma Picasso. 13350 Dallas Pkwy. (phone: 702-7100).

Olla Podrida This classic, albeit unusual Dallas landmark, originally an artisans' showplace, is packed with wonderful boutiques. *The Bunker* has military paraphernalia, while *The Clockworks* has watches and antique timepieces. *De Falco Winemaker* offers a good selection of international wines, as well as homemade varieties. *Earthen Vessels and Treasures* features oddities of Southwestern art, while *The Patchworks* proffers unusual women's clothing. For the small of stature and age, *Through the Looking Glass* presents ornate dollhouses and other miniatures. Lovers of stained glass and hand-blown art should visit the *Kitrell Glassworks.* 12215 Coit Rd. (phone: 934-3603).

SPORTS AND FITNESS

Dallas has enough professional sports to satisfy just about everyone.

BASEBALL The *American League* Texas *Rangers* play at *Ballpark in Arlington* (Nolan Ryan Expwy. at I-30 and Pennant Dr., Arlington; phone: 817-273-5100).

BASKETBALL Dallas's *NBA* team, the *Mavericks,* plays at *Reunion Arena* (777 Sports St.; phone: 939-2800).

BICYCLING Dallas has some pretty trails in the White Rock Lake–East Dallas area and at Bachman Lake, off Northwest Highway near *Love Field.* For maps of the trails, call the *City Parks Department* (phone: 670-4272).

FITNESS CENTERS The *Downtown YMCA* (601 N. Akard at Ross, across from the *Fairmont;* phone: 954-0500) has an indoor and an outdoor pool, tracks, squash and racquetball courts, exercise equipment, and a sauna. Facilities are open to non-members for a fee. *Dr. Kenneth Cooper's Aerobics Center* (12230 Preston Rd.; phone: 386-0306) has a guest lodge available for those who wish to stay overnight.

FOOTBALL The *NFL* Dallas *Cowboys,* 1996 *Super Bowl* champions, play at *Texas Stadium* (Hwy. 183 at Loop 12, Irving; phone: 579-5000). The *Cotton Bowl* is held every *New Year's Day* at *Fair Park* (phone: 638-BOWL).

GOLF There are several municipal courses in Dallas, including the 18-hole course at *Buffalo Creek Golf Club* (Lake Ray Hubbard; phone: 771-4003). *Tennison Memorial* (3501 Samuell; phone: 670-1402) is best known as the home of Lee Trevino. Many hotels also have courses. The *Dallas Convention and Visitors Bureau* (see *Tourist Information* above) has a complete listing.

HOCKEY The Dallas *Stars* of the *NHL* (formerly the Minnesota *North Stars*) play at *Reunion Arena* (777 Sports St.; phone: 467-8277).

ICE SKATING Ice Capades Chalets runs two skating rinks: in the *Galleria Mall* (13350 Dallas Pkwy.; phone: 702-7100) and in the *Prestonwood Mall* (530 Belt Line Rd.; phone: 980-8988). *America's Ice Gardens* also has a huge rink (700 N. Pearle St.; phone: 922-9800).

JOGGING For a 6-mile stint, head north on Akard, right onto Cedar Springs, then take Turtle Creek Boulevard, left onto Avondale, left onto Oak Lawn, left onto Irving, back to Turtle Creek, and retrace your steps home. Or take a bus (40 Bachman Bank or 43 Park Forest) to Bachman Lake for a 3-mile course, or to White Rock Lake (60 White Rock North on Commerce or East St.) for a 10-mile course.

RODEO Professional cowhands compete at the *Mesquite Championship Rodeo* (LBJ Fwy. and Military Pkwy. Exit in Mesquite; phone: 285-8777) on Friday and Saturday evenings, April through September.

SOCCER The *Continental Indoor Soccer League (CISL) Sidekicks* play at *Reunion Arena* (777 Sports St.; phone: 653-0200 or 939-2712).

TENNIS Tennis is a year-round sport here, and it's terrifically popular. Of the more than 200 municipal courts, the best are at *Samuell Grand Park* (6200 Grand

Ave.; phone: 670-1374 or 821-3811) and at *Fretz Park* (Hillcrest and Belt Line; phone: 670-6622).

THEATER

The city has a number of fine regional theater companies. For a complete up-to-date listing on performance schedules, see the publications listed in *Local Coverage.* The following is our favorite place in Dallas for live theater.

CENTER STAGE

Dallas Theater Center Conventional dramas and plays by contemporary authors, many of them premieres, alternate here between the *Kalita Humphreys Theater* and the *Arts District Theater,* the latter a flexible, open performance space. Preston Jones's *A Texas Trilogy* got its start here. Besides the six works presented each season on both stages, the center also produces the *Big D Festival of the Unexpected,* a celebration of new plays in development. Two locations: 3636 Turtle Creek Blvd. (phone: 922-0427) and 2401 Flora St. (phone: 526-8857).

Other major Dallas theaters are *Theatre Three* (2800 Routh; phone: 871-3300) and the beautiful *Majestic Theatre* (1925 Elm; phone: 880-0137). Several "underground" theater companies perform in the Deep Ellum area.

MUSIC

Dallas's $100-million *Morton H. Meyerson Symphony Center* (see *Special Places*) is home to the *Dallas Symphony Orchestra* (phone: 692-0203), which performs in the center's 2,066-seat *Eugene McDermott Concert Hall* (2301 Flora St.; phone: 670-3600). For information on opera, call the *Dallas Opera* (phone: 443-1000), which performs at *Fair Park Music Hall* (First and Parry Sts.). Big-name rock and pop stars (such as Eric Clapton and Janet Jackson) play at *Fair Park*'s *Starplex* (1818 First St.; phone: 421-1111); for information about other pop-rock concerts, call *Rainbow-Ticketmaster* (phone: 787-2000).

NIGHTCLUBS AND NIGHTLIFE

Nightlife in Dallas can be found in major centers. One is Greenville Avenue, a north-south artery chockablock with restaurants and nightclubs on the east side. *Poor David's* (1924 Greenville; phone: 821-9891) in Lower Greenville features every style of music, from reggae to jazz, and *Arcadia* (2005 Greenville; phone: 824-8895) excels in high-energy dance music. *Terilli's* (2815 Greenville; phone: 827-3993) in Lower Greenville is a great jazz spot.

A second center is the West End Historical District, a downtown area of renovated warehouses (one, *Dallas Alley,* contains seven clubs; phone: 988-WEST). *Dick's Last Resort* (1701 N. Market; phone: 747-0001) features live Dixieland jazz. McKinney Avenue is the third major nightlife center. It runs south to downtown and features some of the best restaurants, along with the tourists' favorite, *Hard Rock Café* (2601 McKinney; phone: 855-0007).

For something more avant-garde, head down to the fourth area, Deep Ellum/Near Ellum, a bohemian district where many blues musicians performed in the 1930s. At *Club Dada* (2720 Elm; phone: 744-3232), poetry, classical guitar, rockabilly, and Middle Eastern jazz can be heard. *2826* (2826 Elm; phone: 741-2826) is a jumping joint with alternative dance music. *Club Clearview* (2806 Elm; phone: 283-5358) is the place for a variety of bands. Near *Fair Park,* where some of the uprooted artists moved, is *Bar of Soap* (3615 Parry; phone: 823-6617), a bar/laundromat with live music. Away from those four regions, try *Strictly Tabu* (4111 Lomo Alto; phone: 528-5200), another good choice for jazz lovers; *Schooners* (1212 Skillman at Live Oak; phone: 821-1934) for blues; and *Café Brazil* (6420 N. Central Expwy; phone: 691-7791) for live eclectic, coffeehouse entertainment.

Best in Town

CHECKING IN

As the third-most popular convention city in the country, Dallas has many comfortable accommodations. Some hotels cater almost exclusively to conventions, so it may be difficult to book as an individual. It will save a lot of trouble if you inquire ahead of time. Most of Dallas's major hotels have complete facilities for the business traveler. Those listed below as having "business services" usually offer such conveniences as meeting rooms, photocopiers, computers, translation services, and express checkout, among others. Call the individual hotel for additional information. For something different and a little less expensive, try *Bed & Breakfast Texas Style,* a service that offers lodging in private homes. Contact Ruth Wilson (4224 W. Redbird La., Dallas 75237; phone: 298-5433 or 298-8586) for information. Dallas also has international youth hostel beds available at the *Anchor* motel (10230 Harry Hines Blvd.; phone: 438-6061). At the hotels below, expect to spend $130 or more per night for a double room at those places we describe as very expensive; $105 to $130 at those listed as expensive; and less than $60 at inexpensive places. Unless otherwise noted, hotel rooms have air conditioning, private baths, TV sets, and telephones.

All hotels below are in Dallas and telephone and fax numbers are in the 214 area code unless otherwise indicated.

We begin with our favorite place, followed by recommended hotels, listed by price categories.

A GRAND HOTEL

Mansion on Turtle Creek Dallas's most elegant address is a member of the prestigious Relais & Châteaux group. Custom-made furnishings, opulent bathrooms, attentive service (including a concierge, twice-daily maid service, and complimentary limousine transport), and the superb *Mansion* restaurant (see *Eating Out*) make this the best of the city's deluxe hotels. Twenty-four-hour room service is available, as are a fitness center, a salon, a concierge desk, and business services. 2821 Turtle Creek Blvd. (phone: 559-2100; 800-442-3408 in Texas; 800-527-5432 elsewhere in the US; fax: 528-4187).

VERY EXPENSIVE

Crescent Court Designed by award-winning architect Philip Johnson, this impressive 190-room, 28-suite Rosewood Group property offers high style and excellent service. The soaring Great Hall lobby links an 18-story office tower (with the hottest private club in town) to an elegant courtyard of shops and galleries with a five-story fountain. The spacious, airy rooms were designed for style as well as comfort. There is a lobby lounge, the *Conservatory* for formal dining, and the *Beau Nash* for more casual fare (see *Eating Out*). Among the many amenities are a concierge, 24-hour room service, baby-sitting, a pool, a spa, free shuttle service to downtown, and business services. 400 Crescent Ct. (phone: 871-3200; 800-654-6541; fax: 871-3272).

St. Germain A converted 1906 mansion provides the setting for this luxurious seven-suite inn. Exquisite French antiques, canopied beds, and fireplaces give the rooms an understated elegance, and there's also a lovely courtyard and a fine restaurant (see *Eating Out*). Amenities include room service, a butler, a concierge, a multilingual staff, and access to a nearby health spa. The dining room, library, and parlor are available for meetings. 2516 Maple Ave. (phone: 871-2516; fax: 871-0740).

EXPENSIVE

Adolphus Built in 1912, this elder giant among Dallas hotels is listed in the *National Register of Historic Places.* The decor is turn-of-the-century elegant; rooms are large and individually appointed. Its *French Room* (see *Eating Out*) is one of the city's classiest restaurants, and the *Walt Garrison Rodeo Bar* is a posh watering hole. Also available are 24-hour room service, a concierge, and business services. 1321 Commerce (phone: 742-8200; 800-441-0574 in Texas; 800-221-9083 elsewhere in the US; fax: 747-3532).

Courtyard by Marriott Spacious rooms (with king-size beds) surround pleasant courtyards, each of which has an indoor or outdoor pool. Business services are available. There are seven locations in the Dallas area, including two right in the city (which are more expensive). Call 800-321-2211 for central reservations.

Fairmont This Dallas favorite has a Texas pink granite façade and an elegant entrance and porte cochère. All 550 rooms have been redone, and the restaurants are fine (see the *Pyramid* in *Eating Out*). Room service responds around the clock, and there is a concierge and business services. In the Arts District, within walking distance of the West End, at 1717 N. Akard St. (phone: 720-2020; 800-527-4727; fax: 720-5269).

Four Seasons Numerous awards for its conference facilities have been bestowed on this 365-room, 50-villa property, including 50 new villas. Other amenities on its 400 acres include a spa and sports club, two 18-hole golf courses, four restaurants, a tennis stadium, racquetball, squash, and tennis courts, a jogging track, two pools, and 24-hour room service. Near the airport at 4150 N. MacArthur Blvd., Irving (phone: 717-0700; 800-332-3442; fax: 717-2550).

Grand Kempinski This 529-room hotel with a resort ambience is an attraction in itself. There is 24-hour room service, a concierge floor, tennis and racquetball courts, a spa, indoor and outdoor pools, fine restaurants, and business services. 15201 Dallas Pkwy. (phone: 386-6000; 800-426-3135; fax: 991-6937).

Hyatt Regency One of Dallas's most popular hotels, it has a silver-burnished exterior that mirrors the downtown skyline, 947 rooms and suites, a rooftop restaurant, and a health club. Room service is on call 24 hours a day, and a concierge and business services are available. 300 Reunion Blvd. (phone: 651-1234; 800-233-1234; fax: 742-8126).

Melrose A small, luxury place dating from the 1920s, its 185 rooms give it the feel of a country estate. A cozy, English-style lounge and an Art Deco restaurant, the *Landmark,* add to its appeal. Business services are available. 3015 Oak Lawn Ave. (phone: 521-5151; 800-635-7673; fax: 521-9306).

Omni Mandalay at Las Colinas This 27-story enclave dedicated to luxury is in Las Colinas, a business center west of Dallas. Convenient to both the *Dallas/Ft. Worth Airport* and downtown, it has a fine restaurant, *Enjolie,* a health club, and a heated pool. Among the amenities are 24-hour room service, a concierge desk, and business services. 221 E. Las Colinas Blvd., Irving (phone: 556-0800; 800-843-6664; fax: 556-0729).

Westin Galleria With 440 balconied rooms, this elegant hostelry opens onto the *Galleria.* Amenities include a pool, a jogging track, saunas, exercise facilities, and three restaurants, including *Huntington's,* which serves first-rate continental fare (see *Eating Out*). Convenient to North Dallas business districts, the hotel offers round-the-clock room service, a concierge, and business services. 13340 Dallas Pkwy. (phone: 934-9494; 800-228-3000; fax: 450-2979).

Wyndham Anatole The red brick exterior doesn't look much like a Dallas hotel, but many residents find it a welcome change from the monolithic rectangles of sparkling tinted glass. It has 1,620 rooms and 145 suites, 16 restaurants and lounges, 13 shops, tennis and racquetball courts, and the *Verandah Club Spa.* Around-the-clock room service is available. Other amenities include a concierge desk and business services. 2201 Stemmons Fwy. (phone: 748-1200; 800-235-6397; fax: 761-7520).

INEXPENSIVE

Country Suites One of the city's loveliest inns, it offers 12 one- and two-bedroom suites with microwaves and coffee makers. A good choice for families and businesspeople planning long-term stays. Complimentary airport transportation available. 4100 W. John Carpenter Fwy., Irving (phone: 929-4008; 800-456-4000; fax: 929-4224).

La Quinta Motor Inns If you're looking for a clean, inconspicuous place to sleep, try any of this chain's 14 motels throughout the area, including the airport. They provide nonsmoking rooms and free local calls. Each has a 24-hour adjacent restaurant. Other pluses include a concierge desk and business services. Call 800-531-5900 for central reservations.

EATING OUT

Restaurant dining in Dallas has become as sophisticated as that in any major American city over the last decade, with an emphasis on Southwest cooking. Expect to spend $60 or more for dinner for two in those places we've listed as expensive; between $30 and $60 at those categorized as moderate; and less than $30 at inexpensive places. Prices do not include wine, drinks, tax, or tips. (Parts of Dallas are "dry," but alcoholic beverages generally are available with an inexpensive club membership.) All restaurants are in the 214 area code unless otherwise indicated.

Unless otherwise noted, restaurants are open for lunch and dinner.

EXPENSIVE

Café Pacific An interesting variety of dishes is served in an attractive setting. The lobster and scallop ceviche and polenta with crabmeat are especially good, and this dining spot offers one of the most extensive and reasonably priced wine lists in town. Closed Sundays. Reservations advised. Major credit cards accepted. 24 *Highland Park Village* (phone: 526-1170).

City Café This chic eatery features a distinctive "nouvelle American" menu with such tidbits as warm cabbage salad with bacon, Caesar salad, grilled sweetbreads, and triple chocolate sour cream cake. Reservations advised. Major credit cards accepted. 5757 W. Lovers La. (phone: 351-2233).

Del Frisco's There's no better place in Dallas for steaks. This crowded, club-like eatery offers generous portions of every cut of beef imaginable, along with elegantly cut onion rings. The menu also features a good spinach soufflé. Closed Sundays. Reservations advised. Major credit cards accepted. 5251 Spring Valley Rd. (phone: 490-9000).

East Wind This upscale Vietnamese eatery in the trendy Deep Ellum section of the city offers near-perfect concoctions, including asparagus soup with crabmeat, grilled catfish with lemongrass, and beef dishes with cilantro. Reservations advised. Major credit cards accepted. 2711 Elm St. (phone: 745-5554).

French Room Considered the most elegant dining room in the city, its menu combines American and French fare, such as roasted yellowfin tuna *au poivre* and New Zealand venison with wild mushroom soufflé. Closed Sundays. Reservations advised. Major credit cards accepted. In the *Adolphus Hotel,* 1321 Commerce (phone: 742-8200).

Huntington's This fine restaurant in the *Westin Galleria* presents sumptuous food in an elegant setting. The menu features such American fare as lobster tacos and pan-seared salmon. Closed Sundays. Reservations advised. Major credit cards accepted. 13340 Dallas Pkwy. (phone: 851-2882).

Mansion Though a hotel dining spot, the atmosphere is that of a handsome private mansion. Quiet elegance, Southwestern fare (including baked potato enchiladas and rack of lamb served atop cheese potatoes), polished service, and a VIP crowd make dining here a memorable experience. Reservations necessary. Major credit cards accepted. In the *Mansion on Turtle Creek,* 2821 Turtle Creek Blvd. (phone: 526-2121).

Old Warsaw One of the oldest restaurants in Dallas, it features such continental selections as Dover sole, chateaubriand, and roast quail. Various pâtés also are offered. Open daily for dinner only. Reservations necessary. Major credit cards accepted. 2610 Maple (phone: 528-0032).

Pyramid This dining room in the *Fairmont* hotel serves a four-course *table d'hôte* that has won high praise. Closed Sundays. Reservations necessary. Major credit cards accepted. 1717 N. Akard St. (phone: 720-5249).

Riviera The South of France inspired this gem with a distinct—but not overwhelming—continental atmosphere. Its first-rate menu, featuring roasted-tomato soup with crabmeat and mixed grill of sausage, lamb, and veal, has made it one of the city's best places. Open daily for dinner only. Reservations advised. Major credit cards accepted. 7709 Inwood (phone: 351-0094).

St. Germain The exquisite dining room at the eponymous hotel has brought genteel, refined dining back in style, thanks to nice touches such as Waterford crystal, Limoges china, and white-gloved waiters. The food is as attractive and elegant as the atmosphere: The prix fixe meals may feature pan-roasted snapper with prawns in red curry, warm crab custard, or oysters *velouté.* Open only Fridays and Saturdays for dinner (private dinners at other times may be arranged). Reservations necessary. Major credit cards accepted. 2516 Maple Ave. (phone: 871-2516).

Star Canyon Stephan Pyles's creative "New Texas" fare makes this place one of the most popular in town. Dishes such as arugula salad with sweet vinaigrette, charred pecans, and port-poached pear, and the wood-roasted red onion, eggplant, and red bell peppers with black olive chili are just a couple of the tempting entrées. Leave room for the angel-devil's food cake filled with dark chocolate and peanut butter. Open daily; dinner only Saturdays and Sundays. Reservations advised. Major credit cards accepted. 3102 Oak Lawn at Cedar Springs (phone: 520-7827).

311 Lombardi's This sophisticated Italian trattoria serves risotto with seafood, grilled chicken with gnocchi and garlic, and *focaccia.* Live jazz. Reservations advised. Major credit cards accepted. 311 Market at Ross (phone: 747-0322).

MODERATE

Beau Nash The atmosphere in this small dining room in the *Crescent Court* hotel is stylish but casual; standout dishes include chili with peppery cheese biscuits, calamari, pizza, and grilled fresh fish. Reservations unnecessary. Major credit cards accepted. 400 Crescent Ct. (phone: 871-3240).

Café Madrid Anyone craving excellent *tapas* will find them at this charming, popular European outpost. Menu delights include potato omelette in saffron sauce, fried calamari, mussels in vinaigrette, grilled pork tenderloin, and paella (offered only on weekends). Closed Sundays. Reservations advised. MasterCard and Visa accepted. 4501 Travis (phone: 528-1731).

Deep Ellum Café With an atmosphere that evokes New York's SoHo, this casual, comfortable place is located in Deep Ellum, a onetime hot spot for jazz. The menu is broad, encompassing everything from Vietnamese salads to chicken with dill dumplings, to superb chicken-fried steaks and spinach ravioli. Reservations advised. Major credit cards accepted. 2706 Elm St. (phone: 741-9012).

The 8.0 This hip meeting place has an eclectic menu of burgers, black-eyed pea sandwiches, chili-cured tuna steak, and Southwestern-flavored pasta. Be forewarned: There's an ear-splitting bar scene every night. No reservations accepted. Major credit cards accepted. 2800 Routh St. (phone: 979-0880).

Hard Rock Café The Supreme Court of rock 'n' roll, this restaurant occupies a renovated Baptist church where the walls are hung with such memorabilia as Jimi Hendrix's lead guitar and another that Elvis once strummed. Try the baked potato soup or the grilled *fajitas*—portions are generous. Reservations unnecessary. Major credit cards accepted. 2601 McKinney Ave. (phone: 855-0007).

Yegua Creek Brewing Co. Dallas's first brewpub occupies an old icehouse, where crowds pack in for hearty beers made on-site, and for beer-battered onion rings, venison chili, smoked salmon sandwiches, and fried rabbit. No reservations. Major credit cards accepted. 2920 N. Henderson (phone: 824-2739).

Kathleen's Art Café This hip hangout—with its own bakery next door—begins the day with unforgettable blue corn pancakes, homemade pastries, and eggs scrambled with tortillas and salsa or poached atop *tomatillo* enchiladas. Wait till lunch or dinner for eggplant-garlic-feta pizza or angel-hair pasta with shrimp. The contemporary art on the walls is for sale. Reservations advised. MasterCard and Visa accepted. 4424 Lovers La. (phone: 691-2355).

Matt's No Place The power of Matt Martinez's culinary reputation is uncontested: he packs this restaurant nightly without ever hanging a sign out front. The exceptional fare includes huge shrimp grilled with bacon, onions, and peppers; grilled quail; New York strip steaks; homemade bread; divine salads; and cheesecake with praline sauce. Open for dinner only; closed Sundays. Reservations necessary. Major credit cards accepted. 6310 La Vista (phone: 823-9007).

Mia's A casual, family-run place well known for Tex-Mex specialties, particularly *chiles rellenos.* Closed Sundays. Reservations unnecessary. MasterCard and Visa accepted. 4322 Lemmon (phone: 526-1020).

Patrizio A fashionable Italian trattoria, it serves pizza with eggplant or shrimp, pasta dishes, chicken with Southwestern pesto, and smoked salmon, as well as delicious *tiramisù.* Reservations advised. Major credit cards accepted. 25 *Highland Park Village* (phone: 522-7878).

St. Martin's A well-chosen, reasonably priced wine list coupled with imaginatively prepared seafood make this intimate place a favorite with those who like to linger over a meal. Reservations advised. Major credit cards accepted. 3020 Greenville Ave. (phone: 826-0940).

INEXPENSIVE

Eureka! An inspired menu and stylish ambience make dining here quite a healthful experience. Turkey chili, Vietnamese chicken salad, and couscous with sun-dried tomatoes and chilies are but a few of the low-cal choices. Open daily; lunch only Sundays. No reservations. Major credit cards accepted. 4401 Villanova, Preston Center E. (phone: 369-7767).

Peggy Sue's BBQ Across from *Southern Methodist University* and decorated with memorabilia from the 1950s, this café offers great oak-smoked beef and barbecued chicken. Don't pass up the fried pies for dessert—chocolate, apricot, and peach are the best. No reservations. Major credit cards accepted. 6600 Snider Plaza (phone: 987-9188).

Snuffer's There's no match for this cozy bar's oversized burgers or for its messy cheese fries, which are best with jalapeños and ranch dressing. More virtuous diners can have soft tacos, quesadillas, and chicken Caesar salads—but everyone goes for the strawberry margaritas. The rock music from the jukebox can be a bit loud, but the food is well worth the din. No reservations. Major credit cards accepted. 3526 Greenville Ave. (phone: 826-6850).

Sonny Bryan's Few would argue that this place serves the best barbecue in Dallas, although some might object to the crowds and small, drab interior where school desks serve as tables. Open daily for lunch only. No reservations or credit cards accepted. 2202 Inwood Rd. (phone: 357-7120).

Denver

A few years back, the rage in Denver was a bumper sticker with just one word: NATIVE. But the company making them soon realized it was selling to a limited market and rushed into production with a sequel: SEMI-NATIVE. Most of Denver's population does appear to be from somewhere else. Every section of America is well represented—so much so that many movie studios hold "sneak previews" in Denver to judge how a film will be accepted around the country. The comments of first-time visitors usually include remarks such as "clean," "friendly," and "relaxed." Is it little wonder, then, why so many feel at home here?

The city's population has held steady at about 500,000 over the past few years, but the entire metropolitan area has grown tremendously and now numbers some two million. Today, Denver has 2,000 restaurants, some of them among the country's best; a symphony orchestra; a wide variety of museums; theater companies; the *Denver International Film Festival,* which has attracted world-famous actors, directors, and screenwriters to the city; the Colorado *Rockies* baseball team; the *NBA Nuggets;* the Denver *Broncos;* and the *NHL* hockey team, 1996 Stanley Cup Champions, the Colorado *Avalanche* (formerly Quebec *Nordiques*).

While Denver still suffers from air pollution, it has made tremendous progress in cleaning it up. Denver's infamous "brown cloud" still lingers over the city on cold winter days, sometimes obstructing the view of nearby mountains à la Mexico City. Fortunately, it's more of a visual problem than a health hazard, as a combination of voluntary no-drive days, wood-burning restrictions, and oxygenated gasoline have helped clean the air.

New visitors here will be pleasantly surprised by the weather. Summer in Denver is spectacular, and those who think the city is covered in snow half the year are in for a shock. It does snow ferociously sometimes, but it melts fairly quickly because winter days are often sunny and mild: Temperatures in the 60s are not uncommon. In fact, the weather in Denver itself can be clear and spring-like while the ski resorts, just 75 miles away, are getting a foot of fresh snow. This mild climate makes it possible to enjoy the city's 205 parks (the country's largest municipal park system) year-round.

Another of Denver's pleasant surprises is that shoppers can have a very good time here. The section known as Cherry Creek, southeast of downtown, is popular for its quaint shops and boutiques, and the *Cherry Creek Mall* features upscale department stores and specialty shops. Downtown boasts the *16th Street Mall,* anchored by historic *Larimer Square,* the city's most visited tourist attraction. Once the dregs of the city, the entire area is now a historic center that is gradually being transformed into an enclave of exclusive shops and fine restaurants. Close by is the *Tabor Center,* a unique two-block-long shopping mall that brought Denver its first *The*

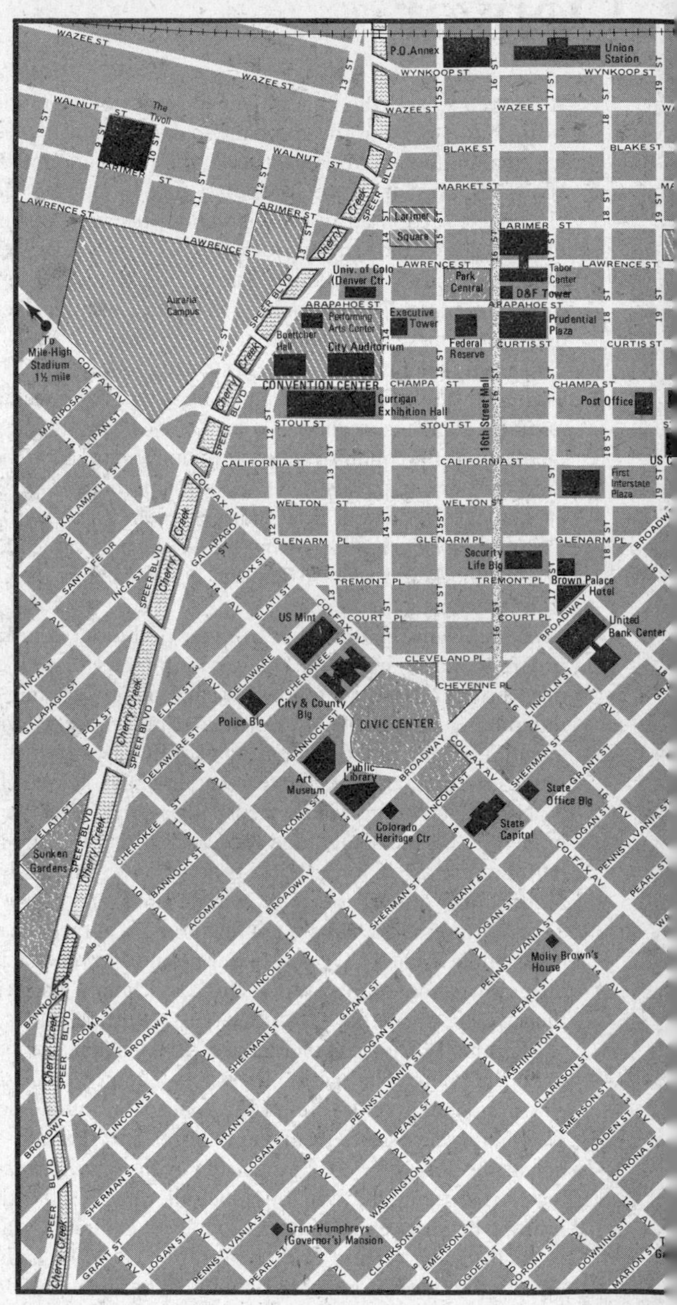
P.O.Annex
Union Station
The Tivoli
Larimer Square
Auraria Campus
To Mile-High Stadium 1½ mile
Univ. of Colo (Denver Ctr.)
Park Central
Tabor Center
D&F Tower
Executive Tower
Performing Arts Center
Boettcher Hall
City Auditorium
Federal Reserve
Prudential Plaza
CONVENTION CENTER
Currigan Exhibition Hall
Post Office
16th Street Mall
First Interstate Plaza
Security Life Blg
Brown Palace Hotel
US Mint
United Bank Center
City & County Blg
Police Blg
CIVIC CENTER
Art Museum
Public Library
Colorado Heritage Ctr
State Capitol
State Office Blg
Sunken Gardens
Molly Brown's House
Grant-Humphreys (Governor's) Mansion
Cherry Creek
SPEER BLVD
COLFAX AV
BROADWAY

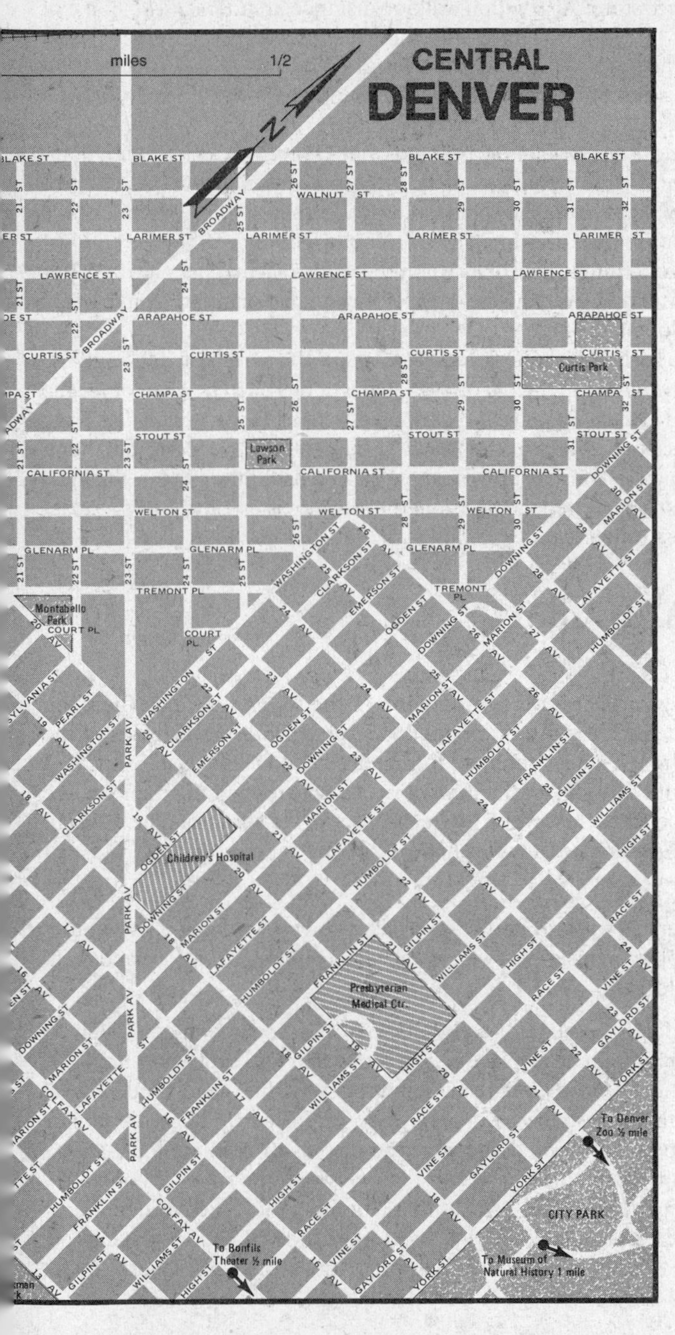
CENTRAL
DENVER
miles
1/2
N
BLAKE ST
WALNUT ST
LARIMER ST
LAWRENCE ST
ARAPAHOE ST
CURTIS ST
CHAMPA ST
STOUT ST
CALIFORNIA ST
WELTON ST
GLENARM PL
TREMONT PL
COURT PL
BROADWAY
21 ST
22 ST
23 ST
24 ST
25 ST
26 ST
27 ST
28 ST
29 ST
30 ST
31 ST
32 ST
Curtis Park
Lawson Park
Montabello Park
PARK AV
WASHINGTON ST
CLARKSON ST
EMERSON ST
OGDEN ST
DOWNING ST
MARION ST
LAFAYETTE ST
HUMBOLDT ST
FRANKLIN ST
GILPIN ST
WILLIAMS ST
HIGH ST
RACE ST
VINE ST
GAYLORD ST
YORK ST
PEARL ST
SYLVANIA ST
COLFAX AV
13 AV
14 AV
16 AV
17 AV
18 AV
19 AV
20 AV
21 AV
22 AV
23 AV
24 AV
25 AV
26 AV
27 AV
28 AV
29 AV
30 AV
Children's Hospital
Presbyterian Medical Ctr.
CITY PARK
To Denver Zoo ½ mile
To Museum of Natural History 1 mile
To Bonfils Theater ½ mile

Sharper Image store. Also within walking distance are *Coors Field,* home of the *Rockies* baseball franchise, and the *Elitch Gardens* amusement park, located to the northwestern edge of downtown.

No discussion of Denver would be complete without a look at the city's favorite excuse for mass hysteria, the Denver *Broncos.* Many *National Football League* cities claim the best fans, but Denver backs it up with numbers. Except for the strike games in 1987 (which still drew some 40,000 each), every home game has been sold out for nearly three decades, in a stadium that holds more than 70,000. You might expect fans to be loyal during the good times (like 1993, when the team reached the playoffs), but they keep attending even during dry spells when the team can't make a first down, let alone a touchdown.

With the arrival of the Colorado *Rockies* in the spring of 1993, and the Colorado *Avalanche* in the fall of 1995, Denver has become a major league baseball and hockey city as well. The sports-crazed Denverites made a large personal sacrifice to attract the *Rockies:* In 1989, they voted to tax themselves to fund the construction of a new baseball stadium. So far, the local citizenry hasn't regretted the decision; the stadium is usually filled to capacity regardless of the team's standing.

Denver At-a-Glance

SEEING THE CITY

The best view of Denver is from the top of the *Capitol* rotunda (between E. 14th and E. Colfax Aves.; phone: 866-2604), with the Rockies to the west, the Great Plains stretching to the east, and Denver itself sprawled below. On the 13th step of the *Capitol* is an inscription noting that you are exactly 1 mile above sea level. The view is also spectacular from the *Museum of Natural History* in *City Park* (phone: 322-7009).

SPECIAL PLACES

It's a pleasure to walk around Denver. The downtown section has a number of Victorian mansions as well as the city's public institutions and commercial buildings.

US MINT Appropriately enough for a city that made its fortune in gold, Denver still has more of it than anyplace else in the country (except *Fort Knox*). On the outside, the *Mint* is a relatively unimpressive white sandstone Federal building with Doric arches over the windows. Inside, you can see money being stamped and printed and view the display of gold bullion—only a fraction of the total stored here. Most impressive is the room full of money just waiting to be counted. Fifteen-minute guided tours are given on weekdays between 8 AM and 2:45 PM. Closed weekends. No admission charge. Delaware St. between Colfax and 14th; tour entrance on Cherokee St. (phone: 844-3582).

DENVER ART MUSEUM Besides having an overall collection that covers the period from 1100 to the present, this museum has top collections of pre-Columbian art and artifacts, Spanish Colonial art, and Asian art. The museum has added modern, contemporary, African, and Oceanic galleries as well. Be sure to visit the American Indian collection on the second floor—it has superlative costumes, basketry, rugs, and totem poles. Some display halls completely re-create another time and place. Stop for lunch or a snack at the terrace restaurant. Closed Mondays. No admission charge on Saturdays or for children under six. 100 W. 14th Ave. and Bannock St. (phone: 640-2793 or 640-2295).

DENVER PUBLIC LIBRARY This remodeled seven-story building houses an expanded collection of books, photographs, and documents related to the history of the West. There is also a splendid children's collection as well as exhibitions on Western life. Rare book lovers will be delighted with the library's special collections. Open daily. 10 W. 14th Ave. Pkwy. (phone: 640-6200).

COLORADO STATE HISTORY MUSEUM This popular attraction features exhibits on people who've contributed to Colorado history, period costumes from the early frontier days, and Indian relics. Many of these authentic costumes were donated by members of old Denver families. Life-size dioramas show how gold miners, pioneers, and Mesa Verde cliff dwellers used to live. Open daily. No admission charge for children under six. 1400 Broadway (phone: 866-3682).

CAPITOL The rotunda looks like the dome of the *US Capitol,* coated with $50,900 worth of Colorado gold leaf; the impressive marble staircases rate a look, even if you don't want to climb them. There are 30-minute tours. Closed Saturdays and Sundays (September through May). No admission charge. Between E. 14th Ave. and Colfax, at Sherman Ave. (phone: 866-2604).

MOLLY BROWN HOUSE When gold miner Johnny Brown and his wife, Molly, moved into their Capitol Hill mansion, Denver society snubbed them as nouveau riche. Ironically, their former house has become a leading attraction. She is particularly remembered for taking charge of a lifeboat when the *Titanic* sank, commanding the men to row while she held her chinchilla cape over a group of children to keep them warm—which is how she came to be known as the "unsinkable Molly Brown." Closed Mondays (September through May). No admission charge for children under six. 1340 Pennsylvania St. (phone: 832-4092).

LARIMER STREET Walk along the *16th Street Mall* to Larimer, Denver's most interesting shopping street, and pass the *Daniels and Fisher Tower,* a 1920s landmark said to be a copy of the campanile in Venice. It used to be the tallest building in town, but it has been overshadowed by more modern edifices. Larimer Street is lined with fascinating art galleries, curio shops, silversmiths, and cafés. Most interesting is *Larimer Square* (between 14th and

15th Sts.), the heart of which is known as "LoDo" (Lower Downtown) where various restaurants, crafts shops, and microbrewery taverns have been restored to reflect the flavor of Denver's past.

CITY PARK This 640-acre park has two lakes, spreading lawns, the *Denver Zoo* (phone: 331-4110), and the *Museum of Natural History* (phone: 322-7009). Known for its exhibitions of animals in natural settings, the museum was the first in the country to use curved backgrounds with reproductions of mountain flowers, shrubs, and smaller animals to give a feeling of nature. There are displays of fossils, minerals, gold coins, and birds; and the *Hall of Life* attempts to unravel the mysteries of the human machine. It's open daily; there's an admission charge. The museum also houses the popular *Gates Planetarium* (phone: 370-6351) and the *IMAX Theatre* (phone: 370-6300). Both are open daily and charge admission. The *Denver Zoo,* which has designed a number of natural mountain environments for its animals, is open daily; there's no admission charge for children under six.

HUDSON GARDENS Sixteen different "garden complexes" comprise this spectacular 30-acre botanical park. Each consists of a theme—roses, wildflowers, fragrances, etc.—and flows seamlessly into the other throughout the rolling, semi-rural topography. It's just 30 minutes south of downtown. Closed November through March. Admission charge. 2888 W. Maplewood Ave., off S. Sante Fe Dr. (phone: 797-8565).

HYLAND HILLS WATER WORLD Colorado is not the place for an ocean vacation, but this is one spot where you can body-surf a mile above sea level. There are 25 exciting rides, two ocean-wave pools, and a special area for small children. Closed September through May. Admission charge. 1850 W. 89th Ave. (phone: 427-7873).

CHILDREN'S MUSEUM A kid-size basketball court, a miniature grocery store, and a real television studio will enthrall youngsters, as will the miniature ski mountain, where kids can try out Colorado trails. Open daily. Admission charge. 2121 Crescent Dr., off I-25 at 23rd Ave. (phone: 433-7444).

ELITCH GARDENS One of America's oldest amusement parks, it was relocated to the northwest edge of downtown last year. The park is clean and the rides will have the kids asking for more. Admission and parking charge. Closed October through April. Speer Blvd. and I-25 (phone: 595-4386).

COORS BREWERY For beer enthusiasts, the Coors Brewery in Golden (just 20 minutes from downtown Denver) will explain the entire brewing process. Visitors can see thousands of six-packs flash by every minute and enjoy an ice-cold mug of—what else?—Coors beer. The 40-minute tour is offered daily except Sundays. No admission charge. For information, contact Coors Brewing Company, Guest Relations/Tours, BC 200, Golden, CO 80401 (phone: 303-277-BEER).

EXTRA SPECIAL

With all the gorgeous places around Denver, it's unfair to single out any particular one. If you have to choose, though, *Rocky Mountain National Park* is one of the most spectacular scenic areas of the US—it makes a perfect day trip. Take I-25 north for 50 miles, then Rte. 34 west. (See *Rocky Mountain National Park,* DIRECTIONS, for more information.)

Sources and Resources

TOURIST INFORMATION

For brochures, maps, and general information, contact the *Denver Metro Convention and Visitors Bureau* (225 W. Colfax Ave., Denver, CO 80202; phone: 892-1112), which is closed Sundays. For information on skiing, contact *Colorado Ski Country USA* (1560 Broadway, Suite 1440, Denver, CO 80202; phone: 837-0793), which is closed weekends.

LOCAL COVERAGE *Denver Post* and *Rocky Mountain News,* dailies; and *5280* magazine, bimonthly. *Westword,* a free weekly newspaper, is the best guide to the Denver area; it's available at newsstands and in grocery and convenience stores. Friday editions of the *Denver Post* and *Rocky Mountain News* have complete entertainment and activity guides.

TELEVISION STATIONS KWGN Channel 2–Independent; KCNC Channel 4–CBS; KRMA Channel 6–PBS; KMGH Channel 7–ABC; KUSA Channel 9–NBC; KBDI Channel 12–PBS; KTVD Channel 20–Independent; and KDVR Channel 31–Fox.

RADIO STATIONS AM: KHOW 630 (talk); KOA 850 (talk/sports); KYGO 1600 (classic country); and KKYD 1340 (children's programming). FM: KCFR 90.1 (NPR/classical); KHIH 94.7 (jazz/new age); KRFX 103.5 (classic rock); KXKL 105.1 (oldies); and KAZY 106.7 (rock).

TELEPHONE The area code for Denver is 303.

SALES TAX The sales tax is 7.2%; the hotel room tax is 11.9%.

CLIMATE Because of its altitude, Denver is pretty dry; the city gets an average of only 15 inches of rain a year. Even when the temperature hits the 90s in summer (it hits 100F every five years!), it's not intolerable. Nights cool to the 70s. In winter, the days are often sunny and in the 40s or 50s, but it does snow occasionally.

GETTING AROUND

AIRPORT *Denver International Airport* is about a 40-minute drive from downtown. *Regional Transportation District (RTD)* buses (phone: 299-6000) travel from the airport to downtown for $6 one way or $10 round trip.

BUS *RTD* runs buses throughout the Denver area. The fare is 50¢ or $1 depending on time of day. Limited *RTD* trains are primarily oriented to commuters who transfer from *RTD* express buses. For information, contact the *Downtown Information Center,* 626 16th St. (phone: 299-6000).

CAR RENTAL All major national firms are represented.

TAXI Taxis cannot be hailed in the streets. Call *Yellow Cab* (phone: 777-7777), *Zone Cab* (phone: 861-2323), or *Metro Taxi* (phone: 333-3333). There are cab stands at the airport, bus station, *Union Station,* and at major hotels.

SPECIAL EVENTS

The *National Western Stock Show and Rodeo* in January lasts two weeks and attracts cowfolk from all over. The *Denver Art Museum*'s annual exhibition of Western art runs from January through March. *Easter* Sunrise Service at *Red Rocks Natural Amphitheater* attracts thousands. In July and August, the *University of Colorado at Boulder* presents its annual *Shakespeare Festival.* And *Larimer Square* is the site of the *Oktoberfest,* held (oddly enough) in September.

MUSEUMS

In addition to those listed in *Special Places,* there are several other museums of note in Denver.

BLACK AMERICAN WEST MUSEUM AND HERITAGE CENTER Exhibits chronicle African-American cowboys, miners, and soldiers, and other black pioneers of the Wild West. Closed Saturdays through Tuesdays. Admission charge. 3091 California St. (phone: 292-2566).

BUFFALO BILL MUSEUM Especially interesting for children, this museum is full of memorabilia relating to the life of one of the wild west's legendary frontiersman, who is buried on the grounds. Open May through October; closed Mondays. Admission charge. Lookout Mountain (phone: 526-0747).

COLORADO RAILROAD MUSEUM For railroad buffs, there are 50 historic cars exhibited outside, as well as railroad artifacts and a model railroad inside. Open daily. Admission charge. 17155 W. 44th Ave. (phone: 279-4591).

MUSEUM OF WESTERN ART Paintings by Georgia O'Keeffe, Thomas Moran, and Alfred Bierstadt, and bronze sculptures by Frederic Remington are featured here. Closed Sundays and Mondays. Admission charge. 1727 Tremont (phone: 296-1880).

SHOPPING

Denver is rapidly becoming a shoppers' paradise and soon may rival Dallas as a regional retail center. *Neiman Marcus, Lord & Taylor,* and *Saks Fifth Avenue* all reside at the *Cherry Creek Mall* (Cherry Creek Drive in east central Denver). Several old favorites are going strong, too, such as downtown's spectacular *Tabor Center* (16th and Lawrence Sts.), home to *The*

Sharper Image, and others; and *Cherry Creek North* (north of First Ave., just across from the mall), featuring dozens of quaint shops, boutiques, restaurants, and one of the world's truly great bookstores—*The Tattered Cover* (2955 E. First Ave.; phone: 322-7727), with over 400,000 titles. Along Larimer Street, *Cry Baby Ranch* (1422 Larimer St.; phone: 623-3979) features Western relics, reproductions, and books with a slant toward the unusual; and the *Squash Blossom Gallery* (1428 Larimer St.; phone: 572-7979) focuses on folk art, crafts (some from Mexico), and jewelry.

SPORTS AND FITNESS

BASEBALL The *National League* Colorado *Rockies* play at *Coors Field* (20th and Wazee Sts.; phone: 292-0200).

BASKETBALL The *NBA Nuggets* play at *McNichols Sports Arena* (1635 Clay St.; phone: 893-3865).

BICYCLING Bicycle tours can be arranged by *Two Wheel Tours* (664 Sage, Highlands Ranch; phone: 798-4601).

FISHING There's good fishing at Dillon Reservoir, 70 miles west of Denver on I-70, and Cherry Creek Reservoir, just 8 miles southeast of the city on I-225. The South Platte River near Deckers, a town 28 miles southwest of Denver, is a good place for fly fishing.

FITNESS CENTERS *Indian Springs Resort* (302 Soda Creek Rd., one block south of Miner St., in Idaho Springs; phone: 623-2050) has relaxing, hot mineral baths. The *International Athletic Club* (1630 Welton; phone: 623-2100) welcomes guests from several downtown hotels; it offers exercise classes, tracks, racquetball and squash courts, a sauna, and massage.

FOOTBALL The *NFL Broncos* play at *Mile High Stadium* (1700 Federal Blvd.; phone: 433-7466).

GOLF Among the area's public golf courses, the best are *Kennedy* (10500 E. Hampden Ave.; phone: 751-0311), *Park Hill* (3500 Colorado Blvd.; phone: 333-5411), and *Wellshire* (3333 S. Colorado Blvd.; phone: 757-1352).

HOCKEY The *University of Denver Pioneers* play at the *DU Arena* (E. Jewell Ave. and S. Gaylord Way; phone: 871-2336). The Colorado *Avalanche*, Denver *NHL* team, plays at *McNichols Arena* (1635 Clay St.; phone: 893-6700).

JOGGING Follow the *Highline Canal Trail,* or run in *Washington Park,* which is 4½ miles from downtown, or in *City Park,* 2 miles from downtown.

RACING HORSE RACING takes place from May through September at *Arapahoe Park* (26000 E. Quincy St.; phone: 690-2400). Greyhounds race at *Mile High Kennel Club* (6200 Dahlia Rd.; phone: 288-1591) from June through August. No one under 21 is admitted.

SKIING Colorado ski country is famous all over the world. The slopes closest to the city are in *Loveland Basin* (60 miles west on I-70; phone: 571-5580).

Keystone and Arapahoe Basin (phone: 970-468-2316), *Breckenridge* (phone: 970-453-5000), and *Copper Mountain* (phone: 970-968-2882) are all from 15 to 25 miles farther on I-70. To reach *Winter Park* (phone: 970-726-5514) drive west on I-70, then north on Route 40, or take the *Ski Train* (phone: 296-4754) to *Winter Park* from Denver's *Union Station,* weekends from late December through early April. The renowned *Vail* and *Beaver Creek* resorts (phone: 970-476-1000) are 100 miles west of Denver on I-70, and equally acclaimed *Aspen* and *Snowmass* (phone for both: 970-925-1220) are about 190 miles southwest of the city (on I-70 and Hwy. 82). *Crested Butte* (237 miles southwest; phone: 970-349-2333) and *Steamboat Springs* (163 miles northwest; phone: 970-879-0740) are also popular (see *Downhill Skiing,* DIVERSIONS).

TENNIS The best public courts are at *Gates Tennis Center* (100 S. Adams St.; phone: 355-4461).

THEATER

For complete up-to-the-minute listings on theatrical and musical events, see the publications listed in *Local Coverage* above. The *University of Colorado at Boulder*—about 20 miles northwest of Denver—hosts a *Shakespeare Festival* every summer (see *Special Events*). The *Denver Center for the Performing Arts* (14th and Curtis Sts.; phone: 893-4000) presents Broadway productions as well as those of local companies. The *Country Dinner Playhouse* (6875 S. Clinton in Englewood, just south of Denver; phone: 799-1410), a dinner-theater, presents light offerings and musicals throughout the year.

MUSIC

Two outdoor amphitheaters feature summer concerts: *Red Rocks,* which provides a spectacular mountain setting (12 miles west of Denver off I-70; phone: 640-7334), and *Fiddler's Green* (12 miles south of downtown, off I-25 in the Denver Tech Center; phone: 220-7000). Most large indoor concerts are held at *McNichols Arena* (1635 Clay St.; phone: 640-7333). The *Colorado Symphony* performs classical and pop concerts November through May at *Boettcher Hall* (14th and Arapahoe Sts.; phone: 595-4388). During summer lunch hours, street musicians give concerts in the financial district, on the plazas outside the Norwest Bank Center and the First Interstate Bank of Denver.

NIGHTCLUBS AND NIGHTLIFE

For jazz try *El Chapultepec* (1962 Market St.; phone: 295-9126). The *Wynkoop Brewing Company* (phone: 297-2700) is the original brew pub in downtown Denver and claims to be the largest in the world. Comedy is king at *Comedy Works* (1226 15th St.; phone: 595-3637). Singles and rockers have an almost limitless array of choices; among the best are *Panama Reds* (2797 S. Parker Rd., Aurora; phone: 695-1750) and *1082* (1082 Broadway; phone: 831-1082).

Best in Town

CHECKING IN

Denver's plentiful hotel facilities often provide great lodging values compared to those in other major US cities. Most of Denver's major hotels have complete facilities for the business traveler. Those listed below as having "business services" usually offer such conveniences as meeting rooms, photocopiers, computers, translation services, and express checkout, among others. Call the individual hotel for additional information. Expect to pay between $100 and $195 per night for a double room at those places listed as expensive; between $60 and $100 at those in the moderate category; and less than $60 at the inexpensive place. Unless otherwise noted, hotels have air conditioning, private baths, TV sets, and telephones.

All hotels below are in Denver and telephone and fax numbers are in the 303 area code unless otherwise indicated.

EXPENSIVE

Adams Mark–Denver Designed by I. M. Pei, this former Radisson property is the largest downtown hotel, with 744 rooms, *Finnegan's* pub, *Windows* restaurant, and a lounge. There are also a rooftop pool, a health club, and business services. At press time, renovations and expansion of the property increasing the number of rooms to 1,230 were ongoing; the scheduled completion date is the beginning of 1998. 16th St. and Court Pl. (phone: 893-3333; fax: 892-0521).

Brown Palace Built in the 1890s, this 231-room hotel was one of the first to have a multistory atrium lobby with balconies on every floor. Throughout the years, it has retained a rather faded glamour. There are three restaurants and business services. 17th St. and Tremont Pl. (phone: 297-3111; fax: 293-9204).

Hyatt Regency Denver In the middle of downtown, this 26-story, 511-room property boasts superior restaurants, a rooftop complex with a pool, a tennis court, and a jogging track, and lavish room amenities. Business services are available. 1750 Welton St. (phone: 295-1200; 800-233-1234; fax: 292-2472).

Loews Giorgio This elegant hotel, the only Colorado member of the Loews chain, boasts 200 rooms and an Italian motif. From the imported Italian marble and original artwork in the public areas to the romantic guestrooms, this is one of Denver's best. The library, bar, and *Tuscany* restaurant are quiet and relaxed. Business services are available. About eight blocks from the *Cherry Creek* shopping area. S. Colorado Blvd. and E. Mississippi Ave. (phone: 782-9300; 800-223-0888; fax: 758-6542).

Marriott Tech Center The Denver Tech Center's largest hotel and one of the city's better values, it has 623 rooms, racquetball courts, a 24-hour deli, and *Compari's* Italian restaurant. Business services are available. There is also a commercial airport shuttle. 4900 DTC Pkwy. (phone: 779-1100; 800-228-9290; fax: 740-2523).

Oxford Located in the center of Lower Downtown's budding restaurant and shopping district—and just three blocks from the magnificent *Coors Field*—this 82-room hotel is a bit of history itself, having opened in 1891. With a restaurant and bar, it is a Denver showplace. 17th St. and Wazee (phone: 628-5400; 800-228-5838; fax: 628-5413).

Westin Tabor Center The centerpiece of the *Tabor Center,* this 420-room complex is in Denver's *16th Street Mall.* Its *Augusta* restaurant (see *Eating Out*) is among the best of a number of excellent downtown dining spots. There is also a pool, a sauna, racquetball courts, and a fitness center. 16th and Lawrence Sts. (phone: 572-9100; 800-228-3000; fax: 572-7288).

MODERATE

Castle Marne An 1889 Victorian mansion has been turned into a lovely bed and breakfast inn with elaborately carved masonry. Its nine rooms are simply furnished (no TV sets or air conditioning), but the ambience is quaint and elegant. Conveniently located three blocks from *City Park,* but the neighborhood isn't the best for walking around at night. Breakfast and afternoon tea are included in the rate. 1572 Race St. (phone: 331-0621; 800-92-MARNE).

Marriott Courtyard A "few frills" entry on the Denver lodging scene that's not to be overlooked. If you can forgo a bellhop and room service, you can secure a Marriott-style room and access to a restaurant for a lot less. Two-room suites are only about $20 more than a standard room. I-25 and Arapahoe Rd. (phone: 721-0300; 800-321-2211; fax: 721-0037).

Merritt House Less than 10 minutes from downtown by car, this Victorian house offers 10 comfortable rooms and the atmosphere of a country inn. There's a pleasant dining room (full breakfast is complimentary). 941 17th Ave. (phone: 861-5230; fax: 861-9009).

Queen Anne Inn Denver's best-known bed and breakfast spot is just four blocks from the downtown *16th Street Mall.* This restored 1879 Victorian home is a 14-room treasure: Each room has a unique decor. The surrounding historic neighborhood is re-emerging after years of decline. No smokers or children under 15. 2147 Tremont Pl. (phone: 296-6666; 800-432-4667).

INEXPENSIVE

Comfort Inn–Downtown Originally part of the *Brown Palace,* this 230-room structure was converted into a separate establishment for budget-conscious travelers. Complimentary breakfast and access to a health club are provided. 17th St. and Tremont Pl. (phone: 296-0400).

EATING OUT

Denver seems to be a magnet for great chefs and adventurous restaurateurs. Beef is king, but there are enough places featuring nouvelle cuisine, Southwestern fare, and pizza to keep everyone happy. Expect to pay $60 or more for dinner for two at restaurants listed as expensive, $40 to $60 at places in the moderate category, and $40 or less at those listed as inexpensive. Prices do not include wine, drinks, tax, or tips. All restaurants are in the 303 area code unless otherwise indicated.

Unless otherwise noted, restaurants are open for lunch and dinner.

EXPENSIVE

Augusta A spectacular view of Denver's skyline accompanies superb American dishes such as rack of lamb, spit-roasted duck, and grilled silver salmon. The atmosphere is elegant, the service excellent. Reservations advised. Major credit cards accepted. In the *Westin Tabor Center,* 16th and Lawrence Sts. (phone: 572-9100).

Buckhorn Exchange Established in 1893 by a former scout for Buffalo Bill Cody, this restaurant is on the *National Register of Historic Places.* A city institution, it is festooned with hunting trophies, and its game dishes—elk, buffalo, and quail, among others—continue to make history. For those who aren't "game," generous beef cuts and other standard fare are available. Don't pass up the navy bean soup or homemade apple pie with ice cream and hard cinnamon sauce. Open daily; dinner only on weekends. Reservations advised. Major credit cards accepted. Near downtown, 1000 Osage (phone: 534-9505).

The Fort Near the foothills southwest of Denver, it gives you a taste of Denver's pioneer spirit. Frontier recipes have been adapted to modern tastes, including elk, Buffalo Boodie Sausage, and Rocky Mountain Oysters (bull's testicles). Try a combination to get a sampling. The restaurant is a replica of Colorado's famous *Bent's Fort.* In warm weather, make sure you get a seat on the patio: the scenery is fantastic. Open daily for dinner only. Reservations necessary. Major credit cards accepted. US 285 at Colorado Hwy. 8 (phone: 697-4771).

Tante Louise The atmosphere of this decades-old Denver dining tradition is intimate, evoking a French country *auberge,* replete with hardwood floors, candlelit tables, and glowing fireplaces. The food is equal to the Gallic ambience, but adds an accent of Colorado with local products such as rack of lamb and veal loin. Closed Sundays. Open for dinner only. Reservations necessary. Major credit cards accepted. 4900 E. Colfax Ave. (phone: 355-4488).

MODERATE

La Coupole The only French bistro downtown, this dining spot is riding a crest of local popularity. Gallic influences prevail, from the Belle Epoque decor to its traditional bistro fare. Try sautéed veal loin medaillons with wild mushrooms and rosemary sauce, grilled sirloin with red wine sauce, or bouillabaisse. Open daily; dinner only on Sundays. Reservations advised. Major credit cards accepted. 2191 Arapahoe St. (phone: 297-2288).

Denver Buffalo Company Dinner at this combination restaurant, deli, and art gallery is dedicated to the buffalo and originates at the restaurant's own 14,000-acre buffalo ranch about 35 miles southeast of Denver. Buffalo prime ribs, roasted in their own juices, and buffalo short ribs are among the most popular offerings. Sample the buffalo chili. Non-buffalo entrées also are available. Open daily; dinner only on Sundays. Reservations advised. Major credit cards accepted. 1109 Lincoln St. (phone: 832-0880).

Fresh Fish Company What's in a name? Everything. The seafood here is so fresh you might think they pulled the swordfish from the Colorado River. In fact, the fish is flown in daily from all over, so the menu includes Maine lobster, Florida stone crab, Canadian walleye, and Hawaiian *ahi.* The food is cooked over imported Mexican mesquite wood. The health- and weight-conscious can choose entrées low in fat, cholesterol, and sodium. Open daily; dinner only on Saturdays. Reservations advised. Major credit cards accepted. 7800 E. Hampden Ave. (phone: 740-9556).

La Loma Here is diverse and authentic Mexican fare, from enchiladas and tacos to the more ambitious sizzling *fajitas.* Try the fried ice cream. The service may sometimes be a bit inattentive, but it's always cheerful and pleasant. Reservations advised for parties of eight or more. Major credit cards accepted. 2527 W. 26th Ave. (phone: 433-8307).

INEXPENSIVE

Bonnie Brae Tavern In a city where most pizza seems to come from a "hut" or a "domino," this is one pizza place Denverites like to boast about. Founded in 1934, its setting is rustic and there's usually a wait for a table, but no one seems to mind. Closed Mondays. No reservations. Major credit cards accepted. 740 S. University Blvd. (phone: 777-2262).

My Brother's Bar Denver's best hamburger is here, just a few blocks north of downtown (try the jalapeño burger). Don't look for a sign out front—there's never been one. Closed Sundays. Reservations advised for six or more. MasterCard and Visa accepted. 2376 15th St. (phone: 455-9991).

Wynkoop Brewing Company This is the first pub in Colorado where beer is brewed on the premises and served directly from aging tanks. The menu features American fare made with fresh ingredients and organically grown produce. Shepherd's pie (braised Colorado lamb with mashed potatoes), and fish and chips are both good choices. Reservations unnecessary. Major credit cards accepted. 1634 18th St. (phone: 297-2700).

Detroit

Though sleek sedans and the sequined sounds of Motown are what come to mind when one thinks of Detroit, this gritty city was actually founded as a French fort in 1701. It seems the oldest city in the Midwest owes its existence to the King of France and his penchant for wearing beaver hats.

The fashion quickly caught on. To develop the fur trade, Antoine de la Mothe Cadillac landed at the narrowest point of the river between Lake St. Clair and Lake Erie and founded an outpost named for the straits—"D'etroit." More than 200 years later, the city returned the favor, naming one of its most famous cars after the explorer.

Following the French and Indian Wars in 1760, the British flag flew over Detroit until the US Army finally arrived in 1796, 13 years after the end of the Revolutionary War.

While its roots are French, subsequent Detroit history is indomitably American. The city's future was charted in 1896 when Charles Brady King and, three months later, Henry Ford, putt-putted their bicycle-wheeled horseless carriages onto the city's brick streets.

King faded into obscurity but Ford went on to apply mass production techniques to car building in uptown Highland Park; today, a plaque marks the factory site where millions of Model Ts sputtered to life.

Well-paying assembly jobs attracted thousands of immigrants and Southerners who left their fields to come north and build cars in a burgeoning metropolis. During World War II, production shifted from wheels to weapons, giving Detroit its nickname the "Arsenal of Democracy."

The population of the city peaked in the 1950s as the middle class began its suburban migration, hastened by new homes and freeways named after auto industry legends. The exodus left a deteriorating downtown and neglected neighborhoods surrounded by a ring of wealthier communities.

Detroit's latest comeback began in 1994 when popular Dennis Archer replaced Coleman Young, the tough-talking longtime mayor.

Rising above downtown just steps from where Cadillac landed is the city's dramatic *Renaissance Center* (known as the *RenCen*): six glass towers surrounding a 73-story *Westin* hotel. Across from the *RenCen* is the *Millender Center* with its shops, restaurants, apartments, and an *Omni International* hotel. Looping around the downtown business district is the elevated automated *People Mover* with its 13 stations.

A few blocks away, the *Atheneum* hotel, built with an eye to being near the city's first gambling casino when city and state officials finally agree on a site, anchors the compact Greektown restaurant district. Here is *Trappers Alley,* a former fur tannery converted into five levels of eateries and shops. The nearby Bricktown and Rivertown areas also offer new restaurants and saloons in old buildings.

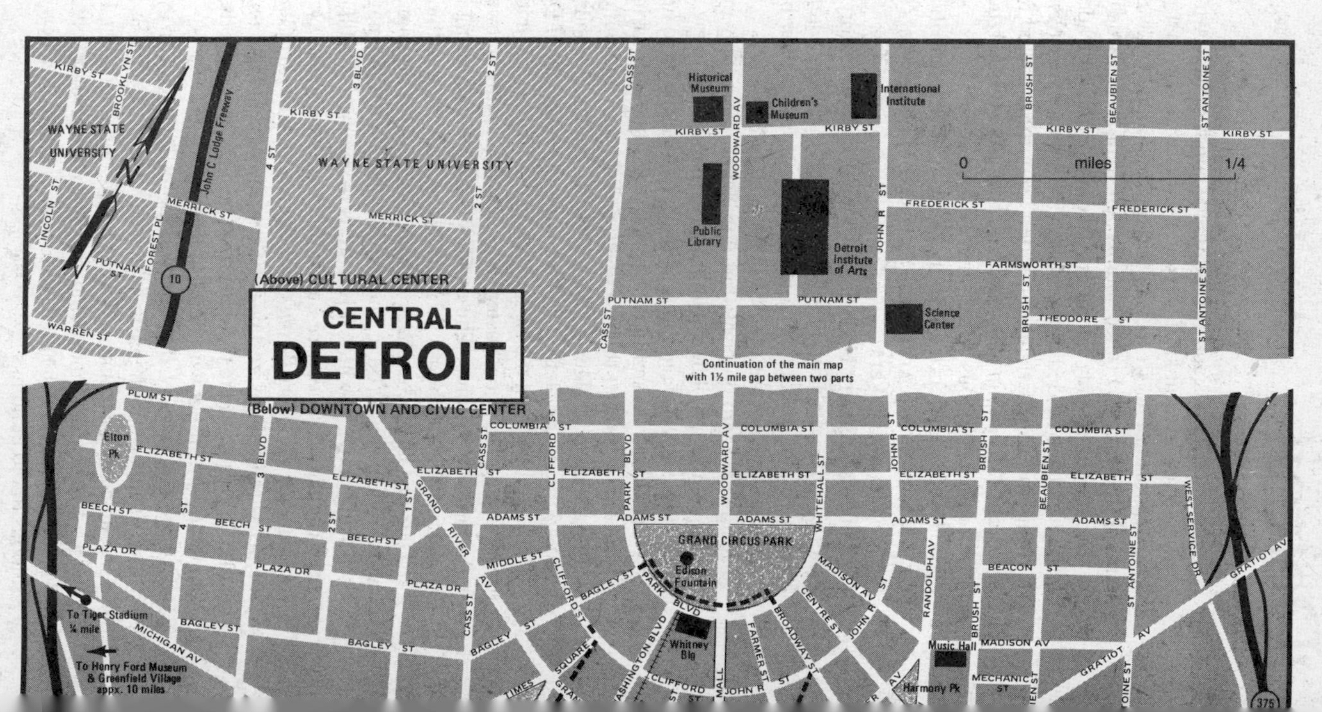
CENTRAL
DETROIT
(Above) CULTURAL CENTER
(Below) DOWNTOWN AND CIVIC CENTER
Continuation of the main map with 1½ mile gap between two parts
0 miles 1/4
Historical Museum
Children's Museum
International Institute
Public Library
Detroit Institute of Arts
Science Center
WAYNE STATE UNIVERSITY
John C Lodge Freeway
10
N
KIRBY ST
BROOKLYN ST
LINCOLN ST
FOREST PL
PUTNAM ST
WARREN ST
MERRICK ST
4 ST
3 BLVD
2 ST
CASS ST
WOODWARD AV
JOHN R ST
BRUSH ST
BEAUBIEN ST
ST ANTOINE ST
FREDERICK ST
FARMSWORTH ST
THEODORE ST
PLUM ST
Elton Pk
ELIZABETH ST
BEECH ST
PLAZA DR
BAGLEY ST
MICHIGAN AV
To Tiger Stadium ¼ mile
To Henry Ford Museum & Greenfield Village appx. 10 miles
1 ST
GRAND RIVER AV
COLUMBIA ST
CLIFFORD ST
PARK BLVD
ADAMS ST
MIDDLE ST
GRAND CIRCUS PARK
Edison Fountain
Whitney Blg
WASHINGTON BLVD
TIMES SQUARE
MALL
FARMER ST
BROADWAY ST
CENTRE ST
MADISON AV
WHITEHALL ST
RANDOLPH AV
Music Hall
Harmony Pk
BEACON ST
MECHANIC ST
GRATIOT AV
WEST SERVICE DR
375

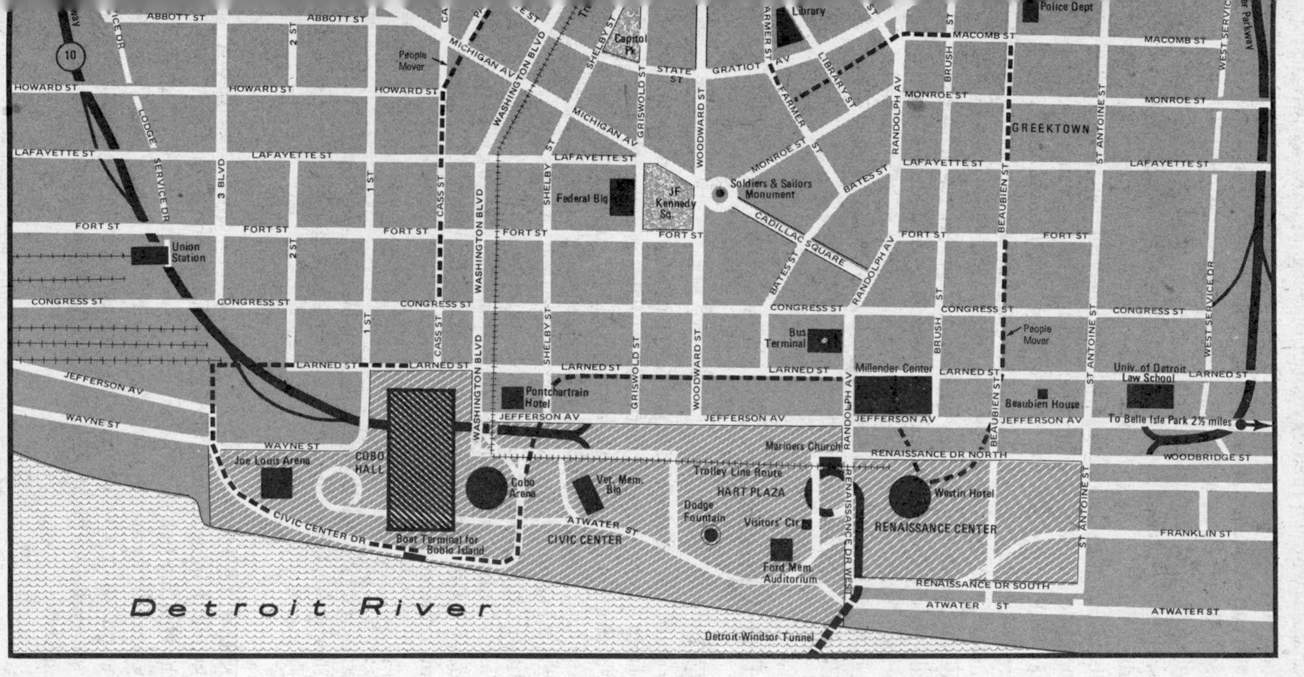
Detroit River
Police Dept
Library
Capitol Pk
GREEKTOWN
People Mover
Union Station
Federal Blg
JF Kennedy Sq.
Soldiers & Sailors Monument
CADILLAC SQUARE
Bus Terminal
Millender Center
Univ. of Detroit Law School
Pontchartrain Hotel
Beaubien House
To Belle Isle Park 2½ miles
Mariners Church
Trolley Line Route
HART PLAZA
Dodge Fountain
Visitors' Ctr
Ford Mem. Auditorium
Westin Hotel
RENAISSANCE CENTER
Joe Louis Arena
COBO HALL
Cobo Arena
Vet. Mem. Blg
CIVIC CENTER
Boat Terminal for Boblo Island
Detroit-Windsor Tunnel
ABBOTT ST
HOWARD ST
LAFAYETTE ST
FORT ST
CONGRESS ST
LARNED ST
JEFFERSON AV
WAYNE ST
CIVIC CENTER DR
ATWATER ST
MACOMB ST
MONROE ST
GRATIOT AV
MICHIGAN AV
WASHINGTON BLVD
CASS ST
1 ST
2 ST
3 BLVD
LODGE SERVICE DR
SHELBY ST
GRISWOLD ST
STATE ST
WOODWARD ST
FARMER ST
LIBRARY ST
BATES ST
RANDOLPH AV
BRUSH ST
BEAUBIEN ST
ST ANTOINE ST
WEST SERVICE DR
RENAISSANCE DR NORTH
RENAISSANCE DR SOUTH
RENAISSANCE DR WEST
WOODBRIDGE ST
FRANKLIN ST
10

A reawakened downtown theater district once again draws crowds to the palatial *Fox,* the cozy *Gem,* and the *Detroit Opera House,* which have spawned restaurants and a *Second City* comedy club. Just north, the world-class *Detroit Symphony* graces historic *Orchestra Hall,* a restored 1919 concert venue with legendary acoustics.

After cars, Detroit is crazy about sports. The downtown *Joe Louis Arena,* named after the town's favorite son boxer, is home to the *Red Wings,* Detroit's pro hockey team. Just west of downtown, the *Tigers* still play in venerable *Tiger Stadium* while officials plot to move to a new ballpark near the *Fox Theatre.* Basketball fans root for the *NBA Pistons* who slam-dunk in suburban Auburn Hills while the *NFL Lions* roar at the *Pontiac Silverdome.*

Although Detroit is downright seedy in spots (crime is an issue as it is in any big city, though downtown has become pretty safe), residents like it here. After all, their city put the world on wheels, gave it Stevie Wonder and the Supremes and the first ice cream soda, not to mention Charles Lindbergh, Lily Tomlin, Madonna, Tim Allen, Robin Williams, Bob Seger, and author Elmore "Dutch" Leonard.

Detroit At-a-Glance

SEEING THE CITY

A great view of the city can be had from the top of North America's tallest hotel, the 73-story *Westin* along the Detroit River. The top of the *Renaissance Center* offers views from its rooftop *Summit* cocktail lounge and revolving restaurant (see *Checking In* for details). Ever-changing views are possible from the *Detroit People Mover* (see *Getting Around*). Across the river, Windsor, Ontario, offers postcard views of Detroit's skyline, particularly from the *Windsor Hilton* and *Compri* hotels (see *Checking In*), and from *Dieppe Gardens,* a flower-filled riverside park at the foot of Ouellette Avenue, Windsor's main street.

SPECIAL PLACES

We've divided the city into Civic Center, Cultural Center, and Other Special Places. The downtown Civic Center is a good place to begin sightseeing.

CIVIC CENTER

RENAISSANCE CENTER Detroit's very own Oz, this city-within-a-city dominates the downtown skyline. Dining, entertainment, shopping, and a soaring hotel have made the *RenCen* tick since it opened in 1977. The huge complex is connected by a maze of walkways and atriums—even an indoor lake. With seven circular buildings to stroll around in, first-timers always get lost. Group tours are available (phone: 591-3611). Jefferson Ave. between Brush and Beaubien Sts.

MILLENDER CENTER Tethered to the *RenCen* by the *People Mover* and a skywalk over Jefferson Avenue, *Millender* is a smaller version of the riverfront complex without all the confusion. Both the *Millender Center* and the adjoining *Omni* hotel boast shops and restaurants.

PHILIP A. HART PLAZA Detroit's 11-acre riverfront plaza was designed by international sculptor Isamu Noguchi, whose spaceship-style *Dodge Fountain* spouts computer-controlled water displays. This paved esplanade is home to Detroit's summer riverfront ethnic festivals, the *Montreaux-Detroit Jazz Festival* and the world's largest annual fireworks display each July which draws a million fans on both sides of the Detroit River. Along Jefferson at Woodward Ave., the city's main drag.

COBO CENTER Named after a former mayor, this sprawling conference and exhibition center contains 700,000 square feet of exhibit area for conventions, trade shows, and events such as the renowned *North American International Auto Show* each January. At Washington Blvd. and Jefferson Ave.

THE FIST Robert Graham's downtown sculpture at Woodward and Jefferson of the fist and forearm of legendary Detroit boxer Joe Louis earns a split decision. Supporters say it symbolizes the city's fighting spirit; others say a city with a crime problem hardly needs a four-ton fist in its midst. At Woodward and Jefferson Aves.

WASHINGTON BOULEVARD TROLLEYS A set of charming antique trolley cars clang their way back and forth from *Grand Circus Park*'s theater district along Washington Boulevard, past *Cobo Center* and *Mariner's Church* on their way to the *Renaissance Center* and back.

CULTURAL CENTER

DETROIT INSTITUTE OF ARTS One of America's top five art museums, its total collection fills 130 galleries. Known for its collections of French Impressionist, German expressionist, Flemish, Italian, African, Egyptian, and 20th Century art, the *DIA* is also home to Diego Rivera's giant "Detroit Industry" frescoes which cover the walls of a central court and depict mythological figures hovering above workers toiling on a 1930s assembly line. Controversial when created, the murals are now much loved as a symbol of this hard-working town. Special exhibitions, lectures, and film, music, and theater performances are held frequently. Closed Mondays and Tuesdays. Admission charge. 5200 Woodward Ave. (phone: 833-7900).

DETROIT PUBLIC LIBRARY Across from the *DIA,* this Italian Renaissance building of white Vermont marble contains not only books but paintings, stained glass windows, and mosaics plus the Burton Historical Collection, an archive of material related to Detroit history. Closed Sundays, Mondays, and holidays. No admission charge. 5201 Woodward Ave. (phone: 833-1000).

DETROIT HISTORICAL MUSEUM Check out the "Motor City Exhibition," a permanent tribute to 100 years of the automobile in Detroit, among this facility's other displays of the city's past. In the basement are the "Streets of Old Detroit," allowing visitors to wander through time among the storefronts of yesteryear. Each *Christmas* season also brings a fine display of antique toys from its collection. Closed Mondays, Tuesdays, and holidays. Admission charge. 5401 Woodward Ave. (phone: 833-1805).

CHILDREN'S MUSEUM This museum features a planetarium and collections of kites, puppets, and small animals. Kids of all ages love *Silverbolt*—the life-size horse sculpture out front made from car bumpers. Closed Sundays; closed Saturdays from June through September. No admission charge. 67 E. Kirby Ave. (phone: 494-1210).

DETROIT SCIENCE CENTER Established in 1978, the center is home to Michigan's only *Omnimax Theater* with its domed three-story screen and 16-speaker sound system. The newer *Discovery Theater* provides programs on inner and outer space plus live science demonstrations and interactive video presentations. There also are more than 50 hands-on exhibits on the main floor. Open daily. Admission charge. 5020 John R St. at E. Warren (phone: 577-8400).

MUSEUM OF AFRICAN-AMERICAN HISTORY Black heritage is explored through art, artifacts, and exhibitions in the museum's new $23-million facility, the largest of its kind in the country. Closed Mondays and Tuesdays. Donation suggested. 315 E. Warren (phone: 833-9800).

OTHER SPECIAL PLACES

BELLE ISLE Legend says this beautiful island in the middle of the Detroit River was originally set aside as pasture by Cadillac himself. The 1,000-acre park designed by Frederick Law Olmsted now hosts the *Detroit Grand Prix* every June along with such regular attractions as the spectacular *Scott Fountain,* a children's zoo, the *Belle Isle Aquarium* (phone: 267-7159), and the *Dossin Great Lakes Museum* (phone: 267-6440), with its displays of ship models and seafaring artifacts. It's also a good place for picnics, biking, canoeing, jogging, and viewing the downtown skyline. South of Jefferson, across the General Douglas MacArthur Bridge (phone: 267-7115).

BIRMINGHAM Detroit's exclusive northern suburb is a good place to hang out if you're looking for pricey stores and eateries. The area is also filled with parks, a theater, and exclusive homes. Fifteen miles north of downtown Detroit, where Woodward forks at Hunter.

CRANBROOK Stroll through 40 rolling acres of gardens surrounding an English manor, catch a laser light show, visit a nature center, or browse through an art museum or science exhibition. It's all part of this internationally known center for the arts, education, and culture designed by Finnish architect Eliel Saarinen where sculptor Carl Milles and designers Harry Bertoia and Charles Eames once taught. Concerts and other special events make

Cranbrook a compelling place to visit, well worth the 25-mile drive north from Detroit. 500 Lone Pine Rd. just west of Woodward, Bloomfield Hills (phone: 810-645-3000).

GREENFIELD VILLAGE AND HENRY FORD MUSEUM The story goes that when Henry Ford couldn't find a copy of McGuffey's Reader, he feared such pieces of Americana would disappear forever unless he founded a museum. The result? A collection of scores of antique automobiles and thousands of 19th- and 20th-century machines housed in a building styled after Philadelphia's *Independence Hall.* Also here is "The Automobile in American Life" exhibit and another, co-produced with the *Motown Museum* on Detroit's sounds of the Sixties. Next door, the 81-acre Greenfield Village boasts 80 historic homes and shops moved here from all over America, including the Wright Brothers' bicycle shop, Thomas Edison's Menlo Park laboratory, and the tiny stable where Ford built his first car. Costumed interpreters, plus rides in an old train, riverboat, and carriages, add to the flavor. Open daily. Separate admissions for the village and the museum; combination tickets also available. 20900 Oakwood Blvd., south of Michigan Ave. just west of the Southfield Fwy., Dearborn (phone: 271-1620).

EASTERN MARKET A carnival of sights, smells, and sounds, this has been Detroit's farmers' market since 1891. Shoppers come from all over the metro area to haggle with merchants selling the freshest produce, meat, fish, cheeses, flowers, and vegetables. Wholesale Monday through Friday; retail Saturdays. Surrounding stores open Monday through Saturday; closed Sundays. Russell at Fisher Fwy. (phone: 833-1560).

FOX THEATRE Part theater, part fantasyland, this $8-million restoration of C. Howard Crane's 1928 movie palace has brought name acts back to the great stage and suburbanites back downtown. The gilded Siamese Byzantine decor is striking with its red faux marble columns in a six-story lobby and a huge stained glass chandelier, resplendent above the theater's 4,800 seats. Two restaurants—*Tres Vite* and *American Pizza Café*—bookend the building with good fare at both. 2211 Woodward Ave. (phone: 396-7600).

GREEKTOWN This downtown enclave of restaurants serving authentic Greek fare (including a flaming cheese dish accompanied by a shout of "Opa!")—plus quaint shops, bakeries, and *Old St. Mary's Church*—makes for an interesting stroll. *Trapper's Alley,* the five-level festival marketplace with its restaurants, specialty shops, and *Attic Theatre,* is also here. Monroe St., between Beaubien and St. Antoine Sts.

MOTOWN HISTORICAL MUSEUM This converted brick-and-stucco house, called *Hitsville USA,* turned out more gold than *Fort Knox*—pop music gold, that is. Motown memories abound here in an early 1960s setting including the original studio where the Supremes, Stevie Wonder, the Temptations, the Four Tops, and Marvin Gaye recorded. Michael Jackson is a big benefactor. Open daily. Admission charge. 2648 W. Grand Blvd. (phone: 875-2264).

PEWABIC POTTERY Founded in 1903, this is the nation's oldest arts and crafts pottery workshop. Many area mansions, churches, and public buildings (including four *People Mover* stations and the Art Deco Guardian Building downtown) are decorated with its unique tiles. Besides a gallery, there is a gift shop featuring old and new patterns (commissions for businesses and clients like lifestyle maven Martha Stewart and Hollywood's Penny Marshall have been created here). Closed Sunday. No admission. 10125 E. Jefferson (phone: 822-0954).

PLANT TOURS Watch luxury Lincolns being built at a Ford assembly plant in Wixom, a suburb west of Detroit. Tours on Fridays; call far ahead for reservations (phone: 810-344-5358). Tours of the *Hiram Walker Canadian Club Distillery* (with free tastings) are held at 2 PM weekdays only (phone: 965-6611 for reservations).

ROYAL OAK This suburb midway between Detroit and Pontiac is home to the *Detroit Zoological Park* (see below). Lately it's become a magnet for the young and trendy, with many coffee houses, restaurants, and art galleries that cater to the upscale and the leather-clad. If it's bistros and boutiques you want, complete with a teeming sidewalk scene on weekends, this is the place.

DETROIT ZOOLOGICAL PARK The first zoo in the US to use natural settings is home to hundreds of species amid small lakes and flower gardens. Don't miss the chimpanzee exhibit and the new walk-through butterfly and hummingbird indoor garden. Open daily. No admission charge for children under two. On Woodward at I-696 (10 Mile Rd.), Royal Oak (phone: 810-398-0900).

EXTRA SPECIAL

Canada lies across the river, only a mile from Detroit. In just a few minutes, you can be across the Detroit River and in a foreign country. You don't even need a passport if you're a US citizen; be prepared to show your birth certificate, though such requests are rare. Windsor's also an auto-making town but one that offers Las Vegas–style gambling at the *Windsor Casino* (445 Riverside Dr. W.; phone: 519-258-7878). You can also roll 'em on the river at the docked *Northern Belle* riverboat casino (350 Riverside E., phone: 519-258-2141). The town's also a good place to buy English woolens, glassware, and china. From Detroit, you can reach Windsor by bus or taxi through the Detroit-Windsor Tunnel or over the Ambassador Bridge.

Sources and Resources

TOURIST INFORMATION

The *Metropolitan Detroit Convention and Vistors Bureau* (Tower 100, *RenCen*, Detroit, MI 48243; phone: 800-DETROIT) maintains a 24-hour "What's Line" directory of events and distributes free brochures and maps. Office closed weekends. Or call the state tourism hotline (phone: 800-543-2937) for maps, calendars of events, and travel advisories.

LOCAL COVERAGE *Detroit Free Press,* morning weekdays; *Detroit News,* morning and afternoon weekdays; combined papers on weekends; *Oakland Press, Royal Oak Tribune and Macomb Daily* (afternoons). *Detroit Sunday Journal* (weekly). *Key* (free) and *Travel Host* magazines available at hotels. *Detroit Visitors Guide* (free from the *Metropolitan Detroit Convention and Visitors Bureau*) is a good guide to the area. Also good is the city magazine *Detroit Monthly.* For around-town happenings and attractions, pick up a free *Detroit Monitor* or the much-hipper *Metro Times* weekly at newsstands.

TELEVISION STATIONS WJBK Channel 2–Fox; WDIV Channel 4–NBC; WXYZ Channel 7–ABC; WXON Channel 20–Warner Bros.; WKBD Channel 50–UPN; WTVS Channel 56–PBS; WWJ Channel 62–CBS.

RADIO STATIONS AM: CKWW 580 (big band); WJR 760 (news/talk); WWJ 950 (news); WDFN 1130 (sports); WXYT 1270 (talk). FM: WCSX 94.7 (classic rock); WJLB 97.9 (urban contemporary); WDET 101.9 (public radio/news/music variety); WOMC 104.3 (oldies); WQRS 105.1 (classical); WJZZ 105.9 (jazz); WGPR 107.5 (urban contemporary).

TELEPHONE The area code for Detroit and Ann Arbor is 313; it's 810 for suburban Oakland and Macomb counties.

SALES TAX The sales tax is 6%; hotel tax ranges from 6% to 14% depending on the size and location of the establishment.

CLIMATE Seasons are changeable in the motor city: It may reach 55F on a winter day and only 40F on *Memorial Day.* The local joke is that if you don't like the weather, wait five minutes—it's sure to change. Temperatures can push into the 90s in summer while subfreezing is often the rule in January and February.

GETTING AROUND

AIRPORT *Detroit Metropolitan Wayne County Airport* handles the city's air traffic and is about a 30-minute drive from downtown. *Commuter Transportation* (phone: 941-3252; 800-351-5466) provides van transport to downtown and area hotels from the airport's north, south, and international terminals. You can also opt for a chauffeur-driven Cadillac or Lincoln from *Metro Cars Inc.* (phone: 946-5700; 800-456-1701). *Kirby Tours* (phone: 278-2224; 800-521-0711) also has shuttle service between *Metro Airport* and city hotels.

CAR RENTAL All major national firms are represented.

PEOPLE MOVER An elevated rail system carries passengers in automated cars around downtown. The complete loop takes 14 minutes with stops at *Joe Louis Arena, Cobo Center, Millender Center, RenCen,* Greektown, and eight other stops. Cost is 50¢ (phone: 962-7245).

RIVER CRUISES Restaurants and bars that are tugboats and sidewheelers are anchored in the Detroit River between Detroit and Windsor. During the summer, *Diamond Jack's River Tours* (phone: 843-7676) operates two-hour narrated boat trips along the river Wednesdays through Sundays from Hart Plaza and *St. Aubin Park.*

TAXI Cabs can be hailed in the street or picked up at stands in front of hotels. Some are licensed to cross over to Canada. If you prefer to call a cab, we suggest Checker (phone: 963-7000).

TOURS *Detroit Upbeat* (phone: 341-6808) and *Kirby Tours* (phone: 278-2224; 800-521-0711) offer tours of Detroit, Ann Arbor, and southeast Michigan.

SPECIAL EVENTS

The *Detroit Grand Prix* (phone: 393-7749) sends Indy-type cars racing around the Belle Isle course every June. It's also the month when hydroplanes roar off Belle Isle in the annual *Thunderfest Gold Cup* races (phone: 259-7760). The friendship between Detroit and Windsor is celebrated annually with the *International Freedom Festival* (phone: 923-7400), a series of events culminating during *Fourth of July* week with spectacular fireworks over the river. Also that weekend, the *Michigan Tastefest* (phone: 872-0188) serves up samples from 30 area restaurants; the celebration includes concerts held in the New Center area (on W. Grand Blvd. west of Woodward). The *Montreaux-Detroit Jazz Festival* (phone: 963-7622) mixes local and international music stars around *Labor Day* weekend with concerts at *Hart Plaza,* the *Chene Park* riverfront amphitheater, and other locations throughout the city. A Detroit tradition since 1926, the Michigan *Thanksgiving Day Parade* (phone: 923-7400) marches down Woodward to Hart Plaza every "Turkey Day."

MUSEUMS

In addition to those described in *Special Places,* Detroit has several other museums of note.

Four of the majestic mansions created by Detroit's auto barons are open to the public: Henry Ford's *Fair Lane* estate (Dearborn; phone: 593-5590); his son Edsel's lakefront mansion (where Henry Ford II grew up) is the *Edsel and Eleanor Ford House* (Grosse Pointe Shores; phone: 884-4222); the ornate riverfront estate of Lawrence P. Fisher, now the *Bhaktivedanta Krishna Cultural Center* (Detroit; phone: 331-6740); and the 100-room *Meadow Brook Hall* (Rochester; phone: 810-370-3140), which cost Matilda Dodge Wilson $4 million to complete in 1929. Both the Edsel Ford home and *Meadow Brook Hall* also have antique auto shows on their grounds each summer.

SHOPPING

Detroit has its share of marketplaces and malls filled with department stores, chain shops, eateries, and entertainment. Perhaps the most opulent is the *Somerset Collection* (phone: 810-643-6360) and *Somerset North,* two glitzy gallerias connected by a walkway over Big Beaver Rd. (16 Mile Rd.) in the suburb of Troy. Enclaves of commerce (such as those listed in *Special Places*) are easy to find and get to and museum shops are also an excellent source of quality gifts and mementos.

SPORTS AND FITNESS

Detroit wouldn't be Detroit without its top major league teams—along with its other recreational opportunities.

BASEBALL Home base for the *American League Tigers* is *Tiger Stadium* (Michigan at Trumbull; phone: 962-4000).

BASKETBALL The *NBA Pistons* shoot hoops at the *Palace of Auburn Hills* (2 Championship Dr.; phone: 810-377-0100).

FISHING Fishing can be good in the Detroit River, especially around Belle Isle. Of the hundreds of other lakes, we recommend Lake St. Clair and Orchard Lake, both in Oakland County.

FITNESS CENTERS *Power House Gym* (2580 N. Squirrel Rd., Auburn Hills; phone: 810-377-3383) is a full-service health club open to non-members for a fee. Check local yellow pages for listings of other facilities.

FOOTBALL The *NFL Lions* play in the covered, 80,000-seat Silverdome (M-59 at Opdyke, Pontiac; phone: 810-335-4151). For top-ranked college ball, try the *University of Michigan Wolverines* in their 104,000-seat stadium in Ann Arbor (phone: 313-747-2583).

GOLF Two of the better public courses are *Kensington Metropark* (2240 W. Buno Rd.; Milford; phone: 810-685-9332) and *Pine Knob* (6925 Royal St. George, Independence Twp.; phone: 810-625-4430).

HOCKEY Action for the *NHL Red Wings* is on the ice at *Joe Louis Arena* (Civic Center Dr.; phone: 396-7600).

HORSE RACING Thoroughbreds race at *Ladbroke DRC* (28001 Schoolcraft, Livonia; phone: 525-7300); *Hazel Park Harness Raceway* (1650 E. Ten Mile, Hazel Park; phone: 810-398-1000); and *Northville Downs* (301 S. Center St., Northville; phone: 810-349-1000). *Windsor Raceway* hosts fall and winter harness racing (Hwy. 18 at Sprucewood, Windsor, Ont.; phone: 961-9545 in Detroit).

JOGGING One ideal spot is *Belle Isle Park.* To get there from downtown, run 2½ miles east along Jefferson and a half mile over the arched bridge; or take the Jefferson bus, then jog around the island's perimeter. One annual rite of fall is the *Detroit Free Press Mazda International Marathon* (phone: 222-6676) which begins in Windsor and runs a unique "underwater mile" through the Detroit/Windsor Tunnel, ending on Belle Isle.

IN-LINE SKATING You can skate in *Belle Isle Park* or in the *Silverdome* (phone: 810-646-7655).

TENNIS The city has several public courts. The best are at *Palmer Park* and Belle Isle. Call the *Detroit Recreation Department* (phone: 224-1100) for information.

THEATER

Detroit's stages offer plenty of choices. There may be a Broadway hit at the *Fisher Theatre* (Second at W. Grand Blvd.; phone: 872-1000) or at the *Masonic Temple Theatre* (500 Temple; phone: 832-2232). Comedy and drama take to the boards at the *Meadow Brook Theatre* on the *Oakland University* campus (University Dr. east of I-75, Rochester Hills; phone: 810-377-3300). The restored *Gem Theatre* (58 Columbia St.; phone: 963-9800) presents small off-beat revues and musicals. Other good venues are the *Hilberry Classic Theatre* on the *Wayne State University* campus (4743 Cass Ave.; phone: 577-2972) for literary classics, and the *Attic Theatre* in Greektown (508 Monroe St.; phone: 963-9339) for off-Broadway productions. Check the Friday Detroit daily papers or the weekly *Metro Times* for other venues.

MUSIC

Just about every kind of music thrives in Detroit—symphonic, jazz, soul, and rock. It's the birthplace of Motown and the home for rockers like favorite son Bob Seger. Rock and soul concerts are played at the *Palace of Auburn Hills* (2 Championship Dr.; phone: 810-377-8200); *Cobo Arena* (Jefferson at Washington Blvd.; phone: 396-7600); *Joe Louis Arena* (Civic Center Dr.; phone: 396-7600); *Pontiac Silverdome* (M-59 at Opdyke, Pontiac; phone: 810-456-1600); *Masonic Temple Theatre* (500 Temple; phone: 832-2232); *Royal Oak Music Theatre* (318 W. 4th St.; phone: 810-546-7610); and the *Fox Theatre* (2211 Woodward; phone: 396-7600). The *Detroit Symphony* concert season runs from September to May at historic *Orchestra Hall* (3711 Woodward; phone: 833-3700), which also offers other classical, dance, and jazz concerts. Another restored movie palace is the new *Detroit Opera House,* home of the *Michigan Opera Theatre* (1526 Broadway; phone: 874-SING). The *Music Hall Center for the Performing Arts* (350 Madison; phone: 963-7680) hosts traveling dance and music concerts. Outdoor venues include *Meadow Brook Music Festival* (*Oakland University* campus; phone: 810-377-0100) for symphonic, pop, and jazz music, and the *Pine Knob Music Theater* (Sashabaw Rd., north of I-75, Clarkston; phone: 810-377-0100) for big name pop and rock entertainers.

NIGHTCLUBS AND NIGHTLIFE

Singles mingle at *Tom's Oyster Bar* (318 S. Main St., Royal Oak; phone: 810-541-1186); *Norm's Eton Street Station* (a former 1931 railroad depot at 245 S. Eton, Birmingham; phone: 810-647-7774); and *Sparky Herbert's* (15117 Kercheval, Groose Pointe Park; phone: 822-0266). Catch the blues at the *Soup Kitchen Saloon* (1585 Franklin; phone: 259-1374) Wednesdays through Sundays, and at *Sisko's on the Boulevard* (5855 Monroe Blvd.,

Taylor; phone: 278-5340) Tuesdays through Saturdays. The *Rhinoceros* (265 Riopelle; phone: 259-2208) has a cool piano bar, while *Charley's Crab* (5498 Crooks Rd., Troy; phone: 810-879-2060) offers the best boogie-woogie pianist in town. Live jazz reigns at *Macon's Music Café* (Fisher Bldg., W. Grand Blvd. at Second; phone: 972-3760) and at *Intermezzo* (1435 Randolph; phone: 961-0707). The *State Theatre* (2115 Woodward; phone: 961-5450) is an old Detroit movie house–turned-arena that features movies, music, and dancing. *Mark Ridley's Comedy Castle* (E. Fourth at Troy, Royal Oak; phone: 810-542-9900) presents national acts with local openers and open-mike night Tuesdays; big-name yucksters also perform at *Chaplin's* (34244 Groesbeck, Clinton Twp.; phone: 810-792-1902), while *Second City-Detroit* (2301 Woodward; phone: 965-2222) stages satirical revues on social and political issues.

In nearby Pontiac, night owls can choose between the *Ultimate Sports Bar and Grill* (40 W. Pike; phone: 810-253-1300), with its boxing ring dance floor, and *Industry* (15 S. Saginaw; phone: 810-334-1999), a music-dance club with factory-style decor.

Best in Town

CHECKING IN

Expect to pay between $125 and $225 per night for a double room at establishments in the expensive category; and from $65 to $125 for those listed as moderate. Inexpensive lodging (less than $65) is available at chain hotels such as Days Inn, Budgetel, Red Roof Inn, and Knights Inn. Most of Detroit's major hotels have complete facilities for the business traveler. Those listed below as having "business services" usually offer such conveniences as meeting rooms, photocopiers, computers, translation services, and express checkout among others. Call the individual hotel for additional information. For downtown bed-and-breakfast accommodations, contact *Blanche House Inn* (506 Parkview; phone: 822-7090) or the *Corktown Inn* (1705 Sixth at Michigan Ave.; phone: 963-6688). The *Metro Detroit Convention and Visitors Bureau* (phone: 800-DETROIT) also maintains a list of area hotels. Unless otherwise noted, hotel rooms have air conditioning, private baths, TVs, and telephones.

All hotels below are in Detroit and telephone and fax numbers are in the 313 area code unless otherwise indicated.

EXPENSIVE

Atheneum Formerly a warehouse, this all-suite hotel sits on the fringe of Greektown. Each of the 174 suites has a living room, bedroom and spacious marble bath; ask for one with a city skyline and a Jacuzzi. Amenities include 24-hour room service and a concierge. Business services are available. 1000 Brush (phone: 962-2323; 800-772-2323; fax: 962-2424).

Hyatt Regency Dearborn Its 771 spacious airy rooms overlook the landscaped park of the Ford World Headquarters in Dearborn. Nearby are *Fairlane Town Center* shopping mall, *Greenfield Village, Henry Ford Museum,* and a satellite *University of Michigan* campus. Amenities include restaurants, room service until midnight, a concierge, and business services. Michigan Ave. and Southfield Fwy., Dearborn (phone: 593-1234; 800-233-1234; fax: 593-3366).

Omni International Abutting the *Millender Center,* this 25-story hostelry with 254 spacious and imaginatively appointed rooms also has exercise facilities, a restaurant, and a lounge. Other amenities include room service until midnight, a concierge, and business services. 333 E. Jefferson, across from the *RenCen* and the Detroit-Windsor Tunnel (phone: 222-7700; 800-843-6664; fax: 222-6509).

Radisson Plaza Hotel This 385-room property has an indoor pool and health club. *T.C. Linguini's* restaurant and *Tango's* bar are popular. Amenities include 24-hour room service, a concierge, and business services. In the *Prudential Town Center* complex, Southfield (phone: 810-827-4000; 800-333-3333; fax: 810-827-1364).

Ritz-Carlton Dearborn From the outside, it looks like a French château; inside, 18th- and 19th-century art and antiques create a warm, elegant atmosphere. Traditional decor defines the 308 guestrooms. A well-trained staff enhances the fine dining at *The Grill.* There's also an exercise room and an indoor pool. Amenities include 24-hour room service, a concierge, and business services. 300 Town Center Dr. across from Ford World Headquarters and *Fairlane Town Center* mall, Dearborn (phone: 441-2000; 800-241-3333; fax: 441-2051).

Townsend This traditional small hotel offers 87 rooms (including executive and two-room suites) in the center of Birmingham's shopping and gallery district. Elegant marble baths boast brass fixtures; there's morning newspaper delivery and afternoon tea. Everything from seafood to beef is served at the first class *Rugby Grille.* Guests have privileges at a local health club (transportation provided). Amenities include 24-hour room service, a concierge, and business services. 100 Townsend St., Birmingham (phone: 810- 642-7900; 800-548-4172; fax: 810-645-9061).

Troy Marriott Located in the booming northern suburb of Troy, this hotel has 350 rooms (including four suites) and a skylighted lobby atrium. It's convenient to the *Pontiac Silverdome. Stacy's Sea Grille* serves up delicious seafood. Other amenities include room service until midnight, a concierge, and business services. 220 W. Big Beaver, east of I-75, Troy (phone: 810-680-9797; 800-777-4096; fax: 810-680-9774).

Westin Renaissance Center This soaring 1,414-room, 73-story round tower features dramatic public areas: The lobby takes up the first eight stories with fountains, trees, aerial walkways, shops, and lounges. Three levels of revolving bars and restaurants highlight the top of the building; downstairs, there's casual dining at the *River Bistro* and more than a dozen eateries in the adjoining retail complex. Amenities include 24-hour room service, a concierge, and business services. At the east end of *Hart Plaza* on Jefferson at St. Antoine (phone: 568-8000; 800-228-3000; fax: 568-8146).

MODERATE

Botsford Inn Originally an 1836 stagecoach stop, it has 65 spacious antiques-filled rooms and serves hearty American fare in the *Coach Room and Lounge.* Amenities include a concierge desk and business services. 28000 Grand River Ave. at 8 Mile, Farmington Hills (phone: 810-474-4800; fax: 810-474-7669).

Dearborn Inn A few blocks from the *Henry Ford Museum* and *Greenfield Village* and only 20 minutes from downtown stands this tasteful Georgian-style hotel. Built by Henry Ford to serve a nearby airfield, it was later expanded with reproductions of five historic homes and two motel-style wings. The 222 rooms and suites have the charm and beauty of a bygone era. Three dining rooms offer tasty American fare; there are also tennis courts to work off the meal. Amenities include valet, laundry, and baby-sitting service. There's room service until midnight plus concierge and business services. 20301 Oakwood Blvd., Dearborn (phone: 271-2700; 800-321-2049; fax: 271-7464).

Doubletree Suites Each of the 239 spacious suites has a bedroom and a parlor. There's *Jacques Demers Bistro,* a pool, a sauna, and a whirlpool bath. Ideally situated for those in the Southfield area. Amenities include room service until 11 PM and business services. 28100 Franklin Rd., Southfield (phone: 810-350-2000; 800-222-TREE; fax: 810-350-1185).

Hilton Suites Auburn Hills Each of this hotel's 224 suites boasts a VCR, wet bar, refrigerator, and microwave oven. It's conveniently located near the new *Chrysler Tech Center,* the *Palace of Auburn Hills,* and the *Pontiac Silverdome.* There's an indoor pool, Jacuzzi, sauna, billiards room, and exercise room, plus the *Great American Grill.* There's limited room service but full business services. 2300 Featherstone at I-75 and M-59 (phone: 810-334-2222; 800-HILTONS; fax: 810-334-2922).

Mayflower Hotel This 73-room inn offers guests a full complimentary breakfast. Amenities include a concierge desk and business services. On the town square in quaint Plymouth, its phone number hails the date of the Pilgrims' landing. 827 W. Ann Arbor Trail (phone: 453-1620; fax: 453-0193).

Windsor Hilton Just across the Detroit River, this hotel commands a sparkling view of Detroit's skyline from each of its 303 rooms. There are three executive floors and mini-bars in every room. Amenities include a restaurant, room service until 11 PM, a concierge, and business services. 277 Riverside Dr. W. (phone: 519-973-5555; 962-3834 in Detroit; 800-463-6655; fax: 519-973-1600).

Wyndham Garden This refurbished hotel has 148 rooms (including 28 suites) in a building with elegant touches of marble and brass; there's also a lovely garden. Amenities include a restaurant, a pool, a sauna, a Jacuzzi and the use of an adjacent health club. Room service until 11:30 PM and business services are available. 42100 Crescent Blvd., Novi (phone: 810-344-8800; 800-822-4200; fax: 810-344-8535).

EATING OUT

Detroit has a large number of moderately priced restaurants serving everything from steaks, crepes, and seafood to natural foods, deep-dish pizza, and deli sandwiches. Nationalities represented range from French and Middle Eastern to Oriental and Ethopian and just about anything else. Expect to pay $75 or more for dinner for two at the restaurants listed as expensive; between $30 and $75 at places categorized as moderate; and less than $30 at those described as inexpensive. Prices do not include drinks, wine, tax, or tips. All telephone numbers are in the 313 area code, unless otherwise indicated.

Unless otherwise noted, restaurants are open for lunch and dinner.

EXPENSIVE

Joe Muer's A Detroit landmark (ca. 1929), this clubby, brick-and-oak family-run place was serving fresh seafood decades before "catch of the day" became a catchphrase. Notable items include Florida stone crabs, Dover sole, and tiny bay scallops. Closed Sundays and holidays. No reservations. Major credit cards accepted. 2000 Gratiot near Eastern Market (phone: 567-1088).

Opus One The finely tuned menu is American with a French flair—try the sautéed breast of Michigan pheasant in basil cream, char-grilled medaillons of veal with truffle Madeira sauce, or grilled salmon steaks. The decor is classical with tapestry-covered banquettes and lots of etched glass and marble. Closed Sundays. Reservations advised. Major credit cards accepted. 565 E. Larned, Bricktown (phone: 961-7766).

Rattlesnake Club This airy, contemporary room with its river-view windows features a highly acclaimed and ever-changing menu with such creative entrées as swordfish grilled with grapefruit, fried ginger, and chives, as well as to die for desserts—chocolate ice cream rolled in cocoa, and white chocolate raviolis with hazelnut *anglaise.* Closed Sundays. Reservations advised. Major credit cards accepted. 300 Stroh River Pl. at Joseph Campau St. (phone: 567-4400).

The Whitney Located in an opulent midtown mansion, circa 1894, this is perhaps the city's most impressive restaurant. High-ceilinged rooms, stained glass, and a sweeping staircase set the stage for an ever-changing menu offering such seasonal dishes as Michigan trout, and filet mignon in peppercorn sauce. Save room for the Chocolate Ugly cake. The third floor bar is a great pre- or après-theater place with live music. Open daily for dinner; lunch on Friday only. Major credit cards accepted. 4421 Woodward at Canfield (phone: 832-5700).

MODERATE

Charley's Crab Stylish seasonal seafood and traditional menu items take the stage in this cross between a manor hall and a dockside tavern which serves business types, visiting *NBA* players, and local residents. Tuesdays through Saturdays the bar swings with an excellent boogie-woogie piano player. Reservations advised. Major credit cards accepted. 5498 Crooks Rd. at I-75, Troy (phone: 810-879-2060).

Cook's Shop Beyond the awning that marks the spot is this romantic hideaway of several small rooms. The fresh pasta sauces and some desserts are prepared at tableside; the grill choices are equally good. Upstairs, the *Pasta Shop* (which has more than pasta) is less formal. Reservations advised. Major credit cards accepted. 683 Ouellette, Windsor (phone: 519-254-3377).

Courthouse Brasserie The 10-table restaurant that lies behind this nondescript exterior is one of downtown's most soothing, especially for lawyers on their way to court nearby. Classical music, dark wood, and antique chandeliers set the mood for such dishes as gingery grilled chicken breast, poached salmon, and marinated rack of lamb. Closed Monday evenings. Reservations advised. Major credit cards accepted. 1436 Brush, just north of Gratiot (phone: 963-8887).

Fishbone's Rhythm Kitchen Café On the edge of Greektown, this renovated warehouse offers a taste of the French Quarter. Diners feast on Cajun and creole dishes—spicy chicken wings and ribs, jambalaya, peel-and-eat shrimp, and *étouffée*. Reservations advised. Major credit cards accepted. 400 Monroe (phone: 965-4600).

Intermezzo In the nascent Harmonie Park loft district near the *Music Hall* and the Detroit *Opera House,* this popular restaurant in an 1898 building has a New York feel: big windows, brick walls, and excellent Italian dishes. Closed Sunday. Reservations advised. Major credit cards accepted. 1435 Randolph just north of Gratiot (phone: 961-0707).

Mario's An old Detroit standby for almost 50 years with checkered tablecloths, mellow wood paneling, and shaded sconces to complement the old-fashioned Italian veal dishes and chateaubriand. It's a great pre- and post-theater or concert spot. Reservations advised. Major credit cards accepted. 4222 Second Ave. (phone: 832-1616).

Tom's Oyster Bar Owner Tom Brandel's casual Grosse Pointe Park hit offers a winning menu chalked on blackboards in a setting of checkered tablecloths and walls decked with sailing pennants. Oysters, of course, are the mainstay here along with delicious varieties of other seafood. No reservations.

Major credit cards accepted. 15402 Mack, Grosse Pointe Park (phone: 884-6030); 318 S. Main, Royal Oak (phone: 810-541-1186); 29106 Franklin Rd. at Northwestern Hwy, Southfield (phone: 810-356-8881).

INEXPENSIVE

Cafe Twingo's Kitty-corner from *Wayne State's Hilberry Theatre,* this demitasse-size place gets its name from a little French car and its colorful ambience from the Left Bank of Paris. Soups, baguette sandwiches, quiche, bagels, and scones vie with cappuccino, latte, and espresso as draws. No reservations. Major credit cards accepted. 4710 Cass near Warren (phone: 832-3832).

Cyprus Taverna This small soothing spot along Greektown's one-block restaurant row puts a fresh Cypriot twist on the Hellenic. The standards are all here—moussaka, spinach pie, and baklava—but so are *sefttalies* (pork-and-lamb sausages blended with onion, garlic, and spices) and *afelia* (pork braised with red wine and spiced with coriander). Reservations advised. Major credit cards accepted. 579 Monroe St. (phone: 961-1550).

Lafayette Coney Island This plain, porcelain-walled storefront has been dishing up the local specialty for 70 years: hot dogs covered in chili, onions, and mustard. They call 'em coneys. Office workers fill the place (and its next-door cousin, *American Coney Island*) at lunch while cops, sports fans, celebs, and urban partyers drop by at night. Reservations unnecessary. No credit cards accepted. 118 W. Lafayette at Michigan (phone: 964-8198).

Mati's Deli This converted 1926 white-tiled gas station in Dearborn serves up good deli sandwiches on crusty hand-cut rye bread as well as lighter fare. Open until 6 PM weekdays and 3 PM Saturdays; closed Sundays. No reservations. No credit cards accepted. 1842 Monroe, Dearborn (phone: 277-3253).

Mexican Town In the Hispanic neighborhood near the Ambassador Bridge west of downtown, this airy brick-walled place offers tasty, affordable Mexican food and relaxing margaritas. For late breakfasts, try the *chilaquiles* (scrambled eggs mixed with tortillas and vegetables). The place can be busy at lunch, weekends, or when the *Tigers* are at home. No reservations. Major credit cards accepted. 3457 Bagley at 24th St. (phone: 841-5811).

Ft. Lauderdale

For many Americans, the mention of Ft. Lauderdale still conjures up the 1960 movie *Where the Boys Are* (or its 1984 remake), which immortalized the seasonal migration of the nation's college students to this sunny city during spring break. That image, however, is out of date. Over the last decade, city leaders have discouraged that much-reported rite of spring in order to improve Ft. Lauderdale's overall appeal to adults and to expand family tourism. Their efforts have been successful—the annual undergraduate migration has diminished dramatically.

Today's collegians set their springtime compasses for Panama City and Daytona Beach while Mom, Dad, and the kids—along with increasing numbers of visitors from Europe and Latin America—populate Ft. Lauderdale's beaches. The players have changed, but the setting remains the same: Ft. Lauderdale still claims to receive 3,000 hours of sun a year—more than anywhere else in the continental US; the year-round average temperature remains in the comfortable mid-70s F; and—as the city's public relations people like to point out—Ft. Lauderdale has never, ever recorded a 100-degree temperature.

In addition to its benign climate, Ft. Lauderdale's proximity to the water has formed its character as a prime resort area. The city is virtually afloat. It (and surrounding Broward County areas) is bordered on the east by 23 miles of Atlantic Ocean coastline and beaches, on the west by that "river of grass," the Everglades. Between the two are 300 miles of the navigable Intracoastal Waterway and an intricate network of canals that is the source of Ft. Lauderdale's nickname, the "Venice of America."

While other resort areas count only their visitors, the Ft. Lauderdale area also counts boats. More than 42,000 are permanently registered, and 10,000 or so more join their ranks during the winter months, as the yachting crowd from as far away as Canada cruises down to the area's warm waters. (Author John D. MacDonald's readers will recognize the *Bahia Mar Marina* as the place where the laid-back sleuth Travis McGee moors his houseboat, the *Busted Flush.*) Moreover, thousands of smaller craft—sailboats and powerboats—knife through these waters throughout the year. In Ft. Lauderdale, even *Christmas* is celebrated in a nautical fashion. In mid-December, hundreds of elaborately decorated and lighted boats and yachts take to the Intracoastal Waterway for the unusual *Winterfest Boat Parade* from Port Everglades to Pompano Beach. Every available waterfront viewing point is packed as waving Santas navigate their water-sleighs past crowded bridges, backyards, and hotel balconies.

Ft. Lauderdale is named after Major William Lauderdale, who arrived in 1838 to quell the Seminole Indians and build a fort on the New River amid mosquito-infested, inhospitable mangrove swamps. Oddly, he was

Ft. Lauderdale
NE 17TH CT.
NE 16TH ST.
DIXIE H
NW 14TH CT.
95
845
NW 22ND AVE.
NW 13TH CT.
CHATEAU PARK
NE 13TH ST.
N ANDREWS AVE.
NW 11TH ST.
NE 11TH ST.
Warfield Park
NW 10TH PL.
W SUNRISE BLVD.
838
Sunland Park
FLAGLER DR.
Holiday Park
NW 22ND ST.
NW 19TH AVE.
NW 8TH ST.
NW 12TH AVE.
NW 11TH TERR.
NW 9TH AVE.
NW 7TH AVE.
NW 5TH AVE.
NW 3RD AVE.
NE 7TH ST.
FEDERAL HWY.
NW 18TH AVE.
NW 6TH ST.
NW 15TH AVE.
NE 6TH ST.
NE 5TH ST.
NE 4TH ST.
NW 4TH ST.
City Hall
NE 3RD ST
NE 2ND S
Public Golf Course
NW 2ND ST.
Bus Station
Bus Station
S ANDREWS AVE.
NE 3RD AVE.
BROWARD BLVD.
Museum of Discovery and Science
NW 1ST AVE.
SW 2ND ST.
LAS OLAS BL
Museum of Art
SW 20TH AVE.
SW 18TH ST.
SE 5TH ST.
SE 6TH ST.
SW 5TH PL.
SE 7TH ST.
SE 9TH
SW 9TH ST.
DAVIE BLVD.
SE 12TH
82
SW 22ND AVE.
SW 15TH AVE.
SW 14TH ST.
SE 14TH
SE 3RD AVE.
1
SW 14TH CT.
S ANDREWS AVE.
SW 15TH ST.
SW 6TH AVE.
SW 4TH AVE.
SE 17TH
SW 17TH ST.
SE 4TH AVE.
SE 20TH ST.
SW 20TH ST.
S FEDERAL HWY.
MIAMI RD.
95
SW 9TH AVE.
SE 22ND ST.
SW 15TH AVE.
SW 3RD AVE.
SW 24TH ST.
84

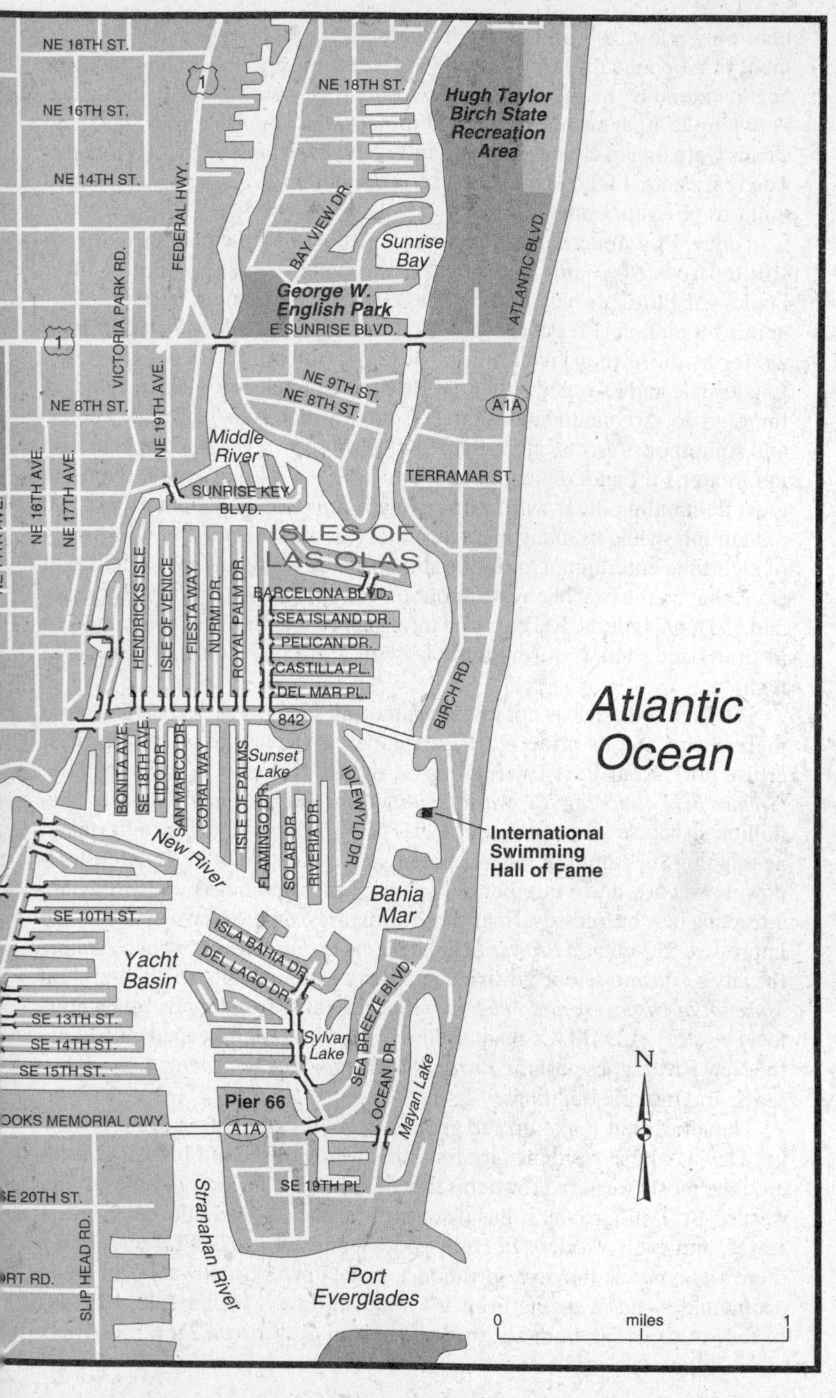
NE 18TH ST.
NE 16TH ST.
NE 14TH ST.
1
NE 18TH ST.
Hugh Taylor
Birch State
Recreation
Area
FEDERAL HWY.
BAY VIEW DR.
Sunrise
Bay
ATLANTIC BLVD.
VICTORIA PARK RD.
George W.
English Park
E SUNRISE BLVD.
1
NE 19TH AVE.
NE 9TH ST.
NE 8TH ST.
NE 8TH ST.
A1A
Middle
River
NE 16TH AVE.
NE 17TH AVE.
TERRAMAR ST.
SUNRISE KEY
BLVD.
ISLES OF
LAS OLAS
HENDRICKS ISLE
ISLE OF VENICE
FIESTA WAY
NURMI DR.
ROYAL PALM DR.
BARCELONA BLVD.
SEA ISLAND DR.
PELICAN DR.
CASTILLA PL.
DEL MAR PL.
BIRCH RD.
Atlantic
Ocean
842
BONITA AVE.
SE 18TH AVE.
LIDO DR.
SAN MARCO DR.
CORAL WAY
ISLE OF PALMS
Sunset
Lake
FLAMINGO DR.
SOLAR DR.
RIVERIA DR.
IDLEWYLD DR.
International
Swimming
Hall of Fame
New River
Bahia
Mar
SE 10TH ST.
ISLA BAHIA DR.
DEL LAGO DR.
Yacht
Basin
SEA BREEZE BLVD.
SE 13TH ST.
SE 14TH ST.
Sylvan
Lake
SE 15TH ST.
OCEAN DR.
Mayan Lake
N
Pier 66
OOKS MEMORIAL CWY.
A1A
SE 19TH PL.
SE 20TH ST.
Stranahan River
SLIP HEAD RD.
ORT RD.
Port
Everglades
0
miles
1

here only a few days and died not long afterward. The door for development first opened during the late 1890s, when entrepreneur Henry Flagler began extending his *Florida East Coast Railroad* south from Palm Beach. A swamp drainage and reclamation project was undertaken in 1906, and canals were dug to create "finger islands," thus maximizing the city's waterside real estate. Ft. Lauderdale was incorporated in 1911 and has welcomed millions of visitors since.

Today, Ft. Lauderdale is the largest of the 28 municipalities that constitute Broward County. Notably, it's the second most populous—after Dade—of Florida's 67 counties. The county's permanent population of about 1.3 million (Ft. Lauderdale itself has 150,000 residents) swells each winter as more than five million tourists pour in. To these guests, Ft. Lauderdale and its vicinity offer a wide choice of places to stay and eat and things to do. Accommodations range from tiny motels to huge luxury hotels and sumptuous resorts; more than 28,000 rooms for visitors can be found in Greater Ft. Lauderdale, many of which are along the ocean. Even the most demanding diner will find satisfaction in one of the county's 2,500 restaurants, while its many nightclubs, discos, and theaters provide plenty of nighttime entertainment. In the sun-splashed daytime, those who tire of frolicking on the beach may work out on the approximately 76 golf courses and 550 tennis courts. Relaxed and informal, Ft. Lauderdale is best enjoyed in shorts and sandals during the day, with attire just a bit more dressy at night.

But Ft. Lauderdale is not just sunshine and surf. It's also a bustling commercial city, and its pride, Port Everglades, is the world's second-busiest cruise port. Near Port Everglades on the Intracoastal Waterway is the *Greater Ft. Lauderdale/Broward County Convention Center,* a nearly $50-million structure that opened in 1991. City leaders also have undertaken an ongoing $670-million refurbishment and expansion of Ft. Lauderdale's downtown core, and a number of high-rise office buildings have sprung up, attracting new businesses. Near those structures, on the New River, sits the impressive $50-million *Broward Center for the Performing Arts,* which anchors the city's arts and science district. Across the street is the new $30-million *Museum of Discovery and Science,* with everything from hands-on exhibits to a five-story, 3-D IMAX theater. *Riverwalk,* a lushly landscaped path along the New River, goes past the *Broward Center for the Performing Arts,* restaurants, and historic buildings.

The cities that make up the greater Ft. Lauderdale area are a diverse lot. Davie, whose residents are fond of cowboy boots and hats, is considered the most "western" town this side of the Pecos; located 14 miles southwest of Ft. Lauderdale, it has dozens of farms, stables, saloons, country stores, and even a rodeo. In Hollywood, 7 miles south of Ft. Lauderdale, there's a Seminole Indian reservation, and the town's Broadwalk—an ocean promenade—has a strong French-Canadian flavor. Hallandale, 10 miles to the south, is the home of the well-known *Gulfstream Park* racetrack.

Some 5½ miles to the south is Dania, whose name reflects its early Danish settlers; it's known for its antiques. Other Greater Ft. Lauderdale communities include: Sunrise, 10½ miles west; Plantation, 9½ miles west; Coconut Creek, 15 miles northwest; Pompano Beach, 8 miles north; Lauderdale-by-the-Sea, 4½ miles north; Oakland Park, 6 miles northwest; Pembroke Pines, 17 miles southwest; Deerfield Beach, 12 miles north; and Margate, 17 miles northwest.

As more and more people discover its enviable lifestyle, the Ft. Lauderdale area continues to grow and change. "The Strip," once party-central for the spring break crowd, has undergone a face-lift. Installed along the beachside are a promenade, a bicycle path, and a low, white, undulating sea wall with a neon-painted ribbon in ever-changing colors running along it. The wall has entryways from street to beach, flanked by spirals that look like sand castles. Though some T-shirt emporiums remain, hotels and shops are being remodeled and spruced up in sherbet colors.

Progress has its price, however, and ecologists and some governmental agencies are sounding alarms as developers draw closer and closer to the last available land in the region—the eastern fringe of the Everglades. The challenge that Greater Ft. Lauderdale now faces lies in controlling development while maintaining the many attractions that make the city appealing.

Ft. Lauderdale At-a-Glance

SEEING THE CITY

The most commanding view of this area is from the *Pier Top Lounge* of the 17-story *Hyatt Regency Pier 66* hotel (see *Checking In*). As the lounge makes one complete revolution every 66 minutes, it affords sweeping vistas of the Atlantic Ocean and its beaches to the east; Port Everglades and the *Greater Ft. Lauderdale/Hollywood International Airport* to the south; the city's many canals, sprawling suburbs, and the Everglades to the west; and more canals and the Intracoastal Waterway to the north.

SPECIAL PLACES

The best way to get around Ft. Lauderdale is by car. It's a sprawling city with a lot to see in all directions, but don't miss the unique water taxi service that cruises the Intracoastal Waterway, enabling passengers to hop on and off at various restaurants and attractions.

DOWNTOWN AREA

PORT EVERGLADES Because it has the deepest water of any port between Norfolk, Virginia, and New Orleans, Port Everglades is a magnet for cargo ships and the marine outfitting business, as well as for luxury cruise ships. In fact, it's the world's second-largest cruise port, after Miami. Thanks to the remodeling of former warehouses and new construction, the port today presents an attractive face, with some of its nine passenger terminals painted in a striking, bold design. An additional terminal under construction at press time should be operational this year. The *Greater Ft. Lauderdale/Broward County Convention Center* occupies the northern end of the grounds. The port presently has one restaurant, *Burt & Jack's,* co-owned by Burt Reynolds (see *Eating Out*). There are no organized tours, but visitors may catch a glimpse of the ships from their cars as they drive along Eisenhower Boulevard, if there's not too much commercial truck traffic. At times, naval vessels in port are open for free tours. State Rd. 84, east of US 1 (phone: 523-3404).

Business travelers and vacationers often combine an area visit with a cruise. More than 32 ships make Port Everglades their home port. Two offer day cruises, while others embark on longer journeys, most often to the Bahamas and Caribbean Islands. Cruise lines that sail from Port Everglades on a variety of itineraries include *Celebrity Cruises* (phone: 800-437-3111); *Crystal Cruises* (phone: 800-446-6620); *Cunard Line* (phone: 800-221-4770); *Discovery Cruises* (phone: 525-7800; 800-937-4477); *Holland America Line* (phone: 800-426-0327); *Norwegian/NCL* (phone: 800-327-7030); *Princess Cruises* (phone: 800-421-0522); *Radisson Seven Seas Cruises* (phone: 800-285-1835); *Royal Olympic Cruises* (phone: 800-468-6400); *Seabourn Cruise Line* (phone: 800-929-9595); and *SeaEscape* (phone: 800-432-0900).

MUSEUM OF DISCOVERY AND SCIENCE One lure of Ft. Lauderdale's 85,000-square-foot museum is its five-story IMAX screen (one of the largest movie screens in the southeastern US), housed in a 300-seat theater. Among the delightful exhibits are a giant outdoor gravity clock whose winding balls captivate onlookers as they twist and turn through an oversized erector-set mechanism. Indoors, exhibits include walk-through simulated Florida ecological habitats with over 100 species of live animals and plants; two simulated space rides; interactive science displays for kids; and "Gizmo City," an area featuring hands-on activities like assembling gadgets and programming robots, as well as workstations that allow visitors to access the Internet and play virtual volleyball and hockey. There are Saturday classes for children (phone: 467-6637, ext. 315). A small restaurant and an excellent museum store are on the premises. Closed *Christmas Day.* Admission charge (additional charge for the theater, which screens up to 11 shows daily). 401 SW Second St., across from the *Broward Center for the Performing Arts* (phone: 467-6637 or 463-IMAX).

HUGH TAYLOR BIRCH STATE RECREATION AREA Just across the street from the beach is this lush, subtropical park. Its 180 acres, two nature trails, and two small playgrounds make it ideal for picnicking, ball playing, canoeing, biking, and hiking. It's a favorite with in-line skaters. A tunnel runs under the highway between the beach and the park. Open daily. Admission charge. 3109 E. Sunrise Blvd. (phone: 564-4521).

STRANAHAN HOUSE The restored 1901 home and Indian trading post of early settler Frank Stranahan, this is Broward County's oldest structure and one of the area's oldest museums. It's hard to imagine the Ft. Lauderdale of those days, but a tour of this house provides some idea of the hardships endured. Closed Mondays and Tuesdays. Admission charge. SE Sixth Ave. at Las Olas Blvd. and the New River Tunnel (phone: 524-4736).

BONNET HOUSE Built in the 1920s as a family retreat for artists Frederick and Evelyn Bartlett, this 36-acre private estate is one of the few remaining oceanfront wildlife areas in South Florida. The two-story house and grounds have been preserved and are on the *National Register of Historic Places.* Guided tours are offered Wednesdays through Sundays. Admission charge. 900 N. Birch Rd. (phone: 563-5393).

INTERNATIONAL SWIMMING HALL OF FAME Many of the world's top swimming and diving competitions are held at this renovated complex, but the Olympic-size pools are open to the public when there's no meet scheduled, and swimming lessons are offered year-round. The adjoining museum houses unusual aquatic memorabilia from more than 100 countries. Open daily. Admission charge. 1 Hall of Fame Dr., off Rte. A1A. (phone: 462-6536).

GREATER FT. LAUDERDALE

EVERGLADES HOLIDAY PARK Savor what the Everglades are all about while on a narrated airboat ride at this small park. You'll see some of the most beautiful birds Mother Nature has ever created (you might even spot an American bald eagle) as well as nesting alligators. (Your tour guide will give you a healthy respect for the power of alligator jaws, even those of the seemingly cute young ones.) There are also special tours offering insights into the lives of the Seminole Indians, a group of Native Americans whose history is little known outside this region. If you're feeling adventurous, rent a boat or an RV for a closer experience with nature. There's also a campground here. Open daily 24 hours. No admission charge to the park; a fee is charged for airboat rides. 21940 Griffin Rd., west of Hwy. 27 (phone: 434-8111).

FLAMINGO GARDENS This 60-acre botanical garden has a flamingo exhibit, a tropical plant house, an Everglades wildlife sanctuary, orange groves, alligators, and river otters. A guided tram tour takes visitors through the groves, wetlands, and an indigenous hardwood hammock with stands of oak, gumbo-limbo, and fig trees. A screened-in aviary re-creates several native settings—including a mangrove swamp and a sawgrass prairie—for those who can't get out to the Everglades. Free-flying local birds, including cormorants and ospreys, can be seen throughout the groves. There's also a snack bar, a gift shop that sells nature books and crafts, a produce stall for purchasing and shipping citrus fruit, and a plant shop. Open daily. Admission charge. 3750 Flamingo Rd., Davie (phone: 473-2955).

LOXAHATCHEE EVERGLADES TOURS Just across the northern Broward County line, visitors can take an airboat trip through the Everglades without traveling great distances to the south. These airboats provide ramps that afford easy access to disabled passengers, and employ improved methods for muffling engine noises. Passengers skim over the "river of grass," spotting alligators and their babies in nests, plus myriad wild fowl such as gallinules. There's a small (and sparsely stocked) snack shop at the park. Open daily. No admission charge to the park, but there's a fee for airboat rides. From Rte. 441 take Loxahatchee Rd. (between Hillsboro Blvd. and Palmetto Park Rd.), then drive 6 miles west to the Everglades (phone: 407-482-0313; 800-683-5873).

HOLLYWOOD BROADWALK This 2¼-mile, 24-foot-wide, concrete ocean promenade is bordered by a bicycle path and lined with inexpensive outdoor cafés often featuring contemporary music. Bikes may be rented at various sites, and there's free music and dancing (the jitterbug and polka are favorites) at the Johnson Street bandstand Monday through Wednesday nights. This area has a strong Quebecois flavor and half the promenade signs are in French. Lifeguard stations are manned year-round. The Broadwalk extends south from *North Beach Park* (near Sheridan St.) to Harrison St. (phone: 921-3404 for information).

SAWGRASS MILLS MALL This 2.3 million-square-foot discount shopping complex, billed as the world's largest outlet mall, boasts such stores as *Saks Fifth Avenue, Neiman Marcus, Brandsmart, JC Penney, Marshall's,* and *Spiegel,* and at least 270 specialty shops. It's so big that you can't see it all in one day; and it draws visitors from around the state (there's a separate entrance for tour buses). Among the temptations are an *Ann Taylor* clearance center, a *Joan & David* shoe outlet, and a newer wing featuring *J.Crew, Mikasa, Waterford,* and *Bernini* outlets. Many stores offer valid savings of 20% to 60%, but this mall is for savvy shoppers: It's important to know what things sell for elsewhere. Several restaurants and two food courts provide respite. An 18-screen movie theater, billed as the largest east of the Mississippi, completes the picture. Open daily. 12801 W. Sunrise Blvd., Sunrise (phone: 846-2350; 800-FL-MILLS).

SWAP SHOP The largest flea market in the South, it claims to be Florida's second-largest tourist attraction after *Walt Disney World.* With over 2,000 vendors, bargains range from electronic equipment to tomatoes. There's also daily entertainment. Open weekdays from 8 AM to 6 PM (outdoor stalls close an hour and a half earlier); on weekends, the complex is open from 7 AM to 7 PM (the outdoor stalls close at 6:30 PM. 3291 W. Sunrise Blvd. (phone: 791-SWAP). A second branch with 625 booths is open Tuesdays, Saturdays, and Sundays from 4:30 AM to 2 PM. 1000 State Rd. 7, Margate (phone: 971-SWAP).

BUTTERFLY WORLD Visitors can walk among the multicolored creatures fluttering freely in this three-acre, re-created jungle habitat. The butterflies are seen in all their stages of life, from larvae and pupae to cocoon and full adulthood. Certain species are attracted to light-colored clothing and certain scents; if you've spent a hot morning in traffic or sightseeing, you may find yourself converted into a temporary perch. There are butterflies from all over the world and a spectacular museum of mounted insects. Closed *Thanksgiving* and *Christmas Day.* Admission charge. Inside *Tradewinds Park,* 3600 W. Sample Rd., Coconut Creek (phone: 977-4400).

JOHN U. LLOYD BEACH STATE RECREATION AREA Many Ft. Lauderdale residents consider this *the* place for picnicking, swimming, fishing, canoeing, and other recreation. There are 244 acres of beach, dunes, mangrove swamp, and vegetation. Park rangers lead nature walks during winter months. Open daily. Admission charge. 6503 N. Ocean Dr., Dania (phone: 923-2833).

TOPEEKEEGEE YUGNEE PARK Locally called "T-Y Park" due to its difficult-to-pronounce Indian name, this is one of the area's more popular parks for families. Visitors can enjoy all kinds of activities—swimming, boating, canoeing, picnicking, barbecuing, hiking, and biking. Open daily. Admission charge on weekends and holidays. 3300 N. Park Rd., just off I-95, Hollywood (phone: 985-1980).

SEMINOLE INDIAN RESERVATION The reservation's *Native Village* includes a historical art exhibit, a gift shop with Indian arts and crafts, demonstrations of alligator wrestling, and snake and turtle shows. The exhibit offers an interesting glimpse into this little-known Native American group. The Seminole gave up their lands reluctantly and never did sign a treaty with the United States. Although bingo games for profit are not legal elsewhere in Florida, they're allowed here. The reservation's bingo hall and 24-hour casino holds up to 1,400 people and often is full; winners have pocketed as much as $110,000 for a single game. There's an admission charge for the village tour, and another for the bingo hall (includes bingo cards). Both are open daily. The village is at 3551 N. State Rd. 7, Hollywood (phone: 961-4519); the bingo hall is at 4150 N. State Rd. 7, Hollywood (phone: 961-3220).

GOODYEAR BLIMP Though tourists may not go for a ride in the *Stars & Stripes* (it's only for corporate clients), they can see the 192-foot-long blimp up close at its hangar at varied times from November through May. Call in advance for schedule. No admission charge. 1500 NE Fifth Ave., Pompano Beach (phone: 946-8300).

GRAND PRIX RACE-O-RAMA A 1990s-style amusement park that's fun for the whole family (and a lifesaver on a rainy day), it features a 24-hour video arcade, five miniature golf courses, batting cages, bumper cars, go-karts, Nascarts, and Sky Coasters. Open daily; extended hours on weekends. Charges per game and attraction. 1500 NW First St., Dania (phone: 921-1411).

EXTRA SPECIAL

To experience fully the subtropical beauty and laid-back ambience that is Ft. Lauderdale, drive east on Las Olas Boulevard past its chic boutiques and palm-lined streets. Continue through the Isles of Las Olas area, which is laced with canals and filled with fancy homes nestled among royal palm trees.

Large, luxurious boats are docked outside many of the homes. Look up and you may spot some of the colorful parrots that nest here. Proceed past the sailboat cove, where towering masts salute the blue sky, and cruise over the small bridge to Route A1A, along the Atlantic Ocean. Drive north, and at about 4 PM, stop at one of the sidewalk cafés or hotel patio bars facing the ocean to watch bicyclists, in-line skaters, joggers, and walkers along the promenade. The ocean will be filled with sailboats returning to safe harbor, and cruise and cargo ships steaming out to distant corners. Take off your shoes, walk along the sand at the water's edge—and let the images soak in.

Sources and Resources

TOURIST INFORMATION

The *Greater Ft. Lauderdale Convention and Visitors Bureau* is downtown (1850 Eller Dr.; Suite 303, Ft. Lauderdale, FL 33316; phone: 765-4466; 800-22-SUNNY; fax: 765-4467). Stop in or call for information on accommodations, activities, attractions, sports, dining, shopping, touring, and special events (closed weekends). Or call in advance for a free, information-filled book (phone: 800-22-SUNNY, ext. 711). There is also a 24-hour hotline that provides local travel directions in English, Spanish, French, German, and Portuguese (phone: 527-5600; cellular phone: #333). *The Broward County Arts and Entertainment Hotline* (phone: 357-5700) provides schedules of events and information about visitor attractions. Contact the *Florida Division of Tourism*'s *Bureau of Visitor Services* (phone: 904-487-1462) for maps, calendars of events, and travel advisories.

LOCAL COVERAGE The *Sun-Sentinel,* a morning daily, carries listings on the following week's events in its "Showtime" section on Fridays; the *Miami Herald,* a morning daily, carries similar information in its "Weekend" section on Fridays. The free weekly alternative newspaper *XS* lists nightclubs, cultural events, and restaurants.

TELEVISION STATIONS WPBT Channel 2–PBS; WTVJ Channel 6–NBC; WFOR Channel 4–CBS; WSVN Channel 7–FOX; and WPLG Channel 10–ABC.

RADIO STATIONS AM: WIOD 610 (news/talk); WINZ 940 (news/talk); WJNO 1230 (news/talk); WKAT 1360 (multilingual); WFTL 1400 (talk). FM: WKPX 88.5 (progressive/alternative rock); WAFG 90.3 (religious); WXEL 90.7 (public radio); WLRN 91.3 (public radio); WTMI 93.1 (classical); WLVE 93.9 (jazz); WZTA 94.9 (rock); WFLC 97.3 (adult contemporary); WKIS 99.9 (country); WHYI 100 (top 40); WLYF 101.5 (easy listening); WMXJ 102.7 (oldies rock); WSHE 103.5 (alternative rock); WHQT 105 (urban adult contemporary); and WRMA 106.7 (easy listening).

TELEPHONE The area code for Ft. Lauderdale is 954.

SALES TAX The sales tax is 6%; there is also a 3% Broward County hotel tax.

GETTING AROUND

AIRPORT The *Greater Ft. Lauderdale/Hollywood International Airport* is 10 to 20 minutes by car from Downtown Ft. Lauderdale, depending on traffic conditions. *Broward County Mass Transit* (phone: 357-8400; TDD: 357-8302) provides bus service between the airport and the downtown bus terminal at Northwest First Avenue and Broward Boulevard; the one-way fare is $1. *Gray Line Airport Service* (phone: 800-244-8252 in Florida; 954-561-8888 elsewhere in the US) offers shared limousine service between the airport and points throughout Broward County for $6 to $20. *Tri-Rail* (phone: 728-8445; 800-TRI-RAIL) operates free shuttle buses between the airport and the airport station in Dania (about halfway between Hollywood and Ft. Lauderdale), where there are commuter trains to Ft. Lauderdale (see "Tri-Rail," below).

BUS *Broward County Transit* serves most of the area. Fares are $1; 15¢ for transfers. Weekly passes cost $8 and are available at selected hotels and motels. For information, call 357-8400.

CAR RENTAL Ft. Lauderdale is served by all the major national firms, one of which has its corporate headquarters in the city: *Alamo* (110 SE Sixth St.; phone: 525-2501; 800-327-9633). There are also several regional agencies; check the phone directory.

TAXI While you can hail a cab on the street, it's best to pick one up at a major hotel or restaurant or to call for one. The major cab company is *Checker/Yellow Cab* (phone: 565-5400). For information on cabs that accommodate wheelchairs, call 565-2800.

TRI-RAIL A double-decker train runs from West Palm Beach south through Ft. Lauderdale to Miami, and connects with Miami's *Metrorail/Metromover* and various county and shuttle bus lines. The train also connects the *Greater Ft. Lauderdale/Hollywood International Airport* with *Miami International* and *Palm Beach International Airports.* Extra trains and shuttles are scheduled for select games at Miami's *Joe Robbie* and *Orange Bowl Stadiums;* special events; and shopping trips to the *Swap Shop, Town Center Mall in Boca Raton,* and Miami's *Bayside Marketplace.* At times, special sightseeing package tours are available. The trains are accessible to the disabled. For information, call 728-8445 or 800-TRI-RAIL.

WATER TAXI Running from the 17th Street Causeway to Atlantic Boulevard in Pompano Beach, *Water Taxi* (651 Seabreeze Blvd.; phone: 467-6677) operates on demand daily and covers more than 100 landings. Some taxis are open-air boats; a couple of the vessels are larger and air conditioned. Vessels are also available for charter.

SIGHTSEEING TOURS

BOAT Dubbed the "Venice of America," Ft. Lauderdale is best seen by boat. The *Jungle Queen* (at the *Bahia Mar Marina,* 801 Seabreeze Blvd.; phone: 462-

5596) offers three-hour sightseeing tours twice daily; it also takes riders down to Miami twice weekly for shopping sprees. The *Carrie B* (docked behind *Hyde Park* supermarket on Las Olas Blvd. at SE Fifth Ave.; phone: 768-9920) runs three one-and-a-half-hour daily trips on the New River down to Port Everglades year-round, and 90-minute sunset cruises daily from February through April. Large families and small business groups can charter the 120-foot *Sir Winston* (on the New River dock; phone: 462-7411), which transports groups along the waterways past millionaires' homes. Two-hour glass-bottom boat tours are conducted on *Pro Diver II,* sailing from the *Bahia Mar Marina* (phone: 467-6030) daily except Mondays.

HORSE-AND-CARRIAGE *Las Olas Horse & Carriage Inc.* (phone: 763-7393; 357-1950, beeper) offers horse-and-carriage tours of Las Olas Boulevard to *Colee Hammock Park* and back.

TRAM Another wonderful way to sightsee is aboard the open-air *South Florida Trolley,* which is available for group tours that can be arranged through a travel agent, tour operator, your hotel concierge, or by calling the company directly (phone: 429-3100). *Ellerworld Tours* picks up cruise ship passengers at the pier in Port Everglades, offering shopping excursions and a two-hour city tour (phone: 525-3381).

WALKING The *Ft. Lauderdale Historical Society* (phone: 463-4431) periodically conducts three-hour walking tours of the historical district from late October through mid-May. Participants learn about the Seminole Wars and early 19th-century farms and trading posts along the then-inhospitable New River.

SPECIAL EVENTS

The *Las Olas Art Fair* takes place on fashionable Las Olas Boulevard on two weekends in January and February, attracting more than 150,000 people (phone: 472-3755). The *Seminole Indian Tribal Fair,* usually held during the first two weeks in February on the reservation, is a showcase of Indian crafts, entertainment, and food (phone: 966-6300). The *Las Olas Art Festival,* hosted by the *Museum of Art,* takes place in early March. The festival attracts 300 artists, whose work is displayed in a juried show at *Bubier Park;* many of these artists are not represented by galleries (phone: 525-5500). The *Honda Golf Classic,* one of the biggest *PGA* tournaments, is held in early March at the *Tournament Players Club at Eagle Trace* in Coral Springs; it attracts the *PGA*'s top players (phone: 346-4000). Also in March, the *Florida Derby Festival* hits town; activities such as the *Derby Ball* culminate in a thoroughbred race (with a purse of about $500,000) at *Gulfstream Park* (phone: 454-7000; 305-931-RACE). The other big March event in town is the annual *Ft. Lauderdale Festival of the Arts,* which brings three days of music to the *Broward Center for the Performing Arts,* with free outdoor concerts along the New River's *Riverwalk* (phone: 468-2687). At the end of February, cowboys kick up their heels at the *Westfest* in Davie, a ten-day affair featuring a rodeo, street fair, concerts, and carnival (phone: 581-0790; 800-962-2420).

In April, seafood is king at the *Ft. Lauderdale Seafood Festival* at *Bubier Park,* where 30 leading restaurants offer samples (phone: 463-4431). In late April, the *Pompano Beach Seafood Festival & Art Show* is held on the beach at East Atlantic Boulevard (phone: 941-2940). In May, anglers test their skill during the *Pompano Beach Fishing Rodeo,* where more than $250,000 in cash is awarded for the largest catches (phone: 942-4513).

September brings the *Las Olas Labor Day Art Fair,* which turns the entire boulevard into a pedestrian mall lined with art exhibits, street performers, and food booths (phone: 472-3755). *Oktoberfest* falls (naturally) in October and features lots of German food, drink, and music in *Bubier Park* (phone: 761-5360). The *Ft. Lauderdale Boat Show,* held in October at four area sites, is the world's largest in-water display of all types and sizes of watercraft (phone: 763-3661). In November, the *Promenade in the Park* features arts and crafts, food, and entertainment at *Holiday Park* (phone: 764-5973). Also held in November are the *Ft. Lauderdale International Film Festival,* with screenings of more than 100 independent films (phone: 563-0500), and the *Broward County Fair* in Hallandale (phone: 963-3247). The year's activities are capped by the December-long *Winterfest;* highlights include the *Ft. Lauderdale* and *Pompano Beach Boat Parades,* with as many as 100 boats festooned with colored lights and *Christmas* decorations plying the Intracoastal Waterway (phone: 767-0686), and a *Light up Lauderdale* laser show in *Bubier Park* on *New Year's Eve* (phone: 767-0686).

MUSEUMS

In addition to those described in *Special Places,* other Ft. Lauderdale area museums include the following:

FT. LAUDERDALE HISTORICAL SOCIETY Located in the historic district, the society headquarters hosts exhibits on Ft. Lauderdale and Broward County history. The society also conducts tours of Downtown Ft. Lauderdale. Closed Sunday mornings and Mondays. Admission charge. 219 SW Second Ave. (phone: 463-4431).

FT. LAUDERDALE MUSEUM OF ART Housed in a 63,800-square-foot building designed by Edward Larabee Barnes, the museum features 19th- and 20th-century European and American art, as well as West African, pre-Columbian, and American Indian works. There are more than 2,000 paintings and 5,000 prints in the collection. Traveling exhibits are housed in three galleries and there's a sculpture garden and auditorium. Open extended hours on Tuesdays; closed Sunday mornings and Mondays. Admission charge. 1 E. Las Olas Blvd. (phone: 525-5500).

GRAVES MUSEUM OF ARCHAEOLOGY AND NATURAL HISTORY This charming complex features some unusual exhibits such as a six-ton quartz crystal, a triceratops skull, and a diorama on the Tequesta Indians. Other highlights include an Egyptian room, African tribal art, marine archaeology, and pre-Columbian art. Closed Mondays. Admission charge. 481 S. Federal Hwy., Dania (phone: 925-7770).

YOUNG AT ART CHILDREN'S MUSEUM Primarily a hands-on museum, children can develop their artistic skills in this creative environment. Closed Sunday mornings and Mondays. No admission charge for children under two. 801 S. University Dr., Plantation (phone: 424-0085).

SHOPPING

For a break from the beach, visit one of the many shopping malls and stores in the Ft. Lauderdale area. The following places are in Ft. Lauderdale unless otherwise noted.

Broward Mall One of the South's largest shopping malls, with 130 specialty shops, this ultramodern mart's main stores are *Burdines, Sears, Mervyn's,* and *JC Penney.* Broward Blvd. and University Dr., Plantation (phone: 473-8100).

Fashion Mall at Plantation This center offers the county's only *Macy's,* plus *Lord & Taylor,* a *Sheraton* hotel, and lots of specialty shops. 321 N. University Dr., Plantation (phone: 370-1884).

Fashion Row Also known as "Shmatte" (Yiddish for garments or rags) Row, it offers an array of discounts. One section of dress and handbag shops is located off Hallandale Beach Boulevard on Northeast First Avenue; the other is on Northeast Second Avenue between Northeast Third and Northeast Fourth Streets. Most Fashion Row shops are open daily from December through March; closed Sundays the rest of the year.

Festival Flea Market Mall At this 400,000-square-foot indoor flea-market-type mall in western Ft. Lauderdale, 650 vendors offer brand-new merchandise as well as antiques and collectibles. There are also eight movie theaters, an amusement arcade, a beauty salon, farmers' market, and an international food court. Many items are discounted. Closed Mondays year-round; closed Tuesdays June through September. Open on all holidays. 2900 W. Sample Rd., Pompano Beach (phone: 979-4555).

Galleria High-fashion clothes and home furnishings are sold at this three-story mall, featuring *Neiman Marcus, Saks Fifth Avenue, Dillard's, Lord & Taylor, Burdines,* and numerous smaller stores, including *Brooks Brothers* and *Cartier.* Valet parking available. 2414 E. Sunrise Blvd. (phone: 564-1015).

Las Olas Boulevard Between Southeast Sixth and 11th Avenues, this street is a window-shopper's delight. There are dozens of trendy specialty shops, galleries, restaurants, and lively sidewalk cafés. Our favorites include *Maus & Hoffman* (800 E. Las Olas Blvd.; phone: 463-1472) for upscale men's clothing; *Sophy Curson* (1508 E. Las Olas Blvd.; phone: 462-7770) for high-fashion women's clothing (open from late October through May only); and

Zola Keller (818 E. Las Olas Blvd.; phone: 462-3222), with more fine fashions for women. Closed Sundays, except for *Zola Keller.*

Lord & Taylor Clearance Center Here you'll find clothing discounted up to 50% initially, with further reductions for special sales. 6820 N. University Dr. (McNab Rd. and University Dr.), Tamarac (phone: 720-1915).

Sawgrass Mills Mall This gigantic, 2.3 million-square-foot shopping center is billed as the world's largest outlet mall. 12801 W. Sunrise Blvd., Sunrise (phone: 846-2350; 800-FL-MILLS). For more information, see *Special Places.*

Swap Shop Indoor and outdoor booths beckon at this massive flea market—the largest in the South and a true bargain-hunter's heaven. 3291 W. Sunrise Blvd. (phone: 791-SWAP). A second branch has 625 booths. 1000 State Rd. 7, Margate (phone: 971-SWAP). For more information, see *Special Places.*

SPORTS AND FITNESS

BASEBALL The *New York Yankees* no longer hold spring training in Ft. Lauderdale, but their rivals, the *Baltimore Orioles,* brought their camp to *Ft. Lauderdale Stadium* (5301 NW 12th Ave.; phone: 938-4980) last year, with an option to return for the 1997 pre-season as well.

BOATING After the sunshine, the water is one of South Florida's greatest draws. The US Corps of Engineers maintains navigational aids, and private and public marinas provide virtually every type of boat for rent. For large charters, power-, or sailboats contact the *Heavy Hitter* at *Bahia Mar Marina* (801 Seabreeze Blvd.; phone: 523-5400) or *Club Nautico* (phone: 920-2796) with docks in Dania (at the *Harbourtowne Marina,* off US 1, 801 NE Third St.; phone: 926-0300); Ft. Lauderdale (2301 SE 17th St. Causeway, Slip A19; phone: 523-0033), and Deerfield Beach (*The Cove Marina,* 1755 SE Third Ct.; phone: 421-4628). Water bikes (jet skis) and power boats may be rented from *Sunrise Watersports* (2025 E. Sunrise Blvd.; phone: 462-8962).

FISHING As in Miami, there's just about every kind of angling you can think of here. For deep-sea adventure, numerous charter boats are available. There are plenty of listings under "Fishing" in the Ft. Lauderdale yellow pages, but we recommend the *Bahia Mar Marina* and *Club Nautico* (see *Boating,* above).

Landlubbers fish 24 hours a day from the 1,080-foot *Pompano Beach Fishing Pier* (two blocks north of East Atlantic Blvd.; phone: 943-1488) and *Anglin's Fishing Pier* (2 Commercial Blvd.; phone: 491-9403). There's an admission charge for each.

FITNESS CENTERS *Nautilus Fitness Center* (1624 N. Federal Hwy.; phone: 566-2222), with certified instructors, offers all the standard Nautilus exercise equipment, plus freeweights and aerobics. It's open to the public for a fee.

GOLF Not surprisingly, Ft. Lauderdale boasts some great greens. Several resorts have excellent golf courses, and many that lack their own links provide access to other clubs. It's usually necessary to call ahead to reserve a tee time, especially during the winter season.

TOP TEE-OFF SPOTS

Bonaventure Two championship 18-hole courses lure golfers to this 500-room resort. The *East* course is considered one of Florida's top ten, and the waterfall hole is certainly challenging. There's also a driving range, putting green, and pro shop. Moonlight golf (for groups of 20 or more) adds to the standard tee-off times. 200 Bonaventure Blvd. (phone: 389-2100; 800-327-8090; fax: 389-2124).

Palm-Aire Courses here have hosted the *Florida Open, US Open* qualifying matches, and the *Florida PGA* tournament. The 1,500-acre resort, which has a 140-room hotel and a residential development, offers four 18-hole championship golf courses (the *Palms, Oaks, Cypress,* and *Pines*) and a shorter 22-hole executive course (the *Sabals*). The *Cypress* will host the *Florida Open* through the year 2004. Instruction is available; combination spa and golf packages can be arranged. 2601 Palm-Aire Dr. N., Pompano Beach (phone: 978-1737; 800-272-5624; fax: 978-6066).

Other courses open to the public include *American Golfers Club* (3850 N. Federal Hwy.; phone: 564-8760); *Rolling Hills* (3501 W. Rolling Hills Cir., Davie; phone: 475-0400; 800-327-7735); *Grand Palms* (110 Grand Palm Dr., Pembroke Pines; phone: 437-3334); and *Jacaranda* (9200 W. Broward Blvd., Plantation; phone: 472-5836). For additional information, call the *Broward County Parks and Recreation Department* (phone: 357-8100).

HORSE AND DOG RACING There's thoroughbred horse racing at *Gulfstream Park* (Hallandale Beach Blvd. and US 1, Hallandale; phone: 454-7000) daily except Tuesdays from mid-January through March, and harness racing at *Pompano Harness Track* (1800 SW Third St., Pompano Beach; phone: 972-2000) from October through early September. Dogs race at *Hollywood Greyhound Track* (831 N. Federal Hwy., Hallandale; phone: 454-9400) from late December to late April. Call for racing dates.

HORSEBACK RIDING Cowboy country awaits in Davie, with many stables in the area offering trail rides and horse rentals. Among the larger ones are *Bar-B Ranch* (4601 SW 128th Ave., Davie; phone: 434-6175), which offers horse rentals, and *Myrland Stables* (5550 SW 73rd Ave., Davie; phone: 587-2285), which has trails and lessons. Both are open daily. On Saturdays and Sundays, Broward County also operates stables at *Tradewinds Park* (3600 W. Sample Rd., Coconut Creek; phone: 968-3880).

JAI ALAI This Basque import is the area's most fast-paced sport, with pari-mutuel betting adding spice. The season is year-round, except for two-and-a-half weeks in April and May. The action takes place at *Dania Jai-Alai* (301 E. Dania Beach Blvd., Dania; phone: 927-2841); it's closed Mondays and Wednesdays.

NATURE HIKES The *Broward County Parks and Recreation Department* sponsors a different nature walk each Friday and Saturday, October through May. Call for a schedule (phone: 357-8100).

PARASAILING Soar like a bird over Ft. Lauderdale with *Watersports Unlimited* (301 Seabreeze Blvd.; phone: 467-1316).

RODEO Cowboys compete in bronco riding, calf roping, and other activities at the *Rodeo Arena* in Davie, just behind the *Davie Town Hall* (6591 SW 45th St.; phone: 797-1166 or 797-1163). There's an admission charge. The arena is also the site of country music concerts and "monster truck" shows, where people gather to watch enormous vehicles leap over one other.

SCUBA DIVING AND SNORKELING Stretching north from the Keys past Ft. Lauderdale, Florida's natural coral reef has suffered from overuse, damage from ships, and pollution. But diving remains popular in this part of Florida, partially due to the practice of sinking freighters and other large objects to create artificial reefs. The most famous sinking in recent years was the tanker *Mercedes,* which was swept by a storm onto socialite Mollie Wilmot's terrace before being scuttled in Ft. Lauderdale. More than 80 other sites also lure fish and coral to varying depths.

Dozens of dive shops offer half-day dive trips, basic resort courses that get neophytes into the water the same day, and certification and specialty courses. *Pro Dive* (*Bahia Mar Marina,* 801 Seabreeze Blvd.; phone: 761-3413; 800-772-DIVE outside Florida) has daily dives and a full range of courses. It also offers snorkeling trips Tuesdays through Sundays aboard the 60-foot glass-bottom boat *Pro Diver II.* Other dive shops offering certification are *Ocean Diving Schools* (750 E. Sample Rd., Pompano; phone: 943-3337) and *Force E* (2700 E. Atlantic Blvd.; phone: 943-3483). Many operators offer package deals with hotels.

SWIMMING The most crowded beach is along "The Strip" (otherwise known as "The Promenade") from Sunrise Boulevard to Bahia Mar. The quaint seaside village of Lauderdale-by-the-Sea is also popular; the beach is just north of Ft. Lauderdale. The Galt Ocean Mile is quieter, with an older crowd. Perhaps the quietest strand is the stretch between Galt Ocean Mile and Northeast 22nd Street, and you may find small pockets of peace in *John U. Lloyd Beach State Recreation Area* (see *Special Places*) or *North Beach Park* (Sheridan Rd. and Rte. A1A, Hollywood; phone: 926-2444). Deerfield Beach, from the border of Broward and Palm Beach Counties south to SE 10th Street, is a favorite of locals.

TENNIS Although most major hotels here have tennis courts, one is a true ace.

CHOICE COURT

Bonaventure The best tennis facilities in Ft. Lauderdale are found at this elegant resort, with its 24 tennis courts—seven clay and most nightlit. There are also five indoor air conditioned racquetball and squash courts, and a pro shop. 357 Racquet Club Rd. (phone: 389-8667; 800-327-8090; fax: 384-0563).

There are also numerous courts open to the public. Among them are *Holiday Park Tennis Center* (701 NE 12th Ave.; phone: 761-5378), where Chris Evert learned to play; *Dillon Tennis Courts* (4091 NE 5th Ave., Oakland Park; phone: 561-6180); *Pompano Beach Tennis Center* (900 NE 18th Ave.; phone: 786-4115); and *George W. English Park* (1101 Bayview Dr.; phone: 396-3620). For more information, contact the *Broward County Parks and Recreation Division* (phone: 357-8100) or the *Ft. Lauderdale Parks and Recreation Department* (phone: 761-5346).

THEATER

Opened in 1991, the $55-million regional *Broward Center for the Performing Arts* (201 SW Fifth Ave.; phone: 462-0222; 522-5334, tickets) stages opera, theatre, ballet, and orchestra productions. The area's other major theaters are the *Parker Playhouse* (707 NE Eighth St.; phone: 763-2444), which features name actors in touring companies of Broadway productions, and *Sunrise Musical Theater* (5555 NW 95th Ave.; phone: 741-7300), which showcases plays, musicals, in-concert performances by musicians and comedians, and children's productions. *Bailey Concert Hall* at *Broward Community College* (3501 SW Davie Rd., Davie; phone: 475-6884) also stages children's theater, as well as plays and musical performances. The *Vinnette Carroll Theater* (503 SE Sixth St.; phone: 462-2424) presents multicultural productions in a converted church.

MUSIC

The *Philharmonic Orchestra of Florida* usually plays at the *Broward Center for the Performing Arts* (see *Theater;* phone: 561-2997; 800-226-1812). The center is also the site for performances by the *Symphony of the Americas* (phone: 561-5882) and the *Florida Grand Opera* (phone: 728-9700; 800-741-1010) during winter months; the latter often features visiting artists. Jazz, opera, and symphonic performances are staged throughout the year at *Broward Community College*'s *Bailey Concert Hall* (see *Theater*).

NIGHTCLUBS AND NIGHTLIFE

Most hotels and larger motels offer music and/or comedy acts nightly. The *Musician's Exchange Café* (729 W. Sunrise Blvd.; phone: 764-1912) is the place to go for jazz, blues, and rock. For dance and billiards, the young and wild go to *Baja Beach Club* (3200 N. Federal Hwy.; phone: 561-2432). *The*

Pier Top Lounge at the *Hyatt Regency Pier 66* hotel attracts romantic couples of all ages (see *Checking In*). At *Squeeze* (2 S. New River Dr. W.; phone: 522-2151), there's dancing to progressive and alternative music. Cowboys and wannabes head to *Desperado's* (2520 S. Miami Rd.; phone: 463-2855), complete with line dancing, western clothing, and a mechanical bull. Jazz lovers flock to *O'Hara's Pub* (722 E. Las Olas Blvd.; phone: 524-1764), and the blues and beer group gathers at *Cheers* (941 E. Cypress Creek Rd.; phone: 771-6337). The hottest gay club remains *The Copa* (624 SE 28th St.; phone: 463-1507). A popular Ft. Lauderdale supper club is *Mario's East* (1313 E. Las Olas Blvd.; phone: 523-4990), which has live entertainment nightly; an elegant waterside spot is *Coconut's* (429 Seabreeze Blvd.; phone: 467-6788). And if you just want to sit at a sidewalk café, watch the waves and the people, and listen to good jazz, *Mistral* (see *Eating Out*) has just the thing every Friday and Saturday.

Best in Town

CHECKING IN

Ft. Lauderdale's busiest period is winter, when reservations should be made as far in advance as possible. During high season, a double room at a hotel in the very expensive category could run $200 to $300 per night; in the expensive category, $155 to $190; in the moderate category, $110 to $150; and in the inexpensive category, $65 to $100. In the summer, occupancy (and room) rates drop. Note that a 3% county tourist development tax and a 6% state sales tax are added to all hotel bills.

Most of Ft. Lauderdale's major hotels have complete facilities for the business traveler. Those hotels listed below as having "business services" usually offer such conveniences as meeting rooms, photocopiers, computers, translation services, and express checkout, among others. Call the hotel for additional information. Unless noted otherwise, hotel rooms have air conditioning, private baths, TV sets, and telephones.

In addition to the establishments listed here, the city has many smaller chain and family-operated hotels and motels. About 90 family-operated properties in the area have been designated "superior small lodgings" by the *Greater Ft. Lauderdale Convention and Visitors' Bureau* and *Nova Southeastern University*'s hospitality department, which conducts inspections of the facilities annually. For more information contact the *Greater Ft. Lauderdale Convention and Visitors Bureau* (see *Tourist Information*).

All the hotels below are in Ft. Lauderdale and telephone and fax numbers are in the 954 area code unless otherwise indicated.

We begin with our favorite place, followed by recommended hotels, listed by price category.

A GRAND HOTEL

Marriott Harbor Beach Ft. Lauderdale's premier resort offers 16 acres of beachfront elegance. Guests think they're in a posh Caribbean retreat, what with the five restaurants (including the outstanding *Sheffield's;* see *Eating Out*), two lounges, a pool bar, five tennis courts, and exercise facilities. There's also a tropically landscaped free-form pool with a waterfall and 50 cabañas. The 624 rooms are undersized for the price; the 35 suites, however, are super. Free transportation to the *Galleria* mall and the shops along Las Olas Boulevard is an added plus; you also can get a ride to the *Bonaventure Country Club* if you're looking to play golf. This place is popular with families due to the year-round "Beach Buddies" supervised camp program for children ages five to 12. Business services are available. 3030 Holiday Dr. (phone: 525-4000; 800-222-6543; fax: 766-6152).

VERY EXPENSIVE

Bonaventure Although it's a long drive to the beach, this resort features one of the area's more popular spas and the best golfing and tennis facilities in town. Set in a lush 1,250-acre residential complex amid waterfalls, lakes, and manicured grounds are two championship 18-hole courses (see *Golf*); a racquet club with 24 tennis courts, five racquetball courts, and a squash court (see *Tennis*); five swimming pools; and a spa that offers a full range of health and nutrition programs in separate facilities for men and women. There are 500 rooms and suites, four restaurants, and two lounges. On weekends, the resort runs supervised activities programs for children ages three to 12. Business services are available. 250 Racquet Club Rd. (phone: 389-3300; 800-327-8090; fax: 984-0563).

Ft. Lauderdale Marina Marriott Located on the Intracoastal Waterway at the 17th Street Causeway, this property offers great views north and south from its 14-story tower and two low-rise sections. Most of the 580 rooms have balconies, and all have in-room safes and two telephones. The focal points here are the free-form pool, with its adjacent bar, and the marina, with slips for up to 35 yachts. There are four tennis courts, a health club, a sauna, an outdoor Jacuzzi, a gift shop, restaurants, lounges, and free shuttle service to the beach. Business services are available. 1881 SE 17th St. Causeway (phone: 463-4000; 800-228-9290; fax: 527-6705).

EXPENSIVE

Double Tree Guest Suites Next to the *Galleria* shopping mall and situated on the Intracoastal Waterway, this hotel's 231 modern suites are good value, with fully equipped kitchens, cable TV, 24-hour room service, and sleep sofas in the living rooms. Facilities include a pool, Jacuzzi, small exercise room, restaurant, lounge, and gameroom. The beach is within walking distance and airport transfers are complimentary. It's also accessible by water taxi. Business services are available. 2670 E. Sunrise Blvd. (phone: 565-3800; 800-222-8733; fax: 561-0387).

Embassy This conveniently located hotel offers 358 suites at prices equivalent to those for deluxe hotel rooms. There is a restaurant and lounge, a pool, a sauna, and a Jacuzzi on the premises. Lots of freebies are included in the room rate—daily full American breakfasts, beach shuttle service, parking, and airport transportation. Saluted by *Consumer Reports* magazine, the rooms are attractive and feature sleep sofas in the living rooms, wet bars with mini-fridges, dining tables, and kitchenettes with microwave ovens and coffee makers. Two children under the age of 12 may stay for free in their parents' suite. Business services are available. 1100 SE 17th St. Causeway (phone: 527-2700; 800-854-6146; fax: 760-7202).

Hyatt Regency Pier 66 Set on the Intracoastal Waterway with 388 rooms and suites in a 17-floor tower and two low-rise sections, this resort just completed a face-lift that has given it a sleek, contemporary look and has restored the property to its former position as one of Ft. Lauderdale's most prestigious hotels. Set on 22 acres, the resort offers a full-service 142-slip marina plus six restaurants and lounges, including the famous *Pier Top Lounge,* which revolves every 66 minutes, offering a 360-degree view of Ft. Lauderdale. Guests keep busy at the aquatics center, tennis courts, three pools, and the full-service *Spa LXVI.* Shopping is nearby, and there's transportation to the beach. Business services are available. 2301 SE 17th St. Causeway (phone: 525-6666; 800-327-3796; fax: 728-3541).

Lago Mar Built in 1952, this beachfront 10-acre complex has been expanded several times and attracts a crowd that has been returning for three generations. There are 32 guestrooms in addition to 138 one- and two-bedroom suites, which feature a tropical-style decor. Guests also enjoy four restaurants including an oceanside grill and bar, two pools, and four tennis courts. Business services are available. 1700 S. Ocean La. (phone: 523-6511; 800-255-5246).

Westin Cypress Creek The Westin group's first foray into Florida, this 14-story, 293-room, luxury property overlooks a five-acre lagoon that's spectacularly lighted at *Christmastime.* It features a health club, a large outdoor pool, and a lakeside pavilion; tennis and golf are a five-minute drive away. The *Cypress Room* restaurant is highly recommended; there is also a bar complex. Free parking and business services are available. 400 Corporate Dr., in the *Radice Corporate Center* (phone: 772-1331; 800-228-3000; fax: 491-6867).

MODERATE

Palm-Aire Home of Ft. Lauderdale's original spa, this resort is part of a residential complex of over 1,500 acres, with 160 rooms. Guests have the use of 37 tennis courts, one executive and four championship 18-hole golf courses (see *Golf*), three pools, a half-mile parcourse running track, two racquetball courts, a squash court, two restaurants, and a lounge. Special packages may be booked at the pricey spa, where health and beauty programs prevail (see *Sybaritic Spas* in DIVERSIONS). Business services are available. 2601 Palm-Aire Dr. N., Pompano Beach (phone: 972-3300; 800-272-5624; fax: 968-2711).

Radisson Bahia Mar This nautically oriented hotel, at the *Bahia Mar Marina* at the southern end of "The Strip," has 298 rooms, one restaurant (the *Bahia Mar Bar & Grill*), a free-form pool, a dive shop, glass-bottom boats for rent, four lighted tennis courts, and several boutiques. There are also 350 slips for fishing boats and pleasure yachts, and the country's largest in-water boat show takes place here (see *Special Events*). Business services are available. 801 Seabreeze Blvd. (phone: 764-2233; 800-327-8154; fax: 524-6912).

Ramada Plaza All 223 rooms (14 of which are suites) at this beachfront property have balconies, some with views of the Atlantic Ocean. The *Ocean Café* offers a mostly continental menu, and the *Polo Lounge* features live music and dancing nightly. Other features include a heated pool, a *tiki* bar for hors d'oeuvres and cocktails, sailboat rentals, and business services. 4060 Galt Ocean Dr. (phone: 565-6611; 800-678-9022; fax: 564-7730).

Sheraton Yankee Clipper "Moored" on the beach, the oldest building at this landmark resort looks like—what else?—a clipper ship. The four-building complex (some buildings are across the street and connected to the beach by an overpass) boasts 502 rooms. There are three heated swimming pools, a restaurant, a beachside bar, a lounge that offers entertainment, and an exercise room with weights and workout machines. Business services are available. 1140 Seabreeze Blvd. (phone: 524-5551; 800-325-3535; fax: 524-5376).

INEXPENSIVE

Bahia Cabana Small, unpretentious, and very Floridian, this informal place is nestled by the *Radisson Bahia Mar* resort. There are 116 rooms and apartments with kitchenettes located in five buildings (request the one most recently renovated). Also on the premises are three swimming pools, a 36-person Jacuzzi, saunas, an indoor sports bar, and an outdoor patio bar/restaurant overlooking the marina—a popular gathering spot for locals. While the standard rooms are reasonably priced, this hostelry is usually noisy, with a lot of young guests. 3001 Harbor Dr. (phone: 524-1555; 800-BEACHES; fax: 764-5951).

A Little Inn by the Sea This 30-room bed and breakfast hostelry on the beach is pleasant, homey, and down-to-earth, with a multilingual staff. Children under 10 stay for free in their parents' room. Nearby restaurants make for great dining. 4546 El Mar Dr., Lauderdale-by-the-Sea (phone: 772-2450; fax: 938-9354).

Riverside Offering 109 rooms and suites, this European-style hostelry has a convenient downtown location as well as a sedate ambience and a cozy lobby with a fireplace. Built in 1936, it is one of the city's oldest structures. There's a restaurant-lounge called *Indigo,* with a distinctive decor that features etched glass, and a swimming pool set amid tropical landscaping on the New River. Note that just a handful of rooms fall into the inexpensive category, and these have only one double bed. Business services are available. 620 E. Las Olas Blvd. (phone: 467-0671; 800-325-3280; fax: 462-2148).

EXTRA SPECIAL

Just 30 minutes north of Ft. Lauderdale, the elegant (and pricey) *Boca Raton Resort & Club* is definitely worth a visit. Old World elegance permeates the *Cloister,* the original 1926 hotel building masterminded by Addison Mizner, a major Florida developer in the 1920s and 1930s. Richly decorated contemporary rooms are found in the 27-story *Tower,* and soft pastels dominate the spacious beachfront *Beach Club* rooms. The club's site on a spit of land between the Intracoastal Waterway and the Atlantic guarantees a watery vista from all but the *Cloister* rooms. Lanais are available for lounging, and there's direct access to the beach on the Atlantic side. Guests also can use four pools, 34 tennis courts, two championship golf courses, three fitness centers, and the myriad other amenities of the sprawling 963-room resort, including several restaurants and lounges, meeting space, and a concierge level. 501 E. Camino Real, Boca Raton (phone: 407-395-3000; 800-327-0101; fax: 407-391-3183).

EATING OUT

There are some 2,800 restaurants in Broward County. Many of these are well known, and most get quite crowded during the winter season, so it's always a good idea to make reservations. In fact, restaurant dining is such a part of the lifestyle that a *Restaurants & Institutions* magazine survey found Ft. Lauderdale restaurants second only to New York City as the country's busiest eating establishments. Casual dress is accepted at most restaurants, though a few of the more expensive ones prefer that men wear jackets. Expect to pay $100 or more for dinner for two at a restaurant in the very expensive category; $55 to $100 in the expensive category; $30 to $55 in the moderate category; and $30 or less in the inexpensive category. Prices do not include wine, drinks, taxes, or tips. All telephone numbers are in the 954 area code unless otherwise indicated.

Unless otherwise noted, all restaurants are open daily for lunch and dinner.

VERY EXPENSIVE

Burt & Jack's Owned by actor Burt Reynolds and his partner Jack Jackson, this beautiful Spanish-style villa offers first-rate lobsters and steaks. Reserve a window table so you can watch the cruise and cargo ships pass by. Jackets are required for men. Open daily for dinner. Reservations necessary. Major credit cards accepted. Berth 23, Port Everglades (phone: 522-5225).

By Word of Mouth This European café–style spot in the heart of Ft. Lauderdale's commercial district serves some of the finest fare in the area. The owner has not advertised since opening the restaurant more than a decade ago, but folks flock here to order abundant salads, hand-size Portobello mushrooms stuffed with brie, duckling soaked in apricot brandy, wild mushroom lasagna, outrageous lobster tarragon pie, and star-quality desserts (of the half-dozen chocolate choices, our favorite is "brownie decadence," followed closely by white chocolate cheese cake with Key lime curd). The menu changes daily. Closed Sundays, Monday and Tuesday dinner, and Saturday lunch. Reservations advised. Major credit cards accepted. 3200 NE 12th Ave. (phone: 564-3663).

Darrel & Oliver's Café Maxx The decor is simple—the focus is on the great, albeit very pricey food. The dishes created here are on the cutting edge of New American cooking; many of the highly praised recipes have appeared in well-known food magazines. Each course is a carefully created visual masterpiece: Oysters are dipped in ground pistachios, fried, placed in their shells atop a bed of corn and tomato salsa, and surrounded by a mound of red and green curly lettuce, *enoki* mushrooms, lemongrass, and a nasturtium blossom. The Peking pork with a honey-sesame glaze and the white chocolate mousse pie with raspberry sauce and a white chocolate truffle are two other examples of the chef's melting-pot inventiveness. Open daily for dinner. Reservations necessary. Major credit cards accepted. 2601 E. Atlantic Blvd., Pompano Beach (phone: 782-0606).

Plum Room A harpist provides the background music at this spot, one of South Florida's more romantic, intimate dining rooms. The menu features beautifully presented continental food. There are classic dishes, including sole Véronique and beef Wellington, as well as such exotica as elk and tenderloin of buffalo. Don't miss the cream of mushroom soup, made with shiitake, *enoki,* and white mushrooms. There's also an extensive—and impressive—wine list. Open for dinner; closed Sundays. Reservations necessary. Major credit cards accepted. 3001 E. Oakland Park Blvd. (phone: 563-4168).

Sheffield's Located in the *Marriott Harbor Beach* resort, this posh dining room offers superb lobster bisque, chateaubriand, and Appalachian free-range chicken. Finish off your meal with one of the scrumptious desserts, especially the three-citrus cheesecake in a white chocolate collar, double chocolate macadamia mousse, and *Marjolaine* (thin layers of crisp hazelnut meringue separated by dark chocolate ganache with hazelnut and Chantilly cream fillings). Open daily for dinner. Reservations necessary. Major credit cards accepted. 3030 Holiday Dr. (phone: 766-6100).

La Vieille Maison The top romantic retreat in South Florida, this award-winning restaurant offers attentive service and classic French fare in a historic home styled by developer Addison Mizner and featuring courtyards, flowing fountains, gaslights, a profusion of fresh flowers, and Old World antiques. The $55-per-person prix fixe winter menu includes an appetizer, sorbet, salad, entrée (the selection includes incomparable venison, sweetbreads with cumin, and filet of snapper in a black and green olive potato crust), baby vegetables, fruit and French cheese, and dessert. An à la carte menu is also available. Open daily for dinner. Reservations necessary. Major credit cards accepted. 770 E. Palmetto Park Rd., Boca Raton, a 20-minute drive from Ft. Lauderdale (phone: 421-7370 or 407-391-6701).

EXPENSIVE

Armadillo Café The chef-owners serve large portions of Southwestern fare in a smoke-free eatery chock-full of cacti, cowboy hats, steer horns, and waiters with skinny bolo ties. The menu items range from flavorful to spicy; favorites include smoked duck quesadillas, Armadillo filet (butterflied beef tenderloin marinated in a special sauce and grilled), and yellowtail snapper seared with roast peppers and garlic. The tequila-grilled shrimp and roasted corn cakes with *chipotle* butter and tomato salsa are fabulous. Delicacies such as fresh rattlesnake, buffalo, and venison occasionally are offered. For dessert, try the deep-fried chocolate cinnamon fritters. Beverages choices include chile beer and excellent wines by the glass. Open daily for dinner; closed major holidays. Reservations necessary. Major credit cards accepted. 4630 SW 64th Ave. (corner of Griffin and Davie Rds.), Davie (phone: 791-4866).

Charley's Crab One of the best of Chuck Muer's seven South Florida restaurants, it has a wonderful location on the Intracoastal Waterway, with dining inside and out. The passing water show can range from a 110-foot Italian-designed yacht to a Labrador retriever, wearing a life vest and sunglasses, skimming along in a Seadoo. Specialties include an excellent Martha's Vineyard salad, a wide range of fresh fish prepared almost every way imaginable, and a terrific apple tart with homemade cinnamon ice cream. This spot can be reached by water taxi. Brunch served on Sundays. Reservations advised. Major credit cards accepted. 3000 NE 32nd Ave. (phone: 561-4800).

Chart House This branch of the chain offers the standard steaks and seafood with unlimited salad and fantastic mud pie for dessert. Its Downtown Ft. Lauderdale location is a knockout. Housed in two homes (ca. 1904) on the New River, it has window tables that offer a passing parade of pleasure craft and working vessels. After dining, stroll along the 2 miles of the lushly landscaped *Riverwalk* to the *Broward Center for the Performing Arts,* or take a water taxi back to your hotel. Open daily for dinner. Reservations advised. Major credit cards accepted. 301 SW Third Ave. (phone: 523-0177).

La Coquille One of Ft. Lauderdale's best-kept secrets, this establishment has been entrancing diners for 14 years with meals that look—and taste—good enough to grace the cover of *Bon Appétit* magazine. The ambience is tropical, with mellow jazz adding to the mood; the fare is Provençal, and bilingual French waiters serve with warmth and humor. Menu highlights include tender and succulent lamb, shrimp grilled to perfection, and salmon with just the right amount of champagne sauce and leeks. Best of all, there's a four-course, $50 prix fixe dinner for two that includes a bottle of French wine, allowing couples to celebrate in style without seriously damaging their wallets. Splurge on the Grand Marnier or chocolate soufflés, the latter served with fresh raspberry sauce—you won't regret it. Open Fridays for lunch, daily for dinner; closed August, and Mondays from May through October. Reservations advised. Major credit cards accepted. 1619 E. Sunrise Blvd. (phone: 467-3030).

Mai-Kai For four decades, this place has been a Ft. Lauderdale landmark, with its huge entranceway torches flanking a rattling plank-bridge entrance. Choose from the main dining room, where you can watch the nightly Polynesian show; smaller, lavishly decorated dining rooms; or outdoor seating by a waterfall. The gardens are lush, with authentic South Seas statuary. The food is interesting, with exotic drinks, such as the famous Mystery Drink (a show in itself), and Polynesian, American, and Cantonese dishes (a specialty is Peking duck). The *Molokai Bar* is filled with old-time nautical memorabilia. The Polynesian show (cover charge) is professional and highly entertaining. Open daily for dinner. Reservations advised. Major credit cards accepted. 3599 N. Federal Hwy. (phone: 563-3272).

Mark's Las Olas Chef Mark Militello's latest venture (his other is *Mark's Place* in North Miami Beach) serves New American cuisine with innovative flair. The menu changes daily, but generally the dishes are simpler here than at Militello's Dade County eatery, with an emphasis on lighter sauces and more grilling. Try the grilled chicken, fish, or beef dishes—they're all superb. Closed for lunch weekends. Reservations advised; a two-week wait isn't uncommon for weekend dates. Major credit cards accepted. 1032 E. Las Olas Blvd. (phone: 463-1000).

Martha's Located on the Intracoastal Waterway, where the passing boat scene provides its own entertainment, this eatery has a split personality—the glitzy downstairs serves dress-up types, while the second-floor deck is less formal, more tropical in flavor. The same courteous service and outstanding menu apply to both. Steaks, chops, and seafood are well prepared; fresh Florida snapper is offered eight different ways—the blackened version is perfectly cooked. Chicken gorgonzola with walnuts is also first-rate. Boat dockage available. Brunch served Sundays. Reservations necessary Saturday nights, advised the rest of the week. Major credit cards accepted. 6024 N. Ocean Dr., Hollywood (phone: 923-5444).

Silverado Café A bit of the Napa Valley has been transplanted to the *University Park Plaza* shopping center, where good cooking and California wines prevail. Dine amid Victorian decor or in a small room designed to look like the gondola of a hot-air balloon. Appetizers include Maryland crab cakes and escargots with mushrooms and anise-flavored liqueur, an outstanding black bean soup, and lobster ravioli. The fresh grilled fish and cashew chicken *à l'orange* are tops for main courses. Closed Mondays and for lunch weekends. Reservations advised. Major credit cards accepted. 3528 S. University Dr., Davie (phone: 474-9992).

MODERATE

Bimini Boatyard There's Bahamian decor and a view of the marina here—plus good food at reasonable prices and lots of singles action at the bar on Fridays. Specialties include conch fritters, pasta, pizza, blackened dolphin, and jerk ribs—along with wonderful Bimini bread. Reservations accepted only for parties of eight or more. Major credit cards accepted. 1555 SE 17th St. Causeway (phone: 525-7400).

Brasserie Max The young and young at heart eat in casual comfort at this affordable spot created (but no longer owned) by noted restaurateur Dennis Max. Creative pizza and pasta dishes are favorites, but the restaurant hits its peak with oak-grilled specialties such as Caribbean pork chops served with homemade applesauce. Reservations advised. Major credit cards accepted. In *The Fashion Mall,* 321 N. University Dr., Plantation (phone: 424-8000).

Brazilian Tropicana Brazilian specialties are dished out here, along with a knockout show replete with soaring headdresses and skimpy outfits (on both the men and women!). Favorite dishes include *mariscada en molho verde* (clams, shrimp, scallops, mussels, and lobster in a garlic and white wine sauce), the all-you-can-eat *rodizio* (skewers of homemade sausage, chicken pork loin, and sirloin steak presented and sliced at your table), and shrimp casserole. Most dishes come with black beans, rice, and fried bananas. Open daily for dinner; shows presented Thursdays through Sundays (cover charge). Reservations necessary. Major credit cards accepted. 410 N. Federal Hwy., Pompano Beach (phone: 781-1113).

Gibby's This enormous eatery offers good value in a pretty setting of natural cedar, brick, and lush greenery. A humongous salad is included with basic steaks, fish dishes, and rack of lamb. Among the country's busiest restaurants, it serves about 1,500 dinners nightly in season. In summer, the lobster specials are unbeatable. Closed for lunch weekdays. Reservations advised. Major credit cards accepted. 2900 NE 12th Ter. (phone: 565-2929).

Mario's East On weekends, be prepared to wait at this ultramodern eatery where cheerful waiters often dance down the aisles. The ambience is loud, noisy, and fun, with a female singer who belts out pop songs. The consistently excellent fare is Italian, with an amazingly large selection of pasta, veal, chicken, and fresh seafood dishes as well as individual pizzas. Garlic lovers will be in heaven with the steamed clams and grilled portobello mushrooms. The veal marsala, homemade ravioli, and shrimp marinara also receive rave reviews. There's a small dance floor and two popular bars. The average cost of a main course runs about $12, making this place a fabulous value. If you prefer a quieter meal come early or sit on the outdoor terrace, which is also great for people watching. Reservations accepted only for parties of six or more. American Express accepted. 1313 E. Las Olas Blvd. (phone: 523-4990).

Sea Watch One of the few South Florida dining spots set on the Atlantic Ocean beach, this woodsy eatery has been here for almost 21 years. The fare is mostly fresh seafood, including those famous stone crabs; escargots with mushroom caps in garlic butter and Gulf garlic shrimp are also favorites. Closed *Christmas.* Reservations accepted only for parties of five or more. Major credit cards accepted. 6002 N. Ocean Blvd. (phone: 781-2200).

Victoria Park Set on a quiet side street, this tiny (only 11 tables) gem, built to resemble a house in St. Barts, produces outstanding French cookery with Caribbean overtones. The pork loin seasoned with Jamaican spices and sliced to resemble a castle is only excelled by the grilled duck breast with ginger cherry sauce. This spot can be reached by water taxi. Open for dinner; closed Sundays and Mondays. Reservations advised. Major credit cards accepted. 900 NE 20th Ave. (phone: 764-6868).

INEXPENSIVE

Brother's This popular place offers bagels and lox and corned beef on rye, as well as roasted chicken dinners and the like, to droves of locals. Save room for the seven-layer cake. Open daily for breakfast, lunch, and dinner. No reservations. Major credit cards accepted. 1325 S. Powerline Rd., Pompano Beach (phone: 968-5881).

Carlos & Pepe's The clientele at this popular hangout is eager and hungry; the setting is crowded but pleasant (light wood, green plants, and tile tables); and the menu is lighthearted Mexican (*fajitas,* chimichangas, and *chiles rellenos*). No reservations. Major credit cards accepted. 1302 SE 17th St. (phone: 467-7192).

Ernie's Bar B Que A local institution for almost 40 years, it serves chicken, pork, and beef prepared in a special barbecue sauce that's famous throughout the area. For something different, try the fiery conch chowder. The decor has a rustic Key West style. Reservations unnecessary. Master Card and Visa accepted. 1843 S. Federal Hwy. (phone: 523-8636).

Mistral This trendy sidewalk café on Ft. Lauderdale's "Strip" also boasts breeze-cooled indoor dining amid Mediterranean decor. People watching is an art form here. A wonderfully addictive black bean dip is served in place of butter. The *tapas* platter (with blackened fish, stuffed mussels, crawfish, and chick-pea dip) is excellent. Repeat diners (and there are plenty of them) come more for the ambience than the food, which tends to be spotty and overly seasoned. Jazz bands play every Friday and Saturday night. Reservations accepted only for parties of six or more. Major credit cards accepted. 201 S. Atlantic Blvd., Rte. A1A (phone: 463-4900).

Shooter's Right at the edge of the Intracoastal Waterway, this is a great luncheon spot to watch the boats breeze by. The Friday night happy hour features a band, and hordes of locals stop in to see, be seen, and end the week with friends. Menu choices range from grilled tuna sandwiches to Mexican pizza to California-style salads. Casual, fun, and always hopping, this place has become a Florida institution. No reservations. Major credit cards accepted. 3033 NE 32nd Ave., off Rte. A1A (phone: 566-2855).

Toojay's This upscale deli offers tasty interpretations of the usual fare, plus interesting sandwich combinations (try the turkey and chopped liver). No reservations. Major credit cards accepted. 4401 Sheridan St., Hollywood (phone: 962-9909).

Ft. Worth

On the banks of the Trinity River, 70 miles south of the Oklahoma state line, and 250 miles north of the Gulf of Mexico, Ft. Worth acts as a geographic and cultural boundary between two very different parts of Texas. To the west of the city is flat prairie, hardly more developed than it was a century ago, while 30 miles to the east is flamboyant, wealthy Dallas. A successful blend of both worlds, Ft. Worth has a natural, rugged charm. Ft. Worth writer Jerry Flemmons describes the difference between the two cities thus: "Dallas grew into a huckster city of contrived haute culture. Ft. Worth became a comfortable, ambitious town with a high society always one generation removed from flour sack underwear."

Comparisons aside, the history of Ft. Worth is interesting in its own right. The city was founded as a frontier army post in 1849 by Major Ripley Arnold for protection against Indian attacks. It was named for the Mexican War hero William Jenkins Worth. The settlers who took refuge in this stronghold considered it the very edge of civilization, since all that existed west of Ft. Worth were hundreds of miles of Indian territory. After the Civil War, Ft. Worth emerged as a key stop on the Chisholm Trail, a route cut through Texas and Oklahoma along which millions of longhorns were driven north to market in Kansas. Enormous stockyards were built in what is now called the North Side, and entrepreneurs wasted no time in building saloons and dance halls to accommodate the weary cowhands and smooth-talking cattle barons who came to trade. These moneyed cattlemen became the first incarnation of Ft. Worth gentry; they built mansions along Pennsylvania Avenue in which entire floors were devoted to ballrooms, and ladies' dressing rooms were filled with gowns bought in the East.

When the first of nine railroads came to Ft. Worth in 1876, the city became a meat packing and shipping center, with millions of cattle processed through the Armour and Swift meat packing plants. Then in 1917, oil was discovered and Ft. Worth experienced a new boom—in population and wealth. And while cattle and oil have remained the bedrock of Ft. Worth's economy, since World War II many technological and defense industries have prospered here; four such corporate giants are the Tandy Corporation, Bell Helicopter, Lockheed, and Pier 1 Imports. In addition, *American Airlines* is headquartered here.

Ft. Worth's broad-based economy is just one example of the city's real drawing card—diversity. Another example is the several different faces of the city. Downtown Ft. Worth has the look of a city being built simultaneously in two different centuries: refurbished turn-of-the-century structures stand just a few feet from modern high-rises. In Ft. Worth's North Side, the stockyards have been declared a National Historic District. Although the stockyard area has been duded up for the tourist trade, it hasn't lost its original Old West charm or its cowboy clientele. Due west of downtown is Ft. Worth's Cultural District, a cluster of museums that are among the best west of the Mississippi. Sustained completely by family money, Ft. Worth's museums grew with the city, supported by the citizenry not by force but by choice. And in spite of numerous business closings, the downtown area is surviving. Local business baron Ed Bass, who launched the *Caravan of Dreams* entertainment complex over a decade ago, has expanded and restored Sundance Square. The number of shops and attractions in the area is rapidly expanding.

Despite its many attractions, "Cowtown" (Ft. Worth's nickname) suffered for many years from a whopping identity crisis, overshadowed by the supposedly more sophisticated Dallas. Then visitors started coming here to see the historic stockyards, the *Amon Carter Museum* and *Kimbell Art Museum* began to garner acclaim in the international art market, and the city's business leaders became acknowledged as"big dogs" by anybody's standards. Suddenly, the people of Ft. Worth realized that their city's idiosyncratic mix of cattle, culture, and commerce is just what makes it so special.

Ft. Worth At-a-Glance

SEEING THE CITY

Panoramic views of Ft. Worth turn up serendipitously over a hill or around a corner, but the best one is from the esplanade at the east entrance of the *Amon Carter Museum.* Get some homemade ice cream from the *Back Porch* (across Camp Bowie Blvd.), and then enjoy the spectacular view of downtown from the rolling lawn of the nearby *Kimbell Art Museum*.

SPECIAL PLACES

One of the nicest things about Ft. Worth is that sightseeing is easy, with most attractions divided into the Stockyards District, the Cultural District, and the Downtown District. The major museums are within walking distance of one another; the Stockyards area is best seen on foot; and the botanical gardens and zoo are just down the street from each other.

STOCKYARDS DISTRICT

FT. WORTH STOCKYARDS Wear your jeans to prowl around the north side of Cowtown. If any area best embodies the city's trademark slogan, "Where the west begins," the Ft. Worth Stockyards is it. Disaster struck the Stockyards many times during the first half of this century, but the district of saloons, hotels, and western outfitters that grew up in the area thrived until the packing industry's demise. In the 1960s and early 1970s, the area deteriorated into a near-slum, but after years of neglect, this isolated enclave of history is in the throes of a renaissance, its integrity preserved with National Historic District status. Today, residents and tourists come to soak up its authentic western flavor.

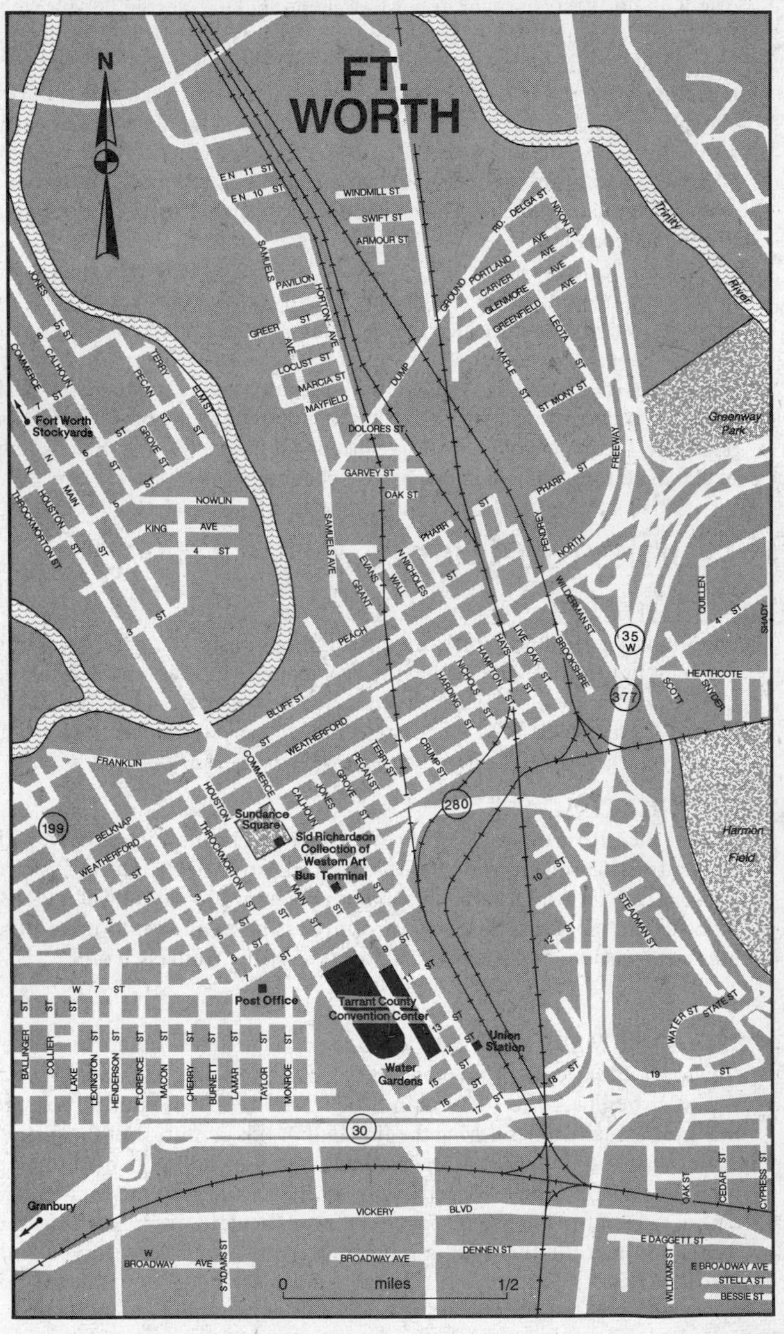
FT. WORTH
N
Fort Worth Stockyards
Greenway Park
Trinity River
Sundance Square
Sid Richardson Collection of Western Art
Bus Terminal
Post Office
Tarrant County Convention Center
Water Gardens
Union Station
Harmon Field
Granbury
FREEWAY
VICKERY BLVD
0 miles 1/2

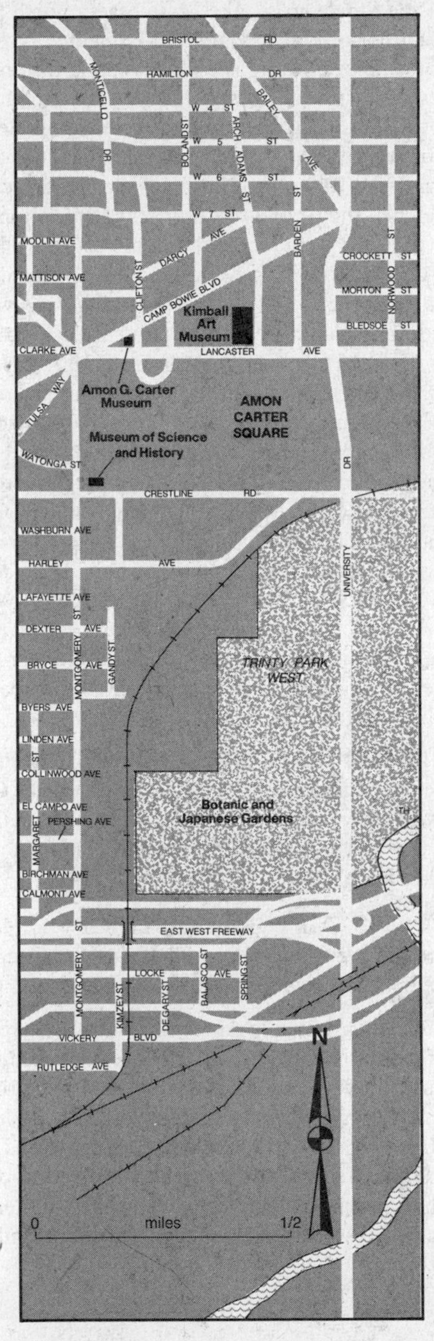
BRISTOL RD
HAMILTON DR
MONTICELLO DR
BAILEY AVE
W 4 ST
W 5 ST
W 6 ST
W 7 ST
BOLAND ST
ARCH ADAMS ST
BARDEN ST
MODLIN AVE
DARCY AVE
MATTISON AVE
CLIFTON ST
CAMP BOWIE BLVD
CROCKETT ST
MORTON ST
NORWOOD ST
BLEDSOE ST
Kimbell Art Museum
CLARKE AVE
LANCASTER AVE
TULSA WAY
Amon G. Carter Museum
AMON CARTER SQUARE
Museum of Science and History
WATONGA ST
CRESTLINE RD
WASHBURN AVE
HARLEY AVE
UNIVERSITY DR
LAFAYETTE AVE
DEXTER AVE
BRYCE AVE
MONTGOMERY ST
GANDY ST
TRINTY PARK WEST
BYERS AVE
LINDEN AVE
COLLINWOOD AVE
EL CAMPO AVE
PERSHING AVE
MARGARET ST
Botanic and Japanese Gardens
BIRCHMAN AVE
CALMONT AVE
EAST WEST FREEWAY
LOCKE AVE
BALASCO ST
SPRING ST
KIMZEY ST
DE GARY ST
VICKERY BLVD
RUTLEDGE AVE
N
0 miles 1/2

To get to the Stockyards, take Main Street north from downtown 2½ miles to the corner of North Main and Exchange Avenue. Park your car anywhere you can; everything is within walking distance. The Stockyards area includes the restored *Cowtown Coliseum,* which hosts live rodeo performances every Saturday night from April through September and other events October through March (phone: 625-1025; 626-2228 for rodeo tickets). Any Monday at 10 AM, you can sit in on a cattle auction at the *Coliseum* or people watch at the *Coliseum*'s *Cattlecar Café* (phone: 624-2241), a tiny place where real Texas traders and other livestock folk lean back and put their boots up while waiting for the café's home cooking. Also in the Stockyards area is the *Livestock Exchange Building,* with several fine art galleries, and dozens of stores where you can pick up a Stetson, a pair of lizard-skin boots, or a bridle for your bronco. *M. L. Leddy's* (2455 N. Main St.; phone: 624-3149) offers leather boots made from ostrich, kangaroo, and sea turtle. The *Stockyards Station Market* (140 E. Exchange Ave.; phone: 625-9715) houses dozens of boutiques, galleries, and eateries in historic buildings where 83 million head of hog and sheep were once sold.

But most people come to the Stockyards to party: On weekend nights, the district is crowded with denim-clad folks meandering from one watering hole or country music dance hall to the next. There are about two dozen nightspots from which to choose, including the century-old *White Elephant Saloon* and *Billy Bob's Texas* (see *Nightclubs and Nightlife,* below). There are also several festivities held here throughout the year (see *Special Events*). And if you get hungry, there's no problem finding a meal—as long as you're satisfied with Tex-Mex or steaks.

STOCKYARDS STATION AND THE FT. WORTH AND WESTERN RAILROAD This 19th-century–style depot greets visitors riding the Tarantula Company's restored *Ft. Worth and Western* cars. The steam excursion train links the Stockyards District with the downtown *Eighth Avenue Station* and the historic Southside District. 140 E. Exchange Ave. (phone: 625-7245).

CULTURAL DISTRICT

In addition to the great museums and attractions listed below, this neighborhood is chockablock with art galleries and upscale boutiques.

AMON CARTER MUSEUM Chronicling America's westward expansion with a huge collection of paintings and sculpture by Frederic Remington and Charles Russell, it also exhibits American art from 1800 to 1950: 19th-century landscapes and genre paintings by such artists as Winslow Homer, Albert Bierstadt, Mary Cassatt, and Thomas Moran, as well as 20th-century works by Georgia O'Keeffe and Stuart Davis. A selection of the 300,000-item American photography collection also is on view. A theater provides a center for films, lectures, and symposiums. Closed Mondays. No admission charge. 3501 Camp Bowie Blvd. (phone: 738-1933).

KIMBELL ART MUSEUM Architect Louis Kahn's last work (1973), this is considered one of the most important and beautiful small art museums in the country. It is the result of a bequest by Kay Kimbell, and today contains an incredible array of works by Caravaggio, Mantegna, Cézanne, Duccio, El Greco, Holbein, Picasso, Poussin, Rembrandt, Velázquez, Watteau, Matisse, and others, not to mention Egyptian, Greek, pre-Columbian, African, and Asian art. Special loan exhibitions and other public programs are regularly scheduled. Closed Mondays. No admission charge except for special exhibits. 3333 Camp Bowie Blvd. (phone: 332-8451).

MODERN ART MUSEUM OF FT. WORTH Opened in 1892, it was the state's first art museum. The collection of 20th-century paintings, drawings, sculpture, and prints features major works by Picasso, Louis, Warhol, Rothko, Stella, de Kooning, Rauschenberg, Motherwell, Pollock, and other modern masters. Loan exhibitions and numerous public programs are prominent features. Closed Mondays and Tuesdays. No admission charge. 1309 Montgomery St. (phone: 738-9215).

FT. WORTH MUSEUM OF SCIENCE AND HISTORY It includes the *Hall of Medical Science, Dino Dig, Man and His Possessions,* and *Computer Technology.* Also part of the museum is the *Omni Theater,* a remarkable computerized 70mm multi-image projection and sound system. The museum is closed Mondays; the *Omni Theater* is open daily. Admission charge. 1501 Montgomery (phone: 732-1631).

CATTLEMAN'S MUSEUM Life-size displays complete with talking figures make an unusual introduction to the history of ranching. Particular emphasis is on the historic and contemporary battles of ranchers and lawmen against cattle rustlers; the museum presents a complete picture of the life of a cattleman. Closed weekends. No admission charge. 1301 W. Seventh St. (phone: 332-7064).

FT. WORTH ZOO Part of *Forest Park,* with picnic tables and a small amusement park, it contains America's largest herpetarium, a lovely rain forest with rare and exotic birds, and an outstanding collection of 4,500 mammals. Exotic exhibits include contemporary-style habitats for primates, big cats, and bears. Also popular is an exhibit called *Texas!* with native flora and fauna such as longhorns, buffalo, and wild boars, as well as a barnyard area of domestic animals and a blacksmithy. Adjacent to the zoo is the longest miniature train ride in the country, a leisurely and scenic 5-mile trip covering the length of *Trinity Park.* Open daily. Admission charge. 1989 Colonial Pkwy., off University Dr. (phone: 871-7050).

LOG CABIN VILLAGE Seven cabins from the 1850s have been restored and furnished with period antiques. Costumed "villagers" demonstrate typical pioneer crafts—weaving, quilting, etc. Open daily. Admission charge. 2100 Log Cabin Village La. near the zoo (phone: 926-5881).

BOTANIC AND JAPANESE GARDENS The *Botanic Gardens* encompass 114 acres for exploring and studying hundreds of different plant species and varieties of roses. Within are the *Japanese Gardens,* tranquil arrangements of trees and shrubs, bridges, pools, waterfalls, and tea houses. A café serves light meals. Open daily. Admission charge for *Japanese Gardens* only. 3220 Botanic Garden Dr., off University Dr. (phone: 871-7686).

THISTLE HILL Built in 1903, this elegant old house is the last one remaining from the days when the cattle barons built their mansions along Pennsylvania Avenue. Closed Saturdays. Admission charge. 1509 Pennsylvania Ave. (phone: 336-1212).

DOWNTOWN DISTRICT

SUNDANCE SQUARE This charming square is formed by Commerce, Houston, Second, and Fourth Streets and is filled with an interesting collection of boutiques, craft shops, restaurants, and art galleries. Main Street, which bisects the square, is notable for its red brick sidewalks, period streetlamps, and turn-of-the-century buildings. Don't miss the wonderful Chisholm Trail mural at Third and Main Streets. Several restaurants, fashionable stores, and two enormous movie complexes indicate the area's growth. The well-known *Sid Richardson Collection of Western Art* (309 Main St.; phone: 332-6554) features 60 original paintings by Western artists Frederic Remington and Charles Russell. *Fire Station No. 1* (201-203 Commerce; phone: 732-1631) houses a museum showcasing the city's history with the exhibition "150 Years of Ft. Worth." Open daily. No admission charge.

CARAVAN OF DREAMS This innovative performing arts center occupies a Victorian-cum-Western building in the heart of Sundance Square. There's a cabaret-style nightclub featuring live performances of jazz, rock, and blues by such big names as Lyle Lovett and Wynton Marsalis. A wide variety of productions is performed at *Stage West,* and there's a rooftop grotto bar with a neon-lit cactus garden. 312 Houston St. (phone: 877-3000).

WATER GARDENS Renowned New York architect Philip Johnson designed this outdoor water park, where some 19,000 gallons of water pour over pebbled concrete sculptures every minute. South of the *Convention Center* between Commerce and Houston Sts.

OLD TYME POSTIQUE The downtown post office has opened this permanent exhibit of memorabilia, information, and merchandise (for sale) for philatelists. The 1930s building has an interior of marble, bronze, and gold leaf. Closed weekends. No admission charge. Lancaster and Houston Sts. (phone: 336-3018).

TARRANT COUNTY COURTHOUSE This masterpiece of pink Texas granite and marble, built in 1895 at a cost of $450,000 (a lot of money back then), resembles the beautiful, Renaissance-style *State Capitol* in Austin. Closed weekends. No admission charge. 100 E. Weatherford St. (phone: 884-1111).

EXTRA SPECIAL

Granbury, an easy 30-minute-drive southwest of Ft. Worth on Highway 377, is a charming little town filled with historic buildings. A limestone courthouse dominates a town square ringed with crafts shops, ice-cream parlors, and restaurants, all in 19th-century structures. In fact, Granbury has so many Old West buildings that the town is entered in the *National Register of Historic Places.* Surrounding Granbury is a manmade lake of the same name with beautiful camping and picnicking facilities; the *Convention and Visitors Bureau* (phone: 573-5548; 800-950-2212) has further information. For a country-style buffet, try the *Nutt House* restaurant (121 E. Bridge St.; phone: 563-9362; closed Mondays). "Country-style" means you go through a line, cafeteria style, pick up some grits, fried or baked chicken, catfish, meat loaf, famous hot-water corn bread, and buttermilk pie, then sit down at a long table.

You might want to spend a day at *Texas Lil's,* a Western dude ranch about 30 minutes north of town. An all-inclusive ticket covers a full day's worth of activities, including an hour-long horseback ride on a 3-mile scenic trail, an all-you-can-eat barbecue, a hayride, swimming, hiking, and fishing. There's also a petting zoo. Closed Mondays. Reservations necessary. Admission charge. Off Hwy. 407, in Justin (phone: 430-0192).

Arlington, about 20 minutes east of Ft. Worth, has several attractions, including *Six Flags Over Texas, Wet 'n' Wild,* and *Ballpark in Arlington,* home of the Texas *Rangers* baseball team (for more information, see *Dallas,* THE CITIES).

Sources and Resources

TOURIST INFORMATION

For brochures, maps, and general information, contact the *Ft. Worth Convention and Visitors Bureau* (415 Throckmorton St., Ft. Worth, TX 76102; phone: 336-8791; 800-433-5747), which is closed weekends. They may also be picked up at the *Sid Richardson Collection of Western Art* (309 Main St., Sundance Sq.; phone: 332-6554); the *Ft. Worth Museum of Science and History* (1501 Montgomery; phone: 732-1631); as well as at the *Visitors' Information Center* (123 E. Exchange in the Stockyards District; phone: 625-9715), which is closed Sundays. For information on special events, call 800-433-5747. Contact the Texas state tourism hotline (800-8888-TEX) for maps, calendars of events, health updates, and travel advisories.

LOCAL COVERAGE The *Fort Worth Star-Telegram* is published mornings, evenings, and Sundays. See Friday's issue for *Star Time,* an insert with entertainment and restaurant listings. *Texas Monthly* magazine publishes reviews of Ft. Worth's best restaurants.

TELEVISION STATIONS KTVT Channel 11–CBS; KXAS Channel 5–NBC; WFAA Channel 8–ABC; and KERA Channel 13–PBS.

RADIO STATIONS AM: KLIF 570 (talk); KKDA 730 (soul); KRLD 1080 (talk/news); and KAAM 1310 (adult contemporary). FM: KSCS 96.3 (country); KEGL 97.1 (Top 40); KLUV 98.7 (oldies); WRR 101.1 (classical); and KVIL 103.7 (adult contemporary).

TELEPHONE The area code for Ft. Worth is 817.

SALES TAX There is a 7.75% sales tax on all purchases except food; the hotel room tax is 13%.

CLIMATE Officially, Ft. Worth's average daily temperature during the spring is 65F; summer, 84F; fall, 66F; and winter, 47F. But don't be fooled by averages: Plan on summer scorchers and some pretty nippy winter days, sometimes (though rarely) with a touch of ice and snow.

GETTING AROUND

AIRPORT *Dallas/Ft. Worth Airport (D/FW),* one of the country's largest, is on the northeast edge of Ft. Worth, a 20- to 25-minute drive from downtown. Bus transportation between *D/FW,* the downtown hotels, and the downtown terminal is provided by the city-owned *Airporter Bus Service and Park & Ride Terminal* (100 Weatherford St.; phone: 334-0092); fare is $7. The *Supershuttle* (phone: 329-2000) also provides airport transportation; reservations are required.

BUS The public transportation system, simply known as the *T,* provides bus service throughout Ft. Worth; travel in the downtown area is free (pick up a pass when you board the bus). A $3 *Visitour* pass allows you to travel throughout the city. To check on routes and schedules, call 871-6200.

CAR RENTAL The major national agencies are represented.

TAXI The best way to get a cab is to phone for one. Try *Yellow Cab* (phone: 534-5555).

SIGHTSEEING TOURS

HORSE-DRAWN CARRIAGES There are also horse-drawn carriage tours of the downtown area year-round, if you'd rather let a Clydesdale show you the sights (phone: 336-0400).

WALKING The *Ft. Worth Convention and Visitors Bureau* suggests two walking tours, the *Western Heritage Trail* and the *Museum and Garden Tour.* Maps are available at their office (see *Tourist Information,* above).

SPECIAL EVENTS

Any child who spent any time at all in the Ft. Worth Independent School District can attest that the highlight of the year comes during three weeks in late January and early February when the *Southwestern Exposition and Livestock Show and Rodeo* comes to town. Schoolchildren have one day designated as *Stock Show Day* and receive free tickets, but the world's oldest indoor rodeo, midway, and stock show are fun for anyone. For more information, contact the *Southwestern Exposition,* PO Box 150, Ft. Worth, TX 76101 (phone: 877-2400 or 877-2420). *Cowtown Goes Green* is a *St. Patrick's Day* celebration held in the Stockyards District; events include a parade, a pub crawl, and a liar's contest. Ft. Worth's restored Main Street becomes a marketplace of food, arts and crafts, and entertainment during the *Main Street Ft. Worth Arts Festival* in April. Other special events are *Mayfest,* a celebration with food, music, and games on the banks of the Trinity River the first weekend in May; the *Chisholm Trail Roundup* (phone: 625-7005), a fair with street dances, chili cook-offs, and gunfights in the Stockyards area the second weekend in June; the *Shakespeare in the Park* series at the *Trinity Park Playhouse* in late June, when spectators bring picnic suppers and enjoy the free performances; *Pioneer Days,* a three-day Western wingding held in September in the Stockyards; *Oktoberfest,* the first weekend in October; and the *National Cutting Horse Futurity,* one of the country's premier Western events, with some of the highest monetary awards outside a racetrack; it's held the first week in December at *Will Rogers Coliseum* (phone: 244-6188).

SHOPPING

Ft. Worth has its share of today's marketplaces, malls filled with department stores, chain shops, eateries, and entertainment. Enclaves of commerce with more individuality, however, also are easy to come by—and get to. Museum shops are another excellent source of quality gifts and mementos.

SPORTS AND FITNESS

BASEBALL The *American League* Texas *Rangers* play at *Ballpark in Arlington* (1700 Copeland Rd., Arlington; phone: 817-273-5100).

BICYCLING The *Department of Parks* (4200 South Frwy.; phone: 871-8700) provides maps of scenic biking trails that circle *Forest Park* and *Trinity Park.*

FITNESS CENTERS The coed *YMCA* (512 Lamar; phone: 332-3281) provides a pool, a track, aerobics courses, weight training, and basketball, racquetball, hardball, and volleyball courts. Another fitness center is *Bally's President's* (6833 Green Oaks Rd.; phone: 738-8910). Both are open to non-members for a fee.

GOLF There are 11 country clubs and nine municipal courses in Ft. Worth. The *Colonial National Invitation* is held in May at the *Colonial Country Club* (3735 Country Club Circle; phone: 927-4278).

HORSE RACING There's parimutuel racing at the new *Lone Star* complex from April through *Labor Day.* Just south of I-30 in Grand Prairie (phone: 214-263-RACE).

JOGGING Maps of the jogging trails around *Forest Park* and *Trinity Park* are available from the *Department of Parks* (4200 South Fwy.; phone: 871-8700). The Trinity trail winds 8.2 miles through three city parks.

TENNIS The *Mary Potishman Lard Tennis Center* at *Texas Christian University* (3609 Bellaire; phone: 921-7960) offers 22 outdoor and five indoor courts to the public. The *McLeland Tennis Center* (1600 W. Seminary Dr.; phone: 921-5134) has 14 outdoor courts, two indoor courts, and one practice court, all lighted. Instruction available.

THEATER

Casa Mañana ("the house of tomorrow") is probably Ft. Worth's best-known playhouse (3101 W. Lancaster at University Dr.; phone: 332-2272). A theater-in-the-round, it mounts a variety of dramatic productions. Others include the *Fort Worth Theatre* (3505 Lancaster; phone: 738-7491), which offers family entertainment as well as avant-garde productions; *Stage West* (3500 S. University; phone: 784-9378), where current and classic comedy and drama are performed; and the outdoor *Hip Pocket Theater* (1620 Las Vegas Trail N.; phone: 927-2833). The *Jubilee Theater* (506 Main; phone: 338-4411) offers a cross-section of African-American theater on Fridays and Saturdays. The *Ft. Worth/Dallas Ballet* performs at the *Ft. Worth/Tarrant County Convention Center* (1111 Houston; phone: 763-0207). The city makes much of the fact that it sustains a major ballet company, something that rival city Dallas has not been able to do.

MUSIC

The *Ft. Worth Opera* (phone: 731-0833) and the *Ft. Worth Symphony Orchestra* (phone: 921-2676) both perform at the *Ft. Worth/Tarrant County Convention Center* (1111 Houston St.). Ft. Worth's Grammy-winning *Texas Boys Choir* (phone: 924-1482) gives concerts in a variety of places. The *Schola Cantorum of Texas* (phone: 737-5788) is a 50-member chorus that also performs in different venues. For more information, call the *Ft. Worth Convention and Visitors Bureau* (see *Tourist Information* above).

NIGHTCLUBS AND NIGHTLIFE

The *White Elephant Saloon* (106 E. Exchange; phone: 624-1887) is a popular watering hole that features "buffalo sweat" margaritas and country music; it's in the historic Stockyards area. *Billy Bob's Texas* (2520 Rodeo Plaza; phone: 624-7117) is a huge honky-tonk place with 42 bars, an arena for bull riding, and live entertainment Friday and Saturday evenings. Also worth visiting in the Stockyards is the *Longhorn Saloon* (121 W. Exchange; phone: 624-4242), a huge bar and the place to hear live country bands. *Caravan of Dreams* (312 Houston; phone: 877-3000), an avant-garde performing arts center, has a jazz and blues nightclub and a theater. It is the preeminent jazz club in the region, and its *Rooftop Garden and Grotto Bar* is the city's most unusual. For variety, try *Hyean's* (604 Main St.; phone:

877-5233), a comedy club in the early evening and disco after 10 PM. Alternative, high energy, and Top 40 dance music is offered at the *Crush Bar* (706 N. Watson, Arlington; phone: 640-5633). *J & J Blues Bar* (937 Woodward; phone: 870-2337) offers the best in regional blues.

Best in Town

CHECKING IN

While Ft. Worth has no shortage of traditional hotels, another alternative, *Bed and Breakfast Texas-Style,* offers lodging and either continental or Texas-style breakfasts in private homes in the city's most desirable neighborhoods. Contact Ruth Wilson, 4224 W. Red Bird La., Dallas, TX 75237 (phone: 214-298-5433). Most of Ft. Worth's major hotels have complete facilities for the business traveler. Those listed below as having "business services" usually offer such conveniences as meeting rooms, photocopiers, computers, translation services, and express checkout, among others. Call the individual hotel for additional information. Expect to pay $100 or more per night for a double room at the hotels listed as expensive, and $50 to $100 at those categorized as moderate; there are no exceptional inexpensive hotels in the city. Unless otherwise noted, hotel rooms have air conditioning, private baths, TV sets, and telephones.

All hotels below are in Ft. Worth and telephone and fax numbers are in the 817 area code unless otherwise indicated.

EXPENSIVE

Hyatt Regency D/FW Big, convenient, and busy, this attractive property in the airport complex is a good place to stay if you're planning to divide your time between Dallas and Ft. Worth—or to visit the amusement parks between the two cities. It has 1,400 rooms, four restaurants, 10 racquetball courts, seven tennis courts (four outdoor lighted, three indoor), an outdoor pool, and access to a nearby club with 36 holes of golf. Ask about summer family rates. Amenities include a concierge and business services. *D/FW Airport* (phone: 214-453-1234; 800-233-1234; fax: 214-615-6826).

Marriott Solana Also in the airport area is this small, pretty complex. It offers 198 well-appointed guestrooms, an outdoor pool, a large health and fitness club, and golf privileges at the nearby *Fossil Creek Club. Cielo,* its restaurant, serves a variety of Mediterranean fare. Other amenities include a concierge and business services. Hwy. 114 at Kirkwood Blvd., Westlake (phone: 430-3848; 800-228-9290; fax: 430-4870).

Radisson Plaza This circa 1921 Texas hotel has retained more original Western flavor than any other in the city. There are 516 guestrooms, including 30 suites, as well as two restaurants, two cocktail lounges, an outdoor pool, a sun deck, a fitness center, and a concierge floor. Business services are available. Facing the *Convention Center,* 815 Main St. (phone: 870-2100; 800-333-3333; fax: 335-3408).

Stockyards Dating to cowboy boomtown days, this place with 44 rooms and eight suites is popular with tourists since the *White Elephant Saloon,* numerous restaurants, and other attractions are within walking distance. Much is made of the time Bonnie and Clyde put up here. Check out the saddles that serve as barstools in the *Booger Red Saloon.* Business services are available. 109 E. Exchange (phone: 625-6427; 800-423-8471 outside Texas; fax: 624-2571).

Worthington This lovely European-style hostelry is across the street from Sundance Square. There are 507 rooms (including 70 luxury suites), two outdoor tennis courts, indoor pools, athletic club, several ballrooms, and the fine *Reflections* restaurant (see *Eating Out*). Other amenities include a concierge desk and business services. 200 Main St. (phone: 870-1000; 800-772-5977 from Texas; 800-433-5677 from elsewhere in the US; fax: 332-5679).

MODERATE

Clarion Hotel and Conference Center This property is located smack in the middle of an older area alongside the *Chisholm Trail,* with a small historic cemetery *in* the parking lot. The 197-room hotel is decorated in light, bright colors and has a spacious lobby. Amenities include a concierge and business services. 2000 Beach St. (phone: 534-4801; 800-221-2222; fax: 536-5384).

Miss Molly's Those who clamor for the flavor of the Old West should check out this eight-room hostelry, previously a bordello. Each room is cleverly decorated and named according to decor (the "Cowboy Room," the "Cattleman's Room"). You can get bountiful bites at the *Star Café.* 109½ W. Exchange (phone: 626-1522; 800-99-MOLLY; fax: 625-2723).

EATING OUT

In a city once called Cowtown, you'd naturally expect good beef, but natives pride themselves more on ferreting out superior Tex-Mex fare and chicken-fried steaks. You also can find some better-than-average continental fare and an assortment of ethnic eats. Expect to spend more than $50 for dinner for two at expensive restaurants; $30 to $50 at those listed as moderate; and less than $30 at inexpensive places. Prices do not include drinks, wine, tax, or tips. All restaurants are in the 817 area code unless otherwise indicated.

Unless otherwise noted, restaurants are open for lunch and dinner.

EXPENSIVE

Balcony Dressy and romantic, it overlooks Camp Bowie Boulevard and serves traditional continental cooking. Broiled lamb chops and veal are the specialties. Closed Sundays. Reservations advised. Major credit cards accepted. 6100 Camp Bowie (phone: 731-3719).

Cacharel Set atop a high-rise, it's appealingly decorated in shades of pale pink and gray, and serves elegant New American fare. Outstanding menu choices include sautéed sea scallops and wild rice cakes with a saffron and Pernod sauce, crabmeat salad, and grilled salmon. The chocolate–Grand Marnier soufflé is unforgettable. Closed Sundays. Reservations advised. Major credit cards accepted. 2221 E. Lamar Blvd., Arlington (phone: 640-9981).

Le Chardonnay A light and airy French bistro with several small dining rooms and a delightful red-brick patio, this place serves imaginative dishes, including sautéed frogs' legs with a creamy *ancho* chili sauce and ginger-laced puffed pastry, fresh grilled salmon with tarragon butter, and roast lamb or veal stuffed with fresh herbs. The extensive wine list presents an array of fine choices. Reservations advised. Major credit cards accepted. 2443 Forest Park (phone: 926-5622).

Michael's Contemporary ranch cuisine and a delightful spin on steaks, veal, pasta, and fresh fish enhanced with *ancho* chilies, polenta, and roasted veggies are the order of the day here. The setting is sophisticated, the crowd trendy. Closed Sundays. Reservations advised. Major credit cards accepted. 3413 W. 7th St. (phone: 877-3413).

La Piazza Italian dishes are elegantly presented in a warm, intimate room decorated with watercolors and fresh flowers. Munch on the fresh-baked bread served with herbed oil, then move on to mozzarella-basil-tomato salad, red snapper, or veal medallions in wine sauce. Jacket and tie required. Closed Sundays. Reservations advised. Major credit cards accepted. 3431 W. Seventh St. (phone: 334-0000).

Reflections An outstanding example of what a hotel restaurant should be. The Art Deco surroundings provide a counterpoint to elegant presentations of coho salmon and game birds, as well as decadent desserts. Closed Sundays. Reservations advised. Major credit cards accepted. In the *Worthington Hotel,* 200 Main St. (phone: 870-1000).

Saint-Emilion Creatively prepared meat, fish, and fowl are featured at this country French bistro. Two- and four-course prix fixe meals are offered for dinner; there's also an extensive wine selection. Reservations advised. Major credit cards accepted. 3617 W. Seventh (phone: 737-2781).

MODERATE

Cattlemen's Steak House The portraits of blue-ribbon beef that grace the walls in this Stockyards stronghold are a little-needed reminder of each T-bone's heritage. Many of the cowboy customers are urban, but look carefully, since old-timers still like to splurge here. Open daily; dinner only on Sundays. No reservations on Saturdays. Major credit cards accepted. 2458 N. Main (phone: 624-3945).

Hedary's Everything is fresh and flavorful at this Lebanese eatery, where customers may watch their dinners being prepared. Try the chicken with lemon, veal sausages, grilled lamb chops, and fresh pita bread. Closed Mondays. No reservations. Major credit cards accepted. 3308 Fairfield in *Ridglea Center* (phone: 731-6961).

Lucile's This piano bar-café occupies a historic building and serves outstanding American favorites, such as wood-burning oven pizza, New York strip steaks, homemade ravioli, Maryland crab cakes, fried green tomatoes, and Maine lobster. The roasted chicken with feta is memorable. Weekend breakfasts are known for scones, beignets, and excellent café au lait. Open daily; breakfast served on weekends. Reservations advised. Major credit cards accepted. 4700 Camp Bowie (phone: 738-4761).

Sardine's This cabaret-like trattoria is more spacious than you might think, given its name. The Old World Italian atmosphere is dark, warm, and cozy, with live jazz music on weekends; the pasta dishes and meat specials are tasty. The warm seafood antipasto is a good choice. Open daily for dinner only. Reservations advised on weekends. Major credit cards accepted. 3410 Camp Bowie (phone: 332-9937).

Szechuan If you hanker for Chinese food in Cowtown, this is the place—heaping portions, helpful service, and an extensive menu. The house specialties are heartily recommended. Open daily. Reservations advised. Major credit cards accepted. 5712 Locke (phone: 738-7300).

INEXPENSIVE

Angelo's Hearty barbecue with the finest of trimmings is all this Ft. Worth institution offers. But what more could one ask for than an icy beer and a paper plate heaped with tangy ribs (served after 4:30 PM only) or barbecued beef plus a scoop of potato salad, coleslaw, a pickle, and bread. Closed Sundays. No reservations or credit cards accepted. 2533 White Settlement (phone: 332-0357).

Benito's The best place in Ft. Worth to sample a variety of Mexican dishes. The standard Tex-Mex combos are available, but the more authentic Mexican fare—homemade tamales and *chiles rellenos*—hasn't been tamed for American taste buds. The restaurant stays open until 3 AM Fridays and Saturdays. Open daily. No reservations. Major credit cards accepted. 1450 W. Magnolia (phone: 332-8633).

Carshon's Split-pea soup, corned beef on rye, and butterscotch pie aren't exactly the stuff of Ft. Worth's fame, but this kosher deli is touted statewide. Closed Mondays. No reservations or credit cards accepted. 3133 Cleburne Rd. (phone: 923-1907).

Joe T. Garcia's This famous North Ft. Worth landmark serves Tex-Mex dishes and *fajitas* to crowds that are willing to line up out front for more than an hour on weekends. The wait may be eased (and the food improved) by a couple of delicious frozen margaritas, and in warm weather, you can eat outside on the patio. Reservations advised only for groups of 20 or more. No credit cards accepted. 2201 N. Commerce (phone: 626-4356).

Kincaid's For decades, this corner grocery has been a popular local spot to grab a big, juicy hamburger. There are some picnic tables for diners who don't want to eat standing up at the counter. Closed Sundays. No reservations or credit cards accepted. 4901 Camp Bowie (phone: 732-2881).

Massey's No theory of evolution has been more often debated here than the origin of its chicken-fried steaks. They're a delight—tender beef and a crunchy crust topped with thick, creamy gravy. No reservations. Major credit cards accepted. 1805 Eighth Ave. (phone: 924-8242).

Paris Coffee Shop Home-style cooking like grits 'n' gravy, homemade soup, and corn bread muffins are definitely de rigueur here. The clanging of dishes and table chatter provide the background music. Open for breakfast and lunch only; closed Sundays. No reservations. Major credit cards accepted. 700 W. Magnolia Ave. (phone: 335-2041).

Hartford

Hartford's modern skyscrapers, rising from the flat Connecticut River Valley, come as a surprise, but this high-rise façade masks one of the most pragmatic urban identities in the country. Some call this "the city that fear built," for Hartford is the insurance capital of the United States. A number of major insurance companies are still headquartered here, making decisions that touch many people's lives, in some way or another, at some time or another. Some 50,000 of the city's citizens work in the insurance business, and even more work for the state government (as Hartford is also the capital of Connecticut). Nearly one million people live in the Greater Hartford area, which includes towns within a 50-mile radius of the city center. Among them are urban centers such as East Hartford and picturebook towns like Avon, Farmington, and Old Wethersfield.

The Dutch first established a trading post in the area in the 1620s, but it was not until 1662 that Hartford was granted independence by Charles II. Sir Edmund Andros, governor of New England, tried to seize the city's charter shortly thereafter, but a local magistrate hid the document in a hollow tree that became known as the Charter Oak. When the tree was blown down in 1856, citizens put up a plaque on Charter Oak Avenue to mark the spot where it once stood.

For many years, Hartford was a lively port, with molasses, coffee, spices, and tobacco stored in its large warehouses, then shipped to other destinations in New England. An important tobacco growing region, the Connecticut River Valley was the site of the first cigar factory in the United States. Even today, the banks of the Connecticut River are checkered with a patchwork of white cloth squares that growers use to shield tobacco leaves from too much light. And Hartford is still the marketing center for Connecticut Valley tobacco.

Hartford also has traces of a historic New England township: Colonial, post-Revolutionary, and 19th-century houses sit in spacious gardens. The *Old State House* is where statesmen gathered to debate issues of the day as far back as 1796. Samuel Clemens (aka Mark Twain) spent many years in Hartford, and his home, as well as the nearby house of *Uncle Tom's Cabin* author Harriet Beecher Stowe, are favorite stopping points along Hartford's literary trail.

Juxtaposed with this historic architecture is a revitalized downtown area. Hartford's *Civic Center* and the restoration of *Union Station* sparked a proliferation of restaurants and cafés, some in ambitiously restored buildings. Streets that used to fold up at nightfall now bustle with barhoppers, diners, tourists, and residents of downtown apartments. Though hard hit by the recession of the early 1990s, Hartford has been making a gradual comeback, taking its place as a lively city with an appeal all its own.

Hartford At-a-Glance

SEEING THE CITY

The top of *Travelers Tower,* 527 feet above the madding crowd in The Travelers Insurance Company building, offers the best view of the city. There are 72 steps to climb before reaching the top. Closed mid-October through April; open weekdays only the rest of the year. No admission charge, but call in advance. 700 Main St. (phone: 277-4208).

SPECIAL PLACES

Walking through Hartford can be highly enjoyable, especially since the city combines classical and contemporary architectural styles. Capitol Hill is a good place to begin.

CONNECTICUT STATE CAPITOL Described as High Victorian Gothic, the *Capitol,* begun in 1874 and opened in 1879, houses the state legislature. Guided tours are given weekdays year-round, and on Saturdays from April through October. 210 Capitol Ave. (phone: 240-0222).

RAYMOND E. BALDWIN MUSEUM OF CONNECTICUT HISTORY Three-and-a-half centuries of Connecticut's heritage are packed into this museum, with exhibitions tracing the growth of major manufacturers in the state. Most notable is the collection of Colt firearms. Closed weekends and holidays. Admission charge. 231 Capitol Ave. (phone: 566-3056).

BUSHNELL PARK Better known as downtown Hartford's "Village Green," *Bushnell Park* is an arboretum for rare and native trees, as well as the home of a delightful 1914 carousel. Frederick Law Olmsted, who designed New York City's *Central Park,* also worked on *Bushnell.* Concerts are often held here during the summer. Carousel closed October through mid-April, weekdays mid-April through mid-May and month of September, and Mondays from mid-May through August. Bounded by Asylum, Elm, Ford, Wells, and Jewell Sts. (phone: 246-7739).

BUTLER-MCCOOK HOMESTEAD Within strolling distance of downtown is the oldest private home in the city, built in 1782. It has an extensive collection of 18th-century furnishings and vintage American paintings, and a fascinating collection of Japanese armor and other curios. Closed mid-October through mid-May; open Tuesdays and Thursdays from mid-May through mid-October. Admission charge. 396 Main St. (phone: 522-1806).

CENTER CHURCH Upon completion in 1807, this was the Meeting House of the original founders of the city. Now a church with stained glass by Tiffany, it is called the *Center Church* because of its location in the middle of town. Outside the church is the *Ancient Burying Ground* (1640–1803), a restored cemetery where the city's founders now rest. The church is open for services on Sundays and by appointment only other times. *Burying Ground* open daily. *First Church of Christ* on Main St. (phone: 249-5631).

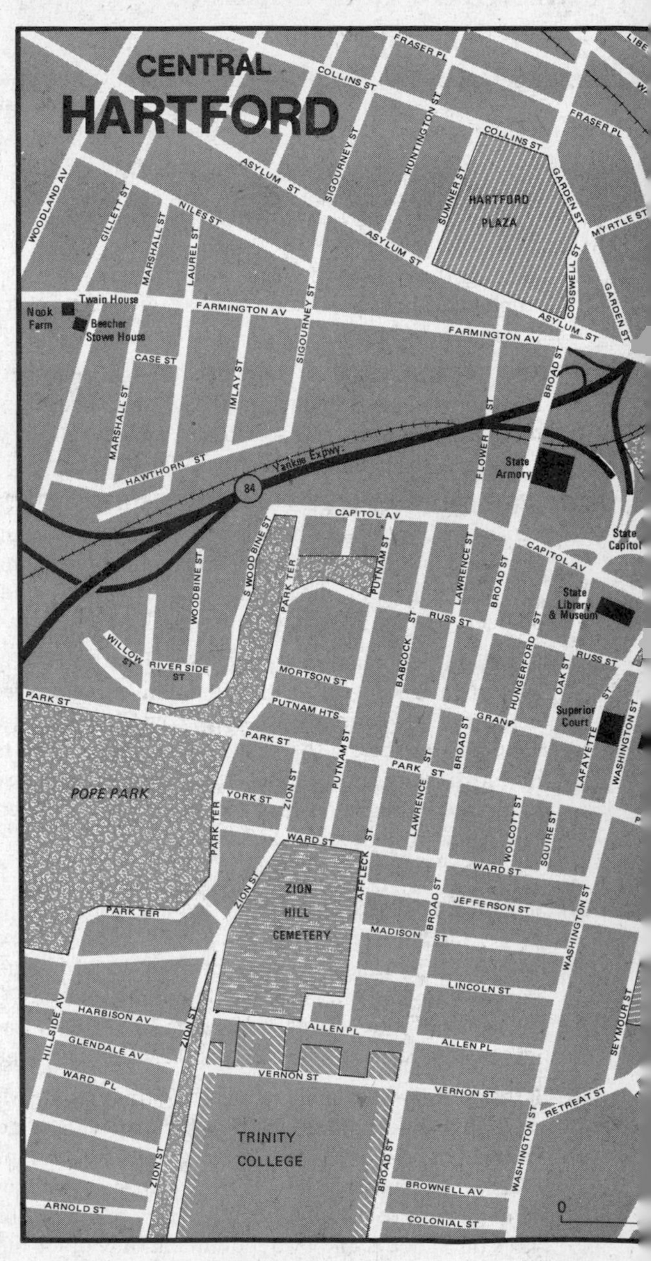

CENTRAL
HARTFORD
Twain House
Nook Farm
Beecher Stowe House
State Armory
State Capitol
State Library & Museum
Superior Court
HARTFORD PLAZA
POPE PARK
ZION HILL CEMETERY
TRINITY COLLEGE
Yankee Expwy.
84
FARMINGTON AV
ASYLUM ST
COLLINS ST
FRASER PL
CAPITOL AV
PARK ST
VERNON ST
ALLEN PL
BROAD ST
WASHINGTON ST
ZION ST

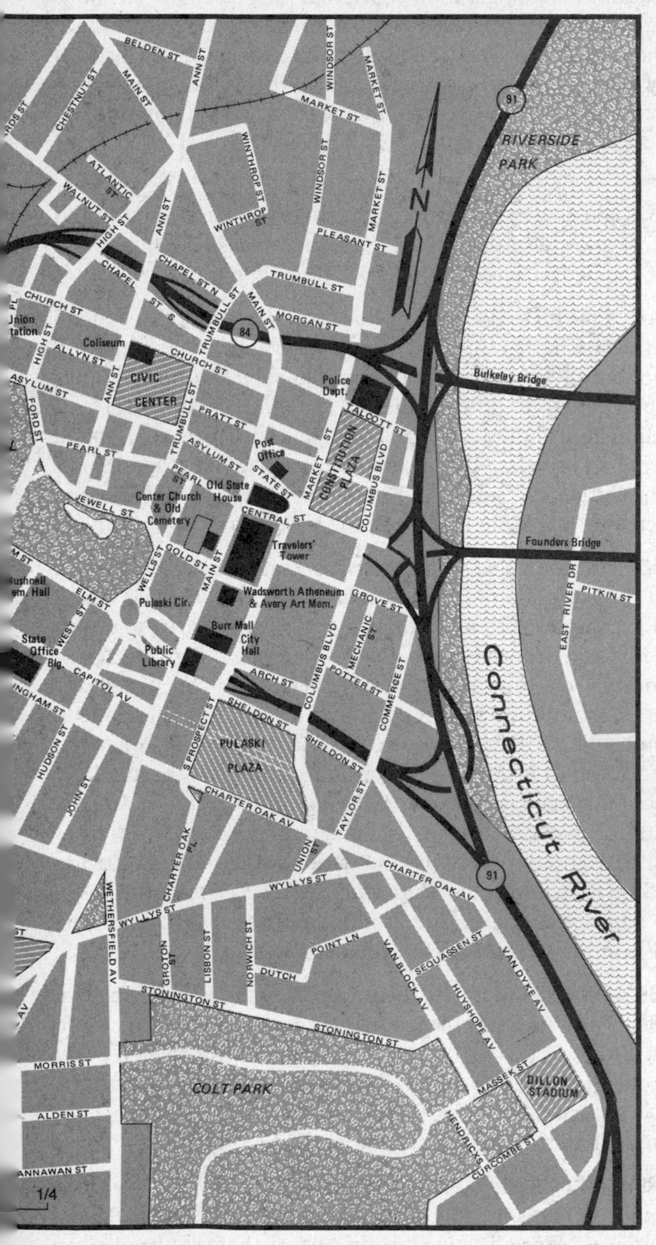
BELDEN ST
CHESTNUT ST
MAIN ST
ANN ST
WINDSOR ST
MARKET ST
MARKET ST
91
RIVERSIDE PARK
WINTHROP ST
WINDSOR ST
MARKET ST
ATLANTIC ST
WALNUT ST
HIGH ST
ANN ST
WINTHROP ST
PLEASANT ST
N
CHAPEL ST N
CHAPEL ST S
TRUMBULL ST
TRUMBULL ST
MAIN ST
CHURCH ST
MORGAN ST
84
Union Station
HIGH ST
ALLYN ST
Coliseum
CHURCH ST
CIVIC CENTER
ASYLUM ST
ANN ST
TRUMBULL ST
Police Dept.
Bulkeley Bridge
TALCOTT ST
PRATT ST
FORD ST
PEARL ST
ASYLUM ST
Post Office
MARKET ST
CONSTITUTION PLAZA
COLUMBUS BLVD
PEARL ST
STATE ST
Old State House
Center Church & Old Cemetery
JEWELL ST
CENTRAL ST
Travelers' Tower
Founders Bridge
GOLD ST
WELLS ST
MAIN ST
Bushnell Mem. Hall
Wadsworth Atheneum & Avery Art Mem.
GROVE ST
EAST RIVER DR
PITKIN ST
ELM ST
Pulaski Cir.
Burr Mall
City Hall
WEST ST
State Office Bldg.
Public Library
COLUMBUS BLVD
MECHANIC ST
Connecticut River
ARCH ST
POTTER ST
CAPITOL AV
COMMERCE ST
SHELDON ST
S PROSPECT ST
HUDSON ST
PULASKI PLAZA
SHELDON ST
JOHN ST
CHARTER OAK AV
TAYLOR ST
CHARTER OAK PL
UNION ST
WETHERSFIELD AV
WYLLYS ST
CHARTER OAK AV
91
WYLLYS ST
GROTON ST
LISBON ST
NORWICH ST
POINT LN
DUTCH
VAN BLOCK AV
SEQUASSEN ST
HUYSHOPE AV
VAN DYKE AV
STONINGTON ST
STONINGTON ST
MORRIS ST
MASSEK ST
DILLON STADIUM
COLT PARK
ALDEN ST
HENDRICKS
CURCOMBE ST
ANNAWAN ST
1/4

HARTFORD CIVIC CENTER This "city within a city" includes a mall with about 50 shops, 20 restaurants including a food court, and the 386-room *Sheraton-Hartford* hotel (see *Checking In*), plus 79,000 square feet of exhibition space for the *Boat Show,* the *Auto Show,* and other large events. The Hartford *Whalers* hockey team plays in a 16,500-seat arena, which hosts other sporting events and concerts in the off-season. 1 Civic Center Plaza (phone: 727-8010 for concert ticket information; 728-3366 or 800-WHALERS for *Whalers'* tickets).

PRATT STREET Located right next to the *Civic Center,* this street has been restored to its former glory as a stylish shopping area. More than 20 boutiques and restaurants line the pedestrian-oriented brick thoroughfare.

OLD STATE HOUSE At one time an active meeting house for statesmen, this Federal building designed by Charles Bulfinch is now a privately owned museum which also has a souvenir and craft shop. The colonial furniture and other artifacts on display date to 1796, when the *Old State House* was built. There is also information here about local attractions and special events, as well as a cannon-firing and fife and drum ceremony carried out several times daily by authentically dressed "soldiers." The souvenir shop is closed Sundays. No admission charge. 800 Main St. (phone: 522-6766).

WADSWORTH ATHENEUM America's oldest continuously operated public art museum was founded in 1842 by philanthropist Daniel Wadsworth, and has grown to a five-building complex with more than 45,000 works of art: American and European fine and decorative arts, 20th-century paintings and sculpture, contemporary art, costumes, and textiles. The highlights of the collection include Hudson River School paintings; works of such European masters as Renoir, Picasso, Monet, Goya, Cézanne, and Miró; American furniture (the *Nutting Collection* of Pilgrim-era furniture is particularly noteworthy); Renaissance and Baroque paintings; the *J. Pierpont Morgan Collection* of European decorative arts; a number of Surrealist works from the 1920s and 1930s; and the Amistad Foundation's collection of African-American art. Stop for a bite at the *Museum Café* (see *Eating Out*). Closed Mondays. No admission charge for groups of 10 or more people on Thursdays and Saturdays. 600 Main St. (phone: 278-2670).

ELIZABETH PARK ROSE GARDENS Another of Hartford's "firsts" is this botanical wonderland, the first municipally owned rose garden in the country. More than 900 varieties of roses, as well as 14,000 other plants, are on view every summer, while the greenhouses stay open year-round. Open-air concerts are performed in summer. In winter, the park's pond is a popular place for ice skating. Prospect and Asylum Aves. (phone: 722-6514).

MARK TWAIN MEMORIAL AND HARRIET BEECHER STOWE HOUSE A 19th-century writers' community here on the former Nook Farm estate contained several authors' houses. Mark Twain lived in one of them, a three-story

Victorian mansion made of brick, stone, and wood. Harriet Beecher Stowe, the author of *Uncle Tom's Cabin,* lived in an only slightly less elaborate painted brick house next door. Both houses are open year-round and offer guided tours. Admission charge. *Mark Twain Memorial* (351 Farmington Ave.; phone: 493-6411); *Harriet Beecher Stowe House* (77 Forest St.; phone: 525-9317).

SCIENCE CENTER OF CONNECTICUT Visitors to this progressive science museum are greeted by a life-size, walk-in replica of a 60-foot sperm whale. There are also traveling exhibitions, a tank with aquatic animals that can be handled, a mini-zoo, and a planetarium-auditorium where the planetarium and laser light shows are presented. Closed Mondays except in summer and on school holidays. Admission charge. 950 Trout Brook Dr., West Hartford (phone: 231-2824).

EXTRA SPECIAL

For a diverting day trip that can include outdoor activities, visits to historic houses, and shopping for antiques, head west on Route 44. This scenic road travels over thickly forested Avon Mountain to the Farmington Valley. There, a great number of outdoor activities awaits you, including canoeing, fishing, and exploring the hiking and cross-country ski trails in the *Talcott Mountain State Park* and along the *Connecticut Blue Trail System.* The area's key landmark, the 165-foot *Heublein Tower,* offers a panorama of five states to those who hike the 1½-mile trail starting at Route 185. Dotted along Route 44 and Route 10 are Avon, Farmington, and Simsbury—cozy New England hamlets with numerous crafts boutiques and antiques shops. Farmington's *Hill-Stead Museum* (35 Mountain Rd.; phone: 677-4787) is an imposing colonial Revival mansion designed by architect Stanford White and the owner's daughter, Theodate Pope Riddle. The superb collection of early French Impressionists amassed by the family, as well as the exquisite furnishings, make it worth a visit. It's closed Mondays; admission charge. In Simsbury, dine in 19th-century elegance at the restored *Simsbury 1820 House* (731 Hopmeadow St.; phone: 658-7658; 800-TRY-1820), which also has 34 guestrooms, each individually decorated with antique furnishings. Farther southwest on Route 202 is Litchfield, a charming town of huge white mansions set around a classic New England village green. Just outside Litchfield, 3½ miles south on Route 63, is *White Flower Farm* (phone: 567-8789), a perennial nursery that is a magnet for countless New England gardeners. Even for non-gardeners, it is worth a visit to see the display gardens, which peak in May and June; in July and August, a greenhouse full of magnificent English tuberous begonias shares the limelight with fields of flowering shrubs and perennials. Open daily.

Sources and Resources

TOURIST INFORMATION

Brochures, maps, and general tourist advice are available from the *Greater Hartford Tourism District* (1 Civic Center Plaza, Hartford, CT 06103; phone: 800-793-4480; fax: 520-4495), the *Greater Hartford Convention and Visitors Bureau* (1 Civic Center Plaza, Hartford, CT 06103; phone: 728-6789; 800-446-7811), both closed weekends, and the tourist information booth at the Center Court of the *Hartford Civic Center* (phone: 275-6456), open daily.

LOCAL COVERAGE *The Hartford Courant* (the oldest American daily newspaper in continuous circulation), morning daily; *Connecticut* Magazine, monthly; and the *Hartford Advocate,* a free alternative news and entertainment publication, weekly.

TELEVISION STATIONS WFSB Channel 3–CBS; WTNH Channel 8–ABC; CPTV Channel 24–PBS; WVIT Channel 30–NBC; and WTIC Channel 61–Fox.

RADIO STATIONS AM: WNEZ 910 (news talk); WTIC 1080 (news); WCCC 1290 (rock); WDRC 1360 (solid gold); and WPOP 1410 (news). FM: WPKT 90.5 (public radio); WWYZ 92.5 (country); WZMX 93.7 (adult contemporary); WKSS 95.7 (adult contemporary); WTIC 96.5 (adult contemporary); WDRC 102.9 (solid gold); WIOF 104 (adult contemporary); WHCN 105.9 (rock); and WCCC 106.9 (rock).

TELEPHONE The area code for Hartford is 860.

SALES TAX The sales tax is 6%; the hotel room tax is 12%.

CLIMATE Hartford's humidity is sometimes a problem in the summer, when temperatures reach the 80s and 90s F; winters are intermittently snowy, generally in the 20s and 30s; spring and fall are delightful.

GETTING AROUND

AIRPORT *Bradley International Airport* is about 12 miles from downtown Hartford. The drive usually takes 20 to 30 minutes. *The Airport Connection* (phone: 627-3400) and *Peter Pan Trailways* (phone: 724-5400) provide bus service between the airport, *Union Station,* and area hotels.

BUS The state-owned *Connecticut Transit Company* (100 Leibert Rd.; phone: 525-9181) operates the municipal bus service. Fare starts at $1.

CAR RENTAL All major national firms are represented at the airport as well as downtown.

TAXI Visitors may either hail a cab on the street or pick one up at *Union Station* and the *Goodwin* and *Sheraton* hotels, or call *Yellow Cab* (phone: 666-6666).

SIGHTSEEING TOURS

BOAT The *Lady Fenwick,* a reproduction of an 1800 steam-powered yacht, takes passengers along the scenic Connecticut River. Organized by *Charter Oak Cruises* (phone: 526-4954), excursions run four times daily from *Memorial Day* through *Labor Day;* three times daily on weekends through October.

SPECIAL EVENTS

Since 1989, *First Night* has been Hartford's way of ringing in the *New Year* with multicultural festivities in the downtown vicinity. *A Taste of Hartford,* New England's largest food festival, is held downtown in June. It's a giant block party with music, dancing, and menu samples from over 60 restaurants. Hartford's *July 4th River Festival* features concerts, sporting events, and fireworks displays along the Connecticut River. *Kidrific* is a two-day event held the weekend after *Labor Day;* specially designed for children and their parents, it features a petting zoo, rides, and games. The *Festival of Lights,* with thousands of tiny white lights illuminating Constitution Plaza, is held every year from the day after *Thanksgiving* until January 6. Santa Claus always starts things off by making a dramatic appearance on top of the Fleet Bank Building in a helicopter and descending in a window-washer's gondola that looks surprisingly like a sleigh.

MUSEUMS

A directory describing several dozen Hartford art galleries is available at the Center Court of the *Hartford Civic Center.* Another good source of information is *Real Art Ways* (56 Arbor St.; phone: 232-1006), a prominent avant-garde arts organization. In addition to those described in *Special Places,* three other museums are worthy of note.

CONNECTICUT HISTORICAL SOCIETY Here is an important collection of American antiques and artifacts. Closed Mondays, Saturdays in summer, and major holidays. Admission charge. 1 Elizabeth St. (phone: 236-5621).

MUSEUM OF AMERICAN POLITICAL LIFE An extensive collection of American political memorabilia (second only to the one at the *Smithsonian*) is handsomely displayed at the *University of Hartford.* Closed Mondays. No admission charge. 200 Bloomfield Ave., West Hartford (phone: 768-4090).

THE WATKINSON LIBRARY This library contains a major collection of rare books, including several Audubon folios and the writings of Hartford resident Samuel Clemens (Mark Twain). Closed when classes are not in session. No admission charge. On the campus of *Trinity College* (phone: 297-2268).

SHOPPING

Hartford has its share of today's marketplaces, malls filled with department stores, chain shops, eateries, and entertainment. Enclaves of commerce with more individuality, however, also are easy to come by—and get to. Museum shops are an excellent source of quality gifts and mementos.

SPORTS AND FITNESS

BASKETBALL The *Huskies* (phone: 486-2724), the nationally ranked men's basketball team of the *University of Connecticut,* divide their home games between the *Gampel Pavilion* at the campus in Storrs and the *Hartford Civic Center* (1 Civic Center Plaza), while the nationally ranked *UConn Women's Basketball Team* (phone: 486-2724) plays exclusively at the *Gampel.* The *Continental Basketball Association*'s *Connecticut Pride* (phone: 547-1747) plays at the *Civic Center.*

FISHING For the best fishing, try Wethersfield Cove, south of Hartford.

FITNESS CENTERS The *YMCA* (160 Jewell; phone: 522-4183) has a pool, squash and racquetball courts, a track, and a masseur. The *YWCA* (135 Broad St.; phone: 525-1163) has a pool, sauna, and weight room. Both are available to non-members for a fee.

GOLF There are 24 golf courses in the Hartford area. The best public courses in the city are located in *Keney Park* and *Goodwin Park. PGA* tour pros compete in the *Canon Greater Hartford Open Golf Tournament* in late June at the *Tournament Players Club* in Cromwell (phone: 635-5000).

HOCKEY The *NHL Whalers* play at the *Hartford Civic Center* (1 Civic Center Plaza; phone: 728-3366; 800-WHALERS).

ICE SKATING Recreational skating is available at the 2,000-seat *International Skating Center of Connecticut,* where it's not uncommon to see many *Olympic* champions cutting the ice as well. Open year-round. Located on Route 10, about 30 minutes northwest of central Hartford. 1375 Hopmeadow St., Simsbury (phone: 651-5400).

JOGGING The perimeter of *Bushnell Park,* across from the *YMCA,* is seven-eighths of a mile; other running courses include *Goodwin Park,* 1½ miles from downtown, with a 2-mile perimeter; and *Elizabeth Park,* 2 miles from downtown, with a 2½-mile perimeter.

SKIING There's excellent cross-country skiing at the *Metropolitan District Commission* reservoir in West Hartford. Downhill enthusiasts like *Mt. Southington* (25 minutes west on I-84), *Powder Ridge Ski Area* (20 minutes south on I-91), *Ski Sundown* (35 minutes west on Rte. 44), and *Mt. Tom* (45 minutes north on I-91).

SWIMMING The Connecticut River is acceptable for boating, but the currents and tides are dangerous for swimming, even though it may look tempting on a hot day. Hartford residents recommend swimming at the *YWCA* or the *YMCA* (See *Fitness Centers*)—both charge a fee.

TENNIS The best public courts are at *Elizabeth Park* (Prospect and Asylum Aves.).

THEATER

Hartford has no shortage of fine theater. For complete performance schedules, check the newspapers listed in *Local Coverage.* The following is our favorite place in Hartford for live theater.

CENTER STAGE

Hartford Stage Company This innovative Tony Award-winning organization presents an assortment of six plays during its season (October through June) in productions that are noteworthy for their style, verve, and aesthetic vision; the focus is on presenting new works and rediscovering—and reinterpreting—the classics. 50 Church St. (phone: 527-5151).

In addition, the 2,800-seat *Bushnell Memorial Hall* (166 Capitol Ave.; phone: 246-6807) features performances by the *Hartford Ballet* (phone: 525-9396) and the *Connecticut Opera* (phone: 527-0713), as well as touring Broadway productions. *TheatreWorks* (233 Pearl St.; phone: 527-7838) offers modern, avant-garde drama, while *The Producing Guild* (at the *Wallace Stevens Theater,* 690 Asylum Ave.; phone: 528-2143) presents both on- and off-Broadway productions.

MUSIC

Concerts, operas, and symphonies are performed at *Bushnell Memorial Hall* (166 Capitol Ave.; phone: 246-6807), American musical revivals are presented at the renowned *Goodspeed Opera House* (East Haddam, 45 minutes south on Rte. 9; phone: 873-8668), while new musicals are presented at the *Goodspeed*'s sister venue, the *Norma Terris Theatre* (Chester, 50 minutes south on Rte. 9; phone: 873-8668). The *Coliseum at the Hartford Civic Center* (1 Civic Center Plaza; phone: 727-8010) features rock concerts. The *Charter Oak Cultural Center* (21 Charter Oak Ave.; phone: 249-1207) has an eclectic mix of zydeco, blues, gospel, and jazz music. The *Hartford Symphony Orchestra* (phone: 244-2999) performs January through May at *Bushnell Memorial Hall.*

NIGHTCLUBS AND NIGHTLIFE

Hartford's nightclubs center around Union Place. At *Mad Murphy's* (22 Union Pl.; phone: 549-1722), a deejay plays oldies but goodies, with live music on weekends. Try *Coach's* (187 Allyn St.; phone: 522-6224), the sports bar owned by *UConn* coach Jim Calhoun features a dance floor with deejay Thursdays through Saturdays, and two large-screen and 32 small TVs for optimum sports watching. Just across from the *Civic Center, The Russian Lady Café* (191 Ann St.; phone: 525-3003) rocks with live music weekends; the rest of the week the club features modern rock. *Bourbon Street North* (70 Union Pl.; phone: 525-1014) is a popular hangout featuring live and recorded alternative music and dancing Thursdays through Saturdays. The *Blue Star Café* (26 Trumbull St.; phone: 527-4557) has live jazz and blues most nights. The *Last Laugh Club* features comedy at *Brown Thomson & Co.* (942 Main St.; phone: 525-1600) on Friday and Saturday nights.

Best in Town

CHECKING IN

The quality of Hartford's lodgings has taken a quantum leap forward as a result of the millions spent on renovations of downtown hotels. Most of Hartford's major hotels have complete facilities for the business traveler. Those listed below as having "business services" usually offer such conveniences as meeting rooms, photocopiers, computers, translation services, and express checkout, among others. Call the individual hotel for additional information. For bed and breakfast listings and referrals, contact *Nutmeg Bed & Breakfast* (PO Box 1117, West Hartford, CT 06127; phone: 236-6698; 800-727-7592). Expect to pay $100 or more per night for a double room at places listed as expensive, and $60 to $100 at those in the moderate category; there are no exceptional inexpensive hotels in the city. Unless otherwise noted, hotel rooms have air conditioning, private baths, TV sets, and telephones.

All hotels below are in Hartford and telephone and fax numbers are in the 860 area code unless otherwide indicated.

EXPENSIVE

Avon Old Farms Only 15 minutes from downtown, this gracious, elegant hotel offers all the benefits of a country setting, along with two fine dining rooms including *Avon Old Farms Inn* (see *Eating Out*), just across the street. Many of the 160 spacious rooms have grand views. Located on 20 acres of manicured grounds, it is near a public golf course. There is an outdoor pool as well as an exercise room and sauna, and hiking trails behind the hotel. Business services are available, and there is live entertainment nightly. Rtes. 10 and 44, Box 1295, Avon, CT 06001 (phone: 677-1651; 800-836-4000; fax: 677-0364).

Goodwin This 124-room European-style luxury boutique hotel, formerly the home of J. P. Morgan, has individual, quirkily shaped rooms with dormer windows, unexpected corners, and lots of space. Genuine antiques and turn-of-the-century reproductions, such as sleigh beds and period-style wallpaper, are combined with contemporary furnishings to produce a quiet elegance. Formal dining is offered at *Pierpont's* restaurant (see *Eating Out*), sandwiches and lighter meals at the *America's Cup* lounge. Room service can be ordered until 1 AM, and business services are available. All rooms have computer-compatible phone lines. Conveniently located across from the *Civic Center.* 1 Haynes St. (phone: 246-7500; 800-922-5006; fax: 247-4576).

Sheraton-Hartford Connected to the *Civic Center,* this 386-room property offers a wider range of indoor sports than any other Hartford hotel. There is an indoor heated pool, and the health club has a whirlpool, a sauna, and exercise and recreation rooms. In-room movies are available, and *93 Church St.,* a casual eatery, serves continental fare. There's a concierge desk, and business services are available. 315 Trumbull St. at the *Civic Center* (phone: 728-5151; 800-325-3535; fax: 240-7247).

MODERATE

Holiday Inn Hartford Downtown On the fringe of downtown, this 343-room high-rise has easy access to I-84 and I-91. The *Rover Lounge* offers cocktails and hors d'oeuvres, and *O'Neill's* is a casual restaurant serving American food. A popular choice among corporate travelers, the hotel has an outdoor pool, a health club with Nautilus equipment, a concierge, and business services. 50 Morgan St. (phone: 549-2400; 800-HOLIDAY; fax: 527-2746).

EATING OUT

The variety of ethnic food—Italian, Greek, Portuguese, Spanish, Brazilian, Peruvian, Indian, Vietnamese, Cajun, and Jamaican—available in the city has increased dramatically in the past few years. The South End is the heart of the old Italian neighborhood, with other ethnic groups represented there and scattered throughout the city and suburbs. Expect to pay between $50 and $100 for dinner for two at restaurants designated as expensive; between $30 and $50 at those we've listed as moderate; and less than $30 at inexpensive places. Prices do not include drinks, wine, tax, or tips. All are in the 860 area code.

Unless otherwise noted, restaurants are open for lunch and dinner.

EXPENSIVE

Avon Old Farms Inn Once a Colonial-era blacksmith shop, this inn has been serving meals since 1757, which makes it one of the oldest restaurants in the nation. It is across the street from the *Avon Old Farms* hotel. In the *Old Forge Room,* you can sit among antique smithy tools, and linger over veal, beef, and seafood specialties, many prepared on an oak-fired grill. An award-winning brunch is offered on Sundays. Reservations advised. Major credit cards accepted. Rtes. 10 and 44, Avon, about a 15-minute drive from downtown Hartford (phone: 677-2818).

Carbone's Thanks to good food and a warm and comfortable atmosphere, this place has been a Hartford tradition for over 50 years. The northern Italian menu features hot spinach salad, veal dishes, and homemade pasta. Desserts are sinfully delicious. Closed Sundays; dinner only on Saturdays. Reservations advised. Major credit cards accepted. 588 Franklin Ave. (phone: 296-9646).

Cavey's For many years, this place has won praise as the most romantic French restaurant in town. In an elegantly appointed room, diners can choose from such seasonal favorites as rack of lamb, cassoulet, and *tarte tatin.* Open for dinner; closed Sundays and Mondays. Reservations advised. Major credit cards accepted. 45 E. Center St., Manchester, about 10 minutes from downtown Hartford (phone: 643-2751).

Pierpont's This elegant dining room in the *Goodwin* hotel features a sophisticated American menu with such specialities as sautéed Maine lobster with forest mushrooms and stuffed loin of lamb. It has consistently won awards for the best hotel dining in Hartford. Open daily; breakfast and brunch only on Sundays. Reservations advised. Major credit cards accepted. 1 Haynes St. (phone: 522-4935).

Ruth's Chris Steak House The place to go for the meat-and-potatoes crowd, this popular eatery specializes in US prime meat. Once you decide on your steak, choose from eight varieties of potatoes. Assorted chops and seafood are also offered. Reservations advised. Major credit cards accepted. 2513 Berlin Tpke. (Rtes. 5 and 15), Newington, about 10 minutes from downtown Hartford (phone: 666-2202).

MODERATE

Bricco This stylish new eatery boasts a staff drawn from the area's best restaurants—which may explain its instant popularity. The American/Mediterranean menu features appetizers such as portobello mushrooms with prosciutto and mozzarella and well-prepared entrées including cedar-planked salmon and linguine with fresh clams. Open daily; dinner only on Sundays. Reservations required for more than six people. Major credit cards accepted. 78 Lasalle Rd., West Hartford, about 10 minutes from downtown Hartford (phone: 233-0220).

Civic Café on Trumbull Delicious American offerings with an Asian flair make this hip eatery one of the city's "in" spots. Popular favorites include herb-crusted rotisserie chicken and fresh tuna. Don't miss the chocolate pâté dessert. Closed Sundays; dinner only on Saturdays. Reservations advised. Major credit cards accepted. 150 Trumbull St. (phone: 493-7412).

Costa del Sol Spanish food is the draw at this inviting spot in the South End. The charming Mediterranean decor with white stucco walls, fresh flowers, and candlelight is set off by an equally fine menu of *tapas*, paella, and crème Catalana. There's also a good selection of Spanish wines. Visit the outdoor patio in summer. Closed Mondays; dinner only on weekends. Reservations advised. Major credit cards accepted. 901 Wethersfield Ave. (phone: 296-1714).

Gaetano's On the mezzanine of the *Civic Center,* but away from its major bustle, this is a businessperson's favorite. Ask for a window seat overlooking Trumbull Street. The chef chooses fresh local and imported produce in his rich, haute Italian creations. The adjacent *Gaetano's Café* offers simpler, less pricey fare. Closed Sundays; dinner only on Saturdays. Reservations advised. Major credit cards accepted. 1 Civic Center Plaza (phone: 249-1629).

Max Downtown Although this restaurant is fashioned as a bistro, the subtly chic, well-heeled clientele indicates it's much more than that. The menu bears this out, with oysters on the half shell, fine champagnes by the glass, and exceptional contemporary American cuisine, with an emphasis on steaks and chops. Open daily; dinner only on weekends. Reservations advised. Major credit cards accepted. 185 Asylum St. (phone: 522-2530).

Museum Café at the Wadsworth Atheneum Decorated with paintings from the museum's collection and overlooking a sculpture garden, this pleasant spot offers an eclectic blend of international flavors in its soups, salads, sandwiches, pasta, and game. Closed Mondays; lunch Tuesdays through Saturdays, brunch Sundays, dinner first Thursday of each month. Reservations advised for lunch and brunch, required for Thursday dinner. Major credit cards accepted. 600 Main St. (phone: 728-5989).

Shish Kebab House of Afghanistan Genuine Afghan food is served here in spacious, tiled, plant-filled rooms. Kebabs are the main attraction—the chicken is excellent, and shrimp and swordfish kebabs are popular. *Bowlani* (a lightly fried crêpe filled with potatoes and scallions) is also recommended, and the unusual desserts are worth a try. Open daily for dinner; closed Sundays. Reservations advised. Major credit cards accepted. 360 Franklin Ave. (phone: 296-0301).

INEXPENSIVE

First and Last Tavern This cozy, South End family-oriented place keeps the locals happy with homemade pasta, terrific breads, and a variety of pizza. Open daily; dinner only on Sundays. Reservations unnecessary. Major credit cards accepted. 939 Maple Ave. (phone: 956-6000).

Oasis Crowd pleasers such as meatloaf and chicken with gravy are the staples at this diner complete with tableside jukeboxes. Downstairs is *Pancho's* a Mexican eatery, which offer burritos, *fajitas,* and enchiladas. There are also excellent margaritas and Mexican beers. Reservations unnecessary. Major credit cards accepted. 267 Farmington Ave. (phone: 241-8200).

Honolulu

Honolulu is the country's most foreign metropolis, an American city that stubbornly refuses to feel quite like America. (Small wonder; just over 100 years ago, it was the capital of a foreign country ruled by a queen.) Yes, there are the designer boutiques, fast-food establishments, and chain stores here as in any other US city. But *haoles* (prounounced *how*-lees, the Hawaiian term for outsiders, meaning Caucasians), are far outnumbered by Asians. Japanese investors own some 25% of the city's real estate, and the 28-mile-long metropolis (pop. 500,000) is flanked by the Pacific Ocean and the Koolau Mountain Range—and within a 15-minute drive are tropical rain forests.

Honolulu residents are unabashedly fond of dubbing their island home "paradise." But it has been a sometimes uneasy Eden, with a violent and often tragic history. Early-19th-century American missionaries experienced severe hardships here, but in battles between missionaries, Western shippers, and merchants for the hearts and minds of the native population, it was the Hawaiians who lost the most. They were converted to Christianity and forced to sacrifice much of their native culture before falling prey to diseases to which they had no immunity. Only today is the long-dormant pride of traditional heritage emerging among descendants of the original Polynesian Hawaiians.

Other groups came to live in the islands, too. When the economy required hard labor for the sugar plantations in the late 19th century, unskilled workers were recruited from all over, especially from Japan, China, and the Portuguese islands of Madeira and the Azores. When their contracts expired, many stayed on, contributing to the racial mix that characterizes contemporary Honolulu society. At the turn of the century, large numbers of Filipino and Korean immigrants joined the melting pot, and in recent years, transplanted mainlanders and South Pacific islanders have arrived in large numbers. More than a third of the marriages in Hawaii today are interracial.

In 1893, Queen Liliuokalani was overthrown by a combined force primarily made up of Americans living in the islands and American troops sent ashore from ships anchored in Honolulu. Seven years later the islands were annexed as a US territory.

With the Japanese attack on Pearl Harbor on December 7, 1941, Honolulu entered the consciousness of most mainland Americans. Martial law was declared throughout the islands, and for millions of American servicemen, Hawaii became the jumping-off point for the Pacific theater.

These days, more than six million visitors a year pour into the Honolulu airport and drop more than $10 billion into Hawaii's coffers. Sugar and pineapple plantations still dot the outback, but no longer support the economy. Tourism is the vital juice of Hawaii, and much of it gets squeezed out in Honolulu. Among the visitors are a good number of former GIs who no longer hate Oahu, which they once called "The Rock"; now the most popular attraction in town is the beautiful memorial that floats over the sunken USS *Arizona.*

By the way, "the mainland" is what residents call the rest of the US—and those who want to keep their respect will never refer to it as "stateside," since Hawaii is our 50th state. In fact, romantic as it may be, with crashing waves, sunny beaches, and balmy breezes, Honolulu is a modern metropolis struggling with modern problems. A few decades ago Waikiki was a sparsely settled peninsula along a swamp, 4 miles southeast of town. There was an unobstructed view of Diamond Head, and the tallest structure in town was the 10-story *Aloha Tower.* No more. Forests of high-rises, the centerpiece of an ongoing major redevelopment for the harbor area, now dwarf the *Tower,* and Waikiki has its share of dope dealers, pickpockets, and prostitutes. It also has something relentlessly exotic about it, like Chinatown for instance, which still has noodle factories and sidewalk stalls, as it did 100 years ago. And within Honolulu is a taste of everything Hawaiian and a flavor of seas far beyond.

Honolulu At-a-Glance

SEEING THE CITY

Honolulu is one of America's most scenic cities, with miles of ocean ending at a photogenic strip of white sand beach, giving way to a wide band of high-rise buildings before ending at the captivating Koolau Mountains. One of the best vantage points for an overview is the country road that spirals up 2,013-foot-high Mt. Tantalus, which offers sweeping views of Waikiki, Diamond Head, and downtown Honolulu. For another eye-popping view of the shoreline, take the outdoor glass elevator to the top of the *Ilikai* hotel (1777 Ala Moana Blvd.; phone: 949-3811). Equally spectacular views await *malihinis* (newcomers) at the *Hanohano Room* atop the *Sheraton Waikiki* (2255 Kalakaua Ave.; phone: 922-4422) and from *Nicholas Nickolas,* atop the *Ala Moana* hotel (410 Atkinson Dr.; phone: 955-4811). For another good perspective, visit the 10th-floor observatory in the *Aloha Tower,* with a panorama that stretches from the airport to Diamond Head (in the *Aloha Tower Marketplace* at the bottom of *Fort Street Mall*). The lookout from Punchbowl Crater offers another panoramic perspective of the city, all the way from downtown Honolulu to Waikiki.

SPECIAL PLACES

Although considerably overbuilt, Honolulu is nonetheless an interesting place to wander.

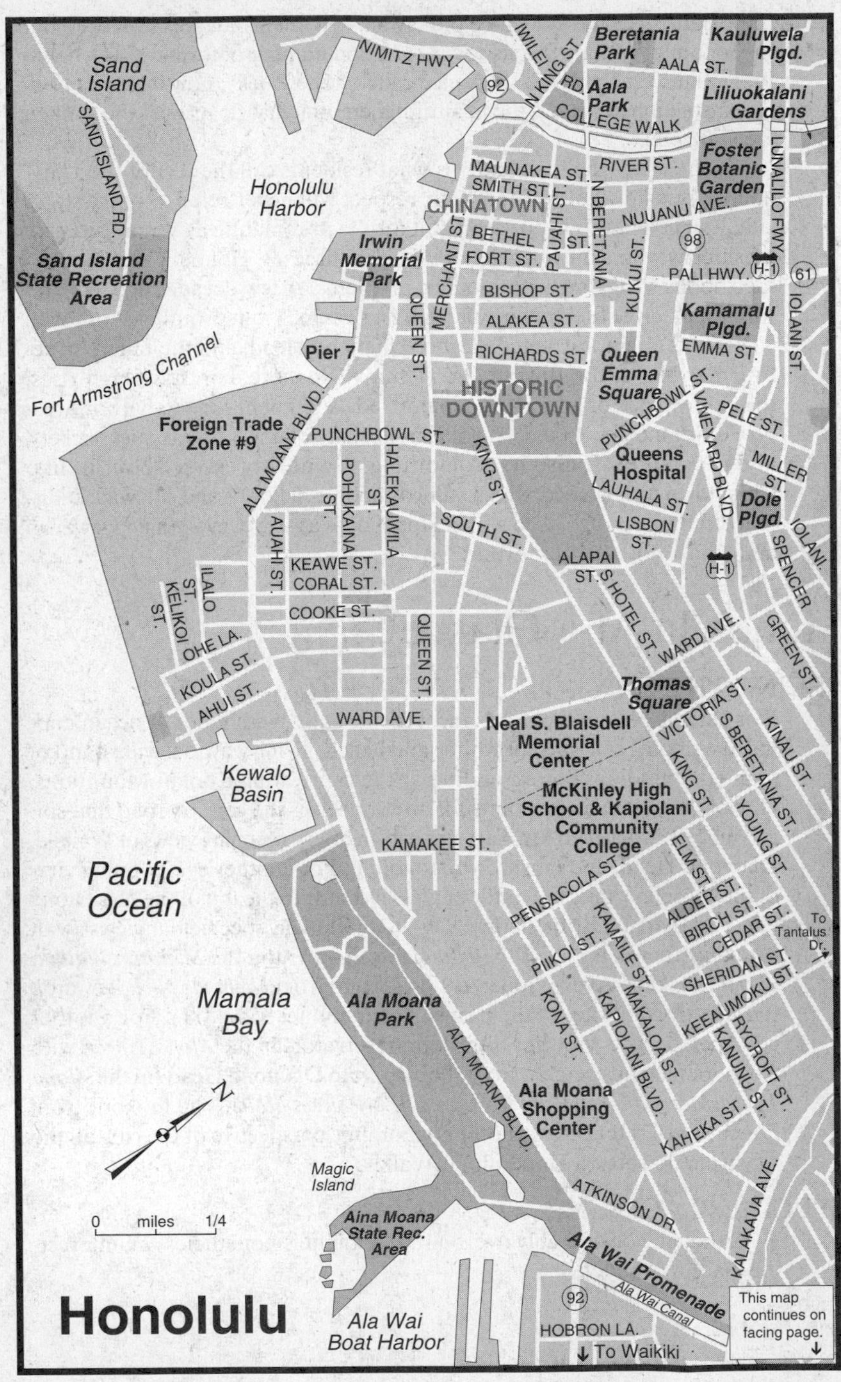
Honolulu
Sand Island
Sand Island Rd.
Sand Island State Recreation Area
Honolulu Harbor
Fort Armstrong Channel
Nimitz Hwy.
Iwilei Rd.
N King St.
Beretania Park
Kauluwela Plgd.
Aala St.
Aala Park
Liliuokalani Gardens
College Walk
River St.
Foster Botanic Garden
Lunalilo Fwy.
Maunakea St.
Smith St.
Chinatown
Pauahi St.
N Beretania St.
Nuuanu Ave.
Irwin Memorial Park
Bethel St.
Fort St.
Merchant St.
Queen St.
Kukui St.
Pali Hwy.
H-1
61
92
98
Iolani St.
Bishop St.
Alakea St.
Kamamalu Plgd.
Pier 7
Richards St.
Queen Emma Square
Emma St.
Historic Downtown
Punchbowl St.
Vineyard Blvd.
Pele St.
Foreign Trade Zone #9
Ala Moana Blvd.
Queens Hospital
Miller St.
Pohukaina St.
Halekauwila St.
King St.
Lauhala St.
Dole Plgd.
South St.
Lisbon St.
Iolani
Spencer
Auahi St.
Keawe St.
Coral St.
Alapai St.
S Hotel St.
Ilalo St.
Kelikoi St.
Cooke St.
Ohe La.
Ward Ave.
Green St.
Koula St.
Ahui St.
Thomas Square
Victoria St.
Neal S. Blaisdell Memorial Center
S Beretania St.
Kinau St.
Kewalo Basin
McKinley High School & Kapiolani Community College
Young St.
Kamakee St.
Elm St.
Pacific Ocean
Pensacola St.
Alder St.
Kamaile St.
Birch St.
Cedar St.
To Tantalus Dr.
Piikoi St.
Sheridan St.
Mamala Bay
Ala Moana Park
Kona St.
Kapiolani Blvd.
Makaloa St.
Keeaumoku St.
Rycroft St.
Kanunu St.
Ala Moana Shopping Center
Kaheka St.
N
Magic Island
Atkinson Dr.
Kalakaua Ave.
0 miles 1/4
Aina Moana State Rec. Area
Ala Wai Promenade
Ala Wai Canal
This map continues on facing page.
Ala Wai Boat Harbor
Hobron La.
To Waikiki

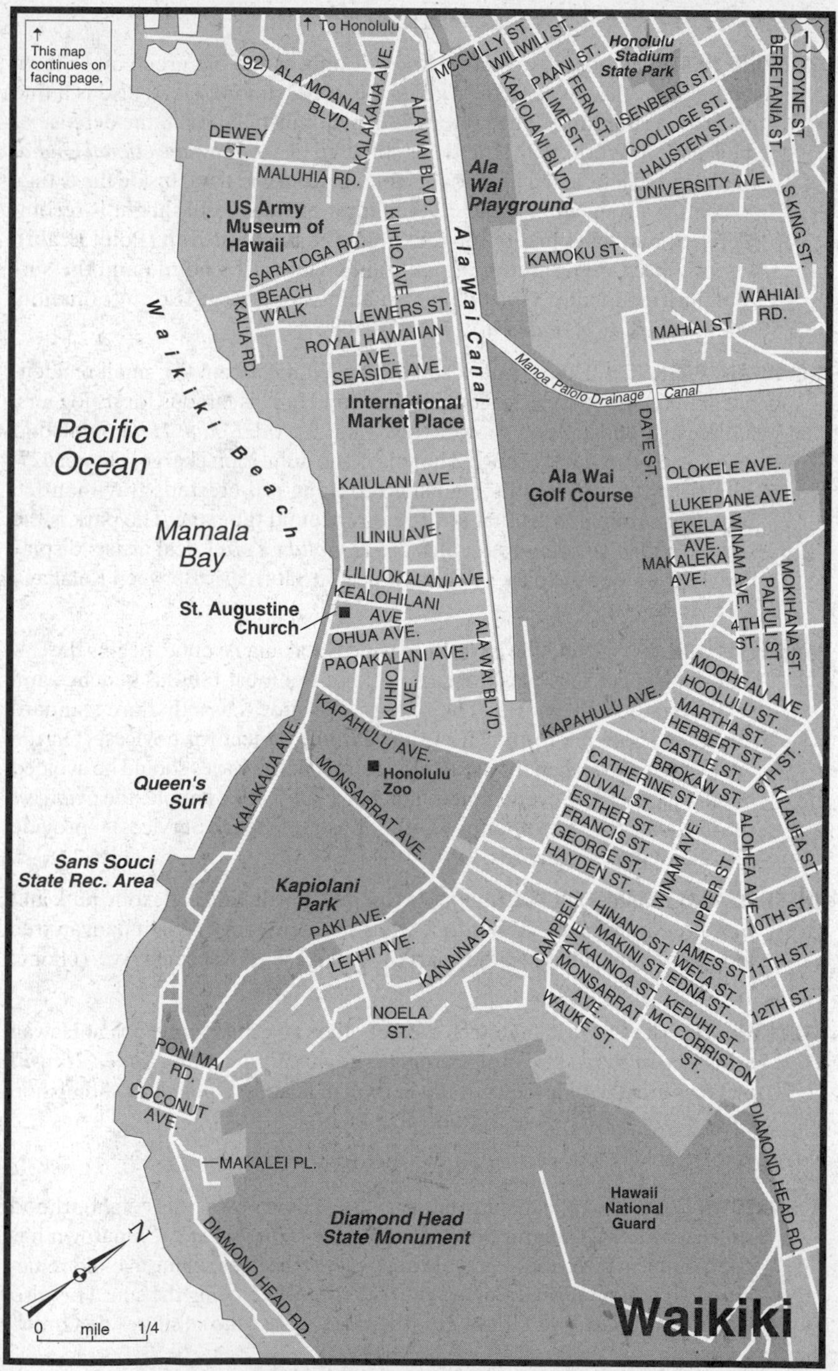

Waikiki
This map continues on facing page.
To Honolulu
Pacific Ocean
Mamala Bay
Waikiki Beach
Ala Wai Canal
Manoa Palolo Drainage Canal
US Army Museum of Hawaii
Ala Wai Playground
Honolulu Stadium State Park
International Market Place
Ala Wai Golf Course
St. Augustine Church
Honolulu Zoo
Queen's Surf
Sans Souci State Rec. Area
Kapiolani Park
Diamond Head State Monument
Hawaii National Guard
ALA MOANA BLVD.
KALAKAUA AVE.
ALA WAI BLVD.
MCCULLY ST.
WILIWILI ST.
PAANI ST.
KAPIOLANI BLVD.
LIME ST.
FERN ST.
ISENBERG ST.
COOLIDGE ST.
HAUSTEN ST.
UNIVERSITY AVE.
BERETANIA ST.
COYNE ST.
S KING ST.
DEWEY CT.
MALUHIA RD.
KUHIO AVE.
SARATOGA RD.
BEACH WALK
KALIA RD.
LEWERS ST.
ROYAL HAWAIIAN AVE.
SEASIDE AVE.
KAMOKU ST.
WAHIAI RD.
MAHIAI ST.
DATE ST.
OLOKELE AVE.
LUKEPANE AVE.
EKELA AVE.
MAKALEKA AVE.
WINAM AVE.
MOKIHANA ST.
PALIULI ST.
4TH ST.
KAIULANI AVE.
ILINIU AVE.
LILIUOKALANI AVE.
KEALOHILANI AVE
OHUA AVE.
PAOAKALANI AVE.
KAPAHULU AVE.
MOOHEAU AVE.
HOOLULU ST.
MARTHA ST.
HERBERT ST.
CASTLE ST.
BROKAW ST.
6TH ST.
KILAUEA ST.
CATHERINE ST.
DUVAL ST.
ESTHER ST.
FRANCIS ST.
GEORGE ST.
HAYDEN ST.
UPPER ST.
ALOHEA AVE.
10TH ST.
11TH ST.
12TH ST.
MONSARRAT AVE.
PAKI AVE.
LEAHI AVE.
KANAINA ST.
NOELA ST.
CAMPBELL AVE.
HINANO ST.
MAKINI ST.
KAUNOA ST.
JAMES ST.
WELA ST.
EDNA ST.
KEPUHI ST.
MC CORRISTON ST.
WAUKE ST.
PONI MAI RD.
COCONUT AVE.
MAKALEI PL.
DIAMOND HEAD RD.
92
1
N
0 mile 1/4

WAIKIKI

DIAMOND HEAD Though most visitors know it only as the big green and brown landmark at the east end of Waikiki Beach, Diamond Head also is a fine place for a short hike. The crater was a major installation in the defense of the Pacific in World War II, and it is still used by the *Hawaii National Guard.* Bunkers, shelters, and gun redoubts remain from war days. Inside the extinct volcano is a trail cut into the crater's interior walls (a flashlight is recommended) that takes hikers 760 feet up to the top of the rim (Point Leahi), where hikers are treated to a panoramic view of Honolulu and the surrounding mountains. Open daily. No admission charge. For information, call the *Division of State Parks* at 587-0300.

KAPIOLANI PARK This 220-acre park separating Waikiki from the small residential area on the southwest side of Diamond Head is famous for its joggers, hibiscus garden, golden shower trees, and for the *Kodak Hula Show* that takes place Tuesdays through Thursdays (no admission charge; phone: 627-3300). Try to spot the distinguished-looking red-crested, gray-mantled Brazilian cardinal birds that strut fussily around the park. The park is the site of the *Waikiki Aquarium* and the *Honolulu Zoo.* Local artists display their wares along the park's eastern fence on Saturdays. Between Kalakaua and Monsarrat Aves.

WAIKIKI BEACH Just outside the park, alongside Kalakaua Avenue, begins the 2½-mile-long curve of Waikiki Beach, one of the most famous beaches and surfing spots in the world. The two- to five-foot waves that are standard along the shoreline for much of the year are perfect for novices. (On the few summer days when they reach 15 feet, Waikiki's waves should be avoided by all but experts.) Several hotels along Waikiki—for example, the *Outrigger* (2335 Kalakaua Ave.; phone: 923-0711; ask for Beach Services)—provide instruction and surfboards.

INTERNATIONAL MARKETPLACE Shoppers can pick up all kinds of exotic junk and treasures at this maze of outdoor stalls situated under a giant banyan tree festooned with lanterns in the heart of Waikiki. 2330 Kalakaua Ave. (phone: 923-9871).

IMAX THEATER The 414-seat, high-tech theater offers an exhilarating look at Hawaii on a screen that's five stories high. The 40-minute film *Hidden Hawaii* includes breathtaking views of the Hawaiian Islands. Open daily. Admission charge. 325 Seaside Ave. (phone: 923-4629).

DOWNTOWN

CHINATOWN Located on the westernmost fringe of downtown, this neighborhood spills across the Nuuanu Stream into *Aala Triangle Park.* Chinatown has open-air meat, fish, and vegetable markets; herb shops selling age-old remedies; and senior citizens playing checkers or just enjoying the sun. This also is the "sin" quarter of Honolulu, where sleazy sex shows sit beside family-style chop suey houses. A gentrification program is under way, however, bringing new shops and galleries into renovated turn-of-the-century buildings. A walking tour of Chinatown with an optional lunch (a real bargain) takes place on Tuesday mornings, starting from the *Chinese Chamber of Commerce* (42 N. King St.; phone: 533-3181).

MAUNAKEA MARKETPLACE At the core of the neighborhood, the marketplace serves as a commercial centerpiece for Chinatown's ongoing renewal. The use of Chinese architectural detail is particularly beautiful. The central courtyard is filled with vendors, shops, restaurants, and food stalls that offer a variety of Asian delicacies. Maunakea and Pauahi Sts.

ALOHA TOWER MARKETPLACE Overlooking Honolulu Harbor, the restored *Aloha Tower* (ca. 1927) now is the centerpiece of a harborside redevelopment that includes shops, restaurants, bars, a museum, cruise ship piers, and a lookout. The tower's 10th-floor observatory is one of the best places to get a perspective of the city from the airport to Diamond Head; it's open until 9 PM on weekdays, 10 PM on weekends. One curious sight is the reflection of Honolulu Harbor in the green glass towers of the Grosvenor Center. The effect is that of a vast Japanese mural, rich with stylized mountains, clouds, seascapes, boats, and cranes (the mechanical kind in this case). There are music and dance performances here Tuesdays through Saturdays, and boat tours of Honolulu Harbor are available. Across from Bishop St., off Nimitz Hwy. (phone: 528-5700).

HAWAII MARITIME CENTER The four-masted square-rigger known as the *Falls of Clyde,* and the voyaging canoe *Hokulea,* both riding at anchor at Pier 7, provide a distinctive look at two aspects of Hawaii's maritime past. The captain's quarters of the *Falls of Clyde* are a nautical masterpiece of teak, birch, and mahogany fittings and furnishings, all set off by an abundance of red velvet upholstery. In contrast, visitors also see the cramped crew's quarters typical of 19th-century shipboard life. The *Hokulea* may not be boarded, but it is berthed to permit viewing from three sides. This now famous voyaging canoe has been used on several occasions to journey among the islands of Polynesia by means of stellar navigation, in order to study the migration routes used by the earliest Hawaiians. The museum itself features a comprehensive look at maritime Hawaii with films, innovative displays, and some hands-on exhibits designed especially for children. There is also an archive, a library, and a gift shop. Open daily. Admission charge. At Pier 7, adjacent to *Aloha Tower Marketplace* and off Ala Moana Blvd. (phone: 536-6373).

MISSION HOUSES MUSEUM This museum complex contains the earliest American buildings in Hawaii. The three frame houses, shipped around Cape Horn in pieces and then reassembled in 1821 by the first missionaries, used to be a school and a minister's home, as well as a mission. They contain furniture and artifacts more reminiscent of New England than Hawaii, as well as a rare archive of the islands' history. The *Printing House* next door, built from coral blocks in 1831, contains a replica of the old-fashioned Ramage handpress used by the printer, Elisha Loomis, to produce a Hawaiian translation of the Bible, schoolbooks, and hymnals. One day each month, the *Living History* program populates the mission grounds with volunteers dressed in 19th-century garb. Walking tours of historic Honolulu leave the museum on Fridays at 9:30 AM. Museum tours are offered Tuesdays through Saturdays. Admission charge. 553 S. King St. (phone: 531-0481).

KAWAIAHAO CHURCH This house of worship likes to think of itself as the *Westminster Abbey* of Hawaii, and indeed, some members of the old Hawaiian families who have retained their Congregational faith do occasionally use the church for baptisms, marriages, and funerals. King Lunalilo is buried near the entrance to the church. The oldest church in Honolulu, it was built in 1820 on the site of Hawaii's first mission established by Reverend Hiram Bingham and his colleagues, which was previously a thatch-roofed hut standing close to an ancient and sacred *hao* (spring). Tall *kahilis* (feather-decorated staffs symbolic of royalty) at the *alii*'s altar testify to its distinguished past. It was here that King Kamehameha III used the expression *Ua mau ke ea o ka aina i ka pono* ("The life of the land is perpetuated in righteousness"), which is now the state motto. For anyone who yearns to hear a church service with Hawaiian hymns, this is the place (the one at 10:30 AM on Sunday is best). 957 Punchbowl St. (phone: 522-1333).

IOLANI PALACE This neo-Florentine edifice, with its stone verandahs and Corinthian columns, is the only former royal palace in the United States. Highly revered by historians and sentimentalists alike, the palace was the residence of monarch and songwriter Queen Liliuokalani. (In fact, she wrote some of her famous songs, including *Aloha Oe,* while imprisoned here in 1895.) It was completed by King David Kalakaua in 1882 and cost over $350,000—a king's ransom at the time. In 1883, he placed a crown on his own head in what is now *Coronation Bandstand,* where, every Friday from 12:15 until 1:15 PM, the *Royal Hawaiian Band* gives free, informal concerts. Palace tours are given every 15 minutes, Wednesdays through Saturdays. Admission charge; children under five years old are not admitted. King and Richards Sts. (phone: 538-1471 for recorded information; 522-0832 for reservations).

STATE CAPITOL The capitol takes its inspiration from the natural history of the islands. It was built in 1969, treated to a multimillion dollar face-lift in the early 1990s, and all of its features—columns, reflecting pools, courtyard—reflect aspects of Hawaii's environment. Outside the capitol stands a beautiful bronze statue of Queen Liliuokalani and the controversial modern statue of Father Damien, founder of the leprosy settlement at Kalaupapa on the island of Molokai. Open daily. No admission charge. 415 S. Beretania St. (phone: 586-0222).

GREATER HONOLULU

ARIZONA MEMORIAL/PEARL HARBOR The *Arizona Memorial,* set in the blue-green water off the tip of Ford Island in Pearl Harbor, is a perfect example of what a tribute to those who died in the service of their country should be: simple, graceful, and intensely moving. The memorial, a 184-foot-long covered white concrete bridge, spans the battleship USS *Arizona,* which was bombed and sank during the Japanese attack on the morning of December 7, 1941. The bridge sags slightly in the middle to represent initial defeat, but is firm and solid at both ends to signify ultimate victory. Buoys mark the bow and stern of the sunken hull, which lies beneath the memorial, entombing the 1,102 servicemen who were aboard the ship when Japanese planes attacked the base. Parts of the battleship's superstructure, eroded by seawater and barnacles, still appear above the waterline.

US Navy pilots operate the short boat trip to the memorial from the *Arizona Memorial Visitors' Center,* which is operated by National Park rangers. Only passengers of the *US Navy* boats are allowed to disembark at the memorial. Within the *Visitors Center* is a bookshop selling souvenirs, among them model kits of the *Arizona* and copies of the front page of the *Honolulu Star-Bulletin* reporting the invasion. Open daily, with 1½ hour-long tours given—first come, first served—between 8 AM and 3 PM. As it is Hawaii's most popular tourist attraction, a wait of one hour or longer for tours to the memorial is not uncommon. The *Arizona Memorial Visitors' Center* is at Arizona Memorial Dr. (phone: 422-0561).

FOSTER BOTANICAL GARDENS Some 20 acres of exotic plants and trees can be found in this arboreal enclave, one of six sites across the island that make up the *Honolulu Botanical Gardens.* The warm, humid climate of downtown Honolulu favors the growth of orchids, and varieties of this exotic plant from both the Old and the New World are cultivated in the popular *Lyn Orchid Garden.* A fascinating glimpse of the earth's past can be experienced in the *Prehistoric Glen,* dwelling place of primitive plants that thrived in the Coal Age. Another inhabitant of the garden is the Indian mongoose, discovered now and again peering from a rock. Guided tours are available at 1 PM on weekdays with reservations. Open daily. Admission charge. 50 N. Vineyard Blvd. (phone: 522-7065).

HONOLULU ACADEMY OF ARTS Across Thomas Square from *Blaisdell Center,* this museum has celebrated Asian art and both prominent and alternative European and American works. Interesting items include a Japanese ink and color handscroll dating to 1250, John Singleton Copley's *Portrait of Nathaniel Allen,* and Segna di Bonaventura's *Madonna and Child.* Lunch is served in the museum garden Tuesdays through Saturdays. Reservations necessary. Closed Mondays. Admission charge. 900 S. Beretania St. (phone: 532-8700).

PUNCHBOWL (THE NATIONAL MEMORIAL CEMETERY OF THE PACIFIC) The ancient Hawaiians called this crater Puowaina, the Hill of Sacrifice, and the name rings true today. More than 38,000 American servicemen and servicewomen (among them 22 recipients of the Medal of Honor) are buried here. In addition, more than 26,000 names of servicemen missing in action are listed on marble walls called the *Court of the Missing.* Every day, but especially on Sundays, visitors and islanders come with leis and small bunches of flowers or blossoms to place against individual graves. Services are held here on *Memorial Day* and *Veterans' Day,* and there's an especially moving and popular service at dawn on *Easter Sunday,* when people by the thousands show up to honor the dead. 2177 Puowaina Dr. (phone: 566-1430).

QUEEN EMMA SUMMER PALACE This royal retreat in the cool highlands of Nuuanu Valley was the summer home of Kamehameha IV and Queen Emma, inherited from the queen's aunt and uncle. Built between 1847 and 1850, the simple building has Doric columns and a roof that overhangs a broad lanai (verandah). It was rescued from wreckers by the *Daughters of Hawaii,* and the civic group has operated it as a museum since 1915. Both furnishings and personal memorabilia are on display, including a Gothic-design cabinet, a gift of Queen Victoria's consort, Prince Albert; a stereopticon presented to the queen by Napoleon III; and a necklace hung with tiger claws decorated with seed pearls embedded in rolled gold. Queen Emma's only son, Albert, died when he was four years old. The simple red jacket and brass megaphone given to the infant prince when he was made an honorary member of the *Honolulu Volunteer Fire Department* hangs in his mother's bedroom. Open daily. Admission charge. 2913 Pali Hwy. (phone: 595-3167).

ROYAL MAUSOLEUM Considered the most sacred burial ground in the islands, this three-acre site serves as the resting place for the monarchs King Kamehameha II through V, Queen Emma, King Kalakaua, and Queen Liliuokalani. (Not buried here are King Kamehameha I, who died on the Big Island and whose remains were never found, and King Lunalilo, who requested a private burial crypt adjacent to *Kawaiahao Church.*) The Gothic-style rock and limestone mausoleum initially was planned by Kamehameha IV and Queen Emma following the death of their son in 1862. Construction, however, did not start until after the king died in 1863. Upon the completion in 1865 of the permanent mausoleum overlooking the beautiful Nuuanu Valley, the remains of the monarchs formerly interred in the *Iolani Palace* were transferred here. Open weekdays. No admission charge. 2261 Nuuanu Ave. (phone: 536-7602).

USS BOWFIN SUBMARINE AND MUSEUM Adjacent to the *Arizona Memorial Visitors Center,* the *Bowfin* provides a firsthand glimpse of the confining reality and technological innocence of World War II submarines. Submarine-related artifacts are displayed in the museum. Open daily. Admission charge. 11 Arizona Memorial Pl. (phone: 423-1341).

EXTRA SPECIAL

Honolulu is the great jumping-off point for island-hopping expeditions. Kauai, the oldest island, is known for golf at the *Princeville* and *Poipu* resort courses, and the spectacular beauty of Waimea Canyon and the Na Pali Coast. Maui has valleys, waterfalls, beaches, and the crater of the dormant Haleakala Volcano. The small *Kapalua/West Maui Airport* offers direct flights to Lahaina, Kaanapali, Kahana, Napili, and Kapalua resorts. Hawaii, also called the Big Island, is the home of Mauna Loa and Kilauea, two of the world's most active volcanoes, as well as some of Hawaii's premier archaeological sites, including *Puuhonua O Honaunau* and *Puukohola Heiau.* All of the other major islands would fit inside 4,038-square-mile Hawaii, and the unique island is home to 21 of the earth's 22 climate zones. On Lanai, only 17 miles long, the main draws are two resort hotels and a sense of away-from-it-all isolation. Molokai, 37 miles long, a relatively untouched ranchers' island, offers tourists the opportunity to see a rural side of Hawaii, or visit the isolated lepers' settlement at *Kalaupapa,* the home of less than 70 victims of Hansen's disease who voluntarily remain at the site to which they were banished more than a century ago. There is also a resort at Kaluakoi and several small condos and hotels along the east coast for those who wish to stay awhile. For information about flights to these islands from Honolulu, see *Getting Around* below.

Sources and Resources

TOURIST INFORMATION

The *Hawaii Visitors Bureau* (2270 Kalakaua Ave., Room 801, Honolulu, HI 96815; phone: 923-1811) has a large number of illustrated guides, brochures, maps, and leaflets for all the islands, including materials distributed by member hotels and tour guide operators. These can be mailed to the mainland on request. The office is closed on weekends.

LOCAL COVERAGE The *Honolulu Advertiser,* a morning daily; the *Honolulu Star-Bulletin,* an afternoon daily, are major newspapers that cover world, national, and local events. *Honolulu* (monthly); *Aloha* (bimonthly); and *Hawaii* (monthly) are magazines that also publish calendars of events. Free visitor publications such as *Guide to Oahu, This Week,* and *Spotlight Oahu Gold* are available in hotel lobbies. At car rental counters you can pick up the *Oahu Drive Guide,* designed for the motorist but with useful information for the tourist on foot as well. In addition, they sometimes contain discount coupons. We immodestly suggest visitors pick up a copy of *Birnbaum's Hawaii 1997* (HarperCollins; $18) as well.

TELEVISION STATIONS KHON Channel 2–FOX; KITV Channel 4–ABC; KGMB Channel 9–CBS; KHET Channels 10 & 11–PBS; and KHNL Channel 13–NBC.

RADIO STATIONS AM: KHNR 650 (CNN news); KSSK 590 (oldies and contemporary); KHVH 830 (news and talk); KCCN 1420 (contemporary Hawaiian). FM: KHPR 88.1 (Hawaii Public Radio, classical); KUMU 94.7 (easy listening); KQMQ 93.1 (soft rock); KPOI 97.5 (rock); KKLV 98.5 (classic rock); and KINE 105.1 (contemporary Hawaiian).

TELEPHONE The area code for Honolulu is 808.

SALES TAX There is a 4% sales tax; the hotel room tax is 6%.

CLIMATE In ancient times, the Hawaiians had no word for weather. They did, however, have words for two seasons—winter and summer. Winter, which runs from about October through April, means daytime highs reaching the mid-70s and low 80s F, dropping into the low 60s at night with brief rain showers common. Daylight lasts for about 11 hours. Summer temperatures hover in the mid-to upper-80s with occasional forays into the low 90s; rain is less frequent, and daylight stretches to 13 hours.

GETTING AROUND

AIRPORT While most of the other islands have at least two airports to service them, Oahu has only one—*Honolulu International Airport.* The largest in the state, it handles all international flights to Hawaii, and most of those from the mainland. Travelers can make connections to the Neighbor Islands—Hawaii, Kauai, Lanai, Maui, and Molokai—at the inter-island terminal or the adjacent commuter terminal. *Hawaiian Airlines* (phone: 838-1555; 800-367-5320) and *Aloha Airlines* (phone: 484-1111; 800-367-5250) both fly to Kaluhui on Maui, Lihue on Kauai, and both Kona and Hilo on the Big Island from Honolulu, with scheduled jet service throughout the day. Flights range from 20 to 35 minutes. In addition, *Hawaiian Airlines* offers jet service to Molokai and Lanai. Commuter carrier *Island Air* (phone: 484-2222; 800-323-3345) offers 18- and 37-passenger prop service to Lanai and Molokai, as well as service to the *Kapalua-West Maui Airport* on Maui and the *Princeville Airport* on Kauai. *Mahalo Air* (phone: 833-5555; 800-462-4256) serves Molokai, Kahului on Maui, Kona on the Big Island and Lihue, Kauai.

Honolulu International is about 6 miles from downtown Honolulu, and nearly 10 miles from Waikiki. Rental cars, taxis, and shuttle buses to all parts of the island are available from both terminals. *Honolulu International Airport* is about a 20- to 25-minute drive from Waikiki (in moderate traffic), slightly less from the downtown area. *Trans Hawaiian Services* (phone: 566-7333) provides van shuttle service for $7 ($12 round trip) from the airport to Waikiki. Vans leave every 20 minutes. Reserve at least 24 hours ahead for the return trip.

BUS *TheBus,* as the municipal transit line is called, is the least expensive way to get around Honolulu. Whether you go one stop or 80 miles around the island, it costs a dollar, which must be paid with exact change. Route maps are available at most hotels, *Ala Moana Center,* and the *Honolulu Department of Transportion, Oahu Transit Services* (*OTS;* 811 Middle St.; phone: 848-5555).

CAR RENTAL All of the major car rental companies have offices at the airport and in Waikiki. In addition, there are *Classic Car Rentals* (2139 Kuhio Ave., Waikiki; phone: 923-6446), which has a vintage fleet that includes a '64 Corvette Stingray, an '88 Porsche 911 and a '28 Roadster; *Courtesy Car and Truck Rental* (3147 N. Nimitz Hwy., Waikiki; phone: 831-2277), one of the few places in town that rents pickup trucks in addition to low-cost economy cars; and *Ferrari Rentals* (1897 Kalakaua Ave. in Waikiki; phone: 942-8725), which features everything from Geo Trackers at $55 a day to $1,300-a-day Lamborghinis as well as the eponymous Italian sports cars. Most of these firms serve four or five islands, and multi-island rates are offered.

MOPED/MOTORCYCLE This is a breezy way to see the island or just to cruise around Waikiki and the southeast for those with the requisite license. Be careful: Pickup truck drivers on the Waianae Coast tend to look askance at riders of these motorized "toys," and driving them on newly wet surfaces can be tricky. *Aloha Funway Rentals* is the best-known motorcycle/moped rental outfit in Waikiki (1778 Ala Moana Blvd.; phone: 926-2277), with mounts ranging from lightweight scooters ($50) to an imposing Harley-Davidson low rider ($149).

TAXI Although taxis sometimes can be hailed on the street, most are on call. To be sure of getting a cab, call for one. Some reliable companies are *State Independent Drivers Association (SIDA;* phone: 836-0011); *Charley's* (phone: 955-2211), which will go to any point on the island from the airport or drive luxury seekers around the island in a Cadillac Fleetwood for about $65 an hour, with a two-hour minimum; and *Aloha State Taxi* (phone: 847-3566), which serves the whole island and is especially popular with military personnel. *Handicabs* (phone: 524-3866) specializes in transport for disabled people and operates vehicles that will accommodate wheelchair-bound passengers (the fare is $2.25 per mile). It's best to reserve a day in advance—and weekends must be scheduled by Friday afternoons.

TROLLEY *Waikiki Trolley* (phone: 591-2561) has launched a fleet of motorized, open-air reproductions of the horse-drawn trolleys that operated at the turn of the century. They provide tour and point-to-point service between Waikiki and such shopping and cultural attractions as the *Bishop Museum, Dole Cannery Square, Ala Moana Center,* Chinatown, and *Aloha Tower Marketplace.* The trolleys run daily; all-day passes are $15 ($5 for children 12 years and under). *The Aloha Tower Express Trolley* (phone: 528-5700) runs between the *Aloha Tower Marketplace* and Waikiki every half hour between 9 AM and 2 AM daily; the cost is $2 each way.

SIGHTSEEING TOURS

HELICOPTER/PLANE *Rainbow Pacific Helicopters* (phone: 971-4900) has been flying 2- and 3-passenger Robinson R22s and R44s since 1992. Highlights are a 15-minute Diamond Head excursion and an hourlong jaunt to Sacred Falls. *Makani Kai Helicopters* (phone: 834-5813) offers 20- to 60-minute helicopter charter tours, as well as night flights from *Honolulu Airport. Original Glider Ride* (phone: 677-3404) features two-passenger gliders that soar over the scenic coastline and foothills of the Waianae Mountains. *Original Glider* also offers open-cockpit rides in a vintage biplane (reservations are recommended).

SPECIAL EVENTS

The *Hula Bowl* takes place during the third week of January at *Aloha Stadium* on the edge of Honolulu, and features all-stars from mainland college teams. The *Chinese New Year,* held between mid-January and late February, is celebrated with traditional lion dances, drums, and firecrackers, in Chinatown and downtown Honolulu. The Irish and would-be Irish celebrate with the wearing of the green and traditional (and not so traditional) varieties of good cheer along Kalakaua Avenue in Waikiki on *St. Patrick's Day* (March 17). A sunrise service is held each year at the *Punchbowl National Memorial Cemetery of the Pacific* on *Easter* morning.

On May 1, a *Lei Day* queen is crowned at the *Waikiki Bandstand* in *Kapiolani Park,* where there is also a lei making contest and, at sunset, an annual music concert. The *50th State Fair* takes place on weekends from late May to mid-June; it features foods, crafts, and entertainment, and is held in the *Aloha Stadium.* The spectacular *Kamehameha Day Parade* is held in downtown Honolulu on the Saturday preceding the king's June 11 birthday. The statue of King Kamehameha the Great that stands opposite the Judiciary Building in downtown Honolulu is festooned with 40-foot leis for the occasion. The Hawaii *State Farm Fair,* held in late June or early July in Honolulu, offers arts and crafts, and a chance to mingle with locals. July also brings the week-long *Festival of the Pacific,* highlighting the songs, dances, arts and crafts, and competitive sports of more than 40 Pacific Rim nations.

The *Honolulu Symphony Orchestra* begins its season at the *Neal S. Blaisdell Center* (777 Ward Ave., Honolulu; phone: 521-2911) in mid-September, with performances running through late April. Internationally renowned soloists often perform. In late September and early October *Aloha Week,* a large-scale, one-of-a-kind celebration, includes a Waikiki floral parade, as well as balls and luaus across the islands. The *Honolulu Orchid Society Show,* held in October at the *Neal S. Blaisdell Center* (see above), features lei making and flower arranging demonstrations as well as stunning floral displays. *Oktoberfest* activities (the best is dubbed "Rocktoberfest" and held on Restaurant Row in downtown Honolulu) abound at the end of the month. In November, free films are offered as part of Honolulu's annual *Hawaii*

International Film Festival. The *Honolulu Marathon* is held in mid-December, with competitors running a 26-mile course from *Aloha Tower* to Hawaii Kai, before returning to the *Kapiolani Park* finish line. *Pearl Harbor Day*, December 7, is commemorated with a service at the *Arizona Memorial.* It is especially moving to see veterans of the attack (along with curious Japanese tourists), who still make the pilgrimage here each December, some from as far away as New England and Florida. Also during early December check out the *Mission Houses Museum's Christmas Fair* and the *Pacific Handcrafters Guild Christmas Fair* in Honolulu's Thomas Square for excellent *raku* pottery, hand-painted fashions, and Hawaiian crafts such as leis, carved woods, and musical gourds. For a very special *Christmas* experience, go to the *Christmas Eve* midnight service at *Kawaiahao Church* (957 Punchbowl St., Honolulu), where carols are sung in Hawaiian. On *New Year's Eve* visitors can rub elbows with locals at the *First Night* street fair in downtown Honolulu, which is held on December 31 from late afternoon through midnight. For more information on these and other events, contact the *Hawaii Visitors Bureau* (phone: 923-1811).

MUSEUMS

In addition to those described in *Special Places,* there are other museums of note.

DAMIEN MUSEUM This museum is dedicated to Father Damien de Veuster, the Belgian priest who worked with the lepers at Kalaupapa on Molokai for 16 years, contracting leprosy himself before he died. On display are his mementos and personal papers. Closed weekends. No admission charge. 130 Ohua Ave. (phone: 923-2690)

PACIFIC AEROSPACE MUSEUM This $1.75-million, high-tech museum traces the history of Pacific exploration from the celestial navigation of the ancient Polynesians to the study of space. There are two flight simulators, a *NASA* space shuttle flight deck, recorded voices of famous aviators, and a mission control exhibit that simulates space launches. At the *Great Skyquest Theater,* a three-dimensional multimedia production re-creates the glory days of such aviators as Amelia Earhart, Charles Kingford-Smith, and US Navy Commander John Rodgers. Open daily. Admission charge. Central Waiting Lobby, *Honolulu International Airport* (phone: 839-0777).

US ARMY MUSEUM OF HAWAII Weapons used by ancient Hawaiians, Japanese soldiers, and US troops are on display here. In addition, there are uniforms worn by US and enemy forces. The most fascinating items are Hawaiian weapons made from shark's teeth and the newspaper accounts of the US involvement in World War II following the invasion of Pearl Harbor. Closed Mondays. No admission charge. Kalia at Saratoga Rds. (phone: 438-2821).

SHOPPING

Those who can drag themselves away from the beach long enough will discover that Honolulu is a tropical shopping heaven—not so much for bargains, but for the incredible diversity of wares that stream into this Pacific capital from Asia, Europe, and the US mainland, as well as from the other South Pacific and Hawaiian islands. With some exceptions, the Honolulu shopping scene is centered around its malls; some have an architectural or commercial theme, usually Asian or Hawaiian, and a few are outdoors. The emphasis is on designer goods; alohawear and other resort clothing; vacation sundries such as lotions, beach towels, and mats; and Polynesian handicrafts. Mixed in are boutiques that carry such famous international names as *Chanel* and *Gucci,* as well as high-fashion sportswear. Most shopping malls are open daily from 10 AM to 9 PM; Sundays until 5 PM, but Waikiki malls have longer hours, usually 9 AM to 11 PM daily.

Shopping Centers

Ala Moana Center The Pacific's major retail outlet attracts 56 million customers a year to 200-plus shops. Large department stores—*Liberty House* (phone: 941-2345), *Shirokiya* (phone: 973-9111), *Sears* (phone: 947-0211)—as well as many European designer boutiques, mainland specialty stores including *Tiffany's* (phone: 943-6677) and *Cartier* (phone: 955-5533), and such local favorites as *Honolulu Book Shop* (phone: 941-2274) are anchored here. 1450 Ala Moana Blvd., opposite *Ala Moana Park* (phone: 946-2811).

Hyatt Regency Waikiki The first three floors of the *Hyatt* complex are dominated by more than 70 shops. 2424 Kalakaua Ave. (phone: 923-1234).

International Marketplace This outdoor market is a bustling, noisy bazaar of shops and booths (see *Special Places*). 2330 Kalakaua Ave. (phone: 923-9871).

Kahala Mall This 84-shop mall, a smaller and less crowded alternative to *Ala Moana Center,* is located in an exclusive neighborhood east of Waikiki. There's also an eight-plex movie theater. 4211 Waialae Ave. (phone: 732-7736).

Kilohana Square Located about a mile from Waikiki's eastern border, this small complex includes Western and Asian antiques shops, art galleries, and specialty stores. 1016 Kapahulu Ave. (no phone).

King's Village This pastel complex of quaint townhouse-style buildings and cobblestone walkways, located behind and across the street from the *Hyatt Regency Waikiki*, offers more than 40 shops, including a branch of the popular sportswear shop *Hawaiian Island Creations* (phone: 971-6715). It is designed to resemble urban Honolulu in the days of the 19th-century monarchs, complete with a changing-of-the-guard ceremony daily at 6:15 PM—although the *Rose and Crown Pub* (phone: 923-5833), with its horse brasses, etched-glass mirrors, and timber beams, manages to be a fair replica of an English country pub. 131 Kaiulani Ave. (no phone).

Rainbow Bazaar Some 30 boutiques sell ethnic handicrafts, jewelry, resortwear, and objets d'art. Elegant gift shops including *Golden Boutique* (phone: 946-4000) and *Elephant Walk* (phone: 946-7380) are worth a browse. At the *Hilton Hawaiian Village*, 2005 Kalia Rd. (phone: 949-4321).

Royal Hawaiian Shopping Center This ultramodern, four-story, three-block-long, six-acre arcade of boutiques and restaurants is touristy, but worth exploring. Here, European and American boutiques, including *Cartier* (phone: 922-7555), *Van Cleef & Arpels* (phone: 923-5889) , *Hermès* (phone: 922-5700), and *Chanel* (phone:923-0255), stand side by side with shops selling Chinese art, beach and sportswear, jewelry, candy, and shave ice, as well as restaurants and the ubiquitous souvenir shops. *The Little Hawaiian Craft Shop* (phone: 926-2662) has a superlative collection of carved-wood objects and museum-quality reproductions of Hawaiian sculpture, as well as crafts made of nuts, gourds, and shells. 2201 Kalakaua Ave. (phone: 922-0588).

Waikiki Shopping Plaza The merchandise in this complex has to compete with a five-story water display that is part fountain and part Plexiglas sculpture. There are a few shops of interest including *Waldenbooks* (phone: 922-4154), as well as nine Asian restaurants on the upper floors. 2250 Kalakaua Ave. (phone: 923-1191).

Ward Centre On Ala Moana Boulevard, across the street from *Ward Warehouse* and *Ala Moana Beach Park,* this low-key mall has a selection of upscale shops and art galleries as well as some popular eateries and the best book store in town, *Borders Books and Music* (phone: 591-8995). 1200 Ala Moana Blvd. (phone: 591-8411).

Ward Warehouse This two-story complex of 71 boutiques and restaurants opposite the *Kewalo Boat Basin* includes *Kamuela Hat Shop* (phone 596-4612) and *Nohea Gallery* (phone: 596-0074). The former features local-style hats, the latter, Hawaiian art and crafts. 1050 Ala Moana Blvd. (phone: 591-8411).

Specialty and Discount Shops

WAIKIKI

Alfred Dunhill The who-can-afford-it prices of this shop, located in the Moana wing of the *Sheraton Moana Surfrider* hotel, are as awesome as the jewelry, leather goods, cigars, and accessories that carry the Dunhill imprint (phone: 971-2020).

Betty's Imports Real bargains can be found here on all kinds of costume jewelry and imported bric-a-brac, often at prices 30% to 50% lower than at other shops. In the *Outrigger Waikiki Surf West,* 412 Lewers St. (phone: 922-3010).

Chanel Here is every Chanel item imaginable at prices that match a Paris boutique. Accessories, perfumes, jewelry, and more. *Ala Moana Center* (phone: 942-5555), 1450 Ala Moana Blvd.

Cotton Cargo This shop offers a refreshing change from alohawear, featuring 100% cotton fashions for women. The clothes have style; most are imported from India, Bali, Turkey, Greece, or Central America. *Ward Warehouse* (phone: 593-2215), 1050 Ala Moana Blvd.

Down Under Honolulu This happens to be one of the best sources for men's swimwear in Hawaii, with designer labels as well as merchandise designed in-house. Everything from nearly revealing to very revealing is here, plus a fine selection of generic shorts, athletic attire and T-shirts. 2139 Kuhio Ave. (phone: 922-9229).

Endangered Species Endangered animals are safely "captured" in art forms—from sculpture to dolls, coffee mugs to T-shirts. 2335 Kalakaua Ave. (phone: 922-6293).

Helen & Suzanne The store carries a unique selection of all that glitters—earrings, belts, pins, necklaces, and bags. At the *Royal Hawaiian* Hotel (phone: 923-7727).

McInerny Galleria This is one of the best places in town for designer clothing for men and women. Some of the labels include Giorgio Armani and Ferragamo. At the *Royal Hawaiian* (phone: 971-4200).

Sawada Golf Everyone can fill all their golf needs at this popular and centrally located duffer's paradise. *Waikiki Shopping Plaza,* 2250 Kalakaua Ave. (phone: 923-0144).

Van Brugge House Designer labels from Australia are found here, as well as a cache of that country's pink, champagne, and cognac colored diamonds. *Royal Hawaiian Shopping Center,* 2201 Kalakaua Ave. (phone: 971-6678).

Wyland Gallery The paintings, sculptures, and multimedia artwork here all share a marine theme created by owner-artist Wyland, and his talented stable of artists. *Hyatt Regency Waikiki,* 2424 Kalakaua Ave. (phone: 924-3133).

Yokohama-Okadaya An international gift shop, it has a fine collection of designer leather goods (phone: 922-5731). Outlets are located in the *Royal Hawaiian Shopping Center; Waikiki Shopping Plaza; Sheraton Waikiki; Princess Kaiulani; and the Hyatt Regency Waikiki.*

DIAMOND HEAD

Apropos The women's clothes available here exhibit European flair. *Kahala Mall,* 4211 Waialae Ave. (phone: 735-1611).

Carriage House The focus at this store is European, Oriental, and American antiques. *Kilohana Square*, 1016 Kapahulu Ave. (phone: 737-2622).

Juma Upscale womenswear is the rage here; the sportswear is well made, if a bit style-conscious. *Kahala Mall*, 4211 Waialae Ave. (phone: 739-5305).

Max Davis High-quality Oriental antiques, art, accessories, and furnishings are the stock-in-trade at this 22-year-old enclave. *Kilohana Square*, 1016 Kapahulu Ave. (phone: 735-2341).

Needlepoint, Etc. This shop sells kits and patterns with tropical flowers and other Hawaii motifs. *Kilohana Square*, 1016 Kapahulu Ave. (phone: 737-3944).

Quilts Hawaii Collectible Hawaiian quilts come in traditional as well as contemporary designs and the shop also carries furniture, jewelry, and other Hawaiiana. 2338 S. King St. (phone: 942-3195).

Vue Hawaii The artwork, clothing, and koa wood items here are created locally. *Kilohana Square*, 1016 Kapahulu Ave. (phone: 735-8774).

MIDTOWN

Artlines Browse through artistic collectibles from all over the globe. *Ala Moana Center*, 1450 Ala Moana Blvd. (phone: 941-1445).

Chocolates for Breakfast The women's clothing sold here is often elegant, sometimes daring, and occasionally counter-chic, but always sophisticated. For the pure of heart there are muslins that *look* innocent enough. *Ala Moana Center*, 1450 Ala Moana Blvd. (phone: 947-3434).

Crack Seed Center Preserved seeds and fruits, including dried cherries, plums, ginger, and lemon peel, are featured. *Ala Moana Center*, 1450 Ala Moana Blvd. (phone: 949-7200).

Iida's The specialty here is things Japanese, from bronze statues to porcelains to back-massage rollers. It's fun to see what's being offered. *Ala Moana Center*, 1450 Ala Moana Blvd. (phone: 973-0320).

Images International The photographs of Japan's Hisashi Otsuka are worth seeing, even if the price tags are high. *Ward Centre*, 1200 Ala Moana Blvd. (phone: 926-5081).

Liberty House At Hawaii's leading department store, which is represented in hotels on all the major islands, the emphasis is on men's, women's, and children's fashions—not quite designer creations, but not simply alohawear, either. The *Ala Moana* branch also has housewares, toys, and books. The staff is, on the whole, extremely helpful. *Ala Moana Center*, 1450 Ala Moana Blvd. (phone: 941-2345).

Pocketbook Man The shop offers an exhaustive selection of very elegant luggage and handbags. *Ala Moana Center*, 1450 Ala Moana Blvd. (phone: 949-3535).

Pomegranates in the Sun The name's a bit far-fetched, but the selection of hand-painted and ethnic clothing for men and women is intriguing. *Ward Warehouse*, 1050 Ala Moana Blvd. (phone: 591-2208).

Products of Hawaii Hawaiian perfume, Hawaiian *tiki* carvings, Hawaiian *lau hala* mats, Hawaiian-designed greeting cards are sold here—as advertised. It's a good spot to do all your souvenir shopping at one time. *Ala Moana Center*, 1450 Ala Moana Blvd. (phone: 949-6866).

Royal Hawaiian Heritage This is the place for the black and gold Hawaiian-style jewelry by many local women. Across from *Ala Moana Center* at 1430 Kona St. (phone: 973-4343).

Royal Hawaiian Mint Numismatists will enjoy watching Hawaiian coins being minted in bronze, gold and silver, then buying them. The process is fascinating and the designs are beautiful, with many royal themes from Hawaii's 19th-century past. Closed on weekends. 1427 Kalakaua Ave. (phone: 949-6468).

Tahiti Imports Polynesian fashions for women, a lot of them quite classy in their brief way, are sold here. The *pareau,* in simple and elegant designs, can be turned into intriguing cover-ups and skirts. *Ala Moana Center* (phone: 941-4539).

Willowdale Gallery Antique furniture, art, and bric-a-brac, most hailing from Europe, is the stock-in-trade here. *Ward Centre*, 1200 Ala Moana Blvd. (phone: 597-8022).

DOWNTOWN

Aala Lei Shop A wide selection of leis and flower arrangements can be found at good prices. 1164 Smith St. (phone: 521-5766).

Honolulu Chocolate Company Chocoholics beware, your taste buds will confirm the initial impulse to surrender to temptation. The prices are steep, but worth it. Restaurant Row (phone: 528-4033), *Ward Centre* (phone: 591-2997), and Manoa Valley (phone: 988-4999).

Jenny's Lei Shop One of a number of downtown shops that specialize in the traditional Hawaiian art of lei making, this outlet has a larger and better-priced selection than that found in Waikiki. 65 N. Beretania St. (phone: 521-1595).

Lai Fong This long-established store features Oriental collectibles, furniture, material, and bric-a-brac. 1118 Nuuanu Ave. (phone: 537-3497).

Mellow's Antiques Fans of antique jewelry will relish shopping here. Closed on weekends. 841 Bishop St. (phone: 533-6313).

Pegge Hopper Gallery This showcase features pricey works in this popular artist's distinctive Hawaiian style. Closed Sundays. 1164 Nuuanu St. (phone: 524-1160).

Penthouse Some real bargains can be found at this reduced-price merchandise outlet for *Liberty House.* Closed Sundays. 1 N. King St. (phone: 945-5151).

Ramsay Galleries Changing exhibits of high-quality watercolors, pen-and-ink drawings, ceramicware, and other art forms are shown here. Closed Sundays. 1128 Smith St. (phone: 537-ARTS).

Robin Buntyn The fine antiques featured here focus on Japanese prints, netsuke, lacquerware, jade, and ivory. Closed Sundays. 848 S. Beretania St. (phone: 523-5913).

SPORTS AND FITNESS

Surfing, canoeing, kayaking, and swimming contests are held often. Also, *Aloha Stadium* (phone: 486-9300) is the site of the *Hula Bowl* college football game each January. Boxing, wrestling, and many other sports events are held at the *Neal S. Blaisdell Center* (777 Ward Ave.; phone: 521-2911).

BICYCLING *Blue Sky Rentals and Sports Center* (1920 Ala Moana Blvd., Waikiki; phone: 947-0101) rents every type of bike including mountain bikes from a low rate of $15 for 12 hours on a road bike to $300 for a week on a top-of-the-line mountain bike.

FISHING Fishing enthusiasts from all over the world flock to Hawaiian waters. Boats can be chartered or are available on a half- or full-day share boat basis from companies like *Ilima V Sport Fishing* (phone: 521-2087), *Coreene C's Sport Fishing Charters* (phone: 226-8421) or *Island Charters* (phone: 536-1555). Most boats leave from Kewalo Basin, at the end of Ward Avenue on Ala Moana Boulevard.

FITNESS CENTERS *Gold's Gym* (phone: 971-GOLD), in the *Pacific Beach* hotel on Waikiki Beach, is open 24 hours a day with staff skilled in weight training and aerobic techniques. The daily rate ($20; half price for guests of many Waikiki hotels as well as coupon holders) includes shower and locker facilities. The *YMCA* (401 Atkinson Dr.; phone: 941-3344) has a pool, racquetball court, sauna, exercise machines, and weights.

GOLF Numerous public courses on Oahu provide gorgeous scenery as well as challenging golfing. More seem always to be in the planning stages.

A TOP TEE-OFF SPOT

Ko Olina Just 30 minutes from downtown Honolulu, this seven-year-old course is one of the best in Hawaii, according to *Golf Digest.* The par 72, 6,867-yard layout is designed to complement 16 spectacular water features—including cascading waterfalls, rock gardens, lakes, and quiet pools. Golf pros are available to give lessons and supervise tee times. There's an enormous practice range for driving balls and practicing chip shots, as well as a putting area. Reservations are accepted up to one week in advance. Proper golf attire is mandatory. 92-1220 Aliinui Dr., Kapolei (phone: 676-5300; fax: 676-5100).

Other courses include *Ala Wai,* the closest to Waikiki (phone: 296-4653); *Pali,* in Kaneohe (phone: 296-7254); *Hawaii Prince* (phone: 689-8361) in Ewa Beach; *Kapolei* (phone: 647-2227), down the road from the *Ko Olina* resort *Makaha West* course (phone: 695-5561) and *Makaha Valley Country Club* (phone: 695-9578), both in Makaha; and *Turtle Bay Hilton* (phone: 293-8811), near Kahuku on the North Shore. In early February, the nationally televised four-day *Hawaiian Open International Golf Tournament* is played at the *Waialae Country Club* in Kahala.

JOGGING Run along Kalakaua Avenue to *Kapiolani Park,* where a group meets at the bandstand at 7:30 AM every Sunday from March through December for a short lecture and a run in preparation for the *Honolulu Marathon*. The distance around the park is 1.8 miles; to tack on more mileage, continue along Kalakaua to Diamond Head Road and circle the base of Diamond Head. The road turns into Monsarrat Avenue, which leads back to Kalakaua (4½ miles altogether). Or take Diamond Head Road as far as Kahala Avenue, one of the island's most beautiful runs. Also popular is the 2-mile perimeter of *Ala Moana Beach Park.*

KAYAKING *Go Bananas* (732 Kapahulu Ave.; phone: 737-9514) offers rentals of single and double kayaks and coastal full- and half-day trips. *Kayak Oahu Adventures* rents gear from its post on the beach in front of the *New Otani Kaimana Beach* Hotel (2863 Kalakaua Ave; phone: 593-4415).

SCUBA DIVING/SNORKELING *Dan's Dive Shop* (660 Ala Moana Blvd.; phone: 536-6181) rents diving gear, offers instructions for beginners, and has brush-up courses for those with some experience. *Aaron's Dive Shops* (98-406 Kamehameha Hwy.; phone: 487-5533) has been taking visitors on boat and shore dives for more than a quarter of a century. Snorkelers can take inexpensive half- and full-day trips to Hanauma Bay Thursdays through Tuesdays with *Hanauma Bay Snorkeling* (phone: 944-8828).

SURFING The quest for the perfect wave attracts surfers from all over the world. Some hotels along Waikiki Beach have surfing instructors and concessions that rent equipment. The most famous surfing beaches are Sunset, Ehukai, and Waimea, on the island's North Shore. Major international competitions are held here in late November through January.

SWIMMING With Waikiki Beach generally very crowded, an alternative is to head to nearby Ala Moana or Diamond Head beach parks, or to beaches on the other side of the island. Spectacular settings include Sandy Beach and Makapuu, where just about everyone body-surfs; Waimanalo and Kailua, where swimming and windsurfing are popular; and the legendary surfing beaches of the North Shore. Many beaches are dangerous for swimming; stick to those with lifeguards.

TENNIS Several public courts are situated at about 40 places around Oahu. Try *Ala Moana Tennis Center* (phone: 522-7031), *Diamond Head Tennis Center* (phone: 971-7150), or *Kapiolani Tennis Courts* (phone: 971-2500). The *Ilikai* hotel (phone: 943-1902) has five courts (one lighted for night play), the *Hawaiian Regent* (phone: 922-6611) has one court, the *Pacific Beach* (phone: 922-1233) has two courts.

THEATER

Tickets may be purchased at the door for most plays and musicals in Honolulu. The main theaters are *Neal S. Blaisdell Center Concert Hall* (777 Ward Ave.; phone: 591-2211); *Diamond Head Theater* (520 Makapuu Ave.; phone: 734-0274); and the *Hawaii Performing Arts Company*'s *Manoa Valley Theatre* (2833 E. Manoa Rd.; phone: 988-6131). Also check for under-the-stars performances at the *Waikiki Shell* (phone: 591-2211).

MUSIC

The *Honolulu Symphony* plays at the *Blaisdell Center Concert Hall* (phone: 591-2211). Rock musicians appear at the *Blaisdell Center Arena* (phone: 591-2211) or sometimes at *Aloha Stadium* (phone: 486-9300) or the *Waikiki Shell* (phone: 591-2211).

NIGHTCLUBS AND NIGHTLIFE

The hottest place to be is the *Aloha Tower Marketplace* at the hub of the redeveloped waterfront area surrounding Honolulu Harbor. There is the state's first microbrewery, the *Gordon Biersch Brewery* (phone: 599-4877), and several nightspots, including *Fat Tuesday* (phone: 528-0004), where daiquiris come in 26 flavors. The Waikiki area swings from 8 PM until 1 AM, (with some clubs open until 4 AM) most nights of the week. For information on hotels listed, see *Checking In* (below).

Headliners in Hawaii usually mean entertainers who have made their name in the islands. One such legend is Don Ho, who performs Tuesdays through Fridays and Sundays the *Waikiki Beachcomber* (2300 Kalakaua Ave.; phone: 922-4646). Don't miss illusionist John Hirokawa at the *Hilton Hawaiian Village* (2095 Kalia Rd.; phone: 949-4321); his mix of magic and Polynesian revue is one of Waikiki's most entertaining shows. The *Society of Seven* offers a Las Vegas-style revue that's become a Waikiki classic at the *Outrigger Waikiki* (2335 Kalakaua Ave.; phone: 922-6408). The *Brothers Cazimero,* the most popular and enduring of Hawaii's musical entertainers, frequently perform at the *Bishop Museum* (phone: 877-3511). Popular discos include *Rumours* (at the *Ala Moana* hotel, 410 Atkinson Dr.; phone: 955-4811); *Wave Waikiki* (1877 Kalakaua Ave.; phone: 941-0424); *Moose McGillicuddy's Pub and Cafe* (310 Lewers St.; phone: 923-0751); and *Moose's University* (1035 University Ave.; phone: 944-5525); *Maharaja Hawaii* (at the *Waikiki Trade Center,* 2255 Kuhio Ave.; phone: 922-3030); and *Hula's Bar and Lei Stand* (2103 Kuhio Ave.; phone: 923-0669), with a predominately gay crowd. At *Studebaker's* (500 Ala Moana Blvd.; phone: 526-9888) in Restaurant Row on the outskirts of downtown Honolulu, crowds line up to enjoy music of the 1950s and 1960s with let-it-all-hang-out dancing by waiters and waitresses as well as patrons. *Anna Bannana's* (2440 S. Beretania St.; phone: 946-5190) packs in local crowds nightly for live performances of rock and reggae Thursdays through Saturdays. The *Honolulu Comedy Club* at the *Aston Waikiki Terrace* (phone: 922-5998) has shows Tuesdays through Sundays. Local comic Frank DeLima performs a consistently funny show at the *Polynesian Palace* (*Outrigger Tower*, 227 Lewers St.; phone: 923-7469), as does international hearthrob Glenn Medeiros. *Legends in Concert* (phone: 971-1400) at the *Royal Hawaiian Shopping Center* features entertainment by Michael Jackson, Madonna, and other such celebrity look-alikes for two shows nightly.

Best in Town

CHECKING IN

Honolulu hotels vary in personality, so check carefully before picking one. Remember, it's not just a place to sleep; it also will serve as a tropical headquarters. Most of Honolulu's major hotels have complete facilities for the business traveler. Those listed below as having "business services" usually offer such conveniences as meeting rooms, photocopiers, computers, translation services, and express checkout, among others. Call the individual hotel for additional information. Expect to pay more than $250 per night for a double room at those places listed as very expensive; $160 to $250 at those rated expensive; between $70 and $160 at those categorized as moderate; and less than $70 at places listed as inexpensive. For bed and breakfast accommodations, contact *Bed & Breakfast Hawaii* (Box 449, Kapaa, HI 96746; phone: 822-7771; 800-733-1632; fax: 822-2723), *Pacific Hawaii Bed & Breakfast* (602 Kailua Rd.; Kailua, HI 96734; phone: 486-8838; 800-999-6026; fax: 487-1228), *Bed and Breakfast Honolulu Statewide* (3242 Kaohinani Dr., Honolulu, HI 96817; phone: 595-7533; 800-288-4666; fax: 595-2030), or *Hawaii's Best Bed and Breakfast* (Box 563, Kamuela, HI 96743; phone: 885-4550; 800-262-9912; fax: 885-0559). Unless otherwise noted, all hotel rooms and condominium units have air conditioning, pools, private baths, TV sets, and telephones. Many have private lanais.

All hotels below are in Honolulu and telephone and fax numbers are in the 808 area code unless otherwise indicated.

We begin with a favorite place, followed by recommended hotels, listed by price category.

A GRAND HOTEL

Halekulani Many generations of Waikiki visitors who have noted the truth in this venerable hostelry's name, which means "house befitting heaven," return yearly to this oasis of calm and refinement adjacent to the beach in the heart of Waikiki. The design incorporates the restored two-story main building of the original hotel into a complex of multilevel structures with a total of 456 rooms surrounding tranquil courtyards and gardens. The *House Without a Key* restaurant, immortalized in one of Earl Derr Biggers's Charlie

Chan novels, has been rebuilt on the same spot, and the old bungalow rooms have been replaced by large, luxurious, expansively balconied rooms facing the Pacific. All three restaurants (including the excellent *La Mer* and *Orchids;* see *Eating Out* for both) overlook the ocean and Diamond Head, and a famous century-old *kiawe* tree continues to preside. The striking tiled orchid design accenting the large oceanside pool has come to be a symbol for the hotel itself. Room service is available around the clock. Other conveniences include a concierge and business services. 2199 Kalia Rd. (phone: 923-2311; 800-367-2343; fax: 926-8004).

VERY EXPENSIVE

Aston Waikiki Beachside Small and sumptuous, this place is perfect for those who appreciate lovely surroundings. Inside, European and Oriental period pieces add to the ambience, while the service is impeccable. A minor drawback is that some of the 79 guestrooms are very small, albeit appealingly appointed. In-room VCRs and French toiletries are just some of the extras. Although there are no restaurants (or pool) on the premises, it's merely a five-minute walk to the *Hyatt Regency Waikiki* and other hotels and restaurants in the area. The hostelry is conveniently located across from the beach. Amenities include a concierge desk and business services. 2452 Kalakaua Ave. (phone: 931-2100; 800-92-ASTON; fax: 931-2129).

Hawaii Prince Attention to detail, panoramic views of the neighboring *Ala Wai Marina,* and fine fare offered at this 521-room hotel's three restaurants (including the *Prince Court;* see *Eating Out*) justify the top-of-the-scale rates. Guests also are offered complimentary shuttle service to the hotel's golf course in Ewa (about 45 minutes away), as well as to Waikiki. It is a short walk from either Ala Moana Beach or Waikiki Beach. There is a concierge and business services. 100 Holomoana St. (phone: 956-1111; 800-321-6248; fax: 946-0811).

Hilton Hawaiian Village With nearly 2,542 rooms on 22 acres, it is Hawaii's largest hotel, Waikiki's most self-contained resort, and the western terminus of Waikiki Beach. Offered here are several executive floors, which include a concierge, complimentary breakfast, cocktails, and *pupus.* It also has a shopping center and post office. The *Rainbow Tower,* famed for its 30-story rainbow mosaic, and the *Tapa Tower,* with 250 corner suites, have the best views, while the *Alii Tower* contains the hotel's most elegant accommodations and features a private pool and concierge services. The village has lots of great features—pools, beachfront setting, fine dining, luaus, showroom entertainment—but lacks serenity. Tropically landscaped grounds surround a stream and pool which lead to a palm-lined beach. "Aloha Friday," a weekly celebration dedicated to King Kalakaua, features crafts displays, hula dancing, and a luau-style dinner, capped off by fireworks after dark. Business services are available. 2005 Kalia Rd. (phone: 949-4321; 800-HILTONS; fax: 947-7898).

Kahala Mandarin Oriental Formerly the *Kahala Hilton*, this property changed hands and received an $80-million face-lift in 1995. Queen Elizabeth II spent a couple of nights here, and King Juan Carlos of Spain came for part of his honeymoon with Queen Sofia. The main structure of this lavish, 371-room hostelry is 10 stories high and overlooks a glorious (though manmade) 800-foot beach. Additional beachside bungalows and a two-story wing watch over a large lagoon in which dolphins and turtles cavort. Rooms in the main building are large and have charming semicircular lanais decorated with bougainvillea. Besides ocean and pool swimming, the hotel provides kayaks and snorkeling equipment and can arrange deep-sea fishing and scuba diving; and there are several fine restaurants (see *Eating Out*). Business services, 24-hour room service, a fitness center and a concierge are also available. 5000 Kahala Ave., Kahala (phone: 734-2211; 800-367-2525; fax: 739-8800).

EXPENSIVE

Aston Waikiki Banyan One of the largest condos in Waikiki, it's a short walk from the beach, the zoo, and the *Ala Wai* golf course. The building features 300 spacious, handsomely decorated units, a sauna, a large recreation area with tennis courts and a swimming pool, laundry facilities on each floor, and daily maid service. From the top floor on the Diamond Head side one can see beyond the crater to Maunalua Bay. Many highly rated restaurants are nearby, although none are on the property. 201 Ohua Ave. (phone: 922-0555; 800-366-7765; fax: 922-0906).

Aston Waikiki Shores Next to the *US Army Museum of Hawaii,* this apartment hotel has an unobstructed view across the museum grounds. From each lanai there is a panorama of both ocean and mountains. Most of the 83 apartments have been refurbished. Linen, cooking utensils, and dishes are provided. There are full kitchens and daily maid service, but no restaurant. Cost and location combine to make this one of the best buys on the beach, especially for budget-conscious families. 2161 Kalia Rd. (phone: 926-4733; 800-367-2353; fax: 922-2902).

Diamond Head Beach This 14-story structure on the beach is one of the more attractive places in terms of price and location in Honolulu, although views are rather limited. The 57 units range from studios to one-bedroom suites. Rooms are smallish but quite comfortable. There are no shops, pools, or tour desks on site, but they are available in the nearby *New Otani Kaimana* (see below). Amenities include unlimited free use of snorkeling and other beach equipment and business services. 2947 Kalakaua Ave. (phone: 922-1928; 800-367-2317; fax: 924-8980).

Hyatt Regency Waikiki The hotel's two octagonal towers are a visual landmark among the concrete high-rises along Kalakaua Avenue. The Great Hall, with its outdoor tropical garden, three-story waterfall, and massive hanging sculpture, is a sightseeing spot in its own right, if often crowded. Each of its 1,230 rooms is handsomely furnished; the artwork that graces the walls is worthy of note. Suites feature some exceptional Japanese and European antiques. Guests in the *Diamond Head Tower* (on floors 35 through 40) have their own complimentary bar and concierge. The pool deck is one of the most attractive in Honolulu, and the bars, cafés, and restaurants—including *Ciao Mein, Musashi* (see *Eating Out* for both), and *Harry's Bar*—are among the best in Waikiki. The service here is exemplary. Amenities include 24-hour room service and business services. 2424 Kalakaua Ave. (phone: 923-1234; 800-233-1234; fax: 923-7839; telex: 7238278).

Ilikai Located at the western edge of Waikiki, this 800-room property has spruced up its spacious guestrooms (some with kitchenettes; many with lovely marina views) and public areas. The hotel has Waikiki's best tennis facilities, with five courts, a pro shop, and a staff of pros available. The open area at the lobby level has pools, terraces, and fountains and at sunset each night a conch is sounded to mark the passage of another day. The beach, Duke Kahanamoku Lagoon, and the yacht marina are just a short walk away. Three fine restaurants including the casual *Canoe's* and more elegant *Sarento's*, as well as two clubs including *Coconut's Nightclub,* complete the picture. Other conveniences include a concierge desk and business services. 1777 Ala Moana Blvd. (phone: 949-3811; 800-245-4524; fax: 947-4523).

Manoa Valley Inn This may be Honolulu's most complete bed and breakfast facility (it's in the *National Register of Historic Places*; with eight bedrooms decorated Victorian-style in a beautifully restored turn-of-the-century Manoa Valley home. The inn comes highly recommended. Rates include an ample continental breakfast and afternoon *pupus*. Bus connections to *Ala Moana Center,* and from there to all other parts of Oahu, are available. About 2 miles from Waikiki, at 2001 Vancouver Dr. (phone: 947-6019; 800-634-5115; fax: 946-6168).

New Otani Kaimana Beach The location is the thing at this 124-room property; it's situated on the Diamond Head side of *Kapiolani Park,* just a few minutes away from Waikiki by foot or bus. The beach is right outside, and beautiful reefs are within easy snorkeling distance. The *Hau Tree Lanai* restaurant overlooks the beach and *Miyako* serves shabu shabu–style cooking (see *Eating Out* for both). All rooms have refrigerators and mini-bars. Oceanside rooms have stunning views. Families and women traveling alone find this a friendly, safe haven. There's a concierge desk, as well as business services and fitness services. 2863 Kalakaua Ave. (phone: 923-1555; 800-356-8264; fax: 922-9404).

Pacific Beach Standing on the site of the summer home of Queen Liliuokalani, this 847-room property is famous for its 280,000-gallon indoor oceanarium, which can be viewed from the *Oceanarium* restaurants. Along with the pool, there are two tennis courts and a Jacuzzi. Other pluses are a concierge and business services. A good value. 2490 Kalakaua Ave. (phone: 922-1233; 800-367-6060; fax: 922-0129).

Royal Hawaiian "The Pink Palace," as this flamingo-colored, six-story Spanish-Moorish landmark is known, is one of the two grand old hotels in Waikiki (the *Sheraton Moana Surfrider* is the other). The pink color scheme runs throughout the hotel, including the 526 guestrooms; (most of the rooms have either a pink sofa, drapes, or quilt). The hotel has palm gardens, a 17-story tower, a pool, and a prime beachront setting. Visit the *Ocean Lawn* for a traditional luau. The *Surf Room* (see *Eating Out*) offers fine dining. Once away from the busy lobby, which attracts spectators as well as guests, this remains the most charming hotel in Waikiki. Business services are available. 2259 Kalakaua Ave. (phone: 923-7311; 800-325-3535; fax: 924-7098).

Sheraton Moana Surfrider This beautifully restored Victorian hostelry has stood at the edge of the Waikiki surf since 1901. Listed on the *National Register of Historic Places,* it features a grand Greek Revival portico while its interior captures a turn-of-the-century elegance and contemporary chic. The *Moana* has been joined with the neighboring *Surfrider* to form a single 793-room hotel, and although the *Surfrider* wing offers rooms with spectacular views of Diamond Head, the historic charm of the original hotel provides guests with a unique experience. These touches, and four delightful ocean-front restaurants, including *Banyan Veranda* and *Ship's Tavern,* help to obscure the more modern iconography of Waikiki outside. Concierge and business services are available. 2365 Kalakaua Ave. (phone: 922-3111; 800-325-3535; fax: 923-0308).

Sheraton Waikiki With 1,852 rooms, this establishment, the second largest in Waikiki (surpassed only by the *Hilton Hawaiian Village*), still has the greatest number of units in one building of any hotel on the beach. Lanais on the Pacific side loom over the ocean as precipitously as a cliff. It's a splendid sensation, if you don't suffer from vertigo, and the sunsets can be memorable. This place has all that's expected of a big hotel: There is never a dearth of taxis, it's a pick-up point for every major tour operator, *TheBus* stops nearby, and there are two pools and four restaurants from which to choose. 2255 Kalakaua Ave. (phone: 922-4422; 800-325-3535; fax: 922-7708).

Waikiki Joy Upscale and contemporary, this 94-room hostelry has a pleasant marble entry and lounge. Avoid the lower-level studios, as they can be a bit noisy; the suites on the upper floors are quieter and larger. A complimentary continental breakfast is served in the lobby each morning, and there is a restaurant serving continental fare. There's a concierge desk, a pool and sauna, and room service is available during meal times. Business services are available. 320 Lewers St. (phone: 923-2300; 800-922-7866; fax: 924-4010).

MODERATE

Alana Waikiki This boutique hotel provides a comfortable Waikiki base for travelers. Both public areas and the 313 rooms are elegantly styled, with plenty of marble, stylish furnishings and artwork. In addition, guests enjoy a pool and two restaurants. Business services and a fitness center open 24 hours a day are available. Located several blocks from the *Hilton Hawaiian Village* and the western end of Waikiki Beach. 1956 Ala Moana Blvd. (phone: 941-7275; 800-367-6070; fax: 949-0996).

Aston Waikikian This low-rise hotel embodies the scale and mood of Waikiki from the 1950s. Rooms are decorated with Hawaiian motifs, ceiling fans, exposed timber ceilings, and wooden lanais, all contributing to a South Seas atmosphere. Some of the 100 units also have kitchenettes. An adjacent six-story building offers more conventional accommodations. The beach, on Duke Kahanamoku Lagoon, and a particularly attractive palm-fringed poolside area with a popular outdoor café called the *Tahitian Lanai* (see *Eating Out*), are just two of the amenities. Room service is available as are a concierge desk and business services. 1811 Ala Moana Blvd. (phone: 949-5331; 800-922-7866; fax: 946-2843).

Coconut Plaza Overlooking the Ala Wai Canal, this small hostelry three blocks from Waikiki Beach offers 80 nicely furnished guest rooms (some with mountain views), a friendly staff, and complimentary continental breakfast served alfresco. Other amenities include exercise equipment and kitchenettes in every room. A particularly good value. 450 Lewers St. (phone: 923-8828; 800-882-9696; fax: 923-3473).

Outrigger Edgewater This 185-room place looks more like a seaside apartment house than a hotel and exudes a quiet, calm air. For those who find the hurly-burly of large establishments either intimidating or just plain exhausting, this is the ideal spot at an ideal price. An added attraction is the *Trattoria,* a well-regarded Italian restaurant (see *Eating Out*). A concierge and business services are pluses. 2168 Kalia Rd. (phone: 922-6424; 800-462-6262; fax: 800-622-4852).

Outrigger Prince Kuhio Quietly set on Kuhio Avenue, just one block from the beach, it feels like a more intimate residence despite its 626 rooms on 37 floors. Rooms are nicely decorated, each with its own wet bar and marble bathroom. The lobby is a graceful and airy place where complimentary coffee is poured from a silver samovar every morning. Rooms high on the Diamond Head side have stunning views of the crater. The top three floors are part of the exclusive *Kuhio Club* (where guests can take advantage of a concierge and other special services). There's a concierge desk and business services. 2500 Kuhio Ave. (phone: 922-0811; 800-462-6262; fax: 800-622-4852).

Outrigger Reef Lanais A small gem, this property has 110 rooms (some with kitchenettes) that look out over the expanse of sandy beach. It is a stylish, reasonably priced alternative to the big hotels that prevail in Waikiki, with a prime location: one block from the beach and convenient to shops and restaurants (there are none on the premises). 225 Saratoga Ave. (phone: 923-3881; 800-462-6262; fax: 800-462-4852).

Outrigger Royal Islander This is another stopping place where smallness is an advantage: The front desk personnel usually manage to remember guests' names. The 100 rooms are on the small side, though not oppressively so, and each has a lanai, refrigerator, and coffee maker on request. Street noise may prove bothersome. Try for one of the recently remodeled upper-floor rooms. The property is located opposite the *Reef* hotel, which is on the beach; the only available pool is located there. 2164 Kalia Rd. (phone: 922-1961; 800-462-6262; fax: 622-4852).

Outrigger Waikiki Village This old standby underwent a face-lift in 1995, and is considerably more attractive than before. The 400-room member of the Outrigger chain is popular with young couples visiting Hawaii for the first time. The poolside area is surprisingly busy, considering that the ocean is two blocks away. Some rooms have kitchenettes. Business services are available. 240 Lewers St. (phone: 923-3881; 800-462-6262; fax: 800-622-4852).

Royal Garden at Waikiki Elegance is the word here, with plush furnishings, frescoed ceilings, chandeliers, and marble providing a sense of European style. The 230 rooms are spacious and nicely furnished. On-site facilities include the excellent *Cascada* restaurant (see *Eating Out*), two pools, business services, and a fitness center. Guests enjoy the complimentary shuttle to various Waikiki locations. Executive level floors receive concierge service. 440 Olohana St. (phone: 943-0202; 800-367-5666; fax: 946-8777).

INEXPENSIVE

Hawaiiana This 95-room, low-rise property, a short walk from the beach and arranged around two pools, has provided a comfortable, friendly base for a Waikiki stay since it opened in 1955. All rooms are air conditioned and have kitchenettes, daily maid service, and a washer/dryer. Ask about renting one of the luxury suites. Guests enjoy a hula show on Wednesdays and Sundays. Continental breakfast is included. 260 Beach Walk (phone: 923-3811; 800-535-0085; fax: 926-5728).

Outrigger Waikiki Surf Truly one of the "finds" of Honolulu, this 303-room hotel in a semi-residential part of Waikiki is friendly, clean, quiet, and delightfully inexpensive. Some rooms have kitchenettes. Perhaps best of all the hotel has two companions—the 102-room *Waikiki Surf East* (422 Royal Hawaiian Ave.) and the 115-room *Waikiki Surf West* (412 Lewers St.)—all owned and run by the Outrigger group. The original *Waikiki Surf* is at 2200 Kuhio Ave. (phone for all three properties: 923-7671; 800-462-6262; fax: 800-622-4852).

Royal Grove An apartment hotel with personality, like the *Royal Hawaiian* it is painted pink. There are 76 very comfortable, cheerful studios as well as 11 one-bedroom units. The ocean, visible from some of the lanais, is a block and a half away, so many people prefer to look out on the pool and tropical gardens. Most rooms have air conditioning and kitchenettes. On the grounds are a sushi bar, a Korean barbecue eatery, and a health food store. There is maid service but no room service. 151 Uluniu Ave. (phone: 923-7691; fax: 922-7508).

EATING OUT

Honolulu now has an emerging regional cuisine that blends the best foods and spices of Asia and the Pacific with European styles and sauces. Today, many restaurants delight visitors with dishes that use local fish and tropical fruits and vegetables in imaginative ways (although finding authentic Hawaiian fare in Honolulu takes some doing). With Hawaii's proximity to Asia, restaurants serving authentic Pacific Rim specialties abound, as do traditional continental restaurants. Expect to pay more than $125 for dinner for two at those places we've described as very expensive; between $60 and $125 at those listed as expensive; between $35 and $60 at moderate places; and under $35 at those rated as inexpensive. Prices don't include drinks, wine, tax, or tip. All restaurants listed are in the 808 area code.

Unless otherwise indicated, all restaurants are open for lunch and dinner.

VERY EXPENSIVE

Café Sistina A quality menu is the major attraction at this high-energy establishment, but a re-creation of a section of the Sistine Chapel above the bar adds to the appeal of the contemporary decor. Plentiful portions of hearty northern Italian fare are served, with numerous antipasti and pasta dishes to tempt and surprise the palate. Open Mondays through Fridays for lunch, dinner nightly. Reservations advised. Major credit cards accepted. 1314 S. King St. (phone: 596-0061).

John Dominis Spectacularly located on a promontory overlooking the Kewalo Basin and the Pacific, this dramatic eatery has floor-to-ceiling windows to showcase the extraordinary views. This is the ideal place to sample island seafood: *Ono* (wahoo), *onaga* (red snapper), and *opakapaka* (white snapper) all are available in season. The cioppino—fresh fish cooked in tomatoes, herbs, and spices—is unbeatable. Open for lunch on Wednesdays, brunch on Sundays, and daily for dinner. Reservations advised. Major credit cards accepted. 43 Ahui St. (phone: 523-0955).

La Mer This fine dining room is elegantly subdued, with fare that is innovative and delicious. Appetizers include lobster salad and Kona crab baked in olive oil. Among the entrées are whole *onaga* baked in a thyme and rosemary rock salt crust, and papillote of *kumu* with shiitake mushrooms and basil—both dishes enhanced with *ogo* (Hawaiian seaweed). Those longing for Paris should order the cheese course; in due time, a cart laden with the finest cheeses this side of the Left Bank arrives for your tasting pleasure. Open daily for dinner only. Reservations advised. Major credit cards accepted. *Halekulani,* 2199 Kalia Rd. (phone: 923-2311).

Michel's At most open-air beachfront restaurants in Honolulu, the cooking takes a back seat to the view. Not here. The dining room is elegant and subdued. Although there are occasionally deft local touches, such as prosciutto served with papaya, the dishes tend to be classic. Even the *opakapaka* is served with champagne sauce and grapes. Reservations necessary. Major credit cards accepted. 2895 Kalakaua Ave. (phone: 923-6552).

Orchids Sliding French doors that open onto a green lawn and expansive views of Diamond Head and the sea create a perfect backdrop for fine dining, which features fresh island seafood and Asian specialties. Breakfast is a highlight, as is the Sunday brunch, although daily lunch and dinner also are first-rate. Reservations advised. Major credit cards accepted. *Halekulani* Hotel, 2199 Kalia Rd. (phone: 923-2311).

Roy's Master chef Roy Yamaguchi has created an eclectic Eurasian menu that has made this one of Honolulu's most popular eateries. The lively ambience, with the kitchen on display, the casually elegant dining room, the prompt service, and specialties such as *kiawe*-roasted Chinatown duck and fresh-seared *opakapaka* (pink snapper) with one of the chef's signature sauces, are first-rate reasons to come here. Open daily for dinner. Reservations necessary. Major credit cards accepted. 6600 Kalanianaole Hwy., Hawaii-Kai (phone: 396-7697).

EXPENSIVE

Bali by the Sea Contemporary elegance, enhanced by a mix of cool whites and Mediterranean pastels, sets the scene for seaside dining. The food is excellent, with appetizers like *coquille* of shrimp and scallops with ginger sauce, enticing entrées such as Kaiwi Channel *opakapaka* with fresh watercress and ginger, and an irresistible dessert tray. Open daily for breakfast and lunch Mondays through Fridays, dinner Mondays through Saturdays. Reservations advised. Major credit cards accepted. Valet parking is available. *Hilton Hawaiian Village Rainbow Tower,* 2005 Kalia Rd. (phone: 949-4321).

Cascada Set facing a garden and a waterfall that provide a calming ambience, the innovative menu features a mix of continental and "Pacific Rim" specialties, including grilled *opakapaka*, Mongolian lamb chops with a cabernet sauce, and a grilled prawns risotto. Service is excellent and attentive without being obtrusive; tables set with linen, china, and crystal add to the sense of elegance and quality. Open daily for breakfast, lunch, and dinner.

Reservations advised. Major credit cards accepted. At the *Royal Garden at Waikiki,* 440 Olohana St. (phone: 943-0202).

Ciao Mein This pleasantly casual restaurant offers an unlikely mix of Italian and Chinese cuisines. The masterful results from either menu are superb. Appetizers include savory sesame asparagus and black mushrooms in oyster sauce, and *antipasto misto* (buffalo mozzarella, copa ham, fried spring rolls, Kalamata olives, roasted onions, and sun-dried tomato croutons). Entrées include broiled prawns with Italian tomato butter sauce, salmon baked in parchment in a sea salt crust, and cake noodles topped with lobster and chicken. Small groups can request one of the semi-private rooms at either a 6:30 or 8:30 PM seating. Open daily for dinner. Buffet brunch on Sundays. Reservations advised. Major credit cards accepted. *Hyatt Regency Waikiki,* 2424 Kalakaua Ave. (phone: 923-1234).

Prince Court Three indisputable facts about this dining establishment are its simple, yet elegant, decor, its polite, unobtrusive staff, and its superb menu, where specialties range from *kiawe* (mesquite) roasted ribs of beef to pan-sautéed tenderloin of veal to blackened blue *ahi* (tuna) to Hawaiian bouillabaisse. Everything is flavorfully prepared, and the fare is so artistically arranged on the plate that one might be tempted to take a photo to preserve the memory. Open daily for breakfast and dinner; Sundays for a knockout brunch. Reservations advised. Major credit cards accepted. In the *Hawaii Prince,* 100 Holomoana St. (phone: 956-1111).

Golden Dragon This is possibly Hawaii's most elegant Chinese restaurant, and the food happily lives up to the surroundings. One specialty, Imperial Beggar's chicken, is wrapped in lotus leaves with spices, then cooked for six hours inside a sealed clay pot to retain natural juices and flavor. Another specialty is the Peking roast duck, and be sure to leave room for the celestial desserts (both of these must be ordered 24 hours in advance). Thanks to the exquisite decorative flourishes, dining indoors is as appealing as alfresco. Valet parking is complimentary. Open Tuesdays through Sundays for dinner. Reservations advised. Major credit cards accepted. *Hilton Hawaiian Village Rainbow Tower,* 2005 Kalia Rd. (phone: 949-4321).

Hau Tree Lanai One of the best alfresco locales in Waikiki, this restaurant takes its name from the ancient tree beneath which it offers beachside patio seating. Soft-shell crabs, New York strip steaks, and Cajun sashimi are some of the dinner offerings. Open daily for breakfast, lunch, and dinner. Reservations advised. Major credit cards accepted. In the *New Otani Kaimana Beach* Hotel, 2863 Kalakaua Ave. (phone: 923-1555).

Hy's Steak House Entering this place is like walking into a magnificent Victorian private library, full of velvet chairs and etched glass. But the difference is the gleaming brass broiler inside a glassed-in gazebo, where steaks and chops are prepared with loving care. Although chicken and seafood are available, the main attraction is steak, which is superb. Valet parking is complimentary. Open daily for dinner. Reservations advised. Major credit cards accepted. 2440 Kuhio Ave. (phone: 922-5555).

Matteo's Low lighting, pleasant decor, and high-backed banquettes all combine to make this a place for quiet dining. The service is good, as is the food. The calamari, chicken, and veal dishes are highly recommended. Open daily for dinner; the bar is open until 1:30 AM. Reservations advised. Major credit cards accepted. In the *Marine Surf* Hotel, 364 Seaside Ave. (phone: 922-5551).

Miyako Shabu-style cooking (meat, vegetables, and seafood prepared in boiling water at the table) is emphasized here. Seating is either in the main dining room with its rooftop, oceanside views, or in small tatami rooms where guests sit on mats on the floor. Two days' advance notice will secure the special *kaiseki* dinner, a set menu of seven, eight, or nine courses, all using the freshest produce and seafood available. Open daily for dinner. Reservations advised. Major credit cards accepted. *New Otani Kaimana Beach* Hotel, 2863 Kalakaua Ave. (phone: 923-1555).

Musashi This very elegant Japanese restaurant in the *Hyatt Regency Waikiki* features *teppanyaki* grill, cooked-in-broth shabu shabu dishes, and cooked-in-sauce sukiyaki dishes, all prepared tableside. There's also an excellent sushi bar. The appealing decor includes rock gardens and pools. Open daily for breakfast, lunch, and dinner. Reservations advised. Major credit cards accepted. 2424 Kalakaua Ave. (phone: 923-1234).

Nicholas Nickolas Fine dining amid soft lights and elegance is featured at this place, plus magnificent views from its location atop the 36-floor *Ala Moana* Hotel. The extensive menu focuses on both American and continental dishes, ranging from veal to lamb, with pasta, soup, salads, as well as catch-of-the-day entrées. Open daily for dinner, with live entertainment nightly. Reservations necessary. Major credit cards accepted. 410 Atkinson Dr. (phone: 955-4466).

Nick's Fishmarket This is one of the best fish restaurants in Honolulu. With a contemporary, casual ambience, guests enjoy live Maine lobsters in addition to other fresh fish including *opakapaka,* mahimahi, and *ono.* Hot Tip: Try the breaded abalone with mushrooms and asparagus with bay shrimp in a wine dill sauce. Open daily for dinner. Reservations advised. Major credit cards accepted. In the *Waikiki Gateway* Hotel, 2070 Kalakaua Ave. (phone: 955-6333).

Restaurant Pier 7 Nestled in a harborside setting at the back of the *Hawaii Maritime Center,* this place serves good seafood, like Hawaiian snapper sautéed with crushed mustard seeds and roasted, and medaillons of mahimahi in tomato coulis. Visa and MasterCard accepted. Reservations advised. At Pier 7 (phone: 524-2233).

Surf Room A beachfront setting with sweeping Diamond Head views and a new menu nightly are two of this restaurant's drawing cards. Favorites are the sauteed *opakapaka* with black bean sauce, and the five-spice rack of lamb; another popular feature is the Friday-night seafood buffet. Open daily for breakfast, lunch, and dinner. Reservations advised. Major credit cards accepted. In the *Royal Hawaiian* Hotel, 2259 Kalakaua Ave. (phone: 923-7311).

3660 on the Rise In residential Kaimuki, this well-acclaimed restaurant sports stylish, contemporary decor, with a nouvelle "Pacific Rim" menu that changes every six weeks. Specialities worth a try include *ahi katsu* (deep-fried seared tuna wrapped in spinach), Chinese steamed *opakapaka* with black bean sauce, and New York steak with Hawaiian rock salt. Open Tuesdays through Sundays for dinner. Reservations necessary. Major credit cards accepted. 3660 Waialae Ave. (phone: 737-1177).

MODERATE

Café Che Pasta Homemade pasta is only one item on a menu that includes fresh grilled fish, calamari, and other nouvelle-style dishes. Open for lunch on weekdays, dinner Tuesdays through Fridays. Reservations advised. Major credit cards accepted. 1001 Bishop Sq. (phone: 524-0004).

Caffèlatte Alfresco seating and the feel of a contemporary bistro complement top-notch traditional northern Italian cuisine. The Milanese owner-chef, Laura Magni, provides a warm ambience and a menu to match. Don't miss the *ravioli burro e salvia* (stuffed pasta with butter and sage), which is memorably delicious, as are many of the other pasta specialities. Closed Tuesdays. Reservations advised. MasterCard and Visa accepted. 339 Saratoga Rd. (phone: 924-1414).

China House The cavernous dining room of this Honolulu favorite is often full. Try shark fin or bird's nest soup; four varieties of the former and three of the latter are served. The dim sum is famous throughout the island, and is served from 10 AM to 2 PM on weekdays, 9 AM to 9 PM on weekends. Reservations advised. Major credit cards accepted. At 1349 Kapiolani Blvd., adjacent to *Ala Moana Center* (phone: 949-6622).

Compadres A comfortable setting, and good prices make this a popular spot. Two of the most often-ordered dishes are *arroz con pollo* (chicken with rice) and steak *a la tampiquena* (flank steak with cheese and onion). Reservations advised. Visa and MasterCard accepted. *Ward Centre* (phone: 523-1307).

Gordon Biersch Brewery Restaurant Honolulu's first microbrewery and restaurant is a popular stop for businesspeople at lunch, when the most popular dish is a grilled *ahi*, and for city dwellers at dinner, when the favored dishes are seafood curry and tenderloin. Don't forget to order a beer, preferably a Marzen. Reservations unnecessary. Major credit cards accepted. At *Aloha Tower Marketplace,* 1 Aloha Tower Dr. (phone: 599-4877).

Hoku's Opened in the remodeled *Kahala Mandarin Oriental*, this continental restaurant cooks lavish dishes in a tandoori oven, a natural-wood oven, and on a charcoal grill. An oyster and sushi bar round out the offerings. Reservations advised. Major credit cards accepted. In the *Kahala Mandarin Oriental*, 5000 Kahala Ave. (phone: 739-8888).

Kincaid's The nautical decor is most appropriate in this tavern overlooking the *Kewalo Boat Basin.* Among the house specialties are island seafood and Nebraska beef. Freshly baked Russian rye bread accompanies each entrée. Reservations advised Fridays and Saturdays. Major credit cards accepted. *Ward Warehouse,* 1050 Ala Moana Blvd. (phone: 591-2005).

Kirin This bustling Hong Kong-style restaurant serves traditional Cantonese and Mandarin fare, including steaming platters of shrimp, crab, and lobster. Don't miss the minced pork with sesame buns and sesame rice balls in *azuki* bean soup. Reservations advised. Major credit cards accepted. 2518 S. Beretania St. (phone: 942-1888).

Legend Seafood Nowhere in Oahu is there such an array of delicacies of the ancient Hunan, Szechuan, and Mandarin cuisines as in this lovely dining room. The decor is intricate and elaborate, influenced no doubt by styles in Hong Kong during the days of Queen Victoria. There are over 100 items from which to choose. Lobster with supreme sauce is outstanding. Beware—many of the dishes are very hot. Also popular are the 80 dim sum dishes that highlight the lunch menu. Reservations advised on weekdays. Major credit cards accepted. Conveniently located in the *Chinese Cultural Plaza,* 100 N. Beretania St. (phone: 532-1868).

Mezzanine "Designer" pizza, topped with everything from goat cheese to cilantro, is the staple here. Less adventurous folks can try the rack of lamb grilled over local *kiawe* wood, as well as numerous pasta and fish dishes. There's indoor and alfresco seating, as well as weekend entertainment. Open daily for breakfast and dinner. Reservations advised. Major credit cards accepted. In the *Aston Waikiki Terrace* Hotel, 2045 Kalakaua Ave. (phone: 955-6000).

Monterey Bay Canners The Waikiki branch of this restaurant, in the *Outrigger Waikiki* hotel, offers a limited number of alfresco tables that take full advantage of the beachfront location. The best bet on the menu is one of the catch-of-the-day specials, which are reasonably priced and delicious. Open daily for breakfast, lunch, and dinner. Reservations advised. Major credit cards accepted. 2335 Kalakaua Ave. (phone: 922-5761).

Murphy's Bar and Grill A pleasant eatery in the revitalized Merchant Square area and a good choice for people who are tired of exotic restaurant grub. From sandwiches, burgers and quesadillas to salads and pasta, the menu offers many tasty specials. Live sports events are beamed in courtesy of a satellite dish. Open for lunch, with *pupus* served until 8 PM; closed Sundays. Lunch reservations advised. 2 Merchant St. (phone: 531-0422).

Orson's Downstairs is a coffee shop called the *Chowder House,* which serves fresh salads as well as seafood; upstairs, a dining room decorated with beautifully stained wood offers fine seafood. Reservations advised. Major credit cards accepted. *Ward Warehouse,* 1050 Ala Moana Blvd. (phone: 591-8681).

Phillip Paolo's Just a five-minute drive from Waikiki and set in an eclectically decorated private home, this establishment receives high praise for its fine Italian fare. Daily specials complement such standard features as *fettuccine Vigario* (pasta with mushrooms and spinach in a light basil cream sauce) and shrimp scampi. Open Tuesdays through Fridays for lunch, daily for dinner. Reservations advised. Major credit cards accepted. 2312 Beretania St. (phone: 946-1163).

Plumeria Beach Cafe New management has taken over what once was the beloved *Hala Terrace* and only time will tell whether or not menu items such as Thai chicken *à l'orange*, garlic-dusted shrimp on a bed of fettuccine marinara or *cioppino* with eggplant salad will be prepared with the care of bygone days. Open daily for breakfast, lunch, and dinner. Reservations advised. Major credit cards accepted. In the *Kahala Mandarin Oriental*, 5000 Kahala Ave. (phone: 739-8888).

Siam Inn High praise has been heaped on this Thai restaurant located in the heart of Waikiki, where imported spices and fresh local produce and seafood are combined to advantage. Normally fiery Thai dishes like five-spice fish and yellow curry shrimp with avocado and peanuts are prepared with Western tastebuds in mind. Open on weekdays for lunch, daily for dinner. Reservations unnecessary. Major credit cards accepted. 407 Seaside Ave. (phone: 926-8802).

Singha Thai This spot serves authentic Thai appetizers, soups, curries, seafood, and noodle and rice dishes, prepared by chef Chai Chaowasaree. Before he came to Honolulu, Chaowasaree owned an award-winning restaurant in Bangkok. Thai dancers and musicians perform Sunday, Monday, and Tuesday evenings. Open daily; no lunch on Sundays. Reservations advised. Major credit cards accepted. 1910 Ala Moana Blvd., across from the *Hilton Hawaiian Village* (phone: 941-2898).

Sunset Grill The style is California-casual; the food is cooked over *kiawe* wood to provide a distinctive flavor. Specialties include chicken, beef, veal, lamb, and fish with rotisserie, oven, and grill preparations. Open daily; breakfast on Sundays only. Reservations advised. Major credit cards accepted. *Restaurant Row*, 500 Ala Moana Blvd. (phone: 521-4409).

Trattoria The chef doesn't overload the menu with tomato paste, and many dishes are cooked *al burro*—delicately, in butter—instead of doused in olive oil. The lasagna in this charmingly decorated restaurant is well worth tasting, as is the *cotoletta di vitello alla parmigiana* (veal cutlet parmesan)—and the cannelloni Milanese is definitely a "don't miss." Open daily for dinner.

Reservations advised. Major credit cards accepted. *Outrigger Edgewater* Hotel, 2168 Kalia Rd. (phone: 923-8415).

INEXPENSIVE

Ba-Le Sandwich Shop Started in Chinatown as a lively hole-in-the-wall eatery, this Vietnamese-run operation now has 16 branches. The menu includes Honolulu's best croissants and espresso, as well as sandwiches, fresh fruit, and some hot entrées. No reservations. No credit cards accepted. 150 N. King St. (phone: 521-3973).

Chiang Mai Tasty, home-cooked northern Thai food—like green curry chicken and spicy clams—is served in this tiny flower-filled restaurant by a large family from the town of Chiang Mai. Open daily; no lunch on weekends. Reservations advised. Major credit cards accepted. 2239 S. King St. (phone: 941-1151).

Chinatown Cultural Plaza This ethnic enclave offers a wide range of good Oriental restaurants and varieties of Asian food—Szechuan, Cantonese, and Mandarin bound to satisfy diverse tastes—as well as shops purveying Oriental bric-a-brac that are fun for browsing. Reservations unnecessary. Major credit cards accepted. 100 N. Beretania at River Sts. (phone: 521-4394).

Hard Rock Café Granted, there's nothing Hawaiian about this cavernous outpost (save for the surfboards providing ambience), but it is one of the hubs of the social scene in Waikiki. And though they're costlier than expected, the signature burgers are tastier than expected, too. Reservations unnecessary. Major credit cards accepted. 1837 Kapiolani Blvd. (phone: 955-7383).

King Tsin Known for its spicy Chinese fare, this eatery serves up very tasty hot and sour soup. The crackling chicken is chopstick-lickin' good, as is the Hunan shrimp sautéed with broccoli. Reservations advised. MasterCard and Visa accepted. 1110 McCully St. (phone: 946-3273).

La Mariana This little-known South Seas–style waterfront hangout is too salty to be a yacht club, even though many of those who eat here are sailors anchored in Keehi Lagoon. All the seafood is just-caught fresh; try the fish and chips made with local mahimahi. No reservations. Major credit cards accepted. 50 Sand Island Access Rd. (phone: 848-2800).

Ono Hawaiian Foods In Hawaiian *ono* means delicious, and for years the search for good Hawaiian food in Honolulu has ended here. Try the chicken long rice soup (slender noodles and chicken in a clear broth) or *kalua* pig (shredded roast pork). Closed Sundays. No reservations. No credit cards accepted. 726 Kapahulu Ave. (phone: 737-2275).

Planet Hollywood Waikiki is a far cry from Beverly Hills, but those who are craving flash and fun are likely to get it here. The food is standard—burgers, pizza, pasta, *fajitas*—but the service is high energy and the atmosphere entertaining. Open daily until 1 AM. Reservations unnecessary. Major credit cards accepted. 2155 Kalakaua Ave. (phone: 924-7877).

Salerno This is like a neighborhood restaurant in New York's Little Italy, where generous amounts of northern Italian food are served (order a half portion if you're not very hungry). Open daily; closed for lunch on Sundays. Reservations advised. Major credit cards accepted. Just over the McCully Bridge from Waikiki. 1960 Kapiolani Blvd., second floor (phone: 942-5273).

Sea Fortune Located in the heart of Chinatown, this popular Cantonese-style eatery has an extensive menu that includes a variety of seafood specialties; the shrimp dishes are particularly tempting. Reservations accepted for dinner only. MasterCard and Visa accepted. 111 N. King St. (phone: 536-3822).

Sloppy Joe's It may be hard to picture Ernest Hemingway knocking them back at this branch of the Key West establishment he frequented, but everybody else will probably enjoy the novelty of wolfing down Jamaican chicken and conch fritters at the edge of Honolulu Harbor. No reservations. Major credit cards accepted. *Aloha Tower Marketplace*, 1 Aloha Tower Dr. (phone: 528-0007).

Woodlands This little Chinese eatery is run by an ex-Hong Kong wigmaker, who also happens to make what nearly everyone in Honolulu agrees are the city's greatest potstickers (dumplings filled with meat or seafood). Closed Tuesdays. Reservations unnecessary. MasterCard and Visa accepted. 1289 S. King St. (phone: 596-8102).

Yanagi Sushi Two Tokyo-style sushi bars serve a sushi lover's abundance of specials. The atmosphere is upbeat, the decor simple but appealing, and the sushi first-rate. Reservations advised. Major credit cards accepted. 762 Kapiolani Blvd. (phone: 537-1525).

Houston

Houston—the biggest city in the Southwest (and, technically, the South)—is dazzling to the newcomer. Its towering downtown skyline rises from the flat coastal plain in a city that stretches for miles in all directions, with no apparent limits.

Often called the "Bayou City" because of its location, Houston is the nation's fourth-largest city, with a metropolitan area population of 3.7 million. Still, it retains the friendly spirit of a small town. And although Houston is more than 150 years old, its past has been all but overrun by an unquenchable entrepreneurial spirit—the 20th century's incarnation of the 19th-century dream of industrial progress.

When Houstonians claim their city is the energy capital of the world, they're not just whistling Dixie. About 60% of the oil and gas wells drilled in this country are within a 500-mile radius of Houston. A quarter of the nation's refining capacity and half of its petrochemical operations are here, and miles of pipelines carrying crude oil, natural gas, or refined products begin or end in this area. The Port of Houston leads the US in foreign trade tonnage, mostly crude oil coming in and oil field equipment going out.

Oil has been both Houston's blessing and its curse. The 1980–81 oil boom brought 1,500 newcomers into Houston every week. But during the boom, the city grew much faster than its civic services, and every sort of urban trauma was magnified as a result. There is still much evidence of a lack of city planning beyond downtown: insufficient mass transit, congested traffic, and often oppressive air pollution. The boom went bust in 1982, and people began to leave the area at almost the same rate at which they arrived. Houston's population began to build again during the late 1980s as oil companies closed offices in other areas and consolidated their operations here—as the recession goes, so goes the oil business (and Houston's prospects). Because of this, city leaders have been working hard to diversify Houston's economy. In recent years, hundreds of companies outside the oil industry have moved their operations here, and the area economy's dependence on oil has dropped from 90% to 60%.

When J. K. and A. C. Allen, brothers from New York, founded the city in 1836, they had no idea just how valuable this humid, marshy swampland would become. The railroads made Houston a vital transportation hub in the late 1800s; and when oil was discovered shortly after the turn of the century 90 miles away at Beaumont, Houston found itself in the middle of its first great oil boom. In 1914, civic leaders built a ship channel 51 miles inland to the city, creating a fair-weather port. By the 1960s the two—oil and shipping—combined to make Houston one of the world's major petrochemical centers, creating the backbone of the city's economic strength.

Pure science, as well as technology, has reinforced Houston's strength. The *Lyndon B. Johnson Space Center* has been the focal point of almost every manned *NASA* flight and has earned Houston the moniker "Space City;" and the revolutionary *Space Center Houston* gives visitors the opportunity to experience the wonders of space travel. The *Texas Medical Center,* noted for cancer research and heart surgery, is one of the largest medical facilities in the country and comprises 49 institutions.

A parallel cultural enrichment has taken place, mainly because of the bullish attitude of those who made their fortunes here. The *Grand Opera, Houston Symphony,* and *Alley Theatre* are nationally acclaimed and locally popular. And the city's emergence as an international business center (about 35 foreign consulates have offices here) gives it a cosmopolitan image unique to the South.

Once more in the process of finding itself, this feisty frontier draws people like a magnet, and despite recent setbacks, Houstonians still think of their city as one of America's greatest. It's hard for a newcomer not to sense this pride even after only a day here, and given the energy of the city and its resources, it's not surprising that Houston is continuing to build upon its own strength and character.

Houston At-a-Glance

SEEING THE CITY

The revolving *Spindletop* restaurant atop the *Hyatt Regency* hotel (1200 Louisiana; phone: 654-1234) turns on the Houston panorama. To the south stands downtown, to the north an industrial area and the Ship Channel, to the east industrial sprawl, and to the west Houston's residential neighborhoods. Open daily.

Stationary, but splendid for a view of the downtown skyline, is *Sam Houston Park* (1100 Bagby St.). Dominating the cityscape are the futuristic *Pennzoil Towers,* designed by Philip Johnson, and the city's other big oil headquarters, Shell and Tenneco.

SPECIAL PLACES

Several of the city's attractions are concentrated in a few areas, so you can park and walk; otherwise, you'll be driving from place to place.

MUSEUM OF NATURAL SCIENCE The enormous, $6-million spectacle has permanent collections housing a 70-foot dinosaur skeleton, a sea shell collection with 2,500 specimens, sensational displays of astronaut suits and space station models, and Native American artifacts. Part of a $23-million expansion, the museum includes the *Cockrell Butterfly Center,* home to 2,000 live butterflies in a tropical rain forest setting with a 40-foot waterfall. The *Burke Baker Planetarium* features astronomy programs and daily laser shows. The museum and the planetarium are open daily. Admission charge; credit

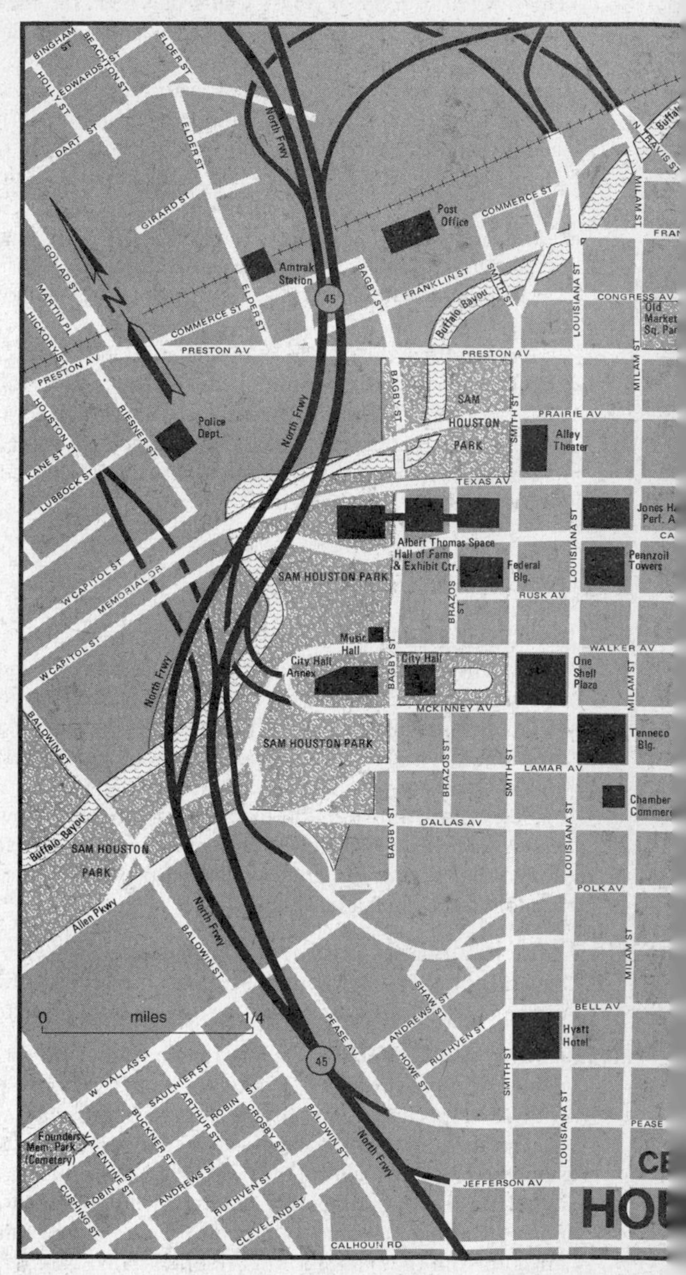

BINGHAM ST
BEACHTON ST
EDWARDS ST
HOLLY ST
ELDER ST
DART ST
GIRARD ST
GOLIAD ST
MARTIN PL
HICKORY ST
PRESTON AV
HOUSTON ST
KANE ST
LUBBOCK ST
RIESNER ST
North Frwy
Post Office
COMMERCE ST
Amtrak Station
45
BAGBY ST
FRANKLIN ST
SMITH ST
Buffalo Bayou
LOUISIANA ST
CONGRESS AV
Old Market Sq. Park
MILAM ST
N TRAVIS ST
Police Dept.
SAM HOUSTON PARK
PRAIRIE AV
Alley Theater
TEXAS AV
Jones Hall Perf. A
Albert Thomas Space Hall of Fame & Exhibit Ctr.
Federal Blg.
Pennzoil Towers
W CAPITOL ST
MEMORIAL DR
BRAZOS ST
RUSK AV
Music Hall
City Hall Annex
City Hall
WALKER AV
One Shell Plaza
MCKINNEY AV
Tenneco Blg.
BALDWIN ST
LAMAR AV
Chamber Commerce
DALLAS AV
Allen Pkwy
POLK AV
BELL AV
SHAW ST
ANDREWS ST
PEASE AV
RUTHVEN ST
HOWE ST
Hyatt Hotel
0 miles 1/4
W DALLAS ST
SAULNIER ST
ARTHUR ST
ROBIN ST
CROSBY ST
BUCKNER ST
Founders Mem. Park (Cemetery)
VALENTINE ST
CUSHING ST
ROBIN ST
ANDREWS ST
RUTHVEN ST
CLEVELAND ST
CALHOUN RD
JEFFERSON AV
PEASE
HOU

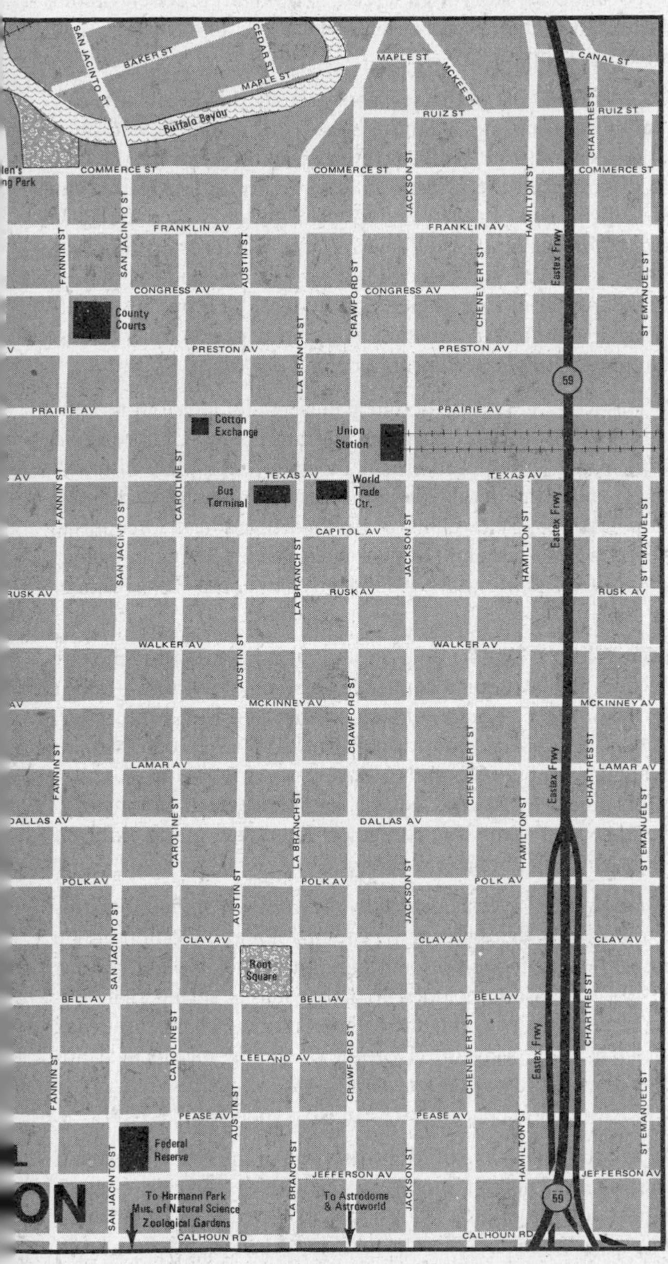

SAN JACINTO ST
BAKER ST
CEDAR ST
MAPLE ST
Buffalo Bayou
MAPLE ST
MCKEE ST
CANAL ST
RUIZ ST
CHARTRES ST
RUIZ ST
COMMERCE ST
COMMERCE ST
JACKSON ST
HAMILTON ST
COMMERCE ST
FRANKLIN AV
FRANKLIN AV
FANNIN ST
AUSTIN ST
CRAWFORD ST
CHENEVERT ST
Eastex Frwy
ST EMANUEL ST
CONGRESS AV
CONGRESS AV
County Courts
LA BRANCH ST
PRESTON AV
PRESTON AV
59
PRAIRIE AV
PRAIRIE AV
Cotton Exchange
Union Station
CAROLINE ST
TEXAS AV
TEXAS AV
Bus Terminal
World Trade Ctr.
CAPITOL AV
RUSK AV
RUSK AV
RUSK AV
WALKER AV
WALKER AV
MCKINNEY AV
MCKINNEY AV
LAMAR AV
LAMAR AV
DALLAS AV
DALLAS AV
POLK AV
POLK AV
POLK AV
CLAY AV
CLAY AV
CLAY AV
Root Square
BELL AV
BELL AV
BELL AV
LEELAND AV
PEASE AV
PEASE AV
Federal Reserve
JEFFERSON AV
JEFFERSON AV
59
To Hermann Park
Mus. of Natural Science
Zoological Gardens
To Astrodome & Astroworld
CALHOUN RD
CALHOUN RD

cards are accepted, but there is a $2 service fee. The *Wortham IMAX Theatre* features an 80-foot-wide, six-story-high screen. Shows start precisely on the hour with no late seating. Open daily. Admission charge. 1 Hermann Circle Dr., in *Hermann Park* (phone: 639-4629).

HOUSTON ZOOLOGICAL GARDENS One of the best zoos around, this has some rarely seen animals in unusual settings: vampire bats, flying squirrels, and bush babies in a red-light district where time is reversed and you can see the bats feeding on blood at 2:30 in the afternoon. The *Tropical Bird House* has more than 200 exotic birds in a rain forest. A welcome addition is the $6.7-million *Wortham World of Primates,* a dense 2.2-acre rain forest habitat that is home to 13 species. There's also a children's zoo where kids can make contact with creatures from four regions of the world. Open daily; children's zoo is closed Mondays. Admission charge except on city holidays. 1513 N. MacGregor in *Hermann Park* (phone: 525-3300).

CHILDREN'S MUSEUM This Robert Venturi–designed museum for kids four months to 14 years old is a hands-on experience and learning center. Children give impromptu performances in a closed-circuit TV station, complete with costumes and sets; go under the hood of a car to learn about auto mechanics; play in a contemporary Spanish dwelling; or dig for artifacts in an Orcoquisac Indian hut. There are environmental exhibits and outside play areas, including a wading stream. Closed Mondays. Admission charge. 1500 Binz (phone: 522-1138).

MUSEUM OF FINE ARTS With neoclassical beginnings and finishing touches by Mies van der Rohe, this structure could house almost anything—and it does, including the *Straus Collection* of Renaissance and 18th-century art, the *Beck Collection* of Impressionist art, with works by Van Gogh, Monet, Matisse, and Gauguin, and the *Glassell Collection* of African gold. A sculpture garden offers pieces by Rodin, Matisse, and Giacometti, among others. Closed Mondays. No admission charge on Thursdays or for children under six. 1001 Bissonnet (phone: 639-7300).

MENIL COLLECTION Though often overshadowed by the *Museum of Fine Arts,* this first-rate museum reflects the discerning taste of John and Dominique de Menil and houses their collection of paintings, sculpture, and antiquities, amassed over a 40-year period. Included are native masks, shrunken heads, and Byzantine, medieval, Cubist, and Surrealist works by such artists as Max Ernst, Salvador Dalí, René Magritte, Dorothea Tanning, and local sculptor Jim Love. The displays are well designed for easy viewing. Closed Mondays and Tuesdays. No admission charge. 1515 Sul Ross (phone: 525-9400).

INTERNATIONAL STRIP On the main drag of Montrose, one of the city's oldest and most bohemian residential neighborhoods, you can browse through antiques shops, foreign bazaars, art galleries, boutiques, flea markets, and offbeat book shops. The art festivals held in October and April are the largest in the South. Sidewalk cafés, restaurants, a wine tasting shop, a tree house bar, and exotic nightspots are just some of the offerings. *Empire Café* (1732 Westheimer; phone: 528-5282) is famous for its breakfast, lunch, and dinner. In the neighborhood is the *Rothko Chapel* (3900 Yupon; phone: 524-9839), a meditation chapel with works by Russian-born painter Mark Rothko. The Strip extends from the 100 to 1800 block of Westheimer.

RIVER OAKS If you're wondering where all that old oil money went, some of it is here, in the palatial mansions and huge estates of Houston's super-rich, who still have it and flaunt it. River Oaks Blvd., between Westheimer and the *Country Club.*

SAM HOUSTON PARK This project of the *Harris County Heritage Society* features a restored country church, homes, and shops, depicting the lifestyle of 19th-century Houstonians. The *Kellum-Noble House,* the oldest brick house in Houston, contains pioneer equipment and furnishings, and the *Nichols-Rice–Cherry House* is a Greek Revival home furnished with American Empire antiques. Tours begin at the office (1100 Bagby St.), but you can explore on your own as well. Open daily. No admission charge, but there is a charge for tours. Allen Pkwy. and Bagby St. (phone: 655-1912).

ASTRODOME Besides serving as home for the *Astros, Oilers,* and the *University of Houston Cougars,* this $36-million domed stadium, big enough to accommodate an 18-story building or 66,000 spectators, is one of Texas's most popular attractions. Guided tours are offered. Open daily. Admission charge. 4¾ miles southwest at I-610 and 8400 Kirby Dr. (phone: 799-9544 or 799-9595).

SIX FLAGS ASTROWORLD This park is big, clean, as glossy as the Space City itself, and rife with rides and attractions (over 100 of them) for the entire family, including a replica of the famous Coney Island *Cyclone*—one of the most exciting roller coasters ever built—a stomach-churning shuttle loop coaster; a wild river-rapids ride; *Sky Screamer;* and the *Ultra Twister,* a unique coaster that dives 92 feet and rotates backward and forward 360 degrees. The *Southern Star Amphitheater* offers performances for fans of contemporary and country music. Next door is *Waterworld,* a 15-acre aquatic recreation park. Closed September through May and weekdays during spring and fall. Admission charge. 9001 Kirby Dr., across from the *Astrodome* (phone: 799-1234 or 799-8404).

SAN JACINTO BATTLEGROUND The 570-foot-tall *San Jacinto Monument*—the world's largest masonry structure—marks the spot where General Sam Houston and his forces defeated the Mexican Army of Santa Anna in 1836 to win Texas's independence. From atop the monument, the view includes the Gulf Coast as well as the Houston skyline. The monument lobby contains the *San Jacinto Museum of History* (phone: 479-2421) with exhibits tracing regional history from Native American civilization to statehood. The museum is open daily; no admission charge. The 460-acre state park is 21 miles east of downtown Houston on Texas Hwy. 134, off Texas Hwy. 225 in La Porte. Next to the battleground, the *Battleship Texas,* forever moored in the Ship Channel, is unique in being a veteran of two world wars. Decommissioned in 1948 and given to the state, it is now a museum (phone: 479-2411) with wartime artifacts and detailed exhibits on its history. Closed Mondays and Tuesdays. Admission charge.

PORT OF HOUSTON From an observation platform atop Wharf 9, see the turning-basin area of this country's third-largest port. To inspect some of the elaborate developments in industrial shipping, take an excursion along the Ship Channel aboard the MV *Sam Houston* (make reservations months in advance). No trips on Mondays or holidays. No admission charge. Gate 12, off Ave. R (phone: 670-2416).

ANHEUSER-BUSCH BREWERY Nine different malt-and-barley beverages are brewed here, and the 45-minute guided tour takes visitors through the process from grains to suds. Also included is the history of the famous American company, from its beginnings in 1861 when Adolphus Busch married Lilly Anheuser in St. Louis and turned her father's weak company into the great American success story. Tours offered daily except Sundays. No admission charge. 775 Gellhorn (phone: 670-1696).

SPACE CENTER HOUSTON AT LYNDON B. JOHNSON SPACE CENTER You may never fly to the moon, but this very popular attraction will give you a taste of what it's like. The $70-million Disneyesque complex is at the *Johnson Space Center.* Visitors begin in *Space Center Plaza,* where there are exhibits, video presentations, *NASA* updates, and lectures by astronauts, scientists, and engineers. During missions, a large video screen allows viewing of live launches and landings. *Starship Gallery* starts with the film *On Human Destiny* and displays space flight artifacts, even a genuine moon rock you can touch. Visitors can walk through *Skylab* and explore a re-creation of the shuttle mid-deck and flight deck. Tram tours of the *Johnson Space Center* guide you through Mission Control and show you how astronauts train for their missions. *To Be an Astronaut,* a film detailing the selection and preparation of astronauts, is shown several times a day on a screen that is five stories tall and 80 feet wide; and *The Feel of Space* lets you attempt to land the shuttle through computer simulation, try the Manned Maneuvering Unit jet pack trainer, and wear a space helmet; you'll also learn how such everyday tasks as eating, sleeping, and showering are accomplished in space. The crowds are often formidably huge. Open daily. Admission charge. 20 miles southeast via I-45 in Clear Lake at 1601 NASA Rd. 1 (phone: 244-2105; 800-972-0369; fax: 283-7724).

EXTRA SPECIAL

Just 51 miles south of Houston along I-45 is Galveston Island, a leading Gulf Coast resort area. *Stewart Beach* is the principal public beach, and

there's good swimming, surfing, sailing, water skiing, and deep-sea fishing (reservations taken at boats on Piers 18 and 19 of the *Galveston Yacht Basin*). Seafood restaurants, art galleries, and restored turn-of-the-century homes are in the former vacation destination of the oil magnates clustered around Strand Boulevard.

Sources and Resources

TOURIST INFORMATION

The *Greater Houston Convention and Visitors Bureau* (801 Congress St., Houston, TX 77002; phone: 227-3100; 800-4-HOUSTON) is the best source for brochures, maps, and general information; it's closed weekends. Many banks also provide free visitor information kits, as does the *Chamber of Commerce* (1100 Milam; phone: 651-1313), also closed weekends. Contact the Texas state tourism hotline (phone: 800-8888-TEX) for maps, calendars of events, health updates, and travel advisories.

LOCAL COVERAGE The *Houston Chronicle* is the daily newspaper available at newsstands. The *Houston Press* is a respected alternative weekly. The revised edition of *Texas Monthly's Guide to Houston* by Joanne Harrison (Gulf Publishing Co.; $8.95) is a comprehensive guide. *Texas Monthly,* the monthly magazine, has extensive and timely dining information.

TELEVISION STATIONS KPRC Channel 2–NBC; KUHT Channel 8–PBS; KHOU Channel 11–CBS; KRIV Channel 26–FOX; and KTRK Channel 13–ABC.

RADIO STATIONS AM: KILT 610 (all news/weather) and KPRC 950 (news/talk). FM: KTSU 90.9 (jazz/urban contemporary); KRTS 92.1 (classical); KLTR 93.7 (adult contemporary music); and KUHF 88.7 (National Public Radio).

TELEPHONE The area code for Houston is 713.

SALES TAX The sales tax is 8.25%; the hotel room tax is 15%.

CLIMATE In the summer, Houston is hot and humid. Winds from the Gulf of Mexico create warm summer nights, and keep the winters and the rest of the year relatively warm. But ice and (more rarely) snow sometimes shut down the city in winter.

GETTING AROUND

AIRPORT The city's main airports are *Houston Intercontinental* and *William P. Hobby Airport.* Those familiar with Houston traffic allow at least 45 minutes to reach either one from downtown (note that it is not unusual for rain, fog, or the nightly rush hour to double this time). *Airport Express* (phone: 523-8888) operates a shuttle service from *Intercontinental* to its three downtown terminals. Buses leave every half hour, and tickets may be purchased at stands outside each terminal.

BUS *Metropolitan Transit Authority of Harris County (Metro)* serves downtown and the suburbs, but the system can be confusing. The fare is 85¢. Minibuses run in the downtown shopping area. For route information contact the main office (1201 Louisiana; phone: 635-4000).

CAR RENTAL A car is a necessity in Houston. Mass transit is unreliable and not always accessible. Try to avoid being caught in Houston's rush hour, when traffic is impossibly snarled. All the major national rental firms serve the city.

TAXI Cabs can be ordered on the phone, picked up in front of hotels and terminals, or—with some difficulty—hailed in the street. Major companies are *United Taxicab* (phone: 699-0000) and *Yellow Cab* (phone: 236-1111). Be warned, however, that taxi rates are rather high.

SIGHTSEEING TOURS

HOT AIR BALLOON The *Rainbow's End Balloon Port* (7826 Fairview; phone: 466-1927) sends them up weekend mornings at dawn when the winds are calm. You can take a ride and watch the balloonists rise to the occasion. If you don't want to get up that early, balloon rides are offered later in the day as well.

LUXURY COACH *Tourworks of Houston* (phone: 320-0713 or 810-0995) offers daily sightseeing tours, with destinations including *Space Center Houston, San Jacinto Battleground,* Old Town Spring, Galveston, and shopping areas. Buses pick up passengers at hotels throughout the city.

SPECIAL EVENTS

Check the publications noted above in *Local Coverage* for exact dates. For two weekends in March, spring explodes along the *River Oaks Garden Club*'s *Azalea Trail,* as thousands visit the gardens at Bayou Bend to see exquisite private homes display their floral finery. In late April, a 10-day multicultural extravaganza called the *International Festival* covers 20 blocks of downtown in a celebration of music, dance, theater, art, and food. The *Texas Renaissance Festival,* held in nearby Plantersville, re-creates 16th-century England from early October through mid-November. But one of the country's major rodeo and livestock shows is held here as well, and it's the event of the year.

A ROLLICKING RODEO

Houston Livestock Show and Rodeo This event, which runs for two weeks beginning in mid-February, features a Texas-size rodeo, complete with musical concert, held in the *Astrodome;* and the world's largest livestock show, which fills up the *Astrohall* and *Astroarena* with horses, sheep, chickens, pigs, and cattle for display and for sale at auction. It isn't unusual to see a grand champion steer sell for a quarter-million dollars. For tickets and information, write to PO Box 20070, Houston, TX 77225 or call 791-9000.

MUSEUMS

In addition to those described in *Special Places,* there are two other notable Houston museums.

BAYOU BEND This museum displays an outstanding collection of Americana. Open daily. Admission charge. 1 Westcott St. (phone: 520-2600).

CONTEMPORARY ARTS MUSEUM Exhibits include a wide variety of works by regional as well as international artists. Traveling exhibitions are featured along with films and lectures. Closed Mondays. Admission charge. 5216 Montrose at Bissonnet (phone: 526-3129).

SHOPPING

The stunning, glass-domed *Galleria Center* is still the most popular local shopping spot, where anything from the best shoeshine in town (a one-chair operation in *Cole's* hair salon on the lower level) to high-priced items at *Tiffany's* and *Neiman Marcus* can be found. Those shopping for real Texan westernwear go to nearby *Stelzig's of Texas* (3123 Post Oak Blvd.; phone: 629-7779), the oldest family-owned store of its kind in Houston, and *Cavender's Boot City* (9525-B Westheimer St.; phone: 952-7102) for a large selection of cowboy boots at reasonable prices. Custom-designed footwear in exotic leathers can be had at *Wheeler Boot Co.* (4115 Willowbend; phone: 665-0224); the store's clients have included Robert Duvall. The suburban malls near such areas as Baybrook, Deer Park, Greenspoint, Memorial City, Seabrook, and Westbrook contain major chain stores including *Sears, Montgomery Ward, JC Penney,* and *Macy's.*

SPORTS AND FITNESS

Tickets to all professional games can be picked up at *Houston Ticket Company,* in the *Galleria* area at 2707 Chimney Rock (phone: 877-1555).

BASEBALL The *National League*'s Houston *Astros* play at the *Astrodome* (I-610 and Kirby Dr.; phone: 799-9555) from April through October.

BASKETBALL The 1995 *NBA* champion *Rockets* play from November through April at the *Summit* (10 Greenway Plaza; phone: 627-0600).

BICYCLING You can rent bikes at *Memorial Park Bicycle Rentals* (5427 Blossom; phone: 864-9335). There's a good bike trail running from the Sabine Street Bridge (just east of *Allen's Landing*) along Buffalo Bayou to Shepherd, and back along the *Memorial* side of the Bayou. The *City of Houston Parks and Recreation Department* (2999 S. Wayside; phone: 845-1000) offers a list of other bike routes.

FISHING Best for fishing is Galveston, where you can wet a line in the Gulf of Mexico off piers or from deep-sea charters that leave from Piers 18 and 19 of the *Galveston Yacht Basin.*

FITNESS CENTER The *YMCA* (1600 Louisiana; phone: 659-8501) has a pool, indoor and outdoor tracks, exercise classes, and handball and racquetball courts. Facilities are open to non-members for a fee.

GOLF The best public 18-hole course is in *Hermann Park* (6201 Golf Course Dr.; phone: 526-0077). Other courses can be found at *Bear Creek Golf World* (16001 Clay Rd.; phone: 859-8188); its *Master's Course* is among the country's top 50 public fairways.

JOGGING Most running is done along a 3-mile loop in *Memorial Park,* 4 miles from downtown and reached on foot from Buffalo Bayou or by taking the No. 16 Memorial or the No. 17 Tanglewood bus. Other possibilities are *Hermann Park* and the well-used trails along Ellen Parkway.

RODEO In nearby Simonton, 45 minutes west of the city, the *Roundup Rodeo* (Westheimer Rd.; phone: 346-1534) offers real live rodeo followed by country music dancing every Saturday night. There's also the *Houston Livestock Show and Rodeo* in February (see *Special Events*).

SWIMMING There are 42 municipal pools in Houston, open from June through *Labor Day.* The *Stude Park* pool (1031 Stude St.; phone: 861-0322) is conveniently located downtown.

TENNIS The municipally run *Memorial Tennis Center* (1500 Memorial Loop Dr.; phone: 861-3765) has 18 Laykold courts, showers, lockers, a tennis shop, and a practice court. There are free courts in most of the city parks.

THEATER

Houston has a wide variety of productions and theater companies; our favorite venue is listed below. For current offerings, check the daily and weekly publications listed under *Local Coverage* above.

CENTER STAGE

Alley Theatre This 50-year-old company produces new plays and musical theater works, unconventional productions of classic and/or neglected texts from the past, and contemporary plays using the talents of the theater's resident company of actors. The shows are presented on a large thrust-stage theater and a smaller arena theater, which are in a stunning concrete and glass structure downtown. Among the country's oldest resident professional theater companies, the *Alley* tours both nationally and internationally. 615 Texas Ave. (phone: 228-8421; 800-259-ALLE).

In addition, the *Miller Outdoor Theater* (100 Concert Dr. in *Hermann Park;* phone: 520-3292) offers free pop concerts during the summer. *Theater Under the Stars* musical extravaganzas are held at the *Miller* or the *Music Hall* (810 Bagby; ticket office is at 4235 San Felipe St.; phone 622-1626). Area colleges and universities also produce plays and musicals. The *Houston Ballet,* one of the nation's top companies, performs year-round at the *Gus S. Wortham Theater Center* (501 Texas Ave.; phone: 237-1439 for general information; 227-2787 for tickets).

MUSIC

Jones Hall for the Performing Arts (615 Louisiana; phone: 227-2787 or 629-3700) is the home of the nationally acclaimed *Houston Symphony Orchestra* and offers concerts and performances throughout the year by internationally renowned guest artists and companies. The *Houston Grand Opera* performs at the *Gus S. Wortham Theater Center* (501 Texas Ave.; phone: 227-2787) from September through May. All give free performances at the *Miller Outdoor Theater* in *Hermann Park* in the summer. Big rock and occasional country-and-western concerts are held at the *Summit* (10 Greenway Plaza; phone: 961-9003) throughout the year.

NIGHTCLUBS AND NIGHTLIFE

Depending on what you want, you can unwind or recharge at one or more of Houston's nightspots. Current favorites are the *Pecos Grill* (2044 E. Jester; phone: 861-0180) or *Wild West* (10086 Long Point; phone: 465-7121) for progressive country music, Texas-style, and local color; *Billy Blues* (6025 Richmond Ave.; phone: 266-9294) for blues; *Al Marks Melody Lane Ballroom* (3027 Crossview; phone: 785-5301) for ballroom dancing; and *Yucatan Liquor Stand* (6353 Richmond Ave.; phone: 789-6055) for rock. *Laffstop* (1952-A W. Grey St.; phone: 524-2333) has a triple bill of comedians on national tour.

Best in Town

CHECKING IN

Even though hotels were overbuilt during the 1970s boom and some are having problems filling their available inventory, rates have not gone down. There are, however, several moderate to inexpensive motel chains scattered about Houston, including *Motel 6, Ramada, Best Western, La Quinta, Days Inn,* and *TraveLodge.* Most of Houston's major hotels have complete facilities for the business traveler. Those listed below as having "business services" usually offer such conveniences as meeting rooms, photocopiers, computers, translation services, and express checkout, among others. Call the individual hotel for additional information. Expect to pay $150 or more a night for a double room at hotels we list as expensive, $90 to $150 at the one that's rated moderate, and $60 to $90 at the one we list as inexpensive.

Unless otherwise noted, hotels have air conditioning, private baths, TV sets, and telephones.

All hotels below are in Houston and telephone and fax numbers are in the 713 area code unless otherwise indicated.

EXPENSIVE

La Colombe d'Or This converted mansion, next to *St. Thomas University* in the heart of Houston's Montrose area, is known for its haute French restaurant of the same name (see *Eating Out*). A member of the prestigious Relais & Châteaux group, it features five antiques-filled suites with private dining rooms, and also has a penthouse for $575 a night. There is a walnut-paneled bar; public areas with original artwork on display; and an obliging concierge desk. Business services are available. 3410 Montrose Blvd. (phone: 524-7999; fax; 524-8923).

Omni Houston In the *Riverway* complex, it overlooks a scenic bayou area populated by swans and features an interesting sculpture garden. Amenities include two restaurants, a lounge, a health club, four tennis courts, and a garage. Twenty-four-hour room service is available. A concierge desk and business services also are offered. In *Riverway* at Post Oak La. and Woodway Dr. (phone: 871-8181; 800-THE-OMNI; fax: 871-8116).

Ritz-Carlton Considered the top of the line in Houston, this establishment offers all the attention and amenities normally found in a top European hotel. There is a restaurant and grill, bar, lounge, heated pool, access to a health club, 24-hour room service, a concierge desk, and business services. 1919 Briar Oaks La. (phone: 840-7600; 800-241-3333; fax: 840-0616).

Westin Oaks and Westin Galleria Smack in the middle of the luxurious *Galleria,* the ideal spot for a shopping spree, the 406-room *Oaks* (5011 Westheimer Rd.; phone: 960-8100; fax: 960-6554) is the older (but no less grand) facility of the two. Really big spenders can splurge on its Crown Suite, a penthouse with two fireplaces and a banquet table for 14—all for only $1,300 a night. Other features include a heated pool, cafés, entertainment and dancing, and access to ice skating, a running track, and indoor tennis. Also available is 24-hour room service, a concierge desk, and business services. At the other end of the mall is the 500-room *Galleria* (5060 W. Alabama; phone: 960-8100; fax: 960-6553), which is every bit as fine. The toll-free reservations number for both properties is 800-228-3000.

Wyndham Warwick Located in the museum district, this Texas institution features marble floors, 17th- and 18th-century French oak and ash paneling, and a 17th-century Aubusson tapestry. There are 307 wonderfully appointed guestrooms, and a 13,000-square-foot conference facility. Additional amenities include room service until 11 PM, a concierge, and business services. 5701 Main St. (phone: 526-1991; 800-WYNDHAM; fax: 639-4545).

MODERATE

Allen Park Inn Just outside the downtown area, this picturesque, antiques-filled property is a favorite of film crews shooting in Houston—although be warned that its neighborhood is pretty rough. There's a 24-hour restaurant, a bar, and health club facilities, plus business services. 2121 Allen Pkwy. (phone: 521-9321; 800-231-6310; fax: 521-9321).

INEXPENSIVE

Rodeway Inn-Southwest Freeway This well-sited property offers 81 modest rooms. The express checkout desk will speed you on your way. 3135 Southwest Fwy. (phone: 526-1071; 800-228-2000; fax: 526-8668).

EATING OUT

Besides fine regional cooking—chili parlors and Mexican restaurants abound—Houston offers a great variety of foods, with the total number of eateries steadily growing. Dining out here is a relative bargain—even the most expensive restaurants cost significantly less than in other similarly sized cities. Expect to spend $75 or more for dinner for two at restaurants in the expensive category, $35 to $75 at those rated moderate, and $35 or less at those listed as inexpensive. Prices do not include drinks, wine, tax, or tips. All restaurants are in the 713 area code unless otherwise indicated.

Unless otherwise noted, restaurants are open for lunch and dinner.

EXPENSIVE

Anthony's This popular restaurant in a superb location offers an innovative menu selection, which typically includes pasta stuffed with truffles, risotto with shrimp and vegetables, and a strawberry–Grand Marnier soufflé. Open daily; dinner only on weekends. Reservations advised. Major credit cards accepted. 4007 Westheimer (phone: 961-0552).

Brennan's A bit of New Orleans's Vieux Carré in Houston, this place is one of the city's most popular dining spots. Patio tables and a lovely pillared dining room are the setting for fine Louisiana-style and creole specialties. Open daily, with wonderful brunches on weekends. Reservations necessary. Major credit cards accepted. 3300 Smith (phone: 522-9711).

Café Annie Another outstanding Houston establishment, this local favorite specializes in original presentations of Southwestern-style dishes. Meat, game, and seafood are grilled over mesquite; good choices are red snapper with avocado-tomato salsa over a black bean and goat cheese quesadilla, and steak with portobello mushrooms and onions. It's a bit noisy, but this is a friendly, lively spot. Closed Sundays; dinner only on Saturdays. Reservations necessary. Major credit cards accepted. 1728 Post Oak Blvd. (phone: 840-1111).

Chez Georges Cozy with charming service and atmosphere, this is *the* place in Houston for fine French country dining. Menu highlights include silky salmon pâté with avocado and mustard sauce; sole and scallops *en brochette;* and profiteroles *au chocolat.* Closed Sundays and Mondays. Reservations advised. Major credit cards accepted. 11920-J Westheimer (phone: 497-1122).

La Colombe d'Or Located in the hotel of the same name, many say this place serves the best French food in Texas. Chef Fabrice Beaudoin, one of four Relais Gourmand chefs in the country, prepares at least four specialties daily, such as roasted red snapper, grilled tuna, and prime ribs, duck, or rabbit. Open daily; dinner only on weekends. Reservations advised. Major credit cards accepted. *La Colombe d'Or Hotel,* 3410 Montrose Blvd. (phone: 524-7999).

La Reserve The *Omni* hotel's elegant dining room offers superb crab cakes, sea scallops with polenta, lamb chops smothered in rosemary and garlic, and lobster bisque. Luxury abounds in the service, decor, and food. Open for dinner only. Closed Sundays. Reservations advised. Major credit cards accepted. 4 Riverway (phone: 871-8181).

Ruth's Chris Steak House This is a true Texas establishment—redolent with the aroma of beef. Decorated with oil company paraphernalia and flashing the latest Dow Jones reports, it's much appreciated for its prime cuts: filet, porterhouse, and strip steaks. Open daily for dinner only. Reservations advised. Major credit cards accepted. 6213 Richmond (phone: 789-2333).

Tony's Owner Tony Vallone is on hand most of the time to oversee this stronghold of elegance in an otherwise purposely informal city. Punctilious service by waiters in black tie, understated wood-paneled decor, and fresh flowers provide the backdrop for excellent continental food. The pâtés, risotto, game, and sauces are impeccable. Jacket and tie required. Closed Sundays; dinner only on Saturdays. Reservations necessary. Major credit cards accepted. 1801 Post Oak Blvd. (phone: 622-6778).

MODERATE

Cadillac Bar This is a Houston favorite for fine Mexican food. Try the *queso flameado con chorizo* (melted white cheese with sausage) with tender tortillas for starters. Ask about house specialties, which include such exotic dishes as mesquite-smoked kid. Reservations advised. Major credit cards accepted. 1802 Shepherd at I-10 (phone: 862-2020).

Ninfa's A must for Mexican fare, this place seems to be on every local's list, so you may have to wait. But it's worth it, particularly for the *tacos al carbón* (tortillas wrapped around barbecued pork or beef) and *chilpanzingas* (ham and cheese wrapped in pastry, fried, and topped with sour cream). There are 14 locations now, but the downtown site is still the best. Reservations advised. Major credit cards accepted. 2704 Navigation (phone: 228-1175).

Nit Noi Extremely popular with the *Rice University* area crowds, this little jewel is representative of Houston's outstanding Asian food selection. Menu favorites are the Thai egg rolls stuffed with cream cheese and grated veggies; soft spring rolls packed with tofu, rice noodles, and cilantro; and for dessert, sticky rice with mango. Open daily; dinner only on Sundays. No reservations. Major credit cards accepted. 2462 Bolsover (phone: 524-8114).

Pappasito's Possibly the only thing more wonderful than this wildly popular cantina's charbroiled swordfish with Mexican spices is the sparkling service—or the spine-tingling margaritas. The roll-your-own *fajitas* also deserve notice. Reservations advised. Major credit cards accepted. Several locations, but the most central is 6445 Richmond at Hillcroft (phone: 784-5253).

Rio Ranch Southwestern fare at its best features chef Robert Del Grande's mix of pork loin in pumpkin-seed mole, quail in a zesty chili sauce, and hot-and-spicy shrimp salsa. The interior is true Texana, with stone walls, iron-work detail, and rodeo-print linen. Open daily for breakfast, lunch, and dinner. Reservations advised. Major credit cards accepted. 9999 Westheimer (phone: 952-5000).

INEXPENSIVE

Goode Company Barbecue Without any doubt, this down-home eatery is the best place in Houston to eat smoked beef, chicken, links, and ribs, along with divine but fattening fixin's and great fresh breads, particularly the jalapeño-cheese. Leave room for pecan pie, too. No reservations. Major credit cards accepted. 5109 Kirby at US Hwy. 59 (phone: 522-2530).

Goode Company Seafood Excellent, fresh Texas seafood, most of it from just 50 miles away, dominates the menu. Among the highlights are oysters, frogs' legs, crawfish, homemade gumbo, and mesquite-grilled rainbow trout and swordfish. No reservations. Major credit cards accepted. 2621 Westpark (phone: 523-7154).

Harlow's Hollywood Café Open daily until 4 AM, this is the place to go after all the other nightspots have closed. Urban cowboys and dance club denizens rub shoulders with the opera set; everything from deli sandwiches to Mexican dishes to Greek food and pre-dawn breakfast is on the menu. Parking is hard to find, and you'll probably have to stand in line if you're not among the first to arrive, but it's worth it for people watching. No reservations. Major credit cards accepted. 3102 Hillcroft (phone: 780-9500).

Indianapolis

Once called "India-no-place," Indianapolis has shed its lackluster image and today boasts a blossoming downtown, a wide array of sporting events, and diverse arts and cultural offerings. With its elegant shopping malls, handsome neighborhoods, and low cost of living, it's the type of city that might seem like a nice place in which to settle down. In fact, *Places Rated Almanac* named it North America's eighth best city in which to live. For more than 20 years, an ongoing revitalization program has turned the city into what the *Wall Street Journal* called the "Star of the Snowbelt."

The once deteriorating downtown has burgeoned with restored charm and fresh vitality. Over the past two decades, historic buildings have been restored, contemporary office buildings and sports facilities constructed, retail enhanced, and downtown housing expanded. The city deliberately maintained the integrity of its downtown heritage by blending the old with the new. Two of the best examples are *Circle Centre,* where eight façades from historic downtown buildings are incorporated into the complex's architecture, and the contemporary *Artsgarden,* an eight-story glass rotunda suspended over a downtown intersection. Crisscrossed by skywalks and tunnels leading to hotels and other retail sites, the mall opened in 1995 bringing a much-needed retail component to downtown Indianapolis. With more than 100 specialty shops, three anchor stores, a virtual-reality gallery, and a cinema, *Circle Centre* has attracted additional retailers, restaurants, and businesses.

This city of 1.4 million is home to the *Children's Museum of Indianapolis*, the largest of its kind in the world. In the summer of 1996, the museum opened the *ScienceWorks* gallery and five-story *IWERKS CineDome* theater, which features large-format nature and science films. Other major attractions include the *Eiteljorg Museum of American Indians and Western Art* and a 64-acre zoo. Also part of the city's fabric are the *Indiana Convention Center* the *RCA Dome*, the *Hyatt Regency* hotel, and *Market Square Arena*, which serves as home court for the Indiana *Pacers* basketball team and Indianapolis *Ice* hockey team as well as the site of concerts and ice shows. The 60,500-seat *RCA Dome*, home of the Indianapolis *Colts*, also hosts sports events, conventions, and trade shows.

These facilities have enhanced Indianapolis's reputation as a major sports center. Since the early 1980s, the city has hosted over 330 national and international sports competitions. This year the city will again welcome the *NCAA Final Four.* Then there is the *Indianapolis 500,* the annual revving of engines at the *Speedway* and the world's largest single-day sporting event.

With all that the city has to offer, add safety to the list. According to the *FBI,* Indianapolis is one of the five safest large cities in the nation.

Indianapolis has come to be recognized as something more than just the town where a big 500-mile auto race is held every year. The quality of local life and its appeal to visitors have grown exponentially—and it looks as if there's more to come.

Indianapolis At-a-Glance

SEEING THE CITY

Although characterized by relatively flat terrain, Indianapolis does afford some breathtaking vantage points. The highest is in *Crown Hill Cemetery* (700 W. 38th St.; phone: 925-8231), at the grave of poet James Whitcomb Riley. (John Dillinger and Benjamin Harrison also are buried at *Crown Hill,* a National Historic Site.) The view from *Teller's Cage,* the restaurant at the top of *One Indiana Square* (1 Indiana Sq.; phone: 266-5211), also is exceptional. Another stunning view is from the 26th floor of the *City—County Building Observatory* (200 E. Washington St. between Delaware and Alabama Sts.; phone: 327-4345).

The 13-by-13-foot model of downtown Indianapolis at the *Indianapolis City Center* (201 S. Capitol Ave.; phone: 237-5200; 800-468-INDY), a visitor and community information center, can help you get your bearings. To find out where a museum or monument is located, press a button on a panel, and the site lights up on the model.

SPECIAL PLACES

Indianapolis is an easy place to get around. Washington Street is the north-south dividing line; Meridian Street is the east-west dividing line. Numbered streets always run east and west, and the number of the street represents the number of blocks north of Washington Street.

CIRCLE CENTRE One of the nation's newest urban shopping malls, *Circle Centre* has boosted the city's retail, dining, and entertainment options. More than a mall, it includes a nine-screen theater complex, a virtual reality gallery, and the glass-domed *Artsgarden,* the showcase for the city's performing and visual arts. 49 W. Maryland St. (phone: 681-8000).

UNION STATION Once a decrepit railroad terminal, *Union Station* was transformed during the mid-1980s into a festival marketplace like *Faneuil Hall Marketplace* in Boston and *South Street Seaport* in New York. Across from the *Indiana Convention Center & RCA Dome,* the three-block structure features nearly 50 shops, restaurants, and nightclubs. Open daily. Attached to *Union Station* is the *Crowne Plaza* (see *Checking In*) at 39 Jackson Place S. Dr.; (phone: 267-0700).

EITELJORG MUSEUM OF AMERICAN INDIANS AND WESTERN ART The $14-million adobe-style building, on the grounds of *White River State Park,* is a work of art in itself, and the collection, considered one of the finest of its kind in

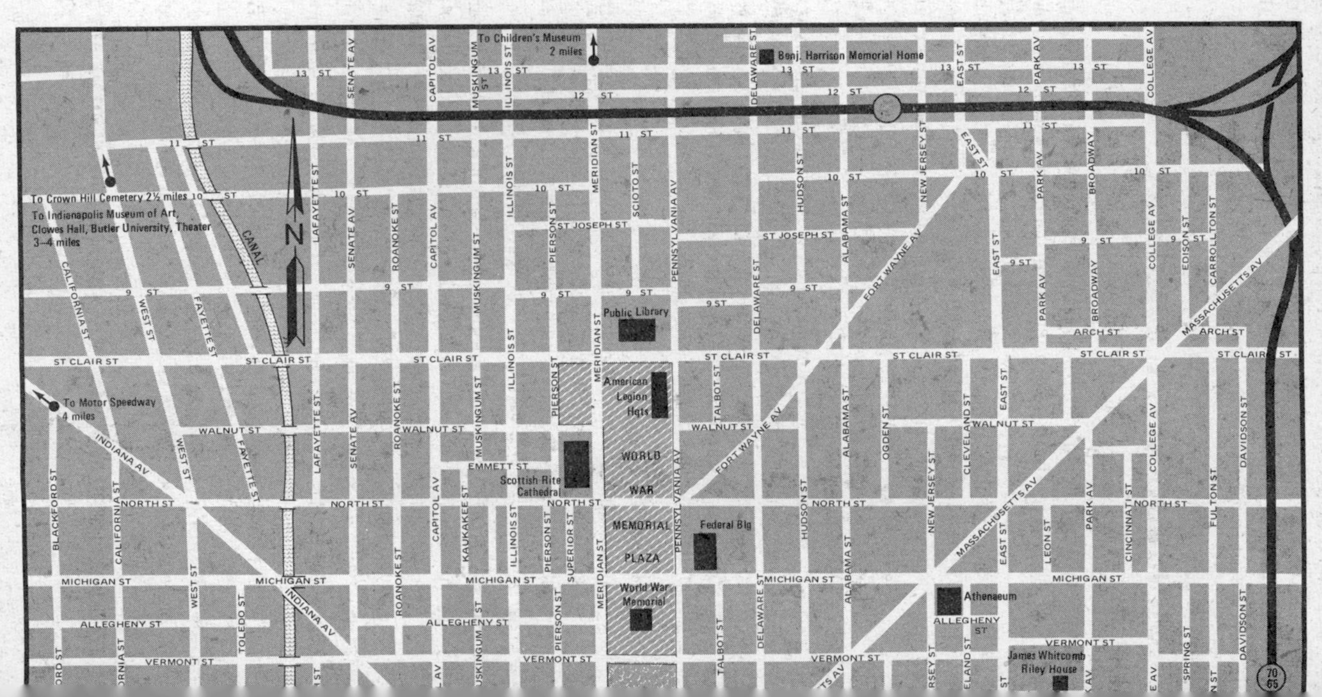
To Children's Museum 2 miles
Benj. Harrison Memorial Home
To Crown Hill Cemetery 2½ miles
To Indianapolis Museum of Art, Clowes Hall, Butler University, Theater 3–4 miles
To Motor Speedway 4 miles
CANAL
N
Public Library
American Legion Hqts
WORLD WAR MEMORIAL PLAZA
World War Memorial
Scottish Rite Cathedral
Federal Blg
Athenaeum
James Whitcomb Riley House
70
65
13 ST
12 ST
11 ST
10 ST
9 ST
ST JOSEPH ST
ST CLAIR ST
WALNUT ST
NORTH ST
MICHIGAN ST
ALLEGHENY ST
VERMONT ST
EMMETT ST
ARCH ST
CALIFORNIA ST
WEST ST
FAYETTE ST
BLACKFORD ST
TOLEDO ST
INDIANA AV
LAFAYETTE ST
SENATE AV
ROANOKE ST
CAPITOL AV
KAUKAKEE ST
MUSKINGUM ST
ILLINOIS ST
PIERSON ST
SUPERIOR ST
MERIDIAN ST
SCIOTO ST
PENNSYLVANIA AV
TALBOT ST
DELAWARE ST
HUDSON ST
ALABAMA ST
OGDEN ST
NEW JERSEY ST
CLEVELAND ST
EAST ST
LEON ST
PARK AV
BROADWAY
CINCINNATI ST
COLLEGE AV
SPRING ST
EDISON ST
CARROLLTON ST
FULTON ST
DAVIDSON ST
FORT WAYNE AV
MASSACHUSETTS AV

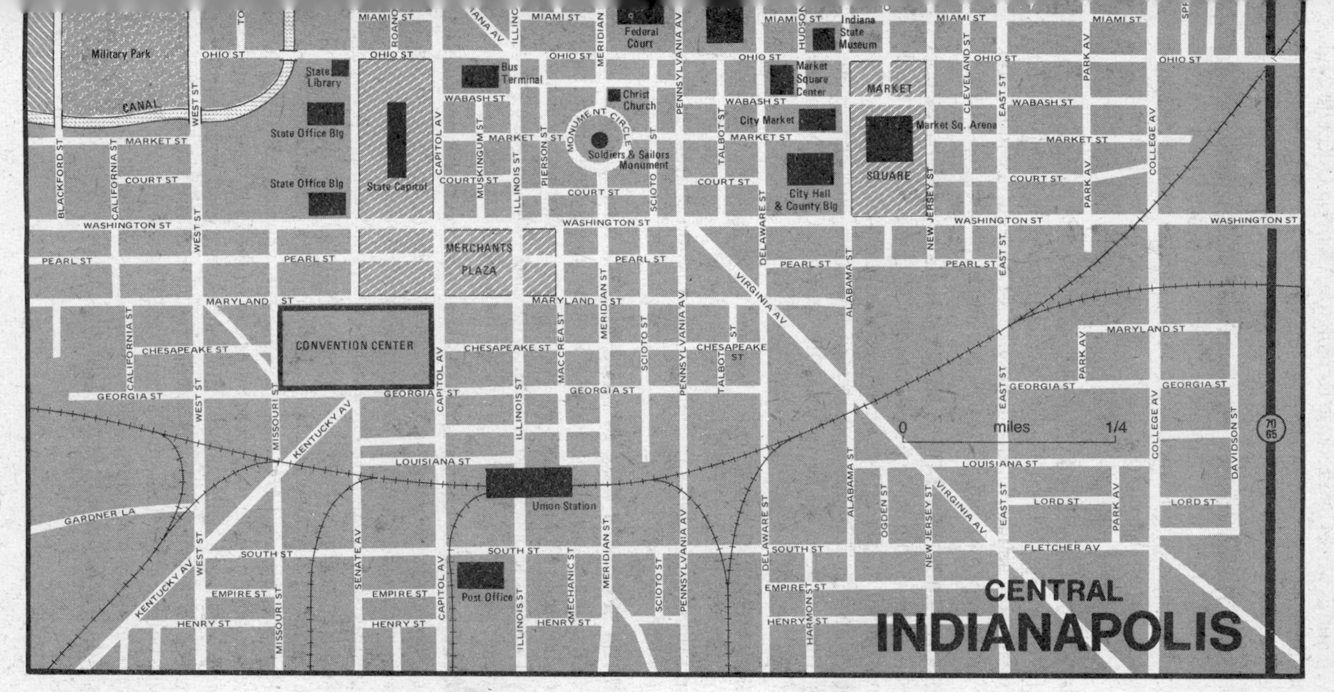
CENTRAL
INDIANAPOLIS
0
miles
1/4
70
65
Military Park
CANAL
State Library
State Office Blg
State Office Blg
State Capitol
Bus Terminal
Christ Church
Federal Court
Soldiers & Sailors Monument
MONUMENT CIRCLE
City Market
Market Square Center
Indiana State Museum
MARKET
SQUARE
Market Sq. Arena
City Hall & County Blg
MERCHANTS
PLAZA
CONVENTION CENTER
Union Station
Post Office
MIAMI ST
OHIO ST
WABASH ST
MARKET ST
COURT ST
WASHINGTON ST
PEARL ST
MARYLAND ST
CHESAPEAKE ST
GEORGIA ST
LOUISIANA ST
SOUTH ST
EMPIRE ST
HENRY ST
LORD ST
FLETCHER AV
DAVIDSON ST
BLACKFORD ST
CALIFORNIA ST
WEST ST
MISSOURI ST
SENATE AV
CAPITOL AV
MUSKINGUM ST
ILLINOIS ST
PIERSON ST
MACCREA ST
MERIDIAN ST
MECHANIC ST
SCIOTO ST
PENNSYLVANIA AV
TALBOT ST
DELAWARE ST
HARMON ST
ALABAMA ST
OGDEN ST
NEW JERSEY ST
EAST ST
CLEVELAND ST
PARK AV
COLLEGE AV
HUDSON ST
ROANO ST
VIRGINIA AV
KENTUCKY AV
GARDNER LA

the country, features works by Frederic Remington, Georgia O'Keeffe, and Ernest L. Blumenschein. Closed Mondays from *Labor Day* through *Memorial Day*. Admission charge. 500 W. Washington (phone: 636-9378).

INDIANA STATE MUSEUM This entertaining five-story museum relates the natural and cultural history of the state. Among the items showcased are a life-size mammoth, a recreation of 1910 Indiana, works by Indiana artists, and sports memorabilia. No admission charge. 202 N. Alabama, at Ohio (phone: 232-1637).

SCOTTISH RITE CATHEDRAL Considered the world's largest building dedicated to Scottish Rite Masonry, this vast Tudor Gothic structure has a 54-bell carillon, two organs, and an interior that looks like 3-D lace turned into wood. Free tours are given on weekdays. 650 N. Meridian (phone: 262-3100).

JAMES WHITCOMB RILEY LOCKERBIE STREET MUSEUM Indiana's underrated poet laureate lived in this comfortable house between 1893 and 1916. The house is considered one of the finest Victorian preservations in the country. The whole Lockerbie Street neighborhood, located downtown, has been restored to look as it might have at the turn of the century. Closed Mondays. Admission charge. 528 Lockerbie (phone: 631-5885).

BENJAMIN HARRISON MEMORIAL HOME This 16-room Victorian-Italianate mansion, built in 1875 for the 23rd president, has many of the original furnishings. Closed first three weeks in January. Admission charge. 1230 N. Delaware (phone: 631-1898).

INDIANAPOLIS MOTOR SPEEDWAY HALL OF FAME MUSEUM Race cars from the early days to the present are displayed at this museum situated in the middle of the *Indianapolis Motor Speedway*. Minibuses take visitors around the 2½-mile oval where the 500-mile race and Brickyard 400 take place annually. Open daily. Admission charge. 4790 W. 16th St. (phone: 241-2500).

INDIANAPOLIS MUSEUM OF ART By any standard, this is a truly remarkable museum. The *Mary F. Hulman Pavilion* houses the *Eiteljorg Collection of African Art,* and the *Krannert Pavilion* contains American, Oriental, primitive, and 18th- and 19th-century European art. The adjacent *Clowes Pavilion* is full of medieval and Renaissance art, plus some watercolors by Turner; there's also a skylit, plant-filled courtyard. In the gardens are modern sculptures, including Robert Indiana's *LOVE,* and a wonderful, geometrical fountain. The grounds originally were the riverview estate of the Lilly family, whose mansion now contains a collection of English, French, and Italian 18th-century art. The 152 beautifully landscaped acres also feature a greenhouse, nature trails, botanical gardens, and a large children's playhouse that has been converted into a restaurant. Closed Mondays. Extended hours on Thursdays. Admission charge for special exhibits. 1200 W. 38th St. (phone: 923-1331).

CHILDREN'S MUSEUM At the world's largest children's museum, kids and adults can explore the galaxies in the planetarium, ride a turn-of-the-century carousel, and see a real mummy and the largest collection of toy trains on public display. Nature and science films are presented in the museum's new five-story *IWERKS CineDome* theater. Opened in 1996, the "ScienceWorks" gallery features exploration stations with special programs held regularly. Closed Mondays from *Labor Day* through *February.* Admission charge. 3000 N. Meridian (phone: 924-5431).

INDIANAPOLIS ZOO Nearly 3,000 animals live in simulated natural habitats at this 64-acre, world class zoo. The downtown zoo features a *Deserts Biome* with free-roaming lizards and birds, daily dolphin shows, and an *Exploration Center* with hands-on interaction with animals. Rides on ponies, camels, and elephants are also available. This year will mark the 28th annual *Christmas at the Zoo* and will feature more than 500,000 festive lights as well as dolphin shows. Open daily. Admission charge. 1200 W. Washington St. (phone: 630-2001).

ZIONSVILLE The streets of this restored mid-19th-century village are now full of ritzy shops. It's a good spot to spend a long afternoon. 86th St. north on Zionsville Rd. Contact the *Greater Zionsville Chamber of Commerce* (phone: 873-3836) for information.

CONNER PRAIRIE Step back in time to 1836 and see the daily life of the era re-created. Interpreters portray villagers in this 32-building settlement: a doctor, a potter, a blacksmith, and an innkeeper talk as they perform their duties. Also featured is a restaurant serving country-style lunches, a new 18-hole golf course, an old-fashioned *Fourth of July* bash, and *Christmas* by candlelight. Closed Mondays; village closed November through March; restaurant open year-round. Admission charge. 13400 Allisonville Rd., about 30 miles northeast of Monument Circle via Rte. 37 and I-465 (phone: 776-6000).

GARFIELD PARK CONSERVATORY In 1996, the conservatory was transformed into a rain forest with more than 500 tropical plants. Environmentally controlled, the exhibit simulates a tropical habitat and features a large collection of bromeliads and epiphytes, a 15-foot waterfall, and fish swimming in exhibit ponds. Closed Mondays. Admission charge. 2450 S. Shelby (phone: 784-3044).

Sources and Resources

TOURIST INFORMATION

The *Indianapolis City Center* (Pan American Plaza, 201 S. Capitol Ave., Indianapolis, IN 46225; phone: 237-5200; 800-468-INDY), which is open daily, and the *Indiana Tourism Development Division* (1 N. Capitol, Suite 700; phone: 232-8860; 800-289-6646) supply brochures and tourist information.

LOCAL COVERAGE *Indianapolis Star,* morning daily and Sundays; *Indianapolis News,* afternoon daily; *NUVO,* weekly entertainment; and *Indianapolis Business Journal,* weekly. Also *This is Indianapolis* and *Where Magazine* visitors guides are available at most hotels.

TELEVISION STATIONS WRTV Channel 6–ABC; WISH Channel 8–CBS; WTHR Channel 13–NBC; WFYI Channel 20–PBS; WTTV Channel 4–local; WXIN Channel 59–Fox; and WNDY Channel 23–local.

RADIO STATIONS AM: WIBC 1070 (news/talk). FM: WFBQ 94.7 (classic rock); WENS 97.1 (adult contemporary); WZPL 99.5 (adult contemporary); WTPI 107.9 (adult contemporary/jazz); and WFMS 95.5 (country).

TELEPHONE The area code for Indianapolis is 317.

SALES TAX There is a 5% sales tax; the hotel room tax is 5%. A 6% beverage tax is imposed in Marion County (Indianapolis).

CLIMATE Indianapolis has typical Midwestern weather—beautiful springs, steamy summers, mild autumns, and moderately cold winters with varying amounts of snow.

GETTING AROUND

AIRPORT *Indianapolis International Airport* is a 15-minute drive from downtown. *Indy Connection Limousines* (phone: 241-7100) offers frequent service ($7 per person when you share a ride), from the airport to most downtown hotels. *Metro Transit*'s No. 9 West Washington Street bus (see below) travels between the airport and downtown; for the return trip, catch the bus on Washington between Illinois and Maryland Streets.

BUSFor schedules and fare information, call *Metro Transit* (phone: 635-3344). The fare is 75¢ off-peak, $1 rush hours; exact change is required.

CAR RENTAL You can get around by public transportation, but a car is more convenient. All the major national companies are represented.

TAXI Call *Yellow Cab* (phone: 487-7777), *A-1 Taxi* (phone: 856-8666), or *Hoosier Cab* (phone: 243-8800).

SPECIAL EVENTS

In March, the city hosts the *NCAA Final Four*. The *Indianapolis 500-Mile Race* is held at the *Indianapolis Motor Speedway* the Sunday before *Memorial Day;* myriad activities surrounding the *Indy 500* take place in May as part of the *500 Festival,* including the nation's largest half-marathon (in 1996 more than 15,000 runners participated in the 13.1-mile race). On the Saturday nearest the summer solstice in June, thousands crowd Monument Circle downtown for the *Mid-Summer Fest,* a music and food fair. During July, *Indiana Black Expo,* the nation's largest exposition of African-American culture, history, and enterprise, takes place at the *Indiana Convention Center* and throughout the city and *Kroger Circlefest,* the city's largest festival of food and live entertainment, is held downtown. August brings the exuberant *Indiana State Fair* and the *Indiana Avenue Jazz Festival,* featuring jazz, blues, and an array of food vendors. The same month, Indianapolis hosts the *RCA Championships,* a men's hardcourt tournament, and the *Brickyard 400,* a *NASCAR* race at *Indianapolis Motor Speedway.* The *National Hot Rod Association* drag races are held at *Indianapolis Raceway Park* every *Labor Day* weekend. September also brings the state's largest art fair, *Penrod,* and the *Brickyard Crossing Championships,* an annual *Senior PGA* tournament. In October, parades, concerts, and fairs lead up to a football matchup during the *Coca-Cola Circle City Classic.* Draped with thousands of twinkling lights, the 284-foot-tall *Soldiers & Sailors Monument* is transformed into the city's holiday showpiece the day after *Thanksgiving.*

SHOPPING

Indianapolis has its share of today's marketplaces, huge malls filled with department stores, chain shops, eateries, and entertainment complexes. The recently opened *Circle Centre* mall (49 W. Maryland St.; phone: 681-8000) houses over 100 stores, including *Nordstrom* and *Parisian* and *Back Home Indiana* featuring upscale, Indiana products. Located just 20 minutes from town is *Fashion Mall* (8701 Keystone Crossing Blvd.; phone: 574-4000), which boasts a number of upscale retailers, including *Jacobson's, The Body Shop, Brooks Brothers, Laura Ashley, Pottery Barn,* and *The Sharper Image.*

SPORTS AND FITNESS

BASEBALL The Indianapolis *Indians* of the *AAA American Association,* the Cincinnati *Reds'* top farm team, play in the 13,500-seat *Victory Field,* which opened in *White River State Park* last year. (201 W. Maryland; phone: 269-3545).

BASKETBALL The *NBA* Indiana *Pacers* play in *Market Square Arena* (300 E. Market St.; phone: 639-2112).

BICYCLING The *Major Taylor Velodrome* (3649 Cold Spring Rd.; phone: 327-8356) has a smooth, 28-degree banked track open year-round (except when sporting events are in progress), depending on the weather. Helmet and bicycle rentals are available for a nominal fee.

FISHING There's good fishing at Eagle Creek Reservoir (7840 W. 56th St.; phone: 327-7130). Farther out of town are Geist and Morse Reservoirs and, about two hours south, the much larger Monroe Reservoir, near Bloomington.

FITNESS CENTERS The *National Institute for Fitness and Sport* (250 N. University Blvd.; phone: 274-3603) welcomes exercise devotees. The pool at the downtown *YMCA* (860 W. 10th; phone: 634-2478) is available to non-members.

FOOTBALL The Indianapolis *Colts* of the *NFL* play in the *RCA Dome* (200 S. Capitol Ave.; phone: 262-3389).

GOLF The 27-hole golf course at *Eagle Creek Park* (8802 W. 56th St.) has been rated one of the top public courses in the country. There are 11 other municipal public courses around the city. For information on all of them, call the *IndyParks and Recreation Department* (phone: 327-0000). The *Brickyard Crossing* course (4400 W. 16th St.; phone: 484-6572) at the *Indianapolis Motor Speedway* has 14 holes outside the track and four inside.

HOCKEY The *Ice,* a farm team of the *NHL* Chicago *Blackhawks,* plays at the *Market Square Arena* (300 E. Market St.; phone: 239-5151 for tickets).

ICE SKATING The *Indiana/World Skating Academy and Research Center* (Pan American Plaza, across from the *RCA Dome*; phone: 237-5565) offers indoor skating and skate rental to the public except during competitions. You can skate mid-September through early April at *Ellenberger City Park* (5301 E. St. Clair; phone: 327-7176) and *Perry City Park* (541 E. Stop 11 Rd.; phone: 888-0070); October through March at the *Pepsi Coliseum* (*State Fairgrounds*; phone: 927-7536); and year-round at the *Carmel Skadium* (1040 Third Ave. SW; phone: 844-8888).

JOGGING Take advantage of the walkways around Canal Walk and the *Indiana Statehouse,* at Capitol and Washington Streets, in the early morning and evening. Joggers also use *Military* and *University Parks* and the *World War Memorial* area downtown. Another possibility is the campus of *Indiana University–Purdue University, Indianapolis* (*IUPUI;* 1100 W. Michigan). The *Indiana University Track & Field Stadium* (901 W. New York St.; phone: 274-3518) has a nine-lane, 400-meter rubber track that's considered one of the world's fastest. It's open to the public for a fee. Still other joggers use the *IUPUI* campus to the half-mile River Promenade, a pedestrian walkway at *White River State Park.*

SWIMMING The *Indiana University Natatorium* (901 W. New York St.; phone: 274-3518), one of the premier aquatic facilities in the world, has two 50-meter pools that are open to the public for a fee.

TENNIS One of the most popular spots is the *Indianapolis Tennis Center* (815 W. New York St.; phone: 278-2100). Most high school courts are open to the public. Municipal courts can be found throughout the city. For specific locations, call 327-0000.

THEATER

The professional *Indiana Repertory Theatre* (140 W. Washington St.; phone: 635-5252), which has grown by leaps and bounds in the last few years, presents everything from musicals to Shakespeare. The *American Cabaret Theatre* offers European-style cabaret in a renovated ballroom at the historic Athenaeum building (401 E. Michigan; phone: 631-0334). Indianapolis also is home to the *Indianapolis Civic Theater* (1200 W. 38th; phone: 923-4597), the oldest continuously active civic theater in the US, offering a varied lineup of drama, comedies, and musicals. Community theater can be found at the *Edyveán Repertory Theatre* (1000 W. 42nd; phone: 923-1516). For dinner-theater, *Beef & Boards Dinner Theater* (9301 N. Michigan Rd. NW; phone: 872-9664) features Broadway plays and musicals. *The Phoenix Theatre* (749 N. Park Ave.; phone: 635-7529) offers issue-oriented contemporary alternatives. The *Indianapolis Ballet Theatre* performs at *Clowes Hall* (4600 Sunset Ave. on *Butler University* campus; phone: 637-8979) and at the *Warren Performing Arts Center* (9301 E. 18th St.; phone: 898-8061).

MUSIC

The *Circle Theatre* (45 Monument Pl.; phone: 639-4300) is where the *Indianapolis Symphony Orchestra* plays most of its concerts. The *Indianapolis Opera Company* performs at *Clowes Hall* (4600 Sunset Ave.; phone: 921-6444; 800-732-0804).

NIGHTCLUBS AND NIGHTLIFE

Like every other aspect of city life, nightlife in Indianapolis has grown. For one admission price, you can visit five clubs at *America Live* (phone: 630-LIVE) in *Circle Centre.* For dancing to the music of the 70s, there's *Flashbaxx* (*Circle Centre;* phone: 632-4553). Sports fans can catch the latest scores at the *Sports City Café* (*Circle Centre;* phone: 630-LIVE). Young singles patronize both locations of *TGI Friday's* (3502 E. 86th; phone: 844-3355; and in the *Courtyard by Marriott,* 501 W. Washington St.; phone: 685-8443). *Crackers Comedy Club* (8702 Keystone Crossing; phone: 846-2500) features nationally known comedians Tuesdays through Sundays; reservations necessary. Comedy is also king (or queen) at the *Broad Ripple Comedy Club* Tuesdays through Saturdays (6281 N. College; phone: 255-4211), reservations advised. Besides the *Circle Centre* nightlife, one of downtown's most popular sites is the *Slippery Noodle Inn* (372 S. Meridian St.; phone: 631-6968), Indiana's oldest—ca. 1850—bar and best venue for live blues. Jazz can be heard at the *Madame Walker Urban Life Center* (617 Indiana Ave.; phone: 236-2099) on Friday nights and at the eclectic *Chatterbox* (435 Massachusetts Ave.; phone: 636-0584). Dozens of cozy pubs, dance clubs, and *The Vogue* (6259 N. College; phone: 255-2828), a renovated movie theater that features live local bands and national acts, are located in Broad Ripple, a quaint and popular Soho-like area, just 25 minutes from downtown. There's country-western-style line dancing at *A Little Bit of Texas* (111 N. Lynnhurst; phone: 487-9065).

Best in Town

CHECKING IN

All the expected national chains are here—most of them immediately off I-465, which rings the city, or I-65, which runs diagonally through it. Most of Indianapolis's major hotels have complete facilities for the business traveler. Those listed below as having "business services" usually offer such conveniences as meeting rooms, photocopiers, computers, translation services, and express checkout, among others. Call the individual hotel for additional information. For a list of local bed and breakfast facilities, contact the *Indiana Tourism Development Division* (phone: 232-8860; 800-289-6646). Expect to pay $150 or more per night for a double room at hotels categorized as very expensive; from $90 to $150 at those listed as expensive; between $45 and $90 at those classified as moderate; and less than $45 at inexpensive places. Rates are usually higher during *Indianapolis 500* and *Brickyard 400* weekends and other major sporting events. Unless otherwise noted, hotels have air conditioning, private baths, TV sets, and telephones.

All hotels below are in Indianapolis and telephone and fax numbers are in the 317 area code unless otherwise indicated.

VERY EXPENSIVE

Canterbury A small, European-style hostelry, with indoor access to *Circle Centre*, it offers 99 rooms and penthouse suites with skylights. Its romantic and highly lauded *Beaulieu* restaurant specializes in continental fare. Among the hotel's amenities are 24-hour room service, a concierge, and business services. 123 S. Illinois St. (phone: 634-3000; fax: 685-2519).

Westin Now the largest hotel in the state (573 rooms), it is connected via skywalk to the *Indiana Convention Center & RCA Dome.* Its restaurant, *Graffiti's,* features an open grill and buffet, and the lobby lounge has a cappuccino bar. The 39,000 square feet of meeting and banquet space can handle receptions for up to 1,500 people. Room service is available around the clock, and there is a concierge desk, an indoor pool, and business services. 50 S. Capitol Ave. (phone: 262-8100; 800-228-3000; fax: 231-3928).

EXPENSIVE

Courtyard by Marriott Convenient to the *Eiteljorg Museum of American Indians and Western Art*, the new baseball stadium, and *Indiana Convention Center & RCA Dome,* this hotel offers guests 233 rooms and *TGI Friday's* restaurant. Facilities include a heated outdoor pool and an exercise room. There is also room service until midnight and business services. 501 W. Washington St. (phone: 635-4443; 800-321-2211; fax: 687-0029).

Crowne Plaza at Union Station Built within the train shed of an existing 1888 railway depot, the hotel has retained a great deal of the original architecture. It also is conveniently connected to the *Union Station* marketplace and the *RCA Dome.* There are 276 rooms (including 26 within restored railway cars), a restaurant, heated pool, Jacuzzi, and exercise facilities. Business services are available. 123 W. Louisiana St. (phone: 631-2221; 800-2CROWNE; fax: 236-7474).

Omni Severin Connected to *Circle Centre* by a skywalk, this renovated, historic 423-room establishment blends historic columns and grand staircases with contemporary architecture. (Don't confuse this hotel with its franchise, the *Omni North,* about 25 minutes from town.) There are two restaurants, an indoor pool, and a health club. Other amenities include room service until midnight, a concierge, and business services. 40 W. Jackson Pl. (phone: 634-6664; 800-THE-OMNI; fax: 687-3612).

Radisson Plaza and Suites Connected to more than a hundred of the city's upscale shops and restaurants, this 552-room hotel is convenient as well as comfortable. Amenities include a restaurant, a pool, a Jacuzzi, and saunas as well as free access to a nearby health club. The hotel offers business services and room service until 1 AM;. 8787 Keystone Crossing (phone: 846-2700; 800-333-3333; fax: 574-6775).

MODERATE

Indianapolis Motor Speedway Motel Next to the racetrack, this 108-room motel has many leisure-time pluses, including an 18-hole golf course (four holes of which are in the infield of the track) and an outdoor heated pool. The *Brickyard* restaurant overlooks the track and the golf course; the *Speedway Museum* is easily accessible. Business services are available. 4400 W. 16th St. (phone: 241-2500; fax: 241-2133).

INEXPENSIVE

Days Inn South A pleasant swimming pool makes the typical low rates at this 104-room motel especially noteworthy. There is no restaurant. On US 31 south and I-465 (phone: 788-0811; 800-325-2525; fax: 788-0143).

EATING OUT

Indianapolis has always had more than its share of steak-and-baked-potato places and very few ethnic eateries, but this situation has greatly improved. The city now boasts an array of ethnic restaurants that specialize in California-style, Cajun, Chinese, French, German, Greek, Italian, Japanese, Mediterranean, and Thai cuisine. Since the 1995 opening of *Circle Centre*, a number of restaurants, coffee shops, and microbreweries have enchanced the downtown scene. You'll pay $40 or more for dinner for two at restaurants listed as expensive, $25 to $40 at places categorized as moderate, and less than $25 at inexpensive places. Prices do not include drinks, wine, tax, or tips. All restaurants are in the 317 area code unless otherwise indicated.

Unless otherwise noted, all restaurants are open for lunch and dinner.

EXPENSIVE

Adam's Rib and Seafood House Prime and barbecued ribs and fresh seafood are the specialties, and the appetizer menu always lists at least one exotic viand such as alligator, black bear, or antelope. Closed Sundays and Mondays; dinner only on Saturdays. Reservations advised. Major credit cards accepted. 40 S. Main, in Zionsville (phone: 873-3301).

Benvenuti Contemporary Italian food is served here in an elegant, yet warm and comfortable setting on the top floor of a downtown office building. The menu changes daily. Open for dinner only; closed Sundays. Reservations advised. Major credit cards accepted. 1 N. Pennsylvania (phone: 633-4915).

Glass Chimney Some of the city's best continental fare appears on the carefully set tables of this consistently fine establishment in a charming old house. Open for dinner only; closed Sundays. Reservations necessary. Major credit cards accepted. 12901 Old Meridian, about 12 miles north of town (phone: 844-0921).

Illusions Magicians perform tableside at this unusual eatery that features seafood, steaks, poultry, fresh fish, and homemade pastries. Open for dinner only; closed Sundays. Reservations necessary. Major credit cards accepted. 969 Keystone Way (phone: 575-8312).

New Orleans House Unless you're ravenous, it's impossible to do justice to the extravagant all-you-can-eat seafood buffet. Allow plenty of time to consume your fill of oysters and clams on the half shell, chowders and creole dishes, crab legs and lobster. Open for dinner only; closed Sundays. Reservations necessary. Major credit cards accepted. 8845 Township Line Rd. (phone: 872-9670).

Peter's Made with local ingredients whenever possible, menu items include American and Midwestern dishes such as Indiana duckling, oven-roasted quail stuffed with corn bread, and sweet potato polenta. This contemporary restaurant also boasts an award-winning wine list. Open for dinner only; closed Sundays. Reservations advised. Major credit cards accepted. 8505 Keystone Crossing (phone: 465-1155).

St. Elmo's A local tradition since 1902 for steaks, chops, the hottest shrimp cocktails this side of Hades, and fine wines. Open daily for dinner only. Reservations advised. Major credit cards accepted. 127 S. Illinois (phone: 635-0636).

MODERATE

Hollyhock Hill One of Indianapolis's several family-style spots, it serves steaks, fried chicken, shrimp, and vegetables in generous portions. Closed Mondays; dinner only Tuesdays through Saturdays; lunch and dinner on Sundays. Reservations advised. Major credit cards accepted. 8110 N. College Ave. (phone: 251-2294).

California Café Colorful, contemporary decor and excellent service make you forget that your table overlooks a shopping mall atrium. Located in *Circle Centre,* this restaurant features salads; mouth-watering pasta dishes; California-style pizza; and entrées such as grilled salmon with artichokes, bacon and plum tomato sauce and cumin-crusted rack of pork. Reservations advised. Major credit cards accepted. *Circle Centre* (phone: 488-8686)

Milano Inn Within easy access of the downtown business district, this restaurant specializes in Italian fare. The succulent specialties include fettuccine Alfredo, chicken marsala and *timballo* (five-layer lasagna with ground beef, sausage, three types of cheese, and homemade noodles). Open daily; dinner only Sundays. Reservations advised. Major credit cards accepted. 231 S. College Ave. (phone: 264-3585) and a second location at 2370 W. 86th St. (phone: 872-7255).

Parthenon Surrounded by the boutiques of *Broad Ripple Village,* this restaurant serves authentic Greek and Middle Eastern cooking. The *spanakopita,* a pastry filled with spinach and feta cheese, and lamb shish kebabs, are especially good. On Friday and Saturday nights, a belly dancer entertains. Reservations advised on weekends. Major credit cards accepted. 6319 Guilford Ave. (phone: 251-3138).

Shapiro's This is Indianapolis's best deli, and the food is served cafeteria-style. The place is lauded by locals for its corned beef sandwiches, homemade soups, and creamy cheesecake. Open daily from 6:30 AM to 8:30 PM. No reservations or credit cards accepted. 808 S. Meridian (phone: 631-4041).

Snax The menu at this sleek, stylish eatery features nothing but appetizers—and not just the usual potato skins and cheese sticks. Good choices include the baked shrimp with fried capers and herb garlic butter, and grilled chicken with cilantro pesto. Open for dinner only; closed Sundays and Mondays. No reservations. Major credit cards accepted. 2413 E. 65th St. (phone: 257-6291).

INEXPENSIVE

Broad Ripple Brew Pub As the name suggests, it's the beer—up to eight varieties—that draws the crowds. Scotch eggs (hard-boiled eggs that are wrapped in sausage, breaded, and deep-fried), fish-and-chips, and shepherd's pie are menu staples. Closed Sundays. No reservations. MasterCard and Visa accepted. 842 E. 65th St. (phone: 253-BREW).

Forbidden City The menu here is several pages long. Chinese fare is the specialty; excellently prepared Hunan, Szechuan, and Mandarin dishes are tastefully served in an elegant Oriental atmosphere. Closed Mondays. Reservations advised for parties of seven or more. Major credit cards accepted. 2605 E. 65th St. at Keystone Ave. (phone: 257-7388).

MCL Cafeterias Ten locations in the city offer homemade fried chicken, vegetables, cinnamon rolls, and pies. No reservations or credit cards accepted. (phone: 257-5425 for information on all locations.)

El Sol de Tala The home cooking in this authentic Mexican eatery is well worth traveling just east of downtown on US 40. Regulars favor *pollo en mole* (boiled chicken with chocolate and spice sauce), guacamole, and *chiles rellenos.* A mariachi band plays every Friday and Saturday evening. Open daily. Reservations advised on weekends. Major credit cards accepted. 2444 E. Washington (635-8252).

Kansas City, Missouri

Surrounded by rich farmlands and grazing fields, Kansas City is in the heart of the "breadbasket of the world," and it owes a lot to its agricultural heritage, which is the backbone of its economy. Yet Kansas City has another side. It is called the City of Fountains because of its hundreds of beautiful fountains, many of them European, some centuries old. It is also a city of public art. J. C. Nichols, developer of the *Country Club Plaza* shopping center and the adjoining residential district, imported more than a million dollars' worth of statuary and other art in the 1920s, not for museums but for the boulevards and parkways. In fact, Kansas City has more boulevards than Paris—140 miles of wide, graceful, tree-lined streets and parkways. But the comparison with Paris does not extend to the condescension that Parisians show to outsiders. A visitor to Kansas City will inevitably be asked—and asked—what he or she thinks of the place. Self-conscious as they are about their city's image, Kansas City folks go out of their way to reassure themselves that you're having a good time.

Dynamic without being frantic, the Kansas City metro area (with a population of nearly 1.5 million) has in recent years been undergoing some growing pains; many civic leaders are concerned about the urban sprawl generated by rapid development to the southwest in upscale Johnson County, Kansas, and to the east in bedroom communities like Blue Springs. The primary effect of this on out-of-towners has been to turn Downtown into a ghost town after dark, with the city's entertainment center shifting a few miles south to the *Country Club Plaza*. Still, this is a town of gracious living and magnificent mansions. The *Nelson-Atkins Museum of Art* is one of the top museums in the United States, and its classical music events, repertory drama, and wide range of pop concerts provide enough entertainment to keep anybody busy.

The city has come a long way from the days of Rodgers and Hammerstein's musical *Oklahoma!* when, according to the song, Kansas City "went and built a skyscraper seven stories high—about as high as a building ought to go." Today's skyline includes complexes like the *Crown Center,* the self-contained "city within a city," and the Westport area, which is filled with young shopkeepers and artisans who have re-created the charm of old Kansas City by restoring the century-old buildings. The nation's first shopping center, *Country Club Plaza,* resembles a tile-roofed Moorish capital rather than an impersonal suburban behemoth of glass and brick. But some things that Rodgers and Hammerstein wrote still apply. Everything is "up to date in Kansas City"—and visitors more often than not are delightfully surprised to find it beautiful as well.

Kansas City At-a-Glance

SEEING THE CITY

One of the best views of Kansas City is from the *Observation Tower* on the 30th floor of *City Hall* (414 E. 12th St.; phone: 274-2000). It's open weekdays; there's no admission charge.

SPECIAL PLACES

Kansas City's three major shopping complexes are self-contained units that can entertain visitors for a whole day.

CROWN CENTER This $300-million development is the brainchild of the late Joyce Hall, founder of Hallmark Cards. Start out from the lobby of the super-elegant *Westin Crown Center* hotel, dominated by a tropical rain forest and waterfall that winds its way down the limestone hillside on which the hotel was built. Then move on to the more than 80 stores that offer everything from fine art to frivolities. 2450 Grand (phone: 274-8444).

WESTPORT The cry of "Westward, ho!" used to echo across the field that is now the *Westport* shopping and entertainment district. Pioneers outfitted themselves here for the great journey west. Although times have changed, the tradition of seeking out supplies at *Westport* is implanted solidly in the consciousness of Kansas City residents. A lot of work has gone into restoring the old buildings, many of which date to the 1850s. Broadway at Westport Rd.

COUNTRY CLUB PLAZA A few blocks south of *Westport,* this plaza is a Midwestern *Disneyland.* Statues, fountains, and murals line the shaded walks of this spectacular Spanish- and Moorish-style shopping center with over 150 shops, restaurants, and nightclubs. West of 47th and Main Sts. (phone: 753-0100).

NELSON-ATKINS MUSEUM OF ART The comprehensive collections here cover eras ranging from the ancient Sumerian civilization (3000 BC) to modern times. Egyptian, Greek, Roman, and medieval sculpture and a reconstructed medieval cloister make this more than just a museum of Old Masters, although there are plenty of classics—Titian, Rembrandt, El Greco, Goya, van Gogh, and the Impressionists. Contemporary works include the largest number of Henry Moore works in the US and the definitive Thomas Hart Benton collection. It also houses a notable Asian art collection. Closed Mondays and major holidays. No admission charge on Saturdays. 4525 Oak St. (phone: 561-4000).

KANSAS CITY ZOO A recent $30-million upgrade has created a sprawling world-class African exhibit where you can watch lions, rhinos, chimps, gazelles, and other wildlife in their natural habitat. Be sure to visit the *Deramus Education Pavilion* with its Disneylike walk-through environmental presentation, *The Journey.* Open daily except major holidays. No admission charge on Tuesday mornings. Swope Park (phone: 816-871-5701).

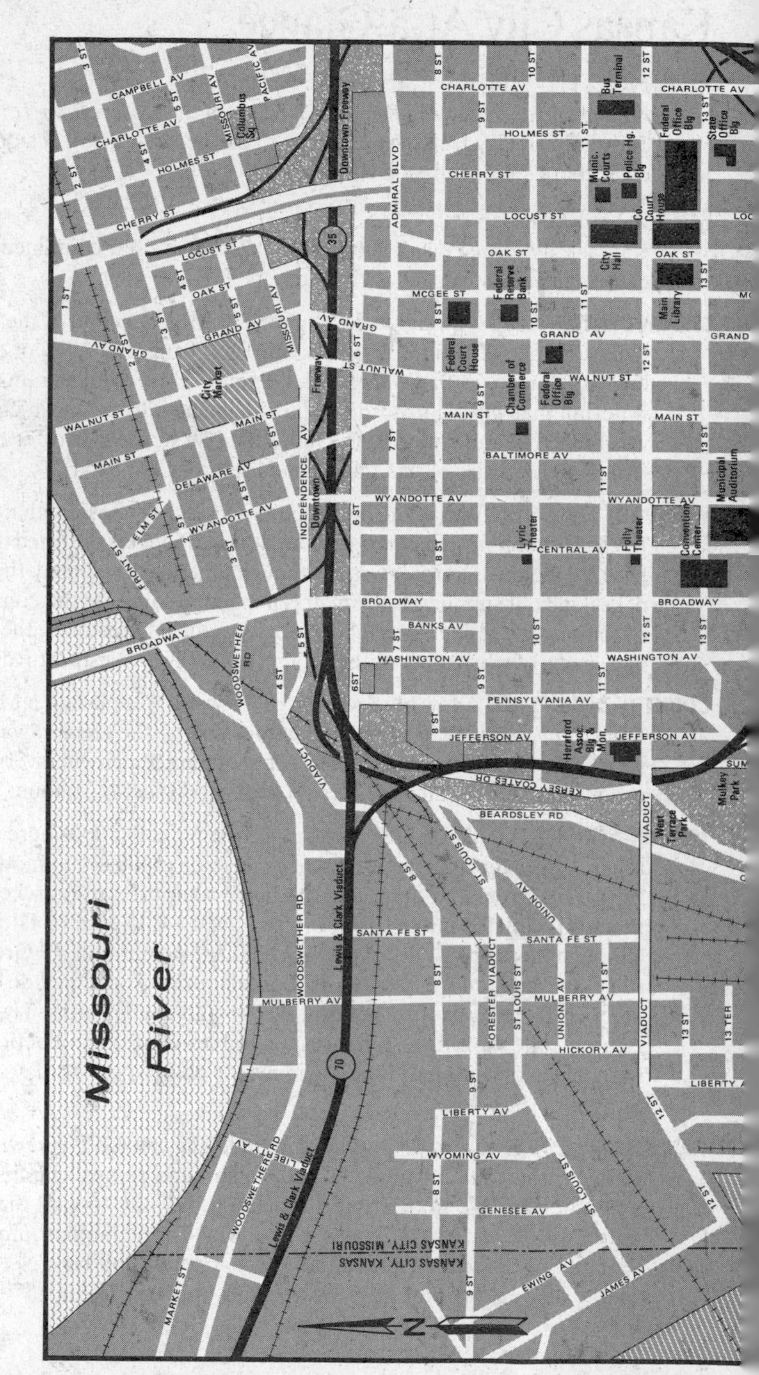
Missouri River
Downtown Freeway
ADMIRAL BLVD
35
CAMPBELL AV
PACIFIC AV
MISSOURI AV
Columbus Sq.
CHARLOTTE AV
HOLMES ST
CHERRY ST
LOCUST ST
OAK ST
GRAND AV
City Market
WALNUT ST
MAIN ST
DELAWARE AV
WYANDOTTE AV
ELM ST
FRONT ST
INDEPENDENCE AV
Downtown Freeway
BROADWAY
WOODSWETHER RD
VIADUCT
1 ST
2 ST
3 ST
4 ST
5 ST
6 ST
7 ST
8 ST
9 ST
10 ST
11 ST
12 ST
13 ST
Bus Terminal
Munic. Courts
Police Hq. Blg
Federal Office Blg
State Office Blg
Co. Court House
City Hall
Federal Reserve Bank
Main Library
MCGEE ST
Federal Court House
Chamber of Commerce
Federal Office Blg
BALTIMORE AV
Municipal Auditorium
Lyric Theater
Folly Theater
Convention Center
CENTRAL AV
BANKS AV
WASHINGTON AV
PENNSYLVANIA AV
JEFFERSON AV
Hereford Assoc. Blg & Mon.
KERSEY COATES DR
BEARDSLEY RD
Mulkey Park
West Terrace Park
ST LOUIS ST
UNION AV
Lewis & Clark Viaduct
SANTA FE ST
FORESTER VIADUCT
MULBERRY AV
HICKORY AV
70
LIBERTY AV
13 TER
WYOMING AV
GENESEE AV
KANSAS CITY, MISSOURI
KANSAS CITY, KANSAS
EWING AV
JAMES AV
MARKET ST
N

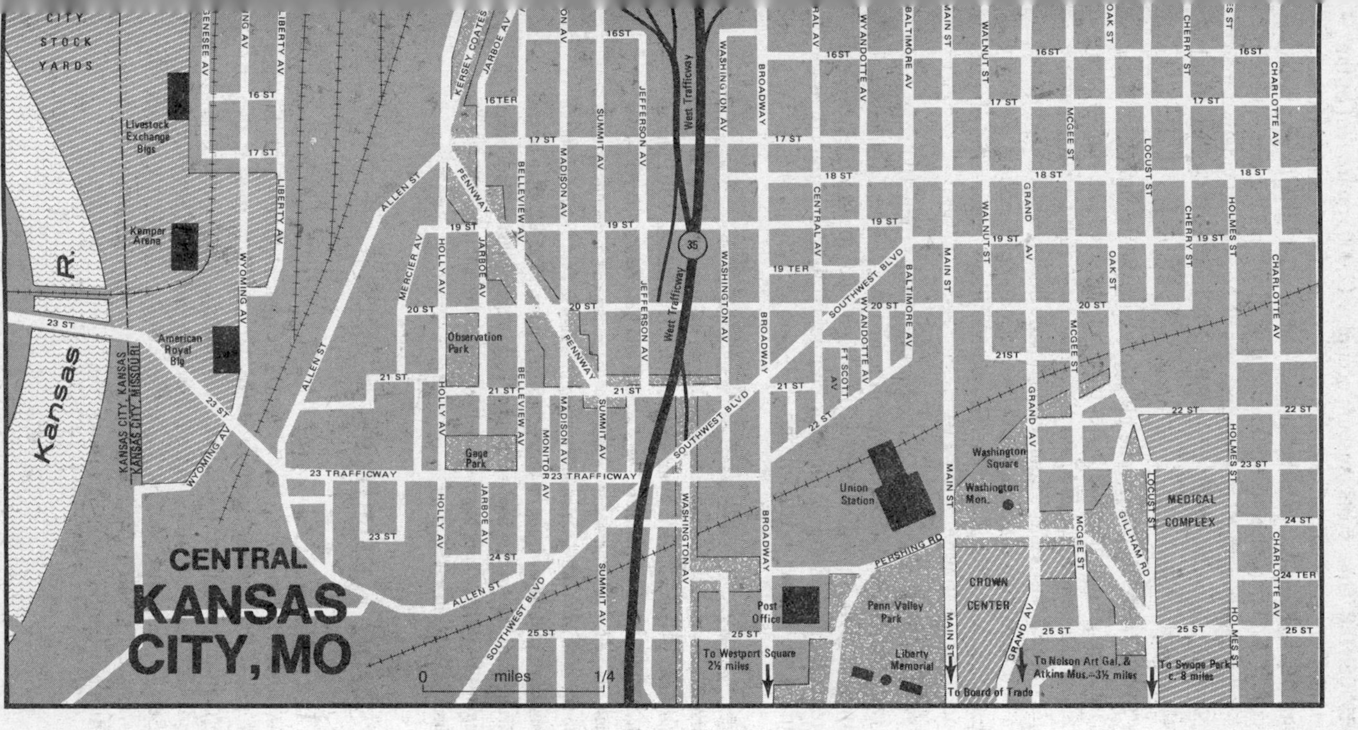
CENTRAL
KANSAS
CITY, MO
CITY STOCK YARDS
Livestock Exchange Blgs
Kemper Arena
American Royal Blg
Kansas R.
KANSAS CITY, KANSAS
KANSAS CITY, MISSOURI
Observation Park
Gage Park
Union Station
Washington Square
Washington Mon.
Post Office
Penn Valley Park
Liberty Memorial
CROWN CENTER
MEDICAL COMPLEX
West Trafficway
35
SOUTHWEST BLVD
PENNWAY
23 TRAFFICWAY
PERSHING RD
GILLHAM RD
To Westport Square 2½ miles
To Board of Trade
To Nelson Art Gal. & Atkins Mus.—3½ miles
To Swope Park c. 8 miles
0 miles 1/4

NCAA VISITORS' CENTER This sports museum occupies 12,000 square feet of the *National Collegiate Athletic Association (NCAA)* national headquarters in Overland Park, Kansas, a nearby suburb. It has photographs and video salutes to *NCAA* champions (both men and women) in 21 sports. There's also a souvenir shop with *NCAA* apparel, sports books, and videos. Open daily. No admission charge for children under five. 6201 College Blvd. (phone: 913-339-1906).

KANSAS CITY STOCKYARDS Although the great packing plants and most of the steers are long gone, there's still plenty of action here. The most recent addition is the *American Royal Visitors' Center* next to *Kemper Arena,* where you can explore Kansas City's equine and bovine heritage in a museum and watch a film about the *American Royal Livestock and Horse Show.* You may even get to see a livestock auction. Closed Mondays. Admission charge. 16th and Genesee (phone: 221-9800).

WORLDS OF FUN This 140-acre theme park contains more than 100 rides and *Oceans of Fun,* a huge aquatic park (summers only). *Worlds of Fun* is open daily June through August; weekends only from mid-April to late May and in September and October. Admission charge. On I-435, just north of the Missouri River, at Parvin Rd. (phone: 454-4545).

EXTRA SPECIAL

Just 8 miles east of downtown Kansas City, in Independence, Missouri, is the *Harry S Truman Library and Museum* (US 24 at Delaware St.; phone: 833-1400). Closed *Christmas, Thanksgiving,* and *New Year's Day.* No admission charge for children under 15 and school-sponsored educational groups. Up the road from the *Truman Library and Museum* is *Fort Osage* (about 15 miles east of Independence on US 24, in Sibley; phone: 795-8200), a reconstruction of the trading post established by explorer William Clark of the famous Lewis and Clark team. Open daily during daylight hours, March 15 through December 15.

Sources and Resources

TOURIST INFORMATION

The *Kansas City Convention and Visitors Bureau* has a 24-hour hotline (phone: 691-3800) for the latest information on city activities. It also provides brochures, maps, and a restaurant and hotel guide. The bureau, which is closed weekends, is in the City Center Square Building (Suite 2550, 1100 Main St., Kansas City, MO 64105; phone: 800-767-7700). Contact the Missouri state tourism hotline (800-877-1234) for maps, calendars of events, health updates, and travel advisories.

LOCAL COVERAGE *Kansas City Star,* daily; *Pitch* and *New Times,* weekly alternative newspapers.

TELEVISION STATIONS WDAF Channel 4–FOX; KCTV Channel 5–CBS; KMBC Channel 9–ABC; KCPT Channel 19–PBS; KSHB Channel 41–NBC; KSMO Channel 62–UPN; and KYFC Channel 50.

RADIO STATIONS AM: WDAF 610 (country music); KCMO 810 (news/talk); and KMBZ 980 (news, talk, sports). FM: KCUR 89.3 (NPR, classic, jazz); KMXV 93.3 (adult contemporary); KLTH 99.7 (adult contemporary); KCFX 101.1 (classic rock, football coverage); KBEQ 104.3 (country); and KLZR 105.9 (alternative rock).

TELEPHONE The area code for Kansas City, Missouri, is 816.

SALES TAX The sales tax is 6.5%; the hotel room tax is 12%.

CLIMATE Kansas City's Midwestern climate is notorious. It's fine in the spring and fall, but the winters are rough (frequently the thermometer doesn't rise above freezing in January), and the summers are hot and humid. Rain is particularly likely in spring.

GETTING AROUND

AIRPORT *Kansas City International Airport* is usually a 30- to 40-minute drive from the city. The green *KCI Airport Express* buses run from the airport to the major downtown and *Plaza* area hotels every 30 minutes. Return schedules vary; ask for a timetable at your hotel or call 243-5000.

BUS The Kansas City *Metro Bus* (phone: 221-0660) covers the downtown area, as well as the *Westport* and *Country Club Plaza* shopping and entertainment districts. The fare is 90¢.

CAR RENTAL The best way to see Kansas City is by car. Major rental firms are represented.

TAXI Call *Yellow Cab* (phone: 471-5000).

SIGHTSEEING TOURS

TROLLEY One of the best ways to see major sites is from the open-air trolleys that go from the *Plaza,* through *Westport* and *Crown Center* shopping centers, to downtown and back again. The trolleys (named Molly, Dolly, Polly, and so on) stop at the special trolley signs. From March through December, drivers will fill you in on sights along the way. Trolley tours don't run in January and February. *Kansas City Trolley Corp.* (phone: 221-3399).

SPECIAL EVENTS

The *Renaissance Festival of Kansas City* runs for seven weekends each fall, beginning *Labor Day.* The *RenFest,* a popular re-creation of 16th-century life, features musicians, courtiers, knights, actors, acrobats, craftspeople, and lots of food and drink. It takes place on 40 wooded acres at the *Agricultural Hall of Fame* (Bonner Springs, just 20 minutes west of downtown on I-70; phone: 561-8005). The *American Royal Horse and Livestock Show* is held from October through early November at *Kemper Arena* (1800 Genesee; phone: 221-9800).

MUSEUMS

In addition to those described in *Special Places,* Kansas City has a number of other noteworthy museums.

ARABIA STEAMBOAT MUSEUM More than a century after it sank near Kansas City, the *Arabia* steamboat was recovered from the Missouri River with nearly 200 tons of cargo intact. Exhibited are pre-Civil war guns, pottery, tools, and other treasures of a bygone era. Open daily. Admission charge. 400 Grand Ave. (phone: 471-4030).

KANSAS CITY MUSEUM OF HISTORY AND SCIENCE In addition to a planetarium, there are several exhibits about the Native Americans who once lived in the region. Closed Mondays. Admission charge. 3218 Gladstone (phone: 483-8300), and a downtown branch at the Town Pavilion (1111 Main St.; phone: 472-9600).

KEMPER MUSEUM OF CONTEMPORARY ART AND DESIGN The city's latest art museum is this Gunnar Birkerts–designed facility at the *Kansas City Art Institute.* Featured are an extensive permanent collection of paintings, sculpture, and photography from well-known artists such as Georgia O'Keeffe, Wayne Thibaud, Jasper Johns, and Frank Stella. There's also a café. Closed Mondays. No admission charge. 4420 Warwick Blvd., two blocks west of the *Nelson Gallery* (phone: 561-3737).

TOY AND MINIATURE MUSEUM OF KANSAS CITY A remarkable collection of toy trains, dolls, dollhouses, and exquisite miniatures is on display here. Closed Mondays and Tuesdays. Admission charge. 5235 Oak St. (phone: 333-2055).

SHOPPING

Kansas City has its share of today's marketplaces, malls, department stores, chain shops, eateries, and entertainment. At the *Crown Center* (see *Special Places*), shoppers can browse in such stores as *Victoria's Secret* (phone: 474-7451), *Baggerie* (phone: 471-3897), *Casual Corner* (phone: 472-0728), and *Waldenbooks* (phone: 474-8774). Museum shops are an excellent source of quality gifts and mementos.

SPORTS AND FITNESS

Kansas City has major league baseball and football teams.

BASEBALL The *American League Royals* take the field at *Ewing M. Kauffman Stadium* at the *Harry S Truman Sports Complex* (I-70 at the Blue Ridge Cutoff; phone: 921-8000).

FITNESS CENTERS *Woodside Racquet Club* (2000 W. 47th Plaza; phone: 831-0034) offers pools, exercise equipment, and aerobics; *Town & Country Health Club,* on the fifth floor of the *Westin Crown Center* hotel (see *Checking In*), has a pool, steamroom, sauna, and coed whirlpool bath.

FOOTBALL The *NFL Chiefs* call *Arrowhead Stadium,* at the *Harry S Truman Sports Complex,* home (I-70 at the Blue Ridge Cutoff; phone: 924-9400).

GOLF The best is at *River Oaks* (140 and US 71, in Grandview; phone: 966-8111).

HOCKEY The Kansas City *Blades* of the *International Hockey League* play at *Kemper Arena* (1800 Genesee; phone: 842-1063).

HORSEBACK RIDING In addition to guided trail rides, *Benjamin Ranch* (6401 E. 87th at I-435; phone: 761-5055) offers hayrides and barbecues.

JOGGING The best places to run are *Penn Valley Park,* at 25th to 33rd Sts. and Pershing Rd. near the *Westin Crown Center* hotel; *Jacob L. Loose Park* inner and outer loops, 1½ blocks south of the *Ritz-Carlton* hotel; and Ward Parkway, a large, lovely boulevard (pick it up at the *Ritz-Carlton* and run south). An excellent jogging and exercise trail is in *Mill Creek Park,* just east of the *Country Club Plaza.*

SOCCER The Kansas City *Attack,* a *National Professional Soccer League* team, plays its home games at *Kemper Arena* (1800 Genesee; phone: 474-2255).

TENNIS There are more than 200 public tennis courts in the Kansas City metro area. Most are free. *Swope Park and the Country Club Plaza* have especially good courts. For information, contact the parks department (871-5600).

THEATER

The city's *Theater League* (phone: 421-7500) presents touring companies of Broadway hits in the *Music Hall* (12th and Wyandotte Sts.) and produces its own shows at *Johnson County Community College.* Dramatic and musical productions are also booked into the *Municipal Auditorium* (200 W. 13th St.; phone: 274-2900) and the *Folly Theatre* (12th and Central; phone: 474-4444). The *Missouri Repertory Theatre* performs both classic and contemporary drama at the *Spencer Theater* (on the *University of Missouri–Kansas City* campus; phone: 235-2700). The *Starlight Theater* (phone: 363-7827) in *Swope Park,* an under-the-stars amphitheater, features musical comedy and concerts with top-name stars from May to mid-September. Musicals and comedies can be found at the *New Theater Restaurant* (92nd and Metcalf Sts., Overland Park, KS; phone: 913-649-7469). Closer to downtown is the *American Heartland Theater* (*Crown Center;* phone: 842-9999), with comedies and musicals. Fans of off-Broadway shows should check out the *Unicorn Theater* (3820 Main; phone: 531-7529). There are two fine children's theaters: *Theater for Young America* (*Mission Mall Shopping Center,* 4811 Johnson Dr., Mission; phone: 913-831-1400) and the *Coterie* (*Crown Center;* phone: 474-6552).

MUSIC

The *Kansas City Symphony* features internationally known conductors and soloists from November through May. Performances are held on Friday and Saturday nights and Sunday afternoons in the *Lyric Theater* (11th and Central; phone: 471-7344). There are two opera seasons, in April and October, at the *Lyric* (the operas are sung in English). A good guide to current musical offerings is the *Concert Connection* (phone: 235-2730), sponsored by the *UMKC Conservatory of Music.*

NIGHTCLUBS AND NIGHTLIFE

Kansas City's after-dark scene is now one of the liveliest in the Midwest. Because of its bistate location, however, liquor laws in Kansas City are a bit confusing. In Missouri, bars may remain open until 1 AM; clubs with cabaret licenses, until 3 AM. Bars are closed on Sundays, but hotels and restaurants may still serve liquor. The state of Kansas legalized the selling of liquor by the drink in the fall of 1986, and more counties are implementing this referendum each year. This means that in Kansas you may encounter taverns selling only 3.2% beer (lower alcohol content), restaurants with full-service bars, or private clubs requiring memberships.

Jazz thrives in Kansas City; call the *Municipal Jazz Commission* hotline (phone: 763-1052) for information. To find out who's playing at the clubs, check the "Preview" section of the Friday *Kansas City Star* or pick up a copy of the *K. C. Pitch* or *New Times,* free at most record stores (see *Local Coverage*). Numerous nightspots feature jazz from both local and national performers. In the downtown area, there's the *Tuba* (333 Southwest Blvd.; phone: 471-6510) and *The Phoenix Piano Bar and Grill* (302 W. Eighth St.; phone: 472-0001). In the midtown and *Plaza* areas, try the *City Light Jazz Club* (4749 Pennsylvania; phone: 444-6969), *The Point* (917 W. 44th St.; phone: 531-9800), *Starker's* (200 Nichols Rd.; phone: 753-3565), or *The Levee* (16 W. 43rd St.; phone: 561-2821). After midnight on Saturdays, stop in at the *Mutual Musicians Foundation* (1823 Highland St.; phone: 471-5212) to hear local musicians play all night long. Famous jazzmen stop in regularly at this spot, which also functions as a nonprofit foundation that provides a support network for local jazz musicians. Blues fans should stop in at *Nightmoves* (5110 NW Vivion Rd.; phone: 452-4393).

For country sounds, try the *Beaumont Club* (phone: 561-2668) in the Manor Square development in *Westport*. Blues and world music (reflecting a variety of international cultures) can be heard at the *Grand Emporium* (3832 Main; phone: 531-1504), and rock and pop are played to enthusiastic crowds at several of the *Westport* clubs. Singles action is liveliest at *Houlihan's Old Place* (4743 Pennsylvania; phone: 561-3141) and at the *Longbranch Saloon* (in nearby Seville Square, 500 Nichols Rd.; phone: 931-2755). The city's hottest gay nightspot is *The Edge* (323 W. 8th; phone: 221-8900). The best bet for out-of-towners is to park in the *Country Club Plaza* or in *Westport* and barhop. There are dozens of clubs and bars—some with live entertainment—within easy walking distance of each other. *Westport* is very casual; the *Country Club Plaza* is a bit more formal, but still pretty relaxed.

A SURE BET

Riverboat gambling is on a roll in Kansas City. A popular pastime both day and night, it brings a whole new level of entertainment to visitors and locals alike. At present, there are three casinos operating: *Harrah's* (203 Armour Rd.; phone: 471-3364), *Argosy Riverside Casino* (I-635 and Hwy. 9, Riverside; phone: 746-7711) and *Sam's Town Casino* (6711 NE Birmingham Rd.; phone: 414-7777). A fourth, the *Hilton Flamingo Casino* (1800 Front St.; phone: 855-7777) opened in 1996. Gamblers typically come aboard for two-hour sessions (though the riverboats are permanently moored and don't actually cruise). Hours of operation generally are 8 AM to midnight; later on weekends. All offer slots, bingo, blackjack, and other games of chance; you must be 21 or over to play.

Best in Town

CHECKING IN

Expect to pay $100 or more per night for a double room at hotels categorized as expensive, and $80 to $100 in moderate places; there are no exceptional inexpensive hotels in the city. Most of Kansas City's major hotels have complete facilities for the business traveler. Those listed below as having "business services" usually offer such conveniences as meeting rooms, photocopiers, computers, translation services, and express checkout, among others. Call the individual hotel for additional information. Unless otherwise noted, hotel rooms have air conditioning, private baths, TV sets, and telephones.

All hotels below are in Kansas City and telephone and fax numbers are in the 816 area code unless otherwise indicated.

EXPENSIVE

Hyatt Regency The queen of Kansas City's hotels, it has 731 rooms and 42 suites. Facilities include a health club, a pool, and tennis courts, plus a covered walkway to the *Crown Center* shops. There are three restaurants, most notably the *Peppercorn Duck Club,* with its diversified menu, and *Skies,* which offers a revolving view of the city. Also available are business services, a concierge desk, and 24-hour room service. South of the downtown loop; McGee at Pershing Rd. (phone: 421-1234; 800-233-1234 or 800-228-9000; fax: 435-4190).

Raphael This charming, European-style place, which bills itself as "Kansas City's elegant 'little' hotel," has a lovely view of the tree-lined, Moorish *Country*

Club Plaza. Its 123 spacious rooms and suites offer hospitality without smothering. There is a restaurant and lounge on the premises, and several excellent dining spots are within walking distance. Amenities include 24-hour room service and complimentary continental breakfast and newspapers each morning. Guests may use the swimming pool at the *Ritz-Carlton* across the street. Business services are available. 325 Ward Pkwy. (phone: 756-3800; 800-821-5343; fax: 756-3800).

Ritz-Carlton Widely regarded as one of the best in town, this hotel has won awards for the quality of its service. Many of the 374 elegantly appointed rooms overlook *Country Club Plaza.* Guests enjoy dining pleasure at the *Top of the Ritz* restaurant. Amenities include marble baths, twice-daily maid service, a concierge desk, 24-hour room service, and business services. 401 Ward Pkwy. (phone: 756-1500; 800-241-3333; fax: 756-1635).

Sheraton Suites on the Country Club Plaza Formerly the *Marriott Kansas City Plaza,* this luxury property has 259 well-appointed suites with French doors separating the bedroom and parlor areas, and a restaurant; amenities include coffee makers and refrigerators. Business services are available. 770 W. 47th St. (phone: 931-4400; 800-325-3535; fax: 931-3352).

Westin Crown Center Built on a huge chunk of limestone known as Signboard Hill because of the commercial embellishments that once hung on it, this 730-room ultramodern property is part of the *Crown Center* complex. It integrates the hill's limestone face into the lobby, where there is a winding stream, five-story waterfall, and tropical rain forest. It has several restaurants, including *Benton's Steak & Chop House.* There's 24-hour room service and business services. 1 Pershing Rd. in *Crown Center* (phone: 474-4400; 800-228-3000; fax: 391-4438).

MODERATE

Doubletree The once-sleepy community of Johnson County, Kansas, is now buzzing with business, thanks to the industrial growth along I-435 and I-35 southwest of downtown Kansas City, and this 356-room hotel is geared to the needs of visitors with business in that part of town. There is a restaurant, and business services are available. 10100 College Blvd. (phone: 913-451-6100; 800-223-TREE; fax: 913-451-3873).

EATING OUT

Kansas City has great steaks and good French food. Its pride and joy, however, is barbecue. Visitors can select a relatively high-price haute cuisine restaurant or one with superb food at more moderate prices—although prices are reasonable everywhere. Expect to pay $60 or more for dinner for two at those places listed as expensive; $35 to $60 at those described as moderate; and less than $35 at inexpensive places. Prices do not include drinks, wine, tax, or tips. All restaurants are in the 816 area code unless otherwise indicated.

Unless otherwise noted, restaurants are open for lunch and dinner.

EXPENSIVE

American This top-end choice, perched high above the *Westin Crown Center,* upholds the loftiest of standards. The atmosphere is Art Deco–style, the menu eclectic. Appetizers include ravioli stuffed with puréed sweet potato and prosciutto, and grilled chicken livers; featured entrées are spiced venison, tuna steak in red bean sauce, and salmon wrapped in seaweed. Reservations advised. Major credit cards accepted. 2450 Grand Ave. (phone: 426-1133).

Jasper's This Kansas City landmark is renowned for its exquisite, French-influenced northern Italian fare. Service hits the heights, though the tuxedoed waiters have a reputation for hovering. Closed Sundays. Reservations advised. Major credit cards accepted. 405 W. 75th St. (phone: 363-3003).

Plaza III–The Steakhouse This place rose from the remains of an establishment that had a far more diverse menu, but the specialization serves the diner well. Premium cuts are served in a setting that recaptures a half-real, half-imagined era of steakhouse opulence. Reservations advised. Major credit cards accepted. 4749 Pennsylvania Ave. (phone: 753-0000).

Savoy Grill No K. C. restaurant has been around longer than this one, which opened in 1903 and has catered to celebrities as diverse as Teddy Roosevelt and W. C. Fields. Seafood has always been a specialty, particularly dishes such as lobster thermidor and shrimp de Jonghe. White-jacketed waiters, stained glass windows, and well-preserved murals complete the classic picture. Reservations advised, especially for parties of four or more. Major credit cards accepted. 219 W. Ninth (phone: 842-3890).

MODERATE

Golden Ox This haven for dedicated steak lovers is located in the heart of the stockyards, near *Kemper Arena.* Real cowboys chow down here and with good reason. Good, solid American cooking and arguably the best steaks in town. Reservations advised. Major credit cards accepted. 1600 Genesee (phone: 842-2866).

Princess Garden Chef Robert Chang's ever-growing Szechuan/Mandarin menu leaves the town's other Chinese restaurants scrambling to keep up. The entire Chang family gets into the act, providing consistently superb service. Reservations advised. Major credit cards accepted. 8906 Wornall Rd. (phone: 444-3709).

INEXPENSIVE

Stroud's The decor at this popular eatery is early roadhouse (which is exactly how the place began). The chicken is fried in big black skillets and served with your choice of equally comforting side dishes, including mashed potatoes, pan gravy, and homemade cinnamon rolls. And the service is appropriately casual. No reservations. Major credit cards accepted. 1015 E. 85th St. (phone: 333-2132), and 5410 NE Oak Ridge Dr. (phone: 454-9600).

A WORD ON BARBECUE

Kansas citizens are a peaceful lot, but you always can start a fight about who has the best ribs in town: There's no doubt that most natives would rather eat barbecue than anything else. Our advice is to check the phone book, snoop around, and ask locals what they prefer—and why. There's a wide choice, from *Gates & Sons* to *Richard's Famous Bar-B-Q, Hayward's Pit, Zarda's,* and a dozen more. Most are differentiated by their sauces, which range from sweet and thick to thin and peppery. There's surely a perfect rib to tickle your taste buds.

Las Vegas

Las Vegas is a glittering desert oasis that never sleeps. A 24-hour city of fantasy for some; an unending nightmare to others. It all depends on how you view casinos with volcanos in the front yard emitting piña colada–scented smoke. But whether it's loved as a vacation paradise or damned as "Sin City," the maze of contradictions that are bred here makes the place fascinating.

Although you'd never know it today, Las Vegas had rather humble beginnings. In 1905, it was incorporated as a town without much fanfare. Even the legalization of gambling by the *Nevada Legislature* in 1931 created only a minor dust storm. The tiny desert town languished until the arrival of one Benjamin "Bugsy" Siegel.

There are no memorials or tributes to Siegel anywhere in the city, but he had more to do with the development of Las Vegas as a sparkling Shangri-la than anyone else. Siegel was enamored of the make-believe world of Hollywood and decided to transform Las Vegas into an equally make-believe, luxurious gambling showplace. In 1945, he began to turn his dream into reality, building a lavish hotel-casino at the south end of what would eventually become the Strip. The *Flamingo*—named for his flamboyant girlfriend, Virginia Hill—opened on *Christmas Day,* 1946. A financial bust, the hotel closed immediately, and Siegel barely outlived his creation (he died in typical gangland style a year later). But he had planted the seed of an idea.

About 20 years later, another fan of Hollywood gave Las Vegas a boost. In 1966, reclusive billionaire Howard Hughes stayed in the penthouse of the *Desert Inn.* He and his entourage did not gamble, and the management requested that he move out to make room for high-rolling guests. Hughes politely declined—and bought the hotel. Others soon followed, including the Hilton group. Although remaining inevitably linked with gambling (and the sometimes seedy characters it attracts), Las Vegas acquired a measure of respectability, which it has attempted—with some measure of success—to enhance ever since.

Even with the success of Atlantic City and the legalization of gambling in other communities across the country, Las Vegas maintains its position as the world's top gambling resort—due in no small part to the city's constant efforts to improve itself. Several of the older hotels have received dramatic face-lifts in recent years, while new structures emphasize unique architecture and offer perks and freebies. This effort seems to have paid off. Estimates put the number of 1995 visitors at more than 29 million, an increase of 2.8% over 1994.

By and large, these visitors see one side of Las Vegas. Throngs of people crowd the cavernous, air conditioned Strip casinos 24 hours a day. In

Las Vegas
Lions Memorial Park
Fantasy Park
WASHINGTON AVE.
Whipple Park
Cashman Field Center
MCWILLIAMS AVE.
1ST ST.
HARRIS AVE.
BONANZA RD.
15
Las Vegas Transit Terminal
WILSON AVE.
MARYLAND PKWY.
ORAN K. GRAGSON EXPY.
95
BONANZA RD.
Las Vegas Club
Post Office
City Hall
Plaza
Binion's Horseshoe
Golden Nugget
Four Queens
Bus Depot
8TH ST.
STEWART ST.
Court House
FREMONT ST.
OGDEN AVE.
N
MAIN ST.
1ST ST.
CASINO CENTER BLVD.
3RD ST.
4TH ST.
6TH ST.
CARSON AVE.
MARYLAND PKWY.
Federal Bldg.
BRIDGER AVE.
7TH ST.
DISCOVERY DR.
CLARK AVE.
9TH ST.
LEWIS AVE.
LAS VEGAS BLVD.
BONNEVILLE ST.
10TH ST.
11TH ST.
HOOVER AVE.
GARCES AVE.
COOLIDGE AVE.
GASS ST.
13TH ST.
14TH ST.
15TH ST.
16TH ST.
CHARLESTON BLVD.
Dutton Park
4TH ST.
LAS VEGAS BLVD.
COLORADO AVE.
CASINO CENTER BLVD.
3RD ST.
9TH ST.
Huntridge Circle Park
NORMAN AVE.
FRANKLIN AVE.
INDUSTRIAL BLVD.
5TH ST.
REXFORD PL.
6TH ST.
7TH ST.
8TH ST.
UTAH AVE.
WYOMING AVE.
BRACKEN AVE.
MAIN ST.
OAKEY BLVD.
NEW YORK ST.
CHICAGO ST.
11TH ST.
MARYLAND PKWY.
15TH ST.
CANOSA AVE.
ST. LOUIS ST.
BONITA AVE.
BOSTON ST.
ST. LOUIS AVE.
BALTIMORE ST.
Baker Park
PHILLIPS AVE.
EXLEY AVE.
FAIRFIELD AVE.
PARADISE RD.
BEVERLY WAY
SAHARA AVE.
589
Downtown
Sahara
This map continues on ↓facing page
0 mile 3/4

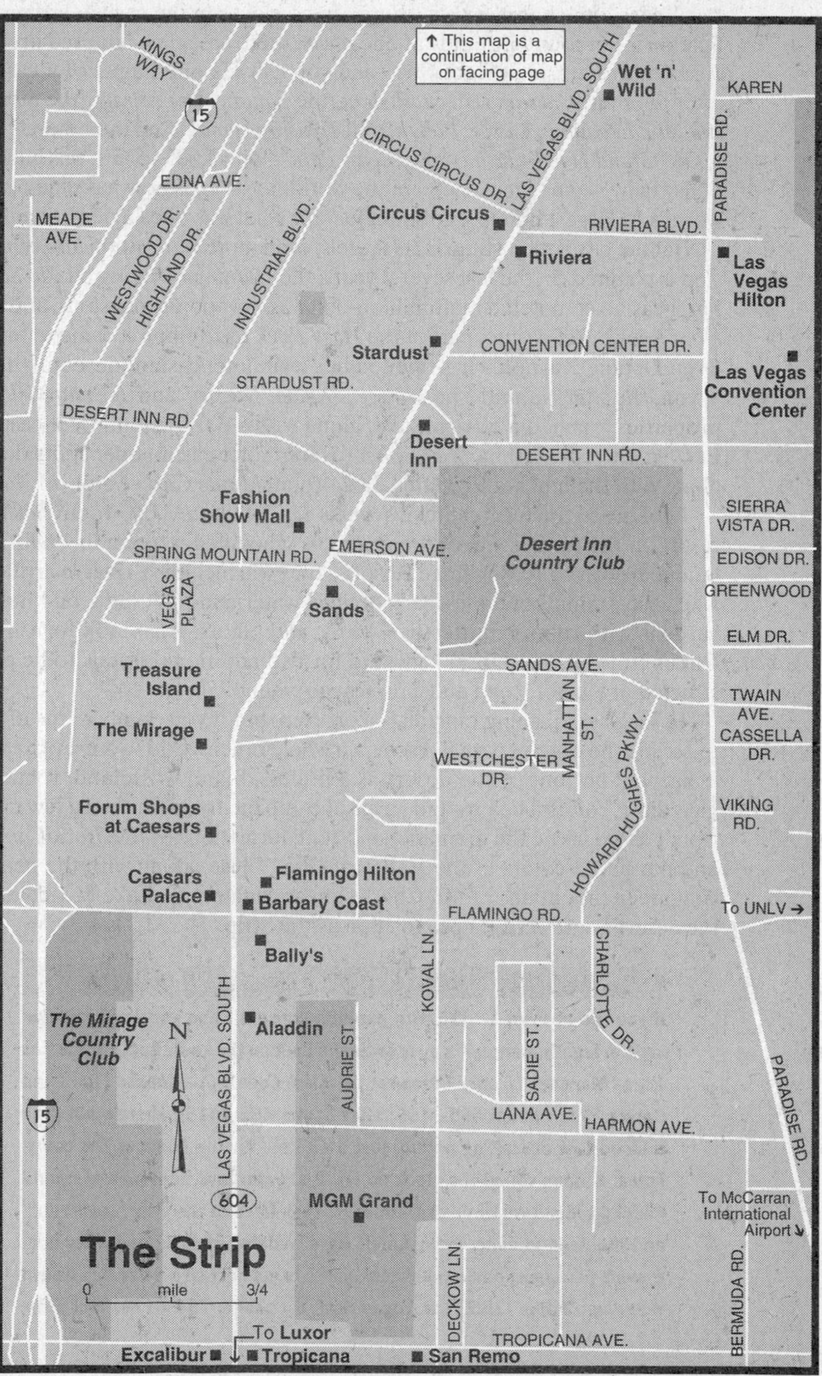

The Strip
This map is a continuation of map on facing page
Wet 'n' Wild
KINGS WAY
15
EDNA AVE.
MEADE AVE.
WESTWOOD DR.
HIGHLAND DR.
INDUSTRIAL BLVD.
CIRCUS CIRCUS DR.
LAS VEGAS BLVD. SOUTH
KAREN
PARADISE RD.
Circus Circus
RIVIERA BLVD.
Riviera
Las Vegas Hilton
Stardust
CONVENTION CENTER DR.
STARDUST RD.
Las Vegas Convention Center
DESERT INN RD.
Desert Inn
Fashion Show Mall
SIERRA VISTA DR.
EDISON DR.
GREENWOOD
ELM DR.
SPRING MOUNTAIN RD.
EMERSON AVE.
Desert Inn Country Club
VEGAS PLAZA
Sands
SANDS AVE.
Treasure Island
TWAIN AVE.
CASSELLA DR.
The Mirage
MANHATTAN ST.
HOWARD HUGHES PKWY.
WESTCHESTER DR.
VIKING RD.
Forum Shops at Caesars
Flamingo Hilton
Caesars Palace
Barbary Coast
FLAMINGO RD.
To UNLV
Bally's
KOVAL LN.
CHARLOTTE DR.
The Mirage Country Club
Aladdin
N
AUDRIE ST.
SADIE ST.
LANA AVE.
HARMON AVE.
PARADISE RD.
604
MGM Grand
To McCarran International Airport
0 mile 3/4
DECKOW LN.
BERMUDA RD.
To Luxor
TROPICANA AVE.
Excalibur
Tropicana
San Remo

Las Vegas, time barely exists (there are no clocks in the casinos). If gratification is not found instantly at one place, there are a few hundred others. Just venture outside on the Strip and you will see one huge hotel-casino after another: *Caesars Palace, Riviera,* the *Sahara, The Mirage,* the *Sands, Aladdin, Excalibur, Luxor, Bally's,* and *Treasure Island.* And then there's the *MGM Grand Hotel–Casino and Theme Park*—with 5,005 rooms, this billion-dollar baby is the biggest hotel in the world. Las Vegas now has nine of the world's 10 largest hotels—no small feat for what was once a desert hamlet.

But the city isn't resting on its laurels; even more renovation and expansion is planned. In the last several years, the *Flamingo Hilton* and *Rio Suite* hotel-casino completed multimillion-dollar renovation/expansions, and the *Hard Rock* hotel-casino, part of the *Hard Rock Café* empire, came to town. Even Debbie Reynolds has opened her own hotel/casino/museum. Steve Wynn, the man behind *The Mirage, Golden Nugget,* and *Treasure Island* properties, opened a 50-acre lake, along with a 3,000-room hotel-casino. In 1996, the 1,500-room *Stratosphere Tower* hotel-casino opened its doors along with the much-anticipated 3,024-room *Monte Carlo* hotel.

Looking to the future, Steve Wynn's $1.25-billion, 3,000-room *Bellagio* resort on the former site of the *Dunes,* is scheduled to open in 1998. The unique resort, built by Mirage Resorts, Inc., will include a 12-acre artificial lake, restaurants, boutiques, a $35-million water-and-light show, and Italian gardens with robotic butterflies, birds, and plants. Also look for Circus Circus Enterprises to break ground for two additional hotels to be constructed at Russel Road and Tropicana Avenue.

In Las Vegas, going outside is a big step, but if you do make the effort to escape the casinos, you'll discover a whole other world. Contrary to preconceived notions of the desert as a lifeless, bland wasteland, it has an incredible, colorful beauty and an air of complete freedom. Just a few miles from Las Vegas lie the dramatic sandstone formations of *Red Rock Canyon* and the subtle colors of the Valley of Fire. These, along with the nearby cool green mountains of Mt. Charleston and manmade Lake Mead, make the desert as attractive a proposition as the Strip.

WEDDING BELLS ARE ALWAYS RINGING

If you are at least 18 (16 with parental consent), and you feel a sudden urge to legally merge, it's easy to tie the knot on the spot. Apply at the *Las Vegas Marriage License Bureau* at the *Clark County Courthouse* (Third and Carson Sts.; phone: 455-3156; after hours, 455-4415); there's not even a blood test or waiting period, just a $35 fee for the license. The courthouse is open round-the-clock on Fridays, Saturdays, and holidays; until midnight Mondays through Thursdays. Then head to the altar, say "I do," and the deed is done. Many hotels have wedding chapels and offer honeymoon packages; other well-known places to get hitched are the *Candlelight Wedding Chapel* (2855 Las Vegas Blvd. S.; phone: 735-4179) and *Little*

Church of the West (3960 Las Vegas Blvd. S.; phone: 739-7971), where Dudley Moore and Clark Gable got married (not to each other). They don't call this place the "Wedding Capital of the World" for nothing.

Las Vegas At-a-Glance

SEEING THE CITY

The *Skytop* restaurant in *Binion's Horseshoe* hotel (128 Fremont St.; phone: 382-1600) offers a panoramic view of Las Vegas. As you ascend in the glass elevator, the entire downtown glitters around you. As you reach the top, the expanse of desert appears, and your eye is drawn to the neon of the Strip and, to the west, the greenery of Mt. Charleston.

SPECIAL PLACES

Gambling is the name of the game in Las Vegas. Just about every type of game of chance known to man (and woman) is available here; from the ubiquitous one-armed bandits and basic games—blackjack, craps, roulette, baccarat, Big Six (wheel of fortune), and poker—to pari-mutuel horse racing bets, bingo, and keno. There are also variations on the basic games, such as "double exposure" blackjack (where the player sees both of the dealer's cards). Poker has recently become permeated with Asian themes that mix the rules of different games. Pai Gow, Super Pan 9, Red Dog, and Caribbean Stud Poker take a little time to learn to play successfully, but all are very exciting once you catch on. House personnel can instruct you about the gaming rules, or you can consult the gaming guidebooks offered at the larger casinos. The legal age for gambling is 21.

Both high- and low-rollers can participate in the action; table limits range from $2 to $5,000, and you can pull on the one-armed bandits for as little as a penny. (By the way, it's considered the height of rudeness to forget to tip the dealer when you win big. Local protocol dictates that you toss a few largish chips his or her way. Never openly hand over cash; the dealer will not be able to accept the gratuity.)

The cultural aspects of the city are limited but expanding, and its history has been all but obliterated by its rapid growth. But the surrounding area is rich in outdoor diversions that can fill your days with a wide variety of non-casino pleasures, leaving the nights for the air conditioned paradise of green felt, dazzling neon, and flashy production numbers.

THE STRIP

If gambling is the game, the Strip (Las Vegas Blvd. S.) is the place. Shining brightly in the desert sun, this 3½-mile stretch of highway (2 miles south of downtown), glows more intensely at night, ablaze with the glittering opulence of a seemingly never-ending stream of hotels. The *MGM Grand, Treasure Island,* and the Egyptian-theme *Luxor* are the latest and greatest entries on the hotel-casino scene (also see *Checking In* for information on these and many of the other Vegas hotels). From production spectaculars featuring superstars to 24-hour dining, it's all here and rolling around the clock. And to make it more convenient to get from one entertainment venue to another, pedestrian skywalks now link major gambling resorts. The first of these are at the *MGM Grand, Luxor, Excalibur,* and *Tropicana* hotels.

Here are a few highlights:

MGM GRAND HOTEL–CASINO AND THEME PARK This is a fantastical coupling of Hollywood icons with the excess of Las Vegas. The 5,005-room, 112-acre property (the world's largest hotel) has a Disneyesque atmosphere, with characters from *The Wizard of Oz* greeting you at the casino door, iridescent neon peacocks, and an 88-foot statue of Leo the Lion, the famed MGM trademark. There is also a huge entertainment complex with a theater, showroom, rides, and other attractions; it's called the Emerald City—an appropriate name, since you'll probably feel as though you've stepped into the Land of Oz. 3799 Las Vegas Blvd. S. (phone: 891-1111).

THE MIRAGE The brainchild of Steve Wynn, developer of the *Golden Nugget,* this 3,000-room property cost $725 million. Its opulent design features a gold-and-white Y-shaped edifice, Polynesian decor, caged animals (including the white tigers used by the hotel's feature act, *Siegfried & Roy*), cascading waterfalls, and a 60-foot volcano that erupts with a piña colada–scented spray every 15 minutes in the evenings. Natural habitats in the lobby display a rain forest and sharks, and there is a dolphin pool near the swimming pool. 3400 Las Vegas Blvd. S. (phone: 791-7111).

EXCALIBUR Though no longer the largest hotel in the world, it's still a wonder to behold. The façade looks like a castle out of a Hans Christian Andersen tale, complete with colorful turrets. Two dinner shows nightly offer Arthurian performances and royal feasting in Renaissance style. 3850 Las Vegas Blvd. S. (phone: 597-7777).

CAESARS PALACE Las Vegas's stab at ancient Rome, with Romanesque names for casinos and a toga-clad staff. Superstars perform here often, and its $40-million *Forum Shops* complex is the most lavish in town. 3570 Las Vegas Blvd. S. (phone: 731-7110).

CIRCUS CIRCUS This is the first Vegas hotel to cater to families with children. In its tent-shaped casino, trapeze and high-wire artists gambol near the gambling, while clowns, acrobats, and dancers perform to the music of a brass band. The observation gallery at circus level is lined with food and carnival stands. Children are permitted in the gallery but not on the casino floor. There's also a carousel, a clown-shaped pool, and an indoor five-acre amusement park with rides, theaters, and restaurants. The circus acts are presented 11 AM to midnight. No admission charge. 2880 Las Vegas Blvd. S. (phone: 734-0410).

HARD ROCK Opened in 1994, this is the world's first rock 'n' roll–themed casino complete with a multimillion dollar showcase of rare memorabilia. The circular casino has 800 slot machines and 33 gaming tables. *The Joint* showroom seats 1,200, while the *Hard Rock Beach Club* features a sandy beach, lush landscaping, whirlpools, spas, and cabañas. 4455 Paradise Rd. (phone: 693-5000; 800-HRD-ROCK; fax: 693-5010).

STAR TREK: THE EXPERIENCE A $50-million joint venture between Paramount Parks and the *Las Vegas Hilton,* this futuristic, interactive entertainment center, which is scheduled to open this year, explores the 24th century through a variety of intergalatic devices. The three-part program includes: "The Exhibit," a museum-like tour of authentic *Star Trek* props, costumes and memorabilia used in the TV and motion picture series; "The Voyage," a 22-minute simulated ride that "beams" you into outer space on the *Enterprise;* and "The Deep Space Nine Promenade," where trekkers interact with virtual reality stations, computer games—and more down-to-earth diversions including restaurants, and gift shops. Admission charge. Located in the north tower of the *Las Vegas Hilton,* 3000 Paradise Rd., (phone: 732-5111).

WET 'N' WILD A 26-acre, family-oriented water playground with a surf lagoon, water chutes, rapids, flumes, a 70-foot water drop called *Der Stuka,* and even pearl diving. Closed November through April. 2600 Las Vegas Blvd. S., next to the *Sahara* hotel (phone: 737-3819).

DEBBIE REYNOLDS This recently opened hotel/casino/museum displays authentic props and costumes from such Reynolds films as *Tammy, Singing in the Rain, Cleopatra,* and *The Wizard of Oz.* On many Monday afternoons, such stars as Ann Miller, Jane Powell, or June Allyson meet with guests between showings of films from the Golden Age of Hollywood. The casino—also decorated with movie sets, props, and posters—features slots, craps, and video poker. The *Hollywood Café* is an ideal spot for casual dining. 305 Convention Center Dr. (phone: 734-0711; 800-633-1777; fax: 734-2954).

CONVENTION CENTER One of the reasons Las Vegas is among the world's major convention destinations is this million-square-foot steel complex next to the *Las Vegas Hilton.* 3150 Paradise Rd. (phone: 892-0711).

DOWNTOWN

GOLDEN NUGGET The most spectacular hotel downtown and one of the most glamorous in Las Vegas. Attractions include a marble-and-brass lobby, the biggest gold nugget in the world (weighing in at about 63 pounds), *Lillie Langtry's* and *Stefano's* restaurants for fine dining, and a 500-seat theater-ballroom. This is the only downtown property that does not use neon to decorate its exterior; instead, the outside of the building is encased in Italian marble. A must-see during any visit. 129 E. Fremont St. (phone: 385-7111).

HOOVER DAM AND LAKE MEAD Completed in 1936, this 726-foot-high structure, the Western Hemisphere's highest concrete dam, was selected by the *American Society of Civil Engineers* as one of the country's Seven Modern Wonders of Civil Engineering; when you take the 528-foot, 52-story elevator ride to the power plant, you'll probably agree. Daily tours. No admission charge for children under 15. Some 115 miles long, with 550 miles of shoreline when full, Lake Mead (behind the dam) is by volume one of the world's largest manmade reservoirs. Fishing (striped bass, crappie, and catfish), swimming, and boating are available year-round. The visitors' center for *Hoover Dam* and the *Alan Bible Visitors Center* (phone: 293-8906 for both) and for *Lake Mead National Recreation Area* is 30 minutes south of the city on Boulder Highway (US 95). For information on guided tours, call the number above.

MT. CHARLESTON Just 35 minutes west of the city, the 12,000-foot mountain exhibits a wide variety of trees and wildlife. With plenty of fresh, cool mountain air, it's an excellent place for camping or hiking. During the winter months, snow covers the ground and temperatures often hover below freezing at the *Lee Canyon* ski slopes while vacationers swim in Las Vegas hotel pools just half an hour away. Take US 95 north to the Mt. Charleston exit, then follow the signs.

RED ROCK CANYON CONSERVATION AREA Featuring red and gold sandstone formations and spectacular views, *Red Rock* is becoming a popular rock climbing area. Just a few miles farther west, the *Spring Mountain State Park* has Old West buildings on a ranch that has belonged to such well-known capitalists as Howard Hughes and the Krupp family (the German armament folks). State rangers lead tours through the old buildings Fridays through Mondays. Admission charge. W. Charleston Blvd., 15 miles west of the city (phone: 363-1921).

EXTRA SPECIAL

Just two hours northwest of Las Vegas lies *Death Valley,* the hottest, driest, and lowest area in the US. It also is starkly beautiful, with a variety of subtle colors and textures. Take US 95 north to Lathrop Wells, then head south on Route 373 to Death Valley Junction, then north on Route 190; follow the signs to the park (phone: 619-786-2331). See also *Death Valley National Monument* in DIRECTIONS.

Sources and Resources

TOURIST INFORMATION

The *Las Vegas Chamber of Commerce* (711 E. Desert Inn Rd., Las Vegas, NV 89109; phone: 735-1616), closed weekends, and the *Las Vegas Convention and Visitors Authority* (3150 Paradise Rd., Las Vegas, NV 89109; phone: 892-0711), open daily, are the best sources for brochures, maps, suggestions, and general tourist information. Contact the Nevada state tourism hotline (800-NEVADA-8) for maps, calendars of events, health updates, and travel advisories. The *Las Vegas Hotline* (phone: 900-446-9797) offers up-to-the-minute tips on events and hotels; the call costs $1.95 a minute.

LOCAL COVERAGE *Review Journal,* morning daily; *Las Vegas Sun,* afternoon daily. Weekly entertainment guides, such as *Showbiz,* are available at newsstands. *What's On,* a weekly entertainment guide available free at hotels and at the *Las Vegas Convention and Visitors Authority,* covers everything from theater to music to nightlife. Also, pick up a copy of *ACCESS Las Vegas* (HarperCollins; $18.50).

TELEVISION STATIONS KVBC Channel 3–NBC; KVVU Channel 5–Fox; KLAS Channel 8–CBS; KLVX Channel 10–PBS; and KTNV Channel 13–ABC.

RADIO STATIONS AM: KDWN 720 (talk); KORK 920 (big band); KNUU 970 (news); KFM 1410 (country); and KENO 1460 (sports). FM: KNPR 89.5 (National Public Radio); KILA 90.5 (Christian music); KUNV 91.5 (jazz); KOMP 92.3 (rock 'n' roll); KEYV 93.1 (country); KXTZ 95.5 (easy listening); KLUC 98.5 (top 40); and KKLZ 103.5 (classic rock).

TELEPHONE The area code for Las Vegas is 702.

SALES TAX There is a 7% tax on all purchases except groceries; the hotel room tax is 8%.

CLIMATE Las Vegas summers are hot and dry. Average daytime temperature can reach 115F, but it usually cools down at night to a comfortable 80–85F. Winters are pleasant and mild (but cold at night); average daytime and nighttime temperatures are in the 50s and 30s, respectively. Outdoor activity takes place year-round.

GETTING AROUND

Although Las Vegas is not a large city, the summer heat makes walking difficult. If you are going any farther than a few hundred yards or so, you'll probably do better on wheels.

AIRPORT *McCarran International Airport* is a 10- to 20-minute drive from the Strip; allow 20 to 25 minutes to get to the downtown area. *Gray Line* (phone: 739-5700) provides van service to Strip and downtown hotels. The service runs daily every 15 minutes. For return service, call 24 hours in advance for reservations. Plan to arrive at the airport at least an hour before flight time, since the distances between the main entrance and the check-in gates are long.

BUS The public bus system covers the entire city ($1.25 fare). A discount commuter ticket offers a real savings if you expect to use the buses frequently. Route information is available at 1550 Industrial Rd. (phone: 384-1234).

Also, *Whittlesea* (phone: 384-6111) operates red and green trolleys that travel along the Strip.

CAR RENTAL The large national firms serve Las Vegas; other companies include *Abbey Rent-A-Car* (3769 Las Vegas Blvd. S.; phone: 736-4042) and *Allstate* (5175 Rent-A-Car Rd., just outside of the airport; phone: 736-6147).

TAXI Cabs can be hailed in the street, ordered on the phone, or picked up at taxi stands in front of hotels. Major companies are *Whittlesea Cab* (phone: 384-6111); *Yellow and Checker Cab* (phone: 873-2000); and *Desert Cab* (phone: 376-2687).

SPECIAL EVENTS

Las Vegas rings in the year with huge *New Year's Eve* bashes at all the big hotels with shows featuring big-name performers such as Barry Manilow, Tony Bennett, Liza Minnelli, and George Carlin. There are also fancy-dress balls with dinner and dancing. The *Las Vegas International Marathon and Half-Marathon* is held the first Saturday in February (phone: 876-3870). In late April, the *Sheraton Desert Inn* hosts the *Senior PGA Golf Tournament;* the *World Series of Poker* is played at *Binion's Horseshoe* (128 Fremont St.; phone: 382-1600) in April or May. During the *Helldorado Festival,* held in mid-May, the city celebrates its western heritage with rodeos, parades, and beauty contests. The *Jaycees State Fair* takes place in October at *Cashman Field* (850 Las Vegas Blvd. N.; phone: 457-8832) and has carnival acts, magic shows, rides, livestock, and craft exhibits.

A ROLLICKING RODEO

National Finals Rodeo In early December, the top 15 money-winners in seven events who have competed in the more than 640 *Professional Rodeo Cowboy Association*—sanctioned rodeos qualify for the *National Finals*—and from there they compete for the championships in the various divisions. At stake are over $2 million in prizes and the *National Finals Rodeo (NFR)* and world titles, and the competition is fierce. Most tickets for the 10 performances, held at the *Thomas and Mack Center* at the *University of Nevada at Las Vegas* (4505 S. Maryland Pkwy.), sell out well in advance (send for tickets at *least* 10 months early). For more information, contact *Las Vegas Events,* 2030 E. Flamingo Ave., Suite 200, Las Vegas, NV 89119 (phone: 731-2115).

MUSEUMS

Though it's not noted for its cultural draw, Las Vegas and its environs do contain a few museums and places of interest. Many of the hotels have commercial art exhibitions with works of well-known artists. *Herigstad's Gallery*

(2290 E. Flamingo Rd.; phone: 733-7366) has art shows as well as works for sale. Closed Sundays. Also worth a visit are *Minotaur Fine Arts Ltd.* (*Fashion Show Mall,* 3200 Las Vegas Blvd. S.; phone: 731-1400) and the *Thomas Charles Gallery* (*Caesars Forum,* 3500 Las Vegas Blvd. S.; phone: 369-8000). Some other museums of note are listed below.

BOULDER CITY, HOOVER DAM MUSEUM This place was established to preserve the historical artifacts relating to the construction of *Hoover Dam* (also known as *Boulder Dam*) in the 1930s. There are exhibits chronicling the workers' lifestyle during the time the dam was being built. A movie detailing the process of building the dam is shown several times daily. Open daily. No admission charge. 444 Hotel Plaza, Boulder City (phone: 294-1988).

CLARK COUNTY HERITAGE MUSEUM Exhibits displayed in several buildings depict the early pioneer and mining history of southern Nevada. On the grounds—located between Las Vegas and Boulder City—is "Heritage Street," a row of houses from the 1920s, 1930s, and 1940s, complete with period furnishings, as well as a 1905 *Union Pacific* steam engine. Open daily. Admission charge. 1830 S. Boulder Hwy., Henderson (phone: 455-7955).

GUINNESS WORLD OF RECORDS MUSEUM A collection detailing many of the world records and feats found in the *Guinness Book of Records.* The museum is divided into six sections: *Sports World; Amazing Humans; Nature's Wonders; Music, Arts, and Entertainment; Amazing Animals;* and *Buildings and Structures.* Exhibits include a model of the world's tallest man (8 feet, 11 inches); displays on *Death Valley,* which holds the record for the highest temperature sustained over a long period of time (120F or more for 43 consecutive days); the *Grand Canyon* (the world's largest land gorge); and videos of some of the records being set. There's also a special display focusing on Las Vegas. Open daily. Admission charge. 2780 Las Vegas Blvd. S., next to the *Circus Circus* hotel (phone: 792-0640).

LAS VEGAS NATURAL HISTORY MUSEUM Exhibits feature animal life—from prehistoric to the present—including woodcarvings, wildlife paintings, artifacts, and more than 2,000 birds, fish, and mammals, preserved and mounted. Open daily. Admission charge. 900 Las Vegas Blvd. N. (phone: 384-3466).

LIBERACE MUSEUM Three buildings house the late, flamboyant entertainer's costumes, pianos, and vintage automobiles (including a Rolls-Royce covered with mirrors), along with other memorabilia. This is the third-most popular attraction in the state, after the casinos and *Hoover Dam.* Open daily. Admission charge (the proceeds go toward music scholarships). 1775 E. Tropicana Ave. (phone: 798-5595).

LIED DISCOVERY CHILDREN'S MUSEUM Youngsters can learn about science and the humanities from the hands-on displays on pollution, weather, computers and electronics, and hot-air balloons. Open daily. Admission charge. 833 Las Vegas Blvd. N., across from the *Natural History Museum* (phone: 382-5437).

MINERAL COLLECTION A display of gems and minerals from the area and around the world. Closed Sundays. No admission charge. At the *University of Nevada at Las Vegas,* Geoscience Hall, Room 103, 4505 S. Maryland Pkwy. (phone: 895-3262).

NEVADA STATE MUSEUM AND HISTORICAL SOCIETY Four galleries contain dioramas depicting the history of southern Nevada, with emphasis on prehistoric humans. Native American culture and lifestyles over the past 13,000 years are shown, as are the area's characteristic plants and animals. Open daily. Admission charge. 700 Twin Lakes Dr., *Lorenzi Park* (phone: 486-5205).

SHOPPING

It doesn't get top billing in Las Vegas; visitors come here to spend their money at the casinos, not to search for the best bargains. However, there are several good shopping spots in the city. *Las Vegas Factory Stores* (9155 Las Vegas Blvd. S.; phone: 897-9090) is ideal for shoppers seeking designer merchandise at 20% to 60% below retail prices; the 70 shops here offer numerous well-known labels. For western-style clothing, try *Sam's Town Western Emporium* (5111 Boulder Hwy.; phone: 454-8017); you'll find a good selection of cowboy boots and hats, jewelry, belt buckles, and string ties. For more upscale designs, the *Forum Shops* at *Caesars Palace* (3570 Las Vegas Blvd.; phone: 893-4800) has 65 different retail outlets under one roof.

There are also a couple of specialty shops focusing on—you guessed it—gambling. *Gambler's Book Club* (630 S. 11th St.; phone: 382-7555) deals primarily in new and used books about gambling history, rules of the games, and the influence of organized crime on its development. Many types of gaming souvenirs and memorabilia can be found at *Gambler's General Store* (800 S. Main St.; phone: 382-9903).

SPORTS AND FITNESS

Las Vegas offers a wide variety of sporting events and fine sports facilities.

BASEBALL The Las Vegas *Stars,* a farm club for the San Diego *Padres,* play from April through September at *Cashman Field* (850 Las Vegas Blvd. N.; phone: 386-7200).

BASKETBALL *The University of Nevada at Las Vegas* has fielded one of the finest (and most controversial) collegiate basketball teams in the nation for several years—the *Runnin' Rebels* were the 1990 *NCAA* Champions. They play from December through March in the *Thomas and Mack Center* (4505 S. Maryland Pkwy.; phone: 895-3900), an 18,000-seat arena on campus. Tickets usually are available, but for really good seats you'll need help from your hotel bell captain or casino pit boss.

BETTING If you want to bet on almost any athletic event taking place outside of Nevada, numerous race and sports bookmakers dot the city. The most lavish facilities on the Strip are in *Caesars Palace, The Mirage, Stardust, MGM*

Grand, and *Las Vegas Hilton. Plaza's Book* (*Plaza Hotel,* 1 Main St.; phone: 386-2110), *Binion's Horseshoe* (128 E. Fremont St.; phone: 382-1600), *Golden Nugget* (see *Special Places*), and *Las Vegas Club* (18 E. Fremont St.; phone: 385-1664) top the downtown locales for laying odds.

BOXING If punching is your bag, you're in luck; the major hotels promote many boxing matches. Bouts between professional contenders are held at *Caesars Palace, Las Vegas Hilton, MGM Grand,* and *The Mirage.*

FISHING You can wet a line all year round at Lake Mead, the manmade body of water created by *Hoover Dam.* Among the types of fish here are striped and largemouth bass, crappie, catfish, and bluegill. Licenses for three or 10 days can be purchased at any of the five marinas around the lake, and there are boats for rent, too (*Lake Mead Marina;* phone: 293-3484).

FITNESS CENTERS Most Las Vegas hotels have fitness centers. Among the best: The health club at *Caesars Palace* has exercise classes, a whirlpool bath, a steamroom, and exercise equipment; the *Aristocrat Health Spa* in the *Las Vegas Hilton* has a sauna, a whirlpool bath, and massage; the multimillion-dollar facility at the *Sheraton Desert Inn Country Club* offers full health club services; *The Mirage* has men's and women's spa facilities, an exercise room, and aerobics studios; and the *Golden Nugget* hotel offers a swank spa and a coed gym with a sauna, a whirlpool bath, and exercise equipment.

FOOTBALL From September through November, the *University of Nevada at Las Vegas*'s *Rebels* play at the *Sam Boyd Silver Bowl* (7000 E. Russell Rd.; phone: 895-3900).

GOLF Dozens of courses dot the desert landscape. The *Sahara Country Club* (1911 E. Desert Inn Rd.; phone: 796-0016) and the *Sheraton Desert Inn Country Club* (phone: 733-4444) are the best. For lower greens fees, try the public courses. Best bet is the *Las Vegas Golf Club* (Washington Ave. and Decatur Blvd.; phone: 646-3003), which offers a reasonable challenge and good greens. *The Mirage* has an 18-hole course on the former *Dunes* property that is open to non-guests. The city has more than 15 additional courses; for information, contact the *Nevada Commission on Tourism* (5151 S. Carson St., Carson City, NV 89710; phone: 702-882-1565; 800-NEVADA8).

JOGGING It's possible to run right along the Strip between Flamingo Road and Spring Mountain, where there are no cross streets to slow the pace (about one-half mile each way); stay on the *Caesars Palace* side. Another possibility is *Squires Park,* one-half mile from downtown; or drive to *Sunset Park,* 7 miles from downtown, or *Bob Baskin Park* (W. Oakey Blvd. at Rancho Dr.). The *University of Nevada at Las Vegas* has a jogging track, as do most of the city's high schools. Note that at the height of the summer, the heat can make running a dangerous sport, even in the morning; however, determined joggers may run inside at the air conditioned *Fashion Show Mall* before its stores open at 10 AM.

SKIING Believe it or not, Las Vegas is only an hour away from the slopes. *Lee Canyon,* a resort at Mt. Charleston, is about 45 miles northwest of the city. The 8,000-foot ski area, with natural and manmade snow, is good for downhill skiing. The season runs from December through February (phone: 593-9500 for snow conditions; 646-0008 for information on free bus).

TENNIS Almost all the Strip hotels have good tennis facilities open to the public. Call first.

THEATER

For current performances, check the publications listed above. *Cirque du Soleil* is a combination of theater, dance, music, comedy, and acrobatics. The whole wild show takes place at *Treasure Island* (see *Checking In*) in a single ring, without animals or spoken communication. Besides the entertainment at the Strip hotels, there are some old standbys, such as the *New West Stage Company* (4033 San Mateo St.; phone: 657-5000), which presents its season at the *Charleston Heights Arts Center* (901 Brush St.; phone: 229-6383), and the *Actor's Repertory Theater,* which performs at the *Clark County Library* (1401 E. Flamingo Rd.; phone: 647-7469); both present a range of contemporary and traditional drama. There also are a number of local theater groups, including the *Repertory Theater* at *Judy Bayley Theatre* (*University of Nevada at Las Vegas* campus, 4505 S. Maryland Pkwy.; phone: 895-3801). The *Clark County Community College* (3200 E. Cheyenne Ave.) and other local companies are featured in *Theatre Under the Stars,* outdoors at the *Spring Mountain Ranch* (Blue Diamond, NV; no phone) in the summer. Productions are usually major musicals; the sets make fine use of the environment, and the acting is first rate. Tickets can be purchased at the ranch (18 miles west on Charleston Blvd.; phone: 875-4141). The *Nevada Dance Theatre* (phone: 732-3838) performs at the *Judy Bayley Theatre* (see above), and the *Nevada Opera Theater* (phone: 737-6373) at *Artemus W. Ham Concert Hall,* both on the *UNLV* campus (4504 S. Maryland Pkwy).

MUSIC

Symphony concerts, opera, and jazz are featured during the school year at *Artemus W. Ham Concert Hall* and the *Judy Bayley Theatre* on the *UNLV* campus (4505 S. Maryland Pkwy.). For tickets, call 895-3801.

NIGHTCLUBS AND NIGHTLIFE

When it comes to nightlife, Las Vegas is king. The city never sleeps and can keep visitors entertained all night. The Strip hotels offer a wide variety of entertainment, with musical and comedy headliners such as Liza Minnelli, George Carlin, and Julio Iglesias. There are nightly production spectaculars, with dancing girls, lavish costumes and sets, and all kinds of specialty acts. *Jubilee* at *Bally's* features a cast of more than 100 singers and dancers performing on one of the largest stages in the world. *EFX,* the *MGM Grand*'s multimillion-dollar, high-tech visual spectacular, starring

Michael Crawford, is the most extravagant. Other notables of this genre are *Siegfried & Roy* at *The Mirage,* featuring the famed illusionists performing magic on a grand and gaudy scale; *Splash* at the *Riviera,* with Esther Williams–style production numbers; the cancan dancing of the *Folies Bergère* at the *Tropicana;* the *Great Radio City Music Hall* spectacular at the *Flamingo Hilton,* featuring dance numbers by the world famous *Rockettes* with actress/singer Susan Anton; and *Enter the Night* at the *Stardust,* with a gymnast/acrobat sharing the stage with some scantily clad showgirls. Smaller-scale productions can be seen at several hotels, including the *Sahara* and the *Rio Suite* hotel and casino, and *Starlight Express* and *Star Trek: The Experience* are at the *Las Vegas Hilton.* The newest act in town is *Pomp Duck & Circumstance* at the *MGM Grand.* This hilarious "out of control" entertainment/gourmet dining experience combines a cast of singers, slapstick comedians, musicians, acrobats, waiters, and chefs who perform and interact with the audience.

In the main showrooms of all the other hotels on the Strip, a constant parade of stars performs for audiences of 800 to 1,200 people. The *Tropicana* and *Flamingo Hilton* serve dinner at the early show. The *Excalibur* serves a Renaissance dinner, with two shows a night depicting the Arthurian legend.

At many of the hotels, you can buy a ticket for a specific seat instead of making a general admission reservation and being seated by the maître d'. Hotel guests get first priority for many shows, so consider staying at the hotel that has the show you most want to see. Always call in the morning or, better still, go in person to buy tickets or make reservations. Most hotels do *not* take show reservations or sell tickets more than one day in advance. The ticket booths open at 10 AM and stay open till show time. If you've been gambling a good deal, ask the pit boss for assistance and, if you haven't, you might try tipping the bell captain and hope for the best. Bring along a sweater or jacket, as powerful air conditioners are at work everywhere. And though dress is casual during the day, you can opt to dress up more for the shows.

Often overlooked are the casino lounges, where lesser-known performers (many of whom—like Wayne Newton, Kenny Rogers, and Don Rickles—soon become better known) entertain for just the cost of your drinks. Comedy clubs are gaining in popularity as well; the best ones are at the *MGM Grand,* the *Riviera,* and the *Tropicana.*

Favorite non-hotel nightspots are the *Shark Club* (75 E. Harmon Ave.; phone: 795-7525) and *L.J.'s Sports Bar* (4405 W. Flamingo Rd.; phone: 871-1424). Try the *Silver Dollar Saloon* (2501 E. Charleston Blvd.; phone: 382-6921), *Sam's Town Western Dance Hall* (5010 Boulder Hwy.; phone: 456-7777), or *Rockabilly's* (3785 Boulder Hwy.; phone: 641-5800) for live country-and-western music.

Las Vegas also presents the best-known striptease artists in the world. Tops (or topless, more likely) is the *Palomino Club* (1848 Las Vegas Blvd.

N.; phone: 642-2984). Other choices are *Crazy Horse One and Two* (4034 Paradise Rd.; phone: 732-1116) and the *CanCan Room* (3155 Industrial Rd.; phone: 737-1161).

SEX TEASE CLUBS

Watch out for brothels masquerading as legitimate nightclubs (some places even advertise in the local yellow pages). Once you enter the club, a "waitress" will offer to perform certain favors if you purchase a $300 bottle of champagne (and we're not talking Dom Perignon). If you find yourself in this situation, keep in mind that although prostitution is legal in some areas of Nevada, it is *not* legal in Las Vegas; your best bet is to steer clear of these clubs.

Best in Town

CHECKING IN

In Vegas, the hotel's the thing. The Strip's 3½-mile stream of hotel-casinos and motels is nearly matched in number—though usually not in quality—by the downtown "Glitter Gulch" area. Competition is fierce among the major hotels, which keeps room costs modest; rates are lowest during the two weeks before *Christmas;* discounts can be as much as 60%, even at the most luxurious hotels. Most of Las Vegas's major hotels have complete facilities for the business traveler. Those listed below as having "business services" usually offer such conveniences as meeting rooms, photocopiers, computers, translation services, and express checkout, among others. Call the individual hotel for additional information. In general, expect to pay $75 or more per night for a double room at those places listed as expensive; $40 to $75 at those categorized as moderate; and $20 to $40 at inexpensive establishments. Unless otherwise noted, hotel rooms have air conditioning, private baths, TV sets, and telephones.

All hotels below are in Las Vegas and telephone and fax numbers are in the 702 area code unless otherwise indicated.

EXPENSIVE

Bally's More grandiose than ever, this 3,000-room hotel has five restaurants—among them *Al Dente* for Italian food and *Seasons* for continental (see *Eating Out* for both)—a 40-store shopping arcade, the *Ziegfeld Room* for lavish production numbers, and the *Celebrity Room* for top-name entertainment. The hotel also features two excellent buffets, the Sterling Brunch on Sundays and the Big Kitchen Buffet daily. Health spas, tennis courts, an Olympic-size pool, 24-hour room service, and business services are some of the amenities. 3645 Las Vegas Blvd. S. (phone: 739-4111; 800-634-3434; fax: 739-4432).

Caesars Palace This is one of the places that immediately comes to mind when the subject of Las Vegas hotels is mentioned. Even the most basic of its 1,520 rooms are ornate, while the high-roller suites are tributes to excess, with large classical statues to make you feel right at home—if you've just flown in from ancient Rome. The service is excellent, and the location—midway on the Strip—puts guests right in the middle of the action. It has big-name entertainment, bars, restaurants (including the fine *Palace Court;* see *Eating Out*), an Olympic-size pool, tennis, golf privileges, the *Forum Shops* complex—which boasts boutiques, art galleries, and restaurants including *Spago, Palm, Bertolini's* (see *Eating Out* for all), and *Planet Hollywood*—and free parking. Business services and 24-hour room service are available. The most recent attraction is *Caesars Magical Empire*—a 66,000-square-foot dining and entertainment complex, where a magical kingdom awaits those who are guided through a catacomb maze. 3570 Las Vegas Blvd. S. (phone: 731-7110; 800-634-6001; fax: 731-6636).

Golden Nugget One of the glitzier of the downtown spots, it combines an overall turn-of-the-century look with mountains of marble, brass, and crystal in its casino, spa, and entertainment room. The 1,908 rooms are attractively decorated, and *Stefano's* and *Lillie Langtry's* feature fine dining. Amenities include 24-hour room service, a health spa, a concierge desk, and business services. 129 E. Fremont St. (phone: 385-7111; 800-634-3454; fax: 386-8362).

Las Vegas Hilton This huge 3,174-room hostelry sits off the Strip next to the *Convention Center.* It offers entertainment, bars, a dozen restaurants including *Le Montrachet, Andiamo,* and *Benihana Village* (see *Eating Out* for all three), a 10-acre rooftop recreation center with a pool, tennis, a health club, putting greens and golf privileges, shops, and free parking. Crystal chandeliers and marble floors glisten in the hotel's refurbished lobby. *Star Trek: The Experience* (see *The Strip*) an interactive, futuristic attraction is worth a visit. Located in the north tower, which also sports the new 22,000-square-foot *SpaceQuest* casino, it's a "Trekkie's" dream-come-true with memorabilia from the original television and motion picture series, simulated rides on the *Enterprise,* and computer and video interactive fun and games. Business services are available, and 24-hour room service makes life easier. 3000 Paradise Rd. (phone: 732-5111; 800-732-7117; fax: 732-5249).

The Mirage This $725-million property has become the talk of the town. The lobby is decorated with lush plants, waterfalls, lagoons, and an aquarium stocked with exotic fish; and then there's that famous volcano—complete with flames and piña colada–scented smoke—erupting outside every 15 minutes after dark. There are 3,049 rooms with light-colored cane and rattan furnishings, bright, cheerful fabrics, and tropical flowers. Other amenities include nine restaurants, 24-hour room service, a spa and salon, shops, and business services. 3400 Las Vegas Blvd. S. (phone: 791-7111; 800-627-6667; fax: 791-7446).

Sheraton Desert Inn This hotel's purchase by Howard Hughes in 1966 sparked the influx of investment that turned the fledgling gambling center into the resort complex it is today. More like a city than a hotel, there are five locations on 2,000 acres with 821 rooms and suites, each offering something unique. There's the Wimbledon, for example, a seven-story pyramid structure which practically sits on the golf course; Augusta Tower overlooks both the Strip and the mountains of Nevada. The rooms include amenities such as wet bars, refrigerators, private patios, and phones in the bathroom. The dining facilities are numerous and just as varied, including the exquisite *Monte Carlo Room* (see *Eating Out*). There are several bars, a health spa, golf courses, a pool, tennis courts, and many shops, including separate golf and tennis pro shops, plus a *Hertz* rental car counter, if you should feel the need (but why?) to leave. Around-the-clock room service and business services are available. 3145 Las Vegas Blvd. S. (phone: 733-4444; 800-634-6906; fax: 733-4774).

MODERATE

Aladdin The original Arabian theme has been replaced by a more modern look for its 1,100 rooms, four restaurants, and public areas. The *Sun Sun* restaurant features Asian fare, and *Fisherman's Port* has a Cajun/seafood menu. Other facilities include a showroom, pools, shops, tennis courts, and business services. 3667 Las Vegas Blvd. S. (phone: 736-0111; 800-634-3424; fax: 736-0491).

Debbie Reynolds This 12-story, 200-room hotel houses more than $30 million of costumes, furniture, artifacts, and other memorabilia from Debbie's own collection and private donations. A number of celebrity-themed suites boast Hollywood-style movie sets complete with sumptuous parlor, dining area, and Jacuzzis. The *Hollywood Café* serves fine continental fare. Other amenities include 24-hour room service. Business services are available. 305 Convention Center Dr. (phone: 734-0711; 800-633-1777; fax: 734-2954).

Excalibur The 4,032 rooms have a castle-like decor, with red and blue fabrics and wallpaper that resembles stonework; baths have oversize showers and tubs. There's a dinner theater, as well as six restaurants including the *Camelot* and *Sir Galahad's*. Room service is available until 11 PM. Business services are offered. 3850 Las Vegas Blvd. S. (phone: 597-7777; 800-937-7777; fax: 597-7009).

Flamingo Hilton The glitz that is Vegas today all started when Benjamin "Bugsy" Siegel opened this hotel as the *Flamingo* in 1946. It now has 4,000 guestrooms, decorated in contemporary style. The *Great Radio City Music Hall* spectacular, one of the few dinner shows in the city, is performed nightly. There are seven restaurants, a fitness center, and business services. 3555 Las Vegas Blvd. S. (phone: 733-3111; 800-732-2111; fax: 733-3528).

Hard Rock The first of its kind ever, this 339-room hotel also features a multimillion dollar collection of rock 'n' roll memorabilia. In addition to the nearby

Hard Rock Café, there are two restaurants to choose from within the hotel: *Mortoni's,* featuring pizza and huge salads indoors or on the garden patio overlooking the pool; and *Mr. Lucky's 24/7,* a 24-hour coffee shop. The *Hard Rock Beach Club,* exclusively for guests and included in the price of a room, features whirlpools, spas, luxury cabañas, and even a sandy beach. The *Athletic Club,* available to guests for a fee, provides an exercise room, and a 2,000-square-foot collectibles store. 4455 Paradise Rd. (phone: 693-5000; 800-473-7625; fax 693-5010).

Luxor A $300-million, Egyptian-style extravaganza under the same ownership as *Circus Circus* (below), the structure resembles an ancient pyramid and sits on 47 acres. In addition to its 2,526 rooms, it offers seven restaurants including the *Isis* and *Papyrus*, a lagoon-like pool and manmade beach, and—its most spectacular feature—a replica of the Nile River that flows between the hotel and casino, complete with barges to transport guests around the property. There's also a full-size model of King Tut's tomb. A concierge desk and 24-hour room service are other pluses. An 1,950-room tower is scheduled to open by the beginning of 1997. 3900 Las Vegas Blvd. S. (phone: 262-4000; 800-288-1000; fax: 262-4404).

MGM Grand Hotel–Casino and Theme Park This is a billion-dollar fantasyland with 5,005 rooms (the largest on the planet). The 30-story building sits on 112 acres and offers a casino (also the world's largest), eight restaurants (including *Charlie Trotter's* and *Coyote Café*—see *Eating Out* for both), and a 15,000-square-foot complex with a theater, showroom, rides, and other attractions. Other amenities include a full health spa, three pools, five tennis courts, and 24-hour room service. 3799 Las Vegas Blvd. S. (phone: 891-1111; 800-929-1111; fax: 891-1000).

Monte Carlo Opened in 1996, this $325-million Victorian-theme resort (a joint venture of Mirage Resorts Inc., and Circus Circus Enterprises, Inc.) features 3,014 rooms, a 90,000 square-foot-casino, dozens of restaurants including the *Market City Café* (for Italian food), *Dragon Noodle Co.* (for Asian cuisine), *Blackstone's Steak House* (for beef specialties). Also within the 43 acres are a large shopping arcade, wedding chapel, and health club. Outdoor fun includes a two-acre pool area with a wave pool, children's pool, and spa. 3770 S. Las Vegas Blvd. (phone: 730-7777; 800-311-8999; fax: 739-9172).

New York–New York When this 2,100-room resort opened in 1996, it unveiled its casino, along with an amazing entertainment center featuring motion-simulation rides and a Coney Island–style roller coaster. Designed to mirror the magnificent Manhattan skyline, the resort re-creates most of the Big Apple's landmarks. There are theme restaurants (*America's Coffee Shop, Gallagher's Steak House, Chin Chin, Il Fornaio)*, as well as *Gotham* nightclub, and an ethnic food court. There's also a major theater, extensive entertainment center, pool and health club, and business center. 3790 Las Vegas Blvd. (phone: 740-6500; 800-693-6763; fax: 740-6510).

Rio Suite Hotel & Casino An all-suite hotel near the Strip, the 860 rooms have floor-to-ceiling windows, separate dressing areas, refrigerators, and coffee makers (with complimentary coffee); some offer views overlooking *Caesars Palace* and the rest Vegas. The pool has waterfalls and a "beach" made of real sand and there are volleyball courts. Other amenities include six restaurants, among them the first-rate *Antonio's* (see *Eating Out*), 24-hour room service, and business services. 3700 W. Flamingo Rd. (phone: 252-7777; 800-752-9746; fax: 253-6090).

Riviera One of the oldest hotels in the city, it has a 100,000-square-foot casino (the second largest in the world since the *MGM Grand* opened). Its 2,100 rooms and 177 suites are decorated in pastel colors and feature a variety of styles, from English Tudor to contemporary. There are five restaurants, a food court, and five showrooms; its *Splash* production is a popular night-time attraction. Business services and 24-hour room service are available. 2901 Las Vegas Blvd. S. (phone: 734-5110; 800-634-6753; fax: 794-9451).

Sahara The first stop on the Strip is notable for its relatively tasteful decor and traditional style. The service at this large (2,100-room) property is personalized and generally excellent. There is also nightly entertainment, *La Terrazza* and the *House of Lords* restaurants, a bar, pools, a health club, and shops. Business services and 24-hour room service are other pluses. 2535 Las Vegas Blvd. S. (phone: 737-2111; 800-634-6666; fax: 791-2027).

Stardust Once the largest resort on the Strip, this 2,461-unit property has been eclipsed by the rise of such gargantuan hotels as the *Excalibur* and the *MGM Grand.* There are accommodations in the high-rise East Tower, as well as Southwestern-style villas. There's a landscaped pool, five restaurants, including *Tony Roma's* and *Ralph's Diner* (see *Eating Out* for both), and *Enter the Night,* a lavish production. Amenities include 24-hour room service and business services. 3000 Las Vegas Blvd. S. (phone: 732-6111; 800-634-6757; fax: 732-6239).

Stratosphere Tower Opened in 1996, this $500-million property features 1,500 well-appointed rooms and suites, a massive casino, and six-themed restaurants including *An Around the World Buffet, Sisters Café,* and the revolving *Top of the World.* Guests also may enjoy the numerous retail shops, or if they prefer, a spa, a pool, and entertainment lounges. The highlights in the complex are the 12-story observation tower, the *High Roller* (the world's highest roller coaster), and the *Big Shot* (the world's highest thrill ride). 2000 S. Las Vegas Blvd. (phone: 380-7777; 800-998-6937; fax: 383-4755).

Treasure Island Steve Wynn, the man behind *The Mirage* and the *Golden Nugget,* has done it again with this $430-million, 2,900-room resort. Named after the famous Robert Louis Stevenson classic, the resort's theme is further expressed with an hourly extravaganza in front of the hotel: pirates battling it out with the HMS *Britannia.* The casino and public areas are decorated in "early pirate," with treasure chests and skull and crossbones. Amenities include four restaurants, a spa, a beauty salon, a pool, and business services. 3300 Las Vegas Blvd. S. (phone: 894-7111; 800-944-7444; fax: 894-7446).

Tropicana Self-billed as "The Island of Las Vegas," it has 1,908 well-appointed guestrooms and is conveniently located near the airport. Many of the suites have hot tubs and large-screen TV sets. The hotel's *Folies Bergère,* modeled after the original French production, with high-stepping cancan dancers, is the longest-running show in the city. There are also six restaurants, a pool (with swim-up blackjack tables), and business services. 3801 Las Vegas Blvd. S. (phone: 739-2222; 800-634-4000; fax: 739-2469).

INEXPENSIVE

Circus Circus Dedicated to family entertainment (at family prices), with an amusement park and a full-scale circus, complete with sideshows, this 2,800-room hotel has plenty for children; for adults, there's *The Steak House* (see *Eating Out*), cafés, bars, a health club, and a sauna. Business services are available. As we went to press, an additional 1,000-room twin tower was scheduled to open by the beginning of this year. 2880 Las Vegas Blvd. S. (phone: 734-0410; 800-634-3450; fax: 734-2268).

EATING OUT

Probably the only sure bet in Vegas is the food. No matter where you go, there's plenty to eat, and the food is much better than standard hotel or nightclub fare. Though the offerings are basically American—steaks and seafood—there are also many good ethnic restaurants. Expect to pay $100 or more for dinner for two at restaurants in the very expensive category; $65 to $100 at places described as expensive; $40 to $65 at those listed as moderate; and less than $40 at those described as inexpensive. Prices do not include drinks, wine, tax, or tips. All restaurants are in the 702 area code unless otherwise indicated.

Unless otherwise noted, restaurants are open for lunch and dinner.

VERY EXPENSIVE

Charlie Trotter's Though the menu is always evolving to accommodate the freshest ingredients available, chef Charlie Trotter features only two options per night—the meat and seafood sampler or the vegetable sampler. The meat and seafood choice might include smoked Maine salmon with pulped avocado, and Japanese yellowtail with red cabbage and sweet-potato gnocchi. The vegetable selection might include such imaginative dishes as truffle potato soup with leeks, artichokes, and black Périgord truffles; and root vegetables and wild mushroom ravioli with white truffle oil. Desserts are luscious. Open for dinner only; closed Tuesdays. Reservations necessary. Major credit cards accepted. 3799 Las Vegas Blvd. (phone: 891-7337).

Le Montrachet Here is European elegance at its best. Flowers are everywhere, and the table settings are extravagant. The menu is seasonal, and everything—from the pheasant-breast mousse appetizer to such entrées as veal chops with mussel purée to the Swiss chocolate soufflé dessert is prepared with a distinctly French flair. Open for dinner only; closed Tuesdays. Reservations necessary. Major credit cards accepted. 3000 Paradise Rd. (phone: 732-5111).

Palace Court This *Caesars Palace* restaurant is considered the ultimate in dining grace in Las Vegas. The menu is French, accompanied by wines from the hotel's distinguished wine cellar. Specialties include Caesar salad, prepared tableside and broiled Dover sole with anchovy butter and capers. The candelabra, vermeil flatware, and hand-blown crystal are the accoutrements of an unforgettable experience. (If asked in advance, the chef will prepare a meal according to your specifications—even if the items are not on the menu.) Open daily for dinner only. Reservations necessary. Major credit cards accepted. 3570 Las Vegas Blvd. S. (phone: 731-7110).

Piero's Northern Italian cooking with an emphasis on veal. The dishes change regularly, but favorites are *vitello del chef* (veal scaloppine sautéed in egg batter and topped with bell peppers and cheese) and *zuppa di pesce* (a seafood stew). A selection from the large wine cellar enhances the experience. The price is very high (about $160 for two), but it's well worth it. Open daily for dinner only. Reservations advised. Major credit cards accepted. 305 Convention Center Dr. (phone: 369-2305).

EXPENSIVE

Andiamo A highly regarded northern Italian restaurant in the *Las Vegas Hilton.* One of the menu's outstanding pasta dishes is *fettuccine all'aragosta e gamberi* (egg noodles with lobster and shrimp in a creamy white wine sauce). Open daily for dinner only. Reservations advised. Major credit cards accepted. 3000 Paradise Rd. (phone: 732-5664).

André's This elegant French restaurant features owner-chef André Rochat's *escargots de Bourgogne* (snails in garlic butter) and *coquilles St. Jacques* (scallops in the shell), plus creative preparations of fillet of beef, veal, lamb, fresh fish, poultry, and stuffed pork tenderloin. The exquisite desserts served here are legendary. Open daily for dinner only. Reservations necessary. Major credit cards accepted. 401 S. 6th St. (phone: 385-5016).

Aristocrat One of a handful of unaffiliated dining rooms, this cozy hideaway with English touches reflects its British owner's homeland. It's a favorite with locals, who dine on such house specialties as mussels vinaigrette, osso buco, beef Wellington, and chicken Oscar (chicken topped with crabmeat, asparagus, and béarnaise sauce). Open daily; dinner only weekends. Reservations advised. 850 S. Rancho Dr. (phone: 870-1977).

Benihana Village The unusual ambience here is as much of a draw as the traditional Japanese fare. This is actually a complex composed of *Hibachi* and the *Seafood Grille,* two eateries built around a re-creation of a small Japanese village. Open daily for dinner only. Reservations advised. Major credit cards accepted. *Las Vegas Hilton,* 3000 Paradise Rd. (phone: 732-5111).

Chin's This expanded version of the original restaurant now nestles in the glittering *Fashion Show Mall* on the Strip. Among the many specialties are *Chin's* beef and "crispy pudding." Reservations advised. Major credit cards accepted. 3200 Las Vegas Blvd. S. (phone: 733-8899).

Coyote Café Just as he did so successfully at the *Coyote Café* in Santa Fe and *Red Sage* in Washington, DC, owner Mark Miller offers a unique menu of Southwestern, Mexican, and Native American cooking that ranges from warm to spicy to red hot. The restaurant and café feature signature dishes such as Southwestern painted soup (a combination of pumpkin and black bean), howlin' *chiles rellenos,* and pumpkin-seed crusted salmon, plus an imaginative dessert menu and impressive wine list. Reservations advised. Major credit cards accepted. *MGM Grand Hotel,* 3799 Las Vegas Blvd. S. (phone: 891-7349).

Ginza This is the place to enjoy true Japanese cuisine. Top choices here include shabu shabu (chicken or beef cooked in a simmering pot of broth with vegetables and noodles), *yosenabe* (bouillabaisse), tempura, and teriyaki all expertly prepared and presented. Closed Mondays. Reservations advised. Most major credit cards accepted. 1000 E. Sahara (phone: 732-3080).

Hugo's Cellar In the *Four Queens* hotel, this is one of the most respected dining rooms in the city. The romantic atmosphere is enhanced by its remote, quiet location (well away from the casino) and the fresh red roses presented to the ladies. The menu features many duck preparations; also recommended are medallions of lobster. Open daily for dinner only. Reservations advised. Major credit cards accepted. 202 Fremont St. (phone: 385-4011).

Jerome's This lively San Francisco–style bar and grill serves up an imaginative menu of mussel-saffron soup topped with puff pastry, veal 49er (with prosciutto and three cheeses in a creamy sage sauce), and—for lunch—beer-cheese soup. The seafood and sourdough bread are flown in from San Francisco daily. There's a wide selection of California wines. Open daily; dinner only Sundays. Major credit cards accepted. 4503 Paradise Rd. (phone: 792-3772).

Michael's A gem in the Times Square section of the Strip. Among the offerings are shrimp served on frosted globes and double-dipped chocolate desserts. Outstanding service. Open daily for dinner only. Reservations necessary. Major credit cards accepted. *Barbary Coast Hotel,* 3595 Las Vegas Blvd. S. (phone: 737-7111).

Monte Carlo Room This dining room overlooks lush poolside vegetation. Hobo steak (New York sirloin sliced thin and served with a sauce of Dijon mustard, shallots, cognac, and herbs) and quail in red wine are just two of the entrées. The pride of the *Sheraton Desert Inn,* it's pricey—but worth it. Open for dinner only; closed Tuesdays and Wednesdays. Reservations advised. Major credit cards accepted. 3145 Las Vegas Blvd. S. (phone: 733-4524).

Morton's of Chicago Carnivores will love the huge portions of beef offered at this steakhouse. Asking for a doggie bag here isn't just accepted—it's expected. The menu does offer lobster for those who don't enjoy red meat, but this definitely isn't the place for vegetarians. Open daily for dinner only. Reservations necessary. Major credit cards accepted. *Fashion Show Mall,* 3200 Las Vegas Blvd. S. (phone: 893-0703).

Palm A branch of the steakhouse group that began in New York, it carries on the tradition of serving first-rate beef, lobster, and veal. The crab cakes are great, too, and the Key lime pie and Jack Daniels chocolate cake finish the meal with a flourish. Reservations advised. Major credit cards accepted. In the *Forum Shops* at *Caesars,* 3500 Las Vegas Blvd. S. (phone: 732-7256).

Pamplemousse This charming, romantic little spot offers a taste of the French countryside (its name translates to "grapefruit") in the glitzy setting of Las Vegas. The menu items change based on what fresh ingredients are available, but they are likely to include innovative presentations of duck, chicken, and veal. Open for dinner only; closed Mondays. Reservations necessary. Major credit cards accepted. 400 E. Sahara Ave. (phone: 733-2066).

Seasons This dining room at *Bally's* has seasonal continental menus featuring everything from filet mignon to Maine lobster. The seafood is outstanding, particularly the Dover sole and mahimahi; other entrées include veal medallions and rabbit served with roasted pine nuts. Closed Sundays and Mondays. Reservations advised. Major credit cards accepted. 3645 Las Vegas Blvd. S. (phone: 739-4651).

Spago of Las Vegas Yet another addition to Wolfgang Puck's line of successful restaurants that began in Beverly Hills. In the attractive dining room, you can enjoy innovative pasta and salads, special dishes such as blackened sea bass with fettuccine in black bean sauce, and fabulous desserts. Puck's signature designer pizza is featured in the café "outside" on the sidewalk, where you can see passersby (and they can see you). Reservations necessary for the dining room; no reservations for the café. Major credit cards accepted. In the *Forum Shops* at *Caesars,* 3500 Las Vegas Blvd. S. (phone: 369-6300).

MODERATE

Al Dente Elegant, modern ambience and impeccable service make this hotel dining room, formerly *Caruso's,* an especially popular setting. Pasta and fresh fish are the menu mainstays. Open for dinner only; closed Sundays and

Mondays. Reservations advised. Major credit cards accepted. *Bally's Hotel,* 3645 Las Vegas Blvd. S. (phone: 739-4111).

Antonio's Flowers brighten the rooms of this hotel dining room featuring well-prepared Italian fare. The staff is friendly and attentive; among the dishes they might recommend are the osso buco and the veal marsala. A tempting appetizer is fresh-baked breadsticks dipped in olive oil. Open daily for dinner only. Reservations advised. Major credit cards accepted. *Rio Suite Hotel & Casino,* 3700 W. Flamingo Rd. (phone: 252-7777).

Bertolini's Among the best Italian eateries in town, it offers heavenly versions of carpaccio, wild mushroom risotto, pasta, Caesar salad, and *tiramisù.* If you can, sit at an "outdoor" table—it's the perfect spot for people watching. Reservations advised. Major credit cards accepted. In the *Forum Shops* at *Caesars,* 3500 Las Vegas Blvd. S. (phone: 735-4663).

Bootlegger Nestled in a quiet area about 3 miles from the Strip, this cozy place specializes in southern Italian dishes. The homemade pasta is especially good; be sure to try the lasagna or the lobster *fra diavolo.* Closed Mondays; dinner only on weekends. Reservations advised. Major credit cards accepted. 5025 S. Eastern Ave. (phone: 736-4939).

California Pizza Kitchen An informal and friendly branch of this national chain known for its pizza with a twist: Instead of pepperoni and anchovies, the pies here are topped with the likes of duck sausage, artichoke hearts, and baby shrimp. Though priced higher than the usual pizza, they're still relatively reasonable. No reservations. Major credit cards accepted. *The Mirage Hotel,* 3400 Las Vegas Blvd. S. (phone: 791-7111); and the *Golden Nugget Hotel,* 129 E. Fremont St. (phone: 385-7111).

China First More elegant than the typical Chinese restaurant, this is one of the city's most popular eateries. One of the reasons is well-prepared dishes such as crystal shrimp (glazed and served with stir-fried vegetables). Open for dinner only; closed Mondays. Reservations advised. Major credit cards accepted. 1801 E. Tropicana Ave. (phone: 736-2828).

Cipriani An exhibition kitchen prepares an unusual, attractively presented Italian menu. Special dishes include salmon and ricotta, *porcini* lasagna, and chicken Frascati (sautéed with artichokes, mushrooms, black olives, and fresh herbs). Imaginative desserts, an extensive wine list, and excellent service are added bonuses. Open daily; dinner only on weekends. Reservations advised. Major credit cards accepted. 2790 E. Flamingo Rd. (phone: 369-6711).

Dive! Direct from Hollywood, where Steven Spielberg's first *Dive!* premiered, this submarine-shaped eatery dishes out sandwiches, pasta, ribs, salads, and super desserts. All this while 64 monitors, placed throughout the room, display undersea adventures. Reservations unnecessary. Major credit cards accepted. *Fashion Show Mall,* 3200 Las Vegas Blvd.S. (phone: 369-3483).

Ferraro's This classic Roman-style dining room features columns, recessed lighting, and dramatic black carpet. Southern Italian cooking predominates, but there are some northern Italian dishes on the menu. Among the specialties are *panzerotti* (potato croquettes with roasted peppers, according to a family recipe), outstanding osso buco, imaginative pasta presentations, and Rosalba Ferraro's *tiramisù.* Open daily for dinner only. Reservations advised. Major credit cards accepted. 5900 W. Flamingo Rd. (phone: 364-5300).

Marrakech Authentic Moroccan fare, including couscous, lamb en brochette, and chicken baked with turmeric and served over rice, is featured here. Diners sit on cushions in an exotic setting, and there's belly dancing. Open daily for dinner only. Reservations advised. Major credit cards accepted. 3900 Paradise Rd. (phone: 737-5611).

Rafters This San Francisco–style restaurant offers some of the best seafood in town. Try the splendid bouillabaisse, which comes topped with a whole soft-shell crab. Open daily for dinner only. Reservations advised. Major credit cards accepted. 1350 E. Tropicana Ave. (phone: 739-9463).

Steak House In the *Circus Circus* hotel, this is one of the best places for steaks. Generous portions of sirloin are served in such a quiet, pleasant atmosphere, you could easily forget that the casinos are right nearby. Open daily for dinner only. Reservations advised. Major credit cards accepted. 2880 Las Vegas Blvd. S. (phone: 794-3767).

Tillerman This pleasant place off the Strip serves fresh fish and seafood flown in daily—at reasonable prices. Open daily for dinner only. No reservations. Major credit cards accepted. 2245 E. Flamingo Rd. (phone: 731-4036).

Tony Roma's Among the best rib joints in the city, this informal eatery offers slabs of pork and beef coated with a spicy barbecue sauce. Try the onion rings on the side. Open daily for dinner only. Reservations unnecessary. Major credit cards accepted. *Stardust Hotel,* 3000 Las Vegas Blvd. S. (phone: 732-6111); the *Fremont Hotel,* 200 Fremont St. (phone: 385-3232); and 620 E. Sahara Ave. (phone: 733-9914).

INEXPENSIVE

Oklahoma Kitchen For nearly two decades, this bare-bones restaurant has been dishing out hearty home cooking, including chicken-fried steak and home-made Mexican food, among other specialties. Pictures of western figures such as John Wayne and Willie Nelson grace the dining room walls. No reservations. Major credit cards accepted. 23 N. Mojave Rd. (phone: 382-2651).

Ralph's Diner Right out of *American Graffiti,* here's a diner that serves burgers, meat loaf, and chocolate malts. The employees sometimes interrupt their duties to sing 1950s hits with a vintage jukebox as backup. No reservations.

Major credit cards accepted. *Stardust Hotel,* 3000 Las Vegas Blvd. S. (phone: 732-6330).

BEST BUFFETS

If all-you-can-eat sounds good to you, Las Vegas is the place to be. Most hotels have buffet breakfasts, lunches, and dinners where, for a few dollars, you can feast to your heart's (or stomach's) content on salads, fish, chicken, pasta, roast beef (occasionally), and dessert. Best bets are the *Golden Nugget, Caesars Palace,* the *MGM Grand,* the *Riviera,* the *Sahara,* and *The Mirage.*

A really special treat is the Sunday Champagne Brunch at *Caesars Palace*—a feast for the eyes as well as the taste buds with its selections of fresh pastries, fresh melons, eggs, bacon, ham, sausage, and all the champagne you can drink. Some locals claim that the Sterling Brunch, served in the *Steakhouse* restaurant in *Bally's,* is the best in town. The food is presented in silver chafing dishes by white-gloved waiters, sushi and omelettes are made to order, and the dessert display is exquisite.

Los Angeles

Los Angeles, like it or not, is a city of dreams, myths, and misunderstandings. It is our nation's Olympus, where certain of our gods live and cavort and where both good and bad are inflated to larger-than-life proportions. Yes, certainly, there is glitter and foolishness and often much about which to chuckle. And, admittedly, there are the curses of snarled traffic and eye-tearing smog.

But much of the rest can be sublime.

To begin with, the 8.6 million people who call the LA metropolitan area home care little about the City of Angels' skewed—and skewered—reputation. They are there, for the most part, not for the glitz and hijinks but for the quality of life.

There is no doubt that Los Angeles is one of the world's most beautifully situated and climate-blessed cities (except for the earthquakes, floods, mudslides, and the smog). The mile-high San Gabriel Mountains skirt Los Angeles to the north and the Santa Monica Mountains bisect it, thus allowing Angelenos to enjoy magnificent vistas and offering the unusual opportunity for secluded hillside living in the midst of a vast metropolis. These lofty ranges also mean that this is one of the few places in the world where it is possible in the same day both to ski and to surf (though you'll want to wear a wetsuit while surfing in winter).

On the other hand, many visitors are stunned to learn that Los Angeles isn't always favored with blue skies and perpetual sunshine. Late summer and early fall usually are the hottest times of year, when the dusty, dry Santa Ana winds blow out of the nearby eastern desert to elevate temperatures into the 90s—and sometimes 100s—and escalate temperaments into the danger zone. This is the time, wrote LA crime novelist Raymond Chandler, that wives finger the sharp edges of knives and study the contour of their husbands' necks. Oddly enough, spring and early summer can bring the dullest weather of the year—chill, fog, and overcast skies. Winter is the rainy season and can be glorious or awful—and normally is both, in spurts. In fact, rainfalls can be quick and violent, giving way to clear, warm days and cool nights.

Despite these vicissitudes, it is virtually inevitable that *New Year's Day* will dawn bright and sunny, with temperatures in the 80s, and that the achingly beautiful panoramas seen by the tens of millions watching the *Rose Bowl* game on television only will reinforce the LA legend.

Los Angeles traces its origins to a dusty little settlement founded in 1781 by order of a Spanish colonial governor. The settlers gave it the monumental name of El Pueblo de Nuestra Señora la Reina de los Angeles (The Town of Our Lady the Queen of the Angels). In 1850, after California was ceded to the United States (following the Mexican-American War), it had a population of only 1,610 and by the year 1900, it was the home of only a few more than 100,000 residents.

Still largely composed of citrus groves and bean fields at the turn of the century, Los Angeles retained much of the character of its Spanish and Mexican roots until the massive American migration to the West Coast began in the 1920s. California was the country's last frontier, a chance to start a new life and make one's fortune, and the city, along with the state, boomed. In the 1930s, the area attracted those rendered homeless and near hopeless by the Great Depression; in the 1940s, servicemen on their way home from World War II stopped here to put the past behind them. The 1950s and 1960s saw LA develop into a center for new businesses—the technological and aerospace industries of the future.

The film industry had begun to develop here in the 1920s, with the arrival of the early movie moguls who were drawn from New York by the sun, which permitted outdoor filming year-round. Later, the city attracted the television and music businesses as well. To much of the rest of the nation, however, Los Angeles was still "the Coast," a place dismissed laughingly and almost automatically as provincial and self-absorbed.

Over the years, Los Angeles also has become a favorite vacation destination and now welcomes more than 60 million visitors annually from all over the world, making *Los Angeles International Airport* the fourth-busiest in the country. Travelers are lured to LA not only by its salubrious weather and the chance of glimpsing a movie or TV personality but also by its theaters, symphony orchestras, opera and light opera companies, dance troupes, museums, and scores of top professional and college sporting events. Specific areas of Los Angeles have become attractions in themselves: Hollywood and its *Mann's Chinese Theatre,* with its footprints and handprints of the stars embedded in cement; Beverly Hills and its expensive shops and Rolls-Royce lifestyle; Westwood, with its footloose university-town ambience; and the casual but wealthy beach communities stretching from Malibu to the Palos Verdes Peninsula. The more traditional tourist sites and activities—*Disneyland, Universal Studios, Knott's Berry Farm,* and so on—continue to draw many visitors to Los Angeles and its surrounding areas as well.

Today, LA is a sophisticated city boasting the kinds of hotels, restaurants, shopping, nightlife, museums, and cultural events that befit the second-largest city in the nation. It also has a state-of-the-art *Metro Rail* that connects downtown with outlining cities. *Metro Rail's* long-term goal is to construct a 400-mile system incorporating a subway and commuter rail throughout Los Angeles County and its surrounding communities. For more information, see *Getting Around* below.

Los Angeles also has the largest convention center on the West Coast, measuring in at an impressive 2.5 million square feet. Located downtown, the *Los Angeles Convention Center* features 685,000 square feet of exhibit hall space, two 400-seat restaurants, food courts, a picturesque plaza land-

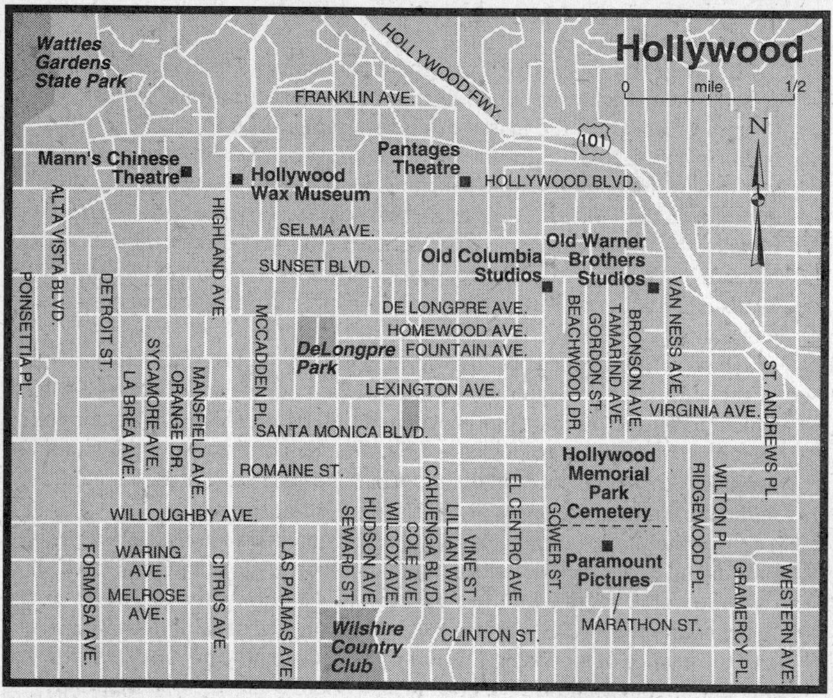

Hollywood

0 mile 1/2

N

Wattles Gardens State Park
FRANKLIN AVE.
HOLLYWOOD FWY
101
Mann's Chinese Theatre
Hollywood Wax Museum
Pantages Theatre
HOLLYWOOD BLVD.
SELMA AVE.
SUNSET BLVD.
Old Columbia Studios
Old Warner Brothers Studios
DE LONGPRE AVE.
HOMEWOOD AVE.
FOUNTAIN AVE.
DeLongpre Park
LEXINGTON AVE.
VIRGINIA AVE.
SANTA MONICA BLVD.
ROMAINE ST.
WILLOUGHBY AVE.
WARING AVE.
MELROSE AVE.
Hollywood Memorial Park Cemetery
Paramount Pictures
MARATHON ST.
CLINTON ST.
Wilshire Country Club
POINSETTIA PL.
ALTA VISTA BLVD.
FORMOSA AVE.
DETROIT ST.
LA BREA AVE.
SYCAMORE AVE.
ORANGE DR.
MANSFIELD AVE.
CITRUS AVE.
HIGHLAND AVE.
MCCADDEN PL.
LAS PALMAS AVE.
SEWARD ST.
HUDSON AVE.
WILCOX AVE.
COLE AVE.
CAHUENGA BLVD.
LILLIAN WAY
VINE ST.
EL CENTRO AVE.
GOWER ST.
BEACHWOOD DR.
GORDON ST.
TAMARIND AVE.
BRONSON AVE.
VAN NESS AVE.
RIDGEWOOD PL.
WILTON PL.
GRAMERCY PL.
ST. ANDREWS PL.
WESTERN AVE.

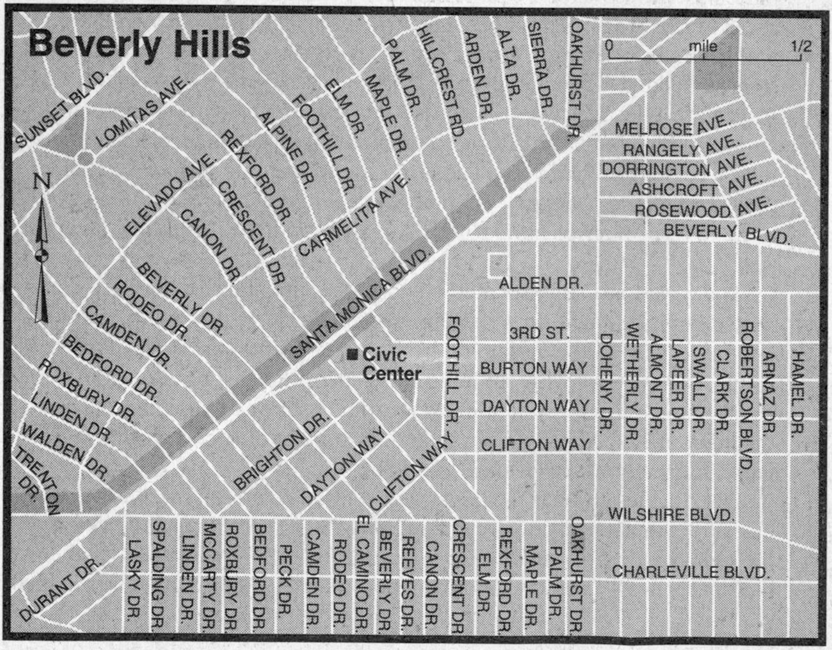

Beverly Hills

0 mile 1/2

N

SUNSET BLVD.
LOMITAS AVE.
ELEVADO AVE.
REXFORD DR.
ALPINE DR.
FOOTHILL DR.
ELM DR.
MAPLE DR.
PALM DR.
HILLCREST RD.
ARDEN DR.
ALTA DR.
SIERRA DR.
OAKHURST DR.
CRESCENT DR.
CANON DR.
CARMELITA AVE.
BEVERLY DR.
RODEO DR.
CAMDEN DR.
BEDFORD DR.
ROXBURY DR.
LINDEN DR.
WALDEN DR.
TRENTON DR.
SANTA MONICA BLVD.
MELROSE AVE.
RANGELY AVE.
DORRINGTON AVE.
ASHCROFT AVE.
ROSEWOOD AVE.
BEVERLY BLVD.
ALDEN DR.
3RD ST.
BURTON WAY
DAYTON WAY
CLIFTON WAY
Civic Center
BRIGHTON DR.
DAYTON WAY
CLIFTON WAY
FOOTHILL DR.
DOHENY DR.
WETHERLY DR.
ALMONT DR.
LAPEER DR.
SWALL DR.
CLARK DR.
ROBERTSON BLVD.
ARNAZ DR.
HAMEL DR.
WILSHIRE BLVD.
CHARLEVILLE BLVD.
DURANT DR.
LASKY DR.
SPALDING DR.
LINDEN DR.
MCCARTY DR.
ROXBURY DR.
BEDFORD DR.
PECK DR.
CAMDEN DR.
RODEO DR.
EL CAMINO DR.
BEVERLY DR.
REEVES DR.
CANON DR.
CRESCENT DR.
ELM DR.
REXFORD DR.
MAPLE DR.
PALM DR.
OAKHURST DR.

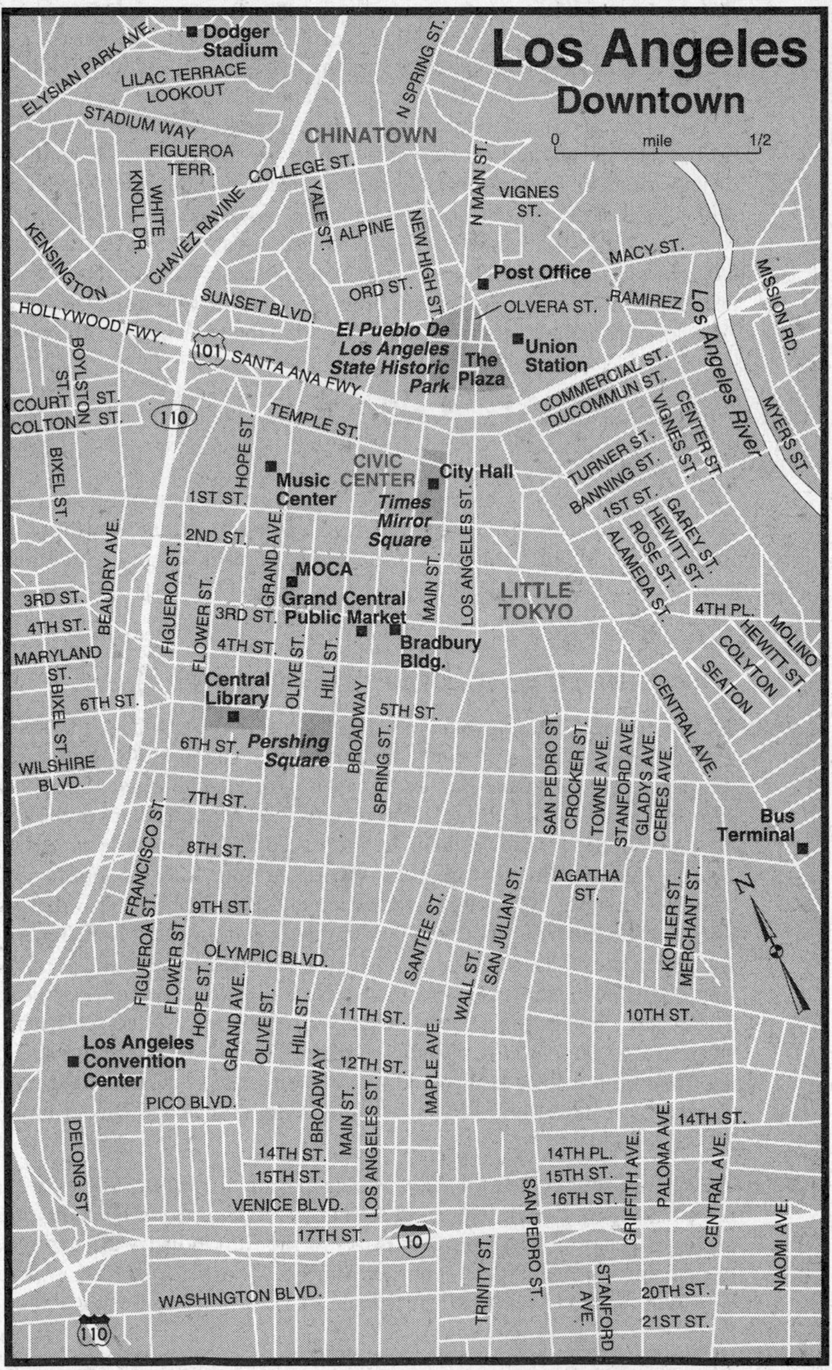
Los Angeles
Downtown
0
mile
1/2
Dodger Stadium
ELYSIAN PARK AVE.
LILAC TERRACE LOOKOUT
STADIUM WAY
FIGUEROA TERR.
KNOLL DR.
WHITE
KENSINGTON
CHAVEZ RAVINE
COLLEGE ST.
CHINATOWN
N SPRING ST.
N MAIN ST.
YALE ST.
ALPINE
NEW HIGH ST.
VIGNES ST.
MACY ST.
Post Office
OLVERA ST.
ORD ST.
SUNSET BLVD.
RAMIREZ
MISSION RD.
Los Angeles River
HOLLYWOOD FWY.
101
SANTA ANA FWY.
El Pueblo De Los Angeles State Historic Park
The Plaza
Union Station
BOYLSTON ST.
COURT ST.
COLTON ST.
110
TEMPLE ST.
COMMERCIAL ST.
DUCOMMUN ST.
VIGNES ST.
CENTER ST.
MYERS ST.
BIXEL ST.
HOPE ST.
Music Center
CIVIC CENTER
City Hall
TURNER ST.
BANNING ST.
1ST ST.
Times Mirror Square
1ST ST.
GAREY ST.
HEWITT ST.
ROSE ST.
ALAMEDA ST.
2ND ST.
GRAND AVE.
BEAUDRY AVE.
FIGUEROA ST.
MOCA
MAIN ST.
LOS ANGELES ST.
LITTLE TOKYO
3RD ST.
FLOWER ST.
3RD ST.
Grand Central Public Market
4TH PL.
4TH ST.
MOLINO
HEWITT ST.
COLYTON
SEATON
MARYLAND ST.
4TH ST.
Bradbury Bldg.
BIXEL ST.
6TH ST.
Central Library
OLIVE ST.
HILL ST.
CENTRAL AVE.
5TH ST.
WILSHIRE BLVD.
6TH ST.
Pershing Square
BROADWAY
SPRING ST.
SAN PEDRO ST.
CROCKER ST.
TOWNE AVE.
STANFORD AVE.
GLADYS AVE.
CERES AVE.
7TH ST.
Bus Terminal
8TH ST.
FRANCISCO ST.
AGATHA ST.
SAN JULIAN ST.
9TH ST.
SANTEE ST.
KOHLER ST.
MERCHANT ST.
N
OLYMPIC BLVD.
WALL ST.
FIGUEROA ST.
FLOWER ST.
HOPE ST.
GRAND AVE.
OLIVE ST.
HILL ST.
11TH ST.
10TH ST.
Los Angeles Convention Center
MAPLE AVE.
12TH ST.
BROADWAY
PICO BLVD.
MAIN ST.
LOS ANGELES ST.
14TH ST.
DELONG ST.
14TH ST.
14TH PL.
15TH ST.
15TH ST.
GRIFFITH AVE.
PALOMA AVE.
CENTRAL AVE.
VENICE BLVD.
16TH ST.
SAN PEDRO ST.
17TH ST.
10
NAOMI AVE.
TRINITY ST.
STANFORD AVE.
20TH ST.
WASHINGTON BLVD.
21ST ST.
110

hall space, two 400-seat restaurants, food courts, a picturesque plaza landscaped with palm trees, and two 150-foot-high glass lobby pavilions.

The City of Angels still has its critics. Its vast size (the city itself is almost half as big as the entire state of Rhode Island) may make it seem uncomfortably spread out and sometimes difficult to negotiate. But most people find LA a pleasant and easy city in which to live and to visit. Beneath the official municipal veneer, away from the sunshine, and removed from the artificial glitter of show biz, Los Angeles has an essentially solid, all-American soul. Add the fascination of the ethnic mix—European, African, and Mexican stock, plus Chinese, Japanese, Korean, Vietnamese, Russian, and Thai—as well as its environmental meld of sea, mountain, and desert, and Los Angeles indisputably retains its status as one of the great cities of the world.

Los Angeles At-a-Glance

SEEING THE CITY

There are at least two great places to go for a fantastic view of Los Angeles. The most famous is Mulholland Drive, a twisting road that winds through the Hollywood Hills. Another is the top of Mount Olympus, in Laurel Canyon, north of Sunset Boulevard.

SPECIAL PLACES

OLD HOLLYWOOD: MEMORIES OF YESTERYEAR

MANN'S CHINESE THEATRE Known to movie fans around the world as *Grauman's Chinese Theatre,* this is probably the most visited site in Hollywood. If you wander down Hollywood Boulevard looking for the *Grauman's* sign, however, you'll never find it. Several years ago, Ted Mann took over the theater, added it to his movie chain, and replaced Syd Grauman's name with his. The *Chinese Theatre* forecourt is world-famous for its celebrity footprints and handprints immortalized in cement. If you join the crowd of visitors outside the box office, you'll probably find imprints of your favorite stars from the 1920s to the present. If you buy a ticket to get in, you'll be treated to one of the world's most impressive and elaborate movie palaces. The ornate carvings, high, decorative ceiling, traditionally plush seats, heavy curtains that whoosh closed when the film ends, and the enormous screen itself are all part of a Hollywood that no longer exists. The less opulent *Chinese Twin* next door also shows films. 6925 Hollywood Blvd. (phone: 213-464-8111).

HOLLYWOOD WAX MUSEUM If the *Chinese Theatre* makes you nostalgic for the faces belonging to celluloid souls, stop in at the *Hollywood Wax Museum.* Here images of many of the immortals of the film industry are captured both in and out of character—in wax. Marilyn Monroe, Jean Harlow, Paul Newman, Raquel Welch, Michael Jackson, Madonna, Sylvester Stallone as Rambo, and many more fill the star-studded display cases. There's also the *Academy Award Film Library,* a horror chamber, and a re-creation of the Last Supper. Open Sundays through Thursdays until midnight, Fridays and Saturdays to 2 AM. No admission charge for children under six. 6767 Hollywood Blvd. (phone: 213-462-8860).

THE HOLLYWOOD BOWL

The natural amphitheater, originally known as *Daisy Dell,* was developed in the 1920s as a concert shell, and now hosts the summer season of the *Los Angeles Philharmonic,* visiting musicians, and jazz and pop concerts. Popular perennials include the *Easter* sunrise service and the *Fourth of July* celebrations, complete with an evening concert capped off with fireworks. The acoustics are spotty, and only subscribers in their box seats can actually *hear* the musicians without amplification. Dress warmly, bring a cushion, and come early for a picnic—the sylvan glades around the *Bowl* fill up quickly. The *Deck* restaurant serves supper alfresco (phone: 213-850-2000, reservations required a week in advance); there's also *The Deli,* a more affordable spot serving fast food, wine, and beer, as well as several refreshment stands. Parking, in lots along Highland Avenue, can be chaotic; a better bet are the 14 park-and-ride buses that serve different parts of LA. On your way in, note George Stanley's statues of music, drama, and dance. Grounds open daily until dusk July through September. 2301 N Highland Ave. (phone: 213-850-2000).

HOLLYWOOD STUDIO MUSEUM If nostalgia is what you seek, you can find it at the largest single historic movie artifact in existence. Called the *De Mille Barn,* it was the production site of the first feature-length film made in Hollywood—Cecil B. De Mille's *The Squaw Man.* Designated a California Cultural Landmark in 1956, it was moved by *Paramount Studios* to the *Hollywood Bowl* parking lot and turned into the *Hollywood Studio Museum* in 1979. Inside are a replica of De Mille's office and stills from silent motion pictures. The outside of the building is interesting, too: When it was on the back lot of *Paramount Studios,* it often was used in Westerns and, for many years, was seen as the railroad station in the "Bonanza" TV series. In addition, there's a gift shop, filled with old autographs, books, and pictures. The museum is open weekends only in winter, also open Friday afternoons in summer. No admission charge for children under six. 2100 N. Highland, across from the *Hollywood Bowl* (phone: 213-874-2276).

PARAMOUNT PICTURES At one time, *RKO Studios* adjoined the *Paramount* lot. After *RKO* folded in 1956, its studio became the home of television's Desilu Productions, which in turn sold its property to next-door *Paramount.* Close to the Bronson Avenue intersection with Melrose is the famous *Paramount Gate,* the highly decorative studio entrance that many people will remember from the film *Sunset Boulevard.* The Gower Street side of today's *Paramount* was the old front entrance to *RKO.* It once featured Art Deco doors and a marquee with distinctive Deco neon letters spelling out *RKO*. Today, it's simply an unimpressive back door to *Paramount,* painted in that dull, flat beige many studios use to protect their exterior walls. *Paramount* extends from Melrose Avenue on the south to Gower Street on the west, Van Ness Avenue on the east, and Willoughby Avenue on the north (phone: 213-956-5000).

GOWER STREET This was once the center for so many small film studios that it became known in the biz as "Gower Gulch." It was also nicknamed "Poverty Row," since so many of its independent producers were perpetually strapped for production money. Poverty Row's most famous studio was *Columbia Pictures,* which ultimately grew healthy enough to acquire most of the smaller parcels of studio real estate in the neighborhood. *Columbia*'s old studios still stand at Gower Street and Sunset Boulevard, although *Columbia* moved out several years ago. (It found a new home in Burbank.)

WARNER BROTHERS During the late 1920s, when Warner's was introducing "talkies" to America, its pictures were filmed here. This also was the home of *Warner*'s radio station at the time, KFWB. Today, the old studio is the headquarters for KTLA-TV and KMPC radio. The stately Southern mansion that served as *Warner*'s administration building still stands on Sunset Boulevard. Sunset Blvd. and Van Ness Ave.

"HOLLYWOOD": LIGHTS. . . CAMERA. . . ACTION!

UNIVERSAL STUDIOS HOLLYWOOD Only during a trip to *Universal Studios Hollywood* can one encounter a 30-foot, 6.5-ton King Kong and/or fly home with *E.T.* The combination movie studio and theme park attracts more than five million people a year. There is a 45-minute guided tram tour past all the attractions on the grounds, which include some of the 500 sets and sound stages. Here you can see the house used in Alfred Hitchcock's *Psycho;* re-created sets from such movies as *All Quiet on the Western Front, Jaws,* and *The Sting;* a collapsing bridge; the parting of the Red Sea; the *Doomed Glacier Expedition,* where you get to plunge down an alpine avalanche; and an earthquake simulation called *The Big One.* If this isn't enough, there is the new *Wild, Wild, Wild West* stunt show, and *Backdraft,* a vivid re-creation of the burning warehouse from the movie. You also can travel through time on *Back to the Future: The Ride.* Fans of the late Lucille Ball will enjoy *Tribute to Lucy,* a dazzling display of memorabilia and highlights of the comedienne's TV and movie career. Meanwhile, Flintstone fans will flip over the new *Flintstone Show,* a fanciful extravaganza with comedic dictabirds, lava-spewing volcanoes, and characters like "Walter Concrete." Don't miss "Casper the Friendly Ghost," a computer generated imaging, high-tech spectacle, and *The Waterworld Sea War Spectacular,* a live action stunt show based on the *Waterworld* motion picture. The biggest attraction though is *Jurassic Park,* guaranteed to delight the whole family with its prehistoric-theme. A *Studio Center* facility features the futuristic *Universal Starway* peoplemover along with the famed *E. T. Adventure.* Food stands and gift stores abound, and there are 50 acres of free parking. Open daily except *Thanksgiving* and *Christmas.* No admission charge for children under three. Hollywood Fwy. to Lankershim exit, Universal City (phone: 818-508-9600).

WARNER BROTHERS STUDIOS To take a look at a real production studio rather than the Universal extravaganza, try these studios in Burbank—home of Warner Brothers, as well as many independent production companies. Nothing on the tour is staged, so visitors watch whatever is happening on that particular day. Not only do you get to see some actual shooting whenever possible, you also witness behind-the-scenes action—scenery construction, sound recording, and prop selection. Since tours are limited to 12 people (children under 10 are not permitted), reservations are required a week in advance. The two-hour tour is offered every hour on the hour weekdays between 9 AM and 3 PM weekdays. Closed weekends and holidays. Admission charge. 4000 Warner Blvd. (phone: 818-954-1744).

UNIVERSAL CITYWALK Rodeo Drive meets Melrose Avenue, Venice Beach, and Hollywood Boulevard at this four-block, open-air retail promenade with its 27 façades, each dedicated to one of the popular architectural styles of the Southern California cityscape. *B. B. King's Blues Club* carries the name of the blues legend who opened this location because his "Lucille" (his guitar) wished to "go Hollywood." Tasty Southern food is dished out with the blues (phone: 818-622-5480). It's worth the trip if only for an affordable pizza at the *Wolfgang Puck Café* (phone: 818-985-9653), where the Italian pies cost a fraction of their higher priced cousins at *Spago,* or for the show at the *Wizard Magic Theater* (phone: 818-506-0066), where the world's top magicians strut their illusionary stuff. You can even walk down a replica of Olvera Street and grab a bite of authentic Mexican fare at *Camacho's Cantina* (phone: 818-622-3333). Then enjoy a cup of coffee with a good book at *Upstart Crow,* a coffee bar/bookstore (phone: 818-763-1811). And if you're too nervous for a real roller coaster ride, you can get your thrills vicariously at *Cinemania* (phone: 818-622-8697), which lets you experience the sensation through visual effects. The complex also houses *Gladstone's 4 Fish* restaurant (phone: 818-622-3474), and a 14-classroom *UCLA Extension Center. CityWalk* is located in the center of Universal City and is accessible from the Universal off-ramps of the Hollywood (101) Fwy. via Lankershim, Cahuenga, or Barham Blvd. entrances; Universal Center Dr. (phone: 818-622-4455).

BEVERLY HILLS Without a doubt the most affluent and elegant neighborhood in Southern California, Beverly Hills is a must-see. If you want to window-shop or purchase high-fashion clothing, stroll along Rodeo Drive between Santa Monica and Wilshire Boulevards. To guarantee that you won't make an impulsive (and expensive) purchase, go during the evening or on Sundays, when many stores are closed. *Gray Line* is one of several companies offering van and limousine tours of the area (phone: 213-856-5900). From June through *Labor Day,* an old-fashioned trolley, which departs from in front of the *Chanel* boutique on Rodeo Drive, tours Beverly Hills daily (phone: 310-271-8174).

DOWNTOWN LOS ANGELES

EL PUEBLO DE LOS ANGELES If you're wondering what LA looked like before shopping centers were created, go to *El Pueblo de Los Angeles,* where the city was born in 1781. Today, the 44-acre Mexican-style site is a state historic park. At the center of the park is the Old Plaza, a wide historic square that is the scene of tours and monthly fiestas. The *Old Plaza Church,* which dates from 1822, has a curious financial history: It was partially paid for by the sale of seven barrels of brandy. The city's first firehouse is here—it is now the *Plaza Firehouse* museum (phone: 213-628-1274). The museum is closed Mondays. No admission charge. Colorful local anecdotes are retold during a narrated 45-minute walking tour of the Plaza, offered hourly Tuesday through Saturday mornings. For information, contact *El Pueblo de Los Angeles State Historic Park* on the Plaza (845 N. Alameda St.; phone: 213-628-1274).

OLVERA STREET The music from the Plaza fiestas spills over to this block-long pedestrian alley filled with colorful Mexican shops, restaurants, and stalls selling spicy food. The oldest house in Los Angeles is here—the 1818 adobe *Avila House* (E10 Olvera; phone: 213-628-1274). It is closed Mondays. No admission charge. The first brick house also is here, but now it's home to *La Golondrina* restaurant (W17 Olvera St.; phone: 213-628-4349). There is a *Visitors' Center* in the 1887 *Sepulveda House* (622 N. Main St.; phone: 213-628-1274). The center, which is closed Sundays, offers a free 18-minute film on the history of Los Angeles.

LOS ANGELES CIVIC CENTER AND MALL An unusually quiet, well-landscaped city mall, it features tropical plants, gently splashing fountains, and sculptures half hidden among the lush greenery. It's the first and only mall of shops and restaurants to be built on LA *City Hall* property. The covered bridge between *East City Hall* and *City Hall* features changing art exhibits. The mall is open daily. *City Hall* is between Main and Spring Sts. (phone: 213-485-2121).

THIRD AND BROADWAY Several places in this area are worth noting. First is the skylit, five-story indoor court of the *Bradbury Building,* now a registered historic landmark (closed weekends). You can ride an old hydraulic elevator to the top balcony and walk down a magnificent staircase guaranteed to evoke visions of bygone splendors. Across the corner from the *Bradbury Building* is the *Million Dollar Theater*—Syd Grauman's first—with a fascinating interior; it's currently a Spanish-language picture palace. Just south of the theater is the entrance to the *Grand Central Public Market,* a conglomeration of stalls selling food from all over the world amid the sounds and smells of a Mexican *mercado.*

LITTLE TOKYO This is the social, economic, cultural, and religious center of the largest Japanese-American community in the US. There are four specialty shopping centers here, as well as the *Japanese Cultural Center* and many fine restaurants. First and San Pedro Sts. (phone: 213-620-8861).

MUSIC CENTER The best time to visit the *Music Center* is during a concert or performance, but it's worth seeing anytime. This large cultural complex encompasses three performance halls (with another in the works). The *Ahmanson Theater* is the base of a branch of the *Center Theater Group;* it stages classical dramas, comedies, and international premieres with big-name stars. The *Mark Taper Forum,* a small, award-winning theater, houses the branch of the *Center Theater Group* that specializes in new works and experimental material. The glittering *Dorothy Chandler Pavilion,* a 3,200-seat auditorium best known as the site of the Academy Awards ceremonies, is the home of the *Los Angeles Philharmonic* and the *Los Angeles Master Chorale.* It's also the setting for most of the season of the *Los Angeles Opera Company.* The orchestra season runs from October through May; musical theater is presented generally in summer, when the orchestra moves to the *Hollywood Bowl.* If you take the free guided tour of the theaters, you will get a sneak preview of the *Walt Disney Concert Hall*—a mega-million-dollar, 2,380-seat, Frank Gehry–designed facility; scheduled to open in 1997, it will house the *Los Angeles Philharmonic.* Made possible by a $50-million grant from Lillian B. Disney in memory of her husband, the hall will contain four theaters, an outdoor park, and gardens. First St. and Grand Ave. (phone: 213-972-7483 for tour information; 213-972-7211 for general information).

NATURAL HISTORY MUSEUM With exhibits illustrating the cultural and technological changes of the 20th century, this museum has a wing devoted to American history, a dazzling hall of gems and minerals, the *Ralph W. Schreiber Hall of Birds,* a large taxidermy collection of North American and African mammals imaginatively posed in picturesque display cases, and ever-changing, traveling exhibitions. The *Ralph M. Parsons Discovery Center* is entertaining and educational. Learning is easy with hands-on exhibits that are as much fun for adults as they are for children. Closed Mondays. No admission charge on the first Tuesday of each month. 900 Exposition Blvd. (phone: 213-744-3466).

CHINATOWN LA's Chinatown has the usual assortment of restaurants, vegetable stores, and little shops selling everything from ivory chess sets to acupuncture charts. The 900 block of N. Broadway.

MUSEUM OF CONTEMPORARY ART (MOCA) This is one museum in two buildings: the *MOCA* building at California Plaza, designed by Arata Isozaki (and a work of modern art in itself), and the *Geffen Contemporary* (named after media mogul David Geffin), a renovated warehouse about 10 blocks away, on Bunker Hill downtown. Both house artworks from the 1940s to the present. In addition, the Media and Performing Arts Program at *MOCA*'s *Ahmanson Auditorium* looks at performance—contemporary dance, theater, film, and video—as an art form. There's also a gift shop, as well as a pleasant café. Closed Mondays. Admission charge (except Thursdays from 5 to 8 PM). One ticket covers admission to both buildings on the same day. *MOCA:* 250 S. Grand Ave. at California Plaza (phone: 213-621-2766; 213-626-6222 for recorded information); *Geffen Contemporary:* 152 N. Central Ave.

MIDTOWN

FARMERS' MARKET A favorite with locals and tourists, this market was established in 1934 as a cooperative where local farmers could sell their produce. Today, more than 160 vendors set up shop every day, including 26 stands offering hot and cold dishes from around the world. Browse, select an appetizer here, an entrée there, but save room for pastry. Several of the fruit and nut stalls will create and ship gift boxes, as will some of the confectioneries, where you can watch candy being made. Open daily. 6333 W. Third St. at Fairfax (phone: 213-933-9211).

LA BREA TAR PITS These pools of sticky, bubbling asphalt, dating back some 40,000 years, are one of the world's most famous fossil sites. Once part of a Mexican land grant called Rancho La Brea, the pits are now part of *Hancock Park,* thanks to oil magnate Captain G. Allan Hancock, who deeded the property to the county in 1916. A natural phenomenon, tar pits develop when asphalt seeps to the earth's surface and forms pools, primarily during warm weather. For thousands of years, unsuspecting animals and at least one human—the 9,000-year-old La Brea Woman—became trapped in the pits, and their skeletons eventually fossilized. Scientists have recovered literally millions of animal and plant fossils from the La Brea site. For two months each summer, visitors can watch a pit excavation. Also in the park near the pits is the colorful *George C. Page Museum of La Brea Discoveries,* which has in excess of one million fossils from the Ice Age, as well as entire skeletons of prehistoric animals that were trapped in the tar pits. There are specimens of plants, reptiles, insects, birds, and mammals. One of the museum's more unusual exhibits is the open paleontological laboratory, where one may observe the cleaning and identification of fossils found in the pits. Also of interest are two films, the *La Brea Story,* which runs every half hour at the *La Brea Story Theater,* and *A Whoppingly Small Dinosaur,* which is shown continuously in the *Dinosaur Theater.* Also near the pits is the *Los Angeles Museum of Art* (see below). Closed Mondays. Admission charge (combination *Museum of Art* and *Page Museum* tickets are available). 5801 Wilshire Blvd. (phone: 213-936-2230).

LOS ANGELES MUSEUM OF ART With five buildings surrounding a spacious central court at the *La Brea Tar Pits* (see above), this is one of the top museums in the country and the largest in the West. The permanent collection features paintings, sculpture, graphic arts, photography, costumes, textiles, and decorative arts from a wide range of cultures and periods from prehistoric times to the present. The museum's holdings include American and European painting, sculpture, and decorative arts; 20th-century arts; pre-Columbian Mexican art; a unique assemblage of glass from Roman times to the 19th century; the renowned Gilbert collection of mosaics and monumental silver; and Indian and Islamic art. Major traveling loan exhibitions also are presented, along with lectures, films, concerts, and other educational events in the 600-seat *Leo S. Bing Theater.* The *Pavilion for Japanese Art* houses the internationally renowned *Shin'enkan Collection* of Japanese paintings, as well as Japanese ceramics, sculpture, lacquerware, screens, scrolls, and prints. Closed Mondays. Admission charge. 5905 Wilshire Blvd. (phone: 213-857-6000).

FARTHER AFIELD

GRIFFITH PARK AND THE LOS ANGELES ZOO The largest municipal park in the country, *Griffith* has three golf courses, a wilderness area and bird sanctuary, tennis courts, three miniature railroads, a carousel, pony rides, and picnic areas within its 4,043 acres. On top of all that, this is where you'll find the famous *Los Angeles Zoo,* home to more than 1,500 mammals, birds, and reptiles. Be sure to check out the *Tiger Fall,* an 18-foot waterfall in the wild cats' enclosure. The zoo is closed *Christmas Day.* No admission charge for children under two (5333 Zoo Dr.; phone: 213-666-4650). If you like railroads, you'll love *Travel Town,* a unique outdoor museum of old railroad engines, cars, railroad equipment, and fire trucks, also located in the park. The *Griffith Observatory* (2800 E. Observatory Rd.; phone: 213-664-1191) near Mt. Hollywood houses a 500-seat planetarium/theater, a twin-refracting telescope, and the *Hall of Science.* Most park facilities are open daily. Admission charge for planetarium shows. The park is in the Las Feliz district; call for details of how to reach it by car (phone: 213-665-5188).

SIX FLAGS MAGIC MOUNTAIN A 260-acre family theme park, featuring 100-plus rides, shows, and other attractions, this is the home of Bugs Bunny and his Looney Tunes friends in *Bugs Bunny World.* In addition to the mighty *Colossus* (a huge, wooden roller coaster) and the spine-tingling *Revolution* (a 360° vertical loop coaster), there's also the challenge of *Roaring Rapids* (a whitewater rafting experience), the *Z Force* mock starship ride, and a magic show run by the wily rabbit himself. *Ninja,* the West Coast's only suspended roller coaster, promises a delightfully terrifying trip. Other attractions include the *Batman Forever* stunt show, a laser and special effects spectacular, and *Batman the Ride,* a 50-mile-per-hour, two-minute romp through Gotham City, complete with hair-raising spins, loops, and turns;

the six-coaster *Psyclone,* a replica of Coney Island's *Cyclone;* and *Flashback,* a thrilling roller coaster that shoots through six 180° dives, fast switchbacks, and a startling 540° spiral. The *Viper* is one of the world's largest—and LA's scariest—multiple-looped roller coasters. The dolphin show and a children's village and petting zoo also are worthwhile. Open daily from *Memorial Day* through *Labor Day,* weekends only the rest of the year. No admission charge for children under three. Twenty-five minutes north of Hollywood on the Golden State Fwy., Magic Mountain exit in Valencia (phone: 818-367-2271 or 805-255-4100; 805-255-4111 or 818-367-5965 for recorded information).

PORTS O' CALL VILLAGE Some 60 specialty shops here feature merchandise from around the world. You can take a boat or helicopter tour of Los Angeles Harbor and dine in your choice of 25 restaurants and snack shops. Open daily. Berths 76–79 at the foot of the Harbor Fwy., San Pedro (phone: 310-831-0287).

REDONDO BEACH MARINA A delightful waterfront recreation showplace, the marina offers boat cruises and sport fishing. Open daily. 181 N. Harbor Dr., Redondo Beach. Take the Harbor Fwy. to the Torrance Blvd. exit and proceed west to the ocean (phone: 310-374-3481).

FOREST LAWN MEMORIAL PARK A major tourist attraction, this huge cemetery is the final resting place of Humphrey Bogart, Walt Disney, W. C. Fields, Clark Gable, and Bette Davis, among others; it advertises on huge billboards overlooking the freeways. The cemetery also contains a major collection of art treasures and marble sculptures including the largest religious painting in the world, Jan Styka's 195-by-45-foot *The Crucifixion.* And don't be surprised if you also find a real live bride and groom—some people like to get married here. Donations suggested. 1712 S. Glendale Ave., Glendale (phone: 818-241-4151).

QUEEN MARY SEAPORT You can explore the 81,000-ton ship, now permanently docked in Long Beach, from stem to stern, either on your own or with one of the daily guided tours; you even can spend the night—some 365 converted staterooms now make up the *Queen Mary* hotel. When she was launched in 1936, the *Queen* was the ultimate transatlantic travel experience of her time. In 1971, after retiring from a long career on the high seas, she was "relaunched" in this picturesque harbor by the Disney Company. After Disney pulled out in late 1992, the behemoth boat closed down for several months before being bought and reopened by a local entrepreneur. Open daily. Admission charge. Long Beach Fwy. to *Queen Mary* exit (phone: 562-435-3511).

CATALINA ISLAND Here you can spend the day wandering around the flower-filled hills, swimming, sightseeing, playing golf, or riding horses. There are places to stay overnight, but be sure to reserve in advance during the summer.

Boats depart for Avalon year-round from Long Beach and San Pedro with five sailings daily between mid-June and mid-September. During peak months, direct service to the Two Harbors/Isthmus area is also available. Reservations for all sailings to the island are advisable; call *Catalina Cruises* (phone: 213-253-9800); the *Catalina Channel Express* (phone: 310-519-1212) offers 55-minute trips from Long Beach year-round to Avalon daily; and *Catalina Passenger Service* (phone: 714-673-5245) operates daily luxury catamarans from *Balboa Pavilion* in Newport Beach to Catalina Island.

GETTY CENTER This $360-million, six-building project now under construction on a dramatic 110-acre hilltop site in the Santa Monica Mountains is slated to open by the end of this year. The 24-acre center will house a museum with seven pavilions, each devoted to a particular period in the history of art. The center will unite the J. Paul Getty Trust's other programs, including art education and conservation, while the original *J. Paul Getty Museum* building (which will be renamed *The Getty Villa*) near Malibu will house the trust's Greek and Roman art in a series of low-scale geometric-shaped buildings in a campuslike design. Natural ridges were bulldozed to create a mesa. Density is somewhat masked because nearly half the project is underground, where all the buildings are connected. Plans call for crisp detailing and rough travertine marble cladding alternated with porcelain steel panels with a metallic finish. Bridges, pergolas, and formal gardens will link the buildings. Viewed from the San Diego Freeway below, which passes east of the hill, drivers will see mostly fortresslike walls. 1200 Getty Center Dr.; phone: 310-395-0388.

ORANGE COUNTY

DISNEYLAND The original dream of Walt Disney, celebrating its 42nd anniversary this year, is spectacular and as magical as Tinker Bell's fairy dust. Thrill rides aren't the big deal. Instead, there are "adventures"—you'll be bombarded by cannonballs fired by *Pirates of the Caribbean,* visit a haunted mansion, explore the frontier, or fly through outer space. The special effects are truly astounding. During summer evenings, the *Main Street Electrical Parade*—floats and creatures outlined in thousands of tiny white lights—is supercalifragilisticexpialidocious, and the fireworks are stupendous. Ditto for *Fantasmic!,* a high-tech battle between the forces of good (led by Mickey Mouse) and several classic Disney villains; and *Fantasyland,* whose old-fashioned kiddie attractions have been treated to some $55 million of Disney's most magical special effects. Speaking of special effects, George Lucas designed a few for one of the park's most popular attractions, *Star Tours,* a flight simulator in which riders experience a *Star Wars*–type journey to the moon of Endor, home of the Ewoks. *Roger Rabbit's Car Toon Spin*, the newest addition, whisks you off on a crazy taxi ride through the streets and dark alleys of *Toontown.* A bit tamer, *Mickey's Toontown,* is "home" to many Disney characters. Then there is *Splash Mountain,* the ultimate flume ride. For thrill-seekers, there's the *Indiana Jones Adventure* archaeological tour and the techno-spectacular *Imagination,* where classic animated Disney films and live performances are staged in an after-dark show on *Tom Sawyer's Island.* Future plans include the addition of *WESTCOT Center*—inspired by Florida's *EPCOT*—that showcases foreign lands and theme pavilions. If you still can't get enough Disney, you can stay at the adjacent *Disneyland* hotel. *Birnbaum's Disneyland* (Hyperion; $10.95) can provide complete details about this still-expanding wonderland. Located 40 minutes from downtown LA, *Disneyland* is open daily. Admission charge. 1313 Harbor Blvd., Anaheim (phone: 714-999-4565).

MOVIELAND WAX MUSEUM More than 270 lifelike replicas of Hollywood stars are displayed in 150 sets of classic movies. Madonna, Kevin Costner, Arnold Schwarzenegger, Mel Gibson, Captain Kirk, and Spock have joined the Marx Brothers, John Wayne, the Keystone Kops, and Shirley Temple. Bring your camera for a close-up of your favorites, quake in the *Chamber of Horrors,* and shop for Hollywood memorabilia in the gift store. Admission charge. 7711 Beach Blvd., Buena Park (phone: 714-522-1154).

MEDIEVAL TIMES An arena set in a castle-like structure is the site of evenings of 11th-century entertainment featuring colorfully attired knights on horseback competing in medieval games, jousting, and sword fighting. The show comes with dinner (whole roasted chicken, spareribs, and various other finger foods, since people in those days didn't use forks). Open daily. Admission charge. Across the street from the *Movieland Wax Museum,* 7662 Beach Blvd., Buena Park (phone: 714-521-4740; 800-899-6600).

KNOTT'S BERRY FARM The theme of this 150-acre amusement park is the Old West. An old-fashioned stagecoach and an authentic steam coach take visitors around the grounds, which are divided into five sections (*Fiesta Village,* a *Roaring Twenties* area, a *Ghost Town,* an early California–Spanish area, and *Camp Snoopy,* a children's park featuring the world's largest Snoopy, a 38-foot-tall replica of the cartoon canine). Among the attractions are rides with such names as *Jaguar!* (a coaster adventure), the *Whirlpool, Mountain Log Ride, Sky Jump, XK-1, Tumbler, Slammer, Slingshot* (a mine train), *Montezooma's Revenge, Boomerang* (the multiple-looped roller coaster), and the exciting *Kingdom of the Dinosaurs.* The *Pacific Pavilion* features delightful aquatic attractions, and you can play games in the largest arcade west of the Mississippi. Top country music artists perform here frequently; there are also marionettes and a great ice show during the *Christmas* season. There's plenty of good eating right on the grounds: Stop in at *Mrs. Knott's Chicken Dinner Restaurant,* which is older than the park, or any of the stands selling Sicilian pizza, extra-juicy hot dogs, and barbecued ribs. Open daily. Admission charge. Located 10 minutes from *Disneyland* at 8039 Beach Blvd., Buena Park (phone: 714-827-1776; 714-220-5200 for recorded information).

EXTRA SPECIAL

For one of the most spectacular drives in California, follow the Pacific Coast Highway (Rte. 1) north about 95 miles from LA to Santa Barbara, a picturesque California mission town facing the Pacific, where bougainvillea bursting with purple and magenta blossoms adorn Mediterranean-style buildings of white adobe. A "red tile" walking tour zigzags through the historic district and runs along downtown State Street—a truly Spanish experience down to the last tile-enclosed trash bin and mailbox. The Spanish-Moorish courthouse is worth a visit for its opulent interior and the incomparable panorama from the tower. The city center owes its harmonious look to the strict architectural guidelines for reconstruction that were imposed after the devastating earthquake of 1925. Overnighters can opt for a hacienda-style hostelry, such as the *Four Seasons Biltmore* (1260 Channel Dr.; phone: 805-969-2261); Charlie Chaplin's favorite hotel, the *Montecito Inn* (1295 Coast Village Rd.; phone: 805-969-7854); an exclusive hideaway such as the *San Ysidro Ranch* (see *Inn Sites: America's Special Havens* in DIVERSIONS), with its excellent French *Stonehouse* restaurant; the Victorian *Upham* hotel (1404 De la Vina; phone: 805-962-0058), which features *Louie's,* a highly regarded restaurant serving California fare; or one of many period bed and breakfast establishments. The *Cold Spring Tavern* (5995 Stagecoach Rd.; phone: 805-967-0066), about 10 miles northwest of Santa Barbara on Route 154, goes back to the old stagecoach days. Chili is popular at lunch. At dinner, the menu tends more toward chicken, steaks, and game.

Sources and Resources

TOURIST INFORMATION

For free information, brochures, and maps, contact the *Los Angeles Visitors' and Convention Bureau* (633 W. Fifth St., Suite 6000, Los Angeles, CA 90071; phone: 213-624-7300). Closed Sundays. For all the latest information on events and happenings, call the *Visitors' and Convention Bureau Events Hotline* (phone: 213-689-8822); the service is available 24 hours a day in English, plus Spanish, French, Japanese, and German. Another information line, run by the *City of Los Angeles Cultural Affairs Department,* provides a recorded events listing covering the fine arts, museum exhibitions, and upcoming festivals (phone: 213-688-ARTS).

Contact the California state hotline (800-TO-CALIF) for maps, calendars of events, health updates, and travel advisories. Also, *West Hollywood Marketing Corporation* provides free brochures, maps, and information (phone: 310-274-7294).

LOCAL COVERAGE The *Los Angeles Times* and the *Daily News,* published in the San Fernando Valley, are daily morning newspapers. *Los Angeles Magazine* is published monthly, and *LA Weekly* and *LA Reader* are free weekly newspapers with local listings of events about town.

For the best (albeit most expensive) maps of the Los Angeles area, as well as travel books, try *Thomas Bros. Maps & Books* (603 W. Seventh St.; phone: 213-627-4018). Another good choice, too, is *ACCESS Los Angeles* (HarperCollins; $18.50). To really get a handle on this massive metropolis, pick up a copy of *50 Maps of LA* (H. M. Gousha; $9.95). This whimsical yet informative tome—a compilation of hot spots from artists, movie stars, and critics in map form—includes such gems as where Nancy Reagan gets her facials and a diagram of celebrity seating at *Laker* games.

TELEVISION STATIONS KCBS Channel 2–CBS; KNBC Channel 4–NBC; KABC Channel 7–ABC; KTTV Channel 11–Fox; and KCET Channel 28–PBS.

RADIO STATIONS AM: KABC 790 (talk); KIIS 1150 (top 40); KGFJ 1230 (country). FM: KXLU 88.9 (electronic synthesized); KCRW 89.9 (public); KKBT 92.3 (urban contemporary); KLOS 95.5 (contemporary); KLSX 97.1 (classic rock/"shock"); KLAX 97.9 (Spanish language); KRTH 101.1 (oldies); KIIS 102.7 (top 40); KOST 103.5 (light rock/pop); KKGO 105.1 (classical); KROQ 106.7 (new wave/rock).

TELEPHONE The area code for central Los Angeles is 213. For Santa Monica, Inglewood, Beverly Hills, and West Los Angeles, the area code is 310. A new area code for Long Beach goes into effect this year and will change from 310 to 562. The 818 area code covers the San Fernando Valley and the upper half of the San Gabriel Valley. The 805 area code covers the Ventura–Santa Barbara area; the 714 area code, Orange County. All telephone numbers in this chapter include area codes.

SALES TAX The sales tax is 8.25%; the hotel room tax is 12.5%.

CLIMATE Summers are hot and dry, with temperatures reaching the 90s during the day, but cool enough for sweaters after sundown. In winter, there are occasional rainy days and hot days, with an average temperature of 68F.

GETTING AROUND

It's always more convenient to have a car for exploring Los Angeles; however, there are buses, taxis, tours, and the *Metrolink* rail service.

AIRPORTS *Los Angeles International Airport* (known as *LAX;* phone: 310-646-5252 for general information) is the city's major airport and handles most international and domestic traffic. The drive downtown from *LAX* takes from a half hour to an hour, depending on traffic. The *Metropolitan Transit Authority (MTA)* provides bus service between *LAX* and downtown Los Angeles at Broadway and Sixth Street; the trip takes about an hour. Scheduled buses running to other parts of the city require one or more transfers; for information, call the *MTA* (phone: 310-273-0910 in the Beverly Hills/West LA area; 213-626-4455 in Hollywood/central LA; and 818-781-5890 in the San Fernando Valley). A more efficient alternative, however, is one of the private transport companies. *Supershuttle* (phone: 213-775-6600 or 310-782-6600) offers transportation by van from *LAX* to downtown hotels. At the airport, *Supershuttle* and several other companies can be summoned through the courtesy phones in the baggage claim area. For the return trip, call at least 24 hours ahead for a pickup at your hotel.

BUS For city bus route and schedule information, call the *MTA* (see above). The bus fare is $1.10. *DASH* minibuses (phone: 213-485-7201 for information), run by the *MTA,* travel through downtown's most scenic areas—from the *Civic Center* district to California Plaza, Broadway, or Pershing Square—24 hours a day, Mondays through Saturdays. The minibus fare is a mere 25¢.

CAR RENTAL All major firms are represented throughout Greater Los Angeles. Offering economical rates throughout the year is *Bob Leech's Auto Rental* (phone: 310-673-2727; 800-635-1240), with free airport pickup and drop-off. *LuxuryLine Rent-a-Car* (phone: 310-659-5555; 800-826-7805) provides a Rolls-Royce, Mercedes, Porsche, BMW, Range Rover, or another suitably esoteric vehicle.

SUBWAY The *Red Line* provides services between *Union Station* and *MacArthur Park/Westlake.* The *Blue Line* operates 22 stations between downtown Los Angeles and Long Beach. And the long-awaited 20-mile *Green Line* is now in operation and services 13 communities between Norwalk and Redondo Beach including a link to *Los Angeles International Airport.* Passengers arriving at *LAX* will be able to hop a free shuttle bus for the approximately 30-minute ride to *Union Station.* Tokens and tickets are available from vending machines at each station and cost $1.10 each.

TAXI Cabs *don't* cruise the streets in LA. Check at your hotel desk; different firms serve different areas. A few companies to try: *Bell Cab* (phone: 213-221-1112); *LA Taxi* (phone: 213-627-7000); and *United Independent Taxi* (phone: 213-653-5050).

TRAIN *Amtrak* provides frequent service from LA to San Diego, with many stops along the way. Day trips are also available by rail to the coastal communities of Santa Barbara and San Francisco. There's also service to *Disneyland* in Anaheim. For additional information, call 800-872-7245.

SIGHTSEEING TOURS

BUS *Oskar J's Tours* (4334 Woodman Ave., Sherman Oaks; phone: 818-501-2217; 800-458-2388) is one of many companies offering tours of downtown LA (including the *Music Center,* Chinatown, Little Tokyo, Olvera St., and more) and of the Hollywood–Beverly Hills area, as well as *Disneyland, Knott's Berry Farm,* and *Universal Studios Hollywood.* There are tours that offer more than the usual sights, including tasteful trips through Southern California wine country given by *Burbury Wine Tours* (30944 S. Mission Rd., Bonsall, CA 92003; phone: 619-631-2007; 800-345-4265) and the ghoulish *Graveline Tours* (PO Box 931694, Hollywood, CA 90093; phone: 213-469-4149), which visits scenes of scandals, crimes, and misdemeanors in a renovated hearse.

SPECIAL EVENTS

There are more special events than we could possibly list here. For complete listings, check the local publications listed above or call the *Los Angeles Visitors' and Convention Bureau* (see *Tourist Information,* above). Annual attractions include: the *Tournament of Roses Parade* and *Rose Bowl,* the traditional *New Year's Day* gridiron spectacle; *Los Angeles Open Golf Tournament,* Pacific Palisades, in February; *Los Angeles Marathon,* in March; *Long Beach Grand Prix Formula One Auto Racing,* in April; *Disneyland*'s *Easter Parade, UCLA*'s *Mardi Gras, Cinco de Mayo* celebrations throughout the area, the *California Strawberry Festival,* and *Manhattan Beach Art Festival,* in May; the *Playboy Jazz Festival,* at the *Hollywood Bowl,* in June; *Fourth of July* fireworks at *Anaheim Stadium* and the *Pasadena Rose Bowl,* as well as at the *Hollywood Bowl* and *Burton Chase Park* in Marina del Rey; *All-Star Shrine Football Game,* usually held in the *Pasadena Rose Bowl,* also in July; *International Surf Festival,* Redondo Beach, in late July or August; *SeaFest,* Long Beach, and *Festival of Arts and Pageant of the Masters,* Laguna Beach, in August; *Los Angeles County Fair,* Pomona, mid-September through early October; *Hollywood Christmas Parade* and the irreverent *DooDah Parade,* Pasadena, in November; and the *Christmas Boat Parade,* Marina del Rey, in December.

MUSEUMS

In addition to those described in *Special Places,* the following are other fine museums in LA:

ARMAND HAMMER MUSEUM OF ART Rembrandts, van Goghs, Cézannes, and Goyas are among the masterpieces that the late industrialist collected during his lifetime. Open daily. Admission charge. 10899 Wilshire Blvd. (phone: 310-443-7000).

CAROLE & BARRY KAYE MUSEUM OF MINIATURES With black-and-gold marble floors and a vaulted ebony ceiling, this 14,000-square-foot museum-cum–gift shop across from the *Los Angeles County Museum of Art* is a dramatic showcase for the world's largest collection of miniatures. Personalties depicted in these tiny creations (all available for purchase) range from First Ladies (Martha Washington to Hillary Rodham Clinton) dressed in their inaugural ball gowns to jazz greats (such as Louis Armstrong, Ella Fitzgerald, and Dizzy Gillespie) to popular celebrities (Bill Cosby and Michael Jackson). There are also more serious works of art by famed miniaturists Eugene and Henry Kupjack, George Stuart, and Gary Mirabelle. Whether you want to browse or buy, this is a fun place to visit. Closed Mondays through Wednesdays. Admission charge. 5900 Wilshire Blvd. (phone: 213-937-MINI).

GENE AUTRY WESTERN HERITAGE MUSEUM The singing cowboy of movies, radio, and television opened this wonderful tribute to the spirit of the West in 1988. Walt Disney Imagineering has brought the memorabilia, artwork, and movie clips to life so that you can get a visceral sense of what it was like to be a settler, a cowboy, or a sheriff. Scholarship and showbiz are fruitfully combined, and the museum presents regular exhibitions along with the permanent collection. Closed Mondays. Admission charge. 4700 Western Heritage Way, Hollywood (phone: 213-667-2000).

JAPANESE AMERICAN NATIONAL MUSEUM Dedicated to preserving the history of Japanese-Americans, this museum is housed in poignant and appropriate quarters. The building, erected in 1925 as the *Hongwanji Buddhist Temple,* was used as a warehouse for the possessions of Japanese-Americans when they were herded into internment camps during World War II. The exhibits, which change quarterly, include photographs, moving images, letters, tools, clothing, works of art, and personal possessions that have been passed from generation to generation. Closed Mondays. Admission charge. 369 E. First St. (phone: 213-625-0414).

LOS ANGELES CHILDREN'S MUSEUM Children and adults alike enjoy this touch-and-play experience, where changing exhibitions on the city's streets, African-American roots, and a kids' television station encourage participation. There are classes and workshops regularly scheduled. Open daily. No admission charge for children under two. 310 N. Main St. (phone: 213-687-8800).

MUSEUM OF FLYING Aeronautical enthusiasts will enjoy the close-up views of vintage planes, including a 1924 Douglas World Cruiser and a DC3 that were built on this site before Douglas Aircraft merged with McDonnell and moved to Long Beach. Also on display here are Spitfires and Mustangs, the workhorse fighters of World War II. Closed Mondays. Admission charge. 2772 Donald Douglas Loop N., Santa Monica (phone: 310-392-8822).

NORTON SIMON MUSEUM OF ART The rich industrialist's multimillion-dollar collection includes five centuries of European art from the Renaissance to the 20th century. There's also Asian sculpture spanning a period of 2,000 years. Closed Mondays through Wednesdays. Admission charge. 411 W. Colorado Blvd., Pasadena (phone: 818-449-6840).

PETERSON AUTOMOTIVE MUSEUM This captivating museum displays the history of cars and motorcycles from Model-T days to the latest in Harley-Davidson wheels. Open daily. No admission charge for children under five. 6060 Wilshire Blvd. (phone: 213-930-2277).

ROY ROGERS AND DALE EVANS MUSEUM An exact replica of a frontier fort features highlights of the lives of this famed Wild West celluloid couple, who trotted their way through dozens of motion pictures. There's a tribute to

Roy's faithful steed Trigger and Dale's Buttermilk—the horses themselves are mounted on pedestals. Open daily. Admission charge. 15650 Seneca Rd., Victorville (phone: 619-243-4547).

SIMON WIESENTHAL CENTER BEIT HASHOAH MUSEUM OF TOLERANCE A $50-million, 165,000-square-foot museum and educational center, it was founded in 1993 to "challenge visitors to confront bigotry and racism and understand the Holocaust in both historical and contemporary contexts." Besides a permanent exhibition level, the center features a multimedia learning facility with 30 workstations from which visitors can access extensive historical data; an extensive archival collection; and the dramatic *Tower of Witness,* which showcases more than 2,000 photographs of victims of Auschwitz-Birkenau. The eight-level complex also features a theater, an auditorium, a memorial plaza, and a temporary exhibit area. Closed Saturdays. Admission charge. 9786 W. Pico Blvd. (phone: 310-553-8403 or 310-553-9036).

SOUTHWEST MUSEUM This museum houses a magnificent collection of Native American art in a Mission-style building on Mount Washington overlooking the Pasadena Freeway. The permanent displays of art and artifacts from the Southwest, Great Plains, Northwest coast, and California have been dramatically improved over time. Notable among the holdings are the *Poole Collections* of American Indian basketry, Navajo blankets, pottery, and a full-size Blackfoot tepee. There is also a well-stocked gift and bookstore and the renowned *Braun Research Library* for scholarly reference. Closed Mondays. Admission charge. 234 Museum Dr., near *Dodger Stadium* (phone: 213-221-2163).

SHOPPING

No single street on this planet so typifies consumer excess as Rodeo Drive in Beverly Hills. Few mortals will be able to afford the prices, but window-shopping along this avenue for the affluent makes for as much fun as studying the boutiques along Paris's Rue du Faubourg-St.-Honoré, London's Bond Street, or New York's Fifth Avenue. In fact, many of the shop names are the same. Only a few are homegrown, such as *Fred Hayman* (see below). Don't miss *2 Rodeo,* a charming enclave of pricey shops and boutiques set on Italianate cobblestone lanes that surround a piazza, travertine fountains, and an elaborate staircase similar to the *Spanish Steps* in Rome. The ritzy retailers who have settled here represent the crème de la crème in high fashion and jewelry including the largest *Tiffany & Co.* store outside of New York. Other tony tenants include *Cole Haan* leather goods, *Rizzoli* books, *José Eber* hair designs, *Pierre Deux* French accessories, and *Charles Jourdan* fashions.

Here are some of the top emporia along and near Rodeo:

Barneys New York A five-level, 108,000-square-foot cathedral of cutting-edge fashion. Also on the premises is the *Chelsea Passage Gift Department,* offering marvelous collectibles from all over the world. 9570 Wilshire Blvd. (phone: 310-888-2200).

Bijan Where the rich and famous shop for men's clothing; by appointment only. 420 N. Rodeo Dr. (phone: 310-273-6544). *Bijan USA,* where no appointment is required, is at 431 N. Rodeo Dr. (phone: 310-285-1800).

Bulgari A long-established purveyor of fine jewelry, also known for exquisitely designed bangles and baubles. 201 N. Rodeo Dr. (phone: 310-858-9216).

Carroll & Co. Ivy League clothing for men. 466 N. Rodeo Dr. (phone: 310-273-9060).

Cartier Internationally renowned jewelers since 1847, with two locations on Rodeo. 370 N. Rodeo Dr. (phone: 310-275-4272) and 220 N. Rodeo Dr. (phone: 310-275-4855).

Chanel Boutique Clothes, scents, and accessories from the famous fashion house, 400 N. Rodeo Dr. (phone: 310-278-5500).

Charles Jourdan Clothes, shoes, and accessories from the French firm. 201 N. Rodeo Dr., in the *2 Rodeo* complex (phone: 310-273-3507).

Dyansen Galleries Fine art. 339 N. Rodeo Dr. (phone: 310-275-0165).

Elliott Katt's Books on the Performing Arts Crammed with a tremendous selection of rare books pertaining to the performing arts, here you'll find biographies of actors and directors, books on film, scores from famous Broadway musicals, as well as how-to books on everything from writing for television to getting a job in the music industry. 8568 Melrose Ave. (phone: 310-652-5178).

Fendi Exclusive leather goods and clothes with an Italian accent. 355 N. Rodeo Dr. (phone: 310-276-8888).

Frances Klein Antique and estate jewelry. 310 N. Rodeo Dr. (phone: 310-273-0155).

Fred Hayman A Beverly Hills shopping landmark, this supposed model for the title store of Judith Krantz's steamy novel *Scruples* sold its popular Giorgio fragrance name to Avon and more recently its "273" and "Touch" fragrances to a Miami-based company. However you'll still find plenty of the striking FHBH signature leather goods and evening bags, and collections from hot, young designers such as Eva Chun, Zang Toi, Christian Francis Roth, and C. D. Greene. There's a stand-up bar with complimentary wine and cappuccino. 273 N. Rodeo Dr. (phone: 310-271-3000).

Fred Joaillier Expensive jewelry, leather goods, and gifts. 401 N. Rodeo Dr. (phone: 310-278-3733).

Giorgio Armani The designer's coveted clothes for men and women. 436 N. Rodeo Dr. (phone: 310-271-5555).

Gucci Italian leather goods, jewelry, clothing, and accessories. 347 N. Rodeo Dr. (phone: 310-278-3451).

Krizia The Italian designer's boutique. 410 N. Rodeo Dr. (phone: 310-276-5411).

Louis Vuitton Famous French handbags, accessories, and luggage. 307 N. Rodeo Dr. (phone: 310-859-0457).

The Rodeo Collection A posh half-block mall; *Gianni Versace, Sonia Rykiel, Merletto, Fogal,* and *Furla* are among the designer boutiques. 421 N. Rodeo Dr. (phone: 310-858-7580).

Samuel French This West Coast outlet for the oldest play publishers in the world (since 1833) has an extensive collection of drama books, biographies of film directors and stars, and a tremendous selection of plays. 7623 Sunset Blvd. (phone: 213-876-0570).

Scriptorium This gallery sells the autographs of a wide variety of famous people—mostly historical figures such as Jimmy Carter, Abraham Lincoln, Lillian Gish, and Andy Warhol, although there are a few signatures of contemporary celebrities as well. Closed Mondays. 427 N. Canon Dr. (phone: 310-275-6060).

Superior Stamp & Coin Gold coins and rare stamps. 9478 W. Olympic Blvd. (phone: 310-203-9855).

Tiffany & Co. Fine jewelry in the famous blue boxes. 210 N. Rodeo Dr. (phone: 310-273-8880).

Yves Saint Laurent Boutique One of only two in the US (the other is in New York City), this Beverly Hills branch of the chic Paris boutique is a must-see (and looking is all most can afford). It is a sensational showcase for the French designer's fashions, jewelry, shoes, furs, fragrances, and cosmetics, framed by a theatrical limestone arch outside. A majestic staircase leads from the plush ground floor to a luminous mezzanine. Closed Sundays. 428 N. Rodeo Dr. (phone: 310-859-2389).

For specialty shopping with a more native character, browse in several burgeoning areas, such as the following:

MELROSE AVENUE This street runs an eastward gamut from upscale to funky to weird, with Gallery Row found roughly between Doheny Drive and Fairfax Avenue. Drop in at *Robert Kuo Ltd* (8686 Melrose Ave.; phone: 310-855-1555), a museum/boutique rolled into one, where cloisonné techniques are used to create dazzling one-of-a-kind pieces such as vases, statuettes, and whimsical animals. *LA Impressions* (8318 Melrose Ave.; phone: 310-659-3336), open by appointment only, specializes in Mexican art. At *Gemini Gel* (8365 Melrose Ave.; phone: 213-651-0513), a superb creator and exhibitor of limited-edition prints, customers watch the printing process through upstairs gallery windows. Or take a magic carpet ride at *Mansour* (8600 Melrose Ave.; phone: 310-652-9999), purveyors of fine Oriental and heirloom-quality carpets. Many businesses are located in the lower rent district to the east with lots to see all the way to Beverly Boulevard and Third to the south. Don't miss *Faux* (7309 Melrose Ave.; phone: 213-931-3763) for jewelry; *Rosso e Nero* (7371 Melrose Ave.; phone: 213-658-6340) and *O'toto* (7119 Melrose Ave.; phone: 213-937-5435) for fine eating; *Caffe Luna* (7463 Melrose Ave.; phone: 213-655-8647) for espresso and dessert; *Aardvark's* (7576 Melrose Ave.; phone: 213-655-6769) for vintage clothing; and *Emphasis* (7361 Melrose Ave.; phone: 213-653-7174) for casual fashions.

MONTANA AVENUE A cornucopia of small shops has sprung up between Seventh and 17th Streets along this Santa Monica thoroughfare, making it a window-shopper's delight. Among the pricey and super-specialized boutiques are *Lisa Norman* (1134 Montana Ave.; phone: 310-451-2026; also at 8595 Sunset Blvd.; phone: 310-854-4422), selling silk lingerie; *Where's My Conga!*(1615 Montana Ave.; phone: 310-451-1879) for funky, retro clothing; and *Private Stock* (1617A Montana Ave.; phone: 310-451-9431), which features unusual men's apparel. After making your selections, quench your thirst with a brew at *Father's Office* (1018 Montana Ave.; phone: 310-393-BEER), a fun, English-style (albeit *nonsmoking*) pub.

LA'S MALLS Lest anyone forgo the rather overwhelming experience of shopping in a mall, LA offers some of the finest, as well as some of the most eclectic, merchandise marts in the country. Among the largest shopping complexes are *Beverly Center* (8500 Beverly Blvd.; phone: 310-854-0070); *Century City Shopping Center* (10250 Santa Monica Blvd.; phone: 310-277-3898); *Del Amo Shopping Center* (Hawthorne Blvd. and Carson St.; phone: 310-542-8525); *Glendale Galleria* (100 W. Broadway; administrative offices: 2148 *Glendale Galleria;* phone: 818-240-9481); *South Coast Plaza* (3333 Bristol St.; phone: 714-435-2000); *One Colorado* (24 E. Union St., Pasadena; phone: 818-564-1066); *Sherman Oaks Galleria* (15301 Ventura Blvd.; phone: 818-884-7090); *Westside Pavilion* (10800 W. Pico Blvd.; phone: 310-474-5940); and *Woodland Hills Promenade* (6100 Topanga Canyon; phone: 818-884-7090).

VINTAGE SHOPPING

It doesn't get any hipper or more happening than *American Rag,* an Art Deco complex of five affiliated shops set along one city block on the east side of La Brea Avenue. The place showcases a mixed bag of high-ticket haute couture, outrageous accessories, and budget-friendly fashions. Even if you're not in a shopping mood, stroll through to see Margot Werts's riveting window displays with their lifelike mannequins. The shops sport a French countryside motif with high, vaulted ceilings and funky flooring. *American Rag* (150 S. La Brea Ave.; phone: 213-935-3154), the main store, proffers new and vintage fashions from designer jeans to outlandish leather jackets priced as high as $8,000; happily, most of the clothes are more affordable. *Maison et Café* (148 S. La Brea Ave.; phone: 213-935-3157), next door and accessible through an inside passageway, is a perky side-

walk café and curio shop rolled into one. Enjoy a cappuccino and baguette or browse among unique bric-a-brac and artifacts. For collectors, there are antique Pernod bottles and rare books, marvelous mosaic tile tables, and hand-picked European dinnerware. A short walk away is *Shoes* (144 S. La Brea Ave.; phone: 213-931-6903), a Moroccan-style bootery featuring everything from French and Italian sandals to sneakers. *Colours* (136 S. La Brea Ave.; phone: 213-937-8816), a super-hip bargain outlet, is popular with rock and rap stars; nothing here costs more than $30. Next door is *Youth* (136 S. La Brea Ave.; phone: 213-965-1404), a stylish kid's shop with unusual togs, accessories, and playthings. And to add new life on old frocks, stop in at the *Button Store* (8344 W. Third St.; phone; 213-658-5473), where you'll find from contemporary to designer-style buttons under one roof.

SPORTS AND FITNESS

There is no question that Southern California is a paradise for sports lovers.

BASEBALL The Los Angeles *Dodgers* play at *Dodger Stadium* (1000 Elysian Park Ave.; phone: 213-224-1500); *Anaheim Stadium* (2000 State College Blvd., Anaheim; phone: 714-937-7200) is the home of the California *Angels.*

BASKETBALL The *NBA Lakers*' home court is at the *Great Western Forum* (3900 Manchester Blvd., Inglewood; phone: 310-419-3100 or 310-419-3182 for tickets). The *Clippers* play at the *LA Memorial Coliseum and Sports Arena* (3939 S. Figueroa; phone: 213-748-6131).

BICYCLING Biking is great around the Westwood *UCLA* campus, *Griffith Park* (see *Special Places*), and on the oceanside, where there is a 19-mile bike path between the cities of Torrance and Pacific Palisades.

FISHING Power and sailboats can be rented from *Rent-A-Sail* (13719 Fiji Way, Marina del Rey; phone: 310-822-1868). Fishermen catch halibut, bonito, and bass off the LA shores. Sport fishing boats leave daily from San Pedro, site of the LA port, about 20 minutes from downtown Los Angeles, and from the Redondo Beach Marina in Redondo Beach.

FITNESS CENTERS *Bally's Sports Connection* (8612 Santa Monica Blvd., W. Hollywood; 310-652-7440) caters to starlets, models, and movie industry types. This branch of a Southern California chain is equipped with Nautilus machines, weight rooms, steamrooms, saunas, a pool, and a Jacuzzi, and offers a full schedule of exercise classes. The shortest membership term is two weeks. *Sports Club LA* (1835 Sepulveda Blvd.; phone: 310-473-1447), a $22-million fitness center complete with state-of-the-art amenities, is where the city's "power" players work out; some regulars are Madonna, Debra Winger, and Brooke Shields. It is open to non-members for a fee. *Nautilus and Aerobics Plus,* on the ground floor of the International Tower Building (888 Figueroa St.; phone: 213-488-0095), offers aerobics classes and has a Jacuzzi and sauna. It also has branches all over the metropolitan area which are open to non-members for a fee. Many hotels have their own health clubs, too (see *Checking In*).

FOOTBALL Champions of the *Big 10* and *Pacific 10* college conferences meet in the *Pasadena Rose Bowl* (1001 Rose Bowl Dr.; phone: 818-577-3100) every *New Year's Day. UCLA* plays its home games at the *Pasadena Rose Bowl,* and *USC* takes the field at the *Coliseum* (3939 S. Figueroa; phone: 213-747-7111 or 213-748-6131).

GOLF The *Industry Hills Golf Club* (1 Industry Hills Pkwy., City of Industry; phone: 818-810-HILL) boasts two 18-hole golf courses, designed by William Bell, with 160 sand bunkers, eight lakes, and miles of astoundingly long fairways. The club also has an ultramodern, lighted driving range and four practice putting greens.

HOCKEY The *Kings* make their home at the *Great Western Forum* (3900 Manchester Blvd., Inglewood; phone: 310-673-1300 or 310-480-3282 for tickets). And the *Mighty Ducks* push their pucks at *The Pond of Anaheim* (2695 Katella Ave.; phone: 714-704-2400 for tickets).

HORSE RACING If you like to spend your nights at the track, make tracks to *Los Alamitos.* There's harness, quarterhorse, and thoroughbred racing year-round. Take the San Gabriel Freeway (605) south to Katella Avenue exit in Orange County (phone: 310-431-1361 or 714-995-1234). If you prefer daytime action, try *Hollywood Park* between mid-April and late July and from early November to *Christmas Eve* (near *Los Angeles International Airport* between Manchester and Century Blvds.; phone: 310-419-1500). From late December to mid-April and in October and November, there's also thoroughbred racing at *Santa Anita Park,* home of the *Breeder's Cup* (Huntington Dr. and Baldwin Ave., Arcadia; phone: 818-574-7223).

JOGGING Downtown, run around *Echo Park Lake* (a little less than a mile) during the day only; get there by going up Sunset and taking a right onto Glendale. In *Griffith Park,* run in the woodsy Ferndale area near the Vermont Avenue entrance; get to the park via the Golden State Freeway and watch for the sign to turn off (also see *Special Places*). In Westwood, *UCLA* has a hilly 4-mile perimeter course and a quarter-mile track. Four blocks from Century City, *Cheviot Hills Park* (at 2551 Motor Ave.) has a runners' course. And in Beverly Hills, jog in *Roxbury Park* (entrance at 471 S. Roxbury Dr. and Olympic) or along the 1½-mile stretch of Santa Monica Boulevard between Doheny and Wilshire. Jogging also is popular along the oceanside bike path between Marina del Rey and the Palos Verdes Peninsula, in Santa Monica's *Palisades Park* on Ocean Avenue, and along San Vicente Boulevard from Brentwood to Ocean Avenue.

SWIMMING AND SURFING For swimming, the best beaches are El Porto Beach in Manhattan Beach, Will Rogers State Beach in Pacific Palisades, and Zuma

Beach, north of Malibu. For surfing, Malibu Surfrider Beach, Hermosa Beach, El Porto Beach, and Zuma Beach are tops.

TENNIS *Griffith Park,* featuring one of the top 25 municipal tennis facilities in the US according to *Tennis* magazine, boasts 12 outdoor courts, all lighted for night play (Riverside and Los Feliz; phone: 213-664-1191). Reservations can be made for a small fee. At the *Racquet Centre* (10933 Ventura Blvd., Studio City; phone: 818-760-2302), there are 20 lighted courts, a tennis shop, and a locker room and showers. The *Tennis Place* (5880 W. Third St.; phone: 213-931-1715), with a prime LA location, has 16 lighted, hard-surface courts; lessons and practice sessions with a ball machine are also available. Top-seeded players on the pro circuit generally show up for the *Volvo/Los Angeles Pro Tournament* held in July at *UCLA* (phone: 310-208-0730).

VOLLEYBALL If volleyball is your game, you won't have any trouble finding a hands-on or a spectator's experience here. There are nets up on most beaches in Los Angeles County, and both amateur and professional tournaments take place year-round. At Manhattan and Hermosa Beaches, 26 professional competitions are held during March and September. For a schedule of the competitions, contact the *Association of Volleyball Professionals* (phone: 310-337-4842). Indoor volleyball is also popular and played regularly by local leagues at most of the area's 150 public parks. For more information, contact the *Southern California Volleyball Association* (phone: 310-320-9440) or the *Valley Municipal Sports Office* (phone: 818-989-8070).

THEATER

There is no shortage of stages in LA, despite the overshadowing presence of the film industry. We begin with one of our favorite venues.

CENTER STAGE

Mark Taper Forum One of the nation's most respected resident theaters, it offers many premieres and an occasional revival; the subject matter tends toward the timely, the currently problematic. The *Mark Taper* production of *Jelly's Last Jam* went on to win Broadway's Tony Awards for best actor, actress, and lighting design in a musical in 1991, and in 1993 and 1994 *Angels in America* (parts I and II) won in the best play, director, actor, and featured actor categories. Also under the *Taper* wing are the *Improvisational Theatre Project,* the intimate *Taper, Too* house, and the Sunday afternoon *Literary Cabaret.* 135 N. Grand Ave. (phone: 213-972-7211).

The *Center Theater Group* performs at the *Music Center*'s *Ahmanson Theater* and *Mark Taper Forum* (see *Special Places*). Also downtown is the *Los Angeles Theatre Center* (514 S. Spring St.; phone: 213-627-6500). The revived *State Theatre of California* is at the *Pasadena Playhouse* (39 S. El

Molina Ave.; phone: 818-356-7529). Other Los Angeles theaters include the *Doolittle Theatre* (1615 N. Vine St., Hollywood; phone: 213-462-6666 or 213-972-0700); the *Shubert Theatre* (in the *ABC Entertainment Center,* 2020 Ave. of the Stars, Century City; phone: 310-201-1500; 800-233-3123 for information and credit card reservations); the *Odyssey Theatre Ensemble,* which performs in three small theaters (all at 2055 S. Sepulveda; phone: 310-477-2055); and the *Pantages Theatre* (6233 Hollywood Blvd.; phone: 310-410-1062). Tickets for all major events can be ordered over the telephone through *TicketMaster* (phone: 213-480-3232).

MUSIC

All kinds of music can be heard in LA's concert halls and clubs. The *Los Angeles Philharmonic* plays at the *Dorothy Chandler Pavilion* at the *Music Center* (see *Special Places*). The *Hollywood Bowl* (2301 N. Highland Ave., Hollywood; phone: 213-850-2000) is a 17,630-seat hillside amphitheater that features famous guest entertainers and is the summer home of the *Philharmonic.* Leading popular performers in a wide range of musical styles play year-round at the *Universal Amphitheatre* (Hollywood Fwy. at Lankershim Blvd.; phone: 818-980-9421). The *Greek Theatre* (2700 N. Vermont Ave.; phone: 310-410-1062) is a 6,200-seat indoor theater with concerts by top names. The *Roxy Theatre* (9009 Sunset Blvd.; phone: 310-276-2222) is also good for concerts. For country music, check out the *Palomino Club* (6907 Lankershim Blvd., N. Hollywood; phone: 818-983-1321). Rock and jazz buffs should try the *Palace* (1735 N. Vine, near Hollywood and Vine; phone: 213-462-3000), where the rock theater–dance club downstairs often has live shows, as well as dancing. Upstairs, the *Palace Court* has live jazz on weekends. Other choices include the *Cinegrille,* an Art Deco cabaret with blues, jazz, and Broadway show performances at the *Radisson Hollywood Roosevelt* hotel (see *Checking In*); and *Kingston 12* (814 Bwy., Santa Monica; phone: 310-451-4423) for reggae.

NIGHTCLUBS AND NIGHTLIFE

Anything goes in LA, especially after dark. Swinging nightspots open and close quickly, since the restless search for what's "in" keeps people on the move. *Doug Weston's Troubadour Club* (9081 Santa Monica Blvd., W. Hollywood; phone: 310-276-6168) has introduced a number of top rock music acts. Another place that seems to be able to hold its own with live rock shows nightly is *Whisky A Go-Go* (8901 Sunset Blvd.; phone: 310-652-4202). *Roxbury* (8225 Sunset, W. Hollywood; phone: 213-656-1750) is popular with celebrities and the wannabe crowd. There are three levels for entertainment, a good restaurant, and an exclusive VIP room. Other hot nightspots include *Hollywood Athletic Club* (6525 Sunset Blvd.; phone: 213-962-6600), with pool tables plus the latest rock groups; and *Café Largo* (432 Fairfax, Hollywood; phone: 213-852-1073), a modern cabaret with a mix of rock 'n' roll, folk, country, and oldies. In downtown LA, step out at the hip

Mayan (1038 Hill St.; phone: 213-746-4287). Since it's not often easy to get in the door at these hot spots, *LA NightHawks* (phone: 310-392-1500) has club-hopping tours conducted in stretch limousines that travel to your choice of 250 popular nightspots. Prices vary depending on destinations and include cover charges and a bottle of French champagne.

For blues buffs there's *Mint* (6010 W. Pico Blvd.; phone: 213-937-9630), a neighborhood bar, and the *House of Blues* (across the street from *The Comedy Club* in W. Hollywood at 8439 W. Sunset Blvd.; phone: 310-652-0247), the 1,000-seat music club/restaurant opened last year by Dan Aykroyd and *Aerosmith.* Another club/restaurant to hit the scene is the *Century Club* (see *Eating Out*) headlining top talent.

With Movietown's pool of talent, comedy clubs here are a better bet than elsewhere. Among the options: *Improvisation* (8162 Melrose Ave.; phone: 213-651-2583, and at 321 Santa Monica Blvd., Santa Monica; phone: 310-394-8664), the grandparent of them all; and the *Comedy Store* (8433 Sunset Blvd.; phone: 213-480-3232), another survivor. If you want to get into the act, head over to *All That Glitz* (1911 Sunset Blvd.; phone: 310-278-7712), where musical comedy comes with a twist—cast members "roast" certain folks in the audience. Comedy is king at the *Groundling Theater* (7307 Melrose Ave., W. Hollywood; phone: 213-934-9700), LA's answer to Chicago's *Second City* and the launching pad for "Saturday Night Live" funny man Phil Hartman.

Best in Town

CHECKING IN

It is not uncommon to find a movie, television, or rock star alongside your mere mortal self when checking into a hotel here. But the privilege will cost you dearly. Especially if your tastes include the *Beverly Hills, Four Seasons,* or *Beverly Regent* hotels. But if you're looking for someplace simply to shower and sleep, you'll be happier at one of the smaller hotels or motels sprinkled throughout the area. Generally speaking, accommodations are less expensive in the San Fernando and San Gabriel Valleys than in Hollywood or downtown. Most of Los Angeles's major hotels have complete facilities for the business traveler. Those hotels listed below as having "business services" usually offer such conveniences as meeting rooms, photocopiers, computers, translation services, and express checkout, among others. Call the hotel for additional information. Expect to pay $250 or more (sometimes *much* more) per night for a double room at hotels we've described as very expensive; between $140 and $240 at those places listed as expensive; between $80 and $140 at places in the moderate category; and less than $80 at places listed as inexpensive. (Be sure to ask about special commercial rates and weekend package deals.) For statewide information on bed and breakfast accommodations, contact *Eye Openers Bed & Breakfast* (PO Box 694, Altadena, CA 91001; phone: 213-684-4428 or 818-

797-2055) or *California Houseguests International* (605 Lindley Ave., Suite 6, Tarzana, CA 91356; phone: 818-344-7878). Unless otherwise indicated, all hotels have air conditioning, private baths, TV sets, and telephones. Twenty-four-hour room service is the norm, unless otherwise noted.

All hotels below are in the Los Angeles vicinity and telephone and fax numbers are included.

We begin with our favorite places, followed by recommended hotels, listed by price category.

GRAND HOTELS

Bel-Air In the fashionable Bel-Air district of Los Angeles, this member of the prestigious Relais & Châteaux group has been a favorite celebrity hideaway since its opening in the 1920s, housing such famous faces as Gary Cooper, Howard Hughes, Grace Kelly, and Sophia Loren. The hotel's exquisitely appointed 92 rooms (39 of which are suites) are in one- and two-story mission-style buildings and bungalows scattered amid 11½ immaculately landscaped acres; privacy prevails. Executive chef Gary Clausen caters to the sophisticated tastes of patrons of *The Bel-Air Dining Room* with "back to basics" culinary artistry: Meat is lightly marinated rather than doused in rich sauces, herbs are grown on the premises, and for the health-conscious, there's a spa cuisine menu. There's also a fitness center, housed in what was once the Marilyn Monroe bungalow. Business services are available, and there's also a very gracious and helpful concierge desk. 701 Stone Canyon Rd. (phone: 310-472-1211; 800-648-4097 outside California; fax: 310-476-5890).

Beverly Hills Nicknamed "the Pink Palace" (but now sporting more of a salmon hue), this sprawling Mission Revival hotel has become an unofficial symbol of the city and its hedonistic lifestyle. The graceful building was constructed in 1912, enhanced in the 1940s with the addition of the *Polo Lounge* (past and future hangout of celebs galore), and purchased by the Sultan of Brunei a few years ago; it has recently undergone an extensive, $100-million renovation. The 12 acres of lush tropical gardens (featuring the legendary pool) have been cleverly landscaped to prevent intrusion from traffic noise and prying eyes. The 194 rooms (including the 21 luxurious bungalows where such luminaries as Chaplin, Garbo, Gable, and Lombard stayed) have been enlarged, modernized, and lavishly decorated using a muted color scheme and designer bed linens and towels. In addition to the *Polo Lounge,* there's a formal dining room and a highly acclaimed *Fountain Room Coffee Shop* where some of the most recognizable people in the world eat breakfast. A fully equipped fitness center and two tennis courts have been added as well. 9641 Sunset Blvd. (phone: 310-276-2251; 800-283-8885; fax: 310-281-2935).

The Argyle Housed in the landmark *Sunset Tower,* originally built in 1929, this 16-story Art Deco architectural gem (formerly the *St. James's Club*) is magnificent. Listed on the *National Register of Historic Places,* the hotel is rich in Hollywood lore (John Wayne was one former tenant of the 12th-floor penthouse—where he reportedly kept a cow on the balcony—and other stars such as Marilyn Monroe, Errol Flynn, Jean Harlow, and Clark Gable were frequent guests). Acquired by the prestigious Lancaster hotel group in 1995, it recently reopened following a complete makeover. The 64 guestrooms, which have also been refurbished have been tastefully appointed in Art Deco style, with striking pieces imported from Italy. The small rooftop pool is a popular gathering place for Hollywood celebs such as Whoopi Goldberg and Sharon Stone; there's also a health club, meeting facilities, a concierge, a bar/lounge, and the *Fenix* restaurant (see *Eating Out*). 8358 Sunset Blvd. (phone: 213-654-7100; 800-225-2637; fax: 213-654-9287).

Century Plaza Divided into two separate buildings, one with 750 rooms, the other a 322-room tower (which boasts spectacular views from spacious rooms and private balconies), both share the same facilities. Completely refurbished accommodations are stunning with a select group of "Westin Guest" rooms offering extras and complimentary services. The *Terrace* restaurant features Italian specialties while at the *Living Room* afternoon tea and drinks are served. The 24,000-square-foot ballroom plays host to major Hollywood spectaculars, while the hotel itself is a favorite spot for conventions. There are plenty of shops and a health club. Located in Century City across the street from the *ABC Entertainment Center,* it offers complimentary town car service for trips within a 5-mile radius. Other amenities include a concierge desk and business services. 2025 Ave. of the Stars, Century City (phone: 310-277-2000; 800-228-3000; fax: 310-551-3355).

Four Seasons Located in a residential area referred to as "Beverly Hills adjacent," this stylish hotel is reminiscent of a grand European manor house. The 285 rooms are large and luxuriously appointed, the decor pleasantly subdued, with an emphasis on comfort. On the fourth-floor rooftop terrace is a heated pool/spa area surrounded by palm trees, with a small exercise area nearby. The *Gardens* restaurant, bright, cheery, and casually elegant, is a delight for lunch, dinner, or a lavish Sunday buffet brunch; it's also known for its oversize club sandwiches. All the rooms have computer modems. Other conveniences include a concierge and business services. 300 S. Doheny Dr. (phone: 310-273-2222; 800-332-3442; fax: 310-859-3824).

Park Hyatt Los Angeles at Century City Acquired by the Hyatt Hotel group several years ago, this former *JW Marriott Hotel at Century City* still looks the same, with its peach pyramid design and softly tinted interior decor, but several special amenities have been added, including personal valet on request, limousine service, and a 24-hour mending and pressing service. Each of the

367 rooms and 189 suites comes with a terry cloth robe, fine toiletries, multiple phones, and a balcony. Also available is a restaurant, a health club with indoor and outdoor pools, sun decks, saunas and whirlpools, and business services. The *Park Grill* is open for breakfast, lunch and dinner. Extensive business services are also available. A limo is available to drop you off at the nearby *Shubert Theater* if you don't feel like walking the block and a half. 2151 Ave of the Stars (phone: 310-277-2777; 800-233-1234; fax 310-785-9240).

Peninsula Beverly Hills A world class hotel, this handsome property has 200 rooms, suites, and villas, but its intimate scale, residential location (complete with lavish gardens and winding gravel pathways), antique furnishings, and fine artworks give it the feel of a private palazzo. Suites are equipped with private fax machines, VCRs, and CD players. Another 16 rooms and suites are located in five villas, some of which offer private terraces and fireplaces. The wonderful rooftop deck has its own lush garden—it even boasts a manicured lawn and Moroccan-style cabañas. A health spa features a weight room, a lap pool, a whirlpool, steamroom, sauna, sun deck, and masseuses. Business services are available. A room attendant is on call 24 hours on every floor. *The Living Room,* a lobby lounge, serves traditional afternoon tea, and *The Belvedere* is a topnotch continental restaurant. 9882 Santa Monica Blvd., Beverly Hills (phone: 310-273-4888; 800-462-7899; fax: 310-788-2319).

Regent Beverly Wilshire Just walk out the front door into the middle of the elegant Beverly Hills shopping district. The mood of this Regent group hotel is more businesslike and subdued (i.e., authentically elegant), less Hollywood flash than at spots like the *Peninsula* (above). In the tower wing, all the rooms are done in different color schemes, furniture styles, and themes. The Wilshire Wing (our favorite) has 147 units, as well as three restaurants (the *Dining Room* is the best) and bars. There are 294 rooms in all, and the marble bathrooms are particularly plush. Other services include a concierge desk and business services. 9500 Wilshire Blvd., Beverly Hills (phone: 310-275-5200; 800-545-4000; fax: 310-274-3709).

Sheraton Grande Pampering on a grand scale—this is the only hotel in town with personal butler service on every floor and other services beyond the call of duty. The 469 spacious rooms are tastefully decorated. There's a pool (but no health club), and each guest receives a complimentary membership to the *YMCA,* right across the street via a pedestrian bridge. For in-hotel dining there are the *Back Porch Café, Marie's Bar and Grill,* and *Scarlatti*'s, which serves Italian and French cuisine. Other amenities include a ballroom, concierge services, and business services. 333 S. Figueroa (phone: 213-617-1133; 800-325-3535; fax: 213-613-0291).

Shutters on the Beach This plantation-style beachfront hotel features 198 tastefully decorated rooms done in dark walnut and blue-and-white Laura

Ashley–style prints, and, naturally, shuttered windows. Other amenities include terry robes, Jacuzzis, a health club, and a pool. For delightful dining, there's *1 Pico* (see *Eating Out*). Business services are available. 1 Pico Blvd., Santa Monica (phone: 310-458-0030; 800-336-3000; fax: 310-458-4589).

Westwood Marquis Civility, luxury, and high standards of service permeate this 258-suite hotel, across the street from *UCLA* and just a short walk from the village. The rooms are spacious and well furnished, plus there's a leafy garden, two pools, and a handsome lounge serving tea. The *Garden Terrace Room* is popular for Sunday brunch, and the elegant *Dynasty Room* (see *Eating Out*) serves California-French food. A concierge, complimentary limousine service, and a health spa are among the amenities. 930 Hilgard Ave., Westwood (phone: 310-208-8765; 800-421-2317; fax: 310-824-0355).

Wyndham Checkers This 188-room property in the center of Los Angeles's financial district is geared to the needs of the business traveler. To ease the stress of the work day, there's a guest library, as well as a rooftop spa with a sauna, a steamroom, and exercise equipment. And for mixing business with pleasure, *Checkers* restaurant, open for "power" breakfasts and lunches, as well as dinners, serves sophisticated American fare. Complimentary limousine service is available to downtown business locations, and guests may choose from six complimentary newspapers each day. Full business services are available, and there's also a concierge desk. 535 S. Grand Ave. (phone: 213-624-0000; 800-426-WYNDHAM, fax: 213-626-9906).

EXPENSIVE

Beverly Hilton It's not quite as convenient to downtown Beverly Hills as the *Regent Beverly Wilshire* (see above), but if you plan to spend a lot of time in the hotel, you'll be happy in this self-contained 579-room establishment. *Trader Vic's* offers superb dining. Other amenities include a concierge desk and business services. 9876 Wilshire Blvd., Beverly Hills (phone: 310-274-7777; 800-922-5432; fax: 310-285-1313).

Biltmore The grande dame of downtown hotels offers dramatic interiors that combine the classical architecture typical of European palaces with contemporary luxury (even more plush after an early 1990s renovation). There are 700 well-appointed rooms, an indoor pool, and a Jacuzzi. Other pluses include the fine French restaurant *Bernard's* and the *Grand Avenue* bar, with great jazz nightly. There's also a concierge and business services. 506 S. Grand Ave. (phone: 213-624-1011; 800-245-8673; fax: 213-612-1545).

Bonaventure Its mirrored towers, with five glass-bubble elevators, are an LA skyline landmark. But despite its exterior glitz, most of the 1,368 rooms are quite compact and even drab. Conventioneers and business travelers wander about trying to make sense of the eight levels of shops, fast-food places, and restaurants. Amenities include a concierge and business services. The revolving rooftop *Top of Five* is notable for its panoramic view. 404 S. Figueroa St. (phone: 213-624-1000; fax: 213-612-4800).

Inter-Continental Los Angeles at California Plaza Downtown's newest hotel, this massive 469-room establishment is geared to business travelers. Business services are available, and two restaurants, a pool, and a health club are also on the premises. 251 S. Olive St. (phone: 213-617-3300; 800-327-0200; fax: 213-617-3399).

Lowell Beverly Hills Formerly *L'Ermitage,* this intimate, luxurious hostelry was scheduled to reopen at press time after undergoing an extensive renovation. The 143 suites are decorated in a variety of styles, accented with contemporary artworks. Wood, marble, and stone permeate both the public spaces and guestrooms. A restaurant, library bar with a fireplace, formal rooftop garden, pool, and lounge area round out the amenities. 9291 Burton Way, Beverly Hills (phone: 310-278-3344; fax: 310-278-8247).

Loews Santa Monica Loews' first venture on the West Coast, this 349-room property provides 20th-century comfort in a 19th-century setting, recalling an era when the area flourished as a resort community. A five-story atrium affords spectacular Pacific views; there's also an extensive fitness center with a personal trainer, an indoor/outdoor pool, and a Jacuzzi. The beach is a few steps away. The decor features antique ironwork, cool Pacific colors, and marine themes in paintings and sculptures by local artists. There are two restaurants, the contemporary Italian *Riva* and the more casual *Coast Café,* and a lobby bar that also serves afternoon tea. A concierge and business services are also available. 1700 Ocean Ave., Santa Monica (phone: 310-458-6700; fax: 310-458-6721).

Mondrian This contemporary 245-room establishment on Sunset Strip pays homage to Piet Mondrian with its checkerboard exterior and original paintings by the Dutch artist. In 1995, hip hotelier Ian Shrager (owner of boutique properties such as New York's *Paramount, Royalton,* and the *Morgan,* as well as Miami's *Delano)* began a restoration of this hotel in an attempt to restore it to its original splendor and popularity. Now completed, accommodations feature a full kitchen with in-room refreshments, entertainment center with color TV sets, telephones with conference and speakerphone capabilities, fax machine, Jacuzzis, and mini-bar. Guests also enjoy the *Patio Garden* restaurant, a lobby lounge and bar, 24-hour room service, and business services. 8440 Sunset Blvd, West Hollywood (phone: 213-650-8999; fax: 213-650-5215).

Nikko at Beverly Hills East meets West in this high-tech, Japanese-style hostelry. The 304-room hotel targeted for business travelers resides on busy La Cienega Boulevard's restaurant row. Part of Japan's largest international hotel chain, it offers both high-tech electronics and Japanese tradition. All rooms have fax machines, computer hookups, and sophisticated remote control gadgetry, as well as deep Japanese soaking tubs. Other amenities include *Panagaea* which specializes in Pacific Rim dishes, a health club, an outdoor pool, and 24-hour room service. 465 S. La Cienega Blvd. (phone: 310-247-0400; 800-NIKKO-US; fax: 310-247-0315).

Sofitel The broad, carved staircase, country French furniture, and gaily patterned wall-and-window treatments create a fittingly homey atmosphere in this 311-room, château-style property. For casual dining, there's the bistro, *La Cajole* (which may change its name), a re-creation of an old Parisian artists' hangout, along with *Cristal,* a charming, garden-like French restaurant (see *Eating Out*). Additional amenities include business services and a 24-hour concierge desk. 8555 Beverly Blvd. (phone: 310-278-5444; 800-521-7772; fax: 310-657-2816).

Sunset Marquis If you're looking for a romantic hideaway, this Mediterranean-style paradise is just the ticket. Lush tropical gardens, dotted with *koi* ponds and inhabited by exotic birds, shelter guests from the outside world; the privacy is just what the many celebrities who stay here are looking for. The 118 luxury suites and villas are furnished with canopy beds, fireplaces, saunas, and Jacuzzis; each has its own butler to cater to guests' needs. Amenities include two restaurants, two pools, a swinging bar called *Whiskey,* a full health club with personal trainers available, a concierge, and full business services. 1200 N. Alta Loma Rd., W. Hollywood (phone: 310-657-1333; 800-858-9758; fax: 310-652-5300).

Wyndham Bel Age Recently refurbished, this 188-suite hotel still retains its European ambience. *La Brasserie* is the hotel's casual café; *Diaghilev,* its more formal dining room, serves Franco-Russe cuisine. Also on the premises is a heated rooftop pool and 400-square-foot health club. A concierge and business services are available. 1020 N. San Vicente Blvd., W. Hollywood (phone: 310-854-1111; 800-WYNDHAM, fax: 310-476-5890).

MODERATE

Beverly Prescott This 140-room boutique hotel is perched on a hilltop overlooking Beverly Hills, Century City, Hollywood, and the Pacific Ocean. The entrance is equally spectacular: a beautiful palm-tree–lined, canopied entrance and garden in its indoor/outdoor lobby. Other highlights include a private balcony, health club, an outdoor pool with cabañas, the newspaper delivered to your door, room service, and *Le Café.* There's also a concierge and business services. 1224 S. Beverwil Dr., W. Los Angeles (phone: 310-277-2800; 800-421-3212; fax: 310-203-9537).

New Otani Within walking distance of the *Music Center,* it has 448 rooms featuring Japanese luxury and service in a lovely garden-like setting—a soothing respite from the madness of downtown LA. The suites have an authentic tatami room and futon bedding, as well as deep bathtubs. *A Thousand Cranes* is its serene Japanese restaurant (see *Eating Out*). For more casual dining, the cheery *Azalea Restaurant & Bar* serves breakfast, lunch, and dinner. There's also a shopping arcade and a Japanese health club that offers shiatsu massage and acupuncture therapy. Other amenities include a concierge and business services. 120 S. Los Angeles St. (phone: 213-629-1200; 800-252-0197 within California; 800-421-8795 elsewhere in the US; fax: 213-622-0980).

Radisson Hollywood Roosevelt Once the social center of old Hollywood, this 322-room establishment has LA-Spanish charm and an essence of thc not so distant past. Traccs of Tinseltown still remain—photographs of movie celebrities grace the walls, the Hollywood sign is up the hill, and the star-studded *Walk of Fame* is right outside. A restaurant, as well as a pool, a Jacuzzi, and a weight room are on the premises. Room service is available from 6 AM to 11PM. Other amenities include a concierge desk and business services. 7000 Hollywood Blvd., Hollywood (phone: 213-466-7000; 800-333-3333; fax: 213-462-8056).

Summit Rodeo Drive Acquired by the Summit hotel group in 1995, the former *Beverly Rodeo* has been completely refurbished; happily, it has retained its intimate European air. Amenities in the 86-room property include terry cloth robes, bottled water, and complimentary continental breakfast served daily in the charming *Café Rodeo,* nightly turn-down service, concierge and room service, a sun deck, and valet parking. Guests here may also enjoy the facilities of the *Bel-Air Summit* (accessible by a complimentary shuttle), including a swimming pool, tennis courts, and a fine restaurant. 360 N. Rodeo Dr. (phone: 310-273-0300; fax 310-859-8730).

INEXPENSIVE

Beverly Garland Holiday Inn Close to *Universal Studios,* this 258-room, California mission–style hotel offers pleasant rooms at very appealing rates (their weekend package features breakfast and free accommodations on Sunday night). Amenities include an outdoor pool, a sauna, a putting green, tennis, free parking, room service from 6 AM to 11 PM, and a restaurant. 4222 Vineland Ave., Studio City (phone: 818-980-8000; 800-HOLIDAY; fax: 818-766-5230).

Courtyard Marriott Formerly the *Chesterfield,* this is a charming find; the 133-room hotel provides guests with all the amenities of higher-priced hostelries such as a concierge, a fine restaurant, and afternoon tea. In the rooms, you'll find complimentary mineral water, bathrobes, hair dryers, and even potpourri sachets. 10320 W. Olympic Blvd., W. Los Angeles (phone: 310-556-2777; 800-321-2211; fax: 310-203-0563).

EATING OUT

Now one of the most exciting restaurant towns in the country, Los Angeles has elevated dining to a fine art. Ethnic places abound in all price ranges, and imaginative chefs meld superb raw materials, international accents, and good nutrition into pots of culinary gold. Though popularity with the show-biz crowd is often inversely proportional to the quality of a kitchen and the maître d's treatment of non-celeb guests, good food and good manners are creeping back at the hot spots. Regrettably, dining in din is still in, even when the food is exquisite, but some new restaurants have rediscovered the joy of calm. Los Angeles has banned smoking in all restaurants in the city proper (alfresco dining places, bars, and nightclubs are exempt, however). For dinner for two, expect to pay $150 or more at those places we've listed as very expensive; $75 to $150 at places in the expensive category; $40 to $70 at moderate places; and $40 or less at restaurants described as inexpensive. Prices do not include drinks, wine, or tips. All telephone numbers below include area codes.

Unless otherwise noted, restaurants are open for lunch and dinner.

VERY EXPENSIVE

Arnie Morton's of Chicago, the Steakhouse Direct from the Windy City comes this LA steakhouse franchise where beef is the name of the game. Although you can get a great lamb or veal chop, porterhouse, New York strip, and rib eye steaks are the raison d'être for eating here. Reservations necessary. Major credit cards accepted. 435 S. La Cienega Blvd. (phone: 310-246-1501) and several other locations around LA.

Citrus Owner Michel Richard's French-Provençal–California fare uses delicate seasonings and creative touches to turn ordinary entrées into masterpieces. Among the highlights are grilled swordfish with lentils, pepper tuna steaks, roast veal, and rack of lamb. Don't miss the tasty fish specialties or his famous signature desserts. Closed Saturday lunch and Sundays. Reservations necessary. Major credit cards accepted. 6703 Melrose Ave. (phone: 213-857-0034).

Fenix Sweeping views of Hollywood coupled with the culinary talent of chef Ken Frank (formerly with *La Toque*) make this dining spot one of the best in town. Hollywood's elite dine here on such signature dishes as Daikon sesame salad with lobster, *rosti* potatoes with caviar, double duck salad, lobster ragout, wild mushroom risotto, and filet mignon with red wine, shallots, bone marrow, and *cepes* (a kind of mushroom). Like its parent hotel, the room is decorated in elegant Art Deco style, with black lacquer furniture, white napery, delicate wineglasses, and an eye-catching purple carpet. Open for breakfast daily; lunch and dinner Mondays through Saturdays. Reservations required. Major credit cards accepted. *Argyle Hotel,* 8358 Sunset Blvd., W. Hollywood (phone: 213-848-6677).

Geoffrey's The wings of Eros beat here, and whether you fall in love with the views of the Pacific, the tasty food, or your dinner companion, it's nigh impossible not to find contentment here. Rich, roasted garlic soup topped with parmesan cheese, addictive rosemary muffins, and hearty braised veal ribs are the stars of the menu. The gallant service continues through the end of the meal, when ladies are offered a rose. Reservations advised. Major credit cards accepted. 27400 Pacific Coast Hwy. (phone: 310-457-1519).

L'Orangerie One of LA's truly elegant French restaurants, this posh, flower-filled, special-occasion spot is among the most beautiful dining places in town. The delicacies served here include coddled eggs with caviar, rack of lamb, roasted squab, lobster fricassee, and scrumptious desserts. Still a favorite for special occasions for Hollywood's high and mighty. Closed weekends for lunch and Mondays. Reservations necessary. Major credit cards accepted. 903 N. La Cienega Blvd. (phone: 213-652-9770).

Polo Grill The *Polo Lounge's* newly opened cousin is smaller and much more formal and intimate, with fresh flowers, paintings of polo players on the walls, and a pleasant, sunny patio for outdoor dining. The food is a daring blend of Californian, Asian, and French influences. The spicy pot-au-feu featuring scallops and lobster, the potato-crusted sea bass, and the warm smoked salmon are just a few of the interesting dishes on one of the most ambitious menus in town. Open for dinner daily. Reservations required. Major credit cards accepted. *Beverly Hills Hotel,* 9641 Sunset Blvd., Beverly Hills (phone: 310-276-2251).

EXPENSIVE

Adriano's High atop the Hollywood hills is this picturesque restaurant decorated with a vaulted ceiling and a brass-trimmed sculpture surrounded by flowers. A favorite with celebrities, it offers tasty northern Italian fare, with perfect pasta and a superb Caesar salad. Reservations advised. Major credit cards accepted. 2930 Beverly Glen Blvd. (phone: 310-475-9807).

La Cachette This charming hideaway, set in a residential area, offers the superb bistro fare of chef/owner Jean François Meteigner (formerly of *L'Orangerie,* he is a favorite of local foodies) in a romantic setting. The dining room is reminiscent of a French country inn, with cedar paneling, wood beams, and Impressionist paintings on the walls. Choice menu items include the Provençal tart (puff pastry topped with *tapenade,* basil, and sun-dried tomatoes and spiced with a hint of garlic and basil), braised lamb shanks, duck cassoulet, and chicken and turkey sausages with black olives. For dessert, the baked chocolate mousse or passion fruit lemon tart are hard to beat. Closed Sundays; dinner only Saturdays. Reservations necessary. Major credit cards accepted. 10050 Little Santa Monica Blvd. (phone: 310-470-4992).

Café Four Oaks This cafe has always been one of the most charming hideaways in town. Its kitchen rests in the talented hands of chef Peter Roelant, who puts his emphasis on vegetarian dishes, including terrine of eggplant, tomatoes, and fresh basil; fresh soups; and vegetable salads. But non-vegans are not forgotten: The menu also includes honey-and-pepper–marinated duck breast and Cajun-roasted catfish with sweet garlic, and pepper-crusted tuna. Closed Mondays. Reservations suggested. Major credit cards accepted. 2181 N. Beverly Glen Blvd., Bel-Air (phone: 310-470-2265).

Campanile Named for the tower that crowns this 1928 Charlie Chaplin–built landmark, this stunning place is run by the husband and wife team of Mark Peel and Nancy Silverton, veterans of *Michael's* and *Spago.* Enter through a delightful, skylit café and walk through a long, cloister-like room with tables on one side and the kitchen on the other to get to the balcony-rimmed dining room in the rear. The food is California-Italian, with other Mediterranean influences. The tastes of Tuscany—like antipasto and poached mozzarella—abound; other specialties include all-American grilled prime ribs and sinfully delicious desserts. Open weekdays for all three meals, Saturdays for dinner only; closed Sundays. Reservations necessary (the farther in advance the better). Major credit cards accepted. 524 S. La Brea Ave. (phone: 213-938-1447).

Century Club This gargantuan space (25,000 square feet) is a combination of swanky restaurant and funky nightclub, with three dance floors and patio and indoor dining areas. There is a lively mix of entertainment styles: For example, on Mondays, it's blues; on Fridays, it's Latin salsa music; on Sundays, African-American musicians are highlighted. This has emerged as the new hot place to see big-name entertainment; recent headliners have included Kid Creole & the Coconuts and Dionne Warwick. The menu features well-prepared continental dishes such as pasta *primavera,* grilled Norwegian salmon, and filet mignon. Open Thursdays through Sundays. Reservations necessary. Cover charge. Major credit cards accepted. 10131 Constellation Blvd. (phone: 310-553-6000).

Chianti Elegantly decked out with etched glass and dark wood booths, this is one of the grande dames of Italian cuisine in Los Angeles. The dishes are as tasty as they are beautiful; favorites include shrimp, lobster, and pasta with *porcini* mushrooms. The tradition of turning amaretto cookie wrappers into flying saucers began here. Next door is the less formal *Chianti Cucina,* which is always filled to capacity with a young, attractive crowd. Open daily for dinner only. Reservations necessary. Major credit cards accepted. 7833 Melrose Ave., W. Hollywood (phone: 213-653-8333).

Chinois on Main It took the Austrian-born owner Wolfgang Puck (proprietor of *Spago,* see below) to combine Oriental and French cooking into a delicious melting pot of superb but unlikely orchestrations, such as goose liver with marinated pineapple and ginger-cinnamon sauce, barbecued squab with scallion noodles, and charcoal-grilled Szechuan beef in a cilantro-shallot sauce. Open daily for dinner, Wednesdays through Fridays for lunch. Reservations advised (but be warned—they're tough to get). Major credit cards accepted. 2709 Main St., Santa Monica (phone: 310-392-9025).

Cicada A menu to delight all palates is offered at this charming, auberge-like dining spot. The Norwegian smoked salmon melts in your mouth; other menu highlights are large, grilled Santa Barbara shrimp, *penne* with *porcini* mushrooms, and linguine with artichoke hearts. Plan on a leisurely evening of fine food and some serious "star-gazing." Closed Saturday lunch and Sundays. Reservations necessary. Major credit cards accepted. 8478 Melrose Ave., W. Hollywood (phone: 213-655-5559).

Cristal Scheduled to open at press time, this grand dining room in the *Sofitel* offers elegant decor and French cuisine. Chef François Meulien's menu features well-designed and beautifully prepared classical French dishes; from time to time, the restaurant also plans to have guest chefs such as Joel Robouchon, Paul Bocuse, Gerard Boyer, and Roger Verge prepare special meals. Closed Sundays. Reservations necessary. Major credit cards accepted. *Sofitel Hotel,* 8555 Beverly Blvd. (phone: 310-854-0883).

Le D9me This Art Deco setting in the heart of the Sunset Strip is great for star watching, especially at lunch on Saturdays and after midnight at the magnificent bar. The food is French-continental; there's also an extensive wine list. Closed Saturday lunch and Sundays. Reservations necessary. Major credit cards accepted. 8720 Sunset Blvd. (phone: 310-659-6919).

Drago One of Santa Monica's trendy spots. Chef-owner Celestino Drago demonstrates his culinary talents with such stylish Sicilian dishes as cannellini beans and tuna and *tramezzino di polenta* with wild mushrooms. The cheesecake accompanied by an espresso ends the meal on just the right note. Closed at lunch on weekends. Reservations necessary. Major credit cards accepted. 2628 Wilshire Blvd., Santa Monica (phone: 310-828-1585).

Drai's Chanel-clad women and Armani-draped men drive up to Victor Drai's hot bistro in Rolls-Royces, Mercedes, and BMWs. They come for the fantastic creations of chef Claude Segal: impeccably prepared whitefish wrapped in phyllo, crabmeat-stuffed pasta, grilled Spencer steaks coated with rich cream, and his signature potatoes *boulangère.* For dessert, there's divine *crème brûlée* or an equally celestial chocolate hazelnut cake. Adding to the dining experience are Villeroy & Boch china with Christofle silver amid an elegantly whimsical setting of mismatched furnishings. Open daily for dinner only. Reservations necessary. Major credit cards accepted. 730 N. La Cienega Blvd. (phone: 310-358-8585).

Dynasty Room It's called "California-fusion" cooking, which translates into such tasty tidings as Chilean sea bass with rock shrimp and spicy green or crisp potato pancakes with smoked salmon and caviar, all of which is served in a charming dining room that showcases original artwork and artifacts from China's Tang Dynasty. The creative fare coupled with an eye-opening Sunday brunch are among the reasons it's remained one of the most popular dining spots in town. Open daily for dinner. Reservations advised.

Major credit cards accepted. In the *Westwood Marquis* hotel, 930 Hillgard Ave., Westwood (phone: 310-208-8765).

Georgia A dark, brooding supper club, it features hand-painted upholstered canvas walls, rich mahogany furnishings, and a très chic celebrity clientele (the latter is not too surprising considering the owners: Debbie Allen, Eddie Murphy, Norm Nixon, Denzel Washington, and Connie Stevens). The food's terrific, too: "Southern comfort" dishes such as charred tomato okra stew, grits, catfish, and hush puppies. Open for dinner only; closed Mondays. Reservations necessary. Major credit cards accepted. 7315 Melrose Ave. (phone: 213-933-8410).

Granita Wolfgang Puck's Malibu entry. Designed by his wife, Barbara Lazaroff, the restaurant has an aquarium theme: mosaics, shells, and a *koi* fishpond. Puck's designer pizza still ranks among the best, and the seafood is superb. But the star-struck staff tends to ignore anybody less famous than the local celebrities who flock from their nearby beachfront homes. Closed Monday and Tuesday lunch. Reservations necessary. Major credit cards accepted. 23725 W. Malibu Rd., Malibu (phone: 310-456-0488).

Ivy–LA Desserts A favorite venue for lunchtime power deals, it is an anomaly—an old brick farmhouse on bustling Robertson Boulevard, bordering Beverly Hills. Its rustic decor is the perfect setting for the eclectic (with a Southern accent) American menu; it's also a great place for outdoor dining. Corn chowder with fresh tarragon, salad with mesquite-grilled chicken or shrimp, and twice-cooked Cajun prime ribs—first oven-seared and then grilled—are standouts on the changing menu. Then there are the desserts—the likes of which mama could only dream of making. Reservations necessary (during evening hours, expect at least an hour's wait even with reservations). Major credit cards accepted. 113 N. Robertson Blvd. (phone: 310-274-8303).

Jimmy's Popular with the Beverly Hills set, this elegant dining place is unbeatable for a romantic dinner or a late-night supper. Try the peppered salmon on a bed of spinach or grilled veal chop with chanterelles. Leave room for the delicious chocolate truffle cake with espresso sauce; insulin shock aside, it's a knockout. Closed Saturday lunch and Sundays. Reservations advised. Major credit cards accepted. 201 Moreno Dr., Beverly Hills (phone: 310-552-2394).

Locanda del Lago A spunky Italian trattoria–style eatery set along Santa Monica's Third Street Promenade, it has oversize windows that afford a great view of the crowd strolling by. Favorite menu selections include wild mushroom polenta, grilled eggplant, *osso buco con risotto alla milanese,* and just about any pasta. Closed weekends for lunch. Reservations advised. Major credit cards accepted. 231 Arizona Ave., Santa Monica (phone: 310-451-3525).

Locanda Veneta A tiny trattoria offering some of the most sophisticated Italian food this side of Rome. Try the arugula, mushroom, and parmesan salad; the veal chop is nearly perfect, juicy and charred just so. For dessert, the *tiramisù* is a must. Closed Saturday lunch and Sundays. Major credit cards accepted. Reservations necessary. 8638 W. Third St. (phone: 310-274-1893).

La Madrague The space that formerly housed *Florian* is now the setting for this romantic French restaurant owned by Yon Idiart (who used to run *Citrus, Patina,* and *La Cachette*). The large dining room is decorated in an intimate, provincial style, with bright white walls, reproductions of paintings by Van Gogh and Monet, colorful tablecloths, and warm wood accents. Chef Martin Herold (also of *La Cachette*) produces a prix fixe menu that changes weekly; the meal may begin with anchovy and onion tart, duck breast and green olives, or eggplant and goat cheese terrine; entrées include rack of lamb prepared tableside and linguine Provençale with red pepper, bacon, tomato sauce, and crème fraîche. Chocolate soufflé and *crème brûlée* are featured desserts. Open daily; dinner only Sundays; special jazz nights Wednesdays through Saturdays. Reservations necessary. Major credit cards accepted. 401 N. La Cienega Blvd. (phone: 310-659-4999).

Maple Drive The comfortable, upscale café-like restaurant features down-home meat loaf and the tastiest chili outside of Texas. Other menu options might include the roast turkey, bouillabaisse, and Caesar salad (made without eggs). And while you're spotting celebrities (such as co-owner Dudley Moore), enjoy the live entertainment nightly. Closed Saturday lunch and Sundays. Reservations necessary. Major credit cards accepted. 345 N. Maple Dr. (phone: 310-274-9800).

Michael's Now that prices have dropped closer to the level of LA's other high-priced restaurants, this pioneer eatery—where California nouvelle was first new—just may be accessible to a few more diners. The gorgeous garden and contemporary art add visual pleasure to the gustatory feats. Try the wild mushroom salad and the grilled Norwegian salmon filet with beurre blanc sauce and steamed vegetables. Closed Mondays, Saturday lunch, and Sunday dinner. Reservations advised. Major credit cards accepted. 1147 Third St., Santa Monica (phone: 310-451-0843).

Modada Sam Marvin, the chef at this trendy Melrose Avenue hangout, is the city's newest superstar. His creations combine culinary flair with originality and wit—for example, "P" soup, which uses every variety of pea under the sun (snow peas, sugar peas, English peas, sweet pea consommé, black-eyed peas, and pea dumplings), and "French Three-Star" (seared scallops and bone marrow served with a leek tart). With its dim, romantic lighting, elegant chandeliers, and warm atmosphere, this is a restaurant worth seeking out. Closed Sundays and Mondays; dinner only Tuesdays and Saturdays. Reservations required. Major credit cards accepted. 8115 Melrose Ave. (phone: 213-653-4612).

Morton's The dining spot of choice for Tinseltown moguls, mavens, and anyone else seeking to dine on good food while basking in the social spotlight.

Although the menu has its local critics, it still offers the standards that made it famous—pasta, pizza, salads, and grilled dishes. Closed Sundays. Reservations necessary. Major credit cards accepted. 8764 Melrose Ave. (phone: 310-276-5205).

1 Pico This cozy, intimate eatery is a perfect showcase for the creative menu featuring mushroom ravioli, fresh fish, and divine desserts such as warm chocolate pudding doused in caramel sauce. Reservations advised for dinner. Major credit cards accepted. Located at *Shutters on the Beach Hotel,* 1 Pico Blvd., Santa Monica (phone: 310-587-1708).

Orso Although the outside decor is extremely unassuming, this popular northern Italian trattoria more than compensates with its interior ambience and its charming patio framed by ficus trees and candlelit tables. Earthy country salads, pizza with all-but-transparent crusts, grilled meat, and delicious calf's liver are served on attractive Italian pottery plates. There is an extensive wine list as well. Well-known actors frequent this spot, and the bar becomes lively after theater hours. Reservations advised. MasterCard and Visa accepted. 8706 W. Third St. (phone: 310-274-7144).

Pacific Dining Car Steaks—cut on the premises from aged, corn-fed beef—are the house specialty, although the menu also offers four types of fresh fish every day. The restaurant is set in a real dining car (plus an additional building) that's been at the same downtown location since 1921. This is a good place for early dinner or late supper when you have tickets for a show at the *Music Center.* Open daily, around the clock. Reservations necessary. Major credit cards accepted. 1310 W. Sixth St. (phone: 213-483-6000).

Patina Superchef Joachim Splichal has really pulled out all the stops with a whimsical menu that includes a corn *blini* "sandwich" filled with marinated salmon; a soufflé (how French) of grits (how American) with Herkimer cheddar and an apple-smoked bacon sauce; or New York duck liver with blueberry pancakes and blueberry sauce. Closed weekends for lunch. Reservations necessary. Major credit cards accepted. 5955 Melrose Ave., W. Hollywood (phone: 213-467-1108).

Pinot *Patina*'s sister bistro, housed in a charming yellow brick building, offers creative fare—also inspired by Splichal—that continues to wow the trendsetters and mega-stars (Warren Beatty for one) who flock here. Closed Sundays. Reservations necessary. Major credit cards accepted. 12969 Ventura Blvd., Studio City (phone: 818-990-0500).

Polo Lounge The bar is jammed during the cocktail hour, and the staff still tends to favor celebrity customers over ordinary folk, but these are only minor drawbacks. The much-ballyhooed restaurant offers the electrifying experience of dining with the rich and famous. The food can be topnotch (try the Dutch apple pancake at breakfast and the Polo club sandwich and interesting salads at lunchtime) and there are several areas in which to eat, including a green and pink dining room with lots of plants and an outdoor patio with a Brazilian pepper tree. Open daily for all three meals. Reservations necessary. Major credit cards accepted. *Beverly Hills Hotel,* 9641 Sunset Blvd. (phone: 310-276-2251).

Remi Evocative of a tony seaside Italian restaurant (even though it's three blocks from the sea), and named for Venetian gondoliers' oars, this eatery serves ambrosial Venetian fare in a casually elegant atmosphere. The rich wood, gleaming brass, and nautical theme provide an airy backdrop for enjoying such dishes as whole fish infused with herbs and the wonderful selection of grappas. The outdoor tables are ideal for people watching on Santa Monica's *Third Street Promenade.* Reservations necessary. Major credit cards accepted. 1451 Third St. Promenade (phone: 310-393-6545).

Spago When you're hot, you're hot. Famed chef Wolfgang Puck (see *Chinois on Main* and *Granita*) turned pizza making into an art form. His are baked in wood-burning brick ovens and topped with shrimp, duck, sausage, and goat cheese. Celebrity diners also munch on Sonoma lamb, Washington oysters, North Pacific salmon, and grilled free-range chicken. Be sure to leave room for one of the incredible desserts. Open daily for dinner only. Since this still is one of the most popular spots in town, make reservations weeks in advance. Major credit cards accepted. 176 N. Canon Dr., Beverly Hills (phone: 310-652-4025).

Water Grill The only oyster bar in the downtown area is located in this handsome spot. Eight varieties of the mollusk are served along with a wide selection of fresh regional seafood: Atlantic soft-shell crabs with cranberries, northern pike with succotash, and California *cioppino* are just a hint of what you can experience. Closed weekends for lunch. Reservations advised. Major credit cards accepted. 523 W. Sixth St. (phone: 213-891-0900).

MODERATE

Benvenuto A tiny trattoria offering friendly service and exquisitely prepared Italian food. This cozy café is a popular hangout for celebs, artists, entertainers, and other assorted Hollywood types. Although chef Mustapha Sadd's menu is the main attraction—designer pizza, fresh fish, pasta, baked rabbit, *tiramisù*—lingering over an espresso in the candlelit dining room or on the patio overlooking Santa Monica Boulevard while watching the celebrity parade pass by, makes this place hard to leave. Closed weekends for lunch. No reservations. Major credit cards accepted. 8512 Santa Monica Blvd., W. Hollywood (phone: 310-659-8635).

Café La Bohème This whimsical West Hollywood eatery attracts a lively crowd that comes mostly for the ambience: The high-ceilinged Nouveau Baroque dining room is draped in faded velvet and adorned with gilded mirrors. The menu has something for everybody—pizza, pasta, salads topped with garlic-seared beef, and filet mignon with shiitake mushrooms. Reservations advised. Major credit cards accepted. 8400 Santa Monica Blvd., W. Hollywood (phone: 213-848-2360).

Café Pierre If you find yourself in the Manhattan Beach area, make it a point to drop in at this neighborhood bistro. Tasty garlic potatoes, pumpkin ravioli and sweetbreads sautéed with cognac and mushrooms are well-worth the trip. Open daily for dinner; lunch Mondays through Fridays. Major credit cards accepted. Reservations advised. 317 Manhattan Beach Blvd., Manhattan Beach (phone: 310-545-5252).

Celestino The young Italian chef draws on his Sicilian roots and Tuscan training for a limited menu with innovative twists, such as the highly praised seafood baked in a paper bag. The restaurant is airy and unpretentious. The art exhibit changes periodically, as does the menu. Closed weekends for lunch. Late-night suppers are served Fridays and Saturdays until 1 AM, with jazz until 2 AM. Reservations advised. Major credit cards accepted. 236 S. Beverly Dr. (phone: 310-859-8601).

Chaya Venice The family responsible for the *Chaya* (Japanese for tea house) chain has been operating tea houses in Japan for three centuries now. Their latest venture blends Japanese and American fare with such dishes as Hawaiian-tuna spring rolls accompanied by a spicy salsa, charred rare tuna *niçoise,* and broiled sea eel with julienned vegetables. The decor is high-tech—an eclectic mix of chrome, copper, stone, and wood, reflecting the diversity of the menu. Open daily for dinner; closed Saturday lunch. Reservations necessary. Major credit cards accepted. 110 Navy St., Venice (phone: 310-396-1179).

Chez Mélange This South Bay eatery is true to its name, offering an international variety of victuals. There is a wine bar for sampling domestic and imported varieties. As an added treat, guest chefs are featured monthly. Open daily for all three meals. Reservations advised. Major credit cards accepted. 1716 Pacific Coast Hwy., Redondo Beach (phone: 310-540-1222).

Il Cielo Set in a brick cottage, with several romantic dining rooms (a fireplace glows in the winter) and a heated patio, this place serves excellent northern Italian food. During quiet hours the staff treats guests as if they were at a family reunion. On a balmy evening, eating in the garden feels like dining in Tuscany. Closed Sundays. Reservations advised. Major credit cards accepted. 9018 Burton Way, Beverly Hills (phone: 310-276-9990).

Cobalt Cantina This former *Babylon* has been transformed into this bustling Mexican cantina with a large dining room decorated with changing exhibits by local artists (the art is for sale). Friendly and inviting, it's a great place to relax and enjoy such creative Mexican dishes as sweet potato tamales and molten Minerva (melted Oaxacan cheese in sizzling tomatillo sauce served with tri-colored corn chips and tortillas). The Cobalt Blue margaritas are tasty, too. The restaurant also offers a terrific Sunday brunch (try the blue corn chocolate waffles). Open daily, Sunday brunch. Reservations advised. Major credit cards accepted. 616 N. Robertson (phone: 310-659-8691).

Epicentre Although some Angelenos fail to see the humor in the faux post-earthquake damage decor presented here, the place attracts a steady clientele. Gimmicky food names—"seismic entrées"—include quesadillas, crab cakes in corn chili sauce, curries, and homemade ice cream. Closed Saturday lunch, Sundays, and Monday dinner. Reservations advised. Major credit cards accepted. *Kawada Hotel,* 200 S. Hill St. (phone: 213-625-0000).

fusion at pdc In addition to offering culinary masterpieces, this restaurant strives to be a work of art in itself. The dining room has a striking design featuring pale beechwood tables on flared silver pedestals, a blond maple bar with stools upholstered in sapphire velvet, and cobalt blue and emerald water glasses. Fortunately, the cuisine, which is described as "Euro-Asian," lives up to the surroundings. Created by super chef Bruce Marder (formerly of the *Broadway, Deli, Rebecca's* and the *West Beach Café*), menu offerings include lobster spring rolls with crunchy green beans, scallop tostadas, chicken breast with shiitake mushroom caps, and great sandwiches made with honey-roasted pork or *pancetta,* arugula, and coleslaw. Open for dinner Mondays through Saturdays: lunch Mondays through Fridays; Sunday brunch. Reservations suggested. Major credit cards accepted. Located at the *Pacific Design Center,* 8687 Melrose Ave. (phone: 310-659-6012).

Gilliland's The owner is Irish but the fare is Californian—with Irish accents (such as soda bread on Sundays). Closed Saturday lunch. Reservations necessary on weekends. Major credit cards accepted. 2425 Main St. (phone: 310-392-3901).

Jones Hollywood Café This hip, club-like restaurant attracts a crowd of young trendies in designer jeans who go for the good food and fun ambience. The menu offers a blend of California and continental fare, including calamari, grilled *ahi* tuna, lamb chops laced with ginger, grilled portobello mushrooms with polenta, and a large selection of salads. The setting is casual, with tables draped in red-and-white–checkered oil cloths, a large banquette adorned with a bandana-like print, a bustling bar serving pricey drinks, and rows of Jack Daniels bottles standing behind chicken wire on a shelf. An eclectic mix of taped music plays in the background. Open weekdays lunch and dinner, Saturdays and Sundays dinner. Reservations required for dinner. Major credit cards accepted. 7205 Santa Monica Blvd. (phone: 213-850-1726).

Joss The austere decor makes this a high-style showcase for unfamiliar regional Chinese delicacies, such as glazed ginger venison with *quei hua* wine. The waiter shows off the whole, perfectly crisped, golden brown Hong Kong Pin-Pei chicken before carving and preparing it in the style of Peking duck on a side table. Closed weekends for lunch. Reservations advised. Major credit cards accepted. 9255 Sunset Blvd. (phone: 310-276-1886).

Mandarin Northern Chinese cooking is presented in elegant surroundings instead of the usual plastic, pseudo-Oriental decor. Not on the menu, but well worth requesting as an appetizer, is the minced squab wrapped in lettuce leaves; also be sure to try the spicy prawns. Closed weekends for lunch. Reservations advised. Major credit cards accepted. 430 N. Camden Dr., Beverly Hills (phone: 213-272-0267).

Matsuhisa The Japanese fare with Peruvian accents (honest!) is described by its chef as "New Wave seafood." The most popular dishes are squid cut like pasta, with an asparagus topping, and seafood with soy, *wasabi,* and garlic. Closed weekends for lunch. Reservations necessary two to three days in advance. Major credit cards accepted. 129 N. La Cienega Blvd. (phone: 310-659-9639).

Mon Kee's Amazing seafood combinations are the draw at this bustling Chinese dining spot, which caters to downtown LA's business crowd as well as to tourists. "Live" lobster, 15 squid dishes (try the crispy squid with special salt), and steamed or fried saltwater and freshwater fish are the mainstays of the seafood menu. For those not compelled by the above or the conch, clams, or oysters, there are dozens of traditional pork, poultry, beef, and vegetable dishes with which to be dazzled. Reservations advised. Major credit cards accepted. 679 N. Spring St. (phone: 213-628-6717).

Musso & Frank Grill It really is a grill, operating in Hollywood since 1919, and apparently not redecorated once (not that its regulars—film people, journalists, the moiling LA middle class—want it to change one iota). The kind of place whose cachet is having none at all, it's fine if you like nostalgia and surly waiters. Traditional American food is served—try the short ribs, chicken pot pie, or macaroni and cheese. Closed Sundays. Reservations advised. Major credit cards accepted. 6667 Hollywood Blvd. (phone: 213-467-7788).

Pane Caldo Bistro An unpretentious Italian *ristorante* with a great view of the city's famed hills. What it lacks in fancy appointments, it more than makes up for with careful food preparation, generous portions, and reasonable prices. A complimentary appetizer and basket of *focaccia* arrive with the menu to ease the difficult task of choosing from among Tuscan specialties such as warm bell-pepper salad, risotto specials, tagliatelle with *porcini* mushrooms, spinach tortelloni with butter and sage, osso buco, and a selection of 14 kinds of individual pizza. Try the ultra-rich *tiramisù* for dessert. Closed Sunday lunch. Reservations advised. Major credit cards accepted. 8840 Beverly Blvd. (phone: 310-274-0916).

Pinot Hollywood Immensely successful LA chef Joachim Splichal, the guiding force behind *Patina, Pinot Bistro,* and *Café Pinot,* has brought his magic touch to this new restaurant (formerly the *Columbia Bar & Grill*). A charming bistro decorated in rich woods, wine-colored velvet drapes, and deep pile carpeting, it offers a lengthy menu of hearty French fare, including butter brioche with chanterelle mushrooms, roasted onion, and parsley sauce; goat cheese terrine; oakwood-grilled New Zealand snapper; and braised veal shanks. Top the meal off with a French pastry, rich chocolate cake, or a trio of fresh fruit sorbets. There's also the comfortable *Martini Bar Lounge,* where you can sip one of more than a dozen varieties of cocktails before a wood-burning fireplace. You're more apt to spy celebrities at lunch, when they are working at or visiting the studios. Valet parking is available. Closed Sundays and weekend lunch. Reservations highly recommended. Major credit cards accepted. 1448 N. Gower St. (phone: 213-461-8800).

Planet Hollywood This branch of the worldwide chain is over-amplified with music and videos, and super-saturated in Hollywood memorabilia hanging from the ceiling and walls—there's even a naked Sly Stallone peering down from a glass cage cemented on the ceiling (his privates covered), the original Val Kilmer *Batman* outfit, the *Ninja Turtles* mingling with the *Alien, Gremlins,* Judy Garland's original *Oz* dress, Jack Nicholsen's ax, and even the train from the *Fugitive.* Check out the theme restrooms. The food is secondary to the atmosphere, but not bad. The menu covers everything from fries, burgers, and shakes, to great salads and pretty good pasta. Don't miss the gift shop. Expect to wait in line unless you're "somebody" Sly and his pals know. Open daily from 11 AM. No reservations. Major credit cards accepted. 9560 Wilshire Blvd. (phone: 310-275-7828).

Provencia This cheerful bistro with its colorful façade and homey interior provides a cozy atmosphere for sampling chef Domenico Manderino's ever-so-delicately spiced, creative Italian fare. Start with the smoked salmon in a French pastry tart, then move on to the black risotto with calamari. Leave enough room for a tasty *tiramisù* or white chocolate mousse. Closed Sundays; dinner only Saturdays. Reservations advised. Major credit cards accepted. 945 Fairfax Ave., West Hollywood (phone: 213-654-4594).

Rockenwagner It's loud, even raucous, but the food's great at this Frank Gehry–designed, high-tech eatery. Set behind a glass façade, it features booths lighted by modern streetlamps and a huge German countryside mural. The creative menu features tasty appetizers such as garlic flan, goat cheese, and beet terrine with grilled radicchio; among the entrées is cilantro fettuccine with chicken, mild chilies, onion, and roasted jalapeño tomato sauce. Dessert highlights include caramelized pear napoleon, crisp warm apple pizza, and scrumptious signature cookies. Open weekdays for all three meals; brunch and dinner on weekends. Reservations advised. Major credit cards accepted. 2435 Main St., Santa Monica (phone: 310-339-6504).

Siamese Princess This Oriental eatery, which predates the Thai proliferation, looks like an antiques shop. European furniture and collectibles vie for space with Siamese gift items and photos of British, Thai, and show-biz royalty. The food, billed as "Royal Thai" and beautifully presented, ranks high above run-of-the-mill. For example, slivers of orange peel turn rice noodles into a delicacy. Closed Saturday through Wednesday lunch. Reservations necessary. Major credit cards accepted. 8048 W. Third St. (phone: 213-653-2643).

A Thousand Cranes Besides having such a beautiful name, this Japanese spot is well versed in the traditional art of serving beautiful food. It has several tatami rooms and a Western dining room. Go for Sunday brunch, a spectacular Japanese buffet accompanied by live music. Reservations advised. Major credit cards accepted. In the *New Otani Hotel,* 120 S. Los Angeles St. (phone: 213-629-1200).

INEXPENSIVE

California Pizza Kitchen *Spago* for the masses, it's Beverly Hills's favorite pizza place. Upscale fast food is served in a sleek black-, white-, and yellow-tiled environment—this is not your average neighborhood pizzeria. Nouvelle cuisine pizza specialties, served straight from a wood-fired oven, include such pizza delights as Original BBQ Chicken, Thai Chicken, Tandoori Chicken, Peking Duck, BLT, and Tuna-Melt. The menu also offers fresh pasta with interesting sauces, and yummy desserts. Open mid-morning to late evening daily. Unlike *Spago,* there's no need for a reservation here—but there'll probably be a line. Major credit cards accepted. 207 S. Beverly Dr., Beverly Hills (phone: 213-272-7878) and several other locations around LA.

Chin Chin Delicious dim sum and traditional Chinese food, cooked without MSG, account for its ongoing popularity as do its quick service and low prices. Takeout also is available. Reservations unnecessary. Major credit cards accepted. Five locations: 8618 Sunset Blvd., Sunset Plaza (phone: 213-652-1818); 11740 San Vicente Blvd., Brentwood (phone: 213-826-2525); 12215 Ventura Blvd., Studio City (phone: 213-985-9090); 16101 Ventura Blvd., Encino (phone: 818-783-1717); and 13455 Maxella Ave., Marina del Rey (phone: 213-823-9999).

Ed Debevic's A treat for the whole family, this retro diner dishes out fun and games along with hearty meals—1950s style. Try the meat loaf, homemade pot roast, chicken-fried steaks, burgers, or hot dogs. A DJ plays favorite rock 'n' roll tunes in the background. Reservations unnecessary. Major credit cards accepted. 134 N. La Cienega Blvd. (phone: 310-659-1952).

DIVE! Yes, LA has another theme restaurant—this one, the brainchild of film director Steven Spielberg, is designed like a submarine and decorated with many appropriate sub parts and gadgets, with underwater sights and sounds appearing on a 210-square-foot video wall. The menu offers more than 20 types of hot, cold, and "nuclear spicy" submarine sandwiches, including ones filled with soft-shell crab, Tuscan steak, and three vegetarian choices. Also on the menu are wood-oven-roasted shrimp and chicken, ribs, main course salads, home fries, and unusual desserts. Inventive drinks are served at the bar, and a retail window sells *DIVE!* T-shirts and the like. Though it looks more like a Hollywood set than a restaurant, the food rates star billing. Open daily (after-theater meals, takeout, and delivery are available). No reservations. Major credit cards accepted. *Century City Shopping Center,* 10250 Santa Monica Blvd. (phone: 310-203-0928).

Emporio Armani Express Café After busting your budget downstairs on Italian designer clothing, head for the balcony and the comfort of a glass of wine and a plate of ravioli *di zucca* (homemade pasta filled with pumpkin and mascarpone cheese) or risotto with artichoke hearts and duck prosciutto. There's also lighter fare, such as a salad of crisp greens tossed in lemon dressing over a bed of sliced oranges and fennel. Open daily for all three meals. Reservations unnecessary. Major credit cards accepted. 9533 Brighton Way (phone: 310-271-9440).

Gladstone's Malibu One of the best beachfront restaurants for casual dining, this funky fish house offers alfresco, picnic-style dining on wooden tables stationed on a floor rife with peanut shells and sawdust (or you can eat indoors, but you'll miss the fresh sea air). The menu offers a variety of seasonal seafood in soups, salads, and an assortment of appetizers and entrées. Bring a hearty appetite because portions are generous. Open daily for all three meals. Reservations unnecessary. Major credit cards accepted. 17300 Pacific Coast Hwy., Pacific Palisades (phone: 310-454-3474).

Hugo's This charming, country-style café with attentive waiters and great coffee is the home of the "power breakfast" for studio heads and major stars (Julia Roberts, Bette Midler, and Geena Davis are regulars). Million-dollar deals are made over pumpkin pancakes, pasta *alla Mamma* (the house specialty: linguine, eggs, garlic, and Hugo's secret seasoning), and smoked salmon omelettes with tomatoes and sour cream. Get here early; window tables go fast. Lunch and dinner have a calmer atmosphere, but the food is equally first-rate: pasta carbonara, fresh fish, veal parmesan, and so forth. No reservations. Major credit cards accepted. 8401 Santa Monica Blvd., W. Hollywood (phone: 213-654-3993).

Nosh of Beverly Hills Stop in for a quick, delicious bite of "authentic delicatessen" at this New York–style eatery, where the sizable portions would make any Jewish mother proud. It's all here—bagels and lox, chicken soup, and incredible cheesecake. No reservations. Major credit cards accepted. 9689 Little Santa Monica Blvd., Beverly Hills (phone: 310-271-3730).

Old Town Bakery A real charmer. Chef-owner Amy Pressman's bakery-cum-restaurant caters to hefty appetites, offering giant country crêpes (filled with chicken, herb pesto, ratatouille, or ricotta), great rotisserie chicken tacos, crisp bow tie pasta, and home-style pan pizza. Leave room for delectable desserts—bittersweet chocolate terrine, orange poppyseed cake, and Amy's hand-spun ice cream. No reservations. No credit cards accepted. 166 W. Colorado Blvd., Pasadena (phone: 818-792-7943).

Pyramids If you're watching fat and calories, this one's for you. Imagine a tasty Caesar salad with only three grams of fat made with egg whites in lieu of yolks, a wild mushroom risotto with just 5.4 grams of fat, and a guilt-free chocolate cake with a paltry 6.5 grams of fat, thanks to restaurateur Bruce Saiber's (an original partner of *Louise's Trattoria)* low-fat interpretations of his signature, higher fat cuisine. The triangular shaped, taupe- and emerald-colored restaurant is as attractive as the food. Open daily; closed weekend lunch. Reservations not required. Major credit cards accepted. 8222½ W. Third St. (phone: 213-653-2121).

Thunder Roadhouse The theme at this trendy bar/restaurant is motorcycles, with a decor that features antique bikes, iron sculptures, motorcycle memorabilia, and mementos of the Old West. The 30-foot brass and copper bar is thick with beer-drinkers after dark, while the restaurant dishes out just what you would expect: burgers, shakes, sandwiches, omelettes, Cajun catfish, grilled pork chops, and hot pecan or sweet potato pie for dessert. Open daily for all three meals. Reservations unnecessary. Major credit cards accepted. 8363 Sunset Blvd. (phone: 213-650-6011).

Whitney's A special little place where chef/owner Whitney Werner and wife, Cheryl Kunitake Werner, work their culinary wonders. Seafood lovers should sample the seared sea bass with tomatillo and black bean salsa or the peppered tuna with crispy wontons and *ponsu* sauce. If pasta is your passion, try the linguine with Norwegian smoked salmon or *arrabbiata penne* (fresh parsley and tomato sauce over quill-shape pasta) with Japanese eggplant smothered with warm goat cheese. Reservations unnecessary. Major credit cards accepted. 1518 Montana Ave., Santa Monica (phone: 310-458-4114).

THE FINAL TOUCH

For dessert, try the luscious ice cream made by *Robin Rose* and sold in the *Robin Rose* shops in Venice (215 Rose Ave.; phone: 310-399-1774) and downtown in the Wells Fargo Center (333 S. Grand Ave.; phone: 310-687-8815). *Mani's Bakery* (8801 Santa Monica Blvd.; phone: 310-659-5955: 3960 Laurel Cyn Blvd., Studio City; phone: 818-762-7200: 2507 Main St., Santa Monica; phone: 310-396-7700: and 519 S. Fairfax Ave.; phone: 213-938-8800) serves delicious guilt-free desserts—fat-free, calorie-reduced baked goods you can't believe can taste this good and still be good for you—from breads to fruit tarts and chocolate cakes, with coffees, lattes, and espressos to wash them down.

Louisville

There are two seasons in Louisville: *Derby Week* (the week preceding the first Saturday in May) and the rest of the year. But there is a good deal to that "other" season, and Kentucky's largest city is too often dismissed as a one-horse-race town.

Pronounced *Loo*-ee-ville by visitors, and *Loo*-a-vul by residents, it combines aspects of big city and small town, of urbanity and provincialism, of tradition and progressivism—resulting from the city's traditional role as fence sitter between North and South.

This dual nature seemed fated by both geography and history. The city was settled in 1778 as an informal military base; from here, George Rogers Clark drove the British and the Indians from the Midwest. The appearance of steamboats on the Ohio in the early 19th century turned a lazy river town into a booming port. And although its setting along the Ohio River placed it south of the Mason-Dixon Line, Louisville's rapid 19th-century growth as a port and manufacturing center aligned it more with the industrial North than with the agrarian South.

Louisville is located on the Ohio River, the boundary between Kentucky and Indiana. Today, more tonnage passes through Louisville than through the Panama Canal, and the city produces more than half the world's bourbon, as well as substantial amounts of such varied products as cigarettes, chemicals, and appliances. Health care and other service industries also have gained increasing economic importance.

Continual building and restoration in the city's downtown area have resulted in a delightfully eclectic mix of old and new. The impressive riverfront *Kentucky Center for the Arts* and the 27-story pink granite *Humana Building* (the result of an international architectural competition) are just two of the structures adding real dimension to the skyline. They share Main Street with beautifully restored 19th-century cast-iron façades and a 120-foot baseball bat, the latter marking *Hillerich & Bradsby's* 1996 return after 22 years of making the famous Louisville Slugger across the river in Jeffersonville, Indiana.

For a city its size, Louisville's cultural cup runneth over. It has its own symphony orchestra, ballet company, opera troupe, and the *Actors Theatre of Louisville,* whose festival of new American plays draws national attention each year. The *J. B. Speed Art Museum,* on the *University of Louisville* campus, may not have a high-profile national reputation (yet), but connoisseurs of fine art should not miss its collection of paintings and sculpture. Don't overlook—as if you could—the *Louisville Falls Fountain,* a water and light show in the middle of the Ohio River. Queen of the city's waterfront is the *Belle of Louisville,* the oldest sternwheeler still operating. And like the rest of Kentucky, Louisville is crazy about basketball; cheering on

OHIO RIVER
G. Rogers Clark Bridge
Port of Louisville Terminal
RIVER RD
Belle of Louisville
To Locust Grove appx. 4½ miles
To Zachary Taylor National Cemetery 5½ miles
64
65
71
ELM ST
ROWAN ST
FRANKLIN ST
WASHINGTON ST
MAIN ST
PIKE ST
MARKET ST
CONGRESS ALLEY
COURT PL
JEFFERSON ST
LIBERTY ST
CEDAR ST
MUHAMMAD ALI BLVD
MADISON ST
CHESTNUT ST
SQUIRE AV
GRAY ST
GUTHRIE ST
ARMORY PL
BALLARD ST
MARSHALL ST
1 ST
2 ST
3 ST
4 AV
5 ST
6 ST
7 ST
8 ST
9 ST
10 ST
11 ST
12 ST
13 ST
BROOK ST
FLOYD ST
PRESTON ST
JACKSON ST
HANCOCK ST
CLAY ST
SHELBY ST
CAMPBELL ST
WENZEL ST
Belvedere
Riverfront Plaza
Kentucky Center For The Arts
Museum of Natural History
Ft. Nelson Monument
Louisville Trust Bank
First Nat. Tower Blg.
Convention Center
Court House
City Hall
Liberty Bank
Citizens Plaza
Union Bus Terminal
Federal Reserve
State Office Blg
Founders Square
Louisville Chamber of Commerce
Bus Terminal
Federal Square
Federal Blg & Post Office
Madison Park
MEDICAL COMPLEX

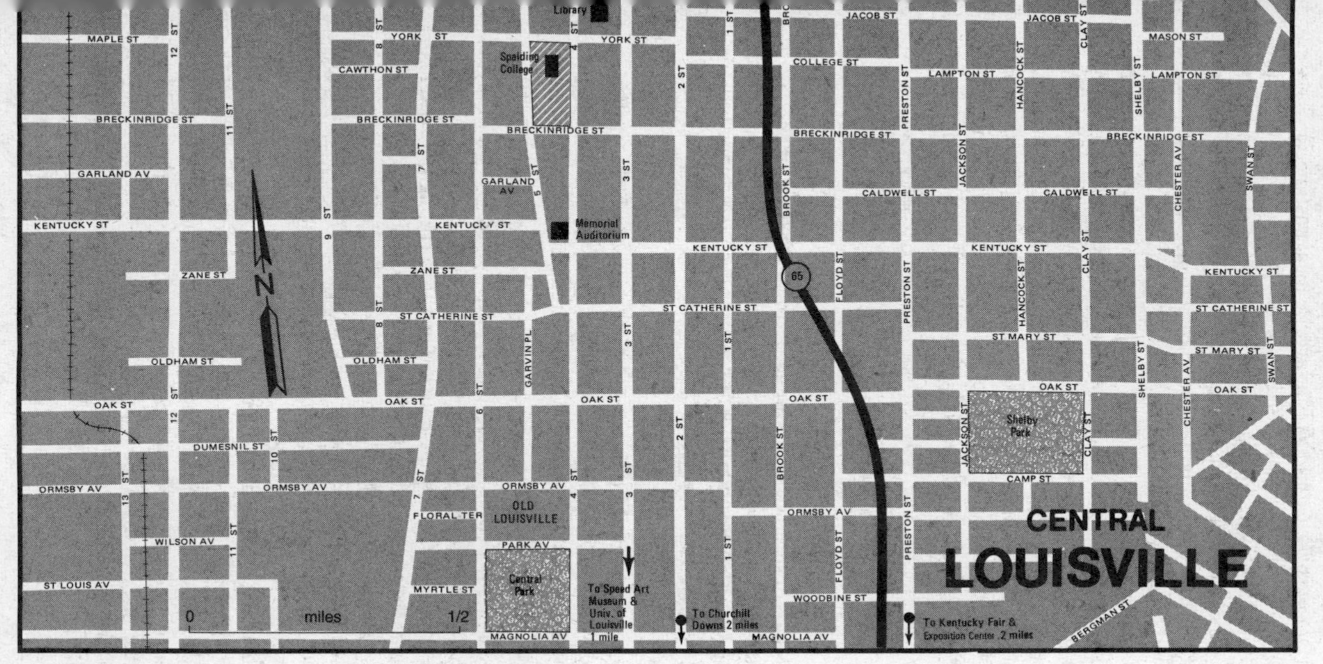
CENTRAL
LOUISVILLE
Library
Spalding College
Memorial Auditorium
OLD LOUISVILLE
Central Park
Shelby Park
To Speed Art Museum & Univ. of Louisville 1 mile
To Churchill Downs 2 miles
To Kentucky Fair & Exposition Center 2 miles
65
N
0
miles
1/2
MAPLE ST
YORK ST
CAWTHON ST
BRECKINRIDGE ST
GARLAND AV
KENTUCKY ST
ZANE ST
ST CATHERINE ST
OLDHAM ST
OAK ST
DUMESNIL ST
ORMSBY AV
FLORAL TER
WILSON AV
PARK AV
ST LOUIS AV
MYRTLE ST
MAGNOLIA AV
WOODBINE ST
GARVIN PL
JACOB ST
COLLEGE ST
LAMPTON ST
CALDWELL ST
ST MARY ST
CAMP ST
MASON ST
BERGMAN ST
13 ST
12 ST
11 ST
10 ST
9 ST
8 ST
7 ST
6 ST
5 ST
4 ST
3 ST
2 ST
1 ST
BROOK ST
FLOYD ST
PRESTON ST
JACKSON ST
HANCOCK ST
CLAY ST
SHELBY ST
CHESTER AV
SWAN ST

like the rest of Kentucky, Louisville is crazy about basketball; cheering on the *University of Louisville Cardinals* is a favorite local pastime.

Being a small/big city does have its drawbacks, however, and there are times when Louisville seems a little too quiet. The entertainment and restaurant scenes have made great strides in recent years—although it's still hard to find a good meal after midnight—and in the city named for Louis XVI of France, good French restaurants are few.

The city has a population of 269,000, but the metropolitan area extends into three Kentucky counties and four in southern Indiana, making Louisville the economic, social, and cultural center for nearly 950,000. The city's diverse economy, modest cost of living, and cultural and recreational amenities combine to earn it consistently high rankings on lists of America's "most livable" cities. The best way to enjoy your visit here is to allow the city to make you feel at home. Relax, dress comfortably, smile—and say "*Loo*-a-vul."

Louisville At-a-Glance

SEEING THE CITY

The *Spire* restaurant and cocktail lounge on the 19th floor of the *Hyatt Regency Louisville* (see *Checking In*) revolves to show views of downtown Louisville, the Ohio River, and, when it's not too hazy, southern Indiana across the river.

SPECIAL PLACES

The best way to get around Louisville is by car. You can hop a trolley or walk around downtown, but attractions like *Churchill Downs,* historic homes, and the lovely surrounding countryside require transportation. But first . . .

CHURCHILL DOWNS By far Louisville's most popular attraction, the *Kentucky Derby* draws close to 140,000 people to *Churchill Downs* on the first Saturday in May. Modeled after England's *Epsom Derby,* this first jewel of the Triple Crown has been run over the same course since 1875 (though the original 1½-mile distance was trimmed to 1¼ miles in 1896). It's a big deal for the horse owners because of the race's prestige, as well as its big purse (usually close to $1 million); for the horses because of the competition and the distance (which is considerable for a three-year-old so early in the season); and for the whole city. The twin-spired track is packed with fans sipping mint juleps, shedding a few tears at the sound of "My Old Kentucky Home," and, if they're lucky, catching a glimpse of some of the world's most expensive horseflesh. If you can stand the unabashed sentimentality, the crowds, and the expense (accommodations are offered at a substantial premium on *Derby* weekend), it's worth the trip—at least once.

Reserved seats for the race are hard to get (most box-holders renew their tickets annually), but all you need to join the general admission party in the infield (no seats) is $20. In addition, a limited number of general admission tickets to the *Clubhouse Gardens* area are sold on the day of the race or by phone after March 1. As for a seat in the *Clubhouse* or *Grandstand,* every year the track gets more than 30,000 requests for the few tickets that become available. Seats are usually sold out by January, so send your written request early (right after the current year's race). Write *Churchill Downs,* Derby Ticket Office, 700 Central Ave., Louisville, KY 40208 (phone: 636-4400).

Most visitors don't mind joining the unseated throngs in the infield or gardens, but those who really want a seat might consider a *Kentucky Derby* tour package. Three companies that offer tours are *Carlson Wagonlit Travel* (400 Metro Place N., Suite 300, Dublin, OH 43017; phone: 800-388-8699); *Delta Queen Steamboat Company* (30 Robin St. Wharf, New Orleans, LA 70130-1890; phone: 800-543-1949); and *Frontier Travel & Tours* (1923 N. Carson St., Suite 105, Carson City, NV 89701; phone: 800-248-4782).

KENTUCKY DERBY MUSEUM Racing memorabilia is on exhibit here, along with hands-on exhibits testing *Derby* trivia skills and the mysteries of pari-mutuel betting. Closed *Oaks Day* (the Friday before the *Derby*), *Derby Day, Thanksgiving,* and *Christmas.* Admission charge. 704 Central Ave. (phone: 637-1111).

LOUISVILLE SCIENCE CENTER *Space Hall,* a panoramic IMAX movie theater, the *Mummy's Tomb,* and *Kidspace,* with hands-on activities for preschoolers, combine with temporary exhibits to give this airy place located in a renovated 19th-century riverfront warehouse consistent appeal. Closed *Thanksgiving, Christmas Eve,* and *Christmas.* Admission charge. 727 W. Main St. (phone: 561-6100).

LOUISVILLE FALLS FOUNTAIN In the middle of the Ohio River, "the world's largest floating fountain" creates 375-foot-high sprays, a watery fleur-de-lis (the city's symbol), and other special water and light effects. It operates daily, spring through fall (dates vary depending on the weather). Best viewing is from Riverfront Plaza/Belvedere, north of Main St., between Fourth Ave. and Sixth St.

STAR OF LOUISVILLE An elegant way to see the area is aboard this 130-foot luxury yacht, which leisurely cruises the Ohio River. Well-prepared, abundant lunch and dinner buffets include dishes such as snow crab and New York strip steaks. Diners can dance nightly to a jazz-pop combo or taped music played by a deejay. Cruises year-round. Fourth St. Wharf at the foot of Second St. on River Rd. (phone: 589-7827).

BELLE OF LOUISVILLE Board an authentic 1914 sternwheeler (and floating National Historic Landmark) for a nostalgic, scenic cruise on the Ohio River. Afternoon cruises daily except Mondays from *Memorial Day* through *Labor Day* weekend, with Saturday evening dance cruises. Tickets are available at the steamer office (Fourth Ave. and River Rd.) or in the boarding line at the foot of Fourth Ave. (phone: 574-2355).

FARMINGTON Built according to Thomas Jefferson's plans, the 19th-century home of Judge John Speed is a fine example of Federal architecture. Open daily. Admission charge. 3033 Bardstown Rd. (phone: 452-9920).

LOUISVILLE ZOOLOGICAL GARDENS The zoo offers a pleasant afternoon outing for the whole family, but be prepared to do some walking. Popular exhibits include an up-close-and-personal polar bear exhibit and a *HerpAquarium,* with amphibians, reptiles, and a simulated rain forest. Open daily. Admission charge. 1100 Trevilian Way (phone: 459-2184).

LOCUST GROVE Fascinating for architecture fans, this Georgian plantation was the last home of George Rogers Clark. Open daily. Admission charge. 561 Blankenbaker La. (phone: 897-9845).

J. B. SPEED ART MUSEUM Here is a particularly noteworthy collection of works by Old Masters—Rembrandt, Rubens, and Tiepolo, among others. In addition, there is an impressive array of contemporary and modern paintings and sculpture. Located south of downtown on the *University of Louisville* campus. Closed Mondays and major holidays. No admission charge. 2035 S. Third St. (phone: 636-2893).

KENTUCKY KINGDOM More than 70 amusements are here at this family theme park on the grounds of the *Kentucky Fair & Exposition Center,* including four roller coasters; *The Quake,* a motion machine that'll get you shaking all over; an international *Grand Carousel;* and the *Hurricane Bay* water park. Open June through August; weekends only April, May, and September. Admission charge. Two miles south of central Louisville off I-264, Watterson Expy. (phone: 366-2231).

HILLERICH & BRADSBY After 22 years of making the Louisville Slugger in Indiana, this famous bat manufacturer returned in 1996 to its namesake city, with a new plant and visitors' center. Exhibits include a display of historic *World Series* bats and other baseball memorabilia. Upon arrival, visitors can order a personalized bat; it will be ready for them when they've completed the 45-minute tour. Closed Sundays. Admission charge. 8th and Main Sts. (phone: 585-5226).

EXTRA SPECIAL

Kentucky history comes to life in Bardstown, about 40 miles south of Louisville. At *My Old Kentucky Home State Park* (501 E. Stephen Foster Ave.; phone: 348-3502), visitors can tour the Federal mansion that inspired Stephen Foster to write what is now the state song. The park is closed *Thanksgiving, Christmas* week, *New Year's Eve,* and *New Year's Day;* admission charge. An outdoor drama, *The Stephen Foster Story,* is presented from June through *Labor Day* weekend in the park. You can see how whiskey is made at *Maker's Mark Distillery* (3350 Burks Spring Rd.; phone: 865-2881). Open daily. Tours are free. Traditional Kentucky food can be found

at the *Old Talbott Tavern* (107 W. Stephen Foster Ave.; phone: 348-3494), whose patrons have included Abraham Lincoln and Andrew Jackson. To get to Bardstown, take I-65 south out of Louisville, exiting to Route 245.

Sources and Resources

TOURIST INFORMATION

The *Louisville Convention and Visitors Bureau* (400 S. First St., Louisville, KY 40202; phone: 584-2121; 800-633-3384 in Kentucky; 800-626-5646 from elsewhere in the US) provides maps and brochures and answers questions. There's also a staffed visitors' information booth at *Louisville International Airport* (phone: 367-4636). Information centers are open daily. Contact the Kentucky state tourism hotline (phone: 800-225-TRIP) for maps, calendars of events, health updates, and travel advisories.

LOCAL COVERAGE *Louisville Courier-Journal,* daily (Friday's *Weekend* section has highlights of the coming week's events); and *Louisville* magazine, a monthly that includes a calendar of events.

TELEVISION STATIONS WAVE Channel 3–NBC; WHAS Channel 11–ABC; WLKY Channel 32–CBS; WDRB Channel 41–Fox; and WKPC Channel 15–PBS.

RADIO STATIONS AM: WHAS 840 (sports/news); WAVG 970 (oldies/news/sports); and WLOU 1350 (urban contemporary). FM: WFPL 89.3 (jazz/information); WUOL 90.5 (classical music); and WQMF 95.7 (rock).

TELEPHONE The area code for Louisville is 502.

SALES TAX There is a 6% state sales tax; the hotel room tax is 4.5%.

CLIMATE The general tendency is toward mild winters, brief but exquisite springs and falls, and long, humid, and polluted summers. But snow in April or a 60F day in December isn't unheard of.

GETTING AROUND

AIRPORT Despite its name, *Louisville International Airport* (5 miles south of downtown via I-65; phone: 367-4636 for airport information) handles only domestic flights. Depending on the traffic, the drive to the airport can take anywhere from 10 to 30 minutes. The airport limousine service makes stops at a few downtown hotels, but most hotels in town offer courtesy vans to pick up registered guests. The city's *TARC* buses stop near the airport's main entrance and travel downtown; for the return trip, buses can be picked up along the southbound side of First Street.

BUS *TARC* bus system serves the downtown area adequately during the day but is limited in the suburbs and after dark downtown. The fare is 75¢ or $1, depending on the time of day. Route information is available at the *Transit Authority Office* (1000 W. Broadway; phone: 585-1234).

CAR RENTAL Most national firms are represented.

HORSE AND CARRIAGE This is a romantic way to see the city. Visitors can pick one up in front of the *Galt House* hotel at Sixth and Main Streets or make arrangements in advance to be dropped off or picked up at downtown hotels and restaurants. The carriages operate evenings April through December; contact *Louisville Horse Trams* (phone: 581-0100).

TAXI Cabs must be ordered by phone and are often slow to respond. The major company is *Yellow Cab* (phone: 636-5511).

TROLLEY The *Toonerville II* (phone: 585-1234) provides free service on Fourth Avenue between Broadway and Main Street. It doesn't operate on Sundays.

SPECIAL EVENTS

The *Humana Festival of New American Plays* takes place in March (sometimes starting in late February or concluding in early April) at the *Actors Theatre of Louisville* (see *Theater*). The week preceding the first Saturday in May, the *Kentucky Derby Festival* unfolds with a parade, music, hot-air balloons, and a race between the *Belle of Louisville* and *Delta Queen* steamboats. Many events are free (write to 137 W. Muhammad Ali Blvd., Louisville KY 40202; phone: 584-6383). The *Kentucky State Fair* is held in mid-August at the *Kentucky Fair & Exposition Center* (2 miles south of central Louisville off I-264, Watterson Expy.; phone: 367-5000).

SHOPPING

The downtown *Galleria* (Fourth Ave. between Liberty St. and Muhammad Ali Blvd.; phone: 584-7170) combines more than 90 stores and restaurants under a glass roof. Pottery collectors will want to stop at *Hadley Pottery* (1570 Story Ave. in Butchertown; phone: 584-2171) and at *Louisville Stoneware* (Barret Ave., off E. Broadway; phone: 582-1900) for hand-crafted dishes and decorative items. Antiques shoppers should try *Joe Ley Antiques* (615 E. Market St.; phone: 583-4014); the 50,000-square-foot *Louisville Antique Mall* (900 Goss Ave.; phone: 635-2852); or the shops along Bardstown Road in the Highlands neighborhood. For authentic, high-quality Kentucky crafts, stop at the *Berea College Crafts* shop (140 N. Fourth Ave. in the *Galt House* hotel; phone: 589-3707) or *Kentucky Art and Craft Gallery* (609 W. Main St.; phone: 589-0102).

SPORTS AND FITNESS

BASEBALL The minor league Louisville *Redbirds,* members of the *American Association,* play April through September at the *Kentucky Fair & Exposition Center* (off I-264, Watterson Expy.; phone: 367-9121).

BICYCLING Rent from *Highland Cycle* (1737 Bardstown Rd.; phone: 458-7832). Nearby *Cherokee Park* has good bike trails over hilly terrain.

COLLEGE SPORTS The *University of Louisville*'s basketball and football teams play at the *Kentucky Fair & Exhibition Center* (off I-264, Watterson Expy.; phone: 852-5151).

FITNESS CENTERS The *Louisville Athletic Club* (Fifth and Muhammad Ali Blvd., at the red awning; phone: 585-6399) offers a steamroom, a sauna, a whirlpool, and basketball, racquetball, and squash courts. The *YMCA* (Second and Chestnut; phone: 587-6700) has a pool, exercise room, gym, racquetball court, and indoor track. Both fitness centers are open to visitors who are guests of a Louisville hotel.

GOLF Two excellent public 18-hole courses are *Quail Chase* (7000 Cooper Chapel Rd.; phone: 239-2110) and *Seneca Park* (Taylorsville Rd. and Cannons La.; phone: 458-9298).

HORSE RACING There's thoroughbred racing from late April through July and during November at *Churchill Downs* (700 Central Ave.; phone: 636-4400; for *Kentucky Derby* information, see *Special Places*). At other times, thoroughbred races at other Kentucky tracks are televised (with wagering) at *Sports Spectrum* (4520 Poplar Level Rd.; phone: 962-2200).

ICE HOCKEY The Louisville *RiverFrogs*, part of the *East Coast Hockey League,* play at the *Kentucky Fair & Exposition Center* (off I-264, Watterson Expy.; phone: 367-9121).

ICE SKATING *Alpine Ice Arena* (1825 Gardiner La.; phone: 459-9500) offers indoor skating. Admission charge.

JOGGING For a 3-mile run, start at the *Hyatt Regency Louisville* on Fourth Avenue. Run north to Main Street, turn right onto Main Street, turn left at Second Street, and head across Clark Memorial Bridge; then retrace your steps.

TENNIS The best outdoor clay courts in the area are at the *Louisville Tennis Center* (Trevilian Way, across from the *Louisville Zoological Gardens;* phone: 239-6000), which is open April through November. Indoor courts are available at the *Louisville Indoor Racquet Club* (8609 Westport Rd.; phone: 426-2454).

THEATER

Considering its size, Louisville is a culturally rich city, offering one nationally recognized theater company and several other fine groups. For current offerings, check the papers listed in *Local Coverage.*

CENTER STAGE

Actors Theatre of Louisville The two stages here have become bright spots on the American theater scene. The annual *Humana Festival of New American Plays,* initiated in 1977, has gained international critical attention and has sent graduates on to successful runs on both coasts: *Agnes of God, Extremities,* and the Pulitzer Prize–winning

Crimes of the Heart premiered here. The 30 productions each season, both classics and innovative new works, are presented in three theaters housed in a grand old columned building that has been designated a National Historic Landmark. 316-320 W. Main St. (phone: 584-1205).

In addition, *Stage One: Louisville Children's Theatre,* the *Louisville Ballet Company,* and touring repertory groups, including Broadway road shows, perform at the *Kentucky Center for the Arts* (5 Riverfront Plaza; phone: 584-7777; 800-775-7777).

MUSIC

The *Louisville Orchestra* and the *Kentucky Opera Association* perform at the *Kentucky Center for the Arts* (see *Theater*).

NIGHTCLUBS AND NIGHTLIFE

Current favorites include the *Phoenix Hill Tavern* (644 Baxter Ave.; phone: 589-4630), which features popular music on three stages, including a large glass-enclosed rooftop beer garden; *Butchertown Pub* (1335 Story Ave.; phone: 583-2242) for a variety of "hot" bands, plus a lively, friendly atmosphere; and *Silo Microbrewery Complex* (630 Barret Ave.; phone: 589-2739) for blues and other live music plus locally brewed specialty beers. For elegant, quiet, after-dinner drinking, try the *Old Seelbach Bar* in the *Seelbach* hotel (see *Checking In*).

Best in Town

CHECKING IN

Louisville's accommodations range from standard large hotels to Victorian-style inns. Most of Louisville's major hotels have complete facilities for the business traveler. Those listed below as having "business services" usually offer such conveniences as meeting rooms, photocopiers, computers, translation services, and express checkout, among others. Call the individual hotel for additional information. The hotels listed as expensive charge $120 to $160 per night for a double room; moderate hotels charge from $70 to $115; and the place in the inexpensive category charges from $50 to $65. (Less expensive weekend rates may be available in all categories.) For bed and breakfast accommodations, contact *Kentucky Homes Bed & Breakfast* (1219 S. Fourth St., Louisville, KY 40203; phone: 635-7341). Unless otherwise noted, hotel rooms have air conditioning, private baths, TV sets, and telephones.

All the hotels below are in Louisville and telephone and fax numbers are in the 502 area code unless otherwise indicated.

EXPENSIVE

Brown Built in the 1920s, this 296-room architectural landmark is a step into Louisville history. From the marble-floored lobby and archway-adorned mezzanine to the *Crystal Ballroom* and warm wood interior of the *English Grille* (see *Eating Out*), it harks to a more gracious time. Amenities include a cocktail lounge, a fitness center, and 24-hour room service. A concierge desk and business services are available. Fourth and Broadway (phone: 583-1234; 800-866-7666; fax: 587-7006).

Hyatt Regency Louisville Contemporary atmosphere, spacious accommodations, and attentive service mark this 388-room hotel in the heart of the downtown business district. Features include an 18-story atrium, the revolving *Spire* restaurant, an indoor pool, a Jacuzzi, and outdoor tennis courts. A concierge and business services are available. 320 W. Jefferson (phone: 587-3434; 800-233-1234; fax: 581-0133).

Seelbach Immortalized by F. Scott Fitzgerald in *The Great Gatsby,* this Beaux Arts showplace from the early 1900s offers the best of modern and period amenities. There are 332 elegantly furnished rooms and suites; fine food in the *Oak Room,* a comfortable bar, and respectful service are standard features here. The hotel offers 24-hour room service, a concierge, and business services. Adjoining the *Galleria* shopping complex. 500 S. Fourth Ave. (phone: 585-3200; 800-333-3399; fax: 585-9239).

MODERATE

Executive Inn English manor decor sets the tone for this comfortable 465-unit motel adjacent to both the airport and the *Kentucky Fair & Exposition Center.* Amenities include indoor and outdoor pools, a health club, and fine food. Business services are available. Watterson Expy. (phone: 367-6161; 800-626-2706; fax: 363-1880).

Galt House The 611-unit hotel, which adjoins the Riverfront Plaza/Belvedere, includes two cocktail lounges, a pool, on-site shops, and three restaurants, one of which, the *Flagship,* has a revolving section to make the most of the wonderful view of the Ohio River. Business services and a concierge desk are available. 140 N. Fourth St. (phone: 589-5200; 800-626-1814; fax: 585-3444).

Old Louisville Inn This elegant bed and breakfast establishment is set in a large Victorian mansion in Old Louisville, complete with 12-foot ceilings, leaded glass windows, and a lobby with massive columns. Most of the 11 guestrooms (including three suites) feature private baths, and all are tastefully furnished with antique furniture. Complimentary breakfast is included in the rates. Business services are offered. Not all rooms have TVs. 1359 S. Third St. (phone: 635-1574).

INEXPENSIVE

Lakeview This resort-style hotel features some unusual extras: an 11-acre lake with boating and fishing, and, next door, a "Wave-Tek ocean" (a huge pool with mechanically created waves). It has 356 rooms and suites, health club access, baby-sitting, and a restaurant and lounge. Business services are available. Two miles north of downtown off I-65 at 505 Marriott Dr., Clarksville, Indiana (phone: 812-283-4411; 800-544-7075; fax: 812-288-8976).

EATING OUT

Our restaurant selections range in price from $60 to $80 for dinner for two at places in the expensive category, $30 to $55 at moderate restaurants, and less than $30 at inexpensive places. Prices do not include drinks, wine, tax, or tips. All restaurants are in the 502 area code unless otherwise indicated.

Unless otherwise noted, all restaurants are open for lunch and dinner.

EXPENSIVE

Café Metro Urbane yet unpretentious, this eatery offers creative entrées such as grilled swordfish with soy sauce, ginger, and sesame seeds. Save room for the Empress Carlotta, a rich chocolate cake with Kahlúa-flavored whipped cream and almonds. Closed Sundays. Reservations advised. Major credit cards accepted. 1700 Bardstown Rd. (phone: 458-4830).

English Grill Chef Joe Castro has taken this historic dining establishment to new culinary heights. The menu combines continental fare and Kentucky tradition; try loin of lamb with hominy cheese grits or the spinach salad with black-eyed peas in country ham vinaigrette. Reservations advised. Major credit cards accepted. In the *Brown* hotel, Broadway and Fourth Ave. (phone: 583-1234).

Lilly's With two guest chef appearances at New York City's *James Beard House* and numerous articles in national magazines, proprietor and chef Kathy Cary has brought national culinary attention to Louisville. The publicity is well-deserved: This is a charming restaurant with a gracious ambience, serving inventive, delicious food. The seasonal menu emphasizes fresh ingredients, and includes such entrees as free-range chicken pot pie, sea scallops in cornmeal stuffed with shrimp, and Kentucky lamb chops with mint pesto. Closed Sundays and Mondays. Reservations advised. Major credit cards accepted. 1147 Bardstown Rd. (phone: 451-0447).

MODERATE

Bristol An informal bar and grill in the heart of downtown. Continental entrées include trout meunière and steak *au poivre* seared in a cognac sauce; lighter fare, including a very popular burger, also is offered. No reservations. Major credit cards accepted. *Kentucky Center for the Arts,* 5 Riverfront Plaza (phone: 562-0158).

Hasenour's Prime rib and sauerbraten are house specialties, but the seafood and daily specials also are reliable in this venerable neighborhood restaurant. The drinks are among the most masterfully mixed in town. Reservations advised. Major credit cards accepted. 1028 Barret Ave. (phone: 451-5210).

Jack Fry's Imaginative food (try the grilled Japanese salmon, black-eyed pea burrito, or grilled-chicken Caesar salad) in a neighborhood-pub atmosphere. Closed Sundays. Reservations advised. Major credit cards accepted. 1007 Bardstown Rd. (phone: 452-9244).

INEXPENSIVE

Ditto's An informal eatery serving scrumptious crab cakes and tasty pizza, this is a great place to take the whole family. Reservations unnecessary. Major credit cards accepted. 1114 Bardstown Rd. (phone: 581-9129).

Lynn's Paradise Café A favorite for the breakfast and lunchtime crowd, this lively spot serves up generous portions of American classics. Don't miss the breakfast burritos—they're tops. Closed Mondays. Breakfast and lunch only Tuesdays and Wednesday. Reservations advised for more than nine. Major credit cards accepted. 984 Barret Ave. (phone: 583-3447).

Memphis

Everyone has heard the cliché that New York City is a great place to visit but you wouldn't want to live there. For quite a while, Memphis was known as just the reverse: a great place to live, but you wouldn't necessarily want to visit. Today, it is a good place to live and an attractive place to visit. It has become one of the nation's top distribution centers.

Sitting high on the bluffs overlooking the Mississippi at the mouth of the Wolf River, the city was one of the busiest ports in the United States in the 19th century. Today, more than one-third of the US cotton crop still is marketed through Memphis. This is basically a conservative town, in both politics and economics. One theory for this, advanced by residents, is that because the wealth in Memphis was accumulated over the decades through cotton, and because this process was so slow, community leaders even now are reluctant to spend.

Fast becoming a popular convention site as well as a tourist destination, Memphis now boasts the *Cook Convention Center;* the *National Civil Rights Museum* (in the former *Lorraine* motel, where Dr. Martin Luther King Jr. was assassinated); Beale Street, where W. C. Handy penned the blues; *Mid-America Mall;* and *Mud Island,* with its exact miniature of the Mississippi River. And don't overlook the *Peabody* hotel ducks, which waddle from their rooftop house (via elevator!) to the lobby fountain for a swim every afternoon. *The Pyramid,* an entertainment complex that features an arena seating 22,500, is a prominent landmark along the riverfront; it can be seen from miles away. A trolley line connects *The Pyramid, Mid-America Mall,* and other downtown attractions. In addition, buses run from Memphis to the Las Vegas–type gambling casinos that are now open 35 miles south of town in Tunica, Mississippi.

Named in 1819 for the ancient Egyptian city, Memphis is a beautiful place, filled with trees, magnificently landscaped lawns, and spacious parks, sitting atop the banks of the Mississippi and surrounded by scores of fishing lakes. Outdoor activities abound (hunting, fishing, golf, water skiing, speedboat racing, auto racing, tennis, and more).

Some uniquely American phenomena hail from Memphis. W. C. Handy, "Father of the Blues," lived here, as did Elvis Presley, the late King of Rock 'n' Roll, who is buried on the grounds of *Graceland,* his Memphis mansion. It draws more visitors to the city than any other single attraction. Holiday Inn and Federal Express got their start in Memphis (Federal Express still makes its home here). These organizations were built on a bedrock of shrewd business judgment and old-fashioned Southern faith—not an unusual combination in this very Southern city.

Memphis At-a-Glance

SEEING THE CITY

The best way to see Memphis is by drifting along the legendary Mississippi. Captain Jake Meanley's *Memphis Queen II* and *Island Queen* paddle wheelers travel along the river. The one-and-a-half-hour cruise leaves daily from *Memphis Downtown Harbor* (Monroe Ave. and Riverside Dr.; phone: 527-5694), March through mid-December. Daylong cruises and private charters are also available.

SPECIAL PLACES

MUD ISLAND Legend has it that *Mud Island,* measuring 1 by 5 miles, was formed by mud deposits clinging to a gunboat sunk during the Civil War. Residents are sure it was a Union gunboat, because, they say, Confederate gunboats were unsinkable. Now the site of a $63-million tribute to the history and heritage of the Mississippi River, the island houses exhibits on the legends, music, and people of the river; a 5,000-seat outdoor amphitheater; a five-block scale model of the Mississippi; and restaurants, shops, a marina, and a picnic area. The *Mud Island Amphitheater* presents the best in local and national music, including rock, hillbilly, and rockabilly. Here also is the *Memphis Belle,* the famed World War II B-17 bomber featured in the movie of the same name. Closed Mondays from April through November. Admission charge. Accessible by monorail. Enter on Front St. between Poplar and Adams (phone: 576-6595).

THE PYRAMID Since Memphis was named after an Egyptian city, it's only right that it should have a pyramid. And it finally got one. This 321-foot structure by the riverfront is an entertainment complex with 85,000 square feet of space inside, part of which contains an arena that seats 22,500. It hosts large-scale concerts, ice shows, basketball games, and anything else that calls for plenty of space. It has become a true Memphis landmark. Located off Front St. (phone: 521-9675).

BEALE STREET Renovated buildings along this historic street, where the blues were born in the early 1900s, contain specialty shops, restaurants, bars, and offices. At the corner of Beale and Third is *W. C. Handy Park,* and at Beale and Main, Elvis Presley Plaza; both feature statues honoring these two musicians from Memphis. Don't miss W. C. Handy's home (Fourth and Beale; no phone), which is open during the summer, or *A. Schwabs* (at 163 Beale), an old dry goods store that stocks a little bit of everything from voodoo potions to 99¢ ties. Another popular attraction is the nightclub at 143 Beale named after B. B. King, the great Memphis-born blues guitarist (see *Nightclubs and Nightlife*).

VICTORIAN VILLAGE Homes and churches in this downtown area date from the 1830s and feature a variety of architectural styles, among them late Victorian,

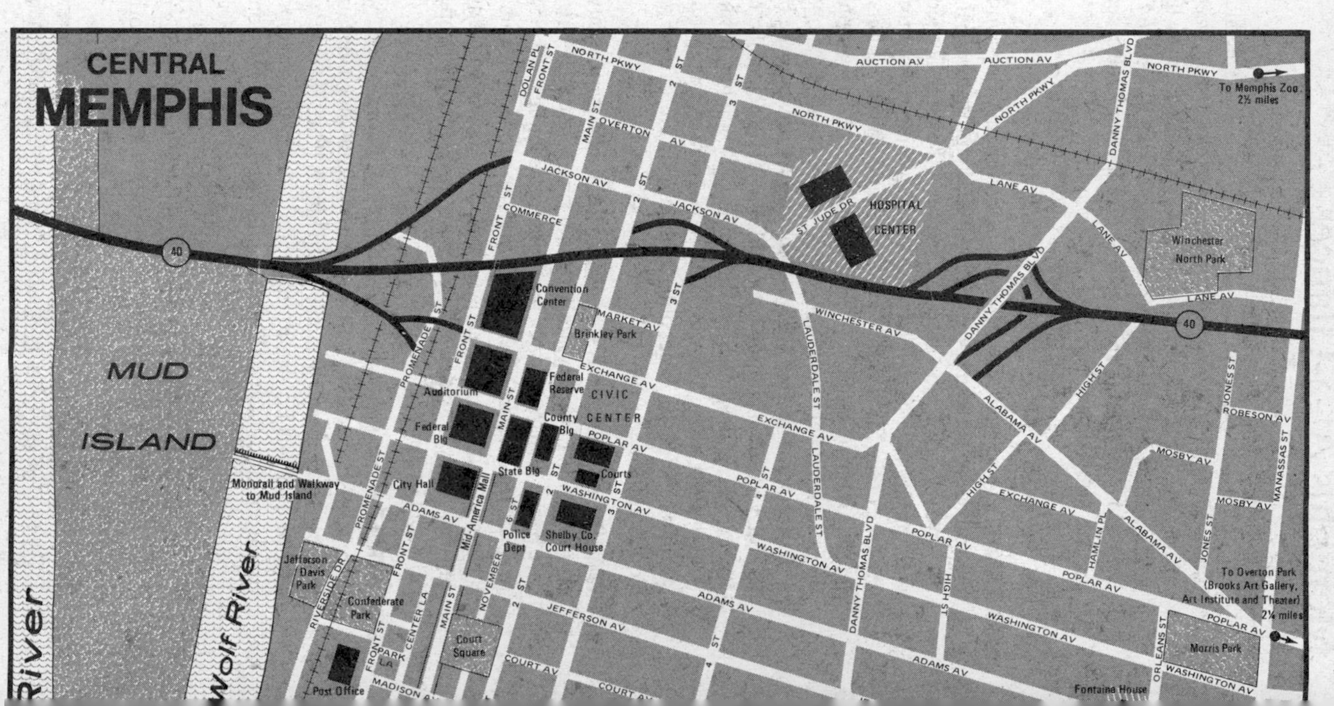

CENTRAL MEMPHIS
MUD ISLAND
Wolf River
River
40
To Memphis Zoo 2½ miles
To Overton Park (Brooks Art Gallery, Art Institute and Theater) 2¼ miles
Winchester North Park
HOSPITAL CENTER
ST JUDE DR
Convention Center
Brinkley Park
Auditorium
Federal Reserve
CIVIC CENTER
County Blg
Federal Blg
State Blg
Courts
City Hall
Police Dept
Shelby Co. Court House
Mid-America Mall
Monorail and Walkway to Mud Island
Jefferson Davis Park
Confederate Park
Court Square
Post Office
Morris Park
Fontaine House
NORTH PKWY
AUCTION AV
DANNY THOMAS BLVD
LANE AV
OVERTON AV
JACKSON AV
COMMERCE
DOLAN PL
FRONT ST
MAIN ST
2 ST
3 ST
4 ST
6 ST
MARKET AV
EXCHANGE AV
POPLAR AV
WASHINGTON AV
ADAMS AV
JEFFERSON AV
COURT AV
MADISON AV
NOVEMBER
CENTER LA
PARK LA
RIVERSIDE DR
PROMENADE ST
WINCHESTER AV
LAUDERDALE ST
ALABAMA AV
HIGH ST
HAMLIN PL
MOSBY AV
JONES ST
ROBESON AV
MANASSAS ST
ORLEANS ST

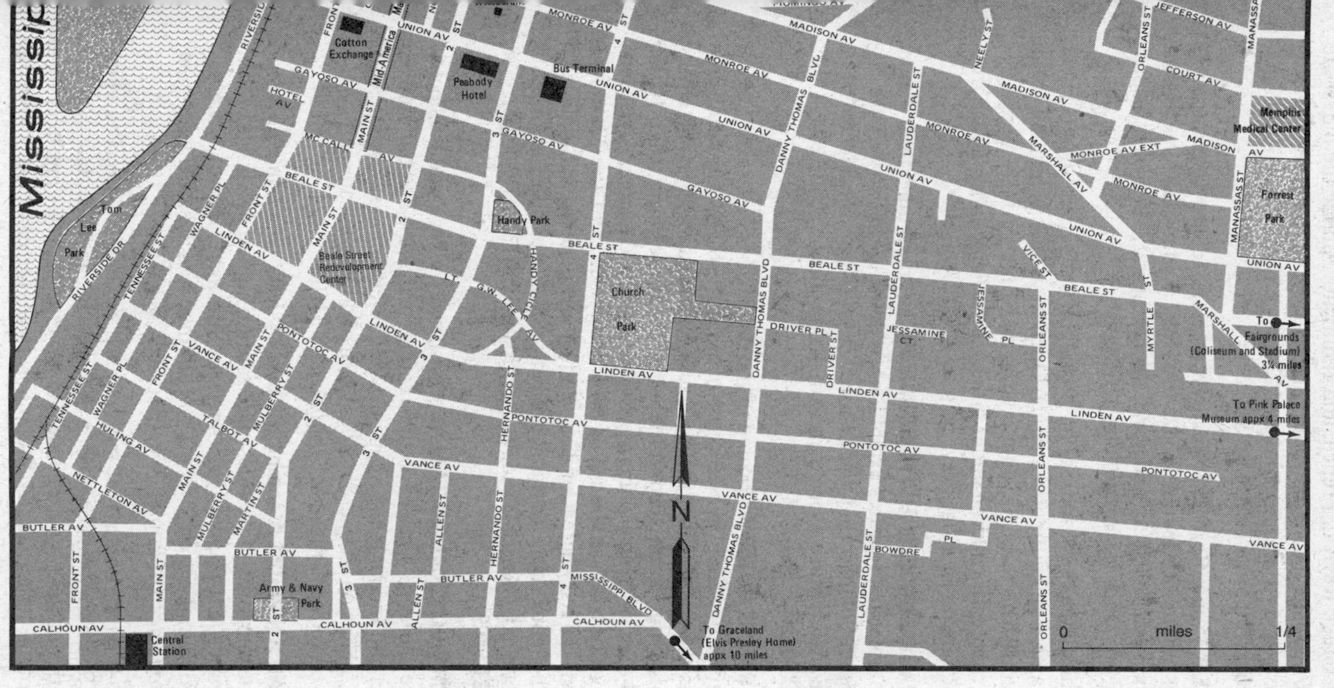
Mississippi
Cotton Exchange
Mid-America Mall
Peabody Hotel
Bus Terminal
Memphis Medical Center
Forrest Park
Handy Park
Beale Street Redevelopment Center
Church Park
Tom Lee Park
Army & Navy Park
Central Station
To Fairgrounds (Coliseum and Stadium) 3¼ miles
To Pink Palace Museum appx 4 miles
To Graceland (Elvis Presley Home) appx 10 miles
0 miles 1/4
N
FRONT ST
UNION AV
MONROE AV
MADISON AV
JEFFERSON AV
COURT AV
MANASSAS ST
GAYOSO AV
HOTEL AV
MAIN ST
MC CALL AV
BEALE ST
2 ST
3 ST
4 ST
DANNY THOMAS BLVD
LAUDERDALE ST
NEELY ST
ORLEANS ST
MARSHALL AV
MONROE AV EXT
VICE ST
MYRTLE ST
HANDY CICLE AV
G.W. LEE AV
LINDEN AV
PONTOTOC AV
VANCE AV
HERNANDO ST
ALLEN ST
BUTLER AV
CALHOUN AV
MISSISSIPPI BLVD
DRIVER PL
DRIVER ST
JESSAMINE CT
JESSAMINE PL
BOWDRE PL
TALBOT AV
MULBERRY ST
MARTIN ST
HULING AV
NETTLETON AV
WAGNER PL
TENNESSEE ST
RIVERSIDE DR

neoclassic, Greek Revival, French, and Italianate. Among the oldest are the *Fontaine House* (680 Adams St.; phone: 526-1469) and the *Mallory-Neely House* (652 Adams St.; phone: 523-1484). Open daily. Admission charge. 100 to 700 block of Adams St.

OVERTON SQUARE A 15-minute drive from downtown, the square has restaurants and bistros, nightclubs featuring jazz trios and rhythm and blues bands, specialty shops, an art gallery, and a professional theater. Madison at Cooper (phone: 274-0671 for information on activities).

LIBERTYLAND This theme park focuses on nostalgia and patriotism (its roller coaster is aptly named the *Revolution*). Open weekends beginning in the spring; Wednesdays through Sundays from mid-June through August. No admission charge for children under three. At the *Fairgrounds,* a mile from Overton Square on East Parkway. (phone: 274-1776).

MEMPHIS PINK PALACE MUSEUM AND PLANETARIUM The museum is built of pink Georgia marble, and features exhibitions on the natural and cultural history of the mid-South, including a restored *Piggly Wiggly,* the country's first self-service grocery store. Open daily. Admission charge. 3050 Central Ave. (phone: 320-6320).

NATIONAL CIVIL RIGHTS MUSEUM Located in the former *Lorraine* motel, where Dr. Martin Luther King Jr. was assassinated in 1968, this museum is the only one in the country that focuses exclusively on civil rights activities, both in this country and around the world. It houses more than 10,000 square feet of exhibits highlighting the bus boycott in Montgomery, Alabama, the landmark *Brown vs. Board of Education* case, and the March on Washington. The cell where King wrote his famous "Letter from Birmingham Jail" and the motel room he was staying in when he was killed are realistically reproduced. Closed Tuesdays. Admission charge. 450 Mulberry St. (phone: 521-9699).

CHUCALISSA ARCHAEOLOGICAL MUSEUM A reconstructed village where Choctaw Indians live and work. Grass huts and a ceremonial house and museum are on the site, and Indian tools, weapons, and pottery are displayed. Closed Mondays. Admission charge. Six miles south of downtown, adjoining *Fuller State Park* on Indian Village Dr. (phone: 785-3160).

MEMPHIS ZOO AND AQUARIUM A complete range of lions, tigers, monkeys, and birds can be found in this well-designed zoo. An aquarium adjoins the animal sections. Closed *Thanksgiving, Christmas Eve,* and *Christmas.* No admission charge Mondays from 3 to 4:30 PM in winter and 3:30 to 5 PM in summer. *Overton Park,* off Poplar Ave. (phone: 726-4787).

GRACELAND Elvis Presley's home is the most popular site in Memphis. The white-columned Southern mansion is open to the public, and Elvis fans can take a bus tour through the 14-acre estate and pay respects at the graves of Elvis and his mother, father, and grandmother. Don't forget to look closely at the *Musical Gate* at the foot of the winding circular driveway. It has a caricature of Elvis with guitar and a bevy of musical notes in ornamental iron. Elvis's plane, the *Lisa Marie,* also is on display. Closed Tuesdays, November through February, and *Thanksgiving, Christmas,* and *New Year's Day*. Admission charge. Make tour reservations in advance. 3764 Elvis Presley Blvd. in Whitehaven, South Memphis (phone: 332-3322; 800-238-2000).

SUN RECORDING STUDIO Elvis, Johnny Cash, Jerry Lee Lewis, Carl Perkins, and other musicians cut their first records here. Restored and operated by the *Graceland Division of Elvis Presley Enterprises.* Tours daily. Admission charge. 706 Union (phone: 521-0664).

MEMPHIS INTERNATIONAL MOTORSPORTS PARK Auto racing is the name of the game at this 600-acre, multimillion-dollar racing park. Races are held March through November. Admission charge. 5500 Taylor Forge Rd. (phone: 358-7223).

EXTRA SPECIAL

About two and a half hours away by car, *Shiloh National Military Park* (off US 64 in Shiloh; phone: 689-5696) lets visitors follow the sequence of the famous Civil War Battle of Shiloh, in 1862. It's closed *Christmas.* Also see *Civil War Battlesites* in DIVERSIONS. In Henning, about 35 miles north on US 51, is the boyhood home and burial place of late author Alex Haley (*Roots*); it's now a museum. Closed Mondays. Admission charge. (200 S. Church St., Henning; phone: 738-2240).

Sources and Resources

TOURIST INFORMATION

The *Memphis Visitor Information Center* (340 Beale St., Memphis, TN 38108; phone: 543-5333), which is open daily; the *Memphis Convention and Visitors Bureau* (47 Union St., Memphis, TN 38103; phone: 543-5300; fax: 901-543-5350) and the *Memphis Area Chamber of Commerce* (22 N. Front St.; phone: 575-3500), which are closed weekends, are all good places for general information. Contact the Tennessee state tourism hotline (phone: 615-741-2158) for maps, calendars of events, health updates, and travel advisories.

LOCAL COVERAGE *Memphis Commercial Appeal,* morning daily; *Memphis* magazine, monthly; and *Memphis Business Journal,* weekly. *Key* magazine and the *Convention and Visitors Guide* are the best sources for information about Memphis activities.

TELEVISION STATIONS WREG Channel 3–CBS; WMC Channel 5–NBC; WKNO Channel 10–PBS; WHBQ Channel 13–FOX; WLMT Channel 30–UPN; and WPTY Channel 24–ABC.

RADIO STATIONS AM: WHBQ 560 (sports); WREC 600 (news/sports/ entertainment); WMC 790 (talk); and WDIA 1070 (rhythm & blues). FM: WKNO 91.1 (classical/news) and WEGR 102.7 (classic rock).

TELEPHONE The area code for Memphis is 901.

SALES TAX The combined city and state sales tax is 8.75%; the hotel room tax is 4.5%.

CLIMATE Memphis humidity is formidable. Even though temperatures seldom drop below the 30s F in winter, it's wet. The worst month is February, when it occasionally snows. July and August get dripping hot, as the temperature climbs into the 90s and 100s.

GETTING AROUND

AIRPORT *Memphis International Airport* is usually about a 30-minute drive from downtown and midtown. The *Airport Limousine Service* (phone: 922-8238) meets incoming flights and takes passengers to the city. When returning to the airport, call in advance for a pickup. Although public bus No. 32 stops at the terminal building, a transfer to bus No. 20 is required to get downtown. The fare is $1.10.

BUS Memphis buses generally run between 4 AM and 11 PM during the week, with limited service on weekends. The fare is $1.10. For information, contact the *Memphis Area Transit Authority* (1370 Levee Rd.; phone: 274-6282).

CAR RENTAL All the major national firms are represented.

TAXI There are taxi stands near the bus station and at the airport. It's best to call *Yellow Cab* (phone: 577-7777).

SPECIAL EVENTS

The *Kroger St. Jude International Indoor Tennis Tournament* takes place in February. The *Memphis in May International Festival* stretches from late April into early June. Highlights of the festival are the *International Children's Festival, International Cooking Contest* (barbecue), *Beale Street Musical Festival,* and a *Sunset Symphony* on the banks of the Mississippi. The *Great River Carnival,* held in early June, has parades, a midway, music, and a riverside pageant. The $1.2-million *PGA–Federal Express St. Jude Classic Golf Tournament* is held in June at the *Southwind* golf course. *Elvis Tribute Week* is observed primarily at *Graceland* around August 17, the day the "King" died. In September one of the largest fairs in the country, the *Mid-South Fair,* takes place at the *Mid-South Fairgrounds.* December heralds college football's *Liberty Bowl* at the *Liberty Bowl Stadium.*

MUSEUMS

In addition to those described in *Special Places,* Memphis has several other museums of note.

CHILDREN'S MUSEUM OF MEMPHIS This discovery museum offers hands-on exhibits and activities for children. Closed Mondays. Admission charge. 2525 Central Ave. (phone: 458-2678).

DIXON GALLERY AND GARDENS French and American Impressionist art is on exhibit here. Closed Mondays. Admission charge. 4339 Park Ave. (phone: 761-5250).

MEMPHIS BROOKS MUSEUM OF ART The collection here encompasses both American and European art. Closed Mondays. Admission charge. *Overton Park* (phone: 722-3500).

WONDER OF WONDERS

***Wonders: Memphis International Cultural Series* is a continuing program that presents art and cultural displays of international significance at various venues throughout the city. Previous exhibitions have included "Splendors of the Ottoman Empire," "The Etruscans—Legacy of a Lost Civilization," and "Napoleon"; for information on current events and locations in the series, call 800-263-6744.**

SHOPPING

Memphis has its share of today's marketplaces, malls filled with department stores, chain shops, eateries, and entertainment. Enclaves of commerce with more individuality, however, also are easy to come by—and get to. Museum shops are an excellent source of quality gifts and mementos.

SPORTS AND FITNESS

BASEBALL The Memphis *Chicks* (short for Chickasaw Indians, who once lived in the area) are a *Southern League* farm club for the San Diego *Padres.* They play at *Tim McCarver Stadium* (*Fairgrounds;* phone: 272-1687), named for the Memphis-born former catcher for the St. Louis *Cardinals,* who is now a sports announcer.

DOG RACING *Southland Greyhound Park* (1550 N. Ingram Blvd.; phone: 501-735-3670) is across the Mississippi in West Memphis, Arkansas. It's closed Wednesdays and Sundays.

FISHING The lakes have bass, bream, crappies, and catfish. Sardis Lake is a good bet; *Meeman-Shelby Forest* is a 14,000-acre park with two large lakes.

FITNESS CENTER The *Peabody Athletic Club* (in the *Peabody* hotel, 149 Union Ave.; phone: 529-4161) offers aerobics classes and a sauna. It's open to non-guests for a fee.

FOOTBALL The *Arena Football League*'s Memphis *Pharaoh's* play in *The Pyramid* (1 Auction Ave.; phone: 527-9595).

GOLF The *PGA–Federal Express St. Jude Classic* is held in June (see *Special Events*). The best public golf course is the 18-hole *Galloway* (3815 Walnut Grove Rd.; phone: 685-7805).

HOCKEY The Memphis *RiverKings* play in the minor league *Central Hockey League* from November through March at *Mid-South Coliseum* (*Fairgrounds;* phone: 278-9009).

JOGGING Run in *Audubon Park* on Park Avenue, and *Overton Park* on Poplar Avenue.

SWIMMING Some of the lakes are polluted. The nearest good swimming pool is *Maywood* (8100 Maywood Dr.; phone: 601-895-2777), just across the state line in Olive Branch, Mississippi.

TENNIS The best year-round public courts are at *Audubon Tennis Center* (4145 Southern; phone: 685-7907).

THEATER

The *Orpheum Theater* (89 Beale St.; phone: 525-3000) offers touring Broadway shows and concerts, while contemporary drama is staged at the *Circuit Playhouse* (1705 Poplar Ave.; phone: 726-5521), the *Playhouse on the Square* (51 S. Cooper; phone: 726-4656), and *Theater Memphis* (630 Perkins Ext.; phone: 682-8323).

MUSIC

Big-name country and rock concerts are held at *The Pyramid* (off Front St.; phone: 521-9675), *Mid-South Coliseum* (*Fairgrounds;* phone: 274-3982), and *Dixon-Meyers Hall* at the *Cook Convention Center* (255 N. Main; phone: 576-1200). Headliners appear from April through November at the *Mud Island Amphitheater* (take the monorail to Front St. between Poplar and Adams; phone: 576-6595) and year-round at the *Orpheum Theater* (see *Theater*).

NIGHTCLUBS AND NIGHTLIFE

Memphis blues originated on Beale Street with W. C. Handy, and is performed nightly at *Rum Boogie* (182 Beale; phone: 528-0150) and at the *B. B. King Nightclub* (143 Beale St.; phone: 527-5464), where the great musician himself plays when he's in town. Other popular downtown nightspots include *Alfred's* (197 Beale; phone: 525-3711) in the *Beale Street Landing* shopping and restaurant complex (at the corner of Beale and Wagner). In midtown, the Overton Square area at Madison and Cooper, try the *Public Eye* (phone: 726-4040). Best bets elsewhere are *Silky Sullivan's* (2080 Madison; phone: 725-0650) and *Willie Mitchel's Rhythm & Blues Club* (326 Beale; phone: 523-7444). Casinos—among them *Splash, Sam's Town,* and *Harrah's*—all within 10 miles of nearby Tunica, Mississippi, combine the romance of riverboat gambling and the excitement of Las Vegas. Buses run the 35 miles from Memphis (phone: 373-7400 for information).

Best in Town

CHECKING IN

There's an abundance of *Holiday Inns* (six, to be exact)—hardly surprising since the chain was founded in Memphis. Other chains, such as Ramada, TraveLodge, Hilton, and Sheraton, also are represented. Most of Memphis's major hotels have complete facilities for the business traveler. Those listed below as having "business services" usually offer such conveniences as meeting rooms, photocopiers, computers, translation services, and express check-out, among others. Call the individual hotel for additional information. Expect to pay more than $100 per night for a double room at the hotel listed as expensive, and between $60 and $100 at those described as moderate. Unless otherwise noted, hotel rooms have air conditioning, private baths, TV sets, and telephones.

All hotels below are in Memphis and telephone and fax numbers are in the 901 area code unless otherwise indicated.

EXPENSIVE

Peabody In 1935, Mississippi author David Cohn wrote that "The Delta begins in the lobby of the *Peabody* and ends on Catfish Row in Vicksburg." Built in 1925, the 13-story, 400-room hotel reopened 17 years ago after a $20-million renovation. A focal point of the elegant Renaissance lobby is a marble fountain to which the *Peabody* ducks—trained mallards—march each day to take a swim. *Chez Philippe* is the hotel's fancy restaurant; *Dux,* its theme restaurant (see *Eating Out* for both). For music and dancing, there's the *Skyway,* a rooftop nightclub. The *Plantation Roof* affords splendid views of the river and city. The hotel's lower level has a pool, snack bar, health club, beauty shop, barber shop, and shoeshine parlor. Room service responds around the clock, there's an obliging concierge desk, and business services are available. 149 Union Ave. (phone: 529-4000; 800-732-2639; fax: 529-3600).

MODERATE

Adams Mark Memphis This circular, 27-story, all-glass structure, known affectionately as "the glass silo," has changed hands a lot—from Hyatt to Omni and now to the Adams Mark hotel group. On the eastern outskirts of town, the 400-room property has a pool, café, and bar with nightly entertainment and dancing, as well as free parking and free cots and cribs. Children under 18 stay for free in their parents' rooms. Meeting rooms hold up to 1,350. A concierge and business services are available. 939 Ridge Lake Blvd. (phone: 684-6664; 800-444-2326; fax: 762-7411).

Holiday Inn Crowne Plaza Focusing on the affluent business traveler and adjacent to the *Convention Center,* it offers 415 rooms, a pool, a health club, and a sauna. *Chervil's* is the ambitious restaurant, and there's a coffee shop, 24-

hour room service, a concierge, and business services. 250 N. Main (phone: 527-7300; 800-HOLIDAY; fax: 526-1561).

EATING OUT

A visitor to Memphis can dine at fancy restaurants, feast on some of the best barbecue anywhere, or enjoy home-cooked meals. Expect to pay more than $40 for dinner for two at restaurants in the expensive category; $25 to $40 at places listed as moderate; and $25 or less at eateries described as inexpensive. Prices do not include drinks, wine, tax, or tips. All restaurants are in the 901 area code unless otherwise indicated.

Unless otherwise noted, restaurants are open for lunch and dinner.

EXPENSIVE

Chez Philippe Decorated in an elegant, French Baroque style, this three-tiered dining room in the *Peabody* hotel is among the best in Memphis. Its sophisticated French menu features such specialties as roast tenderloin of lamb wrapped in goat cheese and served with a caramelized garlic sauce, filet of Dover sole and salmon, and veal medallions. A harpist plays on Friday and Saturday nights. Jacket required for men. Open for dinner only; closed Sundays. Reservations advised. Major credit cards accepted. 149 Union Ave. (phone: 529-4188).

Dux Another delightful place in the *Peabody* hotel, serving excellent seafood specialties. Reservations advised. Major credit cards accepted. 149 Union Ave. (phone: 529-4199).

Folk's Folly This supreme steakhouse serves the largest bites of beef in Memphis. Of the Cajun-style vegetables, try the sautéed mushrooms or fried dill pickles. Reservations advised. Major credit cards accepted. 551 S. Mendenhall (phone: 762-8200).

Ruth's Chris Steak House Often called the "home of serious steaks," visitors and locals alike find superb beef dishes from porterhouse to T-bone to their liking. Desserts are also worth a try. Reservations advised. Major credit cards accepted. 5858 Ridgeway Center Pkwy. (phone: 761-0055).

MODERATE

Western Steak House The fare is traditional: first-rate steaks with fresh vegetables and, not surprisingly, a good variety of delicious seafood, too. The splendid wine list accents regional vintages. Closed Mondays. Reservations advised. Major credit cards accepted. 1298 Madison (phone: 725-9896).

Pete and Sam's Pound for pound, the best all-around restaurant in town; serves dynamite Italian-American food. Order anything: The steaks are as good as the pizza. Reservations advised. Major credit cards accepted. 3886 Park (phone: 458-0694).

Rendezvous In a basement in a back alley, this classic little place is chock-full of Memphis memorabilia. It's as much a museum as a restaurant, and it serves the best barbecued ribs, beef, and pork in town. Closed Sundays, Mondays, and holidays. No reservations. Major credit cards accepted. General Washburn Alley, off S. Second and behind the *Ramada Inn* (phone: 523-2746).

BEST BARBECUE BETS

Memphis is a major league barbecue town, so everyone has his or her own favorite spot. *Gridley's* (6430 Winchester Rd., phone: 794-5997; 6065 Macon Rd., phone: 388-7003; and 1355 Lynnfield Rd., phone: 681-9192); and *Corky's BBQ* (5259 Poplar Ave.; phone: 685-9744) not only serve up great ribs, they'll ship them to your home via Federal Express (but you have to buy $60 to $90 worth). Other good places are *John Wills Bar-Be-Q Pit* (5101 Sanderlin Dr.; phone: 761-5101); *Payne's* (1393 Elvis Prelsey Blvd.; phone: 942-7433 and 1762 Samir; phone: 272-1523); *The Cozy Corner* (745 N. Parkway; phone: 527-9158); and *Willingham's World Champion Bar-B-Que* (6189 Heather Dr.; phone: 767-6759). If you don't mind driving 40 miles for maybe the best barbecue of all (for about $5), try *Bozo's* (in Mason, on Summer Ave. and Hwy. 70; phone: 294-3400).

Miami–Miami Beach

It's difficult to find adults over 30 who actually were born in Miami. Like California, the city—and all of South Florida—seems to be populated by people who have come from somewhere else, and not just another state. Some two million people live in the greater Miami area year-round, and newcomers escaping economic woes overseas and harsh winters in the northeastern states arrive in droves daily. And few are retirees. The myth that Miami is filled with nothing but senior citizens became outdated long ago—in reality, only 15% of the population of Dade County is over 65.

The area's already large population swells tremendously during the winter months, when millions of "snowbirds" arrive. "Snowbird" is a tricky term that refers primarily to tourists escaping the northeastern freeze, but just as easily could describe South Americans in town for a midsummer shopping spree.

Sprawling across 2,054 square miles of land, Miami is a huge and cosmopolitan city. Despite efforts to market it as the gateway to Latin America or a tropical New York, it still retains a somewhat provincial quality. This is due in part to the way in which the metropolitan area is organized. Greater Miami—actually metropolitan Dade County—comprises 27 municipalities and dozens of neighborhoods in unincorporated areas. As a result, residents have a chauvinistic interest in their own enclaves. While they identify with the whole city, their particular neighborhood is what they care about most—even though many of the residents who have this affinity are recent arrivals or part-time snowbirds.

From an early, small settlement consisting primarily of Native Americans living around the US government's Fort Dallas, Miami grew slowly until one Julia Tuttle tickled the fancy of a railroad tycoon with some orange blossoms. Tuttle was an early settler who was eager to see Miami become part of a railroad hookup with the rest of the state. She petitioned railroad magnate Henry M. Flagler to extend his *Florida East Coast Railroad* south from Palm Beach to Miami. He seemed in no great hurry to do so until the Big Freeze of 1894–95 devastated most—but not all—of Florida's fruit and vegetable crops. When Flagler received a box of frost-free orange blossoms from Tuttle, he suddenly got the message. Soon enough Miami had rail access to the rest of the world.

It wasn't long until the rest of the world was glad of access to South Florida. Attracted by year-round warmth and sunshine, thousands of new residents began pouring into the area, only one step behind hundreds of shrewd entrepreneurs. Once a small village stuck on the side of a swamp, Miami and Miami Beach became glittering wintertime destinations and later drew vacationers in the summer as well. While Miami Beach still remains tourist-oriented, the city of Miami has developed into a flourishing international business hub. Together they are an attractive combination that lures a wide variety of visitors.

About 15 years ago, Miami officials—jolted into the realization that their fun-and-sun city had begun to lose its good reputation—launched a series of major programs dedicated to restoration and redevelopment. They began by renewing the beaches, sprucing up oceanfront hotels, dressing up the historic hotel district in Miami Beach, and focusing on clean industry such as international commerce. The Miami River was cleaned up and the parks system was expanded. Ecologists began pushing for strict enforcement of environmental laws to protect the delicate marine ecology, reflecting a determination to keep the good life good in South Florida. Stunning high-rise office towers, bank buildings, and condominiums were built almost overnight to accommodate the Latin Americans and Caribbean islanders who adopted Miami as their capital. The result is truly a new Miami, an exciting place for both residents and visitors—clean, beautiful, and gleaming in the bright Florida sunshine.

That Miami still symbolizes the good life is attested to by the waves of new residents who continue to settle in one or another of Miami's municipalities each year. Many of these new residents are Spanish-speaking, a large number of them refugees from Cuba. Others fled violence in Central America and poverty in the Caribbean; still others are affluent Venezuelans, Brazilians, and Colombians who occupy their Miami homes only part of the year.

This Latin immigration has turned metropolitan Miami into a city where you can buy anything from fried bananas to Chilean wine, and where Spanish is the first language of over 50% of the year-round residents. More recently, the Latin influence has been felt in Miami's art world. An appreciation of and growing demand for the works of such renowned Latin American artists as Rufino Tamayo, Wilfredo Lam, Roberto Matta, and Armando Morales have made the city the undisputed center of Latin American art in the US. A group of galleries featuring the works of both famous and up-and-coming Latin American artists has had an extraordinary impact on the once-struggling Miami art community.

The only slightly smaller tide of newcomers and regular visitors from the Caribbean, Britain, and Europe gives Miami an even more international aspect, with additions like Jamaican restaurants, Haitian grocery stores, and elegant French dining spots. The city today is a tropical mélange of cultures, offering a rich mix of languages and customs, foods and festivals, attitudes and traditions.

Greater Miami's variety is also a product of its many distinct neighborhoods and municipalities. Coral Gables is one of the metropolitan region's most prestigious planned communities, conceived and built by entrepreneur George Merrick in the 1920s. Elegant gates to the city still stand in various spots around the Gables, relics of Merrick's grand scheme to build "a place where castles in Spain are made real." Strict building codes pre-

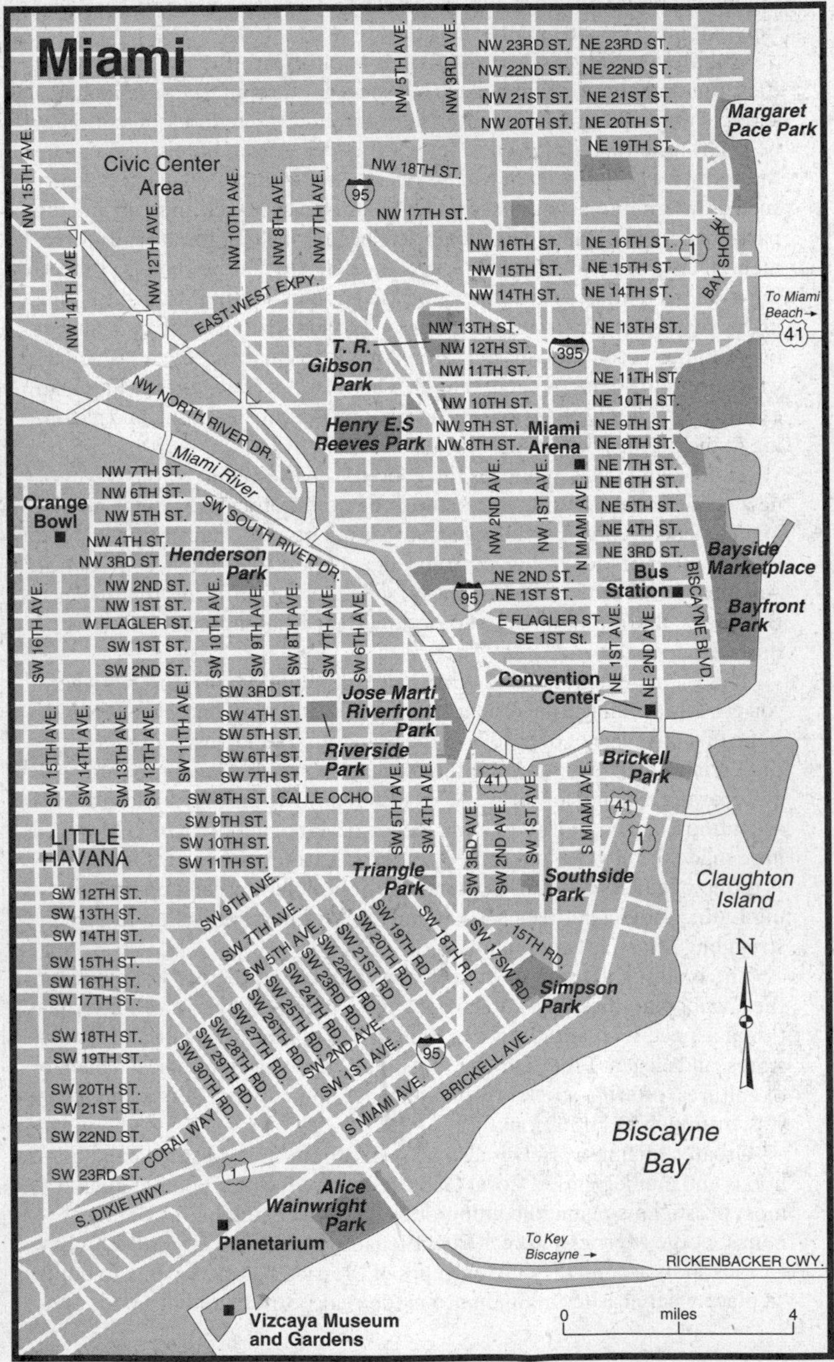
Miami
Civic Center Area
Margaret Pace Park
T. R. Gibson Park
Henry E.S Reeves Park
Miami Arena
Orange Bowl
Henderson Park
Bus Station
Bayside Marketplace
Bayfront Park
Convention Center
Jose Marti Riverfront Park
Riverside Park
Brickell Park
LITTLE HAVANA
Triangle Park
Southside Park
Claughton Island
Simpson Park
Biscayne Bay
Alice Wainwright Park
Planetarium
Vizcaya Museum and Gardens
To Miami Beach
To Key Biscayne
RICKENBACKER CWY.
Miami River
EAST-WEST EXPY.
NW NORTH RIVER DR.
SW SOUTH RIVER DR.
BISCAYNE BLVD.
BAY SHORE
CORAL WAY
S. DIXIE HWY.
BRICKELL AVE.
S MIAMI AVE.
SW 8TH ST. CALLE OCHO
N
miles
0
4

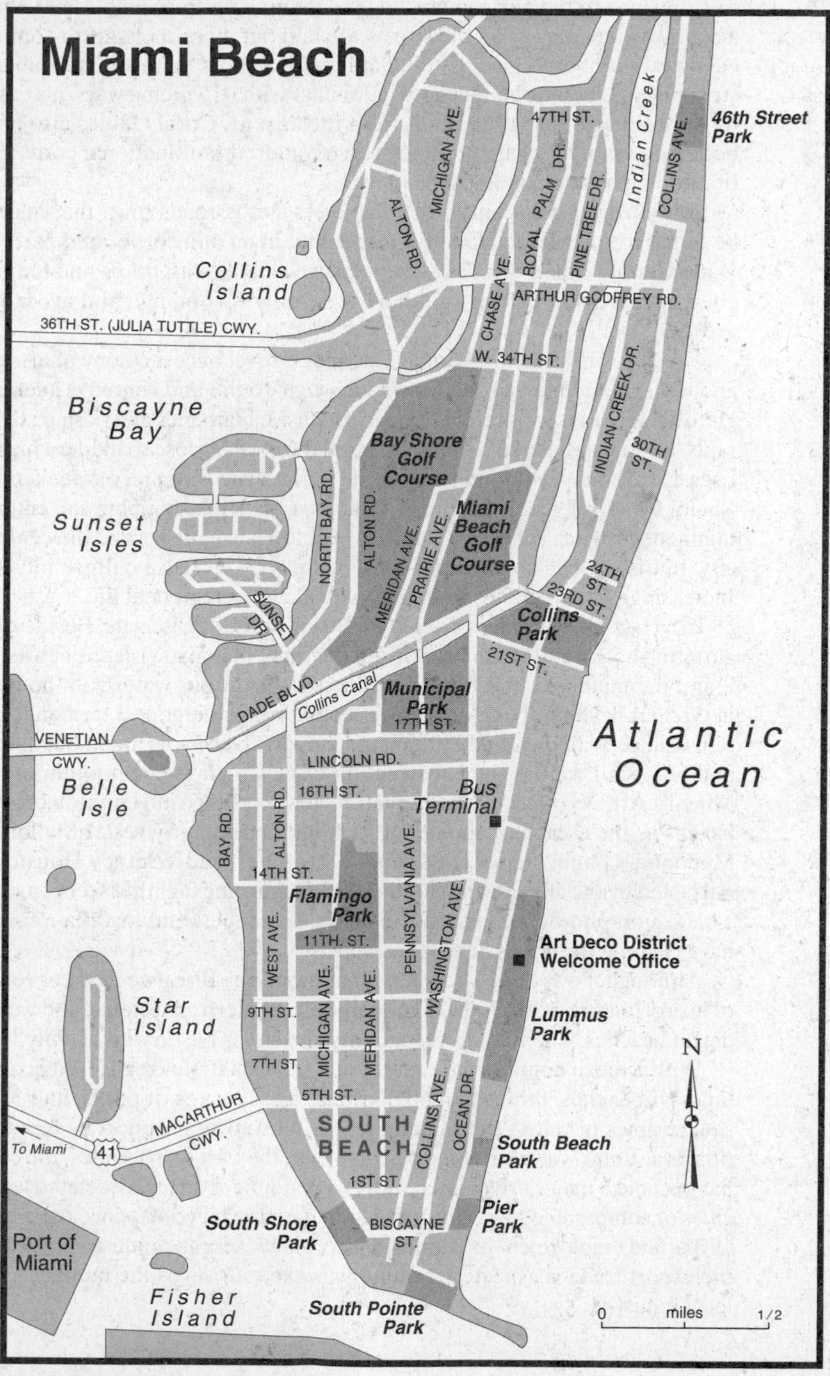

Miami Beach
47TH ST.
46th Street Park
MICHIGAN AVE.
ALTON RD.
ROYAL PALM DR.
PINE TREE DR.
Indian Creek
COLLINS AVE.
Collins Island
CHASE AVE.
ARTHUR GODFREY RD.
36TH ST. (JULIA TUTTLE) CWY.
W. 34TH ST.
INDIAN CREEK DR.
Biscayne Bay
Bay Shore Golf Course
30TH ST.
NORTH BAY RD.
ALTON RD.
MERIDIAN AVE.
PRAIRIE AVE.
Miami Beach Golf Course
Sunset Isles
SUNSET DR.
24TH ST.
23RD ST.
Collins Park
21ST ST.
DADE BLVD.
Collins Canal
Municipal Park
17TH ST.
VENETIAN CWY.
LINCOLN RD.
Atlantic Ocean
Belle Isle
16TH ST.
Bus Terminal
BAY RD.
ALTON RD.
PENNSYLVANIA AVE.
14TH ST.
Flamingo Park
WASHINGTON AVE.
11TH. ST.
WEST AVE.
Art Deco District Welcome Office
Star Island
9TH ST.
MICHIGAN AVE.
MERIDIAN AVE.
Lummus Park
7TH ST.
N
5TH ST.
MACARTHUR CWY.
SOUTH BEACH
COLLINS AVE.
OCEAN DR.
South Beach Park
To Miami
41
1ST ST.
South Shore Park
BISCAYNE ST.
Pier Park
Port of Miami
Fisher Island
South Pointe Park
0
miles
1/2

vail, and woe to the newcomer who tries to put a flat roof on his home. In a county where almost all the streets are laid out in a simple north-south-east-west numbered grid, Coral Gables sticks to its Spanish and Italian street names and layout; for those unfamiliar with its winding ways, it's easy to get lost here. Just 10 minutes from the airport, Coral Gables also has become a favored locale of more than a hundred multinational corporations doing business in Latin America.

South Miami, adjacent to the Gables, is a crossroads town that might be found in Anywhere, USA. Farther south, in an unincorporated part of Dade County called Kendall, lie expensive estates with pools and tennis courts, where not so long ago there were only vast mango and avocado groves.

Closer to Downtown Miami is Coconut Grove, once a colony of artists and writers, and now a base for wealthy year-round and winter residents. Here a few crafts shops remain next to expensive boutiques and posh restaurants, and a handful of old houses of coral rock nestle close to modern high-rises. Luxurious yachts and sailboats lie in Biscayne Bay, and on weekends Miami's younger generation unwinds at the *CocoWalk* shopping and entertainment complex. The area known as Little Havana is part of the center city, but is really a small world unto itself, with its Latin culture intact. Increasingly, it dominates Miami's political and commercial life.

In a class by themselves are Miami Beach and Key Biscayne. Besides its glittering hotel row, Miami Beach and the small manmade islands between it and the mainland house some of the most luxurious waterfront homes in Greater Miami. The South Beach section has undergone a tremendous renaissance, with the rehabilitation of many Art Deco apartment buildings and hotels, as well as the construction of new high-rise condominiums. Miami's Art Deco District has replaced New York's posh Hampton beach havens as the escape of choice for such luminaries as Sylvester Stallone, Madonna, Gianni Versace, Sophia Loren, Cher, and Whitney Houston. Attracted by the climate and South Beach's churning nightlife scene, models, fashion photographers, movie crews, wannabes, and just plain folks have become the area's newest snowbirds.

Although it was once a coconut plantation, Key Biscayne now has rows of luxury high-rises, enclaves of million-dollar waterfront estates, and wonderful beaches. The island's restaurants and shops bustle with activity.

With a mean annual temperature of 75F, 85,000-plus registered boats, miles of beaches, more than 60 marinas, 11,829 acres of parks, and 354 square miles of water, the Miami area's vital statistics support its reputation as a sunny, water-oriented resort. Yet in the past two decades, the city has become a major urban area, with an economic diversity associated with cities of comparable size. The population has grown by 54% since the early 1970s, and employment has doubled in local business and industry. Indeed, the export trade is expected soon to overtake tourism as the number one local industry.

Nonetheless, Miami remains a major tourist destination. As tourist migration from the Northeast slowed during the 1980s and early 1990s (due in great measure to the growing attractions of the Tampa–*Walt Disney World*–Orlando-Daytona axis), increased numbers of travelers from South America, Europe, and the Orient helped to compensate. Although a number of much-publicized incidents against foreign tourists in the past several years has caused a slight drop in the number of visitors from abroad, Miami's efforts to make the area safer apparently have been effective in luring them back (see *A Few Words About Crime,* below). The proof: In 1995, tourism to Greater Miami climbed to record levels, up nearly 10% over 1994.

It's probably not true, as an old Florida legend claims, that a race of giants once lived here, but it certainly is true that Miami today possesses a gigantic will that wants more than anything else to grow—and grow and grow and grow. The new, revitalized—and resilient—Miami is sure to have its way.

A FEW WORDS ABOUT CRIME

Like all large cities, Miami has its share of crime. However—despite the recent murders of several tourists in roadway robberies—crimes against both non-residents and residents of Florida actually declined in 1995, according to the *Florida Department of Law Enforcement.*

In the wake of the roadway murders, South Florida has taken several steps to prevent crimes against tourists. Many hotels now offer guests free transportation from the airport and arrange for rental cars to be delivered to hotels. Easier-to-read road signs bearing orange sunbursts direct travelers to the beach and city areas, and special tourist-oriented police units are now stationed at rental car parking lots and around the airport. In addition, rental agencies are prohibited from putting advertising stickers and special license plates on rental cars (to eliminate the obvious signs that a car is being driven by a visitor). Other measures include establishing undercover police patrols and increasing the number of tourist information centers throughout the Miami area.

Nonetheless, travelers should be aware that criminals may deliberately bump a car from behind and then rob the driver when he or she gets out to check for damage. Another common crime is the "smash and grab," where a robber approaches a car at a traffic light, smashes the window, and then grabs for purses or jewelry. To avoid such crimes, drive alertly, make sure you know where you're going, and carry a map. If your car is bumped or you are told you have a flat tire, don't stop until you have reached a safe and well-lit location. If someone suspicious approaches your car at a red light, check for oncoming traffic, and then drive on quickly. Take taxis if you're going out late at night or to an unfamiliar area, and keep

valuables in your hotel vault. Remember, it's always wise to err on the side of caution to ensure a safe vacation.

Miami–Miami Beach At-a-Glance

SEEING THE CITY

The *Rusty Pelican* (see *Eating Out*) and *Bayside Seafood* restaurant (3501 Rickenbacker Causeway, Key Biscayne; phone: 361-0808) look across Biscayne Bay at the spectacular Miami skyline and have outdoor seating areas with good views. The *South Pointe Seafood House* (see *Eating Out*), on the southernmost tip of Miami Beach, affords spectacular views of Government Cut, the throughway for the dozens of cruise ships that dock at the Port of Miami.

SPECIAL PLACES

The best way to tour Greater Miami is by car.

MIAMI BEACH

MIAMI BEACH From the late 1920s until the 1960s, this 8-mile-long island east of the mainland was renowned for its glittering seaside resorts. But in the mid-1960s, the wide beaches and the distinctive hotels fell into decline. These days, however, Miami Beach's glitzy reputation, along with its unique architecture, has been restored. Several efforts at renewal and redevelopment over the past few years have brought tourists to the flashy *Fontainebleau Hilton* and the other big hotels that line Collins Avenue, the main drag; a $64-million beach renourishment program has created a 300-foot strand extending from Government Cut to Haulover Inlet; and a boardwalk runs 1.8 miles along the beach from 21st to 46th Streets. South Beach, the southern end of the island between Fifth and 20th Streets, has been designated a National Historic District because of its many Art Deco buildings (see below). Ocean Drive, South Beach's main drag, has been widened and spruced up and is now lined with chic outdoor cafés, shops, galleries—and plenty of tanned, attractive, and trendy pedestrians.

ART DECO DISTRICT A drive or stroll through this Miami hot spot will forever banish images of the city as a geriatric center. New and restored buildings, hotels, and cafés with façades of bright pink, turquoise, and peach gleam in the sun. The area's name is actually a bit of a misnomer—the fanciful structures here are a mixture of traditional Art Deco, Art Moderne (a French-influenced hybrid), and Spanish-Mediterranean Revival styles. During the mid-1980s, local preservationists fought to upgrade the South Beach area from Ocean Drive to Lenox Court, which was in a state of decay. More than 800 buildings were rehabilitated and redecorated. Española Way, stretching from Drexel to Washington Avenues between 14th and 15th Streets, also has undergone large-scale renovation. Its Spanish-

Mediterranean Revival–style buildings, many containing eclectic boutiques and art galleries, have been painted in warm coral tones and adorned with gaily striped awnings; gaslight lamps lend a romantic glow.

BASS MUSEUM OF ART The museum building is listed on the *National Register of Historic Places* for its classic Art Deco design. Constructed of Key stone (oolitic limestone), the exterior of the building is adorned with carved nautical figures and features whimsical touches inspired by traditional Maya architecture. Inside, the small museum has several gems in its permanent collection, among them works by Botticelli, Ghirlandaio, and Rubens. Changing exhibitions, lectures, concerts, readings, and a film series complete the picture. Closed Sunday mornings and Mondays. No admission charge for children under six. 2121 Park Ave., off Collins Ave. (phone: 673-7533).

HOLOCAUST MEMORIAL This $3-million memorial park is dedicated to the survivors of the Holocaust in Europe during World War II. At the center of the park is the sculpture *Love and Anguish,* a 43-foot bronze outstretched hand that seems to grow from the ground, symbolic of the concentration camp victims' struggle for survival. A walk surrounding the reflecting pool features touching photographs etched into a granite wall by a special chemical process. Open daily. No admission charge. Meridian Ave. and Dade Blvd. (phone: 538-1663).

DOWNTOWN AREA

PORT OF MIAMI Every week thousands of people depart from here on Caribbean cruises, making Miami the world's busiest cruise port. About three million passengers embark annually; more than 16 cruise ships make this their home port, primarily offering three- to seven-day Bahamas-bound trips, three-day to one-week excursions to the eastern and western Caribbean, and day and evening gambling cruises to the Bahamas.

With the rise of terrorism a few years back, increased security measures were taken that now prevent non-cruising visitors from boarding ships. However, you can park your car on the MacArthur Causeway between Downtown Miami and Miami Beach and watch the ships maneuver. Or have a cool drink at an outdoor café in the Art Deco District and watch the behemoths glide out to sea. Ships generally leave port on Fridays, Saturdays, Sundays, or Mondays between 4 and 7 PM; you'll spot the largest outbound fleets on Saturdays and Sundays around 4 or 5 PM.

Among the cruise lines serving the port are *Carnival Cruise Lines* (phone: 800-327-9501); *Dolphin Cruise Line* (phone: 800-222-1003); *Majesty Cruise Line* (phone: 536-0000; 800-532-7788); *Norwegian Cruise Line* (phone: 800-327-7030); and *Royal Caribbean Cruises* (phone: 800-327-6700). For port information, call 371-7678.

BAYSIDE MARKETPLACE On 16 acres of Biscayne Bay shoreline, this shopping and entertainment complex features 150 stores, restaurants, and outdoor cafés, plus great views of the boats docking at the adjacent *Miamarina.* Charter boats may be hired (see *Boating*), and several sightseeing cruises leave from here (see *Sightseeing Tours*). Stroll past two-story, peach-tinted buildings housing merchandise-filled boutiques, or the adjacent open-air *Pier 5 Market,* which offers crafts displayed on pushcarts, stalls filled with artwork, and vendors selling goods from South and Central America and the Caribbean. Open plazas serve as stages for strolling jugglers, street musicians, and cartoon-costumed characters. Among the hot spots here is the *Hard Rock Café* (phone: 377-3110), where burgers and such are served amid rock 'n' roll memorabilia. It's impossible to miss: A huge neon guitar sits atop its roof. The *Warner Brothers* and *Disney* stores do a vigorous business in movie and television paraphernalia. The marketplace is open daily. Visitors may arrive by *Metrorail*'s "Peoplemover," public bus, hotel shuttlebus, car (parking is available), *Water Taxi,* or boat. 401 Biscayne Blvd., entrance at NE Fourth St. and Biscayne Blvd. (phone: 577-3344).

LITTLE HAVANA, CALLE OCHO (EIGHTH STREET) A real Latin flame burns in this Miami community, founded by Cubans who left their native island after Castro's takeover. A few shops feature handmade jewelry, dolls, and works of art, and fruit stands, bakeries, restaurants, and coffee stalls offer authentic Latin food. Many of the eateries are on Southwest Eighth Street, called Calle Ocho in this part of town. Try *Versailles* (3555 Calle Ocho; phone: 445-7614), *Centro Vasco,* or *Málaga* (see *Eating Out* for the latter two) for a typically Cuban or Spanish lunch or dinner—black bean soup, *tapas* or paella, and flan for dessert—then top off your meal with a quick cup of *café cubano* at a sidewalk stall. Watch cigars being hand-rolled by Cuban experts in exile at *La Gloria Cigar Factory* (1872 W. Flagler St.; phone: 642-1653), but never on Sunday.

METRO-DADE CULTURAL CENTER This huge, $25-million downtown complex, designed by architect Philip Johnson, provides a tranquil Spanish-style oasis in the midst of commercial buildings. It houses the *Center for the Fine Arts,* the *Historical Museum of South Florida,* and the *Miami-Dade Public Library.* 101 W. Flagler St., at NW First Ave.

Center for the Fine Arts Art since World War II and art of the Americas are the focus of this museum, whose name was scheduled at press time to be changed to *The Miami Art Museum of Dade County.* The center hosts major traveling exhibitions of works by artists such as Jasper Johns, but has launched a drive to establish a permanent collection over the next few years. Signs are in English and Spanish. There is a small gift shop. Open extended hours on Thursdays; closed Mondays. Admission charge; voluntary contributions on Tuesdays (phone: 375-1700).

Historical Museum of South Florida The excellent exhibits here chronicle the histories of the various groups that have settled in the region. Numerous displays, including a *chickee* hut, depict Native American life, while the Spanish exploration period comes alive through 17th-century maps and a mock-up of a fort that kids can climb. Maritime history displays include artifacts from treasure fleets. There's also a full-size trolley car that was used in Miami in the 1920s. Exhibitions on the ongoing contributions made by Cubans, blacks, and Jews bring the museum's coverage of the area's history up to date; a sign points out that only "30 years ago, Jews and blacks were barred from part of Dade County." Signs and recorded messages are in both English and Spanish. There's a fine gift shop. Open extended hours on Thursdays; closed Sunday mornings. Admission charge (phone: 375-1492).

Miami-Dade Public Library The main branch of the city's library boasts over one million volumes. In addition, scheduled art exhibitions take place in the first floor auditorium. Open extended hours on Thursdays; closed Sunday mornings October through May; closed all day Sunday June through September (phone: 375-BOOK).

CORAL GABLES

FAIRCHILD TROPICAL GARDEN Founded by a tax attorney with a touch of the poet in him, this just might be one of the most lyrical tax shelters imaginable—83 acres of paradise dotted with lakes and lush with tropical and subtropical plants and trees. Something's always blooming here—it's said to be the largest tropical botanical garden in the continental US. In the wake of Hurricane Andrew, a one-acre plot has been left in its storm-tossed natural state so that students and scientists can observe the natural patterns of regrowth after the fury of the 1992 storm. Other exhibits include the world's largest collection of palms, a rain forest, and a rare-plant house. Complimentary tram rides and walking tours are available, complete with commentary. Visitors also may take a leisurely stroll around the 11 lakes; benches for contemplation are thoughtfully provided. Other features include a snack bar open on weekends from November through April, a gift shop, and a bookstore focusing on horticulture. Closed *Christmas Day.* No admission charge for children under 13. 10901 Old Cutler Rd. (phone: 667-1651).

VENETIAN POOL Once a rock quarry that provided material for many of the stately stone homes in Coral Gables, the *Venetian Pool* is a rare treat. The only swimming pool listed in the *National Register of Historic Places,* this 822,000-gallon free-form lagoon is fed by underground artesian wells. With its varying levels and waterfalls, coral caves, a palm-fringed island, bridges, and painted gaslight poles, it's a place for Esther Williams fantasies. In fact, movie stars such as Williams, the queen of water ballet, and Johnny "Tarzan" Weismuller once backstroked here, and Paul Whiteman's orchestra performed here. A photo exhibit chronicles beauty pageants and celebrities' visits. Visitors may swim here (amenities include lockers and a café, and swimming and scuba lessons are available), but the pool is extremely crowded during the summer, when kids from local camps come here to splash around.

Closed Mondays between *Labor Day* and June 1. Admission charge. 2701 DeSoto Blvd. (phone: 460-5356).

SOUTH MIAMI

VIZCAYA MUSEUM AND GARDENS This palatial estate is where James Deering, the International Harvester magnate, reaped his personal rewards. Built in 1916, the 70-room Venetian palazzo, with 34 rooms open to the public, is furnished with European antiques, precious china, and artwork from the 15th to the 19th centuries. The Roman sculpture, 17th-century Italian marble tables, and a Chinese snuff-bottle collection are particularly noteworthy. The 10 acres of formal gardens, with fountains, grottoes, statuary, and wonderful plant life, exude an ambience of Italian grandeur and are popular wedding sites. Not surprisingly, this is the site of Miami's annual *Italian Renaissance Festival.* Visitors may explore the house on one of the several guided tours given daily and stroll through the grounds at their leisure. Closed *Christmas Day.* No admission charge for children under five. 3251 S. Miami Ave., just off US 1 (phone: 250-9133).

MIAMI MUSEUM OF SCIENCE AND SPACE TRANSIT PLANETARIUM The exhibitions on coral reefs and the Everglades here are especially enlightening; there's also a participatory science arcade, a wildlife center housing more than 150 live animals, and natural history collections with cases of fossils and butterflies. Kids love the hands-on exhibits and mini-shows on Florida natural life, and visitors inspired by the planetarium show may search for the stars themselves with the *Weintraub Observatory's* telescope. Observatory director Jack Horkheimer is somewhat of a "star" himself; he hosts "Star Hustler," a local PBS TV program that explains what's new in the heavens. The planetarium has several shows daily (laser shows with rock music are scheduled on weekends). The observatory is open Friday and Saturday evenings only, weather permitting. The museum is closed *Thanksgiving* and *Christmas Day.* Separate admission charges to the museum and planetarium; no admission charge to the observatory. 3280 S. Miami Ave. (phone: 854-4247, general information; 854-2222, planetarium).

KEY BISCAYNE

BILL BAGGS CAPE FLORIDA STATE RECREATION AREA This 400-acre state park was hit hard by Hurricane Andrew in 1992, but it is on the comeback trail. The coconut plantation is gone, and the fallen Australian pines and other trees non-native to Florida have been turned into mulch to support the native cabbage palms, strangler figs, palmetto stands, and sea grape trees planted here as part of a $4-million revegetation project. There's great fishing all along the seawall, and the park is building several fishing platforms on the ocean (due to be completed at press time); bring your own gear and bait. In addition, the beaches, which stretch for 1¼ miles, are now wider; a man-made coastal wetlands and mangrove area is being constructed (scheduled to open at press time); there are open-air pavilions for picnickers; and the *El Farito* concession sells sandwiches and rents four-wheel surrey bicycles. Snorkelers will enjoy the underwater scenery just off the beach (bring your own gear). This is also the site of Florida's first lighthouse, a 95-foot-tall structure built in 1825 that has just received a complete renovation. Park facilities include the *Lighthouse Café* (phone: 361-8487), a casual eatery next to the historic lighthouse that features good seafood and stunning ocean views; restrooms; changing areas; and four short boardwalks. Open daily. Admission charge. 1200 Crandon Blvd. (phone: 361-5811).

MIAMI SEAQUARIUM Among the 10,000 sea creatures swimming around the tide pools, jungle islands, and huge reef tank (under a geodesic dome) at South Florida's largest tropical marine aquarium are killer whales, sharks, sea lions, and performing seals and dolphins. The biggest stars of the bunch are Lolita, a killer whale, and Flipper, named after the famous TV dolphin (many episodes of the TV series were filmed here). Four different shows are repeated 15 times throughout the day, including one with Salty, star of the TV film *Salty the Sea Lion.* In addition, a "halfway house" for injured manatees is scheduled to open by the end of this year. Snack stands and a café are on the premises. Open daily. Admission charge. 4400 Rickenbacker Causeway (phone: 361-5705).

SOUTH DADE COUNTY

METROZOO Miami's cageless zoo boasts over 250 different species of rare and exotic animals. Pathways lead through re-creations of Asia, the Eurasian steppes, the European forest, the African jungle, and the African plains—each filled with the area's indigenous animals including elephants, chimpanzees, silverback gorillas, and Bengal tigers (some include the rare white kind). Visitors can enjoy a full day's entertainment by roving through the 290-acre site and attending the daily shows, petting zoo, and feedings. Those who prefer riding to walking can hop aboard the elevated, air conditioned, complimentary monorail that runs every 45 minutes. Several stands offer quick snacks and beverages. Open daily. Admission charge. 12400 SW 152nd St. (phone: 251-0401).

PARROT JUNGLE More of the tropics, but this time, screaming, colorful, and talented. Not only do these parrots, macaws, and cockatoos fly, but they also ride bicycles, roller-skate, and solve math problems—all amid a jungle of huge cypress and live oaks. Don't miss the opportunity to pose for photos with brilliantly plumaged red, turquoise, and yellow parrots poised on your arms and head. Other daily wildlife shows feature snakes, bald eagles, and scorpions. There's also a monkey exhibit and a petting zoo with pigs, goats, and miniature deer. The coffee shop here is a great breakfast stop. Open daily. Admission charge. Two miles south of US 1 at 11000 SW 57th Ave. (Red Rd.) and Killian Dr. (phone: 666-7834). The attraction will move 20 miles away to a new location on Watson Island toward the end of the decade.

MONKEY JUNGLE Four hundred monkeys run free, go swimming, swing from trees, and wander about while visitors watch from encaged walkways. Other attractions include orangutans and gibbons, as well as lush gardens. Naturally, some chimp stars perform (four daily shows rotate continuously). In 1994, an archaeological team uncovered the richest fossil deposit in South Florida here, including more than 5,000 specimens dating back 10,000 years. Open daily. Admission charge. 14805 SW 216th St. (phone: 235-1611).

ELSEWHERE

FRUIT AND SPICE PARK Some 30 tropical acres feature over 500 species of fruit, nut, and spice trees and plants. Guided tours by *Dade County Parks Department* naturalists include samplings of seasonal fruits, and you're free to eat anything that's fallen to the ground. This also is the site of the *Redland Natural Arts Festival* each January and the *Tropical Agricultural Fiesta* each July. Tours are conducted Saturday and Sunday afternoons for a nominal charge. A gift shop sells horticulture-related books, canned and dried tropical fruits, and exotic spices. Closed *Thanksgiving, Christmas Day,* and *New Year's Day.* Admission charge. Thirty-five miles southwest of Miami, at 24801 SW 187th Ave., Homestead (phone: 247-5727).

CORAL CASTLE Hand-built in 1923 by a man who was jilted the day before his wedding, this unusual home is testimony to lost love. More than 1,000 tons of coral rock were dug by hand and fashioned into a two-room tower and a walled-in, roofless courtyard divided into several sections containing outdoor furniture and solar-heated bathtubs. Open daily. No admission charge for children under seven. 28655 US 1, Florida City (phone: 248-6344).

MICCOSUKEE INDIAN VILLAGE Just 25 miles west of Miami, descendants of Florida's original settlers are maintaining the lifestyle of their forebears. Among the attractions are alligator wrestling, crafts demonstrations, a small museum featuring the history of the tribe, and airboat rides that will take you deep into the Everglades. Fresh frogs' legs and catfish dinners are served at the restaurant nearby. Music and arts and crafts festivals are held in July and December. Open daily. Admission charge. US 41 (Tamiami Trail) West (phone: 223-8380, weekdays; 223-8388, weekends).

Sources and Resources

TOURIST INFORMATION

The *Greater Miami Convention and Visitors Bureau* (701 Brickell Ave., Suite 2700, Miami, FL 33131; phone: 539-3000; 800-283-2707; fax: 539-3113) is best for brochures, maps, and general tourist information. It's closed weekends. For information on fairs, art shows, and events in the area's parks, call the *Dade County Parks and Recreation Department*'s information line (phone: 857-6868). Call the *Florida State Parks and Recreation Department* (phone: 904-488-9872) for maps, calendars of events, health updates, and travel advisories. *Activity Line* (phone: 557-5600), a visitor information phone guide in six languages, offers updated schedules of events, plus dining, sports, and shopping tips.

LOCAL COVERAGE The *Miami Herald,* a morning daily, publishes its "Weekend" section, with a full schedule of upcoming events, on Fridays. Also of interest are *New Times,* an alternative weekly; *South Florida* and *Ocean Drive* magazines, both monthly; and the *South Florida Business Journal* and *Miami Today,* both weekly newspapers. Spanish publications include the dailies *El Nuevo Herald* and *Diario de las Américas,* and the monthly magazines *Miami Mensual* and *Selecta.*

TELEVISION STATIONS WPBT Channel 2–PBS; WFOR Channel 4–CBS; WTVJ Channel 6–NBC; WSVN Channel 7–Fox; and WPLG Channel 10–ABC.

RADIO STATIONS AM: WIOD 610 (news); and WINZ 940 (news/talk). FM: WLRN 91.3 (public radio); WTMI 93.1 (classical); WLVE 93.9 (mellow jazz); WZTA 94.9 (rock); WKIS 99.9 (country); WMXJ 102.7 (oldies); WSHE 103.5 (alternative); WBGG 106 ('70s); WJQY 106.7 (easy listening); and WQBA 107.5 (Spanish).

TELEPHONE The area code for Miami is 305.

SALES TAX The sales tax is 6.5% in Dade County, 6% in most other counties. There's also a 12.5% Dade County hotel tax, although three municipalities have different rates: the hotel tax is 11.5% in Miami Beach, 9.5% in Bal Harbour, and 10.5% in Surfside. Local meal taxes are generally from 6.5% to 8.5%; in Bal Harbour, the rate is 9.5%, and in Surfside, 8.5%.

GETTING AROUND

AIRPORT *Miami International Airport* is a 15- to 20-minute drive from Downtown Miami and 20 to 30 minutes from Miami Beach—longer during rush hours. Van service between the airport and the city is provided by *Supershuttle* (phone: 800-8-SHUTTL or 871-2000); fares start at $6. *Tri-Rail* (phone: 800-TRI-RAIL in Florida; 305-728-8445 elsewhere in the US) offers free shuttle bus service between *Miami International Airport* and the commuter rail station in Hialeah, a suburb of Miami (also see "Tri-Rail," below).

BUS *Metrobus* serves Downtown Miami, Collins Avenue in Miami Beach, Coral Gables, and Coconut Grove fairly well, but service to other areas tends to be slow and complicated. The fare is $1.25 plus 25¢ for a transfer. For information on routes and schedules, call 638-6700.

CAR RENTAL Miami is served by all the large national firms. Intensive competition makes rates here among the least expensive in the country, but if you want to drive a convertible or minivan during peak season, be sure to reserve one well in advance. For more information, see GETTING READY TO GO.

METRORAIL/METROMOVER *Metrorail,* an elevated rail system, operates from the *Dadeland* shopping mall in the Kendall area to Downtown Miami, and beyond to the *Civic Center* and Hialeah; fare, $1.25. Offering the best views of Miami, the *Metromover* rail system is a 4.3-mile downtown loop; the fare is 25¢, free for those transferring from the *Metrorail.* For information, call 638-6700.

TAXI You sometimes can hail a cab in the street, but it's better to order one on the phone or pick one up in front of any of the big hotels. Major cab companies are *Central Cab* (phone: 532-5555); *Metro Taxi* (phone: 888-8888); *Super Yellow Cab* (phone: 888-7777); and *Yellow Cab* (phone: 444-4444).

TRI-RAIL The 67-mile commuter railroad system began operating in 1989, connecting Dade, Broward, and Palm Beach Counties with increasingly frequent daily routes. The fare ranges from $2 to $5.50 one way and $3.50 to $9.25 round trip, depending on the distance traveled. Passengers board the double-decker trains at any of 15 stops, with connecting passes to *Metrorail/Metromover* and shuttle buses. Transfers to county buses cost 25¢ or less. The train provides access to major sights and, via connecting buses, to the *Miami International, Ft. Lauderdale/Hollywood,* and *Palm Beach International* airports. Extra trains are scheduled for games at the *Joe Robbie* and *Orange Bowl Stadiums* and for special events. There are also guided tours to *Bayside Marketplace* and other attractions. The *Tri-Rail* system is accessible to disabled passengers (phone: 800-TRI-RAIL in Florida; 305-728-8445 elsewhere in the US).

WATER TAXI The *Water Taxi* (phone: 467-6677) runs daily, stopping at major restaurants and other popular landings. The taxis operate on demand as late as 1 AM and must be summoned by phone. Fare is $7 one way; $14 for an all-day pass.

SIGHTSEEING TOURS

Knowledgeable and folksy narrated walking, boat, and *Metromover* rail tours, sponsored by the *Historical Museum of Southern Florida,* are led by Dr. Paul S. George, a local history professor. Itineraries include Little Havana, the Art Deco District, Coconut Grove, Coral Gables, a Miami River boat tour, and a Key Biscayne boat tour (phone: 375-1625).

BOAT Miami is largely a waterfront city, and one good way to get to know it is by boat—excursions range from narrated tours of Millionaires' Row to romantic sunset cruises. Departing from the marina at *Bayside Marketplace* (see *Special Places,* above) are three popular cruises: The *Island Queen* (phone: 379-5119) offers daily hour-and-a-half tours; *Bayside Cruises* (phone: 822-2428) offers six cruises on Fridays, Saturdays, and Sundays on the 49-passenger *Pauhana,* docked next to the *Hard Rock Café;* and the *Heritage of Miami* (phone: 442-9697), a dramatic tall ship, offers daily two-hour tours of Biscayne Bay and also is available for charters. The *Lady Lucille* (phone:

534-7000) docks in front of the *Fontainebleau Hilton Resort & Towers* (see *Checking In*) and offers three 90-minute sightseeing cruises daily.

HELICOPTER/PLANE *Chalk's International Airlines* (phone: 371-8628; 800-4-CHALKS) offers half-hour scenic air tours of Miami on Saturday afternoons, as well as scheduled flights every day to Bimini and Paradise Island in the Bahamas.

WALKING The *Miami Design Preservation League* (phone: 672-1836) sponsors walking tours of Miami Beach's Art Deco District.

SPECIAL EVENTS

On *New Year's Eve,* Miami's annual *Orange Bowl Parade,* which starts from Biscayne Boulevard, serves as a prelude to the *FedEx Orange Bowl,* held on the evening of January 1. This year, the location of the game is scheduled to move from *Orange Bowl Stadium* to *Joe Robbie Stadium* (phone: 371-4600 for information). The *King Mango Strut Parade,* held a few days earlier, pokes fun at the lavish *Orange Bowl* festivities (phone: 444-7270). *Umoja Night—The Lighting of the Community Kinara* is a celebration of *Kwanza,* an African-American holiday that falls just before *New Year's;* it features music, dancing, and food (phone: 836-7344). The annual *Art Miami Fair,* which showcases contemporary art, a good percentage of it Latin American, is held at the *Miami Beach Convention Center* in early January (phone: 673-7311). Also in January, an *Art Deco Weekend* takes place on Ocean Drive, in the heart of South Beach's historic Art Deco District (phone: 672-2014). Miami Beach also hosts the *Festival of the Arts* each February (phone: 673-7733). The *Coconut Grove Art Festival* is also held in February (phone: 447-0401), as is the *Miami Film Festival,* 10 days of national and international film premieres with visiting directors, producers, and stars (phone: 377-3456), and the *International Boat Show,* the largest boat show in the world, which is held at the *Miami Beach Convention Center* (phone: 531-8410).

In March, natives and visitors alike head for Calle Ocho (Eighth St.) in Little Havana for *Carnaval Miami,* a nine-day festival featuring a 23-block street party, Latin foods, conga lines, salsa bands, and lots of people (phone: 644-8888). In April, the *Yamaha Miami Billfish Tournament* attracts more than 300 anglers in pursuit of sailfish, vying for South Florida's richest fishing purse (phone: 365-0497 or 561-2868). May ushers in the *Miami Home Show* at the *Miami Beach Convention Center* (phone: 666-5944). Coconut Grove is the site of the *Miami/Bahamas Goombay Festival* in June, celebrating the area's Bahamian heritage. It's considered the country's largest black heritage festival, with *junkanoo* groups (local citizens who form bands and play calypso and reggae music continuously on homemade instruments) and lots of conch chowder and fritters (phone: 372-9966).

July brings the *Tropical Agricultural Fiesta* at the *Fruit and Spice Park* and the *Annual Everglades Music and Crafts Festival* at the *Miccosukee Indian*

Village (see *Special Places* for information on both sites). For sailboat enthusiasts, the two-day *Columbus Day Regatta* in October attracts more than 300 entrants (phone: 876-0818). In November, the *Miami Book Fair International,* held at *Miami Dade Community College,* welcomes authors, publishers, booksellers, and street vendors to one of the world's largest week-long celebrations of the printed word, considered the country's premier literary event by *The New York Times* and *Publisher's Weekly* (phone: 237-3258). In November, race cars fire up their engines for the *Nascar Busch Series* at the new *Homestead* race track (phone: 379-RACE). The Miccosukee tribe's annual *Arts Festival* in late December draws members from 20 tribes who perform songs and dances, and demonstrate other skills at the *Miccosukee Indian Village* (phone: 223-8380). Also in late December is the *Carquest Auto Parts Bowl*, a top-ranked collegiate football classic (phone: 564-5000) that only adds to Miami's city-wide football mania leading up to the *Orange Bowl* game on *New Year's Day.*

MUSEUMS

In addition to those described in *Special Places,* other museums to see include the following.

AMERICAN POLICE HALL OF FAME AND MUSEUM A marble monument commemorates more than 7,000 slain officers. Exhibits in the three-story building include law enforcement vehicles and equipment, including a guillotine and an electric chair. At a mock crime scene, visitors are encouraged to solve a murder. Closed *Christmas Day.* Admission charge. 3801 Biscayne Blvd., Miami (phone: 573-0070).

ART MUSEUM AT FLORIDA INTERNATIONAL UNIVERSITY The varied exhibits here include painting retrospectives, photography shows, and displays of university graduates' work. Open extended hours on Mondays; closed Saturday mornings and Sundays. No admission charge. University Park, SW 107th Ave. and Eighth St., Miami (phone: 348-2890).

LOWE ART MUSEUM The highlight here is the *Kress Collection of Italian Renaissance and Baroque Art,* a permanent collection of European and American art from antiquity to the present, and Native American, African, Asian, and pre-Columbian art. There also are visiting exhibits. Closed Sunday mornings and Mondays. Admission charge. 1301 Stanford Dr., on the *University of Miami* campus in Coral Gables (phone: 284-3535).

MIAMI YOUTH MUSEUM Hands-on exhibits, including *Kidscape,* a miniature neighborhood with Dr. Smile's dental office, a fire station, and a supermarket, are fun for kids of all ages. There's also a "Metro-Dade Safe Neighborhood" exhibit and a newspaper exhibit called "Hot off the Press." Guided tours are in both English and Spanish. Closed Mondays and holidays. Admission charge. *Miracle Center,* 3301 Coral Way, Level U, Coral Gables (phone: 661-3046).

WOLFSONIAN MUSEUM For decades, multimillionaire Mitchell Wolfson Jr. collected objets d'art, rare books, and everyday items. When the collection grew too large—it now incorporates 60,000 examples of propaganda and the decorative arts—he bought an Art Deco–style warehouse and opened a museum and study center. The result is a rare documentary of American and European cultural history from 1885 to 1945. Closed Mondays. Admission charge. 1001 Washington Ave., Miami Beach (phone: 531-6287).

MAJOR COLLEGES AND UNIVERSITIES

The *University of Miami* in Coral Gables (1200 San Amaro Dr.; phone: 284-2211), with an enrollment of 13,500, has a four-year college and highly regarded graduate schools (medical campus, 1600 NW 10th Ave.; marine science campus, Rickenbacker Causeway, Key Biscayne). *Florida International University* is a four-year college with two separate campuses (SW Eighth St. and 107th Ave., Miami, and NE 151st St. and Biscayne Blvd., North Miami; phone: 348-2000). *Miami Dade Community College* (main campus: 11380 NW 27th Ave.; phone: 237-1093) is the largest junior college in the country.

SHOPPING

In addition to sparkling blue waters and broad wind-swept beaches, Miami offers some sand-free sports—and the best of them is shopping. The places listed below carry a wide variety of items, and many have interesting restaurants and scenic views as well. For general shopping hours, see GETTING READY TO GO.

Aventura Mall One of South Florida's largest malls, with 200 shops and stores on two levels. Anchors are *Lord & Taylor, Macy's, JC Penney,* and *Sears.* A large food court offers a pause that refreshes. 19501 Biscayne Blvd., North Miami Beach (phone: 935-1110).

Bal Harbour Shops Lovely open-air shopping amid gardens and fountains attracts the international jet set and wannabes. The 100 upscale stores include *Saks Fifth Avenue, Neiman Marcus, Cartier, Gucci, Brooks Brothers, Chanel, Cartier, Bally, Louis Vuitton, Mark Cross, A/X Armani Exchange,* and *Tiffany & Co.* Cutting-edge fashion is available at *Gianni Versace, Romanoff Couture, Caron Cherry,* and *Fendi.* Good snack stops include *Bal Harbour Bistro, Coco's Sidewalk Cafe,* and *Carpaccio.* 9700 Collins Ave., Bal Harbour (phone: 866-0311).

Bayside Marketplace From the designers of Boston's *Faneuil Hall,* this shopping and entertainment complex overlooking the water has 150 shops and restaurants. There are also pushcarts where you can buy arts and crafts items from South America, Central America, and the Caribbean. Also see *Special Places.* 401 Biscayne Blvd., Miami (phone: 577-3344).

Books & Books Both locations, one in Coral Gables and the other in Miami Beach, offer frequent readings by authors such as Carlos Fuentes and Susan Sontag.

The Coral Gables store also features a sizable selection of used and out of print books. 296 Aragon Ave., Coral Gables (phone: 442-4408), and 933 Lincoln Rd., Miami Beach (phone: 532-3222).

CocoWalk An exciting open-air, Mediterranean-style shopping complex in the heart of Coconut Grove, it boasts three dozen shops, several eateries (including *Café Tu-Tu Tango;* see *Eating Out*), and entertainment for the young and young-at-heart. Stores are closed holidays. 3015 Grand Ave., Coconut Grove (phone: 444-0777).

Dadeland Mall This large mall in the Kendall section of southwest Miami claims Florida's largest *Burdines,* along with *Saks Fifth Avenue, Lord & Taylor,* and 165 other shops. 7535 N. Kendall Dr., Kendall (phone: 665-6226).

Elite Fine Art Latin American art by masters and emerging artists. Closed weekends. 3140 Ponce de León Blvd., Coral Gables (phone: 448-3800).

Epicure Market *The* place on the Beach for unusual grocery items and take-out goodies for sand or sea, including three types of smoked salmon, imported caviar, fresh-ground coffee, large cooked shrimp, and prepared meals. 1656 Alton Rd., Miami Beach (phone: 672-1861).

Falls Shopping Center More than 60 upscale stores and restaurants set among splashing waterfalls in the Kendall section of Miami. 8888 SW 136th St., Miami (phone: 255-4570).

Florida Keys Factory Shops Excellent bargains amid a Mediterranean setting complete with fountains. More than 50 shops for browsing in addition to an open-air food court. About 30 miles south of Miami, 250 E. Palm Dr., Florida City (phone: 248-4727).

A Likely Story Children's books and educational toys, including easels, games, and specialty items. 5740 Sunset Dr., South Miami (phone: 667-3730).

Mayfair Shops in the Grove High-fashion shops such as *Polo/Ralph Lauren* and *Ann Taylor* are still found here, but now the mix is more mainstream. Newly renovated, the mall has a 10-screen movie theater, new boutiques and shops, and the trendy *Planet Hollywood* restaurant (see *Eating Out*). This mall is worth a visit if only to bask in the fabulous Alhambresque atmosphere. 2911 Grand Ave., Coconut Grove (phone: 448-1700).

Miami Duty-Free Travelers planning to leave the country, even for a short cruise, may buy items at duty-free prices right in Miami, in this clean, uncluttered shop. Drive into the highly secure parking lot and present either your cruise or flight ticket and passport to the security guard. Select and pay for your goods. *MDF* will deliver your purchases to your plane at *Miami International Airport* or to your ship at the Port of Miami on the day of departure. Items include Calvin Klein scents, Cartier watches, and Wedgwood china, as well as jewelry and leather goods. Salespeople speak many languages. Prices are 20% to 40% below retail, and no Florida tax is levied. 125 NE Eighth St., Miami (phone: 358-9774).

Unicorn Village Market This large, trendy shop associated with the *Unicorn Village* restaurant (see *Eating Out*) features enormous displays of organically grown produce, prepared Pritikin Diet items, and wines produced without pesticides or added sulfites. There's also prepared food to go. At *The Shops at the Waterways,* 3595 NE 207th St., North Miami Beach (phone: 933-8829).

Virginia Miller Galleries Features major works by 19th- and 20th-century artists. There's contemporary artwork by Cuban Americans, Latin Americans such as Tamayo and Matta, and European artists such as Karel Appel. Closed Sundays. 169 Madeira Ave., Coral Gables (phone: 444-4493).

SPORTS AND FITNESS

BASEBALL The *National League's* Florida *Marlins* play at *Joe Robbie Stadium* near the north county line (2269 NW 199th St.; phone: 620-2578 or 623-6100). The *University of Miami Hurricanes* play at *Mark Light Stadium* (on campus at 1 Hurricane Dr., corner of Ponce de León and San Amaro, Coral Gables; phone: 284-2655; 800-GO-CANES).

BASKETBALL The *Heat,* Miami's *NBA* entry, burns up the court at the *Miami Arena* (701 Arena Way, Miami; phone: 577-HEAT, tickets; 530-4400, information).

BICYCLING Cyclists have more than 100 miles of bicycle paths at their disposal in the Miami area. A 3½-mile bicycle path on Key Biscayne originates in *Crandon Park* and goes through the beach area, woods, and hammocks of trees and cane grass before ending at *Sundays on the Bay* restaurant. The *Dade County Parks and Recreation Department* has more information (phone: 375-4507). Another favorite spot for cyclists and runners is *Tropical Park.* The 2-mile path winds through a wooded area, along two lakes, and past sports facilities. Pick up a map at the park office (7900 40th Rd., Miami; phone: 226-8315; open weekdays) or the tennis center (same address and phone as the park office; open daily).

Bicycle rentals are available throughout the Greater Miami area. A few places to try: *Dade Cycle Shop* (3216 Grand Ave., Coconut Grove; phone: 443-6075); *Mangrove Cycles* (260 Crandon Blvd., Key Biscayne; phone: 361-5555); and *Miami Beach Bicycle Center* (601 Fifth St., Miami Beach; phone: 673-2055).

BOATING Greater Miami is laced with navigable waters and has many private and public marinas with all kinds of boats for rent. Sailboats and powerboats, along with windsurfers and day sailers, are available from *Easy Sailing* (3400 Pan American Dr., Coconut Grove; phone: 858-4001). Sailboat rentals are available through *Sailboats Miami* (Rickenbacker Causeway, Miami; phone: 361-SAIL) and *Sailboats of Key Biscayne* (*Crandon Marina,* 4000 Crandon Blvd., Miami; phone: 361-0328). The *Pauhana,* a 49-passenger catamaran, is available for charter or sunset tours (401 NE Fourth St. at *Bayside Marketplace,* Miami; phone: 888-3002 or 822-2428). *Club Nautico,* a good choice for powerboat rentals, has docks in Miami (phone: 673-2502) and Coconut Grove (phone: 858-6258). Boat rentals also are available through *Haulover Marine Center* (15000 Collins Ave., Miami Beach; phone: 945-3934). For information on sport fishing charters, see *Fishing,* below.

DOG RACING Greyhound racing is held at the *Flagler Greyhound Track* (401 NW 38th Ct., Miami; phone: 649-3000). Check the racing dates before heading to the track.

FISHING Anglers of every ilk will find their special brand of fishing within reach here. Surf and offshore saltwater fishing is available year-round, and there's also plenty of freshwater action in canals and backwaters, including the Everglades and Florida Bay.

Charter boats offer a choice of half-day or full-day deep-sea fishing. There are dozens of boats listed under "Fishing" in the Miami yellow pages, but the following are among our favorites. *Blue Waters* (16375 Collins Ave., North Miami Beach; phone: 944-4531) rents 50-foot and larger fishing boats with captain, mate, bait, and tackle. Other favorites include the *Kelley Fleet at Haulover* (10800 Collins Ave. Miami Beach; phone: 945-3801 or 949-1173). *Crandon Marina* (4000 Crandon Blvd., Key Biscayne; phone: 361-1281) offers fishing boats; powerboats, speedboats, and overnight cruises are also available. Charter boats for sport fishing are available at *Miami Beach Marina* (300 Alton Rd., phone: 673-6000), where you'll also find the party boat *The Reward* (Haulover Marina, phone: 945-3934) offers rack storage facilities for boats.

The boardwalks on the Rickenbacker and MacArthur Causeways also are popular fishing spots. The *Holiday Inn Newport Pier* (16701 Collins Ave., Miami Beach; phone: 949-1300) is open 24 hours daily and provides equipment rental; there's an admission charge.

Fishing seasons offshore vary by location, as do regulations on kinds and sizes of fish you're allowed to catch. The *Florida Fishing Handbook* is available at no charge by writing to the *Florida Game and Fresh Water Fish Commission* (620 S. Meridian St., Tallahassee, FL 32399-1600; phone: 904-488-1960). Licenses are required for both freshwater and saltwater fishing, and can be obtained from bait and tackle shops as well as some *Kmart* stores. Long-term licenses may be obtained by contacting the state commission.

Competitive fisherfolk may want to enter the *Yamaha Outboard Miami Billfish Tournament,* held in April (see *Special Events*).

FITNESS CENTERS Staying in shape is no problem in Dade County. Try the *YMCA* in the *World Trade Center Building* (90 SW Eighth St.; phone: 577-3091); visitors who are members of a *Y Away Plan* back home (more than 50 miles away) are welcome without charge. The *Cross Training Fitness Centers* (2901 Florida Ave., Coconut Grove; phone: 442-2400); *Downtown Athletic Club*

(200 S. Biscayne Blvd., Miami; phone: 358-9988); *Gold's Gym Miami* (1617 SW 107th Ave., Miami; phone: 553-8878); *Washington's Gym* (95 Hook Sq., Miami Springs; phone: 885-8130); and *World Gym* (3737 SW Eighth St., Coral Gables; phone: 445-5161) are also open to visitors for a fee.

FOOTBALL The *NFL Dolphins* are the team, and *Dolphin*-mania sweeps through the entire city during the pro football season, so for good seats call the *Joe Robbie Stadium* in North Miami in advance (2269 NW 199th St.; phone: 620-2578; fax: 620-6596). The *University of Miami Hurricanes* play at *Orange Bowl Stadium* (1501 NW Third St.; phone: 358-5885 for tickets, 643-7100 for other *Orange Bowl* information; fax: 643-7115). Or contact the *University of Miami* ticket office (5821 San Amaro Dr., Coral Gables; phone: 284-2655 or 1-800-GO-CANES).

GOLF Its almost constant sunshine, balmy breezes, and picturesque fairways make Greater Miami a golfer's dream—witness the preponderance of golf tournaments held here. Resorts and hotels without their own courses usually can provide access to other clubs.

TOP TEE-OFF SPOT

Doral Golf Resort & Spa At the moment, this 667-room resort is the grande golfing dame of the Miami–Miami Beach tourist axis. *The Doral's* superb golf facilities (four 18-hole layouts plus a par 3 executive course) thus far remain unsurpassed. The fabled championship *Blue Monster* course is still one of the most formidable challenges in the state, and the *Gold* course offers little diminution in challenge. The pro is Don Pesant; the *Jim McLean Learning Center* is the pro workshop. 4400 NW 87th Ave., Miami (phone: 592-2000 or 800-71-DORAL; fax: 594-4682).

In addition, Miami has more first-rate courses open to the public than most places you can name. Among the better ones are *Bayshore* (2301 Alton Rd., Miami Beach; phone: 532-3350); *Kendale Lakes* (6401 Kendale Lakes Dr., Miami; phone: 382-3930); *Keys Gate Golf and Tennis Club* (2300 Palm Dr., Homestead; phone: 230-0362); *The Links at Key Biscayne* (6700 Crandon Blvd., Key Biscayne; phone: 361-9129); *Miami Springs* (650 Curtiss Pkwy., Miami Springs; phone: 888-2377); and *Palmetto* (9300 SW 152nd St., Miami; phone: 238-2922). For more information about golfing in Miami, call *Tee Times,* a 24-hour reservation line (phone: 669-9500), or the parks and recreation departments of Dade County (phone: 857-6868), Miami Beach (phone: 673-7730), or Miami (phone: 575-5240).

The *Honda Golf Classic,* played in March at the *Tournament Players Club at Eagle Trace* in Coral Springs (phone: 954-346-4000), is one of the major US events on the *PGA* circuit. You might spot such pros as Nick Price, Nick

Faldo, or Fred Couples attempting a birdie here. The $1.4-million *Doral-Ryder Open* is held annually in late February or early March on the championship *Blue Monster* course at the *Doral Golf Resort & Spa* (see above).

HOCKEY The Florida *Panthers* hockey team is the newest addition to Florida's professional sports teams, and one of the newest expansion teams competing in the *National Hockey League.* Until a permanent stadium is built for them, home games are played at the *Miami Arena* (701 Arena Blvd., Miami; phone: 530-4444).

HORSE RACING The *Hialeah Race Track* (2200 E. Fourth Ave., Hialeah; phone: 885-8000; 800-442-5324), listed on the *National Register of Historic Places,* is worth a visit just to see the beautiful grounds and clubhouse and the famous flock of pink flamingos. Call for racing times. There also is thoroughbred racing at *Calder Race Course* in North Dade County, next to *Joe Robbie Stadium* (21001 NW 27th Ave.; phone: 625-1311 in Dade County; 523-4324 in Broward County). The country's only all-weather racetrack, it's open from May through January. The track's "Family Sundays" feature clowns, games, face painting, and a petting zoo. Dining is available in the *Clubhouse Dining Room, Blinker's Cafe,* and *Turf Club.*

ICE SKATING If it's too hot outside, consider ice skating. *The Miami Ice Arena* (14770 Biscayne Blvd., North Miami Beach; phone: 940-8222) has skate rentals.

JAI ALAI Almost year-round, there's betting nightly on jai alai (a Basque game resembling a combination of lacrosse, handball, and tennis) at the *Miami Jai-Alai Fronton,* the country's largest (3500 NW 37th Ave., Miami; phone: 633-6400). You can buy tickets at the gate or reserve them in advance.

JET SKIING For action-packed water fun, jet skis are available at *Tony's Jet Ski Rentals* (3501 Rickenbacker Causeway, Key Biscayne; phone: 361-8280) and *Fun Watersports* (*Miami Airport Hilton and Marina,* 5101 Blue Lagoon Dr., Miami; phone: 261-7687).

JOGGING In Miami, run along South Bayshore Drive to *David Kennedy Park,* at 22nd Avenue, and jog the Vita Path. In Miami Beach, run on a wooden boardwalk that extends along the ocean from 21st to 46th Street, or run toward the parcourse track on the southern tip of South Beach. The *Miami Mile,* a world class event fashioned after New York's *Fifth Avenue Mile* and San Francisco's *California Mile,* is off and running the third week of January. For more information, call 759-5990.

MOTORCYCLING Harley-Davidson motorcycles are all the rage with the South Beach crowd, so why not cruise Miami on your own "chrome pony"? Harleys are for rent at *The Biker's Place* (12864 Biscayne Blvd., North Miami; phone: 673-2932); delivery to hotels in South Beach is complimentary.

NATURE WALKS There are nature walks at *Fairchild Tropical Garden* and the *Fruit and Spice Park* (see *Special Places*). In addition, the *Dade County Parks and*

Recreation Department (phone: 857-6868) sponsors frequent guided tours through natural hammocks, tree forests, and bird rookeries. For canoe trips and van tours of the Everglades call *The Naturalist Services* (phone: 662-4124).

ROLLER BLADING You'll see in-line skaters all over South Florida, particularly on South Beach and in Coconut Grove. Join them by buying or renting skates at *Skate 2000* (1200 Ocean Dr., Miami Beach; phone: 538-8282). You can skate indoors to a computerized light show—two million lights synchronized to music—at *Hot Wheels Roller Skating Center* (12265 SW 112th St., Kendall; phone: 595-2958).

SCUBA DIVING Diving opportunities abound along the coast, where a three-banded basic reef system extends upward from the Florida Keys, past Miami and Ft. Lauderdale. Although it's broken up in spots, and some areas are polluted, plenty of opportunities exist for spotting elkhorn and brain coral—even bright red soft corals at deeper levels—and colorful tropical fish. The first reef is about 15 feet deep, the second about 40 feet deep, and the third is 60 to 100 feet deep. The practice of sinking freighters and other large objects in the sea to create artificial reefs lures oceans of finny friends at 100- and 200-foot depths. Miami boasts about 150 wrecks, and numerous dive shops operate in this area. Among them are *Diver's Paradise* (*Crandon Marina,* Key Biscayne; phone: 361-DIVE); *The Diving Locker* (223 Sunny Isles Blvd., Miami; phone: 947-6025); and *Team Divers* (300 Alton Rd., Miami Beach; phone: 673-0101; 800-543-7887). Also look in the yellow pages.

SKY DIVING *Skydive Miami* (*Homestead General Airport;* phone: SKYDIVE; 800-759-3483) will fly you up and let you sail down. The company also will provide—for a fee—video or still shots of your dive.

SWIMMING With an average daily temperature of 75F, and miles of ocean beach on the Atlantic, Miami Beach and Key Biscayne offer some great places for swimming, all water sports, and another prime activity: sedentary sun worshiping. A 2-mile stretch of beach is open at *Crandon Park* (Rickenbacker Causeway to Key Biscayne; phone: 361-5421). The southern end of Haulover Beach (A1A north of Bal Harbour; phone: 947-3525) is popular with families, while the northern end is Miami's unofficial clothing-optional beach. There are also a marina, sightseeing boats, charter fishing fleets, kite-flying concessions, and restaurants. Miami Beach has several long stretches of public beach at various places, including South Beach (Fifth St. and Collins Ave.), a favorite of surfers; *Lummus Park* (South Beach on Ocean Ave.), with lots of shade; and North Shore Beach (71st St. and Collins Ave.), with landscaped dunes and an oceanfront walkway. There are also small public beaches at the east ends of streets near major hotels.

TENNIS Mild and sunny weather make South Florida ideal for year-round tennis, as attested to by illustrious part-time residents Gabriela Sabatini and Steffi Graf.

CHOICE COURTS

Doral Golf Resort & Spa A veritable metropolis of a resort, this 2,400-acre establishment offers 15 well-kept clay and hard-surface tennis courts, backboards, ball machines, private lessons, and group clinics. The late Arthur Ashe was director of tennis; the program is currently managed by *Peter Burwash International Clinics.* 4400 NW 87th Ave., Miami (phone: 592-2000; 800-327-6334 or 800-71-DORAL; fax: 594-4682).

Fisher Island Club This exclusive resort's tennis program has two grass, two hard, and 14 clay courts, all lighted. You might bump into a movie star or millionaire working on his or her serve. Private lessons, weekly clinics, and round-robins help tune up your game. There's also a pro shop. 1 Fisher Island Dr., Fisher Island (phone: 535-6021; 800-624-3251 outside Florida; fax: 535-6003).

International Tennis Center The site of the annual *Lipton Championships,* the center is available for play year-round, offering two grass courts, 16 hard courts, and eight clay courts, as well as a pro shop and lessons. 7300 Crandon Blvd., Key Biscayne (phone: 365-2300).

Turnberry Isle Major Pro-Am tournaments, such as the *Fred Stolle Invitational,* are held here There are 26 tennis courts (16 lighted), including 12 clay, 12 hard, and two grass courts. The teaching staff is under the guidance of Fred Stolle, a winner of *Wimbledon* and the *French, US,* and *Australian Opens.* 19999 W. Country Club Dr., Aventura, Turnberry Isle (phone: 932-6200; 800-327-7028; fax: 931-9256).

Most of Miami's major resort hotels have tennis courts for the use of their guests, and there are also public facilities throughout the county, including those at the *Flamingo Stadium* in Miami Beach's *Flamingo Park Tennis Center* (1200 12th St.; phone: 673-7761), with 19 clay courts; *Tamiami* (11201 SW 24th St., Miami; phone: 223-7076); *North Shore Center* (350 73rd St., Miami Beach; phone: 993-2022); *Miami Springs Tennis Courts* (401 Westward Dr., Miami Springs; phone: 885-3654); and *Tropical Park* (7900 SW 40th St., Miami; phone: 553-3161). In addition, there are over 200 public courts in metropolitan Dade County (phone: 857-6868).

The 11-day *Lipton Championships* tournament in March is one of the world's largest tennis happenings, with such top players as Boris Becker and Ivan Lendl on hand. For information and tickets, contact the *International Tennis Center* (see above) or the tournament office (2 Alhambra Plaza, Coral Gables; phone: 446-2200 or 442-3367).

WATER SKIING Those not staying at a beachfront resort can try the sport at *Fun Watersports* (*Miami Airport Hilton and Marina,* 5101 Blue Lagoon Dr., Miami; phone: 261-7687).

WINDSURFING Major beachfront hotels rent equipment, but Windsurfer Beach at Key Biscayne is considered by many to be the prime spot. Bring your own board or rent from *Sailboards Miami* (Rickenbacker Causeway; phone: 361-SAIL), which offers two-hour lessons guaranteed to teach any novice.

THEATER

For current offerings, check the publications listed in *Tourist Information* in this chapter. The *Coconut Grove Playhouse* (3500 Main Hwy.; phone: 442-4000) imports New York stars for its season of classics that runs from November through May. The *Jackie Gleason Theater of the Performing Arts,* referred to locally as *TOPA* (1700 Washington Ave., Miami Beach; phone: 673-7300), offers touring plays and musicals, including some pre- and post-Broadway shows. The *Gusman Center for the Performing Arts* (174 E. Flagler St., Miami; phone: 372-0925) and the *Dade County Auditorium* (2901 W. Flagler St., Miami; phone: 545-3395) book theatrical and cultural events year-round.

MUSIC

Visiting orchestras and artists perform in Miami at the *Gusman Center for the Performing Arts* and the *Dade County Auditorium,* and in Miami Beach at the *Jackie Gleason Theater of the Performing Arts* (see *Theater,* above, for details on all three). The *Florida Grand Opera* (1200 Coral Way, Miami; phone: 854-7890; 800-741-1010) stages a full complement of major productions during the winter season, as does the *New World Symphony* (541 Lincoln Rd., Miami Beach; phone: 673-3331). The *Cameo Theater*, a nightclub and concert venue (1445 Washington Ave., Miami Beach; phone: 532-0922), hosts all manner of performers year-round. Luminaries such as Gloria Estefan, Madonna, and Billy Joel often perform at the *Miami Arena* (701 Arena Way, Miami; phone: 530-4444) and the *Orange Bowl Stadium* (1501 NW Third St., Miami; phone: 643-7100).

DANCE

The *Miami City Ballet* (905 Lincoln Rd., Miami Beach; phone: 532-7713), headed by Edward Villella, is one of the country's best young companies, and performs a full season beginning each fall at four South Florida venues: the *Jackie Gleason Theater* (1700 Washington Ave., Miami Beach), the *Bailey Concert Hall* (3501 SW Bailey Rd., Ft. Lauderdale), the *Broward Center* (201 SW Fifth Ave., Ft. Lauderdale), and the *Kravits Center* (701 Okeechobee Blvd., West Palm Beach). There are numerous performances of *The Nutcracker* throughout the region around *Christmastime.*

NIGHTCLUBS AND NIGHTLIFE

For night owls interested in Miami's myriad after-dark destinations, there are several 24-hour recorded information lines, among them the *Jazz Hotline* (phone: 382-3938); *Blues Hotline* (phone: 666-MOJO); the *PACE Free Concert Line* (phone: 895-5488); and the *Swing Dance Hotline* (phone: 944-9917).

The *Club Tropigala* show at the *Fontainebleau Hilton Resort & Towers* (phone: 672-7469; see *Checking In*) may make customers think they're watching a lavish "flesh and feathers" production in pre-Castro Havana; *Les Violins* (1751 Biscayne Blvd., Miami; phone: 371-8668) also presents a flashy show with a Cuban twist. Latin jazz and salsa bands enliven *Centro Vasco* (see *Eating Out*) late Friday nights, while Las Vegas–style revues fill two stages at the *Holiday Inn Newport Pier* (16701 Collins Ave., Miami Beach; phone: 949-1300) Wednesdays through Sundays. In Little Havana, shout *olé* to flamenco shows at *Málaga* (see *Eating Out*).

For live blues and a bit of history, stop in at *Tobacco Road* (626 S. Miami Ave., Miami; phone: 374-1198), Miami's oldest bar. If jazz is your bag, try *Greenstreet's* (2051 Le Jeune Rd., Coral Gables; phone: 443-2301) or *MoJazz* (928 71st St., Miami Beach; phone: 865-2636). The *Alcazaba* in the *Hyatt Regency Coral Gables* (50 Alhambra Plaza, Coral Gables; phone: 441-1234) features dancing to Top 40, salsa, and merengue music on Wednesdays, Fridays, and Saturdays. The *Baja Beach Club* (3015 Grand Ave., Coconut Grove; phone: 445-5499) and *Hungry Sailor* (3064 Grand Ave., Coconut Grove; phone: 444-9359) offer live reggae or rock 'n' roll nightly.

But the nightlife scene you're most likely familiar with is on the south end of Miami Beach, known as South Beach or SoBe. World-famous for its cutting-edge impresarios who host themed parties, South Beach draws the party crowd from as far north as New York and as far east as London and the Continent, not to mention points south, like São Paulo and Buenos Aires. The only problem: Nightclubs in this hipper-than-thou milieu have an average lifetime of about one year, so be sure to call ahead.

At this writing, supper clubs to see and be seen in (after 10 PM or even later) include *Mezzanotte* (1200 Washington Ave., Miami Beach; phone: 673-4343) on Saturday nights; *Bang* (1516 Washington Ave., Miami Beach; phone: 531-2361) on Sunday nights; *Amnesia* (136 Collins Ave., Miami Beach; phone: 531-5535); *Cheetah Club* (220 21st St., Miami Beach; phone: 532-0042); *Temptations* (1532 Washington Ave., Miami Beach; phone: 534-4288); and *Penrod's Beach Club* (1 Ocean Dr., Miami Beach; phone: 538-1111). A popular dance spot is *Bash* (655 Washington Ave., Miami Beach; phone: 538-2274), which is owned by Mick Hucknall, the lead singer of the pop group *Simply Red,* and actor Sean Penn. South Beach clubs favored by gays include the *Paragon* (245 22nd St., Miami Beach; phone: 534-1235) and the *Warsaw Ballroom* (1450 Collins Ave., Miami Beach; phone: 531-4555).

Best in Town

CHECKING IN

Winter is the busy season in Miami, and reservations should be made well in advance. In winter, a double room at hotels in the very expensive category will run $230 or more per night; in the expensive category, $160 to $210; in the moderate category, $110 to $160; and in the inexpensive category, $55 to $110. Besides those listed below, there are hundreds of other hotels in the Greater Miami area, including those run by such chains as Howard Johnson and Holiday Inn. Check the yellow pages, call the hotel chains' toll-free 800 numbers, or contact the *Central Reservation Service for Greater Miami* (phone: 800-950-0232). In summer, most hotels cut their rates, some quite substantially, so shop around. For information about bed and breakfast accommodations, contact the *Greater Miami Convention and Visitors Bureau* (see *Tourist Information,* above).

Most of Miami's major hotels have complete facilities for the business traveler. Those hotels listed below as having "business services" usually offer such conveniences as meeting rooms, photocopiers, computers, translation services, and express checkout, among others. Call the hotel for additional information. Unless we note otherwise, rooms in the hotels listed below have air conditioning, private baths, TV sets, and telephones.

All hotels below are in Miami–Miami Beach and telephone and fax numbers are in the 305 area code unless otherwise indicated.

We begin with our favorite places, followed by recommended hotels, listed by price category.

GRAND HOTELS

Grand Bay Everything about this consistent winner of Florida and US hotel awards is done in high style. Strains of Mozart and Mendelssohn fill the elegantly appointed, European-style lobby each afternoon and early evening; lavish fresh flower arrangements and stunning crystal chandeliers are everywhere. Rooms and suites boast bleached oak furnishings and elegant appointments. All of its 180 spacious rooms have private balconies (some overlooking Biscayne Bay), stocked bars and mini-fridges, two-poster beds, fax machines, and stereo entertainment centers with VCRs. Eight suites feature in-room Jacuzzis and baby grand pianos. Attention to individual needs is paramount, which makes this a favorite with celebrities from George Michael to Luciano Pavarotti. There are two restaurants, including the famed *Grand Café* (see *Eating Out*), and two lounges; high tea is served in the lobby. Business services are available. 2669 S. Bayshore Dr., Coconut Grove (phone: 858-9600; 800-327-2788; 800-341-0809 in Florida; fax: 859-2026).

Omni Colonnade Built in the 1920s, this Coral Gables hostelry melds its original Spanish Renaissance façade and a two-story, marble-floored rotunda with a late-19th-century decor and European elegance. Luxurious details in its 157 rooms and suites include carved mahogany furniture, king-size beds, stocked mini-bars, marble vanities, and gold bathroom fixtures. No-smoking rooms are available. Upon arrival, guests are greeted with champagne and orange juice in the dark-paneled, intimate lobby with its overstuffed sofas and Oriental rugs. A room-service breakfast can be delivered to outdoor tables set among lovely gardens at the rooftop pool and Jacuzzi that overlook Coral Gables. *Doc Dammers Bar & Grill* is an informal eatery, with interesting early photos of the area and live music most nights. A small health club, a concierge, 24-hour room service, and business services complete the picture. 180 Aragon Ave., Coral Gables (phone: 441-2600; 800-843-6664; fax: 445-3929).

Turnberry Isle Set on 300 verdant acres on the Intracoastal Waterway in North Miami Beach, this complex of two hotels—each with its own distinct personality—offers a total of 340 rooms and suites, all with spacious marble or tile baths complete with sunken whirlpool tubs and separate shower stalls. The *Country Club* hotel is a stunner. The exterior is Mediterranean, with fountains and barrel-tile roofs, and the lobby/lounge is palatial. The guestrooms are oversized and beautifully decorated, and even the meeting rooms are brighter and airier than most, with French doors opening onto the golf course. The *Veranda* restaurant, open only to hotel guests and members of the country club and the yacht club, serves such innovative dishes as rum-glazed shrimp with passion-fruit sauce, plantain-crusted salmon filet, and fire-roasted ranch veal chops. The *Marina* hotel is favored by such notables as Bill Cosby and Elton John for its no-lobby privacy. The design is Mediterranean and all 70 rooms were recently upgraded as part of a $2-million renovation project. Located on the marina, the yacht club attracts those who revel in things nautical—museum-quality ship models enhance the decor. Among the yachts available for charter is the 140-foot *Miss Turnberry* ($10,000 per day). The marina facilities are superb; as many as 117 150-foot boats can moor here. The roster of sports facilities includes five pools, a beach reachable by free shuttle, two Robert Trent Jones Sr. championship golf courses, and 24 tennis courts. The adjacent spa features beauty and stress-management programs, plus the usual compliment of training machines. The complex, linked by a complimentary shuttle, offers a total of 11 restaurants and lounges, a private beach club, 24-hour room service, a concierge, and business services. 19999 W. Country Club Dr., Aventura, Turnberry Isle (phone: 932-6200; 800-327-7028; fax: 937-5736).

VERY EXPENSIVE

Alexander An elegant, yet surprisingly homey place metamorphosed from former luxury apartments into an all-suite condominium hotel. A chandeliered portico, a grand lobby with a curving stairway and antiques from the Cornelius Vanderbilt mansion in New York, and 158 spacious, antiques-filled suites are all impressive; each suite boasts a fully equipped kitchen, a king-size bed, and a sleep sofa in the living room. *Dominique's* restaurant, with a main dining room overlooking the ocean, specializes in rack of lamb and *tarte tatin.* There's also a poolside grill and snack bar and a ballroom. The grounds include an acre of tropical gardens, two lagoon swimming pools—one with its own waterfall—and four soothing whirlpools. A private marina and golf and tennis facilities are nearby. It's actually less expensive for a family to stay in a suite here than to take several rooms in other expensive hotels. Business services are available. 5225 Collins Ave., Miami Beach (phone: 865-6500; 800-327-6121; fax: 864-8525).

Crowne Plaza Miami This recently renovated ($9 million) former *Omni* hotel is located near the bay in Downtown Miami. The lobby's casual, tropical-style elegance is heightened by comfortable public seating areas amid lush greenery, flowers, and floor-to-ceiling windows that offer a view of the almost perpetually bright blue sky. All 528 rooms are furnished in Art Deco style. Guests enjoy a health club, a pool, and sauna facilities. The *Fish Market* (see *Eating Out*) is one of its two restaurants; there's also a sports bar. The hotel sits atop *Omni International Mall,* with 125 stores, and is also convenient to Miami Beach, *Bayside Marketplace,* and the airport. The *Metromover,* with connections to *Metrorail,* stops within walking distance, as does the *Water Taxi* (see *Getting Around*). Business services are available. 1601 Biscayne Blvd., Miami (phone: 374-0000; 800-465-4320; fax: 374-0020).

Delano Famous even before it opened in mid-1995, this refurbished property caters to a sophisticated, glamorous crowd—often celebrities who like to be near other celebrities. And speaking of celebrities, Madonna is a co-owner of the hotel's restaurant, *The Blue Door;* Kelly Klein, wife of Calvin, helped design the spa; and David Barton (the owner of a chain of health clubs based in Manhattan) has opened a branch on the premises, so guests can work out (for an additional fee) next to stars like k.d. lang, Kate Moss, Jack Nicholson, and others. The hotel is owned by Ian Schrager, the New York trendsetter who originated *Studio 54* in the 1970s and who brought in French designer Philippe Starck to reinvent this slim, streamlined tower built in 1947. Most striking is a 150-foot-long swimming pool that is one inch deep at one end and five feet at the other; Starck calls it a *salon d'eau.* Rooms are decorated in minimalist style and all are white, from the linens on the beds to the furniture. Besides the 208 more reasonably priced rooms, eight bungalows are available at $450 a night. The hotel has an eat-in "kitchen" for breakfast and lunch; a terrace for lunch; a lounge, the *Rose Bar;* a concierge desk; room service; and business services. 1685 Collins Ave., Miami Beach (phone: 672-2000; 800-555-5001; fax: 532-0099).

Doral Golf Resort & Spa A luxurious $48-million facility modeled after the Terme di Saturnia in Tuscany, the spa evokes the feeling of its ancient predecessor, with its clay-tile roofs and Roman arches, yet the equipment is thoroughly 20th-century. There's everything needed by those in search of enhanced fitness, health, and stress management. The Tuscan menu, based on the spa's "Fat Point System of Nutrition," is served in the informal *Ristorante di Saturnia* or the luxurious *Villa Montepaldi.* But that's only the beginning: There's also world class golf (four championship courses and a par 3 practice course); 15 tennis courts; and essentially unlimited access (and free transportation) to its sister property, the *Doral Ocean Beach*. The resort itself offers 619 rooms and 48 suites, an Olympic-size pool (heated in winter), six restaurants, three lounges, two Jacuzzis, and a fitness center. Virtually no physical or spiritual need is left unattended. Business services are available. 4400 NW 87th Ave., Miami (phone: 592-2000; 800-71-DORAL; fax: 594-4682).

Doral Ocean Beach Relaxed elegance and a friendly staff are the hallmarks of this 420-room high-rise. The lobby sets the stage, with its European-style gold mosaics, marble, and crystal chandelier. Other highlights include exclusive shops, an Olympic-size pool, water sports, two outdoor Jacuzzis, a disco, a lounge with live piano music, a fitness center, a video gameroom, two lighted tennis courts, and an FAA-licensed helipad. On the 18th floor is *Alfredo the Original of Rome,* a restaurant known for its pasta dishes but also heralded for such entrées as veal stuffed with mushrooms. Not to be overlooked is the stunning view of the ocean, the Intracoastal Waterway, Downtown Miami, and the cruise ships at the Port of Miami. All meals are served indoors and out daily at the *Doral Café* in the hotel and the *Sandbar* at the ocean—more than just another beach bar. Business services are available. 4833 Collins Ave., Miami Beach (phone: 532-3600; 800-22-DORAL; fax: 532-2334).

Inn at Fisher Island Just off the southern tip of Miami Beach, this exclusive 216-acre island was once the Spanish-style private winter playground of William Vanderbilt. It's now a private club and elite residential resort refuge with 55 villas and suites, a nine-hole golf course designed by P. B. Dye, 18 superb tennis courts (see *Tennis* in this chapter), croquet, basketball, a beach, two marinas harboring enormous yachts, seven restaurants (one housed in the original Vanderbilt mansion, with marble floors and mahogany paneling), and several shops. The European-style *Spa Internazionale* is a good place to unwind. Though the cost for a vacation rental is significant, it's worth it to many for the privacy and distance from "the outside world." Business services are available. Accessible only by helicopter, seaplane, private yacht, or private ferry. 1 Fisher Island Dr., Fisher Island (phone: 535-6021; 800-537-3708 outside Florida; fax: 535-6003).

Mayfair House Located in the heart of Coconut Grove, this five-story, all-suite hotel is built around an open-air atrium with lush foliage, mosaic tile staircases, multiple flowing fountains, and reflecting pools. The first level houses the revitalized *Mayfair Shops in the Grove* complex. Each of the 182 oversized suites is beautifully decorated with hand-carved mahogany wood, Viennese Art Nouveau furnishings, French doors, and calming tones that accentuate the eye-appealing angles of the architectural design. Designed for the ultimate in comfort, each suite features a terrace Jacuzzi; kimonos; a fully stocked mini-bar and mini-fridge; a state-of-the-art marble bathroom with a second telephone, TV set, radio, and hair dryer; a central stereo system; and a VCR. There are antique pianos in 52 of the suites. The lobby boasts two original Tiffany windows. Dining and/or drinking options include the highly regarded *Mayfair Grille* (see *Eating Out*); the private (hotel guests and members only) *Ensign Bitters* lounge; the elegant lobby lounge; the bar at the intimate rooftop pool with view of the bay; and more than 70 restaurants in the mall, just steps away. Guests have privileges at the exclusive *Cross Training* gym across the street. Business services are available. Popular among savvy locals seeking weekend getaways, this hotel offers value packages year-round. 3000 Florida Ave., Coconut Grove (phone: 441-0000; 800-433-4555; 800-341-0809 in Florida; fax: 447-9173).

Sheraton Bal Harbour In 1995, this 668-room property located in the exclusive Bal Harbour area completed a $52-million renovation that added a spectacular 17-foot waterfall and a meandering river-like swimming pool with multiple lagoons. The property sits within a lushly landscaped 10-acre garden leading directly to the five-acre beachfront where enticements include a new spa, two tennis courts, a jogging path along the beach, a *Body By Jake* fitness center, volleyball, water sports, beachside cabañas, and a gameroom. For sipping and supping, there are the acclaimed *al Carbón,* a restaurant with an open-hearth kitchen that combines contemporary South American and Mediterranean fare; an oceanside snack and drink bar; three lounges; and a 24-hour deli. Directly across the street are the elegant *Bal Harbour Shops.* Business services are available. 9701 Collins Ave., Bal Harbour (phone: 865-7511; 800-325-3535; fax: 864-2601).

Sonesta Beach Key Biscayne Just minutes away from Miami's action lies this beachside eight-story hotel. The sea-at-sunset color scheme (sea green, lavender, turquoise, and pink) extends from the fashionable lobby to the 300 deluxe rooms, which feature private balconies and stocked mini-fridges and bars. Parents rejoice in the complimentary "Just Us Kids" program of daily supervised activities for children ages five to 13. Adults keep busy by exercising at the fitness center, playing tennis (there are nine courts), or relaxing on the beach or around the Olympic-size pool. Water sports include snorkeling, windsurfing, kayaking, and sailing. Bicycle rentals are available; there's complimentary shuttle service to four popular shopping complexes during the day and a shuttle to *Bayside Marketplace,* South Beach, and Coconut

Grove in the evening. Dining options abound: the innovative *Purple Dolphin* (see *Eating Out*); *Two Dragons*, a Chinese restaurant; a café-deli; and a beachside grill. After dinner, head to *Desire's* disco and lounge, or retire to your room where you can choose from a selection of more than 100 movies. 350 Ocean Dr., Key Biscayne (phone: 361-2021, 800-SONESTA; fax: 361-3096).

EXPENSIVE

Biltmore Originally opened in 1926, this gracious edifice was the creation of George Merrick, who built Coral Gables. Influenced by Seville's Giralda Tower, the 275-room structure is in the ornate, whimsical Mediterranean–Moorish Revival style, which was popular at that time. Now affiliated with Westin hotels, the completely refurbished establishment is listed on the *National Register of Historic Places.* It boasts gold, green, and blue coffered and vaulted ceilings, French doors, gargoyles, hand-carved mahogany elevators, miles of travertine marble floors and columns, original 1920s chandeliers, and poolside statues of Roman gods and goddesses. High-living types may choose the bi-level, two-bedroom *Everglades Suite,* also known as the *Al Capone Suite,* after the mobster who lived here for eight years. At the *Cellar Club* level, guests enjoy complimentary hors d'oeuvres and a 20% discount on dining at the hotel's restaurants (but not for room service); in addition, they may purchase a large selection of wines through the *Cellar Club* at reduced prices. While the rooms feature slightly different layouts, color schemes, and furnishings, all are spacious and boast sitting areas and 10-foot-high ceilings. Deluxe rooms offer balconies, complimentary daily newspapers, and the usual special amenities. There's a 22,000-square-foot J-shaped pool (arguably the country's largest hotel pool), an 18-hole Donald Ross–designed championship golf course, tennis on 10 lighted courts, and the extensive *Biltmore Spa and Fitness Center.* The hotel also has two restaurants, two lounges, a spectacular Sunday brunch (see *Eating Out*), 24-hour room service, business services, conference facilities, historical tours, free airport transportation, and a car rental desk. 1200 Anastasia Ave., Coral Gables (phone: 445-1926; 800-727-1926 or 800-228-3000; fax: 448-9976).

Eden Roc With the addition of a world class spa, a conference center, and the complete renovation of its 350 rooms, this property has been restored to its former dominance on Miami Beach's hotel scene. The facility has two restaurants, five bars, and two swimming pools. The state-of-the-art spa is also the site of an indoor sports club equipped with squash, basketball, and racquetball courts, as well as the only rock-climbing wall in South Florida. Scenes from Sean Connery's 1995 film *Just Cause* were filmed in the lobby area and penthouse suite, and Madonna is shown enveloped in the hotel's aqua bed linen on the cover of her 1995 album "Bedtime Stories." 4525 Collins Ave., Miami Beach (phone: 531-0000; 800-327-8337; fax: 531-6955).

Fontainebleau Hilton Resort & Towers This Miami Beach grande dame, with 1,206 guestrooms on 20 acres of beachfront real estate, is still glamorous. The lagoon-like pool has a grotto bar inside a cave; there are also three whirlpool baths. The 12 restaurants and lounges include *Kamon,* a Japanese steakhouse and sushi bar, and a kosher kitchen. There's also a fully equipped *Spa Pavilion* and seven night-lit tennis courts with pro shop. Business services are available. 4441 Collins Ave., Miami Beach (phone: 538-2000; 800-548-8886 in Florida; 800-HILTONS elsewhere in the US; fax: 532-8145).

Impala One of the best historic renovations on Miami Beach, this 60-year-old Spanish-Mediterranean–style boutique hotel set back one block from the beach boasts fine European service. The 17 rooms and three suites have eclectic furnishings and original artwork; amenities include imported cotton linens, oversized baths, stereos with CD players, speaker phones with voice mail, and computer data ports. *Cafe Impala,* an Italian eatery under separate management, recently opened here. 1228 Collins Ave., Miami Beach (phone: 673-2021; 800-646-7252; fax: 673-5984).

Inter-Continental Miami Built in the grand old hotel tradition, this property is in the city center, near the Brickell Avenue financial district and *Bayside Marketplace.* The 644 rooms in the soaring 34-floor travertine triangle have marble baths and modern furnishings with Oriental accents. Former President George Bush and actor Eddie Murphy are among those who have stayed in the two-story Royal Suite. The lobby, with its 18-foot Henry Moore sculpture, is all beige and bone travertine marble, accented with green rattan furniture and area rugs. There are three restaurants, including the highly regarded *Le Pavillon* and the *Royal Palm Court.* For the fitness-minded there's a swimming pool plus an outdoor jogging trail that takes advantage of the stunning views of Biscayne Bay; three floors are reserved for nonsmokers. Business services are available. 100 Chopin Plaza, Miami (phone: 577-1000; 800-327-0200; fax: 577-0384 or 377-3002).

Marlin This Art Deco District hostelry combines 1930s architecture with 1990s amenities in 12 suites complete with kitchens and VCRs. The decor in the public rooms is "Jam-Deco"—classic Art Deco design with hot Jamaican colors. The hotel was developed by Chris Blackwell, founder of Island Records, who included a recording studio on the premises, attracting lots of show-biz types. The *Shabeen* restaurant serves Jamaican food, the bar specializes in exotic drinks, and the beach is just a block away. 1200 Collins Ave., Miami Beach (phone: 673-8770; 800-688-7678; fax: 673-9609).

Pelican In an area where visual excitement is coin of the realm for hoteliers, this place is true to its fashion roots. Owned by Diesel Jeans International, each of the hotel's 25 rooms has a unique decor, from 1950s subthemes to Hollywood plush; the rooms also have oak floors, ceiling fans, CD players, refrigerators, and safes. The penthouse suite ($2,000 a night) occupies the top floor. Public areas include a bar (with TV sets in the men's room) and the *Pelican Cafe,* serving Mediterranean specialties. 826 Ocean Dr., Miami Beach (phone: 673-3373; 800-7-PELICAN; fax: 673-3255).

MODERATE

Beekman Located in Surfside, a cozy oceanside village north of Miami Beach, this 12-story, all-suite hotel offers lodging options that are ideal for families. Studios and one- and two-bedroom apartments are available, all with balconies and fully equipped kitchens. A 150-foot beach is at your doorstep; shopping, tennis, theaters, and restaurants are within walking distance. Complimentary breakfast is served daily in the *Beekman Cafe.* 9499 Collins Ave., Surfside (phone: 861-4801; 800-237-9367; fax: 865-5971).

Cavalier Built in 1936, this 41-room property has a Jamaican-inspired decor done in tangerine, turquoise, and pink. Many rooms have canopy beds; all feature cable TV, VCRs, CD players, and in-closet safes. There's no restaurant on the premises, but there are plenty of eateries nearby. The beach is just across the street. 1320 Ocean Dr., Miami Beach (phone: 534-2135; 800-338-9076; fax: 531-5543).

Miami Airport Hilton Located on a lagoon, the 500-room hostelry offers a pool, a Jacuzzi, a sauna, jet and water skiing (for a fee), and free use of three lighted tennis courts and a lighted basketball court. There's also a concierge floor, restaurant, café/pool grill, nightclub, and bar. Ten floors are reserved for nonsmokers. Free parking and free transportation to the airport are available. 5101 Blue Lagoon Dr., Miami (phone: 262-1000; 800-HILTONS; fax: 267-0038).

Place St. Michel Charming, cozy, and elegant describe this 27-room European-style bed and breakfast establishment built in 1926. In the heart of Coral Gables, it's favored by international architects who appreciate its Art Deco details and antique furnishings. On the premises is *Stuart's,* a jazz bar; *St. Michel,* an excellent dining spot; and a deli that's popular with the local lunch crowd. Continental breakfast is included, room service is available until 11 PM, and there's an obliging concierge desk. 162 Alcazar Ave., Coral Gables (phone: 444-1666; 800-848-HOTEL; fax: 529-0074).

Sol Miami Beach Originally the *Cadillac* hotel, this 271-room, oceanfront property (ca. 1938) is owned by the Spain-based Grupo Sol. The cool turquoise and blue Deco exterior belies its glitzy interior, which features plum and yellow, with lots of neon. There are two restaurants and two lounges. Some units have kitchenettes; all have cable TV. For action, there's a pool, a fitness center, shuffleboard courts, and water sports. Business services are available. 3925 Collins Ave., Miami Beach (phone: 531-3534; 800-336-3542 or 800-531-3534; fax: 531-1765).

INEXPENSIVE

Leslie Another vintage 1930s hotel in South Beach, this one offers 43 rooms decorated in vivid Art Deco prints and equipped with cable TV, VCRs, and CD players. The *Leslie Cafe* has an eclectic menu. Located across the street from the beach. 1244 Ocean Dr., Miami Beach (phone: 534-2135; 800-338-9076; fax: 531-5543).

Miami River Inn Claiming to be the oldest continuously operating inn south of St. Augustine, this charming bed and breakfast establishment on the Miami River was built in 1906. The 40 antiques-furnished rooms in four wooden buildings and the lushly planted pool and whirlpool area make guests feel like they're in another place and time. Close to the *Center for the Fine Arts, Historical Museum,* and *Bayside Marketplace,* the inn is protected by security gates at night. Complimentary continental breakfast is served. Off-street parking is available. 118 SW South River Dr., entrance on SW Second St., Miami (phone: 325-0045; 800-468-3589; fax: 325-9227).

Paradise Inn Located one block from the beach, this two-story motel with a Key lime façade trimmed in orange is a budgeter's delight, with 45 basic and clean rooms and another 45 efficiency units with kitchenettes. All feature remote-control satellite TV and in-room safes. The quietest rooms face the inner courtyards. There's a pool, free parking, complimentary continental breakfast, and laundry facilities, but no restaurant. 8520 Harding Ave., Miami Beach (phone: 865-6216; fax: 865-9028).

Ritz Plaza This 1940s-style hostelry, with its much-photographed Art Deco squared finial, has been restored to its early splendor, with a soaring lobby featuring the original four-color terrazzo floor and a front desk made of coral—one of the few such pieces extant. The 132 rooms and suites retain a 1940s look and feel, with such period details as the original cast-iron tubs (now modernized). Though a bit small and without any views, the standard rooms are great values. An Olympic-size pool overlooks the ocean, and water sports are also available. Meals are served on the terrace and in the *Ritz Café,* a high-ceilinged dining room with a huge crystal chandelier and a window wall facing the ocean. *Harry's Bar* has a vintage look—with lots of chrome and a jukebox playing 1950s music—and offers a light menu. Guests often include photography crews shooting fashion assignments nearby. Near the *Miami Beach Convention Center,* 1701 Collins Ave., Miami Beach (phone: 534-3500; 800-522-6400; fax: 531-6928).

EATING OUT

Much of Miami's socializing centers on eating out, so be prepared for long lines from December through April, when visitors swell the ranks of restaurant diners. Expect to pay $85 or more for a dinner for two at places in the very expensive category; $65 to $85 at places in the expensive category; $40 to $65 at restaurants in the moderate range; and less than $40 at eateries in the inexpensive range. Prices do not include drinks, wine, taxes, or tips. All telephone numbers are in the 305 area code.

Unless otherwise noted, restaurants are open for lunch and dinner.

Biltmore Café The gastronomic choices are legend at this restaurant's Sunday all-you-can-eat-for-$39.95-a-person brunch ($45 on holidays). To begin with, there are raw oysters, jumbo shrimp, smoked fish, belly lox, three different types of caviar, four types of pâté, raspberry blintzes, eggs Benedict, all types of salads, fresh baked breads and pastries, and pasta. What makes this brunch unique are some unusual extras—grilled Maine lobsters, a sushi and sashimi bar, rack of lamb, a Häagen-Dazs ice-cream sundae station, and a lavishly hedonistic pastry table. Everything is perfect, from the champagne and freshly squeezed orange-juice mimosas to the courtyard setting, complete with ice sculptures, a gurgling fountain, and a jazz-playing trio. Bring your appetite. Open Sundays from 11 AM to 4 PM. Reservations necessary. Major credit cards accepted. At the *Biltmore Hotel,* 1200 Anastasia Ave., Coral Gables (phone: 445-1926; 800-727-1926).

Chef Allen's Chef/owner Allen Susser has won deserved national acclaim for his culinary achievements. Featured here is regional South Florida cooking, using local produce and fresh-caught yellowtail, tuna, and snapper. The menu changes daily and may include whole-wheat linguine with lobster or Florida bay scallop ceviche with cilantro. Even the salad of field greens is beautifully presented, with confetti-like squares of colorful peppers. Among the specialties are roasted veal chops enhanced by the accompanying ginger-baked *calabaza* (a pumpkin-like vegetable). The white-chocolate–macadamia-nut mousse is as rewarding to the eyes as it is to the taste buds. The decor—handmade Italian furniture and pink neon lights—is as upbeat, fresh, and sophisticated as the food. Open daily for dinner. Reservations advised. Major credit cards accepted. 19088 NE 29th Ave., North Miami Beach (phone: 935-2900).

Fish Market Far more elegant than its name implies, this is possibly South Florida's best seafood restaurant. In the *Crowne Plaza Miami* hotel, the two-room dining area gleams with marble and mirrors. You can order just about any kind of fish grilled, with a broad choice of sauces, but the kitchen also performs magic with such specialties as colossal shrimp (Central American crustaceans as large as baby lobster tails, yet succulent and tender) and grilled snapper with buckwheat pasta. The superb sole filets are stuffed with Florida lobster, mussels, and wild mushrooms, and the sumptuous scallops and medaillons of lobster are served with *risotto milanese* (Italian short-grain rice with saffron). For a special treat, try the pâté of tropical fruits and berries with passion-fruit sauce for dessert. Businesspeople love the "executive service" lunch, when a two-course meal is served in less than 30 minutes or there's no charge. Closed Saturday lunch and Sundays. Reservations advised. Major credit cards accepted. In the *Crown Plaza Miami Hotel,* 1601 Biscayne Blvd., Miami (phone: 374-0000).

Forge Once more famous for its 300,000-bottle wine collection and its elegance than for its complex dishes, this ornately decorated restaurant—adorned with antique furniture, stained glass, carved ceilings, and crystal chandeliers—has ditched its stodgy steaks and chops for more imaginative, continental fare, including roast duck with black currant sauce. For dessert, regulars love the famed blacksmith pie—alternating layers of chocolate cake, French vanilla custard, and whipped cream—but don't bypass the chocolate cheesecake. Open daily for dinner. Reservations necessary. Major credit cards accepted. 432 Arthur Godfrey Rd., Miami Beach (phone: 538-8533).

Grand Café This elegantly European bi-level dining room celebrates both romance and business with style, attentive service, and wonderful culinary creations. Recommended appetizers include the renowned fresh spinach risotto with *porcini* mushrooms and mascarpone cheese. Incredible entrées range from black bean–encrusted rare tuna with lemongrass sauce to grilled Maine lobster with cilantro zinfandel sauce. Leave room for the dark chocolate–and-praline *crousillant* (a small round confection consisting of layered hazelnut cake, crisp caramel, dark chocolate mousse, and chocolate *ganache*). Open daily for breakfast, lunch, and dinner; brunch served Sundays. Reservations necessary for dinner, advised for other meals. Major credit cards accepted. In the *Grand Bay Hotel,* 2669 S. Bayshore Dr., Coconut Grove (phone: 858-9600).

Joe's Stone Crab Don't miss this, the ultimate Miami dining experience. Since 1913 the place has been selling tons of the best stone crabs around, along with scrumptious home fries, delectable creamed spinach, and to-die-for Key lime pie. Diners who don't arrive early often have to wait hours to be seated, and service can be rushed and sporadic, but devoted fans say it's well worth the wait—though even that has improved since the completion in 1995 of a multimillion-dollar expansion that includes a parking garage. Besides the crabs, lobster and fresh fish are served. Picnickers can buy lunch from the restaurant's expanded take-out section (with separate entrance) and avoid the lunacy of the dining room. Closed Sunday lunch and from mid-May through mid-October. No reservations. Major credit cards accepted. 227 Biscayne St., Miami Beach (phone: 673-0365; 800-780-CRAB).

Mark's Place The modern interior—dramatized by vibrant contemporary glass sculptures—serves as an exciting backdrop for this Miami "in" spot. Mark Militello, acclaimed as one of the best chefs in the nation, is on the cutting edge of the movement to merge Caribbean and tropical ingredients with classic European techniques. He whips up such imaginative dishes as grilled yellowtail snapper with Mediterranean salsa; West Indian pumpkin and hearts of palm; and salmon with couscous and crispy leeks. The rich desserts include a terrific apple tart. Closed for lunch weekends. Reservations necessary. Major credit cards accepted. 2286 NE 123rd St., North Miami Beach (phone: 893-6888).

Norman's Chef Norman Van Aken's latest venture (he's formerly of *Louie's Back Yard* in Key West and *A Mano* in South Beach) features a split-level dining room washed in earth tones. This intimate setting with a woodburning oven fuses the flavors of the Caribbean, Latin America, Asia, and a few culinary innovations of Van Akens own. The menu changes daily, but popular signature dishes include island French toast (foie gras marinated in liqueur, vanilla bean, and citrus) served with a variety of sauces and Key West yellowtail with asparagus spears, citrus butter, and mashed potatoes. Finish your meal off with a Venezuelan love triangle made with three types of chocolate. Closed for lunch on Saturdays and Sundays. Reservations recommended. Major credit cards accepted. 21 Almeria Ave., Coral Gables (phone: 446-6767).

Osteria del Teatro This trendy, crowded spot consistently serves exquisite Italian food with French overtones, attracting movie stars, models, and locals who consider it one of the best restaurants (if not *the* best) on South Beach. Anything on the menu is sure to be excellent, especially the mixed seafood grill. While the early crowd tends to be older and more conservative, the late crowd is the hippest in town. Open for dinner; closed Tuesdays. Reservations necessary. Major credit cards accepted. 1443 Washington Ave., Miami Beach (phone: 538-7850).

Yuca The name derives from both a Miami acronym for Young Upscale Cuban-Americans and a starchy vegetable ("yucca" in English) that is a staple of Cuban cooking. The award-winning restaurant is decorated in gradations of white to beige, providing a subtle backdrop for the chef's visually spectacular creations. The innovative bilingual menu features nouvelle twists on Cuban standards—sweet plantains stuffed with dried cured beef and *salsa verde* (forget what it sounds like; your mouth will thank you), excellent pan-seared yellowtail filet dusted with cumin and pumpkin seeds and served with *poblano* mashed potatoes, and filet of salmon with pistachio-encrusted coconut rice, sweet corn *arepa,* and avocado vinaigrette. Chocoholics will adore the *tres leches de chocolate,* a milk-soaked cake layered with mousse and covered with chocolate meringue. You can diet tomorrow. Reservations advised. Major credit cards accepted. 501 Lincoln Rd., Miami Beach (phone: 532-YUCA).

EXPENSIVE

Max's South Beach When Miami Beach became too fashionable to be ignored, famed Boca Raton restaurateur Dennis Max looked south. Enlisting chef Kerry Simon, Max soon had another hit on his hands by combining America's popular healthy foods with exotic flavorings from the Far East and Latin America. The restaurant exemplifies the local postmodern style with its dim lighting, mahogany bar, sleek banquettes, high ceilings, and a wait staff of model types. Like most South Beach restaurants, this one is almost painfully noisy, but the food and the experience are worth it. Open daily for dinner. Reservations necessary. Major credit cards accepted. 764 Washington Ave., Miami Beach (phone: 532-0070).

Mayfair Grille Allen Susser of *Chef Allen* fame had a hand in the revamping of this favorite Miami dining spot, and his touch is most evident in the menu. New World fare is served in an elegant atmosphere; specialties are Nantucket bay scallops with lobster polenta and scallion cream, stone crab cassoulet with conch, and rock shrimp with seafood sausage. Open daily for breakfast, lunch, and dinner. Reservations advised for lunch and dinner. Major credit cards accepted. In the *Mayfair House Hotel,* 3000 Florida Ave., Coconut Grove (phone: 441-0000).

Pacific Time Housed in an Art Deco building in Lincoln Road's pedestrian mall, this tall-ceilinged space is a terrific spot for people watching, whether you're inside or at one of the white-linen covered tables set up on the sidewalk outside (where it's quieter). But the real attraction here is the food: Chefs Jonathan Eismann and Yves Picot prepare nouvelle American fare with Asian influences. Among the best entrées are Szechuan grilled black grouper, sweet sake–roasted sea bass, and yellowfin tuna with sushi bar flavors. Open daily for dinner. Reservations necessary. Major credit cards accepted. 915 Lincoln Rd., Miami Beach (phone: 534-5979).

Rusty Pelican For a dynamite view of Downtown Miami across the bay, visit this nautically decorated spot. Meals range from burgers and prime ribs of beef to seafood and tropical fruits. Open daily; brunch served on Sundays. Reservations advised. Major credit cards accepted. 3201 Rickenbacker Causeway, Key Biscayne (phone: 361-3818).

Victor's Café Even in its heyday, Havana didn't offer a restaurant as spectacular as this New Cuban eatery, where Key stone columns, terra cotta tiles, light woods, and a gurgling fountain re-create a Cuban plantation house courtyard—only it's indoors, beneath a three-story-high glass dome. The fare is a blend of the flavors, spices, and dishes of the several cultures that settled in Cuba—traditional Spanish, with Chinese, French creole, African, and Taino Indian influences. Begin with a *mojíto* (a delightful house rum drink with crushed mint) or the white sangria. In season, choose the fresh jumbo stone crabs. Year-round specialties include *maravilla de catibia quesadillas* (yucca flour quesadillas filled with creole spiced shrimp), cassava turnovers filled with Florida lobster fricassee, and yucca French fries served with an out-of-this-world cilantro sauce. Beef dishes include sirloin prepared with adobo (a flavorful herb sauce) and served with creamy polenta, and oak-grilled *churrasco* (skirt steak). Seafood lovers can feast on fresh mahimahi filets marinated in *mojo* (a dark, spicy sauce), shellfish casseroles, and shrimp quenelles. The ambience is both romantic and exotic, with strolling guitarists serenading the guests. A Latin band entertains nightly in the *Rumba* lounge, with its popular happy hour and late night *tapas* bar. The same people own

New York City's *Victor's Café.* Reservations necessary. Major credit cards accepted. 2340 SW 32nd Ave., Coral Gables (phone: 445-1313).

MODERATE

Brasserie L'Entrecôte You'll feel like you're in Paris at this traditional French bistro, which is decorated with hand-painted country tiles and brass and mahogany appointments, and has a terrace that overlooks the *Mayfair Shops in the Grove.* The restaurant, which received a "best French restaurant award" from *South Florida* magazine in 1995, offers an exquisite menu. Favorites are the *L'Entrecôte* steak with mushrooms and *pommes frites,* and blackened swordfish. Leave room for the *crème brûlée*. Reservations advised for dinner on Fridays and Saturdays. Major credit cards accepted. 2901 Florida Ave., Coconut Grove (phone: 444-9697).

Centro Vasco Next to jai alai, this is Miami's favorite Basque import. The present owner's father started this restaurant in Havana, then moved it to Miami when Castro came into power. He replicated the traditional Spanish decor, huge portions, and authentic menu, attracting such notable diners as Ronald Reagan, Jimmy Carter, and John Glenn. Specialties are a classic black bean soup that's arguably the best this side of Cuba, seafood paella (clams, lobster, shrimp, and sea bass in a succulent sauce, served over seasoned yellow rice), *rabo encendido* (braised oxtail simmered in a rich red wine sauce), and sea bass served broiled, grilled, baked, or fried. A great sangria is made right at your table. Save room for the *leche frita* (a flan-like fried milk dessert). On weekends there's entertainment in three different rooms, ranging from Latin-jazz bands to flamenco shows to comedians. Open daily for lunch, dinner, and late night *tapas.* Reservations advised for dinner. Major credit cards accepted. 2235 Calle Ocho (Eighth St.), Miami (phone: 643-9606).

Le Festival Dinner at this French restaurant is to be savored. From the plush decor to the outstanding fare, it's one of Miami's finest. Rack of lamb, veal scaloppine in brandy cream sauce, Dover sole, and chateaubriand are favorites. On Thursdays, wild game such as venison is available. The extensive wine list includes Chilean and Spanish selections. Closed Saturday lunch and Sundays. Reservations advised. Major credit cards accepted. 2120 Salzedo St., Coral Gables (phone: 442-8545).

Kaleidoscope Here fine dining is in a romantic enclosed atrium, on a balcony, or in an air conditioned dining room. Menu high points include Bahamian seafood griddle cakes, grilled grouper, bouillabaisse, and fresh fruit tarts with almond pastry made on the premises. Reservations advised. Major credit cards accepted. 3112 Commodore Plaza, Second Floor, Coconut Grove (phone: 446-5010).

Monty's Stone Crab Casual and known for serving stone crabs year-round (they're brought in from Virginia during the local off-season), this place also offers a wide array of fresh seafood, steaks, and pasta. Guests can eat dockside at picnic tables, or indoors in a setting with lots of glass windows and a view of the bay. Reservations advised. Major credit cards accepted. 2550 S. Bayshore Dr., Coconut Grove (phone: 858-1431).

Las Puertas Here's the place to sample imaginative cuisine in a cozy atmosphere. Dishes have Mexican and Aztec accents: Favorites are lean duck breast *fajitas;* tortilla soup flavored with onion, tomato, carrots, and cilantro and served with *ancho* chili and avocado; and *cochinita pibil,* tender pork stewed in banana leaves with achiote seasoning and sour oranges and topped with chorizo. Open daily for dinner; closed Saturdays and Sundays for lunch. Reservations advised. Major credit cards accepted. 148 Giralda Ave., Coral Gables (phone: 442-0708).

Purple Dolphin Dine either in front of a large mural of frolicking dolphins or on the atrium terrace, which is decked out with potted palms and other tropical greenery. There's live music in the evenings. Hummus and *tapenade* (an addictive black olive, garlic, and anchovy dip) are placed on every table along with freshly baked rolls. Try the seared salmon with black bean salsa and crispy green plantains; meat lovers can choose from rack of lamb with a spinach and goat cheese tart and rosemary sauce, or beef tenderloin medaillons with wild mushroom ragout and potato-leek sauce. Reserve early for Friday's fabulous, reasonably priced, all-you-can-eat seafood buffet. And last but not least, the desserts are to die for. Open daily for breakfast, lunch, and dinner. Reservations advised for weekend dinners. Major credit cards accepted. In the *Sonesta Beach Key Biscayne Hotel,* 350 Ocean Dr., Key Biscayne (phone: 361-2021).

South Pointe Seafood House Seafood lovers will find no disappointments at this casual wood-beamed, wharf-styled, Old Florida eatery with 10 dining rooms, each decked out with Tiffany lamps, Victorian curtains, and rustic appointments. There's jumbo shrimp wrapped in bacon; whitewater clams steamed with garlic, corn relish, and *ancho* chili butter; fresh stone crab claws; and champagne-poached salmon. For those who want to try it all, there are four different seafood combination platters. Sweets include homemade Key lime pie and apple-walnut upside-down pie with cinnamon ice cream. A microbrewery is on the premises. Open daily; brunch served on Sundays. Reservations advised. Major credit cards accepted. 1 Washington Ave., Miami Beach (phone: 673-1708).

Toni's Sushi Bar Japanese interpretations of grilled salmon, chicken, and steaks, along with shrimp teriyaki, are among the highlights here. The sushi is the best on South Beach. Open daily for dinner. Reservations necessary on weekends. Major credit cards accepted. 1208 Washington Ave., Miami Beach (phone: 673-9368).

Café Tu-Tu Tango In the *CocoWalk* complex, this jumping eatery decked out as an artist's loft touts its eclectic *tapas*-style specialties as "food for the starving artist." It offers light, multiethnic dishes such as frittatas (Italian omelettes), pizza, smoked-chicken quesadillas, and kebabs. Entrées are appetizer-sized, so most people order three or more to share. Open daily for lunch, dinner, and late snacks. No reservations. Major credit cards accepted. 3015 Grand Ave., Coconut Grove (phone: 529-2222).

Dan Marino's American Sports Bar & Grill This is a sports fan's heaven, with 41 television screens, football paraphernalia lining the walls, and pool tables, dart boards, and video games. The bill of fare includes steaks, seafood, pasta, burgers, and salads. Occasionally you'll spot the famous Miami *Dolphins* quarterback himself. Reservations unnecessary. Major credit cards accepted. In *CocoWalk,* 3015 Grand Ave., Coconut Grove (phone: 567-0013).

11th Street Diner This 1948 diner traveled from its home in Wilkes-Barre, Pennsylvania, to trendy South Beach. Old-fashioned favorites such as black cows (root beer floats) and meat loaf and gravy are served, as are such modern dishes as Cobb salad and grilled dolphin. Open daily 24 hours. No reservations. Major credit cards accepted. 1065 Washington Ave., Miami (phone: 534-6373).

Málaga Located in Little Havana, this traditional Cuban eatery, a favorite gathering spot for Miami's politicians and business executives, is a good place to get acquainted with the island basics. Best are standards like fried whole red snapper, spiced pork, or *arroz con pollo* (rice with chicken). The fried plantains are a must-try. There's live musical entertainment Fridays and Saturdays. Reservations advised. Major credit cards accepted. 740 Calle Ocho (SW Eighth St.), Miami (phone: 854-9101 or 858-4224).

News Café An international newsstand-cum-sidewalk café that's an ideal spot for people watching or a pre-beach breakfast. The menu is light, with sandwiches, salads, cheeses, and Middle Eastern fare. Open daily 24 hours. Reservations unnecessary. Major credit cards accepted. Located across from the ocean in the heart of South Beach. 800 Ocean Dr., Miami Beach (phone: 538-6397).

Planet Hollywood Hollywood memorabilia, some of it huge (such as Arnold Schwarzenegger's *Terminator II* motorcycle), is suspended from the ceilings, the walls, and the columns, while four giant TV screens show film clips. The food—primarily pizza, sandwiches, and salads—is better than you'd expect and there's often a line on Fridays and Saturdays. Perhaps you'll catch a glimpse of one of the famous owners such as Schwarzenegger, Bruce Willis, or Sylvester Stallone. Reservations necessary for large parties. Major credit cards accepted. In the *Mayfair Shops in the Grove* complex, 3390 Mary St., Coconut Grove (phone: 445-7277).

Rascal House This is one of only two Florida restaurants to make food guru Mimi Sheraton's list of the 50 best US restaurants (the other is *Mark's Place*, above). Lines snaking into the parking lot attest to the delicatessen's popularity for almost 41 years. Try the pastrami on rye or the *rugelach.* Open daily for breakfast, lunch, dinner, and late snacks. No reservations. Major credit cards accepted. 17190 Collins Ave., Miami Beach (phone: 947-4581).

Tap Tap For years, Miami's thriving Haitian community has been overlooked on the culinary scene, but this place may change all that. This small eatery (named for the elaborately decorated buses that ply the countryside of Haiti) is painted with brightly colored Caribbean murals that just plain make you happy. Favorite dishes include grilled fish marinated in chili, blue crab and vegetable soup (in season), and the traditional goat grilled over *boukannen,* the hardwood and charcoal fire that dates from precolonial days. Reservations unnecessary. Major credit cards accepted. 819 Fifth St., Miami Beach (phone: 672-2898).

Tropical Chinese Despite its inauspicious location in a suburban shopping center near an expressway, this place serves the best dim sum in town. Chinese families from all over Miami flock here on weekends to sample these delicate appetizer-size dumplings, which are served one after another as they emerge from the kitchen. Save room for entrées if you can; the baby clams in fresh basil sauce and noodle dishes are first-rate. Reservations advised. Major credit cards accepted. 7991 SW 40th St., west of Palmetto Expressway (phone: 262-7576).

Unicorn Village An outstanding natural-food restaurant and marketplacc, it's on a marina with dockage for diners arriving by boat. Dining is either inside or out. Creative salads, low-fat and low-sodium dishes, vegetarian lasagna and other pasta, plus fish and stir-fry dishes are featured. A large selection of by-the-glass wines includes seven organically produced choices (with no added sulfites). Note: This is a totally nonsmoking place. Open daily; brunch is served Sundays. No reservations. Major credit cards accepted. At *The Shops at the Waterways,* 3595 NE 207th St., North Miami Beach (phone: 933-8829).

Wolfie's A Miami Beach institution since 1947, it might be described as an overgrown deli. The eclectic, 500-item menu carries everything from knishes to chicken parmesan and mountainous desserts. Open daily 24 hours. No reservations. Major credit cards accepted. 2038 Collins Ave., Miami Beach (phone: 538-6626).

Milwaukee

Milwaukee is the sort of place that grows on you gradually, like contentment with a cold glass of beer. And beer is the word you immediately associate with Milwaukee. Miller and Pabst, two of the nation's largest breweries—and several microbreweries—still flourish here, and residents loyally claim they consume more beer than anyone else in America.

The city's role as a lake port was primarily responsible for its early growth. Here, Lake Michigan receives the waters of the Milwaukee, Menominee, and Kinnickinnic Rivers. With so much water around, it's not surprising that Milwaukee used to be a swamp. But the resourceful pioneers who arrived in 1833 discovered plenty of gravel left by a departing glacier 10,000 years earlier. They were fast with a shovel, and before long New Englanders were parceling off Milwaukee real estate and selling it to each other.

Sailing ships brought immigrants in the 19th century—the Irish, fleeing the potato famine; the Germans, including those who left home after the abortive revolutions of 1848; and a variety of other groups, among them the Poles, now Milwaukee's second-largest ethnic community. (The Poles gave the city kielbasa—sausage—a dietary staple on the South Side.)

During the latter half of the 19th century, Milwaukee called itself the German Athens. As late as the 1880s, two out of every three Milwaukee residents chose to read and speak the language of Goethe. The city's Germanic era ended in a flurry of divided loyalties and ill will during World War I. The Deutscher Club changed its name to the Wisconsin Club, sauerkraut became liberty cabbage, and the Germania Building was called the Brumder Building (it took back its original name several years ago).

With a downtown district that seems too small for a metropolitan population of 1.4 million and an Old World respect for homey virtues and tidy streets, Milwaukee seems like an overgrown small town. Where else but at *Milwaukee County Stadium* would a bratwurst be nearly as popular with hungry baseball fans as a hot dog? A bratwurst on a poppy seed roll in one hand, a beer in the other, and the home team hitting homers—now that's Milwaukee living!

But there is lots more to the city than sauerbraten and suds. Milwaukee's lakefront has been compared to the Bay of Naples—not, it must be admitted, by the Neapolitans, but by the people who live here. Much of the shore belongs to the public, and many of the local residents fish there for everything from smelt to coho salmon. When the weather is warm, the beaches within five minutes of downtown are crowded, even though Lake Michigan is generally too chilly for leisurely swimming. (Even in July and August, sweaters are not uncommon.) However, at noon on *New Year's Day,* several hundred members of the *Polar Bear Club* jump, dive, and cavort in the lake—regardless of the temperature.

Everyone celebrates the annual opening of Wisconsin's deer season, with thousands of hunters scurrying toward the woods and North Country taverns. Milwaukee County is proud of its park system, its zoo, its golf courses, and horticultural exhibits in glass domes that rise south of the Menominee Valley. The *Milwaukee Symphony* plays at the *Performing Arts Center,* and there are first-rate repertory and avant-garde drama companies. A downtown natural history museum and an art museum on the lakefront augment the city's cultural life. Milwaukee works hard to uphold its tradition of honest politicians and upright public servants, so urban problems don't seem as severe as they do in many other cities.

Still, Milwaukee is no San Francisco, New Orleans, or New York. And ever since a certain rival lakeport emerged as a major US metropolis, it's been clear it's no Chicago. But the people who live in the city that made beer famous take comfort in that.

Milwaukee At-a-Glance

SEEING THE CITY

Good overviews of the city can be seen from the revolving *Polaris* restaurant atop the *Hyatt Regency* and from the *La Playa* lounge at the *Pfister* hotel (see *Checking In* for details on both hotels).

SPECIAL PLACES

The Milwaukee River divides the downtown area into east and west segments of unequal size (walking east you soon run into the beautiful Lake Michigan shoreline).

DOWNTOWN WEST

WISCONSIN AVENUE WEST Walking west from the river along Wisconsin Avenue, Milwaukee's principal shopping street, you pass *Marshall Field* on the same site that John Plankinton, a pioneer butcher, started his career with one cow and boundless ambition. He became a millionaire, and gave a start to packing tycoons Philip Armour and Patrick Cudahy. The blocks between *Marshall Field* and the *Boston Store* have been converted into the *Grand Avenue* shopping mall.

GRAND AVENUE The center of downtown shopping is the stretch of renovated buildings between Plankinton Avenue and North Fourth Street. The project brought the neighborhood back to life with its airy feel, a hub of fast-food restaurants, and lots of shops. Jugglers, mimes, pianists, choral groups, and other entertainers often perform at various locales (phone: 224-9720).

JOAN OF ARC CHAPEL On the campus of *Marquette University* is the medieval chapel where Joan of Arc prayed before being burned at the stake—not here in Milwaukee but in the French village of Chasse, whence the chapel was transported stone by stone. One of those stones reputedly was kissed by

CENTRAL
MILWAUKEE
NORTH AV
FOND DU LAC AV
GARFIELD AV
LLOYD ST
Carver Park
BROWN ST
RESERVOIR ST
VINE ST
JIRAN PL
North-South Frwy
WALNUT ST
GALENA ST
Schlitz Brewery
CHERRY ST
VLIET ST
WINNEBAGO ST
Martin Luther King Park
MCKINLEY AV
PABST BREWERY
JUNEAU AV
HIGHLAND AV
STATE ST
Court House
Post Office
Auditorium
Arena
KILBOURN AV
Milwaukee Public Museum
Convention Center
Bus Terminal
WELLS ST
State Office Blg
Public Library
Court of Honor
Bus Terminals
WISCONSIN AV
Boston Store
MARQUETTE UNIVERSITY
Joan of Arc Chapel
MICHIGAN ST
MARTIN LUTHER KING ST
CLYBOURN ST
East-West Expwy
ST PAUL ST
Union (Amtrak) Sta
MUSKEGO AV
Menomonee River
FLORIDA ST
VIRGINIA ST
BRUCE ST
43
794
94

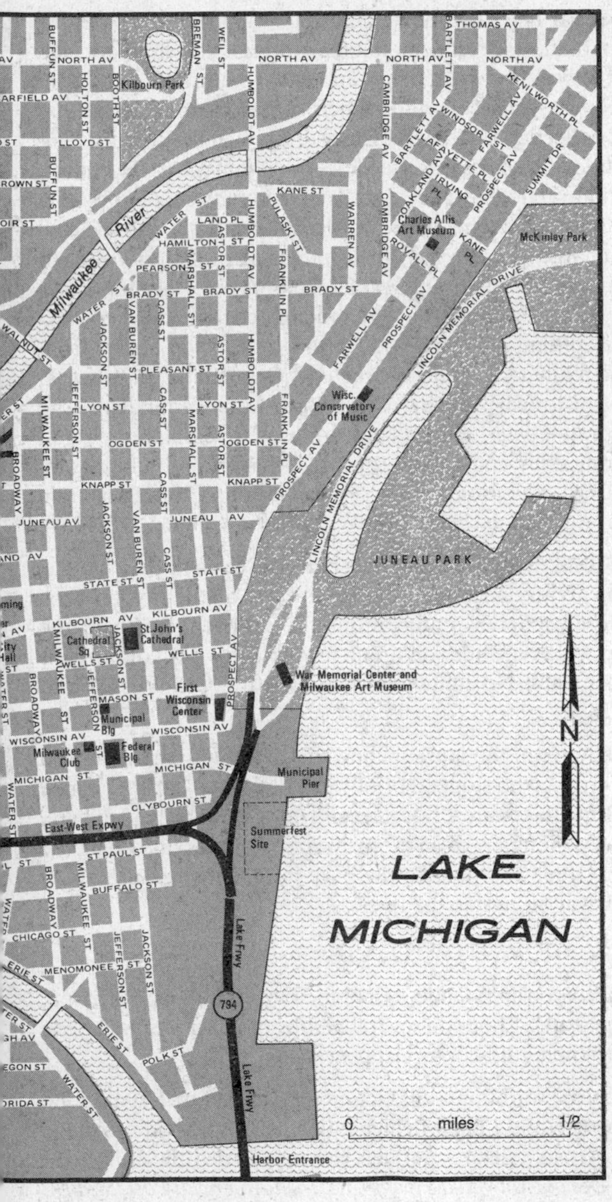
LAKE
MICHIGAN
JUNEAU PARK
McKinley Park
Kilbourn Park
Milwaukee River
Charles Allis Art Museum
Wisc. Conservatory of Music
War Memorial Center and Milwaukee Art Museum
St. John's Cathedral
Cathedral Sq
City Hall
First Wisconsin Center
Municipal Blg
Federal Blg
Milwaukee Club
Municipal Pier
Summerfest Site
East-West Expwy
Lake Frwy
794
Harbor Entrance
LINCOLN MEMORIAL DRIVE
PROSPECT AV
NORTH AV
THOMAS AV
KANE ST
BRADY ST
PLEASANT ST
LYON ST
OGDEN ST
KNAPP ST
JUNEAU AV
STATE ST
KILBOURN AV
WELLS ST
MASON ST
WISCONSIN AV
MICHIGAN ST
CLYBOURN ST
ST PAUL ST
BUFFALO ST
CHICAGO ST
MENOMONEE ST
ERIE ST
POLK ST
WATER ST
HUMBOLDT AV
FARWELL AV
CAMBRIDGE AV
FRANKLIN PL
JACKSON ST
JEFFERSON ST
MILWAUKEE ST
BROADWAY
VAN BUREN ST
CASS ST
MARSHALL ST
ASTOR ST
N
0 miles 1/2

Joan before she went to her death, and is said to be discernibly colder than the others. Open daily except major holidays. Regular Roman Catholic church services are still conducted. 601 N. 14th St. (phone: 288-6873).

MILWAUKEE PUBLIC MUSEUM The basic theme here is how humans and other living creatures adapt to the environment, but there are a lot of variations, and exhibits relate not only to history, geology, and world cultures of the distant past, but also to Native Americans and aspects of American society. It has the fourth-largest collection of natural history displays in the country. This sprawling institution really shines when it comes to dioramas. At a Northwest Coast Indian exhibition, for instance, smells and sounds envelop visitors from all sides. In the Great Plains area, a rattlesnake rattles a warning, and when the buffalo charge, you can hear the thundering of their hooves getting louder and louder. Particularly interesting is the *Streets of Old Milwaukee* section, where the 19th-century city has been re-created, right down to flickering gaslights, telephone poles wrapped with wire to keep horses from chewing them, and a kite tangled in the treetops. One exhibit, *A Tribute to Survival,* features a historical overview of the North American Indians. The *Wizard Wing Discovery Center* offers a hands-on way to learn about water, collecting, pioneering skills, and a variety of natural history and cultural subjects. The *Biology Hall* exhibition is a life-size replica of a Costa Rican rain forest. Open daily. Admission charge. 800 W. Wells St. (phone: 278-2700).

MILWAUKEE COUNTY HISTORICAL CENTER Built in a bank once run by beer barons, the museum has an archive and numerous exhibitions on the city's history, several of which are especially entertaining for children. It is near the *MECCA Complex,* which includes an arena and facilities for conventions and meetings. Open daily. No admission charge. 910 N. Old World Third St. (phone: 273-8288).

PÈRE MARQUETTE PARK Between the museum and the river, this park is named after the explorer-priest who stopped briefly in Milwaukee during a canoe trip through the Great Lakes area. Local legend insists that he landed here, although the site was then part of an extensive tamarack swamp along the Milwaukee River. Other additions to the park in recent years are a new bandshell and walkway alongside the river.

DOWNTOWN EAST

WISCONSIN AVENUE EAST Wisconsin Avenue, east of the river, is a shopper's haven, with numerous fine stores. Shops on several nearby cross streets have been lovingly restored to their 19th-century appearance.

THIRD WARD Formerly an old warehouse district, now bounded by I-794 on the north, N. Water Street, and Lake Michigan, this neighborhood has made a great comeback. Artists' lofts, restaurants, shops, galleries, the *Milwaukee Institute of Art and Design, Milwaukee* magazine, *Irish American Post, Skylight Theater,* and *Theater X* call the place home. Workers on Commission Row haul vegetables and fruit around BMWs and Toyotas owned by the advertising and marketing execs who now live in the district. For walking tour information, call the *Historic Third Ward Association,* 219 N. Milwaukee St. (phone: 273-1173).

CATHEDRAL SQUARE Between Jackson and Jefferson Streets, this square dates to Wisconsin's territorial days. Except for the belltower, *St. John's Cathedral* was nearly destroyed by fire in 1935. If you feel like a snack, turn left on Jefferson to No. 761, where *George Watts & Son's* interesting silver shop has a tearoom on the second floor (phone: 291-5120).

CITY HALL Milwaukee's best-known landmark, this building with its 393-foot tower was designed in 1895 in such a way that taxpayers could drive their buggies up in the rain to pay real estate taxes without getting wet. In the tower above the arched entry, Old Sol, a 20-ton bell, gathers dust. In 1922, citizens complained about the noise of Old Sol's tolling, and the city ordered it stilled. Closed weekends. N. Water St. at Wells St. (phone: 286-3200).

ELSEWHERE

ANNUNCIATION GREEK ORTHODOX CHURCH The last major building designed by Wisconsin-born architect Frank Lloyd Wright. Tours of the saucer-shaped structure are offered for groups of 15 or more on weekdays by appointment only. Admission charge. 9400 W. Congress St. (phone: 461-9400).

WHITNALL PARK At 689 acres, this is one of the larger municipal parks in the country. It includes the 40-acre *Boerner Botanical Gardens* (5879 S. 92nd St., Hales Corners; phone: 425-1132) and the 40-acre *Todd Wehr Nature Center* (9701 W. College Ave., Franklin; phone: 425-8550), a nature preserve with a variety of species. Open daily.

MILWAUKEE COUNTY ZOO Among the most famous zoos in the country, it allows the animals to roam free in their natural habitats. Kids adore the miniature railroad and children's zoo. Open daily. Admission charge. 10001 W. Blue Mound Rd. (phone: 771-5500).

SCHLITZ AUDUBON CENTER The 189 acres of undisturbed forest preserve once provided pasture to brewery horses weary from pulling beer wagons. Its 6 miles of trails through different ecological areas provide a good place to wander and wonder. A 60-foot wooden tower built on a 100-foot bluff offers a bird's-eye view of the city and the Lake Michigan countryside. Be warned—there's no elevator. There is a natural history bookstore. Closed Mondays. Admission charge. 1111 E. Brown Deer Rd. (phone: 352-2880).

EXTRA SPECIAL

For an interesting day trip, take I-94 west 78 miles to Madison, the state capital and home of the *University of Wisconsin.* Drop in at the information center at *Memorial Union* (on Park and Langdon Sts.) to pick up a map and find out what's happening on campus. The university is sure to

offer more than enough to keep you busy, with its art center, geology museum, planetarium, observatory, and arboretum. The four lakes in Madison—Mendota, Monona, Waubesa, and Wingra—as well as Kegonsa in nearby Edgerton—are great for fishing and swimming. If you continue driving west (toward the Iowa border), or due south toward Illinois, you'll find yourself in Wisconsin cheese country.

Sources and Resources

TOURIST INFORMATION

For information, maps, and brochures, contact the *Greater Milwaukee Convention and Visitors Bureau* (510 W. Kilbourn Ave., Milwaukee, WI 53203; phone: 273-3950). It's open daily during the summer; Mondays through Fridays the rest of the year. Also helpful is the *Public Service Bureau* (phone: 224-2120) in the lobby of the Journal Building (Fourth and State Sts.), which is open Mondays through Fridays. Contact the Wisconsin state tourism hotline (800-432-TRIP) for maps, calendars of events, health updates, and travel advisories.

LOCAL COVERAGE The *Milwaukee Journal-Sentinel,* morning daily; *Shepherd Express* and the *City Express,* weekly; the *Irish American Post,* bimonthly; and *Milwaukee* magazine, monthly.

TELEVISION STATIONS WTMJ Channel 4–NBC; WDJT Channel 58–CBS; WITI Channel 6–FOX; WMVS Channel 10–PBS; and WISN Channel 12–ABC.

RADIO STATIONS AM: WTMF 620 (news, Top 40); WBKV 1470 (adult contemporary); and WAUK 1510 (all sports). FM: WUWM 89.8 (jazz/news); WLUM 102.1 (alternative rock); WKLH 96.5 (classic rock); and WMYX 99 (mix of 1960s, 1970s, and 1980s pop music).

TELEPHONE The area code for Milwaukee is 414.

SALES TAX There is a 5.5% state sales tax; the hotel room tax is 9%.

CLIMATE Summer and fall, with average temperatures of 68F and 50F, are generally pleasant, but expect sudden change when the wind shifts to the east. In winter, be prepared for bitter winds. The sub-zero cold is formidable.

GETTING AROUND

AIRPORT *General Mitchell International Airport* handles the city's domestic and international air traffic and is a 15-minute drive from downtown. An economical share-a-ride program is available to those heading to the same destination; make arrangements through the Ground Transportation Coordinator, directly outside the baggage claim area. *Milwaukee County Transit* buses also provide service downtown for $1.35 (exact change required). *A-1 Transportation Airport Shuttle* (phone: 272-1955) leaves every half hour for downtown hotels as well as hotels in the western and northern metro areas.

BUS During major lakefront festivals in the summer, a shuttle bus runs from the lake along Wisconsin Avenue to 10th and Wisconsin. The fare is 50¢. Regular bus service costs $1.35 (exact change required). For information on the schedules, contact *Milwaukee County Transit System* (1942 N. 17th St.; phone: 344-6711).

CAR RENTAL Most major car rental firms are represented.

HARBOR CRUISES *Iroquois Boat Line* (Clybourn St. Bridge dock; phone: 332-4194) offers two-hour trips along the Milwaukee River daily from *Memorial Day* through *Labor Day.* Dinner cruises and private charters on the *Celebration* (502 N. Harbor Dr.; phone: 278-1133) are offered from April through December, and brunch, lunch, and dinner cruises are available on the *Edelweiss* (1110 Old World Third St.; phone: 272-DOCK) from April through October.

TAXI There are taxi stands at most major hotels, but we recommend calling *City Veterans Taxi* (phone: 291-8080) or *Yellow Cab* (phone: 271-1800).

SIGHTSEEING TOURS

WALKING The *Department of City Development* runs *MKE Neighborhood Tours, Ltd.,* a program intended to get visitors out of downtown and into the communities to sample the diversity of restaurants, shops, and cultures of Milwaukee. Its seven itineraries of unescorted walking (or cycling) tours include "The Mitchell Street Express," "Neighborhoods 94 West," "Neighborhood North," and "Riverwest." Discover the *Balkan Trading Company* (938 W. Lapham Blvd.; phone: 643-7372) for homemade *burek* pastries and Serbian smoked sausage; the *Woodland Pattern Bookstore* (720 E. Locust St.; phone: 263-4001), which offers readings and lectures; and *Suzy's Cream Cheesecakes* (5901 W. Vliet St.; phone: 453-2255); as well as other fascinating hideaways. For details, contact the *Greater Milwaukee Convention and Visitors Bureau* (phone: 273-3950).

SPECIAL EVENTS

From mid-December through the end of January, *Winterfest,* Milwaukee's annual winter festival, takes place on weekends with snow sculptures, sporting events, and more. Rock and jazz concerts are part of *Summerfest,* held every June and July on the lakefront. Several ethnic festivals featuring food and entertainment take place at the *Henry W. Maier Festival Park* grounds throughout the summer. *Lakefront Festival of the Arts* is held outdoors near the *Milwaukee Art Museum* in the middle of June with music, food, and arts and crafts exhibits. The *Great Circus Parade* is an annual July event. The *Wisconsin State Fair* takes place for two weeks in mid-August on the fairgrounds adjoining I-94, west of downtown. The weekend before *Thanksgiving,* the *Holiday Folk Fair* features ethnic food, music, and entertainment at the *MECCA Complex* (Kilbourn Ave.).

MUSEUMS

In addition to those described in *Special Places,* Milwaukee has several other museums of note.

BROOKS STEVENS AUTO MUSEUM More than 60 antique cars are on display. Open daily. Admission charge. 10325 N. Port Washington Rd. (phone: 241-4185).

CHARLES ALLIS ART MUSEUM This beautifully preserved mansion is listed on the *National Register of Historic Places.* Closed Mondays and Tuesdays. Admission charge. 1801 N. Prospect Ave. (phone: 278-8295).

CAPTAIN FREDERICK PABST MANSION A Flemish-style mansion built by the famous Milwaukee brewing king, it is listed on the *National Register of Historic Places.* Open daily. Admission charge. 2000 W. Wisconsin Ave. (phone: 931-0808).

DISCOVERY WORLD Visitors can explore science, economics, and technology with hands-on exhibits. Closed weekdays. No admission charge. 818 W. Wisconsin Ave. (phone: 765-9966).

SHOPPING

Milwaukee has its share of today's marketplaces, malls filled with department stores (especially along Grand Avenue), chain stores, eateries, and entertainment. Enclaves of commerce with more individuality, however, also are easy to come by—and get to. Museum shops are an excellent source of quality gifts and mementos.

SPORTS AND FITNESS

Tickets to the city's professional sports events, as well as to *Marquette University* basketball games, are available through *TicketMaster* (phone: 276-4545).

BASEBALL The *American League Brewers* play at *County Stadium* (201 S. 46th St.; phone: 933-9000).

BASKETBALL Milwaukee's *NBA Bucks* and the *Marquette Warriors* play at *Bradley Center* (Fourth and State Sts.; phone: 227-0400).

BICYCLING Bikes can be rented from *East Side Cycle and Hobby Shop* (2031 N. Farwell Ave.; phone: 276-9848) and *Wilson Park Schwinn Cyclery* (2033 W. Howard Ave.; phone: 281-4720).

FISHING Salmon and trout as big as 30 pounds are caught in Lake Michigan, from the shore and breakwaters. You can use launching ramps at *McKinley Marina* and near the private *South Shore Yacht Club.* Half-day boat charters, including bait and tackle, are offered by numerous firms (see the yellow pages).

GOLF The best public 18-hole golf course is *Mee-Kwon Park* (6333 W. Bonniwell Rd., Mequon; phone: 242-1310).

HOCKEY The minor league Milwaukee *Admirals* play at the *Bradley Center* (Fourth and State Sts.; phone: 227-0550).

ICE SKATING In winter, many parks open rinks. For year-round ice skating (indoors), try *Wilson Park Center* (4001 S. 20th St.; phone: 281-4610); *Eble Ice Arena* (19400 W. Blue Mound Rd.; phone: 784-5155); and the *Petit National Ice Center at State Fair Park* (phone: 257-3883).

JOGGING Run along the lakefront near *War Memorial Center,* on the beach, or on the sidewalk.

POLO On Sundays in summer, Milwaukee's polo teams compete at a playing field between North Lake and Merton, about 30 minutes west of the city (no phone).

SKIING *Currie, Dretzka,* and *Whitnall Parks* have ski tows and mostly beginners' trails. Cross-country skiers may use all county parks. The *Whitnall Park* trails are particularly good.

SOCCER The Milwaukee *Wave* professional soccer team plays at the *Bradley Center* (Fourth and State Sts.; phone: 962-9283).

SWIMMING Seven public beaches along the lakefront have lifeguards and dressing facilities. The water is usually chilly, even in August.

TENNIS Try *North Shore Racquet Club* (5750 N. Glen Park Rd.; phone: 351-2900) or *Le Club* (2001 W. Good Hope Rd.; phone: 352-4900). In warm weather, numerous county parks have courts available for a nominal fee.

THEATER

Our favorite Milwaukee theater tops the list below, followed by several other fine venues in the area. For complete listings on theatrical and musical events, see the local publications listed in *Local Coverage.*

CENTER STAGE

Milwaukee Repertory Theater (The Rep) This institution, active since 1954, presents classics and exciting contemporary plays, often with a regional emphasis. Six main-stage productions are presented in its 720-seat *Powerhouse Theater* during its September through May season, and performances also are held at the 198-seat *Stiemke Theater* and the 116-seat *Stackner Cabaret,* both in the three-theater complex. Nearly 200,000 people attend *Rep* productions annually. 108 E. Wells St. (phone: 224-9490).

The *Pabst Theater* (144 E. Wells St.; phone: 278-3663), which stages a variety of shows including the beloved *A Christmas Carol,* is part of the Theater District complex attached to the *Wyndham Milwaukee Center.* The *Marcus Center for the Performing Arts* (929 N. Water St.; phone: 273-7121) is home to *First Stage Milwaukee,* a children's theater. *Riverside Theater* (116 W. Wisconsin Ave.; phone: 224-3000) features stage shows by top performers. Performing companies in the new *Broadway Theatre Centre* (158 N. Broadway; phone: 291-7811) include *Skylight Operatic Theatre, Theatre X* for experimental drama, and *Milwaukee Chamber Theatre* for American and British plays; and the *Milwaukee Irish Arts Theatre Company (MIATC;* phone: 258-9349) presents works throughout the community as well as internationally. This year, MIATC will host the *International Irish Theater Festival,* with troupes from Canada and Ireland.

MUSIC

The *Milwaukee Symphony, Milwaukee Ballet,* and *Florentine Opera Company* perform at the *Marcus Center for the Performing Arts* (929 N. Water St.; phone: 273-7121). *"Music Under the Stars"* concerts are held in *Washington* and *Humboldt Parks* on Friday and Saturday nights in July and August.

NIGHTCLUBS AND NIGHTLIFE

For jazz, visit the *Estate* (2423 N. Murray Ave.; phone: 964-9923). Live country acts can be heard at *Bronco Billy's* (3555 S. 27th St.; phone: 643-9440). *La Playa,* atop the *Pfister* hotel (see *Checking In),* has either dancing, jazz, or a deejay, plus a spectacular view. For Irish music, poetry, and short drama, try the *Black Shamrock* (2311 N. Murray Ave.; phone: 273-5253). On Saturday nights, the *Brown Bottle Pub* (221 W. Galena; phone: 271-4444) has a *karaoke* machine. Located in the old taprooms of a Schlitz brewery, it also has a selection of 103 different ales and beers from which to choose. For blues, there's *Boobie's Place* (502 W. Garfield Ave.; phone: 263-3399).

Best in Town

CHECKING IN

Milwaukee's hotels range from traditional older properties to the modern and the functional. Most of Milwaukee's major hotels have complete facilities for the business traveler. Those listed below as having "business services" usually offer such conveniences as meeting rooms, photocopiers, computers, translation services, and express checkout, among others. Call the individual hotel for additional information. Expect to pay between $80 and $140 per night for a double room at places listed as expensive, and between $55 and $80 at the hotel in the moderate category; there are no exceptional inexpensive hotels in the city. Several offer weekend bargain rates. Unless otherwise noted, hotel rooms have air conditioning, private baths, TV sets, and telephones.

All hotels are below are in Milwaukee and telephone and fax numbers are in the 414 area code unless otherwise indicated.

EXPENSIVE

Hilton Inn Overlooking the Milwaukee River, this spacious 164-room hostelry offers such amenities as king-size beds and an indoor pool. The adjoining *Anchorage* restaurant is noted for its seafood. There's room service daily from 7 AM to 10:30 PM, and business services are available. On the Milwaukee River, near the Hampton Ave. exit of I-43 (phone: 962-6040; 800-HILTONS; fax: 962-6166).

Hyatt Regency This $28-million, 18-story property helped to end what was a chronic shortage of rooms for conventions. And, by no coincidence, it is next to the downtown *Convention Center.* Topping the 485-room structure, with its atrium lobby, is the *Polaris,* a revolving restaurant. Room service continues until 2 AM. Other amenities include a concierge and business services. Fourth and Kilbourn (phone: 276-1234; 800-233-1234 or 800-228-9000; fax: 276-6338).

Milwaukee Hilton The largest hotel in Milwaukee—its 540 rooms have gone through extensive renovation during their almost 70-year career. Facilities include a heated indoor pool and sauna, and the main restaurant is *Benson's, A Place for Steaks.* There is 24-hour room service, as well as a concierge and business services. 509 W. Wisconsin Ave. (phone: 271-7250; 800-HILTONS; fax: 271-8091).

Pfister This 330-room establishment has catered to visiting and local elite since the 1890s. A multimillion-dollar restoration completed in time for its centennial celebration in 1993 brought it back to the level that enchanted Enrico Caruso and every president since McKinley. The bronze lions in the lobby are named Dick and Harry, by the way, and the best views of the lake are from rooms 8, 9, or 10, or from high up in the tower in the romantic *La Playa* lounge. There is also the *English Room,* a fine restaurant (see *Eating Out).* Round-the-clock room service, a concierge, and business services are available. 424 E. Wisconsin Ave. (phone: 273-8222; fax: 273-0747).

MODERATE

Grand Milwaukee Near the airport and next to a convention hall, this property has 400 rooms, two restaurants, a pool, and handball, tennis, and racquetball courts. Room service is available until 10:30 PM. Business services are offered. 4747 S. Howell Ave. (phone: 481-8000; fax: 481-8065).

EATING OUT

Visiting Milwaukee without sampling the Wiener schnitzel would be like going to New Orlean's French Quarter and living on Big Macs. It was once said that visitors could get any kind of food in Milwaukee as long as it was German, but these days it's easy to find Polish, Chinese, Italian, Greek, Japanese, Serbian, and American restaurants as well. Expect to pay between $40 and $60 for dinner for two at those places listed as expensive; between $20 and $40 at restaurants in the moderate category; and under $20 at places in the inexpensive bracket. Prices don't include drinks, wine, tax, or tips. All restaurants are in the 414 area code unless otherwise indicated.

Unless otherwise noted, restaurants are open for lunch and dinner.

EXPENSIVE

English Room If you suddenly develop an overwhelming craving for rack of lamb or cherries jubilee, this is the place to go. Flaming dishes are prepared tableside with appropriate theatrical flourish. Reservations necessary on weekends. Major credit cards accepted. *Pfister* Hotel, 424 E. Wisconsin Ave. (phone: 273-8222).

Karl Ratzch's Ranked as one of Milwaukee's top dining spots for many years, it has specialized in Teutonic fare—schnitzel, sauerbraten, potato pancakes, German sausages, strudel—since the days when the city called itself the German Athens. Reservations advised on weekends. Major credit cards accepted. 320 E. Mason St. (phone: 276-2720).

Mader's A family-run favorite that goes back to shortly after the century's turn. It's decorated in Bavarian style. For years, the late Gus Mader offered a reward to anyone who could finish his 3½-pound pork shank. The prize? Another one, to be eaten at the same sitting. Reservations advised on weekends. Major credit cards accepted. 1037 N. Old World Third St. (phone: 271-3377).

Sanford Several years ago, Sandy D'Amato converted this former grocery store (owned first by his grandparents, then his parents) into a real charmer of a restaurant. His wife, Angie, supervises the dining room, while chef Sandy produces basil-flecked *Cima Kenovese* (a rolled veal roast) and shrimp cakes with caramelized onions and tamarind sauce. He's also a whiz at the grill, and daily specials attest to his skill. Closed Sundays. Reservations advised. Major credit cards accepted. 1547 N. Jackson St. (phone: 276-9608).

MODERATE

Old Town At this Serbian spot you can dine to the tune of guitar-like tamburitzas. Fine, you say, but what is Serbian food like? Well, as prepared here, it features sizzling lamb dishes that are somewhat spicier than similar Greek and Turkish fare. Closed Mondays. Reservations advised on weekends. Major credit cards accepted. 522 W. Lincoln Ave. (phone: 672-0206).

Toy's Chinatown The family that owns this downtown Chinese spot has been serving residents for three generations; when you eat here, you're not just getting egg rolls, you can be sure of fresh Cantonese dishes, like sweet-and-sour shrimp, spareribs, and chow mein. Reservations advised on weekends. Major credit cards accepted. 830 N. Third St. (phone: 271-5166).

INEXPENSIVE

Bavarian Inn Located in a park owned by a consortium of Germans, this informal dining room serves generally good German food. The Sunday buffet is one of the best bargains in town—you can help yourself to as much as you like, so be sure to bring a big appetite. Soccer fields and a festival area on the grounds mean that there's usually something to see, as well. Closed Mondays. Reservations advised on weekends. Major credit cards accepted. Take the Silver Spring exit from I-43 north, turn south on North Port Washington Rd., then west on Lexington to 700 W. Lexington Ave. (phone: 964-0300).

Jake's Delicatessen If corned beef on rye appeals to you, this is the place to go. You can sit at a booth or a counter, or take your sandwich with you in a paper bag. Try the specials—Jake's has giant ¾ pound hot dogs. Closed Sundays. No reservations. No credit cards accepted. 1634 W. North Ave. (phone: 562-1272).

Leon's Frozen Custard Drive-In Besides their passion for cheese and beer, Milwaukeeans also love frozen custard. This place has been in operation since 1942 and is one of the favored spots for indulging in the creamy, frozen treat. 3131 S. 27th St. (phone: 383-1784).

BEERS THAT MADE MILWAUKEE FAMOUS

If you're wondering where the smell of malt is coming from, follow your nose to the big breweries, where you'll be escorted through the facilities and given samples of the wares (unless you're underage, in which case you only get to look). The breweries that offer tours are *Miller* (visitors' center at 4251 W. State St.; phone: 931-2337), *Pabst* (915 Juneau Ave.; phone: 223-3709), and *Sprecher's* (730 W. Oregon St.; phone: 272-BEER). They're all open to visitors daily except holidays, when everyone stays home testing the product.

Minneapolis–St. Paul

The Twin Cities are not twins at all, but very different sister cities that complement and compete with one another. They form the nucleus of a metropolitan area that includes 2.5 million people, and they are the economic and cultural hub of a region that stretches from Wisconsin to Montana.

St. Paul,the state capital and the older of the two cities, began as a railroad and river town and still is a terminal point for the *Delta Queen* tour boat. Its heritage is predominantly German and Irish Catholic, although it has more recently become home to many immigrants from Southeast Asia. It has a compact and relaxed downtown that includes *Town Square Park,* a glass-enclosed atrium with trees and waterfalls, and *Cafesjian's Carousel,* a well-known landmark built in 1914. Grand Avenue and the Ramsey and Crocus Hill areas combine 2 miles of restaurants and innovative shops with restorations of Victorian architecture in F. Scott Fitzgerald's old stomping grounds.

More flamboyant Minneapolis, the largest city within about 400 miles, was a flour milling center that was settled largely by Scandinavian Lutherans. It's the livelier of the Twin Cities, with more night spots downtown and in the adjacent Warehouse District. Downtown also houses more than 400 stores, and the riverfront Mississippi Mile is filled with parks, shops, restaurants, and entertainment areas.

Both cities benefit from a broad economic base that includes such company headquarters as 3M, Honeywell, General Mills, Dayton Hudson, *Northwest Airlines,* and Land O'Lakes. Cargill, the diversified grain-handling company based in suburban Minnetonka, is the nation's largest privately held enterprise. In recent years, the area has seen an upsurge in medical products companies (such as Medtronic) and in the entertainment industry (Paisley Park and other recording studios are major employers, and the Twin Cities area is one of the largest film and commercial production centers in the US).

Settlement of the region began around the confluence of the Mississippi and Minnesota Rivers, where historic *Fort Snelling* now offers summertime reenactments of frontier life in the early 1800s. Discovered by French explorers in the late 17th century, the area remained relatively undeveloped until the 1850s. Situated at the first navigable point on the Mississippi, Minneapolis and St. Paul became major shipping points for timber, flour, furs, and other products. Although St. Paul initially led in population, Minneapolis surpassed its twin around 1880 and has been Minnesota's largest city ever since.

Minnesotans are devoted to their leisure pursuits, and the many lakes and parks provide access to recreation year-round. There are 22 lakes and 6,385 acres of parkland within Minneapolis city limits alone, and more than 900 lakes, 500 parks, and 110 golf courses in the Twin Cities metropolitan area.

The region offers plenty of indoor activities, too. Among the attractions is the *Mall of America* in suburban Bloomington, the largest shopping mall in the nation, which attracts an estimated million visitors a month with more than 350 stores, 40 nightclubs and restaurants, and a seven-acre amusement park. In addition, Minnesota and nearby Wisconsin boast a score of Native American gaming casinos, the largest collection of casinos between Atlantic City and Las Vegas; half a dozen of them are within a two-hour drive of the Twin Cities. Minneapolis is also the home of major league baseball, football, and basketball teams, along with Big Ten teams of the *University of Minnesota.*

The cities have a well-deserved reputation as a cultural center as well, with such institutions as the *Guthrie Theater* in Minneapolis and the restored *F. Scott Fitzgerald Theater* in St. Paul, which hosts Garrison Keillor's "Prairie Home Companion" radio show. Then there are the complementary *Minneapolis Institute of Arts* and *Walker Art Center,* the *Minnesota Orchestra* and *St. Paul Chamber Orchestra,* and a host of other museums and performance groups.

Minneapolis–St. Paul residents don't even mind the rugged winter weather. They enjoy it with a vigor by snowmobiling, ice fishing, and skiing. It is said that executives who have been transferred to the Twin Cities are reluctant to be transferred away—and longtime residents have no trouble understanding why.

Minneapolis–St. Paul At-a-Glance

SEEING THE CITY

Although the IDS and *Norwest Tower* buildings are taller, the best view of the area is from the observation deck of the 32-story *Foshay Tower* (Ninth St. and Marquette Ave., Minneapolis). It's closed October through March. Admission charge. St. Paul's *Cherokee Park,* overlooking the Mississippi River, affords a spectacular panorama of both cities. Another good view is that from *Indian Mounds Park,* also in St. Paul.

SPECIAL PLACES

The most extraordinary feature of downtown Minneapolis and St. Paul is their interior skyways, an interconnected belt of pedestrian malls and escalators lacing in and out of shops, banks, and restaurants at the second-story level. When it's below zero, you can still walk around comfortably without a coat. At street level, courtyards, gardens, fountains, and sculpture form attractive plazas.

MINNEAPOLIS

MINNEAPOLIS INSTITUTE OF ARTS The exterior of this highly esteemed institution is architecturally classic, and inside it houses an equally classic variety of Old Masters and other paintings, sculpture, decorative arts, photographs,

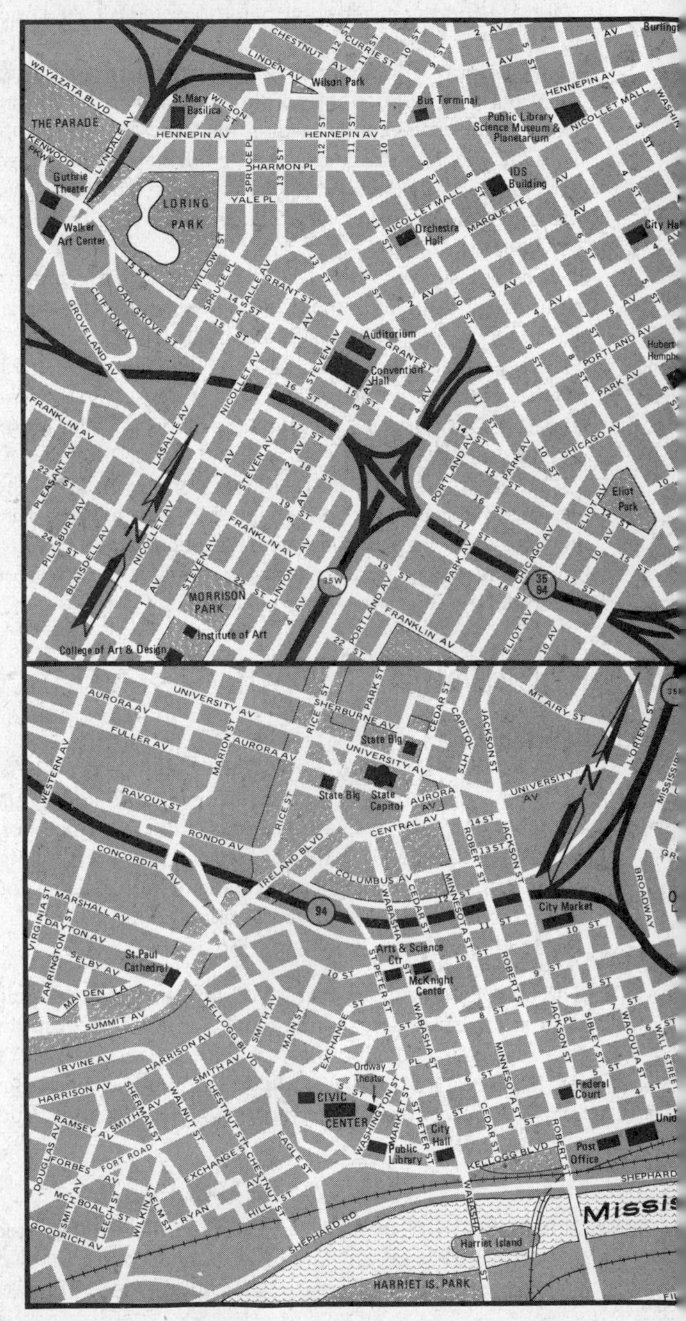

CHESTNUT
CURRIE ST
LINDEN AV
Wilson Park
WAYAZATA BLVD
St.Mary Basilica
WILSON ST
Bus Terminal
HENNEPIN AV
Public Library
Science Museum & Planetarium
NICOLLET MALL
THE PARADE
KENWOOD PKWY
LYNDALE AV
HENNEPIN AV
HARMON PL
SPRUCE PL
YALE PL
Guthrie Theater
LORING PARK
Walker Art Center
IDS Building
MARQUETTE
Orchestra Hall
City Hall
15 ST
OAK GROVE ST
CLIFTON AV
GROVELAND AV
WILLOW ST
SPRUCE PL
LA SALLE AV
GRANT ST
Auditorium
Convention Hall
PORTLAND AV
Hubert Humphrey
PARK AV
STEVEN AV
NICOLLET AV
LASALLE AV
FRANKLIN AV
PLEASANT AV
PILLSBURY AV
BLAISDELL AV
CHICAGO AV
Eliot Park
ELIOT AV
FRANKLIN AV
CLINTON AV
MORRISON PARK
Institute of Art
College of Art & Design
35W
35 94
FRANKLIN AV
AURORA AV
UNIVERSITY AV
SHERBURNE AV
PARK ST
CEDAR ST
CAPITOL HTS
JACKSON ST
MT AIRY ST
L'ORIENT ST
FULLER AV
MARION ST
AURORA AV
RICE ST
State Bldg
UNIVERSITY AV
WESTERN AV
RAVOUX ST
State Bldg
State Capitol
AURORA AV
UNIVERSITY AV
RONDO AV
CENTRAL AV
CONCORDIA AV
IRELAND BLVD
COLUMBUS AV
ROBERT ST
JACKSON ST
WABASHA
CEDAR ST
MINNESOTA ST
BROADWAY
MARSHALL AV
94
City Market
VIRGINIA ST
DAYTON AV
FARRINGTON ST
SELBY AV
St.Paul Cathedral
Arts & Science Ctr
McKnight Center
ST PETER ST
MAIDEN LA
SUMMIT AV
KELLOGG BLVD
SMITH AV
MAIN ST
EXCHANGE ST
JACKSON ST
SIBLEY ST
WACOUTA ST
WALL STREET
IRVINE AV
HARRISON AV
SMITH AV
CHESTNUT ST
WALNUT ST
Ordway Theater
HARRISON AV
SHERMAN ST
CIVIC CENTER
WASHINGTON ST
MARKET ST
ST PETER ST
City Hall
Federal Court
RAMSEY AV
SMITH AV
FORT ROAD
FORBES AV
EXCHANGE ST
CHESTNUT ST
EAGLE ST
Public Library
CEDAR ST
KELLOGG BLVD
Post Office
SHEPHARD
DOUGLAS AV
SMITH AV
MCBOAL ST
LEECH ST
WILKIN ST
ELM ST
RYAN
HILL ST
SHEPHARD RD
WABASHA ST
Missis
GOODRICH AV
Harriet Island
HARRIET IS. PARK

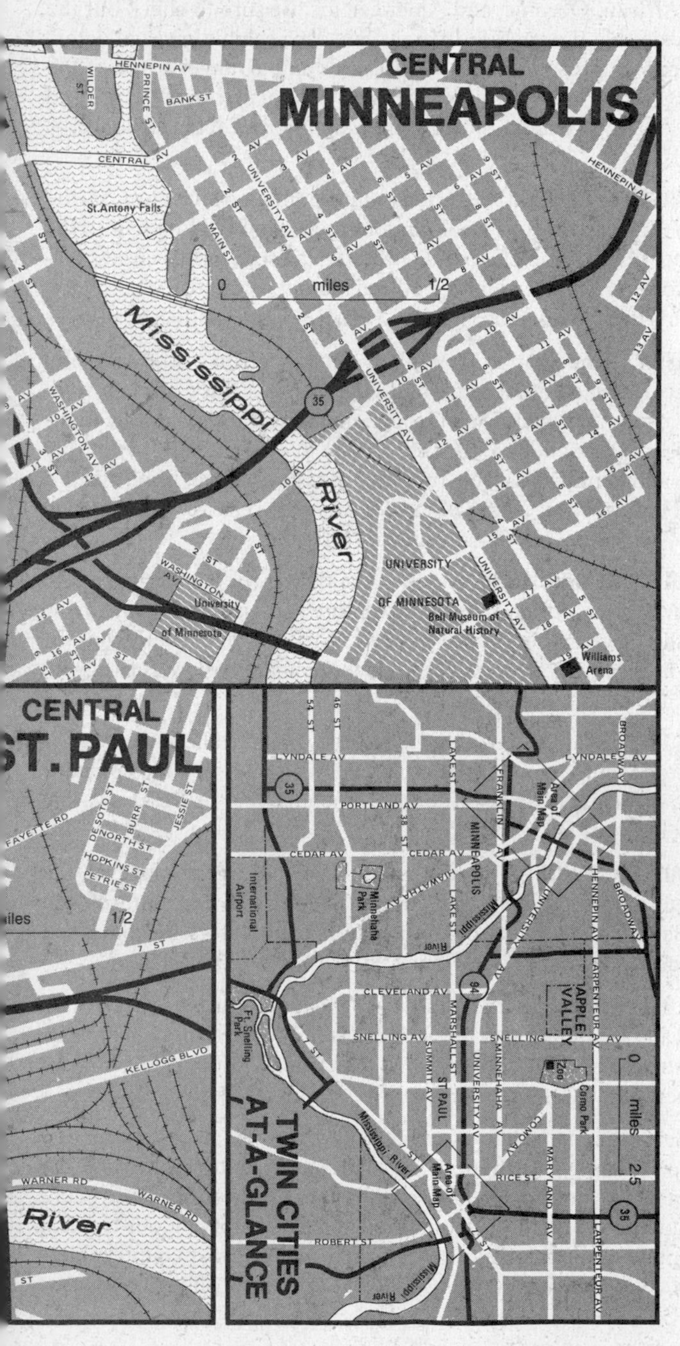
CENTRAL
MINNEAPOLIS
Mississippi
River
St.Antony Falls
UNIVERSITY
OF MINNESOTA
Bell Museum of
Natural History
Williams
Arena
0
miles
1/2
CENTRAL
ST.PAUL
iles
1/2
KELLOGG BLVD
WARNER RD
River
TWIN CITIES
AT-A-GLANCE
MINNEAPOLIS
ST PAUL
International
Airport
Minnehaha
Park
Ft. Snelling
Park
Area of
Main Map
APPLE
VALLEY
Zoo
Como Park
0
miles
2.5

and Asian, African, Oceanic, and American art. Be sure to check out the interactive videos in the galleries that explain each exhibit in visual detail. The museum also presents films and lectures and arranges tours of the *Purcell-Cutts House,* a masterpiece of Prairie School architecture. Closed Mondays. Admission charge for traveling exhibitions. 2400 Third Ave. S. (phone: 870-3131).

FREDERICK R. WEISMAN ART MUSEUM This aluminum-clad museum on the *University of Minnesota's* East Bank campus focuses on the first half of the 20th century, with works by Georgia O'Keeffe and the world's largest collections of works by Marsden Hartley, Alfred Maurer, and B. J. O. Nordfeldt. Closed Mondays. No admission charge. 331 E. River Rd. (phone: 625-9641).

WALKER ART CENTER Named for T. B. Walker, a local patron of the arts, and housed in a striking contemporary building, this art center offers a vivid overview of major 20th-century art, complementing the classic collections of the *Minneapolis Institute of Arts* (see above). It originates many touring exhibitions, and conducts a lively program of music, dance, film, theater, and educational activities. Closed Mondays. Admission charge. 725 Vineland Pl. (phone: 375-7577; 375-7622 for the box office).

MINNEAPOLIS SCULPTURE GARDENS Located at the *Walker Art Center,* this is one of the country's grandest monumental sculpture gardens. Among the many pieces installed throughout this seven-acre park is the delightfully whimsical *Spoonbridge and Cherry* by Claes Oldenburg and Coosje van Bruggen. Open daily. No admission charge.

MINNEHAHA PARK In his poem "Hiawatha," Longfellow immortalized the "laughing waters" of Minnehaha Falls near the Mississippi. Enjoy the splendor of the falls, or picnic near a statue of Minnehaha and brave Hiawatha. Minnehaha Pkwy. at Hiawatha Ave. S.

MINNEAPOLIS GRAIN EXCHANGE An ornate hall the size of a large school gym, the world's largest grain exchange is a loud, hectic place where futures and grain samples are bought and sold. Tours available. Visitors' balcony open daily. No admission charge. 400 Fourth St. S. (phone: 338-6212).

ORCHESTRA HALL This hall houses the *Minnesota Orchestra,* which has been playing classical and symphonic pop music since 1903. Though spartan in appearance, *Orchestra Hall* is renowned for its superior acoustics. 1111 *Nicollet Mall* (phone: 371-5656).

MINNESOTA ZOO Set in the rolling hills of Apple Valley, this 500-acre, state-funded zoological park (among the nation's best) provides a natural environment for Siberian tigers, musk oxen, moose, and other northern animals. There are many aquatic species in the aquarium, and a five-story indoor tropical environment houses jungle fauna and flora. In winter, cross-country skiers can enjoy 6 miles of groomed trails. Closed *Christmas.* Admission charge.

12101 Johnny Cake Ridge Rd., Apple Valley, 25 minutes south of the city on Hwy. 35 (phone: 432-9000).

ST. PAUL

LANDMARK CENTER This castle-like former federal courts building is a cultural center that is host to performing groups, civic events, and the *Minnesota Museum of American Art.* The 1902 building also houses the *Schubert Club Musical Instrument Museum,* with keyboards dating to the 1600s; here, too, are restored courtrooms where mobsters such as Alvin "Creepy" Karpis were convicted in the 1920s and 1930s. Open daily; tours Thursdays and Sundays. No admission charge. 75 W. Fifth St. (phone: 292-3225).

COMO PARK A 70-acre lake, a small zoo, a golf course, a Japanese garden, and children's rides all contribute to the popularity of this, the largest of St. Paul's many parks. In addition, it has special floral gardens, a year-round conservatory, and a lakeside pavilion where summer concerts are held. Open daily. Admission charge to the conservatory. Lexington Ave. at Midway Pkwy. (phone: 488-4041 for the zoo; 489-1740 for the conservatory).

STATE CAPITOL St. Paul is Minnesota's political center, and its Capitol is one of the most important buildings in the state. Its giant dome—similar to one designed by Michelangelo in Rome—is an outstanding state landmark and the largest unsupported marble dome in the world. Free guided tours. Open daily. Cedar and Aurora Sts. (phone: 296-2881).

MINNESOTA HISTORY CENTER Founded in 1849, 10 years before Minnesota became a state, the center houses records of pioneer days. In addition, paintings, sculpture, and other works by contemporary Minnesota artists also are on exhibit. Galleries closed Mondays. No admission charge. 345 Kellogg Blvd. W. (phone: 296-6126).

GOVERNOR'S RESIDENCE This English Tudor residence, built in 1910–11, is on the *National Register of Historic Sites.* It is open for one-hour tours on Thursdays, May through October beginning at 2 PM. Reservations required. No admission charge. 1006 Summit Ave. (phone: 297-8177).

CATHEDRAL OF ST. PAUL Center of the Roman Catholic archdiocese, this cathedral is a replica of *St. Peter's* in Rome. Architecturally notable for its 175-foot dome and central rose window, it has a special *Shrine of the Nations,* where visitors can meditate and pray. 239 Selby Ave. (phone: 228-1766).

SCIENCE MUSEUM OF MINNESOTA AND WILLIAM L. MCKNIGHT/3M OMNITHEATER This immensely popular complex offers hands-on exhibits in science, technology, and natural history. It includes a 635-seat theater for performing arts, a 300-seat auditorium, an art gallery, and the omnitheater. The latter, named for the founder of the 3M Company, has a floor-to-ceiling hemispheric screen and the world's largest film projector. The omnitheater is closed Mondays; the museum is closed Mondays September through

December. Both charge admission; a combination ticket is available. 30 E. 10th St. (phone: 221-9444).

HISTORIC FORT SNELLING The oldest landmark in the Twin Cities is also one of the first military posts west of the Mississippi—but not very far west: *Fort Snelling* sits high on a bluff overlooking the junction of the Mississippi and Minnesota Rivers. See what life was like during the 1820s as people in costume demonstrate early crafts and parade in military formation. Fife and drum bands perform in summer. This history center is closed weekends year-round; the fort is open daily May through October. No admission charge to the history center and museum; admission charge for the fort. Hwy. 5 and 55, 6 miles southwest of downtown (phone: 725-2428).

CITY HALL—COUNTY COURTHOUSE This 20-story Art Deco building offers exterior reliefs and a three-story *Memorial Hall* dominated by the *Vision of Peace,* a 36-foot, 55-ton figure of a Native American that is the world's largest onyx carving. Closed weekends. No admission charge. 15 W. Kellogg Blvd. (phone: 266-8023).

EXTRA SPECIAL

The St. Croix Valley, 25 miles east of Minneapolis–St. Paul, offers several stops for a day's outing. Stillwater, birthplace of Minnesota, is within easy striking distance of the *Afton Alps, Welch Village,* and *Wild Mountain* ski areas. In Stillwater, visit the *Grand Garage and Gallery* (on Main St.) with its shops and galleries. Two good eating stops are *Brine's* (219 S. Main St.; phone: 439-7556), which has great bratwurst, pastrami, and chili; and the *Dock Café* (425 E. Nelson St.; phone: 430-3770), offering fresh fish as well as beef and pasta. On the Wisconsin side of the tour is Somerset, where you can go tubing down the Apple River. You get carted about 4 miles upriver, plunked into an inner tube, and sent drifting back to Somerset. The river flows quickly over rapids at the outset, but widens and slows down, and the ride into town is tranquil.

Sources and Resources

TOURIST INFORMATION

Each Twin has its own source: the *Greater Minneapolis Convention & Visitors Association* (33 S. Sixth St.; Minneapolis, MN 55402; phone: 661-4700) and the *St. Paul Convention and Visitors Bureau* (55 E. Fifth St.; Suite 102, *Norwest Center,* St. Paul, MN 55101; phone: 297-6985: 800-627-6101 outside of the 612 area code). Both are closed weekends. The *GMCVA's City Center Mall's* skyway level information center (40 S. Seventh St.; phone: 348-2453) is open daily. Contact the *Minnesota State Tourism Hotline* (phone: 800-657-3700) for maps, calendars of events, travel advisories, and personalized itinerary assistance.

LOCAL COVERAGE There are two daily newspapers: the *Minneapolis Star Tribune* and the *Saint Paul Pioneer Press.* The *Twin Cities Reader, Skyway News,* and *City Pages* (distributed free in shopping centers, downtown hotels, and many restaurants) list activities in the Twin Cities. For a complete schedule of musical happenings, see the *Saint Paul Pioneer Press* on Thursdays and the *Star Tribune Variety Weekend* on Fridays. *Mpls.–St. Paul,* a monthly magazine, available at newsstands, gives full details on what's going on. A *Metro Area Visitors Guide* is also available from the convention and visitors bureaus in both St. Paul and Minneapolis, as well as from the *Minnesota Office of Tourism* (121 Seventh Pl. E., St. Paul, MN 55101; phone: 296-5029; 800-657-3700). *Minnesota Explorer,* a guide to events throughout the state, is free from the *Minnesota Office of Tourism.*

TELEVISION STATIONS KTCA Channel 2–PBS; WCCO Channel 4–CBS; KSTP Channel 5–ABC; KMSP Channel 9–UPN; KARE Channel 11–NBC; KTIC Channel 17–PBS; KLGT Channel 23–Independent; WFTC Channel 29–FOX; and KXLI Channel 41–Independent.

RADIO STATIONS AM: WCCO 830 (talk/news); KNOW 1330 (public); and KSTP 1500 (talk). FM: KNOW 91.1 (public/news); KS95 94.5 (top 40); and KTCZ 97.1 (jazz).

TELEPHONE The area code for Minneapolis–St. Paul is 612.

SALES TAX The sales tax in Minneapolis–St. Paul is 7%; the hotel room tax is 6.5% in Minneapolis and 6% in St. Paul.

CLIMATE In winter, be prepared for anything. The average temperature is 19F, but it can drop to 35F below zero, and snow has fallen as early as October. Summer temperatures are generally in the 70s and 80s.

GETTING AROUND

AIRPORT *Minneapolis–St. Paul International Airport* is a 15- to 20-minute drive from the downtown area of either Twin City. *Airport Taxi* (phone: 721-0000) provides metered transportation to Minneapolis hotels. *Metropolitan Council Transit Operations* buses run between the airport and Minneapolis–St. Paul. The fare is $1.50 or $2.00, depending on time of day. Limousines travel between the airport and downtown hotels in both cities; one good company is *The Airport Express* (phone: 726-6400).

BUS Minneapolis–St. Paul bus systems are models of efficiency. Express buses make the trip between Minneapolis and St. Paul in 20 minutes. Passengers' queries are handled by an extensive switchboard at the *Metropolitan Council Transit Operations* (560 Sixth Ave. N., Minneapolis; phone: 349-7000). Fares are $1 during off-peak hours; $1.50 peak.

CAR RENTAL All major firms are represented.

TAXI As in many other cities, taxis are difficult to get when you really need them and plentiful when you don't. Most are radio-dispatched. There are some taxi stands. One of the largest taxi companies in Minneapolis is *Yellow Cab* (500 E. 36th St.; phone: 824-4444), which also has an office in St. Paul (1463 Marshall Ave.; phone: 222-4433). For service from the suburbs to the city, there's *Suburban* (phone: 349-9999) and *Town Taxi* (phone: 331-8294).

SPECIAL EVENTS

In July, Minneapolis celebrates summer with a host of sailboat and milk carton boat races, a torchlight parade, and the "Queen of the Lakes" pageant as part of the annual *Minneapolis Aquatennial.* Throughout July and August, the *Minneapolis Orchestra* presents special concerts in the Marketplatz next to *Orchestra Hall* during *Sommerfest* (phone: 371-5656), with vendors and dance performances. The *Minnesota State Fair* at Midway Pkwy. and Snelling Ave., St. Paul) runs for 12 days, ending *Labor Day,* and the *St. Paul Winter Carnival,* 12 days in late January through early February, is a citywide celebration.

MUSEUMS

In addition to those described in *Special Places,* there are several other noteworthy cultural institutions in the Twin Cities.

AMERICAN SWEDISH INSTITUTE Swedish glass and art, along with immigrant memorabilia, are housed in a 33-room Romanesque mansion. Closed Mondays. Admission charge. 2600 Park Ave., Minneapolis (phone: 871-4907).

BELL MUSEUM OF NATURAL HISTORY The focus is on wildlife, with a *Touch and See Room* where you can feel exhibits ranging from a buffalo hide to a live snake. Closed Mondays. No admission charge Thursdays. 10 Church St. SE, Minneapolis (phone: 624-7083).

GIBBS FARM MUSEUM Costumed guides show what life was like at a farm and school in 1900. Closed Mondays and November through April. Admission charge. Outside St. Paul at 2097 W. Larpenteur Ave., Falcon Heights (phone: 646-8629).

MINNEAPOLIS PLANETARIUM Light shows on the stars and planets. Open daily. Admission charge. In the *Minneapolis Public Library,* 300 *Nicollet Mall,* Minneapolis (phone: 372-6644).

MINNESOTA CHILDREN'S MUSEUM A hands-on center where kids can run a TV studio and an electromagnetic crane. Closed Mondays in the winter. Admission charge. Seventh St. between St. Peter and Wabasha, St. Paul (phone: 225-6000).

NATIONAL FIRE FIGHTERS MEMORIAL MUSEUM Kids can climb on old fire trucks, take a ride in a working rig, and try on real firefighting gear. Available for birthday parties. Open Thursdays, Saturdays, the first Sunday of each month, and by arrangement. Admission charge. 1100 Van Buren St. NE, Minneapolis (phone: 623-3817).

PLANES OF FAME More than two dozen World War II–era planes are on display. Closed Mondays. Admission charge. Outside Minneapolis at 14771 Pioneer Trail, Eden Prairie (phone: 941-2633).

SHOPPING

Minneapolis–St. Paul's ethnic diversity is reflected in the interesting variety of shops in its neighborhoods. Several African American–oriented stores are located along University Avenue between Lexington Avenue and Victoria Street in St. Paul. For African crafts, try *Inside Africa* at *Galtier Plaza* (175 E. Fifth St., St. Paul; phone: 224-3508). Tasty Mexican food items can be purchased at *Boca Chica* (11 Concord St., St. Paul; phone: 222-8499) and *El Burrito Mexican Foods and Bakery* (175 Concord St., St. Paul; phone: 227-2192); several other shops along Concord Street offer Hispanic crafts and clothing. In Minneapolis, Native American artworks are sold at the *Two Rivers Gallery* (1530 E. Franklin Ave.; phone: 879-1780).

Bandana Square Filled with specialty and apparel shops and several restaurants in a renovated railroad repair complex, the square (1021 E. Bandana Blvd., St. Paul; phone: 642-1509) is listed in the *National Register of Historic Places.* Be sure to visit the *Twin City Model Railroad Club,* where models of area railroads as they existed in 1950 are on display. Open daily. Donations requested. Bandana Sq. (phone: 647-9628).

Byerly's Offering a food-shopping experience like no other—with carpeted aisles and chandeliers—this is a place where cantaloupe thumpers and tomato squeezers can browse from the cereal aisle over to the imported crystal and jewelry departments, and even take cooking classes. The food store is open 24 hours a day; some of the other departments close at 10 PM. 3777 Park Center Blvd., *St. Louis Park,* west of Minneapolis (phone: 929-2100).

Galtier Plaza Located in St. Paul's historic Lowertown District, the plaza has a marketplace atmosphere, with shops, four movie theaters, underground parking, and a rooftop garden. Sibley Ave. between Fifth and Sixth Sts., St. Paul (phone: 292-0600).

Mall of America Billed as the world's biggest shopping mall, this behemoth has hundreds of retail stores, including *Bloomingdale's, Macy's,* and *Nordstrom.* There also are 14 movie theaters, dozens of restaurants, and the *Camp Snoopy* theme park for kids. In Bloomington, at the intersection of Hwy. 77 and I-494 (phone: 851-3500).

Nicollet Mall Downtown Minneapolis's main shopping area hosts *Dayton's, Neiman Marcus, Saks Fifth Avenue,* boutiques, and other quality shopping outlets. 33 S. Sixth St. (phone: 372-1234).

Vintage Music Co. With more than 250,000 recordings in stock, this is the place for anyone seeking the nostalgic sound of good old vinyl albums. 2931 E. Lake St., Minneapolis (phone: 729-8929).

SPORTS AND FITNESS

BASEBALL The major league Minnesota *Twins* play at the 60,000-seat *Hubert H. Humphrey Metrodome* (500 11th Ave. S., Minneapolis; phone: 375-1116 for ticket information). For outdoor baseball, see the St. Paul *Saints* of the *Northern League* at *Municipal Stadium* (1771 Energy Park Dr., St. Paul; phone: 644-6659).

BASKETBALL The *NBA Timberwolves* play in the *Target Center* (600 First Ave. N., Minneapolis; phone: 337-3865).

BIKING Bike trails wind around Lake Harriet, Lake Calhoun, and Lake of the Isles in Minneapolis; Lakes Como and Phalen in St. Paul. Bicycles may be rented from the *Bike Shop* (213 Oak St. SE, Minneapolis; phone: 331-3442).

COLLEGE SPORTS For *University of Minnesota Big 10* athletic tickets, call 624-8080.

FISHING Of the 12 fishing lakes in the Twin Cities metro area, the best is Lake Minnetonka (15 miles west on Hwys. 394 and 12), which has 177 miles of shoreline. Within the city limits, Lake Calhoun has a fishing dock.

GOLF Minneapolis has five public 18-hole golf courses, one par-3 course, and a 9-hole course (phone: 661-4848 for information); St. Paul has three 18-hole courses and a 9-hole course (phone: 266-6445). Others are in the suburbs.

ICE SKATING The cities clear, test, and maintain outdoor rinks on many of the lakes. Indoor ice arenas offer some free time for public skating. Consult the yellow pages for locations and numbers.

JOGGING An ambitious run leads to Lake of the Isles, 2½ miles from downtown, and from there to Cedar Lake to the west or Lakes Calhoun and Harriet to the south; the perimeter of each lake is about 3 miles. Another route is along the Mississippi on East or West River Road, by the *University of Minnesota.* In St. Paul, joggers take to the trails around Lake Como and Lake Phalen. The most beautiful spot for runners in St. Paul is Summit Avenue and along the Mississippi River.

SKIING The best ski areas in the vicinity are *Afton Alps* in Afton (phone: 436-5245), *Welch Village* in Welch (phone: 258-4567), and *Buck Hill* in Burnsville (phone: 435-7174), all 30 to 45 minutes from town.

SWIMMING There are public beaches at 23 lakes in and around the Twin Cities area that are open during the summer.

TENNIS There are many lighted, outdoor courts as well as indoor courts available throughout the cities. Call for information on public park courts in Minneapolis (phone: 661-4875) and St. Paul (phone: 266-6400).

THEATER

The Twin Cities are filled with great theater companies. Our favorite is listed below, along with several other high-quality choices.

CENTER STAGE

Guthrie Theater After a nationwide search for a hospitable metropolitan environment in which to locate a repertory theater, Sir Tyrone Guthrie selected Minneapolis. His choice has been borne out by the enthusiastic support of audiences and patrons. With 1,309 seats, this is among the largest of the country's regional theaters. It also has one of the longest seasons, and its house, which shares a handsome contemporary building with the *Walker Art Center,* is one of the most unusual; its stage gives audiences access to three sides of the production, and no seat is more than about 50 feet from the stage. The resident acting company performs the classics in rotating repertory. 725 Vineland Pl. (phone: 377-2224).

In addition to the *Guthrie,* the Twin Cities have almost 100 professional and community theaters, with productions ranging from classics or contemporary drama to comedy and experimental theater. The universities and colleges also produce plays and musicals. The options include the *Children's Theatre Company* (phone: 874-0400) and the *Great American History Theatre* (phone: 292-4323), as well as three companies that mount contemporary dramas and the work of new playwrights: *Penumbra Theatre* (phone: 224-4601), *Mixed Blood Theatre* (phone: 338-6131), and the *Cricket Theatre* (phone: 337-0747). You also can be a member of the audience at Garrison Keillor's *Prairie Home Companion* broadcast from the *F. Scott Fitzgerald Theater* (10 E. Exchange St., St. Paul; phone: 290-1221). Since Keillor often takes the show on tour, it's wise to call ahead for tickets; contact either the theater box office or *TicketMaster* (phone: 989-5151). The restored *Historic State* and *Orpheum Theaters* (both at Hennepin Ave. in downtown Minneapolis; phone: 339-7007) offer touring shows.

MUSIC

For a complete schedule of musical happenings, check the newspapers (see *Local Coverage*). *Orchestra Hall* (1111 Nicollet Mall, Minneapolis; phone: 371-5656) is the home of the *Minnesota Orchestra* and presents other concerts as well. The copper-capped, glass-walled *Ordway Music Theatre* (345 Washington St.; phone: 293-5630) presents performances by the *St. Paul Chamber Orchestra,* the *Minnesota Opera,* and the *Schubert Club,* as well as touring Broadway shows and other theater productions. There are outdoor summer concerts at Lake Harriet in Minneapolis and at Lake Como in St. Paul.

NIGHTCLUBS AND NIGHTLIFE

Gallivan's Downtown (354 Wabasha, St. Paul; phone: 227-6688) features professional entertainment. *The Manor* (2550 W. Seventh St., St. Paul; phone: 690-1771) hosts ballroom dancing Thursdays through Saturdays. In the West Bank area near the *University of Minnesota,* there are a number of small clubs and cafés. *America Live!* operates six of the nine bars on the fourth floor of the *Mall of America* (see *Shopping)* in suburban Bloomington, arguably the hottest night scene in the Twin Cities area.

The *Dakota Bar & Grill* (1021 E. Bandana Blvd., St. Paul; phone: 642-1442) hosts the best jazz in the Twin Cities. The former *Greyhound Bus Depot* in Minneapolis now the *7th Street Entry* (701 First Ave. N.; phone: 332-1775), a nightclub featured in local rock star Prince's film *Purple Rain. The Fine Line Music Café* (318 First Ave. N., Minneapolis; phone: 338-8100) presents some of the best local talent to a hip audience. One of the hottest places in town for live music is the *Quest* (110 N. Fifth St., Minneapolis; phone: 338-3383). St. Paul's *Heartthrob Café and Nightclub* (30 E. Seventh St.; phone: 224-2783) draws a young, energetic crowd. Comedy-seekers can find laughs at *Scott Hansen's Comedy Gallery (Galtier Plaza,* St. Paul; phone: 331-4654). The *Gay 90s* (408 Hennepin Ave., Minneapolis; phone: 333-7755) houses eight separate gay bars.

WHEELS OF FORTUNE

Several casinos are only a short drive from the Twin Cities; *Grand Casino Hinckley* (777 Lady Luck Dr., Hinckley; phone: 800-GRAND-21), *Grand Casino Mille Lacs* (Hwy. 169, on the west shore of Mille Lacs Lake, Onamia; phone: 800-626-LUCK), *Jackpot Junction* (in Morton; phone: 800-WIN-CASH), *Mystic Lake Casino* (on the Prior Lake Indian Reservation, 2400 Mystic Lake Blvd., Prior Lake; phone: 800-262-7799), and *Treasure Island Casino* (5734 Sturgeon Lake Rd., Welch; phone: 800-222-7077). All offer slots, bingo, blackjack, and other games of chance; you must be 21 or over to play.

Best in Town

CHECKING IN

There are a number of hotels near the *Minneapolis–St. Paul International Airport,* in the suburb of Bloomington, and downtown. Most of the Twin Cities' major hotels have complete facilities for the business traveler. Those listed below as having "business services" usually offer such conveniences as meeting rooms, photocopiers, computers, translation services, and express checkout, among others. Call the individual hotel for additional information. Expect to pay $100 or more per night for a double room at places we've listed as expensive; $80 to $95 at those in the moderate category. *Days Inn, Best Western, Quality Inn,* and other chains provide inexpensive lodging (around $50). Unless otherwise noted, hotels have air conditioning, private baths, TV sets, and telephones.

All hotels below are in Minneapolis–St. Paul and telephone and fax numbers are in the 612 area code unless otherwise indicated.

We begin with our favorite haven, followed by recommended hotels, listed by price category.

A GRAND HOTEL

Lowell Inn Built more than half a century ago, this gracious colonial-style inn, with its 13 columns and high portico, has been run by the Palmer family since 1930 with an unusual degree of sensitivity to the proper care and feeding of guests. The 21 bedrooms are up-to-date, and each of the three popular dining rooms has a different motif (see *Eating Out).* The inn, a very pricey but rewarding choice, is about 18 miles from St. Paul, and Stillwater is chockablock with antiques shops. 102 N. Second St., Stillwater (phone: 439-1100; fax: 439-4686).

EXPENSIVE

Luxeford Suites This all-suite hotel at the edge of downtown has a European feel. Each of the 230 rooms is equipped with a wet bar, refrigerator, and microwave oven. A complimentary continental breakfast is laid out on the sideboard in the club room off the lobby. Room service is available until midnight. Other amenities include a fitness center, complimentary downtown shuttle service, and business services. 1101 La Salle Ave., Minneapolis (phone: 332-6800; 800-662-3232; fax: 332-8246).

Marquette Connected to the interior skyway in the *IDS Center,* this gracious 281-room inn offers spacious accommodations as well as a bar and restaurant. Among the amenities are room service until 2 AM, a concierge, and business services. 710 Marquette Ave., Minneapolis (phone: 332-2352; 800-328-4782; fax: 376-7419).

Minneapolis Hilton and Towers This 25-story establishment has 814 rooms, including 52 suites. The 71 concierge-level rooms offer private registration and a lounge. Facilities include two restaurants, two lounges, a fitness center, and a pool. Among the other amenities are room service until 2 AM and business services. 1001 Marquette Ave. S., Minneapolis (phone: 376-1000; 800-HILTONS; fax: 397-4871).

Minneapolis Marriott City Center Its 583 rooms include 62 with parlors and wet bars, and 20 two-level suites. Guest amenities include a health club, two restaurants, and a lounge. Room service is available until midnight, and business services are available. 30 S. Seventh St., Minneapolis (phone: 349-4000; 800-228-9290; fax: 332-7165).

Radisson Plaza Minneapolis Emphasizing personal service to the business traveler, this flagship of the Radisson collection has 357 suites and oversize rooms in the heart of downtown Minneapolis and offers two restaurants, two lounges, a fitness center, and concierge services. Other extras include 24-hour room service and business services are available. 35 S. Seventh St. (phone: 339-4900; 800-333-3333; fax: 337-9766).

Regal Minneapolis This former *Park Inn International* hotel features 325 refurbished rooms. The Midwestern modern decor is complemented by a tasteful use of woodwork, floral arrangements, and comfortable furnishings. It is connected to the *Minneapolis Convention Center* via an enclosed skyway. The hotel features a restaurant and lounge, health club with sauna and whirlpool, indoor swimming pool, car rental desk, and even a florist shop. Other amenities include room service and free local phone calls. 1313 *Nicollet Mall,* Minneapolis (phone: 332-6000; 800-522-8856; fax: 359-2160).

Saint Paul At this beautifully restored Victorian hotel, crystal chandeliers sparkle in the lobby, and elegant Biedermeier-style furniture decorates the guestrooms, some of which have lovely views over *Rice Park.* Its restaurants include the *St. Paul Bar & Grill* and *The Café.* The 252-room hotel, across from the *Ordway Music Theatre,* is connected by a skyway to department stores, banks, boutiques, and travel agencies. Room service is on call until 11 PM; other amenities include a concierge desk and business services. 350 Market St., St. Paul (phone: 292-9292; 800-292-9292; fax: 228-9506).

Whitney One of downtown Minneapolis's most deluxe establishments is this renovated turn-of-the-century flour mill overlooking the Mississippi River. Each of its 97 distinctive rooms (some are bi-level suites) is adapted to the old building's unique style. *Whitney's Grill* provides formal dining. Amenities include 24-hour room service. 150 Portland Ave., Minneapolis (phone: 339-9300; 800-248-1879; fax: 339-1333).

MODERATE

Holiday Inn Airport A five-minute drive from the airport, this six-story, 189-room hotel has a restaurant, pool, exercise room, and sauna. Business services are offered. 2700 Pilot Knob Rd., Eagan (phone: 454-3434; 800-EAGAN64; fax: 454-4904).

EATING OUT

Almost any kind of food can be found in the Twin Cities, from high-priced, exquisitely prepared continental dishes to Japanese food or a kosher delicatessen. Prices range from $50 or more for dinner for two at places listed as expensive; $30 to $50 at those in the moderate category; and $30 or less at inexpensive places. Prices do not include drinks, wine, tax, or tips. All restaurants are in the 612 area code.

Unless otherwise noted, restaurants are open for lunch and dinner.

EXPENSIVE

510 Try the pre-theater specials at this elegant place next to the *Guthrie Theater.* The preparation is French, and the results are largely terrific, whether the dish is pork, beef, swordfish, or shellfish. Specials include oven-roasted New Zealand lamb with Dijon crust. Closed Sundays. Reservations necessary. Major credit cards accepted. 510 Groveland Ave., Minneapolis (phone: 874-6440).

Forepaughs French food is served in a gracious 19th-century former home. Try the beef Wellington or the veal medaillons in an apple brandy–cream sauce. Free parking and shuttle service to the *Ordway Music Theatre* are provided. Reservations advised. Major credit cards accepted. 276 Exchange St., St. Paul (phone: 224-5606).

Goodfellow's Beautiful hardwood floors, a roaring fireplace, and a fine collection of contemporary art are almost peripheral to the creative dishes served here. The menu, which changes seasonally, lists farm-raised trout, Minnesota-raised duck, beef—and, on occasion, elk, venison, pheasant, and quail. Specials might include a grilled veal chop with white cheddar–sweet corn pudding and wild mushroom sauce. Closed Sundays; dinner only on Saturdays. Reservations advised. Major credit cards accepted. 800 *Nicollet Mall,* Minneapolis (phone: 332-4800).

Lowell Inn The closest thing to a New England inn that you'll find in the Midwest. The *George Washington Room* and the *Garden Room* offer steaks, seafood, and other American fare. For dessert, try the green grapes with Devonshire cream and brown sugar. The *Matterhorn Room*'s menu features fondues exclusively. Reservations necessary. MasterCard and Visa accepted. 102 N. Second St., Stillwater, a northeast suburb of St. Paul (phone: 439-1100).

Murray's This establishment is well known for its hickory-smoked shrimp appetizers, award-winning steaks, and homemade rolls. The decor recalls the 1940s, and there is music in the evening Thursdays through Saturdays. Reservations advised. Major credit cards accepted. 26 S. Sixth St., Minneapolis (phone: 339-0909).

MODERATE

Aladdin Café Located in the heart of the city, this spacious Middle Eastern restaurant proffers excellent traditional food such as falafel and *makanek* (lamb sausage). Closed Sundays. Reservations advised. MasterCard and Visa accepted. 704 Hennepin Ave. S., Minneapolis (phone: 338-6810).

D'Amico Cucina This eatery offers the chef's modern interpretation of classic Italian dishes as well as live entertainment. The tempting thin-crust pizza might be topped with fennel and orange zest or caramelized onions, golden raisins, and fontina cheese. Other options include sautéed chicken with gnocchi. Open daily for dinner only. Reservations advised. Major credit cards accepted. Butler Sq., 100 N. Sixth St., Minneapolis (phone: 338-2401).

Black Forest Inn Near the *Minneapolis Institute of Arts,* the inn serves bratwurst-and-sauerkraut dinners, Wiener schnitzel, and other honest, substantial

German fare. The restaurant evolved from a tavern that used to serve only beer, and it still offers German brews, which you can enjoy in the outdoor beer garden. Reservations advised. Major credit cards accepted. 1 E. 26th St., Minneapolis (phone: 872-0812).

Cherokee Sirloin Room Sirloins and tenderloins are the specialties at this steakhouse. Reservations advised on weekends. Major credit cards accepted. Two locations: 886 S. Smith, West St. Paul (phone: 457-2729); and outside St. Paul at 4625 Nichols Rd., Eagan (phone: 454-6744).

Dakota Bar & Grill Featuring the Twin Cities' best jazz, this place serves Minnesota-style steaks, lamb with wild rice, and fresh brook trout. Reservations advised. Major credit cards accepted. 1021 E. Bandana Blvd., St. Paul (phone: 642-1442).

Figlio The cooking is Italian via California—pizza and pasta topped with unusual combinations, as well as fresh fish and meat from the wood-fired oven and grill in the open kitchen. Reservations advised. Major credit cards accepted. 3001 Hennepin Ave. S., Minneapolis (phone: 822-1688).

Lexington This landmark spot has attracted politicians and business leaders for over half a century. The decor is formal and the cooking traditional, with short ribs, lamb shanks, and prime ribs. Reservations advised. Major credit cards accepted. 1096 Grand Ave., St. Paul (phone: 222-5878).

Nicollet Island Inn Classic Midwestern cooking with a Mediterranean influence is the staple of this old stone hotel (which also has 24 guestrooms). Delicious cuts of prime New York and tenderloin steaks are served here; another good choice is walleye almondine. It is located on an island in the Mississippi River, only a 10-minute walk from downtown across the Hennepin Suspension Bridge. Reservations advised. Major credit cards accepted. 95 Merriam St., Minneapolis (phone: 331-3035).

INEXPENSIVE

Café Brenda The fare at this sunny downtown health food eatery is so tasty and sophisticated you may forget it's also good for you. Try the Wisconsin rainbow trout or meal-size salads. Closed Sundays. Reservations advised. Major credit cards accepted. 300 First Ave. N., Minneapolis (phone: 342-9230).

Leeann Chin's This cavernous space used to be the *Union Depot.* Now its Oriental decor—stunning vases, jade and ivory carvings, and whimsical modern Chinese paintings—provides a backdrop for buffets that offer everything from cream cheese wontons to lemon chicken to almond cookie ice cream. Reservations advised. Major credit cards accepted. Union Depot Pl. at Fourth and Sibley, St. Paul (phone: 224-8814). A branch, closed Sundays, is located at 900 Second Ave., Minneapolis (phone: 338-8488).

Mickey's Diner This St. Paul institution has been serving world class omelettes 24 hours a day since 1939. Near the *Greyhound Bus Depot,* it attracts regulars from all walks of life. Nothing fancy here, just straight, down-to-earth cookin', four booths, and 17 counter stools. No reservations. Major credit cards accepted. 36 W. Seventh St. (phone: 222-5633). (The family also operates *Mickey's Restaurant,* with more space but the same ambience, at 1950 W. Seventh St.; phone: 698-8387).

BARBECUE BEAT

What's the best place for barbecue? That question always prompts lively debate here. Current favorites include *Market Bar-B-Que* (1414 Nicollet Ave. S., Minneapolis; phone: 872-1111); *Rudolph's Barbecue* (three locations; 1933 Lyndale Ave. S., Minneapolis; phone: 871-8969); 815 E. Hennepin Ave., Minneapolis; phone: 623-3671; and 14601 Hwy. 7, Minnetonka; phone: 938-4800); *The Pickled Parrot* (26 N. Fifth St., Minneapolis; phone: 332-0673); *The Smoke House* (500 E. Lake St., Minneapolis; phone: 824-0558); and *Ted Cook's 19th Hole Barbeque* (2814 E. 38th St., Minneapolis; phone: 721-2023).

Nashville

Nashville has been the country music capital of the world since—forever. Every year thousands of hero-worshiping fans from around the country come to town, taking tours and cruising past the homes of Johnny Cash, Barbara Mandrell, and dozens of other country music stars. In recent years, a rival to Nashville has emerged: Branson, Missouri, a small town in the Ozarks where stars such as Andy Williams, Roy Clark, and Mel Tillis have built their own theaters where they perform on a more or less continual basis. But Nashville has what no rival could possibly top—the "*Opry.*"

The *Grand Ole Opry,* a 2½-hour country music extravaganza, is Nashville's biggest drawing card. Broadcast weekly, it is also the longest-running radio program in the US. Before 1974, the *Opry* was held in the *Ryman Auditorium,* a converted revival temple that lacked air conditioning, and many performers escaped the heat by listening for their cues on the radio at *Tootsie's Orchid Lounge,* conveniently located near the backstage door. In 1974, the *Grand Old Opry* traded this authentic church-meeting atmosphere for the comfort of its present home on the east side of the city, with padded seats, air conditioning, and star-quality dressing rooms. Still onstage, however, are the same guitarists in rhinestoned suits and cloggers stomping in a blizzard of white petticoats.

Nashville is far from the simple hillbilly heaven portrayed in the songs that pour out of the mile-square area of South Nashville known as Music Row. The country music business, which is still concentrated here, is a growing multimillion-dollar industry. Nashville is also the leading center for gospel and bluegrass music. Even pop and rock performers (such as Bob Dylan, Amy Grant, and Linda Ronstadt) come here to record. There are scores of large recording studios, a number of major music publishers, more than a hundred talent agencies, and countless marketing firms and production houses. The *Opry House* is the largest broadcast studio in the world and the home of The Nashville Network (TNN), a country music cable channel. All TNN shows are taped at *Opryland* studios. Scores of other TV shows also are taped in Nashville.

The city has become the base for a number of other industries as well. Nissan and GM have plants nearby, and *American Airlines* has made Nashville its Southeastern hub.

With its various cultural offerings, Nashville has earned the nickname "Athens of the South." The town that goes berserk for the *International Country Music Fan Fair* also has many universities, a number of plantation mansions (including the *Hermitage,* Andrew Jackson's home), and the world's only full-scale replica of the Greek *Parthenon.* There is also a well-regarded symphony orchestra.

Like other American cities of half a million, Nashville has its traffic jams, its slums, and its eyesores: highways lined with fast-food joints, coffee shops with plastic signs, streams of neon lights, and used car lots. But beyond that, and beyond the occasional silliness of the country music mania, there's an unabashed, unpretentious good humor almost everywhere you go. There are dozens of nifty little Southern-cooking restaurants (called "meat 'n' threes" because the meat entrées come with three home-cooked vegetables) and hole-in-the-wall nightclubs with stages so small that the fiddlers can barely keep from bowing the banjo players. And with all the songwriters around, you may just hear a future hit performed before it—or its writer—hits the big time.

Nashville At-a-Glance

SEEING THE CITY

The *Pinnacle* restaurant atop the *Holiday Inn Crowne Plaza* downtown (Seventh and Union; phone: 742-6015) makes a complete rotation every half hour, providing an excellent view of the city, well worth the cost of lunch, dinner, or a drink.

SPECIAL PLACES

Most of the outstanding attractions are within a couple of miles of the downtown area or are along the southern and eastern outskirts of the city.

DOWNTOWN

DOWNTOWN PRESBYTERIAN CHURCH Designed by renowned architect William Strickland and completed in 1848 after a fire destroyed the original (ca. 1808), this church is a rare example of the Egyptian Revival style popular in the mid-1800s. The highly stylized interior, complete with desert clouds painted on the ceiling, was renovated in the 1880s. Closed weekends except for church services. No admission charge. 154 Fifth Ave. N. (phone: 254-7584).

FORT NASHBORO This partially reconstructed pioneer fort overlooking the Cumberland River is where Nashville began back in 1779. Open daily. No admission charge. 170 First Ave. N. For information, contact the *Metro Department of Parks and Recreation* (phone: 225-8192 or 862-8400).

RYMAN AUDITORIUM Home of the *Grand Ole Opry* between 1943 and 1974, the newly renovated *Ryman* now features museum displays, dressing rooms once used by *Opry* performers, and a modernized heating/cooling system—luxuries that were conspicuously absent during the *Opry*'s heyday. Built in 1891 as a revival temple by Tom Ryman, a riverboat captain who found religion, the auditorium has been a tourist attraction and museum since the *Opry* moved to its present home. Now, it once again hosts live country,

CENTRAL
NASHVILLE
0 miles 1/4
To Opryland appx. 8 miles
N
Cumberland R.
FARMER'S MARKET
Municipal Auditorium
Cordell Hull Blg
State Office Blgs
Capitol
State Library & Archives
St. Supreme Ct.
War Memorial Blg
Perf. Arts Ctr
Nat. Life Ctr.
Federal Reserve Bank
Public Library
Metro. Court House
Metro. Gov. Blg
Ft. Nashborough
Belle Carol Excursion Boat
River Terminal
Life & Casualty Tower
Chamber of Commerce
Ryman Auditorium
NASHVILLE CONVENTION CENTER (under construction)
Watkins Park
James Robertson Pkwy
JEFFERSON ST
MEHARRY BLVD
PHILLIPS ST
JACKSON ST
IRELAND ST
HERMAN ST
MORISTON ST
WARREN ST
CLINTON ST
JOHNSTON AV
MILSON ST
GAY ST
PEARL ST
CHARLOTTE AV
TOWNSEND DR
HARRION ST
SECOND AV
THIRD AV
FIRST ST
WOODLAND ST
FIRST AV
DEADERICK ST
UNION ST
PRINTER'S ALLEY
CHURCH ST
CAPITOL BLVD
COMMERCE ST
BROADWAY
MCGAVOCK ST
40

NASHVILLE
Music Row
Union Station
Post Office
Bus Terminal
Country Music Hall of Fame
Music Sq. Park
Toney Rose Park
HOSPITAL COMPLEX
VANDERBILT UNIVERSITY
Cumberland Museum & Science Ctr.
To Tenn. Fairgrounds 1 mile
To Centennial Park (Parthenon) 1 mile
To Stadium ½ mile
40
CHARLOTTE AV
PATTERSON ST
MCMILLIN ST
STATE ST
CHURCH ST
GRUNDY ST
BROADWAY
HAYES ST
WEST END AV
MCGAVOCK ST
DEMONBREUN ST
LAUREL ST
PINE ST
DIVISION ST
SIGLER ST
MUSIC CIR
MUSIC SQ W
MUSIC SQ E
HAWKINS ST
SOUTH ST
GRAND ST
ADELICIA ST
VILLA ST
LYLE ST
TERRACE PL
CLARK PL
SHIRLEY ST
FRANKLIN ST
PEABODY ST
THIRD AV
LEA AV
PALMER ST
LAFAYETTE ST
ELM ST
GLEAVES ST
MAGAZINE ST
OVERTON ST
MIDDLETON ST
EWING ST
ASH ST
FOGG ST
ALLISON ST
VINE ST
9 CT
BASS ST

pop, and bluegrass concerts as well as television tapings and musical theater. Shows highlighting country music's history and stars are regularly featured. Tours daily; shows Tuesdays through Saturdays. Separate admission charge for each. 116 Fifth Ave. N. (phone: 254-1445).

TENNESSEE STATE CAPITOL Completed in 1859, this picturesque hilltop building was a favorite of its designer, architect William Strickland, who is entombed here. Open daily; tours available weekdays. No admission charge. Charlotte Ave. between Sixth and Seventh Aves. (phone: 741-2692).

MUSIC ROW

COUNTRY MUSIC HALL OF FAME AND MUSEUM Memorabilia of country music stars—such as Elvis Presley's solid gold Cadillac, comedienne Minnie Pearl's straw hat with dangling price tag, Chet Atkins's first guitar, and rare film footage of Patsy Cline—celebrate 60-plus years of the *Grand Ole Opry.* Special exhibitions on current country stars or country music history are shown. Open daily. Admission charge. 4 Music Sq. E. (phone: 256-1639). Included in *Hall of Fame* tours is *Studio B,* where Elvis Presley, Charley Pride, Eddy Arnold, and a score of other greats recorded for RCA in the 1950s and 1960s. Guides discuss its history and the Nashville recording industry. Open daily. Admission to *Studio B* is included in the *Hall of Fame* charge. 17th Ave. at Roy Acuff Pl. (phone: 256-1639).

EAST

GRAND OLE OPRY This star-studded country music spectacular is well worth the planning it takes to get tickets. More than a third of the 60-odd acts under contract to the *Opry* will perform on a given night, and you're bound to like some if not all of them. There are shows Fridays and Saturdays year-round. Between *Memorial Day* and *Labor Day,* there are also matinees twice weekly. The first show on Saturday night is aired live on radio. All seats are reserved, and if you don't have tickets, call the *Opry*'s *Information Center* to see if any are available. *Information Center,* 2808 Opryland Dr. (phone: 889-6611).

OPRYLAND USA Full of trees and flowers, this 120-acre site on the banks of the Cumberland River at the edge of the city is a treat to behold. But *Opryland* really shines when it comes to music—not just country and bluegrass, as you might expect, but also rock 'n' roll, gospel, Broadway show tunes, and more; up to a dozen stage shows each day, with more than 400 performers. The complex includes the *Grand Ole Opry* and the *General Jackson* showboat, an entertainment palace that cruises the Cumberland River (see *Eating Out*). There are thrill rides, too: *Chaos,* an eight-story-high ride that incorporates lasers (riders wear 3-D glasses to make images come alive); the *Hangman,* the new heart stopping roller coaster; the wild *Grizzly River Rampage,* a huge and satisfyingly long whitewater rafting adventure; the *Screamin' Delta Demon* bobsled adventure; and more. Every *Memorial Day* weekend, the big *Opryland Gospel Jubilee* attracts some of the country's top-name gospel groups to the park; throughout the year, television specials are taped here (tickets are free to park guests), and top country stars perform from spring to autumn. Closed weekdays in the spring and fall and from November through March. Separate admission charges for *Opryland,* the *Grand Ole Opry,* and the showboat. 2802 Opryland Dr. (phone: 889-6611 or 889-6700).

HERMITAGE Once the home of President Andrew Jackson, this magnificent old plantation home is now a museum devoted to the Jackson family. *Tulip Grove,* a Greek Revival house completed in 1836, is also on the grounds. The museum features artifacts from the time the Jacksons lived in the mansion, details about its restoration, and a 20-minute film on the Jacksons. Tours are available. Open daily. Admission charge. About a 30-minute drive from downtown Nashville. 4580 Rachel's La., Hermitage (phone: 889-2941).

SOUTH

TRAVELLERS' REST The home of John Overton, one of Nashville's first settlers, has been restored, expanded, and filled with furniture, letters, and memorabilia that tell of Tennessee's settlement and civilization. Closed Mondays. Admission charge. 636 Farrell Pkwy., 6 miles south of downtown via Franklin Rd., US 31 (phone: 832-8197).

CIVIL WAR BATTLEFIELDS More Civil War battles were fought in Tennessee than in any other state except Virginia. Markers chronicling the 1864 Battle of Nashville dot the south and west sides of the city, and two battlefields lie just a few miles south. One of the war's bloodiest engagements occurred in Franklin, largely in the front yard of the *Carter House* (1140 Columbia Ave.; phone: 791-1861). This restored antebellum home has a museum on the grounds with an exhibit about the battle, Civil War relics, and other memorabilia. Open daily. Admission charge. About 1 mile southeast of the *Carter House* is *Carnton Plantation,* a beautifully restored Federal-style house set on two acres, with a Confederate cemetery on the grounds. After the battle, the bodies of six slain Confederate generals reportedly were placed on the front porch, and there are tales that several ghosts still haunt the place. Open daily. Admission charge. 1345 Carnton La. (phone: 794-0903). To get to Franklin, take I-65 south to the Franklin exit.

The *Stones River National Battlefield,* where an 1863 struggle set the stage for the Union advance to Chattanooga, is 20 miles southeast of Nashville. Explore the park along hiking trails, either alone or with a guide; there's also a visitors' center and a museum. Open daily. No admission charge. Take I-24 from Nashville to the Stones River/Highway 96 exit, go east on Highway 96 to US Highway 41. Turn north on US 41, then follow the signs. (For information on other battlesites, see "Civil War Battlesites," in DIVERSIONS.)

WEST

BELLE MEADE MANSION Inside the century-old rock walls that edge the 24-acre estate, this house is just a shadow of its former self (it was once the centerpiece of a 5,300-acre plantation), but even the shadow is impressive: immense pillars and ornate plaster cornices outside, and Adamesque moldings and a double parlor inside. Open daily. Admission charge. 5025 Harding Rd. (phone: 356-0501).

PARTHENON This full-scale reproduction of the ancient Greek building celebrates Nashville's reputation as the "Athens of the South." Though the structure is not marble, its four bronze doors are the largest in the world. Inside there is an impressive replica of the statue of Athena that graced the original *Parthenon,* reproductions of the Elgin Marbles, plus pre-Columbian art and various changing exhibitions. Closed Sundays and Mondays. Admission charge. In *Centennial Park* at 25th Ave. N. and West End Ave. (phone: 862-8431).

TENNESSEE BOTANICAL GARDENS AND CHEEKWOOD FINE ARTS CENTER *Cheekwood,* a Georgian mansion built in the 1930s, is now a museum with art shows and traveling exhibitions. Note the elegant Palladian window, the chandelier, and the swooping spiral staircase (which came from Queen Charlotte's palace at Kew, England). Outdoors are formal gardens, a wisteria arbor, wildflower gardens, a Japanese sand garden, greenhouses, and an outstanding boxwood garden. Open daily. Admission charge. On Forrest Park Dr., 7 miles west of town (phone: 356-8000).

EXTRA SPECIAL

You'll see the announcements for tours of the homes of the stars on big billboards on the way into town, and even if you ordinarily hate group excursions, you may like these for a glimpse into what makes Nashville tick. Each of the following offers several all-day, half-day, evening, or nightlife tours: *Country Western/Gray Line* (2416 Music Valley Dr.; phone: 883-5555; 800-251-1864); *Grand Ole Opry Tours* (2810 Opryland Dr.; phone: 889-9490); and *Nashville Tours* (2626 Music Valley Dr.; phone: 889-4646).

Sources and Resources

TOURIST INFORMATION

For brochures, maps, and general tourist information, write the *Nashville Area Chamber of Commerce* (161 Fourth Ave. N., Nashville, TN 37219; phone: 259-4755); or contact the *Convention and Visitors Bureau* (161 Fourth Ave. N.; phone: 259-4700), both closed weekends. The tourist information center at exit 85 on I-65N, just east of downtown (phone: 259-4747), is open daily. Contact the Tennessee state tourism hotline (741-2158) for maps, calendars of events, health updates, and travel advisories.

LOCAL COVERAGE *The Tennessean,* morning daily; the *Nashville Banner,* weekday afternoons. The former publishes a complete events listing on Fridays and Sundays; the latter on Thursdays. Both available at newsstands. The *Nashville*

Scene, a free weekly paper available at many stores and restaurants, publishes a comprehensive listing of area happenings, including a list of every nightspot in town. The *Nashville Visitor's Guide,* on sale at most newsstands, is as comprehensive a city guide as you'll see anywhere.

TELEVISION STATIONS WKRN Channel 2–ABC; WSMV Channel 4–NBC; WTVF Channel 5–CBS; WDCN Channel 8–PBS; and WZTV Channel 17–Fox.

RADIO STATIONS AM: WSIX 980 (country music); WAMB 1160 (big band); WKDA 1240 (contemporary rock); and WLAC 1510 (news/talk). FM: WPLN 90 (classical/public radio); WZEZ 93 (easy listening); WRLT 100 (alternative jazz/rock); and WGFX 104.5 (oldies rock).

TELEPHONE The area code for Nashville is 615.

SALES TAX The city sales tax for most goods is 7¾%; the hotel tax is 11¾%.

CLIMATE Nashville's temperatures hover around the 80s and 90s F in summer, dropping into the 40s and 30s (occasionally into the 20s or lower) between November and March. It gets humid in the summer; expect thunderstorms from March through late summer and rain in the spring and in October and November.

GETTING AROUND

AIRPORT The *Nashville Metropolitan Airport* is a 15- to 20-minute drive from downtown (30 minutes or more during rush hours). Many hotels provide free transportation from the airport; check with your hotel when making reservations.

BUS They are inconvenient at best, but buses are available (phone: 242-4433 for route information). The fare is $1.25.

CAR RENTAL The major national agencies are represented.

TAXI Nashville's principal cab companies are *Yellow* (phone: 256-0101) and *Checker* (phone: 254-5031).

SPECIAL EVENTS

The annual *Tennessee Crafts Fair* (PO Box 120066, Nashville, TN 37212; phone: 665-0502), one of the largest shows of its kind in the South, is held in *Centennial Park* on the first full weekend in May. On the second Saturday in May is the *Iroquois Steeplechase,* the day-long series of eight races that's the oldest amateur steeplechase meet in the US (Old Hickory Blvd. in *Percy Warner Park,* 11 miles south of Nashville; for information contact *Friends of Children's Hospital,* 2424 Garland Ave., Nashville, TN 37212; or call 322-7450, beginning in February). The *Opryland Gospel Jubilee* brings gospel bands, choruses, and lots of extra music to the theme park every year over *Memorial Day* weekend (see *Opryland USA* in *Special Places*). *Summer Lights,* a downtown festival produced by the *Greater Nashville Arts Foundation* (phone: 259-0900) and held the second weekend after *Memorial Day,* lights up 12 city blocks from the historic Second Avenue "Market Street" area to Legislative Plaza. Local musicians are showcased along with street performers, visual arts exhibits, and other entertainment. Many notable restaurants offer specialties from street booths, and area shops have special outdoor stands. The *International Country Music Fan Fair* (2804 Opryland Dr., Nashville, TN 37214; phone: 889-7503), usually scheduled for the first week of June, brings thousands for five days of spectacular shows, autograph sessions, concerts, and a *Grand Masters Fiddling Contest. Independence Day* celebrations include fireworks displays, performances ranging from the *Nashville Symphony* to country and rock bands, and other entertainment in a huge street party in *Riverfront Park.* In late September or October, there's the *National Quartet Convention* (Dept. N, 54 Music Sq. W., Nashville, TN 37203; phone: 800-333-4849), five days of top-name gospel singing at the *Nashville Municipal Auditorium.* The annual *Fall Crafts Fair* (PO Box 120066, Nashville, TN 37212; phone: 665-0502), organized by the *Tennessee Association of Craft Artists,* is held on a September weekend in *Centennial Park.*

MUSEUMS

In addition to those described above in *Special Places,* Nashville has several museums worth noting.

CUMBERLAND SCIENCE MUSEUM AND SUDEKUM PLANETARIUM This children's museum offers live animal shows, science demonstrations, and experiments to try. Closed Mondays except in summer. Admission charge. 800 Ft. Negley Blvd. (phone: 862-5160).

TENNESSEE STATE MUSEUM Located in the *Tennessee Performing Arts Center,* with a branch devoted to military history in the *War Memorial Building,* this museum mounts frequent exhibitions of local arts and crafts. Open daily. No admission charge. Fifth and Union Sts. (phone: 741-2692).

VAN VECHTEN GALLERY Housed here is the *Stieglitz Collection,* more than 100 works of 20th-century art donated to *Fisk University* by artist Georgia O'Keeffe after the death of her husband, photographer Alfred Stieglitz, as well as works by Picasso, Cézanne, Renoir, and O'Keeffe, herself. Closed Mondays. No admission charge. *Fisk University,* 18th Ave. corner of Jackson St. and D.B. Todd N. (phone: 329-8720).

SHOPPING

There's something for all tastes, from small, exclusive shops to large, encompassing malls. The region's largest shopping malls are *Hickory Hollow* (near I-24 at Bell Rd.); *Rivergate* (I-65 at Two Mile Pike); *Bellevue Center* (I-40, Bellevue exit); and *Cool Springs Galleria* (I-65 near Franklin); and the recently renovated *100 Oaks* (719 Thompson La). Brave these on weekends only if you enjoy fighting crowds. The *Mall at Green Hills* (entrances off Hillsboro and Abbott-Martin Rds.) offers upscale shops and two major department stores, and is usually less crowded. Antiques shops are all over the city, but several good ones are clustered on Eighth Avenue near the intersection with Wedgewood. For a fun afternoon of browsing, try *White Way Antique Mall* (1200 Villa Place, behind the *White Way Cleaners* on Edgehill).

Davis-Kidd Booksellers The best—and biggest—bookstore in the state has a pleasant café built into its upper level where you can sip wine or herb tea and read your purchase. 4007 Hillsboro Rd. (phone: 385-2645).

McClure's The city's best department store has clothes you won't find anywhere else in town. 6000 Highway 100, Belle Meade (phone: 356-8822) or 257 Franklin Rd. in Brentwood (phone: 377-3769).

Stanford Square This collection of exclusive stores features clothing shops and *American Artisan* (phone: 298-4691), which sells interesting objets d'art and jewelry by local and national craftspeople. 4231 Harding Rd.

SPORTS AND FITNESS

BASEBALL The Nashville *Sounds,* a Triple-A farm team for the Chicago *White Sox,* play in *Greer Stadium* (Chestnut, between Fourth and Eighth Aves. S.; phone: 242-4371).

FISHING AND BOATING Two manmade lakes—Old Hickory (phone: 822-4846) and Percy Priest (phone: 889-1975)—are a 20-minute drive from downtown, and several others are within an hour or so. Call the Resource Management office at each lake for boat and equipment rental details. The *Tennessee Wildlife Resources Agency* (phone: 781-6500) can provide details about other area lakes.

FITNESS CENTERS The *Centennial Sportsplex* (222 25th Ave. N.; phone: 862-8480), which is open to the public for a fee, offers a fitness center with a pool, weight rooms, aerobics programs, and an ice rink.

GOLF There are 10 public courses in Nashville. The best 18-holers are at *Harpeth Hills* (2424 Old Hickory Blvd., off Rte. 431 S.; phone: 862-8493) and *Nashville Golf and Athletic Club* (Moore's Lane in Franklin; phone: 370-3346). The only 27-hole course is at *McCabe Park* (46th Ave. N. at Murphy Rd.; phone: 269-6951 or 862-8491).

JOGGING Follow Church Street (which turns into Elliston Place) to *Centennial Park,* about 1½ miles from downtown and near *Vanderbilt University;* or drive or take the West End–Belle Meade bus (from Sixth and Church, or Deaderick at Fourth or Sixth) to *Percy Warner Park,* 11 miles south of Nashville. Jogging in either area after dark is not recommended.

STOCK CAR RACING Every Saturday night from April through mid-September, there's local racing at the *Nashville Speedway* located at the *Tennessee State Fairgrounds* (Wedgewood Ave. between Fourth and Eighth Aves. S.; phone: 726-1818).

SWIMMING Open throughout the summer, *Wave Country* (on Two Rivers Pkwy. near *Opryland*; phone: 885-1052) is the Southeast's largest surf-producing pool. Indoor swimming is available year-round at the *Centennial Sportsplex* (25th Ave. N.; phone: 862-8480).

TENNIS The major public facility is at the *Centennial Sportsplex* (25th Ave. N.; phone: 862-8490), where 17 courts are open from March through October and four indoor courts are open year-round. There's indoor tennis year-round at *Nashboro Athletic Club* (2250 Murfreesboro Rd.; phone: 361-3242), which also has outdoor clay courts available in summer.

THEATER

The *Tennessee Performing Arts Center* (505 Deaderick St.; phone: 741-7945) is home to touring Broadway shows and regional companies. Lively children's theater and classics for adults are presented by the *Nashville Academy Theatre* (724 Second Ave. S.; phone: 254-9103), the city's resident professional company. The *Tennessee Repertory Theatre* performs six plays or musicals each year in the *Polk Theater* of the *Tennessee Performing Arts Center.* Two small companies that perform works are *Darkhorse Theatre* (4610 Charlotte Ave.; phone: 297-7113); and *The Circle Players* (phone: 383-7469), both at the *Johnson Theatre* of the *Tennessee Performing Arts Center* (see above). For dinner-theater, try *Chaffin's Barn Dinner Theater* (8204 Hwy. 100; phone: 646-9977). Also, the *Nashville Shakespeare Festival* offers free summer productions in *Centennial Park* weekdays during August.

TV SHOW TAPINGS

The Nashville Network (TNN), a cable TV network originating in *Opryland,* tapes a number of programs before live audiences. For information, contact The Nashville Network, Viewer Services (2806 Opryland Dr., Nashville, TN 37214; phone: 883-7000).

MUSIC

In addition to the omnipresent *Opry,* the *Nashville Symphony* gives concerts from September through May in the *Tennessee Performing Arts Center* (the symphony box office is at 208 23rd Ave. N.; phone: 329-3033). On Friday and Sunday nights from June through August, there are musical programs at *Centennial Park.* For information, call the *Parks and Recreation Department*'s activities number (phone: 862-8400). Chamber music is offered (often at no charge) at *Fisk University,* at the *Blair School of Music* on the *Vanderbilt* campus, and at *Cheekwood Fine Arts Center* on weekends (phone: 356-8000).

NIGHTCLUBS AND NIGHTLIFE

Nashville isn't called "Music City, USA" for nothing. Even motels sometimes turn up good entertainers. Check newspapers and the *Nashville Visitor's Guide* for a rundown of places to hear country music.

Gaylord Entertainment, which runs *Opryland* and the *Ryman Auditorium,* also manages the *Wildhorse Saloon* (phone: 251-1000) on historic Second Avenue. The saloon, which is connected to *Opryland* by two 100-passenger river taxis, is a contemporary country-music dance and performance hall used as a set for TNN (The Nashville Network) tapings. There's a limited-menu restaurant and dance instruction. Up the street is *Club Mere Bulles* (phone: 256-2582), which features modern rock and jazz in the club section and a full-service restaurant. From Second Avenue, it's a four-block walk or a short trolley ride to Printer's Alley, where, along with some striptease joints and seedy-looking bars, there are standouts like the *Captain's Table* (phone: 256-3353), a silver and linen tablecloth sort of place. For bluegrass, try *Station Inn* (402 12th Ave. S.; phone: 255-3307). Hear jazz, rock, country, and folk music at the nationally renowned *Bluebird Café* (4104 Hillsboro Rd.; phone: 383-1461), which frequently hosts Writers' Nights to give local songwriters a chance to try out their compositions; *Boardwalk Café* (4114 Nolensville Rd.; phone: 832-5104); the *Bullpen Lounge* at the *Stock Yard* restaurant (901 Second Ave. N.; phone: 255-6464); and *328 Performance Hall* (328 Fourth Ave. S.; phone: 259-3288). The city's most active dance club is the *Ace of Clubs* (114 Second Ave. S.; phone: 254-2237), with good music (live bands Mondays through Thursdays) and a big dance floor. For blues fans, there's *The Texas Troubadour Theater* (Music Valley Drive; phone: 885-0028) which revives the recordings of Ernest Tubb's legendary midnight jamboree radio program. Most major hotels have entertainment in their lounges; the *Opryland* hotel has three lounges that offer good live country music. The *General Jackson* showboat (phone: 889-6611 for reservations) offers dinner and an excellent musical show as well as entertainment in the lounge before dinner. *Zanies Comedy Showplace* (2025 Eighth Ave.; phone: 269-0221) features stand-up comedians nightly.

Best in Town

CHECKING IN

Along with dozens of motels, there are some venerable (though refurbished) "Southern Belles" in Nashville. Most of Nashville's major hotels have complete facilities for the business traveler. Those listed below as having "business services" usually offer such conveniences as meeting rooms, photocopiers, computers, translation services, and express checkout, among others. Call the individual hotel for additional information. Expect to pay $80 or more per night for a double room at hotels listed as expensive; $45 to $80 at hostelries classified as moderate. Unless noted, hotels have air conditioning, private baths, TV sets, and telephones.

All hotels below are in Nashville and telephone and fax numbers are in the 615 area code unless otherwise indicated.

EXPENSIVE

Hermitage Suites Built in 1910, this luxurious Beaux Arts showpiece has 112 suites, an oak-paneled bar, a fine dining room, and an outrageous Art Deco men's room (a few local ladies have sneaked in for a peek). Business services are available. 231 Sixth Ave. N. (phone: 244-3121; 800-251-1908; fax: 254-6909).

Loews Vanderbilt Plaza This modern tower hotel has 338 luxurious rooms, including 10 parlor suites and three executive suites. There's also a restaurant, café, gameroom, and lounge. Amenities include health club facilities, 24-hour room service, a concierge, and business services. 2100 West End Ave. (phone: 320-1700; 800-23-LOEWS; fax: 320-5019).

Opryland This sprawling hotel has 2,870 rooms and 120 suites near the *Opry* and *Opryland* (but 20 minutes from downtown). The complex includes five lounges, four restaurants, and dozens of specialty shops. An additional wing comprises 979 guestrooms. The *Old Hickory Room* is a good restaurant, serving continental and traditional Southern fare. The hotel also has a beautiful indoor conservatory with suspended walkways. Other amenities include 24-hour room service, a concierge, and business services. 2800 Opryland Dr. (phone: 889-1000; fax: 871-7741).

Regal Maxwell House Located five minutes from downtown, this upscale favorite features 289 rooms. Guests are afforded such amenities as a complimentary full breakfast buffet, afternoon hors d'oeuvres, free local calls, a tennis court, a sauna, and steamroom. *JD's Chop House* offers good American fare along with scenic rooftop dining. Nonsmoking rooms are available. 2025 MetroCenter Blvd. (phone: 259-4343; 800-547-4460; fax: 313-1327).

Renaissance Nashville Next to the *Convention Center* and *Church Street Center,* a mall with shopping and restaurants, this 673-room downtown high-rise has location, location, location. There is casual dining at its *Commerce Street Bar and Grill,* and the *Bridge Deli* offers sandwiches. Other amenities include 24-hour room service, a concierge, and business services. 611 Commerce St. (phone: 255-8400; 800-468-3571; fax: 255-8202).

Union Station Located in the National Historic Landmark building that originally was the city's train station, this property now offers 124 uniquely styled rooms along with 13 suites. There are two restaurants: *Arthur's,* which serves fine continental food (see *Eating Out*), and the *Broadway Bistro* café. Sports facilities are available at a nearby fitness center. Business services are available. 1001 Broadway (phone: 726-1001; 800-331-2123; fax: 248-3554).

MODERATE

Hampton Inn Vanderbilt Among the extras at this comfortable 171-room hostelry are hearty complimentary continental breakfasts, an exercise facility, and an outdoor pool. Business services are available. 1919 West End Ave. and three other area locations (phone: 329-1144; 800-HAMPTON; fax: 320-7112).

Holiday Inn Vanderbilt Though a fairly standard link in the Holiday Inn chain, this 300-room high-rise is a good value. It's conveniently close to *Vanderbilt University,* a horde of good restaurants, the *Parthenon, Centennial Park,* and some good nightspots. Other amenities include a fitness center and business services. 2613 West End Ave. (phone: 327-4707; 800-465-4329; fax: 327-8034).

EATING OUT

Nashville is, as they say, a good eating town, with lots of small, unpretentious restaurants where you'll find fried chicken and shrimp, steaks, homestyle vegetables, and the like. Dinner for two (without drinks, wine, tax, or tips) at places listed as expensive will cost $40 or more. Expect to pay $20 to $40 at those categorized as moderate, and less than $20 at inexpensive places. All restaurants are in the 615 area code unless otherwise indicated.

Unless otherwise noted, restaurants are open for lunch and dinner.

EXPENSIVE

Arthur's Seven-course continental dining (the menu changes daily) and plush decor characterize this chic eating place. Reservations necessary. Major credit cards accepted. *Union Station Hotel,* 1001 Broadway (phone: 255-1494).

Mario's Owner Mario Ferrari serves a variety of Italian veal dishes—try the veal saltimbocca—as well as inventive pasta entrées and seasonal specials. Open for dinner only; closed Sundays. Reservations necessary. Major credit cards accepted. 2005 Broadway (phone: 327-3232).

Wild Boar This is not the place to eat light, but it's a good choice if you want to indulge in nicely cooked game or fish after warming up with one of the many appetizers, accompanied by a fine wine and finished off with a rich dessert. Open daily; dinner only on weekends. Reservations advised. Major credit cards accepted. 2014 Broadway (phone: 329-1313).

MODERATE

Cakewalk This small, pleasant café serves excellent and inventive meals—fish and shrimp dishes, salads, quiche, and an attractive weekend brunch. Try any of the daily specials and soups. Reservations advised for dinner. Major credit cards accepted. 3001 West End Ave. (phone: 320-7778).

General Jackson Based at *Opryland USA,* this showboat offers brunch and dinner cruises on the Cumberland River. Entertainment is topnotch, and the food—particularly brunch—is good. Open daily, but the cruise schedule depends on the time of year. Reservations necessary well in advance. Major credit cards accepted. *Opryland USA* (phone: 889-6611).

La Paz This upscale Mexican restaurant offers an active bar, fireplaces in winter, frozen margaritas, and alfresco dining in the summer. The menu is full of interesting variations on traditional Mexican dishes, with a Southwestern influence. Open daily; dinner only on Saturdays. No reservations. Major credit cards accepted. 3808 Cleghorn Ave. (phone: 383-5200).

Siam Café The place in town for excellent Thai food. If you're in a hurry, go through the cafeteria line and eat in the front section of the restaurant, but we recommend that you take the time to sit in the quiet back section, order one of the day's specials, and try an appetizer or two. Open daily; dinner only on Sundays. No reservations. Major credit cards accepted. Directly off Nolensville Rd. at 316 McCall (phone: 834-3181).

Sunset Grill "Do lunch" or dinner with Music Row moguls and Nashville professionals at this pleasant place, which offers an eclectic range of pasta, vegetarian dishes, and grilled fish and meat. Don't ignore the extensive dessert menu and wine list. Reservations advised for dinner. Major credit cards accepted. 2001 Belcourt Ave. (phone: 386-3663).

INEXPENSIVE

Cooker This chain offers some of the best Southern cooking in town—nothing fancy, but plenty of big salads and stick-to-your-ribs main courses in a pleasant atmosphere. No reservations, and expect a wait at peak hours. Major credit cards accepted. 2609 West End Ave. (phone: 327-2925). Other locations at 4770 Lebanon Rd., Hermitage (phone: 883-9700), 1211 Murfreesboro Rd. (phone: 361-4747), and 317 Blue Bird Rd., Goodlettsville (phone: 859-2756).

Elliston Place Soda Shop Here good lunches and dinners are served by waitresses who look as if they're about to tell you to eat all your vegetables. The tile and chrome decor from the 1940s is beautifully intact. Closed Sundays. Reservations unnecessary. No credit cards accepted. 2111 Elliston Pl. (phone: 327-1090).

Loveless Motel The walls are lined with autographed photos of country music stars who have eaten here. The fried chicken, homemade biscuits, peach and blackberry preserves, and country ham (salty, the way it's supposed to be) with red-eye gravy are famous. Have breakfast anytime. Closed Mondays. Reservations advised. MasterCard and Visa accepted. Rte. 5, Hwy. 100 (phone: 646-9700).

Rotier's A real Nashville tradition, it serves typical bar food in a "Cheers"-like setting. Locals are slavishly loyal to Mrs. Rotier's grilled cheeseburgers, and the milk shakes get rave reviews. Closed Sundays. No reservations or credit cards accepted. 2413 Elliston Pl. near Vanderbilt (phone: 327-9892).

Swett's The excellent Southern cooking here includes home-cooked pork chops, barbecued chicken and ribs, meat loaf, and side dishes that range from traditional Southern green beans to stewed apples. Reservations unnecessary. Major credit cards accepted. 28th and Clifton (phone: 329-4418).

New Haven

To most first-time visitors, New Haven is *Yale,* and *Yale* is New Haven. The university dominates the city center, and as *Yale* is the city's largest single employer, the production of educated, worldly citizens qualifies as New Haven's primary industry.

But there was a New Haven long before there was a *Yale*—the city was established in 1638; *Yale* didn't arrive here until 1716. New Haven has had a diverse population since its founding as an early trading center. The deep waters of New Haven Harbor spurred its progress as a commercial center during the 19th century, and the construction of the *New Haven Railroad* brought many Irish, Italian, Polish, and Jewish immigrants who shaped the city's culture and provided the manpower for heavy industry.

Today, New Haven is a city of strong contrasts. There is the "Hill Section," what many consider an urban eyesore riddled with abandoned and dilapidated buildings; there is also Hillhouse Avenue, once described by Charles Dickens as the loveliest street in America. The avenue is flanked by beautiful Victorian mansions of red brick fronted by spacious landscaped gardens. One of the homes, the *Aaron Skinner House,* is an outstanding example of Greek Revival architecture.

Many of New Haven's neighborhoods have retained their ethnic characteristics. Neat wooden houses line the streets of Fair Haven, where many Irish-Americans live, and the Wooster Square area, with its large Italian population, is also rich in restaurants. Many well-heeled residents live in exclusive homes in Westville and on Wooster Square itself. The efforts of city officials have kept these neighborhoods intact, preventing New Haven from degenerating into a slum surrounding an Ivy League enclave. Nevertheless, the city has undergone a population loss in recent decades, and crime has been a problem, especially in the poorer neighborhoods. The recession of the early 1990s hit the Northeast particularly hard, and the city (like much of the rest of Connecticut) is only slowly getting back on its feet.

Yale's presence is a beneficial one. It brings to New Haven a diversity of architectural styles—modern buildings standing next to genteel 19th-century homes—and an even more distinct mix of cultures. *Yale* also gives the city a number of valuable cultural institutions—the *Peabody Museum of Natural History,* the *Yale Collection of Musical Instruments,* the *Yale Repertory Theatre,* the *University Art Gallery,* and the *Center for British Art.* New Haven, in turn, supplies the university with an efficient work force and complements its collections with three beautiful churches on *The Green,* the *New Haven Historical Society,* and a score of good restaurants.

The bond between the two is hardly perfect, but town-and-gown relations have improved over the past few years, creating a somewhat more relaxed atmosphere. Both "Yalies" and "townies" know that New Haven

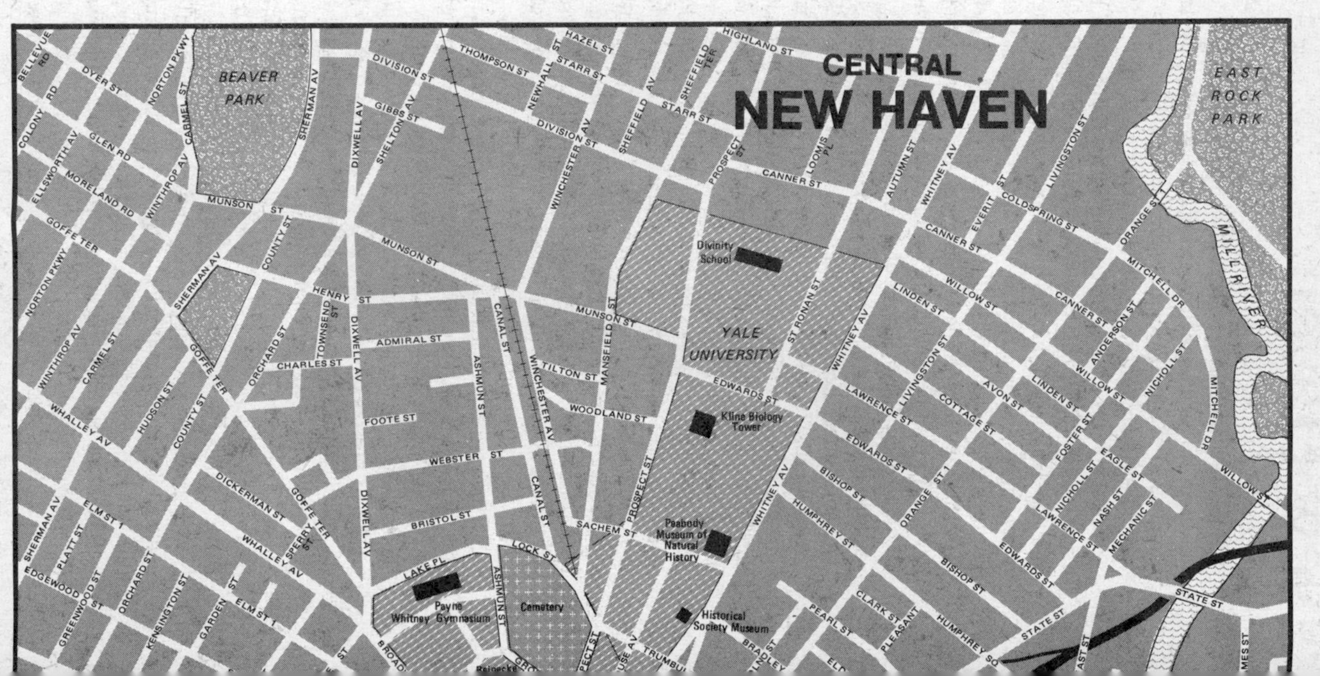
CENTRAL
NEW HAVEN
EAST ROCK PARK
MILL RIVER
BEAVER PARK
YALE UNIVERSITY
Divinity School
Kline Biology Tower
Peabody Museum of Natural History
Historical Society Museum
Payne Whitney Gymnasium
Cemetery
HIGHLAND ST
HAZEL ST
THOMPSON ST
DIVISION ST
NEWHALL ST
STARR ST
SHEFFIELD TER
SHEFFIELD AV
PROSPECT ST
LOOMIS PL
CANNER ST
AUTUMN ST
WHITNEY AV
EVERIT ST
COLDSPRING ST
LIVINGSTON ST
ORANGE ST
MITCHELL DR
GIBBS ST
SHELTON AV
DIXWELL AV
WINCHESTER AV
MUNSON ST
SHERMAN AV
CARMEL ST
NORTON PKWY
DYER ST
BELLEVUE RD
COLONY RD
GLEN RD
ELLSWORTH AV
MORELAND RD
WINTHROP AV
GOFFE TER
COUNTY ST
HENRY ST
TOWNSEND ST
ADMIRAL ST
CHARLES ST
ORCHARD ST
ASHMUN ST
CANAL ST
TILTON ST
MANSFIELD ST
WOODLAND ST
FOOTE ST
WEBSTER ST
BRISTOL ST
SACHEM ST
LOCK ST
LAKE PL
ST RONAN ST
EDWARDS ST
LINDEN ST
WILLOW ST
ANDERSON ST
NICHOLL ST
LAWRENCE ST
AVON ST
COTTAGE ST
FOSTER ST
EAGLE ST
NASH ST
MECHANIC ST
BISHOP ST
HUMPHREY ST
PEARL ST
CLARK ST
PLEASANT
STATE ST
WHALLEY AV
HUDSON ST
DICKERMAN ST
SPERRY ST
ELM ST
KENSINGTON ST
GARDEN ST
PLATT ST
EDGEWOOD ST
GREENWOOD ST
BRADLEY

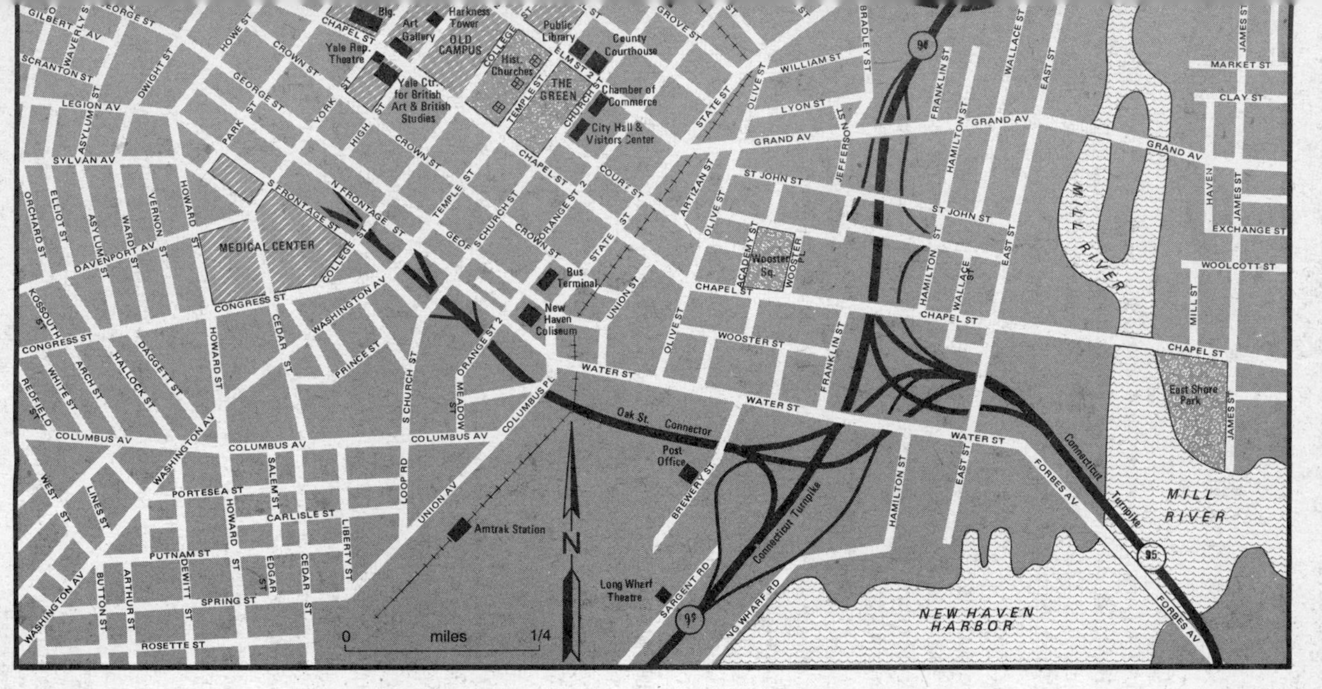

Harkness Tower
Art Gallery
OLD CAMPUS
Yale Rep. Theatre
Yale Ctr. for British Art & British Studies
Public Library
County Courthouse
Hist. Churches
THE GREEN
Chamber of Commerce
City Hall & Visitors Center
MEDICAL CENTER
Wooster Sq.
Bus Terminal
New Haven Coliseum
Post Office
Amtrak Station
Long Wharf Theatre
East Shore Park
MILL RIVER
NEW HAVEN HARBOR
Oak St. Connector
Connecticut Turnpike
95
91
N
0 miles 1/4
CHAPEL ST
CROWN ST
GEORGE ST
HOWE ST
YORK ST
PARK ST
HIGH ST
TEMPLE ST
COLLEGE ST
ELM ST
CHURCH ST
COURT ST
STATE ST
ORANGE ST
GEOF ST
S CHURCH ST
N FRONTAGE ST
S FRONTAGE ST
DWIGHT ST
SCRANTON ST
GILBERT AV
WAVERLY ST
LEGION AV
ASYLUM ST
SYLVAN AV
ORCHARD ST
ELLIOT ST
WARD ST
VERNON ST
HOWARD ST
DAVENPORT AV
CONGRESS ST
KOSSOUTH ST
WASHINGTON AV
CEDAR ST
PRINCE ST
REDFIELD ST
WHITE ST
ARCH ST
HALLOCK ST
DAGGETT ST
COLUMBUS AV
COLUMBUS PL
MEADOW ST
LOOP RD
UNION AV
UNION ST
WATER ST
PORTESEA ST
SALEM ST
CARLISLE ST
LIBERTY ST
PUTNAM ST
DEWITT ST
EDGAR ST
SPRING ST
BUTTON ST
ARTHUR ST
ROSETTE ST
WEST ST
LINES ST
GROVE ST
WILLIAM ST
OLIVE ST
LYON ST
GRAND AV
ARTIZAN ST
ST JOHN ST
JEFFERSON ST
BRADLEY ST
FRANKLIN ST
HAMILTON ST
WALLACE ST
EAST ST
ACADEMY ST
WOOSTER PL
WOOSTER ST
BREWERY ST
SARGENT RD
NG WHARF RD
FORBES AV
MARKET ST
CLAY ST
JAMES ST
HAVEN
EXCHANGE ST
WOOLCOTT ST
MILL ST

wouldn't be New Haven without *Yale,* and *Yale* wouldn't be *Yale* outside New Haven.

New Haven At-a-Glance

SEEING THE CITY

Once used by the Quinnipiac Indians for smoke signals, the 359-foot summit of New Haven's eastern cliff in *East Rock Park* commands a panoramic view of the city, the *Yale* campus, the harbor, and on clear days, 18 miles down Long Island Sound to Bridgeport.

SPECIAL PLACES

New Haven, the first architecturally planned city in the US, was designed for walking. Laid out in nine squares, New Haven radiates from *The Green*; the 30-block area surrounding it has a cultural and historic scope that belies its geographic limits.

THE GREEN This 16-acre square of tree-lined lawns dominates the center of town south of the university. It is as much the city's focal point today as it was in the 1600s, when all public buildings were assembled here, along with the cows and pigs. The only buildings left are three churches—one Georgian, one Federal, and one Gothic Revival in style—all built between 1812 and 1815.

NEW HAVEN COLONY HISTORICAL SOCIETY Drawing on its collections of fine and decorative arts, maritime history, manufacturing, and technology, the society presents a panorama of the city's past and illuminates its development since 1640. Closed Mondays. Admission charge. 114 Whitney Ave. (phone: 562-4183).

YALE CAMPUS AND FACILITIES Named for Elihu Yale, East India trader and donor, the university was founded in 1701 in nearby Old Saybrook. In 1716, it moved to New Haven where it flourished, becoming one of the world's most distinguished educational institutions. The lovely campus, with its ivy-covered Gothic buildings, green courtyards, and mix of classic and contemporary architecture, is best seen by taking a free tour led by student guides well versed in college lore. Tours are given daily, starting at the *Yale Visitor Information Center,* 149 Elm St. (phone: 432-2300).

PEABODY MUSEUM OF NATURAL HISTORY Exhibits on evolutionary history include a huge skeleton of an apatosaurus, the famous *Age of Reptiles* mural by Rudolph Zallinger, habitat dioramas, Native American displays, and the *Hall of Mammals.* Open daily. No admission charge. 170 Whitney Ave. (phone: 432-5050).

YALE CENTER FOR BRITISH ART Designed by Louis I. Kahn, it features works by Hogarth, Constable, Turner, Stubbs, and Blake. There are more British works here than anywhere outside Great Britain. From September through May, the museum sponsors weekly concerts. Closed Mondays. No admission charge. 1080 Chapel St. (phone: 432-2800).

YALE UNIVERSITY ART GALLERY The oldest university art museum in the country, it houses masterpieces from ancient Egypt and Greece, as well as those of artists such as Monet, Picasso, and van Gogh. Of particular interest is the collection of American paintings and decorative arts. Closed Mondays and the month of August. No admission charge. 1111 Chapel St. (phone: 432-0600).

LIGHTHOUSE POINT PARK Located on Long Island Sound on the east end of town, the 1840 lighthouse overlooks 82 acres containing New Haven's best beach, a bird sanctuary with nature trails, areas for fishing, and a beautifully restored antique carousel. Special programs include bird/nature walks and concerts during the summer. Open year-round. Lighthouse Rd. (phone: 946-8005).

EXTRA SPECIAL

Some 60 miles east of New Haven on I-95 is the town of Mystic, where the fastest clipper ships and the first ironclad vessels were built in the 19th century. A section of the town has been restored as a 19th-century seaport. You can stroll along the waterfront of the Mystic River or down the cobblestone streets lined with quaint seaport homes. For more information, see the "New London, Connecticut, to Providence, Rhode Island" route in DIRECTIONS.

Sources and Resources

TOURIST INFORMATION

For general information, contact the *Greater New Haven Convention and Visitors Bureau,* One Long Wharf Dr. (phone: 777-8550; 800-332-7829; fax: 495-6949), the *Greater New Haven Chamber of Commerce* (195 Church St.; phone: 946-6735), or the *Cultural Affairs Department* of the *Mayor's Office* (phone: 946-7821), all of which are closed weekends. You also can visit the *Long Wharf Information Office* (at Exit 46 off I-95; phone: 776-0203), run by the visitors bureau and open daily during the summer. In addition, *Access Line* (phone: 498-5050) provides updates on special events, theater listings, sports, and concerts. *Yale* has its own information center at 149 Elm St. (phone: 432-2300), open daily except major holidays. Contact the *Connecticut Vacation Center* (phone: 800-CT-BOUND) for maps, calendars of events, health updates, and travel advisories.

LOCAL COVERAGE The *New Haven Register,* mornings and Sundays; the *New Haven Advocate* (published Thursdays); and *Connecticut* magazine (published monthly). The Friday *Register* and the *Advocate* list the coming week's attractions. The *Register* is available only at newsstands; the *Advocate* is distributed throughout the city. Recommended reading includes *Harrison's Illustrated Guide: Greater New Haven* (Henry S. Harrison, $13.95) and *Connecticut's Best Dining & Wining* by Patricia Brooks (De Gustibus Press, $8.95), which has many New Haven food listings.

TELEVISION STATIONS WFSB Channel 3–CBS; WTNH Channel 8–ABC; WVIT Channel 30–NBC; and WEDH Channel 65–PBS.

RADIO STATIONS AM: WELI 960 (adult contemporary); WAVZ 1300 (rock); and WNHC 1340 (urban contemporary). FM: WPLR 99.1 (rock).

TELEPHONE The area code for New Haven is 203.

SALES TAX There is a 6% state sales tax; the hotel room tax is 12%.

CLIMATE Since the city is on Long Island Sound, it gets a sea breeze, which gives some relief during the humid summers, the spring, and the fall. However, New Haven usually gets a lot of rain; and that sea breeze often becomes raw during the cold, snowy winters.

GETTING AROUND

AIRPORT *Tweed–New Haven Airport* is a 15-minute drive from downtown. The *Connecticut Transit* bus is located within the airport at the main terminal. A taxi (see below) is another possibility for those with luggage. *Tweed–New Haven* handles only domestic flights. Those with international connections can get to *JFK* and *La Guardia* airports in New York City and *Newark International* in New Jersey by contacting *Connecticut Limousine* (phone: 878-2222; 800-472-5466); the ride to any of the three airports from its terminal (on Brewery St. at Long Wharf, behind the *New Haven Post Office*) will take approximately two hours. *Red Dot Airport Shuttle* (330-1005; 800-6-RED-DOT) also provides limousine service from New Haven to the two New York City airports from the *Holiday Inn* (parking open to the public).

BUS *Connecticut Transit* serves the downtown area and the suburbs. The base fare is $1, which increases by zone. Route information and guides are available at 470 James St. (phone: 624-0151).

CAR RENTAL All the national firms are represented.

TAXI Cabs can be ordered by calling *Metro Taxi* (phone: 777-7777).

TRAIN New Haven is located on the main *Amtrak* line (phone: 773-6177 or 6178; 800-USA-RAIL) between New York and Boston. There is frequent service to those cities and to Hartford. Service to New York City and southern Connecticut is also offered by *Metro North Commuter Railroad* (phone: 800-METRO-INFO). Trains leave from the beautifully restored *Union Station* on Union Avenue.

SIGHTSEEING TOURS

BOAT In season, several vessels ply the Sound. *Schooner Inc.* (60 South Water St.; phone: 865-1737) sails the *Quinnipiack,* a 91-foot wooden schooner, on windjamming nature trips, Wednesdays and Sundays, May through early October. *Liberty Belle Cruises* (Long Wharf Dr.; phone: 562-4163) operates ferry-type power boats for brunch, sunset, and moonlight dancing cruises daily, June through August.

SPECIAL EVENTS

The *New Haven Jazz Festival,* a series of concerts featuring well-known artists, runs from early July through mid-August. In mid-August, the *Volvo International Tennis Tournament* is held at *Yale University*'s *Connecticut Tennis Center* (phone: 776-7331 for information; 772-3838 or 800-54-VOLVO for tickets). The *SNET Linx Street Festival* takes place on a four-block stretch of Chapel Street and coincides with the dates of the *Volvo Tennis Tournament* (above). The 20-kilometer *Road Race* takes place annually on *Labor Day.* The weekend before *Thanksgiving* in odd-numbered years, the *Yale-Harvard* football game is played at the *Yale Bowl,* with all the fanfare of a traditional Ivy League rivalry.

MUSEUMS

With *Yale*'s fine collections and New Haven's *Historical Society* (see *Special Places*), the city touches all cultural bases.

BEINECKE RARE BOOK AND MANUSCRIPT LIBRARY Home of a 1455 Gutenberg Bible, hailed as the first printed volume. There's also an extensive collection of first editions and original letters and manuscripts from William Shakespeare, Charles Dickens, Gertrude Stein, and Eugene O'Neill. Closed Sundays. No admission charge. 121 Wall St. (phone: 432-2977).

YALE COLLECTION OF MUSICAL INSTRUMENTS One of the world's finest collections of historical keyboard instruments, as well as a representative selection of Western European wind and string instruments. Closed Fridays through Mondays, August, and during all *Yale* recesses. There are frequent concerts. Admission charge. 15 Hillhouse Ave. (phone: 432-0822).

SHOPPING

New Haven has its share of today's marketplaces, chain shops, eateries, and entertainment. Enclaves of commerce with more individuality, however, also are easy to come by—and get to. Museum shops are another excellent source of quality gifts and mementos.

SPORTS AND FITNESS

BASEBALL The New Haven *Ravens,* a Double-A expansion team, plays 71 home games at *Yale Field* (252 Derby Ave., West Haven; phone: 782-1666 for information and tickets).

FITNESS CENTERS The *Downtown Health and Racquet Club* (230 George St.; phone: 787-6501) has racquetball and basketball courts, a sauna, and Nautilus equipment. Open to non-members for a fee and to guests of some local hotels.

FOOTBALL The *Bulldogs, Yale*'s popular football team, play at the *Yale Bowl* (Rte. 34, between Derby Ave. and Chapel St.; phone: 432-1400).

GOLF *Alling Memorial Golf Course* (35 Eastern St.; phone: 946-8013) is open to the public.

JAI ALAI Just 20 minutes away in Milford (take Rte. I-95 west), the world's fastest off-the-wall (and the ceiling) ball game is played year-round at *Milford Jai-Alai* (311 Old Gate Ln., Milford; phone: 877-4242).

JOGGING Local joggers prefer the run along Whitney Avenue, which borders the university, between Canner and Temple Streets. Also popular is the beach in West Haven off Captain Thomas Boulevard, just five minutes from the city center.

SKIING The best facilities nearby are at *Powder Ridge* (phone: 349-3454; 800-622-3321) in Middlefield, 21 miles north of New Haven.

TENNIS There are several good outdoor public courts. Municipal courts at *Wilbur Cross High School* (Orange St. and Mitchell Dr.) are free. The same applies to use of the courts at *Edgewood Park* (Edgewood Ave.; phone: 946-8028). Yalies get preference at the university courts (Derby and Central Aves.), but the public can play by paying a nominal fee.

THEATER

The city has an embarrassment of theatrical riches. For up-to-date offerings and performance times, check the publications listed in *Local Coverage* above.

CENTER STAGE

Long Wharf Theatre This prestigious regional theater brings fine ensemble performances by some of America's best actors to "plays of character," produced in two intimate theaters. Numerous *Long Wharf* productions, including *The Gin Game,* Graham Greene's *Travels With My Aunt,* and Arthur Miller's *Broken Glass,* have gone on to New York stages. Closed July through September. 222 Sargent Dr. (phone: 787-4282).

Yale Repertory Theatre The company produces first-rate experimental and classic plays (it earned the 1991 Tony Award for outstanding regional theater). Its productions have received great acclaim in recent years, and many have moved to Broadway, including August Wilson's two Pulitzer Prize winners, *Fences* and *The Piano Lesson.* 1120 Chapel St. (phone: 432-1234).

---

orated in a nautical motif, it sits on a pier built over an old oyster bed. Open Mondays through Saturdays dinner; Sundays brunch. Reservations advised. Major credit cards accepted. 100 S. Water St. (phone: 787-3466).

Delmonaco's The decor is strictly Valentino—Rudolph, that is—from the posters on the wall to an occasional screening of an old silent film starring the sheik. Southern Italian dishes complement the passion on the screen. Closed Sundays; dinner only on Saturdays. Reservations advised. Major credit cards accepted. 232 Wooster St. (phone: 865-1109).

500 Blake Street Café This turn-of-the-century café has been a neighborhood magnet for over 20 years—its cozy bar is reminiscent of the one immortalized on *Cheers*—and rightfully so. It offers both fine- and home-style Italian cuisines and there's something for everyone: pasta, fish, chicken, duck, and beef. There's also a bountiful Sunday brunch. A piano bar adds to the conviviality. Reservations advised. Major credit cards accepted. 500 Blake St. (phone: 387-0500).

Gennaro's Ristorante D'Amalfi A bit away from Wooster Street's Little Italy, it's still considered one of the best Italian restaurants in the city. Diners enjoy well-prepared dishes in the main dining area, two smaller contemporary rooms, or the "greenhouse." Top choices include filet mignon in sherry and cognac sauce, red snapper primavera, and veal chop with asparagus and mozzerella. Closed Sundays; dinner only on Saturdays. Reservations advised. Major credit cards accepted. 937 State St. (phone: 777-5490).

Union League Café A favorite gathering spot, this eatery boasts a stunning, airy dining room enhanced with turn-of-the-century woodwork, marble, and Tiffany-style windows. The menu is just as exciting with chef/owner Jean-Pierre Vuillermet's seasonal Provençal menu of duck-leg *confit* and grilled salmon with French lentils. Open daily; dinner only on weekends. Reservations advised. Major credit cards accepted. 1032 Chapel St. (phone: 562-4299).

MODERATE

Akasaka This interesting spot, which successfully evokes the feeling of a Japanese village, is well known for its house specials including tempura, broiled eel, and Akasaka steak with diced vegetables and teriyaki sauce. Open daily; dinner only Sundays. Reservations advised. Major credit cards accepted. 1450 Whalley Ave. (phone: 387-4898).

Amber Restaurant Families in the mood for great barbecued ribs and chicken head for this family-owned place just north of the city line. Although the ambience may be sparse (unadorned tables and plain decor), the food is good and hearty—a testament to the regulars who keep coming back for more. Closed Mondays; dinner only weekends. Reservations advised. Major credit cards accepted. 132 Middletown Ave., North Haven (phone: 239-4072).

Christopher Martins This casual, darkly lit spot decorated with contemporary artwork turns out reliable Italian fare including venison with pumpkin ravioli, as well as a variety of pizzas. Reservations advised. Major credit cards accepted. 860 State St. (phone: 776-8835).

Consiglio's A popular spot with both students and locals, this restaurant offers a sumptuous continental menu. Try the signature dish of veal with wild mushrooms but leave room for dessert. The pastry ravioli with chocolate-raspberry cream filling and fruit sauce is delicious. Open daily; dinner only on weekends. Reservations advised. Major credit cards accepted. 165 Wooster St. (phone: 865-4489).

Miya A fine Japanese restaurant with great sushi, it also offers fresh fish specials, tempura, and teriyaki. One tatami room can be reserved for four or more. Open for dinner only; closed Tuesdays. Reservations advised. Major credit cards accepted. 68 Howe St. (phone: 777-9760).

The Place This casual steak and barbecue spot 20 minutes east of the city is a summer favorite. Diners sit at picnic tables and feast on mussels, clams, steaks, lobster, and corn in the husk, all cooked on outdoor grills. Open daily from late April through October. Reservations unnecessary. Major credit cards accepted. On Rte. 1, Guilford (phone: 453-9276).

Scoozzi New Haven's hottest trattoria and wine bar, it offers "everything Italian but nothing you've come to expect," with a menu ranging from interesting sandwiches and salads to unusual pasta dishes, in a bright contemporary atmosphere. Located two flights below street level, next to the *Yale Repertory Theatre.* Open daily; dinner only on Sundays. Reservations advised. Major credit cards accepted. 1104 Chapel St. (phone: 776-8268).

Tre Scalini Considered the best new restaurant in town, it features such creative offerings as potato-wrapped red snapper in wild mushroom, tomato, and cognac cream sauce; and veal layered with portobello mushrooms with lobster and gorgonzola sauce. Open daily; dinner only on weekends. Reservations advised. Major credit cards accepted. 100 Wooster St. (phone: 777-3373).

INEXPENSIVE

Bangkok Gardens A light and airy greenhouse setting is the backdrop for this popular Thai restaurant just steps from the *Yale Repertory Theatre.* The menu includes interesting vegetarian delights and noodle dishes, as well as curries and spicy offerings like Thai hot and sour soup or "drunken chicken" stir-fried with chile sauce and vegetables. Reservations advised. Major credit cards accepted. 172 York St. (phone: 789-8684).

Chavoya's Traditional Mexican cookery and fresh seafood are the order of the day at this casual south-of-the-border eatery, enhanced with pastel tablecloths, floral paintings, and lots of plants. Locals rave over the eight varieties of frozen margaritas available at the bar, and the all-you-can-eat salad bar and lunch buffet. Open daily; dinner only on weekends. Major credit cards accepted. 883 Whalley Ave.; (phone: 389-4730).

Claire's CornerCopia A self-proclaimed "gourmet vegetarian" restaurant, this casual place serves pasta, burritos, veggie burgers, and home-style desserts, but best are the daily specials. Perfect for relaxing with a book. No reservations. No credit cards accepted. 1000 Chapel St. (phone: 562-3888).

Frank Pepe's Pizzeria Pepe's claim that he baked America's first pizza in 1925 may be hard to swallow; not true of his variety of pies. In an area where the fine art of pizza making is taken very seriously, the long lines attest to the quality of his efforts. The clam pie is legendary. Closed Tuesdays; dinner only Mondays, Wednesdays and Thursdays. No reservations. No credit cards accepted. 157 Wooster St. (phone: 865-5762).

India Palace An authentically decorated Indian restaurant featuring an all-you-can-eat lunch buffet and a variety of well-prepared Indian dishes. Reservations advised. Major credit cards accepted. 65 Howe St.; (phone: 776-9010).

Libby's At this post-pasta stopover, you can choose from among what seem to be dozens of flavors of gelato and lots of traditional Italian pastries, including over 20 flavors of cannoli. The bright café with its wrought-iron furniture is the perfect place to sip a cappuccino. Closed Mondays. No reservations. No credit cards accepted. 139 Wooster St. (phone: 772-0380).

Louis' Lunch This tiny place, established in 1895 and on the *National Register of Historic Places,* looks like a cross between an English pub and Hansel and Gretel's cottage. It claims to be the birthplace of the hamburger and true or not, the burgers are great—big, juicy, and charcoal-grilled. Don't ask for ketchup—they don't have it, and to ask is considered an affront to the quality of the product. Closed Sundays; lunch only Mondays to Wednesdays. No reservations. No credit cards accepted. 261-263 Crown St. (phone: 562-5507).

Mamoun's Falafel Middle Eastern dishes like falafel and shish kebab are served in this friendly (read: noisy), family-run storefront. Open daily—till 3 AM. No reservations. No credit cards accepted. 85 Howe St. (phone: 562-8444).

Sally's The battle rages on over whose pizza is better—*Sally's* or *Pepe's* (see above). Fans rave about Sally's fresh veggie pies, but the answer is to try both. Closed Mondays. No reservations. No credit cards accepted. 237 Wooster St. (phone: 624-5271).

New Orleans

Romance, mystery, and an almost palpable sense of the past constantly converge on New Orleans. Peek through the wrought-iron gate of a French Quarter carriageway, beyond the cobblestones and into the flower-filled courtyard, and imagine what plots might have been hatched here or what loves might have been consummated 100 years ago. From its *Mardi Gras* madness, boisterous and bawdy Bourbon Street, and listening to all that jazz, the Big Easy pulls people into its steamy embrace with an offer of pleasures not likely to be found elsewhere.

With such a beautiful and timeless setting, your imagination is stimulated at every turn, heightened by the sound of a jazz trumpet coming from who knows where, the pungent taste of a creole remoulade sauce, the arresting beauty of a black iron-lace balcony against tarnished stucco. If all of this seems unreal, that's as it should be—in New Orleans, reality is always put on hold until the final song is sung and the last drop of wine consumed.

Although New Orleans (with a metropolitan-area population of about 1.2 million) lacks manufacturing and heavy industry, throughout its long history it has been a center of trade and a source of great wealth for some. But not even the activity of its port on the Mississippi—once second only to New York City in cargo tonnage—has shaken the city out of a certain Old South torpor (which earned it the nickname "the Big Easy"). This languor has been both a blessing and a curse for New Orleans. It has helped to preserve the city's European, 18th-century charms, where in a different place they might have fallen before the trumpet of civic progress. Thus, for the wealthy the city remains a sophisticated, cultured haven. But for the poor, the city's stasis has offered little hope of improvement over the years. The poverty just seems to roll along like the river; and not much has appeared to change it.

Initially, New Orleans was something of a hot property, traded back and forth between governments. First, the French were attracted in the early 1700s by the area's deep, swift harbor. They named the city for Philippe, Duc d'Orléans, the Regent of France, and it served as the capital of the French territories in America from 1723 to 1763, when a Bourbon family pact transferred it to Spanish rule. It was subsequently ceded to France in 1800. Two important developments resulted from all this swapping and ceding: The creole culture, unique to North America, emerged, created by the influences of the French, Spanish, and Africans; and one of the greatest bargains of the century took place. In 1803 Napoleon sold New Orleans and the entire Louisiana Territory—extending from the Gulf of Mexico up the Mississippi Valley to the Canadian border—to the United States for $15 million, doubling the size of US territory. In 1815, to protect this wily investment, General Andrew Jackson and his Kentucky militiamen teamed with anyone and everyone—including the pirate Jean Lafitte, the Choctaw Indians, numerous Creoles, and some black slaves—and defeated the British in the Battle of New Orleans. The War of 1812, unfortunately, had ended about two weeks earlier, somewhat dampening the victors' spirits. (News of the peace treaty had not yet reached the combatants.) Jackson secured the Mississippi River for America, and New Orleans began to grow as a major port for the cotton, sugarcane, and indigo crops grown on the surrounding plantations, and as a kind of Old World cosmopolitan center in the midst of the deep South.

New Orleans sits on the flat plains of the river delta—a crescent of land with the Mississippi to the south, and the bay-size Lake Pontchartrain to the north. A city of 180 square miles, it's divided into several districts, the most famous of which is the Vieux Carré, or French Quarter. Although still the main area of touristic interest in New Orleans, the French Quarter is having some trouble hanging on to its historic charm—the T-shirt shops, fast-food chains, and glitzy souvenir boutiques seem to multiply monthly. This is despite the fact that the powerful *Vieux Carré Commission,* a state-constituted agency, is supposed to regulate construction and modification of the district's buildings, as well as their commercial or residential usage. Meanwhile, boisterous crowds of partying tourists, college students, and conventioneers seem perpetually to be streaming through the Quarter even when *Mardi Gras* is nowhere near. For those seeking out more tranquil times here, the tawdry, circus aspect dies down a little during *Christmas* and at the height of summer (if you can stand the sodden heat); during the rest of the year, try weekdays from breakfast time to just after lunch.

Nonetheless, the French Quarter's interesting architectural history can still be traced through its many lovely, centuries-old buildings. Near the end of the 18th century, during the Spanish colonial period, two ferocious fires destroyed all but a handful of the district's French colonial structures; the Spaniards' renovation replaced the simple, classical French architecture with "iron lace" balconies and courtyards. The city's architects of the early 19th century borrowed from both cultures to create the creole hybrid found today on almost every block of the French Quarter. Fine examples of the mixture of cultures and styles are the *Cabildo,* once the headquarters of Spanish colonial rule, and the *Presbytère.* Both buildings (now museums) date to the 1790s and flank *St. Louis Cathedral* at Jackson Square. Each building features wide Spanish arches and a French mansard roof. Completing the Jackson Square quadrangle are the *Pontalba Apartments,* twin structures with French-inspired, red brick façades and elegant wrought-iron balconies.

The French Quarter has other attractions as well. The *French Market* dates from the pre-colonial era, when the site was used by the local Indians as a trading post. It still has a colorful atmosphere and some of the best café au lait on either side of the Atlantic. The best way to see the French Quarter is the old-fashioned way—simply by strolling down its pedestrian

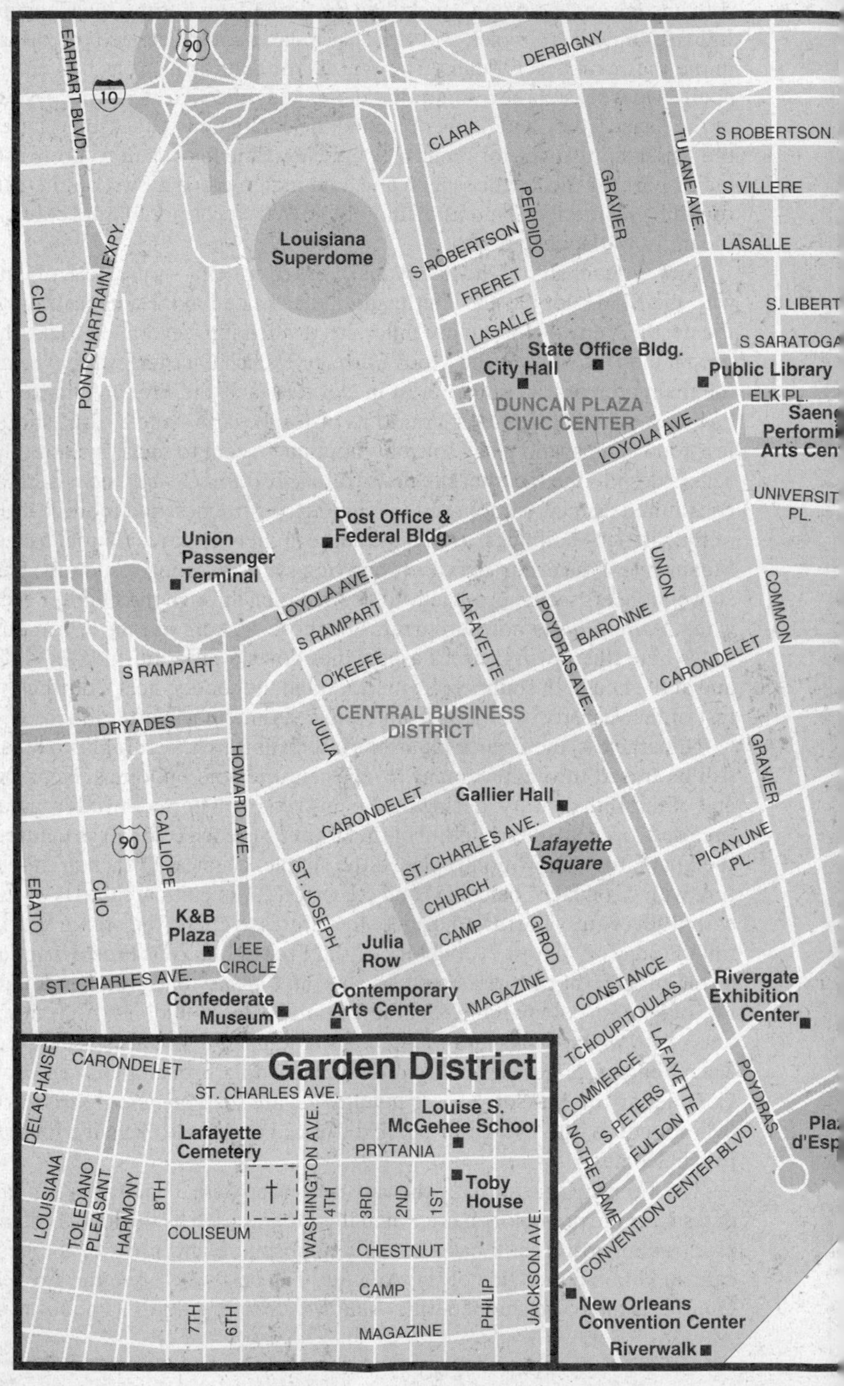

DERBIGNY
EARHART BLVD.
90
10
CLARA
S ROBERTSON
S VILLERE
LASALLE
TULANE AVE.
GRAVIER
PERDIDO
S ROBERTSON
FRERET
LASALLE
Louisiana Superdome
PONTCHARTRAIN EXPY.
CLIO
State Office Bldg.
City Hall
Public Library
ELK PL.
DUNCAN PLAZA CIVIC CENTER
LOYOLA AVE.
UNIVERSIT PL.
Post Office & Federal Bldg.
Union Passenger Terminal
LOYOLA AVE.
S RAMPART
UNION
COMMON
LAFAYETTE
POYDRAS AVE.
BARONNE
S RAMPART
O'KEEFE
CARONDELET
CENTRAL BUSINESS DISTRICT
DRYADES
JULIA
HOWARD AVE.
GRAVIER
Gallier Hall
CARONDELET
CALLIOPE
90
ST. CHARLES AVE.
Lafayette Square
PICAYUNE PL.
ERATO
CLIO
ST. JOSEPH
CHURCH
K&B Plaza
LEE CIRCLE
Julia Row
CAMP
GIROD
ST. CHARLES AVE.
Confederate Museum
Contemporary Arts Center
MAGAZINE
CONSTANCE
TCHOUPITOULAS
Rivergate Exhibition Center
Garden District
CARONDELET
DELACHAISE
ST. CHARLES AVE.
Louise S. McGehee School
Lafayette Cemetery
PRYTANIA
WASHINGTON AVE.
LOUISIANA
TOLEDANO
PLEASANT
HARMONY
8TH
4TH
3RD
2ND
1ST
Toby House
COLISEUM
CHESTNUT
CAMP
7TH
6TH
MAGAZINE
PHILIP
JACKSON AVE.
COMMERCE
LAFAYETTE
S PETERS
FULTON
POYDRAS
NOTRE DAME
CONVENTION CENTER BLVD.
New Orleans Convention Center
Riverwalk

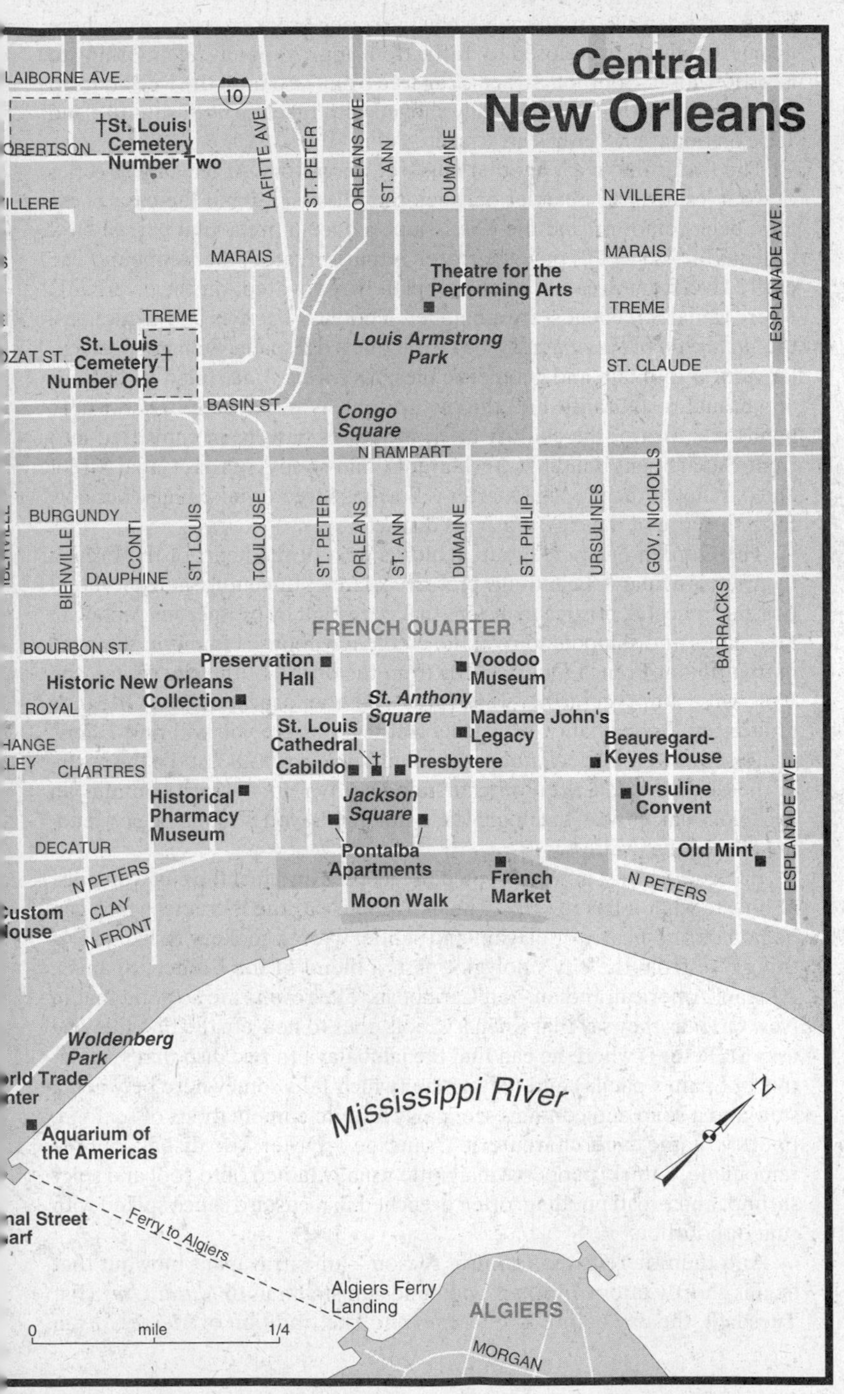

Central New Orleans
LAIBORNE AVE.
10
St. Louis Cemetery Number Two
OBERTSON
LAFITTE AVE.
ST. PETER
ORLEANS AVE.
ST. ANN
DUMAINE
N VILLERE
ILLERE
MARAIS
MARAIS
Theatre for the Performing Arts
ESPLANADE AVE.
TREME
TREME
St. Louis Cemetery Number One
ZAT ST.
Louis Armstrong Park
ST. CLAUDE
BASIN ST.
Congo Square
N RAMPART
BURGUNDY
BIENVILLE
CONTI
DAUPHINE
ST. LOUIS
TOULOUSE
ST. PETER
ORLEANS
ST. ANN
DUMAINE
ST. PHILIP
URSULINES
GOV. NICHOLLS
BARRACKS
FRENCH QUARTER
BOURBON ST.
Preservation Hall
Voodoo Museum
Historic New Orleans Collection
ROYAL
St. Anthony Square
St. Louis Cathedral
Madame John's Legacy
HANGE
LEY
CHARTRES
Beauregard-Keyes House
Cabildo
Presbytere
Historical Pharmacy Museum
Jackson Square
Ursuline Convent
ESPLANADE AVE.
DECATUR
Pontalba Apartments
Old Mint
N PETERS
French Market
N PETERS
Custom House
CLAY
Moon Walk
N FRONT
Woldenberg Park
orld Trade nter
Mississippi River
N
Aquarium of the Americas
nal Street arf
Ferry to Algiers
Algiers Ferry Landing
ALGIERS
0
mile
1/4
MORGAN

malls and sidewalks (preferably when the spring break crowds are nowhere near). Royal Street is closed to traffic from approximately late morning to late afternoon; Bourbon Street is car-free from 7 PM until the wee hours of the morning (although it's usually choked with revelers until sun-up); and Jackson Square never has any traffic.

The riverfront area is another must-see for visitors. At one time, a series of wharves formed a barrier between the Mississippi and the city. These have been removed, and the Mississippi is once more a vital part of New Orleans life—only this time the reason is tourism rather than shipping. The entire riverfront area has been completely renovated; on the riverbank, where Canal Street ends, are a number of noteworthy sites and attractions: the *Aquarium of the Americas;* beautiful Plaza d'España, with its spectacular central fountain and geometric tiles; *Riverwalk Mall,* filled with shops and casual restaurants; and the picturesque Warehouse District, where handsome turn-of-the-century brick structures have been converted into trendy apartment buildings, restaurants, and shops. Across Canal Street and parallel to the French Quarter is Poydras Street, whose high-rises now form the core of the city's business district.

The Garden District, about 30 blocks west of the heart of the French Quarter, is a quaint, beautifully preserved, late-19th-century neighborhood boasting graceful, pristine mansions that were built by prosperous American merchants and shippers to rival the creole townhouses found in the once more affluent French Quarter. Far from the bustle of the city center, the Uptown section, yet farther west, reveals another aspect of New Orleans's multifaceted personality. This leafy district is where you will find *Tulane University* as well as the *Audubon Park* and *Zoological Garden.* To the north, in the direction of Lake Pontchartrain, is *City Park*—which contains an enormous oak grove—the point where tranquil Bayou St. John begins, leading to the lake itself.

In New Orleans, however, you don't just see and feel the city, you must also taste what it has to offer. The indigenous cuisine is creole, which can be homey and hearty or elegant and subtle. Creole cookery is, like everything else from the city's polyglot past, a blend of the French, Spanish, African, American Indian, and Caribbean. The results are so good that in New Orleans they say that when a Creole goes to heaven, the first thing he asks St. Peter is where he can find the jambalaya (a rice dish that's a relative of Spain's paella) and filé gumbo (which falls somewhere between a stew and a soup and contains seemingly infinite combinations of seafood, poultry, game, and charcuterie—sausage). Other key dishes include remoulade, a thick, peppery vinaigrette usually ladled onto cool and spicy shrimp; and bread pudding, often drenched in a custard sauce spiked with rum or bourbon.

And then there is the *Carnival* season—an extravagant blowout that begins shortly after *Christmas* and builds up steam until *Mardi Gras* (Fat Tuesday), the day before *Ash Wednesday.* The tradition of *Mardi Gras* in

New Orleans began in the mid-19th century with spontaneous street parades at the approach of the *Lenten* season. In 1857, a group of locals banded together to form the first *Carnival* parading organization, the *Mystick Krewe of Comus.* Other private clubs picked up the idea, which started the tradition of elaborate balls and parades that continues today. The balls are still major social events for all socioeconomic classes of New Orleans, and with rare exceptions are invitation-only affairs. "Kings" and "queens" are chosen from among the *krewe* (*Carnival* club) membership, and in some *krewes,* the balls serve as formal "coming-out" parties for debutantes. But the parades are decidedly public; about 50 of them—they vary widely in size and complexity—are held in the city and its suburbs during the two weeks preceding *Mardi Gras* itself. In addition to the traditional parade floats, there are marching jazz bands and decorated flatbed trucks. Souvenir doubloons, cups, and beaded necklaces are tossed to onlookers. Beginning on the Friday before *Mardi Gras,* the parade routes along St. Charles Avenue and Canal Street are jammed with revelers, and the French Quarter is closed to vehicular traffic to accommodate the crowds. *Mardi Gras*'s royal personages are Rex, King of *Carnival,* and King Zulu, leader of the city's oldest parading black *krewe,* who shares some of the spotlight with the Big Shot of Africa. Zulu meanders through downtown New Orleans throwing painted coconuts, doubloons, and beads; in its 1909 debut, its antics were meant to satirize the conventions of white society. In the French Quarter, a colorful annual costume competition for transvestites jams the corner of Burgundy and St. Ann Streets, while less competitive maskers in all kinds of outrageous attire roam around. Suburban *krewes* also hold parades on *Mardi Gras;* the principal *krewe* is *Argus,* which conducts its own parade in Metairie.

Another special New Orleans event that's beginning to rival the *Carnival* season in popularity is the *Jazz and Heritage Festival,* usually held during the last two weeks of April at the *New Orleans Fair Grounds* racetrack. Dozens of top local and national performers—Fats Domino, Aaron Neville, and New Orleans native Harry Connick Jr., to name just a few—hold forth in the open air and in tents.

Mardi Gras and the *Jazz and Heritage Festival* are the best and the worst of times to visit New Orleans. The spontaneous fun reaches great heights, but so, too, do the hotel prices and the frenetic pace. Don't expect the more popular restaurants to operate at their best during these periods. There are other festivals that offer New Orleans in a different mood, without the huge crowds of the city's two biggest parties (see *Special Events*).

At any time of year, however, the place that launched such great jazzmen as Louis Armstrong, Buddy Bolden, Joe "King" Oliver, Kid Ory, and Jelly Roll Morton still swings. The *Old US Mint,* which has been renovated, is the permanent home of excellent exhibitions on how it all began with a merging of African-American and European rhythms. At *Preservation Hall,* Dixieland jazz is played every night; and in countless honky-tonks on Bourbon Street the beat goes on.

New Orleans's legendary jazz funerals still are held occasionally, but they're increasingly rare (once or twice a year at the most). In the traditional "celebration," a marching band accompanies the procession from the church to the cemetery, playing solemn marches and hymns. As soon as the burial takes place, however, the rhythm picks up and the theme changes to something like "Didn't He Ramble" or "I'll Be Glad When You're Dead, You Rascal You." The mourners begin prancing and cavorting behind the band, picking up others who join the "Second Line," though they probably don't even know the person who died. But it doesn't really matter, because when you leave the Big Easy, New Orleans folk act as if you are on your way to the Bigger Easy, and send you off easily. If you're lucky enough to see a jazz funeral be sure to join in; the only way to know one is happening is a mention in the local daily newspaper, *The Times-Picayune.*

Another New Orleans tradition that has become more mythical than real is the exotic cult known as voodoo. Based partly on African tribal rites and partly on Catholic ritual, voodoo is believed to have been brought to New Orleans by slaves from the West Indies—Santo Domingo, in particular—in the early 18th century. Voodoo as a functioning religion disappeared from the city long ago, and the occasional report of a "Black Mass" or other bizarre rite always turns out to be something other than the real thing. In *Fabulous New Orleans,* published in 1928, writer Lyle Saxon, a specialist in local color, recounted witnessing a voodoo ceremony. But even in the 1920s, such events were rare. In any case, no tangible evidence of voodoo seems to exist in present-day New Orleans, though most people you ask would know where to find the memento-draped tomb of 19th-century "voodoo queen" Marie Laveau in *St. Louis Cemetery Number One* (see *Special Places*). One spot in the city with tenuous voodoo connections is Congo Square, across North Rampart Street near the French Quarter, where slaves once gathered to socialize. It may at one time have been used for voodoo rites—there's no way of knowing—but it is now a lush public park.

But myth and folklore are part of this city's charm, as vital to its sense of itself as its carefully preserved creole architecture and the mighty Mississippi that rolls right by. New Orleans is a tasty gumbo of Old South elegance and rowdy rockin' and rollin' good times set to the beat of legendary musicians and fed by transcendent chefs. There is an inspired cross-fertilization of cultures and memories here, added to the simple desire just to have fun. The attitude toward life that visitors find in New Orleans can best be summed up in the phrase that has become a kind of axiom: *"Laissez les bon temps rouler!"*—"Let the good times roll!"

A WORD ABOUT CRIME

Although seldom the actual targets of violent crime here, visitors should be on their guard. It's best to keep to the following parts of town: the French Quarter, the Warehouse, Garden, and Central Business Districts,

as well as the Uptown and University areas. Avoid all parks at night, and do not enter any cemetery alone, day or night; finally, avoid housing projects, where one-third of the city's murders take place.

New Orleans At-a-Glance

SEEING THE CITY

The best bird's-eye view of New Orleans is from the *Top of the Mart,* a revolving bar on the 33rd floor of the *World Trade Center,* where Canal Street meets the Mississippi River (phone: 522-9795). An observation deck is on the same floor (open daily; admission charge). There is a grand view of the French Quarter and the river from the 11th floor of the *Westin–Canal Place* hotel (see *Checking In*).

SPECIAL PLACES

Nestled between the Mississippi River and Lake Pontchartrain, New Orleans's natural crescent shape can be confusing. North, south, east, and west mean very little here. Residents keep life simple by using terms such as "lakeside" or "riverside" and "uptown" or "downtown" for directions.

FRENCH QUARTER (VIEUX CARRÉ)

BOURBON STREET Though named for the illustrious French royal family, some say this street now has more in common with the alcoholic beverage that also shares its name. The atmosphere here has been likened to one long, unbroken college spring break. It's legal to drink on the streets throughout New Orleans, as long you are not drinking from metal or glass containers; the legal vessel is the plastic "to-go" cup, offered everywhere. And New Orleans establishments have added many drinks to the bartender's list, with such wicked liquids as the Hurricane and the Absinthe Frappé. Round-the-clock honky-tonks offer live jazz, which can get wild in the wee hours, and late-night booze, which often leads to morning-after regrets. The seven blocks of Bourbon Street extending from Iberville to Dumaine Streets are filled with a hodgepodge of creole restaurants of varying quality, T-shirt stores galore, tacky corn-dog stands and fast-food joints, elegant hotels, sleazy strip joints, jazz clubs, porno shops, and every sort of carny attraction. Often rowdy and raunchy, Bourbon Street has been a hot strip since the postwar years; this is where everybody heads to let it all hang out during the *Carnival* season or after a game in the *Superdome.* The area has a lot of strip joints and peep shows; even if you stay outside, you'll get more of an eyeful than a peep as the hawkers swing the doors open to lure customers. Among the hot spots are *Patout's* (where trumpeter Al Hirt frequently performs) and the *Famous Door.*

PRESERVATION HALL What's recorded in the jazz collection at the *Old US Mint* (see below) still happens live before an audience every night at *Preservation*

Hall. In this ramshackle old creole building at the French Quarter's heart, 60- and 70-year veterans of the city's jazz scene perform nightly for an audience sitting hip-to-haunch on backless benches in a ramshackle double parlor. The New Orleans jazz renaissance—begun in the 1960s—continues to this day here as the small Dixieland bands perform classic renditions of "St. James Infirmary Blues," "Rampart Street Parade," and "When the Saints Go Marchin' In." The surroundings are spartan at best, but this is the real thing. Open nightly. Admission charge. 726 St. Peter St. (phone: 522-2841).

ROYAL STREET There really was a streetcar named *Desire* that used to run along Royal Street to Canal from the late 19th century to the 1950s. Though the streetcar is gone, along this street the desire for the past continues, and a stroll down here will yield views of some of the Quarter's finest examples of cast- and wrought-iron balconies and some of New Orleans's most distinctive architecture. The city's finest antiques shops still dominate the blocks between Bienville and St. Peter Streets, although T-shirt and inexpensive souvenir outlets have proliferated in recent years. The street is a pedestrian mall closed to traffic from late morning to late afternoon every day.

HISTORIC NEW ORLEANS COLLECTION Maintained in two handsome French Quarter buildings—the aristocratic 18th-century *Merieult House* on Royal Street and the *Williams Research Center* in a restored early-20th-century building on Chartres Street—this is one of the South's most impressive depositories of historical and cultural material. All of the materials, dating from the pre-colonial era to the present, relate to the history of New Orleans and Louisiana. They include maps, books, documents, photographs, and artwork that reflect the culture, economy, and politics of the city and the region, all catalogued and available to scholars and researchers (who are advised to call in advance). The *Williams Residence,* immediately adjacent to the *Merieult House* on Royal, was once the home of the *Historic New Orleans Collection*'s major benefactors, General and Mrs. L. Kemper Williams, who bought it in 1938 and lived here in the 1940s. They decorated their elegant French Quarter home with numerous valuable and historic furnishings. There are tours of the house and courtyard (inquire at *Merieult House*). The *Williams Research Center* at 410 Chartres Street was opened in 1995 after a $2.5-million restoration of the massive masonry structure; it also houses temporary exhibitions. All of the facilities are closed Sundays and Mondays. Admission charge for tours of the *Williams Residence* and entry to the *History Galleries* in *Merieult House;* no admission charge to the *Williams Research Center* and the *Williams Gallery* exhibition space in *Merieult House.* 533 Royal St. (phone: 523-4662).

ST. LOUIS CATHEDRAL While it is the oldest cathedral in the United States, the present-day building is actually the third to occupy the site. The first was the parish church erected by Jean-Baptiste Le Moyne, Sieur de Bienville, soon after he founded the colony in 1718. Demolished five years later by a hurricane, the church was rebuilt in 1727, only to be destroyed in the great fire of 1788. In 1793 the parish church was proclaimed a cathedral and the seat of a diocese; a year later, the basic structure existing today was erected, with rounded Spanish-style steeples at the front. The present façade, with its columned entablature and three conical steeples (which took the place of the older ones, which were dismantled) was constructed between 1849 and 1851. This beautiful Spanish-style building also boasts painted ceilings, an altar imported from Belgium, and a bell and clock in the central spire that has marked the hours for the city's inhabitants for more than two centuries. Today it is the seat of the Roman Catholic Archdiocese of New Orleans, where services and rites of the Church still take place. The interior was completely refurbished in the early 1980s. Tours given daily except Sundays. Donations requested. 700 Chartres St., on Jackson Square (phone: 525-9585).

THE CABILDO AND PRESBYTÈRE Together, the *Cabildo* and the *Presbytère,* the twin Spanish colonial buildings flanking *St. Louis Cathedral* on Jackson Square, form the hub of the *Louisiana State Museum* network. They are filled with exhibits—documents, artifacts, portraits, costumes, and furniture—pertaining to the culture and history of the region. The successor to earlier governmental headquarters on the same site, the *Cabildo* (the Spanish word for "council") was built by the Spaniards in 1795 and served as the seat of the colonial governments of both Spain and France. In a large room on the second floor, documents were signed in 1803 that transferred the entire Louisiana Territory—stretching from the Gulf of Mexico to the Canadian border—from France to the United States. The *Cabildo,* which suffered a fire in 1988, reopened in 1994 with a fresh new look and extensive changes in its exhibits, which cover subject matter from the arrival of the first Europeans in the 1500s to the Reconstruction era after the war; popular artifacts are Napoleon's death mask and some items believed to have belonged to the pirate Jean Lafitte. The *Presbytère,* once the offices of colonial church officials, is now devoted to temporary exhibitions on the history of New Orleans and Louisiana. Closed Mondays. Admission charge. 751 Chartres St., Jackson Square (phone: 568-6968).

JACKSON SQUARE This stately plaza, originally the Place d'Armes, was the town square of the original French colonial settlement and the scene of most of New Orleans's history—from hangings to the transfer ceremony commemorating the Louisiana Purchase. It is also where early French settlers worshiped, peddled their wares, and conducted governmental and military ceremonies. It was rebuilt, and the equestrian statue of General Andrew Jackson, the hero of the Battle of New Orleans, was placed at its center in the 1850s. Today it's a pleasant place from which to watch the passing scene against a backdrop of charming cast-iron and brick buildings, or to browse through shops. Heads no longer roll here, but occasional open-air jazz concerts do, and the only hangings are on the iron fence bounding the area, where local artists display their work. Since the early 1970s, this area has been a pedestrian mall. 700 Chartres (pronounced *Chart*-ers) St., bordered by St. Ann, St. Peter, and Decatur Sts.

PONTALBA APARTMENTS Extending along the two sides of Jackson Square perpendicular to the Mississippi River are these twin, block-long, red brick buildings, said to be the first true apartment houses constructed in the United States. The buildings, each of which contains eight row houses, were designed by Henry Howard for the Spanish Baroness Micaela Almonester y Pontalba. (Her family names, Almonester and Pontalba, are preserved in the "AP" monogram set into the original cast-iron balcony railings. Today, the buildings' upper floors are still private apartments, while the arcades below are lined with ice-cream parlors, boutiques, and cafés. The building at 523 St. Ann Street houses the *1850 House,* furnished as it would have been in the mid-19th century (see *Museums*). Jackson Square at St. Ann and St. Peter Sts.

MOON WALK The name of this promenade alongside the Mississippi River may be a bit misleading: It is politically rather than celestially motivated, since it was named for former Mayor Moon Landrieu, whose administration in the early 1970s oversaw numerous physical improvements to the French Quarter's public spaces, including this one. The steps along Decatur Street lead to a landscaped terrace that offers superb views of the river and Jackson Square. Go to the grass-lined walkway right near the river—to the left is the first of many bends the river takes on its way to the Gulf of Mexico; to the right are fine views of the New Orleans skyline and river bridges. Across the levee from Decatur St. at St. Ann and St. Peter Sts.

FRENCH MARKET This is the oldest established marketplace in the Mississippi Valley. Although the five main buildings were erected between 1813 and the end of the 19th century, even before the French explorers arrived in 1718, the site was a trading post used by the Choctaw and other local Indians. The *French Market* still has a colorful atmosphere, with stalls beneath large stone colonnades offering a variety of local produce—try the Louisiana oranges, creole tomatoes, mirlitons (the pale-green, pear-shape squash known in Mexico as *chayote*), sugarcane, and sweet midget bananas—as well as meat and seafood, including live crabs, turtles, shrimp, catfish, and trout. There also are boutiques, cafés, and a large flea market. At Jackson Square and St. Ann Street is the *Café du Monde* (813 Decatur; phone: 581-2914), a bustling New Orleans coffeehouse serving authentic café au lait (half coffee with chicory, half hot milk) and beignets (square, fried crullers dusted with powdered sugar). The café closes only on *Christmas Day,* and the market itself is open daily. On Decatur St. extending from St. Ann St. to Barracks St.

OLD US MINT Designed in the Federalist style by William Strickland, this stately building is the oldest federal mint building still standing. Built in 1835, it minted nearly $300 million in silver dollars and other coins (including Confederate currency) between 1838 and 1909. Later, the building was used as a prison and then as offices of the *US Coast Guard.* In 1982, it became the home of the *New Orleans Jazz Collection* and *Mardi Gras Museum,* both part of the *Louisiana State Museum.* Fine exhibits trace the development of jazz from its origins in African-American rhythms and the European brass band tradition. Jazz lovers also will find souvenirs of the patron saints of jazz—Louis Armstrong's first horn, Bix Beiderbecke's cuff links, and instruments played by members of the *Original Dixieland Jazz Band.* In addition, there are resplendent costumes worn in the hundreds of *Carnival* parades and balls that precede New Orleans's world-famous *Mardi Gras* celebration. The building also houses a *Historical Center* (phone: 568-8214) which contains historical documents from the French and Spanish Louisiana periods; it is open to the public Wednesdays through Fridays by appointment only for on-site research. The *New Orleans Jazz Collection* and *Mardi Gras Museum* are closed Mondays. Admission charge. 400 Esplanade Ave. (phone: 568-6968).

URSULINE CONVENT Constructed in 1734 in French Provincial style, this building was one of the few to survive the two devastating fires that swept through New Orleans during the 18th century. Originally the home of the city's Ursuline nuns—who came from France in 1727 to care for the sick and orphaned and to teach the slaves, Indians, and the colonists' children—it later served as a Catholic school for boys, the Louisiana Legislature, and the official residence of the Archbishop of New Orleans. Today the structure, topped by a mansard roof and surrounded by a brick stucco wall, contains archives of the Archdiocese of New Orleans. Open to the public for tours only on Tuesdays through Fridays at 10 and 11 AM and 1, 2, and 3 PM; weekends at 11:15 AM and 1 and 2 PM; closed Mondays. Admission charge. 1100 Chartres St. (phone: 529-3040).

BEAUREGARD-KEYES HOUSE Although George Washington never slept here, almost everyone else lived in this neoclassical residence, including the legendary chess champion Paul Morphy, Confederate General Pierre G. T. Beauregard, and, in the 1940s, novelist Frances Parkinson Keyes, whose will designated it for use as a museum. It was also here that a local wine maker was shot by a member of the Sicilian Black Hand, a secret organization that operated in the Quarter during the 1920s. Its rooms today are handsomely furnished, with a cozy, un-museum-like atmosphere, and Mrs. Keyes's antique-doll collection is on view. The adjoining formal garden, enclosed by a brick wall and lined with boxwoods, jasmine, and tropical flora, is one of the French Quarter's prettiest. Closed Sundays. Admission charge. It's across the street from the *Ursuline Convent.* 1113 Chartres St. (phone: 523-7257).

MADAME JOHN'S LEGACY This ancient frame cottage is believed to be one of the oldest buildings in the Mississippi Valley, constructed in 1726 by Jean Pascal, a sea captain from Provence who received the site from La Compagnie des Indes, which controlled the Louisiana colony for the King of France. The structure was one of the few to survive the two major fires that all but destroyed New Orleans during the late 1700s. A brick and stucco building, with a sloping roof and colonnaded gallery, it is an excellent example of the West Indies plantation architectural style. The house's name comes from *'Tite Poulette,* a romance novel by 19th-century author George W. Cable that chronicles the lives of New Orleans Creoles in the late 1800s. The book's hero lives in the house and bequeaths it to his mistress, known as Madame John. Although it is one of the *Louisiana State Museum*'s properties and has major historical value, it is not open to the public. 632 Dumaine St.

ST. LOUIS CEMETERY NUMBER ONE About a block from North Rampart Street at the edge of the Vieux Carré, this old New Orleans cemetery, dating back to the early 18th century, is literally a diminutive necropolis. The tombs (the city's marshy ground dictated aboveground burial) are interesting for their structure, inscriptions, and number of remains inside (to solve overcrowding, they are opened and the remaining bones are moved deeper into the vault to accommodate new arrivals). Among the illustrious occupants here are Marie Laveau, who used her charms and spells as a voodoo queen in the 1900s; the two wives of Louisiana's first governor, W. C. C. Claiborne; Jean Etienne de Boré, father of the Louisiana sugar industry and first Mayor of New Orleans; and Louisiana historian Charles Gayarré. Many of the brick-and-stucco tombs have crumbled to near-ruin. The earliest decipherable epitaph is that of Nannette F. de Bailly, dated September 24, 1800. Because of the cemetery's isolation, visitors are strongly advised to visit only in daytime, and in large groups. Open daily. No admission charge to the cemetery, but there is a small charge for guided tours. 400 Basin St.

RIVERFRONT/WAREHOUSE DISTRICT

AQUARIUM OF THE AMERICAS On the bank of the Mississippi, this aquatic adventure has more than 6,000 specimens of marine life on view, including fish, reptiles, birds, and amphibians. The main attractions are the *Gulf of Mexico* exhibit, a two-story, 400,000-gallon tank holding hundreds of species found in the deep waters of the gulf; the walk-through *Amazon Rain Forest,* which re-creates the hot, humid environment of the subtropics with indigenous birds, butterflies, and flora; the *Caribbean Reef,* visible from a see-through, tunnel-shaped walkway; the *Mississippi River Delta Habitat,* featuring the freshwater reptiles and fish that inhabit inland Southern waters; and the sharks and penguins. Don't miss the "petting" tank, where it's possible to get up close to creatures of the sea. There's a large and pleasant cafeteria on the second floor. At the adjacent IMAX theater, interesting documentary films, photographed in striking colors, are shown on a larger-than-life screen. Open daily. Admission charge to both the aquarium and the IMAX theater. 1 Canal St. (phone: 861-2537).

WOLDENBERG PARK Fourteen acres of walkways and park areas bring an oasis-like serenity to the French Quarter riverfront area. Contemporary works by local sculptors are exhibited throughout the park, which also contains benches and a bandstand that is used primarily during festivals. Off Conti St. near the riverfront.

PLAZA D'ESPAÑA The dramatic fountain and intricately patterned tiles that form this huge pavilion along the Mississippi were a gift from the Spanish government in recognition of New Orleans's strong historical Hispanic ties. The pavilion has become a favorite spot for small festivals and band concerts. The *Plaza* is on the riverfront between the *Aquarium of the Americas* (see above) and the end of Poydras St.

ERNEST N. MORIAL CONVENTION CENTER This is the city's primary convention facility, and with more than 700,000 square feet of meeting and exhibition space, it is one of the largest facilities of its kind in the country. Completed in 1985, it was later enlarged. The center's development has spurred a commercial renaissance in the Warehouse District. 900 Convention Center Blvd. (phone: 582-3000).

CONTEMPORARY ARTS CENTER This colorful, lively complex of exhibition and performance spaces is home to the avant-garde—local and regional artists, playwrights, dance groups, composers, and filmmakers. The strikingly contemporary spaces, refashioned from an early-20th-century drugstore and office building, contain no permanent collections, but the galleries are always filled with interesting new works, many by emerging artists. Open daily. Admission charge. 900 Camp St. (phone: 523-1216).

JULIA ROW Built in 1830–32 to accommodate newly arrived immigrants, this handsome set of 13 row houses is the Warehouse District's most important architectural setpiece. These elegant red brick buildings—once the homes of some of New Orleans's most well-to-do and socially prominent families—have graceful cast-iron balconies, ornamented entrances, fanlights, and sidelights, which were considered an architectural innovation at the time. After decades of neighborhood deterioration, the row houses were restored by local preservationists in the 1970s. Today, the street-level spaces hold offices and shops. *Julia Row* is along the 600 block of Julia St., west of Poydras and just south of St. Charles Ave. The nonprofit *Preservation Resource Center* (604 Julia St.; phone: 581-7032) offers information and interesting exhibitions concerning the district. The center also provides architectural tours of various neighborhoods; it's closed weekdays.

K&B PLAZA One of New Orleans's first examples of the sleek, modern "international style" of architecture, this creation of the Skidmore Owings Merrill architectural firm is now the headquarters of a regional drugstore chain. On the surrounding terrace are works by such noted late-20th-century sculptors as George Segal, George Rickey, Henry Moore, Jacques Lipschitz, and Isamu Noguchi. The ground-floor lobby also houses one of the South's most important privately owned collections of contemporary paintings and sculpture. Closed weekends. No admission charge. 1055 St. Charles Ave. at Lee Circle (phone: 586-1234).

CANAL STREET/CENTRAL BUSINESS DISTRICT

CANAL STREET For most of the 19th century, this broad, tree-lined avenue formed the dividing line between the French sector of New Orleans and the newer, Anglo-Saxon part of town. The origin of its name is uncertain, since no canal ever existed here (although there were half-serious plans in the 19th century to dig one). In the 1800s, Canal Street boasted a couple of opera houses and a number of tony residences. Two private men's clubs—the *Pickwick Club* on the corner of St. Charles Avenue and the *Boston Club* at 824 Canal—are among the last vestiges of the street's aristocratic past. From the late-19th to the mid-20th century, Canal Street was New Orleans's shopping hub. While such long-established department stores as *Maison Blanche* and *Krauss* and a few other specialty merchants still operate, other buildings have either been boarded up or turned into office buildings. In recent decades, the river end of Canal has been the site of continuing development, with construction of the *Canal Place* office building and shopping mall, major hotels, and the *Aquarium of the Americas.*

CUSTOM HOUSE Canal Street's most historic structure, the old *US Custom House*—which takes up the entire block bounded by Canal, Decatur, Iberville, and North Peters Streets—is the city's handsomest specimen of Federalist architecture. A fine example of Greek Revival style is the majestic *Marble Hall* (in the center of the building on the second floor), with its 14 columns of pure white marble that rise to a ceiling of huge iron and ground-glass plates. Begun in 1849, the building was still under construction in 1862, at the peak of the Civil War, and was never completed according to the original plans. The *Custom House* is still home to various offices of the *US Customs Service.* Closed weekends. No admission charge. 423 Canal St. (phone: 589-4532).

LOUISIANA SUPERDOME Completed in 1975, this awesome piece of architectural engineering has been described as the largest freestanding room in the world. Twenty-seven stories tall, with a seating capacity of 100,000 people, it is large enough to accommodate all of Rome's St. Peter's Basilica. Host to political conventions, *Super Bowls,* and untold rock concerts, it is primarily a football stadium, and home to the *NFL*'s New Orleans *Saints* as well as to dozens of local high school and college sports teams. Daily tours, lasting 40 minutes, are offered when it's not in use. Admission charge. One Sugar Bowl Dr. at Poydras St. (phone: 587-3810).

GALLIER HALL Considered by many to be the best example of Greek Revival public architecture in New Orleans, the hall was designed by James Gallier Sr. and dedicated in 1853 as *City Hall;* it served in this capacity until the late

1950s. The granite and white-marble building has been restored over the years, and the classically proportioned rooms, separated by a 12-foot-wide central hall, are now used mostly for official receptions. It faces Lafayette Square, which contains a touching monument to John McDonogh, the 19th-century philanthropist who was the principal benefactor of the city's public school system. Closed weekends. No admission charge. 543 St. Charles Ave. (phone: 565-7457).

GARDEN DISTRICT

COLISEUM SQUARE When city planners laid out this rectangular park in the Lower Garden District in the 1830s, they designed it as the campus of a university to be called the Prytaneum. Appropriately, they named the nearby streets for seven of the nine Greek muses—Melpomene, Erato, Terpsichore, Clio, Euterpe, Thalia, and Calliope. The university was never built. Instead, the park became the catalyst for a tony neighborhood of Greek Revival residences, most of which remain today. While the square has lost its aristocratic veneer, many of the old homes have been restored. The Prytaneum survives only in the name of nearby Prytania Street.

TOBY-WESTFELDT HOUSE This imposing residence, a raised-frame cottage with a façade of square, white columns, dates from the 1830s. Typical of the period, it was built by Thomas Toby, a Philadelphian who established a large plantation on the site (it once dominated the area that was eventually to become the Garden District). Enclosed within the white picket fence is a garden filled with such typical New Orleans flora as palm and magnolia. Visible from the street is one of the city's finest oak trees, located at the rear of the house. Not open to the public. 2340 Prytania St.

LOUISE S. McGEHEE SCHOOL "Free Renaissance" was the term used to describe the heavily decorative architectural style of this huge old residence, completed in 1870 and now a private school for girls. Pairs of fluted Corinthian columns define the wide porch at the front of the house. The building contains a fully finished basement, a rarity in New Orleans because of the city's watery substratum. The building is open by arrangement only for groups of 50 or more. 2343 Prytania St. (phone: 561-1224).

LAFAYETTE CEMETERY Fans of New Orleans novelist Anne Rice will find this an especially interesting spot, since it figures prominently in her *Vampire Chronicles.* Before the Garden District became part of New Orleans, it was a suburban town called Lafayette. The community's cemetery, dating from the mid-1850s, was the first one in the area laid out on a grid of symmetrical lanes and driveways. Most of the aboveground tombs hold the remains of prosperous businessmen and traders who inhabited the fancy residences nearby. The gates are open weekdays from 7:30 AM to 2 PM and on Saturdays from 7:30 AM to noon. Visiting the cemetery alone at any time is not advised. For a fee, guided tours are given by *Save Our Cemeteries,* a preservationist organization, on Mondays, Wednesdays, and Fridays. Washington Ave. between Prytania and Coliseum Sts. (phone: 588-9357).

UPTOWN–UNIVERSITY SECTION

AUDUBON ZOOLOGICAL GARDEN Once a neglected, foul-smelling place, the *Audubon Zoo* has been transformed since the mid-1970s into one of the country's best. An exotic white tiger is just one of the 1,500 species housed here in habitats that approximate natural conditions. Some fascinating special exhibits re-create in-the-wild environments: Not to be missed is the *Louisiana Swamp,* with alligators and other indigenous creatures slithering and hopping through marshy terrain. Dozens of tropical and shore birds from Louisiana and around the world flit around the trees and shrubs of the huge, walk-through aviary. The *Asian Domain, Grasslands of the World,* and a large pool of frisky sea lions are other favorites. For children, there is a petting zoo, wildlife theater with live animals, and a hands-on natural history museum. Open daily. Admission charge. 6500 Magazine St. (phone: 861-2538).

AUDUBON PARK Under the leafy umbrella of *Audubon Park*'s immense oaks, joggers now tread ground that was, in the late 18th century, a sugarcane plantation. Occupying the 340 acres extending from St. Charles Avenue to the Mississippi River, the park was named for naturalist John James Audubon, who had lived briefly in New Orleans. In 1884–85, it was the site of the *World's Industrial and Cotton Exposition,* commemorating the 100th anniversary of the first shipment of Louisiana cotton to a foreign port. Today it's a haven, not only for joggers, but for picnickers, golfers, tennis players, and bicyclists. While the park's tranquil lagoons are no longer stocked with fish, they form, along with the graceful oaks, a pleasant backdrop for a morning stroll. Main entrances on the 6400 block of St. Charles Ave. and the 6500 block of Magazine St.

AUDUBON PLACE If New Orleans has a millionaire's row, it is this short, private parkway lined with 28 understated but sumptuous residences, which you can only glimpse from the arched gate on St. Charles Avenue; a security guard admits only residents and their visitors through the gate. It was developed early in the 20th century by a Texas real estate speculator, and all but a few of the homes flanking the elaborately landscaped median date from that period. The immense, white-columned manse to the left of the entry gate is the *Zemurray House,* the traditional residence of the President of *Tulane University.* 6900 St. Charles Ave.

ACADEMY OF THE SACRED HEART In 1889 the nuns of the Order of the Sacred Heart opened this school to educate the daughters of prominent Creole families, and French conversation and grammar remain a major part of its curriculum to this day. Elementary and secondary students attend classes in the three buildings that overlook a large, pleasant garden near St. Charles

Avenue. The red brick façade, with tiers of arched, shuttered windows, columns, and balconies, is one of the most graceful architectural spaces in the city's Uptown section. 4521 St. Charles Ave.

ORLEANS CLUB One of the few buildings on St. Charles Avenue inspired by the creole architecture of the French Quarter, the *Orleans Club* was built in 1868 as a private residence. Since 1925 it's been the headquarters of a local social-cultural women's group, which has carefully preserved the structure's elegant stucco façade, handsome iron lace balconies, and pleasantly manicured gardens. Not open to the public. 5005 St. Charles Ave.

MILTON H. LATTER MEMORIAL LIBRARY None of St. Charles Avenue's mansions exceeds this one for lavishness. Built in 1907 in the Beaux Arts style and occupying an entire block, it was the home in the 1920s of silent-screen star Marguerite Clarke and her husband, aviator Harry Williams; their Jazz Age parties were the talk of the town. In 1948, the house was acquired by a couple who donated it to the *New Orleans Public Library* in memory of their son, a casualty of World War II. Many of the original mantels, murals, and ceiling paintings remain, making this branch of the city's library the most beautiful of all. Open daily. 5120 St. Charles Ave. (phone: 596-2625).

"TARA" As far as we know, Vivien Leigh and Clark Gable never set foot in this plantation-style residence, but Scarlett and Rhett would have felt right at home here. The house was constructed during the 1940s according to the antebellum descriptions of *Tara* in *Gone with the Wind.* Everything is here, from the lofty columns of partially exposed, whitewashed brick to the elegant arched doorway inset with a fan-shaped window. Not open to the public. 5705 St. Charles Ave.

THE LAKEFRONT

CITY PARK Dozens of graceful ancient oaks and quiet lagoons make *City Park*'s 1,500 or so acres an ideal environment for jogging, tennis, fishing, biking and any number of participatory sports and games. Its occasional sculptures and formal gardens, especially the *Botanical Garden* and *Conservatory,* offer a pleasant respite from the city. From late November to early January each year, a large section near City Park Avenue is transformed into a magical place, with hundreds of thousands of lights and holiday decorations strung along the gigantic oaks. For children, there are all sorts of amusements, including pony and buggy rides, a puppet show, a vintage carousel, a miniature train, paddleboats, and the *Storyland* theme park. In the late 18th and early 19th centuries, when the park was part of the Allard Plantation, Creole gentlemen defended their honor here, dueling with swords or pistols under the lacy Spanish moss. Main entrance at Esplanade Ave. and Bayou St. John (phone: 482-4888).

NEW ORLEANS MUSEUM OF ART Built in 1912 by local philanthropist Isaac Delgado, *NOMA* has since become an important American museum. Set in pastoral

City Park, its permanent exhibits include examples of the major European and American art movements as well as specialized collections, including Oriental porcelains and painting, late Gothic and early Renaissance painting from the *Samuel H. Kress Collection,* fine examples of French Impressionism and 20th-century European painting, a wide array of European and American decorative arts (including jewelry, ornamental pieces, exquisite *Easter* eggs, cigarette cases, and boxes created by Peter Carl Fabergé), contemporary photography, and pre-Columbian and African sculpture. Among the more unusual possessions is a portrait by French Impressionist Edgar Degas of his cousin, Estelle Musson; it was painted during the artist's extended 1873 visit to New Orleans, where his relatives were then residing. A major expansion in 1993 added two floors spotlighting African, Asian, Oceanic, and contemporary art. Lectures and other educational programs are presented frequently in the comfortable auditorium. A gift shop and a restaurant are on site. Closed Mondays. Admission charge. *City Park* (phone: 488-2631).

BAYOU ST. JOHN This gently flowing stream extending from *City Park* to Lake Pontchartrain once connected the heart of the Old City with the lake via canals that have long since been filled in or covered over. The local Indians and early settlers used the bayou to transport their wares into town. The bayou's banks have long been a favorite place for outings. A number of family-style resort hotels once dotted the area near the lake known as Old Spanish Fort; it is now the site of seafood restaurants, apartment buildings, and the city's largest marina. Along much of the bayou's length are some of the city's oldest residences, including the Caribbean-style *Pitot House* (see below), home of New Orleans's first mayor.

PITOT HOUSE Designed in the traditional West Indies style, featuring two stories topped by a high-pitched, gently tapering roof, this small plantation house was originally a country home for the aristocratic Ducayet family, who retreated to the cool edge of Bayou St. John on weekend getaways from their French Quarter cottage. Later, it was the home of the family of James Pitot, who served from 1804 to 1805 as the mayor of the newly incorporated city. The outer wall construction is of *briquets-entre-poteaux* ("bricks between posts") covered with stucco; the interior has been furnished by the *Louisiana Landmarks Society* with Louisiana and American antique furniture, and fabrics and bibelots in the style of the early 1800s. Closed Sundays through Tuesdays. Admission charge. 1440 Moss St. (phone: 482-0312).

TAVERN ON THE PARK This handsome two-story structure—dating from 1860—faces two massive trees, known as the Dueling Oaks, across the avenue. Designed as a restaurant from the start, it was built 10 years after New Orleans's city government acquired the *City Park* tract for public use. The place gained considerable notoriety early in the century as a boxing arena, a speakeasy, and, at one point in its history, a bordello. In the late 1980s, the building was extensively restored to its present state. Currently, it is home to a steak and seafood restaurant, with an interesting but unpredictable menu. 900 City Park Ave. (phone: 486-3333).

LAKESHORE DRIVE The parkway that extends along much of Lake Pontchartrain's southern shore begins in the west with the Orleans Marina, where dozens of sailboats and pleasure craft are berthed when they're not plying the lake's gentle waters. Farther along the breezy landscaped roadway are the old *Southern Yacht Club,* and, just past Marconi Drive, the *Mardi Gras* Fountains (memorializing the *krewes* who make the tradition of the pre-*Lenten Carnival* possible), the campus of the *University of New Orleans,* and the *New Orleans Municipal Airport,* now used mostly for private aircraft. On holiday weekends, the miles of grassy strips between Lakeshore Drive and the lake seawall are often filled with picnickers.

LAKE PONTCHARTRAIN CAUSEWAY Stretching more than 24 miles from the Jefferson Parish shoreline to Mandeville, the roadbed—sitting just a few yards above the lake—is advertised as the world's longest bridge. At midpoint, neither shore is visible, but the occasional spectacular sunset or thunderstorm offers respite from the rather monotonous drive. Entrance at the north end of Causeway Blvd. in Metairie. There's a $1.50 toll each way for passenger cars.

OTHER SPECIAL PLACES

JEAN LAFITTE NATIONAL HISTORICAL PARK, BARATARIA UNIT If a trip to the Cajun country of southwest Louisiana is not practical, this beautiful slice of Louisiana wetlands, maintained by the *National Park Service,* is an excellent alternative. Less than an hour's drive from the French Quarter via the Crescent City Connection bridge, the park contains most of the marshy flora that flourish on the Louisiana coastline. There are a couple of pretty bayous surrounded by moss-draped cypress; one of the bayous is carpeted with beautiful water lilies. Wooden walkways lead from the parking area through rows of palmetto, oak, and cypress. Guided walking tours conducted by park rangers are available daily. No admission charge. 7400 La. Hwy. 45, in Marrero (phone: 589-2330).

METAIRIE CEMETERY This aboveground necropolis of towering tombs and memorials pays tribute to some of New Orleans's most illustrious dead, mostly successful business and professional figures of the late 19th and early 20th centuries. The architectural styles of the elaborate stone tombs range from Egyptian to rococo; much of the statuary is monumental. Some bizarre examples of funerary art await at almost every turn along the alleys and walkways through the manicured grounds. A free tape-recorded tour is available at the *Lake Lawn Metairie Funeral Home* (5100 Pontchartrain Blvd.; phone: 486-6331).

LONGUE VUE HOUSE AND GARDENS Although built in the mid-20th century, this handsome estate in the elegant, old suburb of Metairie evokes the grandeur of Edwardian England. It was the residence of the late philanthropists Edith and Edgar B. Stern Jr. Beyond the imposing neoclassical entrance, exquisitely decorated rooms contain a trove of treasures—from rare English furniture and porcelain to paintings by major contemporary artists. Inspiration for the design of the fountains and eight acres of gardens came from Mrs. Stern's frequent trips to Europe. Each of the meticulously maintained flower beds, shrubs, and trees is labeled. Closed Sunday mornings. Admission charge. The house is across from *Metairie Cemetery* at the intersection of Bamboo and Metairie Roads and can be most easily reached by tour bus. 7 Bamboo Rd., near Metairie Rd. (phone: 488-5488).

FREEPORT-McMORAN AUDUBON SPECIES SURVIVAL CENTER Opened in 1994, this institute is dedicated to the breeding and preservation of such endangered species as the Louisiana black bear and the milky stork. Although the center itself is not open to the public, there is a 130-acre *Wilderness Park* with nature trails, an education center, and a picnic site at English Turn, Algiers (Algiers is the section of New Orleans that lies across the Mississippi River). Open daily until dark. No admission charge. The center can be reached in 20 minutes by car from downtown; cross the river via the Crescent City Connection bridge (enter from the Warehouse District), then turn north toward Algiers Point, where Patterson Road begins. Call the center for precise directions. 10004 Patterson Rd., English Turn (phone: 861-2537).

EXTRA SPECIAL

As late as the end of the 19th century, sugarcane was king in Louisiana, and large plantations established commercial empires, as well as an entire social system, around it. A few of these plantations have been restored and are open to visitors, and the life that the Southern gentry created for themselves really is something to see. Just a short drive north of New Orleans, these elegant relics have survived not only the Civil War but countless hurricanes, humidity, and other perils. Among the most impressive are *Oak Alley* (on the west bank of the river at Vacherie), fronted by twin rows of 28 gnarled oaks that form a vast, majestic umbrella; *San Francisco Plantation* (on the river's east bank, north of LaPlace), a combination of mid-Victorian and Steamboat Gothic ornamentation second to none in the state; *Houmas House* (on the east bank near Burnside), which boasts a magnificent setting and charming auxiliary buildings; and *Destrehan Plantation* (on the east bank in Destrehan), said to be the oldest building left intact in the Mississippi Valley. Detailed maps and brochures are available at hotels and the *New Orleans Tourist Information Center* in the French Quarter (529 St. Ann St.; phone: 568-5661). Most of the city's tour companies also offer bus tours of the plantation houses.

Sources and Resources

TOURIST INFORMATION

The *New Orleans Tourist Information Center,* in the French Quarter (529 St. Ann St., New Orleans, LA 70116; phone: 568-5661), provides a wealth of information on the city's attractions, including maps, brochures, and personal help. It's open daily. The *New Orleans Metropolitan Convention and Visitors Bureau* (1520 Sugar Bowl Dr., New Orleans, LA 70112; phone: 566-5011) has information about the outlying areas. It's also open daily. Contact the Louisiana state hotline (phone: 800-33-GUMBO) for maps, calendars of events, health updates, and travel advisories.

LOCAL COVERAGE The city's daily, *The Times-Picayune,* has a special Friday edition that includes "Lagniappe," an arts-and-entertainment section with a comprehensive list of musical, art, theatrical, film, cultural, historical, and recreational activities. The "Eating Out" column covers local restaurants. Other useful local publications include *Gambit,* a free arts-oriented weekly found in local shops and restaurants, and *New Orleans,* a general-interest monthly. Two other monthlies, *Tourist News* and *Where,* are distributed free in hotels, list restaurants, and shops.

Frenchmen, Desire, Goodchildren, by John C. Chase (Robert L. Crager; $12.95), is an entertaining and informative guide to New Orleans's geography and history. Other recommended reading: *The French Quarter,* by Herbert Asbury (Mockingbird Books; $3.50); *Voodoo in New Orleans,* by Robert Tallant (Pelican; $3.95); and *The New Orleans Eat Book* by Tom Fitzmorris (New Orleans Big Band and Pacific Co.; $6.95). Also, pick up a copy of *ACCESS New Orleans* (HarperCollins; $18.50).

TELEVISION STATIONS WWL Channel 4–CBS; WDSU Channel 6–NBC; WVUE Channel 8–Fox; WGNO Channel 26 (UHF)–ABC; WNOL Channel 38–Warner Brothers; and WYES Channel 12 and WLAE Channel 32–both PBS.

RADIO STATIONS AM: WWL 870 (CBS, ABC Information, talk/news); WBYU 1450 (popular music, news). FM: WWNO 89.9 (classical, National Public Radio); WWOZ 90.7 (jazz and folk); and WRNO 99.5 (rock).

TELEPHONE The area code for New Orleans is 504.

SALES TAX State and city sales taxes total 9.5%; the hotel room tax is 11%.

CLIMATE New Orleans weather is subtropical with high humidity, temperatures, and substantial rainfall. Moderated by the Gulf of Mexico winds, summer temperatures hover around 90F, while winter temperatures rarely drop to freezing. Summers can get unbearably sticky.

GETTING AROUND

AIRPORT *New Orleans International Airport* is a 25- to 35-minute drive from the downtown area. The *Louisiana Transit Co.* (phone: 737-9611) runs an

Airport-Downtown Express bus on a 40-minute schedule from downtown at the corner of Loyola and Tulane Avenues; the fare is $1.10. *Airport Shuttle, Inc.* (phone: 592-1991) provides service between the airport and downtown. Its passenger vans depart from the airport every 15 minutes, picking up passengers at most downtown hotels, the Central Business District, French Quarter, and Westbank. The fixed-rate taxi fare to and from the airport is $21 for up to two passengers, and $8 each for more than three.

BUS/STREETCARS The city's *Regional Transit Authority* operates buses throughout the city. The St. Charles Avenue streetcar offers a scenic ride through the Central Business District and Uptown. Board at Canal and Carondelet Streets, or at St. Charles Avenue and Common Street. Special lines include the *Easy Rider,* which circuits the Central Business District and the riverfront; the *French Quarter Minibus,* operating between Elysian Fields Avenue and Poydras Street; and the *Riverfront Streetcar,* which runs along the Mississippi River from Esplanade Avenue to Julia Street. Detailed information is available from *RideLine* (phone: 569-2700). Carfare ranges from $1 to $1.25 (express routes are $1.25).

CAR RENTAL For *Carnival* or the *Jazz and Heritage Festival,* be sure to reserve wheels well in advance. All of the major national car rental companies have offices in New Orleans.

FERRY The Canal Street ferry, operating daily from 6 AM to 11:45 PM, provides free rides back and forth across the river to Algiers.

TAXIS Cabs can be ordered by telephone, hailed in the streets, or picked up at stands in front of hotels, restaurants, and transportation terminals. Major taxi companies are *United* (phone: 522-9771); *White Fleet* (phone: 948-6605); and *Yellow-Checker* (phone: 525-3311).

SIGHTSEEING TOURS

BOAT The very best of the river excursions are those aboard the *Natchez,* one of the five remaining steamboats on the Mississippi. The large sternwheeler departs the Toulouse Street Wharf (behind *Jax Brewery*) twice a day on two-hour runs up and down the river. The scenic tour includes a narrated history of such landmarks as Jackson Square and the Chalmette Battlefield and, for an extra fee, a luncheon buffet of creole specialties. A dinner cruise with live music by the *Crescent City Jazz Band* is also available. For information contact the *New Orleans Steamboat Company* (*World Trade Center;* phone: 586-8777; 800-233-BOAT for reservations).

In addition, the *Bayou Jean Lafitte* excursion boat departs the Toulouse Street Wharf for the bayou country, to Bayou Barataria, home of the famous pirate; a small paddle wheeler, the *Cotton Blossom,* makes three runs daily from the Canal Street docks to the *Audubon Zoo;* and a high-speed catamaran, the *Audubon Express,* makes six trips daily between the *Aquarium of the Americas* and the *Audubon Zoo* (for information on these excursions, call 586-8777). The motorized, three-decker *Cajun Queen* and the stern-wheeler *Creole Queen* offer both daytime and dinner cruises, which depart from behind the *Riverwalk Mall* and the *Aquarium of the Americas* (phone: 524-0814). *Gray Line* (phone: 587-0861) offers river or combined water and land tours of the city aboard the steamboat *Natchez* and coach bus, as well as swamp and bayou cruises and other combination tours.

BUS A variety of itineraries are offered by numerous companies operating bus tours of the French Quarter, Garden District, Lakefront, and major points of interest outside the city proper. Among the companies are *American-Acadian* (phone: 467-1734); *Gray Line* (phone: 587-0861); *Machu Picchu Tours* (phone: 392-5118); *New Orleans Tours* (phone: 592-1991); and *Tours by Isabelle* (phone: 367-3963). All tour companies pick people up, by arrangement, from their hotels.

MULE-DRAWN CARRIAGES Mule-drawn carriages, most with fringed tops and holding as many as 10 passengers, may be hired by the hour from early morning to nighttime on the Decatur Street side of Jackson Square. The carriages roll along the streets of the French Quarter as drivers comment on points of interest. Be aware that while carriages are supposedly licensed by the city, they are de facto unregulated, and practices—and prices—can vary. Many of the drivers have been known to deliver "historical" commentary that is more fancy than fact. Also, some drivers may attempt to give you a subtle sales pitch for some shops or restaurants along the way. Fact or fancy, sit back and enjoy the ride. Two of the companies offering carriage rides are *Charbonnet Transportation* (1615 St. Philip St.; phone: 581-4411), which rents carriages that hold eight to 10 passengers by the hour; and *Gay Nineties Carriage Tours* (1824 N. Rampart St.; phone: 943-8820), which offers a half-hour tour.

VOODOO Voodoo, the ancient African religion once practiced here, first filtered into Louisiana in the early 1700s. When the government refused to recognize it as a religion and suppressed voodoo rites, believers went underground and voodoo became a cult. Although there are no credible signs that voodoo is seriously practiced in present-day New Orleans, several voodoo-oriented tours are available: a voodoo walking tour of the French Quarter, with a stop at the *Voodoo Museum* (see *Museums*), part of the same outfit that runs these tours; a tour that features a voodoo ceremony; a "Voodoo Ritual Swamp Tour"; and other excursions that wind through mysterious bayous, historic plantations, gardens, villages, Indian burial grounds, and fascinating swamp scenery and wildlife. Tours range from two and a half to 10 hours; for information, contact the *Voodoo Museum* (phone: 523-7685).

WALKING The *Friends of the Cabildo* (phone: 523-3939) lead walking tours of the French Quarter that begin at Jackson Square; the price includes admission to two of the four following sites: the *Cabildo,* the *Presbytère,* the *Old US Mint* (see *Special Places*), and *1850 House* (see *Museums and Historic Houses*).

The *National Park Service* (phone: 589-2636) conducts free walking tours of the French Quarter, *St. Louis Cemetery Number One,* and the Garden District, and occasionally offers specialized tours on subjects that range from the story of pirate Jean Lafitte to the history of the Louisiana legal system. *Magic Walking Tours* (phone: 593-9693) offers on-foot explorations of the French Quarter, the port, and other points relating to such special interests as African history, the Civil War, Storyville, and jazz. The walks offered by *Heritage Tours* (phone: 949-9805) focus on the French Quarter's literary history, with commentary on the places where such writers as Tennessee Williams and William Faulkner lived and worked. *Gray Line* (phone: 587-0861), known for its bus tours, also gives walking tours of the French Quarter that begin at the *Old Ursuline Convent.*

SPECIAL EVENTS

The *Sugar Bowl Classic,* one of football's oldest college bowl games, is held *New Year's Day* in the *Louisiana Superdome* (phone: 522-2600). The next celebration of the year is the biggest—New Orleans's famous pre-*Lenten Carnival* during the two weeks or so preceding the final blowout on *Mardi Gras* (Fat Tuesday). Since *Mardi Gras* is 47 days before *Easter,* the date varies from year to year; this year *Mardi Gras* is February 11. A score or more of street parades and dozens of costume balls (mostly private) are held, and the French Quarter, especially Bourbon Street, fills with revelers.

The first of this culturally diverse city's many annual ethnic celebrations is the *Black Heritage Festival* in early March; it features food booths, jazz and church music, and art exhibits (phone: 861-2537). The city's Irish Americans celebrate *St. Patrick's Day* (March 17) with a huge street party Uptown in the old Irish Channel and parades in several parts of the city and suburbs. A tradition that dates back to the turn of the century is the *St. Joseph's Day* parade, held on the weekend night nearest the March 19 feast day of the patron saint of Sicily. Italian-American men of all ages, dressed in tuxedos and carrying canes festooned with red, white, and green carnations, file through the French Quarter's streets amid floats, marching bands, and statues of the saint and the Virgin Mary.

One weekend in early April, the *French Quarter Festival* fills the Vieux Carré with parades, food vendors, artists, musical groups, and other performers (phone: 522-5730). Also in early April is the *Spring Fiesta,* highlighted by tours of private French Quarter patios by daylight or candlelight and a nighttime parade (phone: 581-1367).

The city's other huge annual outdoor event takes place in late April and early May. The two-week *New Orleans Jazz and Heritage Festival* features dozens of bands, vocalists, and gospel groups from nearby and around the world, as well as food and crafts stalls. Performances are held in the mornings to late afternoons on the grassy expanse inside the racetrack at the *New Orleans Fair Grounds;* nighttime concerts take place on riverboats and in nightclubs and concert halls. For festival information call 522-4786.

The Greek residents of the city have their day in late May, when traditional foods, crafts, and music fill the *Hellenic Cultural Center* near Bayou St. John for a *Greek Festival* (phone: 282-0259). Food is the focus of the *Great French Market Tomato Festival,* held inside the colonnades of the *French Market*'s complex of food and gift shops in the French Quarter, usually the first full weekend in June (phone: 522-2621 on weekdays only). In July the city celebrates *Carnaval Latino* (phone: 522-9927) and August brings the *Latino Festival* to Canal Street (phone: 524-0427). A few weeks later, in early September, the *Fiesta Latina* takes place at the *Audubon Zoo* (phone: 861-2537). On an early fall weekend, the *Patio Planters* organization conducts afternoon tours of private French Quarter gardens (phone: 566-5068). Italian-Americans are in the spotlight again in October, when the *Festa d'Italia* takes over the downtown Piazza d'Italia with traditional food, music, and exhibits (phone: 891-1904). The *Gumbo Festival* is another of October's special events; it's held in Bridge City, across the Huey P. Long Bridge from New Orleans (phone: 436-4712).

The *Christmas* season is observed in *City Park* with the *Celebration in the Oaks.* From late November to early January, several acres of the park's shrubbery and huge oaks are festooned with spectacular electrical ornaments. During December, the French Quarter celebrates a New Orleans *Christmas*—the historic homes are decorated in 19th-century creole style and restaurants offer special menus replicating the traditional French-creole *reveillon* holiday meal.

MUSEUMS AND HISTORIC HOUSES

In addition to those described in *Special Places,* other notable New Orleans museums include the following:

CONFEDERATE MUSEUM Louisiana's oldest, this small, red stone museum, just off Lee Circle, dates from 1891. Civil War buffs will find a trove of weapons, uniforms, maps, records, flags, and other memorabilia. Closed Sundays. Admission charge. 929 Camp St. (phone: 523-4522).

1850 HOUSE This townhouse, one of the row houses that comprise the Pontalba Apartments flanking Jackson Square, has been furnished and decorated as a typical home of prosperous Creoles in the mid-19th century, when the Baroness Pontalba had the twin apartment buildings constructed. A lack of ostentation is the principal asset of the furnishings. Closed Mondays. Admission charge. 523 St. Ann St. (phone: 524-9118).

GALLIER HOUSE MUSEUM Upper class New Orleans in the Victorian era is mirrored in the elaborate appointments of this meticulously restored mansion in a quiet section of the French Quarter. Designed by architect James Gallier Jr. as his family's residence, the house now features wall coverings, fabrics, rugs, and fixtures that authentically re-create the lifestyle of 1857. The small, simple garden contains a facsimile of the house's cistern, and a carriage sits ready in the carriageway separating the residence from the gift shop. After each tour, coffee is served on the balcony overlooking an especially picturesque block of Royal Street. Closed Sundays. Admission charge. 1118-1132 Royal St. (phone: 523-6722).

HERMANN-GRIMA HOUSE A small army of historians, botanists, and social scientists took part in the restoration of this aristocratic, red brick residence to its original state. Built in 1831 by a wealthy merchant at the outset of New Orleans's "golden age" (1830 to 1860), the house, with rooms flanking a central hall, was a departure from typical creole design of the era. The details are remarkably authentic, from the cast-iron pots of the creole-style kitchen to the harnesses in the stables and the aromatic plants in the garden. There are creole cooking demonstrations on Thursdays October through May; there's also an annual cooking workshop in the spring. The appointments in the living quarters also are true to the period. Closed Sundays. Admission charge. 820 St. Louis St. (phone: 525-5661).

HISTORICAL PHARMACY MUSEUM In the 1820s, this little shop was the apothecary of Louis J. Dufilho, said to have been the first licensed pharmacist in the US. Its displays of 19th-century jars and equipment may not be as interesting as the quaint old rooms and the charming interior herbal and botanical garden. Closed Mondays. Admission charge. 514 Chartres St. (phone: 524-9077).

LOUISIANA CHILDREN'S MUSEUM More play-school than museum, this cleverly designed spot features all kinds of hands-on fun for kids under 12. It contains a little coffee factory, numerous games and educational exhibits, and miniature versions of a supermarket, TV studio, and hospital. Closed Mondays. Admission charge. 428 Julia St. (phone: 523-1357).

LOUISIANA NATURE AND SCIENCE CENTER Natural sciences are spotlighted at this small museum, which is connected to nature trails on the city's eastern edge. The planetarium offers a number of astronomical programs (usually on weekends) as well as laser rock shows. Raised wooden walkways winding through the surrounding woods afford visitors a short, pleasant hike. Closed Mondays. Admission charge. *Joe Brown Park;* enter at Read Blvd. and Nature Center Dr. (phone: 246-5672; 246-9381 for recorded information).

MUSÉE CONTI WAX MUSEUM Voodoo, *Mardi Gras,* and the pirate Jean Lafitte are represented in the numerous tableaux here, featuring life-size wax mannequins in elaborate stage settings. Major events and personages of New Orleans's colorful history are the focus. There's printed or tape-recorded commentary. Open daily from 10 AM to 5:30 PM. Admission charge. 917 Conti St. (phone: 525-2605).

RIVERTOWN There are several small museums contained in these nostalgically designed buildings situated on the Mississippi River in the New Orleans suburb of Kenner. The *Freeport-McMoRan Daily Living Science Center* has a planetarium and observatory (409 Williams Blvd.; phone: 582-4000). Six working layouts of toy trains, trolleys, and a toy carousel are on display in the *Louisiana Toy Train Museum* (519 Williams Blvd.; phone: 468-7223). The *Louisiana Wildlife and Fisheries Museum* (303 Williams Blvd.; phone: 468-7232) features an aquarium and preserved wildlife specimens and displays. And the *Saints Hall of Fame Museum* (409 Williams Blvd.; phone: 468-6617) contains memorabilia of New Orleans's pro football team. All are closed Sunday mornings and Mondays; admission charge for each, but discount passes also are sold for those intending to visit more than one museum. The *Mardi Gras Museum* (see *Old US Mint* in *Special Places,* above) is also included in this discount pass.

VOODOO MUSEUM Despite its name, this tiny outfit is really more a tourist shop than a museum. It displays African masks and voodoo dolls, and sells souvenirs inspired by the voodoo practices that once flourished in the city. Open daily. Admission charge. 724 Dumaine St. (phone: 523-7685).

SHOPPING

Although the largest shopping centers are found in the surrounding suburbs, downtown New Orleans also contains several major malls offering an immense variety of merchandise, as well as hundreds of specialty shops. The principal malls are the *New Orleans Centre* (just steps away from the *Louisiana Superdome* on Poydras St.), where *Macy's* and *Lord & Taylor* are the main tenants; *Canal Place* (at 333 Canal St. near the Mississippi River), with a three-level branch of *Saks Fifth Avenue* and a large *Brooks Brothers;* and *Riverwalk* (extending along the riverfront near Canal St.), with two levels of restaurants and shops that include *Banana Republic* (casual clothing), *Abercrombie & Fitch* (sportswear and gifts), and *Sharper Image* (electronic gadgets). Canal Street itself still contains a few department stores harking back to its years as the city's shopping artery; the two major ones are the upscale *Maison Blanche* (901 Canal St.; phone: 566-1000) and *Krauss* (1201 Canal St., phone: 523-3311). Each is a full-scale emporium. Antiques hunters should focus their attention on the French Quarter, especially Royal and Chartres Streets, which contain all sorts of antiques shops and art galleries, and, farther out from the city center, Magazine Street, which contains dozens of stores offering moderate to expensive antique furniture, rugs, bric-a-brac, and artwork, from regional to European. Below is a list of New Orleans's favorite shopping places.

Adler's A large selection of jewelry, porcelain, gifts, and bibelots fills the two floors of this plush establishment, now operated by the third generation of the Adler family. 723 Canal St. (phone: 523-5292).

Alfredo's Cameras Expert advice and a wide range of cameras and photographic equipment. 916 Gravier St. (phone: 523-2421).

Arthur Roger Gallery Top contemporary artists from New Orleans and other parts of the country show their paintings and sculpture in this spacious, elegantly designed gallery in the Warehouse District. 432 Julia St. (phone: 522-1990).

Bep's Antiques Modest treasures like old bottles, homey Victorian washstands, and charming little side tables are sold here. 2051 Magazine St. (phone: 525-7726).

Bergeron's Dozens of styles by top designers are the stock-in-trade at the city's preeminent source of fine-quality women's shoes. Unusual handbags are another specialty. *Canal Place,* 333 Canal St. (phone: 525-2195).

Bookstar Two very large floors filled with every type of publication. A good selection of audiotapes, magazines, and maps, too. 414 N. Peters St. (phone: 523-6411).

Central Grocery Co. Known for its *muffuletta* sandwiches and a huge array of Italian food specialties, this is also a good source for a wide variety of non-perishable groceries from around the world. 923 Decatur St. (phone: 523-1620).

Coghlan Gallery This shop features odds and ends to decorate your garden or terrace, including hand-crafted copper fountains and other ornaments. 710 Toulouse St. (phone: 525-8550).

Cuisine Classique You're likely to leave here with something for your kitchen that you didn't know you needed—an oversize stockpot, an apple corer, or a lemon zester. Along with the vast array of cooking tools offered, there is also a wide selection of local cookbooks. 439 Decatur St. (phone: 524-0068).

DeVille Books & Prints This is the place to check for hard-to-find authors and unusual literary works. The art, architecture, and photography sections are especially well stocked. 1 Shell Sq., St. Charles Ave. at Poydras St. (phone: 525-1846) and *Riverwalk Mall,* Poydras St. at the Mississippi River (phone: 595-8916).

Ditto 19th Century Antiques Specializes in clocks, cut-glass, and above-average bric-a-brac. 4838 Magazine St. (phone: 891-4845).

French Market This famous market sells a wide variety of items—souvenirs, sweets (including pralines), toys, candles, spices, and funky clothes, just to name a few. Outdoor vendors' stalls offer a cornucopia of fresh fruits and vegetables, tropical plants, old books and records, and a hodgepodge of cooking spices. Decatur St., between St. Ann and Barracks Sts.

Galerie Simonne Stern Aficionados of abstract expressionism and other 20th-century schools of art should see this prestigious gallery; exhibitions feature emerging local and national artists. 518 Julia St. (phone: 529-1118) and 305 Royal St. (phone: 524-9757).

A Gallery for Fine Photography The work of the world's best-known photographers, from Matthew Brady to Irving Penn, are represented in this vast collection, shown on two floors. Also look for rare and unusual photographs relating to New Orleans, especially its musicians. 322 Royal (phone: 568-1313).

Gasperi Gallery Contemporary folk art and works that have strong ethnic connections. 320 Julia St. (phone: 524-9373).

Henry Stern Antiques A long-established dealer in fine English furniture and paintings from the late 18th and early 19th centuries. 329-331 Royal St. (phone: 522-8687).

Hové Parfumeur Perfumes, colognes, and soaps are produced on the premises of this charming, family-owned boutique, and dried aromatic herbs such as vetiver are also available. 824 Royal St. (phone: 525-7827).

Importicos Showcased here is a wide selection of temple gods (mermaids, fertility angels), carousel horses, wall masks, and other exotica from Mexico, Egypt, Kenya, and India. 517 St. Louis St. (phone: 523-0306).

The Idea Factory Hand-crafted wooden creations—whimsical creatures as well as marquetry boxes and other practical items—can be found here; all are made in a workshop out back. 838 Chartres St. (phone: 524-5195).

Kaboom Books The number and selection of bookseller John Dillman's used volumes are excellent, and he's unusually knowledgeable about various editions. 901 Barracks St. (phone: 529-5780).

Kite Shop From the whimsical to the artistic, all kinds of kites crowd the ceiling and walls of this colorful and fascinating little store on Jackson Square. 542 St. Peter St. (phone: 524-0028).

Lucullus Crowded with antique French and English dining room furniture, crystal, porcelain, and decorative objects relating to food and wine. 610 Chartres St. (phone: 528-9620).

Maison Blanche This fine regional department store in the heart of downtown carries nationally known brands as well as designer clothing. 901 Canal St. (phone: 566-1000).

Maple Street Book Shop If New Orleans has a literary heart, it is this unpretentious uptown cottage crammed with a very selective collection of novels, anthologies, and biographies, from the latest best sellers to the most obscure Southern writers. A bookworm's paradise. 7523 Maple St. (phone: 866-4916). The branch at 2727 Prytania St. (phone: 895-2266) is interesting, too.

Merrill B. Domas American Indian Art The work of the best weavers, potters, and painters from the Southwest is sold here, as well as jewelry in silver and gemstones by some of Santa Fe's leading artisans. 824 Chartres St. (phone: 586-0479).

Mignon Faget Ltd. New Orleans's premier jewelry designer offers elegant pieces inspired by nature in precious metals and stones. *Canal Place,* 333 Canal St. (phone: 524-2973); 710 Dublin St. (phone: 865-7361); and 8220 Maple St. (phone: 865-1107).

Old Town Praline Shop Charmingly old-fashioned, it turns out pecan-studded sugar patties wrapped in the same little waxed-paper bags they've used for decades. They'll pack and ship, as well. 627 Royal St. (phone: 525-1413).

Le Petit Soldier Shoppe Collector or not, you're apt to be charmed by the hundreds of exquisitely crafted and painted lead soldiers sold in this museum-cum-shop. There are also all sorts of antique military memorabilia. 528 Royal St. (phone: 523-7741).

Progress Grocery Co. It's part delicatessen, part fancy grocery store, with a *muffuletta* sandwich take-out counter and a huge variety of exotic edibles on the shelves, including the proprietor's own herbed olive oils. Imported pasta and unusual dried legumes are also available. 915 Decatur St. (phone: 525-6627).

Rapp's Luggage and Gifts Whether you're looking for a plastic carry-on or a briefcase of fine leather, you'll probably find it here; also all sorts of handy travel gear. Minor luggage repairs, too. 604 Canal St. (phone: 568-1953).

Record Ron's Good & Plenty Records Everything from Bing Crosby to heavy metal to baroque, with a specialty in rarities and the offbeat, fills the seemingly endless bins of LPs. 1129 Decatur St. (phone: 524-9444).

Rubenstein Bros. The fashion-conscious man looking for top American and European designers will find them here. So will the follower of the latest trends in casualwear. The choices, from haberdashery to topcoats, are many and varied. 102 St. Charles Ave. (phone: 581-6666).

Serendipitous A wide variety of brightly colored masks can be found here. 831 Decatur St. (phone: 522-9158).

Still-Zinsel Contemporary Fine Art New painters and photographers working in a variety of styles are often introduced here. 328 Julia St. (phone: 588-9999).

Victoria's Designer Discount Shoes From simple pumps to glittery evening shoes, much of the footwear is made by the leading names in fashion—and they're priced to sell. 532 Chartres St. (phone: 568-9990).

Wehmeier's Belt Shop The large inventory of men's and women's leather goods includes shoes and handbags; emergency repairs are made on the premises. 719 Toulouse (phone: 525-2758).

SPORTS AND FITNESS

BICYCLING Bicycles can be rented at *Bicycle Michael's* (618 Frenchmen St., a few blocks from the French Quarter; phone: 945-9505). *City Park* rents bikes at Dreyfous Avenue (phone: 483-9371).

BOATING At *City Park,* you can rent canoes, paddleboats, and skiffs to cruise on the lagoons (phone: 483-9371).

CANOEING The swamps and marshes within an hour's drive from the center of town, teeming with vegetation and wildlife, provide an exotic backdrop for explorations by canoe. *Canoe and Trail Outings* (802 Chapelle St.; phone: 283-9400) specializes in "sunset paddling" excursions to the Manchac Swamp, west of the city, and the Honey Island Swamp to the east, among other places. The company rents all the necessary equipment.

FISHING New Orleans's location on the central Gulf Coast makes it ideal for freshwater and saltwater sport fishing year-round. Full-day excursions from New Orleans to Venice, near the mouth of the Mississippi River, are easily arranged for groups of two to 20. Lakes, bays, inlets, and marshes, less than an hour's drive from the center of town, are filled with redfish, largemouth bass, catfish, and freshwater drum. In the very heart of town, *City Park*'s lagoons are pleasant places to drop a line on a balmy afternoon. Temporary state licenses are required for non-state residents for all fishing, crabbing, and shrimping—saltwater and freshwater licenses are sold by the *Louisiana Department of Wildlife and Fisheries* office in the French Quarter (400 Chartres St.; phone: 568-5636), which is closed weekends. Be sure to inquire about seasonal regulations, too.

FITNESS CENTERS The *New Orleans Athletic Club* (222 N. Rampart St.; phone: 525-2375) has a 60-foot indoor lap pool, exercise equipment and classes, a boxing ring, racquetball and basketball courts, and indoor and outdoor tracks. *Racquetball One Fitness Centers* (1 Shell Sq., 13th Floor, Poydras St. and St. Charles Ave.; phone: 522-2956; and *Canal Place,* Suite 380, 333 Canal St.; phone: 525-2956) offer racquetball courts, aerobics programs, free weights, stair climbers, and exercise cycles. Several hotels also allow non-guests to use their centers for a fee. The *Rivercenter Racquet and Health Club* in the *New Orleans Hilton* (Poydras St. at the Mississippi River; phone: 587-7242) has a jogging track, weight training, saunas, and basketball, racquetball, tennis, and squash courts. *Eurovita Spa* at the *Avenue Plaza Suite* hotel (2111 St. Charles Ave.; phone: 566-1212) offers a fitness room with weights, saunas, steamrooms, a whirlpool bath, and tanning rooms, as well as therapeutic massages. *Le Meridien Sports Center* (*Le Meridien Hotel*, 614 Canal St.; phone: 527-6750) has an outdoor heated pool, Nautilus equipment, Lifecycles, an aerobics program, yoga classes, a sauna, and massage therapists.

FOOTBALL The New Orleans *Saints* play in the *Louisiana Superdome* (Poydras St.; phone: 522-2600). The *Sugar Bowl Classic,* one of football's oldest college bowl games, takes place on *New Year's Day* in the *Superdome.*

GOLF Several public 18-hole courses, all open daily, are short distances from the city center. *City Park* has four courses (phone: 483-9396). *Audubon Park* (in the Uptown section; phone: 861-9511) has its own course. Also check out *Brechtel Park* (on the west bank of the Mississippi River; phone: 362-4761); *Joe Bartholomew Golf Course* (in eastern New Orleans's *Pontchartrain*

Park; phone: 288-0928); and *Plantation Golf Course* (1001 Behrman Hwy.; phone: 392-3363).

HORSEBACK RIDING The 2-mile trail at *Cascade Stables* is shaded by *Audubon Park*'s huge oaks. Horses and ponies are available for adults and youngsters daily (phone: 891-2246).

HORSE RACING The *Fair Grounds* (1751 Gentilly Blvd.; phone: 944-5515), one of the country's oldest thoroughbred-racing tracks, is a 15-minute taxi ride from the city center. It operates from *Thanksgiving* to mid-April. Although a fire in December 1993 destroyed the historic clubhouse and grandstand, as well as other major buildings, the track's owners resumed the races within weeks. At press time, a new clubhouse and grandstand were still under construction.

JOGGING Good routes are in *City Park* at the end of Esplanade Avenue, *Audubon Park* in the Uptown section, *Woldenberg Park* on the French Quarter's edge, and along the Mississippi River levee on Leake Avenue in the Carrollton section.

TENNIS The 39 lighted courts at the *Wisner Tennis Center* in *City Park* are open from 7 AM to past sunset, and the pro shop provides racquet repairs (phone: 483-9383). *Audubon Park*'s 10 courts, near the Mississippi River in the Uptown section, are open at 8 AM (phone: 895-1042). The *Rivercenter Racquet and Health Club* has eight indoor and three outdoor courts; located at the *New Orleans Hilton* (2 Poydras St.; phone: 587-7242), it has river views. All charge court fees; all are open daily.

THEATER

National touring companies of Broadway shows perform regularly in the fall and spring at the *Saenger Performing Arts Center* (143 N. Rampart St. at Canal St.; phone: 524-2490). For those seeking something more daring, contemporary American plays, many of them by local writers and most of them avant-garde, are presented regularly in the arena theater of the *Contemporary Arts Center* (900 Camp St.; phone: 523-1216). In the French Quarter's community theater, the picturesque *Le Petit Théâtre du Vieux Carré* presents modern musical comedies and dramas from Broadway's past, and original plays for children (616 St. Peter St.; phone: 522-2081). Respectable amateur productions, from the spirited performances of the *Dashiki Theatre* group to original spoofs of old Hollywood musicals, are put on in the 100-seat *NORD Theater* space on the ground floor of *Gallier Hall* (543 St. Charles Ave.; phone: 565-7860). Original dramas, some experimental, are the forte of the little *Theater Marigny* (616 Frenchmen St.; phone: 944-2653). Meatier works, from 19th-century classics to contemporary plays, are presented by *Tulane University* (*Dixon Performing Arts Center* on the *Newcomb College* campus; phone: 865-5106, the Drama Department, for theater productions during the year; phone: 865-5269, the

Music Department, for summer stock musicals by the semi-professional *Summer Lyric Theater,* as well as opera and other music concerts); *Loyola University*'s *Lower Depths Theatre* (on the St. Charles Ave. campus; phone: 865-3824); and the *University of New Orleans Performing Arts Center* (near the Lakefront; phone: 834-9774). Lighter fare, in the form of contemporary Broadway comedies and revues, is the stock-in-trade at the *Rivertown Repertory Theatre,* in suburban Kenner's Rivertown entertainment complex (401 Minor St., Kenner; phone: 468-7272).

MUSIC AND DANCE

The demise of the *New Orleans Symphony Orchestra* in early 1990 left the city without a major orchestra of its own for the first time since the 1930s. Later that year, however, a core group of musicians launched a grass-roots movement that resulted in the creation of the *Louisiana Philharmonic Orchestra,* with a limited season in the spring and fall and a roster of guest conductors. The group's concerts are given in the *Orpheum Theater* (129 University Pl., near Canal St.; phone: 523-6530). Aficionados of chamber music should check the schedule of the *Friends of Music* (phone: 895-0690), a group that sponsors several concerts each year by local and nationally known professionals; the performances are usually held at *Tulane University*'s *Dixon Performing Arts Center* on the *Newcomb College* campus. *Loyola University* and *Sophie Newcomb College* at *Tulane University* sponsor occasional recitals and concerts by students, faculty, and visiting performers at *Loyola*'s *Roussel Performance Hall* on the university campus (7214 St. Charles Ave.; phone: 865-2492) and at *Tulane/Newcomb's Dixon Hall* or *Rogers Memorial Chapel* (information from *Tulane*'s Music Department; phone: 865-5269). New Orleans was the first American city to build an opera house, in the early 19th century. The musical tradition continues with several productions yearly by the *New Orleans Opera Association,* featuring internationally known performers offering classical European repertories. They're presented at the *Theatre for the Performing Arts* (N. Rampart St. near the corner of Dumaine St.; phone: 529-2278). Also, the music department of *Xavier University* occasionally stages student opera productions (7325 Palmetto St.; phone: 486-7411, university switchboard; phone: 483-7621, program director's office).

In the 1980s *The New Orleans Ballet* merged with the *Cincinnati Ballet,* but kept its name and locale (phone: 522-0996); it stages several major productions annually in the *Theatre for the Performing Arts* (see above).

The biggest pop and rock stars regularly perform at the *Saenger Performing Arts Center* downtown (143 N. Rampart St.; phone: 524-2490); the *Kiefer UNO Lakefront Arena* (on the *University of New Orleans* campus; phone: 286-7222); the *Louisiana Superdome* (on Poydras St.; phone: 587-3800); and at private halls and clubs around town.

ALL THAT JAZZ

Jazz and Cajun musicians have brought the Big Easy its international reputation as a musical center. New Orleans is a port city, and nowhere is this more apparent than in the flamboyant overlapping of musical influences that have produced the distinctively syncopated swagger and improvisational fire of this city's music. The music is a rich gumbo created from the cross-fertilization of Caribbean music, African rhythms, the blues, zydeco, and traditional Cajun music. New Orleans has exported its music around the globe and has garnered an enthusiastic international following. Some of the current stars of this musical seedbed include the *Neville Brothers,* Dr. John, the *Dirty Dozen Brass Band,* and such zydeco groups as *Buckwheat Zydeco* and *Rockin' Dopsie and the Zydeco Twisters.* At the same time, never forget that Louis Armstrong, Jelly Roll Morton, Sidney Bechet, and other jazz immortals were the New Orleans musicians who brought jazz to a new plateau of improvisational genius, making a major impact on the evolution of this quintessentially American sound.

NIGHTCLUBS AND NIGHTLIFE

No fan of classic New Orleans jazz should miss the authentic music and incomparable atmosphere of *Preservation Hall* (see *Special Places*). More comfortable, and just as much the real thing musically, is the *Palm Court Jazz Café* (1204 Decatur St.; phone: 525-0200), a spacious restaurant in an old French Quarter building where young and old traditionalists play nightly.

Two of the city's most celebrated Dixieland musicians, clarinetist Pete Fountain and trumpeter Al Hirt, have their own clubs, and the seats are always filled when the masters themselves are onstage. Fountain's headquarters is *Pete Fountain's* in the *New Orleans Hilton* (2 Poydras St.; phone: 523-4374), and Hirt holds forth from time to time at *Patout's* in the French Quarter (501 Bourbon St.; phone: 568-0501). Good-quality local bands perform in their absence; if you're interested only in the stars themselves, call ahead. Bourbon Street is lined with Dixieland clubs; one of the best is the *Famous Door* (339 Bourbon St.; phone: 522-7626); another is *Fritzel*'s (733 Bourbon St.; phone: 561-0432); or, off Bourbon, try *Maxwell's Toulouse Cabaret* (615 Toulouse St.; phone: 523-4207). Another especially compatible setting for Dixieland is *LeMoyne's Landing,* near the Plaza d'España and the *Riverwalk Mall* (Canal St. at the Mississippi River; phone: 524-4809).

The music of southwest Louisiana's bayous has an international following and it is certainly not neglected in New Orleans clubs. Authentic Cajun bands, including groups performing in the even earthier and folksier zydeco style, stomp and fiddle every night in the Warehouse District at *Mulate's* (201 Julia St.; phone: 522-1492), which also has a dance floor and a kitchen dispensing spicy Louisiana dishes. Another choice Cajun dance hall–restaurant is *Michaul's,* on the Warehouse District's fringe (701 Magazine St.; phone: 522-5517). Other clubs where Cajun groups often perform are the *Maple Leaf* (8316 Oak St.; phone: 866-9359), with its tiny dance floor, and *Tipitina's* (501 Napoleon Ave.; phone: 895-8477), an earthy spot deep in the heart of the Uptown waterfront. The "New Orleans Sound" and the blues are also featured at *Tipitina's,* where the music is down-and-dirty and the crowd never stops moving—on or off the dance floor.

The New Orleans sound and the blues also are in the spotlight at *Jimmy's* (8200 Willow St.; phone: 861-8200). Blues great Marva Wright can often be found at *Muddy Water's* in Carrollton (8301 Oak St.; phone: 866-7174). A new but already premier blues spot in the Quarter is *House of Blues* (225 Decatur St.; phone: 529-2583), an immense music space and restaurant opened last year by comedian Dan Aykroyd. The $7-million complex holds a vast collection of folk art in addition to its awesome sound system.

At *Snug Harbor* (626 Frenchmen St.; phone: 949-0696), a couple of blocks from the French Quarter, you can hear both the New Orleans Sound, performed by such masters as singers Charmaine Neville and Germaine Bazzle, and contemporary jazz pianist Ellis Marsalis often plays here.

Other nightspots worth visiting include *The Mint* (504 Esplanade Ave.; phone: 525-2000), a large, laid-back gay bar with a floor show in which homegrown talent performs Friday through Sunday nights. The humor usually has lots of local connotations, but out-of-towners seem to catch on quickly. At *Chris Owens* in the French Quarter (502 Bourbon St.; phone: 523-6400), the club's namesake is the sole performer, and if her maraca shaking and fancy footwork aren't the most advanced in town, her showmanship usually fills the place to the rafters. The *Napoleon House Bar* (500 Chartres St.; phone: 524-9752) is an unpolished, bohemian, yet authentically charming spot to sip the house's special Pimm's Cup Cocktail (Pimm's Cup Mix blended with rum) while soaking up the early 19th-century atmosphere; their hearty Italian-style sandwiches are excellent.

Best in Town

CHECKING IN

Hotels in New Orleans usually are more than just places to sleep. Many of them reflect French, Spanish, and/or Louisiana colonial influences, and a good number have serious charm. No matter where you stay or what you pay, make reservations well in advance, particularly during *Sugar Bowl Week* (approximately December 30 to January 2) preceding the annual football classic on *New Year's Day, Carnival* season (in February or early March), and the *New Orleans Jazz and Heritage Festival* (in late April or early May); rates increase by about 25% during these periods. Also note that many hotels have three- or four-day minimum stays during *Carnival.* Most of New Orleans's major hotels have complete facilities for the business traveler.

Those listed below as having "business services" usually offer such conveniences as meeting rooms, photocopiers, computers, translation services, and express checkout, among others. Call the individual hotel for additional information. Expect to pay more than $160 per night for those hotels listed as very expensive; from $110 to $160 for a double room (more for suites) at hotels in the expensive range; $75 to $95 at places in the moderate category; and $50 to $70 at the establishment listed as inexpensive.

For bed and breakfast accommodations, contact *Bed & Breakfast Inc.* (1360 Moss St., Box 52257, New Orleans, LA 70152; phone: 525-4640; 800-228-9711); *Bed & Breakfast of New Orleans* (671 Rosa Ave., Metairie; phone: 838-0071); or the *New Orleans Metropolitan Convention and Visitors Bureau* (1520 Sugar Bowl Dr., New Orleans, LA 70112; phone: 566-5011). Unless we note otherwise, rooms in the hotels listed below have air conditioning, private baths, TV sets, and telephones.

All hotels below are in New Orleans and telephone and fax numbers are in the 504 area code unless otherwise indicated.

VERY EXPENSIVE

Maison de Ville This gem of a hotel in the heart of the French Quarter offers a choice of accommodations: In the *maison* are 16 magnificent rooms and suites furnished with antiques and with balconies offering street or courtyard views. Out back are the remodeled slave quarters (ca. 1742), and a stroll away on Dauphine Street are the seven delightful *Audubon Cottages,* where John James Audubon lived and worked in 1821. Built in the creole brick-and-post style (resembling European half-timbered buildings), the cottages have perhaps the most elegant rooms of all, and come with stocked refrigerators, private gardens, and patios with access to a small swimming pool. There is an omniscient concierge; shoes left outside your door are shined; and a classic French breakfast is served on a silver tray, with newspapers and a rose. Enjoy casual dining at the *Bistro* (see *Eating Out*). Room service is available for lunch and dinner only. 727 Toulouse St. (phone: 561-5858; 800-634-1600).

Soniat House No hostelry in New Orleans captures the city's romantic charm and Old Southern gentility quite like this one does. Proprietors Rodney and Frances Smith refurbished two balconied, early-19th-century creole townhouses in the tranquil lower French Quarter and furnished them with stunning period antiques and exquisite paintings and objets d'art. Each of the 24 rooms and suites is unique, with canopied beds in the larger rooms. A light breakfast is served (for a small additional charge) in the inner courtyards, shaded by aromatic tropical trees and plants. In the downstairs sitting rooms, home-style bars operate after hours on the honor system. Reserve as far in advance as possible. 1133 Chartres St. (phone: 522-0570; 800-544-8808).

Windsor Court The handsome, secluded driveway is an indication of the pleasures that lie within. Delicate Oriental figurines rest in glistening antique cases, sprays of cymbidium orchids crown massive marble tables, and four centuries of art decorate the ground-floor lobby and public rooms. Of the 310 rooms, about 250 are suites with separate living rooms, dressing rooms, and kitchenettes or wet bars. All of the guestrooms have private balconies or bay windows, Italian marble bathrooms, and three telephones equipped with two incoming lines. There are 55 two-bedroom suites and two spectacular penthouse suites on the 22nd floor, each of which includes a library and a large terrace overlooking the Mississippi. In *Le Salon,* a string quartet plays during afternoon tea, and the elegant *Grill Room* (see *Eating Out*) features regional and international delicacies. There is 24-hour room service, a multilingual staff, business services, an Olympic-size pool, a fully equipped health club, and a parking garage. The location, near Canal Street and the Mississippi Riverfront, is another plus. 300 Gravier St. (phone: 523-6000; 800-262-2662).

EXPENSIVE

Fairmont Successor to the legendary *Roosevelt,* which once occupied this same site, this hotel is a delightful blending of the best in San Francisco style and New Orleans charm. The 750 rooms are efficiently maintained (but ask for one in the newer wing). Its location, just a half block from Canal Street and a few blocks from the heart of the French Quarter, makes it convenient for shopping and dining. The *Sazerac,* a luxury restaurant, is frilly and romantic (see *Eating Out*); the more casual *Bailey's,* open 24 hours, offers everything from snacks to good creole fare. There's also a heated pool and two tennis courts. Other amenities include a concierge desk and business services. University Pl. (phone: 529-7111; 800-527-4727; fax: 522-2303).

Hyatt Regency A stone's throw from the *Superdome* and connected to the *New Orleans Centre* shopping mall, this recently renovated 1,200-room link in the Hyatt chain is bunkerlike on the outside, but has an atrium-style lobby, an inner courtyard fountain, lots of greenery, and numerous multilevel public spaces. Some rooms have private patios and balconies; others overlook the heated outdoor swimming pool. The grand view of the city from the *Top of the Dome* restaurant is a plus, and *Hyttops,* the sports bar on the mezzanine level, is always lively, especially during big *Superdome* sports events. Room service and business services are available. 500 Poydras Plaza (phone: 561-1234; 800-233-1234; fax: 587-4141).

Inter-Continental The lustrous wood-paneled mezzanine lobby is decorated with striking works by contemporary New Orleans artists, and is further brightened by the fresh flowers. *Veranda,* a dramatic dining room with a lofty glass ceiling and lush greenery, serves continental fare. Among the 482 guestrooms are several suites luxuriously decorated in 19th-century Louisiana style. On the top floor are a health club and pool. The hotel, which attracts a large concentration of business travelers, is steps away from both the business district and the Mississippi Riverfront. There is butler service on the executive floor, and 24-hour room service is available, as are CNN, a concierge desk, and business services. 444 St. Charles Ave. (phone: 525-5566; 800-327-0200).

Lafayette This stately hotel, just two blocks from Poydras Street, has reemerged as a handsome choice among the hotels of the Business District. Its 144 refurbished guestrooms and 20 suites, all with high ceilings, are elegantly decorated with handsome period-style furniture. Suites contain marble wet bars and refrigerators, and four are equipped with Jacuzzis. Just off the small ground-floor lobby is *Mike's on the Avenue,* a sleekly designed restaurant offering the eclectic cuisine of chef Mike Fennelly (see *Eating Out*). Business services are available. 600 St. Charles Ave. (phone: 524-4441; 800-733-4754; fax: 523-7327).

LaMothe House Built in the early 1800s by a successful planter named Jean LaMothe, this exquisite early New Orleans townhouse, surrounded by moss-draped oaks, is a delightful place to call home while visiting the Big Easy. With its stately foyer, lushly planted courtyard, and antique furnishings, this elegant establishment transports visitors to the city's earlier, gentler days, without exposing them to the discomforts of the past. Continental breakfast, the only meal served, is always an event: Everyone sits at a long banquet table and lingers over chicory coffee. The inn is in the French Quarter, very close to the jazz, good food, and intriguing shops. Note that prices range a great deal due to the very different accommodations offered. 621 Esplanade Ave. (phone: 947-1161 or 800-367-5858; fax: 943-6536).

Le Meridien This classy, sleek member of the French chain has become a major presence on Canal Street's hotel row. The *Jazz Meridien* bar has traditional jazz bands nightly, adding a sassy energy to the atmosphere. *La Gauloise,* a bistro-style restaurant, borrows the look of turn-of-the-century Paris and serves excellent buffets featuring creole and French dishes. Chic understatement characterizes the 497 guestrooms and five bi-level suites. To soothe travel-weary muscles, guests can order a massage in the fully equipped penthouse health club or take a swim in the pool. Amenities also include a concierge, 24-hour room service, and business services. 614 Canal St. (phone: 525-6500; 800-543-4300).

New Orleans Hilton The Mississippi River is almost at the doorstep of this immense and impressive link in the Hilton chain. The lavish marble and polished wood lobby connects directly to the *Riverwalk* shopping mall. Located here is *Pete Fountain's* nightclub, where some of the city's top musicians perform, including Fountain himself. The state-of-the-art *Racquet and Health Club* has 11 tennis courts—eight indoor and three outdoor—as well as two squash courts and a basketball court. All 1,602 guestrooms are soundproofed, and children occupying their parents' room stay free. The 41 meeting rooms contain 127,000 square feet of space for conferences and exhibitions. Other amenities include 24-hour room service, a concierge desk, and business services. 2 Poydras St. (phone: 561-0500; 800-HILTONS).

New Orleans Marriott Unabashedly glitzy, this 1,290-room hotel is tailor-made for those in search of Las Vegas–style ambience. Its spacious but low-ceilinged lobby houses a warren of casual eateries and lounges; and guestrooms are done up in lots of bright colors. On the top floor, the *River View* restaurant offers a pleasant panorama of the Mississippi, the French Quarter, and Canal Street. There's also a health club with Nautilus equipment and a pool. Efficient, affable service is a plus. Business services are offered. Canal and Chartres Sts. (phone: 581-1000; 800-228-9290; fax: 523-6755).

Pontchartrain With 100 tastefully decorated rooms, each furnished with provincial antiques, this is a favorite of celebrities and dignitaries. There are two restaurants, the casual *Coffee Shop* and the lavishly appointed *Caribbean Room* (see *Eating Out*), which offers creole specialties. A jazz pianist performs nightly in the intimate *Bayou Bar.* Around-the-clock room service is offered, as well as business services. 2031 St. Charles Ave. (phone: 524-0581; fax: 524-1165).

Royal Sonesta Somewhere between glitzy and elegant, this swank marble, crystal, and brocade-bedecked French Quarter establishment, with 500 rooms and 35 suites, is right on brassy Bourbon Street. The lobby is surprisingly quiet, however, as are those rooms which overlook the lush interior patio; as you might expect, the rooms with balconies overlooking the frenetic Bourbon Street nighttime revelry are anything but peaceful. *Begue's,* the hotel's prestigious restaurant, offers creole-continental food with occasional lighter, contemporary dishes. Facilities include an outdoor pool, a concierge desk, business services, and a garage. 300 Bourbon St. (phone: 586-0300; 800-343-7170; fax: 586-0335).

Ste. Hélène A carefully preserved historic building, this 18th-century guesthouse has a courtyard pool and three floors with 16 rooms, seven with balconies overlooking the interior garden or busy Chartres Street. An additional 10 rooms on St. Louis Street—next to the famed *Napoleon* restaurant—are exclusively suites complete with hardwood floors and 14-foot ceilings. All accommodations are beautifully appointed with 19th-century antiques. There is no restaurant but room service is available for breakfast and guests enjoy an afternoon Champagne Happy Hour daily. Some business services are available. Conveniently located two blocks from *Jackson Square* at 508 Chartres St. (phone: 522-5014; 800-348-3888; fax: 523-7140).

Westin–Canal Place Its entrance is unassuming, but this hotel located near the French Quarter, Canal Street, and the Mississippi River is as modern and plush as they come. The 11th-floor lobby has a panoramic view of the French Quarter and the river as it begins forming its famous crescent, and public areas are richly furnished with armchairs, antiques, and thick rugs. The glistening marble bar off the lobby—known simply as the *Bar*—is a wonderful place to stop for a drink. Beyond the lobby proper is *Le Jardin* restaurant and bar, serving contemporary creole cuisine, as well as morning coffee and croissants. Most of the 438 spacious rooms and suites, decorated in pastels and accented with prints of the French Quarter, have views of the river. Twenty-four-hour room service is available, as are business services. 100 Iberville St. (phone: 566-7006; 800-228-3000).

MODERATE

Bourbon Orleans On a quiet block of the French Quarter, this 210-room hotel incorporates what was, from 1815 to the late 19th century, a ballroom for Creole ladies and gentlemen. Today it is certainly more luxurious, with its Queen Anne furniture, canopied king-size beds, marble baths, and crystal and brocade accents. An outdoor pool and business services are other pluses. There is a small restaurant. 717 Orleans St. (phone: 523-2222; 800-521-5338; fax: 525-8166).

Dauphine Orleans Almost hidden along one of the French Quarter's more residential streets is this well-run, 109-room establishment that blends modern conveniences with a reasonable amount of creole charm. Across the street is *Dauphine Patios,* a small annex, with pleasant rooms opening onto a courtyard. Amenities include a complimentary newspaper, a fitness room, free parking, continental breakfast, and a lending library; there is no restaurant. A complimentary open-air jitney transports guests around the Quarter and Central Business District. 415 Dauphine St. (phone: 586-1800; 800-521-7111; fax: 586-1409).

Doubletree New Orleans When the small Doubletree chain took over this modern property in the late 1980s, it transformed the once glitzy lobby into a more intimate space and added French country accents to the 363 rooms and 15 suites. The *Chicory Rotisserie and Grill* serves continental fare, and the hotel's location—near the Mississippi River, the *Ernest N. Morial Convention Center,* and the French Quarter—adds to its appeal. 300 Canal St. (phone: 581-1300; 800-223-TREE; fax: 522-4100).

Maison Dupuy Off the French Quarter's beaten track is this modern, handsomely turned out four-story hostelry with a spectacular courtyard and meticulously maintained public spaces. The 195 rooms and suites are decorated in pastels and floral motifs; some suites have three bedrooms. *Sclafani's,* a colorful, casual restaurant and lounge, offers updated creole standards. 1001 Toulouse St. (phone: 586-8000; 800-535-9177; fax: 525-5334).

Le Pavillon Eighteenth-century France was the obvious inspiration for this refurbished Poydras Street place, whose style is locally referred to as "barbecue Baroque." The lobby is filled with a profusion of crystal chandeliers, marble, and brocades. There are 200 rooms, a rooftop swimming pool, and a restaurant on the premises. Business services are available. 833 Poydras St. (phone: 581-3111; 800-535-9095; fax: 522-5543).

Place d'Armes A few steps from Jackson Square, this functional but tastefully decorated hostelry has a lovely courtyard with a pool, fountains, and outdoor tables. There are 79 rooms and eight suites in five renovated 18th-century buildings. The lobby is diminutive, but the place is comfortable and clean, and some rooms have balconies overlooking the Chartres Street corner of Jackson Square. Room service delivers a complimentary continental breakfast only (there is no restaurant on the premises), and business services are available. 625 St. Ann St. (phone: 524-4531).

De la Poste A comprehensive renovation completed several years ago has added sparkle to this sedate hotel on this reasonably quiet section of Chartres Street. Built in 1973 in traditional French Quarter style, the property has 100 rooms and four carriage house suites with private patios; the drive-through, brick-paved carriageway leads to a spacious courtyard with a fountain and a swimming pool. On the ground floor is *Bacco* (see *Eating Out*), a roomy and handsome Italian restaurant. Coffee and fresh fruit in the lobby are complimentary, as is the weekday newspaper delivered to guests' doors. The courtyard can be reserved for receptions; some conference and function rooms open onto the courtyard as well. 316 Chartres St. (phone: 581-1200; 800-448-4927).

Provincial A personal touch is evident throughout this well-designed establishment on lower Chartres Street. A French-country look characterizes the 106 guestrooms, many of which are furnished with canopied beds and old armoires. The small bar and moderately priced *Honfleur* restaurant are especially picturesque, decorated with unpretentious antiques and old prints. There is no charge for children sharing rooms with adults. Convenient to the *French Market,* Jackson Square, and Decatur Street. 1024 Chartres St. (phone: 581-4995; 800-535-7922; fax: 581-1018).

Le Richelieu This 69-room hostelry on the fringes of the French Quarter was the place where former *Beatle* Paul McCartney hung his hat when he came to town. Fans may be surprised at his rather modest taste. Still, the place does have its charms, such as kitchenettes in the 17 suites and, in many of the rooms, such old-fashioned touches as brass ceiling fans and pull-down ironing boards. Other pluses: a pleasant little restaurant overlooking the pool, and cheerful, efficient service. 1234 Chartres St. (phone: 529-2492; 800-535-9653; fax: 524-8179).

St. Pierre A complex of 200-year-old former slave quarters has been restored to create a maze of courtyards, swimming pools, and guest cottages landscaped with tropical plants. French doors open into rooms with high ceilings, exposed brick, and traditional furnishings. Complimentary continental breakfast is included. 911 Burgundy St. (phone: 524-4401; 800-535-7785; fax: 524-6800).

INEXPENSIVE

Château Motor Hotel In a relatively quiet part of the French Quarter, this attractive, serviceable hotel is for the traveler seeking comfort and convenience with a minimum of frills. Access from the small lobby to the 37 rooms and five suites is through a carriageway and patio. While the rooms are not luxurious, they're well maintained and pleasantly decorated. There is also a small restaurant and bar. Jackson Square is a short walk away. 1001 Chartres St. (phone: 524-9636).

EATING OUT

The distinctive regional cuisine—creole cooking—has been shaped through the years by the cultures of France, Spain, America, and the West Indies, and by the influences of Native and African Americans. Seafood is king in creole recipes, and the nearby waters are filled with crab, shrimp, red snapper, flounder, Gulf pompano, and trout. Vegetables in season, fowl, veal, and fresh herbs and seasonings are culinary staples that add to the regional style. Then there's Acadian (known outside the area as Cajun) cooking, the boldly flavored game, pork and fish dishes developed in backwater, southern Louisiana.

Some useful food terms: One traditional Cajun-creole dish is *étouffée* ("smothered" in French), a thick stew made with seafood in a black iron pot. Jambalaya (not unlike Spanish paella) and gumbo (a thick, spicy soup made with myriad ingredients) are two more staples. Remoulade is a peppery vinaigrette; and more humbly, the po-boy is a two-fisted sandwich of thick French bread, slit open and filled with meat, seafood, and vegetables.

There are numerous excellent chefs here, constantly producing new variations on these themes. The result is that you will find find fancy creole food palaces, trendy Cajun bistros, and basic red-beans-and-rice joints. Our selections, below, should help you find the best of them.

Expect to pay $80 or more for two at the places we've noted as very expensive; $65 to $80 at an expensive restaurant; between $40 and $65 at moderate places; and $40 or under at eateries we list as inexpensive. Prices include tax and tips, but not drinks or wine. All telephone numbers are in the 504 area code. Jackets for men are advised for the more expensive restaurants.

Unless other noted, all restaurants are open for lunch and dinner.

VERY EXPENSIVE

Antoine's With a menu that reaches back more than 100 years, and a maze of rooms filled with enough memorabilia for two or three small museums, this place defines the classical creole style in New Orleans. The recipe for oysters Rockefeller was invented here, and it is still excellent. Other good bets are the cool and spicy shrimp remoulade, crabmeat *ravigote* (in a cold, spicy mayonnaise), broiled pompano (a Gulf fish similar to flounder) topped with sautéed lump crabmeat, and baked Alaska emblazoned with the date of the restaurant's founding—1840. Frances Parkinson Keyes's best-selling romance novel *Dinner at Antoine's* (published in the 1940s) used this place as a setting. Closed Mondays. Major credit cards accepted. 713 St. Louis St. (phone: 581-4422).

Arnaud's Old-style creole elegance fairly oozes from this huge French Quarter establishment. An entire wall of the sparkling main dining room is made of antique glass; delicate chandeliers hang from the soaring ceiling. The reliable dishes include shrimp Arnaud (a version of remoulade), oysters in cream, sautéed fish in various seasoned butter sauces, potatoes soufflé, and bread pudding. Major credit cards accepted. 813 Bienville St. (phone: 523-5433).

Bistro at Maison de Ville While the menu at this French Quarter spot changes almost weekly, some things remain predictable—among them the light and herbal seafood soups, beef tournedos with boursin cheese in a subtle wine sauce, unusual pasta dishes, and first-rate *crème brûlée.* The tiny dining room, with lustrous wood paneling and a full-length maroon banquette, holds 40; the charming little courtyard out back is used in pleasant weather, too. Closed lunch Sundays. Major credit cards accepted. 437 Esplanade Ave. (phone: 949-9912).

Brennan's Lavish creole brunches are what put this picturesque French Quarter restaurant on the map. Many of the dining rooms in the early 19th-century building are done up in the high style of the period. The bill of fare is predominantly poached eggs with unusual embellishments: Egg *sardou* (artichoke with cream spinach) and egg *hussarde* (Holland rusk topped with Canadian bacon) are two good choices. Keep in mind, however, that *Brennan's* is not for the budget-minded at any hour. Major credit cards accepted. 417 Royal St. (phone: 525-9711).

Caribbean Room The *Pontchartrain* hotel's exceptional dining room serves French and creole dishes. The menu is imaginative, as is the presentation, highlighting such dishes as red snapper Eugene (in a lemon sauce with crab and shrimp), crabmeat Biarritz (lump crabmeat with whipped cream dressing and topped with caviar), and, if you can go the distance, Mile-High Ice Cream Pie for dessert. Open daily; closed at lunch weekends. Major credit cards accepted. 2031 St. Charles Ave. (phone: 524-0581).

Commander's Palace Few restaurants in the city can match this Garden District dining institution for combining mainstream creole cuisine, a festive atmosphere, and first-rate service. The menu ranges from familiar classics to creative innovations. Among the headliners are a definitive turtle soup, a bountiful seafood and fish bouillabaisse, and excellent remoulades, gumbos, and game dishes. The fried soft-shell crab is superb, as are the sautéed trout with pecans and the bread pudding soufflé. There are several dining rooms in this late-19th-century frame mansion. The glass-walled, second-floor Garden Room overlooks the venerable oak trees in the garden below. Reservations necessary a week in advance for dinner. Major credit cards accepted. 1403 Washington Ave. (phone: 899-8221).

Emeril's Chef Emeril Lagasse's vibrant and original creole-American restaurant, in the trendy Warehouse District, remains one of the hottest meal tickets in town. Among the main attractions are an excellent version of New Orleans–style barbecue shrimp, an *étouffée* of duck with wild mushrooms, soups and salads, and a selection of belt-busting desserts that on some nights number more than a dozen. The hard surfaces of brick, glass, and wood make this contemporary dining room noisy; don't plan on an intimate dinner here. Closed Sundays. Reservations necessary a week or more in advance. Major credit cards accepted. 800 Tchoupitoulas St. (phone: 528-9393).

Graham's Chef Kevin Graham gained an international reputation during his six-year tenure at the *Windsor Court* hotel before opening his own place in 1994. Here Graham aims for "circumstance without the pomp" in a simple gray-and-beige dining room with black granite tables and black lacquer chairs. The menu changes weekly, but past offerings have included *confit* of rabbit with lentils, *udon* noodles with quail and straw mushrooms, roasted monkfish with horseradish-glazed oysters, and napoleon of portobello mushrooms with onion cakes. He also brought along his signature Chinese lacquered duck in a coffee mandarin glaze. To encourage sampling, wines are available by the half glass. Sunday "grunch" is easy on the spirit, a fun mix of food and music. Major credit cards accepted. 200 Magazine St. (phone: 524-9678).

Grill Room Everything about this palatial restaurant—from the Lalique crystal table that stands in the entry to the fresh Japanese oysters—bespeaks money freely spent. The three dining rooms here are decorated with expensive English art, dramatic bronzes, rich fabrics, and more plush than you thought possible. But somehow it's not nearly as intimidating as you'd expect, even with the most precise service in town. And the menu, which changes daily at lunch and dinner, challenges the decor for refinement; a simple but excellent salad of lump crabmeat contrasts with seared foie gras, a glorious shrimp bisque, and smoked blue marlin with zucchini ribbons. And desserts are as spectacular in appearance as they are rewarding in taste. Major credit cards accepted. *Windsor Court Hotel,* 300 Gravier St. (phone: 522-1992).

K-Paul's Louisiana Kitchen Upstairs tables can be reserved, but chances are you'll have to cool your heels outside the door for an hour or more at dinnertime for a sampling of trailblazer Paul Prudhomme's creative Cajun dishes. Once inside the rather rudimentary first-floor dining room, you also may have to share a table with strangers. Still, legions of out-of-towners keep coming back for the Cajun guru's earthy gumbos, peppery *étouffées,* and fish dishes—the ones that started the blackening craze almost a decade ago. Wiser customers come at lunch, when the line is shorter, the prices are lower, and the food is much the same as it is at dinner. Closed Sundays. American Express accepted. 416 Chartres St. (phone: 524-7394).

Louis XVI French classicism reigns in these soft, elegant spaces flanking the pleasant courtyard of a French Quarter hotel. Typical creations are shellfish in puff pastry with cream sauce, beefsteak in wine sauce with mushrooms, Caesar salad, and baroque desserts. The cream soups are especially good. Banks of arched windows and a warm color scheme add to the appealing ambience. Major credit cards accepted. *St. Louis* Hotel, 730 Bienville St. (phone: 581-7000).

EXPENSIVE

Bacco Italian cooking was late in coming to New Orleans. This bright, attractively decorated restaurant, the brainchild of the owners of *Mr. B's Bistro* (see above), fills the bill. The menu is ambitious, with dozens of choices among antipasti, pizza, pasta, and entrées including *pappardelle* with a rabbit ragout, roasted pork loin in a rosemary sauce, and hickory-smoked swordfish in a Mediterranean-style tomato sauce. Decorative accents in the four dining rooms and bar were inspired by several eras, from the Gothic to the contemporary. Major credit cards accepted. *Hotel de la Poste,* 310 Chartres St. (phone: 522-2426).

Bayona Chef Susan Spicer calls her cooking "New World" cuisine, as good a term as any for such creations as tiny medaillons of lamb tenderloin in a pinot noir sauce with fennel seed, rosemary, and three types of peppercorns; or a gratinéed casserole of polenta and thin crescents of artichoke in an Italian cheese sauce of fontina, *grana padano,* and *crescenza.* The intimate, handsomely decorated dining rooms are similarly eclectic, with murals and photos depicting lush Mediterranean landscapes and gardens. Closed Sundays. Major credit cards accepted. 430 Dauphine St. (phone: 525-4455).

Brigtsen's Chef Frank Brigtsen augments the evolution of south Louisiana cooking with his brilliant improvisations, served at this small, unpretentious restaurant in the Carrollton section. Roasted, boned duck in pecan gravy is a tour de force, and the blackened tuna elevates that cooking process to new heights. The cream of oysters Rockefeller soup is better than the dish that inspired it. And the fresh ice cream and bread pudding are unsurpassed anywhere in the city. The setting is a small frame cottage near the Mississippi River, and the mood is informal and friendly. Open for dinner only; closed Sundays and Mondays. Reserve well ahead for Saturday nights. Major credit cards accepted. 723 Dante St. (phone: 861-7610).

Gabrielle Chef Greg Sonnier and Mary Sonnier, his wife and pastry chef, have won a strong local following. Their menu changes weekly to take advantage of the freshest ingredients available at local markets. Preparations vary, but rabbit dishes and blackened tenderloin of beef complemented by caramelized onions, port wine, and stilton cheese sauce are excellent choices. Only the bread is made off premises. The fresh style extends to the decor, which is a crisp ensemble of linen and lace, quiet colors, and plenty of flowers. Although the dining room only seats 40, in warmer weather guests have the option to dine outdoors on a landscaped deck. Closed Sundays and Mondays. Major credit cards. 3201 Esplanade Ave. (phone: 948-6233).

Galatoire's It's been around for almost 100 years, but this classic creole bistro has lost none of its glitter and spunk. The narrow dining room is set off by snowy linen tablecloths, bentwood chairs, wraparound mirror panels, and chandeliers. Choice dishes include a cool and spicy shrimp remoulade, soul-warming eggplant stuffed with shrimp and crab, and lamb chops drenched in béarnaise sauce. Tuxedoed waiters dart around the narrow aisles, adding to the conviviality. Drop in at off-hours and you may not have to wait outside for a table. Closed Mondays. No reservations. Major credit cards accepted. 209 Bourbon St. (phone: 525-2021).

Gautreau's This sophisticated Uptown bistro is a favorite of locals seeking food with a New York spin on such familiar local ingredients as shrimp, crab, and crawfish. The season's menu might contain a terrific reinterpretation of seafood gumbo, along with a napoleon of grilled wild mushrooms, or pan-roasted sea bass with oysters, or grilled beef tenderloin with white-truffle potatoes. Crunchy soft-shell crab arrives under a canopy of matchstick potatoes, and salads are as good as they are adventurous. The downstairs dining room, with its oxblood walls and drugstore-tile floors, is favored by locals. But the brighter, quieter room upstairs is recommended for those who prefer more elegant surroundings. Closed Sundays. Major credit cards accepted. 1728 Soniat St. (phone: 899-7397).

La Provence The name of this French restaurant is most appropriate, both for its idyllic country setting and for the origins of chef/owner Chris Kerageogiu. Born in Port Saint Louis in Provence, he began as a baker and worked to fulfill his dream of opening a restaurant in America. Happily, for Chris and his customers, the restaurant celebrated its 20th anniversary in 1992. It is a charmer, with open fireplaces, warm wood paneling, and the ambience of a country estate. Among the entrées are quail gumbo, *jambalaya des gourmands,* rack of lamb, leg of rabbit, and fish dishes, all among the best in the region. And it's very difficult to keep your eyes off the roving dessert cart. Closed Mondays and Tuesdays. Major credit cards accepted. About 35 miles from central New Orleans, on the north shore of Lake Pontchartrain on US Hwy. 190, Lacombe (phone: 626-7662).

Mike's on the Avenue "Fusion cooking" (dishes influenced by a blend of many different cultures) is taken to new heights by chef/owner Michael Fennelly at his smartly minimal restaurant in a revitalized old hotel on the edge of the Warehouse District. Fennelly draws inspiration from Japan, Thailand, China, the American Southwest, New Orleans, and any other part of the culinary map that strikes his fancy. The results are such concoctions as spring rolls filled with crawfish, a black-bean dip spiked with Cajun seasonings, a casserole of shrimp, mussels, and Cajun sausage, and sautéed cakes of crab and scallops with three sauces zapped with chilies. Somehow, it all works deliciously in the spare, but attractive, whitewashed dining rooms, bathed with light from wide glass walls and hung with the chef's own abstract-expressionist paintings. Closed Sundays. Reservations necessary a week in advance for dinner. Major credit cards accepted. *Lafayette* Hotel, 628 St. Charles Ave. (phone: 523-1709).

Nola Riding the raging success of *Emeril's* in the Warehouse District, this is chef Emeril Lagasse's second restaurant. Dine at the food bar for front-row views of the action around the wood-burning oven that produces great pizza, breads, chicken, and cedar-plank roasted fish. The spinach salad is topped with fried oysters and a creamy dressing. A hefty selection of desserts ranges from deep-dish apple pie with cinnamon ice cream to a bananas Foster drenched in warm caramel sauce. Opens daily at 2:30 PM. Reservations advised, at least a week in advance for dinner. Major credit cards accepted. 534 St. Louis St. (phone: 522-6652).

Palace Café Set in a building that once served as New Orleans's biggest music store, this grand café features "clever creole" cuisine: rabbit ravioli in a Louisiana-style sauce piquant, a red-bean dip with the kitchen's own potato chips, a creamy "napoleon" of seafood, and a yummy white-chocolate bread pudding. The mezzanine, brightened with a large mural of the city's legendary musicians, is reached by a central staircase. Both levels are lively during peak hours, when the bar fills up and things start to sizzle in the open kitchen. Major credit cards accepted. 605 Canal St. (phone: 523-1661).

Pelican Club Innovative New Orleans cooking is the trademark of this stylish dining place located in a stately French Quarter townhouse. Co-chefs Richard Hughes and Chin Ling have combined their talents using Asian influences with contemporary Louisiana techniques. The claypot seafood entrée combines crawfish, scallops, and shrimp seasoned with Thai spices. Also delicious are the Cajun jambalaya and the pecan-crusted seafood of the day with smoked oysters in bourbon sauce. Each of the three dining rooms has its own mood, from the clubby, wood-paneled room in the back to the elegant space overlooking Bienville Street. Closed Sundays. Major credit cards accepted. 312 Exchange Alley (phone: 523-1504).

Sazerac With a dining room as frilly as a dozen wedding cakes, this very upscale hotel restaurant is just the place for a romantic—if expensive—evening. White lace covers the red tablecloths, and a dramatic burst of flowers crowns a central cluster of red-velvet banquettes. The menu, which seems to undergo a complete overhaul annually, is a combination of French, south Louisiana, and regional American cuisines. Foie gras, turtle soup, and fancied-up creole dishes are the mainstays, however. Major credit cards accepted. *Fairmont Hotel,* University Pl. (phone: 529-4733).

MODERATE

Bon Ton Café A strong traditional streak runs through the menu in this rather old-fashioned, but always humming, creole-Cajun bistro at the Central Business District's core. Crawfish is perhaps the biggest seller; the crawfish *étouffée* bisque and the jambalaya are well seasoned. Space is at a premium in the brick-lined dining room, with checkered tablecloths and a cadre of energetic waitresses. Closed weekends. Major credit cards accepted. 401 Magazine St. (phone: 524-3386).

Charley G's "Casual and classy" sums up this large, efficiently run restaurant, a few yards from the boundary line between Orleans and Jefferson Parishes. Spicy south Louisiana cooking is the mainstay of the large menu of hearty appetizers and main courses. Among the better choices are the robustly seasoned crab cakes, the duck and *andouille* sausage gumbo, and fish grilled over mesquite. Desserts, such as the Bullwinkle chocolate mousse pie, are huge and delicious. The uncluttered, contemporary dining spaces are lined in stained woods and warm earth tones, with banquettes flanking the wrap-around windows. Major credit cards accepted. 111 Veterans Blvd., Metairie (phone: 837-6408).

Clancy's If you're tired of the tourist track, consider this likable contemporary bistro deep within an Uptown residential section. It has tuxedoed waiters, very good food, and a decor so simple it's almost nonexistent. The crab bisque and shrimp remoulade are superb. Almost as good are the sautéed fish in cream sauce, sweetbreads with lemon and capers, lamb chops in béarnaise sauce, and home-style lemon icebox pie. Closed Sundays. Major credit cards accepted. 6100 Annunciation St. (phone: 895-1111).

Kelsey's Paul Prudhomme's kitchen has spawned any number of ambitious young chefs. One is Randy Barlow, who has carved out his own niche in this unassuming but attractive second-floor spot in Algiers, just across the Mississippi from central New Orleans. The menu's stars are the gumbos, a superb shrimp stew, and a terrific all-meat jambalaya. The orange-poppyseed cheesecake is addictive, as are the bread pudding and other desserts. Attractive paintings perk up the pleasant dining spaces. Closed Saturday lunch, Sundays, and Mondays. Major credit cards accepted. 3920 Gen. DeGaulle Dr., Algiers (phone: 366-6722).

Odyssey Grill Chef/owner Rosita Skias evokes the sunny climate of the Mediterranean in her cooking that always uses fresh ingredients and lots of olive oil. For starters try the lamb salad, or one of the earthy spreads or dips, especially the *taramasalata* (carp roe dip with olive oil, lemon juice, and garlic). Winning entrées are Moroccan chicken and the shrimp *souv-*

laki. Closed Mondays. MasterCard and Visa accepted. 6264 Argonne Blvd., Lakeview (phone: 482-4092).

Ralph & Kacoo's Even with several locations in the French Quarter and in the suburbs, this casual and very popular Cajun eatery fills up fast. The Cajun theme is carried out with a full-size fishing boat in the bar and a jumble of nostalgic artifacts strewn everywhere. Highlights include a fine crab gumbo, trout meunière, fried shrimp or oysters, and good renderings of sautéed fish. No reservations. Major credit cards accepted. 519 Toulouse St. (phone: 522-5226) and 601 Veterans Blvd., Metairie (phone: 831-3177).

INEXPENSIVE

Casamento's Cleanliness is an obsession in this legendary oyster house on upper Magazine Street, its gleaming white tiles giving the two small dining spaces the look of a large bathroom. Oysters are the stars here, either fried and presented without a trace of grease, freshly shucked and served up on the half shell, or cooked in a homey stew with milk and scallions. The shrimp and oyster "loaves," made with scooped-out white bread, are delicious. The rest of the menu is unimpressive. Closed Mondays and June through August. No reservations. No credit cards accepted. 4330 Magazine St. (phone: 895-9761).

China Blossom What may be the best Chinese-American restaurant in town is tucked away in a small shopping mall across the river. Chef Paul Fung does a great job with shrimp and oysters, grilling or sautéing them before adding marvelous piquant sauces. The pan-Chinese menu covers all the bases from egg rolls to fortune cookies, and it's all reliably good. Closed Mondays. Reservations advised on weekends. Major credit cards accepted. 1801 Stumpf Blvd., Gretna (phone: 361-4598).

Mandina's Once upon a time, every New Orleans neighborhood had its own purveyor of po-boys, red beans, and spaghetti, with a room out back for family gatherings. This place carries on the tradition faithfully. After a wait at the stand-up bar, sit at a Formica-topped table and dig into very good po-boys, garlicky cracked crab claws, butter-drenched trout meunière, or a creditable gumbo. No reservations. No credit cards accepted. 3800 Canal St. (phone: 482-9179).

Taqueria Corona Aficionados of tacos, nachos, and burritos will find exceptionally good renditions here. Try the "tacocado" salad, a fried tortilla filled with guacamole, meat, lettuce, olives, and cheese. Seating is at both the counter and tables. Service is make-do. No reservations. No credit cards accepted. 857 Fulton St. and 5932 Magazine St. (phone: 897-3974 for both locations).

New York City

New York offers an array of distractions unequaled anywhere on earth. Nowhere are there more museums of such a consistently high quality. Nowhere are there restaurants of such striking ethnic diversity. Nowhere is there more varied shopping for more esoteric paraphernalia, and nowhere in the world do the pace of life and the activities of the populace more dramatically accent a city's vitality and appeal.

Just as US citizens hardly ever refer to themselves simply as Americans—they are Southerners, Texans, Californians, and so on—New York's nearly eight million residents are similarly chauvinistic about the specific enclaves of their city.

Though in theory New York is composed of five boroughs—Manhattan, Queens, Brooklyn, the Bronx, and Richmond (Staten Island)—everyone understands that Manhattan is "The City." (New York's daytime population swells to something close to 20 million, which is the total figure of New Yorkers plus residents of the outlying commuter communities.)

Indeed, New York feels like the capital of this country in almost every way, and the presence of the *United Nations* complex in the middle of Manhattan makes it possible to describe the city as the capital of the world. There may be more French people in Paris, more Japanese in Tokyo, and more Africans in Dakar, but in New York, these ethnic entities come together in a single, singular place. And then there are the movers and shakers who live and/or work here; as you sit down to lunch in a midtown restaurant, you may find yourself dining next to people deeply involved in discussing anything from the future of world commerce to maintaining world peace.

New York also is the communications capital of the planet. While the majority of TV production facilities are based in California, a vast number of the decisions about what will be produced (and seen) are made in executive offices in Manhattan—which happens to be the country's advertising hub. New York also dominates radio broadcasting and magazine and book publishing, and though the city is now down to only a handful of citywide daily newspapers, one of them—*The New York Times*—is considered one of the standard-bearers of contemporary journalism. Books, CDs and tapes, not to mention films, often reflect New York values, giving the literary and media world a northeastern US bias of which people elsewhere often do not feel a part.

There is, in addition, a widespread perception that for any creative artist to succeed, he or she must gain recognition in New York. In the theater, every actor, writer, director, designer, singer, dancer, musician, and composer feels the magnetic pull of Broadway. Painters, sculptors, novelists, cartoonists, jingle writers, poets, charlatans—all focus their creative and financial yearnings on New York. Whether one wants to make it on the stage, screen, airwaves, bookshelves, or billboards, the path to success almost always crosses New York.

Just as hard to characterize as the geography of this city is the attempt to stereotype a typical New Yorker. The city is notable, first of all, for its immense ethnic diversity, and there are large areas where the English language is hardly ever heard. From the obvious examples of Spanish Harlem, Chinatown, and Little Italy to the smaller Slavic and Hasidic enclaves, centuries-old traditions are kept up, as are the ethnic ghettos in which they thrive.

New York's cultural and gastronomic leadership is only slightly less important to the nation and the world than its financial ascendancy. Just walking through the Wall Street area dramatically reaffirms that the city has a secure hold on world commerce. Visitors' galleries at the *New York Stock Exchange* and the commodity exchanges provide a unique opportunity to watch capitalism in action, and nowhere is the sense of the enormity of American industry and the scope of financial trading more keenly felt.

Trading has a long history in New York City, where $24 worth of trinkets and baubles bought Manhattan Island from the Native Americans who may (or may not) have been its owners. Depending on one's point of view about this city, the Native Americans were either boldly deceived on the price or made one of the best real estate deals of all time.

The dimensions of the original island of Manhattan—a wilderness traversed by several streams and rivers which is recalled in some of its larger parks—bear little resemblance to the island today. Various landfill and reclamation projects have enlarged it over the years, and just a brief glance at the *Battery Park* area (at Manhattan's southernmost tip) indicates that expanding the island's real estate is still very much an active enterprise.

In all the world, New York has no equal. Its ability to prosper despite monumental problems testifies to its strength and resilience more dramatically than can any analytic essay. That its residents choose to continue to live with its shortcomings shows that New York's excitement and challenges outweigh its imperfections, a formula that also must work for almost all visitors here, whether on a mission of obligatory business or frivolous pleasure.

New York At-a-Glance

SEEING THE CITY

New York is one of the most complex cities in the world. Even people who have lived here all their lives don't know all of it; its size and diversity challenge even the most ambitious. For the visitor who wants to feel the magic of New York and to understand how the city is laid out, the best bet is to take it in from several vantage points.

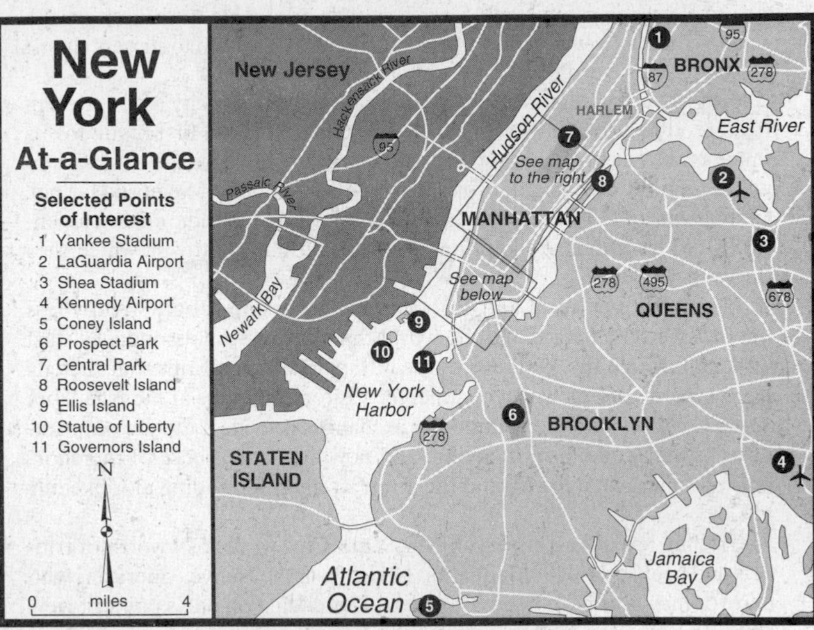

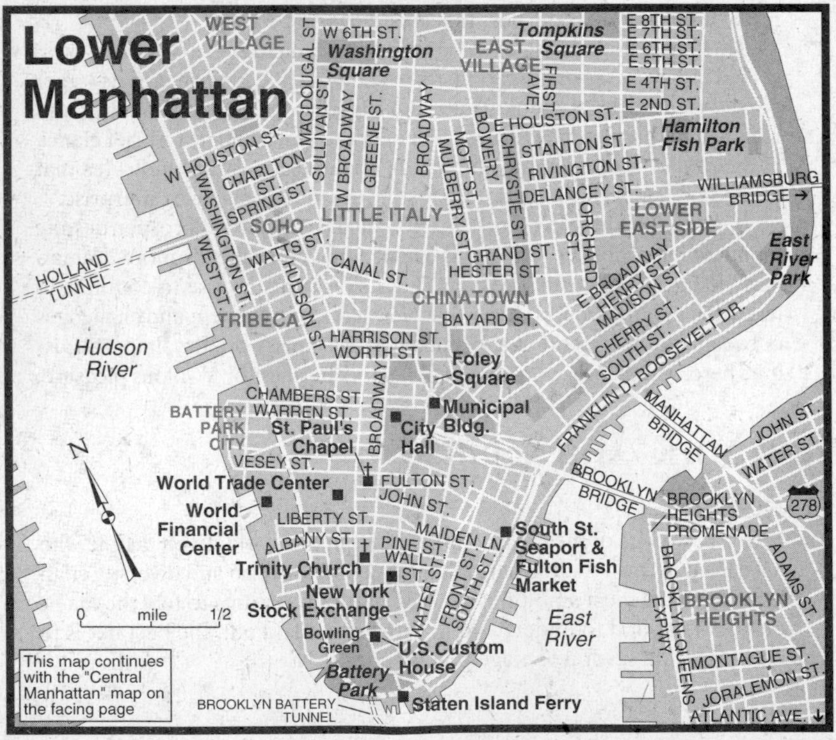

Lower Manhattan

WEST VILLAGE
W 6TH ST.
Washington Square
EAST VILLAGE
Tompkins Square
E 8TH ST.
E 7TH ST.
E 6TH ST.
E 5TH ST.
E 4TH ST.
E 2ND ST.
FIRST AVE
MACDOUGAL ST
SULLIVAN ST
W BROADWAY
GREENE ST.
BROADWAY
BOWERY
MOTT ST.
MULBERRY ST.
CHRYSTIE ST.
ORCHARD ST.
E HOUSTON ST.
Hamilton Fish Park
W HOUSTON ST.
CHARLTON ST.
STANTON ST.
RIVINGTON ST.
DELANCEY ST.
WILLIAMSBURG BRIDGE →
SPRING ST.
WASHINGTON ST.
SOHO
LITTLE ITALY
LOWER EAST SIDE
East River Park
WEST ST.
WATTS ST.
HUDSON ST.
GRAND ST.
HOLLAND TUNNEL
CANAL ST.
HESTER ST.
E BROADWAY
HENRY ST.
MADISON ST.
CHINATOWN
TRIBECA
BAYARD ST.
CHERRY ST.
SOUTH ST.
Hudson River
HARRISON ST.
WORTH ST.
FRANKLIN D. ROOSEVELT DR.
Foley Square
CHAMBERS ST.
BATTERY PARK CITY
WARREN ST.
Municipal Bldg.
St. Paul's Chapel
City Hall
BROADWAY
MANHATTAN BRIDGE
JOHN ST.
WATER ST.
VESEY ST.
World Trade Center
FULTON ST.
BROOKLYN BRIDGE
World Financial Center
JOHN ST.
LIBERTY ST.
BROOKLYN HEIGHTS PROMENADE
278
N
MAIDEN LN.
South St. Seaport & Fulton Fish Market
ALBANY ST.
PINE ST.
WALL ST.
Trinity Church
FRONT ST.
SOUTH ST.
WATER ST.
BROOKLYN-QUEENS EXPWY.
ADAMS ST.
New York Stock Exchange
BROOKLYN HEIGHTS
0 mile 1/2
East River
Bowling Green
U.S.Custom House
MONTAGUE ST.
Battery Park
JORALEMON ST.
Staten Island Ferry
BROOKLYN BATTERY TUNNEL
ATLANTIC AVE. ↓

This map continues with the "Central Manhattan" map on the facing page

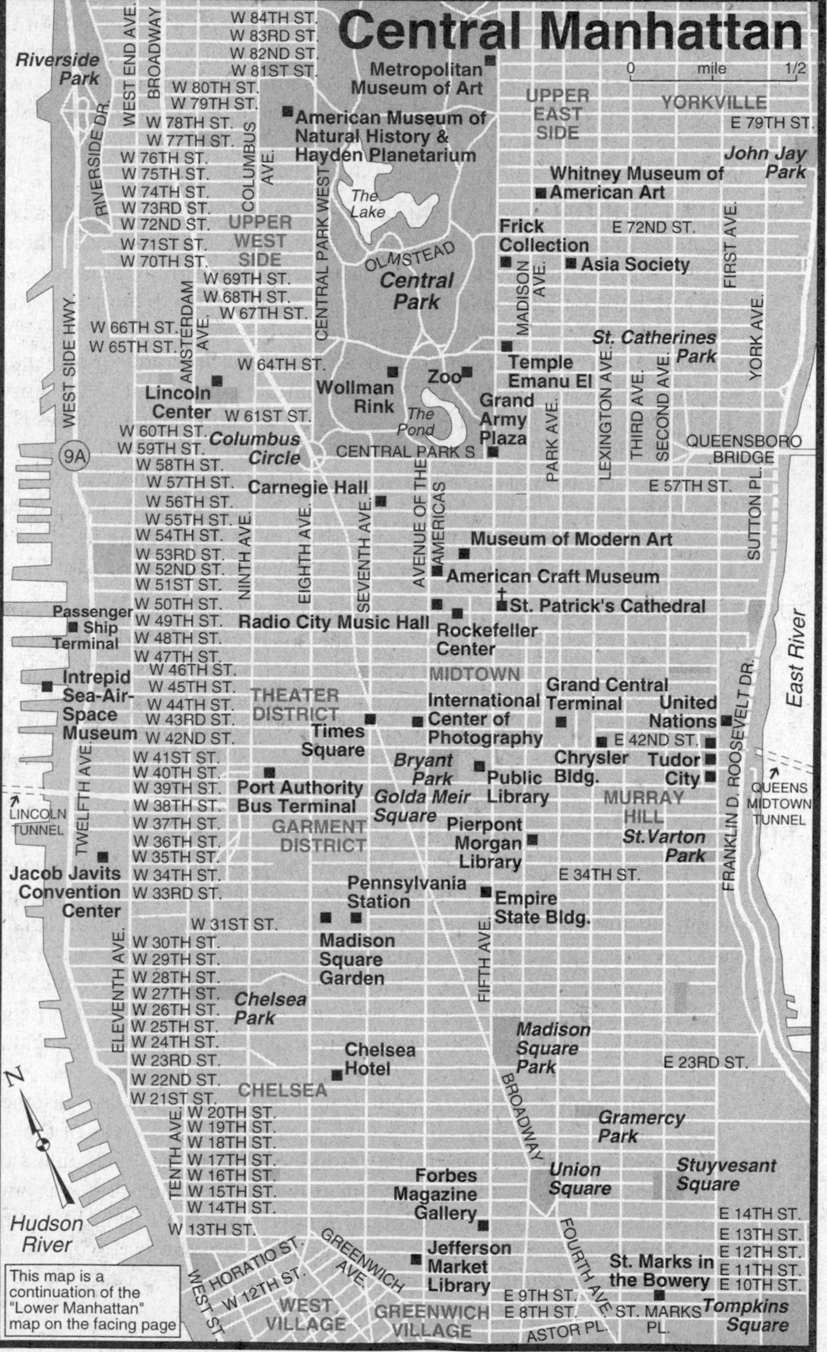
Central Manhattan
0 mile 1/2
Riverside Park
Metropolitan Museum of Art
American Museum of Natural History & Hayden Planetarium
UPPER EAST SIDE
YORKVILLE
John Jay Park
Whitney Museum of American Art
The Lake
UPPER WEST SIDE
Frick Collection
Asia Society
OLMSTEAD
Central Park
St. Catherines Park
Temple Emanu El
Lincoln Center
Wollman Rink
Zoo
The Pond
Grand Army Plaza
Columbus Circle
CENTRAL PARK S
QUEENSBORO BRIDGE
Carnegie Hall
Museum of Modern Art
American Craft Museum
Passenger Ship Terminal
Radio City Music Hall
Rockefeller Center
St. Patrick's Cathedral
East River
Intrepid Sea-Air-Space Museum
MIDTOWN
THEATER DISTRICT
Times Square
International Center of Photography
Grand Central Terminal
United Nations
Chrysler Bldg.
Tudor City
Port Authority Bus Terminal
Bryant Park
Public Library
Golda Meir Square
GARMENT DISTRICT
MURRAY HILL
Pierpont Morgan Library
St.Varton Park
LINCOLN TUNNEL
QUEENS MIDTOWN TUNNEL
Jacob Javits Convention Center
Pennsylvania Station
Empire State Bldg.
Madison Square Garden
Chelsea Park
Madison Square Park
Chelsea Hotel
CHELSEA
Gramercy Park
Union Square
Stuyvesant Square
Forbes Magazine Gallery
Hudson River
Jefferson Market Library
St. Marks in the Bowery
Tompkins Square
WEST VILLAGE
GREENWICH VILLAGE
This map is a continuation of the "Lower Manhattan" map on the facing page

BROOKLYN HEIGHTS PROMENADE Standing on this walkway at dusk, with the lights of Manhattan shimmering across the East River, you'll get an idea of the magnitude and beauty of the city. In lower Manhattan the towers of the *World Trade Center* rise before you, and the Brooklyn Bridge spans the river to your right. Farther north stands the *Empire State Building.* The easiest way to get here is via the *IRT* Seventh Avenue (No. 2 or No. 3), Clark Street stop, or the *BMT* (N or R train), Court Street stop.

WORLD TRADE CENTER It's been four years since the bombing that led to seven fatalities (a memorial now stands in front of the *WTC* to honor them). Luckily, the building itself miraculously escaped structural damage; security within the building is strictly enforced. The elevator to the observation deck of *World Trade Center* whisks you more than a quarter of a mile above the street. There is an enclosed deck on the 107th floor and a promenade on the roof above the 110th floor. Manhattan spreads out to the north, Brooklyn is to the east, to the west is New Jersey, and to the south lies New York Harbor and the *Statue of Liberty.* Open daily from 9:30 AM to 9:30 PM; September to April and 9:30 AM to 11:30 PM from April to September. The roof promenade may be closed during inclement weather and strong winds; check beforehand. Tickets are sold on the mezzanine level of the building. Liberty and West Sts. (phone: 435-7397). See also *Special Places.*

EMPIRE STATE BUILDING Although many visitors prefer the newer and higher *World Trade Center* observation deck, the queen of New York, which turns 66 this year, attracts more than two million people a year. You can feel the breeze from the 86th floor or ascend to the glass-enclosed 102nd floor. Open daily from 9:30 AM to midnight (the last ascending elevator is at 11:30 PM). Admission charge. Fifth Ave. between W. 33rd to W. 34th Sts. (phone: 736-3100). See also *Special Places.*

SPECIAL PLACES

Manhattan is a 12½-mile-long island stretching 2½ miles across at its widest point. Avenues run north and south; streets run east and west. Fifth Avenue is the dividing line between addresses designated east and those designated west. For example, 20 E. 57th Street is in the first block of 57th east of Fifth Avenue; 20 W. 57th Street is in the first block west of Fifth Avenue. New York grew from south to north, street by street and neighborhood by neighborhood; the oldest parts of the city are around the docks in lower Manhattan and in the financial district.

You will want to take taxis or public transport between areas—distances can be great—but, in general, the well-populated, active areas of the city offer an interesting environment for walking, so don't hesitate, unless the neighborhood is unfamiliar or it's late at night. The much-touted reputation of New Yorkers as aloof and unfriendly simply isn't true. Just watch what happens when you ask directions on a bus or subway (except during rush hours, when things are, admittedly, a bit primitive). We suggest a copy of *Flashmaps! Instant Guide to New York* (Flashmaps; $8.95), which has the most accessible and best-organized series of maps of New York neighborhoods we've seen. It's available at bookstores and newsstands around the city. The new 36-by-42-inch *New York Identity Map* ($25), a double-sided, highly detailed map of the upper east and west sides of Manhattan, identifies major buildings by name and provides a color-coded legend for easy identification—yellow for hotel, blue for office, gray for residential, and so on. There are also symbols to pinpoint public sites such as police stations, movie theaters, and courts. Contact the *Identity Map Co.* (55 Bethune St., Suite 1207; phone: 627-1994; fax: 627-5718).

LOWER MANHATTAN

STATUE OF LIBERTY Given by France as a symbol of friendship with the United States, this great lady has been guarding the entrance to New York Harbor since its dedication in 1886. The *Statue of Liberty Ferry* (phone: 269-5755) from *Battery Park* to Liberty Island runs daily from 9:30 AM to 3:30 PM, every 45 minutes on weekdays, every half-hour on weekends. The ferry ticket includes admission to the statue and to the *Ellis Island Immigration Museum* on Ellis Island (see below). You can see the statue from a distance as well as the southern tip of the city by riding the *Staten Island Ferry* (phone: 718-815-2628), still one of the world's great transportation bargains at 50¢. The ferry terminal is next to *Battery Park* (the South Ferry stop on the *IRT* Seventh Ave. subway local line, No. 1 or No. 9 train).

ELLIS ISLAND Visible from the *Statue of Liberty* or *Battery Park*, Ellis Island served as a processing center for more than 12 million immigrants from 1892 to 1954. Their dramatic experience is painstakingly portrayed at the *Ellis Island Immigration Museum* (phone: 363-3200), featuring dozens of exhibits of native costumes, instruments, and household implements as well as an award-winning film and a series of photographs that eloquently document the tension, terror, and joy of the immigrants' ordeal. The *American Immigrant Wall of Honor* is inscribed with the names of more than 420,000 immigrants to the United States who were commemorated by their descendants through a donation. These donations helped pay for the $160 million, six-year Ellis Island restoration project spearheaded by Lee Iacocca. The *Statue of Liberty Ferry* departs from *Battery Park* at regular intervals every day (see *Statue of Liberty* entry, immediately above) for the statue and then Ellis Island. Admission charge is included in the boat fare.

GOVERNORS ISLAND Now a coast guard base, the island's two pre-1800 structures are the *Governor's House* and *Fort Jay; Castle Williams* was completed in 1811 and has been both a fort and a prison. Here you will also find great oceangoing views, oak, hickory, and chestnut trees, and a Gothic stone chapel hung inside with battle flags from the Mexican War. The island is open to visitors once a month (first or second Saturday) only with *Big Onion*

Walking Tours (phone: 439-1090). Off Manhattan's southern tip, it is otherwise accessible only to officials by boat.

BATTERY PARK Twenty-one acres of green overlooking New York Harbor, this is the spot for picnics on hot summer days. There's a statue of Giovanni da Verrazano, who piloted the *Dauphine,* the ship that reached Manhattan in 1524, and there's also a monument to World War II dead. *Castle Clinton,* built as a fort in 1812, has functioned as an opera house, an immigrant landing depot, and an aquarium at various times. Its latest incarnation is as a ticketing center for the *Statue of Liberty Ferry.*

Bordered by State St., Battery Pl., and the harbor (phone: 269-5755). Nearby, in Battery Park City, is *South Cove,* a three-acre park directly on the Hudson River.

BATTERY PARK TO WALL STREET This area is a lovely and usually safe place to wander on weekends, when the empty streets emphasize the incongruity of the Merrill Lynch building, the *World Trade Center,* and the *World Financial Center* (where free concerts are held in a magnificent glass atrium, surrounded by the 17th- and 18th-century buildings on Pearl Street, *Bowling Green,* and Hanover Square. Two buildings of particular note are *India House,* on the south side of Hanover Square (built in 1854), and the old *US Custom House* (the new *Custom House* is in the *World Trade Center*) on *Bowling Green,* which was erected in 1907 in Beaux Arts style and is now the *National Museum of the American Indian.*

NEW YORK STOCK EXCHANGE A tree growing in front of the stock exchange commemorates the one under which the first trading transaction took place in 1792. Today more than 2,500 corporations are listed on the Big Board. You can observe the action from a glass-enclosed gallery reached via the visitors' entrance at 20 Broad Street (south of Wall St.). Open weekdays; no admission charge, but tickets are required and are distributed at 9 AM on a first-come, first-served basis (phone: 656-5168). Large groups should call in advance for special arrangements. Cameras are prohibited. The *American Stock Exchange* (86 Trinity Pl.) no longer has a visitors' gallery. If you want to see real emotion, head for the *Coffee, Sugar, and Cocoa Exchange,* which makes the *New York Stock Exchange* look like a London tea party. The visitors' gallery is open weekdays; no admission charge. *4 World Trade Center* between Liberty and Church Sts. (phone: 938-2025).

TRINITY CHURCH This church was first granted a charter by King William III in 1697. The present rose-colored stone building was completed in 1846 (it got a cleaning in the early 1990s), but the graveyard beside it is even older. For years the *Trinity Church* steeple was the highest point on the New York skyline. Classical concerts are held here on Thursdays at 1 PM from September through June. On Broadway at the head of Wall St. (phone: 602-0800).

ST. PAUL'S CHAPEL The oldest public building in continuous use in Manhattan, this fine example of colonial architecture was erected in 1766 on what was then a field outside the city. George Washington worshiped here. Classical concerts are held in the chapel on Mondays at noon from September through June. Suggested donation for concerts is $2. On the corner of Broadway and Fulton St. (phone: 602-0872).

BATTERY PARK CITY This $4-billion complex includes apartments, tree-lined streets, public parks and squares, and a sumptuous centerpiece, the *World Financial Center* (not related to the neighboring *World Trade Center*). The *WFC* is the home of the *Winter Garden* (not to be confused with the Broadway theater of the same name), a must-visit while in this part of town, where a variety of free concerts are held and artwork displayed amid 15 towering royal palm trees in the soaring atrium. A true city within a city, this landfill development on the Hudson River is logically designed and decidedly not ostentatious. There is a wealth of other diversions, among them a spa, a 1950s rock 'n' roll club, the *Hudson River Club* restaurant (250 Vesey St.; phone: 786-1500), and numerous shops. The views from the 1.2-mile Esplanade are spectacular. The *Winter Garden* is open from 7 AM to 1 AM. No admission charge. For general Battery Park City information, call 416-5328; for *Winter Garden* information, call 945-2600.

VIETNAM VETERAN'S MEMORIAL Not as grand as the one in Washington, DC, but still worth a trip to pay homage to those who lost their lives in Southeast Asia. View letters, diaries, and poems etched into the memorial. Within *Battery Park*.

WORLD TRADE CENTER An unprecedented terrorist bomb attack in the *WTC*'s garage in early 1993 left seven dead and all of New York traumatized. Although there was no structural damage, much reconstruction was necessary, and there is now a higher level of security here than in most New York buildings. The "Twin Towers," at 1,350 feet each, are not quite the tallest buildings in the world (the *CN Tower* in Toronto is, at 1,821 feet), but spectacularly set at the southern tip of Manhattan, they are a must-see landmark. In order to build the center, 1.2 million yards of earth and rock were excavated (subsequently used as landfill). The concourse has a variety of shops and eateries. Open daily. In addition, all three restaurants—*Windows on the World,* the *Hors d'Oeuvrerie,* and *Cellar in the Sky*—are now reopened. Admission charge for the *Observation Deck* (see *Seeing the City,* above). Bounded by West, Church, Liberty, and Vesey Sts. (phone: 435-7000).

CITY HALL This is the third *City Hall* in New York; it was built in 1803 and houses the office of the mayor and the City Council chamber. The original construction cost half a million dollars, and in 1956 the restoration cost some $2 million (times change). The building was a site of great importance to New York and US history: Lafayette visited in 1824; Lincoln's body lay in state here in 1865; and in the 1860s *City Hall* and *Tammany Hall* (Park Row and Frankfort St.) were controlled by Boss Tweed, the powerful, corrupt man who dominated New York politics until the 1870s (phone: 788-3000).

Other city government buildings nearby include the *Municipal Building* on the northeast corner of *City Hall Park,* the *United States Court House,* across from Foley Square, the *New York County Courthouse* next door, the *Federal Office Building* on the other side of Lafayette Street, and the *Hall of Records.*

Within *City Hall Park* is a statue of Nathan Hale, a patriot of the Revolution who was executed here in 1776. Today protestors of every persuasion gather in the park to "fight *City Hall.*" Closed weekends. No admission charge. In the triangle formed by Park Row, Broadway, and Chambers St. (phone: 788-3000).

SOUTH STREET SEAPORT AND THE FULTON FISH MARKET Completed in the 1980s, stage one of the *South Street Seaport* redevelopment program enlivened this historical area with shops and restaurants and additional space for the *South Street Seaport Museum.* The Museum Block is an entire row of rejuvenated buildings (some dating to the 1700s), with room for exhibitions, shops, and offices. The Schermerhorn Row of renovated 19th-century warehouses is also alive with retail outlets and the *South Street Seaport Museum Visitors' Center.* All of these changes have not substantially altered the area's famous old *Fulton Fish Market,* where, from about 2 to 8 AM, trucks still deliver fresh fish to the wholesale outdoor market.

But the old market is now joined by another building called the *Fulton Market,* with restaurants, cafés, and food stalls. Among the many eateries is one of New York's oldest seafood restaurants, *Sloppy Louie's* (92 South St. at Fulton St.; phone: 509-9694). Prices are reasonable, but the portions remain hearty and the fish is as fresh as ever. Also of interest are the historic boats docked at Piers 15 and 16, where summertime pop and jazz concerts are staged. And the three-story *Pier 17 Pavilion* has added even more shops and restaurants. Fulton St. between South and Water Sts.

BROOKLYN BRIDGE You can stroll from Manhattan to Brooklyn by crossing the Brooklyn Bridge on a pedestrian walk. You'll get a good view of the city and a close look at this engineering feat. The 6,775-foot-long bridge, which spans the East River at a height of 133 feet, was completed in 1883 and cost $25 million; it's considered by many to be one of the most beautiful bridges in the world. Take the *IRT* Lexington Ave. subway line (No. 4, No. 5, or No. 6 train) to the Worth St.–Brooklyn Bridge–City Hall station.

CHINATOWN The best way to get the feel of New York's Chinese neighborhood is to hit the streets, especially Mott, Bayard, and Pell. The despair of census takers, this crowded, ever-expanding ethnic neighborhood which seeps into Little Italy is loosely estimated to be home to more than 100,000. Some say the Chinese community here is not as large as the one in San Francisco, but it is equally authentic. You'll know when you reach Chinatown by the pagoda-shaped telephone booths and stores that sell shark fins, duck eggs, fried fungi, and exotic vegetables. Herbs are lined up next to aspirin in the pharmacies. Don't miss the good, inexpensive restaurants, the tea parlors, or the bakeries. At lunchtime try dim sum (steamed or fried dumplings filled with seafood, pork, or beef are just some of the choices). Favorite spots among New Yorkers are the *Golden Unicorn,* whose dim sum are the best in town (see); *Peking Duck House* (22 Mott St.; phone: 227-1810); *Bo Ky* (80 Bayard St.; phone: 406-2292); and *Sun Hop Kee* (13 Mott St.; phone: 285-9856). Sundays are a good time to visit the area, but if you can, come during the *Chinese New Year* (starting on the first new moon after January 21). The celebration is wild and woolly, with fireworks, dancing dragons, and throngs of people.

LITTLE ITALY An occasional aria wafting from tenement windows, old men playing *bocce,* old women dressed in black checking the vegetables in the markets, store windows with religious articles, pasta factories, and the ubiquitous aroma of Italian cooking give character to this ever-shrinking neighborhood, which has the reputation of being one of the safest in the city. Mulberry Street is the center of Little Italy (stop for an espresso at *Caffè Roma,* 385 Broome St.; phone: 226-8413); once stretching for blocks surrounding and blending into parts of SoHo and Greenwich Village, today this area is predominantly Chinese. Farther north, the area of Bleecker Street near the Avenue of the Americas has a decidedly Italian flavor, with bakeries that sell cannoli and cappuccino sandwiched between Middle Eastern restaurants and stores that sell Chinese window shades. Little Italy is thronged during the festivals of *San Gennaro* and *St. Anthony.* In September *San Gennaro* covers Mulberry Street from Spring Street to Park Row; *St. Anthony* fills Sullivan Street from Houston to Spring in June. The festivals attract people from in and out of the city with game booths, rides, and, most of all, enough food and drink (both Italian and "foreign") for several armies. Bordered by Canal and Houston Sts., the Bowery, and the Ave. of the Americas.

THE BOWERY There is nothing romantic about New York's Skid Row. This strip continues to be home for those down on their luck—both old and young. If you drive west on Houston Street, you'll get a look at some of the inhabitants—they'll wipe your windshields whether you like it or not and expect some change for their trouble. The area has a few theaters and music places and some good shopping spots; specialties include lighting and restaurant supplies. The stores have relocated here because of low rents and the proximity to one of the most interesting shopping markets in the world: the Lower East Side. Between Cooper Sq. and Chatham Sq.

LOWER EAST SIDE This area is probably the largest melting pot in the city. Eastern European Jews, many of whom are Hasidim (an ultra-religious sect, recognizable by the men's earlocks, called *peyes,* and their broad-brimmed hats and long black coats), sell their wares—everything from designer fashions to bedspreads—at discounted prices; you'll have to bargain if you want the best deal, and these merchants are formidable opponents. Everything is closed on Saturdays, the Jewish sabbath, but it's business as usual on Sundays, the busiest day of the week. The area also is home to Hispanics, African-Americans, Asian-Americans, and various other minority groups; you will hear an assortment of languages spoken, including Yiddish, Spanish, and even some Yiddish-accented Spanish.

The Lower East Side was where the Eastern European Jews, fleeing czarist persecution and deadly pogroms, first settled during their massive migration from 1880 to 1918. Many of the streets, including Rivington, Hester, Essex, and Grand, still look much as they did then. To get a real taste of the area, try the knishes at *Yonah Schimmel's* (137 E. Houston St.; phone: 477-2858); hot dogs at *Katz's* delicatessen (205 E. Houston St.; phone: 254-2246); or the Romanian "broilings" at *Sammy's Roumanian Steak House* (see *Eating Out*).

SOHO The name stands for "*So*uth of *Ho*uston Street" (pronounced *How*-stun). SoHo leads a double life. On weekends uptown New Yorkers and out-of-towners fill the streets to explore its trendy stores, restaurants, and art galleries. During the week SoHo is a very livable combination of 19th-century cast-iron buildings, spillovers from adjacent Little Italy, off-off-Broadway theater groups, and practicing artists. At night the side streets are empty, and you can see into some of the residential lofts of the old commercial buildings; some are simple, open spaces, others are jungles of plants and Corinthian columns. *Fanelli's* (94 Prince St. at Mercer; phone: 226-9412) is one of the oldest bars around and a hangout for residents. Due to soaring rents, many local artists moved to TriBeCa, which is south and west of SoHo. SoHo is between Canal and Houston Sts., and Broadway and Hudson St.

TRIBECA Once neglected, TriBeCa (the name stands for "*Tri*angle *Be*low *Ca*nal Street") has made a flashy comeback. The current artist residents have spawned a plethora of trendy art galleries on White and Franklin Streets and lower Hudson Street. This is where Robert De Niro has his film production studio, and there are also many discount clothing stores, clubs, restaurants, and theaters here. Historical oddities worth visiting include the *Bond* hotel (125 Chambers St.), reputedly Manhattan's oldest; Stanford White's "Clocktower" building (346 Broadway); and the Art Deco *Western Union Building* (60 Hudson St.). TriBeCa extends from Canal St. to Chambers St. and from West Broadway to the Hudson River.

EAST VILLAGE Still the center of New York's counterculture, this section has become somewhat gentrified, with a growing number of art galleries, restaurants, and nightspots competing for space with poor artists and various ethnic groups (the largest of which is Ukrainian, but there also are Armenians, Czechs, Germans, Russians, Poles, African-Americans, and Hispanics, many of whom live in low-income housing projects). Famous during the 1960s as the city's psychedelic capital, St. Mark's Place, between Second and Third Avenues, is still a lively block, lined with inexpensive restaurants and shops featuring styles from hippie to grunge; it's generally hopping (sometimes with the help of controlled substances) at all hours of the day and night. Two streets south is "India Row," where numerous Indian restaurants line East Sixth Street between First and Second Avenues near Astor Place, on the border of the East Village and Greenwich Village. Also located here is *Cooper Union,* a liberal arts institute (good for free concerts and lectures); nearby is the *New York Shakespeare Festival* (also called the *Joseph Papp Public Theater;* 425 Lafayette St.; phone: 539-8500), where you'll find both contemporary and classical drama as well as experimental theater. You can have a drink at *McSorley's Old Ale House* (15 E. Seventh St.; phone: 473-9148); established in 1854, it is one of the oldest bars still in operation in New York. A few blocks north is the spiritual home of the village, *St. Mark's-in-the-Bouwerie* (Second Ave. and E. 10th St.). The church still sponsors community activities, especially poetry readings by some of the best bards in New York. The East Village has housed many writers, from James Fenimore Cooper (6 St. Mark's Pl.; he also lived at 145 Bleecker St. in Greenwich Village) to W. H. Auden (77 St. Mark's Pl.) to Amiri Baraka, born LeRoi Jones (27 Cooper Sq.). Note: Some parts of the East Village, especially east of Avenue A, remain seedy; don't wander here after dark unless you know where you're going—and don't go unaccompanied. Bounded by Lafayette St. and the East River, Houston and 14th Sts.

GREENWICH VILLAGE You can—and definitely should—stroll around the heart of the Village at night. The area is filled with surprises. You've probably heard of Bleecker Street, the slightly tawdry gathering place of tourists and the high school crowd from the suburbs, or of *Washington Square Park,* with its musicians, chess players, mimes, and street people. But you might not have pictured Grove Court, the lovely and secluded row of 19th-century houses near the corner of Grove and Bedford Streets (where O. Henry lived), or the Morton Street pier on the Hudson River, from which you can see the *Statue of Liberty* on a clear day. There are meat-packing factories from the 1920s, old speakeasies turned into restaurants, a miniature Times Square on West Eighth Street, and immaculate brownstones on quiet, tree-lined streets. Get a map (you'll need it—there's nowhere else in Manhattan where West Fourth Street could bisect West 12th) and wander. Or you can ask directions—Villagers love to help, and it's a nice way to meet them. You can eat, go to the theater, sip cappuccino in an outdoor café, hear great jazz, enjoy an off-Broadway production at the *Players Theater* (115 MacDougal St.; phone: 254-5076), and find your own special places. Bounded by Broadway on the east, the Hudson River on the west, Houston St. on the south, and W. 14th St. on the north.

WASHINGTON SQUARE Actually a park, this is a gathering place for students from the surrounding *New York University* campus, Frisbee aficionados, volleyball and chess players, modern bohemians, and people who like to watch them all. The Fifth Avenue entryway, the *Washington Square Arch,* is New York's answer to the *Arc de Triomphe.* Buildings surrounding the square include the *NYU* library, administration buildings, and law school. The north side of the square has some lovely homes now owned by *NYU,* including No. 7, where Edith Wharton lived. Bounded by extensions of W. Fourth St., MacDougal St., Waverly Pl., and University Pl.

BLEECKER STREET Strolling across Bleecker Street (James Fenimore Cooper once made his home at No. 145) from La Guardia Place to Eighth Avenue, you'll pass outdoor cafés, falafel parlors, jazz clubs, Italian specialty stores, and myriad restaurants. Be sure to wander down some of the side streets, like Thompson, MacDougal (Bob Dylan's old stomping ground), and Sullivan. Have a cappuccino at *Caffè Dante* (79 MacDougal St.; phone: 982-5275), Beyond Seventh Avenue, the side streets become more residential; try Charles Street, West 10th Street, and Bank Street for examples of how the upper middle class lives in the Village. You'll also pass Christopher Street, the original center of gay life in Manhattan.

LOWER FIFTH AVENUE This is the most desirable address in Greenwich Village. The *Salmagundi Club,* built in 1853 (47 Fifth Ave.), is the last of the imposing private mansions that once lined the avenue. On the streets between Fifth Avenue and the Avenue of the Americas (which New Yorkers call Sixth Avenue) are expensive brownstones. The *New School for Social Research* (66 W. 12th St.; phone: 229-5600 or 800-544-1078, ext. 18, for general information) offers courses in everything from fixing a leak to ethnomusicology. From Waverly Pl. to 14th St.

AVENUE OF THE AMERICAS New Yorkers know it as Sixth Avenue. One of the most unusual buildings in the Village is the *Jefferson Market Library* (Sixth Ave. and W. 10th St.), with a small garden alongside. Built in 1874–78 in Italian Gothic style, it once served as a courthouse and prison for many years and today is home to a branch of the *New York Public Library.* Across the street is *Balducci's,* an incredible international food emporium (see *Shopping*). *Famous Ray's of Greenwich Village* (465 Sixth Ave.; phone: 243-2253)—the place on the corner with the long lines—is considered the source of some of the best pizza in the city. (Note that many pizza places in the city have "Ray's" in their names, but this—allegedly the "original"—is the one that gets the raves.) From W. Fourth to W. 14th St.

WEST VILLAGE Farther west (between Seventh Ave. S. and the Hudson River) is a series of small winding streets with some especially interesting places to visit. At 75½ Bedford Street is the house in which Edna St. Vincent Millay and John Barrymore once lived (not at the same time)—it's only nine feet wide. *Chumley's* (86 Bedford St.; phone: 675-4449) used to be a speakeasy during Prohibition and still has no sign on the door—but it does have good food and poetry readings inside. Commerce Street is a small side street lined with lovely old buildings, including the *Cherry Lane Theater* (38 Commerce St.; phone: 989-2020), one of the city's oldest. Two blocks south is Leroy Street with St. Luke's Place, a row of 19th-century houses. No. 6 Leroy was built in 1880 and was once the home of the city's flamboyant Mayor Jimmy Walker. If you walk to the end of the block and north on Hudson, you'll come to the *White Horse Tavern* (567 Hudson St.; phone: 243-9260), Dylan Thomas's hangout on his trips to New York City. Go in and have a drink.

14TH STREET TO 34TH STREET

UNION SQUARE For many years this was a place to avoid—particularly at night, when it was populated by drug pushers and other undesirables. Now, after a major face-lift, it's once again looking as it did in the halcyon days of the 19th century, when the square was the core of upper-crust Manhattan life. The open-air produce market on Mondays, Wednesdays, Fridays, and Saturdays and several new cafés, popular restaurants, and nightspots, fill the side streets and the lower reaches of Park Avenue South; stop in at the trendy *Coffee Shop* (29 Union Sq. W.; phone: 243-7969) or the more upscale *Union Square Café* (see *Eating Out*). E. 14th to E. 17th St. between University Pl. and Fourth Ave.

GRAMERCY PARK A few blocks northeast of Union Square, *Gramercy Park* is one of the few places where visitors can experience the graciousness of old Manhattan. The gem-like park itself is open only to residents on the perimeter streets (they have their own keys), but on a sunny day you can see nannies with their privileged charges sitting on the benches in the shadows of the 19th-century mansions that surround the park. Stop in for a beer on Irving Place, south of the park, at cozy (if frayed), historic *Pete's Tavern* (129 E. 18th St.; phone: 473-7676) where local resident O. Henry is said to have written some of "The Gift of the Magi "; it's one of the oldest bars in New York City. Or if you're in the mood for some exotic fare, try *Patria* (see *Eating Out*), where the menu can be as hot as the music. Teddy Roosevelt's birthplace (28 E. 20th St.; phone: 260-1616) is a museum. Closed Mondays and Tuesdays; admission charge. Other well-known park sons and daughters include Herman Melville and Stephen Crane. A few blocks north of *Gramercy Park* on Lexington Avenue are dozens of little Indian shops selling splendid assortments of spices, saris, cotton blouses, jewelry, and food. E. 20th to E. 21st St. between Park Ave. S. and Third Ave.

CHELSEA In this eclectic residential neighborhood in the West 20s, between Seventh and 10th Avenues, you'll find elegant brownstones next door to run-down, four-story, walk-up tenements. The *Chelsea* hotel (222 W. 23rd St.; phone: 243-3700) has earned an important place in literary history. Thomas Wolfe, Brendan Behan, Dylan Thomas, and Arthur Miller slept and wrote in its rooms. Andy Warhol made a four-hour movie about its raunchier inhabitants. For a sojourn into tranquillity, step into the inner courtyard of the *General Theological Seminary,* a gift to the city in 1817 by Clement C. Moore, author of "A Visit from Saint Nicholas." The grounds are open Mondays through Saturdays in the early afternoons, except during special functions. No admission charge. 175 Ninth Ave. (phone: 243-5150). New to the area but already vitally important to residents and tourists alike is the *Chelsea Piers Sports and Entertainment Complex* (23rd St. and the Hudson River), a 1.7-million–square-foot facility featuring everything from a golf club to a marina (phone: 336-6666).

MIDTOWN (34TH STREET TO 59TH STREET)

WEST 34TH STREET Still a major shopping street, this is the home of *Macy's* (Broadway from W. 34th to W. 35th St.), the mercantile giant; the nearby multilevel mall known as *Manhattan Mall* (Ave. of the Americas from W. 32nd to W. 33rd Sts.; see *Shopping* for both); and scores of stores selling jeans, clothing, shoes, tapes and CDs, and electronic gear. The hub of 34th Street is Herald Square, where Broadway intersects the Avenue of the Americas (Sixth Ave.). The main shopping district runs along 34th Street from Eighth Avenue past the *Empire State Building* to Madison Avenue, with a number of smaller shops lining the street as far east as Third Avenue.

MADISON SQUARE GARDEN, PARAMOUNT THEATER, AND PENNSYLVANIA STATION This is a huge coliseum-arena, office building, and transportation complex. The *Garden*'s seats (19,800 maximum capacity) usually are fully packed when the New York *Knicks* (*NBA* basketball) or the New York *Rangers* (*NHL* hockey) play home games, when the *Ringling Brothers and Barnum & Bailey Circus* comes to town, or whenever there is a major exhibition, concert, or convention. Formerly the *Felt Forum,* the recently renovated *Paramount Theater* (not to be confused with the old movie house of the same name), a 5,600-seat subsidiary hall that's part of the *Garden*, is the site of boxing matches, concerts, and smaller exhibitions. The current *Penn Station,* which dates from the mid-1960s, is *Amtrak*'s major New York terminal and also serves the *Long Island Rail Road (LIRR)* and *New Jersey Transit* commuter lines; the original *Pennsylvania Station* on the same site, a vaulted and columned neoclassical structure, opened in 1910 and was demolished—much to the public's disappointment—in 1963 in the name of progress. No guided tours. W. 31st to W. 33rd St., from Seventh to Eighth Aves. (phone: 465-6741 for *Garden* and *Paramount Theater* information).

GARMENT DISTRICT Here is the nation's center of the fashion design industries (Seventh Avenue street signs here actually say "Fashion Avenue"). The sleek showrooms of America's fashion elite—from Calvin Klein to Donna Karan—are all headquartered here. And although showrooms are not open to the general public, it is possible to catch a preview of next season's styles: On any weekday during office hours, racks of the latest apparel are pushed through the teeming streets. From W. 30th to W. 42nd St. between Seventh and Eighth Aves.

EMPIRE STATE BUILDING The first skyscraper in New York to be attacked by King Kong, this 102-story Art Deco edifice was erected in 1931 and was the symbol of the city for decades. There is an open-air observation deck on the 86th floor, to which millions of tourists have ascended over the years to gaze in awe at the surrounding New York skyline; there is another, glass-enclosed viewing area on the 102nd floor. Don't be surprised if the top of the building is bathed in colored lights in the evening (red, white, and blue on *July 4th,* for example, or orange on *Halloween*—it's the city's way of commemorating holidays and special occasions. Open daily from 9:30 AM to midnight (last elevator up at 11:30 PM). Admission charge. Fifth Ave. from W. 33rd to W. 34th St. (phone: 736-3100).

JACOB K. JAVITS CONVENTION CENTER This glass-and-steel monolith with a 15-story atrium, designed by eminent architect I. M. Pei, hosts the major conventions that outgrew the old *New York Coliseum.* The complex covers five square blocks between 11th and 12th Avenues and encompasses 1.8 million square feet of space, making it one of the world's largest buildings. The kitchens can produce banquet meals for up to 10,000, while the cafeteria serves 1,500 people an hour. State-of-the-art facilities include a sophisticated audiovisual system and soundproofing throughout its 131 separate meeting rooms, with simultaneous interpretation in up to eight languages. There's also a VIP lounge, press room, video information center, and cocktail lounge. The only thing missing is a garage. Located on 11th Ave. between W. 34th and W. 39th Sts. (phone: 216-2000).

TIMES SQUARE The Times Square area is centered from W. 42nd Street to W. 46th Street, where Broadway and Seventh Avenue converge. The building at 229 W. 43rd Street is the home of *The New York Times,* after which the district is named (the newspaper formerly had its headquarters on Times Square). And on *New Year's Eve,* Times Square is indeed the place to be for hundreds of thousands of New Yorkers and visitors who congregate to watch the ball drop at midnight.

In recent years, this once seedy area has experienced a resurgence with the help of the Times Square Redevelopment Project and major industry giants including the Disney Company, who invested millions in restoring the *New Victory* to its former glory. The theater has now become known as the first children's theater, soley deveoted to performances for kids in New York City. Other projects underway are the restoration of the *Amsterdam Theater,* a planned *Madame Tussand Wax Museum,* as well as theme-restaurants and a movie complex.

BROADWAY AND THE THEATER DISTRICT On and just north of Times Square are the colorful marquees and billboards for which New York is famous. The lights are still pretty dazzling, twinkling on and off in a glittering electric collage. On most nights the streets are jammed with theatergoers, taxis, and limos; most curtains go up at 8 PM. The main theaters are between W. 42nd and W. 53rd Streets, east and west of, as well as on, Broadway.

NEW YORK PUBLIC LIBRARY A couple of blocks east of Times Square, this dignified neoclassical building is a good place to relax and catch your breath. Sit on the front steps, between the famous lion statues, or in *Bryant Park,* behind the library. Inside the library is New York's (and one of the world's) largest collection of books and periodicals as well as a gift store; there also are various exhibitions and public programs. Tours are given Mondays through Saturdays at 11 AM and 2 PM. No admission charge. Fifth Ave. from W. 40th to W. 42nd St. (phone: 930-0800).

GRAND CENTRAL STATION This magnificent Beaux Arts relic is worth seeing, and there is a one-hour tour Wednesdays at 12:30 PM conducted by the *Municipal Arts Society* (phone: 935-3960); donations suggested. Otherwise, be sure to check out the illuminated zodiac dotting the immense vaulted ceiling. The *Café at Grand Central,* principally a bar, also offers good food and a great view of the terminal. It is located on the west balcony (phone: 883-0009). The main station entrance is on E. 42nd St., between Vanderbilt and Lexington Aves., although access can be gained from all four sides.

CHRYSLER BUILDING This is the princess of the New York skyline. Its distinctive, graceful spire, decorated with stainless steel, sparkles with more than usual brilliance because of the installation of hand-blown fluorescent lights around its pinnacle. Although it long ago ceded the title of tallest in the city, this Art Deco building completed in 1930 remains, to many New Yorkers, the most beautiful of all. There are no tours and the observatory was closed long ago, but a visit to the small lobby, with its ceiling murals and exquisite inlaid elevator doors, is worth the trip. 405 Lexington Ave. at E. 42nd St.

FORD FOUNDATION BUILDING If you happen to be wandering through New York at sunrise and climb the stairs between First and Second Avenues on 42nd Street, you'll see the bronzed windows of the *Ford Foundation Building* catch the first rays, reflecting copper-colored light into the sky. At other times the building is just as dramatic. Built around a central, glass-enclosed courtyard containing tropical trees and plants, it is the only place in Manhattan where you can feel as if you're in a jungle. It's one of the great New York experiences—especially on snowy afternoons. Open weekdays. No admission charge. 320 E. 43rd St. between First and Second Aves. (phone: 573-5000).

TUDOR CITY A nearly forgotten pocket of Manhattan, this 1920s neo-Tudor apartment complex is one of its most romantic parts. An esplanade overlooks the East River and the nearby *United Nations.* The home of many diplomats and *UN* employees, Tudor City serves as an international campus. (According to local legend, it used to be where executives and industrialists housed their mistresses in the 1930s and 1940s.) The long, curved staircase leading to the sidewalk opposite the *United Nations* is known as the *Isaiah Steps,* because of the biblical quote carved into the wall. Between E. 41st and E. 43rd Sts. at Tudor City Pl. (near First Ave.).

UNITED NATIONS Although the *UN* is open all year, the best time to visit is between September and December, when the General Assembly is in session. Delegates from about 184 nations gather to discuss the world's problems, and there are a limited number of free tickets available to the public. The *Delegates' Dining Room* (phone: 963-7625 for reservations) offers good continental cuisine and spectacular views of the East River. The *UN* is open daily. Charge for a guided tour. The visitors' entrance is on First Ave. between E. 45th and E. 46th Sts. (phone: 963-4440).

ROCKEFELLER CENTER A group of skyscrapers built in the 1930s, *Rockefeller Center* is best known for its giant *Christmas* tree in December; for its ice skating rink open October through May; for *Radio City Music Hall,* a theatrical landmark and home of the *Rockettes* (phone: 247-4777); and for the romantic *Rainbow Room,* where dinner for two becomes a Fred Astaire and Ginger Rogers fantasy. After dinner, visit *Rainbow and Stars* for sophisticated cabaret entertainment (see *Nightclubs and Nightlife*). There are tours of the NBC television studios in 30 Rockefeller Plaza daily except Sundays. Admission charge; children under six not permitted. Bounded by Fifth Ave. and Ave. of the Americas from W. 49th to W. 51st St. (phone: 664-4000).

ST. PATRICK'S CATHEDRAL A refuge from the crowds of Fifth Avenue, this is the most famous church in the city. Dedicated to Ireland's patron saint, it stands in Gothic splendor across the street from *Rockefeller Center* in the shadow of skyscrapers. Resplendent with gargoyles on the outside, stained glass windows and magnificent appointments on the inside, *St. Patrick's* is a good place for rest, contemplation, and prayer. Catholic services are held daily. Fifth Ave. between E. 50th and E. 51st Sts. (phone: 753-2261).

SIXTH AVENUE It's officially known as the Avenue of the Americas, but no true New Yorker calls it that. The stretch of Sixth Avenue between 42nd and 57th Streets is lined with skyscrapers and is particularly imposing at dusk, when the giant glass and steel buildings light up.

MUSEUM OF MODERN ART Possibly the most complete repository of 20th-century art in the world, its permanent collection includes the work of cubists, abstractionists, expressionists, conceptualists, and others. Among the many great paintings housed here are Wyeth's *Christina's World,* Monet's *Water Lilies* (housed in its own gallery), and van Gogh's *Starry Night.* A four-story glass Garden Hall overlooks the sculpture garden. The museum's permanent collection is installed in chronological order, and by following a suggested route, visitors can see the history of modern painting, photography, and sculpture unfold. The *William S. Paley Collection* (Paley was the founder of CBS) consists of 82 major works by Cézanne, Degas, Matisse, and Picasso, among others. The museum's film department and its leadership in film preservation are internationally renowned. Hollywood classics, award-winning foreign films, and the works of lesser-known directors are screened here regularly. Keep your eye out for the shows in the popular "Projects Series," dedicated to installations by contemporary young artists. Closed Wednesdays. Admission charge; on Thursday and Friday evenings, though, when the museum is open until 8:30 PM, admission is on a pay-as-you-wish basis. 11 W. 53rd St. between Fifth and Sixth Aves. (phone: 708-9400; 708-9480 for recorded information).

FIFTH AVENUE Although the street runs from Washington Square straight up to Spanish Harlem, when New Yorkers refer to Fifth Avenue, they usually mean the stretch of the world's most opulent shops between *Rockefeller Center* at 49th Street and the *Plaza* hotel opposite the southeastern corner of *Central Park* at Central Park South (W. 59th St.). *Saks Fifth Avenue, Liz Claiborne, Gucci, Tiffany, Cartier, Henri Bendel,* and *Bergdorf Goodman* make walking along the street an incredible test in temptation. Stop in at *Steuben Glass* on the corner of East 56th Street and marvel at its permanent collection of sculpted glass in mythological and contemporary themes. And whether you decide to go in or not, *Trump Tower* 's golden façade across East 56th Street is quite a spectacle, housing luxury apartments and some of the most exclusive (read: expensive) stores in the city.

GRAND ARMY PLAZA This European-style square, with its central fountain just across the street from the southeast corner of *Central Park,* faces *Bergdorf Goodman,* the regal *Plaza* hotel, the *General Motors Building,* and the hansom cabstand where horse-drawn carriages (some with drivers in top hat and tails) wait to carry clients through the park. If you have a lover, be sure to arrange to meet here at least once. Be sure, too, to take at least one ride through the park in a hansom cab, preferably at dusk. In the southern part of the plaza, Pomona, the Roman Goddess of Abundance, stands atop the *Pulitzer Fountain.* Regilded in 1989, the statue of General Sherman shines brightly (to many New Yorkers, too brightly) in the northern part of the plaza. Three times the quantity of gold used on the flame of the *Statue of Liberty* was used to brighten him. Fifth Ave. and Central Park S.

CENTRAL PARK More than 50 blocks in length but only three lengthy blocks wide, this beloved stretch of greenery, designed by Frederick Law Olmsted and Calvert Vaux in the 1860s, is now a *National Historic Landmark.* New Yorkers use it for everything—jogging, biking, walking, ice skating (at *Wollman Rink*), in-line skating, riding in horse-drawn hansom cabs, listening to concerts (including the *Free Concerts in the Park* series every summer, courtesy of the *New York Philharmonic*) and opera, watching Shakespeare's plays, flying kites, boating, gazing at sculpture, and playing all kinds of ball games. Although city officials claim that the park is now safer due to increased security efforts, you should definitely avoid walking or jogging here at night; and even when you visit it during the day, be cautious, and don't wander into densely wooded areas. In the evenings and on weekends car traffic through the park is reduced or prohibited, leaving the considerable non-vehicular crowd to wend its way around the loop road inside the park much more peacefully. The pretty and very manageably sized *Central Park Zoo,* officially known as the *Central Park Wildlife Center* (entrance on Fifth Ave. at E. 64th St., in the southeast corner of the park), is run by the *Wildlife Conservation Society* (phone: 718-861-6030), which also oversees the Bronx zoo, now called the *Wildlife Conservation Park.* Despite the renamings, to New Yorkers, their zoos will always—and most affectionately—be zoos. Admission charge. *Central Park* is bounded by Central Park S. (W. 59th St.) on the south, W. 110th St. on the north, Fifth Ave. on the east, and Central Park W. (Eighth Ave.) on the west. Urban rangers offer free walking tours (phone: 427-4040), and there are guides who describe which items growing in the park are edible. For information on park events, call 360-1333.

UPPER EAST SIDE

For the art lover, upper Fifth Avenue offers "Museum Mile," including the *Metropolitan Museum of Art* and the *Guggenheim* (see below), and the *Cooper-Hewitt,* the *International Center of Photography,* and the *Jewish Museum* (see *Museums* for all three), plus the *Whitney Museum of American Art,* nearby on Madison Avenue (see below).

METROPOLITAN MUSEUM OF ART Usually considered the finest museum this side of the *Louvre,* it is visited by more than 4.5 million people every year. Here are works by the great masters from the Middle Ages to the present day, a vast assemblage of Greek and Roman sculpture, the most comprehensive collection of Islamic art anywhere, Oriental art, prints and photographs, musical instruments, decorative arts from all ages, and special exhibitions of stunning quality. The *Sackler Wing* contains the *Temple of Dendur;* the *Lila Acheson Wallace Gallery* in the wing of the same name has an extensive Egyptian collection; and an additional 21 more galleries are devoted to 20th-century works. The *American Wing* comprises three centuries of American period rooms, paintings, sculpture, and decorative arts. The *Michael C. Rockefeller Wing* has works from Africa, the Pacific Islands, and pre-Columbian Americas. Asian art galleries include a Buddhist shrine and a Chinese garden court. The *Nineteenth-Century European Paintings and Sculpture Galleries* (formerly the *André Meyer Gallery,* on the second floor) house an unrivaled collection of French Impressionist paintings, including works by Degas and van Gogh. A permanent installation containing 1,300 works created between the third millennium BC and the early 19th century opened in 1994 in 18 of the *Florence and Herbert Irving Galleries for the Arts of South and Southeast Asia.*

A sculpture-filled roof garden offers staggering views. There is also an outdoor sculpture garden overlooking *Central Park* (open May through October). There's a good cafeteria, a restaurant, and two superb, large gift shops. Films and lectures are presented throughout the year, and a distinguished concert series (phone: 570-3949) is held from September through May. The optimum times to visit the museum are Friday and Saturday evenings, when it is open until 8:45 PM. Closed Mondays and some major holidays. (Note: Some wings occasionally close due to lack of funds.) Suggested donation. The main entrance is at Fifth Ave. and 82nd St. (phone: 535-7710 or 879-5500).

SOLOMON R. GUGGENHEIM MUSEUM Designed in 1959 by Frank Lloyd Wright, this white circular building has an interior quarter-mile-long ramp that spirals upward for seven floors, allowing you to travel through the collections—primarily exhibitions of contemporary art (including a large collection of works by Kandinsky, Chagall, and Picasso)—by following the curves of the building. The museum reopened several years ago after extensive renovations, which included a 10-story tower and a redesign of the interior space to bring it more in line with Wright's original vision. The fourth level of this addition was designated the *Robert Mapplethorpe Gallery;* the museum's primary space for photography, it includes periodic exhibitions drawn from the Mapplethorpe collection and other objects belonging to the late controversial photographer, all donated to the museum by the *Mapplethorpe Foundation.* The on-site *Dean & DeLuca Café* (phone: 423-3657) offers a varied menu ranging from full meals to scrumptious desserts. Besides additional gallery space in the annex, the museum also has the *Guggenheim Museum SoHo* gallery (575 Broadway at Prince St.; phone: 423-3500; closed Mondays and Tuesdays; open until 8 PM Saturdays), which features exhibitions from the museum's permanent collection and some traveling shows. The main museum is closed Thursdays; open until 8 PM Fridays and Saturdays. Admission charge for both. 1071 Fifth Ave., between E. 88th and E. 89th Sts. (phone: 423-3500 for both the main museum and the SoHo gallery).

WHITNEY MUSEUM OF AMERICAN ART The permanent collection includes works by Calder, de Kooning, Hopper, Johns, O'Keeffe, Nevelson, Prendergast, Segal, Sheeler, and Warhol, among others. About 15 exhibitions are mounted each year, exclusively featuring 20th-century American art, with the emphasis on the work of living artists. Known locally as the *"Whitney,"* the museum presents an ambitious film and video series focusing on some of the work displayed in the galleries. *Sarabeth's Kitchen* (phone: 570-3670), a branch of the popular Upper East Side eatery, is set in an atrium on the lower level. In addition, there is a branch at 120 Park Avenue, at East 42nd Street (phone: 878-2550). Closed Mondays and Tuesdays. Admission charge. 945 Madison Ave. at E. 75th St. (phone: 570-3600; 570-3676 for recorded information). Closed Mondays and Tuesdays.

YORKVILLE AND GRACIE MANSION In this interesting ethnic neighborhood of mostly German and Eastern European families, a lot of high-rise apartment towers now are diluting the character somewhat. Nonetheless there are still a number of restaurants and delicatessens selling Wiener schnitzel, sauerbraten, goulash, and kielbasa—plus some splendid bakeries. *Gracie Mansion,* the 1799 official residence of the Mayor of New York, sits in a fenced garden in *Carl Schurz Park,* alongside the East River. The park is popular with joggers and dog walkers and is most attractive at dawn, when the eastern sky comes to life. Yorkville stretches from E. 80th to E. 89th St., between Lexington and York Aves. *Gracie Mansion* and *Carl Schurz Park* are at East End Ave. and E. 88th St. The mansion can be visited by appointment only, on Wednesdays from mid-March to mid-November (phone: 570-4751). Donations suggested.

ROOSEVELT ISLAND A self-contained housing development in the middle of the East River, Roosevelt Island is accessible from Manhattan by tramway or subway (the Q train weekdays, the B on weekends), or from Queens by bus and subway. A loop bus encircles the island, which has restricted automobile traffic. Visitors also can stroll the main street from end to end. A landscaped riverside promenade has benches for relaxing while enjoying the unique view of midtown Manhattan. The aerial tramway leaves each side every 15 minutes daily, except during rush hours, when it leaves every seven and a half minutes. The fare at press time was $1.50. The Manhattan terminal is at Second Ave. and E. 60th St. (phone: 832-4543).

UPPER WEST SIDE

LINCOLN CENTER The pulsing water and light of the *Lincoln Center* fountain, the centerpiece of this 14-acre complex, are dramatically framed by the *Metropolitan Opera House,* a contemporary hall with two giant murals by Marc Chagall. The performing arts complex also contains *Avery Fisher Hall,* the *New York State Theater,* the *Vivian Beaumont Theater,* the *Mitzi E. Newhouse Theater, Alice Tully Hall,* the *Juilliard School of Music,* the new *Walter Reade Theatre,* and the *New York Public Library for the Performing Arts* (see *Theater* and *Music and Dance,* below). Guided tours through the major buildings are conducted daily and last about an hour. Admission charge except for children under six. Broadway and W. 65th St. (phone: 875-5400 for *Lincoln Center;* 769-7000 for the *Metropolitan Opera Guild*).

AMERICAN MUSEUM OF NATURAL HISTORY With its $45-million face-lift scheduled for completion by the end of this year, this museum will be an even greater cornucopia of curiosities. The anthropological and natural history exhibitions in the form of life-size dioramas showing people and animals in realistic settings have made this one of the most famous museums in the world. The newly opened dinosaur and fossil halls feature such prehistoric creatures as the baurosaurus (better known as the brontosaurus) and the Tyrannosaurus rex in the largest freestanding dinosaur exhibit in the world.

The popular *Naturemax Theater,* with its four-story screen, often shows double features of nature films (phone: 769-5200 or 769-5650). The museum has three cafeterias and three gift shops. Free guided tours leave from the main floor information desk daily at 15 past each hour. Closed *Thanksgiving* and *Christmas.* Donation suggested. Central Park W. and W. 79th St. (phone: 769-5000; 769-5100 for recorded information).

HAYDEN PLANETARIUM Housed here is an amazing collection of astronomical displays on meteorites, comets, space vehicles, and other galactic phenomena. The sky show, in which constellations are projected onto an observatory ceiling, is one of New York's greatest sights. Subjects include lunar expeditions, the formation of the solar system, and UFOs. There are also special children's shows on weekends. Open daily. Admission charge. W. 81st St. between Central Park W. and Columbus Ave. (phone: 769-5920).

CATHEDRAL OF ST. JOHN THE DIVINE The largest Gothic-style cathedral in the world, it has seating capacity for 10,000. A chronic shortage of funds (and skilled stonemasons) has allowed only two-thirds of the impressive church to be completed since work began in 1892. According to current projections, it may be nearly the 22nd century before construction is completed. Nonetheless, religious services (Episcopal), sold-out concerts, and poetry readings continue, as does the community spirit for which this imposing church has become known. There is a stunning Renaissance and Byzantine art collection as well. Free guided tours of the cathedral and the stone yard are conducted every day except Mondays. Open daily. Amsterdam Ave. between W. 112th St. and Cathedral Pkwy. (phone: 316-7540 or 316-7490).

COLUMBIA UNIVERSITY This is the Big Apple's member of the Ivy League. Although more than 27,000 students attend classes here, the campus is spacious enough to dispel any sense of crowding. Around it are a number of interesting bookstores, restaurants, and bars, including the *West End Gate Café* (2911 Broadway between W. 113th and 114th Sts.; phone: 662-8830), a student favorite. Guided tours of the campus leave from 213 *Low Hall* twice daily; call ahead for schedules. No admission charge. The main gate is at Broadway and W. 116th St. (phone: 854-4900).

RIVERSIDE CHURCH This interdenominational Christian church features a well-known and much-loved carillon tower and an amazing statue of the angel Gabriel blowing his trumpet. The tower is open on Sundays only from 12:30 to 4 PM; free guided tours of the church also are given on Sundays at 12:30 PM. W. 120th St. between Riverside Dr. and Claremont Ave. (phone: 222-5900).

GRANT'S TOMB Who is buried in Grant's tomb? Suffice it to say, the general and his wife are entombed in a gray building topped with a rotunda, set in *Riverside Park.* The interior was inspired by Napoleon's burial place in the *Invalides* in Paris. A word about the park: Don't wander here after dark. Known officially as the *General Grant National Memorial,* the tomb is open daily. No admission charge. Riverside Dr. and W. 122nd St. (phone: 666-1640).

THE CLOISTERS AND FORT TRYON PARK One of the most unusual museums in the country, if not the world, the *Cloisters* is a branch of the *Metropolitan Museum* and consists of sections of cloisters originally belonging to monasteries dating from the 12th through 14th centuries in southern France. It houses an inspiring collection of medieval art from different parts of Europe, of which the *Unicorn Tapestries* are the most famous. Recorded medieval music echoes through the stone corridors and courtyards daily; medieval and Renaissance concerts are held on selected Sundays throughout the year. Set in *Fort Tryon Park* along the Hudson River, the *Cloisters* offers a splendid view of the New Jersey Palisades, the George Washington Bridge, and the Hudson River. Closed Mondays. Suggested admission charge. The closest intersection is Washington Ave. and W. 193rd St. (phone: 923-3700).

HARLEM Some visitors to New York—black or white—are uncomfortable at the thought of entering Harlem, and like any unfamiliar place, it can be intimidating. But there is much to see here, and a visit can dispel the negative image many people have of the neighborhood. Starting at West 120th Street and stretching to about West 160th Street, it is a community of families who are just as concerned about local problems as are people anywhere else in the city.

The most pleasant part of Harlem is "Strivers Row"—West 138th Street between Seventh and Eighth Avenues—two blocks of turn-of-the-century brownstones, some designed by Stanford White. Quite a lot of Harlem, however, is undergoing a revival. *Mart 125* (260-262 W. 125th St.; phone: 316-3340) is a shopping center offering handicrafts, and there is always a constant flow of activities held on Harlem's 10-block waterfront that includes African-American, Latin, and Caribbean arts, music, entertainment, and food stalls. *Harlem Week* is actually 14 days of music, food, and cultural happenings that take place the first two weeks of August; and the famous *Apollo Theater* (253 W. 125th St.; phone: 749-5838) is well worth a visit year-round. Gospel and jazz groups occasionally perform at the *Church of the Intercession* (550 W. 155th St.; phone: 283-6200) once or twice a year. Condos are going up in the area, and a multi-screen cinema has opened.

In the words of a New York police officer: "The best way to see Harlem is by driving or in a cab. Take a bus rather than a subway if you are using public transportation." Among the reliable tour operators are *Harlem Spirituals* (phone: 757-0425) and *Harlem Your Way* (phone: 690-1687 or 866-6997). Worthwhile sights include the *Morris-Jumel Mansion,* once the home of Aaron Burr and Washington's headquarters (Edgecombe Ave. and W. 160th St.; phone: 923-8008); the *Schomburg Center for Research in Black Culture* (515 Malcolm X Blvd.; phone: 491-2200); the *Abyssinian Baptist Church* (132 W. 138th St.; phone: 862-7474), where the late Adam Clayton Powell Jr. preached; the *Studio Museum of Harlem* (144 W. 125th

St.; phone: 864-4500); and the *Black Fashion Museum,* the country's only museum devoted to black contributions to fashion (155-157 W. 126th St.; phone: 666-1320). For more information on Harlem, call the *Harlem Visitors and Convention Association* (phone: 427-3317) or the *New York Convention and Visitors' Bureau* (phone: 397-8222).

BROOKLYN

People who do not know the borough (and that includes many Manhattanites) think purely in terms of the book *A Tree Grows in Brooklyn* or 1930s gangster movies in which Brooklyn-born thugs make snide remarks out of the sides of their mouths while chewing on cigars. Actually, Brooklyn has a lot of trees (more than Manhattan) and some charming neighborhoods that are more European than American in character. Not only is it greener, it is also considerably more rural than Manhattan, even though it has more than four million people and bills itself as the "fourth-largest city in America."

BROOKLYN HEIGHTS The most picturesque streets of classic brownstones (with rents to match those of Manhattan's Greenwich Village) and private gardens are found in this historic district. Not only does the Promenade facing the skyline offer a traditional picture-postcard view of Manhattan, but the area behind it retains an aura of dignity that characterized a more gracious past. Especially convenient for those who work in Manhattan's nearby Wall Street area, this quaint neighborhood is popular with young professionals. Montague Street, a narrow thoroughfare lined with restaurants and shops selling ice cream, candles, old prints, flowers, and clothing, runs from the East River to the *Civic Center,* a complex of federal, state, and municipal government buildings. To get to Brooklyn Heights from Manhattan, take the *IRT* Seventh Avenue line (No. 2 or No. 3 train) to Clark Street station; or better yet, walk across the Brooklyn Bridge and bear right. The district extends from the bridge to Atlantic Avenue and from Court Street to the Promenade. For information on events, contact the *Brooklyn Heights Association* (55 Pierrepont St.; phone: 718-858-9193).

ATLANTIC AVENUE Lebanese, Yemeni, Syrian, and Palestinian shops, bakeries, and restaurants line the street, where purveyors of tahini, Syrian bread, baklava, halvah, other assorted foodstuffs, Arabic recordings, and books are to be found. There is even an office of the *Palestinian Red Crescent,* an official branch of the *International Red Cross* that has been helping victims of the wars in Lebanon. Occasionally, women in veils make their way to and from the shops, some incongruously carrying transistor radios. The most active street scene takes place between the waterfront and Court Street.

PARK SLOPE This restored district resembles London's borough of Chelsea, with its many beautiful shade trees and gardens. A large part of Park Slope has been designated a historic district, and there are some truly impressive townhouses here. Grand Army Plaza, with its colossal arch commemorating those who died in the Civil War, stands at the end of the Slope that extends along the western edge of *Prospect Park.* On Sundays you can climb the inside stairway to the top—the view is stupendous. Seventh Avenue, two blocks from the park, is an intriguing shopping street for old furniture, stained glass, ceramics, housewares, flowers, health food, vegetables, and toys. Saturday afternoons get pretty lively. To get to Park Slope from Manhattan, take the *IRT* Seventh Ave. line (No. 2 or No. 3 train) to Grand Army Plaza, or the *IND* line (D or Q train) to the Seventh Ave. station.

PROSPECT PARK AND THE BROOKLYN BOTANIC GARDENS *Prospect Park,* an Olmsted and Vaux creation (as is Manhattan's *Central Park*), is comprised of more than 500 acres of gracefully landscaped greenery with fields, fountains, lakes, a concert band shell, an ice skating rink in winter, a bridle path, and a zoo. The *Botanic Gardens* (1000 Washington Ave.; phone: 718-622-4433) contain 50 acres of serene rose gardens and hothouses with orchids and other tropical plants, as well as an impressive bonsai collection, cherry trees, an herb garden, and hundreds of other flowers and shrubs. Closed Mondays. No admission charge. From Manhattan, take the *IRT* Seventh Ave. line (No. 2 or 3 train) to the Eastern Pkwy. station, or take the *IND* line (D or Q train) to the Prospect Park station.

BROOKLYN MUSEUM In addition to its outstanding anthropological displays devoted to Native Americans of both the Northern and Southern Hemispheres, the museum's 1.5-million-object permanent collection also includes fine exhibits of Oriental arts, American painting and decorative arts, and European painting by the likes of van Gogh, Rodin, Toulouse-Lautrec, Gauguin, Monet, and Chagall. The recently renovated *West Wing* contains the extensive Egyptian and primitive art collections. This museum hosts excellent traveling exhibitions as well. Closed Mondays and Tuesdays. Suggested donation. From Manhattan take the *IRT* Seventh Ave. line (No. 2 or No. 3 train) to the Eastern Pkwy. station. 200 Eastern Pkwy. and Washington Ave. (phone: 718-638-5000).

BAY RIDGE Although Brooklynites have long been fond of this onetime Scandinavian-dominated waterfront community, it took the 1970s movie *Saturday Night Fever* to bring it to national attention. Bay Ridge is one of the two anchor points for the world's longest suspension bridge, the Verrazano-Narrows Bridge, which connects Brooklyn with Staten Island; the timeless backdrop of the bridge looms over the tops of houses, shops, restaurants, and discos. A bike path runs along the edge of the Narrows (the body of water that connects New York City's rivers to the Atlantic) from Owl's Head Pier, the pier of the now-defunct Brooklyn–Staten Island ferry, all the way to the bridge. The pier has been renovated and is a great place for fishing, watching the ships come in, and catching a wide-angle view of lower Manhattan. To get to Bay Ridge from Manhattan, take the *BMT* line (R train) to the 95th St. station.

CONEY ISLAND Formerly a summer resort where generations of working class New Yorkers came for a day of sun and fun, Coney Island is now a long strip of garish amusement park rides, penny arcades, food stands, honky-tonk bars along the boardwalk where country-and-western singers compete with the sound of the sea, and low-income housing complexes. It is jam-packed in the summer, eerily deserted in winter. Summer weekends are the worst time to visit; weekday evenings are considerably less frenetic. You can ride the *Cyclone,* one of the most terrifying roller coasters on the East Coast, and the *Wonder Wheel,* a giant Ferris wheel alongside the ocean; the parachute jump, a highly visible Coney Island landmark, is no longer operational. The actual amusement park is called *Astroland Park* (phone: 718-265-2100) and is open mid-April through mid-June on weekends only, and from mid-June through early September seven days a week, noon to midnight. The famous belugas (white whales) are the stars of the *New York Aquarium,* officially called the *Aquarium for Wildlife Conservation* (Surf Ave. and W. Eighth St.; phone: 718-265-3400). If you get a sudden craving for Italian food, head for *Gargiulo's* (2911 W. 15th St.; phone: 718-266-4891) for some good Neapolitan dishes. Another New York treat is to have hot dogs at *Nathan's Famous* (1310 Surf Ave.; phone: 718-946-2202). The area's most recent ethnic flavor is provided by a second wave of Russian immigrants, and nearby Brighton Beach has been affectionately dubbed "Little Odessa." From Manhattan take the *IND* line (F, D, or N train) to the Stillwell Ave. station. For further information, call the *Chamber of Commerce* (phone: 718-266-1234).

SHEEPSHEAD BAY This area operates more at the pace of a New England fishing village than a part of New York City. A few anglers sometimes sell their catch on the dock in the early afternoon; charter boats that take people out for the day leave very early in the morning. For the best view of the scene, cross the wooden footbridge at Ocean Avenue and walk along the mile-long esplanade. A few blocks south of the bay is Manhattan Beach, a neighborhood of tree-lined streets and rather elegant homes. Brighton Beach, a few blocks to the east, joins Manhattan Beach with Coney Island. From Manhattan take the *IND* line (D or Q train) to the Sheepshead Bay station.

THE BRONX

With almost two million inhabitants, the Bronx is smaller than Brooklyn, and it's the only New York borough on the mainland. Although all the points of interest listed here are safe for visitors, some sections of the Bronx are among the most dangerous in the city. The South Bronx has been nicknamed "Fort Apache" by the police, and officers advise staying clear of any place south of Fordham Road.

BRONX ZOO (INTERNATIONAL WILDLIFE CONSERVATION PARK) In 1993 this zoo's name, along with those of all the *New York Zoological Society*'s facilities, was changed to include the word "conservation." Whatever you choose to call it, this is one of the most famous facilities of its kind in the world, with over 265 acres inhabited by more than 4,000 animals. Elephants, tigers, chimps, seals, rhinos, hippos, birds, and buffalo are the favorites. Ride the *Bengali Express* monorail through Wild Asia; visit Jungle World or a children's petting zoo; or survey it all from the *Skyfari* tramway. To get here from Manhattan, take the *IRT* Seventh Ave. line express train (No. 2) to the Pelham Pkwy. station; walk west to the Bronxdale entrance (for other routes, call the zoo). Open daily. Admission charge, except on Wednesdays; parking charge. Fordham Rd. and Bronx River Pkwy. (phone: 718-367-1010).

NEW YORK BOTANICAL GARDENS Adjoining the zoo to the north, these 250 acres of flowering hills, valleys, woods, and gardens are set in an unspoiled natural forest. The site comprises the only surviving remnants of the original woodland that once covered the city. The renovated *Enid A. Haupt Conservatory* (closed Mondays), a crystal palace with 11 pavilions—each with a totally different environment—is a special treat. Other highlights include a rose garden, azalea glen, daffodil hill, botanical museum, and restaurant. It's well worth the trip, especially in the spring. From Manhattan take the *IND* line (D train) to the Bedford Park station and walk eight blocks east (for other routes, call the gardens). Closed Mondays. Admission charge. Southern Blvd. and E. 200th St. (phone: 718-817-8705).

BRONX MUSEUM OF THE ARTS This museum has been dedicated since 1971 to serving the ethnically diverse communities of the Bronx and the metropolitan area. Concerts, film programs, poetry readings, and dance performances are held throughout the year. From Manhattan take the *IRT* Lexington Ave. line (No. 4 train) to 161st St., or the *IND* line (C or D train) to 167th St. Closed Mondays and Tuesdays. Donation suggested. 1040 Grand Concourse at E. 165th St. (phone: 718-681-6000).

YANKEE STADIUM The home of the *"Bronx Bombers,"* this 57,545-seat stadium is where Babe Ruth, Lou Gehrig, Joe DiMaggio, and dozens of other baseball stars played the national sport. From Manhattan take the *IND* line (C or D train) or the *IRT* Lexington Ave. line (No. 4 train) to E. 161st St. Open during baseball season. River Ave. and E. 161st St. (phone: 718-293-6000).

QUEENS

Queens is less than a five-minute subway ride from Manhattan's eastern edge and is the largest of the five boroughs. It boasts 118.6 square miles that include major sports facilities, 196 miles of waterfront, numerous parks, cultural centers, universities, two of the metro area's three airports, and even a growing motion picture industry. Queens also is one of the most ethnically diverse areas in the nation, though nationalities tend to congregate in specific pockets. Greeks have settled in Astoria; Hispanics in Corona and Jackson Heights; Asians in Flushing. The largest Hindu temple in North America is found on Bowne Street in Flushing, and Flushing's Chinatown now rivals Manhattan's. These neighborhoods offer a fascinating assortment of restaurants, groceries, and bakeries—Filipino, Irish, Italian, Peruvian, Ecuadorian, Colombian, Argentinean, Greek, German—and also sponsor a number of festivals featuring their own foods, crafts, music, and dancing. For information on these activities, call *Queens Borough Hall* (phone: 718-286-3000).

Queens's architectural ambience can change literally from block to block—from pretty Kew Gardens to elegant Jamaica Estates and Bayside Hills, from the quiet row houses of Flushing to the Victorian homes in Richmond Hill, Old Woodhaven, and College Point. Historical sites abound, including the *Friends Meeting House* (137-16 Northern Blvd., Flushing; phone: 718-358-9636). Built in 1694, it is the oldest house of worship in the US.

Sports buffs flock to Queens to see the *Mets* at *Shea Stadium,* the horse races at *Aqueduct* and *Belmont,* and the *US Open Tennis Championships* at the new *USTA National Tennis Center* in *Flushing Meadows Park.* There are abundant facilities for golf, tennis, swimming, ice skating, horseback riding, boating, hiking, and bird watching. Lovers of the great outdoors enjoy the borough's wetlands and woodlands, including the two-mile Pitobik Trail; Turtle Pond; *Alley Pond Environmental Center* (phone: 718-229-4000); *Forest Park* (phone: 718-235-0684); *Jamaica Bay Wildlife Refuge* (phone: 718-318-4340); and the *Queens Botanical Gardens,* in Flushing (phone: 718-886-3800).

BOWNE HOUSE Dating from 1661, this was the home of John Bowne, a Quaker credited with winning religious freedom in the Dutch colony of New Amsterdam from Governor Peter Stuyvesant. The house is now a museum, featuring 17th- through 19th-century furnishings including many family heirlooms from the Bowne family who lived here from 1661 to 1945. From Manhattan take the *IRT* Flushing line (No. 7 train) to the Main Street station. Officially open 2:30 to 4:30 PM, Tuesdays, Saturdays, and Sundays; call ahead to confirm. Admission charge. 37-01 Bowne St. between 38th Ave. and Northern Blvd., Flushing (phone: 718-359-0528).

KINGSLAND HOMESTEAD The sole survivor of what was once the prevalent architectural style in Queens, this Dutch colonial/English house dating to circa 1785 contains a permanent collection of antique china and memorabilia brought to this country by Captain James King. Next to the house is the *Weeping Beech* tree, planted in 1849 by Samuel Parsons it is considered the city's oldest "living" monument. From Manhattan take the *IRT* Flushing line (No. 7 train) to the Main Street station. Open 2:30 to 4:30 PM, Tuesdays, Saturdays, and Sundays. Admission charge. 143-35 37th Ave. between Parsons Blvd. and Bowne St., Flushing (phone: 718-939-0647).

KING MANOR MANSION Built in the early 18th century, this home was bought in 1805 by Rufus King, one of the signers of the Constitution. Much of the present structure, a fine example of Georgian-Federal architecture, dates from the 19th century. Three generations of King descendants resided here. To get there take the *IND* line (E train) to the Parsons Boulevard station.

Open weekends only from noon to 4 PM, and the second and last Tuesday of each month between noon and 2 PM. Admission charge. Call for updated calendar of events. Located in the 11-acre *Kings Park* at Jamaica Ave. and 153rd St., Jamaica (phone: 718-206-0545).

AMERICAN MUSEUM OF THE MOVING IMAGE A national landmark that pays tribute to New York's revitalized film industry, this museum is located in a building that once housed Paramount Pictures' East Coast facilities and is now home to Kaufmann Astoria Studios. In the 1930s and 1940s the Marx Brothers movies (among others) were produced here; today directors such as Woody Allen, Spike Lee, and Sidney Lumet regularly use this second-largest sound stage in the country. The museum offers lectures and seminars on film and television. An excellent permanent exhibit, "Behind the Screen: Producing, Promoting, and Exhibiting Motion Pictures and Television," displays old movie sets, posters, costumes, and more. From Manhattan take the *BMT* line (G or N trains) to the 36th Street station. Closed Mondays. Admission charge. At 35th Ave. and 36th St., Astoria (phone: 718-784-4520).

FLUSHING MEADOWS–CORONA PARK The site of the *1939* and *1964 World's Fairs* and the original headquarters of the *UN,* the park is now a center for cultural and outdoor activities (phone: 718-760-6565). The *Queens Museum of Art* (phone: 718-592-9700) hosts a variety of changing exhibitions and includes in its permanent collection a 15,000-square-foot scale model of New York City, updated in 1993. Closed Mondays; open afternoons only on weekends. Donations suggested. From Manhattan take the *IRT* Flushing line (No. 7 train) to the 111th Street stop.

NEW YORK HALL OF SCIENCE Located within *Flushing Meadows–Corona Park,* this is the city's only hands-on science and technology center for children. Exhibits include *Seeing the Light,* a journey into the world of color, light, and perception, and *Feedback,* which takes a look at the principles and workings of self-sensing machines. The world's first three-dimensional, dynamic model of a hydrogen atom is present in *Realm of the Atom.* In *Structures,* a playground and construction zone allows visitors to discover the laws of gravity. On weekends, the hall features family workshops through the *Discover Activities Related to Science* program. To get there take the *IRT* (No. 7 train) to the 111th Street station. Open Wednesdays through Sundays. Admission charge. *Flushing Meadows–Corona Park* (phone: 718-699-0005).

STATEN ISLAND

Much closer to New Jersey than New York, Staten Island is the Big Apple's most remote borough and, with only about 375,000 people, its least populous. This is the borough that keeps threatening to "secede" from the others in New York City's union. In 1993 the island's residents voted two to one in favor of secession, but legislators in Albany, the state capital, have yet to agree on or work out what kind of status the borough can be given.

Since the Verrazano-Narrows Bridge opened in 1964, Staten Island has been filling up with suburban housing developments and shopping centers, but a few farms remain in the southern reaches. To find them, you can take the bus marked "Richmond Avenue" at the ferry terminal, but getting around by public transportation takes a long time; driving is recommended if at all possible.

STATEN ISLAND ZOO Considerably smaller than the *Bronx Zoo,* this animal house covers eight wooded acres near a lake in *Barret Park.* Its specialty is reptiles of all descriptions. Open daily. Admission charge. 614 Broadway at Clove Rd. (phone: 718-442-3101).

JACQUES MARCHAIS CENTER OF TIBETAN ART One of the more unusual treasures of the city, this is also one of its best-kept secrets. A reconstructed Tibetan prayer hall, featuring an adjoining library and gardens with Oriental sculpture, the center sits on a hill overlooking a pastoral, un-New York setting of trees. *The Tibetan Book of the Dead,* other esoteric tomes, prayer wheels, statuary, and weavings are on display. Open by appointment only December through March; Wednesday through Sunday afternoons April through November; also open by appointment for group tours. Admission charge. 338 Lighthouse Ave. at Richmond Rd. (phone: 718-987-3500).

CONFERENCE HOUSE Now a national landmark, this manor house was built circa 1680 and hosted such Revolutionary War notables as Benjamin Franklin. Crafts demonstrations are frequently offered; call ahead. Open Wednesday through Sunday afternoons. Admission charge. 7455 Hylan Blvd. at Satterlee St. (phone: 718-984-6046).

RICHMONDTOWN RESTORATION In this 96-acre park, exhibits and crafts demonstrations depict three centuries of local culture, harking back to the early Dutch settlers. Open Wednesday through Sunday afternoons. Admission charge. 441 Clarke Ave. at Richmond Rd. (phone: 718-351-1617).

Sources and Resources

TOURIST INFORMATION

The *New York Convention and Visitors' Bureau Information Center* (2 Columbus Circle, New York, NY 10019; phone: 397-8222) is an excellent source for hotel and restaurant information, subway and bus maps, descriptive brochures, theater discount coupons, and current listings of entertainment, special events, and other activities; the office is staffed by multilingual aides. Look for a new *Visitors' Center* (226 W. 47th St.; no phone at press time) to open later this year. *Big Apple Greeter* (Manhattan Borough President's Office, 1 Centre St., New York, NY 10007; phone: 669-8159) is a program in which New York citizens—from students to seniors—serve as volunteer guides for out-of-towners. Greeters, who are first screened and trained, are matched with a visitor based on the volunteer's expertise and the visitor's interests, needs, and language requirements. During the two- to four-hour neighborhood tours (which usually require at least 24 hours' notice), greeters share their insights and knowledge of their particular slice of the Big Apple. A subscribers-only hotline called *Manhattan Intelligence* provides information on anything from where to pet a lion cub to more mundane data such as cultural events, making restaurant reservations, and finding a parking space for your car (phone: 243-8080 for more information).

The 24-hour *Arts Hotline* (phone: 765-ARTS) is another good source of information on events, up-to-date descriptions of exhibitions at museums and galleries; theater, dance, and music performances; activities at parks and zoos; and festivals and fairs.

Visitors who require assistance in an emergency—anything from a lost wallet to a lost child—should stop at the *Traveler's Aid Services* office (1481 Broadway; phone: 944-0013); open weekdays only from 9 AM to 5 PM (Wednesdays to noon). There is also a branch in the *International Arrivals Building* at *John F. Kennedy International Airport* (phone: 718-656-4870); closed Sundays.

LOCAL COVERAGE *The New York Times,* the *Daily News,* and the *New York Post* all are morning dailies; the *Village Voice* publishes on Wednesdays. Other weeklies include *The New Yorker, New York* magazine, and *TimeOut New York.* Also pick up copies of *ACCESS New York City* (HarperCollins; $18.50) and *ACCESS New York Restaurants 96/97* (HarperCollins; $12).

TELEVISION STATIONS Channel 2–WCBS; Channel 4–WNBC; Channel 5–WNYW (Fox); Channel 7–WABC; Channel 9–WOR; Channel 11–WPIX; Channel 13–WNET (PBS).

RADIO STATIONS AM: WFAN 660 (sports/talk); WOR 710 (news/talk); WABC 770 (talk); WCBS 880 (news). FM: WBGO 88.3 (jazz); WXRK 92.3 (classic rock); WNYC 93.9 (public); WPLJ 95.5 (rock); WQXR 96.3 (classical); WNEW 102.7 (rock); WMXV 105 (contemporary rock); WBLS 107.5 (urban).

TELEPHONE The area code for Manhattan is 212. The area code for the Bronx, Brooklyn, Queens, and Staten Island is 718. The area code for Long Island is 516. Unless otherwise noted, all telephone numbers in this chapter are in Manhattan—area code 212.

SALES TAX New York City's sales tax is 8.25%. The hotel tax is 13.25% plus a $2 per night occupancy tax. Restaurant meals also are taxed 8.25%.

CLIMATE The best times to visit New York are in the spring—April and May—and in the fall—September through mid-November—when temperatures are comfortable, in the high 50s to low 70s F. Winter and summer are extreme, averaging in the 80s and up in July and August, in the 30s or below during the months of hard winter. However, the weather should not determine your visit, since most of what makes New York great takes place indoors, and air conditioning and central heating are standard. New Yorkers dress informally for many events; anything in good taste goes. Remember, there is no rainy season as such—it can happen any day of the year. Be prepared.

GETTING AROUND

AIRPORTS New York City is served by three major airports: *John F. Kennedy International (JFK)* and *La Guardia*—both in the borough of Queens—and *Newark International,* across the Hudson in New Jersey. It takes 50 to 60 minutes to reach *JFK* from midtown Manhattan by cab; *La Guardia* from midtown is a 30- to 45-minute ride. *Newark International* is a 30- to 40-minute drive from midtown.

Quick and relatively inexpensive transportation is available via several bus lines. *Carey Transportation* (phone: 718-632-0500) provides service from *Grand Central Terminal* (arrives at Vanderbilt Ave.; departs from Park Ave., just south of 42nd St.), the *Air Trans Center* at the *Port Authority Bus Terminal,* the *Hilton, Sheraton Manhattan, Marriott Marquis,* and *Holiday Inn Crowne Plaza* hotels in midtown to *JFK* and *La Guardia* airports. Buses leave every 30 minutes (every 20 minutes after 1 PM). *Carey* also runs a shuttle between these two airports. The *Newark Airport Express,* operated by *New Jersey Transit* (phone: 201-762-5100), runs between *Newark Airport* and the *Port Authority Bus Terminal* (Eighth Ave. between W. 40th and W. 42nd Sts.; phone: 212-564-8484). *Olympia Trails* (phone: 964-6233 or 718-622-7700 in New York, 908-354-3330 in New Jersey) provides daily coach service every 20 to 30 minutes from all *Newark International* terminals, the *World Trade Center, Grand Central Terminal,* and *Penn Station.* The *Gray Line Air Shuttle* offers a share-ride van service which operates among all New York airports and most midtown hotels. Arrangements can be made by your hotel, at the *Gray Line Air Shuttle* courtesy telephone by the airline baggage claim areas, or by calling 757-6840 or 800-451-0455. For other information about transportation options to and from the New York area airports, call the *New York/New Jersey Port Authority* (phone: 800-247-7433).

BUS New York City buses run frequently. There are more than 220 routes and over 3,800 buses in operation. Although considerably slower than subways, buses often bring you closer to your destination, stopping about every two blocks, except on express routes, which stop only at major crossings. The main routes in Manhattan are north-south on the avenues and east-west (crosstown) on major cross-streets (such as 14th, 34th, 42nd, 57th, and 72nd Streets), as well as some crisscross and circular routes. Check both the sign on the front of the bus and the one at the bus stop to make sure the bus goes where you want and stops where you are waiting. Be sure to have exact change for the fare or a subway token. *Bus drivers do not make change, nor* *do they accept bills.* The multiple-use *MetroCard* was introduced three years ago and is increasingly accepted at most of the city's 463 subway stations and all of the *New York City Transit Authority*'s 3,600 buses. The size of a credit card, the *Metrocard* is run through a scanner; one fare is deducted each time you use it. Cards are sold at values of $8 to $80. At press time the per-trip transit fare was $1.50, no matter what the length of your trip or method of payment; on buses a transfer is necessary for any change of bus on a continuous journey and is free, but there is no free transfer from bus to subway or vice versa. Most bus routes operate 24 hours a day, seven days a week, but service is less frequent late at night or on Sundays. For information on buses to points outside Manhattan from the *Port Authority Bus Terminal* (Eighth Ave. and W. 42nd St.), call 564-8484 or 564-1114. Free bus maps are available at *Grand Central* and *Penn Stations,* at the *New York Convention and Visitors' Bureau Information Center* (see above), or by sending a self-addressed, stamped legal-size (#10) envelope to the *New York Transit Authority,* Room 875, 370 Jay St., Brooklyn, NY 11201, Attn.: Maps.

CAR RENTAL New York is served by all the major car rental companies, as well as a host of small local firms.

SUBWAY The New York subway system has a reputation for being dangerous, dirty, and confusing. The reality is not quite so harrowing as most people fear. Ongoing renovations, modernizations, and an increased police presence makes this extensive underground network safer than it has been in recent years. Common sense dictates, however, that as in most metropolitan cities, be aware of your surroundings and personal belongings. Still, the system's convenience and speed can't be duplicated by any other form of transportation within the city. Pick up free subway maps at token booths or at the *New York Convention and Visitors' Bureau Information Center* (see above); system maps are displayed in most cars—though not always outside on the platforms. Keep in mind that certain interchange stations are large and confusing, so if you don't find a sign that confirms you are on the right platform, double-check with a transit worker. Also double-check that you don't board an express if you are better served by a local; the map makes the distinctions relatively clear, but even New Yorkers occasionally whiz as many as 50 or more blocks beyond a desired stop when they don't pay attention to which train they are boarding.

The subway system operates 24 hours a day, although most schedules are less frequent between midnight and 6 AM. At night the lights outside many stations indicate accessibility: A red light means the station is closed; a yellow light indicates that the station is open but no one is on duty at the token booth; and a green light means both the station and token booth are open. Whenever possible, try to avoid traveling late at night when stations and train cars are more deserted. For general bus and subway information, call the *New York Transit Authority* (phone: 718-330-1234).

The fare at press time was $1.50 (no matter how far you travel or how many times you change trains without exiting a station). Tokens are required to enter; the multiple-fare *MetroCard* should also streamline subway entry.

TAXI A handy but expensive way to get around the city is by taxi. Expect to pay $2 for the first one-fifth mile, and 30¢ for each additional one-fifth mile. Cabs can be identified by their yellow color and are available if the center portion of the roof light is on (if the *entire* roof light is either on or off, this means that the cab is off-duty, on call, or already occupied). They can be hailed almost anywhere and if on-duty, they are required by law to pick you up and deliver you to your specified destination. New Yorkers generally tip cabbies about 20% of the metered fare. There is a 50¢ surcharge on most cab fares between 8 PM and 6 AM and all day Sundays. Passengers must pay any bridge and/or tunnel tolls. New York City also has dozens of companies that provide conventional sedans with drivers and can be called by phone (known locally as "car services"). Fares run somewhere between those of yellow street cabs and limousines, but are usually cheaper than both for long-distance runs, such as to airports, because a fixed fee is charged. Two such companies are *Dialcar* (phone: 718-743-8383) and *Love* (phone: 718-633-3338).

SIGHTSEEING TOURS

Many of the tour companies in the city will help you get your bearings before setting out on your own.

BICYCLE Join Thomas Ahern on a two-hour *Bite of the Apple's Central Park Tour* (phone: 541-8759). The city's history, culture, and attractions including *Strawberry Fields, Belvedere Castle,* and Edgar Allan Poe's favorite haunts are all covered.

BOAT *Circle Line Sightseeing Yachts* offers an interesting three-hour guided boat trip around Manhattan (two hours from early March through late December). Departures change throughout the year; call for schedule updates. Boats leave from Pier 83 at the foot of W. 42nd Street and the Hudson River (phone: 563-3200). *Spirit Cruises* (Pier 62, Chelsea Piers, West 23rd St.; phone: 727-2789) has dining, dancing, and moonlight cruises, as well as narrated tours.

BUS *Gray Line* (900 Eighth Ave., between W. 53rd and W. 54th Sts., near Seventh Ave.; phone: 397-2600) provides good bus tours in English, French, German, Italian, and Spanish. For a higher perspective, *NY Double Decker Tours* is one of many companies operating double-decker buses from the *Empire State Building* at Fifth Avenue and West 34th Street (phone: 967-6008). *NYC Downtown Tours!* gives minibus tours of areas not usually covered by mainstream tour operators; these include lower Manhattan districts like Little Italy, SoHo, and the Lower East Side, with specialty tours centered around downtown nightlife, art, restaurants, and theater (phone: 932-2744).

HELICOPTER Most spectacular is *Island Helicopter*'s ride around Manhattan. Though the price is steep ($44 to $119 for flights covering from 7- to 34-air miles), the ride is memorable. Tickets are available through most major hotels; flights booked at the heliport have an additional $5 surcharge. At E. 34th St. and the East River (phone: 683-4575).

WALKING Seeing New York on foot is probably the best way to get acquainted with this complex city: You can do it on your own or take a guided tour. A number of excellent walking tours are available, led by guides who are knowledgeable in everything from architecture and ethnic neighborhoods to literary history, the jazz circuit, movie locations, and noshing spots. Try *Adventures on a Shoestring,* which offers 75 walking tours and other activities around Manhattan year-round (phone: 265-2663); *Sidewalks of New York,* which conducts theme tours such as "Ghosts After Sunset," "Writers' New York," and "Hollywood on the Hudson" (phone: 517-0201); *Urban Explorations,* whose walks are organized around such themes as "The Art Deco Era" and "Atriums of New York," with the focus on the city's history, architecture, and ethnic neighborhoods as well as its parks and gardens (phone: 718-721-5254); or *Big Onion Walking Tours,* run by three doctoral candidates in New York history who give lively tours reflecting the history of immigration during trips to Harlem, Chinatown, Ellis Island, and Governors Island, to name a few; Irish and Jewish New York tours are also specialties, as are multiethnic eating tours (phone: 439-1090). Also try the *Municipal Art Society* (phone: 935-3960), the *Museum of the City of New York* (phone: 534-1672), the *92nd Street YM/YWHA* (phone: 996-1105), or the *Lower East Side Tenement Museum* (phone: 431-0233). On weekends, the museum offers the neighborhood heritage walking tours. Call for details.

SPECIAL EVENTS

In late January or early February (held on the first new moon after January 21), *Chinese New Year Celebration and Dragon Parade,* Chinatown; March 17, *St. Patrick's Day Parade,* Fifth Avenue; *Easter Sunday, Easter Parade,* Fifth Avenue; May, *Ninth Avenue International Food Festival;* May, *Washington Square Outdoor Art Show,* Greenwich Village; first Sunday in June, *Puerto Rican Day Parade,* Fifth Avenue; late June to early July, *JVC Jazz Festival; July 4th, Macy's* fireworks along the East River; July and August, free *Shakespeare Festival, Delacorte Theater, Central Park,* and free performances of the *New York Philharmonic* and *Metropolitan Opera,* all boroughs; August, *Harlem Week;* late August and September, *US Open Tennis Championships, USTA National Tennis Center, Flushing Meadows Park,* Queens; September, *African-American Day Parade;* September, the 10-day *Festival of San Gennaro,* patron saint of Neapolitans, Mulberry Street, Little Italy; September and October, *New York Film Festival, Lincoln Center;* October, *Columbus Day Parade,* Fifth Avenue; October 31, *Halloween Parade,* Greenwich Village; November, *NYC Marathon, Central Park,* (finish line); November, *Veterans Day Parade,* Fifth Avenue; November, *Macy's Thanksgiving Day Parade,* Broadway; December, *Christmas Tree Lighting,* Rockefeller Plaza; November through January, the *Great Christmas Show, Radio City Music Hall.*

For borough-by-borough information on parades, festivals, exhibits, and free events, call 360-3456; 718-625-0080 (Brooklyn); 718-590-3505 (Bronx); 718-816-2133 (Staten Island); and 718-291-ARTS (Queens).

MUSEUMS

The city boasts more than 150 museums. In addition to those described in *Special Places,* other notable New York museums include the following:

AMERICAN CRAFT MUSEUM Jewelry, rugs, textiles, metal crafts, and other exhibits. Closed Mondays. Admission charge except for children under 12. 40 W. 53rd St. between Fifth and Sixth Aves. (phone: 956-6047).

ASIA SOCIETY Changing exhibits of ancient and contemporary Asian art. Closed Mondays. Admission charge except Thursday evenings; under 12, free. 725 Park Ave. at E. 70th St. (phone: 288-6400).

CHILDREN'S MUSEUM OF THE ARTS Recently renovated, this museum showcases hands-on, interactive exhibits with arts-related themes. Children are encouraged to design and make their own collages, clay models, and paintings. Closed Mondays. Admission charge except for children 18 months or younger. 72 Spring St. between Crosby and Lafayette Sts. (phone: 941-9198).

COOPER-HEWITT MUSEUM The *National Museum of Design* branch of the *Smithsonian Institution,* featuring a full range of decorative arts. Closed Mondays. Admission charge except for children under 12. 2 E. 91st St. at Fifth Ave. (phone: 860-6868).

FORBES MAGAZINE GALLERIES One of the world's largest collection of Fabergé Imperial Russian *Easter* eggs plus model boats and soldiers. Closed Sundays and Mondays; Thursdays are reserved for guided tours. No admission charge. 62 Fifth Ave. at 12th St. (phone: 206-5548).

FRAUNCES TAVERN MUSEUM This landmark building, the site of Washington's farewell to his officers in 1783, contains memorabilia of the American Revolution (including Washington's hat). In addition, the museum also displays rotating exhibits from around the country. Open weekdays and Saturday afternoons. Admission charge. The *Fraunces Tavern* restaurant (269-0144) occupies the ground floor. 54 Pearl St. at Broad St. (phone: 425-1778).

INTERNATIONAL CENTER OF PHOTOGRAPHY Rotating exhibits of the latest works by internationally renowned photographers; occasionally, these are arranged around particular themes, such as the Holocaust. Closed Mondays. Admission charge. 1130 Fifth Ave. at E. 94th St. (phone: 860-1777) and 1133 Sixth Ave. at W. 43rd St. (phone: 768-4683).

INTREPID SEA-AIR-SPACE MUSEUM This World War II aircraft carrier has exhibits on the navy, pioneers in aviation, and technology. A lightship (a seagoing lighthouse) and a MiG-21 fighter jet are part of the "fleet," which also includes a submarine and a battleship. Open daily from *Memorial Day* through *Labor Day;* closed Mondays and Tuesdays the rest of the year. Admission charge except for children under six. Permanently moored at Pier 86 in the Hudson River, 12th Ave. and W. 46th St. (phone: 245-0072 or 245-2533).

ISAMU NOGUCHI GARDEN MUSEUM Featured here are more than 350 works by the Japanese sculptor, including 12 galleries with works in stone, clay, and wood; paper lamps; and plans for fountains and playgrounds. Open Wednesdays, Saturdays, and Sundays from April through November. Donation suggested. On Vernon Blvd. and 33rd Rd., Queens (phone: 718-204-7088).

JEWISH MUSEUM With a recent $50-million expansion and renovation, this museum houses a permanent collection of more than 27,000 works of art, artifacts, ceremonial objects, and more spanning 4,000 years of Jewish history. Closed Fridays, Saturdays, and major Jewish holidays. Admission charge except for children under 12. 1109 Fifth Ave. at E. 92nd St. (phone: 423-3200).

LOWER EAST SIDE TENEMENT MUSEUM America's first urban "living history" museum features a restored replica of a 19th-century tenement building, as well as photographs, drawings, and documents recounting the lives of immigrants from 1878 through 1930. Walking tours and a Wednesday slide show are also offered. Closed Mondays and Saturdays. Donation suggested; admission charge for the slide show. 97 Orchard St. at Broome St. (phone: 431-0233).

MUSEO DEL BARRIO Dedicated to the arts and culture of Puerto Rico, including painting, sculpture, concerts, photography, and films. Closed Mondays and Tuesdays. Donation suggested. 1230 Fifth Ave. at E. 104th St. (phone: 831-7272).

MUSEUM FOR AFRICAN ART This expanded facility features sculpture, paintings, and crafts in both contemporary and traditional styles. The emphasis is on artisans from Zaire, Cameroon, Ghana, and the Ivory Coast. There are also art-history seminars. Closed Mondays. Admission charge. 593 Broadway between Houston and Prince Sts. (phone: 966-1313).

MUSEUM OF AMERICAN FOLK ART Educational programs, exhibits, and publications devoted to American folk art from the 18th century to the present. Closed Mondays. Donation suggested. Two Lincoln Sq. between Columbus Ave. and W. 66th St. (phone: 595-9533).

MUSEUM OF TELEVISION AND RADIO This repository of over 60,000 radio and television programs and commercials hosts frequent seminars and has excellent research facilities. Closed Mondays. Suggested admission charge. 25 W. 52nd St. (phone: 621-6600).

MUSEUM OF THE CITY OF NEW YORK A free video show, "The Big Apple," is a permanent attraction here; there are also temporary exhibits focusing on the city. Closed Mondays and Tuesdays. Donation suggested. Fifth Ave. and E. 103rd St. (phone: 534-1672).

NATIONAL MUSEUM OF THE AMERICAN INDIAN A comprehensive collection of artifacts linked to the indigenous peoples of all the Americas, this museum, part of Washington, DC's *Smithsonian Institution,* also is known as the *George Gustav Heye Center,* named after a major collector. In 1994, it relocated from West 155th Street to the *Alexander Hamilton US Custom House* in lower Manhattan. The new Beaux Art facility, which features changing displays of its one million objects, also stages educational workshops, film and video festivals, and performances of Native American dance, music, and theater. Although the focus is on North, Central, and South American peoples, there are ethnological materials from as far away as Siberia. Open daily year-round except *Christmas Day.* No admission charge. 1 *Bowling Green* (phone: 668-NMAI).

NEW-YORK HISTORICAL SOCIETY With an ongoing $10-million restoration, this repository of paintings welcomes visitors to exhibits showcasing the Hudson River School. It also houses a library of some 700,000 volumes on the history of New York City and New York State. Closed weekends. Donation suggested. 170 Central Park W. at W. 76th St. (phone: 873-3400).

NEW YORK TRANSIT MUSEUM Old subway cars and other nostalgic and informative metropolitan memorabilia plus changing exhibitions (including some very imaginative ones geared to children), a lecture series, and tours. Closed Mondays. Admission charge except for children under two. Boerum Pl. and Schermerhorn St., Brooklyn (phone: 718-330-5839).

PIERPONT MORGAN LIBRARY AND ANNEX These elegant buildings house Old Master drawings, early printed books, music manuscripts, plus a private research library. A superb collection of medieval and Renaissance illuminated manuscripts is also on display. The facility includes the adjacent *Morgan House;* the two buildings are linked by the beautifully designed, glass-enclosed Garden Court—a pleasant place to take a breather from viewing exhibits. Closed Mondays. Donation suggested. 29 E. 36th St. at Madison Ave. (phone: 685-0610).

STUDIO MUSEUM OF HARLEM An impressive collection of works by African-American artists. Closed Mondays and Tuesdays. Admission charge. 144 W. 125th St. between Lenox and Seventh Aves. (phone: 864-4500).

SHOPPING

This city is like no other for acquiring material possessions. It is the commercial center and the fashion capital of the country, and styles that originate here set the trends for fashionable folk from Portland, Maine, to Portland, Oregon. The scope of merchandise available approaches the infinite, and the best part of all is that there are goodies for every budget.

ANTIQUES "Antiques Row" is a district extending from E. 10th Street to E. 14th Street, from Broadway to University Place, with many former wholesalers now open to the public. Also, the East 60th Street block (between First and

Second Aves.) has recently become the city's center for antiques shoppers, with over 30 dealers now represented. Elsewhere, there is the *Chelsea Antiques Building* (110 W. 25th St.; phone: 929-0909); the year-round, weekends-only *Indoor Antiques Fair* (122 W. 27th St.; phone: 627-4700), with two floors and 65 vendors; and the nearby *Annex Flea Market,* which spreads from W. 24th to W. 26th Street along the Avenue of the Americas (Sixth Avenue), with more than 150 vendors (this is not for ultraserious museum collectors, but a discerning eye can ferret out some exquisite pieces from an extensive collection that includes jewelry, decorative objects, and furniture). Second in size is the indoor/outdoor *Greenflea Market* (Columbus Ave. and W. 77th St.; phone: 721-0900) held every Sunday. Much farther west is *John Koch Antiques* (514 W. 24th St., Third Floor; phone: 243-8625), which sells estate objects from the everyday to the elegant. A down-market, downtown source is the *Soho Antiques Fair and Collectibles* (Broadway and Grand St.; phone: 682-2000); this weekend outdoor flea market sells an enormous variety of trinkets, clothes, photographic and electronic equipment, furniture, art, housewares, and oddities.

BED, BATH, AND TABLE LINEN For good buys on top-quality and designer sheets and pillowcases, New York is definitely the place. At *Bed, Bath, and Beyond* (between Sixth Ave. and W. 18th Ave.; phone: 255-3550), you'll find substantial discounts on bedding, bath items, housewares, and even furniture. *D. Porthault* (18 E. 69th St.; phone: 688-1660) is the French master of extraordinary table and bed linen, many in magnificent floral prints; *L'eron* (750 Madison Ave.; phone: 753-6700) imports exquisite bed and table linen and lingerie. *Pratesi* (829 Madison Ave.; phone: 288-2315) and *Frette* (799 Madison Ave.; phone: 988-5221) offer a wide selection of the finest bed, bath, and table linen manufactured at the companies' factories in Italy. *ABC Carpet & Home* (888 Broadway; phone: 473-3000) is stocked with hundreds of down comforters, blankets, pillows, tablecloths and napkins, and sheets and pillowcases from the most prestigious domestic and European houses; the six-floor emporium, which underwent expansion in 1993, also sells a large selection of rugs, furniture and home textiles and accessories. In the Wall Street vicinity, *Century 21* (22 Cortland St.; phone: 227-9092), which is better known for clothing, has a large collection of discounted linen.

BOOKSTORES The publishing capital of the world, New York is a bibliophile's delight. *Barnes & Noble* (105 Fifth Ave.; phone: 807-0099; 675 Ave. of the Americas; phone: 727-1227; 600 Fifth Ave.; phone: 765-0590; 2289 Broadway; phone: 362-8835; 1280 Lexington Ave.; phone: 423-9900; and various other sites throughout Manhattan and the boroughs) carries wide selections, some at discounted prices. Many of these are now "superstores" and offer *Starbucks Cafés* as you sip and read. *B. Dalton* (666 Fifth Ave.; phone: 247-1740; and 396 Ave. of the Americas; phone: 674-8780) and *Doubleday* (724 Fifth Ave.; phone: 397-0550) carry a broad variety of new titles and trade books, as does *Coliseum Books* (1771 Broadway; phone:

757-8381). The *Strand* (828 Broadway; phone: 473-1452) has eight miles of old and used books and even some rare manuscripts. *Rizzoli* (31 W. 57th St.; phone: 759-2424; 454 West Broadway; phone: 674-1616; and in the *Winter Garden* of the *World Financial Center* at 200 Vesey St.; phone: 385-1400) is best known for its collection of art, music, and photography books. *Kitchen Arts & Letters* (1435 Lexington Ave.; phone: 876-5550) is a bookstore and gallery devoted exclusively to food and wine. *Forbidden Planet* (821 Broadway; phone: 473-1576) has the wackiest bunch of comics, science fiction books, masks, and monsters you're liable to find this side of Mars. The *New York Astrology Center* (350 Lexington Ave.; phone: 947-3603) claims to have the country's largest selection of books on astrology. The *Complete Traveller Bookstore* (199 Madison Ave.; phone: 685-9007) and the *Traveller's Bookstore* (22 W. 52nd St., in *Rockefeller Center;* phone: 664-0995) have enviable troves of travel guides and books. Architecture buffs should head to *Perimeter* (146 Sullivan St.; phone: 529-2275), and bookish toddlers will be delighted by *Books of Wonder* (132 Seventh Ave.; phone: 989-3270).

BOUTIQUES AND SPECIALTY SHOPS Fifth Avenue in the 50s, the adjacent blocks east (especially East 57th Street), and Madison Avenue in the East 60s and 70s are lined with boutiques that carry haute couture at haute prices, but looking is free. The names are an encyclopedia of style: *Armani, Chanel, Daniel Hechter, Emmanuel Ungaro, Gucci, Liz Claiborne, Max Mara, Saint Laurent, Sonia Rykiel, Valentino, Versace,* and the like. Also on the cutting edge of fashion are the styles at *Charivari* (257 W. 72nd St.; phone: 787-7272; and two other locations around town). For the finest in rainwear and traditional British tailoring, there's *Burberrys* (9 E. 57th St.; phone: 371-5010) and *Aquascutum of London* (680 Fifth Ave.; phone: 975-0250). *Ashanti* (872 Lexington Ave.; phone: 535-0740) specializes in stylish clothes for fuller-figured women. *Polo/Ralph Lauren* (867 Madison Ave.; phone: 606-2100), in the 19th-century *Rhinelander Mansion,* is a showcase for the designer's men's, women's, and boys' collections; across the street is *Polo Sport* (888 Madison Ave.; phone: 434-8000). *Fendi* (720 Fifth Ave.; phone: 767-0100) features exclusive leather goods and clothes.

CDS, TAPES, AND RECORDS There are a number of places where you can get good prices. *Tower Records* (692 Broadway; phone: 505-1500; 2107 Broadway; phone: 799-2500; 725 Fifth Ave.; phone: 838-8110; 1535 Third Ave.; phone: 369-2500) has enormous and varied music stores open until midnight every day of the year. *J&R Music World* (33 Park Row, near *City Hall;* phone: 238-9000) has the best selection of new and hard-to-find jazz records at good prices. The *House of Oldies* (35 Carmine St.; phone: 243-0500) specializes in records from the past; the *Gryphon Record Shop* (251 W. 72nd St.; phone: 874-1588) has 60,000 out of print recordings. *HMV* (1280 Lexington Ave.; phone: 348-0800; and 2081 Broadway; phone: 721-5900), another gigantic music retailer, has an extensive selection of jazz, blues, gospel, rock, pop,

New Age, and new and vintage Broadway show music. Opened last year is the *Virgin Megastore* (1540 Broadway; phone: 921-1020) with its multileveled selections of CDs, books, and videos of every type and description. For sheet music try the *Music Exchange* (39th and Broadway; phone: 265-2050) or the *Joseph Patelson Music House* (160 W. 56th St.; phone: 582-5840).

CHINA, CRYSTAL, AND PORCELAIN The retail branch of *Villeroy & Boch* (974 Madison Ave.; phone: 535-2500) carries a full line of elegant tableware. *Royal Copenhagen* (683 Madison Ave.; phone: 759-6457) has all that's best in contemporary Danish crystal and porcelain. *Michael C. Fina* (3 W. 47th St.; phone: 869-5050), suitably located in the diamond district, carries a wide selection of the top names in china, crystal, and silver at reasonable prices. For splendid glass sculpture, bowls, and goblets, head for *Steuben Glass* (717 Fifth Ave.; phone: 752-1441).

DEPARTMENT STORES *Bloomingdale's* (Lexington Ave. from E. 59th to E. 60th St.; phone: 355-5900 or 705-2000), a world unto itself known affectionately to New Yorkers as *"Bloomie's,"* is considered by many to be the ultimate in Upper East Side chic. *Macy's* (Broadway from W. 34th to W. 35th St.; phone: 695-4400) is the largest New York department store, where you can choose from a huge assortment of high-quality goods. *Macy's* basement emporium, *The Cellar,* is designed as a street of shops carrying everything from fruits and vegetables to housewares, plus restaurants, including the *Cellar Grill,* which serves pizza, pasta, and grilled meat. *Lord & Taylor* (Fifth Ave. from W. 38th to W. 39th St.; phone: 391-3344) has stylish, if conservative, clothing and a bright, airy atmosphere that makes browsing enjoyable. *Saks Fifth Avenue* (Fifth Ave. from E. 49th to E. 50th St.; phone: 753-4000) is where you can be sure to get whatever is fashionable this season. *Bergdorf Goodman* (Fifth Ave. and W. 58th St.) is the epitome of elegant shopping for women; *Bergdorf Goodman Men* is directly across the street (phone: 753-7300 for both). *Henri Bendel* (Fifth Ave. and W. 56th St.; phone: 247-1100) carries an impressively stylish yet often whimsical selection of women's clothes, accessories, and miscellany.

Forward-looking *Barneys New York* is a major fashion player, and the flagship Seventh Avenue store's arty *Christmas* windows are a big draw (106 Seventh Ave.; phone: 593-7800; 225 Liberty St., in the *World Financial Center;* phone: 945-1600; and 660 Madison Ave.; phone: 826-8900). *Century 21* (22 Cortland St.; phone: 227-9092) features three floors of top-quality merchandise at discounted prices. And *Filene's Basement* (Sixth Ave. at W. 18th St.; phone: 620-3100; and W. 79th St. and Broadway; phone: 873-8000), offshoots of the original in Boston, features quality fashions at good discounts.

FABRICS AND TRIMMINGS Fabulous silks, imported woolens, and dazzling cotton prints for home decorating or homemade haute couture are available, often at greatly discounted prices, at a number of fascinating and abundant fabric emporiums. *Silk Surplus* (235 E. 58th St.; phone: 735-6511; also E. 19th St. and Broadway; phone: 505-0794); carries closeouts from their parent company, Scalamandre. While discounts generally are only about 15%, better bargains can be had during June and October sales. *Paron*'s (60 W. 57th St.; 247-6451) specializes in discounted designer woolens, cottons, silks, and linen. Even better prices—up to 50% off—can be found on the second floor next door at *Paron* 's super-discount store (56 W. 57th St.; phone: 247-6451). On the Lower East Side, *Interiors by Royale* (289 Grand St.; phone: 431-0170) features fine English linen, tapestries, and cotton prints imported from Italy, Spain, and France at discounts of up to 50%. And to add just the right finishing touch, visit *Tender Buttons* (143 E. 62nd St.; phone: 758-7004). The selection of antique and contemporary buttons here is extraordinary, if pricey. For less costly trim, there are dazzling displays at *G & P Buttons and Novelties* (247 W. 37th St.; phone: 719-5333).

FOOD In a city where one can dine out every night of the year at a different ethnic restaurant, it isn't surprising that delicacies and exotic foodstuffs are staples in a host of upscale grocery shops. Whether you're looking for a little something for a picnic, a snack for back at the hotel, a gift for your host, hostess, or the folks back home, or you merely want to take in a dazzling display of way-beyond-average comestibles, a visit to one of the following shops can be a most memorable part of your trip to New York. *Zabar's* (2245 Broadway; phone: 787-2000) is a Manhattan institution—a huge, noisy emporium with a mock-Tudor exterior where thousands of New Yorkers and suburbanites stock up each day on pastrami, lox, fresh-roasted coffee beans, bread, pungent cheeses, luscious dried fruit, unusual condiments, and the very latest imported delicacies. *Balducci's* (424 Ave. of the Americas; phone: 673-2600) and the flagship of *Dean & Deluca* (560 Broadway; phone: 431-1691) offer pricier fresh fruits and vegetables, plus wonderful imported foods and spices, fresh pasta, and great bread. Worth a visit on the Upper East Side are *Grace's Marketplace* (1237 Third Ave.; phone: 737-0600), for phenomenally fresh produce, imported coffees, spices, jams, and preserves, and *Fraser Morris Fine Foods* (1264 Third Ave.; phone: 288-2727), which features items such as fresh caviar, salmon, and imported chocolates and pastries.

JEWELRY AND GEMS Diamonds are a girl's best friend, but so as not to limit ourselves, we'll include emeralds, rubies, sapphires, pearls, gold, silver, and other precious stones and metals. And so as not to discriminate, we'll include men too. Without a doubt, the most famous of all luxury emporiums is *Tiffany & Co.* (727 Fifth Ave.; phone: 755-8000). If you must have something from *Tiffany's* but can't afford a necklace or ring, purchase a novelty like a sterling silver key ring, bookmark, or toothpaste roller. Across the street, *Bulgari* dazzles in its prestigious corner boutique (730 Fifth Ave.; phone: 315-9000). *Cartier* (653 Fifth Ave.; phone: 753-0111; and in *Trump Tower,* 725 Fifth Ave. at E. 56th St.; phone: 308-0840) is renowned for some of the world's finest jewelry and accessories. *Fortunoff* (681 Fifth Ave.; phone: 758-6660) has a more moderately priced selection of fine gems, sterling, and gold. *Fred Leighton* (773 Madison Ave.; phone: 288-1872) is known for its exquisite antique and Art Deco designs. For pearls of quality in quantity, try *Mikimoto* (730 Fifth Ave.; phone: 586-7153). For watches, go to *Tourneau Corner* (500 Madison Ave.; phone: 758-6098; Madison Ave. and E. 59th St.; phone: 758-6688; and 34th St. and 7th Ave.; phone: 563-6880).

If your budget is limited, do your gem shopping along West 47th Street (the street sign here reads: "Diamond and Jewelry Way") between Fifth and Sixth Avenues. This is the heart of New York's wholesale jewelry district, whose vendors are largely Hasidic Jews of European background, and the best place to find sparkling stuff at mortal prices. If you're planning to get married (or even reaffirm your vows), *1873 Unusual Wedding Bands* (Booth 86 at the *National Jewelery Exchange,* 4 W. 47th St.; phone: 221-1873) is a good place to stop; it has the largest selection of wedding rings in the city.

KITCHEN EQUIPMENT At the *Bridge Co.* (214 E. 52nd St.; phone: 688-4220), you'll find every possible domestic and imported item, from cherry pitters to copper fish poachers, on display on four floors. The *Broadway Panhandler* (477 Broome; phone: 966-3434) has an enormous selection of cookware at affordable prices. *Williams-Sonoma* (110 Seventh Ave.; phone: 633-2203; 20 E. 60th St.; phone: 980-5155; and 1175 Madison Ave.; phone: 289-6832), of catalogue fame, carries first-rate cookware, and master chefs often do demonstrations on the premises. *Zabar's* (see *Food,* above) has a second floor stocked with a huge selection of kitchenware at competitive prices. In the Bowery, New York's kitchenware and lamp district, you'll find stores selling commercial products at reasonable prices.

LEATHER GOODS AND LUGGAGE You'll have no trouble finding a wide selection of both high- and low-priced leather goods and luggage in New York. *Hermès* (11 E. 57th St.; phone: 751-3181) is headquartered in Paris but known the world over for spectacular silk scarves and ties, as well as saddles and other fine leather goods in a variety of exotic skins, all at heart-stopping prices. *Prada Milan* (45 E. 57th St.; phone: 308-2332) has perhaps the best-quality leather goods and shoes from Italy. *Louis Vuitton* (49 E. 57th St.; phone: 371-6111) has a large selection of leather goods, many sporting the famous "LV" logo. If you prefer interlocking "G"s, visit *Gucci* (685 Fifth Ave.; phone: 826-2600). For elegant, high-quality merchandise that's only slightly less costly, try *Crouch & Fitzgerald* (400 Madison Ave.; phone: 755-5888) or *Mark Cross* (645 Fifth Ave.; phone: 421-3000). Along less expensive lines, you will run into several leather goods and luggage stores during your strolls around the West Side, such as the *Westside Luggage Shop* (955 Eighth Ave.; phone: 757-3880) and *Rio Trading* (10 W. 46th St.; phone: 819-0304). The Lower East Side has countless stores offering suitcases at substantial savings, including *Altman Luggage* (135 Orchard St.; phone: 254-7275).

MALLS Indoor urban malls are a relatively recent phenomenon in New York City; they arrived a decade ago with the glitzy *Trump Tower* (725 Fifth Ave.). The vendors in the tower's six-story marble and mirrored atrium are among the world's most opulent (and most expensive): *Abercrombie & Fitch* (men's and women's sportswear and sporting goods); *Kenneth Jay Lane* (high-end costume jewelry); *Ferragamo* (top-quality Italian footwear; also see *Shoes,* below); *Asprey* (one of London's premier jewelers and silversmiths); *Buccellati* (silversmith); *Charles Jourdan* (men's and women's shoes); and *Harry Winston* (diamond jewelry; the main shop is at Fifth Ave. and W. 56th St.).

Close to *Macy's* is *Manhattan Mall* (Ave. of the Americas from W. 32nd to W. 33rd St.; phone: 465-0500), a multilevel complex of specialty shops including *Ann Taylor* and *Oak Tree* (for menswear), and anchored by *Stern's* department store. In lower Manhattan, the *South Street Seaport, World Financial Center,* and *World Trade Center* are a shopper's magnet.

MENSWEAR Manhattan has fashions to fit every man's taste, from the astronomically glitzy at *Bijan* (by appointment only; 699 Fifth Ave.; phone: 758-7500) to westernwear at *Billy Martin* (812 Madison Ave.; phone: 861-3100). *Brooks Brothers* (346 Madison Ave.; phone: 682-8800; and 1 Liberty Plaza, downtown; phone: 267-2400); *Paul Stuart* (Madison Ave. and 45th St.; phone: 682-0320); and *F. R. Tripler* (555 Fifth Ave.; phone: 922-1090) all offer expensive, high-quality, conservative business suits and classic furnishings. *St. Laurie* (895 Broadway; phone: 473-0100) carries similar merchandise with slightly lower price tags. *Barneys New York* (106 Seventh Ave.; phone: 593-7000; 225 Liberty St., in the *World Financial Center;* phone: 945-1600; and 660 Madison Ave.; phone: 826-8900) has an eclectic array of goods but includes top-drawer suits from the world's foremost designers. For Italian *alta moda* in SoHo, try *Di Mitri* (110 Greene St.; phone: 431-1090). *Beau Brummel* (421 W. Broadway; phone: 219-2666) has everything for the fashion-conscious man. *Syms* (42 Trinity Pl.; phone: 797-1199) stocks fine discounted menswear on five floors. *Bergdorf Goodman Men* is a bastion of male chic (745 Fifth Ave.; phone: 753-7300). To top it all off, visit *Worth & Worth* (331 Madison Ave.; phone: 867-6058) for a large selection of hats.

MUSEUM GIFT SHOPS New York's outstanding art and cultural institutions often have equally fine shops stocked with items related to or inspired by their collections. Among the best are those at the *Fraunces Tavern Museum,* with books, reproductions of historic documents, and postcards; the *American Museum of Natural History,* with crafts and jewelry from North America, South America, and Asia, model dinosaurs, and prints of pre-Columbian art; and the *Solomon R. Guggenheim Museum,* with textiles, jewelry, posters, and toys. The *Metropolitan Museum of Art* has two large stores that sell fine-arts prints, jewelry, calendars, stationery, toys, and books, and there is also a more central branch in *Rockefeller Center* (15 W. 49th St.; phone: 332-1360). In addition to the bookstore (with books, posters, stationery, and other smaller gift items) in the *Museum of Modern Art,* there is the *MOMA Design Store* across the street (44 W. 53rd St.; phone: 767-1050), stocked with a large selection of contemporary home and office furnishings and jewelry. The gift shop next door to the *Whitney Museum of American Art* (943 Madison Ave.; phone: 606-0200) purveys toys, jewelry, crafts, and furniture. (See *Special Places* and *Museums* for all addresses and phone numbers not listed above.)

POSTER AND PRINT SHOPS *The Old Print Shop* (150 Lexington Ave.; phone: 683-3950) has a huge collection of early American prints, watercolors, and paintings ranging in price from $10 to $20,000. For contemporary theater posters and some collector's items, try the *Triton Gallery* (323 W. 45th St.; phone: 765-2472). Rare advertising and European movie posters are available at *Poster America* (138 W. 18th St.; phone: 206-0499). The *Gallery at Lincoln Center* (136 W. 65th St.; phone: 580-4673) has the largest collection of limited-edition paintings and photographs celebrating the performing arts—dance, theater, and opera—plus original silk-screen posters.

SHOES All of the top Italian designers of both men's and women's footwear are represented: *Gucci* (685 Fifth Ave.; phone: 826-2600); *Fratelli Rossetti* (601 Madison Ave.; phone: 888-5107); *Tanino Crisci* (795 Madison Ave.; phone: 535-1014); *Ferragamo* (*Trump Tower,* 725 Fifth Ave.; phone: 759-3822); *Bruno Magli* (for men only, 677 Fifth Ave.; phone: 752-7900). Fine European shoes also can be found at *Bally of Switzerland* (Madison Ave. and 59th St.; phone: 751-9082). For well-made men's boots and shoes, stop at *McCreedy & Schreiber* (37 W. 46th St.; phone: 719-1552; and 213 E. 59th St.; phone: 759-9241). *Susan Bennis/Warren Edwards* (22 W. 57th St.; phone: 755-4197) designs outré American shoes.

SPECIAL SHOPPING DISTRICTS—FOR LESS The ultimate shopping experience is on the Lower East Side of Manhattan along Orchard Street, Delancey Street, and all the side streets. If you're up to it, you'll find incredible bargains in all manner of clothing and housewares; but finding them is only half the battle. Then you have to fight for them, and the haggling begins. The merchant says something along the lines of, "I couldn't give you this for a penny less than $12," to which you respond that it's not worth more than 50¢, and usually you come to terms—apparently unsatisfactory to both of you. A lot of the selling is done in a mixture of Yiddish, English, Russian, and Spanish—particularly the counting—and if you know any or all four, you'll do better than wholesale. Most stores are closed Saturdays, open Sundays; they also close early on Fridays and Jewish holidays.

Quintessential basics and classic clothes made of sumptuous fabrics frequently find their way down to Orchard Street. Unpretentious and impossibly noisy, the little shops that line this street proffer fine items of clothing that in other spots are staggeringly expensive. Casual fashion and a wide range of eveningwear are available at *Forman's,* which has three separate shops, for petite, regular, and larger women's sizes (78, 82, and 94 Orchard St., respectively; phone: 228-2500 for all three locations). *Shulie's* (175 Orchard St.; phone: 473-2480) sells Tahari designs at impressive discounts, and *Fine and Klein* (119 Orchard St.; phone: 674-6720) carries an immense selection of handbags by top designers. See *Special Places* for more on the Lower East Side.

SPORTING GOODS The most elegant sporting goods store is *Abercrombie & Fitch* (*South Street Seaport;* phone: 809-9000; and *Trump Tower,* 725 Fifth Ave.; phone: 832-1001). *Paragon* (867 Broadway; phone: 255-8036) is New York's premier sporting goods store. Serious joggers should stop in at the *Super Runners Shop* (416 Third Ave.; phone: 213-4560; and three other locations); tennis players will find good buys at *Mason's Tennis Mart* (911 Seventh Ave.; phone: 757-5374). *Gerry Cosby's* (3 Penn Plaza, above *Penn Station;* phone: 563-6464) outfits professional teams and offers top-of-the-line sporting goods and souvenirs. *Orvis* (355 Madison Ave.; phone: 697-3133) has fishing and hunting gear.

THRIFT SHOPS AND RETRO FASHION Most thrift shops carry a variety of merchandise, from men's and women's clothing to household items and appliances to battered furniture. And unfortunately, many of the secondhand clothes stores in New York carry the price tags of conventional antiques stores. The best area for thrifting in New York is the East 80s along First, Second, and Third Avenues. Two interesting places to try are the *Stuyvesant Square Thrift Shop* (1704 Second Ave.; phone: 831-1830) and *Spence-Chapin Thrift Shop* (1430 Third Ave.; phone: 737-8448). Downtown the clothes get wilder and the prices lower. Go to the *Antique Boutique* (712-714 Broadway; phone: 460-8830) for secondhand clothing from the 1920s through the 1960s. *Alice Underground*'s two shops (380 Columbus Ave.; phone: 724-6682; and 481 Broadway; phone: 431-9067) are other highly affordable havens for a changing collection of casual and dressier clothes. Hats and linen goods are sold as well in the uptown branch.

TOYS, ETC. Once immersed in the enchanting world of toys and stuffed animals at *FAO Schwarz* (GM Bldg., 767 Fifth Ave.; phone: 644-9400), adults have as difficult a time as children leaving empty-handed. It has every kind of plaything—from precious antiques and mechanical spaceships to simple construction sets and building blocks—but some items are very expensive. *Penny Whistle Toys* (448 Columbus Ave.; phone: 873-9090; and 1283 Madison Ave.; phone: 369-3868) offers everything from puppets and bubble machines to wooden blocks and educational toys. The *Enchanted Forest* (85 Mercer; phone: 925-6677) stocks fine toys and craft kits.

Along Fifth Avenue, you'll find the newly opened *Disney Store* (711 Fifth Ave.; phone: 702-0702), where Mickey reigns along with his cartoon character friends. Here you'll find classic Disney videos, T-shirts, watches, all manner of memorabilia, and plenty of stuffed toys. Nearby are two other giants: the *Warner Bros. Studio Store* (1 E. 57th St.; phone: 754-0300) where Bugs Bunny, Daffy Duck, Sylvester the Cat and Tweety, and the Tasmanian Devil take center stage and everything from denim jackets, key chains, mugs, and other novelties bear their images, and the *Coca-Cola* store (711 Fifth Ave.; phone: 418-9260), where you may recapture memories of old-fashioned glass soda bottles, *Christmas* tree ornaments fashioned with a jolly old fellow, and, of course, plenty of T-shirts and the like sporting your favorite cola.

UNIQUELY NEW YORK Probably nowhere else on earth can you find everything from earplugs to fine silver under one roof. *Hammacher Schlemmer* (147 E. 57th St.; phone: 421-9000), the first store to offer the pop-up toaster and microwave oven, has it all. And what it doesn't have, it will try to order.

47th St. Photo is a center for cameras, computers, and other electronic gear with excellent discounts and a huge selection (some 5,000 items in stock). The tiny headquarters (115 W. 45th St.; phone: 398-1530), no longer actually housed on 47th Street, tends to be packed with customers and consequently chaotic. Know what you want before you go, because the brusque manner of the salesmen doesn't lend itself to extended dialogue; however, when they do answer a question, they know what they're talking about. Closed Friday afternoons and Saturdays.

Finally, travel 'round the world in a unique way via a trip to the *United Nations Gift Shop* (*UN Bldg.,* First Ave. and E. 46th St.; phone: 963-7702), featuring handicrafts, ethnic clothing, native jewelry, indigenous toys—lots of beautiful things from the member countries.

SPORTS AND FITNESS

New York is a sports-minded city, offering a great variety of spectator and participatory activities. It is the home of the *Yankees, Mets, Knicks,* and *Rangers.* The *Jets, Giants, Nets,* and *Devils* play about six miles from Manhattan in New Jersey, and the *Islanders* in suburban Nassau County on Long Island. There are racetracks, tennis and basketball courts, bridle and bike paths, pool halls, bowling alleys, skating rinks, running tracks, and swimming pools, to name but a few sporting spots.

BASEBALL The season, April through early October, features the *Mets (National League)* at *Shea Stadium* (Flushing, Queens; phone: 718-507-8499), and the *Yankees (American League)* at *Yankee Stadium* (the Bronx; phone: 718-293-6000). Take the *IRT* Flushing line (No. 7 train) to the Willets Point/Shea Stadium stop to the *Mets;* the *IRT* Lexington Ave. line (No. 4 train) or the *IND* line (C or D train) to the 161st St. stop for the *Yankees.* Tickets can be ordered through *TicketMaster* for *Yankees* games only (phone: 307-7171).

BASKETBALL The *NBA Knicks* play at *Madison Square Garden* (Seventh Ave. and W. 32rd St.; phone: 465-6741); and the *Nets* at the *Continental Airlines*

Arena in the *Meadowlands Sports Complex* in East Rutherford, New Jersey (phone: 201-935-8888), during the regular season from early November to late April. You can order *Nets* tickets through *Ticketmaster* (phone: 307-7171). Buses to the *Meadowlands* leave from the *Port Authority Bus Terminal* (Eighth Ave. and W. 42nd St.; phone: 564-8484 or 564-1114 for ticket and schedule information).

BICYCLING There are over 50 miles of bike paths in the city, with *Central Park* in Manhattan and *Prospect Park* in Brooklyn the two most popular areas. Most roadways within the parks are closed to auto traffic from April through October, except during rush hours on weekdays; they are closed on weekends and holidays year-round. Bikes can be rented in the parks or on nearby side streets, although it's usually less expensive to rent a two-wheeler at one of the many cycling shops around the city. Check the yellow pages for the names of dealers convenient to you. More serious bikers should contact *Transportation Alternatives* (phone: 475-4600) for information on noncompetitive charity events such as bike-a-thons and weekend bicycling tours. For information on competitive cycling events and road races, call Richard Bothwell at the *Toga Bike Shop* (110 West End Ave.; phone: 799-9625).

BILLIARDS Increasingly popular with New Yorkers, pool halls are plentiful throughout the city. Consult the yellow pages (look under "Billiards") for the nearest location.

BOXING Major bouts are still fought at *Madison Square Garden* (see *Basketball,* above), and the *Daily News* continues to sponsor the *Golden Gloves* competition every winter (phone: 210-1952).

FITNESS CENTERS The *Poly Gym* (428 E. 75th St.; phone: 628-6969) offers one-on-one personal training 24 hours a day, seven days a week. *One On One* (31 W. 21st St.; phone: 627-3309) will conduct training sessions at their studio or in your hotel room. Open 24 hours except on Sundays (when it's open from 8 AM to 10 PM) is the *World Gym*'s main location at *Lincoln Center* (1926 Broadway; phone: 874-0942). For information on the various *Y*s around the city, call 308-2899; 755-2410 after 5 PM. New to the fitness scene is *Chelsea Piers Sports Center* (Hudson River and W. 23rd St.; phone: 995-7660). This complex features the world's longest six-lane indoor running track, the largest rock climbing wall in the Northeast, plus 20,000-square feet of exercise machines including cardiovascular, circuit, and freeweight training equipment.

FOOTBALL During the September–December season, the *Jets* and the *Giants* play at *Giants Stadium* in the *Meadowlands Sports Complex* (see *Basketball,* above). Tickets to *NFL* games are hard to get due to the great number of season subscribers. For *Giants* ticket information, call 201-935-8222; for *Jets* tickets, call 516-538-6600. *Columbia University* leads the local collegiate football scene; games are played at *Baker Field* (Broadway and W. 218th St.; phone: 567-0404).

GOLF While there are no public courses in Manhattan, golf enthusiasts can visit the city's outlying boroughs for an invigorating round—there are 13 courses in municipal parks operated by private concessionaires. Tee times and course information can be obtained by calling 718-225-GOLF. For all-weather golfing, *The Golf Club* at the new *Chelsea Piers* (Hudson River and W. 23rd St.; phone: 995-7660) offers a 200-yard fairway.

HOCKEY Tickets are expensive and scarce during the early October to early April season, with the *Islanders* at the *Nassau Coliseum* on Long Island (phone: 516-794-4100), the 1994 *NHL Stanley Cup* Champion *Rangers* at *Madison Square Garden,* and *New Jersey Devils* at the *Continental Airlines Arena* (see *Basketball,* above, for the latter two).

HORSEBACK RIDING Horses can be rented and boarded at the *Claremont Riding Academy* (175 W. 89th St.; phone: 724-5100), close to *Central Park,* where there are about 6 miles of bridle paths.

ICE SKATING You can show off your figure eights from October through April at the famous *Rockefeller Center* rink (phone: 332-7654; from November through March at the *Wollman Rink* in *Central Park* (E. 62nd St.; phone: 396-1010; and from mid-November through February at the *Lasker Rink,* also in *Central Park* (E. 110th St.; phone: 986-1184). The small *Rivergate Ice Rink* (401 E. 34th St. at First Ave.; phone: 689-0035) is open from November through March. Indoor skating year-round is possible at the Olympic-size *Sky Rink* (*Chelsea Piers,* Hudson River and W. 23rd St.; phone: 336-6100).

JOGGING This is undoubtedly the most popular sport in New York, with enthusiastic runners in all the city parks: on the paths at *Riverside Park* (near W. 97th St.); around the *Central Park* reservoir (from 86th to 95th St.); and along the East River promenade (from E. 84th to E. 90th St.). It is recommended that you not run in *any* of these places after dark. The *New York Road Runners Club* (9 E. 89th St.; phone: 860-4455) offers guided runs on weekdays at 6:30 and 7:15 PM from their office and on Saturdays at 10 AM from Fifth Avenue and E. 90th Street; they take scenic routes, including a lap around the *Central Park* reservoir.

ROLLER/IN-LINE SKATING *Central Park* on spring and summer weekends is one huge skating/blading heaven. Rentals are available year-round from *Peck & Goodie* (917 Eighth Ave. between W. 54th and W. 55th Sts.; phone: 246-6123); *Blades West* (120 W. 72nd St.; phone: 787-3911); and *Blades East* (160 E. 86th St.; phone: 996-1644). Don't skate in the park after dark.

SWIMMING Several dozen indoor and outdoor pools are operated throughout the five boroughs by the *Parks Department.* Indoor pools are open most of the year, except Sundays and holidays, usually until 10 PM on weekdays. Call the *Parks Department*'s public information office (phone: 360-8141) for particulars. For information on the pools at the *Y*s, call 308-2899; 755-2410 after 5 PM.

Ocean swimming is a subway or bus ride away. Beaches within the city and maintained by it are Orchard Beach in the Bronx; Coney Island Beach and Manhattan Beach in Brooklyn; and *Riis Park* and Far Rockaway in Queens. *Jones Beach State Park* (Wantagh, Long Island, 30 miles east of the city) is Long Island's most popular public beach. It is a well-maintained, enormous stretch of sand offering surf bathing, swimming and wading pools, lockers, fishing, paddleball, swimming instruction, restaurants, and day and evening entertainment. It can be reached via the *Long Island Rail Road* from *Penn Station* (Seventh Ave. and W. 32nd St.; phone: 718-217-5477) and a connecting bus (the JB62 during the week and the JB24 on weekends; both run from *Memorial Day* through *Labor Day*). A note of advice: On summer weekends, despite its large size, Jones Beach can be crowded as early as 10 AM.

TENNIS Courts maintained by the *Parks Department* require a season permit. Municipal facilities include 26 clay courts in *Central Park* (phone: 360-8131), 10 red-clay courts in *Riverside Park* (no phone), and seven clay and four hard-surface courts on Randall's Island (phone: 534-4845). In the Bronx there are 10 hard-surface courts at *Rice Stadium* in *Pelham Bay Park,* and eight clay and four all-weather courts in *Van Cortlandt Park* (phone: 718-430-1838 or 718-430-1890 for both). In Queens the *USTA National Tennis Center* in *Flushing Meadows Park* (phone: 718-760-6200), home of the *US Open,* has 26 outdoor and nine indoor courts. One of the larger privately owned clubs that will rent by the hour is the *Midtown Tennis Club* (341 Eighth Ave. at W. 27th St.; phone: 989-8572). Check the yellow pages for other locations.

THEATER

New York attracts the best and most accomplished talents in the world. However, there are devoted New York theatergoers who wouldn't dream of stepping inside a Broadway theater. They prefer instead the city's prolific off-Broadway and off-off-Broadway circuit, whose productions are less high-powered and often just as professional as the splashiest shows on Broadway.

Broadway signifies an area—between West 42nd and West 53rd Streets both east and west and on Broadway—and a kind of production that strives to be the smash hit of the season and run forever. The glitter of the area has tarnished a bit since the halcyon days of the Great White Way, but hopes are that a general reconstruction and renovation of West 42nd Street and the entire Times Square area will turn things around. In any case, the productions are getting more stellar (and pricier) than ever.

Off-Broadway and off-off-Broadway signify types of theater, in playhouses strewn from Greenwich Village to the Upper West Side. Off-Broadway productions are usually smaller in scale, with newer, lesser-known talent, than those on Broadway, and are likely to feature revivals of classics or more daring works. Off-off-Broadway is more experimental still:

truly avant-garde productions in coffeehouses, lofts, or any appropriate makeshift arena. Off-Broadway tickets rarely cost as much as those for a Broadway show, while the cost of a seat for an off-off Broadway production is considerably less.

Take advantage of all three during a visit. The excitement of a Broadway show is incomparable, but the thrill of finding a tiny theater in SoHo or the West Village in which you are almost nose to nose with the actors is unforgettable. Planning your theater schedule is as easy as consulting any of the daily papers (they all list theaters and current offerings daily, with comprehensive listings on Fridays or Saturdays), the "Goings On About Town" section in *The New Yorker*, "Cue" section in *New York* magazine, or "Theater" in *TimeOut New York.*

Broadway tickets can be quite expensive (they average $30 to $65, with an occasional musical costing as much as $100, depending on seat and performance), but with a little patience, you can find cheaper tickets. The *TKTS* booths (Broadway and W. 47th St. in Times Square and in *2 World Trade Center* in lower Manhattan; phone: 768-1818) sell orchestra seats at half price, plus a service charge of $2.50 per ticket, for a wide range of Broadway and off-Broadway productions; tickets are sold only for the same day's performance. You must line up—there are no reservations—and payment must be made in cash or traveler's checks. *TKTS* booths are open as follows: On Broadway, sales for Monday through Saturday evening performances are from 3 to 8 PM; for Wednesday and Saturday matinees from 10 AM to 2 PM; for Sunday matinees and evening performances from noon to 8 PM. At *2 World Trade Center* the booth is open weekdays from 11 AM to 5:30 PM and Saturdays from 11 AM to 3:30 PM; tickets for Wednesday, Saturday, and Sunday matinees are available the day *before* the performance. The *Broadway Show Line* (phone: 563-BWAY), sponsored by the *League of American Theaters and Producers,* gives recorded synopses and short reviews of Broadway and off-Broadway plays as well as ticket prices and schedules.

THEATER COMPANIES One of New York's newer repertory companies is the *National Actors Theatre,* founded by actor Tony Randall, which presents revivals of classic plays, often featuring well-known artists, at the *Lyceum Theatre* (149 W. 45th St.; phone: 239-6280 for tickets). Others include the *Classic Stage Company (CSC),* which stages intriguing productions of classics of all centuries (136 E. 13th St.; phone: 677-4210); *Circle Rep* (159 Bleecker St.; phone: 254-6330); *Hudson Guild Theater* (441 W. 26th St.; phone: 760-9800); *INTAR Theater* (420 W. 42nd St.; phone: 695-6134); *Irish Arts Center* (553 W. 51st St.; phone: 757-3318); *Jean Cocteau Repertory* (330 Bowery; phone: 677-0060); *Variety Arts Theater* (Third Ave. and 13th St.; phone: 239-6200); *La Mama ETC* (74A E. Fourth St.; phone: 475-7710); *Manhattan Theatre Club* (*City Center,* 131 W. 55th St.; phone: 581-1212); *National Black Theatre* (2033 Fifth Ave., Second Floor; phone: 722-3800); *Pan Asian*

Repertory (423 W. 46th St.; phone: 505-5655); *Playwrights Horizons Theater* (416 W. 42nd St.; phone: 279-4200); the *Joseph Papp Public Theater,* home of the *New York Shakespeare Festival* (425 Lafayette St.; phone: 539-8500); *Repertorio Español* (138 E. 27th St.; phone: 889-2850); *New Victory Theater* (209 W. 42nd St.; phone: 239-6200); *Roundabout* (1530 Broadway; phone: 869-8400); the *Vivian Beaumont Theater* and the *Mitzi E. Newhouse Theater,* both at *Lincoln Center* (phone: 239-6200); and the *Westside Arts Theater* (407 W. 43rd St.; phone: 307-4100). All can provide a schedule of offerings and performance dates. Alternatively, call the *Theatre Development Fund*'s hotline (phone: 221-0013 or 221-0885) or *New York* magazine's hotline, weekdays from 11 AM to 4 PM (phone: 880-0755).

TV SHOW TAPINGS

Although Los Angeles is more readily associated with the business of television, a large number of popular network and syndicated programs are headquartered in New York, and the public may attend tapings without charge. Although most tickets must be obtained in advance, many programs offer standby seats. The policy for obtaining advance and standby seats varies, and it is best to contact the show you want to see as far ahead of time as possible. Audience members must be 18 or older. For tickets to "Late Night with Conan O'Brien," and "Saturday Night Live," contact NBC (30 Rockefeller Plaza, New York, NY 10112; phone: 664-3056). Other shows taped in New York include "The Late Show with David Letterman" (Tickets, 1697 Broadway, New York, NY 10019; phone: 975-2476); "Geraldo" (CBS Television, 524 W. 57th St., New York, NY 10019; phone: 265-1283); "Live with Regis and Kathie Lee" (Tickets, PO Box 777, Ansonia Station, New York, NY 10023; phone: 456-3537); "The Rush Limbaugh Show" (Unitel Studios, 515 W. 57th St., New York, NY 10019; phone: 397-7367); and "Sally Jessy Raphael" (Tickets, PO Box 1400, Radio City Station, New York, NY 10101; phone: 582-1722). You also can take a tour of the NBC Studios at 30 Rockefeller Plaza; tours leave every 15 minutes throughout the day. For information, call 664-4000.

MUSIC AND DANCE

New York is a world center for performing artists. It presents the best of classical and nonclassical works from all over the world, in a variety of halls and auditoriums filled with appreciative, knowledgeable audiences.

Lincoln Center for the Performing Arts (Broadway and W. 65th St.; phone: 875-5400 for general information) represents the city's devotion to concerts, opera, and ballet. It consists of *Avery Fisher Hall,* home of the *New York Philharmonic* (phone: 875-5030); the *New York State Theater,* featuring the *New York City Ballet* and the *New York City Opera* (phone: 870-5570); the *Metropolitan Opera House* and the *American Ballet Theater* (phone: 362-6000); the *Guggenheim Bandshell* at *Damrosch Park,* an open-air theater used for free concerts in the summertime; the *Juilliard School* for musicians, actors, and dancers (phone: 799-5000); *Alice Tully Hall,* home of the *Chamber Music Society* (phone: 875-5050); and the *Vivian Beaumont* and *Mitzi E. Newhouse Theaters* (see above). In addition, all the auditoriums in *Lincoln Center* present other musical events and recitals. While visiting the city, don't miss the *New York Public Library for the Performing Arts,* a unique repository and museum (phone: 870-1630). Guided tours of *Lincoln Center* are available daily (phone: 875-5000).

Other major venues are *Carnegie Hall,* which celebrated its centennial in 1991 (Seventh Ave. and W. 57th St.; phone: 247-7800), and its *Weill Recital Hall* (phone: 247-7800); *City Center* (131 W. 55th St.; phone: 581-7909); the *Grace Rainey Rogers Auditorium* (in the *Metropolitan Museum,* Fifth Ave. and E. 82nd St.; phone: 570-3949); the *Kaufmann Auditorium* (at the *92nd St. Y,* Lexington Ave. and E. 92nd St.; phone: 996-1100); *Symphony Space* (2537 Broadway at W. 95th St.; phone: 864-5400); and the *Brooklyn Academy of Music* (30 Lafayette Ave., Brooklyn; phone: 718-636-4100). Also check music and dance listings in the newspapers, *New York* magazine, *The New Yorker,* and *TimeOut New York.*

The *TKTS* booth in Times Square, which sells discount theater tickets, has a counterpart on the West 42nd Street side of *Bryant Park* (behind the *New York Public Library,* just east of the Ave. of the Americas; phone: 382-2323) for those interested in buying half-price tickets to music and dance events on the day of the performance (very occasionally, they also have tickets for opera and operetta performed by smaller companies). The booth is open Tuesdays through Sundays from noon to 2 PM and 3 to 7 PM. Full-price tickets for future performances also are available here.

Many pop, rock, rhythm-and-blues, and country artists perform at *Madison Square Garden* (Seventh Ave. and W. 32nd St.; phone: 465-6741) and at several clubs around the city (see below). The *Nassau Coliseum* (Hempstead Tpke., Uniondale; phone: 516-794-9300) holds large concerts on Long Island. The downtown weekly, *The Village Voice,* plus *The New Yorker* and *New York* magazine offer good listings of current and upcoming events.

NIGHTCLUBS AND NIGHTLIFE

The scope of nightlife in New York is as vast as the scope of daily life. Cultural trends strongly affect the kinds of clubs that are "in" at any given time, and their popularity has a tendency to peak, then plunge rather quickly. Old jazz and neighborhood clubs, on the other hand, usually remain intact, catering to a regular clientele. They offer various kinds of entertainment, and many stay open until the wee hours of the morning, serving drinks and food. It's a good idea to call clubs in advance to find out when they are open and what performers or acts are appearing; or, consult the "Cue" section in *New York* magazine. Many of the city's nightclubs with live entertainment and/or dancing have cover charges of $10 and up; most accept major credit cards.

The current focus of the trendy crowd is on clubs that offer a kind of relaxed gentility. This sophisticated atmosphere may include the coveted (or cursed, as the case may be) velvet rope across the entrance, alluring interiors by top designers, elegant cocktails, and ultrachic denizens of the night. Located in the *Elysée* hotel (see *Checking In*) the *Monkey Bar* has become home to the young and beautiful. One of the swankiest places in town continues to be *Nell's* (246 W. 14th St.; phone: 675-1567), a nightclub immortalized by *People* magazine and as popular as ever. Among the city's favored nightspots is *Webster Hall* (125 E. 11th St.; phone: 353-1600), a multitiered dance hall with a lot of Art Deco touches, including antique furniture from local flea markets. Another multilevel club is *Le Bar Bat* (311 W. 57th St.; phone: 307-7228), where you can hear live blues Wednesdays through Saturdays. The quiet nights, Mondays and Tuesdays, have recorded music.

POP AND ROCK The Big Apple's top rock 'n' roll clubs generally feature lavish sound systems, videos, live bands, several bars, and lots of room for dancing. Try *Limelight* (47 W. 20th St.; phone: 807-7850), a late-night favorite for denizens of the downtown scene, and that dance palace *extraordinaire,* the *Palladium* (126 E. 14th St.; phone: 473-7171), with a cavernous interior that attracts an MTV-generation crowd, as does the hip and hot *Mercury Lounge* (217 E. Houston St.; phone: 260-4700). The punk-grunge *CBGB & OMFUG* (315 Bowery; phone: 982-4052) continues to give fringe groups their moment in the spotlight.

For the younger set, the ubiquitous *Hard Rock Café* (221 W. 57th St.; phone: 489-6565) is a monument to rock 'n' roll sporting all manner of memorabilia, a 45-foot guitar-shape bar, and a 1959 Cadillac jutting out from the second floor over the entrance. At *Planet Hollywood* (40 W. 57th St.; phone: 333-7827), owned (but not operated) by Arnold Schwarzenegger, Bruce Willis, Sylvester Stallone, and other Hollywood superstars, you can watch trailers for upcoming movies while you munch on burgers and pizza. Yet another theme entertaiment restaurant, *Motown Café* (104 W. 57th St.; phone: 581-8030), features a deejay, great oldies hits, and a menu featuring everything from burgers to shrimp creole. The more adventurous might opt for the *Tunnel* (220 12th Ave.; phone: 695-7292), a popular nightclub in Manhattan's seamy but exciting meat-packing district.

BLUES AND JAZZ Among popular nightspots that feature live music are *Blue Note* (131 W. Third St.; phone: 475-8592), high ticket but often worth it, and *Dan Lynch* (221 Second Ave.; phone: 677-0911), a bare-bones bar with live bands. The *Bitter End* (147 Bleecker St.; phone: 673-7030) and the *Bottom Line* (15 W. Fourth St.; phone: 228-7880) often feature blues, folk, and jazz groups. The *Village Vanguard* (178 Seventh Ave. S.; phone: 255-4037) and *Sweet Basil* (88 Seventh Ave. S.; phone: 242-1785) also spotlight top jazz artists.

Casual jazz clubs with reasonable prices and a relaxed atmosphere include *Arthur's Tavern* (57 Grove St.; phone: 675-6879) and *Bradley's* (70 University Place; phone: 228-6440). For nostalgic, traditional jazz try the *Iridium Jazz Club* (44 W. 63rd St.; phone: 582-2121) or *Michael's Pub* (211 E. 55th St.; phone: 758-2272), where Woody Allen plays his clarinet on Monday nights.

Birdland (2745 Broadway; phone: 749-2228) serves up dinner and jazz combos nightly. For big band sounds try *Red Blazer Too* (349 W. 46th St.; phone: 262-3112). Order up some gumbo and jambalaya with the Dixieland jazz featured nightly at *Cajun* (129 Eighth Ave.; phone: 691-6174). For down-and-dirty blues head to *Manny's Car Wash* (1558 Third Ave.; phone: 369-2583).

INTERNATIONAL For dancing to a Latin beat, try the *Sounds of Brazil (S.O.B.)* supper club (204 Varick St.; phone: 243-4940) or *Boca Chica* (13 First Ave.; phone: 473-0108), where salsa and other rhythms throb until 3 AM. For avant-garde sounds head for the newly expanded *Knitting Factory* (7 Leonard St.; phone: 219-3055).

SUPPER CLUBS AND CABARETS For a low-key, elegant evening of dancing to live music, a good show, and dinner, try one of New York's supper clubs. Among the city's small, intimate spots with good food and quality entertainment, the *Café Carlyle,* in the hotel of the same name, leads the pack when pianist Bobby Short, a New York institution himself, plays Cole Porter tunes; Harry Connick Jr. made his New York debut tickling the ivories at the *Rose Room* in the *Algonquin;* and *Café Pierre* in the *Pierre* hotel is the city's swankiest supper club spot (see *Checking In* for all three). *Au Bar* offers all the lofty but cozy accoutrements of London's Belgravia (41 E. 58th St.; phone: 308-9455). The *Rainbow Room* (30 Rockefeller Plaza; phone: 632-5100), restored to the splendor of its 1930s heyday, has good cheek-to-cheek dance music and dazzling views of the city from the 65th floor of the GE Building. The adjacent *Rainbow Promenade* is a less expensive café for midnight snacks, and *Rainbow and Stars* showcases cabaret acts (phone: 632-5100 for all three). *Tatou* (151 E. 50th St.; phone: 753-1144) is a cozy supper club with live jazz during dinner; it transforms into a disco later in the evening.

For traditional ballroom fun with American and Latin live dance music, trip the light fantastic at the famous *Roseland* (239 W. 52nd St.; phone: 247-0200)—it holds up to 3,500 dancers. *Laura Belle* (120 W. 43rd St.; phone: 819-1000), an intimate eatery features contemporary music.

SINGLES BARS AND COMEDY CLUBS The largest concentration of bars in New York can be found on First, Second, and Third Avenues between East 61st and East 86th Streets. Walk along any one of these thoroughfares to find a place that suits your fancy. The low-key *Beach Café* (1326 Second Ave.; phone: 988-7299), with its handsome wood bar, is a popular hangout for a beer and burger. Oversize margaritas are the draw for the youngish bar crowd at *Juanita's* (1309 Third Ave.; phone: 517-3800). The bar at *Jim McMullen's*

(1341 Third Ave.; phone: 861-4700), whose owner is a former fashion model, attracts the beautiful people from the top agencies.

The West Side has its strips of bars and restaurants along Broadway, Amsterdam, and Columbus Avenues between West 50th and West 86th Streets. Check out the upstairs jazz room at *B. Smith's* (771 Eighth Ave.; phone: 247-2222) or the ever-crowded *Whiskey* bar in the *Paramount* hotel (see *Checking In*), where the waitresses wear gray leotards.

Lively "showcase" clubs, where comedians, singers, and musicians try out their acts, include *Caroline's* (1626 Broadway; phone: 757-4100); *Comic Strip* (1568 Second Ave.; phone: 861-9386) and *Dangerfield's* (1118 First Ave.; phone: 593-1650).

Best in Town

CHECKING IN

Host to more visitors than any other city in the world, New York can be one of the hardest places to find an empty hotel room from Sunday through Thursday nights, even though a rash of new properties has opened. However, don't expect this increased supply to offset inflation's upward push on room rates in the foreseeable future. Do expect to pay $250 or more—often *lots* more—per night for a very expensive room for two in Manhattan; $175 to $250 for an expensive one; $125 to $175 for a moderately priced room; and less than $125 for an inexpensive one. These prices do not include any meals nor the hefty hotel tax (see "Sales Tax" in the *Sources and Resources* section earlier in this chapter for current rates). *Note:* Many hotels offer relatively low-priced weekend packages which also may include a variety of amenities, such as breakfast and/or dinner, champagne, theater tickets, and parking. Reservations always are necessary, so write or call in advance.

Visitors who yearn to be in the thick of New York's theater district will find a variety of options. Choices include the *Millennium Broadway, Holiday Inn Crowne Plaza, Paramount, Renaissance New York, Sheraton Manhattan,* and *Sheraton New York* hotels (see below for all).

An alternative to a standard hotel room is to try bed and breakfast accommodations in private homes or in an apartment. This option includes continental breakfast and costs from $60 to $125 per night for a double room. Unhosted, fully furnished apartments also are available, starting at $75 per night for a small studio. Weekly and monthly rates are offered by both B&Bs and apartments. For information, contact *Urban Ventures* (PO Box 426, New York, NY 10024; phone: 594-5650; fax: 947-9320); *At Home in New York* (PO Box 407, New York, NY 10185; phone: 956-3125; fax: 247-3294); the *Bed and Breakfast Network of New York* (134 W. 32nd St.; phone: 645-8134); *Bed and Breakfast and Books* (35 W. 92nd St., New York, NY 10025; phone: 865-8740; 800-900-8134); *City Lights B&B* (P.O. Box 20355, New York, NY 10028; phone: 737-7049; fax: 535-2755); or *Abode*

B&B (P.O. Box 20222, New York, NY 10028; phone: 472-2000; 800-835-8880). Other options: Double rooms at many of the coed *Y*s throughout the city run about $45 a night, and the *New York Student Center* (895 Amsterdam Ave.; phone: 666-3619; fax: 666-5012), in cooperation with *American Youth Hostels,* offers students and budget travelers dorm-style accommodations priced as low as $20 to $25 per night.

To reserve a suite in one of nine different all-suite hotels around Manhattan, call the *Manhattan East Suite* hotel (phone: 800-637-8483). These accommodations are located in areas that range from the commercial (the *Southgate Tower* at Seventh Ave. and W. 31st St.) to the posh (the *Surrey* at Madison Ave. and E. 76th St.); this service represents a total of 1,633 suites around the city.

Most of New York's major hotels have complete facilities for the business traveler. Those listed below as having "business services" usually offer such conveniences as meeting rooms, photocopiers, computers, translation services, and express checkout, among others. Call the individual hotel for additional information. All telephone numbers are in the 212 area code unless otherwise indicated. Twenty-four-hour room service and CNN (Cable News Network) are available in all hotels, unless otherwise noted.

VERY EXPENSIVE

Beekman Tower Small and pleasantly old-fashioned, this 171-suite establishment (convenient to the *United Nations*) is perhaps best known for its 26th-floor *Top of the Towers* lounge that provides a spectacular skyline view. Other amenities include a restaurant and a concierge; business services also are available. 3 Mitchell Pl., at First Ave. and E. 49th St. (phone: 355-7300; 800-ME-SUITE; fax: 753-9366).

Carlyle Long the leader among the most luxurious uptown hotels, it's properly noted for its quiet and serenity—with prices that match the high level of service. Predominantly a residential hotel, it provides a homey environment for the rich and respected. The 190 guestrooms (about 35 percent are suites) are tastefully decorated and afford expansive views of the Upper East Side and *Central Park;* in addition, there is also a deluxe for-guests-only spa and a skylit fitness center on the third floor, complete with exercise machines, saunas, and personal trainers. Other delights are the *Café Carlyle* (see *Nightclubs and Nightlife*) and the excellent restaurant. A concierge and business center are available. 35 E. 76th St. at Madison Ave. (phone: 744-1600; 800-227-5737; fax: 717-4682).

Drake Swissôtel Thanks to the grand entrance on Park Avenue, the familiar billing, "the only Swiss hotel on Park Avenue," takes on new meaning. With ongoing renovations, the 615 guestrooms vary in size; however, all feature computer and fax hookups (each of the 78 Swiss Business Advantage Rooms has its own fax machine), marble bathrooms, and even a working fireplace in the Presidential Suite. The *Drake Bar* has its own entrance on Park

Avenue, and the *Café Suisse* is popular for breakfast and lunch. There's an obliging concierge desk and business services, including a daily limousine to Wall Street. 440 Park Ave. at E. 56th St. (phone: 421-0900; 800-DRAKE-NY; fax: 371-4190).

Essex House Overlooking *Central Park,* this 40-story landmark (now owned by Nikko Hotels International) recaptured its original Art Deco grandeur after a $70-million restoration several years ago. Its 595 large guestrooms are tastefully decorated in French and English country styles, although the public areas have a 1920s flavor. The hotel's chi-chi restaurant, *Les Célébrités,* has a fine kitchen featuring French cuisine, while the less formal *Café Botanica* offers a pleasant continental/California menu. Try the *Journey's Lounge Bar* for a relaxing pre-dinner drink. There's a helpful concierge desk and business services. 160 Central Park S. at Seventh Ave. (phone: 247-0300; 800-NIKKO-US; fax: 315-1839).

Four Seasons New York This executive-oriented property opened in 1993 on one of the city's most sought-after shopping streets; it is just steps from Fifth Avenue. The 52-story French limestone building—it's the tallest hotel in the city—was designed in a clean, Art Deco–style by eminent American architect I. M. Pei. The 309 exceptionally spacious rooms and 60 one- and two-bedroom suites feature refrigerators, cable TV and VCRs, modems for personal computer hookup, and large, luxuriously equipped marble bathrooms. There is a bar, a lobby lounge, and the highly-acclaimed *5757* restaurant, where chef Susan Weaver creates culinary magic. Also available are a 24-hour concierge, a spa, and a health club. Business services are available. 57 E. 57th St. between Madison and Park Aves. (phone: 758-5700; 800-332-3442; fax: 758-5711).

Lowell Little expense has been spared in turning this once undistinguished property into an authentic gem, an Art Deco delight—with 66 mostly one- and two-bedroom suites. The cozy rooms are perfect for a modestly proportioned king or queen, and each suite has a working fireplace. The overall feeling is one of being a guest in a well-bred New York townhouse—on what could very well be the most stylish block in Manhattan. The only member of the prestigious Relais & Châteaux group in New York. The hotel's second floor dining room, *The Pembroke,* is elegant and intimate. Room service is available until midnight, and there's a fitness center. A concierge and business services are additional pluses. 28 E. 63rd St. (phone: 838-1400; 800-221-4444; fax: 319-4230).

The Mark A recent $4.1-million renovation on the hotel's public spaces and 180 guestrooms (including 60 suites) further enchanced *The Mark*'s air of elegance. All guestrooms feature overstuffed chairs, credenzas, and sofas, all in a neoclassical Italian motif; cable TV; two-line phones; pantries with refrigerator, sink, and stove; and luxurious bathrooms with heated towel bars and heating lamps, separate glass shower stalls, tub, bidet, and vanity.

Suites are large and offer a library, wet bar, large terrace, and separate living, dining, and bedroom areas. There is now a state-of-the-art fitness center, while the hotel's restaurant, *Mark's,* boasts fine continental cuisine. Other pluses include a concierge and business services. 25 E. 77th St. (phone: 744-4300; 800-THE-MARK; fax: 744-2749)

Mayfair Hotel Perfect for those who stay at the *Gritti Palace* in Venice and the *Hôtel du Cap* in the south of France. Formerly the *Mayfair Regent,* it features 96 rooms and 105 suites (28 with wood-burning fireplaces), plus the nonpareil *Le Cirque* restaurant (see *Eating Out*). Uncompromising elegance and superb service with a focus on detail: Their "Pillow Bank" has a budget of $100,000 merely to amass the finest pillows in the world; and guests can request an in-room putting green, complete with golf balls. A favorite spot for afternoon tea, especially among the social set. A concierge and business services are also available. 610 Park Ave. at 65th St. (phone: 288-0800; 800-223-0542; fax: 737-0538).

Michelangelo The former *Parc Fifty One* provides luxury lodgings in a part of town not traditionally associated with deluxe digs. The 178 large guestrooms come with such amenities as multi-line phones, two TV sets, and computer and fax hookups. There are valets to pack and unpack for you and even an electronic paging service. The hotel's lobby bar is a far more quiet and soothing place to have a drink than the first-rate *Limoncello* Italian restaurant that holds court on the ground floor. The hotel is part of the Italian Star chain, which explains the large number of Italian guests, the stylish Italian ambience, and, of course, the name. Amenities such as a concierge desk and business services are a boon. 152 W. 51st St. at Seventh Ave. (phone: 765-1900; 800-237-0990 outside New York State; fax: 541-6604).

New York Palace This midtown property combines the landmark Henry Villard house with a 51-story high-rise as its backdrop. The historic areas of the building boast the opulent *Madison Room,* considered by art aficionados as one of the most elegantly preserved 19th-century salons in the city—or anywhere else for that matter. The *Gold Room* is richly decorated with mahogany carved designs and paintings by John La Farge. All 957 guestrooms are beautifully appointed. *Le Trianon* serves classic American fare, and during summer months there's an outdoor courtyard café. Later this year, the landmark *Le Cirque* restaurant will open in its new location within this hotel. There are three entrances: one less hectic on East 50th Street, one on East 51st Street, and the third through wrought-iron gates on Madison Avenue. A concierge and business services are also available. 455 Madison Ave., from E. 50th to E. 51st St. (phone: 888-7000; 800-697-2522; fax: 303-6000).

Omni Berkshire Place Built in 1926, the old *Berkshire* has been resuscitated by Omni Hotels with dash and considerable understated flair. A recent $50-million renovation has created a comfortable and intimate atmosphere. Most impressive is the lobby, a mirrored lounge accented in soft pastel hues.

Each of the 396 guestrooms and 14 suites is well appointed and features a mini-bar and two-line phone. Its *Kokachin* restaurant specializes in seafood with a Pacific Rim flair. Business services are available. 21 E. 52nd St. (phone: 753-5800; 800-THE-OMNI; fax: 755-2317).

Le Parker Meridien Billing itself as New York's "first French hotel," this establishment offers 700 rooms and the *Bar Montparnasse,* a lounge in the former formal dining room, where the food includes *tapas* and seafood and there is live music at night. The sports-minded will enjoy *Club La Raquette,* for racquetball, handball, and squash, and the rooftop running track that encircles a glass-enclosed pool—from which the views of *Central Park* are lovely. There's a health club, too. Other pluses are concierge and business services. 118 W. 57th St. between Sixth and Seventh Aves. (phone: 245-5000; 800-543-4300; fax: 307-1776).

Peninsula This 241-room property is a grand hotel in the best Asian tradition (its original namesake is in Hong Kong), featuring Art Nouveau decor, a fitness center and top-rated spa, a rooftop bar, a lounge, and a swank French restaurant and bistro—*Adrienne* and *Le Bistro d'Adrienne,* respectively. Additional pluses are a concierge and business services. 700 Fifth Ave. at W. 55th St. (phone: 247-2200; 800-262-9467; fax: 903-3974).

Pierre The most luxurious stopping place in midtown, with the most august clientele, the elegance at this hotel is low-key, but consistent, and the 202 rooms are furnished with Chippendale pieces and fabrics in subdued tones. Operated by the superb Four Seasons group, on one of the most attractive corners of the city. For many, it is the only place to stay in New York. *Café Pierre* retains all the elegance of a French château, with its low marble balconies, tall candelabra, and gray velvet chairs; the fare is first-rate. The *Rotunda Room* boasts playful cherubim and demigods looking down from immense murals, a white marble staircase, and a high-domed ceiling; try the delectable sandwiches and scones that accompany afternoon tea. There's also a new gym for guests only. Good news for animal lovers: This is one of the few hotels in New York City where small pets are allowed. There's a concierge desk and business services. Fifth Ave. and E. 61 St. (phone: 838-8000; 800-743-7734; fax: 826-0319).

Plaza The only New York City hotel designated a historic landmark, this erratic but mostly elegant hostelry with over 800 rooms affords most guests lovely views of *Central Park.* Hansom cabs can be hired right outside the entrance. The hotel has long been renowned for (pricey) tea in the *Palm Court* and drinks in the *Oak Room,* not to mention dinner in the *Oyster Bar* or *Edwardian Room.* Other amenities include a concierge and business services. Fifth Ave. from W. 58th to W. 59th St. (phone: 546-5493; 800-739-3000; fax: 546-5324).

Plaza Athénée Small and sumptuous, this is the US edition of the celebrated *Plaza Athénée* in Paris. The Forte management strives to make the elegant edifice look as unlike a hotel as possible, and prides itself on personal attention to its guests. The multimillion-dollar enhancement of the 117 rooms and 36 suites, all decorated with paisley fabrics and velvet headboards, make it one of the favorite hotels around. Suites include VCRs (you can request one if you're in a room). There's also *Le Régence* restaurant, which serves French fare in elegant surroundings; a cozy lounge has piano music nightly. Amenities include a multilingual concierge, an exercise facility, and business services. 37 E. 64th St. between Park and Madison Aves. (phone: 734-9100; 800-447-8800; fax: 772-0958).

Regency Where many of the movers and shakers of America stay when they're in New York. The "power breakfast" began here, and more commerce is probably conducted in the dining room at breakfast than in all of the rest of the country during a normal business day. Its modern architecture does not detract at all from its appeal, and the basement-to-roof restoration and refurbishing completed several years ago has only added to its luster. The 374 guestrooms are decorated in mauve, green, and salmon, with tasteful antique reproductions adding to the sense of coziness. Facilities include *The Library* lounge, a newly expanded health club, a concierge desk, and business services. 540 Park Ave. at E. 61st St. (phone: 759-4100; 800-23-LOEWS; fax: 826-5674).

Rihga Royal Standing 54 stories high, this is the most luxurious of the all-suite properties, catering to the corporate traveler. Each of the 500 one- and two-bedroom suites is equipped with two TV sets, a VCR, three telephones, computer hookups, and fax machines. The hotel also boasts fitness centers, a concierge, and a complimentary shuttle to the Wall Street area. The *Halcyon* restaurant serves fine continental fare. 151 W. 54th St. between Sixth and Seventh Aves. (phone: 307-5000; 800-937-5454; fax: 765-6530).

Ritz-Carlton A number of the 214 rooms and 30 suites at this classic property offer wonderful views of *Central Park* and the city skyline. Some of the suites have small terraces. Amenities include twice-daily maid service, terry cloth robes in the rooms, two-line telephones, and personal valet service. Facilities include a fitness center with park views, and *Fantino* restaurant, which offers exceptional northern Italian fare; its bar is a popular meeting place for both guests and New Yorkers. The concierge desk and business services are handy. 112 Central Park S. between Sixth and Seventh Aves. (phone: 757-1900; 800-241-3333; fax: 757-9620).

Royalton The management of ultra-hip *Morgans* (see below) impressed New York once again, this time with a 207-room property not far from Times Square. The block-long lobby, with areas specifically designed for reading, conversation, and board games, is a popular gathering spot for a chic crowd (and the restrooms have to be seen to be believed). Many of the guestrooms, designed by architect Philippe Starck, come with a wood-burning fireplace in the living area, which also includes a VCR and stereo cassette deck. The bar/restaurant *44* fills up with fashionable types from the nearby Condé Nast Building on Madison Avenue. Other amenities include a concierge and business services. 44 W. 44th St. between Fifth and Sixth Aves. (phone: 869-4400; 800-635-9013; fax: 869-8965).

St. Regis Built in 1904 by John Jacob Astor and now under the Sheraton banner, this elaborate, 20-story Beaux Arts landmark, with its prestigious Fifth Avenue address, offers all the sophisticated grandeur of turn-of-the-century Manhattan. Elegant Louis XV furnishings, marble bathrooms with double sinks, and Oriental rugs are wonderful additions to the 222 rooms and 91 suites, all of which also are equipped with fax machines and two-line phones that can deliver messages and information in five languages, operate the TV set and radio, and adjust the room temperature. The famous *St. Regis Roof* ballroom offers spectacular views of midtown Manhattan, and the equally renowned *King Cole* bar retains its look of yesteryear. Also on the premises is *Lespinasse,* an elegant dining room that features French fare (see *Eating Out*), and *Astor Court,* a handsome first-floor salon where afternoon tea, drinks, and light snacks are served. There is a concierge, and business services are available. Fifth Ave. and E. 55th St. (phone: 753-4500; 800-759-7550; fax: 787-3447).

Sherry-Netherland Though a little less renowned than the *Plaza* and the *Pierre* (its immediate neighbors), it is no less luxurious, especially since its complete restoration in 1993. Keep in mind that reservations can sometimes be a problem, because this establishment is largely residential, with only about 60 rooms available for visitors. The *Harry Cipriani* restaurant features a northern Italian menu. 781 Fifth Ave. at E. 59th St. (phone: 355-2800; 800-247-4377 outside New York State; fax: 319-4306).

Stanhope This posh, upper Fifth Avenue place has 140 recently refurbished rooms, most of them one- or two-bedroom suites with views of *Central Park* or Manhattan's spectacular skyline. Guests meet and relax in the opulent public rooms and enjoy a wide range of dining options, including an outdoor café in summer and afternoon tea in the sitting room. The once formal restaurant is now casual brasserie-style. There is a fitness club, and complimentary limousine service is provided to midtown weekday mornings and to *Lincoln Center, Carnegie Hall,* and the theater district in the evenings. The concierge desk and business services are useful. Across from the *Metropolitan Museum of Art* at 995 Fifth Ave. at E. 81st St. (phone: 288-5800; 800-828-1123 outside New York City; fax: 517-0088).

UN Plaza–Park Hyatt In addition to its beautifully integrated modern design, from the sleek, green-tinted glass exterior through the dark green marble reception area to the top 10 floors, this property also offers 425 rooms with magnificent city views. Managed by Hyatt International, it has both a truly international staff and exceptional facilities—including a tennis court, heated pool, and exercise room. Its restaurant is the aptly named *Ambassador Grill,* for the hotel faces the *UN.* Other amenities include a concierge, business services, and complimentary limousine service (to Wall Street and the garment district during the day and to the theater district at night). 1 United Nations Plaza at First Ave. and E. 44th St. (phone: 758-1234; 800-228-9000; fax: 702-5051).

Westbury The tapestries at the entrance are Belgian, the soft pink carpeting in the marble lobby, Irish—as befits this tranquil, European-style hotel (part of the Forte group) with its large international clientele. There are 229 handsome rooms, and the *Polo* restaurant serves fine continental fare. Concierge and business services are easily accessible. 15 E. 69th St. at Madison Ave. (phone: 535-2000; 800-225-5843; fax: 535-5058).

EXPENSIVE

Algonquin Long a favorite among literary types, this 165-room hotel's reputation is most closely connected with the days of the literary "Round Table" in the *Rose Room,* its famous piano bar and cabaret restaurant. Happily its recent $20-million renovation has left intact the legendary lobby, where you can summon a cocktail with the ringing of a bell. The recently unveiled Thurber Suite is proving as popular as the Dorothy Parker Suite. Convenient to both midtown and the theater district. Other amenities include room service until 11:30 PM and business services. 59 W. 44th St. between Fifth and Sixth Aves. (phone: 840-6800; 800-548-0345; fax: 944-1419).

Box Tree Eccentric, unusual, and housed in two East Side brownstones, this place is for those who appreciate detail-oriented luxury. Each of the 13 suites is individually designed with different European furnishings. The restaurant serves very good French fare with an English accent. Or book one of the three party rooms (which seat, respectively, 13, 18, and 35) and host a private dinner. Business services are available. 250 E. 49th St. between Second and Third Aves. (phone: 758-8320; fax: 308-3899).

Doral Court Located on a quaint, tree-lined street in the heart of Manhattan's business and retail districts, this hotel is convenient to such landmarks as the *Empire State Building* and the *United Nations.* The 199 guestrooms, including 48 suites, all feature dressing alcoves and in-room refrigerators. Exercise bikes are available upon request, or enjoy complimentary use of the *Doral Fitness Center* at 90 Park Avenue. Business services are available. 130 E. 39th St. (phone: 685-1100; fax: 889-0287).

Doral Tuscany In the middle of attractive Murray Hill (between 34th and 40th Sts. on the East Side), this 121-room hotel is not widely known outside the city, but guests who know it well treasure the high level of service and discreet atmosphere. It has a restaurant, and guests have free access to a fitness center a block away. A concierge and business services round out the list of amenities. 120 E. 39th St. (phone: 686-1600; 800-22-DORAL; fax: 779-7822).

Doubletree Guest Suites Recently renovated, this 460-suite property has an elegant lobby, well-appointed rooms, and an attentive staff. All suites, some of which overlook Times Square, come equipped with wet bars, microwave ovens, refrigerators, hair-dryers, and irons and ironing boards. Other amenities include room service until 4 AM, a multilingual concierge desk, and business services. 1568 Broadway at W. 47th St. (phone: 719-1600; 800-222-TREE; fax: 921-5212).

Elysée After nearly two years of renovation (and years of neglect), this hotel has gained acclaim as one of New York's more attractive boutique hotels. Although not large, the 99 rooms (some with fireplaces) feature marble baths and VCRs. Guests also enjoy a complimentary continental breakfast as well as afternoon cocktails daily. One of the hottest places in town, the *Monkey Bar* serves fine fare and provides room service. Guests get passes to a nearby cardio-fitness center. 60 E. 54th St. between Madison and Park Aves. (phone: 753-1066).

Grand Hyatt Originally, this was Donald Trump's idea of how a glitzy New York City hotel should look: mirrored exterior glass and lots of shiny chrome. The *Sun Garden* and *Crystal Fountain* restaurants are visible from the lobby. The 1,407 recently renovated rooms are attractive, although some are small, and all feature fax machines and laptop ports. A penthouse health club boasts skyscraper views. Business services and the concierge desk are available. 109 E. 42nd St. at Park Ave. (phone: 883-1234; 800-233-1234 or 800-228-9000; fax: 697-3772).

Holiday Inn Crowne Plaza This razzle-dazzle, 46-story glass tower in the Times Square area offers 770 guestrooms, six Crowne Plaza Club floors (VIP floors with special services), the 15th floor *New York Health Club* (which has a 50-foot pool under a domed skylight); *Samples* and *Broadway Grill* both offer dining pleasure. There's a helpful concierge desk and business services. 1605 Broadway at W. 49th St. (phone: 977-4000; 800-HOLIDAY; fax: 333-7393).

Inter-Continental New York This large, distinguished property with 692 smallish guestrooms on a busy East Side corner is one block south of the *Waldorf.* The well-appointed suites have two-line phones with speaker capabilities. Amenities include a health club, the oak-paneled *Barclay* restaurant, a concierge, and business services. 111 E. 48th St. at Lexington Ave. (phone: 755-5900; 800-327-0200; fax: 644-0079).

Marriott East Side This historic 662-room hotel was built in the 1920s by A. L. Harmon, who designed the *Empire State Building;* it is a mix of Gothic, Byzantine, and Italian architectural styles. The *Shelton Grille* is formal but fun, and the 16th-floor *Fountain Room and Terrace* is the hotel's private meeting room. There also are nonsmoking and Concierge Club floors. Room service is available until 11:30 PM. Business services are available.

525 Lexington Ave. between E. 48th and E. 49th Sts. (phone: 755-4000; 800-228-9290; fax: 751-3440).

Millennium Broadway Formerly the *Macklowe Hotel,* this 52-story hotel in the Time Square area boasts 629 starkly chic guestrooms by well-known designer Bill Durham. Guests have use of a fitness center as well as a 100,000-square-foot conference center, all built around an existing theater (the *Hudson*). Other amenities include business services and a concierge desk. 145 W. 44th St. (phone: 768-4400; fax: 789-7688).

Morgans Without so much as a sign out front, this recently renovated 154-room treasure by Ian Shrager, of *Paramount* and *Royalton* fame, is named for the nearby *Pierpont Morgan Library.* Some unusual standards at this self-proclaimed "boutique hotel" include continental breakfast (at no extra charge) each morning, and, in guestrooms, a stereo cassette player and TV with stereo sound (VCRs and videotapes are available). Bathrooms are pure high-tech, and artwork is by the late avant-garde photographer Robert Mapplethorpe. The suites are reasonably priced. The newly-opened *Morgans Bar* is the place to see and be seen. A fitness club and restaurant/bar are scheduled to open this year. A concierge and business services round out the amenities. 237 Madison Ave. at E. 37th St. (phone: 686-0300; 800-334-3408; fax: 779-8352).

New York Helmsley A shining glass skyscraper on East 42nd Street, this executive-oriented, 730-room facility has special services for the business traveler. For dining there's *Mindy's,* a continental restaurant, and for drinks and piano music try *Harry's New York Bar.* Room service can be called upon until 1 AM, and there's a concierge desk. 212 E. 42nd St. between Second and Third Aves. (phone: 490-8900; 800-221-4982; fax: 986-4792).

New York Hilton and Towers An enormous modern structure near *Rockefeller Center,* this is one of New York's largest properties, and it's about as efficiently run as any hotel with more than 2,041 rooms can be. The well-equipped health club has saunas and even a videocassette player for your own workout tape. Dine at *Grill 53* or *Players* sports bar. Other amenities include a concierge and business services. 1335 Ave. of the Americas between W. 53rd and W. 54th Sts. (phone: 586-7000; 800-HILTONS; fax: 315-1374).

Renaissance New York This 26-story black tower overlooking "The Great White Way" has 305 rooms and 10 suites furnished Art Deco style. In addition to a sybaritic marble bath, there are three telephones in each guestroom, and an exercise room is on the premises. The newly renovated lobbies and restaurants include *Windows on Broadway,* which has a panoramic view of Times Square, a wine bar, and a lobby bar. Business services are available. 714 Seventh Ave. at W. 47th St. (phone: 765-7676; 800-228-9898; fax: 765-1962).

Sheraton Manhattan Formerly the *Sheraton City Squire,* this property underwent an enormous renovation in 1992. The façade now features Art Deco grillwork, tinted windows, and an elegant canopy; the lobby and reception area have been expanded and decorated with contemporary furniture and richly textured carpets and upholstery. In addition, the pool has been refurbished, and there is a fitness club. The 650 comfortable, modern rooms offer such amenities as in-room office supplies, computer and fax connections, coffee makers, cable TV, and express video checkout. Business services are also available. 790 Seventh Ave. at W. 51st St. (phone: 581-3300; 800-325-3535; fax: 315-4265).

Sheraton New York & Towers Part of the same mega-renovation as its Sheraton neighbor (above), this 50-story modern monolith, previously the *Sheraton Centre,* is always busy. The 1,750 rooms are quite comfortable, and it's only a short walk to the theater district or the *Museum of Modern Art.* The top two floors, called the *Sheraton Towers,* are for more exclusive "business class" clients. There is a fitness center, and business services are available. 811 Seventh Ave. at W. 53rd St. (phone: 581-1000; 800-325-3535; fax: 841-6491).

Tudor Located in New York's historic Tudor City district, steps away from the *United Nations* and directly across town from major theaters, this 1931 property, with a unique façade combining Art Deco design with Tudor touches, offers 300 comfortable guestrooms, including 14 suites. Each room has a mini-bar, two-line telephones, outlets for computers and fax machines, and a marble bathroom with towel heaters; some of the suites have Jacuzzis and private terraces. An innovative touch is the addition of six Circadian rooms, whose special features, including the lighting, help jet-lagged travelers adjust. *Cecil's Grill* serves fine American/English fare; there's also *The Regency* lounge. The fitness center is fully equipped with massage rooms. Other amenities include a concierge and business services. 304 E. 42nd St. between First and Second Aves. (phone: 986-8800; 800-TRY-TUDOR; fax: 986-1758).

Waldorf-Astoria and Waldorf Towers A legend on Park Avenue, divided between the basic hotel (with 1,215 rooms) and the more exclusive and opulent *Waldorf Towers* (with 118 rooms, 77 suites, and a number of residential apartments). The degree of comfort delivered here is consistent with the hotel's reputation; it is also a popular convention property. *Peacock Alley* is a lively cocktail rendezvous and excellent French restaurant, and the clock in the middle of the lobby may be one of New York's favorite meeting places. The hotel's *Plus One* fitness center features a wide variety of exercise equipment, health treatments, and consultations and escorted jogs with licensed trainers. There's a helpful concierge desk; butler and business services also are available. 301 Park Ave., from E. 49th to E. 50th St. (phone: 355-3000; 800-HILTONS; fax: 872-6380 for Waldorf-Astoria; 758-9209 or 872-4799 for Waldorf Towers).

MODERATE

Barbizon Recently renovated at a cost of $30 million, this East Side establishment features 314 guestrooms, a new breakfast room, and a lounge serving light fare from 5 PM to midnight. Guests are afforded CD/cassette stereo systems, televisions with computer hookups, and mini-bars. Amenities include 24-hour room service, a concierge, and business services. 140 E. 63rd St. at Lexington Ave. (phone: 838-5700; 800-223-1020; fax: 223-3287).

Gorham The variety of room-and-bed combinations possible in this restored hotel, and the fact that each of the 114 units has a kitchenette, dining table, and color TV set, make this a great choice for families traveling with children. There's also a fitness center. Business services are available. 136 W. 55th St. between Sixth and Seventh Aves. (phone: 245-1800; 800-735-0710; fax: 582-8332).

Holiday Inn Downtown Chinatown's first hotel, this 223-room property (formerly the *Maria*) is reminiscent of Hong Kong: Exotic flowers fill the lobby, and Chinese screens and marble and rosewood furnishings grace the public areas. Although the rooms are not large, many offer fine views of Chinatown and the Hudson River. The *Pacifica Lounge* serves afternoon tea, and the *Pacifica* restaurant features authentic Cantonese cooking as well as continental fare. Additional amenities include valet parking and business services. 138 Lafayette St. between Howard and Canal Sts. (phone: 966-8898; 800-HOLIDAY; fax: 966-3933).

Mayflower This establishment is a favorite with ballet, opera, and concert buffs (it's close to *Lincoln Center*), as well as celebrities from the art world. Ongoing renovations include the refurbishment of 365 guestrooms and a new fitness center. Room service delivers until 10 PM. Business services are available. 15 Central Park W. between W. 61st and W. 62nd Sts. (phone: 265-0060; 800-223-4164; fax: 265-5098).

Mansfield With 131 rooms, this is the largest and the newest member of the Gotham Hospitality Group (the *Shoreham,* the *Franklin,* and the *Wales*). The 129 restored guestrooms and suites feature custom-designed furnishings and a video and CD library is available. There's a complimentary breakfast and after-theater dessert buffet. 12 W. 44th St. between Fifth and Sixth Aves. (phone: 944-6050).

New York Hotel Pennsylvania Once the *Statler,* more recently the *Ramada Madison Square Garden,* this 1,705-room Stanford White landmark building across from *Penn Station* has recently undergone a $15-million renovation of both the public spaces and guestrooms. Business services are available. 401 Seventh Ave. at W. 33rd St. (phone: 736-5000; 800-223-8585; fax: 212-502-8798).

Paramount Another Ian Schrager dazzler, designed by Philippe Starck, this trendy hotel in the middle of the theater district has 600 recently renovated guestrooms. There's a theatrical, dual-level lobby for socializing, the *Whiskey* bar, a mezzanine-level restaurant, and even a playroom for kids. Also available are a concierge and business services. 235 W. 46th St. between Broadway and Eighth Ave. (phone: 764-5500; 800-225-7474; fax: 354-5237).

Quality Inn by Journey's End This 29-story property is noteworthy for its central location (just east of Fifth Avenue, across from the *New York Public Library*) and reasonable rates—well below the city's standard. Each of the 186 guestrooms is equipped with a work area and cable TV set, and guests receive complimentary morning coffee (plus complimentary pastries on weekends) and a copy of *USA Today.* There's a concierge desk, and business services are available. 3 E. 40th St. at Fifth Ave. (phone: 447-1500; 800-221-2222; fax: 685-5214 for reservations, 213-0972 for guests).

Radisson Empire The 375 rooms in this property, located directly across from *Lincoln Center,* all offer compact disc players, VCRs, and heated towel racks. The *West 63rd Street Steakhouse* (see *Eating Out*) is the hotel's restaurant. Business services are available. 44 W. 63rd St. at Broadway (phone: 265-7400; 800-333-3333; fax: 315-0349).

Salisbury Owned by the *Calvary Baptist Church* (thus, no alcohol is permitted on the premises), it has 204 nice-size, pastel-decorated rooms (all with refrigerators and pantries but no stoves). Undergoing a three-year renovation (to be completed this year), it's a favorite with musicians who like the location near *Carnegie Hall.* Complimentary continental breakfast is included in the new breakfast room. Business services are available. 123 W. 57th St. (phone: 246-1300; 800-223-0680; fax: 977-7752).

Sheraton Park Avenue This is one of those "secret" hotels that regulars don't like to share—even with their friends. The 150-room property is convenient to *Grand Central Station* and the garment center, and the comfortable guestrooms boast high ceilings, walk-in closets, three phones, and separate work areas. *Russell's* is a fine dining place, and the *Judge's Chamber* serves buffet lunch in a clubby, book-lined setting. Concierge and business services can lend a hand. 45 Park Ave. at E. 37th St. (phone: 685-7676; 800-325-3535; fax: 889-3193).

Shoreham On a fashionable block off Fifth Avenue and fresh from a stylish restoration, this place has 47 contemporary, good-size rooms and 37 suites, all with modern bathrooms and a refrigerator, a VCR, and cable TV. The hotel has a new lounge (for guests only) where breakfast and specialty coffees are served; there's also an after-theater dessert bar. Continental breakfast is included in the guest rate. A stylish deck with a glassed-in roof has been added; it's available for meetings and private parties. 33 W. 55th St. between Fifth and Sixth Aves. (phone: 247-6700 or 800-553-3347; fax: 765-9741).

Wales Comfortable and reasonably priced, this hotel is in a very appealing residential neighborhood, close to *Central Park* and the *Metropolitan* and

Guggenheim Museums. It offers 90 individually decorated rooms and suites all with VCRs and cable TV. There's a complimentary video/CD library, and one of the city's best breakfasts can be had in the lobby's *Sarabeth's* restaurant. Business services are available. 1295 Madison Ave. at E. 92nd St. (phone: 876-6000; 800-428-5252; fax: 860-7000).

Wyndham This extremely well-located, 125-room property has been fondly described as being like a posh country inn; a fine, small London hotel; and a private club. It takes a certain self-sufficiency to enjoy its special appeal; there's no room service, and *Jonathan's* restaurant is closed on weekends. 42 W. 58th St. between Fifth and Sixth Aves. (phone: 753-3500; 800-257-1111; fax: 754-5638).

INEXPENSIVE

Chelsea At this architectural and historic landmark, Dylan Thomas, Arthur Miller, Lenny Bruce, Diego Rivera, Martha Graham, and others once found their New York home. The down-at-the-heels atmosphere in the 19th-century structure is distinctly unmodern, unhomogenized, and unsterilized. There is a large permanent occupancy in about 250 of the rooms, with some 80 rooms available for short-term guests. Some rooms have a kitchen, a fireplace, and a bathroom; others have none of the above. Service is quirky, and the management is not overly generous with amenities like washcloths and bath mats. For the adventurous only; make reservations well in advance. 222 W. 23rd St. between Seventh and Eighth Aves. (phone: 243-3700; fax: 243-3700).

Larchmont Situated on a quiet Greenwich Village street, this one-time Beaux Arts 77-room residence has been beautifully restored into a cozy, European-style hotel. There's a parlor lobby and great views of the *World Trade Center.* There are no private baths. Each floor does have a common kitchen for guests to whip up late-night snacks, and continental breakfast is included in the rate. 27 W. 11th Street. (phone: 989-9333).

Olcott Comfortable and adequate, this typical New York residential hotel offers some 100 rooms as transient accommodations. Spacious facilities and a homey atmosphere are its advantages. Most rooms are suites, with a living room, bedroom, kitchen, and bathroom. Reservations should be made several weeks in advance. 27 W. 72nd St. between Central Park W. and Columbus Ave. (phone: 877-4200; fax: 580-0511).

Roosevelt Built in 1927, the property enjoyed its heyday when railroads were a means of getting around. Today, it's popular with those doing business steps away from *Grand Central Station.* The newly refurbished 1,013 rooms feature soundproofing and modern decor. Room service is on call until 11 PM. Business services are available. 355 Madison Ave. at E. 45th St. (phone: 661-9600; 800-223-1870 outside New York State; fax: 687-5064).

EATING OUT

New York City is, plain and simply, the culinary capital of the world. There may be more good French restaurants in Paris or more fine Chinese eating places in Hong Kong, but no other city can offer the gastronomic diversity available in New York; it is not unusual for dedicated eaters to make several pilgrimages to New York each year simply to satisfy their sophisticated palates.

Regrettably, the city's tastiest dishes do not come cheap, though there are places to dine around the city where you need not go broke indulging yourself. Currently, a new breed of American bistros is making its presence felt, challenging the reputation of New York restaurants for being uniformly overpriced and intimidating. Their simple approach toward both food and atmosphere is helping to redefine the way New Yorkers dine out. Although prices have leveled off and even dropped in recent years in response to the recession, you can expect to pay top dollar for top establishments here.

Changes are in store for several temples of cuisine including the famed *Bouley,* which is currently closed for expansion and refurbishing, and is scheduled to reopen later this year. And *Le Cirque,* which for many years held court on the East Side, will travel to its new Midtown location and reopen in the *New York Palace Hotel* in November.

For the restaurants we list as very expensive, the tab for two for a three-course dinner will come to $115 or more; at restaurants in the expensive category, $85 to $115; at a moderate restaurant, $60 to $85; and in an inexpensive establishment, $30 to $60. These price ranges do not include drinks, wine, tip, or tax. All telephone numbers are in the 212 area code unless otherwise indicated.

Unless otherwise noted, restaurants are open daily for lunch and dinner.

RESERVATIONS PLEASE

Unless otherwise mentioned, reservations are always necessary; for the higher priced and more popular places, reservations may be necessary several weeks in advance. In addition, men are required to wear jackets and ties at many of the more expensive restaurants.

VERY EXPENSIVE

Aquavit In a landmark Rockefeller townhouse, this Scandinavian dining place is actually two dining spots: a formal dining room set around an atrium and waterfall, with prix fixe and pre-theater menus, and a more casual, less expensive room upstairs featuring simpler fare from a choice of menus. There are many varieties of salmon and game, such as arctic venison (reindeer) and snow grouse. Try the smorgasbord, caviar bank, and "aquavit chiller," consisting of eight flavored vodkas. Jacket required in the dining room; the upstairs café calls for casual but neat attire. Closed Saturdays for lunch and Sundays. Major credit cards accepted. 13 W. 54th St. between Fifth and Sixth Aves. (phone: 307-7311).

Le Bernardin The menu is fiercely seafood-oriented, and no one prepares the products of the world's oceans more imaginatively or deliciously. Since the doors opened here in 1986, such unusual specialties as tuna tartare and sea urchin soup have become staples of the New York restaurant scene, and it's worth a visit just to see what new wonders are swimming out of the kitchen. A prix fixe menu is available at dinner. Closed Saturdays for lunch and Sundays. Major credit cards accepted. 155 W. 51st St. between Sixth and Seventh Aves. (phone: 489-1515).

Chanterelle This SoHo eatery, seriously committed to elegant dining, features an excellent prix fixe meal and a tasting menu, plus a relatively reasonably priced lunch. Begin with seafood sausage, then choose from such entrées as salmon en papillote, rack of lamb, duck in sherry vinegar, or sautéed soft-shell crabs. A cheese board is offered, and dessert might be chocolate pavé, a dense, rich, mousse-like cake. Closed Sundays and Mondays. Make reservations about one month in advance. Major credit cards accepted. 2 Harrison St. at Hudson St. (phone: 966-6960).

Daniel After an illustrious six-year reign at the celebrated *Le Cirque,* Lyonnaise-born Daniel Boulud decided it was time to strike out on his own. Opened in 1993, this airy, sedate dining room offers such culinary creations as nine-herb ravioli, sauced with a *coulis* (purée) of tomato, sage, wild mushrooms, and pine nuts, grilled pepper tuna prepared in a red wine sauce, and for dessert, a warm chocolate soufflé with pistachio ice cream—a gourmand's nirvana. Closed Saturdays for lunch and Sundays. Reservations necessary one month in advance for weekend dining; otherwise, two weeks is recommended. 20 E. 76th St. between Fifth and Madison Aves. (phone: 288-0033).

Four Seasons The Pool Room is perhaps the most beautiful dining room in the city, with a proprietorship that is not only creative but extremely able. This is arguably the best restaurant in the US, not just because of its accomplishments, but because of its innovation and boldness. Although the menu is interesting from top to bottom, desserts deserve special mention, and there's one called Chocolate Velvet that is simply ecstasy. Special "spa cuisine" provides careful calorie and sodium monitoring for the health-conscious. The Grill Room continues to be the luncheon favorite of New York's power elite, and is a good choice for dinner as well. Closed Sundays. Major credit cards accepted. 99 E. 52nd St. between Park and Lexington Aves. (phone: 754-9494).

La Grenouille Soft green walls and glorious floral arrangements provide a romantic setting in which to sample such house masterpieces as frogs' legs, thin, sautéed calf's liver, and roast duck. Be prepared, however, for a slightly condescending attitude if you're not known to the staff. Closed Sundays and Mondays. Major credit cards accepted. 3 E. 52nd St. between Fifth and Madison Aves. (phone: 752-1495).

Lespinasse This serene, formal dining salon in the *St. Regis* hotel gleams with polished marble and gold leaf trim. Gray Kunz, formerly the chef at *Adrienne* in the *Peninsula,* applies his Hong Kong–influenced artistry to such dishes as poached black bass flavored with Asian spices, and gingered chicken with a soy vinegar dressing. Selections on the wine list are surprisingly affordable. Open daily. Major credit cards accepted. 2 E. 55th St. between Fifth and Madison Aves. (phone: 339-6719).

Lutèce Maintaining its mystique for over three decades as one of the world's finest restaurants, it remains what The New York Times dubbed a "culinary cathedral." Although chef-proprietor André Soltner sold the restaurant in 1994, it still retains a classic French touch in a simple East Side townhouse. If you have the option, dine in the comfortable upstairs room, though the garden room downstairs is a treat in New York City. To sample the combination of classic dishes, innovative nouvelle creations, and Alsatian specialties, order the *menu de dégustation,* a tasting of six or seven small courses, or the reasonably priced prix fixe menu. Closed Sundays. Make reservations a month in advance. Major credit cards accepted. 249 E. 50th St. between Second and Third Aves. (phone: 752-2225).

"21" Club The legendary atmosphere and lingering cachet are what lure most visitors, but longtime favorites from the menu, such as the "21" burger and chicken hash, are a treat as well. If you're not a regular or a celebrity, the welcome sometimes isn't quite so warm, but to some, just being here is a true New York experience. The elegant upstairs dining room is open on weekdays for lunch only. Closed Sundays. Major credit cards accepted. 21 W. 52nd St. between Fifth and Sixth Aves. (phone: 582-7200).

EXPENSIVE

Alison on Dominick Street Alison Becker Hurt's romantic spot on the western fringe of SoHo offers guests wonderful French-Mediterranean peasant fare. Chef Daniel Silverman prepares such creative entrées as rabbit stew with white-bean ravioli, seared salmon with braised root vegetables, and roast cod with a fricassee of Yukon gold potatoes, peppers, and olives. For desserts try the frozen praline terrine or warm chocolate timbale with a gratin of oranges and espresso ice cream. The wine list is well chosen and not outrageously priced. Open daily for dinner only. Major credit cards accepted. 38 Dominick St. between Varick and Hudson Sts. (phone: 727-1188).

An American Place Celebrated chef-owner Larry Forgione is regarded as one of the spearheads of the New American food preparation movement; sample his American/continental specialties and you'll discover why. Gastronomic delights include grilled free-range chicken with Jerusalem artichokes in a cream sauce, and pan-roasted lamb with black pepper and cumin. Closed Sundays. Major credit cards accepted. 2 Park Ave. at E. 32nd St. (phone: 684-2122).

Barbetta Opened in 1906, this is the oldest family-managed restaurant in New York City. A romantic old-timer, it boasts a formal dining room with an 18th-century Piedmontese chandelier. The menu changes seasonally, but as has been the custom over the decades, it's the great white truffles (sniffed out by dogs in Tuscany) that create a sensation here. Also on the menu are beef braised in red wine with polenta, charcoal-grilled squab with cranberry beans and red beet olive oil, and veal scaloppine with *porcini.* The dessert tray will entice even the most resolute calorie-counter. The wine list is extenive. In summer, ask to be seated in the beautiful garden. Closed Sundays and Mondays. 321 W. 46th St between Eighth and Ninth Aves. (phone: 246-9171).

Bruno's Pen & Pencil For well over 50 years and three generations of family involvement, this steakhouse has satisfied carnivores in elegant, club-like surroundings. Sports memorabilia makes up the decor, and steaks—aged, marbled, and prepared as you like them—are the stars. Shrimp dishes also are noteworthy. And be sure to leave room for the tangy lemon cheesecake. Open daily except *Labor Day* and *Christmas*. 205 E. 45th St. at Third Ave. (phone: 682-8660).

Café des Artistes From the frolicking wood nymphs of Howard Chandler Christy's rather risqué murals to the leaded-glass windows, this elegant dining place exudes romance. One drawback is that tables practically abut one another, which discourages spontaneous wedding proposals. Owner George Lang periodically tours the dining room and encourages his guests to sample such country French dishes as sweetbread headcheese with cucumber vinaigrette, and the illustrious Ilona torte, a flourless chocolate cake that contains 10 (ah, cholesterol!) eggs. Come here on weekends for the most beautiful brunch in town. Open daily. 1 W. 67th St. between Central Park West and Columbus Ave. (phone: 877-3500).

Il Cantinori A beamed ceiling, terra cotta floor, and chairs of wood and straw create the charming ambience at this Tuscan eatery, located on one of the city's loveliest blocks. Begin with *risotto nero* (a rice delicacy in squid ink) or *ravioli alla fiiorentina* (dumplings filled with spinach and ricotta cheese) before an entrée of excellent fish or game. For dessert try the chef's version of the popular Italian confection *tiramisù,* espresso-soaked ladyfingers and sweet mascarpone cheese. Closed for lunch on weekends. Major credit cards accepted. 32 E. 10th St. between University Pl. and Broadway (phone: 673-6044).

La Caravelle Opened since 1960, this recently refurbished dining spot is considered one of the city's great French restaurants. Owners Rita and André Jammet invite guests to sample classic French cuisine with a modern spin.

Specialties include "French lasagna" (shrimps and scallops tucked inside thin layers of pasta), crispy duck with cranberries, grilled Dover sole with mustard sauce, and medaillons of poached lobster. The extensive French wine list includes some great bottles at predictably steep prices. The pre-theater menu is a relative bargain. Jacket and tie required. Closed Saturdays for lunch and Sundays. Major credit cards accepted. 33 W. 55th St. between Fifth and Sixth Aves. (phone: 586-4252).

Le Chantilly This recently refurbished French restaurant has loosened up quite a bit since chef-owner David Ruggerio arrived. His culinary talents are legendary and here he's infused the predictably classic cuisine with sunny new flavors, as is evident in such dishes as braised salmon in Moroccan spices and pan-seared lamb chop with eggplant tartlet, essence of tomato, and virgin olive oil. Dessert lovers will swoon over the confections, among them dark chocolate versions of a piano, violin, and bowler hat. The extensive wine list features top-quality red Bordeaux, and is generally expensive. Closed Sundays. Reservations necessary. 106 E. 57th St. between Lexington and Park Aves. (phone: 751-2931).

Cascabel Hearty, and robust best describes chef Tom Valenti's fare, which features such dishes as pork tenderloin wrapped in bacon with tomato, oregano, and white bean ravioli, roasted squab with sweet onion barley and carrots, and goat cheese ravioli with tomato. Top the meal with homemade sorbets—the citrus blossom and green apple are delightful. Open for dinner; closed Sundays. 218 Lafayette St. between Broome and Spring Sts. (phone: 431-7300).

Gotham Bar & Grill The space here is cavernous (it was originally a warehouse), but an award-winning bi-level design and lofty decor bring the space down to grand café scale. Chef Alfred Portale's seasonal creations continue to amaze. Sample such dazzlers as grilled Muscovy duck breast with Szechuan peppercorns, apricots, and turnips; grilled salmon; and artichokes *à la grecque.* Open daily. Major credit cards accepted. 12 E. 12 St. between Fifth Ave. and University Pl. (phone: 620-4020).

Grotta Azzurra Neapolitan specialties are served in a basement in the heart of Little Italy. Lobster *fra diavolo* exacts a high price, but it's worth the tariff. The garlic bread (not available on Saturdays) is like none other in this world, and it guarantees that you won't be bothered by vampires for years. Closed Mondays. No reservations, so be prepared to wait in line. No credit cards accepted. 387 Broome St. at Mulberry St. (phone: 925-8775).

Jo Jo Currently a New York hot spot, low fat is the rule here, but don't be fooled: Flavor and innovation are at the top of the list. There might be shrimp with a Thai-accented carrot broth; goat cheese and potato terrine with arugula juice; or rabbit, Swiss chard, and tomato oil enveloped in thin pasta. The desserts are the stuff of dreams. Ask to have coffee served around the fireplace upstairs. Closed Sundays. Major credit cards accepted. 160 E. 64th St. between Lexington and Third Aves. (phone: 223-5656).

Manhattan Ocean Club Both the lower-level and upstairs dining rooms of this fine seafood house have original Picasso ceramic plates and prints displayed behind glass on their white walls, set off by a few Greek columns. This restaurant's appeal is its fresh, delicious fish and shellfish—the Hawaiian *wahoo* and melt-in-your-mouth *kumomoto* oysters are particularly good. The *pâtissier* is winning awards with such sumptuous treats as calvados ice cream on apple tarts, and the service is attentive. Open daily. Major credit cards accepted. 57 W. 58th St. between Fifth and Sixth Aves. (phone: 371-7777).

Montrachet The cooking is best described as nouvelle French, with an emphasis on traditional flavors. Favorite dishes at this chic TriBeCa location include duck in red wine sauce with mission figs or fresh ginger, and roast chicken with garlic and potato purée. In addition to an extensive à la carte menu, there are three excellent prix fixe menus. Jacket requested. Closed Sundays. American Express accepted only. 239 W. Broadway between Walker and White Sts. (phone: 219-2777).

Morton's of Chicago The famous steakhouse chain has hit the Big Apple offering filet mignon, strip steak, and other generous cuts, all perfectly prepared. Side dishes include steaming hash browns, and toasted potato skins. Also on the menu are lobster, whole chicken, and an appetizing assortment of fresh vegetables. Open daily; weekends dinner only. 551 Fifth Ave. (entrance on E. 45th St.; phone: 972-3315) and 90 West St. at Albany St. (phone: 732-5665).

Il Nido A superb menu of northern Italian specialties and the highest standards of service are the hallmarks of Adi Giovannetti's attractive, if somewhat cramped, East Side establishment, especially popular for business lunches. *Crostini di polenta* with a mushroom and chicken liver sauce is the perfect starter, to be followed by mixed fried fish, shellfish in marinara sauce, or any of a host of other specialties. Closed Sundays. Major credit cards accepted. 251 E. 53rd St. between Second and Third Aves. (phone: 753-8450).

Oyster Bar The place for oysters: On any given day, there will be 10 varieties from which to choose. There's also Maine lobster, North Atlantic salmon, Dover sole, mako shark steaks, pompano, pink snapper, swordfish, Florida stone crabs in season, a host of clams, and Mediterranean seafood. The huge volume assures fresh product. Closed weekends. Reservations unnecessary. Major credit cards accepted. Grand Central Station (lower level), E. 42nd St. between Vanderbilt and Lexington Aves. (phone: 490-6650).

Palio Here is an elegant entry in New York's abundant inventory of fine Italian eateries. The street-level bar is surrounded by artist Sandro Chia's mural of Siena's exciting medieval horse race that gives this place its name; the upstairs dining room is spacious, elegant, and perfect for a pre-theater meal. Closed Saturday lunch and Sundays. Major credit cards accepted. 151 W. 51st St. between Sixth and Seventh Aves. (phone: 245-4850).

Palm Good sirloin steaks are served in an atmosphere so unassuming that the draw has got to be the food. Sawdust covers the floor, tables and chairs are refugees from a thrift shop, but the beef is first-rate. The largest (and most expensive) lobsters in New York also are served here. *Palm, Too,* directly across the street at 840 Second Ave. (phone: 697-5198), offers identical food. Reservations advised for lunch; for dinner, they are accepted only for parties of four or more. Closed Sundays. Major credit cards accepted. 837 Second Ave. between E. 44th and E. 45th Sts. (phone: 687-2953).

Patria Miami-born chef Douglas Rodriguez has made news with his exciting Latin American fare. The bi-level restaurant offers red snapper with coconut-conch rice, and a seafood *chupe* (a spicy seafood stew). Desserts are superb, and don't miss the *Patria colada* (a version of the piña). Everything at this place is hot—right down to the pulsating salsa music. Open daily. 250 Park Ave. S. at E. 20th St. (phone: 777-6211).

Peter Luger The best porterhouse and T-bone steaks in the country, lurking in the shadows under the Brooklyn side of the Williamsburg Bridge. The neighborhood is hardly fashionable, but the food is just great. No menu, but try the thick-sliced onions and tomatoes under the special barbecue sauce, and be sure to taste the best home-fried potatoes the city has to offer (served only in the evenings). Open daily. Reservations for weekends should be made a week or two in advance; only on Mondays or Tuesdays can you be seated without a reservation. No credit cards accepted. 178 Broadway, Brooklyn (phone: 718-387-7400).

Remi Beneath a wraparound mural of Venice, diners indulge in such northern Italian fantasies as cuttlefish in its own ink over polenta, smoked prosciutto with greens and truffled olive oil, and ravioli Marco Polo with fresh tuna and ginger. A dessert favorite is *cioccolatissimo,* a chocolate soufflé cake topped with cappuccino parfait. And if you've still got the heart and room, there are 30 different kinds of grappa to follow the meal. Open daily. Major credit cards accepted. 145 W. 53rd St. between Sixth and Seventh Aves. (phone: 581-4242).

River Café Set on a barge on the Brooklyn shore of the East River, with spectacular views of the lower Manhattan skyline, this is one of the top American restaurants, with an especially good weekend brunch menu featuring lobster baked in horseradish oil with oyster risotto, poached eggs on smoked salmon waffles, and duck *confit* with roasted garlic and white beans. Jacket required; tie optional. Open daily. Reservations necessary two weeks ahead. Major credit cards accepted. 1 Water St., Brooklyn (phone: 718-522-5200).

Tavern on the Green The food is less famous than the decor and location (just inside Central Park) at this, one of New York's most beautiful dining establishments. In winter the snow-covered trees trimmed with tiny white lights outside the *Crystal Room* make a dazzling display (and reservations are a must a month in advance). Summer is spectacular, when diners can sit in the outdoor garden. The newly opened *Chestnut Room* showcases big band sounds, jazz trios, and cabaret stars. Open daily. Major credit cards accepted. Central Park W. and W. 67th St. (phone: 873-3200).

Tribeca Grill Stargazers come here in hopes of seeing one of the co-owners: Robert De Niro, Sean Penn, Mikhail Baryshnikov, or Bill Murray. Serious diners flock to sample such temptations as duck *confit* with crisp greens, and cavatelli with plum tomatoes, basil, and pecorino cheese. The changing roster of desserts has gained notoriety. Open daily. Reservations necessary three weeks in advance for weekends. Major credit cards accepted. 375 Greenwich St. at Franklin St. (phone: 941-3900).

Trois Jean The three Jeans of the name refer to owner Jean-Luc Andriot, chef Jean-Louis Dumonet, and the late pastry chef Jean-Marc Burillier (ably succeeded by Bernard Chenivese). Together, they turn out earthy, delicious food in a candlelit, lace-curtained dining room. Among the many good choices are risotto with wild mushrooms and truffle oil, sautéed sweetbreads and artichokes with cumin served on mixed greens with fried leeks, Hudson Valley foie gras terrine, home-smoked salmon, cassoulet, and pan-seared skate with beef broth. For dessert try the warm *crème brûlée* that sets the standard by which all others should be judged. Open daily. Reservations recommended. 154 E. 79th St between Third and Lexington Aves. (phone: 988-4858).

Union Square Café The menu at this informal, perennially popular eatery changes with the seasons, but classic American dishes prepared with a hint of old Italy are always featured. Appetizers may include *bruschetta* (grilled garlic bread with tomatoes), polenta, or a dish of creamed turnips; filet of tuna, fine hamburgers, and calamari often appear as options for the main course. The atmosphere is airy and pleasant, with Italian-style furnishings and oil paintings. Closed Sunday lunch. Major credit cards accepted. 21 E. 16th St. between Union Sq. W. and Fifth Ave. (phone: 243-4020).

Verbena This small dining room of understated beige and khaki is a welcome change from the glitz and glamor of most Big Apple eateries. Here instead all of the drama is soul-satisfying, seasonal fare supplied by chef Diane Forley. Her signature menu might include autumn mushrooms with angel-hair pasta in truffled mushroom broth, butternut-squash ravioli flavored with roasted oranges and sage, or seared venison chop with twice-baked sweet potatoes, chestnuts, and pomegranate seeds. Desserts are excellent—especially the rum-soaked savarin filled with warm bittersweet chocolate,

chocolate soufflé and chocolate-chip ice cream, and *crème brûlée* with lemon verbena. Open daily; Sunday brunch. Reservations necessary. 54 Irving Pl at E. 17th St. (phone: 260-5454).

Water Club The decor at this restaurant/barge in the East River is nautical, but with restraint, since the view is decorative enough: river traffic and the twinkling lights of the Manhattan and Queens skylines. The menu, too, is nautical, with similar restraint. Appetizers range from oysters and smoked salmon to beluga caviar, entrées from Maryland crab cakes to Dover sole and lobster—but diners also can order pâté or filet mignon. Jacket requested. Open daily. Major credit cards accepted. It's tricky to get here, so take a cab. East River at E. 30th St., on the northbound service road of the FDR Dr. (phone: 683-3333).

MODERATE

American Festival Café This place is cheery, very American, and right on the famous ice skating rink in *Rockefeller Center* (in summer tables are available in the rink). The reasonably priced and varied menu includes prime ribs, steaks, roast chicken, and warm and cold seafood. It's also noted for its desserts, including Mississippi mud pie, New York cheesecake, and Key lime pie. The atmosphere is best from November to April, when the rink is open. Open daily. Major credit cards accepted. 20 W. 50th St. (phone: 246-6699).

Arqua This stylish TriBeCa spot specializes in the food of the Veneto, but chef-owner Leonardo Pulito (from the town of Arqua, near Venice) has as fine a touch with grilled salmon and rack of lamb as with artichoke lasagna and game prepared Italian-style. Look into the reasonable prix fixe menu for either lunch or dinner. Closed for lunch on weekends. Major credit cards accepted. 281 Church St. at White St. (phone: 334-1888).

Artusi The former *Cesarina* features good Northern Italian fare, including risotto, pasta, and regional specialties, and pleasant service. If osso buco is on the winter menu, go for it. Very popular at lunch with the executive crowd and a nice choice for pre-theater dinner, it is owned by Italy's renowned and elegant *Villa d'Este* hotel. Closed weekends. Major credit cards accepted. 36 W. 52nd St. between Fifth and Sixth Aves. (phone: 582-6900).

Azzurro This Upper East Side bastion of Sicilian specialties attracts hordes of fans with its grilled fish, fine pasta specials, and delectable *vino santo*. Most members of the staff are related, and Mama Sindoni is in the kitchen. Open daily. Major credit cards accepted. 245 E. 84th St. between Second and Third Aves. (phone: 517-7068).

Bice Excellent northern Italian dishes, a busy atmosphere, and stylish Midtown crowd have made this bistro one of the most popular dining places in the city. Homemade pasta is the mainstay of the ever-changing menu; chef Alessandro Murali's specialties on any given day might include *tagliolini* (thin noodles) with white truffles or grilled tuna with black peppercorns. Open daily. Major credit cards accepted. 7 E. 54th St. between Fifth and Madison Aves. (phone: 688-1999).

Il Bocconcino The celebrity photographs in the window date back to *La Dolce Vita* days, when Gilberto was a paparazzo in Rome. Now he runs this modest but congenial Greenwich Village spot, with lace curtains, white tablecloths, and some murals of Italianate architecture to remind him of home. Sample the *bruschetta* (grilled garlic bread with tomatoes), then follow with pasta, chicken, veal, and seafood. Sidewalk tables are set up in summer. Open daily. Major credit cards accepted. 168 Sullivan St. at Houston St. (phone: 982-0329).

Café Luxembourg The interior here is Art Deco in style, brightly lit, and noisy, with everyone appearing to be looking around for someone famous. Not far from *Lincoln Center,* it is especially popular with concertgoers. The fare is nouvelle, though the specials tend to be uneven. For the best look at the chic crowd, come after 8 PM. There's also a Sunday brunch. Open daily. 200 W. 70th St. between Amsterdam Ave. and West End Ave. (phone: 873-7411).

Café Un Deux Trois In this very lively theater district bistro, whose name is its address, patrons draw on the paper tablecloths with crayons while waiting to sample carefully prepared daily specialties that include fresh sea trout, steak with *pommes frites,* and couscous with chicken, lamb, and chick-peas. Theatergoers should plan to dine very early to be sure to make curtain time. Open daily . Reservations accepted for parties of five or more. Major credit cards accepted. 123 W. 44th St. between Sixth Ave. and Broadway (phone: 354-4148).

Cent' Anni A Greenwich Village gem, it serves down-to-earth northern Italian fare in an unpretentious storefront setting. There are only 60 seats, so evenings tend to be both crowded and convivial as diners enjoy classic pasta. The name comes from the traditional toast "May you live 100 years!" Open daily. Major credit cards accepted. 50 Carmine St. between Bleecker and Bedford Sts. (phone: 989-9494).

Chin Chin This stylish Chinese eatery is somewhat formal at lunchtime, but the atmosphere relaxes in the evening. The three dining rooms are paneled with maple wood, and skylights lend a cheerful brightness. Excellent dishes include Peking duck, Grand Marnier prawns, and cold noodles with sesame sauce. Closed for lunch on weekends. Major credit cards accepted. 216 E. 49th St. between First and Second Aves. (phone: 888-4555).

Contrapunto This modern glass-enclosed dining room is the ideal spot to recover from a splurge at *Bloomingdale's.* Popular favorites include the sumptuous *malfatti* (dumplings filled with crabmeat and tomatoes), and delicate angel-hair pasta with littleneck clams. Located above *Yellowfingers,* the atmosphere is open, airy and ideal for relaxing. The desserts are many—try the rich chocolate torte—and the wine list is very affordable. Open daily. Major credit cards accepted. 200 E. 60th St. (phone: 751-8615).

Dock's Oyster Bar There are two of these huge seafood palaces, and each is packed at lunch- and dinnertime. The sprawling raw bar attracts social nibblers, while others head for the crisply nautical dining area to tackle a lengthy menu that often includes seared and gingered tuna, tangy chowders, and a catch-of-the-day selection, which regulars order with a side dish of sweet potato fries. Open daily. Major credit cards accepted. 2427 Broadway between W. 89th and W. 90th Sts. (phone: 724-5588), and 633 Third Ave. at E. 40th St. (phone: 986-8080).

Hatsuhana Still winning kudos from some of New York's toughest restaurant critics, this Japanese eatery serves some of the best sushi, sashimi, and tempura in town. Closed Sundays. Reservations necessary for dinner only. Major credit cards accepted. 17 E. 48th St. between Fifth and Madison Aves. (phone: 355-3345).

Jean Lafitte As accurate an evocation of a cozy and unpretentious Parisian neighborhood bistro as exists in New York. Go for the excellent tripe, the authentic *choucroute* (on specials only), or steak *au poivre.* Superb soups, which change daily, are a special treat during a cold New York winter. Convenient to *Carnegie Hall.* Closed for lunch on weekends. 68 W. 58th St. between Fifth and Sixth Aves. (phone: 751-2323).

Le Madri Delicacies such as fresh prawns stuffed with wild mushrooms and ricotta cheese, antipasto with caramelized onions, and osso buco are fabulous at this stylish Italian dining spot. The menu changes seasonally, and there is a weekend brunch menu. For dessert try the apple tart with cinnamon ice cream. Open daily. Major credit cards accepted. 168 W. 18th St. at Seventh Ave. (phone: 727-8022).

Mesa Grill The sassy Southwestern fare here, served up by young up-and-coming chef Bobby Flay, surpasses anything of its kind in New York. And the sizzling, noisy social scene adds nearly as much heat as the chilies he uses so liberally. Try the *posole* (a Mexican fish stew made with hominy), the moist, blue corn–encrusted fried chicken, or the grilled swordfish with cilantro pesto. Open daily. Major credit cards accepted. 102 Fifth Ave. between W. 15th and W. 16th Sts. (phone: 807-7400).

Odéon In a gray cast-iron building, this high-style, refurbished cafeteria is in the midst of TriBeCa. Look for seasonal entrées such as squab with shiitake mushrooms and wild rice, and roast loin of lamb with white peppercorns. A dessert worth trying is triple chocolate pudding. Open daily. Major credit cards accepted. 145 W. Broadway and Thomas St. (phone: 233-0507).

Periyali In this cool Aegean oasis, patrons enjoy traditional Greek fare prepared with an exceptionally light touch. Specialties include lima bean salad with skordalia, a tangy potato-based purée; baked sea bass with garlic, tomato, and white wine; and moussaka with grilled zucchini. For dessert, don't miss the luscious custard-filled *galaktoboreko*. Closed Sundays. Major credit cards accepted. 35 W. 20th St. between Fifth and Sixth Aves. (phone: 463-7890).

Pierre au Tunnel Onion soup, mussels, frogs' legs, and grilled steaks typify the French provincial dishes featured in this theater district bistro since 1950. Try the shallots or tripe cooked with white wine and calvados. Closed Sundays. Reservations necessary for pre-theater dinner. Major credit cards accepted. 250 W. 47th St. between Broadway and Eighth Ave. (phone: 575-1220).

Provence At this perfect French dining spot in the Village, the spices and tomato-based sauces of southeastern France are nowhere better utilized, and the roast chicken with garlic gives a whole new meaning to the serving of fowl. A huge vat of aging brandy adorns the bar and provides an excellent digestive at the conclusion of a meal. In summer the back patio is an idyllic dining spot. Open daily. American Express accepted. 38 MacDougal St. between Houston and Prince Sts. (phone: 475-7500).

Sammy's Roumanian Steak House At this last survivor of a long Lower East Side tradition of ethnic meat restaurants, Eastern European favorites are featured, as is Old Country music of a sort you're not likely to hear in any other establishment. The makings for egg creams (milk, seltzer, and chocolate syrup) are set right on the table—an experience you don't usually find anymore in New York. Open daily. Major credit cards accepted. 157 Chrystie St. between Delancey and Rivington Sts. (phone: 673-5526).

Santa Fe Unlike many other Mexican eateries that have sprung up around the city, there are no hanging plants, no neon signs, no ear-splitting noise levels here. Instead, crisp linen and salmon-colored walls hung with Mexican tapestries provide a serene setting for nicely tart margaritas and well-prepared Southwestern dishes. Open daily. Major credit cards accepted. 72 W. 69th St. between Central Park W. and Columbus Ave. (phone: 724-0822).

Shun Lee Palace Owner Michael Tong's recently renovated landmark Chinese restaurant showcases chandeliers and mahogany cases filled with treasures of past dynasties. The menu includes such unlikely named dishes as *ants climb on tree* (a combination of beef, broccoli, and cellophane noodles), or more traditional fare—steamed dumplings, orange beef, or whole poached sea bass with brown-bean sauce. The dessert menu features such Western favorites as chocolate mousse cake. Open daily. 155 E. 55th St. between Third and Lexington Aves. (phone: 371-8844) and 43 W. 65th St. between Central Park W. and Broadway (phone: 595-8895).

Tropica The setting is an amalgam of just about every island in the Caribbean, and the menu is similarly inspired—saucy and piquant, with an emphasis on freshly caught seafood. Its location on the lobby level of the Met-Life Building (formerly the Pan Am Building), in the middle of the traffic path to and from *Grand Central Station,* attracts crowds of expense-account types at lunch; it can be noisy at dinner too. Closed weekends. Major credit cards accepted. 200 Park Ave. between Vanderbilt Ave. and E. 45th St. (phone: 867-6767).

West 63rd Street Steakhouse Located directly across from *Lincoln Center,* this new restaurant offers a clubby atmosphere and a menu of prime cuts of beef enhanced with such excellent sauces as red wine, shallot, herb butter, and chardonnay lemon. The wine list is excellent. Open daily. Major credit cards accepted. 44 W. 63rd St. (phone: 246-6363).

Zarela Among the city's better Mexican eateries, this festive East Sider flourishes under the direction of its high-profile owner, Zarela Martínez. Menu selections range from the familiar to such eclectic dishes as roast duck with tomato and red chili sauce, and shrimp with tomato *poblano* salsa. There are spice levels for every palate, so the cautious needn't fear, and there are great tangy margaritas to shore up everyone's courage. Closed for lunch on weekends. American Express and Diners Club accepted. 953 Second Ave. between E. 50th and E. 51st Sts. (phone: 644-6740).

INEXPENSIVE

Carmine's This eatery lures the hungry hordes to its two locations with oversize portions of home-style food at reasonable prices. There's nothing "nouvelle" about the menu of Italian favorites like fried calamari, spaghetti with meatballs, and chicken Contadina (with sausage, peppers, and lots of garlic). Open daily. Reservations are accepted only for parties of six or more; otherwise, be prepared to wait in a long line. American Express accepted. 2450 Broadway between W. 90th and W. 91st Sts. (phone: 362-2200), and 200 W. 44th St. between Broadway and Eighth Ave. (phone: 221-3800).

Carnegie Delicatessen At this, the quintessential New York deli, the sandwiches are enormous, seemingly too big to put in a normal human mouth, and corned beef and pastrami are king. There are communal tables and no atmosphere, except the frantic Seventh Avenue scene, but waiters provide entertaining banter. Save room for the velvety cheesecake. Open daily from 6:30 AM to 3:30 AM. No reservations or credit cards accepted. 854 Seventh Ave. at W. 55th St. (phone: 757-2245).

Golden Unicorn The dim sum in this Chinatown eatery (served from 8 AM to 4 PM—but try to get here by 10:30 on a Sunday morning) are arguably the city's best. This stylish spot also specializes in Cantonese dishes such as scallops and bean curd in black bean sauce and shrimp with walnuts served with a mayonnaise dressing. If you're unfamiliar with Chinese food, rely on the advice of the courteous and attentive staff. For a special taste treat, try the shark's fin dumpling in its own soup. Open daily. Major credit cards accepted. 18 E. Broadway at Catherine St. (phone: 941-0911).

Hunan House Among Chinatown's best, this pleasant place specializes in the subtly spiced food of the Hunan province. Start off with fried dumplings or hot and sour soup, then have Hunan lamb with scallions; Changsha beef, done in a hot sauce with broccoli; or Confucius prawns with cashews. Open daily. No reservations. American Express and Diners Club accepted. 45 Mott St. between Pell and Bayard Sts. (phone: 962-0010).

Pamir Small and family-run, this spot specializes in Afghan (much like Indian) cooking. The delicately seasoned lamb dishes are very good. Closed Mondays. MasterCard and Visa accepted. 1437 Second Ave. at E. 74th St. (phone: 734-3791). A larger, more comfortable second location is on the corner of First Ave. and E. 58th St. and also accepts American Express (phone: 644-9258).

Serendipity 3 Definitely not for kids only, this East Side classic has been packing them in for as long as most of us can remember. The front room resembles an old-fashioned general store (but the merchandise is cute and trendy); the rear dining room is a cozy jumble of antique oak tables, Tiffany-style lamps, and old-time tin signs. Chocoholics delight in the bathtub-size hot fudge sundaes; other favorites are the foot-long hot dogs and frozen hot chocolate. It's a great place to rest up after a *Bloomingdale's* binge. Open daily. Major credit cards accepted. 225 E. 60th St. between Second and Third Aves. (phone: 838-3531).

SUNDAY BRUNCH

Sunday brunch is a cherished tradition among New Yorkers. Some popular spots—some of which have long lines waiting to get in—are *Sarabeth's Kitchen* (423 Amsterdam Ave.; phone: 496-6280; and 1295 Madison Ave.; phone: 410-7335); *Man Ray Bistro* (169 Eighth Ave.; phone: 627-4220); the *Brasserie* (100 E. 53rd St.; phone: 751-4840); and *Florent, the River Café*, the *Water Club, Odéon,* and *Provence* (see above for all five). One of the few places that takes brunch reservations is *Zoë* (90 Prince St.; phone: 966-6722). Hotel dining rooms with copious—and more costly—brunch buffets are the *Café Pierre* at the *Pierre;* the *Ambassador Grill* at the *UN Plaza–Park Hyatt; Peacock Alley* at the *Waldorf-Astoria;* and the *Palm Court* at the *Plaza* (see *Checking In* for all four). Uptowners head to Chinatown for a dim sum experience in any of the myriad area restaurants, including the *Golden Unicorn* (see above).

On board one of *World Yacht*'s five restaurant-yachts, you can enjoy Sunday brunch ($39 per person) while cruising the Hudson River and New York Harbor past the glittering Manhattan skyline. There are luncheon and dinner cruises as well. Jacket required (no tie). Open daily. Advance reservations and tickets are necessary. Major credit cards accepted. Sailings are from Pier 81 on the Hudson River at W. 41st St. (phone: 630-8100).

TAKING TEA

New Yorkers have become quite fond of the British tradition of afternoon tea, and a number of the city's most posh hotels have jumped on the bandwagon. The *Carlyle's Gallery,* the *Mayfair Hotel,* the *Lowell,* the *Plaza*'s *Palm Court,* the *Rotunda Room* at the *Pierre,* the *New York Palace,* and the *Stanhope* (see *Checking In* for all) offer superlative service and a variety of teas, scones, sandwiches, and condiments. Taking tea is a great way to experience the ambience of these elegant hostelries without having to stay the night. Tea for two usually costs $40 to $50; à la carte service is also available at some hotels. Reservations are usually necessary. Shoppers needing to soothe their nerves can head to the lower level of *Takashimaya* (693 Fifth Ave.; phone: 350-0100) to sip some green tea.

For those who prefer cappuccino to a cup of tea, *Caffè Roma* (385 Broome St.; phone: 226-8413), in the heart of Little Italy, is one of the few remaining old-style coffeehouses still operating. Everything from espresso to egg creams and Italian cookies and pastries are served daily from 8 AM to midnight.

Orlando

Orlando was just another good-size American city until 1971, when Walt Disney's dream park opened nearby. Its unprecedented growth during the last 25 years would impress anyone, even Walt. Today, Orlando fluctuates between first and second place in the neck-and-neck race for the largest number of hotel rooms (Las Vegas is its only rival). The *Orlando International Airport* is in the midst of a constantly ongoing expansion to accommodate the constantly increasing number of tourists who flock here each year. The *Walt Disney World* drawing board is loaded with expansion plans for the late 1990s that include adding attractions to its theme parks, constructing another new hotel, and building yet another theme park.

In short, Orlando, formally established in 1857, has come a long way since its birth as a campground for soldiers fighting the bloody Seminole Indian War in the early 19th century. But despite several growth spurts—in 1880, when a railroad was run from the city of Sanford; in the 1920s, just before the Great Depression; in 1956, with the opening of an important defense plant; and in 1961, when President Kennedy's declaration that the US would place a man on the moon within the next 10 years launched central Florida's space industry—Orlando drifted into and through the 20th century on the commerce of oranges and cows.

All that changed in 1971, and Orlando is now ranked regularly as one of the country's fastest growing cities, and one of its most livable. Many major corporations have set up headquarters here, bringing an ambitious young work force with them. The quality of restaurants and other diversions also has improved dramatically as Orlando matures into a rather cosmopolitan city.

Downtown Orlando continues to be renovated. Just north of town is Winter Park, a lovely suburban neighborhood where the broad, velvety lawns are dotted with palms or huge old oaks. Many of the homes here are sprawling and made of gleaming white stucco, with red-orange ceramic tile roofs in the Spanish style. The shops and restaurants along Park Avenue rival those anywhere in the country. Transplanted executives and their families are putting down roots both here and in other neighborhoods like Windermere and Heathrow.

Moreover, Orlando is an outdoor paradise. The more than 2,000 spring-fed lakes in the area take care of the water sport scene, and the 85 publicly owned and operated parks and recreation facilities offer golf, tennis, jogging, and more. Residents and visitors alike take advantage of the abundant recreational facilities at *Walt Disney World,* about 20 miles southwest of downtown, especially for after-dark entertainment and its six championship golf courses.

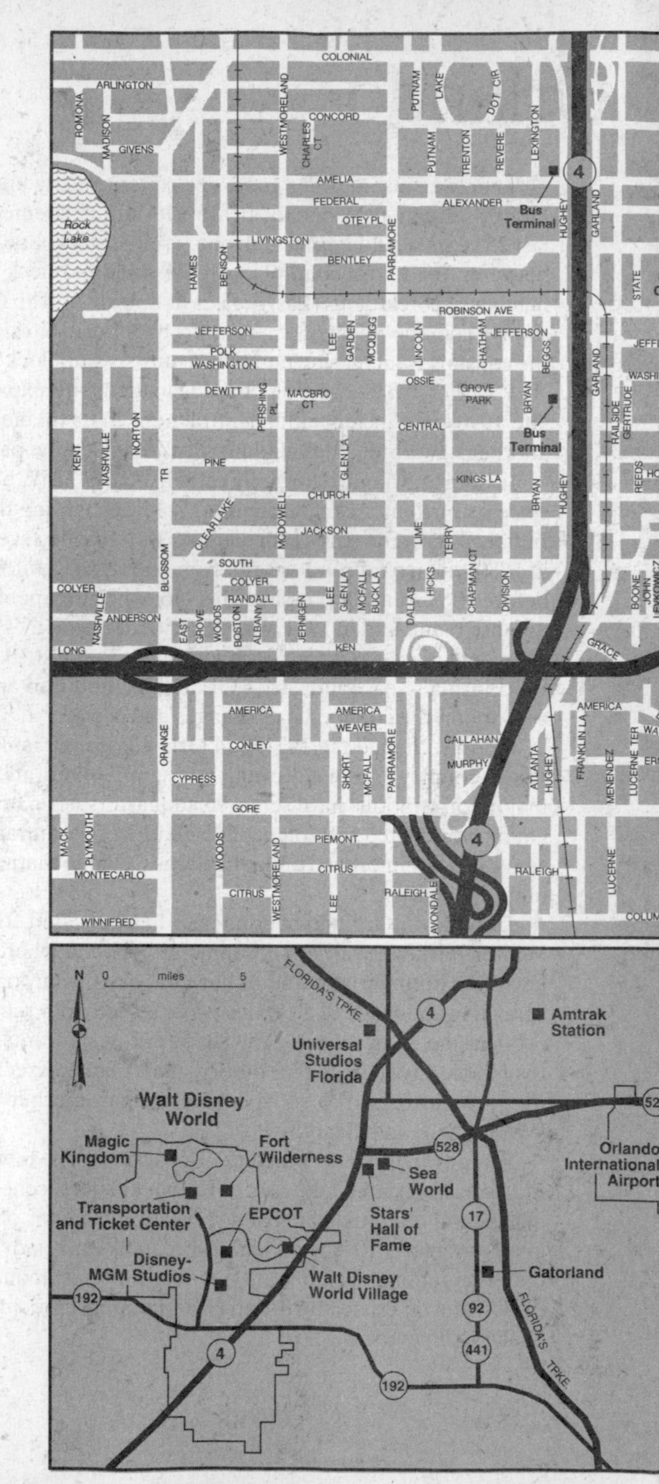

COLONIAL
ARLINGTON
ROMONA
MADISON
GIVENS
WESTMORELAND
CONCORD
CHARLES CT
PUTNAM
LAKE
DOT CIR
TRENTON
REVERE
LEXINGTON
4
AMELIA
FEDERAL
ALEXANDER
Bus Terminal
OTEY PL
Rock Lake
LIVINGSTON
HUGHEY
GARLAND
BENTLEY
PARRAMORE
HAMES
BENSON
STATE
ROBINSON AVE
JEFFERSON
POLK
WASHINGTON
LEE
GARDEN
MCQUIGG
LINCOLN
CHATHAM
JEFFERSON
BEGGS
OSSIE
GROVE PARK
BRYAN
DEWITT
PERSHING PL
MACBRO CT
KENT
NASHVILLE
NORTON
CENTRAL
Bus Terminal
RAILSIDE
GERTRUDE
PINE
TR
GLEN LA
KINGS LA
REEDS
CHURCH
CLEAR LAKE
MCDOWELL
BRYAN
HUGHEY
JACKSON
LIME
TERRY
BLOSSOM
SOUTH
CHAPMAN CT
COLYER
COLYER
RANDALL
NASHVILLE
ANDERSON
LEE
GLEN LA
MCFALL
BUCK LA
DALLAS
HICKS
DIVISION
BOONE
JOHN
LEVKOWICZ
EAST
GROVE
WOODS
BOSTON
ALBANY
JERNIGEN
LONG
KEN
GRACE
AMERICA
AMERICA
AMERICA
WEAVER
ORANGE
CONLEY
CALLAHAN
MURPHY
PARRAMORE
ATLANTA
HUGHEY
FRANKLIN LA
MENENDEZ
LUCERNE TER
CYPRESS
SHORT
MCFALL
GORE
MACK
PLYMOUTH
WOODS
PIEMONT
4
MONTECARLO
WESTMORELAND
CITRUS
RALEIGH
LUCERNE
CITRUS
RALEIGH
LEE
AVONDALE
WINNIFRED
COLUM
N
0 miles 5
FLORIDA'S TPKE.
4
Amtrak Station
Universal Studios Florida
Walt Disney World
528
Orlando International Airport
Magic Kingdom
Fort Wilderness
528
Sea World
Transportation and Ticket Center
EPCOT
Stars' Hall of Fame
17
Disney-MGM Studios
Walt Disney World Village
Gatorland
192
92
FLORIDA'S TPKE.
4
441
192

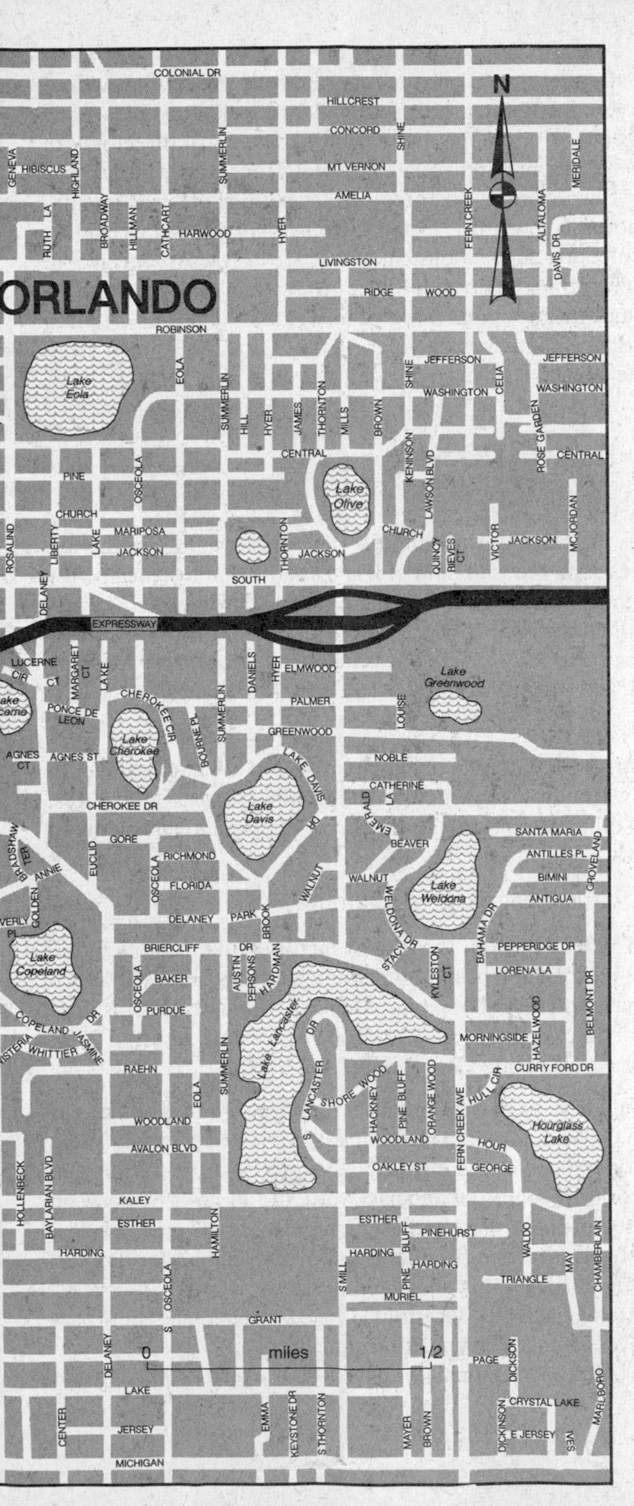
ORLANDO
N
miles
0
1/2
COLONIAL DR
HILLCREST
CONCORD
MT VERNON
AMELIA
HARWOOD
LIVINGSTON
RIDGE
WOOD
ROBINSON
JEFFERSON
WASHINGTON
CENTRAL
PINE
CHURCH
MARIPOSA
JACKSON
SOUTH
EXPRESSWAY
ELMWOOD
PALMER
GREENWOOD
NOBLE
CATHERINE
CHEROKEE DR
GORE
RICHMOND
FLORIDA
DELANEY
PARK
BRIERCLIFF
BAKER
PURDUE
RAEHN
WOODLAND
AVALON BLVD
KALEY
ESTHER
HARDING
GRANT
LAKE
JERSEY
MICHIGAN
Lake Eola
Lake Olive
Lake Greenwood
Lake Cherokee
Lake Davis
Lake Weldona
Lake Copeland
Lake Lancaster
Hourglass Lake
SANTA MARIA
ANTILLES PL
BIMINI
ANTIGUA
PEPPERIDGE DR
LORENA LA
MORNINGSIDE
CURRY FORD DR
OAKLEY ST
GEORGE
PINEHURST
TRIANGLE
MURIEL
PAGE
CRYSTAL LAKE
E JERSEY
GENEVA
HIBISCUS
HIGHLAND
RUTH
LA
BROADWAY
HILLMAN
CATHCART
SUMMERLIN
HYER
SHINE
FERN CREEK
ALTALOMA
MERIDALE
DAVIS DR
EOLA
HILL
JAMES
THORNTON
MILLS
BROWN
KENINSON
LAWSON BLVD
CELIA
ROSE GARDEN
OSCEOLA
ROSALIND
LIBERTY
QUINCY
RIEVES CT
VICTOR
MCJORDAN
DELANEY
LUCERNE CIR
CT
MARGARET CT
DANIELS
LOUISE
PONCE DE LEON
CHEROKEE CIR
BOURNE PL
AGNES CT
AGNES ST
LAKE DAVIS DR
EMERALD LA
BEAVER
WALNUT
WELDONA DR
BAHAMA DR
GROVELAND
BRADSHAW TER
GOLDEN
ANNIE
EUCLID
AVERLY PL
BROOK
AUSTIN DR
PERSONS
HARDMAN
STACY
KYLESTON CT
HAZELWOOD
BELMONT DR
COPELAND DR
JASMINE
WISTERIA
WHITTIER
S. LANCASTER DR
SHORE WOOD
HACKNEY
PINE BLUFF
ORANGE WOOD
FERN CREEK AVE
HULL CIR
HOUR
ORANGE
HOLLENBECK
BAYLARIAN BLVD
HAMILTON
S MILL
WALDO
MAY
CHAMBERLAIN
S OSCEOLA
DICKSON
DICKINSON
MARLBORO
VES
CENTER
EMMA
KEYSTONE DR
S THORNTON
MAYER

And despite the fact that Disney inaugurated the modern growth of Orlando, the city's climate (atypically seasonal for Florida and pleasantly unpredictable), energy, and appeal to corporate boards of directors are sustaining non-amusement park—related growth. Housing has burgeoned to accommodate the growing work force—to say nothing of a vast population of second-home "snowbirds." Orlando ranks among the US's leading convention and meeting destinations, and there are lush resort enclaves in the area that have nothing to do with Mickey or Shamu. And, finally, with the arrival of major league sports a few years ago via the *NBA*'s Orlando *Magic,* the rest of the country is discovering that Orlando is much more than just a theme park gateway.

Orlando At-a-Glance

SEEING THE CITY

For most visitors, the Disney area's premier panoramic vantage points are at the *California Grill* on the 15th floor of *Walt Disney World*'s *Contemporary Resort,* overlooking the *Magic Kingdom* and *Epcot*; and from *Arthur's 27* on the 27th floor of the *Buena Vista Palace*, offering a bird's eye view of *Disney Village Marketplace and Hotel Plaza*, *Pleasure Island*, *The Disney Institute*, the theme parks, and even downtown Orlando in the distance.

SPECIAL PLACES

Walt Disney World alone requires a minimum of four to five days—and even twice that time would not do justice to all its shows, sporting facilities, restaurants, and other attractions. And the rest of Orlando has plenty to offer as well.

ORLANDO AND ENVIRONS

BELZ FACTORY OUTLET WORLD One of the largest factory outlet centers in the world, this "mall-plex" of 180 brand-name merchants is composed of two huge enclosed malls and four shopping centers, all within walking distance of one another. You can "shop 'till you drop" for savings of up to 75%. Open daily. 5401 W. Oak Ridge Rd. (phone: 352-9600).

CYPRESS GARDENS You'd have to visit 90 countries at different times of the year to see all of the 8,000 varieties of plants that can be viewed at this 200-acre attraction developed back in the mid-1930s. Athletes at the "Water Ski Capital of the World" ski barefoot and backward; the all-new "Moscow on Ice Live!" show features Russian skating champions; the *Wings of Wonder* butterfly conservatory houses more than 1,000 free-flying butterflies; the *Masters of the Wind* birds of prey show and the new "Reptile Discovery" show blend entertainment with education; *Variete Internationale* showcases award-winning Russian acrobats performing European circus feats; legendary Southern belles and seasonal floral festivals are picture-perfect; and yuletide *Gardens of Lights* and *Spring Lights* pageantry glitter after dark. Open daily. Admission charge. Rte. 540, Winter Haven (phone: 941-324-2111; 800-282-2123).

SEA WORLD The world's most popular marine park ranks among Orlando's must-sees. Among the fine displays are *Shamu: World Focus,* a show featuring the Shamu family of killer whales and incorporating a video presentation; *Wild Arctic,* a "chilling" adventure featuring flight simulation to a remote North Pole research station of live polar bears, beluga whales, walruses, and harbor seals; and a new *Key West* attraction, featuring dolphins, sea turtles, and stingrays in naturalistic habitats set amidst the park's version of eclectic Duval Street. Other crowd favorites are: *Terrors of the Deep; Manatees: The Last Generation?;* the *"Baywatch"* water ski show; and *Penguin Encounter.* Open daily. Admission charge. 7007 Sea World Dr. (phone: 351-3600).

WET 'N' WILD Among connoisseurs, this aquatic play park full of thrill rides gets top marks. Also, there is a children's water playground. Bring a bathing suit, and prepare for long lines on summer afternoons. Varying hours, depending on the season; open year-round. Admission charge. 6200 International Dr. (phone: 351-1800; 800-992-9453).

UNIVERSAL STUDIOS FLORIDA Along with competing *Disney–MGM Studios,* this attraction lets visitors immerse themselves in the world of movie and television production. A 600-acre resort expansion this decade will include a second theme park, hotels, and an entertainment complex. Currently, there are over 40 rides, shows, and attractions from which to choose, including *Back to the Future ...The Ride, Kongfrontation, Jaws, The E.T. Adventure, Earthquake, The Funtastic World of Hanna-Barbera,Dynamite Nights Stuntacular,* and *A Day in the Park with Barney. Terminator 2 3-D*—a virtual adventure combining live action and 3-D film effects—is the park's newest attraction. Guests can see the soundstages and famous sets of the world's largest production studio outside Hollywood and observe actual filming in progress. Children can watch tapings of Nickelodeon Studios programs. There are about 20 themed eateries, including the popular *Hard Rock Café,* and two dozen shops featuring one-of-a-kind and movie-and television-themed merchandise. Open daily. Admission charge. 1000 Universal Studios Plaza (phone: 363-8000).

WALT DISNEY WORLD

Attracting more than 25 million annual visitors, this legendary park plainly shows its lasting appeal, and year-long 25th anniversary celebrations make this an extra-special time to visit this huge resort. The famous *Magic Kingdom* occupies just 100 of the 27,400 acres here; *Epcot* is more than twice as large, and the *Disney–MGM Studios* has doubled in size during the past decade. The remaining acres are dotted with villas, hotels, retail stores, a nonpareil swimming hole, two state-of-the-art water parks, two entertainment complexes, a cultural/lifestyle enclave, six championship golf courses, tennis courts, lakes, and a huge nature preserve. And there is still plenty of land left for future expansion. The main telephone number at *Walt Disney World* is 824-4321.

MAGIC KINGDOM The glittering *Cinderella Castle*—this year decorated as the world's largest birthday cake—sets the mood for this lushly landscaped fairy tale park full of elaborate sets, robots, sound effects, restaurants, shops, shows, parades, and "adventures"—boat rides, thrill rides, and other amusements. Top attractions include *Pirates of the Caribbean* and *Jungle Cruise* in the park's *Adventureland* section; *Splash Mountain* and *Big Thunder Mountain* in *Frontierland;* the *Haunted Mansion* and the *Hall of Presidents* in *Liberty Square; Space Mountain* and the intense *Alien Encounter* in *Tomorrowland; It's a Small World; Mickey's Toontown Fair* (formerly *Mickey's Starland*), a festive fairground of new pint-size attractions and plenty of Disney characters; and *Legend of The Lion King*, a stage show starring life-size puppets, in *Fantasyland*. During summer evenings and school holiday periods, be sure to see the brilliantly colored *SpectroMagic* light show, presented twice each evening, with an impressive fireworks display between performances.

EPCOT Something like a high-tech world's fair, executed with considerable creative and financial resources, *Epcot* has two "entertainment worlds": *Future World,* which explores the scientific cutting edge; and *World Showcase,* which brings nations of the world to life with ethnic food, entertainment, and lively shops stocked with native wares.

As in the *Magic Kingdom,* there are a few attractions here that visitors simply must not miss. In *Future World,* these include an *Innoventions* display featuring futuristic household appliances, space-age gadgets, and interactive computer games; the entire *Living Seas* pavilion; the ride inside the giant golf ball known as *Spaceship Earth;* the *Honey, I Shrunk the Audience* 3-D adventure at the *Journey into Imagination* pavilion; *Body Wars* and *Cranium Command* in the *Wonders of Life* pavilion; and the newly rehabbed *World of Motion* and *Universe of Energy* pavilions. In *World Showcase,* be sure to see the wide-screen movies in the Canada, China, and France pavilions, which take the travelogue to new heights; also don't miss the show at the *American Adventure,* including an all-new *America Gardens Stage Show,* a salute to 25 years of musical Americana. *IllumiNations 25,* a nightly spectacle of lights, lasers, and fireworks set to music, is also something special.

DISNEY–MGM STUDIOS This major Disney attraction has doubled in size since it opened. Guests can spend a day at the movies—on both sides of the camera—within a fully operating television and motion picture production facility. There's a backlot and soundstage tour where visitors watch a movie or television show being filmed; *Sunset Boulevard,* with Art Deco architecture reminiscent of old Hollywood; *The Great Movie Ride* through famous movie set re-creations that come remarkably to life: Gene Kelly in *Singin' in the*

Rain, Julie Andrews and Dick Van Dyke in *Mary Poppins,* and Sigourney Weaver in *Aliens.* Also, Robin Williams and Walter Cronkite star in a film about the animation process as guests watch actual animators at work; the late Jim Henson's Muppets are featured in the film *MuppetVision 3-D;* there's a live *Beauty and the Beast* show; and *Voyage of the Little Mermaid* blends live and film action. The *Twilight Zone Tower of Terror,* a 13-story, free-fall thrill ride set in a haunted hotel is a must-see, as is *Star Tours;* and a *Hunchback of Notre Dame* stage show, inspired by Disney's latest animated film, is the newest park feature. Other attractions include the *Honey, I Shrunk the Kids Adventure* zone, featuring 30-foot-tall stalks of grass and over-size slides and props; and daily *Toy Story* parades down *Hollywood Boulevard,* where movie characters march to life. A stunt theater, a variety of restaurants, and a sound effects studio are among other offerings.

DISNEY VILLAGE MARKETPLACE Coinciding with the resort's 25th anniversary, this popular shopping and dining complex is in the midst of a major renaissance that represents the largest entertainment expansion in *Disney World* history. Slated to open in phases through this year, the revitalization—which also encompasses neighboring *Pleasure Island* (an adult evening entertainment complex that stays open well past midnight)—will ultimately double the attraction's size. The new "district" will showcase two Disney superstores, an expanded 24-screen movie complex, a 1,500-seat performing arts theater, two celebrity restaurant/nightclubs—*House of Blues*, co-owned by actor Dan Aykroyd, and Gloria and Emilio Estefan's Latin-themed *Lario's*—and star-name restaurants including *Wolfgang Puck's Café,* featuring innovative California cuisine. Recent restaurant additions also include *Planet Hollywood*; *Fulton's Crab House* onboard the former *Empress Lilly*, operated by Levy Restaurants; and *Rainforest Café*, showcasing a jungle motif of waterfalls and thunderstorm special effects.

DISNEY'S BOARDWALK The sights and sounds of Coney Island, Cape Cod and Atlantic City come alive in this new turn-of-the-century, seaside-themed entertainment venue, situated between *Disney–MGM Studios* and *Epcot.* The 45-acre complex features a quaint collection of shops, nightclubs, a pair of whimsically-themed miniature golf courses, and restaurants overlooking the boardwalk. *ESPN World*—a full-service restaurant and sports club—is the linchpin establishment, with over 50 TV monitors, virtual-reality sports games, and live broadcast facilities. A promenade connects *BoardWalk* with five lakeside *Epcot* resort area hotels.

THE DISNEY INSTITUTE This new "discovery" resort for adults and children offers over 80 hands-on, personal enrichment programs ranging from culinary arts and storytelling to topiary gardening and self-defense aerobics. The campus—an eclectic mix of a Midwestern "Smalltown USA" and Caribbean-inspired pastels—includes a 38,000-square-foot sports and fitness center, an amphitheater, a golf course, a youth center, radio and TV studios, a cinema, and a full-service spa (whose services are open to non-resort guests). Participants register for three-, four-, or seyen-night program packages that include single-or double-occupancy stays in renovated on-site town houses or bungalows in the former *Disney Village Resort* complex. For more information call 800-496-6337.

TYPHOON LAGOON A water-fun park set on a 56-acre site that boasts six-foot waves for body surfers and a saltwater reef for snorkeling, as well as pools for swimming, tubing, and sliding.

BLIZZARD BEACH This water park looks like a ski resort in the process of melting. There are lots of slides in the 120-foot-high *Summit Plummet,* as well as flumes and pools.

RIVER COUNTRY The perfect swimming hole, it's full of curvy water chutes that make even blasé grownups roar with delight.

DISCOVERY ISLAND Crisscrossed by footpaths, this tranquil 11½-acre nature preserve on Bay Lake is the home of 120 animal, bird, and reptile species—some in cages or huge aviaries, others running free.

HOOP-DEE-DOO REVUE A lively dinner show with singing, dancing, wisecracking, and country-style vittles. Reservations are required well in advance, as this is one of *Walt Disney World*'s most popular live shows, especially for kids. Pioneer Hall, *Ft. Wilderness* (phone: 934-7639).

POLYNESIAN LUAU This outdoor South Seas revue features an authentic island feast complete with dancing, costumes, and special effects—and the best luau in town. A small-fry version, called *Mickey's Tropical Revue,* features island-garbed Disney characters. *Disney's Polynesian Resort* (phone: 934-7639).

BEHIND THE SCENES There isn't a *Magic Kingdom* visitor around who wouldn't like to see Disney character costumes being made or talk to a Disney artist in person. The *Wonders of Walt Disney World* program makes this happen for youngsters (ages 10 to 15).

Sources and Resources

TOURIST INFORMATION

For details, contact the *Orlando/Orange County Convention and Visitors Bureau* (6700 Forum Dr., Suite 100, Orlando, FL 32821; phone: 363-5800), which is closed weekends; the *Tourist Information Center* (8445 International Dr., *Mercado Mediterranean Village;* phone: 363-5872), which is open daily; the *Chamber of Commerce* (75 S. Ivanhoe Blvd., Orlando, FL 32804; phone: 425-1234), which is closed weekends; and *Walt Disney World Co.* (Box 10,000, Lake Buena Vista, FL 32830; phone: 824-4321), which is open daily. We immodestly believe that the best guides to the area are our own volumes, *Birnbaum's Walt Disney World* and *Birnbaum's Walt Disney World For Kids,*

By Kids (Hyperion and Hearst Business Publishing, Inc.; $12.95 and $9.95 respectively). Also pick up a copy of *ACCESS Orlando & Central Florida* (HarperCollins; $18.50). Contact the *Florida Division of Tourism* (phone: 904-487-1462) for maps, calendars of events, weather updates, and travel advisories.

LOCAL COVERAGE There are what's-doing sections in Friday's *Orlando Sentinel,* a daily, in *Orlando* magazine, a monthly; and in *The Weekly,* an entertainment publication.

TELEVISION STATIONS WESH Channel 2–NBC; WCPX Channel 6–CBS; WFTV Channel 9–ABC; WMFE Channel 24–PBS; and WOFL Channel 35–Fox.

RADIO STATIONS AM: WDBO 580 (news/talk/adult contemporary) and WWNZ 740 (news/talk). FM: WWKA 92.3 (country); WMMO 98.9 (soft rock); WOMX 105.1 (adult contemporary); WOCL 105.9 (oldies); WXXL 106.7 (adult contemporary); and WMGF 107.7 (adult contemporary).

TELEPHONE The area code for Orlando is 407.

SALES TAX The area sales taxes are 6% to 7%; the hotel room tax is 3% to 5%.

CLIMATE Spring and fall temperatures average in the mid-70s F. From November through March, warmer clothing is a must for evening. Summer is hot, rainy, and humid. Always pack something for unseasonably warm or cool weather.

GETTING AROUND

AIRPORT *Orlando International Airport* is 12 to 15 miles from downtown and 20 miles from the gates of *Walt Disney World. Mear's Motor Shuttle* (phone: 423-5566) and *Transtar Airport Shuttle* (phone: 856-7777) provide 24-hour transportation from the airport to most major hotels. Reserve a seat at the airport. *Lynx* city buses (Route No. 11) run on the half hour between the airport and Orlando's downtown terminal at Pine and Central; and (Route 42) between the airport and International Drive; the fare is 75¢ (phone: 841-8240 for information).

BUS *World Transportation* (phone: 826-9999) and *Gray Line* (phone: 422-0744) provide transportation to the major attractions from hotels. For schedule information on *Lynx,* the city bus system, call 841-8240; the fare is 75¢.

CAR RENTAL Most major car rental firms are represented. Orlando has the largest fleet in the US, and the rates (most with unlimited mileage) are relatively modest.

TAXI *Mear's Transportation Group* (phone: 422-4561) has the largest taxi fleet in the city.

SPECIAL EVENTS

The *Orlando Scottish Athletic Games & Festival* in January draws huge crowds for traditional folk dancing, and athletic and bagpipe competitions in kilts and tartans. The *Walt Disney World Indy 200* is raced on a 1.1-mile tri-oval track each January. The *Winter Park Sidewalk Art Festival,* the third weekend of March, and Disney's *Festival of the Masters* each November are two of the Southeast's most prestigious such events. The *Fourth of July* brings a vast array of pyrotechnics. Throughout *Walt Disney World,* lavish decorations make *Christmastime* especially festive and there are parties and extra-large fireworks displays on *New Year's Eve.* The annual *Florida Citrus Bowl Parade,* preceding the traditional clash of Big 10 and Southeastern conference football teams at the *Florida Citrus Bowl,* is always a year-end crowd-pleaser as well.

MUSEUMS

Orlando has a few noteworthy institutions:

CHARLES HOSMER MORSE MUSEUM OF AMERICAN ART The highlight of this turn-of-the-century period museum is its vast collection of Tiffany stained glass. 445 Park Ave. N.; Winter Park (phone: 645-5311).

ORLANDO MUSEUM OF ART In addition to permanent displays of paintings, prints, and sculpture, these newly expanded museum galleries now showcase world class exhibits. 2416 N. Mills Ave. (phone: 896-4231).

ORLANDO SCIENCE CENTER In addition to the recently added *John Young Planetarium,* this newly expanded center offers numerous exhibitions and live shows, some of which explore central Florida's ecosystem, native animals, the physical sciences, and technology. 810 E. Rollins St. (phone: 896-7151).

SHOPPING

Orlando has its share of cosmopolitan marketplaces, factory outlets, and regional malls. Enclaves of commerce with more character, however, also are easy to come by—and get to. The best shopping for gifts and souvenirs, however, can be found in *Walt Disney World,* at *International Drive* factory outlet malls, and at *Orlando International Airport*'s new mall of area attraction shops, where prices are street-competitive.

SPORTS AND FITNESS

BASEBALL The Orlando *Cubs,* a Chicago *Cubs* farm team, play at *Tinker Field* (287 S. Tampa Ave.; phone: 245-2827) during the spring and summer. The *National League* Houston *Astros* hold their spring training for about six weeks beginning in March at *Osceola County Stadium* in Kissimmee (phone: 933-5500). The *American League* Kansas City *Royals* also prepare for the season during six weeks beginning in March at *Baseball City Stadium,* 28 miles southwest of Orlando on US 27 (phone: 813-424-2424).

BASKETBALL The *NBA*'s Orlando *Magic* plays home games at the *Orlando Arena* (600 W. Amelia St.; phone: 896-2442).

FISHING Bass anglers flock to Florida's third-largest lake, Tohopekaliga, and to the St. Johns River network. To find out about nearby fishing camps, contact the *Kissimmee–St. Cloud Convention and Visitors Bureau* (phone: 847-5000), or the *Seminole County Convention and Visitors Bureau* (phone: 328-5770; 800-800-7832).

FITNESS CENTERS *Disney's Grand Floridian* (phone: 824-3000) offers a new full-service spa and health club; and the *Buena Vista Palace* (phone: 827-2727) has a new European-style spa that's also open to non-hotel guests. The *YMCA Aquatic Center* near area theme parks is open to non-members for a fee. The facility offers three indoor pools, wellness and teen fitness centers, weight room, air-conditioned racquetball courts, aerobics, water aerobics, and tae kwon do classes (8422 International Dr.; phone: 363-1911). In addition, many hotels have basic health centers for guests.

FOOTBALL The *Arena Football League*'s Orlando *Predators* play home games at *Orlando Arena*. 600 W. Amelia St. (phone: 872-7362).

GOLF Largely due to the presence of *Walt Disney World,* Orlando has a wealth of outstanding public golf courses. If you long for a round or two after (or instead of) taking in Disney's attractions, these are the best places.

TOP TEE-OFF SPOTS

Walt Disney World Veteran golfers seldom consider this resort complex for their vacations, but this ambitious attempt to be all things to all people has 99 holes of golf designed by three of the world's greatest: Pete Dye, Tom Fazio, and Joe Lee. The newer courses are Fazio's *Osprey Ridge* and Dye's *Eagle Pines.* The 7,190-yard *Magnolia* was named for the 1,000 magnolia trees scattered around its lakes, elevated tees, and greens; the 6,957-yard *Palm* course is rated among the nation's most challenging. The 6,819-yard *Lake Buena Vista* course is the third of the original Lee-designed venues. In addition, the par-36, 9-hole *Oak Trail* course offers fun for the entire family. The *Magnolia, Palm,* and *Lake Buena Vista* courses host the *PGA Tour*'s annual *Walt Disney World/Oldsmobile Golf Classic.* Serious enthusiasts may take lessons and view videotapes to hone their skills. There also are four driving ranges and four practice putting greens, plus three pro shops where clubs and shoes may be rented (phone: 824-2270).

Grand Cypress The original 27 Jack Nicklaus–designed holes transcend a relatively flat terrain with mounded roughs on which high grass grows; the Scottish influence is inescapable. Perhaps the most notable element of the landscape is the number of terraced fairways. Double greens are another unusual aspect. On the other hand, a newer 18-hole course features wide-open meadows and bunkers up to 12-feet deep, creating an entirely different dimension of play. Course access is restricted to resort guests. 1 N. Jacaranda (phone: 239-4700).

HOCKEY The *IHL*'s Orlando *Solar Bears* play at the *Orlando Arena* (see above; phone: 839-3900).

JOGGING Run around *Lake Eola* in downtown Orlando, on a trail at *Ft. Wilderness,* or on the miles and miles of *Walt Disney World* roads.

SWIMMING *Wet 'n' Wild* and *Walt Disney World*'s *River Country, Typhoon Lagoon,* and *Blizzard Beach* (see *Special Places*) are good bets for a dip, and most hotels have pools. There are especially good-size, heated pools at Disney's upper end resorts such as the *Dolphin* and *Swan* resorts, *Yacht* and *Beach Club* resorts, and *Grand Floridian* (see *Checking In* for all five). The pool at *Disney's Wilderness Lodge Resort* is a standout, featuring a Pacific Northwest theme complete with waterfalls, an "Old Faithful"–style geyser, and elaborate rockwork (see *Checking In*). Newly renovated pools at the *Contemporary* and *Polynesian* resorts (see *Checking In* for both) now feature water slides. The *Buena Vista Palace* (phone: 827-2727) offers the nicest pool complex in the *Disney Village Hotel Plaza* (see *Checking In* for both). Off property, the free-form *Hyatt Regency Grand Cypress* pool—with grottoes, waterfalls, and a jungle-style rope bridge (see *Checking In*)—is the cream of the crop.

TENNIS It's possible to play on the many lighted *Walt Disney World* courts (where court reservations, lessons, rental racquets, and even a partner-finding service are available; phone: 824-3578). Or you can play for a small fee on downtown Orlando public clay and hard courts (phone: 246-2161).

The *Grosvenor, Hotel Royal Plaza, Buena Vista Palace, Hilton at Walt Disney World, Hyatt Orlando, Peabody Orlando, Grand Cypress, Marriott's Orlando World Center, Orlando Marriott, Renaissance Orlando* resorts, and, Disney's *Contemporary, Yacht Club, Beach Club, Grand Floridian, Old Key West, Ft. Wilderness, Swan,* and *Dolphin* resorts are among the establishments with courts for guests.

THEATER AND MUSIC

At *Medieval Times* (4510 W. US-192; phone: 396-1518; 800-229-8300), a four-course dinner features jousting knights on horseback and other Middle Ages–themed entertainment. Murder, intrigue, and comedy entertain would-be Sherlocks and Agathas at *Sleuth's Mystery Dinner Show* (7508 Republic Dr.; phone: 363-1985; 800-393-1985). Set in an English drawing room, show themes vary nightly. *Wild Bill's Wild West Dinner Show* (5260 W. US-192; phone: 351-5151) serves up a four-course Southern-style meal, accompanied by western-style hoedown music and a cowboy-and-Indians show.

American Gladiators Orlando Live! (5515 W. US 192; phone: 800-228-8534) showcases athletic prowess by spandex-clad TV superheroes along with a four-course meal. The *Civic Center of Central Florida* (1001 E.

Princeton St.; phone: 896-7365) features musicals, dramas, and mysteries. Programs of dance, music, and theater are often presented at the *Bob Carr Performing Arts Centre* (401 W. Livingston St.; phone: 849-2001). Concerts, ice shows, and touring variety acts are held at the *Orlando Arena* (600 W. Amelia St.; phone: 849-2001). The *Enzian Theater* (1300 S. Orlando Ave.; phone: 644-4662) is Orlando's only art film house, offering independent and foreign films, occasional concerts, and celebrity guest appearances.

NIGHTCLUBS AND NIGHTLIFE

Once a pair of decaying hotels in a depressed downtown area, the *Church Street Station* complex of bars, shops, and restaurants (129 W. Church St.; phone: 422-2434), which charges an admission fee in the evening, has singlehandedly resurrected Orlando business district nightlife. Adjoining it is the *Church Street Station Exchange* (124 W. Pine; phone: 422-2434), a complex of specialty shops, a food court, and a video arcade, which does not charge admission. Cancan and Dixieland keep things lively at *Rosie O'Grady's Good Time Emporium;* specialty cocktails and folk and bluegrass music prevail at the Victorian-style *Apple Annie's Courtyard;* Top 40 and "Nickel Beer Night" Wednesdays make *Phineas Phogg's Balloon Works* a hit; and live rock 'n' roll is played at *Orchid Garden Ballroom.* Meanwhile, traditional American and continental food is served at *Lili Marlene's,* oysters and other seafood at *Crackers Oyster Bar,* and live country music (along with line dancing lessons on weekends), plus barbecue and all the fixings at the *Cheyenne Saloon & Opera House.* Be aware that the charge for most specialty libations here includes the price of the glass.

Among the many other pubs and lounges flourishing nearby is *Pinkie Lee's* (380 W. Amelia St.; phone: 872-7393), a classy downtown Orlando restaurant/nightclub with a Cajun- and Southern-style menu and cool jazz. Adjacent to the *Orlando Arena,* it's a popular celebrity musician and *NBA* player hangout.

Walt Disney World has a variety of nightspots, the most popular of which are at *Pleasure Island.* The *Island Jazz Company* and *House of Blues* (see above) join the Latin nightclub, *Lario's* (see above), along with such established favorites as the *Comedy Warehouse,* the *Neon Armadillo* (country), *8TRAX* (disco), the *Mannequins Dance Palace* (dance club), the *Rock 'n' Roll Beach Club* (golden oldies), and *Planet Hollywood* (movie-themed nightspot/restaurant). Or catch a movie at the newly expanded adjacent 24-screen *AMC* theater.

Best in Town

CHECKING IN

Most Orlando-area accommodations cluster along International Drive and nearby Sand Lake Road at the Orlando city limits, a 10-to 15-minute drive from *Walt Disney World;* along the east-west US 192, which intersects I-4 in Kissimmee near *Walt Disney World;* and within *Walt Disney World* itself. Most of Orlando's major hotels have complete facilities for the business traveler. Those listed below as having "business services" usually offer such conveniences as meeting rooms, photocopiers, computers, translation services, and express checkout, among others. Call the individual hotel for additional information. Expect to pay $300 or more per night for a double room at those places designated as very expensive; $150 to $300 for an expensive hotel; $80 to $150 at those identified as moderate; and less than $80 at those listed as inexpensive. Rates are occasionally less during off-peak periods. Unless otherwise noted, hotel rooms have air conditioning, private baths, TV sets, and telephones.

All hotels below are in Orlando and telephone and fax numbers are in the 407 area code unless otherwise indicated.

WITHIN WALT DISNEY WORLD—WALT DISNEY WORLD–OWNED PROPERTIES

For both facilities and convenience, the hotels and villas owned by the Disney organization can't be beat, and the addition of five inexpensive and moderately priced resorts means that even budget-conscious travelers can enjoy staying right on the *Walt Disney World* property. For details, call *Walt Disney World* Central Reservations (phone: 934-7639). There are meeting facilities at many of the resorts. For details about organizing a *Walt Disney World* meeting or convention, call 828-3200.

VERY EXPENSIVE

Grand Floridian This 900-room, Victorian-style resort, with broad verandahs and gabled roofs, is *Walt Disney World*'s first luxury hotel. A turn-of-the-century theme predominates—in everything from the room decor to the staff's Edwardian costumes. Facilities include nine restaurants and lounges, a pool, a health club, a marina, *Mouseketeer Club,* and business services. Monorail service; near the *Magic Kingdom* (phone: 824-3000).

EXPENSIVE

Beach Club Like its adjacent sister hotel, the *Yacht Club,* this 580-room resort was designed by noted architect Robert A. M. Stern. A beach motif dominates its decor from the spacious rooms to the seafood restaurant. The two hotels share a host of convention and sports facilities, including a marina, tennis courts, a free-form pool, a health club, and business services. Near *Epcot* (phone: 934-8000).

Boardwalk Inn This resort combines a full-service, 378-room motel and 383 *Disney's Old Key West* (formerly *Disney Vacation Club*) vacation ownership *BoardWalk* villas (see below). There are three pools, a health club, tennis courts, a child care facility, and business services. There are restaurants at the hotel and along the boardwalk, plus shops. Near *Epcot* and *Disney–MGM Studios* (phone: 939-5100 and 939-6200, respectively).

Contemporary Resort This bustling 1,050-room hotel offers magical views, a lake's-edge location, three restaurants, two recently renovated pools, a *Mouseketeer Clubhouse*, and one of the biggest gamerooms anywhere. And the monorail runs right through its 90-foot-high lobby. Business services are available. Near the *Magic Kingdom* (phone: 824-1000).

Dolphin The 1,510-room *Dolphin* and its sister hotel, the *Swan* (see below), were designed by Michael Graves and epitomize what is known as entertainment architecture—you can't miss the two 55-foot dolphins atop the hotel. Seven restaurants and three bars, an enormous pool, a state-of-the-art fitness center, and "Camp Dolphin" youth center keep visitors busy. Combined with the *Swan*, the hotels boast the second-largest hotel convention facilities in the Southeast. Business services are available. Near *Epcot* (phone: 934-4000).

Old Key West The tropical-themed studio, one-, two-, and three-bedroom units here are part of a vacation ownership program. Units not occupied by owners are available for nightly rental. There are boat rentals, a gameroom, a playground, two tennis courts, three pools, shops, a fitness center, and two restaurants. Near *Epcot* (phone: 827-7700).

Polynesian This resort's 853 rooms are set in several lakeside buildings on lushly landscaped grounds; the atmosphere is tranquil, the architecture island tropical. The Polynesian motif pervades several eating spots and lounges, and there are two newly renovated pools, a *Neverland* kiddie club, two authentic luaus, and a marina. Monorail service; near the *Magic Kingdom* (phone: 824-2000).

Swan With its two 55-foot swan statues, this distinctive 760-room hotel faces the *Dolphin,* its sister property, across Crescent Lake. Decorated in coral and turquoise, the Michael Graves–designed hotel offers three restaurants, a lobby lounge, eight lighted tennis courts, a large pool, a business center, a *Camp Swan* children's club, and a fitness center. Near *Epcot* (phone: 934-3000).

Wilderness Lodge This comfortably rustic re-creation of US national park lodges boasts 780 rooms, three restaurants, and a lounge, all of which evoke a cross between Pacific Northwest and American frontier themes. Bike and boat rentals are available, and there's an innovative playground and swimming pool (see "Swimming" above). Near the *Magic Kingdom* (phone: 824-3200).

Yacht Club Like its sister property, the *Beach Club,* this 635-room property, designed by architect Robert A. M. Stern, is set on a 25-acre lake. Its nautical theme extends to the guestrooms, two restaurants, and two lounges. The resort shares a wide range of sports and convention facilities with the *Beach Club* (see above), as well as youth club facilities. Near *Epcot* (phone: 934-7000).

MODERATE

Caribbean Beach This 2,112-room resort is composed of five brightly colored villages—each named for a Caribbean island—set on a 42-acre lake. Each has its own pool. The island theme continues throughout the rooms and the central food court. Near *Epcot* and *Disney–MGM Studios* (phone: 934-3400).

Coronado Springs Opened this year, this is Disney's first moderately-priced convention hotel. The hacienda-inspired resort features a white sand beach, a marina, four pools, a health club, a dining court, a lounge, and a full-service restaurant. Near *Disney–MGM Studios* (phone: 934-7639).

Dixie Landings This plantation-style resort, divided into "parishes," evokes the upriver South. Its 2,048 rooms are in either the elegant, columned Mansion homes or the more rustic Bayou buildings. The central food court and restaurant are designed to resemble a cotton mill. There are several pools, boat and bike rentals, and a fishing hole. Near *Epcot* (phone: 934-6000).

Port Orleans Reminiscent of the architectural style of the French Quarter in New Orleans, this 1,008-room resort offers creole cooking in its restaurant. Bike and boat rentals are available, and there's a pool and water slide shaped like a serpent. Near *Epcot* (phone: 934-5000).

INEXPENSIVE

Disney's All-Star Sports Sports is the focus here, with five separate buildings, each devoted to a different sport—tennis, football, surfing, baseball, and basketball. Even the pool is shaped like a baseball diamond. The themed rooms are comparatively small, and there is a food court for informal dining. Near *Disney–MGM Studios* (phone: 939-5000).

Disney's All-Star Music Adjacent to the *All-Star Sports* resort, this 1,920-room hotel celebrates five American music styles—calypso, country, rock, jazz, and Broadway. Larger-than-life icons illustrating the music theme include three-story cowboy boots and a neon-lit walk-through jukebox. There are two swimming pools—one in the shape of a grand piano and the other shaped like a guitar. Near *Disney–MGM Studios* (phone: 939-6000).

Fort Wilderness Campground Accommodations at this 780-acre area of cypress and pine range from campsites to luxurious villa-like trailers, complete with bathrooms, TV sets, and full kitchens (the latter are comparable in price to expensive hotel rooms). There's also a marina, a beach, and a number of waterways for fishing and canoeing. Southeast of the *Magic Kingdom* (phone: 824-2900).

WITHIN WALT DISNEY WORLD—HOTEL PLAZA

The following hotels are not Disney-owned, but they are designated as "official" hotels and are in *Walt Disney World* within walking distance of the *Disney Village Marketplace, The Disney Institute,* and *Pleasure Island.* Reservations for all of these properties can be made through *Walt Disney World* Central Reservations (phone: 934-7639). All are moderate to expensive depending on the season.

Buena Vista Palace Resort & Spa Our favorite in the complex, this hotel has 1,014 handsomely decorated rooms embellished with either a king or two queen-sized beds and voice mail (some rooms even have Mickey Mouse telephones). Twenty guestrooms have been converted into smoke-free, odor-free *EverGreen Rooms,* with such features as filtered tap water, non-allergenic pillows and blankets, and non-dyed bathroom linens. Outstanding sporting facilities, a youth activity program, five restaurants, four lounges, and a new European-style spa (services are open to non-hotel guests, too) are among its amenities. Business services are available. 1900 Buena Vista Dr. (phone: 827-2727; 800-327-2990; fax: 827-6034).

Doubletree Guest Suites Each of the property's 229 suites features a wet bar, a refrigerator, a microwave, and three TV sets. Other amenities include a restaurant, a pool, lighted tennis courts, a fitness center, and a gameroom. Business services are available. 2305 Hotel Plaza Blvd. (phone: 934-1000; 800-424-2900; fax: 934-1011).

Hilton at Walt Disney World Set on 23 acres, rooms at this 813-room hotel include voice mail and data port telephone systems. The tropically-themed property features seven restaurants and lounges, 340 nonsmoking rooms, two pools, and a health club. Business services are offered. 1751 Hotel Plaza Blvd. (phone: 827-4000; 800-782-4414; fax: 827-3890).

OUTSIDE WALT DISNEY WORLD

EXPENSIVE

Grand Cypress Resort The glittering, 750-room *Hyatt Regency Grand Cypress* luxury hotel is the star of a 1,500-acre complex that has more facilities than most visitors can ever use, including one of the largest free-form pools anywhere. The 45-hole Jack Nicklaus–designed course surrounds 146 luxury villas. There are seven restaurants, including the top-rated *Black Swan* and *La Coquina*, a concierge desk, the kiddie *Camp Hyatt,* an equestrian center, junior golf and equestrian academies, an exquisite art collection, and business services. 1 Grand Cypress Blvd., Lake Buena Vista (phone: 239-1234; 800-233-1234; fax: 239-3800; for the villas 239-4700; 800-835-7377; fax: 239-7219).

Marriott's Orlando World Center A 1,503-room, 27-story resort hotel set on nearly 200 beautifully landscaped acres, it's just minutes from *Walt Disney World.* Features include a 12-story lobby atrium, four pools, eight lighted tennis courts, an 18-hole Joe Lee golf course, a miniature golf course, a complete health club, four whirlpools, a gameroom, seven restaurants, two lounges, a concierge desk, a children's clubhouse, and business services. World Center Dr. (phone: 239-4200; 800-228-9290; fax: 238-8991).

Peabody Orlando The sister property of the well-known *Peabody* in Memphis, this elegant 27-story, 891-room hotel is International Drive's most luxurious. Guestrooms include state-of-the-art telephone capabilities. There are 285 nonsmoking rooms. Facilities include a nearly Olympic-length lap pool, four lighted tennis courts, an athletic club, a gameroom, and a concierge desk. The hotel is located directly across from the *Orange County Convention Center;* business services are available. The famous Peabody ducks are here, too: Every day at 11 AM, they waddle into the enormous lobby, down the red carpet, and into the marble fountain—a spectacle that attracts hotel guests and locals. (They return via the same route at 5 PM.) There's also a superb restaurant called *Dux* that serves imaginative international cuisine and has an award-winning wine cellar. 9801 International Dr. (phone: 352-4000; 800-732-2639; fax: 351-0073).

Renaissance Orlando This 780-room property overlooking *Sea World* is built around a 12-story atrium replete with aviary and exotic fish. A fitness center, four tennis courts, a pool, five restaurants, a concierge desk, a children's program, and business services round out the offerings. 6677 Sea Harbor Dr. (phone: 351-5555; 800-327-6677; fax: 351-9991).

MODERATE

Buena Vista Suites Located just minutes away from *Disney* parks, this 280-suite hotel is one of the best deals in town. Each unit has a queen-size sofa bed, a coffee maker, a refrigerator, a microwave, and two televisions. The grounds include exercise rooms, two tennis courts, a pool and whirlpool, a gameroom, a restaurant, and a lounge. Room rates include a free full American breakfast buffet. Nonsmoking rooms are available and there's complimentary shuttle service to *Disney World.* 14450 International Dr., Lake Buena Vista (phone: 239-8588; 800-537-7737; fax: 239-1401).

Park Plaza This bed and breakfast—long a favorite weekend getaway for locals—features 27 quaint bedrooms individually decorated with antiques, brass beds, and hardwood floors. The best rooms include plant-bedecked verandahs overlooking tony Park Avenue. Valet parking available. 307 S. Park Ave., Winter Park (phone: 647-1072; 800-228-7220; fax: 647-4081).

Howard Johnson Park Square Inn & Suites One of the national chain's top-rated properties for several years running, rooms at this property offer either either lake or courtyard views. The hotel is situated less than five minutes from *Disney Village Marketplace.* There are 222 guestrooms and 86 suites, each with an in-room safe. Suites also include a microwave, refrigerator, coffee maker, and sleeper sofa. Smoke-free rooms are available; children 17 and under eat breakfast and dinner free. The complex features two swimming pools, a whirlpool, a playground, a gameroom, and a children's pool. Shuttle service to *Disney World* is free. 8501 Palm Pkwy., Lake Buena Vista (phone: 239-6900; 800-635-8684; fax 239-1287).

Westgate Lakes This full-service escape set on a tranquil lake is about 10 miles from *Walt Disney World* and 2 miles from *Sea World.* There are 370 spacious one- and two-bedroom villas, all with fully equipped kitchenettes.

Located on more than 97 acres, it offers a pool, 11 Jacuzzis, two tennis courts, three children's playgrounds, a gameroom, and a small health club. 10000 Turkey Lake Rd. (phone: 352-8051; 800-424-0708; fax: 345-5384).

INEXPENSIVE

Holiday Inn SunSpree Resort Lake Buena Vista/Holiday Inn Main Gate East These sister properties (507 rooms and 670 rooms, respectively) offer outstanding family programs. Each has a special "Kiddie Check-in" desk; a supervised, licensed Camp Holiday child-care program (ages two to 12, three to 12, respectively); and costumed character bedtime tuck-ins. Kids 12 and under eat free. Pets (under 20 lbs.) are welcome at *Holiday Inn Main Gate East.* New *Kidsuites*—in limited supply—partition standard hotel rooms into parent and child sections at the *Holiday In SunSpree. SunSpree Resort:* 13351 S.R. 535, Lake Buena Vista (phone: 239-4500; 800-FON-MAXX; fax: 239-7713); *Main Gate East:* 5678 US-192, Kissimmee (phone: 396-4488; 800-FON-KIDS; fax: 396-8915).

EATING OUT

Orlando's growth during the last decade has attracted chefs from all over the world, so good dining experiences are easy to find. Expect to pay more than $150 for dinner for two at the restaurant listed as very expensive; between $50 and $100 at those places described as expensive; between $40 and $50 at those categorized as moderate; and less than $40 at those rated inexpensive. Prices do not include drinks, wine, tax, or tips. All restaurants are in the 407 area code unless otherwise indicated.

Unless otherwise noted, restaurants are open for lunch and dinner.

VERY EXPENSIVE

Victoria & Albert's In *Walt Disney World*'s *Grand Floridian Beach,* this intimate, elegant dining room seats only 65 and serves seven-course meals of changing contemporary American cuisine. Special "Chef's Table" seatings and "Royal Wine Pairings" dining options also are available. Jackets required for men. No smoking allowed. Reservations necessary. Major credit cards accepted. *Grand Floridian Beach, Walt Disney World* (phone: WDW-DINE/939-3463).

EXPENSIVE

Arthur's 27 Intimate, romantic, sophisticated, and elegant, this 27th-floor restaurant provides a striking panoramic view and serves fabulous four-, five-, or six-course feasts. Diners select each course from a number of specials, including lobster bisque, red snapper, black sea scallops with a mango salsa, loin of lamb, and amaretto mascarpone cheesecake. This place is popular among local residents because the food and atmosphere are so wonderful. The wine cellar is impressive. Open daily; dinner only. Reservations advised. Major credit cards accepted. *Buena Vista Palace*, 1900 Buena Vista Dr. (phone: 827-2727).

Chalet Suzanne This enchanting European-inspired, country inn—family-owned and operated since 1931—even has its own airplane landing strip. A perennial culinary award winner, the quaint five-room restaurant is a local and celebrity "special occasion" favorite. Servers wear dirndls; decor includes antiques, stained glass, lace tablecloths, and mismatched china. The six-course continental dinners and four-course lunches feature broiled grapefruit with chicken liver and a dash of cinnamon, and Romaine soup—which is also canned on the property and sold in supermarkets—both house specialties. Closed Monday. Reservations advised. Major credit cards accepted. 3800 Chalet Suzanne Dr., Lake Wales (phone: 941/676-6011).

Christini's A local favorite, this upscale Northern Italian restaurant in the attractions neighborhood combines a convivial ambience, strolling musicians, service panache, and stylish Old World dining room appointments—not to mention top-notch food. Open daily, dinner only; reservations advised. Major credit cards accepted. 7600 Dr. Phillips Blvd. (phone: 345-8770).

Manuel's on the 28th This intimate penthouse dining room offers the only panoramic view of downtown Orlando. Its limited à la carte menu changes seasonally and might include such favorites as gingered tuna and pan-seared (farm-raised) bison. No smoking allowed. Closed Mondays. Reservations advised. Major credit cards accepted. Barnett Bank Center Bldg., 390 N. Orange Ave. (phone: 246-6580).

Maison & Jardin Resembling a French château with museum-quality antiques, an enchanting fountain, and formal gardens, this restaurant is considered by many to be the best in the area. The menu features fresh game, fish, meat, and fowl. Pheasant, chateaubriand, and beef Wellington are among the house specialties. Open daily, dinner only; and Sunday brunch. Reservations advised. Major credit cards accepted. 430 S. Wymore Rd., Altamonte Springs (phone: 862-4410).

MODERATE

Bubble Room This place is pure kitsch—from the yellow-brick path leading to the front door to the waiters and waitresses known as Bubble Scouts. Most of the selections at this movie- and toy-themed establishment are classic American: burgers, fish platters, and chili for lunch; steaks, chicken, and seafood for dinner. Portions are obscenely huge, especially the homemade desserts—red velvet cake is the house specialty. Happy hour weeknights. No reservations. Major credit cards accepted. 1351 S. Orlando Ave., Maitland (phone: 628-3331).

Chef Mickey's The dining room's new space-age decor and bright colors are designed to appeal to kids. Relocated to the *Contemporary Resort*, this popular family restaurant now features not only appearances by Chef Mickey and pals, but also a 110-foot-long buffet and a festive dessert and sundae bar. Open for breakfast and dinner. Reservations advised. Major credit cards accepted. *Contemporary Resort, Walt Disney World* (phone: WDW-DINE/939-3463).

Pebbles This café is set amid lots of indoor greenery. The California fare is served à la carte, and regulars often graze on the intriguing tapas such as roasted garlic with sun-dried tomatoes or the nutty cheesy house salad. There are fresh seafood dishes and steaks daily, and a variety of pasta dishes, sandwiches, and soups. No reservations. Major credit cards accepted. Several area locations including Crossroad Plaza, State Rd. 535 (phone: 827-1111).

INEXPENSIVE

Angel's The menu at this new-wave rock 'n' roll diner warns: "This is a bad place for a diet." The family restaurant serves blue plate specials, deli sandwiches, salads, homemade desserts, and breakfast all day. No reservations. Major credit cards accepted. Several locations including 7300 W. US-192, Kissimmee (phone: 397-1960).

Bubbalou's Bodacious Bar-B-Q This unpretentious shack has 20 picnic tables, red ruffled curtains, and baseball caps hanging from the ceiling. The food is hot, fast, fresh, and pit-smoky. Locals consider this the best barbecue in town. Closed Sundays. No reservations. MasterCard and Visa accepted. 1471 Lee Rd., Winter Park (phone: 628-1212).

Captain Appleby's Inn A funky family restaurant, it's loaded with antiques and collectibles, including an old icebox and a player piano. The food isn't particularly memorable, but meals include unlimited trips to the well-stocked salad bar. If you're visiting Florida for the first time, try the traditional Florida Cracker sampler platter, which includes baked chicken, crab cakes, fried petite shrimp, and fried catfish fingerlings. (The term "cracker," by the way, refers to old-time Floridians, not the crunchy stuff you get with your soup.) The fried alligator appetizer is also a good choice for adventurous out-of-towners. Water comes from a pump-it-yourself well and is served in mason jars. Reservations advised. Major credit cards accepted. 549 W. Par (phone: 426-8838).

McDonald's This 24-hour version of the national chain restaurant is an attraction in and of itself, with the world's largest outdoor *Ronald's Playhouse,* a 600-gallon saltwater aquarium, a video arcade, and an audio-animatronic *McDonaldland Theater.* No reservations. Major credit cards accepted. 6875 Sand Lake Rd. (phone: 351-2185).

Planet Hollywood Part of the international chain co-owned by Arnold Schwarzenegger, Sylvester Stallone, and Bruce Willis, this eatery is in a sphere-shaped, three-level building. Such big- and little-screen artifacts as Tom Hanks's costume from *Forrest Gump* and the pistol brandished by Clint Eastwood in *The Good, the Bad and the Ugly* are the focus along with props from movies and shows produced around the Orlando area. At one end of the restaurant, classic clips and trailers from soon-to-be-released movies are shown on a large screen; movie soundtracks provide the background music for your meal. The owners call the food "California New

Classic" cuisine (translation: pizza, turkey burgers, salads, pasta, blackened shrimp, smoked and grilled meat, and the like). No reservations. Major credit cards accepted. *Pleasure Island, Walt Disney World* (phone: 827-7827).

MORE WALT DISNEY WORLD RESTAURANTS

Most first-time visitors are surprised to discover that *Walt Disney World* offers unusual specialties such as amaretto-flavored soufflés along with familiar hot dogs and hamburgers. Even cafeterias and fast-food stops have a bit of atmosphere that makes them a little special. Where you eat at *Walt Disney World* will be determined by where you are; below are a few of the more noteworthy spots.

In the *Magic Kingdom, The Crystal Palace,* an old-fashioned glass-walled and plant-filled eatery on Main Street USA, now presents Winnie the Pooh character buffets, three meals daily. *Tony's Town Square Café* nearby serves delicious pizza. *King Stefan's Banquet Hall* in *Cinderella Castle* has waitress service and a prime rib house special. At *Liberty Tree Tavern*, All-American pot roast, honey-glazed ham, and roasted turkey are served. The *Sleepy Hollow* fast-food eatery offers 100% vegetarian fare such as chili in a scooped out wheat bread "bowl."

Epcot offers even greater variety. In *Future World,* at the *Living Seas* pavilion, try the fresh seafood at the *Coral Reef* restaurant, which affords a panoramic view of a living underwater coral reef. *Pure & Simple* in the *Wonders of Life* pavilion features a limited low-fat menu of yogurts, sandwiches, and salads. *Garden Grill* in *The Land* pavilion, presents three family-style meals with Mickey and Minnie daily in a revolving restaurant setting. In *World Showcase,* don't miss Canada's *Le Cellier,* a buffeteria that specializes in authentic pork and potato pies called *tourtières,* and chicken-and-meatball stew; Italy's *Alfredo's,* home of the original fettuccine Alfredo; Germany's *Biergarten,* with a brand new Bavarian food market concept featuring an on-stage kitchen and freshly prepared regional specialties; China's *Nine Dragons,* where meals are prepared in four provincial cooking styles; *Chefs de France*—supervised by chefs Paul Bocuse, Gaston Le Nôtre, and Roger Verge—noted for such delicacies as red snapper with spinach in puff pastry with sautéed scallops and crab dumplings in lobster cream sauce, and sautéed tenderloin of beef with raisins and brandy sauce; *Restaurant Marrakesh* in Morocco, featuring exotic ethnic food and belly dancers; and Japan's *Tempura Kiku* fresh sushi bar and traditional tableside wizardry at the *Teppanyaki Dining Room.*

The eateries at the *Disney–MGM Studios* offer trendy menus in an atmosphere reminiscent of old Hollywood. The *Hollywood Brown Derby* features the signature Cobb salad created by owner Bob Cobb in the 1930s, and light grapefruit cake dessert, plus a nice wine list. The *50's Prime Time Café* recalls 1950s sitcoms, with decor straight out of yesteryear's kitchen. The menu offers new versions of old standbys, such as Magnificent Meat Loaf, made with fresh veal and shiitake mushrooms and served with mashed potatoes and gravy. Or eat under the stars (indoors) at the *Sci-Fi Dine-In Theater* where diners sit in cut-out 1950s-style cars in a drive-in movie setting (complete with campy movie clips), and order milk shakes, burgers, and stacked sandwiches. *Mama Melrose's*—one of the resort's best-kept secrets—offers all-you-can-eat pasta and brick-oven pizza in a homespun Italian setting with an emphasis on seasonally-fresh ingredients.

Resort hotels also offer outstanding culinary diversity. A show kitchen, extensive wine list, and panoramic resort view complement seasonally fresh, health-conscious cuisine at the new, award-winning *California Grill* on the 15th floor of the *Contemporary Resort.* Oak-fired pizza with smoked salmon, pan-seared yellowfin tuna with black bean and Asian slaw, Sonoma goat cheese ravioli, and jumbo citrus souflées are house specialties. *Artist's Point* at *Wilderness Lodge* features topnotch Northwestern cuisine (venison, lamb, and Northwest salmon) and an excellent wine list; while the hotel's *Whispering Canyon Café* is popular for its generous family-style, oven-roasted, and wood-smoked meals (seating is on a first-come basis). *Ariel's* at the *Beach Club* has a nice wine list to complement its fresh seafood; and the *Yacht Club*s *Yachtsman's Steakhouse* is a good choice for beef. *Ohana* at the *Polynesian Resort* features skewers of fire-grilled beef, pork, sausage, chicken, and shrimp, and pineapple chunks dipped in caramel. *Sum Chows* at the *Dolphin* offers a first-rate Asian menu including sushi and firecracker snapper. Adventurous diners may elect to sample the gator or kangaroo meat at the handsome *Buena Vista Palace*s *Outback Restaurant*.

At *Pleasure Island* there's the *Portobello Yacht Club* for imaginative northern Italian pasta, seafood, and pizza; the *Fireworks Factory* for steaks and robust barbecue; and *Fulton's Crab House* onboard the former *Empress Lilly* riverboat, all operated by Levy Restaurants. Completely renovated, the new nautical restaurant features classic and contemporary fresh seafood preparations—and an oyster bar menu that changes daily. (Seating is on a first-come basis.) The new *Rainforest Café* in *Disney Village Marketplace* serves pasta, chicken, and burgers in a whimsically tropical setting.

Priority seating times, recommended for most resort hotel and theme park sit-down restaurants, can be made up to 60 days in advance (phone: WDW-DINE/939-3463). Same-day seatings may be available; check in-person at the restaurant podium, resort hotel guest services, or park guest relations, or call WDW-DINE. Booking procedures sometimes change, so call on arrival at *Walt Disney World.*

Travelers with children should note the many resort hotel and theme park options for dining with Disney characters, and themed dinner shows outlined elsewhere above (phone: WDW-DINE/939-3463).

Philadelphia

When William Penn founded Philadelphia in 1682, between the Delaware and Schuylkill Rivers, he advertised his colony as a place of religious freedom and named it "The City of Brotherly Love." Thousands of persecuted Europeans came here so they could live in accordance with their beliefs. By 1750, Philadelphia was the leading city in colonial America. In 1752, the *Liberty Bell* was forged in an English foundry to mark the 50th anniversary of William Penn's Charter of Privileges, which declares, "Proclaim liberty throughout all the land, unto all the inhabitants thereof." When the colonies broke away from Great Britain in 1776, the bell cracked and was recast by a Philadelphia foundry. From 1789 until 1800 (when Philadelphia ceded its role as the nation's capital to the newly built Washington, DC), the first *United States Congress* met in *Congress Hall.*

Today, the city has a population of 1.6 million (4.7 million in the metropolitan area), but it still follows Penn's original plans, laid out around four spacious parks (one in each quadrant of the city). Some Philadelphians still live in 18th-century townhouses with cream-colored wooden shutters, and they pray in the same churches as did George Washington, Benjamin Franklin, and John Adams. Philadelphia's red brick sidewalks, narrow alleys, and hidden gardens and courtyards make it look remarkably like 18th-century London.

But Philadelphia is not without modern charm. Between 1986 and 1988, the city spent $14 million restoring its famed but declining Market Street. The street's east end, running from *Independence Mall* at Fifth Street to *City Hall* at Broad Street, was transformed from a seedy, crumbling section into what has been called the "Champs-Elysées de Philly." Junk shops and decaying buildings were replaced by attractive office and retail buildings, while historic edifices were revitalized and reopened by new businesses. One such complex had been owned and operated since the mid-1800s by the once-prosperous *Lit Brothers* department store. After a complete restoration, it was transformed into the *Mellon Independence Center,* a complex of shops, restaurants, and offices, where, in December, a three-quarter-scale colonial village delights visitors with mechanized scenes of an 18th century *Christmas.*

Another historic building worth visiting is *Lord & Taylor* (formerly *John Wanamaker,* one of the city's oldest and most prominent department stores). A delightful place for shopping and browsing, it boasts the city's most famous meeting place—the bronze bald eagle statue on the main floor of the seven-story atrium. Almost directly behind *Lord & Taylor* is the city's most famous landmark, William Penn's statue on top of *City Hall.* The city's founder crowns a dome that, in turn, caps an architectural extravaganza of portholes, turrets, wedding cake statuettes, and Ionic, Doric, and Corinthian columns and pillars. Until 1984, the statue was, by law, the tallest fixture on the skyline. After much debate, the rule declaring that nothing in the city could exceed the 548-foot height of the statue was overturned, and a contractor was allowed to erect two taller buildings. However, the 26-ton, 37-foot bronze Penn has held his own since both he and the historic *City Hall* underwent an $18.5-million restoration several years ago that revealed the original patina of the statue and the beauty of the building.

In addition to the restoration projects, the city has added the *Pennsylvania Convention Center* (the second-largest on the East Coast) to its skyline. The *Center,* part of a $523-million statewide public works project, spans approximately six blocks near *City Hall* in the heart of Philadelphia, and has quickly become the new location for trade shows and special events. It contains exhibition halls, meeting rooms, a huge ballroom, and a grand hall, and encompasses the long-standing *Reading Terminal Market*. The grand hall is actually the historic landmark structure of the 1890s *Reading Terminal* train shed, which has been incorporated into the *Center.* The *Philadelphia Marriott* (the city's newest and largest hotel) is also connected to the complex.

But that's not where the connections end. The city's commuter tunnel, completed in the 1980s, not only links the suburban, airport, and *Amtrak* rail lines to one another, it also connects the rail lines with the city's subway system and indoor malls, the *Gallery I* and *II,* and the major department stores. Concern for keeping the city both liveable and accessible resulted in turning 13 blocks of Chestnut, a popular shopping street, into a pedestrian mall where only buses may pass. This year, visitors can enjoy *Schuylkill River Park* on a narrow slice of riverbank running between the waterworks behind the art museum and Spruce Street. It is hoped that restaurant and boat rental concessions will open here.

The ever-evolving city has focused a great deal of concern on its arts in recent years by redefining the mile of Broad Street extending south from *City Hall* as its Avenue of the Arts. The *Academy of Music, Merriam Theater, Museum of American Arts of the Pennsylvania Academy of Fine Arts,* and *University of the Arts* number among the arts centers already established here; and in 1994 its latest addition, the *Philadelphia Arts Bank*, opened in a renovated building at Broad and South Streets. This newest facility aims to provide technically sophisticated space for the city's myriad smaller performing arts groups. Along the avenue itself, one finds brass stars set into the sidewalks, bearing the names of famous Philadelphians in the arts.

Another aspect of Philadelphia's appeal is its interesting neighborhoods and business districts. The sophisticated Society Hill section near Penn's Landing was named for the *Free Society of Traders*, an early British company. It had deteriorated over the years but was revitalized during the 1970s, blending the historic and the modern in restored townhouses and buildings. An influx of restaurants and, more recently, hotels enlivened the area, too. Near the central business district, Chinatown has survived many city construction projects, including the *Convention Center,* and occupies a small area between Eighth and 11th and Arch and Vine Streets. With between

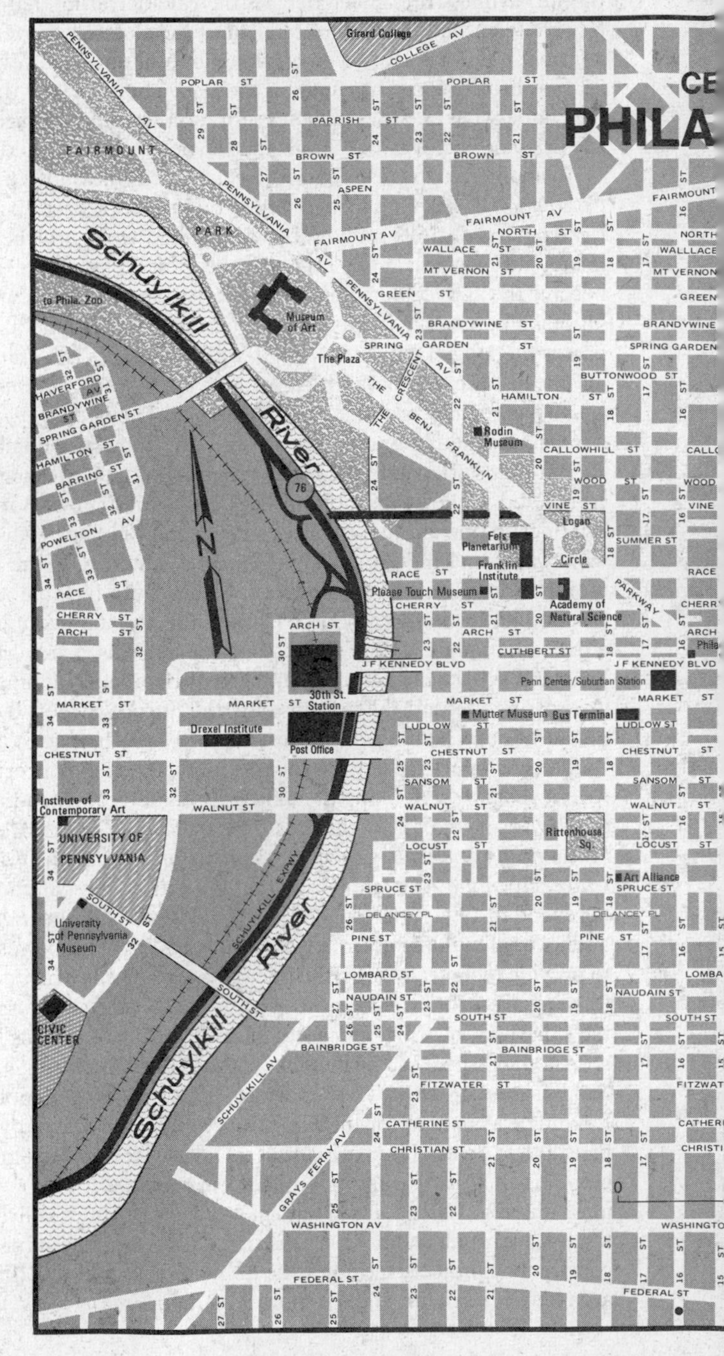
CE
PHILA
Girard College
COLLEGE AV
POPLAR ST
PARRISH ST
BROWN ST
FAIRMOUNT
PENNSYLVANIA AV
ASPEN
PARK
FAIRMOUNT AV
NORTH ST
WALLACE ST
MT VERNON ST
GREEN ST
BRANDYWINE ST
SPRING GARDEN ST
BUTTONWOOD ST
HAMILTON ST
CALLOWHILL ST
WOOD ST
VINE ST
SUMMER ST
RACE ST
CHERRY ST
ARCH ST
CUTHBERT ST
J F KENNEDY BLVD
MARKET ST
LUDLOW ST
CHESTNUT ST
SANSOM ST
WALNUT ST
LOCUST ST
SPRUCE ST
DELANCEY PL
PINE ST
LOMBARD ST
NAUDAIN ST
SOUTH ST
BAINBRIDGE ST
FITZWATER ST
CATHERINE ST
CHRISTIAN ST
WASHINGTON AV
FEDERAL ST
Schuylkill River
to Phila. Zoo
Museum of Art
The Plaza
THE CRESCENT
BENJ FRANKLIN PARKWAY
Rodin Museum
Logan Circle
Fels Planetarium
Franklin Institute
Please Touch Museum
Academy of Natural Science
Penn Center/Suburban Station
30th St. Station
Post Office
Drexel Institute
Mutter Museum
Bus Terminal
Rittenhouse Sq.
Art Alliance
HAVERFORD AV
POWELTON AV
BARRING ST
Institute of Contemporary Art
UNIVERSITY OF PENNSYLVANIA
University of Pennsylvania Museum
CIVIC CENTER
SCHUYLKILL EXPWY
SCHUYLKILL AV
GRAYS FERRY AV
76
N
0

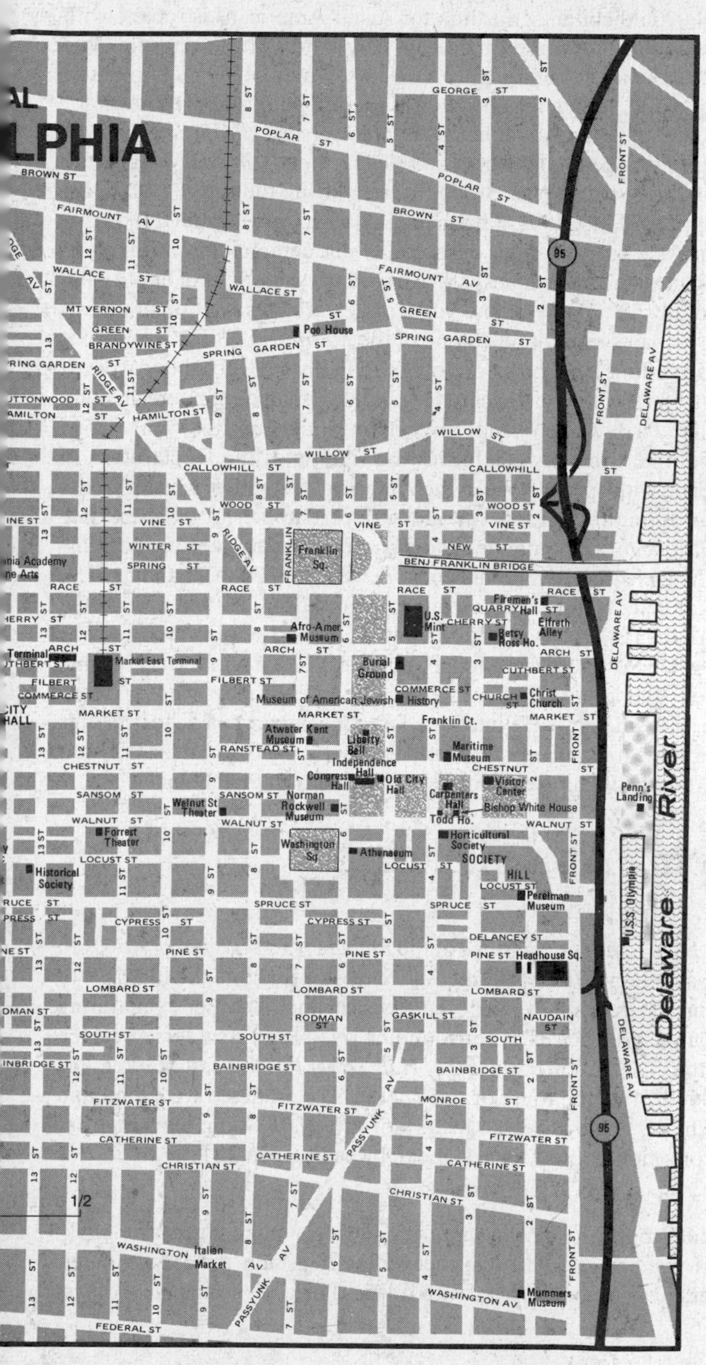

AL
LPHIA
GEORGE ST
POPLAR ST
BROWN ST
FAIRMOUNT AV
WALLACE ST
MT VERNON ST
GREEN ST
BRANDYWINE ST
SPRING GARDEN ST
RIDGE AV
BUTTONWOOD ST
HAMILTON ST
WILLOW ST
CALLOWHILL ST
WOOD ST
VINE ST
NEW ST
WINTER ST
SPRING ST
Franklin Sq.
FRANKLIN
BENJ FRANKLIN BRIDGE
RACE ST
Firemen's Hall
QUARRY ST
Elfreth Alley
CHERRY ST
U.S. Mint
Betsy Ross Ho.
Afro-Amer. Museum
ARCH ST
Terminal
Market East Terminal
CUTHBERT ST
Burial Ground
FILBERT ST
COMMERCE ST
Museum of American Jewish History
CHURCH ST
Christ Church
CITY HALL
MARKET ST
Franklin Ct.
Atwater Kent Museum
Liberty Bell
RANSTEAD ST
Maritime Museum
Independence Hall
CHESTNUT ST
Congress Hall
Old City Hall
Visitor Center
Carpenters Hall
SANSOM ST
Walnut St Theater
Norman Rockwell Museum
Bishop White House
Todd Ho.
WALNUT ST
Forrest Theater
Horticultural Society
Washington Sq.
Athenaeum
SOCIETY HILL
LOCUST ST
Historical Society
Perelman Museum
SPRUCE ST
CYPRESS ST
DELANCEY ST
PINE ST
Headhouse Sq.
LOMBARD ST
RODMAN ST
GASKILL ST
NAUDAIN ST
SOUTH ST
BAINBRIDGE ST
FITZWATER ST
MONROE ST
PASSYUNK AV
CATHERINE ST
CHRISTIAN ST
WASHINGTON AV
Italian Market
Mummers Museum
FEDERAL ST
FRONT ST
DELAWARE AV
Penn's Landing
U.S.S. Olympia
Delaware River
95
1/2

3,000 and 4,000 inhabitants, this hub for Asian-Americans is replete with restaurants, import shops, and Chinese grocery stores. The Friendship Gate at 10th and Arch bids visitors to enter this lively community. In South Philly, as the locals call it, Italian neighborhoods predominate and are known for their small, homey eateries and the *Italian Market* (see *Other Special Places*). Philadelphia's sense of humor cuts loose every *New Year's Day*, when the *Mummers Parade* struts down Broad Street, playing tunes like "Oh, Dem Golden Slippers." Since 1901, it has been Philadelphia's *Mardi Gras,* incorporating the *New Year's* customs of several ethnic communities. Mummers' "suits" (don't call them costumes) are extraordinary fantasies of bright silks, sequins, gold braid, feathers, and veils; prizes are awarded for the best. Parade participants must apply to one of the *Mummers Clubs*—storefront social clubs in ethnic neighborhoods of South Philly. Neighborhood women often design and sew the suits themselves, although some commercial establishments like *Pierre's* (on Walnut Street) also supply outfits.

Every summer, the city celebrates the signing of the Declaration of Independence with special "Welcome America" festivities, which run the last week in June through *July 4th* and with ceremonies at *Independence National Historical Park,* outdoor concerts, and a spectacular fireworks display over the Delaware River that can be viewed from Penn's Landing. The bicentennial celebrations of the country's founding in 1976 and of the Constitution in 1987 focused national attention on the place where it all began. But when the firecrackers stopped and the 200-year anniversary became just another page in the calendar, the bicentennial displays were not torn down here. Instead, they were integrated into the network of historical sites that people come from all over the world to see—yet another indication that the past, present, and future all coexist comfortably in Philadelphia.

Philadelphia At-a-Glance

SEEING THE CITY

You don't have to *run* up the steps of the *Philadelphia Museum of Art* (26th and Parkway; phone: 763-8100) the way Sylvester Stallone did in *Rocky* to get the same far-reaching view of the city's skyline. Another exhilarating view, encompassing the city, its surrounding rivers, and New Jersey, can be had from the observation deck of *City Hall Tower* (Broad and Market Sts.; phone: 686-9074). Free tours of the *Tower* are conducted weekdays and include exhibits and a narrated history of *City Hall*. Some mornings are reserved for school groups (check ahead by calling 686-2840).

SPECIAL PLACES

Philadelphia's tight city blocks and narrow streets make it great for walking, not driving. Streets, laid out in checkerboard fashion, are easy to understand, but they always are choked with traffic. The city's main places of historic interest are clustered in *Independence National Historical Park,* while a variety of museums and other interesting places are found throughout Center City and West Philadelphia's *Fairmount Park.*

INDEPENDENCE HALL HISTORICAL AREA

VISITORS' CENTER This is a good place to launch a tour of the historical area and pick up maps and brochures. There's also a half-hour "Independence" film that provides helpful historical background. You can park your car in the Second Street garage (behind the visitors' center between Chestnut and Walnut Sts.) or the underground garage at Fifth between Arch and Market Streets. Open daily except some winter holidays that change from year to year. Third between Chestnut and Walnut Sts. (phone: 587-8974).

INDEPENDENCE NATIONAL HISTORICAL PARK "The most historic square mile in America," it's what everyone comes to see. Within the park are the major colonial and Revolutionary era buildings, which are listed below. No admission charge. Second to Sixth Sts., between Market and Walnut Sts. (phone: 597-8974) for a 24-hour recording).

INDEPENDENCE HALL The attraction most indelibly associated with the city, its solid tower, massive clock, and graceful spire are unmistakable. Here, the Declaration of Independence was signed and, 11 years later, the Constitution was written. Guided tours are given, beginning in the East Wing. Open daily. No admission charge. Chestnut St. between Fifth and Sixth (phone: 597-8974).

CONGRESS HALL The first *US Congress* met here, between 1789 and 1800. George Washington delivered his final congressional address in these halls; here, too, the Bill of Rights was adopted. Open daily. No admission charge. Sixth and Chestnut Sts. (phone: 597-8974).

OLD CITY HALL The first *US Supreme Court* issued judgments from the bench inside this building from 1789 until 1800, when it moved with the rest of the federal government to Washington, DC. Open daily. No admission charge. Sixth and Chestnut Sts. (phone: 597-8974).

INDEPENDENCE MALL Across the street from the various halls, this leafy stretch of grass, fountains, and tree-lined walks contains the glass pavilion housing the Liberty Bell. It was moved from *Independence Hall* so more people could see it. Open daily. No admission charge. Market and Fifth Sts. (phone: 597-8974).

CARPENTERS' HALL The *Carpenters' Company Guild* was housed here during the colonial era (before unions). The oldest extant trade guild in the US still owns the hall, and early carpentry tools are on display. In 1774, the *First Continental Congress* met here. A 10-minute video explains the hall's history, and volunteer historical interpreters are generally available to answer questions. Closed Mondays; closed Tuesdays in January and February. No admission charge. 320 Chestnut St. (phone: 925-0167).

NEW HALL MILITARY MUSEUM The exhibitions and collections of the *Army, Navy,* and *Marine Corps* branches focus on the years 1775 to 1805. Located on Carpenters' Court (leading back to *Carpenters' Hall*). Open daily. No admission charge. Chestnut and Fourth Sts. (phone: 597-8974).

SECOND BANK OF THE UNITED STATES One of the earliest buildings designed by noted architect William Strickland, this early-19th-century building is a fine example of Greek Revival architecture. It houses *The Portraits of the Capitol City,* which highlights people who were important in government, industry, the arts, and religion during the late 1700s. A brief slide show depicts the life of Charles Willson Peale, who painted most of the portraits. No admission charge. Chestnut between Fourth and Fifth Sts. (phone: 597-8974).

TODD HOUSE Before she became Dolley Madison—wife of fourth president James, famed First Lady, and society hostess—she was Dolley Payne Todd, whose husband, Quaker lawyer John Todd, died of yellow fever in 1793. Their 1775 home is typical of middle class residences of the period. Free guided tours must be arranged in person at the *Visitors' Center* (Third and Chestnut Sts.) on the day of the tour. Fourth and Walnut Sts. (phone: 597-8974).

BISHOP WHITE HOUSE While the *Todd House* reflects a middle class lifestyle, this home displays the affluence of people such as Bishop William White, a politically active Episcopalian minister (from the 1770s to the 1790s) who served as rector of both *Christ Church* and *St. Peter's.* A tour of this house must be combined with the *Todd House* (see above). Third and Walnut Sts. (phone: 597-8974).

CHRIST CHURCH Benjamin Franklin sat in pew 70, George Washington in pew 58. The original church was built in 1695; this larger one was erected in 1745 and is significant both for its architecture and as a national shrine. This Episcopal church remains an active parish with weekly worship services. Tours available. Closed Mondays and Tuesdays from January through early March. Donations suggested. Second St. above Market (phone: 922-1695).

CHRIST CHURCH BURIAL GROUND Throw a penny on the grave of Benjamin Franklin and his wife, Deborah—it's a Philadelphia custom. Tours by appointment only year-round. Enter between Fourth and Fifth Sts. on Arch St. (phone: 922-1965).

BETSY ROSS HOUSE According to tradition, this is where George Washington directed Elizabeth Ross, an upholsterer's widow, in the stitching of the first American flag. The *Philadelphia Historical Commission,* however, says that Betsy Ross never lived here and had nothing to do with the first US flag. Make up your own mind, after you've seen this tiny two-and-a-half story rowhouse with its basement kitchen, all filled with household items and memorabilia allegedly pertinent to the famous seamstress. Closed Mondays, except holidays. Donations suggested. 239 Arch (phone: 627-5343).

ELFRETH'S ALLEY This is America's oldest continuously occupied residential street, dating to 1690. Only one block long and six feet wide, it is lined with nearly 300-year-old houses. Annual *Fete Days* here are usually celebrated with house tours and crafts shows on the first weekend in June. The homes don't open their doors to the public again until the first Friday evening in December for a holiday tour. The *Museum House* (126 Elfreth's Alley) puts on special programs throughout the year—most notably, artisans demonstrate colonial crafts techniques on Sunday afternoons in July and August. Closed Mondays in January and February except national holidays; tours can be arranged by appointment. Off Second St. between Arch and Race Sts. (phone: 574-0560).

HEADHOUSE SQUARE Built in 1775, this sole survivor of the middle-of-the-street markets that once flourished in the city is surrounded by restaurants and shops. In summer, it hosts crafts demonstrations and concerts. Be sure to stop in at *Koffmeyer's Cookies* (Second and Lombard Sts.; phone: 922-0717) to taste some wickedly delicious cookies (especially good is the Headhouse Square, a vanilla brownie peppered with chocolate chips and walnuts) and Philadelphia's famous Bassett's ice cream. Second and Pine Sts.

FRANKLIN COURT Benjamin Franklin came to Philadelphia in 1723. He resided in a brick house on this site in his later years, until his death in 1790. Although the house itself is no longer standing (it was demolished in 1812), three of the surrounding houses designed by Franklin are here, along with an 18th-century garden with a mulberry tree, a print shop, and a post office. An underground museum has Franklin stoves and a phone where you can "dial-an-opinion" from Benjamin Franklin. Open daily. No admission charge. Running from Chestnut to Market between Third and Fourth Sts. (phone: 597-8974).

USS OLYMPIA AND USS BECUNA The oldest steel-hulled American warship afloat, the *Olympia* was Commodore George Dewey's flagship at Manila Bay in the Spanish-American War. Also here is the *Becuna,* a submarine used in the Pacific during World War II. Closed *Christmas* and *New Year's Day.* Admission charge. Penn's Landing between Christopher Columbus Blvd. and Spruce St. (phone: 922-1898).

WEST PHILADELPHIA

BOATHOUSE ROW A collection of Victorian boathouses used by collegiate and club oarsmen, it's the hub of many national competitions. East River Drive, running along the east bank of the Schuylkill River, north of the *Museum of Art.* If you're driving west of the museum after dark on the Schuylkill Expressway (Route 76) or on the West River Drive, don't miss the view across the river of the historic boathouses outlined in white lights.

FAIRMOUNT PARK This huge park—with approximately 8,000 acres of meadows, gardens, creeks, trails, and bridle paths—begins at the *Philadelphia Museum* *of Art* and extends northwest on both sides of the Schuylkill River and Wissahickon Creek. For a free map of the park, stop by the *Fairmount Park Commission* (*Memorial Hall,* Parkside Ave. and 42nd St.; phone: 685-0000). Then be sure to take in the *Japanese House and Garden* where, weather permitting, you can witness a tea ceremony (phone: 685-0104), *Glendinning Rock Garden,* and, if young children are along, *Smith Memorial Playground.* Highlights for many are tours of one or more of the *Park*'s seven mansions—*Cedar Grove, Laurel Hill, Lemon Hill, Mt. Pleasant, Strawberry, Sweetbriar,* and *Woodford* (phone: 684-7922 for a recorded message of seasonal tours and special events). Open daily. No admission charge.

PHILADELPHIA ZOO Established in 1874, this is the nation's oldest zoo and is considered one of the best-run. More than 1,500 mammals, reptiles, and birds live within its 42 acres. There are natural habitat displays, a children's zoo, a safari monorail aerial tram, and America's first white lions. Don't miss the tree house. On *Christmas Day* 1995, a devasting fire completely wiped out the primate population. Zoo officials estimate a new exhibit to be well under way by the end of this year. Closed *Thanksgiving, Christmas Eve, Christmas, New Year's Eve,* and *New Year's Day.* Admission charge except non-holiday Mondays from December through February. 34th St. and Girard Ave. (phone: 243-1100).

PHILADELPHIA MUSEUM OF ART In an imposing Greco-Roman Revival building constructed in 1928, it houses art from the Middle Ages and Renaissance up through the 20th century. On display are outstanding collections of French Impressionist paintings and American furniture, as well as the largest Thomas Eakins collection in the US. Notable holdings include Peter Paul Rubens's *Prometheus Bound,* van Gogh's *Sunflowers,* Cézanne's *Bathers,* Marcel Duchamp's *Nude Descending a Staircase,* Picasso's *Three Musicians,* and the famous statue of Diana that topped New York City's first *Madison Square Garden.* There's a Japanese tea house, designed to convey the atmosphere as well as the art of Japan, a Chinese scholar's study, a large collection of arms and armor, and distinguished collections of china, porcelain, glass, jade, graphics, sculpture, and decorative arts. And year-round on Wednesday evenings, enjoy specially themed cultural programs offering food, entertainment, tours, and more. The museum restaurant serves Wednesday dinner and Sunday brunch. Closed Mondays and holidays. No admission charge on Sundays before 1 PM. N. 26th and The Parkway (phone: 763-8100).

RODIN MUSEUM Sculpture, sketches, and drawings make up the largest collection of Auguste Rodin's work outside France. An afternoon can easily be spent wandering through the halls and gardens. Closed Mondays and holidays. Donations suggested. 22nd and Parkway (phone: 763-8100).

FRANKLIN INSTITUTE SCIENCE MUSEUM This huge, hands-on science museum has all kinds of exhibits on subjects ranging from animals, aviation, and astronomy to human biology, mechanics, and electricity. Watch light bend as it passes through concave and convex mirrors, walk through a 15,000-times-life-size heart, board a T-33 jet trainer, and take a ride on Philadelphia's beloved 350-ton *Baldwin* locomotive. Daily demonstrations show how lightning works and what energy is all about. Planetarium shows discuss black holes, satellite technology, and the constellations, and include laser light shows. The outdoor children's *Science Park* offers interactive displays, such as riding a high-wire tandem bike and playing a step-on organ. The *Institute* also includes the *Mandell Futures Center,* dubbed the "First Museum of the Future," as well as the four-story *Tuttleman Omniverse Theater* with changing shows throughout the year, all preceded by the *Symphony Philadelphia,* which aims to give viewers the visceral experience of soaring and floating about and above the city's famous sites. Closed *Thanksgiving, Christmas Eve, Christmas,* and *New Year's Day.* Admission charge. 20th and Parkway (phone: 448-1200; 448-1292 for the planetarium).

OTHER SPECIAL PLACES

CITY HALL Philadelphia's most distinctive landmark has been called "an architectural nightmare," but some people praise its elaborate decor; sculpture, marble pillars, alabaster chandeliers, gold leaf ceilings, and carved mahogany. The *Tower,* at William Penn's feet, looks out on the Delaware and Schuylkill Rivers. Open to the public on weekdays. No admission charge. Guided one-and-a-half-hour tours of the restored *Conversation Hall,* the Mayor's reception room, City Council chambers and caucus room, and the State Supreme Court are available at 12:30 PM weekdays, as are exterior tours, weather permitting. No admission charge. Broad and Market Sts. (phone: 686-2840).

RITTENHOUSE SQUARE Named after David and Benjamin Rittenhouse, who designed the first astronomical instruments in the US in the 18th century, Rittenhouse Square is one of the city's loveliest, most elegant residential areas. Handsome brownstones and high-rise apartment houses surround a green park, where people from all over town congregate. Art shows, flower shows, and concerts take place here in spring and summer. 18th and Walnut Sts.

US MINT The largest facility of its kind in the world, this mint can produce 10,000 coins per minute. At each observation post, a button activates a taped commentary on the different stages of the minting process. Historic coins are exhibited, and a souvenir shop sells proof sets and medals. Closed Sundays September through June; Saturdays September through April; and all federal holidays. Coinage machines not in operation on weekends. No admission charge. Fifth and Arch Sts. (phone: 597-7350).

EDGAR ALLAN POE HOUSE Known for "The Raven" and his chilling story "The Murders in the Rue Morgue," the famed American writer is said to have written "The Black Cat" and "The Gold Bug" while living here. Closed *Thanksgiving, Christmas,* and *New Year's Day.* No admission charge. 532 N. Seventh (phone: 597-8780).

READING TERMINAL MARKET Multitudes of shoppers come to forage for foods of local origin and international flair, including sushi, lobster, homemade pastas, fresh cheeses, and Amish shoofly pie (a molasses and crumb dessert) and hand-rolled pretzels. Some buy in quantities to take home, while others enjoy sampling as they explore. Stalls added in recent years also sell cookware and tableware, Pennsylvania crafts, including Amish quilts, and a variety of clothing and gift items. Ice cream at *Bassett's* is a must. Closed Sundays except during special events, among them the *Mummers Parade,* the *March Flower Show.* 12th and Arch Sts. (phone: 922-2317).

ITALIAN MARKET Open-air stalls and specialty shops line the sidewalks with their bargain-priced meat, fish, poultry, vegetables, and fresh pasta, cheeses, and spices. Top off the morning's stroll with a Philly cheesesteak at *Pat's* or *Geno's,* the rivals at the south end of the market (see *Say Cheese*). Closed Mondays. Ninth St. between Washington and Passyunk Aves.

NEW JERSEY STATE AQUARIUM This multimillion-dollar aquarium sits across the river in New Jersey. Its state-of-the-art *Ocean Base Atlantic* exhibit turns visitors into explorers as they enter an underwater Caribbean world (complete with a replica of an actual shipwreck and a coral reef) and come face-to-face with 800 species of bright tropical fish, seals, sea turtles, and sharks. This tour concludes at the *Deep Atlantic,* a 760,000-gallon tank with a spectacular 18- by 24-foot viewing window. Daily shows feature divers with scubaphones to answer audience questions. A "petting tank" allows visitors to get in touch with skates, rays, starfish, and even small sharks. The *Riverbus* shuttle (phone: 609-365-1400 for schedule) between Philadelphia and the aquarium leaves regularly from Penn's Landing at Walnut Street and Christopher Columbus Boulevard April through October: the round trip fare is $5 for adults and $3 for children. Closed *New Year's Day, Thanksgiving,* and *Christmas.* Admission charge. 1 S. Riverside Dr., Camden, NJ (phone: 609-365-3300; 800-616-JAWS to order tickets with a credit card).

EXTRA SPECIAL

During the winter of 1777–78, General George Washington and 11,000 Revolutionary troops retreated to *Valley Forge.* The site is now a state park. The visitors' center shows a film in its museum (open daily), and the park itself has a number of interesting historical buildings, including Washington's original headquarters. There also is a self-guided auto tour; information is available at the visitors' center. Closed *Christmas.* Admission charge to the headquarters building April through November. Bus tours can be arranged at the visitors' center daily in summer and on weekends in spring and fall. Take the Schuylkill Expressway (Rte. 76) west to the Valley Forge exit (about 20 miles), then follow Route 363 north to the park (phone: 783-1077).

For another kind of outdoor experience, visit *Longwood Gardens,* a horticultural display in Kennett Square (30 miles west of the city), where more than 11,000 types of plants are carefully tended on 350 acres; some of its trees were planted in the late 1700s. *Longwood Gardens* also hosts more than 300 performing arts events annually, and is renowned for its illuminated fountain displays and concerts in the summer. *Terrace* restaurant has both a dining room and a cafeteria (phone: 610-388-6771). Take Interstate 95 south to Route 322 west, then continue about 8 miles to Route 1 south. From there, proceed another 8 miles to the entrance. Open daily. No admission charge for children under six (phone: 610-388-1000). Just 5 miles north of the gardens on Route 1 is the *Brandywine River Museum and Conservancy,* which houses paintings by three generations of Wyeths (N. C., Andrew, and Jamie), along with works by several other artists including Maxfield Parrish and Howard Pyle. An impressive display of model trains is shown during the *Christmas* season. Closed *Christmas.* Admission charge. Located at the intersection of Rtes. 1 and 100, Chadds Ford (phone: 610-388-2700).

Sources and Resources

TOURIST INFORMATION

Located only steps from *City Hall* is the *Philadelphia Visitors Center* (16th St. at John F. Kennedy Blvd., or write to 1515 Market St., Suite 2020, Philadelphia, PA 19102; phone: 636-1666; 800-537-7676), which is open daily. Ask specifically for the vacation packet containing the *Official Visitor's Guide* to restaurants, hotels, and tours; maps; a "Calendar of Events"; and other helpful information. Visitors may also request the *African-American Historical and Cultural Guide.* For a recording on theater, concerts, and other special events, call the Donnelley Directory 24-hour hotline (phone: 610-337-7777, ext. 2116). For information about current offerings (including same-day, half-price tickets) to more than 40 performing arts groups and theaters throughout the city, contact *Upstage Box Office* (phone: 893-1145).

LOCAL COVERAGE The *Inquirer,* morning daily; the *Daily News,* afternoon daily; *Philadelphia* magazine, monthly. The Friday *Inquirer*'s Weekend section is an excellent source of events. Also see *ACCESS Philadelphia* (HarperCollins; $18.50).

TELEVISION STATIONS KYW Channel 3–CBS; WPVI Channel 6–ABC; WCAU Channel 10–NBC; and WHYY Channel 12–PBS.

RADIO STATIONS AM: WIP 610 (sports); KYW 1060 (news). FM: WHYY 90.9 (news/talk/national public radio); WXTU 92.5 (country); WFLN 95.7 (classical music); WUSL 98.9 (urban contemporary); WBEB 101.1 (soft rock); and WJJZ 106.1 (jazz).

TELEPHONE The area code for Philadelphia is 215. Many surrounding areas are now in the 610 area code.

SALES TAX There is a 7% sales tax on most purchases, excluding many clothing items; the hotel room tax is 13%.

CLIMATE Winter temperatures in Philadelphia generally hover in the 20s and 30s F. Spring and autumn are the best times to visit—temperatures then are usually in the 50s to 70s. Summer tends to be hot and sticky, with thermometer readings in the 80s and 90s.

GETTING AROUND

AIRPORT *Philadelphia International Airport* is a 30-minute drive to Center City (up to an hour in heavy traffic). The *SEPTA (Southeastern Pennsylvania Transportation Authority) Airport Express* train (phone: 587-7800) makes the 20-minute trip to the city's main terminal, *30th St. Station,* for $5. Trains stop at most of the airport terminals every half hour.

BUS/RAIL/SUBWAY *SEPTA (Southeastern Pennsylvania Transportation Authority)* will take you everywhere, by bus, trolley, train, or subway. The fare is $1.60 (this does not include suburban trains); for a savings, purchase tokens at $1.15 each. A good *SEPTA* map showing routes for all public transportation is available at newsstands and rail stations. The *Ben Franklin* line runs from Penn's Landing to the *Museum of Art* and the *Zoo* by way of Market Street and costs 50¢. Buses and stops are marked with red kites (phone: 580-7800). *Phlash* (phone: 4-PHLASH for information and schedules) also runs daily bus service to shops, museums, restaurants, nightspots, hotels, and the *Philadelphia Convention Center.* Fare is $1.50 one way or $3 for an all-day pass. Route maps are available at *SEPTA* stations, visitors' centers, and *Gallery Mall* information booths.

CAR RENTAL Philadelphia is served by all the national firms.

TAXI Cab fare is costly, but worth it for short hops to transport three or four people. Hail taxis in the street or do as Philadelphians do and pick them up in front of the *30th Street* train station, the *Greyhound/Trailways* bus terminal, or the nearest hotel, where most of them wait for customers. Call *Yellow Cab Company* (phone: 922-8400), *Quaker City Cab* (phone:728-8000), or *United Cab Association* (phone: 238-9500).

SIGHTSEEING TOURS

BOAT Take a lunch, dinner, or moonlight cruise on *The Spirit of Philadelphia* (Penn's Landing, on Christopher Blvd. at Lombard Circle; phone: 923-1419; 923-4993 for groups of 20 or more) and sail along the Delaware while enjoying a buffet, musical revue, and narrated sightseeing tour. Cruises run March through January. Check for special theme cruises.

BUS *Gray Line Tours* operates several different sightseeing tours April through mid-November. Three two-and-one-half-hour narrated tours depart twice daily from *30th Street* station and make courtesy hotel stops upon request; tours include both a historic and cultural tour of the city, as well as a visit to *Valley Forge.* Check for tours being added this year and combination train and bus packages that may include a day trip to the Amish country in Lancaster County (phone: 569-3666; 800-577-7745).

HORSE-AND-CARRIAGE Tours depart from the carriage stand on Chestnut between Fifth and Sixth Streets daily, weather permitting. After 6 PM, carriages depart from New Market Square on Second Street between Pine and South Streets (phone: 922-6840).

TROLLEY *American Trolley Tours* (phone: 333-2119) offers daily narrated tours with on/off privileges that take in sights from Rittenhouse Square and Antique Row to Penn's Landing and Society Hill, and include time at *Independence National Historic Park* and the *Betsy Ross House.* The trolley stops at the *Philadelphia Visitors Center* (16th St. and John F. Kennedy Blvd.) and the visitors' center at Third and Chestnut Streets, and will stop at hotels upon request.

WALKING The *Foundation for Architecture* offers a variety of walking and bus tours, organized around a particular theme, such as skyscrapers, Art Deco architecture, taverns, or a specific neighborhood. Tours are conducted April through November. For a brochure, contact the foundation at 1 Penn Center, Suite 1165, Philadelphia, PA 19103 (phone: 569-3187; 569-TOUR for recorded information).

SPECIAL EVENTS

The *Mummers Parade,* a Philadelphia tradition on January 1, is eight hours of string bands strutting up Broad Street, their members dressed in elaborate suits. The *Philadelphia Flower and Garden Show* is held at the *Pennsylvania Convention Center* (12th and Arch Sts.; phone: 625-8250) in early March. From April through mid-May, many residents open their homes and gardens for tours as part of *Philadelphia Open House.* Make arrangements through *Friends of Independence National Historical Park* (313 Walnut St.; phone: 597-7919). The city's *Welcome America* celebration runs the last week in June through *July 4th* and features daily events to showcase Philadelphia's history and culture, culminating with an outdoor concert on the Parkway and a fireworks display over the Delaware River. Come September, join in the *Super Sunday* fun along the Benjamin Franklin Parkway, with folk dancing, flea markets, music and food (phone: 299-1044). The *Philadelphia Craft Show* (phone: 684-7931), held the first or second weekend in November at the *Pennsylvania Convention Center* (see above), displays and sells a variety of crafts by artisans from around the country. *Fairmount Park* holds its *Christmas* tour in early December, during which the mansions and *Horticultural Society* building are decked out in colonial fashion for the holidays (phone: 684-7926; 684-7922 for a seasonal recording of special events tours at park mansions).

MUSEUMS

In addition to those described in *Special Places,* Philadelphia has many other museums of note. All charge admission, unless otherwise indicated.

ACADEMY OF NATURAL SCIENCES Particularly known for its dinosaur exhibits, the museum also offers *Outside In,* a hands-on children's section with live animals. Open daily. 19th St. and Parkway (phone: 299-1000).

AFRO-AMERICAN HISTORICAL AND CULTURAL MUSEUM African-American art in a variety of media is on display, and there are lectures, movies, and musical programs, including monthly jazz concerts. Closed Mondays. Seventh and Arch Sts. (phone: 574-0380).

ATTWATER KENT MUSEUM This small local history museum offers everything from silver miniatures and sketches to artifacts from nearby digs. During the holidays, the three-quarter scale *Colonial Christmas Village* delights visitors with mechanized scenes of 18th-century *Christmas.* Check on expanded daily schedules. Closed Sundays and Mondays. 15 S. Seventh St. (phone: 922-3031).

BARNES FOUNDATION This noted private collection of French Impressionist art exhibits the works of such masters as Manet, Matisse, Monet, Picasso, Renoir, Rousseau, and Seurat. A 12-acre arboretum displays a wide variety of flora. Call ahead for the schedule. Closed Mondays through Wednesdays. 300 N. Latch's La., Merion Station (phone: 610-667-0290).

FIREMAN'S HALL MUSEUM The exhibits here are all about fire fighting and include tools, helmets, a 1730s hand engine probably used by Benjamin Franklin in his Union Fire Company, and an 18th-century hand-drawn pumper. Closed Sundays and Mondays. 147 N. Second St. between Race and Arch Sts. (phone: 923-1438).

INSTITUTE OF CONTEMPORARY AWARENESS Contemporary art by established artists as well as emerging talents is the focus here. Closed Mondays and Tuesdays. *University of Pennsylvania,* 36th and Sansom Sts. (phone: 898-7108).

MUMMERS MUSEUM Exhibits of *Mummers'* memorabilia and history as well as sound recordings showcase a Philadelphia tradition. Tours available. Closed Mondays and holidays. Second St. and Washington Ave. (phone: 336-3050).

MUSEUM OF AMERICAN ART OF THE PENNSYLVANIA ACADEMY OF FINE ARTS This is America's oldest art museum at the nation's first art school. Permanent displays of a variety of media include 18th- through 20th-century American paintings, sculptures, and works on paper in chronological order. Open daily. Broad and Cherry Sts. (phone: 972-7600).

MUTTER MUSEUM Exhibits explore medical history. Closed Saturdays through Mondays. *College of Physicians of Philadelphia,* 19 S. 22nd St (phone: 563-3737).

NORMAN ROCKWELL MUSEUM An extensive collection of *Saturday Evening Post* covers is on display. Open daily. *Curtis Center,* Sixth and Sansom Sts. (phone: 922-4345).

PLEASE TOUCH MUSEUM Terrific hands-on exhibits are made for young children. Admission includes outdoor interactive *Science Park* at *Franklin Institute.* Open daily. 210 N. 21st St. (phone: 963-0667).

ROSENBACH MUSEUM AND LIBRARY This 19th-century townhouse contains thousands of rare books, manuscripts, and original illustrations as well as furniture, silver, paintings, and decorative arts of the time. Tours are available. Closed Mondays, holidays, and August. 2010 Delancey Pl. between Spruce and Pine Sts. (phone: 732-1600).

UNIVERSITY OF PENNSYLVANIA MUSEUM OF ANTHROPOLOGY AND ARCHAEOLOGY History and cultural heritage are seen here through exhibits focusing on archaeology and anthropology. Closed Mondays year-round and summer Sundays. 33rd and Spruce Sts. (phone: 898-4000).

WAGNER FREE INSTITUTE OF SCIENCE This national landmark houses a private natural history collection that exemplifies a rare Victorian-era museum. Highlights include fossils, taxidermy specimens, the first saber tooth tiger bones ever found, rocks, and minerals. Donations suggested. Closed Saturdays through Mondays. 17th St. and Montgomery Ave. (phone: 763-6529).

SHOPPING

For the best in department store shopping, head to *Lord & Taylor* in the landmark *John Wanamaker* building (Chestnut and Market Sts. at 13th St.) or *Strawbridges* (Ninth and Market Sts.), an anchor store at the *Gallery,* one of the largest urban malls in the nation with more than 200 stores and eateries. Running along Market Street from Ninth to 12th, it connects with *SEPTA's Market East* rail stop and several subway stations. The *Mellon Independence Center* (on Market St. between Seventh and Eighth) houses upscale shops, as does the *Bourse,* a restored Victorian building (on Fifth between Market and Chestnut Sts.). *The Shops at Liberty Place* (16th and Chestnut Sts.) is a two-story circular mall located in the heart of the business district and connected to the *Ritz-Carlton* hotel. Its hub is a magnificent marble and skylighted central court where musical entertainment is sometimes provided. The stores here range from the upscale to the practical, and there's a large food court with fast-food eateries and a more formal Italian restaurant.

To see some of Philadelphia's favorite clothing shops and art galleries, walk along Walnut Street between Rittenhouse Square at 18th Street and the *Hotel Atop the Bellevue* building at Broad Street. Nearby, must-see toy shops for all ages include *Einstein* (1627 Walnut Street; phone: 665-3622) and *Past, Present, and Future* (24 S. 18th St.; phone: 854-0444). The area between Second and Fourth Streets (between Market and Arch Sts.) has come to be known as an art district with some 40 galleries that hold an open house each month called *First Friday.* Street flea markets and musical groups add to the evening's atmosphere. Philadelphia is also known for its jewelers' row, which dates from the 1850s and is the second-largest diamond center in the country. Its heart lies between Sixth and Eighth, along Sansom Street. Similarly, an antiques row with both colonial and international crafts runs along Pine Street between Ninth and 12th. An eclectic shopping (and eating) experience can be enjoyed along Main Street in this 19th-century mill section along the Schuylkill River in Manayunk. Renovated factory warehouses and three-story buildings brim with specialty shops and restaurants. For the ultimate funky experience, don't miss a stroll down South Street from 10th to the river. You'll probably enjoy the people watching as much as the many boutiques and small restaurants.

SPORTS AND FITNESS

Whether you like to watch or play, there are plenty of sports around.

BASEBALL From April through early October, the *National League Phillies* chase the pennant at *Veterans Stadium* (Broad St. and Pattison Ave.; phone: 463-1000).

BASKETBALLPro basketball's *76ers* pack them in at the *CoreStates Center* (Broad St. and Pattison Ave.; phone: 339-7676) from November through April.

BICYCLING Some 10.6 miles of *Fairmount Park* are devoted to bike paths. Slated to open this year is a biking-hiking trail from Valley Forge, past the *Philadelphia Museum of Art,* to Penn's Landing at Spruce Street. Though not convenient to the park, *Bike Lane* (1234 Locust St.; phone: 735-1503) rents bikes–and in-line skates—year-round.

FOOTBALL The *NFL Eagles* play at *Veterans Stadium* (Broad St. and Pattison Ave.; phone: 463-5500).

GOLF Try to get invited to a private country club. If you can't your next best bet is *Cobbs Creek,* a public course (72nd and Lansdowne Ave.; phone: 877-8707). Nearby, the *Golf Corp. Sports Center* (7900 City Line Ave.; phone: 879-3536) has a driving range and miniature golf, as well as batting cages.

HOCKEY The *Flyers* play at the *CoreStates Center* (Broad St. and Pattison Ave.; phone: 755-9700) from October through April. Tickets are hard to get, but try *TicketMaster* (phone: 336-2000).

HORSE RACING *Philadelphia Park* has thoroughbred racing (3001 Rd., Bensalem; phone: 639-9000).

ICE SKATING The *Blue Cross River Rink* (Chestnut St. and Christopher Columbus Blvd.; phone: 925-RINK), open from November through mid-March for outdoor skating on the riverfront, offers equipment rentals. Call ahead for time schedules.

JOGGING In *Fairmount Park,* run alongside the Schuylkill River behind the art museum. Also check out the newest trail from the *Philadelphia Museum of Art* (see *Bicycling* above).

SKIING Everybody goes to the Pocono Mountains, two hours away in northeastern Pennsylvania. Best bets: *Camelback Mountain* (Tannersville; phone: 717-629-1661; 800-233-8100 for ski report); *Big Boulder* (Lake Harmony; phone: 717-722-0101); and *Jack Frost* (Whitehaven; phone: 717-443-8425).

TENNIS The nation's number one indoor event, the *US Pro Indoor,* is held annually at the *CoreStates Spectrum* in mid-February. The city runs more than 200 all-weather courts (contact individual recreation centers for availability), and *Fairmount Park* has another 200. Call the *Department of Parks and Recreation* (phone: 685-0052).

THEATER

The Philadelphia theater scene has continued its expansion in the 1990s with Broadway productions presented at the larger houses and many new plays debuting in more intimate settings. The leading theaters for the more extravagant productions are the *Forrest Theater* (1114 Walnut St.; phone: 923-1515; 800-447-7400 for tickets), the *Merriam Theater* (250 S. Broad St.; phone: 732-5446; 336-2000 for tickets), and the *Walnut Street Theater* (Ninth and Walnut Sts.; phone: 574-3550). There is also the *Philadelphia Arts Bank* (Broad and South Sts.; phone: 893-1145) for a wide variety of theater, music, and dance; the *Wilma Theater* (Broad and Spruce Sts.; phone: 963-0249) for contemporary and often controversial offerings; the *Society Hill Playhouse* (507 S. Eighth St.; phone: 923-0210) for musical comedies; the *Arden Theater* (41 N. Second St.; phone: 922-8900) for a variety of plays from Shakespeare to contemporary, September through June; and the *Annenberg Center* (3680 Walnut St.; phone: 898-6791) with its *Dance Celebration Series* and the *Philadelphia Festival Theater for New Plays. The Pennsylvania Ballet* performs at the *Academy of Music* (Broad and Locust Sts.; phone: 551-7000).

MUSIC

The *Philadelphia Orchestra,* under conductor Wolfgang Sawallisch, performs at the stately *Academy of Music* (Broad and Locust Sts.; phone: 893-1999) September through May. In summer, they play under the stars at the *Mann Music Center* (*Fairmount Park;* phone: 567-0707), where rock and pop concerts also are held. A limited number of free tickets to orchestra concerts are available at the *Philadelphia Visitors Center* (16th and John F. Kennedy Blvd.) on the day of a performance. The *Opera Company of Philadelphia* (phone: 928-2110) also performs at the *Academy of Music* throughout the year, while the *Concerto Soloists* perform at the *Walnut Street Theater* (see above).

NIGHTCLUBS AND NIGHTLIFE

To attract people to the city at night, Philadelphia's "Make It a Night," held Wednesday evenings during spring, summer, and fall, extends shopping far beyond normal business hours. Center City shops stay open for the evening, parking rates are reduced, and restaurants and theaters offer special discounts. A monthly event that is sure to please is *First Friday* in the Old City section between Second and Fourth Streets and Market and Vine Streets; here in this growing art district some 40 galleries open their doors to the strolling public. Live music and street flea markets add to the after-dark ambience.

The city's waterfront area along Christopher Columbus Boulevard has become the latest nightlife scene with the national chain *Dave & Buster's* (325 N. Christopher Columbus Blvd.; phone: 413-1951) leading the pack for fun and games. This vast arcade with restaurants also provides amusements for all ages, from traditional shuffleboard and pool to high-tech virtual reality interactive challenges such as simulated golf at North Carolina's prestigious *Pinehurst* or races with competitors seated atop real motorcycles that sway with the motion. *Egypt* (520 N. Christopher Columbus Blvd.; phone: 922-6500), decorated in an Egyptian theme, features dancing to 1980s and 1990s music. *Katmando* (415 N. Christopher Columbus Blvd.; phone: 629-7400) features an open-air nightclub and restaurant with live music nightly and is open April through October. Other samplings around the city include jazz at the American bistro–style *Blue Moon Jazz Café* (Fourth between Market and Chestnut Sts.; phone: 413-2273) and folk music at the *Tin Angel* (20 S. Second St.; phone: 928-0978). Comedy options include the *Comedy Cabaret* (126 Chestnut St.; phone: 625-JOKE) or *ComedySportz* (at the *Brick Playhouse* atop *Montserat* restaurant, 623 South St.; phone: 98-LAUGH), which highlights improvisational acts.

Best in Town

CHECKING IN

Hotels range from famous, durable places to sleek contemporary spots with loud, lively lobbies. Most of Philadelphia's major hotels have complete facilities for the business traveler. Those listed below as having "business services" usually offer such conveniences as meeting rooms, photocopiers, computers, translation services, and express checkout, among others. Call the individual hotel for additional information. Expect to pay $225 or more (sometimes much more) per night for a double room at places we've listed as very expensive; $150 to $225 at those categorized as expensive; and $75 to $150 at those rated moderate; there are no exceptional inexpensive hotels in the city. However, most hotels offer weekend packages at significantly reduced rates. And for bed and breakfast accommodations, which are often quite reasonable, contact *Bed and Breakfast Connection/Bed & Breakfast of Philadelphia* (PO Box 21, Devon, PA 19333; phone: 610-687-3565; 800-448-3619 outside the 610 area code; fax: 610-995-9524), whose listings cover the city as well as outlying areas such as the Main Line, Valley Forge, and the Brandywine River region. Hotel rooms have air conditioning, private baths, TV sets, and telephones unless otherwise indicated.

All hotels below are in Philadelphia and telephone and fax numbers are in the 215 area code unless otherwise indicated.

VERY EXPENSIVE

Four Seasons The height of local elegance, this hostelry has 371 luxurious rooms and suites. Its gracious *Fountain* restaurant (see *Eating Out*) is renowned for fine dining, the *Swann Lounge* serves afternoon tea and cocktails and features weekend entertainment, and a courtyard café is open during the summer. The hotel offers a health spa with a pool, sauna, and whirlpool, and a beauty salon. Special amenities include 24-hour valet and room service, a concierge, and twice-daily maid service. Business services are available. 1 Logan Sq. (phone: 963-1500; 800-332-3442; fax: 963-9506).

Hotel Atop the Bellevue One of the nation's grandest properties early in this century, it fell on hard times in the 1970s. After extensive renovations, however, this landmark now features 154 rooms and 18 spacious suites in a building that also houses three floors of upscale shops and restaurants. The room decor is turn-of-the-century, but there are many modern amenities, including an entertainment center with VCR, stereo, mini-bar, and voice mail. Fine dining and dancing are available in *Founders.* The *Library* lounge, which serves light fare and drinks, and the *Ethel Barrymore Room,* with afternoon tea and weekend entertainment, are perfect for relaxing. Guests receive a complimentary pass to the adjacent health club. There's a courtesy car available to Center City locations. Other amenities include a valet, a concierge, business services, and 24-hour room service. 1415 Chancellor Court (phone: 893-1776; 800-221-0833; fax: 721-8518).

Rittenhouse Appointed in classic European style, it has 87 spacious rooms and 11 suites. There are also 23 "apartments" with fully equipped kitchens and laundry facilities for people who want longer-term accommodations. Amenities include spacious marble bathrooms with TV and phone; two-line speaker phones, fax machines, VCRs, mini-bars, and daily newspaper delivery. *Restaurant 210* provides elegant dining, and *Treetops* offers attractive pre- and post-theater menus as well as picnic baskets to go. The *Cassatt Tea Room and Lounge* serves afternoon tea and cocktails. *Boathouse Row Bar* serves lunch, light dinners, and late-night snacks, and features live Saturday night jazz. An in-house spa offers a pool, steamroom, and sauna. Other conveniences include 24-hour room service, a valet, a concierge, a full service business center, and beauty salon. 210 W. Rittenhouse Sq. (phone: 546-9000; 800-635-1042; fax: 732-3364).

EXPENSIVE

Doubletree of Philadelphia Across from Philadelphia's *Academy of Music,* this contemporary-styled hotel has 419 room and eight suites. The second level

Café Academie overlooks both the atrium lobby and bar, and *Jack's Center City Tavern* serves casual fare. Guests have use of an indoor pool, jogging track, racquetball courts or can simply relax in the sauna or whirlpool. Broad and Locust Sts. (phone: 893-1600; 800-222-TREE; fax: 893-1663).

Latham This hotel is a favorite of businesspeople who seek a central location and first-rate service. Its 137 rooms and two suites are furnished with marble-topped bureaus and graceful French writing desks. Suites feature two-line phones, a laser printer and CD player, and a complimentary *Wall Street Journal* is delivered every business day. Guests have complimentary use of a nearby health club. Both the restaurant, *Michel's* (see *Eating Out),* and *Bar 17,* an English pub–style lounge, are places to see and be seen. Room service, a concierge, a valet, and business services are available. 17th and Walnut (phone: 563-7474; 800-LATHAM-1; fax: 563-4034).

Omni Hotel at Independence Park Its grand marble lobby with working fireplace and its marvelous view of *Independence National Historical Park* make this hotel special. Original watercolors of city scenes adorn the 147 rooms and three suites, which have two-line phones with voice mail. Complimentary coffee makers and mini-bar and a morning newspaper are provided. The *Azalea* restaurant features a regional menu in an elegant atmosphere; more casual meals are served at the lobby bar in the evening. There's twice-daily maid service, 24-hour room service, a valet, a concierge, business services, and a health club with a pool, saunas, and a Jacuzzi. Fourth and Chestnut Sts. (phone: 925-0000; 800-THE-OMNI; fax: 925-1263).

Ritz-Carlton Located in Liberty Place (the first two floors house retail shops, a food court, and a restaurant), this 290-room hotel has been designed and decorated in the style of the city's Federal period, with lots of molding and wainscoting. Rooms have mini-bars and marble bathrooms, and two-line phones with voice mail. Two floors have their own concierge and provide an all-day buffet. The *Dining Room* serves innovative American fare, while *The Grill* offers a more traditional menu; a lounge serves afternoon tea. There is an exercise and fitness center with workout equipment, a massage room, and saunas; guests can arrange to use the pool at a nearby sports club. Other amenities include 24-hour room service, a valet, a concierge, and business services. 17th and Chestnut Sts. (phone: 563-1600; 800-241-3333; fax: 567-2822).

Philadelphia Marriott The city's newest and by far its largest hotel boasts an ideal central location, directly connected by a skywalk to the *Pennsylvania Convention Center* and close to most historic sites. The 1,200 rooms include 57 suites with two-line phones, oversized bathrooms, and in-room movies. There is a fitness center, a whirlpool, a sauna, and an indoor pool. *J. W. Steakhouse* offers upscale dining, while *Allies American Grill* features American fare, *Champion Sports Bar and Restaurant* serves hamburgers and sandwiches, and *Starbucks* offers light meals and specialty coffees.

Other amenities include 24-hour concierge and business services. 1201 Market St. (phone: 625-2900; 800-228-9290; fax: 625-6000).

Sheraton Society Hill A short walk from Penn's Landing and *Independence Mall,* this inn has a brick and wood decor, which lends colonial overtones to its rooms and lobby. Balconies overlook a verdant lobby atrium, where a pianist plays nightly in the *Courtyard Lounge.* There's casual dining at *Hadley's,* the pub-style *Wooden Nickel* lounge, an indoor pool, and a health club with sauna and whirlpool. All 362 guestrooms, including 14 suites, feature coffee makers, and computerized snack bars. Valet service, a concierge, business services, and 24-hour room service are available. 1 Dock St. (phone: 238-6000; 800-325-3535; fax: 922-2709).

Wyndham Franklin Plaza One of the city's best, it's four blocks from *City Hall* and a few steps from the Parkway. Facilities include 720 modern rooms and 36 suites. Amenities include a Nautilus-equipped health club, indoor pool, and sauna. *Between Friends* offers fine dining; *The Terrace* serves more casual American fare; and there's an atrium lobby bar lounge. Amenities include a valet, room service, business services, and a concierge. 17th and Vine Sts. (phone: 448-2000; 800-WYNDHAM; fax: 448-2864).

MODERATE

Best Western Center City In the heart of the museum district and within walking distance of most major attractions, this 183-room and four-suite hotel offers casual comfort following a complete renovation in 1995. Amenities include a restaurant, a lounge, an outdoor pool, valet, and room service. Business services are available. 22nd and Parkway (phone: 568-8300; 800-528-1234; fax: 557-0259).

Holiday Inn–City Line Convenient to City Line shops and restaurants, and a 10-minute drive from Center City, this 343-room inn offers an indoor/outdoor pool, an exercise room, a restaurant, a lounge, valet and room service, and limousine service to and from the airport. A complimentary shuttle bus service provides transportation within a 3-mile radius. There's also a casual, family-style restaurant next door. Business services are available. Free parking. City Line and 4100 Presidential Blvd. (phone: 477-0200; 800-642-8982; fax: 473-2709).

Penn's View Inn Situated in the Old City section, this inn offers European elegance in its 27 rooms, no two of which are alike. Deluxe rooms overlook the Delaware and have fireplaces and Jacuzzis; all receive complimentary breakfast. *Ristorante Panorama* serves northern Italian food in a bustling trattoria atmosphere. The romantic *Il Bar* offers 120 wines by the glass. There is valet and room service, a concierge desk, and business services. Fitness privileges are available nearby for a modest fee. 14 N. Front St. (phone: 922-7600; 800-331-7634; fax: 922-7642).

EATING OUT

The city boasts quite a few outstanding restaurants, some spacious and lively, others intimate and cozy. Expect to pay $75 or more for dinner for two at places we've listed as very expensive; $50 to $75 at those categorized as expensive; $20 to $50 at those rated moderate; and less than $20 at those rated inexpensive. Prices do not include drinks, wine, tax, or tips. All restaurants are in the 215 area code unless otherwise indicated.

Unless otherwise noted, restaurants are open for lunch and dinner.

VERY EXPENSIVE

Le Bec Fin This is the best restaurant in town—and one of the finest in the country. The setting is intimate yet elegant with crystal chandeliers and damask wall coverings. The menu of imaginative French fare—such as *homard à la presse* (pressed lobster sautéed tableside)—changes frequently, but it always offers lavish desserts. Diners can choose the prix fixe dinner (about $102 per person) or lunch (about $36 per person). *Le Bar Lyonnaise* downstairs extends a casual French bistro atmosphere where one can sample dishes à la carte from the main menu. Closed Sundays; dinner only on weekends. Reservations necessary for the restaurant only. Major credit cards accepted. 1523 Walnut (phone: 567-1000).

Deux Cheminées This elegant dining spot in a 19th-century townhouse features old Philadelphia decor, with Oriental rugs and polished hardwood floors. The prix fixe meal is classic French; crab soup and rack of lamb are standouts. Private parties of up to 80 can be accommodated. Open for dinner only; closed Sundays and Mondays. Reservations advised; necessary on Saturdays. Major credit cards accepted. 1221 Locust St. (phone: 790-0200).

Fountain In the *Four Seasons* hotel, this is one of Philadelphia's finest. Experience truly gracious dining accommpanied by attentive service. Rich mahogany walls and picture windows overlooking the stately, flag-draped Benjamin Franklin Parkway add to the elegant setting. A changing menu features fine continental cuisine, emphasizing fresh ingredients. An alternate low-sodium, low-cholesterol menu is available, as are prix fixe selections. Dessert highlights include a rich chocolate soufflé and "the artist's palette" (an assortment of chocolate and fruit). Enjoy an extensive wine selection and after-dinner liqueurs and ports. Sunday brunch offers a buffet or à la carte dining. Reservations necessary (non-hotel guests must call well in advance for Saturday nights). Major credit cards accepted. 1 Logan Sq. (phone: 963-1500).

Kansas City Prime With an ideal location that lends itself to an after-dinner stroll along this neighborhood's 19th-century main street of shops and galleries, this sophisticated steakhouse welcomes diners with a menu of *Kobe* beef, filet mignon, and lobster all accompanied by such interesting side dishes as spinach with raisins and pine nuts. Open daily for dinner only.

Reservations necessary. Major credit cards accepted. 4417 Main St. (phone: 482-3700).

EXPENSIVE

Bookbinder's Seafood House The better of the two restaurants bearing this famous name (see below), this large, bustling eatery offers a casual setting with wood walls. Fresh, well-prepared seafood is the chief attraction—try the snapper soup or the baked crab. Richard Bookbinder's own creamy peanut butter pie and cheesecake are two popular desserts. Reservations advised. Major credit cards accepted. 215 S. 15th St. (phone: 545-1137).

Café Nola A taste of New Orleans in Philadelphia, the selections here are mostly Cajun and creole; the place is known for its seasonal decorations, especially at *Christmas* and during *Mardi Gras.* Crab and lobster cakes, jambalaya, and prime ribs are among the offerings. Reservations advised. Major credit cards accepted. 603-605 S. Third St. (phone: 627-2590).

DiLullo Centro Set in a former theater, this large establishment has world class atmosphere and small restaurant quality. Opulence is everywhere, from the glass elevator to the Impressionist murals. The menu features homemade pasta as well as veal and seafood dishes and fresh pastries. Note that an inexpensive assortment of salads, pasta, pizza, and desserts is served in the *Café Centro* lounge. Closed Sundays; dinner only on Saturdays. Reservations advised. Major credit cards accepted. 1407 Locust St. (phone: 546-2000).

Dock Street Brewery and Restaurant This pub has a thoroughly polished look, with cherry tables, comfortable library chairs, and a long marble bar; the antique billiard tables and dart boards add to the ambience. The glass-enclosed brewery is the focal point and can be toured on Wednesday evenings, Saturday afternoons, or upon request. The menu features pub fare, but with a twist: many dishes are prepared with beer and reflect the foods of the major beer-making countries. Reservations advised for six or more on Fridays and Saturdays. Major credit cards accepted. 18th and Cherry Sts. in 2 Logan Square Building (phone: 496-0413).

Garden Fresh seafood and game in season are served in a stylish old townhouse. Dine outdoors in the courtyard when the weather is good, or sit at the cozy *Oyster Bar.* Two *cruvinets* dispense a variety of French and California wines by the glass. Homemade ice cream is the dessert specialty. Closed Sundays and for lunch on Mondays and Saturdays. Reservations advised. Major credit cards accepted. 1617 Spruce St. (phone: 546-4455).

Michel's Chef Michel Richard has created a California bistro-style eatery with a variety of fish, chicken, steak, and pasta dishes. Save room for one of the fabulous desserts (such as chocolate hazelnut bars or crunchy napoleons with butterscotch sauce). Open daily for breakfast, lunch, and dinner.

Reservations advised. Major credit cards accepted. *Latham Hotel,* 17th and Walnut Sts. (phone: 563-9444).

Old Original Bookbinder's Philadelphia's best-known restaurant, with mahogany and gleaming leather. Many love it; many find it overpriced. The seafood is as much of a legend as many of the celebrities who dine here, but the menu offers meat and chicken as well. Open daily; dinner only Saturdays and Sundays. Reservations advised. Major credit cards accepted. 125 Walnut St. (phone: 925-7027).

Susanna Foo Fine Chinese food in an elegant atmosphere of polished mahogany furniture, fresh flowers, and linen tablecloths. Hunan dishes are prepared with a touch of French flair; the menu changes seasonally but usually features pheasant, quail, and other game in winter, and fresh fish and seafood in summer. The luscious desserts include a variety of mousses, tarts, and fresh fruit in season. Closed Sundays; dinner only Saturdays. Reservations advised weekdays; necessary for dinner on Fridays and Saturdays. Major credit cards accepted. 1512 Walnut St. (phone: 545-2666).

White Dog Café In a Victorian brownstone near the *University of Pennsylvania,* this place offers nourishment for both body and mind, with the charm of a country inn. For the body, the menu has contemporary American fare with influences from Europe, Asia, and Mexico; good entrées include herb-charred leg of lamb with caraway glaze, grilled yellowfin tuna with ginger-basil hot sauce, and stir-fried vegetables served over rice noodles. Don't pass up the restaurant's signature dessert—*crème brûlée* with raspberries. For the mind, the salon *Tails* features live piano music as well as weekly programs in the restaurant's established tradition of political and cultural involvement, offering speakers, storytellers, and the like. Open daily; brunch on weekends. Reservations advised. Major credit cards accepted. 3420 Sansom St. (phone: 386-9224).

MODERATE

Downey's A local favorite for relaxing and partying, this eatery in Society Hill is noted for its Irish stew and liquored cakes. The continental menu features a raw bar as well as steaks, pasta, chicken, and seafood. The wood-and-brass decor is complemented with Irish artifacts, including a mahogany bar brought over from a bank in Cork. In season, patrons can eat on an outdoor deck. Sunday brunch features live entertainment. Reservations advised. Major credit cards accepted. Front and South Sts. (phone: 629-0525).

Marabella's A chain of Italian eateries featuring mesquite-grilled seafood, pizza, and Italian delicacies including homemade pasta. Try veal chops stuffed with ricotta and spinach in a Dijon sauce, rosemary-marinated chicken breast with garlic mashed potatoes, or lobster ravioli. Follow with a chocolate mousse glazed with rum, whipped cream, and shavings. Reservations necessary for lunch only. Major credit cards accepted. Three locations: 1420

Locust St. in *Academy House* (phone: 545-1845); 401 City Ave. (phone: 668-5353); and 1700 Benjamin Franklin Pkwy. (phone: 981-5555).

Sansom Street Oyster House With a large collection of oyster plates displayed overhead and highly polished wooden tables, the casual warmth of this place is a Philadelphia tradition. Among the specialties are Maryland crab cakes, seafood, and oysters (what else?), as well as fruit pies, bread, and rice puddings for dessert. Closed Sundays. Dinner reservations advised for groups of five or more. Major credit cards accepted. 1516 Sansom St. (phone: 567-7683).

Sonoma Derek Davis describes the fare at this eatery as "Italiafornian" (a combination of California and Italian). The blend is well represented in the roast chicken with rosemary, grilled chicken breast with pesto, and garlic rib-eye steaks. The pizza is made with a wonderful thin, flaky crust in a wood-burning oven. One pie is topped with grilled rock shrimp, tomatoes, hot peppers, leeks, fontina cheese, and basil. Reservations accepted for groups of six or more. Major credit cards accepted. 4411 Main St. (phone: 483-9400).

Zocalo Mexican art adorns the walls in this handsome restaurant popular for its contemporary Mexican cuisine. Try the grilled chicken salad with tomato vinaigrette, followed by seared shrimp tacos with red bell peppers and *poblano* peppers with salsa and salad. The menu also offers vegetarian dishes. Open daily; dinner only weekends. Reservations advised. Major credits cards accepted. 3600 Lancaster Ave. (phone: 895-0139).

INEXPENSIVE

Le Bus For years this restaurant operated out of an actual bus parked at the corner of 35th and Sansom Streets. Now a cafeteria in two row houses, it caters to hordes of college students with a menu specializing in huge sandwiches—chicken salad, ham, roast beef—as well as salads, daily entrée specials (often including a decent vegetarian lasagna), and homemade soups. The main attractions, however, are the breads, pastries, and muffins. Open daily for breakfast, lunch, and dinner; closed summer weekends. No reservations. No credit cards accepted. 3402 Sansom St. (phone: 387-3800).

Famous Delicatessen Famous for celebrity customers, as its picture-lined walls prove, this Jewish deli features hot pastrami, roast beef, roast turkey, and corned beef sandwiches, followed by the crowning touch: delicious chocolate chip cookies. Open for breakfast and lunch only. No reservations. Major credit cards accepted. 700 S. Fourth St. (phone: 922-3274).

Imperial Inn One of the best-known spots in Chinatown, this eclectic restaurant features Szechuan, Mandarin, and Cantonese dishes. Cantonese-style dim sum also is offered during the more casual lunch hours; lights are dimmed and linen tablecloths are added at dinner. Reservations advised. Major credit cards accepted. 146 N. 10th St. (phone: 627-5588).

SAY CHEESE

While in Philadelphia, don't forget to sink your teeth into a famous Philly cheesesteak—a sandwich loaded with steak, onions, cheese, and peppers. Try *Pat's King of Steaks* (1237 E. Passyunk Ave., South Philadelphia; phone: 468-1546) for one of the best cheesesteaks in town. It's open 24 hours, seven days a week. Or, if you're in the *Reading Terminal Market,* visit *Rick's Philly Steaks* (12th and Arch Sts.; phone: 925-4320). Another favorite is *Jim's Steaks* (400 South St.; phone: 928-1911), which also has great hoagies (also known as heros or sub sandwiches).

Phoenix

Glittering like a jewel under the bright Southwest sun, Phoenix has drawn people like a magnet: Since 1960, the city's population has soared from 439,000 people to over two million, making it one of the fastest growing metropolises in the country. Most people come here for two things—the eight months of nearly perfect weather and the dazzling surroundings. By day, the sun fairly sparkles; as evening nears, the sunset splashes deep purple and blazing orange across the horizon. This, residents say, is what heaven is all about.

More than 60% of Arizona's population make the Valley of the Sun (as Phoenix's metro area is called) their home. Streets and freeways are clogged with motorists during rush hour, and smog is such a problem in winter that drivers must use gasohol between October and March to cut down air pollution. But that hasn't stopped immigration from places such as California and the Midwest. Suburbs extend for 50 miles: Glendale, Avondale, Sun City, and Youngtown to the west; Scottsdale, Tempe, and Mesa eastward toward the fabled Superstition Mountains. New homes sprout from Peoria to Gilbert, two once-sleepy agricultural towns that are now increasingly active suburbs. It's no mystery why the Valley is a favorite: Just watch one turquoise-and-golden-hued sunset and you're hooked. And don't be surprised by residents' attitude toward distance—they consider it nothing to drive 200 miles for a picnic or a swim. (By the way, you'll need a car to get around. Everything is spread out.)

The rebirth of downtown Phoenix, once a ghost town after 5 PM, is another result of the city's increasing popularity. The *Arizona Center* complex gives workers a reason to stay downtown after quitting time. Amid the high-rises at Van Buren and Third Streets, the conglomeration of restaurants, shops, and nightclubs has exceeded expectations. Just five blocks south is the *America West Arena,* home court for the Phoenix *Suns* basketball team, the Arizona *Rattlers* arena football team and the Phoenix *Coyotes* professional hockey team; you can rub shoulders with local celebrities in the nearby *Copper Club* before, during, and after games. Also nearby is the *Herberger Theater Center,* the home of several local acting troupes.

But the area's awesome natural beauty eclipses any manmade edifice. From the top of nearby South Mountain, a visitor can see the Valley stretching in all directions. To the northeast, there's no mistaking the Valley's most distinctive landmark, Camelback Mountain. And as the eye follows the palisades of the Superstitions along the eastern horizon, it can pick out the Mazatzal mountain chain which cradles the Salt River.

The Salt has been irrigating the Valley for more than 1,000 years, and some of its canals follow water paths created by ancient Hohokam Indians. In fact, new construction is continuously unearthing Hohokam artifacts—

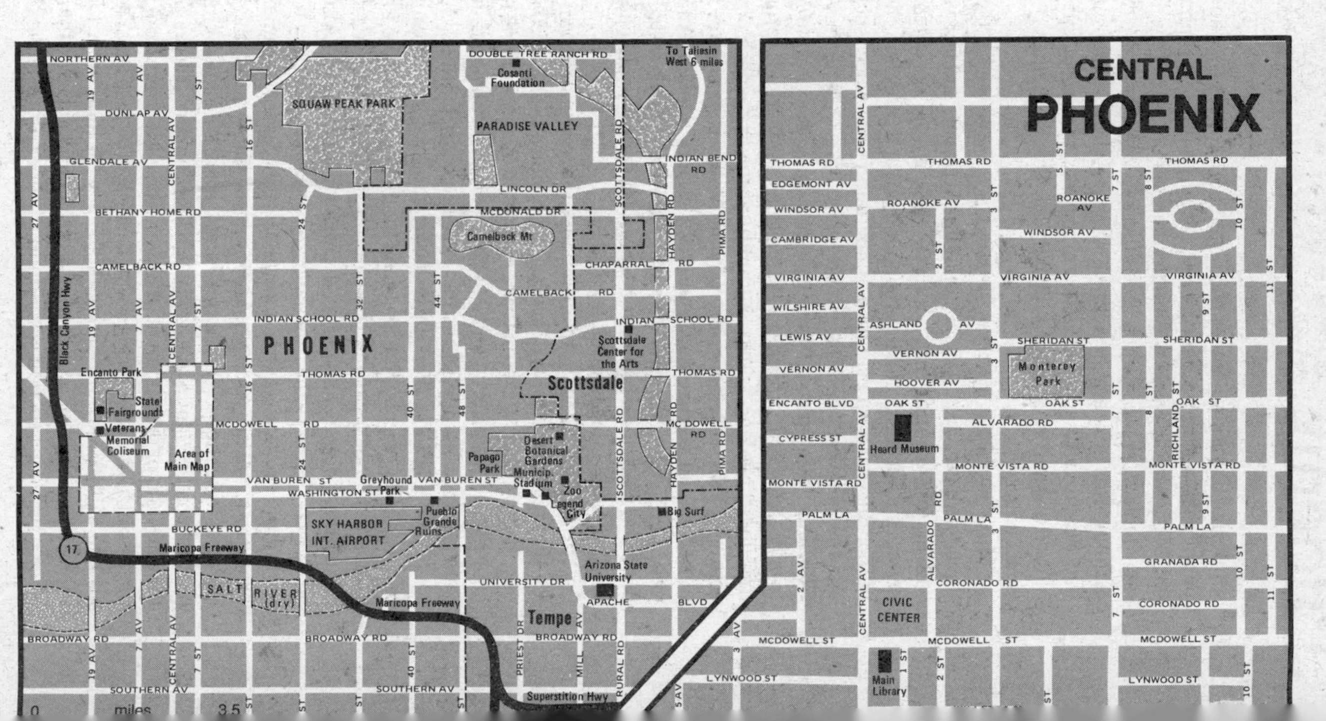

CENTRAL
PHOENIX
PHOENIX
Scottsdale
Tempe
PARADISE VALLEY
SQUAW PEAK PARK
To Taliesin West 6 miles
Cosanti Foundation
Camelback Mt
Scottsdale Center for the Arts
Desert Botanical Gardens
Papago Park
Municip. Stadium
Zoo
Legend City
Big Surf
Arizona State University
Encanto Park
State Fairgrounds
Veterans Memorial Coliseum
Area of Main Map
Greyhound Park
Pueblo Grande Ruins
SKY HARBOR INT. AIRPORT
SALT RIVER (dry)
Maricopa Freeway
Black Canyon Hwy
Superstition Hwy
17
Heard Museum
Monterey Park
CIVIC CENTER
Main Library
NORTHERN AV
DUNLAP AV
GLENDALE AV
BETHANY HOME RD
CAMELBACK RD
INDIAN SCHOOL RD
THOMAS RD
MCDOWELL RD
VAN BUREN ST
WASHINGTON ST
BUCKEYE RD
UNIVERSITY DR
APACHE BLVD
BROADWAY RD
SOUTHERN AV
DOUBLE TREE RANCH RD
LINCOLN DR
MCDONALD DR
CHAPARRAL RD
INDIAN BEND RD
SCOTTSDALE RD
HAYDEN RD
PIMA RD
PRIEST DR
MILL AV
RURAL RD
27 AV
19 AV
7 AV
CENTRAL AV
7 ST
16 ST
24 ST
32 ST
40 ST
44 ST
48 ST
0 miles 3.5
EDGEMONT AV
WINDSOR AV
CAMBRIDGE AV
VIRGINIA AV
WILSHIRE AV
LEWIS AV
VERNON AV
ENCANTO BLVD
CYPRESS ST
MONTE VISTA RD
PALM LA
ROANOKE AV
ASHLAND AV
HOOVER AV
OAK ST
ALVARADO RD
SHERIDAN ST
GRANADA RD
CORONADO RD
MCDOWELL ST
LYNWOOD ST
RICHLAND ST
1 ST
2 ST
3 ST
5 ST
8 ST
9 ST
10 ST
11 ST
2 AV
3 AV
5 AV

SE PHOENIX & VICINITY
SOUTH MOUNTAIN PARK
10
N
Art Museum
MORELAND ST
LATHAM ST
PORTLAND ST
ROOSEVELT ST
GARFIELD ST
MCKINLEY ST
PIERCE ST
FILLMORE ST
TAYLOR ST
POLK ST
VAN BUREN ST
MONROE ST
ADAMS ST
WASHINGTON ST
JEFFERSON ST
MADISON ST
JACKSON ST
HARRISON ST
BUCHANAN ST
GRAND AV
CENTRAL AV
17 DR
18 DR
Hall of Flame Museum
University Park
Ariz. Museum
State Office Blg
State Capitol
Old City Cemetery
Police Dept
Municipal Blg
Federal Blg
Post Office
Union Station
Chamber of Commerce
CIVIC PLAZA
Bus Terminal
Montgomery Stadium
Verde Park
0 miles 1/2

even the remains of entire villages. What ancient history Phoenix has is associated with these original residents; the city itself is little more than 100 years old. Ringed by reservations, the Valley has a number of museums devoted to indigenous cultures, as well as art galleries featuring the work of local Native American artists.

If you think the desert is all sand dunes, you'll be delightfully surprised by the abundance of plant life. There are at least a dozen species of cactus, one of which, the saguaro (pronounced sa-*wha*-ro), is the state symbol. The desert is easy to reach from Phoenix: Just drive for 30 minutes in any direction. Or better yet, go to the 16,000-acre *South Mountain Park,* the nation's largest city park. You won't find the softball fields and tennis courts that characterize most big-city parks; instead, these rolling hills remain in their natural state, criss-crossed by hiking trails. Enjoy the beauty of the native vegetation, but be careful: Rattlesnakes and wild boars are also natives of the park, and they like to roam.

Everything in Phoenix depends on the weather, which is generally fantastic in winter and scorching in summer. In winter, when the "snowbirds" come to escape the cold, it's possible to play tennis and golf, except during the occasional cold snap or cloudburst. But it does get cold after dark, and coats or sweaters may sometimes be needed even during the day. Oddly enough, Phoenix gets most of its minimal rainfall in the summer, when the city turns into an oven. But the sizzling heat has some advantages. The streets are less crowded, and rooms and greens fees at the best resorts are much less expensive. If you visit in summer, you'll also grow to understand why Arizona is one of the few states that don't have daylight saving time: Arizonans can't wait for the sun to go down.

Phoenix At-a-Glance

SEEING THE CITY

There is no view more beautiful than the one from South Mountain, especially when the last rays of sun paint the sky in layers of orange, red, and purple. Drive south on Central Avenue into *South Mountain Park* and stop at one of the lookouts.

SPECIAL PLACES

Street numbers start at zero in the center of downtown. Central Avenue, the business and financial district, runs north and south, bisecting the city into east and west. Numbered avenues lie to the west of Central, numbered streets to the east.

STATE CAPITOL The building shows what granite from the Salt River Mountains looks like when put to constructive use. It has now been restored to the way it originally appeared in 1912, the year of statehood. The murals inside depict Arizona's discovery and exploration in the 16th century, and life in the region through the 1930s. There also is an exhibit displaying an array of bola (string) ties, the official state neckwear. Closed weekends and holidays. No admission charge. W. Washington and 17th Ave. (phone: 542-4675).

HEARD MUSEUM Founded in the late 1920s, this museum focuses on the native cultures of the Southwest. Its award-winning "Native Peoples of the Southwest" exhibit serves as a centerpiece and is the largest display of its kind in North America. Tracing the history of the region from 15,000 BC to the present, it includes everything from prehistoric pottery vessels to contemporary Navajo textiles. There's also a hands-on children's exhibit called "Old Ways, New Ways," which focuses on the Southwest Zuni, Northwest Coast Tsimshian, and the Great Plains Kiowa. A special gallery features a large number of Hopi kachina dolls—perhaps the museum's best-known collection—many of which were donated by Barry Goldwater. The museum also exhibits jewelry, baskets, textiles, ceramics, and artifacts of many Southwestern Native cultures. Of five other galleries devoted to changing shows, one focuses on contemporary Native American fine art; the others feature presentations about native culture both in North America and around the world. Closed major holidays. Admission charge. 22 E. Monte Vista (phone: 252-8840; 252-8848, for recorded information).

PHOENIX ART MUSEUM With renovations completed, this museum specializes in contemporary Southwestern art. The institution also has other collections that cover North American art in general (including Mexican) and a small exhibition of Renaissance, 17th-, and 18th-century work. A planned hands-on interactive gallery is scheduled to open this year. Closed Mondays and major holidays. No admission charge on Wednesdays. 1625 N. Central (phone: 257-1222).

PUEBLO GRANDE MUSEUM AND INDIAN RUINS By climbing to the top of a mound marked into seven stations, you can see the ruins of a former Hohokam Indian settlement, believed to have been occupied from 200 BC until 1400, when the tribe vanished without a trace. Phoenix municipal archaeologists are continuing their excavations. In the museum are excavation photographs and Indian artifacts. Closed major holidays. Admission charge. 4619 E. Washington (phone: 495-0901).

DESERT BOTANICAL GARDENS Half of all the varieties of cactus in the world are planted here, and self-guided tours and booklets help identify the prickly flora. Open daily. Admission charge. *Papago Park* (phone: 941-1217).

PHOENIX ZOO When you've finished exploring the *Botanical Gardens,* take a leisurely drive through desert rock formations to the *Phoenix Zoo,* which covers more than 125 acres in another section of *Papago Park.* (You can stop to picnic in the park.) There are more than 1,200 animals here. One of the most popular attractions is the oryx herd. One exhibit shows off the splendor of Arizona's natural habitats, from its deserts to its 10,000-foot peaks; another focuses on endangered species, not only displaying some of the animals, but also explaining the plight of the environment. Open daily. Admission charge. 455 N. Galvin Pkwy. (phone: 273-1341).

SCOTTSDALE Residents call it "the West's most Western town," and it still has its hitching posts and touches of cowboy mystique, although its face has changed somewhat. The town boasts one of the area's best malls, *Scottsdale Fashion Square,* a bright and airy shopping experience (don't miss the *Museum of Northern Arizona* shop). In addition, Scottsdale's Fifth Avenue is lined with galleries (see *Art Galleries*). The simple act of walking is an aesthetic adventure here. Take McDowell Road east to Scottsdale Road north.

COSANTI FOUNDATION The architect Paolo Soleri maintains a workshop here, with a model of Arcosanti, his megalopolis of the future. His sculpture and windbells are on display, too. Closed major holidays; call for tour information. Donations suggested. 6433 E. Doubletree Rd., Scottsdale (phone: 948-6145).

TALIESIN WEST The future owes much of its shape to master architect Frank Lloyd Wright. His former office and school, *Taliesin* (pronounced Tal-ly-*ess*-en) *West,* offers the chance to see what goes into planning the marvelous, ultramodern structures that students base on Wright's designs. Closed major holidays. Admission charge. Scottsdale Rd. north, to Shea Blvd. east, to 108th St. north, to *Taliesin West* in Scottsdale (phone: 860-8810).

BORGATA Not the place for bargain-priced jeans or a pound of sugar, it's one of the most opulent retail operations this side of Beverly Hills—and one of the most unusual anywhere. There are about 50 boutiques and restaurants in a setting redolent of an old Italian village. It's well worth a visit, even if you can only afford to look. Open daily. 6166 N. Scottsdale Rd., Scottsdale.

HERITAGE SQUARE This Victorian complex in the heart of downtown is a refreshing change in this relatively young city. Spend an afternoon in the museums, shops, and restaurants. *Rosson House* (1894), an open-air lathe house, is particularly notable. Closed Mondays and Tuesdays. Admission charge. 127 N. Sixth St. (phone: 262-5071).

ARIZONA CENTER Shops and restaurants line this L-shaped, two-story center, and fountains, shade trees, and wide lawns help deflect the summer's heat. Open daily. 455 N. Third St. (phone: 271-4000).

RAWHIDE'S 1880S WESTERN TOWN Set in the middle of 160 acres of natural desert is a replica of an entire Old West town. Along the rickety main street are shops, a shooting gallery, a blacksmith, and a general store. You can get arrested by a US marshal (though you don't have to commit a crime, just pay $3). Ride on a stagecoach, pan for gold, ride a burro, and wash hearty, old-fashioned meals down with sarsaparilla. A large collection of antiques is on display throughout the town, and the *Rawhide Museum* has more than 5,000 items of historical interest, including Geronimo's moccasins and items owned by the likes of Diamond Jim Brady and Belle Starr. Children will enjoy *Kid's Territory,* which has a petting ranch. Sunset haywagon rides on Saturday nights and a desert cookout with country dancing complete the Western theme. Open daily. Admission charge for attractions. 23023 N. Scottsdale Rd., Scottsdale (phone: 502-5600).

DOLLY'S STEAMBOAT This is a unique way to tour the desert. Board this replica of a historic steamboat to cruise Canyon Lake, in the breathtaking *Superstition Wilderness.* Guides give an informal history and geography lesson. Cruises daily, with sunset charter rides available. Admission charge. 5106 E. Emilita, Mesa (phone: 827-9144).

EXTRA SPECIAL

For a picturesque day trip through open desert, take the Black Canyon Highway north to Cordes Junction, then travel west through the old territorial capital of Prescott to Sedona, famous for its dramatic red cliffs. At Sedona, take a breathtaking drive up Oak Creek Canyon to Flagstaff, or linger in Sedona before returning via the Black Canyon Highway. Wander through the shopping village of *Tlaquepaque* and enjoy some of the finest "Arizona Style" Mexican cuisine at *El Rincón* (phone: 520-282-4648). This restaurant is famous for their *chimichangas* and first-rate margaritas, dine inside or on the patio under the sycamores. Evening reservations are recommended. Complete the day with a sunset *Pink Jeep Tours' Scenic Sedona* experience, located in uptown Sedona, 204 N. Hwy. 89A (phone: 1-800-8-SEDONA).

Sources and Resources

TOURIST INFORMATION

For maps, brochures, and information, contact the *Arizona Office of Tourism* (2702 N. Third St., Suite 4015., Phoenix, AZ 85004; phone: 230-7733, fax: 277-9289) or the *Phoenix and Valley of the Sun Convention and Visitors Bureau* (1 Arizona Center, 400 E. Van Buren, Suite 600, Phoenix, AZ 85004; phone: 254-6500). Both are closed weekends. Contact the state tourism hotline (phone: 800-842-8257). Contact the state tourism hotline (phone: 800-842-8257) for maps, calendars of events, and travel advisories.

LOCAL COVERAGE *Arizona Republic,* morning daily; *Phoenix Gazette,* evening daily except Sundays; *Scottsdale Progress Tribune,* morning daily; *Mesa, Tempe and Chandler Tribune,* morning daily; *New Times, Business Journal,* and *Arizona Business Gazette,* all weekly; *Phoenix* magazine and *Phoenix Home & Garden,* both monthly.

TELEVISION STATIONS KTVK Channel 3–WB; KPHO Channel 5–CBS; KAET Channel 8–PBS; KSAZ Channel 10–Fox; KPNX Channel 12–NBC; and KNXV Channel 15–ABC.

RADIO STATIONS AM: KTAR 620 (news/talk/sports); KOY 550 (nostalgia); and KFYI 910 (news/talk). FM: KNIX 102.5 (country); KKLT 98.7 (adult contemporary); and KKFR 92.3 (Top 40).

TELEPHONE The area code for metropolitan Phoenix is 602; outside of the city the area code is 520.

SALES TAX The city sales tax is 6.8%; the hotel room tax is 10.6%.

CLIMATE Seasons should be considered when planning trips. Fall, winter, and spring are dry, warm, and sunny. Temperatures range from daytime highs of between 60 and 80F to nighttime lows of about 35 to 50F. Summer is the off-season (hotel prices go down), when it's more than 100F during the day and in the 80s at night.

GETTING AROUND

Getting around Phoenix is next to impossible without a car. Scottsdale traffic lights operate with a "lagging" green left-turn arrow that appears after the standard green light. In contrast, traffic lights in other Valley cities operate with a left-turn arrow that appears before the green light.

AIRPORT *Sky Harbor International Airport* is just a 10-minute drive from downtown. (Taxi fares vary widely, so be sure to agree on a price before getting into a cab.) *Supershuttle* (phone: 244-9000) offers transportation from the airport to downtown and to most other Valley locations. For rides to the airport, call 24 hours in advance. *Valley Metro* (phone: 253-5000) buses stop at terminals 2, 3 and 4 at *Sky Harbor* every half hour. One goes downtown and one to the east Valley. Fare is $1.25; transfers are free.

BUS The system is sketchy, with interminable waiting periods, erratic schedules, limited nighttime and Saturday service, and *Dial-a-Ride* is available to the general public on Sundays and designated holidays. However, you can call *Valley Metro* (phone: 253-5000) for schedule information. Fare: $1.75 on express routes; $1.25 on local routes.

CAR RENTAL All major national firms are represented. Of local companies, *Rent A Wreck* (phone: 252-4897) is among the least expensive.

TAXI Call *Yellow Cab* (phone: 252-5071) or *Triple A* (phone: 437-4000).

SPECIAL EVENTS

The *Fiesta Bowl* starts the *New Year* with a parade, a national high school band pageant, and two of the country's top collegiate football teams playing against each other in a bowl game. The *Phoenix Open Golf Tournament* takes place in mid-January; other golf tournaments are played throughout the year. In March, the *Veterans Memorial Coliseum* (1826 W. McDowell; phone 264-4508) is the site of the *Phoenix Jaycees Rodeo of Rodeos.* In May, one of the city's most vibrant celebrations is the *Cinco de Mayo,* an annual holiday celebrating the Mexican victory over French troops in 1862. In October, the *Arizona State Fair* fills up the *State Fairgrounds* (phone: 252-

6711) and the *Cowboy Artists of America* bring their works to town for the nationally recognized sale and exhibition at the *Phoenix Art Museum* (phone: 257-1222). November finds hundreds of colorful balloons dotting the turquoise skies in the annual *Thunderbird Balloon Race* at *Westworld* in Scottsdale (phone: 978-7208). December brings the *Annual Indian Market* at the *Pueblo Grande Museum* (phone: 495-0901) and the Valley lights up for the holiday season. It is a unique experience to see a saguaro cactus trimmed.

MUSEUMS

In addition to those described in *Special Places,* Phoenix has two other museums of note.

ARIZONA MINING AND MINERAL MUSEUM Polished gems and minerals glitter under spotlights in this warehouse-size museum. Closed Sundays. No admission charge. 1502 W. Washington (phone: 255-3791).

HALL OF FLAME MUSEUM No kidding. This collection of firefighting paraphernalia dates from 1725. Closed Sundays. Admission charge. 6101 E. Van Buren (phone: 275-3473).

ART GALLERIES

Although Phoenix does have some interesting galleries, most of the finest are in Scottsdale. A popular weekly event on Main Street is *Scottsdale Art Walks,* when galleries stay open late for browsers and buyers every Thursday from 7 to 9 PM. They exhibit a rich and vast array of art forms—paintings, sculpture, graphics—and many are devoted to contemporary western and American Indian art.

ELAINE HORWITCH GALLERIES The work of a wide variety of contemporary artists—both sculptors and painters—is on view here. 4211 N. Marshall Way, Scottsdale (phone: 945-0791).

LOVENA OHL GALLERY Indian arts and crafts, from primitive to contemporary, are on display here. 4251 N. Marshall Way, Scottsdale (phone: 945-8212).

MIND'S EYE GALLERY Ceramics, furniture, jewelry, and other crafts can be seen here. 4200 N. Marshall Way, Scottsdale (phone: 941-2494).

SUZANNE BROWN GALLERY The contemporary western art here ranges from abstract to representational. 7160 E. Main St., Scottsdale (phone: 945-8475).

THE LEGACY GALLERY Western art, Southwest landscapes, and bronze sculptures are featured at this gallery. 7178 E. Main St., Scottsdale (phone: 945-1113).

SHOPPING

Phoenix has its share of today's marketplaces, malls filled with department stores, chain shops, eateries, and entertainment. Enclaves of commerce with more individuality, however, also are easy to come by—and get to. Museum shops are an excellent source of quality gifts and mementos.

SPORTS AND FITNESS

The year-round sun makes Phoenix ideal for watching or participating in outdoor athletics.

BASEBALL The eight teams of the *Cactus League* play each other at least once during the pre-season. The Oakland *A's* train at *Phoenix Municipal Stadium* (5999 E. Van Buren, Phoenix; phone: 392-0074); the California *Angels* spend the season at *Tempe Diablo Stadium* (2200 W. Alameda, Tempe; phone: 678-2222); the Milwaukee *Brewers* play at *Compadre Stadium* (4001 S. Alma School, Chandler; phone: 895-6000); and the Chicago *Cubs* at *Mesa Hohokam Park* (1235 N. Center, Mesa; phone: 800-638-4253). Both the San Diego *Padres* (phone: 878-4337) and the Seattle *Mariners* (phone: 784-4444) train at *Peoria Sports Complex* (16101 N. 80 Third Ave., Peoria). The San Francisco *Giants* set up camp at the *Scottsdale Stadium* (7408 E. Osborn Rd., Scottsdale; phone: 990-7972). The *National League*'s Colorado *Rockies* make Tucson their pre-season base. And in 1998, the Arizona *Diamondbacks* will join major league baseball.

BASKETBALL The *NBA* Phoenix *Suns* play in the *America West Arena* (Second and Washington Sts.; phone: 258-6711). The *Arizona State University Sun Devils* play at the *University Athletic Center* in Tempe (phone: 965-2381).

BICYCLING Rent bikes from *Airplane and Bicycle Works* (4400 N. Scottsdale Rd., Scottsdale; phone: 949-1978).

DOG RACING Canines compete at *Greyhound Park* (40th and E. Washington Sts.; phone: 273-7181).

FISHING Trout, bass, and crappie can be caught at Apache Lake and in the Salt River.

FOOTBALL The *NFL* Arizona *Cardinals* (phone: 379-0102) and the *Arizona State Sun Devils* (phone: 965-2381) play at *Sun Devil Stadium* (*Arizona State University,* Tempe). *Arena Football League*'s Arizona *Rattlers* play in the *American West Arena* (Second and Washington Sts.; phone: 514-8383).

GOLF There are about 130 courses in the Phoenix area, many of them at resorts that welcome transient players.

TOP TEE-OFF SPOTS

Boulders Located in the Sonora Desert, this incredible golfing playground has revamped itself into two 18-hole courses, *Boulders' North* (6,731 yards, par 72) and *Boulders' South* (6,589 yards, par 71). Of the two, *Boulders' South* is the more scenic and challenging; the green of No. 5 is set in an amphitheater of boulders, while the tee at No. 6 is at the very foot of a high, boulder-strewn hill. Each course offers dramatic desert scenery. Members of the *Boulders Golf Club* and hotel guests switch courses every other day. In Carefree, about 30 miles north of Phoenix (phone: 488-9009; 800-553-1717).

Scottsdale Princess The *Tournament Players Club* at this resort has both a *Stadium* course (phone: 585-3939) and an adjacent *Desert* course (phone: 585-3800; also see *Checking In*). Both were designed by the team of Weiskopf, Morrish, and Twitty and are operated to the high standards of the *PGA Tour.* The 6,992-yard, par 71 *PGA Stadium* course is the site of the annual *Phoenix Open*, a *PGA Tour* event. The *Desert* course is a challenging 6,525-yard, par 71. There is also a full-service pro shop. 7575 E. Princess Dr. (phone: 585-4848; 800-344-4758).

Another alternative is at *Arizona State University* (1125 E. Rio Salado Pkwy., Tempe; phone: 921-8070) where the Pete Dye–designed 18-hole, par 72 *Karsten* course has the feel of both a links course and a stadium course. Visitors are also welcome at *Papago Park* municipal course (phone: 275-8428).

HORSEBACK RIDING Hourly rentals are available at *Ponderosa Stable* (10215 S. Central; phone: 268-1261), *South Mountain Stable* (10005 S. Central; phone: 276-8131), and *All Western Stables* (10220 S. Central; phone: 276-5862).

HORSE RACING The season runs from October through April at *Turf Paradise* (19th Ave. and Bell Rd.; phone: 942-1101).

JOGGING On scorchingly hot days, the air conditioned *Paradise Valley Mall* (at the intersection of Tatum and Cactus; phone: 996-8840) is an enclosed haven for walkers before it officially opens to shoppers. Run under the sun along the banks of the Arizona Canal (pick it up beside the *Biltmore* hotel) or the Grand Canal, reachable by jogging about a mile north along Central Avenue. *Encanto Park,* about three-quarters of a mile from downtown, also attracts runners.

SWIMMING Tubing down the Salt River is a popular pastime from April through October. *Salt Recreation, Inc.* provides tube rentals and shuttle-bus service in the *Tonto National Forest,* 15 miles north of Hwy. 60, on Power Rd. (phone: 984-3305). There are 23 municipal pools in Phoenix. Every large park has one. Try the pool at Coronado Park (N. 12th St., and Coronado Rd.; phone: 258-7946).

TENNIS In all, there are more than 1,000 courts in the Phoenix area, but two places score high with us.

CHOICE COURTS

Arizona Biltmore This ultra-posh, large-scale, superstar resort (also see *Checking In*) has eight Plexipave courts, plus video replay and ball machines; reservations possible; private lessons and clinics are also available. 24th St. and Missouri (phone: 955-6600; 800-950-0086).

John Gardiner's Some people call this place the most complete and professional training establishment in the world—for good reason. Facilities and services include 22 Plexipave outdoor courts and two Omni courts, video replay and ball machines (plus other instructional aids), tennis clinics, private lessons, and complimentary court time for guests. You can lodge in small casitas or in three- or four-bedroom casas, some with their own pool and court. Champagne is on the house when it rains. 5700 E. McDonald Dr., Scottsdale (phone: 948-2100; 800-245-2051; fax: 483-7314).

In addition, the *Phoenix Tennis Center* (6330 N. 21st Ave.; phone: 249-3712) has 22 lighted courts for night play.

THEATER

There's quite a lot of drama in Phoenix and Scottsdale. Many plays take place on campuses, and world-renowned performers have come to play Shakespeare. Check the local publications listed under *Local Coverage* for schedules. The major theaters include: *Phoenix Theater* (1625 N. Central Ave.; phone: 254-2151); *Herberger Theater Center* (222 E. Monroe St.; phone: 252-8497); *Gammage Auditorium* (a Frank Lloyd Wright building on the campus of *Arizona State University* in Tempe; phone: 965-3434); and *Scottsdale Center for the Arts* (Civic Center Plaza, on the corner of Second St. and Civic Center Blvd., Scottsdale; phone: 994-2787). *Arizona Ballet Theater* performs at *Scottsdale Center for the Arts.* Traveling dance troupes perform at *Gammage Auditorium* and the *Scottsdale Center for the Arts.*

MUSIC

The *Phoenix Symphony* (phone: 264-6363) and *Arizona Opera Company* (phone: 226-7464) play at *Symphony Hall* (225 E. Adams); the *Scottsdale Symphony* performs at *Scottsdale Center for the Arts* (see above). Nationally known rock performers and classical musicians appear at *Gammage Auditorium* (see above). Rock groups also give concerts at *Veterans Memorial Coliseum* (1826 W. McDowell; phone: 258-6711). Good music also is found on college and university campuses.

NIGHTCLUBS AND NIGHTLIFE

After work, professionals belly up to the oyster bar at *Steamers* (*Biltmore Fashion Park;* phone: 956-3631; see *Eating Out*). Another good meeting place is *Timothy's* (6335 N. 16th St.; phone: 277-7634), with live jazz nightly. *Arizona Live!* at the *Arizona Center* (455 N. Third; phone: 271-4636) is a collection of clubs that includes a sports bar, a country-music bar, and a comedy club. If you crave margaritas and music that will knock your socks off, try *Depot Cantina* (300 S. Ash, Tempe; phone: 966-6677).

Best in Town

CHECKING IN

If you're going to Phoenix on business, you'll probably want to stay downtown. If it's a vacation, you can't beat the resorts, which offer full recreational activities and Valley tours. Meals usually are included in the room rate at a resort, but be sure to check first. Most of Phoenix's major hotels have complete facilities for the business traveler. Those listed below as having "business services" usually offer such conveniences as meeting rooms, photocopiers, computers, translation services, and express checkout, among others. Call the individual hotel for additional information. Expect to pay between $120 and $300 per night for a double room at hotels and resorts listed under *Grand Hotels;* between $75 and $120 at hotels categorized as expensive; $30 to $75 at those listed as moderate; and around $30 at the inexpensive place. For bed and breakfast accommodations, contact *Bed & Breakfast in Arizona* (PO Box 8628, Scottsdale, AZ 85252; phone: 995-2831) or *Mi Casa, Su Casa* (PO Box 950, Tempe, AZ 85280; phone: 990-0682). Unless noted otherwise, hotel rooms have air conditioning, private baths, TV sets, and telephones.

All hotels below are in Phoenix and telephone and fax numbers are in the 602 area code unless otherwise indicated.

We begin with our favorite places, followed by recommended hotels, listed by price category.

GRAND HOTELS

Arizona Biltmore Resort & Villas Frank Lloyd Wright was the consulting architect for this grande dame of desert resorts, designed by Albert Chase McArthur, Wright's apprentice. The 600-room resort, which completed a renovation and expansion, sports some very Gatsbyesque features, including the gold leaf ceiling in both dining rooms and the Frank Lloyd Wright glass mural in the lobby. The food is good enough to bring diners from all over the Valley, and there is an endless assortment of facilities—tennis courts (see *Tennis,* above), two first-rate 18-hole golf courses, and five pools (one lined with Catalina tile, comparable to the one at William Randolph Hearst's *San Simeon*). Other amenities include a concierge desk and business services. 24th St. and Missouri (phone: 955-6600; 800-950-0086; fax: 381-7600).

Boulders Set on 1,300 acres of desert foothills, at the base of towering piles of boulders. The resort's 160 adobe-colored casitas blend remarkably well with the surrounding terrain. Walking from any guestroom to any of the five restaurants for a meal is to stroll through an entire spectrum of cactus varieties, to say nothing of sage and desert honeysuckle. The interior landscape is equally impressive: Each casita contains a room with a wet bar and a large oval tub; easy chairs face a juniper wood-burning fireplace in the conversation area. For recreation, there are six tennis courts, first-rate golf (see *Golf,* above), exercise facilities, horseback riding, desert treks, desert jeep tours, hot-air ballooning. Also available is an obliging concierge desk, conference center, and business services. Carefree, about 30 miles north of Phoenix (phone: 488-9009; 800-553-1717; fax: 488-4118).

Marriott's Camelback Inn This resort at the foot of Mummy Mountain, facing its namesake across the Valley, was built in 1936 of adobe mud dug up for the foundation; and in recent years, the total number of rooms on the 125 acres has expanded to 423. There are three outdoor heated swimming pools and whirlpools, eight tennis courts, two 18-hole *USGA* championship golf courses, Ping-Pong, basketball, shuffleboard—or spend the day at *The Spa*, a unique Southwest health spa that blends fitness, beauty, and wellness. 5402 E. Lincoln Dr., Scottsdale (phone: 948-1700; 800-24-CAMEL; fax: 596-7019).

Phoenician An exclusive and secluded retreat on 130 acres at the base of the dramatic Camelback Mountains, its isolation belies its proximity to Scottsdale and Phoenix. The main hotel is marvelously appointed, with geometric fountains, crystal chandeliers, and a ceiling aglitter with gold leaf. The view of the Valley is simply overwhelming. There are 442 rooms, plus 107 luxury casitas, 31 deluxe suites, and two presidential suites. Those with a physical bent can enjoy 11 lighted tennis courts, an 18-hole golf course with a driving range, putting green, seven pools, a whirlpool, two children's pools, and a 165-foot water slide. Other activities include croquet, badminton, volleyball, basketball, biking, lawn bowling, a children's program, and jogging. There's a fully equipped spa and fitness center offering guests weight training, saunas, Swiss showers, massage therapy, and beauty treatments (see *Sybaritic Spas* in DIVERSIONS). Four restaurants offer European and Southwestern cuisine. Other amenities include a concierge desk, 24-hour room service, and business services. 6000 E. Camelback Rd., Scottsdale (phone: 941-8200; 800-888-8234; fax: 947-4311).

Scottsdale Princess This eight-year-old, $90-million property has quickly become one of the premier resort destinations in the Southwest. There are 423 rooms and 21 suites in its main building, plus 125 casitas; all rooms have been designed around the earthy accents of the Southwest, and feature living and working areas, terraces, wet bars, refrigerators, and large bathrooms; casitas offer wood-burning fireplaces. Service is attentive, yet not overbearing, and the facilities are diverse. Activities include two 18-hole championship golf courses (see *Golf,* above), seven world class tennis courts including a 10,000-seat stadium, three heated pools, a spa and fitness center, a nearby polo field, and four restaurants. A recreational program offers volleyball, croquet, biking, hiking, fitness walks, and jogging; during the holidays, there are supervised programs for kids ages five through 12. Adjacent is *Westworld,* Scottsdale's 400-acre horse park. Among the other amenities are a concierge, 24-hour room service, and business services. 7575 E. Princess Dr., Scottsdale (phone: 585-4848; 800-223-1818; fax: 585-0086).

EXPENSIVE

Doubletree Paradise Valley Resort This full-service conference resort in botanical gardens setting has 387 rooms, including 27 suites, as well as two pools, a health club and spa, two restaurants, one bar, and business services. 5401 N. Scottsdale Rd., Scottsdale (phone: 947-5400; 800-222-TREE).

Embassy Suites The goal here is to provide a homey atmosphere, and since 95% of the guests return, it appears that the management is successful. Accommodations are in two-room suites with kitchens; breakfasts and late afternoon cocktails are complimentary. Note: Tipping is *not* permitted. Six locations: 5001 N. Scottsdale Rd., Scottsdale; 1515 N. 44th St., 2333 E. Thomas Rd., 2630 E. Camelback Rd., and 3210 NW Grand Ave., Phoenix; and 4400 S. Rural Rd., Tempe (phone: 800-362-2779).

Hermosa Resort Long one of the Valley's most exclusive guest ranches and tennis resorts, it says it is "not just a resort, it's an attitude." That sounds like hype until you see its 35 charming rooms (with gas-fired fireplaces, wet bars, and Jacuzzis) and its refurbished restaurant; the staff treats every guest like a VIP. 5532 N. Palo Cristi Rd., Paradise Valley (phone: 955-8614).

Hyatt Regency Scottsdale Built at Gainey Ranch, a planned community, this $75-million, 497-room luxury resort offers all the basic recreational facilities (pool with swim-up bar, eight tennis courts, 27 holes of championship golf, health club, and Jacuzzi), as well as a few extras (lawn tennis and croquet). Guests can sate hunger and thirst at the two restaurants, entertainment lounge, or lobby bar. Twenty-four-hour room service is available, as well as a concierge desk and business services. 7500 E. Doubletree Ranch, Scottsdale (phone: 991-3388; 800-223-1234; fax: 483-5550).

Marriott's Mountain Shadows With a 1,500-seat grand ballroom and 10 meeting rooms, it's no wonder this place is popular with convention groups and business travelers. After all those meetings, guests can relax by taking advantage of the three pools, two Jacuzzis, eight lighted tennis courts, and an award-winning 18-hole executive golf course. *Shells Oyster Bar & Seafood Restaurant* offers fresh seafood flown in daily. Other amenities include a concierge and business services. 5641 E. Lincoln Dr., Scottsdale (phone: 948-7111; 800-228-9290; fax: 951-5430).

Pointe Hilton at Tapatio Cliffs Patterned after the successful *Pointe Hilton at Squaw Peak* (above), this mountainside resort has attractive Spanish-Southwestern architecture and luxurious amenities. The dazzling *Etienne's Different Pointe of View* restaurant is a mountaintop facility that serves fine French fare. Room service is available until midnight; also a concierge and business services. 11111 N. Seventh St. (phone: 866-7500; 800-HILTONS; fax: 993-0276).

Radisson Resort A good choice for those who want to go first class, this busy 318-room place borders several golf courses and has three pools, a fitness center, and nightly entertainment. Other amenities include a concierge desk, 24-hour room service, and business services. 7171 N. Scottsdale Rd., Scottsdale (phone: 991-3800; 800-333-3333; fax: 948-9843).

Ritz-Carlton This 281-room hotel looks as if it was plucked right off the East Coast and plunked down in the desert. No cactus, no adobe-style architecture or kachina dolls here. Instead, it remains traditional, from the leaded glass chandeliers overhead to the plush Oriental rugs. And just like other members of its group, the emphasis here is on service for well-heeled corporate travelers and affluent vacationers. Pluses include a restaurant, 24-hour room service, a concierge, and business services. 2401 E. Camelback Rd. (phone: 468-0700; 800-241-3333; fax: 468-0793).

Sheraton Crescent A favorite of businesspeople, this hotel's elegant lobby, meeting rooms, and 342 guestrooms and suites have been given a new look with recent renovation. Also on the premises are a slide pool for children, a family center, and restaurant. 2620 W. Dunlap Ave. (phone: 943-8200; 800-423-4126).

Wyndham Metrocenter This ultramodern hostelry has more original artwork in its 284 luxury rooms and suites than many galleries. Mall shopping, theaters, and *Castle & Coasters,* a family fun park, are within walking distance. Its *Trump* dining room features Southwestern specialties in a pleasant atmosphere. Other amenities include a concierge and business services. 10220 N. Metro Pkwy. E. (phone: 997-5900).

MODERATE

Doubletree Suites Quiet, comfortable, and lushly landscaped, this hotel is only minutes from the airport at *Gateway Center.* Muted Southwestern tones decorate each of its 242 suites. Relax in *Topper's* restaurant, a cozy dining room just off the lobby. Complimentary airport shuttle and health club are included, and business services are available. 320 N. 44th St. (phone: 225-0500; 800-222-TREE).

Fiesta Inn This venerable favorite is a true Southwest delight, with Mexican tiles and room-size fireplaces. In addition to a restaurant, health club, and jogging trails, there's also a concierge desk, business services, and a complimentary airport shuttle. 2100 S. Priest Dr., Tempe (phone: 967-1441; 800-528-6481; fax: 967-0224).

INEXPENSIVE

Travel Inn 9 Smaller and quieter than others in town, this 68-unit motel (with pool) also is kinder to your budget. 201 N. Seventh Ave. (phone: 254-6521).

EATING OUT

Best bets in Phoenix are Mexican restaurants and steakhouses. Expect to pay $60 or more for a dinner for two at places listed as expensive; between $35 and $60 at those categorized as moderate; less than $35 at inexpensive places. Prices do not include drinks, wine, tax, or tips. All restaurants are in the 602 area code.

Unless otherwise noted, restaurants are open for lunch and dinner.

EXPENSIVE

Christopher's Chef and owner Christopher Gross has a well-deserved local reputation for his well-prepared French dishes, and glowing write-ups in several magazines, including *Gourmet,* have given him a high profile nationally as well. Grilled sea scallops with Provençal vegetables, veal chop with carrot and onion potato purée, and sautéed venison with huckleberries and red wine sauce are just some of the selections offered here. Reservations advised. Major credit cards accepted. 2398 E. Camelback Rd. (phone: 957-3214).

Mancuso's The decor at the Scottsdale location will transport you to an Italian Renaissance castle, and the continental dishes and service merit applause. Entrées include soup, salad, and more. Closed major holidays. Reservations advised. Major credit cards accepted. 6166 N. Scottsdale Rd., Scottsdale (phone: 948-9988).

Palm Court Tuxedoed waiters prepare much of the food at your table at this dining room in the *Scottsdale Conference Resort.* While gazing out on Camelback Mountain and Lake McCormick, you can select from the brief but tempting à la carte continental menu. Recommended are the Bibb lettuce salad, the lobster bisque, and the rack of lamb. Sunday brunch here is considered among the Valley's finest. Reservations advised. Major credit cards accepted. 7700 E. McCormick Pkwy., Scottsdale (phone: 596-7700).

Piñon Grill Who said hotel restaurants had to be boring or uncreative? If you hunger for authentic Southwestern fare, head to the grill at the *Regal McCormick Ranch.* Everything from steak, fish, and a few pasta dishes are well prepared. The lakeside setting and the copper and cactus decor only enhance the topnotch fare. No reservations. Major credit cards accepted. 7401 N. Scottsdale Rd., Scottsdale (phone: 948-5050).

RoxSand One of the most talked-about dining spots to open in the Valley in years, this stylish place features "global" dishes that vary widely in price, complexity, and origin. There are enticing entrées from Italy, Korea, Mongolia, Morocco, Sweden, and Russia. Closed on major holidays. Reservations advised. Major credit cards accepted. 2594 E. Camelback Rd. (phone: 381-0444).

Tomaso's This dining spot and its siblings are known for their northern Italian specialties. Closed *Thanksgiving* and *Christmas.* Reservations advised. Major credit cards accepted. 3225 E. Camelback Rd. (phone: 956-0836).

MODERATE

Christopher's Bistro Christopher Gross, chef and owner of *Christopher's* (see above), has extended his talents to the adjacent café. Dishes such as grilled mahimahi with honey, cardamom, and couscous; osso buco with white beans and a roasted tomato; and grilled rib eye steaks with peppercorns and roquefort cheese, as well as dessert soufflés made to order, crown the menu. Reservations advised. Major credit cards accepted. 2398 E. Camelback Rd. (phone: 957-3214).

Don & Charlie's If your appetite is bigger than your budget, try this place. The menu's American dishes may seem standard, but just wait till they arrive at your table. Steaks are huge and perfectly cooked, and the meaty pork ribs are good, too. It boasts one of the best happy hour spreads in town. Closed *Thanksgiving.* Reservations advised. Major credit cards accepted. 7501 E. Camelback Rd., Scottsdale (phone: 990-0900).

Durant's A fashionable place for everyone from politicians to local celebrities for 30 years. Enjoy the traditional appetizers before dinner, then choose steaks or prime ribs. Closed major holidays. Reservations advised. Major credit cards accepted. 2611 N. Central Ave. (phone: 264-5967).

Golden Palace Cuisine of India One of the city's best Indian restaurants, it serves tandoori chicken and fiery specialties such as lamb *vindaloo*. The pace is leisurely, the atmosphere friendly. Reservations unnecessary. Major credit cards accepted. 4320 W. Thomas Rd. (phone: 352-1100).

The Grill In the *Tournament Players Clubhouse* at the *Scottsdale Princess,* score a hole-in-one, with a relaxing view of the course and an all-day menu offering appetizers, soups, salads, sandwiches, and grilled steaks and seafood. Try the baked six-onion soup with glazed Swiss cheese or the fall-off-the-bone baby back ribs. Reservations advised. Major credit cards accepted. 7575 E. Princess Dr. (phone: 585-4848).

Monti's La Casa Vieja A Valley landmark, this spot serves some of the best steaks anywhere. It's always crowded, but the service is good and the side dishes are plentiful. Reservations advised for lunch only. Major credit cards accepted. 3 W. First, Tempe (phone: 967-7594).

Pinnacle Peak Patio No trip to Arizona would be complete without a visit to a real Western cowboy steakhouse. This one's the oldest and most famous, with two-pound porterhouses broiled over mesquite coals and served with sourdough bread and pinto beans. Don't wear a tie! Closed *Thanksgiving, Christmas Eve,* and *Christmas.* Reservations necessary for large groups only. Major credit cards accepted. 10426 E. Jomax Rd., Scottsdale (phone: 967-8082).

Steamers It may seem impossible to find excellent seafood in the Southwest, but here it is. Try the Maine lobster, the Baltimore crab cakes, or the Boston clam chowder. Reservations advised. Major credit cards accepted. 2576 E. Camelback Rd. (phone: 956-3631).

Yamakasa Japanese fare, including a wonderful sushi bar and teriyaki beef and chicken, is presented with great care and style. One section of the restaurant has low tables and legless chairs for diners who want to eat in traditional style. Reservations advised. Major credit cards accepted. 9301 Shea Blvd., Scottsdale (phone: 860-5605).

INEXPENSIVE

Bill Johnson's Big Apple An Arizona landmark since 1956, this ranch-style restaurant serves a country breakfast, plus lunch and dinner. Major credit cards accepted. 3757 E. Van Buren St. (phone: 275-2107). Other locations: 3101 W. Indian School Rd. (phone: 277-6291), 16810 N. 19th Ave. (phone: 863-7921); 950 E. Main St., Mesa (phone: 969-6504), and 3110 E. Arizona Ave., Chandler (phone: 892-2542).

Coffee Plantation This outdoor café in one of the most eclectic neighborhoods in the area is great for people watching. As you sit sipping your cappuccino or hot chocolate, you can see a fantastic assortment of citizenry strolling by. Soups and salads are also available. Closed *Christmas.* No reservations. Major credit cards accepted. 680 S. Mill Ave., Tempe (phone: 829-7878). Other locations: 2468 E. Camelback Rd. (phone: 553-0203); 9636 Metro Parkway East (phone: 997-1527); 6166 N. Scottsdale Rd. (phone: 922-4862).

Ed Debevic's Short Orders Deluxe Step back in time to a 1950s diner, complete with a blue-plate special and wisecracking, gum-snapping, dancing waitresses. Order the meat loaf sandwich with a real cherry Coke. It's as much fun as you remember. Closed *Thanksgiving* and *Christmas.* Reservations unnecessary. Major credit cards accepted. 2102 East Highland St. (phone: 956-2760).

First Watch This is the place for breakfast-hearty omelettes, sizzling skillets, blueberry-wheat germ pancakes and plenty of coffee. Open daily from 6:30 AM to 2:30 PM. Major credit cards accepted. 61 W. Thomas Rd. (phone: 265-

2092). Other locations at 9645 N. Black Canyon Hwy. (phone: 943-3232) and 4422 N. 75th St., Scottsdale (phone: 941-8464).

Honey Bear's BBQ Tender chicken and pork are doused in a sweet spicy sauce. The eatery's motto, "You don't need teeth to eat our meat," is close to the mark. Reservations unnecessary. Major credit cards accepted. 5012 E. Van Buren St. (phone: 273-9148).

Hops Bistro Brewery Pub-style grub—burgers and sandwiches—plus a variety of brews make this a very popular eating den. The owners also offer seasonal beers during the year, including an amber ale and a pilsner along with summer wheat and dark wheat varieties. Closed *Thanksgiving* and *Christmas.* No reservations. Major credit cards accepted. 7000 E. Camelback Rd., Scottsdale (phone: 945-4677); 2584 E. Camelback Rd. (phone: 468-0500); 8668 E. Shea Blvd., Scottsdale (phone: 998-7777).

Los Dos Molinos The New Mexican fare here is expertly prepared and presented. Owners Vickie and Eddie Chavez roast their own green-and-red chilies, which they then add to pizza, beef dishes, and the obligatory (but excellent) salsa. Marinated pork ribs are also first-rate. You can cool your palate with an iced raspberry tea, and *sopapillas* (fried dough) served with honey makes a fine dessert. Closed Mondays. Reservations advised. Major credit cards accepted. 8646 S. Central Ave. (phone: 243-9113).

Los Olivos A family operation for more than three decades, this is the Valley's oldest Mexican eatery. Thoroughly modern decor belies its age, but the food explains its longevity. Try such house specialties as sour cream enchiladas and *carne asada.* Closed major holidays. Reservations accepted. Major credit cards accepted. 7328 E. Second St., Scottsdale (phone: 946-2256).

Pink Pepper A few years ago, the Valley had only one Thai restaurant; now there are about two dozen. This ultramodern spot is the prettiest of the lot, and since it uses moderation when sprinkling on the spices, it's a good place for the uninitiated to try this often fiery food. The soup with lemongrass and coconut milk is tops, as are the meat dishes with Phonaeng curry. Reservations advised. Major credit cards accepted. 2003 N. Scottsdale Rd., Scottsdale (phone: 945-9300). Two other locations: 245 E. Bell Rd. (phone: 548-1333); and 1941 W. Guadalupe, Mesa (phone: 839-9009).

Pittsburgh

For more than a century, Pittsburgh was among the largest steel-producing cities in the country, a one-industry town that eventually succumbed to a changing world economy and fell on hard times. It has since emerged as one of the Mid-Atlantic's most vibrant cities.

Thanks to a progressive urban development program, Pittsburgh is now a high-tech center and a predominant force in the fields of education and health care. A commercial hub for western Pennsylvania and the Ohio River Valley, the city has a large number of Fortune 500 companies' headquarters, seven of them in the downtown area—known as the Golden Triangle. In recent years, more than 220 foreign companies have settled here, making Pittsburgh an international center for the chemical, plastic, and nuclear industries, as well as general scientific research.

Today, the metropolitan area has a population of 1.3 million, spread out around the confluence of the Allegheny, Monongahela, and Ohio Rivers. During the French and Indian War, both the French and English coveted the area for trade and settlement. First surveyed by George Washington, then captured by the French, it finally was reclaimed in 1758 by the British, who built *Fort Pitt* here; both the fort and the city were named after Britain's Prime Minister William Pitt.

Even as *Fort Pitt*'s military importance declined, Pittsburgh developed as a commercial town and river port. As the center for transporting westward-bound pioneers and supplies, the "Gateway to the West" did a thriving business, selling flatboats loaded with glass, home furnishings, hardware, and farm products. A nearby supply of coal helped the city become an industrial center; by the mid-19th century, the city's factories were producing half of the world's glass and iron. During the Civil War, it became the "arsenal of the North" (though a real growth explosion came when World Wars I and II provided a market for its products). It also was a magnet for entrepreneurs like Andrew Mellon, Andrew Carnegie, and Henry Clay Frick. The rise of industry attracted many immigrants. Besides future tycoons like Frick and Carnegie, stonemasons and other Old World artisans also came, creating much of the ornate stone and metal work found in Pittsburgh's older buildings and 1,700 bridges.

Pittsburgh's giants of industry and the wealth they created left behind a rich legacy. Mellon and Carnegie endowed several art institutions; Frick gave the city a museum; and the Heinz family (of the famous "57 varieties") contributed a performing arts center. Today, metropolitan Pittsburgh has seven colleges, three universities, more than 850 high-tech companies, and a renowned symphony. Since the late 1940s, the downtown area has been the focus of an ongoing face-lift. Shopping and office complexes, such as *One Oxford Centre,* have been built; others have been created in classic

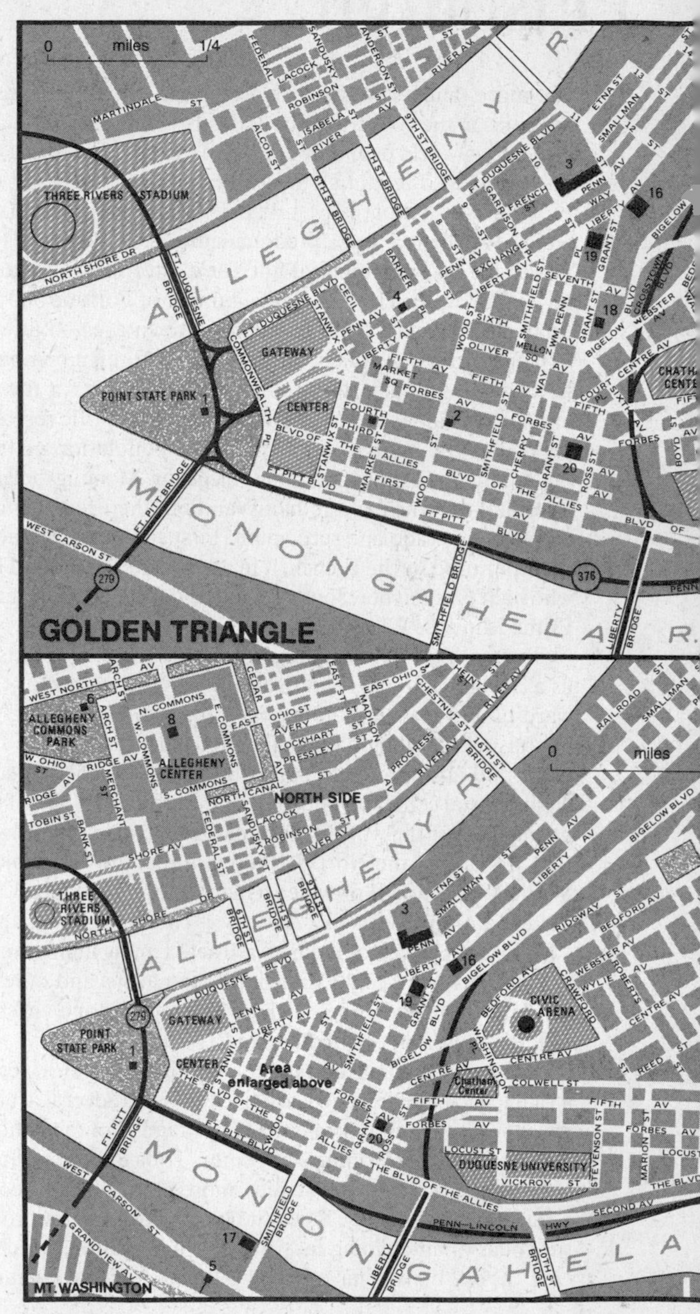

GOLDEN TRIANGLE
0 miles 1/4
THREE RIVERS STADIUM
POINT STATE PARK
GATEWAY
CENTER
ALLEGHENY R.
MONONGAHELA R.
NORTH SHORE DR
FT. DUQUESNE BRIDGE
FT. PITT BRIDGE
WEST CARSON ST
SMITHFIELD BRIDGE
LIBERTY BRIDGE
6TH ST BRIDGE
7TH ST BRIDGE
9TH ST BRIDGE
FT. DUQUESNE BLVD
PENN AV
LIBERTY AV
BLVD OF THE ALLIES
FT PITT BLVD
MARKET SQ
MELLON SQ
CHATHAM CENTER
ALLEGHENY COMMONS PARK
ALLEGHENY CENTER
NORTH SIDE
Area enlarged above
CIVIC ARENA
Chatham Center
DUQUESNE UNIVERSITY
MT. WASHINGTON
GRANDVIEW AV
16TH ST BRIDGE
10TH ST BRIDGE
PENN-LINCOLN HWY

CENTRAL PITTSBURGH

LANDMARKS

1. Fort Pitt Museum
2. Bank Center
3. David L. Lawrence Convention Center
4. Heinz Hall
5. Monongahela Incline
6. West Park Conservatory—Aviary
7. PPG Place
8. Buhl Planetarium
9. Cathedral of Learning
10. Carnegie Museum and Library
11. Mellon Institute
12. Phipps Conservatory
13. Historical Society of Western Pennsylvania
14. Frick Fine Arts Building
15. Pittsburgh Playhouse Theater Center
16. Penn. Central Station
17. Station Square
18. U.S. Steel Building
19. Liberty Center
20. Oxford Center

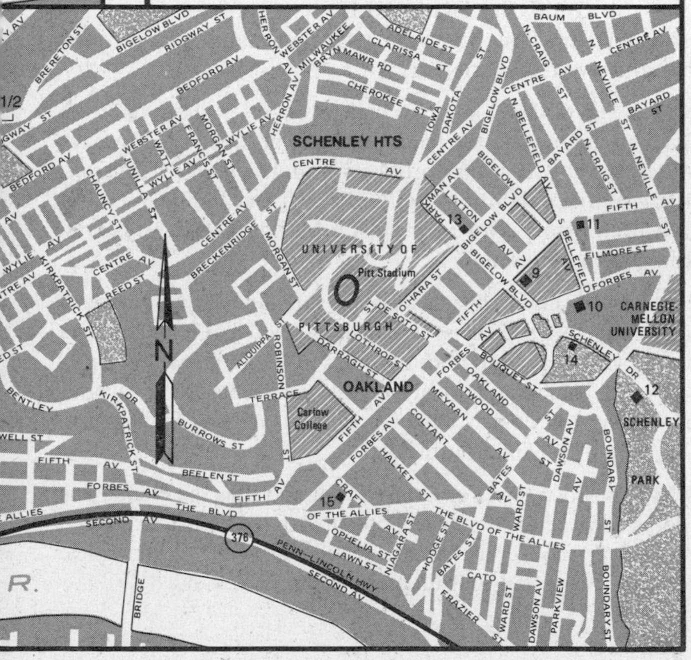

buildings. And the highly rated *Pittsburgh International Airport,* which opened in 1992 at a cost of $800 million (it boasts a shopping mall, an automated tram system, and people movers), is furthering the city's progressive image.

But for all its sophistication, Pittsburgh is an amazingly friendly place. It is not uncommon for strangers to wish each other a good day on their way to work or for visitors asking directions to be escorted personally to their destination—or given an ad lib tour. Pittsburghers are justifiably proud of their city, and it shows.

Pittsburgh At-a-Glance

SEEING THE CITY

Go to the top of Mt. Washington via either of two inclines for a sweeping 17-mile view of the three area rivers. The Duquesne incline (W. Carson St.; phone: 381-1665) and the Monongahela incline (E. Carson St., behind the *Freight House Shops* of *Station Square;* phone: 231-5707), in operation since 1870, cost $1 each way (exact change required).

SPECIAL PLACES

Most of Pittsburgh's places of interest are in four main sections of the city: the Golden Triangle downtown area, the North Side, the East End, and the South Side.

GOLDEN TRIANGLE

Though most major attractions are within walking distance, use the subway for quick crosstown transportation.

POINT STATE PARK At the tip of the Golden Triangle, it covers 36 acres of broad walks and spacious gardens on the banks of the river junction. The park contains *Fort Pitt Blockhouse,* a 1764 fortification; and the *Fort Pitt Museum* (phone: 281-9284), with exhibitions on the French and Indian War and early Pennsylvania history. Museum closed Mondays and Tuesdays. Admission charge to the museum.

PPG PLACE The "crown jewel" in the skyline is a plaza surrounded by six modern Gothic buildings with mirrored glass façades, designed by Philip Johnson and John Burgee. On the ground floor of PPG 1 is the *Wintergarden,* open for civic functions. Several international food establishments and retail boutiques are in buildings 2 through 6. Summer concerts are given in the plaza. Stanwix St. between Third and Fourth Aves.

ONE OXFORD CENTRE This office tower at Grant Street and Fourth Avenue has three lower floors dedicated to designer shops, including *K Barchetti*, *Rodier,* and *Four Winds Gallery*. Several restaurants and nightclubs featuring live jazz are here when you've had your fill of shopping.

DAVID L. LAWRENCE CONVENTION CENTER The city's exposition hall has 131,000 square feet of space and hosts a variety of trade shows. Penn Ave. (phone: 565-6000 for a schedule of events).

BENEDUM CENTER FOR THE PERFORMING ARTS An elegant movie palace in the 1920s, this theater has been restored to a glittering showplace. The backstage is bigger than New York's *Metropolitan Opera,* and is home to the *Pittsburgh Opera* and the *Pittsburgh Ballet,* as well as the *Civic Light Opera.* Penn and Seventh Aves. (phone: 456-6660 for *Benedum;* 281-3973 for *Civic Light Opera*).

HEINZ HALL A very classy movie theater in 1926, the hall is now a stately, acoustically balanced auditorium, home of the *Pittsburgh Symphony* (which enjoys international favor under the baton of Lorin Maazel), and host to performing arts troupes. Worth a look for its ornate decorations and gold leaf. Guided tours by appointment. Admission charge. 600 Penn Ave. (phone: 392-4900 for tickets).

STRIP DISTRICT This noisy, hectic hub where the region's food wholesalers sell their produce can be somewhat overwhelming, especially compared with a supermarket. In addition to the markets, everything from hole-in-the-wall cafés to an Italian espresso bar lines the streets. Stop in at the *Society for Contemporary Crafts,* which displays and sells finely made local and international crafts. Admission charge. 21 Smallman St. (phone: 261-7003). Also nearby is the *Senator John Heinz Pittsburgh Regional History Center,* which houses the *Historical Society of Western Pennsylvania*'s collection of antique glass bottles, hand-carved furniture, and other memorabilia, as well as old documents on Pennsylvania history. The center also houses a theater and a library. Closed Sundays and Mondays. No admission charge. 4338 Bigelow Blvd. (phone: 454-6000).

SOUTH SIDE

STATION SQUARE A beautifully restored 19th-century railroad station, it includes an outdoor museum with antique rail cars and Bessemer converter, an elegant restaurant and saloon, and a shopping mall in the adjacent freight house. The *Gateway Clipper* dock (see "Tours" under *Tourist Information*) also is here.

CARSON STREET DISTRICT Here is a browser's Elysian Fields, home to many antiques shops, art galleries, bookstores, an old-fashioned hardware store, a restored neighborhood movie theater, and numerous good restaurants and nightclubs, where jazz and blues reign supreme. There's plenty of on-street parking. Cross Smithfield Bridge, south of *Station Square.*

NORTH SIDE

To get to the North Side from the Golden Triangle, cross the Sixth Street Bridge, then proceed north to the *Allegheny Center Mall.* Crosstown buses leave from Penn Avenue and Stanwix Street.

ALLEGHENY OBSERVATORY Equipped with a 30-inch-diameter refractory lens—a very powerful telescope—this observatory is acclaimed as one of the world's best. Amateur astronomers can scan the heavens or attend the illustrated lectures. Open April through October by appointment only. No admission charge. Riverview Park off Perrysville Ave. (phone: 321-2400).

LANDMARK SQUARE Almost hidden behind the bunker-like *Allegheny Center Mall* is the restored *Old Post Office,* home to the innovative *Pittsburgh Children's Museum* (phone: 322-5059) and the regional branch of the *Carnegie Library.* In the museum, tots and preteens can play with video equipment, operate puppets they know from TV, and participate in a kids' clinic where they are the doctor to an injured dummy. Open daily; seasonal hours. Admission charge. Just steps away is the first *Carnegie Public Library,* opened in 1890. The building also houses the *Pittsburgh Public Theater.*

CARNEGIE SCIENCE CENTER This riverside museum complex is one of the country's most advanced. Its facilities, designed for both children and adults, include an Omnimax theater with a three-story-high movie screen, a computerized planetarium, a one-of-a-kind science workshop featuring a combination theater and hands-on laboratory, projects for children as young as two, and a vintage submarine from World War II. Closed *Thanksgiving, Christmas,* and *New Year's Day.* Admission charge. Near *Three Rivers Stadium* (phone: 237-3400).

THE NATIONAL AVIARY At the former *Pittsburgh Aviary,* which was designated the *National Aviary* by Congress in 1993, 200 species of birds chatter away in walk-through and enclosed exhibits. A series of educational programs is offered as well. This is a good place to escape from urban America for a while. Open daily. Admission charge. In *West Park* near Arch St., *Allegheny Commons* (phone: 323-7235).

ANDY WARHOL MUSEUM This museum pays tribute to Pittsburgh's favorite son. Mounted in a renovated early 20th-century warehouse, it encompasses seven floors and features the artist's celebrity portrait gallery, an auditorium in which Warhol's films are shown, and a "time capsule" of his personal artifacts. Admission charge. 117 Sandusky St. (phone: 237-8300).

EAST END

CATHEDRAL OF LEARNING Part of the *University of Pittsburgh,* this imposing 42-story Gothic tower is the only skyscraper of classrooms in the country. Of particular interest are the 19 Nationality Rooms on the first floor, devoted to each of the city's major ethnic groups. Open daily. No admission charge. Bigelow Blvd. and Fifth Ave. (phone: 624-6000).

THE CARNEGIE A complex comprising the main branch of the *Carnegie Libraries,* a music hall, a museum with a magnificent collection of French Impressionist art, and the *Carnegie Museum of Natural History,* featuring 10,000 objects from all fields of natural history and anthropology. Closed Sunday mornings and Mondays. Admission charge. 4400 Forbes Ave. (phone: 622-3131).

PHIPPS CONSERVATORY Rare tropical and domestic blossoms flourish in the greenhouses and gardens of this 2½-acre publicly owned conservatory. Annual flower shows take place in spring, fall, and during *Christmas.* The 13 greenhouses are only a fraction of the greenery of surrounding *Schenley Park,* which covers 422 acres and has tennis courts, baseball fields, a golf course, an ice skating rink, picnic areas, and nature trails. Open daily. Admission charge. *Schenley Park* (phone: 422-PHIPPS; *Schenley Park Ice Rink* (phone: 422-6547).

PITTSBURGH ZOO Seventy acres feature open habitats for the more than 2,000 animals. A recent addition is the *Primate House,* with species from South America, Africa, and Asia. There's also an *Aquazoo,* which has tanks full of domestic trout and pike, and esoteric species like penguins and piranhas. Open daily. Admission charge. *Highland Park* (phone: 665-3640).

FRICK ART MUSEUM A magnificent Renaissance-style building houses Old Masters from the Renaissance through the 18th century. Marie Antoinette's furniture is on display in an ornate living room. The eclectic collection comprises Russian silver, Flemish tapestries, and Chinese porcelains. Closed Mondays and Tuesdays. No admission charge, 7227 Reynolds St. and S. Homewood Ave., Point Breeze (phone: 371-0600).

CLAYTON Near the *Frick Art Museum* stands the restored home of its namesake, steel tycoon Henry Clay Frick. Tours are given by reservation only. Closed Mondays. Admission charge. 72 Penn Ave. (phone: 371-0606).

EXTRA SPECIAL

For a change of scene, try the Laurel Highlands, just a 90-minute drive from the city. Take the Pennsylvania Turnpike to the Donhal exit. Follow Route 711 to Ligonier; here is the *Compass Inn* (phone: 238-4983), an old coaching inn used by travelers in the 18th century. Lively tours are given on Sundays from late May through late October, with special candlelight tours in November and December. Admission charge. Also nearby is *Fort Ligonier* (phone: 238-9701), a restored fort from the French and Indian War. Closed November through April. Admission charge. The *Mountain Playhouse* (phone: 814-629-9201 for reservations and information), one of the oldest summer theaters in the country, is a half-mile north of Jennerstown on Route 985 off Route 30. Hungry theatergoers can dine next door at the excellent *Green Gables* restaurant.

Sources and Resources

TOURIST INFORMATION

For information on places of interest and events, contact the visitor information center, open daily in *Gateway Center,* the Golden Triangle. The information center is run by the *Greater Pittsburgh Convention and Visitors Bureau* (4 *Gateway Center,* Pittsburgh, PA 15222; phone: 281-7711; 800-359-0758), which offers a variety of city guides and is closed weekends. Contact the Pennsylvania state tourism hotline (phone: 800-VISIT-PA) for maps, calendars of events, health updates, and travel advisories.

LOCAL COVERAGE *Post-Gazette* and Pittsburgh *Triburne-Review,* morning dailies; *Business Times,* weekly; *Pittsburgh* magazine, monthly.

TELEVISION STATIONS KDKA Channel 2–CBS; WTAE Channel 4–ABC; WPXI Channel 11–NBC; WQED Channel 13–PBS; and WPGH Channel 53–Fox.

RADIO STATIONS AM: KDKA 1020 (contemporary/oldies); WTAE 1250 (talk); and KQV 1410 (news/talk). FM: WQED 89.3 (classical); WDUQ 90.5 (jazz); WLTJ 92.9 (soft rock); and WWSW 94.5 (oldies).

TELEPHONE The area code for Pittsburgh is 412.

SALES TAX There is a 7% sales tax on everything except clothing, shoes, and groceries; the hotel room tax is 5%.

CLIMATE Pittsburgh has a moderate climate with frequent precipitation. Summer temperatures climb into the 80s F; winters drop into the 20s F. About 200 days of the year are cloudy, and winters are wet.

GETTING AROUND

AIRPORT The *Pittsburgh International Airport* (phone: 472-3500) is about 20 minutes from downtown, but in heavy traffic, the ride will take longer. *Airline Transportation Service* (phone: 471-8900) offers frequent connections between the airport and major hotels.

BUS *Port Authority Transit (PAT)* provides efficient bus service (phone: 231-5707 for information). The fare starts at $1.25.

CAR RENTAL All major national firms are represented.

LRT (LIGHT RAPID TRANSIT) SUBWAY *PAT* underground service (phone: 442-2000 for information) operates from downtown to South Hills, through *Station Square,* across the Monongahela River. Ultramodern trains run frequently during the day and every 15 to 30 minutes at night. They are free in the downtown Golden Triangle until 7 PM; all other route fares range from $1.25 to $2, depending on time of day.

TAXIS Call *People's Cab* (phone: 681-3131) or *Yellow Cab of Pittsburgh* (phone: 665-8123).

VAN SERVICE Contact *People's Cab* (phone: 681-3131).

SIGHTSEEING TOURS

BOAT Cruises on ships of the *Gateway Clipper* fleet (phone: 355-7980) leave from the dock at *Station Square.* The captain aboard the two-hour sightseeing cruise will highlight points of interest. The *Good Ship Lollipop* has clowns to amuse children while parents enjoy the sights on its one-hour cruise. Reservations are required for the daily dinner cruise. Specialty cruises include a tour of the river lock system. Some cruises are seasonal.

SPECIAL EVENTS

The *Pittsburgh Marathon,* which draws an international field of runners, is held in early May, as is the *Children's Festival,* a five-day event featuring international performers. The *Three Rivers Arts Festival,* displaying the work of over 600 artists, spans 17 days in June. Performing arts and a film festival are a small part of the Carnegie-sponsored festivities. Allegheny County presents a summer-long schedule of free dance and music events at *Hartwood Acres,* a former country estate. The *Shadyside Arts Festival* takes place in the nearby town of Shadyside in early August. The festive *Three Rivers Regatta,* the first weekend in August, features the *Grand Prix of Formula I Boat Racing, Steamboat Races for the Mayors Cup,* the *Race of the River Belles,* and the not-to-be-missed *Anything That Floats* race. A hot-air balloon race, live music, and water-ski shows enliven the event. The *Great Race,* a 10-kilometer footrace with over 10,000 participants, is held in September; in October, school teams compete in the *Head of the Ohio* crew races and there is *ZooBoo* at the *Pittsburgh Zoo.* In late November, *Light Up Weekend* illuminates the city.

MUSEUMS

In addition to those described in *Special Places,* there are two other museums of note.

OLD ECONOMY MUSEUM AND VILLAGE Several restored buildings recall a 19th-century experiment in communal living. Closed Mondays. Admission charge. 14th and Church Sts., Ambridge (phone: 266-1803).

PITTSBURGH CENTER FOR THE ARTS On display are contemporary paintings, sculpture, photography, and crafts, mostly by local artists. Closed Mondays. Donation suggested. Fifth and Shady Aves. (phone: 361-0873).

SHOPPING

Pittsburgh has its share of today's marketplaces, malls filled with department stores, chain shops, eateries, and entertainment. Enclaves of commerce with more individuality, however, also are easy to come by—and get to. Museum shops are an excellent source of quality gifts and mementos.

SPORTS AND FITNESS

BASEBALL The major league *Pirates* play at *Three Rivers Stadium* (Stadium Circle, North Side; phone: 323-5028).

BICYCLING There are no bike rental shops in town, but the county parks (like *North* and *South Parks*) have rental facilities.

CANOEING/KAYAKING You can canoe and kayak through exciting whitewater rapids in the Laurel Highlands (phone: 800-388-7238). *Three Rivers Rowing Association* (300 Waterfront Dr.; phone: 321-8772) offers lessons. *American Youth Hostels* (5604 Solway St., Squirrel Hill; phone: 422-2282) is another source for lessons and information.

FITNESS CENTER The *YMCA* (330 Blvd. of the Allies; phone: 227-3800) has a pool, racquetball courts, a track, and exercise classes. Facilities are open to non-members for a fee.

FOOTBALL The pro *Steelers'* home grid is at *Three Rivers Stadium* (Stadium Circle, North Side; phone: 323-1200).

GOLF *Schenley Park,* a municipal course in Oakland (phone: 622-6959), has 18 holes, but the *North Park* course (off Rte. 19; phone: 935-1967) and the 27-hole *South Park* course (off Rte. 88; phone: 835-3545) are more challenging. For championship caliber, try the *Quicksilver* course (about 20 miles west of Pittsburgh on Route 980; phone: 796-1594). There are approximately 75 other public courses to choose from within a 90-minute drive of downtown; contact the *Greater Pittsburgh Convention and Visitors Bureau* (phone: 281-7711) for specific information.

HIKING There are quite a few hiking programs. The *Frick Environmental Center* (2005 Beechwood Blvd.; phone: 422-6538) has hiking trails and offers nature programs. For information on hiking, backpacking, canoeing, and camping in the area, contact the *Sierra Club* (phone: 561-0203).

HOCKEY The *NHL* 1991 and 1992 *Stanley Cup* champion *Penguins* play at *Civic Arena* (Washington Pl., Center and Bedford Aves.; phone: 642-1985).

HORSE RACING Fans have a choice of the *Meadows* (in Washington County; phone: 563-1224) or *Mountaineer Race Track and Resort* (Chester, WV; phone: 304-387-2400 or 304-281-2926).

HORSEBACK RIDING *Rolling Hills Ranch* (S. Fayette; phone: 221-9926) offers riding daily from April through October. There are hundreds of miles of riding trails at *Tanglewood Stables* (N. Huntington; phone: 823-5381).

ICE SKATING There are three outdoor rinks in the area: at *North Park* (phone: 935-1780); at *South Park* (phone: 833-1499), about 10 miles outside Pittsburgh; and at *Schenley Park* (phone: 422-6547).

JOGGING *Point State Park,* where the Allegheny and Monongahela meet; *Schenley Park,* east of downtown in Oakland; and *North Park,* 10 miles north of the city, all offer good jogging.

TENNIS The best municipal courts are at *Mellon Park,* east of downtown, and there are excellent suburban courts at *North* and *South Parks,* both about 10 miles outside the city.

THEATER

The city has plenty of professional theater performances all year. The *Public Theater* presents traditional plays in its handsome *Hazlett Theater* (1 Allegheny Sq.; phone: 323-8200), and the *City Theater* offers more avant-garde productions at the corner of 13th and Bingham Streets on the South Side (phone: 431-2489). Smaller companies include the *Upstairs Theater* (phone: 361-5443); listings of scheduled productions can be found in the city's daily newspaper (see *Local Coverage*). The *Benedum Center for the Performing Arts* (207 Seventh St.; phone: 456-6666) and *Heinz Hall* (600 Penn Ave.; phone: 392-4843) present touring musicals and plays. There are also several top-flight professional dance companies; standouts are the internationally renowned *Pittsburgh Ballet Theatre* (2900 Liberty Ave.; phone: 281-0360), *Dance Alloy* (phone: 621-6670) for modern dance, and the *Pittsburgh Dance Council* (phone: 355-0330), which brings in touring companies.

High-quality collegiate productions are presented by the *Carnegie Mellon Theater Company* at *Kresge Theater* (*Carnegie-Mellon University, Schenley Park;* phone: 268-2407), and *Point Park College*'s *Pittsburgh Playhouse* (phone: 621-4445), which stages modern plays and musicals for both adults and children. In the summer, the *Civic Light Opera* re-creates the great Broadway musicals of the past at the *Benedum Center for the Performing Arts* (see above). Also in summer, Allegheny County offers its *Theater at Hartwood* (phone: 767-4738), dramas performed under a tent.

MUSIC

The world-famous *Pittsburgh Symphony Orchestra* performs from September through May at *Heinz Hall* (600 Penn Ave.; phone: 392-4900). In the *Benedum Center for the Performing Arts,* the *Pittsburgh Opera,* in its 52nd year, performs the classics and the not-so-classic in lavish productions. Also try the *River City Brass Band* (phone: 322-7222), based at the *Carnegie Music Hall,* which performs in several locations throughout the city and surrounding area. For fans of pop and rock, the city is a regular stop on the road-show circuit. The *Civic Arena* (phone: 642-2062) and *Palumbo Center* at *Duquesne University* (phone: 391-1111) are venues for popular performing artists. The *Star Lake Amphitheater* (phone: 947-7827) is an outdoor performance area about 45 minutes from downtown where rock groups appear regularly during the summer.

NIGHTCLUBS AND NIGHTLIFE

Long a jazz haven, the city continues that tradition at numerous clubs such as *The Balcony* (phone: 687-0110), and *James Street Tavern* (phone: 323-2222), as well as several spots along Carson Street on the South Side. The top dance places in town are in the vibrant Strip District. Try *Metropol* (phone: 261-4512) for hard rock and *Donzi's* (phone: 281-1585) for riverside dancing. The center for contemporary folk and rock music is *Grafitti* (phone: 682-4210), while the *Decade* (phone: 682-1211) is a local band hangout. *Rosebud* (phone: 261-2221), next door to *Metropol* in the Strip District, presents a European-style coffeehouse atmosphere. And for a quieter evening, the lobby of the *Westin William Penn* hotel (see *Checking In*) offers piano music in an elegant setting.

Best in Town

CHECKING IN

With the city's second renaissance has come an influx of much-needed hotel space, mostly in the nearby suburbs of Green Tree, Coraopolis, and Monroeville. All hotels listed below are downtown. Most of Pittsburgh's major hotels have complete facilities for the business traveler. Those listed below as having "business services" usually offer such conveniences as meeting rooms, photocopiers, computers, translation services, and express checkout, among others. Call the individual hotel for additional information. Expect to pay $95 or more per night for a double room at those listed in the expensive category and $50 to $95 at those described as moderate; there are no exceptional inexpensive hotels in the city. Unless otherwise noted, hotels have air conditioning, private baths, TV sets, and telephones.

All hotels below are in Pittsburgh and telephone and fax numbers are in the 954 area code unless otherwise indicated.

EXPENSIVE

Doubletree Pittsburgh This hotel has a contemporary design, with a four-story atrium lobby, 616 rooms, and a fitness center. Guests can dine informally at the *Orchard Café* or more elegantly at the *Harvest,* where the menu changes seasonally. Indoor parking, 24-hour room service, and business services are just some of the amenities. At Liberty Center on Grant St. (phone: 281-3700; 800-222-TREE; fax: 227-4504).

Pittsburgh Hilton & Towers Standing at the edge of *Point State Park,* this hostelry overlooks the Monongahela and Allegheny Rivers, and some of its 700 rooms have park views. Its lobby is contemporary, and it offers two restaurants, parlor suites with wet bars, and a concierge and business services. *Gateway Center* (phone: 391-4600; 800-HILTONS; fax: 594-5161).

Pittsburgh Marriott Near the *Civic Arena,* this recently refurbished, 700-room property has such amenities as an indoor/outdoor pool, a sauna, and health club. There is a restaurant and business services are available. Chatham Center (phone: 471-1234; 800-228-9290; fax: 281-4797).

Ramada Plaza Suites Downtown's only all-suite property has 300 one-, two-, and three-bedroom units. The *Ruddy Duck* restaurant serves complimentary hors d'oeuvres on weekdays. Other amenities include a health center and business services. One Bigelow Sq. Plaza (phone: 281-5800; 800-225-5858; fax: 281-8467).

Westin William Penn After a recent renovation, this hostelry has 595 enlarged and modernized rooms and a stunning lobby. Because the building was declared a National Historic Landmark, the exterior remains unchanged. The *Terrace Room* offers dinner daily, as well as Sunday brunch. Other conveniences include an on-site day-care center, a concierge, 24-hour room service, a fitness center, and business services. Mellon Sq. (phone: 281-7100; 800-228-3000; fax: 563-5239).

MODERATE

Priory City Inn Built in the 1880s as a residence for priests, this 24-room property has been lovingly restored and converted into an elegant Victorian bed and breakfast inn. There are 12-foot ceilings and a cozy courtyard, and shuttle service to downtown is provided. 614 Pressley Ave. (phone: 231-3338).

EATING OUT

The city offers a wide choice of dining, with a variety of ethnic eateries. These are, for the most part, highly rated, for they offer quality and diversity far greater than those found at anonymous "continental" restaurants. Many places are dressier in the evening. Expect to pay $75 or more for dinner for two at establishments we've described as expensive; and between $40 and $75 at those listed as moderate. Prices don't include drinks, wine, tax, or tips. All restaurants are in the 412 area code unless otherwise indicated.

Unless otherwise noted, restaurants are open for lunch and dinner.

EXPENSIVE

Christopher's Ride the exterior glass elevator up to this unusual place, which has a fantastic view, then dine luxuriously on steak Diane, chateaubriand, seafood, and specialties cooked tableside. It tends to be very dressy and offers live entertainment on Friday and Saturday evenings. Closed Sundays. Reservations necessary. Major credit cards accepted. 1411 Grandview Ave., Mt. Washington (phone: 381-4500).

Common Plea This is one of the best downtown eateries, popular with city officials and lawyers and known for its appetizers. The atmosphere is relaxed;

the array of fresh seafood, splendid. Closed Sundays; dinner only on Saturdays. Reservations advised for lunch. Major credit cards accepted. 310 Ross St. (phone: 281-5140).

Grand Concourse This elegant remake of the old *Pittsburgh and Lake Erie Railroad Terminal,* adorned with beautiful wood, stained glass, and gleaming brass, offers excellent seafood—oysters, shrimp, clams, crab, and especially a tangy seafood chowder. Open daily; brunch on Sundays. Reservations advised for dinner only. Major credit cards accepted. 1 Station Sq. (phone: 261-1717).

Le Mont Classic and contemporary, this restaurant offers French and Italian dishes and a spectacular view of the Golden Triangle. House specialties include prime ribs and veal. Open daily for dinner only. Reservations advised. Major credit cards accepted. 1114 Grandview Ave., Mt. Washington (phone: 431-3100).

Le Pommier Classic French country cooking is beautifully presented in this understated spot on the South Side. The bread is fresh-baked on the premises. Closed Sundays and Mondays. Reservations necessary. Major credit cards accepted. 2104 E. Carson St. (phone: 431-1901).

MODERATE

Abruzzi's The atmosphere of this popular restaurant, just across the 10th Street Bridge on the city's historic South Side, is that of an Old World country inn in the heart of the city. Its menu reflects the Abruzzi region of Italy, and its sauces have garnered excellent reviews. Open daily; dinner only on Sundays. Reservations necessary on weekends. Major credit cards accepted. 52 S. 10th St. (phone: 431-4511).

Café Allegro Mainstream Italian fare—antipasto, pasta, seafood, and veal—is served in this turn-of-the-century building. Try the fettuccine with baby shrimp and garlic. Open daily for dinner. Reservations necessary. Major credit cards accepted. 51 S. 12th St. (phone: 481-7788).

F. Tambellini Situtated in the heart of the cultural district, this homey restaurant offers diners such specialties as fried zucchini, osso buco, and a wide range of pasta dishes. Closed Sundays. 139 7th St. (phone: 391-1091).

Penn Brewery Housed in a renovated 19th-century building, this dining spot with a German accent is the city's only micro-brewery. It offers four different beers on tap, including lagers made only with water, malt, hops, and yeast. Goulash, sauerbraten, and Wiener schnitzel are among the menu items. Closed Sundays. No reservations. Major credit cards accepted. On the North Side at Troy Hill and Vinial (phone: 237-9402).

Portland, Oregon

Portland today is one urban center that has managed to avoid some of the problems burdening other cities. Its residents have not forgotten the reasons they chose to live here in the first place. Parks abound. Jogging and bicycle paths wend their way through the city. Development is strictly monitored, and the waterfront is enjoying a period of closely controlled growth.

The city stretches along the Willamette River (pronounced Will-*am*-it) just below the point where it joins the Columbia River. The confluence provides Portland with a deep, freshwater port that serves oceangoing vessels, and because the city straddles the Willamette, ships dock beneath downtown bridges. Some 110 miles from the ocean, Portland is nonetheless a seaport. And around the whole metropolitan area, like parentheses, are the Northwest's two most imposing mountain ranges—the Cascades to the east, the Coast Range to the west.

As with most cities on rivers, it is divided neatly into its east and west sides by the Willamette; each side has its own atmosphere (east side, homey; west side, posh). It is also divided into five large sections: North, Northeast, Northwest, Southeast, Southwest. Sounds confusing, but it actually makes finding places very easy, since every address includes an area designation (N, NE, NW, and so on).

Greater Portland stretches from the foothills of Mt. Hood to the western plains of the Coast Range; more than a million people live in this four-county area. The city is mostly flat, hugging its major waterways, lakes, and ponds. To the west, a group of forested hills—some of them intentionally undeveloped—raises an imperious eyebrow. In the east, the city holds up three fingers of small, residential mountains, as if pointing to the great mountains to the east, and 11,235-foot Mt. Hood in the Cascades, an hour away. To the north, across the border into Washington, the *Mt. St. Helens National Volcanic Monument* has become a popular tourist draw.

The city was incorporated in 1845 by New Englanders. It's named for Portland, Maine, a decision reached with a toss of a coin—had the coin landed otherwise, Portland would be called Boston today. When the great crash of 1893 closed banks across the country, one pioneer Portland merchant, Aaron Meier, took his bags of gold to banker Henry Corbett. The next morning, as the rest of the nation's banks failed, Corbett stood tall and firm in the middle of his bank's lobby—properly attired in frock coat and top hat—with Meier's gold piled conspicuously around him. There was no bank closure in Portland that day.

When Scottish shipper Donald Macleay bequeathed 107 acres to the city at the turn of the century, it was with the stipulation that no wheeled vehicle ever be allowed to enter the premises. The city agreed, and has even expanded Macleay's trust. *Macleay Park,* part of the densely wooded, 5,000-

CENTRAL
PORTLAND, OR
The city is divided into 5 sectors, by Burnside Rd., The river, and by Williams Av.
All streets within each sector have prefixes: NW, NE, SW, SE and N., respectively.
0 miles 1/4
Port of Portland Terminal
FRONT AV
WILSON ST
VAUGHN ST
UPSHUR ST
THURMAN ST
SAVIER ST
RALEIGH ST
QUIMBY ST
PETTYGROVE ST
OVERTON ST
NORTHRUP ST
MARSHALL ST
LOVEJOY ST
KEARNEY ST
JOHNSON ST
IRVING ST
HOYT ST
GLISAN ST
FLANDERS ST
EVERETT ST
DAVIS ST
COUCH ST
BURNSIDE RD
Medical Center
WESTOVER RD
TRINITY PL
To Pittock Mansion 1 mile
Lewis & Clark Memorial
WASHINGTON PARK
International Rose Test Gardens
To Museum of Science, Western Forestry Center, Portland Zoo (all in the Park) 1 mile
YAMHILL ST
PARK PL
MADISON ST
KING CT
VISTA AV
KING AV
CIVIC STADIUM
MORRISON ST
ALDER ST
WASHINGTON ST
STARK ST
SALMON ST
MAIN ST
TAYLOR ST
JEFFERSON ST
COLUMBIA ST
CLAY ST
MARKET ST
MILL ST
Tunnel
Knight Park
MONTGOMERY ST
HARRISON ST
CARTER LA
MONTGOMERY DR
PROSPECT DR
Public Library
Art Museum
South Park Blocks
PARK AV
BROADWAY
PORTLAND STATE UNIVERSITY
30
405
26

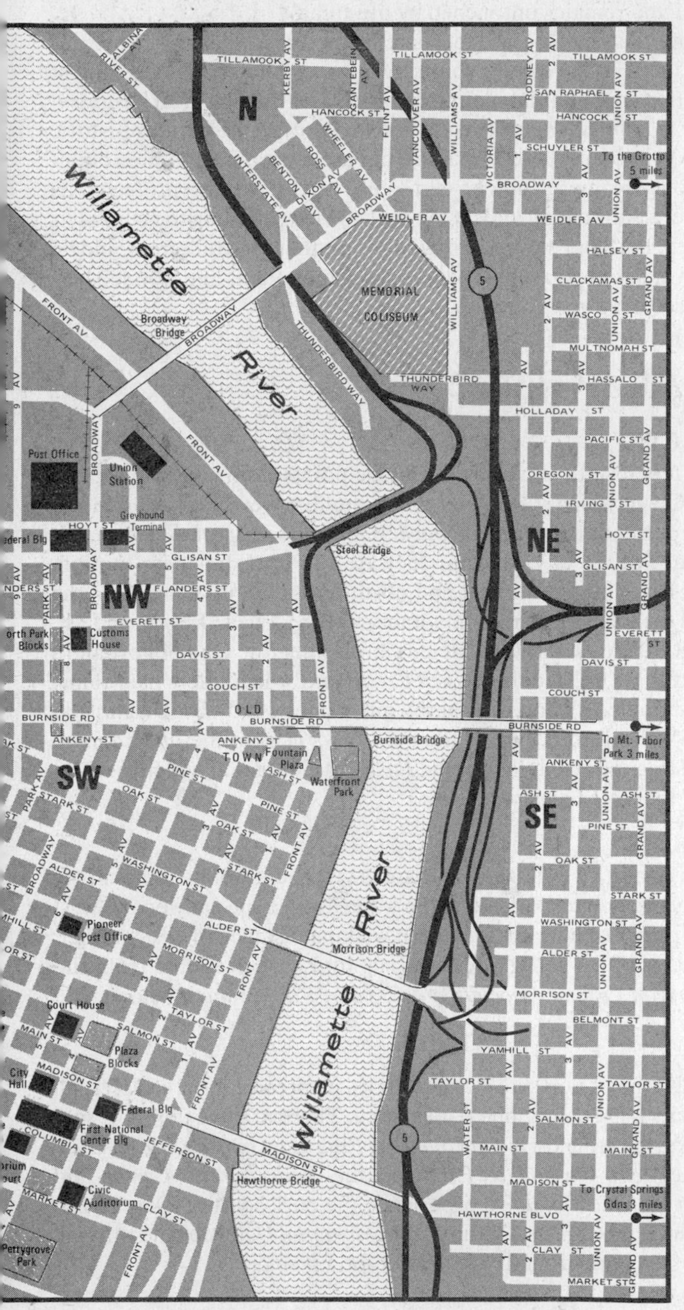

Willamette
River
N
NE
NW
SW
SE
TILLAMOOK ST
HANCOCK ST
SAN RAPHAEL ST
SCHUYLER ST
BROADWAY
WEIDLER AV
HALSEY ST
CLACKAMAS ST
WASCO ST
MULTNOMAH ST
HASSALO ST
HOLLADAY ST
PACIFIC ST
OREGON ST
IRVING ST
HOYT ST
GLISAN ST
EVERETT ST
DAVIS ST
COUCH ST
BURNSIDE RD
ANKENY ST
ASH ST
PINE ST
OAK ST
STARK ST
WASHINGTON ST
ALDER ST
MORRISON ST
BELMONT ST
YAMHILL ST
TAYLOR ST
SALMON ST
MAIN ST
MADISON ST
HAWTHORNE BLVD
CLAY ST
MARKET ST
FLANDERS ST
GOUCH ST
JEFFERSON ST
COLUMBIA ST
RIVER ST
ALBINA AV
KERBY AV
GANTEBEIN AV
FLINT AV
VANCOUVER AV
WILLIAMS AV
VICTORIA AV
RODNEY AV
UNION AV
GRAND AV
WATER ST
FRONT AV
PARK AV
INTERSTATE AV
BENTON
DIXON AV
ROSS
WHEELER AV
THUNDERBIRD WAY
MEMORIAL COLISEUM
Broadway Bridge
Steel Bridge
Burnside Bridge
Morrison Bridge
Hawthorne Bridge
Post Office
Union Station
Greyhound Terminal
Federal Blg
North Park Blocks
Customs House
OLD TOWN
Fountain Plaza
Waterfront Park
Pioneer Post Office
Court House
Plaza Blocks
City Hall
Federal Blg
First National Center Blg
Civic Auditorium
Pettygrove Park
To the Grotto 5 miles
To Mt. Tabor Park 3 miles
To Crystal Springs Gdns 3 miles
5

expanded Macleay's trust. *Macleay Park,* part of the densely wooded, 5,000-acre *Forest Park,* remains untouched by tire tread.

Called the "City of Roses" (for its renowned rose gardens), Portland has been a thorn in the side of some businesses. All new buildings must pass inspection in the initial planning stages, and the powerful *Historical Landmarks Commission* works constantly to protect Portland's historic structures. On its list of protected properties are several iron-fronted buildings—plus one sycamore and one elm tree. The city has also protected its skyline. After taking a long look at the first 40-story building to go up in its business area, Portland moved swiftly to assure that no structure would be built higher. It has thus saved its panorama of mountains and wooded hillsides for succeeding generations.

Portland At-a-Glance

SEEING THE CITY

Portland offers several exceptional vantage points from which to see the city, the valley in which it lies, and the mountains beyond. *Pittock Acres Park,* the grounds of the former *Pittock Mansion* (see *Special Places*), sits 1,000 feet above the city. At your feet are the port, business section, Willamette River, and southwest and northwest residential areas. In the distance are the Cascade Range mountains—Mt. Hood in Oregon, and Mt. Rainier, Mt. Adams, and Mt. St. Helens in Washington. One of Portland's highest points at 1,073 feet is *Council Crest Park*, which offers panoramic views of the whole city and the nearby mountains. And visit *Washington Park* (400 SW Kingston); one of the best views is from the *International Rose Test Gardens* or from the serene *Japanese Gardens* at a higher elevation behind the *Rose Gardens.*

SPECIAL PLACES

Portland was made for walking. Her founders frequently built homes in the west hills and walked to work along the waterfront. Especially on the west side, major points of interest are within walking distance of one another. Brochures describing self-guided walking tours are available from the *Portland, Oregon Visitors Association* (see *Tourist Information* below).

WEST SIDE

WASHINGTON PARK One of Portland's oldest parks, it spreads over 145 acres, all part of the city's 40-square-mile park system. There are five points of special interest on the grounds: the *International Rose Test Gardens,* the *Japanese Gardens,* the *Metro Washington Park Zoo,* the *World Forestry Center,* and the *Vietnam War Memorial.* To experience the park setting, take the zoo train from the *Rose Gardens*—it runs from *Memorial Day* weekend through September. The park grounds are perfect for a picnic.

The *International Rose Test Gardens,* one of Portland's greatest attractions, boasts over 400 varieties of roses. June through October is the best time to see them. The *Japanese Gardens* above the *Rose Gardens* are considered some of the most authentic outside of Japan. Portlanders enjoy sneaking an hour or so to come stroll and meditate in the tranquil and meticulously groomed landscape. Bring a camera: It's impossible to take a poor picture here, rain or shine. Admission charge (phone: 223-4070).

The *Metro Washington Park Zoo* is easily accessible, varied, and well organized. The zoo is best known for the 27 Asian elephants born here, making its breeding herd the most successful in the world. Highlights are the polar bear and penguin exhibits that allow visitors to view the frolicking animals above and below water. No admission charge for children under two. SW Canyon Rd. (phone: 226-1561 or 226-ROAR).

Across from the zoo, and adjacent to the *Vietnam War Memorial*, is the *World Forestry Center* featuring exhibits on the region's forest heritage with a dramatization of a forest fire and a 70-foot "talking tree." Admission charge. Children under six free. 4033 SW Canyon Rd. (phone: 228-1367).

HOYT ARBORETUM An ideal way to spend some leisure time is to ramble along the trails here among hundreds of varieties of trees and enjoy a secluded picnics. Just over the hill from the zoo. 4000 SW Fairview Blvd. (phone: 823-3655).

FOREST PARK This is the nation's largest forested municipal park. With its 5,000 acres and 70 miles of trails, it is home to a variety of wildlife. Trails connect the park to *Macleay Park, Hoyt Arboretum,* the *Audubon House,* and the Collins and Pittock wildlife sanctuaries.

Audubon House is a nature center featuring wildlife exhibits, lectures, tours, and a nature store. It maintains the surrounding sanctuary and wildlife care center. 5151 NW Cornell Rd. (phone: 292-WILD or 292-6855).

IRA KELLER FOUNTAIN This block-wide series of pools and waterfalls faces the *Civic Auditorium.* In hot weather, people splash around in its swirling water. Designed by Lawrence Halprin, it is called "Ira's Fountain." SW Third Ave. at Clay.

PIONEER COURTHOUSE SQUARE The open city block across the street from the *Pioneer Courthouse* has become the hub of downtown. This is a place for music, flowers, food, espresso, and great people watching. Every day at noon the *Weather Machine,* a whimsical mechanical sculpture predicts the weather for the following 24 hours with a trumpet fanfare and a spray of water, then up pops one of three metal sculptures: Look for a gold sun for fair skies, a blue heron for clouds and drizzle, or a copper dragon for stormy weather. Broadway between Morrison and Yamhill (phone: 223-1613).

PIONEER COURTHOUSE Located directly across from *Pioneer Courthouse Square* was the first federal building in the Pacific Northwest; completed in 1875, it has been restored to its original Victorian splendor. The interior includes a working post office, an elegant Victorian courtroom (where the *US Court of Appeals* meets), and adjoining rooms for the judges. Pioneer Courthouse Sq.

PORTLANDIA This sculpture by Raymond Kaskey is the second-largest hammered copper figure in the world (the largest is the *Statue of Liberty*). It's over the main portico of the Portland Building, which was designed by postmodern architect Michael Graves. 1120 SW Fifth Ave.

OLD TOWN When the *Pioneer Courthouse* was brand new, some folks thought it much too far from the downtown business section—a whole six blocks away. Now "downtown" is called Old Town, a restored shopping and restaurant area. From the North Park Blocks west to NW Flanders, bordered by Burnside, is the Pearl District, a working warehouse area. Art galleries, nightclubs, bistros, and brew pubs have made this one of Portland's hot spots. Next door is Chinatown, which formally begins at the ceremonial gate at NW Fourth and Burnside, and where wonderful eating experiences are close at hand. At the northern end of Chinatown is *Union Station.* Built in 1894, this train and bus depot is listed on the *National Registry of Historic Places.*

POWELL'S CITY OF BOOKS Owner Michael Powell says visitors sometimes stop here before they go to their hotel. The reason? About 500,000 new and used books (travel tomes are especially noted). One of the largest bookstores in the country at more than a block long, this funky, cavernous store thoughtfully provides maps so you can find your way around. Besides books, you'll find espresso, pastries, and readings by bestselling authors at the *Anne Hughes Coffee Shop,* which is in the store. Open daily. 1005 W. Burnside (phone: 228-4651; 800-878-7323).

TRYON CREEK STATE PARK This is Oregon's only metropolitan state park, with 643 acres of wilderness for cyclists, hikers, and naturalists. Adjoining Lake Oswego, 2 miles south of central Portland at 11321 SW Terwilliger Blvd. (phone: 636-9886).

EAST SIDE

OREGON MUSEUM OF SCIENCE AND INDUSTRY (OMSI) This $40-million complex covers more than two and a half city blocks and includes six large halls with exhibits focusing on the earth, space, communications, and the life and physical sciences. There's an Omnimax theater, a planetarium, the USS *Blueback* submarine, and a riverfront cafeteria. Among the displays is the *Transparent Woman,* a see-through model whose organs light up; a simulated earthquake; and an exhibit examining the ethical issues surrounding organ transplants, genetic engineering, and the use of life-support systems. A recent addition is the pre-natal exhibit, which traces the growth and development of a human fetus. A special *Discovery Space* allows infants to seven-year-olds to explore the physical worlds of air, sand, and water. Closed Mondays. Admission charge. 1945 SE Water St. (phone: 797-4000; 800-955-6674 for tickets).

THE GROTTO At this shrine, an outdoor chapel has been built in a grotto on one level; on a cliff 10 stories above, there is another level with a monastery and gardens. The 64 acres of grounds are open for contemplation, quiet walks, and solitude. Sunday Mass is celebrated in the chapel and during summer months is offered outdoors. Open daily. Sandy Blvd. at 85th Ave. (phone: 254-7371).

LEACH BOTANICAL GARDEN This nine-acre public garden emphasizes the plants of the Pacific Northwest. Tours are offered on Saturdays and Wednesdays. Closed Mondays. No admission charge. 6704 SE 122nd Ave. (phone: 761-9503).

CRYSTAL SPRINGS RHODODENDRON GARDENS More than 2,000 rhododendron plants are maintained by the Portland chapter of the *American Rhododendron Society.* During April and May the azaleas reach their peak, followed by the rhododendrons. No admission for children under 12. SE 28th Ave. near SE Woodstock (phone: 771-8386).

EXTRA SPECIAL

The Columbia River Highway runs east and west of Portland. Drive northeast along the breathtaking Columbia River Gorge, with its 2,000-foot towering cliffs and 11 waterfalls.

Sauvie Island, the largest island in the Columbia River, is just north of Portland on US 30. Devoted primarily to farmland, it is ideal for biking, bird watching, picnicking, swimming, fruit and berry picking, and boating. Required parking permits can be purchased at any general store on the island. Here, the *Oregon Historical Society* maintains the *Bybee-Howell House,* a restored 19th-century farmhouse on the channel, open from June to *Labor Day* (donations accepted).

Sources and Resources

TOURIST INFORMATION

The visitors' information center at the *Portland, Oregon Visitors Association* (26 SW Salmon St.; phone: 222-2223; 800-345-3214 outside Oregon) is best for brochures, maps, general tourist information, and personal help; if you arrive after hours or on Sunday when it is closed, outdoor map dispensers and kiosks provide a basic orientation. The *Oregon State Welcome Center* (12348 N. Center Ave.; phone: 285-1631) offers tourist information. Another visitors' center, located at the *Oregon Convention Center* (777 NE Martin Luther King Jr. Blvd.; phone: 731-7858), offers self-service information. Contact the Oregon state tourism hotline (phone: 800-547-7842) for maps, calendars of events, health updates, and travel advisories.

LOCAL COVERAGE *The Oregonian,* morning and afternoon daily; *Willamette Week* offers a liberally opinionated study of the city; and *Our Town* is a weekly resource for shopping and city events. *The Portland Guidebook* by Linda Lampman and Julie Sterling (The Writing Works; $9.95) and *Portland's Best Places* by Kim Carlson and Stephanie Irving (Sasquatch Books; $14.95) are comprehensive guides to Portland and its environs.

TELEVISION STATIONS KATU Channel 2–ABC; KOIN Channel 6–CBS; KGW Channel 8–NBC; KOAP Channel 10–PBS; and KPDX Channel 49–Fox.

RADIO STATIONS AM: KXL 750 (news/talk); KBPS 1450 (public radio). FM: KGON 92.3 (classic rock); KUPL 98.5 (country); KWJJ 99.5 (country); and KINK 101.9 (adult contemporary); KBOO 90.7 (eclectic).

TELEPHONE The area code for Portland is 503.

SALES TAX At this writing, there is no sales tax in Oregon. But buyer beware—a sales tax measure is on the ballot in almost every election; the hotel tax is 9%.

CLIMATE The good news: It doesn't get too cold (snow is pretty rare) or too hot (summer temperatures above 90F last only two or three days). However, it certainly does rain. November through May are the wettest months. June through September are fairly clear, and the average temperature is in the 70s; Indian summers are not uncommon. That's prime tourist time, so book ahead.

GETTING AROUND

AIRPORT *Portland International Airport* is a 20- to 25-minute drive from downtown. The *Raz Transportation Dash Airporter* service (phone: 246-4676) provides transportation to major hotels downtown. The trip takes about 35 minutes, 60 minutes during rush hour. *Tri-Met* city bus No. 12 also stops in front of the airport and goes downtown; the fare is $1 to $1.30.

BUS Portland's *Tri-Met* system covers three counties; exact-change-only fare ($1 to $1.30) is zoned except within the 340-block downtown shopping area (including Old Town, major shopping complexes, *Portland Art Museum*, riverfront), which is free and called Fareless Square. Complete route and tourist information is available from the downtown *Customer Assistance Office* (1 Pioneer Courthouse Sq.; phone: 238-4847 or 238-7433); enter under the waterfall.

CAR RENTAL All national firms are represented. *Bee Rent-A-Car* (84 NE Weidler St.; phone: 233-7368; 800-633-7117) is a good local firm; for others, check the yellow pages.

LIGHT RAIL The bus system is complemented by *MAX*, the light rail network of streetcars serving downtown and the eastern suburbs. Schedules are available at light rail stops along the streets as well as at the Pioneer Courthouse Square transit office. Fare is $1 to $1.30.

TAXI Cabs must be called or picked up at taxi stations in front of the major hotels; they *cannot* be hailed. Most hotels have direct phone connections to the two largest companies, *Broadway Cab* (phone: 227-1234) and *Radio Cab* (phone: 227-1212).

TROLLEY Replicas of Portland's grand old "Council Crest" trolleys from the 1890s run on weekends and holidays on the *MAX* light rail tracks. The trolleys feature hand-finished wood paneling and clanging bells. There is no charge (phone: 228-6687).

SPECIAL EVENTS

Something is always happening in Portland, so it pays to check with the visitors' association and read the local paper (see *Local Coverage* above). Among the myriad events that enliven the city are the *Portland Rose Festival,* which features everything from beauty queens to bicycle races and takes place during the first half of June, and the *Mt. Hood Festival of Jazz,* which brings the best jazz musicians to the area every August.

MUSEUMS

In addition to those listed in *Special Places,* Portland has several museums of note.

AMERICAN ADVERTISING MUSEUM One of the nation's best collections of persuasive media, from sandwich boards to videos, is here in the country's only museum dedicated to advertising in all media. Closed Mondays and Tuesdays. Admission charge. 524 NE Grand Ave. (phone: 226-0000).

CHILDREN'S MUSEUM Kids can amuse themselves with a children's grocery store, switchboard, clay workshop, bistro, water exhibit, tunnel, and more. Open daily. Admission charge. 3037 SW Second Ave. (phone: 823-2227).

CONTEMPORARY CRAFTS GALLERY A not-for-profit institution that seeks to support and promote crafts as a fine art. Changing exhibits of work in glass, fiber, wood, metal, and clay by artists worldwide as well as lectures and demonstrations are presented here. The sales gallery concentrates primarily on the works of local Northwest artists. Closed Mondays. No admission charge. 3934 SW Corbett (phone: 223-2654).

OREGON HISTORICAL SOCIETY MUSEUM Housed in the elegant *Oregon History Center* building, the exhibitions concentrate on Oregon history, before and after the arrival of European settlers. There's also a fine series of dioramas on Indian life, a research library with open stacks, and changing exhibitions. Closed Mondays. Admission charge. 1200 SW Park Ave. (phone: 222-1741).

PORTLAND ART MUSEUM This handsome brick edifice in the heart of the city underwent a $3½-million renovation and acquired its next door neighbor, a converted 1915 Masonic temple, now simply called the *North Wing.* With an outstanding permanent collection of Northwest Indian art and Cameroon art, the museum also features a representative group of Oregon's prolific contemporary artists and a wide variety of traveling shows. Also part of the

Institute is the outdoor *Sculpture Mall,* and the *Northwest Film and Video Center.* Closed Mondays. Admission charge. 1219 SW Park Ave. (phone: 226-2811 for museum; 221-1156 for film center).

PICTURE THIS

Portland's burgeoning art scene finds high-caliber expression in downtown galleries and in the Pearl District. On the first Thursday of every month, the *Portland Art Museum* (see above) and participating galleries open their doors for one large art bash. Check *The Oregonian* on Wednesdays for more details.

PARKS AND GARDENS

Even the freeways into Portland are divided by banks of roses and rhododendrons; the city is surrounded by green mountains and garlanded with 7,608 acres of parkland. In addition to those described in *Special Places,* other notable Portland parks include *Council Crest Park,* above Portland Heights (SW Fairmount Blvd.) and *Tom McCall Waterfront Park* in downtown, which runs two miles along the west side of the Willamette River. This is where the Salmon Street Springs' 185 fountain jets are coordinated to change with the day's cycle. A popular venue for summertime events. The city even holds the distinction of having the world's smallest park: *Mill Ends Park,* on SW Front and Taylor Streets, which measures only 24 square inches. Planted with a suitably small evergreen tree surrounded by flowers, it was created to honor the late Dick Fagen, a well-known journalist in Portland during the 1940s.

SHOPPING

The absence of any sales tax makes Portland especially attractive to shoppers. The downtown shopping district is adjacent to Pioneer Courthouse Square. *Pioneer Place* (888 SW Fifth Ave.; phone: 228-5800) includes *Saks Fifth Avenue* among its 80 specialty stores nestled in a glass-enclosed, four-level pavilion. The *Galleria* (921 SW Morrison; phone: 228-2748), one of the city's first historic renovations, offers some 50 stores and restaurants within its three stories. *Lloyd Center* (phone: 282-2511), east of downtown near the *Oregon Convention Center,* features more than 200 stores.

Portland has several charming neighborhoods whose main thoroughfares showcase boutiques and specialty shopping. Bookstores, galleries, bistros, microbreweries (see *Brew Pubs*), film houses, and espresso bars can be found along NW 21st and 23rd Avenues. SE Hawthorne Boulevard between 33rd and 39th Streets has a newly renovated *Powells* branch and other fine bookstores as well as jumping nightspots; its the city's new hot area. Also, see "Old Town" under *Special Places.*

Made in Oregon These shops carry products made, caught, or grown in the state, including filberts, cranberry candy, smoked salmon, Pendleton woolen goods, and Oregon wines. They can be found at several locations: *Portland*

International Airport (phone: 282-7827); *Washington Square Mall* (Tigard; phone: 620-4670); *Galleria* (921 SW Morrison; phone: 241-3630); *Clackamas Town Center* (12000 SE 82nd Ave.; phone: 659-3155); *Lloyd Center* (phone: 282-7636); and Old Town (10 NW First; phone: 273-8354).

Norm Thompson This flagship shop stocks British duffel coats and other luxurious outdoorwear from around the world. 1805 NW Thurman (phone: 221-0764).

Powell's Travel Store A huge selection of books shares space here with all sorts of travel paraphernalia: money belts, journals, maps, and canteens. Owner Michael Powell also operates *Powell's City of Books* (see *Special Places*). At Pioneer Courthouse Sq., 701 SW Sixth Ave. (phone: 228-1108).

The Real Mother Goose A virtual woodland, this place sells finely crafted pieces that range from wooden kaleidoscopes and carved canes to furniture made from exotic woods. There's also hand-crafted jewelry and garments that have been carefully woven, dyed, painted, and/or beaded by hand. 901 SW Yamhill (phone: 223-9510).

Saturday Market Plan to spend the entire morning here. Over 270 artists and food vendors come to sell their work and edibles under the Burnside Bridge between SW First and Front every weekend, March through December 24 (phone: 222-6072).

TAKE SOME PORTLAND HOME WITH YOU

Fresh chinook and silver salmon are two of Portland's best-known exports, and airlines are accustomed to seeing passengers board an outbound flight with a cold fin under one arm. *Irvington Market* (1409 NE Weidler; phone: 284-4537) will supply all kinds of fresh seafood, specially packed to travel.

SPORTS AND FITNESS

Portlanders are dedicated athletes—there are jogging and bike paths all over town—as well as avid basketball fans.

BASKETBALL The *NBA Trail Blazers* play their home games at the *Rose Garden* (One N. Center Ct.; phone: 224-4400) from November through April.

BICYCLING Unique to Portland is its community bike program. About 100 bright yellow bikes, primarily in the downtown area, are set aside for free use. When you've reached your destination, park it in a designated spot; the next user can pick it up there. Rent from *Agape Cycle & Fitness* (2314 SE Division; phone: 230-0317). Mountain bikes can be rented from *Fat Tire Farm* (2714 NW Thurman; phone: 222-3276). Numerous city and country rides are described in *The Portland Guidebook.*

FISHING For chinook salmon, try the lower Willamette or Willamette Slough from March through early May. Steelhead are found in the Clackamas and Sandy Rivers from December through February. For fishing information in the area contact the *Sport Fishing Boating Information Line* (phone: 800-ASK-FISH).

FITNESS CENTERS The *YMCA* has a number of branches: 6036 SE Foster Rd. (phone: 774-3311); 1630 NE 38th St. (phone: 284-3377); and 2831 SW Barbur Blvd. (phone: 294-3366). All are open to non-members for a fee.

GOLF The quality of the public golf courses is considered impressive here, one of which, an 18-hole championship course, is located at the *Pumpkin Ridge Golf Club* (12930 Old Pumpkin Ridge Rd., Cornelius; phone: 647-4747), 20 minutes west of the city. For information on golfing in the area, call the *Oregon Golf Association* (phone: 643-2610).

HORSE/DOG RACING There's horse racing and pari-mutuel betting at *The New Portland Meadows* (1001 N. Schmeer Rd.; phone: 285-9144), with a season from October through April; and *Multnomah Greyhound Park*, 12 miles from the city in Fairview (NE 223 and Glisan; phone: 667-7700), from May through September.

ICE SKATING An enduring Portland tradition is the indoor *Ice Chalet* at *Lloyd Center* (phone: 288-6073). Skates available for rent.

JOGGING Most of the city's parks offer trails or tracks. Contact the *Oregon Road Runners Club* (phone: 646-7867) for suggestions or information on local running events.

SKIING The closest areas, on Mt. Hood, are *Timberline* (phone: 231-7979), *Ski-Bowl* (phone: 272-3206), *Cooper Spur* (phone: 352-7803), and *Mt. Hood Meadows* (phone: 246-7547); better skiing can be found on the slopes of *Mt. Bachelor* (phone: 382-7888), 180 miles from Portland near Bend.

SWIMMING Call the *Portland Parks and Recreation Service* (phone: 823-2223) for public pool information. (See also *Fitness Centers,* above.)

TENNIS The city runs four indoor and dozens of outdoor courts. The indoor courts may be reserved by the *Portland Tennis Center* (324 NE 12th Ave.; phone: 823-3189 or 823-3190).

WALKING This is the town where walking is a sport. Call the *Volksport Hotline* (phone: 243-5725) for up-to-date information on walking tours and other events.

THEATER

Portland has more than a dozen theaters offering musical and dramatic performances, some locally produced, others from out of town. One of the best bets for information is the *Portland Center for the Performing Arts* (1111 SW Broadway; phone: 796-9293), an umbrella organization for many of the city's theaters and companies: *Arlene Schnitzer Concert Hall* (home of the *Oregon Symphony;* phone: 228-1353); *Intermediate Theater; Dolores Winningstad Theatre;* and the *Portland Civic Auditorium,* home of the *Oregon Ballet Theatre* (phone: 222-5538) and the *Portland Opera* (phone: 241-1802).

Other theatrical venues include *Tygres Heart Shakespeare Company* (phone: 222-9220); *Portland Center Stage* (phone: 274-6588), which mounts a range of productions from classical to contemporary; and *Portland Repertory* (phone: 224-4491), where you'll see contemporary dramas and comedies. The area's largest Hispanic arts and culture organization has its own theater, *Miracle Theater* (phone: 236-7253). For children's theater, there's the *Oregon Children's Theatre Company* (phone: 228-9571) and the *Northwest Children's Theater* (phone: 222-4480). For tickets and information for the various theaters contact *Fastixx* (phone: 224-8499) or *Ticketmaster* (phone: 224-4400).

MUSIC

Portland's opera, ballet, and symphony are well respected and their programs ambitious (see *Theater* above for musical offerings at the *Portland Center for the Performing Arts*). There are also free summer concerts in *Washington Park* between mid-July and mid-August; and the always-happening Pioneer Courthouse Square's free concerts that run from June through August (phone: 223-1613).

NIGHTCLUBS AND NIGHTLIFE

Portland has become renowned as a blues town, with jazz not far behind. Homegrown groups like the *Tom Grant Band* and the *Mel Brown Quintet* have gained national attention. Current favorites: *Brasserie Montmartre* (626 SW Park; phone: 224-5552), where the jazz is mellow weeknights and heats up on weekends; the *Roseland Theatre* (8 NW Sixth Ave.; phone: 224-7469) for shows like B. B. King; *Key Largo* (31 NW First Ave.; phone: 223-9919) for blues and rock; and *Berbati's Pan* (231 SW Ankeny; phone: 248-4579) for folk, rock, disco, and even belly dancing.

BREW PUBS

Portland boasts the most breweries of any US city, so it's not surprising that the marriage of microbreweries and public houses has created a mini-industry here. In downtown Portland, there's the *B. Moloch/Heathman Bakery & Pub* (901 SW Salmon; phone: 227-5700), and farther south near the Ross Island Bridge is the *Fulton Pub and Brewery* (618 SW Nebraska St.; phone: 246-9530). On the waterfront downtown, the *Pilsner Room* (0309 SW Montgomery; phone: 220-1873) offers 27 microbrews on tap. Good food and award-winning brews can be found at *Portland Brewing's Brew House Taproom & Grill* (2730 NW 31st Ave.; phone: 228-5269). The McMenamin brothers operate the *Hillsdale Brewery and Public House* (1505 SW Sunset Blvd.; phone: 246-3938). The *Baghdad Theatre & Pub* (3702 SE Hawthorne Blvd.; phone: 230-0895) and the *Mission Theatre & Pub* (1624 NW Glisan St.; phone: 223-4031) are popular places to view films while you quaff a brew and munch on burgers. The brothers' most ambitious addition is *Edgefield McMenamin's,* located in the eastern suburb of Troutdale (2126 SW Halsey St.; phone: 669-8610); the complex includes a brew pub, a winery, a theater, bed and breakfast accommodations, and a restaurant.

Best in Town

CHECKING IN

Portland's choice hotels have made it possible to slumber in splendor as well as in comfort and convenience—although the privilege carries a rather high price tag. Most of Portland's major hotels have complete facilities for the business traveler. Those listed below as having "business services" usually offer such conveniences as meeting rooms, photocopiers, computers, translation services, and express checkout, among others. Call the individual hotel for additional information. Expect to pay $125 or more per night for a double room at hotels we've categorized as expensive; $80 to $125 at lodgings listed as moderate; and about $75 at the inexpensive places. For bed and breakfast accommodations, contact the *Oregon Bed and Breakfast Guild* (PO Box 3187, Ashland, OR 97520; phone: 800-944-6196) or *Northwest Bed & Breakfast* (1067 Hanover Ct. South, Salem, OR 97302; phone: 243-7616). Unless otherwise noted, hotel rooms have air conditioning, private baths, TV sets, and telephones.

All hotels below are in Portland and telephone and fax numbers are in the 503 area code unless otherwise indicated.

EXPENSIVE

Benson Built in 1912 by wealthy logger Simon Benson, this premier hotel has been restored to its original grandeur. The lobby maintains a feeling of Old World luxury, with its white Italian marble floor, Oriental carpets, walnut paneling, and high transom windows. There are 287 rooms and suites, two with gas fireplaces and Jacuzzis. The *London Grill* restaurant is quite good, as is *Trader Vic's.* There is also a coffee shop, a concierge, a health club, 24-hour room service, valet parking, and business services. 309 SW Broadway (phone: 228-2000; 800-426-0670; fax: 226-4603).

Governor Listed on the *National Register of Historic Places,* it is actually two buildings: a 1909 mission-style edifice and an Italian Renaissance–style structure built in 1923. In the mahogany-paneled lobby, massive murals depict the adventures of Lewis and Clark. While the 100 rooms are not as grand as the public areas, they are well appointed and comfortable. The dining room, *Jake's Grill,* serves fine local fare. Business services are offered; there's also access to a health club. SW 10th St. at Alder St. (phone: 224-3400; 800-554-3456; fax: 241-2122).

Heathman Adjoining the *Performing Arts Center* and near the *Portland Art Museum* are 150 of the most conveniently located rooms and suites in town. Listed in the *National Register of Historic Places* and included in the *National Trust for Historic Preservation*'s list of Historic Hotels of America, it has emerged as an authentic first class property. Facilities include a complimentary video movie library, a mezzanine bar, a library with signed editions from authors who have stayed here, a concierge, valet parking, and access to a nearby health club as well as an on-site fitness suite. Its main restaurant (see *Eating Out*) is noted for its fresh Pacific Northwest seafood and game. Additional amenities include around-the-clock room service and business services. SW Broadway at Salmon (phone: 241-4100; 800-551-0011; fax: 790-7110).

RiverPlace One of the city's smallest inns: only 84 rooms and suites clustered on the waterfront (as well as 10 condos available for rent in the complex next door). Six suites have wood-burning fireplaces and wet bars. Guests awaken to views of the marina and to continental breakfast. The *Esplanade* restaurant prepares Northwest regional dishes. A concierge, 24-hour room service, business services, and access to an adjacent health club are also available. 1510 SW Harbor Way (phone: 228-3233; 800-227-1333; fax: 295-6161).

Vintage Plaza Just two blocks from Pioneer Courthouse Square downtown, this charming European-style hotel dates back to 1894. It was designed around a winery theme, complete with an extensive wine cellar and a tasting area where every evening from 5:30 to 6:30 PM guests may sample Oregon wines. The cozy lobby has a fireplace and a baby grand piano. All of the 107 rooms and suites are stylishly decorated and have direct-dial phones and computer hookups; the two-level suites on the seventh floor have a bird's-eye view of downtown. A fitness center, valet parking, and business services are available. *Pazzo,* the adjacent restaurant, serves innovative Italian food. 422 SW Broadway (phone: 228-1212; 800-243-0555; fax: 228-3598).

MODERATE

Red Lion Hotels and Inns One giant complex on the Columbia River, between Portland and Vancouver (Washington) and 10 minutes from the airport, contains three inns with a total of 831 rooms: the *Red Lion/Columbia River* (1401 N. Hayden Island Dr.; phone: 283-2111); the *Red Lion/Jantzen Beach* (909 N. Hayden Island Dr.; phone: 283-4466); and the *Red Lion Inn at the Quay* (on the Washington side at 100 Columbia St., Vancouver; phone: 285-0636 in Portland; 360-694-8341 for all other locations). The *Red Lion/Lloyd Center* (1000 NE Multnomah St.; phone: 281-6111) and the *Red Lion/Coliseum* (1225 N. Thunderbird Wy.; phone: 235-8311) are in Portland itself. All the properties have fine restaurants, live entertainment, grand ballrooms, room service, a pool, tennis, mini-golf, an outdoor Jacuzzi, a concierge, and business services.

INEXPENSIVE

Imperial This recently renovated 1908 hotel boasts locale and comfort for a lot less than its more upscale neighbors. Of the 136 rooms, 88 are accessible to people with disabilities. There is valet parking as well as complimentary transportation to the train station. 400 SW Broadway at Stark (phone: 228-7221; 800-452-2323; fax: 223-4551).

Mallory A comfortable, clean, and quiet 1950s-style hostelry that offers 144 rooms and adequate restaurant facilities at a reasonable price. 729 SW 15th Ave. (phone: 223-6311; 800-228-8657; fax: 223-0522).

EATING OUT

Portland shines brightly as an international dining town. Restaurants put to use the abundant local seafood and game, farm fresh vegetables and fruits, as well as excellent regional wines in unique and satisfying varieties. Our restaurant selections range in price from $60 or more for dinner for two in the expensive category; $30 to $60 in the moderate; and $30 or less in the inexpensive category. Prices do not include drinks, wine, or tips. All restaurants are in the 503 area code unless otherwise indicated.

Unless otherwise noted, restaurants are open for lunch and dinner.

EXPENSIVE

Atwater's Occupying the entire 30th floor of the *US Bancorp Tower,* it offers a 360-degree view over all downtown. The kitchen does justice to the striking panorama, with a seasonal Northwest menu that relies on only the freshest local products, such as seafood and game. Open daily for dinner only. Reservations advised. Major credit cards accepted. 111 SW Fifth Ave. (phone: 275-3600).

Heathman Considered the best restaurant in town, its chef, Philippe Boulot, has won the hearts and stomachs of Oregonians for his culinary delights. Popular choices include tawny braised rabbit, charred rare *ahi* salad, and free-range veal chop. Reservations advised. Major credit cards accepted. 1001 SW Broadway at Salmon St. (phone: 241-4100).

Jake's Famous Crawfish *The* dining spot Portlanders recommend to visitors, it has been around since 1892. Especially delectable are Quilcene oysters on the half shell, grilled chinook salmon with béarnaise sauce, and bouillabaisse. Save room for the famous chocolate truffle cake or hot three-berry cobbler. Open daily; no lunch on weekends. Reservations advised. Major credit cards accepted. 401 SW 12th (phone: 226-1419).

Paley's Place Former New York restaurateurs Vitaly and Kimberly Paley have fused their culinary talents with the region's bounty of seafood to produce a fine menu. One standout is the horseradish-crusted salmon. Desserts are just as tempting and there is a fine wine list. Dinner Tuesdays through Saturdays. Major credit cards accepted. 1204 NW 21st Ave. (phone: 243-2403).

Wildwood Acclaimed as the 1996 restaurant of the year by *The Oregonian,* this American bistro's creative menu in unsurpassed. Top entrée choices include skillet-roasted mussels in garlic broth with tomatoes and saffron, juicy golden wood-roasted duck accented with huckleberries, and lamb roasted in a clay oven. Desserts are equally good: Blood orange sorbet and coffee ice cream sandwiches are two delicious examples. Open daily; Sunday brunch. Reservations advised. Major credit cards accepted. 1221 NW 21st Ave. (phone: 248-9663).

Zefiro With its chic, minimalist decor and inventive continental menu, this has remained the city's most popular dining spot. Entrées often involve presenting native Northwest ingredients in Old World, Mediterranean, and SE Asian dishes, such as grilled Pacific salmon with Javanese sauce. Open weekdays for dinner; lunch only Saturdays. Reservations advised. Major credit cards accepted. 500 NW 21st Ave. (phone: 226-3394).

MODERATE

Bangkok Kitchen This is Portland's reward for being an international port: Thai food at its best. Among the addictive dishes are hot and sour shrimp soup with coconut milk, *pad Thai* (a noodle dish with peanuts and preserved radishes), vegetarian spring rolls, curried peanut sauce, and on occasion, whole red snapper with chili sauce. Closed Sundays and Mondays. No credit cards accepted. 2534 SE Belmont St. (phone: 236-7349).

Café des Amis Lace curtains and candlelight set a romantic tone. The menu is Pacific Northwest with French touches. Filet of beef with port-garlic sauce, grilled halibut in butter sauce, and wild mushroom ravioli are done distinctively. Open for dinner only; closed Sundays. Reservations advised. Major credit cards accepted. 1987 NW Kearney (phone: 295-6487).

Huber's Café Tucked away in the Oregon Pioneer Building, Portland's oldest operating restaurant (1879) has booths, polished mahogany, stained glass, and an atmosphere as appealing as the food. A traditional turkey dinner with all the trimmings is served six days a week. The excellent Spanish coffee is a favorite with the after-theater crowd. Closed Sundays. Major credit cards accepted. 411 SW Third (phone: 228-5686).

Indigine For more than twenty years, chef/owner Millie Howe has been serving up a menu best described as "global." Classic entrées include seafood enchiladas, and roasted chicken with pesto sauce. Every Saturday night she works her magic to produce spicy Indian dishes such as fried lamb chops garnished with a cilantro and tomato chutney. Open for dinner Tuesdays through Saturdays. Reservations advised. MasterCard and Visa accepted. 3725 SE Division St. (phone: 238-1470).

INEXPENSIVE

Berbati More than a Greek restaurant, it's a scene, as lively and crowded as its menu. Especially noteworthy are the fried calamari, stuffed grape leaves, vegetarian moussaka, lamb chops, homemade sweet cookies, and if you are lucky, *crema,* a sybaritic custard. Closed Mondays. Reservations for six or more. Major credit cards accepted. 19 SW Second (phone: 226-2122).

Dan and Louis Oyster Bar A Portland institution with a nautical theme. It opened at a time when restaurants didn't worry about "ambience," and it still doesn't. Shrimp, halibut, and cod are done to perfection in a variety of ways here, and desserts are fresh baked. They offer chicken, steak, and burgers too. And after 80 years of being a "dry" restaurant it now serves beer and wine. Reservations advised for five or more. Major credit cards accepted. 208 SW Ankeny (phone: 227-5906).

Papa Haydn Select dessert first, then order a light meal that won't spoil it. There's almost always a crowd gathered around the pastry case, where delights ranging from "autumn meringue" to *boccone dolce* (a mélange of meringue, cream, strawberries, and chocolate) are on display. Dinners feature light, continental dishes emphasizing seafood and chicken. Closed Mondays; open for Sunday brunch. Reservations only for brunch. Major credit cards accepted. 5829 SE Milwaukee Ave. (phone: 232-9440) and 801 NW 23rd Ave. (phone: 228-7317).

Sweetwater's Jam House Although Portland isn't exactly known for its ribs, this Caribbean eatery is the spot for the Northwest's best pork ribs. Conch fritters, reggae music, and knock-your-socks-off libations will make you think you took a detour down South. Open for dinner only; closed Sundays and Mondays. Major credit cards accepted. 414 N. Broadway (phone: 287-4644).

St. Louis

Back in the 1940s, St. Louis was said to be "First in shoes, first in booze, and last in the *American League*" (referring to the hapless, now defunct St. Louis *Browns*). Today, it is still home to many major league teams: the *NFL Rams,* baseball's *Cardinals* (who celebrated their centennial in St. Louis in 1992), hockey's *Blues,* soccer's *Ambush,* and the hot *Arena Football*'s *Stampede*—but the Gateway to the West also is a major metropolis with more to offer than sports and a scenic view of the *Arch.*

Founded as a fur trading post by Pierre Laclede in 1764, St. Louis is now the 16th-largest metropolitan area in the US, with a population of over 2.5 million. It's also the nation's second-largest inland port, the second-largest rail center, and the eighth-busiest air hub. The city ranks sixth in number of corporate headquarters; ten Fortune 500 companies are based here, and more than 350 others maintain offices in town. Anheuser-Busch, the world's biggest brewer, calls St. Louis home, and the city takes as much pride in its beer as it does in its architecture and sports teams.

Residents hail the achievements of their city's performing artists as well. The *St. Louis Symphony* is the nation's second-oldest symphony orchestra, and the *Opera Theater of St. Louis* consistently receives national and international accolades. The *Fabulous Fox,* a 1920s movie palace restored to all its glitzy greatness, has attracted big-name entertainment and the best of Broadway touring companies to St. Louis's *Grand Center* arts and entertainment district, where seven of the city's own professional companies perform.

The city's modern spirit of revitalization began in the early 1980s. The real estate market boomed, and an infusion of new luxury hotels, office buildings, and shopping malls as well as prominent restorations dramatically changed the downtown skyline (although a strict city ordinance prohibits any building near the famous 630-foot *Arch* to tower above it). The expanded *America's Center,* with its 70,000-seat domed stadium, was designed to enhance the city's reputation as a meetings site. The ultra-modern *Kiel Center* in downtown is located on the former site of *Kiel Auditorium,* built in 1932 as a municipal auditorium for the citizens of St. Louis. The modern *Kiel* is home to St. Louis *Blues* hockey, *St. Louis University Billiken* basketball, and the St. Louis *Stampede.*

While the city looks to its future, many monuments to its past remain prominently in the picture. The centerpiece of St. Louis's rebirth is *Union Station*—an enormous train depot that served passengers from 1894 until the late 1970s and was the busiest station in the world during World War II. Designated a National Historic Landmark in 1976, in the 1980s it was converted in grand style into a shopping and restaurant/hotel complex with its own lake. Old, once-abandoned neighborhoods such as DeBaliviere

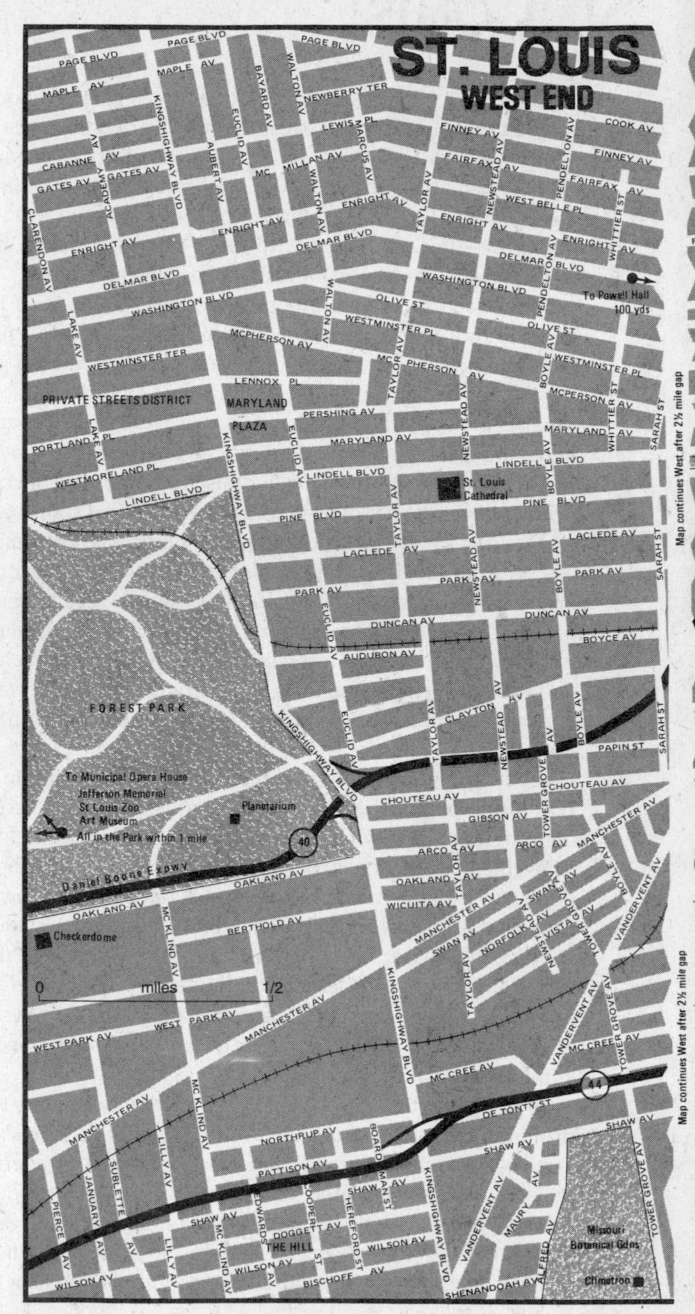
ST. LOUIS
WEST END
PAGE BLVD
MAPLE AV
CABANNE AV
GATES AV
CLARENDON AV
ACADEMY AV
KINGSHIGHWAY BLVD
AUBERT AV
EUCLID AV
BAYARD AV
WALTON AV
NEWBERRY TER
LEWIS PL
MARCUS AV
MC MILLAN AV
ENRIGHT AV
DELMAR BLVD
WASHINGTON BLVD
TAYLOR AV
FINNEY AV
FAIRFAX AV
NEWSTEAD AV
PENDELTON AV
COOK AV
WEST BELLE PL
WHITTIER ST
To Powell Hall 100 yds
OLIVE ST
WESTMINSTER PL
MCPHERSON AV
LAKE AV
WESTMINSTER TER
LENNOX PL
PRIVATE STREETS DISTRICT
MARYLAND PLAZA
PERSHING AV
MARYLAND AV
PORTLAND PL
WESTMORELAND PL
LINDELL BLVD
BOYLE AV
SARAH ST
St. Louis Cathedral
PINE BLVD
LACLEDE AV
PARK AV
DUNCAN AV
BOYCE AV
AUDUBON AV
FOREST PARK
CLAYTON AV
PAPIN ST
TOWER GROVE AV
CHOUTEAU AV
To Municipal Opera House
Jefferson Memorial
St Louis Zoo
Art Museum
All in the Park within 1 mile
Planetarium
GIBSON AV
ARCO AV
MANCHESTER AV
40
Daniel Boone Expwy
OAKLAND AV
WICUITA AV
SWAN AV
NORFOLK AV
VISTA AV
VANDERVENT AV
Checkerdome
MC KLIND AV
BERTHOLD AV
0 miles 1/2
WEST PARK AV
MC CREE AV
44
DE TONTY ST
SHAW AV
NORTHRUP AV
PATTISON AV
BOARDMAN ST
LILLY AV
SUBLETTE AV
JANUARY AV
PIERCE AV
EDWARDS
COOPER ST
HEREFORD ST
DOGGETT AV
WILSON AV
THE HILL
BISCHOFF AV
MAURY AV
ALFRED AV
SHENANDOAH AV
Missouri Botanical Gdns
Climatron
Map continues West after 2½ mile gap

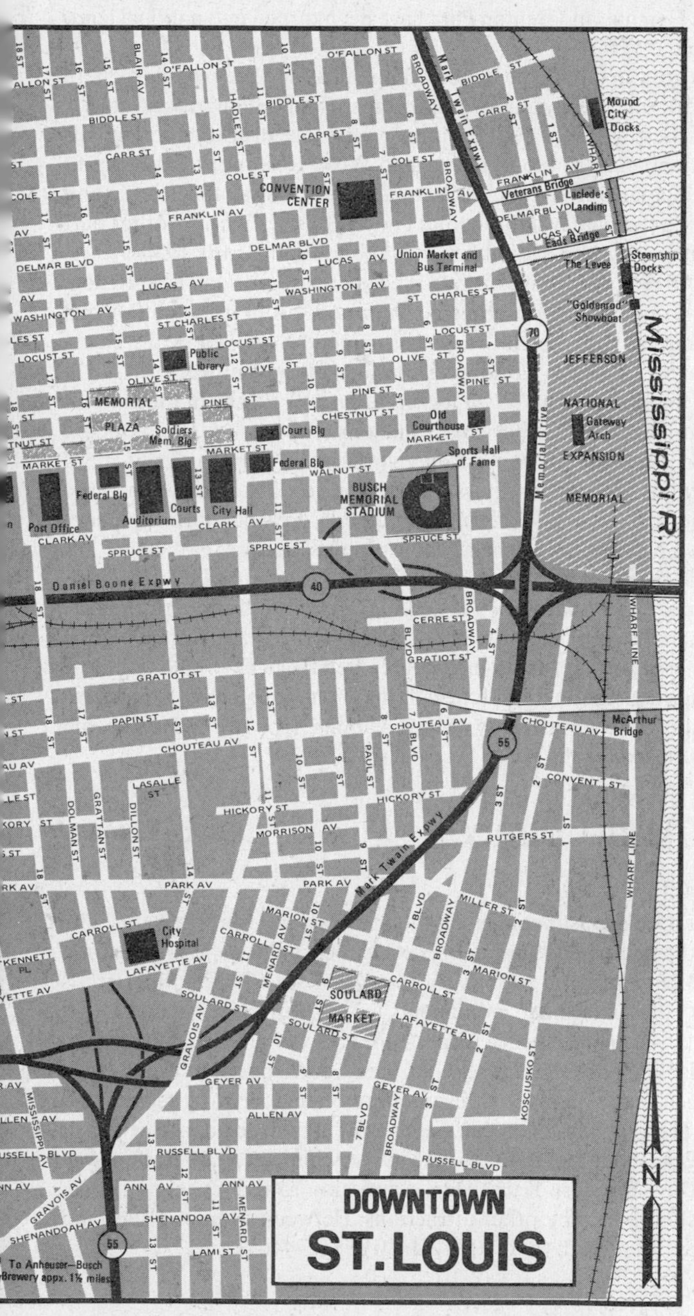

DOWNTOWN
ST. LOUIS
Mississippi R.
O'FALLON ST
BIDDLE ST
CARR ST
COLE ST
FRANKLIN AV
DELMAR BLVD
LUCAS AV
WASHINGTON AV
ST CHARLES ST
LOCUST ST
OLIVE ST
PINE ST
CHESTNUT ST
MARKET ST
WALNUT ST
CLARK AV
SPRUCE ST
CERRE ST
GRATIOT ST
PAPIN ST
CHOUTEAU AV
LASALLE ST
HICKORY ST
MORRISON AV
RUTGERS ST
CONVENT ST
PARK AV
MILLER ST
MARION ST
CARROLL ST
LAFAYETTE AV
SOULARD ST
GEYER AV
ALLEN AV
RUSSELL BLVD
ANN AV
SHENANDOAH AV
LAMI ST
KENNETT PL
BROADWAY
HADLEY ST
BLAIR AV
DOLMAN ST
GRATTAN ST
DILLON ST
PAUL ST
MENARD ST
GRAVOIS AV
MISSISSIPPI AV
KOSCIUSKO ST
7 BLVD
WHARF
WHARF LINE
Memorial Drive
Mark Twain Expwy
Daniel Boone Expwy
70
40
55
CONVENTION CENTER
Union Market and Bus Terminal
Public Library
MEMORIAL PLAZA
Soldiers Mem. Blg
Court Blg
Federal Blg
Post Office
Auditorium
Courts
City Hall
Old Courthouse
Sports Hall of Fame
BUSCH MEMORIAL STADIUM
Mound City Docks
Veterans Bridge
Laclede's Landing
Eads Bridge
Steamship Docks
The Levee
"Goldenrod" Showboat
JEFFERSON NATIONAL EXPANSION MEMORIAL
Gateway Arch
McArthur Bridge
City Hospital
SOULARD MARKET
To Anheuser-Busch Brewery appx. 1½ miles
N

Place, Soulard, the Ville, Lafayette Square, Shaw Park, Compton Heights, Washington Heights, and Benton Park have been turned into national landmarks as well.

St. Louis grew up along the mighty Mississippi, and the river has left an indelible mark on the city's music—jazz, gospel, and bluegrass. Another reminder of the city's river heritage is the warehouse district, where goods once were shipped en route to the rugged West. Restored right down to its original cobblestone streets, *Laclede's Landing* draws office traffic and tourists during the day, restaurant and bar patrons at night. Another part of river heritage, riverboat gambling, was reborn in the early 1990s.

The *1904 World's Fair* gave birth to the ice-cream cone and the hot dog, and St. Louis remains a town obsessed with food. From the tradition-rich Italian restaurants on "the Hill" to sophisticated "New American" eateries, dining in St. Louis is a worldly yet comfortable adventure.

Another important *World's Fair* legacy is *Forest Park,* one of the nation's largest urban parks, with a bevy of attractions (the *St. Louis Zoo,* the *St. Louis Science Center,* and *The St. Louis Art Museum*) that not only are of high quality but have free admission. On the south side of town is the *Missouri Botanical (Shaw's) Garden,* which literally grew out of British immigrant Henry Shaw's generosity and dedication to beauty.

Along the river, where St. Louis began, sits the stately *Old Cathedral—The Basilica of Saint Louis, The King.* Built in 1834 on the site of the first log cabin chapel west of the Mississippi, its museum contains an 800-year-old Spanish crucifix and the original church bell from 1770. The immense and awe-inspiring building stands next to the *Arch.* Together they illustrate the personality of St. Louis, a city where gleaming hopes for the future join a strong reverence for the past.

St. Louis At-a-Glance

SEEING THE CITY

A tour of St. Louis must begin along the Mississippi River, where the city began, and the riverfront offers an irresistible focal point: *Jefferson National Expansion Memorial Park,* with its *Gateway Arch.* At 630 feet, the *Arch* is the nation's tallest manmade monument. Take a tram ride to the observation room at the top for a spectacular 30-mile view of both sides of the river. The park also includes the *Museum of Westward Expansion;* the *Odyssey Theater,* which shows nature and history films on its four-story screen; and the *Tucker Theater,* where you can watch a film about the construction of the *Arch.* Allow about four hours to take in everything. Closed *Thanksgiving, Christmas Day,* and *New Year's Day.* Admission to the museum is free; admission charged to the other attractions. Between Memorial Dr. and Lenore K. Sullivan Blvd. (phone: 982-1410 or 425-4465).

SPECIAL PLACES

Though it's most convenient to get around St. Louis by car, many areas lend themselves to walking. You can park along the riverfront, for example, and explore the levee, *Laclede's Landing,* and downtown.

RIVERFRONT AND DOWNTOWN

THE LEVEE Moored on the river side of the cobblestone levee are St. Louis's most famous riverboats: the *Huck Finn, Becky Thatcher,* and *Tom Sawyer* (phone: 621-4040 or 800-878-7411 for all three), offering sightseeing and dinner cruises on the Mississippi. In this neighborhood even the *McDonald's* is afloat (phone: 231-6725).

On the city side of the levee, next to *Jefferson National Expansion Memorial Park,* is the *Old Cathedral,* aptly named as it is the oldest cathedral west (just west) of the Mississippi. Begun as a log cabin in 1764, the cathedral took its present form in 1834. Its museum contains numerous religious artifacts. Open daily. Second and Walnut Sts. (phone: 231-3250).

LACLEDE'S LANDING In the 50 years after the Civil War, St. Louis became rich as well as famous, and *Laclede's Landing,* a 10-block area just north of the levee on the far side of massive Eads Bridge, was part of that early boom; it contains some fine examples of cast-iron-fronted buildings (*Raeder Place,* formerly the *Old Missouri* hotel, at 806 N. First is best of all). It's now home to a new generation of restaurants and galleries, and is one of the few areas in the city where liquor can be served until 3 AM. Some suggestions of places to visit while wandering the area: *Kennedy's 2nd Street Company* (612 N. Second St.; phone: 421-3655), for a lunch of chili, burgers, and sandwiches, and a great place to hear local bands; *Mississippi Nights* (914 N. First St.; phone: 421-3853), which features local as well as national bands; and the *Old Spaghetti Factory* (727 N. First St.; phone: 621-0276), for inexpensive Italian dishes and old European decor.

OLD COURTHOUSE At one time a site of slave auctions, this building was where an American slave named Dred Scott tested the legality of slavery by suing for his freedom in 1846; the case eventually reached the *US Supreme Court,* which ruled against him. Inside are displays of Old St. Louis and courtrooms where great lawyers such as Thomas Hart Benton tried their cases. Closed *Thanksgiving, Christmas Day,* and *New Year's Day.* No admission charge. Fourth St. at Market (phone: 425-4468).

BOWLING HALL OF FAME Headquarters of the *American Bowling Congress* and the *Women's International Bowling Congress,* it traces the history and development of bowling from 5200 BC to the present. Two interactive children's exhibits use bowling scores to make math more fun. There's also an old-time bowling alley, videodisc program, wide-screen theater, and restaurant. Open daily. Admission charge. Eighth and Walnut, across from *Busch Stadium* (phone: 231-6340).

EUGENE FIELD HOUSE Primarily an antique toy collection, the exhibit also has some artifacts of the famous St. Louis author Eugene Field, who wrote *Little Boy Blue.* In November and December, the house features an elaborate Victorian *Christmas* display complete with a 9-foot tree. Closed Mondays, Tuesdays, and January through February. Admission charge. 634 S. Broadway (phone: 421-4689).

CHRIST CHURCH CATHEDRAL Though the church was built between 1867 and 1911, it beautifully re-creates 14th-century English Gothic architecture. Tours are given on Sundays. 1210 Locust (phone: 231-3454).

MERCANTILE MONEY MUSEUM Here you can learn everything you ever wanted to know about money, including counterfeiting. Open daily. No admission charge. *Mercantile Bank Tower,* Seventh St. and Washington Ave. (phone: 421-1819).

UNION STATION Built in 1894, during the glory days of railroads, this was once the busiest train station in the country. Today, the main lobby and lounge of the *Hyatt Regency* (see *Checking In*) occupy the station's Grand Hall. Shops, restaurants, and a 10-screen movie theater occupy the south end. 18th and Market Sts. (phone: 421-6655).

DENTAL HEALTH THEATRE Three-foot-high fiberglass teeth, a carpeted pink tongue, and a cast of marionettes show kids all about teeth and dental health. Closed weekends. No admission charge. 727 N. First St., Suite 103, on *Laclede Landing* (phone: 241-7391).

ST. LOUIS PUBLIC LIBRARY This 1912 Italianate building contains an art gallery, the *Steedman Architectural Library,* and extensive reference collections. Tours available. Closed Sundays. 1301 Olive St. (phone: 241-2288).

ST. LOUIS MERCANTILE LIBRARY ASSOCIATION Founded in 1846, this is the oldest circulating library west of the Mississippi River. Among its significant photo/print collections are works by George Caleb Bingham and George Catlin, painters who meticulously documented the westward expansion. Closed weekends and national holidays. 510 Locust St. (phone: 621-0670).

ST. LOUIS CARDINALS HALL OF FAME MUSEUM A century of St. Louis sports is celebrated here, including photographs of yesterday's *Browns* as well as soccer and hockey displays. But, as its location in *Busch Stadium* suggests, the main focus is *Cardinals* baseball: Famous first baseman Stan Musial's glove is among the thousands of home team artifacts here. A film about the *Cardinals'* achievements plays continuously. Closed weekends January through March. Admission charge. 100 Stadium Plaza (phone: 421-3263).

SOLDIERS' MEMORIAL MILITARY MUSEUM Dedicated to St. Louis veterans, this museum includes a variety of memorabilia spanning American military history from Civil War days to the Vietnam era. Closed *Thanksgiving, Christmas,* and *New Year's Day.* No admission charge. 1315 Chestnut St. (phone: 622-4550).

SOUTH ST. LOUIS

South St. Louis is primarily German, Italian, and Eastern European. The most determinedly ethnic neighborhood in the area is the Hill (between South Kingshighway and Shaw). From its *bocce* courts and front yard shrines to its green, white, and red hydrants, the Hill is 20 blocks of solid Italian consciousness—great for walking and snacking. Two suggestions: *John Volpi Co.* (5256 Daggett; phone: 772-8550) for salami, prosciutto, and Italian sausage; and *Amighetti Bakery* (5141 Wilson; phone: 776-2855) for fresh bread and carry-out po-boys. And plan to stay for lunch or dinner: The area is packed with excellent Italian restaurants in all price ranges.

ANHEUSER-BUSCH BREWERY The makers of Michelob and Budweiser offer free one-hour tours of the world's largest brewery and grounds. A highlight of the tour is the stable, a registered landmark building and home of the mighty Clydesdale horses. Closed Sundays and holidays. No admission charge. 12th and Lynch Sts. (phone: 577-2626).

CHEROKEE STREET ANTIQUE ROW This six-block historic district is filled with charming mid-19th-century row houses and more than 56 antiques shops offering furniture and collectibles from the Victorian to the Art Deco periods. Cherokee St., between Jefferson and Lemp Aves.

MISSOURI BOTANICAL GARDEN (SHAW'S GARDEN) After Henry Shaw got very rich operating a hardware store in downtown St. Louis, he repaid the city by opening his southside garden estate to the public. Since 1860 its reputation and its collection have grown apace. Highlights of the 79-acre park: the *Climatron,* a tropical geodesic-dome greenhouse; *Seiwa-En,* North America's largest traditional Japanese garden; the *Scented Garden,* a collection of scented plants with descriptions in braille for the blind; and the *William T. Kemper Center for Home Gardening,* an educational resource. Henry Shaw's home is open for tours. Other features include the *Boehm Porcelain Gallery,* a gift shop, and the *Garden View* restaurant. Closed *Christmas Day.* Admission charge. 4344 Shaw Blvd. (phone: 577-5100).

SOULARD MARKET Open for business since 1847, this year-round farmers' market is busiest on Saturday mornings, when everything from live rabbits to homemade apple butter is for sale. The outdoor stalls around the main building open whenever fresh goods—meat or poultry, vegetables, fruit, homemade specialties—come into the city. Closed Sundays through Tuesdays. Seventh St. and Lafayette (phone: 622-4180).

CENTRAL WEST END

Named for its location at the western edge of the city limits, near famous *Forest Park,* the Central West End (CWE) is St. Louis's most cosmopolitan and elegant area. Small specialty shops, restaurants, and ornate mansions dot this historic neighborhood. Private "places" such as Portland and Westmoreland, beautifully maintained by residents, are worth exploring.

Mississippi-born Thomas "Tennessee" Williams set *The Glass Menagerie* in a CWE Westminster Place apartment, where his family lived during the 1920s.

MARYLAND PLAZA Abutting Euclid Avenue, this is a stroller's delight, with the best people watching in town. A potpourri of shops and restaurants makes for good food and great buys. Try *Duff's* (392 N. Euclid; phone: 361-0522) for sandwiches and imported beer; or the *Saint Louis Bread Company* (4651 Maryland Blvd.; phone: 367-7636), which serves delicious sandwiches, fresh bread, pastries, and a variety of piping hot coffees. Sample *Dressel's* (419 N. Euclid; phone: 361-1060) for hearty Welsh pub fare (and the city's best selection of beer and ale). Also worth a stop are *Balaban's* (405 N. Euclid; phone: 361-8085), for seafood, French cuisine, and unusual dinner crêpes; the *Sunshine Inn* (9½ S. Euclid; phone: 367-1413), with an assortment of health food dishes; and *Culpeppers* (300 N. Euclid; phone: 361-2828), known for its spicy chicken wings, club sandwiches, and soups.

SCOTT JOPLIN HOUSE Scott Joplin (1868–1917) was considered one of the masters of ragtime music; his "Maple Leaf Rag" was among the first important examples of the genre. The composer's St. Louis home, listed on the *National Register of Historic Places,* is a museum of his life and work, including a replica of his piano. Open daily. Admission charge. 2658 Delmar Ave. (phone: 533-1003).

ST. LOUIS CATHEDRAL Called the "New Cathedral" to distinguish it from the riverfront basilica, this immense church is one of the world's finest examples of mosaicwork. Mosaics adorn almost the whole interior space—millions of pieces of stone and glass in thousands of shades depicting saints, apostles, and religious scenes. Open daily, with guided tours on Sundays (except *Easter*). Lindell at Newstead (phone: 533-2825).

FABULOUS FOX THEATER This restored 1929 movie palace presents some of the biggest entertainment names in the country—Las Vegas–style shows and pop concerts at Midwestern prices. Tours given Tuesdays, Thursdays, and Saturdays. Admission charge. 527 N. Grand Blvd. (phone: 534-1678).

UNIVERSITY CITY AREA This historic district on Delmar Avenue just west of the Central West End, known as the University Loop (where the streetcars turned around), houses a "strip" of resale shops, modern boutiques, art galleries, and bookstores. Walkers should check out the pavement with stars honoring famous St. Louisans. The *Tivoli Theatre* (6350 Delmar; phone: 862-1100), a restored 1924 movie house, shows art and alternative films. *Blueberry Hill* (6504 Delmar; phone: 727-0880) has Chuck Berry, Elvis Presley, and Bo Diddley memorabilia on the walls, and "Rock 'n' Roll Beer" on the menu. The *High Pointe Theatre* (1001 McCausland; phone: 781-0800) features a foreign, classical, and modern films.

EXTRA SPECIAL

An hour south of St. Louis just off Route 55 is Ste. Genevieve, one of the oldest permanent settlements west of the Mississippi (established in 1735) and a town that has maintained its old homes with admirable care. A number of the oldest are open daily, as is an excellent old inn, *St. Gemme Beauvais* (78 N. Main St.; phone: 883-5744; also see *Inn Sites: America's Special Havens,* in DIVERSIONS). If you are in the area during the second weekend of August, don't miss *Ste. Genevieve's Jour de Fête,* when all the old homes are open for a festive two days.

Take a day trip to *Six Flags Over Mid-America* (I-44 and Allenton Rd. in Eureka; phone: 938-4800 or 938-5300), a 200-acre theme park with rides, unique shows, and interesting shops. It's about a 20-minute drive from downtown. Call for schedule information and see *Amusement Parks,* in DIVERSIONS. Or visit the stomping grounds of Huck Finn and Tom Sawyer—Hannibal, Missouri—about two hours away (phone: 221-1101). Described as the "World's Most Famous Small Town," it was the home of Samuel Clemens, better known as Mark Twain.

Other nearby attractions: *Meramec Caverns* (take I-44 west to the Stanton exit; phone: 468-3166) are some of the largest cave formations in the world and former hideout of Jesse James (closed *Thanksgiving* and *Christmas Day*). Admission charge. Camping and canoeing on the Meramec River are available from April through October. *Cahokia Mounds State Historic Site and Museum* (7850 Collinsville Rd., Collinsville, IL; phone: 618-346-5160) displays artifacts dating from AD 700 to 1450, when Indians inhabited the area; it also conducts tours and offers craft classes and a variety of seasonal events. Open daily. Admission charge.

Missouri has about 25 wineries, many of which offer tasting tours. Several are in Augusta, about 45 minutes from St. Louis, including the internationally renowned *Mount Pleasant Winery* (5634 High St., Augusta; phone: 800-467-WINE). Open daily.

Sources and Resources

TOURIST INFORMATION

The *St. Louis Convention and Visitors Commission* (10 S. Broadway, Ste. 1000, St. Louis, MO 63102; phone: 421-1023; 800-325-7962) publishes a free visitors' guide and can provide maps and other tourist information. A *Visitor Information Center* also is located in *America's Center,* at Seventh and Washington Streets. Both are closed weekends. Contact the *Missouri State Tourism Hotline* (phone: 800-877-1234) for maps, calendars of events, health updates, and travel advisories.

The American Institute of Architects (911 Washington Ave.; phone: 621-3484) sells an inexpensive walking tour of downtown. The *Landmarks Association* (phone: 421-6474) has information on neighborhoods and restoration projects.

LOCAL COVERAGE *St. Louis Post-Dispatch,* daily (Thursday's edition carries a calendar of coming events); the *St. Louis American,* the city's most informative black community newspaper, is published each Thursday. The *St. Louis Business Journal* is a weekly update on the business scene, and the weekly *Riverfront Times* focuses on city happenings.

TELEVISION STATIONS KTVI Channel 2–FOX; KMOV Channel 4–CBS; KSDK Channel 5–NBC; KETC Channel 9–PBS; KPLR Channel 11–Ind.; and KDNL Channel 30–ABC.

RADIO STATIONS AM: WKBG 1300 (contemporary hits); KEZK 590 (sports); KMOX 1120 (news/talk). FM: KWMU 90.7 (national news/music); KSD 93.7 (classic rock); KATZ 100.3 (jazz); KEZK 102.5 (easy listening); and KMJM 107.7 (urban contemporary).

TELEPHONE The area code for St. Louis is 314.

SALES TAX There is a 6% sales tax on general merchandise. In addition, restaurants charge a 1.5% tax, and hotels charge a 3.75% tax, plus $2 extra per night in the city; the hotel tax is 3.5% in the rest of the county.

CLIMATE St. Louis weather is unpredictable, with temperatures ranging from -10F to 103F. From mid-June through September, the heat and humidity are high, particularly in August. Dress coolly, but be aware that most places are air conditioned. Autumn is crisp, cool, and beautiful. Winters are very cold, with snow and ice. Spring is wonderful, but be prepared for occasional rain and very strong winds from April to June.

GETTING AROUND

AIRPORT *Lambert–St. Louis International Airport,* located 18 miles west of downtown via I-70 (phone: 426-8000), usually is a 30-minute drive from downtown (up to an hour during rush periods). Several limo services and hotel vans provide transportation to downtown. You also can take the *MetroLink* light rail service or the *Natural Bridge Airport* bus service, each for $1 one-way fare.

BUS The *Bi-State* bus system (707 N. First St.; phone: 231-2345) serves most of the metropolitan area. The fare is $1, with a 10¢ charge for transfers. Call for route information and maps. From mid-May through December, free *Levee Line* buses run every few minutes between *Union Station* and the riverfront. The *Shutter Bug* provides transportation between downtown St. Louis and *Forest Park* attractions (the fare is $1).

CAR RENTAL St. Louis is served by all the major national companies. A reliable local service is *Enterprise Leasing* (phone: 231-4440), with a dozen locations around the city.

LIGHT RAIL The *MetroLink* aboveground rail system (phone: 231-2345) provides transportation throughout the St. Louis metropolitan area and suburban Illinois. The fare is $1, with a 10¢ charge for transfers.

TAXI Cabs are available at major department stores and hotels, and can be hailed in the streets or ordered by phone. Major companies are *Laclede Cab* (phone: 652-3456); *Yellow Cab* (phone: 361-2345); and *County Cab* (phone: 991-5300).

SIGHTSEEING TOURS

TRAM For the less energetic, *Tour St.Louis* (1100 S. Sixth St.; phone: 241-1400) offers half-day and full-day narrated tram tours of the downtown area.

SPECIAL EVENTS

Fair St. Louis (phone: 434-3434) on the *Arch* grounds is a four-day *Fourth of July* extravaganza, featuring a parade of 20 or more lavishly outfitted floats, fireworks, marathons, music, and air and water events. German food and culture are celebrated during the *Strassenfest* (phone: 842-2652), a weekend celebration usually held in late July or early August. The *Japanese Festival* (phone: 577-5100) at *Missouri Botanical Gardens* is an annual *Labor Day* weekend celebration of Japanese culture through music, dance, food, and crafts. *Labor Day* is also the time to catch top blues performers at the *St. Louis Blues Heritage Festival* at *Laclede's Landing* (phone: 241-2583). The *Great Forest Park Balloon Race* (phone: 821-6724), an annual St. Louis tradition since 1904, takes place in late September. Also in September, look for the annual *Greek Festival* (*St. Nicholas Greek Orthodox Church,* 4967 Forest Park Blvd.; phone: 361-6924), offering ethnic foods, games, and costume pageants. In mid-October, the two-day *International Folkfest* (phone: 773-9090), held at *Queeny Park* in West St. Louis County, features ethnic dance, music, food, and crafts from more than 80 cultures. Caroling by *Sing Out St. Louis* at *Union Station* (phone: 421-6655) is among a bevy of holiday events.

MUSEUMS

In addition to those listed in *Special Places,* there are a number of other museums of interest in St. Louis.

DOG MUSEUM Canines throughout history are depicted in art, photography, and literature. Closed Mondays and holidays. Admission charge. 1721 S. Mason Rd., in *Queeny Park* in West County (phone: 821-DOGS).

THE MAGIC HOUSE Interactive exhibits combine fun and learning at this children's museum. Closed Mondays. Admission charge. 516 S. Kirkwood (phone: 822-8900).

McDONNELL DOUGLAS PROLOGUE ROOM The first *Gemini* and *Mercury* space capsules are among the achievements on display at the world headquarters of the aerospace giant. Closed September through May and Sundays and

Mondays. No admission charge. McDonnell Blvd. and Airport Rd., on the northeast side of the airport (phone: 232-5421).

MISSOURI HISTORICAL SOCIETY AND HISTORY MUSEUM Colorful displays show the history of St. Louis, of Missouri, and of the American West. Exhibits include items from the *1904 World's Fair;* Charles Lindbergh memorabilia; and extensive collections of firearms and period costumes. There's also a public library (225 S. Skinker Blvd., west of the museum). The museum is closed Mondays; the library is closed Sundays. Guided tours by appointment on weekdays. No admission charge. *Forest Park,* Lindell Blvd., and DeBaliviere (phone: 746-4599).

NATIONAL MUSEUM OF TRANSPORTATION Vehicles, from horse-drawn buggies to 1950s singer Bobby Darin's dream car, are on display. The train collection is heralded as one of the greatest in the nation. Closed holidays. Admission charge. 3015 Barrett Station Rd., in West County (phone: 965-7998).

ST. LOUIS ART MUSEUM This turn-of-the-century building is one of a few extant from the *1904 World's Fair*. Note the 47-foot statue of King Louis the Crusader. Closed Mondays. Admission charge for special exhibits. *Forest Park* (phone: 721-0067).

ST. LOUIS SCIENCE CENTER (MCDONNELL PLANETARIUM) The *McDonnell Planetarium* and the *Museum of Science and Natural History* are part of the same entertainment and educational complex. The planetarium features a *Star Theater* and hands-on science and natural history exhibitions. A second building houses the 330-seat *OMNIMAX Theater,* galleries devoted to ecological and technological themes, and a unique structure that shows the physics of highway construction and then plunges downward for a look at a Missouri mine and a city sewer. Closed *Thanksgiving, Christmas Day,* and *New Year's Day.* Admission charge for special exhibits. 5100 Clayton Ave., *Forest Park* (phone: 289-4400).

NATIONAL VIDEO GAME AND COIN-OP MUSEUM This institution will appeal to those pinball wizards and Nintendo fans who wonder where it all started. Here is the first video game, the first pinball machine to use flippers, and other landmarks in the evolution of the video game fad. Visitors are encouraged to try their skills. Open daily. No admission charge, but you can buy tokens to play the machines. 801 N. Second St. (phone: 621-2900).

VAUGHN CULTURAL CENTER Site of many traveling African-American art and photography shows, it is also a resource for research into local and national African-American history. Closed weekends. No admission charge. 524 N. Grand Blvd. (phone: 535-9227).

PARKS AND GARDENS

For information on the *Missouri Botanical Garden,* see *Special Places.* *Forest Park,* which at 1,300 acres is one of America's largest city parks, includes a science center and art museum along with hiking trails and recreational facilities. One must-see *Forest Park* attraction is the 83-acre *St. Louis Zoo,* whose exhibits include *"Big Cat Country,"* the famous *Monkey House,* the walk-through *Bird Cage,* and the grand *Jungle of the Apes House,* as well as a state-of-the-art educational center. No admission charge to main zoo; the *Children's Zoo* has a modest admission charge (phone: 781-0900). *Forest Park* also includes *The Jewel Box,* an immense greenhouse with dozens of species of flowers from all over the world. Admission charge (phone: 531-0100). *Laumeier International Sculpture Park* (12580 Rott Rd.; phone: 821-1209) features huge outdoor sculptures in a woodsy setting. Closed Mondays. No admission charge.

SHOPPING

Denizens and travelers alike marvel at the array of choices that this heartland city has to offer shoppers. *St. Louis Centre,* (downtown between Sixth and Seventh Sts. and Washington and Olive Blvds.; phone: 231-5522) is one of the nation's largest urban shopping complexes, with more than 120 stores and restaurants. The large department stores *Dillard's* and *Famous-Barr* are anchors. *Saks Fifth Avenue, Neiman Marcus, Doubleday Books,* and a plethora of specialty stores can be found at *Plaza Frontenac* (Lindbergh Blvd.; phone: 432-0604). *St. Louis Galleria,* about 12 miles east of downtown in Richmond Heights, is another huge mall including branches of *Dillard's* and *Famous-Barr.*

SPORTS AND FITNESS

St. Louisans love their professional teams, and sports events are well attended.

BASEBALL *Busch Stadium* (Broadway at Walnut St., downtown; phone: 421-3060) is the home of the *National League Cardinals.* Tickets are available at the stadium and from *Schnuck's* grocery stores.

BICYCLING About 13,000 bicyclists wheel through downtown St. Louis during the *Moonlight Ramble,* the world's largest nighttime cycling event. The 20-mile bike ride, a tradition since 1964, starts after midnight and is held the weekend of the full moon in August. Call 644-4660 for information. For recreational biking, pick one of the many trails in the city's *Forest Park;* bikes can be rented at nearby *Touring Cyclist* (1101 S. Big Bend Blvd.; phone: 781-7973). If you want to ride along the *Katy Trail State Park* (phone: 800-334-6946), a premier limestone riding surface that stretches more than 200 miles across the state from St. Charles (just west of St. Louis on I-70) to Sedalia, you can rent from *Tourist Cyclist* in St. Charles (phone: 949-9630) or Augusta (phone: 228-4882).

FITNESS CENTERS The revamped *Downtown YMCA* (1528 Locust St.; phone: 436-4100) has a pool, racquetball courts, a track, and exercise equipment. The *Marquette YMCA* (314 N. Broadway; phone: 436-7070), also downtown, offers a high-tech exercise environment but no pool. Both are open to nonmembers for a fee.

FOOTBALL Since 1995, St. Louis has been home to the *NFL Rams*, who play at the *Dome* at *America's Center* (phone: 425-8830; 800-246-7267). The *Arena Football League*'s St. Louis *Stampede* plays April through August at the *Kiel Center* (14th and Clark Sts.; phone: 622-2547).

GOLF *Quail Creek Golf Course* (6022 Wells Rd. in South County; phone: 487-1988) is a challenging 72-par 18-hole public course designed and managed by golfer Hale Irwin's company. *Forest Park Municipal Golf Course* (phone: 367-1337) is a fairly tough 18-hole, 70-par course.

HOCKEY The *Blues* play *NHL* hockey at the *Kiel Center* (14th and Clark Sts.; phone: 622-2500).

HORSE RACING Depending upon the time of year, there's either thoroughbred or harness racing at *Fairmount Park* (Rte. 40 East, Collinsville, IL; phone: 436-1516).

JOGGING Start at Wharf Street below the *Gateway Arch* and run the 2-mile stretch along the river; jog the 6-mile perimeter of *Forest Park;* or follow Wydown Road by the *Washington University* campus for about a 2-mile run.

SOCCER The St. Louis *Ambush* play major league soccer at the *Kiel Center* (14th and Clark Sts.; phone: 291-7600).

TENNIS The St. Louis *Aces* play professional team tennis at *Dwight F. Davis Tennis Center* in *Forest Park* (phone: 762-ACES). Visitors can obtain permits to play at the center, which is open during daylight hours (phone: 361-0177).

THEATER

Numerous theaters and art galleries are located in the eight square blocks of St. Louis's Grand Center arts and entertainment district. For information about events, contact the main office (634 N. Grand Ave.; phone: 533-1884). There's also the fine *Repertory Theatre of St. Louis* (136 Edgar Rd.; phone: 968-4925), offering a range of contemporary drama; and the attractive *Westport Playhouse* (600 Westport Plaza; phone: 275-8787), for productions ranging from plays to well-known entertainers. The *Muni* (*Forest Park;* phone: 361-1900) offers a summer stock program of musicals in a 12,000-seat outdoor amphitheater. *St. Louis Black Repertory Company* (*Grandel Square Theatre,* 3601 Grandel Sq.; phone: 534-3807) performs theater and dance reflecting African-American culture.

MUSIC

Concerts and opera are performed by the *St. Louis Symphony* at *Powell Hall* (Grand and Delmar; phone: 533-2500); by the *Opera Theater of St. Louis* at *Loretto-Hilton Theater* (539 Garden Ave., in the suburb of Webster Grove; phone: 961-0171); and at *Sheldon Arts Foundation Concert Hall*

(3648 Washington; phone: 533-9900), one of the country's most acoustically perfect auditoriums. *American Theater* (416 N. Ninth; phone: 231-7000) is a cabaret setting that hosts topnotch entertainment acts and musical groups.

NIGHTCLUBS AND NIGHTLIFE

After dark, from *Laclede's Landing* to the suburbs, night crawlers can enjoy a variety of activities. *Mississippi Nights* (914 N. First St.; phone: 421-3853), on *Laclede's Landing,* features a large dance floor and national and local rock and alternative bands. For jazz try *Hannegan's* (719 N. Second St.; phone: 241-8877). Popular happy-hour venues include *Balaban's* (405 N. Euclid in the Central West End; phone: 361-8085), where St. Louis's old money rubs elbows with the nouveau riche; the *Links Club* (408 N. Euclid Ave.; phone: 367-1900), just across the street, with reggae on Wednesdays, rock bands and DJs on other nights; and *Cardwell's* (8100 Maryland, in the suburb of Clayton; phone: 726-5055), for both business and cocktail chatter. More live music and displays of the work of local artists liven up the *Hi-Pointe Café/Bar* (1001 McCausland Ave.; phone: 781-4716). *Mike & Min's* (Tenth and Geyer in historic Soulard neighborhood; phone: 421-1655) features live blues Wednesdays through Saturdays.

RISKY BUSINESS

Riverboat gambling returned to the St. Louis area in the early 1990s. The *President Casino* on the *Admiral* riverboat (phone: 800-772-3647) is docked just north of *Gateway Arch,* offering an array of games including blackjack and poker. On the Illinois side of the Mississippi, the *Casino Queen* (phone: 800-777-0777) offers several cruises a day, with slots, craps, roulette, blackjack, and other casino games, as does the *Alton Belle Riverboat Casino* (219 Piasa St., Alton; phone: 800-336-SLOT). A few miles west of the airport off I-70 is *Casino St. Charles* (1355 S. Fifth St., St. Charles; phone: 940-4300). You must be 21 or over to play.

Best in Town

CHECKING IN

High-quality hotels are available throughout the city. Most of St. Louis's major hotels have complete facilities for the business traveler. Those listed below as having "business services" usually offer such conveniences as meeting rooms, photocopiers, computers, translation services, and express checkout. Expect to pay $120 or more per night for a double room at places in the expensive category (though less expensive weekend and special rates may be available); from $80 to $120 at those rated moderate. There are no exceptional inexpensive hotels in the city. Unless otherwise noted, hotels have air conditioning, private baths, TV sets, and telephones.

All hotels below are in St. Louis and telephone and fax numbers are in the 314 area code unless otherwise indicated.

EXPENSIVE

Adam's Mark In the shadow of the *Gateway Arch,* this is one of the city's best. With 17th-century Flemish tapestries, French crystal chandeliers, Russian lithographs, and an Italian marble lobby, it reflects the grand tradition of Europe's finest hotels. Along with the 968 rooms and 96 suites, there are several restaurants, business services, a concierge, and 24-hour room service. Fourth and Chestnut (phone: 241-7400; 800-444-ADAM; fax: 241-6618).

Airport Marriott At *Lambert–St. Louis International Airport,* half an hour from downtown, this 602-room hotel features extensive sports facilities—two pools, tennis courts, putting greens, a sauna, and exercise rooms—and is good both for businesspeople and for families who'd like to relax after a busy day. There is a restaurant, as well as business services, a concierge, free parking, and a parking lot shuttle service. I-70 at the airport (phone: 423-9700; 800-228-9290; fax: 423-0213).

Hyatt Regency More than just a hotel, it's an event—part of the complex that includes the beautifully restored *Union Station.* Of its 538 rooms, 68 are in *Head House,* which actually was part of the station; the rest are located under the original roof of the train shed. There are two restaurants, the casual *Aldo's* and the formal *Station Grille,* as well as the *Grand Hall* bar. Surrounded by more than 11 acres of fine shops and marketplaces, it is truly an experience. Business services, exercise facilities, a pool and a concierge are available. 1820 Market St. (phone: 231-1234; 800-233-1234; fax: 923-3970).

Majestic Distinctively European, this National Historic Landmark built in 1913 sets the standard for personal service in downtown St. Louis. Each of the 91 guestrooms and mini-suites is unique in design and appointments. Guests can use nearby *YMCA* fitness facilities. There are business services, as well as a concierge and 24-hour room service. 1019 Pine St. (phone: 436-2355; 800-451-2355; fax: 436-0223).

Marriott Pavilion "Pavilion" refers to the *Spanish Pavilion,* jewel of the *1964 New York World's Fair,* dismantled and moved to downtown St. Louis by former mayor Alfonso Cervantes amid great controversy. The *Pavilion* is now the two-story lobby of this 671-room property. Among the facilities are a coffee shop, two restaurants, a bar, a pool, a sauna, and a fitness center. There's also a concierge and business center. 1 Broadway (phone: 421-1776; 800-228-9290; fax: 331-9029).

Ritz-Carlton Halfway between downtown and the airport, this world-class establishment has 302 rooms, including 30 executive suites and one Ritz-Carlton Suite. Though built in 1990, its decor features 18th- and 19th-century art and antiques. Private concierge service is available, as is a fitness and exercise center with an indoor climate-controlled pool. *The Restaurant* and *The Grill* are both full-service dining rooms. Business services are available, and there is also 24-hour room service. Located in the suburb of Clayton at 100 Carondolet Plaza (phone: 863-6300; 800-241-3333; fax: 863-3525).

Seven Gables Inn With 32 charming European-style guestrooms and suites in the heart of Clayton's business district, this Tudor-style, vintage 1920s inn, originally modeled after the house in Nathaniel Hawthorne's *House of the Seven Gables,* is listed in the *National Register of Historic Places.* There are two restaurants, the formal *Chez Louis* and the more casual *Bernard's* bistro, as well as business services and a concierge desk. 26 N. Meramec (phone: 863-8400; 800-433-6590; fax: 863-8846).

MODERATE

Cheshire Inn Located one block west of *Forest Park,* this 105-room hotel is part English country inn, part "Fantasy Island"—five theme suites offer settings ranging from a Treehouse and Safari Rainforest to a Roman Bathhouse. Amenities include a pool and a good restaurant. Business services are available, and there are double-decker airport shuttle buses. Clayton Rd. at Skinker (phone: 647-7300; 800-325-7378; fax: 647-0442).

Doubletree Guest Suites Listed on the *National Register of Historic Places,* this 1925 structure in the heart of downtown has been restored to its original elegance. The 184 suites are refined and comfortable; the three penthouse suites have fireplaces and Jacuzzis. Amenities include an on-site fitness center, a rooftop pool, and a fine restaurant. 806 St. Charles St. (phone: 421-2500; 800-222-TREE; fax: 421-6254).

Drury Inn Retaining the elegance of the 1907 railroad *YMCA* building adjacent to *Union Station,* this downtown hostelry with above-average service is a favorite of vacationers as well as businesspeople. There are 180 guestrooms and mini-suites as well as an indoor pool and a Jacuzzi; guests receive continental breakfast. Business services are available. 201 S. 20th St., southwest of *Union Station* (phone: 231-3900; 800-325-8300; fax: 231-3900).

Regal Riverfront Directly across from the *Gateway Arch, Busch Stadium,* and the *Old Courthouse,* this hotel's two towers encompass 800 rooms and 54 executive suites, three restaurants (one revolving 27 stories above the city), and the largest hotel ballroom in the state. There's also a health club, a gameroom, and both indoor and outdoor pools. Business services are available. 200 S. Fourth St. (phone: 241-9500; 800-325-7353; fax: 241-6171).

EATING OUT

St. Louis has a host of good restaurants offering wide variety at reasonable prices. Expect to pay $60 or more for dinner for two at places listed as expensive; $30 to $60 at those categorized as moderate; and less than $30 at inexpensive places. Drinks, wine, tax, and tip are not included. All restaurants are in the 314 area code unless otherwise indicated.

Unless otherwise noted, restaurants are open for lunch and dinner.

EXPENSIVE

Giovanni's On the Hill This romantic restaurant is one of the finest of the many eateries on "the Hill," St. Louis's traditional Italian neighborhood. Well-prepared classic pasta, veal, and seafood dishes are served in an Italian Renaissance setting. Closed Sundays. Reservations advised. Major credit cards accepted. 5201 Shaw (phone: 772-5958).

Nantucket Cove Fresh seafood in the Midwest? At this fashionable Clayton eatery with cozy New England–style decor, Maine lobster, swordfish, red snapper, and other delicious catches are flown in daily. Reservations advised. Major credit cards accepted. 101 S. Hanley at Carondelet (phone: 726-4900).

Painted Plates Since it opened in 1993, this casual yet sophisticated restaurant has been recognized by *Bon Appetit* magazine and other national observers of the culinary scene. Its "New American" fare offers interesting twists on comfort-food classic. Seasoned fried chicken with sage gravy and meat loaf with garlic mashed potatoes are favorites. Dinner only. Closed Sundays through Tuesdays. Reservations advised. Major credit cards accepted. Delmar and Eastgate (phone: 725-6565).

Tony's According to the *Wall Street Journal,* owner Vince Bommarito is the Vince Lombardi of the restaurant world—a stickler for detail and a perfectionist. What began as a spaghetti house in 1949 has grown into a nationally acclaimed first-rate Italian eatery, long a contender for "best in town." Open for dinner only; closed Sundays and Mondays. Reservations strongly advised; weekends can fill up a month in advance. Major credit cards accepted. 410 Market St. (phone: 231-7007).

MODERATE

Busch's Grove Solidly American and owned by the same family since the 1890s, this clublike county landmark is a great place for prime ribs and chicken. Weather permitting, sit outdoors under the cabaña. Closed Sundays and Mondays. Reservations necessary. Major credit cards accepted. 9160 Clayton at Price Rd. (phone: 993-0011).

Café Zoe The decor at this informal and trendy spot suggests Southern California, and the menu lists contemporary versions of classic American seafood and pasta dishes. Risotto, prepared a different way every day, is the specialty. Closed Sundays. Reservations advised. Major credit cards accepted. 12 N. Meramec (phone: 725-5554).

Cardwell's Here, seasonal dishes are served in an atmosphere of relaxed elegance. Specialties include meat grilled over pecan wood, and mouth-watering pasta. There is a daily happy hour with complimentary hors d'oeuvres. Reservations advised. Major credit cards accepted. 8100 Maryland, in the suburb of Clayton (phone: 997-8885).

INEXPENSIVE

Cunetto's House of Pasta Located on the Hill, where everything Italian prospers, and where the heart and soul of good food is pasta, this place serves it hot, fresh, and in a variety of styles. The menu also lists veal, steaks, and other Italian specialties. Closed Sundays; dinner only on Saturdays. No reservations for dinner. Major credit cards accepted. 5453 Magnolia (phone: 781-1135).

Riddles Penultimate Café Modern American cooking with a dash of Cajun and an emphasis on fresh, locally grown ingredients are the hallmarks of this casual, imaginative eatery located in the University Loop. Some people make a meal of the unusual appetizers (everything from wild mushroom caps and smoked trout to focaccia bread with goat cheese and black olive pesto). Open for dinner only; closed Mondays. Reservations advised on weekends. Major credit cards accepted. 6307 Delmar in University City (phone: 725-6985).

St. Louis Brewery, Inc. Taproom The production of beer and ale is the backdrop at this brew pub near *Union Station*, but the food goes well beyond standard pub fare. From the goat-cheese rarebit to the popular beer-battered fish and fresh-cut fries, the emphasis is on quality ingredients and preparation. Ten beers and ales, all made on-site, are on tap; selections vary seasonally. Missouri wines also are served. Reservations unnecessary. Major credit cards accepted. 21st St. between Olive and Locust (phone: 241-2337).

Salt Lake City

Salt Lake City was born when two mighty forces, history and geology, came together. For both residents and visitors, it was a fortuitous cosmic collision. This kind of epic overview has particular appeal for residents of this gleaming oasis, since Salt Lake City is the headquarters of the Church of Jesus Christ of Latter-Day Saints (better known as Mormons). Members of this church believe in divine revelation, and they believe God was guiding Brigham Young when he led the persecuted, desperately weary Mormons here across 1,000 miles of prairie and mountains in search of refuge. When they arrived, Salt Lake City was barren desert; its transformation into a habitable city was the Mormons' major task, and their history is the area's legacy.

Although the church tries to keep a low profile, evidence of its influence is everywhere. All the streets, for example, begin at the center point of Temple Square, according to the plan ordered by Brigham Young in 1847. Following the vision of Mormon prophet Joseph Smith, Young designed the city so its wide streets and tree-lined boulevards would be its most prominent features. His foresight has stood the test of time, although the home of the Mormon pilgrims, like most other places, has yielded somewhat to the tyranny of progress. The face of Salt Lake City has changed; Main Street has been redesigned with sparkling fountains, patterned sidewalks, new trees, and flower planters. Buildings like the *Delta Center,* the *Convention Center,* and *ZCMI* and *Crossroads* malls have transformed other formerly run-down areas. The *Salt Palace*'s squat dome has been replaced by a new $85-million structure, enhancing downtown Salt Lake City's sophisticated ambience. Still, some delightful old Victorian mansions remain, while portions of others have been relocated to *Trolley Square,* a shopping center patterned after San Francisco's *Ghirardelli Square.*

The excitement is palpable as Salt Lake City, Utah's largest metropolis, gears up to host the 2002 *Winter Olympics.* Game venues will include nearby ski areas and a new skating oval. The city has a population in excess of 168,000; over 900,000 more live in the larger Wasatch Front metropolitan district, nestled between the mountains to the east, the Great Salt Lake, and its desert to the west.

Utah—and Salt Lake City—lead the West in economic growth. Not to be overlooked is that the city's Mormon dominance is being diluted by a strong influx of new residents. Ethnic communities also exert cultural influences. The *Guadalupe Center* is the base for the area's Mexican-Americans, and Japanese and Greek communities also contribute to the city's eclectic flavor.

The city itself is arid (with an average annual rainfall of only 16 inches), but the nearby 11,500-foot mountains are a different story: They get about 450 inches of snow per year, which makes for terrific skiing. The peaks at the region's eight ski areas become covered with a fine powder that reaches depths of more than 100 inches. The hottest ski area these days is *Park City,* an old mining town about 30 minutes from the airport along I-80. *Deer Valley, Snowbird,* and *Alta* are world class resorts as well. The building of the brand-new *Winter Sports Park,* just off I-80 on the Park City exit, was financed by Utah taxpayers as the site of the 2002 *Winter Olympics. US Olympic* athletes and others train year-round on the park's eight ski jumps and state-of-the-art freestyle jumping pool. Spectators are welcome, and you can even try out the ski jumps if you're brave enough. In addition, a $17-million-plus bobsled-luge run is now under construction.

An attractive, well-organized city of good-natured people should be enticing enough for these qualities alone, without the added incentive of the Great Salt Lake, without which nothing would be the same. Swimming in its briny, warm water is as much a part of the Salt Lake City experience as getting immersed in its architecture and attractions. This city is unquestionably a splendid collaboration of nature and civilization, with idealistic, independent residents who refuse to accept the notion that kindness and what we commonly refer to as progress are mutually exclusive.

Salt Lake City At-a-Glance

SEEING THE CITY

For a panoramic view, go to the top of Capitol Hill, where you can look out over the entire city.

SPECIAL PLACES

Salt Lake City's grid pattern is simplicity itself. Everything radiates from Temple Square. For example: 18 blocks south is 18th South, five blocks west is Fifth West. Most of the city's attractions are within walking distance of the square, except for the lake and the university.

CENTRAL CITY

TEMPLE SQUARE The logical place to start a tour of the city is the heart of the worldwide Mormon church. The 10-acre grounds draw about four million visitors a year. Enclosed behind a 15-foot wall are the granite *Salt Lake Temple,* which took 40 years to build; the dome-shaped, acoustically perfect *Tabernacle,* home of the *Mormon Tabernacle Choir;* and an information center, where you can join any one of many free, daily guided tours.

FAMILY HISTORY LIBRARY It houses the world's largest genealogical collection, parish registers, and biographies; the friendly staff will be glad to help you search for your ancestors. Closed Sundays. No admission charge. 35 N. West Temple (phone: 240-2331).

MUSEUM OF CHURCH HISTORY AND ART This building houses art exhibits and Mormon memorabilia. Open daily. No admission charge. 45 N. West Temple (phone: 240-3310).

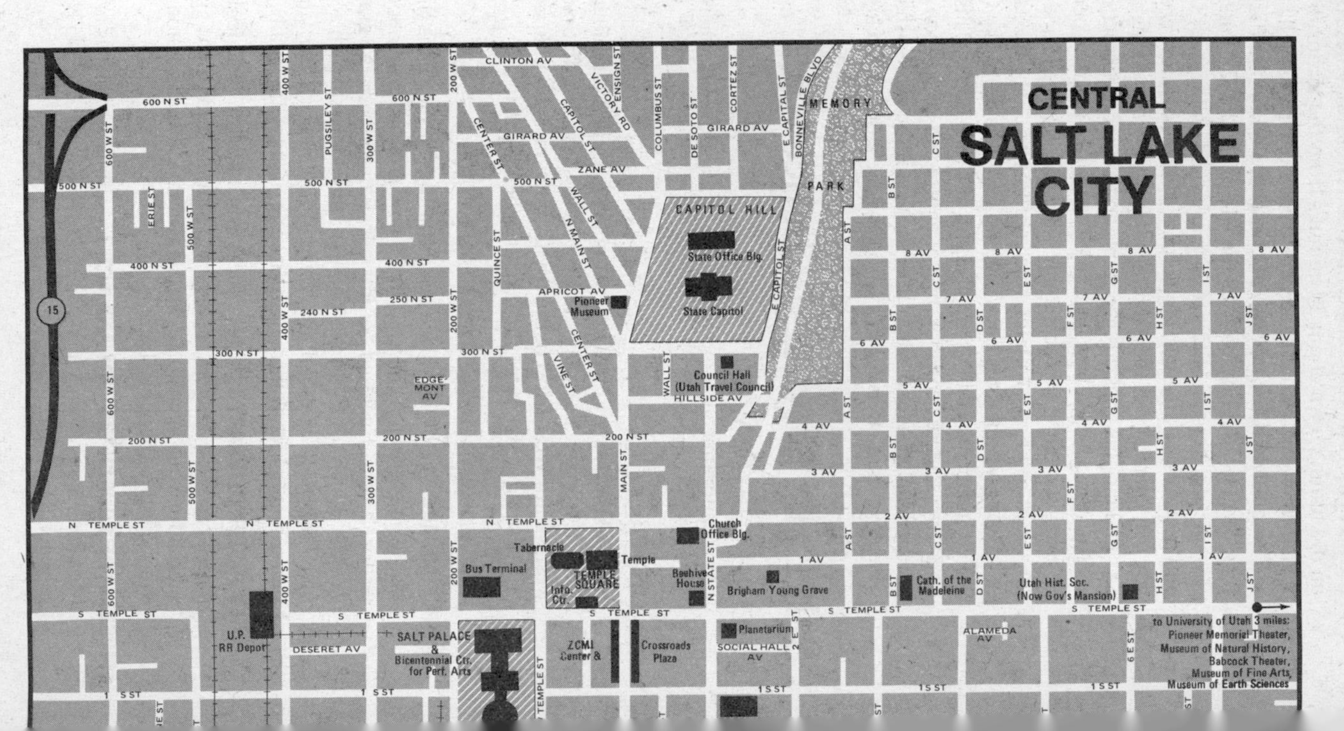
CENTRAL
SALT LAKE
CITY
MEMORY
PARK
CAPITOL HILL
State Office Blg.
State Capitol
Pioneer Museum
Council Hall (Utah Travel Council)
Church Office Blg.
Tabernacle
Temple
TEMPLE SQUARE
Info. Ctr.
Beehive House
Brigham Young Grave
Bus Terminal
Planetarium
ZCMI Center &
Crossroads Plaza
SALT PALACE & Bicentennial Ctr. for Perf. Arts
U.P. RR Depot
Cath. of the Madeleine
Utah Hist. Soc. (Now Gov's Mansion)
to University of Utah 3 miles: Pioneer Memorial Theater, Museum of Natural History, Babcock Theater, Museum of Fine Arts, Museum of Earth Sciences
CLINTON AV
VICTORY RD
ENSIGN ST
CAPITOL ST
COLUMBUS ST
DE SOTO ST
CORTEZ ST
GIRARD AV
E CAPITAL ST
BONNEVILLE BLVD
ZANE AV
CENTER ST
WALL ST
N MAIN ST
QUINCE ST
APRICOT AV
VINE ST
HILLSIDE AV
EDGE-MONT AV
PUGSLEY ST
ERIE ST
600 N ST
500 N ST
400 N ST
250 N ST
240 N ST
300 N ST
200 N ST
N TEMPLE ST
S TEMPLE ST
DESERET AV
1 S ST
600 W ST
500 W ST
400 W ST
300 W ST
200 W ST
MAIN ST
N STATE ST
2 E ST
SOCIAL HALL AV
ALAMEDA AV
6 E ST
A ST
B ST
C ST
D ST
E ST
F ST
G ST
H ST
I ST
J ST
1 AV
2 AV
3 AV
4 AV
5 AV
6 AV
7 AV
8 AV
15

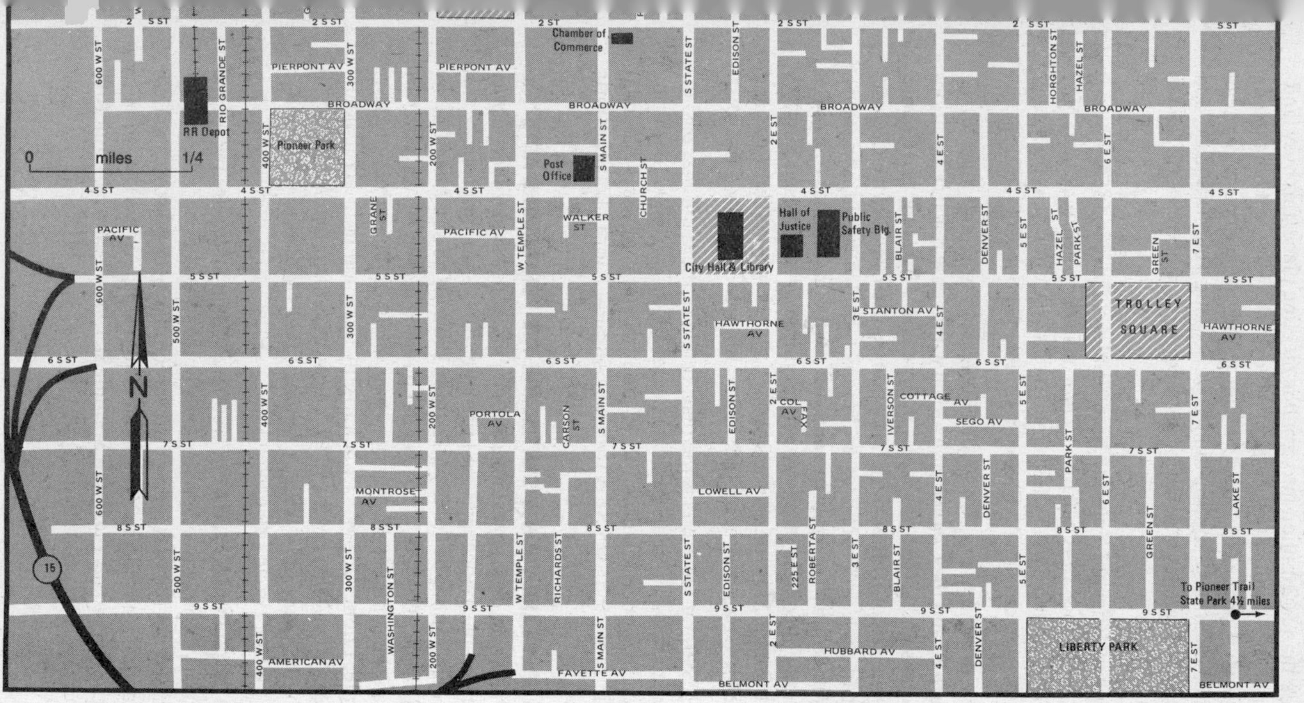

Chamber of Commerce
Post Office
RR Depot
Pioneer Park
City Hall & Library
Hall of Justice
Public Safety Blg.
TROLLEY SQUARE
LIBERTY PARK
To Pioneer Trail State Park 4½ miles
0 miles 1/4
N
15
2 S ST
4 S ST
5 S ST
6 S ST
7 S ST
8 S ST
9 S ST
BROADWAY
PIERPONT AV
PACIFIC AV
HAWTHORNE AV
STANTON AV
COTTAGE AV
SEGO AV
COL FAX AV
PORTOLA AV
CARSON ST
MONTROSE AV
LOWELL AV
HUBBARD AV
AMERICAN AV
FAYETTE AV
BELMONT AV
WALKER ST
GRANE ST
600 W ST
500 W ST
400 W ST
300 W ST
200 W ST
RIO GRANDE ST
WASHINGTON ST
W TEMPLE ST
RICHARDS ST
S MAIN ST
CHURCH ST
S STATE ST
EDISON ST
2 E ST
225 E ST
ROBERTA ST
3 E ST
IVERSON ST
BLAIR ST
4 E ST
DENVER ST
5 E ST
HORGHTON ST
HAZEL ST
PARK ST
6 E ST
GREEN ST
7 E ST
LAKE ST

JOSEPH SMITH MEMORIAL BUILDING Formerly the *Hotel Utah,* now renovated at a cost of more than $42 million into a public meeting place, this busy landmark is ornately beautiful in the grand pre-World War I style. Outstanding features are free showings of *Legacy,* a film telling the pioneer story (call 240-3893 for reservations), rooftop dining overlooking Temple Square, and computer-assisted searches of genealogical records. Corner of South Temple and Main Sts.

BEEHIVE HOUSE Built by Brigham Young as his official residence in 1854, it is now a museum run by the church. Closed *Thanksgiving, Christmas,* and *New Year's Day.* The patriarch himself is buried half a block northeast in a quiet park. No admission charge. 67 E. South Temple (phone: 240-2671).

CAPITOL HILL The Corinthian-style *Capitol Building* of granite and marble, the *Pioneers Museum,* and the *Council Hall* are all within easy reach. Exhibitions of Utah products and art are on display in the *Capitol Building;* the *Council Hall,* across the street to the south, now houses the *Utah Travel Council,* where you can pick up brochures and maps (see *Tourist Information*). *Daughters of the Utah Pioneers Museum,* west of the *Capitol,* has one of the most complete collections of pioneer relics in the West. Closed Sundays September through May, on major holidays, and between *Christmas* and *New Year's Day.* Donations accepted. 300 N. Main St. (phone: 538-1050).

DELTA CENTER This $90-million arena is the playground of the Utah *Jazz* basketball team. In addition, it treats capacity crowds of up to 20,000 to touring concerts and other performances. 301 W. South Temple (phone: 325-2000 for general information; 325-SEAT or 800-358-SEAT for tickets to sports and concerts).

SALT PALACE AND SALT LAKE COUNTY CENTER FOR THE PERFORMING ARTS The hub of downtown activity, sparkling new *Salt Palace and Convention Center* (100 S. West Temple; phone: 363-7681 or 534-6370) hosts a variety of events, from major conventions to home and garden shows. The *Salt Lake County Arts Center* (phone: 328-4201), a triangular building displaying traveling art exhibits, is on the same block. *Maurice Abravanel Symphony Hall* (123 W. South Temple; phone: 533-6683), beautifully designed both acoustically and architecturally, is also here, and a block away is the *Capitol Theater* (50 W. 200th South; phone: 355-ARTS), home of *Ballet West* and other dance groups and touring Broadway productions.

ZCMI CENTER AND CROSSROADS PLAZA Off tree-lined Main Street are two of the largest downtown covered shopping malls in the West. The *ZCMI Center* (15 S. Main St.), on the east side of the street, has over 60 stores and 20 fast-food stands clustered around a main dining area. Across the street to the west is the *Crossroads Plaza* (18 S. Main St.) with 70 stores, numerous theaters, and fast-food eateries.

MID-CITY

SOUTH TEMPLE Start at the beautifully restored *Cathedral of the Madeleine* (331 E. South Temple), a Roman Gothic church completed in 1909, featuring lovely German stained glass windows. Farther along the street are dozens of exquisite turn-of-the-century mansions.

TROLLEY SQUARE In 1972, in a project that garnered national acclaim, several old, abandoned trolley barns were ingeniously transformed into a collection of shops, theaters, restaurants, and boutiques using architectural components from historic structures throughout the city. Fifth S. and Seventh E. Sts. (phone: 521-9877).

LIBERTY PARK Three blocks south of *Trolley Square* on Seventh East is 80-acre *Liberty Park,* with bowers, picnic areas, tennis and horseshoe courts, a pond, a playground, the *Tracy Aviary,* an amusement park, and a boating center. Between Ninth and 13th S., and Fifth and Seventh E. Sts. (phone: 972-6714).

ELSEWHERE

THIS IS THE PLACE STATE PARK Presently undergoing major renovations, with the addition of numerous pioneer buildings and a new visitors center, this is where Brigham Young first caught a glimpse of the Valley of the Great Salt Lake and said, "This is the Place." The park contains *Old Deseret Village,* some two dozen renovated pioneer buildings including *Brigham Young Farm Home, This Is The Place Monument,* and a handsome new visitors' center with an audiovisual exhibit showing the Mormon trek from Illinois to Utah. Grounds open daily, attractions closed Mondays. Tours of *Old Deseret Village* are given during the summer. Admission charge. Wagon rides are included; chuck wagon dinner. Emigration Canyon, 2601 Sunnyside Ave. (phone: 584-8391)

HOGLE ZOOLOGICAL GARDENS Across from *Pioneer Trail State Park,* this 50-acre zoo draws about 790,000 visitors a year. About half of the 1,300 animals are housed outdoors in simulated natural surroundings. Other exhibits include *Discovery Land,* with a nursery for young animals, hands-on displays, and animals from various climates. Closed *Christmas* and *New Year's.* No admission charge for children under three. 2600 Sunnyside Ave. (phone: 582-1631).

GREAT SALT LAKE A popular tourist attraction, this marshy, salty, 73-mile-long lake is the most important natural feature of the region. Although the rising waters have diluted the salt concentration over the years, floating on these briny waters is still a unique experience. Showers, food, and sailboat and paddleboat rentals are available. (For more information, see *Great Salt Lake, Utah,* DIRECTIONS.) 17 miles west on US 40, I-80.

EXTRA SPECIAL

One of the busiest forests in the country, the 848,000-acre *Wasatch National Forest* contains the *High Uintas Primitive Area,* full of mountain lakes, rugged spruce, dramatic canyons, and mountain peaks as high as 13,400 feet; a winter elk feeding ground at *Hardware Ranch* in Logan (phone: 245-3131); and camping and picnic grounds at Little Cottonwood and Big Cottonwood Canyons (picnicking only at Mill Creek). Call the *Salt Lake Ranger District* for information (phone: 943-1794). Trout fishing is excellent, and deer and elk can be hunted in the fall; for details, call the *Utah Division of Wildlife Resources* (phone: 538-4700 for general information; 596-8660 for recorded fishing, wildlife viewing, and hunting information). In winter, skiers flock to *Alta,* 25 miles southeast of the city on Route 210; *Brighton,* 27 miles southeast on Route 152; and *Snowbird,* in Gad Valley, 2 miles from *Alta* (see *Sports*). To get to the eastern section of *Wasatch,* take US 40 and Routes 152 and 210; to reach the northern part, follow US 89 and 91. For further information, contact the Supervisor's Office, *Wasatch-Cache National Forests* (125 S. State St., Salt Lake City, UT 84138; phone: 524-5030 for campground information; 364-1581 for avalanche information).

Sources and Resources

TOURIST INFORMATION

Brochures and maps are available through the *Salt Lake County Convention and Visitors Bureau* (180 S. West Temple, Salt Lake City, UT 84101; phone: 521-2822), which is closed Sundays except during the summer. Information centers also are at *Salt Lake City International Airport* and *Great Salt Lake State Park.* Contact the *Utah Travel Council* (*Council Hall,* Capitol Hill, Salt Lake City, UT 84114; phone: 538-1030) for city and state information. For information on winter skiing and summer recreation, call 521-8102. For current road conditions, call 964-6000. Contact the Utah state tourism hotline (801-538-1030) for maps, calendars of events, and travel packets.

LOCAL COVERAGE *Salt Lake Tribune,* morning daily; *Deseret News,* evening daily; *Salt Lake City,* bimonthly magazine. The *Salt Lake Visitor's Guide,* a free magazine available from the convention and visitors bureau, is the best city reference guide.

TELEVISION STATIONS KUTV Channel 2–CBS; KTVX Channel 4–ABC; KSL Channel 5–NBC; KUED Channel 7–PBS; KBYU Channel 11–PBS; KSTU Channel 13–Fox; KJZZ Channel 14–Independent; and KOOG Channel 30–Independent.

RADIO STATIONS AM: KALL 910 (adult contemporary); KSL 1160 (CBS news/talk); KSOP 1370 (country); and KSUN 1490 (news/talk). FM: KUER 90.1 (NPR, classical); KISN 97.1 (adult contemporary); KCPX 98.7 (Top 40); and KSOP 104.3 (country).

TELEPHONE The area code for all of Utah is 801.

SALES TAX The sales tax is 6.25%; the hotel room tax is 3%.

CLIMATE Wintertime is for skiing. Spring is beautiful but fickle, with apricot blossoms sometimes covered in snow. Summer is hot and dry, with temperatures in the 90s F and above. Fall is gorgeous, especially in the nearby canyons.

GETTING AROUND

AIRPORT *Salt Lake City International Airport* is a 15- to 20-minute ride from downtown. *Utah Transit Authority* buses run hourly from airport terminals into the city center for 65¢. Special *Downtowner* buses run from the airport to downtown hotels on a regular basis.

BUS For information on schedules in and around Salt Lake, call *Utah Transit Authority* (phone: 287-4636). The fare is 65¢. There is a free fare zone downtown; consult any bus map for details.

CAR RENTAL All major firms are represented. An inexpensive local alternative is *Payless Car Rental* (1974 W. North Temple; phone: 596-2596; 800-327-3631).

HORSE-DRAWN CARRIAGES Carriages will pick up customers anywhere in the downtown area. Contact *Carriage Connection,* 428 W. 200 North (phone: 363-8687).

TAXI The best way to get a cab is to call *Yellow Cab* (phone: 521-2100) or *Ute Cab* (phone: 359-7788).

TROLLEY In the summer months, an old-fashioned trolley circles the downtown area and major hotels, with pick-up points at Trolley Square and Temple Square. Fare is 65¢. Contact the *Utah Transit Authority* (phone: 287-4636).

SPECIAL EVENTS

In May, a huge multi-cultural festival takes place on *Washington Square,* site of the magnificently restored *Renaissance-Revival City.* On July 24, a huge parade and other events mark *Pioneer Day,* celebrating the arrival of the Mormon pioneers. Also in July, the *Japanese Obon Festival* is held at the Buddhist temple (211 W. First South). In September, the *Greek Festival* takes place at the Hellenic Memorial Building (279 S. 300 West). For information on other special events, call 521-2868.

MUSEUMS

In addition to those described in *Special Places,* Salt Lake City has a number of museums worthy of note.

HANSEN PLANETARIUM Exhibitions on astronomy and natural sciences, along with laser and star shows. Open daily. Admission charge. 15 S. State St. (phone: 538-2104).

MUSEUM OF CHURCH HISTORY AND ART Features exhibits on the heritage of the Mormons, including paintings, artifacts, and rare documents dating from 1820 to the present. Open daily. No admission charge. 45 N. West Temple (phone: 240-3310).

SALT LAKE ARTS CENTER Traveling exhibits of works by regional and national artists in a sculpture court and two bi-level galleries. Closed Mondays. No admission charge. 20 S. West Temple (phone: 328-4201).

UTAH MUSEUM OF FINE ARTS The only public art gallery in the state, featuring American and European art from the 17th century to the present, as well as some ancient Egyptian pieces. Open daily. No admission charge. On the *University of Utah* campus (phone: 581-7332).

UTAH MUSEUM OF NATURAL HISTORY Dinosaur bones, dioramas on the Great Basin area, and displays of minerals and rock paintings. Open daily. Admission charge. On the *University of Utah* campus (phone: 581-6927).

SHOPPING

Salt Lake City has its share of today's marketplaces, malls filled with department stores, chain shops, eateries, and entertainment. Enclaves of commerce with more individuality, however, also are easy to come by—and get to. Museum shops are an excellent source of quality gifts and mementos.

SPORTS AND FITNESS

BASEBALL The Triple A Salt Lake *Buzz* play from mid-April through *Labor Day* at the new *Franklin Quest Field* (65 W. 1300 South; phone: 485-3800).

BASKETBALL The *NBA* Utah *Jazz* play at the *Delta Center* (301 W. South Temple; phone: 325-SEAT; 800-358-SEAT). Tickets usually sell out quickly, so try to reserve well in advance.

FITNESS CENTERS The *Deseret Gym* (161 N. Main; phone: 359-3911) has a pool, sauna, steamroom, track, Nautilus exercise rooms, plus basketball, racquetball, and squash courts. It is open to the public for a fee.

GOLF There are eight public courses in the Salt Lake Valley. The best is *Mountain Dell* (Parley's Canyon; phone: 582-3812).

ICE SKATING AND SLEIGH RIDING Skate at *Bountiful Recreation Center* (150 W. Sixth North, Bountiful; phone: 298-6120) year-round, or at *Triad Center* outdoor ice rink (350 W. South Temple; phone: 575-5423) or the *John W. Gallivan Plaza* (Second South and State Sts.) during the winter. Visit *Sugarhouse Park* (21 S. 16th East; phone: 467-1721) for sledding.

JOGGING Run in *Memory Grove Park,* half a mile from downtown, or in *Liberty Park* (1-mile perimeter), about 2 miles from downtown.

SKIING Utah claims to have the "Greatest Snow on Earth," and downhill and cross-country skiers from all over the world enthusiastically attest to the excellence of the ski conditions here. The season runs from mid-November through April or May. For a ski report, call 521-8102. For details on the major ski resorts within half an hour's drive of Salt Lake City (*Alta, Deer Valley, Park City, Snowbird,* and *Sundance*), see *Downhill Skiing* in DIVERSIONS. Other local favorites include *Brighton* (at the top of Big Cottonwood Canyon, 27 miles southeast of Salt Lake City on Rte. 152; phone: 943-8309), with an average annual snowfall of 430 inches; *Solitude,* also in Big Cottonwood Canyon (phone: 534-1400); and *Wolf Mountain,* located 3 miles from *Park City* (east of Salt Lake City on I-80; phone: 649-5400).

SWIMMING Beaches are open at the Great Salt Lake (take I-80 west of town). For freshwater swimming try *Raging Waters* (1200 W. 1700 South; phone: 973-9900), a huge aquatic park with 40 water attractions, picnic areas, arcades, and gift shops. Closed September through May.

TENNIS There are 17 parks in the city with tennis courts. The most popular are the 16 courts (14 lighted) at *Liberty Park.* Lessons are available spring and summer only (phone: 596-5036). The *University of Utah* has quite a few outdoor public courts.

THE CALL OF THE WILD

At *Wasatch-Cache National Forest* (phone: 524-5030), you can fish, hunt, camp, and backpack (see *Extra Special*). For hunting and fishing regulations, contact the *Utah Division of Wildlife Resources* (1596 W. North Temple; phone: 596-8660). For information on backpacking, river running, and primitive wilderness areas in general, call the *Bureau of Land Management Office of Public Affairs* (324 S. State St.; phone: 539-4001).

THEATER

The *Pioneer Theater Company* on the *University of Utah* campus is an important regional theater. The *Babcock Theater,* in the same building, stages more intimate productions (phone: 581-6961 for both). Downtown, the *Salt Lake Acting Company* (168 W. 500 North; phone: 363-7522) produces lively drama. *Salt Lake Repertory Theatre* (688 S. State St.; phone: 532-6000) performs musicals. *Ballet West, Ririe-Woodbury Dance Company, Repertory Dance Theater,* and touring Broadway shows appear at the *Capitol Theater* (phone: 355-ARTS for tickets). Check local listings for other groups.

MUSIC

Salt Lake City has many concerts. For information, call 521-2868 or 325-7328. The *Mormon Tabernacle Choir*'s rehearsals on Thursdays at 8 PM are free and open to the public, as are its Sunday morning performances, which are broadcast nationally on radio and television. If you're planning to attend the Sunday program, show up by 9:15 AM. Recitals on the great *Tabernacle* organ are given daily. *The Mormon Youth Symphony* presents free mini-concerts on Tuesdays at 8 PM; the *Mormon Youth Chorus* performs similar programs at the same time on Wednesdays. All of these events take place at Temple Square (phone: 240-4872). The *Utah Symphony Orchestra* performs at *Maurice Abravanel Symphony Hall* (123 W. South Temple; phone 533-6407). Big-name rock and country artists take the stage at the *Delta Center* (301 W. South Temple; phone: 325-SEAT; 800-358-SEAT).

NIGHTCLUBS AND NIGHTLIFE

Room at the Top in the *Salt Lake Hilton* (150 W. Fifth South; phone: 532-3344) has a piano bar and fine food. The *Zephyr* (301 S. West Temple; phone: 355-2582) features blues and rock music. More comfortable but less trendy is Salt Lake City's oldest private club, *D. B. Cooper's* (19 E. 200 South; phone: 532-2948). Utah liquor laws require that you buy a two-week membership ($5) for clubs; you may bring up to five friends.

Best in Town

CHECKING IN

More than 10 million people a year visit Utah, making tourism the state's largest industry. Accommodations are plentiful and varied. Most of Salt Lake City's major hotels have complete facilities for the business traveler. Those listed below as having "business services" usually offer such conveniences as meeting rooms, photocopiers, computers, translation services, and express checkout, among others. Call the individual hotel for additional information. Expect to pay between $80 and $130 per night for a double room at those places listed as expensive; and between $55 and $70 at those categorized as moderate; there are no exceptional inexpensive hotels in the city. Unless otherwise noted, hotels have air conditioning, private baths, TV sets, and telephones.

All hotels below are in Salt Lake City and telephone and fax numbers are in the 801 area code unless otherwise indicated.

EXPENSIVE

Inn at Temple Square This place has a posh, old English atmosphere. Meals are served in the *Carriage Court* restaurant (see *Eating Out*), and there is a complimentary breakfast buffet. Its 90 rooms are equipped with refrigerators, and suites come with Jacuzzis in oversize tubs. An ice-cream parlor located downstairs is a perfect spot for a snack. No liquor, wine, or beer is served on the premises. Room service is available until 10 PM. Other conveniences include a free airport shuttle and business services. 71 W. South Temple (phone: 531-1000; 800-843-4668; fax: 536-7272).

Little America On the city's main thoroughfare, within walking distance of downtown shopping and the *Convention Center,* this 850-room hotel covers an entire block. Accommodations range from luxury tower suites to garden-view rooms to less expensive motel units. It has year-round swimming in an indoor-outdoor pool, plus an outdoor pool, saunas, a Jacuzzi, and an exercise center. Children under 12 stay free. Room service is available until midnight. Other amenities include a concierge desk, free bus service to the airport, and business services. 500 S. Main St. (phone: 363-6781; 800-453-9450; fax: 596-5911).

Red Lion A sophisticated hostelry convenient to downtown attractions, it offers 500 rooms, an indoor/outdoor pool, and an exercise room. The 18th-floor Executive Level provides guests with a complimentary continental breakfast and afternoon refreshments. In addition, there are two restaurants serving American fare, including the elegant *Maxi's.* Business services are available. 255 SW Temple (phone: 328-2000; 800-547-8010; fax: 532-1953).

Salt Lake Marriott With 515 rooms, it has two restaurants, a lounge, an indoor-outdoor pool, saunas, and direct access to *Crossroads Plaza.* Guests have privileges at an adjoining health spa. Room service is available until midnight. Other amenities include a concierge and business services. The 16-story structure is opposite the *Salt Palace* on the corner of West Temple and First South (phone: 531-0800; 800-228-9290; fax: 532-4127).

MODERATE

Comfort Inn–Salt Lake Airport/International Center Conveniently located 7 miles from downtown and 2 miles from the airport, it has 152 rooms (some of which are nonsmoking). Other features: a heated pool (open in season), a hot tub, a 24-hour restaurant, and complimentary morning coffee in the lobby. Room service is available until 10 PM. Business services and an airport shuttle are also offered. 200 N. Admiral Byrd Rd. (phone: 537-7444; 800-535-8742; fax: 532-4721).

Peery The city's oldest hotel, it is small (just 77 rooms) but elegant, with the charm of the early 1900s. Amenities include a restaurant, complimentary continental breakfast, newspaper, shoeshine, a Jacuzzi, a tanning salon, and an exercise room. Room service is available until 10:30 PM. Other amenities include a concierge, business services, and free airport transportation. 110 W. Third South (phone: 521-4300; 800-331-0073; fax: 575-5014).

EATING OUT

Salt Lake Valley restaurants offer a variety of cuisines. In a major concession to the tourist trade, Utah's liquor laws were revised a few years ago. The old practice of "brown bagging," where customers brought their own alcohol to a restaurant, has been eliminated; twice as many restaurants now have liquor licenses, and drinks are served after 1 PM. Expect to pay $80 or more for dinner for two at the restaurant listed as very expensive; between $40 and $50 at those places listed as expensive; between $20 and $40 at places designated as moderate; and less than $20 at inexpensive places. Prices do not include drinks, wine, tax, or tips. All restaurants are in the 801 area code.

Unless otherwise noted, restaurants are open for lunch and dinner.

VERY EXPENSIVE

La Caille at Quail Run One of Utah's finest dining spots, it occupies a building that resembles a French country house; the dining room overlooks formal gardens. The French menu is as inspired as the atmosphere. Although the prices are high, the quality of the fare and the ambience make it worthwhile. Open for dinner only Mondays through Saturdays; brunch only on Sundays. Reservations advised. Major credit cards accepted. 9565 Wasatch Blvd. (phone: 942-1751).

EXPENSIVE

Chart House This member of the popular upscale chain is located in an elegant Victorian mansion, where small rooms offer intimate dining. The extensive menu includes hand-cut steaks, fresh seafood, and prime ribs. Open daily for dinner. Reservations advised. Major credit cards accepted. 334 W. South Temple (phone: 596-0990).

MODERATE

Cedars of Lebanon A favorite among locals for over 15 years, this exciting eatery serves exceptional Middle East cuisine. For added enjoyment, belly dancers on weekends. Reservations suggested. Major credit cards accepted. 152 E. 200th St. (phone: 364-4096).

Lamb's The oldest restaurant in Utah, open since the early 1900s, this downtown institution is where the city's power brokers power lunch. The extensive menu includes such hearty favorites as stews and puddings. Closed Sundays. Reservations unnecessary. Major credit cards accepted. 169 S. Main St. (phone: 364-7166).

Market Street Grill A popular gathering spot, especially at lunchtime, it's in a handsomely renovated old building. The menu features fresh seafood (flown in daily) as well as steaks, prime ribs, and lamb. There's also an oyster bar that serves liquor (but you must buy a membership for $5). No reservations. Major credit cards accepted. 60 Post Office Pl. (phone: 322-4668; 531-6044, oyster bar).

INEXPENSIVE

Marianne's Delicatessen The menu features German specialties, from homemade sausages to scrumptious desserts. There are daily specials and a long list of sandwiches as well as a deli that is open all day. Be prepared to wait if you arrive between noon and 1 PM. Open for lunch only; closed Sundays and Mondays. No reservations. Major credit cards accepted. 149 W. Second South (phone: 364-0513).

Old Spaghetti Factory One of the more popular eating places in town, it has lots of friendly ambience. You may find yourself dining on an old brass bed or in a trolley car with turn-of-the-century furnishings. Be sure to try the clam sauce with your spaghetti. No reservations. Major credit cards accepted. 189 Trolley Sq. (phone: 521-0424).

San Antonio

More than 300 years ago, Father Massenett, a Franciscan friar, came across a tiny Indian village along the banks of a river in what then was solid Spanish territory. Because his discovery took place on the feast day of Saint Anthony, the spiritual traveler called the village San Antonio. It wasn't until 1718, when Spanish missionaries came to convert the Indians, that the first permanent colony and the *San Antonio de Valero Mission*—better known as the *Alamo*—were established.

Over the next several centuries, that sleepy village emerged into what is today the nation's 10th-largest city, boasting 1.3 million residents. Happily, the old San Antonio, with its classic Spanish missions and rustic adobe buildings, has not been lost among the steel skyscrapers and fancy hotels. The *Alamo*—the Spanish word for "cottonwood"—attracts hundreds of thousands of visitors annually, most of whom come to relive Texas's struggle for independence from Mexico. Inside the Texas shrine, memories of the 1836 Battle of the *Alamo* spring to life. Visitors are reminded of the 189 *Alamo* defenders who fought for 13 days until they were overrun and killed on March 6, 1836, by Mexican general Santa Anna's huge army. But their efforts were not in vain. Just a few weeks later (at the Battle of San Jacinto), Santa Anna and his army were defeated by a small Texan army, a victory that led to Texas's independence.

Thousands of pioneers from around the world were drawn to Texas during its early days, and many ethnic groups remain today. Mexican-Americans, who make up over half of the city's total population, have gained political clout and influence in recent years. Beyond this mix of cultures, however, lies a great economic disparity: Posh suburbs rub shoulders with deep pockets of poverty.

Military tradition runs deep here, and provides jobs. Teddy Roosevelt is said to have recruited his famous Rough Riders in the bar of the *Menger* hotel. Several aviation "firsts" were established at *Fort Sam Houston* in 1910, when Lieutenant Benjamin D. Foulouis reported, "My first takeoff, my first solo, my first landing, and my first crash on the same day." San Antonio's current military record is somewhat more stable. Five military installations with more than 50,000 active duty personnel and civilian employees make the federal government the city's major employer. The armed forces contribute more than $3 billion to the economy annually (though this figure is expected to drop). *Lackland Training Center* is the cradle of the *Air Force,* and *Fort Sam Houston* is home to *Brooke Army Medical Center* and the *Academy of Health Sciences,* which trains all army medical personnel. *Randolph Air Force Base,* considered one of the *Air Force*'s most beautiful, lives up to its reputation with a stately, pristine white water tower that locals call the "Taj Mahal."

The tourism and convention industry is particularly impressive these days: In 1994, it brought a little over $2 billion into San Antonio's coffers. In fact, the city has been a tourist magnet since 1968, the year it marked its 250th birthday with *HemisFair.* The celebration left behind a *Convention Center,* the *Tower of the Americas,* the *Institute of Texan Cultures,* and the *Mexican Cultural Institute,* as well as focusing attention on the city's forgotten architectural treasures. La Villita, San Antonio's oldest residential neighborhood, was restored with lovely adobe buildings. Also restored were many homes in the King William District, where the local German community lived in grandeur during the 19th century; they feature German stonemasonry as well as almost every notable style of American architecture of the past century.

The city is home to the nation's only Mexican market, and the *Old Ursuline Academy,* once a cloistered convent, houses the *Southwest Crafts Center.* San Antonio's cultural legacy also includes several offbeat museums, such as the *San Antonio Museum of Art* and the *Witte Museum.* One of the city's newer museums is *Echoes from the Past,* a collection of Elvis Presley memorabilia. *German Heritage Park* is a downtown development with restored historic German structures.

To walk on the *Paseo del Río* (the *River Walk*) is to enter a people-scale tropical paradise of banana palms and bougainvillea only steps away from apartments, shops, hotels, cafés, and San Antonio's business center. San Antonio is home to *Sea World of Texas,* the world's largest marine-life theme park, and *Fiesta Texas,* a musical theme park developed by Nashville's *Opryland USA* and San Antonio-based USAA, a major financial services company. The city is also proud of its *Alamodome,* a $182-million, state-of-the-art, multipurpose domed facility with a cable-suspended roof; the *Hyatt Hill Country* resort, its latest luxury hotel complex; and the $55-million *Retama Park* racecourse, a former polo field in Selma, just north of San Antonio. This city is truly a work-in-progress.

San Antonio At-a-Glance

SEEING THE CITY

The 750-foot *Tower of the Americas,* San Antonio's most visible landmark, offers the best vantage point from which to view the city and the surrounding countryside. From the revolving observation deck, you see flatland stretching south and gently rolling hills northwest, leading to the Texas Hill Country. Directly below are the buildings of *HemisFair Urban Water Park,* the site of the *HemisFair* in 1968, and a tributary of the San Antonio River that cuts a horseshoe path through town and branches into *HemisFair Urban Water Park* and *Rivercenter Mall.*

CENTRAL
SAN ANTONIO
San Antonio Museum Of Art
To Mc Nay Art Institute 4 miles
To Brackenridge Park 2½ miles Texas Ranger Museum, Witte Museum, Zoo
Municipal Auditorium
Travis Park
Nat. Bank of Commerce
Milam Blg
Post Office
Emily Morgan Hotel
Alamo Plaza
The Alamo
City Hall
Spanish
Columbus Park
SANTA ROSA MEDICAL CENTER
Milam Square Park
MEXICAN MERCADO
PRODUCE
ROW
San Antonio River
San Pedro Creek
PanAm Expwy
110-W
10
35
ELMIRA AV
QUINCY AV
JACKSON ST
MAIN AV
CAMDEN ST
RICHMOND AV
DALLAS ST
REYNOLDS ST
BALTIMORE AV
LEXINGTON AV
AUGUSTA ST
MCCULLOUGH AV
BROOKLYN AV
MOLINO ST
ST MARYS ST
7 ST
AVENUE B
8 ST
AVENUE A
6 ST
5 ST
4 ST
3 ST
6ST
TAYLOR ST
BROADWAY
ALAMO ST
AVENUE E
BONHAM ST
HOUSTON ST
STARR ST
BOWIE ST
ALAMO ST
CROCKETT ST
COLLEGE ST
JEFFERSON ST
NAVARRO ST
SOLEDAD ST
GIRAUD ST
FANNIN ST
CONVENT ST
MARTIN ST
PECAN ST
TRAVIS ST
SALINAS ST
FLORES ST
GALLITZEN ST
CALIFORNIA ST
KINGSBURY S.
CAMARON ST
LAREDO ST
SANTA ROSA AV
SAN SABA ST
PECOS ST
LEONA ST
MORALES ST
FRIO ST
PEREZ ST
MEDINA ST
COMMERCE ST
BUENA VISTA ST

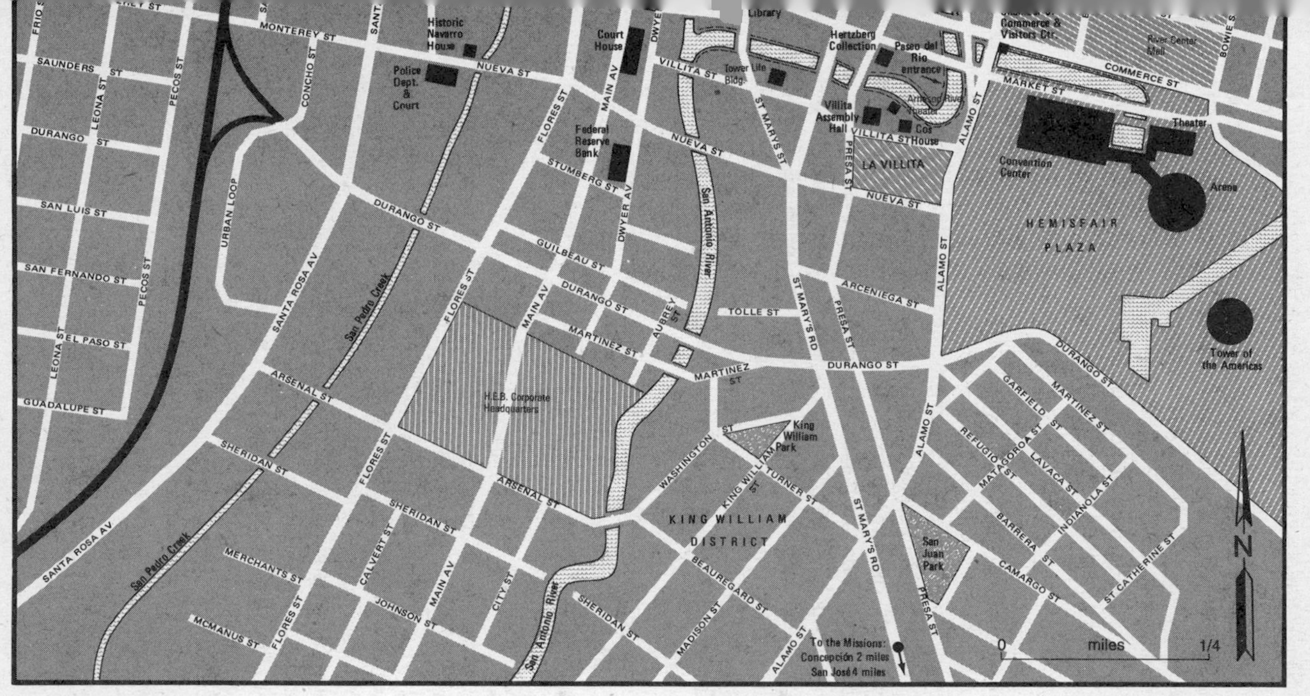

Historic Navarro House
Court House
Library
Hertzberg Collection
Paseo del Rio entrance
Commerce & Visitors Ctr.
River Center Mall
COMMERCE ST
MARKET ST
BOWIE ST
Theater
Convention Center
Arena
HEMISFAIR PLAZA
Tower of the Americas
Police Dept. & Court
Federal Reserve Bank
Tower Life Bldg
Villita Assembly Hall
Cos House
VILLITA ST
LA VILLITA
NUEVA ST
MONTEREY ST
SAUNDERS ST
LEONA ST
PECOS ST
DURANGO ST
SAN LUIS ST
SAN FERNANDO ST
EL PASO ST
GUADALUPE ST
FRIO ST
CONCHO ST
URBAN LOOP
SANTA ROSA AV
San Pedro Creek
FLORES ST
MAIN AV
DWYER AV
STUMBERG ST
GUILBEAU ST
San Antonio River
ST MARYS ST
PRESA ST
ALAMO ST
ARCENIEGA ST
TOLLE ST
ST MARY'S RD
AUBREY ST
MARTINEZ ST
H.E.B. Corporate Headquarters
ARSENAL ST
SHERIDAN ST
WASHINGTON
King William Park
KING WILLIAM ST
TURNER ST
KING WILLIAM DISTRICT
BEAUREGARD ST
MADISON ST
MERCHANTS ST
CALVERT ST
JOHNSON ST
CITY ST
MCMANUS ST
GARFIELD ST
REFUGIO ST
MATAGORDA ST
LAVACA ST
BARRERA ST
INDIANOLA ST
CAMARGO ST
ST CATHERINE ST
San Juan Park
To the Missions: Concepción 2 miles San José 4 miles
0 miles 1/4
N

SPECIAL PLACES

The heart of San Antonio is great for walking, with the lovely *Paseo del Río (River Walk)* tracing the course of the river, and short distances between many of the attractions. Visitors can also take a slow-paced, horse-drawn carriage tour of downtown and the King William District, or catch a 10¢ trolley ride between the *Alamo* and Market Square (see *Getting Around*). Jump on the trolley one block south of the *Alamo* at the corner of Commerce and Alamo Streets. Other sights, including the missions along *Mission Trail* and the zoo, are best reached by car or bus.

CENTRAL CITY

THE ALAMO Established in 1718 by Spanish priests as the *Misión San Antonio de Valero,* this is where Davy Crockett, James Bowie, William B. Travis, and 186 other Texans fought against Mexican general Santa Anna and his force of 5,000 in Texas's 1836 struggle for independence. The original mission has been restored and the site turned into a block-square state park that includes a museum with displays on the *Alamo* and Texas history as well as an excellent weapons collection featuring derringers, swords, and an original bowie knife. Open daily. No admission charge. Alamo Plaza (phone: 225-1391).

After visiting the *Alamo,* it's an easy stroll along the *Paseo del Río,* which now reaches the west side of S. Alamo Street, directly across from the park; the steps from street level are bounded by a series of waterfalls that lead to the *Hyatt* hotel.

IMAX THEATER *Alamo: The Price of Freedom,* a first-rate 45-minute docudrama, is shown on a six-foot-high screen with a six-track magnetic sound system. Viewers are drawn into the action, while learning about the history of the *Alamo.* Open daily. Admission charge. *Rivercenter Mall,* 849 E. Commerce St. (phone: 225-4629).

LA VILLITA This little Spanish town in the center of the city looks very much as it did more than 250 years ago, when it was San Antonio's first residential area. Girded by a stone wall and surrounded by banana palms and bougainvillea, the stone patios and adobe dwellings have been restored and now house artisans' shops where many of the old crafts—glass blowing, weaving, doll-making, and pottery—still are practiced. *A Night in Old San Antonio* is an annual, four-day fiesta held here in April. Among the buildings are the restored *Cos House* (1835), where General Perfecto de Cos, commander of the Mexican forces, surrendered to the Texans prior to the siege of the *Alamo.* Open daily. No admission charge. One square city block bounded by the river on the north, Nueva St. on the south, S. Alamo St. on the east, and Villita St. on the west. Main office, 418 Villita St. (phone: 299-8610 or 224-INFO).

PASEO DEL RÍO A branch of the San Antonio River winds like a horseshoe through the central business district. Stone stairways lead down to the *River Walk* which, only 20 feet below street level, is as far from the world of the business district as you can get. Tall trees, tropical foliage, and banana palms line the walks, stretching 21 blocks, dotted with curio and crafts shops, hotels, nightspots, and cafés, and an increasing number of fashionable apartments. You can experience the 1½-mile-long section of river on a barge and, on some, dine aboard by candlelight (see *Getting Around*).

HEMISFAIR URBAN WATER PARK A legacy of the *1968 HemisFair,* the area features a dramatic water design at the base of the *Tower of the Americas.* The *Institute of Texan Cultures* examines the influence of 26 different ethnic groups—including Mexicans, Germans, Poles, Hungarians, and the Irish—who developed the state. There are films, slide shows, and exhibitions of artifacts including Mexican stone-cooking equipment and examples of the dress of each group. Closed Mondays. No admission charge. 801 S. Bowie St. (phone: 558-2300).

SAN ANTONIO MUSEUM OF ART Rapidly gaining recognition as one of the Southwest's best museums, *SAMA* occupies the buildings that once housed the Lone Star Brewery Company. On display is *Con Cariño* (which means "with affection"), a Mexican folk art collection. Nelson A. Rockefeller's extensive private collection comprises the bulk of *Con Cariño* and is said to be the largest in the US. Open daily. Admission charge. 200 W. Jones Ave. (phone: 978-8100).

EL MERCADO Though the original marketplace has been renovated, it is lined with Spanish buildings and retains its old market flavor, with Mexican merchants who do their best to lure you into shops offering hand-crafted baskets, piñatas, pottery, and silver jewelry. Open daily. Market Square, 514 W. Commerce St. (phone: 299-8600).

SPANISH GOVERNOR'S PALACE Built in 1749 for the Spanish governors, the palace is the only Spanish colonial mansion remaining in Texas. It has three-foot-thick walls, a keystone above the door bearing the Hapsburg coat of arms, original Spanish furnishings, and a floor of native flagstone. Open daily. Admission charge. 105 Military Plaza (phone: 224-0601).

HERTZBERG CIRCUS COLLECTION If you're a circus fanatic, you'll go ring-crazy here with displays of more than 20,000 artifacts tracing the development of the circus from its English origins to P. T. Barnum and the American three-ring extravaganza. The collection is particularly strong in miniatures, including the original carriage of Tom Thumb and an entire circus in one room. Closed Sundays. Admission charge. 210 W. Market St. in *Library Annex* (phone: 299-7810).

KING WILLIAM HISTORIC DISTRICT On the southern edge of downtown, this elegant area was established in the late 1800s by successful German merchants whose graceful and sometimes colorful mansions have been meticulously restored. Among the finest is the *Steves Homestead,* a Gothic Revival masterpiece with fascinating appointments. Open daily for tours. Admission charge. 509 King William St. (phone: 224-6163).

VIETNAM VETERANS MEMORIAL This outdoor sculpture portrays a moment from a Vietnam War battle: a soldier radioing for help for a wounded comrade. Local residents often leave flowers, letters, poems, drawings, and photos in memory of loved ones who died in the war. In front of the *Municipal Auditorium,* at the corner of E. Martin and Jefferson Sts.

SOUTH SIDE

MISSIONS The *Alamo* was the first of five missions established under Spanish rule. All except the *Alamo* are still active parish churches and are located along the well-marked *Mission Trail,* starting at the southern tip of the city. *VIA Metropolitan Transit,* the city's public transportation system, runs shuttles along the trail every half hour starting at Alamo Plaza. The most notable missions are the following:

Misión Concepción Established in 1731, the oldest unrestored church in the country is nonetheless remarkably well preserved, with original frescoes painted by the padres and Indians using a mixture of vegetable and mineral dyes. Open daily. 807 Mission Rd. (phone: 229-5732).

Misión San José Established in 1720 and called the Queen of the Missions, it's the finest and largest example of early mission life. The original parish church, built of limestone and tufa, features Rosa's Window, an impressive stone carving, and is surrounded by a six-acre compound including a restored mill, former Indian quarters, and a granary. Check out the colorful mariachi mass on Sundays at noon. Open daily. 6539 San José Dr., 6 miles south on US 281 (phone: 229-4770).

BUCKHORN HALL OF HORNS AND TEXAS HISTORY WAX MUSEUM Once an old shoot-'em-up saloon, *Buckhorn Hall* was transported to tamer grounds. The collection is as wild as ever—some of the fastest guns in the West, and hunting trophies of everything from horns and antlers of elk, buffalo, and antelope to whole polar and grizzly bears. The *Texas History Wax Museum,* in an adjacent building, features 14 dioramas of Wild West history. Open daily. Admission charge. At the Lone Star Brewing Company, 600 Lone Star Blvd. (phone: 270-9467).

NORTH SIDE

BRACKENRIDGE PARK This 433-acre park includes the Southwest's largest zoo (3903 N. St. Mary's; phone: 734-7184) with about 700 species. Cliffs provide a backdrop for fine displays of animals in their natural settings. The best attractions are *Monkey Island,* an outdoor hippo pool, open bear pits, and a $3-million children's zoo. Open daily. Admission charge. There's also the *Brackenridge Eagle,* a mini-railway that makes a 3½-mile tour, and *Skyride* cable cars, which give a panoramic view of the city (additional charge for both; phone: 736-9534). A good place to relax and meditate is the Japanese tea garden (no admission charge; 3800 N. St. Mary's; phone: 821-3000).

SAN ANTONIO BOTANICAL CENTER A living museum of diverse plant life, ranging from desert to tropical, is presented in lovely formal gardens on this 38-acre site near downtown. The centerpiece is the *Lucile Halsell Conservatory,* a 90,000-square-foot below-ground courtyard surrounded by greenhouses. Closed Mondays. Admission charge. 555 Funston (phone: 821-5115).

McNAY ART MUSEUM Set in a lovely Spanish-Mediterranean building, this small but fine collection includes works by Picasso and Chagall. The museum also mounts shows of international scope and exhibitions of regional artists. Closed Mondays. No admission charge. 6000 N. New Braunfels (phone: 824-5368).

WEST SIDE

SEA WORLD OF TEXAS This expanded marine entertainment showplace is considered the world's largest, on 250 acres of rolling hills 20 miles west of San Antonio. It features spectacular performances of killer whales, sea lions, and dolphins, as well as professional water skiing and speed boat shows, concerts, and other events. Closed in winter and on weekdays in spring and fall; open daily *Memorial Day* through *Labor Day.* Admission charge. 10500 Sea World Dr., reached by city bus service (phone: 523-3611).

FIESTA TEXAS A 200-acre, uniquely Texan theme park, 15 miles northwest of downtown, it focuses on the state's history and culture, including the contribution of ethnic groups that have lived in the region. Musical productions, rides, food stands, and shops are set in four different areas of the park, labeled Rockville, Spassburg, Los Festivales, and Crackaxle Canyon. Among the attractions are the *Rattler,* billed as the world's fastest, highest, and steepest wooden roller coaster; the *Gully Washer,* a rapid river ride; *Power Surge,* a combination roller coaster and water slide; and *Motorama,* which allows you to drive replicas of classic 1950s cars. Closed in winter and on weekdays in spring and fall; open daily *Memorial Day* through *Labor Day.* Admission charge. 17000 I-10 at Loop 1604 (phone: 697-5000).

EXTRA SPECIAL

Two day trips from the city can introduce you to the state's European heritage. Gruene (pronounced *green*) is a 150-year-old German settlement about 45 minutes north of San Antonio on I-35. The meticulously restored area includes art galleries, shops, a winery, rafting on the Guadalupe River, and several good cafés. For more information, call the town's visitors' center (phone: 625-0684). Castroville, a village 20 minutes west of the city via US 90, boasts 19th-century homes, antiques shops, walking tours, and several Alsatian restaurants. For details, contact the *Castroville Chamber*

***of Commerce* (PO Box 572, Castroville, TX 78009; phone: 538-3142 or 800-778-6775).**

Sources and Resources

TOURIST INFORMATION

General tourist information, brochures, maps, and events calendars are available at the *San Antonio Convention and Visitors Bureau* (121 Alamo Plaza, San Antonio, TX 78205; phone: 270-8700; 800-447-3372; or write: PO Box 2277, San Antonio, TX 78298), which is closed weekends. More convenient is the *San Antonio Visitor Information Center* (317 Alamo Plaza, San Antonio, TX 78205; phone: 270-8700), which is directly across from the *Alamo* and open daily. Contact the Texas state tourism hotline (phone: 880-8888-TEX) for maps, calendars of events, health updates, and travel advisories.

LOCAL COVERAGE The *San Antonio Express-News,* morning and afternoon daily; the *San Antonio Current,* weekly. *Paseo del Río Association*'s *Reflexiónes* lists upcoming events and is available at the convention and visitors' bureau and in hotel lobbies. The free *San Antonio Convention & Visitor's Guide* is a good area source.

TELEVISION STATIONS KMOL Channel 4–NBC; KENS Channel 5–CBS; KLRN Channel 9–PBS; and KSAT Channel 12–ABC.

RADIO STATIONS AM: KTSA 550 (news); KKYX 680 (country); and WOAI 1200 (news/talk). FM: KCYY 100.3 (country); KQXT 102.7 (adult contemporary); and KMIX 106.7 (soft rock).

TELEPHONE The area code for San Antonio is 210.

SALES TAX The sales tax is 8%; the hotel room tax is 15%.

CLIMATE San Antonio winters are sunny and mild with temperatures averaging above 50F; summers are blistering and humid, with temperatures over 90F and lots of sunshine except for an occasional tropical storm from the Gulf of Mexico.

GETTING AROUND

AIRPORT *San Antonio International Airport* is about a 20-minute drive from downtown. Public buses run between the airport and downtown during certain hours in the morning and afternoon for 75¢; call *VIA Metropolitan Transit* (phone: 227-2020) for schedules. Another option is the *Star Shuttle* (phone: 366-3183), which travels to the downtown area. Limousine service is provided by most major hotels.

BUS *VIA Metropolitan Transit System* serves all sections of the city. The basic fare is 40¢; second-zone (outside I-410) is an additional 10¢; and express buses are 75¢. Complete route and tourist information is available from the transit office, 800 W. Myrtle St. (phone: 227-2020).

CAR RENTAL All national firms are represented.

STREETCAR Attractive reproductions of antique trolleys (on rubber wheels) follow four distinct tourist and traffic loops to and through major points of interest around the city. The fare is 10¢. Free maps are available from any visitors' center.

TAXI Cabs may be ordered by phone or picked up at taxi stations in front of major hotels. Some will answer a hail in the street, most will not. Two of the largest firms are *Checker* (phone: 222-2151) and *Yellow* (phone: 226-4242).

SIGHTSEEING TOURS

BUS *Gray Line* (phone: 226-1706 or 240-2826) offers a selection of guided tours.

HORSE-DRAWN CARRIAGES Old World and romantic, these open carriages are most abundant at the *Alamo.* The companies running them include *H.R.H.* (phone: 225-6490); *Lone Star* (phone: 656-7527); and *Yellow Rose* (phone: 225-6490).

RIVER TAXI The *Paseo del Río* boat company (430 E. Commerce St; phone: 222-1701) operates a river taxi from hotels and various points along the river to the commercial center. They also offer a 45-minute boat tour, during which a commentator describes the historical points of interest along the way.

SPECIAL EVENTS

In early February at *Freeman Coliseum* is the city's popular *Livestock Show and Rodeo.* The most elaborate blowout in this city of fiestas is the 10-day *Fiesta San Antonio* in mid-April, celebrating Sam Houston's victory over Santa Anna with parades, the *Battle of the Flowers,* the *Fiesta Flambeau* in the streets, and the *Fiesta River Parade* with lighted floats on the river, a king and queen, and lots of food and drink. The *Starving Artists Show* in early April has works of art by hungry local artists, with nothing priced much higher than $20. San Antonio celebrates the Mexican defeat of the French in the Battle of Puebla in true Mexican form during the *Cinco de Mayo* festival, at Market Square during the first weekend in May. The *Texas Folklife Festival,* staged the first weekend in August at the *Institute of Texan Cultures,* showcases ethnic customs and foods, crafts and games, and 30 cultures that helped shape Texas. Also in August is the *Carver Jazz Festival,* held at the *Carver Cultural Center.* In early December, *Las Posadas* is a Hispanic folklore drama re-enacting the Holy Family's search for shelter in Bethlehem. It is set against a dazzling *River Walk* backdrop of 60,000 red, blue, and green *Christmas* lights; mariachis herald the arrival of the pilgrims and a choir sings the traditional *posada* songs. *Fiesta de las Luminarias* takes place on the first three weekends of December. Nearly

2,000 candles placed in sand-filled paper bags line the *River Walk,* symbolizing the lighting of the Holy Family's way to Bethlehem.

MUSEUMS

In addition to those described in *Special Places,* there are several other museums of note in San Antonio.

COWBOY MUSEUM AND GALLERY A collection of artifacts and memorabilia illustrate life in an Old West town. Open daily. Admission charge. 209 Alamo Plaza (phone: 229-1257).

ECHOES FROM THE PAST This collection of Elvis Presley memorabilia, including photos, records, and other souvenirs, belongs to a local woman who is related to the King's former drummer. Adjacent to the museum is a vintage musical instrument and machine exhibit. Open daily. Admission charge. 517 E. Houston St. (phone: 225-3714).

FORT SAM HOUSTON MUSEUM Exhibits display the history of the *US Army* in San Antonio since 1845 and the fort's role in national military activities. Closed Mondays and Tuesdays. No admission charge. *Fort Sam Houston,* Bldg. 123 (phone: 221-1886).

INSTITUTE OF TEXAN CULTURES The artifacts here represent various ethnic groups that helped establish Texas culture; exhibits describe Indian, French, Spanish, German, Jewish, and African-American influences. Closed Mondays. No admission charge. 801 S. Bowie (phone: 558-2300).

PIONEER MUSEUM The history of the Texas Rangers since their inception in 1823 is explained. Closed Mondays. Admission charge. 3805 Broadway (phone: 824-2537).

WITTE MEMORIAL MUSEUM This museum offers award-winning special exhibits about Texas history. Open daily. Admission charge. 3801 Broadway (phone: 820-2111; 829-7262 for recorded information).

ZOOLOGICAL GARDENS AND AQUARIUM Located in a rock quarry by the river, the zoo has a wonderful exhibit of koalas, as well as an African antelope collection and a variety of exotic birds. Elephant and camel rides are offered for children, and the zoo has the only whooping crane in captivity in the US. Open daily. Admission charge. 3903 N. St. Mary's St. (phone: 734-7184).

ART GALLERIES

Artists and craftspeople from all over the world have found that San Antonio is an accommodating place to live and work; the artistic community has grown rapidly, and galleries are numerous. Try the *Raul Gutierrez Gallery of Fine Arts* (8940 Wurzbach; phone: 614-3897) for Western oils, acrylics, and bronze sculptures; *Blue Star Art Space* (116 Blue Star; phone: 227-6960) for paintings and photographs; and *Rattlesnake and Star* (209 N. Presa;

phone: 225-5977). At the *Southwest Craft Center* (300 Augusta; phone: 224-1848), you can watch art objects being created.

SHOPPING

San Antonio has its share of today's marketplaces, malls filled with department stores, chain shops, eateries, and entertainment. Enclaves of commerce with more individuality, however, also are easy to come by—and get to. Museum shops are an excellent source of quality gifts and mementos.

SPORTS AND FITNESS

BASEBALL The LA *Dodgers'* minor league team, the San Antonio *Missions,* plays at *V. J. Keefe Field* (*St. Mary's University;* phone: 675-7275).

BASKETBALL The *NBA Spurs* play from November through April at the *Alamodome* (near I-37 at Market; phone: 223-DOME).

FITNESS CENTER The *YMCA* (903 N. St. Mary's and Lexington; phone: 246-9600), which is open to non-members for a fee, has a pool, track, weights, and handball and racquetball courts.

GOLF There are 25 courses in the city, all open year-round. Best for visitors are *Olmos Basin Municipal Course* (7022 McCullough; phone: 826-4041) and *Pecan Valley Golf Club* (4700 Pecan Valley; phone: 333-9018).

JOGGING Run along the *River Walk* early or late in the day; up Broadway to *Brackenridge Park;* or follow the *Mission Trail,* along Mission Road (the marathon route), to the missions.

RIDING *Brackenridge Stables* (840 E. Mulberry; phone: 732-8881) are ideal for urban cowboys wishing to ride along bridle paths in *Brackenridge Park.*

SWIMMING There are 21 municipal pools open from May through *Labor Day* (phone: 821-3000). Best is *Alamo Heights Pool* (229 Greeley St.; phone: 824-2595). For serious lap swimmers, two 50-meter pools are open year-round: *Northside Aquatics Center* (7001 Culebra; phone: 681-4026) and *Northeast Aquatics Center* (12002 Jones-Maltsberger; phone: 491-6136).

TENNIS *McFarlin Tennis Center* (1503 San Pedro Ave.; phone: 732-1223) is a municipal facility. Reservations advised.

THEATER

A variety of traveling and locally produced shows is offered by more than a dozen theaters, the most impressive of which is the *Majestic Performing Arts Center* (216 E. Houston St.; phone: 226-3333). This ornate structure has been restored to its 1920s grandeur and hosts everything from traveling national theater companies to rock concerts. The area's colleges and universities also produce plays. For shows: *San Antonio Little Theater* (800 W. Ashby; phone: 733-7258); *Harlequin Dinner Theater* (2652 Harney Rd.; phone: 222-9694); *Carver Cultural Center* (226 N. Hackberry; phone: 225-

6516), where musical theater often focuses on African-American life; *Alamo City Theater* (339 W. Josephine; phone: 734-4646); and *Arneson River Theater* (Villita St.; phone: 299-8610), where the audience is separated from the stage by the river, and an occasional passing barge upstages the actors.

MUSIC

The *San Antonio Symphony* performs at the *Majestic Performing Arts Center* (216 E. Houston St.; phone: 226-3333) with guest stars from September through May. *Fiesta Noche del Río,* a program of Mexican and Spanish music, dance, and theater, is offered by local professionals from June through August at *Arneson River Theater* (*River Walk* at La Villita; phone: 226-4651). The *Fifth Army Band* stages free gazebo concerts at *Fort Sam Houston* on the third Sunday of each month, May through August (phone: 221-6896).

NIGHTCLUBS AND NIGHTLIFE

Pop music, jazz, Dixieland, folk, rock, and country-western are all offered at San Antonio's many pubs, taverns, and nightclubs. For a little country, try *Bluebonnet Palace* (16842 I-35 North; phone: 651-6702). For jazz, try *Jim Cullum's Landing* (*Hyatt Regency;* phone: 223-7266). You may want to try piano sing-alongs at *Durty Nelly's Irish Pub* (*Hilton Palacio del Río;* phone: 222-1400).

Best in Town

CHECKING IN

San Antonio's hotels offer comfortable and convenient accommodations. If you're looking for a good bed and breakfast establishment, *Bed & Breakfast Hosts of San Antonio* (166 Rockhill; phone: 824-8036) will make reservations for you at historic homes and guest cottages in the area. Most of San Antonio's major hotels have complete facilities for the business traveler. Those listed below as having "business services" usually offer such conveniences as meeting rooms, photocopiers, computers, translation services, and express checkout, among others. Call the individual hotel for additional information. Expect to pay $100 or more per night for a double room at establishments listed as expensive; $65 to $100 at those in the moderate category; and $65 or less at the inexpensive place. Unless otherwise noted, hotels have air conditioning, private baths, TV sets, and telephones.

All hotels below are in San Antonio and telephone and fax numbers are in the 210 area code unless otherwise indicated.

EXPENSIVE

Bed and Breakfast on the River A small, lovely inn nestled into the historic district near the San Antonio River, it has seven guestrooms with private sun decks. Hot-air balloon rides are available from the innkeeper, a licensed balloonist.

A fine continental breakfast is included, and business services are available. 129 Woodward Pl. (phone: 225-6333; 800-730-0019; fax: 225-6337).

Crockett Built in 1909, it has emerged as one of the nicest of San Antonio's "old" hotels. Some of the 202 rooms are small, but all are beautifully decorated. The most impressive accommodations are the luxurious seventh-floor suites overlooking the *Alamo. The Landmark* serves breakfast and dinner. Business services are available. 320 Bonham (phone: 225-6500; 800-292-1050; fax: 225-6251).

Fairmount This cozy little landmark offers 37 elegantly appointed rooms and a staff whose pampering makes you feel as if you've landed in Europe. Once a derelict building situated in a downtown renewal area, the hotel made moving history when it was rolled—all of its 3.2 million pounds intact—to its present site across the street from La Villita and HemisFair Plaza. *Polo's* is a fine restaurant and bar (see *Eating Out*), and there's another dining room as well. A concierge desk, 24-hour room service, and business services are available. 401 S. Alamo (phone: 224-2767; 800-642-3363; fax: 224-2767).

Hilton Palacio del Río Right on the riverside, at the liveliest corner of *Paseo del Río,* this attractive Spanish-style place makes the best use of its prime location. The dining room serves alfresco on the *River Walk;* half of the 482 rooms have river views; and there is an elevator that lets you off at river's edge. Also featured is a rooftop pool, free coffee in the rooms, shops, and *Durty Nellie's* pub, where you can let loose. Business services are offered; other pluses are a concierge and a car rental desk. 200 S. Alamo St. (phone: 222-1400; 800-HILTONS; fax: 226-4123).

Hyatt Hill Country Resort This remarkable $100-million luxury establishment features 500 guestrooms, two pools with waterfalls, an outdoor spa, tennis courts, exercise and massage facilities, an 18-hole golf course designed by Arthur Hill, and a picnic pavilion. The structure is made of native Texas materials, and there are wide wooden verandahs and deeply gabled windows. The hotel has seven restaurants and lounges, as well as business services. Located near *Sea World of Texas* and *Fiesta Texas.* 9800 Hyatt Resort Dr. (phone: 647-1234; 800-233-1234; fax: 681-9681).

Hyatt Regency Most of the 632 rooms in this 16-story establishment have views of the San Antonio River and Old San Antonio. For dining and drinking, there's the *Riverbend Saloon, Chaps,* and the multilevel *River Terrace* lounge in the atrium. There is also a pool, business services, and a concierge desk. 123 Losoya (phone: 222-1234; 800-233-1234; fax: 277-4925).

La Mansión del Río This hotel combines a Spanish-style building with a restored 1852 building that originally was part of *St. Mary's University.* Its 337 rooms overlook either the river or an inner courtyard and pool. Two restaurants, the *Capistrano Room* and *Las Canarias,* and *El Colegio* bar provide food and drink; room service delivers around-the-clock. Other conveniences include a concierge desk and business services. 112 College St. (phone: 225-2581; 800-531-7208; fax: 226-0389).

Menger To the right of the *Alamo,* this 19th-century gem is where Teddy Roosevelt is said to have recruited his Rough Riders. The historic 320-room building has been restored and features a pool, a restaurant, and business services. An extra special amenity is the excellent spa with sauna, herbal scrubs, and full beauty treatments. 204 Alamo Plaza (phone: 223-4361 or 223-5772; 800-345-9285; fax: 228-0022).

Ogé House An elegant bed and breakfast inn along the river in the King William Historic District. The renovated 1857 mansion offers 10 rooms, some with fireplaces, all furnished with period French and English antiques. Amenities include refrigerators in all the rooms, and an expansive continental breakfast. Business services are available. 209 Washington St. (phone: 223-2353; 800-242-2770; fax: 226-5812).

Plaza San Antonio Locally known as "The Plaza," this is a garden property on nearly five acres, accented by tropical gardens, tall native Texas trees, and sparkling fountains. Its 252 rooms have balconies overlooking La Villita Historic District. The *Anaqua Grill* (see *Eating Out*) has a distinctive international menu, and incorporated into the complex are three restored 19th-century bungalows, which house the hotel's entertainment facilities. Features include a pool, exercise rooms, a sauna, and tennis courts. Additional amenities include 24-hour room service, a concierge, and business services. 555 S. Alamo (phone: 229-1000; 800-421-1172; fax: 223-6650).

St. Anthony The richness of this thoroughly restored landmark is reflected in the lobby, decorated with Empire chandeliers, Oriental rugs, marble, and hand-painted Mexican tiles, and a rosewood and gold leaf grand piano. The *Café* offers pasta, steaks, and sandwiches; and there is 24-hour room service, business services, and a pool. 300 E. Travis St. (phone: 227-4392; 800-355-5153; fax: 227-0915).

San Antonio Marriott Rivercenter Directly across the street from the *Convention Center* and nestled in a bend of the San Antonio River, it is one of the city's largest properties with 1,000 rooms. Most striking is its seven-story atrium with an indoor-outdoor heated swimming pool. *Gambits* on the *River Walk,* a two-story nightclub, opens onto the river across the street; the *Garden Café* offers casual fare, the *River Grill* is for more formal dining, and there is also a lobby bar. Other pluses are 24-hour room service, a concierge, airline and car rental desks, and business services. 101 Bowie (phone: 223-1000; 800-228-9290; fax: 223-4092).

Sheraton Gunter This place originally opened in 1909 and has twice been declared a Texas landmark. A turn-of-the-century atmosphere still pervades the lobby, with its crystal chandeliers, marble floor, and dark mahogany paneling. More modern are the 326 high-ceilinged rooms. Continental and Texas specialties are served in the *Café Suisse; Pâtisserie Suisse* is a European-style bakery; and *Padre Muldoon's* is a Victorian saloon. Amenities include business services, 24-hour room service, and a concierge desk. 205 E. Houston St. (phone: 227-3241; 800-22-CHARM; fax: 227-3299).

Sheraton Fiesta In the midst of the business district and near the airport, this hotel has 284 rooms and seven suites. The Spanish colonial architecture and Mexican-style furnishings lend charm and grace. There is a beautifully landscaped courtyard, a restaurant, a lobby lounge with live piano music nightly, a pool, and an exercise room. Other amenities include a concierge, complimentary shuttle service to and from the airport, and business services. 37 NE Loop 410 (phone: 366-2424; 800-535-1980 from Texas; 800-325-3535 from elsewhere in the US; fax: 341-3140).

MODERATE

Beauregard House Conveniently located in the King William District, this four-room inn offers comfortable accommodations at reasonable rates. There's a pool and small café. 215 Beauregard St. (phone: 222-1198; 800-841-9377).

Emily Morgan This establishment's 177 rooms, which include 11 plush suites with Jacuzzis, overlook the *Alamo. The Yellow Rose* is a modern coffee shop–style restaurant that serves good food. In addition, there are health club facilities and a pool. Business services are available. 705 E. Houston St. (phone: 225-8486; 800-824-6674; fax: 225-7227).

INEXPENSIVE

Bullis House Inn/San Antonio International Hostel Historic surroundings, lovely appointments (oak wainscoting, paneling, and staircases), and a friendly atmosphere make this seven-room inn popular with travelers who want to stay somewhere comfortable without busting their budgets. There's a restaurant and a pool, and functions for up to 150 can be held in the two parlors and two dining rooms, which are connected. Limited business services can be arranged. 621 Pierce St. (phone: 229-1479 or 223-9426; fax: 299-1479).

EATING OUT

Some 26 ethnic groups pioneered Texas, and its current military population has brought back a taste for exotic dishes from remote areas of the globe. As a result, San Antonio enjoys a variety of restaurants. The best, however, are Mexican. Non-Texans (outlanders, as they're called down here) generally are pleasantly surprised by the prices. Expect to pay from $50 to $100 for dinner for two at places in the expensive category, $25 to $50 at those listed as moderate, and $25 or less at inexpensive places. Prices do not include drinks, wine, tax, or tips. All restaurants are in the 210 area code unless otherwise indicated.

Unless noted otherwise, restaurants are open for lunch and dinner.

EXPENSIVE

Anaqua Grill Etched glass partitions give this place an elegant ambience, and the culinary influences are Mediterranean, Asian, and Southwestern. *Tapas* are standouts, as are cold shrimp with herbed white beans and honey-drizzled duck on noodles. Diners also may order margaritas made with either fresh lime or kiwi. Reservations advised. Major credit cards accepted. *Plaza San Antonio Hotel,* 555 S. Alamo St. (phone: 229-1000).

Biga This fashionable bistro in a restored 100-year-old mansion combines Mediterranean, Southwestern, and California dishes. Soft-shelled crab with sweet potato, oak-smoked pork loin, and risotto with smoky lobster are among the favorites. The on-site bakery produces heavenly breads. Closed Sundays. Reservations advised. Major credit cards accepted. 206 E. Locust (phone: 225-0722).

Boudro's This popular *River Walk* place magically blends flavors from New Orleans and New Mexico. A smoked shrimp and peppered-bacon club sandwich, black and white bean soup, and crab and shrimp tamales are among the offerings. Reservations necessary for riverside tables only. Major credit cards accepted. 421 E. Commerce St. on the *River Walk* (phone: 224-8484).

Chez Ardid French nouvelle cuisine is highlighted by such delightful choices as boneless duck breast with raspberry sauce, and turbot with white wine and caviar on champagne cream. The atmosphere reflects the opulence of the mansion that this restaurant used to be. Jacket and tie required. Closed Sundays. Reservations necessary. Major credit cards accepted. 1919 San Pedro (phone: 732-3203).

L'Etoile This lively bistro turns out the kind of solid cooking that has given French continental food a good name—curried shrimp on a bed of couscous, and sweetbreads with mushrooms and olives, for example. Inside, it's light wood and soft colors under a cathedral ceiling. There's also dining outdoors. Reservations advised for dinner. Major credit cards accepted. 6106 Broadway, Alamo Heights (phone: 826-4551).

Grey Moss Inn To get to this historic inn in Texas hill country, you have to drive through some of the loveliest scenery around. Located in a wildlife sanctuary called *Grey Forest,* it offers outdoor dining on a shaded patio. Specialties include mesquite-grilled steaks and fish served with herbed tomato salad or shrimp cocktail. Open daily for dinner only. Reservations—and directions—necessary. Major credit cards accepted. 19010 Scenic Loop Rd., about 15 miles northwest of town (phone: 695-8301).

Little Rhein This is the city's priciest (but most romantic) steakhouse. Texas caviar, a black-eyed pea dish, is complimentary, while pepper steaks and lamb chops are top menu offerings. Its terraced riverside setting in an 1847 limestone house is a big draw. Open daily for dinner only. Reservations advised. Major credit cards accepted. 231 S. Alamo St. (phone: 225-2111).

La Louisiane When it opened in 1935, this French and creole place offered full dinners for 75¢ to $1.25 (and was immediately criticized for its high prices). Today, a couple willing to pay about 100 times that much can feast on snapper in artichokes, chicken with asparagus and wild rice, and steak Diane. The wonderful *Courtyard* offers casual dining, too. Reservations advised. Major credit cards accepted. 2632 Broadway (phone: 225-7984).

Polo's The fine dining room of the *Fairmount* hotel presents a predominantly Southwestern menu. Service is efficient, and the linguine with wild boar sausage and duck breast or the grilled rack of lamb with herb-berry sauce make this an excellent dining choice. Reservations advised. Major credit cards accepted. 401 S. Alamo (phone: 224-8800).

Stetson There's a distinctive air here, and the outdoor seating with a river view is hard to beat. What's more, the menu delivers sensational fare, including chorizo-stuffed ravioli; tequila-sizzled shrimp; and medallions of tender buffalo. Open for dinner only; closed Sundays. Reservations advised. Major credit cards accepted. In the *Hilton Palacio del Río,* 200 S. Alamo St. (phone 222-1400).

MODERATE

Clubhouse Pit Bar-B-Que A lively, local barbecue place. The menu features pork and other meat dishes with a spunky sauce, smoked chicken salad, and Southern-style veggies including collard greens and yams. Live jazz keeps the joint jumping on Fridays. Closed Sundays. No reservations. Major credit cards accepted. 2218 Broadway (phone: 229-9945).

Cappy's The kind of place where folks head after work on Fridays to let down their hair. It's upscale but comfy, with exposed brick walls and lots of natural wood; the menu includes shrimp and scallops, shellfish, and Italian sausage with pasta. No reservations. Major credit cards accepted. 5011 Broadway, Alamo Heights (phone: 828-9669).

County Line A cheery 1940s roadhouse, it serves some of Texas's best barbecued ribs, beef, pork loin, and chicken, smoked throughout the day. Just as sinful are the beans, potato salad, giant loaves of homemade bread, and fruit cobblers à la mode. No reservations. Major credit cards accepted. 607 W. Afton Oak, near Loop 1604 and US 281 (phone: 496-0011).

Crumpets A soothing atmosphere is enhanced by classical music, a quietly elegant decor, and superlative desserts turned out by the restaurant's pastry shop next door. Try the buttercream cake or fresh fruit tart. Preceding dessert is some very good continental fare, including beef Wellington. No reservations. Major credit cards accepted. 5800 Broadway, Alamo Heights (phone: 821-5454).

Diva Seafood Bar and Grill Here's a boisterous nightspot with inspired cooking. Most enjoyable are the generous, flavorful smoked salmon appetizer; bouillabaisse; shrimp cloaked in coconut; and fresh, tender salmon entrées. Closed Sundays; dinner only on Saturdays. No reservations. Major credit cards accepted. 720 E. Mistletoe (phone: 735-3482).

Liberty Bar Down-home yet trendy, it is a favorite of locals as well as visitors. No wonder, given such eclectic, well-presented menu items as lamb burgers, grilled snapper filet with thick cilantro sauce, and salads topped with edible flowers. Reservations unnecessary. Major credit cards accepted. 328 E. Josephine (phone: 227-1187).

Luna Notte Very contemporary and stylish, this place offers great innovations in Italian fare. The sumptuous *bagna cauda*, or melted cheeses on bread with onions and pepper, is sublime, as are crab cakes with sun-dried tomato aiole and lemon-basil sauce. Open daily; dinner only on weekends. Reservations advised. Major credit cards accepted. 6402 N. New Braunfels (phone: 822-4242).

INEXPENSIVE

La Fogata Outstanding and authentic Mexican recipes—such as *tacos chiveros* (tacos filled with goat cheese and guacamole) and seafood served with avocados—may sound exotic, but the prices are down to earth. In nice weather, try to sit on the cheery patio. No reservations. Major credit cards accepted. 2427 Vance Jackson (phone: 340-1337).

Mi Tierra Café and Bakery When you tire of souvenir hunting at *El Mercado,* head for the heart of the market square for great Mexican food at low prices. The cheese enchiladas are terrific, and the *cabrito* (kid) is good, too. Open 24 hours a day. No reservations. Major credit cards accepted. 218 Produce Row (phone: 225-1262).

El Mirador Locals say the best, most authentic Mexican food in the city is served here. It's a favorite at lunchtime on Saturdays, when the entire citizenry seems to visit. *Caldo Xochitl* (a chicken-cum-vegetable soup served Saturdays only) is special, and *chilaquiles* (eggs, tortillas, and chilies) makes a great breakfast. Open for breakfast and lunch only; closed Sundays. No reservations or credit cards accepted. 722 S. St. Mary's (phone: 225-9444).

Schilo's Delicatessen This downtown favorite has been around since the 1920s, and locals still come for stick-to-your-ribs German fare. Don't miss the potato pancakes or the heavenly cheesecake. Closed Sundays. No reservations. Major credit cards accepted. 424 E. Commerce (phone: 223-6692).

San Diego

Sunlit, clean, and glowing, San Diego is archetypal Southern California. Residents really do call it paradise, and strangers in paradise usually are flabbergasted by the remarkable climate. Here is the land of eternal spring (70F is the average daytime temperature), and residents tend to gripe when even the merest wisp of cumulus mars the sky. You can get spoiled living in Eden.

More than a million people live in the city, while the San Diego metro area has a population of more than 2.6 million. With a vibrant, revitalized central core, a dramatic waterfront convention center that opened in 1995, and a good public transportation system, San Diego is becoming the ultimate city. Ideally situated between the sea and the mountains, it also offers all the benefits of a sophisticated urban culture. No wonder some 35 million people visit San Diego every year.

Tourism is the city's third-largest industry. The largest is the aerospace equipment and missile industry. About 1,000 firms manufacture aviation equipment. The US government ranks number two, with more than 20% of San Diego's labor force working for Uncle Sam. (However, this segment of San Diego's economy may well be affected by military base closings and other federal spending cuts implemented by the Clinton administration.)

San Diego is California's birthplace. In 1542, Portugal's Juan Rodríguez Cabrillo, sailing under a Spanish flag, pulled into the natural shelter formed by San Diego Bay. The first settlement was not established until more than two centuries later, however, when explorer Gaspar de Portolá and a group of Spanish settlers planted San Diego's first European roots. One of this city's original settlers was the legendary Franciscan, Fray Junípero Serra, founder of the 21-mission trail known as El Camino Real. The first of his missions, *San Diego de Alcalá,* forms the southern end of the chain that follows the coast as far as Sonoma, north of San Francisco. The missions were established in the 18th century with the aim of proselytization, but there were military objectives as well. As the Russians pushed into Alaska, the Spanish government looked toward its string of religious settlements and outposts as potential strategic bulwarks. Spaced about a day's journey apart, each mission housed about 1,000 Indian converts to Catholicism. The Indians worked as farmers and craftspeople. The priests gave them food, clothing, and medical care, and taught them how to irrigate the fields.

In 1810, Mexicans gained control of San Diego during a revolution against Spain that began in the northern Mexican town of Querétaro. In 1846 during its expansionist "manifest destiny" period, the United States seized the land from Mexico. Under American rule, San Diego grew slowly, remaining an insular village until the turn of the century, when the population followed industrialist Alonzo Horton from "Old Town" (today's his-

OLD TOWN
SAN DIEGO
SAN DIEGO RIVER
0 miles 1/4
Junipero Serra Museum
PRESIDIO PARK
Historic District
Casa De Estudillo
Old Town Plaza
Heritage Park
Mormon Memorial
To El Campo Santo 200 Yds
SAN DIEGO
DOWNTOWN
SAN DIEGO ZOO
Balboa
Park
El Prado
Cabrillo Bridge
Plaza Panama
All in this section of Balboa Park
Timken Art Gallery
Fine Arts Gallery
Shakespearean Theater
Museum of Man
Aerospace Museum
R.H.Fleet Space Theater
Museum of Natural History
Balboa Stadium
US Customs
County Blg
Chamber of Commerce
"Star of India"
SAN DIEGO
AT-A-GLANCE
University of California
Scripps Institute of Oceanography
Sea Caves
Seal Rock
Torrey Pines St. Park
Whale Point
LA JOLLA

N
Sea World
Mission Bay Park
Old Town
8
163
Harbor Island
Shelter Island
Balboa Park
Area of the Main Map
MILITARY RESERVE
NORTH ISLAND (US Navy)
CORONADO
75
5
Cabrillo Nat. Monument
Pt Loma
0 miles 2
BROADWAY
Carnegie Library
Post Office
HARBOR DR
PACIFIC HWY
CALIFORNIA ST
KETTNER BLVD
INDIA ST
COLUMBIA ST
STATE ST
UNION ST
FRONT ST
MARKET ST
ISLAND AV
IMPERIAL AV
COMMERCIAL AV
NATIONAL ST
NEWTON ST
BEARDLEY ST
CROSBY ST
GULL ST
SWITZER ST
WATER ST
San Diego Bay
CORONADO
SOLEDAD ST
PROSPECT ST
EL CHICO RD
0 miles 1/2

toric district) to the "New Town" (today's downtown). Modern San Diego has since expanded more than 20 miles to the north, south, and east.

San Diego County contains lots of fertile land. In fact, agriculture is San Diego's fourth-largest industry. Nursery and flower products—cuttings, seeds, and the plants themselves—are now the county's most valuable crops, with avocados running a close second (most of the avocados grown in California come from here). Many eventually find their way into guacamole—only one of the many Mexican dishes and customs that permeate city life. San Diego's Mexican-Spanish heritage also is reflected in its large Mexican-American population, and in both its modern architecture and its remarkable old buildings. The Mexican border is only 17 miles to the south, and because of it, San Diego retains a unique character, blending American hospitality and traditional border-town sensuality.

San Diego At-a-Glance

SEEING THE CITY

The *Cabrillo National Monument,* where Juan Rodríguez Cabrillo first saw the West Coast, still offers the best view of San Diego. It's the second-most visited national monument in the US—right after the *Statue of Liberty.* Museum and visitors' center open daily. Admission charge. Catalina Blvd. on the tip of Point Loma (phone: 557-5450).

SPECIAL PLACES

San Diego stretches from the fashionable northern suburb of Del Mar to the Mexican border, a span of more than 30 miles along the Pacific Coast. It's advisable to concentrate your sightseeing efforts in one area at a time. There's no way you can see everything in just one day. Each of the Big Four (*Balboa Park, Old Town,* the *San Diego Zoo,* and *Sea World of California*) is an all-day proposition.

SAN DIEGO

SHELTER ISLAND This manmade resort island in the middle of San Diego Bay is lined with boatyards, marinas, and picturesque neo-Polynesian restaurants. Between July and November, marlin sport fishers haul their giant catches into port here. Stop at Marlin Club Landing (2445 Shelter Island Dr.; phone: 222-2502), where the marlin and tuna are weighed in. If the sight of these monsters makes you yearn for the tug of a giant fish on the line, sign up for a marlin expedition at any of the sport fishing marinas two blocks away on Fenelon Street. You also can fish for albacore and yellowtail. To get to Shelter Island from downtown, take Harbor Drive north past the airport and turn left on Scott Street, which feeds into Shelter Island Drive.

HARBOR ISLAND This superdeluxe resort island started as a landfill project in 1961, when the *US Navy,* deepening a channel through the bay, offered surplus harbor muck to the Port of San Diego. Port officials used the three-and-a-half-million tons of waste to create Harbor Island. These humble beginnings have yielded fancy beachside promenades, traffic-free malls, restaurants, and hotels. Take Harbor Drive north from downtown, then follow the signs to Harbor Island.

MISSION BAY PARK A 4,600-acre waterfront park, it features manmade tropical islands, channels, and areas where you can water-ski, swim, and sail. There are golf courses, hotels, and restaurants here, too. The 2-mile stretch of Mission Beach, along the western edge of the park, is one of San Diego's oldest beach communities. The visitors' information center is open daily. Take Route 5 to the Mission Bay Drive exit. The information center is right off the exit ramp (phone: 276-8200).

SEA WORLD OF CALIFORNIA This 150-acre oceanarium is the highlight of the *Mission Bay* recreation complex. Performing dolphins; Shamu, the three-ton killer whale; and Baby Shamu entertain regularly. The shows include performing sea lions and otters. *Penguin Encounter* is a glassed-in bit of Antarctica, where penguins from Emperors to fledglings flourish in zero-degree cold. You also can feed the dolphins and meet the walruses. Yes, there are sharks, too—a multimillion-dollar exhibit features a tankful of them. Open daily. Admission charge. *Mission Bay Park* (phone: 226-3901).

OLD TOWN SAN DIEGO STATE HISTORIC PARK Historic buildings mix with commercial re-creations on the site of California's first permanent Spanish settlement, preserved by the *State Department of Parks and Recreation.* Tours leave from the park headquarters. A diorama of Old Town as it looked 100 years ago is on display. Buildings include the *Seeley Stables,* with exhibits on Californian and western history and children's displays; the *Stuart House,* an early adobe structure where volunteers demonstrate candlemaking, spinning, and weaving; the *Machado-Silvas House,* another adobe structure; and an early dentist's office. (Buildings are closed on *Thanksgiving, Christmas,* and *New Year's Day.*) Living history programs take place on the fourth Saturday of each month. The *Bazaar del Mundo,* an area of shops and restaurants, is also here, plus an old-fashioned general store, tobacconist, and confectionery. For further information, contact the visitors' information center in *Robinson-Rose House* (Old Town Plaza; phone: 220-5422). *Old Town San Diego State Historic Park* is bounded by Wallace, Juan, Twiggs, and Congress Streets. Some of the park's other highlights:

Old Town Plaza The best way to see Old San Diego is by walking through it. Old Town Plaza (also known as Washington Square) used to be the scene of violent cockfights, bullfights, and duels. San Diego Ave., Mason, Calhoun, and Wallace Sts.

Casa de Estudillo A former *comandante* of San Diego, José María Estudillo, lived here while the city was under Mexican control. It was built in 1829. Open daily. Admission charge. San Diego Ave. and Mason St. (no phone).

WHALEY HOUSE The first brick house in San Diego, it was built by New Yorker Thomas Whaley, and became the scene of many lively high society parties in its day. Ornate 19th-century furnishings still fill the halls, and the house is supposedly haunted by a man who was hanged on the grounds in 1852. Closed Mondays and Tuesdays. Admission charge. 2482 San Diego Ave., Old Town (phone: 298-2482).

EL CAMPO SANTO At the southern end of San Diego Avenue is a cemetery containing the graves of many pioneers, soldiers, and bandits. One of the latter, Antonio Garra, was executed next to his grave. Many of the headstones are missing, but there's enough history here to merit a visit. San Diego Ave. and Noell St., Old Town.

HERITAGE PARK VILLAGE A pocket of preserved Victoriana mansions. The *County Parks and Recreation Department* has its offices in the *Sherman-Gilbert House*. Open daily. No admission charge. Afternoon tea served Tuesdays through Saturdays. Heritage Park Row, Old Town (phone: 299-6832).

MORMON BATTALION MEMORIAL VISITORS CENTER This military museum commemorates the longest infantry march in US history: from 1846 to 1847, when 500 Mormons in a battalion of the *US Army* left Illinois to trek more than 2,000 miles to San Diego. Only 350 made it. It also has exhibits about the Church of Jesus Christ of Latter-Day Saints. Open daily. No admission charge. In *Heritage Park* at 2510 Juan St., Old Town (phone: 298-3317).

JUNÍPERO SERRA MUSEUM Built in 1929 and named after Fray Junípero Serra, it contains artifacts from San Diego's early Spanish and Mexican periods. The tower gallery is especially fascinating. The museum is on the site of the first European settlement and mission in California. Closed Mondays. Admission charge. *Presidio Park,* Old Town (phone: 297-3258).

BALBOA PARK A definite must, this is the cultural heart of the city. Within its 1,200 acres of lawns, groves, lakes, and paths are the world-famous *San Diego Zoo,* a complex of fine museums in an area of the park known as El Prado (each is listed separately below), restaurants, and a theater. Open daily. No admission charge to the park. The *Balboa Park Visitors' Center,* located in the *House of Hospitality,* provides a free map to the many museums, shops, restaurants, theaters, and sports facilities in the park. Many *Balboa Park* museums close at 4:30 PM, and some have no admission charge on Tuesdays. Be sure to call ahead. Park Blvd. (phone: 239-0512). Here are some highlights of the park:

San Diego Zoo One of the world's finest zoos for more than 75 years, it covers over 125 acres, with 4,000 animals ranging from Australian koalas to the only New Zealand kiwis in captivity in the country to Indonesian Komodo dragons. Don't miss the *Tiger River* exhibit, a re-creation of a Southeast Asian rain forest. Few of the animals are caged. The *Skyfari Aerial Tramway* offers a bird's-eye view of everything. Guided bus tours leave frequently from the gate. Open daily. Admission charge (except on *Founder's Day,* the first Monday in October). *Balboa Park* (phone: 234-3153 or 231-1515).

Timken Museum of Art Controversial when it was built in 1965 because some people felt its modern bent clashed with its Spanish Baroque architecture, this gallery has French, Spanish, Flemish, and Italian Renaissance art and a world-famous collection of Russian icons. Works by Rembrandt, Brueghel the Elder, and Cézanne adorn the walls. Closed in September and on Mondays and major holidays. No admission charge. 1500 El Prado, *Balboa Park* (phone: 239-5548).

San Diego Museum of Art Donated by the Appleton Bridges family in 1926, the gallery was built to resemble the university at Salamanca, Spain; two other wings were added later. Diego Rivera, Rubens, Dalí, and Rembrandt are represented. There's also the *Sculpture Garden Café* for casual dining. Closed Mondays. Admission charge. 1450 El Prado Way, *Balboa Park* (phone: 232-7931).

San Diego Museum of Man Concerned primarily with anthropology and archaeology, this museum is the only remaining permanent structure from San Diego's 1915 *Panama-California Exposition.* Its Spanish colonial tower is remarkable in itself. Exhibitions focus on the Southwest Indians, pre-Columbian Maya, and Early Man. There's also an ethnic arts shop. Open daily. Admission charge except the third Tuesday of every month. El Prado, *Balboa Park* (phone: 239-2001).

Aerospace Historical Center Containing the *San Diego Aerospace Museum* and the *International Aerospace Hall of Fame,* it has a notable collection of aircraft and spacecraft. Open daily. Admission charge except the fourth Tuesday of every month. 2001 Pan American Plaza, *Balboa Park* (phone: 234-8291).

Reuben H. Fleet Space Theater and Science Center Simulated space travel is the attraction here. Images projected on the 360° screen give you the impression you're moving in zero-gravity conditions. The *Science Center* also has exhibitions on astronomy and technology, and a free demonstration of lasers. Open daily, and evenings, too. Admission charge. 1875 El Prado, *Balboa Park* (phone: 238-1233).

San Diego Natural History Museum More than a century old, this museum has a collection of birds that nest in the San Diego area, and sharks, whales, and fish who make their home in the surrounding seas. A Sefton seismograph measures tremors and earth movement, and a desert discovery laboratory features live reptiles. Open daily. Admission charge. Across from the *Fleet Space Theater, Balboa Park* (phone: 232-3821).

Japanese Friendship Garden These 11½ acres contain a lake, tea garden, stone garden, meadow, and terrace. Closed Mondays, Wednesdays, and Thursdays. Admission charge. *Balboa Park,* near the *Spreckels Organ Pavilion* (phone: 232-2721).

SEAPORT VILLAGE Built around three main plazas edging San Diego Bay, this 14-acre waterfront complex of restaurants and specialty shops resembles a New England fishing village. A main attraction is the wonderful *Flying Horses Carousel* with its hand-carved wooden animals, constructed at the turn of the century for the amusement park at Coney Island, New York. It's nice to stroll through the village in the evening and have dinner overlooking the water. 849 Harbor Dr. at Pacific Hwy. (phone: 235-4014).

EMBARCADERO This is another interesting place to walk. From the pier you can see the activities on *North Island Naval Air Station* across the bay, and watch cruise ships at anchor and the hundreds of sailboats cruising.

SAN DIEGO MARITIME MUSEUM The oldest square-rigged merchantman afloat, the 125-plus-year-old *Star of India* is berthed here, along with the turn-of-the-century ferryboat *Berkeley* and steam yacht *Medea.* Open daily. Admission charge. Ash St. at Harbor Dr. (phone: 234-9153).

LA JOLLA

MORMON TEMPLE This 190-foot stone-and-glass structure looms over the highway between San Diego and La Jolla. Built to serve the area's 85,000 Mormons, it is used for marriage ceremonies and other sacred rites. Non-Mormons can admire the exterior architecture, which resembles a sparkling Baroque cathedral, but they are not allowed inside. Off Interstate 5, 12 miles north of downtown.

TIDE POOLS Visit the tide pools just beyond Alligator Head at La Jolla Cove at low tide to see a veritable profusion of hermit crabs, sea anemones, and starfish clambering over one another. Wear tennis shoes, since the jagged rocks can cut your feet. From San Diego, take Route 5 to Ardath Road exit. Follow Ardath west until it becomes Torrey Pines Road. Take Torrey Pines west, turn right on Prospect and follow it to Coast Boulevard. Follow signs to La Jolla Cove.

WHALE POINT Every year in late December, January, and February, giant whales migrate south past this point (at least, they have for eight million years or so). Follow the shore south from Alligator Head. Opposite the only large building on the beach is a small cove known as Seal Rock. From Seal Rock, you'll be able to see another cove, marked by a lifeguard stand and a wall. That's Whale Point.

MUSEUM OF CONTEMPORARY ART, SAN DIEGO Situated near the beach between Seal Rock and Whale Point, the gardens and building are well worth a look. Recently expanded, the museum exhibits fine contemporary paintings and sculpture from all over the world. Closed Mondays. Admission charge. Prospect and Silverado (phone: 454-3541). A second location is at 1001 Kettner (phone: 234-1001).

SEA CAVES North of Seal Rock is a natural formation of seven caves hollowed out by waves. To reach it walk along the cliffs facing the ocean. Take Coast Boulevard to the tunnel leading to Coast Walk.

SCRIPPS INSTITUTION OF OCEANOGRAPHY One of the most highly esteemed marine study research centers and graduate schools in the world, it is part of the *University of California, San Diego.* Stroll through the grounds or relax on the Scripps beach. You can't walk on the pier, but you can enjoy the tide pools nearby. 8602 La Jolla Shores Dr. (phone: 534-3624).

STEPHEN BIRCH AQUARIUM-MUSEUM Overlooking the Pacific Ocean, this facility affiliated with the *Scripps Institution* displays an array of fascinating marine life in 34 tanks (including a 50,000-gallon kelp forest filled with marine specimens indigenous to the waters off La Jolla). There's also an interactive oceanographic museum and an outdoor artificial tide pool. Open daily. Admission and parking charge. 2300 Expedition Way (phone: 534-FISH).

TORREY PINES STATE RESERVE This 2,000-acre park within the city limits is an oasis of wilderness in an urban environment. The pine trees date to the period when Southern California was less arid and forests flourished. On the northern side of the park, Los Penasquitos Lagoon offers a spectacular vantage point for watching blue herons and rare egrets. Mule deer feed in the southern part of the lagoon. The visitors' center is in a 1923 adobe building. Try to arrive early in the day; the number of admissions is limited. Open daily. Parking charge. N. Torrey Pines Rd. (phone: 755-2063).

EXTRA SPECIAL

No tour of San Diego would be complete without a visit to Mexico. The border city of Tijuana is 17 miles south. Many San Diego visitors and residents drive there, park on the US side of the border, and walk into Tijuana. (The Tijuana taxis are notorious for overcharging. Be sure to agree upon the fare before you start.) If you plan to drive in Mexico, rent a car once you're across the border. Also, purchase insurance at one of the many insurance offices near the border. It can prevent unpleasant detention should you have an accident while in Mexico, as US auto insurance is not valid there.

San Diego's trolley system is a good alternative to driving. The trip to Tijuana takes about 40 minutes and costs $1.75 each way. The trip originates at the *Amtrak* terminal (C St. and Kettner Blvd.) and terminates at San Ysidro (200 feet from the border). *Tijuana City Tour* buses pick up passengers at the trolley stop and, for an additional charge, will tour the Mexican city's main attractions. Trolleys leave the main stations (in either direction) every 15 minutes from 5 to 1 AM daily; tickets are purchased at vending machines at all pick-up points.

Tijuana has many crafts shops selling finely wrought ironwork, pottery, and jewelry at prices that are a fraction of those in the US. You may bring back $400 worth of goods duty-free, once every 30 days. Goods must be declared at retail value at the checkpoint for re-entering the US, but certain items—such as Mexican national treasures—are prohibited. The *Tijuana Cultural Center* (Paseo de los Héroes; phone: 52-66-841111 in Tijuana) has an Omnimax theater which depicts Mexico's cultural heritage, a museum, a performing arts center, shopping, and a restaurant. Tijuana also offers year-round thoroughbred racing at the *Hipódromo Agua Caliente* track, dog racing, jai alai, and bullfighting. The *Tijuana Trolley* picks up passengers on the Tijuana side and makes a round-trip journey between the two cities. The $5 ticket allows you to get on and off as often as you like. For more information, call the *Tijuana Tourism and Convention Bureau* (phone: 52-66-840537; 800-252-5363 in the US and Canada).

You need a tourist card to travel more than 75 miles south of the border, or if you plan to stay in Mexico longer than 72 hours. It's a good idea to carry your passport, birth certificate, or voter registration card at all times, as you are in a foreign country; a driver's license alone is not enough. Also, upon re-entering the US, you may be asked for proof of citizenship. Be sure that your documentation is in order *before* crossing the border.

Sources and Resources

TOURIST INFORMATION

The *San Diego Convention and Visitors Bureau* (401 B St., Suite 1400, San Diego, CA 92101; phone: 232-3101; fax: 232-1707), which is closed weekends, distributes maps and brochures. The main *International Visitor Information Center* is at First Avenue and F Street (11 Horton Plaza, San Diego, CA 92101; phone: 236-1212). It is open daily in summer, closed Sundays the rest of the year. There is another information center, which is open daily, at 2688 East Mission Bay Drive, off Route 5 (phone: 276-8200). For maps and brochures on walking tours of the historic district, stop at the *State Park Visitor Center* (Old Town Plaza; phone: 220-5422), which is open daily. Contact the California state tourism hotline (phone: 800-TO-CALIF) for maps, calendars of events, health updates, and travel advisories.

LOCAL COVERAGE *Union-Tribune,* daily; *San Diego Reader,* weekly; *San Diego* magazine, monthly. The *San Diego Official Visitors Guide* is available through the visitors' bureau (above); *The San Diegan* (San Diego Guide; $1.95) is the most complete guide to the area; write to *The San Diegan,* PO Box 99127, San Diego, CA 92169, or call 453-1633. *K-Lynn Restaurant Guide,* by Lynn Heller and Kathy Glick (AM/PM Publishing; $6.50), has listings of the best eateries in town.

TELEVISION STATIONS KFMB Channel 8–CBS; KGTV Channel 10–ABC; KPBS Channel 15–PBS; and KNSD Channel 39–NBC.

RADIO STATIONS AM: KFMB 760 (talk); KSDO 1130 (news/talk/sports); and KSON 1240 (country). FM: KFSD 94.1 (classical); KIFM 98.1 (soft jazz); and KCBQ 105.3 (classic rock).

TELEPHONE The area code for San Diego is 619.

SALES TAX The city sales tax is 7.75%; the hotel room tax is 10.5%.

CLIMATE Rainstorms are few and far between, and almost invariably occur in December, January, and February. During these months, the temperature might drop into the high 40s F at night. Daytimes generally are in the 60s. The rest of the year, you can expect bright days and cool evenings with daytime highs in the 70s, lows at night in the 50s (so be sure to pack a sweater or jacket). Bathing suits and tennis shoes are de rigueur year-round. For beach weather and surf reports call 221-8884.

GETTING AROUND

AIRPORT *San Diego International Airport* at *Lindbergh Field* is within sight of downtown. *San Diego Metropolitan Transit* bus No. 2 leaves from the airport every 20 minutes and runs along Broadway, downtown (phone: 233-3004). *Peerless Shuttle* (phone: 554-1700) and *Cloud 9 Shuttle* (phone: 278-5841) also operate airport transfer service by mini-van.

BUS The *San Diego Metropolitan Transit System* operates frequent buses connecting downtown with the suburbs. Fares range from $1 to $3, depending on distance (phone: 233-3004).

CAR RENTAL The best way to see everything conveniently is by car. Most major national car rental firms are represented.

TAXI Call *Yellow Cab* (phone: 234-6161) or *American Cab* (phone: 292-1111).

TROLLEY The *San Diego Trolley* originates at the *Amtrak* terminal (C St. and Kettner Blvd.). The *South Line* runs from the restored Spanish-style depot to the Mexican border, the *East Line* to the town of El Cajón, and the *Bayside Line* to the *Convention Center* and bayside hotels and attractions. Tickets, available from machines at all 27 stops, cost $1 to $1.75, depending on distance (phone: 231-8549).

WATER TAXI/FERRY The *Harbor Hopper* (phone: 234-4111) makes regular trips between *Sea World of California,* several of the major hotels, El Camino Point, and other places of interest daily except Mondays. The 22-foot "water limousines" can carry up to 24 passengers and are equipped with TV sets, VCRs, and stereos. There is a ferry (phone: 435-8895) between the Broadway Pier in San Diego and the Old Ferry Landing on Coronado (the fare is $2 each way).

SIGHTSEEING TOURS

HORSE-DRAWN CARRIAGES *Cinderella Carriage* (phone: 239-8080) picks up passengers at *Seaport Village* and takes them on 30-, 45-, or 60-minute drives through different areas of the city.

HOT-AIR BALLOON A unique way to see the city is by hot-air balloon. *Balloon Adventure* (phone: 800-373-3359) can set it up for you—the trip includes champagne in the air and a certificate upon landing. Another choice is *Skysurfer Balloon* (phone: 481-6800).

TROLLEY *Old Town Trolley Tours* (phone: 298-8687) offers sightseeing loop tours of central San Diego with all-day on-and-off privileges, stops at or near many hotels, and provides additional travel on extension shuttles to Hotel Circle.

SPECIAL EVENTS

San Diego holds a summer festival almost all year. The following is only a selection of events. In January (sometimes in December), the *San Diego Marathon* (phone: 792-2900) is run along 14 miles of coastline in Carlsbad. Also in January is the *Mercedes Championships,* a *PGA* golf tournament held at *La Costa Resort and Spa* (Costa del Mar Rd., Carlsbad; phone: 800-918-4653). Another professional golf tournament, the *Buick Invitational of California* tees off in February at *Torrey Pines* (La Jolla; phone: 281-4653). March sees the *St. Patrick's Day Parade* (phone: 299-7812). April heralds the *San Diego Crew Classic* (West Mission Bay; phone: 488-1039) and the *La Jolla Grand Prix Bicycle Race* (phone: 579-5723). The Mexican-American community hosts the *Cinco de Mayo Festival* (phone: 296-3161) in early May. In July, the *Festival of the Bells* (phone: 281-8449) celebrates the founding of *San Diego de Alcalá*, and the *Mission San Luis Rey Fiesta* (phone: 757-3651) does the same for *Mission San Luis Rey*. September's *Cabrillo Festival* (phone: 557-5450) marks the discovery of the West Coast, and *Oktoberfest* (phone: 465-3653) is held along La Mesa Boulevard for several days in October. A number of events herald the *Christmas* holiday season: the *Mission Bay Christmas Boat Parade of Lights* (phone: 488-0501), from Quivira Basin to *Sea World of California; San Diego Harbor Parade of Lights* (phone: 297-5917); *Posadas and Luminarias* (*Mission San Luis Rey;* phone: 297-1183), a Mexican *Christmas* ceremony; Old Town's *Las Posadas* (phone: 220-5422), a *Christmas* candlelight procession honoring the Holy Family; *Christmas on the Prado* (*Balboa Park;* phone: 239-0512), and the *Holiday Bowl* college football (phone: 283-5808).

MUSEUMS

In addition to those described in *Special Places,* other museums include the *Museum of San Diego History, Centro Cultural de la Raza, San Diego Automotive Museum, San Diego Museum of Photographic Arts, San Diego Hall of Champions,* and *San Diego Model Railroad Museum*—all in *Balboa Park.* Hours and days vary; many *Balboa Park* museums close at 4:30 PM, and some have special days when there is no admission charge. Be sure to call ahead (phone: 239-0512) for information. In addition, *Palomar Observatory*'s giant telescope, for many years the most powerful in the world, is still in use. Photographs of the cosmos are on display there. Open daily. No admission charge. County Rd. S6, east of Escondido (phone: 742-2119).

SHOPPING

San Diego has its share of today's marketplaces, huge malls filled with cookie-cutter department stores, chain shops, eateries, and entertainment. Enclaves of commerce with more individuality, however, also are easy to come by—and get to. Museum shops are an excellent source of quality gifts and mementos. Theme "villages" have sprouted near other city attractions, including the following:

Bazaar del Mundo Locals as well as tourists patronize this Old Town shopping center. Be sure to check out *Ariana* (phone: 296-4989) for brightly colored hand-crafted jewelry, and ethnic and hand-painted silk and cotton apparel. 2754 Calhoun St., between Taylor and Mason Sts. (phone: 296-3161).

Horton Plaza This complex is a glittering, multicolored labyrinth with passages and galleries, odd angles and curves, banners, awnings, whimsical sculptures, and plantings, in addition to nearly 150 shops and eateries, seven movie theaters, and two live theaters. *Nordstrom, Robinson's,* the *Broadway,* and *Mervyn's* are the department store anchors; and designer boutiques include *Louis Vuitton* and *Jessica McClintock.* Between Broadway and G St., and First and Fourth Aves. (phone: 238-1596).

Paladion An upscale mall, it features such tony shops as *Tiffany & Co., Ferragamo, Cartier,* and *Alfred Dunhill.* There are also two fine restaurants, valet parking, and concierge service. 777 Front St. (phone: 232-1627).

Promenade at Pacific Beach and Belmont Park Located in Mission Beach, these two shopping spots are handy to beach resort hotels. The *Promenade* is at Ventura and Mission Blvds. (phone: 490-9097); *Belmont Park* is at 3146 Mission Blvd. (phone: 491-2988).

Other regions around the city provide a variety of shopping enclaves, with specialty shops as well as national chains. In La Jolla, two streets vie for the title of San Diego's Rodeo Drive. Prospect Street runs on a bluff overlooking the Pacific and is the city's most pleasant street for shopping on foot. Art galleries and restaurants predominate. A fashion parade of boutiques on Girard Avenue, which intersects Prospect, culminates with *Saks Fifth Avenue* to the east. Among the intriguing establishments:

C. J. Felcher This shop features a unique collection of antique and estate jewelry. 1237 Prospect (phone: 459-5166).

Jacques LeLong Stop here for the Southern California–Western look: studs and sequins on leather duds. 1141 Prospect St. (phone: 454-7760).

London Associates Shells The seashells and fossils sold here are polished, and often hand-crafted into jewelry. 1137 Prospect St. (phone: 459-6858).

Ports International This shop is an oasis of classic women's fashions. 7844 Girard Ave. (phone: 454-9151).

SPORTS AND FITNESS

There's something here for just about everybody.

BASEBALL The *National League Padres* play at *Jack Murphy Stadium* (9449 Friars Rd.; phone: 283-4494).

BICYCLING Bikes may be rented at *Hamel's Action Sports Center* (704 Ventura Pl., Mission Beach; phone: 488-5050); *Reid's Bike Rentals* (711 Pacific Beach Dr.; phone: 275-0765); *Bike San Diego* (1775 E. Mission Bay Dr.; phone: 232-4700); or *Bicycle Barn* (746 Emerald St.; phone: 581-3665).

FISHING The Oceanside Pier is one of America's longest wooden piers; there also are piers at Mission Bay, San Diego Harbor, and Shelter Island. You need a permit for deep-sea fishing; contact the *California Department of Fish and Game Resources* (1350 Front St., Room 2041, San Diego, CA 92101; phone: 467-4201). Marlin, yellowtail, and sailfish run in the spring. A fishing license is required for those 16 and older. Licenses can be obtained for less than $10 a day at sporting goods stores and at many lakes.

FITNESS CENTERS *Shiley Sports and Health Center of Scripps Clinic* has a comprehensive fitness center (10820 N. Torrey Pines, La Jolla; phone: 554-FITT); the *YMCA* has a pool and weight room (5505 Friars Rd.; phone: 298-3576). Both are open to visitors for a fee.

FOOTBALL The *NFL Chargers* play home games at *Jack Murphy Stadium* (9449 Friars Rd.; phone 280-2111). The *San Diego State Aztecs* (phone: 283-7378) play at *San Diego State University*'s *Aztec Bowl.*

GOLF San Diego is a golfing capital of Southern California, with nearly six dozen public courses in the area to satisfy local and visiting golfaholics alike. One of these is well above par.

A TOP TEE-OFF SPOT

Torrey Pines Both the *North* and *South* courses at *Torrey Pines* (11480 N. Torrey Pines Rd., La Jolla; phone: 800-985-4653) are highly acclaimed and worth the attention of serious golfers.

Two other fine courses are the *Mission Bay,* which is lighted for night-time play (*Mission Bay Park;* phone: 490-3370), and the *Coronado Municipal* (2000 Visalia Row; phone: 234-4111).

HORSE RACING Thoroughbreds race at *Del Mar Race Track,* July through September (I-5 to Fairgrounds exit; phone: 755-1141), or contact *Del Mar Thoroughbred*

Club (phone: 792-4242). The racetrack at Del Mar is closed on Tuesdays. There's also seasonal racing at *Hipódromo Agua Caliente* racetrack in Tijuana (phone: 231-1910; see *Extra Special*).

ICE SKATING Try the ice at *Ice Capades Chalet* (4545 La Jolla Village Dr.; phone: 452-9110) and *San Diego Ice Arena* (off Hwy. 15, 1001 Black Mountain Rd.; phone: 530-1825).

JAI ALAI This Basque import is played at *Fronton Palacio,* Tijuana (phone: 52-66-863958 in Tijuana; 231-1910 in San Diego), nightly except Wednesdays.

JOGGING Run along Laurel Street to *Balboa Park,* where there are six different courses, ranging from less than half a mile to 9 miles. It's possible to jog along Harbor Drive in the direction of the airport, but avoid rush hours because of the fumes. Mileage is marked around Mission Bay. In La Jolla, run along the shore and boardwalk or the La Jolla Cove.

SAILING AND BOATING The *City Lakes Department* rents motorboats and rowboats for use on lakes (phone: 465-3474 for information, 390-0222 for reservations). *Mission Bay Sportcenter* also gives sailing courses (phone: 488-1004). *Seaforth Mission Bay Boat Rentals* (1641 Quivira Rd., Mission Bay; phone: 223-1681) has sailboats, rowboats, and power boats as well as boats rigged for water skiing; they also rent fishing gear and windsurfing equipment. You can rent sailboats and take sailing lessons at *Harbor Island Sailboats* (2040 Harbor Island Dr., Harbor Island; phone: 291-9568) and at many beach resort hotels.

SKIING The *Torrey Pines Ski Club* (write PO Box 82087, San Diego, CA 92138; phone: 583-8832) organizes trips to nearby mountains.

SOCCER The San Diego *Sockers* of the *Continental Indoor Soccer League (CISL)* kick a few balls around at the *San Diego Sports Arena* (3500 Sports Arena Blvd.; phone: 224-4171).

SCUBA DIVING Diving gear and lessons are available at *Diving Locker* (1020 Grand Ave.; phone: 272-1120), and the San Diego area has one of our very favorite dive spots.

BEST DEPTHS

La Jolla Cove Starting at this 50-yard-deep, 100-yard-wide notch in the Southern California coastline, the *San Diego–La Jolla Underwater Park* takes in about 7 miles of underwater scenery up the coast as far as *Torrey Pines;* within the park there's a look-but-don't-touch area where you can see vast quantities of kelp, abalone, and lobster. One of the best sites is at the edge of a 20-mile-long submarine canyon that borders the underwater park; the drop-off is 11,000 feet. For more information, contact the *Parks and Recreation Department, Coastline Parks Division* (phone: 221-8900).

SURFING *Boomer Beach,* so named because of the rumbling sound of surf crashing to shore, is the body-surfer's first choice. Surfboarders ride the waves at *La Jolla Shores.*

SWIMMING There are 70 miles of public beaches, not to mention *Mission Bay Park*'s manmade lagoons. La Jolla and *Torrey Pines State Park* beaches are especially beautiful (see *Special Places*). There are 10 municipal swimming pools; for information call the *Aquatics Department* of the *City Recreation Office* (phone: 685-1322). Don't miss the *Plunge* water slide at Belmont Shores.

TENNIS San Diego itself has plenty of courts for public use, but just outside the city limits is a *primo* tennis resort.

CHOICE COURTS

Rancho Valencia This resort got its start as a tennis camp, and it's a wonderful place to stay even if you don't like tennis. There are 18 tennis courts, a staff of pros to help you refine your strokes, a pro shop, and a clubhouse; week-long intensive tennis clinics are offered through the well-respected John Gardiner program. If you come without a partner, the staff can set up a game for you with someone who matches your level of expertise. The location, just inland from Del Mar and La Jolla, is ideal (5921 Valencia Circle; phone: 756-1123; 800-548-3664).

In the city, there are public courts at *Balboa Tennis Club,* Morley Field (2221 Morley Field Dr., *Balboa Park;* phone: 295-9278); *University City Racquet Club, Standley Park* (3585 Governor Dr.; phone: 452-LOVE); and *Peninsula Tennis Club,* Robb Field (2525 Bacon St.; phone: 226-3407).

WHALE WATCHING Watch the migrating sea mammals from *Cabrillo National Monument,* Whale Point in La Jolla, or go on a whale watching excursion from *H & M Landing* (2803 Emerson St.; phone: 222-1144) or *Fisherman's Landing* (2838 Garrison St.; phone: 221-8500), in late December, January, and February. The *Scripps Institution of Oceanography* offers weekend whale watching trips in January and February.

THEATER

The *Old Globe Theatre* stages summer festivals featuring contemporary productions, as well as Shakespeare; the rest of the year, the company performs modern classics, musicals, and dramas at both the *Old Globe* and next-door *Cassius Carter Center Stage* (*Balboa Park;* phone: 239-2255). During the summer, some productions are staged at the outdoor *Lowell Davies Festival Theater. San Diego Repertory Theatre* performs in the *Lyceum Theater*—two stages (*Horton Plaza;* phone: 231-3586). *Gaslamp Quarter Theatre Company* offers cabaret theater at the *Hahn Cosmopolitan Theatre*

(444 Fourth Ave.; phone: 234-9583 or 232-9608). The well-regarded *La Jolla Playhouse,* at the *Mandel Weiss Center* on the *University of California–San Diego* campus, presents a variety of plays from May through November (phone: 550-1010). The *California Ballet* performs the *Nutcracker Suite* at *Christmas* and other classics the rest of the year, at venues around the metro area (phone: 560-5676). Discount tickets for theater and other cultural events are available at the *ARTSTIX* booth (*Horton Plaza;* phone: 238-0700) on the day of the performance (cash only).

MUSIC

Copley Symphony Hall (1245 Seventh Ave.; phone: 699-4205) is the home of the *San Diego Symphony*. The *San Diego Opera Company* performs at the *Civic Theatre* (202 C St.; phone: 232-7636). Free organ concerts are played every Sunday afternoon at the *Spreckels Organ Pavilion* (*Balboa Park;* phone: 226-0819). Most rock concerts take place at the *San Diego Sports Arena* (3500 Sports Arena Blvd.; phone: 225-9813).

NIGHTCLUBS AND NIGHTLIFE

In Cahoots (5373 Mission Center Rd.; phone: 291-8635) features country-and-western music. The *Cannibal Bar* at the *Catamaran* hotel (3999 Mission Blvd.; phone: 488-1081) is a lively, young dance club. *Elario's* in La Jolla features top jazz performances on the top floor of the *Summerhouse Inn* (7955 La Jolla Shores Dr., La Jolla; phone: 459-0541). *Croce's* restaurant (802 Fifth Ave.; phone: 233-4355) features live jazz seven nights a week; jazz is also presented frequently at the *Palace Bar* at the *Horton Grand* hotel (311 Island Ave.; phone: 544-1886). *Dick's Last Resort* (345 Fourth Ave., between J and K Sts.; phone: 231-9100), in the Gaslamp Quarter, is a rowdy restaurant-bar with live Dixieland jazz. For comedy, try *The Comedy Store* (916 Pearl St., La Jolla; phone: 454-9176).

Best in Town

CHECKING IN

The presence of the *Convention Center* and the redevelopment of downtown have caused an increase in the number of fine hotels and resorts in the city. Visitors seeking comfortable, reasonably priced accommodations will find them in all parts of San Diego. Those listed below are special in quality, character, or value. Most of San Diego's major hotels have complete facilities for the business traveler. Those listed below as having "business services" usually offer such conveniences as meeting rooms, photocopiers, computers, translation services, and express checkout, among others. Call the individual hotel for additional information. Expect to pay $130 or more per night for a double room at those places categorized as expensive; between $90 and $130 at those rated moderate; and less than $90 at places listed as inexpensive. For accommodations at bed and breakfast establishments, contact *Bed & Breakfast Directory for San Diego* (PO Box 3292, San Diego, CA 92163; phone: 297-3130; 800-619-7666). One option is to spend the night at sea. The *Dockside Inn* (1450 Harbor Island Dr.; phone: 296-8940) can arrange for you to sleep on board a yacht at one of San Diego's marinas. A continental breakfast is included; catered dinners can be ordered as well. Hotel rooms have air conditioning, private baths, and TV sets.

All hotels below are in San Diego and telephone and fax numbers are in the 619 area code unless otherwise indicated.

We begin with our favorite places, followed by recommended hotels listed by price category.

GRAND HOTELS

Inn at Rancho Santa Fe Here, you'll find a sedate and very restful complex of unpretentious cottages nestled on 20 acres of luxuriant grounds surrounding the original building. There are three tennis courts, a heated swimming pool, an English croquet lawn, and, nearby, two championship golf courses and *Del Mar Beach* (7 miles away). The inn will pack a box lunch for you. There's a wonderful library and a high-ceilinged living room, both with fireplaces, as well as maid service, a fine dining room, and business services—and all just 25 miles north of San Diego. 5951 Linea del Cielo, Rancho Santa Fe (phone: 756-1131; 800-654-2928; fax: 759-1604).

Rancho Valencia Reminiscent of an early California hacienda, this secluded resort—a popular romantic hideaway among Southern Californians—near Del Mar and La Jolla offers accommodations in 21 Spanish-style casitas, comprising 34 spacious suites with fireplaces, large tiled baths, and terraces; "The Hacienda" suite has its own pool. The decor in both the public areas and the suites combines rustic charm and elegance; the rosebud delivered each morning with your newspaper and fresh-squeezed orange juice is just one extra touch. Known for its extensive tennis facilities and clinics (see *Tennis*), the property also boasts a pool, two Jacuzzis, a croquet lawn, a fitness center, and access to nearby golf courses. Spa treatments and fitness programs round out the on-property diversions. The *Rancho Valencia* dining room (see *Eating Out*) provides fine American fare, and room service is always on call. There's also a concierge desk and business services. Transportation to some of Southern California's most beautiful beaches is available. 5921 Valencia Circle, Rancho Santa Fe (phone: 756-1123; 800-548-3664; fax: 756-0165).

EXPENSIVE

L'Auberge Del Mar The defunct *Tudor Del Mar* hotel, a favorite pre-World War II seaside hangout of Hollywood stars and *Del Mar Race Track* fans, has been reincarnated as a 123-room luxury resort (now managed by the Bel-Air company) in a cozy, French provincial mode. Located in the heart of Del Mar, it's across the street from *Del Mar Plaza*'s chic boutiques and eateries and only a short stroll from the Pacific. Special treats include award-winning fare at *Tourlas* restaurant, afternoon tea, and weekend dinner dances. Pools, a full health and beauty spa, tennis courts, and chic shops are on the premises. Other amenities include a concierge and business services. 1540 Camino Del Mar, Del Mar (phone: 259-1515; 800-553-1336; fax: 755-4940).

Bahia Situated on its own 14-acre peninsula on Mission Bay and great for families, this resort has a tropical feel; it boasts its own beaches, a seal pond, and a plethora of exotic palm trees. Many of its 325 rooms have not only their own kitchens, but also private patios overlooking Mission Bay. Two paddle wheel riverboats ferry guests around the bay on cocktail cruises complete with music and dancing; the boats double as meeting facilities and ballrooms. Amenities include a restaurant/comedy club, a piano bar, an Olympic-size pool, an oversize Jacuzzi, and two lighted tennis courts. Business services are also available. 998 W. Mission Bay Dr. (phone: 488-0551; 800-288-0770).

Catamaran Resort South Pacific in feeling, this 315-room property features a lobby with a waterfall, ponds filled with *koi,* and a museum-quality collection of Polynesian artifacts. More than 100 varieties of trees, many exotic birds, and a whimsical hippopotamus fountain lend a special ambience to the resort's eight-and-a-half acres. Many rooms have kitchens. The *Cannibal Bar* jumps at night with live entertainment and dancing, while *Moray's Bar* is quieter. One of San Diego's finest restaurants, the *Atoll* (see *Eating Out*) is also here. The *Bahia Belle,* an authentic paddle wheel riverboat, links the *Catamaran* with its sister hotel, the *Bahia.* Business services are available, and there's also a concierge desk. 3999 Mission Blvd. (phone: 488-1081; 800-288-0770; fax: 488-1081).

Del Coronado When it opened in 1888, it was the largest wooden building in the country and the first hotel in the world to have electric lighting and elevators. Today, the 691-room resort is a National Historic Landmark and one of the world's most picturesque hotels. The first floor ocean-view lanai rooms are extraordinary, but other rooms in the historic building are less impressive than the exterior architecture, and there is a modern annex that's downright pedestrian. Then there are those rather noisy early morning flights out of the naval air station. Facilities include a small spa, two pools, tennis courts, three restaurants, and a deli. A concierge desk is also available, as are business services and 24-hour room service. On the Coronado

Peninsula, 1500 Orange Ave. (phone: 522-8000; 800-468-3533 or 800-HOTEL-DEL; fax: 522-8238).

Doubletree at Horton Plaza Adjacent to the *Horton Plaza Shopping Center,* it has 450 rooms, an outdoor pool, and two tennis courts, plus a health club. The interior is done in soft tones, the menu at the *Café San Diego* features regional California cooking, the early bird dinner at the coffee shop is a tasty bargain, and 24-hour room service is available. There's also a concierge desk and business services. 910 Broadway Circle (phone: 239-2200; 800-222-TREE; fax: 239-0509).

Hyatt Islandia This 423-room property sits on four-and-a-half lush acres overlooking Mission Bay and the Pacific, not far from *Sea World* and other San Diego attractions. A 17-story tower offers 260 spacious rooms with glass-enclosed patios. Upper floors boast terrific nighttime views. The Regency Club, on the top two floors, provides concierge service and complimentary continental breakfast and hors d'oeuvres. The Marina Suites are in a three-story building overlooking the marina. The resort offers a huge, California-shaped pool, an outdoor Jacuzzi, workout room, whale watching, deep-sea fishing, sailboat rental, and a jogging path; golf and tennis are nearby. There are two restaurants, two lounges, a concierge and business services. 1441 Quivira Rd. (phone: 224-1234; 800-233-1234; fax: 224-4880).

Loews Coronado Bay Resort This $80-million, 440-room seaside property sits on a 15-acre private peninsula surrounded by San Diego Bay. Every room offers views of the marina, the bay, or the city skyline. Facilities include a health club, five tennis courts, three pools, and there are sunken tubs in many of the rooms. The hotel has three restaurants (including *Azzura Point;* see *Eating Out*), two lounges, a poolside grill, and an upscale food and gift store. Equipment for bicycling, sailing, and water sports can be rented. Other amenities include a concierge and business services. 4000 Coronado Bay Rd., Coronado (phone: 424-4000; 800-81-LOEWS; fax: 424-4400).

Le Meridien San Diego at Coronado It's a fresh, airy, luxury resort in a South Seas island setting, with tropical plants, lagoons, and exotic birds. The 300 rooms are bright, the atmosphere relaxing. An on-site spa soothes the strains of a full range of resort activities, and a spa menu is always available. Food at the elegant *Marius* and the casual brasserie, *L'Escale,* is exquisite (see *Eating Out* for both). Room service is available around the clock. There are also business services and a concierge desk. 2000 Second St., Coronado (phone: 435-3000; 800-543-4300; fax: 435-3032).

San Diego Marriott Two elliptical towers rise 25 floors above San Diego Bay and the hotel's own 19-acre marina. Inside are 1,355 rooms and suites, a shopping arcade, and six restaurants and bars. A fitness center, six lighted tennis courts, and a large outdoor pool provide plenty of workout opportunities, and the marina offers boats for rent. Other pluses are 24-hour room service, a concierge, and business services. 333 W. Harbor Dr. (phone: 234-1500; 800-228-9290; fax: 234-8678).

Sheraton Grande Torrey Pines Next to the two *Torrey Pines* golf courses, this casually elegant, white Mediterranean-style establishment has 400 rooms overlooking the greens and the Pacific beyond. Facilities include a fitness center, a pool with Jacuzzi, privileges at the *Shiley Sports and Health Center of the Scripps Clinic* next door, plus a butler on each floor. The view alone is worth the price of admission. Complimentary transportation within a 5-mile radius. Room service is available around the clock. There's also a concierge desk and business services. 10950 N. Torrey Pines Rd. (phone: 558-1500; 800-325-3535; fax: 558-1131).

U. S. Grant Restored to its 1910 ambience, this grand property is listed on the *National Register of Historic Places.* The lobby has pillars and a green and white marble floor, and the public rooms glitter with gold leaf and chandeliers. The 280 rooms are discreetly luxurious and equipped with modern amenities, but vestiges of the past remain, such as windows that open. Light lunch and tea are served in the *Grant Grill Lounge;* meals also are served in the *Grant Grill.* The central downtown location is unbeatable. Complimentary van transportation to and from the airport. There is a health club, a concierge desk, 24-hour room service, and business services. 326 Broadway (phone: 232-3121; 800-334-6957 in California, 800-237-5029 elsewhere in the US; fax: 232-3626).

La Valencia The venerable pink building on La Jolla's browseable Prospect Street is a handsome Spanish *doña* with wrought iron, tiles, and flowers. Both an international 100-room hotel and a local meeting place, it offers three restaurants and the popular *Whaling Bar,* garden dining, a sauna, a fitness room, a Jacuzzi, and a pool. The 10th-floor *Sky Room* provides panoramic views. Around-the-clock room service is available. Other amenities include a concierge and business services. 1132 Prospect St., La Jolla (phone: 454-0771; 800-451-0772; fax: 456-3921).

Westgate A 223-room property, it has a convenient downtown location and an excellent reputation. Consistent with the $1 million worth of antiques decorating the premises, the hotel also offers superb service. The *Fontainebleau* is one of the city's most elegant eateries (see *Eating Out*). Additional conveniences are 24-hour room service, a concierge, and business services. 1055 Second Ave. (phone: 238-1818; 800-522-1564 in California; 800-221-3802 elsewhere in the US; fax: 557-3737).

MODERATE

Horton Grand Ironically, a former bordello is considered the city's most romantic hostelry. In fact, it is two hotels joined by a sunny courtyard, with 132 guest units, some with fireplaces. Gilded mirrors swing open to reveal TV sets, and toilets have pull-chains, but the amenities are modern, the service cheerfully solicitous. The *Ida Bailey* restaurant (named for the original madam) has jazz Thursdays through Sundays. Room service is offered until 11 PM, and there are business services. 311 Island Ave. (phone: 544-1886; 800-542-1886; fax: 239-3823).

Somerset Suites Close to *Balboa Park* and the lively restaurant row on Fifth Avenue, this 80-suite hotel features a pool, a Jacuzzi, complimentary continental breakfast, and cable TV. Each evening, there is a social hour with complimentary beer, wine, and snacks. There's shuttle service for guests within a 5-mile radius of the hotel, as well as the train and bus stations and the airport. Concierge service is on call, and business services are available. 606 Washington St. (phone: 692-5200; 800-356-1787 in California; 800-962-9665 elsewhere in the US; fax: 299-6065).

Town and Country One of the best hotels in Mission Valley and among the city's largest, with over 1,000 rooms, this is a popular convention spot. Facilities include pools, saunas, a barber shop, a beauty parlor, and a 24-hour coffee shop. Other amenities include a concierge and business services. 500 Hotel Circle (phone: 291-7131; 800-542-6082 in California, 800-854-2608 elsewhere in the US; fax: 291-3584).

INEXPENSIVE

Torrey Pines Inn A 74-room property with a spectacular location overlooking the Pacific and right on the two famous *Torrey Pines* golf courses. Surfers and hang gliders can be spotted from the hotel, and La Jolla's beaches are just out the door. A pool and a lounge provide other options. There is a concierge desk, and business services are available. 11480 Torrey Pines Rd., La Jolla (phone: 453-4420; 800-448-8355 in California, 800-777-1700 elsewhere in the US; fax: 453-0691).

Travelodge at the Zoo The huge columns at the entrance to this 139-room hotel (formerly the *Lafayette*) near *Balboa Park* resemble those of a Southern plantation; bargain rates that include breakfast and transportation to and from the airport make up for a bit of wear around the edges. Bob Hope was the first registered guest when the hotel was built in 1946, and although the hotel may have seen better days, the pastel rooms are comfortable and many are spacious (room 328 has a long, broad porch and costs $39 a night). There is a whirlpool and a restaurant. Business services are available. 2223 El Cajón Blvd. (phone: 296-2101; 800-423-1935 in California, 800-843-9988 elsewhere in the US; fax: 296-2101).

EATING OUT

San Diego's range of restaurants has become more innovative and international. Naturally, seafood stars on many menus, and both locals and out-of-towners go for Mexican food here. Expect to pay about $125 for dinner for two at the restaurant in the very expensive category; $60 or more at those places listed as expensive; $30 to $60 at those described as moderate; and less than $30 at those rated inexpensive. Prices do not include drinks, wine, tax, or tips. All restaurants are in the 619 area code unless otherwise indicated.

Unless otherwise noted, restaurants are open for lunch and dinner.

VERY EXPENSIVE

Marius The great atmosphere and award-winning cooking evoke Provence. The menu changes three times a year but usually features fine seafood and lamb entrées concocted with a light hand and a touch of whimsy; desserts are sensational. The price is dear, but it costs much less than a trip to France. Closed Sundays and Mondays. Reservations advised. Major credit cards accepted. *Le Meridien San Diego,* 2000 Second St. (phone: 435-3000).

EXPENSIVE

Anthony's Star of the Sea Room One of the best on the West Coast, it overlooks San Diego Harbor and serves fresh-from-the-ocean abalone, as well as other fish dishes. The clams *genovese* often are ordered as an entrée. Jackets and ties required for men. Open for dinner only; closed major holidays. Reservations necessary a day or two in advance. Major credit cards accepted. 1360 N. Harbor Dr. at the foot of Ash St. (phone: 232-7408).

Azzura Point This trendy spot at *Loews Coronado Bay* is a don't-miss dining experience. Since it opened a few years ago, it has been earning raves for its outstanding seafood. The atmosphere is friendly and informal (although that casual attitude sometimes extends to the service). Still, the freshness of the ingredients and the attractiveness of the presentations make eating here more than worthwhile. Open for dinner only. Reservations advised. Major credit cards accepted. 4000 Coronado Bay Rd. (phone: 424-4000).

Delicias This eatery puts everything together perfectly—delicious food, pleasant atmosphere, and great service. Pasta, soups, and pizza baked in a wood-burning oven are among the treats offered in a cheerful room decorated with tapestries, fresh flowers, and French-country fabrics. Diners may also choose to eat outdoors under giant umbrellas. Closed Mondays. Reservations advised. Major credit cards accepted. 6106 Paseo Delicias, Rancho Santa Fe (phone: 756-8000).

Fontainebleau One of San Diego's best restaurants, it offers continental food in palatial surroundings served by waiters wearing white gloves. The dessert cart is fabulous. Closed Sundays. Reservations necessary. Major credit cards accepted. *Westgate Hotel,* 1055 Second Ave. (phone: 238-1818).

Mille Fleurs This French restaurant tucked into a charming courtyard has received considerable acclaim over the years. Chef Martin Woesle creates a complex menu of Gallic specialties; the selections change daily, but diners can expect elegant dishes such as grilled Hawaiian swordfish, roast loin of rabbit, sautéed veal sweetbreads, and Norwegian salmon in puff pastry. There's a lounge with live piano music Wednesdays through Saturdays. Open daily; dinner only on weekends. Reservations advised. Major credit cards accepted. 6009 Paseo Delicias, Rancho Santa Fe (phone: 756-3085).

Rainwater's This popular spot is a favorite of the power-lunch set who enjoy its classic American chophouse fare. Soul-satisfying steaks, melt-in-your-mouth ribs, and fish dishes top the menu. Don't miss the perfect filet mignon, steamed mussels in Champagne, Maine lobster, or chicken potpie. Delicious desserts include Southern-style pecan pie and profiteroles. Reservations advised. Major credit cards accepted. 1202 Kettner Blvd. (phone: 233-5757).

Rancho Valencia Here is award-winning fare served indoors and out. The menu changes frequently, but the food is consistently excellent, and there are always fabulous desserts plus an extensive wine list. On summer evenings, diners can dance under the stars. Reservations necessary. Major credit cards accepted. *Rancho Valencia Resort,* 5921 Valencia Circle, Rancho Santa Fe (phone: 756-1123).

Top o' the Cove Looking out onto La Jolla Cove, this restaurant is a favorite with show-biz types from LA, and is consistently voted the area's most romantic. It features squab, venison, and fresh pasta dishes. Reservations advised. Major credit cards accepted. 1216 Prospect St., La Jolla (phone: 454-7779).

MODERATE

Atoll Loudly applauded by local restaurant critics, this dining spot offers such dishes as lamb potstickers, and spinach salad with marinated scallops. The outrageously rich desserts, such as the Southwestern lemon citrus tart, are not to be missed. Reservations advised. Major credit cards accepted. *Catamaran Resort Hotel,* 3999 Mission Blvd. (phone: 488-1081).

Café Pacifica An alternative to Mexican in Old Town, this is among the city's best seafood spots. The fish is fresh, the seasoning sophisticated. The mustard catfish is especially noteworthy; also, save room for dessert. Valet parking available. Open daily; dinner only on weekends. Reservations advised. Major credit cards accepted. 2414 San Diego Ave. (phone: 291-6666).

Cindy Black's Dynamic, award-winning chef Cindy Black consistently turns out exciting dishes that have attracted a large local following. The huge, grilled portobello mushroom with rosemary oil is an appetizer that could very well be a meal in itself; risotto and Dover sole are other outstanding offerings. Desserts are deliciously sinful. Reservations necessary. Major credit cards accepted. 5721 La Jolla Blvd., La Jolla (phone: 456-6299).

Dobson's Downstairs, the pub is crowded and cozy. The dining room above the bar serves delicious seafood and grilled dishes with French flair, and the house specialty—mussel bisque topped with a pastry toque—is a big hit. Closed Sundays; dinner only on Saturdays. Reservations necessary for the dining room. Major credit cards accepted. 956 Broadway Circle (phone: 231-6771).

L'Escale Located in *Le Meridien* hotel, this place offers fabulous outdoor dining under umbrellas overlooking the bay during the summer. The emphasis is on fresh seafood and "Fitness Specials" (115 to 282 calories), but you'll have a hard time resisting the cheese twists and fresh bread. There's also a popular Sunday brunch. Reservations advised. Major credit cards accepted. 2000 Second St. (phone: 435-3000).

Fio's This northern Italian spot has been packed practically from the instant its doors opened. One of the two dining rooms features stunning murals of Siena's famous *Palio* by local artist Debra Sievers. There's an ever-changing menu, plus homemade pasta and pizza. Don't miss the *tiramisù.* Valet parking is a plus. Open daily for dinner; lunch weekdays. Reservations advised. Major credit cards accepted. 801 Fifth Ave. (phone: 234-FIOS).

Il Fornaio The menu here is as authentically Tuscan as the Carrara marble on the counters, and it includes homemade pasta and pizza from wood-burning ovens. Diners gaze at the Pacific from the terrace or window tables, or at a huge open kitchen with a genuine *girarrosto* spit from the counter seats. Coffee comes in many varieties, and the breads and pastries are delectable. Reservations advised. Major credit cards accepted. 1555 Camino Del Mar (phone: 755-8876).

George's at the Cove Pleasant, with big windows overlooking La Jolla cove, this dining spot features regional California cuisine which uses local produce, and an excellent California wine list. Entrées include prawns with *tapenade* (an olive paste), and tuna with *wasabi* (a hot Japanese mustard). Upstairs, *George's Ocean Terrace* offers the same wonderful view and similar food at more moderate prices (no reservations). Reservations advised. Major credit cards accepted. 1250 Prospect St., La Jolla (phone: 454-4244).

Pacifica Grill & Rotisserie This downtown sibling of the *Café Pacifica* (see above) overlooks the ground level of a warehouse fetchingly converted into a mini-mall next to the *Amtrak* terminal. There's something for everyone on its regional American menu, including Maryland crab cakes, mustard catfish, pizza, pasta, and ribs. Open daily; dinner only on weekends. Reservations advised. Major credit cards accepted. 1202 Kettner Blvd. (phone: 696-9226).

Sfuzzi This made-up word (pronounced *foozi*) means "fun food," and that's what is dished up here. Pizza, pasta, grilled meat, and seasonal specialties are presented in an old brick building in the Gaslamp Quarter; its walls are decorated with peeling Pompeii-like frescoes. High ceilings, wood floors, and contemporary lighting complete the picture. There's also a bar and an outdoor patio. Reservations advised. Major credit cards accepted. 304 Fifth Ave. (phone: 231-2323).

Alfonso's of La Jolla The Mexican dishes here are probably the most popular in town. Try *carne asada Alfonso* or one of the burrito or taco combination plates. Ask about Alfonso's Secret—it changes every day, and it's not on the menu. Reservations advised. Major credit cards accepted. 1251 Prospect St., La Jolla (phone: 454-2232).

Anthony's Fish Grotto If you're looking for a burger, don't come here, as this casual place serves mostly seafood (the only respite from the sea is a chicken sandwich). This is the flagship link in the popular chain of "grottoes." Others are located in La Mesa, Chula Vista, and Rancho Bernardo. No reservations. Major credit cards accepted. 1360 N. Harbor Dr. (phone: 232-5103).

Hob Nob Hill One of the most delightful places to have breakfast in the entire city. Offerings include "The Three Musketeers," a slice of ham encased in three buttermilk pancakes; eggs Florentine; and delectable pecan waffles. Closed Saturdays. Reservations advised. Major credit cards accepted. 2271 First Ave. (phone: 239-4990).

Old Town Mexican Café y Cantina A perennial local favorite; *carnitas* are the specialty. The bar stays open to 2 AM. Open daily; Sunday brunch. Reservations advised for parties of 10 or more. Major credit cards accepted. 2489 San Diego Ave. (phone: 297-4330).

Taco Auctioneers Bidding isn't necessary, but this hip café warns diners that food fights are not allowed. Despite the place's eccentricities, the food is very, very good. *Enfrijoladas,* three corn tortillas with jack cheese, ranchero beans, and avocados, is a favorite, as is the *sopa mazatleca,* excellent shrimp in tomato broth. Reservations unnecessary. MasterCard and Visa accepted. 1951 San Elijo Ave., Cardiff-by-the-Sea (phone: 942-8226).

San Francisco

According to author William Saroyan, in San Francisco "every block is a short story, every hill a novel." As you wander around and through its full-of-character (and character-filled) streets, you can watch its stories unfold: A mime acting out a scene at the cable car turntable, a motorist trying to maneuver through the throngs along Chinatown's Grant Avenue, a couple from the East catching their first look at *Golden Gate Bridge.* A place where not only Tony Bennett "left his heart," San Francisco is more than just a magnificient, multi-hilled city surrounded by water—it's an experience that stays with you long after the song has ended.

Shaped something like a crooked thumb pointing north, the city occupies a hilly peninsula of 47 square miles. On its western border is the Pacific Ocean; to the east is huge, beautiful San Francisco Bay. The waters of the bay join the Pacific through the narrow northern strait that the *Golden Gate Bridge* spans so majestically. When the bay fills with fog, as it often does, the bridge becomes a single strand of lights riding over clouds. By choosing an inland suburb or an area along the coast, residents can have either the Sunbelt warmth of California's eternal spring or the sharper, foggier weather of the shoreline.

The city's climate is universally desirable for walking, if you can handle some incredibly steep hills. Even casual strollers can chance upon hidden lanes, small houses circled by picket fences and surrounded by large commercial buildings, stately Victorian façades, stunning murals and other public art, and historical plaques. Grant Avenue provides a tour of Chinatown; Columbus Avenue, a glimpse of Italian North Beach and the birthplace of the Beat Generation; and Post Street, a taste of San Francisco's fashionable shops and art galleries.

To live uphill in any part of town is more prestigious than downhill, and to live on a famous hill tops all. Nob Hill, originally the home of railroad and mining nabobs and now the site of several of the city's luxury hotels, is an elegant address, and Russian Hill offers renowned views of the city and the bay. Along Telegraph Hill's eastern side, Filbert and Greenwich Streets create a series of steps that become wooden sidewalks fronting New England–style cottages, surrounded by gardens and filled with an impressive quiet.

For a city so generously endowed with views, vistas, and vantage points, San Francisco took its time being discovered. Explorers seeking a northern strait and new lands, among them Sir Francis Drake and Juan Rodríguez Cabrillo, sailed up and down the California coast without spying the great, but hidden, inner bay. In 1769, a Spanish land expedition led by Gaspar de Portol blundered onto San Francisco Bay on a trek north from Mexico. Their goal had been Monterey, and their excitement at discovering one of

George R. Moscone Recreation Center
Fort Mas
BAY ST.
FRANCISCO ST.
CHESTNUT ST.
LOMBARD ST.
GREENWICH ST.
FILBERT ST.
UNION ST.
GREEN ST.
VALLEJO ST.
BROADWAY
DIVISADERO ST.
SCOTT ST.
PIERCE ST.
STEINER ST.
FILLMORE ST.
WEBSTER ST.
BUCHANAN ST.
LAGUNA ST.
OCTAVIA ST.
GOUGH ST.
FRANKLIN ST.
VAN NESS AVE.
POLK ST.
LARKIN
101
PACIFIC HEIGHTS
PACIFIC AVE.
Alta Plaza Park
JACKSON ST.
WASHINGTON ST.
CLAY ST.
SACRAMENTO ST.
CALIFORNIA ST.
PINE ST.
BUSH ST.
SUTTER ST.
POST ST.
Lafayette Park
JAPAN CENTER
AUSTIN ST.
FERN ST.
HEMLOCK ST.
CEDAR ST.
MYRTLE ST.
OLIVE ST.
WILLOW ST.
NOB
HYDE ST.
Gra
Cathed
GEARY EXPY.
St Mary's Cathedral
Jefferson Square
Hayward Playground
Great American Music Hall
GEARY ST.
O'FARRELL ST.
ELLIS ST.
EDDY ST.
TURK ST.
GOLDEN GATE AVE.
Curran Theater
MCALLISTER ST.
FULTON ST.
GROVE ST.
HAYES ST.
FELL ST.
OAK ST.
War Memorial Opera House
City Hall
CIVIC CENTER
Main Library
Federal Bldg.
Louise M. Davies Symphony Hall
Civic Auditorium
United Nations Plaza
Golden Gate Theater
MARKET ST.
Old Mint

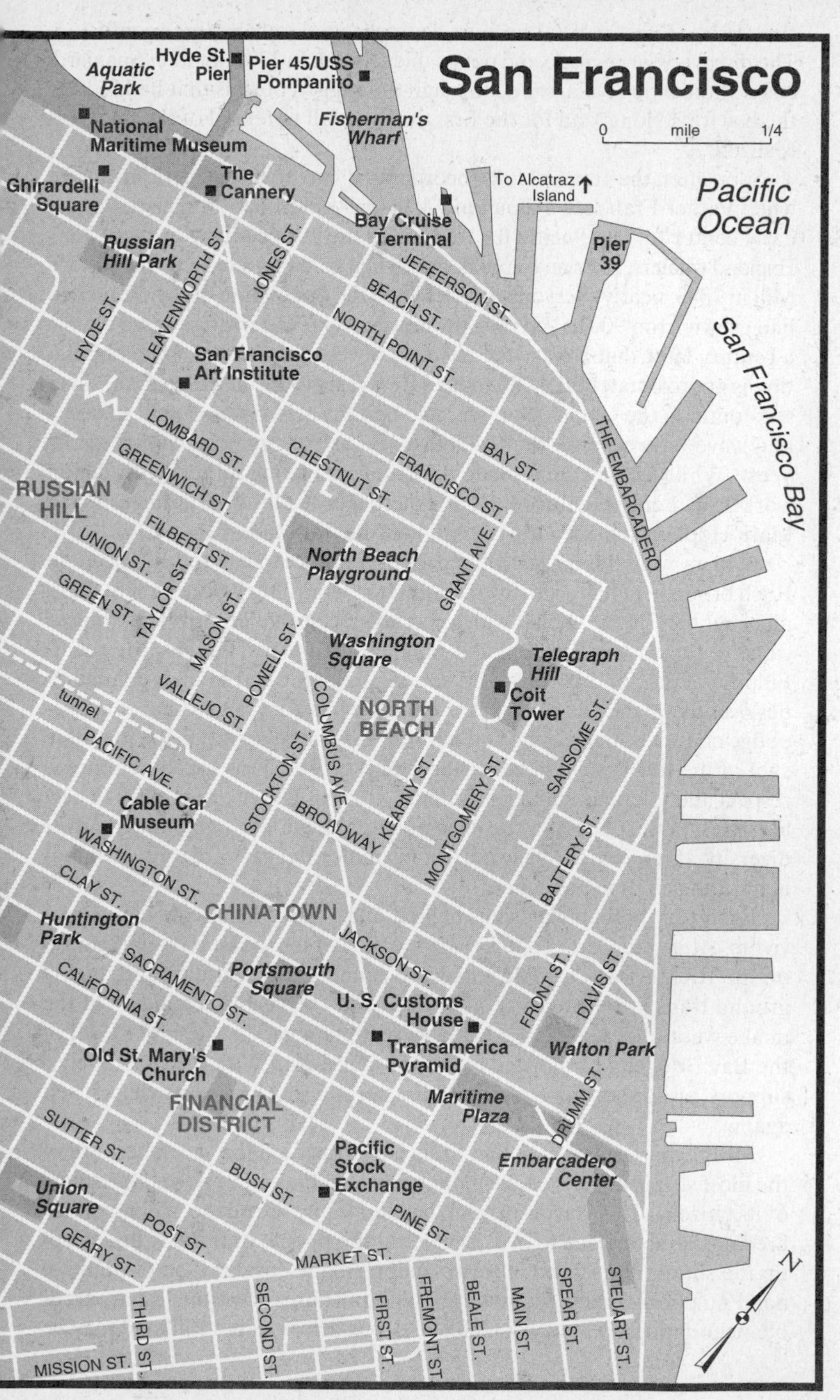

San Francisco
0 mile 1/4
Hyde St. Pier
Pier 45/USS Pompanito
Aquatic Park
National Maritime Museum
Fisherman's Wharf
Ghirardelli Square
The Cannery
To Alcatraz Island
Pacific Ocean
Bay Cruise Terminal
Pier 39
Russian Hill Park
JEFFERSON ST.
BEACH ST.
NORTH POINT ST.
San Francisco Bay
HYDE ST.
LEAVENWORTH ST.
JONES ST.
San Francisco Art Institute
LOMBARD ST.
GREENWICH ST.
CHESTNUT ST.
FRANCISCO ST.
BAY ST.
THE EMBARCADERO
RUSSIAN HILL
FILBERT ST.
UNION ST.
GREEN ST.
TAYLOR ST.
MASON ST.
North Beach Playground
GRANT AVE.
POWELL ST.
Washington Square
Telegraph Hill
Coit Tower
VALLEJO ST.
tunnel
COLUMBUS AVE.
NORTH BEACH
STOCKTON ST.
SANSOME ST.
PACIFIC AVE.
KEARNY ST.
MONTGOMERY ST.
Cable Car Museum
BROADWAY
BATTERY ST.
WASHINGTON ST.
CLAY ST.
CHINATOWN
Huntington Park
JACKSON ST.
SACRAMENTO ST.
Portsmouth Square
CALiFORNIA ST.
U. S. Customs House
FRONT ST.
DAVIS ST.
Transamerica Pyramid
Walton Park
Old St. Mary's Church
FINANCIAL DISTRICT
Maritime Plaza
DRUMM ST.
SUTTER ST.
Pacific Stock Exchange
Embarcadero Center
BUSH ST.
Union Square
PINE ST.
POST ST.
GEARY ST.
MARKET ST.
THIRD ST.
SECOND ST.
FIRST ST.
FREMONT ST.
BEALE ST.
MAIN ST.
SPEAR ST.
STEUART ST.
MISSION ST.
N

the world's finest natural harbors was exceeded only by their confusion. The discovery, once made, did not go unexplored. In 1775, another Spaniard, Juan Manuel de Ayala, sailed through the rugged portals that had hidden the bay for so long, and for the first time the full potential of the inlet was realized.

Soon after, the area was fully incorporated into Spain's American empire when Father Francisco Palou built *Misión Dolores.* San Francisco was an early center for the Pacific fur trade, and the 19th century brought New England whalers, Russian trappers, and, when gold was discovered at Sutter's Mill in 1848, nearly everyone else. By 1850 the population of San Francisco had grown from 900 to 25,000—prompting Will Rogers to observe almost a century later that it was "the city that never was a town." (The population is approximately 725,000 today.) Ten years after the gold strike, silver was found in the Comstock Lode, and San Francisco was caught in a second wave of prosperity that established it as the financial capital of the West. While Levi Strauss made a fortune providing miners with denim workwear, Leland Stanford, Charles Crocker, Collis P. Huntington, and Mark Hopkins financed the transcontinental railroad.

In many ways this history influences the city's character today. The Gold Rush brought adventurers from around the world; they were violent, hard men, but they lived together with a certain graceless tolerance. The Chinese came to the city, followed by the Japanese, Russians, Greeks, Mexicans, Filipinos, Irish, and Italians—all settling in larger and smaller communities over the years. The result is an admirable harmony, and a kind of hodgepodge culture both pleasing and natural: In what other city is the longtime chef of the town's best pizza parlor Chinese? The basis for this culture is respect and tolerance among individual citizens. The city gives birth to new lifestyles, in part because the civic body politic doesn't get choleric over diversity. It is a center of gay life, for example, and gays are a vital component of the city's mainstream.

Its history probably also has helped make San Francisco a city of survivors. After the October 1989 earthquake (which measured a jarring 6.9 on the Richter scale), cable cars were running the next day, and underground transportation never stopped at all. The visible reminders of the quake were few: a collapsed highway section; a gap in the upper level of the Bay Bridge; a few unsafe buildings shut down. With the help of civic support, just a short time after the disaster, the city looked its elegant self again.

Most experts agree that San Francisco withstood the shock because of the most stringent earthquake building code in the country—and the spunk of its citizens. The Marina district, hardest hit by the quake, still is considered a desirable place to live. In general the people of this city just swept up the shards and stayed in town, undeterred. Consider it an example of San Franciscan mettle: In this city of hills, full buses occasionally have trouble negotiating the steepest inclines. A bus driver with a full load may be forced to stop before beginning an ascent, to ask a few passengers to get off. Remarkably enough, some always do. Though absolutely true, this also is a parable of sorts, a conundrum to contemplate when standing on the Golden Gate Promenade. From there you will see the fine spires of the bridge, with the golden dome of the *Palace of Fine Arts* shining below, and in the distance, framing the picture, the blue Pacific. If that's not a sight worth getting off the bus for, you're just not resident material.

San Francisco At-a-Glance

SEEING THE CITY

Coit Tower, on the summit of Telegraph Hill, offers a spectacular panorama of San Francisco and the surrounding area: to the north are the waterfront and San Francisco Bay, the *Golden Gate Bridge,* Alcatraz Island, and on the far shore, Sausalito; downtown San Francisco lies to the south; to the east are Berkeley and the East Bay hills; and Nob Hill and Russian Hill rise to the west. The tower itself, a 212-foot cylindrical column built in 1933 with funds from a bequest by local eccentric and socialite Lillie Coit "to add beauty to the city she loved," is a striking landmark against the skyline. In the lobby are restored Depression-era frescoes depicting scenes of California in political, economic, and social vignettes. Open daily. Admission charge to ride the elevator to the top of the tower. (From Lombard St. follow Telegraph Hill Blvd. to the top; phone: 362-0808.) Twin Peaks, at nearly 1,000 feet, is the city's highest vantage point. (Follow Twin Peaks Blvd. to the top.) Several cocktail lounges offer fine views, too; among the highest, at 779 feet, is the *Carnelian Room,* the restaurant (don't go for the food) and bar atop the Bank of America building (555 California St.; phone: 433-7500). Another unsurpassed 360° panorama is afforded from high atop the *San Francisco Marriott* (777 Market St.; phone: 896-1600) and from the *Top of the Mark Lounge* of the *Mark Hopkins Inter-Continental* (see *Checking In*).

SPECIAL PLACES

San Francisco is a compact city and easy to get around. Most of the attractions are concentrated within a few areas, and the mild weather year-round makes walking pleasant, but you can sightsee by almost anything that rides, flies, or floats, from cable cars and their motorized facsimiles to buses, bicycles, carriages, trains, boats, helicopters, and hot-air balloons to a beautifully preserved DC-3 (see *Tours*).

DOWNTOWN

CIVIC CENTER This 15-square-block area contains the best collection of Beaux Arts–style buildings in America. Among the buildings are *City Hall,* a notable example of Renaissance grandeur with a 300-foot-high dome; the *War Memorial Opera House,* site of the signing of the *UN* Charter in 1945 and current home of the *San Francisco Opera* and *Ballet* (at press time the *Opera House* was undergoing a $7-million renovation and scheduled to reopen by the end of this year); *Bill Graham Civic Auditorium,* scene of cultural and political events since 1915; the modern *Louise M. Davies Symphony Hall*; and the new *San Francisco Public Library* which opened in 1996. Wednesdays and Sundays look for the *Heart of the City Farmer's Market* (at the eastern edge of the *Civic Center*), a colorful place rife with exotic fruits and vegetables. Bounded by Franklin, Golden Gate, Leavenworth, and Hayes Streets, the *Civic Center* is a good place to start the *49-Mile Drive,* a well-marked trail that takes in many of the city's highlights. Just follow the blue, white, and orange sea gull signs. *San Francisco Quick Guide* publishes a map of the trail and is available free in most hotel lobbies.

UNION SQUARE Right in the shopping area, Union Square offers a respite from the crowds of people (though not from the hordes of pigeons). You can feed the birds and relax on the benches in good weather. On holiday weekends bands play on the steps. The elegant *Westin St. Francis* hotel is on the west side of the square, while the surrounding area contains sidewalk flower stands and the city's finest department stores and shops, including *Gucci, Hermès, Chanel,* and *Tiffany*'s. Bordered by Geary, Post, Powell, and Stockton Sts.

EMBARCADERO CENTER Between the financial district and the waterfront, this 10-acre area of shopping malls, restaurants, hotels, and offices features several notable sculptures, including the controversial *Vaillancourt Fountain* (100 abstractly arranged concrete boxes with water spouting from them, often described by locals as the intestines of a square dog) in Justin Herman Plaza and a 60-foot sculpture by Louise Nevelson. At the foot of Market St.

SAN FRANCISCO WATERFRONT Once a world class working port, the city's waterfront now is more like a world class promenade thanks to the *Embarcadero.* Outstanding views of Treasure Island and the light-festooned Bay Bridge draw an admiring audience. Pier 7 is a gaslamp-lined walkway out over the bay for strolling, fishing, or sightseeing. A farmers' market held on Saturdays at the foot of Market Street bustles with people and is chockablock with stalls of fresh produce, bread, and ready-to-eat food from local restaurants. Walking south along the *Embarcadero* you pass the *Harbor Court Hotel*'s brick façade, the *Gordon Biersch Brewery* bar and restaurant at Harrison Street, and the *Embarko* restaurant in the Bay Village complex at Brannon Street. In addition, tracks for the *MUNI* (*Municipal Transit*) extension have been laid from Pier 39 to South Beach Harbor connecting the north and south waterfront; streetcars are set to begin operation this year. The waterfront area runs about half a mile along the *Embarcadero,* from Market Street south to Brannon Street.

CHINATOWN One of the largest Chinese communities outside of Asia, Chinatown is an intriguing 24-block enclave of pagoda-roofed buildings, excellent restaurants, and fine import shops featuring ivory carvings and jade jewelry. There are also several temples and museums here. Grant Avenue is the main thoroughfare—enter through an archway crowned by a dragon (Grant at Bush St.). It's best to go on foot or take the California Street cable car, because the area is too congested for easy parking. If you must drive, try the *Portsmouth Square Garage* (at Kearny St., north of Clay St.). The *Old St. Mary's Church* (Grant Ave. and California St.) built in 1854 of granite from China and bricks from New England, is the city's oldest cathedral. It survived the 1906 and 1989 earthquakes, perhaps because of its warning on the façade above the clock dial: "Son, Observe the Time and Fly from Evil." More words of wisdom, as well as regional artifacts, including pipes from old Chinatown opium dens and photographs of some famed telephone operators who memorized the names and numbers of 2,400 Chinatown residents in the old days, can be found at the *Chinese Historical Society of America*'s museum, the largest Chinese-American collection in the US (650 Commercial St., between Kearny and Montgomery; phone: 391-1188). Open Tuesdays through Saturdays, afternoons only. No admission charge. For information on walking tours of Chinatown, contact the *Chinese Cultural Center,* Tuesdays through Saturdays (750 Kearny St., inside the *Holiday Inn;* phone: 986-1822).

NORTH BEACH There is no longer a beach here, but this traditional neighborhood remains colorful and diverse—Italian, Basque, and Chinese. The area's great for strolling and eating—bakeries sell cannoli, rum babas, and panettone (a sweet bread filled with raisins and candied fruit). Numerous restaurants and cafés serve anything from espresso and cappuccino to complete dinners. *Caffè Trieste* (Vallejo and Grant Sts.; phone: 392-6737), the granddaddy of San Francisco's coffeehouses, serves an unsurpassed cappuccino. A jukebox plays arias from Puccini's operas daily (except Sundays, when local opera singers perform). One of the best times of year to visit North Beach is in early June, during the street bazaar, when local artists display their wares along Upper Grant Avenue. This trendy area is also good for window shopping. Boutiques with Victorian façades sell vintage clothing, collectibles, and furnishings, among other interesting items. *The Open Door* (548 Union St.; phone: 765-0488), which sells the creations of local designer Shawn E. Hall, is especially worth a peek. Hall's works are ecologically sensitive, recycling old objects into new. Washington Square is a nice place to sit in the sun or have lunch with the locals under the statue—ironically, not of the square's namesake, but of Benjamin Franklin (Columbus Ave. and Union Sts.). North Beach extends north and northwest from Chinatown to Bay Street.

JAPANTOWN This neighborhood, the focal point of culture and trade for San Francisco's substantial Japanese community, is the area where the Japanese have lived since before World War II. Within Japantown is *Japan Center* (Geary Blvd. and Post St.; phone: 922-6776), a modern five-acre complex of movie theaters, tea houses, restaurants, sushi and tempura bars, art galleries, shops selling everything from pearls to stereo equipment, and a school that offers classes in Japanese doll making and flower arranging. Nearby, with its five-tier *Peace Pagoda,* the elegantly landscaped Peace Plaza is the scene of the April *Cherry Blossom Festival* and traditional Japanese celebrations, like the *Mochi-Pounding Ceremony* (in which much preparation and even more pounding result in delicious rice cakes). Speaking of pounding, the *Kabuki Hot Spring and Japanese Spa* offers shiatsu massage, traditional Japanese baths, whirlpool baths, saunas, steambaths, and other services; the works will leave you feeling as fresh and crisp as a newly made rice cake (1750 Geary Blvd.; phone: 922-6000). The *Kinokuniya* bookstore, a large, well-appointed place with books and periodicals in English as well as Japanese, offers browsers an unparalleled look at contemporary Japan. Japantown is bounded by Octavia and Fillmore Sts. and California St. and Geary Blvds.

FISHERMAN'S WHARF AND VICINITY

FISHERMAN'S WHARF This rambling waterfront section, formerly the center of the city's commercial fishing industry, is California's largest tourist attraction after *Disneyland.* On the wharf at Jefferson Street, you walk through an open-air fish market. Locals find it more convenient to shop for fish in their own neighborhoods, but you can create the ultimate urban picnic by buying a loaf of freshly baked sourdough bread at *Boudin* (156 Jefferson St.; phone: 928-1849) and adding Dungeness crab purchased at one of the numerous sidewalk stalls. The boats return in the afternoon and hoist their crates of fish onto the pier at the foot of Jones and Leavenworth Streets. The wharf restaurants often are crowded and expensive, but try the huge *Alioto's;* the menu has been upgraded with Sicilian seafood recipes, and the cappuccino is as good as the best in Italy (at the foot of Taylor St.; phone: 673-0183). The area has many sidewalk vendors selling hand-crafted items.

PIER 39 Reconstructed with wood salvaged from other (demolished) piers and looking more like Gloucester, Massachusetts, than the West Coast, *Pier 39* is a popular entertainment complex on the northern waterfront. A pleasant hour or two can be spent moving with the crowds through the plethora of shops—craft, bakery, import, clothing, specialty, toy, jewelry, camera, fine food, crystal and silver, and many others. While here, stop in at *Underwater World,* a 50,000-square-foot aquarium exhibiting California marine life. Other attractions include a double-deck Venetian carousel and the multimedia presentation of *San Francisco Experience.* For lunch or dinner, there's an international roster of restaurants from which to choose—French, Italian, Chinese, Swiss; grab a bite at one of the numerous stand-up, take-out fresh seafood booths; or simply indulge your sweet tooth at *Breyer's Ice Cream.* The *Eagle Café* (phone: 433-3689) still attracts enough longshoremen to lend a working class aura not otherwise evident in this part of the waterfront. Weekend sailors and anglers can charter boats at the marina, and landlubbers can watch the more than 300 sea lions that sun themselves on the docks. *Pier 39* is on the *Embarcadero,* just east of *Fisherman's Wharf.* (There's a parking garage across the way on Beach St.)

AQUATIC PARK–MARITIME NATIONAL HISTORICAL PARK Overlooking the bay, *Aquatic Park* sits in front of *Ghirardelli Square.* Within the park is the *National Maritime Museum,* a treasure trove of memorabilia documenting shipping development from Gold Rush days to the present: with photographs, figureheads, massive anchors, shipwreck relics, and beautiful model ships. Open daily. No admission charge (phone: 556-3002).

Berthed off nearby Hyde Street Pier, three old ships welcome the public aboard. The *Balclutha* was a British cargo ship that rounded Cape Horn 17 times carrying rice and wine to San Francisco, worked as an Alaskan salmon trader, and even did a stint in Hollywood as a rather oversize prop in films. The *Eureka* used to shuttle passengers and cars across the bay during the early decades of this century. The antique automobiles displayed on deck are sure to delight car buffs. Aboard the schooner *CA Thayer,* old salts sing chanteys some evenings. All open daily. Admission charge (phone: 556-1871). Also here—though unavailable for boarding—are the *Alma,* a scow schooner built in 1891; the *Eppleton Hall,* a 1914 British tugboat; and the *Hercules,* a 1907 oceangoing steam tug that hauled logs to mills down the coast. *The Maritime Store* is full of books about the sea, plus maps and posters (phone: 775-BOOK). The World War II submarine USS *Pampanito* (phone: 929-0202) is at *Fisherman's Wharf* and the Liberty ship *Jeremiah O'Brien* (phone: 441-3101) at the foot of Brannan Street.

ALCATRAZ ISLAND This famed escape-proof former federal penitentiary stands out grimly in the bay, 1½ miles from *Fisherman's Wharf.* Such notorious criminals as Al Capone, "Machine Gun" Kelly, and Doc Barker never returned from their stays here. The prison was closed in 1963 because of exorbitant operating costs and has been open to the public since 1973. The *National Park Service* runs tours of the prison block, where you see the "dark holes" in which rebellious prisoners were confined in solitude, and the tiny steel-barred cells. Two-hour tours depart daily on the *Red & White Fleet* (see *Bay Cruises,* above) on a first-come, first-served basis; tickets may be purchased in advance (strongly recommended for the summer and holiday weekends and over holiday weekends). Ferries sail from Pier 41 (phone: 546-2700).

ANGEL ISLAND Shaped like a candy kiss, this island is a premier urban playground with a 360° vista at its tip. Originally used by the federal government as an immigration station (similar to New York's Ellis Island), in later years it also served as a Civil War encampment and a World War II stopover. Today, visitors can see Fort McDowell, whose mess hall once dished out 20,000 meals a day to its soldiers; and the immigration block house, covered with graffiti painted on or scratched into the walls by weary travelers. Mountain bikes and sea kayaks can be rented at the *Cove Café* (phone: 897-0715) at Ayala Cove. Tours depart on weekends February through mid-March and daily mid-March through mid-November on the *Red & White Fleet* (see *Bay Cruises,* above).

GHIRARDELLI SQUARE Pronounced *Gear*-a-*del*-li. Originally a woolen mill that turned out Union Army uniforms during the Civil War, then later a chocolate factory, the stately, landmark, red brick buildings here now house import shops that sell anything from Persian rugs to Chinese kites, plus outdoor cafés, art galleries, and fine restaurants. The *Mandarin* (phone: 673-8812) serves excellent Chinese food; *McCormick & Kuleto's* restaurant (phone: 929-1730) serves seafood in a flashy setting with stunning bay views; but perhaps sweetest of all is the *Ghirardelli Chocolate Manufactory* (900 North Point St.; phone: 474-3938), where you can watch chocolate being made and then eat the spoils afterward. If you're truly inspired, try the Golden Gate banana split. Open daily, on weekends until midnight. The square is bounded by Beach, Larkin, North Point, and Polk Sts.

THE CANNERY Inspired by *Ghirardelli Square,* this former Del Monte cannery is now a three-level arcade featuring chic boutiques, restaurants, and the *Museum of the City of San Francisco* (see *Museums*). Street musicians and mimes strut their stuff in the olive tree–shaded central courtyard. Open daily. Bounded by Beach, Leavenworth, and Jefferson Sts.

LOMBARD STREET Take the time to appreciate the residential façades and colorful flowers that line what is often referred to as the most twisting urban street in the world (between Hyde and Leavenworth Sts.).

GOLDEN GATE—FROM THE PROMENADE TO THE PARK

GOLDEN GATE PROMENADE This 3½-mile shoreline trail is among the most spectacular walks (or jogging paths) in America. You meander from *Aquatic Park* past wind-shaped Monterey cypress, eroding rocky points, a classy yacht harbor in front of the *St. Francis Yacht Club,* a grassy park beside an old cobbled seawall, all the while approaching that ultimate span, the *Golden Gate Bridge.* A number of interesting museums line the way. *Fort Point,* completed in 1861 as the West Coast's only Civil War outpost, is now a National Historic Site. Closed Mondays and Tuesdays. No admission charge (at the base of the *Golden Gate Bridge,* Presidio; phone: 556-1693). The history of the *Presidio,* established in 1776 as a Spanish garrison, is traced in the exhibits of the *Presidio Army Museum,* housed in the Old Station Hospital. Closed Mondays and Tuesdays. No admission charge (Lincoln Blvd. and Funston Ave.; phone: 561-4331). Most unusual is the *Palace of Fine Arts,* a grand Beaux Arts building constructed for the 1915 *Panama-Pacific International Exposition.* It houses the *Exploratorium,* a collection of 800 displays on science, technology, and the reaches and limits of human perception (see *Museums*).

GOLDEN GATE BRIDGE The loftiest and one of the longest single-span suspension bridges ever constructed, the bright-orange *Golden Gate* offers pedestrians a stunning vista. Yes, you can walk across the bridge, and under it to the Coastal Trail. Follow the handicapped-accessible walk up to the toll plaza level where you'll find gardens landscaped with native flowering plants. From here you have several options: catch a bus back downtown; turn around, and retrace your steps along the promenade with the view of the city skyline before you; or follow in the footsteps of great coast trekkers across the bridge and beyond–north along trails on the ridges and shoreline for 60 miles to Tomales Point. If you are driving, take the very first exit across the bridge, park, and gaze upon not only the bridge but the entire cityscape.

SAN FRANCISCO ZOO *Gorilla World* and an ultramodern $7-million *Primate Discovery Center* make a visit here particularly worthwhile. More than a thousand birds and animals can be viewed on foot or from aboard the motorized tour train. Adjacent to the main zoo is the *Children's Zoo,* a seven-acre nursery where children can stroke barnyard animals or watch baby lions being bottle fed. An outstanding *Insect Zoo* brings kids face to face with an impressive collection of creepy crawlers. The spectacular primate center has dozens of exotic and/or endangered species, as well as hands-on experiments and informative, fun-to-do computer/slide programs. Don't miss the big cats—leopards, jaguars, and lynxes—roaming in the safari-like natural habitat. Open daily. Admission charge. Sloat Blvd. and 45th Ave. (phone: 753-7080).

GOLDEN GATE PARK Developed from 1,000 acres of rolling sand dunes, *Golden Gate Park* has all the amenities of a large recreation area: bike paths, hiking and equestrian trails, three lakes (where you can sail model boats or rent paddleboats and rowboats), sports fields, and a 25-acre meadow. The park also features a rose garden, the lovely *John McLaren Rhododendron Dell,* the *Strybing Arboretum and Botanical Gardens*—over 70 acres rich with 5,000 species of plants and trees from all over the world—and the *Conservatory of Flowers,* a Victorian greenhouse with lush tropical growth is closed indefinitely. (Arboretum and conservatory open daily. No admission charge to arboretum. Along Martin Luther King Jr. Dr. and John F. Kennedy Dr., respectively.) The *Japanese Tea Garden* is a masterpiece of Oriental landscaping. Open daily. Admission charge. (At the intersection of Martin Luther King Jr. Dr. and Tea Garden Dr., just west of the *de Young Museum.*) No such lyrical setting could be complete without music, and the Music Concourse offers free open-air *Municipal Band* concerts on Sundays at 1 PM when the weather is good (between the *de Young Museum* and the *California Academy of Sciences;* see below for both).

CALIFORNIA ACADEMY OF SCIENCES The state's oldest scientific institution offers a wide variety of exhibitions ranging from the *Steinhart Aquarium,* with dolphins, piranhas, talking fish, penguins, and 14,000 other species; to the

Natural History Museum, with exhibits on dinosaurs, earthquakes, and meteors; to the farthest reaches of space in the *Morrison Planetarium*'s changing shows. Be sure to check out the *Far Side Gallery,* which displays several of Gary Larson's hilarious and original cartoons, all focusing on prehistoric life. Open daily from 10 AM to 5 PM; open to 7 PM from *July 4* through *Labor Day;* admission charge. On the Music Concourse (phone: 750-7145).

M. H. DE YOUNG MEMORIAL MUSEUM An outstanding collection of American art from the colonial era through the 20th century, and including major contributions by Mr. and Mrs. John D. Rockefeller III, hangs on the walls of the 22 galleries in this fine arts museum. Works by John Singer Sargent, Mary Cassatt, and George Caleb Bingham are among those exhibited. Also featured is art from ancient Egypt, Greece, Oceania, and Africa; plus a large textile collection. Docent tours are conducted daily. The original building was constructed for the *1894 California Midwinter Exposition,* which was backed and publicized by *San Francisco Chronicle* founder M. H. De Young. Lunch and refreshments are served in the *De Young Café.* Closed Mondays and Tuesdays; admission charge (good for admission to the *Asian Art Museum* on the same day—see below). Music Concourse, *Golden Gate Park* (phone: 750-3600; 863-3330 for recorded information).

ASIAN ART MUSEUM Created to accommodate the collection of Asian art donated by Avery Brundage, this museum is known for the scope of its works, which span a 6,000-year period. More than 500 masterpieces—including the earliest dated bronze Chinese Buddha (AD 338) from his Chinese collection—are on permanent exhibit, as is a 2,000-year-old bronze rhinoceros wine vessel. Also on display is one of the world's most extensive exhibits of Gandharan sculpture (from northern India). Housed in a specially constructed wing of the *De Young Museum,* the *Asian Art Museum* is operated separately. Closed Mondays and Tuesdays; admission charge (good for admission to the *De Young Museum* on the same day). Across from the Music Concourse, *Golden Gate Park* (phone: 668-7855).

CALIFORNIA PALACE OF THE LEGION OF HONOR A gift to the city from Alma and Adolph Spreckels, this recently renovated museum features paintings, sculpture (in a skylit atrium), and decorative arts presented in a chronological sequence, illustrating the development of European art from the medieval periods through the beginning of the 20th century. The museum café has outdoor seating on the terrace. Closed Mondays and Tuesdays. Admission charge. *Lincoln Park* at 34th Ave. and Clement St. (phone: 863-3330).

SOUTH OF MARKET STREET

SOMA Formerly the city's gritty warehouse district (the name stands for "*So*uth of *Ma*rket"), this area has been transformed into a vibrant, lived-in, artistic neighborhood of street markets and performers, shops, galleries, small theaters, gay bars, and nightclubs. Even as housing prices have veered upward, it remains one of San Francisco's most accessible, most colorful districts. Some once-elegant residential buildings still stand on Third Street, and living lofts are slowly being fashioned out of the former warehouses. South Park, at the heart of the district, is flanked by several clubs and restaurants. SoMa also is home to the *Moscone Convention Center* (named in memory of the assassinated San Francisco mayor) and the adjacent *Center for the Arts at Yerba Buena Gardens* (see below). There are also enough discount clothing outlets and boutiques to satiate even the most obsessed shopper (see *Shopping*). *Shopper Stopper* (PO Box 535, Sebastopol, CA 95473; phone: 707-829-1597) offers a 6½-hour shopping tour of the area, stopping at wholesalers not usually open to the public. The area is roughly bounded by Market, the *Embarcadero,* China Basin, and Division Sts.

CENTER FOR THE ARTS AT YERBA BUENA GARDENS A sprawling complex of galleries, theaters, gardens, a walk-behind fountain, plus a café and gift shop, the center showcases the city's culture and traditions. Offerings on this theme run the gamut from painting to electronic music, from ballet to video, from sculpture to CD-ROM. Purchase theater tickets at the *Center*'s *Ticket Office* (phone: 978-2787). 701 Mission St., between Third and Fourth Sts.

SAN FRANCISCO MUSEUM OF MODERN ART California's first museum devoted to modern art is housed in the $60-million Mario Botta–designed facility across from the *Center for the Arts at Yerba Buena Gardens.* It has a distinguished permanent collection of photography and American abstract expressionist art, with paintings by Jackson Pollock and Clyfford Still, and contemporary works by Bay Area artists such as Wayne Thiebaud and Richard Diebenkorn. Music, lectures, and film events are frequently scheduled; there's also a small, selective bookshop and a café. Closed Mondays. Admission charge; the first Tuesday of every month is free; Thursday evenings, half price. 151 Third St. at Howard St. (phone: 357-4000).

EXTRA SPECIAL

Within an hour's drive of San Francisco (north along US 101, east on Rte. 37, then north on Rte. 121) begins the number one wine-producing region in the US, the gently rolling Sonoma County and the Napa Valley. (For more information on wine tours and tastings, see *Visitable Vineyards* in DIVERSIONS.) The mild weather encourages not only grape production but outdoor activity. Pick up some bread and cheese along Highway 29 en route to *Bothe–Napa Valley State Park.* Its thousand acres of broad-leaved trees, pines, and redwoods are a lovely backdrop for picnicking, biking, and swimming in summer.

If time permits, try one of the Napa Valley's charming bed and breakfast establishments, such as *La Residence* (4066 St. Helena Hwy. N., Napa; phone: 707-253-0337) or *Maison Fleurie* (6529 Yount St. Yountville; 707-944-2056). Two resorts with beautiful rooms and renowned restaurants

are *Meadowood* (900 Meadowood La., St. Helena, CA 94574; phone: 707-963-3646) and *Auberge du Soleil* (180 Rutherford Hill Rd., Rutherford, CA 94573; phone: 707-963-1211). (Also see *America's Special Havens* in DIVERSIONS). Or you may find you don't want to move from Sonoma County, with its rugged coastline, deep woods, and picturesque farms. Be sure to take a meal at *John Ash & Company* (4330 Barres Rd.; Santa Rosa, CA 95403; phone: 707-527-7687), one of Sonoma's best restaurants. If you want the elegance of a 1920s luxury hotel plus a fitness spa, try the *Sonoma Mission Inn & Spa* (PO Box 1447, Sonoma, CA 95476 or 18140 Hwy. 12, Boyes Hot Springs, CA 95416; phone: 707-938-9000; 800-358-9022); see *America's Special Havens* and *Sybaritic Spas* in DIVERSIONS.

South of San Francisco and about two hours away (via Rte. 101, then Rte. 156, then Rte. 1, or via the slow, scenic coastal Rte. 1 all the way) lies the Monterey Peninsula, rich in history and natural beauty. For more information about the area, see *Big Sur and the Monterey Peninsula* in DIRECTIONS.

Sources and Resources

TOURIST INFORMATION

The *San Francisco Convention and Visitors' Bureau* (*Visitor Information Center,* PO Box 429097, San Francisco, CA 94142; phone: 391-2000) is best for brochures, maps, general tourist information, and other assistance. If you call, they will send you (for $2) a valuable package of information, including a three-month calendar of events. Call 391-2001 anytime for the lowdown on what's going on in town. The bureau's downtown *Visitor Information Center* on the lower level of *Hallidie Plaza* (just downstairs from the cable car turntable, at 900 Market St. at Powell St.) provides multilingual services. Contact the California state hotline (phone: 800-TO-CALIF) for maps, calendars of events, health updates, and travel advisories.

LOCAL COVERAGE The *San Francisco Chronicle* is a morning daily; the *San Francisco Examiner,* an evening daily. On Fridays, both list events and places to go on weekends. Sundays the two publish a joint edition, including a comprehensive entertainment section, the "Datebook."

For information on area dining, consult *Best Restaurants of San Francisco: The San Francisco Chronicle Guide to Fine Dining* (Chronicle Books, $10.95) and *Exploring the Best Ethnic Restaurants of the Bay Area* by Sharon Silva and Frank Viviano (S.F. Focus Books, $9.95). A good general guide to the city is *ACCESS San Francisco* (HarperCollins; $18).

TELEVISION STATIONS KRON Channel 4–NBC; KPIX Channel 5–CBS; KGO Channel 7–ABC; KQED Channel 9–PBS; KTVU Channel 17–CNN.

RADIO STATIONS AM: KFRC 610 (oldies); KCBS 740 (news); KGO 810 (news/talk); FM: KQED 88.5 (National Public Radio); KALW 91.7 (National Public Radio); KCSM 91.1 (jazz); KKHI 100.9 (classical); KDFC 102.1 (classical); KKSF 103.7 (New Age music).

TELEPHONE The area code for San Francisco, Marin, and south to Los Altos is 415. The area code for Oakland and Berkeley is 510.

SALES TAX Sales tax is 8.5%; the hotel room tax is 12%.

CLIMATE Daytime temperatures average 60F to 65F in summer and 45F to 57F in winter (downpours are common between November and March). In summer, morning and evening fog make parts of the day very cool; and while it is 65F in San Francisco, it can be in the 80s in the suburbs.

GETTING AROUND

AIRPORTS *San Francisco International Airport* is about 15 miles south of the city, a 20- to 30-minute drive when it's not rush hour. A number of shuttles operate to and from the airport for a more economical fare. *SFO Airporter* buses run every 20 minutes between the airport and a number of downtown hotels for $9 one way, (phone: 495-8404). *San Francisco Supershuttle* (phone: 558-8500) offers transportation between the airport and anywhere in San Francisco. The one-way fare to a downtown hotel is $10; for the return trip, reservations must be made 24 hours in advance. *SAMTRANS* and *CalTrain* buses (phone: 800-660-4287 in San Francisco; 800-508-6200 elsewhere in the US) serve both the peninsula and downtown San Francisco (the *Transbay Terminal* at Mission and 1st Sts.). Buses depart from the upper levels in North and South Terminals every half hour during the day, hourly at night; the fare is $1. For more information on the airport's facilities, call 761-0800. Also, contact the *Transportation Hotline* (phone: 800-SFO-2008) for helpful information concerning all types of transportation to and from the airport.

Oakland International Airport is a 30- to 45-minute drive from San Francisco's financial district during non-commuter hours; cab fare runs about $45. Rail service is available via the *Bay Area Rapid Transit* (*BART*) system (phone: 788-2278 or 510-464-6000); take an *Air BART* shuttle bus to the *Oakland Coliseum Arena* ($2), and then pick up *BART* to Montgomery Street in downtown San Francisco ($2.15). For airport information, call 510-577-4000.

BART If you really want to move, this ultramodern, high-speed railway will whisk you from San Francisco to Oakland, Berkeley, Richmond, Concord, Daly City, and Fremont at up to 80 miles an hour. The system is easy to use, with large maps and signboards in each station clarifying routes and fares (which vary according to distance traveled). For information, contact *Bay Area Rapid Transit (BART),* 800 Madison St., Oakland (phone: 992-BART in San Francisco).

BUS Efficient buses serve the entire metropolitan area; maps appear at the front of the yellow pages in the telephone book. *MUNI (Municipal Transit)* Passports ($6 for one day, $10 for three days, and $15 for seven days) are good for rides on *MUNI* buses, streetcars, and cable cars. *MUNI* street and transit maps are available at bookstores for $2. For detailed route information, contact the *Municipal Railway of San Francisco,* 949 Presidio Ave. (phone: 673-*MUNI* daily during business hours).

CABLE CAR The best way to travel up and over the hills of downtown is aboard these famous trademarks, which are pulled along at 9½ miles an hour. There are three lines, the most scenic being the *Powell-Hyde* route, which you can pick up at the turntable at Powell and Market Streets. It will take you over both Nob and Russian Hills to gaslit *Victorian Park.*

CAR RENTAL There are a few things to remember if you plan to drive in San Francisco: Cable cars and pedestrians always have the right-of-way; curb your wheels when parking on a hill to prevent runaway cars. The national firms all serve San Francisco. Least expensive, however, is *Bob Leech Auto Rental* (at 435 S. Airport Blvd., South San Francisco—five minutes from the airport; phone: 583-3844).

FERRY For outstanding views of the city, ride the *Golden Gate Ferry* (phone: 332-6600) from the terminal under the clock tower at the foot of Market Street. The 30-minute ride to Sausalito (slightly longer to Larkspur) takes you right past Alcatraz and almost within reach of the *Golden Gate Bridge.* For other service see "Bay Cruises and Attractions" in *Special Places.*

STREETCAR Five lines of the *MUNI Metro* streetcar system, which branch off toward various parts of the city, run under Market Street. Colorful vintage street cars from the 1930s (F-line) run along Market Street. For route information, call 673-MUNI.

TAXI Cabs can be hailed on downtown streets, especially near hotels, or summoned by phone. Major companies are *Luxor Cab* (phone: 282-4141), *Veterans Cab* (phone: 552-1300), and *Yellow Cab* (phone: 626-2345).

SIGHTSEEING TOURS

CRUISES The *Blue & Gold Fleet* (Pier 39; phone: 705-5444) offers daily cruises, and evenings from April through December passengers can dine and dance across the bay. The *Red & White Fleet* uses Piers 41 and 43½, near *Fisherman's Wharf,* for its cruises and services to the north bay (phone: 546-2628; 800-229-2784). Choose among Alcatraz (reserve ahead in summer and on holiday weekends), Sausalito, Angel Island, and Tiburon, with optional tours to the redwoods at *Muir Woods National Monument.* The *Blue & Gold Fleet* provides ferry service to Vallejo, with bus extension to *Marine World Africa USA* (phone: 707-644-4000; fax 707-644-0241). The latter features an enormous and exotic collection of sea, air, and land creatures and visitor participation such as playing tug-of-war with the elephants, giraffe feeding, getting close to prairie dogs and pygmy goats in the petting *kraal,* and learning about newborn animals like Bengal tiger cubs in the *Animal Nursery;* the marine area includes a killer whale and dolphin show, a shark habitat, and a walrus cove. Admission charge is included in the cruise fee. Or, if you want to go on your own, *Marine World Africa USA* can also be reached from downtown San Francisco via high-speed catamaran in one hour, by car in 30 minutes, or by public transport; call the number above for more information. The *Red & White Fleet* also offers a three-winery cruise visit to the Napa Valley. And *Hornblower Dining Yachts* offers brunch, lunch, and dinner on its sails around the bay (Pier 33; phone: 394-8900). The gray whale migration can be witnessed off the Pacific coastline; *Oceanic Society Expeditions* (phone: 474-3385) and *Bay and Delta Charters* (phone: 332-6811) both conduct tours from January through April.

BUS/CAR One of the largest operators of sightseeing tours, the *Gray Line,* runs from two locations: at Union Square, opposite the *Westin St. Francis* hotel (Powell St, between Geary and Post Sts); and from the bus terminal (First and Mission Sts). For reservations call 558-9400. Also, for a unique look at San Francisco's nightlife join *3 Babes and a Bus* (phone: 552-CLUB) on Friday or Saturday. Party-goers can dance the night away at four hot clubs and then be whisked back to their hotel for much-needed R&R. *Roger's Custom Tours* (phone: 742-9611) provides a closer look at San Francisco by car. Roger F. Erickson guides visitors to all the high points of the city, as well as to specialized destinations such as small museums off the beaten path. He also offers scenic suburban excursions, as well as an afternoon of architectural appreciation.

PLANE *San Francisco Seaplane Tours* (phone: 800-973-2752) offers spectacular views high above the Bay Area with a 30-minute *Golden Gate Tour* which soars over Alcatraz and the Golden Gate Bridge, and along the Pacific Coast. There is also a "Sunset Champagne" tour.

WALKING The best way to see San Francisco is on foot. *City Guides* (phone: 557-4266) offers free neighborhood walking tours daily that focus on the city's historical diversity. For example, the "Gold Rush City" trek explores the haunts of the original 49ers, and the "Haight-Ashbury" walk details the history of this area which was a resort in the 1890s and the haunt of the psychedelic street culture in the 1960s. (Pick up schedules at city libraries, at the Visitor Information Center on the lower level of Hallidie Plaza, or send a self-addressed, stamped envelope to *Friends of the Library, Main Library, Civic Center,* San Francisco, CA 94102.) The history of the gold miners who once flooded this town and their legendary vices—gambling, drinking, and women—is traced by *A. M. Walking Tours* (phone: 928-5965) through Nob Hill, Chinatown, the old Barbary Coast, Union Square, and Maiden Lane. "Cruisin' the Castro" is a walking tour of "the heart of gay

America" (Castro Street); contact Trevor Hailey (phone: 550-8110). *Wok Wiz Chinatown Walking Tours* (phone: 355-9657) provides an insider's view of this city within the city—with stops at Chinese markets, herbal shops, a pastry shop that makes rice noodles, an art gallery, a tea shop, and along the narrow streets and alleys of Chinatown for a dim sum lunch. *Javawalk* (phone: 673-WALK) offers a two-hour tour of San Francisco's coffeehouse culture.

SPECIAL EVENTS

San Franciscans know how to throw a party, and anyone lucky enough to be in town during one—which is usually every week—is welcome to join in the fun. Some are big, some are unusual, and everyone has a favorite reason for celebrating. To find out what's happening in any given week, call the *Visitor Information Center* (phone: 391-2000) or check the "Datebook" section of the Sunday *San Francisco Examiner and Chronicle.*

For nine days each year, Chinatown is even noisier and more crowded than usual when the *Chinese New Year* is celebrated in January or February (based on the lunar calendar). Fireworks explode day and night; the streets and storefronts are rife with red paper envelopes and other symbols of good luck. Hundreds of thousands of onlookers come to see the parade on the final day, when block-long dragons steered from within by more than a hundred people wind through the narrow streets, leading floats and marching bands to a festival in Portsmouth Square. The final celebration runs from 8 AM to midnight; fireworks are shot off at the end of the parade. For further information contact the *Chinese Chamber of Commerce* (phone: 982-3000).

The *Cherry Blossom Festival,* held on two weekends in April at the *Japan Center* (Post and Buchanan Sts.), features traditional tea ceremonies, flower-arranging and doll-making demonstrations, bonsai displays, and performances by folk dancers from Japan. A crosstown parade highlights the events with over 50 Japanese performing groups and intricate floats of shrines and temples.

The *Carnaval Parade and Festival,* a two-day event held the last weekend in May, celebrates Caribbean, Latin, and Brazilian culture. Highlights include parade with music and dancing, a street festival, and a costume contest. The festivities take place in the mission district (24th and Mission Sts.).

Fleet Week celebrates the October birthday of the *US Navy* with a parade of ships under the *Golden Gate Bridge* and several days of open houses on the vessels, plus aerial stunts by the *Blue Angels,* fireworks, and boat rides.

MUSEUMS

The city's major museums are all described in *Special Places.* Other institutions worth a visit include the following:

AFRICAN-AMERICAN HISTORICAL AND CULTURAL SOCIETY A museum and library honoring black history and culture. Open Wednesdays through Sundays, afternoons only. Admission charge. *Fort Mason,* Bldg. C (phone: 441-0640).

ANSEL ADAMS CENTER Changing exhibitions are devoted to the extraordinary photographs of this San Francisco native and environmentalist and to the works of other great photographers. Closed Mondays. Admission charge. 250 Fourth St., between Howard and Folsom Sts. (phone: 495-7000).

CABLE CAR MUSEUM This lovely brick building is the powerhouse for the current system and a repository of cable car history. On display here are the first cable car, invented in 1873 by Andrew Hallidie, and exact scale models of cars servicing all the various lines. Open daily. No admission charge. 1201 Mason St., near Chinatown (phone: 474-1887).

CARTOON ART MUSEUM Original cartoon art is exhibited: editorial, newspaper, and magazine cartoons, as well as animation boards, plus five 1789 works from British artist William Hogarth, considered among the first cartoons ever created. Special events include lectures and Saturday conversations with cartoonists (call the hotline at 227-8666 for schedules). Closed Mondays and Tuesdays. Admission charge. 814 Mission St. near Fourth St. (phone: 546-3922).

CRAFT AND FOLK ART MUSEUM Exhibitions of contemporary crafts and folk art; small museum shop. Closed Mondays. Admission charge. *Fort Mason,* Bldg. A (phone: 775-0990).

EXPLORATORIUM Expect to hear such sophisticated reactions as "wow" and "cool" when visiting the *Exploratorium.* Touching is a "must" here—more than 650 exhibits require pushing, pulling, throwing, or some other participation to explore the forces of the physical world. Light, sound, gravity, and perception are just four of the subjects examined. The *Tactile Dome*—a hit with kids and adults—is a touchy-feely experience; crawl through a series of pitch-black tunnels, using your sense of touch to guide you. (Because of its popularity, advance reservations are required for the *Tactile Dome,* but there is no additional admission charge.) Closed Mondays. Admission charge. 3601 Lyon St. (inside the *Palace of Fine Arts*; phone: 561-0360 for recorded information; 561-0362 for *Tactile Dome* reservations).

JEWISH MUSEUM OF SAN FRANCISCO Devoted to a lively exploration of Jewish traditions and art as they relate to current affairs, the galleries and shop are open Sundays through Thursdays, with an 8 PM closing on Thursday; closed holidays. Admission charge. 121 Steuart St., near the *Embarcadero BART Station* (phone: 543-8880).

MEXICAN MUSEUM Colorful displays of handicrafts and paintings from south-of-the-border artists. Closed Mondays and Tuesdays. Admission charge. *Fort Mason,* Bldg. D (phone: 441-0404).

MUSEUM OF THE CITY OF SAN FRANCISCO Rotating art exhibits depict the wide diversity of this city by the bay and the struggles of its people. Closed Mondays and Tuesdays. No admission charge. *The Cannery,* 2801 Leavenworth, third floor, (phone: 928-0289).

SAN FRANCISCO ART COMMISSION GALLERY Emerging Bay Area artists exhibit paintings, sculpture, and nontraditional art forms. Open Wednesdays through Saturdays, afternoons only. No admission charge. 401 Van Ness Ave. (phone: 554-6080).

SAN FRANCISCO PERFORMING ARTS LIBRARY AND MUSEUM Displays and an extensive research collection of posters, programs, reviews, and other memorabilia. Closed Sundays and Mondays. No admission charge. 399 Grove St., near the *Civic Center* (phone: 255-4800).

SHOPPING

In the various neighborhoods as well as downtown, shopping is easy in this relatively compact city. For Japanese wares one can go to Japantown; for Chinese, Chinatown. With *Ghirardelli Square, The Cannery,* the *Anchorage* on *Fisherman's Wharf,* and *Pier 39,* San Francisco revived the age-old combination of marketplace and fun fair. *Embarcadero Center,* between the waterfront and the financial district, is filled with shops and restaurants. *San Francisco Centre,* on Market Street near Powell Street, is a stunning, polished-stone structure with a huge, retractable skylight and spiral escalators; *Nordstrom* is the anchor department store here. The highly decorative *Rincon Center,* on Mission Street between Main and Spear Streets, was once an Art Deco–style post office; it now has a restored lobby, a 90-foot rain column, 30 shops, and several good restaurants. When serious buying is the object—and money is not—the place to be still is Union Square and the streets that frame it. On the square are three major department stores: *Macy's, Saks Fifth Avenue,* and *Neiman Marcus.* Nearby specialty shops include firms from Britain, France, Germany, Italy, and Switzerland, plus US competitors. Victorian Union Street (not to be confused with Union Square), a strip on the old dairy land of Cow Hollow, has exotic and unusual gift shops and designer boutiques featuring European fashions. Another good shopping thoroughfare is Fillmore Street, whose shops feature new and vintage fashion and home furnishings. For bargains in high fashion, explore the factory outlets south of Market Street (SoMa). A number of discount stores have opened up in this area; clothing prices are great, but shop decor is usually threadbare.

Note: Serious book browsers should check out both sides of the bay. In San Francisco, don't miss North Beach's *City Lights* (261 Columbus Ave. phone: 362-8193). Launched by Beat poet Lawrence Ferlinghetti in 1953, the bookstore stocks hard-to-find and esoteric titles, an excellent selection of contemporary poetry, and an unusual selection of Third World literature. *A Clean, Well Lighted Place for Books* (601 Van Ness Ave., near the *Civic Center,* phone: 441-6670) borrows its name from an Ernest Hemingway short story; it is San Francisco's largest independent bookstore, with particularly strong fiction, science fiction, mystery, and music sections, and frequent book signings and readings. Countering as "A dirty, poorly lit place for books," *McDonald*'s (48 Turk St.; phone: 673-2235) is the largest used bookstore in town; located in the Union Square district, it has or can find out of print titles; it also offers a selection of secondhand magazines.

Across the bay in Berkeley, waiters have master's degrees and auto mechanics have PhDs, and the bookstores reflect that. Look for *Cody's Books* (phone: 510-845-7852) and *Moe's* (phone: 510-849-2087), both on Telegraph Avenue, and *Black Oak Books* on Shattuck Avenue (phone: 510-486-0698).

Here's a window shopper's view of the classic and the unusual:

UNION SQUARE

Emporio Armani Boutique Beautiful day- and eveningwear by the famed designer can be found in this opulent multimillion dollar shop. 1 Grant Ave. (phone: 677-9400).

Dorothy Weiss Gallery Ceramic sculptures are the stock in trade at this upscale gallery two blocks east of Union Square. 256 Sutter St. (phone: 397-3611).

Giants Dugout Store Paraphernalia for followers of the orange and black and other sports teams; ticket sales, too. 170 Grant Ave. (phone: 982-9400).

Gump's Famous for its jade, art, jewelry, crystal, china, sculpture, furniture, antiques, stationery, and food. 135 Post St. (phone: 982-1616).

Obiko One-of-a-kind women's clothing with an artistic bent by contemporary designers. 794 Sutter St. (phone: 775-2882).

La Parisienne Fine jewelry designed and made in Paris, as well as genuine French lithographs, all well priced. 460 Post St. (phone: 788-2255).

Shreve & Co. One of San Francisco's oldest purveyors of the finest silver, crystal, and jewelry. 200 Post St. (phone: 421-2600).

Wilkes Bashford High-priced men's and women's clothing. 375 Sutter St. (phone: 986-4380).

HAYES STREET

F. Dorian, Inc. Hand-crafted collectibles of many cultures including Mexican, African, and Asian. 388 Hayes St. (phone: 861-3191).

Richard Hilkert Books Books on art, music, design, and architecture. 333 Hayes St. (phone: 863-3339).

Star Classics Browse through 50,000 hard-to-find CDs, all musical masterpieces. 425 Hayes St. (phone: 552-1110).

de Vera Italian and Swedish glassware from the 1950s and 1960s, as well as several stunning pieces of glass art from the collection of Federico de Vera. 384 Hayes St. (phone: 861-8480).

Victorian Interiors Everything necessary from decorative wall moldings to brass bath fixtures to spiff up (or create) your Victorian-era dream home. 575 Hayes St. (phone: 431-7191).

Worldware Products from around the world are the specialty here, including Neal's Yard essential oils, organic cotton socks, and knit clothing made from recycled cotton yarn. 336 Hayes St. (phone: 487-9030).

Zonal Metal and other materials are fashioned into unique sculptures and other artworks. 568 Hayes St. (phone: 255-9307).

MID-MARKET

Bell'occhio A unique and whimsical collection of dried flowers, antique and hand-dyed ribbons, unusual soaps, sachets, and eccentric little boxes. 8 Brady St. (phone: 864-4048).

Red Desert A wide range of cacti and succulent plants, which can be shipped throughout the country, and other finds from the desert. 1632 Market St. (phone: 552-2800).

UNION STREET

John Wheatman & Assoc. English- and Japanese-style antiques and contemporary furniture. 1933 Union St. (phone: 346-8300).

Kenneth Cole The place to shop for chic shoes. 2078 Union St. (phone: 346-2161).

Oggetti Marbleized Florentine papers sold by the sheet, or used on picture frames, or to cover treasure boxes and photo albums. Other gift items, too. 1846 Union St. (phone: 346-0631).

Paris 1925 Antique watches and Art Deco jewelry. 1954 Union St., Second Floor (phone: 567-1925).

Three Bags Full Fabulous sweaters hand-knit with luxurious yarns. 2181 Union St. (phone: 567-5753).

Zuni Pueblo A tribe-owned store featuring contemporary Zuni arts. 1749 Union St. (phone: 567-0941).

FILLMORE STREET

Cedanna Arts and crafts by Northern California artists, as well as pottery, a selection of fine foods, and interesting housewares. 1925 Fillmore St. (phone: 474-7152).

Fillamento Three floors of decorative items, locally designed glassware, and trendy furniture. 2185 Fillmore St. (phone: 931-2224).

Paint Effects Painted wood and metal artwork are the rage here as are the regularly scheduled classes for would-be artists. 2426 Fillmore St. (phone: 292-7780).

R.H. Reminiscent of an English cottage, this quaint shop is known for its excellent selection of topiary creations. 2506 Sacramento St. (phone: 346-1460).

Zoe Far-out, expensive women's clothes. 2400 Fillmore St. (phone: 929-0441).

OUTER SACRAMENTO STREET

Forrest Jones Everything you might need for the well-accessorized kitchen and dining table. 3274 Sacramento St. (phone 567-2483).

Jasper Byron French and English antiques, reproductions, and accessories in the classic style. 3364 Sacramento St. (phone: 563-8122).

Sue Fisher King Elegant linen and accessories for bed and table. 3067 Sacramento St. (phone: 922-7276).

V. Breier Contemporary and traditional crafts, including neon sculpture and colorful ceramics, imaginative furniture, and baskets made of handmade papers, leaves, pine cones, and seed pods. 3091 Sacramento St. (phone: 929-7173).

SOUTH OF MARKET STREET (SOMA)

Baker Hamilton Square A dozen shops selling antiques, art, and furnishings share space in a historic warehouse. Near the train station at 7th and Townsend Sts. (phone: 861-3500).

Basic Brown Bears At this teddy bear lair you can watch the cuddly creatures being made, then pick out one who's ready to travel. 444 De Haro St. (phone: 626-0781).

Discount Bridal Brides-to-be travel cross-country for wedding dresses at sensational savings. 300 Brannon St. (phone: 495-7922).

Jessica McClintock Outlet Original beaded, lacy fashions for women at outlet prices. Also sells Scott McClintock and Gunne Sax lines. 35 Stanford St., off Brannan St. (phone: 495-3326).

LIMN Company Avant-garde art and furniture. 290 Townsend St. (phone: 543-5466).

Six Sixty Center Eight discount outlets under one roof selling everything from sweaters and jeans to jewelry and cosmetics. 660 Third St. (phone: 227-0464).

SPORTS AND FITNESS

Any successful local professional team plays to a full house, especially the *Giants* (their fans are awarded an icicle-draped "Croix de Candlestick" pin for surviving an extra-inning night game), at windy *Candlestick Park.* However, mild year-round weather and varied terrain lures bikers, boaters, and joggers away from arenas, stadiums, and television sets.

BASEBALL The San Francisco *Giants* play from April to October in *Candlestick Park* (Gilman Ave., on the southern edge of the city east of US 101; phone: 467-8000). The Oakland *A's* play at the *Oakland Coliseum* (7000 Coliseum Way; phone: 510-638-0500).

BASKETBALL The *NBA*'s *Golden State Warriors* play from November to April at the *Oakland Coliseum Arena* (phone: 510-638-6300 for information; 510-762-*BASS* for tickets).

BICYCLING A general tour of San Francisco on a bicycle is not the safest way to see the sights, but there are some fine routes that offer grand views with less risk. Cycles and mountain bikes can be rented from *Magic Skates and Bikes* at *Golden Gate Park* (3038 Fulton St. at Sixth Ave.; phone: 668-1117), and *American Bicycle Rental* (2715 Hyde St.; phone: 931-0234). Pedaling along the city's scenic shoreline between the zoo and *Cliff House* is breathtaking. On Sundays, roads through the middle of *Golden Gate Park* are off limits to automobiles, which provides a respite from the treachery of riding side by side with cars. Another favorite route is past the Presidio and over the *Golden Gate Bridge.* More ambitious riders head to Sausalito or through the (very hilly) Marin Headlands to the beaches of Marin County. Bike route maps are available at most bicycle shops.

FISHING There is fine salmon fishing in the sea beyond the bay. The season spans mid-February to mid-October; afternoon trips are available June through October. Charter boats leave daily early in the morning and return in the afternoon. For information contact *New Easy Rider Sport Fishing* (phone: 285-2000). You also can cast off San Francisco's municipal pier at *Aquatic Park,* anytime. No license required.

FITNESS CENTERS The *YMCA* (169 Steuart St.; phone: 957-9622) has a pool, sauna, and weight room (including Nautilus, Cybex, and cardiovascular exercise equipment), along with racquetball and handball courts and aerobics classes. Facilities are available to non-guests at a nominal charge.

FOOTBALL The San Francisco *49ers* play from August to December (and sometimes in January) at *Candlestick Park* (Gilman Ave., on the southern edge of the city east of US 101; 468-2249). The Oakland *Raiders* play at the *Oakland Coliseum Arena* (phone: 510-569-2121 for information).

GOLF There are fine public courses at *Lincoln Park* (34th Ave. and Clement St.; phone: 221-9911) and *Harding Park* (Skyline Blvd. and Harding Rd.; phone: 664-4690).

HOCKEY The *NHL*'s San Jose *Sharks* play at the 18,000-seat *San Jose Arena,* on The Alameda near Guadalupe Pkwy. (phone: 408-287-7070 for ticket information).

HORSE RACING *Bay Meadows* is the place, in San Mateo (phone: 574-7223). The racing season begins in August and runs into January. In the East Bay *Golden Gate Fields* features thoroughbred racing from March through late June (phone: 510-559-7300).

HORSEBACK RIDING Guided trail rides and lessons are available at *Golden Gate Stables* at *Golden Gate Park* (John F. Kennedy Dr. at 36th Ave.; phone: 668-7360). Twelve miles of bridle paths wind through the park. Reservations necessary.

JOGGING Run from the *Ferry Building* along the *Embarcadero* to *Fort Point* beneath the *Golden Gate Bridge* (6 miles one way); jog back and forth across the

Golden Gate Bridge (1½ miles each way) and enjoy the fore and aft views, as well as the one directly below. From Market Street via the *Civic Center* the 21 Hayes bus goes to *Golden Gate Park,* where there are numerous dirt and concrete trails, not to mention plenty of other joggers. (Do not run alone in secluded areas of the park.)

SKATING Roller-skating/roller-blading is very popular in San Francisco, especially in *Golden Gate Park* on Sundays, when traffic is detoured off the park's main roads. You can rent skates from *Magic Skates* (3038 Fulton St. at 6th Ave.; phone: 668-1117) right across from the park.

SWIMMING Though much of San Francisco's waters are too rough and cold for swimming, China Beach (at Sea Cliff Ave. and El Camino del Mar) is good when the weather permits and the current is safe. The *Sheehan* hotel pool and work-out area (620 Sutter St.; phone: 775-6500) are open to the public daily.

TENNIS The *San Francisco Recreation and Parks Department* (phone: 666-7200) maintains more than a hundred tennis courts around the city. Free to the public, they are available on a first-come, first-served basis. *Golden Gate Park* has 21 courts, which can be reserved in advance on weekends for a nominal fee. *Golden Gate Park* at *McLaren Lodge* (Fell and Stanyan Sts.; phone: 753-7101).

YACHT RACING The *Yacht Racing Association* holds most of its races between April and mid-October, but midwinter regattas also are held. Races start and end off the Marina Green and turn at Blossom Rock Buoy beyond Pier 39 (phone: 771-9500 for information).

THEATER

San Francisco abounds in great theater; among its treasures is one of the best repertory groups in the country.

CENTER STAGE

American Conservatory Theatre (ACT) A bit of Shakespeare, some Chekhov, some Shaw, works by Lanford Wilson, Sam Shepard, and Terence Rattigan—these, as well as world premieres by a slew of others, have been performed by this company, which started out in Pittsburgh and moved to the West Coast in the mid-1960s. The annual year-end production of *A Christmas Carol* is now a Bay Area tradition. Severely damaged in the 1989 earthquake, the *Geary, ACT*'s home theater, is reopened and more splendid than ever. 450 Geary St. (phone: 834-3200).

In addition, the *Curran Theater* (445 Geary St.; phone: 474-3800) is a venue for musicals and often stages traveling Broadway productions. The

Orpheum Theater (1192 Market St.; phone: 474-3800) and the *Golden Gate Theater* (Golden Gate and Taylor Sts.; phone: 474-3800) also feature Broadway shows. At *Club Fugazi* (678 Green St.; phone: 421-4222), an old North Beach landmark, the camp cult classic *Beach Blanket Babylon* has been running for 20 years. If you have an urge to see the world through celluloid, visit the *Castro* (Castro St. near Market St.; phone: 621-6120), a 1922 landmark theater—complete with an organist—that shows classic films. Or try the *Paramount,* which holds a Friday "Classic Nights" film series. The theater itself is a prize; tours are offered on the first and third Saturdays of the month, at 10 AM. Meticulously maintained, this Art Deco building is in the *National Register of Historic Places* (2025 Broadway near the *19th St. BART Station* in Oakland; phone: 510-465-6400). The *San Francisco Ballet,* the country's oldest company and among its finest, moves into the *War Memorial Opera House* in the *Civic Center* with its *Nutcracker* production in December, followed by a repertory season from January through May (phone: 703-9400).

MUSIC

The *San Francisco Opera Association* is a world class opera company. It performs at the *War Memorial Opera House* (*Civic Center,* Van Ness Ave. and Grove St.; phone: 864-3330) from September to early December; the summer season is May and early June. Since it is undergoing a multimillion-dollar face-lift (scheduled for completion by the end of this year), all opera performances have been moved to the *Bill Graham Civic Auditorium* and *Orpheum Theater.* Since tickets are difficult to get, it's best to reserve in advance (*War Memorial Opera House* Box Office, San Francisco, CA 94102). The *San Francisco Symphony* season runs from September through May at *Louise M. Davies Symphony Hall* in the *Civic Center* (phone: 431-5400), but the orchestra can be heard at other times, too, such as during its June *Beethoven Festival* or its July *Pops Concerts* in the *Civic Auditorium.* The *Midsummer Music Festival* is a free Sunday series of symphony, opera, jazz, and ethnic programs from mid-June to mid-August at *Sigmund Stern Grove* (19th Ave. and Sloat Blvd.; phone: 252-6252).

Tickets for most music, dance, and theater events can be obtained through *BASS* ticket centers (phone: 776-1999). In addition, half-price as well as full-price tickets to many events can be bought (cash or traveler's checks only for half-price seats) on the day of performance at the *TIX* booth on the Stockton Street side of Union Square, Tuesdays through Saturdays from 11 AM to 7:30 PM (phone: 433-7827; you must go to the booth for information on half-price tickets).

NIGHTCLUBS AND NIGHTLIFE

San Francisco is alive at night and can keep you going whether you're inclined toward jazz, pop, swing, salsa, or alternative rock. The nightlife glitters all around the city. Current favorites: the *Great American Music*

Hall (859 O'Farrell St.; phone: 885-0750), for major jazz and folk artists, and *Eleven* (374 11th St. at Folsom St.; phone: 431-3337), for jazz. For comedy: *Cobb's Comedy Club* (2801 Leavenworth St., in *The Cannery;* phone: 928-4320) and *Punch Line* (444 Battery St.; phone: 397-7573). For cabaret try the *Coconut Grove Supper Club* (1415 Van Ness Ave.; phone: 776-1616) and the *Plush Room* (940 Sutter St.; phone: 885-2800). For a view of San Francisco at night try the *Top of the Mark* in the *Mark Hopkins Inter-Continental* hotel; *Oz,* a nightclub atop the *Westin St. Francis* hotel (see *Checking In* for both); or the *Starlight Room* in the *Sir Francis Drake* hotel (Powell St. at Sutter St.; phone: 395-8595). Dance to rhythm and blues at *Harry Denton's* (161 Steuart St.; phone: 882-1333). The younger crowd heads to SoMa—the district south of Market Street. On lower Haight *Nickies* (460 Haight St.; phone: 621-6508) is popular—the music ranges from hip-hop to Latin. The *Elbo Room* (647 Valencia St.; phone: 552-7788) has a hip crowd, with live music upstairs. *Johnny Love's* (1500 Broadway at Polk; phone 931-6053) appeals to a wide range of tastes with offerings of R&B, jazz, American rock, world beat, and reggae. Rock headliners perform at the historic *Fillmore* (1805 Geary St., near Japantown; phone: 346-6000 for recorded information), a combination of restaurant, bar, and performance hall. Tickets to performances can be purchased at *BASS* outlets (see *Music*). Another option is to take San Francisco's only nightclub tour, a bus excursion bearing the unlikely name *3 Babes and a Bus* (phone: 552-CLUB for reservations).

Best in Town

CHECKING IN

President Taft called San Francisco "the town that knows how," and though he probably wasn't talking about hotels, his statement nonetheless applies. A pleasant embarrassment of riches confronts visitors, from luxurious mammoths to ritzy mid-size establishments to dozens of intimate "boutique" hotels, which mimic European small hotels in character. Expect to pay more than $200 per night for a double room in the very expensive bracket; $140 to $200, expensive; $80 to $140, moderate; and under $80, inexpensive. Most of San Francisco's major hotels have complete facilities for the business traveler. Those hotels listed below as having "business services" usually offer such conveniences as an English-speaking concierge, meeting rooms, photocopiers, computers, translation services, and express check-out, among others. Call the hotel for additional information.

For B&B lodgings contact *American Family Inn/Bed & Breakfast San Francisco* (PO Box 420009, San Francisco, CA 94142; phone: 931-3083); *Bed & Breakfast International* (PO Box 282910, San Francisco, CA 94128-2910; phone: 696-1690; 800-272-4500; fax: 696-1699); *Dockside Boat & Bed* (phone: 392-5526) or *Vinspirations* (phone: 788-7062), both of which offer lodging on boats at Pier 39; or *East Brother Isle* (phone: 510-820-9133), which can put you up in a Victorian lighthouse. For daily, weekly, or monthly rentals of condominiums, townhouses, apartments, and homes, contact *American Property Exchange* (170 Page St., San Francisco, CA 94102; phone: 863-8484; 800-747-7784). Always ask about special packages and discounts. All telephone numbers are in the 415 area code unless otherwise indicated.

VERY EXPENSIVE

ANA San Francisco This elegant 36-floor establishment is the epitome of commercial luxury on the inside (apparently nothing can be done about the concrete box it comes in). Located in the trendy SoMa area, just a block from the *Moscone Convention Center,* most of the 677 rooms have floor-to-ceiling windows with city views. It features a fine restaurant, *Café 53,* which serves classic California, Italian, and Japanese dishes; calories can be burned off in the hotel's health club. Business services are available. 50 Third St. (phone: 974-6400; 800-262-4683; fax: 543-8268).

Campton Place Half a block north of Union Square, this small property in the European tradition has 126 sumptuously decorated (but smallish) rooms and suites fitted with armoires, writing desks, cable TV, marble and brass baths, and even padded coat hangers. The service is impeccable. The location—close to shopping, the financial district, and Chinatown—can't be beat. There's a roof garden for sunning and small receptions, and two conference rooms. On the lobby level, wonderfully innovative and well-prepared American dishes are served at breakfast, lunch, and dinner in the *Campton Place* restaurant (see *Eating Out*); cocktails and coffee are available in the adjacent bar. Business services are available. 340 Stockton St. (phone: 781-5555; 800-235-4300 in California; 800-647-4000 elsewhere in the US; fax: 955-5536).

Clift Hotel The warmth of rich wood paneling is matched by the warm, personalized service of the staff at this refined, 329-room property. Some of its employees have been on staff long enough to serve return guests for decades. Attention to detail can be seen in every corner—each room is individually decorated, and even at 2 AM room service can deliver a perfect cheeseburger in 20 minutes. The antiques-filled lobby harkens to another, more gracious time, and a Viennese dessert buffet is served in the *French Room* in the late evening until midnight. Built from a single giant sequoia, the *Redwood Room* has an altogether different ambience; its selection of cognacs and ports is one of the city's best. Meanwhile, the hotel's "Very Important Kids" program pampers children and teens. Playtime offerings include computer and board games, books, toys, and a VCR and tape library. Business services are available. 495 Geary St. (phone: 775-4700; 800-65-CLIFT; fax: 441-4621).

Fairmont New owner Saudi billionaire Prince Alwaleed has embarked on a much-needed refurbishing project for this grand hotel. Adjoining the distinctive old-fashioned main building is a 22-story modern tower with a total of 600 rooms and suites plus six restaurants, six lounges (including the *Fairmont Crown,* the highest public-observation point in the city, and the *New Orleans Room,* with nightly live jazz), two orchestras, international supper-club talent, and an almost one-to-one ratio of guests to employees. In addition, guests enjoy such other amenities as a health club, room service, and twice-daily maid service. Business services are available. California and Mason Sts. (phone: 772-5000; 800-527-4727; fax: 837-0587).

Hyatt Regency Inside this futuristically designed structure is a 17-story atrium lobby with all the activity of a three-ring circus, including a classical guitarist most afternoons and a jazz trio nightly. Glass elevators whisk you to the top, where a revolving restaurant looks out on San Francisco. The 803 rooms are attractive and modern; nonsmoking floors are available. There are numerous services for the business traveler. 5 *Embarcadero Center* (phone: 788-1234; 800-233-1234 outside California; fax: 398-2567).

Mandarin Oriental This luxurious hostelry occupies the top 11 floors of the 48-story *First Interstate Center* towers in the heart of the financial district, affording each of the 158 rooms unobstructed views of the city and portions of the bay. Glass "sky bridges" connect the two towers. The rooms are graced with Oriental-motif art and marble bathrooms, each one complete with a choice of terry cloth and lightweight kimono robes, slippers, and a digital scale. Larger rooms include screened sitting areas and expansive windows. (All offer "On Command Video," a choice of 80 children's and adults' films for a fee). The marble-walled reception area, the lounge (where a complimentary breakfast buffet is set up on weekends) and the Business Center are all on the ground level. An outstanding restaurant, *Silks,* is on the second floor. Room service is on call 24 hours a day. Business services are available. 222 Sansome St. (phone: 885-0999; 800-622-0404; fax: 433-0289).

Mark Hopkins Inter-Continental At the height of elegance, crowning Nob Hill, this hotel has a guest list that has included everyone from Haile Selassie to Frank Sinatra. The 391 suites and rooms feature either classical or contemporary decor, commodious baths and closets, and possibly a grand piano (the Presidential Suite has one). The tower rooms have especially fine views, and the glass-walled *Top of the Mark* lounge offers the best 360° panorama of the city. The *Nob Hill* restaurant (open daily) serves noteworthy California and international fare, with outstanding lamb and duck dishes and wines from 34 states. Twenty-four-hour room service is available. Business services are available. 1 Nob Hill (phone: 392-3434; 800-327-0200; fax: 421-3302).

Palace A San Francisco landmark since 1875 and one of America's first grand hotels, this property has 550 rooms. The *Garden Court,* a Victorian atrium with a domed, leaded glass ceiling, crystal chandeliers, and marble columns and floors, serves all meals, plus afternoon tea. Guestrooms are distinguished by antique furnishings and fixtures, along with such modern conveniences as robes, hair dryers, hookups for personal computers, and fax machines. The spa features an indoor pool, whirlpool bath, and sauna. Nonsmoking floors and handicapped-accessible rooms are available. There are also business services. 2 New Montgomery St., adjacent to the financial district (phone: 392-8600; 800-325-3535; fax: 543-06711).

Pan Pacific Glowing with rosy marble, brass, chrome, and glass, this 330-room property combines an American look with Asian-style service. Three valets per floor are on call to unpack, press clothes, polish shoes, draw baths, and prop matchsticks against room doors (a toppled match signals that the guests may be out and their rooms should be tidied up). Exercise machines for in-room use are complimentary, and computers with software can be rented. The menu at the elegant *Pacific* restaurant emphasizes California-style fare prepared with a French influence. From 7 AM to 11 PM, Rolls-Royces shuttle guests free of charge to the financial district or to dinner and the theater, and limousines can be rented for airport trips. Business services are available. 500 Post St. (phone: 771-8600; 800-533-6465; fax: 398-0267).

Ritz-Carlton Originally built in 1909 as the home of the Metropolitan Life Insurance Company, this historic landmark, with its white Greek columns and Ionic architecture, looks like the *United States Treasury.* And it is indeed a treasure; the entire interior has been restored to create 336 guestrooms, a full fitness center with an indoor pool, two restaurants and two lounges, and over 22,000 square feet of meeting space, including an outdoor courtyard. Throughout the public areas are fine collections of 18th- and 19th-century artwork and antiques, as well as Aubusson tapestries and Persian carpets. It has 336 beautifully furnished rooms and suites, including a Club Floor with such amenities as private concierge and complimentary continental breakfast and afternoon tea. Room service is on call 24 hours. Business services are available. California and Stockton Sts. (phone: 296-7465; 800-241-3333; fax: 291-0288).

Sherman House Once the home of music store owner Leander Sherman, this 14-room Pacific Heights mansion is the only San Francisco member of the prestigious Relais & Châteaux group. Interior designer Billy Gaylord created the decor, featuring French Second Empire and Biedermeier design elements. Guestrooms are furnished with handwoven Persian carpets, fireplaces, feather beds, and down comforters. Some suites have terraces that afford a view of the Golden Gate Bridge. Built in 1876, in the Victorian Italianate style, it has a three-story music room where Sherman used to entertain his famous guests (among them, Lillian Russell and Enrico Caruso). French-inspired food is served in the simply named *Dining Room;* room service is available around the clock. 2160 Green St. (phone: 563-3600; 800-424-5777; fax: 563-1882).

Westin St. Francis San Francisco's second-oldest hotel, a landmark since 1904, has entertained royalty, presidents, and international celebrities with its Old World charm. The recently refurbished 1,200-room establishment still keeps to its traditional theme of red velvet, glimmering crystal, and polished rosewood. The spacious lobby was—and still is—the busiest rendezvous spot in the city for those who "meet under the clock." The great Magneta clock—the first master clock of its kind introduced to the western US and dedicated following the fire in 1907—has remained here ever since. At the top of the 32-story tower is the chick *Oz* disco which offers panoramic views of the city. There are three restaurants including the *Compass Rose* serving California cuisine. A fitness center is open daily, room service is available 24 hours a day, and business services are available. 335 Powell St. (phone: 397-7000; 800-228-3000; fax: 774-0124).

EXPENSIVE

Archbishop's Mansion This stately structure built in 1904 once served as the home of San Francisco's Archbishop Riordan. Now a romantic bed and breakfast establishment, each of its 15 rooms (all named for operas) have fireplaces and private baths. Antiques and Oriental carpets grace the rooms; fine embroidered linen dresses the beds. Breakfast is delivered to your door each morning, and complimentary wine is served in the parlor every evening. Business services are available and parking is free. 1000 Fulton St. (phone: 563-7872; 800-543-5820; fax: 885-3193).

Donatello One block west of Union Square, this elegant hotel offers 94 spacious rooms (including nine suites), a serene atmosphere, and special touches such as plants, terry cloth robes, valet parking, and a concierge. Its mezzanine level restaurant serves fine northern Italian fare. Room service may be ordered until midnight. Business services are available. 501 Post St. (phone: 441-7100; 800-227-3184; fax: 885-8842).

Harbor Court Parallel to the waterfront, this landmark property, built right after the 1906 earthquake, offers Old World charm; 30 of the 131 rooms have bay views (enhanced by the demolition of the Embarcadero Freeway after the 1989 earthquake). The vaulted ceilings and architectural details have been retained throughout the large, club-style lobby and the small, subtly colored guestrooms. Amenities include limousine service to the financial district each morning, coffee, tea, and apples served throughout the day, and complimentary wine served each evening from 5 to 7 PM. All rooms have refrigerators. Room service is available for dinner. There's also a business center; business services are available. 165 Steuart St. (phone: 882-1300; 800-346-0555; fax: 882-1313).

Huntington The gold and burgundy antiques-filled lobby exudes elegance in this former apartment building on Nob Hill. A sleek, chauffeured Lincoln Town Car provides complimentary transportation within downtown. Each of its

140 spacious rooms is distinctively decorated and comfortable, and many have outstanding views. The *Big Four* restaurant (the name refers to the four railroad magnates) looks like a turn-of-the-century men's club and serves fish, game, and steaks. Deliveries from room service arrive until midnight. Business services are available. 1075 California St. (phone: 474-5400; 800-652-1539 in California; 800-227-4683 elsewhere in the US; fax: 474-6227).

Petite Auberge Near Union Square but closer to the heart of France, this less pricey Gallic sister of the *White Swan Inn* (see below), complete with an antique carousel horse in the foyer, manages to be both cozy and elegant. A sweeping staircase (and a small elevator for the less athletic) leads to 26 rooms (many with fireplaces) on five floors, furnished in country French style. Full concierge service, a buffet breakfast, afternoon tea, and valet parking are provided; business services are also available. Reserve a month or more in advance. 863 Bush St. (phone: 928-6000; 800-365-3004; fax: 775-5717).

Prescott A long Oriental carpet on an Italian marble floor leads guests into the reception area of this 167-room establishment, one block from Union Square. Though in the heart of the city, the lobby has the ambience of a gracious Southwestern living room, with its country hearth fireplace and displays of Native American artifacts. The *Postrio* restaurant is hot, with the clientele clamoring for chef Wolfgang Puck's interpretations of classic San Francisco fare (see *Eating Out*). Other amenities include complimentary wine and cheese in the lobby, complimentary limousine service to the financial district on weekday mornings, plus cable TV and stocked refrigerators in the rooms; room service until midnight. Business services are available as well. 545 Post St. (phone: 563-0303; 800-283-7322; fax: 563-6831).

Radisson Miyako This 218-room establishment in Japantown is the place for a plunge into the Orient—and a Japanese bath—especially during the *Cherry Blossom Festival.* The decor is Japanese, but both Japanese- and Western-style suites with saunas are available. The standout fare at the award-winning *YoYo Tsumami* restaurant is California produce, poultry and seafood cooked the French way but with Asian seasonings. Business services are available. 1625 Post St. (phone: 922-3200; 800-533-4567; fax: 921-0417).

Renaissance Stanford Court Set back from the street, the entryway of this 402-room hostelry includes a Beaux Arts fountain and Tiffany-style glass dome. Built on the site of 19th-century Governor Leland Stanford's mansion, this property is now a link in the Stouffer Renaisssance hotel chain. A stay here can include coffee and the newspaper with your wake-up call, afternoon tea and/or wine in the lobby bar, and dinner in the hotel's *Fournou's Oven* restaurant. No details are overlooked: Breads are baked fresh, on the premises, each morning; soaps are hand-milled. Elizabeth Taylor makes her San Francisco home-away-from-home in the Presidential Suite, as does

Mary Tyler Moore. The hotel is conveniently located, with two cable car lines crossing just steps from the main entrance; there's also complimentary car service from 7 AM to 3 PM. Business services are also available. 905 California St. (phone: 989-3500; 800-227-4736; fax: 391-0513).

White Swan Inn Converted from an old hotel, this 26-room English-style inn offers a personal welcome, a lounge and library with fireplaces, plus card rooms and a garden. Rooms are spacious and bright, and the amenities luxurious. Full buffet breakfast and afternoon tea, which also includes wine, sherry, and hors d'oeuvres, are complimentary. Valet parking and business services are available. 845 Bush St. (phone: 775-1755; 800-999-9570; fax: 775-5717).

MODERATE

Andrews This renovated 1905 Victorian building has retained some original brass fixtures and beveled-glass windows, as well as a sense of old-fashioned hospitality, in its 48 rooms. Continental breakfast is included. *Fino,* located off the lobby, serves Italian favorites at dinner. The front desk personnel double as concierges. 624 Post St. (phone: 563-6877; 800-926-3739; fax: 928-6919).

Diva Italianate meets high-tech on seven floors with 108 stunning guestrooms, all furnished with chrome, glass, and brightly lacquered furniture and fixtures. Traditional down comforters and pillows soften the effect. Complimentary California breakfast (fresh fruit and multigrain breads, muffins, and cereals along with coffee). Each room is equipped with a VCR, and there is an extensive library of classic and current videos. The *California Pizza Kitchen* serves "designer" pizza. Perhaps best of all is the location: right near the theaters and just a couple of blocks from Union Square. Complimentary limousine service runs to the financial district on weekdays, and other business services are available. 440 Geary St. (phone: 885-0200; 800-553-1900; fax: 885-3268).

Inn at the Opera This small, European-style, 48-room hostelry affords easy access to the culturally rich *Civic Center* area, which has improved since the demolition of the nearby elevated freeway. International luminaries like Mikhail Baryshnikov and Luciano Pavarotti stay here, sleeping in rooms with canopy beds and fresh-cut flowers. Pre- and post-performance dinners and desserts are served in the fireplace-cozy *Act IV* restaurant. Promotional packages to arts performances are sometimes available. Small-scale but luxurious rooms have kitchenettes with microwaves and mini-bars. Business services are available, there's a concierge on duty 24 hours a day, and free limousine service to downtown is provided weekdays. 333 Fulton St. (phone: 863-8400; 800-325-2708; fax: 861-0821).

Hotel Monoco An American Beaux Arts beauty, three blocks from Union Square, this hotel is for visitors looking for a port to call home. Each of the 200 rooms and suites boast decorative details from all over the world. The furniture of black lacquer, mahogany and satinwood is set off by striped fabrics. The lobby has a two-story inglenook fireplace where guests gather for complimentary wine and hors d'oeuvres. The whirlpool and sauna is located in the health club. Business services are available. 501 Geary St. (phone: 292-0100; 800-214-4220; fax: 292-0111).

Milano A 1919 Beaux Arts–style structure, this 108-room hotel affords its guests an elegant stay in Italian-inspired style. Amenities include a health club with a sauna, hot tub, and exercise equipment, as well as room service from the hotel's restaurant, *Bistro M* (see *Eating Out*). Its proximity to the *San Francisco Shopping Centre* and the *Museum of Modern Art* make this the perfect base for shoppers and art aficionados. Business services are available. 55 Fifth St. (phone: 543-8555; 800-398-7555; fax: 543-5843).

Nob Hill Lambourne This business-oriented hotel features 20 contemporary rooms and suites with kitchenettes, spacious baths with deep tubs, exercise equipment, and VCRs. Complimentary continental breakfast is available; there's a spa that offers facials, massage, and aromatherapy. Business services are available. 725 Pine St. (phone: 433-2287; 800-BRIT-INN).

Triton Definitely hip, this 140-room, pastel-decorated establishment in the heart of the gallery district showcases local San Francisco artists. Sophisticated design shows up everywhere—from the hand-painted wall murals to the custom-designed furniture to the staff uniforms. Amenities include CD players and a music library for guests staying in the hotel's moderate-sized ("junior") suites, complimentary wine each evening, bars that serve up plenty of free snacks, and room service. The hotel has a small conference room. Business services are also available. 342 Grant Ave. (phone: 394-0500; 800-433-6611; fax: 394-0555).

Victorian Inn on the Park Known as the *Clunie House,* it was built in 1897 in honor of Queen Victoria's *Diamond Jubilee* and now has guests reserving up to a month in advance for one of its 12 bedrooms. Inlaid oak floors, mahogany woodwork, charming period pieces, a handsome oak-paneled dining room (the complimentary continental breakfast features breads baked on the premises), a lavish parlor (complimentary afternoon wine), and a concierge desk. Some business services are available. Across from *Panhandle Park* near *Golden Gate Park* at 301 Lyon St. (phone: 931-1830; 800-435-1967; fax: 931-1830).

Vintage Court Everything is up-to-date in this 106-room boutique property, established in 1913. (A glass etching of the original building is in the mauve lobby with a cheerful fireplace.) A night's lodging for two costs less than dinner next door at the famed *Masa's* French restaurant (see *Eating Out*); note, however, that the hotel's complimentary continental breakfast is served at *Masa's.* Every afternoon in the lobby, the hotel serves complimentary

California wine. Outside rooms (named for Napa Valley wineries) have bay-window seats, padded headboards, and bedspreads in floral or wine-grape motifs. Business services are available. 650 Bush St. (phone: 392-4666; 800-654-1100; fax: 433-4065).

Washington Square Inn Within walking distance of *Ghirardelli Square* and Chinatown, the turn-of-the-century apartment house–turned-hotel in North Beach has only 15 rooms (10 with private baths), each individually decorated. Three rooms face Washington Square and are more expensive. Complimentary breakfast and afternoon tea are served; there's also a concierge desk. No smoking is permitted in the hotel. 1660 Stockton St. (phone: 981-4220; 800-388-0220; fax: 397-7242).

INEXPENSIVE

Beresford Here is British charm at a reasonable price: old-fashioned service, a writing parlor off the Victorian lobby, flower boxes in the street windows, and 114 pleasant rooms. Even the lamppost in front has a blue-and-white Wedgwoodesque frieze. Meals served at the *White Horse* tavern here feature fresh vegetables from the hotel's garden. 635 Sutter St. (phone: 673-9900; 800-533-6533; fax: 474-0449).

Carlton Just five blocks from Union Square, this 165-room property has all the charm of a large home. The hotel's café serves breakfast and dinner daily; complimentary wine is served each evening in the 1920s-style lobby; and room service may be ordered during meal hours. Business services are available. 1075 Sutter St. (phone: 673-0242; 800-227-4496; fax: 673-4904).

Cornell Everything but the name is French—atmosphere, furnishings, the manager's accent—in this lovingly spruced-up antique, with flower beds behind a picket fence, old reproductions of Cluny tapestries, a cage elevator, and rustic furniture in 55 rooms that have private bathrooms, phones, and cable TV. The *Restaurant Jeanne d'Arc,* filled with memorabilia honoring its namesake, serves dinner six days a week and complimentary breakfast. Smoking is prohibited. Some business services are available. Ask about the special weekly rate. 715 Bush St. (phone: 421-3154; 800-232-9698; fax: 399-1442).

Hotel Boheme This one-time Victorian building has been transformed by interior designer Candra Scott into a hotel that captures the true bohemian spirit of North Beach. Look for such touches as handmade light fixtures (some fashioned from parasols found in Chinatown) and furnishings. Each of the 15 guest rooms has a private bath and a queen-sized bed. There is no restaurant; some business services are available. 444 Columbus Ave. (phone: 433-9111; fax: 362-6292).

San Remo The only budget-priced hotel in North Beach, this lovingly restored Italianate Victorian building was constructed in 1906 by A.P. Giannini, Bank of America's founder. Although there are no private baths, each of the 62 guestrooms is comfortably furnished (some have sinks). There are no telephones or TVs, and the hotel lacks a restaurant. 2237 Mason St. (phone: 776.8688; fax: 776-2811).

EATING OUT

San Francisco has about 4,300 eating places, serving a wide variety of food, from haute cuisine to ethnic fare, and taking fine advantage of the wonderful seafood and fresh produce so readily available from the ocean and the surrounding valleys. Along with such longtime favorites as *Tadich Grill* and *Jack's,* San Franciscans welcome new restaurants that show up on the horizon at an astonishing rate. One notable trend is toward first-rate food in hotels, starting with *Campton Place* and extending to even newer establishments like *Boulevard*. At the other end of the spectrum are the neighborhood places that specialize in Chinese, Japanese, Vietnamese, Thai, or Mexican food at very affordable prices. Our restaurant selections range in price from $75 or more (sometimes much more) for dinner for two in the expensive category; to $45 to $75, moderate; to less than $45, inexpensive—excluding drinks, wine, and tip. All telephone numbers are in the 415 area code. Unless otherwise noted, all restaurants are open for lunch and dinner.

EXPENSIVE

Aqua In the financial district, this dramatic dining place—peach-colored walls, huge floral arrangements—features innovative seafood dishes such as ravioli stuffed with a creamy lobster salad, and medallions of *ahi* tuna. Valet parking. Closed Saturdays for lunch and Sundays. Reservations necessary. Major credit cards accepted. 252 California St. (phone: 956-9662).

Bistro M Chef Michel Richard's highly stylized eatery works culinary magic in this French bistro. Try foie gras served with sweet corn polenta, or five-spice grilled seafood with caramelized fruit. For a cooling finish, the homemade ice creams and sorbets, and the apple tart are just perfect. In the *Milano* Hotel, 55 Fifth St. (phone: 543-8555).

Boulevard Chef Nancy Oakes has won acclaim for her new restaurant which features three distinct areas: the bar, defined by a domed brick ceiling and an intricate peacock-patterned tile floor; the informal central section, with an open kitchen and a counter; and the dramatically lit, more formal dining area. The menu changes often but staples include wood-oven roasted chicken served on a bed of golden chanterelle mushrooms; grilled range-fed veal T-bone served with mashed potatoes, yellow turnips, and roasted shallot sauce. Open daily for dinner; Mondays through Fridays for lunch. Reservations advised. Major credit cards accepted. One Mission St. at Steuart St. (phone: 543-6084).

Campton Place Although it's in the *Campton Place* hotel, this is a legitimate magnet for diners in its own right. The relatively small room is decorated in soft shades of rose and gray, while the menu is an outstanding example of American dishes done to perfection—without excessive fuss or fanfare. Breakfast (arguably the best in the city), lunch, and dinner are served daily, and each is marvelous. The prix fixe dinner menu, served from 5:30 to 7:30 PM, is popular with theatergoers. Reservations necessary. Major credit cards accepted. 340 Stockton St. (phone: 781-5555).

Chez Panisse The oft-called "guru of California cookery," Alice Waters, opened this landmark restaurant in the early 1970s. Set in a house in Berkeley, it has a sparse, redwood-beamed dining room where the limited menu offerings reflect the southern French and northern Italian influences on West Coast dishes. Since only one meal is served in the downstairs dining room each evening, you may want to call ahead to know whether it will be spring lamb, grilled salmon, ravioli stuffed with potatoes, or something even more innovative. Upstairs the more casual and less expensive *Chez Panisse Café* specializes in pizza, calzones, salads, and soups. Closed Sundays. Reservations necessary at least a month in advance. Major credit cards accepted. 1517 Shattuck Ave., Berkeley (phone: 510-548-5525).

Fleur de Lys One of the oldest French restaurants in the city, it boasts an incredibly romantic setting, with murals and 700 yards of red and green floral fabric decorating the dining area. The fare is French, with California influences, and excellently presented. Chef Herbert Keller's latest innovations include lamb wrapped in zucchini and served with black olive and sun-dried-tomato *jus,* Maine lobster, and truffle cappuccino. Open for dinner only; closed Sundays. Valet parking is available. Reservations advised. Major credit cards accepted. 777 Sutter St. (phone: 673-7779).

Harris' Dark oak paneling and leather banquettes create the aura of an elegant men's club with a meat-and-potatoes menu: thick steaks and prime ribs aged for 21 days in a refrigerator to intensify their flavor. For dessert, the chocolate decadence torte is sinful. Open for dinner daily, for lunch on Wednesdays only. Reservations advised. Major credit cards accepted. 2100 Van Ness Ave. (phone 673-1888).

Masa's Creative combinations, extravagant sauces, and perfect presentation enhance a menu that changes daily. Highlights might include grilled scallops with saffron sauce, sautéed medallions of fallow deer with caramelized apples and zinfandel sauce, or roast squab with risotto. For dessert order the sublime white and dark chocolate mousse with raspberry sauce or the unique baked apple in phyllo pastry with cinnamon-rosemary ice cream. Open Tuesdays through Saturdays, 6 to 9:30 PM. Reservations necessary; call three weeks ahead. Major credit cards accepted. 648 Bush St. (phone: 989-7154).

Moose's Popular with the city's elite for power lunches and dinners, it's modern and airy, with windows overlooking the street, and has an expansive open kitchen, arches separating the bar from the dining area, and live jazz at dinnertime. Chef Fabrice Canelle creates such dishes as Mediterranean fish soup with rouille; and small gnocchi with smoked salmon, *pistou* sauce, and crème fraîche and caviar. Desserts are heaven. Open daily. Reservations required. 1652 Stockton St.(phone: 989-7800).

Postrio Elegant and airy (and expensive), this dining place in the *Prescott* hotel was dreamed up by chef-restaurateur Wolfgang Puck of *Spago* fame. Specials feature California's freshest ingredients, prepared with Asian and Mediterranean influences: grilled baby lamb chops on wilted salad with cilantro honey vinaigrette, and roast salmon with almond–black pepper crust and warm spinach salad. Pizza, salads, and sandwiches are served upstairs at the bar. Lighting fixtures, which incorporate hand-blown glass ribbons, were created by a former jewelry designer. Service is impeccable. Open daily for all three meals. Reservations necessary, as far in advance as possible (reservations unnecessary for bar or for breakfast). Major credit cards accepted. 545 Post St. (phone: 776-7825).

Square One Joyce Goldstein, an alumna of *Chez Panisse* (see above), brings together flavors from around the Mediterranean in this Bay City dining place. The à la carte menu changes regularly, depending on what's fresh. An open cooking area makes it easy for guests to watch chefs at work. Bread, desserts, and ice cream are made on the premises, and the wine list is extensive. Closed for lunch on weekends. Reservations advised. Major credit cards accepted. 190 Pacific Ave. (phone: 788-1110).

Stars Colorful, energetic, and sometimes noisy, this is a gathering place for the city's rich and famous. Jeremiah Tower, another graduate of *Chez Panisse,* prepares American classics with contemporary flair—veal shanks, venison, fish (even hamburgers, hot dogs, and pizza). Though the setting is elegant, the mood is casual, and diners come dressed in everything from black tie to blue jeans. Sit at the long, long bar (48 feet), listen to the piano player, and watch the chefs in the open kitchen prepare your meal. Similar fare is presented at *Stars Café,* located a block away and under the same management. Both restaurant and café are open late and are within walking distance of the *Opera House* and *Symphony Hall.* Open daily. Reservations advised. Major credit cards accepted. Main restaurant: 150 Redwood Alley, between Polk St. and Van Ness Ave. (phone: 861-7827); *Café:* 500 Van Ness Ave. and McAllister (phone: 861-4344).

Tommy Toy's The owner of this luxurious dining establishment describes the food as "haute cuisine *chinoise*"—and, indeed, it does represent an East/West melding of tastes presented in a palatial setting. The main dining room is fashioned after the 19th-century reading room, with ancient powder paintings framed in sandalwood. Dishes include such cross-cultural offerings as breast of duckling smoked with camphorwood and tea leaves served with a plum-wine sauce, whole fresh Maine lobster shelled and sautéed with pine nuts and mushrooms in a peppercorn sauce, and prawns in vanilla-flavored sauce with raisins and fresh melon. Closed weekends. Reservations advised. 655 Montgomery St. (phone: 397-4888).

Zuni Café The fare at this casual brick and glass, California-Mediterranean–style dining spot (with sidewalk tables, too) changes daily; it's based on the seasonal ingredients chef Judy Rodgers finds at the market each morning. The eclectic menu features the cuisine of southern France with an emphasis on braised meat and poultry and grilled seafood; pasta is also a favorite, and there is an oyster bar. Closed Mondays; open for all three meals the rest of the week. Reservations advised. Major credit cards accepted. 1658 Market St. (phone: 552-2522).

MODERATE

Bizou In a romantic old fashioned bistro with hanging light fixtures and glazed mustard-colored walls, chef Loretta Keller creates such favorites as tempura-fried green beans, Catalan shrimp, and fresh grilled sardines. The slow-simmered and gently baked dishes are just the thing on a foggy day. Desserts are memorable, especially the summer berry pudding, with its dense, moist, cakey texture and plenty of fruit. Vacherin is a bittersweet chocolate and coffee confection that stops conversations when it emerges from the kitchen. Open for lunch and dinner Mondays through Fridays and for dinner on Saturdays. Closed Sundays. Reservations advised. Major credit cards accepted. 598 Fourth St. at Brannan St. (phone: 543-2222).

China Moon In a cleverly disguised coffee shop setting, owner/chef Barbara Tropp has succeeded in presenting her singular brand of Chinese food. In what other "Chinese" restaurant would you expect to find such appetizers as chili-spiked spring rolls, spicy lamb, fresh water chestnuts, and Peking antipasto plates side by side with a California wine list and Western-style desserts? Portions are small; no smoking is permitted. Closed Sunday lunch. Reservations advised. MasterCard and Visa accepted. 639 Post St. (phone: 775-4789).

Fog City Diner Not your usual diner, this 1930s Pullman-style eatery is sleek, unique, and perennially packed. Created by chef Cindy Pawlcyn (who also opened *Mustard's* in Napa and several Carmel Valley restaurants), the food and the ambience—dazzling chrome and neon—are dramatically different from that found in a traditional American diner. Chicly dressed patrons like to order appetizer-size plates of red curry mussel stew and crab cakes and play smorgasbord, but milk shakes and hamburgers are also offered. Open daily. Reservations advised. Major credit cards accepted. 1300 Battery St. (phone: 982-2000).

Flying Saucer Out of this world in more ways than one, this restaurant is decorated with UFO-style memorabilia and dishes out huge salads and such heavenly entrées as duck *confit* in coconut-lemongrass lentil sauce and sautéed black sea bass. Open daily. Reservations advised. Major credit cards accepted. 1000 Guerrero St. (phone: 641-9955).

Fly Trap In the trendy SoMa district, this place is named after a long-closed but once popular Financial district eatery. Among the popular choices are sautéed chicken Raphael Weill, or many of the delicious pasta dishes. Valet parking. Closed Saturdays for lunch and Sundays. Reservations advised. Visa and Mastercard accepted. 606 Folsom St. (phone: 243-0580).

Gordon Biersch Brewery The financial district meets South of Market at this classy bar and restaurant on the *Embarcadero.* Featured are pitchers of house ales and a bar menu that's long on pizza; restaurant fare ranges from braised lamb shanks to wild mushroom risotto. Open daily. Reservations advised for dinner. Major credit cards accepted. 2 Harrison St. (phone: 243-8246).

Hayes Street Grill In a city famous for its seafood restaurants, this is one of the best—a quintessential San Francisco dining experience. Everything is fresh; nothing is overcooked. There always is a long list of daily specials, along with great sourdough bread and an unusually good *crème brûlée* for dessert. Closed for lunch on weekends. Reservations advised; consider dining here after performances start at nearby venues. Major credit cards accepted. 320 Hayes St. (phone: 863-5545).

John's Grill Dashiell Hammett used this restaurant near Union Square as one of the settings of *The Maltese Falcon,* and the 1920s ambience is still evident. Sepia photographs of San Francisco are the main decoration, but people come here for the fresh, excellently prepared seafood. The crab cakes are the best in town. Closed Sunday lunch. Reservations advised. Major credit cards accepted. 63 Ellis St. at Powell St. (phone: 986-DASH).

Pane e Vino The extension of a Santa Barbara establishment, this authentic-looking trattoria features such northern Italian fare as *vitello tonnato* (sliced veal with a sauce of tuna, mayonnaise, and capers), risotto, and grilled fish. It's close to the Triangle area of singles bars, so parking spots are at a premium. Closed Sundays for lunch. Reservations necessary. MasterCard and Visa accepted. 3011 Steiner St. (phone: 346-2111).

Splendido's Evoking the look of a centuries-old Mediterranean village, this exciting restaurant features sophisticated, innovative cuisine in a rustic setting. All dishes are made to order and may vary from seared peppered tuna with chive potatoes to grilled lamb served with fried shallots and white bean–garlic flan. Chef Christopher Majer opts for food presentations that look "architectural" and don't just lie flat on a plate. Those who don't want full meals can opt for the good pizza, made in a handsome wood-fired oven. Award-winning desserts and breads are baked on the premises. Open daily. Reservation necessary. 4 *Embarcadero Center* (phone: 986-3222).

Tadich Grill San Francisco's oldest restaurant (ca. 1849) is still going strong with what folks maintain is the freshest seafood in town. Best bets: baked avocado with shrimp *diablo,* rex sole, salmon, and sea bass. Don't pass up the homemade cheesecake for dessert. Open only until 9 PM; closed Sundays and major holidays. No reservations. MasterCard and Visa accepted. 240 California St. (phone: 391-1849).

Yoshida-Ya This stunning Japanese spot is known for its excellent yakitori—a selection of meat, fish, and vegetables, all marinated, skewered, and grilled over charcoal. Upstairs is less crowded, as are weekends. Open daily. Reservations necessary. Major credit cards accepted. 2909 Webster St. at Union St. (phone: 346-3431).

INEXPENSIVE

Angkor Borei Adventurous diners might enjoy the unusually prepared seafood at this Cambodian eatery. Open daily. Reservations advised on weekends. Major credit cards accepted. 3471 Mission St. (phone: 550-8417).

Burma's House Among the myriad of Chinese dishes listed on the extensive menu, there are some unusual—and delicious—Burmese specialties, such as *pat dok* (a salad of fermented tea leaves, toasted lentils, ground shrimp, green chilies, garlic, and sesame seeds) and *moo hing nga* (a traditional Burmese fish chowder with rice noodles, chilies, tamarind, hard-boiled egg, and kernels of corn). Open daily. Reservations necessary on weekends. MasterCard and Visa accepted. 720 Post St. (phone: 775-1156).

Casa Aguila At this haven of south-of-the-border warmth in the fog-shrouded Sunset district, try seafood prepared tableside on the *parrilla* (small grill); portions are large enough to fill several doggie bags. Open daily. No reservations; you wait outside on the street. Major credit cards accepted. 1240 Noriega St. between 19th and 20th Aves. (phone: 661-5593).

Far East Café Don't let the neon-lit exterior fool you—inside are ornate Chinese lanterns and private, curtained booths. The extensive Cantonese and Mandarin menu features all the old classics and, if you call in advance, an excellent family banquet. Open daily. Reservations advised. Major credit cards accepted. 631 Grant Ave. (phone: 982-3245).

Jackson Fillmore Garlicky, steamy, cozy, and informal, this Pacific Heights trattoria is a favorite among locals for early Sunday evening meals. Specialties include osso buco (braised veal shanks); chicken sautéed with tomatoes, olives, onions, and anchovies; and a wide variety of pasta. Open daily for dinner only. Reservations advised for parties of three or more; let them know if you will take a place at the counter. Major credit cards accepted. 2506 Fillmore St. (phone: 346-5288).

San Francisco Bar-B-Q The aroma of Thai spices wafts over Potrero Hill when the cooks fire up the grill to barbecue spareribs, chicken, salmon, trout, lamb, or even oysters. The meat can be ordered à la carte or as part of a dinner that includes sticky rice, grated carrot salad, and sourdough bread. A bowl of noodles comes cooked in sesame and soy, with crisp grilled pieces of duck. Just about everything on the menu can be ordered to go. Closed Sunday lunch and Mondays. No reservations. No credit cards accepted. 1328 18th St. (phone: 431-8956).

Sears Fine Food A line forms outside on summer mornings at this San Francisco institution serving old-fashioned breakfasts. The pancakes are Swedish; the French toast is made with sourdough bread. The standard lunch menu includes such nonstandard items as lemon soufflé. Open for breakfast and lunch, Wednesdays through Sundays. No reservations. No credit cards accepted (avoid a wait by sitting at the counter). 439 Powell St. (phone: 986-1160).

Ti Couz Crêpes are the specialty here, prepared in large iron skillets in an open kitchen. You can order them either as an entrée (filled with meat or fish) or as a dessert (filled with a sweet confection such as sauteéd pears and vanilla ice cream). There's not much atmosphere, but the food is great. Open daily. No reservations. Major credit cards accepted. 2108 16th St. (phone: 252-7373).

Santa Fe

The Pueblo Indians had a village on the site of Santa Fe several centuries before Europeans settled in the New World. According to legend, they called the town "the dancing ground of the sun," an apt description of a splendid setting. The city sprawls across a 7,000-foot-high plateau in the middle of the vast, sagebrush-swept Southwestern desert. To the east rise the massive, forested peaks of the Sangre de Cristo Mountains; to the west, those of the Jemez Mountains. The sky is a shimmering turquoise blue and the air, clear and dry. Sunlight, which is dazzling in intensity, dominates the perspective, casting ever-shifting patterns of light and shadow across the monumental landscape.

The ancestors of the Pueblo, the Anasazi, settled in this area thousands of years ago. Anthropologists are uncertain of their origins, but the Pueblo believe they came from a world beneath the earth's surface. This place was dark, ugly, and damp, and they struggled to get out. After many and various trials, finally they emerged through the earth's navel onto the land and into the light. The point of emergence is represented by a small opening, or *sipapu,* in the sacred underground ceremonial chambers called kivas, which still are found in pueblos today.

The Spanish established modern Santa Fe a decade before the Pilgrims landed at Plymouth Rock. In contrast to the English settlers, who came to America to escape poverty and religious persecution at home, the Spanish came to the New World to reshape it in the image of the Old. Their interests were, quite simply, God, gold, and glory; their settlement here, however, was a serious miscalculation. La Villa Real de la Santa Fe de San Francisco (the Royal City of the Holy Faith of St. Francis) yielded little gold or glory, and the Pueblo took to the Spanish manner of worshiping God in only limited and frustrating ways. When Spanish demands and oppression became too great, the Indians rose up in the Pueblo Revolt of 1680, driving the Spanish away and reducing most of Santa Fe to ashes. The Spaniards did not return until 12 years later, and even then the Reconquest, led by Don Diego de Vargas, was bloody and many Indians were killed. Although the *Palace of the Governors* was intact and the walls of the *San Miguel Mission* were standing, everything else had been razed. The Spanish colonists had to rebuild Santa Fe totally, using construction concepts borrowed from the Pueblo. Many of these early 18th-century structures have survived to the present.

The frontier period—also called the Mexican Period—of Santa Fe life, which began in 1821 with the opening of the *Santa Fe Trail,* had less influence on the city than the Spanish, but it looms large in America's mythology of the West. At its peak of activity, trade on the *Santa Fe Trail* employed 10,000 men a year and grossed millions of dollars. When American traders

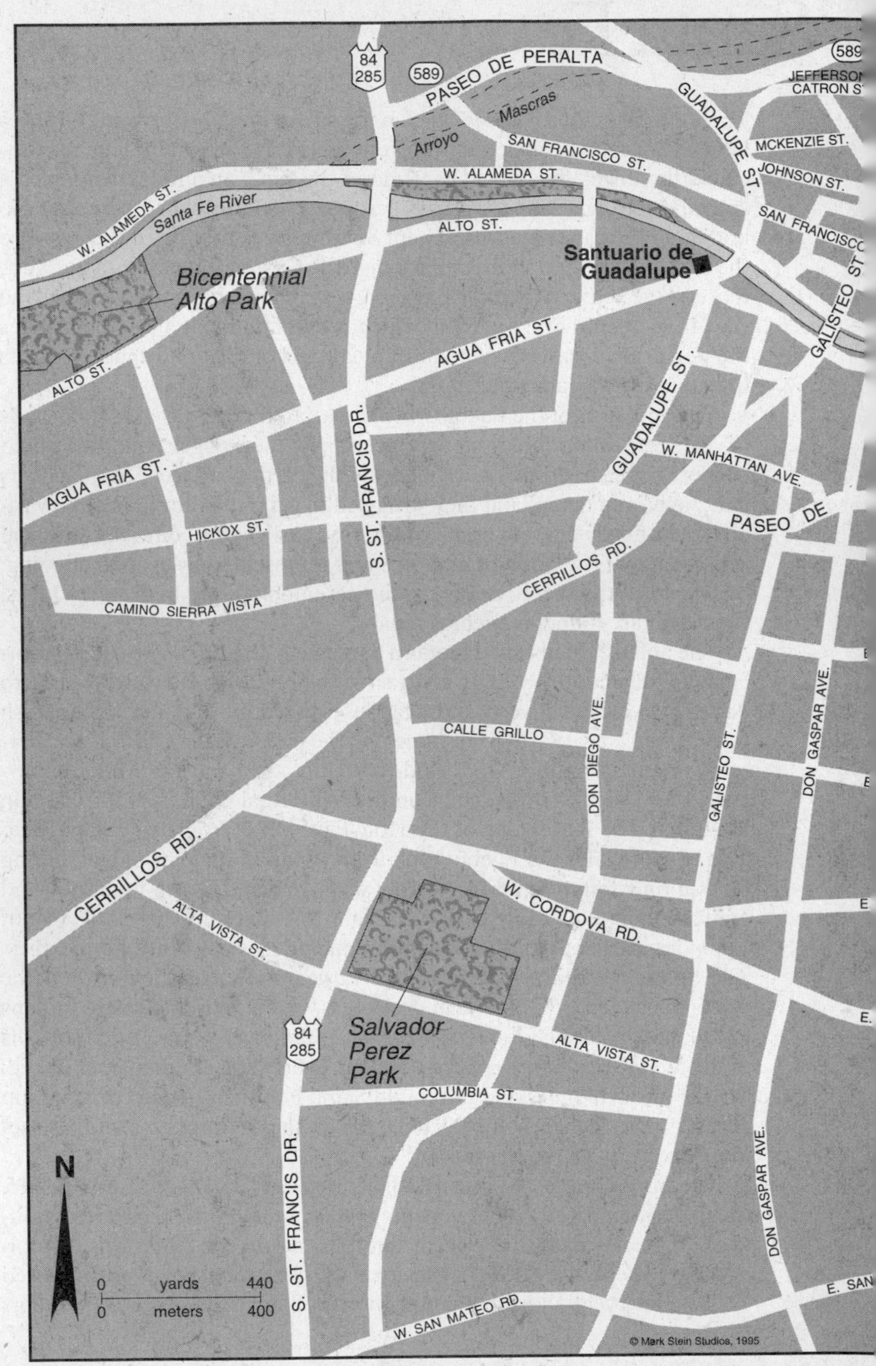

84
285
589
PASEO DE PERALTA
Arroyo
Mascras
JEFFERSON
CATRON ST
GUADALUPE ST.
MCKENZIE ST.
JOHNSON ST.
SAN FRANCISCO ST.
W. ALAMEDA ST.
Santa Fe River
ALTO ST.
SAN FRANCISCO
Santuario de Guadalupe
Bicentennial Alto Park
GALISTEO ST.
AGUA FRIA ST.
ALTO ST.
S. ST. FRANCIS DR.
W. MANHATTAN AVE.
PASEO DE
HICKOX ST.
CERRILLOS RD.
CAMINO SIERRA VISTA
CALLE GRILLO
DON DIEGO AVE.
GALISTEO ST.
DON GASPAR AVE.
W. CORDOVA RD.
ALTA VISTA ST.
Salvador Perez Park
ALTA VISTA ST.
COLUMBIA ST.
N
0 yards 440
0 meters 400
W. SAN MATEO RD.
E. SAN
© Mark Stein Studios, 1995

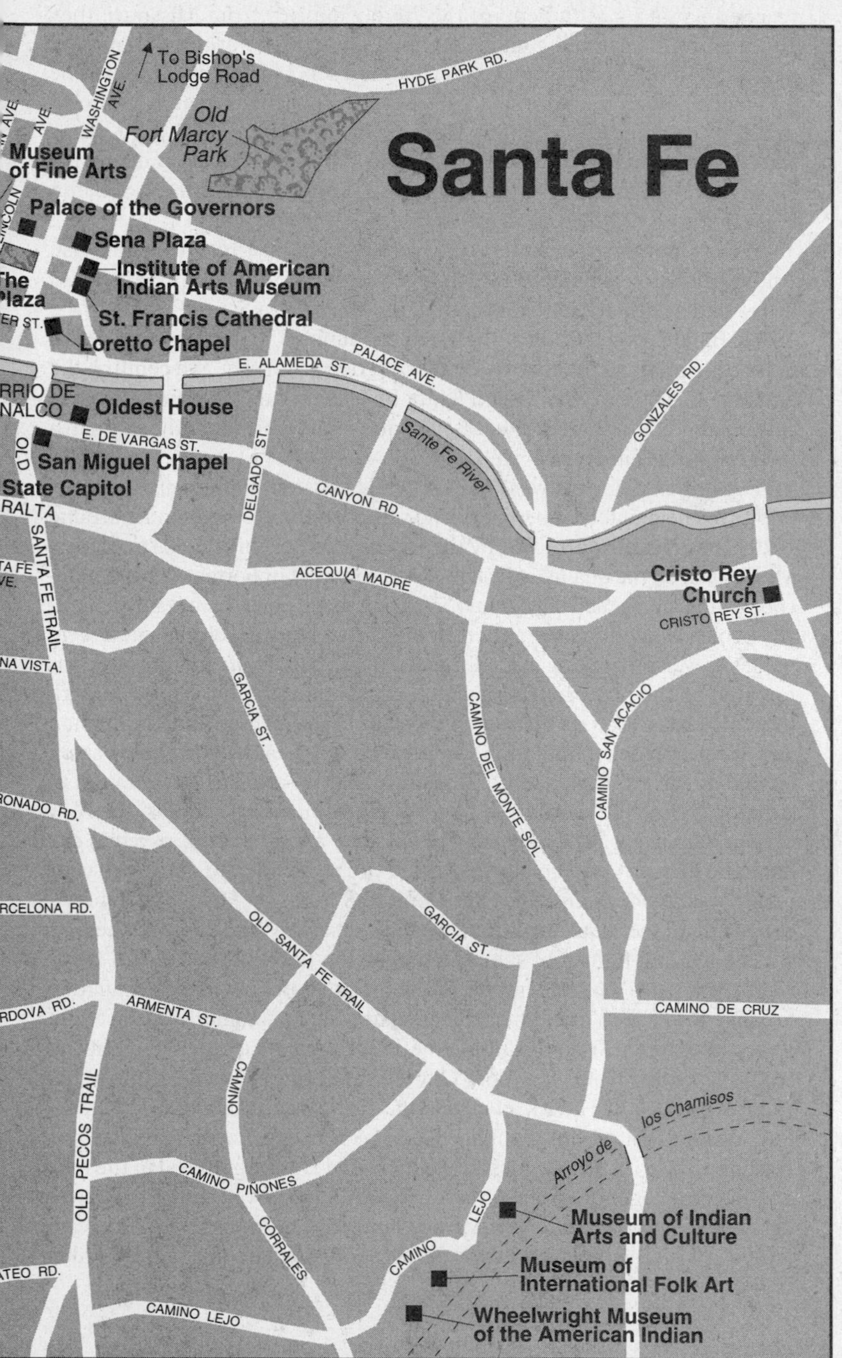

Santa Fe
To Bishop's Lodge Road
HYDE PARK RD.
Old Fort Marcy Park
WASHINGTON AVE.
Museum of Fine Arts
Palace of the Governors
Sena Plaza
Institute of American Indian Arts Museum
The Plaza
St. Francis Cathedral
Loretto Chapel
E. ALAMEDA ST.
PALACE AVE.
Oldest House
E. DE VARGAS ST.
San Miguel Chapel
State Capitol
DELGADO ST.
Sante Fe River
CANYON RD.
GONZALES RD.
ACEQUIA MADRE
Cristo Rey Church
CRISTO REY ST.
SANTA FE TRAIL
OLD SANTA FE TRAIL
GARCIA ST.
CAMINO DEL MONTE SOL
CAMINO SAN ACACIO
CAMINO DE CRUZ
ARMENTA ST.
CAMINO
OLD PECOS TRAIL
CAMINO PIÑONES
CORRALES
CAMINO LEJO
Arroyo de los Chamisos
Museum of Indian Arts and Culture
Museum of International Folk Art
Wheelwright Museum of the American Indian

reached Santa Fe at the end of the 70-day journey from Missouri, they poured into the gambling halls that lined the Plaza to drink, play monte, and dance fandangos with lavender-scented señoritas in black veils. The trail made Santa Fe a natural target for the *US Army* in its march westward to fulfill the country's Manifest Destiny. In 1846, General S. W. Kearny seized the city from Mexico, and two years later the Treaty of Guadalupe Hidalgo was signed, giving the territory of New Mexico to the US. Santa Fe at first resisted, then gradually adapted to the change.

Shortly thereafter, a new breed of settler began to arrive from the East. Anthropologists came here to continue the work of Adolph Bandelier, a Swiss scholar of international reputation who lived in Santa Fe during the 1880s. Bandelier's studies of the Pueblo stimulated considerable interest in North American prehistory. By the first decade of the 20th century, the anthropologists had established Santa Fe as a research center for Indian culture and had initiated a successful campaign to preserve the city's historic adobe architecture as well.

The anthropologists were energetically assisted in their preservation efforts by the painters and writers who settled in the area beginning around 1910. These artists, attracted by the serenity and primitive charm of New Mexico and by the quality of its light, were the most important outside influence on the city in the 20th century. Through them, Santa Fe became nationally known as an art colony, where young artists were developing new techniques as well as working in traditional styles. The *Museum of Fine Arts* was founded on the premise that any local artist might exhibit his or her work there. These days Santa Fe remains a major US art center. With more than 250 galleries (for a population of only 60,000), it ranks third in art sales, behind only New York and Los Angeles. The city also has a reputation as a major "New Age" center: A handful of acupuncture schools, the *New Mexico Academy of Massage and Healing Arts,* and numerous psychics call Santa Fe home. A good place to begin if you're inclined to delve into your metaphysical side is *The Ark* (133 Romero St.; phone: 988-3709), a bookstore with all the requisite paraphernalia—an aviary, crystals, and the like.

The leading figures of the area during the first decades of the 1900s were the artists Robert Henri and John Sloan, both of whom continued to live mainly in New York, though Sloan maintained a summer home in Santa Fe for more than 30 years. During the 1920s, Mabel Dodge Luhán moved her radical salon from New York City to Taos, bringing such visitors as the English novelist D. H. Lawrence and the early American modern painters Max Weber, John Marin, Georgia O'Keeffe, Marsden Hartley, and Andrew Dasburg. Two of Luhán's guests, O'Keeffe and Dasburg, stayed in the area and became legendary presences. O'Keeffe, who lived in Abiquiu, was known for her elemental New Mexico landscape paintings. Dasburg, who settled in Taos, once compared the pureness of its light to that in the Garden of Eden.

These days, that garden has gotten a little overcrowded. Longtime residents have seen a steady proliferation of new shops aspiring to capture that Old West feeling, and, as a result, cheap imitations of Indian and Mexican jewelry abound, along with other cutesy replicas of Western icons. But Santa Fe's charm is not easily ruined by crowded streets. Even for those who visit in the high season, the fine architecture and incredible wilderness vistas are still there to inspire, which caused D. H. Lawrence to write: "The moment I saw the brilliant, proud morning shine high up over the deserts of Santa Fe, something stood still in my soul and . . . the old world gave way to a new." These same glorious surroundings inspired Marsden Hartley's claim that this was the only place in America where true color exists; and indeed, for artists, or anyone else who cares to linger, Santa Fe remains "the dancing ground of the sun."

Santa Fe At-a-Glance

SEEING THE CITY

Visitors with lots of time and stamina should hike the trail up Lake Peak (12,040 feet) from the *Aspen Vista Picnic Area.* The trailhead is on the paved road to the *Santa Fe Ski Area,* a drive that also provides fine views for those who prefer to stay in the car. Another vantage point, the top of Martyr's Hill, affords spectacular views of the city and the mountains; it's about a 15-minute walk from the Plaza.

SPECIAL PLACES

The downtown area of Santa Fe is compact and can be explored on foot easily. A car is helpful for visiting the museums on Camino Lejo or for taking day trips to Taos, *Bandelier, Pecos,* and other nearby places of interest.

THE PLAZA The Plaza has been the center of Santa Fe life for almost four centuries, ever since the day in 1610 when mounted Spanish soldiers in armor first used it as a parade ground. Throughout the centuries it has been the scene of the most important public events in the city: markets, fiestas, proclamations, parades, and even, at one time, bullfights. An obelisk now marks the center of the lovely, tree-shaded square. Along the footpaths emanating from the obelisk are benches where weary shoppers rest, sightseers fiddle with their cameras, and office workers enjoy picnic lunches. The *Palace of the Governors* dominates the north side of the square; the three other sides are lined with shops, restaurants, and galleries.

PALACE OF THE GOVERNORS Built by Spanish settlers in 1609–10, 11 years before the Pilgrims landed at Plymouth Rock, this is the oldest public building in the US, having served as a seat of government for four nations: Spain, Mexico, the Confederacy, and the US. Originally, the entire palace was made of mud except for the roof beams, or vigas. The walls, then as now, were adobe. The dirt floor was mixed with animal blood to pack it down and produce a sheen. Following the Pueblo Revolt of 1680, the Indians enlarged the structure and used it as a large pueblo. It again was occupied and further enlarged by the Spanish following the Reconquest in 1692. The palace became a museum in 1909, housing historical exhibitions for the *Museum of New Mexico.* This makes it a natural starting point for a tour of the city. Closed Mondays in January and February; open daily except major holidays the rest of the year. No admission charge for children under 16. On the Plaza (phone: 827-6483).

MUSEUM OF FINE ARTS Next door, moving west from the palace, this museum houses a permanent collection of more than 8,000 works of art. Changing exhibitions throughout the year feature 20th-century photography, prints, and sculpture, with a strong emphasis on the Southwest. Completed in 1917, some 300 years after the *Palace of the Governors,* the building is an outstanding example of Pueblo Revival architecture. It became a model for the style that still dominates Santa Fe, combining traditional adobe design and materials with modern comfort and efficiency. Closed Mondays and Tuesdays in January and February. No admission charge for children under 16. On the Plaza, W. Palace Ave. (phone: 827-4455).

MUSEUM OF INTERNATIONAL FOLK ART Housing the world's largest such collection from around the globe, the museum was founded in 1953 by Florence Dibell Bartlett, who believed folk art to be a bond among the peoples of the world. The collection includes traditional costumes and textiles, masks, toys, items of everyday use, and folk art from the Spanish Colonial period. The famed *Girard Foundation Collection,* with items from more than a hundred countries, is on permanent exhibit. Closed Mondays in January and February. No admission charge for children under 16. 706 Camino Lejo, about 4 miles south of the Plaza off the Old Santa Fe Trail (phone: 827-6350).

MUSEUM OF INDIAN ARTS AND CULTURE As the exhibition facility for the adjacent *Laboratory of Anthropology,* its collection includes more than 50,000 pieces of prehistoric and historic basketry, pottery, textiles, jewelry, clothing, and other items crafted by the native peoples of the Southwest. Artifacts from this collection are shown in rotation. The museum also offers numerous demonstrations of crafts and traditional arts, lectures, and dance performances. Native American jewelry, pottery, textiles, and baskets are available in the gift shop. Closed Mondays in January and February. No admission charge for children under 16. 710 Camino Lejo, about 4 miles south of the Plaza off the Old Santa Fe Trail (phone: 827-6344).

MUSEUM PASSES

True museum enthusiasts can get a bargain by purchasing three-day passes to the *Palace of the Governors, Museum of Fine Arts, Museum of International Folk Art,* and *Museum of Indian Arts and Culture.* The cost

of the pass is substantially less than the combined regular admission prices to the four institutions.

WHEELWRIGHT MUSEUM OF THE AMERICAN INDIAN Indian arts and artifacts are the attractions here. *Note:* The *Case Trading Post* downstairs sells high-quality, award-winning Indian pottery, jewelry, and weavings. Open daily. No admission charge, but donations are accepted. 704 Camino Lejo, about 4 miles south of the Plaza off the Old Santa Fe Trail (phone: 982-4636).

SEÑA PLAZA East of the *Palace of the Governors* is this charming, tree-shaded, and flower-brightened courtyard surrounded by the four wings of the 19th-century home of Major José Seña. The 33-room adobe structure now is divided into shops and offices. E. Palace Ave. (phone: 988-5792).

ST. FRANCIS CATHEDRAL Directly across Palace Avenue, this structure built between 1869 and 1886 is the legacy of the French bishop Jean-Baptiste Lamy, the most influential person in local history. (He was buried in front of the high altar in 1888.) The Romanesque style of the building is, like many of Lamy's ideas, a little out of place. Its most interesting feature is the adobe chapel that existed here before the cathedral, most of which was incorporated into the larger structure; it is built of local quarry stone. In continuous use since 1718, the chapel is dedicated to *La Conquistadora* (Our Lady of the Conquest), protector of the early Spanish settlers. In 1992 parishioners renamed her, so that she now is known as *Nuestra Señora de la Paz* (Our Lady of Peace). The carved wooden statue, said to be the oldest representation of the Madonna in North America, was brought here from Mexico by the Spanish in 1625 and is carried in religious processions throughout the year. 131 Cathedral Pl. (phone: 982-5619).

INSTITUTE OF AMERICAN INDIAN ARTS MUSEUM One block east of the Plaza, this museum is housed in a spacious, Pueblo Revival–style, former federal office building facing *St. Francis Cathedral.* Federally funded schooling in the visual arts is offered here free to the most talented Native American students from around the US. (Founded in the 1930s, the institute has been one of the strongest forces in establishing Santa Fe as a major artists' community.) Contemporary paintings and sculptures donated to the school over the years by such renowned alumni as Allan Houser, R. C. Gorman, and Jaune "Quick-to-See" Smith are on display. Closed Mondays in January and February. No admission charge for children under 6. 108 Cathedral Pl. (phone: 988-6211 or 988-6281).

BARRIO DE ANALCO The Santa Fe River is as slow, irregular, and inexpedient as the town it crosses, yet because it was the main source of water in the early days, almost all the homes were built along it. Many of the old houses on the narrow streets in the Barrio de Analco (as the quarter on the south side of the river was called) have been preserved, particularly on East De Vargas Street.

LORETTO CHAPEL Also known as the *Chapel of Our Lady of Light,* this graceful neo-Gothic stone masterpiece was built in 1873 as a private place of worship for Santa Fe's first nuns. It is famed for its "miraculous staircase," which makes two 360-degree turns with no central support, defying all engineering principles. Open daily. No admission charge for children under 12. 219 Old Santa Fe Trail (phone: 988-5531).

"OLDEST HOUSE" The foundations of this structure are thought to have been laid by the Pueblo people in the 13th century, although the tree rings in the ceiling beams date only to about 1600. However accurate its claim of being the "oldest house in the US," the western portion of this structure is a good example of primitive adobe construction. Most early Santa Fe residents had similar dwellings, with low, log-beamed ceilings, dirt floors, thick mud walls, and a corner fireplace for heating and cooking. Closed Sundays. No admission charge. 215 E. De Vargas St. (no phone).

SAN MIGUEL MISSION Built in 1610, this historic church is as old as the *Palace of the Governors.* Much of the structure was destroyed by the Pueblo Indians in the 1680 Revolt. Rebuilt in 1710, its chapel boasts the massive, 800-pound *San José Bell,* thought by some to have been cast in 1356 in Spain and hauled to its present home via Mexico hundreds of years later. (The *Historic Santa Fe Foundation,* however, counters that a local bellcaster did a poor job, and that the date appearing to read 1356 should be 1856.) The most prominent feature of the interior is a fine old reredos, or colonial Spanish altar screen, made in 1798. Most of the paintings on the altar screen were done in Mexico in the 18th century. Closed Sunday mornings, *New Year's Day, Easter, Thanksgiving,* and *Christmas.* 401 Old Santa Fe Trail at E. De Vargas St. (phone: 983-3974).

STATE CAPITOL A bit south of the *San Miguel Mission* is this unusual structure, which residents call the "Round House." With a floor plan in the shape of the Zia sun symbol that graces the state flag, its architects intended to evoke a Pueblo kiva (the ceremonial chamber in which religious rites are performed). No admission charge. Old Santa Fe Trail at Paseo de Peralta.

CANYON ROAD One of the most romantic and picturesque streets in the US, it's also the oldest still in use; it was well established as a Pueblo trail long before the Spanish arrived. By the 18th century residents were building adobe homes and cultivating farms along Canyon Road, which follows the river east from downtown. Sections of some of the current buildings date from that period, and the style of the street's architecture was established in a way that has not changed substantially since. In the early 20th century, Canyon Road became the center of the Santa Fe art colony. Though few struggling artists can afford to live here today, the street still is zoned for residential arts and crafts, limiting its use to galleries, studios, restaurants, and homes. It's an ideal place to see both the residential character of the old city and the latest work of Santa Fe artists.

CRISTO REY CHURCH Built in 1940, this church was designed by architect John Gaw Meem in classic Spanish mission style. Nearly 200,000 adobe bricks were used in its construction, all using soil from the site—the traditional practice. One of the largest adobe structures in existence, it was scaled to house the most famous piece of Spanish Colonial art in New Mexico, an ornately carved stone reredos (altar screen), commissioned in 1760. 1107 Cristo Rey (phone: 983-8528).

EL SANTUARIO DE NUESTRA SEÑORA DE GUADALUPE This frontier church, built by Franciscan missionaries in the late 18th century, contains a painting of Our Lady of Guadalupe as well as outstanding woodcarvings and the *Plants of the Holy Land* botanical garden. It is located four blocks west of the Plaza in the Guadalupe historic district, a restored area of restaurants and trendy shops. Closed Sundays year-round and Saturdays November through April. 100 Guadalupe St. at Agua Fria St. (phone: 988-2027).

EXTRA SPECIAL

The Sangre de Cristo mountain range, the southernmost part of the Rockies, runs for 300 miles between the Rio Grande Valley to the eastern plains, and from Santa Fe to central Colorado. Santa Fe's own piece of this majestic range is *Pecos Wilderness,* a 167,000-acre expanse of roadless territory with ancient forests of spruce and fir, broad meadows, alpine lakes, secluded valleys, and exquisite summits such as Santa Fe Baldy (elevation 12,622 feet) and Truchas Peak (13,103 feet). This is New Mexico's ultimate recreation area for hiking, backpacking, pony trekking, and cross-country skiing; there is a network of hundreds of miles of trails suitable for anything from a pleasant summer-morning walk to week-long camping expeditions.

The most popular trailhead into *Pecos* begins at the lower parking lot of the *Santa Fe Ski Area,* located 15 miles east of downtown Santa Fe via the winding, steep Hyde Park/Ski Basin Road. On the way you pass the popular *Hyde Memorial State Park* picnic area and *Aspen Vista* overlook, where another trail leads through a shimmering aspen forest. There are many other places to explore within the *Pecos Wilderness.*

To venture deeper into *Pecos,* take Interstate 25 east for about 25 miles to the old Spanish village of Pecos. From there, a paved road runs up the wonderfully scenic Pecos River Canyon, a popular area for catch-and-release trout fishing during the summer months. After 14 miles, the paved road ends, and a dirt road continues for several more miles into campgrounds and trailheads.

A few miles south of the village of Pecos is *Pecos National Historical Park,* a 300-acre national preserve that includes the ruins of a 12th-century Indian pueblo as well as a 17th-century mission church. This area is

now being expanded, thanks to a gift by actress Greer Garson; to protect the region from commercial development, she signed over her 5,500-acre ranch to the *Mellon Foundation,* which turned the land over to the *National Parks Service.* The ranch land contains a beautiful 2-mile stretch of the Pecos River (which was not open to the public at press time, though the rest of the park is). For information, including maps of the *Pecos Wilderness* area, contact *Pecos National Historical Park,* Pecos, NM 87552 (phone: 757-6032 or 757-6414).

Sources and Resources

TOURIST INFORMATION

For a free copy of the *Santa Fe Convention and Visitors' Bureau*'s *Visitors' Guide,* call 800-777-CITY, or pick one up at the bureau's office in the *Sweeney Convention Center* (201 W. Marcy St.; phone: 984-6760). A better but more expensive alternative is the newsstand at *La Fonda* hotel (100 E. San Francisco St.), just off the Plaza, which carries all available guides and major works of fiction and nonfiction about the area. For a lively literary introduction to the city and vicinity, pick up Willa Cather's *Death Comes for the Archbishop* and John Nichols's *The Milagro Beanfield War;* the latter was adapted for the screen by Robert Redford and is available on videocassette. Contact the *New Mexico State Information Hotline* (phone: 800-545-2040) for maps, calendars of events, health updates, and travel advisories.

LOCAL COVERAGE The *New Mexican* is published daily; look at Friday's "Pasatiempo" section for information on events of the coming week. Do not, however, rely on the paper for restaurant recommendations. There also are listings in the weekly *Santa Fe Reporter.* And we immodestly recommend *Access Santa Fe/Taos/Albuquerque* (HarperCollins; $18).

TELEVISION STATIONS KOB Channel 4–NBC; KNME Channel 5–PBS; KOAT Channel 7–ABC; KGGM Channel 13–CBS.

RADIO STATIONS AM: KZSS 610 (rock); KSWV 810 (Spanish); KREO 920 (oldies); KFMG 1080 (rock); KRZY 1450 (country). FM: KUNM 89.9 (public radio); KSFR 90.7 (classical); KNYN 95 (country); KHFM 96.3 (classical); KISS 97 (rock); KBAC 98.1 (contemporary); KIOT 102.3 (progressive adult music); KLSK 104 (jazz); KBOM 107 (rock); KFMG 108 (rock).

TELEPHONE The area code for Santa Fe is 505.

SALES TAX The city sales tax is 5.75%; the hotel room tax is 3%.

CLIMATE Santa Fe's climate is shaped by both the Rocky Mountains and the Southwestern desert. The sun usually is shining, the air is very dry, and the sky is clear and turquoise blue. During the day, the air temperature always feels warm, even when there's snow on the ground, although as soon as the sun sets, the air cools quickly. The average daily temperature is about 80F in summer and about 40F in winter. Note, however, that the high altitude can slow you down a bit until you get used to the thinner air. Take a day or two to acclimate, especially if you're contemplating any serious hiking (and go easy on drinking alcoholic beverages).

GETTING AROUND

Although the downtown area is small enough to see enjoyably by foot, a car or other transportation is needed to visit the farther-flung points of interest.

AIRPORT *Santa Fe Municipal Airport* is serviced by *Mesa Airlines* (phone: 800-MESA-AIR), which flies from Albuquerque and Denver to Santa Fe. Visitors usually fly into *Albuquerque International Airport,* about 65 miles south, and then either rent a car or rely on one of several bus services; one is *Shuttlejack* (phone: 243-3244 or 982-4311), and departures are from *Southwest Airlines*'s baggage claim area approximately every two hours. The trip takes about 80 minutes.

BUS *Santa Fe Trails* (phone: 984-6730), the city's first public bus service, was inaugurated in 1993. Six routes, with both early-morning and late-evening service, link destinations throughout the city limits, including the museums on Camino Lejo, suburban shopping malls, and residential areas. The main transfer area for all routes is located near the intersection of Sheridan Street and Palace Avenue, just off the Plaza.

CAR RENTAL Although cars can be rented in Santa Fe, the rental offices are scattered. All the major car rental agencies are represented at *Albuquerque International Airport.*

TAXI There is no central taxi stand, but you can call *Capital City Cab Co.* (1107 Early Rd.; phone: 989-8888). If you're in a hurry, though, walking may be a better option; it may take anywhere from 20 minutes to an hour for a cab to appear.

SIGHTSEEING TOURS

WALKING Daily walking tours of the city depart from *La Fonda* hotel and the *Inn at Loretto;* contact *Santa Fe Walks* (phone: 988-2774), *Afoot in Santa Fe* (phone: 983-3701), or *Santa Fe Detours* (phone: 983-6565).

SPECIAL EVENTS

Summer is the performing arts season, with cultural events staged most nights of the week in July and August by the *Santa Fe Opera* and the *Santa Fe Chamber Music Festival* (see *Music,* below). The annual *Indian Market* is held the weekend after the third Thursday in August in the Plaza; at this very popular event (the country's oldest and largest Indian arts and crafts fair), Indians from the surrounding pueblos and across the US sell a wide variety of crafts—jewelry, pottery, sand paintings, weavings, kachina figurines, and so on. *Las Fiestas de Santa Fe,* celebrated the weekend after *Labor Day,* originated in 1712. The festivities open with the ritual burning of a 40-foot marionette, called a *Zozobra,* representing Old Man Gloom. After two days of fireworks, parades, dancing, eating, and partying, the fiestas end with mass at *St. Francis Cathedral.* Also part of the festivities are performances by the *Santa Fe Community Theater* (phone: 988-4262), the oldest theater group in New Mexico, founded in the 1920s. The theater's *Fiesta Melodrama,* performed during *Las Fiestas* in the fall, has received national notice for its irreverent satire, poking fun at some of Sante Fe's more prominent citizens. The pueblos near town have very different but equally interesting celebrations; the *Santa Fe Chamber of Commerce* (510 N. Guadalupe St.; phone: 983-7317) usually has information about the events visitors are allowed to attend; or contact the *Eight Northern Pueblos Council* (phone: 852-4265).

SHOPPING

Santa Fe is the best place in New Mexico (and perhaps in the entire Southwest) to shop for Indian art: jewelry, pottery, weavings, paintings, beadwork, baskets, and carved kachina figurines representing principally Hopi ancestral spirits who are said to visit the pueblos intermittently and are represented by masked impersonators at agricultural ceremonies. Decorative pottery has been made by the Pueblo Indians and traded between villages for over 1,200 years; today it commands high prices. Each of the pueblos has its own unique style that has developed over many centuries, such as the micaceous pottery (made from clay laced with mica) found at the Taos Pueblo.

Traditional Spanish crafts can be found in small villages throughout New Mexico. Decorative wool blankets, less expensive than Navajo rugs, are made using designs and techniques that date to the colonial era. Spanish woodcarvers are famed for their *bultos* (also called *santos*), statues of saints made for household chapels. Other crafts include tinwork and decorative wrought-iron items. Silver and turquoise jewelry made by both Navajo and Pueblo artisans is also a Santa Fe hallmark.

We recommend that you begin your education in native crafts by visiting Santa Fe's museums, including the *Millicent Rogers Museum,* 4 miles north of Taos (Museum Rd.; phone: 758-2462). They all display the very distinctive works produced by the various tribes, and you'll soon learn to recognize the traditional patterns and techniques each employs. You also will become familiar with the names of certain families or individuals who have become well known for a particular style. The museum shops at the *Palace of the Governors,* the *Museum of Indian Arts and Culture,* and the *Wheelwright Museum* all carry fine Indian art as well as numerous books on the subject. They also are usually attended by salespeople who are willing to part with a few pointers about how to distinguish quality, what's special about the pieces they carry, and how to care for what you buy.

Visitors can purchase pottery and jewelry directly from Native Americans in front of the *Palace of the Governors,* at a market known as *Under the Portal.* The vendors, from nearby pueblos, are licensed by the *Museum of New Mexico,* which sets high standards for the wares they display. It's also possible to buy while visiting any of several pueblos in the area. Two final bits of advice: Buy what you like when you see it—each piece is handmade and unique, so you are unlikely to find it elsewhere. And bring lots of cash if you shop in the pueblos, because many of the people who sell from their homes won't accept credit cards.

But traditional Indian art is only one aspect of Santa Fe's ever-growing gallery and boutique scene. The city's principal shopping districts are the downtown Plaza area, Canyon Road, and Guadalupe and San Francisco Streets. Some establishments exhibit weaving and woodcarving from remote mountain villages; a growing number are starting to sell folk art from other parts of the world as well. More than 250 art galleries show a wide variety of paintings, sculptures, photographs, and objets d'art; much of the work is by local artists.

In addition, Canyon Road studios and shops sponsor community open houses called *Art Walks,* which are listed weekly in the *Santa Fe Reporter* and the *New Mexican*'s Friday "Pasatiempo" section. Art enthusiasts also should contact longtime Santa Fe resident Linda Morton, who runs *Studio Entrada Tours* (Box 4934, Santa Fe, NM 87502; phone: 983-8786). This outfit takes groups of up to six adults on a two-and-a-half-hour tour around several local studios for a peek behind the gallery glitz; participants can meet the artists, see works in progress, and make purchases on the spot. Morton picks up visitors at their hotels and drives them around the city and its environs. Tours must be arranged by appointment a week in advance.

Any day of the week, big spenders and browsers alike will discover the chic, the exotic, and the highly unusual along the stylish streets of Santa Fe.

PLAZA DISTRICT

Andrew Smith Fine American Photography Offering selections of prints by Edward Curtis, Ansel Adams, Eliot Porter, and others. 76 E. San Francisco St. (phone: 984-1234).

The Chile Shop Stop in here for tasty, albeit mouth-searing, souvenirs and fine dinnerware. 109 E. Water St. (phone: 983-6080).

Cristof's Fine-quality Navajo rugs. 106 W. San Francisco St. (phone: 988-9881).

Davis-Mather Folk Art Gallery For browsing or buying, there's a jungle of traditional animal woodcarvings. 141 Lincoln Ave. (phone: 983-1660).

Elaine Horwitch Galleries Contemporary art, much of it done by Native Americans, selected with a sense of whimsy. 129 W. Palace Ave. (phone: 988-8997).

Fenn Gallery Featured here are classic regional artworks. 1075 Paseo de Peralta (phone: 982-4631).

La Fonda Indian Shop The best traditional Native American arts gallery in town. In *La Fonda Hotel,* 100 E. San Francisco St. (phone: 988-2488).

Glenn Green Galleries Works in stone and bronze by renowned Apache sculptor Allan Houser. 50 E. San Francisco St. (phone: 988-4168).

Móntez Gallery Traditional Spanish woodcarvings, tinwork, weaving, jewelry, and furniture. In Seña Plaza, 125 E. Palace Ave. (phone: 982-1828).

Nambé Foundry Outlet Contemporary housewares crafted of metal alloys. 112 W. San Francisco St. (phone: 988-3574).

Origins No Southwest staples here. Elegant fashions and jewelry, as well as some imported antiques. 135 W. San Francisco St. (phone: 988-2323).

Owings-Dewey Fine Art High-quality 19th- and 20th-century American paintings. 74 E. San Francisco St., upstairs (phone: 982-6244).

Peyton-Wright Gallery Contemporary paintings. 131 Nusbaum St. (phone: 989-9888).

Prairie Edge Lakota (Sioux) Indian artifacts, jewelry, and contemporary art. 102 E. Water St. (phone: 984-1336).

Rainbow Man Stop here for rare Indian artifacts, especially antique trade blankets (which were made specifically for barter). 107 E. Palace Ave. (phone: 982-8706).

Santa Fe East Museum-quality classic and contemporary American art. 200 Old Santa Fe Trail (phone: 988-3103).

Wadle Galleries Ltd. Traditional Western paintings, especially landscapes. 128 W. Palace Ave. (phone: 983-9219).

CANYON ROAD

Bellas Artes An eclectic assortment of paintings, works in clay, and other curiosities makes this shop an adventure in itself. 653 Canyon Rd. (phone: 983-2745).

Canyon Trading Post Handmade belts, handbags, and one-of-a-kind buckles. 670 Canyon Rd. (phone: 988-5012).

Copeland-Rutherford Fine Arts The works of contemporary New Mexico painters, sculptors, and photographers are represented here. 403 Canyon Rd. (phone: 983-1588).

David Ross Studio Wonderful hand-crafted furniture is made on the premises in this working studio. 610 Canyon Rd. (phone: 988-4017).

Expressions in Fine Art Stylish Southwestern art and handmade furniture. 225 Canyon Rd. (phone: 988-3631).

Gerald Peters Gallery More quality works by New Mexico artists. 439 Camino del Monte Sol (phone: 988-8961).

Gypsy Alley This cluster of small studios/galleries is reminiscent of the way Canyon Road used to be. 708 Canyon Rd. (no phone).

Kania-Ferrin Gallery Traditional souvenirs plus Indian art, weavings, and kachinas. 708 Canyon Rd. (phone: 982-1186).

Laurel Seth Gallery Southwestern contemporary art is exhibited in this historic building. 1121B Paseo de Peralta (phone: 988-7349).

Linda McAdoo Galleries One of Santa Fe's oldest galleries, featuring traditional artwork. 503 Canyon Rd. (phone: 983-7182).

Meyer Gallery Canyon Road's largest sculpture gallery. 225 Canyon Rd. (phone: 983-1434).

Morning Star Gallery This gallery shows antique Native American art and artifacts, including Pueblo pottery, Navajo chief blankets, and basketry. Especially interesting are the bold, unforgettable ledger drawings made by Plains warriors—and this is the only place in the area that displays them. 513 Canyon Rd. (phone: 982-8187).

Project Tibet You probably won't bump into the Dalai Lama, but Santa Fe's sizable Tibetan refugee community offers a good selection of folk art and gift items here. 403 Canyon Rd. (phone: 982-3002).

Running Ridge Gallery Contemporary glassware, ceramics, sculpture, and paintings. 640 Canyon Rd. (phone: 988-2515).

Spider Woman Designs Stylish handwoven fashions are on display here—wearable art at its best. 225 Canyon Rd. (phone: 984-0136).

Zaplin-Lambert Gallery Paintings by early Taos artists and historical prints reflecting 19th-century Indian life. 651 Canyon Rd. (phone: 982-6100).

GUADALUPE DISTRICT

Hand Graphics Gallery and Atelier Whether you're looking to shop or just looking, stop to see fine printmakers at work in this studio-cum-gallery. 418 Montezuma Ave. (phone: 988-1241).

Woodrow Wilson Fine Art This long-established gallery exhibits paintings by Blumenschein, Nordfeldt, Hurd, and other early New Mexico artists. 319 Read St. (phone: 983-2444).

Worldly Possessions To satisfy the hippie in you—imported beads, silk blouses, peacock feathers, plus a folk art gallery. 330 Garfield St. (phone: 983-6090).

ELSEWHERE

Jackalope Folk Art Center A favorite among locals as well as visitors, this giant complex of interconnected buildings covers six and a half acres. Inside, artisans from all over the world—including Europe, Africa, Mexico, Central America, China, the Philippines, and Indonesia—display and sell their wares. Items include pottery, jewelry, clothing, baskets, candles, and furnishings. A café serves Mexican and Southwestern fare. In addition, there is a greenhouse, an aviary, a goldfish pond, and a prairie dog village (a manmade replica of the rodents' natural habitat). 2820 Cerrillos Rd. (phone: 471-8539).

Santa Fe Flea Market Indian and frontier artifacts dealers, importers from all parts of the world, and local farmers make this one of the most intriguing public marketplaces around. Open Fridays through Sundays. Located 6 miles north of the city on Hwy. 84, near the *Santa Fe Opera* amphitheater (no phone).

Shidoni Art Foundry This vast outdoor sculpture garden displays dozens of large pieces, with indoor galleries for smaller works. On Saturdays visitors can observe the bronze-casting process; call ahead for times. Located 5 miles north of the city on Bishop's Lodge Rd. (phone: 988-8001).

SPORTS AND FITNESS

CAMPING AND HIKING For maps and advice about the Santa Fe area, write to the *US Forest Service* (PO Box 1689, Santa Fe, NM 87504; phone: 988-6940). For information about the *Bandelier National Monument,* write to the *Visitors' Center* (*Bandelier National Monument,* HCR 1 Box 1, Suite 15, Los Alamos, NM 87544-9701; phone: 672-3861). Also refer to the book *Day Hikes in the Santa Fe Area,* published by the local chapter of the *Sierra Club.*

FISHING Among other wilderness areas where fishing is allowed by permit are the *Jemez Pueblo* lands, an 88,000-acre parcel with two spring-fed lakes at the *Holy Ghost* and *Dragonfly* recreation areas. Permits are available for fishing on weekends from sunrise to sundown for a small fee. The waters are stocked with trout, catfish, and bass. Cycling and hiking trails also are open to the public (no fee). *Jemez Pueblo* residents are expanding their recreational facilities. For more details, call the *Jemez Pueblo Visitors' Center* (northwest of Bernalillo, off State Hwy. 44; phone: 834-7235 or 834-7265).

FITNESS CENTERS *Santa Fe Spa* (786 N. St. Francis Dr.; phone: 984-8727); *Carl and Sandra's Conditioning Center* (560 Montezuma Ave.; phone: 982-6760).

GOLF The *Santa Fe Country Club* (Airport Rd.; phone: 471-0601) is popular, as is the *Cochiti Lake* golf course (5200 Cochiti Hwy., Cochiti Lake; phone: 465-2239).

HORSE RACING The season at the *Downs,* just south of the city on Interstate 25, extends from early June through *Labor Day,* with races on Fridays and weekends (phone: 471-3311).

HORSEBACK RIDING *Pool Wells* (phone: 852-2013 or 800-882-3024), 4 miles north of Española on the way to Taos, offers trail rides and overnight pack trips into the *Pecos Wilderness, Carson National Forest,* and the *Sebastian Martin Land Grant.*

JOGGING The most pleasant run is along the Santa Fe River, on Palace Avenue or Canyon Road. A more strenuous route is up Bishop's Lodge Road, into the Tesuque Valley.

SKIING Northern New Mexico usually has good powder from mid-December until early March and sunny spring skiing for several weeks after that. The *Santa Fe Ski Area* (phone: 982-4429 or 800-776-7669) is close (just 15 miles from town), moderate in size and challenge, and relatively uncrowded. At *Ten Thousand Waves* (Hyde Park Rd.; phone: 988-1047 or 982-9304), a Japanese bathhouse in the mountains, you can enjoy an après-ski soak in one of the outdoor hot tubs, along with a variety of beauty treatments (including herbal wraps, facials, saunas, and massage). The *Southwest Adventure Group* (*Sanbusco Market Center,* 500 Montezuma Ave; phone: 984-2080; 983-0111; or 800-723-9815) offers full- and half-day cross-country and downhill packages for groups of 10 or more; *Southwest Wilderness Adventures* (phone: 471-0589) offers packages to individuals.

TENNIS There are 32 courts at nine locations around town (phone: 473-7236 for information). Non-guests sometimes are allowed to use the courts at the *Rancho Encantado* resort (see *Checking In*) for a fee.

MUSIC

The *Orchestra of Santa Fe* performs at the *Lensic Theater* downtown (phone: 988-4640) from September through May; in February, the orchestra stages a *Bach* or *Mozart Festival,* alternating composers every year. The *Santa Fe Symphony* (phone: 983-3530) performs a similar season. In July and August the *Santa Fe Chamber Music Festival,* widely recognized by its posters reproducing the work of Georgia O'Keeffe, takes place at the *St. Francis Auditorium* in the *Museum of Fine Arts* (W. Palace Ave.; phone: 983-2075). The six-week festival features eminent artists from around the world. The internationally acclaimed *Santa Fe Opera* offers lavish, adventuresome performances in a dramatic outdoor theater from late June through late August (phone: 986-5900 or 986-5955). Lectures and backstage tours are available to the public. The theater is on US 285/84, about 6 miles north of town.

NIGHTCLUBS AND NIGHTLIFE

Santa Fe is not known for its throbbing nightlife; the summertime arts festivals can be exciting, but, for the most part, it's a pretty quiet town. There are, however, some diversions. María Benítez, one of the world's great flamenco artists, has a dance company performing June through September (phone: 983-8477). At the *Mañana Bar* (Don Gaspar Ave. and Alameda St.; phone: 982-4333), Broadway tunes and cabaret shows are featured at the piano bar. At *El Farol* (808 Canyon Rd.; phone: 983-9912), jazz, blues, and other live entertainment draw in the crowds. *Vanessies* (434 W. San Francisco St.; phone: 982-9966) has a piano bar for those who want to sing along, and at *La Casa Seña* (125 Palace Ave.; phone: 988-9232) singing waiters and waitresses perform Broadway songs. Live country music and dancing can be found at *Rodeo Nights* (2911 Cerrillos Rd.; phone: 473-4138). Live salsa music and Latin jazz keep the dance floor lively at *Salsa's* (3347 Cerrillos Rd.; phone: 438-0691). If you're not up for dancing, while away the evening soaking in a hot tub and contemplating the stars at *Ten Thousand Waves* (see *Skiing*).

Best in Town

CHECKING IN

Santa Fe sees a tremendous influx of visitors every summer, so it's best to book well in advance. Most of Santa Fe's major hotels have complete facilities for the business traveler. Those listed below as having "business services" usually offer such conveniences as meeting rooms, photocopiers, computers, translation services, and express checkout, among others. Call the individual hotel for additional information. Expect to pay more than $200 a day for a double room (with private bath, TV set, and phone, unless otherwise indicated) in hotels listed as very expensive; $100 to $195 in expensive places; and $60 to $100 in moderate listings. During the winter, however, rates usually are 10% to 25% lower. We list a few of the better bed and breakfast establishments; for other recommendations, call *Bed & Breakfast de Santa Fe* (phone: 982-5942).

All the hotels below are in Santa Fe and telephone and fax numbers are in the 505 area code unless otherwise indicated.

We begin with our favorite places followed by recommended hotels listed by price category.

GRAND HOTELS

Inn of the Anasazi Opened in 1991, this Pueblo Revival–style hotel fulfills ideals of classic Santa Fe architecture. It is beautifully appointed, from the wood and stone floors, vigas (roof beams), and kiva fireplaces to the four-poster beds and hand-painted furnishings. Small yet elegant, the 59 rooms have all the comforts and charms of a small inn. There's also a library and a cozy living room. The caring staff members (including masseuses) are at your beck and call. An excellent restaurant, *Anasazi,* is on the premises (see *Eating Out*), and room service is always available. There is a concierge desk and business services. 113 Washington Ave. (phone: 988-3030; 800-688-8100; fax: 988-9005).

Rancho Encantado Bordered by the *Tesuque Indian Reservation* and the *Santa Fe National Forest,* this topnotch Old Southwest resort hotel came into being in the 1930s as a very ordinary sort of desert lodge. Today it is a luxurious Western guest ranch—more than a hotel, more than an inn, this is the sort of establishment where you expect to find cowbells, dried peppers, and Indian weavings hanging here and there, the occasional rawhide chair, and lots of red tile. The 26 guestrooms, furnished with antiques and Southwestern Indian art and artifacts, have their own patios; most have fireplaces. Across the road are another 60 guestrooms in two-bedroom villas. The tri-level dining room, walled in white adobe, looks out across the desert, nearly 170 acres of which make up the ranch's spread. You can swim in a heated outdoor pool, play tennis, take escorted trail rides, or join in many other indoor or outdoor activities. The food is Mexican, American, and continental. (Be sure to try the sour cream–chicken enchiladas.) There are big feasts for *Thanksgiving* and *Christmas.* Business services are available. Rte. 592 in Tesuque, 8 miles north of Santa Fe (phone: 982-3537; 800-722-9339; fax: 983-8269).

VERY EXPENSIVE

Las Brisas de Santa Fe This quiet, Southwestern-style compound with 11 beautifully furnished one- and two-bedroom rental condominiums is within walking distance of the Plaza. All units have fireplaces. 624 Galisteo (phone: 982-5795).

EXPENSIVE

Bishop's Lodge Originally Bishop Lamy's retirement home in the late 19th century, this quiet retreat nestled in the Sangre de Cristo Mountains is surrounded by beautiful gardens and orchards on a thousand acres of privately owned land. The comfortable lodge has 88 spacious rooms, its own stables, tennis courts, a pool and sauna, trap and skeet shooting, and an all-day program for children during the summer. The Modified American Plan (MAP) rate in the summer includes two meals a day from the excellent kitchen; room service also is available. For those inclined to tie the knot, there's a tiny, but historic, chapel located on the property. Business services are available. Open April through December. Bishop's Lodge Rd. (phone: 983-6377; 800-860-9257; fax: 989-8739).

Don Gaspar Compound Inn Set in a cluster of adobe and Spanish mission–style buildings, this charming inn is conveniently located in the Don Gaspar Historic District, a short walk from the Plaza and Canyon Road. The six units (including a double room, two suites, and three separate casitas or small houses) are decorated in classic Southwestern style with antique furnishings and feature plenty of luxury amenities, including mini-refrigerators, plush robes, and stereos (but no TV sets). The larger suites and casitas also have full kitchens and fireplaces, and one has its own courtyard and garden. Although there's no restaurant, a full breakfast is included in the rate, and there are several good dining spots in the neighborhood. 623 Don Gaspar Ave. (phone: 986-8664; fax: 986-0696).

Eldorado This 218-room property has handsomely furnished rooms with mini-bars; many suites boast wood-burning fireplaces and porches. There are remarkable mountain and city vistas, and guests can find everything from local art to *The New York Times* to real estate offerings in the extensive shopping gallery. Other pluses are masseuses, saunas, and the heated rooftop Jacuzzi. Meeting rooms can accommodate up to 600. There's a restaurant, a concierge desk, and business services. 309 W. San Francisco St. (phone: 988-4455; 800-955-4455; fax: 988-5376).

La Fonda A Santa Fe landmark on the Plaza, it's less notable for service than for its striking appearance and historical character: Though the present hotel was built in 1920, an inn (with the same name) has existed on this site since the opening of the *Santa Fe Trail,* almost 200 years ago. The 153 guestrooms have Spanish Colonial accents. There's an outdoor pool, two indoor Jacuzzis, and massages by appointment. An outdoor bar, located in a bell tower, is open seasonally and offers sunset views of the city. Other conveniences include a concierge desk and business services. 100 E. San Francisco St. (phone: 982-5511; 800-523-5002; fax: 988-2952).

Inn of the Animal Tracks This homey bed and breakfast establishment, just a five-minute walk from the Plaza, offers six guestrooms, each individually decorated in a wild-animal motif—wolf, otter, eagle, and other predators. A spacious Southwestern-style living room with fireplace and a peaceful backyard make this a great downtown haven. The inn's superior breakfasts (with changing menu) are one of Santa Fe's secret treasures. 707 Paseo de Peralta (phone: 988-1546).

Inn of the Governors Don't let the motelish exterior dissuade you, for this cozy, 100-room property has an extremely attentive staff and thoughtfully appointed accommodations. Classical music plays continuously in the inviting lobby. Rooms are furnished with contemporary yet rustic Southwest furniture and local art; many have balconies and wood-burning fireplaces. *Mañana* serves dinner nightly, and has a piano bar and intimate outdoor dining around a huge fireplace. There's also an outdoor heated pool and complimentary coffee, newspapers, and parking. A concierge desk attends to guests, and business services are available. 234 Don Gaspar Ave. (phone: 982-4333; 800-234-4534; fax: 989-9149).

Inn at Loretto The exterior of this modern, 137-room hostelry near the Plaza is distinctively Spanish Pueblo in style, although the rooms are quite standard, with no surprises. It's named for the historic spot it occupies, that of the old *Loretto Academy,* established in the 1850s by Bishop Lamy and the Sisters of Loretto. Other amenities include business services and a concierge. 211 Old Santa Fe Trail (phone: 988-5531; 800-727-5531; fax: 984-7988).

Inn on the Alameda Located just two blocks from the Plaza, this abobe-style hostelry features 66 charming rooms (ask for one with a fireplace), personal service, and elaborate buffet breakfasts. There's no restaurant, but guests enjoy the wonderful bar. Other amenities include hot tubs and massages, a concierge desk, and business services. 303 E. Alameda (phone: 984-2121; 800-506-9206; fax: 986-8325).

Picacho Plaza and Cielo Grande Condominiums This hostelry offers 133 Southwestern-style guestrooms with hand-carved furnishings; many have private terraces. The hotel also manages 38 fully equipped condominiums with fireplaces and outdoor spas. Highlights are a landscaped garden and a pool. The *Petroglyph* restaurant provides stunning views of the mountains. Guests can use the 19,000-square-foot health club, which has racquetball courts, a lap pool, aerobics classes, and weights. Additional amenities include room service until 10 PM and business services. 750 N. St. Francis Dr. (phone: 982-5591; 800-441-5591; fax: 988-2821).

Plaza Real Located a half block from the Plaza, this intimate establishment has 56 rooms decorated in muted Southwestern tones. Most are demi-suites with fireplaces and sitting areas, and some have balconies. Although there is no restaurant on the premises, the kitchen delivers a continental breakfast to your room. The cozy lobby has a fireplace. Business services are available, and there's a concierge desk and underground parking. 125 Washington Ave. (phone: 988-4900; 800-279-7325; fax: 988-4900).

La Posada A few blocks from the Plaza, this 116-room inn is spread out over six landscaped acres. The center of the complex is the *Staab House,* a Victorian home dating from 1882 that's been tastefully converted into a good restaurant and a popular lounge. Rates depend on the size and charm of the rooms, some of which are fairly conventional and others romantically Southwestern, with adobe fireplaces and Indian rugs. A concierge desk responds to guests' needs, and business services are available. 330 E. Palace Ave. (phone: 986-0000; 800-727-5276; fax: 982-6850).

St. Francis Built in the 1920s and restored to its original style, this small downtown place features 83 rooms decorated with period furnishings, the whole reflecting a simple, romantic elegance; afternoon tea is served. Business services are available, and there's also a concierge desk. 210 Don Gaspar Ave. (phone: 983-5700; 800-529-5700; fax: 989-7690).

Santa Fe This hotel, designed in the Pueblo Revival style, is located in the Guadalupe district, less than a 10-minute walk to the Plaza. Run by a partnership between the Picuris tribe of northern New Mexico and the Santa Fe Hospitality Company, it is the first joint venture of its kind off the reservation trust lands. The 131 rooms include 91 suites, each with a separate bedroom and living area, a microwave oven, and a mini-bar. Complimentary shuttle service to the Plaza also is provided, as well as a concierge desk and business services. Paseo de Peralta at Cerrillos Rd. (phone: 982-1200; 800-825-9876; fax: 984-2211).

MODERATE

Preston House Another good bed and breakfast option downtown. Five of the 15 rooms have fireplaces; two Queen Anne–style cottages also are available. 106 Faithway (phone: 982-3465).

Pueblo Bonito Bed & Breakfast Inn This downtown compound with 14 rooms and four suites is decorated in Southwest style. All units have kiva fireplaces. Continental breakfast and afternoon tea are included in the room rate. 138 W. Manhattan Ave. (phone: 984-8001; 800-461-4599).

El Rey Inn This is the best bargain in town for Santa Fe charm; if it were located downtown (rather than on "motel row"), prices would be at least double. Many of the individually decorated rooms have adobe fireplaces, decorated vigas, and tile murals; some are solar heated and overlook a garden. A continental breakfast is included. There's also a playground, an outdoor pool, a coin-operated laundry, and a hot tub, which is open year-round. 1862 Cerrillos Rd. (phone: 982-1931; 800-521-1349; fax: 989-9249).

EATING OUT

Northern New Mexico's distinctive regional fare is a variation on Mexican and Spanish dishes such as enchiladas and tamales, with less familiar local favorites like *chiles rellenos* (battered whole green chili peppers stuffed with cheese) and *carne adovada* (beef or pork strips grilled with red chili marinade). The special ingredients include blue corn, which the Indians of the nearby pueblos believe to be the sacred corn of the gods, and green chili peppers, which are roasted, peeled, and served in a stew or sauce. (Avoid the common mistake of assuming that green chilies are milder than red chilies.) Many restaurants serve conventional northern New Mexican fare, as well as "new Southwestern" cuisine, creative dishes prepared with distinctively local ingredients such as green chilies, piñon nuts, blue corn, or *posole* (Mexican hominy).

With more than 200 dining establishments, Santa Fe's restaurant scene is highly competitive. Expect to pay $40 or more for a meal for two (without drinks, wine, or tip) in restaurants listed below as expensive; between $20 and $40 in those listed as moderate; and around $15 in inexpensive places. All telephone numbers are in the 505 area code unless otherwise indicated.

Unless otherwise noted, restaurants are open for lunch and dinner.

EXPENSIVE

Anasazi The menu here, described by the restaurant as "foods of the earth from the Native American, foods of the soul from the northern New Mexican, and foods of substance from the American cowboy," includes unusual dishes such as ginger shrimp dumplings in red chili oil, grilled shrimp *gorditas* (little tortilla pockets), and grilled pork chops on sun-dried tomato flecked with polenta. Reservations advised. Major credit cards accepted. In the *Inn of the Anasazi,* 113 Washington Ave. (phone: 988-3236).

Antiquity Built as a honeymoon cottage almost a century ago, this secluded restaurant provides two intimate dining areas lined with traditional brick floors and bordered by walls clad in regional art. The open kitchen and grill proffers well-prepared filet mignon, chateaubriand for two, and a variety of seafood and pasta entrées, plus a selection of equally delicious appetizers. Open for dinner only; closed Sundays. Reservations advised. Major credit cards accepted. 112 Romero St NW (phone: 247-3545).

Babba Ganzo If you need a break from all the chilies and tortillas, run—don't walk—to this endearing, Tuscany-inspired trattoria. Airy and rustic, the "Dapper Daddy" (the English translation of the Florentine name) rewards with exceptional rosemary *focaccia;* pizza with goat cheese and garlic; ravioli stuffed with veal and ricotta in sage butter;.and charbroiled rack of lamb marinated in wine and herbs. Do save room, somehow, for the chocolate torte, the lemon custard tart sprinkled with pine nuts, or the *tiramisù.* Open daily. Reservations advised. Major credit cards accepted. 130 Lincoln Ave. (phone: 986-3835).

Café Escalera This light, airy café upstairs in Lincoln Place has attracted a local following because of its tasty health-conscious dishes. The culinary offerings include salads, pasta, grilled Moroccan lamb sausages, and even rib-eye steaks with roquefort butter and sinfully caloric desserts (for those with fewer health worries). There's an extensive wine list. Open Mondays through Saturdays for all three meals; for dinner only on Sundays. Reservations advised. Major credit cards accepted. 130 Lincoln Pl. (phone: 989-8188).

La Casa Seña This elegant yet cozy dining spot offers outdoor seating in historic Seña Plaza. Begin with a chilled margarita, then segue into fantastic blue-corn muffins and *trucha en terracotta,* a fresh Rocky Mountain trout wrapped in vine leaves and baked in a clay dish that's cracked open at tableside. Reservations advised. Major credit cards accepted. 125 Palace Ave. (phone: 988-9232).

Coyote Café Chef/owner Mark Miller, who established a national reputation in the San Francisco Bay area and helped pioneer Southwestern cuisine, runs this fashionable place that uses regional ingredients in imaginative ways. Signature dishes include buttermilk corn cakes with *chipotle* (roasted jalapeño) shrimp; rib chops with chili onion rings; and sour-lemon bread pudding. Closed for lunch on weekdays, November through April; brunch menu on weekends. Reservations advised. Major credit cards accepted. 132 W. Water St. (phone: 983-1615).

Encore Provence A lovely private home has been remade into the city's only French dining room by a relocated French couple who successfully create such haute cuisine as shrimp beignets with seaweed salad, swordfish with oyster mushrooms, and halibut with Niçoise olives. Landlubbers may opt for rabbit with sage stuffing and risotto, or lamb noisettes with eggplant Provençale. Reservations advised. Major credit cards accepted. 548 Agua Fria St. (phone: 983-7470).

Geronimo Housed in an adobe-style building built in 1756 by Geronimo Lopez, this popular dining spot serves unusual dishes with spicy flair. The menu changes often, but be sure to try the salmon piñon sticks with sambuca butter sauce and smoked tomato glaze, an appetizer that will linger in your memory. Closed Mondays for lunch. Reservations necessary. Major credit cards accepted. 724 Canyon Rd. (phone: 982-1500).

Pink Adobe One of the city's best for many years, "the Pink" (as it's known) features an unusual menu that includes steaks, creole dishes, and New Mexican specialties. Try the steak Dunnigan with green chili peppers, or the chicken enchiladas with green chilies and sour cream. For dessert the hot French apple pie with rum sauce is hard to resist. The locals congregate in the *Dragon Room* bar over margaritas and other libations. Closed for lunch on weekends. Reservations advised. Major credit cards accepted. 406 Old Santa Fe Trail (phone: 983-7712).

Santacafé Locally popular for its casual elegance and fine food, it offers a sophisticated, "adaptive Southwestern" menu (which changes daily) drawing on Thai, Japanese, Chinese, Greek, Spanish, and Italian influences. Closed for lunch on weekends. Reservations advised. MasterCard and Visa accepted. 231 Washington Ave. (phone: 984-1788).

Thao This Thai place (pronounced *Tay*-oh) has become a favorite, offering a tasty counterpoint to the usual Santa Fe fare. The three small dining rooms are filled with authentic Asian artifacts: wooden crosses from the Philippines, colorful Burmese sashes, and an antique Chinese ceremonial chest. For an appetizer, try *som tom* (juliennes of papaya, greens, and peppers with dried shrimp-and-lime salad dressing). Entrées include Thai lacquered duck with turmeric and cassava. Coconut milk *crème brûlée* with palm sugar and cashew cookies ends the meal with a flourish. Closed Sundays. Reservations advised. Major credit cards accepted. 322 Garfield St. (phone: 988-9562).

MODERATE

Corn Dance Café Loretta Barrett Oden, a member of the Potawatomi Indian Tribe and owner of Santa Fe's only Native American restaurant, has created one of the most unusual menus in town. A house specialty is Little Big Pies, a low-cal version of Indian tacos with a choice of such toppings as Potawatomi prairie chicken and barbecued buffalo brisket. Open daily from March through September; Mondays, Wednesdays through Sundays from October through February. Reservations advised. No credit cards accepted. 409 W. Water St. (phone: 986-1662).

El Farol This longtime local favorite serves Spanish and Mediterranean *tapas* (hors d'oeuvres), as well as curried chicken, pasta with *manchego* cheese, grilled cactus, and salmon. The cozy bar is frequently crowded with locals. Nightly entertainment is eclectic: anything from jazz and flamenco to country blues. Reservations advised. MasterCard and Visa accepted. 808 Canyon Rd. (phone: 983-9912).

Maria's At this domain of powerful margaritas and mariachi music, not to mention delicious New Mexican food, diners can watch tortillas being patted out in the front room or head to the cozy cantina in back for chicken *fajitas, chiles rellenos,* homemade *posole,* green chili stew, and barbecued ribs. An excellent wine list and scrumptious desserts are not easily forgotten. Reservations advised. Major credit cards accepted. 555 W. Cordova Rd. (phone: 983-7929).

Paul's A local secret right in the heart of downtown, this neighborhood spot is bright, airy, and filled with folk art. Chef/owner Paul Hunsicker offers some of the city's best cookery. Try the baked salmon with pecan-herb crust and sorrel cream sauce. Closed Sundays. Reservations advised. Major credit cards accepted. 72 W. Marcy St. (phone: 982-8738).

Shohko Café One of several Japanese spots that have become popular in Santa Fe, it serves what could be the only green chili tempura in the world. The rest of the menu includes more traditional dishes—sukiyaki, teriyaki, and so on—and there's a large, crowded sushi bar. Closed weekends for dinner. Reservations advised for dinner. Major credit cards accepted. 321 Johnson St. (phone: 983-7288).

INEXPENSIVE

Blue Corn Café This cheery downtown place features local art, friendly service, and plentiful food at most reasonable prices. A real taste treat is the lavish burrito drizzled with both red and green chilies (just ask for the "*Christmas* version"). The restaurant stocks more than 25 brands of tequila. Reservations unnecessary. Major credit cards accepted. 133 Water St., upstairs (phone: 984-1800).

Café Pasqual's Just a block southwest of the Plaza, this bright, bustling room is homey and merry, with frilly Mexican decorations, bold murals, and friendly service. Breakfast is a celebration of chorizos, eggs, tortillas, whole-wheat pancakes, and pastries—and it's served all day. Fill up on a lunch of salmon-and-goat cheese quesadillas, or go for dinner's heavier Mexican plates with Asian touches. Nothing will disappoint. Open daily for all three meals. No reservations. Major credit cards accepted. 121 Don Gaspar Ave. (phone: 983-9340).

La Choza Obscure, yet cozy, this place in a turn-of-the-century adobe ranch house on a side street just northeast of Cerrillos Road and St. Francis Drive is worth searching out. It has been operated by the same family for generations, and New Mexican cooking doesn't come any more authentic than here. Diners can savor the ambience of Old Santa Fe on the lovely open-air patio. No reservations. Major credit cards accepted. 905 Alarid St. (phone: 982-0909).

Josie's Casa de Comida A rare example of a dying breed—the small, plain, downtown luncheon café. The *chiles rellenos,* enchiladas, and other regional dishes are terrific. This place is so popular that people will line up and wait patiently on the street for a table. Lunch only. Closed weekends. No reservations or credit cards accepted. 225 E. Marcy St. (phone: 983-5311).

Old Santa Fe Trail Books and Coffeehouse Combine a light meal, a cappuccino, and a good read at this bookstore/café in a cozy Victorian house. Soups and sandwiches are the mainstays. Open daily for breakfast and lunch. No reservations. Major credit cards accepted. 613 Old Santa Fe Trail (phone: 988-8878).

Shed At this popular place for lunch, there's usually a line after 11:30 AM, but the wait is pleasant in the front courtyard, originally the central patio of a large hacienda. The red chili served on blue-corn enchiladas, tacos, or burritos is unmatched, the *posole* and beans are very good, and the desserts are fine. Open Mondays through Saturdays for lunch. No reservations or credit cards accepted. 113½ Palace Ave. (phone: 982-9030).

Tia Sophia's A longtime downtown favorite of locals and visitors, this casual eatery showcases some of the best green chili cookery in town. Try the breakfast burrito, a popular Southwest dish that was invented right here. Daily lunch specials include *carne adovada* (beef marinated in red chili sauce) and blue-corn enchiladas. Open Mondays through Saturdays for breakfast and lunch. No reservations. Major credit cards accepted. 210 W. San Francisco St. (phone: 983-9880).

Tomasita's At another local favorite, the menu selection runs from stuffed *sopaipillas* to *chalupas* and tacos and steaks to vegetarian dishes. Chili—hot and spicy—is emphasized; portions are large. Unless you arrive early, the wait for a table can easily last as long as your meal. Closed Sundays. No reservations. MasterCard and Visa accepted. 500 S. Guadalupe St. (phone: 983-5721).

Tortilla Flats Don't let the fast-food exterior deceive you; the New Mexican food is delicious, and the service is friendly. Open daily for all three meals. No reservations. MasterCard and Visa accepted. 3139 Cerrillos Rd. (phone: 471-8685).

Zia Diner and Bakery Nestled in a converted warehouse is a version of a 1950s diner decorated with pink and turquoise Southwestern accents. It's a very popular luncheon spot with the locals. Burgers, homemade soups, and daily specials are featured. The affiliated bakery around the corner offers homemade muffins, pies, and cappuccino in the morning and pot pies, meat loaf, and pizza in the evening. Closed Sundays for lunch. No reservations. Major credit cards accepted. 326 Guadalupe St. (phone: 988-7008).

THE JOY OF SOUTHWEST COOKING

For those with an urge to create their own Southwestern and New Mexican culinary masterpieces, the *Santa Fe School of Cooking and Market* (116 W. San Francisco St., Upper Level, in *Plaza Mercado;* phone: 983-4511) conducts two-and-a-half-hour classes where you can learn to make a variety of native dishes such as *posole,* blue-corn enchiladas, and *sopaipilla* (pillow-like pastry). Happily, you then get to consume the fruits (or in this case, enchiladas) of your labor and take home the recipes. Reservations advised. MasterCard and Visa accepted. A good place to buy the materials for practicing your newfound culinary skills is the *Farmers' Market,* held Tuesday and Saturday mornings at *Sanbusco Market Center.* Everything from fresh chilies to homemade preserves can be found here.

Savannah

New Englanders trace their bloodlines to the *Mayflower;* Georgians trace theirs to the good ship *Anne,* which sailed up the Savannah River in 1733 carrying General James Edward Oglethorpe and 114 English colonists. Ashore on Yamacraw Bluff, the general planned the seat of His Majesty's Crown Colony of Georgia—today's Savannah, population 150,000—in an orderly grid of broad thoroughfares. They were punctuated by 24 squares to be used as safe havens by outlying settlers in times of danger.

During the halcyon days before the 1861–65 War Between the States, cotton bound for northern states and foreign ports flowed through Savannah's busy harbor to create a thriving mercantile class. Wealthy brokers and merchants transformed the utilitarian squares into lush public parks and surrounded them with splendid mansions in English, Regency, Georgian, Italianate, and neo-Gothic styles.

Fate and benign neglect conspired to preserve Savannah's unique layout, elegant architecture, and beguiling beauty. Near the close of the War Between the States, with the rapacious Union army hammering at the gates, civic officials surrendered so the town wouldn't be put to the torch as Atlanta had been. During ensuing decades, the citizenry was too poor to raze or renovate the slowly deteriorating downtown, and developers set their sights on the burgeoning suburbs. During the mid-1950s, however, "progress" made an abrupt about-face and toppled a few treasured landmarks in the city's genteel core. A group of outraged Savannahians formed the *Historic Savannah Foundation,* turned "reclamation" into a 20th-century Rebel yell, and spearheaded the salvation and restoration of close to 2,000 endangered structures. The present 2.2-square-mile National Historic District is one of the largest in the country, and gentrification is slowly spreading through surrounding Victorian-era neighborhoods.

The 19th-century brick warehouses paralleling the Savannah River have traded their bales of cotton for convivial pubs, seafood eateries, art galleries, boutiques, and museums. Between the buildings and the waterfront, *Riverfront Plaza* stretches like a front porch for watching mammoth freighters steam upstream to the nation's tenth busiest port. The brick esplanade is a focal point for many of the festive events that keep Savannah bustling year-round. Condos, hotels, and shops occupy the former offices of cotton brokers on Factors Walk, behind and above the warehouses on old Yamacraw Bluff.

Two blocks south of the river, *City Market* encompasses four strollable blocks of sidewalk cafés, nightspots, and crafts shops. The *City Market Art Center* has resuscitated yet more old warehouses and stores, turning them into art galleries and studios. Some of the city's most gracious old mansions have been resurrected as elegantly furnished inns and guesthouses.

Tours of private homes are given in spring and at *Christmas,* and at six historic house museums year-round.

For summer fun, beachside Tybee Island lies 18 miles due east.

Savannah At-a-Glance

SEEING THE CITY

The ebb and flow of tides and vessels give Savannah the sense of excitement and adventure connected with port cities. Benches along *Riverfront Plaza* offer ringside seats of the busy, oceangoing traffic on the Savannah River that makes the city the nation's tenth largest port. More elegant perches for lunch, dinner, or drinks are *M. D.'s* lounge and *Windows* restaurant, both in the *Hyatt Regency Savannah* hotel (2 W. Bay St.; phone 238-1234).

SPECIAL PLACES

Historic Savannah is appealingly negotiable on foot, by bicycle, and via a wide variety of tours. Count on a minimum of three days to see everything. Here are some of the city's favorite stops and routes.

RIVERFRONT PLAZA Bordering the thriving seaport's 40-foot-deep channel, this wide, 11-block walkway complements the lively collection of restaurants, watering holes, and tourist shops across cobbled River Street. Parades, concerts, and other special events enliven the atmosphere. The "Waving Girl" statue commemorates Florence Martus, who between 1887 and 1931 greeted every ship by waving a cloth from the lighthouse on Cockspur Island in the hopes that her long-lost lover would be aboard. In the olden days, ships would return her greeting with a blast of their horn. Some still do.

BULL STREET A favorite stroll is along Bull Street, historic Savannah's principal north-south artery. The route stretches from the stately *City Hall,* built in 1905, 16 blocks south to *Forsyth Park,* and encompasses five of the city's most beautiful squares. Boutiques, bookstores, antiques shops, and art galleries line the thoroughfare. Shops cluster especially around Madison Square, where the *Savannah College of Art and Design* inhabits an eye-catching, red brick Romanesque Revival edifice.

SQUARES AND PARKS In addition to the river, Savannah's outstanding feature is its picturesque squares. Each is a heady fusion of monuments, fountains, flowering plants, magnolias, and inviting benches. (Forrest Gump awaited his bus while sitting on a Hollywood version placed in Chippewa Square for the opening sequence in the film of the same name.) Most of the squares are canopied by the Low Country's distinctive live oaks, their limbs shawled with curly garlands of Spanish moss. Twenty-one of the original 24 squares remain as "outdoor living rooms" where neighbors chat, lovers meet, office workers picnic, bookworms read, strollers rest, and sightseers pause to admire the townhouses, the churches, and the government, commercial,

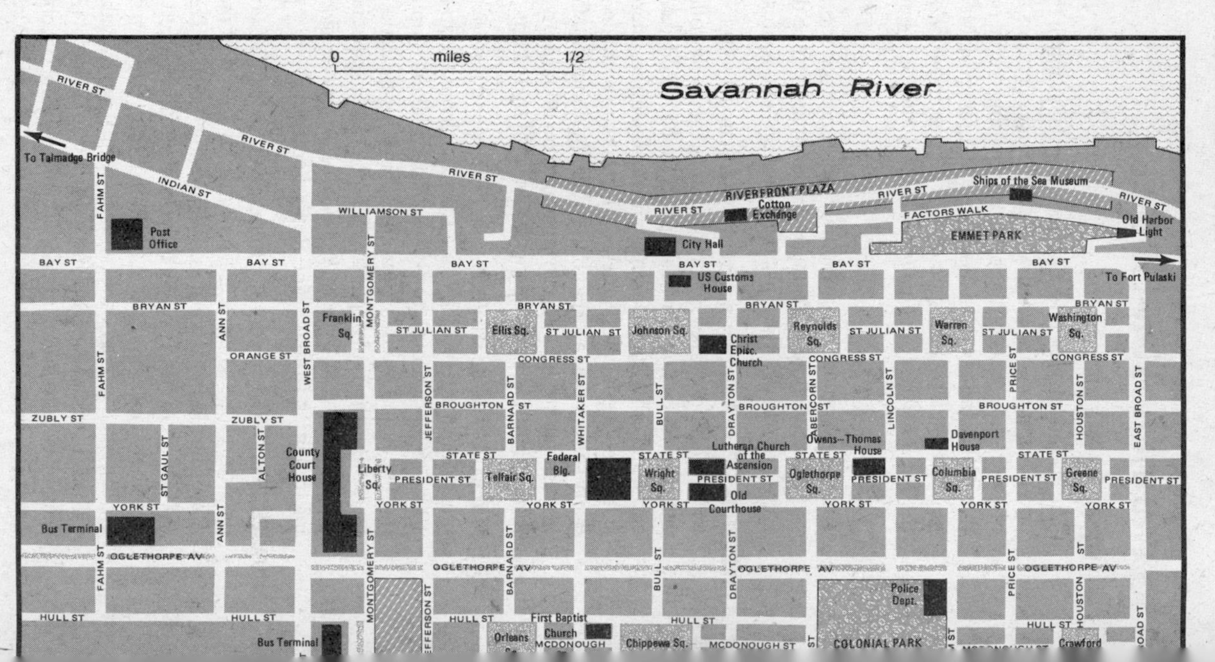
Savannah River
0 miles 1/2
To Talmadge Bridge
To Fort Pulaski
RIVER ST
INDIAN ST
WILLIAMSON ST
FACTORS WALK
RIVERFRONT PLAZA
Ships of the Sea Museum
Cotton Exchange
City Hall
EMMET PARK
Old Harbor Light
Post Office
BAY ST
US Customs House
BRYAN ST
ST JULIAN ST
CONGRESS ST
ORANGE ST
BROUGHTON ST
ZUBLY ST
STATE ST
PRESIDENT ST
YORK ST
OGLETHORPE AV
HULL ST
MCDONOUGH ST
FAHM ST
ANN ST
ST GAUL ST
ALTON ST
WEST BROAD ST
MONTGOMERY ST
JEFFERSON ST
BARNARD ST
WHITAKER ST
BULL ST
DRAYTON ST
ABERCORN ST
LINCOLN ST
PRICE ST
HOUSTON ST
EAST BROAD ST
Franklin Sq.
Ellis Sq.
Johnson Sq.
Reynolds Sq.
Warren Sq.
Washington Sq.
Christ Episc. Church
Liberty Sq.
Telfair Sq.
Wright Sq.
Oglethorpe Sq.
Columbia Sq.
Greene Sq.
County Court House
Federal Blg.
Lutheran Church of the Ascension
Old Courthouse
Owens-Thomas House
Davenport House
Bus Terminal
Police Dept.
COLONIAL PARK
First Baptist Church
Orleans Sq.
Chippewa Sq.
Crawford

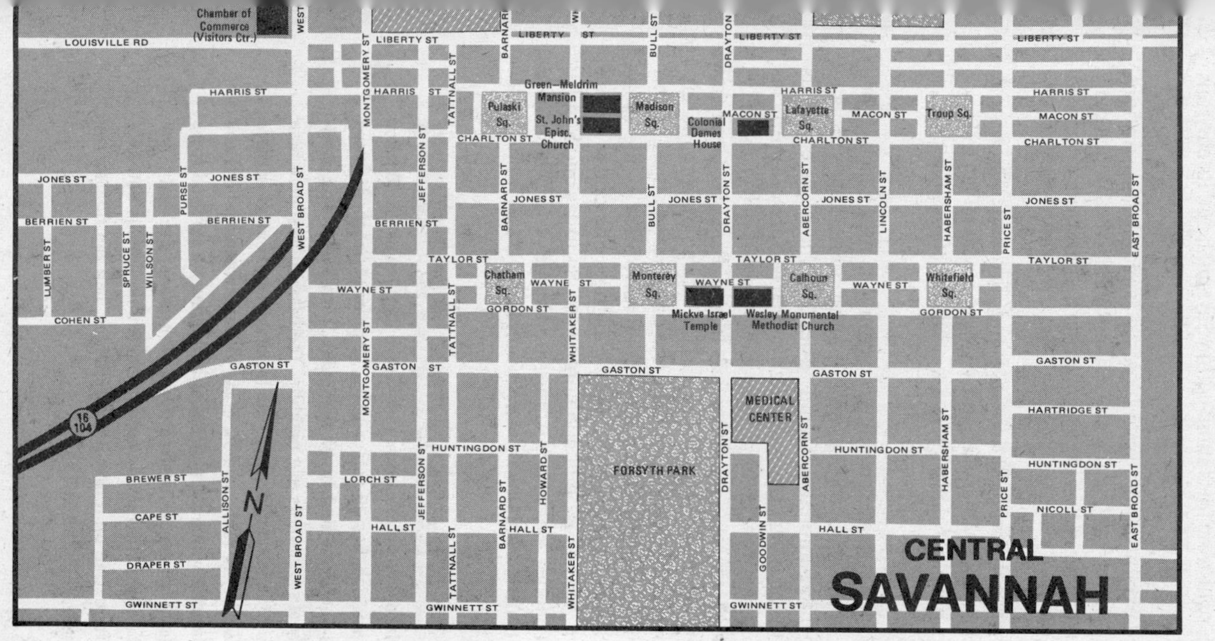
CENTRAL
SAVANNAH
Chamber of Commerce (Visitors Ctr.)
LOUISVILLE RD
LIBERTY ST
HARRIS ST
MACON ST
CHARLTON ST
JONES ST
BERRIEN ST
TAYLOR ST
WAYNE ST
GORDON ST
GASTON ST
HARTRIDGE ST
HUNTINGDON ST
NICOLL ST
HALL ST
GWINNETT ST
PURSE ST
LUMBER ST
SPRUCE ST
WILSON ST
COHEN ST
BREWER ST
CAPE ST
DRAPER ST
ALLISON ST
LORCH ST
WEST BROAD ST
MONTGOMERY ST
JEFFERSON ST
TATTNALL ST
BARNARD ST
HOWARD ST
WHITAKER ST
BULL ST
DRAYTON ST
GOODWIN ST
ABERCORN ST
LINCOLN ST
HABERSHAM ST
PRICE ST
EAST BROAD ST
Pulaski Sq.
Green–Meldrim Mansion
St. John's Episc. Church
Madison Sq.
Colonial Dames House
Lafayette Sq.
Troup Sq.
Chatham Sq.
Monterey Sq.
Mickve Israel Temple
Wesley Monumental Methodist Church
Calhoun Sq.
Whitefield Sq.
MEDICAL CENTER
FORSYTH PARK
16
104
N

admire the townhouses, the churches, and the government, commercial, and other structures that surround them.

FORTS Several 19th-century historic forts stand within Savannah and its environs. Among them are:

Fort Jackson Year-round exhibits and displays, plus seasonal demonstrations, occupy this brickwork fort built on the Savannah River in 1809. Open daily. Admission charge. President St. Extension, about 3 miles from downtown (phone: 232-3945).

Fort Pulaski National Monument Completed in 1847 and surrounded by a moat, this five-sided brick bastion witnessed battle only once, when it fell to Union forces in 1862. Open daily. Admission charge. Off US 80, 15 miles east of Savannah near Tybee Island (phone: 786-5787).

TYBEE ISLAND Bordered by marsh and six miles of Atlantic-lapped beach, Tybee is a favorite local getaway. Cottages, motels, guest houses, eateries, and amusements are gently rumpled and family-oriented. The island claims its share of history, too, having been inhabited by early Native Americans (Tybee derives its name from the Euchee Indian word for "salt") to the US military. Visitors may climb 178 steps for views from *Tybee Light,* Georgia's tallest and oldest lighthouse (portions date to 1773), and explore the surrounding compound as well as the six concrete batteries of adjacent *Fort Screven* (1897-1945). Battery Garland has been retrofitted as the *Tybee Museum,* with exhibits of local and military history. The duo is closed Tuesday. Other weekdays it is open noon until 4 PM, Saturday and Sunday 10 AM until 4 PM (phone: 786-5801). Admission charge. The *Tybee Island Visitors Center* is 18 miles from downtown Savannah via US 80 (phone: 786-5444 or 800-868-BEACH).

EXTRA SPECIAL

Hilton Head Island, a luxury resort area in South Carolina about 40 miles northeast of Savannah, has 29 golf courses, 12 miles of beach, deep-sea fishing, tennis courts, an airstrip, bicycle paths, horseback riding, marinas, and plenty of restaurants and nightlife. The island offers more than 9,000 rooms in 27 hotels, motels, and villa (condominium) enclaves; there also is a wide variety of rental homes. Many of the accommodations and facilities are located within 11 residential developments referred to as plantations. Reservations are advised if you plan to stay overnight, and may be made through *Hilton Head Central Reservations* (phone: 800-845-7018). For information on Hilton Head activities, call the *Chamber of Commerce* (phone: 803-785-3673).

Sources and Resources

TOURIST INFORMATION

For an all-inclusive visitors' guide and/or lodgings reservations, contact the *Savannah Area Convention and Visitors Bureau* (PO Box 1628, Savannah, GA 31402; phone: 944-0456; 800-444-2427). Once in town, stop first at the *Savannah Visitors Center* (301 Martin Luther King Jr. Blvd.; phone: 944-0455), which is open daily. Housed in the former 1860s railway station, the center has maps, information, trained staff, and parking; it also is the starting point for city tours. You may contact the Georgia state tourism hotline as well (phone: 404-656-3590).

LOCAL COVERAGE *Savannah Morning News* and *Savannah Evening Press,* dailies. *Historic Savannah Visitors Guide,* published annually by the *Savannah Area Convention and Visitors Bureau;* free of charge. *Savannah Scene* magazine and *Savannah Tourist Guide* newspaper are free and published quarterly.

TELEVISION STATIONS WSAV Channel 3–NBC; WVAN Channel 9–PBS; WTOC Channel 11–CBS; WJCL Channel 22–ABC; and WTGS Channel 28–FOX.

RADIO STATIONS AM: WBMQ 630 (news/talk); WSOK 1230 (gospel music); WCHY 1290 (country). FM: WSVH 91.1 (classical/jazz); WCHY 94.1 (country); WAEV 97.3 (adult contemporary); WIXV 95.5 (rock); and WGCO 98.3 (oldies); WLVH 101.1 (soft soul).

TELEPHONE The area code for Savannah is 912.

SALES TAX Combined state and local sales tax is 6%; the hotel room tax is 5%.

CLIMATE In spring and fall, temperatures hover in the 70s F, but the mercury drops into the 50s and 40s from December through March and climbs to the high 80s or low 90s in summer. Humidity is usually high and afternoon thunderstorms are frequent from June through September.

GETTING AROUND

AIRPORT *Savannah International Airport* is 15 miles from the downtown Historic District. The on-site *Savannah Regional Visitors Center* has maps, brochures, and orientation personnel. It is open daily from 10 AM to 6 PM and provides fax and photocopying services (phone: 964-1109). *McCall's Transportation Services* (phone: 966-5364; 800-673-9365) operates shuttle vans between the airport and downtown. *Low Country Transportation* (phone: 966-2112; 800-845-5582) operates between the airport and the Hilton Head Island, SC resort area.

BUS *Chatham Area Transit Authority* (*CAT;* phone: 233-5767) operates the municipal bus system (the fare is $1). It also operates electrically powered shuttle buses within the downtown Historic District Monday through Saturday from 7 AM to 10:30 PM and on Sundays 9:30 AM to 5 PM. One-way fare is 50 cents; $1.50 for full day ticket.

CAR RENTAL All the major firms are represented at or near the airport. The office for *Savannah Car and Van Rental* is in town.

CRUISES Sightseeing, cocktail, dinner, and Sunday brunch cruises on the Savannah River are offered on the paddle wheel riverboat *Savannah River Queen* (phone: 232-6404; 800-786-6404).

PEDI-CABS Foot-powered tri-wheelers scoot about the Historic District daily between noon and midnight. They can be hailed or reserved (phone: 232-7900).

TAXI Cabs can be hailed downtown or obtained at stands outside the major hotels. For radio dispatch, call *Adam Cab* (phone: 927-7466) or *Yellow Cab* (phone: 236-1133).

SIGHTSEEING TOURS

BUS/TROLLEY *Gray Line Historic Savannah* (phone: 234-8687), *Old Town Trolley Tours of Savannah* (phone: 233-0083), *Tapestry Tours of Savannah* (phone: 233-7770; 800-794-7770), and *Hospitality Tours of Savannah* (phone: 233-0119) all offer tours of the city; some offer tours of sites mentioned in the best-selling book, *Midnight in the Garden of Good and Evil,* and/or wildlife and other excursions to nearby islands.

HORSE-DRAWN CARRIAGE Guided tours of the compact Historic District are available from *Carriage Tours of Savannah* (phone: 236-6756; 800-442-5933).

WALKING *Ghost Walk, Ghost Talk* (phone: 233-3896) and *Walking Tours by BJ* (phone: 233-2335; 800-962-6595) offer educational and entertaining excursions by foot of the Historic District.

SPECIAL EVENTS

Georgia Heritage Celebration, the first two weeks of February, commemorates the colony's founding on February 12. The *First Saturday Festival on the River,* held every month except January, brings themed performances and food booths, arts, and crafts to *Riverfront Plaza.* In March, look for the largest *St. Patrick's Day* parade (March 17) south of Manhattan. Also in March, *Savannah Onstage* recognizes talented international vocal and instrumental artists in its annual *American Traditions* competition. The *Savannah Tour of Homes* (phone: 234-8054) allows visitors a glimpse of three dozen private mansions in late March. May brings *Arts on the River* to *Riverfront Plaza* and the *Hidden Gardens Tour* (phone: 238-0248), which offers a peek at seldom-seen nooks. Savannah's July bursts *Fourth* with the southeast's largest fireworks display. During the month of September, sites throughout the city host the *Savannah Jazz Festival,*. In October, food fests are sponsored by the city's large Greek, Jewish, German, and other ethnic communities. The entire month of December finds city streets, squares, and shops garbed in colonial holiday finery, with strolling carolers, special children's events, and a tour of decorated homes and inns.

MUSEUMS

Savannah has a number of notable museums, as well as visitable historic houses (see below).

HISTORIC RAILROAD SHOPS The pre-Civil War roundhouse complex, a National Landmark Site, contains the nation's oldest and most complete railroad repair shops and the oldest wheeled portable steam engine. Open daily. Admission charge. 601 W. Harris St. (phone: 651-6823).

KING-TISDELL COTTAGE The 1896 cottage, heavy with gingerbread trim, houses a museum of African-American history, and of the culture of Savannah and Georgia's Sea Islands. Closed Sundays and Mondays. Admission charge. 514 E. Huntingdon St. (phone: 234-8000).

RALPH MARK GILBERT CIVIL RIGHTS MUSEUM Less than a year old, this museum chronicles the history and achievements of African Americans in Savannah. Open daily. Admission charge. 460 Martin Luther King Jr. Blvd. (phone: 231-8900).

SAVANNAH HISTORY MUSEUM A 19th-century steam locomotive, a cotton gin (invented in Savannah), tributes to such notable Savannahians as musician Johnny Mercer and author Flannery O'Connor, and films on the city's history are among items and artifacts displayed in the restored train shed area adjacent to the *Savannah Visitors Center.* Open daily. Admission charge. 303 Martin Luther King Jr. Blvd. (phone: 238-1779).

SAVANNAH SCIENCE MUSEUM Chock-full of models and nautical artifacts, this waterfront warehouse chronicles maritime history throughout the world. Open daily. Admission charge. 503 E. River St. and 504 E. Bay St. (phone: 232-1511).

SKIDAWAY ISLAND AQUARIUM Operated as a teaching facility by the *University of Georgia,* the aquarium displays hundreds of Georgia's offshore inhabitants. *Skidaway Island State Park* is nearby. Closed Sundays. Admission charge. Skidaway Island, six miles southeast of Savannah via Diamond Causeway. (phone: 598-FISH; 598-3474).

TELFAIR MUSEUM OF ART The South's oldest public art museum displays American and European paintings and sculpture in an exquisite 1818 mansion. Closed Mondays. Admission charge (free on Sundays). 121 Barnard St. (phone: 232-1177).

WORMSLOE STATE HISTORIC SITE An avenue of gracious live oaks leads to the ruins of a fortified home built in 1739. The visitors center contains artifacts and an audiovisual presentation. Closed Mondays. Admission charge. 7601 Skidaway Rd. on Isle of Hope (phone: 352-2548).

HISTORIC HOUSES

A number of beautiful old homes open their historic doors for a walk into the lives of yesteryear's Savannahians.

ANDREW LOW HOUSE While living in this handsome, classical, 1848 mansion as the wife of William MacKay Low (the son of Andrew Low), Juliette Gordon Low founded the *Girl Scouts of America* in 1912. Closed Thursdays. Admission charge. 329 Abercorn St. (phone: 233-6854).

GREEN-MELDRIM HOUSE Headquarters for Union General William T. Sherman during his occupation of the city in December, 1864, this 1851–53 Gothic Revival beauty now is the parish house for *St. John's Episcopal Church.* Open Tuesdays, Thursdays, Fridays, and Saturdays from 10 AM to 4 PM. Closed mid-December to mid-January. Admission charge. 14 W. Macon St. (phone: 233-3845).

HAMILTON-TURNER MANSION The privately-owned, Second Empire–style house dates to the Victorian era. Open daily. Admission charge. 330 Abercorn St. (phone: 233-4800).

ISAIAH DAVENPORT HOUSE The near-destruction of this fine Federal home, built by its namesake in 1820, generated the flurry of restoration activity that continues to this day. Open daily. Admission charge. 324 E. State St. (phone: 236-8097).

JULIETTE GORDON LOW BIRTHPLACE This English Regency townhouse, built 1818–21 and known also as the *Wayne-Gordon House,* was the 1860 birthplace of the *Girl Scouts'* founder. Now a national program center for the organization, it has been restored to the period of 1886. Closed Wednesdays. Admission charge. 142 Bull St. (phone: 233-4501).

OWENS-THOMAS HOUSE Renovated former slave quarters, the 1816 mansion is considered among the finest examples of Regency architecture in America. Interior architectural details are unique and many of the antiques are original to the house. A short video is shown. Closed Mondays. Admission charge. 124 Abercorn St. (phone: 233-9743).

SHOPPING

Greater Savannah has its share of chain shops and department stores. Enclaves of commerce with more individuality, however, distinguish the Historic District. River Street has gift, novelty, and souvenir shops. *City Market* is the section for arts and crafts. Bull Street, especially the area around Madison Square, is lined with book, clothing, and antiques emporiums. Museum shops are excellent sources of quality gifts and mementos.

SPORTS AND FITNESS

BICYCLING The flat, shady historic district lends itself to biking. *Cycle Logical* (322 W. Broughton St.; phone: 233-9401) rents bicycles.

FITNESS CENTER Facilities at the *Downtown Athletic Club* (7 E. Congress St.; phone: 236-4874) and *YMCA* (6400 Habersham St.; phone: 354-6223) are available to non-members for a fee.

GOLF The best golf clubs open to the public are *Bacon Park* (Skidaway Rd. and Shorty Cooper Dr.; phone: 354-2625); *Black Creek* (Bill Futch Rd., Ellabell, GA; phone: 858-4653); and *Southbridge* (415 Southbridge Blvd.; phone: 651-5455).

JOGGING Run the mile perimeter of *Forsyth Park,* or along the waterfront in the early morning or evening when traffic dies down. A jogging map is available at the *Savannah Visitors Center;* several historic district hotels and inns have prepared their own. Lake Mayer (Montgomery Crossroad and Sallie Mood Dr.), a 15-minute drive from downtown, has a lighted jogging trail.

SAILING *Sail Harbor* (618 Wilmington Island Rd.; phone: 897-2896) rents sailboats and equipment.

SWIMMING AND FISHING Tybee Island, 18 miles from downtown Savannah, is a longtime favorite for its swimming, fishing, surfing, sunning, crabbing, boating, and picnicking.

TENNIS The best public tennis courts are at *Bacon Park,* Lake Mayer, *Forsyth Park,* and *Daffin Park.*

THEATER

For complete performance schedules, check the publications listed under *Local Coverage* above. The *Savannah Civic Center* (Orleans Sq.; phone: 651-6556) is the largest auditorium in the city, presenting touring Broadway productions, ballet, and other dance performances. In addition, there are the *Savannah Theatre* (Chippewa Sq. downtown; phone: 233-7764); the intimate *City Lights Theater* (125 E. Broughton St.; phone: 234-9860); and the *Lucas Theater for the Arts* (24 Abercorn St.; phone: 232-1696).

MUSIC

The *Savannah Symphony Orchestra* performs during the spring and fall at the *Savannah Civic Center* (Orleans Sq.; phone: 651-6550).

NIGHTCLUBS AND NIGHTLIFE

Riverfront Plaza/River Street and the *City Market* area are alive with taverns and clubs. Among the most popular are *Kevin Barry's Irish Pub* (117 W. River St.; phone: 233-9626); *Bernie's River Street* (115 E. River St.; phone: 236-1827); and *Hannah's East* in the *Pirate's House* restaurant (20 E. Broad St.; phone: 233-5757).

Best in Town

CHECKING IN

Savannah has a range of excellent vintage inns in the downtown Historic District. For reservations at many of them, call these central services: *Savannah Historic Inns and Guest Houses* (phone: 233-7666; 800-262-4667); *R.S.V.P. Savannah* (phone: 232-7787; 800-729-7787); and *Historic Savannah Reservation Service* (phone: 800-444-2427). Most of Savannah's major hotels have complete facilities for the business traveler. Those listed below as having "business services" usually offer such conveniences as meeting rooms, photocopiers, computers, translation services, and express checkout, among others. Call the hotel for additional information. Expect to pay $150 or more per night for a double room at those places classified as very expensive; between $100 and $145 at those categorized as expensive; and under $100 at those listed as moderate; there are no exceptional inexpensive hotels in the city. Rates can vary seasonally, peaking March through June and September through October. Unless otherwise noted, hotels have air conditioning, private baths, TV sets, and telephones, and accept major credit cards.

All hotels below are in Savannah and telephone and fax numbers are in the 912 area code unless otherwise indicated.

VERY EXPENSIVE

Ballastone Inn Charming and romantic, this inn has a total of 17 rooms. All are uniquely furnished with canopy beds, ceiling fans, 19th-century antiques, and fireplaces. A complimentary continental breakfast is served in the room, the downstairs parlor, or the cozy courtyard. Other amenities include a 24-hour concierge and complimentary beverages. 14 E. Oglethorpe Ave. (phone: 236-1484; 800-822-4553; fax: 236-4626).

Gastonian The grand Caracalla Suite with a Roman bath is one of 13 rooms in these two connected 1868 townhomes. Guests are provided with terry robes and a split of wine; a full Southern breakfast is served each morning. 220 E. Gaston St. (phone: 232-2869; 800-322-6603; fax: 232-0710).

Hyatt Regency Savannah Overlooking *Riverfront Plaza* on the Savannah River, this 346-room property recently underwent an extensive renovation. The sixth floor is reserved for business travelers who have use of the state-of-the-art center featuring desks, copiers, fax machines, and computer hookups. Views from the *Windows* restaurant and *M. D.'s* lounge make this hotel a favorite gathering spot. Other amenities include an indoor pool and a health club. 2 W. Bay St. (phone: 238-1234; 800-233-1234; fax: 944-3673).

Kehoe House Awesome best describes this Victorian four-story brick mansion run as a small hotel. The 12 rooms are sumptuously decorated, as are three suites in an adjacent townhouse. A full breakfast, evening hors d'oeuvres, and a 24-hour concierge are included in the rate. Business services are available. 123 Habersham St. (phone: 232-1020; 800-820-1020; fax: 231-0208).

Magnolia Place Inn Bounded by wrought iron and framed by magnificent magnolias, this three-story inn provides a whiff of the decadent South. Some of the 13 rooms have floor-to-ceiling windows that open onto a verandah, the perfect place for a complimentary continental breakfast (served on a silver tray) overlooking *Forsyth Park.* Others are fitted with Jacuzzis. Tea time brings complimentary refreshments; nighttime brings port and pralines. 503 Whitaker St. (phone: 236-7674; 800-238-7674; fax: 236-1145).

EXPENSIVE

Foley House Inn A new owner has imbued this 1896 townhouse, overlooking one of Savannah's loveliest squares, with fresh style and decor. The central parlor is sumptuously furnished and the dining room, where a complimentary continental breakfast is served, is reminiscent of a sophisticated European cafe. Amenities include gas log fireplaces that light at the flip of a wall switch, and Jacuzzis in some of the 19 rooms. 14 W. Hull St. (phone: 232-6622; 800-647-3708).

Joan's on Jones Two suites on the garden level of this 1883 townhouse are furnished with antiques. One suite has a living room, the other a walled garden. Small kitchens are stocked with breakfast essentials. No credit cards accepted. 17 W. Jones St. (phone: 234-3863; 800-407-3863; fax: 234-1455).

Savannah DeSoto Hilton A total renovation has given this centrally located hotel a new lease on life. The windows in all 245 rooms open for fresh air, and the rooms on the upper floors of the 15-story property offer good views of the city. Among the amenities are a heated outdoor pool, a nearby health club, a restaurant serving innovative fare, and a lounge with live music on weekend evenings. Business services are available. 15 E. Liberty St. (phone: 232-9000; 800-426-8483; fax: 231-1633).

Planters Inn Built in 1913, this 56-room, seven-story hotel has been restored to a 19th-century–style inn, with reproduction Georgian furnishings. Executive suites are available. A complimentary continental breakfast and afternoon tea are served. 29 Abercorn St. (phone: 232-5678; 800-554-1187; fax: 232-8893).

River Street Inn Consisting of 44 rooms, this hotel occupies three floors of a restored 19th-century warehouse alongside the Savannah River. Some rooms have small balconies. There is no restaurant, but morning coffee and pastries are available in the lobby and there are a number of restaurants nearby. Business services are available. 115 E. River St. (phone: 234-6400; 800-253-4229; fax: 234-1478).

MODERATE

Bed and Breakfast Inn Two restored 1853 row houses offer historic charm at reasonable rates. Seven of the 14 rooms have private baths; garden suites have full kitchens and living/dining areas as well. A full Southern breakfast is served each morning. 117 W. Gordon St. (phone: 238-0518; fax: 233-2537).

Foret Screven Inn This 1902 house, once part of the US military's former *Fort Screven* complex, has been remodeled to hold four individually decorated guestrooms and a living/dining/library area with a fireplace. Homemade breads are among breakfast offerings and complimentary wine is served in the evenings. 24 Van Horne St., Tybee Island (phone: 786-9255).

EATING OUT

With their menus ranging from elegant to home-style, the city's chefs are turning Savannah into a culinary landmark. Expect to pay $50 or more for dinner for two at restaurants listed as expensive; between $30 and $50 at those categorized as moderate; and less than $30 at inexpensive places. Prices do not include drinks, wine, tax, or tips. All restaurants are in the 912 area code unless otherwise noted.

Unless otherwise indicated, restaurants serve lunch and dinner.

EXPENSIVE

Elizabeth on 37th Set in a turn-of-the-century mansion outside the Historic District, chef Elizabeth Terry has won acclaim for innovative Southern fare such as fried grits, black-eyed pea relish with shrimp, and country ham with red-eyed gravy. Desserts are exceptional. Wine tastings are held Thursdays. Open for dinner; closed Sundays. Reservations advised. Major credit cards accepted. 105 E. 37th St. (phone: 236-5547).

45 South Located in an 1852 cottage, this modern dining room serves contemporary American fare. The menu changes monthly but entrées might include broiled grouper in burgundy butter sauce or rack of lamb with garlic cream and Madeira sauce. Closed Sundays. Reservations advised. Major credit cards accepted. 20 E. Broad St. (phone: 233-1881).

The Olde Pink House In the antique-filled rooms of Savannah's only 18th-century mansion, traditional "Old South" recipes from land and sea are the staple. Try the signature dish of crispy scored flounder with apricot shallot sauce. The downstairs *Planters Tavern* serves the same food in clubby surroundings with a bar, huge fireplaces, and a singer/pianist. Open daily for dinner. Reservations advised. Major credit cards accepted. 23 Abercorn St. (phone: 232-4286).

MODERATE

Bistro Savannah Bordering *City Market,* this popular and convivial spot offers something for almost every palate. The fare encompasses meat, seafood, pasta, and a choice of delicious "small plates" such as the grilled mini-cheese sandwich (a purée of goat and cream cheeses, sun-dried tomatoes, and wild mushrooms in a cabernet-and-sage sauce). Dinner only; closed Monday.

Reservations advised. Major credit cards accepted. 309 W. Congress St. (phone: 233-6266).

Garibaldi's Some twenty years ago, this 1870s firehouse was magically transformed into an Italian café and ranks among Savannah's most popular dining establishments. It serves first-rate pasta, seafood, and grilled duck, lamb, and lobster; the specialty is veal chop *au poivre* with cognac sauce. Open daily for dinner only. Reservations advised. Major credit cards accepted. 315 W. Congress St. (phone: 232-7118).

Il Pasticcio The floor-to-ceiling windows of this smart, contemporary Italian bistro afford diners a view of the city while they feast on dishes from a menu that is changed each day. Try the pasta, sauces, bread, and desserts—all of which are superbly prepared. Reservations advised; required on weekends. Major credit cards accepted. 2 E. Broughton St. (phone: 231-8888).

INEXPENSIVE

Mrs. Wilkes' Boarding House This is *the* place for home cooking, recognizable only by a small sign and the long lines that form well before opening hours. Once seated, help yourself to endless portions of grits, biscuits, sausage, bacon, and eggs for breakfast; fried chicken, swordfish steaks, potatoes, rice, peas, and more for lunch. Open for breakfast and lunch; closed weekends. No reservations or credit cards accepted. In the basement of 107 W. Jones St. (phone: 232-5997).

Seattle

People who live in Seattle love it. In fact, the city's newest "natives" want to keep it to themselves. Some have been known to tell visitors, "See our city, but please don't move here." The city's attraction is based at least in part on its accessibility. Several lakes, Elliott Bay, and Puget Sound offer a variety of water activities. Imposing mountain ranges—the Olympic Mountains to the west, and to the east, the Cascades, with their jagged peaks crowned by the snow-capped summit of 14,411-foot Mt. Rainier—attract skiers, climbers, and hikers. The area's many parks and greenbelts offer recreation as well, and at the same time, testify to the abundance of steady rainfall, in which the city takes a somewhat ironic pride (T-shirts proclaim that Seattleites don't tan, they rust).

Seattle makes the most of its location, a half-day closer to Asian markets than any other US port. The Port of Seattle, the fourth-largest container cargo port in the country, does 95% of its business with Asia. Tourism, computer software, bioengineering, apparel, and manufacturing all contribute to the local economy, but the wood product industry is in a steep decline, and Boeing has laid off thousands of workers. Still, there's more to Seattle than meets the eye.

Downtown Seattle is booming. On the waterfront, the *Bell Street Pier* is set to open this year, and will include facilities for fishing vessels and fish processing, as well as a short-term marina and cruise ship terminal. Also in the works, a new $99-million *Symphony Hall* is scheduled to open by the end of 1998.

Ironically, Seattleites, who have long been described as mellow and outdoorsy, have recently given their city the unofficial title of coffee consumption capital of the country. There are coffee bars all over town, selling the national drink in every imaginable form—"Make mine a single, short decaf, non-fat to go." Residents now debate the finer points of brands like Starbucks, a company started by former Boeing workers, SBC (Seattle's Best Coffee), headquartered on Vashon Island, and the myriad others that are available.

The earliest inhabitants of the region were the Northwest Coast Indians, who generally were more content to trade than to make war with their neighbors. They lived harmoniously with the thick forests and the waters of Puget Sound and Lake Washington. They had fish and clams, a moderate (albeit rainy) climate year-round, and plenty of cedar for the construction of their superb long canoes. The European settlers who came in the early 1850s couldn't leave well enough alone. They harvested timber and sent it south to San Francisco. Then they leveled a couple of the more prominent hills in Seattle to make north-south travel easier. One of those hills, now a concrete downtown canyon, was a principal source of timber. When teams of oxen skidded logs down the street to the sawmill, a new American expression was born—Skid Road (this evolved into Skid Row, the name given to the rough part of town frequented by the loggers). *Pioneer Square,* where the city was founded, was renovated and designated a historic preservation area in the 1970s. Today, galleries, boutiques, and restaurants lie behind the 19th-century façades.

Seattle seems to owe its 19th-century rise to having been in the right place at the right time. There was nothing inevitable about its growth, and other towns in the area seemed to have more to offer. But in 1897 gold was brought back from Alaska via Seattle's deep-water harbor, and the town was, well . . . golden. The fever spread, and Seattle naturally became a boomtown because of its easy access to riches—a protected inland passage to Alaska. After the Alaskan Gold Rush ended, Seattle almost seemed ashamed of itself for its extravagances. It embraced Prohibition in 1916, three years before the rest of the nation capitulated. It was now a conservative town, and after World War II it became a one-industry town, heavily dependent on airplane production.

Things began to change in 1962, when a group of businessmen put together an audacious undertaking, a *World's Fair* in Seattle. Even the backers had their doubts, but the venture succeeded, leaving the city with a different attitude—a feeling that it could be first class in more ways than it thought possible. The *World's Fair* gave the city a real boost culturally, leaving behind the *Seattle Center,* a complex that includes an opera house, a playhouse, the *Bagley Wright Theater,* the *Pacific Science Center,* and the futuristic *Space Needle.* In addition, the *Seattle Repertory Theater* is a strong professional group; the *Seattle Symphony* under the direction of Gerard Schwarz is world class; and the *Seattle Opera* is considered one of the country's foremost Wagner companies. Thanks to the *Seattle Art Museum* and the *Seattle Asian Art Museum,* the city is poised to assert its position as a premier art center as well. And Seattle plays in the big leagues when it comes to sports, with basketball's *SuperSonics* and baseball's *Mariners.* Top all this with the city's reputation for a distinctive, innovative brand of hard rock music. No wonder Seattle is healthy and growing.

Seattle At-a-Glance

SEEING THE CITY

The best view of Seattle and the magnificent Washington landscape is from the top of the *Space Needle* (phone: 443-2111) in the *Seattle Center* (see *Special Places*). The observation deck and revolving restaurant offer 360-degree views of the city, Puget Sound, Lake Washington, and the snow-covered peaks of the Cascade and Olympic Mountains. There is an admission charge unless you are dining.

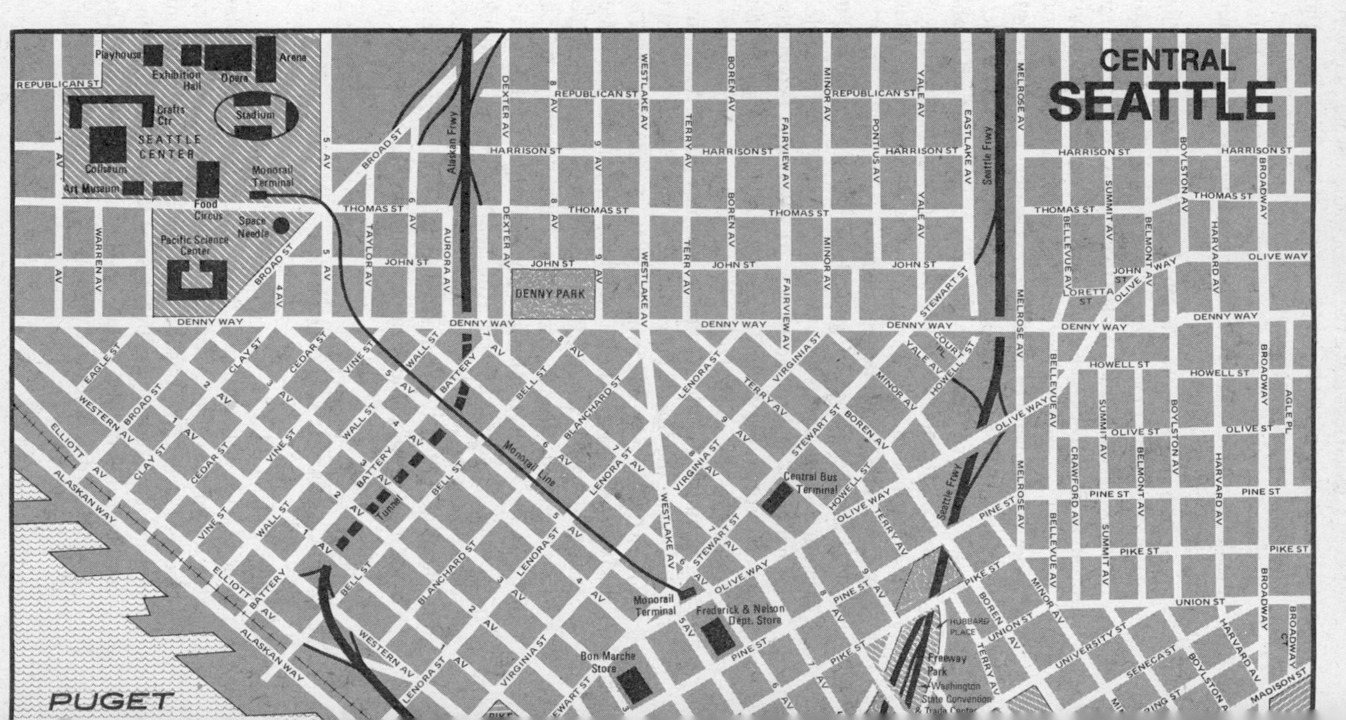

CENTRAL
SEATTLE
Playhouse
Exhibition Hall
Opera
Arena
Stadium
Crafts Ctr
SEATTLE CENTER
Coliseum
Art Museum
Monorail Terminal
Food Circus
Space Needle
Pacific Science Center
DENNY PARK
Alaskan Frwy
Seattle Frwy
Monorail Line
Tunnel
Central Bus Terminal
Monorail Terminal
Frederick & Nelson Dept. Store
Bon Marche Store
HUBBARD PLACE
Freeway Park
Washington State Convention & Trade Center
PUGET
REPUBLICAN ST
HARRISON ST
THOMAS ST
JOHN ST
DENNY WAY
BROAD ST
WARREN AV
DEXTER AV
WESTLAKE AV
TERRY AV
BOREN AV
FAIRVIEW AV
MINOR AV
PONTIUS AV
YALE AV
EASTLAKE AV
MELROSE AV
BELLEVUE AV
SUMMIT AV
BELMONT AV
BOYLSTON AV
HARVARD AV
BROADWAY
OLIVE WAY
LORETTA ST
TAYLOR AV
AURORA AV
STEWART ST
COURT PL
HOWELL ST
OLIVE ST
AGLE PL
CRAWFORD AV
PINE ST
PIKE ST
UNION ST
UNIVERSITY ST
SENECA ST
MADISON ST
BROADWAY CT
EAGLE ST
CLAY ST
CEDAR ST
VINE ST
WALL ST
BATTERY
BELL ST
BLANCHARD ST
LENORA ST
VIRGINIA ST
WESTERN AV
ELLIOTT AV
ALASKAN WAY

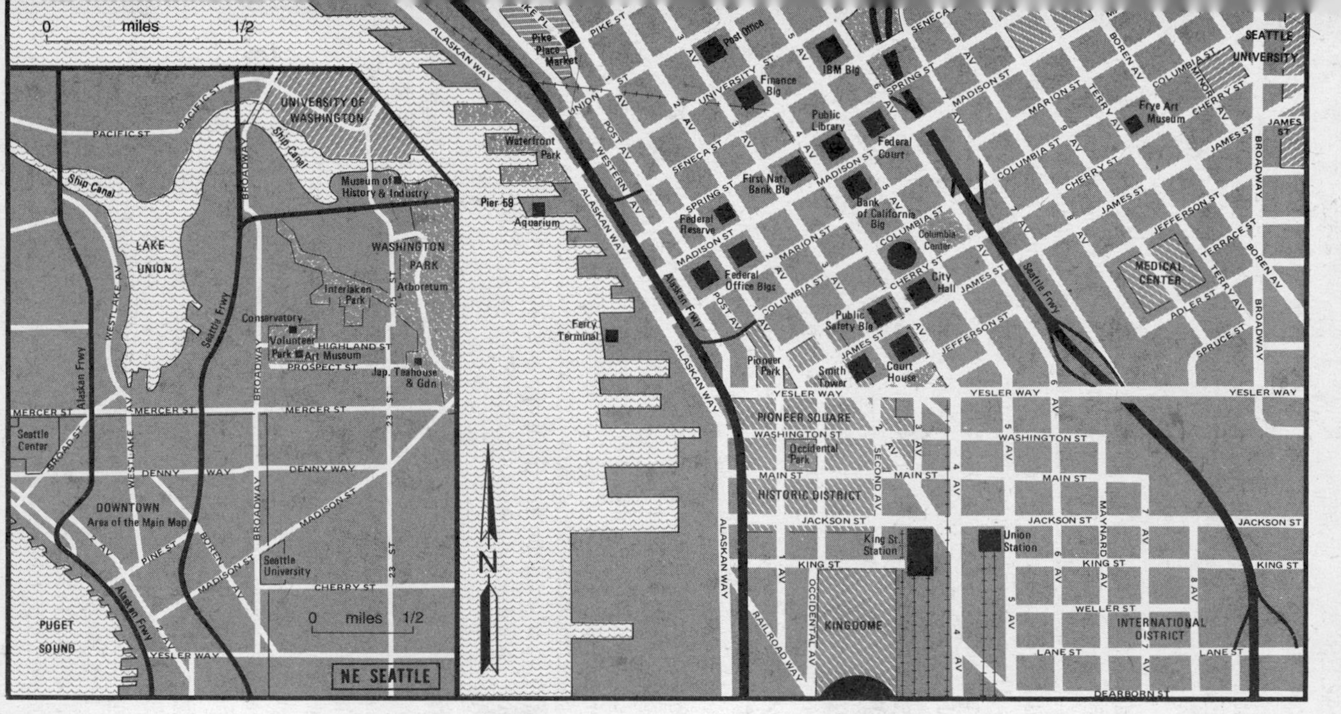

0 miles 1/2
NE SEATTLE
UNIVERSITY OF WASHINGTON
Ship Canal
Museum of History & Industry
WASHINGTON PARK
Arboretum
Interlaken Park
Conservatory
Volunteer Park
Art Museum
HIGHLAND ST
PROSPECT ST
Jap. Teahouse & Gdn
LAKE UNION
PACIFIC ST
WESTLAKE AV
BROADWAY
Seattle Frwy
Alaskan Frwy
MERCER ST
Seattle Center
BROAD ST
DENNY WAY
DOWNTOWN
Area of the Main Map
PINE ST
BOREN AV
MADISON ST
Seattle University
CHERRY ST
23 ST
25 ST
2 AV
YESLER WAY
PUGET SOUND
N
ALASKAN WAY
Pike Place Market
Waterfront Park
Pier 59
Aquarium
Ferry Terminal
PIKE ST
Post Office
IBM Blg
Finance Blg
Public Library
Federal Court
First Nat. Bank Blg
Bank of California Blg
Federal Reserve
Federal Office Blgs
Columbia Center
City Hall
Public Safety Blg
Court House
Smith Tower
Pioneer Park
Frye Art Museum
MEDICAL CENTER
SEATTLE UNIVERSITY
UNION ST
UNIVERSITY ST
SENECA ST
SPRING ST
MARION ST
COLUMBIA ST
JAMES ST
JEFFERSON ST
TERRACE ST
ADLER ST
SPRUCE ST
MINOR AV
TERRY AV
WESTERN AV
POST AV
PIONEER SQUARE
WASHINGTON ST
Occidental Park
MAIN ST
HISTORIC DISTRICT
SECOND AV
JACKSON ST
KING ST
King St. Station
Union Station
KINGDOME
OCCIDENTAL AV
RAILROAD WAY
MAYNARD AV
WELLER ST
INTERNATIONAL DISTRICT
LANE ST
DEARBORN ST

SPECIAL PLACES

Don't be confused by the geographical designations in Seattle street addresses. The directions that follow avenue names and precede street names (Fifth Ave. N. or N. Fifth St.) indicate location in relation to downtown (where only street names and numbers are used).

DOWNTOWN

SEATTLE AQUARIUM Next to the fishing pier at *Waterfront Park,* the aquarium offers a close view of what's swimming in Puget Sound. In the domed viewing room—actually a 400,000-gallon tank—you are surrounded by octopus, starfish, dogfish sharks, rock cod, red snapper, scallops, shrimp, and anemones. There also are tropical fish and a captivating family of sea otters. All along the waterfront, there are seafood bars where you can pick up a good lunch. Open daily. Admission charge. Pier 59 (phone: 386-4320).

PIKE PLACE MARKET Founded in 1907, this public market is now a historic site full of lively vendors selling produce, flowers, and fresh fish. There also are musicians, craftspeople, and specialty restaurants. Closed Sundays except in summer. First Ave. between Pike St. and Virginia St.

SEATTLE ART MUSEUM In the heart of downtown Seattle, the $62-million facility, designed by architect Robert Venturi to great acclaim, houses an extensive array of African, Asian, and Northwest Coast Native American art. Also on display are European and American works, which span the centuries from ancient to contemporary. Besides its beautiful galleries and its imaginative use of videotape, the museum features a large auditorium for films and performances, an art studio, a lecture hall, classrooms, a café, and a shop with one of the best selections of art books anywhere. Closed Mondays. No admission charge on the first Thursday of each month. 100 University St. between First and Second Aves. (phone: 625-8900; 654-3100 for recorded information).

WESTLAKE CENTER This $110-million retail and office project forms the heart of downtown Seattle. The airy four-level glass and steel retail pavilion features upscale shops, pushcarts, and the *Pacific Picnic* food court, offering ethnic dishes. It is flanked by a 25-story office tower and *Westlake Park,* an urban space with a granite plaza designed in contrasting colors to resemble a woven Indian basket. The center, open daily, is connected to the city's main department stores and is served by a monorail terminal. Pine St., between Fourth and Fifth Aves.

PIONEER SQUARE The site where the city was founded in 1852 has become a historic preservation area. The Victorian brick buildings house some of the city's favorite boutiques, galleries, and restaurants. When fire ravaged the district in 1889, the city rebuilt atop the rubble, leaving the remnants of an underground town 10 feet below what is now *Pioneer Square. Bill Speidel's Underground Tours* (610 First Ave.; phone: 682-4646) guides visitors through the subterranean eight-block area, which has some storefronts, interiors, and old waterlines intact. Tours daily. Admission charge. Reservations advised. For Gold Rush nostalgia, visit the *Klondike Gold Rush National Historic Park* (117 S. Main; phone: 553-7220), a museum that traces the history of Klondike gold fever with murals, exhibitions, movies, and a slide show. Open daily. No admission charge.

OTHER SPECIAL PLACES

SEATTLE CENTER A legacy of the *1962 World's Fair,* this 74-acre area contains some of the city's finest facilities. Dominating the 50 buildings and the grassy plazas is the *Space Needle,* a steel structure that spires 605 feet upward from its tripod base. The *Food Circus* (Center House, 305 Harrison St.) offers international fare in the fast-food arena. There are also three playhouses—the *Opera House,* the *Bagley Wright Theatre,* and the *Charlotte Martin Theatre*—as well as the *Fun Forest Amusement Park* (370 Thomas St.). Information about theater tickets and activities is available at a booth in the Center House (Fifth Ave. N. between Denny Way and Mercer St.; phone: 684-7200).

Pacific Science Center In the *Seattle Center,* this museum designed by Minoru Yamasaki features astro-space displays, an operating oceanographic model of Puget Sound that simulates waves, a laserium that uses laser beams to form images, a reconstruction of a Northwest Indian longhouse, and a popular science playground with hands-on exhibitions for children. Open daily. Admission charge. 200 Second Ave. N. (phone: 443-2001).

INTERNATIONAL DISTRICT Seattle has a large Chinese and Japanese community concentrated in this interesting old neighborhood. Among its points of interest are a Buddhist temple, many crafts shops, and Asian restaurants. Shop at *Uwajimaya* (Sixth Ave. S. and S. King; phone: 624-6248), the West Coast's largest Asian retail store, for gifts and specialty foods. The *Wing Luke Memorial Museum* (407 Seventh Ave. S.; phone: 623-5124) features a permanent exhibition tracing the immigration of the Chinese to the Northwest beginning in the 1860s, a folk arts gallery, and a fine arts gallery. It's closed Mondays; there's an admission charge.

MUSEUM OF HISTORY AND INDUSTRY This extensive collection of Pacific Northwest artifacts traces the history of Seattle's first century after European settlement. A mural depicts the fire that leveled the city in 1889, and the displays include almost everything that came afterward—mementos of the Gold Rush, old fire fighting equipment, a maritime display, and a Boeing exhibit that follows the company's development over the past 60-odd years. Open daily. 2700 24th Ave. E. (phone: 324-1125).

BURKE MUSEUM Here is an extraordinary collection of Northwest Coast Indian art, as well as an Alaskan arctic collection that includes over 6,000 examples of basketry, ivory carvings, and beadwork. There are artifacts from the

Western subarctic, the Plains, the Great Lakes, and the Southwest, as well as from Asia, Southeast Asia, and Oceania. The Northwest Coast Indian masks are especially haunting. Open daily. Donation suggested. At the northwest corner of the *University of Washington* campus (phone: 543-5590).

WASHINGTON PARK ARBORETUM Some 200 lakeside acres contain over 5,000 plant species from all over the world. It also features one of the largest Japanese tea gardens outside Japan. Open daily. Admission charge to *Japanese Garden.* Lake Washington Blvd. between E. Madison and Montlake (phone: 543-8800).

EXTRA SPECIAL

Just an hour and a half south of Seattle is the spectacular *Mt. Rainier National Park,* with over 300 miles of trails; two hours south of the city is Mt. St. Helens, which erupted in May 1980 (also see *Mt. Rainier National Park and Mt. St. Helens National Volcanic Monument,* DIRECTIONS). On Route 161, an hour south of town, is the *Northwest Trek Wildlife Park* (phone: 360-847-1903), where moose, elk, buffalo, mountain goat, and caribou roam free. The zoo belongs to the animals; visitors tour from a tram and are not allowed off. Admission charge.

Northeast of Seattle, near Sedro Woolley, Washington, is *North Cascades National Park.* Ice falls and waterfalls, hanging valleys and ice caps, some 300 glaciers, plus canyons, granite peaks, and mountain lakes and streams make this a rugged 789 square miles. In addition to the park, there's the 184-square-mile *Ross Lake National Recreation Area* (which lies between the park's north and south units); the 97-square-mile *Lake Chelan National Recreation Area* (adjoining the south unit on its southern border); and, surrounding the four units, the *Mt. Baker-Snoqualmie, Wenatchee,* and *Okanogan National Forests.* You'll find especially interesting rooms at the rustic *North Cascades Lodge* (phone: 509-682-4494) in Stehekin, at the north end of Lake Chelan. For park information, contact *North Cascades National Park,* 2105 Hwy. 20, Sedro Woolley, WA 98284 (phone: 360-856-5700); for information on backpacking and permits, contact *Wilderness Permits System,* Wilderness District Office, 728 Ranger Station Rd., Marble Mount, WA 98267 (phone: 360-873-4500, ext. 39).

Sources and Resources

TOURIST INFORMATION

The *Seattle/King County Convention and Visitors Bureau* (*Washington State Convention Center,* 8th Ave. and Pike St.; phone: 461-5840) offers daily events schedules, maps, and information. It is open daily during the summer; closed weekends the rest of the year. Contact the Washington state tourism hotline (phone: 800-544-1800) for maps, calendars of events, health updates, and travel advisories.

LOCAL COVERAGE *Seattle Post-Intelligencer,* morning daily, publishes *What's Happening* on Fridays with coming week's events; *Seattle Times,* afternoon daily, publishes *Tempo* magazine on Fridays. *The Weekly* is an opinionated yuppie-oriented newspaper. All are available at newsstands. The visitors' bureau offers the *Seattle Visitors Guide,* which is also available at hotels, some restaurants, and newsstands. *The Seattle Guidebook* by Archie Satterfield (Globe Pequot; $12.95), available at the *Elliott Bay Book Company* (phone: 624-6600) and elsewhere, is a good guide to Seattle and the surrounding area. *Seattle's Best Places* by Stephanie Irving (Sasquatch Books; $16.95) has restaurant listings. *ACCESS Seattle* (HarperCollins; $18.50) is a popular and useful guidebook.

TELEVISION STATIONS KOMO Channel 4–ABC; KING Channel 5–NBC; KIRO Channel 7–UPN; KCTS Channel 9–PBS; and KSTW Channel 11–CBS.

RADIO STATIONS AM: KIXI 880 (big band/swing); KING 1090 (news); and KMPS 1300 (country). FM: KLSY 92.5 (adult contemporary); KING 98.1 (classical music); and KNDD 107.7 (alternative rock).

TELEPHONE The area code for Seattle is 206; for other parts of western Washington, including Tacoma and Everett, the area code is 360.

SALES TAX The city sales tax is 8.1%, except on groceries; the hotel room tax is 7.1%.

CLIMATE Seattle's proximity to Puget Sound keeps the climate mild and moderately moist. Winters are relatively warm, with temperatures averaging around 40F; it seldom snows. The wet season is from October through April. Seattle is best in summer and early fall.

GETTING AROUND

AIRPORT *Seattle-Tacoma International Airport* (known as *Sea-Tac*) is about a 25-minute drive from downtown. *Gray Line Airport Express* (phone: 626-6088) offers service to major hotels. *Shuttle Express* (phone: 622-1424) offers round-trip service between downtown and the airport. *Metro* buses No. 174 and No. 194 leave for *Sea-Tac* from Ninth Avenue and Stewart Street via Second Avenue; the fare ranges from 85¢ to $1.60 depending on distance and time of day. For more information, contact *Metropolitan Transit* (phone: 553-3000).

BUS *Metropolitan Transit* provides extensive service in the metropolitan area with an added attraction: *Metro*'s Free Ride Service in the downtown-waterfront area. Bus fare ranges from 85¢ to $1.60 depending on distance and time of day. Route information is available at its office, 821 Second Ave. (phone: 553-3000).

CAR RENTAL Seattle is served by the major national firms.

FERRY RIDE If looking out at Puget Sound isn't enough, you can enjoy the full experience by taking a 30-minute ride to Winslow or a 45-minute ride to Bremerton. *Ferry Terminal* (phone: 464-6400).

MONORAIL The quickest way to get from downtown to the *Seattle Center,* the *World's Fair* monorail leaves every 15 minutes from *Westlake Center.*

TAXI Cabs can be hailed in the street but are best ordered on the phone. Major companies are *Farwest* (phone: 622-1717) and *Yellow Cab* (phone: 622-6500).

SIGHTSEEING TOURS

BOAT Take a lunch, dinner, or moonlight cruise on the *Spirit of Puget Sound* (Pier 70 at Broad St.; phone: 443-1442) and sail along Elliott Bay as waiters serve your meal and then perform a musical revue.

TRAIN The *Spirit of Washington* dinner train (phone: 800-876-RAIL) features a scenic excursion departing from Renton, southeast of Seattle. The train follows the eastern shore of Lake Washington; passengers feast on fine food and Northwest wines. There's a 45-minute stop at the *Columbia Winery* in Woodinville, where visitors can take a winery tour, visit the tasting room and gift shop, and stroll the lovely grounds (also see *Visitable Vineyards,* DIVERSIONS). The round-trip journey takes 3½ hours. The train does not run on Mondays. Reservations necessary. Major credit cards accepted.

SPECIAL EVENTS

The *Folklife Festival,* featuring folk music and crafts, is held over *Memorial Day* weekend at the *Seattle Center*. *Seattle Seafair* is a citywide celebration in late July and early August featuring everything from hydroplane races, a torchlight parade, a beauty contest, and a marathon, to a special appearance by ships of the Pacific Fleet. Check newspapers for exact dates. Over *Labor Day* weekend, the *Seattle Center* hosts *Bumbershoot,* a festival featuring a wide variety of live music (the name comes from the British slang term for "umbrella").

MUSEUMS

In addition to those described under *Special Places,* Seattle has a number of notable museums.

BELLEVUE ART MUSEUM This third-floor museum hosts five or six rotating exhibits of contemporary and regional art and crafts each year. Open daily. Admission charge. *Bellevue Sq. Shopping Center* (phone: 454-3322).

FRYE ART MUSEUM Founded by Charles and Emma Frye, this museum contains 19th-century European paintings and sculpture as well as contemporary regional works. Open daily. No admission charge. Terry Ave. and Cherry St. (phone: 622-9250).

MUSEUM OF FLIGHT This aviation museum features a soaring glassed-in gallery with more than 20 full-size planes, including a DC-3 and the first supersonic jet, suspended from the ceiling. Open daily. Admission charge. 9404 E. Marginal Way S., near *Sea-Tac Airport* (phone: 764-5720).

ROSALIE WHYEL MUSEUM OF DOLL ART More than two thousand dolls are on display in a building resembling an oversized Victorian dollhouse. Open daily. Admission charge. 1116 108th Ave. NE, Bellevue (phone: 455-1116).

SEATTLE ASIAN ART MUSEUM When the *Seattle Art Museum* moved from *Volunteer Park,* the building underwent a major gallery renovation and reopened as an Asian art center. This branch museum houses more than 7,000 traditional art objects from China, Japan, Korea, and Southeast Asia. Closed Mondays. Admission charge. 14th St. and E. Prospect (phone: 654-3100).

SHOPPING

Westlake Mall encompasses a number of upscale specialty shops, including *Fireworks Gallery* (400 Pine St.; phone: 682-6462), and access to Seattle's two major department stores, the *Bon* and *Nordstrom.* At the *Pike Place Market* (First Ave. between Pike and Virginia Sts.), shoppers can buy home-grown fresh and dried herbs, locally produced honey, and jams made from mountain berries. Fresh seafood can be packed in ice to be taken on the plane. Craftspeople sell silk-screened T-shirts, hand-painted jackets, and hand-crafted jewelry. At *City Center* (1420 Fifth Ave.; phone: 623-4818), shoppers find the latest in fashions at *Ann Taylor* and *Europa,* among others. *Pioneer Square* is an eight-block area that features a concentration of art galleries. Among its other shops are the following:

Banana Republic The former *Coliseum Theater* has been transformed into this clothing emporium. The area's flagship store features casualwear for men and women amid antiques and towering columns. 5th Ave. and Pike St. (phone: 622-2303).

Boston Sox For those who appreciate wildly designed stockings and socks, this is a shoppers' paradise. A great place to find Christmas stocking stuffers. *Westlake Center,* Fourth Ave. and Pine St. (phone: 625-1663).

Biagio Pricey but excellent leather accessories for the status-conscious shopper can be found at this emporium, where the smells alone are worth a stop. At *Rainier Square,* 1200 Fourth Ave. (phone: 623-3842).

Elliott Bay Book Company The staff here is extremely knowledgeable about the store's growing collection of new titles and its expanded children's literature section. At the *Elliott Bay Café* downstairs, authors give lectures and readings weekly. 101 S. Main St. (phone: 624-6600).

Fireworks Gallery Browse through one-of-a-kind ceramic pieces, *raku* pottery, and a large selection of unique pins and earrings. 210 First Ave. (phone: 682-8707).

Glass House The city's oldest working glass studio open to the public, it showcases blown-glass art pieces. 311 Occidental Ave. S. (phone: 682-9939).

Great Winds Kite Shop It's like a bigger-than-life kaleidoscope with kites, wind socks, and kite-flying accoutrements available in almost as many brilliant colors as styles. 402 Occidental Ave. S. (phone: 624-6886).

SPORTS AND FITNESS

Seattle is in the big leagues, with three professional teams. The best bet is to order tickets by phone and pick them up later at the team's ticket office.

BASEBALL The *Mariners'* season runs from April through early October at the *Kingdome* (201 S. King St.; phone: 628-3555).

BASKETBALL The *NBA SuperSonics* play from November through April at the *Seattle Center Key Arena* (ticket office, at the west entrance; phone: 281-5800).

BICYCLING Rent from *Gregg's Green Lake Cycle* (7007 Woodlawn Ave. NE; phone: 523-1822). *Green Lake Park* and *Burke-Gilman Trail* are good biking areas.

FISHING Seattle provides plenty of sport fishing for the dedicated angler.

WHERE THEY BITE

Puget Sound Stalk the wild king salmon, quill-back rock fish, black cod, and sole, as well as the true cod and Pacific flounder, while you take in the breathtaking Northwest scenery. During the late summer or early fall, you might just be lucky enough to see a pod of killer whales. Contact *Sportfishing of Seattle* (Pier 54 on the waterfront; phone: 623-6364) for information on tackle, boats, and trips.

You also can wet a line from the public pier of *Waterfront Park* or go after the big salmon by renting a boat or taking a charter into the deep sea from *Ballard Salmon Charters* (2620 NW 63rd St.; phone: 789-6202).

FITNESS CENTERS *Fitness Limited* (across from the *Westin* hotel, see *Checking In*) has a pool, a Jacuzzi, a sauna, a steamroom, exercise equipment, and weights; athletic clothing is provided. The *YMCA* (909 Fourth Ave. and Madison; phone: 382-5000) has a pool, weight room, and track. Both are open to non-members for a fee. The private *Seattle Club* (2020 Western Ave.; phone: 443-1111) is open to guests of several downtown hotels. Among its many facilities are racquetball courts, a track, a pool, Nautilus equipment, massage, tanning rooms, exercise classes, and a restaurant.

GOLF The city has three good 18-hole public courses: *Jackson Park* (1000 NE 135th St.; phone: 363-4747); *Jefferson Park* (4101 Beacon Ave. S.; phone: 762-4513); and *West Seattle Municipal Course* (4470 35th Ave. SW; phone: 935-5187).

JOGGING Run the 3-mile course at *Myrtle Edwards Park* on the waterfront, at Alaska Way between W. Bay and W. Thomas. Or follow many Seattle residents and run around Green Lake (2.8 miles); to get there, take the No. 6 or No. 16 northbound bus from Third and Pine.

SAILING Seattle has more boats per capita than any other US city. Off Puget Sound, there are hundreds of islands, miles of secluded waterways, marine state parks, and waterside resorts for every type of boat. The season begins in early May and continues until the end of the salmon fishing season in late fall. Many charter outfits rent both bareboats and full crews. For more information, contact *Sportfishing of Seattle* (Pier 54 on the waterfront; phone: 623-6364) or the *Convention and Visitors Bureau* (see *Tourist Information*).

SKIING Popular ski areas include nearby *Alpental* (on the Snoqualmie Pass via I-90; phone: 434-6112) and *Crystal Mountain* (120 miles away near Mt. Rainier; phone: 360-663-2265).

TENNIS Many of the city parks have outdoor courts. Call the *Seattle Department of Parks and Recreation* (phone: 684-4075) for information.

THEATER

Seattle has the highest ratio of resident equity theater companies per capita in the nation. Listed below is our favorite, along with several other options. For current offerings check the publications listed under *Local Coverage.*

CENTER STAGE

Seattle Repertory Theatre Modern and contemporary comedies and dramas, both classics and premieres, are performed at the 856-seat *Bagley Wright Theatre* at *Seattle Center* (Fifth Ave. N. between Denny Way and Mercer St.; phone: 443-2222) and in the *PONCHO Forum* (155 Mercer St.; phone: 443-2222), an intimate studio theater seating 133, where controversial plays often are presented.

The *Intiman Theatre Co.* performs works by playwrights as diverse as Noël Coward and Athol Fugard at the *Seattle Center Playhouse* (201 Mercer St.; phone: 269-1900) May through October. Now housing the *Contemporary Theater,* the *Eagles Auditorium* (Seventh Ave. and Union St.; phone: 285-5110) offers works by up-and-coming playwrights; the theater features two main stages and a smaller alternative venue. *Seattle Children's Theater* performs at the *Charlotte Martin Theater* (Second Ave. N. and Thomas St.: phone: 443-0807) at *Seattle Center.* Productions range from classics to contemporary plays for children of all ages. The *Fifth Avenue Theater* (1308 Fifth Ave.; phone: 625-1900) features top concert artists and touring Broadway plays. The *Empty Space Theatre at First Stage* (3509 Fremont Ave. N.; phone: 547-7500) showcases new plays. The *Bathhouse Theatre*

(7312 W. Green Lake Dr. N.; phone: 524-9108) stages experimental productions of classics; the *New City Theatre* (1634 11th Ave.; phone: 323-6800) features works by cutting-edge playwrights, local writers, and visiting artists; and the *Group Theatre* in the *Center House* (305 Harrison Ave.; phone: 441-1299) at *Seattle Center* focuses on ethnic plays.

MUSIC

The *Seattle Symphony* and the *Seattle Opera Association* perform at the *Opera House* from September through April. The *Wagner Ring Festival* is held every four years in August; the next production is in 1999. The ticket offices for both are in the *Center House* at *Seattle Center*, 305 Harrison Ave. (phone: 443-4747 for symphony; 389-7676 for opera). The restored *Paramount Theater* (907 Pine St.; phone: 682-1414) has pop concerts. The touted *Symphony Hall* (Second Ave. and University St.) is slated to open in 1998.

NIGHTCLUBS AND NIGHTLIFE

Seattle has enjoyed a national reputation as a leading center of "grunge" music (reminiscent of 1960s and 1970s rock 'n' roll). The city is still crawling with clubs where the music has a distinctive sound: aggressive, loud, and moody. In the past few years, several local bands have made it to the big time: *Queensrÿche* is a heavy metal group, and *Nirvana,* the kicky grunge band founded by the late Kurt Cobain, has earned several Grammy nominations. Among the area's hottest nightspots are *Dimitriou's Jazz Alley* (Sixth and Lenora; phone: 441-9729) for jazz, and *Swannie's* (222 S. Main St.; phone: 622-9353) for headline comedy acts. Good live music—especially alternative rock groups—can be heard at *Crocodile Café* (2200 Second Ave.; phone: 441-5611), and the *Off Ramp Café and Lounge* (109 Eastlake St. E.; phone: 628-0232). Hip-hop, disco, and other sounds can be heard live at the *Re-Bar* (1114 Howell St.; phone: 233-9873). The *Virginia Inn Tavern* (1937 First Ave.; phone: 728-1937) entertains its art- and ale-loving patrons with recorded jazz, blues, and rock, and the *Vogue* (2018 First Ave.; phone: 443-0673) features jazz, rock, and reggae music on various nights.

Best in Town

CHECKING IN

Seattle has an abundance and wide variety of accommodations. Most of Seattle's major hotels have complete facilities for the business traveler. Those listed below as having "business services" usually offer such conveniences as meeting rooms, photocopiers, computers, translation services, and express checkout, among others. Call the individual hotel for additional information. Expect to pay $180 or more per night for a double room in hotels listed as expensive; $110 to $180 at those listed as moderate; and between $75 and $110 at places described as inexpensive. For information about bed and breakfast accommodations, contact the *Pacific Bed & Breakfast Agency,* 701 NW 60th St., Seattle, WA 98107 (phone: 784-0539). Unless otherwise noted, hotels have air conditioning, private baths, TV sets, and telephones.

All hotels below are in Seattle and telephone and fax numbers are in the 206 area code unless otherwise indicated.

EXPENSIVE

Alexis For the sophisticated traveler who needs to be pampered, this renovated 109-room hotel (including 44 suites) may fit the bill. From the optional butler who will do your unpacking to the complimentary shoeshines, the service is attentive and enthusiastic, if not completely polished, *and* there is a no-tipping policy. *The Painted Table* is a special dining place. Additional amenities include 24-hour room service, a concierge, and business services. First and Madison (phone: 624-4844; 800-426-7033; fax: 621-9009).

Four Seasons Olympic A splendid restoration of an Italian Renaissance–style building, this 450-room hotel seamlessly blends old and new. Highlights include the elegant public rooms; the *Solarium,* a sparkling health spa; and the *Georgian Room* restaurant (see *Eating Out*), a favorite for special occasions. Many of the city's most popular attractions are within walking distance. Room service is always on call. Other amenities include a concierge and business services. 411 University (phone: 621-1700; 800-821-8106; fax: 682-9633).

Seattle Sheraton and Towers A $6.5-million renovation has made this one of the city's best locations for those who enjoy culture along with their comfort. It boasts an extensive collection of contemporary Northwestern art works, many of which are displayed in the public areas of the hotel. There are great views as well from many of the 840 rooms. Try out the pool room on the 35th floor, or any of its three restaurants (including *Fullers;* see *Eating Out*). Also available is 24-hour room service. The top four floors have their own lobby and concierge. Other amenities include a concierge and business services. Sixth and Pike (phone: 621-9000; 800-325-3535; fax: 621-8441).

Vintage Park With 129 rooms, this European-style property is conveniently located downtown, across from the *Seattle Public Library.* The rooms are decorated with cherry furniture, and the lobby resembles an elegant but cozy study, with comfortable furniture and a fireplace. The hotel celebrates the state's excellent local wines with evening tastings and guestrooms named for Washington wineries; guests dine at *Tulio's* Italian restaurant. Amenities include health club access, a concierge, business services, and 24-hour room service. 1100 Fifth Ave. (phone: 624-8000; 800-624-4433; fax: 623-0568).

Warwick The 229 rooms are comfortable and large, with balconies that offer decent downtown views. There's a pool in the health club, albeit a shallow one, and the piano lounge provides entertainment nightly. The staff is friendly and efficient. Other amenities include a 24-hour courtesy van, and the

Liason restaurant serving continental fare. 401 Lenora St. (phone: 443-4300).

Westin The circular design allows for a maximum number of the 865 rooms, all equipped with balconies. (The best views are from above the 20th floor.) Guests enjoy spacious accommodations, a large pool, an exercise room, and three restaurants including the newly reopened *Palm Court.* Business services are available. 1900 Fifth Ave. (phone: 728-1000; 800-228-3000; fax: 728-2259).

MODERATE

Inn at the Market A French country–style hostelry with 65 rooms above the *Pike Place Market.* Rooms with a view of Elliott Bay are more expensive but worth it. Guests enjoy complimentary coffee and limousine service around downtown, and the nearby *Campagne* restaurant (see *Eating Out*) offers French country cuisine. There is a coffee shop and athletic facilities nearby. Business services are available. 86 Pine St. (phone: 443-3600; 800-446-4484; fax: 448-0631).

Mayflower Park In the downtown shopping district, adjacent to *Westlake Center,* it provides 178 guestrooms in a convenient, quiet setting. Children under 17 stay free with their parents. *Clipper's,* a small restaurant, and *Oliver's,* a cocktail lounge, are on the premises. Room service is available around the clock, and there are business services. Fourth Ave. and Olive Way (phone: 623-8700 or 382-6990; 800-426-5100; fax: 382-6997).

Sorrento This small (just 76 rooms), first class spot, designed to resemble an Italian Renaissance castle, offers many extras: terry cloth bathrobes, plants and potpourri in every room, a hot water bottle in your bed in winter, and complimentary limousine service. Dine at the *Hunt Club* or enjoy English afternoon tea in the mahogany lobby. Amenities such as a concierge desk and business services are offered. Terry Ave. and Madison St. (phone: 622-6400; 800-426-1265; fax: 625-1059).

INEXPENSIVE

Pacific Plaza An older hotel, it appeals to businesspeople and others who want to be in the center of downtown at a reasonable price. It features 168 quiet rooms and complimentary continental breakfast. Business services are available. 400 Spring St. (phone: 623-3900; 800-426-1165; fax: 623-2059).

Williams Located on the east side of town, this turn-of-the-century inn features five spacious guestrooms (most with private bath). Nearby are plenty of restaurants and shopping. 1505 Fourth Ave. N. (phone: 285-0810).

EATING OUT

Seattle's restaurant scene is sophisticated and wide-ranging. Several of the top places showcase fresh local ingredients, and Seattle's position as a gateway to the Pacific has encouraged superb Asian culinary influences. Dinner for two costs $70 or more at restaurants listed in the expensive category; $50 to $70 at places classified as moderate; and less than $50 at inexpensive spots. Prices do not include drinks, wine, tax, or tips. All restaurants are in the 206 area code unless otherwise indicated.

Unless otherwise noted, restaurants serve lunch and dinner.

EXPENSIVE

Campagne Romantically decorated with Oriental rugs and a satisfying view of Elliott Bay, this restaurant offers seasonal French fare featuring such dishes as pan-roasted monkfish, lamb salad, herb chicken filled with goat cheese, and rack of pork served with small, light dumplings. The staff is gracious and knowledgeable. Open daily for dinner. Reservations advised. Major credit cards accepted. At the *Inn at the Market,* 86 Pine St. (phone: 728-2800).

Fullers In the *Sheraton,* this is one of Seattle's best dining rooms. Elegant booths showcase original artwork by Northwest artists. The seasonal menu celebrates Northwest specialties with Pacific Rim enhancements. Entrées include osso buco with green peppercorn gnocchi. The wine list showcases the best the state has to offer. Closed Sundays; dinner only on Saturdays. Reservations advised. Major credit cards accepted. Sixth and Pike (phone: 621-9000; 800-325-3535).

Nikko This Japanese dining place in the *Westin Seattle* offers wonderful Asian specialties such as Kasuzuke cod (marinated black cod), sashimi, and a wide variety of sushi. The sushi happy hour features complimentary California rolls. Closed Sundays. Reservations advised. Major credit cards accepted. 1900 Fifth Ave. (phone: 322-4641).

Rover's In a romantic little house with a garden, this delightful restaurant serves seasonal French-Northwest fare, featuring salmon, pheasant, quail, venison, and rabbit. It's an excellent choice for a special occasion or romantic dinner. Closed Sundays and Mondays. Reservations advised. Major credit cards accepted. 2808 E. Madison St. (phone: 325-7442).

MODERATE

Dahlia Lounge Chef-owner Tom Douglas's romantic restaurant features a creative menu with entrées such as grilled salmon with a ginger-sake butter and Asian-spiced seafood. The desserts are incredible—coconut cream pie, strawberry-rhubarb crisp, pear tart with caramel sauce—all worth putting calorie-counting on hold. Reservations advised. Major credit cards accepted. 1404 Fourth Ave. (phone: 682-4142).

Elliott's Oyster House As you might expect, the menu here features fresh seafood (although steaks are also available). Choose from mahimahi (in season), salmon, and *cioppino* (fish stew). The restaurant smokes its own seafood on the premises. The large windows afford a wonderful view of seafaring boats and ferries traveling along Elliott Bay, off Puget Sound. Reservations necessary. MasterCard and Visa accepted. 1203 Alaskan Way, Pier 56 (phone: 623-4340).

Georgian Room This elegant showcase for the *Four Seasons Olympic* and English chef Kerry Sear offers sophisticated dining and tasty fare. Sear, a vegetarian himself, is best-known for his sophisticated and tasty vegetarian fare, such as russet potato gnocchi with sautéed crêpes with mushrooms, cheese, and parsley. Meat and seafood dishes also are served. Open for breakfast daily; closed Sunday dinner. Reservations recommended. Major credit cards accepted. Fourth Ave. and University St. (phone: 621-7889).

Kaspar's Chef Kaspar Donier's creative menu features fresh, local salmon, mussels, lamb, quail, and duck. A popular dish is sea scallops in a spicy bacon sauce served with a spinach and mushroom couscous. Closed Sundays and Mondays. Reservations advised. Major credit cards accepted. 19 W. Harrison St. (phone: 298-0123).

Metropolitan Grill Aged beef is this upscale steakhouse's specialty, but the salmon's great, too. There's a special *Seahawks* brunch during football season. Closed Saturdays; dinner only on Sundays. Reservations advised. Major credit cards accepted. 820 Second Ave. (phone: 624-3287).

Palomino The place to be seen is here in this sophisticated Euro-bistro serving Northwest seafood and beef with a Mediterranean flair. Its openness and warmly decorated interior are complemented by a menu that includes delicious seafood, pasta, and pizza dishes. Especially good is the red snapper grilled over applewood and served with a raspberry-currant sauce. Top it all off with the extraordinary *tiramisù.* Closed Sundays lunch. Reservations necessary. Major credit cards accepted. 1420 Fifth Ave. (phone: 623-1300).

Ray's Boathouse On the waterfront at Shilshole Bay, this is a great place to have a leisurely dinner while watching the sun go down behind the Olympic Mountains. The seafood offerings are excellent and varied. The more moderate upstairs café is also good. Reservations advised. Major credit cards accepted. 6049 Seaview Ave. NW (phone: 789-3770).

Wild Ginger Owners Ann and Rick Yoder spent two years traveling through Southeast Asia before opening this wildly successful restaurant. Most notable entrées include the seafood, particularly the scallops, beef curry, and a sweetly flavored duck. The satay bar, where skewered meat or vegetables are grilled and served with a variety of sauces, is the main event. Reservations advised. Major credit cards accepted. 1400 Western Ave. (phone: 623-4450).

INEXPENSIVE

Café Flora This airy neighborhood eatery features strictly vegetarian fare. Roasted beet salad with goat cheese, and four-onion pizza with blue cheese are just a few of the artistically presented dishes. Closed Mondays. Reservations necessary. MasterCard and Visa accepted. 2901 Madison St. (phone: 325-9100).

du jour Salads, soups, and sandwiches form the cornerstone of the menu here, but there are also chicken and seafood entrées. The selections change daily; outstanding dishes include chicken pecan salad, chicken breast glazed with saffron, and an unusual version of tortellini salad made of three flavors of pasta (pumpkin, spinach, and egg). Open for breakfast and lunch only; closed Sundays. Reservations advised for large groups only. Major credit cards accepted. 1919 First Ave. (phone: 441-3354).

Ivar's Indian Salmon House With views of Lake Union, this is a favorite stop for out-of-towners. Designed to look like an Indian longhouse, it features heavy timbers, canoes hanging overhead, and totem poles. The menu includes alder-smoked salmon and black cod, prepared in Northwest Indian style, as well as prime ribs. Reservations advised. Major credit cards accepted. 401 NE Northlake Way (phone: 632-0767).

Viet My This no-frills eatery on the fringes of *Pioneer Square* and the International District serves up great noodle dishes such as grilled pork and peanuts, seasoned with mint and lemongrass. Closed Saturdays and Sundays. Reservations advised. No credit cards accepted. 129 Prefontaine Pl. S. (phone: 382-9923).

JAVA JIVE

To the true coffee connoisseur, Seattle is heaven on earth. Whether your preference is espresso, cappuccino, or *caffè latte* (coffee mixed generously with steamed milk), you can find it here; feel free to experiment until you've discovered the perfect blend. A few places to begin your search are *Starbucks* (1912 Pike Pl.; phone: 448-8762), whose proprietors started Seattle's coffee craze in the late 1960s; *Uptown Espresso* (525 Queen Anne Ave. N.; phone: 281-8669), quaintly decorated with antique mirrors and furniture; and *M. Coy Books and Espresso* (117 Pine St.; phone: 623-5354), where you can enjoy a good book and a good cup of espresso at the same time.

Washington, DC

Back in the 1950s, during one of the thaws in the Cold War, President Eisenhower was showing the visiting Nikita Khrushchev around Washington. Every time Eisenhower pointed out a government building, the Soviet leader would claim that the Russians had one bigger and better that had taken only half as long to build. Eisenhower, so the story goes, got pretty weary of this civic one-upmanship, and when they passed the *Washington Monument* he said nothing, forcing Khrushchev to ask what the structure was. Eisenhower replied, "It's news to me. It wasn't here yesterday."

The story may be apocryphal, but it does indicate something important about Washington: It is a city filled with imperial architecture—grand, expansive, deliberate—of a kind that simply doesn't happen overnight or by chance. And yet it is a city that did, indeed, happen almost by chance; a city that until World War II seemed to resist almost in its bones being what it has become today: the international showplace of the United States.

A walk along the *Mall* will remove any doubts you have about the quality of Washington's cityscape. The *Mall* is the grand promenade of the capital, connecting the *Capitol* to the *Lincoln Memorial* with 2 miles of open green and reflecting pools, lined by several of the superb *Smithsonian* museums. Familiar to everyone from picture postcards, the massive, columned buildings take on real dimensions and fulfill the promise of grandeur (particularly at night, when they are bathed in floodlights). But this city of wide tree-lined avenues offers enough open space for varied architectural styles to appear highly consistent. Newer government buildings of modern design and neat rows of townhouses fit in with Greek Revival and Federal architecture (the latter, featuring solid geometry and refined decorations and proportions, was the dominant style in the early 19th century, when much of Washington was built). And Washington will retain its impressive mien into the future. A city ordinance limits the height of buildings to 13 stories, so the *Capitol* remains the city's tallest building. Though others approach it, none surpasses the splendor of this domed edifice.

The fact that Washington is so impressive is especially remarkable when you consider its stormy birth. The selection of the site of the new nation's capital was preceded by years of wrangling between north and south. It wasn't until 1790 that both sides agreed upon a marshy site on the Potomac shore. Neither too far north nor too far south, it was far enough inland to protect against surprise attack, yet accessible to ocean vessels and at the head of a tidewater. Maryland agreed to give 69.25 square miles of land and Virginia 30.75 square miles to form the square to be known as the District of Columbia. The city was named for George Washington, who as first president was authorized to oversee its development.

Washington appointed Major Pierre L'Enfant, a French engineer, to lay out the city. L'Enfant arrived on the scene in 1791 and on viewing Jenkins Hill, the present *Capitol Hill,* he pronounced it "a pedestal waiting for a monument." He also set about designing avenues 160 feet wide that were to radiate from circles crowned with sculpture. The city's two focal points were to be the *Capitol* and the president's house, with Pennsylvania Avenue the principal ceremonial street between.

L'Enfant became involved in a controversy over the sale of lots that were to have raised money to finance construction of government buildings, and was fired before the year was out. George Washington died in 1799 before the development of the federal city was assured. But President John Adams's resolve was firm, and in 1800, Congress was moved to the howling wilderness of Washington. Abigail Adams was displeased by the *White House,* and nobody was pleased with the city. The streets were unpaved and mud-rutted, the sewers nonexistent, and the swampy surroundings infested with mosquitoes.

During the War of 1812 the city suffered a devastating setback when British troops burned the *White House* and gutted the *Capitol.* A torrential thunderstorm saved the city from total destruction, but much was burned beyond repair.

In 1901 the McMillan Commission was instituted to resurrect L'Enfant's original plans. Railroad tracks were removed from the *Mall,* plans were made for the construction of the *Lincoln Memorial* and *Arlington Bridge,* and 640 acres of swampland were converted into Potomac parklands. Unfortunately, things did not turn out as well for L'Enfant himself. He died a pauper in 1825; his remains were later transferred to a grave in *Arlington National Cemetery* overlooking the city that still bears the stamp of his magnificent design.

First-time visitors to Washington may well wonder if there's a life in Washington beyond the monuments, buildings, fountains, and statues. Behind the handsome façades lie many Washingtons, but it would take the combined skills of a historian, political analyst, city planner, expert on international, race, and social relations, and master satirist to explain each one.

All that, plus something else Washington has that no other city can claim—the federal government. The District is something of a one-industry town, but the industry is government, and that makes all the difference. Nearly half of the 600,000 people living in Washington and its immediate surroundings work for some branch of government (the population of the entire metropolitan area is over 3.5 million). As civil servants, they earn relatively high incomes, a factor that provides a solid economic base for the city. In addition to the permanent government employees, diplomats from more than 150 countries serve in Washington–considered to be the world's top post. The embassies lend a cultural sophistication to the capital and further diversify the population.

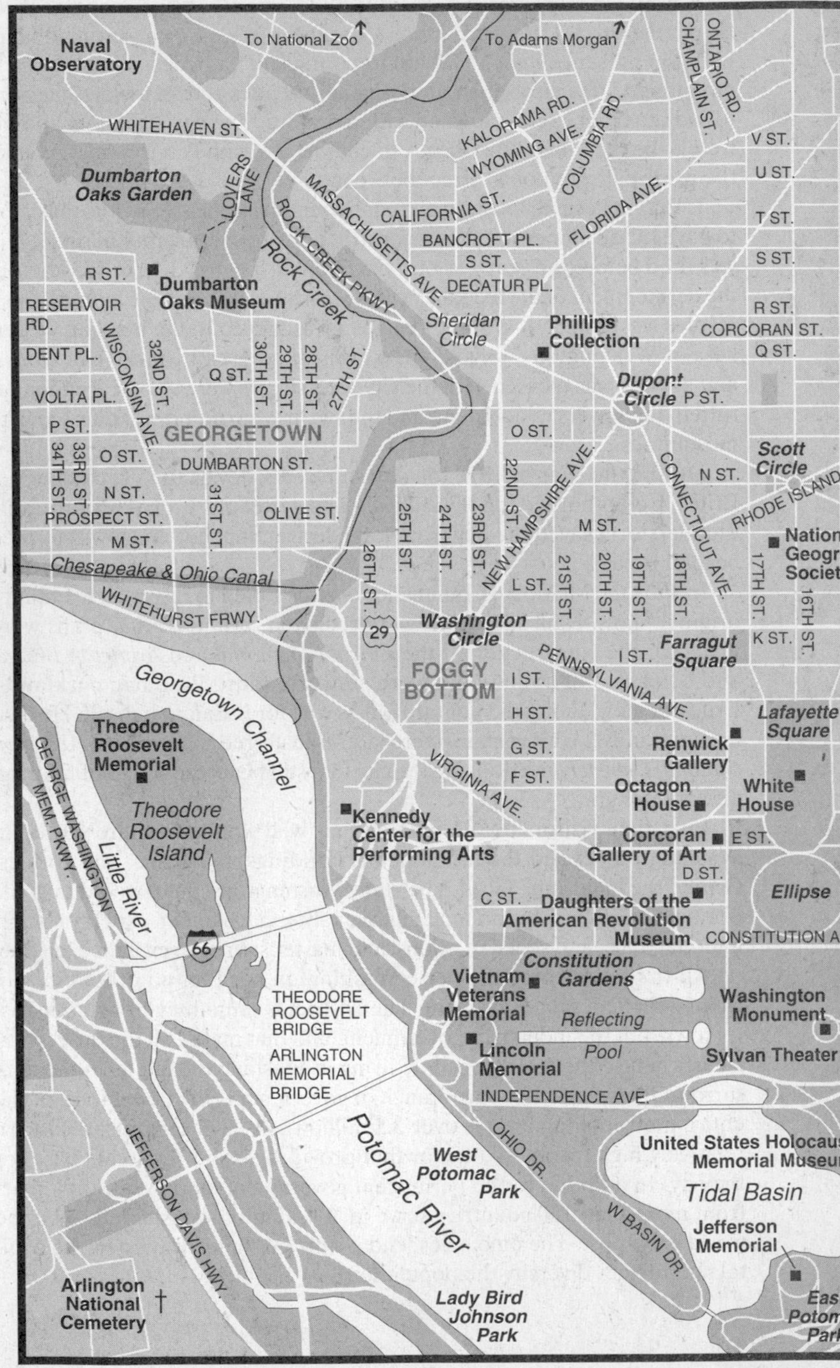

Naval Observatory
To National Zoo
To Adams Morgan
CHAMPLAIN ST.
ONTARIO RD.
KALORAMA RD.
WYOMING AVE.
COLUMBIA RD.
V ST.
U ST.
T ST.
S ST.
R ST.
CORCORAN ST.
Q ST.
WHITEHAVEN ST.
Dumbarton Oaks Garden
LOVERS LANE
MASSACHUSETTS AVE.
ROCK CREEK PKWY
Rock Creek
CALIFORNIA ST.
BANCROFT PL.
FLORIDA AVE.
S ST.
DECATUR PL.
R ST.
Dumbarton Oaks Museum
RESERVOIR RD.
Sheridan Circle
Phillips Collection
DENT PL.
WISCONSIN AVE.
32ND ST.
Q ST.
30TH ST.
29TH ST.
28TH ST.
27TH ST.
Dupont Circle
P ST.
VOLTA PL.
P ST.
GEORGETOWN
O ST.
34TH ST.
33RD ST.
O ST.
DUMBARTON ST.
22ND ST.
NEW HAMPSHIRE AVE.
CONNECTICUT AVE.
Scott Circle
N ST.
N ST.
PROSPECT ST.
31ST ST.
OLIVE ST.
25TH ST.
24TH ST.
23RD ST.
M ST.
RHODE ISLAND A
M ST.
National Geogra Society
Chesapeake & Ohio Canal
26TH ST.
L ST.
21ST ST.
20TH ST.
19TH ST.
18TH ST.
17TH ST.
16TH ST.
WHITEHURST FRWY.
29
Washington Circle
K ST.
Farragut Square
I ST.
PENNSYLVANIA AVE.
Georgetown Channel
FOGGY BOTTOM
I ST.
H ST.
Lafayette Square
Theodore Roosevelt Memorial
GEORGE WASHINGTON MEM. PKWY.
G ST.
Renwick Gallery
VIRGINIA AVE.
F ST.
Octagon House
White House
Theodore Roosevelt Island
Kennedy Center for the Performing Arts
Corcoran Gallery of Art
E ST.
Little River
D ST.
C ST.
Ellipse
Daughters of the American Revolution Museum
66
CONSTITUTION AVE
Constitution Gardens
Vietnam Veterans Memorial
THEODORE ROOSEVELT BRIDGE
Washington Monument
Reflecting Pool
ARLINGTON MEMORIAL BRIDGE
Lincoln Memorial
Sylvan Theater
INDEPENDENCE AVE.
Potomac River
OHIO DR.
United States Holocaust Memorial Museum
JEFFERSON DAVIS HWY.
West Potomac Park
Tidal Basin
W BASIN DR.
Jefferson Memorial
Arlington National Cemetery
Lady Bird Johnson Park
East Potomac Park

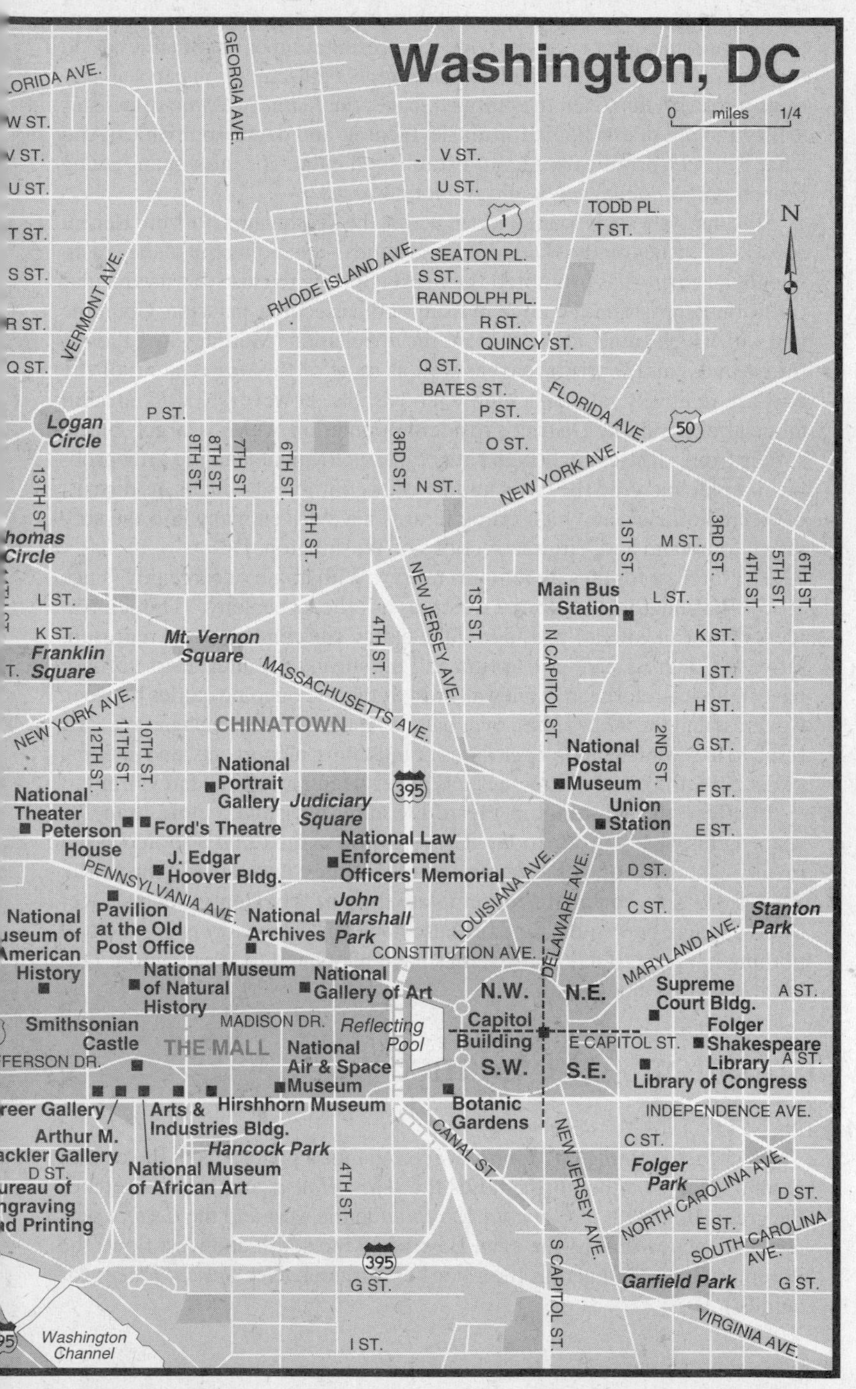

Washington, DC
0 miles 1/4
N
FLORIDA AVE.
W ST.
V ST.
U ST.
T ST.
S ST.
R ST.
Q ST.
GEORGIA AVE.
VERMONT AVE.
RHODE ISLAND AVE.
V ST.
U ST.
TODD PL.
T ST.
SEATON PL.
S ST.
RANDOLPH PL.
R ST.
QUINCY ST.
Q ST.
BATES ST.
P ST.
O ST.
N ST.
FLORIDA AVE.
NEW YORK AVE.
Logan Circle
P ST.
13TH ST.
9TH ST.
8TH ST.
7TH ST.
6TH ST.
5TH ST.
3RD ST.
Thomas Circle
L ST.
K ST.
Franklin Square
Mt. Vernon Square
MASSACHUSETTS AVE.
NEW JERSEY AVE.
4TH ST.
1ST ST.
N CAPITOL ST.
Main Bus Station
1ST ST.
M ST.
L ST.
3RD ST.
4TH ST.
5TH ST.
6TH ST.
K ST.
I ST.
H ST.
G ST.
F ST.
E ST.
NEW YORK AVE.
12TH ST.
11TH ST.
10TH ST.
CHINATOWN
National Portrait Gallery
Judiciary Square
National Theater
Peterson House
Ford's Theatre
J. Edgar Hoover Bldg.
National Law Enforcement Officers' Memorial
National Postal Museum
2ND ST.
Union Station
PENNSYLVANIA AVE.
Pavilion at the Old Post Office
National Museum of American History
National Archives
John Marshall Park
LOUISIANA AVE.
DELAWARE AVE.
D ST.
C ST.
Stanton Park
MARYLAND AVE.
CONSTITUTION AVE.
National Museum of Natural History
National Gallery of Art
N.W.
N.E.
Supreme Court Bldg.
A ST.
Smithsonian Castle
MADISON DR.
Reflecting Pool
Capitol Building
E CAPITOL ST.
Folger Shakespeare Library
THE MALL
JEFFERSON DR.
National Air & Space Museum
S.W.
S.E.
A ST.
Library of Congress
Freer Gallery
Arts & Industries Bldg.
Hirshhorn Museum
Botanic Gardens
INDEPENDENCE AVE.
Arthur M. Sackler Gallery
Hancock Park
CANAL ST.
C ST.
D ST.
Bureau of Engraving and Printing
National Museum of African Art
4TH ST.
NEW JERSEY AVE.
Folger Park
NORTH CAROLINA AVE.
D ST.
E ST.
SOUTH CAROLINA AVE.
395
G ST.
S CAPITOL ST.
Garfield Park
G ST.
VIRGINIA AVE.
Washington Channel
I ST.
1
50

As a result of these influences, Washington is a major cosmopolitan center. Restaurants offer nearly as wide a representation of nationalities as do the embassies. In the *Smithsonian Institution*'s museums you can see anything and everything. On the cultural scene, the *Kennedy Center* draws star artists and provides a home for music, theater, and dance companies. And what is better proof of being an established cultural center than having branches of *Bloomingdale's* and *Neiman Marcus?*

Still, there are some long shadows across the Washington horizon. Recent security breaches on the *White House* grounds—including the plane crashing on the lawn—has prompted the Secret Service to close down vehicular traffic on Pennyslvania Avenue in front of the executive mansion. Combine that with a high crime rate to warrant the appellation "Murder City," though the business and tourist areas, as well as most of the western end of the city, are relatively safe. It is highly inadvisable, however, to walk around alone after dark. The District's resident population, which is largely black, suffers from a distressingly high rate of unemployment, and the drug problem is epidemic. And the city's middle class continues to shrink, as distrust of elected officials and high crime figures have driven many into the suburban Maryland and Virginia sections of Washington, DC.

The forecast for the city remains murky. With home rule a reality (since 1973), Washington abandoned its status as "the last colony." Though residents now can vote for president, a mayor, a city council, and a representative to Congress, civic corruption and the shrinking middle class tax base have impeded reform and renewal. Add to this the ongoing battles between Congress and the *White House* over balancing the budget, which has recently resulted in several temporary closures of museums, monuments, and national parks. Still, the city a visitor sees has never been more vital and vibrant.

In effect, the Washington Pierre L'Enfant envisioned more than 200 years ago is what you see today. Every visitor to the *Capitol* should stand on its west terrace and appreciate one of the finest cityscapes in the world. And as you gaze, you might contemplate the words of Henry Adams. Over a century ago, he wrote, "One of these days this will be a very great city if nothing happens to it." Many things have happened to Washington, DC, but it is a great city nonetheless.

Washington At-a-Glance

SEEING THE CITY

The 555-foot *Washington Monument* commands a panorama of the capital in all its glory. To the north stands the *White House,* and below stretches the green *Mall,* with the *Lincoln Memorial* in the west and the *Capitol* perfectly aligned with it to the east. Beyond to the south and west flows the Potomac River, and across the river lies Virginia. (See *Special Places* for details.)

SPECIAL PLACES

In Washington, all roads lead to the *Capitol.* The building marks the center of the District. North-south streets are numbered in relation to it, east-west streets are lettered, and the four quadrants into which Washington is divided (NW, NE, SW, and SE, designated after addresses) meet here. *Note:* A surprising number of remarkable attractions in this city have no admission charge, as they are funded by federal monies.

An easy way to get around the principal sightseeing area, which includes *Arlington National Cemetery* (across the Potomac in Arlington, Virginia), is by *Tourmobile;* for details on this shuttle bus and other tours see "Tours" in *Getting Around.*

CAPITOL HILL AREA

THE CAPITOL The Senate and House of Representatives are housed in the *Capitol,* which is visible from almost every part of the city. The 258-foot cast-iron dome, topped by Thomas Crawford's statue of *Freedom,* was erected during the Civil War; beneath it, the massive *Rotunda* is a veritable art gallery of American history featuring Constantino Brumidi's fresco *The Apotheosis of Washington* in the eye of the dome, John Trumbull's Revolutionary War paintings on the walls, and statues of Washington, Lincoln, Jefferson, and others. The rest of the building also contains much artwork. You may join one of the excellent 40-minute guided tours that leave from the *Rotunda* every 20 minutes in order to gain access to the visitors' galleries of Congress (congressional sessions start at noon). You also can ride the monorail subway that joins the House and Senate wings with the congressional office buildings and try the famous bean soup in the Senate dining room. Closed *Christmas, New Year's Day,* and *Thanksgiving.* The last tour is at 3:45 PM; from the first week of May through *Labor Day,* the *Rotunda* is open until 8 PM. No admission charge. First St. between Constitution and Independence Aves. (phone: 224-3121). *Metro: Capitol South* or *Union Station.*

SUPREME COURT BUILDING This neoclassical white marble structure, surrounded by Corinthian columns and with the inscription on its pediment "Equal Justice Under Law," was designed by Cass Gilbert and completed in 1935. The impressive courtroom is flanked by Ionic columns. Court is in session intermittently from the first Monday in October through June. Actual court proceedings may be viewed by the public on a first-come, first-served basis. In addition, there is a 20-minute courtroom presentation on the history and function of the *Court* presented every hour on the half hour from 9:30 AM to 3:30 PM except when court is in session. Closed weekends. No admission charge. First St. between Maryland Ave. and E. Capitol St. NE (phone: 479-3030 or 479-3395). *Metro: Capitol South* or *Union Station.*

LIBRARY OF CONGRESS Three buildings—the *Jefferson,* the *Adams,* and the *Madison*—house the world's largest and richest library. Originally designed as a research aid to Congress, the *Library* serves the public as well with 84 million items in 470 languages, including manuscripts, maps, photographs, motion pictures, and music. The exhibition hall displays include Jefferson's first draft of the *Declaration of Independence* and Lincoln's first two drafts of the *Gettysburg Address.* Among the *Library*'s other holdings are one of three extant copies of the Gutenberg Bible, Pierre L'Enfant's original design for Washington, and the earliest surviving copyrighted film—the 14-second *Sneeze* by Thomas Edison. The main reading room is capped by a magnificent 160-foot dome. Forty-five-minute guided tours of the *Jefferson* building are offered on weekdays from 10 AM to 4 PM, Saturdays from 10 AM to 3 PM, and Sundays at 1, 2, and 3 PM. Open daily, with evening hours on Mondays, Wednesdays, and Thursdays. No admission charge. First St. between E. Capitol St. and Independence Ave. SE (phone: 707-5458). *Metro: Capitol South* or *Union Station.*

FOLGER SHAKESPEARE LIBRARY The nine bas-reliefs on the façade depict scenes from Shakespeare's plays; inside is the world's finest collection of rare books, manuscripts, and research materials relating to the foremost English-language playwright. The library, an oak-paneled, barrel-vaulted Elizabethan palace, also has a model of the *Globe Theatre* and a full-scale replica of an Elizabethan theater complete with a trapdoor called "the heavens," used for special effects. Visitors can see how productions were mounted in Shakespeare's day and how they are done today. The bookstore features the fine Folger series on the Elizabethan period as well as editions of Shakespeare's plays. Tours are at 11 AM; closed Sundays. No admission charge. 201 E. Capitol St. SE (phone: 544-4600). *Metro: Capitol South* or *Union Station.*

BOTANIC GARDENS If you feel as if you are overdosing on history, the *Botanic Gardens* provide a pleasant antidote of azaleas, orchids, and tropical plants. Open daily. No admission charge. First St. and Maryland Ave. SW, at the foot of Capitol Hill (phone: 226-4082). *Metro: Federal Center Southwest.*

NATIONAL POSTAL MUSEUM Opened in the summer of 1993, this museum occupies a dramatic atrium area of the *City Post Office Building,* which served as Washington's main post office from 1914 to 1986. It features the world's largest collection of stamps and philatelic materials, which was formerly housed in the *National Museum of American History* (see below). A variety of exhibits traces the colorful history of the ways the mail has been collected, sorted, and delivered over the years. Also included is an extensive, historical stamp collection. Be sure to take a stroll through the old post office's main lobby, with its marble floors and columns restored to their original luster. Also here are an educational *Discovery Center* and the *Library Research Center* (open by appointment from 10 AM to 4 PM on weekdays), specializing in philatelic and postal history. Closed *Christmas.* No admission charge. First St. and Massachusetts Ave. NE (phone: 357-2700). *Metro: Union Station.*

UNION STATION This early 20th-century Beaux Arts landmark was modeled after the *Baths of Diocletian* and the triumphal *Arch of Constantine* in Rome; its marble floors, granite walls, bronze grilles, and classic statuary dazzle visitors. In front of *Amtrak*'s rail terminal is a complex of chic boutiques and dining areas. (*Sfuzzi* is one of our favorites; see *Eating Out.*) The main concourse, once the largest room under a single roof, has been divided into a series of levels and mezzanines for stores and eateries. The lower level houses movie theaters and a score of fast-food outlets. 50 Massachusetts Ave. NE (phone: 289-1908). *Metro: Union Station.*

THE WHITE HOUSE AREA

WHITE HOUSE Probably the most historic house in America; even though George Washington never slept here, every president since has. Designed originally by James Hoban, the *White House* still looks like an Irish country mansion from the outside; inside there are elegant parlors decorated with portraits of the presidents and first ladies, and antique furnishings of many periods. The five state rooms on the first floor are open to the public, and though you actually won't see the business of government going on, you'll be very close to it.

Note: Security breaches at the *White House* have prompted the Secret Service to close the streets around the *White House* to vehicular traffic. The area, however, is still accessible to pedestrians. From late spring through summer, visitors may now secure free, timed same-day tickets for touring the presidential mansion at the new *White House Visitors' Center* (1450 Pennsylvania Ave. NW; phone 208-1631). The center is open daily from 7:30 AM to 4 PM; closed *Thanksgiving, Christmas,* and *New Year's Day.* Throughout the year tours are conducted Tuesdays through Saturdays from 10 AM to noon. No admission charge. Congressional tours of seven rooms, instead of the usual five, are available by writing to your congressperson at least three months in advance. Be sure to specify alternate dates. 1600 Pennsylvania Ave. NW (phone: 456-7041). *Metro: McPherson Square.*

LAFAYETTE SQUARE If you do not enter the *White House,* you can get a fine view of it from this square, which was originally proposed by city planner L'Enfant as the mansion's front yard. Statues commemorate Andrew Jackson and the foreign heroes of the American Revolution—Lafayette, de Rochambeau, von Steuben, and Kościuszko. Flanking the square are two early 19th-century buildings designed by Benjamin Latrobe, Washington's first public architect. *St. John's Church* (16th and H Sts. NW; phone: 347-8766), constructed along classically simple lines, is better known as the *Church of Presidents* because every president since Madison has attended services here. It's open to the public daily. The *Decatur House* (748 Jackson Pl. NW; phone: 842-0920), built for Commodore Stephen Decatur and occupied after his death by a succession of diplomats, is a Federal-style townhouse featuring handsome woodwork, a spiral staircase, and furniture of the 1820s.

It's closed Mondays; admission charge. Near the southwest corner of the square is *Blair House* (1651-1653 Pennsylvania Ave. NW), the president's official guesthouse since 1942; it is not open to the public. *Metro: McPherson Square* or *Farragut West.*

ELLIPSE This grassy 32-acre expanse is the location of the zero milestone from which all distances in Washington are measured. It's the site of everything from demonstrations and ball games to the national *Christmas* tree. 1600 Constitution Ave. NW. *Metro: Farragut West.*

CORCORAN GALLERY OF ART One of the finest collections of 18th-, 19th-, and 20th-century American art anywhere is displayed in this museum's gracious, skylit halls. (It's privately funded, and despite its location is not a *Smithsonian* museum.) Among the distinguished works are paintings by Sargent, Bierstadt, and Copley. You'll also find European paintings and sculpture (some by Corot, some by the animal sculptor Antoine Barye), as well as Renaissance drawings, and a variety of changing exhibitions of contemporary art and photography. Closed Tuesdays; open until 9 PM on Thursdays. No admission charge. One block from the *White House* at 17th and E Sts. NW (phone: 638-3211). *Metro: Farragut West.*

RENWICK GALLERY The nation's first art museum, this beautiful French Second Empire building was designed by *Smithsonian Castle* architect James Renwick in 1859 to house W. W. Corcoran's art collection. Now run by the *Smithsonian Institution,* it is worth a visit for its changing exhibitions of contemporary American crafts and design. The gallery's other noteworthy sights are the entrance foyer, with its impressive staircase, and the 1870 Grand Salon, a wonderful, opulent room where visitors can enjoy a respite on overstuffed Louis XV sofas. Open daily. No admission charge. Pennsylvania Ave. at 17th St. NW (phone: 357-2531). *Metro: Farragut North* or *West.*

DAUGHTERS OF THE AMERICAN REVOLUTION MUSEUM Though any member of the DAR must prove that she is descended from those who served the cause of American independence with "unfailing loyalty," the museum is open to everyone. Exhibitions feature more than 30 period rooms, including the parlor of a 19th-century Mississippi River steamboat, and the *Oklahoma Room,* with a prairie farm kitchen's utensils. *Continental Hall,* the building that houses the museum, is also one of the world's largest genealogical archives (there's a small charge to do research here). The museum is open and tours are given on a walk-in basis; closed all day Saturday, and Sunday morning. No admission charge. 1776 D St. NW (phone: 628-1776). *Metro: Farragut West.*

OCTAGON HOUSE This stately red brick townhouse, a notable example of Federal architecture, is where President James Madison and his wife, Dolley, lived for six months after the British burned down the *White House* (and the *Capitol*) in 1814. The British may have spared this structure because the

French ambassador had been living here since the outbreak of the War of 1812, and the French tricolor was flying over the house. Today it is maintained as a museum; the American antique furnishings from the Federal period give visitors an idea of the high style of the early 19th century. Tours are available. Closed Mondays. Donations suggested. 1799 New York Ave. NW (phone: 638-3105). *Metro: Farragut West.*

ORGANIZATION OF AMERICAN STATES Architects Paul Cret and Albert Kelsey blended the styles of North and South America in this building of imposing formality and inviting elegance. The *OAS* links the US with the countries of Latin America and the Caribbean, and through its symposiums, lectures, and general precepts tries to promote better political and trade relations. For example, the *OAS* was involved in planning the celebration of the 500th anniversary of Columbus's voyage to the New World. Note the statue of Queen Isabella I as you enter. Also inside are the *Hall of Heroes and Flags;* the *Hall of the Americas;* several Louis Tiffany chandeliers; and the *Aztec Gardens,* a year-round tropical spot that is overgrown with exotic plants sent here from the member nations of the *OAS.* Closed weekends. No admission charge. The *Art Museum of the Americas* is just behind the *Aztec Garden.* Closed Sundays and Mondays. No admission charge. In the *Pan American Union Building,* 17th St. and Constitution Ave. NW (phone: 458-3000 for *OAS;* 458-6016 for the art museum). *Metro: Farragut West.*

THE MALL AREA

This 2-mile stretch of green from the *Lincoln Memorial* to the *Capitol* forms something of the grand avenue envisioned by Pierre L'Enfant in his original plans for the city.

WORK IN PROGRESS

Due to extensive repairs to the *Lincoln* and *Jefferson Memorials,* visitors might see more scaffolding than monuments for the next year or so. The statues themselves, however, will not be obstructed. Although both will remain open to the public, walking entirely around the colonnades will be prohibited until repairs are completed, sometime next year.

LINCOLN MEMORIAL From the outside, this columned white marble building looks like a Greek temple; inside, the spacious chamber with its colossal seated statue of Lincoln, sculpted by Daniel French, is just as inspiring. Carved on the walls are the words of the *Gettysburg Address* and *Lincoln's Second Inaugural Address. National Park Service* guides present brief talks at regular intervals. Open 24 hours a day, with park rangers on duty until midnight. No admission charge. *Memorial Circle* between Constitution and Independence Aves. (phone: 426-6841 or 426-6895). *Metro: Foggy Bottom.*

WASHINGTON MONUMENT Dominating the *Mall* is the 555-foot marble and granite obelisk designed by Robert Mills (completed in 1888) to commemorate

George Washington. The top, reached by elevator, commands an excellent panoramic view of the city. On *National Park Service* tours on weekends, you can walk down the 897 steps, where you see many stones donated by such groups as the "Citizens of the US residing in Foo Chow Foo, China." Open daily, 8 AM to midnight, from the first Sunday in April through *Labor Day;* 9 AM to 5 PM the rest of the year. No admission charge. 15th St. between Independence and Constitution Aves. (phone: 426-6841 or 426-6839). *Metro: Smithsonian.*

VIETNAM VETERANS MEMORIAL Maya Ying Lin, while a *Yale* architecture student, designed this simple memorial, which evokes complicated feelings about the American soldiers who died or are missing as a result of the Vietnam War. The two arms of the long, V-shaped, polished black granite walls point toward the *Washington Monument* and the *Lincoln Memorial.* On the 492-foot-long wall are inscribed the names of more than 58,000 men and women killed in the war or still missing. A sculpture by Frederick Hart, depicting three soldiers, stands a short distance from the memorial. Also nearby is a memorial honoring the estimated 10,000 women who served in the Vietnam War. The memorial, a bronze sculpture by Gienna Goodacre, depicts two women in uniform attending a wounded male soldier. Many make pilgrimages here to find the names of lost friends and family members, some of them quietly etching an inscribed name onto a piece of paper to take home with them. Constitution Ave. NW and Henry Bacon Dr. (phone: 634-1568). *Metro: Foggy Bottom.*

FRANKLIN DELANO ROOSEVELT MEMORIAL Scheduled to open this year is Washington's newest presidential memorial, and a fitting tribute to the man who spent more years in the *White House* than any other chief executive. Designed by San Francisco architect Lawrence Halprin, it's a short walk from the *Washington, Jefferson,* and *Lincoln Memorials,* and is bordered by the Tidal Basin and the Potomac River. Despite efforts by members of the disabled community to portray Roosevelt in a wheelchair, he is depicted in a standing position. The memorial's design features four "outdoor rooms," each dedicated to one of FDR's four terms in office including moving remembrances of the Depression and World War II. *West Potomac Park,* along W. Basin Dr. (phone: 619-7222) *Metro: Smithsonian.*

KOREAN WAR VETERANS MEMORIAL Opened in 1995, this tribute to the men and women who served in the "Forgotton War" is located on the south side of the Reflecting Pool, complementing the *Vietnam Memorial* on the north side. There are two intersecting geometric components to the memorial: The "Field of Service" and the "Pool of Remembrance." Scattered on the field are statues, sculpted by Frank Gaylord, of 19 military personnel. Walkways lead pedestrians along two sides of the triangle to a point, which intersects with the pool. Bordering one walkway is a granite wall with bas-relief images of the war (phone: 634-1568). *Metro: Smithsonian.*

JEFFERSON MEMORIAL Dominating the south bank of the Tidal Basin, this domed temple-like structure (designed by John Russell Pope) is a tribute to our third president and the drafter of the *Declaration of Independence.* The bronze statue of Jefferson was executed by Rudolph Evans, and inscribed on the walls are quotations from Jefferson's writings. This is the place to be for the most dramatic view of the cherry blossoms in early spring. Open daily. No admission charge. South Basin Dr. SW (phone: 426-6822). *Metro: Smithsonian.*

UNITED STATES HOLOCAUST MEMORIAL MUSEUM Opened in 1993, this museum is dedicated to educating visitors about one of the twentieth century's darkest periods: the persecution and systematic execution by the Nazis of Jews, Gypsies, homosexuals, and other "undesirables" during World War II. Located between the *Washington Monument* and the *Jefferson Memorial,* the red brick and sandstone building was designed by James I. Freed. Upon entering, you are given an ID card bearing the picture and name of an actual victim; as you wend your way through exhibits about book burning, *Kristallnacht,* and the "Final Solution," you discover the eventual fate of "your" victim. There is also a library, archives, and the *Learning Center,* an interactive exhibit that allows visitors access to maps, documents, videos, and music via touch screens. A limited number of (free) same-day tickets is available when the museum opens at 10 AM, but demand has been very high and people line up early. Advance tickets (a much better idea), with a fixed date and time of entry, can be ordered through *Ticketmaster* (phone: 432-7328); there is a small service charge per ticket when ordering. Closed *Yom Kippur* and *Christmas.* No admission charge. 100 Raoul Wallenberg Pl. SW, between 14th and 15th Sts. (phone: 488-0400). *Metro: Smithsonian.*

BUREAU OF ENGRAVING AND PRINTING At the world's largest securities manufacturing establishment, you can watch the making of currency on 25-minute self-guided tours. Open weekdays from 9 AM to 2 PM only. Closed weekends, federal holidays, and from *Christmas* through *New Year's Day.* No admission charge. 14th and C Sts. SW (phone: 874-3019). *Metro: Smithsonian.*

J. EDGAR HOOVER BUILDING If you want to find out a little more about an organization that already knows everything about you, take a tour of the *Federal Bureau of Investigation (FBI).* In addition to a film on some past investigative activities, you'll get to see the laboratory and a firearms demonstration. One-hour tours start every 20 minutes on weekdays from 8:45 AM to 4:15 PM. Line up early. No admission charge. Pennsylvania Ave. between Ninth and 10th Sts. NW (phone: 324-3447). *Metro: Metro Center* or *Archives/Navy Memorial.*

NATIONAL ARCHIVES The repository for all major American records. The 76 Corinthian columns supporting this handsome building designed by John Russell Pope are nothing compared to the contents. Inside, in special helium-filled glass and bronze cases, reside the very pillars of our democracy—the

Declaration of Independence, the *Constitution,* and the *Bill of Rights.* A fascinating array of history-related lecture and art films are free to the public. Visitors may also research their family's history by accessing the vast genealogical data that includes immigration files and military service records. Open daily; there are evening hours from April through *Labor Day.* No admission charge. Constitution Ave. between Seventh and Ninth Sts. NW (phone: 501-5205). *Metro: Archives/Navy Memorial.*

US NAVY MEMORIAL PLAZA The plaza has a statue of a lone US sailor overlooking the US portion of a granite world map. The visitors' center includes a gift shop, and museum. An IMAX theater shows the 36-minute film *At Sea* daily for a small charge. Military bands perform during spring and summer evenings; pick up a brochure at any hotel or call for schedule. Open daily. No admission charge. Pennsylvania Ave. between Seventh and Ninth Sts. NW (phone: 737-2300; 800-821-8892). *Metro: Archives/Navy Memorial.*

NATIONAL GALLERY OF ART In a John Russell Pope building whose 500,000 square feet make it one of the world's largest marble structures, this museum, built to introduce Americans to the cream of European art, is what one local critic called "the sort of place paintings would aspire to if masterpieces went to heaven." Columns of Tuscan marble, floors of green marble from Vermont and gray marble from Tennessee, and walls of Indiana limestone and Italian travertine create an unadulteratedly sumptuous effect. Leonardo da Vinci's *Ginevra de' Benci* (America's only Leonardo), Jan Vermeer's *Woman Holding a Balance,* a Rembrandt *Self-Portrait,* Jean-Honoré Fragonard's *A Young Girl Reading,* Pierre-Auguste Renoir's *Girl with a Watering Can,* and Claude Monet's *Rouen Cathedral, West Façade* are among literally thousands of breathtaking canvases and sculptures housed in the original building and the striking *East Building,* designed as a grouping of interlocking triangles by I. M. Pei. It all can be a bit bewildering, so, as an introduction, you might want to join one of the regular tours, rent a taped tour, or pick up the excellent *Brief Guide.* A monthly calendar of events includes free films, lectures, and concerts. Closed *Christmas* and *New Year's Day.* No admission charge. Fourth St. and Constitution Ave. NW (phone: 737-4215). *Metro: Judiciary Square, Federal Center Southwest,* or *Archives/Navy Memorial.*

SMITHSONIAN INSTITUTION Completed in 1855, the red Gothic castle on the *Mall,* built to house the institution's collections, is now the site of the *Smithsonian*'s *Information Center* and the offices of the staff that oversees the *Smithsonian*'s scattered museums and galleries. There are nine *Smithsonian* properties on the *Mall,* five (including the *National Zoo*—see below) in other parts of DC, two in New York City (the *Cooper-Hewitt National Museum of Design* and the *National Museum of the American Indian*), and a half-dozen scientific research facilities around the country. The total collection contains over 137 million items and gains almost one million more every year; only an infinitesimal percentage is displayed at any given time, so there's always something new to see. The *Smithsonian*'s $73-million, three-floor complex just south of the *Castle* on Independence Avenue SW at 10th Street is a bit controversial because it is underground. It houses two museums—the *Arthur M. Sackler Gallery,* featuring Asian art, and the *National Museum of African Art*, which was moved from its former *Capitol Hill* location (see below for details on both). The third floor houses the *International Center* for exhibitions, and atop it all is the *Enid A. Haupt Garden,* a $3-million Victorian delight built around a century-old linden tree. The *Castle* is at 1000 Jefferson Dr. SW (phone: 357-2700).

The following are the *Smithsonian Museums* on the *Mall;* they are listed in clockwise order, starting from the *Smithsonian Castle.* All are closed on *Christmas Day;* hours are slightly longer in summer. There's no admission charge for any of the *Smithsonian* museums.

National Museum of African Art The most extensive collection of African art in this country, and the only one dedicated exclusively to the arts of sub-Saharan Africa. Exhibitions include figures, masks, and sculptures in ivory, wood, bronze, and clay from 20 African nations; also color panels and audiovisual presentations on the people and environments of Africa. One gallery has an intriguing display concerning the influence of Africa's cultural heritage on modern European and American art. There's also a delightful gift shop. 950 Independence Ave. SW, next to the *Sackler Gallery of Art* (phone: 357-4600). *Metro: Smithsonian.*

Arthur M. Sackler Gallery Donated by Dr. Arthur M. Sackler, a New York medical researcher, the extensive collection of over 1,000 pieces of Eastern art includes Chinese bronzes from the Shang (1523–1028 BC) through Han (206 BC–AD 220) dynasties, Chinese jade that dates from 3000 BC, and Near Eastern works in silver, gold, bronze, and lesser ores. There are also Persian and Indian paintings, Chinese Ming Dynasty furniture, and more. 1050 Independence Ave. SW (phone: 357-4880). *Metro: Smithsonian.*

Freer Gallery An eclectic collection of Asian art, plus late-19th- and early-20th-century American art. Wealthy Detroit businessman Charles Lang Freer donated the works from his personal collection. *The Peacock Room,* designed by Freer's friend, James McNeill Whistler, is a must-see. Jefferson Dr. at 12th St. SW (phone: 357-4880). *Metro: Smithsonian.*

National Museum of American History The wealth of Americana that fills this uniquely austere *Mall* museum includes George Washington's false teeth, the original Star-Spangled Banner that inspired the Francis Scott Key poem (that inspired the national anthem), the desk on which Thomas Jefferson wrote the *Declaration of Independence,* Eli Whitney's cotton gin, Alexander Graham Bell's telephone, and other prized possessions—such as the gowns worn by First Ladies from Martha Washington to Hillary Rodham Clinton, modeled by mannequins standing in authentic reproductions of rooms in the *White House.* The museum's ground floor traces the role of machines in our nation's history, from railroad locomotives and a 1913 Model T to atom smashers and computers. The second floor focuses on our nation's people, our home life, our community life, and our relationship to the world beyond. The third floor is packed with exhibits ranging from musical instruments to instruments of war. One of the more interesting exhibits is an entire pre–Civil War post office taken from Headsville, West Virginia, that is still in operation and accepts letters for mail, franking them with a unique *Smithsonian* seal. The various galleries, from the *1776 Gallery* to the *Pain Gallery* (in the *Medical Gallery*), offer a variety of demonstrations—visitors can learn about the workings of the ham radio, methods of type founding and printing, and much more. The *Smithsonian Bookstore* (phone: 357-1784) has the area's best selection of American history books. Constitution Ave. between 12th and 14th Sts. NW (phone: 357-2700). *Metro: Smithsonian* or *Federal Triangle.*

National Museum of Natural History This massive museum on the *Mall* is filled with 118 million items (only a fraction of which are on display) that tell the story of human beings and their environment. The exhibits cover the entire spectrum of the life sciences, from anthropology to marine zoology. Among the more popular exhibits are the *Dinosaur Hall,* exhibits on the evolution of humans, fossils, a collection of beasts bagged by Teddy Roosevelt on his African adventures, the *Insect Zoo,* and displays on birds, plants, rocks, and gems. The gem collection contains the legendary Hope Diamond, smuggled out of India in the 17th century and reputed to bring tragedy to its owners; at 45.5 carats, this blue diamond is the largest in the world. The largest elephant on record, a giant Fenkovi African bush elephant more than 13 feet tall, greets visitors in the museum's octagonal rotunda, where banners point the way to the worlds of fossils, birds, mammals, bones, and the geology of the Earth. Another favorite occupant is "Uncle Beazly," the life-size model of a triceratops dinosaur. The *Sea Life Hall* contains live aquatic specimens and a living coral reef, and the *Discovery Room* is a godsend to parents, with its touchable exhibits of elephant tusks and arrowheads, plus a costume room (in which children can try on costumes from around the world). The museum's gift shops and *Associates Court* cafeteria are good bets. Constitution Ave. at 10th St. NW (phone: 357-2700). *Metro: Smithsonian* or *Federal Triangle.*

National Air & Space Museum This member of the *Smithsonian* complex, housing a fascinating assortment of aerodynamic treasures, draws more visitors annually than any other museum in the world; consequently, a visit here often means braving crowds. But in exchange for a little jostling and waiting, you will learn about the history of flight from people's earliest yearnings and attempts to fly, to World War II rockets, to the modern space probes that now explore the outer reaches of our solar system and beyond.

In addition to the mechanics of flying, the 23 galleries in this lofty building explore the politics, physics, and art linked to man's dreams of flight. The entry hall's *Milestones of Flight Gallery* holds Charles Lindbergh's *Spirit of St. Louis,* the Wright brothers' *Kitty Hawk Flyer,* and the *Gossamer Albatross,* the first human-powered plane to cross the English Channel, but this is just the beginning. In all, there are 240 aircraft and 50 missiles in the collection. The museum's *Albert Einstein Planetarium* is truly a cosmic experience and the *Langley Theater,* which projects films onto a towering five-story-high screen, is the next best thing to having your own wings. Different films are featured periodically but the historic mainstay of the theater is *To Fly,* a hell-for-leather romp through the skies in everything from a hot-air balloon to a fighter jet. Other exhibits allow visitors to design aircraft, observe the history of aerial photography, and inspect a model of Skylab. There's an admission charge for movies. Sixth St. and Independence Ave. SW (phone: 357-2700). *Metro: L'Enfant Plaza.*

Hirshhorn Museum and Sculpture Garden This is the most modern of the city's museums of modern art. The *Hirshhorn* houses the ever-astonishing collection amassed by Joseph H. Hirshhorn (1899–1981), who grew up in such poverty that he never even owned a toy. The collection focuses on American art and includes works by Estes, Golub, Gorky, Henri, Hopper, de Kooning, Noland, and Stella; modern European masters such as Bacon, Balthus, Kiefer, and Magritte also are represented. The extraordinary vitality of the sculpture collection reflects the genius of Calder, Degas, Matisse, Moore, Rodin, Serra, and David Smith—many of whose works are displayed in the sculpture garden—plus the innovations of more recent artists. For this variety alone the museum is fascinating; the building itself—circular and fortress-like—is intriguing as well. Seventh St. and Independence Ave. SW (phone: 357-1300). *Metro: L'Enfant Plaza.*

Arts and Industries Building Just east of the *Castle,* this is the second-oldest *Smithsonian* building on the *Mall.* The *Centennial Exhibition,* displayed in Philadelphia in 1876, has been re-created with marvelous displays of fashions, furnishings, and machinery. Jefferson Dr. and Independence Ave. at Ninth St. SW (phone: 357-1300). *Metro: Smithsonian.*

CHILD'S PLAY

The beautiful early 20th-century carousel set in the shadow of the *Smithsonian Castle* operates in the warm weather between 10 AM and 5:30 PM. *Metro: Smithsonian.*

DOWNTOWN

NATIONAL PORTRAIT GALLERY AND NATIONAL MUSEUM OF AMERICAN ART In the *National Portrait Gallery,* an excellent example of Greek Revival architecture, many Americans who have gone down in the history of this country have gone up on the walls (in portrait form, that is). Among those hanging are all the American presidents, Pocahontas, Horace Greeley, and Harriet Beecher Stowe. The *National Museum of American Art* features American painting, sculpture, and graphic arts, including Catlin's paintings of Indians and a choice group of works by the American Impressionists. The museum has recently acquired a major collection of 274 turn-of-the century daguerreotypes and photographs. Both museums (also administered by the *Smithsonian Institution*) are open daily. No admission charge. Eighth St. at F and G Sts. NW. (phone: 357-2700). *Metro: Gallery Place.*

FORD'S THEATRE The site of Abraham Lincoln's assassination by John Wilkes Booth is a national monument, restored and decorated as it appeared on the fatal night of April 14, 1865. In the basement is a museum of Lincoln memorabilia, including displays showing his life as a lawyer, statesman, husband, father, and president; the clothes he was wearing when he was shot; the flag that covered his casket; the derringer used by the assassin; and Booth's personal diary. Theater performances are held throughout the year. Open daily. Admission charge for shows only. 511 10th St. NW (phone: 426-6924; 347-4833 for theater tickets). *Metro: Metro Center* (11th St. exit).

PETERSON HOUSE Directly across the street from *Ford's Theatre* is the house in which Lincoln died the morning after the shooting. The small, sparsely furnished home appears much the way it did in 1865. Open daily. No admission charge. 516 10th St. NW (phone: 426-6830). *Metro: Metro Center* (11th St. exit).

NATIONAL LAW ENFORCEMENT OFFICERS' MEMORIAL Dedicated in late 1991, this monument honors federal, state, and local law enforcement officers who have died in the line of duty, dating as far back as 1794. The enclosed plaza has walled pathways that encircle a terraced pool, and are guarded on each side by majestic bronze lions. Between Sixth and Seventh Sts. NW (phone: 737-3400). *Metro: Judiciary Square.*

ADAMS MORGAN

This funky, international neighborhood is now rivaling Georgetown as the area for after-hours fun and frolicking in the nation's capital. Long the bohemian section of town (though a few fast-food outlets and chain stores have arrived on the scene), it has been home to many Salvadoran, Ethiopian, and African immigrants. Surrounding the intersection of Columbia Road and 18th Street NW are foreign-language book and record stores, clothing boutiques with products from Asia and Africa, Ethiopian and Vietnamese restaurants, reggae bars, and hot nightspots. *Adams Morgan Day,* an annual cultural street fair held in early September, is alive with music from all over the world; local restaurants provide a host of international foods to satisfy any palate. Metro: *Dupont Circle.*

GEORGETOWN

Though it was once the Union's major tobacco port, the only tobacco left in Georgetown is in the smoke shops. Still holding fast to its own identity, this neighborhood is particularly nice in the spring when it's pleasant to walk along the Chesapeake and Ohio Canal. The whole area's great for strolling (though too much tourism has produced the occasional tacky stretch). In summer, it's possible to catch a slow barge up the canal. Tickets can be purchased at the *Foundry Mall* (1055 Thomas Jefferson St. NW; phone: 301-299-2026). Beside the canal (between Jefferson and 31st Sts.), the streets off Wisconsin Avenue house the city's social and political elite in beautifully restored townhouses with prim gardens and lovely magnolia trees. Many of the buildings are on the *National Register of Historic Places* and are well worth seeing. The main drags—Wisconsin Avenue and M Street–are where most of the action is. In addition to boasting a shopping mall and some of the hottest nightlife in town (including sports and blues bars), the area is rich with boutiques, movie theaters, and restaurants offering a vast variety of food—from Vietnamese to Indian to French.

At the northern edge of Georgetown (along R St. east of Wisconsin Ave.), large 18th-century country estates mingle with smaller, more modern row houses. The *Dumbarton Oaks Garden* has beautiful formal grounds, and the *Dumbarton Oaks Museum* contains a fine collection of early Christian and Byzantine art. The museum is open Tuesdays through Sundays from 2 to 5 PM; no admission charge. The gardens are open daily from 2 to 5 PM; admission charge from April through October (phone: 342-3200 or 338-8278). The entrance to the museum is at 1703 32nd Street NW; the entrance to the gardens is at 31st and R Streets NW.

At 37th and O Streets is the campus of *Georgetown University.* Established in 1789, it is the oldest Jesuit university in the United States and is renowned for its schools of foreign service and languages, as well as one of the best law schools in the country.

ELSEWHERE IN DC

ROCK CREEK PARK New York has its *Central Park,* Chicago its *Grant Park,* and Philadelphia its *Fairmount Park.* Washington's premier city park, where one can escape the traffic, the noise, the concrete, and (mostly) the crowds, is found in a 1,700-acre swath of green in the northwest section of town. From its narrow south tip just outside Georgetown, *Rock Creek Park* (named for the meandering stream that bisects it) widens gradually until it's big enough to contain the *National Zoo* (see below) and, a few miles farther north, a modest 18-hole golf course (see *Golf*). There are bike and jogging trails, picnic tables, even riding stables, but mostly untended greenery, which covers the park's steep hills. A two-lane road meanders down its spine; the northern section of the park is closed to automobiles on Sundays to allow cyclists, Rollerbladers, and strollers free reign. In the northwest quadrant of the city (phone: 282-1063). *Metro: Fort Totten* or *Van Ness* (though it's a bus ride or long walk from either station).

NATIONAL ZOO The *Smithsonian Institution* is best known for its museums on the *Mall,* but its largest facility is located in the midst of verdant *Rock Creek Park* (see above) in the northwest quadrant of the city. Created in 1889 for "the advancement of science and the instruction and recreation of the people," this 163-acre zoological park clings to the side of a gently rolling hill. The *Amazonia* exhibit re-creates a tropical river and rain forest, while the *Reptile Discovery Center* allows visitors to meet reptiles and amphibians up close and personal. The *Great Flight Cage* features exotic birds. Sadly, the zoo's female panda, Ling-Ling, died in late 1992, leaving her male companion, Hsing-Hsing, the only panda in the zoo; there are no children (although the pair's numerous tries at parenting are documented in a photo display!). There are, however, many infant animals born each year to such species as giraffes, orangutans, and elephants. The *Panda Café* serves refreshments, and souvenir shops are filled with, among other things, panda paraphernalia. Closed *Christmas.* No admission charge. 3301 Connecticut Ave. NW (phone: 673-4800). *Metro: Woodley Park/Zoo* or *Cleveland Park* (the easier walk is from *Cleveland Park;* it's a stiff uphill climb from *Woodley Park/Zoo*).

VANTAGE POINTS

ARLINGTON NATIONAL CEMETERY Overlooking the Potomac is this solemn reminder of the more turbulent parts of our country's history. Here lie the bodies of many who served their country, both in the military forces and in other ways, among them Admiral Richard Byrd, General George C. Marshall, Robert F. Kennedy, Justice Oliver Wendell Holmes, and John F. Kennedy, whose grave is marked by an *Eternal Flame.* Former First Lady Jacqueline Bouvier Kennedy Onassis is interred beside her husband. The *Tomb of the Unknown Soldier,* a 50-ton block of white marble, commemorates the dead of World Wars I and II and the Korean, Vietnam, and Persian Gulf Wars and is always guarded by a solitary soldier. Changing of the guard takes place every hour on the hour (every half hour during summer months). The beautifully landscaped grounds of the cemetery once were part of Robert E. Lee's plantation but were confiscated by the Union after Lee joined the Confederacy. Lee's home, *Arlington House,* has been restored and is open to the public. Cars are not allowed in the cemetery, but you can park at the visitors' center and go on foot or pay and ride the *Tourmobile* (phone: 554-7950). Both *Arlington House* and the cemetery are open daily. Directly west of Memorial Bridge in Arlington, Virginia. *Metro: Arlington Cemetery.*

MOUNT VERNON Just 16 miles south of Washington on George Washington Memorial Parkway is *Mount Vernon,* George Washington's home from 1754 to 1799 and his final resting place. This lovely 18th-century plantation shows a less familiar aspect of the military-political figure. An exhibit entitled

“George Washington: Pioneer Farmer” features costumed interpreters demonstrating colonial farming methods. The mansion, overlooking the Potomac, and the outbuildings housing the shops that made *Mount Vernon* a self-sufficient economic unit have been authentically restored and refurnished. Some 500 of the original 8,000 acres remain; all are well maintained, and the parterre gardens and formal lawns provide a magnificent setting. There’s also a museum with Washington memorabilia; the tomb of George and Martha lies at the foot of the hill. During spring and summer, come early to avoid the crowds. Bicycle paths lead from the DC side of Memorial Bridge to *Mount Vernon*—a lovely ride along the Potomac. Open daily. Admission charge (phone: 703-780-2000).

Sources and Resources

TOURIST INFORMATION

The *Washington, DC Convention and Visitors Association* (*WCVA;* 1212 New York Ave. NW, Suite 600, Washington, DC 20005; phone: 789-7000; fax: 789-7037) coordinates all Washington tourism information and provides free maps and information on where to stay, eat, and shop, and on events.

LOCAL COVERAGE The *Washington Post* and the *Washington Times* are the city’s morning daily newspapers. The *Post*’s “Weekend” section (available on Fridays) is an excellent source for arts and entertainment listings. *Washingtonian* magazine is published monthly. All are available at newsstands. *Museum and Arts Washington* lists current museum exhibits. The *City Paper,* a free weekly tabloid published on Thursdays, is an excellent source of cultural and clubs listings; it’s available in shops, restaurants, and *Metro* stations. We also recommend *ACCESS Washington DC* (HarperCollins; $18.50).

TELEVISION STATIONS WRC Channel 4–NBC; WTTG Channel 5–Fox; WJLA Channel 7–ABC; WUSA Channel 9–CBS; Cable Channel 11 or 42–CNN; and WETA Channel 26–PBS.

RADIO STATIONS AM: WTEM 570 (sports); WMAL 630 (news/talk/sports); WWRC 980 (talk); and WTOP 1500 (all news). FM: WPFW 89.3 (jazz/community radio); WETA 90.9 (classical/National Public Radio); WKYS 93.9 (urban contemporary); WMZQ 98.7 (country); WGAY 99.5 (easy listening); WBIG 100.3 (oldies); and WGMS 103.5 (classical).

FOOD *Best Restaurants and Others* by Phyllis Richman (101 Productions; $8.95) lists fine dining places in Washington, DC, and environs.

TELEPHONE The area code for the District is 202; for Maryland, 301; and for Virginia, 703. The telephone numbers in this chapter are in the 202 area code unless otherwise indicated.

SALES TAX The city sales tax is 6.75%; the hotel room tax is 11%.

CLIMATE Washington has four distinct seasons. Summer can be hot and sweltering, fall New Englandish and lovely, winter cold with some snow and lots of slush, and spring—when the cherry blossoms bloom—sublime.

GETTING AROUND

AIRPORTS Washington is served by three major airports. *Washington National Airport* is the city's primary facility. The *Washington Flyer* (phone: 703-685-1400) provides express bus and van service from *National* to 1517 K St. NW (at the rear of the *Capital Hilton*). Free shuttle service is available to several downtown hotels. The *Metro*'s *Blue* and *Yellow* lines connect downtown with the airport. The *Blue* line stops include *Metro Center* (11th and G Sts. NW; phone: 637-7000) and Foggy Bottom (23rd and I St. NW); the *Yellow* line can be boarded at *L'Enfant Plaza* (Seventh St. and Maryland Ave. NW).

Dulles International Airport is about 25 miles west of the city, in Virginia. The ride from *Dulles* to downtown DC at 1517 K St. NW usually takes 45 minutes to an hour. The *Washington Flyer* leaves *Dulles* about every half hour and travels to 1517 K St. NW. Free shuttle service to several downtown hotels is available. The *Washington Flyer* also offers bus service between *Dulles* and *National Airports* and between *Dulles* and the nearest *Metro* stop, *West Falls Church.*

Baltimore/Washington International Airport (*BWI*) also serves the DC area and is a 1-hour drive from downtown. *BWI Airport Connection* (phone: 301-441-2345). The *Super Shuttle* (phone: 800-809-7080) also offers bus service. Buses depart daily every 90 minutes from 1517 K St. NW.

BUS The *Metro Bus* system serves the entire District and the surrounding area. Transfers within the District are free; the rates increase when you go into Maryland and Virginia. For complete route information call the *Washington Metropolitan Area Transit Authority* office (phone: 637-7000). *Greyhound/Trailways* runs to and from its main bus station (First St. and L St. NE; phone: 800-231-2222).

CAR RENTAL All the national firms serve Washington.

METRO The fastest way to get around Washington is by *Metrorail,* the nation's premier subway system. The lines provide a quick and quiet ride, for $1.10 to $3.25 depending on the route and time of day. (Fare schedules are posted in each station.) You need a fare card to enter and exit platform areas; they are on sale inside the stations. Transfers to the bus system are free. *Note:* Be sure to pick up a transfer at your boarding station (not the exiting station). Children ages five and under ride free. *Metro* hours are weekdays from 6 AM to midnight; Saturdays and Sundays from 8 AM to midnight. Inquire about discount passes; for example, a two-day *Family/Tourist Pass,* which costs $5, is good for unlimited travel on the *Metro* buses and subway for up to four persons. For complete route and travel information and a map of the system, contact the *Washington Metropolitan Area Transit Authority* office (600 Fifth St. NW; phone: 637-7000).

TAXI Cabs in the District charge by zone. Sharing cabs is common, but ask the driver whether there is a route conflict if you join another passenger. Cabs may be hailed in the street, picked up outside stations and hotels, or ordered on the phone, but there is an extra charge of $1.50 for phone dispatch. By law, basic rates must be posted in all taxis. The major cab companies are *Yellow* (phone: 544-1212) and *Diamond* (phone: 387-6200).

TRAIN More than 50 *Amtrak* trains daily pull into historic *Union Station* on *Capitol Hill,* including the *Metroliner,* linking the capital to New York and other Northeast Corridor cities. For reservations and information, call 800-872-7245.

SIGHTSEEING TOURS

BOAT *Spirit Cruises* runs tours such as the "Spirit of Washington" (March through December) and the "Spirit of Mt. Vernon" (March through mid-October) aboard sightseeing boats on the Potomac (Pier 4, Sixth and Water Sts. SW; phone: 554-8000 or 548-9000). The *Potomac Riverboat Company* also offers cruises to monuments along the waterways of the capital area from April through October (phone: 703-684-0580). *Odyssey Cruises* (phone: 488-6010) features dinner cruises on the Potomac River aboard the *Odyssey III* (Gangplank Marina, Seventh and Waters Sts. SW; phone: 488-6010).

BUS *Gray Line* offers guided, narrated bus tours of the District and outlying areas (phone: 289-1995); another bus touring company is *All About Town* (phone: 393-3696). Also, *Eyre Bus Service* (phone: 442-1330) offers "Executive Club" tour service for 20 passengers, which includes food and beverages.

TRAM/TROLLEY The *Tourmobile* operates in the downtown sightseeing area between the *Lincoln Memorial* and *Capitol* area (the *Mall*), and also goes to *Arlington National Cemetery.* These 88-passenger shuttle trams make 18 stops, and passengers may get on or off as they wish (*Tourmobiles* pass each stop every 30 minutes). Commentary about the sights also is provided. Tickets can be purchased from the driver or from a booth near the tour sites. For complete information contact the *Tourmobile* office (1000 Ohio Dr. SW; phone: 554-7950). *Old Town Trolley Tours* offers two-hour excursions around the District (phone: 682-0079).

SPECIAL EVENTS

A town that knows how to throw presidential inauguration parties is a town that knows how to celebrate. There's plenty to keep the District going between inaugurations, too. Late March brings the annual *Smithsonian Kite Festival* on the *Mall.* The first sighting of white single blossoms and a flood of pink double blossoms means it's *Cherry Blossom* time in Washington. In early April, a big festival celebrates the coming of the spring blossoms and the spring with concerts, parades, balls, and the lighting of the *Japanese Lantern* at the Tidal Basin.

Around the same time (give or take a few blossoms) is the *Easter Monday Egg Rolling,,* when scads of children descend on the *White House* lawn, usually to be greeted by the First Family; adults are admitted only if accompanied by a child. In mid-April, The *White House* spring garden tours allow visitors a free stroll through the West Lawn and *Jacqueline Kennedy Rose Gardens.*

Historic houses, gardens, and embassy tours of some of Washington's most elegant interiors are given April and May, allowing entrance to some of Washington's most elegant interiors. For information on the tours, see the "Weekend" section in Friday's *Washington Post.*

During the summer, the *Festival of American Folklife,* sponsored by the *Smithsonian Institution,* sets up its tents on the *Mall* near the *Museum of American History,* and groups from all regions of the country do their stuff; jug band concerts, blues performances, Indian dances, and handicraft demonstrations are just a few of the possibilities. In midsummer the *Twilight Tattoo* features military pageantry. From June through September, US military service bands perform free outdoor concerts several nights a week at 8 PM on the *Mall* and at other locations. And the *Fourth of July* celebrations in the capital are among the best in the country, with a parade, a *National Symphony Orchestra* concert, fireworks, and other entertainment.

In early September, *Adams Morgan Day* is celebrated in the Adams Morgan neighborhood. The festival, which reflects Spanish, Ethiopian, and African influences, features music, crafts, and food. The city is especially festive at *Christmas,* when the streets are trimmed with holiday decorations. Special music programs are presented at the *Kennedy Center* and at many other spots around town. The president lights the national *Christmas* tree in mid-December at the *Ellipse,* in a ceremony complete with music and caroling.

MUSEUMS

In addition to those described in *Special Places,* other notable museums include the following:

ANACOSTIA MUSEUM Founded in 1967 as a branch of the *Smithsonian Institution,* this museum celebrates African-American culture and history through exhibitions, educational lectures, films, concerts, and demonstrations of black music, art, and dance. There is a picnic area with tables and grills. Groups of 15 or more may arrange tours by calling in advance. Open daily. No admission charge. 1901 Fort Pl. SE (phone: 287-3369).

HILLWOOD Exquisite 18th- and 19th-century French and Russian icons, portraits, and Fabergé creations are housed in the elegant former home of cereal heiress Marjorie Merriweather Post. Other buildings on the 25-acre site include a dacha, or Russian country house, with a small collection of Russian art; the C. W. Post collection of paintings, sculpture, and furnishings; and a lodge housing Native American artifacts. Be sure to stroll around the *Rose Garden, French Garden,* and *Japanese Garden.* Closed Sundays and Mondays. Open to the public only via tours, which must be arranged by appointment; call well in advance for reservations. Admission charge. 4155 Linnean Ave. NW (phone: 686-5807). *Metro: Van Ness–UDC.*

HISTORICAL SOCIETY OF WASHINGTON, DC A museum devoted to Washington history, housed in the spectacular Victorian mansion of brewer Christian Heurich. There is also a library and a bookstore. Tours are offered on the hour on Wednesdays through Saturdays starting from noon; the last tour leaves at 3 PM. The museum is closed Mondays. The library is open to the public Wednesdays, Fridays, and Saturdays from 10 AM to 4 PM. Admission charge. 1307 New Hampshire Ave. NW (phone: 785-2068). *Metro: Dupont Circle.*

NATIONAL BUILDING MUSEUM Housed in the old and wonderful *Pension Building,* this museum has permanent and changing exhibits relating to architecture, building, engineering, and design. Presidential inaugural balls are held in its *Great Hall.* Open daily. No admission charge. 401 F St. NW (phone: 272-2448). *Metro: Judiciary Square.*

NATIONAL GEOGRAPHIC SOCIETY EXPLORERS HALL Headquarters for the society; exhibits here document research and discoveries made by its explorers and documentarians. Open daily. No admission charge. 17th and M Sts. NW (phone: 857-7588). *Metro: Farragut North.*

NATIONAL LEARNING CENTER/CAPITAL CHILDREN'S MUSEUM A hands-on museum where children can dress up in period costumes, feed animals, and work on high-tech equipment. Closed Mondays and Tuesdays. Admission charge. 800 Third St. NE (phone: 543-8600). *Metro: Union Station.*

NATIONAL MUSEUM OF AMERICAN JEWISH MILITARY HISTORY This museum chronicles the contributions of Jewish-Americans who served in the Armed Services through exhibits and films. Open daily. No admission charge. 1811 R St. NW (phone: 265-6280).

NATIONAL MUSEUM OF WOMEN IN THE ARTS In a former Masonic temple, this permanent collection of 500 pieces of pictorial, sculpted, and ceramic art spans 400 years of women's work. Open daily. Admission charge. 1250 New York Ave. at 13th St. NW (phone: 783-5000). *Metro: Metro Center* (13th St. exit).

PHILLIPS COLLECTION Opened in 1918, this is America's oldest museum of "modern art." Set in an elegant Victorian brownstone, the works of such masters as El Greco, Manet, and Chardin are shown together with their artistic progeny: Cézanne, Monet, Klee, O'Keeffe, Rothko, and many others. The pièce de résistance is Renoir's *Luncheon of the Boating Party.* The mahogany-paneled *Music Room* features a long-standing Sunday evening concert series of chamber music from September through May at 5 PM; (admission charge). Closed Mondays, *New Year's Day, July 4, Thanksgiving,* and *Christmas.* Admission charge weekends. 1600 21st St. and Q St. NW (phone: 387-0961). *Metro: Dupont Circle.*

TEXTILE MUSEUM A diverse collection of fabrics from around the world, in a former mansion with a charming garden. Featuring woven goods of both artistic and archaeological significance, it is one of only two museums in the world devoted entirely to woven rugs and fabrics. Even if your interest in the field runs no deeper than getting a good buy on something to cover that stain on the den rug, this may be the place (although goods for sale in the shop are high-priced). A museum shop sells tablecloths, fabrics, jewelry, and books. Open daily. Admission charge. Donations suggested. 2320 S St. NW (phone: 667-0441). *Metro: Dupont Circle.*

WASHINGTON DOLL'S HOUSE AND TOY MUSEUM Featured here is the private collection of dollhouse historian Floragill Jacobs. On display are antique dollhouses and toys, including a section of presidents' games that includes the "Game of Politics or Race for the Presidency," a board game published in 1887, and the "Game of Presidents," a card game dating from the early 20th century. Closed Mondays. Admission charge. 5236 44th St. NW, one block west of Wisconsin Ave., between Jennifer and Harrison Sts. (phone: 244-0024). *Metro: Friendship Heights.*

WOODROW WILSON HOUSE Home to Woodrow Wilson (from 1921 to 1924) and Mrs. Wilson (from 1921 to 1961), this is now a memorial to our 28th president and his wife. Gifts of state, presidential memorabilia, and other items from the 1920s are displayed. Considering Wilson's tireless effort in establishing the *League of Nations* and in expanding America's role in international affairs, it is altogether fitting that he relocated to the Embassy Row district. Visitors may view the library, the dining room, bedrooms, a solarium overlooking a garden, and many personal effects such as the typewriter he used to compose speeches. Only guided tours—which take approximately 45 minutes—are available; the house is closed Mondays. Admission charge. 2340 S St. NW (phone: 387-4062). *Metro: Dupont Circle North.*

SHOPPING

When you've had your fill of monuments, the nation's capital has enough shopping venues to satisfy even "shop-till-you-drop" appetites. Following the sprucing up of Pennsylvania Avenue some years ago, Washington is now home to a number of excellent shopping malls. For unique gifts, however, the city's impressive museums are the best bet. Most museums, shrines, and churches have their own shops, some offering reproductions of priceless treasures at very affordable prices. Here's a capital shoppers' guide:

SHOPPING MALLS

Connecticut Connection This three-story shopping and dining complex is conveniently located atop the *Farragut North Metro* station. Connecticut Ave. and L St. NW (no main phone number).

Eastern Market An open-air extravaganza on weekends with fresh produce, flowers, and crafts. North Carolina Ave. and Seventh St. SE.

Georgetown Park The centerpiece of Georgetown shopping, this handsome brick complex, with its magnificent Victorian interior, houses more than 100 elegant shops—including *Ann Taylor, FAO Schwarz,* and *Williams-Sonoma*—and restaurants. 3222 M St. NW at Wisconsin Ave. (phone: 298-5577).

International Square In this 12-story atrium with a cascading fountain are 30 retail shops, restaurants, and fast-food eateries. 1850 K St. NW (phone: 223-1850).

Mazza Gallerie On the north end of Wisconsin Avenue, this enclosed four-level mall features all kinds of high fashion shops and specialty stores, as well as department stores such as *Neiman Marcus, Filene's Basement,* a cineplex theater, and a number of restaurants. 5300 Wisconsin Ave. NW (phone: 966-6114).

Pavilion at the Old Post Office The city's oldest Federal building has been newly renovated with even more stores and restaurants to browse. 12th St. and Pennsylvania Ave. NW (phone: 289-4224).

Shops at National Place This mall includes such national chains as *Victoria's Secret, Sharper Image,* and *B. Dalton.* F St. between 13th and 14th Sts. NW (phone: 783-9090).

2000 Pennsylvania Avenue On the edge of the *George Washington University* campus, this mall, located within a brick townhouse complex, has a variety of specialty shops. Between 20th and 21st Sts. NW (phone: 452-0924).

Union Station The capital's train station is worth a visit simply for its stunning Beaux Arts interior: The main waiting room with its 96-foot ceiling (encircled with 46 statues) is often used as a ballroom. Now restored to its former glory, it contains numerous shops, a nine-screen movie theater, as well as unique casual and elegant eating spots. 50 Massachusetts Ave. NE (phone: 371-9441).

Washington Harbour This expansive office/retail/residential complex on the Potomac River features unique architectural designs, with fountain-filled courtyards and specialty shops and restaurants. 3000 K St. NW, next to the Whitehurst Freeway in Georgetown (phone: 944-4140).

Watergate A prestigious shopping arcade in the Watergate complex, including *Yves Saint Laurent, Gucci, Valentino,* and *Guy Laroche.* (It also has excellent restaurants and a hotel; see the *Watergate* listing in *Checking In.*) New Hampshire and Virginia Aves. NW (phone: 338-6630).

BARGAIN CITY

Thirty minutes south of Washington is *Potomac Mills,* one of the world's largest outlet malls, and a big attraction for Washington shoppers on weekends. Among the almost 200 discount stores are outlets of such well-known retailers as *Eddie Bauer, Laura Ashley, Nordstrom's, Saks Fifth Avenue,* and *IKEA.* Open daily. On I-95S, exit 52, in Prince William, Virginia (phone: 703-643-1770; 800-VA-MILLS).

DOWNTOWN SHOPS

Border's Books and Music One of downtown's superstores, this print and music emporium has a wide selection, plus a café. 18th and L Sts. NW (phone: 466-4999, books; 466-6999, music).

Britches of Georgetown Casual menswear and womenswear. 1219 Connecticut Ave. NW (phone: 347-8994).

Earl Allen Office clothing for women. *International Sq.,* 1825 I St. NW (phone: 466-3437).

Hecht's One of Washington's top department stores. 12th and G Sts. NW (phone: 628-6661).

Kramer Book Stores A wide selection of classics and books on diverse subjects. Two locations: *Kramerbooks and Afterwords,* with a cozy café in the rear of the store, open until 1 AM Sundays through Thursdays; all night Fridays and Saturdays (1517 Connecticut Ave. NW; phone: 387-1400); and *Sidney Kramer Books* (1825 I St. NW; phone: 293-2685).

The Newsroom In the heart of the embassy district, this newsstand has a wide selection of international newspapers and magazines. 1753 Connecticut Ave. NW (phone: 332-1489).

Political Americana Two blocks from the *White House,* this shop sells mugs, pens, T-shirts, hats, ties, lapel pins, and other items that proudly indicate Democratic or Republican allegiance. It's the place to go for a vintage Teddy Roosevelt campaign button or a "Wee Publican" baby bib. 685 15th St. NW (phone: 547-1871). Other locations at *Union Station* (West Hall; phone: 547-1685); and Georgetown Park (3222 M St. NW; phone: 543-7300).

Post Office Exchange Designer and souvenir Washington T-shirts. *Pavilion at the Old Post Office,* 12th St. and Pennsylvania Ave. NW (phone: 842-0504).

Woodward and Lothrop A popular, traditional department store. 11th and F Sts. NW (phone: 347-5300).

American Hand Plus Stunning ceramics, design objects, and glassware for home and office. 2906 M St. NW (phone: 965-3273).

Appalachian Spring Handmade crafts, quilts, pottery, and jewelry from all over the US. 1415 Wisconsin Ave. NW (phone: 337-5780).

Barnes & Noble An extensive three floors of books and a *Starbucks Café* make this a popular spot for browsing. 3040 M St. NW (phone: 965-9880).

Britches of Georgetown Casual clothing for men and women. 1247 Wisconsin Ave. NW (phone: 338-3330).

Dean & Deluca New York's trendy food emporium features a fabulous array of packaged goods, as well as fresh meat, fish, and cheeses. There's also a good selection of housewares. The prices may astound, but the aromas will certainly entice. An adjoining café serves light fare. 3276 M St. NW (phone: 342-2500).

Hats in the Belfry Funny, unusual, elegant, and antique toppers for all occasions. 1237 Wisconsin Ave. NW (phone: 342-2006).

Little Caledonia Unusual furnishings, fabrics, china, and stationery. 1419 Wisconsin Ave. NW (phone: 333-4700).

Orpheus Records Specializes in vintage and rare recordings. 3249 M St. NW (phone: 337-7970).

Phoenix Mexican jewelry, crafts, and clothing. 1514 Wisconsin Ave. NW (phone: 338-4404).

Santa Fe Style Crafts and art from the American Southwest. 1413 Wisconsin Ave. NW (phone: 333-3747).

Threepenny Bit Irish items—including hand-knit sweaters, shorts, shirts, ties, and shoes. 3122 M St. NW (phone: 338-1338).

SPORTS AND FITNESS

BASKETBALL The *NBA*'s *Wizards* hold court from November through April at the *USAir Arena* (1 Harry S Truman Dr., Landover, Maryland; phone: 301-350-3400). It can be reached via signposted access roads off the Beltway; either take Beltway exit 18 and go east on MD Route 214/Central Avenue for about 100 yards, or take exit 17 and go south about half a mile on MD Route 202. Tickets can be ordered by calling NBA-DUNK.

BICYCLING Rent from *Metropolis Bike & Scooter* (709 Eighth St. SE; phone: 543-8900); *Big Wheel Bikes* (1034 33rd St. NW, Georgetown; phone: 337-0254); or *Thompson's Boat Center* (Virginia Ave. at Rock Creek Pkwy. NW; phone: 333-4861). The latter also has mountain bikes, beach bikes, and tandems available. The towpath of the Chesapeake and Ohio Canal, starting at the barge landing in Georgetown, is a good place to ride.

FITNESS CENTERS Most major hotels have health and fitness centers (see *Checking In*).

FOOTBALL The *NFL Redskins* play at *Robert F. Kennedy Stadium* (E. Capitol and 22nd Sts. SE; phone: 547-9077) from September through December. Tickets are hard to come by during the season; it's much easier to get into pre-season games, held in late July and August. Try *Ticketmaster* (phone: 432-7328) or the stadium box office.

GOLF The most convenient public golf courses in the city are at *East Potomac Park* (phone: 554-7660) and *Rock Creek Park* (phone: 882-7332).

HOCKEY The *Capitals,* Washington's pro hockey team, play at the *USAir Arena* (see *Basketball*) from October to April. Tickets are available at *TicketCenter* outlets or by calling the arena.

JOGGING Join plenty of others in making a round trip from the *Lincoln Memorial* to the *Capitol* (4 miles); also run in *Rock Creek Park* and in Georgetown, along the Chesapeake and Ohio Canal.

SKATING From November through March you can ice skate on the rink on the *Mall.* Seventh St. and Constitution Ave. NW (phone: 371-5340).

SWIMMING Year-round facilities are available at the *East Capitol Natatorium* (635 North Carolina Ave. SE; phone: 724-4495). Many of the hotels also have pools (see *Checking In*).

TENNIS Washington has some fine public courts; the best bets are the *Washington Rock Creek Park Tennis Center* (16th and Kennedy Sts. NW; phone: 722-5949) and the *Hains Point* complex (1090 Ohio Dr.; phone: 554-5962).

THEATER

Washington is America's third city of theater (after New York and Boston), according to *Variety,* the bible of showbiz. The following is Washington's most outstanding stage.

CENTER STAGE

Arena Stage One of the oldest and most consistently admired American theater companies and the first outside New York to receive a Tony for theatrical excellence, the *Arena Stage* is noted for developing American drama and for introducing foreign (particularly Eastern European) plays to the US. The theater's three stages seat 827, 514, and 180; the last is used for small musical revues and experimental works. Sixth St. and Maine Ave. SW (phone: 488-3300, box office; 484-0247, TTY number for hearing-impaired patrons).

The *Kennedy Center for the Performing Arts* is another weighty cultural presence in the District, attracting world-renowned dance, theater, and musical companies to its five theaters and concert halls (off Virginia Ave. on New Hampshire Ave. NW; phone: 467-4600 or 800-444-1324 for all theaters). The center's *Eisenhower Theater* offers musical and dramatic productions, including Broadway previews and road shows; and the *Terrace Theater* offers many different productions—modern dance, ballet, dramas, poetry recitals, and so on. The *National Theatre* (1321 Pennsylvania Ave. NW; phone: 628-6161) presents major productions throughout the year. *Ford's Theatre* (511 10th St. NW; phone: 347-4833) offers American productions. The *Shakespeare Theater Group* offers innovative interpretations of the bard's plays as well as more contemporary works at the *Shakespeare Theater* (450 Seventh St. NW; phone: 547-3230, information; 393-2700, box office). Note: In the summer (usually August), the troupe also performs a free outdoor play at the *Carter Barron Amphitheater,* in *Rock Creek Park* near Kennedy Street NW; call the above number for information. For half-price, same-day performance tickets, try *Ticketplace* (*Lisner Auditorium,* 21st and H Sts. NW; phone: TIC-KETS). If all else fails, a hotel concierge might have some pull. Washington also has what one theater critic calls the "off-off *Kennedy Center* movement"—a network of small avant-garde houses on or near the stretch of 14th Street NW above Thomas Circle: *Studio Theater* (1333 P St. NW; phone: 332-3300); *Woolly Mammoth Theater Company* (1401 Church St. NW; phone: 393-3939); and *Source Theater* (1835 14th St. NW; phone: 462-1073). During the summer the *Olney Theater* (2001 Rte. 108, Olney, Maryland; phone: 301-924-3400), about a half-hour drive from the District, offers summer stock with well-known casts. In winter, the *Barns at Wolf Trap,* a 350-seat theater at *Wolf Trap Farm Park for the Performing Arts* (1624 Trap Rd., off Rte. 7 near Vienna, Virginia; phone: 703-255-1868), holds performances indoors. To get there, take the *Dulles Airport* toll road Route 267, or the *Metro* to West Falls Church, Virginia, where there's a connecting shuttle bus. For a unique dinner-theater experience, see *Mystery on the Menu.* Held only on Saturday evenings, it's a participatory play that takes the form of a Georgetown wedding reception for a senator and his bride. During the reception, a murder occurs and all the audience members ("guests") get a chance to solve the crime. A three-course meal with a glass of champagne is included in the ticket price. Locations vary and reservations are necessary; call for details (phone: 333-6875).

MUSIC

The *National Symphony Orchestra* performs at the *Kennedy Center Concert Hall* (phone: 467-4600) from September through June; in June the concert hall also hosts a *Mostly Mozart Festival.* In addition, concerts are presented at the city's *former* premier venue, *Constitution Hall* (18th and C Sts. NW; phone: 638-2661), which is renowned for its acoustics. The *Washington*

Opera (phone: 416-7800) presents seven operas a year, between November and March, at the *Kennedy Center Opera House.* The *Juilliard String Quartet* and other notable ensembles usually perform chamber music concerts on Stradivarius instruments in the *Library of Congress*'s *Coolidge Auditorium* Thursday and Friday evenings in the spring and fall. However, at press time concerts were temporarily being held at the *National Academy of Sciences* (2100 C St. NW), while the *Coolidge* undergoes renovations, scheduled for completion later this year; for tickets, call 707-5502. During the summer, *Wolf Trap Farm Park for the Performing Arts* near Vienna, Virginia (see *Theater,* above), presents musicals, ballet, pop concerts, and symphonic music in a lovely outdoor setting—bring a picnic basket. There are often free concerts by the service bands on the plaza at the West Front of the *Capitol* or in front of the *Jefferson Memorial.* Consult newspapers for where and when. *Army and Navy Band* concerts are presented at different locations in the winter (phone: 703-696-3643 for Army; 433-2525 for Navy). The *British Embassy Players* delight audiences with old-fashioned music hall performances; the *British Embassy Rotunda* (3100 Massachusetts Ave. NW) is magically transformed into a cabaret, with some embassy staff and other area Britons providing the entertainment. There are four productions beginning in the fall and ending with three *Music Hall* weekends in June. Tickets are limited and must be reserved well in advance (phone: 703-271-0172).

NIGHTCLUBS AND NIGHTLIFE

For some, Washington is an early-to-bed town, but there's plenty of pub crawling, jazz, bluegrass, soul, rock, and folk music going on after dark—you just have to know where to look for it. Best bets are the Georgetown, Adams Morgan, Dupont Circle, and *Capitol Hill* areas. For up-to-the-minute listings of DC's ever-shifting club scene, consult the weekly *City Paper* (see *Local Coverage*). Some sure favorites: *Blues Alley* (1073 Wisconsin Ave. NW; phone: 337-4141), for mainstream jazz and Dixieland; *Tortilla Coast* (400 First St. SE; phone: 546-6768), decorated with hot tropical murals and featuring killer margaritas; the *Dubliner Restaurant and Pub* (520 N. Capitol St. NW; phone: 737-3773), the place to hear old Irish and Celtic tunes and jigs; *Market Inn* (200 E St. SW; phone: 554-2100), a popular steak and seafood house near *Capitol Hill* where live jazz is featured Friday and Saturday nights; and *Cities* (2424 18th St. NW; phone: 328-7194), which changes its "city theme" every six months, is located in the heart of Washington's newest nightlife scene–Adams Morgan, a funky mélange of bars, dance clubs, ethnic restaurants, and shops radiating from the intersection of Columbia Road and 18th Street NW.

On Saturday nights the satirical (and sometimes political) revue called *Gross National Product* (phone 783-7212 for locations and reservations) targets two Washington politicians in the shows *Clintoons* and *Newt World*

Order. Shows are often presented at the *Bayou* in Georgetown (3135 K St. NW; phone: 333-2897) and reservations are required. Political satirist Mark Russell also performs occasionally in local nightspots (check local newspapers for details). Watch local listings, too, for performances by the *Capitol Steps,* a satirical singing group. The *Comedy Café* (1520 K St. NW; phone: 638-5653) features nationally known comedians in an informal, downtown club.

Déjà Vu (2119 M St. NW; phone: 452-1966) is a lively dance club with music from the 1960s to today. *West End Café* at the *One Washington Circle* hotel (One Washington Circle; phone: 293-5390) is a popular piano bar where classical and jazz music are featured. Two ever-popular chains have Washington branches: the rock 'n' roll–centered *Hard Rock Café* (999 E St. NW; phone: 737-7625), and the movie world's *Planet Hollywood* (11th St. and Pennsylvania Ave. NW; phone: 783-7827), both brasserie-style bar restaurants.

SPORTS BARS

Because Washingtonians are serious about their sports teams, especially the *Redskins,* sports bars are scattered around the area and are prime spots for viewing the game (if you don't have seats at *RFK Stadium*). Try *Champions* (1206 Wisconsin Ave. NW; phone: 965-4005), a Georgetown favorite; *Bottom Line* (1716 I St. NW; phone: 298-8488), a rugby bar popular with local players and their cheering squads; *Poor Robert's* (3419 Connecticut Ave. NW; phone: 363-1839), which offers satellite TV for special sporting events; and *Joe Theismann's* (1800 Diagonal Rd., Alexandria, Virginia; phone: 703-739-0777), a sports bar owned by the former, fabulous *Redskins* quarterback. The capital is also a major saloon town, and some of the best stomping grounds are on the "Hill." *Bullfeathers* (410 First St. SE; phone: 543-5005), where the Congressional crowd hangs out, has a bar that's always hopping. The *Hawk 'n' Dove* (329 Pennsylvania Ave. SE; phone: 543-3300), a dark, rustic bar, is perfect for after work (or after play), and crowded with both Capitol Hillers and law students. *Hamburger Hamlet* in Georgetown (3125 M St. NW; phone: 965-6970), offers a casual, warm atmosphere, great summer drinks, and crayons for drawing on the paper tablecloths. The *Capital City Brewing Company* (1100 New York Ave. NW; phone: 628-2222) serves up nine kinds on beer made on the premises.

Best in Town

CHECKING IN

Washington enjoys a wealth of good-quality hotel establishments because of a building boom in the late 1980s. Still, accommodations at the best places can dwindle fast, so reservations should be made in advance. Visitors in town for only a few days should stay downtown to make the best use of their limited time; weekends offer the best package deals. Inexpensive taxis, the *Metro* system, and buses facilitate getting around without private cars, which can be difficult and expensive to park (although some hotels offer reasonable valet parking). If you're traveling by car, it may make more sense to stay at one of the major motel chains located at the principal entry points to the district—Silver Spring and Bethesda in Maryland, and Arlington, Rosslyn, and Alexandria in Virginia. Expect to pay $175 or more (sometimes much more) per night for a double room at a hotel described as expensive, $100 to $175 at a place in the moderate category, and $70 to $100 at a hotel listed as inexpensive. For information about bed and breakfast accommodations, contact *The Bed and Breakfast League/Sweet Dreams & Toast* (PO Box 9490, Washington, DC 20016; phone: 363-7767). *Washington, DC, Accommodations* (phone: 289-2220; 800-554-2220) provides assistance with hotel reservations at no charge. *Capitol Reservations* (phone: 800-554-6750) offers a free reservation service and discount rates at Washington area hotels.

Most of Washington's major hotels have complete facilities for the business traveler. Those hotels listed below as having "business services" usually offer such conveniences as meeting rooms, photocopiers, computers, translation services, and express checkout, among others. Call the hotel for additional information. Unless otherwise noted, hotel rooms have air conditioning, private baths, TV sets, and telephones.

All hotels below are in Washington, DC and telephone and fax numbers are in the 202 area code unless otherwise indicated.

EXPENSIVE

ANA This outstanding hotel is as elegant inside as it is outside. There is a lovely interior garden, and 415 luxuriously appointed rooms, including 36 "Executive Club" rooms and 26 suites; three "Executive Premier King" suites. Accommodations include cable TV, three phones, voice mail, and terry cloth robes. The *Colonnade* is a fine restaurant for formal dining, and there's a more casual brasserie, and a lobby lounge in a glass loggia is just off the garden. A professionally staffed fitness center, complete with a pool, a Jacuzzi, saunas, squash courts, an aerobics room, weights, and state-of-the-art exercise equipment, plus a mini-spa and juice bar, are on the premises. Business services are available. Children under 18 stay free in their parents' rooms. 24th and M Sts. NW (phone: 429-2400; 800-228-3000; fax: 457-5010).

Canterbury Near the downtown business district and not far from the *White House,* this place features 99 suites each with a sitting area, dressing room, and wet bar. A complimentary continental breakfast greets guests every morning, and fine fare is served at *Chaucer's* restaurant. Other pluses include nightly turn-down service; business services are available. Inquire about weekend package rates. 1733 N St. NW (phone: 393-3000; 800-424-2950; fax: 785-9581).

Capital Hilton One of Washington's most luxurious hostelries is also one of the most conveniently located, just a few minutes from the *White House.* It has 549 expansive rooms, each with a marble foyer, two telephones, a fully stocked mini-bar, and terry cloth robes. The Deluxe Towers' rooms on the top four floors also have VCRs and a separate concierge and check-in area. Restaurants include *Fran O'Brien's Steakhouse,* which serves steak, seafood, and pasta in a sports-bar setting; the sophisticated *Twigs Grill,* and the lobby bar. There's also a state-of-the-art fitness center. Business services are available. 1001 16th at K St. NW (phone: 393-1000; 800-445-8667; fax: 639-5784).

Carlton Host to many presidents and dignitaries, this hotel has an elegant Italian Renaissance lobby, 197 comfortable rooms, and a bar that's good enough to win approval from feisty *New York Newsday* columnist Jimmy Breslin. The *Allegro* dining room is excellent and has a terrific Sunday brunch (see *Eating Out*); there's also a cocktail lounge. Business services and 24-hour room service are available. 923 16th St. NW (phone: 638-2626; 800-325-3535; fax: 638-4231).

Four Seasons If the difference between a good and a great hotel is in the details, this is one of the capital city's very best. The property is flanked by the Chesapeake & Ohio Canal (a run along the canal is a Washington ritual) and by *Rock Creek Park,* Washington's premier parkland; in fact, most of the 197 rooms overlook the tranquil green space. The *Seasons* restaurant deserves high praise (see *Eating Out*), as does *Desirée,* a private nightclub for guests and members. There's also afternoon tea in the sunlit indoor *Garden Terrace.* A traditional concierge offers many personal services including mail delivery. Around-the-clock room service and business services are available. Body-conscious guests can use the fitness club with a skylit lap pool, a whirlpool bath, a sauna, and a steamroom. 2800 Pennsylvania Ave. NW (phone: 342-0444; 800-332-3442; fax: 342-1673).

Grand Hyatt Washington Located in the heart of downtown DC, across from the *Washington Convention Center,* this renovated property has 947 rooms, including 58 suites, and a Regency Club floor with a private lounge and concierge service. The suites, all with living areas, wet bars, and lots of greenery, also feature saunas and marble baths. All rooms have turn-down service, free cable television with HBO and ESPN, and full-service honor bars. Dining facilities include the New York–style *Zephyr Deli;* the *Grande Café,* an informal eatery for breakfast, lunch, and dinner; the more formal *Hamilton's; Palladio's,* a three-level lobby bar; and *Grand Slam,* a sports bar with two large-screen TV sets. Business services are available. There's also a health club with an exercise room, a sauna, a Jacuzzi, a lap pool, and aerobics classes. 1000 H St. NW (phone: 582-1234; 800-233-1234; fax: 637-4781).

Hay-Adams At an incomparable location just off Lafayette Square, within a silver dollar's throw of the *White House.* This 143-room hotel retains its Old World dignity and maintains the standards of the neighborhood with antique furnishings, a paneled lobby, and three fine dining rooms—the formal *Adams Room* for breakfast and lunch, the *John Hay Room* with traditional English decor and original paneling from *Warwick Palace* for afternoon tea and cocktails, and the informal *Eagle Bar & Grill* for soup and salad. Room service is available 24 hours a day. There's also a concierge desk and business services. 16th and H Sts. NW (phone: 638-6600 or 800-424-5054; fax: 638-2716).

Jefferson A clubby place and a favorite of many politicians. Located near the *White House* and the shops on Connecticut Avenue, it has a low-key, traditional atmosphere and outstanding service. Acclaimed chef Andrew Roche oversees the French cuisine at the *Jefferson* restaurant. The 69 rooms and 35 suites offer stereos with CD players, mini-bars, and at least two phone lines that are fax and computer compatible. Business services, a concierge, and 24-hour room service round out the amenities. 1200 16th St. NW (phone: 347-2200; 800-368-5966; fax: 331-7982).

J. W. Marriott A significant step above other members of the Marriott chain, this property is connected to a mall complex of 160 stores and the *National Theatre.* There are 772 rooms, an indoor pool, and a health club; the "Marquis Level" (14th and 15th floors) are especially comfortable with private concierge and complimentary continental breakfast, hors d'oeuvres, and a private lounge. There is also a *Grand Ballroom* for up to 2,000 people, and the *Capital Ballroom,* which can accommodate up to 800. Restaurants include the *Allies American Grille* for American cuisine and *Celadon,* serving continental fare. Room service is available around the clock. Business services are available. 1331 Pennsylvania Ave. NW (phone: 393-2000; 800-228-9290; fax: 626-6991).

Madison With 374 luxurious rooms, this property features gracious Federal decor and excellent service by a well-trained staff. Extras include interpreters, refrigerators, and bathroom phones; there is also a health club. The *Montpelier Room* is quite a good restaurant; it serves a buffet on weekdays and brunch on Sundays. The *Retreat* restaurant is open for afternoon tea on weekdays and for dinner daily; the lobby bar has nightly entertainment. Business services are available. 15th and M Sts. NW (phone: 862-1600; 800-424-8577; fax: 785-1255).

Renaissance Mayflower This historic property, one of the city's treasures, has earned laurels over the years for catering to the world's movers and shakers with elegance and style. The yellow brick-and-limestone Beaux Arts building boasts a block-long lobby adorned with Italian marble, glittering chandeliers, and intricately carved, 23-karat gold leaf ceilings. Its central location in the heart of downtown is ideal for sightseers (not far from the *White House* and the *Mall*) and its nearly 700 rooms can accommodate legions of them. The *Grand Ballroom* recalls the splendor of a bygone era, and the *Café Promenade* restaurant is a fitting place to feast on Mediterranean fare (a jacket and tie are required for men). Guests also can enjoy a health center, round-the-clock room service, valet parking, and full concierge service. Business services are available. 1127 Connecticut Ave. NW (phone: 347-3000; 800-HOTELS-1; fax: 466-9082).

Ritz-Carlton This is as close to a classic European hostelry as exists in Washington. There are 206 rooms, the *Jockey Club* restaurant (see *Eating Out*), and the *Fairfax Bar,* as well as a ballroom and a health club with weights and cardiovascular machines. Other amenities include 24-hour room service, a concierge, and business services. 2100 Massachusetts Ave. NW (phone: 293-2100; 800-241-3333; fax: 293-0641).

Sofitel Washington This link in the French hotel chain boasts 145 spacious, elegantly decorated rooms with such extras as fax and computer hookups, mini-bars, safes, and coffee makers. There is a restaurant, and business services are available. There's also a multilingual concierge, access to a health club, tennis, and golf, and 24-hour room service. Located in the heart of the embassy district. 1914 Connecticut Ave. NW (phone: 797-2000; 800-424-2464; fax: 462-0944).

Washington Vista François Mitterrand and Elizabeth Taylor are among those who have stayed at this 399-room hostelry, only six blocks from the *White House.* Its six very expensive one-bedroom suites, designed by Givenchy, feature full-length mirrors, large private balconies, and bathrooms with Jacuzzis; they are completely separate from the rest of the hotel—sharing no walls with any other rooms. Favorite recipes of past presidents are on the menu at the *American Verandah* restaurant; cardiovascular fitness gear is available at the health club along with treadmills and a sauna. Business services are available, as is 24-hour room service. 1400 M St. NW (phone: 429-1700; 800-847-8232; fax: 785-0786).

Watergate Though this modern hotel-apartment-office complex doesn't look too historic, appearances can be deceiving (as can small pieces of tape). This property boasts 235 large contemporarily furnished rooms, an indoor swimming pool, and health club. There is a cocktail lounge and *The Watergate Shopping Mall* (offering many dining possibilities), all at a location adjacent to the *Kennedy Center.* There's a concierge desk and 24-hour room service, and business services are available. 2650 Virginia Ave. NW (phone: 965-2300; 800-424-2736; fax: 337-7915).

Westin A distinctive copper dome wedged between walls of brick and granite marks this West End hostelry. In architecture and ambience it is reminiscent of a small European hotel: A white marble staircase cascades down into the center of the lobby, the inner courtyard is meticulously landscaped, and all 263 recently refurbished rooms (including 22 suites) feature Italian marble baths and three phones; there are working fireplaces in some suites. *Cafe on M* serves light fare in a clubby atmosphere, while the *Promenade* features fine dining in a romantic setting. Besides a multilingual concierge, accommodating staff, and currency conversion service, there is 24-hour room service, valet and dry cleaning, and valet parking. Business services are available. 2350 M St. NW (phone: 429-0100; 800-848-0016; fax: 429-9759).

Willard Inter-Continental Ten presidents-elect stayed at this Beaux Arts landmark while awaiting inauguration, and Charles Dickens, Julia Ward Howe (who wrote the "Battle Hymn of the Republic"), and Dr. Martin Luther King Jr. are other prominent past guests. The carpeting, columns, and furnishings reproduce the original decor, and the 341 rooms are decorated in turn-of-the-century style. The hotel dining room, the *Willard Room,* is one of DC's most prestigious eateries, as is the nearby *Occidental Grill* (see *Eating Out* for both); *Peacock Alley,* its grand central corridor. The hotel lobby was once a favorite brandy-sipping spot for Ulysses Grant. Additional amenities include 24-hour room service, a concierge, an exercise room, a café, two lounges, and business services. 1401 Pennsylvania Ave. NW (phone: 628-9100; 800-327-0200; fax: 637-7326).

Wyndham Bristol There are 239 newly renovated rooms (37 of which are suites) in this English-style hostelry; guests also have complimentary access to a health club. The *Bristol Grill* offers fine food. Business services and 24-hour room service are available. 2430 Pennsylvania Ave. NW (phone: 955-6400; 800-822-WYNDHAM; fax: 955-5765).

MODERATE

Morrison-Clark Inn This popular bed and breakfast–style inn served as the hostel for the *Soldiers', Sailors', Marines', and Airmen's Club* from 1923 to 1984. A 1988 addition to the two historic buildings comprises 41 of the 54 tastefully decorated rooms, some furnished with Victorian antiques. The hotel has an excellent restaurant; a continental breakfast is included in the rate. There's also a concierge desk, and business services are available. Located three blocks from the *Convention Center* and four blocks from *Metro Center* (*Metrorail* stop) at Massachusetts Ave. and 11th St. NW (phone: 898-1200; 800-332-7898; fax: 289-8576).

Radisson Barcelo This 297-room hotel's best feature is its lovely location, west of Dupont Circle on the verge of *Rock Creek Park.* An outdoor pool, a sauna, an exercise room, and valet and concierge services are among the amenities. Nonsmoking accomodations are available. Its restaurant, *Gabriel,* has an upscale, nightclub decor and an inventive Southwestern American menu. 2121 P St. NW and 21st St. (phone: 293-3100; 800-333-3333; fax 857-0134).

Tabard Inn On a charming semi-residential street near the heart of the business district, this establishment offers guests an ambience rare in an American city. The 40 rooms are furnished with antiques and some of them share baths (23 have private baths); there are no in-room TV sets. A restaurant serves breakfast, lunch, and dinner, and brunch on weekends (see *Eating Out*); there's also a library. Business and concierge services are available. 1739 N St. NW (phone: 785-1277; fax: 785-6173).

Washington One of the city's older properties, this comfortable hotel offers an incomparable view from its rooftop restaurant (which makes it a particularly good place to be from early April through late October). The 370 rooms feature such luxury amenities as telephones in the bathrooms; downtown shopping is nearby. Room service is available until 11 PM. 15th St. and Pennsylvania Ave. NW (phone: 638-5900; 800-424-9540; fax: 638-4275).

INEXPENSIVE

Harrington A 265-room, older establishment in the center of Washington's commercial area, it has seen better days but provides clean accommodations and is within walking distance of the *Mall* and the *White House.* Popular with high school and family groups. There are two restaurants and a gift shop. 11th and E Sts. NW (phone: 628-8140; 800-424-8532; fax: 347-3924).

Windsor Inn Small and unpretentious, near the trendy Adams Morgan district. A magnet for relocating embassy employees as well as government workers who prefer a modest, homey atmosphere. There are 46 rooms; the staff is personable and attentive. Continental breakfast comes with a newspaper; and for a European touch, afternoon sherry is served. 1842 16th St. NW (phone: 667-0300; 800-423-9111; fax: 667-4503).

Windsor Park It's modest, but this 43-room property is within walking distance of the *Woodley Park/Zoo Metro* station and near the French diplomats' residence and the *Chinese Embassy.* Continental breakfast buffet is included in the rate. 2116 Kalorama Rd. NW (phone: 483-7700; 800-247-3064; fax: 332-4547).

EATING OUT

Considering the international aspects of Washington—2,000 diplomats and a large number of residents who have lived abroad and brought back a taste for foreign fare—it's not too surprising that the District can provide an international gastronomic tour de force. But though it's always helpful to have an ermine-lined wallet or, better yet, a generous expense account, those who have only a yen for good food needn't go hungry. Expect to pay $100 or more for a dinner for two at places described as very expensive; between $60 and $80 at places listed as expensive; $30 to $60 at restaurants in the moderate category; and less than $30 at dining spots described as inexpensive. Prices do not include drinks, wine, or tips. Reservations are a must at the top-flight restaurants. All telephone numbers are in the 202 area code.

Unless otherwise noted, restaurants are open for lunch and dinner.

VERY EXPENSIVE

Galileo *Washingtonian* magazine ranked this as not only the capital's best Italian dining spot, but possibly the best restaurant in town recently awarded this northern Italian dining spot a blue ribbon, and ranked it among the best restaurants in the entire country. Try the risotto or the homemade *agnolotti,* a pasta filled with spinach and ricotta. The sautéed rack of veal with mushroom and rosemary and wild mushrooms in a marsala sauce are also popular menu choices. The city's finest breads, fresh-baked, accompany each meal. Closed at lunch on weekends. Reservations advised. Major credit cards accepted. 1110 21st St. NW (phone: 293-7191).

Le Lion d'Or This establishment is reputed to have the finest French food in town, although some say that the service is unpredictable. Selections from the long and exquisite menu by chef Jean-Pierre Goyenvalle include duck sausage with a port sauce and a hot pâté of quail in puff pastry, lobster stew, filet of lamb, roasted pigeon, and red snapper. Don't leave without tasting one of the spectacular desserts. Closed Saturdays. Reservations necessary at least two weeks in advance. Major credit cards accepted. 1150 Connecticut Ave. NW, near 18th and M Sts. (phone: 296-7972).

Seasons This handsome dining room in the *Four Seasons* hotel is distinguished by stylish service and a highly creative menu that changes daily, specializing in *cuisine courante*—a mixture of French and California food. Specialties include breast of quail stuffed with woodland mushrooms in a zinfandel sauce with wild rice and scallion cake, and stuffed lamb with pistachio crust and risotto fritters in a minted madeira glaze. Reservations advised. Major credit cards accepted. 2800 Pennsylvania Ave. NW (phone: 342-0810).

EXPENSIVE

L'Auberge Chez François This Alsatian country inn, 30 minutes west of the District in northern Virginia's hunt country, is a perennial favorite. The service is attentive, and the setting cozy yet refined. There are several working fireplaces, antique grandfather clocks, a mounted elk's head, and a staff dressed in Alsatian garb. The fare blends the hearty proportions of Germanic cooking with French touches like superb sauces, fine cheeses, and artistic presentation. The reasonably priced menu includes a number of Alsatian specialties, among them the famed *choucroute garnie,* a collection of sausages and duck served atop heavily seasoned sauerkraut; gruyère tart; an Alsatian version of cassoulet with sausages and lentils; stuffed rabbit; and chicken stewed in Alsatian riesling salmon soufflé. The assortment of pâtés is renowned, and for dessert, we recommend the lime tart. Open for dinner; closed Mondays. The reservation book is always filled, so plan far in advance (a well-kept secret among the regulars is that no reservations are necessary for dining in the garden during the warm months). Major credit cards accepted. 332 Springvale Rd., Great Falls, VA (phone: 703-759-3800).

Bice This northern Italian eatery, owned by the proprietors of the New York establishment of the same name, specializes in risotto, fresh pasta, fish dishes, and duck entrées. Only Italian and California still wines are served, but the champagne is French. Closed Saturdays and Sundays for lunch. Reservations advised. Major credit cards accepted. 601 Pennsylvania Ave. NW, between Sixth and Seventh Sts.; enter on Indiana Ave. (phone: 638-2423).

Jockey Club This *Ritz-Carlton* restaurant is a favorite meeting and eating spot for local movers and shakers. Beyond the soft-shell crabs, the menu is French-influenced. Specialties include roasted rack of lamb and filet of beef tenderloin. Reservations necessary. Major credit cards accepted. 2100 Massachusetts Ave. NW (phone: 659-8000).

Kinkead's Chef Robert Kinkead offers a creative international cuisine with an emphasis on seafood. Try the grilled swordfish with potatoes and olives; crab cakes; or the restaurant's signature dish, pumpkin seed–crusted salmon garnished with shrimp, chilies, and corn. The desserts are heavenly. Downstairs there's a lively bar and informal café. Reservations advised. Major credit cards accepted. 2000 Pennsylvania Ave. NW (phone: 296-7700).

Maison Blanche This elegant French dining room is so close to the *White House* that even a snail could crawl over on its lunch hour. Washington's famous and powerful (such as assorted Kennedys, lobbyists, and Art Buchwald) meet here. Classical French dishes are served, but there are touches of "nouvelle" as well. Chef Christian Gautrois is well known for his exquisite escargots; other favorites are his nouvelle version of Norwegian salmon in a vegetable sauce and shrimp with angel-hair pasta. The prix fixe menu (available nightly from 6 to 9:30 PM) is a bargain. The *Kennedy Center* is a short drive or an eight-block walk away. Closed Sundays. Reservations advised. Major credit cards accepted. 1725 F St. NW (phone: 842-0070).

Prime Rib Arguably Washington's premier steakhouse, this first-rate establishment serves a spectacular rib that is perfectly cooked throughout its two-inch thickness. The menu also includes a wide choice of fresh seafood dishes, as well as rack of lamb. Perhaps the city's best lunch value is an on-the-bone cut of prime ribs served with two vegetables for $15. An elegant atmosphere is accompanied by impeccable service. Closed Saturday lunch and Sundays. Reservations advised. Jacket and tie required. Major credit cards accepted. 2020 K St. NW (phone: 466-8811).

Red Sage This trendy dining spot is accented with a whimsical decor of hand-blown chandeliers, silver and gold decor; the food is as exquisite as the surroundings. Chef Mark Miller creates dishes with a Southwestern flavor; among the selections is a stew of lobster, scallops, mussels, and clams. Also try plum *ancho* (glazed quail with jalapeño slaw and spoonbread). Reservations necessary. Major credit cards accepted. 605 14th St. NW at F St. (phone: 638-4444).

I Ricchi One of the city's hottest eateries, here chef Francesco Ricchi concocts fabulous Florentine fare, such as broad noodles tossed with hare sauce, leg of rabbit with rosemary, and quail stuffed with homemade sausage. This trattoria has a warm homey feeling. Closed Saturday lunch and Sundays. Reservations necessary. Major credit cards accepted. 1220 19th St. NW (phone: 835-0459).

1789 Situated on two floors of an 18th-century house, this restaurant boasts early-American furnishings and etchings, a fireplace in the main dining room, and a menu that changes with the seasons. Chef Ris Lacoste's all-American menu changes daily and might include such entrées as Shenandoah brook trout, Maryland crab cakes, Virginia quail, or Alaska salmon. Landlubbers will find rack of lamb with merlot sauce very appealing. Desserts include a pistachio cannoli with bitter-orange sauce. Reservations advised. Major credit cards accepted. 1226 36th St. NW (phone: 965-1789).

Willard Room Chef Guy Reinbolt presides over the regional American–European cuisine in this opulent Edwardian dining room. Try the rack of lamb, Dover sole, or Chesapeake Bay fish. Open Mondays through Fridays for breakfast, lunch and dinner; Saturdays and Sundays dinner only; Sunday brunch. Reservations advised. Major credit cards accepted. In the *Willard Inter-Continental* Hotel, 1401 Pennsylvania Ave. NW (phone: 637-7440).

MODERATE

Allegro This lovely dining room of the *Carlton* hotel is known for its fabulous business buffet lunch featuring jumbo shrimp, salmon, pâté, and carved roast of the day, and is perfect for those under time constraints. Afternoon tea is accompanied by a harpist and Sunday brunch by a pianist. Breakfast might include assorted breads, healthy options such as Bircher muesli and honey yogurt, and international offerings such as miso soup and grilled salmon à la Japanese. Dinner highlights include saffron ravioli with shiitake-morel sauce and asparagus tips, and curry oyster tempura with sake herb sabayon. Open daily for breakfast, lunch, and dinner. Reservations advised, especially for the business lunch and brunch. Major credit cards accepted. 16th and K Sts. NW (phone: 879-6900).

La Colline Charming and reasonably priced, it serves adventurous French food and daily specials as well as wonderful desserts. Try the bouillabaisse and *choucroute alsacienne* (sauerkraut, sausages, pork). Reservations advised. Major credit cards accepted. 400 N. Capitol St. NW (phone: 737-0400).

Ernie's Original Crab House Across the Potomac in Alexandria, this is an old favorite of crab lovers. Reservations advised on weekends. Major credit cards accepted. Two locations: 1623 Fern St. (phone: 703-836-1623) and 7929 Richmond Hwy. (phone: 703-780-0100).

Germaine's The varied Pan-Asian menu includes Japanese, Korean, Vietnamese, and Indonesian fare. Specialties are pinecone fish, scallop salad, *satay,* and squirrelfish. Closed at lunch on weekends. Reservations advised. Major credit cards accepted. 2400 Wisconsin Ave. NW (phone: 965-1185).

Jaleo Located in the thriving Seventh Street corridor, this restaurant offers delicious *tapas,* appetizers that can be ordered in combinations to create a meal. Also good are the *gambas al ajillo* (garlic shrimp). There are, of course, main entrées—fish of the day and the paella—generous enough to share. Major credit cards accepted. 480 Seventh St. NW (phone: 628-7949).

I Matti *Galileo* owner Roberto Donna's popular eatery in the Adams Morgan section of town offers both northern Italian dishes and Italian nouvelle cuisine. Aromatic stews, pizza with a paper-thin crust, and meltingly wonderful ricotta cheesecake are the highlights. Closed Sundays. Reservations necessary. Major credit cards accepted. 2436 18th St. NW (phone: 462-8844).

Mr. K's Excellent food from four regions of China, including Peking, Hunan, both spicy and milder Szechuan, and classic Cantonese; favorites include beef mimosa, Peking duck, and any of several lobster dishes. This bustling place has four private dining rooms—very private, for the high-powered lawyers and lobbyists who have lunch or dinner here—decorated with impressive jade statues of dragons and a phoenix. At the end of the meal, a high-tech coffee urn is wheeled out and delivers a delicious brew (they serve tea, too). Reservations advised. Major credit cards accepted. 2121 K St. NW (phone: 331-8868).

Occidental Grill Though this historic Washington eatery has shed its stuffy, formal atmosphere, fortunately, its first-rate fare hasn't changed: Specialties of chef Jeff Ruben include a swordfish sandwich, escalope of salmon *au poivre* with black bean purée, crab cakes, and varied meat, fish, and sausage dishes. There is an impressive wine list and a tempting dessert menu. The walls of this clubby brass and leather dining room are covered with more than 3,000 signed photographs of statesmen dating back to the early 1900s. Reservations advised. Major credit cards accepted. 1475 Pennsylvania Ave. NW (phone: 783-1475).

Old Ebbitt Grill This bustling Victorian-style restaurant saloon is loaded with old-time Washington charm. First established as a boarding house in 1856, the Old Ebbitt has drawn the likes of presidents Grant, Andrew Johnson, Cleveland, and Teddy Roosevelt, and still brings in political insiders and celebrities. Etched-glass panels separate the velvet banquettes of the main dining room from the long mahogany bar. The American fare includes mouth-watering burgers, meat loaf, fish, pasta, and salads. Reservations advised. Major credit cards accepted. 675 15th St. NW (phone: 347-4801).

Au Pied de Cochon An informal place for a good meal at a decent price 24 hours a day. If *pieds de cochon* (pigs' feet) aren't your style, try asparagus vinaigrette, coq au vin, and other bistro specialties. No reservations. Major credit cards accepted. 1335 Wisconsin Ave. NW (phone: 333-5440).

Sfuzzi Northern Italian food with an American touch is served in this *Union Station* dining establishment, founded by the owners of New York City's *Sfuzzi* restaurant. The grilled salmon is recommended, as are the pizza and pasta. Try the chicken *romano tagliatelle* (grilled chicken with gorgonzola cheese and noodles). There's an outdoor café in the summer and a happy hour on weekdays. Reservations advised. Major credit cards accepted. 50 Massachusetts Ave. NE (phone: 842-4141).

Tabard Inn The nouvelle-influenced menu at this charmingly quirky inn is strong on fresh seafood such as grilled tuna and swordfish. Breads and desserts are homemade, and the vegetables are shipped fresh daily from a nearby farm in Virginia. The Saturday and Sunday brunch is a popular affair. There's a fire in the hearth in winter and in summer enjoy dining on the garden patio. Reservations advised. MasterCard and Visa accepted. 1739 N St. NW (phone: 833-2668).

INEXPENSIVE

America The menu at this eatery (whose sister restaurant is in New York City) offers choices from all regions of the United States, from grits to Cajun shrimp to grilled tuna salad. Reservations advised. Major credit cards accepted. In *Union Station,* 50 Massachusetts Ave. NE (phone: 682-9555).

Clyde's of Georgetown Over 30 years old, this archetypal fern bar has matured nicely, thank you. It's the place's classics that bring people back: the quintessential cozy-pub decor, good thick burgers, excellent crab cakes, and brunch–still among the best omelettes and Bloody Marys around. Don't miss the ice cream shakes and homemade desserts. Open daily. 3236 M St NW (phone: 333-9180)

Madurai Vegetarian Indian food is the specialty of this Georgetown establishment. Try the eggplant curry or the vegetable *biryani* (mixed vegetables cooked with rice). Reservations advised. Major credit cards accepted. 3316 M St. NW (phone: 333-0997).

Peyote Café This Southwestern bar and grill is located below *Roxanne's* (see below) in the heart of Adams Morgan. Try the chuck wagon beef and pinto bean chili, the mashed potatoes (with skins), and the Texas yardbird (barbecued chicken with melted Monterey jack cheese). Reservations advised. Major credit cards accepted. 2319 18th St. NW (phone: 462-8330).

Roma A solid Italian family-style place, best in warm weather when the large outdoor garden is open and musicians and singers add to the relaxed ambience. All the old favorites, from pizza to pasta, are here. Reservations advised. Major credit cards accepted. 3419 Connecticut Ave. NW (phone: 363-6611).

Roxanne's Chef Phil DeMott worked with New Orleans's Paul Prudhomme for five years before coming to this Cajun-style eatery in Adams Morgan. Try the barbecued shrimp, the blackened tuna, or the grilled lamb with white bean salad. Reservations advised. Major credit cards accepted. 2319 18th St. NW (phone: 462-8330).

Star of Siam This is the best Thai restaurant in the district. Try one of the 10 different kinds of curries, the crispy noodles, or the fish cakes. Reservations necessary for parties of four or more. Major credit cards accepted. 1136 19th St NW, between L and M Sts. (phone: 785-2838/9). There are two other locations: in Rosslyn, Virginia, across the Key Bridge from Georgetown (1735 N. Lynn St.; phone: 703-524-1208), and in Adams Morgan (2446 18th St. NW; phone: 986-4133).

Vietnam Georgetown Small and intimate, this simple place serves the best Vietnamese food in town. Specialties include deep-fried crispy spring rolls, shrimp with sugarcane, and beef in grape leaves. Reservations unnecessary. MasterCard and Visa accepted. 2934 M St. NW (phone: 337-4536).

COOL TREATS

Washington has a homegrown ice cream empire founded by renegade attorney Bob Weiss. *Bob's Famous Ice Cream* has stores on Capitol Hill (236 Massachusetts Ave. NE; phone: 546-3860), near the *Cleveland Park Metro* station (3510 Connecticut Ave. NW; phone: 244-4465), and in Bethesda, Maryland (4706 Bethesda Ave.; phone: 301-657-2963). *Bob's* ice cream also is sold at the *Ice Cream Shop* (2416 Wisconsin Ave. NW; phone: 965-4499).

Diversions

Unexpected Pleasures and Treasures

Introduction

If you selected 1,000 Americans at random and asked them to briefly describe their homeland, you could easily receive 1,000 different answers. Although the United States defies easy characterization, there is one common trait that applies to both the country and its people: diversity. America's geographical characteristics run the gamut from arid deserts to fertile pastures to frozen tundra. These landscapes can be admired from a distance, but they also provide a handy setting for any number of outdoor activities. Adventurous athletes can climb the dizzying heights of Mt. McKinley or explore the depths of the *Grand Canyon;* those who prefer scaling fish to scaling mountains have numerous lakes and rivers at their disposal, not to mention the Atlantic and Pacific Oceans; and nature watchers can get their fill of wildlife at the hundreds of thousands of national parks and campsites across the land.

The makeup of America's population is even more varied than its topography. Almost from the beginning of its history, the United States has been a conglomerate nation of people from other countries who came in search of a new and better life. Although most abandoned their homelands for what they hoped would be greener pastures, they clung steadfastly to their heritage; their disparate languages, music, art, food, and customs indelibly influenced the developing character of their new home.

As a result, the US offers a veritable smorgasbord of culture, history, and entertainment. You can observe a traditional Navajo ritual dance, tour vineyards in California's wine country, relive the Battle of Gettysburg, or play roulette in Atlantic City. And if you're in the mood for something a bit more highbrow, there's bound to be at least one noteworthy music festival, regional theater, or museum wherever you are visiting.

With all these activities from which to choose, deciding what to do with your spare time can be difficult at best. If the city you're visiting is covered in THE CITIES, check the respective chapter for our choices of where to stay and what to do in that area. To further help you sort through your options, the following section lists what we think are the best diversions elsewhere in the United States. We don't presume to define any particular experience as quintessentially "American"; that opinion will vary for each individual. Therefore, this section has been organized into 32 categories ranging from the physical to the cerebral to the unusual. All are designed to guide you to the most interesting, eclectic, and exhilarating places the country has to offer, whether you want to enjoy the ultimate golfing vacation, explore America's rich history, or indulge in the sybaritic pleasures of a spa. With planning and a little luck, your travel experience will give you an opportunity to develop a fresh viewpoint for your exploration of the US—and perhaps discover a few aspects of this country's extraordinarily multifaceted character that will surprise and delight you.

For the Experience

Amusement Parks and Theme Parks

About 80 years ago, the American Sunday changed forever. Until then, the country's amusement parks were run as sedate adjuncts to picnic groves, usually owned by the companies that ran trolleys and interurban train lines. At some unrecorded moment, a trolley line executive realized that people loved the rides a lot more than the picnics, and before long picnicking as a Sunday afternoon pastime went the way of oil lamps. Huge entertainment complexes sprang up beside piers and boardwalks across the country. Roller coasters didn't go very fast, but even then they stirred the masses.

Today, more time, money, and talent is going into the business than ever before—and the results are spectacular. Not only are the parks clean, green, and flowering, but you can take in zippy, chills-down-the-spine shows and even top-name entertainers after you've whirled over some of the scariest roller coaster tracks in history.

Throughout this book, we have described amusement parks in our US city chapters: *Walt Disney World* and *Universal Studios Florida* in Orlando; *Six Flags Over Georgia* in Atlanta; *Opryland USA* in Nashville; *Astroworld* in Houston; *Six Flags Over Texas* in Arlington, Texas (near Dallas); *Kings Island,* near Cincinnati; and *Disneyland, Knott's Berry Farm, Six Flags Magic Mountain,* and *Universal Studios Hollywood,* all in or around Los Angeles. For detailed descriptions, see the individual chapters in THE CITIES; listed below are additional playgrounds for thrill seekers. Admission fees—usually between $25 and $35, with reductions for children—generally buy all the rides and shows you want, though occasionally you'll have to pay extra to play games of skill.

EAST

SIX FLAGS GREAT ADVENTURE, Jackson, New Jersey Located between New York City and Philadelphia, this 2,000-acre facility includes a 350-acre drive-through safari, with 1,500 free-roaming animals representing more than 60 species. Here, guests can drive their own vehicles or take an air conditioned bus ride for a nominal charge. The park contains 55 amusement rides, a special children's area called *Bugs Bunny Land,* celebrity concerts, four live water shows, and six other live shows for your enjoyment. For those who like to get wet, there are 14 water rides, including *Movietown Water Effect,* and the *Adventure Rivers* theme area featuring *Skull Mountain,* an indoor thrill ride. At a height of 17 stories, the *Great American Scream Machine* is one of the world's tallest and fastest roller coasters. Information: *Six Flags Great Adventure,* PO Box 120, Jackson, NJ 08527 (phone: 908-928-2000).

HERSHEYPARK, Hershey, Pennsylvania A Hershey Bar and a Reese's Cup are two of the friendly characters strolling the grounds of the 100-acre theme park. *Chocolate Town, USA,* has nine theme areas. Be sure to visit the general store in the Old West theme area, *Pioneer Frontier.* Pennsylvania's German and English heritage is woven through an artfully reconstructed Tudor castle and food shops offering local specialties like Belgian waffles and funnel cakes; also on hand are candlemakers, blacksmiths, and leathercrafters. The fast, old wooden roller coaster, known as the *Comet,* is among the best in the US; the *SooperdooperLooper*—a thrill ride that shoots passengers around steeply banked turns and upside down through one enormous 360-degree vertical loop—was the first of its kind on the East Coast. *The Wildcat* coaster ride has become the focal point of a new theme area called *Midway America.* Try the exciting *Sidewinder,* a multi-looped coaster. The *Canyon River Rapids* ride gives the exhilarating feeling of whitewater rafting on a less dangerous scale, and there are over three dozen other rides. Also included in the basic admission charge is a trip through *ZooAmerica*, a high-quality, 11-acre zoo. Open from *Memorial Day* through *Labor Day;* some rides and concessions operate during *Christmas Candylane,* held from mid-November through December. Information: *Hersheypark,* 100 W. Hersheypark Dr., Hershey, PA 17033 (phone: 717-534-3090; 800-HER-SHEY).

SESAME PLACE, Langhorne, Pennsylvania This nine-acre "Sesame Street" affiliate 30 minutes north of Philadelphia caters to families with children ages three through 13. In addition to educational science attractions, there's live entertainment with "Big Bird & Company," a musical revue; *Sesame Neighborhood,* a full-size, interactive replica of the TV show's stage set; and regular appearances by Big Bird, Ernie, Bert, Count von Count, the Cookie Monster, and the Honkers. *Slimey's Chutes,* named for Oscar the Grouch's best friend, is the park's newest water ride. Twiddlebug Land is a play area where everything is so enormous it makes both children and grownups feel bug size. Information: *Sesame Place,* PO Box L579, Langhorne, PA 19047 (phone: 215-752-7070).

SOUTH

BUSCH GARDENS, Tampa, Florida Africa is the theme of this 300-acre family entertainment center, where even the names of the amusement areas evoke the exotic—*Nairobi, Marrakech,* the *Congo,* and so forth. Last year, *Egypt* made its debut, complete with King Tut's tomb and a state-of-the-art inverted roller coaster. Rare white Bengal tigers and cubs are among the more than 3,400 animals here, many of whom roam freely among the park's plains and waterways. A three-acre primate habitat called *Myombe Reserve: The Great Ape Domain* is home to six lowland gorillas and eight chimpanzees.

There are bird gardens, bazaars, belly dancers, Broadway-style musical revues, an interactive play area called *Land of the Dragons,* an animal nursery, and snake charmers; and, of course, there are rides, including the *Phoenix,* a looping boat swing; the *Questor,* a state-of-the-art flight simulator; and the *Python, Scorpion,* and *Kumba* roller coasters. Information: *Busch Gardens,* PO Box 9158, Tampa, FL 33674 (phone: 813-987-5082).

PARAMOUNT'S CAROWINDS, Charlotte, North Carolina Now owned and operated by Paramount Studios, this amusement park boasts 10 theme areas on 91 acres. There are more than 35 rides; its six coasters include a stand-up roller coaster and one that turns riders upside down four times. There's also a wild whitewater rapids ride, shows, shopping, plus *Animation Station* and *Hanna-Barbera Land* for children. Camping is adjacent to the park. Information: *Paramount's Carowinds,* PO Box 410289, Charlotte, NC 28241 (phone: 704-588-2600).

PARAMOUNT'S KINGS DOMINION, Richmond, Virginia This 400-acre playground includes eight theme areas, over 44 rides, live shows, and top-name concert performers every season. Recent additions include the *Days of Thunder* motion-simulation theater, which makes audience members feel as though they're driving a race car; *Paramount on Ice,* a professional ice-skating show that salutes the studio's films; and the Nickelodeon-themed *Splat City,* a three-acre children's play area. In *Splat City,* kids climb, crawl, and slide over obstacles, run through a maze, and twist and turn a variety of valves and levers, all the while getting soaked with the trademark Nickelodeon "green slime" (bathing suits are a good idea here). A 30-minute audience-participation show—also featuring lots of green slime—is presented regularly in a 1,300-seat arena. The park has seven roller coasters, including the *Anaconda,* a giant steel ride featuring a vertical loop and an underwater tunnel; the wooden *Grizzly,* patterned after Coney Island's *Wildcat* and a favorite of roller-coaster aficionados; the *Rebel Yell,* a wooden coaster in which one train travels backward while another goes forward; and *Shockwave,* a standing-up coaster that sends riders through a 360-degree loop. *Hurricane Reef,* a water park, features six major water attractions, including the *White Water Canyon* raft ride and a children's water-play area. Klingons and other "Star Trek" characters as well as such Hanna-Barbera cartoon favorites as Scooby Doo and Yogi Bear can be seen walking around the park, which is 20 miles north of Richmond. Information: *Paramount's Kings Dominion,* PO Box 2000, Doswell, VA 23047 (phone: 804-876-5000).

BUSCH GARDENS, Williamsburg, Virginia A charming re-creation of Old World Europe nestled on 360 acres of rolling, wooded hills, the park offers a vast array of exciting rides, shows, entertainment, shops, restaurants, and exhibits. There are nine authentically detailed European settings: *Banbury Cross* and *Hastings* (England); *Aquitaine* (France); *Rhinefeld* and *Oktoberfest* (Germany); *Heatherdowns* (Scotland); *San Marco* (Italy); *Festa Italia* (Italy);

and *New France. Questor,* the world's largest flight simulator, is a 35,000-pound "theme" machine that takes riders on a thrilling fantasy mission of sight, sound, and motion. The *Loch Ness Monster*—an absolutely terrifying double-looped, upside-down roller coaster that drops riders 114 feet in five seconds—is one of the best rides in the country, and the *Big Bad Wolf* roller coaster travels seemingly out of control before plunging 80 feet to a splashing finish. *Drachen Fire,* the world's largest steel roller coaster, is designed to produce a feeling of total weightlessness in its victims—er, passengers. *Haunts of the Olde Country* is a state-of-the-art "4-D" film experience where members of the audience feel mist, fog, and cold air as they "wander" through historic and haunted castles. *Escape from Pompeii* is a new water ride that includes simulated earthquakes and volcanic eruptions. A mouth-watering array of pricey European delicacies, such as Italian cannelloni, German bratwurst and sauerkraut, and European pastries, are abundant throughout the park. There are over 16 hours of continuous live entertainment daily, including musical revues, oompah bands, Italian operas, strolling street entertainers, and concerts by top-name performers. Visiting the *Old Country* makes a fine complement to sightseeing around *Colonial Williamsburg.* Information: *Busch Gardens,* One Busch Gardens Blvd., Williamsburg, VA 23187 (phone: 804-253-3350). See also T*idewater Virginia,* DIRECTIONS.

MIDWEST

SIX FLAGS GREAT AMERICA, Gurnee, Illinois This popular link in the Six Flags chain has plenty of rides and attractions—*Batman, The Ride,* a suspended, outside-looping thrill ride; *Iron Wolf,* a stand-up coaster; *Power Dive,* a looping starship thrill ride; *Bugs Bunny's Yukon Adventure,* a children's playground; and *Splashwater Falls,* a giant water ride. However, the Americana theme remains in its five areas, including *Orleans Place* and *Yukon Territory.* There's also a *Farmers' Market;* a reproduction of an antique 100-foot-high double-decker carousel; the *Pictorium,* an IMAX movie theater that projects a 70-foot by 96-foot image; plus a variety of shows, games, and shops. Other highlights include an exciting whitewater raft ride and the *American Eagle,* one of the world's largest double-racing wooden roller coasters. Information: *Six Flags Great America,* PO Box 1776, Gurnee, IL 60031 (phone: 708-249-1776).

SIX FLAGS OVER MID-AMERICA, Eureka, Missouri Like the other parks in the chain, this one near St. Louis will show you a something-for-everyone good time. The 200-acre park also features *Thunder River,* a whitewater raft ride; *Colossus: the Giant Wheel;* and the *Screamin' Eagle* roller coaster—no longer the highest and fastest of all, but still exciting. A popular attraction at the park is *Tidal Wave,* a log flume ride. Information: *Six Flags Over Mid-America,* PO Box 60, Eureka, MO 63025 (phone: 314-938-5300).

CEDAR POINT, Sandusky, Ohio A host of nifty one-of-a-kind rides makes this Great Lakes–area park one of the most unusual in the US: *Gemini* (a traditional racing wooden coaster whose 125-foot-high first hill drops 118 feet at a 55-degree angle); one of the tallest Ferris wheels in the world; an IMAX movie theater; four theaters with live stage shows; three hand-carved carousels; an enormous arcade; a marine-life complex. There are 12 roller coasters (more than anywhere else in the world): At 205 feet, the *Magnum XL-200* is one of the world's tallest coasters, while the *Mean Streak* is one of the world's tallest (161 feet) and fastest (65 mph) wooden scream machines. *Snake River Falls* is one of the tallest (82 feet) and fastest (more than 40 mph) water rides in the world. The newest addition is *Raptor,* an inverted roller coaster (137 feet high and 57 mph). Especially enjoyable for the family is the adjacent *Challenge Park,* where a water park, miniature golf course, and go-cart speedway are draws. Also popular with young children is *Berenstain Bear Country.* Stay at the big, rambling *Breakers* hotel, built in 1905 and fitted out with Tiffany windows and chandeliers, and which now has a new wing with 206 units, or the *Sandcastle Suites* lakeside resort. Information: *Cedar Point Resort,* PO Box 5006, Sandusky, OH 44871 (phone: 419-627-2350 or 419-627-2106 for hotel reservations).

WEST

PARAMOUNT'S GREAT AMERICA, Santa Clara, California Now part of Paramount Studio's growing chain of theme parks, this 100-acre place—the largest family entertainment center in northern California—offers a combination of live stage shows, games, shops, and thrill rides. The *Drop Zone* stunt tower, a 224-foot free-fall ride; the *Demon,* a steel-loop and corkscrew coaster; the *Vortex,* a stand-up steel roller coaster; and *Rip Roaring Rapids,* a thundering whitewater raft ride that is just one of five water thrills, are a few of the popular attractions. Among the other crowd-pleasers are a wooden roller coaster called the *Grizzly,* a double-decker carousel, an ice skating show, and an IMAX film projected onto a screen that's seven stories high and 96 feet wide. Hanna-Barbera characters entertain the tots. Information: *Paramount's Great America,* PO Box 1776, Santa Clara, CA 95052 (phone: 408-988-1776).

PONDEROSA RANCH, Incline Village, Nevada Once the summertime filming site for the TV series "Bonanza," this 600-acre ranch is a re-creation of the Wild West. About 300,000 people visit each year to take a guided tour of the ranch house where the honorable Ben Cartwright lived with his sons, Adam, Hoss, and Little Joe, and then explore an entirely reconstructed 15-acre Western town. Among the highlights are a shooting gallery with a fine antique gun collection, and a petting farm and pony rides for children. The highlight event is *Shootout at High Noon,* a 20-minute gunfight. For those who don't mind a little hay with their meals, there's the Hayride breakfast; otherwise, visitors can partake heartily of the tasty Western grub served at the ranch.

Closed November through April. Information: *Ponderosa Ranch,* 100 Ponderosa Ranch Rd., Incline Village, NV 89451 (phone: 702-831-0691).

America's Best Resort Hotels

American resorts are playgrounds—full of golf courses, tennis courts, horseback riding trails, bike paths, hiking paths, pools, beaches, and other facilities. In addition to offering all these things, our favorite places provide just a bit more—more activities, better service, or simply just a bit more panache than their competitors. Several are located in or near major cities, and we have described them in detail in the specific chapters in THE CITIES. The places listed below are our selections of those unexpected treasures off the beaten track that make for delightful detours.

For any resort you will pay more than you would for a hotel or motel. But remember that rates are usually reduced—sometimes halved—during off-season (which will vary depending upon the resort). Be sure to ask whether meals, greens fees, tennis court fees, and the costs of other activities are included in the price of your room.

EAST

BALSAMS, Dixville Notch, New Hampshire This fairy-tale castle—immense and white, with red tile roofs and 230 rooms—sits at the base of 800-foot cliffs alongside a manmade lake and is surrounded by 15,000 acres of the forests and stony peaks of northernmost New Hampshire. The 6,804-yard Donald Ross 18-hole golf course, built against the side of a mountain and full of sloping fairways, is a challenge; even the nine-hole executive course will require every club in your bag. There's also tennis, swimming, hiking, trout fishing, and, in winter, downhill and cross-country skiing. Information: *The Balsams,* Rte. 26, Dixville Notch, NH 03576 (phone: 603-255-3400; 800-255-0800 in New Hampshire or 800-255-0600 in the US and Canada for reservations; fax: 603-237-4221).

THE SAGAMORE RESORT, Bolton Landing, New York This 70-acre private island resort and conference center, nestled between Lake George and the Adirondack Mountains, offers recreational pleasures throughout the seasons. The 1883 grande dame is listed on the *National Register of Historic Places.* The 350-room property retains the best 19th-century charms—plant-filled sun porches with white wicker rockers, a vintage wooden yacht used for lake cruises, and sunny rooms overlooking the sparkling sapphire lake—but adds such 20th-century touches as the contemporary *Trillium* restaurant, an executive-level conference center, a championship 18-hole golf course, and a spa/fitness complex. Information: *The Sagamore Resort,* Bolton Landing, NY 12814 (phone: 518-644-9400; 800-358-3585 for reservations; fax: 518-644-2626).

OTESAGA, Cooperstown, New York The building's fine turn-of-the-century Georgian exterior, with large columns and a stately colonnaded lobby, is much more formal than the resort itself, which is mannerly but not straitlaced. It has 136 rooms. You can swim in Lake Otsego, at the foot of the resort's lawns, go sailing or fishing, and play golf or tennis. There's a wonderful noontime buffet, a heated pool, and nightly dancing. Cooperstown itself is a village of museums, including the *Farmers' Museum, the Baseball Hall of Fame,* and the *Fenimore House.* The resort is open from April through late October. Information: *Otesaga,* PO Box 311, Cooperstown, NY 13326 (phone: 607-547-9931; 800-348-6222; fax: 607-547-9675).

MOHONK MOUNTAIN HOUSE, New Paltz, New York A 19th-century American original, this 273-room National Historic Landmark is majestically perched along the cliffs overlooking Lake Mohonk and the surrounding Shawangunk Mountains in New York's Catskills region, 90 miles north of Manhattan. The same Quaker family has owned the resort since 1869, and they have preserved its Old World traditions. You'll find Victorian decor and dark wood throughout, corridors full of nooks and crannies, claw-foot bathtubs, and rooms with fireplaces or balconies. Ask for Room 571, a favorite of Teddy Roosevelt. Outside on the 7,500-acre grounds, horse-drawn carriages meander through the gardens and nearly 127 gazebos. Guests can also enjoy boating, fishing, six tennis courts, and a nine-hole Scottish-designed golf course. Information: *Mohonk Mountain House,* 1000 Mountain Rest Rd., New Paltz, NY 12561 (phone: 914-255-1000; 800-772-6646 for reservations; fax: 914-256-2161).

BASIN HARBOR CLUB, Vergennes, Vermont In its 110th year of summer resort operation and in the fourth generation of Beach family proprietorship, the *Basin Harbor Club* sits on the banks of Lake Champlain some 20 miles from the *Shelburne Museum* in Shelburne (see *Restored Towns and Reconstructed Villages*). It's geared for a well-heeled clientele. Lodging is in 77 cottages (beautifully appointed and continually refurbished) and two historic lodges. You'll find a 3,200-foot airstrip, five tennis courts, a pool, boats for rent, and a children's program. The adjacent *Lake Champlain Maritime Museum* (phone: 802-475-2022) features a broad spectrum of educational programs; and there's a full-scale replica of the *Philadelphia,* Benedict Arnold's gunship sunk during the American Revolution. There is an 18-hole championship golf course, and the large rocks along Lake Champlain are great for sunning. On *July 4th,* the resort celebrates with a buffet breakfast, brass band concerts, and a big fireworks display. Open from May to mid-October. Information: *Basin Harbor Club,* Vergennes, VT 05491 (phone: 802-475-2311; for reservations, 800-622-4000 outside Vermont; fax: 802-475-6545).

WOODSTOCK INN, Woodstock, Vermont The town, a picture-postcard affair the village green of which is rimmed by colonial homes and presided over by church steeples boasting three Paul Revere bells (the fourth bell is in the garden), deserves an inn like this. It has 144 rooms. On the grounds, you can swim indoors and out, play tennis on any of 12 courts (two indoors), play racquetball or squash in the sports center, golf on a Robert Trent Jones Sr. course, or bike; nearby, you can shop for antiques, go horseback riding, or hike through the woods on beautifully maintained trails. In winter, there is downhill skiing at Suicide Six or the resort's ski touring center. Sleigh rides, ice skating, and sledding also are available. Information: *Woodstock Inn & Resort,* 14 The Green, Woodstock, VT 05091 (phone: 802-457-1100; 800-448-7900 for reservations; fax: 802-457-6699).

SOUTH

MARRIOTT'S GRAND HOTEL AND GOLF CLUB, Point Clear, Alabama A rambling structure of weathered cypress, which was once a Confederate hospital, occupies a corner of a 550-acre expanse of live oaks and spreading pines that grow right down to the soft white sand that edges Mobile Bay. The extensive facilities at this 307-room resort include 36 holes of golf, a swimming beach and a freshwater pool, sailboats and fishing boats, 10 tennis courts (two lighted), bikes, horseback riding, croquet, and card rooms. But the atmosphere is low-key, and nobody feels obliged to scurry around to take advantage of it all. Information: *Marriott's Grand Hotel and Golf Club,* Scenic Hwy. 98, Point Clear, AL 36564 (phone: 334-928-9201; 800-544-9933 for reservations).

RITZ-CARLTON, Naples, Florida Set on 19 acres of oceanfront property, this Mediterranean-style hotel has 463 rooms (including 28 suites). The huge lobby harks back to the Old World, with English Georgian and French Regency furnishings, Italian marble floors, and paintings by European artists. All guestrooms have a gulf view, and the Club rooms, on the 12th and 14th floors, feature concierge services, complimentary continental breakfast, in-room afternoon tea, and after-dinner digestifs. (Afternoon tea for all guests is also served in the downstairs lobby.) There are five restaurants—offering menus that range from pheasant and venison to chili and sundaes—plus a health club and spa, six tennis courts, and a heated pool. Golfers can play on the nearby *Pelican's Nest* course. Information: *Ritz-Carlton,* 280 Vanderbilt Beach Rd., Naples, FL 33963 (phone: 813-598-3300; 800-241-3333 for reservations; fax: 813-598-6690).

BREAKERS, Palm Beach, Florida In 1926, the heirs of Florida pioneer developer and Standard Oil co-founder Henry Flagler built this great palace by the sea, the third on the property, to be the best resort in the world. Crystal chandeliers, hand-painted frescoes, vaulted ceilings, and polished marble floors combine with 15th-century Flemish tapestries and Italian Renaissance–influenced architecture to create an atmosphere worthy of the 572-room hotel's listing on the *National Register of Historic Places.* Also on the 140-acre property are the recently renovated *Ocean* golf course, 14 tennis courts, two croquet lawns, an oceanfront pool, a fitness center, and a private beach. Another 18-hole golf course and seven other tennis courts are available for guests at *Breakers West,* 10 miles west of the resort. Supervised youth programs are available. Information: *The Breakers,* 1 S. County Rd., Palm Beach, FL 33480 (phone: 407-655-6611; 800-833-3141 for reservations; fax: 407-659-8403).

PALM-AIRE SPA RESORT, Pompano Beach, Florida This low-slung white stucco hotel and spa, whose sweeping lawns are brightened by an explosion of begonias, impatiens, and orange trees, is just 15 minutes from the beach. It has 180 rooms, and its spa facilities range from the Olympic-size pool and exercise equipment to the steamrooms, saunas, whirlpool baths, and Swiss showers. Guests also can keep busy on four 18-hole golf courses and one 22-hole course, 37 tennis courts, and squash and racquetball courts. Also see *Sybaritic Spas.* Information: *Palm-Aire Spa Resort,* 2601 Palm-Aire Dr. N., Pompano Beach, FL 33069 (phone: 954-972-3300; 800-2-PALM-AIR for reservations; fax: 954-968-2711).

THE CLOISTER, Sea Island, Georgia This famous old Georgia shore resort is the kind of clubby place to which young people who came here originally on vacation with their parents return on their honeymoons, then come back time and time again, bringing their own youngsters; where, even when guests don't know each other at the start, conversations come easily. The resort's old-fashioned style means dressy evenings of dinner and dancing, and afternoons on the 17 tennis courts or the links (absolutely superb; see *Golf*), or riding, shooting, fishing, boating, cycling, or swimming (either at the beach or in two lovely pools). The facilities are first class, the grounds are immaculate, and the 262 rooms look so fresh that even regulars marvel. The *Beach Club Spa* offers a full range of fitness services. Information: *The Cloister,* Sea Island, GA 31561 (phone: 912-638-3611; 800-SEA-ISLAND for reservations; fax: 912-638-5823).

PINEHURST, Pinehurst, North Carolina Founded by a Yankee soda fountain manufacturer named James Tufts, *Pinehurst* quickly became known as a golf center (there are seven courses; also see *Golf*). But it offers a lot more: the 10,000 acres of grounds, laid out by the firm of Frederick Law Olmsted (who gave New York its *Central Park*); the sailing on 200-acre Lake Pinehurst; hayrides; carriage tours; tennis clinics and 24 courts; jogging trails; free bicycles; and croquet and lawn bowling. It all adds up to one of the most invigorating—and friendliest—grand resorts around. Accommodations are in a gracious hotel and in more than 130 well-appointed condominiums. The resort also manages 50,000 square feet of conference and exhibit space. Information: *Pinehurst Resort & Country Club,* PO Box 4000, Pinehurst, NC 28374 (phone: 910-295-6811; 800-487-4653 for reservations).

HOMESTEAD, Hot Springs, Virginia One of the finest American resorts, this historic complex of impressive red brick buildings has immense colonnaded salons where music offered by a tuxedoed trio accompanies afternoon tea every day. At the health clubs and mineral baths you can soak, take saunas, or get a massage. Swim (indoors or out), play tennis, or golf on any of three wooded courses (two of which are championship), try skeet or rifle shooting, go riding, or hike along the well-marked trails on the 15,000 acres of Allegheny Mountain forests that belong to the resort, or go dining and dancing in dressed-up style. During winter months, there's downhill and cross-country skiing, as well as ice skating. This is a big hotel (521 rooms), but it's so well run that you won't notice the crowds even when the house is full. Information: *The Homestead,* Hot Springs, VA 24445 (phone: 540-839-1766; 800-838-1766 for reservations; 540-839-2970).

GREENBRIER, White Sulphur Springs, West Virginia Staying here will take you back to the Ginger Rogers–Fred Astaire era: You can't help but feel like dressing for dinner and going dancing in the *Old White Club* afterward—despite the fact that it's also difficult not to wear yourself out on the riding trails, hiking paths, tennis courts, and three 18-hole golf courses that cover the hotel's 6,500 acres. Everything about this place is elegant, from the endless string of parlors ornamented with Chinese vases and priceless screens, centuries-old oil paintings, and English antique furniture; to the menu with every conceivable fish, fowl, meat, salad, appetizer, and dessert; to the accommodations in the 650 comfortable bedrooms and "cottages," a short walk away from the hotel. A European-style spa features mineral baths, steamrooms, a sauna, therapeutic showers, and massage. For the history buff, there's the little known Eisenhower-era underground bunker, which was designed to house all members of Congress during a surprise nuclear attack. Information: *The Greenbrier,* White Sulphur Springs, WV 24986 (phone: 304-536-1110; 800-624-6070 for reservations; fax: 304-536-7854).

MIDWEST

GRAND, Mackinac Island, Michigan The fact that there are no cars on this island gives it a turn-of-the-century feel seldom found elsewhere in the US today. A rambling white structure with 320 rooms, set on 500 acres of lawns, gardens, and trees—adjoining a 2,000-acre state park that makes up nearly 85% of the island—and overlooking the Straits of Mackinac, the hostelry is fiercely old-fashioned, from the long pillared verandah to the horse-drawn surreys that meet guests at the ferry, the afternoon teas, the ornate staircase, and the 19th-century furnishings. By some accounts, this is the world's largest summer resort. There's a big heated pool, whirlpool, and sauna; cycling, horseback riding, golf on an 18-hole course, and tennis are major activities. Closed from November to mid-May. Information: *Grand Hotel,* Mackinac Island, MI 49757 (phone: 906-847-3331; 800-33-GRAND for reservations; fax: 906-847-3259).

WEST

WIGWAM, Litchfield Park, Arizona One of the top resorts in the country, this establishment offers 331 rooms in one- and two-story adobe casitas (some with fireplaces) surrounded by palm- and eucalyptus-shaded gardens. Golf is the main activity because of the two excellent Robert Trent Jones Sr. courses—the 7,200-yard *Gold Course,* cleverly filled with sand traps, and the much easier 6,107-yard *Blue Course,* par 70, which offers well-bunkered fairways and many water holes. A third course, designed by Robert Lawrence, plays 6,861 yards (par 72). There also are nine lighted tennis courts, plus ball machines, practice alleys, and a good program of clinics and private instruction. Other activities: horseback riding, steak broils, shuffleboard, lawn sports, swimming, and workouts at a full health club. Open year-round. Information: *The Wigwam,* PO Box 278, Litchfield Park, AZ 85340 (phone: 602-935-3811; 800-327-0396 for reservations; fax: 602-935-3737).

LOEWS VENTANA CANYON RESORT, Tucson, Arizona Guests approach the 93-acre resort via a winding road dotted with towering saguaro cacti (the state symbol) amid the chirping of more than 132 species of birds. With vertically textured masonry, emulating the ribbing of the saguaro, the expansive resort subtly emerges from the foothills of the Santa Catalina Mountains. At the entrance, there's a two-level lake formed by an 80-foot waterfall that rushes down from the Catalinas. Nearby sits a 300-year-old saguaro cactus. Everything blends with the desert theme—from the outdoor activities to the earth tones used in the rooms. There are miles of nature trails for hiking and biking to secluded picnic areas. There also are two outdoor pools with adjacent hot tubs; two 18-hole golf courses (see *Golf*); 10 lighted tennis courts; a croquet lawn; and a newly expanded health spa with exercise rooms, saunas, and weight training equipment. Each of the 398 guestrooms and suites has a mini-bar, a stocked refrigerator, a giant bathtub, two TV sets, three phones, and a terrace with a spectacular view. Information: *Loews Ventana Canyon Resort,* 7000 N. Resort Dr., Tucson, AZ 85715 (phone: 520-299-2020; 800-234-5117 for reservations; fax: 520-299-6832).

CARMEL VALLEY RANCH, Carmel, California This intimate (100 suites) resort hotel is just 6 miles from Carmel-by-the-Sea, home to major cultural and sporting events like the *Monterey Jazz Fesitval* and The *AT&T Celebrity Pro-Am Golf Tournament,* and numerous other local attractions. Suites feature cathedral ceilings, woodburning fireplaces, and wraparound decks. The *Oaks* restaurant serves local California specialties and has an outstanding wine list. Along with teeing off on a Pete Dye–designed 18-hole golf course, guests can play tennis on 12 courts (two are clay), or go horseback riding. There are jogging and hiking trails, along with nearby fishing and sailing. Information: *Carmel Valley Ranch,* One Old Ranch Rd., Carmel, CA 93923 (phone: 408-625-9500; 800-422-7635; fax: 408-624-2858).

RITZ-CARLTON, RANCHO MIRAGE, Palm Springs, California Located at the gateway to a 900-acre wildlife preserve, this may be the hotel group's most activity-filled resort. Besides utilizing the 10 lighted tennis courts, swimming pool, fitness center, and nearby golf, guests can indulge in croquet, nature walks, desert drives, horseback trail riding, cross-country skiing, or even hot-air ballooning. While dining outdoors, you may be joined by the occasional bighorn sheep. The 210 rooms and 21 suites are, as one would expect, decorated in deluxe style. Dining options include the Southwestern-style *Mirada* restaurant, along with the more formal *Dining Room*. There are monthly Sunday jazz concerts in the *Lobby Lounge*. Information: *Ritz-Carlton, Rancho Mirage,* 68-900 Frank Sinatra Dr., Palm Springs, CA 92270 (phone: 619-321-8282; 800-241-3333 for reservations; fax: 619-321-6928).

LODGE AT PEBBLE BEACH, Pebble Beach, California The California coast—"the finest meeting place of land and water in existence," according to one admirer—deserves no less than this magnificent 161-room hotel. The interior is only a part of the charm. The *Pebble Beach Golf Links* and *Spyglass Hill* golf courses are among the most famous in existence, and for good reason: They're also among the few tournament class courses open to the public (see *Golf*). And there are still other courses at Pebble Beach. If you don't like golf, you can go shopping in the Lodge arcade and in nearby Carmel, or sightseeing along the celebrated Seventeen Mile Drive, with its magnificent views of the rocky shore. Or ride horseback in the private 5,328-acre Del Monte Forest, swim, or play tennis at the nearby *Beach & Tennis Club.* Information: *The Lodge at Pebble Beach,* Seventeen Mile Dr., Pebble Beach, CA 93953 (phone: 408-624-3811; 800-654-9300 for reservations; fax: 408-644-07955).

MEADOWOOD, St. Helena, California Located 65 miles north of San Francisco, in the center of the Napa Valley, this secluded Relais & Châteaux resort has only 85 rooms and suites that are strategically scattered about its 256 acres. Guestrooms are divided among the *Croquet Lodge,* in the woods near the pool, or in accommodations by the tennis courts and the fairway. A recent addition are the more-secluded *Hillside Terrace Lodges.* There are two regulation English croquet courts (and a pro is on hand to teach the sport in private or group lessons), a nine-hole golf course, seven tennis courts, two pools, and a wine-tasting school. Other options include bicycling, horseback riding, glider rides, a spa, a fitness center, and an outdoor hot tub. The romantic *Restaurant at Meadowood* has a first-rate California wine list, and the *Grill* is perfect for casual lunches. The resort's proximity to the Napa Valley's wineries and restaurants will inspire any vacationing gourmand. *Meadowood* has recently opened a nearby "sister" property, the 21-room *Inn at Southbridge.* Guests can use *Meadowood*'s facilities for a daily fee. Information: *Meadowood Resort,* 900 Meadowood Lane, St. Helena, CA 94574 (phone: 707-963-3646; 800-458-8080 for reservations; fax: 707-963-3532); *Inn At Southbridge,* 1020 Main St. (phone: 707-967-9400, 800-520-6800).

FOUR SEASONS BILTMORE AT SANTA BARBARA, Santa Barbara, California Any of the hotel's 22 Montecito acres not taken up with the Spanish mission–style buildings that house the guestrooms are filled with gardens of eucalyptus, junipers, rare Australian Kentia palms, and oaks. The 234 rooms are luxurious—with oversize beds, oversize showerheads, and thick bath towels. Many of the rooms have fireplaces, private balconies, and vaulted ceilings. There's an Olympic-size pool across from the hotel, plus an additional one on the property, three lighted tennis courts, and a ¼-mile-long beach. The hotel boasts an extensive children's program. In the area, there's golf, fishing, horseback riding, wineries, and four fine restaurants. Prime season is summer, when daytime temperatures in the 80s are moderated by a constant ocean breeze. Information: *Four Seasons Biltmore,* 1260 Channel Dr., Santa Barbara, CA 93108 (phone: 805-969-2261; 800-332-3442 for reservations; fax: 805-969-5715).

THE RITZ-CARLTON, ASPEN, Aspen, Colorado Although skiing is the activity that springs to mind in this part of the country, Aspen is equally invigorating when the snow takes a vacation. This hotel combines the luxury of a fine hotel (elegant dining, marble baths, full concierge services) with the qualities of a top-flight outdoor-oriented resort property. Its 257 guestrooms and suites boast the usual luxurious amenities, while the *Terrace* restaurant features local specialties, along with health-conscious cuisine. There's a weightroom, outdoor heated pool, and basic "spa" services on the premises; nearby are major ski and golf destinations such as Buttermilk, Snowmass, and Aspen Highlands. The knowledgeable staff can easily arrange a variety of activities, including hot-air ballooning, hiking, and rafting. The resort is also within walking distance of Aspen's shopping and dining districts. Information: *The Ritz-Carlton, Aspen,* 315 East Dean Street, Aspen, CO 81611 (phone: 970-920-3300; 800-241-3333; fax: 970-925-8998).

BROADMOOR, Colorado Springs, Colorado When mining magnate Spencer Penrose and Charles Tutt built this magnificent hostelry in 1918, it was intended to be one of the world's most fashionable hotels, "permanent and perfect." It is. In the foothills of the Rocky Mountains and at the edge of a small manmade lake, it offers the appealing combination of grand-hotel luxury, a stunning natural setting, and a wide range of facilities that make it possible to do something different every day of your vacation without ever leaving the property. The three championship golf courses are the main draws: the *East Course* was designed by Donald Ross in 1918 and later redesigned by Robert Trent Jones; the *West Course* is also the work of Trent Jones; and the *South Course* was created by Ed Seay and Arnold Palmer. The resort's first-rate spa and sports center offers 13 tennis courts (including a stadium court), an indoor pool, an outdoor lap pool and Jacuzzi, a fitness center, and a complete range of health and beauty treatments. Other facilities include a second outdoor pool and Jacuzzi, riding stables, trap and skeet shooting grounds, a movie theater, numerous shops, a hair salon, a travel agent, a car rental desk, and extensive meeting and conference facilities. The nine restaurants offer a wide range of dining options, and there are six bars and lounges, some offering nightly entertainment. As for the venerable main building itself, it's everything you'd expect of a structure built with the assistance of hundreds of European craftsmen; the public rooms feature incredible handcrafted ornamentation and art objects from around the world. The 700 guest rooms are roomy and well equipped; many offer views of Cheyenne Mountain, which overlooks this self-contained vacation spot. Information: *The Broadmoor,* 1 Lake Ave., Colorado Springs, CO 80906 (phone: 719-634-7711; 800-634-7711 for reservations; fax: 719-577-5700).

MAUNA LANI BAY, Kohala Coast, Big Island of Hawaii, Hawaii Built on 3,200 acres atop a prehistoric lava flow where the early Hawaiians settled in approximately AD 750, this 341-room arrow-shaped hotel is one of Hawaii's most luxurious. Arriving guests are greeted with fresh orange juice and leis. The lobby resembles a rain forest, complete with palm trees, waterfalls, and saltwater lagoons adorned with colorful fish. The guestrooms are no less striking. The same goes for the property's restaurants, including the unique *Canoe House,* located on the beach near the private two-bedroom villas and featuring Pacific Rim specialties. For those for whom privacy is everything—and money is no object—ask about one of the five "bungalows" that offer two spectacular bedrooms, a huge living room, a private pool, all for only $2,500 to $3,500 a night. Some 27 acres of the property have been preserved as a historic park and can be explored on a number of walking trails. Fifteen acres of ancient spring-fed fishponds offer wonderful picnic grounds, a private swimming hole, and more quiet walking paths. Those of a more sociable bent may opt for swimming at the pool or beach, helicopter tours, tennis at the *Tennis Garden* or the *Racquet Club,* or golf on 36 holes where green fairways snake through black lava broken by coastal inlets (see *Golf*); though the course is not quite as fierce as it may first appear, the occasional cavorting of migrating whales not half a mile from the sixth tee can be distracting. An interesting children's program, *Camp Mauna Lani,* is run at various times each year. Information: *Mauna Lani Bay Hotel,* 68-1400 Mauna Lani Dr., Kohala Coast, HI 96743-9796 (phone: 808-885-6622; 800-356-6652 for reservations; fax: 808-885-6183).

THE ORCHID AT MAUNA LANI, Kohala Coast, Big Island of Hawaii, Hawaii With 541 attractive, oversize rooms, including 54 suites with marble baths, guests are afforded ocean-view lanais in distinctive lodgings. Facilities on the hotel's 32 acres include an 11-court tennis complex, a fitness center, two white sand beaches, and two 18-hole golf courses. Information: *The Orchid at Mauna Lani,* 1 N. Kaniku Dr., Kohala Coast, HI 96743 (phone: 808-885-2000; 800-241-3333 or 800-845-9905 for reservations; fax: 808-885-5778).

LODGE AT KOELE, Lanai, Hawaii This is Hawaii's first upscale, up-country resort hotel. Located adjacent to Lanai City at Koele, at the base of Lanaihale's mountainous heights, its setting is every bit as appealing as the palm tree–and–beach-lined Hawaiian surroundings. With each of its 102 rooms situated in garden surroundings, the *Lodge* provides a sophisticated version of a country inn. A massive living room at the center of the main floor—complete with two 50-foot fireplaces, high-beamed ceilings, and an impressive collection of Pacific art and artifacts—sets a decorative theme that recalls the island's ranching and plantation eras. There's easy access to an 18-hole, par 72 championship golf course (designed by Greg Norman and Ted Robinson) and to an older nine-hole layout, croquet, garden walks, lawn bowling, horseback riding, and an 18-hole putting course. All rooms have cable TV, but there's also a large projection set in the library. Shuttle service links the *Lodge* with Lanai City (1 mile away), the *Manele Bay* hotel at Hulopoe Beach (20 minutes away), and the airport. Information: *The Lodge at Koele,* PO Box 774, Lanai City, HI 96763 (phone: 808-565-7300; 800-321-4666 for reservations; fax: 808-565-4561).

FOUR SEASONS WAILEA, Maui, Hawaii At an average of 620 square feet each, the 380 guestrooms (including 91 suites) are among the largest conventional accommodations in Hawaii. More than 85% of the rooms boast ocean views, and every one has its own lanai, oversize closets, deluxe bathroom, and in-room VCR (with films available from the hotel's sizable video library). Other facilities include a huge, heated pool with a large fountain in the center and whirlpool baths at each end. Tennis courts, a putting green, and croquet also are available. Six golf courses are less than 20 minutes away. The exterior design is neo-Georgian Hawaiian; the interior design and decor are open, airy, and first-rate. The *Seasons* dining room is among the best eating places in all the islands. There also is an aerobic fitness center. The hotel offers a children's program, "Kids for All Seasons," which includes an activities center for children from five to 12 years old; there are also special activities for teens. Information: *Four Seasons Resort Wailea,* 3900 Wailea Alanui Dr., Maui, HI 96753 (phone: 808-874-8000; 800-334-6284; fax: 808-874-6449).

KAPALUA BAY, Kapalua, Maui, Hawaii Its name means "arms embracing the sea." With its fringe of pineapple fields bordered by neat rows of Cook pines, a view of Molokai and Lanai, and the landscapes distinguished by banyan trees and delicate yellow oleanders, this northwestern Maui resort hotel with 194 hotel rooms and 99 villa units is the centerpiece of a 23,000-acre property. And from the latticework of white pillars and bougainvillea-decked crosspieces out front to the grand, open-air, multilevel lobby full of hanging plants, it is as quietly luxurious as the landscape is beautiful. In addition to water sports, there are 20 tennis courts, three 18-hole golf courses that rank among the most distractingly scenic in existence, and a beach right on the doorstep. Exercise classes, wine tastings, afternoon tea, and inviting food and settings for lunch or dinner round things out. Information: *Kapalua Bay Hotel & Villas,* 1 Bay Dr., Kapalua, Maui, HI 96761 (phone: 808-669-5656; 800-367-8000 for reservations; fax: 808-669-4694).

SUNDANCE, Sundance, Utah Robert Redford's heavenly resort is snuggled in a canyon at the base of Mt. Timpanogos in the Wasatch range. The 71 cottages and six mountain homes blend into the 5,000 acres of wilderness that surround them, embodying harmony, peace, and a sense of aesthetics. The Native American decor, stone fireplaces, and handmade furnishings reflect rustic elegance and comfort. Although best known as a great ski resort (see *Downhill Skiing*), it's also popular with hikers, naturalists, anglers, and equestrians, as well as vacationers who just want to unwind in a truly unspoiled, organic American getaway. There are two restaurants—the elegant *Tree Room* and the more casual *Grill Room*—and a summer outdoor musical theater. The resort also houses the *Sundance Institute,* a center for promising filmmakers. Information: *Sundance,* RR3, PO Box A-1, Sundance, UT 84604 (phone: 801-225-4107; 800-892-1600 for reservations; fax: 801-226-1937).

Inn Sites: America's Special Havens

When standardization finally overtook the hotel industry, at least one great anxiety—where to stay—was removed from travel. Travelers could be assured of finding acceptable accommodations in even the most remote corners of the country. But a new worry arose: What happened to those special places, the inns and hostelries with special charm, with atmosphere, with a personal spirit and style and history all their own?

They still exist. The trend toward cookie-cutter construction simply increased the number of hotel and motel rooms; it didn't destroy those unique lodgings that still grace this country from Maine to California. They tend to become the secret pleasures of lucky patrons who would publish their credit card numbers before they would broadcast the name and location of their favorite hideaway. But being made of sterner stuff, we offer a listing of our treasured "finds." Some are traditional New England inns, perfect for a ski weekend or a trip through the woods when the foliage is at its most brilliant; some are luxurious havens; some are rugged Western lodges where the horses are spirited and the campfire stories tall.

EAST

GRISWOLD INN, Essex, Connecticut For true devotees of traditional New England fare, there is no better place than this inn with its 14 rooms and 12 suites. Built in 1776, the "Gris" is a favorite port of call for Connecticut River sailors, who may tie up just a few steps from the front door. Landlubbers are just as welcome, and all are quickly infused with the inn's friendly spirit. There's an outstanding collection of historic lithographs, steamboat relics, historic firearms, ships' name plaques, and a fine group of marine oils by Antonio Jacobsen. Guests enjoy unpretentious but outstanding New England fare, with an emphasis on beef and fresh seafood delivered daily. At the inn's famous Hunt Breakfast on Sunday, children six years and under are served free, ages seven through 12 at a reduced rate. Nightly entertainment ranges from sea chanteys to Dixieland, and throughout December "A 1776 Country Inn *Christmas*" gives guests a taste of an earlier era, with a special game menu, magicians and madrigal singers, and the staff outfitted in colonial costumes. Information: *Griswold Inn,* 36 Main St., Essex, CT 06426 (phone: 860-767-1776; fax: 860-767-0481). The Paul Brothers, innkeepers.

COPPER BEECH INN, Ivoryton, Connecticut The decor of this elegant, charming, and immaculate inn in a turn-of-the-century Victorian home looks more like your rich old aunt's country estate than a commercial enterprise. There are four airy rooms in the main house, and several of the bathrooms have huge, old-fashioned, claw-footed bathtubs; an additional nine rooms are in a restored carriage house, each with its own Jacuzzi, bathtub, and TV set; some have French doors leading out onto decks. A gallery displays fine antique Oriental porcelain, and the three dining rooms are full of fresh flowers, crystal, gleaming silver, and the incredible smells of rabbit, pâté, lobster bisque, bouillabaisse, and other culinary delights. Breakfasts are light, which is just as well because dinner is so good (no dinner served Mondays). Information: *Copper Beech Inn,* 46 Main St., Ivoryton, CT 06442 (phone: 860-767-0330). Eldon and Sally Senner, innkeepers.

MAYFLOWER INN, Washington, Connecticut After years of neglect, this 1894 inn (which began as a private boys' school) has been reborn as a charming, country-style haven. Nestled on 28 well-landscaped acres, the five buildings that comprise the property are decorated with 18th- and 19th-century art and antiques collected by the inn's owners during their travels throughout Europe and the US. It recently became a member of Relais & Châteaux group. Guests can enjoy afternoon tea in front of the fireplace in the cozy parlor, and the library offers a wide selection of books. The 17 rooms and eight suites feature four-poster beds with down comforters and linen sheets, fireplaces, and large marble baths with brass accents; and although there are modern amenities, such as TV sets and air conditioning, they don't spoil the old-fashioned atmosphere. The dining room has received great acclaim for its continental fare prepared with fresh local ingredients. You can work off excess calories at the inn's extensive fitness facilities, including a pool, a tennis court, and health club. Here, European elegance combines with attentive, friendly service to create a "home away from home" feeling. Information: *Mayflower Inn,* PO Box 1288, Washington, CT 06793 (phone: 860-868-9466; fax: 860-868-1497). Robert and Adriana Mnuchin, innkeepers.

THE INN AT NATIONAL HALL, Westport, Connecticut This 1873 riverfront building has been lovingly restored to a gleaming aerie of polished woods, glass, and architectural "surprises." Last year, it became a member of Relais & Châteaux group. Each of the 15 rooms and suites is furnished in lavish style with such features as canopy beds and whimsical stencil detailing. There are modern comforts, too, such as stocked refrigerators and VCRs. Most bathrooms feature separate showers and tubs. The elegant restaurant *Zanghi* has European-inspired cuisine. Information: *The Inn At National Hall,* Two Post Rd. W., Westport, CT 06880 (phone: 203-221-1351, 800-628-4255, fax: 203-221-0276). Nick Carter, innkeeper.

GREENVILLE INN, Greenville, Maine Built by a wealthy lumber baron in 1895, this rambling Victorian mansion sits on a hill overlooking Moosehead Lake, the Squaw Mountains, and the town of Greenville. Both inside and out, the focal point is a large leaded and stained glass window that depicts a spruce tree. The six rooms and one suite are furnished with intricately carved cherry mahogany and oak woodwork and fireplace mantels, gaslight fixtures, and embossed wallcoverings. Many of the elegantly appointed guestrooms have queen- or king-size beds; some have original baths with deep ceramic tubs and pull-chain toilets; one has a unique needle-spray marble shower. There are also six single-occupant cottages available during the summer. The menus vary daily; a "European continental" buffet breakfast featuring cereal, fruit, ham, and cheeses is included. Dinner may include fresh Maine seafood, veal, lamb, duck, and choice steaks. Since this area boasts the largest moose population in the state, guests are almost guaranteed to see at least one during their stay. Information: *Greenville Inn,* PO Box 1194, Greenville, ME 04441 (phone: 207-695-2206). Elfie, Michael, and Susie Schnetzer, innkeepers.

ISLAND INN, Monhegan Island, Maine The century-old frame structure on a picturesque bluff overlooking the tiny harbor between Monhegan and its satellite island of Manana is open summers only. Ferry service from June through September is provided by the *Balmy Days* from Boothbay Harbor and the *Laura B* from Port Clyde Harbor year-round (phone: 207-372-8848). The 40-room inn has a large, bright dining room where boiled lobster is the specialty, and fresh, simply prepared fish—striped bass, haddock, bluefish—fills the menu. An all-you-can-eat buffet on Sunday nights draws scores of Monhegan visitors who have spent the day exploring the awesome, 150-foot cliffs that face the pounding surf to the east. Although most of the island goes without electricity (kerosene lamps are de rigueur here), the inn has its own generator. More than 600 varieties of flowering plants—including the trailing yew, unique to the island—and up to 200 species of birds may be seen along the many woodland trails. Information: *Island Inn,* Monhegan Island, ME 04852 (phone: 207-596-0371; 813-763-5007 in winter). Bob and Mary Burton, innkeepers.

HANCOCK INN, Hancock, Massachusetts Now that the old wooden structure of this hostelry is like new again, owner-manager Chester Gorski has turned his full attention to culinary matters, earning quite a reputation in the process. Dinner offerings are elaborate and tasty. There's billi-bi (a cream of mussel soup) and medallions of fresh veal and jumbo shrimp in Dijon mustard sauce, duckling braised in port wine with grapes, and fresh lemon sole wrapped around a bay scallop and served in a shallot and muscadet wine sauce. Ellen Gorski has a way with salads, and her white wine vinaigrette dressing is a standout; her cheesecake, whipped-cream-filled chocolate mousse torte, and frozen white chocolate mousse rank among guests' favorites. The six guestrooms are modest but comfortable. Information: *Hancock Inn,* Rte. 43, Hancock, MA 01237 (phone: 413-738-5873). Chester and Ellen Gorski, innkeepers.

BLANTYRE, Lenox, Massachusetts Set on 85 scenic acres in the heart of the Berkshire Mountains, this former private mansion built at the turn of the century (a member of the Relais & Châteaux group) resembles a baronial Scottish estate. Sir Walter Scott would feel right at home entering the oak-paneled main hall. Some of the 23 guestrooms and five suites are furnished with period antiques and a four-poster bed, and some have large fireplaces. A complimentary continental breakfast is served in your room and a full breakfast also is available. Dinner is a formal affair (jacket and tie required), now finally worth the expense thanks to chef Michael Roller's inventive cuisine. Before heading off to nearby *Tanglewood* (summer home of the Boston Symphony), guests can use the pool, four tennis courts, two croquet lawns, a sauna, and a Jacuzzi. Open mid-May through early November. Information: *Blantyre,* PO Box 995, Lenox, MA 01240 (phone: 413-637-3556 in summer; 413-298-3806 in winter; fax: 413-637-4282 year-round). Roderick Anderson, managing director; Jack and Jane Fitzpatrick, owners.

WHEATLEIGH, Lenox, Massachusetts This expansive Italianate palazzo, built in 1893 by an American railroad man and banker, ranks as one of the finest inns in New England. Surrounded by formal gardens and lawns, the structure is all blond bricks and terra cotta and limestone detailing. There are loggias and arcades, stained glass windows, a magnificent swooping staircase, lovely fireplaces, and ornately carved ceilings, moldings, mantelpieces, and walls. Travelers with a fondness for good food have reason to rejoice at the inn's fine restaurant. The five front bedrooms upstairs are extra special and commensurately costly; all 17 recently refurbished guestrooms are air conditioned and nine have working fireplaces. There's also a pool and tennis court. Information: *Wheatleigh,* PO Box 824, Lenox, MA 01240 (phone: 413-637-0610; fax: 413-637-4507; 800-321-0610). Susan and Linfield Simon, innkeepers.

JARED COFFIN HOUSE, Nantucket, Massachusetts The gas lamps ornamenting the façade of this inn have been converted to electricity, but they still cast a flattering glow on the 1845 brickwork—and give you an inkling of the marvels inside: high ceilings; wonderfully ornate moldings; elegant chests and desks in Chippendale, Sheraton, and American Federal style; canopied beds, Oriental rugs; scrumptious seafood; and, most important, the extraordinary warmth and friendliness evinced by every staff member from the chambermaid to the desk clerk to the waitresses to the innkeepers themselves. With 60 rooms in four buildings, this is the island's best-known and most popular inn, so you'll need reservations well in advance. Information: *Jared Coffin House,* PO Box 1580, Nantucket, MA 02554-1580 (phone: 508-228-2400; 800-248-2405; fax: 508-228-8549). Philip Whitney Read, innkeeper.

OLD FARM INN, Rockport, Massachusetts When Antonio Balzarini, originally from northern Italy, rented the property that now surrounds this inn, he must have known about its long history and its several owners (the initials of one of them, one James Norwood, are chiseled in an old granite gate post together with a date, 1799); however, he could not have foreseen its future as one of the most prosperous and popular establishments in the area. He himself purchased the farm down the road, but one of the dozen children he raised later came back to the property, which by then was known as the Babson Farm, and began restoring the farmhouse, filling it with antiques and converting the erstwhile barn into guest accommodations. The 10 rooms are cozy, the atmosphere very peaceful and private, and the proprietors as helpful as can be, providing guests with sightseeing pointers and dining suggestions. For extended stays, a housekeeping cottage is also available. Closed from November through March. Information: *Old Farm Inn,* 291 Granite St., Rte. 127, Rockport, MA 01966 (phone: 508-546-3237; 800-233-6828). The Balzarini family, innkeepers.

RED LION INN, Stockbridge, Massachusetts This old rambling four-story clapboard structure occupies a prominent place on Main Street, which looks as if Norman Rockwell ought to have painted it—and he did. His home was just across the road, and the country's largest and finest collection of his paintings can be seen in the *Norman Rockwell Museum* on the edge of town. Still, there's more to Stockbridge than Rockwelliana—the *Berkshire Theater Festival, Tanglewood,* and the *Jacob's Pillow Dance Festival* at Lee, among other things—and the inn hums throughout the hot-weather months with overnight guests, diners, and other folk who have simply stopped in to ogle the high-ceilinged Victorian parlors and their gleaming embellishments, or to sit on the long front porch, where two rows of rocking chairs bob back and forth from early morning until well after dusk. The inn has 109 rooms and suites and is well worth seeing, even if you can't get a bed for the night (call well in advance for reservations). The inn's dining areas—the flower-laden courtyard; the cozy *Widow Bingham's Tavern,* with its candles and checkered tablecloths; and the main dining room—are among the most charming spots in a region full of appealing eateries. Live music fills the *Lion's Den Pub* nightly. Information: *Red Lion Inn,* Main St., Stockbridge, MA 01262 (phone: 413-298-5545; fax: 413-298-5130). Brooks Bradbury, innkeeper.

PUBLICK HOUSE, Sturbridge, Massachusetts This is not one of those cozy country inns where it's you and the innkeeper against the rest of the world. Instead, this hostelry—which opened as a fine restaurant in 1770—is most popular for its food; legions of hungry people pour in for fresh fish and lobster pie and the wonderful sticky buns served here. After sating themselves on the savory offerings, inn guests can simply waddle up the creaky, crooked stairs to one of the cozy rooms—or step outside to the *Country Motor Lodge* and collapse in one of the colonial-style rooms. The 100-room *Lodge* also offers an outdoor pool, tennis court, and jogging course. The 17-room *Publick House* holds *Yuletide* celebrations modeled on those of Merrie Olde England, with a Boar's Head Feast, a *Yule* Log Procession, and the telling of moving tales of the season; held thrice daily on the two Saturdays and Sundays preceding *Christmas,* the event now sells out well in advance. Another event, "Yankee Winter Weekends," keeps the inn filled during January and February. You're welcomed with syllabub (chablis with cream) and Joe Froggers (giant ginger cookies), then fed goodies nearly around the clock. Winter or summer, you can visit *Old Sturbridge Village* (see *Restored Towns and Reconstructed Villages*). Information: *Publick House,* PO Box 187, Sturbridge, MA 01566 (phone: 508-347-3313). David Lane, innkeeper. *Country Motor Lodge, Publick House,* PO Box 187, Sturbridge, MA 01566 (phone: 508-347-3313; fax: 508-347-1246). Ronald Merry, innkeeper.

LONGFELLOW'S WAYSIDE INN, Sudbury, Massachusetts In the mid-1950s, after standing some two-and-a-half centuries, the building in which Longfellow set his work "Tales of a Wayside Inn" (whose most celebrated poem begins, "Listen, my children, and you shall hear . . . ") was partially destroyed by fire. With help from the Ford Foundation it soon was restored, and many of the original rooms were turned into museum-like displays showing how the inn probably looked in the early 18th century; eight other rooms were added and fitted out with fine bathrooms and reproduction furnishings in Early American color schemes. The surrounding 106 acres insulate guests from the highway hubbub, and, because the 10-room inn's principal trade is its fine food, when the diners are gone you feel as though you're on your own private estate. Meals consist of sturdy New England fare, including fresh-baked breads, cakes, and pies made from flour ground by the gristmill on the premises. Also on the grounds is the schoolhouse that inspired "Mary Had a Little Lamb" and a classic New England chapel complete with white clapboards and a soaring steeple, where countless sweethearts have tied the knot. Information: *Wayside Inn,* Sudbury, MA 01776 (phone: 508-443-8846; fax: 508-443-2312). Robert H. Purrington, innkeeper.

HANCOCK INN, Hancock, New Hampshire Despite the inn's name, John Hancock never slept here; however, its 1789 opening makes it New Hampshire's oldest inn operating in the same building. In the Monadnock region, the "Currier and Ives corner of the Granite State," the inn is located in one of those quintessentially New England towns with a white-steepled church, a bandstand on the green, and a half dozen bright clapboard houses. It is full of small neat rooms with twin canopy beds, white ruffled curtains, and tiny-print wallpapers. There are 11 rooms (for some unknown reason they bear numbers up to 24); No. 16 happens to be more beautiful than nearly any other room in any other inn in the region. The murals that are its most striking feature, creations of an itinerant artist named Rufus Porter, depict scenes of the area in heavenly blues and greens. The only other remnant of Porter's work is found inside the closet of one of the rooms down the hall. Each room now has its own phone. The restaurant's offerings include roast duckling, New York sirloin steaks, prime ribs, Shaker cranberry pot roast, loin of pork, and venison. A cozy study with comfortable wing chairs also houses the bar. Information: *Hancock Inn,* Main St., Hancock, NH 03449 (phone: 603-525-3318; 800-525-1789; fax: 603-525-9301). Linda and Joe Johnston, innkeepers.

NEW LONDON INN, New London, New Hampshire New London is a delightful discovery—the perfect New England college town, not so much restored, one senses, as preserved. And in the middle of it sits this three-story clapboard inn furnished with antiques. Built in 1792, it has 30 rooms, all with private baths. There are wide porches, complete with rocking chairs, and fireplaces in the living rooms and dining room to ward off the New England chill. The dining room is beautifully decorated, and the food, considered the area's best by many, is extraordinary. Each meal is prepared to order using fresh, seasonal ingredients. All of the breads and desserts are made at the inn. The homemade egg bread is used for the French toast, which is one of the breakfast selections included in your room rate. There's plenty to keep you busy: golf, tennis, hiking, water sports on three lakes, and downhill and cross-country skiing. Information: *New London Inn,* PO Box 8, New London, NH 03257 (phone: 603-526-2791; fax: 603-526-2749). Jeff and Rose Follansbee, innkeepers.

MAINSTAY INN, Cape May, New Jersey Cape May, one of the country's oldest seaside resorts, is a treasure trove of Victorian architecture, and this inn—just a few blocks from the Atlantic—is one of its gems. From the inn's buff-colored picket fence to the green wicker chairs that sit on its verandah, to the 12-foot mirror in the entrance hall, this 1872 former gambling house has been lovingly restored, its nine rooms and three suites exquisitely furnished in pure Victorian style by a dedicated young couple. Your quarters might be one of the "front rooms," which means you'll enjoy 12-foot ceilings and a splendid view. Or you might choose a room in the "new wing," which was built in 1896 to accommodate the six housemaids. In addition, there's the World War I–era house across the street with four suites and more modern amenities like whirlpool tubs and VCRs. Information: *Mainstay Inn,* 635 Columbia Ave., Cape May, NJ 08204 (phone: 609-884-8690). Tom and Sue Carroll, innkeepers.

VIRGINIA, Cape May, New Jersey Those searching for accommodations just a notch above the typical local Victorian bed and breakfast establishment will delight in this 24-room hostelry. It occupies a carefully restored, 117-year-old landmark building that is close to the beach and shopping, and is staffed by young and talented people. Its Ebbitt dining room is a must, even for non-guests. Lunch and dinner menus are extensive and the dishes do the place proud, but it's the Sunday breakfasts—fresh-baked muffins, frittatas, apple cinnamon pancakes, and down-home porridge—that had us coming back for more. Closed January. Information: *Virginia Hotel,* PO Box 557, Cape May, NJ 08204 (phone: 609-884-5700; 800-732-4236; fax: 609-884-1236). Patrick Logue, innkeeper.

INN AT THE SHAKER MILL FARM, Canaan, New York The very simple but comfortable rooms in what was an early-19th-century mill reflect the austere heritage of the Shakers, an ascetic, communal sect that originated in England in the mid-18th century and lived in this area. (At Old Chatham, New York, there's an extraordinary museum collection on display, and just across the state line in Hancock, Massachusetts, is the popular *Shaker Village.*) Set beside a hillside waterfall, the 20-room inn is located 10 miles from *Tanglewood* and 12 miles from the Jiminy Peak ski area. The inn's setting in the foothills of the Berkshires is lovely and it attracts an interesting crowd. No smoking is permitted in the dining room. Information: *Inn at Shaker Mill,* Canaan, NY 12029 (phone: 518-794-9345; fax: 518-794-9344). Ingram Paperny, innkeeper.

OLD CHATHAM SHEEPHERDING COMPANY INN, Old Chatham, New York The eight-room inn boasts six luxury, antique-filled guestrooms in the main building and adjacent cottage, which feature soaking tubs, American antiques, and wonderful views of the surrounding greenery, and sheep! There is a fresh-water swimming pond and croquet on the property; mountain bikes are available for riding around the area. Guests can also enjoy nearby horse-back riding, fishing, tennis, and golf. The inn's restaurant receives high praise from locals and visitors alike. The area is also close to the *Shaker Museum,* and other Berkshire area attractions. Information: *Old Chatham Sheepherding Company Inn,* Shaker Museum Rd., Old Chatham, New York 12136 (phone: 518-794-9774; (fax: 518-794-9779). George Shattuck, innkeeper.

OLD DROVERS INN, Dover Plains, New York A member of the prestigious Relais & Châteaux group, this romantic inn at the foot of the Berkshires has been in business since 1750. Originally the *Clearwater Tavern,* it was a rest stop for New England cowboys driving cattle to market in New York City (they were called "drovers," thus the name). The five guestrooms feature private baths, antiques, satin comforters, and polished wood wainscoting; three of them have fireplaces. Five additional "cabins" feature fireplaces and entertainment centers. The *Federal Room* serves excellent game, poultry, and seafood. A cozy library is filled with plush chairs and a wide variety of books. It doesn't take much imagination to picture the dusty cattlemen, soldiers, and statesmen of the past swapping stories around a roaring fire in the parlor. Closed first three weeks in January. Information: *Old Drovers Inn,* Old

Rte. 22, Dover Plains, NY 12522 (phone: 914-832-9311; fax: 914-832-6356). Alice Pitcher and Kemper Peacock, innkeepers.

GURNEY'S INN, Montauk, Long Island, New York If you define an inn as a colonial hostelry on an elm-shaded New England street, this may not be the place for you. You won't find one antique lamp, patchwork quilt, spinning wheel, or stenciled wall. Instead, you'll lodge in cottages with fireplaces or in comfortable rooms with ocean-view balconies, set among trees and country gardens. Dress up for dinner and dance to live music in the lounge after you've supped or just hole up in your room, enjoy the sunset, and gaze at the mighty ocean. The spa center gives you a choice of two spa experiences; together they're good (and chic) enough to attract the rich and famous (see *Sybaritic Spas*). This 109-room inn is a personable place, and when you go out on the endless, surf-pounded beach, civilization feels as if it's thousands of miles away. The shore is delightful for jogging or sunbathing in summer, and even better for walks in the fall—if you don't mind the whip of the wind and the tingle of the cold spray. Information: *Gurney's Inn Resort & Spa,* Old Montauk Hwy., Montauk, NY 11954 (phone: 516-668-2345; fax: 516-668-3576). Nick Monte, owner. Angelo Monte, innkeeper.

THE POINT, Saranac Lake, New York This extraordinary Adirondack lodge was built in the 1930s by William Rockefeller. Some of the 11 rooms, with hardwood floors, fireplaces, and spectacular lake views, are now decorated in "rustic" Ralph Lauren fabrics. *The Boathouse,* separate from the main building (and closed in winter), has a king-size bed plus two daybeds, a large fireplace, and a wraparound porch. With the appointment of executive chef Sam Mahoney (formerly of three-Michelin-star kitchen of London's *Le Gavroche* restaurant), the fine French food now equals the setting and scenery. Guests can swim, canoe, and sail on the lake. Tennis and golf facilities are available nearby. Ice skating and cross-country and downhill skiing are popular in winter. A member of the prestigious Relais & Châteaux group, the inn is closed mid-March to mid-April. Information: *The Point,* HCR 1, PO Box 65, Saranac Lake, NY 12983 (phone: 518-891-5678; 800-255-3530; fax: 518-891-1152). David and Christie Garrett, owners. Jacques and Pam Brouchier, managers.

1740 HOUSE, Lumberville, Pennsylvania This Bucks County inn was built around an early 18th-century stable by two refugees from urban America. The secret of its charm is not that it's particularly quaint, because it isn't: The 24 rooms are air conditioned, the floors are carpeted wall to wall, the baths are tiled, and the furnishings are period reproductions, although each room has a terrace or balcony with a view of the Delaware River. Rather, the inn prospers because it is one of those well-managed places where everything works, and because it stands in the kind of countryside where everyone dreams of making a second—or permanent—home: a woodsy region that shelters antique houses and is run through by a mighty river and a placid canal where you can canoe or ice skate. Hearty breakfasts and dinners are available at the inn, but you'll have to go elsewhere for lunches, and BYOB. If you must do business, comfortable meeting rooms for small groups (up to 22) also are available. Information: *1740 House,* River Rd., Lumberville, PA 18933 (phone: 215-297-5661). Robert John Vris, owner and innkeeper.

1661 INN & HOTEL MANISSES, Block Island, Rhode Island The charm of this pretty, 38-room building (open year-round) comes mostly from the beauty of its site, perched above a village on the harbor on a meadow 12 miles off Point Judith, an hour's ferry ride away. But the atmosphere figures strongly as well—informal enough that before-dinner wine-and-nibbles hours seem to make perfect sense. And the special house drinks—the Mohegan Moro, a wild combination of sweet and dry vermouth, and the Island of the Little Gods Mind Boggler, white wine with cranberry juice—are something else again. An abundant breakfast buffet offers eggs, ham, corned beef hash, homegrown potatoes, fresh fish, muffins and breads, and fruit. Lunches and dinners are served at the owners' other property, the mansard-roofed, Victorian *Manisses* hotel, inside the *Garden Terrace* or on the breezy deck outside. That sister establishment (open year-round) boasts 17 rooms, all with private baths and four with Jacuzzis. The new *Nicholas Ball House* is a romantic three-room winter hideaway with fireplace and Jacuzzi. Information: *1661 Inn and Hotel Manisses,* PO Box 1, Block Island, RI 02807 (phone: 401-466-2421; 800-626-4773; fax: 401-466-2858). Joan and Justin Abrams, innkeepers.

OLD TAVERN, Grafton, Vermont Refurbished, along with some 50 other Grafton buildings, by the Windham Foundation as a part of one of the country's most extensive restoration projects, this inn is one of America's most beautiful. (Its guest list is more than impressive: Ralph Waldo Emerson, Rudyard Kipling, and Henry David Thoreau are only a few of the entries.) Everything shines: the wooden floorboards throughout the main building and the annex across the street, the furniture, the tabletops in the dining room, the silverware, the glasses, and the china. The 35 rooms and six guesthouses are furnished with the loveliest of antiques—lace tester beds, chintz-covered wing chairs, and Chippendale highboys. When you consider all that, and the delightful setting in picture-postcard Grafton, you may call the *Old Tavern* one of your favorite inns even though it's more elegant than cozy; so many people love the place, in fact, that you'll be hard put to get a room at the last minute. Reserve well in advance, and ask the desk clerk carefully about the rooms: No two are alike, and some are more wonderful than others. Cross-country ski on 18¾ miles of trails along Grafton Ponds and enjoy two tennis courts (plus a heated platform tennis court), a natural spring-fed pond, and mountain bikes. Information: *Old Tavern,* Grafton, VT 05146 (phone: 802-843-2231; 800-843-1801). Thomas List, innkeeper.

GOVERNOR'S INN, Ludlow, Vermont Built in 1890 by Vermont governor William Wallace Stickney, this inn retains the intimate feeling of a comfortable and elegant country house. Its nine delightful guestrooms (all with private baths) are furnished in the manner of the Victorian period with heirloom antiques, Oriental rugs, brass beds, and highly polished oak. House guests and the public enjoy full English breakfasts, complimentary afternoon tea, and elegant six-course candlelit dinners. Meals are prepared from fresh and preferably indigenous ingredients such as pumpkin, blueberries, New England seafood, and cranberries. The award-winning kitchen also prepares wonderful picnic hampers on just a few hours' notice. All of this, coupled with friendly and accommodating innkeepers, make a stay here a personal experience akin to what the governor's guests may have experienced. Guests also are invited to take cooking classes. Information: *Governor's Inn,* 86 Main St., Ludlow VT 05149 (phone: 802-228-8830; 800-GOVERNOR). Charlie and Deedy Marble, innkeepers.

INN AT SHELBURNE FARMS, Shelburne, Vermont Set on a bluff overlooking Lake Champlain is a 24-room country inn that refuses to conform to today's idea of an all-purpose resort: No TV sets or air conditioning will be found in the guestrooms; no pool or golf course will be found on the surrounding 1,400 acres (landscaped by Frederick Law Olmsted, of *Central Park* fame). But there are miles of meandering walks, a bright garden, sailing on the lake, croquet, a clay tennis court, and on summer evenings, concerts on the lawn by the *Vermont Symphony Orchestra* and the *Vermont Mozart Company.* Built in 1899 by railroad baron Dr. William Seward Webb and his wife, Lila Vanderbilt, this three-story summer "cottage" was converted into an inn 10 years ago. The ambience of a gilded age permeates the oak-paneled Main Hall; the North Wing houses the yellow Tea Room where afternoon tea is served. The formal dining room with its marble floor is where the chef creates contemporary American fare with emphasis on Vermont products. No two of the bedrooms (17 with private baths) are alike: The Overlook Room has the best view, but all the deluxe rooms overlook Lake Champlain and the Adirondacks; the Louis XVI Room is the most ornate. Open from mid-May through mid-October. Information: *Inn at Shelburne Farms,* Shelburne Farms, Shelburne, VT 05482 (phone: 802-985-8498; fax: 802-985-8123). Kevin O'Donnell, innkeeper.

SOUTH

CHALET SUZANNE, Lake Wales, Florida The style of many places can be suggested in a word or phrase—Victorian, Early American, motel modern. The best word to describe this 30-room inn is eclectic. Left to her own devices in the depths of the Depression, with two children to care for, a tiny young widow named Bertha Hinshaw decided to start serving meals to the public. Talent and energy made this central Florida endeavor a huge success over the years, and by the time she died, the inn had its own orange groves, a private airstrip, one of the finest and most original kitchens in the state, and a reputation for being one of the oddest-looking inns this side of paradise. The *Chalet Suzanne* (named after Mrs. Hinshaw's daughter) eventually came to reflect Mrs. Hinshaw's passion for collecting anything and everything and her penchant for combining elements of many architectural styles, everything from turrets to bare-wood decks. What could have been garish is simply exquisite. Information: *Chalet Suzanne,* 3800 Chalet Suzanne Dr., Lake Wales, FL 33853 (phone: 941-676-6011; 800-433-6011; fax: 941-676-1814). Carl and Vita Hinshaw, innkeepers.

SHAKER VILLAGE OF PLEASANT HILL, Harrodsburg, Kentucky The Shakers went west in the 19th century and eventually settled in Kentucky, at Auburn and near Harrodsburg at Pleasant Hill (see *Utopias and Religious Settlements*). As part of the nationwide revival of interest in the Shakers, particularly in their architecture and design, 33 surviving buildings at Pleasant Hill have been restored, 15 of them fitted out with 81 guestrooms with appropriate reproductions of Shaker furniture—chairs and trundle beds, sconces, mirrors, and, everywhere, pegs on which to hang things as the Shakers did. The nonprofit organization that administers Pleasant Hill has provided every room with its own tiled bath, air conditioning, and a TV set; but otherwise authenticity has been retained. A dining room offers big Kentucky-style breakfasts with grits, eggs, sausage, and biscuits; lunches and dinners are also belt-looseners. Information: *Shaker Village of Pleasant Hill,* 3501 Lexington Rd., Harrodsburg, KY 40330 (phone: 606-734-5411). Chris Brassfield, innkeeper.

HOUND EARS LODGE AND CLUB, Blowing Rock, North Carolina Skiing down south? Yep, up in the Blue Ridge Mountains the powder can be pretty good, both here at the lodge and nearby. Open all year, this friendly resort has a fine 18-hole golf course as well as swimming, tennis, and other outdoor activities—for children as well as adults. The 29-room lodge operates on the Modified American Plan, and meals are served to overnight guests and club members only. Information: *Hound Ears Lodge and Club,* PO Box 188, Blowing Rock, NC 28605 (phone: 704-963-4321; fax: 704-963-8030). Lillian Smith, manager.

NUWRAY INN, Burnsville, North Carolina If you get high on mountains and you're east of the Rockies, this is the place. Nearby are the *Pisgah National Forest,* one of the wildest woodlands in the East (don't miss Linville Gorge), and Mt. Mitchell, which at 6,684 feet is the highest peak east of the Mississippi. The 32-room inn, at about half that altitude, will keep your feelings on the up side with its good food (featuring fried chicken and country ham served family style) and friendly atmosphere—despite the fact that you're awakened every morning at 8 by the ringing of a bell and summoned to breakfast a half hour later by that same bell. The call to dinner Mondays through Saturdays (reservations suggested) is less jarring: the sound of a

Reginaphone, an old-fashioned music box that is just one of the many Wray family antiques scattered around the inn. Open year-round. Information: *NuWray Inn,* PO Box 156, Burnsville, NC 28714 (phone: 704-682-2329; 800-368-9729). Chris and Pam Strickland, innkeepers.

SNOWBIRD MOUNTAIN LODGE, Robbinsville, North Carolina As the name implies, this is a place for the birds—and the bird watchers. From the inn's 3,000-foot setting bordering the *Nantahala National Forest,* the views are breathtaking. Birders and hikers have their choice of trails, from the gentle to the rugged. The forest covers 450,000 acres, including a 50,000-acre Cherokee reservation with a restored village and exhibits and demonstrations for visitors. Moreover, there are some spectacular driving tours, most notably to the 30-mile-distant Fontana Dam and its 30-mile-long lake. The 22-room inn serves all meals but no liquor, as the county is dry (brownbagging is allowed, however). Closed from mid-November to mid-April. Information: *Snowbird Mountain Lodge,* 275 Santeetlah Rd., Robbinsville, NC 28771 (phone: 704-479-3433). The Lenz Family, innkeepers.

RHETT HOUSE INN, Beaufort, South Carolina The former home not of Rhett Butler but of Thomas Rhett and his wife, Caroline Barnwell, is now a warm and gracious inn, with fresh flowers in the rooms, hand-stitched quilts, and the aromas of baking bread and fresh coffee in the morning. Historic Beaufort and its waterfront are nearby, with tennis, golf, and swimming. The 10-room inn is convenient for day trips to Charleston, Hilton Head, and Savannah. Information: *Rhett House Inn,* 1009 Craven St., Beaufort, SC 29902 (phone: 803-524-9030; fax: 803-524-1310). Marianne and Steve Harrison, innkeepers.

EXCELSIOR HOUSE, Jefferson, Texas In the 19th century, this community 170 miles east of Dallas on the Louisiana border was a booming cotton-shipping center. But then the railroad passed it by, business suffered, and "progress" ceased. As a result, Jefferson came into the 1950s virtually unscarred by the wrecker's ball. The brick and timber, grillwork-embellished *Excelsior House,* a New Orleans–style building that was one of the town's most prominent, was bought in 1961 by the *Jesse Allen Wise Garden Club,* and its members set about restoring the hotel to the grandeur it knew back when it welcomed the wealthy and the famous (even a few presidents). The 13 rooms are now furnished with warm walnut, mahogany, and maple dressers, and sleigh beds, canopy beds, and Jenny Lind–style spool beds. In the public rooms, there are Oriental rugs and chandeliers of crystal and porcelain. Some of the ceilings are pressed tin, some are plaster. The windows are draped in the Victorian style. Breakfast, served on the sun porch, is the only meal (and you need a reservation)—but what a meal it is: ham and eggs, grits, and heaps of the fluffy, bite-size Orange Blossom muffins for which the hotel is famous. Also memorable are a visit to turn-of-the-century railroad financier Jay Gould's luxurious private railway car, restored by the garden club after it was found rotting away in a field, and a leisurely tour of the town's several other historical sights. Information: *Excelsior House,* 211 W. Austin St., Jefferson, TX 75657 (phone: 903-665-2513). Gloria Bennett, manager.

RED FOX INN, Middleburg, Virginia Washington surveyed the land; Civil War rebels used the building, constructed in 1728, as their headquarters; and later, because Middleburg lies in the heart of Virginia hunt country, the inn prospered as a social center for the horsey set. Lovingly restored by a local woman who wanted to preserve that tradition, the 24-room inn was decorated with Williamsburg wallpapers, antique furniture, and paintings that speak of horses as if there were no other subject. In the dining room, where many locals still enjoy their hunt breakfasts, the innkeeper serves classic Southern breakfasts and wonderful lunches and dinners that mix local specialties like crab cakes and peanut soup with steaks, chops, and continental offerings. Music and lighter fare are available in *Mosby's Tavern,* out back. There's plenty to watch—if not the *National Beagle Trials,* then plenty of races and shows. Information: *Red Fox Inn,* 2 E. Washington St., PO Box 385, Middleburg, VA 22117 (phone: 540-687-6301; 800-223-1728; fax: 540-687-3338). Turner Reuter Jr., innkeeper.

INN AT LITTLE WASHINGTON, Washington, Virginia This colonial gem (and member of the Relais & Châteaux group) boasts nine rooms and three suites, each individually designed with a separate sitting room and some with window seats. Some duplex rooms offer views of the courtyard and moat from balconies on both levels. Other rooms look out over the Virginia mountains. Dining is intimate, and the menu changes daily. Tennis, horseback riding, and golf facilities are available nearby. Information: *The Inn at Little Washington,* PO Box 300, Washington, VA 22747 (phone: 703-675-3800; fax: 703-675-3100). Patrick O'Connell and Reinhardt Lynch, innkeepers.

GENERAL LEWIS INN, Lewisburg, West Virginia What began as a private home on a hilltop back in 1834 and grew over the years into a magnificent mansion, with columns in the front and beautiful lawns all about, has been a classic inn in a lovely, old-fashioned town since 1929—much to the delight of traveling Americans enamored of the 25 antique-filled rooms and hearty country meals. Information: *General Lewis Inn,* 301 E. Washington St., Lewisburg, WV 24901 (phone: 304-645-2600; 800-628-4454). Mary Noel and Jim Morgan, innkeepers.

MIDWEST

COLUMBUS INN, Columbus, Indiana Columbus is in an industrially oriented region of Indiana, but the town itself is well known for distinctive architecture: Its public buildings were designed by such renowned masters as I. M. Pei and Robert Venturi. In the heart of downtown, this former *City Hall,* erected in 1895, has a formidable-looking brick exterior, but it is one of the area's most unusual and elegant inns, decorated with beautiful hand-carved oak woodwork, Victorian tin ceilings, brass chandeliers, and the original terra cotta floors. The 29 guestrooms and five suites have carved Victorian beds, large, overstuffed chairs, and tassled lamps; the Charles Sparrell Suite (named after the inn's architect) has high ceilings and 12-foot windows. A complimentary buffet breakfast is served in the dining room downstairs, and there is an 18-hole golf course nearby. Information: *Columbus Inn,* 445 Fifth St., Columbus, IN 47201 (phone and fax: 812-378-4289). Paul Staublin, innkeeper.

ABE MARTIN LODGE, Nashville, Indiana Like many other Indiana state park facilities, this rustic stone and log lodge at *Brown County State Park* is short on antiques and fancy cuisine. Guest quarters, both in the 84-room lodge and in the 76 surrounding cabins, tend toward the plain but comfortable, and food toward the home-style—fried chicken and biscuits are the order of almost every day. But few far more sumptuously furnished hostelries can boast of such a setting—in the midst of 15,000 acres of wooded hills. The scenery is gorgeous in the spring, when dogwoods and redbuds cover the landscape in a rosy blizzard, and in the autumn, when the hardwoods turn blazing scarlet, yellow, and all the colors in between. Nearby Nashville, a small town gone touristy with galleries and antiques shops, is quaintly and distinctively Hoosier. Information: *Abe Martin Lodge,* PO Box 547, Nashville, IN 47448 (phone: 812-988-4418; fax: 812-988-7334). Andy Rogers, manager.

NEW HARMONY INN, New Harmony, Indiana Associated with a restoration of two 19th-century communes that flourished here (see *Utopias and Religious Settlements*), this 90-room inn may be among the most beautiful hostelries in America. The lines are spare and clean, like those of a Shaker building, and the variety of woods used as furniture, floors, stairways, and moldings provides a visual treat, especially in combination with the natural colors and subtle, serene shades of blue and green used to decorate the inn. Amenities include a unique glass-roofed pool, tennis courts, and a health spa, sauna, and Jacuzzi. The *Bayou Grill* offers excellent meals, including breakfast. You also can get a terrific lunch or dinner at the *Red Geranium* (phone: 812-682-4431), a couple of minutes' walk away. Information: *New Harmony Inn,* PO Box 581, New Harmony, IN 47631 (phone: 812-682-4491; 800-782-8605; fax: 812-682-4491). Gary Gerard, manager.

NATIONAL HOUSE INN, Marshall, Michigan The one-man preservation drive launched over a half century ago by Harold Brooks, a former Marshall mayor, is finally bearing fruit, and hundreds of people are now actively involved in breathing new life into the town's beauty spots. Brooks bought several choice homes—the finest examples of 19th-century architecture in the area—and held them until he found buyers willing to restore and preserve them in their original style. Later, thanks to an enlightened zoning code and community cooperation, even more homes were saved, so that the town itself was designated a National Historic Landmark District in 1991. The 16-room *National House* (1835) is the oldest operating inn in Michigan. It started as a hotel, served as a stop on the Underground Railroad (evidenced by abandoned tunnels and a hidden cellar room), went through several transformations, and has in recent years been restored in the Victorian style of its distinguished neighbors. From the doorknobs to the bed linen, everything has been done with a reverence for the original. The highlight of the year is the town's annual *Historic Home Tour,* the first weekend after *Labor Day,* when thousands come here to inspect the restored houses. Information: *National House Inn,* 102 S. Parkview, Marshall, MI 49068 (phone: 616-781-7374; fax: 616-781-4510). Barbara Bradley, innkeeper.

ST. GEMME BEAUVAIS, Ste. Genevieve, Missouri A number of the late-18th- and early-19th-century buildings in this surprising town, which is less than an hour and a half from St. Louis and whose founding in 1732 makes it Missouri's first permanent settlement, have been restored—among them the 1790 *Green Tree Tavern,* the town's first inn; and *St. Gemme Beauvais,* its only operating country inn. As befits the town's French heritage, the hostelry's breakfasts and lunches (the only meals served—although dinner is provided on request) feature such continental concoctions as quiche, crêpes, and omelettes. In keeping with the age of the structure, the parlors and seven guestrooms (five of which are suites) are almost entirely done in Victorian antiques, including immense carved bedsteads, ornately framed mirrors, dressing tables with marble tops, and a handsome old dining table and chairs. Lace curtains, flowered wallpaper, and draperies in the Victorian manner complete the charming effect. Afternoon tea and wine are served daily. Open all year. Information: *St. Gemme Beauvais,* 78 N. Main, Ste. Genevieve, MO 63670 (phone: 573-883-5744; 800-818-5744). Mike and Connie Emerson, owners. Janet Joggerst, innkeeper.

GOLDEN LAMB INN, Lebanon, Ohio Midway between Cincinnati and Dayton in a town of 10,000, Ohio's oldest operating inn has, since its founding in 1803, provided lodging to 10 presidents, as well as DeWitt Clinton, Henry Clay, Mark Twain, and a very cross Charles Dickens (who visited when the *Golden Lamb* was a temperance hotel and complained that he couldn't get a drink). It is smack in the middle of town on a beautiful, wide, tree-lined street that also offers a number of antiques shops and quaint stores. The 18 antiques-furnished rooms, some with four-poster beds, are among the most pleasant in the area, and the inn makes a fine base for a couple of days' canoeing or fishing on the Little Miami River or visiting the nearby museums or *Kings Island* theme park. The food at the inn is good, and overnight guests get preferred seating. Try some of the Shaker items on the menu, such as sugar pie, beef stew, and chicken with cider sauce. Information: *Golden Lamb Inn,* 27 S. Broadway, Lebanon, OH 45036 (phone: 513-932-5065; fax: 513-932-5065, ext. 21). Paul Resetar, innkeeper.

WHITE GULL INN, Fish Creek, Wisconsin Fish Creek is just what it sounds like: Door County's gift to those who want a small, far-out-of-the-way place near water where things are fairly quiet and the eating's good, something like Montauk or Cape Cod. The inn's 14 rooms, remodeled in 1994, are filled with antiques; 13 have fireplaces, as do the five cottages; and the dining room has a brick floor, open beams, and a wood ceiling. The atmosphere is country warm. You can't beat the Fish Boil dinner, the best of the day's catch from Lake Michigan, with boiled potatoes, tasty coleslaw, and homemade cherry pie. Wash it down with a beer and walk to the harbor and then back to bed for a good night's sleep. Information: *White Gull Inn,* PO Box 160, Fish Creek, WI 54212 (phone: 414-868-3517; fax: 414-868-2367). Andrew and Jan Coulson, innkeepers.

WEST

ARIZONA INN, Tucson, Arizona When Isabella Greenway (a bridesmaid of Eleanor Roosevelt) opened this inn in 1930, it was primarily a desert oasis for the mighty, the mighty rich, and the mighty well known—Rockefellers, Windsors, movie stars, and such. Surrounded by Tucson, the inn is no longer alone in the desert and no longer beyond the reach of lesser souls, yet it endures in the luxurious manner and spirit in which it was conceived. The gardens will astonish you: Flourishing amid the arid desert environment are 14 acres of lawns and flowers scattered with bushes and trees and crisscrossed by lovely footpaths. Inside, the color scheme used in the 83 rooms and nine suites is a Mexican-American symphony of corals, beiges, grays, and reds that harmonize with the desert surroundings. A vivid blue heated pool is shaded on one side (to the delight of those who want to escape the glaring sun). You can play tennis on floodlit courts or, not far away, go horseback riding or enjoy a round of golf. A good portion of the staff has worked here for a couple of decades or more, and this longevity is reflected in their unfailingly professional service. The menu, with a Southwestern touch, attracts diners from all over the state. Information: *Arizona Inn,* 2200 E. Elm St., Tucson, AZ 85719 (phone: 520-325-1541; 800-933-1093 for reservations only; fax: 520-881-5830). Mrs. Greenway's granddaughter, Patty Doar, is the innkeeper.

TANQUE VERDE RANCH, Tucson, Arizona When is a dude ranch a country inn? When the dude ranch is situated, like this one, 12 miles outside Tucson on the edge of the 1.4-million-acre *Coronado National Forest* and the lovely 63,000-acre *Saguaro National Monument,* and is the last word in luxury and charm. The ranch, part of which used to be a stagecoach stop, has five tennis courts, indoor and outdoor pools and a therapy pool, saunas, exercise rooms, and other luxuries. Most of the 64 rooms (and the three units that accommodate groups of six) have fireplaces and patios, and all have phones (but no TV sets). Antiques are scattered throughout the inn. Some 220 species of birds, from the bridled titmouse to the bald eagle, have been identified in the area, and the inn is so popular with bird watchers that bird banding is a regular activity. Riding, however, is still the preferred sport, and you can do it to your heart's content (or your bottom's protest); you have your choice of some 100 horses, and supervised trail rides take place several times daily. And when all is said and done, there's the *Dog House* bar, a bunkhouse converted to a bottle club. Information: *Tanque Verde Ranch,* 14301 E. Speedway, Tucson, AZ 85748 (phone: 520-296-6275; 800-234-DUDE; fax: 520-721-9426). Bob Cote, innkeeper.

VENTANA INN, Big Sur, California Boasting a setting as stupendous as any in the country—an expanse of staggeringly beautiful meadows in the rugged Santa Lucia Mountains, which drop precipitously down to the rocky shoreline of the California coast 150 miles south of San Francisco—the 59-room *Ventana Inn* is quintessentially California modern. That means pale natural cedar, plenty of wicker, patchwork quilts, Franklin stoves and window seats, patios and private balconies, cathedral ceilings, pools long enough for healthful laps, Japanese hot baths, a fitness center, and a sauna. Sybarites can choose one of the rooms with a hot tub or indulge in a full menu of spa services. Hiking in the woods is literally right outside the door, and the beach is a healthy hike away. A complimentary continental breakfast featuring home-baked goods and fresh fruit is served on a tray in your room or buffet-style in the lobby in front of the fireplace. But perhaps best of all are the sweeping vistas that take in all that splendid natural scenery. The silence—broken only by classical music and the ticking of the clock in the breakfast rooms and, in the guest quarters, by the rush of the wind through the redwoods—is not bad, either. Information: *Ventana Inn,* Hwy. 1, Big Sur, CA 93920 (phone: 408-667-2331; 800-628-6500; fax: 408-667-2419). Lisa Mitchell, innkeeper.

SONOMA MISSION INN AND SPA, Boyes Hot Springs, California This 170-room wine country landmark just outside Sonoma, in operation since 1927, includes a world class spa (see *Sybaritic Spas*). The guests' quarters are inviting and contemporary (many feature fireplaces and balconies), the service is friendly, and the ambience is casual yet distinctly luxurious. The cheery, sunlit Grille restaurant is almost as famous as the celebrities the resort attracts: Kurt Russell and Goldie Hawn, Tom Selleck, Gregory Hines, and Tom Cruise among them. The culinary focus is an innovative "wine country" style of cooking. Information: *Sonoma Mission Inn and Spa,* PO Box 1447, Sonoma, CA 95476 (phone: 707-938-9000; for reservations, 800-862-4945 in California; 800-358-9022 elsewhere in the US; fax: 707-938-4250). Jack Burkam, general manager.

STONEPINE, Carmel Valley, California Simplicity is the key to the beauty of this luxurious place, located on 330 secluded acres. The French country house, Château Noël, has eight rooms with Jacuzzis and fresh flowers replenished daily, and the Paddock House has four rooms in a quiet, intimate environment. Briar Rose Cottage, the latest addition, has two rooms and overlooks a beautiful rose garden. The charming little cottage, with fireplace and full kitchen, makes for a private, secluded retreat from the world. There is a pool, a tennis court, and a full equestrian center where resident trainers give lessons in English and Western riding, as well as carriage driving. Information: *Stonepine,* 150 E. Carmel Valley Road, Carmel Valley, CA 93924 (phone: 408-659-2245; fax: 408-659-5160). Daniel Barduzzi, managing director.

ST. ORRES, Gualala, California A renaissance of interest in fine workmanship quietly has been taking place in America. For example, consider this eight-room inn on the northern California coast, a Russian palace built of redwood and salvaged materials around a tumbledown old guesthouse by a couple of carpenters with a dream, then named for the family that homesteaded the land. The interior is an exercise in woodworking virtuosity. Redwood paneling on the bedroom walls is meticulously tongue-and-grooved and laid in intriguing patterns; equally interesting are the quilted comforters hand-stitched by a local craftswoman. And the three-story dining room—walled partially in redwood-framed stained glass and topped by a copper onion dome—may be more arresting than any other restaurant in the country. In such a setting, you expect (and get) original meals; some people drive all the way from San Francisco for co-owner/chef Rosemary Campiformio's wonderful variations on continental classics. The "chocolate decadence" dessert may make a chocoholic of you even if you don't have a sweet tooth. There is also a spa next to the 11 creekside cottages. The peaceful setting among the beaches, coves, and redwoods is just icing on the cake. Information: *St. Orres,* PO Box 523, Gualala, CA 95445 (phone: 707-884-3303). Eric Black, Ted Black, Rosemary Campiformio, owners.

HERITAGE HOUSE, Little River, California Because so many early California settlers were homesick when they first arrived here from New England, they built their houses in East Coast styles; as a result, they left this part of the West liberally sprinkled with New Hampshire cottages and Down East farmhouses like the main building of this inn on California's northern coast (which, incidentally, gangster Baby Face Nelson once used as a hideout). Over the years, however, the original structure has been expanded many times over. Most of the 68 rooms are not in the farmhouse but in cottages of various sizes surrounding it. Each set of quarters is different. Some of the old ones, originally sited elsewhere in the coast region, were knocked down, transported to Little River, reassembled with varying fidelity to the originals, and then luxuriously furnished; others were built from salvaged lumber. All rooms have private baths; many have fireplaces or potbellied stoves; and—most important of all—most have ocean views, which is why you came here. As for the kitchen, it eschews the continental in favor of the best American cooking—the dinner menu changes daily, and the inn takes pride in the fact that mostly local ingredients are used. Breakfast and dinner are included. Information: *Heritage House,* 5200 N. Highway 1, Little River, CA 95456 (phone: 707-937-5885; 800-235-5885; fax: 707-937-0318). Gay Jones, innkeeper.

UNION HOTEL AND VICTORIAN MANSION, Los Alamos, California This old property, originally built in 1880 and rebuilt after a fire in 1915 to re-create the façade of the first *Union* hotel, is filled with antiques. Here are 19th-century gaslights from Mississippi and hand-carved chairs from Alabama, antique chandeliers that once graced an actor's home, a lamp used in the film *Gone With the Wind*, a 150-year-old bar made of African mahogany, and an ivory-inlaid Brunswick pool table. The 13 guestrooms boast such treasures as a mahogany armoire that conceals a Murphy bed; a brass and iron bedstead inset with cloisonné work; and countless antique four-posters, quilts, and crocheted bedspreads. After all this Victorian clutter, the spacious dining room featuring unpretentious home cooking and the rough-paneled Western bar are a welcome change. The inn and restaurant are now open seven days a week. A hundred feet west of the hotel is the *Mansion,* a three-story Victorian structure (1864) that was moved to the site, gutted, and rebuilt into six sybaritic fantasy suites that are available year-round. In the Fifties Room, guests can sleep in a 1956 Cadillac and eat at a table made from the Caddy's trunk or soak in a hot tub while watching a James Dean movie on a big screen. You also can choose from an Egyptian room, a Parisian artist's garret, a pirate ship, a Roman emperor's digs, and a Gypsy wagon. There's a privet-hedge maze between the hotel and the *Mansion.* Information: *Union Hotel and Victorian Mansion,* 362 Bell St., PO Box 616, Los Alamos, CA 93440 (phone: 805-344-2744; fax: 805-344-3125). Bill Bubbel, innkeeper.

MacCALLUM HOUSE INN, Mendocino, California East is East and West is West, but they meet here, three hours north of San Francisco. Mendocino—Nantucket West to many—is another example of how the early California settlers brought New England to the coast, and this inn is one of the prettier expressions of the Easterners' homesickness. Built in 1882 by lumber magnate William H. Kelley as a wedding present for his daughter Daisy and her husband, Alexander MacCallum, this three-story Victorian mansion, trimmed with jigsaw-cut woodwork and fronted by a wonderful expanse of windows, has almost all of the original furnishings; you can browse through the library (with some handsome leatherbound books and a good many romantic novels) and admire the Tiffany lamps, Persian carpets, and carved footstools that belonged to the MacCallums themselves. Some of the 20 guestrooms are in the main building (some have shared baths), but most are in the rebuilt old carriage house, the barn, and the greenhouse. The elegant continental dinners devised by Rob Ferrero have become a tradition. A short walk from town are the headlands at *Russian Gulch State Park* that can be described by only one word—spectacular. Information: *MacCallum House Inn,* 45020 Albion St. (PO Box 206), Mendocino, CA 95460 (phone: 707-937-0289). Melanie and Joe Reding, innkeepers.

SAN YSIDRO RANCH, Montecito, California Originally owned by the Franciscan Missions, this 540-acre resort near Santa Barbara, which opened in 1893, enjoyed a long season as the choice vacation spot of the rich and famous: Here, Laurence Olivier married Vivien Leigh; John F. Kennedy honeymooned with Jackie; and John Galsworthy, Aldous Huxley, Sinclair Lewis, Winston Churchill, Somerset Maugham, Bing Crosby, and Jack Benny stayed. Ronald Colman owned the place from the mid-1930s until his death in 1958. But during the 1960s, the inn started to fall apart; it was well down the road to total ruin when Jim Lavenson, once president of New York's famed *Plaza* hotel, put up the money to clean up, fix up, and paint up. Today, the two tennis courts, stables, restaurant, and pool are as spiffy as they were when Galsworthy revised his *Forsyte Saga* here (if not more so: 12 of the 42 guest cottages have their own Jacuzzis). You can hole up in front of your fireplace, order room service, and never see the light of day, mix with fellow guests in the hacienda and dining room, or hike along trails in the area; there are nearby golf facilities as well. As for the food, among those who drop in to say "Hi!" to the chef is none other than Julia Child. Special meals grace the tables on holidays. The ranch is one of only 21 American hostelries to be made a member of the prestigious Relais & Châteaux group. Information: *San Ysidro Ranch,* 900 San Ysidro La., Montecito, CA 93108 (phone: 805-969-5046; 800-368-6788; fax: 805-565-1995). Janis Clopoff, general manager.

AUBERGE DU SOLEIL, Rutherford, California When this highly acclaimed restaurant in the Napa Valley evolved into an inn in 1985, it was quickly accepted as a member of Relais & Châteaux, with valid reasons. The 48 charming and romantic Mediterranean-style rooms within 11 villas, Olympic-size pool, three tennis courts, exercise room, Jacuzzi, and beauty salon offer the best in amenities and personal service. The grounds are beautifully manicured and feature flower gardens galore. And then there's the restaurant, still the epitome of gracious, first-rate dining under the direction of chef Andrew Sutton. The menu changes often, and it always features tasty, elegantly presented dishes such as pan-seared foie gras and lobster medallions, smoked American river sturgeon, rack of Sonoma lamb with eggplant pesto lasagna, and espresso–chocolate chip ice cream sandwiches with Grand Marnier sauce. Room service is available 24 hours for those who don't want to make the journey to the dining room. Information: *Auberge du Soleil,* 180 Rutherford Hill Rd., Rutherford, CA 94573 (phone: 707-963-1211; fax: 707-963-8764). George Goeggel, general manager.

WINE COUNTRY INN, St. Helena, California Here in Napa Valley, some 70 miles from San Francisco, is a rarity: a recently constructed, built-from-scratch, old-fashioned country inn. Ned and Marge Smith spent years dreaming, talking, sketching, and planning; they traveled to classic inn country, lived there as guests, and picked the brains of innkeepers. And when they were ready a few years ago, they built their own, a marriage of the old and new made in inn heaven. Each of the 24 rooms is different; most have fireplaces, all have character. There's also a pool and Jacuzzi. Breakfast is the only meal, and it's served in a large, attractive common room. There are many fine restaurants in the area; the menus for most of them are available for your perusal. Information: *Wine Country Inn,* 1152 Lodi La., St. Helena, CA 94574 (phone: 707-963-7077; fax: 707-963-9018). Jim Smith and Diane Horkheimer, innkeepers.

EL ENCANTO HOTEL AND GARDEN VILLAS, Santa Barbara, California Tucked away in the hills above Santa Barbara, this 1915 hostelry has been completely restored to its original state, though the cottages have modern conveniences. Most of the guest quarters have an ocean view and a fireplace; on the grounds are a heated pool, a tennis court, a library, a lounge, and 10 acres of lush gardens. Each of the 84 cottages and villas is surrounded by a themed garden. It has been said that the hotel's terrace has been the site of more marriage proposals than anywhere else in Santa Barbara. The menu, which changes daily, is famous for its bouillabaisse and the use of local products such as miniature Ojai snails, spiny lobster and shrimp, and tomatoes and raspberries from Carpinteria. Information: *El Encanto Hotel and Garden Villas,* 1900 Lasuen Rd., Santa Barbara, CA 93103 (phone: 805-687-5000; fax: 805-687-3903). Thomas Narozonick, general manager.

SONOMA, Sonoma, California This old wood and adobe structure, which started out in the 1870s as a dry goods store and meeting hall, was carefully restored in 1976 by the present owners and now has a delightful Gay Nineties ambience. All of the 17 rooms are furnished in turn-of-the-century European and American antiques. In the morning, when you go downstairs for continental breakfast in the inn's charming lobby, the management will help you plan a tour of the surrounding wine country and such nearby points of interest as the *Jack London State Historic Park* at Glen Ellen. There you can see the ruins of London's own *Wolf House* as well as the home of his widow, which is filled with London memorabilia. They also can help you arrange horseback or hot-air balloon rides, picnics, and spa appointments. Information: *Sonoma Hotel,* 110 W. Spain St., Sonoma, CA 95476 (phone: 707-996-2996; fax: 707-996-7014). Dorene and John Musilli, innkeepers.

SUTTER CREEK INN, Sutter Creek, California One of the oldest country inns in the West, this green-shuttered bit of New England in California was built in 1859 by a wealthy merchant for his Eastern bride. It came into the possession of Jane Way, a palm reader and graphologist, in 1966, and she turned it into an inn, which today has 18 rooms. She installed canopy beds and beds that swing, ever so gently, by chains from the ceiling. (If you can't get used to the motion, you can stabilize your bed.) Some of the bathtubs were sunk into the floors, fireplaces were installed, and outbuildings were converted to guestrooms, with hidden patios and gardens scattered about. Chintz by the yard was swathed around squashy sofas, draped over beds, and hung at the windows. There are plenty of antiques, and the place feels comfortable, reflecting the personality of the innkeeper herself. Jane doesn't serve lunch or dinner, but she does offer her guests the chance to congregate over a country breakfast. When the conversation lags, Jane might be persuaded to tell you how she came to terms with the ghost she encountered when she first arrived at the inn, or about her father, who is known locally for having brought France's colombard grape to California. Or she might tell you the sad tale of John Sutter, who had built up one of the state's biggest ranches when a carpenter discovered gold in one of his streams in 1848 and set off a gold rush that had prospectors killing his cattle, destroying his land, and ruining his hopes for a comfortable old age. Only the memory remains: *Sutter Creek* today is beautifully kept, an antiquer's delight. Information: *Sutter Creek Inn,* 75 Main St., PO Box 385, Sutter Creek, CA 95685 (phone: 209-267-5606). Jane Way, innkeeper.

AHWAHNEE, Yosemite National Park, California Built in 1927 in a deep, wide valley guarded by granite mountains, ostensibly to accommodate the growing number of visitors arriving in the park by automobile, this marvelous establishment is rustic but luxurious, with slate floors, beamed ceilings, a cavernous lobby, and immense windows in even the smallest sitting rooms to give you views into the park. The *Ahwahnee* is the kind of place where dressing for dinner is the order of the day, yet the inn harmonizes with the surroundings so well that even Frank Lloyd Wright admired it. Meals in the vast and imposing dining room, especially notable for its towering picture windows and heavily beamed ceiling, are highlighted by salmon and prime ribs. Like the park, the hotel, with 99 rooms and 24 cottages, is open all year. But you'd be hard-pressed to say which season is best for a visit. In summer, there's hiking all through the Sierras, and you can sign up for rock climbing schools or special programs dealing with high-altitude ecology. In winter, the favored pastimes include downhill and cross-country skiing, snowshoeing to some of the frozen waterfalls, or races and winter games sponsored by the park concessionaire. At *Christmastime,* usually the high point of the *Ahwahnee*'s season, the hotel hosts the annual Bracebridge Dinner, wherein a section from Washington Irving's *Sketch Book* is reenacted in song and drama, accompanied by a fabulous seven-course dinner that includes a flaming plum pudding and a peacock pie. The pageantry is gorgeous, so tickets (a limited number) are hard to come by. Currently, they're sold by lottery from mid-December through mid-January, with a drawing in February; the procedure changes occasionally, however, so write or call in advance for particulars. (Tickets to *New Year*'s festivities are also sold by lottery.) Information: *Yosemite Reservations,* 5410 E. Home Ave., Fresno, CA 93727 (phone: 209-372-1407; 209-252-4848 for reservations; fax: 209-372-1463). Debbie Price, manager.

MAISON FLEURIE, Yountville, California Now under new management, this inn was built in 1873 and probably used as a bordello and a rumrunners' headquarters at various times during its checkered past. The small, stylish, stone-walled wine country establishment is fitted out with marble-topped tables, brass or walnut beds covered with crocheted lace bedspreads, and other French antiques; about a third of the 13 rooms have fireplaces, and all have private baths. The breakfasts of French toast (with a special port wine syrup) or various egg dishes are excellent. The Jacuzzi and large swimming pool complete the experience. Select a bottle from the extensive wine cellar (14,000 bottles, including over 200 California selections). Information: *Maison Fleurie,* 6529 Yount St., Yountville, CA 94599 (phone: 707-944-2056; 800-788-0369). The Post Family, owners and innkeepers.

LODGE AT CORDILLERA, Edwards, Colorado This European-inspired, auberge-style resort in the Rockies strives to harmonize with its surroundings. Designed by Belgian architect Leon Lambotte, the resort/residential community contains buildings of native stone, stucco, and forged iron. Fifteen of the 28 rooms in the lodge have stone fireplaces and spectacular views of the New York Range. French chef Fabrice Beaudoin brings his expertise to the lodge's *Picasso* restaurant, whose menu features wild game, seafood, and local produce; there's a spa menu as well. Recreational facilities include a spa and a health club, 15 miles of cross-country ski trails, and trout fishing on a private 3-mile stretch of Eagle River, while downhill skiing at Vail and Beaver Creek is only 10 minutes away. Information: *Lodge at Cordillera,* PO Box 1110, Edwards, CO 81632 (phone: 303-926-2200; 800-548-2721; fax: 303-926-2486). Cary Brent, general manager.

HARRISON HOUSE INN, Guthrie, Oklahoma Guthrie is a museum of a town, filled with Victorian architectural gems. The finest example is this 30-room inn, one of the largest of its kind listed on the *National Register of Historic Places.* Built in 1893, it sits in the heart of the historic district. The guestrooms, many of which have sitting rooms and views of the charming town, are decorated with turn-of-the-century antiques, but all have modern conveniences and private baths. Each room is named after someone who was part of Guthrie's colorful history: Tom Mix, Carrie Nation, Will Rogers, Lon Chaney, and O. Henry, to name just a few. Information: *Harrison House Inn,* 124 W. Harrison, Guthrie, OK 73044 (phone: 405-282-1000; 800-375-1001). Helen Machtolff, innkeeper.

SALISHAN LODGE, Gleneden Beach, Oregon At this unusual modern resort on the Oregon coast about 90 miles west of Portland, everything harmonizes with the spectacular landscape of lagoons, woods, beach, and ocean. Every bedroom, lounge, and dining room testifies to the complex's tasteful design, architectural and environmental integrity. The creation of Oregon manufacturer John D. Gray, *Salishan* proves that reverence for the environment can also be good business. The 205 rooms and three suites—all with fireplaces, big bathrooms, and oversize windows that frame forest or bay and ocean views—are in 15 villas connected by bridges and covered walkways.

The dining room (dinner only) also is exceptionally handsome, and the kitchen is noted for its way with seafood, particularly salmon. The wine list is so extensive that it has an index, offering everything from an unpretentious beaujolais to a Lafite-Rothschild that costs more than a whole weekend's stay at some very nice places. The wine cellar is available for tours, tastings, and even catered dinner parties. The resort has its own art gallery and publishes a botanical guide to the flora on the grounds and in the area. And every guest is assigned his or her own parking space (very handy for the Cadillac-Mercedes-BMW crowd that gravitates here). To round things out, there is an indoor swimming pool, therapy pool, health club facilities, an 18-hole putting course, and tennis courts (both indoors and outdoors). Bird and whale watching, deep-sea fishing, collecting driftwood, and studying the trees and the wildflowers on the nature trails can keep you plenty busy. Information: *Salishan Lodge,* PO Box 118, Gleneden Beach, OR 97388 (phone: 541-764-2371; 800-452-2300; fax: 541-764-3681). Pierre Alarco, general manager.

COLUMBIA GORGE, Hood River, Oregon The Columbia River Gorge, the chasm that separates Oregon and Washington, offers heartstopping vistas, hiking, windsurfing, fishing, skiing at Mt. Hood, winery hopping, viewing the full-scale replica of *Stonehenge* near the curious *Maryhill Museum,* and rafting on the Salmon and Deschutes Rivers (see *Touring America's Waterways*). And this hotel, sitting above a cliff and waterfall 200 feet above the gorge, is a good jumping-off place for all of these activities. Built in 1921, it has been restored with great care. All of the 41 rooms have breathtaking views; however, ask for one that looks out on the gorge itself. The dining room has a menu featuring imaginative uses for local products, wines from the Northwest, and a great view of the gorge. The "World Famous Farm Breakfast," included in the rate, has proved to be so popular the hotel has trademarked the name; the bounteous feast includes fruit, apple fritters, oatmeal, eggs, bacon, and trout, with various breads and muffins on the side. Information: *Columbia Gorge Hotel,* 4000 Westcliff Dr., Hood River, OR 97031 (phone: 541-386-5566; 800-345-1921 from elsewhere in the US; fax: 541-387-5414). Allen Guiberson, manager.

SALISH LODGE, Snoqualmie, Washington Overlooking the 268-foot Snoqualmie Falls, this modern, elegantly appointed lodge about 35 minutes from Seattle is managed by the same group that runs *Salishan Lodge* (see above). Its 87 rooms and four suites have fireplaces, huge bathrooms with whirlpool tubs, and luxurious goosedown bedding. The furnishings in the lodge were designed to accent the country atmosphere complemented by original Northwest art and Native American crafts. Full room service is available, as are a library stocked with books and games, a fitness center, a rooftop hot tub, and a recently opened spa center. There's volleyball, badminton, pickleball (a combination of tennis and Ping-Pong), and mountain biking. The area offers great skiing at Snoqualmie Pass, five golf courses, and wineries worth exploring, but the real draw is for hikers. There's a wonderful trail that starts at the lodge and leads to the top of the falls, as well as a satisfying four- to six-hour hike (round trip) to the summit of Mt. Si. The dining room's menu features local seasonal dishes and an extensive wine list that includes many local vintages. Information: *Salish Lodge,* PO Box 1109, Snoqualmie, WA 98065 (phone: 206-888-2556; 800-826-6124; fax: 206-888-2533). Loy Helmly, general manager.

Visitable Vineyards

Whether you're in search of the perfect cabernet or the perfect vacation, you'll find it in American wine country. A dozen years ago, you might have flown to Europe. Today US wines are grabbing gold medals in blind tastings against the finest French bordeaux, burgundies, and many others, and winery touring is an entrenched American sport.

America's wine capital is the dynamic Napa–Sonoma area in northern California, with more than 150 wineries open to the public within a one-and-a-half-hour drive from San Francisco. The past decade or so has witnessed a burgeoning wine industry in southern California as well, particularly in Santa Barbara County. In the Pacific Northwest, particularly Oregon, you can taste fine wines in spectacular surroundings. New York State has several beautiful wine routes, some right near New York City.

Outside the "big three" grape-growing regions, wineries drop off sharply in number and scale, but there are still plenty to see in other parts of the US. The rolling hills of Virginia's Albemarle wine country, where Jefferson planted European vines at *Monticello,* are within easy driving distance of Washington, DC. In Pennsylvania, you can taste and tour near the place where Washington crossed the Delaware. The Texas hill country now invites visitors to taste both premium reds and whites. There's a flourishing wine route on the shores of Lake Erie. In more than 25 states, visitors can watch vintners make wines from the acclaimed European varietals and the sturdier French-American hybrids, as well as from the traditional native American grapes and local fruits and berries.

What makes wine touring the ideal travel diversion is the vine's own finicky nature. Grapes thrive in protected valleys and on gentle hillsides that are warmed by long hours of sunshine and cooled by the mists from rivers, lakes, and coastlines—dream settings for day-trippers and vacationers as well as serious oenophiles.

Furthermore, wine makers—from the giant conglomerate to the lone vintner in a four-car garage—are anxious to showcase their products. At small wineries, you'll probably be taken through by the owner, who'll taste with you and share production secrets down to the last barrel stave. These visits require planning, since appointments usually must be made in advance. For more casual visits, try larger wineries with tasting rooms open to drop-ins (a souvenir-shop atmosphere often comes with the territory here).

They're apt to be better organized for touring the vineyards, the crushing pads, and the fermentation rooms, with their giant steel tanks, endless rows of aging barrels, and clattering bottling lines.

Winery tours are generally complimentary, but there is frequently a charge for wine tastings. Some wineries pour grape juice for children and for whoever is driving. Start with the whites and work up through the full-bodied reds and sweet dessert wines. Don't hesitate to spit (as professional tasters do) or to empty unconsumed wine from your glass into the crocks set along the tasting bar.

Bus trips sometimes are offered out of larger cities, but generally you'll need a car for wine touring. Bring low-heel, rubber-sole shoes for climbing up observation ramps and stepping over hoses on wet floors. Bring a sweater, too, for chilly, damp aging cellars. Since many wineries are open only from around 10 AM to 4 PM and there may be a wait for tours, don't plan more than four winery stops a day. Note that some wineries will ship a half- or full case of wine to your home via UPS—a plus for vacationing tasters who don't have room in their suitcases.

MAJOR WINE REGIONS

CALIFORNIA

You'll find pockets of scenic wine country from Mendocino County, well to the north of San Francisco, all the way down to the Mexican border, with some good visiting in the Monterey–Carmel areas, around Santa Barbara, and inland in the Temecula Valley between Los Angeles and San Diego. But the ultimate are superchic Napa Valley and country-gentleman Sonoma County, both an hour north of San Francisco.

For general information on California wines and for free wine country regional maps, contact the *Wine Institute,* 425 Market St., Suite 1000, San Francisco, CA 94105 (phone: 415-512-0151; fax: 415-442-0742).

Napa Valley

Some 30 miles long and 6 miles across at its widest point, cozy Napa Valley, with 25,000 acres of microclimates and soil variations at every turn, is the promised land for cabernet sauvignon, pinot noir, chardonnay, sauvignon blanc, johannisberg riesling, and many other varieties. It's also a playground for winery touring, ballooning, cycling, hiking, picnicking, and boutiquing, complete with fine dining and charming inns. Its main road, Highway 29, runs the length of the valley, chockablock with vineyards and wineries, and winds through the gussied-up country towns of Napa, Yountville, St. Helena, and Calistoga. One of the best wine-country maps is *Wineries of the Napa Valley,* which also gives the telephone numbers of more than 150 wineries. It is available without charge in major hotels and from the *Napa Valley Vintners Association* (phone: 707-963-0148). The *Wine Spectator Maps* and the *Napa Valley Guide* are on sale throughout the valley.

Napa is California's biggest tourist attraction after *Disneyland,* so big that there's a *Napa Valley Wine Train* (1275 McKinstry St., Napa, CA 94559; for reservations, phone: 707-253-2111; 800-427-4124) that makes the 36-mile round trip, offering luncheon and dinner excursions and champagne brunch trips on weekends aboard elegant 1915 vintage Pullman parlor cars. If you drive, time your visit for spring to avoid the July-through-September vacation crowds and the October weekend stampedes. With autumn's arrival, the tempo quickens, the grapes hang heavy, and the trucks line up to dump their gleaming harvest onto the crushing pads. If you come in summer, you'll face bumper-to-bumper traffic, crowds jostling for places at the tasting bar, and no room at the inns, unless you do San Francisco on the weekend and Napa midweek. The following list provides a sampling of the range of experiences offered in Napa's wineries.

BEAULIEU VINEYARD Founded in 1900 by Bordeaux native Georges de Latour, this is the third-oldest continuously operated winery in Napa Valley. Beaulieu (French for "beautiful place"), produces world class award winners served to every president since FDR. The vineyard is also known for its legendary enologist André Tchelistcheff, who revolutionized California wine with contributions such as cold fermentation and vineyard frost-protection methods. Visitors are greeted with a complimentary glass of chardonnay in the newly remodeled brick-and-redwood tasting room. More serious wine drinkers should head for the Private Reserve Tasting Room nearby, where for a small fee you can taste reserve wines and browse BV's historic memorabilia. A free full-production tour explains the wine making process and the rich history of the vineyard. Information: *Beaulieu Vineyard,* 1960 South St., Helena Hwy., Rutherford, CA 94573 (phone: 707-967-5200).

BERINGER VINEYARDS It's hard to miss this turreted Rhineland mansion from the road. Stop at its lavish, paneled tasting rooms and take the fascinating tour of hand-dug caves still showing the pickax marks left by Chinese laborers in the 1800s. Beringer doesn't make its wines right here, but there's a lot to see. Information: *Beringer Vineyards,* 2000 Main St., PO Box 111, St. Helena, CA 94574 (phone: 707-963-7115).

CHÂTEAU MONTELENA You have to ask the way to this century-old stone palace shrouded by woods at the north end of the valley. After a tour and tasting, visitors can purchase a bottle of the winery's famous chardonnay or cabernet sauvignon and picnic among the black swans on the island in the château's pond. Picnic reservations are required months in advance, but the tasting room is always open (there is a charge). Information: *Château Montelena,* 1429 Tubbs La., Calistoga, CA 94515 (phone: 707-942-5105).

CLOS DU VAL WINE COMPANY This unpretentious modern French château faces Napa's *Silverado Trail,* the road that runs along the quieter, eastern edge of the valley, where pasturelands recall a time when Napa was dairy country. In the vineyards that lead up from the road, a rose bush has been planted (a French custom) at the end of each row of vines. Tours are informal, and you can taste a range of European varietals as well as zinfandel, a California mainstay. Information: *Clos du Val Wine Company,* 5330 Silverado Trail, PO Box 4350, Napa, CA 94558 (phone: 707-259-2200).

CLOS PEGASE WINERY A Napa eyebrow raiser, this stolid, many-columned, ocher-and-rust-colored complex was designed by the postmodern architect Michael Graves. It's been called a cross between a nuclear reactor and a Greek temple. The tour, not surprisingly, devotes as much attention to architecture as to the process of making the winery's well-received chardonnay, merlot, and cabernet sauvignon. Tours are twice daily. Information: *Clos Pegase Winery,* 1060 Dunaweal La., PO Box 305, Calistoga, CA 94515 (phone: 707-942-4981).

DOMAINE CARNEROS WINERY Partly owned by Champagne Taittinger, this winery was inspired by the family's 18th-century Château de la Marquetterie in France's Champagne region. It's located near both the Napa and Sonoma Valleys. Tours are free, but there is a charge for a glass of sparkling wine with hors d'oeuvres. Tours are hourly in summer and on weekends, by appointment only in winter. Information: *Domaine Carneros,* 1240 Duhig Rd., PO Box 5420, Napa, CA 94581 (phone: 707-257-0101).

DOMAINE CHANDON Tours of this glamorous arm of the French firm of Moët et Chandon begin in an underground wine museum and proceed through a high-production sparkling-wine making operation. You'll see the unusual sight of high fermentation tanks lying on their sides, and inspect the latest automatic riddling machines (for periodic turning of the bottles). There's no tasting with this tour, but you can buy a glass of bubbly (try the *réserve*) in a sunny sit-down café. The winery also has an internationally known restaurant, which requires reservations well in advance. Information: *Domaine Chandon,* California Dr., PO Box 2470, Yountville, CA 94599 (phone: 707-944-2280).

FLORA SPRINGS WINE COMPANY Nestled in the western foothills of the valley only a mile from the highway, this winery is a real family business. If you make an appointment, the owners will show you how they saved and updated an ancient winery. Information: *Flora Springs Wine Co.,* 1978 W. Zinfandel La., St. Helena, CA 94574 (phone: 707-963-5711).

FREEMARK ABBEY WINERY After the tour here, sip cabernet in a spacious tasting room, complete with fireplace, Oriental carpet, and concert grand. Information: *Freemark Abbey Winery,* 3022 St. Helena Hwy. N., PO Box 410, St. Helena, CA 94574 (phone: 707-963-9694).

GRGICH HILLS CELLAR Connoisseurs come to this attractive hacienda for its whites, particularly the handsome chardonnays. The tasting room welcomes drop-ins, but tours with the wine makers are by appointment only. Information: *Grgich Hills Cellar,* 1829 St. Helena Hwy., PO Box 450, Rutherford, CA 94573 (phone: 707-963-2784).

HESS WINERY On the hillside of Mt. Veeder stands this stone winery built in 1903. Swiss entrepreneur and art collector Donald Hess acquired the property in 1978 from the Christian Brothers. After years of producing impressive chardonnays and cabernet sauvignons, Hess commissioned architect A. H. Jordi to redesign his winery. Completed in 1989 and a favorite among visitors and locals alike, the state-of-the-art building astutely maintains its original integrity while exhibiting Hess's impressive contemporary art collection along with the wine making facilities. A free self-guided tour ends at the tasting room, where three varieties are offered for a nominal fee. Information: *Hess Winery,* 4411 Redwood Rd., Napa, CA 94558 (phone: 707-255-1144).

THE INGLENOOK CHÂTEAU AT NIEBAUM-COPPOLA Film director Francis Ford Coppola has been producing fine wines for nearly as long as he has been making movies. Several years ago, he purchased the old *Inglenook* and restored it to its former glory. The building now houses a museum that chronicles the wine making history of the estate, along with memorabilia from Coppola's films, including Vito Corleone's desk and chair from *The Godfather,* and costumes from his production of *Dracula*. Visitors can taste and purchase wines at the adjacent retail store, sip an espresso at the outdoor café, or picnic on the grounds. The château is open daily except on *Thanksgiving, Christmas,* and *New Year's Day.* Admission charge for tastings. Information: *Ingelnook Château at Niebaum-Coppola,* 1991 St. Helena Hwy. Rutherford, CA 94573 (phone: 707-963-9099).

MERRYVALE VINEYARDS Located on the site of the first winery built in the valley following the repeal of Prohibition, it offers a free Saturday wine tasting seminar. Visitors are welcome in the tasting room daily; tours by appointment only. Information: *Merryvale Vineyards,* 1000 Main St., St. Helena, CA 94574 (phone: 707-963-7777).

MUMM This *méthode champenoise* sparkling wine producer offers a public tour that gives visitors a distinctive taste of sparkling wine making. Guided tours are offered daily. In the tasting salon, visitors may purchase wine by the glass or by the bottle, and leisurely sip and nibble complimentary hors d'oeuvres on the large porch, which overlooks the vineyards and the Mayacamas Mountains. Information: *Mumm Napa Valley,* 8445 Silverado Trail, Napa, CA 94558 (phone: 707-942-3434).

PRAGER WINERY & PORT WORKS In a winery behind the main highway, this dedicated wine maker is championing a port revival; the modest output is available on the premises. The tasting room is in a laboratory behind the minuscule barrel room. Visits by appointment only. There are also two bed and breakfast suites. Information: *Prager Winery & Port Works,* 1281 Lewelling La., St. Helena, CA 94574 (phone: 707-963-PORT; 707-963-3720 for bed and breakfast accommodations).

ROBERT MONDAVI WINERY The best guided tour in the valley takes place at this white, V-shaped, mission-styled winery surrounded by flower gardens. Tours paced with the precision of a TV game show give comprehensive walk-throughs from vineyard to bottling line and end with a tasting that's a learning experience. Reservations by phone are advised. Tours are given every hour on the hour by appointment, but the winery does try to accommodate drop-ins. Information: *Robert Mondavi Winery,* 7801 St. Helena Hwy., PO Box 106, Oakville, CA 94562 (phone: 707-259-9463).

ST. SUPERY This wine museum in a restored Queen Anne (ca. 1880s) house offers free self-guided tours. Call ahead to make an appointment. Information: *St. Supery,* 8440 St. Helena Hwy., Rutherford, CA 94573 (phone: 707-963-4507).

STERLING VINEYARDS When locals grumble about the Disneyfication of Napa, they point to the wildly popular white sky trams that lift visitors from the parking lot to the white building of this imposing winery, which was modeled after a hilltop monastery in Greece. Once aloft, you get breathtaking views down-valley and a well-organized self-guided tour (follow the signs) along ramps overlooking the works. There's a sit-down tasting of cabernets, chardonnays, pinot noirs, sauvignon blancs, and merlots in a luxurious tower room. Information: *Sterling Vineyards,* 1111 Dunaweal La., PO Box 365, Calistoga, CA 94515 (phone: 707-942-3344).

VICHON WINERY Plan to be at this hillside boutique winery around lunchtime. The shady picnic tables at the edge of its best cabernet vineyard afford a sensational view of the valley. Tours are small and personal, and a tasting will include the winery's proprietary chevrignon, a blend of semillon and sauvignon blanc. Information: *Vichon Winery,* 1595 Oakville Grade, PO Box 363, Oakville, CA 94562 (phone: 707-944-2811).

VILLA ENCINA This tiny, unpretentious place is one of the oldest wineries in the area, having produced its first grapes in 1881. They don't stand on ceremony here; you can drop in any morning or afternoon and taste the outstanding wares for no charge. There are picnic areas where wine-happy visitors can eat their lunch. Information: *Villa Encina,* 8711 Silverado Trail, St. Helena, CA 94574-9795 (phone: 707-944-2414).

Sonoma County

Just over the mountains, less than a half hour from the Napa Valley, a whole new wine country offers rural calm, uncrowded roads, plentiful accommodations, and a chance to soak up California history. The Sonoma town square, for instance, was the site of the Bear Flag uprising that declared California's independence from Mexico. Sonoma County's vineyard-filled valleys—Alexander, Dry Creek, Sonoma, and Russian River—still have room for pear and apple orchards, truck farms, and chicken ranches. There's even an organized "farm route" that leads to farmstands, llama- and pony-petting corrals, and cheese and jam making enterprises that offer a break between wineries—ideal if you're touring with children. The *Sonoma County Wineries Association* has a visitors' center (5000 Roberts Lake Rd., Rohnert Park 94928; phone: 707-586-3795; fax: 707-586-1383) that features an interactive video terminal to help plan a tour of area wineries, a facsimile of a winery, and a wine tasting bar. And a few companies offer tours of wine country by horse-drawn carriage and picnics ranging from chuck wagon–style to fancy fare. *Carriage Charter* (3325 Gravenstein Hwy. N., Sebastopol, CA 95472; phone: 707-823-7083) takes visitors to vineyards and wineries in turn-of-the-century, private horse-drawn conveyances; also, depending upon the season, to *Christmas* tree and berry farms and apple orchards. *Wine Country Wagons* (PO Box 1069, Kenwood, CA 95452; phone: 707-833-2724) offers seasonal trips to several wineries and ends with a picnic lunch at a private ranch.

BENZIGER WINERY The Benziger family migrated to Sonoma from New York City in 1980, purchased the land neighboring *Jack London State Park,* and dubbed it the *Glen Ellen Winery.* Under the management of two generations of Benzigers, the family business blossomed into an empire and in less than a decade became the valley's second-largest winery. Recently, they sold the rights to the Glen Ellen label, but continue to produce award-winning wines under the Benziger name. The property is user friendly, offering a self-guided tour, a rose garden, and an array of picnic spots. A free tram tour takes visitors through the wine making process, wine producing techniques, and the vineyards, and stops at the winery's architectural trademark—the Parthenon—for a sweeping view of the estate and a glass of bubbly. The tasting room offers a cornucopia of gifts and merchandise, as well as chardonnay, cabernet sauvignon, fumé blanc, pinot noir, merlot, zinfandel, and the "Imagery Series," a combination of unusual wines; there's also an eye-catching gallery housing labels developed by commissioned artists. Information: *Benziger Winery,* 1883 London Ranch Rd., Glen Ellen, CA 95442 (phone: 707-935-3000).

BUENA VISTA WINERY AND TASTING ROOM A short drive into the hills of Sonoma leads to the place where the scoundrel adventurer Agoston Haraszthy planted the first European wine grapes in California during the 1860s. The romantic ivy-covered stone buildings house tasting areas, a gift shop, an art gallery, and a wine museum; the fine Buena Vista wines tasted here are made at the winery's Carneros estate. There's picnicking under giant eucalyptus trees along the creek out front. Information: *Buena Vista Winery and Tasting Room,* 18000 Old Winery Rd., PO Box 1842, Sonoma, CA 95476 (phone: 707-938-1266; 800-926-1266).

CHÂTEAU ST. JEAN Take a self-guided tour through a fanciful winery building set well back in the vineyards. Taste its premium whites in a charming villa across a flower-filled courtyard. Information: *Château St. Jean,* 8555 Sonoma Hwy., PO Box 293, Kenwood, CA 95452 (phone: 707-833-4134).

CHÂTEAU SOUVERAIN A most impressive winery building dominates a Dry Creek Valley hillside and offers tastings, plus lunches with a view, at moderate prices. Information: *Château Souverain,* 400 Souverain Rd., PO Box 528, Geyserville, CA 95441 (phone: 707-433-8281).

FERRARI-CARANO VINEYARDS & WINERY This Italianate winery is surrounded by vineyards and five acres of manicured lawns bordered by Old World rock and flower gardens. Stop by for tastings, which include a popular chardonnay. Tours of the shiny facilities can be arranged by appointment. Information: *Ferrari-Carano Vineyards & Winery,* 8761 Dry Creek Rd., PO Box 1549, Healdsburg, CA 95448 (phone: 707-433-6700).

GLORIA FERRER CHAMPAGNE CAVES This offshoot of Spain's *Freixenet* winery offers an informative tour through its lavish Catalonian-contemporary complex, with panoramic views of Sonoma County from the wine bar terrace. There's a charge for tasting. Information: *Gloria Ferrer Champagne Caves,* 23555 Hwy. 121, PO Box 1427, Sonoma, CA 95476 (phone: 707-996-7256).

HOP KILN WINERY Located on a National Historic Landmark site, this stone building provides a look at the days before the wine boom, when Sonoma's vineyards were hop fields for a thriving beer industry. The building's three square towers are chimneys for the old hops-drying furnaces that stand alongside the wine making tanks and barrels. Try the zinfandel in the tasting room while viewing the ongoing display of art by local artists. A picturesque duck pond surrounded by tables is ideal for picnicking. Information: *Hop Kiln Winery,* 6050 Westside Rd., Healdsburg, CA 95448 (phone: 707-433-6491).

IRON HORSE VINEYARDS Call ahead for an appointment and enjoy the understated elegance of this privately owned estate winery on its own hilltop, reached by a rutted narrow road. Surrounded by vine-covered hills that shut out the world, you'll stroll the winery, a glass of fumé blanc in hand, as a wine maker shows you around. You'll be given more samples of cabernet, chardonnay, and sparkling wine in the tasting room. Information: *Iron Horse Vineyards,* 9786 Ross Station Rd., Sebastopol, CA 95472 (phone: 707-887-1507).

KORBEL CHAMPAGNE CELLARS The biggest champagne maker in the US conducts one of the most thorough guided tours, ending with a generous free tasting at a block-long bar made from old barrels. Korbel, founded in 1882 near the Russian River, has its original buildings in place and an antique rose garden to visit. Information: *Korbel Champagne Cellars,* 13250 River Rd., Guerneville, CA 95446 (phone: 707-887-2294).

RAVENSWOOD On a hillside five minutes from Sonoma Plaza, a stone building headquarters a tasting room and declares, "No Wimpy Wines." Although the vineyard takes this lighthearted approach to a serious business, it lives up to its word—producing gold-medal–winning zinfandels four years running. Tours include a barrel tasting of unreleased wine and a walk through production facilities. This winery also offers a fine merlot, cabernet sauvignon, and small amounts of chardonnay. Information: *Ravenswood,* 18701 Gehricke Rd., Sonoma, CA 95476 (phone: 707-938-1960).

SEBASTIANI VINEYARDS There's constant hubbub in the tasting room–gift shop of this winery, which has operated in Sonoma since 1904. The giant Sebastiani company offers more than a dozen varieties for tasting. Tours of the vineyards and winery are well guided and include a look at a fascinating collection of hand-carved casks. Information: *Sebastiani Vineyards,* 389 Fourth St. E., PO Box AA, Sonoma, CA 95476 (phone: 707-938-5532).

VIANSA WINERY This luxurious Tuscan-style hillside villa brings the charm of the Italian wine country to California. Surrounded by a grove of olive trees, the villa has beautiful hand-painted murals, frescoes, stone fermentation tanks, and a vaulted aging cellar. The winery also has its own kitchen, where meals are prepared daily. You can sip the superb wine and eat at picnic tables, which afford a stunning view of the valley. Open daily for wine and food tasting and self-guided tours; groups must make an appointment for tours, tastings, and dining. Information: *Viansa Winery,* 25200 Arnold Dr. (Hwy. 121), Sonoma, CA 95476 (phone: 707-935-4700).

Santa Barbara County

About 250 miles south of Napa and Sonoma, the wineries of Santa Barbara County are giving northern California's wine industry a run for its money. The number of vintners here has grown from a mere handful with less than 100 acres in the 1970s to more than 30 with 10,000 acres under cultivation.

The soul of Santa Barbara wine country is its two grape-growing valleys: the Santa Ynez, 15 miles northwest of Santa Barbara, and the Santa Maria, directly north. Sixteen wineries make their homes here. The coastal mountain range runs east to west rather than north to south as it does in Sonoma and Napa, so cool ocean breezes blow straight into the valleys. Therefore, the daytime temperature is 15 degrees cooler here than in the wine valleys farther north, making for a longer growing season; consequently, the wine produced has a less sweet, more natural taste. The region is particularly noted for its chardonnay, riesling, and pinot noir. The wineries' output is small (8,000 cases a year is average for a Santa Barbara vintner), so these wines generally are not widely marketed. Oenophiles who have discovered the area's wines must either buy them directly at the winery or by mail order.

During the summer, when crowds are flocking to Napa and Sonoma, Santa Barbara wine country is relatively tourist-free. The wineries here are more likely to be open to walk-in visitors; many have lovely picnic areas. You may even meet a wine maker who will share the secrets of his or her craft. (It's a good idea to call ahead to the winery to ask if reservations are necessary.) The *Los Olivos Tasting Room and Wine Shop* in Los Olivos (phone: 805-688-7406) is a good place to get an overview of Santa Barbara wines; many of the local wineries stock their wares here. Los Olivos also has one of the best places to stay in the valley—the *Grand* (2860 Grand Ave., Los Olivos, CA 93441; phone: 805-688-7788; 800-446-2455; fax: 805-688-1942), a 21-room inn with a blend of ranch charm and French provinciality. The *Ballard Inn* (2436 Baseline Ave., Ballard, CA 93463; phone: 805-688-7770; 800-638-2466; fax: 805-688-9560), a 15-room bed and breakfast hideaway, is another good choice.

What follows is a short list of the more interesting wineries located in the Santa Barbara area. For a free map and more information, contact the *Santa Barbara County Vintners Association* (3669 Sagunto St., Suite 103, PO Box 1558, Santa Ynez, CA 93460; phone: 805-688-0881; fax: 805-686-5881).

BRANDER VINEYARD In the east-central Santa Ynez Valley, this winery produces a lean, crisp chardonnay. Visitors can sample the product daily in the tasting room, decorated in the style of a French château. Information: *Brander Vineyard,* PO Box 92, Los Olivos, CA 93441 (phone: 805-688-2455).

CAREY CELLARS In what used to be a dairy barn, Carey's La Questa vineyard now produces one of the area's best cabernet sauvignons. A yellow farmhouse nearby serves as the tasting room. Information: *Carey Cellars,* 1711 Alamo Pintado Rd., Solvang, CA 93463 (phone: 805-688-8554).

FIRESTONE VINEYARD Founded in 1974 by Brooks Firestone (of the tire family), this is the oldest and largest winery in the area. It produces 75,000 cases a year of varietals, but it is best known for its johannisberg riesling. Visitors can tour the handsome wood-and-brick winery building on top of a hill at the northern Santa Ynez Valley and observe the wine making process. Information: *Firestone Vineyard,* 5017 Zaca Station Rd., Los Olivos, CA 93441 (phone: 805-688-3940).

GAINEY VINEYARD The wines produced here have won many awards—in particular, the 1989 johannisberg riesling and the 1987 pinot noir. Tours of the Spanish-style winery and tasting rooms are offered along with a comprehensive explanation of the wine making process. Information: *Gainey Vineyard,* PO Box 910, 3950 E. Hwy. 246, Santa Ynez, CA 93460 (phone: 805-688-0558).

ZACA MESA WINERY Just down the road from the *Firestone Vineyard,* this vintner has produced award-winning chardonnays and pinot noirs. It has a lovely redwood-paneled tasting room. Information: *Zaca Mesa Winery,* PO Box 899, 6905 Foxen Canyon Rd., Los Olivos, CA 93441 (phone: 805-688-9339).

NEW YORK STATE

You get your choice of ambience here. Take a rural vacation in the mountainous Finger Lakes region of central New York, between Rochester and Syracuse, take a day trip from Manhattan to the quiet Hudson Valley, or combine a visit to the state's newer wineries on eastern Long Island with a weekend at a stylish Hamptons beach town.

New York's prodigious wine output depended on native American labrusca grapes until the mid-1970s, when small farm wineries succeeded in making European varieties and hardy French-American hybrids (mostly whites). In the Finger Lakes area, there are 45 wineries, most of them small, within minutes of each other along uncrowded roads that rim the hills around a group of glacier-cut lakes. In the Hudson Valley, grape farmers on both sides of the river produce premium wines with European varietals and such French-American hybrids as seyval blanc and baco noir. Long Island's vineyards, planted in what used to be potato fields, all specialize in the big-name European varieties.

For a free New York winery guide, send a self-addressed, stamped 52¢ envelope to the *New York Wine and Grape Foundation,* 350 Elm St., Penn Yan, NY 14527 (phone: 315-536-7442; fax: 315-536-0719).

Finger Lakes

BULLY HILL VINEYARDS This lively winery/restaurant complex also includes an interesting wine museum. The winery is open all year, but call for tour information; the restaurant and museum are closed November through April. Information: *Bully Hill Vineyards,* 8843 Greyton H. Taylor Memorial Dr., Hammondsport, NY 14840 (phone: 607-868-3210).

GLENORA WINE CELLARS There's a gorgeous view of Seneca Lake, but no tour, only a video. You can, however, look into the working winery and taste the firm's fine chardonnay, johannisberg riesling, and seyval blanc, sparkling wines, *blanc de blancs,* and brut champagne. Information: *Glenora Wine Cellars,* 5435 Rte. 14, Dundee, NY 14837 (phone: 607-243-5511).

SONNENBERG GARDENS Visitors can sample wines made by the Canandaigua Wine Co. and tour a late Victorian garden estate–mansion and showpiece gardens all in one stop. Tasting room and gardens (and picnic area) are closed mid-October through early May. Information: *Sonnenberg Gardens,* 151 Charlotte St., Canandaigua, NY 14424 (phone: 716-394-4922).

WAGNER VINEYARDS Estate-bottled whites, notably johannisberg riesling and chardonnay (the reds and pinks), draw oenophiles here, but the octagonal winery building looking over the vineyards to Seneca Lake below is an attraction in itself. There is a good guided tour and a leisurely tasting of European varietals and native wines. Picnic or enjoy a meal in a pretty café. Information: *Wagner Vineyards,* 9322 Rte. 414, Lodi, NY 14860 (phone: 607-582-6450).

Hudson Valley

Wine country begins an hour from Manhattan and meanders upstate on both sides of the river, with farm wineries and colonial towns along the way.

BENMARL VINEYARDS The jewel of the Hudson River is this pioneer farm winery high on the west bank. Visitors can chat with artist and wine maker Mark

Miller, who started the premium-wine renaissance in the Hudson Valley. Tours through Miller's chalet-style buildings include a look at his 3,800-bottle collection of fine old European wines and examples of his own sculpture and painting. The tour includes tasting his premium estate-bottled reds and whites and his red table wines as well as wines from Long Island and the Finger Lakes, or enjoying a view clear to the foothills of the Berkshires. There are lovely picnic groves on the grounds. Open daily. Information: *Benmarl Vineyards,* 156 Highland Ave., Marlboro, NY 12542 (phone: 914-236-4265).

BROTHERHOOD WINERY Its unrivaled 157 years of continuous operation (even during Prohibition, when it made sacramental wines) make a tour of this landmark fieldstone winery and its underground storage caves a must, especially if you're visiting nearby *West Point.* Open daily May through October; closed weekdays November through April. Information: *Brotherhood Winery,* 35 North St., Washingtonville, NY 10992 (phone: 914-496-3661).

CASCADE MOUNTAIN WINERY AND RESTAURANT A tiny winery among the vines at the end of a lane has intimate tours and tastings—and funky names like Pardonnay-Moi for its wines. Local cheeses, sausages, and game—some highlights of the menu—are served at its restaurant. Information: *Cascade Mountain Winery and Restaurant,* Flint Hill Rd., Amenia, NY 12501 (phone: 914-373-9021).

Long Island

DUCK WALK VINEYARDS The most spectacular of Long Island's dozen wineries, this beauty is housed in a 17,000-foot copper-roofed building patterned after a Normandy château. The tasting rooms and terrace overlook the vineyards. Weekend tours and tastings are free. Information: *Duck Walk Vineyards,* PO Box 962, 231 Montauk Hwy., Water Mill, NY 11976 (phone: 516-726-7555).

WASHINGTON STATE

No matter where you are in Washington, you're always no more than an hour's drive from a winery. You're most likely, however, to base your touring around Seattle, a major wine center despite the fact that wine grapes don't do well in its cool, damp climate. Washington's acclaimed white and red wines come from vines grown in the sunny farmlands on the eastern side of the snow-crowned Cascade Mountains. Grapes are crushed right in the fields, and their juice is trucked over the hills to Seattle wineries. For country winery visiting, tour the Yakima Valley, three hours from the city. More than 20 wineries are open to visitors along Highway 82, running down the center of the valley.

For a complimentary Washington winery guide, write to the *Washington Wine Commission,* PO Box 61217, Seattle, WA 98121 (phone: 206-728-2252).

CHÂTEAU STE. MICHELLE Seattle's major winery welcomes visitors to a graceful, French-style château surrounded by 87 acres of manicured grounds and lush picnic areas. The vineyards here are for experimental purposes and decoration—visitors throw grapes to the ducks in the ponds. There is an expert tour of the white wine process (the reds are made in eastern Washington) and a tasting from among a dozen red and white varietals, including the popular chardonnay and johannisberg riesling. Information: *Château Ste. Michelle,* 14111 NE 145th St., Woodinville, WA 98072 (phone: 206-488-1133).

COLUMBIA CREST WINERY Surrounded by 2,000 acres of estate vineyards, Washington's largest winery was founded in 1983 on the eastern side of the mountains. Known for its state-of-the art facility (90% underground) and for its elegant French country château architecture, it is also well known for its merlot, chardonnay, cabernet sauvignon, and a unique semillon-chardonnay blend. Self-guided tours and tastings are offered daily. Information: *Columbia Crest Winery,* State Rte. 221, Columbia Crest Dr., Paterson, WA 99345 (phone: 509-875-2061).

COLUMBIA WINERY The blue Victorian building across the road from *Château Ste. Michelle* is a touch of luxury for this respected winery, which was formerly in a warehouse. The winery offers tastings of varietals, including merlot, chardonnay, semillon, and its specialty, cabernet sauvignon. Information: *Columbia Winery,* PO Box 1248, Woodinville, WA 98072 (phone: 206-488-2776).

SNOQUALMIE WINERY A short excursion from Seattle into the wooded western foothills of the Cascades (no grapes grow here either) takes you past spectacular waterfalls to this modern chalet winery with an eagle's eye view of the Snoqualmie River Valley and the Cascades. You can sample their unique, dry, Alsatian-style gewürztraminer by a comfy fire in the tasting room. Information: *Snoqualmie Winery,* 1000 Winery Rd., Snoqualmie, WA 98065 (phone: 206-888-4000).

OREGON

The hard-to-please pinot noir grape is the pride of Oregon, having found ideal growing conditions in vineyards next to the familiar hazelnut groves, berry patches, and orchards. In fact, wine is being made all up and down the state. From Portland it's an easy and picturesque drive to the lush Willamette Valley to taste pinot, chardonnay, and riesling in small, friendly wineries.

For a complimentary Oregon winery guide, contact the *Oregon Winegrowers Association,* 1200 NW Front Ave., Suite 400, Portland, OR 97209 (phone: 541-228-8403).

HILLCREST VINEYARD Richard Sommer, the father of Oregon's modern wine-growing industry, is famous for his bottle-aged cabernet sauvignon and riesling. Tastings of these and other varietals are held in his modern-rustic winery in the rolling hills of the Umpqua Valley in southern Oregon. Visitors can take daily guided tours or look down on the winery operation from the deck. There's also a lovely picnic area. Information: *Hillcrest Vineyard,* 240 Vineyard La., Roseburg, OR 97470 (phone: 541-673-3709).

KNUDSEN ERATH WINERY Even at one of Oregon's biggest wineries, you need an appointment for a guided tour, but drop-in visitors may sample the prize-winning pinot and traditional whites and admire the vine-covered hillsides from the tasting room patio. Information: *Knudsen Erath Winery,* Worden Hill Rd., PO Box 667, Dundee, OR 97115 (phone: 541-538-3318; 800-539-9463).

SOKOL BLOSSER WINERY Noted architect John Storrs designed this concrete winery built into the hillside. A picnic pavilion offers a sweeping view of the Willamette Valley. There are daily tastings, but tours are by appointment only. Information: *Sokol Blosser Winery,* 5000 NE Sokol Blosser La., PO Box 399, Dundee, OR 97115 (phone: 541-864-2282; 800-582-6668).

ELSEWHERE AROUND THE COUNTRY

The welcome mat is out at wineries in half the states in the US. Check with state and local tourism organizations for winery guides. Some places close in winter, many receive visitors on weekends only, and some require appointments; call ahead for information.

CONNECTICUT

The Litchfield Hills has a number of small vineyards where the wines, while hardly competitive with those of primary growing regions like California, are pleasant enough to merit a stop or two while enjoying the other scenic delights in this part of the state. Many offer free tastings and tours. Notables in this region include *The Hopkins Vineyard* (Hopkins Rd., New Preston, CT 06777; phone: 860-868-7954).

Wineries near *Mystic Seaport* include *Stonington Vineyard* (PO Box 463, Taugwonk Rd., Stonington, CT 06378; phone: 860-535-1222) and the *Haight Vineyard and Wine Education Center* (Coogan Blvd., Olde Mystick Village, CT 06355; phone: 860-572-1978).

MISSOURI

To the German immigrants who settled here in the 1830s, the banks of the Missouri River resembled their beloved Rhine Valley. They planted the fertile hills with grapes, wine making flourished, and by the latter half of the 19th century Missouri ranked as America's second-largest wine producing region. The long arm of Prohibition swiftly buried Missouri's wine industry; vineyards were plowed into farmlands, and cellars and natural caves were given over to the cultivation of mushrooms. But the wine dreams revived in the early 1960s, and today the state has more than 30 vineyards. Names to note: outside St. Louis, *Stone Hill Winery* (*mailing address:* Rte.

1, PO Box 26, Hermann, MO 65041; phone: 314-486-2221); and *Mount Pleasant Winery* (5634 High St., Augusta, MO 63332; phone: 314-228-4419). Information: *The Grape and Wine Program* (phone: 314-751-6807; 800-392-WINE).

OHIO

Fairs and festivals are a traditional part of wine touring in a state that has produced native American grapes for generations. To tour wineries that specialize in European varietals, drive along Lake Erie between Sandusky and Conneaut. Picturesque pre-Prohibition wineries can be found in the "wine islands" (Bass Islands) on Lake Erie, reachable by ferry from Port Clinton. Names to note: in the Lake Erie area, *Chalet Debonné Vineyards* (7743 Doty Rd., Madison, OH 44057; phone: 216-466-3485); in the wine islands, *Lonz Winery* (Middle Bass Island, OH 43446; phone: 419-285-5411) and *Heineman Winery at Put-in-Bay* (*mailing address:* PO Box 300, Put-in-Bay, OH 43456; phone: 419-285-2811); and in the Cincinnati area, *Meier's Wine Cellars* (6955 Plainfield Rd., Cincinnati OH 45236; phone: 513-891-2900).

PENNSYLVANIA

The bucolic southeast corner of the state is the home of beautiful old wineries making native American wines and newcomer European varietals. Names to note: in the Brandywine River Valley, *Chaddsford Winery* (Rte. 1, PO Box 229, Chaddsford, PA 19317; phone: 610-388-6221); and in Amish Country, *Mount Hope Estate and Winery* (Rte. 72 in Manheim; *mailing address:* PO Box 685, Cornwall, PA 17016; phone: 717-665-7021).

TEXAS

Fine red and white varietal wines are making news in the hill country near Austin and San Antonio and on the high plains around Lubbock in West Texas. Names to note: *Bell Mt./Oberhellman Vineyards* (Hwy. 16, north of Fredericksburg; *mailing address:* HC 61, PO Box 22, Fredericksburg, TX 78624; phone: 210-685-3297); *Fall Creek Vineyards* (85 miles north of Austin; call for directions; *mailing address:* 1111 Guadalupe St., Austin, TX 78701; phone: 512-476-4477); *Slaughter Leftwich* (1 mile south of Mansfield Dam, Ranch Rd. 620, Lake Travis; *mailing address:* 107 RR 620 South, PO Box 22F, Austin, TX 78734; phone: 512-266-3331); and *Llano Estacado Winery* (Farm Rd. 1585, 3.2 miles east of US 87 South; *mailing address*: PO Box 3487, Lubbock, TX 79452; phone: 806-745-2258).

VIRGINIA

From Washington, DC, it's less than a two-hour drive to Albemarle wine country near Charlottesville, where small vintners produce fine varietals, including some of the East Coast's better cabernets and merlots. At least 30 wineries from the Alleghenies to the eastern shore welcome visitors. Names to note: *Oakencroft Vineyard and Winery* (3½ miles west of Rte. 29

on Barracks Rd., Rte. 654; *mailing address:* Rte. 5, PO Box 429, Charlottesville, VA 22901; phone: 804-296-4188); *Montdomaine Cellars Winery* (Rte. 20 south of Charlottesville to Rte. 720; *mailing address:* Rte. 6, PO Box 188A, Charlottesville, VA 22902; phone: 804-971-8947); and *Meredyth Vineyards* (Rte. 776 from Middleburgh to Rte. 628; *mailing address:* PO Box 347, Middleburgh, VA 22117; phone: 703-687-6277).

Vacations on Farms and Ranches

In the country, city people rediscover the sound of songbirds and the smell of freshly cut grass. Suburbanites get the chance to poke around an area where the nearest neighbors live miles away. Parents can say to their children, "No, eggs do not start out in waffle-shaped cartons"—and then prove it. Youngsters can see people who live differently, think differently, and have different values. But even if there were no lessons to be learned, a stay at a farm or ranch would be a pleasant vacation, so it's no wonder that all over the country there are hundreds of farms and ranches welcoming guests.

No two are quite alike. On the one hand, there are guest farms and dude ranches with tennis courts, fancy pools, square dances, hayrides, and jam-packed recreation programs, where guests are the main business. On the other hand, there are family farms and working ranches where raising animals or crops is the main activity, and the owners take guests only to bring in extra money.

Rates generally range from about $500 to $1,500 per adult per week. Often three meals a day, unlimited horseback riding, and use of all facilities are included, but some activities may cost extra. Be sure to find out exactly what's included when you price the ranches.

For a comprehensive description of farms and ranches of all kinds, plus addresses, phone numbers, rates, size, activities, and previous guests' comments, see Pat Dickerman's *Adventure Guides* (7550 E. McDonald Dr., Suite M, Scottsdale, AZ 85250; phone: 800-252-7899) or *Ranch Vacations* by Eugene Kilgore (John Muir Publications, 1995, $19.95; 800-888-7504); for Western ranches, Dickerman also can dispense advice and make reservations. Herewith, a short list of some of the most typical.

FAMILY FARMS

WILSON'S PINTO BEAN FARM, Yellow Jacket, Colorado Everything at this southwestern Colorado establishment is comfortable and homey—but don't expect luxury: The three guestrooms in the farmhouse are not large. Yet to visit the Wilson family is to experience real, honest-to-goodness farm life—1,200 acres of pinto beans, wheat, and alfalfa; an assortment of farm animals; and a shed with the huge modern farm machinery used for planting and harvesting crops. The Wilsons grow much of their own food, and home-baked bread, kosher dills, sweet pickle chips, apricot jam, and chokecherry jelly turn up on the big family table like clockwork, along with apple, cherry, and plum pies. Dancing, biking, and horseshoe pitching are favorite activities, as is hiking to Canyon Pasture, where you can see the remains of a settlement that once housed more people than the similar, although better-preserved, structures at nearby *Mesa Verde National Park.* Also nearby in the red earth country of the Four Corners region are the *Hovenweep National Monument* and *Anasazi Heritage Center.* Closed November through March. Information: *Arthur and Esther Wilson, Wilson's Pinto Bean Farm,* PO Box 252, Yellow Jacket, CO 81335 (phone: 303-562-4476).

APPLEWOOD FARMS INN, Ledyard, Connecticut It's hard to believe that this bucolic farmhouse is only a few minutes from the bustling seaport town of Mystic, Connecticut. Built in 1826, it has six guestrooms, four with fireplaces and private baths. Guests may explore the scenic 33 acres, where they can get up close and personal with horses, sheep, and goats. Information: *Frankie and Tom Betz, Applewood Farms Inn,* 528 Colonel Ledyard Hwy., Ledyard, CT 06339 (phone: 203-536-2022).

RODGERS DAIRY FARM, West Glover, Vermont About 35 miles from the Canadian border in Vermont's unspoiled Northeast Kingdom, the Rodgers family runs a 350-acre dairy farm on the same property that their Scottish ancestors settled in the early 1800s—and provide lodgings to city folk in a century-old, five-room, white clapboard farmhouse that's surrounded by maple-shaded lawns ringed with an old-fashioned split-rail fence. You can watch the cows being milked by machine, or learn to do it yourself by hand. You also can learn to ride a horse, reach under the clucking hens to gather eggs, and, if it's haying time, go on a hayride. Or, if you prefer, drive a few miles to Shadow Lake for a swim; or to Barton, 12 miles away, to see what it's like to be in a town with 900 inhabitants (many more than in the villages of Glover and West Glover, pop. 650, combined); take in an auction or two; or just sit in lawn chairs under the maple trees. Information: *James and Nancy Rodgers, Rodgers Dairy Farm,* RFD 3, PO Box 57, West Glover, VT 05875 (phone: 802-525-6677).

GUEST RANCHES

WHITE STALLION, Tucson, Arizona You get the feeling of wide-open spaces on this 3,000-acre spread northwest of Tucson, at the foot of the rugged Tucson Mountains, within a 100,000-acre game preserve. The *White Stallion* is the only guest ranch in the area that can also claim a longhorn cattle operation—but riding is the point here. Owner Cynthia True stages weekly cowboy rodeos in the ranch arena. Wranglers will take you into the saguaro-dotted desert around the ranch house up to four times a day. Other activities include hayrides, barbecues and cookouts, shuffleboard, and hikes. Or you can stake out a spot poolside or in the cozy library, visit the hot tub therapy room, play a round of golf nearby, or try some tennis on the ranch's two Laykold courts. There's even a petting zoo. Everyone is on a first-name basis; the place is friendly and very informal, despite the size (about 60 guests). Closed from the end of April through September. Information: *Cynthia True, White Stallion Ranch,* 9251 W. Twin Peaks Rd., Tucson, AZ 85743 (phone: 520-297-0252; 800-782-5546; fax: 520-744-2786).

RANCHO DE LOS CABALLEROS, Wickenburg, Arizona Visitors can take their pick of 70 horses to lead and speed along the sandy desert trails of Wickenburg. A country club atmosphere pervades "Los Cab," with its 7,000-yard golf course, four tennis courts, and pool. Accommodations in 74 two- and four-unit casitas. Information: *Rancho de los Caballeros,* 1551 South Vulture Mine Rd., Wickenburg, AZ 85390 (phone: 520-684-5484; fax: 520-684-2267).

WICKENBURG INN, Wickenburg, Arizona This 20-year-old operation has 80 horses, including seven gaited equines. Other facilities include 11 all-weather tennis courts, a nature museum, and two nearby golf courses. Nature hikes and arts and crafts make this a great place for kids. There are nine lodge rooms and 44 whitewashed casitas, with fireplaces and kitchenettes. Information: *Wickenburg Inn,* PO Box P, Wickenburg, AZ 85358 (phone: 520-684-7811; 800-WICKENBURG; fax: 520-684-2981).

HOME, Clark, Colorado A member of the Relais & Châteaux group, it offers six rooms in the main lodge and eight log cabins with wood-burning stoves, private porches, and hot tubs. All rooms are furnished with antiques, Indian rugs, and Western art. Summer activities include hiking, fly fishing, horseback riding, and swimming. Children can feed barn animals, swim, hike, and picnic with counselors. Wintertime guests either cross-country ski on the ranch's groomed trails, ski at nearby Steamboat Springs (see *Downhill Skiing*), or take a sleigh ride. The food is hearty and wonderful. Information: *Home Ranch,* PO Box 822, Clark, CO 80428 (phone: 303-879-1780; fax: 303-879-1795).

COLORADO TRAILS, Durango, Colorado See the Old West, hear its tales, and get the flavor of cowboy life—and at the same time lodge in a tidy little cabin with your own bath and electric heat—at this 525-acre mountain ranch just outside Durango, in the southwestern corner of Colorado. With up to 65 other vacationers, you can take riding lessons (the horse operation is one of the best of its kind, with certified instructors in both English and Western riding); go on trail rides; swim in a heated pool; lounge in the whirlpool; play tennis; fish for trout; shoot arrows, shotguns, and rifles; and water-ski on 10-mile-distant Vallecito Lake. The staff puts on chuck wagon dinners, variety shows, dances, hayrides, and powwows around the campfire. But there's never any pressure to do anything, and though sing-alongs may at first seem corny, somehow everyone ends up enjoying them. Counselors take groups of kids off for riding and other activities each day; the arrangement seems to give each generation just the right amount of time together and apart. Closed early October to late May; plan to reserve several months in advance. Information: *Ginny and Dick Elder, Colorado Trails Ranch,* 12161 CR240, Durango, CO 81301 (phone: 970-247-5055; 800-323-3833; fax: 970-385-7372).

C LAZY U, Granby, Colorado This establishment, at about 8,200 feet just west of the Continental Divide, is the real thing: a working ranch as well as a country inn, with warm hospitality and all the amenities. The emphasis is on horseback riding, and guests are given their own personal mounts. But there's plenty more horsing around: ranch riding competitions and rodeos, to be specific. The *C Lazy U* also is a guest ranch, so you'll find a heated pool, a whirlpool bath and sauna, two tennis courts and a racquetball court, a skeet- and trap-shooting range, Ping-Pong tables, and miles of trails for hiking (and cross-country skiing in winter). And if that won't keep you busy, you can always go fishing—or just take a drive through the mountains. The large lodge, which faces a lake where you can ice skate in winter, is surrounded by guest cottages. All the rooms are cozy and comfortable, the food is solid and plentiful, and evenings are convivial. Information: *C Lazy U Ranch,* PO Box 379, Granby, CO 80446 (phone: 970-887-3344; fax: 970-887-3917).

CHEROKEE PARK, Livermore, Colorado Believed to be the first guest ranch in Colorado, it was also occasionally used during the late 1880s as a stagecoach stop between Ft. Collins, Colorado, and Laramie, Wyoming. At 7,000 feet, it sits in its own valley on the Cache Le Poudre River and is surrounded by pine forests. The small ranch accommodates up to 35 guests in cabins (some with fireplaces). In the main lodge, four suites are available with private baths (no TV sets or telephones). Rooms are nicely appointed with pine paneling, oak furniture, and Indian rugs; meals are served family-style—all the traditional ranch fare you can eat. Individual instruction by experienced wranglers, who take care to match the rider's experience with the right horse, make the horseback riding program a real treat. Guided trail rides are available from one-hour to all-day rides and overnight pack trips. If riding isn't your game, you can choose activities such as whitewater rafting, trap shooting, fishing in the river or the ranch's trout pond, four-wheel-drive rides, and hiking. Children can also be happily occupied: There's an extensive activities program supervised by counselors, as well as a wonderful baby-sitting service. Information: *William and Elizabeth Elfland, Cherokee Park Ranch,* PO Box 97, Livermore, CO 80536 (phone: 970-493-6522; 800-628-0949).

VISTA VERDE, near Steamboat Springs, Colorado Owned by a couple of displaced Hoosiers, this 540-acre working ranch provides "dudes" with such creature comforts as a Jacuzzi and mints on the pillows. The ranch is open year-round; activities change with the season. In summer, there's horseback riding, Colorado River rafting, hot-air ballooning from nearby Steamboat Springs, rock climbing (taught by a certified instructor), gold panning, guided hikes to the high-altitude lakes, mountain bike touring, and if that doesn't suit, there's an artificial pond for fly fishing and a beach for swimming. In winter, cross-country skiing, sleigh rides, snowshoeing, dog sledding, and a school for ice climbing are enough to keep you active. Children can visit a petting zoo where they gather eggs and feed the livestock, and an old fire engine takes them on fishing trips where they learn to cast a line, pan for gold, and go on nature walks. The ranch also offers nightly entertainment, and once a week during the summer, guests can troop into Steamboat to watch a rodeo. There are eight roomy log cabins with daily maid service. Information: *John and Suzanne Munn, Vista Verde,* PO Box 465, Steamboat Springs, CO 80477 (phone: 970-879-3858; 800-526-RIDE; fax: 970-879-1413).

LONE MOUNTAIN, Big Sky, Montana A 100-horse guest ranch in summer, a cross-country ski resort in winter, *Lone Mountain* is surrounded by the *Spanish Peaks Wilderness Area.* Trail rides, limited to seven riders, vary in difficulty and often lead up into remote wilderness settings for campfire lunches beside a lake. On site are 25 cabins with fireplaces, electric heat, private baths, and queen-size beds, plus a 12-person hot tub and a saloon. On any given night, dinner might feature barbecued steaks with a flambéed dessert. During the summer, restless dudes have several options: group excursions to *Yellowstone,* trout fishing on the Gallatin River, float trips on the Madison and Yellowstone Rivers, and tours of the *Museum of the Rockies* in Bozeman. The pace doesn't let up any in winter, either; the ranch has 47 miles of professionally groomed ski trails and organizes guided backcountry ski trips into *Yellowstone,* as well as snowcoach excursions into the park to peek at the wildlife. Information: *Bob Schaap, Lone Mountain Ranch,* PO Box 160069, Big Sky, MT 59716 (phone: 406-995-4644; fax: 406-995-4670).

LAZY HILLS, Ingram, Texas The proud proprietors have dubbed this "The Family Ranch," and have been welcoming families from around the globe since 1959. Set in the heart of Texas hill country, the 750-acre spread offers such activities as horseback riding, swimming in an Olympic-size pool, tennis, volleyball, basketball, hiking, fishing, and bird watching. There is supervised child care for kids two to eight years old during the summer season. Open year-round. Information: *Bob and Carol Steinruck, Lazy Hills Guest Ranch,* PO Box G, Ingram, Texas 78025 (phone: 210-367-5600; 800-880-0632; fax: 210-367-5667).

PARADISE, Buffalo, Wyoming Nestled in a valley at the edge of the *Big Horn National Forest,* this aptly named ranch offers "accessible seclusion." Guests here are assigned a horse suited to their riding ability for the duration of their stay. Scheduled rides—with wranglers—range from one-hour, half-, and full-day outings to three- or four-day pack trips. There is a dining room with a lively atmosphere that serves ample portions of stick-to-your-ribs home-style cooking, a saloon with live entertainment, and a spacious meeting room. Cozy one-, two-, and three-bedroom log cabins have outdoor decks, fireplaces, and dining and kitchen areas. Activities include hiking, fishing, swimming in a heated pool, spa visits, chuck wagon cookouts, talent shows, history and nature talks, square dances, and special programs for children, including a campout in the hills ("parents' night off"). Minimum stay is one week; ask about special rates for children. Information: *Jim and Leah Anderson, Paradise Guest Ranch,* PO Box 790, Buffalo, WY 82834 (phone: 307-684-7876).

WORKING RANCHES

GRAPEVINE CANYON RANCH, Pearce, Arizona The Dragoon Mountains provide an imposing backdrop to this working ranch. Once you've settled in, you might choose to help owners Gerry and Eve Searle round up a herd of cattle, or spend the day on a guided trail ride exploring the rugged 64,000 acres surrounding the ranch. Twelve guest cabins and casitas nestle comfortably in a grove of Arizona oak. There's also an outdoor pool and a hot tub. The kitchen prepares three hearty meals a day. No children under 12. Information: *Gerry and Eve Searle, Grapevine Canyon Ranch,* PO Box 302, Pearce, AZ 85625 (phone: 520-826-3185; fax: 520-826-3636).

HALTER, Big Sandy, Montana In the center of the *Missouri River Wilderness Waterway,* 80 miles east of Great Falls, Montana, the Halter family raises cattle, horses, hay, and barley on 3,000 acres of meadows and rugged breaks along the White Cliffs of the Missouri River, described in Lewis and Clark's journal. Gay Halter Pearson and her husband, Ron, will teach you to ride or take you on overnight trail rides. Gay's father, Jerry Halter, can regale you with tales of the homesteads, forts, and Indian ruins in the area. Summertime youth vacations are available for those ages nine through 17 without parents. Closed November through March. Information: *Gay Halter Pearson, Halter Ranch,* PO Box 408, Big Sandy, MT 59520 (phone: 406-378-2549).

G BAR M, Clyde Park, Montana One of the few remaining cattle ranches in the West to cleave to the old lifestyle and welcome vacationers (it's been in business for nearly 60 years), this establishment in the Bridger Mountain foothills just east of Bozeman has 3,300 acres mainly given over to cattle. There are four rooms in the ranch house and two outlying log cabins fitted out for visitors. Riding, of course, is the main feature; you'll go out to check fence and water holes, help doctor calves that got too curious about porcupines, carry salt to the cattle, and help in herding; and George Leffingwell, the owner, puts even the most inexperienced rider at ease. You can go for an all-day ride and be met at lunchtime with a well-stocked picnic basket. Because part of the ranch is a private game sanctuary, you'll often see mule deer, golden eagles, and coyotes, along with moose, elk, and bear on occasion. You also can go fishing or hiking, hunt fossils or photograph wildflowers. There are daily tours of the area on horseback, and on Friday or Saturday nights there's a steak fry. Otherwise, you won't find much of an activities program—and most people like it that way. Everyone—

the family, vacationers, and ranch hands—eats together (including breakfasts of sourdough pancakes and chokecherry syrup). Closed October through mid-May. Information: *The Leffingwells, G Bar M Ranch,* PO Box 29, Clyde Park, MT 59018 (phone: 406-686-4423).

DEER FORKS, Douglas, Wyoming It takes about an hour to drive through the rangelands of eastern Wyoming from the town of Douglas to the 5,900-acre spread where the Middleton family grazes cows, grows hay, and welcomes guests. The two rustic housekeeping cabins with private baths and full kitchens are quite comfortable. You can eat in these cabins or, if you prefer, share some meals with Ben and Pauli Middleton and their college-age children; the fare usually includes beef from the family's cattle, garden-grown vegetables, and homemade breads and pies. Besides the milk cow, there are plenty of animals here to delight children—lambs, cats, and two dogs. If you can ride, you may be rounding up cows—and if you can't, you'll soon learn how. Hiking, arrowhead-hunting, and trout fishing will also keep you busy. In addition, depending on the season, you may find yourself stacking bales of hay, separating steers from heifers, or helping the vet do pregnancy tests. One day you may drive in to see the rodeo, or state fair, or a cattle auction; another, you may join the Middletons and their friends and relatives for a branding. Open from May through October. Information: *Ben and Pauli Middleton, Deer Forks Ranch,* 1200 Poison Lake Rd., Douglas, WY 82633 (phone: 307-358-2033).

COTTONWOOD RANCH, Riverton, Wyoming The owners raise corn, oats, barley, and alfalfa as well as cattle and sheep. The simple 13-room house is an expansion of the original log house that was homesteaded in 1937. The three guestrooms share a bath and family room. Guests can accompany Earl Anglen on his farm chores or go hiking. Horseback riding and fishing are available nearby. The food, prepared by Earl's wife, Judy, is sumptuous—sourdough pancakes topped with honey from the ranch's own hives, scrambled eggs with homemade salsa, and biscuits with gravy. Information: *Earl and Judy Anglen, Cottonwood Ranch,* 951 Missouri Valley Rd., Riverton, WY 82501 (phone: 307-856-3064).

A Short Tour of Indian America

When people discuss early American history, their starting point is usually the 17th or 18th century, and the founding of Jamestown, the colonial settlements, or George Washington and the American Revolution. But the real history of this country, occurring long before Europeans ever arrived, is the story of the American Indian. During the last glaciation, some 15,000 to 25,000 years ago, the area that now is the Bering Strait was a broad plain about 1,000 miles wide. Nomadic peoples wandered across this land bridge from Siberia into what now is Alaska. Before them stretched a vast, diverse land, from the frozen ice caps of the north to the primordial swamp of the southeastern tropics. These people roamed freely over the land and discovered what is now North America. In the Far North, they became ice hunters. In rich northern forests, hunting bands tracked the caribou, deer, beaver, and small fur-bearing animals. In the eastern woodlands and warm southeastern region, agriculture developed and became the center of ceremonial life. The farmers and hunters who inhabited the Great Plains would become great warriors after the introduction of the horse in 1750. Along the Pacific Coast were tribes who primarily fished. Native North American culture reached its most sophisticated point among the Pueblo, who lived in villages in the Southwest and developed a strain of maize that could survive in this arid region.

All of these peoples came to be known as Indians, for no better reason than that Christopher Columbus, who "discovered" these lands, thought he was in the Indies, off the coast of Asia. As the Indians settled, they adopted diverse lifestyles; but they remained similar in many ways. They were remarkably resourceful; isolated from the rest of the world, they created rich cultures around the mysteries and miracles of nature. In addition to the varieties of maize grown by different tribes, Indians developed pumpkins, beans, squash, tobacco, potatoes, sweet potatoes, chocolate, tomatoes, vanilla, and peanuts. Each tribe spoke its own language; during this period in history, at least 200 mutually unintelligible languages were spoken by the Native American people. In these languages, the Indians told stories of the wonders of creation. The Navajo story of emergence from the Black World that was "darker than the darkness of all the moonless nights of many winters" is as beautiful and rich as the story of Adam and Eve. Other tribes created their own legends, songs, dances, and ceremonies. Some feared nature, others praised its benevolence, but they all channeled tremendous amounts of physical and emotional energy into their rituals. In New Mexico, the Indians painted a series of murals with iron oxide to glorify nature. Elsewhere in the Southwest, they built subterranean chambers of worship, called kivas. In the Southeast, immense ceremonial mounds of earth were filled with sculpture, and many stand today, still protecting the secrets of the rituals for which they were created.

With the arrival of European explorers, the story of the American Indian becomes, to a great extent, a tragic tale of exploitation. In 1492, Columbus sailed to the New World and encountered the Indians, remarking on their "artless and generous quality." In return for their good will, Columbus sent 600 Indians back to Spain as slaves. During the following centuries, the Spanish, British, and Americans waged nearly constant war against the Indians. There was outright massacre, exemplified by the 1890 incident at Wounded Knee, when 300 unarmed Sioux men, women, and children, gathered to celebrate a Ghost Dance (which the Indians ironically believed would save them from decimation by the white invaders), were gunned down by the Seventh Cavalry of the *US Army.* Less openly horrific, but just as pernicious, was the Indians' systematic subjugation by the US government. In 1835, the Five Civilized Tribes of the East (Cherokee, Seminole, Creek, Choctaw, and Chickasaw) were forcibly relocated to Indian Territory in Oklahoma, only to have most of the land taken away by the government for white homesteading after the Civil War. From 1887 to 1934 the General Allotment Act divided communal Indian lands, and reduced the total number of Indian-owned acres in America from 138 million to 48 million. Even in pathetic reservation enclaves, civil rights were denied the Indians. (Not until 1968, with the Civil Rights Act, were the provisions of the Bill of Rights extended to reservation Indians.)

Though many tribes have become extinct, 950,000 American Indians still survive, a testament to human dignity and endurance. Except in the Southwest, the Indian tribes no longer occupy their original lands, and their members are beset with problems—discrimination, extremely high unemployment, and high alcoholism and suicide rates. But the story of the real discoverers of America is not finished. In the past 25 years or so, many young Native Americans have become politically active and have brought about international recognition of their plight.

But improvement in Indian affairs demands more than recognition; this gap in understanding can be bridged only by direct contact. In recent years, this has become possible with the growth of tourism in Indian communities. Even more militant members of Indian society believe that tourism is a positive trend that will allow their tribes to practice their own unique lifestyles while sustaining themselves economically. From commercialized Seminole reservations in Florida to settlements in the Southwest, where tribes still inhabit their ancestral lands—some of the most beautiful country in America—you can glimpse the complex dances and ceremonies and examine the magnificent hand-crafted baskets, jewelry, patchwork, and painting of these ancient civilizations. Though the cultures of this Indian America lie at the root of our nation's heritage, they are as foreign to most of us as those of remotest Egypt and the Far East. When you enter Indian America, meet the people on their own terms. Do not photograph ceremonies, rituals, or individuals without express permission; do not use recording devices, sketch pads, or notebooks. In general, behave as unobtrusively as possible, refraining from applause, loud talking, or even questions about the significance of rituals. In some cases, explanations may be offered. Otherwise it is best to watch what is going on around you and do research before or afterward. Keeping these few things in mind, you will undoubtedly find an adventure in Indian America truly rewarding.

Described below are several highlights of Indian America—reservations and other Indian lands, ceremonies, beautiful natural settings, and excellent museums. For information about arts and crafts businesses owned and operated by Native Americans, get a copy of the free *Source Directory* published by the *Indian Arts & Crafts Board* (*US Dept. of the Interior,* Room 4004 MIB, Washington, DC 20240; phone: 202-208-3773).

For an overview of American Indian heritage, consult the following: *America in 1492,* by Alvin Josephy Jr. (Knopf; $17, paperback); *I Have Spoken: American History Through the Voices of the Indians,* edited by Virginia I. Armstrong (Swallow Press; $12.95, paperback); *Indian America: A Traveler's Companion,* by Eagle-Walking Turtle (John Muir Publications; $18.95, paperback; 800-888-7504); *Indian Heritage of America,* by Alvin Josephy (Houghton Mifflin; $12.95, paperback); and *Indians of North America,* by Harold E. Driver (University of Chicago Press; $24.95, paperback), a reconstruction of the Native American culture with an emphasis on the 20th century and the post-1960s era.

SOUTH

MICCOSUKEE INDIAN VILLAGE, near Miami, Florida Some 550 members of the Miccosukee tribe (which was not recognized officially until 1962) live on this reservation on the northern border of the *Everglades National Park.* A museum has exhibits tracing the history of the tribe, which shares a language and hunting and fishing techniques with another tribe living in Florida, the Seminole. Craftspeople demonstrate dollmaking, woodcarving, and basketweaving; daily alligator-wrestling shows are presented as well. The lifestyle on the reservation is still fairly traditional. In the school system, English takes second place to Mikasuki, the tribal language. You'll see the traditional *chickees,* which are palmetto thatch-roofed dwellings, and some Miccosukee artists at work, making baskets, cypress woodcarvings, and clothing of patchwork cloth (available at the cultural center). A quarter-mile east of the museum is the tribe's restaurant, which serves traditional Indian fare—frybread, pumpkin bread, and catfish—as well as hot dogs, burgers, and such. One of the best times to visit is at the end of December during the annual *Indian Arts Festival,* when musicians, artists, and craftsmen from many tribes around the world converge to play everything from traditional music to Indian rock. On US 41, 26 miles west of Miami. Information: *Miccosukee Tribal Enterprise,* PO Box 440021, Miami, FL 33144 (phone: 970-223-8380), or *Florida Dept. of Commerce, Div. of Tourism,* 107 W. Gaines St., Tallahassee, FL 32399-2000 (phone: 904-487-1462).

CHEROKEE, North Carolina Adjacent to the *Great Smoky Mountains National Park,* this beautiful area is the country where the Cherokee lived before they were forcibly relocated to Oklahoma in 1838 along a route now called the Trail of Tears. But some Cherokee remained, hiding in the mountains, and others returned later. Today, this is the center of the Cherokee people, and many work here in the tribal government, in factories that produce moccasins and quilts, and in tourist businesses. One of the best times to visit is in the fall during the *Fall Festival,* when Cherokee from all over return to participate in traditional dances, games, and arts and crafts demonstrations. The event customarily begins the Tuesday of the first full week in

October. Information: *Cherokee Visitors Center,* PO Box 460, Cherokee, NC 28719 (phone: 704-497-9195; 800-438-1601). Of interest at Cherokee are the following:

Oconaluftee Indian Village This replica of a Cherokee village depicts 18th-century life, with guided tours. Included are a seven-sided council house, ceremonial chambers, and lectures where tribal members dressed in authentic costumes demonstrate crafts, cooking, and weapon making. Closed November through mid-May. Off Rte. 441 on Drama Rd. For a little more history come to life, see the drama *Unto These Hills,* which recounts the story of the Cherokee people in an amphitheater—*Mountainside Theater* (on Drama Rd.)—during the summer (also see *Outdoor Dramas*). Information: *Oconaluftee Indian Village,* PO Box 398, Cherokee, NC 28719 (phone: 704-497-2111).

Museum of the Cherokee Indian Owned by the Eastern Band of Cherokee Indians, it has multimedia theaters and innovative exhibitions, including examples of clothing and implements used for farming, hunting, and fishing from the Ice Age to the present, as well as an exhibit on the Cherokee language. Open daily. Admission charge. On Drama Rd. Information: *Museum of the Cherokee Indian,* PO Box 1599, Cherokee, NC 28719 (phone: 704-497-3481).

Qualla Arts and Crafts Mutual The best of the area's many crafts shops, this is the official cooperative marketing center of the Cherokee. The work is authentic, and many items here are rarely available elsewhere, such as white oak, river cane, and honeysuckle vine baskets; animal sculptures made of buckeye, walnut, and wild cherry; pottery; and beadwork. Write or call for their $2 color catalogue. Rte. 441 near the museum. Information: *Qualla Arts and Crafts Mutual,* PO Box 310, Cherokee, NC 28719 (phone: 704-497-3103).

WEST

Some 17 million acres in northeastern Arizona and neighboring New Mexico and Utah form the Navajo Nation, the largest Indian reservation in America. The Navajo are the most populous of the Indian tribes, with over 200,000 members, many of whom live in traditional dwellings called hogans, octagonal houses built of logs, cemented with clay, and covered with earth. The Navajo primarily were a pastoral rather than agricultural people, but they did pick up farming, weaving, and sand painting from the Pueblo.

Nowhere in the United States do you get a better sense of the Indian past than among the Pueblo, the desert peoples of New Mexico. The arid climate has left many ancient ruins intact, and the tribes live among them on the land of their ancestors in pueblos, communal villages of adobe or sandstone dwellings that blend unobtrusively into their surroundings. The pueblos described below are within driving distance of Santa Fe or Albuquerque. Other reservations described below include those of the Hopi and Sioux.

When exploring on a reservation, rules are stringent for non-tribal members. In Navajoland, for example, you must be accompanied by a Navajo guide in most areas and you must sign an agreement not to deface or remove artifacts.

FIRST, SECOND, AND THIRD MESA, Arizona The Hopi are exceptional jewelry makers and farmers and live in a close communal relationship in apartment villages on three isolated ridges of land high above the northeastern Arizona desert. The best place to stay is on the Second Mesa, at the *Hopi Cultural Center,* which has a motel, museum, and restaurant where traditional Hopi foods such as hominy stew, frybread, and *piki* are served along with hamburgers and such. At the *Hopi Arts and Crafts Guild,* you can purchase the finest Hopi crafts—silver jewelry, pottery, kachina dolls, and baskets. The studio of Charles Loloma, the most prominent contemporary Indian jeweler, and Old Oraibi, the oldest continuously occupied village in the US, are on the Third Mesa. A variety of ceremonies are open to visitors, such as the Ladies Society's *Basket Dance,* but the exact dates usually are not announced until very close to the event, so check at the cultural center. Motel reservations should be made at least three weeks to two months in advance, especially during the summer. Rte. 264 at Piñon Rd., 4 miles northwest of Rte. 87. Information: *Hopi Cultural Center,* PO Box 67, Second Mesa, AZ 86043 (phone: 520-734-2401).

WINDOW ROCK, Arizona The town is the seat of Navajo tribal government and the hub of a reservation that spreads across Arizona, New Mexico, and Utah. It's a good place to begin a trip into Navajoland. You can view displays about the tribe's history and culture at the *Tribal Museum;* learn a bit about how the Navajo live in harmony with their environment at the *Navajo Zoological Park;* shop at the *Navajo Arts and Crafts Enterprise;* tour the *Tribal Council Chambers* and learn about the history of the Navajo government; and take excursions into the surrounding countryside. Most notable are the Anasazi ruins in *Canyon de Chelle* near Chinle. The *Navajoland Tourism Development*—within the *Division of Economic Development*—can suggest destinations and give you dates for various events and activities. Among the biggest festivities are the *Navajo Nation Fair,* staged in Window Rock the first Wednesday through Sunday after *Labor Day,* and the *Fourth of July* celebration and *PRCA Rodeo,* held annually during *July Fourth* weekend. The *Shiprock Navajo Fair* in Shiprock, New Mexico, is considered the oldest and most traditional Navajo fair in the US. There is also a monthly rug auction in Crownpoint, New Mexico. Both towns are part of the reservation; Crownpoint is a one-hour drive east of Window Rock on Route 66, and Shiprock is 45 minutes farther in the same direction. The *Navajo Nation Inn*'s restaurant in Window Rock offers hearty native dishes like Navajo tacos, frybread, and lamb stew. The inn, the only lodging for miles around, is pleasant and comfortable (phone: 602-871-4108). Alcoholic beverages are not allowed on the reservation. Information: *Navajoland Tourism Dept.,*

PO Box 663, Window Rock, AZ 86515 (phone: 520-871-6659; 520-871-6436).

MONUMENT VALLEY NAVAJO TRIBAL PARK, Arizona and Utah The valley is a classic western scenic wonder with high mesas, sculptured buttes, natural bridges, earth arches, chiseled canyons and gorges, and huge sandstone monoliths; it has been used in filming innumerable Westerns, including a few early John Wayne films. A 14-mile road (a one-and-a-half- to two-hour drive) winds its way through the valley and can be negotiated by most cars, except during the winter, when four-wheel-drive vehicles are advisable. You may either take your own car or join a group tour with a Navajo guide; if you drive yourself, however, you may not get out of your car during the tour. There are also two campgrounds; permits for both are available at the visitors' center, where there is also a Navajo arts and crafts shop. 25 miles north of Kayenta off Rte. 163. Information: *Monument Valley Tribal Park,* PO Box 360289, Monument Valley, UT 84536 (phone: 801-727-3353).

HUBBELL TRADING POST NATIONAL HISTORIC SITE, Ganado, Arizona Dating to the 1870s, this is the oldest continuously active trading post on the Navajo reservation. The post and Hubbell home depict the life of an unusual trader and his family, and have displays on the history of the area, as well as a beautiful Western art collection, handwoven rugs, silver work, and other jewelry. Prices are reasonable and the craftsmanship excellent. The *National Park Service* runs guided tours, and there are usually weaving and silversmithing demonstrations at the visitors' center; you may also try your hand at the ancient art of weaving. Located 1 mile west of Ganado on Rte. 264. Information: *Hubbell Trading Post National Historic Site,* PO Box 150, Ganado, AZ 86505 (phone: 520-755-3475).

NAVAJO NATIONAL MONUMENT, Tonalea, Arizona The largest and most intricate of Arizona's cliff dwellings are preserved in this rugged country. There are two areas, each of which contains a remarkable 13th-century pueblo ruin. Betatakin is the more accessible of the areas, and the ruin across the canyon may be viewed from a ½-mile-long foot trail or visited on a 5-mile (round trip), four- to six-hour guided hike given daily in summer. The other area, Keet Seel, may be reached on horseback (reserve in advance at headquarters) or by a strenuous 8½-mile hike (one way), in summer only. At the monument headquarters, the visitors' center offers exhibitions on the Anasazi culture, a slide show and film, and a Navajo arts and crafts shop. There are also campgrounds for RVs, tents, and group camping. Call first for tour information and winter weather conditions. 28 miles west of Kayenta off Rte. 160 to 564. Information: *Navajo National Monument,* HC-71, PO Box 3, Tonalea, AZ 86044 (phone: 520-672-2366).

MESA VERDE NATIONAL PARK, near Durango and Cortez, Colorado More than 1,400 years ago, Indians built homes on the mesa tops and elaborate dwellings set into the cliffsides of area canyons. Today, visitors can explore some of the most dramatic of the cliff dwellings, including Long House and Step House on Wetherill Mesa; the 200-room Cliff Palace, the largest cliff dwelling in North America; Spruce Tree House, amazingly well preserved; and Balcony House. Whether you tour these on your own or with a ranger will depend upon which site, and when, you are visiting. All the sites except Spruce Tree House close after the first big snowfall and reopen in the spring. Other area attractions include the old *Durango & Silverton* narrow-gauge railroad (phone: 970-247-2733 for train information), which runs from Durango, through deep forested canyons, to the quaint old mining town of Silverton; and the *San Juan National Forest,* great for hiking and fishing. The area offers a variety of other national monuments, such as the *Aztec Ruins, Chaco Canyon,* and other nearby prehistoric remains, pueblos, and cliff dwellings scattered around the Four Corners area, as well as *Canyon de Chelly* (pronounced *Shay*), near Chinle, Arizona, on the Navajo reservation. Lodgings are available in the park at *Far View Lodge* (phone: 970-529-4421), which is modern, beautifully situated, and aptly named. Generally, it is closed during the winter, as are parts of the park. In Durango is the famous 108-year-old, 93-room *Strater* hotel (phone: 970 247-4431; 800-247-4431), lavishly furnished with authentic Victorian walnut antiques (the largest collection in the US), yet with all modern conveniences. Eighteen miles north of Durango is *Tamarron* (phone: 970-259-2000; 800-678-1000), a 412-room luxury resort on 760 acres. Information: *Superintendent,* PO Box 8, *Mesa Verde National Park,* CO 81330 (phone: 970-529-4461); for details about the area, write the *Cortez Chamber of Commerce,* PO Box 968, Cortez, CO 81321 (phone: 970-565-3414).

ACOMA, New Mexico Perhaps the most spectacular of the pueblos, this village sits on a 367-foot-high mesa, commanding a panoramic view of the New Mexico plain. The pueblo has been inhabited for some 1,000 years, and though many of the families live in nearby farming villages, Acoma is open to visitors year-round except during religious ceremonies. Among the buildings are the mission of San Esteban, established in 1629 and constructed of adobe walls 10 to 14 feet thick; a subterranean ceremonial chamber known as a kiva on the main plaza (off-limits to visitors); and several small craft shops where delicate Acoma pottery with geometric and bird pattern motifs can be purchased for prices lower than at trading posts elsewhere. Tribal members lead tours daily; admission charge and photographic fee. On I-40, Exit 108, 60 miles west of Albuquerque. Information: *Acoma Tourist Center,* PO Box 309, Acoma, NM 87034 (phone: 505-470-4966).

TAOS, New Mexico Sitting at the base of the Sangre de Cristo range, which culminates in New Mexico's highest point, the Taos pueblo is a stronghold of tribal tradition. The people are devout in their religious observances, and subsist as farmers. Near the multi-storied adobe dwelling, craftsmen display moccasins and drums as well as mica clay pottery. There is an admission charge and an additional charge for sketching and/or painting. The

San Geronimo Fiesta in late September is open to the public and features extraordinary dancing, a greased-pole climbing contest, and other festivities. The town of Taos, 2½ miles south, is primarily an artists' colony, and the work of residents and of other artists is displayed at some 80 galleries all over town. Area information: *Taos County Chamber of Commerce,* Drawer I, Taos, NM 87571 (phone: 505-758-3873; 800-732-8267).

OGLALA SIOUX TRIBE, PINE RIDGE RESERVATION, South Dakota This 1.4-million acre reservation—the site of the 1890 Wounded Knee massacre (a tragedy later commemorated by a simple gravesite)—is now the home of nearly 19,000 Lakota. Once dominant on the northern plains, the Sioux—nomadic buffalo hunters who lived in conical tents of animal hide called tepees—were the prototypical American Indians. Today, the buffalo no longer roam, and the tribe is beset with economic problems, but the Sioux remain. The area is not highly developed commercially, but the rewards for visitors are great. You can visit the *Red Cloud Indian School,* 4 miles north of Pine Ridge, where there are exhibits on the Lakota culture and fine art: beadwork, quillwork (an intricate type of weaving employing porcupine quills), and magnificent paintings on buffalo hide that display a visionary quality, depicting a happy life that might again be. The tribal office can provide information about powwows to which the public is welcome, among which is the *Oglala Nation Fair.* Held the first weekend in August, it is a celebration of both honor and achievement that involves traditional drumming, dancing, and a parade. There also are other powwows and rodeos throughout the summer. The reservation is 120 miles south of Rapid City on Rte. 18. Information: *Oglala Sioux Tribe,* PO Box H, Pine Ridge, SD 57770 (phone: 605-867-5821).

MUSEUMS

The *Heard Museum* in Phoenix, the *Wheelwright Museum of the American Indian* in Santa Fe, the *National Museum of the American Indian* in New York City, and the *Burke Museum* in Seattle are each described in detail in the appropriate city chapters. The institutions below also provide extensive information and perspectives about Native American history and culture.

ANCHORAGE MUSEUM OF HISTORY AND ART, Anchorage, Alaska This municipal museum is dedicated to the collection, preservation, and interpretation of material pertinent to the art, history, and cultures of native Alaskans. The cultures of the Athapaska, Aleut, Tlingit, Haida, and Eskimo peoples are described in dioramas and models. Information: *Anchorage Museum of History and Art,* 121 W. Seventh Ave., Anchorage, AK 99501 (phone: 907-343-4326).

SIOUX INDIAN MUSEUM, Rapid City, South Dakota This fine facility, operated by the *Indian Arts and Crafts Board* of the *Department of the Interior,* transmits a feeling for the Sioux past with its collection of 19th-century Sioux artifacts—clothing, games, moccasins, pipe bags, and baby carriers. Another gallery broadens the scope with changing exhibitions, usually shows of contemporary artists from many different regional tribes. Information: *Sioux Indian Museum,* PO Box 1504, 515 West Blvd., Rapid City, SD 57709 (phone: 605-348-0557).

Civil War Battlesites

At the outset of the Civil War, much of America expected that the conflict would be settled after a single battle. This idea proved tremendously naïve, perhaps the greatest folly of the 19th century. As congressmen picnicked with their wives and watched the first battle at Manassas (Bull Run), they could not possibly anticipate the gruesome bloodbaths that would sorely challenge their patriotism and take the lives of well over half a million men.

The ethics and morality of slavery were not originally at the forefront of the Civil War; as in all wars, economics and politics were the true driving forces. In 1860, the North was becoming highly industrialized and favored a strong central government, whereas almost all the South's profits derived from agriculture. Blacks were deliberately uprooted from their homes in Africa and enslaved to white landowners, who used them to harvest their immense crops. The North's system of tariffs, freight rates, and other government intervention irritated southerners, who advocated states' rights and eventually proposed a separation from the Union. The secession of the Southern states, under the aegis of Jefferson Davis, the newly elected President of the Confederate States, prompted the Union to declare war.

The North attempted to coerce the Southern states back into the Union by advancing along two corridors—toward the Confederate capital at Richmond, Virginia, and along vital waterways through Tennessee—with the goal of splitting the Confederacy in two at the Mississippi River. At first, the Confederacy adopted a defensive posture, but later it unleashed retaliatory offenses. General Robert E. Lee successfully defeated a series of fierce Union attacks before President Abraham Lincoln appointed General Ulysses S. Grant commander-in-chief of the Union forces. Grant began an unswerving war of attrition against the Confederate forces, while General William Tecumseh Sherman forced western Confederate armies backward, captured Atlanta, and burned a bloody swath to the sea at Savannah. Southern civilian homes were routinely occupied by northern troops, who took brief respites before the inexorable march moved onward, then looted them and burned them to the ground. After the Union victory at Petersburg, Grant finally forced Lee to abandon his Richmond-Petersburg fortifications and accept terms for surrender at *Appomattox Court House.* The Union had regained its brother states at the cost of 624,500 lives, not including the countless thousands of civilians who also perished.

Casualties were unparalleled; although weapons technology was considered at its peak, bullets were ejected from guns at a low velocity. If a bone was struck, it would shatter completely, rendering the limb virtually useless. Medieval medical procedures and the constant shortage of surgical supplies resulted in routine amputations without anesthesia. Teeming masses of soldiers died waiting for medical care on the field hours after a battle had concluded, frequently entangled with dead comrades.

Since 1913, when war veterans reenacted Pickett's Charge at Gettysburg on the 50th anniversary of that battle, a Civil War cult following has steadily gained momentum. Tactical demonstrations of weaponry used during the war, re-created battles with simulated casualties, and "living history" weekends, where volunteers dress in authentic period costumes and re-create the lifestyle of the soldiers and their families, have become immensely popular. There are also annual luminaries (candle-lighting ceremonies) at major battlesites; at Antietam, for example, 23,000 lighted candles are placed across the battlefield in remembrance of the dead on the anniversary of the battle. All of the national parks listed below have interpretive programs, demonstrations, and reenactments of Civil War life; contact each park directly for schedule information.

Although most visits to Civil War sites consist of tours of individual sites, an escorted package tour is offered by the *Smithsonian Institution.* It covers a number of sites in Virginia, including *Manassas (Bull Run)*, *Fredericksburg* and *Chancellorsville,* the *Wilderness* and *Spotsylvania* battlefields, Richmond and *Richmond National Battlefield Park, Petersburg National Battlefield, Appomattox Court House, Lexington,* and various battlefields in the Shenandoah Valley. The tour continues to Harpers Ferry, West Virginia, Antietam Creek (near Sharpsburg, Maryland), and Gettysburg, Pennsylvania. For more information, contact the *Smithsonian Institution, Study Tours and Seminars* (1100 Jefferson Dr. SW, Suite 3045, Washington, DC 20560; phone: 202-357-4700; fax: 202-786-2315). For a listing of Civil War battlesites in Virginia, write to *Virginia Tourism* (1021 E. Cary St., 14th Floor, Richmond, VA 23219; phone: 804-786-4484; 800-321-1965; fax: 804-786-1919). In addition, the *Civil War Courier,* a newspaper that comes out every two months, lists battlefield reenactment sites and other Civil War–related events, such as balls, commemorations, and memorabilia sales. For information and a free sample copy, write or call *Civil War Courier* (2503 Delaware Ave., Buffalo, NY 14216; phone: 716-873-2594).

Released two years ago by the *National Parks and Conservation Association,* in cooperation with the National Park Experience, is the *Civil War Battlefields Vacation Kit.* It provides facts on every battlefield park and includes information on how to trace your Civil War ancestors. It costs $39.95, plus $4.95 for shipping and handling. Information: *National Parks and Conservation Assn.,* c/o NPE, PO Box 5794, Bethesda, MD 20814 (phone: 800-PARK-KIT, ext. 89).

And for an overview of the Civil War, consult *Battle Cry of Freedom, The Era of the Civil War,* by James M. McPherson (Oxford University Press; $16.95, paperback) or *The Civil War: A Narrative,* by Shelby Foote (Random House; $72, three volumes in hardcover).

GETTYSBURG, Pennsylvania This watershed battle, fought from July 1 to July 3, 1863, proved the demise of the Confederate army. Gettysburg was the locus of a network of roads that led from Pennsylvania and Maryland; General Robert E. Lee's strategy was to gain control of the area and then further infiltrate the North. Union forces held firm, despite the courageous attempts of the Confederate Pickett's Charge. Twelve thousand infantrymen charged Cemetery Ridge, and were systematically cut down by Union fire. On November 19, 1863, President Lincoln delivered a brief speech honoring the dead (later called the *Gettysburg Address*), affirming ". . . that this nation, under God, shall have a new birth of freedom; and that government of the people, by the people, for the people, shall not perish from the earth." Today the site covers 25 square miles. More than 1,300 monuments and 400 cannon are located throughout the park, along 40 miles of scenic roads. *Gettysburg Civil War Heritage Days* are a major annual event; the festivities include a living history encampment, band concerts, a lectures series, and a battle reenactment. In the park's *Cyclorama Center* hangs the *Cyclorama,* painted by Paul Philippoteaux, which depicts the Battle of Pickett's Charge. There's also an enormous topographical electric map in the visitors' center, which provides basic information on the battle and the park. Visitors can take a self-guided, three-hour auto tour with a map provided by the visitors' center or obtain a detailed battlefield guide that outlines another, two-hour driving tour. The *Gettysburg Museum of the Civil War* also is located in the visitors' center. Displayed here is the premier collection of Civil War and *Gettysburg* artifacts in the country. A descriptive audiotape tour and cassette player can be rented at the *National Civil War Wax Museum* (phone: 717-334-6245). Bus tours of the battlefield are offered by *Gettysburg Tours* (778 Baltimore St., Gettysburg, PA 17325; phone: 717-334-6296). The park is closed *Thanksgiving, Christmas,* and *New Year's Day.* No admission charge to the park; there is a fee for the *Cyclorama* and electric map. Information: *Superintendent, Gettysburg National Military Park,* 97 Taneytown Rd., Gettysburg, PA 17325 (phone: 717-334-1124) or the *Gettysburg Travel Council,* 35 Carlisle St., Gettysburg, PA 17325 (phone: 717-334-6274).

ANTIETAM CREEK, Sharpsburg, Maryland The astounding beauty of the Maryland countryside, with its rolling, verdant hills and towering cornfields, belies the carnage that once littered these grounds. September 17, 1862 was considered the bloodiest one-day battle in American history, with casualties totaling more than 23,000. The battle eventually concluded as a tactical draw. In the sunken road, dubbed "Bloody Lane," the dead were piled high; the combat was so intense that Union troops steadied themselves on the dead to get a better shot at retreating Confederate soldiers. Ironically, thousands might never have perished had Union General George McClellan decided to attack Lee's army sooner. There is an 8½-mile driving tour, which covers the three phases of the conflict, as well as a visitors' center with a small museum, which features Captain James Hope's panoramic painting of the battle. The museum also offers a 26-minute film re-creating the battle and Lincoln's visit a fortnight later, as well as a wintertime lecture series that hosts authors and historians of the Civil War. During the year, the park offers living history presentations, which include an evening tour conducted by torchlight in September that shows the impact of the war on the surrounding town. The *Christmastime* candle-lighting ceremony is staggering; at dusk on the first Saturday in December, a candle is lit across the field for each casualty, and the field fairly blazes with light. Closed *Thanksgiving, Christmas,* and *New Year's Day.* No admission charge for children under 16 and senior citizens. Information: *Superintendent, Antietam National Battlefield,* PO Box 158, Sharpsburg, MD 21782 (phone: 301-432-5124) or *Washington County Convention and Visitors Bureau,* 1826 Dual Hwy., Hagerstown, MD 21740 (phone: 301-791-3130; 800-228-7829).

HARPERS FERRY, West Virginia In 1859, the ardent anti-slavery activist John Brown made an unsuccessful raid on the town's arsenal and armory. Three years later, in September 1862, General "Stonewall" Jackson captured the army garrison and won a small victory for the South. You can visit the *Master Armorer's House,* now a museum on the history of gunmaking, or the reconstructed garrison, arsenal, and mills. A walking trail on Bolivar Heights reveals the remains of Union earthworks, and the trail on Maryland Heights leads to Civil War defenses and to the confluence of the Shenandoah and Potomac Rivers. In the *John Brown Building,* located near the visitors' center, there is a brief 12-minute slide show depicting the conflict, as well as an exhibit that contains the sledgehammer used to break down the doors of the arsenal that Brown had captured. The visitors' center offers lectures given in period costume from May through late August. Closed *Christmas.* No admission charge for children under 16; there's a fee for parking. Information: *Superintendent, Harpers Ferry National Historical Park,* PO Box 65, Harpers Ferry, WV 25425 (phone: 304-535-6029).

MANASSAS (BULL RUN), near Centreville, Virginia The Civil War was originally expected by both the North and South to be short-lived, culminating in one tremendous battle. Yet the first major conflict of the war—the Battle of Bull Run—on July 21, 1861, proved but a precursor to bloodshed. An equestrian statue of General Thomas Jackson marks the site where the imperturbable Confederate leader first achieved fame for his staunch conduct on the field. As Brigadier General Barnard Bee approached Jackson's troops, who were patiently awaiting the Union troops on Henry House Hill, he quipped, "There is Jackson standing like a stone wall"; hence his nickname, "Stonewall" Jackson. There are trails on Henry House and Matthews Hills leading to the reconstructed Stone Bridge across Bull Run. Markers and trails identify tactical positions in the second battle fought here, including an unfinished section of railroad grade that the Confederates held, throwing rocks at the enemy when they temporarily ran out of ammunition. Today the site is the largest contiguous battlefield park in the country, covering 5,100 acres. The visitors' center, located on Henry House Hill, contains an aerial-view map of the battle, as well as a brief slide show. From June through *Labor Day,* a field history walking tour of the conflict is offered several times daily from the visitors' center. Guided van tours are available on weekends during the summer to visit the grounds of the second battle. Closed *Christmas*. No admission charge for children under 17 and senior citizens over 61. Information: *Superintendent, Manassas (Bull Run) National Battlefield Park,* 6511 Sudley Rd., Manassas, VA 22110 (phone: 703-361-1339).

ARLINGTON HOUSE, THE ROBERT E. LEE MEMORIAL, Arlington National Cemetery, Virginia In 1864, the military cemeteries in Washington and Alexandria were already packed with the dead. Secretary of War Edwin Stanton charged Quartermaster General Montgomery Meigs with the task of choosing a new site. Meigs, who had once served under Robert E. Lee before the war and now was allied with the North, chose the lawn in front of Lee's home and built the *Tomb of the Unknown Dead,* a monument that houses the bones of 2,110 soldiers originally buried in unmarked graves. The 1818 house now stands in the middle of *Arlington Cemetery* (see *Washington, DC,* THE CITIES), and has panoramic views of Washington and the Potomac River. The cemetery contains the dead from many military conflicts, as well as statesmen and other prominent Americans. Self-guided tours begin at the front portico. Closed *Christmas* and *New Year's Day.* Admission charge. Information: *Site Manager, Arlington House,* c/o *Turkey Run Park,* McLean, VA 22101 (phone: 703-557-0613).

FREDERICKSBURG, Virginia On December 13, 1862, despite General Ambrose Burnside's plan to cross the Rappahannock River and seize the heights beyond Fredericksburg, Lee's army crushed the determined Union attack. Telegraph Hill (later dubbed Lee Hill) lies along a 5-mile driving tour that shows remnants of the Confederate frontline. Also, visitors can see miles of well-preserved Confederate infantry trenches; artillery strongpoints; Marye's Heights, where thousands were slaughtered by Lee's men; and the Sunken Road and the stone wall at the base of the hill, which sheltered Confederate marksmen.

Three other battles were fought around Fredericksburg during the following 18 months. At *Chancellorsville,* which was considered Lee's most masterful campaign, "Stonewall" Jackson lost an arm when his own soldiers mistakenly fired on him; later he died of pneumonia. (The house in which he died lies 25 miles south of the battlefield, just off I-95.) Remnants of trenches and earthworks, as well as cannon, delineate the battle. On May 5 and 6, 1864, Lee and Lieutenant General Ulysses S. Grant met in the Wilderness, a series of dense thickets and scrub that lay 10 miles west of Frederickbsurg. Union troops turned southward and renewed the fighting at Spotsylvania Courthouse on May 8, 1864. A section of these Confederate earthworks became known as the Bloody Angle; the 20 hours of combat in the pouring rain were so fierce that wounded Confederate soldiers fell on top of the dead. The visitors' center at *Fredericksburg* displays artwork completed by both Union and Confederate soldiers. Other artifacts include a sword and scabbard as well as a Zouave uniform (adapted from uniforms worn by French colonial soldiers). Closed *Christmas* and *New Year's Day.* No admission charge. Information: *Superintendent, Fredericksburg and Spotsylvania National Military Park,* 120 Chatham La., Fredericksburg, VA 22405 (phone: 703-371-0802).

RICHMOND-PETERSBURG, Virginia Since the Confederate capital of Richmond was only 100 miles from Washington, its capture was the ultimate objective of most of the battles fought in Virginia. *Richmond National Battlefield Park,* which stretches in an arc east of the city, contains sites of General George McClellan's Seven Days campaign (a series of bloody battles that took place in 1862) and the Battle of Cold Harbor, Lee's last major victory. The park preserves remnants of Beaver Dam Creek, Gaines' Mill, as well as Malvern Hill, where the last of the Seven Days battles were fought. At Cold Harbor, a battlefield drive follows the Union and Confederate earthworks where Grant's army lost a staggering 7,000 men in half an hour. *Fort Harrison,* 5 miles south of Richmond, has earthen fortifications and a 7-mile battlefield tour. At Drewry's Bluff, located above the James River, a fortification attacked by the famous *Monitor* and other Union ships in 1862 is well preserved. Just as Grant foresaw, the final campaign for Richmond was fought at Petersburg. The most prominent battlefield feature here is the Crater, a costly Union attempt to blow up the Confederate line by digging a tunnel to the enemy lines and exploding a mine. In the visitors' center, there is a 17-minute show that depicts the battle. Guided tours and special living history programs are offered from mid-June to mid-August. The *Richmond Convention and Visitors Bureau* (Sixth St. Marketplace, 2nd Fl.; *mailing address:* 550 E. Marshall St., PO Box C25023219, Richmond, VA 23219; phone: 804-782-2777; 800-365-7272) can provide a list of battlefield locations in the area. Guided tours are available through *Historic Richmond Foundation Tours* (707-A E. Franklin St., Richmond, VA 23219; phone: 804-780-0107), which offers a four-hour Civil War battlefields tour on selected Sundays from April through October, and a Civil War city tour on Mondays through Saturdays. *Richmond Park* is closed *Thanksgiving* and *Christmas.* No admission charge. Information: *Superintendent, Richmond National Battlefield Park,* 3215 E. Broad St., Richmond VA 23223 (phone: 804-226-1981). *Petersburg Battlefield* is closed *Christmas* and *New Year's Day.* No admission charge for senior citizens. Information: *Superintendent, Petersburg National Battlefield,* PO Box 549, Petersburg, VA 23804 (phone: 804-732-3531).

APPOMATTOX COURT HOUSE, Virginia On April 9, 1865, Lee finally surrendered his army to Grant. Three days later, as Confederates marched up the Old Richmond–Lynchburg Stage Road to stack their weapons, the Union ranks were called to attention and saluted their foes. The *McLean House,* where the surrender document was drafted, is part of this restored village, which includes the *Clover Hill Tavern, Meek's Store,* and the *Woodson Law Office.* A visitors' center is located in the courthouse, which houses photographs, drawings, and uniforms. Closed all federal holidays between November and February. No admission charge for children under 16 and senior citizens. Information: *Superintendent, Appomattox Court House National Historical Park,* PO Box 218, Appomattox, VA 24522 (phone: 804-352-8987).

SHILOH, near Crump, Tennessee Fighting around a church here, Confederate forces tried to roust Grant's army, which was waiting for reinforcements before continuing to Mississippi. Most of the men who participated in the battle had never been in combat before, and some tried to flee before they could be asked to fight. The firing in the peach orchard was so intense that the bullets striking blooming buds created the illusion of falling snow. *Shiloh Church* survived the battle but was shortly destroyed; the present church is the third on this site near the initial Confederate assault. There is a 9½-mile driving tour of the battlefield, which includes the peach orchard and Sunken Road, where Union defenders bought Grant enough time to organize a new defensive line; Water Oaks Pond, where the Confederates made a last desperate attack on the second day of battle; and the site where one of the South's most respected military men, General Albert S. Johnston, died. Across the battlefield, a Confederate burial trench (one of 10) was a mass grave for over 700 men. At the visitors' center, a 25-minute film delineates the battle. The small museum exhibits artifacts of the rank-and-file soldiers, company commanders, and equipment. Closed *Christmas* and *New Year's Day*. Admission charge. Information: *Superintendent, Shiloh National Military Park,* Rte. 1, Box 9, Shiloh, TN 38376 (phone: 901-689-5275; 901-689-5696).

VICKSBURG, Mississippi Grant's nine-month campaign to capture the major Confederate stronghold began with the back-breaking work of digging canals across river bends to bypass defenses. While this tactic ultimately failed, Grant's troops eventually succeeded because of sheer determination. Grant finally marched down the west side of the Mississippi, and crossed the river below the city. After a 47-day siege, the city surrendered. When the Confederate forces at Port Hudson received news of the defeat, they, too, surrendered. Thus, the Union army gained control of the Mississippi River from Cairo, Illinois, to the Gulf. In joyous response, President Abraham Lincoln stated, "The Father of Waters again goes unvexed to the sea." The *Vicksburg National Military Park* stretches in an arc around the city. A 16-mile driving tour follows the wooded, hilly contours of the Union siege line and Confederate defenses, where numerous artillery batteries, forts, and earthworks are marked by more than 1,600 memorial plaques and other monuments. In the park's visitors' center, there is a mock-up of the caves in which civilians hid to escape Union bombardment. Located at the *Cairo Museum* is a reconstructed gunboat, the USS *Cairo,* which includes the 15-ton bow section recovered from the Yazoo River—mine hole and all. (The *Cairo* was the first ship to be sunk by a mine.) Also at the museum are displays of the soldiers' personal effects, which include pocket combs, toothbrushes, razors, and knives. No admission charge for senior citizens. Closed *Christmas.* Information: *Superintendent, Vicksburg National Military Park,* 3201 Clay St., Vicksburg, MS 39180 (phone: 601-636-0583).

CHICKAMAUGA, Georgia, and CHATTANOOGA, Tennessee Some historians claim that the Confederates might easily have retaken Tennessee and prolonged the war following the Battle of Chickamauga if General Braxton Bragg had aggressively pursued the Union forces. By the time Bragg acted, however, the Union army was entrenched in Chattanooga and reinforcements were on the way. Nevertheless, it was still considered a major victory for the South. You can almost hear the faint echoes of the thunderous cannon and groans of dying men in this tranquil, forest setting. A 7-mile driving tour includes the sparsely furnished Brotherton log cabin, where Confederates breached the center of the Union line, and the cabin on Snodgrass Hill, where Union General George H. Thomas's unyielding stand earned him the sobriquet "Rock of Chickamauga." The drive along Missionary Ridge and a visit to the visitors' center to see James Walker's 13-by-30-foot painting, *Battle of Lookout Mountain,* are recommended. Also in the visitors' center is a multimedia film presentation that documents the progression of the battles. It includes photographs, letters, and artwork, with voice-overs of a Confederate and a Union "ghost" narrating the course of the conflict. Closed *Christmas.* Admission charge only for the film. Information: *Superintendent, Chickamauga and Chattanooga National Military Parks,* PO Box 2128, Fort Oglethorpe, GA 30742 (phone: 706-866-9241).

FORT SUMTER, Charleston, South Carolina The very first shots of the Civil War were fired on this fort on April 12, 1861, by Confederate General Pierre Gustave Toutant Beauregard's troops. The minor damage the fort sustained during the bombardment gave little indication of the traumatic conflict to follow. Later Union bombardment reduced the fort to a battered hulk, destroyed by seven million pounds of shells. The fort, which resides on a manmade island, has been renovated and houses 11 Parrott cannon. The three Union shells embedded in one wall show how the rifled cannon eventually rendered this type of large fortification obsolete. A mountain howitzer guards the exterior esplanade, and the small museum contains a variety of dioramas, pictoral displays, and relics. The original flags taken by Major Robert Anderson when he surrendered the fort are still on display. *Fort Sumter* can be reached either via ferryboat from Patriot's Point in Mt. Pleasant outside Charleston or from Lockwood Boulevard in Charleston. Closed *Christmas. Fort Moultrie* (a fort that dates back to the Revolutionary War), where Union troops were stationed before they retreated to *Fort Sumter,* is also closed *Christmas.* Information: *Superintendent, Fort Sumter National Monument,* 1214 Middle St., Sullivan Island, SC 29482 (phone: 803-883-3123).

Dam Nation

The politics of water and the ecological impact of America's "big dams" are just beginning to be understood, but the bane of environmentalists can, for all that, make quite a pleasant vacation experience. First of all, dams are clean-lined and beautiful to look at; they're impressively huge. All the bigger ones offer tours of the powerhouses of pumping stations, or at least have visitors' centers with exhibits that explain what the dams do. Often you also can watch boats being locked through navigation systems, or see fish fighting their way up fish ladders to their upstream spawning grounds. And after you've seen the dam, you can enjoy yourself on the huge reservoirs they impound.

Note that the *Hoover Dam* is described in detail in *Las Vegas,* THE CITIES. Listed below are several other water spots worth checking out.

GLEN CANYON, near Page, Arizona Five million cubic yards of concrete, 1,560 feet across, rise 710 feet above the bedrock across the Colorado River between sheer walls of red Navajo sandstone. Behind it lies Lake Powell, 186 miles long and with more than 1,900 miles of shoreline. You can fish for crappie or striped and largemouth bass; the largest stripers are nearing 48 pounds. Around the lake is the 1¼-million-acre *Glen Canyon National Recreation Area.* Information: *Glen Canyon Visitors Center,* PO Box 1507, Page, AZ 86040 (phone: 520-608-6404).

OROVILLE, Oroville, California Rising 770 feet above Oroville's business district, this is one of the highest dams in the US. Lake Oroville, with 162 miles of shoreline, backs up behind the dam and provides good camping, boating, and fishing—for king salmon, rainbow and brown trout, largemouth and smallmouth bass, crappie, bluegill, and catfish. There's a visitors' center with an observation tower at 900 Kelly Ridge Rd. Information: *Lake Oroville State Recreation Area,* 400 Glen Dr., Oroville, CA 95966 (phone: 916-538-2200).

KENTUCKY, near Gilbertsville, Kentucky Its 206-foot height and 8,422-foot length make this structure across the Tennessee River the largest in the *TVA* system; together with the *Barkley Dam* on the Cumberland River nearby, it impounds some 220,000 acres of water with 3,400 miles of forested, cove-notched shoreline. Both Kentucky Lake and Lake Barkley are great for crappie and bass fishing as well as catfish, sauger, and bluegill from March until late October. A multitude of activities are available at Kenlake, *Kentucky Dam State Park and Marina,* and *Lake Barkley State Resort Parks,* and at the *TVA*'s own 170,000-acre *Land Between the Lakes.* Information: *Kentucky*

Dam Village, PO Box 69, Gilbertsville, KY 42044 (phone: 502-362-4271) or *Kentucky Department of Travel Development,* Capitol Plaza Tower, 500 Mero St., 22nd Floor, Frankfort, KY 40601 (phone: 502-564-4930; 800-225-TRIP).

FORT PECK, near Glasgow, Montana The largest earth-filled hydraulic dam in the world, this 21,026-foot-long structure rises 250½ feet above the Missouri River. Fort Peck Lake, with 1,520 miles of shoreline, is the world's fourth-largest reservoir and home of the *Montana Governor's Cup Walleye Tournament* the second weekend in July. Information: *Chamber of Commerce,* 740 Hwy. 2E, PO Box 832, Glasgow, MT 59230 (phone: 406-228-2222).

JOHN DAY, near Biggs, Oregon For this $487-million project, the *US Army Corps of Engineers* rerouted highways and moved a pair of towns and parts of two others (Boardman, Roosevelt, Arlington, and Umatilla). The most impressive part of a visit is a viewing window in the fish ladder by which adult salmon and steelhead make their way upstream to spawn. This is called the "counting season," generally from April through October, when everything that comes through the ladder is counted. All kinds of superlatives apply. Lake Umatilla stretches for about 75 miles behind the dam. Don't miss the tour by train (flatbed and caboose) of the *Dalles Dam* (*John Day*'s sister dam) just 24 miles away. The tour runs from April to October; there are two fish ladders, a lovely park with ducks, and plenty of picnic areas (phone: 541-296-9778). Information: *John Day Dam,* PO Box 564, The Dalles, OR 97058 (phone: 541-296-1181).

FLAMING GORGE, near Vernal, Utah In the Green River's Red Canyon, this 502-foot-high dam impounds a 91-mile-long reservoir in the *Flaming Gorge National Recreation Area*—185,645 acres of bright red and orange rock canyons, rust-colored chimneys and spires, and pine-clad mountains. The recreation area offers three marinas, nine boat ramps, river floating, fishing, numerous campgrounds, etc. Open year-round; the main season is from *Memorial Day* to *Labor Day.* Information: *Flaming Gorge National Recreation Area, Ashley National Forest,* PO Box 157, Dutch John, UT 84023 (phone: 801-784-3433).

GRAND COULEE, Coulee Dam, Washington The world's second-largest concrete dam (the largest is *Itaipa,* on the border of Brazil and Paraguay), it is higher than a 46-story building and nearly a mile long, with a spillway twice as high as Niagara Falls. Yet it's dwarfed by the immense granite cliffs on either side. On summer nights, there is a laser light show. Recreational opportunities are available in the 100,059-acre *Coulee Dam National Recreation Area.* Information: *Visitors Center, Bureau of Reclamation:* PO Box 620, Grand Coulee, WA 99133 (phone: 509-633-9265) or *Superintendent, Coulee Dam National Recreation Area,* 1008 Crest Dr., Coulee Dam, WA 99116-1259 (phone: 509-633-9441).

Historic Canals

When Charles Dickens visited Ohio in the 1840s, he traveled on a canal boat; he wrote a tale of cramped quarters and odoriferous mules brought aboard between stints of pulling. But these canals that linked inland cities to lakes and rivers from Maine to Chicago provided the fastest possible transportation until the railroad. Then canal boomtowns died out, and many canals (like much of the original *Erie Canal,* which linked Lake Erie and the Atlantic Ocean) were filled in and paved over or left to crumble.

Still, canals have not been forgotten. Cruising on these wave-free waterways is relaxing, and several short trips are available for only a few dollars a person. Also, *Mid Lakes Navigation Co.* (PO Box 61, Skaneateles, NY 13152; phone: 315-685-8500; 800-545-4318) has sightseeing day trips from mid-May to mid-October, as well as two- and three-day cruises on the canals of New York State—*Champlain, Erie, Oswego,* and *Cayuga-Seneca.* The same firm leases canal boats as well; all supplies except food are provided. *American-Canadian-Caribbean Line* (PO Box 368, Warren, RI 02885; phone: 401-247-0955; 800-556-7450; fax: 401-245-8303) runs 12-day trips from the first of June to mid-October between Warren, Rhode Island, and Montreal, Quebec, via the *Erie* and *Oswego* canals, the Saquenay River, and the St. Lawrence Seaway. There are some canals and several canal-related places you can visit. For further information about events taking place along the Canal System, call 800-4-CANAL-4.

EAST

C&D CANAL MUSEUM, Chesapeake City, Maryland This old stone pumphouse on the *Chesapeake and Delaware Canal* has working models of a lock, and a brief video that relates the story of the still-busy 150-year-old canal for which it is named. Also on display are a wooden waterwheel—a mechanical marvel fitted out with buckets that transferred water from Back Creek into the canal at the rate of 1.2 million gallons an hour—and the original steam engines. Open year-round. Information: *US Army Corps of Engineers, Chesapeake City Project Office,* 815 Bethel Rd., Chesapeake City, MD 21915 (phone: 410-885-5622).

CANAL TOWN MUSEUM, Canastota, New York This museum, in a yellow clapboard building directly across the street from the canal, is filled with artifacts related to canal days, models of canal boats, and displays on Canastota history. Closed Sundays and Mondays. Information: *Canal Town Museum,* PO Box 51, 122 Canal St., Canastota, NY 13032 (phone: 315-697-3451).

OLD ERIE CANAL STATE PARK, DeWitt to Rome, New York Some 35 miles of the celebrated *Erie Canal* are maintained by the state for recreational use. You can go hiking and biking in summer and snowmobiling in winter. Picnic areas and connecting paths to nearby recreation areas are strategically placed. Information: *Central Region–New York State Office of Parks, Recreation and Historic Preservation,* Rte. 173, Jamesville, NY 13078 (phone: 315-492-1756).

ERIE CANAL VILLAGE, Rome, New York A re-created 1840s canal village, featuring period buildings such as the *New York State Museum of Cheese, Bennett's Tavern,* and the *Harden Carriage Museum,* with over 30 carriages on view. Visitors may enjoy a horse-drawn packet boat ride down a restored section of the *Old Erie Canal.* Closed early September through late May. Information: *Erie Canal Village,* 5789 New London Rd., Rome, NY 13440 (phone: 315-337-3999).

ERIE CANAL MUSEUM, Syracuse, New York Changing exhibitions of life on the canals are set up in the 1850 *Weighlock Building,* the only surviving canal boat weigh station, where canal boats were weighed to determine the tolls they'd pay. A full-size canal boat has been reconstructed, participatory exhibitions organized, and a weighmaster's office re-created. There's even a sculpture of a mule and hogee (mule driver) on the tow path. The archival materials are extensive. Closed *Christmas*. Group tours and research library available by appointment. Information: *Erie Canal Museum,* 318 Erie Blvd. E., Syracuse, NY 13202 (phone: 315-471-0593).

ALLEGHENY PORTAGE RAILROAD NATIONAL HISTORIC SITE, Cresson, Pennsylvania The eastern and western divisions of the state-run *Pennsylvania Canal* were linked by this railroad. Visitors see some of the stone railroad ties, a quarry where they were made, one of the engine house foundations, a stone bridge, and a full-scale model of a locomotive. Demonstrations of stonecutting are presented in summer. A film at the visitors' center tells the story. Closed *Christmas*. Information: *Allegheny Portage Railroad National Historic Site,* PO Box 189, Cresson, PA 16630 (phone: 814-886-8176).

CHESAPEAKE AND OHIO CANAL NATIONAL HISTORICAL PARK, Washington, DC, to Cumberland, Maryland A 1924 flood put an end to the uneven career of this 184-mile-long waterway between Georgetown and Cumberland, Maryland. The woodsy towpath is ideal for hiking and biking; the sections of the canal that aren't dry (22 miles above Georgetown) are great for canoeing. Exhibitions in the visitors' center, in an old tavern at Great Falls, Maryland, tell the story. Visitors' centers also are in Hancock and Cumberland. Open daily. Information: *C&O Canal National Historical Park,* PO Box 4, Sharpsburg, MD 21782 (phone: 301-739-4200).

MIDWEST

ILLINOIS AND MICHIGAN CANAL HEADQUARTERS BUILDING, Lockport, Illinois What some people call the best-preserved canal town in America has a number of old canal locks (as well as a modern one), a fine 19th-century block of storefronts, some stone sidewalks—and the only canal museum in the US that illustrates the construction, operation, and demise of a single waterway. The *Pioneer Settlement,* the *Illinois State Museum, Lockport Gallery, Department of Conservation* facilities, and a recreation trail are additional offerings to visitors. Exhibitions relating to the history of the settlement and pioneer lifestyles round out the extensive display. Information: *Will County Historical Society,* 803 S. State St., Lockport, IL 60441 (phone: 815-838-5080).

CANAL FULTON, Canal Fulton, Ohio A full-size replica of the mule-drawn canal barges that once plied the *Ohio-Erie Canal* takes you up and down that same waterway today. A small museum adjoins the boat dock. Information: *Canal Fulton Heritage Society,* 103 Tuscarawas St., Canal Fulton, OH 44614 (phone: 216-854-3808).

ROSCOE VILLAGE, Coshocton, Ohio This once-busy 1800s community on the *Ohio-Erie Canal* is a fine place to get a sense of rough-and-ready canal life. The restored village is open year-round and offers unique shops, old-time crafts, exhibit buildings, fine dining, and a 51-room country inn. Visit a blacksmith shop, a general store, a restored period home, and an old-fashioned ice-cream parlor. In warm weather, you also can ride a horse-drawn canal-boat replica. Many lively special events all year. Information: *Roscoe Village,* 381 Hill St., Coshocton, OH 43812 (phone: 614-622-9310; 800-877-1830).

America's Military Academies

From the establishment of *West Point* in 1802 to the opening of the *Air Force Academy* in April 1954, the academies have always provided a variety of spectacles, from full-dress parades to museums of military equipment and guns. The grounds are manicured, delightful for walking; the settings usually breathtaking. Be sure to time your visit to catch a parade; and ask about athletic events and guided tours, which are often available.

US AIR FORCE ACADEMY, Colorado Springs, Colorado After you've seen the visitors' center (open year-round) and its displays about cadet life, take a self-guided tour of the 18,000-acre grounds (guided tours are offered throughout the summer), which should include the Academy's chapel—a "chapel of the future" when it was built between 1959 and 1963 in the shape of a 17-spired tetrahedron pyramid 150 feet high, with separate chapels inside for various faiths. Every weekday at noon, weather permitting (except during summer vacations and some other breaks), the uniformed cadets assemble and march in formation to the dining hall to the accompaniment of martial music. You can lodge in Colorado Springs at any number of motels or hotels; most prestigious is the *Broadmoor* (phone: 719-634-7711; see *America's Best Resort Hotels*). Information: *HQ USAFA/PAV, US Air Force Academy,* 2346 Academy Dr., Colorado Springs, CO 80840 (phone: 719-472-2025; 719-472-2555 for recorded information).

US COAST GUARD ACADEMY, New London, Connecticut A visit to this pretty campus begins at the modern visitors' center, where you can browse through exhibits and watch a multimedia show depicting cadet life, then pick up a map for a self-guided tour that takes in the chapel; the academy's museum, notable for its intriguing collection of vessel models; and, when it's in port, the sailing bark *Eagle,* now used for cadet training cruises. Once weekly in spring and fall, usually on Friday afternoons, cadets parade in review. An added attraction of this nautically minded corner of Connecticut is the interesting selection of inns, the best of which includes the venerable *Griswold Inn* in Essex (phone: 203-767-1812) and the *Copper Beech Inn* in Ivoryton (phone: 203-767-0330). See *America's Special Havens* for detailed information about both. Information: *US Coast Guard Academy,* Public Affairs Office, 15 Mohegan Ave., New London, CT 06320 (phone: 860-444-8270).

US NAVAL ACADEMY, Annapolis, Maryland On certain Wednesday afternoons during April and October, the 4,500 spit-and-polished midshipmen have a 3 PM dress parade on Worden Field. There's more to see: the crypt of John Paul Jones, somewhat like Napoleon's in Paris; the chapel, really a large cathedral, complete with stained glass windows; a museum full of naval history exhibits; and various monuments on the grounds. Pamphlets outlining a self-guided walking tour are available, as are guided tours. Information: *Visitors Center, US Naval Academy,* Halsey Field House, Annapolis, MD 21402 (phone: 410-263-6933).

US MERCHANT MARINE ACADEMY, Kings Point, New York On Long Island's picturesque North Shore, and overlooking Connecticut, Long Island Sound, and New York City and its bridges, this academy occupies what used to be the Chrysler estate (as well as parts of others on Long Island's Gold Coast). At the Main Gate, you can get maps and information; there are displays about the history of the *Merchant Marine* and their ships at the *American Merchant Marine Museum,* as well as regimental reviews, held on some Saturdays in fall and spring at 10 AM. Information: *US Merchant Marine Academy,* Steamboat Rd., Kings Point, NY 11024 (phone: 516-773-5000).

US MILITARY ACADEMY, West Point, New York Founded on March 16, 1802, with an initial enrollment of 10, this academy is probably the most famous and most visited of the service schools, and for good reason: It epitomizes military tradition. The campus is beautiful, as manicured as any parkland, full of Gothic buildings, and magnificent views like the one from Trophy Point, above the Hudson River. The *Cadet Chapel,* a lofty granite Gothic structure overlooking the cadet parade field, houses the largest church pipe organ in the country. The museum—filled with military artifacts from the Stone Age to the present—is the world's largest military museum. At Trophy Point, you can see a few links of the heavy iron chains the Americans stretched across the river to block British ships during the Revolution. Cadet parades are held during spring and fall; for times and dates, call ahead. The *Thayer* hotel is on the grounds (phone: 914-446-4731). Among the area's nicest country inns are the *Bird and Bottle Inn* (in Garrison; phone: 914-424-3000) and the *Beekman Arms* (in Rhinebeck; phone: 914-876-7077). First-rate fare at reasonable prices is served at the *Culinary Institute of America*'s *Escoffier Room, American Bounty, Caterina,* and *St. Andrew's* restaurants in Hyde Park, where future top chefs train (phone: 914-471-6608; closed for three weeks in July). Guided tours are available for prospective cadets and for groups of 20 or more. Check the visitors' center for times and fees. Information: *Visitors' Information Center, US Military Academy,* Bldg. 2107, West Point, NY 10996 (phone: 914-938-2638).

Great Horse Races

Ever since President Washington closed Congress on October 24, 1790, so that he and the senators could attend the races at this country's first racetrack, Baltimore's *Pimlico,* Americans have been competing against each other on horseback.

Every breed has its set of competitive events. Standardbreds, bred to trot (with diagonal legs moving in synch) or, more commonly, to pace (with lateral legs moving together), pull sulkies around dirt ovals. Thoroughbreds ridden by jockeys in brightly colored silks charge down flat tracks or leap their way over steeplechase courses. Quarter horses run for million-dollar purses, while Western horses work out at rodeos.

There are complicated systems for the way the thoroughbreds and standardbreds race; an understanding will help you enjoy the races more and make wiser bets. The *Thoroughbred Racing Associations* (420 Fairhill Dr., Suite 1, Elkton, MD 21921; phone: 410-392-9200) publishes lists of major races in its *Stakes Schedule.* The *US Trotting Association* (750 Michigan Ave., Columbus, OH 43215; phone: 614-224-2291) publishes a history of the sport and free booklets that tell you how to pick a winner, purchase a horse, or pursue a career in racing. To learn about steeplechasing, contact the *National Steeplechase and Hunt Association* (400 Fairhill Dr., Elkton, MD 21921; phone: 410-392-0700).

ALL ABOUT HORSES

KENTUCKY HORSE PARK, Lexington, Kentucky World-renowned *Kentucky Horse Park* is the only one of its kind in the world and possibly the best place in the country to get a feeling for American horse life. This facility, on 1,032 acres in the heart of the Kentucky bluegrass country, represents not just the thoroughbreds born and bred in the area but also Morgans, Arabians, Appaloosas, and just about any other breed you can name. There's a stirring 25-minute film on the history of man and horse, and a 40,000-square-foot museum full of dioramas, computers, and various displays about horses the size of dogs, horses and Roman chariots, horses in the Wild West, and more. Tours by horse-drawn buggy give you an overview and take you through the back paddock areas. On the "Walking Farm Tour," you can see a farrier and a harnessmaker and learn about the horses' day-to-day care. The tour also features two live shows daily: the *Hall of Champions Presentation,* with such champions as thoroughbred gelding John Henry (the winningest thoroughbred ever), Forego, American saddlebred top show horse Imperator, and standardbred Rambling Willie (known as "the horse that God loved"); and the ever-popular and most colorful *Parade of Breeds Show,* where riders and horses are in full costume and tack. You can ride horses and ponies, cruise the grounds in horse-drawn trolleys and surries, watch appropriately costumed drivers hitch up landaus, and take in dozens of special events: polo matches, steeplechase meetings, dressage exhibitions, horse pulling contests, quarter horse sprints, cross-country races, and more.

From June through October, polo is played on any one of the park's six polo fields. A covered arena that seats 5,600 people offers competition in any weather. Also available are 260 sites for camping, tennis and basketball courts, recreation areas, a fine lively activities program, and a junior Olympic-size swimming pool. Information: *Kentucky Horse Park,* 4089 Iron Works Pike, Lexington, KY 40511 (phone: 606-233-4303; 800-678-8813; fax: 606-254-0253).

HUNT COUNTRY STABLE TOUR, Upperville and Middleburg, Virginia On *Memorial Day* weekend each year, many of America's premier thoroughbred racing and breeding stables open their doors to visitors. The self-drive tour in this area of Virginia, which bills itself as "the horse capital of the world," features stops at Blue Ridge Farm, one of the oldest thoroughbred breeding farms in the US; Kent Farm, the stables of Washington *Redskins* owner Jack Kent Cooke; Oakley, a famous breeding stable whose grounds encompass two Civil War battlesites; and Takaro, where Andalusian horses are bred for dressage. In addition, training facilities are open to the public, including the Middleburg Equine Swim Center, where horses exercise by swimming laps in a heated indoor pool and relax in hydropools (equine Jacuzzis). Visits to a local vineyard/stable and *Trinity Episcopal Church,* a beautiful adaptation of a 13th-century French country church, are also included in the tour. A catered luncheon may be purchased on either day; there are ample picnic grounds, as well. Admission charge. Information: *Hunt Country Stable Tour, Trinity Episcopal Church,* Upperville, VA 22176 (phone: 540-592-3711; fax: 540-592-3408).

GREAT RACES

Along with the *Kentucky Derby* in Louisville and the *Preakness* in Baltimore (both described in detail in the appropriate city chapters), there are hundreds of races held in the US every year; horse racing enjoys the largest paid attendance of any US sport. The following races are some of the biggest.

BLUE GRASS STAKES, Lexington, Kentucky With a $500,000-added purse, this is the biggest event of the three-week spring meeting at *Keeneland Race Course*—famous, rustic, and very beautiful at this time of year with the dogwoods and flowering crabs in full bloom. Because the race is run three weeks before the *Kentucky Derby,* and because it's just an eighth of a mile shorter than the *Derby*'s mile and a quarter, it often serves as a steppingstone to the Triple Crown. The $300,000-added *Spinster,* for fillies and mares three years old and up, highlights a three-week October season and determines, at least in part, which horse will be named champion in her respective division. Five times a year there are thoroughbred sales—two-year-olds in April, yearlings in July and September, breeding stock in November, all ages in January. The highest price ever paid for a horse at public auction—$13.1 million—was paid here at *Keeneland* in 1985 for a colt by Nijinsky II. Tickets and information: *Keeneland Assn.,* PO Box 1690, Lexington, KY 40592 (phone: 606-254-3412; 800-456-3412; fax: 606-288-4348).

KENTUCKY FUTURITY, Lexington, Kentucky The *Kentucky Futurity*—a mile-long, $200,000 race that is the third leg of the Triple Crown for three-year-old trotters—comes at the end of September or early October. The fact that the fillies and colts who enter have raced against each other for months by the time they get here makes for exciting races. The *Red Mile,* named for the color of the clay on the track, is known as the world's fastest standardbred track. Right in the middle of the October meeting is the *Tattersalls Sale* (the equivalent of *Keeneland*'s big yearling sale). On *Show Day,* the Sunday halfway through the October meeting, all the horse farms in the area hold open houses, complete with burgoo (a stew with various meats and vegetables) and music. Information: *Red Mile Race Track,* PO Box 420, Lexington, KY 40585 (phone: 606-255-0752).

HAMBLETONIAN, East Rutherford, New Jersey Named for the greatest sire of them all (every trotter and pacer is said to be related to this famous horse), this jewel in the Triple Crown for trotters was moved to the *Meadowlands* in 1981 from its home of 25 years at the *Illinois Du Quoin State Fair.* Usually held the first Saturday in August, it is one of the most prestigious races of them all, with a purse of more than $1 million. Information: *Meadowlands Racetrack,* East Rutherford, NJ 07073 (phone: 201-935-8500).

WOODROW WILSON PACE, East Rutherford, New Jersey The richest event in harness racing, this contest for two-year-old pacers—held every year at the *Meadowlands* in late summer—carries a purse of about $1 million. Information: *Meadowlands Racetrack,* East Rutherford, NJ 07073 (phone: 201-935-8500).

ALL-AMERICAN FUTURITY, Ruidoso Downs, New Mexico This is the richest quarter horse race in the world, with a purse in excess of $2 million ($1 million of which goes to the winner). Quarter horses, originally bred primarily for ranch work, have powerful hind quarters that make them superb sprinters. Every summer, between 10,000 and 15,000 people make their way to southern New Mexico to watch over 300 horses go through eliminations that leave the 10 fastest to compete on a quarter-mile dash down a straight track. Held on *Labor Day.* Information: *Ruidoso Downs Race Track,* PO Box 449, Ruidoso Downs, NM 88346 (phone: 505-378-4431).

BELMONT STAKES, Elmont, New York This is the third and final leg of the Triple Crown for three-year-old thoroughbreds (the first two are the *Kentucky Derby* and the *Preakness*). Called "The Test of the Champion," it is held every year in the first half of June and is the longest (1½ miles) of the Triple Crown events. Secretariat, who won the race in 1973 by an astounding 31 lengths, holds the record at 2:24. The regular racing season at *Belmont Park,* where the race is held, is early May through July, and late August to mid-October. No races on Tuesdays. Information: *New York Racing Assn.,* PO Box 90, Jamaica, NY 11417 (phone: 718-641-4700).

TRAVERS, Saratoga Springs, New York Run at 1¼ miles, the nation's oldest continuous stakes race for three-year-olds is held at the oldest active racetrack in the country, the *Saratoga* racecourse, where they've been racing almost every year since 1864. Many US tracks have been designed after *Saratoga.* The *Travers,* known as "the Midsummer Derby," usually draws the top three-year-olds from the Triple Crown series. The season runs for five weeks, starting the last week in July, and there are stakes races of one sort or another almost every day, with big races on weekends: the *Alabama,* for three-year-old fillies; the *Whitney,* for three-year-olds and up; and the *Hopeful,* a race for two-year-olds whose winner, historically, has often gone on to compete successfully in the Triple Crown the following year. No races on Tuesdays. Information: *New York Racing Assn.,* PO Box 90, Jamaica, NY 11417 (phone: 718-641-4700).

CANE PACE, Yonkers, New York This $500,000-plus race, held in August, with the *Little Brown Jug* (*Delaware County Fair,* Delaware, Ohio) and the *Messenger Stakes* (see below), is the opening leg of pacing's Triple Crown. This race attracts the finest sophomore (three-year-old) pacers annually to the Westchester County oval. Information: *Yonkers Raceway,* Central Ave., Yonkers, NY 10704 (phone: 914-968-4200).

INTERNATIONAL TROT, Yonkers, New York In Europe, where trotters are more popular than pacers, trainers are particularly concerned with gait and style. At this world trotting classic held in August, which annually draws the finest high steppers, you can watch the European and American trotters compete. The race used to be held at *Roosevelt Raceway*; the purse is now $500,000. Information: *Yonkers Raceway,* Central Ave., Yonkers, NY 10704 (phone: 914-968-4200).

YONKERS TROT, Yonkers, New York Worth an estimated $400,000, this is one of the three glamour events of trotting (along with the *Kentucky Futurity* and the *Hambletonian,* above), held in July at the end of the *Yonkers Trot Week* festival. It is the cornerstone event of *Empire City Stakes'* night, where each race is a stakes event. The total purse is more than $1.4 million. Information: *Yonkers Raceway,* Central Ave., Yonkers, NY 10704 (phone: 914-968-4200).

MESSENGER STAKES, Meadow Lands, Pennsylvania This is the second of the three legs of the Triple Crown for three-year-old pacers, and it is one of the key races to decide both the divisional honors and horse of the year. Held in September, the race has a purse of $400,000. Information: *Ladbroke at the Meadows,* Racetrack Rd., PO Box 409, Meadow Lands, PA 15347 (phone: 412-225-9300).

MARION DU PONT SCOTT COLONIAL CUP INTERNATIONAL STEEPLECHASE, Camden, South Carolina The $60,000 cup makes this late fall event, first held in 1970, one of the very biggest in steeplechase racing. The participants come from around the world. The horses compete over special "Colonial Cup fences" made of fresh pine brush—17 obstacles in all. The *Carolina Cup,* held in the spring, is older and draws bigger crowds (though the purse is smaller). Information: *Colonial Cup,* PO Box 280, Camden, SC 29020 (phone: 803-432-6513).

Rodeos

Beyond the fact that the rodeo cowboy's skills are rooted in the life of the Wild West, the rodeo system today has very little to do with that romantic era. In the first place, there's big money involved—hundreds of thousands of dollars in prizes for all the different events. Then, too, the cowboys are more like Olympic athletes: They train hard and work hard to get where they are. All rodeos sanctioned by the *Professional Rodeo Cowboys Association (PRCA)*—the larger of the two cowboy "leagues"—include bareback, saddle bronc, and bull riding; calf roping and team roping; and steer wrestling. Often there's also barrel racing (for women), sanctioned by the *Women's Professional Rodeo Association (WPRA)*; plus chuck wagon races and the like. Information: *Professional Rodeo Cowboys Association* (*PRCA,* 101 Pro Rodeo Dr., Colorado Springs, CO 80919; phone: 719-593-8840); this association is the sanctioning body of more than 600 professional rodeos annually.

The *National Western Stock Show and Rodeo* in Denver, the *National Finals Rodeo* in Las Vegas, the *Southwestern Exposition and Livestock Show and Rodeo* in Ft. Worth, and the *Houston Livestock Show and Rodeo* in Houston are described in the respective chapters in THE CITIES; several other noteworthy rodeo events across the country are listed below.

TUCSON RODEO, Tucson, Arizona One of the largest midwinter outdoor rodeos on the *PRCA* circuit takes place in February for five days at the *Tucson Rodeo Grounds.* This is the main event of the annual *La Fiesta de los Vaqueros* (Celebration of the Cowboys), with a parade and other entertainment. About 700 contestants from the US and Canada vie to prove they are the best at bareback bronc riding, steer wrestling, and barrel racing. Information: *Tucson Rodeo Office,* PO Box 11006, Tucson, AZ 85734 (phone: 520-741-2233).

MESQUITE ARENA, Mesquite, Texas Every Friday and Saturday night from April through September, the *Mesquite Arena* explodes with two hours of traditional rodeo events, including saddle bronc riding, steer wrestling, barrel racing, calf roping, and bareback riding (the bull riding is a real crowd-pleaser). Only 15 minutes from downtown Dallas, this rodeo offers fans Texas-style buffets, pony rides, and a petting zoo. An event especially designed for children is the calf scramble, in which kids compete to remove a ribbon tied to a calf's tail. Information: *Mesquite Arena,* 1818 Rodeo Dr., Mesquite, TX 75149 (phone: 214-222-BULL).

CHEYENNE FRONTIER DAYS RODEO, Cheyenne, Wyoming The largest outdoor rodeo in the world and the "Daddy of 'em all" is a long-standing tradition in Wyoming. In addition to the usual competitive events, there are night shows (generally featuring country-and-western performers like Reba McEntyre, Tanya Tucker, or Garth Brooks), chuck wagon races, parades, Indian dancers, and various exhibitions and entertainments at the associated nine-day celebration (nine rodeos and nine evening shows). Last full week in July. Information: *Cheyenne Frontier Days,* PO Box 2477, Cheyenne, WY 82003 (phone: 307-778-7200; 800-227-6336).

Wheels of Fortune: Gambling in the US

From medieval times in Europe, when a free man could gamble himself and his descendants into a state of servitude, to 19th-century riverboat gambling on the Mississippi, gaming has emerged as an intoxicating and sometimes ruinous obsession. In the US, betting once was considered a gracious and gentlemanly sport. Today's casino experience is a cross between a palace tour and a visit to temple ruins. Sprawling, multi-story buildings covered in imported marble, lamé, and jittery neon boast exotic themes—from orgiastic Roman times to Scheherazade's *A Thousand and One Nights.* House personnel are almost painful in their attentiveness to the whims of players, and when a sizable jackpot is won, it is a full-blown paparazzi event. Fabulously extravagant shows, where Houdini-like stunts are performed and mega-stars sing for million-dollar salaries, are part of the nightly scene, as well as revues with female dancers clad in huge feather headdresses and little else.

Casinos try to convince players that perks abound for anyone willing to risk a few dollars. Complimentary extras, or "comps," are accrued by a complicated system of ratings that could tax the most advanced intellect. Almost every casino issues a credit card–size identification card for players to use while they gamble. Rewards ranging from a free meal or casino show to a lavish suite at the hotel and first class airfare are frequently awarded to players who are willing to spend a great deal of time (and, most likely, money) at the gaming tables. Casinos also offer other premiums in the form of contests and sweepstakes; discount coupons on hotels, T-shirts, and tote bags are routinely given to players. And casinos routinely offer junkets, which are planned excursions offering free airfare, hotel rooms, meals, and drinks to gamblers who agree to wager a certain amount at the gaming tables.

Until the latter part of the 1970s, Las Vegas reigned supreme as the leader of the casino industry. But as soon as gambling was legalized in New Jersey in 1976, Atlantic City became a betting boomtown. Reno and Lake Tahoe also do quite well for themselves. Although these cities rack up the largest profit margins and numbers of visitors in the business, they have recently come up against competition. Gaming houses have rolled through the Midwest like tumbleweeds. Mining towns formerly in hibernation in South Dakota and Colorado now boast Wild West gambling houses aptly named "Miss Kitty's" or "Rotten Luck Willie's." Riverboat gambling has once again become the rage; elaborate paddle wheelers leisurely ply the Mississippi from ports in Iowa and Illinois. And other states are trying to get into the act as well: In the last few years, gambling has been made legal in 15 states.

For details on the gambling frenzy that is Las Vegas, see *Las Vegas,* THE CITIES. Listed below are the other big casino spots.

BEST BETS: GAMBLING RESORTS

LAKE TAHOE

Perched on the California-Nevada state line, Lake Tahoe is home to a group of expensive resorts that just happen to house casinos. While the choices of chance on the gaming floors are on a par with those in Las Vegas, even the most fervent gambler might be lured away temporarily from the slots to enjoy the calm lake and outstanding ski slopes. Headliners also make occasional appearances in the casinos' nightclubs. The legal age for gambling in Tahoe is 21.

BILL'S LAKE TAHOE Colored craps tables assist newcomers in learning the rules of the game, and Billie Jean, the world's largest free-pull slot machine, is not to be missed. Table limits go no higher than $300. Information: *Bill's Lake Tahoe Casino,* US Hwy. 50, Stateline, NV 89449 (phone: 702-588-2455).

CAESARS TAHOE After a $16-million remodeling job, this hotel casino makes a grand Roman statement to equal that of *Caesars Palace* in Vegas. Mid-range gamblers can indulge their fancy at the tables with a $2 minimum, while other tables can play up to $3,000 per hand. Other games include roulette, keno, and craps. Information: *Caesars Tahoe Resort,* US Hwy. 50, Stateline, NV 89449 (phone: 702-588-3515; 800-648-3353 for reservations).

HARRAH'S TAHOE This casino is one of the most tasteful in the US, where glitter and glitz are usually lauded. Everything from baccarat to keno and bingo is offered here, and table bets reach as high as $2,000 per hand. Information: *Harrah's Tahoe Hotel & Casino,* US Hwy. 50, Stateline, NV 89449 (phone: 702-588-6606; 800-648-3773 for reservations).

RENO

Casinos have been operating here since gambling was legalized in Nevada in 1931. Most of the major gaming spots are as flamboyant as those in Lake Tahoe or Las Vegas, but a touch of small-town atmosphere remains. Some establishments also have entertainment, but with less flash and fewer luminaries than Las Vegas. Many Reno casinos are "branches" of their Vegas counterparts: *Circus Circus* (500 N. Sierra; phone: 702-329-0711; 800-648-5010 for reservations); *Fitzgerald's* (255 N. Virginia St.; phone: 702-785-3300; 800-648-5022 for reservations); *Harrah's* (219 N. Center St.; phone: 702-786-3232; 800-HARRAHS for reservations); and the *Sands Regency* (345 N. Arlington Ave.; phone: 702-348-2200; 800-648-3553 for reservations). The legal age for gambling here is 21.

PEPPERMILL The neon lighting and cigarette girls shrilly proclaiming their wares contribute to the frantic, noisy atmosphere. Gamblers seem to voice their elation and frustration loudest at the gambling tables, although there are plenty of disappointed sighs and shrieks of happiness emanating from the vicinity of the slot machines. All the customary gambling equipment, including roulette, Pai-Gow, and keno. Information: *Peppermill Hotel & Casino,* 2707 S. Virginia St., Reno, NV 89502 (phone: 702-826-2121; 800-648-6992 or 800-282-2444).

RENO HILTON Originally a Bally property, this largest casino in northern Nevada recently underwent a massive renovation and is bedecked with impressive chandeliers. Slots progress from a nickel up to $1, and table limits range from $2 to $1,000. Information: *Reno Hilton,* 2500 E. Second St., Reno, NV 89595 (phone: 702-789-2000; 800-648-5080 for reservations).

ATLANTIC CITY

When New Jersey legalized gambling in 1976, Atlantic City decided to forgo the quiet (albeit long-faded) pleasures of its seaside hostelries and quickly erected a series of casinos that rivaled the glitter palaces in Las Vegas. While many people still travel to Atlantic City to breathe in the wonderful sea air and enjoy the amusement booths, thousands more cram the gaming establishments with wild hopes of returning home with increased bankrolls. Busloads of folks arrive daily from Pennsylvania, New Jersey, and New York to chance some or all of their modest earnings. Headliners like Liza Minnelli, Frank Sinatra, and Diana Ross hold hundreds in thrall at the nightclubs—but very rarely. The evening shows are as flamboyant as those in Las Vegas, and entertainment ranges from Broadway shows to championship boxing. Hoping to change its image, Atlantic City is building a new convention center to draw more business visitors and to achieve a much-needed face-lift. (For more information on the area, see *Atlantic City to Cape May, New Jersey* in DIRECTIONS.)

You must be 21 to play at any table, or pull on a slot machine. The *New Jersey Casino Control Commission* allows casinos to operate around the clock. Traditional games, such as blackjack, craps, roulette, baccarat, and Big Six (wheel of fortune) have been joined by such innovations as video poker machines, inter-casino slot systems that offer huge jackpots, and the $1 Mega-bucks and 25¢ Quartermania systems. Surrender blackjack (where you can relinquish half your bet if you think you're going to lose) is now offered on many gambling floors. A five-card "21" is frequently paid double, and you can now bet five times the odds on the craps tables.

While the slot machines will accept anything from a nickel to a $100 token, the sky is truly the limit at the table games. On a busy Saturday night, you will be hard pressed to find a table under the $25 minimum, although $5 minimums are the rule on weekdays. Maximum bets can extend up to a staggering $10,000 with special prior arrangements with the house.

BALLY'S PARK PLACE A high-tech theme of neon and confetti makes this gaming spot one of the brightest around. The usual gaming paraphernalia—from 25¢ slot machines to Big Six wheels—line the casino. Other games include mini-baccarat, Pai-Gai, and Sic Bo. Information: *Bally's Park Place Hotel-Casino,* 1900 Boardwalk, Atlantic City, NJ 08401 (phone: 609-340-2000; 800-BALLYS7 for reservations).

CAESARS This East Coast cousin of Vegas fame is considered *the* casino for high rollers. Baccarat is pursued with a vengeance, and the $100 minimum bets for blackjack are not for the faint of heart. Information: *Caesars Hotel and Casino,* 2100 Pacific Ave., Atlantic City, NJ 08401 (phone: 609-348-4411; 800-443-0104 for reservations).

CLARIDGE Diminutive and downright homey in comparison to most gambling houses, this casino is located in a turn-of-the-century hotel. A veritable maze of escalators takes you from one gaming floor to the next. This place introduced surrender blackjack. Information: *Claridge Casino Hotel,* Indiana Ave. and the Boardwalk, Atlantic City, NJ 08401 (phone: 609-340-3400; 800-257-8585 for reservations).

THE GRAND At this establishment, one of the most luxurious near the Boardwalk, players can pull on slot machines that take everything from nickels to $100 tokens; games such as red dog, blackjack, baccarat, mini-baccarat, and craps keep the crowds absorbed. Information: *The Grand,* Boston and Pacific Aves., Atlantic City, NJ 08401 (phone: 609-347-7111; 800-257-8677 for reservations).

HARRAH'S ATLANTIC CITY This may be the only casino where players can tell if it's day or night. The huge skylight in the lobby, spacious gaming floor, and miles of plants lend a cheerful note. Once one of Atlantic City's most progressive casinos, its gaming equipment has become as old as the vintage machines in the lobby (some of the wooden models date as far back as 1900). The first $100 slot machines in Atlantic City were introduced here. Information: *Harrah's Atlantic City,* 777 Harrah's Blvd., Atlantic City, NJ 08401 (phone: 609-441-5000; 800-2-HARRAHS).

MERV GRIFFIN'S RESORTS CASINO Now splashier than ever, this renovated property boasts a lavish turn-of-the-century–style lobby and beautifully appointed guestrooms. And gamblers can indulge in a variety of table games in more than 60,000 square feet of casino space. Information: *Merv Griffin's Resorts Casino Hotel,* 1133 Boardwalk, Atlantic City, NJ 08401 (phone: 609-344-6000; 800-336-MERV for reservations).

SANDS This cavernous casino is very popular with daytime bettors who like to stop in after a walk along the Boardwalk. As in most Atlantic City casinos, the jackpots here are progressive, and slot machines accept coins from a quarter all the way up to $100 tokens. Blackjack is the favored game here, and there is a baccarat pit for those who wish to play for high stakes. Information: *Sands Hotel & Casino,* S. Indiana Ave. and Brighton Pk., Atlantic City, NJ 08401 (phone: 609-441-4000; 800-257-8580 for reservations).

SHOWBOAT Although this establishment is reminiscent of a Mississippi riverboat, its seaworthiness is to be seriously doubted. Gamblers vie for high stakes at the tables, and even the nickel slot machine players can get very excited. Information: *Showboat Casino Hotel,* 801 Boardwalk, Atlantic City, NJ 08401 (phone: 609-343-4000; 800-621-0200).

TROPICANA The casino claims to have just about every type of slot machine ever invented, and we would be hard pressed to argue. This immense gaming retreat is second in size only to the *Trump Taj Mahal.* Roulette, baccarat, craps, video poker, and blackjack are the highlights, although most people hang out at the slot machines. Information: *Tropicana Hotel and Casino,* Brighton and the Boardwalk, Atlantic City, NJ 08401 (phone: 609-340-4000; 800-257-6227 for reservations).

TRUMP PLAZA There are over 1,700 slot machines and 100 table games here, including the increasingly popular Pai-Gow poker. High stakes gamblers will appreciate the secluded and luxurious baccarat room here. At these tables, bets regularly climb into the thousands. Information: *Trump Plaza*

Hotel & Casino, Mississippi Ave. and the Boardwalk, Atlantic City, NJ 08401 (phone: 609-441-6000; 800-677-7378 for reservations).

TRUMP TAJ MAHAL This ostentatious gambling palace makes the original Circus Maximus seem tame by comparison. Donald Trump's controversial four-million-square-foot casino was designed as a facsimile of the famous 17th-century mausoleum built by Mogul Emperor Shah Jahan. A bearded man on stilts will probably ask you to rub his lantern as you enter the marble-tiled lobby, but we suggest you save your luck for yourself. The *Taj* has the second-largest casino floor in the world (the *Riviera*'s in Las Vegas is the biggest). Information: *Trump Taj Mahal Casino Resort,* 1000 Virginia Ave., Atlantic City, NJ 08401 (phone: 609-449-1000; 800-825-8786 for reservations).

SOUTH DAKOTA

In 1988, voters in Deadwood, South Dakota, rallied to legalize gambling in their state, and following a flurry of casino openings, the number of gambling "saloons" in this Wild West town has stabilized at about 80. These are typically small, hospitable places, and many of the historic buildings have benefited from substantial renovation earned from gambling dollars. However, Hollywood hero Kevin Costner may change the face of gambling in Deadwood with a new $50-million luxury conference center, resort, and casino he is developing with his brother, Dan. The facility in the Black Hills will be a follow-up to the brothers' *Midnight Star* casino (phone: 605-578-1555; 800-999-6482), also in Deadwood. If all goes according to plan, the complex will be located near the site where the final scene of *Dances with Wolves,* Costner's multi-Oscar-winning film of a few years ago, was shot, and a $13-million, 53-mile railroad line will connect it to the *Rapid City Airport* and local ski areas.

You must be 21 or older to play at the slot machines or gaming tables. Games of chance offered in Deadwood are blackjack, poker, and slot machines. There is a $5 bet limit and the slot machines accept donations from a nickel to $5. Information: *Deadwood-Lead Chamber of Commerce,* 735 Main St., Deadwood, SD 57732 (phone: 605-578-1876) or the *State of South Dakota Commission on Gaming,* 118 E. Missouri, Pierre, SD 57501 (phone: 605-773-6050).

RIVERBOAT GAMBLING

Many 19th-century explorers traversed the United States in search of a river of gold; their aspirations soundly thwarted, they turned homeward. Those who remained staked their claim, settled in their new homeland, and looked for ways to drive off the inevitable ennui when they stopped panning for gold or working in the fields. Saloons became the social hub of small towns, where the pastimes of drinking and poker playing were firmly entwined. Along the Mississippi River, riverboats offered gamblers an opportunity to risk high stakes, and the romantic legend of the dashing riverboat gambler was born. The days of Gaylord Ravenal disappeared along with hoop skirts and crinolines, but private industry has sought to recreate a genteel version of those times. It has been responsible for the furious development of floating paddleboat casinos and has transformed a dozen dozing farming towns into lively ports of call. Casino gambling in Iowa and Illinois is restricted to boats moored on the Mississippi River, many of which put out for two-hour cruises.

You must be 21 to board a riverboat gambling cruise and try your luck at the games of chance. Daily sailing schedules are posted by the individual cruise companies, and games include blackjack, craps, poker, roulette, Big Six (the wheel of fortune), slot machines, and video poker. In Iowa there is a $200 cap on losses on gambling cruises, bettors purchase chips before boarding, and table bets are limited to $5 per hand.

The *President Riverboat Casino* (President's Landing, 130 W. River Dr., Davenport, IA 52801; phone: 800-BOAT-711) departs once a day from President's Landing in Davenport and paddles up and down the Mississippi for two hours from June through October; during the winter and on weekends it is dockside, but the gambling continues. *Casino Rock Island* (Rock Island, IL 61204; phone: 800-477-7747) cruises on the river, weather permitting, and there are no betting limits.

Dockside casino gambling can be found at the *Isle of Capri* (151 E. Beach Blvd., Biloxi, MS 39530; phone: 800-THE-ISLE). For 24 hours a day you can indulge yourself with slots and a variety of table games—bets can range from $5 up to $1,000.

One of the fastest-growing casino gambling areas is Tunica County, Mississippi, less than an hour's drive from Memphis, TN. You'll find branches of familiar names like *Circus, Circus; Bally's; Harrah's;* and *Sam's Town* on this stretch of Delta farmland. All the usual games such as craps, roulette, poker, and blackjack are here, along with—you guessed it—lots of slots. Entertainment, as one might expect, is strong on country and blues. For information, contact individual casino hotels, or The *Memphis Convention & Visitors Bureau* (47 Union Ave., Memphis, TN 38103; phone: 901-543-5303).

GAMBLING ON INDIAN RESERVATIONS

In a number of states, more than 100 Indian tribes have been licensed to engage in gaming activities on their land. The revenue that is generated (not to mention the hundreds of people who will be employed because of the casinos) is expected to improve each tribe's quality of life. Wagering is usually limited to high-stakes bingo and video games; however, in some cases, traditional Vegas-type games such as roulette, blackjack, and craps are allowed. Don't expect to find the glamour of Las Vegas or Atlantic City. The most reliable source of information about gambling on reservations in a particular state is its tourism office. For example, the *Minnesota Office of Tourism* (100 Metro Sq., 121 Seventh Pl. E., St. Paul, MN 55101; phone: 612-296-5029; 800-657-3700; 800-766-8687 in Canada) has a list of about

16 bingo and gaming facilities, noting the type of gambling that each offers; *Oklahoma Tourism* (PO Box 60789, Oklahoma City, OK 73146-0789; phone: 405-521-2409; 800-652-6552) has an "Indian Bingo" list that indicates facilities and which Indian tribe runs them; the *Native American Tourism Center* (4130 N. Goldwater Blvd., Suite 114, Scottsdale, AZ 85251; phone: 602-945-0771) has information on bingo and video-game parlors.

Also, the first casino established in New England is run by Native Americans. *Foxwoods Resort Casino* on the Mashantucket Pequot reservation in Connecticut (Rte. 2 in Ledyard, about 7 miles from Mystic; phone: 860-885-3000; 800-PLAY-BIG) offers visitors slot machines and 173 gaming tables for craps, roulette, baccarat, blackjack, and poker. There are also 11 restaurants, two bars, and valet parking. Employing 2,300 workers, the enterprise promises to boost the economic status of the 200-member tribe—and of the local area as well—to the tune of $900 million a year.

GAMBLING IN HISTORIC MINING TOWNS

In Colorado, casinos also can be found in three historic mining towns. Central City, Black Hawk, and Cripple Creek, all near Denver, have added poker, blackjack, and slot machines to their Old West attractions. For more information, contact the *Denver Metro Convention & Visitors Bureau,* 225 W. Colfax St., Denver, CO 80202 (phone: 303-892-1112).

Shopping Spree

Browsing through the department stores, street markets, small shops, craft centers, and discount stores of America will undoubtedly be one of the highlights of your trip. There is plenty of value for the money and enough quality and craftsmanship to make many an item irresistible. If the city you're visiting is covered in THE CITIES, check "Shopping" in the respective chapter for detailed listings of stores in that area.

REGIONAL SPECIALTIES In New England, New York, and Pennsylvania, look for good antiques. In addition to shops on Madison Avenue in New York City or Pine Street in Philadelphia, you can find good buys in small antiques stores along country roads if you are prepared to weed through the junk and have a good sense of what items are worth. For those interested in edible treasures, Vermont cheese and maple syrup, saltwater taffy along the New Jersey shore, and shoofly pie and pretzels in the Pennsylvania Dutch country are all worth seeking out.

In the South there are interesting crafts, especially in the inland mountains. West Virginia is noted for hand-stitched quilts and quilted clothing and toys. In Williamsburg, Virginia, reproductions of pewter, furniture, and other 18th-century items are justly famous. Georgia offers basketware, woodcarvings, handwoven wool, and ceramics. In the Blue Ridge Mountains, look for cornhusk dolls and a small wooden musical instrument called the Gee-Haw-Whimmy-Diddle.

In the Great Lakes region, consider homemade jams, relishes, and other canned goods (especially in Iowa's country stores). Other regional specialties include American antiques in Illinois; hand-painted ceramics in Clay County, Indiana; wheel cheese, summer sausage, and lace in Wisconsin; and pipes, moccasins, and handwoven Indian tribal rugs in Minnesota.

In the Southwest, Mexican, Indian, and "Old West" items are especially good buys. Serapes, tree-of-life candlesticks, and wool rebozos from across the border make nice gifts. Indian specialties are pottery, Kaibab squaw boots, Navajo rugs, and silver and turquoise jewelry, as well as drums, dolls, and headdresses. Cowboy items include hats, boots, and other ranch clothes from Arizona, New Mexico, and Texas. In the Rockies, the same "Old West" focus prevails in many of the shops. Consider buckskin jackets or pants and tooled leather belts, boots, or hats. The region is not without its Indian specialties, but most special is Rocky Mountain jade jewelry.

The Far West, Alaska, and the Northwestern states are the places to buy Eskimo crafts, which include ceremonial masks, dolls, carved whalebone sculpture, and jade items. American Indian crafts also are available in Oregon and Idaho, as well as in northern Nevada. Many specialty seafood stores in Seattle and Portland are happy to ship your salmon purchases anywhere in the world; it's always worth asking. Merchandise from the Far East is available in New York's and San Francisco's Chinatowns and in Hawaii.

Ask any store about mailing your purchases home; it may save on local sales tax and will mean that you'll have less to carry with you.

MANUFACTURER AND DESIGNER OUTLETS Outlets are huge warehouse stores where companies unload their overruns and canceled orders at dramatically reduced prices—from 20% to 75% off the retail price. They also sell irregulars (slightly flawed pieces) and seconds (more severely flawed or damaged goods). These will be appropriately marked. Some companies, like *Bass* shoes and *Dansk* housewares, have many stores, others just one or two. Factory outlets tend to be outside major urban areas, and several cities around the country have become known for having clusters of outlets nearby.

Among the best-known and largest outlet centers (certainly worth a stop for bargains if you're traveling in the area) are the following: Louisville, Kentucky; Freeport, Maine; Fall River, Massachusetts; Rochester, Minnesota; Secaucus and Flemington, New Jersey; Cohoes, New York; Westchester, New York; Sylvania, Ohio; Lincoln City, Oregon; Reading, Pennsylvania; Chattanooga and Pigeon Forge, Tennessee; Manchester, Vermont; and Williamsburg, Virginia. Two urban areas known for outlets are Orchard Street in Lower Manhattan, New York City, and Fashion Row in Miami, Florida. The New England states are famous for blankets, leather, linen, and textiles; the Carolinas for furniture, linen, textiles, and towels; and Virginia and West Virginia for glassware and pottery.

At any manufacturer outlet (or factory store), be prepared for crowds, especially on Saturdays and during peak travel periods. Also, when planning a side trip, bear in mind that outlets often are not centrally located and may take some time to find, although they are increasingly common along major highways between cities. (Usually you will need a car.)

With the demise of a number of the country's major department stores, designer clothing companies are joining the outlet market in force. The bargains range anywhere from 20% to 50% off for top-quality merchandise—as opposed to the seconds often found in factory outlets—and the list of designer names keeps growing. As with most factory outlets, these specialty outlets tend to be located either in clusters of outlet stores or in low-rent locations well away from major shopping centers, and often are hard to find. For information on locations of outlets along your route, you can call the designer's headquarters (most of which are in New York City). Another alternative is to consult *The Joy of Outlet Shopping,* which lists outlets of all types, including designer shops. To order a copy, send $6.95 (plus $1.50 for shipping and handling) to *The Joy of Outlet Shopping,* PO Box 17129, Clearwater, FL 34622-0129 (phone: 800-344-6397).

Another source of information for bargain shoppers is *OUTLET BOUND,* which provides a toll-free hotline (800-33-OUTLET) that you can call for information on outlets coast to coast; free brochures on the individual stores are available on request. This company also publishes a useful book, *OUTLET BOUND's Guide to the Nation's Best Outlets,* which lists over 10,000 outlets nationwide. To order, either call the toll-free number or send $7.95 (plus $3.50 for shipping and handling) to *OUTLET BOUND,* PO Box 1255, Orange, CT 06477.

FLEA MARKETS A growing phenomenon, all across the country, is that of flea markets, where all kinds of goods are offered in open stands. Found in country fields or empty parking lots, stadiums, or skating rinks, some are occasional events advertised locally (watch the daily or weekly paper in the area in which you are traveling); others, usually in larger cities, are run on a permanent or semi-permanent basis and advertised regularly in local papers. Among the books on flea markets in the US are the following:

Price Guide to Flea Market Treasures, published by Chilton Book Co. (attention: Customer Service; 1 Chilton Way, Radnor, PA 19089; phone: 800-695-1214), is by Harry Rinker Jr. and costs $19.95. This is a useful guide for determining what is a fair price to pay as well as to charge.

U.S. Flea Markets Directory describes in detail over 500 regularly scheduled flea markets across the country, ranging in size from under 50 to over 1,000 dealers. It also offers practical advice on how to shop at flea markets, when to haggle, and how to become a seller. Published by the House of Collectibles (a division of Random House) for $6, plus $4 for shipping and handling; to order call 800-733-3000.

For the Mind

Regional American Theaters

A note in the program tells you to keep the aisles free of obstructions, and when the lights go down and the actors come whooping down the aisles around you, you know why.

Regional theater isn't always so exuberant, but it's not provincial either. The old situation, in which all you had in the hinterlands was dinner theater and summer stock of varying quality, no longer exists. Regional theater—theater outside New York City—has entered its prime, and some of the most exciting and innovative productions, the kinds that "lower the drawbridge between actor and audience," in the words of one critic, are presented on stages across the country. Regional theaters provide actors with an opportunity to get back to the basics, and give talented local authors and first-timers a chance to get their works produced. Meanwhile, whether the play ends up on Broadway or never gets more than a reading, audiences get some lively dramatic experiences. Throughout this book, we have described the best theaters in the major US cities in individual chapters in THE CITIES. The following is a list of other "boards" in places that are a bit out-of-the-way—but well worth the trip.

GOODSPEED OPERA HOUSE, East Haddam, Connecticut Works of Cole Porter, George Gershwin, Rodgers and Hart, and Frank Loesser are among the classics regularly played here, as American musicals comprise this theater's repertoire. The *Goodspeed* puts on three shows during its season, April through December. Information: *Goodspeed Opera House,* Rte. 82, East Haddam, CT 06423 (phone: 860-873-8668, box office).

STEPPENWOLF THEATRE COMPANY, Chicago, Illinois Originally founded in the mid-1970s by actors from the *Illinois State University* community, the company has become one of this country's most vital regional theater ensembles. Productions such as Frank Galati's adaptation of John Steinbeck's *The Grapes of Wrath* have moved from here to Broadway and London's West End. Major names like Gary Sinise (a founding member), Glenne Headly, and John Malkovich have all taken part in *Steppenwolf* productions. Recently, the company moved into a new 500-seat theater. Information: *Steppenwolf Theatre Company,* 1650 N. Halsted St., Chicago, IL 60614 (phone: 312-335-1650).

TRINITY REPERTORY COMPANY, Providence, Rhode Island Eleven major productions of modern, classic, and original dramas are staged annually in two theaters. *Trinity Rep* makes headlines as much for its vigorous ensemble style as for the plays themselves. The theater won a Tony Award as the nation's best repertory company in 1981 and, in 1984, it was awarded its first Ensemble Grant from the *National Endowment for the Arts.* Since it began in 1964, the company has aimed to provide permanent employment for its resident artists and to involve the audience as participants in the theater experience. Information: *Trinity Repertory Company,* 201 Washington St., Providence, RI 02903 (phone: 401-521-1100; 401-351-4242, box office).

Outdoor Dramas

Paul Green, the dramatist who wrote some of the best of the American outdoor epics, called this dramatic form "a people's theater" and anticipated the day when it would ripen into something like the outdoor drama of the Greeks. Whether or not we ever see that day, close to two million travelers make an annual pilgrimage to woodland amphitheaters across the country to watch these spectacles of war and peace, statesmen and villains, heroes and plain folk, prejudice, feuds, murder, night riders, love and suffering—the very stuff of American history acted out a lot larger than most of it was lived. The passion play, which has survived since the Middle Ages, recounts the suffering, death, and resurrection of Jesus and is a genre unto itself.

Outdoor drama is not a subtle art form, since it employs many pageant elements. These summer epics have two compelling virtues. With the exception of the passion plays, they are uniquely American, based on legends, tall tales, and real history performed in the original settings; and they are exciting—colorfully and enthusiastically performed with horses charging, guns and cannon exploding, flames leaping, extravagant costuming, and good music. They are also generally inexpensive; reserved seats (which you should consider) usually cost $10 to $12; unreserved even less. For a complete directory of American outdoor dramas (there are about 80), send $5 to the *Institute of Outdoor Drama, University of North Carolina,* CB #3240, NationsBank Plaza, Chapel Hill, NC 27599 (phone: 919-962-1328). Below is a sampling of some of the best.

SOUTH

GREAT PASSION PLAY, Eureka Springs, Arkansas The quaint hillside town where Carrie Nation made her last temperance speech also puts on a pageant about Christ's last days, complete with camels, horses, sheep, donkeys, doves, and a cast of over 200. Last Friday of April through last Saturday of October; closed Mondays and Thursdays. Information: *Great Passion Play,* PO Box 471, Eureka Springs, AR 72632 (phone: 501-253-8559).

CROSS AND SWORD, St. Augustine, Florida Paul Green's production of Pedro Menéndez de Avilés's founding of St. Augustine, the oldest permanent settlement in the US, was first seen in 1965, the year the city celebrated its 400th birthday; it continues to play from mid-July through August.

Information: *Cross and Sword,* PO Box 1965, St. Augustine, FL 32085 (phone: 904-471-1965). Also see *Restored Towns and Reconstructed Villages.*

STEPHEN FOSTER STORY, Bardstown, Kentucky A musical about how the composer wooed and won his Jeanie with the light brown hair (whose real name, it turns out, was Jane). Early June to *Labor Day.* Information: *Stephen Foster Story,* PO Box 546, Bardstown, KY 40004 (phone: 502-348-5971; 800-626-1563).

LEGEND OF DANIEL BOONE, Harrodsburg, Kentucky This popular drama focusing on the history of the great pioneer is performed at the *James Harrod Amphitheatre* in *Old Fort Harrod State Park*—a 28-acre preserve set up to honor the first permanent white settlement in Kentucky. Mid-June through late August. Information: *Legend of Daniel Boone,* PO Box 365, Harrodsburg, KY 40330 (phone: 606-734-3346).

HORN IN THE WEST, Boone, North Carolina This story of how the earliest American pioneers rebelled against the royal governor and went west was written by Kermit Hunter, a celebrated creator of outdoor dramas. Late June through mid-August. Information: *Horn in the West,* PO Box 295, Boone, NC 28607 (phone: 704-264-2120).

UNTO THESE HILLS, Cherokee, North Carolina Kermit Hunter also wrote this piece about the Cherokee Indians from 1540 until 1838, when they were herded westward over the Trail of Tears; it's presented mid-June through late August at the *Mountainside Amphitheater,* near the *Oconaluftee Indian Village,* a replica of a Cherokee settlement of 200 years ago (see also *A Short Tour of Indian America*). Information: *Unto These Hills,* PO Box 398, Cherokee, NC 28719 (phone: 704-497-2111).

TEXAS, Canyon, Texas The struggle between farmers and cattlemen in the 1880s is presented by a cast of 80, with sound-and-light effects, at *Palo Duro State Park,* near Amarillo, from mid-June through late August in a 1,000-foot-deep, 100-mile-long canyon so impressive that in many ways it turns out to be the star of the show. Information: *Texas Panhandle Heritage Foundation, Inc.* PO Box 268, Canyon, TX 79015 (phone: 806-655-2181).

TRAIL OF THE LONESOME PINE, Big Stone Gap, Virginia The love story of a mountain girl and a mining engineer from the East, set in the days when coal and iron discoveries were changing the lives of the mountain people. It's based on a true story, presented not far from where the couple wooed, in a part of the state deeply affected by mining. Mid-June through August. Information: *Trail of the Lonesome Pine,* PO Box 1976, Big Stone Gap, VA 24219 (phone: 703-523-1235).

HATFIELDS AND MCCOYS, Beckley, West Virginia The saga of the most famous feuding families in America (complete with a runaway daughter, a stillborn baby, killings, bounties, and betrayal) alternates in repertory with other productions, including a musical. Late June through late August.

Information: *Theatre West Virginia,* PO Box 1205, Beckley, WV 25802 (phone: 304-256-6800; 800-666-9142).

MIDWEST

SHEPHERD OF THE HILLS, Branson, Missouri Harold Bell Wright's novel is reenacted on the homestead where the 1902 Ozarks drought it depicts actually took place. The drama is staged from late April through October. Information: *Shepherd of the Hills Historical Society,* 5586 W. State Hwy. 76, Branson, MO 65616 (phone: 417-334-4191).

TECUMSEH!, Chillicothe, Ohio The Shawnee war leader's struggle with William Henry Harrison over the Northwest Territory involves a cast and crew of 80, a dozen horses, and 13 stages. Mid-June through early September. Information: *Tecumseh!,* PO Box 73, Chillicothe, OH 45601 (phone: 614-775-0700 from March 1 until the end of the season).

TRUMPET IN THE LAND, New Philadelphia, Ohio This outdoor drama spectacular features missionaries, Indians, soldiers, and the Revolutionary War on America's first frontier, complete with horses, a massacre, dances, and music. It's presented from mid-June through August about a mile from *Schoenbrunn Village* (see also *Utopias and Religious Settlements*), a restoration of the settlement where many of the events took place. Information: *Trumpet in the Land,* PO Box 450, New Philadelphia, OH 44663 (phone: 216-339-1132).

BLACK HILLS PASSION PLAY, Spearfish, South Dakota, and Lake Wales, Florida Under the direction of Josef Meier, an ensemble of some 200 players presents the last seven days in the life of Christ. Performances from June through August in Spearfish and mid-February through mid-April in Lake Wales. Information: *Black Hills Passion Play,* PO Box 489, Spearfish, SD 57783 (phone: 605-642-2646; 800-457-0160), or PO Box 71, Lake Wales, FL 33859 (phone: 813-676-1495; 800-622-8383).

WEST

RAMONA PAGEANT, Hemet, California This love story is set among the rolling hills in the colorful Hemet–San Jacinto Valley and uses an entire mountainside as a setting. Some consider the beauty of this dramatization of Helen Hunt Jackson's novel to be unparalleled. Since 1923, tourists from all over the world have found it a fascinating journey into the California of yesteryear. Six performances are presented in late April and early May. Tickets go on sale in January. Information: *Ramona Pageant Assn.,* 27400 Ramona Bowl Rd., Hemet, CA 92544 (phone: 909-658-3111 from January 1 until the end of the season).

TRAIL OF TEARS CHEROKEE HERITAGE CENTER, Tahlequah, Oklahoma The story of the Cherokees from the end of the tragic march over the Trail of Tears until the beginning of this century. The story is presented at the *Tsa-La-Gi*

Amphitheatre, where you also can tour a re-creation of a 17th-century Cherokee village, where Cherokees in costume make baskets, weapons, pottery, and tools. Mid-June through mid-August. The *Cherokee National Museum* uses state-of-the-art technology to tell the Cherokee story from the white man's arrival in North America to the present; it is closed Saturdays and Sundays from mid-December to early February. Information: *Trail of Tears, Cherokee Heritage Center,* PO Box 515, Tahlequah, OK 74465 (phone: 918-456-6007).

Music Festivals: Summers of Sound

All over the country, throughout the summer audiences gather to be enraptured by the glorious sounds of live music—not just symphonies, string trios, chorales and cantatas, but also breakdowns, rags, gospel choruses, and a lot of country fiddling and picking. The music is played in mansions and amphitheaters, rustic gardens and antique opera halls, huge band shells, and even California vineyards. Some festivals are one-day happenings; others mean round-the-clock music for a weekend or more.

State tourist organizations can tell you about the ones in the area you want to visit. Or, for a list of bluegrass events, you can contact *Bluegrass Unlimited* magazine for its annual festival edition published in January ($2.25; PO Box 111, Broad Run, VA 22014; phone: 703-349-8181).

Expect to pay from about $15 to $65 for tickets. Should you order in advance? By all means, especially if the object of your trip is to hear a specific performance. Usually, you will be able to get seats at the last minute (and at many of the big festivals you can sit on the lawn), but planning ahead will ensure you'll sit where you want. Remember, too, that tickets for seats under a roof eliminate the chance that rain will wash out your enjoyment. Throughout this book, we have described festivals that take place in the major US cities in individual chapters in THE CITIES. The following is a list of worthwhile festivals largely located outside the major urban areas.

EAST

NATIONAL FOLK FESTIVAL, based in Silver Spring, Maryland A moveable feast of traditional arts, through 1998 this festival will be held in Dayton, Ohio. An annual event since 1934, it is the oldest multicultural folk festival in the US. Crafts demonstrations and storytelling are part of the goings-on, but the real emphasis is on the music—bluegrass, blues, gospel, Cajun, zydeco, rhythm and blues, old-time, Tex-Mex, ethnic, and country—played by the nation's best performers. Joint sponsors are the *National Council for the Traditional Arts,* the *National Park Service,* and local not-for-profit concerns. The site changes every three years, as do the dates—anytime from late July through late September. Information: *NCTA,* 1320 Fenwick Lane, Suite 200, Silver Spring, MD 20910 (phone: 301-565-0654).

TANGLEWOOD, Lenox, Massachusetts The *Boston Symphony Orchestra* (with music director Seiji Ozawa) summers at this old, 500-acre estate in the Berkshires. During July and August, the orchestra and various student and chamber groups perform Friday and Saturday evenings and Sunday afternoons in the *Seiji Ozawa Hall,* an enormous open-sided pavilion, with seating on the huge surrounding lawn as well. In addition to these concerts, there are Thursday evening chamber music concerts, prelude concerts, open rehearsals, recitals by world class musicians, the annual *Festival of Contemporary Music,* and concerts by the gifted young musicians from the *Tanglewood Music Center* most other evenings. The *Boston Pops Orchestra* gives an annual concert as well. The Popular Artists Series brings various performers to *Tanglewood,* and the *Jazz Festival* closes the season. For lodgings, see *America's Special Havens.* Information: *Boston Symphony Orchestra, Symphony Hall,* 301 Massachusetts Ave., Boston, MA 02115 (phone: 617-266-1492), before mid-June; *Tanglewood,* Lenox, MA 01240 (phone: 413-637-1899), from mid-June to *Labor Day.*

CHAUTAUQUA INSTITUTION, Chautauqua, New York Founded in 1874, this 750-acre National Historic Landmark about 65 miles from Buffalo is a lakeside Victorian community where cars are restricted. Here, learning keeps company with performances; the institute offers operas, symphony concerts, dance, popular entertainment, and theater along with lectures and courses in fine arts, psychology, politics, philosophy, crafts, and just about any other subject you can name. Late June to late August. Information: *Chautauqua Institution,* PO Box 28, Chautauqua, NY 14722 (phone: 716-357-6200; 800-836-ARTS).

GLIMMERGLASS OPERA, Cooperstown, New York Established in 1975, this summer festival presents four operas either in English or in the original language with supertitles in English. The company is renowned for its staging of rarely performed works as well as unusual stagings of standard pieces by such acclaimed directors as Martha Clarke, Mark Lamos, and Jonathan Miller. The 900-seat *Alice Busch Opera Theater* is surrounded by 25 acres of meadows that provide a perfect location for relaxing, walking, or picnicking. Free opera previews are held an hour before every performance. Throughout the season (July and August), behind-the-scenes tours of the theater are given. Information: *Glimmerglass Opera,* PO Box 191, Cooperstown, NY 13326 (phone: 607-547-5704; 607-547-2255, box office; fax: 607-547-6030).

LAKE GEORGE OPERA FESTIVAL, Glens Falls, New York Favorite operas and American premieres are sung in English by internationally recognized performers in this most delightful of American vacation areas. The productions, which are fully staged with a professional orchestra, take place in August; and on the last Sunday evening in July, there is an Opera-on-the-Lake cruise. Information: *Lake George Opera Festival,* PO Box 2172, Glens Falls, NY 12801 (phone: 518-793-3858).

HUNTER MOUNTAIN FESTIVALS, Hunter, New York From April through October, this upstate New York ski area is big on ethnic festivals and events, offering the *German Alps Festival,* the *International Celtic Festival,* a *Rockstalgia* gathering full of 1950s and 1960s rock 'n' roll, and a celebration of Native Americans with traditional festivities. In addition, there are two country festivals (past performers have included Garth Brooks and Alan Jackson). Information: *Hunter Mountain Festivals,* PO Box 295, Hunter, NY 12442 (phone: 518-263-3800).

CARAMOOR FESTIVAL, Katonah, New York On weekends from mid-June through mid-August, chamber and orchestral concerts are presented on an Italian Renaissance–style estate an hour's drive from Manhattan. The large works are performed in an outdoor theater surrounded by 15th-century Venetian columns, the chamber concerts in a Spanish-style courtyard. Information: *Caramoor,* PO Box 816, Katonah, NY 10536 (phone: 914-232-5035).

SARATOGA PERFORMING ARTS CENTER, Saratoga Springs, New York The watering hole of the horsey set, this genteel old town also is the home of the giant amphitheater where the *New York City Ballet* performs in July and the *Philadelphia Orchestra* in August. The *New York City Opera,* in its 10th season here, performs in June. Popular special events, including the *Newport Jazz Festival–Saratoga,* are presented from June through September. In August, the *Saratoga Chamber Music Festival* is held in *SPA*'s *Little Theatre.* Information: *SPAC Box Office,* Saratoga Springs, NY 12866 (phone: 518-587-3330).

JVC JAZZ FESTIVAL, Newport, Rhode Island Jazz comes to Newport the second weekend in August when a lineup of well-known musicians and bands perform at *Fort Adams State Park.* Jazz buffs picnic on the grassy waterside slopes while they listen. Information: *JVC Jazz Festival,* PO Box 605, Newport, RI 02840 (phone: 401-847-3700, June through September only).

NEWPORT MUSIC FESTIVAL, Newport, Rhode Island Three times daily, for two weeks every July, first-rate international artists perform chamber music in the gilt and marble ballrooms of Newport's glorious mansions. It is one of the most prestigious musical festivals in the country. For lodgings, see *America's Special Havens.* Information: *Newport Music Festival,* PO Box 3300, Newport, RI 02840 (phone: 401-846-1133).

MARLBORO MUSIC SCHOOL AND FESTIVAL, Marlboro, Vermont Fine musicians play such glorious chamber music every weekend from mid-July through mid-August that most tickets sell out within a couple of weeks of an early April mailing. You may latch onto one of the 100 available for seating under an outdoor canopy by presenting yourself at the box office about an hour before curtain time. Information: *Marlboro Music School and Festival,* 135 S. 18th St., Philadelphia, PA 19103 (phone: 215-569-4690), before mid-June and after mid-August; or Marlboro, VT 05344 (phone: 802-254-2394), in the summer.

SOUTH

MOUNTAIN DANCE AND FOLK FESTIVAL, Asheville, North Carolina Square dancers and cloggers keep time to the music of mountain pickers, fiddlers, ballad singers, and dulcimer players at this festival. The oldest of its type in the country, it's been going strong since 1927. The first weekend in August. Information: *Asheville Convention and Visitors Bureau,* PO Box 1010, Asheville, NC 28801 (phone: 704-258-6107; 800-257-5583).

OLD FIDDLERS' CONVENTION, Galax, Virginia This traditional music festival, one of the oldest, largest, and best-known in the country, is held annually during the second full weekend in August. Information: *Old Fiddlers' Convention,* c/o Tom Jones, PO Box 655, Galax, VA 24333 (phone: 703-236-8541).

HAMPTON JAZZ FESTIVAL, Hampton, Virginia The *Hampton Coliseum,* where this event is held, sells out well in advance for performances by top soul and jazz artists the last full weekend in June. Information: *Hampton Jazz Festival,* PO Box 7309, Hampton, VA 23666-0309 (phone: 804-838-4203).

FILENE CENTER AT WOLF TRAP FARM PARK, Vienna, Virginia At this national park for the performing arts, you'll get a cross section of what's happening on the American and international music scene. Big-name performers from the worlds of classical and popular music, ballet, opera, and modern dance draw audiences to the park's lawns and big open-air pavilion. The air also reverberates with the music of bluegrass musicians like Bill Monroe, rock and blues performers like Bonnie Raitt and Ray Charles, and entertainment by the likes of comedian Jay Leno and even tap-dance groups. Late May into September. Information: *Wolf Trap Foundation for the Performing Arts,* 1624 Trap Rd., Vienna, VA 22182 (phone: 703-255-1916).

MIDWEST

RAVINIA FESTIVAL, Highland Park, Illinois The *Chicago Symphony Orchestra* holds forth in the open-air pavilion of a 36-acre woodland park beginning in early June, and stands as the star attraction of this international festival of all the arts. Visiting orchestras, recitals and chamber music programs, ballet and dance, a jazz and popular music series, and a New Perspectives series also are part of a long and varied summer season that lasts into September. There is also a recital and chamber music series in *Bennett Hall,* year-round. Information: *Ravinia Festival,* 1575 Oakwood Ave., Highland Park, IL 60035 (phone: 312-RAVINIA).

BEANBLOSSOM BLUEGRASS MUSIC FESTIVAL, Beanblossom, Indiana This blink-and-you-miss-it settlement in the hilly southern part of the state really hops in June, when festival organizer James Monroe (son of bluegrass music star Bill Monroe) brings musicians to town for a bluegrass marathon. Thousands come to hear the concerts in the wooded amphitheater, setting up tents and parking their campers in a nearby field, and the air rings with the fiddling and picking of their jam sessions into the wee hours. Information: *Monroe Enterprises,* 3819 Dickerson Rd., Nashville, TN 37207 (phone: 615-868-3333; 812-988-6422, festival park).

BLOSSOM MUSIC CENTER, Cuyahoga Falls, Ohio When the *Cleveland Orchestra* isn't playing at this cedar-shingled shell halfway between Akron and Cleveland, the center hosts everything from *Van Halen,* Diana Ross, and Julio Iglesias to jazz and ballet. All in all, some 80 musical events are held every year from mid-May through mid-September. Full banquet facilities are available. Information: *Blossom Music Center,* PO Box 1000, Cuyahoga Falls, OH 44223 (phone: 216-920-8040).

WEST

CARMEL BACH FESTIVAL, Carmel, California For three weeks from mid-July to early August, works by Bach and others are performed at the *Sunset Cultural Center* and the *Carmel Mission Basilica* in this lovely village on the northern California coast. Information: *Carmel Bach Festival,* PO Box 575, Carmel, CA 93921 (phone: 408-624-1521; 408-624-2046, tickets). Information about the many interesting hotels and restaurants in the area is available from the *Carmel Business Association,* PO Box 4444, Carmel-by-the-Sea, CA 93921 (phone: 408-624-2522).

MONTEREY JAZZ FESTIVAL, Monterey, California The oldest continuously presented jazz festival in the nation, this event, held on the third full weekend in September, features some of the biggest names in the business. Season tickets (for all five weekend shows), which cost between $115 and $150 depending on the seats, sell out by the end of July; ground admission is available through the festival weekend. Information: *Monterey Jazz Festival,* PO Box JAZZ, Monterey, CA 93942 (phone: 408-373-3366; 800-307-3378, box office).

ASPEN MUSIC FESTIVAL, Aspen, Colorado Daily musical activity of one sort or another—jazz, choral, orchestral, and operatic pieces, chamber works, and about anything else you can name—makes this festival, which is held annually from late June through late August, one of the nation's liveliest. Sometimes the performers are name soloists on the order of Pinchas Zukerman and Arleen Augér; sometimes you'll be hearing gifted students from the *Aspen Music School,* whose sessions run concurrently. Information: *Aspen Music Festival,* 2 Music School Rd., Aspen, CO 81612 (phone: 970-925-3254).

NATIONAL OLD-TIME FIDDLERS' CONTEST, Weiser, Idaho Parades, barbecue dinners—and near-nonstop fiddling at daytime and nighttime competitions, and jam sessions in between—keep this town of 4,000 hopping during the third full week in June. Weiser is the self-styled "fiddling capital of America" and the home of the *Fiddlers' Hall of Fame.* The competition attracts some 300-plus contestants ages three through 92 and nearly 5,000 spectators from all over the US and Canada. Information: *Chamber of Commerce,* 8 E. Idaho St., Weiser, ID 83672 (phone: 208-549-0450).

PETER BRITT FESTIVALS, Jacksonville, Oregon The Northwest's oldest music festival, founded to honor pioneer vintner, horticulturist, and daguerrotypist Peter Britt, now offers six festivals every summer in the spectacular outdoor *Britt Music Pavilion:* classical, country folk, jazz, pop, dance, and musical theater. Arrange lodgings well in advance because of the concurrent *Oregon Shakespeare Festival,* some 15 miles away in Ashland. Information: *Peter Britt Festivals,* PO Box 1124, Medford, OR 97501 (phone: 541-773-6077; 800-88-BRITT, tickets).

GRAND TETON MUSIC FESTIVAL, Teton Village, Wyoming Along with the Orchestral Seminar, starting in mid-June and running until late August, for 11 weeks you'll find great music in these oft-climbed mountains—small ensembles during the week, and a full symphony orchestra on Fridays and Saturdays. Sometimes the artist or composer discusses the pieces beforehand. *Festival Hall* is known for its fine acoustics. Information: *Grand Teton Music Festival,* PO Box 490, Teton Village, WY 83025-0490 (phone: 307-733-1128).

NASHVILLE IN THE OZARKS

Since its beginnings, country music has had its roots in Nashville. But in recent years, it's had a steady migration toward a new home—Branson, Missouri. This small town in the Ozarks has more live country music shows than anywhere else in the US. With 32 indoor theaters and three outdoor amphitheaters, the town is giving Nashville a real run for its money. Celebrities such as Glen Campbell, Barbara Mandrell, Ray Stevens, Jim Stafford, Mickey Gilley, Crystal Gayle, Kenny Rogers, Andy Williams, and Tammy Wynette have been featured performers in these family-oriented, often patriotic shows. Roy Clark, Boxcar Willie, and Mel Tillis have built their own permanent theaters and perform here regularly. Tourists have gotten the message: About five million of them visited the area in 1992 and spent more than $675 million. As a result of this influx of country music fans, there is a bumper crop of hotels, restaurants, and camping areas from which to choose. There also can be bumper-to-bumper traffic jams getting into or out of town. For more information, contact the *Branson/Lakes Area Chamber of Commerce* (PO Box 1897, Branson, MO 65615; phone: 417-334-4136; 900-884-BRANSON, $1.50 per minute for a recorded message or operator; fax: 417-334-4139).

Restored Towns and Reconstructed Villages

Williamsburg, Virginia, is only the most famous of America's restored towns: All over the country historical villages have been reconstructed—some simply repaired and restored, others pieced together with brand-new buildings or from original structures collected from numerous sites—to graphically re-create the day-by-day life of earlier periods in American history. At the best of these, curators hire craftspeople to demonstrate everyday tasks of the era, and provide lectures, walking tours, and special events. In general, the larger the restoration, the wider the variety of special activities.

Unless otherwise noted, all town/villages are open year-round.

EAST

MYSTIC SEAPORT, Mystic, Connecticut Gulls wheel and cry overhead while you're walking around this 17-acre maritime museum. Included is a re-created 19th-century coastal community; along with blacksmithing, woodcarving, and fireplace cooking, there's a ship's chandlery, sail loft, ship model shop, printers' shop, general store, tavern, and more. You may see shipwrights at work on 19th-century ships and boats, and the restored, 151-year-old *Charles W. Morgan,* America's last surviving wooden whaling ship and a National Historic Landmark, towers proudly over it all. And there's more: the US's largest collection of small boats; exhibits of scrimshaw, marine art, and figureheads; steamboat cruises; children's games; a planetarium; demonstrations of sail-setting and furling and other marine skills; special events all year; and, at *Christmas,* a lively program of lantern-light tours and other period merriment. Information: *Mystic Seaport,* 75 Greenmanville Ave., Mystic, CT 06355 (phone: 860-572-5315; 800-522-1841 for brochures only). See also *New London, Connecticut, to Providence, Rhode Island,* DIRECTIONS.

PLIMOTH PLANTATION, Plymouth, Massachusetts This re-creation of the first permanent settlement in the northeast lets visitors step back in time to the year 1627, six-and-a-half years after the Pilgrims' arrival on the *Mayflower.* There are small, thatch-roofed clapboard houses that line the road overlooking Cape Cod Bay. Herb and vegetable gardens are cultivated, and foods such as roasted fowl and "minc't" pies are prepared in season from 17th-century recipes and sold at the *J. Barnes Bake Shop.* Every detail is authentic to the period, right down to the farm animals. Men and women in period dress engage visitors in conversation, and speak in any one of 17 dialects. Adjacent to the village is *Hobbamock's Homesite,* named for a Wampanoag Indian who lived near the Pilgrims and acted as their guide and interpreter. There are two gift shops specializing in 17th-century reproductions, as well as a cafeteria. Closed December through March. Information: *Plimoth Plantation,* PO Box 1620, Plymouth, MA 02362 (phone: 508-746-1622).

As for actual colonial landmarks, nearby Duxbury and Kingston have street upon street of old homes. In Plymouth itself, visit the houses of the Pilgrims, their burial sites, a gristmill, and a winery (which aptly enough, produces only cranberry wine). *Thanksgiving* is a particularly good time to come; there's a reenactment of the Pilgrims' Progress to church. Information:

Plymouth Area Chamber of Commerce, 225 Water St., Suite 500, Plymouth, MA 02360 (phone: 508-830-1620).

OLD STURBRIDGE VILLAGE, Sturbridge, Massachusetts Things are so authentic at this re-created village that sheep help to trim the grass on the village green, and the general store is stocked with just those items an early-19th-century shopper would have expected. Hardworking ladies cook up savory goodies, using early-19th-century "receipts," and blacksmiths, broom makers, coopers, printers, shoemakers, and other artisans go about their work the traditional way. The purpose is to demonstrate the transformation of rural America into industrial America, so in addition to the farm and the gristmill, there are exhibits like the water-powered wool carding mill and the 1830s sawmill. *Sturbridge* is one of the most respected establishments of its type and the largest living history center in the Northeast; you could come back many times and still not see everything. At *Thanksgiving, Bullard Tavern* puts on a traditional feast. Reservations are necessary well in advance. Information: *Old Sturbridge Village,* 1 Old Sturbridge Village Rd., Sturbridge, MA 01566 (phone: 508-347-3362). Note: At the *Publick House,* a nearby quaint inn, *Christmas* brings an Edwardian *Yuletide Pageant* and feast (phone: 508-347-3313; see *America's Special Havens*).

STRAWBERY BANKE MUSEUM, Portsmouth, New Hampshire Beginning in the 1600s, this neighborhood flourished for some 200 years, only to sink into what seemed a lasting decline in the mid-1800s. But a 10-acre area was rescued from demolition in the 1950s and has been largely restored. Of the 42 historic houses, nine are furnished in different period styles, six contain museum exhibits, three house crafts workshops, and the remainder are in various stages of completion. Open from April through early November. Information: *Strawbery Banke Museum,* PO Box 300, Portsmouth, NH 03802 (phone: 603-433-1100).

FARMERS' MUSEUM AND VILLAGE CROSSROADS, Cooperstown, New York *The Farmers' Museum,* along with *Fenimore House,* a museum of folk, decorative, academic, and American Indian art, provides a center for the study of America's rural heritage. Founded in 1943, it is one of the oldest open-air sites in the US. The *Main Barn,* built as a dairy barn in 1918, today is a visitors' orientation area with displays on farm technology, village life, domestic economy, 19th-century trades, and amusements. Craftspeople work at broom making, cabinetmaking, spinning, and weaving. A dozen buildings were moved to the site from the surrounding region to re-create a 19th-century farm community. The buildings, including a schoolhouse, general store, blacksmith shop, print shop, pharmacy, doctor's office, lawyer's office, tavern, and church, were erected along a roadway in a typical New York village arrangement. There is a presentation of typical domestic life at the *Lippitt Farm,* where household chores are performed, sheep, cattle, and fowl are kept, and fields are planted. Special programs include a *Harvest Festival* in the fall, a 19th-century–style *Fourth of July* celebration, seminars on American culture, a *Junior Livestock Show,* and craft workshops for amateurs as well as professionals. Lodgings in the area include the comfortable Georgian-style *Otesaga* (phone: 607-547-9931; see *America's Best Resort Hotels*). Information: *Farmers' Museum,* PO Box 800, Cooperstown, NY 13326 (phone: 607-547-1400).

GENESEE COUNTRY MUSEUM, Mumford, New York Some 55 19th-century American buildings gathered from upstate New York and restored on this rolling 125-acre site reflect American life in the early 1800s. Among them are an elegant Italianate home, with a two-story carriage house and handsome sunken formal gardens; a gunsmith shop; and a two-story Shaker building. You'll also see pottery, a bandstand, a farm, a parsonage, a pioneer settlement, a variety of homes, an inn, a Methodist church, a score of working crafts shops, and offices, all peopled by costumed "villagers." There are special events most weekends. The unusual *Gallery of Sporting Art* explores man and his animals. Next to the museum complex is the *Nature Center,* 200 acres of trails exposing visitors to the flora and fauna of the region. Closed from the end of October through mid-May. Information: *Genesee Country Museum,* PO Box 310, Mumford, NY 14511 (phone: 716-538-6822).

HOPEWELL FURNACE NATIONAL HISTORIC SITE, near Elverson, Pennsylvania This community, dating to 1771, is the most far-ranging restoration of the cold-blast, charcoal-burning iron furnaces that flourished in this corner of southeastern Pennsylvania during the 18th and 19th centuries. The ironmaster's home, charcoal house, waterwheel, blast machinery, casting house, cold-blast furnace, tenant houses, and barns are all open year-round. Molding and metal casting skills of the early 19th century are demonstrated from late June through *Labor Day.* Information: *Hopewell Furnace National Historic Site,* 2 Mark Bird Ln., Elverson, PA 19520 (phone: 610-582-8773).

SHELBURNE MUSEUM, Shelburne, Vermont These collections of Americana housed in 37 historic buildings were moved to the 45-acre site from all over New England. Among the more than 80,000 folk art objects and artifacts you'll find carousel figures, cigar store Indians, cradles, dolls, dresses, horse-drawn vehicles, quilts, rugs, ship figureheads, shop figures, tin bathtubs, tools for farming and woodworking, toys, and more. The museum features the largest public collection of waterfowl decoys in the world. The massive steamship *Ticonderoga,* now landlocked, presides over it all. Visit between May and October; only a few buildings are open in winter—and only on Sundays. Information: *Shelburne Museum,* Shelburne, VT 05482 (phone: 802-985-3344). Note: Two of the best area lodgings are at the classy *Basin Harbor Club* on Lake Champlain, open from May through October (phone: 802-985-3346; see *America's Best Resort Hotels*) and the *Inn at Shelburne Farms* (phone: 802-985-8498; see *America's Special Havens*); eat at the handsome, antiques-filled *Dog Team Tavern* (phone: 802-388-7651)—and don't miss those great sticky buns.

HISTORIC ST. AUGUSTINE, St. Augustine, Florida The Spanish settled in St. Augustine in 1565, making this the US's oldest permanent settlement. The plain stucco houses of the restored section line a narrow street across from the *Castillo de San Marcos* (the fort that protected the town) and fill a couple of side streets as well. At work are a candlemaker, a carpenter, and a weaver who crafts marvels out of lovely wools. The settlement's story is told at the visitors' information center—a good place to begin—and at the outdoor drama *Cross and Sword,* performed during summer months (see *Outdoor Dramas*). Special events include an annual *Blessing of the Fleet* on *Palm Sunday* weekend and, on *Easter Sunday,* a parade of horse-drawn carriages. Other events include a maritime festival the first weekend in October, and reenactments of various historic events year-round. Information: *St. Augustine–St. Johns County Chamber of Commerce,* 1 Castillo Dr., St. Augustine, FL 32086 (phone: 904-829-5681).

WESTVILLE 1850, Lumpkin, Georgia Life in the South wasn't all barbecues and 17-inch waistlines. Some people lived in modest homes, gathered eggs in the baskets they crafted, made pottery jugs and bowls, repaired buggies, dried fruits, stored vegetables, made syrup from sugarcane, and ginned and baled cotton—all of which you'll see demonstrated at this nifty re-created village. Extra craftspeople are on hand for the *Fair of 1850,* held during the first week in October, and there are Maypole dances on *May Day,* a barbecue on *July 4,* and *Christmas* activities every Saturday in December. Information: *Westville 1850,* PO Box 1850, Lumpkin, GA 31815 (phone: 912-838-6310).

JAMESTOWN, Jamestown, Virginia Foundations, property ditches, a church tower dating to 1639, and a few streets in the *Jamestown National Historical Site* are all that remain of the city that served as Virginia's capital and cultural center for 92 years. The glasshouse has been reconstructed so that craftsmen can make glass as they did here three centuries ago. The museum contains one of the largest collections of 17th-century artifacts in the country, part of which is on display at the visitors' center (phone: 804-229-1733). Also, 3- and 5-mile drives provide access to the marshes and pine forests of Jamestown Island. Information: *Colonial National Historical Park,* PO Box 210, Yorktown, VA 23690 (phone: 804-898-3400).

Nearby, at the 25-acre *Jamestown Settlement,* are a re-created 17th-century fort and Indian village; as well as full-scale replicas of the three famous ships that, though hardly bigger than yachts, transported 104 men and boys to Virginia in 1607. In the three areas, costumed interpreters carry out typical 17th-century tasks. There is also an indoor museum which features an orientation film and exhibitions that tell the story of Jamestown's beginnings in the Old World, the Powhatan Indian culture encountered by the colonists, and the first 100 years of the colony. Open year-round. Information: *Jamestown Settlement,* Jamestown Yorktown Foundation, PO Drawer JF,

Williamsburg, VA 23185 (phone: 804-253-4838). See also *Tidewater Virginia* in DIRECTIONS.

COLONIAL WILLIAMSBURG, Williamsburg, Virginia All the superlatives apply to this restoration of Virginia's 18th-century colonial capital which was the political and cultural center of Britain's largest colony in the New World. Its living history program is staggering. There is an active practice of 36 colonial crafts and trades, ranging from apothecary to wigmaking. Exhibitions come to life with interesting and informative presentations. Throughout the year, interpreters representing 18th-century people appear at exhibition sites to provide insights into the attitudes, problems, and opinions of the time. In an attempt to re-create the African-American experience, there are slave quarters reconstructed on their original sites with some of their original furnishings, as well as music performances and presentations showing what slavery was like on the plantations. On the 173-acre grounds are more than 500 restored and reconstructed buildings, homes, shops, taverns, public buildings, gardens and greens, and hundreds of costumed townspeople. There are some buildings you won't want to miss: the *Governor's Palace,* as it was called by the disgruntled colonists whose taxes paid its bills; the *College of William and Mary,* built in 1693 and the second-oldest college in America; and two jovial and famous meeting places, *Raleigh* and *Wetherburn's* taverns. In addition, there is the *Abby Aldrich Rockefeller Folk Art Center* and the *DeWitt Wallace Decorative Arts Gallery.* Every day in summer, spring and autumn weekends, and *Christmas* are the busiest times, which means you may have to wait to get into the taverns. Note: No smoking is allowed in any buildings in Williamsburg. Information: *Colonial Williamsburg,* PO Box 1776, Williamsburg, VA 23187 (phone: 804-229-1000; 800-HISTORY for reservations); *Williamsburg Area Convention & Visitors Bureau,* PO Box 3585, Williamsburg, VA 23185 (phone: 804-253-0192; 800-368-6511). See also *Tidewater Virginia,* DIRECTIONS.

YORKTOWN, Yorktown, Virginia The final major conflict of the War of Independence was fought here in 1781, when the British general Lord Cornwallis led his army into Virginia in the hope of conquering the southern colonies. Opposing him was the smaller American force led by the Marquis de Lafayette. After several skirmishes, Cornwallis received orders to fortify Yorktown as a base for contact with the British fleet. Meanwhile, General George Washington decided that a combined land and naval battle in Virginia now was possible. On September 5, the French fleet intercepted the British outside the Virginia capes and forced them to retire: Washington and Rochambeau arrived later in the month and laid siege to the town. The *Celebration of Victory,* held here every October, commemorates this historic event. Like neighboring Williamsburg and Jamestown, Yorktown offers sites that portray the Revolutionary War period and the climactic siege; they are open year-round. Of particular interest is the *Yorktown Victory Center* (phone: 804-887-1776), which features a film, exhibits, and living history re-creations of the American Revolution. Information: *Colonial National Historic Park,* PO Box 210, Yorktown, VA 23690 (phone: 804-898-3400). See also *Tidewater Virginia,* DIRECTIONS.

MIDWEST

LINCOLN'S NEW SALEM STATE HISTORIC SITE, Petersburg, Illinois Edgar Lee Masters's hometown of Petersburg, the setting for his *Spoon River Anthology,* is a mere 2 miles from the town where Abraham Lincoln tended store, worked as a postmaster, studied law, learned surveying, and, in 1837, was elected to the legislature. A variety of buildings have been reconstructed next to the *Onstot Cooper Shop* (an original structure that has been restored) on a site presented to the state by William Randolph Hearst. There are craftspeople on hand in summer and for special events throughout the year. Information: *Lincoln's New Salem State Historic Site,* RR1, PO Box 244A, Petersburg, IL 62675 (phone: 217-632-4000).

HENRY FORD MUSEUM & GREENFIELD VILLAGE, Dearborn, Michigan The *Henry Ford Museum*'s phenomenal collection of American decorative arts, tools, household furnishings and appliances (washing machines, vacuum cleaners, and sewing machines, for instance), and implements of agriculture, communications, lighting, power, and, especially, transportation covers 12 acres—but that's only what you'll see in the museum. Set in *Greenfield Village,* on an adjacent 240 acres (81 acres are developed; the rest is pastureland) are, for starters, a courthouse where Abe Lincoln practiced law as a circuit rider; Thomas Edison's Menlo Park, New Jersey laboratory; homes or birthplaces of the Wright brothers, Luther Burbank, Noah Webster, Harvey Firestone, Henry Ford, and William Holmes McGuffey (of *McGuffey's Reader*); and nearly 80 other structures that tell the story of American life from the colonial period into the 20th century. The emphasis is on the changes that occurred in America with the new processes and inventions of the Industrial Revolution. Depending on the season, you can ride in a horse-drawn carriage or sleigh, an antique car, a steam train, or a steam-powered paddle wheel boat—or even take a spin on a 1913 carousel. Information: *Henry Ford Museum and Greenfield Village,* PO Box 1970, Dearborn, MI 48121-1970 (phone: 313-271-1620; 800-343-1929). Note: Best lodgings in the area are at the Georgian-style *Dearborn Inn* (phone: 313-271-2700).

LUMBERTOWN USA, Brainerd, Minnesota The town that calls itself Paul Bunyan's home also is the site of a re-created 1870 logging center with bunkhouse, mess hall, saloon, and nearly 30 other buildings. Closed mid-September through late May. Information: *Brainerd Lakes Area, Chamber of Commerce,* 124 N. Sixth St., Brainerd, MN 56401 (phone: 218-829-2838; 800-450-2838).

STUHR MUSEUM OF THE PRAIRIE PIONEER, Grand Island, Nebraska The cottage in which native son Henry Fonda was born is one of some 60 structures on 200 acres of indoor and outdoor displays (including an extensive seven-acre railyard exhibit) that give a vivid impression of what life was like for the ordinary pioneers here on the south-central Nebraska prairie. The village is closed mid-October through April, but two museums on the property are open year-round. Nearby are *Harold Warp Pioneer Village* (see below) and the *1864 Fort Kearny State Historical Park,* once an important stop on the *Oregon Trail.* Information: *Stuhr Museum,* 3133 W. Hwy. 34, Grand Island, NE 68801 (phone: 308-385-5316).

HAROLD WARP PIONEER VILLAGE, Minden, Nebraska This antiques collection, installed in a group of 26 buildings compactly arranged on a 20-acre site, shows "man's progress since 1830." That means, in part, that you'll see not one old kitchen setup but several (from 1830, 1860, 1890, 1910, 1930, 1950, and 1980) as well as living rooms and bedrooms—22 rooms in all. Stoves, refrigerators, 350 autos and trucks, farm machinery, tractors, bikes, boats, planes, fire engines, streetcars, steam engines, locomotives, and many other familiar objects get the same thorough treatment; there are 50,000 historic items at this 42-year-old institution. Information: *Harold Warp Pioneer Village,* PO Box 68, Minden, NE 68959 (phone: 308-832-1181; 800-445-4447).

WEST

BODIE STATE HISTORIC PARK, near Bridgeport, California Within 20 years of the discovery of gold in 1859, Bodie was, in the words of its pastor Reverend F. M. Warrington, "a sea of sin lashed by the tempests of passion." It had 30 mines, breweries, 65 saloons, ale stoops, pothouses, restaurants, gin mills, and opium dens; and, on Maiden Lane and Virgin Alley, plenty of ladies—Eleanor Dumont (alias Madame Mustache), Nellie Monroe, French Joe, and Rosa May. The 170 buildings that are still standing are maintained by the California State Park system in a state of "arrested decay"—that is, minor repairs are made and walls are shored up, but no attempt is made to make Bodie look any different than it did when it was abandoned. As you take the mapped-out walking tour, you'll spot old-fashioned condiments and canned goods on a general store shelf; caskets inside the morgue; a pipe organ in the Methodist church. It all can be enormously eerie. Open year-round, but call ahead for snow reports and road conditions. Information: *Bodie State Historic Park,* PO Box 515, Bridgeport, CA 93517 (phone: 619-647-6445).

COLUMBIA STATE HISTORIC PARK, Columbia, California The "gem of the southern mines" never quite died out like Bodie had, so restoration was relatively simple. Mapped-out walking tours take you past all the important structures. After your tour, pan for gold, ride a stagecoach, or sip sarsaparilla. Plenty of camping and hiking is available in the surrounding *Stanislaus National Forest,* and there are lively special events during *Easter,* the first weekend in May, the *Fourth of July* weekend, and the first two weekends of December. Open year-round, except for *Thanksgiving* and *Christmas Day.* Information: *Columbia State Historic Park,* PO Box 151, Columbia, CA 95310 (phone: 209-532-0150); *Tuolumne County Visitors Bureau,* PO Box 4020,

Sonora, CA 95370 (phone: 209-984-4636); *Tuolumne County Chamber of Commerce,* 222 S. Shepherd St., Sonora, CA 95370 (phone: 209-532-4212); and *Stanislaus National Forest,* 19777 Greenley Rd., Sonora, CA 95370 (phone: 209-532-3671). Note: Best lodgings are at the restored 1851 *Gunn House Motel,* in Sonora (phone: 209-532-3421) and at the restored 1857 *Fallon* hotel, in the park (phone: 209-532-1470), and its associate, the very Victorian *City* hotel (phone: 209-532-1479).

POLYNESIAN CULTURAL CENTER, Laie, Oahu, Hawaii Studying at the Mormon-operated *Brigham Young University* Hawaii campus, students from all over the South Pacific put themselves through school by working at this 42-acre reconstruction of traditional villages from Fiji, Hawaii, New Zealand's Maori culture, Samoa, Tahiti, the Marquesas, and Tonga. The crafts, singing, dancing, and food preparation are all things the students have grown up with, so it couldn't be more authentic. Information: *Polynesian Cultural Center,* 55-370 Kamehameha Hwy., Laie, HI 96762 (phone: 808-293-3333).

Utopias and Religious Settlements

Ever since the Pilgrims fled England for the New World, Americans have been leaving settled areas for wildernesses where they could set up their own civilizations, far from corrupting influences. Sometimes the new settlements survived. For instance, the Amana Colonies in Iowa—founded over a century ago—still thrive, even though the communal ownership of property was dissolved in the 1930s. In parts of Ohio, Pennsylvania, and Maryland, the Amish still live by the old ways.

A good many others were less successful, but often the physical settlements they built withstood the ravages of time, and a number of them have been restored as museum villages. Some are open year-round, some only in summer; it's wise to call before you go. Admission fees are under $15 for passes that will allow you to tour all the buildings, or a reasonable $1 or so for each restored structure. Some are free.

BISHOP HILL, near Galesburg, Illinois The first major Swedish settlement in the US, this community near the Mississippi River was not a big success. Erik Jansson, the dissident Swede who brought some 1,200 of his fellows here in 1846, was assassinated in 1850—and it was all downhill after that. In 1861, communal ownership of property was dissolved. Dissidents among the dissidents withdrew, and the remaining property was mismanaged. Drowning in debt, Bishop Hill crumbled. However, many of the descendants of the original settlers stayed on, so the buildings did not all decay. By the 1960s, when people got interested in the colony, 13 of the 16 original structures still stood, among them the *Colony* hotel, the blacksmith shop, the *Steeple Building* (topped by a one-handed clock), and the *Colony Church,* which could seat 1,000 worshipers. Early every *Christmas* morning, a traditional Julotta service is held by candlelight in the church sanctuary. The nearest motels are in Galesburg, where you can visit Carl Sandburg's birthplace, see the granite boulder under which his ashes were placed, and, on the campus of *Knox College,* tour the site of the Lincoln-Douglas debates. Information: *Bishop Hill State Historic Site,* PO Box 104, Bishop Hill, IL 61419 (phone: 309-927-3345).

NAUVOO, Nauvoo, Illinois Chicago was little more than a one-horse town when the followers of Mormon leader Joseph Smith arrived here and started building simple frame houses with wood from Wisconsin forests and brick they were soon manufacturing themselves. By 1844, the town was 20,000 strong, full of gardens, and topped by an immense white limestone temple. Schisms developed within the group, partly because of disagreement about polygamy. Joseph Smith ended up shot by a mob at the jail in Carthage, and Brigham Young, another Mormon, led the group westward. Over the years, while Salt Lake City was abuilding, the houses in Nauvoo were falling down. But the neat grid of streets remains, and scattered here and there are enough restored and reconstructed buildings to provide a pretty good idea of how it all was. Most are open for free tours and manned by Mormon missionaries. Jonathan Browning, maker of the famous rifles, was a Mormon; you'll tour his studio and home and see a device he invented that would churn butter and rock a baby in a cradle at the same time. Over 20 re-created shops have daily demonstrations of horseshoe making, candlemaking, and pottery. In 1849, a group of French Utopian thinkers called Icarians settled here, but most left after about 10 years. Following them came a very traditional group of Germans, as well as some Swiss and Irish, who, finding that the land would grow grapes, built 35 wine cellars. In 1937, these were discovered to be perfect for ripening blue cheese (Illinois' oldest winery, built in 1857, stands here). These businesses flourish in Nauvoo today, and if you eat at the *Nauvoo* hotel (open mid-March through mid-November; phone: 217-453-2211), you can sample their products. A good time to visit—plan for lodgings well in advance—is *Labor Day* weekend, when the annual *Grape Festival* takes place. Among the parades and other small-town doings, there's a ceremony called the *Wedding of the Wine and Cheese. City of Joseph,* a free outdoor musical, is presented the last week in July on a hillside overlooking the Mississippi. Information: *Nauvoo Chamber of Commerce,* PO Box 41, Nauvoo, IL 62354 (phone: 217-453-6648, from May 1 to October 31).

NEW HARMONY, Indiana This quiet little town in southwestern Indiana near the confluence of the Wabash and Ohio Rivers witnessed two experiments in Utopian living. The first was led by Harmonist (a believer in common property) George Rapp, who, with his 800-plus followers, turned the forests and swamplands they found here in 1814 into 30,000 acres of farms, factories, and homes in a mere 10 years. The later venture was led by Robert Owen, a Scottish intellectual who, with geologist William Maclure, drew distinguished scholars, writers, and educators to New Harmony. Their pioneering contributions to education, geology, trade schools, and women's suffrage had national impact. Tours of the sturdy Harmonist buildings and exhibits are offered daily from April through October and on a limited basis from November through March. All tours begin at the striking *Atheneum* visitors' center, designed by architect Richard Meier. Particularly fascinating are the *Workingmen's Institute,* founded in 1838 as a trade school and now filled with Indian artifacts, lacy antique underwear, and what we'll wager is the oddest lot of knickknacks you've ever seen; also, you can try to find your way through the re-created *Labyrinth,* a maze made out of hedges. The original, built by the Harmonists, was supposed to represent the difficult journey to perfection. The carefully designed *New Harmony Inn* (phone: 812-682-4491; see *America's Special Havens*)—modern, but Shaker-simple, a real symphony of polished woods—is alone worth the trip, and there's good food at the *Red Geranium* (phone: 812-682-4431) and the *Bayou Grill* (phone: 812-682-4491). Information: *Historic New Harmony,* PO Box 579, New Harmony, IN 47631 (phone: 812-682-4488).

AMANA COLONIES, Iowa The Community of True Inspiration, a Lutheran splinter group, founded this group of seven villages—now a National Historic Landmark—in 1855 as a communal society in which everybody shared all goods and all gains, and even ate together. Reorganized some three quarters of a century later in 1932, the Amana Colonies today have a good deal more community feeling than normally is found in other parts of the US. The story of life in the good old days is told at the *Barn Museum* in South Amana (a scale-model village) and at the *Museum of Amana History* in Amana, which houses exhibitions of potting, ice-cutting, bookbinding, woodworking, wine making, and soap making, along with a schoolhouse and an Amana doctor's washhouse and woodshed. There are various festivals throughout the year. Amana, West Amana, South Amana, Middle, High, and Homestead all have interesting little shops where you can buy local produce—fruit wines, woolens, furniture, baked goods, sausages, and other foods and crafts. And several have atmospheric restaurants that are great for German-American food served family style; *Bill Zuber's* is one (phone: 319-622-3911). Information: *Amana Colonies Convention & Visitors Bureau,* PO Box 303, Amana, IA 52203 (phone: 319-622-3828).

SHAKER VILLAGE OF PLEASANT HILL, near Harrodsburg, Kentucky The third largest of 19 Shaker communities stretching from Maine to Kentucky, Pleasant Hill flourished in the early 19th century. Members of this celibate, communal society were devoted to a life of simplicity and purity. The Shaker conviction that religion should not be separated from the secular concerns of human life meant that much effort and ingenuity were expended on the tiniest details; every object was considered a prayer, and engineered for perfection. The tools and furniture that resulted fetch high prices at auctions today; they're bound to impress you when you see them in this restoration's 30 original buildings. There are many crafts demonstrations and special events, as well as daily paddle wheel riverboat rides on the Kentucky River (except during winter). Dining, crafts, conference facilities, and 80 guestrooms are available in the original buildings. Closed *Christmas*. Information: *Shaker Village of Pleasant Hill,* 3501 Lexington Rd., Harrodsburg, KY 40330 (phone: 606-734-5411).

HANCOCK SHAKER VILLAGE, near Pittsfield, Massachusetts The best place in the East to see Shaker architecture. The standout is the three-story *Round Stone Barn,* designed for efficiency but beautiful enough to bring Le Corbusier and other great architects to mind. In all, 20 buildings on the property are filled with Shaker furniture and artifacts. The five-story *Brick Dwelling House* once held 100 men and women; and there's a laundry and machine shop, washhouse, and icehouse. Working crafts shops include basketry, cabinetmaking, oval box making, spinning, and weaving, as well as cooking in an 1830s kitchen. A working farm has livestock, vegetable and herb gardens cultivated as they would have been in the 19th century, and daily talks about Shaker agriculture. Almost every Saturday from July through October, there are candlelight dinners and tours led by "interpreters" in period costumes. Country inns are plentiful nearby. Open from April through November, closed *Thanksgiving*; the rest of the year, tours are by appointment only. Information: *Hancock Shaker Village,* PO Box 927, Pittsfield, MA 01202-0927 (phone: 413-443-0188).

CANTERBURY SHAKER VILLAGE, Canterbury, New Hampshire A community of 300 Shakers once lived in the 24 white frame structures here. Meeting House Lane is lined with enormous sugar maples planted for the orphans taken in by the Shakers. The historic buildings sit on 694 acres surrounded by fields, forests, and ponds. Guided tours of the village lead through the *Ministry, Sisters' Shop,* laundry, infirmary, schoolhouse, and meetinghouse (with separate entrances for men and women). Self-guided nature trails lead to mill sites and ponds. Craft making in the Shaker tradition is demonstrated. Closed January through March, and on weekdays in April, November, and December. Candlelight dinners and tours of the village are offered Fridays and Saturdays by reservation. Authentic Shaker food is served at the *Creamery* restaurant. Information: *Canterbury Shaker Village,* 288 Shaker Rd., Canterbury, NH 03224 (phone: 603-783-9511).

OLD SALEM, Winston-Salem, North Carolina Founded in 1766 by a group of Moravians from Pennsylvania, Salem's church directed not just spiritual life but also secular doings—and business prospered. At the restoration, there are demonstrations of domestic skills practiced in early Salem, decorative arts and household items, plus crafts shops and the immense *Single Brothers House,* where 14-year-old boys came to live while they learned a craft. Special events are planned throughout the year. Information: *Director of Information, Old Salem, Inc.,* Drawer F, Salem Station, Winston-Salem, NC 27108 (phone: 910-721-7300).

SCHOENBRUNN VILLAGE STATE MEMORIAL, near New Philadelphia, Ohio Concerned about spreading the Gospel to the Indians, the Moravian church sent missionaries into the wilderness, and this was the first of six separate settlements that were established in this area. David Zeisberger and his force of Christian Indians, converts, and missionaries cleared the wilderness and within a couple of years had put up some 60 log structures. But by that time, England and the colonies were at war, and Schoenbrunn was caught between the firing lines. The missionaries and their congregations departed, leaving the settlement to crumble. What you see now—a church, a school, and a baker's dozen other structures—is a re-created area built by the *Ohio Historical Society* since the 1920s. On occasional special weekends, craftspeople are on hand to demonstrate woodworking or candle-dipping. *Trumpet in the Land,* an outdoor drama presented mid-June through August in an amphitheater nearby, tells the story (see *Outdoor Dramas*). Information: *Schoenbrunn Village State Memorial,* PO Box 129, New Philadelphia, OH 44663 (phone: 216-339-3636).

ZOAR VILLAGE STATE MEMORIAL, Zoar, Ohio This was founded by another group of German Separatists who, like New Harmony's George Rapp, refused to accept the Lutheran doctrine and found themselves alternately ignored and persecuted until it seemed easier to leave the Old World than to stay. Following Rapp's example, they crossed the ocean and bought a tract of land on the Tuscarawas River. The system of communal ownership under which the community eventually flourished in Zoar was not inspired by the Bible so much as by the very lean times of the settlement's first years. Today, the red brick houses with their tile roofs and bright trim are spic and span; the bakery, tin shop, and garden house look as if they still were open for business; and the fantastic community garden, with a neat geometric design, seems to have been laid out by some Prussian drill sergeant. A good time to see it all is during the *Zoar Harvest Festival,* held on the first weekend in August, with antiques, crafts, and music shows. *Zoar Village State Memorial* is closed from November through March. There are small shops and several bed and breakfast establishments in private historic houses open all year. Information: *Zoar Village State Memorial,* PO Box 404, Zoar, OH 44697 (phone: 216-874-3211). Note: The *Atwood Lake* resort hotel near *Atwood Lake Park,* open year-round, is modern, comfortable, beautifully situated, and quite reasonable (phone: 216-735-2211; 800-362-6406 for reservations).

OLD ECONOMY VILLAGE, Ambridge, Pennsylvania When Father George Rapp left New Harmony, Indiana, in 1824, he came here—and proceeded to create something even grander than the settlement he had left. There was, first of all, his own home, which was as imposing as the domicile of the society's leader should be. Then there was the *Feast Hall,* a single room that could seat 500 diners. Both structures, plus the wine cellar, shoe shop, cabinetmakers' shop, store, community kitchen, and two dwellings, as well as the gardens (all plant species here were grown by the Harmonists) have been restored and are open year-round. Why did this enormously successful settlement finally die out? The policy of celibacy eventually rang the death knell, and the society was dissolved in 1905. Information: *Old Economy Village,* 14th and Church Sts., Ambridge, PA 15003 (phone: 412-266-4500).

EPHRATA CLOISTER, Ephrata, Pennsylvania This religious experiment in the heart of Pennsylvania Dutch country, begun in 1732 by a German Seventh-Day Baptist named Conrad Beissel, lasted until 1813—despite celibacy and the rigorous lifestyle: Members slept on beds that were more like narrow benches, laid their heads on wooden pillows, walked down straight and narrow hallways and through doorways so low they had to stoop. There may have been plenty of symbolism behind all of it—and that, among other things, is what you learn about when you tour the handsome buildings. Open year-round. Information: *Ephrata Cloister,* 632 W. Main St., Ephrata, PA 17522 (phone: 717-733-6600).

Space Centers: The Future Now

The *Saturn V* rocket on display at the *US Space and Rocket Center* in Huntsville, Alabama—one of three such space centers in the US—is longer than a football field and as wide as a two-lane highway; the sheer size of it is adequate testimony to the scope of the space program. There are plenty of reasons to visit. At each center you will be given facts and figures that may give you pause the next time you start to agree with someone who calls the space exploration program a waste of money. You'll be offered the opportunity to take over the controls of a rocket, and in a dozen other ways retrace the small steps that were such giant leaps for mankind. Outside there are "rocket parks"—greenswards where mammoth spacecraft grow like so many monster asparagus stalks. In addition to *Space Center Houston* (described in detail in *Houston,* THE CITIES,) there are two other centers where you can boldly go where many of your fellow men have gone before.

US SPACE AND ROCKET CENTER, Huntsville, Alabama The feature attractions at *Earth's Largest Space Museum* tell you what's happening on the space scene—and look into the future as well. The current emphasis is on the space shuttle and the space station, scheduled for orbit during this decade. Visitors can see *NASA*'s full-scale mock-up of the space shuttle orbiter: the 122-foot *Pathfinder* used for clearance and engineering tests at the nearby *Marshall Space Flight Center,* where *NASA* develops rockets for the space program. The full-size replica of *NASA*'s Hubble Space Telescope is now on permanent display in the main hall. The audience in the *Spacedome Theater* will grab their seats as they soar over mountains and hug sharp curves during presentations of the Omnimax film *Speed.* An action-packed adventure awaits visitors via a simulated journey to Jupiter. Because the

Saturn V rocket that launched Neil Armstrong to the moon was made in Huntsville, *Apollo* spacecraft, space suits, and astronaut training gear are popular museum displays. The original moon rocket—which has been designated a National Historic Landmark—dominates the 10-acre park of *NASA* rockets and army missiles. Bus tours that depart from the museum enter the space station development center and various astronaut training facilities. From March to *Christmas,* the center holds the US Space Camp for children from fourth grade through high school, as well as for adults, with weekly astronaut training activities and simulated space shuttle missions; activities can be viewed in the *US Space Camp Training Center.* Information: *US Space and Rocket Center,* PO Box 070015, Huntsville, AL 35807 (phone: 205-837-3400; 800-63-SPACE for recorded information).

SPACEPORT USA, Kennedy Space Center, Florida The *Kennedy Space Center* is on Merritt Island and is the home of all space shuttle launchings; *Cape Canaveral,* across the Banana River, is the site for launchings of *Department of Defense* flights and *NASA* unmanned launchings. Tour the facility by bus (Red Tour) or the *Cape Canaveral Air Force Station* (Blue Tour). *Spaceport USA,* where you meet the tours, offers abundant attractions, including a lunar roving vehicle, a replica of an *Apollo Lunar Module,* and a baker's dozen theaters, mini-theaters, and tape programs that describe flights past and future. A popular facility is the *IMAX Theater,* where viewers can watch *The Dream Is Alive*, *Blue Planet,* and *Destiny in Space* on a screen five stories high and 70 feet wide; six-track stereo delivers the audio sensation of actual takeoff. Another featured attraction is *Satellites and You,* a 55-minute walk-through of a simulated space station of the future. The *Astronauts Memorial,* a collection of exhibits dedicated to astronauts who have died in the course of their duties, is the latest installation. Cocoa Beach, where most motels are just a shell's throw from the Atlantic, is the place to lodge. Information: *Spaceport USA,* Visitor Center, TW Recreational Services, Kennedy Space Center, FL 32899 (phone: 407-452-2121).

TO SEE A LIFT-OFF

"Your entire body shakes, your bones and organs shake, the earth shakes." That is an eyewitness description of watching a launch: They're definitely worth seeing. A good place to view a shuttle launch is from the beach in Cocoa Beach, between *Cape Canaveral* and *Patrick Air Force Base.* (For launch information, call 407-867-4636.) It's hard to plan a vacation around a launching, since variable weather conditions make a strict schedule impossible. There is a special viewing area, 3 miles from the launching pads, for which you can make reservations through the *Kennedy Space Center* (phone: 407-452-2121).

For the Body

Downhill Skiing

You don't have to be particularly athletic, or even particularly rich, to ski. All sorts of people have flocked to some 1,200 ski areas around the country to practice their art. For no other reason than the sheer number of runs, knowing just where to go can be a problem.

If you're going for only a day or a weekend, the primary consideration will be to find a nearby resort that meets your budget and doesn't have long lift lines. For a list of those near you, write to the state travel directors or consult magazines like *Ski* and *Skiing; Skiing*'s "Travel Advisory" monthly is full of information on lift rates, kids' programs, how to avoid lift lines, and more. If you have a week to spend, the problem of choosing an area becomes more difficult. California, Colorado, Idaho, Montana, New Hampshire, New Mexico, Utah, Vermont, and Wyoming all have resorts with diverse terrain and abundant nightlife, restaurants, and other amenities. The *White Book of Ski Areas: U.S. & Canada* (Inter-Ski Services, PO Box 9595 Friendship Station, Washington, DC 20016; phone: 202-342-0886) lists all the ski areas in the US and Canada, with detailed information. It's revised annually and can be found in ski shops and bookstores ($16.95) or obtained by mail from the publisher ($21.95).

The first decision involves choosing the particular part of the country—East, Midwest, Rockies, or the Far West. California and the Pacific Northwest generally get hundreds of inches' accumulation every year, but because of the high moisture content of the clouds that bring it from the sea, the snow is often heavy and slushy. The East has the best snowmaking in the world, so even when Mother Nature doesn't cooperate, there is always some snow. It also has some of the coldest skiing around, so slopes tend to get icy.

Mountains are smallest in the Midwest, where vertical drops (the height from the highest lift-served point to the base of the ski area) may amount to only a few hundred feet, but Midwestern resorts are just the place if you are learning. Also good for newer skiers—especially southeastern residents with limited time to spare—are the somewhat greater vertical drops (up to 1,600 feet) of the resorts scattered from West Virginia all the way down to Alabama.

The mountains are highest in the West; the vertical drops are steeper and the runs somewhat longer. In the West, too, you will find wide-open bowls. In the East, trails have been cut narrow to keep snow from blowing off and to provide shelter from the wind. As a result, skiing that is already difficult because of the snow conditions can be even more demanding—

but often more fun and challenging—because the skier often must ski the fall line.

Eastern mountains range in size between the hills of the Midwest and the Western giants. As a rule, if you're just learning to ski, you won't need access to difficult terrain; what matters will be whether the resort has good beginner ski programs and schools and whether the beginners' area has well-groomed terrain that is varied enough to keep you interested. In fact, small ski areas are a good place to start. The friendly atmosphere and less-hectic slopes make for a pleasant experience.

Where you go also will depend on what sort of lodging you like. Not all resorts have condominiums. Not all have inexpensive ski dorms or, for that matter, those friendly, rustic old inns where everybody eats in the lodge every night. Most resort towns have modern motels and ski lodges with private baths, saunas, pools, and the like. In New England, in addition, you'll find old country inns—long on charm but not as convenient as some people like. Some resorts are better for families. Many resorts make a special effort for families and often offer all kinds of amenities. Consider these factors: complimentary children's lodging, ski lifts tickets, and, in most cases, day-care centers.

Many ski areas are beginning to cater to the exceptionally expert skier as well. All across the country, resorts are adding acreage of advanced and extreme terrain to meet what they hope is an untapped demand for more difficult runs.

The trend in recent years has been toward developing snowboard terrain for the increasing numbers of snowboarders. All across the country, ski areas are building snowboard parks and snowboard-only slopes for these "new" athletes.

The resorts listed below include a few of the major destinations in the country. At all of them, you'll find an abundance of lifts, with rates from $30 to $45 a day (considerably less when you purchase a full week's pass), lodging places in all price ranges, a variety of packages, and seasons that run generally from mid-November into April. Note that most resorts are extremely crowded at *Christmastime,* over *Presidents' Day* weekend, and in March during college spring break. Always reserve well in advance.

EAST

SUNDAY RIVER, Bethel, Maine The emphasis at this western Maine resort is skiing, skiing, and more skiing. It is constantly upgrading and adding sections to keep things new and fresh. The resort claims that its White Heat is the longest, steepest, and widest lift-served mogul run. The 102 trails make this area's network second in size only to *Killington* (see below) among Eastern ski resorts. Its 200-bed ski dorm isn't elegant, but it is practical—and a bargain. Other accommodations include slopeside condos, the 67-room *Snow Cap Inn* (phone: 207-824-7669), and the 230-room *Summit Hotel* (phone:

207-824-7605). For more atmosphere, restaurants, and nightlife, skiers have to travel to the town of Bethel, 6 miles away. *Holidae House* (phone: 207-824-3400), a small, charming Victorian inn decorated with antiques, and the more traditional *Bethel Inn & Country Club* (phone: 207-824-2175) are lodging options here. Information: *Sunday River Ski Resort,* PO Box 450, Bethel, ME 04217 (phone: 207-824-3000; 800-543-2SKI).

SUGARLOAF USA, Carrabassett Valley, Maine With a 2,816-foot vertical drop, plus 101 trails and slopes and above-timberline lift service, this is the third-largest ski mountain in the East. There are 430 acres of skiable terrain, almost evenly divided among novice, intermediate, and expert trails—this area has the lowest skier-acre ratio in New England. There are two high-capacity quad chair lifts, increased snowmaking, covering 90% of its trails, and a half-pipe for snowboarding. The gondola now runs from mid-station to the summit, making it the only lift service to snowfields in the US. More emphasis has also been placed on recreational racing. Best skiing is from *Christmas* to April. The *Sugarloaf Inn* has a definite Down East feel, and you can stay right on the mountain in any of more than 700 condos or comfortable lodges. *Riverbend Express* (phone: 207-628-2877) offers van shuttle service between Portland jetport and *Sugarloaf.* Information: *Sugarloaf USA,* PO Box 5000, Carrabassett Valley, ME 04947-9799 (phone: 207-237-2000; 800-THE-LOAF for reservations; 800-THE-AREA for the *Sugarloaf Chamber of Commerce* reservation service).

ATTITASH, Bartlett, New Hampshire The *US Ski Team* uses *Attitash* as one of its official training sites and with good reason. The area concentrates heavily on its snowmaking, covering 98% of the mountain. It even uses a computer-controlled system that measures dew point, wind direction, and temperature—all of which help to improve the quality of manmade snow. The 28 trails are mainly intermediate and novice. Its *Smart Ticket* value concept allows skiers to pay per ride. There's a secluded beginner area with its own lift and special ski school programs, including women's clinics and senior groups. The full-service day-care center also offers lessons and the Adventure Kids school. For lodging, there are 250 condos slopeside or nearby (phone: 800-223-SNOW). The *Bernerhof* (phone: 603-383-4414) down the road has a cozy inn atmosphere with elegant sit-down dining and luxury suites—some with saunas and Jacuzzis. If you want to get away from it all, try *Wentworth*'s (phone: 603-383-9700), a 125-year-old resort run by a Swiss hotelier in the nearby town of Jackson. It has a modern yet quaint decor and a continental restaurant. Information: *Attitash,* PO Box 308, Bartlett, NH 03812 (phone: 603-374-1960; fax: 603-374-1960).

WATERVILLE VALLEY, Waterville Valley, New Hampshire Known for its snowmaking and its carefully groomed slopes with 48 trails, this resort also boasts varied terrain on a maximum 2,020-foot vertical; a self-contained "village" full of country inns and lodges; daytime shuttle bus service; reciprocal lift privileges with eight other New Hampshire ski areas midweek; and a friendly ski week program for adults as well as children. The village has a five-building retail and commercial center, with 37 shops and seven restaurants, plus offices and condominiums. The resort also has the *High Country Express*—a high-speed detachable quad lift—which carries 3,000 skiers an hour over a distance of 7,000 feet. And there's the *Golden Eagle Lodge* (phone: 603-236-4551; 800-468-2553 for reservations), a 139-suite property designed to resemble New Hampshire's grand old resort hotels, and a children's ski center, which offers various programs for youngsters age three and up, as well as nursery care for ages six weeks and up. Information: *Waterville Valley Ski Areas,* Waterville Valley, NH 03215 (phone: 800-468-2553 for reservations and for snow information).

KILLINGTON, Killington, Vermont The home of the longest ski lift in North America and the longest trail in the US, this trail-veined basin offers a huge variety of terrain. There are long wide runs, steep and narrow ones (107 in all), six interconnected peaks, six base lodge facilities, one of the best novice slopes in the East, and Vermont's longest vertical drop (3,175 feet). The Bear Mountain area, where the *US Alpine Ski Team* trained for the *1980 Olympics,* offers New England's steepest skiing terrain. *Killington* also has fantastic snow conditions (which mean skiing from October through late May), and the standout snowmaking operation, now the world's most extensive, has been expanded so that 75% of the skiable terrain now is covered, 43 miles in all. *Killington* also has some of the East's best learn-to-ski weeks, a children's center, and good packages. The *Inn of the Six Mountains* (phone: 802-422-4302; 800-228-4676 outside Vermont) has 103 rooms. Shuttle bus service to the slopes is available. Information: *Killington Ski and Summer Resort,* Killington, VT 05751 (phone: 802-422-3333; 800-372-2007 or 800-621-6867 for travel and lodging information).

OKEMO MOUNTAIN, Ludlow, Vermont In just 10 years, *Okemo* has become one of Vermont's top ski resorts. Its accessible location in south central Vermont and its family friendly environment bring skiers back here year after year. There's free skiing for children six and under and two free beginner lifts. A new ticket for teens saves them $7—enough for lunch. Most of the 83 trails are geared to beginners and intermediates. *Okemo* also has one of the highest vertical drops in southern Vermont at 2,150 feet; but even beginners can enjoy the long runs on the scenic 4½-mile beginner trail from the top. Snowmaking facilities fill in where Mother Nature lets off, covering 95% of the terrain. The mountain recently added a snowboard park with a half-pipe and other terrain challenges—rails, slides, spines, and so on. The resort also has an exchange ticket program with *Stratton.* Located in the quaint New England town of Ludlow, *Okemo* offers a good selection of restaurants and shops, as well as a variety of lodging choices (including inns, bed and breakfast establishments, and condos). A couple of noteworthy lodges in nearby Proctorsville include the *Okemo Lantern Lodge* (phone: 802-226-7770), a classic Victorian home with individually decorated rooms and fireside dining, and the *Castle Inn* (phone: 802-226-7222), an enchanting English mansion overlooking the Okemo valley that has intimate candlelit dinners and a hot tub/sauna. Information: *Okemo Ski Resort,* RFD 1, Ludlow, VT 05149 (phone: 802-228-4041; 800-78-OKEMO; fax: 802-228-4558).

STOWE, Stowe, Vermont When one journalist poked fun at *Stowe*'s lift lines and its variable snow conditions, letters of indignation poured in. This is the East's premier ski resort, and its regulars don't take that position lightly. Nowadays, they have even more to puff up about. A massive snowmaking installation covering 72% of the resort's terrain, 10 lifts, a four-passenger high-speed quad, an eight-passenger gondola (the fastest in the world), and 45 trails have resolved situations that most skiers were willing to tolerate only because the skiing on the 2,360-foot vertical was so good. A well-coordinated children's ski school–day-care setup has terrific appeal; the famous tough runs share the limelight with the 75% of the slopes and trails rated for novices and intermediates; and the largest cross-country skiing network in the East also is here. The restaurants, nightlife, and accommodations are as varied and lively as ever. *Stowe* is close to an airport and interstate highways and is served by *Amtrak.* Information: *Stowe Area Association,* Main St., Stowe, VT 05672 (phone: 802-253-7321; 800-24-STOWE outside Vermont); *Stowe Mountain Resort,* Stowe, VT 05672 (phone: 802-253-7311; 800-253-4SKI for lodging and reservations).

STRATTON, Stratton, Vermont With its 2,003-foot vertical drop, *Stratton*'s mountain, in the Green Mountains of southern Vermont, is the tallest in the region. It is a smooth classic cone divided into two separate areas, each with steep sections that are wide, interestingly contoured, and unfailingly well groomed. Its improved snowmaking system, 92 trails, and 14 lifts offer something for skiers at every level. There are four lodges within walking distance of the base and a number of condominiums in the area. Snowboarding is allowed, and this was the site of the sport's *1992 US Open Championships.* The *Stratton Mountain Village* features a hotel, luxury villas and townhouses, conference facilities, covered parking, 30 shops and restaurants along a pedestrian mall, and two additional restaurants. The *Starship XII* is a futuristic, French-designed gondola. The first of its kind in the US, it has 64 snug units, each of which can hold 12 passengers, that zip from base to summit in eight minutes, transporting 2,400 passengers per hour—sightseers as well as skiers. The Sun Bowl area has its own lodge with such facilities as a ski shop, rentals, and a cafeteria. Other fine lodgings include the *Stratton Mountain and Village Lodge* (phone: 802-297-2500) and *Birkenhaus* (phone: 802-297-2000), a nearby Austrian-style inn. Information: *Stratton Corporation,* Stratton Mountain, VT 05155 (phone: 802-297-2200; 800-787-2886 for lodging information, reservations, and group sales).

SUGARBUSH RESORT, Warren, Vermont One resort with two lift-laced mountains, it offers some of the best expert terrain in the East. It also boasts some of the nicest scenery, as many of the 75 intermediate and novice runs wind through the glades of the *Green Mountain National Forest. Sugarbush South* includes the original 3,975-foot-high mountain of *Sugarbush Resort.* Its sister mountain, *Sugarbush North,* formally known as Mount Ellen, adds a 2,600-foot vertical and 139 acres of skiable terrain. Free shuttle buses transport skiers between the two mountains—which are separated by 4 miles of road—as well as to and from the *Sugarbush Inn* (phone: 802-583-2301) and nearby condominiums. On weekends and holidays there's free transportation to quaint Waitsfield and its popular eating and drinking establishments. There's also cross-country skiing, snowboarding, children's programs, day-care, sleigh rides, and ice skating. Information: *Sugarbush Resort,* RR1, PO Box 350, Warren, VT 05674 (phone: 802-583-2381; 800-53-SUGAR).

MOUNT SNOW, near West Dover, Vermont Mt. Snow is a big, 3,600-foot mountain with 1,700 vertical feet of skiing. A network of 127 trails is spread over five separate areas. There are 24 lifts, including a high-speed quad chair. Snowmaking covers 84% of all skiable terrain, ensuring reliable skiing from early November through early April. With the recent addition of Haystack Mountain (accessible via a complimentary shuttle), *Mount Snow* boasts the most trails and lifts of any Eastern resort. Especially popular are its theme weeks. EXCL (Express Customized Learning) is an accelerated program for intermediate and advanced skiers. The area includes a ski school, ski rentals, and child care. Cross-country skiing, snowmobiling, and sleigh rides are nearby. Dozens of restaurants and nightspots provide plenty of après-ski entertainment. *Mount Snow*'s location in southern Vermont makes it the closest major ski resort to eastern metropolitan centers. One of the classiest country inns is the *Inn at Sawmill Farm* (phone: 802-464-8131), located about 3 miles south. Information: *Mount Snow Resort,* Mount Snow, VT 05356 (phone: 800-245-SNOW; 802-464-2151 for a ski report).

WEST

LAKE TAHOE, near Lake Tahoe, California Within an hour's drive of incredibly deep-blue Lake Tahoe are 16 ski resorts, together offering the greatest concentration of skiing available in America. The five largest are *Heavenly, Alpine Meadows, Kirkwood, Northstar-at-Tahoe,* and *Squaw Valley.* Alone, each of the five resorts offers magnificent, varied terrain; the combination is simply mind-boggling. *Heavenly* (phone: 800-2-HEAVEN), straddling the California-Nevada state line, is America's largest ski resort, covering 20 square miles. The intermediates' haven is on the Nevada side, the beginner/intermediate terrain mainly in California, with plenty of expert terrain on each. A high-speed gondola in the heart of the South Shore is being planned. This is also the resort closest to big-time gambling and low-cost, high-quality lodging in South Lake Tahoe. *Alpine Meadows* (phone: 916-583-4232; 800-441-4423 for ski school reservations) offers over 2,000 skiable acres, with a smooth lift layout, a respectable 1,800-foot vertical rise, 125 acres covered by snowmaking machines, and the longest ski season at Tahoe—through *Memorial Day.* The upper mountain is full of steep bowls and narrow chutes, but there's usually enough space for traversing; the lower slopes are wide, gentle, beautifully groomed. *Kirkwood* (phone: 209-258-6000; 800-967-7500; 209-258-3000 for snow conditions), with a 2,000-foot vertical, has become one of Tahoe's fastest-growing ski resorts with 150 condos in seven separate complexes. It also has a Nordic operation with 45 miles of groomed track. Olympic and Sentinel bowls and the snow-filled saddles of the ridges have established *Kirkwood*'s reputation as a place for experts and intermediates. *Northstar-at-Tahoe* (phone: 916-562-1010; 800-466-6784 for reservations), with a 2,200-foot vertical, is a self-contained resort community with ski-in/ski-out condominiums, excellent beginner and intermediate terrain, and a full-service cross-country and telemark center. Information: *Tahoe North Visitors & Convention Bureau,* PO Box 5578, Tahoe City, CA 96145 (phone: 916-583-3494; 800-824-6348 for lodging information and reservations; fax: 916-581-4081); *Lake Tahoe Visitors Authority* (for South Shore), 1156 Ski Run Blvd., S. Lake Tahoe, CA 96150 (phone: 916-544-5050; 800-ATTAHOE for lodging only; 916-541-8900 for ski report); for rental of houses, cabins, and condominiums, contact *Lake Tahoe Accommodations,* 2048 Dunlap Dr., Suite No. 4, S. Lake Tahoe, CA 96150 (phone: 800-544-3234).

MAMMOTH MOUNTAIN, Mammoth Lakes, California Mammoth it is. This 11,053-foot blown-out volcano is skiable from late October until early June. The 3,500 acres of terrain is 30% beginner, 40% intermediate, and 30% expert. There are rugged runs designed to chill experts on 3,100 feet of vertical slopes, served by 30 lifts, and 150 trails. Facilities include three day lodges, two ski shops, two rental shops, a ski school, and a race department as well as two restaurants and cafeterias and on-hill snack bars. The complex also has three indoor spas, day-care facilities, a free shuttle, and 213 lodging rooms. The town of Mammoth Lakes at the base has 34 miles of cross-country ski trails, horse-drawn sleighs, hot-air balloon rides, snowmobiling, dogsled rides, and ice skating, in addition to shopping, dining, and lodging. The *Mammoth Lakes Visitors Bureau* (PO Box 48, Mammoth Lakes, CA 93546; phone: 619-934-2712; 800-367-6572) will send brochures and information on ski packages. Information: *Mammoth Mountain,* PO Box 24, Mammoth Lakes, CA 93546 (phone: 619-934-2571).

SQUAW VALLEY, Olympic Valley, California Experts, intermediates, and novices enjoy 4,000 acres of wide-open bowl skiing, with 33 lifts, including a 150-passenger aerial cable car and a six-passenger gondola. The *Opera House* is a complex at the base of the mountain housing a 250-seat movie theater, a general store, conference rooms, and the *Back Stage Bistro.* At the top of the mountain is the *High Camp Bath & Tennis Camp,* with year-round ice skating, as well as six tennis courts, a pool and spa, three restaurants, seven sun decks, and even a bungee-jumping tower. Senior citizens and children under 13 receive significant discounts on lift tickets. Information: *Squaw Valley Ski Corp.,* PO Box 2007, Olympic Valley, CA 96146 (phone: 916-583-6985; 800-545-4350 for reservations; 916-583-6955, 24-hour snow phone).

ASPEN, Aspen, Colorado The "Aspens" are a community of four ski mountains, one town, and one village. The biggest action town in ski-dom, an old mining center, and the granddaddy of American ski resorts, *Aspen* has a little something for almost everyone. There are no beginner trails at Aspen Mountain, with its 3,267-foot vertical rise; it's known worldwide for its deep powder, its steep runs, and celebrated trail toughies like Silver Queen. Aspen Highlands, with its 3,800-foot vertical, has runs of up to 3½ miles. Its terrain is well balanced, with half intermediate and the other half divided equally between beginner and expert. Tiehack/Buttermilk Mountain, with its 2,030-foot vertical, is a beginners' and intermediates' paradise, not only for the quality of the snow, but also for its wide, gentle trails. Nearby is the skiers' nirvana called *Snowmass* (see below). And there's nightlife and good eating in a quantity and variety that you'll find at few other ski resorts in the world, as well as excellent family packages. *Little Nell* (phone: 970-920-4600) is a 92-room hotel at the foot of the *Silver Queen Gondola,* right at the base of Aspen Mountain. Decorated in the style of a European ski chalet, it offers all manner of luxury amenities. Another elegant choice is the *Ritz-Carlton, Aspen* (phone: 970-920-3300; 800-241-3333; see *America's Best Resort Hotel*). The *Aspen Bed and Breakfast* (phone: 800-36-ASPEN) offers modern rooms and facilities for the budget-conscious. The *10th Mountain Trail,* which connects *Aspen* and *Vail,* has created a rugged back-country track reminiscent of Switzerland's famed *Haute Route. Paragon Guides* (PO Box 130, Vail, CO 81658; phone: 970-926-5299; fax: 970-926-5298) runs three- to eight-day trips along this route for skiers of all abilities (except rank novices). The company rents equipment, and the package includes fine meals, lodging, and instruction. Information: *Aspen Skiing Company,* PO Box 1248, Aspen, CO 81612 (phone: 970-925-1220; 800-525-6200 for reservations).

BRECKENRIDGE, Breckenridge, Colorado Some 85 miles (90 minutes) west of Denver and associated with *Copper Mountain* and *Keystone* (see below) through a lift ticket exchange program, *Breckenridge,* one of Colorado's first great skiing finds, does a brisk business among skiing families—and everybody else lucky enough to have discovered it. There are three mountains; three base areas; a 3,398-foot vertical rise; 1,600 skiable acres comprising over 70 miles of trails (which even on the busiest days can seem empty); 430 acres of snowmaking; and a half-pipe for snowboarding. Snowmobiling, ice skating, dogsledding, a Nordic center, and other winter activities are nearby. *Breckenridge* resort is part of a 135-year-old town with its own history and character. The town boasts 350 Victorian structures in the *National Register of Historic Places,* as well as many newer homes designed to harmonize with their older neighbors—perfect for a walking tour. There are a variety of available lodgings, including bed and breakfast establishments, and an active nightlife. In town, free public transportation is plentiful, but a car is better for real mobility. Information: *Breckenridge Ski Resort,* PO Box 1058, Breckenridge, CO 80424 (phone: 970-453-5000; 800-789-7669 for reservations and lodging information).

COPPER MOUNTAIN, Copper Mountain, Colorado About 75 miles west of Denver, the mountain soars above a compact condominium village, including the only cold-weather *Club Med* (phone: 303-968-2161) in North America. Three base lift areas, within walking distance of accommodations, lead to beginner, intermediate, and advanced terrain. The vertical rise is 2,760 feet; and there are two high-speed quad chair lifts. There is a total of 96 trails and 1,330 acres as well as a 300-foot half-pipe for snowboarding and racing competitions. *Copper Mountain* offers a $3-million racquet and athletic club and extensive cross-country activities. Together with *Breckenridge* and *Keystone,* this resort is part of the "Ski the Summit" (Summit County) exchange program. Information: *Copper Mountain Resort,* PO Box 3001, Copper Mountain, CO 80443 (phone: 970-968-2882; 800-I-LUV-FUN).

KEYSTONE AND ARAPAHOE BASIN, Keystone, Colorado Only 68 miles from Denver, *Keystone* offers five unique skiing experiences: Keystone Mountain, North Peak, Arapahoe Basin, the Outback, and *Keystone Night Ski.* Even the easy slopes, like the 3-mile "Schoolmarm," are interesting, and the difficult slopes, while tough, are not impossible. The snowmaking system, which can cover 100% of Keystone Mountain and 50% of North Peak, is the Rockies' most extensive. Top-to-bottom night skiing is available on 40% of the mountain, reached via gondola. Arapahoe Basin, the longtime favorite of Denver daytrippers, is the highest lift-served area in North America. It offers a long skiing season (into June). Its vertical is 1,640 feet; Keystone's is 2,340. *Keystone*'s third mountain, North Peak, has 200 acres of advanced intermediate and expert terrain, and the Outback has 256 acres of advanced and higher intermediate terrain—in keeping with the current trend of catering to the expert skier. The resort's skiable acreage has been increased to 2,200. Keystone and North Peak can be reached by six-passenger gondola. All three areas participate in the "Ski the Summit" lift exchange program with *Copper Mountain* and *Breckenridge.* Shuttle buses are available, but a car is helpful. The *Olympic* medal–winning Mahre twins, Phil and Steve, run the training center here. The five-day programs are held for recreational racers or for skiers who just want to improve their skills. Information: *Keystone Resort Reservations,* PO Box 38, Keystone, CO 80435 (phone: 970-468-2316; 800-222-0188).

CRESTED BUTTE MOUNTAIN, Mt. Crested Butte, Colorado Lots of skiing, no crowds, and friendly people are the reasons this has become one of Colorado's most popular mid-size resorts. It offers over 1,150 acres of skiing with 13 lifts and 85 trails, including "Extreme Limits," 550 acres of ungroomed black-diamond-level, experts-only slopes. The surrounding mountains offer a vast system of ski touring trails and groomed tracks for both traditional cross-country skiing and "ski skating," which is similar to speed skating. The mining town of Crested Butte is a National Historic District with beautiful Victorian buildings. Lodging choices include condominiums and the luxurious 261-room *Grande Butte* hotel (phone: 303-349-7561), just 20 yards from the base lifts. Information: *Crested Butte Mountain Resort,* PO Box A, Mt. Crested Butte, CO 81225 (phone: 970-349-2333; 800-544-8448 for reservations).

SNOWMASS, Snowmass Village, Colorado *Snowmass* is the ideal ski resort for an intimate getaway or a family vacation. It has one of North America's largest mountains, offering immense diversity for every level of skier, and 95% of the accommodations are located slopeside. There are three high-speed SuperChairs on the Big Burn; kids' half-price lift tickets; Snow Cubs, a play program for toddlers up to four years; and a children's ski school called the Big Burn Bears. In addition, three other ski mountains—Aspen, Aspen Highlands, and Piehack/Buttermilk—are within a 12-mile radius and are linked by an interchangeable multi-day lift ticket as well as free shuttle bus service. Everything is easy at *Snowmass,* with slopeside lodging, a pedestrian mall, a complete self-contained community, and free village shuttle service. Its 20-plus restaurants offer a variety of food, and shopping options include furriers, boutiques, jewelry stores, children's shops, and T-shirt outlets. In case the aforementioned aren't adequate, visitors will find a transit plaza, an 8,000-square-foot day-care center for children from 18 months to three-and-a-half years, and 40 shops and restaurants. There's a full health spa at the *Silvertree* hotel (phone: 970-923-3520; 800-525-9402). Other activities range from sleigh-ride barbecues, dogsled rides, cross-country skiing, and snowmobiling to hot-air ballooning. Information: *Aspen Skiing Company,* PO Box 1248, Aspen, CO 81612 (phone: 970-925-1220; 800-525-6200 for reservations).

STEAMBOAT, Steamboat Springs, Colorado This relaxed family area is on the outskirts of an archetypal Old West town named for its whistling hot springs. The runs (110 of them) are roomy and varied. There are trails, bowls, and powder fields for skiers of all skills; good children's programs; and a 3,685-foot vertical. An eight-passenger, high-speed gondola shoots skiers up to *Thunderhead Terminal* (where there is also a restaurant and barbecue sun deck) in just nine minutes. Last year, two high-speed quad lifts were added. *Steamboat*'s celebrated, ultra-light "champagne powder" is best in January and February; March and April are good for sunny, warm skiing. Snowboarding is allowed; rentals and lessons are available. Accommodations at the base of the mountain for easy ski-in/ski-out can be found at *Bearclaw Condominiums* (phone: 970-879-6100; 800-232-7252). Information: *Steamboat,* 2305 Mt. Werner Circle, Steamboat Springs, CO 80487 (phone: 970-879-0740; 800-922-2722).

TELLURIDE, Telluride, Colorado This former mining town, a National Historic District, is more than 100 years old. One of Colorado's fastest growing resorts, *Telluride* offers not only great skiing but a beautiful natural setting and accommodations in lovely Victorian-style buildings. Since 1985, it has almost doubled both its accommodations and its ski facilities. About 85% of the lodgings are within walking distance of either of the two base facilities. As for the skiing, 1,050 acres of terrain are divided among 62 trails: 32% expert, 47% intermediate, and 21% beginner. The See Forever run, the longest, extends 2.85 miles. There is a 2½-mile beginners' run, the Galloping Goose, and a 31-mile Nordic ski track; snowboarding also is available. The vertical is 3,165 feet. For accommodations, try *The Peaks Resort and Spa* (phone: 970-728-6800) or the *San Sophia* (phone: 800-537-4781); either one will spoil you. Information: *Telluride Ski Resort,* 562 Mountain Village Blvd., PO Box 11155, Telluride, CO 81435 (phone: 970-728-4424; 800-525-3455 for reservations).

VAIL-BEAVER CREEK, Vail, Colorado One of the most magnificent ski complexes in the US, this pioneer of modern American skiing takes up 10 square miles with a 3,250-foot vertical slope. There's so much skiing that even experts can spend a week at *Vail* and continue to find new challenges. The area includes six bowls—China, Tea Cup, Siberia, Sun Up, Sun Down, and Mongolia—making *Vail* the largest single-mountain resort in North America. The six double lifts, three triple lifts, nine high-speed quads, and the gondola at Lionshead make all areas of the mountain easily accessible. *Beaver Creek,* Vail's sister resort, about 7 miles down the valley, is a multimillion-dollar development. Trails with Western mining town themes take skiers through tepees, mines, and mogul gardens. There's also Grouse Mountain, a seven-run advanced ski area that the resort describes as "1,800 vertical feet of churning, burning, hair-raising, mogul-covered slopes." A unique *Vail* experience is an overnight stay at the isolated (and expensive) *Trapper's Cabin* in Beaver Creek. Guests either ski to the rustic log cabin or are chauffeured by Snowcat. Area lodging ranges from small, simple inns and lodges to full-service hotels within skiing distance of the lift bases. If Cadillac limousines and complimentary champagne at the end of the day are more to your taste, the Vail Valley has some of the most elegant mountain resorts in the nation. One of them, the *Hyatt Regency Beaver Creek* (phone: 970-949-1234), offers "Single Share," a unique program that allows solo skiers to share a room with another skier without paying the usual double occupancy price (the hotel even tries to match similarly skilled roommates). There's also ice skating, sleigh rides, cross-country skiing, snowmobiling, and more. Information: *Vail Valley Tourism & Convention Bureau,* 100 E. Meadow Dr., Vail, CO 81657 (phone: 970-476-1000; 800-525-3875; 970-476-4888 for snow reports; fax: 970-476-6008).

SUN VALLEY, Sun Valley, Idaho The "*ne plus ultra*" of destination ski resorts, this grande dame offers something for everyone—steilhangs for the brave and ballroom slopes for the tyro—on its 3,400 vertical feet. Baldy, famous for steep-bowl skiing, now boasts an equal variety of intermediate terrain, more like that of Dollar (*Sun Valley*'s other mountain—accessible by shuttle bus). The news here is that *Sun Valley* has been modernized to enable hard-core skiers to get to the top quicker and easier. Four high-speed quads ferry skiers to the top of Baldy, dropping them near the *Lookout* restaurant. The *Christmas* quad carries skiers from the *Roundhouse* restaurant. Lodging is in Sun Valley proper, at the base of Dollar, where there's a self-contained village full of shops and restaurants, and at Baldy's base, in the old mining town of Ketchum. Information: *Sun Valley,* Sun Valley, ID 83353 (phone: 208-622-4111; 800-SUN-VALY for reservations; 800-635-4150 for snow reports).

BIG MOUNTAIN, Whitefish, Montana It's often been said that the farther you have to go to get to a resort, the friendlier it's bound to be. And though it's remarkably accessible, thanks to decent transportation, *Big Mountain* is a good example. Singles can have a great time because of the cozy lodges (within walking distance of lifts) and a schedule of parties; families enjoy it because of the centralized, manageable layout of its 55 miles of runs. Because the mountain is in the northern Rockies, it gets enough snow so that you can ski from *Thanksgiving* until mid-April. Whitefish, 28 miles from the west entrance to *Glacier National Park,* is an old logging town turned resort; the après-ski scene can be lively. Accommodations are in the cozy *Garden Wall* (phone: 406-862-3440), a bed and breakfast inn located in town; *Kandahar Lodge* (phone: 406-862-6098), with 50 pine-paneled rooms, a sauna, and a hot tub; and the much-touted *Grouse Mountain Lodge* (phone: 406-862-3000; 800-321-8822), a resort hotel with 144 rooms and a pool. Information: *The Big Mountain Ski Resort,* PO Box 1400, Whitefish, MT 59937 (phone: 406-862-1960; 800-858-5439 for reservations).

TAOS SKI VALLEY, Taos, New Mexico Featherlight powder, brilliant sunshine, notably absent lift lines, and some startlingly steep expert runs have made *Taos* famous. Beginner, intermediate, and expert slopes are accessible from the top of each lift. The vertical drop is 2,613 feet, base elevation is 9,207 feet, and the 72 runs encompass powder glades, bowls, chutes, and well-manicured expanses. Snowmaking covers 85% of the beginner and intermediate terrain. There are après-ski centers in several cozy American-plan lodges at the mountain's base. A large resort center offers shops, galleries, cafeteria, and bar—all with views of the slopes. Its ski school carries a fine reputation that is well earned. Among the best places to stay in the area are *The Inn at Snakedance* (phone: 505-776-2277; 800-322-9815), *Thunderbird Lodge* (phone: 505-776-2280), and *St. Bernard* (phone: 505-776-2251); all have cozy rooms, excellent meals, and are close to the lifts. Information: *Taos Ski Valley,* PO Box 90, Taos Ski Valley, NM 87525 (phone: 505-776-2291; 800-776-1111 for reservations; 505-776-2916 for snow reports).

ALTA, Alta, Utah Two things generally are known about this rustic resort hidden away in Little Cottonwood Canyon since 1938, not far from *Snowbird* and Salt Lake City. First, this is the mother lode for powder skiers (snowfall averages 500 inches yearly); second, the famous Alf's High Rustler run, a ¾-mile chute with a 40-degree slope, no trees, and challenging terrain, is possibly the most sought-after expert trail in the West. However, not all the runs on these 2,200 skiable acres are steep, and the novice and intermediate bowls offer wonderful views of jagged peaks and forests. The base is at 8,550 feet and the top is over 10,550 feet. *Alta* is also one of the cozier American ski resorts, since all après-ski life revolves around the several lodges at the base. Closed May through mid-November. Information: *Alta Ski Lifts,* PO Box 8007, Alta, UT 84092 (phone: 801-742-3333; 801-942-0404 for lodging information; 801-572-3939 for snow reports).

DEER VALLEY, Park City, Utah This highly unusual ski resort believes that skiers care as much about the flakiness of their croissants as they do about the grooming quality and steepness of their slopes; it's like a superb big resort at which a major ski mountain is just one of the amenities. Accordingly, the base lodge and the mid-mountain lodge are tastefully done up with pine, cedar, fir, and real antiques; the restrooms are fitted out with pink Carrara marble and brass fixtures. Accommodations are in the luxurious fieldstone and stucco *Stein Eriksen Lodge* (phone: 801-649-3700; 800-453-1302) and in superb condos; and *Deer Valley Lodging* (phone: 801-649-4040), with hillside views, big Jacuzzis, sun porches, and more. As for the skiing, it's ideal—thanks to an annual 300 inches of the type of powdery snow only Utah can deliver, trails that unfold like a good novel, and a limited lift ticket sales policy that keeps lift lines down to a maximum wait of five minutes. The vertical here is 2,200 feet. Add the great food (both *Snow Country* and *Ski* magazines rated *Deer Valley* as offering the best food found on any US mountain), and you've got a ski vacation option like no other in the US. Information: *Deer Valley Resort,* PO Box 889, Park City, UT 84060 (phone: 801-649-1000; 800-424-3337).

PARK CITY, Park City, Utah With its many varied trails, night skiing, and snowmaking, *Park City* always has been terrific for skiers of all levels, with some of the steep snowfields a particular challenge to experts. It's the home of the *US Ski Team.* On the eastern slopes of the Wasatch Mountains, it is Utah's largest ski area, with some 2,200 acres of skiable terrain—including 650 acres of open bowls. The maximum vertical is now 3,100 feet. The town is an erstwhile mining settlement full of shops, health food emporiums, saloons, fancy steak joints—and atmosphere to spare. Information: *Park City Ski Area,* PO Box 39, Park City, UT 84060 (phone: 801-649-8111; 800-222-PARK for lodging reservations; 801-649-9571 for snow reports).

SNOWBIRD, Snowbird, Utah Like *Alta, Snowbird* is well known for powder skiing, but where *Alta* is old-fashioned and homegrown, *Snowbird,* just a mile to the west, is high-tech and elegant. Its slick condominium lodges of unadorned concrete add to the aura of luxury that surrounds the whole scene. As for the 1,900 acres of skiing, there are superb runs for experts on *Snowbird*'s 3,100 vertical feet, and a respectable quota of runs for novices and intermediates as well. Among the resort's special programs offered by the ski school are the Mountain Experience (five hours of steep going off-trail for experts), free guided skiing tours, and helicopter skiing in the backcountry with the *Wasatch Powderbird Guides* (phone: 801-742-2800). There's also a full-service health and beauty spa housed in the elegant, massive (532-room) *Cliff Lodge* (phone: 801-742-2222; 800-453-3000). Information: *Snowbird Ski and Summer Resort,* Snowbird, UT 84092 (phone: 801-521-6040; 800-453-3000 for reservations; 800-882-4766 for groups and conferences).

SUNDANCE, Sundance, Utah Owned by Robert Redford, this intimate, environmentally conscious community blends arts with recreation. At the base of majestic Mt. Timpanogos, the resort offers 41 ski trails spread over 450 acres and a 2,150-foot vertical drop. The new ski lift takes more advanced skiers to expert terrain. There are also 14 acres of cross-country skiing. Overnight guests may stay in the *Sundance Cottages,* which have rustic, yet elegant one-, two-, and three-bedroom suites; or in a private mountain home. For evening entertainment, *Sundance Indoor Theatre* produces a musical each winter. Information: *Sundance,* RR3, PO Box A-1, Sundance, UT 84604 (phone: 801-225-4107; 800-892-1600).

JACKSON HOLE, Teton Village, Wyoming That the resort has America's greatest vertical drop (4,139 feet) as well as its longest runs does not explain why it also ranks among the country's least crowded. That is because the first lifts here went up on redoubtable Rendezvous Mountain, and its early reputation marked it as not only the steepest, but also the toughest. Energetic development of the 2,200 vertical feet of Après Vous, the resort's other, far more forgiving giant, is only beginning to dispel the scare stories. And it's high time: Half of *Jackson Hole*'s skiable acreage is rated for experts, its intermediate terrain covers 40%, and 10% is just perfect for beginners. That, plus a compact lift-base arrangement of resorts (so that cars are optional), makes *Jackson Hole* a good vacation bet. Information: *Jackson Hole Ski Resort,* PO Box 290, Teton Village, WY 83025 (phone: 307-733-2292; 800-443-6931 for lodging and airfare information).

Cross-Country Skiing

You can go striding and gliding across almost anywhere when there's even a little snow on the ground. Or you can spend an afternoon tooling down a frozen river or canal, around the edge of a cemetery, or through a city park. You can cross-country in most forests, national and state parks, and even in wildlife management areas; all you need is a pair of cross-country skis. As long as snow covers the grass, the pavement, or the underbrush, those long, skinny skis will glide right along.

The special cross-country skiing centers springing up around the country not only offer lessons and cross-country ski rentals but also suggest marked trails that are tracked by machines to make the going easier and distribute trail maps. In very wild areas, some will also provide guides. With the boom in snowmobiling, cross-country skiers are finding it harder to keep out of the way of these motorized vehicles. However, many national parks have designated large areas where snowmobiles are forbidden. In general, commercial areas offer amenities such as lessons, rentals, groomed terrain, and warming huts along the trails. Wilderness areas are a different experience. While they don't have the extras, they offer natural beauty and exploration for the adventurous. If you're just starting out, though, the commercial spots are a better bet.

EAST

ACADIA NATIONAL PARK, Bar Harbor, Maine The 44 miles of carriage roads on Mt. Desert Island, which are not plowed in winter, take you up and down the rugged mountains of the interior, and when conditions are right, this is a winter wonderland par excellence. The total trail coverage is 120 miles (30 miles of which are also open to snowmobiles). However, because the ocean moderates the temperatures, you can't count on snow; call before traveling. Information: *Acadia National Park,* PO Box 177, Bar Harbor, ME 04609 (phone: 207-288-3338).

SUGARLOAF AREA, Kingfield, Maine Two miles from *Sugarloaf USA,* Maine's largest downhill skiing area, the *Sugarloaf Ski Touring Center* has some 52 miles of trails along old logging roads, through forests, down an old narrow-gauge railroad track, to a pond surrounded by hills and mountains, and around some condominiums. Lodgings are in cabins, condominiums, and motels nearby. A subsidiary trail connects with the alpine trail system, which enables skiers to ski directly to their lodgings at *Sugarloaf.* Information: *Sugarloaf Ski Touring Center,* Carrabassett Valley, ME 04947 (phone: 207-237-2000; 800-THE-LOAF).

BERKSHIRES, around Lenox, Massachusetts Miles and miles of trails wind through the forests here, some in state parks, some at resorts, and some maintained by special touring centers. Country inns here are like hotels with personality, intimate resorts, or parties at somebody's exceptionally wonderful country home. You'll find a number of major touring centers with ski rental shops and special activities—some of them adjoining state forest lands that also have trails. Information: *Berkshire Visitors Bureau,* Berkshire Common, Pittsfield, MA 01201 (phone: 413-443-9186; 800-237-5747).

JACKSON, New Hampshire The tradition of ski touring in the village of Jackson dates back to the turn of the century when skiing was used as a means of transport. But it's come a long way since then. With 64 trails, it is now the largest trail system in New England, and its network spans three river valleys, several open vistas, scenic woodland terrain, and a number of the routes within the boundaries of the *White Mountain National Forest.* Skiers will find a good variety of gentle and wooded trails near the village, too. This is also an ideal spot for cross-country skiers. The village revolves around skiing and offers schussboomers a number of eating and drinking destinations. In fact, the system links up 15 inns and lodges, five pubs, nine eateries, and several art galleries. For a longer tour, the *Ellis River Trail* is an enjoyable ski route that winds along the river and through the woods. Next to the center is the *Jack Frost Nordic Shop,* which has rentals and lessons. Information: *Jackson Ski Touring Center,* PO Box 216, Jackson, NH 03846 (phone: 603-383-9355; fax: 603-383-0816).

ADIRONDACKS, around Lake Placid, New York This six-million-acre region offers some of the most varied touring in the eastern US, and the area around the site of the *1980 Olympics* at Lake Placid is one of its centers. The *Bark Eater*—a small country inn (PO Box 139, Alstead Hill Rd., Keene, NY 12942; phone: 518-576-2221)—offers rentals and skiing on its own 9-mile trail system. The *Adirondak Loj* (spelling attributed to Dr. Melvil Dewey, originator of the Dewey Decimal System) is a rustic mountain lodge offering backcountry ski packages, workshops, seminars, lodge-to-lodge tours, rentals, and instruction (PO Box 867, Lake Placid, NY 12946; phone: 518-523-3441). Various sections of the *Northville–Lake Placid Trail,* a famous wilderness hiking trail through the valleys between the two towns, are suitable for cross-country skiing, and there are well over 100 miles of backcountry trails. For trail maps and information, call the *New York State Department of Environmental Conservation* (phone: 518-457-7433). Also contact the *Lake Placid/Essex County Visitors Bureau, Olympic Center,* 216 Main St., Lake Placid, NY 12946 (phone: 518-523-2445; 800-447-5224 for central reservations).

STOWE, Vermont The *Trapp Family Lodge* (42 Trapp Hill Rd., Stowe, VT 05672; phone: 802-253-8511; 800-826-7000), owned by the *Sound of Music* von Trapp family, is the oldest cross-country ski center in the US and one of the finest. Linking up with its 37 miles of especially well-groomed trails are the paths at prim and proper *Edson Hill Manor* (1500 Edson Hill Rd., Stowe, VT 05672; phone: 802-253-7371; 800-621-0284); those at the *Mt. Mansfield Touring Center* at the base of the alpine facilities; and the 20 miles of trails at *Topnotch at Stowe Resort and Spa* (4000 Mountain Rd., PO Box 1458, Stowe, VT 05672; phone: 802-253-8585; 800-451-8686), perhaps Vermont's premier luxury resort. Stowe visitors can "live on their XC skis," using the recreational path that connects everything in the village to *Topnotch.* Information: *Stowe Area Association,* PO Box 1320, Stowe, VT 05672 (phone: 802-253-7321; 800-24-STOWE for reservations).

WOODSTOCK, Vermont Located in central Vermont in the picturesque town of Woodstock, the *Woodstock Ski Touring Center* offers 40 miles of groomed trails for both classical and skating techniques. The *Mt. Peg Trail* network is accessible directly from the Touring Center and provides gentle, easy grades on terrain that serves as a golf course in summer. In town across the green are the *Mt. Tom Trails,* which treat skiers to 20 miles of scenic terrain through Vermont's first tree farm and over century-old carriage roads. Skiers who opt to stay at the *Woodstock Inn and Resort* (phone: 802-457-1100; also see *America's Best Resort Hotels*) will enjoy first class luxury only an eight-minute run from the ski area. Lessons, rentals, and guided tours are available at the *Touring Center,* as well as a retail/repair shop and the *Fireside Lounge and Restaurant.* The historic town of Woodstock features many fine restaurants, markets, antiques and gift shops, and a good selection of art galleries. Information: *Woodstock Touring Center,* 14 The Green, Woodstock, VT 05091 (phone: 802-457-2114).

MIDWEST

SUPERIOR NATIONAL FOREST, north of Duluth, Minnesota Some of Minnesota's most concentrated touring opportunities are on the eastern edge of this vast forestland on the Canadian border. There are hundreds of miles of groomed and ungroomed trails in the forest, most of them maintained by ski clubs or the rustic lodges and inns of the region. Many are connected; the *Gun Flint Trail,* an extensive network of trails, lets you travel from inn to inn while the owners take care of your luggage. *Bear Track Outfitting* has a lodge-to-lodge ski program; contact the company for more details (PO Box 937, Grand Marais, MN 55604; phone: 218-387-1162). For a list of lodges and details, contact *Minnesota Office of Tourism,* 100 Metro Sq., 121 Seventh Pl. E., St. Paul, MN 55101 (phone: 612-296-5029; 800-657-3700; 800-766-8687 for Canada).

CHEQUAMEGON NATIONAL FOREST, Park Falls, Wisconsin This north-central Wisconsin woodland has about 64 miles of mapped and marked loop trails, ranging in length from about 1 to 10 miles, designed primarily for cross-country skiers. But it's also possible to set out along hundreds of miles of unplowed roads or along the 60-mile section of the *North Country National Scenic Trail* that runs through the forest. This is a straight-line affair, but you can camp en route at Adirondack-style shelters; the scenery certainly warrants the effort. Information: *Chequamegon National Forest,* 1170 Fourth Ave. S., Park Falls, WI 54552 (phone: 715-762-2461).

WEST

ROYAL GORGE, Soda Springs, California The largest cross-country ski area in the world, it boasts nearly 180 miles of groomed track skiing. It is located in the Sierras on the Donner Summit, where the average snowfall is 450 inches per year. But just in case the weather doesn't cooperate, there's snowmaking on about 10 miles of trails. *Royal Gorge* offers skiing for everyone—28 novice trails, 44 intermediate trails, and 16 advanced trails. For skaters, there are skating lanes on all trails. The Interconnect trail is the longest (14 miles) and takes skiers from inn to inn. Another fun experience is the *Palisade Trail,* which travels gentle, winding paths through the pine-clad Mirkwood forest. The resort offers two hotels, 10 warming huts, and four cafés. There are the usual amenities—rentals and lessons—plus night skiing, guided tours of the area, ski patrol, and even day-care. And for those who crave action after a day in the wilderness, the resort is only 30 minutes away from the action at Lake Tahoe's gambling resorts or 45 minutes from Reno. Information: *Royal Gorge,* 9411 Hillside Dr., PO Box 1100, Soda Springs, CA 95728 (phone: 916-426-3871; 800-500-3871; fax: 916-426-9221).

SEQUOIA AND KINGS CANYON NATIONAL PARKS, near Visalia, California *Sequoia Ski Touring*'s extensive trail network leads through groves of giant, magnificent sequoia trees, across white-carpeted meadows, and to overlooks that give you wonderful vistas of the Sierra high country. The season runs from December through March. Two-hour lessons for beginners are available, as well as ski rentals. Information: *Sequoia Ski Touring,* Sequoia & Kings Canyon Guest Services, *Sequoia National Park,* CA 93262 (phone: 209-565-3134 for Sequoia; 209-335-2856 for Kings Canyon; 209-561-3314 for lodging in both areas).

YOSEMITE NATIONAL PARK, Yosemite, California The sequoias drown in the snow, the waterfalls freeze into fantastic sculptures, and everything sparkles. From *Thanksgiving* to *Easter, Yosemite Cross-Country Ski School* (phone: 209-372-1244) takes groups on easy overnight trips through these wonderlands. Special clinics teach you touring, winter camping, racing techniques—and how to handle that cross-country anathema, a real downhill run. The first weekend in March, the whole place is overrun for two days of anyone-can-do-it "citizens' races," part of the *Nordic Holiday Race.* The ski school is at the Badger Pass downhill ski area. Lodgings range from the primitive cabins at *Curry Village* to the posh *Ahwahnee* (also see *America's Special Havens*). Information: *Yosemite Reservations Office,* 5410 E. Home Ave., Fresno, CA 93727 (phone: 209-252-4848).

STEAMBOAT SPRINGS, Colorado Some of the best groomed and backcountry tours in the state can be found with the *Steamboat Ski Touring Center* (phone: 970-879-8180); Sven Wiik, the former *US Olympic Nordic Team* coach who set it up, knew what he was doing. Especially on Rabbit Ears Pass, you've got the advantage of being up at 10,000 feet—the great views and November-to-May powder—and none of the steep pitches or, for that matter, avalanche danger. Stay at any of the fine cross-country skiing ranches in the area, such as *Vista Verde* (phone: 970-879-3858) and the *Home Ranch* (phone: 970-879-1780). For information on other ski ranches in Colorado, contact

Colorado Tourist Information, 3554 N. Academy Blvd., Colorado Springs, CO 80917 (phone: 800-433-2656; fax: 719-591-7068).

VAIL–BEAVER CREEK, Colorado The *Golden Peak at Vail,* directed by Jean Naumann, has been the focus of ski touring in the area; it now shares the spotlight with its companion resort 10 miles west, *Beaver Creek Cross Country Center* (phone for both: 970-845-5313); both have complete ski schools. At *Vail,* there are easy marked and packed trails on a golf course east of town. Guides take beginners through the aspen forests in the valley not far away, and lead better skiers up the valley to the high country of the *White River National Forest* for half- and full-day tours. At *Beaver Creek,* there's an 18-mile double machine-set track with a skating lane at *McCoy Park* and a complete instruction and touring program. Rental equipment is available at both locations. Equipment also may be rented at the *Vail Nordic Center,* which has tracks available for cross-country skiing; instruction is available there, too (phone: 970-479-4391). Information: *Vail Associates,* PO Box 7, Vail, CO 81658 (phone: 970-476-5601), and the *Vail Resort Assn.,* PO Box 915, Avon, CO 81620 (phone; 970-476-4888 for snow reports; 800-525-2257 for lodging and reservations).

SUN VALLEY, Idaho This is one place where you don't have to climb to get to the high country: Helicopters operated by *Sun Valley Heliski* (phone: 208-622-3108) take you up to the Douglas fir–covered mountains for trips to Boulder Basin or Corral Creek, or you can go on your own to the *Pioneer Cabin* near Hyndman Peak, where you can picnic in the sun. In addition, there are some 112 miles of marked trails that you can do on your own or with guides. At *Elkhorn* resort, with up to 150 annual inches of snow on 756 acres of trails, daily skiing is an adventure for every level of skier. *Elkhorn* has its own cross-country ski tracks, providing skiing for the novice and the expert. Information: *Sun Valley Nordic Center,* Sun Valley, ID 83353 (phone: 208-622-2251; 800-SUN-VALY, ext. 2250); *Elkhorn Resort,* PO Box 6009, Sun Valley, ID 83354 (phone: 208-622-4511; 800-ELKHORN for reservations).

LONE MOUNTAIN, Big Sky, Montana Just an hour north of *Yellowstone National Park* is the *Lone Mountain Ranch,* which maintains 47 miles of groomed trails for all types of skiing. Here you can take a naturalist-guided ski tour to Yellowstone or an overnight backcountry tour. For those who don't want to venture off, there's plenty of skiing and sightseeing right around the ranch, which is near the *Gallatin Canyon,* home to bald eagles, elk, moose, and bighorn sheep. The ranch offers 24 private cabins, all with fireplaces or wood-burning stoves. The cuisine is ranch style with a continental flair. Off-trail activities include old-fashioned, horse-drawn sleigh ride dinners, massage, and hot tub. *PSIA*-certified lessons, a ski wax room, rentals, and a retail shop round out the picture. Information: *Lone Mountain Ranch,* PO Box 16069, Big Sky, MT 59716 (phone: 406-995-4644; fax: 406-995-4670).

GRAND TETON NATIONAL PARK, near Jackson, Wyoming This park has miles and miles of touring along roads as well as on countless trails (skier-groomed only) around and in the Jackson Hole Valley. You'll ski up gentle hills and across frozen flatlands, and enjoy splendid views of the jagged-tooth mountains. More experienced skiers may register at park headquarters for trips into the canyons, up the steeper slopes, and through high-country tundra. *Flagg Ranch Village* (phone: 307-543-2861), at the south entrance of nearby *Yellowstone National Park,* is open for lodging, meals, and cross-country skiing from December 15 to March 15. The Jackson Hole Valley contains a handful of special cross-country ski areas, with lodges, restaurants, rentals, tours, and instruction. You can also find helicopter skiing through *High Mountains Helicopter Skiing* (PO Box 173, Teton Village, WY 83025; phone: 307-733-3274). *Teton Pines Country Club* (phone: 307-733-1005) and *Spring Creek Nordic Center* (phone: 307-733-1004) have good terrain and facilities for beginners. Annual snowfall averages 500 to 600 inches, and there is unlimited backcountry and telemark skiing in the surrounding *Bridger-Teton National Forest* (PO Box 1888, Jackson, WY 83001; phone: 307-739-5500). You can stay in a sleek condominium in Teton Village at the base of *Jackson Hole* ski resort, 12 miles north of town, which also has a cross-country touring center (PO Box 290, Teton Village, WY 83025; phone: 307-733-2292 for ski information; 800-443-6931 for lodging information and reservations). Information: *Jackson Hole Chamber of Commerce,* PO Box E, Jackson, WY 83001 (phone: 307-733-3316); *Jackson Hole Visitors Council,* PO Box 2618, Jackson, WY 83001 (phone: 800-782-0011); *Grand Teton National Park,* PO Drawer 170, Moose, WY 83012 (phone: 307-739-3300).

YELLOWSTONE NATIONAL PARK, Yellowstone, Wyoming There's an otherworldly look to the place in winter—partly because of the clouds of steam rising from the flats, partly because of the overwhelming emptiness: Geysers roar, fumaroles rumble, and blue pools mild as morning glories explode into showers of scalding water. Bison, Canada geese, and elk are so prevalent that you stop noticing them after a while. You can make cross-country tours out of the *Old Faithful Snow Lodge* in the southern section of the park or *Mammoth Hot Springs* hotel (phone: 307-344-7311 for both) in the northern section. Rental snowmobiles are available as well as snow coaches and van shuttles to get you to more distant trailheads. Information: *TW Recreational Services, Yellowstone National Park,* WY 82190 (phone: 307-344-7311 for reservations).

The Best Tennis Vacations

Got some vacation time coming and want to work on your game? Hole up at a resort with good tennis facilities or visit a tennis camp, and play away.

Resorts are probably the most relaxing places to spend a tennis vacation. Sign up for a couple of lessons, play tennis when you want, and use the resort's saunas, whirlpool baths, pools, golf courses, and activity programs the rest of the time. In other than clinic situations, larger resorts catering to groups often attract so many beginners that advanced players may be bored, while older, more established resorts attract more advanced players and may not be much fun for beginners. And a high courts-to-rooms ratio and the presence of a tennis host who arranges games usually means that the tennis program is organized well enough that you won't spend all your time waiting around for a court.

Find out where the resort you're considering fits into this scheme. Also look into the court situation. How many are there, and what kinds? How many are lighted? (In some areas, it's just too hot to play during the day.) Can you reserve courts? How far in advance? Can you do it on the phone or must it be done in person? Is there any limit to how long you can play? And if you're not taking your own partner, is it easy to scare up a game?

The five-to-eight-hour-a-day programs known as camps are particularly intensive. Usually held at colleges, private schools, or camps that cater to children in other seasons, they don't offer much choice of accommodations, but there's always plenty of tennis. Cost for room, board, and instruction is about $125 per day. Clinics, usually held at hotels or resorts, are special weekend or week-long programs with instruction provided by the establishment's own pros or by visiting experts. An all-inclusive tennis clinic may cost $65 to $125 per day more than camps. But in either case you're guaranteed a certain number of hours of daily court time. At the beginning of the program you're graded, grouped with others of similar ability, and then worked—hard—by instructors. Usually you tackle one stroke at a time. First there will be a demonstration, then simple hitting drills, then more complicated hitting drills in which the stroke is made part of a more complex sequence of moves. You'll end each day with varying degrees of sunburn, blisters, and sore muscles. How successful the course is will depend on your original level of prowess—and how hard you work at improving.

For a complete and up-to-date list of clinics, camps, and places to play, check the annual February issue of *Tennis* magazine. In even-numbered years, its November issue lists the 50 greatest tennis resorts in the US. Reprints of articles from back issues may be ordered for a fee from *Tennis,* 5520 Park Ave., Trumbull, CT 06611-0359 (phone: 203-373-7000; 800-666-8336 for subscription department).

TENNIS RESORTS

Described below are some good bets for a first-rate tennis vacation.

EAST

NEW SEABURY, Cape Cod, Massachusetts With 16 all-weather courts, this waterfront resort community is the largest tennis venue on the Cape, and its designers cleverly placed the courts within a sunken wooded area to protect players from sou'westers that could throw off their strokes. Information: *New Seabury Company,* PO Box 549, Mashpee, MA 02649 (phone: 508-477-9400; fax: 508-477-9790).

MT. WASHINGTON, Bretton Woods, New Hampshire This classic grand resort, housed in a turn-of-the-century, white Edwardian structure, gives you spectacular views into the Presidential Range of the White Mountains. Private and group lessons (some using video) are available, and facilities include 12 clay courts. The resort is closed from mid-October through mid-May. Information: *Mt. Washington Hotel and Resort,* Rte. 302, Bretton Woods, NH 03575 (phone: 603-278-1000; 800-258-0330, outside New Hampshire).

WATERVILLE VALLEY, Waterville Valley, New Hampshire Condominiums and country inns, snuggled in the *White Mountain National Forest,* are popular with families. Facilities include clinics and private instruction, 18 clay courts, and two indoor courts; court reservations are possible. Information: *Waterville Valley Resort,* Waterville Valley, NH 03215 (phone: 603-236-8371; 800-468-2553 for reservations).

CONCORD, Kiamesha Lake, New York With 1,200 rooms scattered through several high-rise hotel structures on 4,000 acres in the Catskills, this place is like a city—but you can play all winter long. There are 40 hard courts, 16 of them indoors and open 24 hours a day, as well as ball machines and other teaching aids. Courts are available by reservation only; private and group lessons can be arranged. Information: *Concord Resort Hotel,* Kiamesha Lake, NY 12751 (phone: 914-794-4000; 800-431-3850 for reservations).

TOPNOTCH AT STOWE, Stowe, Vermont The instruction at this elegant, modern resort is considered among the best in the country by *Tennis* magazine. Facilities and services include 10 outdoor courts and four indoor; ball machines; videotapes and written critiques of performance; and tennis camps and packages. Reservations advised. Information: *Topnotch At Stowe Resort and Spa,* PO Box 1458, Stowe, VT 05672 (phone: 802-253-8585; 800-451-8686).

SUGARBUSH INN, Warren, Vermont At this gracious yet casual country inn in the heart of the Green Mountains, facilities and services include 24 outdoor courts (eight clay, 10 Har-Tru, six Deco-Turf), video replay and ball machines, and indoor tennis with private instruction. Clinics are available at the *Sugarbush Sports Center* and *The Bridges.* Reservations advised. Information: *Sugarbush Inn,* RR1, PO Box 350, Warren, VT 05674 (phone: 802-583-2391 for the tennis pro shop; 800-451-4320 for reservations).

SOUTH

AMELIA ISLAND PLANTATION, Amelia Island, Florida This 1,250-acre development appears consistently on *Tennis* magazine's biannual list of America's top 50 tennis resorts. You'll find 19 clay courts (three lighted), two Deco-Turf hard courts, four Omni courts, video replay and ball machines, clinics, and private and group lessons led by the pros on the premises. Court reservations are available. See also *Golf* in this section. Information: *Amelia Island Plantation,* PO Box 3000, Amelia Island, FL 32034 (phone: 904-261-6161; 800-874-6878).

GRENELEFE, Grenelefe, Florida This 1,000-acre resort development in the pines and citrus country a half-hour southwest of *Walt Disney World* offers 19 courts (nine Har-Tru, eight clay, two grass, 11 lighted); videotape and ball machines; and clinics and private lessons led by talented pros. Information: *Grenelefe Golf & Tennis Resort,* 3200 State Rd. 546, Grenelefe, FL 33844 (phone: 813-422-7511; 800-237-9549 for reservations).

INNISBROOK, Tarpon Springs, Florida Near the famous sponge market, a thousand acres of pine woods, citrus groves, moss-hung cypress trees, and 1,000 condo suites make this quite a big place—but it's well managed and friendly all the same. Among the facilities and services are 15 courts (11 clay, four hard), seven of which are lighted; video replay and ball machines; backboards; clinics; and private and group lessons. Information: *Innisbrook,* PO Drawer 1088, Tarpon Springs, FL 34688 (phone: 813-942-2000; 800-456-2000).

HILTON HEAD ISLAND, South Carolina Along with its stunning white beaches; quietly elegant villas, homes, and marinas; and subtropical forests, this island also has lots of tennis. You'll find most of it at two resorts: the *Palmetto Dunes* and *Sea Pines. Palmetto Dunes* has 25 courts, 19 of them clay and six of them lighted, and offers clinics in addition to private and group instruction; professional exhibition matches are played here as well. At *Sea Pines Racquet Club*—the largest tennis-oriented resort in the world—there are 43 courts (most Har-Tru) clustered primarily in three locations. Private lessons are available if you don't want to join one of the resort's tennis clinics, which include a "Tiny Tots" program for children ages four through seven, and clinics that focus on singles and doubles strategy, the contact point, preparation, and the like. There are full-time tennis hostesses at both resorts and frequent round-robin tourneys for players of all ages and skill levels. Stan Smith is *Sea Pines'* touring pro. The difference is mainly a matter of style and layout: *Sea Pines* is big, spread out enough so that you need at least a bike to get around, whereas at the *Hyatt Regency* (phone: 803-785-1234) and the *Hilton Head Island Hilton Resort* (phone: 803-842-8000) at *Palmetto Dunes,* nearly everything is within walking distance. Information: *Palmetto Dunes,* PO Box 5606, Hilton Head Island, SC 29938 (phone: 803-785-1161; 800-845-6130); *Palmetto Dunes Tennis Center,* PO Box 4798, Hilton Head Island, SC 29938 (phone: 803-785-1152; 800-972-0257); and *Sea Pines,* PO Box 7000, Hilton Head Island, SC 29938 (phone: 803-785-3333; 800-925-4653).

WORLD OF TENNIS AT LAKEWAY, Austin, Texas Here, townhouses cluster around groups of courts in the Texas hill country. Facilities include 26 Laykold courts—12 lighted, two indoors; reservations necessary. Private lessons and clinics are available. Information: *World of Tennis at Lakeway,* 1 World of Tennis Sq., Austin, TX 78738 (phone: 512-261-7222).

JOHN NEWCOMBE'S TENNIS RANCH, New Braunfels, Texas At this quiet and unpretentious resort located in Texas hill country, the lodging is courtside in comfortable condos or cottages, and the video replays are in color. Other facilities include 29 Laykold courts—eight lighted and four covered; practice alleys; and many clinics, including junior clinics. Information: *John Newcombe's Tennis Ranch,* New Braunfels, TX 78131 (phone: 210-625-9105; 800-444-6204 for reservations).

MIDWEST

FRENCH LICK SPRINGS, French Lick, Indiana This restored resort is located in the hills of the southern part of the state in what was once *the* spot to sip mineral water and take the cure, and the first place in America where a chef served tomato juice. It now does a booming business in conventions, golf—and tennis. Facilities include 18 courts (eight indoor, 10 outdoor, all lighted), ball machines, and video aids. Private and group lessons are available. Information: *French Lick Springs Resort,* Hwy. 56, French Lick, IN 47432 (phone: 812-936-9300; 800-457-4042 for reservations).

AMERICAN CLUB, Kohler, Wisconsin The guests at this hotel and spa, which is one of the Midwest's most elegant, enjoy full privileges at *Sports Core,* a private racquet facility and spa with six climate-controlled indoor courts and six outdoor hard courts, tournaments, and group and private lessons under the direction of *Peter Burwash International.* The hotel is a member of Historic Hotels of America. Information: *The American Club,* Highland Dr., Kohler, WI 53044 (phone: 414-457-8000; *Sports Core,* 414-457-4444).

WEST

LA QUINTA, La Quinta, California Built in 1926, this retreat is one of the oldest hotels in the Palm Springs area, and according to Hollywood gossip, it inspired Frank Capra's *It Happened One Night.* Its tennis club, consistently rated among the top resorts in the US, offers 30 courts (hard, grass, and Har-Tru surfaces), rigorous three-hour clinics, a maximum of four students per instructor, programmable ball machines, video analysis, and unlimited play. Each day the lesson focuses on a different aspect of the game. Round robins and special lessons also can be arranged. Information: *La Quinta Hotel, Golf, and Tennis Resort,* 49-499 Eisenhower Dr., La Quinta, CA 92253 (phone: 619-564-4111; 800-472-4316 from California; 800-854-1271 from elsewhere in the US).

WAILEA TENNIS CLUB, Maui, Hawaii This club is one of the best in the country for tennis, according to *Tennis* magazine. (It proudly refers to itself as "Wimbledon West" because of its three grass courts—a rarity even at private tennis resorts.) In addition, there are 11 Plexipave courts (three lighted) and daily private instruction. Several excellent hotels are nearby, including the *Maui Inter-Continental* (phone: 800-367-2960); *Stouffer Renaissance Wailea Beach Resort* (phone: 800-9-WAILEA); and the *Destination Resort at Wailea* (phone: 800-367-5246). Information: *Wailea Tennis Club,* 131 Wailea Iki Pl., Wailea, Maui, HI 96753 (phone: 808-879-1958).

SUN VALLEY, Idaho Guests at the *Sun Valley Inn,* the *Sun Valley Lodge,* and condominiums in *Sun Valley* and at *Elkhorn* (the smaller resort community a mile away) have access to more than 50 Laykold courts. *Elkhorn* offers year-round tennis to guests—weather permitting—with clinics and lessons conducted by a staff of professional instructors during the summer. Reservations are available, as are videotaping and closed-circuit TV facilities. Information: *Elkhorn Sun Valley Resort,* PO Box 6009, Sun Valley, ID 83354 (phone: 208-622-4511; 800-355-4676 for reservations); *Sun Valley Resort,* Sun Valley, ID 83353 (phone: 208-622-4111; 800-786-8259 for reservations).

TENNIS CAMPS AND CLINICS

These organizations sponsor clinics and camps at a number of resorts, schools, and college campuses.

HARRY HOPMAN/SADDLEBROOK INTERNATIONAL TENNIS, Wesley Chapel, FL A well-respected camp for both adults and juniors at all levels of the game. The five-hour daily instruction sessions include many imaginative drills as well as fitness and agility training exercises. The program guarantees that there will be no more than four players per instructor. The accommodations here are first class, too: The *Saddlebrook* resort has 36 holes of golf, three pools, and a Nautilus center to complement its 45 tennis courts. Information: *Harry Hopman/Saddlebrook International Tennis,* 5700 Saddlebrook Way, Wesley Chapel, FL 33543 (phone: 941-973-1111, ext. 4214; 800-729-8383 for reservations; fax: 813-973-2936).

JOHN GARDINER'S TENNIS RANCHES The celebrated ranches in Scottsdale, Arizona (see *Phoenix,* THE CITIES) and Carmel Valley, California (where there is a junior summer day camp) have clinics where you hit lots of balls under the supervision of well-trained and well-disciplined instructors who hammer the basics into you as you hammer balls. Both ranches are luxurious; for top-of-the-line instruction and superlative resort amenities, either will restore your spirits as well as your backhand. Information: *John Gardiner's Tennis Ranches,* 5700 E. McDonald Dr., Scottsdale, AZ 85253 (phone: 602-948-2100; 800-245-2051; fax: 602-483-7314); or PO Box 228, Carmel Valley, CA 93924 (phone: 408-659-2207; 800-453-6225; fax: 408-659-2492).

NICK BOLLETTIERI TENNIS ACADEMIES, based in Bradenton, Florida The largest and most ambitious tennis school in the country, *NBTA* has summer camps in California, Wisconsin, Massachusetts, and Connecticut, as well as at its home base in Florida (reportedly the world's largest tennis training facility). The features in Florida are extensive: 75 outdoor courts, five indoor courts, several types of sports training centers, and a pro shop. There are also affiliates in numerous other US locations, in addition to operations in Canada and Europe. The academy trains both recreational and professional players; it boasts Andre Agassi, Jim Courier, and Monica Seles among its graduates. Information: *Nick Bollettieri Tennis Academies,* 5500 34th St. W., Bradenton, FL 34210 (phone: 813-755-1000; 800-USA-NICK; fax: 813-758-0198).

RAMEY TENNIS SCHOOLS, based in Owensboro, Kentucky This organization puts on spring and summer clinics for youth and adults in stroke development; for more advanced players it offers tournament camps and competitive play and drill programs at its headquarters in Owensboro. Adult weekend programs and women-only programs are held at an indoor club, with deluxe hotel housing. There are junior "tournament camps." One of the program's unique features is that campers are housed in cottages in a rural setting that includes horseback riding. Computer stroke charting and videotape analyses are other special features. Information: *Ramey Tennis Schools,* 5931 Hwy. 56, Owensboro, KY 42301 (phone: 502-771-5590; fax: 502-771-4723).

VAN DER MEER TENNIS UNIVERSITY Billie Jean King's onetime coach Dennis Van der Meer, one of the most knowledgeable and influential teaching pros in the US, personally supervises programs for players at all skill levels at his Hilton Head Island, South Carolina, headquarters. Programs also are conducted at *Sweet Briar College* and *Randolph-Macon Women's College,* both in Virginia; *Gray Rocks Inn,* Canada; *Four Seasons Lake Ozark Resort,* Missouri; and in Europe and Asia. Information: *Van der Meer Tennis University,* PO Box 5902, Hilton Head Island, SC 29938 (phone: 803-785-8388 in South Carolina; 800-845-6138 elsewhere).

VIC BRADEN TENNIS COLLEGE, Coto de Caza, California The licensed psychologist and tennis ace holds forth here, delivering pre-drill lectures that some stand-up comics would envy ("Get to know your navel," "Air your armpits"). The facilities are impressive: six hard courts—four lighted; ball machines; specially designed hitting lanes; a tall tower where the teacher can view students on several courts simultaneously; video screening rooms; and a huge array of high-tech teaching devices. Classroom lectures also are part of the program. Information: *Vic Braden Tennis College,* 23335 Av. la Caza, Coto de Caza, CA 92679 (phone: 714-581-2990; 800-CALL-VIC in California; 800-42-COURT elsewhere).

Golf: The Greening of America

Golf can be a most frustrating sport for travelers in America, especially for those who've spent any appreciable time watching televised matches where the pros cavort on some of the world's finest courses. Not only are the courses attractive to the point of distraction, but seeing them so temptingly displayed only heightens their allure.

One would think that being willing to travel to a course would be the only requirement for a golfer who wanted to satisfy his or her fondest longings. Not so. The fact is that only about half a dozen of the golf courses listed by *Golf Digest* magazine among the country's top 50 are open for public play on any regular basis.

Nonetheless, some top courses are open to traveling players. What follows is a list of a few of those that are truly worth traveling a great distance to experience.

EAST

NEW SEABURY, Cape Cod, Massachusetts *Golf Digest* ranked the par 72 *Blue* course here among the best 75 resort courses in the country and one of the top 5 in Massachusetts; the *Green* course (par 70) is also challenging. The 36 holes are set amidst invigorating seascapes, salt marshes dotted with roses, and inland waters. Information: *New Seabury Company,* PO Box 549, Mashpee, MA 02649 (phone: 508-477-9400; fax: 508-477-9790).

CONCORD, Kiamesha Lake, New York One of the very best courses in the country is part of the three-course *Concord* resort hotel complex on Kiamesha Lake in the Catskill Mountains. It is a track well worth its nickname, "the Monster," for it is nearly unconscionably long and almost intolerably difficult—and that's probably why great numbers of masochistic golfers from New York City and points north trudge up to its first tee every weekend. The golfing season is generally from the end of April through September. Information: *Concord Resort Hotel,* Kiamesha Lake, NY 12751 (phone: 914-794-4000; 800-431-3850 for reservations).

WOODLOCH SPRINGS, Hawley, Pennsylvania Guests at the *Woodloch Pines* resort can try their luck at this tough, par 72, 6,579-yard layout in the northern Pocono Mountains. Designed by Rocky Roquemore, it was named one of the top 10 new courses in 1993 by *Golf* magazine, perhaps because of the par 5 14th hole—577 demanding yards over Hell's Gate Gorge with a winding brook below. The 18 holes are set amid mosses, meadows, and mountains. Between the challenging fairways and lovely scenery, this private course is one of the finest layouts in the East. Information: *Woodloch Pines,* RR1, PO Box 280, Hawley, PA 18428 (phone: 717-685-7121; 800-572-6658).

SOUTH

AMELIA ISLAND PLANTATION, Amelia Island, Florida Golf is just one of the many activities to be pursued here, and it is quite a challenge. The courses are a definite contrast in styles. *Amelia Links,* the original 27-hole, par 107 layout, designed by Pete Dye in 1972, is composed of three nines, none of which stretches much more than 3,000 yards from the regular men's tees. But golfers must contend with overhanging trees, narrow fairways, and small greens perched along salt marsh or tucked behind sand dunes. The golf course is played in different rotations, and guests should reserve tee-off times prior to arriving at the resort. At Amelia's second layout, the *Long Point* course, golfers will find as much water as terra firma. Still, the Tom Fazio design is one of the best anywhere. See also *Tennis.* Information: *Amelia Island Plantation,* PO Box 3000, Amelia Island, FL 32034 (phone: 904-261-6161; 800-874-6878).

WALT DISNEY WORLD, Lake Buena Vista, Florida See *Orlando,* THE CITIES.

DORAL, Miami, Florida See *Miami,* THE CITIES.

GRAND CYPRESS, Orlando, Florida See *Orlando,* THE CITIES.

PGA NATIONAL RESORT AND SPA, Palm Beach Gardens, Florida This is the headquarters for the *Professional Golfers Association of America,* and home to many important tournaments. For starters, there's a choice of five 18-hole courses including the *Championship* with its 15th, 16th, and 17th holes dubbed *The Bear Trap* by members of the *PGA Senior Tour.* Three of the courses were designed by George and Tom Fazio, others wear the seal of Arnold Palmer, Karl Litten, and Jack Nicklaus. Taking up the sport here can be enjoyable since *PGA*'s *Academy of Golf* has well-respected top instructors. It also has been garnered the most "women friendly" by *Golf for Women* magazine. If you want a break from golf, there's an impressive tennis program (19 clay courts), six croquet courts, a *Spa* with outdoor mineral pools and a wide range of beauty and health services, three swimming pools, and a private beach with a marina. There are 339 rooms and 80 cottages, and a variety of restaurants for formal to casual dining. Information: *PGA National Resort & Spa,* 400 Ave. of the Champions, Palm Beach Gardens, FL 33418, (phone: 407-627-2000, 800-633-9150 for reservations, fax: 407-622-0261).

TOURNAMENT PLAYERS CLUB, Ponte Vedra Beach, Florida This well may be Pete Dye's masterpiece. The 17th hole became a classic in 1982 after the first professional tournament here, and it remains one of the most famous holes in golf. It won't treat you any better than it treats the pros, so bring enough golf balls when you attempt to conquer the sculptured fairways and unkindly undulating greens. You probably won't score very well, but it's a comfort to know the pros do only a little better. The *Valley* course was also designed by Pete Dye, with Jerry Pate as *PGA Tour* player consultant. Though a private club, this establishment allows resort guests and visiting golfers to play through reasonably priced associate memberships and guest fees. Getting a tee-time can be difficult, unless you're a registered guest at the *Marriott at Sawgrass* hotel. Information: *Tournament Players Club at Sawgrass,* 110 TPC Blvd., Ponte Vedra Beach, FL 32082 (phone: 904-285-7777).

EMERALD DUNES, West Palm Beach, Florida Here you'll find golf holes set in landscapes reminiscent of the old links courses in Scotland. Each of the 18 holes of this Tom Fazio–designed course has five tees that allow players of all abilities to pursue a challenging game. The course's potential Waterloo is the 50-foot-high Super Dune, surrounded by waterfalls and lakes. Information: *Emerald Dunes,* 2100 Emerald Dunes Drive, West Palm Beach, FL 33411 (phone: 407-684-4653).

SEA ISLAND, Sea Island, Georgia This is only the most important part of the 10,000-acre resort complex known as the *Cloister.* The 36 holes of golf (divided into four distinct nines) all have ocean views, and the landscape is dominated by magnolias and pampas grass. The *Seaside* nine is probably the most challenging of the available four, which may be played in any combination. The neighboring *St. Simons Island Club,* which has its own 18-hole course and a low country–style clubhouse, is also a part of the *Cloister* complex. Information: *Sea Island Golf Club,* c/o *The Cloister,* Sea Island, GA 31561 (phone: 912-638-3611; 800-SEA-ISLA).

PINEHURST, Pinehurst, North Carolina There is no golf community in the US more devoted to the game than *Pinehurst.* Non-golfers often can't grasp what all the hushed reverence is about, but believers happily play two rounds a day on the eight courses here, and attend golf clinics at the *Pinehurst* hotel after dinner. Donald Ross's *Pinehurst No. 2,* ranked ninth in the US by *Golf Digest* in 1995, is indicative of the class of the circuits here; George and Tom Fazio built a tough (and scenic) *No. 8,* and Rees Jones designed *No. 7.* Instruction is available. See also *America's Best Resort Hotels.* Information: *Pinehurst Resort and Country Club,* PO Box 4000, Pinehurst, NC 28374 (phone: 910-295-6811; 800-487-4653 for reservations).

HARBOUR TOWN, Sea Pines, Hilton Head Island, South Carolina Golfers have long known what the general public is just discovering: This island, the second largest (after New York's Long Island) in the East Coast's barrier chain, holds some of the country's best resort terrain. Golfers have their choice of two dozen courses; but the magnet usually is the *Harbour Town Golf Links,* a public resort course which is part of the marvelous *Sea Pines* development (see also *Ocean Beaches* and *Tennis*) and the site of the annual *PGA MCI Heritage Classic.* With a whopping course rating of 74—one of the highest in the country—its difficulty needs no elaboration. Only the laid-back environment provides some small salve to soaring scores. It was designed by Pete Dye with Jack Nicklaus consulting; Dye is our personal choice for the game's most creative craftsman, and his talent and handiwork are nowhere better displayed (except possibly at the *Tournament Players Club,* above). Information: *Harbour Town Golf Links,* Sea Pines, Hilton Head Island, SC 29928 (phone: 803-842-8484; 800-925-4653 for reservations).

HOMESTEAD, Hot Springs, Virginia Three superior courses are the focus of attention at this magnificently kept dowager resort, and the fact that the redoubtable Sam Snead learned to play the game here gives you an idea of just how good they are. The *Cascades* course, 4 miles from the hotel's front door, is the best of the trio. The *Lower Cascades* course is longer. Only a nine-iron from the front door of the hotel, the *Homestead* course, designed by Scotsman Donald Ross and built in 1892, is Virginia's oldest and among America's oldest as well. See also *America's Best Resort Hotels.* Information: *Homestead,* Hot Springs, VA 24445 (phone: 703-839-5500; 800-336-5771 for reservations).

KINGSMILL RESORT, Williamsburg, Virginia Minutes away from *Colonial Williamsburg* is Virginia's largest golf community, with four layouts: The newest, *The Woods,* is a par 72 course designed by Curtis Strang and Tom Clark; there's also the Pete Dye–designed *River* course, home to the annual *PGA Anheuser-Busch Classic;* the 18-hole *Plantation* course, which winds through the original *Kingsmill* grounds, was designed by Arnold Palmer. There is also a 9-hole course, *The Bray Kinks.* There is an academy, several clubhouses, and a well-stocked pro shop. This 2,900-acre property has 352 villas, extensive meeting and conference facilities, 15 tennis courts, and a marina. The facility has won recent accolades from *Golf* magazine and other publications. Information: *Kingsmill Resort,* 1010 Kingsmill Rd., Williamsburg, VA 23185 (phone: 804-253-1703; 800-832-5665).

GREENBRIER, White Sulphur Springs, West Virginia Anyone who regularly attends business meetings or seminars inevitably will trip over this immense and elegant resort, but golfers tend to look forward to these conferences with particular relish. The resort's three courses provide a more than adequate variety of play. See also *America's Best Resort Hotels.* Information: *Greenbrier,* White Sulphur Springs, WV 24986 (phone: 304-536-1110; 800-624-6070).

MIDWEST

TIMBER RIDGE, East Lansing, Michigan Designed by Jerry Matthews, this 18-hole, 6,497-yard, par 72 "forest" course, located in a natural wooded setting, is only 10 minutes away from the state capital. Instruction is available, and there is a snack bar and lounge. Information: *Timber Ridge Golf Course,* 16339 Park Lake Rd., East Lansing, MI 48823 (phone: 517-339-8000; 800-T-RIDGE-2 in Michigan).

WEST

BOULDERS, Carefree, Arizona See *Phoenix,* THE CITIES.

SCOTTSDALE PRINCESS, Scottsdale, Arizona See *Phoenix,* THE CITIES.

TROON NORTH, Scottsdale, Arizona See *Phoenix,* THE CITIES.

LOEWS VENTANA CANYON, Tucson, Arizona Designed by Tom Fazio to blend easily with the natural surroundings, *The Canyon* is both a work of art and a stiff challenge. Golfers will find greens tucked against whaleback rocks as well as high grounds that provide 100-mile views south into Mexico. The front nine leads a player through the beautiful Esperero Canyon; down the No. 1 handicap, par 5, 552-yard seventh hole; to the challenging ninth hole, with its sweeping "hidden" green. The pièce de résistance, however, is the 18th; the approach shot on this par 5 must carry a gulley and land softly on a green with water guarding the right side. Behind it, a waterfall gently splashes. See also *America's Best Resort Hotels.* Information: *Loews Ventana Canyon Resort,* 7000 N. Resort Dr., Tucson, AZ 85715 (phone: 520-299-2020; 800-234-5117).

LA COSTA, Carlsbad, California At this famous Southern California resort and health spa, Dick Wilson and Joe Lee created courses that bedevil even the pros, so you'll probably welcome the opportunity to repair to the steamroom after your first foray. The *North* and *South* courses make a total of 36 holes. Information: *La Costa Resort and Spa,* 2100 Costa Del Mar Rd., Carlsbad, CA 92009 (phone: 619-438-9111; 800-854-5000 for reservations).

TORREY PINES, La Jolla, California See *San Diego,* THE CITIES.

MORENO VALLEY RANCH, Moreno Valley, California Located halfway between Palm Springs and Los Angeles, this 27-hole desert facility was designed by Pete Dye. The *Valley Nine,* the *Mountain Nine,* and the *Lake Nine* are all par 36. There's a lighted driving range and a pro shop. *PGA* instructors are available for lessons. Information: *Moreno Valley Ranch Golf Course,* 28095 John F. Kennedy Ave., Moreno Valley, CA 92555 (phone: 909-924-4444).

PEBBLE BEACH GOLF LINKS, Pebble Beach, California If there is a leading contender for the title of Most Photographed Golf Course, it has to be the ocean-hugging *Pebble Beach Golf Links* on the windswept Monterey Peninsula. Its reputation as a first-rate course is supported by a flood of accolades: In 1991, *Golf* magazine placed it fifth on the list of the world's best courses; in 1992, *Golf Digest* rated it the top resort course in the US. This is one of the rare instances where a truly first class US tournament track actually is accessible to the public, and it's an opportunity not to be missed. Information: *Pebble Beach Golf Links,* Seventeen Mile Dr., Pebble Beach, CA 93953 (phone: 408-625-8518; 800-624-3811 for lodging reservations).

SPYGLASS HILL, Pebble Beach, California Consistently rated as one of the most challenging courses in the country, *Spyglass Hill* combines elements of oceanfront play with the challenge of long, tree-lined holes through the woods and lakes of the back nine. Just 1 mile from *Pebble Beach Golf Links,* this 18-hole beauty was designed by Robert Trent Jones Sr. and is the home course for the annual *Pebble Beach Invitational* and for the *AT&T Pro-Am.* Information: *Spyglass Hill,* Stevenson Dr., Pebble Beach, CA 93953 (phone: 408-625-8563; 800-654-9300 for lodging reservations).

KEYSTONE, Keystone, Colorado At first glance, the *Keystone Ranch* course looks like something out of a John Wayne movie. The first class golf course is laid out on a 9,300-foot plateau framed by snow-capped peaks; several holes run around old ranch buildings. Some are tree-lined like those at Hilton Head, while the water hazards resemble those at *Pebble Beach.* Perhaps the greatest attraction of all is the thin air; you'll find your shots going considerably farther than at sea level. Depending on the snowfall, the course is generally playable from the end of April through September. Information: *Keystone Resort,* PO Box 38, Keystone, CO 80435 (phone: 970-468-4242; 800-222-0188).

MAUNA KEA BEACH, Kohala Coast, Big Island of Hawaii, Hawaii The course is built on ancient lava flows that have somehow solidified to give it a linksland character. This is a warm, arid corner of the islands, and much care (and water) is needed to keep the terrain green and true. The spectacular volcanic peak that gives the resort its name is the backdrop for nearly every shot, and the *Mauna Kea* fairways are among the most scenic in the world. Information: *Mauna Kea Beach Hotel,* 62-100 Kaunaoa Dr., Kamuela, HI 96743 (phone: 808-882-7222; 800-882-6060 for reservations).

MAUNA LANI BAY, Kohala Coast, Big Island of Hawaii, Hawaii Built atop jagged black lava flows, using thousands of tons of imported topsoil, this home of the popular annual *Senior Skins Game* is considered one of the most beautiful courses in the islands. The resort offers two 18-hole courses called *North* and *South,* set amidst breathtaking scenery. Black lava rock borders the lush fairways. Beauty aside, the courses provide a true test of golfing skill. Hazards range from the conventional complement of sand traps to huge lava boulders that evoke images of Japanese gardens (see also *America's Best Resort Hotels*). Information: *Mauna Lani Bay Hotel,* 68-1400 Mauna Lani Dr., Kohala Coast, HI 96743 (phone: 808-885-6622; 800-367-2323 for reservations).

PRINCEVILLE, Hanalei, Kauai, Hawaii The garden spot of the Garden Island, *Makai* affords three spectacular nines (*Ocean, Woods,* and *Lake*) in the same terrain seen in the film *South Pacific.* About a mile away is the challenging *Prince* course (phone: 808-826-5000), an 18-holer designed by Robert Trent Jones Jr., which brings the total number of holes to 45 and makes Princeville one of Hawaii's biggest golf resort cities. Information: *Princeville Golf Course,* PO Box 3040, Princeville, HI 96722 (phone: 808-826-3580).

KAPALUA, Maui, Hawaii The *Plantation* is the latest course on this resort that was once a pineapple plantation. Located on Maui's scenic northwest coast, this 18-hole, par 73, 7,100-yard course is the site of the prestigious *Lincoln-Mercury Kapalua International. Kapalua* is currently the only resort on Hawaii with three top-quality 18-hole golf courses (*Bay* and *Village* are the others). The course retains natural terrain features, and boasts fabulous vistas and native vegetation, and can be enjoyed on all skill levels. Information: *The Plantation at Kapalua,* 500 Bay Drive, Lahaina, HI 96761 (phone: 808-669-0244; fax: 808-669-4480).

EAGLE BEND, Bigfork, Montana Dramatically placed among large rock outcroppings, pines, and white birch thickets, this course is also bordered by farmland, the Flathead River, and a federal waterfowl reproduction area. The 18-hole course on the north shore of Flathead Lake has an eight-month golfing season, and it's not uncommon for golfers to play until 9 or 10 PM on the long summer evenings. They've recently added a second, 9-hole course. Information: *Eagle Bend Golfing Community,* PO Box 960, Bigfork, MT 59911 (phone: 406-837-7311; 800-255-5641).

HARBOUR POINTE, Mukilteo, Washington You can clearly see Puget Sound and the southern tip of Whidby Island on the elevated tees as you play this wonderful 18-hole course. It was designed by Arthur Hills and lauded as one of the best new public courses by *Golf* magazine in 1990 and by *Golf Digest* in 1991. The landscape includes many steep drop-offs that surround fairways and should inspire doubt in the stoutest of hearts. Information: *Harbour Pointe Golf,* 11817 Harbour Pointe Blvd., Mukilteo, WA 98275 (phone: 206-355-6060).

GOLF CLINICS

Regular practice under the supervision of a pro on your own home course can't be beat for reducing your handicap. But there's no substitute for an occasional look at your weaknesses from a new point of view. That's the purpose of the golf clinics that have sprouted up all over the country.

SPORTS ENHANCEMENT ASSOCIATES (SEA), headquartered in Sedona, Arizona Formed in 1983 by Chuck Hogan, guru to many *PGA* and *LPGA* players and the author of several books on golfing technique and strategy, the organization's purpose is to help amateurs as well as professionals to achieve peak performance. Instruction blends the game's mental and physical aspects; sessions are held in clinics at top golfing resorts around the country. Information: *Sports Enhancement Associates,* 8055 N. 24th Ave., Suite 112, Phoenix, AZ 85021 (phone: 602-864-2951; 800-345-4245).

GOLF DIGEST INSTRUCTION SCHOOLS, headquartered in Trumbull, Connecticut The "Harvard" of golf schools holds its classes—taught by some of the best teaching pros in the business—at 17 resorts all across the country, year-round. Information: *Golf Digest Instruction Schools,* 5520 Park Ave., PO Box 395, Trumbull, CT 06611-0395 (phone: 203-373-7130; 800-243-6121).

INNISBROOK GOLF INSTITUTE, Tarpon Springs, Florida Training more than 1,000 students annually, this year-round intensive golf school is one of the largest resort-owned and -operated institutes in the country. During a four-day, three-night program, the instructors put you through your paces from 7:30 AM to 6 or 7 PM. With a 4:1 student/teacher ratio, students begin with an evaluation of their current status and then participate in drills, exercises, videotape analysis, and four hours of on-course supervision. Information: *Innisbrook Golf Institute,* PO Drawer 1088, Tarpon Springs, FL 34688 (phone: 800-456-2000).

GOLF SCHOOL AT MT. SNOW, Mt. Snow, Vermont Started in 1978, the *Golf School* has become one of the most popular golfing programs in the country. Keys to the school's success are small teaching groups with a maximum of four students per instructor. The Accelerated Teaching Method incorporates the use of videotape, special practice areas, and a building-block approach. The school offers two-day weekend programs and five-day midweek sessions that include lodging, meals, and five hours of daily instruction. Offered at the *Plantation Inn & Resort* in Crystal River, Florida (phone: 800-632-6262), during the fall and winter. Information: *Golf School at Mt. Snow,* Mt. Snow, VT 05356 (phone: 800-451-4211).

STRATTON GOLF SCHOOL, Stratton Mountain, Vermont This school, one of the oldest in New England, now teaches year-round by moving to Scottsdale, Arizona, during the winter months. In summer, this unique, 22-acre Vermont training site, designed by noted golf course architect Geoffrey Cornish, allows students to simulate all golf shots. Director Keith Lyford and his staff focus on the basics—grip, stance, alignment, and swing—during two- and five-day sessions from mid-May to September. Lodging packages are available. Information: *Stratton Golf School,* Stratton Mountain, VT 05155 (phone: 802-297-2200; 800-787-2886 outside Vermont; 800-238-2424 for Scottsdale information).

Sailing America's Coastal Waters

WINDJAMMER CRUISES

There's no better way to get a feeling for the great age of sailing than on one of the big windjammers that were built during the first quarter of this century—mostly for oystering, fishing, or cargo—and later converted to handle passengers. You spend your days swimming off the side or dozing in the sun, and you eat big family-style meals that may include muffins and pastries cooked on old-fashioned wood stoves. You cruise at least a few hours every day, sometimes all day, then stop for a while—to go sightseeing, to have a cookout, or to take hot showers at a marina. When you fall asleep at night, it's to the creaking of the ship's oak beams.

Otherwise, what a specific cruise is like depends a lot on the boat. On smaller vessels, the atmosphere is bound to be chummy (or confining, depending on your psyche) and somewhat more informal; each passenger has more say about where you go, what you do, and when you do it.

When considering the different windjammers, a selection of which follows, look into their size, ports of call, price (usually from $495 to $635 per person for six days), means of power, and the policy about children (there may be minimum ages of, say, 10 or 16, but talk to the captain; he or she may make an exception). Also investigate the plumbing facilities: Many boats simply supply wash water on deck, while others have washbasins or showers in their cabins. In general, the season runs from *Memorial Day* weekend through September.

MAINE WINDJAMMER CRUISES, Camden, Maine The historic vessels of this line make three- and six-day coastal sailings in the vicinity of Penobscot Bay. Itineraries are loosely structured; they go "where the wind goes." Information: *Maine Windjammer Cruises,* PO Box 617, Camden, ME 04843 (phone: 207-236-2938; 800-736-7981).

MARY DAY, Camden, Maine This 90-foot schooner accommodates 28 in single, double, and triple cabins on week-long and three- and four-day cruises among Maine's coastal islands. Noted for her sailing ability and speed, *Mary Day* has no engine. A small powerboat provides access to shore and power in calm weather. Each cabin has fresh water; there is a shower on deck. Cruises organized around special interests such as photography, folk music, and natural history are scheduled each season. Several nonsmoking cruises are also scheduled. Information: *Coastal Cruises,* PO Box 798, Camden, ME 04843 (phone: 207-236-2750; 800-992-2218).

ROSEWAY, Camden, Maine One of the largest windjammers that sails off the Maine coast, the 137-foot *Roseway* was built as a yacht and used for many years as a pilot boat in Boston Harbor. Today, it cruises the Maine coast as well as the Virgin Islands and carries 30 to 36 passengers (no children under 16). Hot and cold showers are available on all cruises. In addition, there are photography and watercolor painting "theme" sailings. Information: *Yankee Schooner Cruises,* PO Box 696, Camden, ME 04843 (phone: 207-236-4449; 800-255-4449; fax: 207-236-3269).

AMERICAN EAGLE, Rockland, Maine A former fishing vessel launched in 1930, this two-masted, 92-foot schooner takes 28 guests (no small children) on three- and six-day trips along the coast of Maine from May to October. Cabins have reading lights and sinks; there is a shower on board. The food is good, and the craft swift. Information: *American Eagle,* PO Box 482, Rockland, ME 04841 (phone: 207-594-8007; 800-648-4544).

HERITAGE, Rockland, Maine Constructed of native Maine oak and pine in the design of a 19th-century coasting schooner, *Heritage* was built by her captains in 1983. Cruises depend on tide and weather, and though there is no set route, each cruise features a lobster bake on an island. Passengers can help with sailing, and there are small rowboats handy for exploring islands and harbors. Information: *Captains Douglas K. and Linda J. Lee,* PO Box 482, Rockland, ME 04841 (phone: 207-594-8007; 800-648-4544).

ISAAC H. EVANS, Rockland, Maine Built in 1886, this 64½-foot, two-masted schooner spent most of its life oystering and freighting in Delaware Bay. (It has been designated a national landmark.) Now completely rebuilt, it has fresh running water in the cabins, a potbellied heating stove in the public room aft, one hot-and-cold-water shower, and a small push boat for going ashore (or getting to safe harbor) if there's no wind: The ship has no engine. Up to 22 passengers are allowed (minimum age 16). Information: *Captain Edward Glaser,* PO Box 482, Rockland, ME 04841 (phone: 207-594-8007; 800-648-4544).

STEPHEN TABER, Rockland, Maine Now a national landmark, this family-operated, two-masted, 68-foot gaff-rigged schooner, built in 1871, is the oldest continuously active US merchant vessel. It used to carry bricks and cord wood, but it has been cruising Maine's Penobscot Bay region with up to 22 passengers (no children under 14) since 1946. There's running water in the cabins. Information: *Schooner Stephen Taber,* 70 Elm St., Camden, ME 04843 (phone: 207-236-3520; 800-999-7352).

SCHOONER WOODWIND, Annapolis, Maryland Even dedicated landlubbers can experience the exhilaration of schooner sailing on this 74-foot replica of a classic turn-of-the-century ship. The *Woodwind* makes several daily two-hour cruises (depending on the weather and time of year), and longer, three- to six-day voyages during May, October, and November. Guests can participate by hoisting sails or simply relax and take in the Chesapeake views. The schooner, which can carry up to 48 passengers, departs from Pusser's Landing in downtown Annapolis. Information: *Schooner Windward,* Running Free, Inc., PO Box 3254, Annapolis, MD. 21403 (phone: 410-263-7837).

GREAT SAILING AND CRUISING

Some parts of the US coastline are so sail-happy that you'd think everybody there owns a boat; if you don't, you can usually charter. Most rental boats are handled by brokers for private owners. Your level of sailing experience will determine what you get, but ask for a good-size boat if you plan a long cruise, since boats under 26 feet can be a little too cozy for a week on the water.

MARINA DEL REY, California Ever since this marina, the largest manmade recreational-boat harbor in the world, was built in the 1960s, pleasure boaters have been passing through in droves; there are 6,000 slips and plenty of docks and sailing schools. In addition to boat rentals, transient boat dock rentals are available for overnight or up to one week. Information: *Dept. of Beaches and Harbors,* 13837 Fiji Way, Marina del Rey, CA 90292 (phone: 310-305-9503; 310-305-9545 for recorded information).

NEWPORT BEACH, California Local celebs are among the 10,000 folks who keep boats in this big, beautiful, busy Southern California harbor, the largest pleasure-boat harbor in the world. There are dozens of marinas. Information: *Newport Harbor Area Chamber of Commerce,* 1470 Jamboree Rd., Newport Beach, CA 92660 (phone: 714-644-8211).

SACRAMENTO–SAN JOAQUIN RIVER DELTA, surrounding Stockton, California Better than 1,000 miles of sloughs, cuts, canals, and other streams tunnel through the tules (pronounced "two-lees," the tall rushes that give this flatland its distinctive appearance), and for some local folk, weekend cruising is a way of life. Three great rivers help form the delta labyrinth—the Mokelumne, San Joaquin, and Sacramento. The delta's banks are sprinkled with over 100 handy marinas, restaurants, and river rat hangouts where you can stop to wet your whistle, take on fuel or water, buy supplies, or merely mingle with the locals. Most rentals are houseboats, which just about anyone can handle. Information: *Stockton–San Joaquin Convention and Visitors Bureau,* 46 W. Fremont St., Stockton, CA 95202 (phone: 209-943-1987; 800-350-1987).

SAUSALITO, California This is the yachting center for San Francisco Bay, with space for over 2,000 boats in its marinas. For information on the area and yacht rentals, contact the *Sausalito Chamber of Commerce & Visitors Center,* PO Box 566, Sausalito, CA 94966 (phone: 415-332-0505; fax: 415-332-0323).

LONG ISLAND SOUND, Connecticut and New York Between the notched shoreline of Connecticut and the rocks and sand edge of Long Island, there are literally hundreds of square miles of protected cruising water. The Sunday *New York Times* classified section always contains an extensive listing of boats available for charter. For information on crewed yachts and charters, contact *Sparkman & Stephens,* 529 Fifth Ave., New York, NY 10017 (phone: 212-661-6170; fax: 212-661-1235).

HAWAIIAN ISLANDS The boating opportunities are as varied and imaginative as the islands and islanders themselves. From outrigger canoe rides to moonlight cruises, even those who cling to terra firma will be hard pressed to resist embarking on these blue waves. Here is just a sampling of some of the boating opportunities in the islands: On Oahu, *Jada Classic Sailing Adventures* (1860 Ala Moana Blvd., Suite 402, Honolulu, HI 96815; phone: 808-955-0772) offers morning and afternoon sails. Outrigger canoe rides can be arranged by *Waikiki Beach Services* at two locations: the *Outrigger Reef Hotel* (2169 Kalia Rd., Honolulu, HI 96815; phone: 808-923-3111); and the *Sheraton Waikiki* (2255 Kalakaua Ave., Honolulu, HI 96815; phone: 808-922-4422). On the Big Island, *Ocean Sports Waikoloa* (PO Box 5000, Kohala Coast, HI 96743; phone: 808-885-5555) arranges snorkeling, scuba diving, whale watching trips, and sunset sails; *Kona Coast Activities* (74-381 Kealiakehe Pkwy., Kailua-Kona, HI 96745; phone: 808-329-7529; 800-648-7529) is a sports complex that offers cruises on vessels such as an 85-foot Polynesian glass-bottomed canoe and a 50-foot trimaran equipped with a water slide and a bar. *Ocean Activities Center* on Maui (1325 S. Kihei Rd., Suite 212, Kihei, HI 96753; phone: 808-879-4485) offers just about every conceivable type of boating; and *Captain Zodiac* (PO Box 456, Hanalei, HI 96714; phone: 808-826-9371; 800-4-CAPTAIN) explores the Na Pali Coast in large inflatable rafts. With a little luck, you'll see dolphins, flying fish, humpback whales, and sea caves.

MAINE COAST Straight and bold in the southwest, deeply notched near Boothbay Harbor, and dotted with islands like Matinicus (ultra-wild) and Monhegan (crisscrossed with walking paths that take you to bluffs and boulders where you can sun yourself)—the Maine coast offers enough variety to make it among the country's best spots for cruising—provided, that is, you can handle the frequent fogs, tides, rocky shores, and scarcity of marinas. Information: *Robinhood Marine Center,* Robinhood Rd., Robinhood, ME 04530 (phone: 207-371-2525); *Bay Island Yacht Charters,* 120 Tillson Ave., Rockland, ME 04841 (phone: 207-596-7550); *Maine Sport Outdoor School,* PO Box 956, Rte. 1, Rockport, ME 04856 (phone: 800-722-0826); and *Sparkman & Stephens,* 529 Fifth Ave., New York, NY 10017 (phone: 212-661-6170; fax: 212-661-1235), for crewed yachts.

CHESAPEAKE BAY, Maryland and Virginia The sine qua non of cruising in America, 185-mile-long Chesapeake Bay, America's largest estuary, is broken by river mouths, little coves, and harbors where you can tie up and go ashore for a walk through 300-year-old towns. Scattered alongside are quaint islands like Smith and Tangier, where the people started losing their Elizabethan accents in the 1960s. The cruising season, which begins in April, continues well beyond October, when the Annapolis *In-the-Water Boat Show,* the largest in the world, is held. Information and charters (bareboats from 27 to 40 feet): *Hartge Chesapeake Charters,* Church Lane, Galesville, MD 20765 (phone: 410-867-7240).

SAILING SCHOOLS

OFFSHORE SAILING SCHOOL, Ft. Myers, Florida Founded by former Olympian and 12-meter sailor Steve Colgate, this school has seven locations offering three-day and/or week-long Learn to Sail courses, with classroom and on-water sailing instruction. The courses cover all the basics, including navigation and some spinnaker work on 27-foot extra-stable Olympic class Solings. Packages include accommodations. Advanced courses are offered on the same schedule and include Performance Sailing, Bareboat Preparation, Introductory Racing, Advanced Racing, and Live Aboard Cruising for Bareboat Certification. Locations include Stamford, Connecticut; Captiva Island, and St. Petersburg, Florida; Newport, Rhode Island; Jersey City, New Jersey; Tortola, the British Virgin Islands; St. Lucia; and the Sea of Cortez, Mexico. Information: *Offshore Sailing School,* 16731 McGregor Blvd., Suite 110, Ft. Myers, FL 33908 (phone: 941-454-1700; 800-221-4326).

ANNAPOLIS SAILING SCHOOL, Annapolis, Maryland Based in Annapolis, America's first and largest sailing school has branches in all parts of the country and on St. Croix in the US Virgin Islands. The basic two-day beginners' course includes four hours in the classroom and eight hours on the water; the three- and five-day beginners' courses give you extra time to practice your skills. Several other programs are available, including many advanced courses (handling auxiliary cruising boats, coastal navigation and piloting, and preparation for bareboat chartering), but not at all locations. Information: *Annapolis Sailing School,* PO Box 3334, Annapolis, MD 21403 (phone: 410-267-7205; 800-638-9192).

America's Most Surprising Ocean Beaches

Along America's thousands of miles of lake and ocean shores, you'll find beaches for everyone. Most of the East Coast between the brief, busy coast of New Hampshire and Miami Beach is beach-edged, and a dotted line of slim barrier beaches, which protect the mainland from the brunt of the ocean's force, extends from Long Island to Florida. There, and along the Gulf Coast of Florida, Texas, and Mississippi (which has bluer, warmer waters, more gently sloping bottoms, and less surf than East Coast shores), beach grass backs the sand; behind that, further inland, grow scrubby trees and, in the South, tropical vegetation. Often, incredible as it may seem, the deep roots of these fragile plants are all that keep the islands from washing away in storms.

Beaches up and down the Pacific Coast are, as a rule, better for beachwalking and fishing than for swimming because of riptides, heavy undertow, and cold water temperatures. However, there are exceptions. Water at beaches below Santa Barbara generally is warm enough for dips (above Santa Barbara, it's for the hardy only because of the proximity of the Alaska Current). Around Carmel, the shore is scalloped with coves; north of Ft. Ross, it's gravelly and driftwood collecting is terrific. Still farther up the coast, the beaches are edged by forests. The coastlines of Oregon and southern Washington make up one solid strip of beach cut by occasional headlands; but the best concentrations are between Pacific City and Florence, Oregon. Storm watching and whale watching in winter are popular there, as is beachwalking afterward to pick up the leavings—driftwood, most commonly, and luminous agates. And Hawaii has some of the best beaches of all; *Waikiki* is only the most famous.

In addition to the beaches described below, which are some of the country's best, there are still others described in the DIRECTIONS chapters elsewhere in this book. Consider, for instance, *Acadia National Park,* in Maine; Cape Cod, Massachusetts; the New Jersey coast, from Atlantic City to Victorian Cape May; the Outer Banks of North Carolina; Padre Island, off the Texas Gulf Coast; Carmel, California; and the entire western edge of Oregon.

EAST

OGUNQUIT, Ogunquit, Maine This little harbor town is also the site of a 3-mile stretch of beach that is one of the best in New England—partly for its length, partly for its gentle drop-off. It's also considered a good surfing beach. The Atlantic is "refreshing," as you must expect in Maine. Information: *Chamber of Commerce,* PO Box 2289, Ogunquit, ME 03907 (phone: 207-646-2939).

OLD ORCHARD BEACH, Old Orchard Beach, Maine This 7-mile, 700-foot-wide strand is the state's longest; the low surf makes it one of the safest on the Atlantic for swimming. Information: *Chamber of Commerce,* PO Box 600, Old Orchard Beach, ME 04064 (phone: 207-934-2500).

CRANE BEACH, Ipswich, Massachusetts Ipswich, a historic town with several hundred colonial homes, also boasts a wonderful 7-mile-long sweep of dune-backed sand (called *Crane's Beach* by locals). There's not much surf, so swimming is possible. There are lots of activities in town, too. Information: *Crane Beach & Castle Hill,* PO Box 563, Ipswich, MA 01938 (phone: 508-356-4354 in summer; 508-356-4351 in winter).

FIRE ISLAND, New York Walk-on ferries from Patchogue, Sayville, and Bay Shore, Long Island, take passengers to this slip of land, where there are communities for families and for both gay and heterosexual singles. In the 19,587-acre *Fire Island National Seashore,* you can camp (by reservation), swim, hike, take a guided nature walk, surf, or just sun yourself. Information: *Fire Island National Seashore,* 120 Laurel St., Patchogue, NY 11772 (phone: 516-289-4810).

THE HAMPTONS, QUOGUE, AND MONTAUK, Long Island, New York These various East End towns have some of the most attractive ocean beaches in the nation; they also have crowds and accommodations ranging from loud and tacky to regal and refined. Though many of the beaches require seasonal or temporary passes (most inns and motels provide these for guests), the restrictions often have to do with parking rather than foot access. Quogue is among the most sedate (and the nearest to Manhattan). Southampton and East Hampton are the most expensive in terms of dining and lodging, and are the best locations for catching sight of favorite celebs; West Hampton, Hampton Bays, and Montauk (the farthest east) have the highest concentration of inexpensive motels; the latter two also offer the best opportunities for boating and fishing. On weekends, from *Memorial Day* through the end of September, be prepared for lots of traffic. But when the sun shines on the miles of pristine sand and the various village greens and amazing homes nearby, there's nothing to beat it. Information: *Long Island Convention & Visitors Bureau,* 350 Vanderbilt Motor Pkwy., Suite 103, Hauppauge, NY 11788 (phone: 800-441-4601).

WATCH HILL BEACH, Watch Hill, Rhode Island Its fine surf beach is about the only thing open to the public in this exclusive town. Presiding over the entrance to the beach is the century-old *Flying Horse Carousel,* one of the oldest in the nation, in use since 1850. More beaches can be found nearby at Misquamicut and Weekapaug, with their picturesque rocky overlooks. Rentals and information: *Westerly Chamber of Commerce,* 74 Post Rd., Westerly, RI 02891 (phone: 401-596-7761).

GULF STATE PARK, Gulf Shores, Alabama These 2½ miles of sugary sand, lapped by the aquamarine gulf, make up only one short section of the 32-mile stretch between Alabama and Mobile Points—but it's the best section for vacations because of the quality of the facilities (which include cabins, campsites, an 18-hole golf course, and a saltwater fishing pier) at the well-run, modern 144-room *Gulf State Park Resort Hotel* (PO Box 437, Gulf Shores, AL 36547; phone: 205-948-4853; 800-544-4853). Information: *Gulf State Park,* 20115 State Hwy. 135, Gulf Shores, AL 36542 (phone: 205-948-7275; 800-ALA-PARK for reservations at the campground or motel).

FERNANDINA BEACH, Amelia Island, Florida Along the eastern coast of Amelia Island, this lovely 13-mile beach boasts one of the finest resorts in existence, the *Amelia Island Plantation* (phone: 904-261-6161; 800-874-6878; also see *Tennis* and *Golf*), nestled among groves of live oak and surrounded by salt marshes and dunes on the south end of the island. On the north end of the island is *Fort Clinch State Park,* offering beachside camping, and the *Municipal Fishing Pier* that juts 1,500 feet into the ocean. The *Ritz-Carlton Amelia Island* hotel (phone: 904-277-1100; 800-241-3333 for reservations) has received rave reviews for its 449 luxurious beachfront rooms, as well as its tennis and golf facilities. The nearby historic town of Fernandina Beach is worth a visit, too. Information: *Amelia Island–Fernandina Beach Chamber of Commerce,* 102 Centre St., PO Box 472, Fernandina Beach, FL 32035-0472 (phone: 904-261-3248; 800-2-AMELIA).

NORTHWEST COAST, Florida This may be the whitest sand you'll ever see; it's white like snow, white like sugar. West of Panama City, in the panhandle, US 98 runs next to these beaches (but dunes protect sunbathers from traffic noise). One US government–owned 6-mile stretch, between greater Ft. Walton Beach (pop. 69,000) and Destin (pop. 9,300), is completely undeveloped; there's no parking lot—you just stop your car anyplace along the road. Between Destin and Panama City, there are all kinds of handsome new hotels, motels, and condos, many available for rent in summer. Some of the towns east of Panama City are just being discovered to be great tourist destinations. St. George Island, near Apalachicola, has 20 miles of beaches, a state park, and a couple of hundred beach houses on stilts, some of which are available for rent through *Collins Vacation Rentals* (HCR Box 16, St. George Island, FL 32328; phone: 904-927-2900) and *Suncoast Realty* (HCR Box 2, St. George Island, FL 32328; phone: 904-927-2247; 800-341-2021). Surf fish in the gulf or pick up oysters along the bay. Not far away, the *T. H. Stone State Memorial–St. Joseph Peninsula State Park* has another 20 miles of pure white sand, nice campsites in a grove of trees, and facilities for biking, boating, clamming, and fishing. Late March and early April begin the warm-weather season, and especially around Ft. Walton Beach, the crowds (such as they are) stay until *Labor Day.* But even on *July 4* you can find empty patches of beach. September and October are the best months for deep-sea fishing, and November through March is known as snowbird season, when northerners come to worship the sun and swim in waters that rarely get below 58F. Information: *Destin Chamber of Commerce,* PO Box 8, Destin, FL 32540 (phone: 904-837-6241), and *Greater Ft. Walton Beach Chamber of Commerce,* PO Drawer 640, Ft. Walton Beach, FL 32549 (phone: 904-244-8191); *Emerald Coast Convention and Visitors Bureau,* PO Box 609, Ft. Walton Beach, FL 32549 (phone: 800-322-3319).

SANIBEL-CAPTIVA ISLANDS, Florida The 20-mile stretch of white sand on this two-island chain off the coast of Ft. Myers offers some of the best (if not *the* best) seashell collecting in the US, especially after storms with heavy northwest winds between January and March. Some good areas to search are around the lighthouse at the eastern tip of Sanibel; at *Bowman's Beach* at the island's western end; and on the southern and northern tips of Captiva. The water averages about 55F in winter, 89F in summer. Temperatures range between 65F and 86F in April, between 61F and 77F in November. Motels on the island are hidden away in groves of trees, so the atmosphere is low-key, even during the busy *Christmas* and spring school holidays. Always reserve in advance, however. Information: *Sanibel-Captiva Chamber of Commerce,* 1159 Causeway Rd., Sanibel, FL 33957 (phone: 813-472-1080).

CUMBERLAND ISLAND NATIONAL SEASHORE, Cumberland Island, Georgia The interior of this 20-mile-long, 3-mile-wide barrier island, the most southerly of Georgia's Sea Islands, is covered with marshes alive with fiddler crabs, oysters, long-legged wading birds like ibis and wood stork, and groves of weirdly contorted live oak, magnolia, holly, and pine. The 18 miles of beaches that rim these wildlands are golden and (since the ferry that serves the island from St. Marys, Georgia, makes the 45-minute trip on a fairly limited basis) fairly empty as well. The ferry operates daily, April through September, and is closed on Tuesdays and Wednesdays the rest of the year. To get off by yourself, all you have to do is walk a bit farther from the dock than anybody else. Be sure to visit *Plum Orchard Mansion,* an intact plantation home on the island with period furniture, clothing, and pictures. Bring a picnic to enjoy on the grounds. Plan well in advance and reserve one of the handful of campsites on the island or a room at the small *Greyfield Inn* (closed in August; phone: 904-261-6408). Camping and boat reservations are accepted by phone only. Information: *Cumberland Island National Seashore,* PO Box 806, St. Marys, GA 31558 (phone: 912-882-4336 for information; 912-882-4335 for reservations).

GULF ISLANDS NATIONAL SEASHORE, near Ocean Springs, Mississippi and Pensacola, Florida In the Mississippi District of the *National Seashore* there are 52 miles of sugary sand beaches on the barrier islands of Horn, Petit Bois, and East and West Ship. The first two islands, once national wildlife refuges because of the plentiful wildlife inhabiting their brackish and freshwater ponds and marshes, are now classified as Wilderness Areas. Like East Ship Island, they are accessible only by private or chartered boat; overnight visitors camp in their own boats or on the shore. Primitive island camping (and we mean bring your own everything, including water!) is very popular, especially during fall and spring. Charter boats are available through concessions in Biloxi and Ocean Springs. West Ship Island is accessible for day use (there's a boardwalk, a fishing pier, swimming, and picnic facilities, but no overnight camping) by private craft. From March through November, a ferry shuttles to and from the island daily from Gulfport and Biloxi; each boat accommodates 250. That may sound like a lot of people, but once on the island the crowds scatter, and you can end up practically alone. Regularly scheduled tours are given during the summer months. For those who prefer more company, the mainland in Ocean Springs, Mississippi, has a 51-site campground with water and electrical hookups, a boat ramp, visitors' center, picnic areas, and recreational equipment. The Florida District, which consists of Santa Rosa Island, Perdido Key, and other spots surrounding Pensacola, is accessible by car and offers a 200-site campground and historic forts. Take plenty of sunscreen, a lightweight long-sleeve shirt, and trousers: You'll need the protection, since there's hardly any shade on the islands. Information: *Gulf Islands National Seashore,* 3500 Park Rd., Ocean Springs, MS 39564 (phone: 601-875-9057) or 1801 Gulf Breeze Pkwy., Gulf Breeze, FL 32561 (phone: 904-934-2600).

HILTON HEAD ISLAND, South Carolina The 12 miles of sugar sand beach here are clean, gently sloping, and almost completely free of crushing waves. They're also wide—600 feet at low tide—and hard-packed. You can bicycle along them as well as watch birds, beachcomb (best after fall and winter storms), jog, and swim (April into October). When it's too cold for splashing in the surf, you can always swim in a pool at one of the several resort developments that make this island famous; among them are *Sea Pines* (woodsy and spread out, so you will need to rent a car; phone: 803-785-3333; 800-925-4653 for reservations) and *Palmetto Dunes* (everything in walking distance; phone: 803-785-1161; 800-845-6130). Some of the country's best golf and tennis facilities are also here, along with sailing and fishing schools, bike paths, stables, shops, restaurants, and much more. Information: *Chamber of Commerce,* PO Box 5647, Hilton Head Island, SC 29938 (phone: 803-785-3673).

KIAWAH ISLAND, South Carolina On this barrier island southwest of historic Charleston, natural sand dunes border 10 miles of wide, sandy beach. You can stroll or bike on hard ocean beach (among the best spots on the East Coast for shelling), or pick up elegant disks, stiff pen shells, lettered olives, whelks, and such. Or play tennis (30 courts) or golf (four 18-hole courses); bike along the 12 miles of paths; or swim in the ocean or any of three large resort pools. From May through August, loggerhead turtles lay their eggs on the beach in the dark of night. The climate is subtropical and balmy, with average highs in the 80s in August and September and in the 60s in February and March. Lodgings are available in the posh *Kiawah Island Resort.* Information: *Kiawah Island Resort,* 12 Kiawah Beach Dr., Charleston, SC 29455 (phone: 803-768-2121; 800-654-2924).

GRAND STRAND, Myrtle Beach, South Carolina Stretching for 60 miles from the North Carolina border to Georgetown, South Carolina, this strand of white beaches is one of the most popular seaside resorts on the Atlantic Coast and similar to the Maryland and Jersey shore. Accommodations range from modest motels to plush oceanfront villas and condominiums to dozens of hotels and motels along the boardwalk—something for everyone. The recreational possibilities are broad, with 78 golf courses, 200 tennis courts, seven fishing piers, 1,350 restaurants, 2,100 shopping outlets, and all sorts of other amusements. If that doesn't appeal, the *Grand Strand* also has nine campgrounds and two state parks, with more than 7,000 campsites. The peak activity period here is in summer, but a mild year-round climate makes it pleasant in fall and early spring as well. Although a lot of the development behind it is pretty tacky, the beach itself is one of the world's wonders. Information: *Chamber of Commerce,* PO Box 2115, Myrtle Beach, SC 29577 (phone: 803-626-7444; 800-356-3016 to order literature only).

WEST

HUNTINGTON BEACH, California "The Surfing Capital of the USA," with its 1,800-foot-long pier (built in 1902 as the Pacific's answer to Atlantic City), is one of the top spots on the coast to watch surfers catching some of the Pacific's best waves, sometimes right under the barnacle-spiked pilings. A good surfer can stay on top for the equivalent of two city blocks. Information: *Los Angeles Convention and Visitors Bureau,* 633 W. Fifth St., Suite 6000, Los Angeles, CA 90071 (phone: 213-624-7300; 800-228-2452).

PISMO BEACH, California The giant Pismo clams, once found in such numbers that farmers fed them to their hogs and cattle, now are scarce on this wide, 21-mile-long strand. But you can swim (best from August through November) and go surfing, fishing, shelling, or just drive down the beach. ATCs (all-terrain cycles) can be rented nearby, and there are dozens of special events. Motels are mainly at the north end of the strand, atop rocky cliffs; some have their own narrow beaches, accessible by twisty wooden staircases. The monarch butterfly also makes its winter home here from late October through February. Information: *Pismo Beach Chamber of Commerce and Visitors Center,* 581 Dolliver St., Pismo Beach, CA 93449 (phone: 805-773-1661; 800-443-7778 in California).

POINT REYES NATIONAL SEASHORE, Point Reyes, California The westernmost point of this triangle of land 40 minutes north of San Francisco holds the *US Weather Bureau*'s record for the foggiest, windiest station between Mexico and Canada. So, even though people swim at 4-mile *Drake's Beach* (where there's a beautiful visitors' center) and at 3-mile *Limantour, Point Reyes* is not where you come for fun in the sun—or swimming, either; there are no lifeguards and the water is frigid year-round. Rather, you come for the solitude and great walks, especially along Pacific-pounded *Point Reyes* and *McClure's* beaches. People stop for picnics on the former, the more sheltered of the pair, then move on; *McClure's* is nearly deserted most of the time because of its more difficult access (a steep, though navigable, trail). Inland, where weather is less changeable, 140 miles of hiking trails show off wildflowers, marshes, and wildlife. Also visit the self-guided *Earthquake Trail, Bear Valley Visitors' Center, Kule Loklo (Miwok Indian Exhibition)*, the Morgan horse ranch, and the historic *Point Reyes Lighthouse,* a prime spot for watching the migration of the gray whales from January through March. There are motels and bed and breakfast accommodations in Inverness and at Point Reyes Station, where heavenly fried oysters are sold from a beach shack restaurant that has no name. Information: *Point Reyes National Seashore,* Point Reyes Station, CA 94956 (phone: 415-663-1092).

KAANAPALI, Maui, Hawaii The longest of all Hawaii's great beaches, this one takes in about 3 miles of golden sand near Lahaina, the old whaling port; flat water makes it good for swimming. Edging the beach: an area full of hotels and golf courses on land owned by the Amfac Corporation, whose careful master plan has kept the architecture handsome and harmonious. Information: *Maui Visitors Bureau,* 1727 Wili Pa Loop, Wailuku, Maui, HI 96793 (phone: 808-244-3530).

OREGON COAST, Oregon It seems an impossible task to pinpoint a particular beach or section of this spectacular and multifaceted coastline. There are the northern coast's broad beaches, cozy towns, and pine forests; the central coast resort areas with golf, horseback riding, and dune buggies; and the southern coast's isolated, rugged seascapes and wildlife. The shoreline offers unlimited amounts of solitude, fresh seafood (try the geoduck), animal watching (the gray whale migration is a favorite local pastime), fishing in the deep-green sea, hiking, camping, and bird watching. Although the sun and the swimming are not always predictable, you might be surprised in the summer by just how perfect the beaches are. Take Highway 1 at any point and drive until you reach a good stopping place. Information: *Oregon State Parks and Recreation Department,* 1115 Commercial St. NE, Salem, OR 97310 (phone: 541-378-6305; 541-731-3411 from March through August only; 800-452-5687 in Oregon).

Scuba: The Wild Blue Under

Just about anyone can use a snorkel, mask, and flippers (invented, incidentally, by Benjamin Franklin), but scuba diving is something else. Handling everyday procedures and emergencies with equal aplomb takes training and practice. To buy scuba gear, refill tanks, and rent equipment at any dive shop, you have to show a scuba card proving you have passed special certification courses which require no less than five lessons or a full certification course of 35 hours, depending on the skill level. You also can get your certification on your vacation if you work at it every day. Many places nationwide offer short courses, with a good deal of work in the clear warm waters around the coral reefs.

For details on certification, contact the following organizations: the *National Association of Underwater Instructors (NAUI),* 4650 Arrow Hwy., Suite F1, Montclair, CA 91763 (phone: 909-621-5801); *PADI International,* 1251 E. Dyer Rd., Suite 100, Santa Ana, CA 92705 (phone: 714-540-7234; 800-729-7234); or your local branch of the *YMCA.*

SOME GREAT DIVING SPOTS

Throughout the city chapters of this book, we list the best dive sites for scubaphiles who find themselves near major US cities. In addition, here are some great out-of-the-way depths worth delving into. Check local diving shops for up-to-the-minute particulars.

PFEIFFER BIG SUR STATE PARK, Big Sur, California Some 30 miles south of Monterey, where the mountains shoulder down to the sea, divers in wet suits watch sea lions, some 50 varieties of fish, and the occasional whale coming by to scrape barnacles from its back on rocky chimneys in the sea floor—all this and kelp beds, too. Partington Cove, where the diving takes place, is extremely rugged, so only experienced divers should venture in. *Nepenthe* (phone: 408-667-2345), 30 miles south of Carmel, a redwood pavilion designed by a Frank Lloyd Wright disciple on a cliff 800 feet above the sea, is the place to eat and see what's going on in the area. Information: *Pfeiffer Big Sur State Park,* Big Sur Station No. 1, Big Sur, CA 93920 (phone: 408-667-2315).

JOHN PENNEKAMP CORAL REEF STATE PARK AND KEY LARGO NATIONAL MARINE SANCTUARY, Key Largo, Florida Key Largo is the first and the longest of the Florida Keys, but what is most interesting here is underwater. Running parallel to the Key for 21 miles is the country's only underwater state park, and the largest living coral reef in the continental US. The park is a scuba diver's heaven, encompassing 165 square miles of the Atlantic Ocean, hundreds of species of tropical fish, and 55 different varieties of coral. The *Florida Keys National Marine Sanctuary,* of which the *John Pennekamp Coral Reef State Park* is part, is the largest protected underwater reef system in this hemisphere. Seasoned divers rank more than 27 dives as outstanding along this reef from Key Largo to Key West; beginners and snorkelers can find magic just about anywhere they put their masks to task. A special program, "Diver into History," lets serious divers participate in an archaeological program that is salvaging centuries-old ships sunk off Islamorada. Laws forbid taking anything from the water, to preserve the area for future visitors. You also can take scuba diving tours of the reef. Gear can be rented at one of Key Largo's many dive shops or at park headquarters. Information: *John Pennekamp Coral Reef State Park,* PO Box 487, Key Largo, FL 33037 (phone: 305-451-1202; 305-451-1621 for concession and equipment rental information).

FLORIDA'S SOUTHEAST COAST, Palm Beach to Miami, Florida This 120-mile Gold Coast is rapidly becoming a gold mine, thanks to the proliferation of artificially created underwater reefs. There's everything down there—from the freighter that a hurricane once tossed into a Palm Beach socialite's front yard to a derelict Boeing 727 to scrapped sailboats and confiscated drug-running vessels—all cleaned up and deliberately scuttled to create a new habitat for marine life (not to mention great new sites for recreational divers). Information: *Greater Ft. Lauderdale Convention & Visitors Bureau* (phone: 305-765-4466).

HAWAII'S KONA COAST, Big Island of Hawaii, Hawaii On the leeward side of Hawaii Island, there's good diving in the Pine Trees area (lava-tube caves big enough to drive a Volkswagen through, plus lionfish, lobsters, and a spectacular canyon) and the Red Hills area (good caves, including one in which you'll almost always see a shark, shrimp, and banded coral). Everywhere there are arches, coral, clear warm water, and fish. *Kona Coast Divers* sponsors weekly night dives. Information: *Kona Coast Divers,* 75-5614 Palani Rd., Kailua-Kona, HI 96740 (phone: 808-329-8802).

MAUI'S SOUTHERN COAST, near Wailea, Hawaii The off-shore sunken volcano known as Molokini Crater is, by far, Maui's best-loved dive site. The portion of crescent-shaped ridge that remains above water creates a protected bay-like area that forms a natural aquarium filled with diver-friendly fish. Thrill seekers can leave the protected lee and drift-dive the vertical wall on the crater's outer edge.

Closer to Maui's shore the site known as Five Caves provides scenic shallow diving (45 feet) famous for the sightings of green turtles, along with plentiful rainbows of reef fish. Information: *Maui Hawaiian Pleasure Divers,* Wailea, HI (phone: 808-874-8611).

BONNE TERRE MINE, Bonne Terre, Missouri That's right, a century-old lead mine in landlocked Missouri boasts some of the most astounding diving in the entire US. What is now the largest freshwater dive resort in the world, with over a billion gallons of water and 17 miles of shoreline, was once a mine that became flooded with clear springwater after operations shut down in 1962. Divers liken the mine-dive experience to diving a huge shipwreck or a ghost town. Submerged relics left behind include pickaxes, shovels, ore carts, a rail system, even a timekeeper's shack, everything illuminated by the more than 300,000 watts of lighting installed by the owner/divers Doug and Cathy Goergens. The Goergens have also transformed the land above the lake into a complete dive destination, converting the mansion that once belonged to the mine's president into a posh inn and restaurant, and the old train depot into a bed and breakfast inn and saloon. There's even a petting zoo for the kids. Information: *Bonne Terre Mine,* 60 miles south of St. Louis (phone: 314-731-5003).

DIVING TRIPS

The establishments that sponsor scuba courses for beginners usually also run extensive dive trip schedules to sites accessible only by boat, for experienced divers; for lists of these operators in the area you want to visit, write the national scuba-instruction certification organizations, *PADI* and *NAUI* (above), or the *YMCA.* The following outfits also sponsor trips.

CALIFORNIA *The Diving Locker* (1020 Grand Ave., San Diego, CA 92109; phone: 619-272-1120) sponsors dive trips to San Clemente Island and Coronado Island as well as offering scuba classes, rentals, and local beach dives.

FLORIDA Diving trips in the Keys are sponsored by the *Reef Shop Dive Center* (84771 Overseas Hwy., Islamorada, FL 33036; phone: 305-664-4385; 800-741-4385); the *Diving Site* (12399 Overseas Hwy., Marathon, FL 33050; phone: 305-289-1021; 800-634-3935); *Hall's Diving Center* (1994 Overseas Hwy., Marathon, FL 33050; phone: 305-743-5929; 800-331-HALL); and *Key West Pro Dive Shop* (3128 N. Roosevelt Blvd., Key West, FL 33040; phone: 305-296-3823; 800-426-0707), specializing in personal scuba instruction and reef, wreck, and night dives, as well as equipment rental and repair. In the Palm Beach area, contact *The Scuba Club* (4708 Poinsettia Ave., West Palm Beach, FL 33407; phone: 407-844-2466; 800-835-2466) for trips to colorful reefs and to sunken ships full of eagle rays and other exotic fish. Sea turtles are seen on almost every dive. Around *Ft. Lauderdale Beach,* where there are 50 different coral reefs and several wrecks, contact *Pro Dive* (801 Seabreeze Blvd., Ft. Lauderdale, FL 33316; phone: 305-761-3413; 800-772-DIVE).

TEXAS Along the coast of South Padre Island near the Mexican border, you can dive off oil platforms, three sunken Liberty ships, or the more natural surface of coral and fossil reefs; the water is warm but becoming murkier with each passing year. Information: *American Diving,* 1807 Padre Blvd., South Padre Island, TX 78597 (phone: 210-761-2030).

Touring America's Waterways

In the days before cities were strung together by highways, people traveled from one settlement to another along rivers and chains of lakes. Quite a few have been dammed up, polluted, or defaced by highways and factories. But there are still enough open and visible water courses to suit the needs of most recreationists, and you don't have to be an expert paddler to enjoy them. Some are easy enough for beginning canoeists in open-deck canoes. Others—whitewater torrents as wild now as they were 200 years ago—are serviced by experienced boaters who will take you down in big rubber rafts.

FLATWATER CANOEING

The following waterways offer extensive opportunities for paddling trips easy enough for almost anyone—though you should check on conditions before you put in, since recent rainfalls or strong winds can turn normally navigable lakes and streams into trouble spots. Canoes usually are available at about $25 to $50 a day, with packages and reductions available for multi-day tours. Liveries usually are your best source of information about campsites en route. Most provide shuttle services from point of entry to final landing.

EAST

ALLAGASH, Maine As much a region as a 92-mile-long river and chain of lakes, the Allagash sweeps and swirls through one of the most extensive wooded areas in New England as it heads north from Telos Lake near *Baxter State Park* to its confluence with the St. John River along the Canadian border. Countless other lakes and streams, in equally wild country, are accessible by portages, so you can canoe and fish to your heart's content. May and June are high-water months; fall foliage, which flames bright in late September and early October, changes the scene once again. Guided canoe trips can be arranged through *Allagash Canoe Trips* (PO Box 713, Greenville, ME 04441; phone: 207-695-3668) or *North Woods Ways* (RR2, PO Box 159-A, Guilford, ME 04443; 207-997-3723). Information: *Maine Bureau of Parks and Recreation, Department of Conservation,* Station 22, Augusta, ME 04333 (phone: 207-287-3821).

ADIRONDACK CANOE ROUTES, New York You feel like a 19th-century woodsman as you paddle through this 100-mile-long chain of river-and-portage-connected lakes in New York's North Country. The waters are on the cold side, but still lovely for swimming and fishing. You can camp in a three-sided log lean-to on the shore of one of the lakes or on the islands in the middle. The terrain along the route is mountainous, rocky, forested, and, except for the shelters, virtually undeveloped. *Wild/Waters Outdoor Center* (Warrensburg, NY 12885; phone: 518-494-7478) offers clinics for both canoeing and kayaking. Information: *New York State Department of Environmental Conservation, Bureau of Preservation, Protection, and Management,* 50 Wolf Rd., Suite 412, Albany, NY 12233-4255 (phone: 518-457-7433).

DELAWARE RIVER, Pennsylvania, New York, New Jersey From the foothills of the Catskill Mountains in southern New York State to the *Delaware Water Gap* on the border of Pennsylvania and New Jersey, the Delaware ripples through some 120 miles of dense woodlands—the sort you wouldn't expect to find so close to big Eastern cities. Liveries include *Bob & Rick Lander's Delaware River Canoe and Raft Trips* (1336 Rte. 97, Narrowsburg, NY 12764; phone: 914-252-3925; 800-252-3925); *Jerry's Three River Canoe Corp.* (Rte. 97, PO

Box 7, Pond Eddy, NY 12770; phone: 914-557-6078); and *Kittatinny Canoes* (SR Box 360, Silver Lake Rd., Dingmans Ferry, PA 18328; phone: 717-828-2338; 800-FLOAT-KC).

SOUTH

BUFFALO NATIONAL RIVER, Arkansas This 148-mile-long stream in northern Arkansas is speckled by gravel bars and edged by forests and cliffs full of waterfalls, caves, and fern falls. The seasons—from pink and white springs to lush summers and stunning orange and red autumns—make each trip down the Buffalo a delight. Current is no problem; long pools alternate with rapids and riffles. Camping is permitted on the gravel bars and at most river accesses; hiking is available in *Wilderness Areas* and on developed day-use trails. Information: *Buffalo National River,* PO Box 1173, Harrison, AR 72602 (phone: 501-741-5443).

WHITE RIVER, Arkansas With its ghostlike morning fogs, cave-pocked shoreline bluffs, mountains, wildlife, and good trout fishing, this 100-mile stream provides a beautiful trip. Information: *Batesville Area Chamber of Commerce,* 409 Vine St., Batesville, AR 72501 (phone: 501-793-2378).

EVERGLADES NATIONAL PARK, Florida In still water, the paddling is more strenuous, but the scenery—mangroves, big buttonwood trees, bays, and tunnels—is worth the effort. There are several short trails and one 100-miler that will keep you paddling for days. Winter months are best; there are fewer bugs, you see more birds, and the weather is more invigorating. You need a backcountry use permit for overnight stays. And if you venture in by boat, you must follow a float plan. Information: *Everglades National Park,* 40001 State Rd. 9336, Homestead, FL 33034 (phone: 305-242-7700). Also see *Everglades National Park* in DIRECTIONS.

OKEFENOKEE NATIONAL WILDLIFE REFUGE, Georgia Leachings of decaying vegetation stain these still south Georgian waters black as a moonless night; they reflect every twig of the moss-veiled cypress forests through which many of the canoe trails will take you. (Others cut through "prairies"—water-rooted versions of those in Kansas.) A limited-permit system ensures that you'll have a campsite all to yourself each night. Information: *US Fish and Wildlife Service,* Rte. 2, PO Box 338, Folkston, GA 31537 (phone: 912-496-3331).

BLACK CREEK, Mississippi Canoeing this stream through forests of cypress, pines, and oaks, you can simply float along on the gentle current; at night, you can camp on snow-white sandbars. The longest trip is about 40 miles, starting at Big Creek; it takes about three days. Nearly 75% of the trip runs through the *National Forest.* Information: *De Soto National Forest,* Black Creek Ranger District, PO Box 248, Wiggins, MS 39577 (phone: 601-928-4422); *Black Creek Canoe Rentals,* PO Box 414, Brooklyn, MS 39425 (phone: 601-582-8817).

SHENANDOAH RIVER, Virginia Snaking between the Massanutten Mountains and the Blue Ridge on this majestic stream, you will almost always have a panorama of forested hills in view—though occasionally the banks are given over to farmlands or summer homes. This goes on for nearly 100 miles, but the most popular trip is the 45-mile stretch between Luray and Front Royal, which can be paddled in a long weekend. The foliage peaks in mid-October, while the fish are most active in early June. Tube rentals also are offered from June through September. Information: *Shenandoah River Outfitters,* Rte. 3, PO Box 144, Luray, VA 22835 (phone: 703-743-4159).

MIDWEST

BLUE RIVER, Indiana From Fredericksburg to this southern Indiana stream's confluence with the Ohio, there are 58-plus miles of clear, deep green water edged by forests of redbud, oak, maple. There's good rock bass fishing, especially in early summer. Information: *Old Mill Canoe Rental,* PO Box 60, Fredericksburg, IN 47120 (phone: 812-472-3140).

AU SABLE RIVER, Michigan Along the 240 canoeable miles of this twisting midwestern waterway you'll find quiet wooded shores, some in the *Huron National Forest,* and plenty of good fishing. Information: *Oscoda–Au Sable Visitors Bureau,* 4440 N. US Hwy. 23, Oscoda, MI 48750 (phone: 517-739-7322; 800-235-4625).

BOUNDARY WATERS CANOE AREA WILDERNESS, Minnesota Wild and vast, this system of streams, narrows, and island-dotted lakes created by glaciers eons ago offers—with surrounding *Superior National Forest* (of which it is a part), nearby *Voyageurs National Park,* and Ontario's *Quetico Provincial Park*—some of the most extensive canoeing on the continent. For information on the many guides, liveries, and complete outfitting services widely available, contact the local chamber of commerce in Grand Marais, Ely, or Crane Lake, Minnesota. Information: *Superior National Forest,* PO Box 338, Duluth, MN 55801 (phone: 218-720-5324; 800-745-3399 for entry permits and reservations). Also see *Voyageurs National Park and Boundary Waters Canoe Area,* in DIRECTIONS.

OZARK NATIONAL SCENIC RIVERWAYS, Missouri The Current River and its tributary the Jacks Fork together offer some 140 miles (80,000 acres) of woods, caves, springs, sinkholes, and pleasant, easy-to-negotiate pools and riffles. Information: *Ozark National Scenic Riverways,* PO Box 490, Van Buren, MO 63965 (phone: 314-323-4236).

WEST

RUSSIAN RIVER, California Fast enough to be fun, but not too fast, the 60 miles of this California stream from the Lake Mendocino Dam to the Pacific are safe almost year-round and understandably popular. The waters—deep pools, small riffles, and moderate rapids—swirl you between steep forested banks, past shores full of vineyards, orchards, and stands of redwood that hide summer cottages, to open spaces where you can smell the salt air. And it's all just an hour north of San Francisco. Information: *Burke's Russian River Canoe Rentals,* PO Box 602, Forestville, CA 95436 (phone: 707-887-1222).

MISSOURI RIVER, Montana Central Montana's wonderfully stark sagebrush-and-sandstone-cliff wilderness encompasses the 149-mile length of this *National Wild and Scenic River*. It's a great place for sun, and it's also among the best in the West for easy canoeing on free-flowing water. May, June, and September are best for wildlife watching; the cottonwoods turn to gold in late September and October. Information: *Missouri River Outfitters,* PO Box 762, Ft. Benton, MT 59442 (phone: 406-622-3295).

WHITEWATER RAFTING

After you've knifed through the 20-foot-high waves of a river racing downstream at the rate of 50,000 or 60,000 cubic feet per second, with the spray drenching your clothes and the noise of the river (something like the roar of a dozen freight trains) drowning out the screams of your companions, even the wildest roller coaster seems like a day at the beach.

But even when the same river is flowing at its normal 5,000 cubic feet per second, and even in the East, where the torrential stretches of wilderness rivers are so short that whitewater trips usually last only a day, it's not hard to understand why river-running can get into your blood. Few other means of wilderness travel put you so close to the forces of nature. And if you're not the rugged, hardy type, it's the only way to get deep into the wilderness without using a noisy motor. Many of the following have been designated *National Wild and Scenic Rivers.* This means that their routes pass through true wilderness, and it is advisable to apply for a permit (or sign up with an outfitter) well in advance—at many, early in the preceding winter—as access is strictly limited; to true river-runners, "crowd" is a dirty word. Most of the country's mightiest rivers are accessible through trips run by commercial operators—both small outfits who take their craft down one or two streams in a given region, and larger organizations that have developed regional or nationwide programs. A few are the *Sierra Club* (730 Polk St., San Francisco, CA 94109; phone: 415-776-2211); the *American River Touring Association* (24000 Casa Loma Rd., Groveland, CA 95321; phone: 800-323-ARTA); and *OARS* (PO Box 67, Angels Camp, CA 95222; phone: 209-736-4677; 800-346-6277), which specializes in *Grand Canyon* and western river trips.

Depending on where and when you go and who takes you, you may wield a paddle (with the guide in the rear shouting out instructions) or you may be just a passenger. In the very wildest waters, you'll probably go in big catamaran rafts. On trips down other rivers, the outfitter will pack along inflatable canoes or kayaks. You can get out and do some paddling on your own, even closer to the water level, when you tire of watching the cliffs, rocky banks, and forests go by—that is, if you're not worn out from the swimming, picnicking, hiking, fishing, and other diversions that the outfitters normally program into excursions. With the river action, the sourdough pancake breakfasts, the steaks and spuds dinners, the companionable evenings around campfires, and the lullaby the river sings to you through the quiet canyon nights, a trip down a great waterway is a memorable adventure that will bring out the poet in you.

COLORADO RIVER (GRAND CANYON SECTION), Arizona The most challenging of all river trips, and one of the most popular, is also, some people will tell you, one of the great moments of human experience. You shoot some 100 rapids—Badger Creek, Soap Creek, 25 Mile, House Rock, Unkar, Nevills, Crystal, Lava, Sockdolager, and Grapevine among them—as you run the 277 miles between the put-in area at Lee's Ferry and the headwaters of Lake Mead. The soaring sculptured walls and the glowing colors of their rock layers are as grand when seen from below as they are when you stand on the *Canyon* rim. And though the flow is controlled by the Glen Canyon Dam upstream, the river itself changes all the time. Summers are busy and hot; in spring you'll find comfortable temperatures in the 70s and 80s, blooming desert plants, and smaller crowds. *River Travel Center* (PO Box 6, Point Arena, CA 95468; phone: 800-882-7238) is a specialty agency handling 16 canyon outfitters. Information: For a complete list of outfitters (who go downstream in everything from dories to motor-powered rafts) and permits, contact the *River Permits Office, Grand Canyon National Park,* PO Box 129, Grand Canyon, AZ 86023 (phone: 520-638-7843; 520-638-7888 for recorded information on lodging, mule rides, river trips, and weather).

MAIN SALMON, Idaho A good trip for beginning your river-running career, Lewis and Clark's "River of No Return" offers enough deep-rolling rapids to keep you interested, but not so many that you'll spend your river hours in terror. On the 100-mile stretch between Corn Creek and Spring Bar, not far from Riggins—the stretch most commonly floated by commercial outfitters—there are warm springs and quiet pools where you can get out and splash, sandy beaches, spectacular canyons, bighorn sheep and other wildlife, and, on the north-facing slopes, stands of Douglas fir. Runs during high water in May or June are wildest; the following months through *Labor Day* are quieter. Actually, the river is floatable for 237 miles between North Fork and the confluence of the Salmon and the Snake. Private parties require permits to float the Wild section, from Corn Creek to Long Tom Bar, but only from June to September. Information: For a list of outfitters, including some who will take you the whole route, contact the *Idaho Outfitters and Guides Association,* PO Box 95, Boise, ID 83701 (phone: 208-342-1919), or the *Salmon National Forest,* PO Box 180, North Fork, ID 83466 (phone: 208-865-2383).

MIDDLE FORK OF THE SALMON, Idaho This 105-mile stretch, floated by numerous private individuals and 29 outfitters, is a National Wild and Scenic River that flows between Boundary Creek and the Main Salmon. It takes you through the *Frank Church River of No Return Wilderness,* over 80 or more wild rapids, and into the second deepest gorge on the continent (Hell's Canyon on the Snake is the deepest). During rest stops and overnights, you can explore creeks, waterfalls, side canyons, petroglyphs, historic sites, and hot springs. From June through September, *Echo* (6529 Telegraph Ave., Oakland, CA 94609; phone: 510-652-1600) arranges rafting trips along the Middle Fork and Main Salmon. Information: *Middle Fork Ranger District, Challis National Forest,* PO Box 750, Challis, ID 83226 (phone: 208-879-5204), and the *Idaho Outfitter and Guides Association,* PO Box 95, Boise, ID 83701 (phone: 208-342-1919).

SELWAY RIVER, Idaho From Paradise Guard Station at the mouth of White Cap Creek to Selway Falls, this river drops an average of 28 feet per mile. Too rocky for floating most of the time, it is among the most challenging white-water courses in the country during peak spring runoff in the last week in May and the first two in June. (Applications for permits to float from May 15 to July 31 should be submitted to the West Fork Ranger Station for random drawing the first week in February; applications *must* be received between December 1 and January 31.) Novices wouldn't want to pit themselves against the Selway, but it's a good bet for veterans. The river takes you through the 1,239,840-acre *Selway-Bitterroot Wilderness,* among the country's largest, most of which is passable only on foot or by boat. The *Idaho Outfitters and Guides Association* (PO Box 95, Boise, ID 83701; phone: 208-342-1919) provides information and can direct you to a program that will suit your needs. Information: *Bitterroot National Forest,* West Fork Ranger Station, 6735 W. Fork Rd., Darby, MT 59829 (phone: 406-821-3269) and *Nez Perce National Forest,* Moose Creek Ranger Station, PO Box 464, Grangeville, ID 83530 (phone: 208-983-2712).

SNAKE RIVER, Idaho This river in Hell's Canyon, the deepest gorge in North America (one-third deeper than the *Grand Canyon*), offers some of the most powerful whitewater in the Northwest. On the border between Oregon and Idaho, you can float 32 miles in two to four days, or take the longer, 81-mile trip to the confluence of the Grande Ronde River (five or six days). While in camp, you can hike well-maintained trails, swim, take photographs, explore ancient Indian pit houses and burial grounds, or fish—smallmouth bass and rainbow trout abound here. *Idaho Afloat* specializes in upscale family trips and short excursions for busy executives (wryly entitled "Mental Health Escapes"). Information: *Idaho Afloat,* PO Box 542, Grangeville, ID 83530 (phone: 208-983-2414).

CHAMA RIVER, New Mexico The scenic and rapids portion of this river starts at El Vado Ranch with takeout at Big Eddy above the Abiquiu Reservoir. Rio Chama includes the canyon made famous by artist Georgia O'Keeffe and is popular because of its long season (approximately mid-April through mid-September). This river hosts rafts, canoes, and kayaks, and it is a favorite for families with small children because of its relatively benign rapids and the frequent peeks at wildlife it offers. Permits are required; apply by mid-January at the latest, since only a limited number are available. The following commercial outfitters are recommended: *Randall Davey Audubon Center* (PO Box 9314, Santa Fe, NM 87504; phone: 505-983-4609), which focuses on natural history and bird watching; and *New Wave Rafting* (Rte. 5, PO Box 302-A, Santa Fe, NM 87501; phone: 505-984-1444). Information: *Bureau of Land Management,* Taos Resource Area, 224 Cruz Alta Rd., Taos, NM 87571 (phone: 505-758-8851).

DESCHUTES RIVER, Oregon An intermediate water rat will enjoy the roller coaster rapids, lots of flat water, and the warm, sometimes hot, weather usually not found elsewhere in Oregon. The river cuts through a high desert canyon, with its painted cliffs and wildlife, and is topnotch for camping, fishing, and swimming. Information: *Oregon Guides and Packers Association,* PO Box 10841, Eugene, OR 97440 (phone: 503-683-9552).

ROGUE RIVER, Oregon A *National Wild and Scenic River*, the 33 miles between Grave Creek and Watson Creek, about 25 miles from the Pacific, offer Class III rapids, high canyons, rock gorges, wildlife, good fishing (for steelhead, chinook, and silver salmon), and historic sites—Zane Grey had a cabin at Winkle Bar. There's whitewater on rapids like Mule Creek Canyon and Blossom Bar, but since there are long stretches of smooth water between them, commercial trips on the Rogue are good for families. Apply *before* February for permits. Most operators run between Grave Creek and Foster Bar. Information: *River Permits/Information,* 14335 Galice Rd., Merlin, OR 97532 (phone: 541-479-3735) or *Rogue Excursions Unlimited,* PO Box 2626, White City, OR 97503 (phone: 541-826-6222). *Oregon Guides and Packers Association,* PO Box 10841, Eugene, OR 97440 (phone: 541-683-9552) is a good source for information and advice on guides.

YOUGHIOGHENY RIVER, Pennsylvania The trip down the 7½-mile wild section of this famous Eastern whitewater stream lasts only a little over half a day, but you get quite a run for your money. The scenery is beautiful: laurel and rhododendron in the spring, wraith-like mists and lush forests in summer, and bright leaves in autumn. Information: *Ohiopyle State Park,* PO Box 105, Ohiopyle, PA 15470 (phone: 412-329-8591).

CHATTOOGA, South Carolina This *National Wild and Scenic River*, considered to be among the most beautiful in the world, can be rafted from March through October. After seeing *Deliverance,* which was filmed here, a lot of people who didn't know any better tackled the whitewater in metal canoes, which usually ended up on the river bottom, torn to pieces, or wrapped around rocks. In other words, this is no trip for beginners. But in a raft, and with a guide, almost anyone can shoot the rapids. *Wildwater Ltd.* (PO Box 309, Long Creek, SC 29658; phone: 803-647-9587) has guided over 200,000 people on the Chattooga since 1971 and will show you how to run the rapids. There are stretches suitable for any level of skill in these 47 miles, which span two national forests. Overnight trips are available. *Nantahala Outdoor Center* (13077 Hwy. 19W, Bryson City, NC 28713; phone: 704-488-6900) offers whitewater rafting trips on four more rivers in the Southeast, including the Ocoee River, one of the most popular recreational rivers in the US. Another outfitter is *Southeastern Expeditions* (50 Executive Park S., Suite 5016, Atlanta, GA 30329; phone: 404-329-0433). Canoe and kayak trips are available from all three outfitters; day outings are offered for groups.

RIO GRANDE, Texas A stretch of the Rio Grande within *Big Bend National Park* takes you through some of the most isolated country in America. You won't find much whitewater, but the floating is spectacular. Most trips run through either Santa Elena Canyon, Boquillas Canyon, or Mariscal Canyon. Santa Elena is deepest, and, because of Rockslide Rapids, it is also the wildest; Mariscal is the most remote; and Boquillas, 16 miles from end to end (although it is a 33-mile trip from put-in to pull-out), is the longest and great for sunsets. Raft trips of at least 30 miles include non-canyon stretches. Go in the spring to see a spectacular wildflower display and the bird migrations (in April), or in October, which is the residents' favorite time because of the great weather and the ordinarily reliable water flows. One portion of the river, designated the *Rio Grande Wild and Scenic River,* offers an 84-mile raft trip through the extremely remote "Lower Canyons," where "you can go for two weeks and never see another soul." A permit is required. *Far Flung Adventures* (PO Box 377, Terlingua, TX 79852; phone: 915-371-2489; 800-359-4138) explores the Rio Grande, as well as other rivers in Mexico. Information: *Superintendent, Big Bend National Park,* TX 79834 (phone: 915-477-2251). Also see *Big Bend National Park* in DIRECTIONS.

COLORADO RIVER (CATARACT CANYON SECTION), Utah In all of the immense Colorado River system, this stretch of water in *Canyonlands National Park* offers some of the most technically demanding whitewater and some of the most exciting rafting in the country—even if you don't go in the spring, when the flow is many times faster than normal. *Cataract Canyon* lies just downstream of the Green's confluence with the Colorado; trips through the canyon begin either on the Green or the Colorado and continue downstream to Lake Powell. Permits required for camping inside the park as well as rafting on certain sections of the river. Information: *Canyonlands National Park,* 125 W. 200 South, Moab, UT 84532 (phone: 801-259-7164).

GREEN RIVER (GRAY AND DESOLATION CANYONS), Utah Were you to put in on the Green below Flaming Gorge and float all the way to Lake Powell, several hundred miles later, you wouldn't find more interesting river country than this stretch between Sand Wash (about 42 miles southwest of Myton) and Green River City (some 96 miles later). *Gray Canyon* generally has the bigger rapids, but there are some in Desolation that, in the words of one river rat, will "eat you up if you don't know what you're doing." The scale of the canyon landscape is impressive. At Rock Creek, about halfway through the trip, it is as deep as the *Grand Canyon.* Views from the boat take in stands of Douglas fir, cottonwood groves, and petroglyphs from the Fremont culture of 1,200 years ago. Floating season is April through October; spring is wildest, and July and August are hottest. Permits and reservations are required year-round. Information: *Bureau of Land Management,* 900 North 700 East, Price, UT 84501 (phone: 801-637-4584).

GREEN MOUNTAIN NATIONAL FOREST RIVERS, Waitsfield, Vermont Here flow the Mad, White, Connecticut, and Winooski Rivers—calm and manageable Class I-III waterways. *Clearwater Sports* operates full-day canoeing and kayaking trips from April through October; fall foliage season is the best time for checking out the scenery, but it's pretty in the summertime, too. Information: *Clearwater Sports,* Rte. 100, Waitsfield, VT 05673 (phone: 802-496-2708).

WHITEWATER STREAMS, West Virginia The Mountain State's geographical position and topography conspire to dump abundant rain and snow on the Allegheny Highlands, a region of misty mountains, ridges, and deep gorges cut by eons of runoff. Major streams born here include the Cheat, Tygart, Greenbrier, Elk, Gauley, and Meadow, and the three sisters of the *Monongahela National Forest*—the Cherry, Williams, and Cranberry Rivers. All feature whitewater stretches suitable for various skill levels. In spring and late fall, the Gauley surges to Class III and IV whitewater levels. In the south, the New River and its rowdy tributary, the Bluestone, drain a huge, sparsely populated, and ruggedly beautiful watershed. In eastern West Virginia, the gentle Shenandoah and the Potomac and its tributaries, the South Branch and the Cacapon, combine whitewater and stunning landscapes rich in American history. Professional outfitters run trips on many of these streams in spring, summer, and fall, and also teach paddling and kayak skills. Information: *Travel West Virginia, Tourism and Parks,* 2101 Washington St. E., Charleston, WV 25305 (phone: 800-CALL-WVA).

Goin' Fishing: The Best Spots in America

America's number one participation sport has hooked 25% of the US population, so it's no wonder that huge amounts of money, not to mention bureaucratic time and effort, go into massive stocking programs. Just where you'll find all these fish at any given time can vary from year to year, depending on water conditions, weather, chemicals, and season.

A long familiarity with the habits of fish in a single lake is almost a guarantee of hefty stringers. However, as the professional bass fishermen who fish many different lakes can tell you, it's enough to have reliable knowledge of the species' habits, the water temperatures, bottom conformations, shoreline, and so on, of the area you're fishing. This information is obtained easily from local fish and game authorities, and also from area marinas and bait and tackle shops. A noteworthy angling book is *Fishing: An Angler's Dictionary* by Henry Beard and Roy McKie (Workman Publishing Co.; $5.95, paperback).

WHERE THEY BITE

EAST

Ocean fishing is big in all the coastal states—mainly for bluefish and stripers that seek out congenial water temperatures up and down the coast. Inland, fishermen work the lakes and stalk the wily trout in streams and rivers.

MOOSEHEAD LAKE, Greenville, Maine A sport fishing resort for over a century, the largest body of water in Maine provides landlocked salmon and brook and lake trout. Deep waters (246 feet) and good oxygenation make the fishing excellent throughout the season (*Memorial Day* weekend through September). Despite a variety of fishing camps in this area, at least half of the shoreline remains undeveloped. The steamer *Katahdin* cruises the lake daily in season. Call the *Moosehead Marine Museum* for reservations (phone: 207-695-2716). Information: *Moosehead Lake Region Chamber of Commerce,* PO Box 581, Greenville, ME 04441 (phone: 207-695-2702).

OCEAN CITY, Maryland The white marlin capital of the world sends fishermen out to the Baltimore and Washington Canyons, about 65 miles offshore, for dolphin, bonito, tuna, wahoo, shark, porgy, bluefish, sea bass, and blue marlin. Surf casting and jetty fishing can also yield good results. Information: *Chamber of Commerce,* 12320 Ocean Gateway, Ocean City, MD 21842 (phone: 410-213-0552; 800-62-OCEAN for recorded information).

LAKE WINNIPESAUKEE, near Laconia, New Hampshire The largest body of water in New Hampshire (72 square miles) offers some of the best stringers of lake trout and landlocked salmon in New England. Some 283 miles of shoreline on the mainland, and still more on 274 scattered islands, provide good habitat for bass and pickerel. Salmon are most active in April, May, and June (at the surface); later you've got to fish deeper. Lake trout are liveliest in April and May. There's ice fishing (for lake trout only) from the time the lake freezes through March. Information: *Lakes Region Association,* PO Box 589, Center Harbor, NH 03226 (phone: 603-253-8555), and the *New Hampshire Fish and Game Department,* 2 Hazen Dr., Concord, NH 03301 (phone: 603-271-3211), which has excellent literature on the area.

BATTENKILL RIVER, near Manchester, Vermont This famous Vermont fishing stream, a forest-edged, sun-dappled angler's idyll, is heavily fished, but its long, slow, waist-deep pools give the brookies and browns who inhabit it "a two-day look at every visitor" (according to one veteran), and since the fish are not hatchery-bred, they don't regard man as a friend. The upshot is that the average fisherman doesn't get much. *Orvis,* a nationally known tackle company based nearby, can answer questions about when and where (see also *Fishing Schools,* below). Information: *Orvis,* Historic Route 7A, Manchester, VT 05254 (phone: 802-362-3622; 800-235-9763).

SOUTH

The Southern angler heads for the Gulf or the Atlantic, where offshore oil rigs and artificial reefs draw huge populations of big fish, or for the huge Arkansas, Kentucky, and Tennessee impoundments, which are managed with fishing in mind. Crappie and largemouth bass are usually available, but depending on the area, you'll also get smallmouth, trout, stripers. Try western North Carolina and northern Georgia for trout.

LAKE EUFAULA, near Eufaula, Alabama One of the country's finest largemouth fisheries, not just for the quantity of available fish but also for their size. This impoundment of the Chattahoochee River along the Georgia-Alabama line is the site of many annual tournaments. Spring and fall are best. Information: *Chamber of Commerce,* PO Box 697, Eufaula, AL 36072-0697 (phone: 205-687-6664).

WHITE RIVER, Lakeview, Arkansas Local fishermen call this wilderness Ozarks stream the trout capital of the world; the lake water released below the Bull Shoals Dam is ideal for trout propagation, and record catches of rainbows and browns are not uncommon. Information: For a list of outfitters, request the *Ozark Mountain Region Guide* from the *Arkansas Department of Parks and Tourism,* 1 Capitol Mall, Little Rock, AR 72201 (phone: 501-682-7777; 800-NATURAL).

BOCA GRANDE PASS, Boca Grande, Florida One of the world's most famous fishing grounds, for the silvery legions of fighting tarpon that invade the Gulf every summer, will give you the liveliest action in June; the season extends from March through October. Information: *Boca Grande Area Chamber of Commerce,* PO Box 704, Boca Grande, FL 33921 (phone: 813-964-0568).

DESTIN, Florida Residents call Destin "the world's luckiest fishing village," and with more than 125 party boats and charters (the state's largest fishing fleet) charging into the Gulf every day, they just may be right. The quarry: pompano, grouper, king mackerel, sailfish, and blue marlin. The *Destin Seafood Festival* takes place the first weekend of October; the popular *Deep Sea Fishing Rodeo* consumes the entire month of October. Information: *Chamber of Commerce,* PO Box 8, Destin, FL 32540 (phone: 904-837-6241); or *Emerald Coast Convention and Visitors Bureau* (phone: 800-322-3319).

EVERGLADES, Everglades City, Florida This national treasure offers year-round freshwater and saltwater fishing. Freshwater fish include largemouth bass and some exotic species, such as oscars (a popular aquarium fish that some people like to eat). The real fishing, however, is on the edge of the park, where brackish water is created by mixing fresh and saltwater. Here, the favorite sport is reeling in redfish (there's a limit of one fish per person per day). Other species include bonefish, snook, tarpon, four varieties of snapper, flounder, and grouper. Information: *Everglades National Park,* 40001 State Rd. 9336, Homestead, FL 33034 (phone: 305-242-7700). Also see *Everglades National Park* in DIRECTIONS.

THE KEYS, Florida Islamorada, Marathon, and Key West are the three main centers in the area for bonefish, permit (a kind of pompano), and tarpon; Islamorada's sport fishing fleet is one of the US's largest. And that doesn't include the deep-sea fishing—for marlin, sailfish, grouper, and the other big ones. Information: *Chamber of Commerce,* 1222 Overseas Hwy., Marathon, FL 33050 (phone: 305-743-5417; 800-842-9580); *Greater Key West Chamber of Commerce,* 402 Wall St., Key West, FL 33040 (phone: 305-294-2587; 800-LAST-KEY); and *Chamber of Commerce,* PO Box 915, Islamorada, FL 33036 (phone: 305-664-4503; 800-322-5397). Also see *Florida Keys and John Pennekamp Coral Reef State Park* in DIRECTIONS.

LAKE TOHOPEKALIGA, Kissimmee, Florida A vast 19,000-acre expanse that experts consider one of the hottest bass lakes in the state. Expect to net fish in the seven- to 13-pound range. The best season is late winter to early spring. Information: *Game and Fresh Water Fish Commission,* 620 S. Meridian St., Tallahassee, FL 32399-1600 (phone: 904-488-4676).

TEN THOUSAND ISLANDS, near Naples, Florida This mangrove wilderness of creeks, oyster-bottomed coves, and rivers, stretching 60-odd miles along the Gulf Coast, is one of the best spots in the US for snook, a battling tropical fish found only in southern Florida; May through July is the season. Information: *Naples Area Chamber of Commerce,* 3620 Tamiami Trail N., Naples, FL 33940 (phone: 813-262-6141).

LAKE OKEECHOBEE, Okeechobee, Florida Some of the world's finest speckled perch (crappie) fishing can be found at this inland sea, the second largest body of fresh water entirely within the US; you also can take bluegill and bass, plus catfish that sometimes take two hands to display. The season runs from November to April, but the crappies bite year-round. Every year, the *Speckled Perch Festival, Parade, and Rodeo* has its heyday on the second weekend in March. Information: *Okeechobee County Chamber of Commerce,* 55 S. Parrott Ave., Okeechobee, FL 34972-2970 (phone: 813-763-6464).

LAKE BARKLEY AND KENTUCKY LAKE, near Cadiz, Kentucky The 220,000 acres of water shared by these two impoundments offer some of the state's most consistently fine bass fishing—with an abundance of largemouth, smallmouth, and spotted bass (the last two are especially plentiful in Kentucky Lake). The area has also been called the "crappie capital of the world." March through November is the season. Information: *Land Between the Lakes, TVA,* 100 Van Morgan Dr., Golden Pond, KY 42211 (phone: 541-924-5602).

GRAND ISLE, Louisiana Internationally known for its deep-sea fishing, especially around offshore oil rigs. The surf fishing—for trout, flounder, sheepshead, tarpon, reds, and mackerel—is also great. There's crabbing, too. Information: *Chamber of Commerce of Lafourche and the Bayou Region,* PO Box 1462, Larose, LA 70373 (phone: 504-693-6700).

OUTER BANKS, North Carolina The proximity of the Gulf Stream to this slender finger of sand has brought good fishing close to shore. There are blue and white marlin, flounder, weakfish, bonito, tuna, dolphin, barracuda, wahoo, sailfish, Spanish and king mackerel, and bluefish aplenty. Best fishing is from April through November. Information: *Outer Banks Chamber of Commerce,* PO Box 1757, Kill Devil Hills, NC 27948 (phone: 919-441-8144).

LAKES MARION AND MOULTRIE, near Santee, South Carolina This 171,000-acre impoundment of the Santee and Cooper Rivers, the first in the country with a landlocked striped bass program, offers some of the best fishing for these fighters, and has produced world-record channel catfish and warmouth as well as black crappie, and bowfin. Crappie and largemouth are especially plentiful. An Arkansas bluefish weighing 109 pounds, 4 ounces (biggest in the world) was caught here in 1991. Information: *Santee-Cooper Country,* Drawer 40, Santee, SC 29142 (phone: 803-854-2131; 800-227-8510).

NEW RIVER, near Hinton, West Virginia Considered *the* finest smallmouth bass fishing stream in the eastern US, it also is renowned for its channel and flathead catfish. It produces good creels of trophy white bass, hybrid striped bass, muskellunge, walleye, and rock bass. Best spots are downstream at the Bluestone Dam and 10 miles above Bluestone Lake. Primarily a whitewater river, it's not for the inexperienced boater, but it is an assured thrill for the practiced canoeist. There are pools for flat-bottomed boats, and it is suggested that the eager angler learn where to put-in safely. Information: *Division of Natural Wildlife Resources Section,* State Capitol Complex, Bldg. 3, Charleston, WV 25305 (phone: 304-558-2771) or *New River Gorge National River,* 104 Main St., PO Box 246, Glen Jean, WV 25846 (phone: 304-465-0508).

MIDWEST

Michigan, Minnesota, and Wisconsin together boast nearly five million fishing license holders, so it's not surprising that the angling is lively. The best fishing is for trout on Michigan's Au Sable, Manistee, Pine, Rifle, and upper Muskegon Rivers; for steelhead in April; and for smallmouth bass in lakes in the northwest part of the lower peninsula.

In Minnesota, on the other hand, walleye is the fish—but you can also get smallmouth on the waters along the Canadian border; pike in the north, muskie in the Boy River chain, the Mantrap chain, and Big Lake and Leech Lake; and kamloops and native steelhead in the streams that empty into Lake Superior.

Missouri's fishing is mainly in the big southwestern reservoirs, but there's also float fishing for bass and panfish on the Jack's Fork, Meramec, Eleven Point, Niangua, James, Big Piney, and Current Rivers. Ohio's western basin produces some of the US's best walleye fishing in spring and summer, off reefs, island shorelines, and submerged shoals. Wisconsin produces salmon beginning in August around Kenosha, Milwaukee, and Racine. Fishermen troll for lake trout in summer and go for cohos and brown trout between Bayfield and Washburn. There are smallmouth in all the northern lakes, especially on the Door County peninsula in July and August.

LAKE MILLE LACS, near Brainerd, Minnesota The fact that between opening day and late July the harvest of walleyes allegedly runs to two-and-a-half tons of fish a day (or about 400,000 over a one-year period) gives you an idea of the scope of the fishing here. Information: *Brainerd Chamber of Commerce,* 124 N. Sixth St., Brainerd, MN 56401 (phone: 218-829-2838; 800-450-2838).

WEST

Salmon fishing in Alaska is the standard by which all other salmon fishing is matched; you can get kings in May and June and silver salmon in autumn. But California is the bigger fishing state, with over two million holders of fishing licenses and 500 charter boats leaving from ports up and down the coast—for salmon in the north, and for yellowtail, albacore, and bonito in the south.

Trout is king in Colorado, Idaho, the Black Hills of South Dakota, western Montana, and the mountain lakes of California and Washington. Idaho's Snake, Clearwater, and Salmon Rivers are visited every year by huge quantities of steelhead and chinook in October, November, March, and April. Hawaiian catches hold more than half of the *International Game Fish Association* records for blue marlin–but there's also adventure to be had in going for bonefish (not in the flats as in Florida but in deep water) and surf casting.

In Oregon and Washington, charters go for salmon and tuna from June through September. Chinook and silver run in summer and early fall, and steelhead in winter. Meanwhile, there are walleye in Missouri River impoundments in South Dakota, and in North Dakota, smallmouths around islands and flooded butte tops of the various impoundments. In Utah, 200-mile-long Lake Powell has crappie, striped bass, and walleye; bass are active March through May and late September and early November.

SACRAMENTO RIVER, Red Bluff, California Especially downstream from Redding to Hamilton City (July through December), this river offers excellent king salmon fishing. Hefty 25- to 30-pounders are common, and 40-pounders are occasionally pulled out. The Balls Ferry area south of Redding and the mouths of the American and Feather Rivers are also good, as is the steelhead fishing in the Klamath and Trinity Rivers, to name just a few.

Information: *Sports Wild,* 327 Walnut St., Red Bluff, CA 96080 (phone: 916-527-3225).

KONA COAST, Big Island of Hawaii, Hawaii All but one of those record fish caught in Hawaii were pulled in off the Kona Coast. Charters are plentiful around the port of Kailua. Information: *Hawaii Visitors Bureau,* 75-5719 Kona Plaza W., Alii Dr., Kailua-Kona, HI 96740 (phone: 808-329-7787).

GREATER YELLOWSTONE AREA, West Yellowstone, Montana Here flow the Madison, Henry's Fork, Gallatin, and Firehole Rivers—all blue-ribbon streams. Wild rainbows and browns tempt the angler from late May and June, when the salmon fly hatch occurs (some are as long as four inches) and the big trout go crazy. Some catches have been as long as 27 inches. From August until late October, the mayfly and caddis fly hatch and there's more action. Information: *Bud Lilly's Trout Shop,* 39 Madison Ave., PO Box 698, West Yellowstone, MT 59758 (phone: 406-646-7801).

COLUMBIA RIVER, Oregon May and June shad runs are so huge that nearly everyone catches one of these strong-running, high-leaping fish; stringers of 25 (the limit) are not uncommon. Walleye fishing is a major attraction as are salmon and steelhead. Information: *Chamber of Commerce, Port Marina Park,* Hood River, OR 97031 (phone: 541-386-2000; 800-366-3530).

DESCHUTES RIVER, Central Oregon This blue ribbon expanse, which is divided into the Upper Deschutes and the Lower Deschutes, offers excellent and abundant fishing. Delicious wild trout crowd the Upper, and summer steelhead cavort in the Lower. There's also lots of flatwater on the river for easy put-in. The camping is great, as is the weather, although it does get hot in July and August. The fishing is so good that unfortunately you can expect quite a bit of river traffic, especially in summer. Information: *Oregon Outdoors Association,* PO Box 10841, Eugene, OR 97440 (phone: 541-747-9688).

PORT ARANSAS, Texas Some 70 charter boats operate out of this small town on Mustang Island, one of a handful of long, skinny islands that skim Texas's Gulf Coast. Sportsmen come by the dozen to cruise out to sea in search of finned fighters such as tarpon, sailfish, tuna, and marlin. But you don't have to be a diehard fisherman to have a great time here. Party boats accommodating anywhere from 18 to 100 passengers sail out to the snapper banks, about one-and-a-half hours offshore, allowing anglers to haul in fish by the basketful. The so-called electric reels provided on the boats going out after snapper may take away some of the sport—just press a button and the reel whirls into action, bringing in a hooked fish in a trice. If you don't want to have to give away all your catch, stay in a motel with housekeeping facilities. Information: *Tourist Bureau,* PO Box 356, Port Aransas, TX 78373 (phone: 512-749-5919; 800-45-COAST). Also see *Padre Island* in DIRECTIONS.

ILWACO, Washington Each summer, a fleet of charter boats goes out into the Pacific for kings and silvers at the Salmon Capital of the World; several thousand salmon are caught offshore every year. Some fishermen, in fact, complain that they get their limit almost as soon as they leave shore and don't know what to do with the rest of the day. The area also is famous for its razor clam digging. If, however, you have no luck, try the wonderful *Ark* restaurant (phone: 206-665-4133) in Nahcotta for great seafood. Information: *Long Beach Peninsula Visitors Bureau,* PO Box 562, Long Beach, WA 98631 (phone: 206-642-2400; 800-451-2542 in the US and Canada).

FISHING SCHOOLS

In the last few years, a number of fishing pros and tackle manufacturers have taken it upon themselves to teach the bumbling angler the fine art of filling up a stringer, so even if you didn't grow up in a fishing family, you can quickly begin acquiring the skills necessary to keep you hauling them in with the best. Some provide instruction in fly-fishing and concentrate on trout; others teach you bait- and spin-casting techniques.

BUD LILLY'S FLY-FISHING SCHOOL, West Yellowstone, Montana Complete one-, three-, and five-day programs are offered. More informal programs are run daily in and around *Yellowstone National Park;* special classes are offered for women. Information: *Bud Lilly's Trout Shop,* 39 Madison Ave., PO Box 698, West Yellowstone, MT 59758 (phone: 406-646-7801).

JOAN AND LEE WULFF FISHING SCHOOL, Lew Beach, New York Although Lee Wulff passed away in 1991, Joan continues to share her expertise with anglers of all skill levels at this school in the Catskills, just 120 miles from New York City. The Beaverkill is one of several productive waters where you can practice. Weekend courses (which include fly casting instruction) are offered in trout fishing, or you may take a course devoted entirely to just fly casting. Weekends in May and June only. Information: *Joan and Lee Wulff Fishing School,* HCR 1, PO Box 70, Lew Beach, NY 12753 (phone: 914-439-4060).

SPORTFISHING SCHOOL, Cape Hatteras, North Carolina This is one of the few places in the country that teaches saltwater fishing. The week-long curriculum includes two Gulf Stream charter boat excursions and a surf casting course on the beach. Classroom instruction on sound and inlet fishing, tackle, and fish identification also is featured. Held in the spring, the course fills up very quickly, so register early. Information: *Sportfishing School, North Carolina State University,* Continuing Education and Professional Development, PO Box 7401, Raleigh, NC 27695 (phone: 919-515-2261).

ORVIS FLY-FISHING SCHOOL, Manchester, Vermont This manufacturer of fine fishing gear, in business since 1856, has taught the intricacies of the sport to such luminaries as the late Supreme Court justice Potter Stewart, and in the opinion of some who know the field, its program—which includes practice in the company's stocked ponds, dry runs on the famous Battenkill (see above), and classroom sessions—is one of the best of its kind. Students stay at the colonial *Equinox* hotel (phone: 802-362-4700). In November, the school moves to Florida. Contact them for their complete *Guide and Outfitter Program,* which lists available fishing vacations around the country. Information: *Orvis,* Historic Route 7A, Manchester, VT 05254 (phone: 802-362-3900; 800-235-9763).

Mountain Climbing and Mountains

Like all great sports, mountaineering allows the participant to choose the severity of the test—from matching one's skills to challenging them. Climbs can range from simple but rugged hikes requiring some technical work (the use of chocks, nuts, ropes, ice axes, and crampons to get over vertical rock faces and icy surfaces) to high-altitude expeditions lasting weeks and requiring specialized skills, great reserves of strength and endurance, and sophisticated equipment. But two rules always apply: You are only as safe as your judgment and training are good, and the experience always is exhilarating.

Note: Because of severe floods and fires, many trails and sections of America's National Parks have been closed down. Therefore, we advise travelers to call first before planning a trip.

AMERICA'S MOUNTAINS FOR THE CLIMBING

ALASKA RANGE, Alaska From climbing to the summit of Mt. McKinley to experiencing Ruth Glacier (adjacent to the *Denali Preserve*), this wilderness offers enough exhilarating challenges to last a lifetime. Information: *Alaska-Denali Guiding,* PO Box 566, Talkeetna, AK 99676 (phone: 907-733-2649).

LONGS PEAK, near Estes Park, Colorado One way to reach this 14,255-foot summit in *Rocky Mountain National Park* involves a long, challenging trek from the Longs Peak Ranger Station through aspen stands and conifer forests, tundra, alpine meadows, and boulder fields through the Keyhole (about 8 miles). This is the only part that can be climbed by novices. Meltout is usually mid-July through September, but snow squalls do happen occasionally. The north face route is less crowded, but advanced technical climbing skills are required. There are over 100 designated technical routes. Permits are required year-round for overnight camping or bivouacking; reservations are accepted by phone or mail. Information: *Backcountry Office, Rocky Mountain National Park,* Estes Park, CO 80517 (phone: 970-586-1242).

MT. KATAHDIN, near Millinocket, Maine The 5,267-foot peak in *Baxter State Park,* the northern terminus of the *Appalachian Trail,* rises sharply as you get close to the 4,000-foot timberline. Most routes don't require ropes, and the climb takes a day—but slopes full of loose rock can make the going tough. Advance reservations required for camping. Information: *Baxter State Park,* 64 Balsam Dr., Millinocket, ME 04462 (phone: 207-723-5140).

MT. MARCY, near Lake Placid, New York This 5,344-foot Adirondack peak (the highest in the state) can be reached in a day over a variety of routes—most of them steep trails that make many climbers wish they were in better shape. The area offers ice and rock climbing challenges as well. The forests at the bottom—full of ferns and trees whose foliage seems almost electric green—may remind you of the Pacific Northwest rain forests. A permit is required if you are camping for more than three days in a single location or with more than nine in a group. Information: *New York State Department of Environmental Conservation,* Rte. 86, Ray Brook, NY 12977 (phone: 518-897-1200; 518-576-4796 for permits).

MT. HOOD, near Government Camp, Oregon The 11,245-foot summit of this active volcano has been conquered by many, but the climb takes considerable technical know-how and preparation; it is the inexperienced, poorly equipped climber who is most apt to be injured (and well over a hundred people have lost their lives on this mountain). Most people follow the southside route, which departs from the *Timberland Lodge* (phone: 503-231-7979; 800-547-1406), where you can register and get current conditions at a 24-hour climbing station. Then you're off for the beautiful trip—beginning at midnight, past scenic glaciers and fumaroles. The best climbing is from mid-May to mid-July. Information: *Mt. Hood Visitors Center,* 65000 E. Hwy. 26, Welches, OR 97067 (phone: 503-666-0771).

MT. RAINIER, near Ashford, Washington Visible on a clear day for over 100 miles in all directions, this 14,410-foot mountain, the fifth highest in the lower 48 states, is lush with wildflowers and giant forests below the timberline, heavily glaciated above it. The two-day trip to the top, which takes you over glaciers and crumbling lava, is long, strenuous, demanding, and not without hazards—but anyone in good condition can do it with a guide and the proper equipment. Information: *Mt. Rainier National Park,* Tahoma Woods, Star Route, Ashford, WA 98304-9751 (phone: 206-569-2211). Also see *Mt. Rainier National Park* in DIRECTIONS.

GRAND TETON, near Jackson, Wyoming Looking at it from below, you'd never think that relatively inexperienced climbers could safely scale the awe-inspiring 13,770-foot summit. However, the granite rock offers plenty of hand- and footholds—everything you need to climb a mountain, one step at a time, with some training, the proper equipment, and a guide (which more experienced climbers may be able to do without). *Exum Mountain Guides,* which operates the *School of American Mountaineering* (PO Box 56, Moose, WY 83012; phone: 307-733-2297 from June to mid-September), and *Jackson Hole Mountain Guides* (PO Box 7477, Jackson, WY 83001; phone: 307-733-4979) will take you on the four-day Grand Teton course and climb, as well as offer a three-week teen climbing camp. Information: *Grand Teton National Park,* PO Drawer 170, Moose, WY 83012 (phone: 307-739-3300). Also see *Grand Teton National Park and Jackson Hole* in DIRECTIONS.

CLIMBING SCHOOLS

Climbing is not a forbidding sport, even for beginners, but the only way to start is with training. A beginner's one-day course is helpful; in the West, such courses are offered by *Exum Mountain Guides* in *Grand Teton National Park* (PO Box 56, Moose, WY 83012; phone: 307-733-2297, seasonal) and the *Yosemite Mountaineering School* in *Yosemite National Park* (Yosemite, CA 95389; phone: 209-372-8344, June to mid-September; 209-372-1244, rest of the year). In the East, the *Eastern Mountain Sports Climbing School* (PO Box 514, North Conway, NH 03860; phone: 603-356-5433) offers all levels of instruction year-round. *Outward Bound* (Rte. 9D, R2, Box 280, Garrison, NY 10524-9757; phone: 914-424-4000; 800-243-8520) conducts training programs nationwide. A one-day course will give a not too strenuous introduction to belaying, anchoring, rappelling, and moderate-angle climbing; and even with these modest skills you will be able to take rocks that you'd have judged unclimbable in your pre-course life.

Better than a one-day course (which is really more orientation and encouragement than adequate training for rigorous climbs) is a week-long or multi-week course, which provides an active, exciting vacation. The one you pick should depend on where you want to be and what you want to learn—rock work, snow and ice techniques, or expedition planning. Some courses concentrate on one subject; others combine the three.

COLORADO MOUNTAIN SCHOOL, Estes Park, Colorado Basic to advanced ice, snow, and rock climbing courses and climbs in *Rocky Mountain National Park*, lasting from one to seven days—as well as 11- to 26-day expeditions to Alaska, Africa, Mexico, Bolivia, Argentina, and countries of the former Soviet Union—are offered year-round by this establishment. Information: *Colorado Mountain School*, PO Box 2062, Estes Park, CO 80517 (phone: 970-586-5758).

NANTAHALA OUTDOOR CENTER, Bryson City, North Carolina This wilderness adventures center, the largest whitewater canoe and kayak instruction facility in the US, also offers a program of weekend and five-day rock climbing clinics for beginners and intermediates, plus regional bicycle tours in the area around the Great Smokies. Information: *Nantahala Outdoor Center*, 13077 Hwy. 19W, Bryson City, NC 28713 (phone: 704-488-2175).

AMERICAN ALPINE INSTITUTE, Bellingham, Washington One of the most comprehensive guide, training, and expedition centers for alpine, rock, and expedition climbing, waterfall ice, winter mountaineering, glacier travel, crevasse rescue, and backcountry skiing. The institute offers a rich mix of courses and guided trips that last anywhere from two days to six weeks and are designed for students at all ability levels. Alaska, Washington, Oregon, California, Nevada, Colorado, and New Hampshire are the US locations; foreign destinations include Mexico, Equador, Bolivia, Chile, Argentina, the Alps, Nepal, and occasionally India. Information: *American Alpine Institute*, 1515 12th St., Bellingham, WA 98225 (phone: 206-671-1505).

RAINIER MOUNTAINEERING, Tacoma, Washington Seminars in snow and ice climbing and guided summit climbs of Mt. Rainier are offered at this Northwestern institution. Information: *Rainier Mountaineering,* 535 Dock St., Suite 209, Tacoma, WA 98402 (phone: 206-627-6242).

Wilderness Trips on Foot

Building your backpacking skills to the point that you can go deep into a trackless wilderness for a few weeks and come out none the worse for wear takes some time, but it's not impossible. Day hikes are a good introduction, and all the national and state parks and forests and various other public lands have trails that are perfect for simple walks. You'll be breaking in your boots so that blisters will be less likely to develop over extended treks, and you'll be building up your stamina.

From there, short trips close to home are your best bet. Or you can sign up for one of the many outdoor programs that school tenderfeet in wilderness and hiking skills. Guided trips build confidence and provide companionship. A few areas of the US have the counterparts of the hikers' huts scattered all over the Alps; you don't have to carry a tent or even food.

Then there are thousands of square miles of hikeable terrain throughout the country, with easy trails for novices, steeper and less well maintained ones for more experienced hikers, and huge wildernesses where you can hike cross-country with just a topographic map and compass. For casual hikers, *500 Great Rail Trails* (published by *Rails-to-Trails Conservancy;* $7.95 for members; $9.95 for non-members, plus $1.50 for postage) is a directory to paths created on old rail corridors. Listings are by state, and there are a map and resource list for each state covered. For more information, contact *Rails-to-Trails Conservancy,* 1400 16th St. NW, Suite 300, Washington, DC 20036 (phone: 202-797-5400).

Note: Because of severe floods and fires, many trails and sections of America's National Parks have been closed down. Therefore, we advise travelers to call first before planning a trip.

EASY LONG TRIPS

On these trips, you don't have to pack anything more than the clothes you'll need for the time you're away from home. Hikers' huts and inns provide your shelter.

YOSEMITE NATIONAL PARK, Yosemite, California The High Sierra camps in this park are among the few places in the US where you can stay in the mountains overnight without having to camp out. The five tent-dormitory groups are roughly 9 miles apart. Hot showers, linen, blankets, soap, towels, and breakfast and dinner are provided. Reservations are now by lottery. Applications are due between October 15 and November 30. In early December only 1,000 names (usually out of 4,000) will be chosen. The longer the season the better the chances of getting a shot—depending on snowfall and meltout, the dormitory operates from the end of June to mid-September. If there's too much snow on your designated date, you miss your turn for that year. Information: *Yosemite Concession Services,* 5410 E. Home Ave., Fresno, CA 93727 (phone: 209-454-2002). Also see *Yosemite National Park* in DIRECTIONS.

HAWAII VOLCANOES NATIONAL PARK, near Hilo, Hawaii Hiking here is dramatic for the simple reason that you can walk over the hot floor of an active volcano. Many trails of varying lengths traverse the park—some are less than 1 mile, while one trip is a four-day excursion to the summit of Mauna Loa and back. The park provides basic cabins for shelter, but you can bring a tent to sleep in if you choose—a good idea if it gets cold. For hiking in Hawaii in general, contact the *Sierra Club* (1111 Bishop St., Suite 511, Honolulu, HI 96803; phone: 808-538-6616). Information: *Hawaii Volcanoes National Park,* PO Box 52, Hawaii National Park, HI 96718 (phone: 808-967-7311). Also see "Hawaii Volcanoes National Park," *Hawaii (The Big Island), Hawaii* in DIRECTIONS.

GLACIER NATIONAL PARK, West Glacier, Montana You can't exactly backpack from *Sperry,* one of two rugged stone chalets in this park, to *Granite Park,* the other, but you can do separate overnight trips to both. Only the restrooms, in separate buildings, and the kitchens at both chalets have been modernized, so they're much as they were when built around World War I. Both are lit after dark by candlelight, both are in the *National Register of Historic Landmarks,* and both are open only in July and August; rates include three meals. Reserve well in advance (in writing only). Information: *Belton Chalets,* PO Box 188, West Glacier, MT 59936 (phone: 406-888-5511 from mid-May to mid-September). Also see *Glacier National Park* in DIRECTIONS.

WHITE MOUNTAINS NATIONAL FOREST, around North Conway, New Hampshire In the heart of the Presidential range, a system of nine hikers' huts maintained by the *Appalachian Mountain Club* gives you almost unlimited hiking variety—both above and below tree line. No two are quite alike: Lakes of the Clouds, situated at the edge of two icy blue lakes above tree line, seems relatively new; the Madison Hut, just above tree line, is built of stone and seems almost ancient. Blankets (but not linen), dinners, and breakfasts are provided for the nightly charge (non-members pay a higher fee). Various packages are available. Reservations are essential. Information: *AMC,* PO Box 298, Gorham, NH 03581 (phone: 603-466-2727).

INN-TO-INN HIKING, around Vermont A group of country inns along a 100-mile section of Vermont's *Long Trail* have teamed up to offer special trips during which you sleep in big brass beds under antique quilts, soak your sore muscles in claw-footed bathtubs, and bring your gear and car to the selected finish each morning, where staff members will await your later arrival as the innkeeper drives you back to the day's starting point. The season begins in May and continues through October (or until the first big snowfall, whichever comes first). Reservations required. Information: *Country Inns Along the Trail,* c/o *Churchill House Inn,* RR3, PO Box 3265, Brandon, VT 05733 (phone: 802-247-3300; fax: 802-247-6851).

BEST BACKPACKING SPOTS

There's good backpacking all over the country—even in the Midwest, where most of the forests have given way to farms and pastures. The best hiking and backpacking, however, lie in 11 general regions—Alaska, the Northwest Coast ranges, the Cascade range (slightly inland in Washington, Oregon, and northern California), the Columbia Plateau (just slightly inland from the Cascades), the Rockies (swooping through Idaho, western Montana, most of Wyoming and Colorado, and northern New Mexico), the Great Desert (covering most of Nevada), the Sierra (in California), the Colorado Plateau (northern Arizona, northwestern New Mexico, the southern two-thirds of Utah), the Ozarks of northern Arkansas and southern Missouri, the Appalachians (extending from northern Maine through Tennessee and Virginia), and the north woods of northern Michigan, Wisconsin, and Minnesota. Each area has its particular characteristics.

Alaska's mountains, valleys, forests, and oceans are all wilderness. The climate is wet and temperate in the southern part of the state, drier and much colder (with winters that fall to 50F below) north of the Alaskan range, and drier and colder yet north of the Brooks range, where large trees simply do not exist and the vegetation has to hug the ground to survive the winds. Trails and cross-country travel are both possible, but mosquitoes sometimes make the wilds unpleasant (particularly in June).

The Northwest Coast ranges, with peaks of less than 8,000 feet, are primarily distinguished by their weather—wet, with about 200 inches of rain each year—and the resultant lush growth of cedars, firs, hemlocks, spruces, redwoods, ferns, moss, and shrubs. Summer is the driest season; trail use is usually moderate. The Cascade range, paralleling the Northwest Coast range, has peaks up to 10,000 feet, somewhat lighter precipitation, dense forests except in areas covered by relatively recent lava flows, good trails, and all-around fine wilderness. The Sierras, made famous by John Muir, are known for their good hiking. Not only are there awesome glaciated granite peaks (which are characteristic), but the climate is somewhat drier than along the coast, with low-altitude forests of ponderosa, yellow and lodgepole pine, and white and red fir that give way to alpine lakes and lichen-covered granite boulders as you follow the numerous uphill trails. In addition, mosquitoes and other pests are usually absent. It's not hard to understand why the area is heavily trafficked.

The Columbia Plateau, on the other hand, gets relatively little use. Home of some of the largest populations of cougar in the country, as well as eagles, hawks, salmon, and sturgeon, it is relatively insect-free because of the overall aridity. The landscape ranges from areas of recent volcanic activity that resemble moonscapes, to ponderosa pineland, alpine terrain, and canyons such as the celebrated Hell's Canyon and Snake River Canyon. Many people float the streams, but scarcely anyone ventures uphill. The Great Desert area, cut by mountain ranges of sculptured rock, is the wildest and least used. People think of it as hot and boring. Actually, it boasts a wide variety of terrain: handsome stands of the weird Joshua tree (in the Mojave Desert), the cactus of the Sonora Desert (archetypal desert), and sagebrush and cottonwood country in its Great Basin section. There aren't many designated backpacking trails, but if you've got the experience to go cross-country, this is a good place to do it.

The Colorado Plateau is characterized by its weirdly shaped buttes, canyons, mesas, and a range of environments from desert to alpine. It's hikeable so long as you're prepared. The Rockies, on the other hand, require less experience. More than 40 monuments, forests, and parks make this a Valhalla for foot travelers; there are snow-capped peaks, fields of wildflowers, alpine lakes, icy streams, and slopes full of conifers and deciduous trees. Along with the Sierra, this is the US's prime backpacking territory.

The Ozarks offer some backpacking through dense forests in low mountains and shallow valleys, scattered with caves and underground rivers. This is especially good if you want to travel cross-country, though long trails recently have become more abundant. The north woods, on the other hand, are full of trails. Flat and rolling countryside makes the going fairly easy as well, and huge numbers of lakes offer fine campsites.

In the East, the Appalachians make for the best backpacking. The peaks are lower and more rounded than those in the West, but many of the grades are just as steep as those in the rest of the country. The *Appalachian Trail* runs the length of the chain for 2,147 miles from Maine to Georgia (it takes about five to six months to hike the full distance). The oldest long-distance trail in the US, the *Long Trail,* runs for 265 miles along the spine of the Green Mountains in Vermont. For details about these long trails, contact the *Appalachian Trail Conference* (PO Box 807, Harpers Ferry, WV 25425; phone: 304-535-6331) or the *Green Mountain Club* (RR1, PO Box 650, Rte. 100, Waterbury Center, VT 05677; phone: 802-244-7037).

In addition to these long trails, there is yet a third—the *North Country National Scenic Trail.* The country's longest, it runs for 3,246 miles from Crown Point, New York, across seven northern states to the *Lewis and Clark National Historic Trail* at Lake Sakakawea in North Dakota. For details, contact the *National Park Service,* 700 Rayovac Dr., Suite 100, Madison, WI 53711 (phone: 608-264-5610).

TONTO NATIONAL FOREST, Phoenix, Arizona This is the largest national forest in the state, with more than 2.8 million acres, an 800-mile trail system, and eight *Wilderness Areas* that go from an elevation of 1,500 feet to nearly 8,000 feet. You'll find desert, grassland, piñon, a maze of box canyons, and arid mountains covered with chaparral, as well as some ponderosa pine and mixed conifer at the higher elevations. Experience in desert travel and a sufficient supply of water are needed. Trail conditions vary from excellent to very poor. Several *Recreation Opportunity Guides and Maps* are available, which give detailed information on the specific area and its trails. Information: *Tonto National Forest,* 2324 E. McDowell Rd., Phoenix, AZ 85006 (phone: 602-225-5200).

OUACHITA NATIONAL FOREST, Hot Springs, Arkansas Some of America's best year-round hiking is to be found along the ridge-climbing, scenic, 192-mile-long *Ouachita National Recreation Trail* and its 40-odd miles of spurs. Information: *Ouachita National Forest,* PO Box 1270, Hot Springs, AR 71902 (phone: 501-321-5202). Also see *Hot Springs National Park* in DIRECTIONS.

OZARK–ST. FRANCIS NATIONAL FOREST, Russellville, Arkansas The *Ozark Highlands Trail* stretches for 166 miles across the forest, which is most beautiful in spring, when dogwoods and redbuds bloom by the thousands, and during fall foliage season. Information: *US Forest Service, Ozark National Forest,* PO Box 1008, Russellville, AR 72801 (phone: 501-968-2354). Also see *The Ozarks* in DIRECTIONS.

KLAMATH NATIONAL FOREST, Yreka, California Below the California-Oregon border, this region has vast forests that are largely unvisited because the many other national forests one must pass through on the way tend to absorb the majority of tourists. Here are river activities and outstanding backpacking possibilities in a state that's full of them. The forest is immense (almost 1.7 million acres) and has fine forests of pine, cedar, Douglas fir, and hemlock covering mountains than range up to 8,000 feet. You can hike 1,100 miles of trails, most only moderately steep, and cross-country ski in the roadless tracts of five established *Wilderness Areas: Salmon-Trinity Alps, Russian, Siskiyou, Red Buttes,* and *Marble Mountain.* The wildlife population includes elk, pronghorn antelope, black bear, cougar, and wild horses. During the spring and fall, you'll see a spectacular wildfowl show, as birds from Canada and Alaska, moving along the Pacific flyway, converge on the eastern part of the forest. The *Pacific Crest Trail* also runs through the Klamath. Information: *Klamath National Forest,* 1312 Fairlane Rd., Yreka, CA 96097 (phone: 916-842-6131).

KALALAU TRAIL, Kauai, Hawaii Considered to be one of the most spectacular hiking destinations on the planet, this trail snakes above the sheer cliffs of the Na Pali Coast and then through lush rain forests and stands of wild fruit trees. Hikers then continue to the Hanakapiai Falls and into the Hanakoa Valley, where a steep climb begins; the reward to those hardy enough to make it to the top is a view of Hanakoa Falls and the beautiful coastline. Open from May to September. Permits are required. Apply at least six months in advance. Access is on a first-come, first-served basis. Information: *State Parks,* Division of Forestry, 3060 Eiwa St., Rm. 306, Lihue, HI 96766 (phone: 808-241-3444).

NEZ PERCE NATIONAL FOREST, Grangeville, Idaho An incredible trail system—over 2,300 miles—makes this 2.2-million-acre forest one of the best for backpacking in the Rockies. Trails are open as well to pack stock. An elevation range from 1,000 feet to 10,000 feet makes for plenty of variety, from deep river canyons to rolling prairies and rugged mountain peaks. Three *Wilderness Areas* (covering almost a million acres) and four *Wild and Scenic Rivers* fall within national forest boundaries. Information: *Nez Perce National Forest,* Rte. 2, PO Box 475, Grangeville, ID 83530 (phone: 208-983-1950).

SUPERIOR NATIONAL FOREST, Duluth, Minnesota This is one of the finest forest areas in the country. Its three million acres take in a million acres of wilderness scattered with lichen-covered granite outcrops and about 2,000 lakes—many larger than 10 acres—with rocky shorelines, islands, and occasional sand beaches. There are over 250 miles of maintained hiking trails varying in length and difficulty. The fishing—for walleye, northern pike, trout, and bass—is superb; some people come for that alone. Information: *Superior National Forest,* PO Box 338, Duluth, MN 55801 (phone: 218-720-5324).

TOIYABE NATIONAL FOREST, Sparks, Nevada The largest national forest in the lower 48 states, the *Toiyabe* is scattered across central, southern, and western Nevada and the eastern slopes of the Sierra Nevada in eastern California. It has high sierra environments with alpine lakes, icy streams, spectacular granite formations, and coniferous forests, as well as desert-like country with cactus, creosote bush, yucca, and juniper and piñon stands. Hundreds of miles of trails poke into every corner of its 3.8 million acres; those in California's *Hoover Wilderness* near Yosemite and Mt. Charleston in the Las Vegas district are heavily used, while trails in the *Carson-Iceberg* and *Mokelumne Wildernesses* and the high desert ranges of central Nevada are quiet. Temperatures are less forbidding than you might expect, although snow may occur anytime. For a few brief weeks, generally in October, you can gather the tasty piñon pine nuts, long an important food staple for the Native Americans of Nevada and California, and a great delicacy nowadays. Information: *Toiyabe National Forest,* 1200 Franklin Way, Sparks, NV 89431 (phone: 702-331-6444).

MT. WASHINGTON, near Gorham, New Hampshire The view from the 6,288-foot summit—the "second greatest show on Earth," according to no less than P. T. Barnum—attracts hikers by the thousands. The trails up are steep, but not that steep. The danger, instead, lies in the weather, reputedly the worst in the world. It is treacherous, and ferocious snowstorms do blow up on a regular basis with practically no warning—even in summer. Information: *Appalachian Mountain Club,* PO Box 298, Gorham, NH 03581 (phone: 603-466-2725).

WILLAMETTE NATIONAL FOREST, Eugene, Oregon You can do outstanding backpacking on good trails through over 1,675,000 acres, 379,000 of which have been designated as wilderness. These include the *Diamond Peak Wilderness,* a cluster of volcanic peaks covered with fir, hemlock, pine, and meadows, scattered with lakes; the *Bull of the Woods Wilderness,* a terrain of rocky ridgetops and forested dells; the *Mt. Jefferson Wilderness,* which surrounds an extinct, glacier-covered volcano; the *Three Sisters Wilderness,* whose extensive trails take you through vast forests, sub-alpine terrain, meadows, and expanses of basalt and obsidian left from recent volcanic activity; and the *Mt. Washington Wilderness,* much of which is lava flow. Information: *Willamette National Forest,* PO Box 10607, Eugene, OR 97440 (phone: 541-465-6521).

SISKIYOU NATIONAL FOREST, Grants Pass, Oregon The low mountains in the southwestern corner of the state are covered by wonderful flowering bushes—wild lilac, azaleas, and rhododendrons among them—and crossed by fine fishing streams, including the celebrated Rogue. You can hike along the *Rogue River Trail,* a part of the 36,038-acre *Wild Rogue Wilderness,* through the rugged Coast Range; along the *Boundary Trail* to Hanging Rock on the *Panther Ridge Trail;* or through the rugged *Kalmiopsis Wilderness* (named after the rare Ice Age flower, *Kalmiopsis leachiana*), 179,650 acres of rocky hills and low canyons where you'll see interesting hardwoods and shrubs, some quite rare. Hornets, yellow jackets, poison oak, and rattlesnakes are common but not usually a problem if you are careful. The fishing is superb in the Rogue River during fall's massive salmon and steelhead migration. *Siskiyou* is also the gateway to *Oregon Caves National Monument* on the coast. Details on specific trails may be obtained from the following Ranger Districts: Chetco (phone: 541-469-2196); Galice (phone: 541-476-3830); Gold Beach (phone: 541-247-3600); Illinois Valley (phone: 541-592-2166). Information: *Siskiyou National Forest,* PO Box 440, Grants Pass, OR 97526 (phone: 541-471-6500).

ASHLEY NATIONAL FOREST, Vernal, Utah The 460,000-acre *High Uintas Wilderness*—a wonderful expanse of lakes, forests, meadows, and rocky mountains, which the *Ashley National Forest* shares with the *Wasatch-Cache National Forest*—is what most people come to hike from July through September. Similar environments can be found throughout the more than 1.3 million acres of this national forest, particularly on the east, which is far less crowded. Lakes, streams full of trout, and many exposed geologic formations are also here. Information: *Ashley National Forest,* 355 N. Vernal Ave., Vernal, UT 84078 (phone: 801-789-1181).

OLYMPIC PENINSULA, near Port Angeles, Washington It's been dubbed the "rain forest" by the locals, and it's easy to see why: With the rains come the awesome vegetation of ancient Sitka spruce, vine maple, and myriad species of ferns which give this damp area of the state a lush, velvety environment. The streams and rivers fed by frequent rains and melting snow as they rush to the sea produce unexpected and dramatic falls. Black bears can be seen everywhere. Hurricane Ridge is one of the most famous destinations for hiking; there's a 7½-mile hike on Grand Ridge, where you can see the entire Olympic Range from one side of the ridge and the Straits of Juan de Fuca and Vancouver Island from the other. The national park can offer all sorts of trail suggestions. *Mountain Madness* (4218 SW Alaska, Suite 206, Seattle, WA 98116; phone: 206-937-8389; fax: 206-937-1772) leads mountain climbers and backpackers into *Olympic National Park* from May through September. Information: *Olympic National Park,* 600 E. Park St., Port Angeles, WA 98362 (phone: 206-452-4501). See also *Olympic National Park* in DIRECTIONS.

GUIDED HIKES

Not all organizations that sponsor trips for groups furnish the gear you'll need; some provide everything, while some will set you up with everything but a sleeping bag. Make sure to confirm this in advance, and find out whether the rates—usually $70 and up per day—include food, sleeping gear, lodging the night before the trip begins, guides, equipment, and the like. For extensive lists of organizations offering group backpacking trips and hiking trips with pack stock carrying your gear, read *Outside* magazine.

DENALI NATIONAL PARK WILDERNESS CENTERS: CAMP DENALI AND NORTH FACE LODGE, Denali National Park, Alaska Spectacular vacations in view of 20,320-foot Mt. McKinley, North America's highest peak, where moose, caribou, grizzly bears, wolves, and white mountain sheep thrive. Enjoy bird watching and wildflowers in early June, fall color and migrating sandhill cranes in late August and early September. There's naturalist-guided hiking, canoeing, gold-panning, rafting, and fishing. *Camp Denali* offers individual cabins and a central shower facility for stays of three to five nights, sometimes longer. There are also periodic seminars on natural history and nature photography. *North Face Lodge* offers two- and three-night stays, sometimes longer. Fees at both lodges include accommodations, transportation, meals, and access to all the activities and equipment. "Flightseeing" in small planes that offer passengers terrific views of the mountains is available at an additional charge, weather permitting. Information: Summer: *Denali National Park Wilderness Centers,* PO Box 67, *Denali National Park,* AK 99755 (phone: 907-683-2290); Winter: *Denali National Park Wilderness Centers,* PO Box 369, Cornish, NH 03746 (phone: 603-675-2248; fax: 603-675-9125). Also see *Denali National Park and Preserve,* in DIRECTIONS.

SIERRA CLUB, based in San Francisco, California The conservation organization offers a variety of trips nationwide. Information: *Sierra Club,* Outing Dept., 730 Polk St., San Francisco, CA 94109 (phone: 415-776-2211).

WILDERNESS SOUTHEAST, Savannah, Georgia This active organization offers adventures for the inquisitive via naturalist-led hiking, flatwater canoeing, sailing, and snorkeling programs in southeastern woodlands, islands, coral reefs, and swamps. Designed for all ages, year-round, and lasting three to 14 days, these programs cover the Great Smoky Mountains, coastal Georgia, the Everglades, Okefenokee Swamp, and several foreign countries. Information: *Wilderness Southeast,* 711 Sandtown Rd., Savannah, GA 31410 (phone: 912-897-5108).

APPALACHIAN MOUNTAIN CLUB (AMC), Gorham, New Hampshire This group's guided overnight hikes give you insight into the White Mountains' natural and social history (see above). Information: *AMC,* PO Box 298, Gorham, NH 03581 (phone: 603-466-2727).

OUTDOOR TRAINING SCHOOLS

Some adults are lucky enough to have learned how to handle themselves in the wilderness when they were young—in the company of backpack-loving relatives. Others acquire camping skills on their own, and learn about everything from tree identification to backcountry first aid from books. For those who want more structured guidance, however, there's no better introduction to woodcraft than one of the outdoor training schools offered by a number of organizations around the country. The *National Outdoor Leadership School (NOLS)* and *Outward Bound,* listed below, are among the most important. You can find out about others in magazines like *Backpacker* (733 Third Ave., New York, NY 10017; phone: 212-697-2040) and *Outside* (Outside Plaza, 400 Market St., Santa Fe, NM 87501; phone: 505-989-7100), where most advertise their services.

NATIONAL AUDUBON SOCIETY ECOLOGY CAMPS, based in Greenwich, Connecticut These June, July, and August programs held in Connecticut, Maine, and Wyoming focus on area ecosystems. You lodge in cabins and bungalows in each area and do your learning on field trips. One-week workshops also are scheduled throughout the year. Two sessions for children are offered. Information: *National Audubon Society,* 613 Riversville Road, Greenwich, CT 06831 (phone: 203-869-2017).

OUTWARD BOUND USA, based in Garrison, New York At schools in Maine, Colorado, Minnesota, North Carolina, and Oregon, the aim is to help you move beyond your self-imposed limits as well as to provide an enjoyable wilderness experience. Information: *Outward Bound,* Rte. 90, R2, PO Box 280, Garrison, NY 10524 (phone: 914-424-4000; 800-243-8520).

BOULDER OUTDOOR SURVIVAL SCHOOL (BOSS), Escalante, Utah The mountains, deserts, and canyonlands of Utah are the setting for this small but venerable institution's 7-, 14-, 21-, and 27-day programs. You learn primitive fire building techniques, trap-and-snare construction, plant identification, direction finding, shelter construction, and more. But increased self-confidence and personal awareness, and enhanced interpersonal relationships, are equally important benefits. Information: *BOSS Booking Offices,* PO Box 3226, Flagstaff, AZ 86003 (phone: 208-359-2400).

AMERICAN HIKING SOCIETY, based in Washington, DC This nonprofit hikers' association sponsors two-week trail maintenance and construction trips from January until the end of September. It publishes *Helping Out in the Outdoors* (available for $5), a directory of volunteer work and internships on America's public lands—an unusual vacation idea whose popularity is growing steadily.

Information: *American Hiking Society,* PO Box 20160, Washington, DC 20041 (phone: 703-255-9304).

NATIONAL WILDLIFE FEDERATION CONSERVATION SUMMITS Week-long programs with self-designed schedules in several states (each year the states vary), held in the summer months, focus on natural history and outdoor recreation. The programs and activities are wonderful for families, and wildlife camps for kids are available in North Carolina and Colorado. Information: *National Wildlife Federation,* Conservation Summits Department, 1400 16th St. NW, Washington, DC 20036-2266 (phone: 703-790-4363; 800-245-5484).

NATIONAL OUTDOOR LEADERSHIP SCHOOL (NOLS), based in Lander, Wyoming This organization was originally established to school wilderness-trip leaders in outdoor skills, wilderness safety, survival methods, and teamwork with an emphasis on conservation. It offers year-round courses in cross-country skiing, sea kayaking, and climbing in Alaska, Washington, Wyoming, Mexico, Chile, and Africa. Information: *NOLS,* 288 Main St., Lander, WY 82520 (phone: 307-332-6973).

Sybaritic Spas

Eternal youth and spiritual rejuvenation have been on folks' minds ever since the days of ancient Rome. The curative properties of mineral springs, from Germany's *Baden-Baden* to Arkansas' *Hot Springs* (see *Hot Springs National Park* in DIRECTIONS), have been loudly lauded, but the definition of a spa vacation has been infused with a whole new meaning since the days when taking the waters at *Saratoga Springs* was thought of as the height of fashion. Today, a new legion of spas motivate and inspire folks who want to lose a few pounds or escape from a stressful environment to a more healthful one for a few days (or weeks).

The traditional European spa, where pure, unadulterated mineral water is believed to possess magical restorative powers, has been modernized to suit a fast-track clientele that doesn't have weeks to devote to the leisurely ceremony of "taking the waters." Today, sophisticated equipment and specialized treatments, such as aromatherapy (where the skin is treated with herbal oils and then wrapped in dry sheets), are combined to relax the mind as well as strengthen the body. In addition to such old standbys as massages, herbal wraps, and facials, many spas and wellness centers now offer such treatments as fruit showers (hot water scented with citrus) and sound massages, where classical or New Age music is played in the background. Most spas also have a beauty salon.

In general, spas appear allergic to cigarette smoke, although many permit guests to smoke in their rooms or in outside areas. While no one will snatch the offending article from your hand, it's probably wiser to call beforehand to find out the operative restrictions. In some cases, you can reserve a "smoker's room" for your stay.

Many spas will send you a medical evaluation sheet to be filled out before your visit, and some do a thorough medical exam once you arrive. If you are nervous about the program or just want a listing of daily activities and exercise classes, call the spa to arrange for a consultation and in-depth information on their programs. You can then map out a personal fitness program with which you will be the most comfortable.

The *Doral Saturnia* in Miami, the *Bonaventure* in Ft. Lauderdale, and the *Spa at Marriott's Camelback Inn* in Phoenix are described in detail in the respective chapters in THE CITIES; listed below are several other self-indulging spots across the country with marvelous massages, wonderful whirlpools, and super saunas. Most offer curricula that last from a day to a week.

EAST

CANYON RANCH IN THE BERKSHIRES, Lenox, Massachusetts The gamut of spa services are offered at this sister of *Canyon Ranch* in Arizona (see below); among them are hydrotherapy, underwater massage, clay and salt treatments, and a relaxation course that purports to "heal life's hurts." When you've sufficiently healed, submit to an aromatherapy session or a deep muscle massage. There are two pools for laps or aquatic aerobics, indoor and outdoor tennis courts, racquetball courts, and a squash court, as well as hiking trails, biking paths, and cross-country skiing in the winter. There are 120 rooms, 24 of which are well-appointed suites. The elegant *Belle Fontaine Mansion* houses one of the most sophisticated spa dining rooms in the country. No smoking is permitted. Information: *Canyon Ranch in the Berkshires,* 165 Kemble St., Lenox, MA 01240 (phone: 413-637-4100; 800-742-9000).

GURNEY'S INN, Montauk, Long Island, New York This resort is renowned for its international program of thalasso and marine therapies (seawater and seaweed treatments), featuring Roman baths with powerful Jacuzzis and an indoor heated seawater pool overlooking the Atlantic. Additional therapies include massage, aromatherapy, reflexology, fango packs, Swiss showers, herbal and seaweed body wraps, and biofeedback therapy. The facilities are prodigious; a comprehensive medical evaluation is available, and you can pedal until dusk on a stationary bicycle or use other machines. Eleven types of massage are available; other pursuits include yoga, aerobics, and aquatic classes in the seawater pool. There's also a full-service beauty salon. The 109 studios, suites, and cottages have private sun decks and views of the Atlantic Ocean. The food is very good and uncomplicated (spa cuisine is also available). The kitchen will pack up a picnic basket for an impromptu lunch at the beach. Also see *America's Special Havens.* Information: *Gurney's Inn Resort & Spa,* Old Montauk Hwy., Montauk, NY 11954 (phone: 516-668-2345; fax: 516-668-3576).

TOPNOTCH, Stowe, Vermont Nature lovers can enjoy exercise and views of the exquisite Stowe countryside simultaneously when they take a dip in the pool. Aerobics, stretching classes, free weights, and stationary bicycles are offered, and guests thirsty to build stamina can also try a mountain hike, uphill bicycle racing, or even snowshoeing in winter (akin to jogging on snow). There are also ski and tennis clinics at the connecting *Topnotch* hotel, where you can arrange for private lessons. Guests who find ordinary massages too painful can try polarity therapy, where gentle strokes, instead of kneading motions, are used to relax tense muscles. The spa is linked to the *Topnotch* hotel by an enclosed walkway, and accommodations include 92 hotel rooms, as well as 17 condo units on the premises. Specially prepared spa meals also are served. There are three-, five-, and seven-night packages available. Information: *The Spa at Topnotch,* PO Box 1458, Stowe, VT 05672 (phone: 802-253-8585; 800-451-8686).

SOUTH

ARLINGTON, Hot Springs, Arkansas You can choose between soaking in the mountainside outdoor mineral hot tub and swimming in one of the two heated outdoor pools at this luxury hotel. The mineral waters come directly from the eponymous hot springs. Thermal baths, whirlpool, heat packs, and massage are given at the Bath House. Try to reserve a room with its own mineral bath so you can experience the treatment in privacy. (Make reservations well in advance, especially in February and March.) There's also an exercise room, as well as golf and tennis at the nearby *Hot Springs Country Club.* Information: *The Arlington Hotel,* 239 Central Ave., Hot Springs, AK 71901 (phone: 501-623-7771; 800-643-1502 from outside Arkansas; fax: 501-623-6191).

PALM-AIRE, Pompano Beach, Florida This super-posh resort (see *America's Best Resort Hotels* in this section) offers the latest in spa facilities. Full 45-minute body massages, reflexology, aromatherapy, hydrotherapy, body wraps, and scrubs are available. Aerobics classes (both in and out of the water) are led by certified instructors. What makes this spa stand out is its knack for personal service, from the individualized fitness/lifestyle evaluation you receive upon arrival to providing all the clothes you'll need during your stay. Information: *Palm-Aire Resort, Spa and Club,* 2601 Palm-Aire Dr. N., Pompano Beach, FL 33069 (phone: 954-972-3300; 800-2-PALM-AIR for reservations; fax: 954-968-2711).

SAFETY HARBOR SPA, Tampa, Florida Following a multi-million-dollar renovation, this is one of the biggest and best destination spas on the east coast. Located in a tiny village on Old Tampa Bay, the 182-room facility provides innovative fitness options, healthy meals, and plenty of pampering. In addition to walking, aerobics, yoga, and stretching, spa-goers can play tennis. Accommodations are comfortable but hardly luxurious, the spa cuisine is first-rate, and both the beauty and fitness staff are extremely knowledgeable. Information: *Safety Harbor Spa,* 106 N. Bayshore Dr., Safety Harbor, FL 34695 (phone: 813-726-1161; 800-237-0155).

GREENBRIER, White Sulphur Springs, West Virginia One of the most elegant resorts in the country (also see *America's Best Resort Hotels*), it has its own private mineral baths, hydrotherapy tubs for underwater massage, and seaweed treatments. There are both indoor and outdoor pools, an aerobics studio, tennis courts, three championship 18-hole golf courses, and a fully equipped gym. Information: *The Greenbrier Hotel,* White Sulphur Springs, WV 24986 (phone: 304-536-1110; 800-624-6070 for reservations; fax: 304-536-7854).

MIDWEST

THE HEARTLAND SPA, Gilman, Illinois About 80 miles from Chicago is an oasis of calm in the center of a Midwest farmland. The atmosphere is rustic and casual with many of the facilities located in a converted barn. The emphasis is on vegetarian nutrition and fitness through exercise, including swimming (there's an indoor pool) and race walking. Men are welcome, although the majority of guests are women. The spa supplies workoutwear. Information: *The Heartland Spa,* Kam Lake Estate, RR1, PO Box 181, Gilman, IL 60938 (phone: 815-683-2182; 800-545-4853).

WEST

PHOENICIAN, Scottsdale, Arizona This self-contained spa offers the perfect antidote to stressful living. Medically supervised packages zero in on mind and body in a peaceful environment—130 sprawling acres at the base of Camelback Mountain. Housing is in the gorgeous 580-room hotel. Although nutritional guidance is provided, you'll need willpower to avoid the tempting menus offered alongside the spa cuisine. Information: *The Phoenician,* 6000 Camelback Rd., Scottsdale, AZ 82551 (phone: 602-941-8200; 800-888-8234).

CANYON RANCH, Tucson, Arizona The *Canyon Ranch* program combines exercise, health education, stress reduction, and total well-being, and there are personalized programs to take home—including anti-stress and arthritis control—so that the positive effects linger. More than a dozen types of massage, hydrotherapy, and a full-service skin and beauty salon are available. Aside from the numerous fitness classes, there are also mountain hiking, biking, yoga, and tai chi. You also can play an unhurried game of tennis at one of the eight lighted courts. Men's programs are now offered, featuring basketball, calisthenics, volleyball, water polo, and discussion groups with guest speakers. Or you can do nothing but gaze at the Catalina Mountains. Information: *Canyon Ranch Health and Fitness Resort,* 8600 E. Rockcliff Rd., Tucson, AZ 85715 (phone: 520-749-9000; 800-742-9000 for reservations).

SONOMA MISSION INN AND SPA, Boyes Hot Springs, California A plethora of pampering awaits guests under the pink roof of this well-known Spanish-style resort 2 miles outside Sonoma. Massages range from a refreshing aromatherapy session to a vigorous rubdown, or you can submit to a relaxing seaweed, mud, or herbal wrap. Water enthusiasts can swim in the two outdoor heated pools; the water is naturally warmed from underground wells. The inn offers low- and non-impact exercise for those with specific injuries, and the usual array of weight machines and aerobics classes is available. Guests also can elect to receive a nutritional evaluation. The decor in the 170 guestrooms (some of which have wood-burning fireplaces) is very attractive, but you'll probably fall happily asleep before you've had a chance to notice your surroundings. Best bet: Since practically everything at Sonoma costs extra, try to book a package which will include many services. Also see *Inn Sites: America's Special Havens.* Information: *Sonoma Mission Inn and Spa,* PO Box 1447, Sonoma, CA 95476 (phone: 707-938-9000; for reservations: 800-862-4945 in California, 800-358-9022 elsewhere in the US; fax: 707-938-4250).

TWO BUNCH PALMS, Desert Hot Springs, California A world away from the glitzy image promoted by neighboring Palm Springs, this 45-room mineral water spa prides itself on pampering its guests in privacy. Film stars who wish to remain almost anonymous come to be rubbed at this highly touted center for massage therapy. From shiatsu to *watzu* (Japanese acupressure and massage), which is enhanced by enriching oils, candlelight, and the reverberation of gongs, this spa seriously concentrates on the release of body energy. You can do as much or as little as you please; schedules, evening programs, and crash courses on counting calories do not exist at this sanctuary. The retreat does get high marks for its healthful cuisine. No children are allowed. Information: *Two Bunch Palms Resort,* 67-425 Two Bunch Palms Trail, Desert Hot Springs, CA 92240 (phone: 619-329-8791; 800-472-4334).

ASHRAM, Calabasas, California Only the fittest survive the intensive week-long program at this no-frills facility where six to 10 coed guests live dormitory-style in a cozy, three-bedroom house. "We're mean, lean, hard, and hungry," is the motto of founder–exercise guru Anne-Marie Bennstrom, who runs the transcendental-style spa. The regimen is rigorous with miles and miles of tough daily hikes, calisthenics, aerobics classes, weight training, water exercises, and only a spartan, vegetarian diet for fuel. Except for a much-needed daily massage, no other pampering is provided. But the results are awesome. Pounds and inches melt with each grueling day. For those who don't collapse by then, after-dinner programs are offered—mostly spiritualistic sessions by guest speakers. Information: *Ashram,* PO Box 8009, Calabasas, CA 91302 (phone: 818-222-6900).

LA COSTA, Carlsbad, California A glitzy haven for the Hollywood set who go to be pampered, this multi-million-dollar spa provides the ultimate in salubrious treatments along with a daily diet of fitness options. Keep in mind that this is a hotel first, with 100 rooms set aside for spa guests. There are separate, elegant facilities for men and women—whirlpools, saunas, steam- and therapy baths. A variety of all-inclusive packages offer pampering options from facials to foot reflexology. The spa cuisine is good and guests may order lighter fare from the regular menu. For serious weight watchers, a major drawback is the proximity to higher-calorie restaurants and bars located near the resort. Information: *La Costa,* 2100 Costa del Mar Rd., Carlsbad, CA 92009 (phone: 619-438-9111; 800-854-5000).

GOLDEN DOOR, Escondido, California A commitment of at least seven days is required at this grande dame of US spas. Only 39 guests at a time are privy to the concentrated program of fitness, nutrition, and pampering. They can meander through 177 meticulously kept acres, with orchards, brooks, and a precision-raked sand garden. Although the spa is devoted exclusively to women most of the year, it does offer five weeks for men only and four weeks for both men and women. This oasis of health, created by Deborah Szekely (the doyenne of spas), provides a nurturing cocoon to inspire an overall sense of well-being. Designed to reflect the tranquillity and care proffered by Japanese *honjin* (similar to a very attentive bed and breakfast inn), the program revolves around structured periods of relaxation and exercise. Guests receive personal supervision at all classes. There are two lighted tennis courts and two heated outdoor lap pools. Many guests participate in the "Inner Door," a day-long course that promotes creative problem solving and behavior change. Information: *The Golden Door,* PO Box 463077, Escondido, CA 92046 (phone: 619-744-5777; 800-424-0777 for reservations; fax: 619-471-2393).

THE OAKS AT OJAI, Ojai, California Owner Sheila Cluff has cultivated a loyal clientele, which practices fitness with fervor. Evening programs and special interest theme weeks, such as high-energy workshops and celebrity chefs who prepare spa fare, are so numerous that Cluff publishes a quarterly magazine for guests on the latest spa news. Classes include high-and low-impact aerobics, toning, and stretching, and there are programs to help guests stop smoking or learn how to cook low-calorie dishes. The 44 rooms are decorated simply and are very comfortable and cozy; you'll probably feel so relaxed that you'll rarely change out of a T-shirt and shorts. The chef is a whiz at transforming locally grown herbs, organic produce, and fruit into wonderous, calorie-defying delights. Information: *The Oaks at Ojai,* 122 E. Ojai Ave., Ojai, CA 93023 (phone: 805-646-5573).

THE PALMS, Palm Springs, California Sister spa of the *Oaks at Ojai* (see above), this is one of the best spa buys around. Founder Sheila Cluff offers more than a dozen daily fitness options—everything from a morning hike around residential Palm Springs to aerobics, step, yoga, body toning, and pool workouts. The healthy, low-calorie diet is tasty and satisfying—and even fairly creative. There is no alcohol on the premises. Beauty treatments are offered à la carte, but don't expect too much. Information: *The Palms,* 572 N. Indian Canyon Dr., Palm Springs, CA (phone: 619-325-1111).

CAL-A-VIE, Vista, California About an hour north of San Diego, this flower-filled retreat hosts only 24 guests at a time, to ensure sufficient pampering and in-depth nutrition counseling. The regime begins at 6 AM with a walk on the golf course or a hike, followed by an aerobics workout. Meals feature low-calorie but tasty dishes. There's an afternoon massage daily, as well as body wraps, facials, hair treatments, pedicures, and manicures. Occasional lectures on nutrition are available, and other diversions include tennis, swimming, and golf. Husbands and wives may be lodged separately if preferred (for better sleep, the spa claims). Information: *Cal-a-Vie,* 2249 Somerset Rd., Vista, CA 92084 (phone: 619-945-2055).

THE PEAKS RESORT AND SPA, Telluride, Colorado Combining indulgence with a reverence for the great outdoors, *The Peaks* (formerly *Doral Telluride*) offers 44 treatment rooms, an indoor lap pool, saunas, and Jacuzzis, as well as fitness classes from rock climbing to yoga. In addition, there are facials and massages, and an unusual use of Eastern healing techniques. The spa's most unusual aspect, however, is that it actually welcomes children. Besides daycare and baby-sitting services, there are all sorts of outdoor activities, including horseback riding, hot-air ballooning, panning for gold, and nature walks. Information: *The Peaks Resort and Spa,* PO Box 2702, Telluride, CO 81435 (phone: 303-728-6800; 800-789-2220 for reservations; fax: 303-728-6175).

IHILANI, Kapolei, Hawaii This 340-room deluxe oceanfront spa resort is situated along Oahu's beautiful southern shore, just 17 miles west of Waikiki in the *Ko Olina Resort.* A fitness fanatics nirvana, it offers a range of aerobics classes; as a reward you can indulge in any of several types of massage including Lomi Lomi (Hawaiian-style), thalasso or hydrotherapies; and afterward, slip into an herbal wrap. Also take advantage of the spa's complete range of skin care and beauty programs. Both body and mind are further pampered in the dining room, where chef Katsuo Sugiura uses only fresh seafood and vegetables from the region in his healthful, low-fat menu. Information: *Ihilani,* 92-1001 Olani St., Kapolei, HI 97707 (808-679-0079; 800-626-4446; fax: 808-679-0080).

KOHALA SPA AT THE HILTON WAIKOLOA, Kohala, Hawaii This spa offers a multidimensional, holistic program that includes extensive beauty and skincare treatments, nutrition, and health and meditation counseling. Guests begin the day with a brisk walk at sunrise, followed by a class in tai chi, then continue to toning and low-impact aerobics classes, stress management talks, and aquatic aerobics, and finish with a session of high- and low-impact aerobics. Information: *Kohala Spa at Hilton Waikoloa,* 1 Waikoloa, Kohala Coast, Kohala, HI 96743 (phone: 808-885-1234; 800-228-9000 for reservations).

SPA GRANDE AT THE GRAND WAILEA, Wailea, Maui, Hawaii This spa claims to be the largest health facility in the Pacific; without a doubt, it offers everything for the world-weary. From cardiovascular fitness, weight training, and lectures, to massages, facials, body wraps, and masks, to authentic Hawaiian treatments—it's all here. Unique to this spa is the Terme Wailea Hydrotherapy Circuit: A round of water immersions from hot to cool; a stop under a waterfall; a choice of one of five specialty baths; a Swiss jet shower; and use of a *furo* (a Japanese bath, similar to a Jacuzzi), steamroom, sauna, and sonic relaxation room. Private consultations with trainers, nutritionists, and stress management instructors are available. Most of the massage rooms overlook the beautiful beach and ocean. Information: *Spa Grande at the Grand Wailea Resort,* 3850 Wailea Alanui, Wailea, HI 96753 (phone: 808-875-1234; 800-888-6100 for reservations).

NATIONAL INSTITUTE OF FITNESS, Ivins, Utah Founder Marc Sorensen has developed a well-seasoned program of strenuous exercise coupled with a closely monitored meal plan for those who intend to make a serious commitment to health while losing weight. At an elevation of 2,800 feet, the majestic scenery in the mild desert climate is impressive. This program hardly leaves time to catch your breath as you race from aerobics to calisthenics to uphill walking. When your courage fails, there are enrichment programs to keep you on the right track. Within driving distance of *Zion* and *Bryce Canyon Parks,* as well as the *Grand Canyon.* Information: *National Institute of Fitness,* 202 N. Snow Canyon Rd., PO Box 938, Ivins, UT (phone: 801-673-4905).

Directions

Introduction

Ever since the pioneer days, traveling throughout the United States has been something of a mania. Perhaps it's the intriguing diversity that compels savvy travelers to seek out a remote spot in their own country to rename Paradise. Exploring a land so rich in archaeological treasures, history, and spectacular scenery has proved pure pleasure for those folks willing to do a bit of roaming.

To tell the truth, our favorite parts of the US are those that attract the fewest camera-toting tourists; our idea of a superlative travel experience doesn't include hand-to-hand combat for a chaise longue beside a crowded pool, or wasting half an afternoon languishing in a line. We've concocted creative touring itineraries that more often than not will make you drop your jaw in wonder rather than sigh with exasperation.

What follows are prime driving routes through the US—the East, West, North, and South. We have charted the Hawaiian Islands, the best paths to and through Death Valley, itineraries throughout New England, and the best of the Midwest. Each entry discusses the highlights of the route, and throws in a pinch of history and a dash of insider's information on sights worth seeking (or avoiding altogether). You can fall asleep to the wail of a distant coyote, travel on horseback to the bottom of a treacherous canyon, or gaze on the crimson and violet glory of bougainvillea. After you weary of these delights, consult the *Best en Route* section, which provides recommendations on where to stay in the area. Frankly, there's no effort to cover absolutely everything in these selections; our choices are made on the basis of which places offer the most memorable experiences.

Route selections are based on our opinions of the most fascinating sites and sights in the States, and it's certainly possible to string two or more of these itineraries together for more extensive roaming. For those with less time or inclination, following any single itinerary will help you to see the most notable points of interest in a given area.

Note: This year nearly 240 million people are expected to visit America's national parks. However, park officials strongly advise travelers to call ahead since there will be closures of campsites, curtailment of programs and other activities this summer due to budget cuts.

Finally, as anywhere, picking up strangers, camping on a lonely beach, or sleeping in a car in an isolated area can sometimes invite serious trouble. It takes only a little common sense, and some very basic planning, to ensure your safety and make your travel adventure both memorable and momentous.

East

New London, Connecticut, to Providence, Rhode Island

This stretch of coastline is full of American maritime history, from the *US Coast Guard Academy* in New London to the *Mystic Seaport Museum* to the luxe summer houses of Watch Hill. Along the way are plenty of fishing villages full of antiques shops, restaurants, and country inns.

This tour begins in New London, Connecticut, about 150 miles northeast of New York City and about 100 miles southwest of Boston. The principal route from New London (just west of Mystic) to Providence is I-95, but Route 1 runs parallel for most of the journey and offers better views of the ocean and more interesting detours through little seaside towns.

En Route from New York City The quickest route is to follow I-95 northeast to New London. For a more scenic drive, take the Hutchinson River Parkway north to the Merritt Parkway (Route 15). Follow the Merritt Parkway to the Milford, Connecticut, exit, then take I-95 to New London.

NEW LONDON, Connecticut An 18th- and 19th-century whaling port, New London has a rather faded air. A prime attraction is the *US Coast Guard Academy* (exit 83 off I-95; phone: 860-444-8270 or 860-444-8511), where the three-masted *Eagle* is in port at various times during the year. It's open for visits daily. Other sights include *Connecticut College* (270 Mohegan Ave.; phone 860-439-4636), a lovely hilltop campus with a 425-acre arboretum open for hiking and nature walks; the *Lyman Allyn Museum* (625 Williams St.; phone: 860-443-2545; closed Mondays), which features New England art and furniture, as well as ancient and Asian art; *Monte Cristo Cottage* (325 Pequot Ave.; phone: 860-443-0051; closed *Labor Day* through *Memorial Day*), the boyhood home of playwright Eugene O'Neill; and the *1833 Robert Mills US Customs House Museum* (150 Bank St.; phone: 860-447-2501), the country's oldest customs house still in use; it's open only Monday, Wednesday, and Friday afternoons. The *Garde Arts Center* (329 State St.; phone: 860-444-7373) presents Broadway and family theater as well as classical and pop concerts. Nearby *Ocean Beach Park* (south of New London, off I-95; phone: 860-447-3031; 800-510-SAND) has a beach, boardwalk, rides, and a pool. Just over the city line is the *Eugene O'Neill Theater Center* (305 Great Neck Rd., Waterford; phone: 860-443-5378), which showcases the work of up-and-coming playwrights and performers in a summer series of drama, musical theater, cabaret, and puppetry.

En Route from New London Take I-95 to exit 87 and follow Route 1 to Groton, about 3 miles away.

GROTON, Connecticut At *Fort Griswold Battlefield State Park* (Monument St.; phone: 860-445-1729), the site of the 1781 massacre of American troops by the British under Benedict Arnold, there is a battle monument and museum. Also in Groton is the *USS Nautilus Memorial and Submarine Force Library and Museum* (off I-95's exit 86; phone: 860-449-3174; 800-343-0079), the official submarine museum of the United States, featuring the world's first nuclear-powered vessel. Designed by the staff of the *Smithsonian Institution,* the museum exhibits periscopes, World War II memorabilia, and miniature subs. It's closed Tuesdays in winter; there's no admission charge. From late June through early September, the *Enviro-Lab* at *Project Oceanology* (Avery Point; phone: 860-445-9007) offers two-and-a-half-hour oceanographic cruises to study local marine life.

En Route from Groton Follow Route 1 to Route 215 (Noank Road) and continue on to Noank, about 5 miles away.

NOANK, Connecticut This tiny, 300-year-old village has long been a favorite of connoisseurs of traditional craft. The *Noank Historical Society Museum* (17 Sylvan Street; phone: 860-536-3021) traces the town's shipbuilding heritage, and the harbor is full of beautiful wooden-hulled sailboats. Views of the fleet can be enjoyed from the outdoor picnic tables of *Abbott's* (117 Pearl St.; phone: 860-536-7719). The best place in the state for lobster—and shrimp, oysters, clams, and mussels—in the rough, *Abbott's* is open daily May through *Labor Day,* then weekends through *Columbus Day.*

En Route from Noank Head back north on Route 215 to I-95, take exit 90, and follow Route 27 to Mystic, less than 3 miles away.

MYSTIC, Connecticut Ideally, you should allow a full day's visit to see everything here, including the community of Mystic (separate from *Mystic Seaport Museum* and the Historic Downtown Mystic), with its interesting shops and sparkling white buildings along the banks of the Mystic River. Leaving the interstate you'll pass the *Mystic Marinelife Aquarium* (55 Coogan Blvd.; phone: 860-572-5955), home to whales, dolphins, sea lions, seals, penguins, and more than 6,000 other species of marine life. It's closed the last week of January and major holidays. Across the street is *Olde Mistick Village* (Coogan Blvd.; phone: 860-536-4941), a nicely landscaped shopping center consisting of stores, businesses, and restaurants built to resemble a colonial New England village.

About half a mile south of I-95 on Route 27 is *Mystic Seaport Museum* (75 Greenmanville Ave.; phone: 860-572-5315), a re-created 19th-century New England coastal community complete with craftspeople, a working shipyard, formal exhibition galleries, and four major historic ships. Open daily, the museum is popular year round, especially during the crowded summer season, when there are daily demonstrations of sail setting and furling, chantey singing, and other maritime skills, along with boat rentals, and horse and carriage rides. The *Mystic Seaport Planetarium* has daily shows. On display are ships' figureheads and exhibitions of scrimshaw; museum events and parades, including *Yuletide* and *Lantern Light* tours, are held year-round (also see *Restored Towns and Reconstructed Villages* in DIVERSIONS).

En Route from Mystic Take Route 27 north to Route 1 east to Alternate Route 1 to Stonington, about 4 miles away.

STONINGTON, Connecticut An 18th-century fishing village and artists' and writers' colony, present-day Stonington epitomizes a New England coastal community. Main and Water Streets are lined with elegant clapboard houses, antiques shops, and cafés. At No. 7 Water is the *Old Lighthouse Museum,* built in 1823. The first federal government lighthouse built in Connecticut, it features a collection reflecting life in the coastal community settled in 1649 and offers views of Long Island Sound from its tower. It's closed Mondays (phone: 860-535-1440). Around 5 PM, stroll down to the water to watch Connecticut's last remaining commercial fishing fleet put in at the town dock, at the foot of High Street. Other amusements in the area include *Stonington Vineyards* (Taugwonk Rd.; phone: 860-535-1222), with winery tours and tastings daily; and horse-drawn hay- and surrey rides at *Oakbrook Farm* (576 Greenhaven Rd., off Rte. 1 in Pawcatuck; phone: 860-599-5859), which are offered daily year-round; reservations necessary.

En Route from Stonington Head north to I-95, go east to exit 92, and take Route 2 north to the intersection of Route 214 and the *Foxwoods* casino outside Ledyard, Connecticut.

LEDYARD, Connecticut *Foxwoods Resort* (Rte. 2; phone: 860-885-3000; 800-PLAY-BIG) is the largest casino in the Western Hemisphere. Owned and run by the Mashantucket Pequot Indians, this huge complex on a pretty wooded site includes a casino with the usual games, plus pari-mutuel horse-race betting, keno, high-stakes bingo, two hotels (see *Best en Route*), and a full roster of shows. Also see *Wheels of Fortune* in DIVERSIONS.

En Route from Ledyard Head south past I-95 on Route 2 to Westerly, about 12 miles away just across the Rhode Island border. This town of white colonial mansions stretches to Block Island Sound. *Westerly Hospital* (Wells St.; phone: 401-596-6000) proudly displays Florence Nightingale's nurse's cap. Westerly has only five main streets, but it's easy to get lost and end up in Pawcatuck, Connecticut. Keep bearing right around the circle to avoid this. Take Route 1A south of town to Watch Hill.

WATCH HILL, Rhode Island An arm of land dotted with huge summer houses, Watch Hill was built by Yankee aristocrats whose wealth was a rung or two below that of the Newport crowd. The main street is lined with little shops offering antiques, curios, candy, and homemade ice cream; at the end is an antique carousel for the kids. Best is Misquamicut State Beach (entrance just behind the carousel), a long, broad, sickle-shaped swath of soft sand. Another nice beach on the other side of town is accessible via a path next to the *Ocean House* hotel on Bluff Avenue (see *Best En Route*).

En Route from Watch Hill Take Route 1-A to Route 1, a delightfully empty road that hugs the coast, and drive east about 50 miles. At the Providence line, pick up Route I-95 east.

PROVIDENCE, Rhode Island The skyline of Rhode Island's capital city features the tall, pointed spires of historic churches, plus the capitol building's white marble dome. To see the sights, take exit 22 and follow downtown signs to Memorial Boulevard. On the left side of the boulevard are State House, *Waterplace Park,* and, just below street level, the scenic riverwalk. Turn left onto College Street and continue up the hill to Benefit Street, stopping at the *Museum of Art* (224 Benefit St.; phone: 401-454-6500). Here is a fine collection of world class art, ranging from ancient Greece, Rome, and Egypt through 20th-century US and Europe. Closed Mondays.

This area, known as College Hill, includes *Brown University,* an Ivy League school whose main gate is on Prospect Street (phone: 401-863-1000), and the *Rhode Island School of Design* (2 College St.; phone: 401-454-6100), familiarly known as *RISD*—pronounced *Riz*-dee. Both campuses schedule concerts, films, plays, lectures, and cultural exhibitions. Interspersed with college buildings are a number of splendid colonial homes, columned mansions, and gardens, some of which are open daily. By the way, George Washington really did sleep in the *Stephen Hopkins House* (10 Hopkins St. at Benefit St.; phone: 401-331-2134 for tour reservations).

If hunger strikes, stop in at the popular *Al Forno* (577 S. Main St.; phone: 401-273-9760), which serves Italian-inspired dishes including pizza grilled over a hardwood fire. Reservations are unnecessary.

En Route from Providence Follow Thayer Street to I-195. It feeds into I-95, which will take you south to New York or northeast to Boston.

BEST EN ROUTE

It is possible to find clean, basic motels along Route 1 that are inexpensive, but the more interesting choices along the way fall into the moderate or expensive category. Expect to pay $150 or more per night for a double room during high season (May through October) in those hotels listed as expensive, and $100 to $150 in those rated moderate. Unless otherwise indicated, hotels are open year-round and rooms have air conditioning, private baths, TV sets, and telephones. For each location, hotels are listed alphabetically by price category.

NEW LONDON

Lighthouse Inn The refurbished 50 rooms in this turn-of-the-century mansion and carriage house are decorated in the Victorian style. Mansion rooms feature whirlpool baths, and there's a private beach a block away. There's also a restaurant. 6 Guthrie Place (phone: 860-443-8411). Expensive.

NORWICH

Norwich Inn and Spa Twenty minutes north of New London on Route 32, this hostelry has 65 rooms in a country inn and another 65 private villas with fireplaces and kitchens. On the premises are a restaurant, a full fitness spa, tennis, swimming, and hiking trails; golf is nearby. On the Thames River, 607 W. Thames St. (phone: 860-886-2401; 800-ASK-4SPA). Expensive to moderate.

MYSTIC

The Inn at Mystic This combination inn, motor inn, and gate house on a bluff overlooking the Mystic River has 68 rooms, all decorated with antiques or reproductions. Some also come with a whirlpool and a fireplace. There's also a pool, a tennis court, and a restaurant. Rte. 1 (phone: 860-536-9604; 800-237-2415). Expensive to moderate.

Steamboat Inn This hostelry's 10 rooms all feature whirlpool baths, and some have four-poster beds and fireplaces. No restaurant, but continental breakfast is served. On the river in downtown Mystic, 77 Steamboat Wharf (phone: 860-536-8300). Expensive to moderate.

LEDYARD

Foxwoods Resort This luxurious property features 312 well-appointed rooms. With the added bonus of the adjoining famous casino, guests also enjoy an indoor pool, health club, saunas, and whirlpools. There are two restaurants, a deli, and headline entertainment nightly. Rte 2 (phone: 860-885-3000; 800-75209255; fax: 860-885-4040). Expensive to moderate.

Two Trees Inn at Foxwoods The charm of a New England country inn is captured in 280 rooms and 60 suites adjacent to *Foxwoods.* Extras include an indoor pool, exercise room, and whirlpool. A restaurant is on the premises, and 24-hour transportation is provided to the casino. Lantern Hill Rd. (phone: 860-885-3000; 800-752-9244; fax: 860-885-4050). Expensive to moderate.

WATCH HILL

Ocean House Perched on a bluff above the Atlantic, this carryover from a more genteel era (the 59-room hotel was built in 1868) retains the air of an old-time summer resort. Taking in the sun and salt air while sitting on the verandah is lovely. Breakfast and dinner are included in the rate; a European plan is also available. Open from the end of June to the day after *Labor Day.* 2 Bluff Ave. (phone: 401-348-8161). Expensive.

PROVIDENCE

Westin The city's newest hotel is also its most exclusive. This 363-room neoclassical high-rise sits adjacent to the *Rhode Island Convention Center,* making it very convenient for business travelers. Amenities include a complete health spa, indoor pool, and two fine restaurants. 1 W. Exchange St. (phone: 401-598-8000; 800-228-3000; fax: 401-598-8200). Very expensive.

Providence Biltmore A renovated, gracious old hotel downtown. Many of its 217 rooms have views of the Rhode Island capitol, which is particularly beautiful at night, when it is floodlit. *Stanford's* restaurant features an open kitchen that produces New England seafood specialties plus steaks, pasta, and salads. 11 Dorrance St. (phone: 401-421-0700; 800-437-4824; fax: 401-455-3050). Expensive to moderate.

Providence Marriott With 345 rooms, the city's second-largest hotel boasts a sleek contemporary decor and amenities that include a restaurant, pool, exercise room, sauna and whirlpool, and nightclub. 1 Orms St. (phone: 401-272-2400; 800-822-2722; fax: 401-273-2686). Expensive to moderate.

The Maine Coast and Acadia National Park, Maine

To drive along Maine's coastline is to spend some time with nature on its own forceful terms. To watch the fundamental power of the Atlantic pounding the rocky coastline—perhaps at *Acadia National Park,* where the process is dramatically apparent—is to understand that the continent is being constantly altered, continually worn away. Possibly the best route east of the California/Oregon coastal road for witnessing this clash of stone and sea and the wild beauty that results is Maine's Route 1, which stretches along the Maine coast (called "Down East" in local parlance) from Kittery to the Canadian border. The nation's history is evident all along this craggy coast—not because of famous battlesites or monuments, but because the region reflects uniquely American traditions.

The most interesting section of Route 1 for a two- or three-day drive is from Kennebunkport, about 30 miles north of the New Hampshire border, to *Acadia National Park,* midway up the coast. Along the route are a number of villages and towns whose character is distinctly "Down East."

En Route from New York or Boston Follow I-95 to Kennebunkport.

KENNEBUNKPORT A booming shipbuilding center in the mid-18th century, this small seaside town with its five distinct beaches is best known as former president George Bush's favorite retreat. (His grandfather, George Herbert Walker, bought 11 acres of land on a Kennebunkport peninsula in 1903, built two large homes there, and dubbed the site "Walker Point." It's closed to the public, but visitors often stroll along the adjoining road, which provides a glimpse of the grounds and compound.) A walking or bicycling tour of the town should include *Dock Square,* with its many shops; Maine Street, for a look at the Federal-era houses built with the profits of trading and ship building; and Ocean Avenue, which offers views of the harbor and the Atlantic. Stop at the beautiful and isolated Cleaves Cove and at Cape Porpoise, a bona fide commercial fishing harbor. The *Seashore Trolley Museum* (Log Cabin Rd.; phone: 207-967-2712) displays more than 100 vintage trolleys and may have four or five running each summer day. It's open daily from late April through early October; other times by appointment. Beach Street is the setting for the shingled *White Barn Inn,* a charming way station (see *Best en Route*). For more information contact the *Kennebunk–Kennebunkport Chamber of Commerce,* PO Box 740, Kennebunk, ME 04043 (phone: 207-967-0857).

En Route from Kennebunkport Take Route 9A to Route 1, then head north for about 30 miles to Portland.

PORTLAND Once a gritty seaport town, Portland is now one of New England's liveliest and most beautiful cities. Stroll through the Old Port district, with its cobblestone streets, colorful stores and boutiques, and restaurants that serve everything from clam chowder to authentic Thai food. The *Portland Museum of Art* (7 Congress Sq.; phone: 207-775-6148) is worth a visit, particularly for its extensive collection of paintings and watercolors by Winslow Homer. The museum is closed Mondays.

En Route from Portland Back on Route 1, continue north for about 35 miles to Bath.

BATH A shipbuilding center for centuries, Bath is the site of the *Maine Maritime Museum* (243 Washington St.; phone: 207-443-1316), which includes a historic shipyard and an apprentice boat shop. The museum is closed *Thanksgiving, Christmas,* and *New Year's Day.* Visitors also can explore the antique fishing schooner *Sherman Zwicker* during the summer, when it's in port. There is an admission charge.

En Route from Bath About 15 miles farther north on Route 1 is Wiscasset.

WISCASSET This town makes it easy to envision life as it was during the late 1800s: Many of the homes of that era, built by wealthy merchants and shippers, are still occupied and lovingly maintained today. The *Nickels-Sortwell House* (Main and Federal Sts.; no phone), one of several homes open to the public, is a good example of 19th-century Federal elegance.

En Route from Wiscasset Just north of Wiscasset on Route 1 is Route 27; follow it south for about 14 miles to Boothbay Harbor.

BOOTHBAY HARBOR This town, which was discovered by tourists years ago, is a tribute to the Yankee ingenuity that recognized the marketability of picture-postcard scenes, lobster suppers, and singular charm. Be sure to eat your fill of the local delicacy, lobster. You'll find it served in a variety of ways, all delicious and relatively inexpensive. Enjoy the appealing (albeit commercial) attractions, among them the *Railway Village* (just north of town on Rte. 27; phone: 207-633-4727; open daily June through *Columbus Day*), with its narrow-gauge passenger train. There's also a public aquarium at *Marine Resources* on McKown Point Road on the waterfront (phone: 207-633-9500; fax: 207-633-9579). It's open daily from *Memorial Day* weekend through *Columbus Day* weekend; closed the rest of the year; there's an admission charge.

There are several fine places to stay right in Boothbay Harbor, but for a memorable experience, head for Monhegan Island, just across the bay. There's a sort of time-stood-still feeling about this tranquil island—most of it, in fact, has no electricity. Stay at the *Island Inn* (see *Best en Route*), which is family-owned and over a century old, and explore the island in solitude, discovering the wildflowers and birds only a short ferry ride from the mainland.

En Route from Boothbay Harbor Head back to Route 1 and continue about 35 miles north to Rockland. This modern port city is the world's largest lobster distribution hub and the departure point for the ferry to two very special islands, North Haven and Vinalhaven.

NORTH HAVEN AND VINALHAVEN The island of North Haven is a quiet community with a number of summer estates; Vinalhaven is a fishing village of about 1,200 Down East residents. Neither island has tennis courts, swimming pools, or movies; but there are church suppers (with baked beans, brown bread, and homemade pies), walks along the often foggy shores, and the constant comings and goings of fishermen. Both islands are accessible via the *Maine State Ferry Service* from Rockland (PO Box 645, Rockland, ME 04841; phone: 207-596-2202; 800-491-4883).

En Route from North Haven or Vinalhaven Return to Rockland and proceed north on Route 1 to Camden, about 10 miles away.

CAMDEN This beautiful harbor town is surrounded by high hills, with good skiing and other winter sports at *Camden Snow Bowl* (phone: 207-236-3438) and a number of beautiful old homes. It's an ideal spot if you want to go for a walk, take a long lunch, or go shopping—especially if you're in the market for one of Maine's 3,344 islands. Camden is something of an island real estate center, and the place to start looking is in the advertising pages of *Down East* magazine, published in neighboring Rockport.

En Route from Camden Follow Route 1 north to Ellsworth, then take Route 3 south to Mt. Desert Island.

MT. DESERT ISLAND One of the most wildly beautiful spots in the country, this island devotes 40,000 acres to spectacular *Acadia National Park.* The park is the site of Mt. Cadillac (named by the French explorer Samuel de Champlain in 1605), the highest spot on the Atlantic coast. At 1,532 feet it's hardly gargantuan, but there's a marvelous view of Frenchman Bay from the summit.

Bar Harbor, the island's major town, was too posh for most folks in its heyday—from the 1890s through the 1940s. The old wealth is still here (as you will see when you peek at the mammoth estates in the hills from the park's loop road), but today Bar Harbor is far too open, raucous, and egalitarian to appeal to its original crowd. It opens and closes with the summer season, and for people en route to *Acadia,* it offers trendy shops (especially the *Rock Shop* on Main Street), many motels and inns, and a host of good seafood restaurants.

The real attraction of Mt. Desert, however, is *Acadia,* New England's only national park. *Acadia* is also the only national park purchased with private funds, an effort organized by Dr. Charles W. Eliot of *Harvard* and George Bucknam Dorr when lumber interests threatened the island. The nation accepted the gift in 1916. Parts of the park are off the island, on Isle au Haut and on Schoodic Point on the mainland, but the main attractions are accessible from Mt. Desert's 20-mile Park Loop Road. Start a tour at the visitors' center (at the entrance near Bar Harbor), where there are exhibitions on the ecology and history of the island. You also can pick up information there on camping and on golf, cycling, horseback riding, hiking, swimming, and an array of winter sports, as well as maps of the driving routes and the hundreds of trails that score the island's mountains. The Ocean Drive loop culminates at the crown of Mt. Cadillac; along the way there are ample opportunities to stop for a descent straight to the rocky shore. For park information, contact *Acadia National Park* (PO Box 177, Bar Harbor, ME 04609; phone: 207-288-3338).

Cruises among the nearby islands, directed by naturalists, depart from the harbors of all of the island's towns (Bar Harbor, Northeast Harbor, Bass Harbor). You may search for eagles' nests or signs of porpoises and seals, go whale watching, learn about the lobster trade, or make a foray to the *Islesford Historical Museum* on Little Cranberry Island to see maritime and other historical items from the island's past. Information about cruises is available at the *Acadia Visitors' Center* two miles north of Bar Harbor in Hulls Cove (phone: 207-288-3338). It's closed November through April.

BEST EN ROUTE

The three weeks from late September to mid-October are foliage season here, a magical (but crowded) period. The optimal time to visit is from mid-

October to mid-November, when life has returned to normal, the weather (with luck) is fine, and rates are often cut in half at those inns that remain open. Expect to pay $185 to $360 per night during high season (June through October) for a double room in those places we've listed as very expensive; $130 to $185 in those rated expensive; $85 to $130 in those rated moderate; and less than $85 in the inexpensive ones. For each location below, hotels are listed alphabetically by price category. They're open year-round unless otherwise noted.

KENNEBUNKPORT

Captain Lord Mansion This Federal-style inn combines the informality of a home—the kitchen is always open to guests—with extra amenities such as room refrigerators and a gift shop. The 16 rooms (14 with fireplaces) are decorated with fine antiques; all have air conditioning, phones, and private baths. A full breakfast is included in the rate. No restaurant. On the corner of Pleasant and Green Sts. (phone: 207-967-3141). Expensive.

White Barn Inn A restored 19th-century boardinghouse, this gray-shingled and white-shuttered member of the prestigious Relais & Châteaux hotel group has 24 rooms (including seven suites) with period furnishings. The suites have fireplaces and whirlpool baths; all have air conditioning, TV sets, and phones. The restaurant is one of the area's best, featuring fine New England cooking. 37 Beach St. (phone: 207-967-2321; fax: 207-967-1100). Moderate.

MONHEGAN ISLAND

Island Inn Surrounded by 10 miles of open sea, this 45-room inn provides a total getaway, with no telephones, TV sets, or air conditioning—indeed, only limited electricity for lighting and hot water. Rates include breakfast. Open late-May through mid-October. Also see *America's Special Havens* in DIVERSIONS. 10 Ocean St. (phone: 207-596-0371; 800-722-1269 in winter). Expensive.

NORTH HAVEN

Pulpit Harbor Inn This pleasant place on a small, quiet island has four rooms. All rooms have air conditioning, but no telephones or TV sets; some have private baths. There's no restaurant, but breakfast is included in the rate. Crabtree Point Rd. (phone: 207-867-2219). Moderate to inexpensive.

VINALHAVEN

Fox Island Inn This 100-year-old house in the village has six guest rooms, all with comfortable country decor. Rooms do not have air conditioning, telephones, private baths, or TV sets, and there's no restaurant. Breakfast, which is included in the rate, is homemade every morning. Complimentary bicycles are available. Closed mid-October through mid-May. Carver Rd. (phone: 207-863-2122). Inexpensive.

Libby House Bed and Breakfast Just minutes from Main Street, this 19th-century house offers five no-smoking rooms, some with harbor views. Two rooms have private baths, but there are no TVs, telephones, or air conditioning. Open late June to *Labor Day.* No credit cards. Water St. (phone: 207-863-4696). Inexpensive.

Tidewater Motel This 11-room motel has a view of the main harbor. There's no restaurant, and the rooms have no air conditioning or phones, but all have private baths and TV sets. Open year-round. Main St. (phone: 207-863-4618). Moderate to inexpensive.

CAMDEN

Nurumbega Inn This turreted fieldstone Victorian summer "cottage" (actually more like a castle) is one of Maine's most beautiful bed and breakfast establishments. There are 12 large bedrooms, each decorated with reproduction furniture, including a king-size bed. Some rooms have spectacular views of Penobscot Bay, and all have phones. Full breakfast is served each morning; there is a wine and cheese hour in the afternoon. No restaurant. The penthouse suite is air conditioned. 61 High St. (phone: 207-236-4646). Very expensive.

Edgecombe-Coles House The best of the six rooms in this converted 1890s Camden summer house overlook Penobscot Bay. Some rooms have fireplaces, king-size beds, and TV sets, but there's no air conditioning. There's no restaurant either, but a full breakfast is included. 64 High St. (phone: 207-236-2336). Expensive.

Whitehall Inn A classic Maine house, it has several deep, cool, wraparound porches decorated with potted plants. Edna St. Vincent Millay, a resident of the town from the time she was 18, gave the first public recitation of "Renascence" here. There are 50 guestrooms and a restaurant. No air conditioning or TV sets, but the rooms have phones. Open May through October. 52 High St. (phone: 207-236-3391; 800-789-6565 for reservations; fax: 800-236-4427). Expensive to moderate.

Blue Harbor House There are 10 rooms with private baths in this New England Cape–style hostelry, unique for its large glass-walled dining and living rooms. Afternoon tea and full breakfast are included in the rate. All rooms offer air conditioning, TV sets, and phones. 67 Elm St., Rte. 1 (phone: 207-236-3196; 800-248-3196). Moderate.

MT. DESERT ISLAND

Asticou Inn The proprietors of this elegant but comfortable 113-year-old resort like to get to know their visitors. There are no TV sets, but each room has a phone. Breakfast and dinner are included in the rate during high season. The inn is open year-round. During the winter season it operates as the

Cranberry Restaurant and Lodge. Located in the very backyard of *Acadia National Park,* Asticou Way, Northeast Harbor (phone: 207-276-3344; 800-258-3373 for reservations; fax: 207-276-3373). Very expensive.

HULLS COVE

Inn at Canoe Point Located near the *Acadia National Park Visitors' Center,* midway between Hulls Cove and Bar Harbor, this Tudor-style stone mansion offers an elegant alternative to the motels along Route 1. All five rooms feature views of Frenchman Bay. No air conditioning, TV sets, telephones, or restaurant, but a full breakfast is included in the rate. No credit cards accepted. On the coast, off Rte. 3 (phone: 207-288-9511). Very expensive.

Maryland's Eastern Shore

Separated from the larger portion of Maryland by the Chesapeake Bay is a peninsula known as the Eastern Shore. Lying between the bay and the Atlantic Ocean, this genteel region is one of the first settled by the British; Lord Baltimore and his followers established their settlements here in 1634.

The Eastern Shore is characterized by rolling farmland, stately manors whose grounds stretch to the water's edge, picturesque towns, broad tidal rivers, and creeks. In this part of the country, "the bay" means only one thing: the Chesapeake, 200 miles long and from 4 to 30 miles wide. The Eastern Shore's renowned oysters, crabs, clams, and fish are brought in on utilitarian workboats that cruise the bay alongside luxurious yachts and sailboats.

Our route starts on the north end of the Eastern Shore in Chesapeake City and winds its way down to Smith and Tangier Islands, the latter being in Virginia.

En Route from Baltimore Take US 40 or I-95 northeast about 35 miles, then head 5 miles south on Route 213 to Chesapeake City.

CHESAPEAKE CITY Located on the Chesapeake and Delaware Canal, this restored historic village features antiques, gift, and specialty shops, charming bed and breakfast inns, local artists' exhibits, and fine dining. The canal, built in 1829, shortened the water route between Baltimore and Philadelphia by more than 275 miles. It was purchased by the US government in 1919 and later lowered to sea level. Used by commercial and pleasure craft, it is an important link in the inland waterway system connecting Maine to Florida. One of the world's largest waterwheels, used to control water levels until the early 1900s, can be seen in the *Old Lock Pump House* (phone: 410-885-5621 or 410-885-5622), along with a scale model of the original canal. It's open daily; there's no admission charge.

En Route from Chesapeake City Continue south for 8 miles on Route 213, turn right at Route 282 west, and drive about 2 miles to Grove Neck Road. Turn left and then, almost immediately, right, and then follow Grove Neck about a mile to the *Mount Harmon Plantation,* which overlooks the Sassafras River.

MOUNT HARMON PLANTATION On this 18th-century tobacco plantation are a restored 1730 brick mansion (closed indefinitely), formal boxwood and wisteria gardens, and a tobacco house. Drive through the 386-acre property, which is surrounded almost entirely by water and evocative of 17th- and 18th-century life on the Eastern Shore. The site is now owned by the *Natural Lands Trust* and more than 200 acres are still farmed, although tobacco no longer is grown. The plantation is closed November through March; for information contact *Mount Harmon Plantation* (PO Box 65, Earleville, MD 21919; phone: 410-275-8819).

En Route from Mount Harmon Plantation Continue about 20 miles south on Route 213 to Chestertown.

CHESTERTOWN This charming and tranquil town on the banks of the Chester River, founded in 1706, contains many colonial and Victorian houses, sophisticated shops, and bed and breakfast inns, along with brick sidewalks and a town square with a large ornamental cast-iron fountain. Across town, away from the river on Washington Avenue, *Washington College* spreads over 20 acres. Founded in 1780, this small liberal arts school is the only college George Washington permitted to use his name. Pre-Revolutionary buildings include the *Wickes House* (100 E. High St.); *Palmer House* (532 W. High St.); *Geddes-Piper House* (Church Alley); and *Widehall* and the *Customs House* (both at High and Water Sts.). You can obtain a self-guided walking tour map from the shops or at the *Kent County Chamber of Commerce* (400 S. Cross St., PO Box 146, Chestertown, MD 21620; phone: 410-778-0416). On the third Saturday in September, a candlelight walking tour leads past sweeping lawns into 18th-, 19th-, and 20th-century sites including colonial homes decorated with ornate, carved mantelpieces and unusual Americana. Admission charge for tour. For more information, call the *Historical Society of Kent County* (phone: 410-778-3499).

En Route from Chestertown Go south for about 25 miles on Route 213 to Route 662 and Wye Mills.

WYE MILLS This tiny colonial town grew up around an early 18th-century gristmill, which ground flour for Washington's Valley Forge troops. The mill is now restored and again in use. *Wye Church,* built in 1721, is also in use. Nearby stands the Wye Oak, the official state tree. It has provided shade for more than 450 years, and is one of the largest white oaks in the country.

En Route from Wye Mills Head south for 12 miles on US 50 to Easton.

EASTON The self-proclaimed "Colonial Capital of the Eastern Shore," Easton is known for its fine local antiques, artwork, and artifacts. Historic attractions include the *Talbot County Historical Society and Museum* (25 S. Washington St.: phone: 410-822-0773) and two old houses on its grounds: *Joseph's Cottage* (1795); the *James Neall House* (1810). A few blocks south on Washington Street is the *Third Haven Meeting House,* built in 1682; and the *Ending of Controversy,* a house representative of the 17th century. During the second weekend in November the town celebrates the *Waterfowl Festival,* which attracts wildfowl artists and carvers from all over the East Coast. For information contact the *Talbot County Chamber of Commerce* (PO Box 1366, Easton, MD 21601; phone: 410-822-4606; fax: 410-822-7922).

En Route from Easton Take Route 322 (the Easton Parkway) south to Route 333 south. Route 333 becomes Morris Street in Oxford, which is about 10 miles from Easton. Continue on 333 until you reach water. The *Oxford-Bellevue Ferry* (phone: 410-745-9023) shuttles across the Tred Avon River, offering a fine view of the enclosed port and the small boating community of Oxford, founded in 1683. On the other side of the river, take Route 329 north to Route 33 northwest and continue about 8 miles to St. Michaels.

ST. MICHAELS At the *Chesapeake Bay Maritime Museum* (Maritime Rd.; phone: 410-745-2916) are an authentic 19th-century lighthouse, maritime exhibitions, a boatbuilding workshop, and Chesapeake Bay sailing craft. Open weekends and holidays only from *January 1* through the first week of March; open daily the rest of the year. Admission charge. Narrated cruises of the Miles River can be taken from the museum aboard the 65-foot-long, steel-hulled *Patriot* from April through October (phone: 410-745-3100).

En Route from St. Michaels Continue southwest on Route 33 to the Knapp's Narrows drawbridge, one of the busiest in the world, and cross over to Tilghman Island.

TILGHMAN ISLAND Scenic and remote, Tilghman Island is home to a portion of the Chesapeake Bay skipjack fleet, seafood packing houses, and a number of good restaurants, including *Harrison's Chesapeake House* (phone: 410-886-2121); *Bay Hundred* (phone: 410-886-2622); and *Island Grill* (phone: 410-886-2330). Fishing boats are available for charter; *Harrison's Sport Fishing Center* (phone: 410-886-2121) has the largest fleet on the island.

En Route from Tilghman Island Return to Easton and continue on Route 50 south past Cambridge to Route 16. Follow Route 16 southwest to Route 335, then head south to the *Blackwater National Wildlife Refuge.*

BLACKWATER NATIONAL WILDLIFE REFUGE *Blackwater* is a winter refuge for Canada and snow geese, ducks, and birds of prey, and home to the American bald eagle, the Delmarva fox squirrel, and other endangered species. A visitors' information center (2145 Key Wallace Dr.; phone: 410-228-2677) offers maps for driving and walking tours; it's open daily from *Labor Day* through *Memorial Day;* weekdays only during the rest of the year. There's an admission charge.

En Route from Blackwater National Wildlife Refuge Return to Cambridge, then drive about 55 miles south on Route 50, picking up Route 13 south at Salisbury and Route 413 soon after Princess Anne. Continue south on 413 to Crisfield, from which several boats take passengers, mail, and freight to two unusual retreats, Smith and Tangier Islands.

SMITH AND TANGIER ISLANDS Chesapeake Bay watermen live and work on these islands, both of which are flat, sandy, and surrounded by marshland.

Smith Island, Maryland, where many residents still speak with the hint of a British accent, features wharves, crab shanties, tiny frame houses with gardens, and very little commercialism. There's no town hall here because there's no local government: Nearly everything is part of the United Methodist Church.

Tangier Island, Virginia, is more developed, with an anchorage for visiting sailors, a high school, and a local government headed by a mayor. Still, it's not unusual to see gravestones and vaults smack-dab in the small front yards of the houses. For more information, contact *Somerset County Tourism* (PO Box 243, Princess Anne, MD 21853; phone: 410-651-2968; 800-521-9189).

BEST EN ROUTE

For a double room during tourist season, expect to pay $149 or more per night in those places we've listed as expensive; $90 to $149 at places in the moderate category; and less than $90 in the one rated inexpensive. Unless otherwise noted, hotels are open year-round and rooms have air conditioning, private baths, TV sets, and telephones. For each location, hotels are listed alphabetically by price category.

EASTON

Tidewater Inn Almost a legend and certainly a landmark, this renovated colonial inn is the center of the town's activities, especially during the *Waterfowl Festival.* Its 113 rooms include eight suites. The restaurant is famous for its crab cakes and snapper soup. 101 E. Dover St. (phone: 410-822-1300; 800-237-8775). Moderate.

OXFORD

Robert Morris Inn Built in the early 1700s, this 35-room hostelry is furnished with period antiques. Its large dining room is open to non-guests. The inn is close to tennis, golf, sailing, swimming, and bicycling. From mid-January through mid-March, the inn and restaurant are closed. 314 N. Morris St. (phone: 410-226-5111). Moderate.

ST. MICHAELS

Inn at Perry Cabin The first of the stateside inn projects established by Sir Bernard Ashley (of the Laura Ashley empire), this 41-room property is located on the Chesapeake Bay side of the Eastern Shore. The Ashley touch is evident throughout—on the wallpaper, bed and bath linen, and in the cozy sitting room. Afternoon tea is served in the library, other meals in the inn's restaurant. 308 Watkins La. (phone: 410-745-2200; 800-722-2949). Expensive.

St. Michaels Harbor Inn This modern hotel sits alongside the marina. There are 38 suites with balconies and eight rooms; all but four of the rooms and suites have a water view, as does the restaurant. 101 N. Harbor Rd. (phone: 410-745-9001; 800-955-9001). Expensive.

PRINCESS ANNE

Washington Hotel and Inn Built in 1744, this full-service property has two restaurants and 12 rooms, six of which are decorated with period furniture and accessories. 11784 Somerset Ave. (phone: 410-651-2525). Inexpensive.

TANGIER ISLAND, VIRGINIA

Chesapeake House A charming eight-room guesthouse, it's close to many nautical activities. The restaurant serves generous portions of homemade family fare. Room rates include breakfast and dinner. Open April 15 to October 15. On Main St., five minutes from the ferry dock (phone: 804-891-2331). Moderate.

The Berkshires, Massachusetts

Nestled in a 20-mile-wide strip along the western border of the state, Berkshire County stretches from Connecticut to Vermont along the border Massachusetts shares with New York. However, the Berkshires—more correctly referred to as the Berkshire Hills (although you'll swear they look just like mountains)—start in earnest west of I-91, beginning from Sheffield in the south to the Mohawk Trail on Route 2 and Vermont in the north. The Berkshires are famous for art and music in the summer, foliage in the fall, and downhill and cross-country skiing in the winter.

Summer is prime time for artistic offerings here. From the world-famous *Tanglewood* concerts and the *Jacob's Pillow* dance performances to other theatrical offerings and art galleries, the area is synonymous with both excellence and innovation. During the summer months there's so much going on that even residents have to consult the newspaper; local papers run comprehensive lists of events at all locations.

A formidable rival to summer is autumn, when the Berkshire Hills explode into color. The leaf-peeping season starts in late September, and most trees are in their full regalia in early October. Finding foliage at its absolute peak is about as unlikely as finding perfect snow on a ski trip—Nature rarely cooperates—but the trees are pretty for at least a couple of weeks before and after what the experts consider their peak.

In the winter, snow is the Berkshires' main attraction. Mt. Greylock, the state's highest peak, provides a glorious setting for cross-country skiing and snowmobiling.

For lodging referrals or general information, write to the *Berkshire Visitors Bureau* (Berkshire Common, Pittsfield, MA 01201; phone: 413-443-9186; 800-237-5747). Request the *Discover the Berkshires* guidebook and the *Circle Tours* booklet, which describes nine trips through the area. For information on the Mohawk Trail area, contact the *Mohawk Trail Association* (PO Box 722, Charlemont, MA 01339; phone: 413-664-6256). Ask for the *Mohawk Trail Region Visitors Guide,* a directory of the region's accommodations.

Our route mainly follows Route 7, which runs straight through the Berkshires, then merges into the Mohawk Trail. The perfect introduction to the area, it covers all the major towns (Pittsfield is the only city of any size): Great Barrington, Stockbridge, Lenox, Pittsfield, and Williamstown. If you'd like to explore the region further, keep in mind that the outside boundaries of the Berkshires form an almost perfect rectangle, which in turn makes an almost perfect driving route. Follow the rectangle (Route 8 to the east, Route 22 in New York on the west, Route 23 along the south, and Route 2 at the north) and you can take in all the significant cultural, educational, and historical activities that give the Berkshires area its special cachet.

En Route from Boston Follow the Massachusetts Turnpike (I-90) west for about 125 miles. If you're a dance fan and the season is right (see below), take exit 2 at Lee, head east on Route 20, then north to Becket, about 6 miles from the turnpike.

BECKET This is the home of *Jacob's Pillow,* America's oldest dance festival. From late June through August, it draws dance groups from all over the world. For a schedule and reservations, contact *Jacob's Pillow Dance Festival* (PO Box 287, Lee, MA 01238; phone: 413-243-0745).

En Route from Becket Backtrack toward I-90 and head west to Stockbridge on Route 20.

STOCKBRIDGE This beautiful town is the archetypal Berkshire village, in part because of the work of its late resident Norman Rockwell. Stockbridge's buildings and people graced the covers of the *Saturday Evening Post* dozens of times. Many of Rockwell's famous paintings can be seen at the *Norman Rockwell Museum* at the edge of town (on Rte. 183; phone: 413-298-4100); it's closed on *Thanksgiving, Christmas,* and *New Year's Day.* On Main Street is the marvelous *Red Lion Inn* (see *Best en Route*), one of New England's most famous hostelries. The *Berkshire Theatre Festival,* the oldest summer theater in the country, takes place in *The Berkshire Playhouse* (E. Main St.; phone: 413-298-5536), a landmark building designed by Stanford White. Among the many tempting stores in town is the *1884 House* (Main St.; phone: 413-298-5159), which features classic British countrywear for men and women.

Two interesting stops are *Chesterwood* (2 miles west of town off Rte. 183, Glendale; phone: 413-298-3579), the home of sculptor Daniel Chester French, and *Mission House* (Main and Sergeant Sts.; phone: 413-298-3239). At *Chesterwood,* you can visit the home, its studio, barn gallery, and garden. The *Mission House* was built in 1739 by the Reverend John Sergeant, who preached to the Stockbridge Indians. Sergeant, a charismatic minister, was remarkable in his time for accepting Indian cultural values; a few blocks from the *Mission House,* a marker reads: "The Ancient Burial Place of the Stockbridge Indians, Friends of Our Fathers." Today the house is a museum of early colonial life. Both houses charge admission and are closed from November through April. Another interesting site in Stockbridge is *Naumkeag* (Prospect Hill; 413-298-3239), a gem of a Victorian mansion set on sweeping lawns trimmed with gardens designed by Fletcher Steele. It's closed Mondays (except on holidays) and from the day after *Columbus Day* to *Memorial Day.* There's an admission charge.

En Route from Stockbridge Take Routes 7 and 7A north to Lenox.

LENOX Generally acknowledged as the star town of the Berkshires, Lenox is the summer home of the *Boston Symphony Orchestra.* In July and August, the *Tanglewood Music Festival* draws crowds of thousands each weekend. The new 1,200-seat *Seiji Ozawa Hall* has an open back to allow patrons to picnic on the lawn while enjoying a performance. You can tour the manicured grounds and the *Hemlock Gardens* as well. For more information, see *Music Festivals: Summers of Sound* in DIVERSIONS. *The Mount* (south junction of Rte. 7A and Plunkett St.; phone: 413-637-1899), once the home of Pulitzer Prize–winning novelist Edith Wharton, is closed from November through May and Mondays from June through October. House and garden tours are offered. It's also the summer home of *Shakespeare & Company,* which offers outdoors performances of the Bard's plays and matinee performances of plays based on Wharton's stories and novels during July and August (phone: 413-637-1197).

Nearby is the *Pleasant Valley Wildlife Sanctuary* (472 W. Mountain Rd.; phone: 413-637-0320), maintained by the *Massachusetts Audubon Society.* Marked trails show you western Massachusetts flora and fauna, including a beaver colony. It's closed Mondays; there's an admission charge.

En Route from Lenox Head north for about 7 miles on Route 7 to Pittsfield.

PITTSFIELD The biggest town in the Berkshires, Pittsfield is a sprawling commercial center; its main attractions are out of town. In late August and early autumn, the *South Mountain Concerts* series features chamber music (phone: 413-442-2106). *Hancock Shaker Village* (5 miles west of town on Rte. 20; phone: 413-443-0188) is an original Shaker community, built around 1790. It contains 20 restored buildings on some 1,200 acres. (Also see *Utopias and Religious Settlements* in DIVERSIONS.) Open daily April through November; a special *Christmas* festival takes place the first weekend in December. The *Berkshire Museum* (39 South St.; phone: 413-443-7171) has an impressive collection of Old Masters, early American works, and modern pieces as well as natural history displays and children's exhibits; it's open daily during July and August and closed Mondays the rest of the year. If you loved *Moby Dick,* visit *Arrowhead* (780 Holmes Rd.; phone: 413-442-1793), Herman Melville's home from 1850 to 1863, to see Melville memorabilia, furniture, and period clothing. It's open daily from *Memorial Day* through *Halloween;* remainder of the year by appointment only. If hunger strikes, *Elizabeth's* (1264 East St.; phone: 413-448-8244) offers tantalizing pizza, sandwiches, and salads. It's closed Mondays; no credit cards accepted.

En Route from Pittsfield Continue north on Route 7 until it ends in Williamstown, 20 miles away.

WILLIAMSTOWN This is the home of *Williams College* (phone: 413-597-3131); the *Williamstown Theatre Festival* (Main St.; phone: 413-597-3400) in the summer; and the *Clark Art Institute* (South St.; phone: 413-458-9545), a jewel box of a museum with outstanding examples of work by the French Impressionists, in addition to old silver, porcelain, and sculpture. The *Williams College Museum of Art* (Main St.; phone: 413-597-2429) houses prehistoric and contemporary art, as well as works by the American Impressionists Maurice and Charles Prendergast.

En Route from Williamstown Turn the "corner" of the Berkshire route, leaving Route 7 for the Mohawk Trail (Route 2) east toward Greenfield. To the south, nature provides some spectacular attractions along the way: Mt. Greylock and its war memorial; the Natural Bridge formation, which has been around for an estimated 55 million years; and the *Savoy Mountain State Forest,* with its host of camping, picnicking, swimming, hunting, and fishing spots.

BEST EN ROUTE

Below are our choices from a wide variety of eating and lodging places. The Berkshires have some of the best inns in the country—truly an embarrassment of riches. Expect to pay $175 to $250 or more (sometimes much more) per night during high season (June through October) for a double room in those places we call very expensive; $130 to $175 in those rated expensive; and $75 to $130 in those listed as moderate. There are no extraordinary hotels here in the inexpensive category. Unless otherwise indicated, hotels are open year-round and rooms have air conditioning, private baths, TV sets, and telephones. For each location, hotels are listed alphabetically by price category.

STOCKBRIDGE AND WEST STOCKBRIDGE

Williamsville Inn Dating from 1797, this former farmhouse is on a 10-acre property with a pool, a tennis court, and skiing and antiquing nearby. The 16 rooms include two with fireplaces and four with wood stoves; none have TV sets or telephones. The inn is known for its fine country homemade fare. Route 41, West Stockbridge (phone: 413-274-6118). Moderate.

Red Lion Inn The atmosphere here is homey, friendly, and full of small-town charm—complete with rocking chairs on the wide front porch. The 108 rooms and 10 suites are filled with antiques. There's also an outdoor pool, an exercise room, and three dependable restaurants. Also see *America's Special Havens* in DIVERSIONS. Main St., Stockbridge (phone: 413-298-5545). Moderate.

LENOX

Blantyre Right out of America's golden age, this country house has 23 rooms and five suites. Amenities include sports facilities, a pool, a sauna, a Jacuzzi, and an excellent restaurant. Also see *America's Special Havens* in DIVERSIONS. Closed October through April. On Blantyre Rd. off Rte. 20 (phone: 413-637-3556 in summer; 413-298-3806 in winter). Very expensive.

Canyon Ranch A contemporary retreat. The main buildings consist of a two-story inn with 120 guestrooms, an extensive spa, and the *Bellefontaine Mansion.* Facilities include an indoor lap pool, indoor tennis, racquetball, and squash courts, herbal and massage rooms, saunas, Jacuzzis, and steamrooms, as well as an outdoor pool, tennis courts, and extensive hiking and cross-country ski trails. All rooms have TV sets and phones, and are air conditioned. Kemble St., Lenox (phone: 800-326-7080; fax: 413-637-0057). Very expensive.

Wheatleigh An Italianate palazzo surrounded by formal gardens and lawns, with an equally elegant restaurant. Of the 17 rooms, we recommend those that face the lake. There are no TV sets. The hotel has a pool, a tennis court, and a steamroom. Also see *America's Special Havens* in DIVERSIONS. On Hawthorne Rd. (phone: 413-637-0610; fax: 413-637-4507). Very expensive.

SOUTH LEE

Federal House A few miles east of Stockbridge, this small, cozy inn built in 1824 has six rooms, all decorated with period furniture and fresh flowers (there are no TV sets or telephones). Its restaurant serves excellent continental food for dinner only; a continental breakfast is included in the rate. In the heart of town on Rte. 102 (phone: 413-243-1824). Expensive.

Orchards Just outside Williamstown center, this inn captures Old English–style ambience complete with fresh flowers in all 47 rooms. All rooms have TV sets, phones, and air conditioning. The inn also has an exercise room with Jacuzzi and sauna. Its restaurant specializes in continental cuisine serving breakfast, lunch, and dinner. 222 Adams Rd. (phone: 413-459-9611; 800-225-1517; fax: 413-458-3273). Expensive.

Cape Cod, Martha's Vineyard, and Nantucket, Massachusetts

On a map of Massachusetts, Cape Cod resembles a squat foot—wrapped in a slipper that curls up at the toes—stepping into the Atlantic. The cape is 70 miles long from Buzzards Bay, where it leaves the mainland, to the tip of its toe at Provincetown. It juts about 30 miles into the Atlantic, far enough to be washed by the warmer waters of the Gulf Stream; consequently, the cape has cooler summers and milder winters than inland areas—and the beaches on its south side are usually about 10 degrees cooler than the northern and eastern beaches.

Below the cape, accessible by ferry and plane, are the famous islands of Martha's Vineyard and Nantucket, where the homes and villages of America's 19th-century seafaring community are still bustling.

The sea provides the sailing, swimming, and beaches that make the area so attractive in summer: Cape Cod has 300 miles of clean, beautiful coastline. The sea—and the sand it constantly rearranges—also makes Cape Cod one of the most interesting ecological studies a layman is likely to stumble across.

The sea is responsible for the region's history. Pilgrims landed at Provincetown about a month before they reached Plymouth, and the cape's beautiful, perfectly preserved 19th-century homes and villages are products of the area's successful ventures into worldwide shipping 150 years ago: There was a time when Nantucket captains were as likely to meet one another in the Banda Islands as on the streets at home.

Commercialism has corrupted much of the area's tranquillity, filling up open spaces with fast-food chains, and assaulting the eyes and ears with concrete and cacophony. But, thankfully, the assault is not universal. Protected by law from 20th-century excesses are the *Cape Cod National Seashore,* with its 40-mile stretch of untamed shoreline; and old Route 6A (or Old Kings' Highway Historic District) along the north coast of the cape. Village elders must okay even the smallest changes within the historic district; consequently, very few changes take place. For a look at what might have happened without these protective laws, take a drive along the south shore on Route 28, which is lined on both sides with drive-ins, stores, and restaurants with names like *Leaning Tower of Pizza.*

Sightseeing on Cape Cod can be adapted to fit your preference: For up-to-the-minute action, follow Route 28; for peace and a sense of history, take Route 6A; and for a quick route to Provincetown, take Route 6, which bisects the cape. One further consideration: In peak season, Cape Cod groans under the weight of all its adoring visitors. (Provincetown's population, about 4,000 in the off-season, leaps to 45,000 during the summer.) If you plan your trip for either spring or late fall, you'll find it easier to enjoy nature and to find some local folks with time to sit and chat; if you want crowds and excitement (and weather suitable for swimming and sunning), July and August are your time.

Our tour of Cape Cod and the neighboring islands sweeps up the northern shore to Provincetown on Route 6A and returns via the outer shore along the southern coast as far as Hyannis on Route 28. Here, you pick up the ferry (summers only) for the two offshore islands. The trip ends with a return to the cape at Woods Hole in Falmouth.

En Route from Boston Follow Route 3 south to Route 6A and Sandwich, about 60 miles away.

SANDWICH The first town along Route 6A is rich in history. The *Sandwich Glass Museum* (Rte. 130, 129 Main St.; phone: 508-888-0251) has remarkable examples of the town's famous glass; closed January. The *First Church of Christ* (136 Main St.; phone: 508-888-0434), which dates from 1848, features a spire copied from a design by Sir Christopher Wren. American artifacts from antique cars to a Civil War gristmill can be seen at the *Heritage Plantation* (Grove and Pine Sts.; phone: 508-888-3300), and children will be delighted with the *Yesteryears Doll Museum* (River and Main Sts.; phone: 508-888-1711). Both are closed in the off-season (November through April).

En Route from Sandwich Continue on 6A to Yarmouth Port.

YARMOUTH PORT Three original restored houses are located here: the 18th-century *Captain Bangs Hallet House* (11 Strawberry La.; phone: 508-362-3021 for information on hours); the 1680 *Colonel John Thatcher House* (Rte. 6A); and the 1780 *Winslow Crocker House* (250 Main St.; phone: 508-362-4385 for information on hours). Only the *Bangs Hallet* and *Crocker* houses are open to the public; both charge admission.

En Route from Yarmouth Port Continue on 6A to Dennis and East Dennis. To explore South and West Dennis, head south on Route 134 and then backtrack to the west on Route 28.

"THE DENNISES" Four towns—South, East, and West Dennis, and Dennis Port—offer a combination of old and new. Scattered throughout the four towns, mostly along Route 6A and around Yarmouth Port, are historical houses open to tourists. From June through mid-September, there's contemporary theater at the *Cape Playhouse* on Main Street in Dennis (Rte. 6A; phone: 508-385-3911), and the *Dennis Pines* golf course has two 18-hole courses (Rte. 134 in East Dennis; phone: 508-385-8347).

En Route from The Dennises Continue for about 5 miles on 6A to Brewster, the next stop after East Dennis.

BREWSTER The main attraction here is the *Cape Cod Museum of Natural History* (Main St.; phone: 508-896-3867; 800-479-3867 from Massachusetts), with live animals and marine exhibits. It's closed Sunday mornings; there's an admission charge.

En Route from Brewster Continue on 6A until it merges with Route 6; then follow Route 6 to Eastham, about 10 miles away.

EASTHAM This is the gateway town to the *Cape Cod National Seashore* (see below). The old (1793) *Eastham Windmill* on Route 6 still works, and the *Historical Society* maintains several restored homes for touring. The society's office is just off Route 6, in an 1869 schoolhouse with exhibits (phone: 508-255-0788).

En Route from Eastham To the right off Route 6, half a mile north of *Eastham Town Hall,* is the entrance to the *Cape Cod National Seashore.*

CAPE COD NATIONAL SEASHORE Cape Cod is a peninsula without bedrock—it is all sand. Before the first settlers came, stands of hardwood and topsoil protected the Atlantic shoreline from the sea's fury. Over time the sea and the wind played havoc with the sand—shores around Truro and Wellfleet were devoured, and the sand was deposited along the moors surrounding Provincetown. The *Cape Cod National Seashore* was created in 1961 after years of appalling neglect had almost eradicated this 27,000-acre chunk of the cape. The national seashore runs 40 miles from Chatham to Provincetown and includes six towns, much private property, and five public beaches with parking lots (Herring Cove, Head of the Meadow, Race Point, Marconi, and Nauset). No camping is allowed except on privately owned campgrounds. There are four picnic areas. From June through the fall, the *National Park Service* conducts guided tours and evening lectures. There are many self-guided trails, bike trails, and working lighthouses, plus braille markers and trails suitable for blind travelers with canes. For more information, contact Superintendent, *Cape Cod National Seashore* (South Wellfleet, MA 02663; phone: 508-349-3785); *Race Point Rangers Station* (Race Point Rd., Provincetown; phone: 508-487-2100); or *Salt Pond Visitors Center* (Rte. 6, Eastham; phone: 508-255-3421).

En Route from Cape Cod National Seashore Back on Route 6, continue up the coast to Wellfleet, about 2 miles from the headquarters building.

WELLFLEET Numerous beaches for swimming and a wealth of inland freshwater ponds dot the area. Fishing and sailing are also well provided for here—the town marina can accommodate 150 boats. *Wellfleet Bay Wildlife Sanctuary* (off Rte. 6 in South Wellfleet; phone: 508-349-2615) runs a summer day camp for kids with an emphasis on natural history and features nature trails, one of which is self-guided.

En Route from Wellfleet Drive north on Route 6 to Truro.

TRURO A real contrast to Provincetown's hustle, sparsely settled Truro is known for its excellent fishing and swimming and for the *Highland Light* (also known as the *Cape Cod Light*). The *Light,* which dates to 1795, can be seen 20 miles out to sea. For additional information contact the *Truro Chamber of Commerce* (phone: 508-487-1288).

En Route from Truro Continue on Route 6 until it widens into a highway and leads you to Provincetown, about 12 miles away.

PROVINCETOWN This is the town most familiar to first-timers on the cape. It attracts artists, writers, celebrities, and a large gay population and is exceedingly liberal and easygoing—in startling contrast to its early history as the first landing site of the Pilgrims.

In 1899 Charles Hawthorne established the *Cape Cod School of Art* in Provincetown, and the town's reputation as an art center was established. Several leading artists summer here, and the town's long Commercial Street has at least a dozen good galleries. Side by side with these are several museums: the *Heritage Museum* (corner of Commercial and Center Sts.; phone: 508-487-7098); and the *Provincetown Museum,* which adjoins the *Pilgrim Monument* overlooking the town (Monument Hill; phone: 508-487-1310). The *Provincetown Art Association & Museum* (460 Commercial St.; phone: 508-487-1750), founded in 1914, is *the* place in town to see the work of contemporary artists along with its sizable permanent collection. It's open daily from *Memorial Day* through September; open Saturdays and Sundays in winter. Admission charge for non-members.

En Route from Provincetown To return via the south shore, you must backtrack for a period of time on Route 6, the only main road here. Continue on Route 6 to Orleans, then switch to Route 28 and continue to Chatham.

CHATHAM The three sights here are the *Chatham Light* and the fish pier, both on Shore Road about half a mile from Route 28, and the *Railroad Museum* (Depot Rd. near the fire/police station). For more information, contact the *Chatham Chamber of Commerce* (phone: 508-945-5199).

En Route from Chatham About halfway down the south shore on Route 28 is Hyannis.

HYANNIS It's now synonymous with the Kennedy family, but long before it was home to the clan and its compound, Hyannis drew visitors for its marvelous beaches. It hosts an annual *Antiques Fair* (*National Guard Armory,* South St.; phone: 508-775-7857) in July, and musical theater-in-the-round is performed in the *Melody Tent* (W. Main St.; phone: 508-775-5630). Hyannis also is a terminus for ferry services to Nantucket and Martha's Vineyard, with day trips for sightseeing as well as auto ferry service.

En Route from Hyannis You must reserve well in advance for ferry space if you're traveling by car. The only line that ferries vehicles to the islands is the *Steamship Authority* (Wood's Hole; phone: 508-477-8600). It operates year-round, but goes only to Nantucket from Hyannis. *Hy-Line* (Pier 7, Ocean St., Hyannis; phone: 508-778-2600), a passenger-only ferry, serves both Nantucket and Martha's Vineyard from Hyannis from mid-May through late October. A passenger-only ferry runs in summer months only between the two islands. (There is also ferry service to Martha's Vineyard from Falmouth, Woods Hole, and New Bedford).

NANTUCKET Some 30 miles south of Cape Cod and about two hours away by ferry, this little island boasts 50 miles of sand-dune–protected beaches. The Gulf Stream warms the waters to 70F or more during much of the summer. Most of the eight beaches have lifeguards, bathhouses, and food facilities, and sailing enthusiasts can rent all sizes of boats. Bicycle lanes coexist peacefully with roads for cars.

It is not by chance that both Captain Ahab and First Mate Starbuck of Melville's ill-fated *Pequod* were Nantucket men. Nantucket once was the whaling capital of the world, and one Captain George Pollard of Nantucket lost a ship to an enraged sperm whale. Main Street is lined with elegant 19th-century homes, one of which is open for viewing, and the *Whaling Museum* (Broad St.; phone: 508-228-1736; 508-228-1894 for hours) has an authentic whaling boat, among other exhibits. It's open daily from *Memorial Day* through *Labor Day* and intermittently from *Labor Day* through mid-December.

MARTHA'S VINEYARD If you don't believe that New Englanders are independent and feisty, consider this tale about Martha's Vineyard. In 1977, the state legislature decided to incorporate the island into a single district with Cape Cod. The residents didn't take too kindly to this. Forming a group to push for secession, they considered offers of annexation from other US states—including Hawaii—before a compromise was finally worked out.

To see all of this island, which is a sprawling 10 miles wide and 20 miles long, you need wheels. You can rent cars, bikes, or mopeds; shuttle buses scurry between the main resort towns; and taxis and tour buses are available. The main towns are Vineyard Haven, the island's main port; Gay Head, famous for its multicolored clay cliffs looming above the ocean; Oak Bluffs; Menemsha; and Edgartown. Edgartown is the oldest settlement on the island, a fact well documented by the *Vineyard Museum* (School and Cooke Sts.; phone: 508-627-4441). Built in 1765, the building that houses the museum has some marvelous examples of colonial architecture, a Jacobean fireplace, and seven open fireplaces. It's open weekdays during summer; closed Sundays through Tuesdays in winter.

En Route from Martha's Vineyard Take the ferry back to Wood's Hole and follow Route 28 north to Mashpee.

MASHPEE This is the heart of cranberry country, and descendants of the Mashpee Indians still gather cranberries from the many bogs. Among the places of interest is the *Mashpee Wampanoag Indian Museum* (Rte. 130; phone: 508-477-1536; open daily in summer), with a diorama and exhibitions of Indian lore. The *Old Indian Meeting House* in the center of town (Meeting House Rd. at Rte. 28), built in 1648, is not open to the public, but you may visit the Mashpee burial grounds on the land surrounding the meeting house.

En Route from Mashpee Continue on Route 28 south to Falmouth. From here, Route 28A leads northward and back to mainland Massachusetts.

BEST EN ROUTE

Expect to pay $175 to $275 per night for a double room during high season (June through October) in those places we list as very expensive; $125 to $175 in those rated expensive; and $75 to $125 in those rated moderate. There are no extraordinary hotels in the inexpensive category in this area. Unless otherwise indicated, hotels are open year-round and rooms have air conditioning, private baths, TV sets, and telephones. For each location, hotels are listed alphabetically by price category.

YARMOUTH PORT

Yarmouth Inn The oldest place on the cape, dating from 1696, this inn doesn't advertise anywhere. It doesn't need to; its delighted clientele do the job for it. There are five rooms, including two suites, and the price of an overnight stay includes a full breakfast. There are no phones in the rooms. The inn has a pub with jazz performances on Wednesday through Saturday nights. There's also *Le Trajet,* a restaurant serving French country fare. Closed January to mid-February. 223 Old King's Hwy. (phone: 800-833-5125). Moderate.

DENNIS

Isaiah Hall Bed and Breakfast Inn This charming, secluded 1857 farmhouse is named for the renowned builder and cooper (barrel maker) who patented the cranberry barrel for transport. There are 11 cozy period rooms (no TV sets or phones) in the *Main House* and *Carriage House,* an antiques-filled dining room, a country New England–style parlor with wood stove, a TV lounge, a shaded porch, and extensive landscaped gardens. A continental breakfast is included in the rate. Open April to mid-October. Ten minutes from the beach and village, 152 Whig St. (phone: 508-385-9928; 800-736-0160). Moderate.

PROVINCETOWN

Land's End Inn A romantic Victorian hilltop mission retreat, it offers panoramic views of the town, harbor, bay, and dunes. There are 16 rooms, including a loft duplex with a deck and whirlpool and two tower suites with 360° views. The rate includes a continental breakfast. There's no restaurant, air conditioning, TV sets, or telephones in the rooms. 22 Commercial St. (phone: 508-487-0706; 800-677-8696). Expensive to moderate.

NANTUCKET ISLAND

Wauwinet Set between the Atlantic Ocean and Nantucket Bay, this 19th-century inn was named one of the historic hotels of America by the *National Trust for Historic Preservation.* Its 35 high-ceilinged rooms are decorated with such 1920s memorabilia as antique armoires, wicker headboards, wainscoting, and brass fixtures in the bathrooms; most of the rooms have water views. The room rate includes tennis, boating, and the use of the hotel's bicycles, as well as a full breakfast. Guests are encouraged to leave their cars on the mainland; they are met at the ferry, and the hotel offers hourly jitney service to downtown Nantucket. *Toppers* restaurant—complete with a bay-view terrace for lunch and cocktails—offers a casual but sophisticated setting and innovative new American dishes. Open from May through October. 120 Wauwinet Rd. (phone: 508-228-0145; 800-426-8718; fax: 508-228-6712). Very expensive.

Jared Coffin House Built in 1845 and tastefully restored, the inn offers a formal dining room and *The Taproom,* which serves hearty New England fare. There are 28 rooms in the main house (with another 32 rooms in several other buildings); a few are air conditioned, and all have TV sets. Also see *America's Special Havens* in DIVERSIONS. 29 Broad St. (phone: 508-228-2400; 800-248-2405; fax: 508-228-8549). Expensive.

MARTHA'S VINEYARD

Charlotte Inn A member of the renowned Relais & Châteaux hotel group, this 24-room, three-suite inn is old-fashioned and elegant. Its seclusion amid beautifully maintained gardens and trees make it an ideal romantic hideaway. A good French restaurant is on the premises, and tennis and golf facilities, museums, and sailing are nearby. Not all rooms have air conditioning, TV sets, and telephones. S. Summer St., Edgartown (phone: 508-627-4751; fax: 508-627-462). Very expensive.

White Mountains, New Hampshire

Just north of the Lakes Region, which is smack in the center of New Hampshire and some 140 miles north of Boston on I-93 and Route 3 (the two roads parallel each other closely, but I-93 bypasses many of the towns), the White Mountains region is New England countryside at its best. One of the oldest ranges in the Appalachian chain, stretching across 3,600 square miles, these mountains have been smoothed over time into rounded formations. During the fall, you'll be overwhelmed by their foliage—reds and oranges fanning out in all directions like spectacular flames—and you might wonder why they're called the White Mountains (they're named for the white granite in their hills, which gleams in the sunshine). In summer, the subtle green leaves of the white birch ripple beside those of the sugar maple, giving the mountains an unforgettable depth and richness. For general information, contact *White Mountain National Forest* (PO Box 638, Laconia, NH 03247; phone: 603-528-8721; on weekends, call the *Saco Ranger Station* in Conway; phone: 603-447-5448) or *White Mountains Attractions Association* (phone: 603-745-8720; 800-346-3687; fax: 603-745-6765). For information about the area's 22 campgrounds, contact the *Appalachian Mountain Club Huts System,* which is headquartered in Pinkham Notch (phone: 603-466-2727; fax: 603-466-2721).

Our route starts at Plymouth, about 60 miles north of Manchester on Route 3, and wanders up Route 3 to Route 302, over to Route 16 and then west along Route 112, through some of the best sightseeing and skiing areas in the state.

En Route from Concord Follow Route 3 north to Plymouth, then take a brief detour about 5 miles west on Route 25 for a look at *Polar Caves Park* (phone: 603-536-1888; fax: 603-536-1887). The caves were carved out by the great glaciers that passed this way around 50,000 years ago, then retreated to the north. The Hanging Boulder, an 80-ton rock that seems to be suspended in air, has been that way for countless thousands of years.

Then head back east on Route 25 to Route 3 north. Just past North Woodstock, Route 3 joins I-93 to form the Franconia Notch Parkway. Get off at Parkway exit 1 to see the Flume, at the southern end of *Franconia Notch State Park.*

FRANCONIA NOTCH STATE PARK Known as "the Switzerland of America," Franconia Notch extends for about 7 miles between the Kinsman and Franconia mountain ranges. Southeast of the Franconia Range, the Presidential Range stretches across the horizon, as noble as those grand men of history for whom it is named. Mt. Lincoln and Mt. Lafayette are the closest to Franconia.

The Flume is a narrow natural granite gorge set in the fir, spruce, and birch forest of *Franconia Notch State Park.* The park is open from mid-May through October; there's an admission charge. A major visitors' center is located here (phone: 603-745-8391), and intertwined along the cliffs is an intricate set of boardwalks that allow you to get several perspectives of the Flume Brook and its waterfall.

From there, drive slowly up the Parkway to take in the view of Mt. Liberty on the right. Just 3 miles north of the Flume is the *Old Man of the Mountains.* A magnificent, craggy, Lincolnesque profile carved naturally into the side of a mountain, it is New Hampshire's most famous landmark and the state symbol. Skiers are familiar with this part of the world as the site of the *Cannon Mountain Aerial Tramway* (phone: 603-823-5563; fax: 603-823-8088).

En Route from Franconia Notch Proceed northeast on Route 3, after it splits off from I-93, past Mt. Cleveland, then follow Route 302 southeast to Bretton Woods.

BRETTON WOODS Four miles after joining 302, a sign at Base Road leads you to the *Mt. Washington Cog Railway* (Rte. 302, Bretton Woods; phone: 603-846-5404; 800-922-8825, ext. 5; fax: 603-846-5830), 5 miles to the east off Route 302. In operation since 1869, the railway runs from May to November. At 6,288 feet, Mt. Washington is the tallest peak in the Northeast. It is known for foul weather—there's the chance of snow no matter when you go, and August temperatures have been as low as 27F and never rise above 72F. Ascending this mountain is an adventure. Only rugged paths lead to its stark, wind-swept peak, and some spots can be slippery and dangerous. Unless you're an experienced climber, we recommend going up by the railway or in your car (see below). From Mt. Washington, you'll see Mts. Jefferson, Adams, and Madison to the north; and Monroe, Franklin, Eisenhower, Pierce, Jackson, and Webster to the south.

En Route from Bretton Woods Back on Route 302, continue southeast for less than a mile to the historic *Mt. Washington Hotel* (see *Best en Route*), one of the last of the turn-of-the-century grande dames that made the White Mountains famous. For camping, fishing, hiking, or picnicking, exit into *Crawford Notch State Park* (phone: 603-374-2272). Farther down Route 302, just past Bartlett, is the *Attitash Ski Area;* when the snow has melted, the *Attitash Alpine Slide* offers a 4,000-foot-long ride down the mountainside in the summer and fall (phone: 603-374-2368; fax: 603-374-1960). A few miles farther east, Route 302 crosses Route 16. If you want to drive up Mt. Washington, turn north on Route 16 through Jackson, with its picturesque covered bridge, and go 15 miles to the Mt. Washington Auto Road. While descending the mountain, stop frequently to let your brakes cool. If you don't want to risk damaging them, you may take a chauffeured van (*Mt. Washington Auto Road Stages,* Rte. 16, Glen House; phone: 603-466-3988; fax: 603-466-5225).

If you detoured to drive up the mountain, head back south on Route 16 to North Conway; if you stayed on Route 302, continue on for a few miles past Bartlett.

NORTH CONWAY This is the home of the *Mt. Cranmore Ski Area* (phone: 603-356-5543; fax: 603-356-8526). The restored Victorian *Conway Scenic Railroad* (Rte. 16, North Conway Village; phone: 603-356-5251; 800-232-5251; fax: 603-356-7606) runs an 11-mile round trip south to Conway, a resort town of shopping centers, designer outlet stores, and motels, and in summer and autumn months through Crawford Notch's spectacular scenery. Trains run daily from late May to late October; weekends mid-April and May, November to mid-December.

En Route from North Conway If this part of the state is overdeveloped for your taste, head 5 miles south on Route 16 to Conway, then west on Route 112, known as the Kancamagus Highway. One of 10 designated Scenic Byways in the nation, this glorious drive goes deep into the recesses between the mountains, then returns to Route 3 and I-93 about 35 miles later near Lincoln, after passing *Loon Mountain,* a premier ski area (phone: 603-745-8111; 800-227-4191; fax: 603-745-8214).

BEST EN ROUTE

Expect to pay $100 or more per night in season (winter and summer) for a double room in those places we've listed as expensive; and $70 to $95 in the moderate category. Unless otherwise indicated, hotels are open year-round and rooms have private baths, TV sets, and telephones.

FRANCONIA

Franconia Inn Situated on 107 acres of lush greenery, this turn-of-the-century inn faces Mt. Lafayette and Franconia Notch. With 31 rooms and three suites (none with phones or TV sets), it features an outdoor pool and hot tub, four tennis courts, horseback riding, cross-country skiing, ice skating, equipment rentals, and a glider port. The service is attentive and the dinner menu is excellent. Closed April. Rte. 16 S. (phone: 603-823-5542; 800-473-5299; fax: 603-823-8078). Moderate.

BRETTON WOODS

Mt. Washington Hotel Built in 1902, this is one of the few remaining turn-of-the-century hotels in the White Mountains. Facilities in the 200-room hotel include indoor-outdoor pools, tennis courts, a golf course, riding stables, a restaurant, and nightly entertainment. Open mid-May through mid-October. Rte. 302 (phone: 603-278-1000; 800-258-0330; fax: 603-278-3457). Expensive.

LINCOLN

Mountain Club on Loon Right at the foot of the *Loon Mountain* ski area in Lincoln, this resort has easy access to the gondola that travels 7,000 feet to the summit. The 117 contemporary suites all have air conditioning and balconies; half face the mountain. There are three restaurants, a fitness center, a pool, and tennis courts. Kancamagus Hwy. (phone: 603-745-2244; 800-433-3413; fax: 603-745-2317). Expensive.

JACKSON

Christmas Farm Inn Here are 24 rooms and 11 suites (all with phones and many with TV sets) in a comfortable country inn on 14 acres surrounded by forest. Two-room suites in The Barn, Log Cabin, Sugar House, and cottages are ideal for families. There's an outdoor pool, putting green, and sauna. Breakfast and dinner is included in the rates. Rte. 16B (phone: 603-383-4313; 800-443-5837; fax: 603-383-6495). Expensive.

Atlantic City to Cape May, New Jersey

While New Jersey's 127-mile-long Atlantic Ocean shoreline is edged with a ribbon of sandy beaches, the most celebrated stretch is the 50-mile portion of seashore and gentle surf that begins just south of Atlantic City and ends at Cape May Point, stretching along what is called the Jersey Cape. It boasts some of the best beaches on the eastern seaboard, numerous campgrounds, and a geographic conformation that makes for fabulous deep-sea fishing: The oceanfront land is a series of narrow islands that run parallel to the mainland, with a tidal bay in between.

This stretch of Jersey shore was *the* place to summer in the late 1800s for anyone who was anyone. Its popularity—exemplified by Atlantic City and made famous by the Depression-era board game Monopoly—ultimately led to overexposure. After World War II, as successive waves of the rich and famous flocked to Florida, Europe, and the Caribbean rather than to prosaic New Jersey, the major resorts suffered severe setbacks.

In desperate attempts to lure tourists back, many of these towns began casting about for other attractions, from convention facilities to amusement parks and other special activities. While the shore, with its quiet surf and wide beaches, is still a great place to take small children, this flurry of commercialization has caused the best aspect of some shore towns—with their lovely Victorian and Edwardian houses—to be lost behind flashy boardwalks.

For more information about the area, contact *Atlantic City Convention and Visitors Bureau* (2314 Pacific Ave., Atlantic City, NJ 08401; phone: 609-348-7100); *City of Wildwood Information Center* (PO Box 609, Wildwood, NJ 08260; phone: 609-522-1407; 800-WW-BY-SEA east of the Mississippi); *Cape May County Dept. of Tourism* (PO Box 365, *Cape May Courthouse,* NJ 08210; phone: 609-886-0901; 800-227-2297); or *Cape May Welcome Center* (405 Lafayette St., Cape May, NJ 08204; phone: 609-884-9562); or call the *New Jersey Division of Travel and Tourism* information number: 800-JERSEY-7.

Our route follows Ocean Drive—actually a series of bridges designed as a scenic, efficient beltway up and down the cape. A stop at any of the towns along Ocean Drive will prove entertaining, but the high points are Atlantic City, the East Coast's gaudiest gambling center; Wildwood, with its inviting beach and lively boardwalk; and captivating Victorian Cape May. Our route begins in Atlantic City and heads south.

ATLANTIC CITY On November 2, 1976, New Jersey legalized casino gambling, and Atlantic City became the East Coast's answer to Las Vegas. The project continues to receive mixed reviews. While the casinos generate high revenues and compete successfully with their Vegas counterparts, community benefits—such as a bolstering of the local economy and a face-lift for sections outside the famous boardwalk area—are slow in materializing. Nonetheless, Atlantic City attracts everyone from the tuxedoed high roller to the blue-collar slots player. For more information on gambling here, see *Wheels of Fortune* in DIVERSIONS.

The city's most popular non-casino attraction is *Ocean One,* a shopping complex built to resemble an ocean liner with open decks and a nautical motif, which juts out over the water on one of the boardwalk's former piers. Then there's the rest of the boardwalk, all 6 miles of it—teeming with tacky amusement centers, souvenir shops, and food stands (don't forget to pick up some saltwater taffy). This is also the home of the *Miss America* pageant, held annually in September.

En Route from Atlantic City For a drive that's scenic—but *slow,* in tourist season—hug the shoreline on Ocean Drive, which passes through a series of picturesque old resort towns. If you're more interested in speed than in setting, take the Atlantic City Expressway west to the Garden State Parkway (a toll road), then continue on the Parkway until exit 4B and follow the signs to Wildwood.

WILDWOOD This town strikes a balance between the quieter, gentler, pleasures of a visit to Cape May and the glitz, swank, and swizzle of Atlantic City. Wildwood actually consists of four distinct but linked areas. West Wildwood, the smallest of the four, is a residential section. The other three—Wildwood, Wildwood Crest, and North Wildwood—all have wide, white beaches on the Atlantic that are lined with hotels and motels. The famous boardwalk, with its six amusement piers featuring carnival-type rides and mostly fast-food eateries, runs through all of Wildwood's beachfront and into about half of North Wildwood's. Evening entertainment is offered by an array of nightclubs with comedians and singers, jazz bands and Dixieland groups.

En Route from Wildwood Head south on Ocean Drive to Cape May, less than 10 miles away.

CAPE MAY It seems as if the clocks here all stopped somewhere toward the end of the 19th century. In fact, there are so many original Victorian frame buildings, colorfully restored and in mint condition, that the entire town has been declared a national landmark—and that suits the townsfolk just fine, since it has proved to be a gold mine for tourism.

Because much of Cape May was rebuilt after a fire in 1878, today it has 600 Victorian buildings, all constructed within a few years of each other; they stand side by side, resplendent in gingerbread excess, from scalloped widow's walks traced along scalloped rooftops to columned verandahs with latticework trims. Many of the buildings are now guesthouses and inns, the most famous of which is the *Mainstay Inn* (see *Best en Route*), known locally as the "Victorian Mansion." A stay at a Victorian guesthouse might well feature afternoon tea served on the verandah, a room with an antique four-poster bed, and a tour of the house. The town also has a number of excellent restaurants, including the *Washington Inn* (801 Washington St.; phone: 609-884-5697) and the *Mad Batter* (19 Jackson St.; phone: 609-884-5970), which both feature seafood and continental fare, and the *Lobster House* (Fisherman's Wharf; phone: 609-884-8296) serving seafood specialties.

The *Mid-Atlantic Center for the Arts* (in the *Emlen Physick Estate,* 1048 Washington St., Cape May, NY 08204; phone: 609-884-5404; 800-ASK-4-ART) offers a variety of tours, including one of the *Emlen Physick Estate,* an 18-room mansion in the eclectic Stick style popular in the late 19th century. The building, which dates from 1879, is attributed to Philadelphia architect Frank Furness. An hour-and-a-quarter-long walking tour through town, offered four days a week, leaves from the information booth at Washington and Ocean Streets; an enclosed tourist trolley covers a similar route. There are also special tours for children. Mid-October heralds *Victorian Week,* with guided tours of Victorian homes and lectures on architecture and decorative arts of the period. The *Christmas Candlelight* tour of more than 10 historic houses, decorated in the Victorian style, is also very popular. The *Washington Street Mall* (Ocean to Perry Sts.), lined with shops, art galleries, and restaurants, is delightfully Victorian as well.

Just off the mall is a bandstand where free weekly concerts are presented. *Convention Hall* (714 Beach Ave.; phone: 609-884-9565) sponsors weekly entertainment ranging from free ballroom dancing, teen dances, and concerts to antiques shows from *Memorial Day* through *Labor Day.* The *Mid-Atlantic Center for the Arts* also sponsors a music festival held at various locations in Cape May for six weeks each spring. For more information, consult the calendar of events posted at the information office just outside the hall on the promenade at Beach Drive or call the city's *Department of Civic Affairs* (phone: 609-884-9565).

At the very tip of the cape is *Cape May Point State Park.* The working lighthouse here is open to the public. The arduous climb to the top of its 199 steps is rewarded by a grand view of the shoreline and the surrounding sea. Although no swimming is allowed here due to the insidious currents, called "Cape May rips," visitors may search through the pebbles of nearby Sunset Beach for "Cape May diamonds"—bits of wave-washed quartz that shine brilliantly when polished. The park also offers a small museum (no admission charge) that houses exhibits on the natural and cultural resources of the Cape May region, and a bird sanctuary, where hundreds of species find rest and food while on their spring and fall migrations. Cape May is among the best places in the nation for bird watching; more than 400 species have been counted here.

Also at the tip of the cape is the *Cape May–Lewes, Delaware Ferry.* The 17-mile ride to Lewes takes about 75 minutes. Make reservations in writing (PO Box 827, North Cape May, NJ 08204; phone: 609-886-2718) or call *Lewes Terminal* (phone: 302-645-6313).

BEST EN ROUTE

Expect to pay $140 or more per night for a double room in high season (June through August) in those place we've listed as expensive; $85 to $140 in those listed as moderate; and less than $85 in places described as inexpensive. Unless otherwise indicated, hotels are open year-round and rooms have air conditioning, private baths, TV sets, and telephones. For each location, hotels are listed alphabetically by price category.

ATLANTIC CITY

For information about hotel-casinos in Atlantic City, see *Wheels of Fortune* in DIVERSIONS.

The Flagship Resort Each of the 440 rooms in this non-casino resort hotel features a private balcony and a kitchenette with a refrigerator and microwave oven. There's an indoor pool, a health club, and a restaurant; free indoor parking and free shuttle service to and from the casinos are provided. 60 N. Maine Ave. (phone: 609-343-7447; 800-824-4953). Expensive to moderate.

Quality Inn One block from the boardwalk and casinos, this hotel offers 203 rooms, including seven suites. There's a restaurant. On S. Carolina Ave. at Pacific Ave. (phone: 609-345-7070; 800-356-6044). Moderate to inexpensive.

WILDWOOD

Aqua Beach Resort One block from the boardwalk on the beach, this resort hotel has 123 rooms, including 11 two-room apartments. Amenities include a pool, a poolside Jacuzzi, beach volleyball, barbecue grills poolside, and a video gameroom. Amenities include free parking, and laundry facilities. Open April through the third weekend of October. 5501 Ocean Ave., Wildwood Crest (phone: 609-522-6507; 800-247-4776). Expensive to moderate.

Ocean Holiday Motor Inn This 58-room hotel, which includes a number of efficiency units with refrigerators and stoves, is directly on the beach. Pluses include an oceanfront sun deck, Ping-Pong tables, and laundry facilities. Open from the first weekend after *Easter* through mid-October. 6501 Ocean Ave., Wildwood Crest (609-729-2900; 800-321-6232). Expensive to moderate.

El Coronado Motor Inn This modern 113-room resort motel offers one- and two-room efficiency units, each with a refrigerator and a private balcony affording a view of the ocean. Other features include a video gameroom, beach and pool volleyball, a sauna, a sun deck with a pool, a hot tub, gas barbecue grills, and laundry facilities. Open May through mid-October. 8501 Atlantic Ave., Wildwood Crest (phone: 609-729-1000; 800-227-5302). Moderate.

CAPE MAY

Angel of the Sea This award-winning mansion has 26 guestrooms, most overlooking the sea. Guests have use of porches and verandahs. Afternoon tea and wine and cheese are offered; there are also bikes, beach equipment, and parking. There's no restaurant, but breakfast is included in the rate. 5 Trenton Ave. (phone: 609-884-3369; 800-848-3369). Expensive.

Mainstay Inn and Officers' Quarters Built in 1872, the 12-unit *Mainstay Inn* features original furnishings, a grand dining room, and a verandah. Directly across the street, the inn's owners have transformed a World War I naval officers' residence into *Officers' Quarters,* with four deluxe one- and two-bedroom units, each with a whirlpool, fireplace, and private porch. *Mainstay Inn* is open April through October and weekends in November and December; *Officers' Quarters* is open year-round. Rates for both include continental breakfast in summer, full breakfast the rest of the year, and afternoon tea. No credit cards accepted at either. Also see *America's Special Havens* in DIVERSIONS. 635 Columbia Ave. (phone: 609-884-8690). Expensive.

The Queen Victoria This restored villa has 23 rooms in two main buildings, which were constructed in 1880 and 1881. There are period Victorian furnishings throughout, and pieces from the Arts and Crafts Movement decorate the public areas. Complimentary house bicycles are available to guests; afternoon tea and breakfast are included in the rate. No restaurant. 102 Ocean St. (phone: 609-884-8702). Expensive.

Virginia Set in a restored 1879 Victorian house a block from the beach, this is a cut above the typical bed and breakfast establishment. The 24 rooms are elegantly furnished, and the food is excellent—especially the breakfasts. Closed January. Also see *America's Special Havens* in DIVERSIONS. 25 Jackson St. (phone: 609-884-5700; 800-732-4236; fax: 609-884-1236). Expensive.

The Abbey Just a block from the beach, this Gothic Revival villa, now a bed and breakfast establishment, comprises two buildings: the main house, built in 1869, and a cottage constructed in 1873. Each has seven rooms with refrigerators and period Victorian antiques. Most rooms are air conditioned. Limited on-site parking is available. Open April to mid-December. 34

Gurney St. at Columbia Ave. (phone: 609-884-4506). Expensive to moderate.

Windward House In the heart of the historic district just half a block from the beach, this shingled cottage has eight rooms. There's a third-floor sun deck. No restaurant. Open mid-February through December. 24 Jackson St. (phone: 609-884-3368). Moderate.

Brass Bed Conveniently located just two blocks from the beach, this eight-room (six with private bath) inn features antiques-filled guestrooms complete with brass beds. Guests enjoy lovely views from the wide front porch. No restaurant. 719 Columbia Ave. (phone: 800-884-2302). Moderate to inexpensive.

Adirondack Park and Mountains, New York

Adirondack Park and the Adirondack Mountains encompass just under 10,000 square miles, nearly filling the northeastern section of New York State, from close to the Canada border to as far south as the town of Glens Falls. In winter, the area draws both downhill and cross-country skiers (Lake Placid was the site of two *Winter Olympics*), as well as snowmobilers and ice fishing aficionados; in spring, visitors come to hike and look for birds; in summer, folks enjoy the lakes, mountains, forests, fishing, golfing, and whitewater rafting; in autumn, they hunt and look at the spectacular foliage.

Adirondack Park, over 100 years old, offers almost unlimited opportunities for outdoor activity. Nearly half of its six million acres are protected by law from "modern improvements." It encompasses wonderful mountain trails, a section of the Hudson River, more than 125 canoe routes, campsites, and several famous lakes—Saranac Lake, Lake George, Lake Champlain, and Lake Placid. Parts of the park are surprisingly wild, home to bear and coyote and an astonishing array of birds. Among the lakes and mountains are small villages that can be visited or avoided, depending on your preference.

The deliberate underdevelopment of the *Adirondack Park* is the very foundation of its charm and appeal. Roads are few, and they don't always follow a straight route. But with some backtracking and patience you can circle the entire park in a few days, allowing plenty of time for stopping, looking, enjoying, and relaxing.

For general information, contact the *Adirondack Regional Tourism Council* (PO Box 51, West Chazy, NY 12992; phone: 800-ITS-MTNS); for camping information, write to *New York State Dept. of Environmental Conservation* (50 Wolf Rd., Albany, NY 12233-4250; phone: 518-457-2500). Detailed topographic maps and hiking guides can be purchased from the *Adirondack Mountain Club* (RR 3, PO Box 3055, Lake George, NY 12845; phone: 518-668-4447; 800-395-8080; fax: 518-668-3518). The *Adirondack*

North Country Association (*ANCA;* phone: 518-891-6200) has a driving trail system marked with special signs; call for maps.

The Adirondack Mountains are about four hours from New York City. Our route starts at Lake George, about 60 miles north of Albany on I-87, heads northwest to Blue Mountain Lake and two other lakes nearby, then makes a clockwise loop through the mountains on smaller roads; along the way you will have ample opportunity for exploring on your own.

LAKE GEORGE VILLAGE This town, the most populous and most commercial in the area, sits on a 32-mile jewel of a lake ringed by mountains and dotted with dozens of state-owned islands. Although it's a great place for swimming and fishing, Lake George Village's natural pleasures have almost been superseded by more profitable ventures like parasailing outfitters, miniature golf courses, honky-tonk tourist shops, and the *Great Escape* theme park (5 miles south of town on Rte. 9; phone: 518-792-6568; fax: 518-792-3404). The amusement park is open May through September; there's an admission charge.

Of historic interest is *Fort William Henry* (Canada St.; phone: 518-668-5471), a reconstructed 235-year-old fort with displays of muskets, cannon, and other war relics. A 45-minute version of *The Last of the Mohicans* is part of the tour. The fort is open May to mid-October; there's an admission charge. Many companies offer daily sightseeing trips on Lake George, as well as dinner, jazz, and moonlight cruises; one is *Lake George Steamboat Cruises* (phone: 518-668-5777). For an eagle's-eye view of the lake, take Route 9 half a mile south to Prospect Mountain State Parkway. At the end of a 5-mile climb up the 2,100-ft. mountain is a view of the southern Adirondack Mountains and the upper Hudson Valley.

En Route from Lake George Village Take Route 9 north to Route 28, then head northwest about 50 miles to the town of Blue Mountain Lake, on a lake of the same name.

BLUE MOUNTAIN LAKE In addition to the glorious scenery in this village, the *Adirondack Lakes Center for the Arts* (Rte. 28; phone: 518-352-7715) is a major attraction, with an art gallery, concerts, films, and exhibitions. The center is open year-round; gallery exhibits are shown from *Memorial Day* through December. There's no admission charge except for special events. The *Adirondack Museum* (1 mile north on Rte. 30; phone: 518-352-7311) has 20 buildings of treasures, mostly on the history of the area, including a wonderful collection of lake boats. It's open from *Memorial Day* through mid-October; there's an admission charge. Nearby Blue Mountain has nature trails and some lookout points at its peak.

En Route from Blue Mountain Lake For a scenic boat or plane tour, take a detour southwest on Route 28. The first stop is Raquette Lake, about 12 miles away.

RAQUETTE LAKE Along this lake's shoreline—about 70% of which can be reached only by boat—are several grand turn-of-the-century camps built as rural retreats by the Vanderbilts, Morgans, Carnegies, and other wealthy former summer residents. *Bird's Marina* (phone: 315-354-4441) arranges tours of the camps on request, and also offers daily trips from July 1 through *Labor Day* aboard the 36-passenger boat that has been delivering the mail to summer residents of the lakeside camps for more than 50 years. Another option is to take a dinner cruise on the 150-passenger double-decker boat operated by the *Raquette Lake Navigational Company* (phone: 315-354-5532).

En Route from Raquette Lake For a dramatic view of the Fulton Chain Lakes and the sea of surrounding wilderness, continue southwest on Route 28 to the town of Inlet. There, seaplane rides are offered by *Bird's Seaplane* (phone: 315-357-3631) and *Payne's Air Service* (phone: 315-357-3971). Then backtrack to Blue Mountain Lake on Route 28 and take Route 30 north, past Long Lake and Moody, to Tupper Lake.

TUPPER LAKE This old logging town hasn't been changed by tourism nearly as much as most Adirondack villages. A chief attraction is *Big Tupper Mountain* (phone: 518-359-7902; 800-824-4754), with excellent skiing facilities. There are also golfing, boating, swimming, and camping.

En Route from Tupper Lake Continue north on Route 30 to Paul Smiths, northwest of Saranac Lake.

PAUL SMITHS The *Adirondack Park Visitor Interpretive Center* (Rte. 30; phone: 518-327-3000) in this small community has 5½ miles of hiking trails, environmental exhibits, and a computerized travelers' assistance system that provides information on camping, hiking, food, and lodging in the park. Visiting the center is a must if you don't have time to tour the park extensively: Scenic hiking trails, naturalist-led walks, and informative exhibits provide a good overview of the region. The center is open year-round, and there's no admission charge.

En Route from Paul Smiths Take Route 30 south to Lake Clear, then follow Route 86 to Saranac Lake.

SARANAC LAKE Saranac's world-famous spas have been visited by a host of celebrities, including Robert Louis Stevenson, whose cottage (Stevenson La.) is open to the public in July and August. The area is also a winter and summer sports resort. In winter there's a wonderful festival featuring a huge lakeside ice castle; in the summer there are boat races, art exhibitions, and outdoor concerts. The *Charles Dickert Memorial Museum* (in the *Saranac Lake Free Library,* 100 Main St.; phone: 518-891-4190) houses some marvelous mounted specimens of local wildlife. It's open July to *Labor Day;* there's no admission charge. For an offbeat excursion, visit the *Six Nations Indian Museum* in nearby Onchiota (10 miles off NY 3; phone: 518-891-

0769). It's open May through September and whenever else manager John Fadden decides to open it; there's an admission charge.

En Route from Saranac Lake Take Route 86 east through Ray Brook to Lake Placid.

LAKE PLACID Host to two *Winter Olympics,* Lake Placid is an upscale resort that mixes superior sports facilities with a Main Street lined with designer boutiques and cozy cafés. The *Olympic Arena and Convention Hall* (Main St.; phone: 518-523-1655; 800-462-6236) offers year-round skating as well as ice shows, concerts, and other performances. Those looking for winter adventure can ride on an Olympic-type bobsled or luge at Mt. Van Hoevenberg (7 miles southeast on Rte. 73; phone: 518-523-1655; 800-462-6236). This is also an excellent cross-country ski area. Downhill skiers don't want to miss nearby *Whiteface Mountain,* with its challenging slopes and a lift ticket that costs less than at most other major areas (phone: 518-946-2223).

Lake Placid Center for the Arts (Saranac Ave. at Fawn Ridge; phone: 518-523-2512) offers first-rate concerts, repertory performances, and art exhibitions. The nearby *John Brown Farm Historical Site* (John Brown Rd. off Rte. 73; phone: 518-523-3900) gives you a glimpse into the famous abolitionist's world—his furnishings, his home, and his gravesite. It's closed November through April; no admission charge. Lake Placid also offers a variety of lake cruises. Trips leave from Holiday Harbor (drive north on Rte. 86 to Mirror Lake Dr.). General tourist information is available from the *Lake Placid/Essex County Visitors Bureau* (*Olympic Arena,* Lake Placid, NY 12946; phone: 800-447-5224).

En Route from Lake Placid Follow Route 86 east to Route 9N, then continue to Ausable Chasm on Route 9, 12 miles south of Plattsburgh near Lake Champlain.

AUSABLE CHASM This scenic wonder is not to be missed. (Just to settle any arguments, it's pronounced Oh-*say*-bull.) An incredible gorge, it ranges from 100 to 200 feet deep; footbridges cross its 20- to 50-foot width. You can take a self-guided walking tour and see the quaintly named rock formations: "Pulpit Rock," "Elephant's Head," "Cathedral Rock." Or take a guided boat ride down a natural flume through the rapids. The chasm is closed from October through April; there's an admission charge (phone: 518-834-7454).

En Route from Ausable Chasm Take Route 9 south through Whallonsburg, then pick up Route 9N and follow it to Fort Ticonderoga.

FORT TICONDEROGA This fort played a strategic part in our nation's history. Originally built in 1755 by the French, it was captured by the British four years later and held until 1775, when Ethan Allen and his Green Mountain Boys won it for good. Restored according to the original French plans, it now houses a museum with many original weapons, uniforms, and other war relics from the period. Live fife and drum performances and cannon firings add realistic touches in July and August. The fort is closed late October through mid-May; there's an admission charge (phone: 518-585-2821).

En Route from Fort Ticonderoga Take Route 9N south to Lake George, then follow I-87 south to Albany or New York City.

BEST EN ROUTE

Expect to pay $120 or more per night for a double room in those hotels we've listed as expensive and less than $75 at places in the inexpensive category. Unless otherwise indicated, hotels are open year-round and rooms have air conditioning, private baths, TV sets, and telephones. For each location, the hotels are listed alphabetically by price category. Also below is a list of some area campgrounds; for general information on camping in the region, contact the *Division of Tourism, Dept. of Economic Development, Parks, and Recreation* (1 Commerce Plaza, Albany, NY 12245; phone: 518-474-4116 or 518-474-0456; 800-CALL-NYS; 800-456-CAMP for reservations at any state-run campground).

LAKE GEORGE

Sagamore Omni Resort Built in 1883 on a private island, this elegant 100-room Victorian hotel is listed in the *National Register of Historic Places.* It's the center of a year-round sports playground. There's a restaurant on the premises. Also see *America's Best Resort Hotels* in DIVERSIONS. 110 Sagamore Rd., Bolton Landing (phone: 518-644-9400; 800-358-3585; fax: 518-644-2626). Expensive.

SARANAC LAKE

The Point This extraordinary Adirondack hunting lodge was built in the 1930s by William Rockefeller. The log-hewn compound includes 11 luxurious guestrooms (most with stone fireplaces) and a convivial pub lounge; a staggering variety of sports activities are available year-round. Rates include all meals, wine and spirits, and recreational facilities. Closed April. Also see *America's Special Havens* in DIVERSIONS. Star Rte., Upper Saranac Lake (phone: 518-891-5678; 800-255-3530; fax: 518-891-1152). Expensive.

Saranac Owned and operated by *Paul Smiths College,* this is a laboratory for students of hotel administration, with 92 rooms and a dining room, lounge, bakery, and gift shop. Comfortable and pleasant, it offers good food and service. 101 Main St. (phone: 518-891-2200; 800-937-0211; fax: 518-891-5664). Inexpensive.

LAKE CLEAR

The Lodge at Lake Clear The ambience is pure old Adirondack, with mounted moose heads on the walls, at this property with four guestrooms and three two-bedroom chalets. German fare is featured in the rustic dining room. The menu is fixed and food is served family-style, so everyone can get to know everyone else. On Rte. 30, just north of Lake Saranac, at the junction of Rte. 186 (phone/fax: 518-891-1489). Inexpensive.

CAMPGROUNDS

Ausable Point There are 123 sites at this remote area near the Ausable Chasm rapids. Near Peru (phone: 518-561-7080).

Cranberry Lake On these grounds are over 50 miles of wilderness trails, some with rustic lean-tos; 173 sites for tents and RVs; shower facilities; a store; and access to 20 miles of the Oswegatchie Inlet for boaters and beach lovers. At Cranberry Lake (phone: 315-848-2315).

The Glen Island Group Register at this tents-only site and boat to any of 55 islands. Each of the 213 sites has a fireplace, tent platform, and semiprivate dock. No shower facilities. At Bolton Landing (phone: 518-668-5441).

Lewey Lake Here are 206 sites for tents and RVs, along with shower facilities. From base camp, you can climb Snowy and Blue Ridge Mountains. On Indian Lake (phone: 518-648-5266).

Luzerne Swim and hike while staying at one of this camp's 174 sites for tents and RVs. Shower facilities available. On Fourth Lake (phone: 518-696-2031).

Moffit Beach This 258-site camp for tents and RVs bordering both Lake Pleasant and Sacandaga Lake has shower facilities (phone: 518-548-7102).

Putnam Pond Miles of trails branch out from this camp to forest ponds and lakes. Also available are shower facilities and 72 sites for tents and RVs. Six miles from Ticonderoga (phone: 518-585-7280).

Rogers Rock Enjoy the view of Lake George and hike up the 1,000-foot Rogers Rock from this base. There are 314 sites for tents and RVs, and shower facilities. At Hague (phone: 518-585-6746 or 518-585-9728).

Hudson River Valley, New York

In its 315-mile course from the Adirondacks to the sea, the Hudson changes from a shimmering, 3-mile-wide expanse (called Tappan Zee by the early Dutch; *zee* is Dutch for "sea") to a serpent squeezed by the towering Palisades downriver, nearer New York City. Thomas Cole, Frederick Church, and others of the Hudson River School of landscape painters were inspired by its beauty, while Romantic poets and just plain folk have compared the Hudson to Germany's Rhine. In the 19th century, wealthy families whose names (Vanderbilt, Roosevelt, Rockefeller) are synonymous with America's Gilded Age built palatial estates along its banks. Many of Hudson Valley Gothic pseudo-villas and châteaux are open to the public, and they're well worth a look.

British and American forces fought for this area inch by inch during the Revolutionary War. The Hudson was the key to holding the great northern territories beyond, and the valley's towns held patriots and king's men in turn. And in addition to the echoes of historical events, an air of folklore and mystery—the delicious shiver of the supernatural—cloaks the mountains and the heavily forested valleys. There's the goblin who sits atop Dunderberg and whose churlish moods, it is said, control the winds whipping up the river below. And, of course, there's the Headless Horseman.

Our route follows the east bank of the Hudson along Route 9 from New York City to Rip Van Winkle Bridge, about 20 miles south of Albany near Hudson—almost as far as English explorer Henry Hudson made it in his ship *Half Moon* in 1609. This is the entry point to the Catskill Mountain area to the west and the Adirondacks to the north. At the bridge, the route crosses from the east to the west bank, and heads back toward New York City.

En Route from New York City From Manhattan drive north on Route 9 (the Henry Hudson Parkway) for about 25 miles to Washington Irving's "Sleepy Hollow" country.

TARRYTOWN AND NORTH TARRYTOWN A prime attraction in Tarrytown is Washington Irving's home of 24 years, *Sunnyside* (W. Sunnyside La., off Broadway/Rte. 9; phone: 914-591-8763). Here you can see the author's books, manuscripts, and household furnishings, as well as statues of some of his characters. The house is closed Tuesdays; there's an admission charge. Nearby is *Lyndhurst* (635 S. Broadway; phone: 914-631-4481), built in 1838 by Alexander Jackson Davis and the home of railroad tycoon Jay Gould from 1880 to 1893. The 67-acre estate, now run by the *National Trust for Historic Preservation,* offers stunning interiors and vistas as well as outdoor concerts and festivals in the warm months. It's closed Mondays; open weekends only November through April. There's an admission charge. For general information on attractions in this area, call *Historic Hudson Valley* (phone: 914-631-8200; 800-448-4007).

A bit farther up Route 9 is North Tarrytown, whose *Philipsburg Manor* (Rte. 9, Upper Mills; phone: 914-631-8200), dating from the mid–17th century, is one of the first "industrial complexes" in the country. A perfect stop for children weary of touring palatial mansions, it has a gristmill where a period-costumed miller will let kids help grind the corn. There are also sheep—and, in the springtime, lambs. It's closed Tuesdays December through March; there's an admission charge. Recently opened to the public is the Rockefeller estate, *Kykuit,* built in 1907. The 40-room mansion and its grounds overlook the river. On display are antiques, carriages, cars, and some magnificent 20th-century paintings and sculpture from Nelson Rockefeller's collection. Transportation to the mansion leaves from the *Philipsburg Mansion Visitors Center* (phone: 914-631-8200). The mansion is closed November through April. Reservations (at least three months in advance) are required to tour *Kykuit;* there's an admission charge.

En Route from North Tarrytown Continue north about 20 miles to Garrison, just off Route 9 via Route 403 to Route 9D.

GARRISON The highlight here is *Boscobel* (Rte. 9D; phone: 914-265-3638), a glorious villa built in 1806, which houses a collection of rare and beautiful antiques. The grounds are manicured in English formal style, and the view of the Hudson is spectacular. It's closed January and February, and on Tuesdays during the rest of the year; there's an admission charge. The *Manitoga Nature Center* (on Rte. 9D; phone: 914-424-3812), the former estate of industrial designer Russell Wright, features 200 acres of forests and trails overlooking the Hudson. It's closed weekends November through April; an annual membership fee entitles you to the combination to the gate lock for winter hiking and cross-country skiing.

En Route from Garrison Back on Route 9, continue for another 20 miles or so to Poughkeepsie.

POUGHKEEPSIE There are several beautiful old houses in town, including the *Glebe House* (635 Main St.; phone: 914-454-0605), which was built in the late 1760s as a rectory for the Episcopal church. Also worth a stop is the *Clinton House* (549 Main St. at White St.; phone: 914-471-1630), home of the governor during the brief period in 1777 when Poughkeepsie was the state capital. Both houses are closed weekends and holidays and have admission charges.

Two Poughkeepsie families have immortalized their names: the Vassars, for their prestigious college, and the brothers Smith, for their cough drops. The grounds and gatehouse at *Springside* on Academy Street, which was Matthew Vassar's summer home, were built by renowned landscape architect Andrew Jackson Downing; the site is now a National Historic Park. Also nearby is the *Young-Morse Historic Site* (Locust Grove; phone: 914-454-4500), once the home of Samuel Morse, inventor of the telegraph. It's open Wednesdays through Sundays from *Memorial Day* through September.

En Route from Poughkeepsie Just north of Poughkeepsie on Route 9 is Hyde Park.

HYDE PARK Franklin Delano Roosevelt spent most of his life here, at *Springwood* (519 Albany Post Rd.). He and his wife, Eleanor, are buried in the rose gardens on the estate, which was designed by Stanford White and built in 1895. Visitors may browse through FDR's books, collections, and other personal treasures in the estate's museum and library. The Eleanor Roosevelt retreat and homestead, *Val-Kill,* is just a short (2½-mile) drive away. One admission charge covers both houses. FDR's home is closed Tuesdays and Wednesdays from November through April; *Val-Kill* is closed *Thanksgiving* through February and weekdays in November, March, and April. Down the road is the *Vanderbilt Mansion,* the spring and fall retreat of the railroad mogul Frederick Vanderbilt. Built in the Beaux Arts style at the end of the 19th century, it is furnished with European imports. The grounds feature formal gardens, a steel-and-concrete bridge, and a pond. Visits to the house are by tour only; there's an admission charge. The grounds are open daily; the mansion is closed Tuesdays and Wednesdays November through March. For information on any of the three estates, call 914-229-9115. Another prime Hyde Park attraction is the *Culinary Institute of America* (on Rte. 9), a cooking school for serious chefs whose final phase includes cooking for the public in one of four dining rooms. The formal *Escoffier* restaurant offers haute cuisine; the *American Bounty* has American regional fare; the *St. Andrews Café* features spa cuisine; and the *Caterina de Medici* offers northern Italian food. (Dinners, it should be noted, are meticulous three-hour affairs; reservations are necessary, and should be made well in advance; phone: 914-471-6608 for all four.) The institute restaurants are closed *Good Friday, Easter* weekend, *Memorial Day* weekend, *Labor Day* weekend, *Christmas, Thanksgiving,* and two weeks in July.

En Route from Hyde Park About 10 miles north on Route 9 is Rhinebeck.

RHINEBECK Rhinebeck is a lovely 300-year-old town. Don't miss the *Old Rhinebeck Aerodrome* (off Rte. 9 on Stone Church Rd.; phone: 914-758-8610). In addition to housing a spiffy collection of World War I aircraft, it stages air shows complete with simulated dogfights on Saturday and Sunday afternoons from June 15 through October 15. The aerodrome is closed November through mid-May; there's an admission charge. The *Rhinebeck Chamber of Commerce* (phone: 914-876-4778) has free maps for self-guided walking and driving tours; they're available May through October at the visitors' booth between 17 and 19 Mill Street.

En Route from Rhinebeck About 40 miles north on Route 9 is Kinderhook.

KINDERHOOK Here is the birthplace and burial site of Martin Van Buren, eighth president of the United States. The *Martin Van Buren National Historic Site,* along Route 9H, showcases Van Buren's retirement home (open from May through early December). Not far from here is the *Luykas Van Alen House,* a 1737 Dutch farmhouse with mid–18th century furnishings. This site was used in Martin Scorsese's film *The Age of Innocence.* The *James Vanderpoel House,* along Route 9, in the village of Kinderhook, is a circa-1820 Federal period mansion. Both the Van Alen and Vanderpoel houses are open Wednesdays through Sundays, *Memorial Day* through *Labor Day.* East of Kinderhook is the *Shaker Museum and Library* (off Rte. 13, Old Chatham;

phone: 518-794-9100), featuring Shaker artifacts. Open early May through October. Admission charge.

En Route from Kinderhook Backtrack about 20 miles to the exit for the Rip Van Winkle Bridge (take Route 23A off Route 9 near Hudson), cross the river, and head south on Route 32.

CATSKILL The famous mountain resort area of the northern Catskills offers over 170 accommodations and a variety of family attractions. The *Catskill Game Farm* (12 miles west, off Rte. 32; phone: 518-678-9595) can be delightful for kids, with its petting areas inhabited by tame deer, antelopes, gazelles, giraffes and exotic birds. It's open mid-April through October. *Catskill State Park* is a forest preserve with six campgrounds, marked trails, and all the glories of nature.

Summer celebrations begin with the *East Durham Irish Festival* (phone: 518-634-2286) during the *Memorial Day* weekend and end with the *Leed's Irish Festival* (phone: 518-943-3736) on *Labor Day*. In addition, *Hunter Mountain Ski Bowl* (phone: 518-263-3800) is the site of Native American- and Celtic-themed entertainment.

During winter months *Hunter Mountain* (Rte. 23A, Hunter; phone: 518-263-4223) is a popular ski area and claims it makes more snow than any other in the country. In addition, there are *Ski Windham* (phone: 800-729-SKIW) and *Ski Cortina* (phone: 518-589-6500). For more information on the Catskills contact the *Greene County Tourism Department* (PO Box 527, Catskill, NY 12414; phone: 800-355-CATS).

En Route from Catskill Take 32 south to 212 west to Woodstock.

WOODSTOCK Still associated with the flower children of the 1960s, the town was established in 1895 by a wealthy Englishman as a colony for intellectuals and artists. The *Art Students League of New York* set up a summer program here a few years later. Each summer numerous cultural events are presented to the public. The *Woodstock Artists Association Gallery* (28 Tinker St. at Village Green; phone: 914-679-2940), open Thursday through Monday, features traveling shows by local and nationally known artists.

En Route from Woodstock Take Route 375 south to Route 28, then head east to Kingston.

KINGSTON One of New York's oldest towns (settled in 1652), it was first a Dutch trading post, then an English colony, and finally American (the state constitution was signed here in 1777). Over the years, the city suffered attacks by various parties—Indians, Dutch, British, and Americans. This town has more than 15 original early American homes in the old stockade area (built in 1658). Some of the houses on the self-guided tour made up a segment of the underground railroad for escaped slaves headed for Canada. Afterward, visitors can peek into the *New York State Senate House and Museum* (269 Fair St.; phone: 914-338-2786). Open from mid-April to late

October; closed Mondays and Tuesdays. During the winter season, open by appointment. No admission charge.

En Route from Kingston Take I-87 south to the New Paltz exit (Route 299 west).

NEW PALTZ Six restored homes and a church from the original settlement, founded by French Huguenots in 1678, are open from the end of May through October. Closed Mondays and Tuesdays. Another area attraction is the marvelous *Mohonk Mountain House,* a fine resort (see *Best en Route*).

En Route from New Paltz Continue south on I-87 to Newburgh.

NEWBURGH Between April 1782 and August 1783 George Washington and the Continental Army made their headquarters here, and it was from here that the successful conclusion of the war was announced. See both the *Jonathan Hasbrouck House* (Liberty St.; phone: 914-562-1195), where Washington stayed, and the *New Windsor Cantonment* (Temple Hill Rd., off Rte. 32; phone: 914-561-1765), a reconstruction of the army's winter camp. These sites are closed Mondays, Tuesdays, and October to mid-April (except to groups); there's no admission charge.

En Route from Newburgh Take Route 32 south to Mountainville.

MOUNTAINVILLE The *Storm King Art Center* (Old Pleasant Hill Rd.; phone: 914-534-3190), a cut-stone French château, features works by world-famous sculptors on 400 acres of land. The distant vistas call to mind the Alps. It's closed December through March; there's an admission charge. For a change in perspective, visit the *Brotherhood Winery* in nearby Washingtonville (35 North St.; phone: 914-496-9101). The winery is closed weekdays January through April. (Also see *Visitable Vineyards* in DIVERSIONS.)

En Route from Mountainville Take Route 9W south to West Point.

WEST POINT The *US Military Academy,* founded in 1802, was the training ground for some of our nation's top military leaders. Be sure to see the chapel with its stained glass windows, the museum, the kissing rock, and Trophy Point, which offers a bird's-eye view of the Hudson. Also see *America's Military Academies* in DIVERSIONS.

En Route from West Point Just south on Route 9W is Highland Falls.

HIGHLAND FALLS From May through October, sail aboard the *Commander* into the Highlands to view the region's dramatic precipices and the gray grandeur of the fortress at West Point. *Hudson Highlands Cruises and Tours, Inc.* (South Dock, West Point; phone: 914-446-7171) offers one-and-a-half-hour and three-hour trips.

BEST EN ROUTE

Expect to pay $120 or more for a double room at those places we've listed as expensive, and $75 to $120 at places in the moderate category. Unless otherwise indicated, hotels are open year-round and rooms have air conditioning, private baths, TV sets, and telephones. For each location, hotels are listed alphabetically by price category.

POUGHKEEPSIE

Old Drovers Inn Several miles east of Poughkeepsie in Dover Plains, near the Connecticut border, this romantic colonial inn is worth a detour for those in search of a quiet, intimate getaway. Built in 1750, it has four guestrooms decorated with antique cherry wood furniture. Guests can lunch on the scenic patio surrounded by beautiful gardens; the candlelit *Tap Room* serves lunch and dinner. A buffet breakfast is included in the rate. Closed for the first three weeks of January. See also *America's Special Havens* in DIVERSIONS. Old Rte. 22 near E. Duncan St. (phone: 914-832-9311; 914-832-6356). Expensive.

Inn at the Falls A multimillion-dollar property, it combines the amenities of a luxury resort with the ambience of a bed and breakfast inn. Fourteen of the 36 rooms are suites, with decor ranging from English manor house to American country, Oriental, and contemporary. Many rooms have four-poster, wrought-iron, or canopy beds, armoires, and rolltop desks. There's no restaurant, but breakfast is brought to the rooms each morning. 50 Red Oaks Mill Rd. (phone: 914-462-5770). Moderate.

RHINEBECK

Beekman Arms This may well be the oldest continuously operating inn in the US. Constructed on the site of a stone tavern (ca. 1700), the main portion was built in 1766. During the Revolution it was known as *Bogardus Tavern* to its regulars—among them Washington and Lafayette. Today, 59 rooms are distributed among the original building, an American Gothic guesthouse, a renovated carriage house, and several newer buildings. All feature country decor; 23 have fireplaces. The restaurant is outstanding. Rtes. 9 and 308 (phone: 914-876-7077). Moderate.

HIGHLAND FALLS

DePuy Canal House Adding to the historic ambience of this three-room, 18th-century inn are the restored canal locks nearby. The dining room offers creative American fare. Southwest of Kingston, off Rte. 209 on Rte. 213 (914-687-7700). Moderate.

Niagara Falls and Buffalo, New York

If you're searching for an unspoiled vacation paradise far from crowds and confusion, Niagara Falls is not for you. It is a major tourist attraction, second only to New York City in the entire northeastern US. Big and bawdy, Niagara Falls makes things seem larger than life—its commercialism is tackier and somehow more annoying than in other areas, its industrial pollution more offensive. Yet the falls themselves, with their massive beauty, manage to rise above all these excesses.

The single most ominous threat to the future of the falls comes not from the abuses of man but rather from a fact of nature: The shale and limestone foundations of the riverbed are slowly being washed away by the sheer force of the water rushing toward the falls. As this erosion continues, the falls will be forced backward until they flatten out altogether and become little more than a series of rapids in the river. Scientists estimate that this won't take place for another few thousand years, however, so there's still time to pack the car and drive to the Canadian border at the far western end of New York State to see the famous waterfalls.

Afterward, head south on I-190 and seek some urban stimulation in nearby Buffalo, an upstate cultural oasis complete with major art galleries, museums, and a symphony orchestra—not to mention five professional sports teams (including the *Bills* of the *National Football League*) and plenty of places to shop.

NIAGARA FALLS The world-famous falls are formed as the waters of Lake Erie race downhill to join Lake Ontario, becoming the Niagara River en route. A small island in the river splits this whitewater juggernaut at the point of its mighty dive, dividing it into two falls: the American Falls, 190 feet high and 1,100 feet wide; and the Horseshoe (Canadian) Falls, 185 feet high and 2,500 feet wide. (There is a minor falls, much smaller, called Bridal Veil.) The indomitable little chunk of land responsible for this twofold masterpiece is Goat Island, named for its former residents. On its 70 acres are scenic walks almost at the brink of the falls, a heliport for sightseeing choppers, and an elevator that takes visitors to the falls' base. From here the fearless may don the heavy-weather gear provided by the tour leader and walk along the path just behind the incredible wall of water—as drenching as it is deafening.

Aerial views of the falls may be had from cable cars, called *Spanish Aerocars,* that cross over the whirlpool and rapids; helicopter rides; and observation towers. On the US side, the *New York State Park Observation Tower,* adjacent to the falls, provides spectacular views 200 feet above the base of the Niagara Gorge. The tower is part of the *Niagara Reservation State Park,* designed by famed landscape architect Frederick Law Olmsted, who created New York City's *Central Park.* Also on the grounds is a *New*

York State Park Visitors Center (phone: 716-278-1796). Here, a wide-screen movie theater features one star—the falls—while exhibitions provide an overview of the area's history, natural history, and geography, and describe some of the amazing stunts that have been performed near the falls. Outdoors, a formal garden has a map of the Great Lakes made entirely from plants. Adjacent to the park is the *Schoellkopf Geological Museum* (phone: 716-278-1780; fax: 716-278-1744), which offers audiovisual presentations on area rock formations and the future of the falls. The museum also has a lovely rock garden and a nature trail. Closed Monday through Wednesday from November through *Memorial Day;* open daily the rest of the year. No admission charge for children under four.

There are a number of ways to view the falls from ground level as well. *The Viewmobile* offers miniature trams that run a 30-minute course between Prospect Point and Goat Island, allowing passengers to get on and off at any of several stops along the route. Of the various boat trips, the *Maid of the Mist* (phone: 716-284-8897) is the most famous. Fortunately, there are four sightseeing boats named *Maid of the Mist,* so there's never too long a wait. Boats operate May through October; waterproof gear is provided.

For a northern view of the falls, shuttle across the Niagara River and see the whole thing from Canada. Several bridges span the river, and crossovers are made as hassle-free as both countries' Customs Bureaus can manage. There are two viewing towers on the Canadian side, on a 250-foot escarpment across from the falls. They are the *Skylon Tower* (viewing height about 770 feet above the falls) and the *Panasonic Tower* (viewing height about 665 feet). In addition, the Canadian side offers a wide range of falls-oriented attractions. The *Niagara Falls Museum,* at the foot of the Rainbow Bridge, contains daredevils' barrels and other artifacts tracing the falls' history. The *IMAX Theatre* (6170 Buchanan Ave.; phone: 905-358-3611 or 374-4629) offers continous 45-minute armchair tours of the falls, while lovely *Victoria Park,* which extends along Niagara Parkway south of the bridge, provides picturesque real-life views of the falls from a garden setting.

Then there's the night view. Horseshoe Falls and the upper rapids are lighted by four billion candlepower in rainbow colors every night, with the energy for this Technicolor extravaganza provided by the falls itself. *Victoria Park* is a favorite place from which to view the nighttime show.

Many festivals and special events are held in the area during the peak summer months. Concerts, dance and theater performances are frequently presented at the 200-acre *Artpark* (Robert Moses Pkwy. at Lewiston, 7 miles north of town; phone: 716-754-4375; 800-659-7275; fax: 716-754-8655). Those interested in Native American heritage should visit the *Native American Center for the Living Arts* (25 Rainbow Blvd. S.; phone: 716-284-2427), known as "The Turtle" because of the building's shape. It features cultural displays, art, and theatrical performances prepared or created by Native Americans; there's an admission charge.

The *Rainbow Centre* (302 Rainbow Blvd. N.; phone: 716-285-9758), just a block from the American Falls, is a one-stop fashion, dining, and entertainment experience, with dozens of factory outlet and specialty stores. Next door is the *Wintergarden,* a majestic, glass-enclosed tropical park with ponds, waterfalls, and 7,000 trees, connected to the *Niagara Falls Convention Center* and open year-round (phone: 716-285-8007). In winter, this is the site of the *Festival of Lights,* an annual celebration that includes thousands of lights and animated displays. A few miles away is the *Factory Outlet Mall* (1900 Military Rd.; phone: 716-297-2022), one of the largest shopping centers of its type in the nation, with over 80 stores that sell brand-name and designer clothing, jewelry, and household items at discounted prices.

Old Fort Niagara State Park is a 15-minute drive north from the falls (off Rte. 18F). The fort, built by the French in 1725, changed hands between the Americans and the British several times over the course of its history. Today it's one of the most colorful and best preserved of all the historic Great Lakes forts. Battles and troop musters are reenacted on weekends (phone: 716-745-7611). The park is open daily; there is an admission charge.

To learn more about the falls, visit the *Niagara Power Project* (4 miles north of town, Rte. 104; phone: 716-285-3211; fax: 726-285-0809), which has displays and demonstrations that explain how the falls' power is harnessed and utilized. For more information about the area, contact *Niagara Falls Convention and Visitors Bureau* (345 3rd St., Suite 101, Niagara Falls, NY 14303; phone: 716-285-2400). A 40-page travel brochure is available free by calling 800-338-7890.

En Route from Niagara Falls Take I-190 south to Buffalo (you'll pay a toll to cross Grand Island's bridges).

BUFFALO The second-largest city in New York (pop. about 328,000), Buffalo is known as a financial and industrial center. Less well known are its cultural attractions and its physical beauty. The city is virtually surrounded by parks, the most notable of which is *Delaware Park,* designed by Frederick Law Olmsted. *Delaware Park* boasts not only spectacular grounds and landscaping but also a golf course, a zoo (complete with buffalo), and three museums. The *Albright-Knox Art Gallery* (1285 Elmwood Ave.; phone: 716-882-8700; fax: 716-882-1958) has an impressive collection of contemporary American and European art as well as works by 18th-century English and 19th-century French and American artists. It's closed Mondays; there's an admission charge. The *Buffalo and Erie County Historical Society* (25 Nottingham Court at Elmwood Ave.; phone: 716-873-9644; fax: 716-873-8754) features exhibits that plunge visitors into the rich history of the area. It's closed Mondays; there's an admission charge.

History buffs might enjoy the *Millard Fillmore Landmark House and Museum* (24 Shearer Ave., East Aurora; phone: 716-652-8875), which focuses on the life and times of the 13th US president, a native of the area.

It's closed Mondays, Tuesdays, Thursdays, and Fridays; there's an admission charge. Fillmore is buried in Buffalo's *Forest Lawn Cemetery* (1411 Delaware Ave.; phone: 716-885-1600; fax: 716-881-6482). The *Theodore Roosevelt Inaugural National Historical Site* (641 Delaware Ave.; phone: 716-884-0095), in one of the city's stately mansions, is where Roosevelt took the presidential oath of office after President William McKinley was assassinated in Buffalo during the 1901 *Pan American Exposition.* It's closed holidays; there's an admission charge.

For more insight into Buffalo's past, stroll through the Allentown section, about a mile north of downtown. It comprises 40 blocks of antiques and arts and crafts shops, boutiques, galleries, restaurants, and Victorian homes. The annual *Allentown Art Festival* (phone: 716-881-4269) attracts thousands in June. Also pleasant to walk through are the *Erie County Botanical Gardens* (in South Park; phone: 716-828-1040), whose buildings and grounds have been restored to their 1898 appearance. The park, the last to be designed by Olmsted, has a 30-foot waterfall and 12 greenhouses filled with tropical and exotic trees, plants, and flowers. Spring and fall flower shows and a *Christmas* show are held here.

Waterways have always played an important role in Buffalo, which was the terminus of the Erie Canal—so a boat trip is a great introduction to the city. *Miss Buffalo Cruise Boats* (*Buffalo Naval & Servicemen's Park;* phone: 716-856-6696; fax: 716-856-8901) offers summer tours. There's also boating and fishing on nearby waters, including Lake Erie, and skiing within an hour of the city.

For those who prefer spectator sports, Buffalo has five professional teams: the *NFL Bills,* who play football in *Rich Stadium* (Abbott Rd. and US 20 in suburban Orchard Park; phone: 716-649-0015); the *Bisons,* a triple-A baseball team based at *Pilot Field* (275 Washington St.; phone: 716-846-2000); the *NHL Sabres,* who play hockey in *Marine Midland Arena* (Main St.; phone: 716-856-7300; 800-333-PUCK); the *Bandits* of the *Major Indoor Lacrosse League* (phone: 716-856-7300); and the *Blizzards* of the *Professional Indoor Soccer League* (phone: 716-856-2500).

Up-and-coming artists have found a haven in Buffalo, which has a lively downtown theater district and numerous galleries scattered throughout the city. *Metro Rail,* a 6-mile light-rail line (phone: 716-855-7211) carries passengers from the theater district to downtown hotels and shopping, and connects with the city's excellent bus system. For classical music lovers, the *Buffalo Philharmonic Orchestra* plays in the *Kleinhans Music Hall* (370 Pennsylvania St.; phone: 716-885-5000; fax: 716-885-5064).

Last, but by no means least, sample some Buffalo chicken wings. This Tabasco-hot finger food is said to have been born during a blizzard when a local bar ran low on ordinary snacks. Now wings are served all over the city—and the nation—properly accompanied by celery sticks and blue cheese dressing.

For more information on the city, contact the *Greater Buffalo Convention and Visitors Bureau* (107 Delaware Ave., Buffalo, NY 14202; phone: 716-852-0511).

BEST EN ROUTE

Expect to pay $80 or more per night for a double room during high season (June through September) at those places we've listed as expensive; $55 to $80 at places in the moderate range; and less than $55 at places in the inexpensive category. Unless otherwise indicated, hotels are open year-round and rooms have air conditioning, private baths, TV sets, and telephones. For each location, hotels are listed alphabetically by price category.

NIAGARA FALLS, NEW YORK

Best Western Inn on the River Some of the 150 rooms have private patios overlooking the Niagara River (here, an island strait). There's an outdoor pool, a restaurant, and entertainment on weekends. 7001 Buffalo Ave. (phone: 716-283-7612; 800-245-7612). Moderate.

Radisson The falls are only a block away. There are 401 rooms (some with kitchenettes), an indoor pool, a health club, and a restaurant. Pets are welcome. Third St. at Old Falls St. (phone: 716-285-3361; 800-333-3333; fax: 716-285-3900). Inexpensive.

NIAGARA FALLS, ONTARIO

Ameri-Cana About 2 miles from the hustle and bustle of downtown, amid spacious grounds with a play area, this resort and conference center has 100 rooms and 20 suites with Jacuzzis. The sports center features an indoor pool, whirlpool, saunas, a gameroom, and indoor tennis, basketball, volleyball, and squash courts. There are also two restaurants. It makes a great base for families. 8444 Lundy's La. (phone: 905-356-8444). Inexpensive.

BUFFALO

Buffalo Hilton Located on the waterfront, this 468-room hotel offers lovely views of the harbor. There are indoor and outdoor pools, indoor tennis and racquetball courts, a weight room, a running track, saunas, and six restaurants, as well as meeting facilities and a business center. 120 Church St. (phone: 716-845-5100; 800-445-8667; fax: 716-845-5377). Expensive.

Hyatt Regency The theater district is just outside the door; inside there's a restaurant, health club, pool, gift shop, and 393 rooms. 2 Fountain Plaza (phone: 716-856-1234; 800-233-1234; fax: 716-856-6734). Expensive.

Pennsylvania Dutch Country

The Pennsylvania Dutch aren't Dutch at all; they are actually German ("Dutch" is an Americanized version of *Deutsch,* the German word for "German"). Their ancestors emigrated to the United States from Germany in the 18th century seeking the freedom to worship and live as they chose. In south-central Pennsylvania they found that freedom, as well as acres of green land perfect for farming, which became their mainstay. Pennsylvania Dutch country encompasses Lancaster, York, Dauphin, Lebanon, Berks, and Lehigh counties. Its center is Lancaster, a medium-size city in southern Pennsylvania almost halfway between Philadelphia and Harrisburg.

"Pennsylvania Dutch" is applied generically to the members of three distinct faiths: the Amish, the Mennonites, and the Moravians. Of the three, the Amish, members of a religious sect founded by Mennonite minister Jacob Amman in the late 17th century, are the most rigid in their interpretation of the Bible. The Amish settlement in Lancaster County is the second-largest in the US. They live simple, family-centered lives, dress in modest, old-fashioned clothing, travel in horse-drawn buggies, and shun all modern conveniences. Some Amish will not speak to strangers, and most will not allow themselves to be photographed. In fact, tourists are asked not to take pictures of the Amish out of respect for their religious beliefs. They are superior farmers, and many of their distinctive foods are now famous, including shoofly pie (a rich molasses crumb pie), chow-chow (a blend of marinated vegetables), scrapple (a spicy, fried blend of cornmeal and pork products), and chicken-corn soup. Eating in Pennsylvania Dutch country is an experience in overabundance as well as plain good cooking, in a culture that traditionally equates being well stuffed with good health. In the region's family-style restaurants, you'll be as dazzled by the sheer size of the spread as by the wonderful flavors; your table is sure to be crowded with an array of appetizers, assorted meats and vegetables, and several desserts.

The Mennonites, known as the "plain people," also live and dress simply, but they are more liberal than the Amish in their biblical interpretations and mingle more with the outside world. The Moravians, the most liberal of the three, are mainly German Lutherans and Reformed Church members; they are known as the "fancy Dutch." Their farms are distinguished by the hex signs on their barns.

Touring Lancaster County is easy. Most of the little towns—which have colorful names like Bird-in-Hand, Intercourse, Paradise, and Smoketown—are within a few minutes' drive of one another. For an overall view of the area, many commercial sightseeing tours offer planned itineraries, or you can take a self-guided auto tape tour. Tapes and players can be rented from many commercial establishments; ask at the *Pennsylvania Dutch Convention and Visitors Bureau* (501 Greenfield Rd., Lancaster, PA 17601; phone: 717-299-8901; 800-PA-DUTCH for free maps and guides). At the visitors' bureau, you can pick up a copy of guides and scan the racks of brochures for places to explore. Then take in the multi-image show about the area, *There Is a Season.*

Enjoy a scenic drive through Pennsylvania Dutch country on Route 30 (Lincoln Hwy.). This route also strings together most of the area's main attractions, and the others are all close by, most of them on Route 741 to the south or Route 340 to the north as well as along Route 896, which bisects all three. When traveling these roads, be prepared to brake suddenly for the Amish in their horse-drawn carriages. Our route ends in a detour to Hershey, a picturesque and fun-filled site outside Lancaster County that shares its Pennsylvania Dutch roots.

A couple of other places nearby host interesting special events that merit a detour. A few miles northwest of Lancaster is Manheim, where the *Pennsylvania Renaissance Faire* takes place on weekends early July through *Columbus Day* weekend; also Mondays until *Labor Day.* Held on the grounds of the *Mount Hope Estate and Winery* (Rte. 72; phone: 717-665-7021), it takes visitors back to the 16th century with jousting, juggling, jesting, magic, music, and dancing. During the end of June and first week of July, visitors flock to Summit Station, a small town between Allentown and Harrisburg, for the *Kutztown Folk Festival* (at the Schuylkill County fairgrounds, off I-78 on Rte 895), which features 18th- and 19th-century Pennsylvania Dutch life and culture in theatrical presentations, polka bands, square dancing, folk arts and crafts including quilt and antiques shows and, of course, lots of food. For more information contact *Festival Associates* (461 Vine La, Kutztown, PA 19536; phone: 610-683-8707).

En Route from Philadelphia Take the Pennsylvania Turnpike west to exit 23 at Route 100. Follow Route 100 east briefly to Route 113 south, which soon connnects with Route 30. Head west about 17 miles to the intersection of Route 30 and Route 896, the heart of Pennsylvania Dutch country.

LANCASTER AND ENVIRONS The largest concentration of authentic Pennsylvania Dutch sights is clustered just outside Lancaster along Routes 30 and 340. The *Amish Farm and House* (2395 Rte. 30 E.; phone: 717-394-6185) features a tour of a working farm and a 10-room house built in 1805. Open daily, it provides a good overview of Amish religious beliefs and customs. The *Amish Village* (Rte. 896, 2 miles south of Rte. 30; phone: 717-687-8511) has a tour through a 150-year-old farmhouse furnished in the Amish tradition. Visitors may inspect a blacksmith shop, a one-room school, a smokehouse, a springhouse, and a windmill with a working waterwheel. Closed weekdays from January through mid-March; open daily the rest of the year. *Abe's Buggy Rides* (Rte. 340, a half-mile east of Rte. 896; phone: 717-392-1794; closed Sundays) offers a 2-mile countryside tour in an Amish family carriage, and *Ed's Buggy Rides* (Rte. 896, about 2 miles south of Rte. 30; phone: 717-687-0360) offers a 3-mile tour on back roads.

To learn more about the Mennonite people, visit the *Mennonite Information Center* (2209 Millstream Rd., Lancaster; phone: 717-299-0954). Here visitors can arrange to rent rooms in a Mennonite farmhouse or at a bed and breakfast. They also can hire a Mennonite guide for a customized tour that can include visits to less commercial Amish quilt, woodworking, and other craft shops. The *Pennsylvania Dutch Convention & Visitors Bureau* also can provide lists of Mennonite bed and breakfast establishments and tour guides.

The *Landis Valley Museum* (2451 Kissel Hill Rd., Lancaster; phone: 717-569-0401) gives visitors a look at 19th-century Pennsylvania Dutch farm buildings, orchards, gardens, and animals. Crafts and living history demonstrations are given, and there is a tavern, a country store, and a hotel built in the 1850s. To get to the museum, take Route 30 west to Route 272 (also known as Oregon Pike), and continue north 2 miles. The museum is closed Mondays and major holidays. The *Landis Valley Fair* in early June and *Harvest Days* on *Columbus Day* weekend, both held on the museum grounds, are among the special activities that provide a taste of Pennsylvania Dutch culture.

The area's farmers' markets are another attraction for their vegetables, flowers, potted plants, homemade baked goods, canned relishes, and Old Country–style sausage and bologna. The oldest is Lancaster's *Central Market* (Queen and King Sts.; phone: 717-291-4739), which has been held at this site since the 1730s. Open year-round, the market operates Tuesdays, Fridays, and Saturdays.

Lancaster County also provides ample opportunity for bargain hunters. Brand-name and designer clothing, leather goods, cosmetics, china and glassware, linen, and toys can be found, often at very reasonable prices, at the many factory outlet stores along Route 30 near the intersection of Route 896.

For children, *Dutch Wonderland and Family Fun Park* (2249 Rte. 30 E., Lancaster: phone: 717-291-1888) has rides, shows, a picnic grove, and gardens. It's open daily in summer; weekends only in spring and fall. Its *Castle Gift Shop* is open year-round. Next door, the *National Wax Museum of Lancaster County Heritage* (2249 Rte. 30 E., Lancaster; phone: 717-393-3679) offers displays, including an animated scene of an Amish barn raising; it's open daily. South of town is *Mill Bridge Village* (on S. Ronks Rd., Strasburg; phone: 717-687-6521), where visitors can walk across a covered bridge and explore a 1728 mill with a functioning waterwheel. There's also a movie about Amish ways, as well as demonstrations of candle dipping, broom making, and blacksmithing. It's open daily from April through October, and on weekends in November and December.

En Route from Lancaster From the intersection of Routes 30 and 896, head north on 896 and then take 340 east to Bird-in-Hand. Note: Most shops here and in surrounding areas are closed on Sundays.

BIRD-IN-HAND One of the region's best farmers' markets operates here. The *Bird-in-Hand Farmers Market* (Rte. 340; phone: 717-393-9674) is open Fridays and Saturdays year-round; also on Wednesdays April through November and Thursdays July through October. While there, visit the adjoining *Glass Factory,* offering an array from cut crystal to everyday ware, and *Snyder's Crafts*, which features pine and oak furniture as well as handicrafts. Across the street, select Pennsylvania Dutch treats at the tempting *Bird-in-Hand Bakery,* then head upstairs to *Fisher's Handmade Quilts* for a fine selection of quality quilts and other handmade goods. Also notable is the 1877 *Weavertown One-Room Schoolhouse* (Rte. 340E.; phone: 717-768-3976; 717-291-1888 during the winter), which served the Amish community until 1969. It's closed from *Thanksgiving* to *Easter.* Outside *Bird-in-Hand* is the excellent *Plain 'n' Fancy Farm* restaurant (on Rte. 340E.; phone: 717-768-8281; 800-621-4945), where you can get a complete family-style meal of Pennsylvania Dutch favorites at a reasonable price. The farm has opened *Amish House,* a nine-room building where visitors can learn about Amish customs and family life and view authentic clothing and furnishings. *The Amish Experience Theater* lets viewers hear of one family's personal experience in deciding to preserve its lifestyle and culture. Then, take a ride in an Amish buggy at *Aaron and Jessica's Buggy Rides,* located on the premises, and complete your stopover with a stroll through the shops just outside the restaurant.

En Route from Bird-in-Hand Continue east on Route 340 to Intercourse.

INTERCOURSE With a cluster of shops and museums, this is a good place to buy locally made crafts and needlework and learn more about the Amish and Mennonites. The *Old Country Store* (Main St.; phone: 717-768-7101) sells homemade goods from hundreds of consignors and features a fabric room as well as a quilt room where the handiwork of Amish and Mennonite women is sold. On the second floor, the *Quilt Museum* features a changing exhibit of quilts from various collections and time periods. The *People's Place* (Main St.; phone: 717-768-7171) shows films on the Amish and the Mennonites and has a bookshop and crafts gallery. Next door is the *People's Place Gallery* which displays and sells works of local artists.

En Route from Intercourse Return to the intersection of 340 and 896 and head south on 896 for several miles to its intersection with 741, Strasburg's town center. Head east about 1 mile to all the railroad attractions.

STRASBURG Lovers of trains—either models or the real thing—will love this town. The *Strasburg Rail Road* (Rte. 741; phone: 717-687-7522), the nation's oldest operating short line steam train, was chartered in 1832. It offers a 45-minute narrated round trip through the Pennsylvania Dutch countryside in well-maintained wooden cars. Check in-season schedules for on-board lunch and dinner. The train operates daily from April through October, and weekends the rest of the year; closed January. The station gift shop has every kind of train toy and souvenir. Across the street is the *Railroad Museum of Pennsylvania* (Rte. 741; phone: 717-687-8628), which houses four tracks of historic engines and coaches; it's closed Mondays November through March and winter holidays; there's an admission charge. The *Choo Choo Barn* (Rte. 741 E.; phone: 717-687-7911) features an outstanding hand-built, 1,700-square-foot display of the Amish country in miniature with a dozen operating O-gauge trains. It's closed January through March; admission charge. The *Strasburg Train Shop* in the adjoing *Shops of Traintown* is well-stocked with model train supplies. Both are open year-round; there's an admission charge for the *Choo Choo Barn.* Children will enjoy the *Toy Train Museum* (Paradise La.; phone: 717-687-8976), which has hands-on displays and cases of toy trains from around the world. There is a good reference library for train buffs. It's open daily May through October, and on weekends in April, November, and December; there's an admission charge. At the *Red Caboose* (Paradise La.; phone: 717-687-6646), guests may eat at the restaurant, seated in renovated coaches that simulate the sound and motion of a train (but not enough to upset sensitive stomachs), or spend the night at the motel, in a refurbished caboose. For miniature golf aficionados, don't miss the 24-hole challenge course at *Village Greens* (phone: 717-687-6933), off 741 about a mile west of 896. Before departing this hamlet, the *Strasburg Country Store and Creamery* is a must for savoring homemade ice cream and penny candy (corner of Rtes 896 and 741; phone: 717-687-0766).

En Route from Strasburg Return to the intersection of Routes 30 and 896 and head west on 30, which turns into Route 283. Continue to the Hershey exit and follow Route 743 north into town (approximately 32 miles in total).

Sample excellent Pennsylvania Dutch fare prepared with fresh ingredients at *Groff's Farm* in nearby Mt. Joy (650 Pinkerton Rd.; phone: 717-653-2048). For this stop, leave 283 at the Mt. Joy exit and follow 230 west about one-half block beyond the second light to 772 west. Then proceed four blocks to Pinkerton Road on the left. This is also one of the few restaurants in the area to serve alcohol. It's closed Sundays and Mondays; dinner reservations are essential.

HERSHEY Milton Hershey was a Mennonite whose lifestyle appears to have been pretty worldly—and whose sweet tooth has affected just about every American since the *Hershey Chocolate Factory* was built in 1903. The streetlights are giant candy kisses in this company town, and in summer the very air seems laced with chocolate. Visitors may take a *Disney World*–like ride through *Chocolate World* (phone: 717-534-4900) to see the candy making process in a simulated factory setting. Many of the area's other attractions bear Hershey's name. *HersheyPark* is an amusement park with an array of rides, performances, and gift shops. It's open *Memorial Day* through *Labor Day,* and some rides, shows, and all the shops operate during *Christmas Candylane,* a large light display held mid-November through December. No admission charge to the park; rides are pay as you go. Also see *Amusement Parks* in DIVERSIONS.) The *Hershey Museum* (phone: 717-534-

3439) features antique furniture and fire fighting equipment, as well as a *Discovery Room* where kids can try on clothes and handle kitchen utensils and other artifacts dating from the 1830s to the 1880s. The museum is closed on winter holidays; there's an admission charge. The stately *Hershey Gardens* (phone: 717-534-3492) covering 23 acres with botanical displays are known for dazzling roses; they're open daily from mid-April through October. There is an admission charge. Also *ZooAmerica* (phone: 717-534-3860), an 11-acre park features a wide variety of North American animals. Open year-round; admission charge. For more information about any of the Hershey attractions, call 800-HERSHEY.

BEST EN ROUTE

Accommodations in the area run the gamut from full-service resorts to back-road inns and roadside motels. For an up-to-date listing of Mennonite farms that take in overnight guests, contact the *Mennonite Information Center* or the *Pennsylvania Dutch Convention & Visitors Bureau* (addresses above); a double room at a Mennonite farm can range from $35 to $60 per night. During tourist season, (May through October) expect to pay $150 or more per night for a double room at hotels we've listed as very expensive; $100 to $150 at those rated expensive; $50 to $100 at places in the moderate range; and less than $50 at hotels in the inexpensive category. Unless otherwise indicated, hotels are open year-round and rooms have air conditioning, private baths, TV sets, and telephones. For each location, hotels are listed alphabetically by price category.

LANCASTER

Holiday Inn Lancaster Host and Conference Center Across from *Dutch Wonderland,* the area's prime golf resort offers a driving range, a lighted putting green, 27 holes of golf, indoor and outdoor tennis courts and pools, a fitness center, a sauna, and supervised children's activities daily in summer and on weekends the rest of the year. The 330 rooms have cable TV and VCRs upon request. There are two restaurants, a lounge, a nightclub, two seasonal outdoor grills, meeting facilities, a gift shop, and a gameroom. 2300 Lincoln Hwy. E. (phone: 717-299-5500; 800-233-0121; fax: 717-295-5112). Expensive.

Willow Valley Family Resort and Conference Center This family-oriented property with 350 rooms and suites has a nine-hole golf course, outdoor lighted tennis courts, indoor and outdoor pools, Jacuzzis, saunas, fitness rooms, a playground, two buffet-style restaurants, a coffee shop, a bakery, and two gift shops. It offers a complimentary weekday three-hour tour of Pennsylvania Dutch country. 2416 Willow St. Pike (Rte. 222; phone: 717-464-2711; 800-444-1714; fax: 717-464-4784). Expensive.

BIRD-IN-HAND

Bird-in-Hand Family Inn In a country setting only minutes from the factory outlet stores on Route 30, the 100-room inn includes lighted tennis courts, indoor and outdoor pools, a hot tub, a gameroom, a playground, and conference rooms. The restaurant features Pennsylvania Dutch specialties and an assortment of sweets. Wonderful goodies to take home from the even larger selection at their bakery across the street. A complimentary two-hour tour of the area is offered. 2740 Old Philadelphia Pike (Rte. 340; phone: 717-768-8271; 800-537-2535; fax: 717-768-1117). Moderate.

STRASBURG

Historic Strasburg Inn This lovely hideaway on 58 acres is a short drive from most sightseeing attractions. The 100 rooms (including eight suites) are decorated in colonial style. There's a restaurant and tavern, gift and bake shops, an exercise room, an outdoor pool, a gameroom, bicycling, volleyball court, and meeting rooms. Continental breakfast is included in the rate. Rte. 896 (phone: 717-687-7691; 800-872-0201; fax: 717-687-6098). Expensive.

Fulton Steamship Inn Named after Robert Fulton, who built the first successful passenger steamship, this riverboat hotel actually lies outside the town of Strasburg and is located within walking distance of the factory outlet stores on Route 30. The inn has been set in a manmade "river" and has three upper decks of 95 "staterooms" with refrigerators and microwave ovens. Rooms on the top floor also have balconies and whirlpool tubs. There's a restaurant, a coffee shop, an enclosed pool, a spa, exercise and gamerooms, a gift shop, and meeting facilities. Rtes. 30 and 896 (phone: 717-299-9999; 800-922-2229 from outside Pennsylvania; fax: 717-299-9992). Moderate.

HERSHEY

Hotel Hershey Grand enough to have played host to presidents and celebrities, this establishment is renowned for its formal gardens and European ambience. There are 241 rooms and suites, some with computer hookups; twice-daily maid service; and complimentary daily newspapers; as well as a restaurant, a café, an outdoor café in season, a lounge, and meeting facilities. Other amenities include indoor and outdoor pools, a whirlpool bath, saunas, an exercise room, tennis courts, bicycling, lawn bowling, a nine-hole golf course with privileges at four area courses, horse and carriage rides, and children's activities. During the winter, cross-country skiing, sledding, and tobogganing are available. There's a free shuttle to area attractions in summer and between *Thanksgiving* and *New Year's Day,* and complimentary transportation to the airport and train station year-round. Off Route 39 on Hotel Rd. (phone: 717-533-2171; 800-533-3131; fax: 717-534-8887). Very expensive.

Hershey Lodge & Convention Center This 457-room complex is situated on 30 acres. There are three restaurants, two lounges, nightly deejay music, and meeting facilities. Other amenities include indoor and outdoor pools, a whirlpool bath, saunas, an exercise room, a gameroom, lighted tennis courts, cycling, and pitch-and-putt golf, with golfing privileges at four area courses. A cinema on the premises shows first-run movies. Complimentary shuttle bus service to airport or train station. W. Chocolate Ave. and University Dr. (phone: 717-533-3311; 800-533-3131; fax: 717-533-9642). Expensive.

Newport and Block Island, Rhode Island

Newport, America's first resort town, has many personalities, each rooted in a different period of time. There is colonial Newport, a refuge from religious intolerance; 18th-century Newport, a bustling and prosperous seaport; and late–19th-century Newport, the summer playground of the superrich. They all coexist in 20th-century Newport, where a visitor can take a leisurely stroll past a row of 19th-century millionaires' mansions; stop by a tavern that has been in business since 1673; see the *Old Colony House,* where George Washington conferred with French strategists during the Revolutionary War; and admire some of the oldest houses of worship in America. Add a pleasant shoreline and snug harbor in Narragansett Bay and you have a place where history and recreation are in fine balance.

Founded in 1639 by victims of the Massachusetts elders' religious intolerance, Newport attracted settlers of all religious convictions, including Quakers and Jews. In the 17th and 18th centuries the town prospered as a seaport, and merchants built fine homes with the profits they made from transporting rum to the West Indies and slaves from Africa. In the 1720s, wealthy planters and merchants from the Carolinas and West Indies began to spend their summers here. The British occupation during the Revolution put an end to Newport's first golden age; the second did not begin until after the Civil War, when people like the Astors, the Belmonts, and the Vanderbilts began to build their summer "cottages" here, modeling them after the grand palaces and châteaux of Europe.

A center for yachting and all kinds of sea sports, Newport is on the tip of Aquidneck Island, the largest in Narragansett Bay. It has several excellent beaches, but even better ones are on Block Island, about 12 miles south of the mainland. Ferries connect Block Island to Newport and to Point Judith, about 15 miles west. There is also ferry service from Providence, Rhode Island, and New London, Connecticut. For information on ferry service, contact *Interstate Navigation* (phone: 401-783-4613). The Newport/Block Island area is a morning's drive from Boston or New York.

En Route from Providence Take Route 195 east to Route 24 south. When Route 138 and Route 24 diverge, follow Route 138 south to Newport.

NEWPORT To get oriented, stop at the *Gateway Visitors Center,* home of the *Newport County Convention and Visitors Bureau* (23 America's Cup Ave., Newport,

RI 02840; phone: 401-849-8048; 800-326-6030), for a free visitors' guide, maps, and information on current happenings. The town is the site of popular jazz, folk, blues, and classical music festivals, and there are frequent musical programs, especially in summer. Newport's bookstores carry many guidebooks to the town; an excellent one is *Exploring Newport,* by Terrence Gavan, which includes walking tours and restaurant information. Newport is so compact that you can walk or bicycle just about everywhere, but if you like your sightseeing sitting down, *Viking Tours* (phone: 401-847-6921) offers an hour-and-a-half city bus tour and a one-hour harbor/bay boat ride in addition to walking tours.

For a very good tour of some of Newport's most stunning "summer cottages," visit the home of the *Preservation Society of Newport County* (424 Bellevue Ave.; phone: 401-847-1000). *Hunter House* (54 Washington St.), built in 1748, is the only colonial mansion on the tour. This stately home once served as the headquarters of the commander of the French forces that assisted in the American Revolution. *The Breakers* (Ochre Point Ave.), a 70-room mansion overlooking the Atlantic, is the most splendid of Newport's greathouses. Built in 1895 for Cornelius Vanderbilt, the building resembles a northern Italian Renaissance palace. Bellevue Avenue is the site of a magnificent line of "cottages" from the Gilded Age. *The Elms,* built in 1901 for a Philadelphia coal magnate, was modeled after the *Château d'Asnières* near Paris. After touring the house, which is completely furnished with museum pieces, walk around the grounds and see the formal French gardens and rare trees and shrubs from all over the world. Marble of all kinds and colors was used to build *Marble House,* completed in 1892 for William K. Vanderbilt. This palatial home contains all of its original furnishings. *Château-sur-Mer,* built in 1852, is one of the finest examples of ornate Victorian architecture in America. *Beechwood,* built in 1851 and rebuilt by William Astor in 1881, has 40 rooms. *Rosecliff,* where scenes from Paramount's *Great Gatsby* were filmed, was designed by Stanford White after the *Grand Trianon at Versailles* and was built in 1902. Another way to see Newport's mansions is to take the Cliff Walk, a 3-mile trail between the mansions and the sea.

Also on Bellevue Avenue are the *International Tennis Hall of Fame and Tennis Museum* (phone: 401-849-3990), an 1881 casino where the first US tennis matches were played, and *Belcourt Castle* (phone: 401-846-0669), with the largest collection of 13th-century stained glass in America. Away from mansion row, you step back in time to the Federal and colonial eras. The *Old Colony House* (Washington Sq.), where Washington conferred with Rochambeau, is not open to the public, but you can see it from the street. The *Wanton-Lyman-Hazard House* (17 Broadway; phone: 401-846-0813 for hours), built in 1675, is the oldest residence in Newport. Operated by the *Newport Historical Society* (82 Touro St.; phone: 401-846-0813), it is open to the public during the summer. The *Museum of Newport History at Brick Market* (Thames St. at Washington Sq.; phone: 401-841-8770), in a recently renovated 1762 building, uses recordings, models, decorative arts, and original documents to illustrate Newport's past. Closed Tuesdays. Nearby is the *Touro Synagogue* (85 Touro St.; phone: 401-847-4794), considered an architectural gem as well as a symbol of religious liberty. Built in 1763, the synagogue is the oldest in the US. It's closed Saturdays and religious holidays.

At the corner of Church and Spring Streets, *Trinity Church,* built in 1726, is the most perfectly preserved wooden colonial structure in the country. The church, modeled after the London churches of Christopher Wren, contains many artifacts of early American life. On the harbor, the *Rhode Island Fisherman and Whale Museum* (18 Market Sq.; phone: 401-849-1340) encourages parents and kids to touch starfish, tie sailor's knots, and learn about New England's marine life. At the *Samuel Whitehorne House* (416 Thames St.), you can see some of the exquisitely crafted furniture, silver, and pewter that once graced the homes of wealthy Newport merchants. It's open by appointment only; call the *Newport Restoration Foundation* (phone: 401-849-7300) for reservations.

If you crave a few of Newport's treasures for yourself, antiques shops line Franklin and Spring Streets, and the boutiques on cobblestoned Bannister's and Bowen's wharves at the waterfront (off Thames St.) carry everything from sweaters to scrimshaw. And before you leave, be sure to try at least one of the town's seafood restaurants.

En Route from Newport Take an hour-long ferry ride from Newport Harbor 12 miles across Block Island Sound to Block Island.

BLOCK ISLAND This pear-shaped bit of rolling meadowland is an antidote to too much shopping and sightseeing. You can leave your car on the mainland and rent a bike or moped to get around; the whole island is only 11 square miles. There are a few historical things to see on Block Island: Settlers Rock, where the first settlers landed in 1661; the *Block Island Historical Society* (Old Town Rd.; phone: 401-466-2481), with exhibitions on the island's history; and the *Palatine Graves,* a memorial to the victims of a tragic shipwreck commemorated in a poem by Whittier. (The island has a bad reputation with sailors. The site of over 200 shipwrecks, it was an 18th-century haven for pirates, smugglers, and sea thieves.) But mostly this is a place to loll on the beach, take long walks by the sea, or do some serious fishing. In the waters off Block Island are tuna, bluefish, cod, and flounder, and there are over 300 inland ponds. On the Atlantic flyway, Block Island is an excellent vantage point for bird watching in fall and spring. And Mohegan Bluffs, 200 feet above sea level at the southeastern end of the island, offer long ocean vistas.

En Route from Block Island Take the ferry back to Newport.

BEST EN ROUTE

In Newport and on Block Island, prices for lodging and meals tend to be high, especially in the summer. Expect to pay $150 or more per night during tourist season for a double room at a place we've rated as expensive, and $100 to $150 at a hotel described as moderate. Unless otherwise indicated, hotels are open year-round. For each location, hotels are listed alphabetically by price category.

NEWPORT

Inn at Castle Hill Formerly the home of Alexander Agassiz, the son of the famous 19th-century naturalist, this inn has been declared a national monument. There are no TV sets or phones in the guestrooms, very few of which are air conditioned. Most of the 10 rooms have excellent views of Narragansett Bay, and some have private baths. The restaurant is quite good. The kitchen closes for the winter season and reopens in late April. Ocean Dr. (phone: 401-849-3800). Expensive.

The Inntowne This nicely restored inn is within walking distance of many Newport sites. The 26 rooms are decorated in cheerful chintz. All have air conditioning, private baths, and telephones; none have TV sets. Continental breakfast and afternoon tea are served in a pleasant sitting room, but there's no restaurant. 6 Mary Street (phone: 401-846-9200). Expensive to moderate.

BLOCK ISLAND

The 1661 Inn and Hotel Manisses A Block Island tradition, these two properties with a total of 38 rooms share ownership and dining facilities for lunch and dinner. Some guestrooms have private baths, TV sets, and phones; none have air conditioning. The newest rooms are up the street in the *Nicholas Ball House,* a replica of an old Episcopal church, complete with fireplaces and Jacuzzis. Breakfast is included in rates. Dinner is served at the hotel mid-March through November; the inn is open year-round. Also see *America's Special Havens* in DIVERSIONS. Spring St. (phone: 401-466-2421; 800-626-4773; fax: 401-466-2858). Expensive.

Vermont: A Short Tour

Vermont is one of the most exquisite, unspoiled pieces of real estate in the United States. On offer are winter skiing, springtime blossoms and greenery, summer hiking and water sports, and stupefying autumn foliage. It's still a primarily rural state, and local lore has it that only recently have humans outnumbered cows. Vermont's holsteins seem more contented than bovines elsewhere—which is hardly surprising, considering that they're grazing in the lea of the Green Mountains or Lake Champlain.

This route starts at Woodstock/Quechee on I-89. From there it makes a loop north on Route 100, stopping in Stowe to see (and, perhaps, hike or ski) Mt. Mansfield, the state's highest at 4393 feet, and then continues via Route 12 to Montpelier, the state capital, with a quick jag over to the wilds of the Northeast Kingdom on Route 2. From there the route heads west to I-89 and Burlington, Vermont's largest city, on Lake Champlain. The way back south via Route 7 includes stops in Shelburne, Middlebury, Manchester/Arlington, and Bennington.

For general information about visiting Vermont, contact the *Department of Travel and Tourism* (134 State St., Montpelier, VT 05602; phone: 802-828-3236).

En Route from Boston Take I-93 to I-89 and Woodstock/Quechee.

WOODSTOCK/QUECHEE This pair of early 18th-century towns oozes charm from every antiques and craft shop—and there are many. For history buffs there's *Billings Farm and Museum* (Rte. 12, Woodstock; phone: 802-457-2355), a re-created 19th-century farm. It's open daily May through October and weekends in November and December; there's an admission charge. Nature lovers will enjoy the *Quechee Gorge,* a mile-long chasm with waterfalls and nature trails (Rte. 4; phone: 802-295-7600), and the *Vermont Institute of Natural Science* (Church Hill Rd., Woodstock; phone: 802-457-2779), whose raptor center houses spectacular birds of prey. It's closed Sundays November through April; open daily the rest of the year. There is an admission charge.

En Route from Woodstock Head west on Route 4 to Route 100, then head north.

ROUTE 100 This road follows the eastern fringe of *Green Mountain National Forest,* through cow pastures and little towns with white-spired churches and general stores. En route is *Killington* ski area, Vermont's largest, which stretches across six mountains (phone: 800-621-MTNS). Just west of Hancock on Route 125 is *Texas Falls Recreation Area,* with falls, hiking, and picnicking. Continuing on Route 100, follow the Mad River through Warren and Waitsfield, covered-bridge towns serving two ski resorts, *Sugarbush Resort* (phone: 802-583-2381) and *Mad River Glen* (phone: 802-496-2001 for snow reports; 802-496-3551 for lodging information). The *Warren-Sugarbush Airport,* just off Route 100, offers glider rides (phone: 802-496-2290). There are also lots of good swimming holes along this stretch of Mad River—look for groups of parked cars. Waitsfield is also the home of the *Vermont Icelandic Horse Farm* (phone: 802-496-7141; fax: 802-496-5124), which offers a variety of riding programs and trips on Icelandic horses, a small, gentle, and sturdy breed that dates to the Viking era.

One of the state's premier indulgences awaits in Waterbury: *Ben & Jerry's Ice Cream Factory* (1 mile north of I-89 on Route 100; phone: 802-244-5641). A modest admission fee covers a factory tour and tasting. The company also sponsors films and shows for children here.

Ten miles north of Waterbury on Route 100 is Stowe.

STOWE AND ENVIRONS Stowe is one of the most famous ski areas in New England. Even if you don't ski, it's worth a trip to see this beautiful region. There are downhill ski areas at the *Village at Smugglers Notch* (phone: 802-644-8851), *Stowe Mountain Resort* (5781 Mountain Rd.; phone: 802-253-3000), and nearby *Bolton Valley* (phone: 802-434-2131). When the sun is shining behind Mt. Mansfield's snow-covered peak in winter, it is, in the words of one resident, "most amazing." Marking the end of the Green Mountains, Mt. Mansfield (4,393 feet) is laced with trails and caves. Every January, the town celebrates the season with the *Stowe Winter Carnival,* which features a snow sculpture contest, cross-country ski races, fireworks, and other events. You can ride a plastic sled down Mt. Mansfield on an exciting alpine slide at *Stowe Mountain Resort* (it's open daily from mid-June through *Labor Day,* and on weekends from mid-May through mid-June and *Labor Day* through mid-October). In August, you can pick blueberries as you hike.

En Route from Stowe North of Stowe, Route 100 passes near Moss Glen Falls, with its silvery cascades thundering through the forest, then on to Morrisville and Cambridge Junction–Jeffersonville, the prettiest part of the state, according to many residents. A few miles south of the turnoff, you'll pass through Smugglers Notch, an important hideout for contraband goods passing between the US and Canada during the War of 1812.

Return to Morrisville on Route 15, then pick up Route 12 south and follow it to Montpelier.

MONTPELIER AND THE NORTHEAST KINGDOM Montpelier is a pleasant mix of state capital and small town, with the gilt dome of the *State House* (115 State St.; phone: 802-828-2228) glittering in front of a forested slope. There are *State House* tours July through mid-October. Antiques, photographs, and other memorabilia at the *Vermont Historical Society* (109 State St.; phone: 802-828-2291; closed Mondays) trace the social and political evolution of the state. Thanks to the *New England Culinary Institute,* Montpelier also has an impressive array of eateries.

The Northeast Kingdom is a vast, compelling landscape of evergreen forests and mountain-ringed, glacier-chiseled lakes stretching north to Canada. Little towns like Craftsbury Common (off Route 14), with its music festivals, and Glover (on route 16), home of the annual summertime circus and pageant provided by the resident *Bread and Puppet Theater,* offer one-of-a-kind artistic events. In the far north, on Route 242, is *Jay Peak* (phone: 802-988-2611), a top ski area the crowds have yet to discover; it provides gondola rides and mountain biking in summer. Just north of Route 58 is Brownington Village, with its *Old Stone House Museum* (phone: 802-754-2022), an 1830s school dormitory now housing American decorative arts. It's closed mid-October to mid-May; there is an admission charge. St. Johnsbury to the south, on I-91, is rich in possibilities for a modest-sized town. The *Fairbanks Museum and Planetarium* (Main and Prospect Sts.; phone: 802-748-2372; open daily) focuses on natural history, while the *St.*

Johnsbury Atheneum and Art Gallery (30 Main St.; phone: 802-748-8291; closed Sundays) houses fine arts. The performing arts—dance, film, drama, music—are well represented by *Catamount Arts* (60 Eastern Ave.; phone: 802-748-2600).

En Route from Montpelier and the Northeast Kingdom Backtrack to Burlington, heading west on Route 2 and north on I-89.

BURLINGTON This town dates back to the Revolution, and Revolutionary War hero Ethan Allen is buried here in *Greenmount Cemetery,* which also was the site of a major naval battle during the War of 1812. From *Battery Park* you can get a marvelous view of the tranquil lake and the Adirondacks on the far shore. Lake Champlain is famous for its elusive Loch Ness–type monster, "Champ." Try to spot it on the *Spirit of Ethan Allen* sunset cruise. The voyages are offered from May through October; they depart from the *Burlington Boat House* at the foot of College Street (phone: 802-862-8300). There's also a swimming area at North Beach. The *University of Vermont* (phone: 802-656-3480), *Trinity College* (phone: 802-658-0337), and *St. Michael's College* (phone: 802-655-2000) offer films, concerts, plays, and sports throughout the year.

If you're traveling during the fall, we recommend an excursion to South Hero, a town just north of Burlington on one of Lake Champlain's islands. From late September through early October, when the foliage is at its height, you can pick your own apples at *Allenholm Farms* (South St.; phone: 802-372-5566). To get to South Hero, take Route 7 north to Route 2 west. Along the way you'll pass through *Sand Bar Wildlife Area and State Park,* a good picnicking spot.

En Route from Burlington Head south on Route 7 to Shelburne.

SHELBURNE This is the home of the *Shelburne Museum* (Rte. 7; phone: 802-985-3346). A terrific trek through American history, the museum is actually a collection of 37 buildings. Highlights include an antique toy shop; a mansion with fine Impressionist paintings; a shop with rugs, quilts, and antique clothing; and a working blacksmith shop and weaving shed. A favorite with children is a building that has beautiful, brilliantly carved miniatures representing a circus parade. The entire complex is open from May through October; during the rest of the year, six buildings are open daily for guided tours. There's an admission charge. Also see *Restored Towns and Reconstructed Villages* in DIVERSIONS.

If you're fortunate enough to be here at sunset, go to Shelburne Point, the tip of a finger of land pointing northwest on the shores of Lake Champlain, where you can catch a view of the sun sinking behind the Adirondacks.

En Route from Shelburne Wandering south along Route 7, you'll encounter a number of good restaurants and inns. South of Vergennes, you can detour east on Route 17 through Bristol to Lincoln Gap, a winding passageway. The Long Trail crosses the road at the summit, with good hikes north and south. Then head back west on Route 17 to Route 7 south to Middlebury.

MIDDLEBURY Otter Creek Falls, a 30-foot cascade in the center of town, provides a spectacular sideshow for a place dominated by *Middlebury College.* The college has a formidable cultural schedule, including lectures, dance, theater, music, film, and fine-arts exhibitions (phone: 802-388-3711). Not to be missed is the *Vermont State Craft Center* (in town just below the falls at Frog Hollow, 1 Mill St.; phone: 802-388-3177), which sells the finest work of Vermont artisans. Also worth seeing is the *Sheldon Museum* (1 Park St.; phone: 802-388-2117), which is located in an 1829 house with period furnishings and relics of local history. It's closed weekends in winter; there's an admission charge. Just north of the town center on Horse Farm Road is the *Morgan Horse Farm* (phone: 802-388-2011), showcasing the sturdy breed that Justin Morgan developed in the state. The *University of Vermont* offers tours of the farm daily May through October; there's an admission charge. The western boundary of the *Green Mountain National Forest* is just a short drive away, south on Route 7 and then east on Route 125. Up the mountain on Route 125 is the site of the *Bread Loaf Writers' School,* where Robert Frost taught. Also in the area are Robert Frost Mountain, a *Robert Frost Wayside Recreation Area,* and *Middlebury College Snow Bowl* (phone: 802-388-4356), a popular family ski area.

En Route from Middlebury There are several pleasant route options for the drive south. From east to west—and busiest to quietest—these are Routes 7, 30, and 22A (crossing over to 30 at Poultney). All three roll through dairy farms and traditional towns with village greens, arriving in the Manchester area.

MANCHESTER Once a quiet, genteel town, Manchester has become a victim of its own charm, now hemmed in by fast-food restaurants and factory outlets. (For a saner experience—and some great antiquing—try Dorset just up Route 30.) Nonetheless, Manchester has many diversions. *Hildene* (Rte. 7A; phone: 802-362-1788), the home of President Lincoln's descendants, is a Georgian Revival mansion with turn-of-the-century furnishings and formal gardens. It's closed November to mid-May; there's an admission charge. The *Southern Vermont Art Center* (West Rd.; phone: 802-362-1405) is a gallery and performance venue (indoors and out) on a 400-acre estate. It's closed Sundays.

En Route from Manchester South of Manchester, just off Route 7A, is a scenic toll road climbing up Mt. Equinox. At the summit are a lodge and panorama—and quite a few tourists. Farther south on 7A in Arlington is the *Norman Rockwell Exhibition,* a gallery of the *Saturday Evening Post* cover artist's work (phone: 802-375-6423). It's open daily; there is an admission charge. Running through, and westward from, Arlington is the

Battenkill, a swift-flowing stream, complete with covered bridge, that is favored for fishing, canoeing, and inner tubing (several places in town rent tubes).

From Arlington, take Route 7A south to Bennington.

BENNINGTON Another college town artistically livened by its academic community, Bennington is also famous for a Revolutionary War battle commemorated by the 306-foot *Bennington Battle Monument* (Monument Ave.; phone: 802-447-0550). The monument is open daily to climbers. On display at the *Bennington Museum* (West Main St.; phone: 802-447-1571) are exhibits of Americana, including Bennington pottery and Grandma Moses paintings. Closed *Christmas* through *New Year's Day;* there is an admission charge. There are several major ski areas nearby, all east of Route 7: *Bromley Mountain* (Rte. 11; phone: 802-824-5522), *Stratton Mountain* (off Rte. 30 in Bondville; phone: 802-297-2200), and *Mt. Snow/Haystack* (off Rte. 100; phone: 802-464-3333).

En Route from Bennington To return to Boston, take Route 9 east to I-91, then head south to I-93.

BEST EN ROUTE

High season in Vermont lasts nearly all year: summer, fall, and winter. Expect to pay $150 or more per night for a double room in high season at those hotels rated as expensive, $100 to $150 at those described as moderate, and less than $100 at inexpensive places. Unless otherwise indicated, hotels are open year-round and rooms have air conditioning, private baths, TV sets, and telephones. For each location, hotels are listed alphabetically by price category.

QUECHEE

The Quechee Inn at Marshland Farm This 24-room establishment with river views is home to the *Vermont Fly Fishing School* in the summer and to cross-country skiing in winter. Guests can enjoy biking, canoeing, swimming, and tennis, as well as golfing privileges at the nearby *Quechee Club.* Rates include breakfast and dinner. There's no air conditioning. Clubhouse Rd. (phone: 802-295-3133; 800-235-3133). Expensive to moderate.

ROUTE 100

Cortina Inn This 98-room resort is best known for its tennis instruction on eight clay and Plexipave courts, but there's also a fitness center and swimming pool and lots of hunting, fishing, golf, horseback riding, and skiing nearby, plus snowmobiling and sleigh rides in winter. Breakfast is included in the rate. About 8 miles east of Rutland on Rte. 4 (phone: 802-773-3333; 800-451-6108; fax: 802-775-6948). Expensive.

Inn at the Round Barn Farm The farmhouse was built in 1810; its round barn, 100 years later. The 11 guestrooms, all furnished with antiques and some with fireplaces and Jacuzzis, are in the farmhouse. Picturesque meadows, mountains, and a pond provide a lovely setting, and there's an indoor pool. Breakfast is included in the rate. No restaurant. East Warren Rd., Waitsfield (phone: 802-496-2276; fax: 802-496-8832). Expensive to moderate.

Lareau Farm A country inn on a picturesque working farm with congenial owners and an authentic 1832 Greek Revival farmhouse. The 13 guestrooms (including a deluxe suite) have antique beds, plush handmade quilts, and plank floors—but no TV sets, phones, or air conditioning. Swim or fish in the Mad River, or take one of the farm's hay or sleigh rides. Breakfast is included in the rate. On Friday and Saturday nights, "flatbread" (wonderful thin-crust dough grilled over a wood fire) is served in a big barn. Rte. 100, Waitsfield (phone: 802-496-4949; 800-833-0766). Moderate.

Newtons' 1824 House Inn This lovely clapboard farmhouse with six elegant guestrooms sits on 52 acres of land. The Mad River meanders through the property, and there's a swimming hole. Breakfast is included in the rate. There's no restaurant. Rte. 100, Waitsfield (phone: 802-496-7555). Moderate.

STOWE

Trapp Family Lodge Maria von Trapp, of *The Sound of Music* fame, opened a singing camp here in the 1940s. Surrounded by sensational mountain scenery, the Tyrolean-style lodge has 93 rooms with TV sets but no air conditioning. There are three pools (one indoor), four clay tennis courts, and cross-country skiing. Its location is ideal for downhill skiers, too; the slopes are only 10 minutes away. Rates include breakfast and dinner. 42 Trapp Hill Rd. (phone: 802-253-8511; 800-826-7000; fax: 802-253-5740). Expensive to moderate.

Edson Hill Manor This laid-back lodge is one of Stowe's hidden treasures. There are 25 rooms, trout ponds, riding stables, and hiking trails. There's no air conditioning, and not all rooms have TV sets. The restaurant serves breakfast and dinner daily; breakfast is included in the room rate. 1500 Edson Hill Rd. (phone: 802-253-7371; 800-621-0284; fax: 802-253-4036). Expensive to moderate.

MONTPELIER AND THE NORTHEAST KINGDOM

Inn on the Common In the center of Craftsbury, a gem of a Northeast Kingdom town, this hostelry's 16 rooms are decorated with simple elegance. Some have fireplaces. There are also sweeping views from the inn and its lovely gardens, as well as a pool, a tennis court, a sports center, and fine dining. Rooms have no telephones, TV sets, or air conditioning. Rates include breakfast and dinner. Main St., Craftsbury Common (phone: 802-586-9619; 800-521-2233; 802-586-2249). Expensive.

The Inn at Montpelier A country inn with capital city amenities, and just steps from the *State House* on a quiet tree-lined street. Six of the 19 rooms have fireplaces. There is an elegant restaurant, and breakfast is included in the rate. Breakfast is included in the rate. 147 Main St., Montpelier (phone: 802-223-2727; fax: 802-223-0722). Expensive to moderate.

BURLINGTON

Marble Island Ten minutes north of Burlington on a quiet cove of Lake Champlain, this resort offers 34 modern rooms, most with balconies overlooking the lake. There are two pools, tennis, golf, two restaurants, and two bars. Breakfast is included in the rate. 150 Marble Island Rd., Colchester (phone: 802-864-6800; 800-331-2093; fax: 802-865-3620). Moderate.

North Hero House A 23-room inn with tennis and water sports facilities, this has an ideal lakefront location, across the bridge from South Hero. There's a restaurant. Rooms have no TV sets, telephones, or air conditioning. Open mid-May through mid-October. Rte. 2 (phone: 802-372-8237 from May through October; 908-439-2837 the rest of the year). Inexpensive.

SHELBURNE

Inn at Shelburne Farms Built in 1899 by railroad baron Dr. William Seward Webb and his wife, Lila Vanderbilt, this three-story summer cottage was converted to a 24-room inn. On the 1,400-acre grounds are a garden, a tennis court, and, occasionally on summer evenings, classical music concerts. The dining rooms serve classic American fare; breakfast is included in the rate. There are no TV sets or air conditioning in the spacious rooms; some have shared baths. Open from mid-May through mid-October. Also see *America's Special Havens* in DIVERSIONS. Shelburne Farms, Bay Road (phone/fax: 802-985-8498). Expensive.

MIDDLEBURY AND ENVIRONS

Blueberry Hill Inn This inn on a secluded hillside overlooking the Champlain Valley, about 20 minutes from Middlebury and just outside the *Green Mountain National Forest,* specializes in hiking and cross-country skiing. It has a sauna and a spring-fed pond for swimming and trout fishing. Its 12 rooms are decorated with antiques and quilts; the rooms do not have TV sets or air conditioning. The restaurant is superb, and rates include breakfast and dinner. RD 3, Goshen (phone: 802-247-6735; 800-448-0707; fax: 802-247-3983). Expensive.

Middlebury Inn Close to the college, this 75-room inn is also near golf, tennis, bicycling, skiing, and swimming. Be sure to ask for a room in the original, older part of the hotel. The dining room is open to the public. 14 Courthouse Sq., Rte. 7, Middlebury (phone: 802-388-4961; 800-842-4666; fax: 802-388-4563). Moderate to inexpensive.

Swift House Inn A former governor's estate on the outskirts of town, this hostelry manages to combine elegance with a feeling of home. Its three buildings comprise 21 rooms, some with fireplaces and whirlpools; not all have TV sets. There's a steamroom, a sauna, and an excellent restaurant. Room rates include breakfast. 25 Steward La. (phone: 802-388-9925; fax: 802-388-9927). Moderate to inexpensive.

Waybury Inn Built in 1810 as a stagecoach stop, this inn has 14 rooms, some with air conditioning; none have TV sets or telephones. It is a popular spot for fine country dining, with a good selection of international beers and ales, even if you don't plan to stay here. Room rates include breakfast. Rte. 125, East Middlebury (phone: 802-388-4015; 800-348-1810). Moderate to inexpensive.

MANCHESTER VILLAGE

The Equinox This recently refurbished resort disguised as a country inn opened in 1769. It's set on the green, and its 163 rooms are furnished with reproduction antiques. Golf, tennis, swimming, hiking, skiing, complete spa facilities, and a restaurant are available. Rte. 7A (phone: 802-362-4700; 800-362-4747; fax: 802-362-4861). Expensive.

ARLINGTON

Inn on Covered Bridge Green Norman Rockwell's former home and studio offers a picture-perfect setting in a building more than 200 years old, with the Battenkill River and a covered bridge just outside. There's a tennis court as well as swimming, fishing, and canoeing on the Battenkill. No smoking allowed; the five guestrooms have no TV sets, telephones, or air conditioning. There's no restaurant, but a generous breakfast is included in the rate. River Rd. (phone: 802-375-9489; 800-726-9480). Expensive to moderate.

South

Hot Springs National Park, Arkansas

If you think that Hot Springs, Arkansas, is just a place to bring your aching joints, you're in for a huge surprise. Hot Springs is the hottest tourist attraction in Arkansas—at least when President Clinton isn't visiting his former home in Little Rock.

A city of some 32,000, Hot Springs is partially located in *Hot Springs National Park.* (This is unusual in itself, since most national parks are miles from large, populated centers.) The place has come a long way from when it was christened "the valley of vapors" by explorer Hernando de Soto in 1541. At that time, it was secluded Indian territory, and it was supposedly the Indians who led de Soto and his exhausted team to the bubbling pools of water, where they were rejuvenated after a bath. The legendary curative properties of these 47 thermal springs became known all the world over. In 1832, four sections of Hot Springs were declared a federal reservation. In 1921 they became a national park, which now covers almost 5,000 acres.

The fabled Bathhouse Row has been offering regimens of baths and massages for long enough to be designated a National Historic Landmark. There are six operating bathhouses, one of them on Bathhouse Row (the others are in nearby hotels and a health spa). *Fordyce Bathhouse* (369 Central Ave.; phone: 501-623-1433), a former bathhouse now listed on the *National Register of Historic Places,* is open for tours and serves as a visitors' information center. Before stepping into a mineral bath, it's recommended (not required) that you be examined by a physician, and you must have a physician's referral for physiotherapy sessions at any of the hydrotherapy facilities.

The springs themselves are on the western slope of Hot Springs Mountain. A reservoir collects the 850,000 gallons flowing through 44 of the thermal springs daily and channels them to the bathhouses. (You can see two of the bubbling springs behind the *Maurice Bathhouse* on Central Avenue; another flows down the hillside above Arlington Lawn at the north end of Bathhouse Row. The rest are not visible to the public.) The springs puzzle geologists: They theorize that rain seeps through an aquifer and then rises along layers of rock to bubble out through a fault at the base of Hot Springs Mountain, but they don't understand how the water is heated. The answer may be molten rock, radioactive minerals, inner seismic friction, or unexplained chemical reactions.

There also are plenty of activities here that have nothing to do with the springs. Thoroughbred horses race from late January to mid-April at *Oaklawn Park* (2705 Central Ave.; phone: 501-623-4411), a handsome track. The season's climax is the week-long *Racing Festival of the South* in the third week of April, which culminates in the running of the *Arkansas Derby* on the final day. The local races kick off a lively, diversified summer and fall season, during which races from around the country are simulcast at *Oaklawn Park.* Other annual events include the city-wide *Arkansas Celebration of the Arts* (phone: 501-321-0234), usually held the first week of November and the highly acclaimed *Hot Springs Documentary Film Festival* (phone: 501-321-4747) held in October.

Art lovers will appreciate the *Gallery Walk,* beginning at 5 PM on the first Thursday and Friday of each month. For details, get a brochure from any downtown art gallery or look for the crowds on Central Avenue. Performances of *The Witness,* an outdoor drama similar to the *Passion Play* are staged in summer at the 1,600-seat *Mid-America* amphitheater (phone: 501-623-9781). To get there, turn right from 270W onto 227 and follow the signs. The *Hot Springs Arts Center* (405 Park Ave.; phone: 501-624-0489) hosts changing art displays and community arts programs.

Kids will especially enjoy the sights at the *Arkansas Alligator Farm* (847 Whittington Ave.; phone: 501-623-6172); *National Park Aquarium* (209 Central Ave.; phone: 501-624-3474); and *Magic Springs Family Theme Park* (1701 E. Grand Ave. 70 E.; phone: 501-624-5411). Other attractions include the *Josephine Tussaud Wax Museum* (250 Central Ave.; phone: 501-623-5836); *Belle of Hot Springs* riverboat cruises (5200 Central Ave.; phone: 501-525-4438); *Tiny Town* (374 Whittington Ave.; phone: 501-624-4742), billed as the world's greatest indoor display of mechanical wooden figures and buildings; the *Museum of Hot Springs* (201 Central Ave.; phone: 501-624-5545); and the *Mid-America Science Museum* (500 Mid-American Blvd.; phone: 501-767-3461). In October, there's the *Arkansas Oktoberfest* (134 Convention Blvd.; phone: 501-321-3802); in November, the *Healthfest/Spa 10K Run* (phone: 501-321-3802).

Tour the town in mule-drawn carriages operated by *Mule Line Trolley* (264 Central Ave.; phone: 501-624-2202) or on amphibious vehicles, used by the military in World War II, that cruise the area by land and then take to the waters of Lake Hamilton. Amphibious tours are offered by several companies including the *Ducks in the Park* (310 Central Ave.; phone: 501-321-9667). Or simply take a stroll down the Central Avenue Historic District opposite Bathhouse Row.

For a touch of tranquillity, follow Route 270 west to the gently rolling Ouachita Mountains, one of the oldest mountain ranges on the continent. There are three manmade lakes in the Hot Springs area on the Ouachita River: Ouachita (west of town on Route 270 east), Hamilton (south on Hwy. 7), and Catherine (on Hwy. 171 southwest of town). Each offers fishing, swimming, water skiing, sailing, and scuba diving, and there are campsites along the southern shores of Lake Ouachita and miles of hiking trails through the forests. *Lake Catherine State Park* (on Hwy. 171 southwest of town) and *Lake Ouachita State Park* (off US 270 or Hwy. 7) offer camping and hiking.

For complete information on accommodations and facilities, call the *Hot Springs Visitor Information Center* (phone: 501-321-2277; 800-SPA-CITY). For a free travel kit, write to the *Hot Springs Convention and Visitors Bureau* (PO Box K, *Hot Springs National Park,* Hot Springs, AR 71902), or contact the *Arkansas Department of Parks and Tourism* (1 Capitol Mall, Little Rock, AR 72201; phone: 501-682-7777; 800-NATURAL). For general information, contact the Superintendent, *Hot Springs National Park* (PO Box 1860, Hot Springs, AR 71902; phone: 501-623-1433).

BEST EN ROUTE

Expect to pay $80 or more per night for a double room in those places we have listed as expensive, and $50 to $80 in those rated moderate. Unless otherwise noted, hotels are open year-round and rooms have air conditioning, private baths, TV sets, and telephones.

HOT SPRINGS

Arlington In the middle of the city, this grand old lady of Hot Springs hotels has 486 rooms, its own hot mineral water bathhouse and spa, two pools, a mountainside hot tub, a sun deck, an exercise room, three restaurants, and a lounge. Some of the rooms have private mineral baths. Breakfast is included in the rate. Also see *Sybaritic Spas* in DIVERSIONS. 229 Central Ave. (phone: 501-623-7771; 800-643-1502 outside Arkansas; fax: 501-623-6191). Expensive to moderate.

Majestic Another grand old Hot Springs hotel, this has 225 rooms, a heated outdoor pool, hot tubs, a spa, and thermal baths and massages. There's a restaurant, and breakfast is included in the price of the more expensive rooms. 101 Park Ave. (phone: 501-623-5511; 800-643-1504). Moderate.

The Ozarks, Arkansas

They call it "the Natural State"—down-home, pickin' and strummin', come-as-you-are Arkansas. A center of American folk myth and heritage, the Ozarks are an unpretentious part of the world. Country roads lead through gentle, blue-green mountains, twisting along the edges of gorges that catapult into frothy rivers. If you can imagine a banjo or fiddle playing in the background, you've got the picture.

Our route starts in Jacksonport, just a few miles north of Newport in the northeastern quarter of the state, then heads northwest through the heart of the Ozarks on Routes 14 and 62, past forests, lakes, folk centers, and old-fashioned towns. At the state's northwestern border, the route heads south, past a Civil War battlefield and the university town of Fayetteville, then east on I-40 to the *Ozark National Forest.*

JACKSONPORT This spot on the banks of the White River is famous for its fishing. Stop at *Jacksonport State Park* (phone: 501-523-2143), just north of Newport, to picnic. If you have enough confidence in your casting ability, you can fish for your meal. Jacksonport was once a rough-and-ready frontier river town, and its old *Courthouse,* which is near the entrance to the park, is now a local history museum, with various artifacts dating from the 1820s through the turn of the century. The museum is closed Mondays from April through October, and Mondays and Tuesdays from November through March; there's an admission charge. The *Mary Woods II,* a White River paddle wheel steamboat, is on display at the park, with exhibits on the history of riverboats in the area; there's an admission charge. According to local history, Jacksonport citizens liked the river city so much they refused to let the railroad come in; so the station was built in nearby Newport instead. As a result, Jacksonport declined.

En Route from Jacksonport Return to Newport by heading south on Highway 69. Then follow the river northwest along Route 14 to Route 167, which heads north to Batesville.

BATESVILLE Stop here and you'll step back into the 19th century: The downtown area has barely changed since the days when the paddle wheelers steamed into dock along the majestic White River, full of passengers and cargo.

En Route from Batesville Head back to Highway 14 on 167 south, then continue northwest for about 40 miles to Mountain View.

MOUNTAIN VIEW This is the home of the *Ozark Folk Center* (phone: 501-269-3851), which is located a few miles north of town off Highways 5, 9, and 14 on Spur 382. A good place for first-timers to get acquainted with the Ozarks, the 80-acre center features mountain craft displays and workshops. It's also alive with music. Visit on the third weekend in April and you'll be swept up in a crowd of about 100,000 people, all flocking to town for the *Arkansas Folk Festival,* a weekend of jug band, fiddle, Jew's harp, mountain dulcimer, and banjo strummin' sessions. If you don't like crowds but hanker after that foot-stompin' music, stop by between late spring and October, when the center's 1,042-seat auditorium holds concerts nightly except Sundays. There also are free concerts at the county courthouse every Saturday night, special theme weekends, and, in October, a two-week *Harvest Festival* at the center. You can always see traditional pottery, quilting, shucking, spinning, and weaving at the folk center; most of the handiwork is for sale at the center's shop.

En Route from Mountain View Follow Highway 14 west about 15 miles to *Blanchard Springs Cavern.*

BLANCHARD SPRINGS CAVERN In the Sylamore district of the *Ozark National Forest,* about 8 miles west of Allison, *Blanchard Springs Cavern* is considered one of the most spectacular underground natural environments in the country.

Walk along *Dripstone Trail* (open year-round), a labyrinth that crisscrosses the palatial subterranean caverns, past dramatic stalactites. More difficult is the *Discovery Trail,* with a Christmas tree–shaped stalagmite, a frozen waterfall, and a cavern called the Ghost Room (open *Memorial Day* to *Labor Day*). Above ground, there are nature trails and camping areas. To see the cavern during the summer months, make reservations (phone: 501-757-2213) well in advance, even if you only want a tour. The caverns are closed Mondays and Tuesdays from November through March; open daily the rest of the year.

En Route from Blanchard Springs Cavern Take Highway 14 east to Allison, where it intersects with Highway 5. Then head north on 5 to Mountain Home, about 35 miles away.

MOUNTAIN HOME Some fabulous river and lake country lies here between Norfork and Bull Shoals, two of the Ozarks' most famous lakes. Both lakes are great for canoeing, swimming, and water skiing. Bass, bream, crappie, catfish, stripers, and rainbow trout swim around in the clear water just waiting to be caught, and there are Ozark guides who can lead anglers to where the fish are biting. Night fishing expeditions on a pontoon boat can also be arranged. On the shores of Bull Shoals Lake and the White River is *Bull Shoals State Park* (phone: 501-431-5521), which has campsites and a dock. To enter the park, head 6 miles north of Mountain Home on Highway 5, then go 8 miles west on State Highway 178.

En Route from Mountain Home Take Highway 62 west to Yellville. In Yellville, take Highway 14 about 17 miles south to Buffalo Point on the river.

BUFFALO POINT For an unforgettable canoe trip, ride the wild Buffalo River through the *Buffalo Point National Recreation Area,* located 3 miles east of Highway 14 on Spur 268. The 132-mile river flows through spectacular blue mountains, and there are no artificial dams to obstruct the water's flow. The *National Park Service* (phone: 501-741-5443) maintains cabins at Buffalo Point and campsites along the riverbanks. For information on the park, cabins, and canoe rentals, call 501-449-4311.

En Route from Buffalo Point Return to Highway 62 via Highway 14 north, then continue west through the heart of the Arkansas Ozarks to Eureka Springs, which is just north of 62 on State Highway 23. There is a state tourist information center on Highway 62/65 in Harrison.

EUREKA SPRINGS This delightful Victorian town, a fashionable health spa in the 1880s, has 63 natural springs within the city limits. During the summer, there's an occasional concert at the *Basin Spring Park* band shell. From late April through October, the *Great Passion Play* is performed daily except Mondays and Thursdays near the seven-story-tall *Christ of the Ozarks* statue in a 4,400-seat amphitheater (phone: 501-253-9200; also see *Outdoor Dramas* in DIVERSIONS).

En Route from Eureka Springs Follow Highway 62 as it loops around the north shore of 28,000-acre Beaver Lake. Just west of town, you'll find *Eureka Springs Gardens,* a 33-acre park filled with blooming greenery (phone: 501-253-9244). From there, continue west and then south on 62 to *Pea Ridge National Military Park,* 10 miles north of Roger.

PEA RIDGE NATIONAL MILITARY PARK This was the site of a decisive 1862 Civil War battle, after which Missouri stuck firmly to the Union. At the visitors' center are military exhibits and a slide show. Audiocassette guides may be rented for a self-guided automobile tour, which visits the major battle areas. Open daily except *Thanksgiving, Christmas,* and *New Year's.* Admission charge (phone: 501-451-8122).

En Route from Pea Ridge National Military Park Take Highway 62 west, then Highway 71 south, to Fayetteville, home of the *University of Arkansas's* main campus (phone: 501-575-2000). Follow Highway 71 south, past *Devil's Den* (on Rte. 74) and *Lake Fort Smith* state parks, to I-40. (There's a state travel information center at *Fort Smith,* west of the intersection of Highway 71 and I-40.) Then take I-40 east to Clarksville, gateway to the 1.1-million-acre *Ozark National Forest.*

OZARK NATIONAL FOREST Get off the interstate at Clarksville and wander north along Highway 21 through dense, uninhabited woods. This is just the place to enjoy the sounds of the forest and have a picnic lunch near a cascading creek—or stay a little longer and go swimming, canoeing, hiking, camping, or fishing. For information, contact the Forest Supervisor, *Ozark National Forest* (PO Box 1008, Russellville, AR 72801; phone: 501-968-2354).

BEST EN ROUTE

Expect to pay $120 or more per night for a double room in those places we have listed as expensive; $75 to $120 in those rated moderate; and less than $75 in those listed as inexpensive. Unless otherwise noted, hotels are open year-round and rooms have air conditioning, private baths, TV sets, and telephones. For each location, hotels are listed alphabetically by price category.

MOUNTAIN VIEW

Ozark Folk Center Lodge In woodsy surroundings right next to the folk center, this 60-room lodge is a good place if you want a rustic environment and a chance to be where it's all happening. There's a restaurant. On Spur 382 off Hwy. 5 (phone: 501-269-3871; 800-264-3655). Inexpensive.

Wildflower–A Vintage Comfort Guest House This historic "bed and bakery" is located in the town square. Many evenings, local folk musicians gather on the porch;

musical types can usually join in. The fabulous on-premises bakery serves lunch, and the hotel offers continental breakfasts. Some of the eight rooms have shared baths. On the corner of Peabody and Washington Sts. (phone: 501-269-4383; 800-591-4879). Inexpensive.

EUREKA SPRINGS

Dairy Hollow House Considered one of the best bed and breakfast establishments in the country, this is actually two houses, with six rooms and suites with wood-burning fireplaces. A bountiful "breakfast in a basket" is delivered to guests' rooms and there is a fine restaurant that serves daily lunch and dinner. Inn and restaurant closed January. 515 Spring St. (phone: 501-253-7444; 800-562-8650). Expensive.

New Orleans Hotel From the wrought-iron balconies of this historic hotel, guests can look down on winding Spring Street in the heart of this popular tourist town. There are 18 double-Jacuzzi suites; there's no restaurant. 63 Spring St. (phone: 501-253-8630; 800-243-8630). Moderate.

Everglades National Park, Florida

In most of America's national parks there's little more to do than arrive and open your eyes to be impressed. *Everglades National Park* is far more demanding. Here it helps to know something about ecology, and something about what you're looking at, in order to appreciate the full splendor of this magnificent marshy wilderness. Or, at least, it helps to have a child-like curiosity that aches to see that fabled reptile, the alligator.

Fed by the waters of huge Lake Okeechobee, the entire southern tip of the state was once more or less as the Everglades are today—a huge tract of mangrove swamps, seas of sawgrass, hammocks of hardwood trees, and millions of birds, fish, snakes, alligators, and insects (including 43 species of mosquitoes). As South Florida developed, the slow-draining waters of Okeechobee were channeled for irrigation and most of the swamps were drained. Bit by bit, South Florida dried out.

In 1947, alarmed by the destruction of these unique wetlands, the federal government set aside 1.5 million acres 30 miles southwest of Miami as *Everglades National Park.* Despite various (and continuing) environmental threats from urbanization, industry, and farming, the park survives. It's the third-largest of the continental US's national parks—2,510 square miles stretching to Florida's southern and western Gulf coasts. Although the Everglades are considered the nation's most threatened natural area by the *National Park Service* and various environmental agencies, there is reason to be at least cautiously optimistic about their future. Congress has extended the national park eastward by more than 107,000 acres to include and protect the northeast Shark River Slough (pronounced *slew*), whose flow of water had been chopped out of the water-starved park's original boundaries. In addition, South Florida's water management system of canals, levees, and dams is being modified to restore natural water flow and marsh conditions to this critical wildlife habitat to the extent possible. Park managers also are hoping that filtration marshes being created north of the park will cleanse pollutants out of the water that passes through them before entering the Everglades. There is still controversy, however, over whether preservation efforts thus far have been effective enough.

You must understand the delicacy of the Everglades to enjoy the wetlands' understated pleasures. The area is actually a freshwater river (its Indian name is Pa-Hay-Okee, "River of Grass") 100 miles long, several dozen miles wide, and just inches deep during much of the year. This strange stream travels along an incline of only three inches a mile, moving so slowly that a single drop of water takes years to reach the Gulf from Lake Okeechobee. The slow river provides nourishment for a vast and complex system of life, and is a great laboratory in which to see the interdependence and sensitivity of an ecosystem. Where the earth rises a few inches, the plant life in the Everglades changes from sawgrass to hardwood forest. Where ripples appear in a pond, a small fish is eating mosquito larvae; a larger fish, a bream perhaps, will dine on the larva-eater; bass hunt the bream; gar will feed on the bass; and the gar is fodder for the alligator who originally made (or deepened) this pool by digging with his tail.

About 200 miles north of the Tropic of Cancer, the Everglades are the meeting point of subtropical and temperate life forms. In this, the region is unique in the US: Here you see mangrove, West Indian mahogany, and the poisonous manchineel tree, and in a nearby hammock rising from the sawgrass, pine and hardwood trees. Alligators, the rarely seen American crocodile, and white-tail deer share the same ecosystem, and schools of dolphins can sometimes be spotted from the coastal shorelines. Recreational fishing is permitted, but all plants and animals are protected by law from any molestation or harm by humans. (For general information, write or call *Everglades National Park,* 40001 State Rd. 9336, Homestead, FL 33034-6733; phone: 305-242-7700).

Plan to visit the Everglades during the winter to avoid being consumed by mosquitoes. In summer, some areas are so infested by these offensive insects that a pleasant visit is nigh impossible. Always carry insect repellent, regardless of the time of year (if you forget, you can buy it at the visitors' centers).

Serious visitors to the Everglades should plan to spend most of their time out of their cars. For the less hardy, marked foot trails (usually boardwalks, some as short as half a mile) are a comfortable way to have an intimate experience in the 'glades; there are also tram rides available at Shark Valley (phone: 305-221-8775) and Flamingo (phone: 305-253-2241). More intrepid visitors may want to join a "swamp tromp" or "slough slog" into the very heart of the marshes. These walking expeditions led by park naturalists are offered frequently from December through March. They really get you into things—quite literally. You'll need old clothes and shoes that you don't mind getting muddy and wet; waterproof, high boots are a good idea, for you'll be going into the water up to your knees. Bring plenty of mosquito repellent. There are several possible destinations, among them a 'gator hole, a tree island, and a major mangrove stand. Ask for schedules at the *Flamingo Visitors Center.*

For exploring the waterways that begin at Everglades City and extend to Flamingo, small outboard motorboats may be rented. Any serious nature observer, however, will opt instead for the canoe and the serenity it offers en route. There are minimally outfitted campsites, each wryly nicknamed, along the water lanes: "Hell's Bay" ("hell to get into and hell to get out of"); "Onion Key" (the bare-bones remains of a 1920s land developer's dream); and a crude pit outhouse and fireplace campsite known as "the Coming Miami of the Gulf." There are also shorter canoe trails, complete with camping sites. The somewhat less athletic and daring boater might prefer to take a guided boat cruise.

The Shark Valley area of *Everglades National Park* is most accessible from Miami and Ft. Lauderdale (about 20 miles west along the *Tamiami Trail*) and offers year-round tram tours (phone: 305-221-8455). Several ranger-led walks are offered from January through the beginning of April, and riding a rented bike along a path is a nice way to see the place. Lucky visitors will spot otters in early morning or around dusk, and alligator sightings are virtually a sure bet.

To reach the park's main entrance, drive about 30 miles south on Route 1 to Homestead, and then about 10 miles southwest on Route 9336. Stop at the *Robert Is Here Fruit Stand* (phone: 305-246-1592) along the way for the best strawberry shake on the East Coast; fruits and vegetables are also available. (This and snacks from vending machines are the only food to be found between Homestead and Flamingo, so pack a picnic lunch before leaving.) From the park's entrance follow the main park road for a 38-mile journey to Flamingo, on Florida Bay. Don't skip this drive; Florida Bay is a jewel worth the trek. There are several ways to see the 'glades: By car, driving to various stops along the road; on foot, following trails (some as short as half a mile) into the heart of things (with or without ranger guides); and by small outboard or canoe, following the water routes. Most of the park is under water, so it's a canoeist's paradise.

Our route explores the southern end of the Everglades, starting at the park's main entrance on Route 9336 and following the main park road for a 38-mile journey to Flamingo, on Florida Bay.

En Route from Miami Follow Route 1 south to Homestead. The only food to be found between Homestead and Flamingo consists of snacks and drinks from vending machines, so it's a good idea to pack a picnic lunch or eat in Homestead before leaving. Then pick up Route 9336 and take it about 10 miles southwest to the park's main entrance. Stop at the temporary visitors' center here (the main visitors' center suffered severe damage from Hurricane Andrew in 1992 and, at press time, repair work had not yet begun); this is the place to see exhibitions on park wildlife and ecology and pick up information on guided tours, winter "swamp tromps," and park activities and rules. Then continue about 2 miles to *Royal Palm Station.*

ROYAL PALM STATION Don't miss the exhibit on indigenous flora and fauna at the *Royal Palm Visitor Center* (phone: 305-242-7700). Here, on the *Anhinga Trail,* is a pond rich in animal life: Anhingas and ibis regularly hang out in the trees, alligators waddle out of the water and loll a few feet from visitors, snakes sun themselves on the grass, gars float in the clear water, and raccoons stroll by. Another well-known trail, the nearby *Gumbo Limbo Trail,* is missing its canopy of trees—it was destroyed by Hurricane Andrew but it's starting to grow back. A bit farther, Mahogany Hammock (see below) resembles the way the *Gumbo Limbo Trail* used to look; comparing these two places over time will reveal the often miraculous ways in which nature can replenish itself.

En Route from Royal Palm Station Beyond the *Royal Palm Visitor Center,* the road runs through pine forests. Continue to the *Pinelands Trail* (beginning about 2 miles from Long Pine Key).

PINELANDS TRAIL Here you might be lucky enough to spot the delicate Virginia white-tailed deer. The prey of the Florida panther, they have been dwindling in number here in recent years. Note the pines along the *Pinelands Trail.* They manage to survive only because they are sturdily fire resistant. You may see a number of them with fire-blackened trunks. In both summer and winter, fires often sweep through parts of the 'glades. Many trees are killed, primarily the hardwood trees. It's nature's way of keeping a balance here; without the fires, the hardwood trees would soon gain ground over the pines and push them out. The pines survive as they burn only on the outside; their corky bark protects them. In summer, the saltwort marshes that flank many of the forests dry out and are torched by lightning, but since it is the rainy season, when water levels are relatively high, these fires do little damage. Fires caused by humans during the winter dry season do the most harm here.

En Route from Pinelands Trail Continue on the main park road to the *Pa-Hay-Okee Overlook,* the next stop along the route.

PA-HAY-OKEE OVERLOOK From here, you can see the expanse of sawgrass that makes up Shark River Slough, where alligators and fowl gather. ("Sawgrass" is actually a misnomer; it is not a grass but a fine-toothed sedge. Despite its delicate appearance, it has mean, serrated edges on three sides that easily slice clothes or flesh, so be careful.) The alligators are an important link in the chain of life in the Everglades. During the dry season—autumn through spring—they settle into sloughs and dig deep holes with their tails. In late winter, as the marshes dry out, fish get caught in these 'gator holes. This is crucial for the wading birds, which nest near these natural fishbowls and are thus assured a food supply. The dead-looking trees here are dwarf bald cypresses, some of them 100 years old, which sprout leaves at the onset of the rainy season.

En Route from Pa-Hay-Okee Overlook Follow the main road for 7 miles to Mahogany Hammock.

MAHOGANY HAMMOCK Located here is the largest stand of mahoganies in the US and site of the country's largest mahogany tree. Boardwalks allow visitors to wander into it. You'll still see some Vriesia (bromeliads with red bracts) and Spanish moss growing on trees. The air plants, including orchids, are making a comeback after the 1992 hurricane. Beyond this point, the park was virtually untouched by the storm.

En Route from Mahogany Hammock Drive about 4 miles farther to Paurotis Pond.

PAUROTIS POND Here salt and fresh water begin to mix, and mangrove trees first appear. The mangrove is the only tree that thrives in salt water. It is a great colonizer and lives in a constant drama of creation and destruction all along the Gulf shore. It settles into the swampy salt water of the coast, and as it drops seeds and throws out breathing roots it captures material and actually begins "building" earth bulwarks against the sea. As seagulls and other sea birds collect around it, dropping guano, this earth becomes rich and fertile. Eventually, however, hurricanes sweep the coast, and everything is ripped out of the swampy ground and thrown inland.

En Route from Paurotis Pond Follow the main road until you see the signs for Mrazek and Eco Ponds; other ponds and trails beckon all along the road.

MRAZEK and ECO PONDS At Mrazek Pond, the water level ebbs as the dry season approaches, and hundreds of birds gather to eat the plentiful fish. Beautiful roseate spoonbills, with bright pink feathers, share tree limbs with egrets, white ibis, and tricolored herons, among other species.

Just before Flamingo is Eco Pond, an eight-acre manmade body of water drawn from the Flamingo Sewage Treatment Plant. The pond is the final stage of sewage treatment; the water is then evaporated and later returns to the Everglades as rain. Meanwhile, it provides a stop-off point for alligators and a variety of fowl, including gallinules and egrets.

En Route from Mrazek and Eco Ponds Return to the main road and follow it until it ends at Flamingo.

FLAMINGO Here you'll find another visitors' center (phone: 813-695-3092), a hotel, campgrounds, and bicycle rentals. Excursions aboard the open-sided catamaran *Bald Eagle* or the schooner *Windfall* depart daily from Flamingo and sail among Florida Bay's islets or keys. They provide a fine opportunity to view Florida's blazing sunsets and watch the indigenous birds returning to roost for the evening; contact the *Flamingo Lodge* for reservations and information (phone: 305-253-2241; 800-600-3813). But the craft most visitors associate with the Everglades is the airboat. Though banned from *Everglades National Park* (the noise and gas fumes disturb the fragile environment), airboats may be operated outside the park. Near the Shark Valley park entrance, daily airboat rides are offered year-round at *Everglades Safari Park* (Rte. 41, about 9 miles west of Krome Ave.; phone: 305-226-6923).

BEST EN ROUTE

Note: Visitors who plan to use Miami as their base should see *Miami–Miami Beach* in THE CITIES for complete information on hotels and restaurants.

Flamingo Lodge If you tire of your tent and camping, this is the only place to stay right in the Everglades. It offers modern, clean, and rustic accommodations in 24 cottages with kitchenettes (but no TV sets) and 102 motel rooms (all with TV sets). All of the rooms are air conditioned, and there's a screened-in swimming pool. The restaurant and gift shop are closed from May through October. It's reasonably priced; a double room in high season costs less than $90 a night. On Florida Bay, 38 miles from the entrance of *Everglades Park.* 1 Flamingo Lodge Hwy., Flamingo (phone: 305-253-2241).

Florida Keys and John Pennekamp Coral Reef State Park, Florida

Curving 150 miles out into the Gulf of Mexico from the southern tip of mainland Florida, the Florida Keys dot the waters like an ellipsis following a phrase. And in many ways this archipelago is an afterthought to that great landmass above, centered on Miami, with its glittering nightlife and crowded swimming beaches. The 45 principal islands (a "key" is a low island, or reef) that make up the Keys have very few sandy beaches despite miles of coastline, and few glamorous resorts. It's a low-key place and guests are generally tucked soundly away by 11 PM. A seven-story hotel—a midget by Miami standards—is a skyscraper hereabouts.

What the Keys do have, however, are some of the finest seascapes anywhere in the world—the blue waters of the Atlantic to the east and south and the green seas of the Gulf of Mexico on the northwestern side. As you drive along the Overseas Highway (US 1), a toll-free road that spans the islands with 43 bridges (some only 100 feet long, one stretching more than 7 miles), you are surrounded by sea and sky on all sides. Even on the Keys themselves, many of which are only a few hundred yards wide, you can see through the mangroves, Caribbean pine, and silver palmetto to the water, which is the overwhelming presence here. And though you can't see it from a car, the view is even more dramatic below the ocean surface.

The Keys are bordered by an offshore coral reef averaging 5 to 8 miles offshore. The *Florida Keys National Marine Sanctuary,* measuring 2,800 square nautical miles, extends from Dade County west to the Dry Tortugas (it's actually the same reef that continues northward past Ft. Lauderdale, with some gaps along the way). All along the route, there are dive shops (most indicated by the red-and-white-striped "divers down" flag), which arrange private or group snorkeling expeditions to nearby reefs. The best section of the reef that can be seen close up is at the *John Pennekamp Coral Reef State Park* in Key Largo. It is a slightly hallucinogenic underwater scene, as bright blue and green tropical fish move in and out of the sculptured reefs of white, pink, and orange coral. No boat is needed if you just plan to snorkel; though the sights offshore are even more marvelous.

The story of the Overseas Highway is interesting. During the late 1880s, Henry Flagler, an associate of John D. Rockefeller, aimed to establish a "land" route to Cuba by extending the *Florida East Coast Railroad* line to Key West. From there he planned a ferry shuttle for the final 90 miles to Havana. He invested some $20 million in the construction of tracks, but the line never showed a profit and the *Labor Day* hurricane of 1935 wiped out the tracks and roadbed. At that point, the government stepped in and began building the Overseas Highway along the same route. In 1982, 37 bridges were replaced with wider, heavier spans. Many of the old bridges remain open for pedestrians and fisherfolk, among them the well-known Seven-Mile Bridge at Marathon (featured in the 1995 Arnold Schwarzenegger film *True Lies*).

Of the 45 Keys linked by the highway, several are major islands with accommodations, restaurants, shops, and their own unique character. Much of this local flavor has to do with the natives of the area. They're Floridians, but they call themselves "Conchs" (pronounced *konks*). Descended from London Cockneys who settled in the Bahamas, the Conchs also have Cuban, Yankee sailor, and Virginia merchant blood. Not surprisingly, Conchs always have been people of the sea—fisherfolk, boaters, sponge divers, and underwater salvagers.

Fishing is king in these parts, with over 300 varieties of fish in the surrounding waters. Besides attracting anglers, the abundance of fresh fish has stimulated Keys chefs to dream up such creations as conch fritters alongside their land-bound flights of fancy such as Key lime pie. (Made from limes native to the Keys, the pie must be yellow, not green, to be genuine.)

For general information about the Keys, contact the *Florida Keys Visitors Bureau* (PO Box 1147-PR, Key West, FL 33041; phone: 800-FLA-KEYS).

Depending on which key you're visiting, a trip to the Keys can be an easy day's excursion from Miami. The drive from the city to Key West via the Overseas Highway takes about three hours. A fun way to both save driving time and view the multicolored water from the air is provided by *Chalk's International Airlines* (phone: 800-424-2557), whose seaplanes depart from Miami and Ft. Lauderdale and splash down right off of Duval Street in Key West.

En Route from Miami Take Route 1 south and cross the Blackwater Sound to the *John Pennekamp Coral Reef State Park.*

JOHN PENNEKAMP CORAL REEF STATE PARK and KEY LARGO NATIONAL MARINE SANCTUARY, Key Largo Key Largo is the first of the Keys and the longest, but what is most interesting here is under water. Running parallel to the Key for 21 miles is *John Pennekamp Coral Reef State Park* (PO Box 487, Key Largo, FL 33037; phone: 305-451-1202; 305-451-1621, concession and equipment rental information), the country's first underwater state park, and the largest living coral reef in the continental US. The park is a snorkeler's and scuba diver's heaven, encompassing 165 square miles of the Atlantic Ocean, hundreds of species of tropical fish, and 55 different varieties of coral. Laws forbid taking any coral, tropical fish, lobsters, or conch shells from the water, so the area will be preserved for generations to come.

To get an overview of the reef and surrounding ocean, take the glass-bottom boat tour operated by the park. The tour, offered three times a day, weather permitting, provides valuable insights into the ecological balance of the reef. The boat journeys several miles out onto the high seas to the reef's most spectacular section, where you'll see beautifully colored coral formations and other marine life, including barracuda, giant sea turtles, and sharks.

You also can venture into the water for snorkeling and scuba diving tours of the reef. The park offers snorkeling and scuba excursions and rents equipment; gear and tours are also available at Key Largo's many dive shops. If you dive, be sure to see the nine-foot-tall bronze statue *Christ of the Deep,* situated 20 feet beneath the sea in the *National Marine Sanctuary.* The statue, which was dedicated in 1966, symbolizes peace for mankind.

The park has a beach with a roped-off swimming area that is good for a dip or some casual snorkeling. For those who want to stay above water, there are trails for canoeing in the mangrove hammock. The water is so crystal clear that you can look down from your canoe and see spectacularly colored fish darting in and out of the mangrove roots. In addition, the park offers 47 campsites, all with tables, charcoal grills, electrical hookups, and water. Reservations for the sites should be made up to 60 days in advance—this is a very popular destination. (Private campgrounds are scattered throughout the Keys if you can't get into *Pennekamp.*) Be warned if you camp in a tent: The ground is usually rocky or gravel-covered. The park is open daily; there's an admission charge. Stop by the visitors' center for information on the reef and park programs. Information on Key Largo may be obtained by calling the *Key Largo Chamber of Commerce* (phone: 800-822-1088).

En Route from John Pennekamp Coral Reef State Park and Key Largo National Marine Sanctuary Follow the Overseas Highway for about 25 miles to Islamorada.

ISLAMORADA, Upper Matecumbe Key This is a sport fishing center in an area that's famous for fishing. Its many coral reefs in the surrounding shallow waters attract scuba and skin divers as well. The *Underwater Coral Gardens,* which feature two colorful coral deposits and the wreck of a Spanish galleon, are good for underwater exploration and photography and can be reached by charter boat. For information on Islamorada and also Long Key (see below), call the *Islamorada Chamber of Commerce* (phone: 800-322-5397).

En Route from Islamorada About 10 miles farther on the Overseas Highway is Long Key.

LONG KEY Stop here in season (the last Wednesday and Thursday of July and from August 6 through the middle or end of March) for underwater hunting of Florida lobsters. The *Long Key State Recreation Area* (Long Key Park, mile marker 67.5; phone: 305-664-4815) features 60 campsites, picnic areas with tables, barbecue grills, fresh water, and nature trails through the mangrove swamps.

En Route from Long Key Follow the Overseas Highway about 20 miles further west to Marathon.

MARATHON Marathon, midway down the archipelago, has been developed as a tourist center and has an airport and an 18-hole golf course, *Sombrero Country Club* (phone: 305-743-2551). Nevertheless, Marathon retains much of its original fishing-town character. There are more than 80 species in the gulf and ocean waters that can be taken with rod and reel or nets from charter boats or the Key's bridges. For information on the many fishing tournaments held throughout the year, contact the *Marathon Chamber of Commerce* (12222 Overseas Hwy., Marathon, FL 33050; phone: 305-743-5417; 800-842-9580). The competition is tough and the fish are smart. *Hall's Diving Center* (1994 Overseas Hwy.; phone: 305-743-5929) is a good place to rent gear or arrange dive and snorkel trips.

En Route from Marathon Bahia Honda Key is about 15 miles west on the Overseas Highway.

BAHIA HONDA KEY The 524-acre *Bahia Honda State Park* (near mile marker 33; phone: 305-872-2353) has 80 campsites, six cabins, picnicking, nature trails, and coral-free swimming. You can see a cross-section of Henry Flagler's old railroad bridge suspended high over the water. Other parts of the old road bed parallel the highway and are used as fishing piers.

En Route from Bahia Honda Key Just 5 miles west on the Overseas Highway is Big Pine Key.

BIG PINE KEY The largest of the Lower Keys, contains 6,300 acres thick with mangroves, silver palmetto, and Caribbean pine. Tiny Key deer, once close to extinction, now number about 300 here; it also is possible to spot the endangered great white heron here. For more information on Big Pine Key, or any of the Keys between Marathon and Key West, call the *Big Pine Chamber of Commerce* (phone: 800-872-3722).

En Route from Big Pine Key Continue west on the Overseas Highway until it ends in Key West, about 30 miles away.

KEY WEST The southernmost community in the US and the point closest to Cuba, it combines Southern, Bahamian, Cuban, and Yankee influences in a unique culture that can be seen in its architecture, tasted in its often quirky food, and felt in its relaxed, individualistic atmosphere. Traditionally, fishermen, artists, and writers have been drawn to this tranquil slip of sand and sea. Ernest Hemingway, among the island's early devotees, lived here during his most productive years, when he wrote *To Have and Have Not, For Whom the Bell Tolls, Green Hills of Africa,* and one of his greatest short stories, "The Snows of Kilimanjaro." His Spanish colonial–style house of native stone, surrounded by a lush tropical garden, is now a museum with many original furnishings and Hemingway memorabilia, along with several six-toed cats alleged to be descendants of Hemingway's own pets. The *Ernest Hemingway Home and Museum* (907 Whitehead St.; phone: 305-294-1575) is open daily; admission charge. Among others who have been attracted to Key West are John James Audubon, Tennessee Williams, John Dos Passos, Robert Frost, and President Harry S Truman. Now a museum, Truman's *Little White House* (111 Front St.; phone: 305-294-9911) is filled with original furniture and artifacts. It's open daily; admission charge.

At the *Welcome Center* in Key West (3840 N. Roosevelt Blvd.; phone: 305-296-4444; 800-352-8538 or 800-284-4482) you can make hotel reservations, sign up for tours, arrange to go skydiving, or even make wedding arrangements.

To get your bearings, take the *Conch Tour Train* (phone: 305-294-5161), a 90-minute narrated tram ride that covers 14 miles, passing all the Key West highlights. The train leaves from Mallory Square and North Roosevelt Boulevard, next to the *Welcome Center* (see above), where there's free parking. Purchase tickets at the bright red-and-white kiosk on the corner of Duval and Front Streets. *Old Town Trolley Tours* (phone: 305-296-6688) also provides a great orientation. The narrated tours pick up passengers daily at 12 stops; the full-day ticket permits on-again, off-again privileges until the loop is completed.

Since Key West is best explored on foot, after your tour stroll past the houses whose wooden gingerbread architecture reflects the influence of

Bahamian settlers and New England sea captains, and browse through the many galleries and crafts, shell, and souvenir shops. (Key West has the dubious distinction of having more T-shirt shops per square foot than any place outside of Orlando.) The best walking tours are offered daily by *Lowder Tours and Travel* (phone: 800-354-1961). Knowledgeable guides lead participants through streets and into hidden gardens while dispensing colorful anecdotes.

Visitors can choose from a number of boat excursions, including the *Fireball* and the *Pride of Key West,* which sail daily from the foot of Duval Street (phone: 305-296-6293 or 305-294-8704). The catamaran *Stars & Stripes* offers daily, six-hour excursions to a deserted island that include off-boat snorkeling, beachcombing, and bird watching; there's also a sunset sail. The boat departs from *Land's End Marina* (phone: 305-294-PURR; 800-634-MEOW—as in *cat*-amaran).

Unlike glass-bottom boats, *Discovery Tours*' craft have below-deck viewing rooms where passengers observe the coral reef and its inhabitants through eye-level windows lining the hull. The boats leave from *Land's End Marina* (phone: 305-293-0099) for thrice-daily trips. On the way back from the reef, the boat cruises by Mallory Dock, where an onboard sunset celebration takes place every night, beginning one hour before and lasting until one hour after the sun sinks below the horizon. Artisans, jugglers, flame swallowers, a high-wire act, an escape artist, and trained house cats are all part of the festivities.

At the *Lighthouse Museum* (938 Whitehead St.; phone: 305-294-0012), visitors can climb the 90-foot-tall 1847 lighthouse for panoramic island views and visit the furnished *Lighthouse Keeper's Quarters.* It's closed *Christmas Day;* admission charge. The *Audubon House & Gardens* (205 Whitehead St.; phone: 305-294-2116), where the artist John James Audubon worked on paintings of Florida Keys wildlife in 1831 and 1832, has original Audubon engravings, some of which appeared in his *Birds of America.* The lovely gardens showcase numerous tropical plants. Restored by the philanthropic Wolfson family, who hail from these parts, *Audubon House* also encompasses the home and belongings of a wealthy 19th-century sea captain and wrecker. It's open daily; admission charge.

Wrecking was an important industry among early Conchs. Wreckers were licensed salvagers who saved lives, ships, and cargo in the event of a shipwreck; the practice is explained through talks and pictures at the *Wrecker's Museum* (322 Duval St.; phone: 305-294-9502). The oldest house in Key West (dating from 1829 and also owned by a sea captain), it harbors furniture, documents, a charming furnished dollhouse, and ship models. The museum is open daily; admission charge.

The island's oldest house of worship, the *Cornish Memorial A.M.E. Zion Church* (702 Whitehead St., Bahama Village; phone: 305-294-2350), dates from 1864. The *East Martello Museum* (3501 S. Roosevelt Blvd; phone: 305-296-3913), housed in a Civil War fort, details colorful island history, including tales of weird inhabitants such as "the mad scientist of Key West," who "reconstructed" his dead girlfriend using wax and wire, hoping to bring her back to life. The museum is open daily; admission charge. Also of interest is the *Mel Fisher Maritime Heritage Society Museum,* set in a former navy warehouse (200 Greene St.; phone: 305-294-2633). It displays treasures and artifacts salvaged from the Spanish ships *Atocha* and *Santa Margarita,* sunk in a 1622 hurricane. On view are silver bars, gold chains, emerald and diamond jewelry, plus trade beads and shackles from the *Henrietta Marie,* an English merchant slaver, which sank in 1701. The museum is open daily; admission charge. The *Key West Aquarium* (1 Whitehead St. on Mallory Sq.; phone: 305-296-2051) has a collection of colorful local marine animals. It's open daily; admission charge.

As elsewhere in the Keys, fishing dominates the sporting life here. Both the *Gulfstream III* (phone: 305-296-8494) and *Back Country Fishing and Deep Sea* (phone: 305-296-8673) offer a variety of excursions in and around the Keys. But there are other options for active visitors. For snorkeling and scuba diving around the coral reefs, the *Key West Pro Dive Shop* (3128 N. Roosevelt Blvd.; phone: 305-296-3823; 800-426-0707) sponsors trips and rents gear. Golfers can tee off at the 18-hole *Key West Resort Golf Course* (6450 Junior College Rd.; phone: 305-294-5232). There's a resident pro. The area also boasts nine public tennis courts: The six at *Bayview Park* on Truman Avenue are lit at night; the three at Atlantic Boulevard and Reynolds Street do not have lights.

Kelly's Caribbean Bar, Grill & Brewery (301 Whitehead St.; phone: 305-293-8484) is one of Key West's most popular eateries. Owned by actress Kelly McGillis, its menu offers a wide selection of Caribbean fare and micro-brewed beers. Outstanding meals also are served at *Louie's Backyard* (700 Waddell Ave.; phone: 305-294-1061), either inside or on the spacious deck under a large shade tree, overlooking the ocean, and at the *Pier House* restaurant (see *Best en Route*), where the Key lime pie may be the best anywhere. Fans of Jimmy Buffett can stop at his *Margaritaville Café* (500 Duval St.; phone: 305-292-1435) for the famous thirst-quencher, a light meal, and the possibility of bumping into the singer, who appears here from time to time. And Hemingway fans never miss a pilgrimage to *Sloppy Joe's* (201 Duval St.; phone: 305-294-5717), the bar said to be once frequented by the writer himself; current regulars are not of the literary persuasion.

For information on Key West, contact the *Key West Chamber of Commerce* (402 Wall St., Key West, FL 33040; phone: 305-294-2587; 800-648-6269). For general information about the Keys, contact the *Florida Keys Visitors Bureau* (PO Box 866, Key West, FL 33041; phone: 800-FLA-KEYS).

BEST EN ROUTE

Expect to pay $250 or more per night in tourist season for a double room in those places we have listed as very expensive, and $180 to $250 in the one rated expensive. Unless otherwise noted, hotels are open year-round and rooms have air conditioning, private baths, TV sets, and telephones. For each location, hotels are listed alphabetically by price category.

KEY LARGO

Ocean Reef Club Once a private fishing camp and now a posh tropical paradise, this 300-room exclusive—and expensive—resort boasts two 18-hole championship golf courses, terrific fishing, 11 tennis courts, and 145 hotel rooms plus accommodations in condominiums and villas spread out over 4,000 acres of land. There are seven restaurants, five lounges, and an Olympic-size pool; a daily supervised children's program is offered year-round. If you're into high-style living and have the pocketbook to back it up, this is the place for you. 31 Ocean Reef Dr. (phone: 305-367-2611; 800-741-REEF; fax: 305-367-2224). Very expensive.

ISLAMORADA

Cheeca Lodge Low-key elegance makes this 27-acre seaside hideaway a romantic pleasure. There are 203 rooms and suites; facilities include a dining room and open-air grill, two pools, a manmade lagoon with a sand beach and waterfalls, six lighted tennis courts, and a nine-hole, par-3 golf course designed by Jack Nicklaus. "Camp Cheeca" has won awards for its environmentally conscious program for kids. Water activities—such as fishing, snorkeling, diving, and parasailing—also are available. Mile Marker 82, PO Box 527, Islamorada (phone: 305-664-4651; 800-327-2888; fax: 305-664-2893). Very expensive.

LITTLE PALM ISLAND

Little Palm Island On a secluded island just off Little Torch Key, this charming, romantic hideaway, a member of the prestigious Relais & Châteaux group, is popular with honeymooners and couples. The 30 private, one-bedroom, thatch-roofed cottages have rustic but elegant furnishings. Other attractions include a pool, water sports, and a fine restaurant. No children under age 12 are allowed. Between Islamorada and Key West, Rte. 4, PO Box 1036, Little Palm Island (phone: 305-872-2524; 800-343-8567; fax: 305-872-4843). Very expensive.

KEY WEST

Key West Hilton Located in the heart of the Old Town, this newly opened property features 178 well-appointed guestrooms with an elegant Victorian decor. All rooms have private terraces offering views of spectacular sunsets. Guests enjoy *Bistro 245,* which offers fine continental cuisine.

245 Front St. (phone: 305-294-4000; 800-221-2424; fax: 205-294-4086). Very expensive.

Hyatt Key West With its own private beach and marina, this four-story, 120-room hostelry in town offers a pool, a Jacuzzi, a small exercise facility, and two restaurants. 601 Front St. (phone: 305-296-9900; 800-233-1234; fax: 305-292-1038). Very expensive.

Marriott's Casa Marina Built in 1921 by Henry Flagler, this is a charming full-service resort whose past guests have included Rita Hayworth, Ethel Merman, Al Jolson, and Gregory Peck. Along with its own beach, it offers 311 rooms, two restaurants, two pools, a whirlpool bath, three lighted tennis courts, a health club, and water sports. 1500 Reynolds St. (phone: 305-296-3535; 800-228-9290; fax: 305-296-4633). Very expensive.

Pier House In the heart of the restored Old Town area, this comfortably upscale yet unpretentious deluxe property has 142 rooms, five bars, and three dining rooms (the *Pier House* restaurant is first-rate). Twenty-two of the rooms are in a separate health spa available to resort guests (also see *Sybaritic Spas* in DIVERSIONS). Other features include a manmade sand beach (with a section for topless bathers), a pool, a Jacuzzi, and a deck for sunset watchers. 1 Duval St. (phone: 305-296-4600; 800-327-8340; fax: 305-296-7569). Very expensive.

La Concha Holiday Inn In the heart of the Old Town, this restored 160-room, seven-story Art Deco hotel first opened in 1926. Chintz bedspreads, four-poster beds, lace curtains, and antique furnishings abound, although plumbing and electronic equipment are modern. There are two restaurants, four bars, a gift shop, and a pool. A daily sunset celebration (weather permitting) takes place at the rooftop bar. Rates in winter season run less than $250 a night—but not much less. 430 Duval St. (phone: 305-296-2991; 800-745-2191 or 800-HOLIDAY; fax: 305-294-3283). Expensive.

Golden Isles and Okefenokee Swamp, Georgia

If you've ever hummed the line "Way down upon the Swanee River," from Stephen Foster's tune "The Old Folks at Home," you already have a connection to the *Okefenokee Swamp,* where the wandering waterway that inspired Foster's song begins. The mysterious marshland of watery caverns lined with elegant, cypress trees dripping with moss was called "land of the trembling earth" by its early Native American inhabitants.

The 100-mile Georgia coast is rich in history, sun-dappled peacefulness, relaxing getaways, and natural phenomena.

Thousands of years ago, the Atlantic Ocean covered half the state. When the salt water began receding, a reef trapped some of it, transforming 630 square miles into the *Okefenokee Swamp.* Within this pristine wilderness, which since 1947 has been known as the *Okefenokee National Wildlife Refuge,* treeless prairies intersperse the stands of cypress that cover most of the territory. Other than 60 or so pine-forested islands, most of the *Okefenokee* (Oh-kee-feh-*no*-kee) isn't firmly anchored. It consists of a sandy bottom, several feet of water, and layers of spongy peat.

Some 50 miles to the east, barrier islands protect the mainland from the ocean's wild churnings. In the 1600s and 1700s, they attracted pirates, Native Americans, Spanish missionaries, French settlers, and English colonizers. From the 1880s until World War II, wealthy industrialists and their families escaped wretched Northern winters during sojourns on then–privately owned Jekyll Island or at the legendary *Cloister* resort on Sea Island. A number of low-key retreats now cater to vacationers from all walks of life. Excellent sports facilities, coupled with sophisticated shopping and dining opportunities, augment the basic beaching and basking. Brunswick, which has grown into a "full service" city, is the gateway to four of the best-known barrier islands: St. Simons, Sea, Little St. Simons, and Jekyll. Separated from the mainland by salt marshes threaded with creeks and rivers, each of the islands, collectively known as the Golden Isles, possesses a unique ambience and lifestyle.

Our route follows I-95 south from Savannah, stopping in at Midway, Darien, Sapelo Island, Brunswick, and the Golden Isles. After returning to the mainland, you can pick up Route 82 west of Brunswick and head west to the North Entrance of the *Okefenokee National Wildlife Refuge*. Our route, however, continues south to St. Marys and Cumberland Island, then follows Route 40 west to Folkston, where it turns southwest to the east entrance to the wildlife refuge.

En Route from Savannah Head south about 30 miles along I-95 to Exit 13. Turn west (right) for Midway, where a somnolent crossroad is dominated by the *Midway Congregational Church* and cemetery, dating from the 1700s. The adjacent *Midway Museum* (phone: 912-884-5837) contains period furnishings and exhibits. It is closed Mondays and holidays; admission charge. Five miles east of Exit 13, *Seabrook Village* (phone: 912-884-7008) portrays the turn-of-the-century African-American culture and environment of a rural coastal community. It is closed Sundays and Mondays; admission charge. Return to I-95 and drive south for about 30 miles. At Exit 10, the *Magnolia Bluff Factory Shops* complex (phone: 912-437-2700) contains designer outlets among its 60 discount stores. Take Exit 10 east to Darien.

DARIEN A flourishing banking, timber, and shipping center in the 18th century, the small community retains vestiges of its important past. The *Darien Welcome Center* (PO Box 734, Darien, GA 31305; phone: 912-437-6684) has self-guided tours of Old Town Darien and information on nearby *Fort*

King George (phone: 912-437-4770), a state historic site that replicates the British compound erected in 1721 overlooking the Altamaha River.

En Route from Darien The *Darien Welcome Center* (see above) handles the required reservations (preferably in advance) and tickets for early morning excursions to nearby Sapelo Island. Operated by the *Georgia Department of Natural Resources (DNR)* and limited to 35 people, the four-hour tours depart on Wednesdays and Saturdays year-round and Fridays from June through *Labor Day*.

SAPELO ISLAND Known officially as the *Sapelo Island Estuarine Research Reserve* (phone: 912-485-2251), the unspoiled island is a test tube for the study and protection of salt marshes and marine life. A ferry plies to and from the island; once there, tours travel by air-conditioned school bus through the forest habitats of deer and birds to beaches and to a small community populated by the descendants of slaves. Participants also see the mansion built by the late tobacco magnate Richard J. Reynolds, who once owned Sapelo, and outbuildings that house *University of Georgia Marine Research Institute* laboratories.

En Route from Sapelo Island Return through Darien to Highway 17 and travel five miles to the turnoff to the *Hofwyl-Broadfield State Historic Site* (phone 912-264-7333), a coastal rice plantation that flourished during the 1800s. The grounds, the Low Country–style house, and a museum are open for touring. It is closed Mondays; admission charge.

Return to Highway 17 and head south 14 miles to Brunswick, a scenic shrimping port with a charming Victorian residential district and a bustling downtown commercial area. From here, causeways lead over the marshes and Intracoastal Waterway to St. Simons, Sea, and Jekyll Islands. The *Brunswick/Golden Isles Visitors Center* (phone: 912-264-5337; 800-933-COAST) is open daily and situated at the entrance to the St. Simons Causeway, which charges a toll. The *Jekyll Island Welcome Center* (phone: 912-635-3636; 800-841-6586) is open daily and is located across the Jekyll Causeway. For an information packet, contact the *Brunswick & The Golden Isles of Georgia Visitors Bureau* (4 Glynn Ave., Brunswick, GA 31520; phone: 912-265-0620; 800-933-COAST; fax: 912-265-0629); it's open daily.

GOLDEN ISLES Enjoying a temperate climate year-round, these islands between the Marshes of Glynn and the Atlantic Ocean are relaxing vacation havens, with outstanding golf, tennis, fishing, skeet and trap shooting, and horseback riding. During December, they are festive with holiday events and thousands of twinkling white lights.

Jekyll was for decades the private winter retreat of Rockefellers, Morgans, and other wealthy families. Their stables now house the *Museum Orientation Center* (phone: 912-635-4036 or 912-635-2762; open daily); their 33 "cottages" form a unique historic district, and their clubhouse has been revived as the *Jekyll Island Club* hotel (see *Best En Route*). Three of the restored mansions are open to visitors who take the tram tours that operate daily;

there is a charge. A state-owned "playground" since 1946, Jekyll has 9 miles of beach, 63 holes of golf, a tennis center, a water park, a fishing pier, and historic ruins. A parking fee is collected for cars arriving on the island.

The greatest number of restaurants, boutiques, and historic sites are found on St. Simons, the largest of the Golden Isles. At the southern end, a 104-foot, brick lighthouse, built in 1872, rises alongside the *Museum of Coastal History* (phone: 912-638-4666), in the former lighthouse keeper's cottage. It is closed Mondays; there is an admission charge. Toward the northern end, the *Fort Frederica National Monument* (phone: 912-638-3639) encompasses the remains of houses, public buildings, and a fort, all built by British settlers in the 1730s. The monument is open daily; there is an admission charge. Island-wide trolley tours (phone: 912-638-8954) operate daily except Sunday and Monday; there is a charge.

Like Jekyll's historic mansions, the imposing homes on Sea Island also are called cottages. The focal point for visitors, however, is *The Cloister* resort (see *Best En Route*). Sea Island is accessible by car from St. Simons Island, which is connected to the mainland by a causeway.

A marina on St. Simons is the gateway to Little St. Simons, a privately-owned retreat (see *Best En Route*).

En Route from the Golden Isles Follow Highway 17 south. About 30 miles from Brunswick, take Route 40 east to the town of St. Marys. A number of imposing historic homes include the 1829 *Orange Hall,* a house museum that also is the *St. Marys Welcome Center* (Osborne and Conyers Sts.; phone: 912-882-4000). From St. Marys, a ferry takes daytrippers back and forth to Cumberland Island twice a day. Reservations can be made through the *National Park Service/Cumberland Island National Seashore* (PO Box 806, St. Marys, GA 31558; phone: 912-882-4335).

CUMBERLAND ISLAND NATIONAL SEASHORE Georgia's largest barrier island is about 18 miles long and 2 miles wide. By foot (no autos are allowed), visitors may explore miles of deserted beaches and see more than 200 kinds of birds, as well as wild horses, deer, and armadillos. Overnight guests may camp out or stay at the *Greyfield Inn* (see *Best En Route*).

En Route from Cumberland Island National Seashore Return to St. Marys and take Route 40 approximately 22 miles west to Folkston. Then follow Route 121/23 south for 8 miles to the east entrance of the *Okefenokee National Wildlife Refuge.*

OKEFENOKEE NATIONAL WILDLIFE REFUGE Alligators always have the right-of-way along the watery trails that lace the *Okefenokee Swamp.* Keep that in mind and all will be fine within this primeval preserve that in the late 1940s came under federal oversight. Its other denizens include hundreds of rare species of birds, reptiles, and amphibians; its flora is varied, and some of it is carnivorous. Until the creation of the refuge, the *Okefenokee* also was inhabited by early settlers, called swampers, a rugged, self-sufficient lot. So were the loggers who, impracticably, attempted to drain the swamp in the 1890s. For general information, contact the *Okefenokee National Wildlife Refuge* (Rte. 2, Box 3330, Folkston, GA 31537; phone: 912-496-7836), which maintains a visitor center at the east entrance. Here, visitors may take guided boat trips or rent a boat (phone: 912-496-7156). Or, they may head to designated campsites within the swamp (phone: 912-496-3331 for required advance permits). There are also hiking trails, a wildlife observation drive, and the *Chesser Island Homestead,* where interpreters explain what life was like for the early swampers. The nonprofit *Wilderness Southeast* (phone: 912-897-5108; fax: 912-897-5116) offers guided, four- and five-night canoe trips.

At the western entrance of the refuge, near Fargo, Georgia, is *Stephen C. Foster State Park* (phone: 912-637-5274), which offers camping, picnicking, fishing, furnished cottages, and boat tours and rentals. At the north entrance, ten miles south of Waycross, Georgia, is *Okefenokee Swamp Park* (phone: 912-283-0583), a privately-operated microcosm of the swamp, with boat tours, wildlife exhibits, a wilderness walkway, a pioneer homestead, an otter preserve, and Oscar, a "pet" alligator that is 14 feet long and weighs in the neighborhood of 900 pounds. Outside the north entrance is *Laura Walker State Park* (phone: 912-287-4900), which offers swimming, water skiing, and 18 holes of golf.

BEST EN ROUTE

Expect to pay $250 or more for a double room during high season (mid-March through November) in those places we have classified as very expensive (note that meals, beverages, and leisure activities may be included) and from $100 to $175 for those listed as expensive. Unless otherwise noted, hotels are open year-round and rooms have air conditioning, private baths, TV sets, and telephones.

JEKYLL ISLAND

Jekyll Island Club During the island's "Gilded Age" (1885-1942), its four-story, turreted clubhouse was the center of social activities. Today, it continues to shine with 135 recently refurbished guestrooms and suites. Its fine restaurant and public rooms are adorned with fluted columns, century-old stained glass, and other priceless architectural details. A swimming pool, regulation croquet court, tennis courts, and a ballroom are among the many amenities. Business services are available. 371 Riverview Dr. (phone: 912-635-2600; 800-535-9547; fax: 912-635-2818). Expensive.

LITTLE ST. SIMON'S ISLAND

Lodge at Little St. Simon's Island Occupying 10,000 acres of unspoiled natural beauty, this privately-owned, island-wide haven is exceptional for its migratory birds, its wildlife, and for its privacy; it accommodates only 24 guests at a time. Ceiling fans cool the guestrooms, most of which are in modern, rustic-style cottages, and the dining room, in the 1917 lodge, where meals are served family style. Telephones and TV sets are absent. Days may be spent swimming in the pool, sunning or shelling on 7 miles of deserted beach, hiking, horseback riding, canoeing, fishing, and on field trips guided by a trained naturalist; all are included in the rate, as are meals and beverages. Day trips to the island can be arranged. PO Box 21078, St. Simons Island, GA 31522 (phone: 912-638-7472). Very expensive.

SEA ISLAND

The Cloister The fabled, virtually impeccable, grande dame of a resort has reigned over Sea Island and the Golden Isles since 1928. Built in Spanish Mediterranean style, it is a perennial favorite spot for honeymoons, anniversary celebrations, and family vacations. The resort's 262 deluxe rooms include a variety of sizes, locations, and rates, which include three sumptuous meals each day at one of four restaurants. Fifty-four holes of superb golf are complemented by a state-of-the-art golf learning center. Within the oceanside *Beach Club* are two swimming pools and a full-service spa. There's tennis, also horseback riding, skeet and trap shooting, and an orchestra that plays nightly. A business center is on the premises. No credit cards accepted. (Also see *America's Best Resort Hotels* in DIVERSIONS.) Sea Island Dr., Sea Island, GA 31561 (phone: 912-638-3611; 800-SEA-ISLAND; fax: 912-638-5159.) Very expensive.

CUMBERLAND ISLAND

Greyfield Inn Built by the Carnegie family around the turn of the century, this is the only non-camping lodgings on the *Cumberland Island National Seashore.* The dining room and guest cottage are air conditioned, but the nine guestrooms in the main house are cooled by ceiling fans; there are no telephones or TV sets in the guestrooms, and some share a bath. Three daily meals, transportation to and from the island (from Fernandina Beach, Florida), bicycles, and naturalist-led tours are included in the price. Closed August. (Also see *America's Special Havens* in DIVERSIONS.) PO Box 900, Fernandina Beach, FL 32035 (phone: 904-261-6408; fax: 904-261-0964). Very expensive.

Mammoth Cave National Park, Kentucky

An ancient Chinese sage, believing that it is better to be soft and yielding than hard and inflexible, was fond of pointing out that stone always gives way to water. A perfect example of his teachings is *Mammoth Cave,* a huge system of underground chambers and passageways in central Kentucky's *Mammoth Cave National Park* that has been hollowed out of stone entirely by the seepage of rainwater and the dissolving action of underground streams.

The world's longest cave, *Mammoth* has chambers that are two-thirds the length of a football field. Its tallest dome is 192 feet high; its deepest pit is 106 feet deep; and its known passageways and chambers wind and twist through five separate levels for more than 336 miles. If its size alone isn't enough to impress you, consider the cave's fantastic formations, Disney-like shapes in stone that twist and turn, ripple and flow. Most of these natural sculptures, like strange yet familiar objects in a dream, remind you of a hundred different things at once, but some—usually the larger ones—so strongly suggest particular objects that they have been named: *King Solomon's Temple,* the *Pillars of Hercules, Frozen Niagara,* the *Giant's Coffin,* and the *Bridal Altar* (which actually has been used for weddings). Adding to the dreamlike effect, clusters of gypsum crystals, like rare flowers, hug many of the cave's walls, turning them into exotic hanging gardens.

The origins of *Mammoth Cave* go back more than 280 million years, when a shallow sea covered this part of the country. The sea left layers of mud, shells, and sand that hardened into limestone and sandstone. After the sea drained away, rainwater, containing small amounts of carbonic acid, seeped into the limestone layers, dissolving some of the stone. Over time, the cracks widened and a system of underground streams hollowed out the cave. As the streams cut deeper and deeper into their beds, they lowered the floor of the cave, allowing more of the upper regions to dry.

Water not only carved out this mammoth house of stone, it furnished and decorated it as well. As it seeped through the limestone, the water evaporated, leaving a mineral deposit called travertine (also known as cave onyx). Water dripping from the ceiling of the cave over centuries formed chemical icicles of travertine, or stalactites. Water flowing over rock formed waterfalls of travertine, or flowstone. In a similar way, water shaped the cave's pillars, temples, and altars. Even today, water seeping through the limestone and flowing in underground streams through this vast underground palace continues the process begun eons ago.

Human beings knew about *Mammoth Cave* about 4,000 years ago. The remains of a man who apparently was killed by a falling boulder while chipping minerals from the cave walls indicate that the woodland Indians used to mine gypsum here. Kentucky pioneers discovered the cave in 1798; since then it has had a varied history. As a principal source of saltpeter, an ingredient in gunpowder, the cave played an important role in winning the War of 1812; the mineral was extracted from the dirt of the cave floor. Throughout the 19th century, the curious came from far and near to see the cave's wonders by the flickering light of oil lamps. Edwin Booth, the celebrated Shakespearean actor, recited Hamlet's soliloquy in a chamber of the cave now called *Booth's Amphitheater.*

When you've finished admiring the park's subterranean wonders, aboveground are more than 52,830 acres of beautiful Kentucky woodlands to roam, as well as many special wildlife, hiking, and children's programs. For general information about the park, contact *Mammoth Cave National Park* (Mammoth Cave, KY 42259; phone: 502-758-2328).

En Route from Louisville Head south 90 miles on I-65 to the entrance to the main cave, which is about 9 miles west of Cave City, Kentucky.

MAMMOTH CAVE NATIONAL PARK There are four main entrances to the cave: the natural *Historic Entrance* and three manmade entrances known as *Frozen Niagara, Carmichael,* and *New Entrance. National Park Service* rangers conduct daily tours (except on *Christmas*) of the most interesting parts of the cave. No solo exploring is allowed. You can purchase tickets for a variety of different tours at the visitors' center near the *Historic Entrance* or through *Destinet* (phone 800-967-2283). Advance tickets are strongly recommended by the park if you're planning to visit on a holiday or summer weekend. All tours require sturdy shoes and a sweater or jacket, as the cave temperature hovers in the mid-50s to low 60s F.

The tours offered vary somewhat from season to season, but there is enough variety to suit just about every age and level of endurance. The easiest is the Travertine Tour (¼ mile), which takes you to a variety of formations, the largest of which is *Frozen Niagara.* The Frozen Niagara Tour (¾ mile), a more strenuous version of the Travertine Tour, is also worth taking—though it's not for those with claustrophobia or acrophobia. It descends 280 stairs, past impressive pits and domes, to *Grand Central Station,* and from there proceeds to the stalactites and stalagmites of the dripstone formation area.

On the Historic Tour (2 miles), you will see the *Rotunda Room,* where mineral-laden dirt was processed into saltpeter during the War of 1812, and *Mammoth Dome,* one of the highest domes in the cave. The Gothic Tour (1½ miles, two hours) combines part of the Historic Tour with a foray into a section of the cave where humans have left their mark—tour guides call it the "historic graffiti" area. To learn more about the cave's geology and formation, take the strenuous 2½-mile Making of Mammoth Tour. If you're really daring, try the Wild Cave Tour, where you crawl, climb, and squeeze your way through passages off-the-beaten path.

The Violet City Lantern Tour (3 miles), usually offered only in spring and summer, allows you to see *Mammoth Cave* in an entirely different light. While electricity makes it easy to see everything, only lantern light casts the atmospheric shadows that emphasize the cave's awesome grandeur.

A special tour of the cave (½ mile) is available for persons in wheelchairs.

When you finally emerge, blinking, in the sunlight, you can restore your senses with a short (1 mile) walk on the *Cave Island Nature Trail,* which begins and ends near the *Historic Entrance.* Lined with giant sycamores and beech trees, this trail leads to the bottomlands of the Green River, where underground streams emerge.

If you have had enough hiking for the day, you can board the *Miss Green River II* for a leisurely cruise (April through October). The twilight cruise is the best for seeing wildlife: As you sit in comfort, you glide past beaver, turtles, deer, and snakes on the riverbank. It's not as exciting as the *African Queen,* perhaps, but a very pleasant way to pass an hour. Buy tickets at the visitors' center. For more information about the cruise, contact Captain Don Gore (511 Grinstead Mill Rd., Cave City, KY 42127; phone: 502-758-2243).

BEST EN ROUTE

There are numerous hotels and motels in Cave City and Bowling Green, but none that are especially noteworthy. Farther afield in central Kentucky, in the general direction of Louisville and Lexington, are a couple of reasonably priced inns of interest that could be comfortably incorporated into a *Mammoth Cave* visit. Expect to pay $50 to $90 per night for a double room in those places listed as moderate, and less than $50 in those rated inexpensive. Unless otherwise noted, hotels are open year-round and rooms have air conditioning, private baths, TV sets, and telephones.

MAMMOTH CAVE NATIONAL PARK

Mammoth Cave Hotel Unpretentious and moderately priced, the park's 42-room hotel and 20-room motor lodge overlook a scenic ravine. Its dining room specializes in regional foods such as country ham and fried chicken. Rental cottages also are available. About 10 miles from the highway on the main park road (phone: 502-758-2225). Moderate.

BEREA

Boone Tavern Run by *Berea College* and staffed by students, this hostelry offers 59 rooms, two dining rooms (one for private parties) serving excellent traditional Kentucky dishes, and access to the college's pool, tennis and racquetball courts, and running track. The small town of Berea is considered the crafts capital of Kentucky; it has more than 50 shops with everything from pottery to handmade furniture. About 40 miles south of Lexington via I-75 and four hours from *Mammoth Cave,* Main St. and Prospect (phone: 606-986-9358). Moderate.

BRANDENBURG

Doe Run Inn This inn incorporates the remains of an early Kentucky mill, and its 12 rooms are simple, unadorned, and comfortable; some have shared baths. One reason for visiting is to eat traditional Kentucky fare—chicken, ham, biscuits—skillfully prepared. Near the Ohio River, about 70 miles from *Mammoth Cave* and 4 miles east of Brandenburg on Hwy. 448 (phone: 502-422-2982). Inexpensive.

Bayou Country, Louisiana

A bayou is a waterway that has wandered away from—or been left by—a main river. A huge, slow river will create bayous as it flows across any flat plain, cutting new waterways as rising sediment changes its course, then abandoning them when it changes direction again.

But that technical definition doesn't begin to describe the bayou country of southern Louisiana. Here the Mississippi River flows so slowly, and over such a wide and meandering course, that it has bred bayous by the dozen, patrolled by alligators and filled with swamp grass and cypress trees festooned with Spanish moss. Bayou country—called Acadiana—is in south-central Louisiana, west of Baton Rouge. It starts west of New Orleans and covers 15 parishes (counties) from Avoyelles Parish to the Gulf Coast.

Bayou actually is the French mispronunciation of the Choctaw word "bayuk," meaning creek or stream. The Choctaw Indians were the first inhabitants of this region. In the mid-1700s they were joined by the Acadians, French inhabitants of Nova Scotia whom the British exiled from Canada. (You may remember *Evangeline,* Longfellow's tragic poem about their trek.) These "Cajuns," as they came to be known down here, adapted to the temperate climate and gradually turned the bayou country into a French-American enclave.

Today the culture remains unique, though tempered by other influences. Cajun French crops up everywhere: Horse races at *Evangeline Downs* begin with the cry *"Ils sont partis"* instead of "They're off." Conversations may be prefaced with *"cher,"* which means "dear." The unofficial motto of this part of the country is *"Laissez les bons temps rouler,"* which, if not authentic French, nonetheless translates into an accurate summary of Cajun attitudes: "Let the good times roll."

Acadiana includes a few largish cities, some spectacular gardens, some local oddities like salt islands, and a lot of history kept alive by the Cajuns. There are dozens of little towns, each with its own festival or its special claim to fame. The people are very outgoing—friendly and willing to sit for a spell and chat—and the pace of life is far from hectic. Add to this Southern hospitality and French charm, and you'll wind up with a memorable vacation. Try some of the regional cuisine, like crawfish *étouffée,* gumbo, or jambalaya, and join in the local festivals. In short . . . *Laissez les bons temps rouler!*

Due to its sprawling size, Acadiana does not lend itself to an organized driving route. Part of the charm of a visit here is in meandering like the bayous themselves, traveling wherever highways lead you. A good way to start is by exploring Atchafalaya Basin, which runs down the eastern third of Acadiana, in the Mississippi River flood plain west of Baton Rouge between the Mississippi and Atchafalaya Rivers. This is the largest river basin swamp in North America (1,300 square miles). From season to season, it offers the opportunity to observe a tremendous variety of wildlife: deer, foxes, coyotes, bears, nutria, beavers, mink, egrets, eagles, and tropical birds, among others—not to mention alligators and succulent crawfish. You'll also enjoy the peace and quiet of the beautiful moss-draped forest in the swamp. Numerous boat trips through the swamp are offered by *McGee's Landing Tours* (Hwy. 352, McGee's Landing, near Henderson; phone: 318-228-2384) and by *Atchafalaya Experience* (phone: 318-233-7816), with treks for up to 12 people run by Coerte Voorhies, a professional geologist. Voorhies designs tours according to the participants' interests; at least 24 hours' notice is required.

Our route starts west of Baton Rouge in Washington, just off I-49, then meanders southward, ending up in Thibodaux, southeast of Baton Rouge. Some of the roads here will not even show up on large state maps, so before setting out, request a tour guide brochure from the *Lafayette Convention and Visitors Commission* (PO Box 52066, Lafayette, LA 70505; phone: 318-232-3737; 800-346-1958).

En Route from Baton Rouge Take Route 190 west toward Opelousas. At Port Barre, about 6 miles east of Opelousas, turn north on Highway 103. At the first stop sign on Highway 103, turn left toward Washington.

WASHINGTON Just off the highway is the *Washington Museum* (phone: 318-826-3627), with artifacts dating from this town's glory days in the steamboat era. Located on the formerly navigable Bayou Courtableau, Washington was once the busiest steamboat port between New Orleans and St. Louis. The arrival of the train in 1880 ended the shipping business. Now this quiet, picturesque area has many historic homes that can be toured, as well as antiques shops and bed and breakfast establishments.

En Route from Washington Head south on Highway 49 to Opelousas, then west on Hwy. 190 to Eunice.

EUNICE Louisiana's Cajun Prairie capital regularly broadcasts a live radio show Saturday nights from the restored *Liberty Theatre* (200 W. Park Ave.; phone: 318-457-6575), built in 1924. The show, a joint project of the city and the *Jean Lafitte National Historical Park and Preserve,* is a combination of the *Grand Ole Opry* and Cajun folk music. It runs from 6 to 8 PM, but doors open at 4 PM and you can't make reservations, so arrive early to get a good seat. Tickets (the minimal charge goes toward a fund for maintaining the theater) are available at the door. Another *Jean Lafitte* project is the *Prairie Acadian Cultural Center* (250 W. Park; phone: 318-457-8499), which features permanent and rotating exhibits of Cajun cooking, crafts, music, and folklore. It's open daily except on *Christmas;* there's no admission charge. In addition, Cajun musicians, many of whom have performed nationally, can be heard at various entertainment spots around town.

En Route from Eunice Follow Highway 190 east to I-49, then head south to Lafayette.

LAFAYETTE At the intersection of US 167, US 90, I-10, and I-49, this is the undisputed center of Acadiana. A city with a population of some 90,000, it boasts the usual municipal auditoriums, centers, and museums. But there are also special Cajun places and events here you'll not want to miss. The *Acadian Village* (200 Green Leaf Dr.; phone: 318-981-2364; 800-962-9133) is a relocated and restored 19th-century bayou town. To get there from I-10, take the Ambassador Caffrey Parkway exit south to Ridge Road and follow the signs. Among its attractions are a general store; open houses; a trading post; a blacksmith shop; the *Missionary Museum,* with its displays of Indian artifacts; and the *Chapel of New Hope,* at the heart of the village. Open daily except on major holidays. There's an admission charge; profits raised by the village help support the *Alleman Center* for Louisiana's disabled citizens. *Vermilionville* (1600 Surrey St.; phone: 318-233-4077; 800-99-BAYOU) is a 22-acre open-air living history museum depicting Cajun and Creole life in the 18th and early 19th centuries. You'll hear Cajun music, see crafts demonstrations, and sample such delicacies as gumbo, *boudin,* jambalaya, and pralines. It's closed *Christmas* and *New Year's Day;* there's an admission charge.

Lafayette holds its own *Mardi Gras* celebration, the second largest in the US. The week or so of parades, live music, and general revelry culminates in the *Annual Southwest Louisiana Mardi Gras Association Pageant and Ball;* free tickets are available from the *Lafayette Chamber of Commerce* (PO Drawer 51307, Lafayette, LA 70505-1307; phone: 318-233-2705).

In March and April, Lafayette holds the *Azalea Trail* festivities, when antebellum homes throughout the area are open to the public and millions of azaleas burst into bloom. The *Festival International de Louisiane,* also in April, celebrates Louisiana's cultural heritage, with exhibits and performances by artists from French-speaking cultures around the world. And the annual *Festivals Acadiens,* held the third weekend of September, feature Cajun music, bayou food, native crafts, and other regional specialties. *Cajun Christmas* is a series of 24 events held throughout December. For details about all of these festivals, contact the *Lafayette Convention and Visitors Commission* (PO Box 52066, Lafayette, LA 70505; phone: 318-232-3737; 800-346-1958). From April through September, thoroughbred horse racing takes place at *Evangeline Downs* (on I-49; phone: 318-896-7223).

En Route from Lafayette Head east on I-10 to Highway 31 and Breaux Bridge.

BREAUX BRIDGE This "crawfish capital of the world" is a picturesque Acadian town on the banks of the Bayou Teche. Here the annual *Crawfish Festival* is held the first weekend of May. Up to 50,000 hungry visitors come to enjoy this delicacy that restaurants serve in dozens of different ways, all Cajun and all delicious.

En Route from Breaux Bridge Follow Highway 31 south to St. Martinville.

ST. MARTINVILLE This is the area where a great many Acadians first settled, and the town is filled with references to that epic story and Longfellow's poem *Evangeline,* a tale of two star-crossed lovers that commemorates the fate of the Acadians. (Reading the poem before you visit will heighten your appreciation of the town.) You can visit Evangeline's grave, and the city has a life-size bronze statue of her, a gift from actress Dolores del Rio after filming the movie *Evangeline* here. Many refugees from the French Revolution settled here, and the courthouse has a small, intriguing display of early French aristocratic coats of arms. Even more interesting is the 157-acre *Longfellow-Evangeline Commemorative Area* (just north of town on Hwy. 31; phone: 318-394-3754), which has a Gallic museum. Also on the grounds are a French-Creole plantation house and an Acadian cabin, both furnished in the style of the early 19th century; a blacksmith shop; and a barn. The area is open daily; no admission charge for senior citizens and children under 13.

En Route from St. Martinville Take Highway 31 south to New Iberia.

NEW IBERIA The center of Louisiana's sugarcane industry, this is also the home of the romantic Bayou Teche. Here, too, is *Shadows-on-the-Teche* (317 E. Main St.; phone: 318-369-6446), a stately old mansion, vintage 1834. It is one of 18 properties owned and maintained by the *National Trust for Historic Preservation,* which conducts guided tours daily. There's an admission charge.

Just outside of town are two geographical oddities, called islands although they are landlocked. Both Jefferson and Avery Islands were formed by salt domes that pushed up from the sea-level marshlands millions of years ago; salt from here served the entire Confederate Army for the duration of the war. There is also an abundance of other natural resources, including oil reserves and some of America's most fertile earth.

En Route from New Iberia Drive west for 6 miles on Highway 14, past I-49 and US Highway 90, to Jefferson Island. At Rip Van Winkle Drive, near the town of Delcambre, turn right and follow the signs to Jefferson Island and *Live Oak Gardens.*

JEFFERSON ISLAND This is the site of *Live Oak Gardens,* the 20-acre estate of the famed 19th-century actor Joseph Jefferson. The large, frame house is furnished with 19th-century antiques; a separate building houses an antique decoy exhibit. In the surrounding gardens are azalea, camellia, and other blooming shrubs and trees. The buildings and gardens are open daily; there's an admission charge (phone: 318-365-3332).

En Route from Jefferson Island Return to Highway 14 and head east toward New Iberia. At Highway 329, head south to Avery Island.

AVERY ISLAND The highway will take you to the entrance of Avery Island (phone: 318-369-6243), a private estate, most of which is open to the public. Though small, this salt dome is packed with marvels. *Jungle Gardens* is a 200-acre landscaped paradise, featuring exotic plants from all over the world, and the *Bird Sanctuary* is famous for its huge rookery for egrets. Enormous flocks of egrets, herons, and other protected birds can be seen in warm months; ducks and other migrating fowl can be seen in winter. The island is one of the primary US producers of nutria (furbearing mammals, also known as coypus, originally from South America). Several years ago during a hurricane, some domestic nutria escaped from their cages. Finding the bayou a hospitable habitat, they proceeded to overpopulate. Here also grow all those fiery little peppers that go into the supersecret recipe for Tabasco sauce. You can tour the Tabasco plant if you like, but the secret formula is diligently guarded (phone: 318-365-8173). No admission charge.

En Route from Avery Island Return via Highway 329 to US Highway 90 and head south, through Morgan City. Pick up Highway 20 east near Gibson and follow it to Thibodaux.

THIBODAUX In this small town is the *Jean Lafitte National Historical Park and Preserve Wetlands Acadian Cultural Center* (314 St. Mary St.; phone: 504-448-1375), another park with exhibits about swamps and wetlands and demonstrations of boat building and other crafts. It's closed *Christmas;* there's no admission charge.

BEST EN ROUTE

With the exception of the *Acadiana* and the *Hilton* (see below), Lafayette is basically an ordinary city when it comes to lodgings. Staying in nearby New Iberia offers two pluses: a picturesque little inn (see below) and a central location for short driving trips. Expect to pay $120 or more per night for a double room in those places we've listed as expensive; $75 to $120 in those rated moderate; and under $75 in those listed as inexpensive. Unless otherwise noted, hotels are open year-round and rooms have air conditioning, private baths, TV sets, and telephones. For each location, hotels are listed alphabetically by price category.

LAFAYETTE

Acadiana This modern six-story, 300-room property has a restaurant and a lounge, an outdoor swimming pool, and other amenities, including hot tubs. 1801 W. Pinhook Rd. (phone: 318-233-8120; 800-874-4664 in Louisiana, or 800-826-8386 elsewhere in the US; fax: 318-234-9667). Expensive.

Hilton Here are 327 rooms (including suites with Jacuzzis), a restaurant, a lounge, and an outdoor pool. 1521 W. Pinhook Rd. (phone: 318-235-6111; 800-332-2586). Expensive.

Bois des Chênes Bed and Breakfast Inn An Acadian plantation mansion (ca. 1820) with architecture typical of the period, this establishment is listed in the *National Register of Historic Places.* Its Victorian carriage house has two bedrooms and one suite; two additional suites are located in the main house.

There's no restaurant, but a full breakfast is included. 338 North Sterling (phone: 318-233-7816; 800-749-1928). Moderate.

NEW IBERIA

The Inn at Le Rosier Old-fashioned charm fills the four rooms of this guesthouse, a traditional raised Acadian cottage. The building is set behind a large main house, which dates from 1870, with a rose garden, an elegant parlor, and a much-praised restaurant. A country-style breakfast is included in the room rate. 314 E. Main St. (phone: 318-367-5306). Moderate.

Natchez Trace Parkway, Natchez, Mississippi, to Nashville, Tennessee

For several hundred years before white people settled in the Mississippi and Ohio valleys, the Natchez, Choctaw, and Chickasaw Indians used one major trail to pass north and south. Worn down to a permanent roadbed, the trail—or trace—wandered for 500 miles from the lower Mississippi River into what was to become central Tennessee. When Kentucky and Tennessee filled up with European hunters and trappers, then settlers, the Natchez Trace entered the history of commerce. Between the late 1700s and the early 1800s, the trace was a constant thoroughfare, as "Kaintuck" boatmen floated their goods downriver on flatboats carried by the Mississippi's currents, returning on foot or on horseback. That era ended with the coming of steamboats. By 1819 steam-driven ships were plying the Mississippi, eliminating the need for overland portage.

Parts of the Natchez Trace still exist, and today the entire route is commemorated by the Natchez Trace Parkway, a modern highway that now runs almost the full 445 miles from Natchez, Mississippi north through a slip of Alabama to Pasquo, Tennessee, just outside Nashville. (Note: Two short stretches of the parkway, one near Jackson and the other at the southern terminus near Natchez, are still under construction.) The parkway does not replace the trace, but it follows the original route as closely as possible, and there are numerous spots along the way where travelers can park and walk on the trace.

Today the significance of the Natchez Trace is the history that is buried on or near it. The parkway offers a way of following the trace while having the most significant aspects of it pointed out as you go. Indian mounds, remains of inns (or "stands," as they were called), and talks presented by rangers give a sense of what the trace was like when it was a footpath winding through steaming swamps and flatlands, plagued by insects, disease, and roving bands of cutthroats preying on passing boatmen. Much of the country around the trace also saw action during the Civil War, and markers note points of historical interest.

The parkway is completely free of hotels, restaurants, and other signs of commercialism. No commercial vehicles are allowed. You can pull off the highway to eat or spend the night in many towns and cities along the route. There are picnicking facilities at frequent scenic spots, and campsites at three campgrounds (but no utility hookups).

The parkway's longest continuous section stretches from Jackson, Mississippi, to State Highway 96 near Franklin, Tennessee, approximately 350 miles of quiet two-lane highway with numerous points of interest, including Indian mounds, sites of Civil War battles, craft centers, and pastoral countryside. For more information, contact the Superintendent, *Natchez Trace Parkway* (RR 1, NT 143, Tupelo, MS 38801; phone: 601-680-4025). Call in advance of your trip and ask for a map of the parkway pinpointing where you can find historical sites, parks, picnic and natural areas, and other attractions. In addition, *Lincoln Limited B&B Reservations* (phone: 800-633-6477) arranges private tours of the trace from Nashville, New Orleans, or anyplace in between.

Our itinerary starts, as did that of the boatmen who used the trace, at Natchez, then travels north to Tennessee.

NATCHEZ, Mississippi Before beginning the journey north, spend some time in Natchez itself. When the boatmen ended their downriver journeys here in the early 19th century, they found a city on its way to getting rich, supported by the profitable cotton trade and obsessed with elegance and style. The rivermen saw little of this opulence, however. With their wages stuffed in their pockets, they spent most of their time in Natchez-Under-the-Hill, everything a shantytown river city should be. Gamblers, prostitutes, killers, adventurers, and traders gathered there to pursue their respective businesses.

Much of this activity disappeared from Natchez-Under-the-Hill without a trace long ago, but riverboat gambling has returned. The *Lady Luck* (phone: 601-445-0605 or 601-445-0550; 800-722-LUCK), the largest riverboat casino on the Mississippi, is docked at the foot of Silver Street. It offers slot machines, blackjack, craps, and roulette, as well as live entertainment, a steakhouse, and a coffee shop.

In Natchez itself, there is plenty to see and do. The *Spring Pilgrimage,* held from early March to early April, features six half-day tours of 30 beautifully restored antebellum homes, with a *Confederate Ball* each evening. The old South is evoked by gracious ladies in hoopskirts greeting guests in spacious homes and flower-filled gardens. Most of the homes are listed on the *National Register of Historic Places,* and a number are National Historic Landmarks. More than a dozen may be toured year-round (hours and admission prices vary).

Of special interest are four of these antebellum homes: *Stanton Hall* (401 High St.; phone: 601-442-6631; 800-647-6742), an 1857 house that is the site of the excellent *Carriage House* restaurant (phone: 601-445-5151); *Rosalie* (100 Orleans St.; phone: 601-446-6631; 800-647-6742); *Melrose* (at the intersection of Melrose and Montebello Blvds.; phone: 601-446-5790), an 1845 estate, now a national park, that is an outstanding example of preserved Greek Revival architecture; and *Longwood* (140 Lower Woodville Rd., near Homochitto St. and John R. Junkin Dr.; phone: 601-442-5193), whose construction was interrupted by the Civil War. Although only the basement is completed, you can see how the architecture and landscaping blend Egyptian, American, and Oriental influences in an interesting way, and the Japanese trees on the grounds are especially lovely. To find out more about the other historic homes and special events, contact *Natchez Pilgrimage Tours* (Canal and State Sts., PO Box 347, Natchez, MS 39121; phone: 601-446-6631; 800-647-6742) or the *Natchez Convention & Visitors' Bureau* (422 Main St., PO Box 1485, Natchez, MS 39121; phone: 601-446-6631; 800-647-6742).

The town's other activities include the *Opera Festival* in May, the *Fall Pilgrimage* of antebellum homes in early October, and the *Christmas Festival* throughout December. Also of interest is the *Grand Village* of the Natchez Indians (US 61, at 400 Jefferson Davis Blvd.; phone: 601-446-6502), a National Historic Landmark and archaeological site that has yielded evidence that Natchez was the site of the Natchez Indians' largest village. The Natchez culture peaked in the mid-1500s and ended in 1730, when the French wiped out most of the tribe.

En Route from Natchez Head 12 miles north on the parkway to Emerald Mound (mile marker 10.3).

EMERALD MOUND, Mississippi This is the second-largest Indian ceremonial mound ever found in the US. Built around AD 1400 by the ancestors of the Natchez Indians, *Emerald Mound* covers nearly eight acres. You can hike along a trail that leads to the top.

En Route from Emerald Mound Head 5 miles north to *Mount Locust.*

MOUNT LOCUST, Mississippi Now restored to its original 1810 appearance, *Mount Locust* (mile marker 15.5; phone: 601-445-4211) once served as both a home and an inn along the Old Trace. From March through November you can tour the house, which has exhibits and a ranger station with maps and parkway information.

En Route from Mount Locust Continue north past *Grindstone Ford/Mangum Mound* (mile marker 45.7), where artifacts of the area's prehistoric inhabitants have been found, and the *Ridgeland Craft Center* just outside Jackson (mile marker 102; phone: 601-856-7546), where Mississippi crafts are demonstrated and sold. Then exit the parkway onto State Highway 6 at mile marker 259.7 and drive 1 mile east to the *Tupelo National Battlefield.*

TUPELO NATIONAL BATTLEFIELD, Mississippi Here some 10,000 Confederate cavalry met 14,000 Union troops. The horsemen engaged the Union forces three times on July 14, 1864, and were defeated each time, paying a ghastly price in men and horses. Finally the Union troops retreated, after buying enough time for General Sherman to begin his attack on Atlanta. A small monument and two cannons may now be seen there. It's open daily; no admission charge (phone: 601-680-4025 for information).

En Route from Tupelo National Battlefield Return to the parkway for the 2-mile drive north to *Chickasaw Village,* at mile marker 261.8.

CHICKASAW VILLAGE, Mississippi Once the site of a fortified Chickasaw camp, it now features exhibits describing the daily lives and early history of the Chickasaw people and a fine nature trail with plants they once used. Open daily; no admission charge (phone: 601-842-1572).

En Route from Chickasaw Village Head north on the parkway to the *Tupelo Visitors Center* (mile marker 266; phone: 601-842-1572), the parkway's headquarters. Here you may get maps and information before continuing north to mile marker 375.8, where you can stop at a special segment of the parkway 109 miles beyond Tupelo. Called the Old Trace Loop Drive, this is a short section of the actual trace that can be driven. About 2½ miles of the trace have been paved and turned into a (very narrow) one-way loop drive for automobiles, featuring several scenic overlooks. Trailers are not recommended on the loop. Back on the parkway, head north to Franklin, Tennessee.

FRANKLIN, Tennessee Here you'll find good antiques shopping in several malls, a picturesque downtown area, and many pleasant cafés. Several Civil War battlefields are located around Franklin. More Civil War battles were fought in Tennessee than in any other state except Virginia, and one of the war's bloodiest engagements occurred in Franklin, largely in the front yard of the *Carter House* (1140 Columbia Ave.; phone: 615-791-1861). This restored antebellum home has a museum on the grounds with an exhibit about the battle, Civil War relics, and other memorabilia. It's open daily; there's an admission charge. About a mile southeast of the *Carter House* is *Carnton Plantation* (1345 Carnton La.; phone: 615-794-0903), a beautifully restored Federal-style house set on two acres of grounds. After the battle, the bodies of six slain Confederate generals reportedly were placed on the front porch of this house, which was being used as a hospital. A Confederate cemetery is on the grounds, and there are tales that several ghosts from the war still haunt the place. It's open daily; there's an admission charge.

En Route from Franklin Follow the parkway north until the end of the trace, at Highway 100 in Pasquo, Tennessee.

PASQUO, Tennessee Here, on the outskirts of Nashville, the famous *Loveless Café* features down-home country cooking (for a complete listing, see *Nashville* in THE CITIES).

BEST EN ROUTE

In Natchez there are more than 30 excellent historic bed & breakfast homes available year-round; several are listed below. For information and reservations, contact *Natchez Pilgrimage Tours* (Canal and State Sts., PO Box 347, Natchez, MS 39121; phone: 601-446-6631; 800-647-6742); *Lincoln Limited B&B Reservations* (PO Box 3479, Meridian, MS 39303; phone: 601-482-5483). Expect to pay $125 or more per night in season (October through May) for a double room in those places we've listed as expensive; $90 to $125 in those rated moderate; and under $90 in those listed as inexpensive. Unless otherwise noted, hotels are open year-round and rooms have air conditioning, private baths, TV sets, and telephones. For each location, hotels are listed alphabetically by price category.

NATCHEZ

Monmouth Plantation Bed & Breakfast Antebellum elegance is the hallmark of this 25-unit establishment; the building has been designated a National Historic Landmark. Dinner is available by advance reservation; breakfast is included in the rate. John Quitman Pkwy., 36 Melrose (phone: 601-442-5852; 800-828-4531). Expensive to moderate.

The Burn This beautifully furnished bed and breakfast inn in an antebellum home has seven guestrooms (none with phones). Breakfast is included in the rate, but there's no restaurant. 712 N. Union St. (phone: 601-442-1344; 800-654-8859). Moderate.

Sweet Olive Tree Manor Bed & Breakfast This elegant restored Victorian home has four guestrooms and a charming, Old World atmosphere. There's a pleasant TV room on the second floor, but no in-room TV sets or phones. No restaurant, but breakfast is included in the rate. 700 Orleans Street (phone: 601-442-1401). Moderate.

Texada Pronounced Tay-*ha*-da, this fully restored 1792 townhouse is part of the *Spring Pilgrimage* and offers overnight accommodations. There are four rooms in the main house, one of which has twin sleigh beds, and a three-bedroom guest cottage; most rooms have private baths. TV sets are available upon request, and breakfast is included in the rate. There's no restaurant. 222 S. Wall St. (phone: 601-445-4283). Moderate.

FRANKLIN

The Magnolia House Built in 1905, this pleasant home is within easy walking distance of the town square and antiques shopping. There are three guestrooms (no in-room TV sets). Breakfast is included in the room rate, but there's no restaurant. 1317 Columbia Ave. (phone: 615-794-8178). Inexpensive.

Outer Banks and Cape Hatteras National Seashore, North Carolina

The elements reign supreme on the Outer Banks, a 175-mile ribbon of sandy islands (north to south: Bodie, Pea/Hatteras, Ocracoke, and Cape Lookout) that runs roughly parallel to the North Carolina coast. The ocean and the wind constantly lash at the shoreline here, washing away and replacing sand. Storm waves falling across the sand at a particularly narrow point can split one island into two, and there are spots where only a few hundred feet separate a crashing Atlantic from the calm Pamlico Sound on the inland side. Except for some small island villages that existed before the *National Park Service* took over, and one commercialized stretch of road—the "motel row" from Kitty Hawk to Nags Head, a developed area tolerated only for the tourists it brings—the Outer Banks are America's seaside wilderness, a fragile ecosystem protected from development.

Ghosts haunt the Outer Banks. More than 500 ships have sunk within just a few miles of its shores, earning it the title "Graveyard of the Atlantic." This grim legacy began with Sir Richard Grenville's *Tiger* in 1585 and continues today; its most recent victim was the *Lois Joyce* in 1982. The most famous ship lost here was the Federal gunboat *Monitor;* it survived a match with the Confederacy's *Merrimac* in March of 1862, but on December 31 of that same year it went under in a Hatteras storm. The irregular coastline also made these shores the perfect lair for pirates. In the early 1700s, Edward Teach (Blackbeard) and his band holed up in Ocracoke; he was killed here in 1718.

This section of ocean offers excellent sport, with scores of drum, bluefish, trout, and mackerel to be caught. (During the summer, park rangers teach novices how to surf cast; just bring your own bait.) Birds stop here by the thousands on their seasonal migrations north and south, making the Outer Banks one of the country's prime bird watching spots, although the trees that held the sands in place centuries ago are gone, having been felled for New England shipbuilding by the fishermen who lived here. Today, several picturesque fishing villages remain, accented by clusters of sea oats and wildflowers. For general Outer Banks information, contact the *Outer Banks Chamber of Commerce* (PO Box 1757, Kill Devil Hills, NC 27948; phone: 919-441-8144) or the Superintendent, *Cape Hatteras National Seashore* (Rte. 1, PO Box 675, Manteo, NC 27954; phone: 919-473-2111).

Our route starts at Kitty Hawk, the northernmost entry point to the Outer Banks from the North Carolina mainland, and heads south to *Cape Lookout National Seashore.*

En Route from Norfolk Take Route 168 south to Route 158. Cross the bridge at Point Harbor near the end of Route 158 to Kitty Hawk.

KITTY HAWK In this little town, the Wright Brothers introduced a new era one day in 1903. Commemorating the two bicycle makers from Dayton, Ohio, is the majestic *Wright Brothers National Memorial,* on the Route 158 bypass in the town of Kill Devil Hills. The memorial has a visitors' center that displays full-scale reproductions of the 1902 glider and the 1903 "flying machine"; nearby are the reconstructed hangar and living quarters. The center is closed *Christmas;* there's an admission charge (phone: 919-441-7430).

En Route from Kitty Hawk Go west across the bridge to Manteo on Roanoke Island.

ROANOKE ISLAND Just north of Manteo is the *Fort Raleigh National Historic Site* (phone: 919-473-5772), commemorating the English colonies that were settled here in 1585 and 1587 by Sir Walter Raleigh and found abandoned in 1590. Historians still are puzzled by the disappearance of the colony and the single word "croatoan," found carved on a palisade post. Today, visitors can tour a reconstruction of the earthwork fort (closed *Christmas;* no admission charge), and a nature trail by Roanoke Sound. Next to the site is the *Elizabethan Gardens,* a memorial to the colonists featuring herb and flower gardens and sculpted lawns. A presentation of the historical drama *The Lost Colony* takes place at the *Waterside Amphitheater* at *Fort Raleigh* in summer (no Sunday performances; also see *Outdoor Dramas* in DIVERSIONS). The gardens are open year-round; there's an admission charge (phone: 919-473-3234). Across from Manteo's waterfront is the *Elizabeth II State Historic Site,* with a full-scale replica of the wooden ship *Elizabeth,* which sailed in the 1585 expedition. It's closed *Christmas Day* and Mondays in winter; admission charge (phone: 919-473-1144). A good eatery on the island is *Queen Anne's Revenge* (Old Wharf Road, about 5 miles south of Manteo; phone: 919-473-5466), which serves steaks and seafood for dinner only. It's closed Tuesdays.

En Route from Roanoke Island Head east across the causeway to Route 12; follow Route 12 south to Nags Head. Try to ignore the motels that line the road and anticipate the scenery to come.

NAGS HEAD This is the last town before the *Cape Hatteras National Seashore* officially begins. The beach just south of town boasts beautiful natural landscapes. While in the area, visit *Port O' Call* (Rte. 158 at milepost 9; phone: 919-441-7484), an especially good seafood restaurant with daily specials; it's closed January and February.

En Route from Nags Head Drive past the built-up strip and onto Bodie Island, once separate from Nags Head but now joined.

BODIE ISLAND The *Bodie Island Lighthouse* stands near the southern end of Bodie (prounounced body) Island; signs point the way. Nearby is a nature trail with an observation platform for viewing the local bird life.

En Route from Bodie Island Continue south on Route 12, across the Oregon Inlet, to Pea/Hatteras Island, the next bit of land you'll come to.

PEA AND HATTERAS ISLAND Home of the 5,800-acre *Pea Island National Wildlife Refuge,* this is one of the East Coast's most populated avian roosting places year-round. Expect to see great snow geese, gadwalls, Canada geese, loons, grebes, herons, brant, whistling swans, and countless other species of aquatic and migratory birds.

The drive south on Route 12 deserves unhurried attention; each spot is worth a stop. Markings along the road indicate places for swimming, fishing, viewing hulls of wrecked vessels, and spying on wildlife. At the "elbow" of the island is the village of Buxton, and just south is the 208-foot *Cape Hatteras Lighthouse,* America's tallest. After extensive restoration, it has been reopened for visitors during the summer. Because of the encroaching ocean, however, the lighthouse may soon be declared too dangerous to visit; call the *Cape Hatteras National Seashore* number above for hours and admission information. If you spend enough time here watching the waves and the shifting sands, you'll feel that you're actually seeing the shape of the island change. Nearby is the *Hatteras Island Visitors Center,* with programs and displays on the island's centuries of maritime activity and industry (closed *Christmas*).

Hatteras, southwest of Buxton on Route 12, is mostly known as the spot to catch the ferry to Ocracoke Island, although you may want to stop for a bite to eat or a quick look around. Listen for the cockney-like accent of the natives; the story goes that Hatteras Village was settled by the survivors of a ship from Devon, England, that capsized off the coast.

En Route from Pea/Hatteras Island Free ferry service runs from the village of Hatteras to Ocracoke Island. For more information on the ferry call 919-986-2353 from Hatteras. No reservations; the ferry runs once an hour in winter and four times an hour in summer.

OCRACOKE ISLAND Ocracoke is the final and most beautiful island in the *Cape Hatteras National Seashore* chain. Its only town is Ocracoke Village, at the island's southern tip, where ferries from Cedar Island and Swan Quarter dock and pick up passengers. The village's shops, inns, and restaurants surround a sheltered inlet called Silver Lake. Stop in the visitors' center there (open *Memorial Day* to *Labor Day;* phone: 919-928-4531) to pick up brochures on the island's many walks and sights. A good place to eat is the dining room at the *Island Inn* (phone: 919-928-4351), with seafood and Southern-style fare; its breakfasts are especially good. It's closed in December and January.

En Route from Ocracoke Island Nature lovers who prefer wild oceanfront to restaurants and gift shops will want to visit *Cape Lookout National Seashore,* the next set of islands to the south. To get there from Ocracoke, take a boat charter (phone: 919-928-4361 or 919-928-5921).

CAPE LOOKOUT There are no roads, so the best way to explore the unfettered vegetation and the remains of fishing villages is on foot (some ferries will transport four-wheel-drive vehicles). Of all the areas in the Outer Banks, this is one of the most fascinating; there is little to do, but so very much to see and experience. Most visitors walk along the natural seashore and visit the interpretive center near the lighthouse. For information, contact the *Cape Lookout National Seashore* (PO Box 690, Beaufort, NC 28516; phone: 919-728-2250).

BEST EN ROUTE

Nags Head and Kill Devil Hills have a wide range of lodgings and restaurants; Hatteras and Ocracoke islands offer far fewer options. For information about lodging, contact *Dare County Tourist Bureau* (PO Box 399, Manteo, NC 27954; phone: 919-473-2138; 800-446-6262).

Expect to pay more than $125 per night during high season (June through August) for a double room in hotels we've listed as expensive; $85 to $125 in those rated moderate; and under $85 in those rated inexpensive. Unless otherwise noted, hotels are open year-round and rooms have air conditioning, private baths, TV sets, and telephones. For each location, hotels are listed alphabetically by price category.

KITTY HAWK

Sanderling Inn This deluxe beachfront resort and restaurant is in a quiet, undeveloped area north of Kitty Hawk. There are 60 guestrooms, and amenities include golf and tennis, hot tubs, and a health club. 1461 Duck Rd., Duck (phone: 919-261-4111). Expensive.

KILL DEVIL HILLS

Quality Inn Sea Ranch Amenities at this 48-room motel include a restaurant, an indoor-outdoor pool, indoor tennis, golf privileges, and a nightclub with entertainment. Rte. 158 at milepost 7 (phone: 919-441-7126). Moderate.

Chart House You'll find comfortable accommodations and a selection of recreational activities here, as well as a private beach, a pool, golf, and picnic facilities. There are 18 rooms, none with phones. There's no restaurant. Open April through November. Rte. 158 at milepost 7.5 (phone: 919-441-7418). Inexpensive.

NAGS HEAD

Quality Inn Sea Oatel On its own beach, this pleasant two-level motel has an outdoor pool and a restaurant. Many of the 140 rooms overlook the sea. Rte. 158 at milepost 16.5 (phone: 919-441-7191). Expensive.

Blue Heron This no-frills motel has 87 rooms (including 10 efficiencies), indoor and outdoor pools, a Jacuzzi, and its own beach. There's no restaurant. Rte. 158 at milepost 16 (phone: 919-441-7447). Moderate.

HATTERAS ISLAND

Hatteras Island Resort This place offers 32 rooms, cottages with two-, three-, and four-bedroom apartments, and a pool, playground, fishing pier, restaurant, and lounge. There are no phones in rooms. Open April through November. On the north end of the island on Rte. 12 (phone: 919-987-2345). Inexpensive.

OCRACOKE

Berkeley Center Country Inn Overlooking the harbor, this gable-roofed retreat has nine comfortable rooms decorated with works by local artists (no in-room TV sets or phones). It's in a good location for exploring the village. Continental breakfast is included, but there's no restaurant. Closed November through *Easter.* Within sight of the ferry terminal (phone: 919-928-5911). Moderate.

Boyette House This complex offers 22 rooms and two suites. Those in the newer building have queen-size beds and in-room breakfast bars. There are no phones in the room and no restaurant. Free pickups from the ferry terminal. On the main street, about half a mile north of the ferry terminal (phone: 919-928-4261). Moderate to inexpensive.

Great Smoky Mountains National Park, Tennessee

The 800 square miles of Great Smoky mountains are named for the bluish veil they almost always wear, which the Indians once called "smoke." (We now know that this mist is formed by a mixture of water vapor and oils secreted by plants.) Spread across the southwestern corner of North Carolina and the southeastern tip of Tennessee, the *Great Smoky Mountains National Park* offers 800 square miles of quiet beauty: virgin forest; ancient, rounded mountains; winding drives with inspiring views; marked trails for hiking and horseback riding, many of which can be covered easily in a day or less; streams for fishing; and lush vegetation.

The oldest mountains in America and among the oldest on earth, they were formed during the Appalachian Revolution, a period that began about 230 million years ago. Whipped, worn, and shaped by eons of storms, winds, and rains, the Smokies are no longer as high as they once were, but their altitude is still more than 5,000 feet for 36 miles along the main crest. Clingmans Dome, the highest peak, arches 6,643 feet.

The Smokies support an incredible variety of plants, including more than 130 species of trees. Some trees here, now giants with trunks measuring 25 feet around, were seedlings when the Europeans came to America. Hemlocks, pines, oaks, yellow poplars, mountain laurel, and rhododendrons can be seen as you drive along US 441, which becomes Newfound Gap Road as it bisects the park.

As for wildlife, there are many black bears in the Smokies, but chances are you won't come across any, since they tend to shy away from humans. You are more likely to see other species, such as the 200 bird species that frequent the park, or white-tailed deer, commonly seen at Cades Cove at dawn and dusk. The black bear is the smallest species of North American bear, weighing 200 to 300 pounds. Occasionally, backcountry bears will raid hikers' packs and food supplies, so when camping at night, hang your pack at least ten feet off the ground, on a tree no less than four feet from its nearest neighbor. Bolder bears will sometimes beg for food from tourists, but don't give in to the temptation; bears that rely on handouts forget how to forage for food when the tourist season ends. Certainly do not imitate the man who tried to push a bear into his car so that he could take a picture of the bear sitting next to his wife. As gentle as bears may seem, they can suddenly turn mean.

The park has three visitors' centers, at Sugarlands (near the Tennessee entrance), Cades Cove, and Oconaluftee (near the North Carolina entrance), where helpful staff offer maps and brochures on available trails. A wide variety of interpretive programs are led by rangers from May through October. For motorists, there are miles of paved or graded gravel roads. The main one, Newfound Gap Road, affords splendid views of the mountains as they wind across the park between Gatlinburg, Tennessee, and Cherokee, North Carolina. But a mountain is more than a big thing to be seen from a car window. To fully appreciate the beauty of the Smokies, you must get out of your car and onto one of the park's many hiking trails.

The *Great Smoky Mountains National Park* is open year-round, as are its visitors' centers—except Cades Cove, which is open only from mid-April through October. The blue mist is thickest in summer, but the mountains are smoky and majestic anytime. The park broadcasts informational messages on AM radio station 1610. For additional information contact the Superintendent, *Great Smoky Mountains National Park* (107 Park Headquarters Rd., Gatlinburg, TN 37738; phone: 615-436-1200).

The North Carolina side of the park has a number of attractions, including the Cataloochee historic district and part of the north shore of Fontana Lake. With the exception of the town of Cherokee, however, the attractions listed below are all in the state of Tennessee.

Our route enters the park via the bustling towns of Pigeon Forge and Gatlinburg, then exits to the southwest and heads across the border to the town of Cherokee, North Carolina. Those who want to avoid the hubbub of the tourist centers may prefer to enter the park via Townsend, west of Gatlinburg on Route 321 South.

En Route from Knoxville Take Route 441 south through Sevierville to Pigeon Forge, just outside Gatlinburg.

PIGEON FORGE, Tennessee A steady attraction in this touristy town is *Dollywood* (700 Dollywood La.; phone: 615-428-9401). Named after singer and native Tennessean Dolly Parton, the park includes a living museum that depicts her "rags to riches" story, along with country music entertainment, crafts, and rides. The park is closed January through April; admission charge.

En Route from Pigeon Forge Continue south on 441 to Gatlinburg, the northern entrance to the park.

GATLINBURG, Tennessee A small town stretching for a mile along a creek, Gatlinburg sees a large share of the park's visitors. With a population of just 3,600, the town is wall-to-wall hotels and tourist attractions; it can handle more than 30,000 visitors per night in accommodations ranging from family-operated cabins and cottages to 400-room hotels.

En Route from Gatlinburg Follow 441 into the park. Stop at the visitors' center for a trail map and information about horseback riding or other special activities. Back on the main road, head into the park; the highlights of its 800 square miles are described below.

GREAT SMOKY MOUNTAINS NATIONAL PARK, Tennessee Cades Cove, a tranquil spot that can be toured entirely by car, is a green Tennessee valley in the park's western reaches. A one-way road circles past cabins, barns, and a gristmill from pioneer days. Many of the 19th-century pioneers who settled this area now rest in the Cades Cove church graveyard and other graveyards in the area.

Mt. Le Conte (6,593 feet) may be ascended only by foot or on horseback; there is no road. At its base, southern plants such as dogwood abound; higher up, New England sugar maples and yellow birches appear; and thriving near the top are Canadian spruce and fir trees. On the way up Mt. Le Conte, you can follow *Alum Cave Trail* or choose less traveled "quiet walkways." Crossing Alum Cave Creek on *Alum Cave Trail,* you confront one of the park's mysteries: the laurel hells, areas where laurel and rhododendron tangle together so inextricably as to be almost impenetrable. No one knows why no trees grow here, but getting out of a hell can be tricky off the paths. *Alum Cave Trail* leads not to Alum Cave (there is no such place) but to a bluff with a good view. Legend has it that Confederate soldiers came here to mine alum for gunpowder. There is an overhang of black slate 150 feet high and about 300 feet long. On the summit are a glorious view and a resting spot—*Le Conte Lodge*—well worth the trek (see *Best en Route*).

Clingmans Dome, the highest peak in the Smokies at 6,643 feet, is another worthwhile climb. The winding road up leads to a parking lot. From there a paved ½-mile trail goes to the summit, spirals up the ramp of an observation tower, and ends in a serene and beautiful view from the Smokies' highest point. The smooth asphalt trail provides access to the view for those in wheelchairs, but both the path and ramp to the tower are steep.

Gregory Bald, which can be climbed only on horseback or foot, is a good example of the kind of wide, green, open meadowlands that are typical of the Smokies' mountaintops. The balds are something of a mystery; there is no obvious reason for these grassy areas, and none of the traditional explanations put forward by park naturalists—wind, fire, or prolonged dry spells killing tree life, and thus making way for meadows—is entirely satisfactory.

En Route from Great Smokies National Park On the main road on the park's south side is the town of Cherokee.

CHEROKEE, North Carolina Like Gatlinburg, Cherokee has been heavily exploited for tourism. The capital of the Cherokee Indian Reservation, it has more than 70 campgrounds and motels, as well as a variety of attractions. Among the best are the *Oconaluftee Indian Village* (Off Rte. 441 on Drama Rd.; phone: 704-497-2111), where demonstrations of Indian arts and crafts are given from mid-May through October 25 (admission charge); the *Qualla Arts and Crafts Mutual* (Rte. 441; phone: 704-497-3103), which sells high-quality crafts made by several Indian tribes; and the *Museum of the Cherokee Indian* (Drama Rd.; phone: 704-497-3481), which traces the tribe's history. The museum is open daily; there's an admission charge. Also see *A Short Tour of Indian America* in DIVERSIONS.

BEST EN ROUTE

For accommodations outside the park, visitors to Tennessee can contact the chambers of commerce in Gatlinburg, TN 37738; Sevierville, TN 37864; or Townsend, TN 37882; information about accommodations also may be obtained from the privately run *Smoky Mountains Accommodations* (Rte. 4, PO Box 538, Gatlinburg, TN 37738; phone: 800-231-2230), which books reservations at 40 properties. For North Carolina accommodations, try the *Haywood County Visitors' Information Center* (PO Box 87, Maggie Valley, NC 28751; phone: 704-926-5426; 800-334-9036) and, on the Cherokee Reservation, *Cherokee Visitors' Center* (PO Box 465-18, Cherokee, NC 28719; phone: 704-497-9195; 800-438-1601).

Visitors have several lodging options inside the park. There are nine developed campgrounds; reservations are recommended in summer at those at Cades Cove, Elkmont, and Smokemont, which are open year-round. Reservations can be made through *Destinet* (phone: 800-365-2267). Permits, which are required for all overnight use of the backcountry, can be reserved up to 30 days in advance by contacting *Great Smoky Mountains National Park* (107 Park Headquarters Rd., Gatlinburg, TN 37738; phone: 423-436-1231). The park has nearly 90 primitive backcountry campsites, most of which are simply clearings with water; there are also 17 shelters (with chain-link fencing fortified against bears) along the *Appalachian Trail* and other trails. Listed below are other lodgings inside the park. Expect to pay about $60 per night for a double room at either.

Le Conte Lodge This secluded retreat atop Mt. Le Conte is accessible only by foot. A primitive hiking lodge, it has no electricity. The lodge is on park grounds but is privately run; it can accommodate up to 50 people with plenty of fresh mountain air and hearty mountain fare. Rates include breakfast and dinner. Open March to mid-November; reservations essential. PO Box 350, Gatlinburg, TN 37738 (phone: 615-429-5704).

Wonderland Hotel Accessible by car, this quiet, rustic inn is modeled on the old *Wonderland,* which was run by the same owner. The atmosphere is old-fashioned, with rocking chairs on the porch, and there's good service and generous portions of country-style cooking. None of the 29 rooms has air conditioning, a TV, or a phone. Closed January through mid-March. 3889 Wonderland Way, Sevierville, TN 37862 (phone: 615-436-5490).

Big Bend National Park, Texas

If the call of the wild is your kind of music, strike out for *Big Bend National Park,* as remote a part of the Southwest as you can find without going to the more obscure sections of northern Mexico. Set in that little pocket of Texas that sags slightly to the left of the main body, it attracts only about 300,000 visitors every year, making it the third least-visited national park in the country. Not that the folks and wildlife in *Big Bend* mind—they adore having these isolated, 801,163 acres of canyons and desert all to themselves. The park, which came under federal jurisdiction in 1944, is only part of a mammoth, exquisite stretch of land, the last surviving huge wilderness of Texas. It's still as raw here today as it was when the frontiersmen and women arrived to conquer the Wild West. The closest town is Marathon, Texas, about 41 miles north of the park's northern entrance. And the only thing really noteworthy about Marathon—aside from the wonderful *Gage Hotel* (see *Best en Route*)—is that you have to go through it to get to *Big Bend.*

Big Bend is just that—a big bend in the Rio Grande in southwestern Texas. A hundred million years ago, the entire area was covered with water. Layer upon layer of sand filtered to the bottom, forming sedimentary rock—in some places, more than 1,000 feet thick. When the ocean dried, the Rio Grande began winding its way through the rocky plains, wearing a groove in the earth along its path. The shallow Rio Grande now cuts its way through the gorges of Boquillas Canyon and the 1,500-foot-deep Santa Elena Canyon. The park also takes in an entire mountain range—the Chisos Mountains.

In the springtime, rocky cliffs overflow with white, blue, and crimson blossoms (more than 1,000 types of plants can be found here). Although the scenery is a knockout, we can't promise balmy breezes; *Big Bend*'s climate is notoriously unpredictable. In February, it may hit the 90s and snow three inches or more in the same week. In summer, it is almost too hot to breathe in the park's lower elevations. Thermal conditions create frequent "sand devils" (swirling cones of dust) and keep vultures circling overhead. The occasional thunderstorm can turn gullies to rivers and leave broad shallow lakes, but these quickly disappear. Because the park's altitude ranges from 1,750 to 7,835 feet, there are always places where you can cool off, but the park is at its greenest and prettiest after the early spring rains.

Although many people prefer the greater intimacy of traveling on foot, you don't have to walk to see *Big Bend*'s sights—in fact, you can drive for 187 miles through *Big Bend.* A good driving road leads to Santa Elena and Boquillas Canyons. But be aware that there have been incidents over the years of travelers getting lost or trying to hike for help after their cars were stuck or disabled, with fatal results. The daytime heat can be hard on those in poor health or unused to high temperatures—especially the elderly. Carry plenty of nonalcoholic liquids with you, and always make sure your car is in good repair before setting out.

The other way to travel the park is by water. *Big Bend River Tours* (phone: 915-424-3219; 800-545-4240); *Far Flung Adventures* (phone: 915-371-2489; 800-359-4138); and *Outback Expeditions* (phone: 915-371-2490; 800-343-1640) can arrange rafting or canoeing excursions on the Rio Grande, ranging from half-day trips with lunch to camping trips that last several days.

Some dangers have been connected with the park in the past. Visitors should remember this vast area is sparsely populated and has been a traditional entry point for smugglers and illegal aliens. In fact, in the early part of this century the *US Army* and the Texas Rangers mounted a mini-war against border bandits here. Hunting (indeed, even bringing in any type of firearm) and open containers of alcoholic beverages are prohibited within the park.

The entrance fee is good for seven days in the park. Three main campgrounds and an area for trailer hookups are available for an additional charge on a first-come, first-served basis. For additional information contact the Superintendent, *Big Bend National Park* (Big Bend, TX 79834; phone: 915-477-2251).

The route below enters the park at the *Persimmon Gap Ranger Station* just south of Marathon and continues along the main road, past most of the park's major attractions. Just past Lajitas on the park's western end, the national park merges into *Big Bend Ranch State Park.*

En Route from Dallas/Ft. Worth Take I-20 west to Route 18 south at Monahans. At Ft. Stockton, Route 18 runs into Route 385 south, which takes you through Marathon to *Persimmon Gap Ranger Station.* Continue to the administration building and visitors' center at *Panther Junction,* your first stop in *Big Bend National Park.*

PANTHER JUNCTION Stop in for maps and information about ranger-led activities. If you want to hike, the rangers will tell you about the trails: There's one to Lost Mine Ridge that takes about three hours, round trip, and another good one to the South Rim.

En Route from Panther Junction From here, continue along the road to the following points.

CHISOS BASIN You can camp at the *Chisos Basin* campground. (Since the Chisos Basin is more than 5,000 feet high, bring a sleeping bag even in the summer.) Sunsets here are spectacular, as the sky cascades into a medley of pink, orange, and purple in the clear desert atmosphere. White-tailed deer occasionally wander past; skunk and javelina also live here. You can hear the coyote wail as it gets dark, an eerie, echoing prelude to the harmonious songs of night birds. Lizards come out in the morning, which is the best time for human exploration, too. *Chisos Remuda Stables* (phone: 915-477-2374) offers daily trips on horseback; the minimum age is six years, and the maximum weight permitted is 210 pounds. Schedules and prices vary.

LAJITAS General Pershing had a camp at Lajitas, at the western gate of the park, and Pancho Villa is said to have stopped here as well. Lajitas is now a flourishing re-created western town and resort (phone: 915-424-3471), complete with a bunkhouse, hotels, and condominiums outfitted with period reproduction furniture as well as two restaurants, a bar, a drugstore and soda fountain, and a gift shop and trading post with a resident beer-guzzling goat. There's also a nine-hole golf course, stables, tennis, and an art gallery. Just east of Lajitas, at the entrance to *Big Bend Ranch State Park,* is the *Warnock Environmental Education Center* (Farm Road 170; phone: 915-424-3327), a repository of archaeological, historical, and natural artifacts found in the region.

BIG BEND RANCH STATE PARK A private ranch deeded to the state in the late 1980s, *Big Bend Ranch State Park* (phone: 915-358-4444 or 915-229-3416) is growing in popularity. Land has been added recently, making it Texas's largest state park at 265,000 acres. The extraordinary scenery includes mountains, canyons, rivers, geological formations, and exotic plants; there is also a wide variety of wildlife, as well as Texas longhorns. This is prime hiking and rafting country, with primitive camping areas and hiking trails. For rafting information, contact the rafting outfitters listed above. Monthly bus tours include a chuck wagon lunch; call well in advance to reserve seats (phone: 915-424-3327). The park is open daily; there's an admission charge.

BEST EN ROUTE

For a list of lodgings in the area, contact the national park superintendent well in advance of your trip. It's best to call ahead for overnight accommodations, which are few and far between. The Chisos Basin is the only place inside the park with lodging and dining, but a variety of accommodations, from bunkhouses to condos, are available in Lajitas (phone: 915-424-3471 for reservations). Expect to pay $75 or more per night for a double room in those places we've listed as expensive, and $50 to $75 in those rated moderate.

MARATHON

Gage Hotel This 1927 re-creation north of the park looks and feels like the Old West. It's simple and brown and charming, with trendy *rancho* decor in its 37 rooms and truly exceptional Southwestern fare in the dining room. Some rooms have shared baths; others have fireplaces. Open year-round. West Hwy. 90 (phone: 915-386-4205). Expensive to moderate.

BIG BEND NATIONAL PARK

Chisos Mountains Lodge, Chisos Basin A small lodge with 72 motel-type units, a restaurant, and a supply store, dramatically situated within the park at 5,400 feet. Reservations are necessary year-round. Basin Station (phone: 915-477-2291; fax: 915-477-2352). Moderate.

Padre Island, Texas

Like the coasts of New Jersey and the Carolinas, Texas's Gulf of Mexico shoreline is blessed with a series of islands that lie just offshore and follow the great arc of the Gulf Coast. The last and longest of these is Padre Island, 113 miles of sand and grass that stretch along the south Texas coast, roughly from Corpus Christi to Port Isabel, where Mexico and Texas meet like two lips puckering to kiss the Gulf.

Padre Island is really two islands separated by a tiny channel of sea: South Padre Island, the southernmost 34 miles of the island; and North Padre Island, covering about 80 miles and designated as the *Padre Island National Seashore.* The national seashore is the longest stretch of undeveloped ocean beach in the US; there are no towns or other signs of man's existence. Here, you stand a good chance of witnessing nothing but the work of nature—ocean waves, grasslands, sand dunes, thousands of birds, and other wildlife—and, if you're lucky, not another human being.

Development is predominantly confined to the northern and southern tips of Padre Island, with the hotels, restaurants, resort communities, condominiums, and highways that have made the South Texas coast famous. These two radically different environments—virgin coastline and developed beach resort—coexist peacefully, complementing each other.

En Route from Corpus Christi Before setting out, visit the new and spectacular *Texas State Aquarium* (2710 N. Shoreline Blvd. on Corpus Christi Beach; phone: 512-881-1300; 800-477-GULF), which features plenty of marine life indigenous to the Caribbean and the Gulf of Mexico. Then take Park Road 22 east to Texas Highway 361 north to Port Aransas.

PORT ARANSAS This unpretentious seaside town is actually on Mustang Island, an "adopted" part of the Padres that adjoins—and is virtually indistinguishable from—Padre Island. The *University of Texas Marine Science Institute* is here, a reminder of the area's primary, if not only, industry, the sea. Charter trawlers and deep-sea fishing charters crowd the small harbor, waiting to plow the Gulf in search of tarpon, sailfish, snapper, tuna, and countless other breeds of fighters. A hefty catch is almost guaranteed, as many of the deep-sea boats are equipped with motorized reels: Get a nibble, flick the switch, and land your catch. In July, anglers come here for the *Deep-Sea Roundup,* a contest to see who can land the biggest and the most fish. Other activities center on the 18 miles of sparkling white beach, a focal point for surfing, surf casting, swimming, and surfside drives. In March, Port Aransas is a popular destination for students on spring break, although South Padre Island attracts even more of the rowdy revelers. Plenty of fine restaurants are on hand, including *Pelican's Landing* (Alister St.; phone: 512-749-6405), which prepares excellent seafood; the *Crazy Cajun* (315 S. Alister St.; phone: 512-749-5069), which serves Louisiana-style stone crab and shrimp with new potatoes and corn; and the *Quarterdeck* (914 Tarpon; phone: 512-749-4449), which couples a beachfront location with fine presentations of oysters, crab salad, and onion rings. For more information, contact the *Port Aransas Chamber of Commerce and Tourist Bureau* (PO Box 356, Port Aransas, TX 78373; phone: 512-749-5919; 800-452-6278).

En Route from Port Aransas Take Route 35 through Aransas Pass and go just beyond the tiny hamlet of Lamar to the *Aransas National Wildlife Refuge*.

ARANSAS NATIONAL WILDLIFE REFUGE The 55,000 acres of this wildlife refuge have been set aside for the endangered whooping crane, visible in the colder months when they migrate south from Canada. There is an observation tower and an information station, as well as trails for spying on the birds by foot or car. The refuge is open daily; there's an admission charge. For less obstructed views of the cranes, you can cruise up Aransas Bay past the water side of the refuge. Four-hour cruises leave from just south of the refuge in Rockport, and must be arranged at its harbor; for a list of tour operators, contact the *Rockport-Fulton Chamber of Commerce* (phone: 512-729-6445).

En Route from Aransas National Wildlife Refuge Return to Port Aransas and take Route 53 south to North Padre.

PADRE ISLAND NATIONAL SEASHORE One of the first sights in North Padre is Malaquite Beach, which has a visitors' center; inquire here about ranger-led nature activities. There's also an excellent campground for trailers and the hardy few who tent on the beach. Beaches are open for overnight guests, but camping is not allowed in the dunes or grasslands. Malaquite is open year-round; there's an admission charge.

Near Malaquite Beach is the *Grasslands Trail,* a well-marked trek through the tall grasses (visitors are forbidden to walk on the dunes). The walk offers a look at the island's native growth, including sea oats, railroad vines, croton, wild indigo, and a last vestige of Virginia live oak. The walk is also impressive for its museum-like representation of how dunes are formed, using real drifts shaped entirely by nature, in every stage of formation from small mounds to hills. For *Grasslands Trail* information, call 512-949-8068.

At one time, the grasslands that cover the inland portions of the island were grazing land for cattle. Padre Nicholas Bali, the Spanish monk after whom the island chain is named, started raising livestock here in 1800, but the cattle, cowboys, and monks are gone, and the grasses are returning.

Other men have been here during the last 500 years, mostly Spaniards in the 16th, 17th, and 18th centuries, chasing or being chased by Indians. The shallow waters of the Gulf side have taken their share of vessels over the years, including many a royal treasure ship. As a result, millions of dollars in silver and gold are thought to be buried in the sand or lost just off the coast. (Potential fortune seekers should note that the seashore is off limits to metal detectors and treasure hunting.)

You may explore the seashore either on foot or in a four-wheel-drive vehicle, but driving on the dunes and in the grasslands is prohibited. However you go, watch for the diverse, fascinating collection of animal life, including coyote, ground squirrels, gophers, and kangaroo rats. At least 12 different types of snakes are known to reside in the tall grasses, including two species of rattlers: Watch out for these unfriendly fellows. (Campgrounds and other areas designated for two-legged guests can be assumed safe from potentially dangerous visitors.) Also keep a sharp eye out for Kemp's Ridley sea turtles, which seashore personnel are trying to save from extinction. If you see a turtle, report its location to park rangers immediately. In the air are hundreds of herons, willets, black skimmers, marsh hawks, pelicans, avocets, horned owls, peregrine falcons, sanderlings, and other birds. Year-round, Padre is an avian amusement park.

Wherever you go, there is fishing. The beaches of Padre are regarded as among America's best for the variety and sheer volume of fish in their surf. You may be the only person for miles, with not another soul to hear your victory shout after a half-hour fight with a hammerhead shark—a not unheard of catch in this part of the Gulf.

For more information about camping and other activities on North Padre, contact the Superintendent, *Padre Island National Seashore* (9405

S. Padre Island Dr., Corpus Christi, TX 78418; phone: 512-937-2621 or 512-949-8068; 512-949-8173 for the ranger station).

En Route from Padre Island National Seashore Because no road runs the full length of either North or South Padre, you'll have to get back on Highway 77 to reach South Padre.

SOUTH PADRE ISLAND South Padre Island is fully developed as a vacation haven. While relaxed in spirit, it is packed with shoppping centers, high-rise hotels and condos, some low-rise (but expensive) condos, and miles of sporting pleasures. Among the best restaurants in the area are *Blackbeard's* (103 E. Saturn; phone: 210-761-2962), with its outstanding blackened shrimp *fajitas; Jetties* (in *Isla Blanca State Park*; phone: 210-761-6461), which specializes in stuffed shrimp and crab; and *Louie's Backyard* (2305 Laguna Blvd.; phone: 210-761-6406), which offers lavish seafood buffets and a bayside view.

The causeway to Port Isabel originates on South Padre Island near *Isla Blanca Park.* There you'll find a bathhouse and cabañas, plus overnight accommodations under the stars. There also are food concessions, shopping centers, miniature golf courses, tennis courts, water skiing facilities, a trailer park, and a children's recreation area. Tens of thousands of teenagers and college students from across the US and Canada flock here during spring break in March; this is a wild time, not recommended for families.

For more information on accommodations and activities on South Padre, contact *South Padre Island Visitors and Convention Bureau* (600 Padre Blvd., South Padre Island, TX 78597; phone: 210-761-6433; 800-343-2368).

En Route from South Padre Island Just across the Laguna Madre and connected to South Padre by the Queen Isabella Causeway (Texas's longest bridge) is Port Isabel.

PORT ISABEL Port Isabel, a peaceful resort town, was a favorite vacation spot of Texas society from about the turn of the century until a few decades ago. It is primarily a fishing town, with the world's largest shrimping fleet tying up here and at the port of Brownsville; the harbor is home port for many deep-sea charter fishing boats, and fresh fish markets are abundant.

Just west of town on Route 100 is the *Port Isabel Lighthouse Historic Site,* the smallest state park in this state famous for big things. The lighthouse dates to the 1850s, when gold rush fever made Port Isabel a popular stop for folks on the way west. It's open daily; there's an admission charge. The lighthouse overlooks the site of *Fort Polk,* a Mexican War camp and depot that was commanded by General Zachary Taylor. The last land battle of the Civil War also was fought in the neighborhood, at Palmito Hill.

While in Port Isabel, take a half-hour drive across the Mexican border to Matamoros, a town featuring markets for jewelry, leather, and clothing as well as several popular restaurants and nightclubs. Merchants here accept American currency, and only informal proof of citizenship, such as a driver's license or voter's registration card, is necessary to cross the border if you are traveling within 12½ miles of the border and plan to return home within 24 hours. US automobile insurance is not valid in Mexico, however, so if you plan to drive you should get the proper insurance. Several insurance firms handle Mexican insurance if yours does not; *Sanborn's Mexico Insurance Service* (PO Box 310, McAllen, TX 78502; phone: 210-686-0711) is a particularly reputable and reliable company.

BEST EN ROUTE

Expect to pay $100 or more per night for a double room in those places we've listed as expensive; $75 to $100 in the places described as moderate; and less than $75 in those rated inexpensive. Unless otherwise noted, hotels are open year-round and rooms have air conditioning, private baths, TV sets, and telephones. For each location, hotels are listed alphabetically by price category.

PORT ARANSAS

Island Retreat A fisherman's delight, it offers fish cleaning and freezing facilities and access to the ocean. Most of the 111 apartments have balconies on the gulf, kitchen appliances, and a washer-dryer. There are two pools and other recreational activities, but no restaurant. 700 Island Retreat Court (phone: 512-749-6222). Expensive to moderate.

Sand Castle Set in the middle of the beach with a boardwalk connecting the pool to the shore, this establishment features 116 luxurious one-, two-, and three-bedroom condos with private balconies and a wealth of modern conveniences, and two tennis courts. There's no restaurant. 800 Sand Castle Dr. (phone: 512-749-6201; 800-727-6201). Expensive to moderate.

Beachhead Just a boardwalk away from the beach, here are 40 two-bedroom, two-bath condos with kitchens and balconies overlooking the Gulf. There's also parking, a coin laundry, and a heated pool. 1319 11th St. (phone: 512-749-6261). Moderate.

MUSTANG ISLAND

Port Royal This beachfront condominium resort offers 175 units and deluxe amenities, including a lagoon-style pool with waterfalls, a restaurant, a lounge, meeting rooms, and a gift shop. Park Road 53 at Highway 361 (phone: 512-749-5011; 800-847-5659). Expensive.

SOUTH PADRE ISLAND

Bridgepoint Condominiums Sleek, contemporary, and elegant, this high-rise property on the beach has 114 units, a pool, tennis courts, a fitness room, and a restaurant. 334 Padre Blvd. (phone: 210-761-7969; 800-221-1402). Expensive.

Bahia Mar This establishment has two pools, a Jacuzzi, tennis courts, a putting green, and a restaurant. The 347 units range from rooms to suites to condos. 6300 Padre Blvd. (phone: 210-761-1343; 800-292-7502 from Texas; 800-531-7404 from elsewhere in the US). Expensive to moderate.

Radisson Resort Part of the worldwide chain, this beachfront hotel has 182 rooms, five pools, a health club, eight tennis courts, two restaurants, and several meeting rooms. 500 Padre Blvd. (phone: 210-761-6511; 800-333-3333). Expensive to moderate.

Shenandoah National Park, Virginia

For 80 miles along the spine of the Blue Ridge Mountains in northwestern Virginia, extending from the town of Front Royal in the north to just east of Waynesboro in the south and overlooking the beautiful Shenandoah River valley, lies *Shenandoah National Park.* More than 95% of the park's 194,327 acres are wooded—stands of deciduous hardwood (oak, hickory, maple) that turn salad green in the spring, darken in summer, and explode into bright colors in autumn. Through the park runs the 105-mile Skyline Drive as well as a 95-mile section of the *Appalachian Trail,* which winds from Maine to Georgia.

Bounded on the east by the Blue Ridge Mountains—the most southeasterly wave of the Appalachians—and on the west by the Alleghenies, the Shenandoah Valley is in the heart of the mighty Appalachian Mountain chain. The area was revered for centuries by Native Americans (Shenandoah is an Indian word meaning "daughter of the stars") and by subsequent settlers of the region. George Washington surveyed land here and was so awed by its splendor that he claimed a large tract for himself. It is said that he required each of his tenants to plant at least four acres of apple trees. Today, the park's overlooks and trails provide views of the glorious apple orchards in the valley.

Though almost entirely forest, the park has very little virgin woodland left. Generations of farmers practiced the time-honored method of quick-burning to clear forests and prepare fields for planting, and further woodland was lost as the result of a natural calamity—about 85 years ago, a fungus deadly to the area's native chestnut trees decimated the forests. The park was established in 1935 to ensure that a good portion of the Shenandoah area would remain untouched. For additional information about the park, contact the Superintendent, *Shenandoah National Park* (Rte. 4, PO Box 348, Luray, VA 22835; phone: 540-999-2266 for taped information on weather, campground, lodge, and activities; 540-999-3500 for further details). Park headquarters are on US 211, 4 miles west of Thornton Gap.

Our route starts at Front Royal, just off I-66 at the northern end of the park, and proceeds south on the park's main road.

FRONT ROYAL Here are nature walks, picnic facilities, and crafts shops, among other attractions. The *Warren Rifles Confederate Museum* (95 Chester St.; phone: 540-636-6982) houses relics of the Civil War, including furniture, rare photographs, weapons, and other memorabilia. If you're visiting in the fall, plan to attend the annual *Blue Ridge Oktoberfest,* held the third weekend in October (when the foliage usually is at its peak). The festival includes crafts sales and a show featuring the works of more than 50 artists. For information contact the *Front Royal Chamber of Commerce* (414 E. Main St., Front Royal, VA 22630; phone: 540-635-3185; 800-338-2576).

If you find yourself seduced by the beauty of the Shenandoah River and want to get to know it better before entering the park, a short drive north into West Virginia's eastern panhandle will bring you to Harpers Ferry, where you can join a Shenandoah River whitewater rapids expedition. Each trip takes about five hours, including a Southern-style picnic. Whitewater tours are run from April through October by *Blue Ridge Outfitters* (phone: 304-725-3444), *Front Royal Canoe Co.* (phone: 540-635-5440), and *Downriver Canoe Co.* (phone: 540-635-5526). For additional details, see the *Harpers Ferry and Monongahela National Forest* route in this section, below.

En Route from Front Royal Enter the park at *Dickey Ridge,* just within the northern entrance at Front Royal.

SHENANDOAH NATIONAL PARK *Shenandoah Overlook,* a free newspaper that lists daily activities, park services and facilities, and points of interest, is available at the entrance station. Rangers lead nature walks, advise on trails, and provide information on camping and fishing. *Shenandoah* has two lodges, three campgrounds, a primitive group camping area, and a policy allowing backcountry camping (see *Best en Route*). However, campers must have permits, which are available at entrance stations, visitors' centers, or park headquarters.

From the center, head south on Skyline Drive along the crest of the Blue Ridge for the length of the park, surrounded by successive waves of Appalachian hills rising and falling into the distance. Park vistas are gorgeous in the autumn, but they're just as beautiful in the spring and summer, when the road is far less crowded. Skyline Drive has numerous stops and overlooks, many with short trails, which allow visitors to drive the park's length, stopping where they wish. (Some people believe that the most beautiful section starts at Rockfish Gap, just east of Waynesboro.)

You can enjoy the many beautiful vistas along Skyline Drive, and with luck even see some wildlife; however, with the *Appalachian Trail* and more than 500 miles of hiking trails and paths—some quite arduous, others little more than strolls—*Shenandoah* is made for hiking. The river lures plenty of trout fisherfolk as well.

The caverns in the region reveal the underpinnings of the entire mountain chain; they are formed of ancient lava that cooled and separated nearly a billion years ago. *Luray Caverns* (on the US 211 Bypass, 10 minutes from the central entrance to Skyline Dr.; phone: 540-743-6551 for information) are the most outstanding example; there's an admission charge.

A walk around Stony Man Mountain also displays the results of this process. The high cliffs along Stony Man (and elsewhere in the park) break into great columns of stone, called columnar jointings, which developed as gas percolated through the cooling lava, creating strange, circular bubbles of color in the rock.

At Limberlost, in Whiteoak Canyon, is a stand of original hemlock trees and some 350- to 400-year-old white oaks.

The trail up Hawksbill Mountain is rigorous (from 1.1 to 3 miles, round trip), but along the route—if you go by way of the *Appalachian Trail*—are numerous stopping points that offer spectacular views of the valley.

BEST EN ROUTE

In addition to the lodges listed below, *Shenandoah* has three major campgrounds for the general public, one youth campground, and seven picnic areas. It also has a backcountry "camp where you like" system (all backcountry campers must have permits that specify how many people are allowed in the party and how long they will be out). For information on accommodations outside the park, contact the following: *Front Royal Chamber of Commerce* (phone: 540-635-3185; 800-338-2576); *Page County Chamber of Commerce* (phone: 540-743-3915); *Waynesboro/East Augusta Chamber of Commerce* (phone: 540-949-8203); or *Shenandoah Valley Travel Association* (phone: 540-740-3132). The state of Virginia also supplies excellent tourist information through the *Virginia Division of Tourism* (901 E. Byrd St., Richmond, VA 23219; phone: 804-786-2051; 800-VISIT-VA).

Expect to pay $120 or more per night for a double room at those places we've listed as expensive; $75 to $120 at hotels in the moderate category; and under $75 at places in the inexpensive range. Unless otherwise noted, hotels are open year-round; rooms do not have air conditioning or telephones, but all have private baths and most have TV sets. For each location, hotels are listed alphabetically by price category.

SHENANDOAH NATIONAL PARK

Big Meadows With 102 rooms it's somewhat smaller than *Skyland* (below), but this lodge with rustic cabins otherwise offers the same features. Reservations must be made about two months in advance (for a stay during foliage season, 10 months in advance!). For reservations, write to *Aramark Virginia Sky-Line Co.* (PO Box 727, Luray, VA 22835; phone: 800-999-4714; fax: 540-743-7883). Open March through November. On the Skyline Dr. at milepost 51.3 (phone: 540-999-2221). Moderate.

Skyland This hotel, a *Shenandoah* tradition, was founded in 1894 and has 186 rooms, a dining room, a stable, and crafts shops. For reservations, write to

Aramark Virginia Sky-Line Co. (see above). Open from mid-March through the day after *Thanksgiving.* On the Skyline Dr. at milepost 41.7 (phone: 540-999-2211). Moderate.

Lewis Mountain South of *Big Meadows* (above), this complex offers 14 cabins with baths, heat, electric lights, linen, and a cooking and eating area outside. Open mid-May through October. On the Blue Ridge Parkway at milepost 57.5 (phone: 540-999-2255). Off-season, contact the *Aramark Virginia Sky-Line Co.* (see above). Inexpensive.

WINTERGREEN

Wintergreen Resort Set on 11,000 acres in Wintergreen, near the park, this luxury establishment includes 350 suites and condos, as well as two award-winning golf courses, a golf school, 25 tennis courts, horseback riding, hiking trails, a pool, and six restaurants. On the Blue Ridge Pkwy. between mileposts 13 and 14, via Rte. 151 (phone: 804-325-2200). Expensive.

HOT SPRINGS

Homestead A blend of Old World charm and modern luxury in the *George Washington National Forest* not far from the park, this famous resort has 600 rooms, a wide range of activities, and a spa. For more information, see *America's Special Havens* in DIVERSIONS. Rte. 220 (phone: 540-839-5500; 800-838-1766; fax: 540-839-7656). Expensive.

Tidewater Virginia

One of the historically richest areas in the country is Virginia's coast—traditionally called Tidewater Virginia—on the Chesapeake Bay. Here are *Colonial Williamsburg, Jamestown,* and Yorktown; the beautiful 18th-century plantation homes along the James, York, Rappahannock, and Potomac Rivers; and Richmond and other Civil War sites. Hardly a period of early American history, from initial exploration to the War Between the States, is not represented by some vital detail here.

For further information on the Virginia coast contact *Hampton Visitors Center* (710 Settlers Landing Rd., Hampton, VA 23669; phone: 804-727-1102); *Norfolk Convention and Visitors Bureau* (236 E. Plume St., Norfolk, VA 23510; phone: 804-441-5266; 800-368-3097); *Newport News Tourist Information Center* (13560 Jefferson Ave., Newport News, VA 23603; phone: 804-886-7777); *Virginia Beach Visitor Information Center* (2700 Parks Ave., Virginia Beach, VA 23451; phone: 804-451-8888; 800-822-3224); or *Virginia Beach Pavilion* (1000 19th St., Virginia Beach, VA 23451; phone: 804-428-8000).

Our tour of Tidewater Virginia begins in the state capital, Richmond. From there it heads south to the "historic triangle" between the James and the York Rivers, one of the country's most highly concentrated area of sites from American history. The three points of the triangle, all conveniently linked by the Colonial Parkway, are *Jamestown,* where America began; Williamsburg, where patriots plotted America's future; and Yorktown, where the Revolutionary War ended and the nation was born. From there, we visit several of the stately plantations along the James River, then head south to the Port of Hampton Roads and Virginia Beach.

RICHMOND You'll find history in every block of Virginia's capital. Reminders of the American Revolution, the Civil War, and the Victorian era all coexist in this genteel city.

Begin your tour at the city's newest attraction, *Valentine Riverside* (500 Tredegar St.; phone: 649-0711), a branch of *The Valentine: The Museum of the Life and History of Richmond.* Set in the buildings of the 19th-century Tredegar Iron Works, the museum traces the history of Richmond through a variety of high-tech exhibits. The museum complex is located in a park along the James River, which skirts the southern edge of the city. Bicycles are available for rent, and whitewater rafting trips run by the *Richmond Raft Company* (phone: 804-222-RAFT) depart from the park (also see *Touring America's Waterways* in DIVERSIONS). The museum offers a variety of bus and walking tours, and shuttle buses provide transportation to several of the city's main tourist areas, enabling visitors to leave their cars in the parking lot while they explore. After sunset, a sophisticated sound-and-light show tells the city's story through an artful combination of music and historic images projected on the brick wall of one of the iron works buildings (the show is a bit skimpy on narration, though, so be sure to visit the museum first). The *Valentine Riverside* is closed Sunday mornings; there's an admission charge.

Richmond's most popular attraction is the *Virginia State Capitol* (Ninth and Grace Sts.; phone: 804-786-4344). The neoclassical structure, designed by Thomas Jefferson in 1785, was the site of Aaron Burr's treason proceedings and served as the *Capitol of the Confederacy* during the Civil War. Its rotunda houses Jean Antoine Houdon's life-size sculpture of George Washington, the only statue for which Washington posed. The capitol building is open daily, although from December through March it's closed Sunday mornings; there's no admission charge.

Two blocks north of the capitol is the Court End District, with numerous historic structures and several interesting museums. *Valentine Court End* (1015 E. Clay St.; phone: 804-649-0711), the second branch of *The Valentine: The Museum of Life and History of Richmond,* is set in the newly refurbished *Wickham House* (1812). Through exhibits, period furnishings, and recordings of the types of conversations that might have taken place in each of the rooms, the museum describes how the Wickhams and their slaves interacted and offers insight into family life and race relations in the antebellum South. The museum is closed Sunday mornings; there's an admission charge. Just east of the museum are the *White House and Museum of the Confederacy* (1201 E. Clay St.; phone: 804-649-1861). The *White House* served as the executive mansion of the Confederacy and the home of Confederate president Jefferson Davis and his family from 1861 to 1865; it has been restored to appear as it was during the Civil War and features many original Davis furnishings. The museum houses the most comprehensive collection of military, political, and domestic items and art from the Confederate period. Both are closed Sunday mornings; there's an admission charge.

Among the city's other Civil War sites is the *Richmond National Battlefield Park & Visitor Center* (3215 E. Broad St.; phone: 804-226-1981), east of the city center, which offers an overview of the city's battlefields (see the "Richmond-Petersburg" entry in *Civil War Battle Sites* in DIRECTIONS). *Hollywood Cemetery* (Cherry and Albemarle Sts.; phone: 804-648-8501), located west of downtown, is the final resting place of Confederate President Jefferson Davis, several other Civil War heroes, and 18,000 Confederate soldiers, as well as Virginia-born US presidents James Monroe and John Tyler. A visit to the cemetery is highly recommended, even for those who are not history buffs. Laid out in 1849, the tranquil tree-filled grounds are beautiful, as are the elaborate Victorian tombs, statuary, and ironwork.

Five statues of Civil War heroes dominate Monument Avenue, a 130-foot-wide boulevard lined with trees and Victorian mansions northwest of the city center. It's the main thoroughfare of the Historic Fan District—an 85-block neighborhood so named because it "fans" out from *Monroe Park.* Home to *Virginia Commonwealth University,* this lovely and lively residential area is notable for its Victorian townhouses in a variety of architectural styles; there are a number of shops and restaurants, too.

Located near the Fan District is the *Virginia Museum of Fine Arts* (2800 Grove Ave.; phone: 804-367-0844), which features a large collection of Fabergé Russian Imperial eggs, as well as a broad range of other collections, from ancient Greek and Egyptian art to Impressionist paintings to Art Deco and Art Nouveau works. The museum is closed Mondays; there's no admission charge. Nearby is the home of the *Virginia Historical Society* (428 N. Boulevard; phone: 804-342-9676), with permanent displays that chronicle the state's history. The society also mounts interesting temporary exhibits; a recent show explored the life and legend of Pocahontas. The society's headquarters is closed Sunday afternoons; there is an admission charge.

Other interesting Richmond districts include Church Hill, at the east end of the city, which is lined with 18th- and 19th-century structures, most notably *St. John's Church* (2401 E. Broad St.; phone: 804-648-5015). Built in 1741, the church was the venue of the Second Virginia Convention in March 1775, during which Patrick Henry delivered the rousing speech that ended "give me liberty or give me death!" Guide tours are conducted daily (donation requested); reenactments of Henry's speech are presented on

Sunday afternoons in summer. Another neighborhood, Jackson Ward, became an African-American cultural and entrepreneurial center after the Civil War. It's the site of the *Black History Museum and Cultural Center of Virginia* (00 Clay St.; phone: 804-780-9093) and the *Maggie Walker National Historic Site* (110½ E. Leigh St.; phone: 804-780-1380), home of the first woman bank president in the US. The museum is closed Mondays, Wednesdays, and Sundays; there's an admission charge. Shockhoe Slip and Shockhoe Bottom, in the southeastern section of the city, are once-decaying commercial and warehouse districts that have been rejuvenated with trendy shops, restaurants, and bars. Richmond's outdoor *Farmer's Market* (17th and Main Sts.; no phone) has been operating in Shockhoe Bottom since 1775; it's open daily. Gardening and architecture fans will want to visit *Maymont* (1700 Hampton St.; phone: 804-358-7166), a Victorian Romanesque mansion set on a 100-acre park in the southwestern part of the city. The grounds are complete with formal gardens, a nature center, and a children's farm. The mansion is closed Mondays; the park is open daily. Donations are requested.

For an overview of the city, *Historic Richmond Tours* (phone: 804-780-0107) offers daily guided van tours with pickups at most downtown hotels. Additional information about Virginia's capital city is available from the *Metro Richmond Convention and Visitors Bureau* (550 E. Marshall St., Richmond, VA 23219; phone: 804-782-2777 or 800-365-7272; fax: 804-780-2577).

En Route from Richmond Take I-64 east to Exit 242A. Follow Rte. 199 and the Colonial Parkway to *Jamestown.*

JAMESTOWN John Smith (who became president of the Colonial Council) and his group of 103 settlers arrived in *Jamestown* in May 1607, forming the first successful English settlement in America. The first years of the colony were extremely hard. The London Company, which sponsored the journey, offered the fledgling community little assistance, and fate dealt it a rather hard hand. By 1699, when the Virginia capital was moved to Williamsburg, *Jamestown*'s state house had burned to the ground; years later the town was eventually abandoned.

Today the area is part of the *Colonial National Historical Park* off Colonial Parkway (phone: 804-229-1733; admission charge). In the 17th century, it was connected to the mainland by a narrow isthmus but the James River eventually ate the isthmus away, making the site of Jamestown an island. For the most part, all that remains of the colony are diggings indicating where buildings once were. The one remaining building is the church tower of 1639, around which the church has been reconstructed. Also rebuilt on its original site is the *Jamestown Glasshouse* (off Jamestown Rd. and Colonial Pkwy.; phone: 804-229-2437; admission charge), which is occupied, as it was originally, with glass blowers. But history comes most vividly alive on the harbor of the James River at nearby *Jamestown Settlement* (phone: 804-

229-1607), which is not part of the national park. Here are full-scale replicas of the three tiny ships on which the first settlers sailed: the *Susan Constant,* the *Godspeed,* and the *Discovery.* You can board one of them and see the cramped quarters that housed the courageous pioneers. There is also a re-creation of *James Fort* here, which visitors can tour, as well as a re-created Powhatan Indian village and exhibitions showing *Jamestown*'s origins. It's open daily; admission charge. Also see *Restored Towns and Reconstructed Villages* in DIVERSIONS.

En Route from Jamestown Continue north on the Colonial Parkway to *Colonial Williamsburg.*

COLONIAL WILLIAMSBURG The first restoration of a historical area ever undertaken in the US (it was begun in 1926), *Colonial Williamsburg* is still the best. A good introduction to the town can be found at the visitors' center (Colonial Pkwy. and Rte. 132Y; phone: 804-220-7645). In a daily re-creation of colonial life, craftsmen ply their trades, sheep graze on the green, and horse-drawn carts carry passengers down Duke of Gloucester Street, with its array of taverns and shops all busy at their 18th-century businesses. Stroll over to Market Square and watch the militia train and drill, or admire examples of English and American pottery, paintings, ceramics, and housewares at the *DeWitt Wallace Decorative Arts Gallery* (325 W. Francis St.; phone: 804-220-7554; admission charge). Although there are many motels and hotels near town, you need to make reservations well in advance, for *Colonial Williamsburg* is a popular family destination; more than a million people visit each year. For information, contact the *Williamsburg Area Convention & Visitors' Bureau* (PO Box 3585, Williamsburg, VA 23187; phone: 804-253-0192). Also see *Restored Towns and Reconstructed Villages* in DIVERSIONS.

En Route from Colonial Williamsburg While you're in the area, consider a visit to *Busch Gardens, The Old Country,* a theme park 5 miles south of Williamsburg (Rte. 60; phone: 804-253-3000; admission charge). For additional details on the park, see *Amusement Parks and Theme Parks* in DIVERSIONS. Then return to the Colonial Parkway and head east to Yorktown.

YORKTOWN Still a functioning city, Yorktown was an important tobacco shipping port until the Revolutionary War. In the autumn of 1781, British commander Charles Cornwallis got boxed in by a combination of the French fleet along the coast and French and American troops, led by George Washington, on land. A siege began, and 10 days later Cornwallis surrendered, ending the Revolutionary War on October 19. Stop in at the state-managed *Yorktown Victory Center* (Rte. 1020, off Rtes. 238 and 17; phone: 804-887-1776; admission charge) for information and brochures. Visit the *American Revolution Museum* here, with Revolutionary War exhibitions and a display of archaeological material raised from one of Cornwallis's ships, which sank in the York River during the war. Walk through the re-created Continental Army encampment and an 18th century farmsite. Visitors can take part in military drills, learn about 18th-century medical practices, and help with farm chores. Open daily except *Christmas* and *New Years Day*; admission charge.

Of special interest is the *Moore House* (on Rte. 238; phone: 804-898-3400 for information), where the capitulation papers were drawn up (they were signed in the adjacent trenches), and the *Swan Tavern* (300 Main St.; phone: 804-898-3033), a reconstruction of an early 18th-century tavern that is now an antiques shop. For general information, contact the *Yorktown Visitors' Center* at the *Colonial National Historic Park* (PO Box 210, Yorktown, VA 23690; phone: 804-898-3400). Also see *Restored Towns and Reconstructed Villages* in DIVERSIONS.

En Route from Yorktown From Highway 17, take Route 238 west to Highway 60, then head north toward Williamsburg. A couple of miles down the road on the left is the exit to *Carter's Grove* plantation.

TIDEWATER PLANTATIONS Along all of the rivers, inlets, bays, and peninsulas of Tidewater Virginia and the Chesapeake Bay, you will find lovely Georgian homes, fully restored and inhabited, which date from the tobacco trading days of the mid-1800s. And from Williamsburg west along the north shore of the James River are a number of the most famous plantation homes in America. Most are open to visitors; even if a house is closed, the grounds always are open. Most charge admission.

The first you'll come to is *Carter's Grove* (phone: 804-229-1000, ext. 2973), built in the 1750s and restored as part of the *Colonial Williamsburg* project. Across the river from *Jamestown* is *Smith's Fort Plantation* (phone: 804-294-3872), built almost 100 years earlier, on land given by the Indian Chief Powhatan to his daughter Pocahontas and her groom John Rolfe. Nearby is *Bacon's Castle* (phone: 804-357-5976), which claims the oldest documented garden in America. Just east of *Smith's Fort* lies *Chippokes Plantation State Park* (phone: 804-294-3625), a plantation dating from 1619.

Cross back over the river on the Colonial Parkway and then follow Route 5 north for the James River's north shore route. Along the way are *Sherwood Forest* (phone: 804-829-5377), the home of President John Tyler; *Westover*, the home of William Byrd II, built in the 1730s as the focal point of his 179,000-acre fiefdom; *Evelyntown* (phone: 800-473-5075), home of the man who fired the first shot of the Civil War at Fort Sumter; *Berkeley* (phone: 804-829-6018), the birthplace of President William Henry Harrison; and *Shirley* (phone: 804-829-5121), the home of Robert E. Lee's mother, Anne Hill Carter.

En Route from the Tidewater Plantations Take Highway 295 north to I-64 south and the Port of Hampton Roads.

PORT OF HAMPTON ROADS This port incorporates three cities—Newport News, Portsmouth, and Norfolk—and is a center for shipping and shipbuilding.

It is also the entry point to Virginia's beaches, either around Cape Henry to Virginia Beach or through the Chesapeake Bay Bridge–Tunnel to the peninsula of Virginia that hangs below Maryland.

An appropriate stop is the *Mariners' Museum* in Newport News (100 Museum Dr.; phone: 804-596-2222; admission charge), which exhibits a wealth of ships' fittings, models, cannon, maps, and instruments. In Newport News or Hampton you can take a harbor cruise that sails around Hampton Roads harbor and historic *Fort Monroe,* in the very waters where the USS *Monitor* met the *Virginia Merrimac.* The trips leave from the boat harbor (917 Jefferson Ave.) in Newport News, and from Settlers Landing Road in Hampton, April through October.

At Norfolk's *Nauticus National Maritime Center* (232 E. Main; phone: 804-664-1000; 800-664-1080), visitors may see exhibits or films on marine life, shipbuilding, and other nautical subjects; tour the ships moored at the pier outside; try a computer simulation of landing a jet fighter on a carrier deck; or explore an underwater world via virtual reality. There's also a marine *Exploratorium* for children. It's open daily; there's an admission charge.

En Route from Hampton Roads Follow Highway 44 (the Virginia Beach Expressway) east to Virginia Beach.

VIRGINIA BEACH With 29 miles of shoreline, this is one of the premier resorts on the East Coast. Summer vacationers and students on spring break flock to its boardwalk and wide beach, and downtown is a mass of hotels, restaurants, gift shops, and night spots. Its *Adam Thoroughgood House* (1636 Parish Rd.; phone: 804-622-1211, Ext. 238), ca. 1680, is purportedly the oldest brick home in the United States; it's open daily in summer and closed Sundays and Mondays in winter. At the *Virginia Marine Science Museum* (717 General Booth Blvd.; phone: 804-437-4949), visitors can touch live sea animals or create a hurricane. It's open daily year-round; there's an admission charge. For deep-sea fishing or whale watching, call *Virginia Beach Fishing Center* (phone: 804-422-5700).

BEST EN ROUTE

Expect to pay $120 or more per night for a double room at those hotels we've listed as expensive; $75 to $120 at places in the moderate category; and less than $75 at those rated inexpensive. Unless otherwise noted, hotels are open year-round and rooms have air conditioning, private baths, TV sets, and telephones. For each location, hotels are listed alphabetically by price category.

RICHMOND

Jefferson Dating from 1895, this grand establishment was modeled after a Spanish palace. There are 274 rooms; two restaurants, including the elegant *Lemaire,* offering fine French fare; and a handsome lobby bar. Local couples pose for wedding photos in front of the ornate lobby's sweeping stairway, said to have been the model for the one in *Gone With the Wind.* Franklin and Adams Sts. (phone: 788-8000; 800-424-8014). Expensive.

Linden Row Inn Set in a row of Greek Revival townhouses seven blocks from the *Virginia State Capitol,* this inn is the embodiment of Richmond charm. The Registered Historic Landmark has 70 rooms furnished with antiques, a lovely brick-walled courtyard, and a restaurant. First and Franklin Sts. (phone: 804-783-7000; 800-348-7424). Expensive to moderate.

WILLIAMSBURG

Kingsmill Resort A family-oriented luxury resort on the James River with 407 private villas, it offers a championship golf course, a marina, and an excellent restaurant. 1010 Kingsmill Rd. (phone: 804-253-1703; 800-832-5665; fax: 804-253-8264). Expensive.

Williamsburg Inn In the center of town, this 95-room inn offers genteel luxury in an 18th-century atmosphere, complete with candlelight dining. There's history outside the front door and a golf course outside the back. For reservations, contact Reservations Office, *Colonial Williamsburg Foundation,* PO Box 1776C, Williamsburg, VA 23187 (phone: 804-229-1000; 800-HISTORY for reservations; fax: 804-220-7729). Expensive.

NORFOLK

Omni Norfolk Adjacent to the *Waterside Marketplace* downtown, this 442-room property has water views, lounges, and an outdoor pool. Its *Riverwalk Café* is popular. 777 Waterside Dr. (phone: 804-622-6664; 800-THE-OMNI). Moderate.

NEWPORT NEWS

Omni Newport News Just 15 miles from Williamsburg, this 183-room member of the popular chain is one of the most luxurious properties in the area. There's a glassed-in pool, an exercise room, a sauna, an Italian restaurant, a bar, and a nightclub. 1000 Omni Way Blvd. (phone: 804-873-6664; 800-THE-OMNI; fax: 804-873-1732). Moderate.

VIRGINIA BEACH

Founders Inn Named in honor of America's first presidents—Washington, Adams, Jefferson, and Madison—this gracious hostelry is best known for its old-fashioned hospitality. The 240 guestrooms are located in three separate buildings featuring antiques and elegant period furnishings. Other amenities include a two-story health club, two pools, tennis and racquetball courts, and jogging trails. There's also a fine restaurant. 5641 Indian River Rd. (phone: 800-926-4466). Expensive.

Harpers Ferry and Monongahela National Forest, West Virginia

West Virginia really is the stuff of which country music is made—country roads, Blue Ridge Mountains, almost heaven. But it's much more than mountaintops and John Denver lyrics. The small towns built into these old hills are strongholds of America's history. This is where John Brown's ill-fated raid on Harpers Ferry took place, where one of the bloodiest and most crucial battles of the Civil War was fought, and where hundreds of mule-drawn barges navigated the Chesapeake and Ohio Canal (in Maryland), carrying coal to fuel the young nation. The towns are within a few hours' drive of each other through beautiful backcountry, including the 200-mile *Allegheny Trail* and the *Monongahela National Forest.*

The forest covers more than 900,000 acres in the heart of the Alleghenies, stretching southwest from near the Maryland border for 100 miles through the West Virginia backcountry, a region of rounded mountains and twisting valleys. Much of the *Monongahela* is a regrown forest; fires and indiscriminate logging practices stripped it of its original timber around the turn of the century, but the region is blanketed once again with deep forests inhabited by white-tailed deer, black bear, turkey, and other wildlife. The *Monongahela National Forest* now has 19 campgrounds, about 700 miles of streams with excellent trout and bass fishing and wild whitewater canoeing, and 600 miles of hiking trails. In season, there is hunting for bear, deer, grouse, cottontail rabbit, snowshoe hare, squirrel, and wild turkey. Ranger district headquarters are at Petersburg, Parsons, Bartow, Marlinton, Richwood, and White Sulphur Springs; for information, contact *Monongahela National Forest Headquarters* (200 Sycamore St., Elkins, WV 26241; phone: 304-636-1800). For information on other West Virginia State facilities, call 800-CALL-WVA.

Our route starts with three historic sites to visit near the juncture of Virginia, West Virginia, and Maryland, then heads northwest to the spa town of Berkeley Springs and south to *Lost River State Park,* the *Monongahela National Forest,* and *Wahoga State Park.*

CHARLES TOWN, West Virginia Charles Washington, brother of George, founded and designed this town in 1786. Here are numerous historic homes as well as the *Jefferson County Courthouse* (N. George and E. Washington Sts.), the site of the 1859 trial of John Brown, and the site of his gallows (at S. Samuel and Hunter Sts.). The *Jefferson County Museum* (N. Samuel and E. Washington Sts.; phone: 304-725-8628) has everything of John Brown's that is not moldering in the grave. It's open April through November; there's no admission charge.

En Route from Charles Town Backtrack on Route 340 east for 4 miles to Harpers Ferry.

HARPERS FERRY, West Virginia Though this lovely hillside town overlooking the confluence of the Potomac and Shenandoah rivers appears tranquil, it was the site of John Brown's raid on the federal arsenal in 1859 as part of his plan to arm a slave rebellion and to establish a free state in the Blue Ridge Mountains. The 21-man abolitionist force succeeded in capturing the arsenal, but it was then surrounded by the local militia, and Brown was captured by Colonel Robert E. Lee and hanged for treason and murder a month and a half later. A 30-minute walking tour along the brick streets of *Harpers Ferry National Historical Park* (Shenandoah St.; phone: 304-535-6223) links several restored homes, a gunmaking museum, the engine house where Brown was apprehended, a blacksmith shop, a confectionery, a tavern, and Jefferson Rock, which commands a fine view of the area's rivers and hills. The park is closed *Christmas* and *New Year's Day;* there's a parking fee. For more information on Brown's raid and the area's Civil War history, see *Civil War Battlesites* in DIVERSIONS.

En Route from Harpers Ferry Take Route 340 west for 2 miles, then head north on Route 230 and follow it to Shepherdstown. Go northeast on Route 480, crossing the Maryland state line, where the road becomes Route 34. Continue to Route 65 and head north to Sharpsburg.

SHARPSBURG, Maryland The headquarters of the *Chesapeake and Ohio Canal National Historical Park* is here (the park itself extends from Cumberland, Maryland, to Georgetown in Washington, DC, paralleling the Potomac along Rte. 65). The 185-mile canal was begun in 1828 to link Washington, DC, with Pittsburgh. It never reached its final destination: Construction was halted at Cumberland, Maryland, in 1850 because the railroad had become a more efficient means of transportation. Still among the longest and best preserved of the canals built during the early 1800s, it was used until 1924 to carry coal, crops, and lumber from the mountains to Georgetown. At its peak, some 500 mule-drawn barges navigated the waterway and were raised and lowered through its 75 locks. Some of the locks and aqueducts have been restored, and interesting old buildings line the banks of the canal, now run by the *National Park Service.* Trails and campsites are available for hikers and bicyclists.

The *Antietam National Battlefield and Cemetery Site* lies a mile north of Sharpsburg on Route 65. Here the Union forces stopped the first Confederate invasion of the North in one of the bloodiest battles of the war. Iron markers and battlefield maps describe the events. The visitors' center at the entrance (phone: 301-432-5124) houses a museum; musket and cannon demonstrations, historical talks, and bicycle tours are scheduled throughout the year. There's an admission charge. Also see *Civil War Battlesites* in DIVERSIONS.

En Route from Sharpsburg Backtrack to Sheperdstown via Routes 65, 34, and 480. Take Route 45 west to Martinsburg, then follow Route 9 west to Berkeley Springs.

BERKELEY SPRINGS, West Virginia For many years, this resort city was called Bath, after the English spa. George Washington made note of the mineral springs while surveying the region for Lord Fairfax, who donated the springs to Virginia in 1756; they have been public property ever since. Not wanting to mix with commoners, Fairfax bathed in a private hollow that's known as the *Fairfax Bathtub.* Today, however, just about anyone can bathe at the center of town in the *Berkeley Springs Park.* A state-run facility, it offers health baths, massage, warm springs, a swimming pool, and even a Roman bathhouse (phone: 304-258-3738; 800-447-8797). It's open year-round; admission is free except for Roman baths and massages.

Cacapon Park, 10 miles south of town (off Rte. 522), is a 6,155-acre park at the base of Cacapon Mountain with lodging and excellent facilities for golf, tennis, horseback riding, fishing, swimming, and boating. Panorama Point, about 10 miles west, offers a stirring view of Maryland, West Virginia, and Pennsylvania.

En Route from Berkeley Springs Take Route 9 south to Route 29, and continue south. At Slanesville, stop and see Ice Mountain, which has ice at its base even on the hottest days (it is honeycombed with cold underground passages that keep the ice frozen). Soon after Route 29 merges with Route 259, you'll reach Mathias and the entrance to *Lost River State Park.*

LOST RIVER STATE PARK, Mathias, West Virginia Once a vacation spot of the Lee family of Virginia, this park has 24 cabins and facilities for swimming, tennis, picnicking, and riding. One of the original cabins has been restored and turned into a museum (Rte. 2; phone: 304-897-5372), with furniture, clothing, tools, and other 19th-century artifacts on display. It's open *Memorial Day* through *Labor Day;* there's no admission charge.

En Route from Lost River State Park Head back north on Route 259 to Route 55 west. At Moorefield, take Route 220 south to Petersburg and the entrance to the 900,000-acre *Monongahela National Forest.*

MONONGAHELA NATIONAL FOREST, West Virginia A popular route through this vast forest follows Route 28 southwest to Bartow, paralleling the North Fork of the South Branch of the Potomac River. Seneca Rocks, towering 900 feet above the river, is a major landmark. Mountain climbers come to claw their way up the rugged face of this immense rock cliff. The *Forest Service* manages the *Seneca Rocks Visitor Center* (phone: 304-567-2827) and the large, modern *Seneca Shadows Campground.* Nearby is Spruce Knob, at 4,861 feet the highest peak in West Virginia. This area of the forest is being managed as a *National Recreation Area.* The 100,000 acres are open for hiking, camping, fishing, and hunting. There's whitewater canoeing for 15 miles along the headwaters of the Potomac (best sampled in the spring).

Route 28 continues south past *Seneca State Forest* to Huntersville. Along the way, just north of Green Bank, is the *National Radio Astronomy Observatory* (Rte. 28/92; phone: 304-456-2011), site of a huge radio telescope with which astronomers are recharting the heavens. Tours of the complex are given during the summer, and a film explains the work done at the observatory. The facility is open daily from mid-June through *Labor Day;* weekends only from *Memorial Day* to mid-June and in September and October. There's no admission charge. Just south of Green Bank at Cass, on Route 7, is the depot of a state-owned railroad with a steam locomotive that runs through the rugged mountains along an old logging track up to the summit of Bald Knob, the second-highest mountain in the state. The trip to the top of the mountain takes 4½ hours. A shorter trip also is available. The train operates from *Memorial Day* through *Labor Day;* there's an admission charge. Also nearby are the jointly operated ski resorts of *Snowshoe* and *Silver Creek* (off Rte. 219 between Marlinton and Huttonsville; phone: 304-572-1000), with more than 50 downhill slopes and trails and a 1,500-foot drop. (West Virginia's average altitude is the highest of any state east of the Mississippi, and ski resorts are cropping up to take advantage of it.)

From here, Route 39 leads to Marlinton and US 219 north. The 44-mile Highland Scenic Highway (Routes 55 and 150) loops from US 219, 7 miles north of Marlinton, to the *Cranberry Mountain Visitor Center* (WV 150; phone: 304-653-4826), and on to Richwood (WV 39-55). The visitors' center, which offers instructive displays and programs, is open daily from *Memorial Day* through *Labor Day;* it's closed in December and open weekends and occasional weekdays during the rest of the year. There's no admission charge. The byway includes several scenic overlooks and short hiking trails, and passes *Cranberry Glades Botanical Area* (a large outdoor botanical laboratory with an interpretive boardwalk) and *Falls of Hills Creek Scenic Area.* Both are open in summer; there's no admission charge.

En Route from Monongahela National Forest Head south on 219 at Mill Point, just south of Marlinton, for *Watoga State Park.*

WATOGA STATE PARK, West Virginia A state facility here offers 88 campsites, cabins, a restaurant, a swimming pool, picnicking, fishing, and hiking. For information and reservations, write HC 82, PO Box 252, Marlinton, WV 24954 (phone: 304-799-4087 or 304-799-7421; 800-CALL-WVA).

BEST EN ROUTE

For a list of inns and bed and breakfast establishments in Charles Town and Sheperdstown, call the *Jefferson County Visitors Bureau* (phone: 800-848-8687). Expect to pay $120 or more per night for a double room in those places we've listed as expensive; $75 to $120 in those listed as moderate; and under $75 in those rated inexpensive. Unless otherwise noted, hotels are open year-round, and all rooms have air conditioning, TV sets, and telephones. For each location, hotels are listed alphabetically by price category.

HARPER'S FERRY

Hilltop House Over a century old, this stone inn overlooks the village and the Potomac River from a hill. It offers simple, clean accomodations, with 73 rooms and a buffet restaurant. Not all rooms have TV sets. Ridge St. (phone: 304-535-2132; 800-338-8319). Inexpensive.

BERKELEY SPRINGS

Coolfont Resort This comfortable, unpretentious resort and conference center emphasizes fitness and relaxation. The 240 rooms are distributed among several separate chalets on 1,200 acres of land. It offers a lake, an indoor pool, a health spa, a dining room, weekend and week-long health programs, and mountain hiking. Not all rooms have TV sets or phones. Off Rte. 522 on Quarry Rd., 6 miles north of *Cacapon Lodge* (phone: 304-258-4500; 800-296-8768; fax: 304-258-5499). Moderate.

Country Inn A cozy, modern inn with 70 rooms and one of the nicest spas in the area, as well as a pleasant restaurant. Not all rooms have phones or private baths. Adjacent to the tiny *Berkeley Springs State Park,* on the main road through town (phone: 304-258-2210; 800-822-6630). Moderate.

Cacapon Lodge This state-run facility in *Cacapon State Park* near Berkeley Springs provides good standard accommodations and easy access to all the park activities. There are 49 rooms in the main lodge, 11 with shared baths in the inn, and 30 cabins. The cabins do not have telephones, TV sets, or air conditioning. Facilities include a dining room, an 18-hole golf course, tennis, a six-acre lake, paddleboats, and fishing. Eleven deluxe cabins and the lodge rooms are available year-round; the inn is open only weekends in September and is closed from the last week of October through April. Off Rte. 522 (phone: 304-258-1022; fax: 304-258-5323). Inexpensive.

MONONGAHELA NATIONAL FOREST

Greenbrier Originally a mineral spa, it has been a grand resort for more than 200 years. There are 700 rooms, golf, tennis, two Olympic-size pools, and plenty of other activities, as well as a restaurant. Also see *America's Best Resort Hotels* in DIVERSIONS. Station A, just outside the state forest and west of White Sulphur Springs on Rte. 60 (phone: 304-536-1110; 800-624-6070; fax: 304-536-7853). Expensive.

Midwest

The Lincoln Heritage Trail, Illinois, Indiana, and Kentucky

The *Lincoln Heritage Trail* blazes hundreds of miles along the folkloric roads of Illinois, Indiana, and Kentucky, Abraham Lincoln's home states. Here, his voice still echoes: eloquently in government chambers, softly in great Victorian mansions, and jokingly in the backwoods cabins of his close friends. Along the trail, memories of Mr. Lincoln are recollected vividly through reenactments of scenes from America's past and reconstructions of stately buildings, quaint homesteads, and entire 19th-century towns.

The following route traces Lincoln's footsteps through frontier America, covering much of the ground included in the *Heritage Trail.* Starting at the heart of Lincoln country in Springfield, Illinois, 200 miles southwest of Chicago, it briefly jogs northeast and northwest before snaking through southeast Illinois, across southern Indiana, and into north-central Kentucky.

SPRINGFIELD, Illinois There's more to see and hear about Abraham Lincoln here than anywhere else in the US. Start with Lincoln's own residence—the only house he ever owned—at Eighth and Jackson Streets, where he lived from May 1844 until he became president in 1861. One of a row of handsome period homes, it has been repainted in its original colors of Quaker brown and apple green and furnished with some Lincoln family possessions. Informative tour guides minutely detail Lincoln's home life. There's no admission charge. (413 S. Seventh St.; phone: 217-492-4150).

The *Old State Capitol* (phone: 217-785-7961) on the town square, where Lincoln gave his famous "House Divided" speech, has been rebuilt, and the stunning second-floor legislative chamber looks as if a session had just adjourned. The *Illinois State Historical Library* is on the lower level; donation suggested. Across the street are the *Lincoln-Herndon Law Offices* (phone: 217-785-7289; admission charge), which have been restored to the way they were when Lincoln worked here with his law partner, William Herndon, from 1843 to 1861. Guided tours are given of the law offices.

A 117-foot granite obelisk marks the *Lincoln Tomb* site in *Oak Ridge Cemetery* (off N. Grand Ave. on the north end of town). The tomb's rotunda contains a single statue of Lincoln and a few bronze plaques; at the rear of the memorial, a monument to Lincoln is enclosed in a semicircular chamber, flanked by flags. On the opposite wall are the crypts of Mary Todd Lincoln and three of the couple's four sons. Closed *Thanksgiving, Christmas,* and *New Year's Day.*

Although it has nothing to do with Lincoln, the *Dana-Thomas House State Historic Site* (310 E. Lawrence Ave.; phone: 217-782-6776) is well worth seeing, as it is one of the best-preserved of architect Frank Lloyd Wright's early Prairie-style houses in the US. The house was built between 1902 and 1904, and contains a virtually complete collection of original decorative arts material, including over 100 pieces of furniture. Guided tours are given. It's closed Mondays and Tuesdays; there's an admission charge.

For information and assistance in planning a visit to the Springfield area, contact the *Springfield Convention and Visitors Bureau* (109 N. Seventh St., Springfield, IL 62701 (phone: 1-800-545-7300).

En Route from Springfield Head north for 30 miles on I-55 to exit 123 and the town of Lincoln.

LINCOLN, Illinois The *Lincoln College Museum* (300 Keokut St.; phone: 217-732-3155, ex. 295) houses an impressive array of Lincoln's memorabilia ranging from books to furniture. At the historic *Postville Courthouse* (914 5th St.; phone: 217-732-8930), the walls are covered with maps and documents from the days when Lincoln traveled as a lawyer of the Eighth Judicial Circuit. Hours for both attractions vary, so call ahead.

En Route from Lincoln Head southeast 11 miles on Highway 121 to Mt. Pulaski.

MT. PULASKI, Illinois Unlike *Postville Courthouse,* which is a reproduction of the original 1840 structure Lincoln visited, the *Mt. Pulaski Courthouse* is the real thing. It's one of only two surviving courthouses in Illinois where Lincoln practiced law (the second is in Decatur, see below). Built in 1848, today it is restored and furnished to look as it did during the 1850s. Closed Sundays, Mondays, and major holidays.

En Route from Mt. Pulaski Take the interstate access road (this road is not numbered; ask for directions from the courthouse) 10 miles to Ekhart to I-55. Then proceed on I-55 south and exit at Williamsville, following signs to *Lincoln's New Salem State Historical Site,* near Petersburg, about 25 miles from Ekhart.

LINCOLN'S NEW SALEM STATE HISTORIC SITE, Illinois Another site on the *Heritage Trail* is *Lincoln's New Salem State Historic Site* (phone: 217-632-4000). The town where Lincoln lived in the 1830s, it is reconstructed to look as it did then. Mammoth oxen pull covered wagons along dirt roads lined with tiny log cabins, and a visit to the cabins finds women in period costumes kneading dough, cooking over flaming hearths, and spinning wool. Open daily. Donations are suggested. Also see *Restored Towns and Reconstructed Villages* in DIVERSIONS.

In Lincoln's time, the steamboat *Talisman* sailed up and down the Sangamon River. Excursions aboard a re-created *Talisman* depart from *Lincoln's New Salem* Tuesdays through Sundays from May through August and weekends in September and October. For details contact *Sangamon Packet Company* (PO Box 207, Petersburg, IL 62675; phone: 217-632-2219). Also during the summer, there's outdoor drama, including plays relating to Lincoln. Performances are given Thursdays through Saturdays from mid-June to mid-August. For more information contact *Lincoln's New Salem* (phone: 217-632-4000).

For additional information on Lincoln's New Salem, contact the *Springfield Convention and Visitors Bureau* (see *Springfield,* above).

En Route from Lincoln's New Salem Return to Springfield via Highway 97, then head east on I-72 about 39 miles to Decatur.

DECATUR, Illinois The *Macon County Historical Society Museum* (5580 North Fork Rd.; phone: 217-422-4919) here houses several historic buildings, including the first Macon County courthouse, where Lincoln practiced law. Closed Mondays; there is an admission charge. At the museum and elsewhere in town are several Lincoln statues. For information, contact the *Decatur Convention and Visitors Bureau* (phone: 800-252-3376).

En Route from Decatur Take Highway 121 south to Clarksville and State Highway 1. Follow Highway 1 south to Lawrenceville, then take US Highway 50 east to Vincennes, about 110 miles from *Lincoln's New Salem Historic Site.*

VINCENNES, Indiana The original capital of Indiana, Vincennes is called "the Birthplace of the West." Visit the *George Rogers Clark Memorial and Visitors Center* (401 S. Second St.; phone: 812-882-1776), an awesome structure that contains several massive murals by Ezra Winter. Headsets, distributed at the entrance, explain each mural and its relevance to American history. It's closed *Thanksgiving, Christmas,* and *New Year's Day.*

En Route from Vincennes Head 54 miles south on Highway 41 to Evansville. If you want to take a side trip to *Historic New Harmony,* head west for about 25 miles on Highway 66. Otherwise, take Highway 66 east for 26 miles, then head 25 miles north on US 231 to Lincoln City (see below).

HISTORIC NEW HARMONY, Indiana Originally a tract of wilderness on the banks of the Wabash, this village grew from settlements of religious and utopian communal sects. First came the Rappites (or Harmonists) in 1814, led by Father George Rapp; later came the Owenites, a group of experimenting intellectuals looking to improve the quality of life. Today, many Harmonist buildings survive and are open year-round.

Begin at the visitors' center in the *Atheneum* at the corner of North and Arthur Streets. Tickets to many of the historic buildings may be purchased there. There's no admission charge to the *Roofless Church* (North St.) or the *Opera House* (Church St.). Wander through the "labyrinth" on Main Street, a reconstruction of the Harmonist sect's maze symbolizing the twisting road of life that leads to perfect harmony. The *Atheneum* is open year-round; other historic sites are closed during January and February. For information contact *Historic New Harmony,* New Harmony, IN 47631 (phone: 812-682-4474). Also see *Utopias and Religious Settlements* in DIVERSIONS.

En Route from New Harmony Return to Evansville and take Highway 66 east to US 231, then head north to Lincoln City, about 50 miles from New Harmony.

LINCOLN CITY, Indiana The *Heritage Trail* continues at the *Lincoln Boyhood National Memorial* (Rte. 162, off US 231; phone: 812-937-4541) and *Lincoln State Park* (phone: 812-937-4710). The memorial features a museum, a working pioneer farm on the site of the farm Lincoln's father owned from 1816 to 1830, and his mother's burial place. A visitors' center is open year-round; the farm operates from April through October; there is an admission charge. The state park has many recreational facilities, and both areas have self-guided history and nature trails. *Young Abe Lincoln,* an outdoor drama about Lincoln's boyhood years, is presented mid-June through August at the 1,500-seat *Lincoln State Park Amphitheater.*

En Route from Lincoln City Get on I-64 just north of Lincoln City and head east. At exit 92, take a side trip to the *Wyandotte Cave* near Leavenworth.

WYANDOTTE CAVE, Indiana One of the largest cave complexes in North America, *Wyandotte Cave* (Rte. 62; phone: 812-738-2782) offers six guided tours daily; there are spelunking tours on weekends, by reservation only. The cave is closed Mondays from *Labor Day* through *Memorial Day* and on winter holidays; there is an admission charge.

En Route from Wyandotte Cave Return to I-64 and head east toward Jeffersonville, which is just across the river from Louisville and about 60 miles from Lincoln. Continue and cross the Ohio River on I-65 south into Louisville.

LOUISVILLE, Kentucky For a complete report on the city and its attractions, see *Louisville* in THE CITIES.

En Route from Louisville Continue on I-65 to Highway 61 and Hodgenville, about 50 miles south.

HODGENVILLE, Kentucky Here is the *Abraham Lincoln Birthplace and National Historic Site* (2995 Lincoln Farm Rd., Hodgenville; phone: 502-358-3874), where Abe Lincoln's life began in a tiny cabin nestled among the bluish-green "knob" hills of north-central Kentucky. A section of this national park actually is *Sinking Springs Farm,* where Lincoln was born in 1809. An elaborate memorial building has been erected around a reproduction of the original family cabin, which is closed *Thanksgiving* and *Christmas.*

En Route from Hodgenville Take Highway 61 about 10 miles north to Elizabethtown, then head east on the Bluegrass Parkway for about 25 miles for a pleasant stop at Bardstown.

BARDSTOWN, Kentucky Here is the site of the estate better known as "My Old Kentucky Home" (E. Stephen Foster Ave.; phone: 502-348-3502). Tour the grounds and the mansion that supposedly inspired Stephen Foster to write the famous song. Dine at the *Old Talbott Tavern* (107 W. Stephen Foster Ave.; phone: 502-348-3494), where you can enjoy your meal in a room where Lincoln and Jesse James once sat. Also see *Outdoor Dramas* in DIVERSIONS.

En Route from Bardstown Take US 150 south to Perryville, where you can tour the Civil War battlefield at *Perryville Battlefield State Historic Park* (2 miles north of Hwy. 150 at Hwy. 192; phone: 800-85-BOONE). It's closed November through March; there's no admission charge except to a museum in the park. From Perryville, take US 68 north to Harrodsburg, 43 miles from Bardstown.

HARRODSBURG, Kentucky Here is *Old Fort Harrod State Site* (phone: 606-734-3314), a reproduction of the fort, built circa 1774, that was the first permanent pioneer settlement west of the Alleghenies. In the fort is a museum of pioneer artifacts. The *Lincoln Marriage Temple,* the cabin where Abraham Lincoln's parents were married, is also on the grounds. The historical drama *The New Legend of Daniel Boone* is performed in the amphitheater in summer (for information about performances contact PO Box 365, Harrodsburg, KY 40330; phone: 606-734-3346; also see *Outdoor Dramas* in DIVERSIONS). The state park is closed *Thanksgiving, Christmas week,* and Mondays in January; the museum and the temple are closed December through February.

En Route from Harrodsburg Take Highway 68 east to Pleasant Hill, 7 miles away.

PLEASANT HILL, Kentucky In the mid-1800s, this was a flourishing community of the United Society of Believers in Christ's Second Appearing, who were also known as "Shakers" because of their ecstatic movements during worship. Today, 2,700 acres have been preserved, along with 30 buildings, making this the largest restored Shaker community in the country. Village tours are given year-round. Photogenic historic buildings, crafts demonstrations, sleigh rides in winter, and cruises on the Kentucky River from April through October are among the attractions (phone: 606-734-5411). There also are overnight accommodations and a fine restaurant (see *Best en Route*). Also see *Utopias and Religious Settlements* in DIVERSIONS.

En Route from Pleasant Hill Follow US 68 about 25 miles east to Lexington. This extremely scenic drive takes you past the breathtaking limestone cliffs known as the Palisades along the Kentucky River and past classic bluegrass horse farms.

LEXINGTON, Kentucky Off Route 68 (which becomes Broadway) on West Main Street is Mary Todd Lincoln's childhood home (578 W. Main St.; phone

606-233-9999). This grand house, with its antiques, exquisitely detailed carpets, and polished wooden floors, reflects the troubled First Lady's aristocratic background, so different from her husband's humble beginnings. The house is closed Sundays, Mondays, and from mid-December through mid-March. There's an admission charge.

BEST EN ROUTE

Expect to pay more than $80 per night for a double room in those places listed as expensive, $40 to $80 in those rated moderate, and less than $40 at those listed as inexpensive. Unless otherwise indicated hotels are open year-round and rooms have air conditioning, private baths, TV sets, and telephones.

NEW HARMONY

New Harmony Inn The 90 rooms here all have simple wood furnishings. There's a quiet atmosphere, and the *Red Geranium* next door serves excellent regional specialties and homemade baked good. Also see *America's Special Havens* in DIVERSIONS. 508 N. Main (phone: 812-682-4491). Moderate.

HARRODSBURG

Beaumont Inn The main building of this lovely old inn, built in 1845, was once a girls' school. There are 33 guestrooms, an outdoor pool, tennis courts, shuffleboard, and a gameroom. Three country-style full-course meals a day are served in the dining room; breakfast is for guests only. Closed from mid-December through February. 638 Beaumont Dr. (phone: 606-734-3381; 800-352-3992 for reservations). Expensive.

PLEASANT HILL

Shaker Village This is the only lodging in America where you can sleep in original 19th-century Shaker buildings. The 80 guestrooms are furnished with period reproductions, and there is an excellent dining room that serves Shaker lemon pie and other regional specialties. Closed *Christmas Eve* and *Christmas.* 3501 Lexington Rd. (phone: 606-734-5411). Expensive to moderate.

St. Croix River, Minnesota and Wisconsin

Many people say the territory around the St. Croix River is haunted by spirits of the Indians who lived here for many generations. Some even say that shadowy birchbark canoes still travel through the tributaries and creeks feeding into the St. Croix, and that the rustle of paddles breaking water can be heard in the silence.

More prosaic travelers also are enchanted by the St. Croix, a 164-mile river separating Minnesota and Wisconsin. It's surprising to find such relatively unspoiled country close to a big city: The lower St. Croix, which is dotted with attractive villages, is just 25 miles northeast of St. Paul on Route 36. Wilder yet is the untamed upper St. Croix, which hasn't changed much from Indian times. In fact, the Ojibwa (or Chippewa), descendants of the Algonquin, still harvest wild rice from the small inlets lacing the surrounding marshes.

But the placid waters bear a history of conflict. The Dakota Indians lived here first, treasuring the river for its fish, the land for its wild rice, and the forest for its game. (Otter, beaver, raccoon, fox, and deer still inhabit these woods.) After more than 350 years of living here, the Dakota were driven out by the Ojibwa, who had moved in from the East after unsuccessfully trying to defend their land from Iroquois attack. While the Ojibwa and Dakota battled, the French explorers and traders arrived. The French, and the British settlers who followed on their heels, called the Dakota by a derogatory Ojibwa name, Sioux. After the Ojibwa victory, the Dakota fled south and west, eventually to be vanquished by the white settlers.

The French used the St. Croix as a fur connection, establishing many trading posts and developing the waterway into a flourishing commercial route. Beaver pelts were shipped to Canada and from there to Europe, where they found their way to the clothiers of the fashionable.

The British were just as avid for control of this resource-rich territory. In 1763, when the French and Indian wars were finally over, the Union Jack flew from the masts and flagpoles along the St. Croix. The Hudson Bay Company and other trading enterprises of the period conducted a brisk business until the War of 1812, when the US imposed a ban on foreign trading activity.

Then the loggers arrived. Thousands of men felled hundreds of thousands—perhaps even millions—of trees, mostly white pine, and the river was used to float logs. The logging industry died out when there were no longer enough trees to support it. Since then, the region has been marked for conservation.

For general information on the St. Croix River area, contact *St. Croix National Scenic Riverway/National Park Service* (401 Hamilton St., St. Croix Falls, WI 54024; phone: 715-483-3284).

Our route starts in Minneapolis–St. Paul, then follows the river north.

MINNEAPOLIS–ST. PAUL, Minnesota For a complete report on the Twin Cities and their attractions, see *Minneapolis–St. Paul* in THE CITIES.

En Route from St. Paul Take I-94 east to State Highway 95 north to Afton, about 20 miles away on the Mississippi River.

AFTON, Minnesota Though only a few blocks long, this hamlet features a toy shop, antiques stores, boutiques, and a deli. Named after the river Afton (made famous by poet Robbie Burns), it was founded during the 1850s. About 4 miles south of town is *Afton Alps* (phone: 612-436-5245) for downhill skiing and *Afton State Park* (phone: 612-436-5391) for cross-country skiing. Houseboats can be rented from *Afton Cruise Lines* (3291 S. St. Croix Trail, Afton, MN 55001; phone: 612-436-8883), which also offers Sunday brunch cruises.

En Route from Afton Head north for about 10 miles on State Highway 95 to Stillwater.

STILLWATER, Minnesota The birthplace of Minnesota, this riverfront town is the kind of place where they consider you a newcomer unless at least one generation of your family is in the town cemetery. But it's still a great place for visitors—full of charming old buildings, fine antiques shops and other emporiums, and cafés. At the Stillwater Levee in *Lowell Park*, you can buy tickets for a lunch or dinner ride on a reproduction paddlewheel boat, either the 110-passenger *Andiamo* or the 150-passenger *Andiamo Showboat* (phone: 612-430-1234; 800-950-2028). There are daily rides, with Dixieland bands on weekends. For walking tours of the Victorian homes and other historic sites in Stillwater, call *Valley Tours* (phone: 612-439-6110). *Valley* also arranges motor coach tours of the upper and lower St. Croix for groups of 15 or more. Or you may combine dinner and a tour on the elegant *Minnesota Zephyr* (phone: 612-430-3000) dining train, which departs from downtown Stillwater for a three-and-a-quarter-hour ride through the scenic St. Croix River Valley. Reservations are necessary.

If you're visiting in May, be sure to take in the *Rivertown Arts Festival,* at which artists from all across the US display their works; it's held on the third weekend in May in *Lowell Park* on the banks of the St. Croix. For information on the logrolling contests, fireworks, and the pageantry of Stillwater's annual *Lumberjack Days* in July, contact the *Stillwater Area Chamber of Commerce* (323 S. Main, Stillwater, MN 55082; phone: 612-439-7700).

En Route from Stillwater Ten miles north on State Highway 95 is Marine–on–St. Croix.

MARINE–ON–ST. CROIX, Minnesota At one time a dynamic lumberjack town, Marine–on–St. Croix has lost much of that rip-roaring, free-wheeling atmosphere. Stop at *William O'Brien State Park* (phone: 612-433-0500), overlooking the river on the north side of town, to hike, camp, picnic, or bird watch—and muse about what the old days must have been like.

En Route from Marine–on–St. Croix Continue north on State Highway 95 to the junction of US Highway 8 and head east to Taylors Falls and St. Croix Falls, two towns that sit across the river from each other about 28 miles north of Stillwater.

TAYLORS FALLS, Minnesota, and ST. CROIX FALLS, Wisconsin These two towns sit on the dividing line between the upper and lower St. Croix. The picturesque, tranquil southern stretch yields to swifter waters here, tempting canoe enthusiasts with occasional spots of mostly moderate whitewater in a great gorge known as the Dalles. The land is relatively unsettled from this point north, which makes it ideal for back-to-the-woods types. For a list of outfitters and other information, contact the *State of Wisconsin Department of Development* (PO Box 7606, Madison, WI 53707; phone: 608-266-2161; 800-432-TRIP).

Those unwilling to tackle the frothy, churning waters of the northern St. Croix in a canoe might consider a paddle wheel excursion on the Dalles as a safer alternative. *Taylors Falls Scenic Boat Tours* (PO Box 225, Taylors Falls, MN 55084; phone: 612-465-6315) runs trips daily from May through October on the *Taylors Falls Queen* and the 250-passenger *Taylors Falls Princess,* both authentic paddle wheelers. The excursions pass geological formations while guides explain what each is and how it was formed. Beyond the 1½-mile Dalles rapids at Taylors Falls—which should only be handled by experts—most of the northern St. Croix is fairly placid. For information about a houseboat vacation on the St. Croix, write to *Great River Houseboats* (1009 E. Main, PO Box 106, Wabasha, MN 55981; phone: 612-565-3376). For information about canoe routes on the St. Croix River and throughout Minnesota, contact the *Minnesota Office of Tourism* (100 Metro Sq., 121 Seventh Pl. E., St. Paul, MN 55101-2112; phone: 612-296-5029; 800-657-3700 from Minnesota).

En Route from Taylors Falls and St. Croix Falls Those who enjoy looking at the great outdoors but don't care to spend the night may head back to Minneapolis–St. Paul, which is about 40 miles away. To get there, take Route 8 west to I-35 south.

BEST EN ROUTE

Expect to pay $150 or more per night for a double room in hotels listed as very expensive, $100 to $150 in those rated expensive, and $60 to $100 in those listed as moderate. Unless otherwise noted, hotels are open year-round and rooms have air conditioning, private baths, TV sets, and telephones.

AFTON

Afton House Inn Some of this inn's 15 rooms have Jacuzzis, fireplaces, or balconies with river views; all have an antique decor. The restaurant features tableside cooking. 3221 St. Croix Trail (phone: 612-436-8883). Expensive to moderate.

STILLWATER

Lowell Inn This red brick colonial-style country inn is known as the "Mount Vernon of the West," because of its resemblance to George Washington's Virginia home. Run by members of the same family for more than 50 years, it has 21 guestrooms; some have Jacuzzis and some have circular French provincial showers, but not all have TV sets. There are three dining rooms, all serving American cuisine. Weekend rates are considerably higher but include dinner, breakfast, and complimentary wine in the room. 102 N. Second St. (phone: 612-439-1100). Very expensive to expensive.

Voyageurs National Park and Boundary Waters Canoe Area, Minnesota

Centuries before there were roads in North America, the Indians traveled a network of lakes, streams, and connecting portage trails that stretched from the Rocky Mountains to the St. Lawrence River. In the heyday of the great fur trade, French Canadian voyageurs plied this natural highway, paddling and portaging huge quantities of furs east to Montreal, and great numbers of soldiers, explorers, and missionaries west to the frontier. The last of the voyageurs disappeared in the 1830s, but *Voyageurs National Park* and the *Boundary Waters Canoe Area (BWCA)* in northern Minnesota offer a taste of what it was like on the old voyageur highway, when the wilderness stretched as far as the eye could see.

Voyageurs National Park and the *BWCA* are part of the oldest landmass in the world. Glaciers shaped this land, scooping out its lake basins, scoring its surface with an intricate maze of waterways, and polishing its ancient boulders smooth. Except for an occasional beach or cliff, a canopy of trees—spruce, pine, fir, balsam, aspen, and birch—covers the land.

Voyageurs National Park, established in 1975, extends almost 50 miles along Minnesota's northeast border. Numerous streams and 30 lakes—ranging in size from Rainy Lake, 35 miles long, to Quarterline Lake, about 350 yards across—make up a third of the park's 219,000 acres. At the heart of the park lies the wild and scenic Kabetogama Peninsula. There is hiking, fishing, and boating here, and accommodations that range from tent sites accessible only by water to fine lakeside resorts. As in the days of the voyageurs, wild rice grows in the shallow waters of the park, and deer, moose, wolves, beaver, and bear inhabit its deep woods. No fees are charged for using the park and no permits are required. While it is possible to drive to the edge of this 219,000-acre park, no cars are allowed inside. Access to most of the forests, bogs, and lakes is almost entirely by motorboat, float plane, or canoe. Motorboats are the park's most popular means of transportation; there are no restrictions on their use.

Just east of *Voyageurs National Park* lies the vast *Boundary Waters Canoe Area,* a million acres of Minnesota's *Superior National Forest,* most of which have been reserved for canoeists. The *BWCA* stretches nearly 100 miles along the border between Minnesota and Ontario's million-acre *Quetico Provincial Park,* another protected canoeing area. With its myriad lakes interconnected by innumerable streams and portage trails and its access to *Quetico*'s waters, the *BWCA* offers a seemingly infinite number of route possibilities. Motorboats and cars are allowed only in certain parts of this canoeist's paradise, and even the air space is restricted. Reservations for entry permits into the *BWCA* are strongly recommended, due to increased demand. These permits, required for overnight trips in the *Boundary Waters* area, are available for a small fee from district rangers, some canoe outfitters, and some resorts that have outfitting operations. Outfitters in Ely and Grand Marais can supply everything needed for a canoe trip, including guides, food, and the canoe itself. Maps of all major canoeing trails in Minnesota and *Quetico Provincial Park* in Ontario are sold at *W. A. Fisher Co.* (123-25 Chestnut St., or PO Box 1107, Virginia, MN 55792; phone: 218-741-9544).

While you're in the neighborhood, you may want to visit *Superior National Forest,* where the voyageurs used to have their central trading post, and Michigan's *Isle Royale National Park.* But remember: The broad expanse of trackless wilderness that allows you to lose yourself in nature could spell trouble if you actually got lost. Check in with a ranger upon entering and leaving any of the four parks. And if you're driving, be sure to fill your gas tank and pack emergency flares, a spare tire, and blankets before setting out.

En Route from Duluth Take US 53 north to International Falls, then follow route 11 east to the park. You may also enter the park from the Crane Lake, Ash River, or Kabetogama Lake resort areas east of US 53. You can't travel by car within the park, so rent a boat or float plane at any of the surrounding resorts. In the winter, only ice roads, snowmobiles, and skis provide access.

VOYAGEURS NATIONAL PARK, International Falls, Minnesota *Voyageurs* is unique to the national park system in that it allows visitors to motorboat and camp at primitive campsites scattered throughout the park. More than 125 primitive, boat-in island campsites await, as do two wilderness trails that offer access to inland lakes. At the east end of Rainy Lake is the well-preserved *Kettle Falls* hotel (see *Best en Route*). Because of a quirk in the boundary line here, you can stand at Kettle Falls on the Minnesota side and look *south* to Canada.

When Rainy Lake freezes to more than 18 inches thick, the park plows a 7-mile road across it, allowing visitors to explore the lake by car from the intersection of US Highways 71 and 53, State Highways 332 and 11, and Canadian Highway 11. In winter, snowmobiling, cross-country skiing, and ice fishing are the park's main activities. Year-round, the waters of Lakes Rainy, Namakan, Sand Point, and Kabetogama are known for their walleye, northern pike, and smallmouth bass. In the smaller lakes and streams are lake trout, and Shoepack Lake on Kabetogama Peninsula has the famed muskellunge. A 75,000-acre, roadless wilderness, the Kabetogama Peninsula also is home to timber wolves, moose, bear, and numerous other animals, including a large beaver population.

You may canoe in the park, but pay attention to the weather: Fast-rising storms can generate dangerous waves on the larger lakes. Experienced canoeists use islands for shelter from the winds and avoid crossing the largest open stretches of water. Maps are available and the services of a guide can be arranged at local resorts; canoes and supplies can be obtained from outfitters at a number of locations.

Local businesses also will arrange a variety of other activities, from water skiing to backcountry fishing via float plane. For information on naturalist-guided activities, camping, and recreational facilities in and adjacent to the park contact Superintendent, *Voyageurs National Park* (3131 Highway 53, International Falls, MN 56649; phone: 218-283-9821).

En Route from Voyageurs National Park By canoe, you can enter the *BWCA,* which is directly southeast of *Voyageurs,* through the eastern end of Rainy Lake. Other main gateways are through Ely, Minnesota, and through Grand Marais on the *Gunflint Trail.* Outfitters can provide maps to the area, or a guide can be hired.

BOUNDARY WATERS CANOE AREA, Ely or Grand Marais, Minnesota By paddle and portage, it is possible to follow the Canada-US border from Rainy Lake to the western end of *BWCA* and beyond to Grand Portage, on the shores of Lake Superior. This 275-mile route retraces the final leg of the 2,000-mile journey made annually by the northwestern voyageurs, who transported furs from the northwest trading posts in the Rockies to the central depot in Grand Portage. Here, Montrealers, who paddled across the Great Lakes to meet the voyageurs, collected the furs to be taken east. The voyageurs used to paddle 18 hours a day, but visitors looking for a less grueling trip may rent houseboats from *Minnesota Voyageur Houseboats* (10326 Ash River Trail, Orr, MN 55771; phone: 218-374-3571) or *Voyagaire Houseboats* (Gold Coast Rd., Crane Lake, MN 55725; phone: 218-993-2333).

Like *Voyageurs,* the *BWCA* doesn't offer many whitewater thrills. (The few rapids are generally too rough to navigate and canoeists have to take a portage trail around them.) What it does offer is the chance to canoe in solitude: Those who choose one of the less-traveled routes that require longer portages may find that they have almost the whole route to themselves. The area's peak months are July and August, but the prime canoeing season runs from May through September. (Unfortunately, May and June also are prime months for mosquitoes and blackflies.) Dogsled trips are available in the winter, including a Winter Wolf Odyssey that features winter camping, snowshoeing, and tracking wild wolves by air. For information on canoe routes, write to *Superior National Forest Boundary Waters Reservations, Forest Service, US Dept. of Agriculture* (PO Box 338, Duluth, MN 55801; phone: 218-720-5324). For brochures and listings of adventure trips, contact the *Minnesota Office of Tourism* (100 Metro Sq., 121 Seventh Pl. E., St. Paul, MN 55101-2112; phone: 800-657-3700).

En Route from Boundary Waters Canoe Area *Superior National Forest* is connected to the eastern edge of the *Boundary Waters Canoe Area* by several lakes, including Farm, Burnside, Fourtown, and Snake Lakes. To reach *Superior* by car, head north from Duluth on Highway 61.

SUPERIOR NATIONAL FOREST, Ely, Minnesota Here you can follow up a canoeing adventure with something that requires a little less exertion, like a scenic drive on *Gunflint Trail* or *Sawbill Trail* (off Highway 61 in Tofte). Or you can get around by boat; wherever you travel in this huge and magnificent wilderness preserve, you won't be far from one of its 2,000 lakes. In the forest is Grand Portage, the last town in Minnesota before the Canadian border. Also here, on the Pigeon River just south of Canada, is the *Grand Portage National Monument,* where historical plaques mark the site of the central trading depot of the voyageurs. There are a few lodges around Vermilion Lake, but most people who stay here overnight camp out. For information on campgrounds, hiking trails, and wildlife, contact *Superior National Forest* (phone: 218-720-5324).

En Route from Superior National Forest From Grand Portage you can take a ferry (phone: 715-392-2100) to Michigan's remote *Isle Royale National Park.* Ferry reservations must be made in advance.

ISLE ROYALE NATIONAL PARK, near Houghton, Michigan, in Lake Superior With some 166 miles of trails, this 571,790-acre park on the largest island in Lake Superior is one of the best places for hiking in the US—and certainly in the Midwest. You can also go boating, or fish in inland waters and Lake Superior for trout, northern pike, or perch. There is no lodging in *Isle Royale,* but campsites are available; no advance reservations can be made. The park is closed from November through mid-April. Information: *Isle Royale National Park* (800 East Lakeshore Dr., Houghton, MI 49931; phone: 906-482-0984).

BEST EN ROUTE

The area surrounding *Voyageurs National Park* abounds with fishing camps, lodges, and resorts (the park service will provide lists of local accommodations), but *Kettle Falls* (below) is the only lodge within park boundaries. For reservations in the *Boundary Waters Canoe Area,* contact *Boundary Waters Canoe Area,* PO Box 338, Duluth, MN 55801 (phone: 218-720-5324; 800-745-3399); reservations are taken by phone only from February 1 through September. Expect to pay $100 or more per night for a double room or cabin in those places listed below as expensive, $70 to $100 in those rated moderate, and less than $70 in those listed as inexpensive.

INTERNATIONAL FALLS

Island View Lodge The central lodge has nine rooms, a restaurant, and a bar. There are also 12 cabins, all but two of them lakeside. Open year-round. Twelve miles east of town on Rte. 8 (phone: 218-286-3511). Moderate to inexpensive.

Thunderbird Lodge This 15-room lodge has tennis courts, a restaurant, and a bar. There are also 10 cabins. Open year-round. Ten miles east of town on Highway 11 E. (phone: 218-286-3151). Moderate to inexpensive.

VOYAGEURS NATIONAL PARK

Kettle Falls Long a favorite of fisherfolk, this hotel, built in 1913, recalls the days when only trappers, traders, fishermen, and lumberjacks passed through these parts. On the east end of Rainy Lake and the northwest end of Lake Namaken, which stretch along the US-Canada border, it's accessible only by boat, plane, and snowmobile. There are 12 rooms in the hotel; in the summer, 10 more are available in villas about 1/4 mile away. It's pricey, but rooms in the villas have private baths and access to kitchens, and there's a restaurant in the hotel. Hotel room rates include breakfast and dinner. Open from mid-May through September and from December 31 to the end of March. *Ash River Trail* (phone: 218-374-4452; 800-322-0886). Expensive.

West

Denali National Park and Preserve, Alaska

With the passage of the Alaska Lands Bill in 1980, this park's name was changed from *Mt. McKinley National Park* to *Denali National Park and Preserve.* Denali, an Athapaskan Indian word meaning "High One," refers, of course, to the commanding peak, Mt. McKinley.

Mt. McKinley is North America's giant. Nothing on the continent is higher, and at 20,320 feet, Mt. McKinley approaches—admittedly just barely—Himalayan altitudes. Just a couple of hundred miles from the Arctic Circle, Mt. McKinley is the heart and soul of surrounding *Denali National Park and Preserve,* about six million acres of austere, wild tundra country that is one of the greatest natural wonders in the US.

McKinley actually is two peaks, its double summits separated by 2 miles of glacial ridge. It is an imposing sight: North Peak rises 19,470 feet, South Peak, 20,320. No matter how many pictures you see or how many articles you read, nothing quite prepares you for it. Be forewarned, however, that Mt. McKinley makes its own weather and can be cloud-hidden during as much as 65% of the summer.

Climbers have been on the South Peak since the early 1900s when "sourdoughs" (gold prospectors with some free time) decided to get to the top to see what the country looked like from up there. But the last 7,000 feet are covered by sheer ice and snow, which make for very difficult climbing. Parties interested in scaling McKinley or Mt. Foraker, which is farther west, must register with the *National Park Service* first. Because of the difficulty—and a fatality rate of 1 in 200—only experienced, healthy climbers with tested skill and proper equipment should consider the challenge. The *Park Service* is considering major changes in its management of mountaineering on Mt. McKinley and Mt. Foraker; for further information contact the *Talkeetna Ranger Station* (PO Box 588, Talkeetna, AK 99676; phone: 907-733-2231).

Only about 600,000 people visit *Denali National Park* each year. There is one navigable road through the park; most of it is closed to private traffic, and the rest is limited to park shuttles and tour buses. The park is open year-round, but its access road is closed from October until late May due to snow.

Mt. McKinley is just one of the attractions of this huge, isolated world. The park was set aside in 1917 for the protection of wildlife: caribou, grizzly bear, surefooted Dall sheep, wolf, and a huge variety of smaller, furred, warm-blooded beasts. One of the area's surprises is its array of flora—

including a variety of miniature trees, such as one-foot willows and knee-high birch—that have adapted to the incredible cold of winter and the limited availability of water by growing down instead of up, developing root systems that reach yards into the earth, where the temperature may be 50F warmer than that on the surface. Moss and lichen also grow, like tufts of beard on the tundra's rough face, providing vital food supplies to caribou and other non-hibernating winter creatures.

Spring arrives late in this part of the world—it's not until late June or early July that the wildflowers, nesting birds, and mosquitoes come out in full force. During the warm season sunlight lasts more than 20 hours each day, and many activities are scheduled for early morning to take advantage of the light, when the mountain shimmers cold-blue and ice-white.

Denali National Park and Preserve is not a place to visit casually. The only road into the interior begins in the small community known as Denali Park, 123 miles south of Fairbanks and 240 miles north of Anchorage. For years after the park was established, it remained without direct road access to these main cities; a railroad and private aircraft linked it to the outside world. Today, in addition to the trains and planes that bring visitors to the park, Highway 3 passes the park entrance on its run from Anchorage to Fairbanks. The road into the park is almost 90 miles long, running due west past valleys, passes, and riverbanks. Only the initial 15 miles are paved. The first sight of Mt. McKinley occurs a few miles in, but it isn't until mile 60, at Stony Dome, that you get a full view of its peaks. To help protect wildlife, private vehicles are not allowed on the park road after Savage River Bridge, at mile 14.5.

Campsites are spread intermittently along the road with regular shuttle bus available. The bus also is something of a mobile social center, a place for picking up the latest on wildlife sightings. The shuttle bus runs from the *Visitor Center* to Wonder Lake daily from the end of May through mid-September. More comfortable buses run on the shuttle route now than in the past, and a charge has been instituted for shuttle trips. For bus and camping tickets, call 800-622-PARK.

The *Eielson Visitor Center* sits just off the park road some 65 miles from the entrance. At an elevation of 3,730 feet, it offers good views of the mountain's twin peaks and the awesome spectacle of the Muldrow Glacier, which stretches from McKinley to within a mile of the park road. Exhibitions at the center explain geology as well as plants and animals of the tundra. Make a point of stopping at the center, especially if you plan to hike or stay overnight. Information on weather conditions, animal activity, and other backcountry conditions are available from the rangers stationed there.

Along the park road you're sure to pass a number of places worthy of a stop. The Teklanika River is a classic example of the glacial rivers that flow north from the Alaska Range. Dall sheep, those surefooted mountain climbers, can be spotted as mere dots on the sides of Igloo Canyon. Grizzly bear activity centers around Sable Pass. (No matter where you spot grizzlies and other animals throughout the park, don't frighten them or attempt to pet or feed them. They only *look* friendly.) Wildflowers spreading across the vast fields of Stony Hill Overlook are a summer contribution to the scene.

Hikers and backpackers must obtain a backcountry-use permit in person (no charge) before setting out on their treks (see address below). Check at the *Visitor Center* for fishing regulations (though the fishing here is far from Alaska's best due to silty lakebeds and streams and shallow ponds). Tours can be arranged at the *Denali National Park* hotel (see *Best en Route*) for a full day's excursion into the park. For information on all aspects of park life and visiting, contact the Superintendent, *Denali National Park and Preserve* (PO Box 9, *Denali National Park,* AK 99755; phone: 907-683-2294).

BEST EN ROUTE

A choice of several campgrounds along the park road offers the best opportunity to experience tundra life in *Denali National Park.* The camps are *Sanctuary River, Teklanika, Igloo Creek, Wonder Lake, Savage,* and *Riley Creek.* Campground registration may be done by calling 800-622-7275 or in person at the *Visitor Center.* Motorists can drive to the *Savage* and *Riley Creek* sites without road permits, but other sites are on the controlled-access portion of the road. Bring warm clothing, a waterproof shelter, mosquito netting and/or repellent, and camp stoves.

Accommodations in the area fill up quickly, so reserve early. Lodging at *Denali Park* hotel and *McKinley Chalets* can be arranged through *Denali Park Resorts* (241 W. Ship Creek, Anchorage, AK 99501; phone: 907-276-7234). Expect to pay $140 or more per night for a double room at places listed as expensive. Unless otherwise indicated, rooms have private baths, but no air conditioning, phones, or TV sets. For each location, hotels are listed alphabetically by price category.

DENALI NATIONAL PARK

Camp Denali This wilderness vacation lodge 90 miles inside the park, with a commanding view of Mt. McKinley, offers three- and four-night all-inclusive stays in 17 log cabins with outhouses, shower houses, and communal dining. The emphasis is on natural history, canoeing, fishing, bicycling, and guided hiking. In summer, contact PO Box 67, *Denali National Park,* AK 99755 (phone: 907-683-2290); in winter, PO Box 216, Cornish, NH 03746 (phone: 603-675-2248). Expensive.

Denali National Park Hotel This 100-room hotel has a restaurant, snack bar, and gift shop. For information contact *Denali Park Resorts* (see above). Expensive.

McKinley Chalets These are luxurious lodgings near the park. The 219 mini-suites feature separate sitting rooms. There is a pool, sauna, deli, and cappuccino bar, as well as a dining room with some of the best food in the park. For information contact *Denali Park Resorts* (see above). Expensive.

North Face Lodge In the heart of the park, this place offers 15 modern rooms and a dining room with a country-inn flavor for two- and three-night stays. There's also a commanding view of you-know-what. Guided hiking, canoeing, bicycling, and fishing are available. In summer, contact PO Box 67, *Denali National Park,* AK 99755 (phone: 907-683-2290); in winter, PO Box 216, Cornish, NH 03746 (phone: 603-675-2248). Expensive.

Tongass National Forest, Alaska

John Muir, the Scottish naturalist who wrote eloquently about *Yosemite* and this country's western wilderness, was rendered almost speechless by the beauty of the southeastern panhandle of Alaska. "Never before this had I been embosomed in scenery so hopelessly beyond description," he wrote in *Travels in Alaska.* His words capture the nature of this area, much of which is still preserved as a wilderness in *Tongass National Forest.* It is the largest of the national forests, encompassing 16.9 million acres, reaching nearly the entire length of the rugged 500-mile coastline of southern Alaska from north of Juneau to south of Ketchikan, east from the outermost islands of the Alexander Archipelago to the border of British Columbia in the west. The panhandle also is bordered by two parallel mountain ranges. To the west, the peaks of the submerged Fairweather Range form the islands of the archipelago; to the east looms the Coast Range, with many peaks between 5,000 and 10,000 feet and numerous glaciers. In between is enough land to leave even the most blasé visitor breathless: America's only remaining frontier—more than 11,000 evergreen-covered islands, fjords whose flanks rise precipitously from the water's edge, huge walls of moving ice, glaciers carving and molding the coastline, and lush, moss-blanketed rain forests rising toward the Coast Range.

The Inside Passage runs the entire length of the *Tongass.* This waterway, which once provided gold seekers with access to the Klondike, is well protected from the bitter northwesterly winds by the outlying islands, and it's a pleasant passage by ferry along the foot of the Coast Range. Rivers flow into the passage, and the surrounding lowlands are blanketed by thick stands of hemlock, cedar, and spruce. In the summer, wildflowers abound: Fireweed, shooting stars, iris, and anemone color the marshes and meadows.

This region does not conform to stereotyped notions of Arctic harshness. If you expect huskies pulling sleds and boundless snow, the weather will disappoint you. Sitka, a city with a climate typical of the region, has an average temperature of 56F in August and 32F in January. This moderation is caused by the Japanese Current, which brings warm temperatures and plenty of rain. During the summer it doesn't get dark until around midnight, so there is plenty of light for exploration.

The *Tongass* is a "working forest" managed for a variety of uses, such as providing timber and minerals for domestic and international markets, food and shelter for wildlife and fish, and a variety of recreational opportunities and facilities for the enjoyment of thousands each year. It's also a rich wildlife area. Brown and black bear, trumpeter swans, deer, wolf, and mountain goats roam many of the islands and coastal regions. The bald eagle, a bird that is close to extinction in the lower 48 states, thrives in Alaska and can be seen readily. Fishing is outstanding, with salmon up to 35 pounds not uncommon. In addition, many varieties of trout inhabit the freshwater lakes and streams.

Even bigger and better than a 35-pound salmon is another natural phenomenon of the *Tongass*—the glacier. Alaska possesses the largest expanse of glacial ice in the world outside Greenland and Antarctica. The glaciers that exist in Alaska today are reminders of a "Little Ice Age" that began around 2,500 years ago and lasted until about 200 years ago. Due to a warming trend from the latter half of the 19th century right up to the present, many Alaskan glaciers are receding. But there is some evidence that this warming trend is slowing, and some glaciers, such as the Taku Glacier near Juneau, are advancing. The ice in most southeast Alaska glaciers is only a couple of hundred years old—the time it takes for the snow to change to ice.

The only glacier in southeast Alaska accessible by highway, Mendenhall Glacier is reached by the Egan Expressway (also called the Glacier Highway), the primary route going north out of Juneau, and Mendenhall Loop Road, just 13 miles from downtown Juneau. Mendenhall is over 12 miles long and 1½ miles wide at its face. The *USDA Forest Service* has a visitors' center (open daily in summer and on weekends the rest of the year) at the glacier and also maintains trails alongside so that you can view the river of ice from excellent vantage points. If you're lucky, you'll see an example of calving: when a large slab of turquoise blue ice plummets from the glacier's face into Mendenhall Lake.

The retreat of Mendenhall Glacier has left behind rocky deposits (glacial moraines), illustrating how virgin forest grows on seemingly barren soil. Only lichens and moss can survive in the most recently exposed regions. However, in the areas exposed during earlier years, small willows take hold and are followed by spruce and hemlock that mature into a forest. When the glacier moves inexorably forward during the next Ice Age, the forest will be swept aside.

The few major cities in the panhandle serve as excellent departure points for fishing, camping, and hiking forays into the *Tongass,* and also provide comfortable modern accommodations. Ketchikan, Sitka, and Juneau (described below) are inaccessible by highway; they can be reached only by air, cruise ship, or the *Alaska Marine Highway System* (PO Box 25535, Juneau,

AK 99802 (phone: 907-465-3941; 800-642-0066 from the US, not Canada), a state-run ferry service linking Bellingham, Washington, and Prince Rupert, British Columbia, with the panhandle. From Juneau, travelers can also take an excursion to *Glacier Bay National Park,* which is in the panhandle area and surrounded by the *Tongass.*

For further information on the *Tongass National Forest,* contact the *USDA Forest Service Information Center* (101 Egan Dr., Juneau, AK 99811; phone: 907-586-8751), which has exhibits, displays, and audiovisual programs on the resources and management of the forest. It's open daily in summer. Information on the cities and the rest of the panhandle is available through the *Southeast Alaska Tourism Council* (369 S. Franklin St., Suite 205, Juneau, AK 99801; phone: 907-586-4777).

KETCHIKAN Southernmost Ketchikan is renowned for its salmon fishing, and the many sport fishing lodges in the area offer anglers a chance to go after king salmon. The *Tongass Historical Society Museum* (629 Dock St.; phone: 907-225-5600) has a collection of Indian artifacts and items used by southeastern Alaska pioneers. It's closed Mondays; there is an admission charge.

Wrangell and Petersburg are the next stops on the *Marine Highway* ferry service. The *Clausen Memorial Museum* (Second and Fram Sts.) in Petersburg has a good collection of historical fishing gear. The *Bear Tribal House* of the Tlingit Indians has a fine totem pole collection.

SITKA West of Petersburg on Baranof Island is Sitka, known as the "Paris of the Pacific" during the 19th century, when it was the major trading outpost of the Russian Empire. *St. Michael's Russian Orthodox Cathedral* (Lincoln St.; phone: 907-747-8120) is one of the best surviving examples of Russian peasant cathedral architecture outside of the former Soviet Union and contains ecclesiastical art. The *Sitka National Historical Park* and the *Russian Bishop's House* (both at 106 Metlekela St.; phone: 907-747-6281; by appointment only) interpret this Russian-American period and the interaction between the Russians and the Tlingit natives of Sitka. The *Sheldon Jackson Museum* (*Jackson College* campus; phone: 907-747-8981) has an outstanding collection of Aleut, Eskimo, and Indian artifacts. In mid- to late June, the city hosts the *All-Alaska Logging Championships* (phone: 907-747-5940).

JUNEAU The state capital, at the northern end of the Inside Passage, has the widest range of accommodations. A walking tour links 15 points of historic interest. The *Alaska State Museum,* in downtown Juneau (395 Whittier St.; phone: 907-465-2901), has extensive collections of pioneer memorabilia from the Russian-American period and Gold Rush era as well as Aleut, Eskimo, and Indian crafts and artifacts. The museum is closed Sundays and Mondays; there is an admission charge. Bus tours of the Mendenhall Glacier region are available from Juneau. For details contact the *Juneau Visitor Information Center* (phone: 907-586-2201).

Those who want to continue their exploration of Alaska can travel on to spectacular *Glacier Bay National Park,* which is surrounded by the *Tongass National Forest,* northwest of Juneau. It can be reached by airplane, cruise ship, or boat from Juneau.

GLACIER BAY NATIONAL PARK The park's 5,000 square miles encompass rugged mountains; glaciers flowing and calving into a deep, fjord-like bay; and a variety of landscapes ranging from terrain just recovering from glacial retreat to lush temperate rain forest. Brown and black bears, whales, and seals, as well as eagles and another 2,000 species of birds, may be observed here. Although the park is open year-round, most visitors come between May and September—the weather is very cold and damp in winter and spring. The *Glacier Bay Lodge* (phone: 800-622-2042), on the grounds, is a good hotel choice. For national park information, contact the Superintendent, *Glacier Bay National Park* (Gustavus, AK 99826; phone: 907-697-2230).

BEST EN ROUTE

The *USDA Forest Service* maintains campgrounds near the cities of the panhandle. In addition, about 150 cabins in the outlying areas, on the seacoast, or near rivers or lakes offer excellent opportunities to get back to nature. They have no bedding, plumbing, or electricity, but most of the lakeside cabins include a skiff. Cabins, which must be reserved in advance, cost $25 per night per party. When traveling this way you see the *Tongass* for what it is—a spectacular and productive rain forest. For information and reservations, write *USDA Forest Service Information Center* (101 Egan Dr., Juneau, AK 99811; phone: 907-586-8751).

For those who prefer a few more creature comforts, the panhandle's major cities, which are reached by *Marine Highway* ferries, offer modern lodgings. Expect to pay $120 or more per night for a double room at those places described below as expensive, and $75 to $120 at those rated moderate. Unless otherwise indicated, rooms have private baths, TV sets, and telephones but no air conditioning. For each location, hotels are listed alphabetically by price category.

KETCHIKAN

Westmark Cape Fox Lodge This 72-room hotel is a large, beamed building at the top of Cape Fox Hill, accessible by tram from the marina. The decor features totems and other native artifacts; there is a restaurant and lounge as well. 800 Venetia Way (phone: 907-225-8001; 800-544-0970; fax: 907-225-8286). Expensive.

Best Western Landing Here are 76 rooms with a restaurant and lounge, across from the *Marine Highway* ferry. There's also a conference room and exercise area. A complimentary shuttle will take guests anywhere within the city limits. 3434 Tongass Ave. (phone: 907-225-5166; 800-528-1234). Moderate.

SITKA

Westmark Shee Atika Lodge Built by the Shee Atika Native Corporation on the waterfront, this hostelry incorporates native tapestries and crafts into its decor—there's even a Tlingit motif in the wallpaper. Facilities include 98 guestrooms, a seafood restaurant, and a marina. 330 Seward St. (phone: 907-747-6241; 800-544-0970; fax: 907-747-8456). Expensive.

JUNEAU

Baranof In the center of the city, this 200-room quaint hotel built in the 1930s has a restaurant and a coffee shop. Old photographs and historical displays depict Alaska's early days. 127 N. Franklin St. (phone: 907-586-2660; 800-544-0970; fax: 907-586-8315). Expensive.

Westmark Juneau This hostelry offers 104 rooms (some with mountain or water views), a restaurant, and a lounge. 54 Egan Dr. (phone: 907-586-6900; 800-544-0970; fax: 907-463-3567). Expensive.

Grand Canyon National Park, Arizona

From atop the *Desert View Watchtower,* a panoramic view of the Colorado plateau spreads out into the Painted Desert, the San Francisco Peaks, and the Grand Canyon. Looking across the horizon and into the depths of this huge chasm, level upon level of rock in intricate and seemingly infinite formations display two billion years of the earth's history. Yet the force that created the vast expanse of beautiful sculptures lies just one mile below, a thin stripe of blue that seems to meander across the canyon floor—the wide and mighty Colorado River. With the combined forces of a regional uplift and the river rushing to the Gulf of California, the Grand Canyon legacy began.

Located in northwest Arizona, about 220 miles north of Phoenix, the canyon is 277 miles long, from less than 1 mile to 18 miles wide, and more than a mile deep.

The story told by the multiple layers of the Grand Canyon is extraordinary. Initially, the area surrounding the canyon was flat. Over millions of years, heat and pressure buckled the land into mountains, which were then flattened over more millions of years by erosion. Mountains formed again, eroded, and were covered by shallow seas, which deposited layers of sediment. This sequence was repeated continuously over the ages. The Colorado River began eroding the layers of sediment to form the canyon about 10 to 20 million years ago, and its present course is no more than 6 million years old.

All of this is recorded in the canyon walls by the rock layers exposed to view; they are like steps in a staircase of natural history. At the bottom of the gorge is the first step, the 1.7 billion-year-old *Vishnu Schist,* hard shiny black rocks of Precambrian Age mountains, which are among the oldest exposed rocks on earth. As you proceed up the canyon, the differences in the hue, texture, and fossil remains of the rock layers are truly incredible: There is Redwall limestone, a 500-foot-thick deposit of gray-blue limestone stained by higher layers, outstanding because of its sheer cliffs and traces of fossils from a warm, shallow sea; above that is Coconino sandstone, the solid remains of sand dunes in which fossilized footprints indicate lizard life. And at the top is pale gray Kaibab limestone (at 250 million years, the toddler of the Grand Canyon rock family), a rich exhibition case for fossils of sponges, sharks' teeth, corals, and bivalves from the shallow sea that once covered the area.

Though geologists could spend lifetimes exploring the area, the canyon has attractions that appeal to other visitors as well. Hikers, bikers, river adventurers, naturalists, and just plain tourists find equal enjoyment here. Between the South Rim and North Rim, there is a vast expanse with something to see at every point, from the magnificent views to four distinct climatic zones to many species of plants and animals. The South Rim is the more heavily visited side and the best place for an introduction to the Grand Canyon. Crowded in the summer but open year-round, it has extensive facilities for visitors amid a lovely background of juniper and piñon forest and open fields of Arizona blue lupine, yellow wild buckwheat, and purple asters. Less accessible from major highways and cities, and closed from late October to mid-May, the North Rim also is less crowded and offers different views of the canyon from a magnificent setting.

For more information about the park, contact the Superintendent, *Grand Canyon National Park* (PO Box 129, Grand Canyon, AZ 86023; phone: 520-638-7888), and *Grand Canyon North Rim TW Services* (PO Box 400, Cedar City, UT 84720; phone: 801-586-7686).

SOUTH RIM The *South Rim Visitors' Center* (South Entrance Rd.), *Yavapai Observation Station* (South Entrance Rd. near the visitors' center) and *Tusayan Ruin and Museum* (East Rim Dr.) offer exhibits on the geological history of the area and the peoples who lived in the canyon. The museums are open daily; there is no admission charge beyond park admission. At the center you can pick up information on all the daily and weekly activities, from nature hikes along the rim led by rangers to more strenuous excursions into the canyon. South Rim roads (West Rim Dr. and East Rim Dr.) cover 35 miles and have excellent overlooks. The 8-mile West Rim Drive provides the best overview of the canyon. It's closed to automobile traffic from *Memorial Day* weekend through September, but frequent (and free) shuttle buses linking key points run from early morning till evening and allow visitors to enjoy the sights at their own pace.

Trails for hiking into the canyon start at the South Rim and, if you know your limits, can provide more intimate acquaintance with the canyon's wonders. The 9.5-mile *Bright Angel Trail,* with rest stations at 1½ and 3 miles, and the steep *South Kaibab Trail,* a 6.4-mile hike with no water facilities, are best. You can take supervised nature walks or go on your own, but remember that the canyon gets hotter as you descend and is hottest at midday. Begin in the early morning or late afternoon, be sure to have plenty of water and food and a hat for protection from the sun, and remember that going down is the easy part. Leave twice as much time for the return trip. Note that hiking to the Colorado River and back in one day is *not* recommended and nearly impossible. Instead, take the *Bright Angel* 6 miles down to a windswept overlook where you can see the Colorado snake in each direction for several miles. And don't forget your wide-angle camera lens.

One of the most interesting ways to see the canyon is on muleback. There are one-day rides and overnight trips into the Inner Gorge; riders stay overnight at *Phantom Ranch,* a small guest ranch alongside Bright Angel Creek, where comfortable cabins can soothe even the worst saddlesores.

Of all the ways to see the canyon, none is more exciting than rafting the roaring Colorado. Not only are you rewarded with a magnificent view of the canyon above you, but you also experience the thrill of shooting some of the most powerful rapids in the world. Many outfitters offer raft trips, letting you choose from kayaks (experience is a must) to four-person rafts to large, motor-driven pontoon boats. On many tours, your boat will stop along the way for hikes up the side canyons. On these, you get to see the canyon from the bottom up—from the cat's claw, yucca, and blackbrush at your feet to the sheer cliffs of rock almost older than time itself rising above them. Or strap on a life vest and float down the small rapids and chutes of the Little Colorado, known for its brilliant turquoise color.

You also can glimpse the canyon from on high aboard one of the many airplanes or helicopters that offer tours. There are daily flights out of Tusayan and the *Grand Canyon* and Las Vegas airports. Due to safety requirements and noise restrictions, aircraft are no longer allowed to fly below the rim, but even from greater heights, the view remains unmatched. Also, at the historic depot in Williams, Arizona, visitors may board a restored 1923 Harriman train pulled by a turn-of-the-century steam engine for a delightful 65-mile narrated journey to the South Rim. Refreshments, strolling musicians, and cowboy entertainment are provided on board for the two-hour trip. Trains leave daily at 9:30 AM from mid-March through January. For further information contact *Grand Canyon Railway* (phone: 800-843-8724).

A list of air, bus, mule, train, and river tours is available at the *South Rim Visitors' Center,* or contact the superintendent of the park (see above).

NORTH RIM The distance between the South Rim and the North Rim of the canyon is only about 12 miles as the crow flies, but to get from one rim to the other requires almost 23 miles of hiking on the rugged *Kaibab Trail,* or a more than 200-mile drive. There is no airport on the North Rim.

Tall blue-green firs, scarlet gilias, and roaming deer can be seen on the quieter, more remote North Rim. The 26-mile Cape Royal Drive has magnificent overlooks including Point Imperial, which at 8,801 feet is the highest point on the canyon rim and features spectacular views of the subtle hues of the Painted Desert, Marble Canyon, and Colorado River. The North Rim has some organized activities (trail walks, talks, evening programs led by rangers, muleback trips) but is more a place for solitary communion with nature. The most outstanding vista is from Toroweap Point; far off the beaten track (reached only by 60 miles of dirt road, sometimes impassable in wet weather), it offers an amazing view 3,000 feet down a sheer vertical wall to the snake-shaped Colorado. The North Rim is closed from mid-October until mid-May.

BEST EN ROUTE

There are a variety of accommodations at the South Rim. The *National Park Service* runs *Desert View Campground* on a first-come, first-served basis. However, *Mather Campground* on the South Rim can be reserved through *Mistix* (phone: 800-365-2267) from *Memorial Day* through *Labor Day* weekends. For overnight hikes you need a permit and should make reservations by contacting the Backcountry Office (PO Box 129, Grand Canyon, AZ 86023). Reservations must be made in person at the park or by mail; no phone requests are accepted. The eight lodges, including *Phantom Ranch* at the bottom of the canyon, should be booked well in advance, particularly for a summer stay. Contact *Grand Canyon National Park Lodges at South Rim* (PO Box 699, Grand Canyon, AZ 86023; phone: 520-638-2401 for advance reservations; same-day reservations may be made at the front desk of any lodging facility on a space-available basis.

Below are our favorite *Grand Canyon* lodging spots. Expect to pay $110 or more per night for a double room at a place in the expensive category; $75 to $110 at one in the moderate category; and less than $75 at the place listed as inexpensive. Unless otherwise indicated, rooms have air conditioning, private baths, TV sets, and telephones. Hotels are listed alphabetically by price category.

GRAND CANYON

El Tovar This 78-room lodge is the oldest and most luxurious of the *Grand Canyon* accommodations. Some suites have balconies overlooking the canyon, and there is a good dining room serving Southwestern fare. South Rim (phone: 520-638-2401). Expensive to moderate.

Grand Canyon Lodge This 201-room lodge sits on the very edge of the North Rim. Although the lodge does not have air conditioning, it does offer fantastic views, a solarium, and a dining room. Open mid-May through mid-October. North Rim (phone 520-638-2611; 801-586-7686 for reservations). Inexpensive.

Petrified Forest National Park, Arizona

The 147-square-mile *Petrified Forest* is not a forest at all but a semi-arid desert and shortgrass prairie region in northeastern Arizona near the New Mexico border. Desolate and inhospitable, yet strangely beautiful, its vastness is as compelling as its treasures. Few living trees stand, and the dominant forms of vegetation are saltbush and sedges growing sparsely around mesas and buttes that bake in the unrelenting sun. But there are thousands of trees, or at least the remains of them, lying supine and glowing in the desert landscape. The park contains the richest collection of petrified wood in the world, ranging from huge prone logs to small chips. The wood is brilliantly hued—burning oranges, deep reds, rusts, and yellows mixed with shades of black, blue, purple, white, gray, and tan—the only color you won't see much of is green.

In the dawn of its history, the *Petrified Forest* actually was a coastal plain of marshes and swamps. About 225 million years ago, what now is a high desert plateau was a low-lying swamp basin with dense beds of ferns, mosses, and trees growing in marshlands and along streams. Groves of conifers flourished on hills and ridges above this basin. Over long periods of time, natural forces felled the trees, and flooding streams transported them to the floor of the floodplain, where they gradually were buried under thousands of feet of mud, sand, and silica-rich volcanic ash. Water carrying the silica and other minerals seeped through the sediment and filled in each wood cell, retaining the details of the wooden mold. The silica left glass-like deposits of white, gray, and tan, while traces of iron in the water colored the logs yellow, orange, red, and rust, and manganese created the blacks, blues, and purples. During a period of mountain building activity 70 million years ago, an upheaval lifted the layer high above sea level, and gradual erosion left the rainbow logs exposed.

Though more logs will surface in the continuing evolutionary process, those that presently are strewn across the *Petrified Forest* floor are truly remarkable. The park's major features—five separate "forests" with concentrations of chips and huge chunks of onyx, agate, and jasper—are linked by a 28-mile road that stretches between I-40 and US 180. The two visitors' centers (closed *Christmas* and *New Year's Day*), one at each end of this road, are good places to stop first to see specimens of polished petrified wood and displays explaining the petrification process. At the visitors' center at the south entrance is the *Rainbow Forest Museum,* where displays include maps, castings of prehistoric animals, and dioramas of area flora and fauna. Open daily; no admission charge.

The best way to see the park is on foot; it can be covered in half a day. Several trails loop out from the parking lots; one of the prettiest paths passes through Crystal Forest, where walkers can see logs jutting from the ground at odd angles. At sunset, filtered light strikes the logs, illuminating them with fiery beauty and creating the illusion that they glow from within.

Behind the *Rainbow Forest Museum* is the Giant Logs site, which is a magnificent highlight for its beautiful colors and the evidence of the petrification process; many trunks exceed 100 feet in length, and brilliant chips of onyx, agate, carnelian, and jasper tint the sand. At Long Logs, logs are piled on top of one another, and a partially restored Indian pueblo built of petrified wood chunks overlooks the area. One of the park's most unusual sights is Agate Bridge, which is actually a huge single log that fell across a chasm. According to one tall tale, in the 1880s a cowboy rode his horse across the bridge on a $10 bet. The log bridge has since been reinforced with concrete, increasing its safety but reducing its mysticism. A parking lookout on a ridgetop above Jasper Forest provides a view of masses of logs strewn on the valley floor. Be sure to stop at Blue Mesa, where a 1-mile loop of paved trail leads along a blue-gray ridge carved by the wind into intricate sculptures. Also of interest is Newspaper Rock, a mammoth chunk of sandstone with intriguing uninterpreted picture writings of prehistoric Indians. The rock is closed permanently due to rock slides, although an overlook with free telescopes allows visitors to inspect the rock art.

The northern portion of the park contains part of the Painted Desert. This series of plateaus, buttes, and low mesas truly lives up to its name, except that the bright reds, oranges, browns, blues, and purples in the layers of sandstones, shales, and clays were painted by nature, making the area something of an outdoor gallery. The colors and forms change from minute to minute with the intensity of sun and the formidable shadows of late afternoon or early morning. They appear most vivid at these times, or after rain, a most uncommon event. After stopping at the visitors' center at the northern entrance (off I-40) where displays show how traces of iron have stained the layers of clay and sandstone many shades from bright red to pale blue, drive to one of the several overlooks and see it for yourself.

The *Petrified Forest National Park* is a treasure trove for paleontologists, archaeologists, and geologists. Teams of scientists from around the world often come here to try to unearth this region's vivid history. Geologists believe that petrified logs may be buried as far as 300 feet below the surface. Since 1981, fossils of at least 35 animals that lived in the area have been discovered, as well as petroglyphs that acted as solar calendars. In 1985, one of the oldest dinosaur skeletons in the world was excavated from the Painted Desert.

Exploration of the vast unmarked surroundings should be arranged with park rangers; without natural water sources or trails, the *Petrified Forest* is not for casual hiking. Modern explorers should carry hats to shade themselves from the sun and plenty of drinking water. Backpack camping is allowed with a permit from one of the visitors' centers.

Unfortunately, the uniqueness of the *Petrified Forest* is leading to its slow destruction. Although removing petrified wood from the park is strictly forbidden, rangers estimate that the park loses 12 tons of wood each year to visitors who give in to the temptation to take "just one" piece as a souvenir. The *Painted Desert Visitor Center* off I-40 has a display of apologetic letters, in some cases long confessions written as many as 20 years later, from people who have found that the wood weighs more heavily on their minds than on their bookshelves. The park's survival depends on the kindness of strangers; instead of taking a sample, buy one. Some gift shops in the area sell pieces of petrified wood from private lands outside the park for only a few dollars.

For the sake of future generations of visitors, be sure to leave the park intact as federal law, nature's law, and, as many have found, the law of one's conscience dictate. The beauty of the *Petrified Forest* is there for all to behold. For additional information, contact the *Petrified Forest National Park Headquarters* (PO Box 2217, *Petrified Forest National Park*, AZ 86028; phone: 520-524-6228).

BEST EN ROUTE

The park has no overnight facilities, but there are about 20 motels in Holbrook, 25 miles to the west, and one in Chambers, 21 miles east. Expect to pay about $60 per night for a double room at those places we've listed as inexpensive. Unless otherwise indicated, rooms have air conditioning, private bath, TV sets, and telephones. For each location, hotels are listed alphabetically.

CHAMBERS

Best Western Chieftain This 52-room hotel has a pool and a playground. The restaurant next door features some authentic Native American dishes including Navajo tacos, which are "frybread" (deep-fried bread) sandwiches with beans and other vegetables. Reservations advised in summer. On I-40 near the Navajo Reservation (phone: 520-688-2754; 800-528-1234). Inexpensive.

HOLBROOK

Best Western Arizonian Inn This 70-room motel offers a pool and a casual restaurant on the property. Reservations advised April through October. 2508 E. Navajo Blvd. (phone/fax: 502-524-2611; 800-528-1234). Inexpensive.

Comfort Inn This 83-room motel has a pool and complimentary coffee, tea, or cocoa in the lobby. There's a restaurant next door. Reservations advised. 2602 E. Navajo Blvd. (phone: 520-524-6131; 800-228-5150; fax: 520-524-2281). Inexpensive.

Big Sur and the Monterey Peninsula, California

Big Sur is a 90-mile stretch of the Pacific Coast south of the Monterey Peninsula and Carmel-by-the-Sea; its name is a corruption of a Spanish phrase meaning "big south." California Highway 1 hugs the rugged coastline from Monterey, through Big Sur, to Morro Bay, 125 miles south. Convict chain gangs spent almost two decades carving the twisting highway out of solid cliffs, creating what is unquestionably the most dramatic road on the entire Pacific Coast.

The Monterey Peninsula and Carmel lie 120 miles south of San Francisco via Highway 1, and 340 miles north of Los Angeles via US 101 and Highway 1.

MONTEREY California's first capital has more than 40 buildings built before 1850. The *Old Custom House* (Custom House Sq.), the oldest government building in California, dating from 1827, has historic material on display. The *Royal Presidio Chapel* (Church St.), built in 1794, is Monterey's oldest building, dating back to Spanish colonization. California's first constitution was drafted in *Colton Hall* in 1849; the building dates from 1848. Today it is the *Colton Hall Museum and Jail* (Pacific St. and *Colton Hall Park*; phone: 408-646-5640); it is open daily; no admission charge. Enamored of what he sensed as "the haunting presence of the ocean," Robert Louis Stevenson in 1879 lived and worked at the *French* hotel, now called *Robert Louis Stevenson House* (530 Houston St.; phone: 408-649-7118); call ahead for hours; admission charge. Cannery Row, the site of John Steinbeck's famous novel, has long since given way to chic shops and elegant eateries. Also on Cannery Row is the *Monterey Bay Aquarium* (886 Cannery Row; phone: 408-648-4800), which has 100 major exhibitions and galleries, including a three-story kelp forest and daily feeding shows. A new wing illuminates the mysteries of the outer bay, where Monterey Bay meets the open sea. The aquarium is open daily; there's an admission charge. The state-of-the-art *Maritime Museum of Monterey* (5 Custom House Plaza; phone: 408-373-2469) has exhibits on the region's maritime history. It's open daily; there's an admission charge. The *Monterey Bay National Marine Sanctuary* (the country's largest), encompassing 5,312 square miles, extends along California's coast from just north of San Francisco to William Randolph Hearst's castle at *San Simeon* and contains the largest submarine canyon in North America. Boat trips which cruise part of the area are run by *Monterey Sports Fishing* (96 Fisherman's Wharf; 408-372-2203). Kayak trips with *Monterey Bay Kayaks* (phone: 408-373-KELP) offer a close look at sea lions and otters. The *Monterey Jazz Festival,* a must for music lovers, is held in late September (see *Music Festivals* in DIVERSIONS). For more information on Monterey, contact the *Monterey Peninsula Visitors & Convention Bureau* (PO Box 1770, Monterey, CA 93942; phone: 408-649-1770).

En Route from Monterey Head northwest along the north side of Monterey Peninsula to Pacific Grove.

PACIFIC GROVE Nicknamed "Butterfly Town USA" because hundreds of monarch butterflies arrive here every year between October and March, Pacific Grove celebrates the event with a *Butterfly Parade.* Held in October, it features butterfly-related floats, marching children dressed as butterflies, and music. The area is beautiful, with beaches and plenty of cypress trees. Another attraction here is the tiny *Pacific Grove Museum* (165 Forest Ave.; phone: 408-648-3116), which has natural history exhibits about local mammals, birds, marine life, and plants. The geology and early inhabitants of the region are also explored. The nearby *Point Piños Lighthouse* is part of the museum as well. The museum is closed Mondays; the lighthouse is closed weekdays. There's no admission charge to either.

En Route from Pacific Grove Despite its name, 17-Mile Drive, which goes from Pacific Grove to Carmel, is only 12 miles long. Along the way stop off to see the seals at Seal Rock and the Lone Cypress Tree at scenic Cypress Point. Other points of interest include the *Pebble Beach Golf Links,* site of the *AT&T–Pebble Beach National Pro-Am* (also see *Golf* in DIVERSIONS), and Pebble Beach, enclave of the super-rich.

CARMEL-BY-THE-SEA In this picturesque seaside artists' colony, working artists comprise about 25% of the permanent population. Its quaint, untouched quality is attributable to some of the most stringent zoning laws in the country, which prohibit neon signs, traffic signals, and other garish accoutrements. Carmel's narrow streets are lined with intriguing boutiques, shops, art galleries, and some excellent restaurants. The *Carmel Mission* (Lasuen Dr. and Rio Rd.; phone: 408-624-1271), the most perfectly restored of all the California missions, was founded in 1770 by Father Junípero Serra, who loved it so much he arranged to be buried here. In 1960, Pope John raised the mission to the status of a minor basilica. The *Carmel Bach Festival* takes place every July (see *Music Festivals* in DIVERSIONS). For information on events in Carmel-by-the-Sea, contact the *Carmel Business Association* (Carmel, CA 93921; phone: 408-624-2522).

From Carmel, a drive into Carmel Valley makes for an enjoyable detour.

CARMEL VALLEY Follow the Carmel Valley Road east into the land of strawberry fields, orchards, grazing pasture, and artichoke farms. Because of its sunny, warm climate, the valley is an ideal choice for vacationers. You can play golf, ride horses, swim, play tennis, hunt wild boar and deer in season, or fish for trout in the Carmel River. *Carmel Valley Begonia Gardens* (9220 Carmel Valley Rd.; phone: 408-624-7231) are ablaze with the colors of 15,000 flowers. For information on accommodations and events in the area, contact the *Carmel Valley Chamber of Commerce* (PO Box 288, Carmel Valley, CA 93924; phone: 408-659-4000).

From here, return to Highway 1.

En Route from Carmel-by-the-Sea Thirty-mile Drive (yes, it is 30 miles long), between the Monterey-Carmel area and Big Sur, is one of the most dramatic stretches of road in the country. It takes about an hour to drive along the coast-hugging, twisting highway, which parallels the line where the Santa Lucia Mountains encounter the sea. Just south of Carmel is *Point Lobos State Preserve,* a 1,255-acre park with some of the most beautiful scenery along the California coast. Be sure to visit China Cove, Bird Island, and the wonderful stands of cypress. Colonies of seals and sea lions live on the rocks. Though there are no wolves in the area, the Spanish called it *lobos* (meaning "wolves") because the seals' barking reminded them of wolves baying. The park has a visitors' center and hiking trails. Farther south, Bixby Creek Bridge is a 260-foot-high observation point where you can park, watch the ocean pound the beach, and gaze hypnotically at the *Point Sur Lighthouse,* which flashes every 15 seconds.

BIG SUR This most famous piece of shoreline on the continent is so familiar to TV and movie audiences, it's almost unnecessary to talk about it. The rolling grassy hills of Big Sur end abruptly at cliffs towering high above the sea. There are many places to stop and watch sea otters, seals, and sea lions near the shore. You even might see whales spouting farther out to sea between December and March. Below the cliffs, waves crash over the boulders. You won't need to be told what spots are especially scenic; when you round a hairpin curve and find yourself grabbing your camera, you'll know you've found one.

In the town of Big Sur, stroll along the beach, have a picnic overlooking the water, browse in the art galleries, or visit the redwood trees. Be sure to stop at *Nepenthe* (phone: 408-667-2345), a restaurant that was built by a student of Frank Lloyd Wright on an 800-foot cliff. It has evolved over the years into Big Sur's main hangout and social center. *Pfeiffer–Big Sur State Park* (phone: 408-667-2315), a deep forest of redwood and other trees, provides a change of scenery from the grassy hills of Big Sur. It has horseback riding, hiking trails, fishing spots, picnic areas, campgrounds, food service, and a lodge. At Jade Cove, you can hunt for jade at low tide. For additional information contact the *Big Sur Chamber of Commerce* (PO Box 87, Big Sur, CA 93920; phone: 408-667-2100).

En Route from Big Sur Continue 67 miles south on Highway 1 to *San Simeon.*

SAN SIMEON William Randolph Hearst's fabled castle, *San Simeon* contains sections of castles from other parts of the world which the newspaper tycoon shipped to his Pacific estate. Amazingly reconstructed, the majestic rooms, halls, courtyards, and swimming pools are no less than stunning. Tours will take you through this regal $50-million treasure house, now a 123-acre state historical monument overlooking the ocean. Tickets may be purchased in advance through *Mistix* reservation service, by mail or phone (PO Box 85705, San Diego, CA 92138; phone: 800-444-PARK from California; 619-452-5956 from elsewhere in the US).

En Route from San Simeon Continue 28 miles south to the end of Highway 1 at Morro Bay.

MORRO BAY Morro Bay is named for the massive volcanic spire jutting out almost 600 feet above the sea. *Morro Bay State Park* (phone: 805-772-2560), a 1,483-acre tract with horseback riding, hiking trails, picnic areas, and campsites, also has a natural history museum on local marine biology and ecology.

BEST EN ROUTE

This area is replete with high-quality accommodations; listed below are only some of the best. Expect to pay $200 or more per night for a double room at places we've listed as very expensive; $120 to $200 at those in the expensive category; and $75 to $120 at those described as moderate. Unless otherwise indicated, rooms have private baths, TV sets, and telephones, but no air conditioning. For each location, hotels are listed alphabetically by price category.

MONTEREY

Spindrift Inn This intimate, elegant inn is a delightfully romantic hideaway right on Cannery Row. Its 41 rooms boast canopy feather beds and fireplaces; half have Monterey Bay right outside the window. Continental breakfast and afternoon wine and cheese are included. There is a restaurant unrelated to the inn in the building. 652 Cannery Row (phone: 408-646-8900; 800-232-4141). Very expensive.

Hotel Pacific Arranged in clusters around four landscaped courtyards, this hotel's 103 adobe-style guestrooms offer separate sitting and sleeping areas, fireplaces, and individual balconies or patios. Breakfast and afternoon tea are included. There is no restaurant, but room service from local restaurants is available. 300 Pacific St. (phone: 408-373-5700; 800-232-4141). Expensive.

Old Monterey Inn This 1929 English Tudor–style country house is a romantic hideaway, with fireplaces and either stained glass windows or skylights in the 10 guestrooms, each decorated according to a theme. Choose the Library Room, Tattersall Room, or, if you feel adventurous, the Serengeti Room, complete with mosquito netting atop Ralph Lauren bedding. There is no restaurant, but a full breakfast is included. 500 Martin St. (phone: 408-375-8284; 800-350-2344). Expensive.

PACIFIC GROVE

Martine Inn This turn-of-the-century oceanfront inn offers 20 rooms in a lovely Mediterranean-style villa and a separate carriage house. Each room is furnished with museum-quality antiques. A full breakfast (included in the rate) is served in a parlor complete with old Sheffield silver, Victorian china, crystal, and lace doilies. There is no restaurant. 255 Ocean View Blvd. (phone: 408-373-3388; 800-852-5588). Expensive.

PEBBLE BEACH

The Inn at Spanish Bay Owned by the Pebble Beach Company, this property on 17-Mile Drive offers the same high level of amenities as its sister lodge (see below) but has a different tone. Its 270 rooms are decorated with contemporary furnishings; all have oil-burning fireplaces, and most have decks or patios. There are spa facilities, golf, and three restaurants. 2700 17-Mile Dr. (phone: 408-647-7500; 800-654-9300). Very expensive.

The Lodge at Pebble Beach Frequented by the rich and famous, this place is the height of luxury on the Monterey Peninsula. The 160 rooms, which have large fireplaces, are decorated with antique furnishings and king-size beds with down quilts. There are four restaurants. Though situated on the edge of the 5,300-acre *Del Monte Forest,* it is better known for the world-famous golf links and the *Pebble Beach and Tennis Club.* See also *Best Resort Hotels* in DIVERSIONS. 17-Mile Dr. (phone: 408-624-3811; 800-654-9300). Very expensive.

CARMEL

Carmel Valley Ranch Set on a forested hillside overlooking the adjacent golf course, this property offers 100 air conditioned one- and two-bedroom suites with high ceilings and large decks (some with private hot tubs) as well as a restaurant. In addition to the 18-hole course, there are 12 tennis courts, two pools, five outdoor spas, and hiking trails through the ranch's 1,700 acres. 1 Old Ranch Rd. (phone: 408-625-9500; 800-422-7635). Very expensive.

Highlands Inn With the Santa Lucia Mountains as a backdrop, this is the place for a romantic retreat. Most of the 142 accommodations are "spa suites," which contain large living rooms with fireplaces, full bar-kitchens, and sleeping/bathing areas dominated by huge hot tubs. Amenities include two restaurants, a pool, and more hot tubs. Bicycles are available, and nearby golf and tennis facilities can be used by prior arrangement. Hwy. 1, 4 miles south of Carmel (phone: 408-624-3801; 800-538-9525; 800-682-4811 in California). Very expensive.

Stonepine This property offers a French château manor house, an equestrian center, a pool, and the Carmel River. Situated on 330 acres, the manor house has eight rooms and the *Paddock House* has four; there is an additional cottage with its own rose garden. Other activities include fishing, croquet, and tennis; there's also a fine restaurant. Also see *America's Special Havens* in DIVERSIONS. 150 East Carmel Valley Rd. (phone: 408-659-2245; fax: 408-659-5160). Very expensive.

Quail Lodge Offering one of the valley's best golf courses, this resort sits amid 241 lush acres. Some of the 100 rooms have fireplaces and decks, and overlook the lakes on the property. The four- and five-bedroom cottages have central living rooms, wet bars, and fireplaces. The *Covey* restaurant offers dinner nightly. You can hike and fish on the 600 adjoining acres. 8205 Valley Greens Dr. (phone: 408-624-1581; 800-538-9516). Very expensive.

Tickle Pink Inn at Carmel Highlands Set behind the *Highlands Inn* (see above), this 41-year-old hotel has 35 rooms and suites, some with hand-hewn stone fireplaces; most open onto spectacular ocean views. A continental breakfast and wine and cheese reception are included, but there is no restaurant. 155 Highlands Dr. (phone: 408-624-1244; 800-635-4774). Expensive.

La Playa This landmark hostelry is a gracious, Mediterranean-style establishment offering well-priced lodging and excellent food. There are 75 rooms—those facing the ocean are best—or try one of the five cottages with a fireplace. The one- and two-bedroom units boast full kitchens, sitting rooms with fireplaces, and private patios. There also is a pool. Located a few blocks from Carmel Beach at Eighth Ave. and Camino Real (phone: 408-624-6476; 800-582-8900). Expensive to moderate.

Pine Inn This Victorian establishment is decorated with stained glass, electrified gas lamps, marble-topped tables, and wooden chests. Each of the 48 guestrooms is furnished differently, and a penthouse area has five suites, one with a fireplace. There's also a restaurant. Ocean Ave. between Lincoln and Monteverda Sts. (phone: 408-624-3851). Moderate to expensive.

Sea View Inn Although the sea view is partially blocked by tall pines, this inn built around 1906 has retained much of its original atmosphere—if not its original $3 nightly rate. There are eight bedrooms, six with private baths; several have window seats (none have TV sets or telephones). A delicious breakfast is included in the rate. There is no restaurant. On Camino Real between 11th and 12th Aves. (phone: 408-624-8778). Moderate.

Vagabond's House Inn The 11 rooms in this charming English Tudor country inn surround a flower-filled stone courtyard. The rooms have fireplaces, and continental breakfast is included in the rate, but there is no restaurant. Fourth and Dolores Sts. (phone: 408-624-7738; 800-262-1262; fax: 408-626-1243). Moderate.

BIG SUR

Post Ranch Inn Big Sur's luxury property sits on 40 lovely acres overlooking the sea. It has earned raves since its opening four years ago for both its environmental correctness (only one tree was felled in the hotel's construction) and its services. The 30 rooms feature fireplaces and Jacuzzis; one guestroom is in a house by the Pacific and another is set in a tree house. Continental breakfast is included, and the dining room serves dinner. There is air conditioning but the rooms do not have TV sets. West Hwy. 1 (phone: 408-667-2200; 800-527-2200). Very expensive.

Ventana Inn Exposed beams, high ceilings, balconies, patios, and views of the mountains and ocean provide dramatic, contemporary elegance. All 59 rooms are air conditioned and have hand-painted headboards; some have hot tubs. Other features include a restaurant, two breakfast rooms, two pools, a sauna, a Jacuzzi, a fitness room, and hiking trails. Also see *America's Special Havens* in DIVERSIONS. Located on Hwy. 1 (phone: 408-667-2331; 800-628-6500; fax: 408-667-2419). Very expensive.

MORRO BAY

Inn at Morro Bay This 96-room inn overlooks the harbor and the massive volcanic spire that gave Morro Bay its name. The rooms are decorated in country French style, and many have bay views and fireplaces; amenities include a fine restaurant and a heated pool. In *Morro Bay State Park* (phone: 805-772-5651; 800-321-9566). Expensive to moderate.

Death Valley National Park, California

One of the largest of the US national parks, *Death Valley National Park* now covers 5,250 square miles, 550 of which are below sea level. Covering an area as large as the state of Connecticut, it is 140 miles west of Las Vegas and 300 miles northeast of Los Angeles in the Mojave Desert, primarily on the California side of the California-Nevada border. *Death Valley*'s size increased by one third when it was elevated from a national monument to a national park as part of the Desert Protection Act of 1994. The recreational area and tourist facilities have not been affected by this change, which was enacted to protect the desert plants and such dwindling desert animals as the land tortoise and the big horn sheep. However, its glamorous new status is bound to bring an increase in visitors to the national park.

According to legend, the 140-mile valley originally was called Tomesha ("ground afire") by the Paiute Indians, but was given its present name by a party of pioneers who got lost in the valley during the Gold Rush. To the '49ers and the early settlers, *Death Valley* was a potentially deadly obstacle between them and the riches of California. Modern travelers find it an exciting, dramatic place that can be explored in relative safety.

Death Valley is part of a region of extremes. At 282 feet below sea level, it is the lowest point in the Western Hemisphere. Only 70 air miles away stands the highest point in the 48 contiguous states—Mt. Whitney, 14,494 feet above sea level. It is also among the hottest places on earth, with temperatures recorded as high as 134F in the shade (the world record is 136F, recorded in Libya in 1922). Don't come in the summer unless you are well prepared. The tourist season runs from mid-fall to mid-spring, and the weather is pleasant during the winter. If you're hiking, remember that *Death Valley* got its name for a reason; always carry plenty of extra water.

The valley actually is the floor of what once was a large inland lake—fed primarily by increased precipitation in the Sierra Nevada range during the last Ice Age. With the prevailing warming trend and decreasing rainfall—little precipitation makes it past the formidable barrier of the Sierras—the supply of new water couldn't keep up with the evaporation rate.

Despite its great heat and minuscule rainfall (less than two inches annually), *Death Valley* has springs and several streams that flow—or at least trickle—all year. There's even a small marsh at Saratoga Springs. And while the idea of studying fish here may seem strange, several species found in the streams here do not exist anywhere else. There are, in fact, more than 40 species of plant and animal life indigenous only to this area. In addition, during migration periods the valley is visited by such unlikely guests as Canada and snow geese, herons, and ducks.

In addition to its valid claims to things that are the highest, the lowest, the hottest, and the biggest, *Death Valley* also might be the richest. There are many legends about the fabulous lost mines of *Death Valley.* They may or may not be true, but at one time it certainly had some of the nation's most lucrative mines. There were boomtowns with colorful names like Bullfrog and Skidoo; today you'll pass what remains of these once-vibrant mining centers en route to the *Furnace Creek Visitors' Center* (on Hwy. 190 in Furnace Creek; phone: 619-786-3244), where you can pick up brochures and maps explaining how to take self-guided auto tours. There also are slide shows, nature exhibitions, and other activities run by the rangers.

Death Valley also is famous for its borax. The borax mines were established in the 1880s, when roads were built for the 20-mule team wagons that hauled the borax out of the valley. At the Harmony Borax Works, 1½ miles north of the visitors' center, are the remains of one of the first borax processing plants.

One of the most famous valley landmarks is *Scotty's Castle* at the northern end of the valley. The structure is named for one Walter Scott (or "Death Valley Scotty," as he was known), a onetime cowboy and performer in *Buffalo Bill's Wild West* show. He claimed to have built an elaborate, lavishly furnished castle in Grapevine Canyon; moreover, he said he had paid for it with gold from a secret mine. But while the castle does stand in an oasis on the edge of the desert, the romantic tale of a secret gold mine is, unfortunately, false. The castle was actually built by Albert M. Johnson, a wealthy Chicago businessman who came to *Death Valley* to check on Scotty's nonexistent mine and later became friends with the flamboyant ex-cowboy.

Among the valley's most spectacular sights are the fantastically eroded golden badlands of Zabriskie Point; the Sahara-like Sand Dunes; the Devil's Golf Course, a craggy white salt flat where the pinnacles reach as high as two feet—and still growing; and Dante's View, from which you look down at Badwater, the lowest point in *Death Valley* and up at Telescope Peak, the highest point at 11,049 feet. The latter is definitely a must-see.

Each of the canyons and mountains surrounding the lowlands of *Death Valley* seems to have its own special colors. Golden Canyon has bright golds and rich purples; Mustard Canyon is various shades of ocher. The Black Mountains have reds, greens, and tans. A particularly interesting attraction is Mosaic Canyon, with walls of smooth beige dolomite marble and eroded surfaces embedded with brilliantly colored pebbles.

The valley's stark visual appeal evokes a strong emotional response. While other western national parks and monuments allow visitors to view the beauty of the West, *Death Valley* invites you to experience something of the spirit of the Old West. The original pioneers knew that they faced the very real possibility of death as they started out across this valley. Most of them made it and went on to new lives in California. You can't visit *Death Valley* without thinking about these settlers—and about the determination, drive, and sense of hope that made this part of America what it is today. For additional information about *Death Valley* contact the Superintendent, *Death Valley National Park* (Death Valley, CA 92328; phone: 619-786-2331).

BEST EN ROUTE

Campgrounds are scattered throughout the valley, among them *Furnace Creek, Mesquite Springs,* and *Wildrose,* which is open only during summer months. Reservations are accepted at *Furnace Creek* only, through *Destinet* (phone: 800-365-2267), but there's almost always plenty of room for everyone, except on holiday weekends and the second weekend in November (the annual *Death Valley '49er Encampment*). Expect to pay $100 to $325 per night for a double room at those places we've listed as expensive; $65 to $100 at those in the moderate category; and less than $65 at those described as inexpensive. Unless otherwise indicated, hotels are open year-round and rooms have air conditioning, private baths, TV sets, and telephones. Hotels are listed alphabetically by price category.

DEATH VALLEY

Furnace Creek Inn This luxurious, 68-room property has two restaurants, a lounge with entertainment, a pool, tennis courts, and palm-lined gardens. Open mid-October to early May. One mile south of the visitors' center on Hwy. 190 (phone: 619-786-2345; fax: 619-786-2307). Expensive.

Furnace Creek Ranch This 240-room place has casual accommodations in rustic cottages (no air conditioning or TV sets) and motel units, with three restaurants, a cocktail lounge, a pool, facilities for golf, tennis, and horseback riding, and a service station. It's adjacent to a trailer park and landing strip for light planes. Next to the visitors' center on Hwy. 190 (phone: 619-786-2345; fax: 619-786-2514). Moderate.

Stovepipe Wells Simply furnished, this motel has 82 rooms, a heated pool, a restaurant, a cocktail lounge, and a landing strip. Twenty-five miles north of Furnace Creek on Hwy. 190 (phone: 619-786-2387; fax: 619-786-2389). Inexpensive.

Lake Tahoe, California and Nevada

The largest alpine lake in North America, Tahoe is 22 miles long, 12 miles wide, and has 72 miles of shoreline. Just south of Reno, it is nestled at the notch in the California-Nevada state line where California's eastern boundary starts to slant southeast. Actually, two-thirds of the lake belongs to California, one-third to Nevada. At an altitude of 6,229 feet, it is 1,664 feet deep and contains enough water to cover the state of California to a depth of more than one foot. Despite the lake's size and the heavily populated sections of its shoreline, the water is pure enough to drink. In fact, it could supply every person in the US with five gallons of water every day for five years.

There are two theories about Lake Tahoe's origins. One argues that the lake was a huge crater gouged out of the crown of the Sierra Nevada range during the Ice Age. Another says the lake began three million years ago, when volcanic lava hardened, trapping water in a deep, geological cup.

Lake Tahoe is also a resort, equally famous for its incomparable outdoor sports facilities, especially skiing, and for its gambling casinos which offer top entertainers. Luxury-seekers will find ultramodern hotels and casinos at both ends; sports enthusiasts will find boating, swimming, fishing, hiking, golf, tennis, and skiing (for detailed information about Tahoe's ski areas, see *Downhill Skiing* in DIVERSIONS). Campers seeking solitude and untrammeled nature have access to any of the three national forests around the lake—*Tahoe,* 696,000 acres north of the lake; *Toiyabe,* four million acres on the eastern edge in Nevada; and *Eldorado,* 590,000 acres to the southwest.

South Lake Tahoe is 198 miles from San Francisco, on I-80 to Sacramento, then US 50. At South Lake Tahoe you have a choice: US 50 and Highway 28 along the undeveloped eastern shore in Nevada, or Highways 89 and 28 around the western edge of the lake in California.

The following route circles the lake from the California to the Nevada side, starting in South Lake Tahoe at the southern tip of the lake. The corkscrew road through the ponderosa pine and spruce along the western edge is considerably more rugged than the strip facing the eastern shoreline. California offers much better sightseeing, since Highway 89's intricate twists and turns reveal dramatic, panoramic views. You'll have to take it easy—the road is peppered with 10 mph zones, and, on weekends, it's clogged with people. And take it very slow if the weather is foggy, rainy, or snowy—Highway 89 can be treacherous; it is often closed during winter months.

SOUTH LAKE TAHOE, California Before circling the lake, stop by the *US Forest Service Visitors' Center,* 1 mile north of Camp Richardson (open weekends from *Memorial Day* to June 28, daily from June 29 to *Labor Day;* phone: 916-573-2674). Skiers can get lift tickets for *Heavenly* and *Kirkwood,* two ski areas south of South Lake Tahoe, at the resorts. At *Heavenly* ski resort, try the *Top of the Tram* restaurant (Keller Rd.; phone: 702-586-7000) for chicken marsala or fresh poached salmon. Sunday brunch is served from *Memorial Day* through the third week of September. Drive about 10 miles northwest on Highway 89.

EMERALD BAY, California As you approach the bay, you might well experience déjà vu—the feeling you've been here before. This is one of the most photographed sites in the state. Eagle Falls, a canyon above the bay, has crystal-clear pools for swimming. Cruises of Emerald Bay are available aboard the *Tahoe Queen,* a glass-bottom paddle wheeler (phone: 916-541-3364) and the MS *Dixie II* (see "Zephyr Cove," below).

En Route from Emerald Bay In startling contrast to Emerald Bay's fairyland splendor, *Desolation Wilderness,* 63,469 forbidding acres of lake-dotted granite west of the bay, form a barren landscape laced with dozens of hiking trails. (Experienced hikers have been known to gripe that the trails are as mannerly as a city park's.) About 20 miles from Emerald Bay on Highway 89 is Tahoe City.

TAHOE CITY, California This is ski country. You can pick up interchangeable lift tickets for slopes at *Northstar, Alpine Meadows, Squaw Valley, Sugar Bowl, Diamond Peak, Boreal, Ski Homewood,* and *Mt. Rose.* For information, call *Ski Tahoe North* (phone: 800-TAHOE-4-U). The *Tahoe North Visitors and Convention Bureau* (950 N. Lake Blvd., Tahoe City, CA 96145; phone: 916-583-3494; 800-824-6348) offers a central reservations service for all North Tahoe ski resorts.

En Route from Tahoe City Squaw Valley is five miles north.

SQUAW VALLEY, California *Squaw Valley* is one of the world's most famous ski areas, with 32 chair lifts, cable cars, and complete accoutrements. The aerial tram operates year-round, as do the outdoor *Olympic* ice-skating rink and the *High Camp Bath and Tennis Club* (phone: 916-583-6985).

En Route from Squaw Valley Return to the junction of Highways 89 and 28; take Highway 28 north past the state line to Incline Village.

INCLINE VILLAGE, Nevada This Nevada town is at the northern end of the lake. Skiing is available from December through April at *Diamond Peak,* formerly *Ski Incline* (phone: 702-832-1177). Also, Incline Village has a $6.4-million recreation complex (980 Incline Way; phone: 702-832-1300) with an Olympic-size pool that is open to the public daily; admission charge. Every year more than 350,000 people visit *Ponderosa Ranch* (phone: 702-831-0691), once used as the set of the old TV series "Bonanza"; you can glimpse it from the *Incline* golf courses as well. A haywagon ride leaves the *Ponderosa Stables* at 8 AM; breakfast is served. The ranch is closed October through May (also see *Amusement Parks* in DIVERSIONS).

En Route from Incline Village Detour north on Highway 431 for a bird's-eye perspective of the lake and environs from Mt. Rose. In winter, there's skiing at the *Mt. Rose* ski area (phone: 702-849-0704); in summer, 24 campsites are made available in the *Mt. Rose Campground* (phone: 702-882-2766). North and slightly to the east of the shoreline is *Toiyabe National Forest,* known for its challenging hiking trails—so "uncontrolled" that inexperienced hikers are cautioned to stay away. Advance reservations must be made for five of the campsites; 18 are available on a first-come, first-served basis. For information, contact *Toiyabe National Forest* (1200 Franklin Way, Sparks, NV 89431; phone: 702-331-6444). Head south on Highway 28 and US 50. About 8 miles north of Stateline, Nevada, is Cave Rock. Once used as a natural barrier against enemy attack by the Paiute Indians, today the cave is a tunnel for cars, with a lookout point. Beyond the tunnel are Zephyr Cove and Stateline.

ZEPHYR COVE, Nevada From here you can cruise to Emerald Bay on the MS *Dixie II,* Tahoe's largest paddle wheeler. Breakfast, cocktail, and dinner dance cruises are available; the ship also can be hired for special charter cruises year-round. Reservations are advised (phone: 702-588-3508).

STATELINE, Nevada This Nevada town is gambling country, what Tahoe is most famous for. You'll find slot machines, craps and keno tables, and roulette wheels, as well as giant names in nightclub entertainment, all over town. *Harrah's, Lake Tahoe Horizon, Harvey's,* and *Caesar's Tahoe* are the most famous casinos. *Bill's,* next to *Harrah's,* has a smaller casino and gives discount coupons to guests at other hotels. For information and reservations, contact the *Lake Tahoe Visitors Authority* (1156 Ski Run Blvd., South Lake Tahoe, CA 96150; phone: 916-544-5050; 800-AT-TAHOE). Also see *Wheels of Fortune* in DIVERSIONS.

BEST EN ROUTE

Expect to pay $200 or more per night for a double room at those places we've listed as very expensive; $120 to $200 at those described as expensive; $75 to $120 at those in the moderate category; and less than $75 at those listed as inexpensive. Unless otherwise indicated, rooms have private baths, TV sets, and telephones, but no air conditioning. For each location, hotels are arranged alphabetically by price category.

SOUTH LAKE TAHOE

Christiana Inn A mere 100 yards from the ski lifts at *Heavenly,* this two-room, four-suite European-style chalet offers quiet accommodations close to the slopes. An extensive continental menu and wine list are available in the dining room. There are no TV sets or telephones in the rooms. 3819 Saddle Rd. (phone: 916-544-7337). Expensive.

Embassy Suites This 400-suite property opened as part of the redevelopment plan to spruce up South Lake Tahoe. The Swiss-style mountain chalet has a two-level atrium, an indoor pool, a spa, a fitness center, and a restaurant and lounge. Complimentary breakfasts are made to order. 4130 Lake Tahoe Blvd. (phone: 916-544-5400; 800-EMBASSY). Expensive.

Tahoe Seasons Resort This all-suite hotel has 180 guestrooms with kitchenettes; most also have fireplaces. There's a restaurant (hours limited in summer, so check ahead), an outdoor pool, a spa, a cozy lounge, and rooftop tennis courts. Located across from *Heavenly* ski resort (phone: 916-541-6700; 800-551-2044). Expensive.

Lakeland Village A condominium resort with 211 units, it has just about the best location in town: on the lake near skiing and gambling. There are two pools, a spa, a clubhouse, and a long stretch of beach. There is no restaurant, but all rooms have kitchens. Some units are air conditioned. Located 1 mile from *Heavenly* ski resort and 2 miles from the casinos (phone: 916-544-1685; 800-822-5969). Moderate to expensive.

HOMEWOOD

Rockwood Lodge This luxurious bed and breakfast establishment, 6 miles south of Tahoe City, is stylishly decorated with antiques, featherbeds, and pedestal sinks. Built in the 1930s, the mansion is constructed of wood, knotty pine, and stone featuring five rooms (three of which have private baths; there are no TV sets or telephones) offering views of either the lake or lush, green forest. Complimentary wine and cheese are served in the parlor during a daily cocktail hour. There is no restaurant. 5295 West Lake Blvd. (phone: 916-525-5273; 800-538-2463). Moderate to expensive.

TAHOE CITY

Sunnyside Lodge All of the 23 lakeview rooms here have private decks; some also have fireplaces. The restaurant and bar are popular. This is an especially good place to stay, both in summer, when people dock their boats at the marina, and in winter, for après-ski cocktails, dinner, and entertainment. 1850 West Lake Blvd. (phone: 916-583-7200; 800-822-2754). Expensive.

OLYMPIC VALLEY

Resort at Squaw Creek This luxury establishment, 5 miles north of Tahoe City, offers 405 rooms and suites, three pools, hot tubs, a water slide, an ice skating rink, fitness clubs, a tennis center, an 18-hole Robert Trent Jones Jr. golf course, and four eateries, including an outstanding French restaurant. 400 Squaw Creek Rd. (phone: 916-583-6300; 800-3-CREEK-3). Very expensive.

TAHOE VISTA

Tahoe Vista Inn and Marina This small, elegant place, located 1.5 miles from the state line at the head of the lake, has six suites with Jacuzzis, fireplaces, and a great view of the lake. *Captain Jon's,* the inn's restaurant, is one of the best in the region. 7220 North Lake Blvd. (phone: 916-546-1515; 800-662-3433). Expensive.

INCLINE VILLAGE

Hyatt Regency Lake Tahoe This 458-room resort offers lots of casino and nightclub activity, plus three restaurants, water sports, tennis, golf, and skiing nearby. 111 Country Club Dr. (phone: 702-831-1111; 800-327-3910). Very expensive to expensive.

STATELINE

Caesar's Tahoe In addition to its 440 rooms, this resort provides four restaurants, a showroom, a cabaret, and complete gambling facilities. 55 Hwy. 50 (phone: 702-588-3515; 800-648-3353). Expensive.

Harrah's Tahoe This world-famous 533-room super-resort offers a 150-yard-long casino, famous entertainers, four lounges, and a full range of activities 24 hours a day. There are seven restaurants, including the *Summit,* which has lake views and fine California-style fare. Hwy. 50 (phone: 702-588-6611; 800-648-3773). Expensive.

Harvey's More than 2,300 slot machines, complete gambling facilities, and eight restaurants complement this hotel's 740 rooms. Hwy. 50 (phone: 702-588-2411; 800-648-3361). Expensive.

Lake Tahoe Horizon Nonstop action is the name of the game at this 539-room luxury facility: The casino has more than 1,200 slot machines; and there is a superstar nightclub, a lounge, and *Josh's* restaurant, where steaks, seafood dishes, and pasta are on the menu. Hwy. 50 (phone: 702-588-6211; 800-648-3322). Expensive.

Palm Springs and Joshua Tree National Park, California

Palm Springs, once an important stop on the stagecoach route from Prescott, Arizona, to Los Angeles, is in the Coachella Valley, 100 miles east of LA. The sun shines an average of 330 days a year here, the desert air is dry, and the sky brilliantly clear (except on rare days when light smog hangs over the area as a reminder of its proximity to Los Angeles). Daytime highs range from about 70F in January to over 100F from June through September. At night, the temperature drops about 30 degrees, so sweaters and jackets are sometimes necessary. Since the humidity always is low, you can enjoy the heat without suffering from that muggy, clammy feeling that can accompany high humidity.

Palm Springs was discovered hundreds of years ago by the Agua Caliente Indians. Agua Caliente means "hot water" in Spanish; in fact, the discovery of hot springs in the earth led to the area's development into a spa and, later, a resort, for the Indians considered the springs to have miraculous healing powers. They were opened to the public around the turn of the century, and, whether or not they healed anyone, they have provided a miracle for the Agua Caliente tribe, the largest single landowner in Palm Springs. The tribe owns more than 10 square miles of valuable land within the city limits.

Today, people are more attracted to Palm Springs's warm, dry climate, its desert scenery, the area's four Indian-owned casinos, and superb resort facilities than to the springs themselves. For the rich, Palm Springs offers all the goods and services money can buy (some of the more famous denizens have had streets named after them—Hope, Autry, Sinatra, Shore, and Waring, among others). For anyone, rich or poor, it offers what money cannot buy—a sparkling environment and a delightful climate.

The following route begins in Palm Springs, proceeds south to the lands of the Agua Caliente Indians, and then heads east to the *Joshua Tree National Park,* a 792,000-acre preserve for the Joshua tree and other desert flora and fauna. The drive to Palm Springs from Los Angeles takes about two and a half hours on I-10, which in LA is the San Bernardino Freeway. Visitors also can fly in on major airlines' commuter planes.

PALM SPRINGS Although the Palm Springs area has more than 200 hotels and welcomes about two million visitors annually, it still is a very small town, with a permanent population of approximately 42,000. It probably has the world's highest number of swimming pools per capita—over 10,000, one for every four people. Not everyone in Palm Springs is wealthy, although sometimes it seems that way. It has long been a retreat for celebrities and zillionaires, especially in winter, when the prices soar as high as Mt. San Jacinto, the peak that overlooks the city. During the summer, temperatures rise and prices drop. For a glimpse of the rich and famous—and their estate walls, mailboxes, and country clubs—several tour companies offer "insider" forays around the area.

No matter when you visit, you'll find active nightclubs, hundreds of fascinating (and expensive) boutiques, and sports activities that range from horseback riding through the nearby canyons to balloon trips above the desert. Known as "the Golf Capital of the World," the area has about 90 golf courses and is the site of more than 12 major golf tournaments each year, including the *Bob Hope Chrysler Classic* and the *Nabisco–Dinah Shore Invitational.* There are about 600 tennis courts and an increasing number of important annual tennis championships. In January, the *Palm Springs International Film Festival* showcases new films. Other events and festivals include rodeos, horse shows, art festivals, charity balls, and designer fashion shows. Check out the elegant specialty shops and art galleries on Palm Canyon Drive, the principal thoroughfare, and on El Paseo in nearby Palm Desert.

The main places of interest include the *Palm Springs Desert Museum* (101 Museum Dr.; phone: 619-325-7186), a lavish cultural center with an excellent art museum, a history museum with unusual Indian artifacts, and outstanding facilities for the performing arts. The museum is closed Mondays; there's an admission charge. The *Living Desert* (47900 Portola Ave.; phone: 619-346-5694) has wild animals and plants in natural settings with landscaped paths; there is an admission charge. Another interesting stop for plant-lovers is the *Moorten Botanical Gardens* (1701 S. Palm Canyon Dr.; phone: 619-327-6555), which boasts more than 3,000 kinds of desert plants from all over the world; there is an admission charge. *San Jacinto Wilderness State Park,* atop the 10,780-foot mountain, has more than 50 miles of hiking trails, picnic areas, and six campgrounds. Its 13,000 acres can be reached only by an aerial tram ride. Part of the larger *San Bernardino National Forest,* the park is the site of numerous activities—some serious and some purely fanciful—throughout the year. For additional information about Palm Springs, contact the *Palm Springs Desert Resorts Convention and Visitors Bureau* (69-930 Hwy. 111, Suite 201, Rancho Mirage, CA 92270; phone: 619-770-9000 or 619-770-1992) or *Palm Springs Visitors Information Center* (2781 N. Palm Canyon Dr., Palm Springs, CA 92262; phone: 619-778-8418; 800-347-7746).

En Route from Palm Springs Directly south of Palm Springs, at the end of South Palm Canyon Drive, is the Agua Caliente Cahuilla Indian Reservation and the Indian Canyons.

INDIAN CANYONS Filled with plants, bubbling hot springs, magnificent waterfalls, ancient Indian cliff dwellings, and pictographs on the walls, the three canyons may remind you of Shangri-la. In fact, the original movie version of *Lost Horizon,* James Hilton's novel about the fabled hidden paradise, was filmed here. Open daily; there is an admission charge. The canyons are administered by the Tribal Council (phone: 619-325-5673).

En Route from the Indian Canyons Head southeast on Highway 111 for about 20 miles to Indio.

INDIO "The Date Capital of the World" (the kind that grows on trees), Indio is also the site of the *National Date Festival* in February. The festival's ambience is neo–Arabian Nights, complete with camel and ostrich races. A movie called *The Sex Life of a Date* plays regularly at *Shields Date Gardens* (80225 Hwy. 111; phone: 619-347-0996). The snack bar here is a popular place to sample one of the area's distinctive date milk shakes.

En Route from Indio Head for the *Joshua Tree Park,* 25 miles east of Indio off I-10.

JOSHUA TREE NATIONAL PARK Upgraded from a national monument by the *Desert Protection Act* in 1994, the park is a haven for the spiky Joshua tree, a type of yucca, and other desert life. The Joshua tree was named by early pioneers who felt that it resembled the prophet Joshua raising his arms in supplication to God or perhaps pointing the way for them to go. More than 80% of the park is designated as wilderness, so far off-road that most of the park's 1.3 million visitors each year never get to explore it.

Start at the *Cottonwood Visitor Center,* 7 miles north of I-10 at the south entrance to the park. There is another visitors' center, the *Oasis Visitor Center,* at the park's northern entrance and headquarters about a mile south of Twentynine Palms on Utail Trail off Highway 62. Each center has a cactus garden, and offers brochures of the area. At the *Oasis Visitor Center,* a short trail takes hikers to the *Oasis of Mara,* an area of cottonwoods, mesquite, and palm trees. This park has become one of the world's most popular rock climbing areas from October through May, when temperatures are mildest. More than 3,500 climbs of varying stages of difficulty have been established on the decomposing granite pillars and boulders throughout the park.

There is plenty to do besides scaling the rocks. Drives along the park's two-lane roads offer panoramic vistas of distant mountains. Take water and food; the park has no stores. At *Cholla Cactus Gardens,* 10 miles south of Wye, a nature trail winds among the species known as jumping cholla, named for the way it seems to jump out at you to give you a painful sting. (It's probably a good place to skip if you have young children with you.) *Wonderland of the Rocks* in Hidden Valley is the most popular site on park grounds. Thousands of years of desert winds have carved the rocks into bizarre shapes resembling sailing ships, monsters, cabbages, kings, and assorted other oddities. The best examples of Joshua trees stand at *Keys View,* which offers impressive views of the San Bernardino Mountains, Mt. San Jacinto, and the distant waters of the Salton Sea. Camping is available on park land. For information contact the Superintendent, *Joshua Tree National Park* (74485 National Park Dr., Twentynine Palms, CA 92277; phone: 619-367-7511).

BEST EN ROUTE

Expect to pay $165 or more per night in winter for a double room at those places we've listed as expensive; and $100 to $165 at those in the moderate category. Summer rates generally are half the winter rates or less. Unless otherwise indicated, rooms have air conditioning, private baths, TV sets, and telephones. Hotels are listed alphabetically by price category.

PALM SPRINGS

Hyatt Grand Champions In addition to 316 suites and 20 villas, facilities include two restaurants, four pools, two Jacuzzis, a health center, and golf clinics.

Children's programs are also available. 44600 Indian Wells La. (phone: 619-341-1000; fax: 619-568-2236). Expensive.

Palm Springs Hilton This luxury resort has 260 rooms and suites, a restaurant, a swimming pool with poolside café, desert gardens, six lighted tennis courts, a piano bar, and an extensive art collection. 400 E. Tahquitz Canyon Way (phone: 619-320-6868; 800-522-6900). Expensive.

Palm Springs Marquis Features here include 267 deluxe rooms and suites, two restaurants, a lounge, two pools surrounded by palms, two tennis courts, and free airport shuttle service. All rooms have balconies, and the suites have kitchenettes, fireplaces, and wet bars. 150 S. Indian Canyon Dr. (phone: 619-322-2121; 800-262-0186; fax: 619-322-2380). Expensive.

Spa Resort Owned by the Agua Caliente Indians, the hotel has 210 rooms and 20 suites, many with private balconies, plus a restaurant, lounge, and pool. However, the big attraction is the luxury spa with 34 marble tubs brimming with the therapeutic hot springs water for which Palm Springs was named. 100 N. Indian Canyon Dr. (phone: 619-325-1461; 800-854-1279). Moderate.

Wyndham Palm Springs This 410-room luxury property boasts the largest hotel swimming pool in town, plus a full health club, two Jacuzzis, two restaurants, and live entertainment in its nightclub. 888 E. Tahquitz Canyon Way (phone: 619-322-6000; 800-872-4335; fax: 619-322-5351). Moderate.

Redwood National and State Parks and Lassen Volcanic National Park, California

Millions of years ago, redwoods grew throughout vast areas of North America. Now they're found only in a narrow band of land along the coast of northern California and southern Oregon, and they rarely grow more than 30 miles inland since the conifer needs the moisture of the coastal fog.

Nature designed the redwood to last. Although redwoods are related to the giant sequoias of the High Sierra, the sequoia's trunk is larger, and the dark brown bark of a redwood is easily distinguished from the sequoia's bright reddish brown color. The scientific name for the coast redwood is *Sequoia sempervirens.* It can grow either from seeds or sprout from the roots and stumps of old trees. Its bark often is more than a foot thick, and natural chemicals in the fiber of the tree resist decay, disease, and fire. The durability of redwood trees is, ironically, the main reason for their demise; their wood is superb for items like picnic benches and the siding of houses, and it has incredible insulation properties.

For over a century commercial logging has been active in this region of the northwest, and more than 95% of the original redwood forest has been cut down. Efforts have been made to preserve the trees, however. Today, there are about 250,000 acres of redwood parks in California.

The following route goes through 110,000-acre *Redwood National and State Parks* (as the area is now known), which hugs the northern California coastline for 50 miles along US 101 from above Eureka almost to the Oregon border. Travelers can then drive 200 miles southeast to *Lassen Volcanic National Park,* home of one of the most recently active volcanoes in the continental US.

En Route from San Francisco The *Redwood National and State Parks* is 326 miles north of San Francisco via US 101. Forty-five miles south of Eureka, there are 33 miles of majestic redwood groves on the Avenue of the Giants in *Humboldt Redwoods State Park.* Enter *Redwood National and State Parks* about 30 miles north of Eureka near Orick.

REDWOOD NATIONAL AND STATE PARKS Home of the world's tallest tree, *Redwood National Park* has been designated a World Heritage Site and International Biosphere Reserve. Within its borders are three state parks, which existed for many years before the national park was established. The "State Parks" was recently added to its official name. There are visitors' centers at Orick, Hiouchi, and Crescent City.

Because it encompasses woodlands and seashore, the area offers a wide range of activities, including camping, hiking, and trail riding through majestic forests; spectacular views from bluffs along 33 miles of rugged shoreline; and access to remote beaches. For a leisurely drive through the redwoods, take the Newton B. Drury Scenic Parkway off US 101 between Orick and Klamath.

Just north of Orick on Bald Hills Road stands *Lady Bird Johnson Grove,* a group of immense trees named in honor of the former First Lady. The world's tallest tree, 367.8 feet high and 44 feet in circumference, stands in *Tall Trees Grove* among fellow behemoths averaging more than 300 feet high. You can visit the record-holder via a steep 3-mile (round trip) hiking trail. In summer you can get a shuttle to the trailhead, leaving from the *Redwood Information Center* at Orick. If you drive yourself, you will need to get a trailhead parking permit at the information center.

North of *Lady Bird Johnson Grove* is *Prairie Creek Redwoods State Park,* which gets as much rain as an Amazon rain forest (about 100 inches a year, most of which falls in winter). The park is filled with redwood, big-leaf maple, Douglas fir, and luxuriant foliage and flowers; Fern Canyon's 50-foot-high walls are swathed with moss and lichen. Forty miles of trails stretch through the area's 12,000-acre forest, and in the broad meadows of the state park, a herd of about 200 Roosevelt elk roams free. Gold Bluffs, at the western edge of *Prairie Creek Redwoods State Park,* faces the sea. Rugged promontories jut into the Pacific and huge waves break over the jagged rocks. There are more than 100 campsites at *Gold Bluff Beach* and *Elk Prairie.*

Take the Newton B. Drury Scenic Parkway as far as Klamath. About 20 miles farther north on US 101 is *Del Norte Coast Redwoods State Park.* It is unusual because its virgin redwood forest extends right to the steep bluffs overlooking the rocky shore. The best views are from the coast-winding *Damnation Creek Trail.* In late spring, this section is ablaze with rhododendrons. There are campsites at *Mill Creek.*

Jedediah Smith Redwoods State Park is at the northeastern edge of the coastal redwood belt, 9 miles northeast of Crescent City. *Redwood National and State Parks* maintains its headquarters and a visitors' center here. The park contains redwoods as well as such inland species as Jeffrey pine. The largest trees are in *Stout Grove,* the star attraction being the 340-foot Stout Tree. There are campsites and good swimming at a sandy beach along the Smith River.

For additional information, contact *Redwood National and State Parks* (1111 Second St., Crescent City, CA 95531; phone: 707-464-6101).

En Route from Redwood National and State Parks Drive south on US 101 to the junction with Highway 299 (about 10 miles north of Eureka). Follow Highways 299 and 44 to *Lassen Volcanic National Park,* about 200 miles southeast of Eureka. Highway 44 will take you to the visitors' information center at Manzanita Lake. The park headquarters is in Mineral, on Highway 36, 9 miles from another park entrance.

LASSEN VOLCANIC NATIONAL PARK Lassen Peak last erupted from 1914 to 1921, making it one of the most recently active volcanoes in the continental US. After centuries of peace, Lassen's 20th-century eruptions were highlighted by a massive explosion in May 1915 that mowed down all life on the northeast side of the mountain for several miles. Volcanic dust fell as far away as Nevada. In 1916, the volcano and the surrounding area were designated a national park. (You could say it opened with a bang.) *Lassen* is a tiny *Yellowstone,* with bubbling mud pots, boiling hot springs, and hissing steam vents known as fumaroles. An example of every type of volcano can be found here. Like *Yellowstone,* most of *Lassen*'s major sites are easily accessible by car. The 30-mile Lassen Park Road winds through the park's western section, which contains the major attractions, including 10,457-foot Lassen Peak. More than 150 miles of hiking trails lead to thermal areas and lakes. *Lassen Peak Trail* will take you on a 2½-mile climb to the top of Lassen Peak; a shorter, easier trail leads to *Bumpass Hell,* a section of boiling hot springs, mud pots, and fumaroles in the southwest corner. (Bumpass is named for an early guide who plunged a leg into a steaming mud pot.) Heed warning signs and stay on the trail. Nearby is the *Sulphur Works,* another hydrothermal area of bubbling pools, mud pots, and fumaroles. It is accessible by car.

Summit Lake, in the park's center, is the starting point for backpacking trips to the eastern areas. *Cinder Cone,* in the northeast corner, was set aside as a national monument several years before *Lassen* became a park.

The stark cylindrical cone is surrounded by colorful formations of volcanic ash called the *Painted Dunes.* To the east of *Cinder Cone* lie the aptly named *Fantastic Lava Beds,* a mass of black volcanic stone deposited when *Cinder Cone* erupted in the late 1700s. Keep in mind that though *Cinder Cone* is considered dormant, new eruptions are still possible. *Lassen* has about 400 campsites available on a first-come, first-served basis. The only lodging in the park is *Drakeshead Guest Ranch* (phone: 916-529-1512). Private campgrounds and lodging are available in surrounding areas. For additional information contact the Superintendent, *Lassen Volcanic National Park* (PO Box 100, Mineral, CA 96063; phone: 916-595-4444).

BEST EN ROUTE

Expect to pay $85 to $135 per night for a double room at those places we've listed as expensive. Unless otherwise indicated, rooms have air conditioning, private baths, TV sets, and telephones.

EUREKA

Eureka Inn This National Historic Landmark English Tudor building is the social center of the Victorian town of Eureka, which stands midway between *Redwood National and State Parks* and the Avenue of the Giants in *Humboldt Redwoods State Park.* The 105-room inn has a traditional, wood-paneled lobby with a fireplace, as well as a splendid restaurant, a rathskeller with nightly entertainment, a pool, and a Jacuzzi. There is no air conditioning. Seventh and F Sts. (phone: 707-442-6441; 800-862-4906; fax: 707-442-0637). Expensive.

REDDING

Red Lion Inn This comfortable, modern 194-room motel features a dining room, coffee shop, pool, Jacuzzi, and putting green. Guests have access to the nearby 18-hole *Gold Hills* golf course and the *Sun Oaks Racket Club* in town. Redding is less than an hour's drive from *Lassen Volcanic National Park* and a few minutes from the Lake Shasta recreational area. 1830 Hilltop Dr. (phone: 916-221-8700; 800-547-8010; fax: 916-221-0324). Expensive.

Sequoia and Kings Canyon National Parks, California

Sequoia and *Kings Canyon National Parks* are the backpackers' highway into the majestic Sierra Nevada of California. By car you can see some views of the high country, particularly the giant sequoias, for which *Sequoia* is named, and the forests that surround them. What you don't see by car is almost everything but the trees: the largest mountain peaks, especially Mt. Whitney, which at 14,494 feet is the tallest peak in the 48 contiguous states;

animals; streams; and hundreds of miles of mountain trails for hiking, camping, horse and mule packing, and fishing.

Geographically and administratively, *Sequoia* and *Kings Canyon* are one park, covering about 860,000 acres. But the two boast some different physical features. *Sequoia,* the western edge of which is accessible by car, is the site of the largest of the world-renowned giant *Sequoiadendron giganteum* trees, among the largest living things known on earth (and not to be confused with coastal redwoods—*Sequoia sempervirens*—which are taller but not nearly so broad). Ancestors of the giant sequoia used to cover much of this hemisphere's landmass; now they are found only between 5,000- to 7,000-foot elevation on the western slopes of the Sierra Nevada. East of the stands of sequoia, the park rises with the Sierra Nevada, culminating at the park's eastern edge in Mt. Whitney, Mt. Muir (14,015 feet), and Mt. Langley (14,042 feet). The western slope is a gradual climb, but on the eastern heights, as quickly as the steep peaks rise they drop off again to lower elevations, and outside the parks the country breaks into deep, long valleys.

Kings Canyon stretches north of *Sequoia,* sharing with it one entire border. Made a national park in 1940, *Kings Canyon* has the same wild, rugged mountain beauty, with the additional attraction of the sheer canyon walls for which it gained its fame. Mountains of 13,000 feet are not at all uncommon in the eastern region of *Kings Canyon,* and running through them, from the northern reaches of *Kings Canyon* to Mt. Whitney in *Sequoia,* is the *John Muir Trail,* the much-traveled 220-mile walking path that threads through the most spectacular vistas of both parks. Immediately to the east and north of the parks are the *John Muir Wilderness* and part of the *Inyo National Forest.*

There is no more fitting tribute to the naturalist than the trails and protected areas that bear his name. It seems that most of America's beautiful parks and natural wonderlands have at some time in their histories required the guardianship of farseeing and usually heroic protectors—in this case it was naturalists John Muir and George Stewart who fought the government and the lumber companies to protect the sanctity of *Sequoia* and *Kings Canyon* in the late 1880s, long before most people recognized their beauty and spiritual importance. In 1890, *Sequoia National Park* was officially created, the country's second such refuge. (*Yellowstone* had been established 18 years earlier; *Yosemite* followed *Sequoia* by a mere six days.)

Sequoia National Park is 236 miles north of Los Angeles and 268 miles southeast of San Francisco. Cars are given limited access to the parks; only two major roads—Highway 180 and Generals Highway—enter their 1,300 square miles. Both roads are kept open when weather permits, but may require tire chains in the winter. During this time, heavy snow can close the section of road that connects the parks for weeks at a time. The drive through the parks takes patience and time, but the rewards are great. Generals Highway is a beautiful road; 46 miles long, it runs from the park entrance, 7 miles north of Three Rivers, winds through the mighty stands of sequoia in the park's western portion, and ends at Grant Grove in *Kings Canyon National Park.* From there, travelers can continue their explorations on Highway 180.

A number of stores and supply stations, located near the park campsites, can outfit visitors for a hike or camping overnight. They also sell California state fishing licenses, which are required if you plan to try your luck in the park's lakes and streams. Mules and horses can be rented at Wolverton, Cedar Grove, and Mineral King for day or overnight trips through both parks, and at Grant Grove for day use only. For additional information contact the Superintendent, *Sequoia and Kings Canyon National Parks* (Three Rivers, CA 93271; phone: 209-565-3134 for park visitor information; 209-565-3351 for road and weather conditions; 209-565-3708 for backcountry information; 209-561-3314 for cabin or motel reservations).

SEQUOIA NATIONAL PARK If you start the driving tour at the western corner of *Sequoia,* you will pass some of the most magnificent examples of sequoia in the world—several named for American generals. Based on total volume, the sequoias are the largest living things on this planet. The General Sherman Tree rises 274.9 feet on a 102.6-foot circumference, it weighs 1,385 tons, and it is estimated to be between 2,300 and 2,700 years old. Almost as tall as the *Capitol* in Washington, it's no less a national treasure. Although the tree has been photographed thousands of times, no picture expresses the sheer awe you'll feel standing next to its thick, reddish-brown trunk. The General Sherman Tree is part of Giant Forest, of special interest because it has four or five of the biggest sequoias anywhere and it offers a view of the sequoia in every stage of development, from seedling (they grow from seeds about the size of a flake of oatmeal) to huge adulthood.

Halfway along Generals Highway is the *Lodgepole Visitor Center,* with displays on the trees and other aspects of park life; the center also has information on the variety of activities available to visitors and is one of the many starting points for guided hiking tours. (There's also a visitors' center in Grant Grove and one at Ash Mountain, the *Foothills Visitor Center,* near the Highway 198 entrance; visitors' contact stations at Cedar Grove in *Kings Canyon* and at *Mineral King* in Sequoia are open summers only.) The best way to see the parks is on foot with a backpack, a tent, and plenty of time. Ranger-guided trips through the sequoia forests provide visitors with a feeling for the land that is impossible to get from the road.

In the Giant Forest, rising some 6,725 feet above sea level (4,000 feet above the Kaweah River) is Moro Rock, which offers a magnificent view of some of the treasures *Sequoia* has to offer. The eastward view is most impressive, looking toward the spiny Great Western Divide. A short drive from the rock is Crescent Meadow and *Tharp's Log,* the log cabin summer headquarters of 19th-century cattleman Hale Tharp. A stroll to Beetle Rock is best saved for late afternoon, for the experience of watching the sunset. The strong-winded should hike down the steep ½-mile trail to Crystal Cave, a marble cavern accessible only by guided tours. (It is a 9-mile drive to where this hike begins. The road is not accessible to buses or trailers. Tickets for cave tours must be purchased in advance at *Lodgepole* or *Foothills Visitor Centers*, see above.)

KINGS CANYON NATIONAL PARK As you drive along the Generals Highway into *Kings Canyon* you will pass several other magnificent trees. Particularly noteworthy are those in Grant Grove, where the road joins Highway 180. There stands the General Grant Tree, a full seven feet shorter than Sherman, but five feet larger in circumference, and considered by many to be the more awe-inspiring spectacle. The Robert E. Lee Tree is nearby, and a short drive (about 5 miles) from the grove is Big Stump Basin, where you can see what remains of these colossi after loggers get to them, as they did in the late 19th century. Another well-known tree in the range is the Hart Tree, standing in the Redwood Mountain Grove, west of Generals Highway in *Kings Canyon National Park.*

The center of activity in *Kings Canyon* is Cedar Grove, reached by Highway 180. This area has three family campgrounds with 314 sites and one group campground, and the ranger station at Cedar Grove has the most current information on hikes. From Cedar Grove, hikers can go in almost any direction, usually up, on miles of trails. The least explored areas are to the north, into the heart of the park. You will find lakes of all sizes and mountain after mountain. Visitors can set out on foot or horse or mule-back.

BEST EN ROUTE

There are park lodges and campsites throughout the national parks. *Guest Services* (PO Box 789, Three Rivers, CA 93271; phone: 209-561-3314; fax: 209-561-3135) has information about the parks' four lodges: *Giant Forest Lodge* in *Sequoia Park* (see below), *Cedar Grove* and *Grant Grove* lodges in *Kings Canyon,* and *Stony Creek Lodge* between *Sequoia Park* and *Kings Canyon.*

The big *Lodgepole Campground* in *Sequoia Park* is run on a reservation basis from a week before *Memorial Day* through September. Reservations can be made through *Destinet* (phone: 800-365-2267). The rest of the year it's first-come, first-served. Other campsites are available in the *Sequoia National Forest* (south and west of *Sequoia* and *Kings Canyon* parks). These include sites at *Hume Lake,* where boating, swimming, and fishing are among the attractions, and *Stony Creek Campground* on the Generals Highway between *Sequoia* and *Kings Canyon*. Camping is also available in nearby *Inyo National Forest* south and east of *Sequoia*. Many campgrounds are closed in winter.

Outside the parks, hotel and motel accommodations are available in three nearby towns: Three Rivers, just south of *Sequoia;* Visalia to the west; and also to the west, Fresno, by far the biggest city, where there's a large choice of national hotel and motel chains.

Expect to pay $80 to $115 per night for a double room at those places we've listed as expensive; $55 to $80 at those in the moderate category; and less than $55 at those described as inexpensive. Unless otherwise indicated, rooms have private baths, but no air conditioning, TV sets, or telephones.

SEQUOIA NATIONAL PARK

Giant Forest Lodge Location is everything, so this 103-room national park–style complex of simple rustic cottages and motel-type rooms fills up fast. Reserve early. Don't expect the amenities of a city hotel, though some rooms do have radios. There is a restaurant and lounge. Open May through October. For reservations, contact *Guest Services* (see above). Moderate.

GRANT GROVE

Grant Grove Lodge In this complex of 52 extremely rustic cabins (a few have private baths), almost all have wood-burning stoves and some have patios. There's a coffee shop and lounge. Open year-round. In Grant Grove Village, Hwy. 180, Kings Canyon. For reservations, contact *Guest Services* (see above). Moderate.

Montecito-Sequoia Lodge Eleven miles south of Grant Grove, this private lake resort offers 32 rooms, most of which are in the central lodge, but there are also some cabins (without private baths). There's a dining room and lounge, as well as facilities for tennis, canoeing, water skiing, and sailing. Open year-round. PO Box 858, Kings Canyon, CA 93633 (phone: 209-565-3388; 800-227-9900; fax: 415-967-1540). Expensive.

Yosemite National Park, California

A good many of California's finest physical resources are the product of the Sierra Nevada, the mountain range that runs for 500 miles parallel to the Nevada border. The gem in this mountainous necklace is *Yosemite National Park,* 1,170 square miles of mountains, valleys, granite spires and monoliths, waterfalls, and forests in central-eastern California, 309 miles north of Los Angeles and 190 miles east of San Francisco.

The natural history of the park spans millions of years, starting during an ancient age when a shallow arm of the Pacific covered a section of western Nevada, the Sierra Nevada, and the great Central Valley of California. The outer crust of the earth was shifted and pushed up by molten rock that welled up beneath it and eventually cooled. In time, these layers were eroded and the igneous rock, granite, was exposed. Later upheavals of the earth tilted these layers to the west, creating the steep eastern flank and long western slope of the mountains we know today. As a consequence of the angle of the mountains, the flow of streams became more rapid, cutting deep V-shaped valleys into the granite. Then, during Ice Ages two million years ago, glaciers gouged the valley into a U-shaped trough with a round bottom and sheer sides. As the glaciers melted, rocks and other debris that had mixed with the ice were released; the resulting dam created Lake Yosemite. Scientists estimate that the lake was originally 2,000 feet deep, but sediment from the high country filled it in to the present valley floor level.

Yosemite was established as a national park in 1890 and, with its impressive scenery and numerous recreational possibilities, it continues to attract millions of visitors year-round.

Yosemite Village, the center of activities in the park, with campgrounds, lodging, shops, and restaurants, is a good place to begin a visit (if possible, come in the off-season to avoid the huge summer crowds). The *Yosemite Valley Visitors' Center,* open year-round, offers exhibits on the geological development of the area and information on the wide range of activities offered—ranger-guided walks, lectures, and demonstrations (the *Yosemite Guide* provides a schedule of the week's activities). After a stop at the visitors' center, a tour of the valley via tram will introduce you to the park's wonders.

The valley is *Yosemite*'s main attraction. Carpeted with meadows and forests and watered by the Merced River, the valley is 7 miles long and up to a mile wide. Its walls rise 2,000 to 4,000 feet from the valley floor, featuring some of the geological wonders of the world. First and foremost is El Capitan which, at 7,569 feet high, is among the largest single blocks of granite in the world. Towering above the lower end of the valley, directly across from El Capitan, are the Cathedral Spires. The left one is 5,907 feet high; the right, 6,118 feet. On the north side of the valley stand the Three Brothers, a trio of leaning peaks piled on top of one another to a height of 7,779 feet. Beyond, the upper valley broadens with a semicircle of granite domes—Sentinel, Basket, North Dome, and the massive Half Dome. These granite deposits were sculpted by glaciation and exfoliation; in the latter process, the surface layers of rock peel, chip, and crumble into rounded contours on their way toward ultimate dissolution. Though this shaping force is completely imperceptible, the valley's magnificent waterfalls demonstrate the process still at work. The most spectacular of the valley's falls is Yosemite, noted for its height; the Upper Fall plunges 1,430 feet over the north wall (a height equal to nine Niagara Falls), and the Lower Fall immediately below is a drop of more than 300 feet. Combined with the cascades in between, the fall's double leap measures 2,425 feet, making Yosemite the highest waterfall on this continent. With the valley's other waterfalls—Ribbon, the misty Bridalveil, Nevada, Vernal, and Illilouette—*Yosemite* offers one of the most amazing water spectacles anywhere.

But Yosemite Valley is by no means all the park has to offer. More than 800 miles of trails beyond the valley can be covered by horse, mule, or foot. No matter how you see them, there are several other park highlights you should not miss. Glacier Point offers a sweeping 180° panorama of the High Sierra. Half Dome rises in front of you, Nevada and Vernal Falls are prominent, and in the background are the snowy peaks of Yosemite's backcountry. The road to Glacier Point (closed in winter) winds through red fir and pine forest and meadow.

Tuolumne Meadows is a major trailhead to the high country and, at 8,600 feet, the largest subalpine meadow complex in the High Sierra. Though the Tioga Road to Tuolumne Meadows is closed in the winter, during the summer the park operates a campground here and a full-scale naturalist program exploring high-altitude ecological systems.

The Mariposa Grove, at the southern end of the park, is the largest of the park's three groves of mammoth sequoia. Over 200 of the beautiful old trees here measure more than 10 feet in diameter. Among them is the tunnel tree (now supine), which was so large that people used to drive through the hollow area at the base. The Grizzly Giant is not hollow; but if it were, a Mack truck carrying the tunnel tree could drive straight through it.

You also can hike to the valley floor along one of several trails. *Four-Mile Trail* (really 4.6 miles) zigzags down steeply, while *Pohono Trail* skirts the south rim and descends to the valley floor near Bridalveil Falls, a total of 13 miles.

In addition to its scenic attractions, *Yosemite* offers a wide variety of summer and winter recreational activities. The miles of trails offer hiking for everyone from tenderfoot to trailblazer. Wilderness permits are required for overnight backcountry travel and are issued at the ranger station on a first-come first-served basis, or by mail reservation February through May. *Tuolumne Meadows* stables rent horses and mules and offer a variety of guided trips from one-day excursions to six-day saddle trips through the High Sierra. If you're afraid of mules and horses, bike rentals at *Yosemite Lodge* and *Camp Curry* provide wheels. For those who like to live dangerously, the vertical granite walls of the valley beckon with some of the finest climbing challenges in the world. Both *Yosemite Mountaineering School* (phone: 209-372-8444) and *Curry Village Cross-Country Ski School* (phone: 209-372-1244) give lessons for all levels of expertise; also see "Climbing Schools" in *Mountain Climbing and Mountains,* DIVERSIONS.

In wintertime, *Yosemite* becomes a snow-covered paradise, with *Badger Pass* for downhill skiing, over 90 miles of marked trails and about 24 miles of groomed track for cross-country skiing (see *Cross-Country Skiing* in DIVERSIONS), an outdoor ice skating rink at *Camp Curry,* and magnificent mountainous vistas. Call 209-372-0200 for recorded road and weather conditions.

Though not strictly in the park itself, a trip to *Yosemite* should include a meal at *Erna's Elderberry House* (48688 Victoria La., Oakhurst; phone:

209-683-6800). This restaurant offers California fare with a European twist, providing an eclectic and sophisticated dining experience that you would expect to find in a large city, not a tiny hamlet just outside the south gate of the park. The restaurant is part of *Château du Sureau,* an elegant country inn (see *Best en Route*).

For additional information contact the Superintendent, *Yosemite National Park* (PO Box 577, Yosemite, CA 95389; phone: 209-372-0265 for general information during business hours; 209-372-0200 for recorded information on road conditions, weather, skiing, camping, and permits; 209-252-4848 for lodging).

BEST EN ROUTE

The *National Park Service* runs 17 developed campgrounds in the park. Group and individual campsites in the Yosemite Valley must be reserved (phone: 800-365-2267 in the US and Canada). In addition, there are a number of campgrounds (including those in the high country, which are open only in the summer) that are available on a first-come, first-served basis. Expect to pay $200 or more per night for a double room at the place we've listed as very expensive; $120 to $200 at those described as expensive; $75 to $120 at those in the moderate category; and less than $75 at places listed as inexpensive. Unless otherwise indicated, rooms have air conditioning, private baths, TV sets, and telephones. For each location, hotels are listed alphabetically by price category.

YOSEMITE NATIONAL PARK

Ahwahnee This classy structure of stone and native timber dates from 1927. It has 99 lodge rooms, 24 cottages (not air conditioned), a magnificent dining room, a bar, entertainment, and well-designed, spacious public areas. Also see *America's Special Havens* in DIVERSIONS. Yosemite Valley (phone: 209-372-1407; 209-252-4848 for reservations). Expensive.

Wawona The 104 rooms in this century-old Victorian structure are furnished with antiques. The dining room serves all meals; there's also a nine-hole golf course, tennis courts, and a pool. Roughly half the rooms have private baths; there are no in-room telephones, TV sets, or air conditioning. Open April to *Thanksgiving,* for the *Christmas* holiday season, and Thursdays through Sundays from January through March. 27 miles south of Yosemite Valley (phone: 209-252-4848). Moderate to inexpensive.

Yosemite Lodge A combination of cabins and modern hotel rooms built around a central area, this property has 200 rooms (no TV sets or air conditioning) plus two restaurants, a cafeteria, a pool, bike rental, shops, and, in summer, an ice-cream cone stand. Yosemite Valley (phone: 209-252-4848 for reservations). Moderate to inexpensive.

Camp Curry The 200 units here are in rustic tents, cabins, and hotel rooms. Guests have access to a cafeteria, a public lounge, fast-food service, a pool, and a bike rental facility. The *Mountaineering School* has its headquarters here in the spring and autumn (in summer at Tuolumne Meadows), and in the winter there's an ice skating rink. Yosemite Valley (phone: 209-252-4848 for reservations). Inexpensive.

FISH CAMP

Marriott's Tenaya Lodge at Yosemite Just 2 miles from the park's south entrance, this 242-room resort offers deluxe accommodations. The rooms are decorated in western and Native American designs. The *Sierra* restaurant, which operates seasonally, offers California/northern Italian food; the *Parkside Deli* serves breakfast, lunch, and dinner in a casual setting. There also are indoor and outdoor pools, whirlpool baths, an aerobic center, a fitness salon, and a sauna. Golf, horseback riding, mountain climbing, bicycle rentals, skiing, fishing, and water sports are available nearby. There's a children's day camp program available as well. 1122 Hwy. 41 (phone: 209-683-6555; 800-635-5807). Expensive.

OAKHURST

Château du Sureau This nine-room hotel on a seven-and-a-half-acre estate evokes the ambience of a country inn in the south of France. Antiques and fine artwork combine with touches of French limestone and hand-painted tile to create a luxurious atmosphere; the service is first-rate. *Erna's Elderberry House* restaurant offers unusually fine food; a full breakfast is included in the room rate. TV sets are available on request. Located in the Sierra foothills, about 30 minutes from *Yosemite*'s south gate. 48688 Victoria La. (phone: 209-683-6860). Very expensive.

Rocky Mountain National Park, Colorado

The North American Rocky Mountains stretch from northern New Mexico and southern Colorado to the Columbia Range and the Rocky Mountain Trench in Canada, 300 miles north of the US-Canada border. And this massive range is part of an even larger series of mountains, the North American Cordillera, which includes the Brooks Range in Alaska and Mexico's Sierra Madre, the mountains that follow Mexico's eastern and western coasts.

In the US, the highest peaks in the Rockies are those of the Front Range, so named because it is the first range of the chain to rise from the Great Plains in north-central Colorado. Some 415 square miles of the Front Range have been set aside as *Rocky Mountain National Park,* and within its 265,700 acres are 113 named peaks over 10,000 feet, 67 above 12,000 feet, innumerable mountain valleys (averaging 8,000 feet above sea level), and Longs

Peak at 14,255 feet. It is a spectacular area of glacial moraines (piles of rocks where the advance of glaciers finally stopped), mountain lakes, and alpine meadows. The area has five small glaciers, hiking and horse trails, peaks, canyons, and roads.

The Colorado Rockies began forming around 70 million years ago; they rose and were worn down by wind and water erosion over the next 30 million years. A 15-million-year period of volcanic activity and faulting tossed them up once again. The mountains that appeared were at the mercy of wind and water for eons, but their present form was stamped on the chain during the past two million years, when the first of four glacial periods began. Portions of mountains were leveled by the incredible force of the glaciers; chasms appeared as mountain walls were cut through; cirques dug where the glaciers' heads buttressed against unyielding mountain faces. Many of the beautiful mountain lakes that dot the park today are the remnants of deep gouges dug by the inexorable force of glaciers grinding against bedrock.

The US government bought this land as part of the Louisiana Purchase in 1803. The first Americans to explore the region, Colonel Stephen Long (1820), William Ashley (1825), and John C. Frémont (1843) paved the way for others. The mountains became the goal of many Easterners seeking gold in the late 1850s and early 1860s. In 1859, Joel Estes saw the Front Range and within a year had settled there, in Estes Park, the town now named for him (just 3 miles from the main entrance to the park). Estes loved the beauty and abundance of the area, but several years after he arrived, he became weary of the isolation and moved farther west. Within a year he was back, unable to live without the rugged spectacle of the mountains. He was not alone in his appreciation. An English earl built a huge estate in the Front Range and publicized the area's beauty. In 1915, the region became a national park, thanks largely to the hard work and constant writing of Enos Mills, a great naturalist and author. He believed that this wonderful wilderness should be maintained as a park in order to preserve the clean air and lofty peaks. He once wrote: "He who feels the spell of the wild, the rhythmic melody of falling water, the echoes among the crags, the bird songs, the wind in the pines . . . is in tune with the universe."

The entire park is a wildlife refuge, natural habitat of elk, deer, black bear, coyote, moose, and mountain lions and bobcats, which are increasing in number. You may see bighorn sheep—called Rocky Mountain sheep—which are the park's emblem, and if you do any hiking, especially in spring (which comes late here), you will see the alpine wildflowers that flourish in the meadows above and below treeline. Above treeline, flora is that of the tundra—lichen, tiny flowers, scrub trees with deep roots that can survive the fierce winds, deep snows, and rocky, barren terrain above 11,000 feet. Summer is brief in the mountains—a few weeks in late July and August—and the winters are long and harsh. You should always carry a warm jacket—even in summer, there can be snow showers.

Rocky Mountain National Park is open all year, though many facilities—and roads—within the park close during the snows, between October and May. The wilderness will not necessarily be bereft of people—about 3.1 million visit each year. For the best chance of spending some time with nature relatively alone, visit the western and southwestern portions of the park; they are the least populated because they're the hardest to reach by road.

For additional information contact the Superintendent, *Rocky Mountain National Park* (Estes Park, CO 80517; phone: 970-586-1206; 970-586-1333 for recorded information; 800-365-2267 for camping reservations from June to *Labor Day*); *Estes Park Area Chamber of Commerce* (PO Box 3050, Estes Park, CO 80517; phone: 303-586-4431; 800-443-7837); or *Grand Lake Chamber of Commerce* (Grand Lake, CO 80447; phone: 970-627-3402; 800-531-1019).

En Route from Denver *Rocky Mountain National Park,* a two-hour drive northwest of Denver, is approached through the beautiful Estes Valley. In the town of Estes Park you can take an aerial tramway to the top of Prospect Mountain (8,900 feet) for your first, overwhelming view of the Rockies to the west. From Estes Park, there are two possible entrances to the park—via US 34 through the Fall River entrance onto Trail Ridge Road, or via US 36 through the more southerly entrance at Beaver Meadows and directly onto Trail Ridge Road.

BEAVER MEADOWS If you are visiting for the first time, by all means take the slightly more direct and shorter route through the Beaver Meadows entrance, where you will be able to stop at the visitors' center. Rangers at the visitors' center have information on hikes, camping and campgrounds, activities, and facilities in the park. There are more than 355 miles of trails here, designed for amateurs as well as experienced hikers, one of which is the half-mile trail (at the end of the short drive south from Beaver Meadows) that circles Bear Lake. If you are a serious hiker you may want to try the 16-mile (round trip) route to and from the top of Longs Peak, the highest in the range. The view is unsurpassed.

TRAIL RIDGE ROAD AND OLD FALL RIVER ROAD There are two roads across the park: Trail Ridge Road, the park's main road, which starts at the Deer Ridge Junction and meanders west and then south to Grand Lake; and the shorter Old Fall River Road, which runs slightly north of Trail Ridge Road. Old Fall River Road is a narrow, one-way dirt road with a 15 mph speed limit that is strictly enforced, but it offers marvelous opportunities for photographs, both of mountain peaks and of park wildlife.

Trail Ridge Road offers an exquisite view of Longs Peak and passes by the Mummy Range, where you rise above the treeline and lose sight of the stands of spruce, pine, and fir. The road, which climbs above 12,000 feet, is billed as "the highest continuously paved highway in the United States." At Fall River Pass, where the road turns gradually southward, you can stop at the *Alpine Visitors' Center,* where exhibits explain the alpine tundra through which you are driving. The *Trail Ridge Store* has a snack bar for light meals. If you follow Trail Ridge Road to its end at Grand Lake you will cross the Continental Divide at Milner Pass (10,760 feet). The Divide is the weaving line that defines a basic North American watershed: All precipitation falling to the west of this ridge eventually winds up in the Pacific; to the east, in the Atlantic or the Gulf of Mexico. Farther north the Divide often appears as no more than a gentle rise in the road, but at Milner Pass, where the north fork of the Colorado River begins, you get a real sense of its significance. From here, Trail Ridge Road follows the Colorado to the western entrance and egress point of the park at Grand Lake and Lake Granby, which border the park on its southwest edge.

GRAND LAKE For a truly personalized guide to what's in the park, stop at the *Kawuneeche Visitor Center* at Grand Lake, at the park's western entrance point (US 34). The recently expanded center offers a computerized list of activities based on visitors' interests and time constraints. Grand Lake also has a good marina.

BEST EN ROUTE

Expect to pay $60 or more per night for a double room or cabin at places we've listed as expensive; $40 to $60 at those in the moderate category; and less than $40 at those described as inexpensive. Unless otherwise indicated, rooms have private baths, TV sets, and telephones but no air conditioning. Hotels are listed alphabetically by price category.

ESTES PARK

Machin's Cottages in the Pines Here are 17 comfortable, well-appointed cottages, which accommodate groups of up to 10 people. They have full kitchens, fireplaces, and cozy living rooms, but no telephones. Closed October through April. 2450 Eagle Cliff Rd. (phone: 970-586-4276). Expensive.

McGregor Mountain Lodge At the park entrance, overlooking Fall River Canyon, this lodge offers 28 one- and two-room units and an outdoor hot tub. There are no in-room telephones or dining facilities. 2815 Fall River Rd. (phone: 970-586-3457). Expensive to moderate.

Hobby Horse Motor Lodge Adjacent to a stable and golf course, with riding trails in the surrounding area, this 56-room inn has a heated pool as well as its own trout pool for children. There's no dining room, but there are restaurants within walking distance. Closed November through April. 800 Big Thompson (phone: 970-586-3336). Moderate to inexpensive.

Hawaii (The Big Island), Hawaii

With more than 4,038 square miles and a population of 125,000, Hawaii is truly the Big Island. It is also the youngest Hawaiian island—it's the only one still growing—a living text of how, and of what, the entire chain was formed. Hawaii is the island of volcanoes—periodic eruptions of Kilauea and Mauna Loa in *Hawaii Volcanoes National Park* have poured tons of lava across the countryside and into the sea. The natural forces gradually shaping and reshaping the entire chain have wrought a variety of landscapes here: the rich earth of the sugarcane fields, the coffee fields of the south Kona Coast, the verdant eastern coast, and the strange, sparse, moon-like rock beds of lava in the park. The island, larger in landmass than all of the major Hawaiian Islands combined, is home to 21 of the earth's 22 major climate zones as well.

The attractions of the Big Island are manifold. It has glittering resort areas on the Kona (west) and Kohala (northwest) Coasts offering accommodations and activities of every sort; many small agricultural communities practically untouched by commercialism; and numerous areas of lava-torn landscape that are both austere and impressive.

Allow at least four days to see the Big Island. There really are three major areas that beg to be explored: Hilo and the northern Hamakua Coast; the Kona Coast, famous for game fishing and golf; and *Hawaii Volcanoes National Park.* The route described below starts at Hilo, circles counterclockwise past the Hamakua area to the Kona Coast, and ends at the park. Both *Hilo Airport,* on the northeastern coast, and *Keahole-Kona Airport,* north of Kailua-Kona on the western coast, serve as entrance or exit points for travelers.

HILO The seat of Hawaii County, the focal point of Hawaii's thriving orchid industry and the gateway to *Hawaii Volcanoes National Park* just 28 miles away, Hilo has a funky charm. Several of its Plantation-era buildings—particularly along its main streets—have been faithfully restored.

The *Lyman Mission House and Museum* (276 Haili St.; phone: 808-935-5021), built in 1839 as the home of an early missionary, has exhibits on the ethnic makeup of the islands, as well as artifacts of early Hawaiian culture. It is open daily; there's an admission charge. Nearby is a very large artifact: the *Naha Stone,* which adorns the front yard of the *Hilo Library* (300 Waianuenue Ave.; phone: 808-933-4650). The stone weighs more than two tons. According to an ancient legend, the man who could lift the stone would become king of all the islands. The man who did so was King Kamehameha I—known to history as Kamehameha the Great because he did indeed conquer all the islands (although he depended more on cannons than brute strength).

A few blocks away, the *East Hawaii Cultural Center* (141 Kalakaua St.; phone: 808-961-5711) offers exhibits by many fine local artists. It is closed Sundays; no admission charge.

The most intriguing tropical gardens include *Nani Mau Gardens* (421 Makalika St.; phone: 808-959-3541), which is open daily and charges admission; *Hilo Tropical Gardens* (1477 Kalanianaole Ave.; phone: 808-935-4957), which is open daily and charges no admission; and *Orchids of Hawaii* (2801 Kilauea Ave.; phone: 808-959-3581), which is open weekdays and charges no admission.

Be sure to tour Banyan Drive, named for the numerous banyan trees planted by celebrities visiting the island. *Liliuokalani Gardens,* a 30-acre park with an Oriental theme, lies just off Banyan Drive. The park offers panoramic views of Hilo, Mauna Kea, and the Hamakua Coast. At the end of Banyan Drive is the *Suisan Fish Market,* where fishermen auction their morning catch Mondays through Saturdays beginning at 7:30 AM.

En Route from Hilo Head north on Highway 19, following the Hamakua Coast.

HAMAKUA COAST Atop high *pali* (cliffs), Highway 19 overlooks the windward coast and the not-very-peaceful Pacific Ocean. The views are staggering. This road was constructed to accommodate nature, not man, but drivers soon develop a rhythm as they curve, plunge, curve, and climb around waterfalls and valleys. All along the route are state Hawaiian Warrior signs indicating scenic overviews. Don't fail to stop. When Hawaiians think a view is good enough to warrant special note, take them at their word. Off the highway 15 miles north of Hilo at the small village of Honomu is *Akaka State Park,* with two of the island's most beautiful waterfalls. The highest is Akaka Falls itself—a 442-foot ribbon of water that plunges daintily down a jungle cliff; the other is Kahuna Falls, which drops 400 feet. Nearby are jungle walks among lush, if eerie, plants. Laupahoehoe Point—a small "leaf of lava" that pushes into the brutal Pacific—is an excellent spot for lunch alfresco. The picnic area is bathed in a fine sea spray, and the sometimes terrifying fury of the sea smashing against the rocks is a sight to see. In 1946, 20 school children and three teachers were swept away when a giant tidal wave washed over the point. A monument commemorates the spot.

WAIPIO VALLEY At its northernmost point Highway 19 joins Highway 240, which ends after 10 miles at Waipio Valley. The largest valley on the Big Island, Waipio was once home to some of old Hawaii's most powerful kings—Kamehameha, Liloa, and Umi. There is a scenic overlook there with fine views of the northeastern end of the island, and tour companies with four-wheel-drive vehicles offer tours along the rough roads.

En Route from Waipio Valley Return to Highway 19 and head west about 16 miles to Waimea/Kamuela and *Parker Ranch.*

PARKER RANCH At the base of the Kohala Mountains lies Hawaii's cattle industry capital, 225,000-acre *Parker Ranch,* in the quaint, rural community of Waimea/Kamuela. Unlike what most people expect of a Hawaiian town, Waimea has rustic charm, crisp mountain air, and lush, rolling hills dotted with grazing cattle. The *Parker Ranch Visitor Center* in Kamuela (*Parker Ranch Shopping Center;* phone: 808-885-7655) has a museum and provides tours that include several historic buildings. The center and museum are open daily; there's an admission charge.

En Route from Parker Ranch Continue west on Highway 19, crossing the base of the Kohala Mountains. Where the road turns south to follow Hawaii's western coast stands the *Puukohola Heiau National Historic Site* (off Hwy. 270 at Kawaihae; phone: 808-882-7218). Here you'll see an ancient temple (approximately 15th-century) and altar that young King Kamehameha I rebuilt between 1790 and 1791 and dedicated to the god of war. Behind this act of piety was cold and cunning ambition. He invited his chief island rival to the dedication ceremony and there had him killed. With that act, Kamehameha came closer to fulfilling his goal to conquer not just the island of Hawaii but all the major islands in the chain. The site is open daily; no admission charge.

Five miles south is Puako, a small village with several Hawaiian petroglyphs. At Puako, Highway 19 becomes the Queen Kaahumanu Highway, cutting across a lava desert and skirting a number of relatively undeveloped beaches. Just down the road from the Puako lies perhaps the most elegant strand of beachfront resorts in Hawaii (see *Best en Route*). The area also offers some of Hawaii's best golf. Just 5 miles north of *Keahole-Kona Airport,* along the Queen Kaahumanu Highway, is the unique Polynesian hideaway *Kona Village Resort.* Less than 10 miles south of the airport is Kailua-Kona, the major town on the Kona Coast.

KAILUA-KONA This is the starting point of a condominium-lined coast that stretches 8 miles to Keauhou. Kailua-Kona's principal contemporary attractions—hotels, shops, restaurants, and bars—are on Alii Drive. There, also, is *Hulihee Palace* (75-5718 Alii Dr.; phone: 808-329-1877), a summer residence built in 1838 for the Hawaiian royal family, now a museum featuring furnishings and memorabilia of the period. It's open daily; there's an admission charge. Directly across the street is the *Mokuaikaua Church,* the first Christian church in the Hawaiian Islands, built in 1837.

Worth visiting on the grounds of *King Kamehameha Kona Beach* hotel near Kailua Pier is the restored Kamakahonu compound—headquarters of King Kamehameha the Great, who died here in 1819. Also part of the compound is *Ahu'ena Heiau,* a former temple used during the final seven years of Kamehameha's reign. Kailua-Kona is a major deep-sea fishing center along the Kona Coast (one of the world's best big-game fishing grounds), and there are numerous charter operations, most of them based at Honokohau Harbor between the town and *Keahole-Kona Airport.* Another of Kailua-Kona's attractions is the *Atlantis* submarine (Kailua Pier; phone: 808-329-6626), a 65-foot vessel that explores Kailua-Kona's reef to depths of 100 feet.

En Route from Kailua-Kona Take Kuakini Highway (Hwy. 11) 14 miles south through the coffee producing uplands to Kealakekua. Turn right on Napoopoo Road.

KEALAKEKUA Kealakekua is famed as the site where British captain James Cook, the first Westerner to explore the Hawaiian Islands, was killed in 1779. Cook discovered the islands (which he called the Sandwich Islands) when he sailed into Kauai's Waimea Bay in 1778 in search of fresh water. He was greeted joyfully by the Hawaiians, who regarded him as their god returned. Cook's expedition stayed for only a few weeks but returned in January 1779 to Kealakekua Bay on the Big Island. Here, too, he was accorded great respect. On February 4, 1779, Cook and his crew set sail but ran into a storm that damaged one ship and forced them to return. This lapse in godliness, as well as new demands for food and supplies, strained relations between the islanders and Cook, and eventually a battle erupted, ending with Cook's death. Legend says that the islanders dismembered and ate Cook. In reality, they gave him a hero's burial, which involved dismemberment and special interment in the earth. The spot where Cook fell is marked by a monument. Today the bay is a marine preserve noted for excellent snorkeling.

En Route from Kealakekua Continue south on Puuhonoa Road (Hwy. 160) for 3 miles to *Pu'uhonua o Honaunau—City of Refuge.*

CITY OF REFUGE NATIONAL HISTORICAL PARK This ancient and sacred area once provided sanctuary for those who had broken *kapu* (sacred laws) or were prisoners of war. Fugitives had to swim the perilous Honaunau Bay to the City of Refuge, but then they were entitled to pardons from the resident priest and could return home, free from stigma and the threat of death. Today visitors can explore this bit of antiquity; watch craftsmen carve canoes with the same tools and methods used by early Hawaiians; marvel at the remains of the six-foot-thick lava walls cemented in place without mortar; and visit the royal palace grounds, *heiaus* (temples), and formidable *tikis* (hand-crafted copies of the 16th-century originals). At sunset, a peaceful silence descends on the area, and the spirit of old Hawaii prevails. Brochures are available at the visitors' center (phone: 808-328-2326); open daily; there's an admission charge.

En Route from the City of Refuge National Historical Park Continue on Highway 160 (now called Keala O Keaue Rd.) for 3 miles.

HAWAII VOLCANOES NATIONAL PARK Dedicated to collecting and disseminating information on volcanic phenomena, this park is the home of Mauna Loa (13,680 feet) and Kilauea (4,078 feet), among the world's most active volcanoes.

Kilauea Volcano, youngest of the Big Island's five volcanic mountains, started erupting in 1983 and is still active today. It's the longest eruption series ever recorded in Hawaii (records have been kept since the early 1800s). Half a million yards of lava continue to flow into the sea daily, running downhill through channels beneath the solidified crust and emerging at a temperature of about 2,000F. The eruptions occur in a rift zone that encompasses the entire eastern flank of the volcano. Though the eruption area is inaccessible by road, thousands of people—sightseers, photographers, journalists, and the idly curious—have flown over to the island to try to glimpse the volcanic activity. Aerial tours of the park are offered by many helicopter companies, including *Volcano Heli-Tours* (phone: 808-967-7578).

Scientists living in the park constantly monitor the moods of Kilauea and Mauna Loa, and the visitors' center (at the entrance to the park) has volumes of material on the effects of the two volcanoes, as well as information on such park activities as ranger-led hikes and special events. A $3.5-million observatory with working seismological equipment is set up in the adjacent *Thomas A. Jaegger Museum* (phone: 808-967-7643). At *Volcano House* (phone: 808-967-7321) the park's inn and restaurant, just across from the visitors' center, you can spend the night on the edge of Kilauea Crater and have a box lunch packed for a day's hike the next morning. For additional information, contact the Superintendent, *Hawaii Volcanoes National Park* (PO Box 52, *Hawaii National Park,* HI 96718; phone: 808-967-7184).

BEST EN ROUTE

In addition to its many fine hotels, the Big Island offers an ever-growing number of bed and breakfast establishments. Locations include the fern forests of *Hawaii Volcanoes National Park,* grassy ranchlands of Waimea, and oceanfront properties along the Kona Coast. For information and reservations, contact *Hawaii's Best Bed & Breakfast,* PO Box 563, Kamuela, HI 96743 (phone: 808-885-4550; 800-262-9912).

Expect to pay $175 or more per night for a double room at the properties described as expensive; $95 to $175 at those in the moderate category; and less than $75 at those listed as inexpensive. Hotels are listed alphabetically by price category. Rooms have air conditioning, private baths, TV sets, and telephones, unless otherwise indicated.

KOHALA COAST

Aston's Shores at Waikoloa This 66-unit luxury condominium resort is a favorite with golfers because of its setting on the *Waikoloa Beach* course. But spacious, attractive one- and two-bedroom units and villas, and such amenities as a pool, a Jacuzzi, two tennis courts, and barbecue grills, make it an appealing choice for any visitor seeking a tranquil, low-rise resort setting. There is no restaurant, but units have kitchens. 69-1035 Keana Pl. (phone: 808-885-5001; 800-922-7866; fax: 808-885-8414). Expensive.

Hapuna Beach Prince This 350-room hotel (adjacent to the *Mauna Kea Beach* hotel) offers guests an open-air lobby and spacious accommodations. Nearly all rooms have ocean views, with lanais and easy access to the white expanse of Hapuna Beach, one of Hawaii's best. Guests can enjoy the *Mauna Kea* and *Hapuna Prince* golf courses, a fitness center, and a tennis pavilion. In addition, there are five restaurants and lounges; choices include seafood, Japanese dishes, and Mediterranean fare. 62-100 Kaunaoa Dr. (phone: 808-882-1111; 800-321-6248; fax: 808-882-1174). Expensive.

Hilton Waikoloa Village One of the most lavish properties in Hawaii, this self-contained resort spreads along 62 acres on the sunny Kohala Coast. It features 1,241 rooms, six restaurants, three lounges, three pools, two championship golf courses, eight tennis courts, horseback riding facilities, a spa, shops, a pool where guests can swim with dolphins, and more. The only drawback is that it tends to overpower its surroundings. 1 Waikoloa Beach Dr. (phone: 808-885-1234; 800-HILTONS; fax: 808-885-2900). Expensive.

Mauna Lani Bay The 350 refurbished guestrooms radiate extravagance. There are three restaurants, including the elegant *Canoe House.* Amateur archaeologists will enjoy exploring the nearby *King's Trail* and petroglyph field, remnants of Hawaii's Polynesian past. Those of a less studious bent should head for the pool, the 10-court tennis garden, the health club, or (most popular of all) the golf links. 68-1400 Mauna Lani Dr., Kohala Coast (phone: 808-885-6622; 800-367-2323; fax: 808-885-6183). Expensive.

The Orchid at Mauna Lani Situated just north of the airport, this luxurious resort boasts 541 large guestrooms (including 54 suites), with marble baths and lanais. Facilities include four restaurants, two golf courses, a 10-court tennis complex, a fitness center, and white sand beaches. Also see *America's Best Resort Hotels* in DIVERSIONS. 1 N. Kaniku Dr. (phone: 808-885-2000; 800-845-9905; fax: 808-885-5770). Expensive.

KONA COAST

Four Seasons This newly opened luxury resort features 243 ocean view bungalows, including five suites. The 16,000-square-foot *Hualalai Sports Club and Spa* offers massages, a beauty salon, and a pool. The Jack Nicklaus–designed 18-hole golf course is the site of the *Seniors PGA Tournament* held in January; there also are eight-lighted tennis courts. Three dining rooms offer everything from sandwiches to elegantly served continental cuisine. The resort is just 3 miles north of the airport at mile marker 87 in Kaupulehu, adjacent to the *Kona Village* (phone: 808-325-8000; fax: 808-325-8100). Expensive.

Kona Village Some 125 bungalows dot the 65-acre expanse of this village, each decorated in the style of one of the islands of the South Pacific. Facilities include two restaurants (rates include all meals), two pools, tennis courts, water sports, and sailing, but the magic lies in the sound of balmy breezes blowing through your thatch-roofed *hale* (house) and across the lagoon and beach. There are no in-room telephones, TVs, or air conditioning. Off Queen Kaahumanu Hwy. (phone: 808-325-5555; 800-367-5290). Expensive.

Holualoa Inn This large estate, formerly the retreat of newspaper publisher and art patron Thurston Twigg-Smith, is now a six-room bed and breakfast inn. Set on 40 acres of coffee plantation and cattle ranchlands in the hills overlooking Kailua-Kona, it offers superior views from the rooftop. The *Hibiscus Suite,* complete with a Jacuzzi, is a perfect honeymoon hideaway. There are no in-room telephones, TVs, or air conditioning. 76-5932 Manalahoa Hwy., Holualoa (phone: 808-324-1121; 800-392-1812; fax: 808-322-2472). Moderate.

VOLCANO VILLAGE

Kilauea Lodge A mile from the entrance to *Hawaii Volcanoes National Park,* this rustic inn built in 1938 is now a noteworthy bed and breakfast establishment. Each of the four rooms has a fireplace and a view of either the fern forest or the parking lot. Seven additional rooms are in a separate building; there's also a one-bedroom cottage. The restaurant serves excellent breakfasts (included in the room rate) and dinners. There are no in-room telephones, TVs, or air conditioning. Off Old Volcano Rd. (phone: 808-967-7366; fax: 808-967-7367). Moderate.

Kauai, Hawaii

Kauai is spectacular by any standards. The 533-square-mile island on the northwestern edge of the main cluster of the Hawaiian Islands is the oldest in the Hawaiian archipelago—first formed, and, therefore, first to cool—and, with its nutrient-rich soil, the most lush and verdant. Almost anything can grow here—from papaya, mango, and other tropical fruits to hundreds of varieties of exotic plants.

On the island's windward side are the razor-sharp pinnacles of the volcanic fissures along the Na Pali coast and the spectacular rock chasms that spill down the windward side of the island into dense jungle valleys are covered with lichen. And whatever is not green is red—the ferrous red of iron-permeated soil, further evidence of the now extinct volcanoes that heaved this island thousands of feet from the sea bed.

Kauai is known as one of the wettest spots on earth. But while it may rain 80 to 100 inches a year on the northern, windward side of the island, rainfall is only 15 to 20 inches a year leeward. Kauai's reputation for unfavorable weather is mostly due to Mt. Waialeale (pronounced Why-ali-*ali*), which receives some 500 inches of rain per year. But Waialeale is in the middle of the island, 5,000 feet up, and it actually acts as a rain barrier for the southern half of Kauai. Spring and summer bring good vacation weather to the entire island.

Kauai is a slightly dented and bashed circle, 32 miles across. The following route circles the island—almost. The road would make a complete circle except for the interruption by the impassable Na Pali Coast. Most vacationers begin their visit to Kauai in Lihue, the island's commercial center and the site of its main airport (a 25-minute flight from Oahu), although it is possible to fly into the don't-blink-or-you'll-miss-it *Princeville Airport* on the North Shore. Whether tourists come for a week (advised) or a day (popular, but a pity), Lihue is the most common point of arrival and offers the first glimpse of the marriage of sugarcane and tourism that characterizes Kauai.

LIHUE The best thing about Lihue is its location on Kauai's eastern coast, midway on the road that circles the island. A unique attraction is *Kilohana Estate* (3-2087 Kaumualii Hwy.; phone: 808-245-5608), a legendary plantation estate and former home of Gaylord Wilcox, Kauai sugarcane king. Built in the 1930s, this estate features horse-drawn carriage rides throughout its lush gardens, working farm, old plantation camp, shops selling products of the islands, and restaurant. The estate is open daily. Also worth seeing in Lihue is the *Kauai Museum* (4428 Rice St.; phone: 808-245-6931) with exhibits of island history and missionary memorabilia. It is closed Saturdays and Sundays. *Grove Farm Homestead* (Nawiliwili Rd.; phone: 808-245-3202), once the center of a thriving cane plantation, is now a museum featuring a group of historic houses that date from 1864. Reservations are required to visit the site (PO Box 1631, Lihue, Kauai, HI 96766); there's an admission charge. Five miles north of Lihue is *Wailua State Park* (phone: 808-822-5065) and the *Fern Grotto,* a fern-draped cave with lush tropical foliage. Guided boat tours are available to this enchanting spot, a popular site for weddings.

En Route from Lihue Head west on Highway 50, then turn south on Highway 520 toward Poipu Beach. Once beyond Lihue, the terrain changes almost instantly into old Hawaii. The towns and villages still live in the grip of the two monoliths of island life, the missionary church and the plantation. The road to Poipu travels through a tunnel of trees, and back 150 years to Old Koloa Town, Hawaii's first sugar plantation town, now authentically restored and featuring modern shops, restaurants, and services. Nearby, at *Koloa Baseball Field,* the *Sunshine Farmers Market* (Mondays only, from noon to 1 PM) allows visitors to meet local farmers and purchase vegetables and fruits, some of which are seldom seen on the mainland.

POIPU BEACH Its waters (like those along most of the island's beaches) are shallow a long way out and there are rocks along the seafloor where sand ought to be, but it's still a lovely beach for swimming and sunning. (All island beaches, even at resorts, are public, open, and free.) Poipu Beach has several posh resorts, including the *Hyatt Regency Kauai* (see *Best en Route*).

SPOUTING HORN This out-jutting of volcanic rock reached by Lauai Road, west along the coast from Poipu is so eaten by the sea that when a strong roller comes in, the sea water spurts through a hole 10 to 15 feet into the air, accompanied by a sad sigh. It provides a good illustration of the power the sugarcane companies have traditionally held on Kauai. Years ago, the spout shot as high as 80 feet into the air, high enough to fling salt spray across the cane fields—perhaps 200 yards away—killing patches of cane. The plantation managers dynamited the horn, widening the hole so that the spout stayed within a reasonable height. Now the horn is protected by the state.

En Route from Poipu Beach Return to Highway 50 and continue west. Little towns like Hanapepe (which means "crushed bay"), the sugar village of Kaumakani, and Kakaha are part of a genuine frontier plantation culture. Along this south and west side of Kauai, more people speak Hawaiian than in any other district in the state. *Salt Pond Beach Park* lies near the west end of Hanapepetown. Near the east side of Waimea are the remains of the Russian Fort Elizabeth, built in 1817 by a German physician who dreamed of taking over the island for the Russians. Waimea, the site where Captain James Cook first explored the islands, has a statue of Cook and numerous buildings listed in the *National Register of Historic Places.* Here Highway 50 joins Highway 550, which runs north paralleling Waimea Canyon (the Grand Canyon of the Pacific), a "must-see."

WAIMEA CANYON Nowhere on Kauai seems so close to the staggering power of the earth as this 3,600-foot-deep, 10-mile-long canyon. The original Hawaiians believed this was the work of Pele, goddess of fire. That belief seems understandable when contemplating the force necessary to have left these huge wedges of mountain hanging just so; to have honed these cliffs to such sharp precision; to have etched such regular and undeviating patterns across miles of rock.

En Route from Waimea Canyon Highway 550 ends at *Kokee State Park*—literally perched over a 1,000-foot drop into the westernmost valley of the Na Pali. This is the final destination of the 42-mile drive south and west of Lihue.

KOKEE STATE PARK The 4,345-acre park (phone: 808-335-5871) has a lovely, tiny museum, a large picnic area, and a restaurant serving hamburgers and other sandwiches. *Kokee Lodge* (PO Box 819, Waimea, HI 96796; phone: 808-335-6061) offers comfortable cabins. It's a good place to stay after Waimea Canyon and before going the few miles more to the road's end at Kalalau Lookout, which is 4,000 feet above the ocean and offers a magnificent view of the Na Pali Coast and the Kalalau Valley which opens out to the sea. Kalalau Beach, at the foot of the valley, is not accessible from Kalalau Lookout. The beach is at the end of an 11-mile trail that leads from *Haena State Park* on the northern side of the island. In addition to having a spectacular view, Kalalau Lookout also marks the starting point of miles of nature walks and hiking trails that will be irresistible to botanists and backpackers.

En Route from Kokee State Park Since access to the Na Pali Coast is from the north side of the island, it is necessary to circle back to Lihue, and take Highway 56, Kauai's main road around the island north to Hanalei and then 9 miles farther to Haena. Between the 22- and 24-mile markers of Highway 56 lies the turnoff to *Kilauea Lighthouse* and *Kilauea Point National Wildlife Refuge* (closed weekends), known for its rugged coastline, monk seals, and sea birds such as shearwaters and frigates.

HANALEI *South Pacific* was filmed in this marvelous old plantation town, which in the 1990s has become a haven of funky clothing, antiques, and sports shops clustered with trendy bars and restaurants. The *Waioli Mission House* (phone: 808-245-3202), built in 1846 and filled with period furnishings, is a piece of genuine New England Hawaii. Closed Mondays, Wednesdays, Fridays, and Sundays; donations suggested. It's affiliated with *Grove Farm Homestead* in Lihue (see above). The area also offers good scuba diving and snorkeling.

En Route from Hanalei From Hanalei, a weaving, mountainous road takes travelers along spectacular sea cliffs. About 2 miles outside Hanalei, park and walk down a steep path to the spectacular Lumahai Beach (where many beautiful hala trees were destroyed by Hurricane Iniki). Nine miles from Hanalei, the road ends at *Haena State Park,* where there is a nice swimming beach when there is no surf. *Haena* is the jumping-off point for hikers and campers visiting the Na Pali Coast.

NA PALI COAST This 14-mile stretch of coastline is the highlight of any trip to Kauai. Here the windward side of the island breaks into a series of jagged jungle valleys which are thousands of feet deep and stretch from the mountains to the sea.

Numerous legends and superstitions surround Na Pali. It was here that an entire Hawaiian tribe disappeared several centuries ago, and the legendary Menehune—a race of dwarfs credited with building much of the stonework on the island—are said to have hidden here, where they also disappeared. Some islanders believe they still live in Na Pali. (If you don't quite believe in the existence of the Menehune, Captain James Cook, who landed here in 1778, mentions in his report to the British Admiralty seeing a group of very light-skinned, diminutive women.) Late last century, a victim of leprosy named Koolau fought off the entire state militia using guerrilla warfare waged from the jungles of Na Pali. He refused to go to the leper colony on Molokai and took his family into the depths of the jungle, where they lived and died.

Because there are no paved roads to the coast, it is accessible only on foot, or by air or sea. Hike from *Haena State Park,* hire a helicopter from Lihue or Princeville (near Hanalei on Hanalei Bay) to see the valleys, or take a coastal tour from Hanalei by raft or powerboat. There are a number of helicopter tour companies, including *Safari Helicopters* (phone: 808-246-0136; 800-326-3356); *Will Squyres Helicopter Tours* (phone: 808-245-

8881); and *Ohana Helicopters* (phone: 808-245-3996). *Captain Zodiac* (phone: 808-826-9371) and *Na Pali Adventures* (phone: 808-826-6804) are among the companies offering boat tours. Those who want to hike the Na Pali Coast have a choice of various destinations. Among them is a 2-mile trek for day hikers and, the longest, and a 22-mile round trip to Kalalau Beach, a vigorous hike only for the hardy. Either way, hikers will encounter tropical valleys and pristine beaches, all of which are isolated and dazzlingly beautiful.

BEST EN ROUTE

Expect to pay $120 or more per night for a double room at those places we've listed as expensive; from $60 to $120 for those described as moderate; and less than $60 at those described as inexpensive. Rooms have air conditioning, private baths, TV sets, and telephones, unless otherwise indicated.

POIPU BEACH

Hyatt Regency Kauai This 605-room luxury resort gleams with *koa* wood, and has five acres of saltwater swimming pools that are dotted with islands. Other pluses: four restaurants, four Plexipave tennis courts, an 18-hole Robert Trent Jones Jr. golf course, and a full health club. 1571 Poipu Road (phone: 808-742-1234; 800-233-1234). Expensive.

Outrigger Kiahuna Plantation The 340 handsome one- and two-bedroom apartments, excellent sports facilities, superb beachfront, and first-rate restaurant are reasons enough for the loyal clientele at this condominium resort. But what really sets this place apart are the grounds, 50 lushly landscaped acres. There's a pool, and facilities and equipment for sailing and snorkeling. There's also a very attractive tennis complex across the street. The *Kiahuna* and the nearby *Hyatt Regency* golf courses provide first-rate tee-time options. 2253 Poipu Rd., Poipu (phone: 808-742-6411; 800-462-6262; fax: 808-742-1698). Expensive.

Aston's Waimea Plantation Cottages True Hawaiiana is reflected in this gracious collection of 48 restored plantation homes from the 1920s, 1930s, and 1940s. Many of the homes were transported to the site from other parts of Kauai as part of a comprehensive preservation plan. Ranging from one to six bedrooms, all of the cottages are tastefully furnished and are situated in an expansive, beachfront palm grove where an Art Deco–style pool and clubhouse (in a restored plantation manager's home) are located. Adjacent to the cottages is the *Grove* restaurant. At the edge of Waimea, on Hwy. 50 (phone: 808-338-1625; 800-992-4632; fax: 808-338-2336). Moderate.

PRINCEVILLE

Hanalei Bay Resort More like a hotel than the condominium complex it is, this resort features a full-service front desk, shops, a free-form swimming pool complete with waterfalls and lush landscaping, and the *Bali Hai* restaurant and lounge overlooking eight tennis courts. All 280 guestrooms are decorated in vibrant shades of pink, green, teal, and mauve to complement Kauai's surrounding natural beauty. 5380 Honoiki Rd., Princeville (phone: 808-826-6522; 800-827-4427; fax: 808-826-6680). Expensive.

Princeville Reopened after Hurricane Iniki at a cost of $30 million, this ITT Sheraton hotel is now one of Hawaii's most elegant. Cooled by green and white marble and given a European flavor with classic furnishings, this 252-room property offers luxurious but soothing surroundings both inside and out. The views from its beautifully appointed rooms are nothing short of spectacular. All rooms feature such extra niceties as soaking tubs, terry robes, and toiletries, as well as mini-bars. Guests enjoy paths that lead to an inviting pool, a small health spa, and a beach on Hanalei Bay. First-rate restaurants (*La Cascata* and *Café Hanalei*), and the *Living Room* lounge, where afternoon tea and sunset cocktails are served, make this hotel a truly outstanding destination. 5520 Kahaku Rd., Princeville (phone: 808-826-9644; 800-826-4400; fax: 808-826-1166). Expensive.

Lanai, Hawaii

The least populated of the major Hawaiian Islands, pear-shaped Lanai is a mere 13 miles across at its widest point, and 18 miles long. According to ancient legends, it was cursed and haunted by evil spirits until Kaululaau, the precocious son of a West Maui king, was exiled to its shores. Local lore has it that he killed or drove off the demons, making the isle safe for habitation.

But even rid of its resident demons, the island remained sparsely populated due to its unfavorable geography. The western mountains of the east side had deep gulches and were uninhabitable, while the remainder of the island was extremely dry and unsuited for agriculture or vegetation. After sailing past the island late in the 18th century, Captain James Cook's expedition (which continued after Cook's death) described Lanai as a brown, barren, and inhospitable place.

Lanai's history is somewhat less eventful than that of the other islands. Battles were fought here during Kamehameha's drive to unify the Hawaiian Islands. *Heiaus* (ancient temples and shrines) were built and petroglyphs left behind. In the mid–19th century, Mormons came to colonize the island and farmed in the Palawai Basin. The group gave up and left a decade later.

The biggest single event in Lanai history—the one that changed the face of the barren isle—was Jim Dole's purchase of almost the entire island in 1922. After brief, unsuccessful attempts to raise cattle and grow sugarcane, pineapples were determined to be the ideal crop for the island's climate. With water pumped from underground and piped in from the mountains, these prickly plants grew rapidly and helped transform the island into one of the world's largest pineapple plantations. Lanai quickly became known as the Pineapple Island. Today, however, less than a hundred of the 16,000 acres of pineapple fields remain, as Dole has transferred its operations to Guam and the Philippines.

The island has been focusing more on tourism since the opening of two deluxe properties (see *Best en Route*), which employ most of the 2,600 residents on Lanai.

The island has two main roads which intersect at the center of the island (there is no circular route): Highway 440 (Kaumalapau Highway) runs from the west coast town of Kaumalapau to Lanai City and then turns south to Manele Bay (on this southward leg it is called Manele Road); the other less developed route, Keomuko Road (Hwy. 441), heads northeast and then south, skirting the coast.

LANAI CITY Located almost dead center of the 141-square-mile island, this town has rows of single-story wooden homes and buildings that are clustered in a grid pattern around a central park square. At 1,650 feet above sea level, it lies above the pineapple fields and below the 3,370-foot peak of Lanaihale, the island's highest point. Founded by Dole in 1923, Lanai City is home to nearly all of the island's residents, most of whom have been involved in the pineapple industry and now are working in the burgeoning tourist trade.

MUNRO TRAIL New Zealander George C. Munro was manager of the ill-fated Lanai Ranch in the early 1900s. Also an amateur botanist, he imported seeds from New Zealand and planted Norfolk pines along the 9-mile ridge above what today is Lanai City. The ridge now has a rugged trail bearing his name that winds through Norfolk pine, ironwood, silver oak, *koa* trees, and eucalyptus. From *Munro Trail,* a clear day offers views of all the Hawaiian Islands except Niihau and Kauai. En route is the 3,370-foot Lanaihale peak, the island's highest point. The trail requires a four-wheel-drive vehicle (unless one goes on foot), as well as detailed directions on how to find the trail's beginning.

LUAHIWA PETROGLYPHS These fascinating rock carvings are located a mile from Lanai City off Manele Road (Hwy. 440) toward Hulopoe and Manele Bays. Difficult to find, these boulders climb up a steep hillside next to pineapple fields and are deeply etched with likenesses of animals, men, and ships. Since the area requires driving on dirt pineapple roads, clear directions are necessary.

GARDEN OF THE GODS An almost eerie *Garden of the Gods* is located off the beaten path near Kanepuu, about 7 miles from Lanai City. Resembling a scene from a prehistoric movie, it has a severe beauty and spectacular colors that make this hard-to-find spot worth seeking.

HULOPOE BAY This is the most swimmable beach on Lanai, with beautiful white sand in a small, protected cove on the south end of the island at the end of Manele Road (Hwy. 440). It has gentle waves for swimming, good snorkeling, showers, a campsite, and picnic tables. A short trail leads from the eastern end of the beach to beautiful views of the hills, the emerald and sapphire sea, and legend-haunted Puupehe (Sweetheart Rock).

MANELE BAY Tour boats from Maui dock in this small marina and harbor adjacent to Hulopoe.

KAUNOLU BAY Kamehameha the Great kept his summer home here and built a small village around it in the early 19th century. Located at the southwestern tip of the island, the historical site—which is only stone foundations now—is fascinating. Adjacent is Kahekili's Leap, where the king put his warriors to a test of bravery and loyalty by demanding that they jump 62 feet past a protruding ledge into the sea. The road is difficult, even with a four-wheel-drive vehicle.

SHIPWRECK BEACH Drive along Keomuku Road (Hwy. 441) from Lanai City until it turns toward the southeast near the shoreline. The next 6-mile stretch of sand has decent diving and very good beachcombing, but the sea here is shallow and dangerous. The beach earned its name because of the breezy northern coastal winds of Lanai that have driven numerous ships onto the reefs, where some hulks remain visible today.

BEST EN ROUTE

Expect to pay $225 or more per night for a double room at properties listed as expensive; and less than $120 at those described as moderate. Rooms have air conditioning, private baths, TV sets, and telephones, unless otherwise indicated.

LANAI CITY

Lanai This 11-room hotel was built in 1923 as a boardinghouse for Dole supervisors and temporary lodging for visitors. The simple one-story structure features nicely decorated rooms and a cottage, as well as a restaurant and bar. There are no TV sets (except in the cottage) or air conditioning. Lanai Ave. (phone: 808-565-4700; 800-321-4666; fax: 808-565-4713). Moderate.

Lodge at Koele One mile from Lanai City, set amid 21 acres in the island's cool central highlands, some 1,700 feet above sea level, the 102-room property resembles a grand country estate. Activities include golf, croquet, tennis, horseback riding, jeep rides, swimming, garden walks, and both an 18-hole course and a putting course. There are two restaurants, but no air conditioning. Also see *America's Best Resort Hotels* in DIVERSIONS. Keomoku Hwy. (phone: 808-565-7300; 800-321-4666; fax: 808-565-4561). Expensive.

HULOPOE BEACH

Manele Bay Overlooking Lanai's finest stretch of white sand beach at Hulopoe Bay, the 250-room hotel evokes 1920s Hawaiian design. The beachfront property features luxurious suites and guestrooms with private lanais affording sweeping ocean views. A two-level main dining room, an assortment of fine boutiques and shops, a spa, meeting rooms, and a lush courtyard with waterfalls and reflecting pools enhance the site. There's also tennis, snorkeling, scuba diving, sailing, and kayaking; a Jack Nicklaus–designed 18-hole golf course is just next door. Hulopoe Beach (phone: 808-565-7700; 800-321-4666; fax: 808-565-2483). Expensive.

Maui, Hawaii

The second-largest—and third-most populated—island in the Hawaiian chain (729 square miles) has a modified hourglass shape, an interesting history, and topography that accounts for some of the most beautiful country in the islands. Given only a day or two, most visitors end up on the beaches of West Maui, where beautiful hotels and condominiums stretch from Kaanapali to Kapalua, or on the resort strip farther south, from Kihei to Makena. But with just a couple more days, and a car to help negotiate the long distances (in island terms) between stops, visitors can also see the lush valleys around Wailuku and Kahului, the heights of *Haleakala National Park,* and the wilds of Hana. The result would be a mini-survey of Hawaii's geologic and cultural history—a dormant volcano; verdant, fertile valleys devoted to cane and pineapples; and a west coast village that was a standard stop on the whaling route more than 150 years ago, when missionaries and New England whalers literally fought for the hearts and minds of the Hawaiian people.

Maui has several distinct geographic areas in its 729 square miles. Picture the island as a steer's head facing east. West Maui, with the gold coast strip of hotels and beach, and the town of Lahaina, forms the ear. Inland, West Maui is mountainous, wild, and, in part at least, unexplored. Where the ear joins the head, at Wailuku and Kahului, the mountains give way to flat and fertile farmland. To the east the island rises steadily along the slopes of the dormant volcano Mt. Haleakala, its summit 10,023 feet above the sea. At the steer's snout is the village of Hana.

Most tourists begin their visit to Maui at *Kahului Airport* (a 20-minute jet flight from Oahu). From this central hub, travelers can head west to Lahaina and the resorts beyond; south to Kihei, Wailea, and Makena; or east to visit *Haleakala National Park* or to take the scenic drive along the Hana Highway (depending on time constraints, travelers can opt for any or all of the four legs of this route).

WEST MAUI

En Route from Kahului From *Kahului Airport,* take Kaahumanu Avenue to Highway 30 for the drive to West Maui and Lahaina, about 24 miles.

LAHAINA This city was the capital of the Hawaiian Islands from 1795 until 1843, when King Kamehameha III moved the court to Honolulu. Of far greater impact on the town and its people, however, were the whaling ships, which made Lahaina a regular stop from the early 1800s until petroleum replaced whale oil as a source of light in the 1860s. During the 50-year whaling period, life here was constant turmoil. Missionaries saved souls and sailors seduced and drank, and in general the Hawaiians were harassed and harangued on all sides. A great deal of the original whaling town still exists, in part due to the hard work of Lahaina's contemporary citizens, who have spent a good deal of time on restoration. An interesting place to visit is *Baldwin House Museum* (Front St.; phone: 808-661-3262), the home of the medical missionary Dr. Dwight Baldwin in the mid–19th century. The museum is open daily; there is an admission charge. A huge, spreading banyan tree stands in the town square nearby. It was planted in 1873 to commemorate 50 years of missionary work on the island. Across the street from the tree is the town's most famous manmade landmark, the *Pioneer Inn* (Hotel and Wharf Sts.; phone: 808-661-3636), which opened in 1901 and now is a restored restaurant and hotel; in the harbor in front is the *Carthaginian II,* a ship of more recent vintage that functions as a museum.

With more than a dozen galleries, Lahaina has emerged as the art capital of Hawaii; on Friday nights, many of them offer visitors *pupus* (hors d'oeuvres) and beverages, as well as the chance to meet local artists.

Winter visitors can choose from a wide variety of whale watching cruises. The whales breed in Hawaiian waters in the winter (in summer they live much farther north, in Arctic seas); from December through April landlubbers can stand on the dock and watch them cavorting between Maui and Lanai.

The *Lahaina Cannery,* a replica of the original Baldwin Packers Pineapple Cannery, is just a 10-minute walk north of town. It features 50 modern shops and restaurants, and an oil-fired turn-of-the-century steam locomotive that traverses 6 miles of narrow-gauge track between Lahaina and Kaanapali. Here also is the *Lahaina, Kaanapali & Pacific Railroad* (phone: 808-661-0089).

En Route from Lahaina Kaanapali is 4 miles north of Lahaina on Highway 30 (Honoapiilani Hwy.).

KAANAPALI This 4-mile stretch of beach has been compared to Waikiki, and even if the beach is not quite so spectacular as Waikiki, the resorts that line it have been far more sensitively and sensibly developed. At the north end of the beach is a huge outcropping of black volcanic rock, called Black Rock in English and Puu Kekaa in Hawaiian; at its base is the remodeled *Sheraton Maui.* Six other hotels and five condominium complexes make up the Kaanapali Beach resort, which also includes the two famous 18-hole *Royal Kaanapali* golf courses (two of 14 good 18-hole courses on the island) and the *Whalers Village* shopping area. The full impact of the whaling industry on Maui is described in detail in a museum at the shopping center, where there are whale exhibits, including a huge skeleton at the *Whalers Village* entrance.

NAPILI AND KAPALUA Beyond Kaanapali, the coast of West Maui is almost one uninterrupted 6-mile stretch of holiday condominiums to the northwest tip of the island. Two lovely beaches can be found here at Napili Bay and Kapalua Bay. Kapalua Bay is surrounded by the exquisite scenery of another of Maui's planned resort developments, Kapalua, set on panoramic acreage once used to grow pineapples. The *Kapalua Bay* and *Ritz-Carlton Kapalua* hotels (see *Best en Route*), condominium communities, three acclaimed golf courses (including two designed by Arnold Palmer), 10 tennis courts, and a small shopping center are the central features of the resort.

En Route from Kapalua Unimproved and secondary highways continue around the northern tip of the island and then south to Wailuku. Otherwise backtrack south on Highway 30.

WAILUKU On the northern coast, close to Kahului and the airport, Wailuku boasts remnants of early Hawaii. A staunch emblem of Maui's missionary past is *Kaahumanu Church* (103 S. High St.; phone: 808-244-5189), the first version of which was built in 1832 (the present structure dates from 1876). The simple building reflects much of the spirit and the form of early church work here and throughout the islands.

An interesting attraction near Wailuku is *Maui Tropical Plantation* (off Hwy. 30 at Waikapu; phone: 808-244-7643), 60 acres of Hawaiian agriculture including bananas, mangoes, papayas, ginger, pineapples, sugar, avocados, and macadamia nuts. There's a tram ride, and the visitors' center features a Hawaiian marketplace as well as a restaurant, nursery, display pavilion, and special "Hawaiian Country Barbecue." It is open daily; there's no admission charge.

En Route from Wailuku Take Highway 320 through the mountains of inland West Maui. Along the way is the *Bailey House Museum* (2375A Main St.; phone: 808-244-3326), with exhibits on all aspects of Maui history.

IAO VALLEY Iao Valley's *Kepaniwai Park* at road's end pays tribute to Maui's ethnic groups. The park also contains the dramatic Iao Needle—a lava pinnacle rising 1,200 feet from the valley floor. Pegged as "the Yosemite of the Pacific" by Mark Twain, the park is also the approximate point where King Kamehameha the Great finally trapped his Mauian enemies in the basin of Iao Valley and decimated them, assuring the loyalty of all the major islands in the chain. The carnage was so great that the stream that runs through the valley was named Wailuku, "Water of Destruction." On Iao Valley Road is *Tropical Gardens of Maui* (phone: 808-244-3085), with orchids, a palm garden, lily ponds, and gift shops.

En Route from Iao Valley To continue on to Southwest Maui, drive 9 miles south on Highways 30 or 311 and 31 to Kihei (see below). Or return to Kahului and go from there.

SOUTHWEST MAUI

En Route from Kahului From *Kahului Airport,* head south on Highway 350 to Kihei and connect with Highway 31.

KIHEI, WAILEA, and MAKENA The southwestern coast of Maui is on the dry leeward side of Haleakala. Six miles of the coast are known as Kihei—and better known as "sunny" Kihei because of the sparse average annual rainfall. Kihei is almost one long strip of golden beach from beginning to end, and not two decades ago the land fronting the beach—the same land that is now chockablock with low- and high-rise condominiums—was virtually virgin territory. Kihei often is cited as a prime example of the ravages of unchecked development, while the *Wailea* resort, just south, is considered a model of the way to go. Its three 18-hole golf courses, an 11-court tennis center, a shopping center, condominium villages, and five first class hotels complement—rather than intrude on—the landscape. South of Wailea, the *Makena* resort includes two 18-hole golf courses and the luxury 300-room *Maui Prince* hotel. The area's 18-hole public course is Kihei's *Silversword Golf Club* (phone: 808-874-0777).

EAST MAUI

En Route from Southwest Maui Return to Kahului. From there to the summit of Haleakala is only 38 miles, but it takes two hours to climb from sea level to 10,023 feet. Take Highway 37 and, just above Pukalani, Highway 377 south. On the way to the entrance is the *Kula Botanical Gardens* (Hwy. 377; phone: 808-878-1715), where experts will explain how Maui's unique climate is used to grow simple garden vegetables (the best in the islands) beside exotic tropical orchids. It's open daily; there's an admission charge. Maui's only vineyard, the *Tedeschi Vineyard and Winery* (phone: 808-878-6058), is just past the headquarters to the 18,000-acre *Ulupalakua Ranch,* which dates from the 1850s. A tasting room (open daily) is in the ranch's 19th-century jailhouse.

HALEAKALA NATIONAL PARK "The House of the Sun"—Mt. Haleakala—dominates the skyline on two-thirds of Maui. The approaches from the west are a peaceful contrast to the tourist frenzy of the coastal resort areas. Here is countryside virtually untouched by commercialism, a series of pastoral scenes that could represent almost any mountainous region in the world. Because of the mountain, Maui enjoys a unique climate system, hot on the coasts, fertile and moist on the flat plains between West Maui and the mountain, and progressively cooler as the altitudes increase. The 10,023-foot-high mountain's dormant crater is one of the world's largest—a 19-

square-mile hole 3,000 feet deep, honeycombed with trails and designated a national park.

Park headquarters, a mile from the entrance at about 7,000 feet, is a necessary stop for information on campgrounds, the mountain, and activities like horseback riding, hiking, and renting simple cabins in the crater maintained by the *National Park Service.* For general park information, contact the Superintendent, *Haleakala National Park* (PO Box 369, Makawao, Maui, HI 96768; phone: 808-572-9306 for recorded reports on weather conditions and cabin/camping information).

Early morning and late afternoon are the best times for visiting the crater, since there's less chance of cloudiness. No matter how warm it may be at the base of Haleakala, warm clothes are needed, especially at the summit and at sunrise (a popular excursion). The view from the top is spectacular. From there West Maui and the neighboring islands of Hawaii (Lanai and Molokai) are visible. According to Hawaiian legend, it was from the summit of Haleakala that the god Maui lassoed the sun to force him to make his daily trip across the sky more slowly. And dawn atop the mountain is one of the finest experiences a traveler can have.

The Kipahulu District of the park is a single 8-mile strip that extends to Maui's eastern coast. It encompasses a stretch of ecologically delicate rain forest, where the rangers are struggling to maintain a nurturing environment for tropical growth, as well as the *Pools at Kipahulu,* a series of pools and streams that spill into one another like a pyramid of champagne glasses filled to overflowing. To reach the Kipahulu District, which encompasses the Kipahulu Valley, it is necessary to approach it from the coast via the Hana Highway (see below).

En Route from Haleakala National Park Return to Kahului, or head northeast from Highway 37 to Highway 365 (Makawo Hwy.) to pick up the Hana Highway (Hwy. 360) along the island's northeast coast.

HANA HIGHWAY This scenic route is a sightseeing attraction in itself. The road is rough, winding, and very narrow—with an estimated 617 curves and 56 bridges—which is why the 52-mile drive takes about three to four hours and why it's difficult to stop to enjoy the views. But there are three lookout points along the way before it ends in Hana, a tiny village populated mainly by workers at the Hana Ranch and by out-of-town celebrities seeking seclusion. Beyond Hana, another 10 miles of rutted road lead to the park again, at the spot where the lowest of the *Pools at Kipahulu* spills into the sea.

BEST EN ROUTE

Expect to pay $150 or more per night for a double room at those properties listed as expensive. Rooms have air conditioning, private baths, TV sets, and telephones, unless otherwise indicated.

Cabin rental in the national park can be reserved only through a lottery. Three months before visiting, send a letter detailing your name, address, and date preference to *Haleakala National Park* (PO Box 369, Makawao, HI 96768); lottery winners will be notified. Camping is strictly controlled and limited to three 12-person cabins and two campgrounds, with a three-day minimum stay.

KAANAPALI

Hyatt Regency Maui Besides the 815 elegant rooms in three seven- to nine-story towers and five restaurants, the hotel's 20 landscaped acres contain tropical gardens, waterfalls, and one of Maui's largest pools, with a 130-foot lava tube water slide. The hotel also boasts $2 million worth of Asian and Pacific art and a staff ornithologist to care for the property's many exotic birds. 200 Nohea Kai Dr. (phone: 808-661-1234; 800-233-1234; fax: 808-677-4499). Expensive.

Kaanapali Alii This 264-unit beachfront condo complex is one of the island's best. The rooms are large, tastefully furnished, and have fully supplied kitchens; the grounds are well maintained, and the central location (near golf, shopping, and restaurants) is especially convenient. 50 Nohea Kai Dr. (phone: 808-667-1400; 800-642-MAUI; fax: 808-661-1025). Expensive.

KAPALUA

Kapalua Bay Beautifully situated on a privately owned 23,000-acre pineapple plantation on the northwest coast of Maui, the resort offers 194 hotel rooms and 128 villas, three 18-hole championship golf courses (two designed by Arnold Palmer), 10 tennis courts, pools, secluded beaches, water sports, five distinctive restaurants, and posh boutiques. Also see *America's Best Resort Hotels* in DIVERSIONS. 1 Bay Dr. (phone: 808-669-5656; 800-367-8000; fax: 808-669-4679). Expensive.

Ritz-Carlton Kapalua This elegant 550-room hotel offers a magnificent oceanfront setting with panoramic views of mountains and sea from nearly every room. The 18th- and 19th-century antique furniture is complemented by art with a Hawaiian theme, including a number of impressive landscape paintings. Rooms feature marble baths. Adjacent to the hotel are the dramatic West Maui Mountains, and Fleming Beach, with a 10-court tennis complex. On-site facilities include a two-level pool, four restaurants, three lounges, a health spa, and jogging and walking trails. 1 Ritz-Carlton Dr. (phone: 808-669-6200; 800-242-8400; fax: 808-665-0026). Expensive.

WAILEA

Aston Wailea Formerly the *Maui Inter-Continental,* this elegant link in the Aston chain boasts 516 rooms set on 22 lush oceanfront acres, two restaurants, three pools, and a jogging path. 3700 Wailea Alanui Dr. (phone: 808-879-1922; 800-367-2960; fax: 808-874-8331). Expensive.

Four Seasons Wailea The majority of the 380 particularly spacious guestrooms (and 91 suites) boast ocean views, and each has its own lanai, deluxe bath, and VCR. Facilities include a huge pool with a large fountain in the center and whirlpool baths at each end. The *Seasons* dining room is among the best in the islands. There also is a health and fitness center. Also see *America's Best Resort Hotels* in DIVERSIONS. 3900 Wailea Alanui Dr. (phone: 808-874-8000; 800-334-6284; fax: 808-874-6449). Expensive.

Grand Wailea This astounding $500-million, 767-room property has five restaurants, seven spectacular gardens and marvelous lagoons, a whale-shaped pool that winds through acres of the hotel grounds, and a superb art collection, as well as the most comprehensive spa in the islands. There also is a separate 20,000-square-foot play facility for children, with a kid-size theater, as well as a soda fountain and a computer learning center. 3850 Wailea Alanui Dr. (phone: 808-875-1234; 800-888-6100). Expensive.

Stouffer Renaissance Wailea Beach This beachfront resort features 365 rooms, three championship 18-hole golf courses, 14 tennis courts (three grass), and a 15-acre tropical garden with waterfalls, ponds, and streams surrounding a pool and three whirlpool baths. There also are four restaurants and two lounges. 3550 Wailea Alanui Dr. (phone: 808-879-4900; 800-992-4532). Expensive.

MAKENA

Makena Surf The 50 units—spacious, nicely decorated one-, two-, and three-bedroom apartments—and a private beachfront setting make this condominium one of the Makena area's most appealing. On-site facilities include tennis courts and a large pool and lounge area, but no restaurant. There is a three-night minimum stay. 96 Makena Alani Dr. (phone: 808-879-0616; 800-367-5246; fax: 808-661-5875). Expensive.

HANA

Hana-Maui This intimate 96-room hotel spreads across 66 acres on the east coast; the only distractions from the perfectly blue Pacific are tennis courts, hiking trails, a spa, riding stables, and two heated outdoor pools. Rates include all meals and activities. Hana (phone: 808-248-8211; 800-321-4262; fax: 808-248-7202). Expensive.

Molokai, Hawaii

Most of the major Hawaiian Islands—Maui, Hawaii, Kauai, Lanai, Molokai—have depended on agriculture at one time or another during this century. And the failure of that industry has forced each island to develop tourist facilities to replace its lost income. For example, Kauai had a thriving sugarcane industry for years, but over the last decade, it repeatedly lost business to the

Far East, where cane is produced at perhaps one-tenth the cost. So Kauai began depending on tourism to replace the vacuum left by sugarcane.

Similar developments evolved with the pineapple industry on Molokai. Molokai—known to many people as the site of Father Damien's leper colony—was dubbed "the Forgotten Island" until early in the 20th century, when Dole and Del Monte bought large chunks of the island for pineapple fields. A gradual renaissance began, and the island and its people flourished. But as with sugarcane on Kauai, pineapples could be grown much less expensively in the Far East, where labor was far cheaper. Ever mindful of their bottom lines, Dole and Del Monte ceased operations in Molokai in 1975 and 1983, respectively.

At present, Molokai has only one full-fledged resort, the *Kaluakoi,* though the *Molokai* hotel in Kaunakakai is a pleasant alternative. More resorts are on the drawing boards, but for the time being the island seems almost in a state of suspended animation. For visitors at least, this solitude is splendid and serene, along the jagged, wild, inaccessible cliffs east of Kalaupapa Peninsula, for example, or at the many coves and beaches that swimmers and sunbathers have entirely to themselves for hours on end.

Molokai can easily be visited on a day trip from Oahu; the visitor flies either to *Molokai Airport* (well outside the town of Kaunakakai) to see the whole island or to Kalaupapa to visit the Kalaupapa Peninsula, now the *Kalaupapa National Historic Park* and site of a historic leper colony. But Molokai has wild roads and beautiful vistas as yet unmapped on any standard tourist itinerary, and a two- or three-day visit will offer a feeling of Hawaii that can't be found on the more developed islands.

En Route from Molokai Airport Eight miles southeast of *Molokai Airport,* where most tourists enter Molokai, is the island's main town, Kaunakakai.

KAUNAKAKAI With its main street and the wooden storefronts, Kaunakakai is remarkably like a western frontier town. It has the distinct "cowboy" atmosphere typical of many towns throughout the islands—although in this case the atmosphere is more a reflection of the general character of Molokai towns than of its proximity to the island's huge *Puu O Hoku Ranch.* With a population of less than 1,000, the town has few tourist facilities, but much about it speaks of the island's recent history: For example, the fine, long—but almost empty—wharf extending a half mile into the sea was built to accommodate the huge barges on which pineapples were shipped. Today only the *Maui Princess* ferry and a few fishing and cruise boats dock here.

En Route from Kaunakakai Proceed on Highway 460 toward the western end of the island and Papohaku Beach. Along the way former Dole plantation town of Maunaloa, where artists and craftspeople have settled and glacial development progresses. It is well worth a look as a living museum of contemporary company towns in Hawaii.

PAPOHAKU BEACH This is the west coast site of the *Kaluakoi* resort, with 103 hotel rooms and approximately 350 condominium units in four properties. The coast tends to be rocky, with occasional underwater coral reefs that can be an unpleasant surprise for swimmers. The beach is better for sunning than swimming. Adjacent to *Kaluakoi* is the 400-acre *Molokai Ranch Wildlife Conservation Park* (phone: 808-552-2681); part of the 53,000-acre *Molokai Ranch,* it is home to some 100 African and Asian animals. It is closed Tuesdays through Thursdays.

En Route from Papohaku Beach Return east via Highway 460, then north to *Palaau State Park.*

PALAAU STATE PARK On Molokai's northern coast, the park overlooks Kalaupapa Peninsula and the Kalaupapa leper settlement. The peninsula is 2,000 feet below the park, at the base of a series of jagged, wild cliffs that become inaccessible farther along the eastern coastline.

En Route from Palaau State Park The *Kalaupapa Trail,* navigable by foot or mule, is the only route to the leper colony from the state park; otherwise, visitors may fly in from *Hoolehua Airport* outside Kaunakakai. Call *Molokai Shuttle* (phone: 808-567-6847) for reservations. The *Molokai Mule Ride* (phone: 808-567-6088; 800-567-7550; fax: 808-567-6244) is once again operating with daily round-trip treks down the precipitous 3-mile trail. Hikers must be experienced and ready for a strenuous climb on the return trip; before heading down the trail visitors are required to make arrangements in advance with *Damien Tours* (PO Box 1, Kalaupapa, HI 96742; phone: 808-567-6171). Usually led by the company's owner and resident curmudgeon, Richard Marks (whose family has lived in Kalaupapa for three generations), the tours are interesting, informative, and enjoyable. Remember to bring your own lunch.

KALAUPAPA In 1866 the entire Kalaupapa Peninsula was declared a leper colony by royal decree, and islanders who sufferered from the disease (now called Hansen's disease) were exiled here. The suffering inflicted on victims was intense: No provisions were made for food, shelter, clothing, or other basic necessities; people with the disease were dumped on the island and left to die (often with whichever family members consented to care for them). But in 1873 a Belgian priest, Father Damien Joseph de Veuster, chose to live and work here, and for the next 16 years he labored to build a living community where previously only disease and despair had ruled. In 1889 Father Damien died of leprosy, but he had largely succeeded in reaching his goal. Today the peninsula is a national historic park, and fewer than 80 people with Hansen's disease live here. It is their peninsula, but visitors are welcome (children under 16 are not allowed) on scheduled tours. Thanks to various sulfone drugs, Hansen's disease now can be rendered noncontagious and controlled; adult visitors are completely safe.

En Route from Kalaupapa To reach Halawa Valley, which fills Molokai's northeastern end, it is necessary to return to Kaunakakai. The valley is accessible only by Highway 450, which begins in Kaunakakai and follows the island's coast east and north. It is at least a half-day's excursion from the airport. The road narrows as it heads north, twisting and turning along the mountains that rise like a ship's prow along the island's northern coast. Immediately outside Kaunakakai on Highway 450 are a number of ancient fish ponds. Dating as far back as the 15th century, they were built to assure the availability of fresh fish whenever the royal whim so desired. All the major islands have ruins of these royal fish ponds, but the ones on Molokai are in the best state of preservation and are therefore worth a stop.

HALAWA VALLEY At the end of Highway 450 is the near-deserted Halawa Valley. It offers a real sense of Molokai today—and the best views of the magnificent cliffs at road's end. Once a thriving community valley patchworked with taro farms, in 1946 a giant tidal wave (tsunami) forced an evacuation after which few residents returned. Once quite popular with hikers and nature lovers, the valley remains a tranquil, very tropical place, but is presently closed to visitors as landowners resolve a lawsuit filed by an injured hiker. The beach is still accessible and makes a great place for an afternoon picnic.

BEST EN ROUTE

Expect to pay $120 or more per night for a double room at those properties we've listed as expensive; $75 to $120 at those in the moderate category; and less than $75 at those listed as inexpensive. Rooms have air conditioning, private baths, TV sets, and telephones, unless otherwise indicated.

KAUNAKAKAI

Hotel Molokai Located on the island's south shore, this resort sits in a palm grove about 2 miles from town. Its 50 simple rooms are distributed among buildings throughout the grounds. There are no telephones, TVs, air conditioning, or restaurant. On Hwy. 5, east of Kaunakaki (phone: 808-553-5347; 800-423-MOLO; 808-531-4004). Inexpensive.

KEPUHI BEACH

Colony's Kaluakoi This Polynesian-style hotel is part of the 6,800-acre Kaluakoi resort, which includes three resort condominium projects, *Ke Nani Kai, Paniolo Hale,* and *Kaluakoi Villas.* The 103-room Colony-operated property is beautifully set along secluded white sand beaches and has four tennis courts, an 18-hole golf course, a pool, shops, and a restaurant and lounge. There is no air conditioning. About 13 miles west of the airport (phone: 808-552-2555; 800-777-1700; 808-552-2821). Moderate.

Oahu, Hawaii

Oahu, the 608-square-mile island that's home to four-fifths of Hawaii's 1.8 million population, is appropriately nicknamed "the Gathering Place." Since Kamehameha III moved the royal court to Honolulu from Lahaina in 1843, Oahu has been Hawaii's social, political, and industrial center. Since World War II it has also been the center of tourism, and several Oahu sites and cities have become synonymous with Hawaii itself: Honolulu, Diamond Head, Waikiki, and Pearl Harbor. (For a detailed report on these, see *Honolulu* in THE CITIES.)

Just as one must get off Oahu to see all of Hawaii, one must get out of Honolulu to see all of Oahu. Over the past several years, there has been a major effort to develop resort areas outside the tourist magnet of Honolulu. Ko Olina, a resort development, is under construction near Ewa Beach, west of Waikiki. Eventually, the complex will include marinas, several golf courses, beaches, condos, houses, and hotels; for now, it consists of one lush, palm-dotted golf course and a clubhouse, the *Ihilani* hotel, and the Paradise Cove luau grounds.

En route from Honolulu From Honolulu and Waikiki, the route follows the windward and northern shores in a 110-mile loop. Take the H-1 Freeway to Highway 72 which runs along the eastern tip of Oahu, from Diamond Head to Kailua. Ask at any hotel or car rental agency for the *Drive Guide,* a booklet of Oahu itineraries which contains helpful maps.

SOUTHEAST OAHU Highway 72 starts near Diamond Head, the spectacular volcanic crater that has become a symbol of Hawaii. The volcano that formed this perfect crater has been extinct for at least 150,000 years; the crater was just as much of a landmark for early Hawaiians (who thought it resembled a fish head) as it is today. A very popular hike that begins off Diamond Head Road near 18th Avenue leads through a tunnel to the Crater Rim (flashlights are recommended).

Highway 72 passes through two affluent neighborhoods beyond Diamond Head: the Kahala District and Hawaii Kai, a development begun by Henry Kaiser. During World War II Kaiser devised production procedures that turned out troop- and cargo-carrying Liberty ships in only five weeks; Hawaii Kai was constructed with the proceeds. *Hanauma Bay Beach Park* is where part of the Elvis Presley movie *Blue Hawaii* was filmed. It has one of the most beautiful underwater parks in the country and is an excellent place for snorkeling or scuba diving because the waters are so clear, especially in the early morning (the park is closed to visitors on Wednesdays). Nearby is Halona Blow Hole, a submerged lava tube that turns sea water into a geyser as the waves roll in.

Two miles farther is *Sea Life Park* (off Kalanianaole Hwy. at Makapuu Pt.; phone: 808-259-7933), with a number of standard aquatic displays (dolphins, seals, whales) as well as the *Hawaiian Reef,* a 300,000-gallon tank which houses a re-creation of the Pacific reef. At feeding times, scuba divers plunge into the water to lead a parade of turtles, multicolored fish, manta rays, eels, and small and larger sharks happily intent on the food being distributed. For confirmed landlubbers it is a fascinating performance. The park is open daily; there is an admission charge. The easternmost point on the island is Makapuu Point, marked by a lighthouse. Here, the trade winds divide, some continuing north, some south. Less than half a mile west is *Makapuu Beach Park*, a top spot for summer surfers, with diabolical shorebreakers.

At Kailua, to the north, it is possible to cut inland and return to Honolulu through the Koolau Mountains via the Pali Highway (Hwy. 61). En route are the Nuuanu Pali Tunnels that cut through the mountains and the scenic Pali Lookout. This is where Kamehameha I drove the defenders of Oahu over the steep cliffs to their deaths. Today the view from these heights is as grand as it is frightening. The mountainous Pali Highway leads through lush tropical rain forests, makes numerous curves, and arrives abruptly in urban Honolulu.

En route to the North Shore The coastal loop continues beyond Kailua as Highway 83, Kamehameha Highway. The road goes along the windward coast and North Shore.

THE NORTH SHORE On Maui there is the John F. Kennedy profile in Iao Valley, and on Kauai, Queen Victoria's profile. Oahu's major profile is the Crouching Lion, visible from Highway 83 (Kamehameha Hwy.), just beyond *Swanzy Beach Park.* Like all these figures, the resemblance is not exact and depends as much on the viewer's perspective and good will as on the actual shape of the formation. Five miles north of the Crouching Lion is the lovely Sacred Falls, an 87-foot waterfall that plunges into a pool in *Sacred Falls State Park* (phone: 808-587-0300). Explorers may swim in the pool and cavort in the falling water, but it is a hard mile's hike beyond the parking spot, and hikers should be prepared for about an hour's tramp. (*A caveat:* Don't even attempt this hike in rainy weather, because of the very real danger of flash floods.)

The culmination of the drive along the eastern shore is the *Polynesian Cultural Center* in Laie (phone: 808-293-3333; 808-923-1861 in Waikiki). Though commercial, the center has excellent reconstructions of villages of all the major Pacific societies—Marquesas, Samoan, Tongan, Hawaiian, Tahitian, Fijian, Maori—with cultural performances and arts and crafts demonstrations in each village. There are lunchtime and evening Polynesian shows. A mixture of museum and *Disneyland,* the center is informative and fun.

After Highway 83 rounds the top of the island and turns southwest, it runs into a spot guaranteed to raise goose pimples on any surfer—Sunset Beach, home of the Big Waves, including the notorious Banzai Pipeline.

Here, every winter, international competitions are held. Ahead on the North Shore is *Waimea Falls Park* (phone: 808-638-8511), another natural wonder gone commercial. The famous and incredibly beautiful waterfall is now easily seen on a round-trip tram ride. The 1,800-acre park features archaeological sites and 3,500 varieties of plants, including 100 endangered species.

Five miles farther southwest, sightseers will pull into the surfers paradise known as Haleiwa, where sunset viewing from the bridge at the center of town with a shave ice from *Matsumoto Store* (66-087 Kamehameha Hwy.; phone: 808-637-4827) is a hallowed tradition. And 9 miles past Haleiwa on Oahu's northwest edge is Kaena Point, a magnet for hikers and mountain bikers.

From here the highway turns south and heads toward Honolulu.

BEST EN ROUTE

For a full list of accommodations and restaurants, see *Honolulu* in THE CITIES.

Craters of the Moon National Monument, Idaho

Everyone wants to know what the moon really looks like. For centuries we lived with intense speculation, but since 1969 we have lived with reality: those incredible pictures of a flat, gray, pockmarked surface scarred by flying space debris and flanked by strange, craggy rocks; and the astronaut in front, looking as awkward and out of place as a snowman learning to walk. But what did the astronauts feel? What would it be like to visit the moon?

To get an idea, you have to go no farther than Idaho: When scientists wanted to familiarize prospective astronauts with the lunar surface, they brought them to *Craters of the Moon National Monument* on the Snake River Plain. *Craters of the Moon* is a land of lava on lava—stark, black, and cinder-blown. Its visual impact is stunning: miles of black lava rising and falling over the otherwise broad, flat valley, with abrupt, jagged peaks and huge cinder and lava cones—one 800 feet high—dotting the landscape. The area was created by a series of volcanic explosions that occurred over eons, for the monument sits atop a 60-mile fissure in the earth known as the Great Rift. In eight great epochs of upheaval dating from 2,000 to nearly 15,000 years ago, the Great Rift exploded in waves upon waves of white-hot magma—spewing molten rock at 2,000F out of the fissure and throwing tons of debris and rock into the air to form volcanic cones.

The monument's human history is nowhere near as intriguing as its natural history. Trail markers and cairns piled in various spots are Indian artifacts, though we do not know exactly how they were used. But this does not seem to have been an important part of the world for the Indians. Discovered by white men in 1833, the area was proclaimed a national monument in 1924.

In winter, the entire area is covered in deep snow and turns into marvelous cross-country ski terrain. Many visitors to *Craters of the Moon National Monument* also visit the year-round resort towns of Ketchum and Sun Valley, some 70 miles to the northwest. Famed Sun Valley is one of Idaho's finest skiing centers.

The following route heads south from Sun Valley to the *Shoshone Ice Caves* and Shoshone Falls, then turns northeast toward the *Craters of the Moon National Monument.*

En Route from Sun Valley Follow Highway 75 south about 43 miles to the *Shoshone Ice Caves,* which are 15 miles north of Shoshone.

SHOSHONE ICE CAVES The caves here (actually one three-block-long cavern) remain constantly cold; no matter how hot it is outside, the temperature inside is 32F. (Be sure to bring a jacket.) Tours are conducted every half hour from May through September; there's an admission charge. On the grounds are a rock and gem museum and a statue of Chief Washakie of the Shosone tribe.

En Route from the Shoshone Ice Caves Continue south on Highway 75 to Shoshone, then take US 93 21 miles south to Shoshone Falls. They are well worth the drive.

SHOSHONE FALLS Taller than Niagara, the falls drop 212 dramatic, turbulent feet into the Snake River. Like all parts of the Snake, the falls are affected by the flow of water, which is, in its turn, affected by rainfall and, more important, the amount of irrigation along the river's course through Idaho. During the summer, irrigation is at its height and the falls are at their nadir. They can be seen from US 93, but if you want a really close look, there is a platform right above the falls, which offers a bird's-eye view for a nominal charge. For more information, contact the *Twin Falls Chamber of Commerce* (phone: 208-733-3974).

En Route from Shoshone Falls Head north again on US 93 to Shoshone, then take US 93/26 to *Craters of the Moon National Monument,* 60 miles northeast of Shoshone.

CRATERS OF THE MOON NATIONAL MONUMENT The place to start any tour is at the visitors' center (phone: 208-527-3257; closed on major holidays), where there are detailed displays on the area's amazing formations and natural history. From there, a 7-mile loop drive will take you past most of the monument's best-known landmarks. Don't miss the *Indian Tunnel,* an 830-foot lava tube used as a cave by the Indians on treks through the lava fields, and *Devils Orchard,* one of the younger lava formations. Be sure to take along water, even when you are driving; in summer, the sun bakes the lava and parches the throat.

More adventurous visitors may hike numerous trails and walks that bring them face to face with the lava. There is much to recommend this approach. Since large parts of the monument can't be reached by car, this is the only way to see the vast lava fields that are virtually unexplored. And by venturing into the (relative) unknown on foot, visitors discover the monument's great secret: Far from being a sterile, hostile, bleak landscape, it is alive with plants, birds, and animals. Hundreds of species of flora grow; there are mountain bluebirds, nighthawks, and sparrows galore; and in the backcountry, hikers can see mule deer, hear coyote, and perhaps even spot a distant bobcat.

For information about the national monument, contact the Superintendent, *Craters of the Moon National Monument* (PO Box 29, Arco, ID 83213; phone: 208-527-3257).

BEST EN ROUTE

Overnight camping is allowed in wilderness areas of *Craters of the Moon National Monument.* Between October and May campgrounds have no running water (but no entrance fee, either). Contact the monument superintendent (see above) for details.

The most popular accommodations are in the Sun Valley/Ketchum area, however; Hailey (70 miles south of Ketchum) on Highway 75 provides an economical alternative. Expect to pay $160 or more per night for a double room at those places listed as very expensive; $110 to $160 at those rated expensive; and less than $110 at those listed as moderate. Unless otherwise indicated rooms have private baths, TV sets, and telephones, but no air conditioning. Hotels are listed alphabetically, by price category.

SUN VALLEY

Sun Valley Lodge This Sun Valley resort consists of both a lodge and an inn. The lodge is a classic, rustic ski lodge (of recent vintage) with 141 rooms, some with fireplaces; there are also two good restaurants. The inn is more family-oriented, with 115 rooms in a rambling, neo-Tyrolean building. In a mall separating the two buildings are shops and restaurants. Sun Valley Rd. (phone: 208-622-4111; 800-632-4104 in Idaho, 800-635-8261 elsewhere in the US; fax: 208-622-2030). Very expensive to expensive.

Heidelberg Inn A sort of Austrian Alps–style motel, this is a good choice for families. It has 30 rooms (some with fireplaces and kitchenettes), a pool, and a hot tub. Mountain bikes also are available for guests' use. Breakfast is included in the rate, but there's no restaurant. 1908 Warm Springs Rd. (phone: 208-726-5361; 800-284-4863; fax: 208-726-2084). Expensive to moderate.

KETCHUM

Knob Hill Inn This centrally located inn has 24 luxuriously appointed rooms and suites with private balconies. Amenities include a pool, a Jacuzzi, a sauna, and an exercise room. *Felix's* restaurant features gourmet dinners; the *Konditorei* serves moderately priced meals—breakfast, afternoon tea in winter, and lunch in summer. 960 North Main St. (phone: 208-726-8010; fax: 208-276-2712). Very expensive.

River Street Inn This English country–style bed and breakfast establishment offers nine suites, luxurious Japanese soaking tubs, and full homemade breakfasts, but no restaurant. 100 River St. (phone: 208-726-3611). Expensive.

HAILEY

Airport Inn This reasonably priced motel features 30 air conditioned units, many with microwaves and coffeemakers. For the sports minded, there's plenty of fishing, hunting, hiking trails, and skiing in the winter. Visitors to the area flock to *The Mint* restaurant, owned by actor Bruce Willis. 820 Fourth Ave S. (phone: 208-788-2477). Moderate.

Flint Hills, Kansas

For decades travelers viewed the Flint Hills, among the last surviving examples of the tallgrass prairie that once covered the Great Plains, only from car windows as they zipped along I-35 or I-70 on their way to someplace else. Now, however, that situation may be changing. *PrairyErth,* William Least Heat Moon's best-selling chronicle of life in Chase County, Kansas, has familiarized Americans with the region's history and people.

Running through much of the eastern half of Kansas, from the Oklahoma border into the northern third of the state, the Flint Hills got their name from the chunks of flint in their soil. Although at one time the plains ran from Chicago to the edge of the Rockies and from Canada to Texas, now scarcely 1% of the original 400,000 square miles of tallgrass remains. Most of the prairie has been tamed by a century of plowing, cattle grazing, and highway building. But when the pioneers first settled here, the bluestem prairie grass, Indian grass, switch grass, and buffalo grass grew so high that someone on horseback could be lost for days.

Once the plains were subject to long droughts and brush fires—the stereotypical picture of this area of Kansas. But modern technology has changed that image with the planting of fire lines and the building of large reservoirs. Also, the Flint Hills are not as dry and devoid of plant life as you might think. Trees line the area's streams; wildflowers thrive on the grassy banks with blooms for every warm season; and Fremont's clematis, towering sunflower, evening primrose, larkspur, cornflower, indigo, and clover mingle on the hillsides.

For the most part, this section of Kansas looks much as it did when pioneers passed through on their way west. Cowboys still ride the hills on horseback and in four-wheel-drives, searching for the stragglers of their grazing herds. You can join these lone sailors in a sea of golden grass by driving through Flint Hills. If you have a jeep, you can get away from the paved highways that cross the plains here, but even if you stick to the civilized paths, you cannot help being transported, for a moment, to the simpler life of the past.

The route we suggest leads south through Flint Hills from Topeka, just west of Kansas City, to Wichita and then into Oklahoma.

TOPEKA The state capital since 1861, Topeka was the site of bitter conflict between abolitionists and proslavery factions during the Civil War. After years of being known as Bleeding Kansas, the state joined the Union. Sites in town include the *State House* (Capitol Square; phone: 913-296-3966), which features murals by the great regionalist painter John Stuart Curry. Exhibits at the zoo (*Gage Park;* phone: 913-272-5821) include a tropical rain forest and a gorilla encounter. Nearby, the *Reinisch Memorial Rose and Rock Gardens (Gage Park)* provide an oasis of fragrant tranquillity in spring, summer, and autumn. The *Kansas State Historical Society* has the multimillion-dollar *Kansas Museum of History* (phone: 913-272-8681), with displays on the state's history (take the Wanamaker North exit off I-70, west of Topeka).

En Route from Topeka Take I-335 from Topeka about 50 miles southwest to Emporia.

EMPORIA This is the heart of the Flint Hills region and its major cattle market. Tens of thousands of cattle are sent to the slaughterhouse from this town every year. Emporia was the home of William Allen White, publisher of the *Emporia Gazette* and one of America's most respected editors. His bust stands in *Peter Pan Park. Emporia State University* (1200 Commercial) presents concerts, plays, and films year-round. *Lyons County Lake and Park,* a 528-acre recreation area (11 miles north of town on Hwy. 170), has swimming, boat launching, fishing, and camping (campsites do not have hookups). For park information, call the *State Forestry, Fish and Game Commission* office in Emporia (phone: 316-342-0658). For activities information, call the *Emporia Convention and Visitors Bureau* (phone: 316-342-1600).

En Route from Emporia Take Highway 99 south for about 3 miles. After you cross the river bridge, you'll see an unnumbered county road running east to Hartford. Follow it for about 20 miles to the *Flint Hills National Wildlife Refuge.* Or take US 50 about 20 miles west to Cottonwood Falls, heart of Chase County and of Kansas cowboy culture. If time permits, consider a visit to the *Z-Bar Ranch* (phone: 316-273-8494), an 1880s cattle spread just 2 miles north of Cottonwood Falls on Highway 177. It's operated by the National Park Trust and offers tours of the ranch, an 1882 farmhouse, and a one-room prairie school, and hikes along a tallgrass trail.

FLINT HILLS NATIONAL WILDLIFE REFUGE About 5,000 acres form this refuge (phone: 316-392-5553), which is primarily devoted to waterfowl. In winter, as many as 20 bald eagles nest on the grounds, as well as snow geese, blue geese, greater and lesser Canadian geese, mallard ducks, and great horned and snowy owls. Whitetail deer, coyote, red fox, and rabbit live here too. The refuge is open daily year-round. The best time to visit is fall; call ahead to check on hunting season closures. There's no admission charge.

En Route from Flint Hills National Wildlife Refuge Return to Highway 99 and head south for about 52 miles, then head west for 32 miles on Highway 96 to US 54 and Wichita, on the western edge of the Flint Hills.

WICHITA Kansas's largest city, this is a leading manufacturing center and the headquarters of four aircraft companies. Places of interest include the *Wichita Art Museum* (619 Stackman Dr.; phone: 316-268-4921), exhibiting American and European canvases and sculpture; *Wichita Center for the Arts* (9112 E. Central; phone: 316-634-2787), containing a gallery and a theater; *Sedgwick County Historical Museum* (204 S. Main; 316-265-9314), with displays on home life in the 1800s and the *Chisholm Trail;* and the *Ulrich Museum* (N. Hillside and 17th Sts.; phone: 316-689-3664), a contemporary art museum. Kids will enjoy the *Old Cow Town Museum* (1871 Sim Park Dr.; 316-264-6398), a restored frontier village with Wyatt Earp's jail. It's closed weekdays November through February; admission charge. For a look at the flora and fauna of the Flint Hills, visit the *Wichita Gardens* (701 Amidon; phone: 316-264-9799), which are closed weekends January through March. There is an admission charge.

En Route from Wichita Head east on US 54 and Highway 96 about 56 miles to Highway 99. Turn south on Highway 99 and drive about 50 miles into Oklahoma. Seventeen miles north of Pawhuska, Oklahoma, is the *Tallgrass Prairie Preserve.*

TALLGRASS PRAIRIE PRESERVE Recently opened by the *Nature Conservancy,* the 36,000-acre *Tallgrass Prairie Preserve* (phone: 918-287-4803) is home to 300 bison. The drive-through preserve is open year-round, and features numerous turnouts for watching the shaggy beasts. There's no admission charge.

BEST EN ROUTE

Motels are easy to find in both Topeka and Wichita, where the major chains are represented. Emporia has at least 10 motels as well as two charming bed and breakfast establishments, the *White Rose Inn* and the *Plumb House.* For information contact the *Topeka Chamber of Commerce* (phone: 913-234-2644); the *Wichita Chamber of Commerce* (phone: 316-265-7771); and the *Emporia Convention & Visitors Bureau* (phone: 316-342-1600).

Glacier National Park, Montana

Montana's *Glacier National Park* is measured in millions: one million acres carved by the movement of massive glaciers millions of years ago, visited by about two million people every year. These 1,600 square miles shared by the US and Canada are officially named *Waterton-Glacier International Peace Park.* The US section of the park is located in the northwest region of Montana (just west of St. Mary); West Glacier, at the western entrance to the park, is 427 miles from *Yellowstone National Park* in Wyoming and 197 miles from Great Falls, Montana. Although the giant ice sheets to which the park owes its name and its geology have long since disappeared, there are still some 50 small glaciers in the park—snow masses so deep that their lower levels have been compacted into ice, and so heavy that they creep downhill. The largest of these, Grinnell, covers 300 acres and contains ice 400 feet thick. In the summer, streams of water from Grinnell and the other glaciers cascade down the mountainsides, gathering volume as they merge and tumble into the deep cold lakes. This spectacular descent is one of the many reasons that this alpine wilderness merits at least a one-week visit.

Glacier National Park's six large lakes (each at least five miles long) stretch from the park's edges into its interior; it has 650 smaller lakes and glacial ponds, 1,000 waterfalls, more than 550 streams, and more than 700 miles of maintained trails and paths for hiking and horseback riding as well. The Blackfeet Indians considered the area sacred and called it the backbone of the world.

The park is open all year long, although most interior roads are closed in winter due to heavy snow. Late fall brings visitors who come to observe the brilliant foliage, snow-capped mountains, and various wildlife; winter brings cross-country skiers and snowshoers. Others come merely to enjoy a snowball fight in summer, fish in a mountain stream, or watch a mountain goat appear to defy gravity in search of vegetation along a mountain slope.

Within park boundaries, you will be required to follow regulations, not only because of the geology of the park, which can be treacherous, but to protect its rich and abundant animal and plant life. The 57 species of animals include the wolverine, lynx, mountain goat, deer, moose, elk, beaver, muskrat, mink, bighorn sheep, coyote, wolf, mountain lion, and grizzly bear. *Glacier* is one of the few US parks that is home to grizzlies (more than 200); hikers are encouraged to talk or sing loudly or make load noises along the trail to indicate their presence in order to avoid surprising and frightening the bears. For the past decade, wolves have been making a comeback as they migrate south from British Columbia. In addition, there are at least 200 types of birds, from hawks and eagles that swoop overhead to grouse and dippers that inhabit the woods and streams. As in any wildlife preserve, however, these creatures are difficult to spot; it is likely that you will leave having seen only an occasional mountain goat or sleepy marmot.

For information about the park, contact the Superintendent, *Glacier National Park* (West Glacier, MT 59936; phone: 406-888-5441; 406-888-5551 for recorded information on weather, road conditions, camping, and park activities). For general information about the park and the surrounding area, contact the *Flathead Convention and Visitors Association* (15 Depot Park, Kalispell, MT 59901; phone: 800-543-3105).

GLACIER NATIONAL PARK Enter from West Glacier or East Glacier off US 2, or from St. Mary off US 89. Once inside, the best way to see the sights is either on short walks from the visitors' centers at Logan Pass (in the center of the park), St. Mary (on the east side), or Apgar (on the west side), or on longer treks, some of which are guided. Check at the park visitors' centers for a schedule of nature walks and hikes. In some areas you can rent horses for riding through the park. But if you have a few days to spare, the best way to get a taste of the park's resources and attractions is to camp in any of the 10 campgrounds and hike from there. What you discover on your own can be augmented by one of the daily walks or campfire programs conducted by rangers at the visitors' centers or campgrounds. Rangers point out the myriad plants and explain how the knife-edged ridges and glacial peaks were formed eons ago.

If you choose just to drive through *Glacier* instead, you will experience one of the most scenic routes in America. The park's Going-to-the-Sun Road between St. Mary and West Glacier is an unforgettable 52 miles of twisting, cliff-hanging mountain roadway linking the east and west sides of the park. (No vehicles more than 21 feet long or eight feet wide, including mirrors, are allowed.) Along the way, you skirt the edge of St. Mary Lake, with its backdrop of snow-capped peaks and Douglas firs, reaching the first of numerous parking turnouts about 5 miles beyond the lake. Here you can see Triple Divide Peak, where—as the name implies—mountain waters divide and enter three larger water systems: the Arctic via Hudson Bay, the Gulf of Mexico via the Mississippi system, and the Pacific Ocean via the Columbia River.

After many other magnificent vistas and views of the park's towering peaks (including 10,014-foot Mt. Siyeh), you reach the highlight of the drive, the crossing of the Continental Divide at Logan Pass. From this 6,664-foot elevation there's a 100-mile view of the countryside—a spectacular panorama that justifies *Glacier*'s reputation as the Alps of America. Get directions to the Hidden Lake overlook at the visitors' center here. The 1½-mile hike, which begins at the *Logan Pass Visitors' Center* and is part boardwalk and part trail, offers a fine view of the calm, deep blue lake 800 feet below—a perfect finale to a lovely walk.

Your drive on the Going-to-the-Sun Road eventually leads into McDonald Valley. For more hiking, head west to *Avalanche Campground* and pick up an easy 2-mile trail that leads to Avalanche Basin. Technically called a "glacial cirque," this is a natural amphitheater with 2,000-foot walls and several waterfalls—a spectacular sight that gives you a sense of the park's interior. The park's largest lake, McDonald, is a center of activity. Here visitors can swim, take a boat tour from the dock at the historic *Lake McDonald Lodge* (see *Best en Route*), or embark on a strenuous hike to Sperry Glacier.

There is fishing at Two Medicine Lake in Two Medicine Valley, in the southeast area of the park, where rainbow, brook trout, mackinaw, and northern pike may be caught. Two Medicine Lake is a good place for camping, hiking, and boating as well. For horseback riding, stay in Many Glacier Valley long enough to join one of the popular all-day trips through wildflower-filled alpine meadows to Cracker or Poia Lakes. Horseback riding also is available at *Lake McDonald Lodge* and in the Apgar area. Arrangements for riding can be made through *Mule Shoe Outfitters* (phone: 406-732-4203); *Lake McDonald Corral* (phone: 406-888-5121); or *Apgar Village Lodge* (phone: 406-888-5010).

Among the park's other noteworthy sites are Red Eagle Lake, with spectacular falls and an impressive gorge; Grinnell Lake, where a trail leads to Grinnell Glacier, the largest in the park; and Flattop Mountain, near Logan Pass. Rafting the north and middle fork of the Flathead River, the park's western and southern borders, is also popular. Half-day to six-day float, whitewater, fishing, and camping trips are offered by *Glacier Rafting* (phone: 800-332-9945); *Glacier Wilderness Guides* (phone: 800-521-RAFT); *Great Northern Rafting* (phone: 800-735-7841); and *Wild River Adventures* (phone: 406-888-5539). Combination raft and horseback riding trips also are available.

En Route from Glacier National Park For even more wildlife adventure and/or isolation in the mountain pines, take Chief Mountain International Highway (Hwy. 17) to *Waterton Lakes National Park* in Alberta, Canada.

WATERTON LAKES NATIONAL PARK This park, across the US-Canada border, is the Canadian section of *Waterton-Glacier International Peace Park.* It offers more of the same, with fewer crowds.

BEST EN ROUTE

If you prefer sheets and blankets to the stars above, there are several good accommodations at the park. Early reservations are suggested for all in-park lodging places. Information is available through *Glacier Park, Inc.*, headquartered during the season at the southeast corner of the park in the *Glacier Park Lodge* (Hwy. 49, East Glacier, MT 59434). For reservations dial *Tower* (PO Box 147, Station 0928, Phoenix, AZ 85077; phone: 602-207-6000). Expect to pay $110 or more per night for a double room at hotels described as expensive; and $60 to $110 at those listed as moderate. Rooms in the places below have private baths and telephones, but no air conditioning or TV sets. Hotels are listed alphabetically by price category.

GLACIER NATIONAL PARK

Lake McDonald Lodge Built in 1913 in a lakeside setting of giant cedars, it has a cozy (although sometimes dingy) atmosphere with Old West flair, 100 rooms, a lobby with a giant fireplace, a lounge, a restaurant, a coffee shop, a camp store, and gift shop. A good choice for fishing, boating, or riding. Open from early June to late September. 10.6 miles northeast of West Glacier on Going-to-the-Sun Rd. (phone: 602-207-6000). Moderate.

Many Glacier Hotel Sitting on the shore of Swiftcurrent Lake, this Swiss-inspired 208-room lodge built in 1914 features a restaurant, a snack bar, a gift shop, and lounges; entertainment is provided by students from more than 200 US colleges. Open from early June to early September. About 12 miles west of Babb off US 89 (phone: 602-207-6000). Moderate.

EAST GLACIER

Glacier Park Lodge Huge Douglas fir timbers with intact bark support the lobby of this 1913 lodge that sits right on the boundary of the park. It has 154 rooms as well as a steakhouse, gift shop, pool, and nine-hole golf course. Open from late May to late September. Just outside the southeast corner of the park on Hwy. 49 (phone: 602-207-6000 off season). Expensive.

Carlsbad Caverns National Park, New Mexico

If you're driving across the eastern part of New Mexico and those vast horizontal plains are beginning to appear endless rather than beautiful, there's relief nearby: the bat flight at *Carlsbad Caverns.* Every sunset from May through September, 5,000 bats per minute spiral out of the dark cave—as many as a million in one viewing. For an hour or more, the bats, on their way out to feed, create a blackening vortex against the sky, which widens into a gray streak as they set off into the stillness of nightfall.

Carlsbad Caverns National Park is in New Mexico's southeastern corner, 16 miles north of the Texas state line and 285 miles southeast of Santa Fe. As you approach the caverns, the monotony of the terrain is broken by the rise of the Guadalupe Mountains. (*Guadalupe Mountains National Park,* just over the border in Texas, is an easy side trip from here.) But the truly spectacular sights at *Carlsbad Caverns* are all underground. Below the 73 square miles of the national park are many caves, and the main cavern is one of the world's largest known underground cavities. With its stalagmite and stalactite formations—some joining and creating monumental pillars, others densely clustered in fragile and delicate patterns—it is a testament to nature's artistry.

In the late 1800s, New Mexico residents noticed the nightly bat flights from a nearby cave and named it Bat Cave. But they left the bats and the cave alone until 1903, when the deposits of bat guano near the cave's entrance attracted commercial interest. A mining operation was set up and, over the next 20 years, 200 million pounds of guano were extracted from the cave for fertilizer. During that time, James Larkin White, a cowboy and guano miner, discovered the cave's marvelous limestone formations. Inside lie acres of caverns; even now, some areas still have not been completely explored.

The beginnings of this subterranean gallery go back more than 200 million years, to a time when a vast inland sea covered the entire area. At the edge of this sea, limestone-secreting organisms and mineral precipitates built the massive Capitan Reef. In the course of millennia, the sea dried up and the reef was buried under several thousand feet of sediment. Then, approximately 20 million years ago, cracks appeared in the rock. Slightly acidic rainwater seeped into the cracks and worked its way down to the water table. The acid eroded the rock, creating the caverns. Additionally, hydrogen sulfide escaped from oil and gas reservoirs and combined with oxygen-carrying water to form sulfuric acid that dissolved the rock.

When subterranean pressure pushed the caverns above the water table, the erosion accelerated as massive blocks of porous rock, no longer supported by water, collapsed. The seepage of surface rain and melted snow continued, carrying dissolved limestone to the walls. Drop by drop, eon by eon, the water deposited more limestone, creating many formations—stalactites that hang like icicles from the ceiling, stalagmites that reach up from the ground, and massive pillars where the two have fused.

The park is open daily year-round except on *Christmas Day.* For additional information contact the Superintendent, *Carlsbad Caverns National Park* (3225 National Parks Hwy., Carlsbad, NM 88220; phone: 505-785-2232).

CARLSBAD CAVERNS NATIONAL PARK To gain an appreciation of nature's work at *Carlsbad Caverns,* you will need about half a day. After stopping at the visitors' center to consult displays on the caverns' history, follow a short trail to the entrance, where a self-guided tour begins (visitors can rent portable radio receivers for a recorded description of the sites). Remember to wear a sweater or jacket, as the cave stays a pleasantly cool 56F year-round. The walk starts at the imposing Natural Entrance to the cave—an arch 90 feet wide and 40 feet high—and continues for 3 miles, beginning with a relatively steep descent down switchback trails to a depth of 829 feet. Lighting hidden in underground cables brings out the subtle hues in the limestone formations. Walk along the *Main Corridor* to the aptly named *Big Room,* an area the size of 14 football fields, with a 255-foot ceiling, pillars, domes, and the tall (and also appropriately named) *Totem Pole* stalagmite. If you are pressed for time or cannot make the descent by foot, you may descend in an elevator for a shorter tour (about 1¼ miles) of the *Big Room.* Park rangers also lead tours through the *King's Palace,* with its ornate limestone formations and curtains of glittering cave onyx; the *Queen's Chamber,* noted for its delicate "elephant ear" formations; and the *Papoose Room,* a low-ceilinged chamber with numerous stalactites.

Incongruous as it may seem after walking through the cavern's natural chambers, there is a lunchroom at the bottom. Except for the underground lunchroom and the elevator, little has been done to alter the natural state of the caverns.

Flashlight tours are available at *Slaughter Canyon Cave,* 23 miles southwest of the visitors' center. The trip involves a trek up a steep half-mile trail to get to the cave. During the tour, which lasts from one-and-a-half to two hours, you discover spectacular formations with only the help of the lights you are carrying. Tours of *Slaughter Canyon Cave* are given daily from *Memorial Day* through *Labor Day* weekend; weekends the rest of the year. Reservations are required (phone: 505-785-2232). You needn't be an experienced spelunker, but rangers advise that you should be in good physical condition, wear sturdy walking shoes, and carry your own flashlight.

Visitors may explore *Carlsbad Caverns National Park* aboveground as well. A self-guided nature trail begins at the visitors' center (in summer, there are occasional guided tours). Along the trail you may see arid desert vegetation and a large variety of cacti—and, with luck, some of the area's wildlife, such as mule deer and lizards. Walnut Canyon Desert Drive, a one-way gravel road of 9.5 miles, begins half a mile from the visitors' center and travels to the edge of Rattlesnake Canyon and back down through upper Walnut Canyon to the main entrance road. For the more adventurous, there is backcountry camping, offering plenty of contact with the wilderness. The trails are poorly defined, and the desert rugged and dry.

At dusk, no one should miss the bat flight from *Carlsbad Caverns.* Visitors sit in the amphitheater at the cave's mouth, waiting for the bats, as park rangers explain what's about to happen; however, they are usually interrupted in mid-sentence when thousands of bats pour out of the cave into the darkening sky.

En Route from Carlsbad Caverns National Park While in the area, you might want to follow Highway 62 about 35 miles south of Whites City to the *Guadalupe Mountains National Park,* just south of the Texas border.

GUADALUPE MOUNTAINS NATIONAL PARK, near Pine Springs, Texas This 86,416-acre park preserves what some geologists consider the world's most significant and extensive fossil reef. Guadalupe Peak, Texas's highest point (8,749 feet, accessible by trail), is here, as are the landmark cliffs of El Capitan. The rugged countryside takes in desert vegetation and high-country forests of ponderosa pine, southwestern white pine, and Douglas fir that offer 80 miles of hiking trails. The last two weeks in October and the first week in November, when the canyon maples, oaks, and walnuts take on their autumn colorations, are particularly beautiful times to visit. Be sure to stop at the *McKittricle Canyon Visitor Center* and *Frijole Ranch Museum* to see the exhibits on the park's geology and flora and fauna as well as artifacts from the area's first settlers. There are three self-guided nature trails within the park. For camping information, contact *Guadalupe Mountains National Park* (HC60 Box 400, Salt Flat, TX 79847; phone: 915-828-3251).

BEST EN ROUTE

Although you can get a permit at the *Carlsbad Caverns* visitors' center for rugged backcountry camping, the park has no developed overnight facilities. The town of Carlsbad, 27 miles northeast of the park's visitors' center, offers a wide range of motels, hotels, and camping facilities; White's City, a privately owned town 7 miles east of the visitors' center, has a motel and a few shops as well. Expect to pay $75 or more per night for a double room at hotels described as expensive; $50 to $75 at those listed as moderate; and less than $50 at those in the inexpensive category. Rooms have air conditioning, private bath, TV sets, and telephones, unless otherwise indicated. Hotels are listed alphabetically by price category.

WHITE'S CITY

Best Western Cavern Inn This motel has 105 rooms, a restaurant, and two pools with spas. 17 Carlsbad Caverns Hwy. (phone: 505-785-2291; 800-CAVERNS). Expensive.

CARLSBAD

Holiday Inn A pool, a restaurant, a lounge, and a fitness center and spa are among the amenities at this 101-room motel. 601 S. Canal St. (phone: 505-885-8500; 800-465-4329). Expensive to moderate.

Crater Lake National Park, Oregon

The Klamath Indians have their own explanation for the creation of this spectacular, brilliant blue, deep lake in the Cascade Mountains of southern Oregon. According to their legends, Llao, the god of the underworld who lived here, and Skell, the god who dwelt on Mt. Shasta, had a battle over an Indian maiden. Skell won and collapsed Llao's mountain. It was later filled with water to prevent Llao from escaping.

Geologists offer an equally splendid story to explain the formation of the caldera, which now attracts more than 500,000 visitors each year. At least half a million years ago, a series of eruptions of magma (hot molten rock) from several miles underground began to form Mt. Mazama, which eventually reached an estimated 12,000 feet. A massive eruption of the mountain about 7,700 years ago virtually emptied the magma chamber and weakened the structure of the volcanic cone. The cone then collapsed into the chamber, forming a caldera about 6 miles wide and nearly 4,000 feet deep. Continuing lesser eruptions within the caldera created smaller cones and helped seal off the basin with lava flows, and rain and snow began filling the basin, eventually forming a lake.

Whichever version you believe, Crater Lake—and the park that surrounds it—is a sight not to be missed. Oregon's only national park (established in 1902 after long years of lobbying), *Crater Lake National Park,* 256 miles from Portland, is a 286-square-mile tract surrounded on almost every side by national forests. It boasts a rich variety of animal and plant life, miles of hiking trails, countless beautiful vistas, a scenic road running 33 miles around the rim of the caldera, and the lake itself—at 1,932 feet, the deepest in the US.

Until 1853, Crater Lake was unknown to white men. Then a gold prospector, John Wesley Hillman, and a party of gold diggers stumbled upon it while searching for the famous Lost Cabin Mine. The few who knew of it dubbed it Deep Blue Lake, and its discovery wasn't made public for 31 years.

The man most crucial to the lake's fate first saw it in 1886. William Gladstone Steel was a Kansan transplanted to the great new West. Once he laid eyes on this spectacle, he committed his life to its preservation, leading a crusade to save it from homesteaders, lumber interests, and prospectors. Teddy Roosevelt made Crater Lake a national park on May 22, 1902; Steel was later rewarded for his work with an appointment as the park's second superintendent.

The following route circles Crater Lake clockwise from the south entrance on 33-mile Rim Drive.

CRATER LAKE NATIONAL PARK There are two reasons to go to Crater Lake. One is to take a boat tour on it (no private craft allowed), and the other is to look at it from above. Rim Drive is the best possible manmade vantage point for viewing the lake: Almost 70 miles of trails, many starting from the road, snake through the park, up adjacent mountains, or down to the lake's shores. At the lakeside, boats depart for trips around the lake and to its two islands, Phantom Ship and Wizard.

Begin at the *Rim Visitors' Center* in Rim Village (open June through September), where there are three restaurants and a store. (The other visitors' center, *Steel Information Center* at Munson Valley, is open year-round). Daily talks on the lake's origin are given here in summer. In addition, two walking tours worth investigating start here. The first, a 1½-mile trail, runs south to the top of Garfield Peak, 1,900 feet above the lake; the second leads to *Discovery Point,* where John Wesley Hillman first saw the lake. Next to the visitors' center is *Sinnott Memorial,* another excellent vantage point.

From the visitors' center at Rim Village, you enter Rim Drive, where you'll have to struggle to keep your eyes on the road and off the scenery.

Fortunately, numerous stopping places mark the circular route. There also are many trails that lead from stopping places up nearby summits (for even broader vistas).

The first stop on the mountain is called the Watchman. A 4/5-mile trail leads to its summit, overlooking the lake from 1,800 feet. Farther along, on the northeast side of the mountain, is *Cleetwood Trail* and its 1-mile path down to the lake's shores. It's steep going down and even steeper coming back up; don't take more than you can comfortably carry. But do go down, for at the end of the trail you can take a two-hour boat trip around Crater Lake and to the islands. Rangers on board explain what you pass and what to look for. Inquire at one of the park visitors' centers for schedules.

Other stops along the route include the 2½-mile trail up Mt. Scott, the highest point in the park, and, a little farther on, the turnoff for the drive to the top of Cloudcap, 1,600 feet above the lake. Each path or road gives a different perspective on the vastness of the lake below, the Cascade Range to the north, and the Oregon scenery all around.

Swimming is permitted; the lake's surface temperature gets as warm as 60F in summer, but its depths remain very cold, and rangers advise visitors not to drink the water. The lake has trout and Kokanee salmon, and fishing is allowed without a license. Nightly campfire programs, which include slide shows and ranger talks, are held at *Mazama Campground.* Mazama Village, 7 miles south of Rim Village, has a store, a gas station, coin-operated showers, and a laundromat.

Although things at the park slow down in winter, *Crater Lake* does appeal to cross-country skiers, who get a good look at its pristine beauty. Ski rentals are available; ask at the visitors' center at Munson Valley. Snow generally begins to accumulate in mid-October, reaches a depth of 13 to 15 feet by early April, and doesn't disappear until early July. Many roads and facilities close during the winter, but the roads to the lake overlook at Rim Village are plowed daily. From mid-October to mid-June, only the park's south and west entrances are open.

A last note: Although you'll undoubtedly have the experience of sneaking up on "tame" wild animals like deer, squirrels, chipmunks, marmots, and foxes, don't feed or try to pet them.

For additional information about the park, contact the Superintendent, *Crater Lake National Park* (PO Box 7, Crater Lake, OR 97604; phone: 503-594-2211).

BEST EN ROUTE

Two campgrounds in the park—*Mazama* in the south-central area and the primitive *Lost Creek* off East Rim Drive—offer a variety of facilities. Both are run on a first-come, first-served basis.

Expect to pay $80 or more per night for a double room at hotels listed as expensive; and less than $80 at those categorized as moderate. Rooms have air conditioning, private baths, TV sets, and telephones, unless otherwise indicated.

CRATER LAKE

Crater Lake Lodge This place resembles the original 1912 lodge, but it has been renovated in the style of the 1920s. The lobby features walls of stone and ponderosa pine slabs from the original building, heavy beams, a large fireplace, and period furnishings. The 71 guestrooms have views of either the lake or the mountains. There's a fine restaurant, a café, and a cafeteria. The lodge is open mid-May through mid-October. Rim Village Dr. (phone: 503-594-2511). Expensive.

DIAMOND LAKE

Diamond Lake Resort Five miles north of the park's northern entrance, this lakefront lodge has 93 rooms including two-bedroom cabins in a mountain setting, and motel rooms (some with kitchen units), as well as a dining room, a restaurant, and a pizza parlor. There is no air conditioning or in-room telephones. Diamond Lake (phone: 503-793-3333). Moderate.

JACKSONVILLE

Jacksonville Inn Built in 1863, this inn has been through several incarnations: It has served as a bank, a hardware store, professional offices, and a repair shop. Today it offers eight bedrooms and a cottage, all lovingly furnished with antiques; a dining room, open for lunch and dinner; and a wine and gift shop. Prices include a full breakfast. It's located in Jacksonville, an interesting 19th-century town in the heart of what was once gold rush country, about 85 miles southwest of Crater Lake and just west of Medford. 175 E. California St. (phone: 503-899-1900; fax: 503-899-1373). Expensive.

The Oregon Coast

One of the most awe-inspiring drives in the country is along Oregon's Pacific Coast, from Astoria at the mouth of the Columbia River to the California border at Pelican Beach. Here you can see how land has been—and is still being—sculpted by the enormous, slow force of the sea. Very little of the land along the coast is privately owned, so you can stop at hundreds of points along the road that are part of state and federal forests. Most of the coast is lined with steep cliffs; 20 million years ago, when the coastline was formed, the land was level with the Pacific. Some commercial blight has appeared here and there, but don't despair: it doesn't extend all the way down the coast. If urban, touristy havens turn you off, just keep driving. For more information on the Oregon Coast, contact the *Oregon Department of Tourism* (775 Summer St. NE, Salem, OR 97310; phone: 800-547-7842).

Our route starts at the coast's northernmost point, Astoria—which is 100 miles northwest of Portland—and heads south along the coast road, US 101.

ASTORIA At the mouth of the Columbia River, known for its salmon, Astoria is both a river fishing and a commercial deep-sea fishing center. On the waterfront, the *Columbia River Maritime Museum* (at the foot of 17th St.; phone: 503-325-2323) has ship models, artifacts, and—moored outside—a restored lightship. It is closed *Thanksgiving* and *Christmas;* there's an admission charge. *Astoria Column,* a 125-foot observation tower on Coxcomb Hill, is a monument to those who explored and settled the area. From the top you can see the harbor, ocean, and wooded mountains. It's open daily except *Thanksgiving* and *Christmas;* there's an admission charge.

En Route from Astoria Just 2 miles west of town off US 101 is the major charter fishing port of Warrenton. *Fort Clatsop National Memorial,* 4 miles south on US 101, replicates the fort where Lewis and Clark spent the winter of 1805–6. Ten miles farther south, the small town of Gearheart has two fine 18-hole golf courses, *Gearheart* (phone: 503-738-3538) and *Highlands at Gearheart* (phone: 503-738-5248). Two miles south of Gearheart is Seaside.

SEASIDE This is one of Oregon's busiest shore resorts. A seawall along the coast forms a 2-mile boardwalk above the beach.

En Route from Seaside Tillamook Head, 5 miles south of Seaside on an old logging road that juts west to the ocean, stands more than 1,200 feet above sea level, and provides a sweeping view of the northern territories and the offshore *Tillamook Lighthouse.* From here, US 101 turns east along the Necanicum River, through green lowlands where commercial farms grow lettuce and peas. At Cannon Beach Junction, a road lined with towering hemlocks leads to Cannon Beach.

CANNON BEACH One of the most popular beaches on the coast, it is known for its surf fishing, clam digging, and for Haystack Rock, a huge offshore rock formation that attracts photographers and artists. Also popular are the shops and galleries in the community of Cannon Beach.

En Route from Cannon Beach From here, continue south on US 101 for 5 miles to Arch Cape, carved into a bluff at Neah-kah-nie Mountain. Eight miles down the road, Manzanita is both a beach and mountain resort, tucked in a cove protected by rugged headlands to the north. From here the road cuts inland with Nehalem Bay, crosses the Nehalem River, and passes through Wheeler. Another 8 miles south, Rockaway has broad beaches, the arched Twin Rocks, an offshore formation, and attractive resort facilities. Just south is Tillamook Bay.

TILLAMOOK BAY The bay's main town is Tillamook, a center of Oregon's inland dairy region. The *Tillamook Cheese Factory* here (4175 Hwy. 101N; phone: 503-842-4481) has a viewing area and interpretive exhibits that draw more than 800,000 visitors each year. Closed *Thanksgiving* and *Christmas.* Cape

Meares, just west of town, offers a broad view of the ocean from a 700-foot-high overlook.

En Route from Tillamook Bay Cape Meares is the first stop on the Three Capes Scenic Drive; follow this drive south to Cape Lookout and Cape Kiwanda, near Pacific City. Rejoin US 101 at Pacific City and proceed to Neskowin, about 30 miles south of Tillamook.

NESKOWIN The beaches here attract beachcombers who hunt for Japanese floats, colored glass balls used as net supports by Asian fishermen. The floats cross the Pacific on the Japan Current. Cascade Head, southwest of Neskowin, stands 1,400 feet high and juts out to sea.

En Route from Neskowin Head south about 10 miles to Lincoln City.

LINCOLN CITY Here are a 7-mile beach and a hodgepodge of shops, galleries, and vendors, including *Factory Stores,* Oregon's largest outlet mall, as well as a large number of resort facilities. Just east of Lincoln City off US 101 is *Devil's Lake State Park,* which offers the *Blue Heron Landing,* a marina with boat rentals and good fishing; and claims to be the source of the world's shortest river, "D" River, which flows only 400 yards from Devil's Lake to the Pacific.

En Route from Lincoln City Go south for 13 miles to Depoe Bay.

DEPOE BAY The harbor is nearly always filled with trawlers, and charter boat fishing is available, as are sightseeing and whale watching cruises. Offshore, water sprays from an aperture in the rocks known as Spouting Horn. Look for the geyser shooting skyward from the ocean. The *Depoe Bay Aquarium,* in the middle of town (US 101; phone: 503-765-2259), has displays of local marine life. It's closed *Christmas;* there's an admission charge. About 4 miles south, the Cape Foulweather viewpoint overlooks an impressive stretch of ocean, and just south of that, *Devil's Punch Bowl State Park* looks out to Otter Rock, a seabird rookery that was once the home of thousands of sea otters. At the base of a sandstone bluff, waves rush through two openings and boil up inside the rocky caldron, receding in a wash of foam—this is the Devil's Punch Bowl. For information on Depoe Bay parks, contact *Oregon State Parks* (525 Trade St. SE, Salem, OR 97310; phone: 503-378-6305).

En Route from Depoe Bay Continue south for about 10 miles from the Devil's Punch Bowl to Newport.

NEWPORT Newport spreads across a steep, ridged peninsula between the ocean and Yaquina Bay. The resultant sheltered harbor offers year-round surfing, scuba diving, fishing, clamming, and crabbing. Be sure to sample the delicious Dungeness crab and Yaquina Bay oysters. Across the bay (via US 101) is the newly renovated *Mark O. Hatfield Marine Science Center* (2030 S. Marine Science Dr.; phone: 503-867-0100); with a variety of exhibitions, it is especially popular with kids for its "handling pools." It's closed *Christmas;* there's an admission charge. Also on the south side of the bay, the 23-acre *Oregon Coast Aquarium* (2820 SE Ferry Slip Rd.; phone: 503-867-3474) educates visitors about environmental preservation. Exhibits include the popular whale "Keiko" of *Free Willy* movie fame; a walk-through aviary; a display that follows a drop of rain as it travels from the Coastal Range to the ocean; and several caves, cliffs, and dunes. It's closed *Christmas;* there's an admission charge.

En Route from Newport Continue south on US 101 to Waldport and cross the Alsea Bay Bridge (built in 1991 to replace the original 1937 structure). Three miles south is Cape Perpetua, with hiking trails along the rocky coast and into the lush forest and a visitors' center. Continue south to the *Sea Lion Caves,* which are 11 miles north of Florence.

SEA LION CAVES A modern elevator here takes visitors down to one of the world's largest sea caves (phone: 503-547-3111). Sea lions can be seen inside primarily during the fall and winter; they live outside on the rocks in front during spring and summer. The caves are closed *Christmas;* there's an admission charge.

En Route from the Sea Lion Caves Follow US 101 south to Florence.

FLORENCE Here, the coastline alters in character. The steep, craggy headlands give way to a 50-mile stretch of sand dunes extending to the Coos Bay area. Behind the low foredunes along the shore stretches a chain of freshwater lakes. Beyond the lakes are huge dunes, some reaching as high as 250 feet and extending as far as 3 miles inland. Half-buried pine and spruce mark the dunes' eastward march. *Jessie M. Honeyman State Park* contains Cleawox Lake, locked in by the dunes, and a dense evergreen forest laced with trails.

En Route from Florence Head south to Honeyman, at the northern boundary of the *Oregon Dunes National Recreation Area.*

OREGON DUNES NATIONAL RECREATION AREA The 41-mile-long *Oregon Dunes National Recreation Area* is part of *Siuslaw National Forest.* You can take a dune buggy ride or hike over the dunes in the recreation area, but be careful: It's easy to get lost. Winds can whip up and become blinding in a short time, covering your footprints. Dune hiking is also more taxing than hiking on hard-packed ground. Trail access and platforms for viewing some of the highest dunes are available at the *Dunes Overlook,* 10 miles south of Florence and 10 miles north of Reedsport, the headquarters for the *Oregon Dunes National Recreation Area.* The overlook is well marked, with signs along the highway pointing the way. Near Reedsport is Winchester Bay, which has one of the Oregon coast's largest sport fishing fleets.

En Route from Oregon Dunes National Recreation Area South of the dunes area, mile-long McCullough Bridge crosses Coos Bay.

COOS BAY The largest bay in Oregon and home to the lumber and shipping town of North Bend, the Coos Bay region is the West's main lumber port. *Shore Acres, Sunset Bay,* and *Cape Arago State Parks,* west of Coos Bay on Cape Arago Highway off US 101, overlook protected coves and Simpson's Reef offshore. *Shore Acres* (in *Sunset Bay State Park* off Cape Arago Hwy.; phone: 503-888-3732; 800-824-8486) is a large formal botanical garden at a former estate. From the headland, sea otters and sea lions can be seen playing on offshore reefs.

En Route from Coos Bay Some 17 miles south of Coos Bay is Bandon.

BANDON This town features a restored Old Town, a cheese factory, and a spectacular beach. Summer stern-wheeler rides are offered up the Coquille River. A few miles south is the *West Coast Game Park,* a petting zoo/walk-through safari featuring more than 70 species and more than 450 animals. It's open year-round, weekends only in January and February; there's an admission charge (phone: 503-347-3106).

En Route from Bandon About 23 miles south of Bandon is Cape Blanco, the most westerly point in Oregon.

CAPE BLANCO A flat, grassy peninsula that juts 2 miles into the Pacific, Cape Blanco overlooks Blanco and Orford Reefs to the south. The *Cape Blanco Lighthouse* on the headland was built in the 1870s. It is not open to the public.

En Route from Cape Blanco Port Orford, 6 miles south of the Cape Blanco turnoff, is a small harbor town protected by a cape to the north called the Heads. Many trails lead through underbrush to secluded beaches and tidal pools. Six miles farther south, Humbug Mountain rises 1,750 feet; *Humbug Mountain State Park* (part of *Siskiyou National Forest*) has fishing, swimming, and camping facilities. Another 22 miles south of Humbug Mountain is Gold Beach.

GOLD BEACH This beach lies at the mouth of the Rogue River, which can be toured by jet boat. During the 1850s a good deal of gold was dredged from the Rogue, but in 1861 floods swept the deposits into the ocean. (Small amounts of gold can still be found along the beach.)

En Route from Gold Beach The stretch of coastline from here to the California line is probably the most rugged in Oregon. Innumerable coves and tidal pools remain virtually untouched. Cape Sebastian, 7 miles south of Gold Beach, is a 700-foot promontory reaching out to the sea, with many trails branching inland from the coast. *Harris State Park,* 6 miles north of California, has miles of beach and a view of offshore bird rookeries.

BEST EN ROUTE

Expect to pay $120 or more per night for a double room at those places we've listed as expensive, $75 to $120 at those listed as moderate, and less than $75 at those rated inexpensive. Unless otherwise indicated, rooms have private baths, TV sets, and telephones but no air conditioning.

ASTORIA

Crest Located on two-and-a-half acres of woods and lawns, it offers a panoramic hilltop view overlooking the Columbia River, with mountains on the far shore. There are 40 rooms located in four buildings (one is nonsmoking). Amenities include an outdoor hot tub and in-room coffee makers. There is no restaurant. 5366 Leif Erickson Dr. (phone: 503-325-3141; 800-421-3141). Inexpensive.

GLENEDEN BEACH

Salishan Lodge This spectacular, first class resort, located 8 miles south of Lincoln City in Gleneden Beach, is designed to harmonize with the surrounding woods, lagoons, beach, and ocean. Its 200 rooms and three suites are in 15 villas; resort facilities include almost the entire list of possibilities. Also see *America's Special Havens* in DIVERSIONS. 7760 Hwy. 101N (phone: 503-764-2371; 800-452-2300; fax: 503-764-3681). Expensive.

GOLD BEACH

Tu Tu Tun Lodge On the banks of the Rogue River, it offers fishing, wild river jet boat trips, a four-hole pitch-and-putt course, and hiking trips. The 16 rooms and two suites overlook the water; there's also a garden house and a river house, separate units that accommodate from two to six people each. Also on the premises are a pool and a dining room (open to non-guests from May through October; reservations necessary). There are no TVs. 96550 N. Bank Rogue (phone: 503-247-6664). Expensive.

Badlands National Park, South Dakota

Badlands National Park covers more than 380 square miles in southwestern South Dakota, its awesome, irregular hills carved in hues of gold, pink, and green are brilliant enough to eclipse even Dorothy's magical rainbow. French Canadian explorers and trappers labeled the barren buttes *"les mauvaises terres"*—bad lands—and General Alfred Sully took one look at the place and called it "a part of hell with the fires burned out." The Lakota Indians called the region Maco Sica, or "land bad," probably translating the French characterization into their own language.

Until about 65 million years ago, this area was submerged under a shallow sea. Silt and clay accumulated on the sea bottom; as time passed, these sediments hardened into the rock known as the Pierre Shale. Eventually, the same forces that pushed up the Black Hills also lifted the seabed. Between about 37 to 23 million years ago, the area was a floodplain resembling today's Gulf Coast. Animals roamed here in great numbers; many later suffered extinction, but some, such as the tiny three-toed horse, evolved into species still seen today. Frequent flooding buried mammal bones with mud, permitting them to fossilize. Then millions more years rolled by, and the climate became cooler and drier. Finally, in the last few thousand years, a semiarid climate punctuated by downpours set off erosion.

Now the land is a sweeping garden of nature's sculpture, with fantastic buttes rising above zigzag gullies. Colored layers representing ancient soils are vivid reminders of the long-lost Golden Age of Mammals, and each scouring rain uncovers fossil skulls, exposed to sunlight after millennia of darkness. Occasionally, you can spot a juniper or red cedar among the stark surroundings. Yucca and rabbit brush thrive on the slopes and valleys, which hold greater moisture. Most animals in the area seek refuge in the moist prairies on the park's circumference; here you may see buffalo, herds of deer and antelope, or jackrabbits, cottontails, or chipmunks attempting to avoid their predatory neighbor, the coyote. Occasionally, the golden eagle, cliff swallow, rock wren, and snowy owl make appearances as well.

During the late 1800s, the badlands were overrun with geologists seeking fossils. In an attempt to preserve the area, Congress passed legislation creating *Badlands National Monument* in 1929. In later years, presidential proclamations set aside nearly 250,000 acres to be administered by the *National Park Service.* Collecting fossils in the park is now forbidden.

Our journey starts in Rapid City, continues through the *Badlands National Park,* and ends at the small town of Wall.

RAPID CITY Settled in the late 1870s after gold was discovered in the Black Hills, Rapid City now has a population of more than 54,000 and spreads across a section of Black Hills plateau. Main sites in town include the *South Dakota School of Mines & Technology* (St. Joseph St.; phone: 605-394-2511), with displays of fossils and geological artifacts, including specimens of local minerals; *Dahl Fine Arts Center* (713 Seventh St.; phone: 605-394-4101), with giant murals showing scenes of US history and assorted Americana; and *Marine Life* (2 miles south on Rte. 16; phone: 605-343-7400), with aquariums and dolphin and seal shows.

On the outskirts of town are *Bear Country USA* (8 miles south on Rte. 16; phone: 605-343-2290), home of black and brown bears, roaming buffalo, wolves, moose, deer, mountain lion, and various smaller furry native creatures, and *Black Hills Reptile Gardens* (6 miles south on Rte. 16; phone: 605-342-5873), where you can see rattlesnakes being milked, alligators being wrestled, and snakes from all over the world. *Chapel in the Hills* (Chapel Rd. off Hwy. 44; phone: 605-342-8281) is a replica of an 800-year-old Norwegian church set among rolling hills in a tranquil valley. And then there's *Mt. Rushmore,* 25 miles south on Route 16 (see *Black Hills,* below).

Before heading for the national park, look at the surrounding countryside from Skyline Drive, a scenic route in the southwest part of town. For additional information, contact the *Rapid City Chamber of Commerce* (PO Box 747, Rapid City, SD 57709; phone: 605-343-1744; fax: 605-343-1916) or the *Rapid City Convention and Visitors Bureau* (PO Box 747, Rapid City, SD 57709; phone: 800-487-3223).

En Route from Rapid City Take I-90 east about 70 miles to Cactus Flat. The park's northeast entrance is south of Cactus Flat on Highway 240.

BADLANDS NATIONAL PARK The northeast entrance takes you to park headquarters and the visitors' center, which are farther down the road on the left, near Cedar Pass. Inside are displays and a video program; in the summer, nature hikes are conducted and evening programs take place in the amphitheater. From here you can drive through the park for 30 miles, along a paved road lined with parking areas and lookouts with markers describing geological and botanical phenomena, before exiting at the western Pinnacles entrance. With ongoing construction along 7 miles of roadway, delays are inevitable.

There are eight main hiking trails in the park, including the ¾-mile *Door Trail* and the shorter *Cliff Shell Nature Trail,* both of which take you into the middle of the multicolored plateaus and soft clay surroundings. If you are a photographer, be sure to set out in the early morning or late afternoon, when the slanting light intensifies the hues of the jagged hills. There are 96 campsites at Cedar Pass and 24 at Sage Creek. Open year-round. For additional information, contact the Superintendent, *Badlands National Park* (PO Box 6, Interior, SD 57750; phone: 605-433-5361; fax: 605-433-5404).

En Route from Badlands National Park Exit at the western Pinnacles entrance, which is 9 miles south of exit 110 on I-90 and the town of Wall.

WALL This little town in the shadows of South Dakota's *Badlands* is home to the *Wall Drug Store* (510 Main St.; phone: 605-279-2715; fax: 605-279-2699), an emporium famous for its 5¢ cup of coffee. The store's *Western Art Gallery* dining rooms are the repository of 210 original Western oil paintings. Also on Main Street is the 4,500-square-foot *Buffalo Gap National Grasslands Visitor Center* (phone: 605-279-2125), with exhibits on the prairie, rangelands, grasslands, and federal forests of the West. The *Wild West Historical Wax Museum* (601 Main St.; phone: 605-279-2915) has figures of Jesse James, Wild Bill Hickok, Buffalo Bill Cody, and Calamity Jane. It's open daily; admission charge.

BEST EN ROUTE

There is only one lodge in *Badlands National Park.* Accommodations there are inexpensive—expect to pay less than $50 per night for a double room. There also are numerous motels in the surrounding area (there are 13 in Wall) and three bed and breakfast establishments. For information, contact the *Wall Chamber of Commerce* (phone: 605-279-2665).

Cedar Pass Lodge This lodge is in the heart of the rugged badlands. Accommodations consist of 24 cabins and a main building with a restaurant and a gift shop. Rooms have private baths, but no air conditioning, TV sets, or telephones. On Hwy. 240 off I-90 next to the park's visitors' center (phone: 605-433-5460). Inexpensive.

Black Hills and Mt. Rushmore National Memorial, South Dakota

The fabled Black Hills, famous for mineral deposits and pure grazing land, cover about 6,075 square miles of southwestern South Dakota along the Wyoming border. The ominous-sounding name was bestowed upon the hills by the Lakota Sioux Indians, who called them "Paha Sapa,"or "Hills That Are Black." The Black Hills are actually dark green, predominantly ponderosa pine.

The Lakota believe the Black Hills to be the center of the spiritual universe. According to tribal legend, the Black Hills were a reclining female figure from whose breasts flowed life-giving forces, and to them the Lakota went as a child to its mother's arms. Native Americans and others still visit the Black Hills in search of communion with the universe.

Our route, forming a very rough oval, heads south from Rapid City to Hot Springs, stopping at *Mt. Rushmore* and *Wind Cave National Park,* before heading north again through *Black Hills National Forest* to Lead and Deadwood, South Dakota.

RAPID CITY For details on the city, see the *Badlands National Park, South Dakota* route, above.

En Route from Rapid City Drive southwest on US 16 about 13 miles to Rockerville.

ROCKERVILLE Now a veritable ghost town, Rockerville was in its glory during the late 1870s, when $1 million worth of gold was mined out of the surrounding hills, but its supply of the valuable mineral ran dry as suddenly as it was found. By 1882, most residents moved farther west, leaving empty saloons and cabins. Nowadays the town comes alive in summer, when tourists come to spend some time at the *Gaslight* (phone: 605-343-9276; 605-343-6924), a combination dining saloon, antique shop, and old-fashioned soda fountain and candy shop.

En Route from Rockerville Continue southwest on US 16 for about 5 miles. Turn left on US 16A and drive about 2 miles to Keystone.

KEYSTONE One of the first pioneer towns in the area, this is the official address of *Mt. Rushmore National Memorial,* 3 miles south of town. You can see the carvings from the *Rushmore Aerial Tramway* (one-half mile south of Keystone, on US 16A; phone: 605-666-4478). North of town on Highway 40, you can mine for gold ore—and keep anything you find—at *Big Thunder Gold Mine* (phone: 605-666-4847). And 5 miles east of town on Highway 40 is *Rushmore Cave* (13622 Hwy. 40; phone: 605-255-4467), with more stalactites and stalagmites than any other cave in the region. Open daily, it can be explored on guided tours only. There's an admission charge.

En Route from Keystone Head southwest on Highway 16A to *Mt. Rushmore.*

MT. RUSHMORE NATIONAL MEMORIAL Here, carved into the granite cliffs, the faces of Presidents Washington, Jefferson, Lincoln, and Theodore Roosevelt rise above all else.

The idea of creating a shrine here was not readily accepted. In 1923, Doane Robinson, South Dakota state historian and poet, proposed building a monument dedicated to famous western heroes such as Lewis and Clark, Kit Carson, and the famous Lakota Sioux Red Cloud. The citizens were reluctant, but Robinson managed to win the support of two influential South Dakotans, Representative William Williamson and Senator Peter Norbeck. Both agreed that the giant sculpture would bring fame and fortune to the state. In 1924 Robinson and his colleagues called in a designer named Gutzon Borglum to survey the terrain and discuss the project. Intrigued by the challenge, Borglum left the *Confederate Memorial,* which he was carving at Stone Mountain outside Atlanta, Georgia, and headed for the Black Hills.

Borglum's idea was to create a national memorial that would embrace the merits and symbolize the ideals of our most celebrated presidents. "American history shall march along the skyline," he exclaimed. But many people felt that a manmade sculpture would destroy the beauty of the rich Black Hills, and supporters found fund-raising difficult. Traveling extensively, Borglum finally collected enough money to begin his greatest work. On August 10, 1927, President Calvin Coolidge rode a horse 3 miles from nearby Keystone for a ceremony marking the beginning of *Mt. Rushmore's* construction.

Due to sporadic funding the project took 14 years—six-and-a-half for the actual construction. Borglum and his son, Lincoln, supervised throughout, overseeing a crew that averaged 30 members. More than 450,000 tons of rock were removed. Drillers blasted away stone to rough out the faces, and then the remaining rock was chipped away by hand and smoothed with air hammers. Borglum painstakingly inscribed the hard granite surface, but more than its fine detail, the dimensions of the monument are what make it so impressive. *Mt. Rushmore* ranks as one of the world's largest sculptures, comparable to the ancient Egyptian pyramids and sphinxes: The faces measure 60 feet from top of head to chin, the mouths stretch more than 18 feet across, and the average nose is 20 feet long.

Gutzon Borglum died in March 1941, but his son and the remaining workers finished the project by the following October.

The symbolism of this "Shrine of Democracy," as the monument is known, is as grand as its physical dimensions, as William Williamson pointed out in a speech to his congressional peers in 1928. "Washington symbolizes the founding of our country and the stability of our institutions," he said. "Jefferson, our idealism, expansion, and love of liberty; Lincoln, our altruism and sense of inseparable unity. Roosevelt typifies the soul of America—its restless energy, rugged morality, and progressive spirit."

The memorial is currently undergoing a $40-million expansion and renovation to insure that natural cracks in the faces do not expand and cause instability. It also has a new walking trail leading to the base of the faces. The visitors' center is open daily year-round; in the summer it remains open till 10 PM.

In summer there is a nightly lighting ceremony which begins at 9 PM, and the faces are lit from 9:30 to 10:30 PM; the lighting schedule varies according to the season, so call ahead. No camping or picnicking is permitted at the site. For additional information, contact *Mt. Rushmore National Memorial* (PO Box 268, SD 57751; phone: 605-574-2523; fax: 605-574-2307).

En Route from Mt. Rushmore National Memorial Head south on US 16A to the junction with US 16; follow US 16 west through *Custer State Park*, about 10 miles.

CUSTER STATE PARK Within the 73,000 acres of *Custer State Park* roams one of the largest publicly owned buffalo herds in the world numbering between 1,400 and 1,500 head. The park has four lodges leased to the *Custer State Park Resort* (phone: 800-658-3430) that offer accommodations and meals (see *Best en Route*), as well as seven campgrounds with 320 sites (run by the state); four lakes; mountain streams; and 12 hiking, mountain bike, and horseback riding trails. Daily interpretive programs are held from *Memorial Day* through *Labor Day.* The park is open year-round; an entrance fee is charged year-round. For additional information contact the *Custer State Park* (HC 83, PO Box 70, Custer, SD 57730; phone: 605-255-4515; 800-710-2267 for reservations).

En Route from Custer State Park Take Highway 87 15 miles south to *Wind Cave National Park.*

WIND CAVE NATIONAL PARK Designated a national park by President Theodore Roosevelt in 1903, the cave got its name from the strong wind currents that blow through its entrance. Most of the 28,292-acre park consists of woodlands and open prairies. Elk, bison, and prairie dogs wander freely among the wildflowers and trees, making the area a favorite of photographers. For additional information contact *Wind Cave National Park* (RR2, PO Box 190 WCNP, Hot Springs, SD 57747; phone: 605-745-4600).

En Route from Wind Cave National Park Continue about 8 miles south along US 385 to Hot Springs.

HOT SPRINGS Named for the springs that flow year-round through the city's downtown, this community of 5,000 is the home of two fascinating natural phenomena. In 1974, a bulldozer operator accidentally unearthed the *Mammoth Site* (1800 Hwy. 18 Bypass; phone: 605-745-6017), a prehistoric sinkhole containing the remains of huge Columbian mammoths; to date, 40 mammoths have been discovered here. A visitors' center, which features miniature digs for children, encloses the site, and guided tours lead you among bones and tusks that have been hidden for 26,000 years. The site is open daily; there's an admission charge. Also here is *Evans Plunge* (Hwy. 385; phone: 605-745-5165), dubbed the world's largest natural warm water indoor pool. Spring-fed water at 87F rises from a pebble bottom at the rate of 5,000 gallons a minute, causing a complete change of water 16 times a day. Visitors may swim in the pool; there's also an outdoor pool and slide.

En Route from Hot Springs Take US 385 32 miles north to Custer.

CUSTER Custer is one of the oldest towns in the Black Hills. Though quartz, mica, beryl, and gypsum are mined in the immediate area, it was gold that brought the town its prosperity. In fact, the first gold strike in the state occurred in 1874 in nearby *Custer State Park* (see above). During the last weekend in July, the *Gold Discovery Days Pageant* (phone: 800-992-9818 for information) attempts to re-create the time of the great gold discovery of 1874. Celebrations include a carnival, a rodeo, and a reenactment of Gold Rush events. For information contact *Custer Chamber of Commerce* (phone: 605-673-2244).

En Route from Custer Go about 13 miles west on US 16 to *Jewel Cave National Monument.*

JEWEL CAVE NATIONAL MONUMENT Myriad crystal formations here create beautiful images and designs. Walking tours and more rigorous spelunking tours are conducted in summer, but participants should be in good physical condition. The visitors' center and exhibition room (off US 16; phone: 605-673-2288) provide background on local geology. They're open daily June through August.

En Route from Jewel Cave National Monument Return to Custer and head 3 miles north on US 385.

CRAZY HORSE MEMORIAL This memorial to Oglala Sioux chief Crazy Horse was originally begun by sculptor Korczak Ziolkowski in 1947. When the sculptor died in 1982, his family adopted the project, which is still under construction. When completed, the monument will be 563 feet high and 641 feet long, so massive that all of *Mt. Rushmore* could easily fit into one section of it. The blasting and sculpting can been seen from the 70-room *Crazy Horse Visitor Complex,* which houses displays on the creation of the memorial and on its importance as a tribute to all Native Americans. The memorial and visitor complex are open year-round. For additional information, contact the *Crazy Horse Memorial* (Ave. of the Chiefs, Crazy Horse, SD 57730; phone: 605-673-4681).

En Route from Crazy Horse Memorial Head north about 11 miles on US 385 to Hill City.

HILL CITY An 1880s steam train (1880 Circle Dr.; phone: 605-574-2222) takes you from here through the Black Hills, past the settings used in the old TV series "Gunsmoke." You can go by train to Keystone Junction and back, but be sure to make reservations in advance. About 5 miles south of town stands 7,242-foot Harney Peak, the highest point in the state. Two popular trailheads are located at *Willow Creek Horse Camp,* an unattended campground in *Custer State Park* to the north, and *Sylvan Lake* to the south. From either you can hike to the summit of Harney Peak, which provides an elegant view of "the Needles," a group of granite pinnacles.

En Route from Hill City There is a *Black Hills* visitors' center at Pactola Lake, about 13 miles north of Hill City.

BLACK HILLS NATIONAL FOREST The forest covers more than a million acres of dense stands of pines and open meadows, which are seemingly wedged into the crevices of the jagged hills. Established in 1897, *Black Hills National Forest* is home to elk, deer, antelope, and mountain goats. Camping, hiking, fishing, and picnicking facilities are available. A visitors' center at Pactola Lake is open from *Memorial Day* to *Labor Day.* For information, contact the Forest Supervisor, *Black Hills National Forest* (RR2, PO Box 200, Custer, SD 57730; phone: 605-673-2251).

En Route from Black Hills National Forest Drive about 24 miles north on US 385 to Lead.

LEAD Unlike its neighbors, Lead (pronounced *Leed*) never ran dry of gold. Here is the largest working mine in the Western Hemisphere, Homestake Mine (on US 14A and US 85; phone: 605-584-4653), which has been in operation since 1877. It offers tours from May through October. In winter, skiers flock to *Terry Peak Ski Area* (phone: 605-584-2165), about 10 miles west of Lead. At 7,076 feet, it is the highest ski mountain east of the Rockies. The chair lift to the summit affords an unparalleled view of Montana, North Dakota, Nebraska, and Wyoming. Nearby, the *Deer Mountain Ski Area* (phone: 605-584-3230) offers 25 trails and 200 acres of skiing, and southwest of Lead is Cheyenne Crossing, lauded nationally for *Eagle Cliff Cross-Country Ski Area* (unattended), and nearby snowmobile trail, which gets more than 15 feet of snow annually.

En Route from Lead Less than 5 miles east on US 85 is Deadwood.

DEADWOOD Deadwood is primarily a town for tourists and gamblers. Known as a "get rich quick" spot after Custer ran dry, it saw such legends as Wild Bill Hickok, Calamity Jane, Colorado Charlie Utter, and Potato Creek Johnny roam the streets and carouse at the well-attended saloons. *Old Saloon No. 10,* where Wild Bill Hickok lost not only a game of poker but his life, still stands on Main Street. Hickok and other Wild West characters are buried at *Mt. Moriah Cemetery* (Lincoln Ave.). Every summer, the trial of Wild Bill's killer is reenacted at the *Old Town Hall* (Lee St.) in a play called *The Trial of Jack McCall.*

Legalized gambling reappeared in 1989, when Deadwood voted to allow casinos; since then, 88 licenses have been issued, resulting in 53 establishments. One of the most popular of these is the recently renovated *Midnight Star* casino (677 Main St., Deadwood; phone: 605-578-1555; 800-999-6482; fax: 605-578-2739), partly owned by film star Kevin Costner and his brother, Dan. Along with slot machines, wheels of fortune, and card games, it houses two restaurants: *Jake's* for fine dining, and *Diamond Lil's* sports bar, which displays a collection of memorabilia from Costner's movies. A portion of all gambling profits goes to the city for the historic preservation of the downtown district; already completed is a brick street that spans two blocks and is lined with several restored turn-of-the-century gas street lamps.

During the first weekend of August, Deadwood holds a rodeo and a parade on Main Street to celebrate the *Days of '76.* For information, call the *Deadwood Chamber of Commerce* (phone: 605-578-1876; 605-578-1033).

BEST EN ROUTE

Expect to pay $100 or more per night for a double room at those places we have categorized as expensive; $65 to $100 at those listed as moderate; and less than $65 at those described as inexpensive. Unless otherwise indicated, rooms have private baths, telephones, and TV sets but no air conditioning. Hotels are listed alphabetically by price category.

CUSTER STATE PARK

Blue Bell Lodge and Resort Hayrides, chuck wagon cookouts, hiking, and fishing are among the activities offered here. There are 29 cabins (none with phones) and a restaurant. Open year-round. On US 87 (phone: 605-255-4531; 800-658-3530 for reservations). Expensive to moderate.

Sylvan Lake Lodge and Resort This popular resort area overlooking the lake offers fishing, boating, biking, hiking, swimming, and rock climbing. There are 35 lodge rooms and 31 cabins (some of the cabins have fireplaces and some have kitchenettes). There's a restaurant on the premises. Open from May through mid-September. On US 87 (phone: 605-574-2561; 800-658-3530 for reservations). Moderate.

Legion Lake Resort Here are 25 cottages near buffalo herds, summer theater, and horse and hiking trails. Some of the cottages have kitchens, but none have telephones or TV sets. There is a restaurant. Open late May to late September. On US 16A (phone: 605-255-4521; 800-658-3530 for reservations). Inexpensive.

State Game Lodge Resort Here are seven rooms in a historic lodge, 40 motel units, and 21 cabins, some with cooking facilities. There are stocked fishing streams, hiking trails, and the popular *Buffalo Safari* four-wheel-drive–vehicle rides. Guests also enjoy a restaurant and cocktail lounge. Open May through early October. On US 16A (phone: 605-255-4541; 800-658-3530 for reservations). Moderate.

HILL CITY

Best Western Golden Spike Inn This member of the world-wide chain has 61 comfortable rooms, a restaurant, an outdoor heated pool, and a hot tub. In addition, guests enjoy plenty of outdoor activities including horseback riding, fishing, tennis, and strolling in the garden area. Open April through November. Located 8½ miles from Mt. Rushmore on Hwy. 16 and 385 (phone: 605-574-2577; 800-528-1234). Expensive to moderate.

Mt. Rushmore KOA, Palmer Gulch Resort Here are down-home ranch accommodations with horseback riding, fishing, hiking, and swimming. There are 30 furnished housekeeping cabins (some of which have phones and TV sets) and 40 camping cabins. RV hookups and tent space are available, as are nightly entertainment programs and movies. Open May through September. Five miles from *Mt. Rushmore* on Hwy. 244 (phone: 605-574-2525). Inexpensive.

LEAD

Best Western Hills Situated a mile from the *Homestake Mine,* the historic district, two ski areas, and snowmobile trailheads, this 100-room hotel has a restaurant, an indoor pool, a racquetball court, and full gym facilities. There's also a courtesy shuttle to Deadwood gambling and nearby ski areas. 900 Miners Ave. at the intersections of Hwy. 14A and Hwy. 85 (phone: 605-584-1800; 800-528-1234; fax: 605-584-3933). Moderate.

Great Salt Lake, Utah

Located west of Salt Lake City in the northwest corner of Utah is the Great Salt Lake, set in the desert like a gray-blue inland sea. This 40-by-80-mile body of water does not teem with life, as one would expect; it is North America's dead sea because of its high salt concentration (in its northern reaches, the lake is as much as 27% salt, about seven times as salty as sea water). The lake supports no life but primitive algae, bacteria, a quarter-inch-long brine shrimp used for tropical fish food, and stingless brine flies that blacken the shores from June to September. Naturally, the water is unfit for drinking, not exactly an angler's dream, and hardly ideal for swimming—put your face in or under the water and you'll feel a burning sensation that will make you wish you had never set eyes on the Great Salt Lake. But it does offer 4.8 billion tons of salt; deposits of magnesium, lithium, gypsum, potash, boron, sulfur; and chloride compounds that have lured chemical firms to this liquid mine—not to mention some of the most fantasy-fulfilling floating and wading imaginable.

The arid and desolate area around the lake appears so inhospitable because it once also was covered by salty waters. Today's Great Salt Lake is merely a drop in the bucket compared to this earlier sea. Only 23,000 years ago, freshwater Lake Bonneville (formed from the melting snows of successive Ice Ages) stretched from Salt Lake City west into Nevada, north into Idaho, and south into Cedar City, Utah; it reached depths exceeding 1,000 feet and encompassed 20,000 square miles. (The terraced striations marking its former shorelines are still visible today on the flanks of the Wasatch Mountains of the Rockies.) When the last glaciers waned and the ice retreated northward, weather in this region became hotter and drier. Lake Bonneville shrank below the level of its outlet, Red Rock Pass in southeast Idaho, and its feeder streams continued to bring in minerals that could not escape. Some water continued to flow in, but not enough to offset evaporation, and the lake grew saltier and saltier.

Today, the remnant of this once vast inland sea is so salty that it's impossible for a person to sink in it. The *Southern Pacific*'s rail causeway, built in 1903, divides the lake into two sections of differing salinities. To the south of the dike-supported track, the lake appears bluer because the freshwater inflow dilutes the salinity, while the north side approaches saturation. Either side provides ample testing grounds for experiments in human buoyancy—but keep your face out of the water.

Sixteen miles west of Salt Lake City (for a full report on the city, see *Salt Lake City* in THE CITIES) off I-80 at the southern end of the lake is *Great Salt Lake State Park.* Here you'll find a 300-boat marina and Saltair Beach, with its snack bar, rides (in summer), and souvenir shops. The water gets quite warm, around 80F in summer (in winter it can go below freezing, though, of course, the saltwater doesn't freeze). At the marina, there is a boat ramp, and small sailboats may be rented; ask the rangers how to reach some of the lake's islands. Because the lake's high salt concentration will corrode motors and metal, the majority of boats on the lake are fiberglass sail boats (there is a facility for washing motorboats if necessary). The park is open year-round.

Antelope Island State Park, off I-15's Exit 335 south of Ogden, is the other point for public access to the lake. The park, which has a resident buffalo herd, is a good jumping-off point for boat trips. Because most of the lake islands are privately owned, visits are limited to viewing from off shore. Fremont, for example, is a private island, where you can see birds and other animals, including horses and sheep that are brought here for summer grazing. Another private island, Gunnison, in the northwest quadrant of the lake, is a nesting site for the great white pelican. From a boat you can scan the island's scrubby bushes and rock heaps for this magnificent bird, as well as terns and gulls. The best time to see pelicans is spring, when they literally cover the island.

For more information on the Great Salt Lake, contact the Superintendent, *Great Salt Lake State Park* (GSL, PO Box 323, Magna, UT 84044; phone: 801-250-1898 or 801-250-1849).

The Great Salt Lake area holds one last surprise: Within an hour's drive, in the Wasatch Mountain Range east of Salt Lake City, there are a dozen well-developed ski resorts. The base elevation is 8,000 feet and the season stretches from November to May, so when it gets too cold for all but the hardiest to float, there is plenty of time—and plenty of places—for skiing. For information, contact *Ski Utah* (phone: 801-534-1779).

BEST EN ROUTE

For information on camping in the Salt Lake area, contact *Utah State Parks and Recreation* (1636 W. North Temple, Salt Lake City, UT 84116; phone: 801-538-7221). For a full range of accommodations and restaurants in Salt Lake City, see *Salt Lake City* in THE CITIES.

Utah's National Parks

Ten percent of all the 51 national parks in the US are in southern Utah. The following route (about 375 miles long) covers all five, including two of the most spectacular, *Zion* and *Bryce Canyon National Parks,* which are less than 90 miles apart.

Both Zion Canyon and Bryce Canyon are geologically part of the area that includes the Grand Canyon, 125 miles south of Zion. From the air, the three canyons look like a series of steps, with Grand Canyon the bottom, Zion the middle, and Bryce Canyon the top. The middle sibling of this vast natural canyon-scape, Zion is younger than the Grand Canyon and older than Bryce. It dates to the Mesozoic era, the time when dinosaurs stalked the earth. (You can see dinosaur footprints in the rocks at *Zion National Park;* ask at a visitors' center.) *Bryce Canyon National Park* is laced by a network of tributaries (usually dry) of the Paria River. Technically, *Bryce's* canyons are not canyons at all, but breaks in the earth, tremendous pink and white limestone amphitheaters as deep as 1,000 feet. The Paiute Indians called the stone formations at Bryce Canyon *"angku-ku-wass-a-wits,"* or "red, painted faces" and thought the twisted shapes had been cast into stone by a vengeful god.

Our route begins at *Zion National Park,* which is 320 miles south of Salt Lake City via I-15, and 160 miles northeast of Las Vegas via I-15 and Route

9. It then continues across the state, stopping at *Bryce Canyon National Park; Capitol Reef National Park,* a beautiful, isolated area near Torrey with Indian rock art and rich-hued canyons; *Arches National Park,* home to a variety of majestic natural stone arches; and *Canyonlands National Park,* where two rivers meet.

ZION NATIONAL PARK The 229 square miles of *Zion National Park* were named by a 19th-century Mormon, Isaac Behunin. To the Mormons, Zion means "heavenly resting place." A series of dramatic gorges and canyons, the area was first a sea and then a desert; its layered buttes and canyons are actually the scars of incredibly harsh climatic changes. These shifts created the psychedelic purple, lilac, yellow, and pink rock walls and gorges, shimmering in the clear light, for which the area is called "the land of rainbow canyons." Geologists believe Zion Canyon was formed by the Virgin River, which carved a gorge out of deep layers of sediments left from the shallow seas and windblown sand dunes that once covered the area.

A good way to begin your visit is at *Zion Canyon Theater* (Springdale; phone: 801-772-2400). Then stop at the *Zion Canyon Visitors' Center* (Hwy. 9; phone: 801-772-3256), where there's a museum of geological exhibitions and an information desk. You'll have an excellent view of multicolored Zion Canyon from the lobby. For a breathtaking overview of rugged canyons (some of which are just as impassable today as they were when explorers began visiting the area in the 19th century) and incandescent rock formations, drive the Zion–Mt. Carmel Highway. The highway runs along the east section of the park, connecting with Canyon Drive and zigzagging up Pine Creek Canyon and through a 5,607-foot-long tunnel that goes through Bridge Mountain.

Overnight hikes on any of the park's 65 miles of trails require permits, which you can pick up at either of the visitors' centers before setting out. And be sure to check weather conditions—the trails around the canyon rim are sometimes closed by snow. From the *Zion Park Lodge* (see *Best en Route*), you also can embark on horseback trips on *Sandbench Trail.*

Take the shuttle from *Zion Park Lodge* to the *Temple of Sinawava,* 8 miles from the south entrance of the park. It is a natural formation shaped like an amphitheater. Inside are the two giant pillars for which the temple got its name: *The Altar* and *The Pulpit.* Once you reach the temple, the road stops. From here, it's a mile-long hike to the *Narrows,* where the Virgin River—sometimes no more than 20 feet wide—races through the giant walls of rock, and columbine and shooting star flowers bloom in spring.

During the summer, you can join a guided nature hike (locations vary), or camp along the ash-, cottonwood-, and moonflower-lined riverbanks in the two designated camping areas. From this area there's a strenuous 2½-mile hike to *Angels Landing* at the top of the canyon, but the view is worth it.

For additional information, contact the Superintendent, *Zion National Park* (Springdale, UT 84767; phone: 801-772-3256).

En Route from Zion National Park Highway 9 east, US 89 north, and scenic Highway 12 east take you to *Bryce Canyon National Park,* 86 miles away. Before heading north on US 89, you might want to detour south on US 89 to Kanab, a town of about 19 motels and a handful of restaurants 3 miles from the Arizona border. It has the distinction of being near a set of coral pink sand dunes that were used as a location for many a Hollywood movie.

BRYCE CANYON NATIONAL PARK As at *Zion,* the best place to start your explorations of *Bryce Canyon National Park*'s 35,835 acres is the visitors' center, where you'll find geological, natural history, and archaeological exhibits. Guided naturalist activities are offered during summer; horseback rides are available spring, summer, and fall. In summer, there is also a park tour in a restored 1938 White Motors original touring limousine, which leaves from *Bryce Canyon Lodge* (see *Best en Route*).

There are 20 miles of driving roads along the rim of the canyon and 61 miles of hiking trails for exploring either the top or the bottom of the canyon. The most popular hiking trail is the *Navajo Loop Trail,* a one- to two-hour excursion that takes you more than 500 feet into the canyon, past *Thor's Hammer* and other rock formations. The trail intersects with the *Peekaboo Loop Trail* (a 3½-mile loop) and *Queen's Garden Trail.* Don't miss the 18-mile–rim drive from Farview Point to the 9,105-foot-high Rainbow Point, where you can get a great view of the splintered rock plateau stretching to the north. Southward, from adjacent *Yovington Point,* you may look across southern Utah toward the North Rim of the Grand Canyon. In general, we recommend taking it easy at *Bryce Canyon,* as the 8,000- to 9,000-foot altitude will tire you quickly.

Although *Bryce* stands at the eastern edge of the Paunsaugunt Plateau, and Paunsaugunt means "home of the beaver," there are no beavers in the park. You should, however, be able to spot skunks, deer, marmots, chipmunks, and squirrels easily. Hawks, swallows, and ravens are among the more prevalent winged creatures that can be seen above Bryce Canyon. This is also one of the best places in the country for photography. Light sparkles here, illuminating the canyons so that they seem to glow from an inner fire. Dawn and dusk are the best times to take pictures.

Winter activities include cross-country skiing, snowshoeing (snowshoes are on loan at the visitors' center), and winter camping. There are two campgrounds in the park, and part of one of them stays open all winter. For additional information, contact the Superintendent, *Bryce Canyon National Park* (Bryce Canyon, UT 84717; phone: 801-834-5322).

En Route from Bryce Canyon National Park Follow Highway 12 east and north through *Dixie National Forest* about 106 miles to Highway 24. *Capitol Reef National Park* is just east of the junction.

CAPITOL REEF NATIONAL PARK This is a geologist's paradise, especially the uplift known as the *Waterpocket Fold,* with layer upon layer of exposed rock formations. The Fruita historic district, around the visitors' center and campground, is the site of a pioneer Mormon settlement. In the midst of the desert, the district forms a green oasis where visitors may pick cherries, apricots, peaches, and other fruit in season. Other attractions include a variety of desert flora and fauna; prehistoric Fremont Indian rock art; and sheer-walled sandstone cliffs, canyons, and monoliths whose rich, rainbow hues seem almost luminous in the late-afternoon sun. You may travel by car, on the 25-mile–round-trip Scenic Drive, or by foot, along short hiking trails or on carefully planned backpacking trips. The park is open all year, but most campers prefer visiting in spring and fall, when the weather is best for hiking. There are three campgrounds, two of which have only limited (dirt road) access by car. For additional information, contact *Capitol Reef National Park* (Torrey, UT 84775; phone: 801-425-3791).

En Route from Capitol Reef National Park Continue along Highway 24 east and north about 70 miles to I-70. Take the Interstate 34 miles east, then head south on US 191 28 miles to *Arches National Park.*

ARCHES NATIONAL PARK Through some of the numerous arches here, you can see vast canyons and, off in the distance, the snow-capped peaks of the La Sal Mountains. Awe-inspiring *Delicate Arch,* the 73,379-acre park's most celebrated landmark, is higher than most houses, while *Landscape Arch* is among the world's longest known natural stone arches. Though only a few miles north of *Canyonlands* (see below), the formations here have their own distinct character; a visit to both parks will teach you a lot about how the earth came to be what it is. The park is open year-round, but spring, fall, and winter are the best times to visit. *Devil's Garden* campground is 18 miles from the main entrance. For information, contact *Arches National Park* (PO Box 907, Moab, UT 84532; phone: 801-259-8161) or the *Moab Information Center* (PO Box 550, Moab, UT 84532; phone: 801-259-8825; 800-635-MOAB).

En Route from Arches National Park Take US 191 a few miles north to Highway 313, which leads south into the Island in the Sky section of *Canyonlands National Park.*

CANYONLANDS NATIONAL PARK The Green and Colorado Rivers, which meet here, have carved deep and winding gorges into the reddish-orange sandstone. The relatively untrammeled 337,570 acres are scattered with juniper and piñon trees and dotted with fantastic buttes, cliffs, mesas, spires, columns, and pillars. It can all be seen on jeep tours out of Moab; on float trips down the Green and Colorado Rivers (see *Touring America's Waterways* in DIVERSIONS); by foot, mountain bike, or four-wheel-drive; and by car from a number of overlooks. There are two campgrounds in the more developed part of the park; occupancy is on a first-come, first-served basis. Go early, as sites are limited, and bring your own water. The park is open year-round, but spring and fall are the most pleasant times to visit. Private rafting and canoeing trips require permits. For information, contact *Canyonlands National Park* (2282 S. West Resource Blvd., Moab, UT 84532; phone: 801-259-7164) or *Grand County Travel Council* (PO Box 550, Moab, UT 84532; phone: 801-259-8825; 800-635-MOAB).

BEST EN ROUTE

Expect to pay $90 or more per night for a double room at places we have listed as expensive; $65 to $90 at those described as moderate; and less than $65 at those categorized as inexpensive. Unless otherwise indicated, rooms have private baths, air conditioning, TV sets, and telephones. Hotels are listed alphabetically by price category. There are a number of motels and bed and breakfast establishments in Torrey, near *Capitol Reef.* For general reservations in the Moab area, near *Canyonlands* and *Arches National Parks,* call *Canyonlands Central Reservations* (phone: 800-748-4386) or *Grand County Travel Council* (phone: 800-635-MOAB).

ZION NATIONAL PARK

Zion Park Lodge This group of motel units and cabins with gas fireplaces has a total of 121 rooms (there are no TV sets). Horseback riding facilities, a snack bar, and a restaurant are also on the premises. Open year-round. In the park (phone: 801-772-3213; 303-297-2757 for reservations; fax: 801-772-3060). Expensive to moderate.

BRYCE CANYON NATIONAL PARK

Bryce Canyon Lodge There are 110 rooms and four suites here, set in motel units and cabins with gas fireplaces. There's a restaurant in the main building. Open from mid-April through October. Hwy. 12 in the park (phone: 801-586-7686; 303-297-2759 for reservations). Expensive to moderate.

Best Western Ruby's Inn One mile from the entrance to *Bryce Canyon,* this motel offers 410 rooms (two with kitchenettes), a restaurant, conference facilities, a gift/grocery store, and an indoor pool. Open year-round. Hwy. 63 (phone: 801-834-5341; 800-528-1234). Moderate.

Bryce Canyon Pines Facilities at this motel about 6 miles from the park include a restaurant, coffee shop, and heated pool. Some of the 51 rooms have fireplaces. Open year-round. Hwy. 12 (phone: 801-834-5441; fax: 801-834-5330). Moderate.

CAPITOL REEF NATIONAL PARK

Capitol Reef Inn Just a few miles west of *Capitol Reef* in Torrey, this rustic inn offers 10 comfortable rooms, a good restaurant, and a gift/book shop. Open year-round. 360 W. Main (phone: 801-425-3271). Inexpensive.

Mt. Rainier National Park and Mt. St. Helens National Volcanic Monument, Washington

Swathed in glaciers, Mt. Rainier reaches 14,411 splendid, icy feet into the sky. The tallest peak in Washington State, it dominates the surrounding area, while the 235,404 acres of *Mt. Rainier National Park* provides a setting of firs, wildflowers, and lakes against which the solitary giant can be seen to best advantage. Exploring Mt. Rainier's perilous slopes might not be your idea of a holiday, but regardless of what form it takes, your first encounter with Mt. Rainier is sure to be unforgettable.

A curious combination of glacial and volcanic activity, Mt. Rainier is the product of momentous eruptions that occured within the last million years. The same eruptions were also responsible for Mt. Baker, near the Canadian border; Lassen Peak in northern California; and the other peaks in the Cascade Range, to which Rainier belongs.

Mt. Rainier offers visitors the chance to simultaneously observe icy and subterranean thermal forces in action. Climbers approaching Columbia Crest, Mt. Rainier's summit, have reported tiny geysers of steam spurting through the ice, a sign of volcanic activity below. The steam has carved intricate mazes in the mountain's ice, forming a labyrinthine network of ice tunnels and caves. In 1870, the first team to reach the summit of Mt. Rainier spent the night nestled in one of these burrows, without whose shelter they probably would have died from exposure.

Mt. Rainier's glacial system, the most extensive "single peak" network in the continental United States, consists of 26 named glaciers and about 50 smaller, unnamed ones. Their age is estimated to be a mere 10,000 years, a legacy of the last, massive Ice Age Retreat. Carbon Glacier is Mt. Rainier's longest, at 6 miles; Emmons Glacier, almost 4½ miles long and a mile wide, the largest. The Nisqually Glacier may move as much as 50 to 400 feet a year.

Declared a national park in 1899, *Mt. Rainier* is surrounded by national forests. *Mt. Baker–Snoqualmie National Forest* forms its eastern, northern, and western boundaries. This forest stretches 160 miles from the Canadian border to White Pass. Spruce and fir trees cover the 1.7 million acres that include Mt. Baker, a 10,778-foot dormant volcano, 390 glaciers, and 1,200 miles of trails, including sections of the *Pacific Crest Trail.*

South of *Mt. Rainier National Park* is *Gifford Pinchot National Forest,* site of Mt. St. Helens, a volcano that stirred to life in March 1980 after having stood dormant since 1842. A series of earthquakes and minor eruptions culminated in a massive explosion that blasted more than 1,300 feet off the top of the 9,677-foot mountain in May 1980. In August 1982, Mt. St. Helens was named a *National Volcanic Monument* and 110,000 acres of its surrounding area were designated for recreation and research.

Our route extends from Seattle to *Crystal Mountain,* a resort area in *Mt. Baker–Snoqualmie National Forest,* to *Mt. Rainier National Park,* and then south to *Mt. St. Helens National Volcanic Monument.*

En Route from Seattle Take I-90 east and I-405 south, exiting onto Highway 169 and following it for 25 miles to Enumclaw. From Enumclaw follow Highway 410 for about 30 miles around the northeast side of Mt. Rainier to *Crystal Mountain.*

CRYSTAL MOUNTAIN A year-round resort in the *Mt. Baker–Snoqualmie National Forest, Crystal Mountain* (Hwy. 410; phone: 360-663-2265) is particularly noted for its excellent downhill skiing facilities. There are 10 chair lifts at 3,000 vertical feet. The lifts offer a breathtaking panorama from Mt. Rainier to Mt. Hood in Oregon. For additional information on *Mt. Baker–Snoqualmie National Forest,* contact forest headquarters (21905 64th Ave. W., Montlake Terrace, WA 98043; phone: 206-775-9702).

En Route from Crystal Mountain Head south on Hwy. 410 (Mather Memorial Parkway) to the White River entrance to *Mt. Rainier National Park.*

MT. RAINIER NATIONAL PARK At the park's White River entrance head west to the *Sunrise Visitors' Center* or continue south on Hwy. 410 to 123 to the Stevens Canyon entrance and the *Ohanapecosh Visitors' Center.* Here you can pick up Stevens Canyon Road, a section of the mountain's 117-mile network of paved roads, which travels along the park's southern boundary, past the Tatoosh Range and 5,955-foot Eagle Peak, then crosses the park, climbing to the *Paradise Visitors' Center* at 5,400 feet, continuing down to the *Longmire Visitor's Center* at 2,700 feet, and arriving finally at the Nisqually entrance and ranger station, in the southwest corner of the park. The visitors' centers distribute free information on hiking and climbing. Guides conduct interpretive walks throughout the park in summer, and in winter the Paradise section of the mountain is headquarters for snowshoe walks and cross-country skiing. Note that the eastern entrance to the park is closed in winter, as is the Sunrise section, which at 6,400 feet is the highest part of the mountain that can be reached by car. Keep in mind, too, that winter lasts a long time on Mt. Rainier; with an average annual snowfall of 620 inches in the Paradise section of the mountain, there may still be 100 inches of snow in late May, and the road to the Sunset area may not open until late June. The Nisqually entrance is open year-round, weather permitting. At the *Paradise, Longmire,* or *Sunrise Visitors' Centers,* you can pick up the *Wonderland Hiking Trail,* a 90-mile route that circles the base of Mt. Rainier. *Wonderland* takes you past Box Canyon, waterfalls, fields of wildflowers (in season), Golden Lakes, Carbon River, Carbon Glacier, and the Mowich Glaciers. Campsites (available on a first-come, first-served basis) are spaced about 12 miles apart along the trail. From mid-June until the end of

September, it's a good idea to come during the week and before 3 PM to grab a site. (You'll also need to pick up a permit at a visitors' center if you intend to camp overnight.) *Northern Loop Trail* extends 17½ miles from *Wonderland Trail* through backcountry meadows to Crescent Mountain, at an elevation of 6,400 feet. Throughout the park there are also numerous hiking and walking trails of varying lengths and degrees of difficulty (some are only a half-mile long and on level ground), making the mountain accessible to nature lovers of all levels of fitness and experience.

But the ultimate climb up Mt. Rainier is the one that leads to the peak; you should take this climb seriously. Even in good weather, sudden storms can envelop the mountain in gales of Himalayan ferocity, and on quiet days, the glacial movements sometimes form new crevasses. At any moment, sudden rockfalls can tear out hunks of trail. Several climbers have died due to avalanches and storm conditions. Before setting out, you may want to take a one- or five-day course in mountain climbing techniques given by *Rainier Mountaineering* (RMI, Paradise, WA 98398; phone: 360-569-2227) at the national park's *Paradise Guide House.* All climbers must register at one of the visitors' centers before departing, and there are restrictions on the number of people allowed in each party, as well as requirements for health, equipment, and leadership qualifications. The best time to climb is mid-July, after the summer storms have passed but before the constant summer heat wears down the ice, causing unstable mountain conditions. Generally, the climb takes two days, with an overnight stop at *Camp Muir,* at 10,000 feet. You can rent or buy climbing gear at *Paradise Guide House.*

For additional information, contact the Superintendent, *Mt. Rainier National Park* (Tahoma Woods, Star Rte., Ashford, WA 98304; phone: 360-569-2211).

En Route from Mt. Rainier National Park There are two possible approaches to *Mt. St. Helens National Volcanic Monument* from Mt. Rainier. To reach the west side of the mountain, site of two visitors' centers with exhibits and presentations on the volcano and the May 1980 eruption, take Highway 706 west. At Elbe, head south on Highway 7 to Morton, then west on Highway 12 to I-5 south. Exit at Castle Rock (Exit 49) and drive east on Highway 504 five miles to the *Silver Lake Visitors' Center.*

To visit the western side of Mt. St. Helens, which has only a tiny information station but offers the best views of the devastation caused by the 1980 eruption, head southeast from Mt. Rainier on Forest Road 52 to Packwood and US 12. Continue on US 12 south and west to Randle. Here you can pick up Highway 25 heading south along the eastern side of Mt. St. Helens. *Woods Creek Information Station,* operated by the *National Forest Service,* is six miles south of Randle.

Keep in mind that the *Silver Lake Visitors' Center* on the west side and the *Woods Creek Information Station* on the east side of Mt. St. Helens are separated by a two-hour drive (you have to go around the mountain); also note that some of the park roads are closed from November through May because of snow.

MT. ST. HELENS NATIONAL VOLCANIC MONUMENT The story of the volcano is presented at two visitors' centers west of the mountain. The *Silver Lake Visitors' Center* is the original visitors' center; it focuses primarily on the area's history and geology, and the events leading up to the eruption, and also shows a 22-minute video of the volcano's blast. Continue east on US 504 to the *Coldwater Visitors' Center,* which opened in 1993. It offers panoramic views of the area, the crater, and the dome inside, as well as exhibits focusing on returning plant and animal life.

On the east side of the mountain, the road from the *Woods Creek Information Center* leads past green forest to the dramatically stark landscape created by the volcanic eruption. Thousands of dead, grey tree trunks lie like so many toothpicks on the tan volcanic ash. There's a good view of Mt. St. Helens from Cascade Peaks; you can get a great look at the crater from Windy Ridge, which is inaccessible from November through May.

For additional information, contact *Mt. St. Helens National Volcanic Monument* (42218 Northeast Yale Bridge Rd., Amboy, WA 98601; phone: 360-750-3900 or 360-247-5800).

Also in *Gifford Pinchot National Forest* is Mt. Adams. The Pacific Northwest's second-highest peak, the mountain is a 12,307-foot monster with glaciers, forests, and lava flows. From its base on the western side, the *Pacific Crest Trail* heads through *Goat Rocks Wilderness.* There are several campgrounds in different parts of the forest, which are open most of the year but closed to vehicles. For information, call 360-274-2103.

BEST EN ROUTE

Expect to pay $120 or more per night for a double room at those places we've listed as expensive; $75 to $120 at those described as moderate; and less than $75 at those rated inexpensive. Unless otherwise indicated, hotels are open year-round and rooms have private baths but no air conditioning, TV sets, or in-room telephones. Hotels are listed alphabetically by price category.

CRYSTAL MOUNTAIN

Crystal Mountain There are a number of accommodations options at this self-contained alpine village, including the *Silver Skis Chalet* and *Crystal Chalets* condominiums, with a total of 96 units; the nonsmoking *Quicksilver Lodge,* with 25 units (11 with sleeping lofts); and the slightly older *Village Inn,* with 20 rooms. All rooms have TV sets. Although there is no restaurant on the premises, there are several dining establishments within a five-minute walk. Other amenities include a heated pool and a grocery store. Off Hwy. 410 (phone: 360-663-2558). Expensive to moderate.

National Park Inn Near *Longmire Visitors' Center,* it has 25 nonsmoking rooms (18 with private baths) and offers meal service. For reservations, write *Mt. Rainier Guest Services,* PO Box 108, Ashford, WA 98304 (phone: 360-569-2275; fax: 360-569-2770). Moderate to inexpensive.

Paradise Inn Near the *Paradise Visitors' Center,* this nonsmoking inn has 125 rooms (95 with private baths), a lodge-type lobby with two open fireplaces, a dining room, a cocktail lounge, and a snack bar. Open from mid-May through early October. For reservations, write *Mt. Rainier Guest Services* (see *National Park Inn,* above). Moderate to inexpensive.

Olympic Peninsula and Olympic National Park, Washington

Directly west of Seattle, across Puget Sound, is the Olympic Peninsula, dominated by the Olympic Mountains in general, and by Mt. Olympus in particular. At the heart of the peninsula is *Olympic National Park,* covering 1,441 square miles of diverse terrain, including rugged coastline, temperate rain forest, and mountain peaks. On the western edge of the peninsula lies a 57-mile stretch of wild Pacific Ocean coastline studded with giant rocks and home to seagulls, eagles, seals, and sea lions. Hundreds of offshore islands nestle among the coast's inlets and coves, sheltering many communities of seals and other marine and amphibious creatures. Inland, the landscape is dotted with numerous small lakes—glacial pits formed when alpine glaciers retreated 13,000 years ago. The lakes are part of a thriving water system, and the western slope of the Olympic Peninsula is the wettest spot in the continental US, with an average annual precipitation of more than 130 inches and cloudy weather more than 220 days a year (temperatures are in the 70s F in summer, in the 30s F in winter). Also on the peninsula are complex and primeval rain forests—the most well known being the Huh—and not far from them glacier-capped mountains. The biggest is Mt. Olympus, a 7,965-foot peak in the center of the park. All told, 60 glaciers cover some 25 square miles of mountainous terrain, in frosty juxtaposition to the lush vegetation nearby.

Possibly discovered in 1592 by the Spanish explorer Juan de Fuca, for whom the strait connecting the Pacific with Puget Sound was later named, the Olympic Peninsula was the home of the coast Salish and the Makah Indians, an artistic civilization with an intense economic and spiritual kinship to the sea. A stream of trappers and traders found their way to the peninsula in the early 1800s, bringing germs to which the Indians were not immune. A series of epidemics and conflicts with the white settlers wiped out many of the original inhabitants. Today, many of the descendants of the survivors live on reservations. The Quillayute and Hoh Indian reservations are adjacent to *Olympic National Park*'s coastal area. The Ozette and Makah reservations are in the northwestern corner of the peninsula; the Skokomish and Nisqually reservations, in the southeast; and the S'klallam reservation may be found in the northeast.

The economy of the peninsula is diversifying. With a decline in the timber industry a few years ago, many residents found themselves out of work. Reluctant to leave their homes, however, several have developed services catering to tourists, such as llama trekking, fishing charters, guided backpacking trips and bed-and-breakfast establishments. The S'klallum reservation features a native art gallery, and a casino. From the *Forks Chamber of Commerce* (PO Box 1249, Forks, WA 98331; phone: 800-44-FORKS), you can request a brochure for *Olympic West ArtTrek,* a self-guided tour to several galleries and artists' studios including that of a chainsaw carver, marble sculptor and four Indian art outlets.

Our route leaves from Seattle, then circles the Olympic Peninsula, visiting *Olympic National Park* along the way. For a detailed report on the city, its hotels, restaurants, and attractions, see *Seattle* in THE CITIES.

En Route from Seattle One option—which is the faster and more scenic—is to take a *Washington State Ferry* across Puget Sound to Bainbridge Island or Bremerton, cross the Hood Canal floating bridge, and pick up US 101 north to Port Townsend. The other entails driving to Olympia via I-5 south and then picking up US 101 north to Port Townsend.

PORT TOWNSEND In the northeast corner of the peninsula, off US 101 on Highway 20, Port Townsend was a bustling harbor at the turn of the century. Many of the Victorian mansions here have been converted to charming bed and breakfast establishments, and the number of good art galleries, shops, and restaurants is impressive for such a small, out-of-the-way town. For more information, contact the *Port Townsend Chamber of Commerce* (2437 E. Sims Way, Port Townsend, WA 98368; phone: 360-385-2722).

En Route from Port Townsend Return to US 101 and drive 48 miles west along the north coast to Port Angeles, site of the largest of *Olympic National Park*'s three visitors' centers.

OLYMPIC NATIONAL PARK Stop at the visitors' center in Port Angeles to see the exhibits on local fauna and flora, then drive into the park on Heart of the Hills Road, a 17-mile paved road that ascends to an elevation of nearly a mile. Halfway up, at *Lookout Point,* you can see across the Strait of Juan de Fuca to British Columbia and to Mt. Baker when visibility is good. Perched at the top of the road, *Hurricane Ridge Visitors' Center* (not always accessible during the winter) is a good place to catch your breath and pick up more information. You can embark on *Big Meadow Nature Trail* on foot, or drive along an unpaved mountain road to *Obstruction Point,* at 6,450 feet. Unless it's shrouded in fog, Mt. Olympus should be staring you smack in the face: Named after the mythological home of the Greek gods and covered by six glaciers, some as thick as 900 feet, the 7,965-foot mountain gets about 200 inches of snow and rain a year. A number of hiking trails begin at *Obstruction Point.* One leads to *Deer Park Campground,* one of 17 campgrounds in the park.

Another spot worth visiting is Lake Crescent, about 20 miles west of Port Angeles on US 101 and still in mountain country. From the *Shadow Mountain General Store,* visitors can take one of five 75-minute interpretive cruises of Lake Crescent offered May through October aboard the same kind of paddle wheeler used decades ago on the lake (phone: 360-452-4520). West of the lake, you can pick up the road to *Sol Duc Hot Springs and Sol Duc Campground.* On the western edge of the park stands the Hoh rain forest with many walking and hiking trails. It has numerous species of shrubs, fungi, mosses, and trees, including the giant Sitka spruce, which often grows as high as 190 feet. Roosevelt elk, deer, bear, raccoon, and dozens of different species of birds also live in this area.

For additional information, contact the Superintendent, *Olympic National Park* (600 E. Park Ave., Port Angeles, WA 98362; phone: 360-452-0330) and the North Olympic Peninsula Visitor and Convention Bureau (PO Box 670, Port Angeles, WA 98362; phone: 800-942-4042; fax: 360-452-3959).

En Route from Olympic National Park About 17 miles west of Lake Crescent, pick up Highway 113 running north from Sappho, bearing left onto Highway 112 northwest to Clallam Bay. Continue 20 miles to Neah Bay and the Makah Indian Reservation on the northwesternmost tip of the peninsula.

MAKAH INDIAN RESERVATION Neah Bay is a fishing village where the Makah Indians operate motels and crafts shops. The *Makah Cultural and Research Center* (Bay View Ave.; phone: 360-645-2711) across from the *Coast Guard Station* at Neah Bay displays canoes, longhouses, tools, and clothing; exhibits include the archaeological material excavated by teams from *Washington State University.* Open daily May through September; closed Mondays and Tuesdays during winter. There's an admission charge.

En Route from the Makah Indian Reservation Return to US 101 at Sappho (via Highways 112 east and 113 south) and head south toward Aberdeen, where you will pick up Highway 12 and complete the circular route around the peninsula. On the way, you'll travel through parts of the *Olympic National Forest.*

OLYMPIC NATIONAL FOREST With 651,000 acres of rain forest vegetation, the forest forms the eastern, northern, and southern borders of *Olympic National Park.* Farther south, La Push offers two excellent trails to Second Beach and to Third Beach on the Pacific Ocean. Campsites in the Quinault Lake and Hood Canal area are open in summer; those at Brown Creek and Falls View, among others, are open year-round, but there are no services. The

Quilcene and Hood Canal areas east of the park are laced with popular hiking trails, and there are lots of lakes and rivers for fishing. For information, contact *National Forest Headquarters* (1835 Block Lake Blvd. SW, Olympia, WA 98502; phone: 360-956-2400).

BEST EN ROUTE

You can't reserve space at any of the campsites in the park. The maximum stay permitted at any site is 14 days. If you plan to explore the wilderness or camp, you must first get a permit at a ranger station or visitors' center. Reservations can be made for group sites at two area campgrounds by calling the respective ranger stations (phone: 360-374-5460, Mora; 360-962-2283, Kalaloch; 360-374-6925, Hoh).

There are also several pleasant lodges and motels in the area. Expect to pay $125 or more per night for a double room at those places we've listed as expensive; $70 to $125 at places described as moderate, and less than $70 at those rated inexpensive. Unless otherwise indicated, hotels are open year-round and rooms have private baths, but no air conditioning, TV sets, or telephones. For each location, hotels are listed alphabetically by price category.

PORT TOWNSEND

Old Consulate Inn Perched on a bluff overlooking the town and the water, this turreted mansion (the *F. W. Hastings House*) has five rooms and three suites, plus friendly owners, antique furnishings, and a lot of Victorian charm. A generous, family-style breakfast is included in the room rate. 313 Walker at Washington St. (phone: 360-385-6753). Expensive to moderate.

OLYMPIC NATIONAL PARK

Kalaloch Lodge This complex offers 58 rooms in a lodge, a motel, and cabins, as well as a dining room, coffee shop, cocktail lounge, library, store, and service station. On US 101 on the ocean beach, 36 miles south of Forks. For information or reservations: HC 80, PO Box 1100, Forks, WA 98331 (phone: 360-962-2271). Expensive to moderate.

Lake Crescent Lodge There is a total of 54 rooms here in a lodge (built in 1916), motel units (some with mountain or lake views), and cottages. Five rooms do not have private baths. The property also has a dining room and a cocktail lounge. Open from May through October. About 21 miles west of Port Angeles on Lake Crescent off US 101. For information or reservations: 416 Lake Crescent Rd., Port Angeles, WA 98363 (phone: 360-928-3211; fax: 360-928-3253). Moderate.

Log Cabin Offering 28 standard motel units and cabins (four without private baths), this place also has a restaurant, a cocktail lounge, a grocery store, an RV park, camping spaces, boat rentals, a boat launch, fishing tackle, and a coin-operated laundry. Open from April through October. Some 18 miles west of Port Angeles on the northeast end of Lake Crescent, 3 miles off US 101. For information or reservations: 3183 E. Beach Rd., Port Angeles, WA 98363 (phone: 360-928-3245). Moderate to inexpensive.

Devils Tower National Monument, Wyoming

In the film *Close Encounters of the Third Kind,* François Truffaut holds up a picture of Devils Tower, asking, "Have you ever seen anything like this?" "Sure," says Richard Dreyfuss. "I've got one just like it in my living room." In the movie, the 867-foot-high, tree-stump–shaped rock tower is the site chosen by beings from another planet for encounters with humans, and one aspect of the initial contact is the implantation of an image of Devils Tower in the minds of American men and women. They then become obsessed with visions of the tower, which they are driven to reproduce by sketching, painting, or even creating replicas.

After your first encounter with Devils Tower, you may develop a certain amount of sympathy for that obsession. A gargantuan landmark suddenly rising up in the middle of a vast Wyoming plain, near the western edge of the *Black Hills National Forest,* Devils Tower is the only outstanding physical feature in the northeastern sector of the state. On a clear day you can see it from as far as 100 miles away. *Devils Tower National Monument* covers 1,347 acres of land between the towns of Sundance and Hulett.

Pioneers traversing the Great Plains by horse and wagon used the tower as a guidepost, as did the first white explorers and, before them, the Indians. Some of those Indians called it Mateo Tepee, meaning Grizzly Bear Lodge. The army misinterpreted Mateo Tepee to mean Bad God's Tower, and it was by this name the first US Geological Survey party became acquainted with it in 1875, later changing its name to Devils Tower. According to one legend, the Bad God (Satan) beats on the top of the tower as on a drum to frighten the land during thunderstorms. A Kiowa Indian myth, however, ascribes the tower's origin to an incident in which several bears attacked seven Indian maidens. The Great Spirit saved them by lifting the rock on which they were standing to a great height—thus, the tower. In this version, those deep, vertical ridges on the sides of the tower were formed by the bears' frustrated scratching in an attempt to reach their prey. When the animals died from exhaustion, the Great Spirit transformed the girls into the constellation Pleiades. Three Indian tribes consider the tower sacred, which is emphasized in an orientation program given within the park.

In 1906, President Theodore Roosevelt declared Devils Tower and the surrounding area the country's first national monument. Since then, it has intrigued visitors from all over the world. Geologists have come to its base at the Belle Fourche River, fascinated by the layers of sedimentary rock and vegetation. According to scientific estimates, the tower dates back about 60 million years, the product of a geological process involving molten rock bubbling up from the earth's center and then cooling.

Although the fluted, strangely symmetrical sides of the monolith hardly seem hospitable to botanical life, the rock attracts lichens that slowly erode the solid mineral surface into tiny fragments. As dust blows in from the prairie, little pockets of soil nestle in the cracks, attracting moss and liverwort. As the soil deepens, grass and wildflowers grow. Sagebrush and other shrubs cluster closer to the base while aspen and pine trees take root at the very bottom. About a half-mile from the base, prairie dogs burrow intricate underground mazes. Because it is on the grounds of a national monument, the colony here is one of the few protected prairie dog communities in the US.

Begin your visit at the visitors' center, which is at the base of the tower, and pick up a color brochure with a map you can follow as you hike. If you want to climb to the top of the tower, you must be an experienced climber and you must register at the visitors' center (from May through October) or at the administrative building (the remainder of the year), which is 2 miles from the base.

If you're not up for an assault on the tower itself, you can take advantage of any of the 200 other climbing and hiking trails in the area, or wander along the *Tower Trail,* a 1½-mile paved road at the base of the tower, and watch the prairie dogs burrow. You'll also catch glimpses of rabbit, chipmunk, and, if you're lucky, white-tailed and mule deer. (Deer come out to feed at sunset.) There are wayside exhibits on park trails, and educational programs in summer.

Devils Tower National Monument is open year-round. Because of its isolated location—Rapid City, the nearest city of any size, is 100 miles away—you're likely to find yourself alone with the staff members if you visit the park between October and March. Early morning and late afternoon are the best times to visit from June through August, as parking is limited. Cross-country skiing is permitted, but there are no signed or groomed trails.

For additional information, contact the Superintendent, *Devils Tower National Monument* (Devils Tower, WY 82714; phone: 307-467-5283; fax: 207-467-5350).

BEST EN ROUTE

In addition to the places listed below, reasonable motel accommodations are available near the park in the towns of Hulett, Sundance, and Moorcroft. The *Belle Fourche River Campground,* operated by the *National Park Service* within monument boundaries, has 51 campsites, some accommodating 36-foot trailers (no reservations taken). Supplies are available at three convenience/souvenir stores within a mile of the campground. For information, contact *Devils Tower National Monument* (Devils Tower, WY 82714; phone: 307-467-5283; fax: 307-467-5350).

Expect to pay $60 to $70 per night for a double room at the moderately priced places described below. The rooms have private baths, air conditioning, TV sets, and telephones unless otherwise indicated.

DEVILS TOWER NATIONAL MONUMENT

R-Place This bed and breakfast establishment at the foot of Devils Tower is within walking distance of wildlife trails and cross-country skiing. The place has only one guestroom, which accommodates three people and has a private entrance and a deck; consequently, reservations are required. It's also the premier place to view Devil's Tower. There is a complimentary continental breakfast, but no TV or in-room telephone. PO Box 8, Devils Tower, WY 82714 (phone: 307-467-5938). Moderate.

GILLETTE

Best Western Tower West Lodge Here are 188 rooms, a restaurant, a lounge, a pool, and a fitness center with a sauna, weight room, and Jacuzzi. Children under 12 stay free with their parents. Located 60 miles west of the monument at 109 N. US Hwy. 14–16 (phone: 307-686-2210; 800-528-1234; fax: 307-682-5105). Moderate.

Grand Teton National Park and Jackson Hole, Wyoming

Grand Teton National Park encompasses more than 310,000 acres just south of *Yellowstone National Park* in northwestern Wyoming. Within its bounds is the most spectacular part of the Teton Range, the youngest stretch of peaks in the Rockies at less than 10 million years of age. Early French Canadian fur trappers gave the Tetons their name, French slang for "big breasts." Perhaps the name represented wishful thinking, for there is nothing smooth, soft, or voluptuous about the jagged, irregular spires of the Teton Range. The name is doubly ironic since there are three mountains named Teton: Grand, Middle, and South Teton.

According to legend, John Colter, a trapper and guide, explored the Jackson Hole–*Yellowstone* region during the winter of 1807–8. He brought back fantastic tales of boiling springs, powerful geysers, and sulfurous fumes spouting from the earth. People back East didn't believe him and nicknamed the place "Colter's Hell." If *Yellowstone* is Colter's Hell, then by rights the Tetons, with their tranquil, majestic beauty, should be called Colter's Heaven.

Although there are higher mountains in North America, the Tetons have a special visual impact because their sheer mass rises abruptly without foothills from the peaceful flat valley of Jackson Hole, Wyoming. Jackson Hole ("hole" is an old fur trappers' term for an enclosed mountain valley) is about 40 miles long and 8 to 12 miles wide, with highways leading to different parts of the valley. Most of the valley is accessible by automobile year-round.

JACKSON HOLE Unparalled natural beauty is the backdrop for this unique year-round resort area. To the north is *Yellowstone National Park,* and to the south is the western town of Jackson, with boardwalks, swinging-door saloons, and elk antler arches decorating the town square.

One of this area's main attractions is skiing—and not just because of its impressive ski facilities, excellent food, and après-ski entertainment. Its most important feature is something other ski areas often lack: snow. One year, the *US Forest Service* had already recorded 161 inches of new snow by the opening day of the ski season—more than most ski resorts get in an entire year. With the longest continuous vertical drop in the US (4,139 feet) and the longest runs anywhere in the US, two world-famous ski resorts attract people each winter to the Jackson Hole area: *Jackson Hole Ski Resort at Teton Village* (phone: 307-733-2292), on Rendezvous Mountain overlooking Jackson Hole, and *Grand Targhee* (phone: 800-TARGHEE), on the west side of the range, both of which are in the *Grand Targhee National Forest. Teton Village,* 12 miles northwest of Jackson, has more extensive beginner and intermediate slopes than those found at 90% of the major ski resorts in the country as well as some of the toughest expert slopes around. It's an excellent place for a family whose members ski at different levels. *Jackson Hole Ski Resort* has 2,500 acres of available skiing: 10 percent beginners, 40 percent intermediates, and 50 percent expert. *Grand Targhee* is an hour's drive from Jackson over Teton Pass, on Highways 22 and 33, but it offers excellent skiing from mid-November through mid-April.

In summer, more than a million people come to Jackson Hole for quiet, leisurely Snake River floating excursions or more exciting whitewater trips. There are more than 15 float trip operators in the area. Three of the best are *Barker-Ewing* (PO Box 100, Moose, WY 83012; phone: 307-733-1800; 800-365-1800 for scenic tours; 800-448-4202 for whitewater rafting); *Triangle X* (PO Box 120W, Moose, WY 83012; phone: 307-733-5500), which is also a first-rate working dude ranch; and *Jack Dennis Float Trips* (PO Box 3369, Jackson, WY 83001; phone: 307-733-3270), only guided fishing trips. This area also has the best fishing in the Rockies; local cutthroat trout are legendary. For additional information, contact the *Jackson Hole Area Chamber of Commerce* (PO Box E, Jackson, WY 83001; phone: 307-733-3316; fax: 307-733-5585) or the *Jackson Hole Visitors Council* (PO Box 982, Dept. 8, Jackson Hole, WY 83001; phone: 800-443-6931; fax: 307-733-1286).

En Route from Jackson Hole From the town of Jackson, head north for 13 miles on the John D. Rockefeller Jr. Memorial Parkway, which runs beside the Snake River south of *Yellowstone,* to *Grand Teton National Park* headquarters at *Moose Visitors' Center.*

GRAND TETON NATIONAL PARK As you enter the park, be sure to stop at the spectacular Snake River Overlook. Then head for the visitors' center, where you'll find information on hiking, fishing, camping, and the history of the Tetons. (The *Colter Bay Visitors' Center* and *Jenny Lake Ranger Station* distribute the same information.)

There are more than 200 miles of hiking trails in the park. One three-hour excursion, the most popular tour, includes a boat ride across Jenny Lake and a moderate hike of 2 miles round trip to Hidden Falls and Inspiration Point. More difficult is the *Teton Crest Trail,* which climbs to an elevation of 2 miles above sea level. Another strenuous hike, along the *Indian Paintbrush Trail,* is known for its resplendent wildflowers and wonderful views of the lakes and mountains. Both *Teton Crest* and *Indian Paintbrush* trails are suitable for people in reasonably good physical condition. (Be warned, however, that the park rangers' idea of "reasonably good physical condition" might well be considerably more rigorous than your own.)

There are over a dozen routes to the summit of Grand Teton Mountain, the highest of the three Tetons at 13,770 feet. Some of the climbs are relatively easy, but one is considered to be among the most difficult in the nation. Climbing permits are no longer required. However, back country permits are necessary and can be obtained at any ranger station throughout the area. At Jenny Lake and Teton Village, *Exum Mountain Guides* (PO Box 56, Moose, WY 83012; phone: 307-733-2297) offers a two-day mountain climbing course, with guides to take you up many peaks in the summer. *Jackson Hole Mountain Guides* at Teton Village (PO Box 744, Jackson, WY 83001; phone: 307-733-4979) provides three-week climbing courses for teenagers and four-day climbs for beginners in the summer.

You can rent canoes and boats on Jackson and Jenny Lakes or launch your own (you must buy a permit, available at either of the visitors' centers). There are scheduled boat rides on Jackson Lake, the biggest lake in the valley. Guided rubber raft trips down the Snake River leave from *Jackson Lake Lodge* (see *Best en Route*) as well as other valley locations, including Colter Bay. You may also take a guided horseback ride at *Colter Bay Corrals* (Colter Bay; phone: 307-543-2811) or *Jackson Lake Lodge.* There are five *Park Service* campgrounds at Colter Bay (phone: 307-543-2811) and *Flagg Ranch* (phone: 307-543-2861). For information, contact the Superintendent, *Grand Teton National Park* (PO Drawer 170, Moose, WY 83012; phone: 307-739-3300; fax: 307-739-3304).

En Route from Grand Teton National Park Continuing north on Rockefeller Parkway, *Grand Teton National Park* is flanked on the east by *Bridger-Teton National Forest* and on the west by *Grand Targhee National Forest.*

BRIDGER-TETON NATIONAL FOREST This forest extends north to flank *Yellowstone National Park,* taking in more than 3.4 million acres of forest, river, mountain, and wilderness. Trout fishing in streams and mountain lakes, hunting, skiing, rafting, 2,900 miles of hiking trails, and the Teton and Bridger wildernesses are the major attractions. Boat launches at Fremont, Willow, New Fork, and Green River Lakes. There are 42 campgrounds, with a total of 600 sites, and an aerial tramway that rises to 10,450 feet—great for sightseeing in summer and skiing in winter. For information, contact the Forest Supervisor, *Bridger-Teton National Forest* (FS Building, PO Box 1888, Jackson, WY 83001; phone: 307-739-5500; fax: 307-739-5010).

TARGHEE NATIONAL FOREST Often called the back door to *Grand Teton* and *Yellowstone National Parks* because it borders them, *Targhee* covers 1,854,240 acres, most of it in southeast Idaho. Fishing, rafting, swimming, horseback riding, backpacking, and camping are the activities in summer; there are 33 campgrounds. The *Jedediah Smith* and *Winegar Hole Wilderness Areas* (on the west side and in the southwest corner of the park, respectively) allow hiking, skiing, fishing, and no-trace camping. In winter, there's snowmobiling on 500 miles of groomed trails and cross-country as well as downhill skiing at *Grand Targhee Winter Sports Area* in Alta, Wyoming (phone: 307-353-2300). For information, contact the Forest Supervisor, *Targhee National Forest* (PO Box 208, St. Anthony, ID 83445; phone: 208-624-3151).

BEST EN ROUTE

Expect to pay $200 or more per night for a double room at places we've listed as very expensive, $100 to $200 at those described as expensive, $50 to $100 at those categorized as moderate, and less than $50 at places described as inexpensive. Unless otherwise indicated, rooms have private baths, but no air conditioning, TV sets, or telephones. For each location, hotels are listed alphabetically by price category.

JACKSON

Spring Creek Resort Here are 36 hotel rooms and 80 condominiums on a secluded mountaintop with a fabulous view. All have TV sets and telephones. A heated pool, Jacuzzis, two tennis courts, cross-country skiing, nature trails, horseback riding, and winter sleigh rides keep guests busy. There is a first class restaurant, *The Granary,* plus room service, and free transportation to the airport. 1800 Spirit Dance Rd. (phone: 307-733-8833; fax: 307-733-1524). Very expensive to expensive.

Best Western Lodge Just 20 minutes from *Yellowstone National Park,* this hotel offers a rustic setting complete with a pine interior, fireplaces, and Jacuzzis in most of its 100 rooms, as well as mini-bars and an indoor/outdoor pool. 80 Scott Lane (phone: 307-739-9703; 800-528-1234). Expensive.

TETON VILLAGE

Alpenhof This chalet-style mountain lodge at the base of the *Jackson Hole* ski area has 42 rooms (with telephones and TV sets), a pool, a sauna, fireplaces in the lounge, and a good American and continental restaurant. Closed April through mid-May, and early October through early December. 3255 W. McCollister Dr. (phone: 307-733-3242; 800-732-3244; fax: 307-739-1516). For all reservations in Teton Village, contact *Jackson Hole Central Reservations* (phone: 307-733-2811; 800-443-6931). Expensive.

GRAND TETON NATIONAL PARK

Jenny Lake Lodge Thirty-seven log cabins in a secluded, rustic setting surround the lodge here. Although breakfast and dinner are included—as well as horseback riding and bicycles—the rate is high. Also available are boating and fishing at nearby Jenny Lake, hiking trails, and an excellent restaurant. Inner Loop Rd. (phone 307-733-4647). For reservations, contact *Grand Teton Lodge Co.,* PO Box 240, Moran, WY 83013 (phone: 307-543-2855; fax: 307-543-2869). Very expensive.

Jackson Lake Lodge There are 42 guestrooms in the lodge, and 343 located in cluster buildings on either side of it along tree-lined avenues. It's an excellent base for boating and fishing expeditions, float trips, swimming, or horseback riding. There are spectacular views across Willow Flats to the skyline of the Tetons, and there are two restaurants (the lodge's chef will cook your catch of the day). Rooms have telephones. Open late May through mid-September. Five miles south of Colter Bay. For reservations, contact *Grand Teton Lodge Co.* (see *Jenny Lake Lodge,* above). Expensive.

Colter Bay Cabins Here are 209 log cabins and 72 tent cabins. Water sports, scenic float trips on the Snake River, and horseback riding are available. There are also 112 RV spaces and a restaurant. US 89N (phone: 307-543-2811). For reservations, contact *Grand Teton Lodge Co.* (see *Jenny Lake Lodge,* above). Moderate to inexpensive.

Yellowstone National Park, Wyoming

Founded in 1872, *Yellowstone* was the first national park to be established anywhere in the world. It is the largest national park in the contiguous states, covering 3,472 square miles—larger than Rhode Island and Delaware combined—in northwestern Wyoming, Montana, and Idaho. In 1988, forest fires in *Yellowstone* destroyed about 794,000 acres—just over a third of the park. Thanks to the fertilizing effects of the ashes, however, the grasses and wildflowers in the park have been more productive than ever after the fires, and the park's facilities, as well as its most famous features—geysers, hot springs, and magnificent scenery—are still in place.

The park has the greatest concentration of mammals in the lower 48 states, with bison, grizzlies, elk, and moose; it is also home to North America's only colony of white pelicans. Don't forget that it is illegal and dangerous to feed the animals, especially the bears, which can turn from seemingly tame creatures to the unpredictable wild animals they are in a split second. Buffalo, too, are swifter and more dangerous than they appear. The number of buffalo gorings has been increasing at an alarming rate—graphic evidence that these animals are not to be trifled with. Some visitors may be lucky enough to hear the howl of the gray wolf which is, by Congressional order, being reintroduced to the park. Their howl was last heard in these parts in the 1930s.

The superstar of *Yellowstone* is, of course, *Old Faithful.* Though not the largest geyser in *Yellowstone, Old Faithful* is among the most dependable. Ever since it was discovered over 100 years ago, the geyser has been erupting on an average of once every 70 minutes (ranging from a record low of 30 minutes to a record high of two hours between performances), shooting thousands of gallons of steaming water into the air for periods of two to five minutes. With almost 200 active geysers, *Yellowstone* is the greatest geyser region in the world. (Only three other areas in the world—Iceland, New Zealand, and Siberia—have concentrations of geysers.) *Yellowstone* also has an estimated 10,000 hot springs, mud pots, and fumaroles (natural vents in the earth that shoot out superheated steam).

The heat source for all this thermal activity is thought to lie just 2 to 3 miles below the earth's surface, where a chamber of magma (molten rock) heats the overlying layers of stone. A geyser occurs where groundwater seeps into underground crevasses in the red-hot rocks and is superheated to over twice its boiling point. At first, the pressure of the thousands of gallons of overlying water prevents the superheated liquid from turning to steam. Finally the pressure becomes so great that some of the water is pushed out through the cone of the geyser. As the pressure drops, the water instantly distills into steam and blasts out of the geyser's cone.

Even without its geysers, *Yellowstone* would be important. The Grand Canyon of the Yellowstone River, with a waterfall twice as high as Niagara and canyon walls splashed with multicolored rock, deserves that status by itself. There's also a petrified forest, with trees that remain upright, just as they were when they were covered with volcanic dust and turned to stone millions of years ago. Yellowstone Lake is the largest mountain lake above 7,000 feet in North America, and one of the highest lakes of its size in the world, second only to Lake Titicaca in Peru. Plan on a minimum of two or three days to see all of the park's major attractions.

Yellowstone presents the park service with a dilemma. It is one of the most popular national parks, and the millions of people who visit each year cause traffic jams and leave behind tons of litter. Some visitors want the park service to expand the facilities, while others would prefer a moratorium on further development. The last major expansion program took place from 1955 to 1965. Midway through the process, *Yellowstone* was shaken by a series of huge earthquakes that knocked down half a mountain—almost as if the earth were reasserting its sovereignty and cautioning those who wanted to commercialize this region that they should regard the park with awe and treat it with respect.

Many of *Yellowstone*'s major attractions are accessible by car via the famous Grand Loop, a 142-mile-long road that traces a circular route around the park. You may enter the park from Gardiner, Montana, on US 89 to the north; from West Yellowstone, Montana, via US 20 and 191 to the west; from Jackson, Wyoming, or the *Grand Teton National Park* along the John D. Rockefeller Jr. Memorial Parkway to the south; from Cody, Wyoming, along US 20 to the east; or from Cooke City, Montana, on US 212 to the northeast. The entrance at Gardiner is open all year; the others are closed to cars from early November through April. All are open in winter to snowmobiles, and heated snow coaches (vans that hold 10 to 15 people) are available at the south, north, and west entrances. During winter months, snowmobiling in *Yellowstone National Park* has become even more popular than ever with the completion of the 360-mile *Continental Divide Snowmobile Trail* from Lander, through both *Yellowstone National* and *Grand Teton National Parks* to West Yellowstone, Montana. For more information, contact the *Lander Chamber of Commerce* (phone: 307-332-3892; 800-433-0662) for trail information.

The park's headquarters and museum and the *Mammoth Hot Springs Terraces* are near the north entrance. At the springs you will see bizarre-looking terraced pools formed on the side of Terrace Mountain by mineral-rich water from the hot springs. Some of the terraces are growing at the rate of a foot a year as the hot springs dissolve the subterranean limestone beds under the mountain and redeposit the minerals on the surface, literally turning Terrace Mountain inside out. The *Norris Geyser Basin,* 21 miles south of *Mammoth Hot Springs,* is dotted with geysers and hot springs. A museum here offers exhibitions and guided walks through the main basin, and there are trails through both the Upper and Lower Basins.

The west entrance joins the Grand Loop at Madison Junction. Heading south from here, the Grand Loop follows the banks of the Firehole River, a stream that's fed by dozens of hot springs in its bed. At *Old Faithful,* just 16 miles south of Madison Junction, there is a visitors' center, where changing exhibits and a video are shown, in addition to the famous gusher. The surrounding geyser basins—Midway and Lower—have some of the best geysers, hot springs, and mud pots in the park.

The south entrance road joins the Grand Loop 17 miles east of *Old Faithful.* From there, the road hugs the shore of Yellowstone Lake all the way up to its northern end. Yellowstone Lake has great fishing for cutthroat trout (although there are strict catch limitations). Boats and tackle are available at Bridge Bay Marina (phone: 307-344-7901) on the northwest shore.

North of Fishing Bridge Junction at the northern tip of Yellowstone Lake, the Grand Loop leads to the 20-mile-long Grand Canyon of the Yellowstone, where the river has carved a twisting canyon 800 to 1,200 feet deep. The dominant color of the stone face of the canyon walls is, of course, yellow, but the canyon is also tinted with colors ranging from pale saffron to bright orange. At the Upper Falls of the Yellowstone, which mark the beginning of the canyon, the water moves with such force that it appears to arch through the air rather than fall. Farther along is the magnificent Lower Falls, which are twice as high as Niagara. The Upper Falls are easy to see; the best view of the Lower Falls is from a trail leading to them. About 16 miles north of Fishing Bridge Junction, *Inspiration Point,* which juts far out into the canyon, offers incredible views of the river raging below. Observation points along the road are well marked.

At Tower Junction, the northeast entrance road joins the Grand Loop. Nearby, the spectacular Tower Falls drop 132 feet. Follow the Grand Loop Road west back to the north entrance.

For additional information, contact the *National Park Service, Yellowstone National Park* (PO Box 168, WY 82190; phone: 307-344-7381; fax: 307-344-2104).

BEST EN ROUTE

Keep in mind that *Yellowstone* is packed to the treetops with tourists in the summer, especially during July and August. If you would like to stay at one of the accommodations listed below at that time, make reservations well in advance; they must be made through *TW Recreational Services* (Yellowstone Division, *Yellowstone National Park,* WY 82190; phone: 307-344-2104 or 307-344-7901; fax: 307-344-7456). *TW Recreational Services* offers lodging in nine properties in the park, as well as restaurants, horseback riding, chuck wagon cookouts, snowcoach rides in winter, and tours around the park. For more information on facilities in *Yellowstone,* contact the *National Park Service* (PO Box 168, *Yellowstone National Park,* WY 82190; phone: 307-344-7381).

For reservations at Madison, Grant, Canyon, Fishing Bridge, and Bridge Bay campgrounds (phone: 307-344-7311). All other campgrounds in the park are on a first-come, first-served basis.

Expect to pay $200 or more per night for a double room at places listed as very expensive, $100 to $200 at those described as expensive, $50 to $100 at those listed as moderate, and less than $50 at places in the inexpensive category. Rooms have private baths, but no air conditioning, TV sets, or telephones, unless otherwise indicated. For each location, hotels are listed alphabetically by price category.

YELLOWSTONE NATIONAL PARK

Lake Yellowstone Columns, dormers, and decorative moldings give the hotel a charming colonial look. Opened in 1891 and remodeled several times, this matriarch has 194 rooms, lakeview dining, a lobby bar, a gift shop, and easy access to boating and fishing. In addition, there are 102 cabins nearby. Open from mid-May through late September. Two miles south of Fishing Bridge Jct. (phone: 307-344-7311). Very expensive to inexpensive.

Mammoth Hot Springs Here are 96 rooms and 126 cabins (some with view of the springs, most with private baths), two restaurants, a fireside lounge, and a gift shop. The immense, limestone terraces overlook the area. Open from mid-May through mid-September, and from mid-December through February. Five miles south of the north entrance on Loop Rd. (phone: 307-344-7311). Very expensive to inexpensive.

Old Faithful Inn A National Historic Landmark, this 325-room (many with private baths) log hotel, built in 1904, has a massive roof peak that rises 86 feet; a huge, four-sided stone fireplace; and a unique hand-crafted clock made of copper, wood, and raw iron parts. There also is a dining room, lounge, and gift shop. Open early May through mid-October. Loop Rd. next to *Old Faithful* (phone: 307-344-7901). Very expensive to expensive.

Flagg Ranch Village This lodge features 100 rooms in addition to 175 campsites. *Bear's Den* restaurant features buffalo burgers. Guests enjoy a variety of activities including rafting expeditions and horseback riding. There is a gift shop and food store on the premises. PO Box 187, Moran, WY 82013 (phone: 307-543-2861; 800-443-2311; fax: 307-543-2356). Moderate.

Grant Village The six condo-style buildings have a total of 300 rooms, as well as a separate dining room and lakeview steakhouse. Open from early June through late September. Nineteen miles from *Old Faithful* on Loop Rd. (phone: 307-344-7311). Moderate.

Canyon Village Centrally located, ½ mile from the Grand Canyon of the Yellowstone River, the village has 588 cabins (most with private baths). There's a dining room, snack shop, cafeteria, and lounge. Open from mid-June through late August. Loop Rd. at Canyon Jct. (phone: 307-344-7311). Moderate to inexpensive.

IMMIGRANT, MONTANA

Mountain Sky Guest Ranch Located 30 miles from the park's north entrance, this ranch has 27 secluded units and spectacular scenery. Activities include fishing, horseback riding, tennis, hiking, swimming in a heated pool, and western dancing; there also is a sauna. Guests can dine on barbecue at poolside or more formally on continental fare in the ranch's dining room. There is generally a minimum stay of one week, for an all-inclusive charge. PO Box 317, Immigrant, MT 59027 (phone: 406-587-3977; 800-548-3392). Very expensive.

Index